Ernst and Peter Neufert

Architects' Data

Third Edition

Edited by

Bousmaha Baiche
DipArch, MPhil, PhD
School of Architecture, Oxford Brookes University

and

Nicholas Walliman
DipArch, PhD, RIBA
School of Architecture, Oxford Brookes University

Blackwell
Science

© 2000 English language edition
by Blackwell Science Ltd, a Blackwell Publishing Company

Editorial Offices:
Blackwell Science Ltd, 9600 Garsington Road, Oxford OX4 2DQ, UK
    Tel: +44 (0) 1865 776868
Blackwell Publishing Inc., 350 Main Street, Malden, MA 02148-5020, USA
    Tel: +1 781 388 8250
Blackwell Science Asia Pty, 550 Swanston Street, Carlton, Victoria 3053, Australia
    Tel: +61 (0)3 8359 1011

First English language edition published by Crosby Lockwood Staples 1970
Reprinted 5 times
Second (International) English language edition published by Granada Publishing 1980
Reprinted 3 times
Reissued in paperback by Collins Professional and Technical Books 1985
Reprinted by Blackwell Science Ltd 12 times
Third English language edition published by Blackwell Science Ltd 2000
9 2010
Original German edition published by Friedr, Vieweg & Sohn, Braunachweig, Wiesbaden,
    as Bauentwurfslehre (35th edition)

ISBN: 978-0-632-05771-9

Library of Congress Cataloging-in-Publication Data
Neufert, Ernst
    (Bauentwurfslehre. English)
    Architects' Data/Ernst and Peter Neufert – 3rd ed./ed by Bousmaha Baiche and Nicholas Walliman.
        p. cm.
    Includes bibliographical references and index
    1. Building – Handbooks, manuals, etc. 2. Building –
Planning – Handbooks, manuals, etc. 3. Architecture –
Handbooks, manuals etc.   I. Neufert, Peter. II. Baiche,
Bousmaha. III. Walliman, Nicholas. IV. Title

TH151 .N513 2000
    721 – dc21
                                            00-042905

A catalogue record for this title is available from the British Library

Printed and bound in Singapore
by Markono Print Media Pte Ltd

The publisher's policy is to use permanent paper from mills that operate a sustainable forestry policy, and which has been manufactured from pulp processed using acid-free and elementary chlorine-free practices. Furthermore, the publisher ensures that the text paper and cover board used have met acceptable environmental accreditation standards.

For further information on Blackwell Publishing, visit our website:
www.blackwellpublishing.com/construction

CONTENTS

About This Book   viii
Acknowledgements   ix

Introduction
Introduction   1

Draughting Guidelines
Units and symbols   2
Documentation and drawings   4
Construction drawings   7
Construction drawings: CAD   10
Construction drawings: symbols   12

Measurement Basis
Man: the universal standard   15
Man: dimensions and space requirements   16
Man: small spaces   18
Man and his housing   19
Room climate   20
Building biology   21
The eye: perception   24
Man and colour   26
Dimensional relationships   27
Basic measurements   31
Modular system   34
Coordinate system and dimensioning   35

Design
Building details: functional use of materials   36
Form: the result of construction   37
Form: modern construction techniques and forms   38
The design of houses: expression of the period   39
Design method: working process   40
Building design: preparatory work   41

Construction Management
Construction management   43

Building Components
The building site: foundations, excavation, trenches   51
Excavations: site and building measurements   52
Earthworks and foundations structures   53
Building and site drainage   55
Damp-proofing and tanking   59
Masonry: natural stone   62
Masonry: bricks and blocks   63
External walls: low-energy building construction   66
Masonry bonds   67
Fireplaces   68
Chimneys and flues   69
Ventilation ducting   70
Services: connections   71
Roof structures   72
Roof forms and coverings   75
Dormers   77
Loft space   78
Roof slopes and flat roofs   79
Flat roofs: warm roof construction   80
Flat roofs: cold roof construction   81
Roof gardens   82
Roof gardens: roof construction   84
Roof cultivation   85
Tensile and inflatable structures   86
Cable net structures   87
Suspended and tensioned structures   88
Space frames: principles   89
Space frames: applications   90
Multistorey structures   92

Suspended floors   93
Flooring   94

Heating and Ventilation
Heating   95
Heating: oil storage tanks   100
Solar architecture   101
Solar energy   104
Ventilation and air conditioning   105
Cold storage rooms   109

Thermal and Sound Insulation
Thermal insulation: terminology and mechanisms   111
Thermal insulation: water vapour diffusion   112
Thermal insulation: types of construction   113
Thermal insulation: exterior walls and roofs   114
Sound insulation   117
Vibration damping   121
Room acoustics   122

Fire Protection and Means of Escape
Fire detection   125
Fire spread   126
Smoke and heat extraction systems   127
Extinguisher systems   128
Fire protection: closures and glazing   130
Fire protection: glazing   131
Fire protection: water cooling   132
Means of escape from fire   133
Access for firefighters   137

Lightning Protection and Aerials
Protection from lightning   138
Aerials   140

Artificial Lighting and Daylight
Lighting: lamps and fittings   141
Lighting: provision   143
Lighting: arrangement   144
Lighting: requirements   147
Daylight   151
Daylight: insolation   164
Glass   166
Plastics   174

Windows and Doors
Skylights and dome rooflights   175
Windows: sizes   176
Windows: arrangement   177
Windows: shading   178
Windows: types and dimensions   179
Loft windows   180
Windows: construction   181
Windows: cleaning   183
Doors: internal   184
Doors: sizes and frames   185
Revolving and sliding doors   186
Garage/warehouse doors   187
Locking systems   188
Security of buildings and grounds   189

Stairs, Escalators and Lifts
Stairs   191
Ramps and spiral staircases   194
Escalators   195
Travelators   196
Lifts   197
Small goods lifts   199

Hydraulic lifts   200
Panoramic glass lifts   201

Refurbishment, Maintenance and Change of Use
Renovation of old buildings   202
Maintenance and restoration   207
Change of use   210

Roads and streets
Road dimensions   212
Road design   213
Intersections   215
Roadside paths   216
Paths and paving   217
Bicycle parking   218
Bicycle parking and cycle paths   219
Motorways   220
Tramways/urban light railways   221
Traffic layout   222
Traffic noise   225
Securing embankments   226

Gardens
Garden enclosures   227
Pergolas, paths, steps, retaining walls   229
Earthworks   230
Gardens: planting methods   231
Tendril and climbing plants   233
Banked and raised beds   234
Greenhouses   235
Gardens: trees and hedges   236
Garden ponds   237
Gardens: use of rainwater   238
Garden equipment   239
Garden swimming pools   240
Private swimming pools   242

Houses and Residential Buildings
Porches, entrance halls and corridors   245
Landings and hallways   246
Storage space   247
Utility rooms   248
Pantries, larders and storage   250
Kitchens   251
Dining rooms   255
Bedrooms   257
Bathrooms   262
Carports   268
Holiday homes   269
Sheds/summer houses   270
Timber houses   271
House orientation   272
Housing types   273
Terraced houses   277
Semi-detached houses   278
Courtyard houses   279
Detached houses   280
Houses with conservatories   281
Three-level houses   282
Square, cubic and tent-shape forms   283
Ecological building   284
House types: examples   285
Houses on slopes   288
Large houses   289
International examples   290
Multistorey housing   292
Balconies   295

Access corridors/decks   296
Stepped housing   297
Building for disabled people   298
Barrier-free living   301
Old people's accommodation   302
Laundries   305

Educational and Research Facilities
Schools   307
Further education colleges   314
Colleges and universities   315
Drawing studios   320
Laboratories   321
Child daycare centres   325
Playgrounds   326
Libraries   327
Museums and art galleries   333
Museums: examples   334

Office Buildings
Principles   336
Principles of typology   340
Calculations: construction   343
Calculations: building technology   344
Calculations: division of space   345
Calculations: floor area requirements   346
Calculations: space for furniture   348
Calculations: archive space   350
Calculations: workstations with computers   351
Office buildings: examples   352
Banks and building societies   359

Arcades
Glazed arcades: typology   363
Glazed arcades: historical examples   364
Glazed arcades: applied examples   366
Transparent roofs and canopies   367

Retail outlets
Shops   368
Food courts   370
Department stores and supermarkets   371
Supermarkets/hypermarkets   374

Workshops and Industrial Buildings
Workshops: woodworking   375
Workshops: metalworking   379
Workshops: showrooms and vehicle repairs   381
Vehicle repair shops   382
Vehicle company workshops   384
Workshops: bakery etc.   385
Wholesale butchers   387
Meat processing centre   388
Industrial buildings: planning   389
Warehouse design   391
High-bay warehouses   392
Warehousing technology: planning/logistics   393
Warehousing technology: safety regulations   394
Warehousing technology: rack systems   395
Handling   396
Industrial buildings: sheds   397
Multistorey industrial buildings   398
Toilet facilities   399
Washing facilities   400
Sanitary installations   401
Changing rooms, lockers   402
Power stations   403
Hydro-electric power stations   404

Agricultural Buildings
Small animal stalls 405
Poultry farms 408
Pig sheds: fattening 409
Pig sheds: breeding 411
Stables/horses 412
Cattle 414
Cattle: store bulls 415
Buildings for farm vehicles 416
Farm facilities 417
Ventilation systems 421

Public Transport
Railways: track installations 422
Railways: European structure gauges and clearances 424
Railways: UK structure gauges and clearances 425
Railway freight yards 427
Railway stations 428
Bus stations 430

Designing for Vehicles
Vehicle dimensions 432
Loading bays 434
Turning and parking 436
Garages and car-parking 439
Car-parks 440
Filling stations 443
Service stations 445

Airports
Airports: planning 446
Airports: terminals 448
Airports: runways and aprons 450
Airports: examples 451

Fire stations
Fire stations 452

Restaurants
Restaurants: space requirements 455
Restaurants: arrangements 456
Restaurant cars 457
Restaurant types 458
Restaurant kitchens 459
Large kitchens 462

Hotels/Motels
Hotel layout and area requirements 464
Hotel kitchens 467
Hotels: examples 468
Motels 469
Youth hostels 470

Zoos and Aquariums
Zoos and aquariums 473

Theatres/Cinemas
Theatres: historical summary 476
Theatres: auditoriums 478
Stages and secondary areas 481
Cinemas 486
Drive-in cinemas 488

Sport and Recreation
Sports: stadiums 489
Sports halls 491
Outdoor pitches 497

Indoor pitches 499
Athletics facilities 500
Conditioning and fitness rooms 504
Tennis facilities 506
Miniature golf 508
Golf courses 510
Sailing: yachts and marinas 512
Sailing: harbours/marinas 514
Rowing 515
Water sports 516
Riding facilities 517
Ski jumps 519
Ice rinks 520
Roller-skate/skateboarding 522
Cyclecross/BMX 523
Shooting ranges 524
Indoor sports 526
Skittle and bowling alleys 528
Indoor swimming pools 529
Open air swimming pools 534
Indoor/open air swimming pools 535
Sauna 537
Amusement arcades 540

Healthcare Buildings
Group practices and healthcare centres 541
Hospitals: general 543
Hospitals: construction planning 544
Hospitals: planning conception 545
Hospitals: forms of building 546
Hospitals: dimensional co-ordination 548
Hospitals: corridors, doors, stairs, lifts 550
Hospitals: surgical department 551
Hospitals: main surgical rooms 552
Hospitals: post-operative facilities 553
Surgery safety requirements 554
Hospitals: demarcation 555
Hospitals: intensive care area 556
Hospitals: care areas 557
Hospitals: treatment areas 561
Hospitals: laboratories; functional diagnosis 564
Hospitals: supplementary disciplines 565
Day clinics; outpatient surgery 566
Hospitals: supplies areas 567
Hospitals: general areas 571
Hospitals: teaching and research 572
A&E and outpatients department 573
Hospitals: maternity and neonatal care 574
Hospitals: mortuary, pathology, service yard 575
Special hospitals 576
Special care area safety 678

Places of Worship
Churches 579
Church organs 581
Churches: bells, towers 583
Synagogues 584
Mosques 585

Cemeteries and Crematoria
Cemeteries and crematoria 586
Cemeteries and graveyards 587

Bibliography 589
Related Standards 595
Conversion Factors/Tables 611
Index 629

This book provides architects and designers with a concise source of core information needed to form a framework for the detailed planning of any building project. The objective is to save time for building designers during their basic investigations. The information includes the principles of the design process, basic information on siting, servicing and constructing buildings, as well as illustrations and descriptions of a wide range of building types. Designers need to be well informed about the requirements for all the constituent parts of new projects in order to ensure that their designs satisfy the requirements of the briefs and that the buildings conform to accepted standards and regulations.

The extended contents list shows how the book is organised and the order of the subjects discussed. To help readers to identify relevant background information easily, the Bibliography (page 589) and list of related British and international standards (page 595) have been structured in a way that mirrors the organisation of the main sections of the book.

To avoid repetition and keep the book to a manageable length, the different subjects are covered only once in full. Readers should therefore refer to several sections to glean all of the information they require. For instance, a designer wanting to prepare a scheme for a college will need to refer to other sections apart from that on colleges, such as – draughting guidelines; multistorey buildings; the various sections on services and environmental control; restaurants for the catering facilities; hotels, hostels and flats for the student accommodation; office buildings for details on working environments; libraries; car-parks; disabled access (in the housing and residential section); indoor and outdoor sports facilities; gardens; as well as details on doors, windows, stairs, and the section on construction management, etc.

Readers should note that the majority of the material is from European contributors and this means that the detail on, for example, climate and daylight is from the perspective of a temperate climate in the northern hemisphere. The conditions at the location of the proposed building will always have to be ascertained from specific information on the locality. A similar situation is to be seen in the section on roads, where the illustrations show traffic driving on the right-hand side of the road. Again, local conditions must be taken into consideration for each individual case.

The terminology and style of the text is UK English and this clearly will need to be taken into account by readers accustomed to American English. These readers will need to be aware that, for example, 'lift' has been used in place of 'elevator' and 'ground floor' is used instead of 'first floor' (and 'first floor' for 'second', etc.).

The data and examples included in the text are drawn from a wide range of sources and as a result a combination of conventions is used throughout for dimensions. The measurements shown are all metric but a mixture of metres, centimetres and millimetres is used and they are in the main not identified.

Readers will also find some superscript numbers associated with the measurements. Where these appear by dimensions in metres with centimetres, for instance, they represent the additional millimetre component of the measure (e.g. 1.26^5 denotes 1 m, 26 cm, 5 mm). Anybody familiar with the metric system will not find this troublesome and those people who are less comfortable with metric units can use the Conversion Tables given on pages 611 to 627 to clarify any ambiguities.

The plans and diagrams of buildings do not have scales as the purpose here is to show the general layout and express relationships between different spaces, making exact scaling unnecessary. However, all relevant dimensions are given on the detailed drawings and diagrams of installations, to assist in the design of specific spaces and constructions.

ACKNOWLEDGEMENTS

The Publishers wish to thank, in particular, Dr Bousmaha Baiche, of the Postgraduate Research School, School of Architecture, Oxford Brookes University, for his enormous efforts and patience in overseeing the final English language edition. They would also like to thank his colleague, Dr Nicholas Walliman, also of the Postgraduate Research School, for his valuable contribution on questions of content and terminology.

The Publishers are also especially grateful to Paul Stringer for his efforts in managing the editorial and production work on the new edition and for his exceptional attention to detail.

They would also like to thank Mark Straker of Vector for his work on the illustrations and text, Richard Moore for proof-reading, and the following for their work on the translation: Bantrans Services, Chris Charlesworth, Chiltern Language Services, Katharina Hesse, Jeff Howell, Keith Murray, Amy Newland and Wordswop.

Finally, they would like to thank the following for contributing information and illustrations to this edition:

Martin Pugh, Trevor Fish, Group Property Services, Barclays Bank Plc
Peter J. Clement, Group Property, NatWest Group
Mary Heighway and members of staff, Public Relations, Environment Agency
Pick Everard, Graham Brown, Andrew Robinson, Pick Everard (Architects, Surveyors, and Consulting Engineers) and J. Sainsbury's Plc
Asda/WCEC Architects
Lesley Baillie, Office of Health Economics
Simon Marshall, railway expert
Stanley Partnership, Architects, Cheltenham
Malcom Lee, National Small-Bore Rifle Association (NSRA)
British Steel Strip Products
Matthew Foreman, Katy Harris, Jo Olsen and members of staff, Foster and Partners, London
Liza Kershaw and colleagues at RIBA Publications, the Royal Institute of the British Architects for permission to reproduce forms on page 48 (copyright RIBA Publications 1999)
Derek Wolferdale, Principal Track and Gauge Engineer at Railtrack, and members of staff of Railtrack
Graeme Loudon, The Met. Office
Pam Beckley (Copyright Administrator), the Controller, and members of staff of the Copyright Unit, HMSO for permission to reproduce illustrations (Fig. 1, page 541 and Fig 8, page 542) from *Health Building Note 36* (Crown copyright material is reproduced with the permission of the Controller of Her Majesty's Stationery Office)
Addison-Wesley Longman for permission to reproduce illustrations (Fig. 1, page 101 and Fig. 15 page 154) from *The Climate of the British Isles* (Chandler & Gregory)
Dr Ray Ogden, Professor Mike Jenks, Margaret Ackrill, Postgraduate Research School, School of Architecture, Oxford Brookes University
Chris Kendrick, School of Architecture, Oxford Brookes University.
The illustrations on pages 134–7 are reproduced from *The Building Regulations Explained and Illustrated* (Powell-Smith & Billington), Blackwell Science Ltd.

Throughout history man has created things to be of service to him using measurements relating to his body. Until relatively recent times, the limbs of humans were the basis for all the units of measurement. Even today many people would have a better understanding of the size of an object if they were told that it was so many men high, so many paces long, so many feet wider or so many heads bigger. These are concepts we have from birth, the sizes of which can be said to be in our nature. However, the introduction of metric dimensions put an end to that way of depicting our world.

Using the metric scale, architects have to try to create a mental picture that is as accurate and as vivid as possible. Clients are doing the same when they measure rooms on a plan to envisage the dimensions in reality. Architects should familiarise themselves with the size of rooms and the objects they contain so that they can picture and convey the real size of yet-to-be designed furniture, rooms or buildings in each line they draw and each dimension they measure.

We immediately have an accurate idea of the size of an object when we see a man (real or imaginary) next to it. It is a sign of our times that pictures of buildings and rooms presented in our trade and professional journals are too often shown without people present in them. From pictures alone, we often obtain a false idea of the size of these rooms and buildings and are surprised how different they appear in reality – frequently, they seem much smaller than expected. One of the reasons for the failure of buildings to have cohesive relationships with one another is because the designers have based their work on different arbitrary scales and not on the only true scale, namely that of human beings.

If this is ever to be changed, architects and designers must be shown how these thoughtlessly accepted measurements have developed and how they can be avoided. They have to understand the relationship between the sizes of human limbs and what space a person requires in various postures and whilst moving around. They must also know the sizes of objects, utensils, clothing etc. in everyday use to be able to determine suitable dimensions for containers and furniture.

In addition, architects and designers have to know what space humans need between furniture – both in the home and in the workplace – as well as how the furniture can best be positioned. Without this knowledge, they will be unable to create an environment in which no space is wasted and people can comfortably perform their duties or enjoy relaxation time.

Finally, architects and designers must know the dimensions for minimum space requirements for people moving around in, for example, railways and vehicles. These minimum space requirements produce strongly fixed impressions from which, often unconsciously, other dimensions of spaces are derived.

Man is not simply a physical being, who needs room. Emotional response is no less important; the way people feel about any space depends crucially on how it is divided up, painted, lit, entered, and furnished.

Starting out from all these considerations and perceptions, Ernst Neufert began in 1926 to collect methodically the experiences gained in a varied practice and teaching activities. He developed a 'theory of planning' based on the human being and provided a framework for assessing the dimensions of buildings and their constituent parts. The results were embodied in this

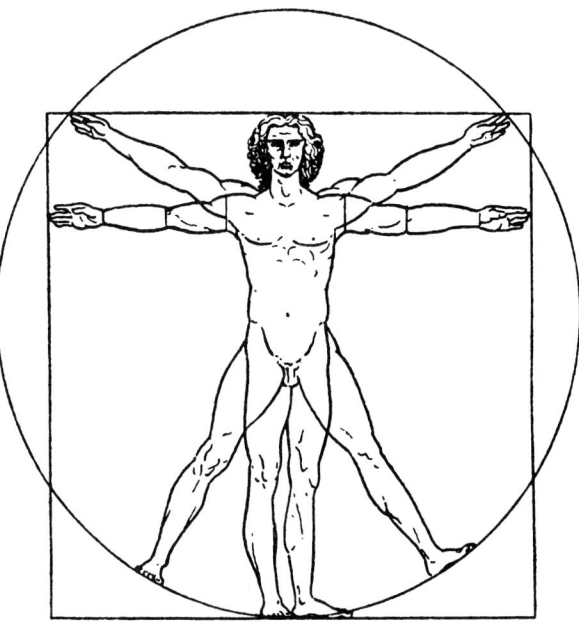

Leonardo da Vinci: rules of proportion

book. Many questions of principle were examined, developed and weighed against one another for the first time.

In the current edition up-to-date technical options are included to the fullest extent and common standards are taken into consideration. Description is kept to the absolute minimum necessary and is augmented or replaced as far as possible by drawings. Creative building designers can thus obtain the necessary information for design in an orderly, brief, and coherent form, which otherwise they would have to collect together laboriously from many reference sources or obtain by detailed measurement of completed buildings. Importance has been attached to giving only a summary; the fundamental data and experiences are compared with finished buildings only if it is necessary to provide a suitable example.

By and large, apart from the requirements of pertinent standards, each project is different and so should be studied, approached and designed afresh by the architect. Only in this way can there be lively progress within the spirit of the times. However, executed projects lend themselves too readily to imitation, or establish conventions from which architects of similar projects may find difficulty in detaching themselves. If creative architects are given only constituent parts, as is the intention here, they are compelled to weave the components together into their own imaginative and unified construction.

Finally, the component parts presented here have been systematically researched from the literature to provide the data necessary for individual building tasks, checked out on well-known buildings of a similar type and, where necessary, determined from models and experiments. The objective of this is always that of saving practising building planners from having to carry out all of these basic investigations, thereby enabling them to devote themselves to the important creative aspects of the task.

	basic unit	unit symbol	definition based on	SI units in the definition
1 length	metre	m	wavelength of krypton radiation	
2 mass	kilogram	kg	international prototype	
3 time	second	s	duration period of caesium radiation	
4 electrical current	ampere	A	electrodynamic power between two conductors	kg, m, s
5 temperature	kelvin	K	triple point of water	
6 luminous intensity	candela	cd	radiation from freezing platinum	kg, s
7 quantity of matter	mole	mol	number of carbon atoms	kg

(1) **SI basic units**

The statutory introduction of SI Units took place in stages between 1974 and 1977. As from 1 January 1978 the International Measurement System became valid using SI Units (SI = Système Internationale d'Unités).

prefixes and their abbreviations are:

T	(tera)	$= 10^{12}$	(billion)	c	(centi)	$= 1/100$	(hundredth)
G	(giga)	$= 10^9$	(US billion)	m	(milli)	$= 10^{-3}$	(thousandth)
M	(mega)	$= 10^6$	(million)	μ	(micro)	$= 10^{-6}$	(millionth)
k	(kilo)	$= 10^3$	(thousand)	n	(nano)	$= 10^{-9}$	(US billionth)
h	(hecto)	$= 100$		p	(pico)	$= 10^{-12}$	(billionth)
da	(deca)	$= 10$		f	(femto)	$= 10^{-15}$	(US trillionth)
d	(deci)	$= 1/10$	(tenth)	a	(atto)	$= 10^{-18}$	(trillionth)

no more than one prefix can be used at the same time

(2) **Decimal multipliers**

area	$1\,m \times 1\,m = 1\,m^2$
velocity	$1\,m \times 1\,s^{-1} = 1\,ms^{-1} = 1\,m/s$
acceleration	$1\,m \times 1\,s^{-2} = 1\,ms^{-2} = 1\,m/s^2$
force	$1\,kg \times 1\,m \times 1\,s^{-2} = 1\,kg\,ms^{-2} = 1\,kg\,m/s^2$
density	$1\,kg \times 1\,m^{-3} = 1\,kg\,m^{-3} = 1\,kg/m^3$

(3) **Examples of deriving SI units**

quantity	unit (symbol)	dimensions (M = mass, L = length, T = time)	relationships
area A	m^2	L^2	–
volume V	m^3	L^3	–
density ρ	kgm^{-3}	ML^{-3}	–
velocity v	ms^{-1}	LT^{-1}	–
acceleration a	ms^{-2}	LT^{-2}	–
momentum p	$kgms^{-1}$	MLT^{-1}	–
moment of inertia I,J	kgm^2	ML^2	–
angular momentum L	kgm^2s^{-1}	ML^2T^{-1}	–
force F	newton (N)	MLT^{-2}	$1\,N = 1\,kgm/s^2$
energy, work E, W	joule (J)	ML^2T^{-2}	$1\,J = 1\,Nm = 1\,Ws$ $1\,kcal = 4186\,J$, $1\,kWh = 3.6\,MJ$
power P	watt (W)	ML^2T^{-3}	$1\,W = 1\,J/s$
pressure, stress p, σ	pascal (Pa)	$ML^{-1}T^{-2}$	$1\,Pa = 1\,N/m^2$
			$1\,bar = 10^5\,Pa$
surface tension γ	Nm^{-1}	$ML^{-1}T^{-2}$	–
viscosity η	$kgm^{-1}s^{-1}$	$ML^{-1}T^{-1}$	–

(4) **Summary of main derived SI units**

symbol	name (unit)	meaning and relationships
I	ampere (A)	current
V	volt (V)	potential difference: $1\,V = 1\,W/A$
R	ohm (Ω)	resistance: $1\,\Omega = 1\,V/A$
Q	coulomb (C)	charge: $1\,C = 1\,As$
P	watt (W)	power
G	siemens (S)	conductance: $1\,S = 1/\Omega$
F	farad (F)	capacitance: $1\,F = 1\,As/V$
H	henry (H)	inductance: $1\,H = 1\,Vs/A$
Φ	weber (Wb)	magnetic flux: $1\,Wb = 1\,Vs$
B	tesla (T)	magnetic flux density: $1\,T = 1\,Wb/m^2$

(5) **Symbols and units: electromagnetism**

symbol	(unit)	meaning
t	(°C, K)	temperature (note: intervals in Celsius and kelvin are identical)
Δt	(K)	temperature differential
q	(J)	quantity of heat (also measured in kilowatt hours (kWh))
λ	(W/mK)	thermal conductivity (k-value)
λ'	(W/mK)	equivalent thermal conductivity
Λ	(W/m²K)	coefficient of thermal conductance (C-value)
α	(W/m²K)	coefficient of heat transfer (U-value)
k	(W/m²K)	coefficient of heat penetration
$1/\Lambda$	(m²K/W)	value of thermal insulation
$1/\alpha$	(m²K/W)	heat transfer resistance (R-value)
$1/k$	(m²K/W)	heat penetration resistance
D'	(m²K/W cm)	coefficient of heat resistance
c	(Wh/kgK)	specific heat value
S	(Wh/m³K)	coefficient of heat storage
ß	(1/K)	coefficient of linear expansion
P	(Pa)	pressure
P_o	(Pa)	vapour pressure
g_o	(g)	quantity of steam
g_k	(g)	quantity of condensed water
ν	(%)	relative atmospheric humidity
μ	(–)	coefficient of diffusion resistance
$\mu \cdot d$	(cm)	equivalent atmospheric layer thickness
Λ_o	(g/m²hPa)	coefficient of water vapour penetration
$1/\Lambda_o$	(m²hPa/g)	resistance to water vapour penetration
$\mu\lambda$	(W/mK)	layer factor
$\mu\lambda'$	(W/mK)	layer factor of atmospheric strata
P	(£,$/kWh)	heating cost

(6) **Symbols and units: heat and moisture**

symbol	(unit)	meaning
λ	(m)	wavelength
f	(Hz)	frequency
f_{gr}	(Hz)	limiting frequency
f_η	(Hz)	frequency resonance
E_{dva}	(N/cm²)	dynamic modulus of elasticity
S'	(N/cm³)	dynamic stiffness
R	(dB)	measurement of airborn noise reduction
R_m	(dB)	average measurement of noise reduction
R'	(dB)	measurement of airborn noise suppression in a building
L_n	(dB)	impact noise level standard
a	(–)	degree of sound absorption
A	(m²)	equivalent noise absorption area
r	(m)	radius of reverberation
ΔL	(dB)	noise level reduction

(7) **Symbols and units: sound**

UNITS AND SYMBOLS

quantity	symbol	SI unit name	SI unit symbols	statutory unit name	statutory unit symbols	old unit name	old unit symbols	relationships
normal angle	α, β, γ	radian	rad					1 rad = 57.296° = 63.662 gon
				perigon	pla			1 pla = 2π rad
						right angle	L	1^L = 1/4 pla = (π/2) rad
				degree	°	old degrees		1° = 1^L/90 = 1 pla/360 = (π/180) rad
				minute	′			1′ = 1°/60
				second	″			1″ = 1′/60 = 1°/3600
				gon	gon	new degrees	g	1 gon = 1 g = 1^L/100 = 1 pla/400 = π/200 rad
						new minute	a	1 c = 10^{-2} gon
						new second	cc	1 cc = 10^{-2}) c = 10^{-4} gon
length	l	metre	m	micron	μm	inch	in	1 in = 25.4 mm
				millimetre	mm	foot	ft	1 ft = 30.48 cm
				centimetre	cm	fathom	fathom	1 fathom = 1.8288 m
				decimetre	dm	mile	mil	1 mil = 1.609 km
				kilometre	km	nautical mile	sm	1 sm = 1.852 km
area: cross-section of land plots	A	square metre	m^2					square foot (= 0.092 m^2); acre (0.405 ha) still in use
				are	a			1 a = 10^2 m
				hectare	ha			1 ha = 10^4 m
volume	V	cubic metre	m^3	litre	l			1 l = 1 dm^3 = 10^{-3} m^3
normal volume						normal cubic metre	Nm^3	1 Nm^3 = 1 m^3 in norm condition
						cubic metre	cbm	cbm = 1 m^3
time, time span, duration	t	second	s	minute	min			1 min = 60 s
				hour	h			1 h = 60 min = 3600 s
				day	d			1 d = 24 h = 86400 s
				year	a, y			1 a = 1 y = 8765.8 h = 3.1557×10^7 s
frequency reciprocal of duration	f	hertz	Hz					1 Hz = 1/s for expressing frequencies in dimensional equations
angular frequency	ω	reciprocal second	1/s					ω = 2 × f
angular velocity	ω	radians per second	rad/s					ω = 2 × n
no. of revs, speed of revolutions	n	reciprocal second	1/s	revs per second	r/s	revs per second	r.p.s.	1/s = t/s = r/s
				revs per minute	r/min	revs per minute	r.p.m.	
velocity	v	metres per second	m/s	kilometres per hour	km/h			1 m/s = 3.6 km/h
						knots	kn	1 kn = 1 sm/h = 1.852 km/h
acceleration due to gravity	g	metres per second per second	m/s^2			gal	gal	1 gal = 1 cm/s^2 = 10^{-2} m/s^2
mass: weight (as a result of weighing)	m	kilogram	kg	gram	g			1 g = 10^{-3} kg
				tonne	t			1 t = 1 Mg = 10^3 kg
						pound	lb	1 lb = 0.45359237 kg
						metric pound		1 metric pound = 0.5 kg
						ton	ton	1 ton = 2240 lb = 1016 kg
force thrust	F, G	newton	N					1 N = 1 kg m/s^2 = 1 Ws/m = 1 J/m
						dyn	dyn	1 dyn = 1 g cm/s^2 = 10^{-5} N
						pond	p	1 p = 9.80665 × 10^{-3} N
						kilopond	kp	
						megapond	Mp	
						kilogram force	kg/f	
						tonne force	t/f	
stress strength	σ	newtons per square metre	N/m^2	newtons per square millimetre	N/mm^2	kiloponds per square cm/mm	kp/cm^2 kp/mm^2	1 kp/cm^2 = 0.0980665 N/mm^2 1 kp/mm^2 = 9.80665 N/mm^2
energy	W, E	joule	J					1 J = 1 Nm = 1 Ws = 10^7 erg
				kilowatt hour	kWh			1 kWh = 3.6 × 10^6 J = 3.6 MJ
						h.p. per hour	h.p./h	1 h.p./h = 2.64780 × 10^6 J
						erg	erg	1 erg = 10^{-7} J
quantity of heat	Q	joule	J			calorie	cal	1 cal = 4.1868 J = 1.163 × 10^{-3} Wh
torque bending moment	M, M_b	newton metre or joule	Nm J			kilopond metre	kpm	1 kpm = 9.80665 J
power energy current	P	watt	W					1 W = 1 J/s = 1 Nm/s = 1 kg m^2/s^3
						horsepower	h.p.	1 h.p. = 745.7 kW
thermodynamic temperature	T	kelvin	K			deg. kelvin	°K	
						deg. Rankine	°R, °Rk	°R = ^{5}/9 K
Celsius temp.	θ			degrees Celsius	°C			θ = T − T$_o$ (T$_o$ = 273.15 K)
temperature interval and differential	ΔT or θΔ		K					Δθ = ΔT, therefore 1 K = 1°C = 1 deg.
Fahrenheit temperature	θ$_F$					deg. Fahrenheit	°F	θ$_F$ = ^{9}/5 θ + 32 = ^{9}/5 T − 459.67
Réaumur temp.	θ$_R$					deg. Réaumur	°R	θ$_R$ = ^{4}/5 θ, 1°R ^{5}/4°C

(1) **SI and statutory units for the construction industry**

Mathematical symbols

>	greater than
≥	greater than or equal to
<	smaller than
≤	smaller than or equal to
Σ	sum of
∠	angle
sin	sine
cos	cosine
tan	tangent
cotan	cotangent
‖	on average
=	equals
≡	identically equal
≠	not equals
≈	roughly equals, about
•	congruent
~	asymptotically equal (similar) to
∞	infinity
‖	parallel
#	equal and parallel
⧣	not identically equal to
×	multiplied by
/	divided by
⊥	perpendicular
V	volume, content
ω	solid angle
√	root of
Δ	final increment
≡	congruent
△	triangle
↑↑	same direction, parallel
↓↓	opposite direction, parallel

Greek alphabet

A α	(a) alpha
B β	(b) beta
Γ γ	(g) gamma
Δ δ	(d) delta
E ε	(e) epsilon
Z ζ	(z) zeta
H η	(e) eta
Θ θ	(th) theta
I ι	(i) iota
K κ	(k) kappa
Λ λ	(l) lambda
M μ	(m) mu
N ν	(n) nu
Ξ ξ	(x) xi
O o	(o) omicron
Π π	(p) pi
P ρ	(r) rho
Σ σ	(s) sigma
T τ	(t) tau
Y υ	(u) upsilon
Φ φ	(ph) phi
Ξ χ	(ch) chi
Ψ ψ	(ps) psi
Ω ω	(o) omega

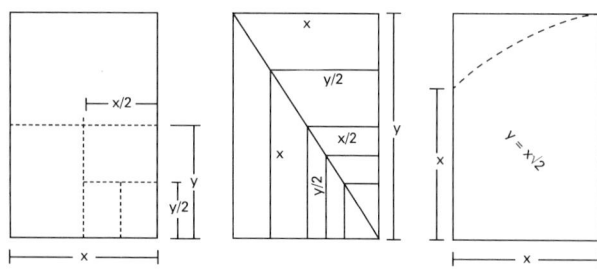

(1) – (3) **Basis of paper formats**

format	A series	B series	C series
0	841 × 1189	1000 × 1414	917 × 1297
1	594 × 841	707 × 1000	648 × 917
2	420 × 594	500 × 707	458 × 648
3	297 × 420	353 × 500	324 × 458
4	210 × 297	250 × 353	229 × 324
5	148 × 210	176 × 250	162 × 229
6	105 × 148	125 × 176	114 × 162
7	74 × 105	88 × 125	81 × 141
8	52 × 74	62 × 88	57 × 81
9	37 × 52	44 × 62	
10	26 × 37	31 × 44	
11	18 × 26	22 × 31	
12	13 × 18	15 × 22	

(4) **Sheet sizes**

format	abbre-viation	mm
half length A4	1/2 A4	105 × 297
quarter length A4	1/4 A4	52 × 297
one eighth A7	1/8 A7	9 × 105
half length C4	1/2 C4	114 × 324
etc.		

(5) **Strip formats**

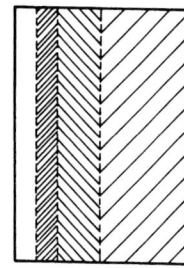

1/8 1/8 1/4 1/2 A4

A4

(6) **Format strips in A4**

(7) **Loose-leaf binder**

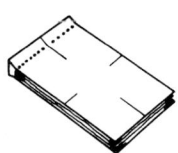

(8) **Pads (including carbonless)**

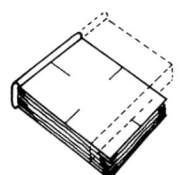

(9) **Bound and trimmed books**   (10) → (11)

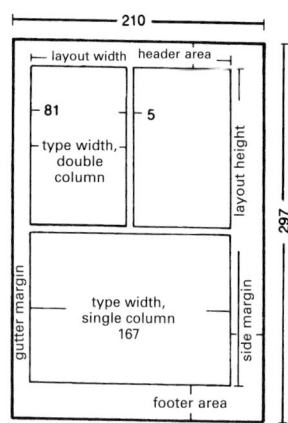

DOCUMENTATION AND DRAWINGS

The format of documentation (whether in the form of plans, reports, letters, envelopes etc.) has, apart from in the USA, generally been standardised to conform to the internationally accepted (ISO) series of paper sheet sizes in the 'A', 'B', 'C' and 'D' ranges. These standard paper formats are derived from a rectangular sheet with an area of $1\,m^2$. Using the 'golden square', the lengths of the sides are chosen as $x = 0.841\,m$ and $y = 1.189\,m$ such that:

$$x \times y = 1$$
$$x{:}y = 1{:}\sqrt{2}$$

This forms the basis for the A series. Maintaining the same ratio of length to width, the sheet sizes are worked out by progressively halving (or, the other way round, doubling) the sheet area, as would happen if the rectangular sheet was repeatedly folded exactly in half → (1) – (3).

Additional ranges (B, C, and D) are provided for the associated products that require larger paper sizes, i.e. posters, envelopes, loose-leaf file binders, folders etc. The formats of range B are designed for posters and wall-charts. The formats in ranges C and D are the geometric mean dimensions of ranges A and B and are used to manufacture the envelopes and folders to take the A sizes. → (4) The extra size needed for loose-leaf binders, folders and box files will depend on the size and type of clamping device employed.

The strip or side margin formats are formed by halves, quarters, and eighths of the main formats (for envelopes, signs, drawings etc.) → (5) + (6).

Pads and duplicate books using carbonless paper also have standard formats but may have a perforated edge or border, which means the resulting pages will be a corresponding amount smaller than the standard sheet size → (8).

During book-binding, a further trim is usually necessary, giving pages somewhat smaller than the standard format size. However, commercial printers use paper supplied in the RA or SRA sizes and this has an allowance for trimming, which allows the final page sizes to match the standard formats.

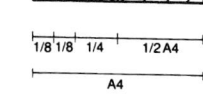

	picas		mm	
type area width	39.5	40.5	167	171
type area, height (without header/footer)	58.5	59	247	250
space between columns	1		5	
max. width, single column	39.5		167	
max. width, double column	19		81	
inside (gutter) margin, nominal			16	14
outer (side) margin, nominal			27	25
top (head) margin, nominal			20	19
bottom (foot) margin, nominal			30	28

(11) **Layouts and type area with A4 standard format**

DOCUMENTATION AND DRAWINGS

The use of standard drawing formats makes it easier for architects to lay out drawings for discussion in the design office or on the building site, and also facilitates posting and filing. The trimmed, original drawing or print must therefore conform to the formats of the ISO A series. → ③ – ⑥

The box for written details should be the following distance from the edge of the drawing:

for formats A0–A3	10 mm
for formats A4–A6	5 mm

For small drawings, a filing margin of up to 25 mm can be used, with the result that the usable area of the finished format will be smaller.

As an exception, narrow formats can be arrived at by stringing together a row of identical or adjacent formats out of the format range.

From normal roll widths, the following sizes can be used to give formats in the A series:

for drawing paper, tracing paper	1500, 1560 mm
(derived from this	250, 1250, 660, 900 mm)
for print paper	650, 900, 1200 mm

If all the drawing formats up to A0 are to be cut from a paper web, a roll width of at least 900 mm will be necessary.

Drawings which are to be stored in A4 box files should be folded as follows: → ⑧

(1) The writing box must always be uppermost, in the correct place and clearly visible.

(2) On starting to fold, the width of 210 mm (fold 1) must always be maintained, and it is useful to use a 210 × 297 mm template.

(3) Fold 2 is a triangular fold started 297 mm up from the bottom left-hand corner, so that on the completely folded drawing only the left bottom field, indicated with a cross, will be punched or clamped.

(4) The drawing is next folded back parallel to side 'a' using a 185 × 298 mm template. Any remaining area is concertina-folded so as to even out the sheet size and this leaves the writing box on the top surface. If it is not possible to have even folds throughout, the final fold should simply halve the area left (e.g. A1 fold 5, A0 fold 7). Any longer standard formats can be folded in a similar way.

(5) The resulting strip should be folded from side 'b' to give a final size of 210 × 297 mm.

To reinforce holes and filing edges, a piece of A5 size cardboard (148 × 210 mm) can be glued to the back of the punched part of the drawing.

① **Standard drawing**

uncut drawing sheet, depending on requirement, is 2–3 cm wider than final trimmed original drawing and print

box for written details and parts list

sheet sizes in acc. with ISO A series	ISO A0	ISO A1	ISO A2	ISO A3	ISO A4	ISO A5
uncut blank paper (mm)	880×1230	625×880	450×625	330×450	240×330	165×240
format trimmed, finished sheet (mm)	841×1189	594×841	420×594	297×420	210×297	148×210

② **Sheet sizes**

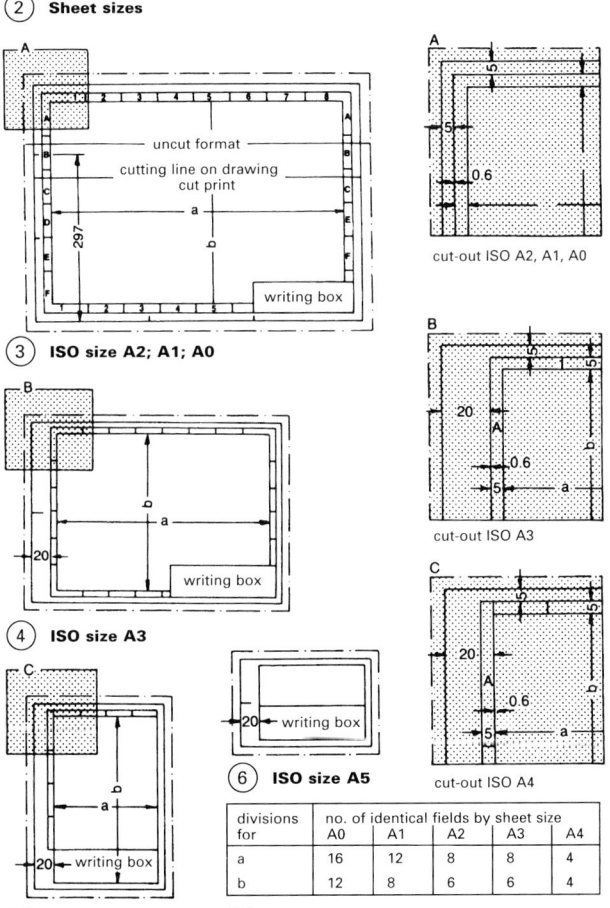

③ **ISO size A2; A1; A0**

④ **ISO size A3**

⑤ **ISO size A4**

⑥ **ISO size A5**

cut-out ISO A2, A1, A0

cut-out ISO A3

cut-out ISO A4

divisions for	no. of identical fields by sheet size				
	A0	A1	A2	A3	A4
a	16	12	8	8	4
b	12	8	6	6	4

⑦ **Field divisions (grid squares)**

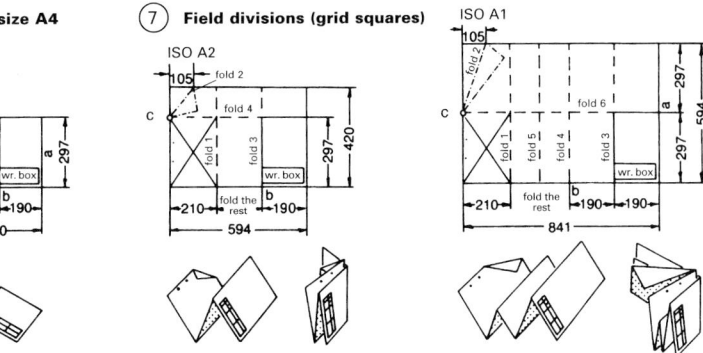

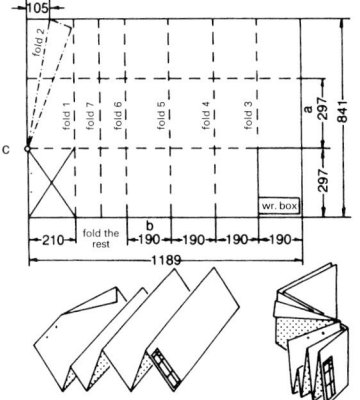

⑧ **Dimensions and scheme for folding**

5

DOCUMENTATION AND DRAWINGS

Arrangement

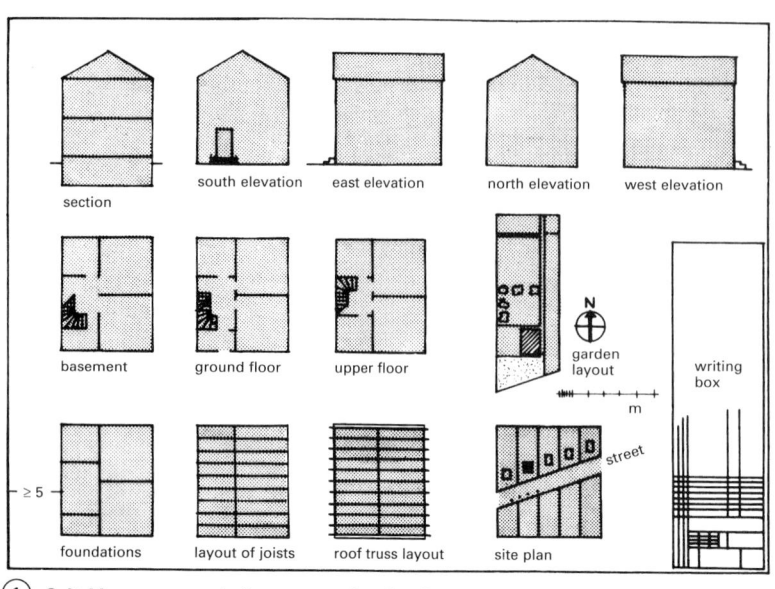

(1) **Suitable arrangement of a construction drawing**

(2) **Suitable arrangement of scale details**

Leave a 5cm wide blank strip down the left-hand edge of the sheet for binding or stapling. The writing box on the extreme right → ① should contain the following details:

(1) type of drawing (sketch, preliminary design, design etc.)
(2) type of view or the part of the building illustrated (layout drawing, plan view, section, elevation, etc.)
(3) scale
(4) dimensions, if necessary.

On drawings used for statutory approvals (and those used by supervisors during construction) it might also contain:

(1) the client's name (and signature)
(2) the building supervisor's name (and signature)
(3) the main contractor's signature
(4) the building supervisor's comments about inspection and the building permit (if necessary on the back of the sheet).

A north-point must be shown on the drawings for site layouts, plan views etc.

Scales

The main scale of the drawing must be given in large type in the box for written details. Other scales must be in smaller type and these scales must be repeated next to their respective diagrams. All objects should be drawn to scale; where the drawing is not to scale the dimensions must be underlined. As far as possible, use the following scales:

for construction drawings: 1:1, 1:2.5, 1:5, 1:10, 1:20, 1:25, 1:50, 1:100, 1:200, 1:250
for site layouts: 1:500, 1:1000, 1:2000, 1:2500, 1:5000, 1:10 000, 1:25 000.

Measurement Figures and Other Inscriptions

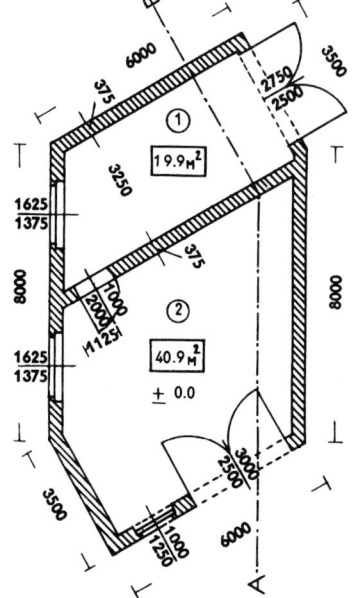

(3) **Standard method of dimensioning an oddly shaped plan (measurements given are structural dimensions)**

In continental Europe, for structural engineering and architectural drawings, dimensions under 1 m are generally given in cm and those above 1 m in m. However, recently the trend has been to give all dimensions in mm, and this is standard practice in the UK.

Chimney stack flues, pressurised gas pipes and air ducts are shown with their internal dimensions as a fraction (width over length) and, assuming they are circular, by the use of the symbol Ø for diameter.

Squared timber is also shown as a fraction written as width over height.

The rise of stairs is shown along the course of the centre-line, with the tread depth given underneath (→ p. 13).

Window and door opening dimensions are shown, as with stairs, along the central axis. The width is shown above, and the internal height below, the line (→ p. 13).

Details of floor heights and other heights are measured from the finished floor level of the ground floor (FFL: zero height ±0.00).

Room numbers are written inside a circle and surface area details, in m², are displayed in a square or a rectangle → ③.

Section lines in plan views are drawn in chain dot lines and are labelled with capital letters, usually in alphabetical order, to indicate where the section cuts through the building. As well as standard dimensional arrows → ⑤ oblique arrows and extent marks → ⑥ + ⑦ are commonly used. The position of the dimensional figures must be such that the viewer, standing in front of the drawing, can read the dimensions as easily as possible, without having to turn the drawing round, and they must be printed in the same direction as the dimension lines.

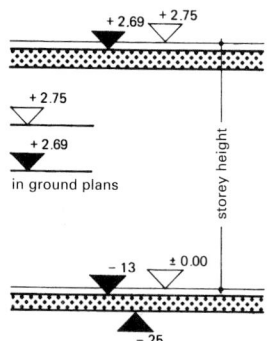

(4) **Heights as shown in sections and elevations**

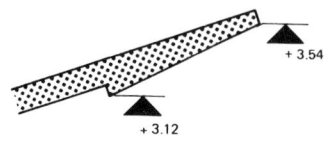

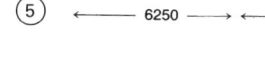

(5) ←——— 6250 ——→ ←

(6) ⊬——— 6250 ——⊬ ⊬

(7) ⊦ 6250 / 5250 ⊦

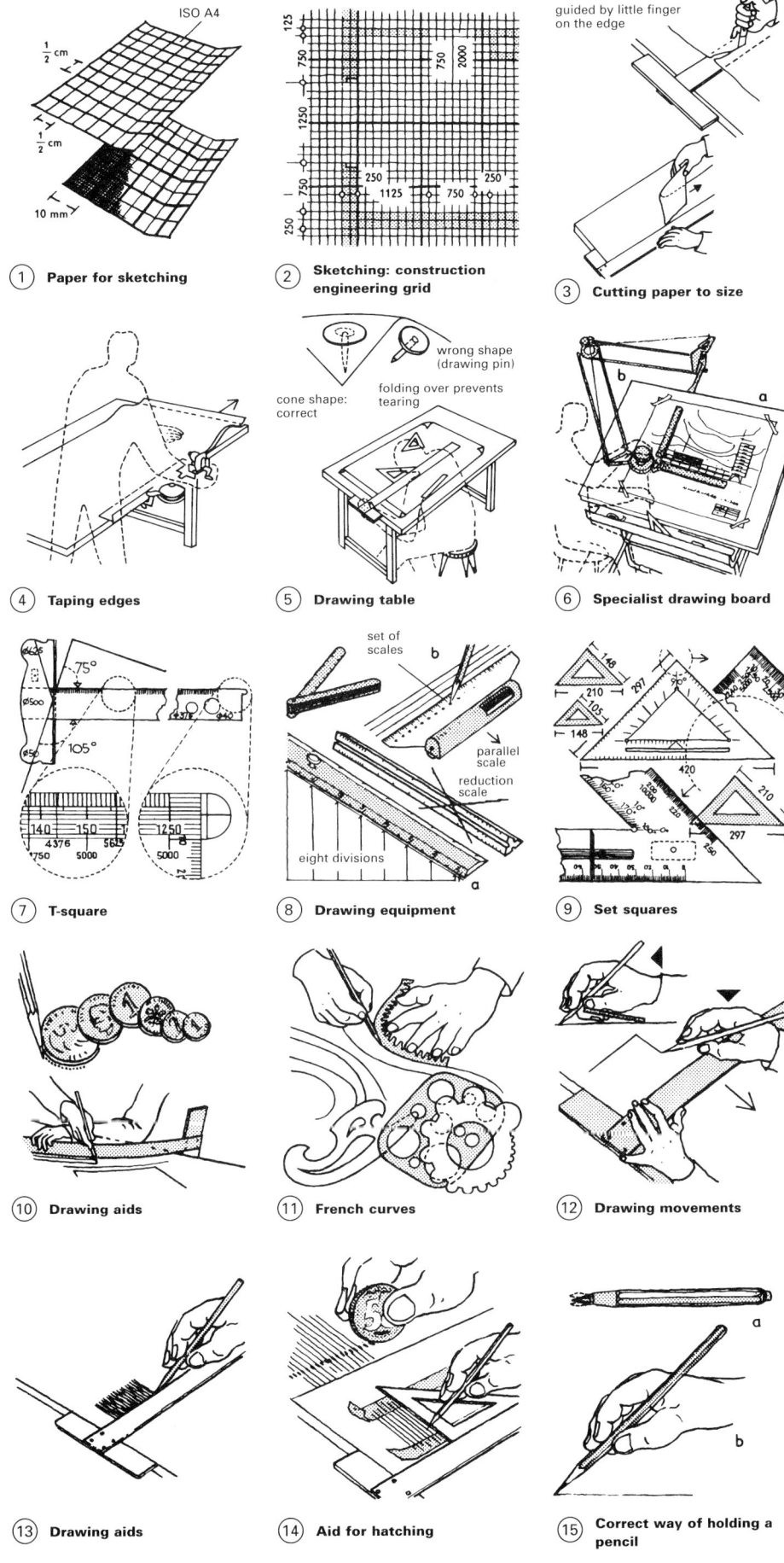

(1) **Paper for sketching**

(2) **Sketching: construction engineering grid**

(3) **Cutting paper to size** — guided by little finger on the edge

(4) **Taping edges**

(5) **Drawing table** — wrong shape (drawing pin); cone shape: correct; folding over prevents tearing

(6) **Specialist drawing board**

(7) **T-square**

(8) **Drawing equipment** — set of scales; parallel scale; reduction scale; eight divisions

(9) **Set squares**

(10) **Drawing aids**

(11) **French curves**

(12) **Drawing movements**

(13) **Drawing aids**

(14) **Aid for hatching**

(15) **Correct way of holding a pencil**

Designers use drawings and illustrations to communicate information in a factual, unambiguous and geometric form that can be understood anywhere in the world. With good drawing skills it is simpler for designers to explain their proposals and also give clients a convincing picture of how the finished project will look. Unlike painting, construction drawing is a means to an end and this differentiates diagrams/working drawings and illustrations from artistic works.

Sketch pads with graph paper having 0.5 cm squares are ideal for freehand sketches to scale → (1). For more accurate sketches, millimetre graph paper should be used. This has thick rules for centimetre divisions, thinner rules for half centimetres and fine rules for the millimetre divisions. Different paper is used for drawing and sketching according to standard modular coordinated construction and engineering grids → (2). Use tracing paper for sketching with a soft lead pencil.

Suitable sheet sizes for drawings can be cut straight from a roll, single pages being torn off using a T-square or cut on the underside of the T-square → (3). Construction drawings are done in hard pencil or ink on clear, tear-resistant tracing paper, bordered with protected edges → (4) and stored in drawers or hung in vertical plan chests.

Fix the paper on a simple drawing board (designed for standard formats), made of limewood or poplar, using drawing pins with conical points → (5). First turn over 2 cm width of the drawing paper edge, which can later be used as the filing edge (see p. 4), for this lifts the T-square a little during drawing and prevents the drawing being smudged by the T-square itself. (For the same reason, draw from top to bottom.) The drawing can be fixed with drafting tape rather than tacks → (6) if a plastic underlay backing is used.

The T-square has traditionally been the basic tool of the designer, with special T-squares used to draw lines at varying angles. They are provided with octameter and centimetre divisions → (7). In general, however, the T-square has been replaced by parallel motion rulers mounted on the drawing board → (6). Other drawing aids include different measuring scales → (8), 45° set squares with millimetre and degree divisions, drawing aids for curves → (10), and French curves → (11).

CONSTRUCTION DRAWINGS

To maintain accuracy in construction drawings requires practice. For instance, it is essential to hold the T-square properly and use pencils and pens in the correct manner. Another important factor in eliminating inaccuracy is keeping a sharp pencil point. There are various drawing aids that can help: grip pencils, for example, are suitable for leads with diameters of 2mm or more and propelling pencils are useful for thinner leads. Lead hardnesses from 6B to 9H are available. Many models of drafting pens are available, both refillable and disposable, and offer a wide range of line thicknesses. For rubbing out ink use mechanical erasers, erasing knives or razor blades whereas non-smear rubbers should be used for erasing pencil. For drawings with tightly packed lines use eraser templates → ①.

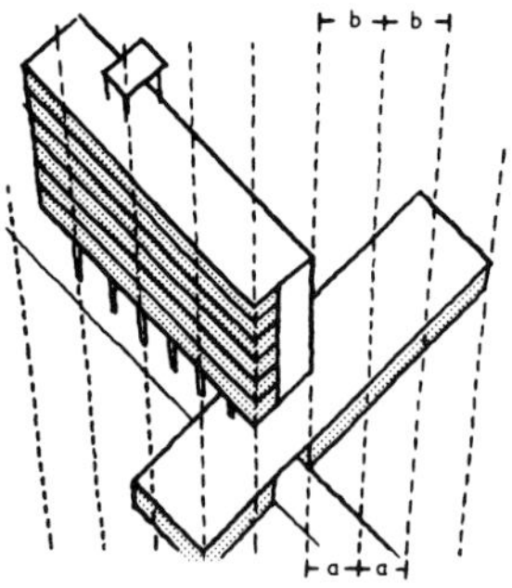

Write text preferably without aids. On technical drawings use lettering stencils, writing either with drafting pens or using a stipple brush → ②. Transfer lettering (Letraset etc.) is also commonly used. The international standard for lettering ISO 3098/1.

To make the designer's intentions clear, diagrams should be drawn to convincingly portray the finished building. Isometry can be used to replace a bird's eye view if drawn to the scale of ≤1:500 → ⑬ and perspective grids at standard angles are suitable for showing internal views → ⑯.

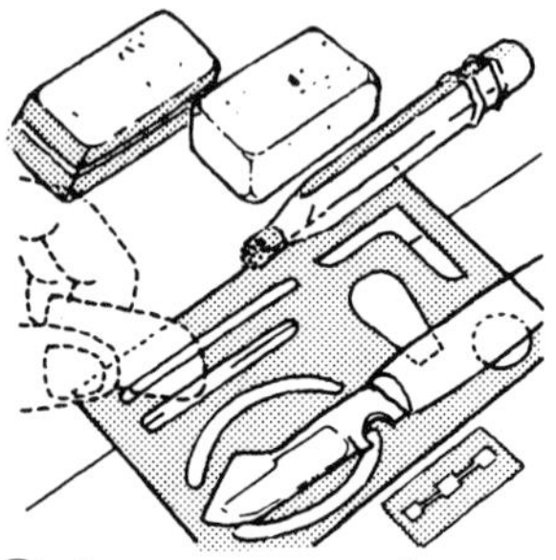

① Erasers, eraser template, eraser blades, etc.

② Lettering stencils

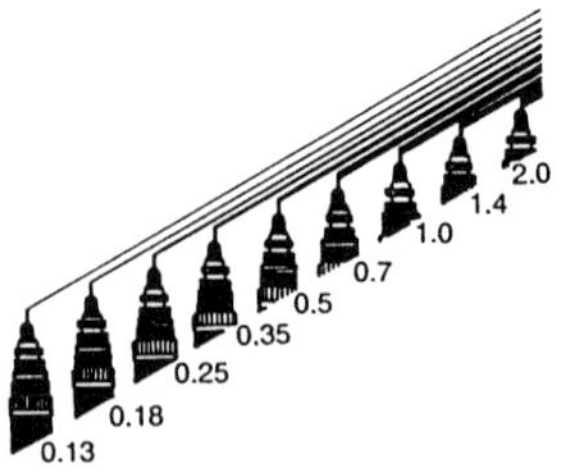

③ Drafting pens

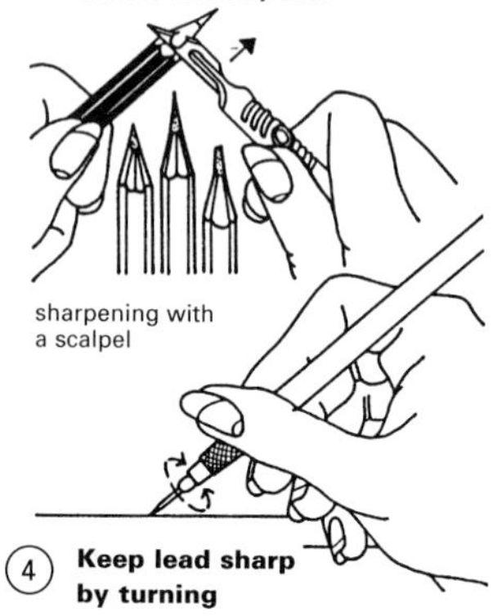

2.0
1.4
1.0
0.7
0.5
0.35
0.25
0.18
0.13

sharpening with a scalpel

④ Keep lead sharp by turning

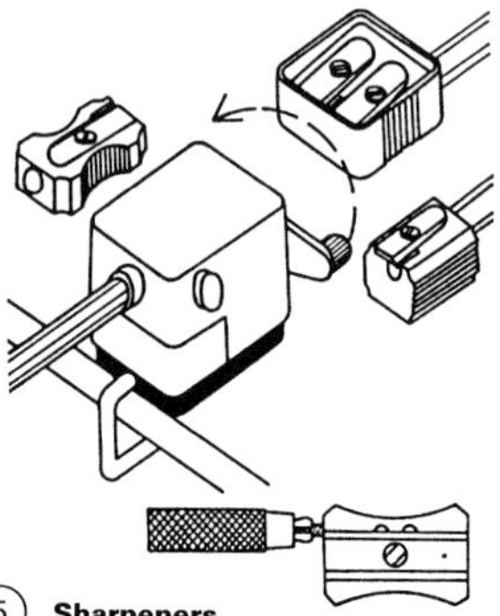

⑤ Sharpeners

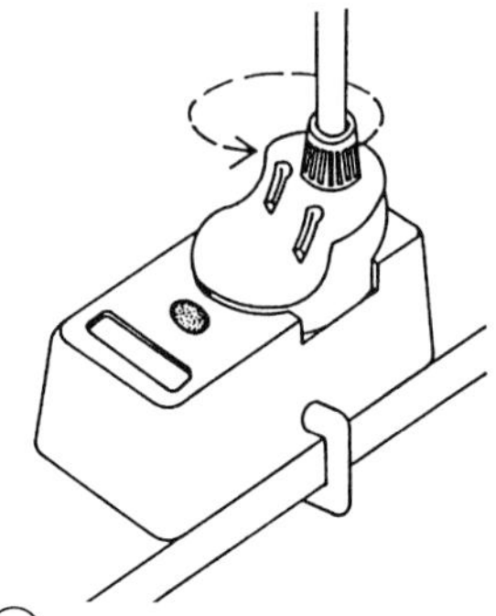

⑥ Rotary pencil sharpener

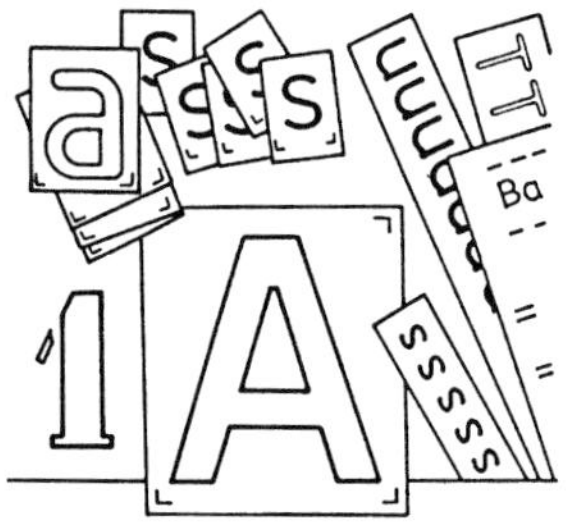

⑦ Self-adhesive or Letraset lettering

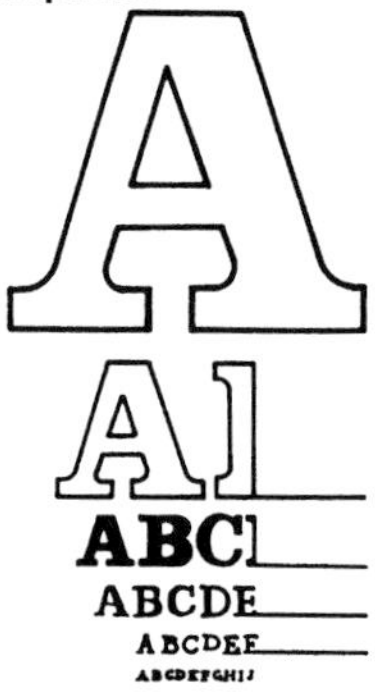

⑧ Lettering sizes measured in points

⑨ Typewriter for lettering

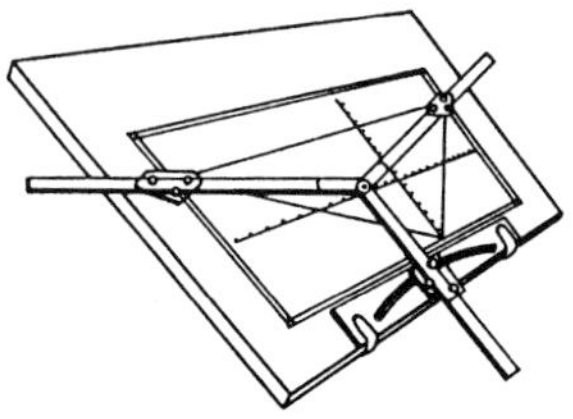

⑩ Three-armed drawing instrument

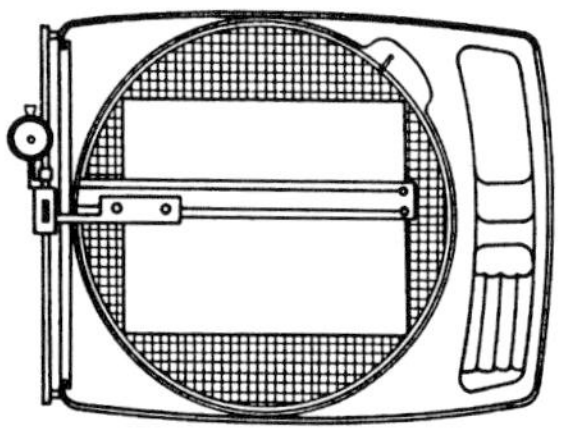

⑪ Circular drawing board for perspective drawing

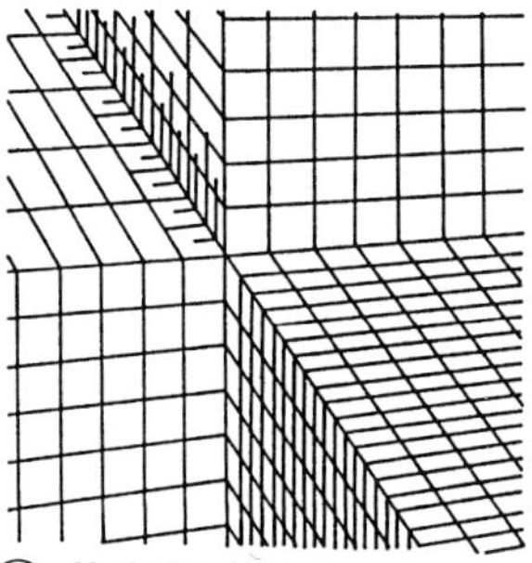

⑫ Underlay for perspective drawing

⑬ Isometry

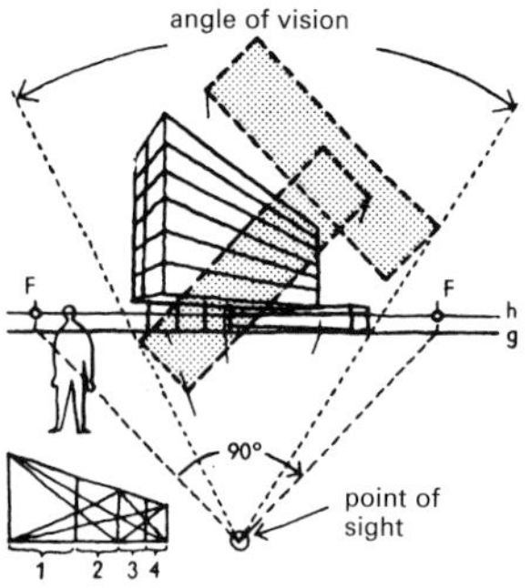

b + b
a + a

angle of vision

F   F
h
g

90°

point of sight

1 2 3 4

⑭ Perspective method

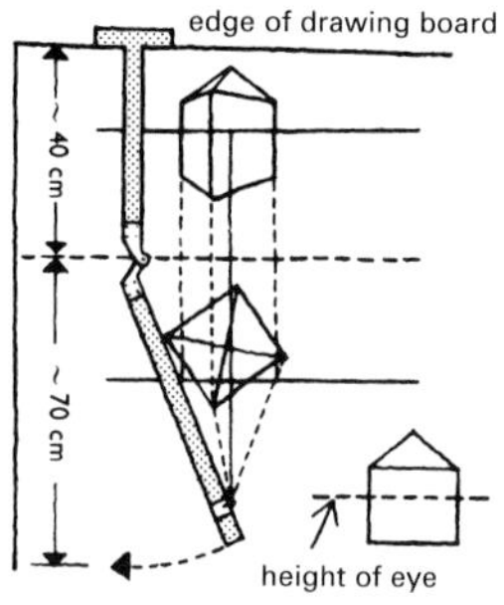

edge of drawing board

40 cm

70 cm

height of eye

⑮ Reilesch's perspective apparatus

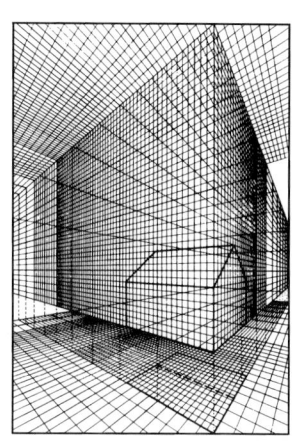

⑯ Perspective grid

line types (weight)	primary application	scale of drawings		
		1:1 1:5 1:10	1:20 1:25 1:50	1:100 1:200
		line thickness (mm)		
solid line (heavy)	boundaries of buildings in section	1.0	0.7	0.5
solid line (medium)	visible edges of components; boundaries of narrow or smaller areas of building parts in section	0.5	0.35	0.35
solid line (fine)	dimension guide lines; dimension lines; grid lines	0.25	0.25	0.25
	indication lines to notes; working lines	0.35	0.25**)	0.25
dashed line*) (medium)	hidden edges of building parts	0.5	0.35	0.35
chain dot line (heavy)	indication of section planes	1.0	0.7	0.5
chain dot line (medium)	axes	0.35	0.35	0.35
dotted line*) (fine)	parts lying behind the observer	0.35	0.35	0.35

*) dashed line – – – – – dashes longer than the distance between them
dotted line .... dots (or dashes) shorter than the distance between them
**) 0.35 mm if reduction from 1:50 to 1:100 is necessary

note: for plotter drawings using electronic data processing equipment and drawings destined for microfilm, other combinations of line widths may be necessary

(1) **Types and thicknesses of lines to be used in construction drawings**

In some European countries the measurement unit used in connection with the scale must be given in the written notes box (e.g. 1:50 cm). In the UK, dimensions are given only either in metres or millimetres so no indication of units is required. Where metres are used it is preferable to specify the dimension to three decimal places (e.g. 3.450) to avoid all ambiguity.

		1	2	3	4
unit		dimensions			
		under 1 m e.g.			over 1 m e.g.
1	m	0.05	0.24	0.88	3.76
2	cm	5	24	88.5	376
3	m, cm	5	24	88^5	3.76
4	mm	50	240	885	3760

(5) **Units of measurement**

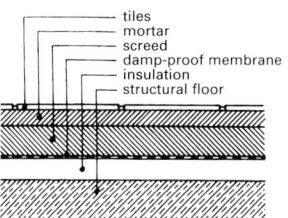

tiles
mortar
screed
damp-proof membrane
insulation
structural floor

(6) **Indication lines to notes**

dimension figure
dimension line
extension line
dimension arrow

– 3.76 –

(7) **Designation for dimensioning**

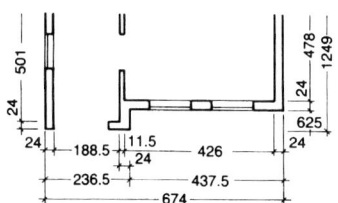

(2) **Dimensions given around the drawing**
(drawn at 1:100 cm; units = cm)

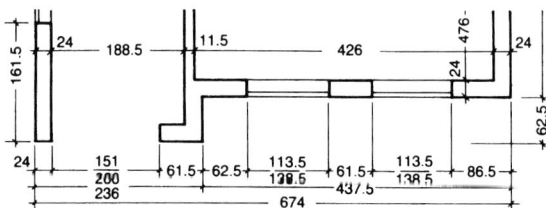

(3) **Dimensions of piers and apertures**
(drawn at 1:50 cm; units = cm)

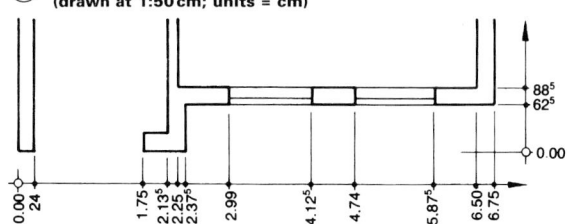

(4) **Dimensions given by coordinates**
(drawn at 1:50 cm, m; units = cm and m)

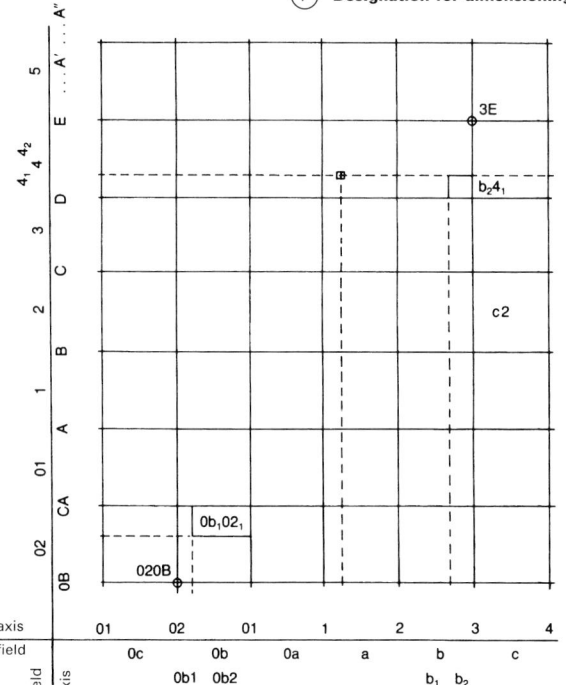

(8) **Axis-field grid**

CAD application in architectural design

The acronym CAD usually means either computer-aided design or computer-aided draughting. CADD is sometimes used to mean computer-aided draughting and design. Computer-aided design is a highly valued technique because it not only enables a substantial increase in productivity but also helps to achieve neater and clearer drawings than those produced using the conventional manual drafting techniques described in the preceding pages. Standard symbols or building elements can be compiled as a library of items, stored and used to create new designs. There is also a possibility of minimising the repetition of tasks by linking CAD data directly with other computer systems, i.e. scheduling databases, bills of quantities etc.

Another advantage of CAD is that it minimises the need for storage space: electronic storage and retrieval of graphic and data features clearly requires a fraction of the space needed for a paper-based system. Drawings currently being worked on may be stored in the CAD program memory whereas finished design drawings that are not immediately required may be archived in high-capacity electronic storage media, such as magnetic tapes or compact disks.

A drawback relating to the sophisticated technology required for professional CAD has been the high expense of the software packages, many of which would only be run on large, costly computer systems. However, various cheap, though still relatively powerful, packages are now available and these will run on a wide range of low-cost personal computers.

CAD software

A CAD software package consists of the CAD program, which contains the program files and accessories such as help files and interfaces with other programs, and an extensive reference manual. In the past, the program files were stored on either 5¼" or 3½" floppy disks. The low storage capacity of the 5¼" floppy disks and their susceptibility to damage has rendered them obsolete. Besides their higher storage density, 3½" disks are stronger and easier to handle. Nowadays, the program files are usually stored on compact discs (CD-ROM) because of their high capacity and the ever increasing size of programs; they are even capable of storing several programs.

When installing a CAD program onto the computer system, the program files must be copied onto the hard disk of the computer. In the past, CAD was run on microcomputers using the MS-DOS operating system only. New versions of the CAD programs are run using MS-DOS and/or Microsoft Windows operating systems.

Hardware requirements

Once the desired CAD software has been selected, it is important to ensure that the appropriate hardware (equipment) needed to run the program is in place. A typical computer system usually includes the following hardware:

Visual Display Unit (VDU): Also called a screen or monitor, these are now always full-colour displays. The level of resolution will dictate how clear and neat the design appears on the screen. For intricate design work it is better to use a large, high-resolution screen. The prices of such graphic screens have fallen substantially in recent years making them affordable to a wide range of businesses and they are hence becoming commonplace. In the past, using CAD required two screens, one for text and the other for graphics. This is not necessary now because some of the latest CAD programs have a 'flip screen' facility that allows the user to alternate between the graphics and text display. In addition, the Windows version of some CAD programs also has a re-sizable text display that may be viewed in parallel with the graphics display.

Disk drives and disks: The most usual combination of disk drives for desktop CAD systems initially was one hard drive and one 3½" floppy drive. The storage capacity of hard disks increased rapidly throughout the 1990s, from early 40 MB (megabyte) standard hard drives to capacities measured in gigabytes (GB) by the end of the decade. The storage capability of floppy disks is now generally far too restrictive and this has led to the universal addition of compact disc drives in new PCs. These can hold up to 650MB. This storage limitation has also led to the use of stand-alone zip drives and CD writers (or CD burners) to allow large files to be saved easily.

Keyboard: Virtually every computer is supplied with a standard alphanumeric keyboard. This is a very common input device in CAD but it has an intrinsic drawback: it is a relatively slow method of moving the cursor around the screen and selecting draughting options. For maximum flexibility and speed, therefore, the support of other input devices is required.

Mouse: The advantage of the mouse over the keyboard as an input device in CAD is in speeding up the movement of the cursor around the screen. The mouse is fitted with a button which allows point locations on the screen to be specified and commands from screen menus (and icons in the Windows system) to be selected. There are several types of mouse, but nowadays a standard CAD mouse has two buttons: one used for PICKing and the other for RETURNing.

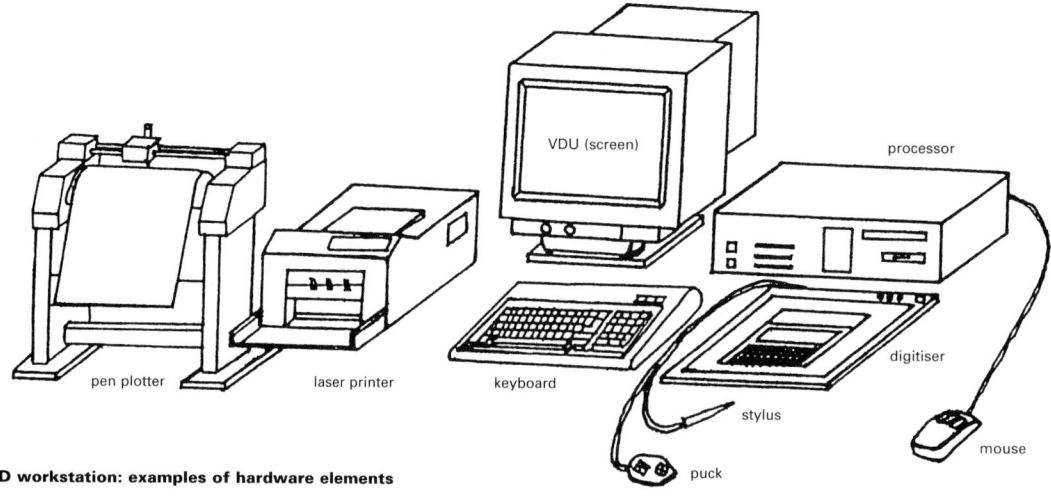

1 **CAD workstation: examples of hardware elements**

Graphic tablet, digitising tablet (digitiser): A digitiser consists of a flat plate with a clear area in the centre, representing the screen area, the rest divided into small squares providing menu options. An electric pen (stylus) or puck is used to insert points on the screen and to pick commands from menus. The selection of a command is made by touching a command square on the menu with the stylus (or puck) and at a press of a button the command is carried out. Data can be read from an overlay menu or a document map or chart. The document should first be placed on the surface of the digitiser and its boundaries marked with the stylus or puck. The position of the puck on the digitiser may be directly related to the position of the cursor on the screen.

Most pucks have four buttons: they all have a PICK button for selecting the screen cursor position and a RETURN button for completing commands but, in addition, they have two or more buttons for quick selection of frequently used commands.

Printers: Hard-copy drawings from CAD software can be produced by using an appropriately configured printer. Printers are usually simple and fast to operate, and may also be used for producing hard copies from other programs installed in the computer. There are several types of printer, principally: dot-matrix, inkjet, and laser printers. The graphic output of dot-matrix printers is not of an acceptable standard, particularly when handling lines that diverge from the horizontal or vertical axes. Inkjet and laser printers are fast and quiet and allow the production of high-quality monochrome and coloured graphic diagrams up to A3 size. Colour prints are also no longer a problem since there is now a wide range of printers that can produce high-quality colour graphic prints at a reasonably low cost.

Plotters: Unlike printers, conventional plotters draw by using small ink pens of different colours and widths. Most pen plotters have up to eight pens or more. Usually the CAD software is programmed to enable the nomination of the pen for each element in the drawing.

Flat-bed plotters hold the drawing paper tightly on a bed, and the pens move over the surface to create the desired drawing. Although they are slow, their availability in small sizes (some with a single pen, for instance) means that a good-quality output device can be installed at low cost.

Rotary (drum) plotters operate by rolling the drawing surface over a rotating cylinder, with the pens moving perpendicularly back and forth across the direction of the flow. They can achieve high plotting speeds. With large-format drafting plotters, it is possible to produce drawings on paper up to A0 size. Depending on the plotter model, cut-size sheets or continuous rolls of paper can be used.

Modern printer technology has been used to develop electrostatic plotters, inkjet plotters and laser printer/plotters. These are more efficient and reliable, and produce higher line quality than pen plotters. As well as drawing plans and line diagrams, they can also be used to create large colour plots of shaded and rendered 3D images that are close to photographic quality.

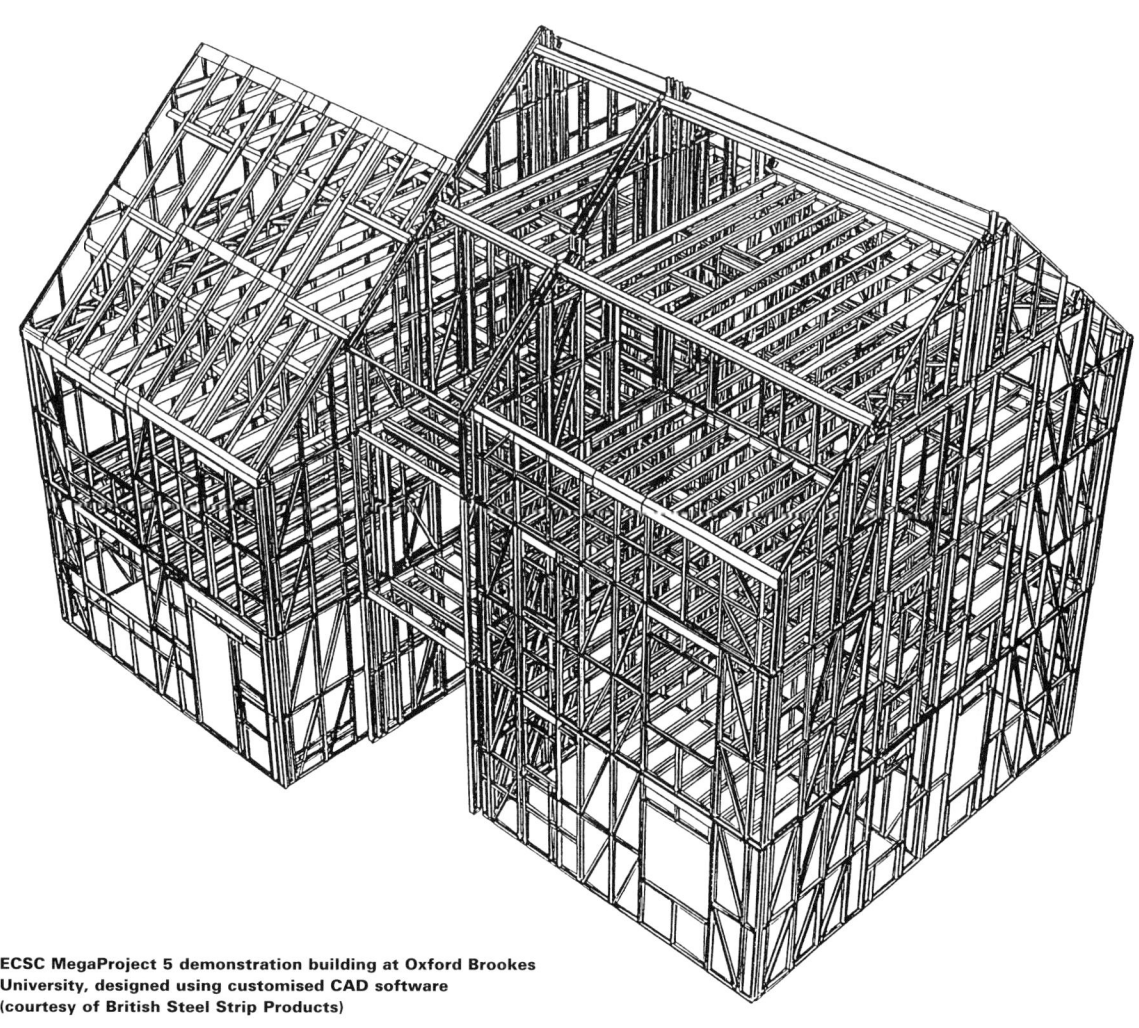

① **ECSC MegaProject 5 demonstration building at Oxford Brookes University, designed using customised CAD software (courtesy of British Steel Strip Products)**

CONSTRUCTION DRAWINGS: SYMBOLS

Living room

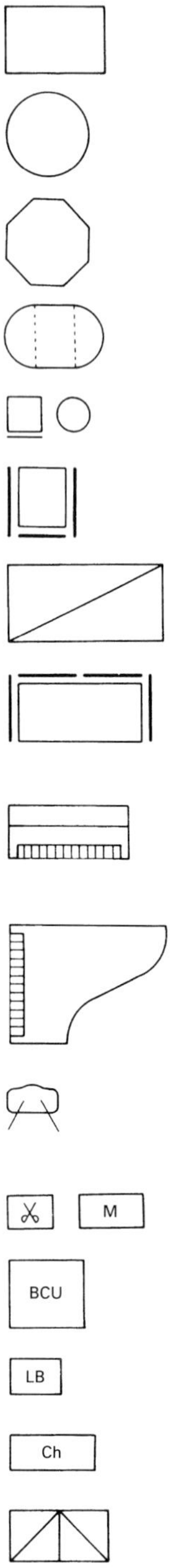

1. table 85 × 85 × 78 = 4 people / 130 × 80 × 78 = 6 people
2. round table Ø 90 = 6 people
3. shaped table 70–100
4. extending table
5. chair, stool Ø 45 × 50
6. arm chair 70 × 85
7. chaise-longue 95 × 195
8. sofa 80/1.75
9. upright piano 60/1.40–1.60
10. grand pianos baby 155 × 114 / drawing-room 200 × 150 / concert 275 × 160
11. television
12. sewing table 50/50–70 / sewing machine 50/90
13. baby's changing unit 80/90
14. laundry basket 40/60
15. chest 40/1.00–1.50
16. cupboard 60/1.20

Cloakroom

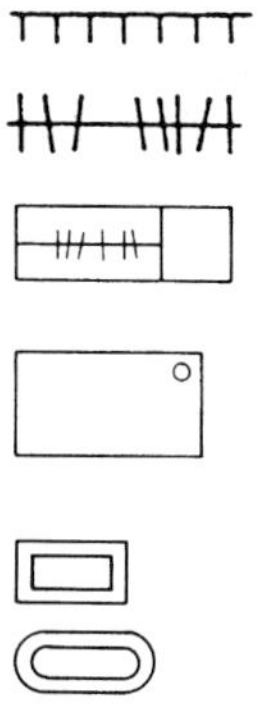

17. hooks, 15–20 cm apart
18. coat rack
19. linen cupboard 50 × 100–180
20. desk 70 × 1.30 × 78 / 80 × 1.50 × 78
21. flower stands

Bedroom

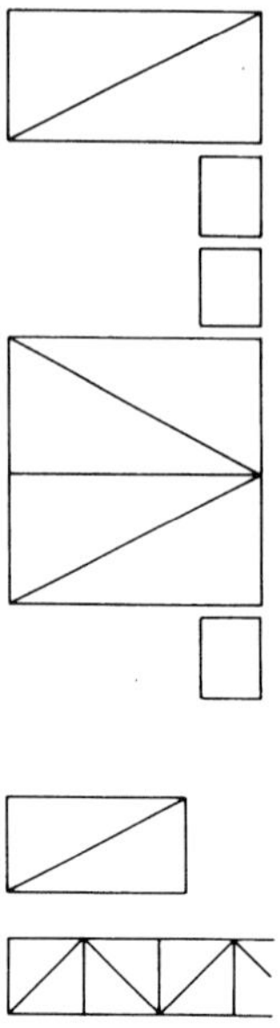

22. bed 95 × 195 bedside table 50 × 70, 60 × 70
23. twin bed 2(95 × 195, 100 × 200)
24. double bed 150 × 195
25. child's bed 70 × 140–170
26. wardrobe 60 × 120

Bathroom

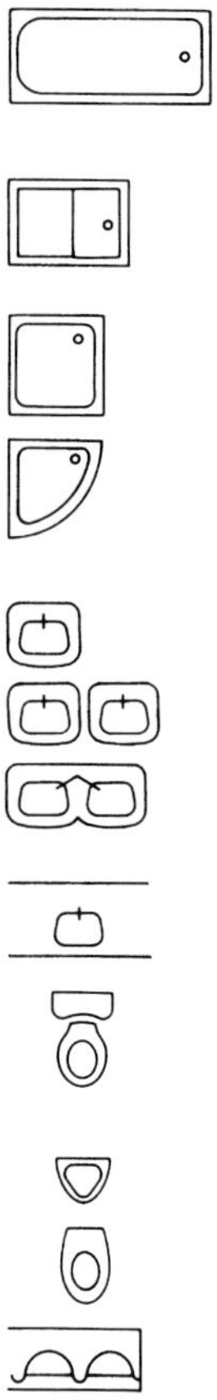

27. bath 75 × 170, 85 × 185
28. sit-up bath 70 × 105, 70 × 125
29. shower 80 × 80, 90 × 90, 75 × 90
30. corner shower 90 × 90
31. wash-basin 50 × 60, 60 × 70
32. two wash-basins
33. twin wash-basins 60 × 120, 60 × 140
34. built-in wash-basin 45 × 30
35. toilet 38 × 70
36. urinal bowl 35/30
37. bidet 38 × 60
38. row of urinals

Kitchen

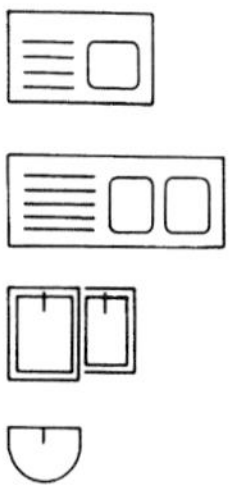

39. single sink and drainer 60 × 100
40. twin sinks, single drainer 60 × 150
41. stepped sinks
42. kitchen waste sink

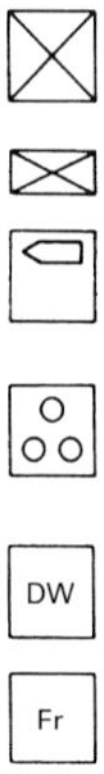

43. cupboard/base unit
44. top cupboard
45. ironing board
46. cooker
47. dishwasher
48. refrigerator
49. freezer

Other symbols

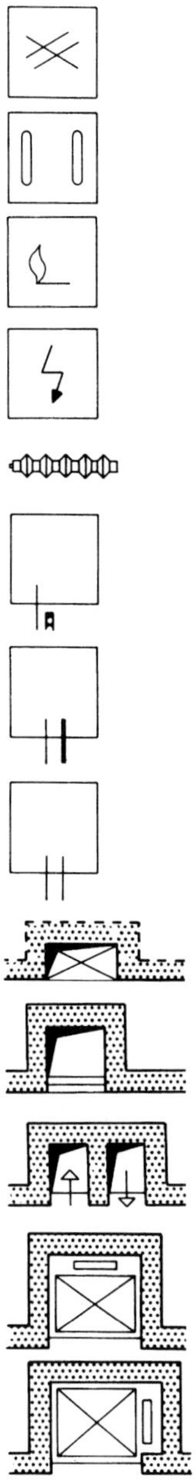

50. cookers/hobs fuelled by solid fuels
51. cookers/hobs fuelled by oil
52. cookers/hobs fuelled by gas
53. electric cooker/hob
54. central heating radiator
55. boiler (stainless)
56. gas fired boiler
57. oil fired boiler
58. refuse chute
59. laundry chute
60. ventilation and extraction shaft
61. GL = goods lift / PL = passenger lift / FL = food lift / HL = hydraulic lift

12

Windows set in reveals

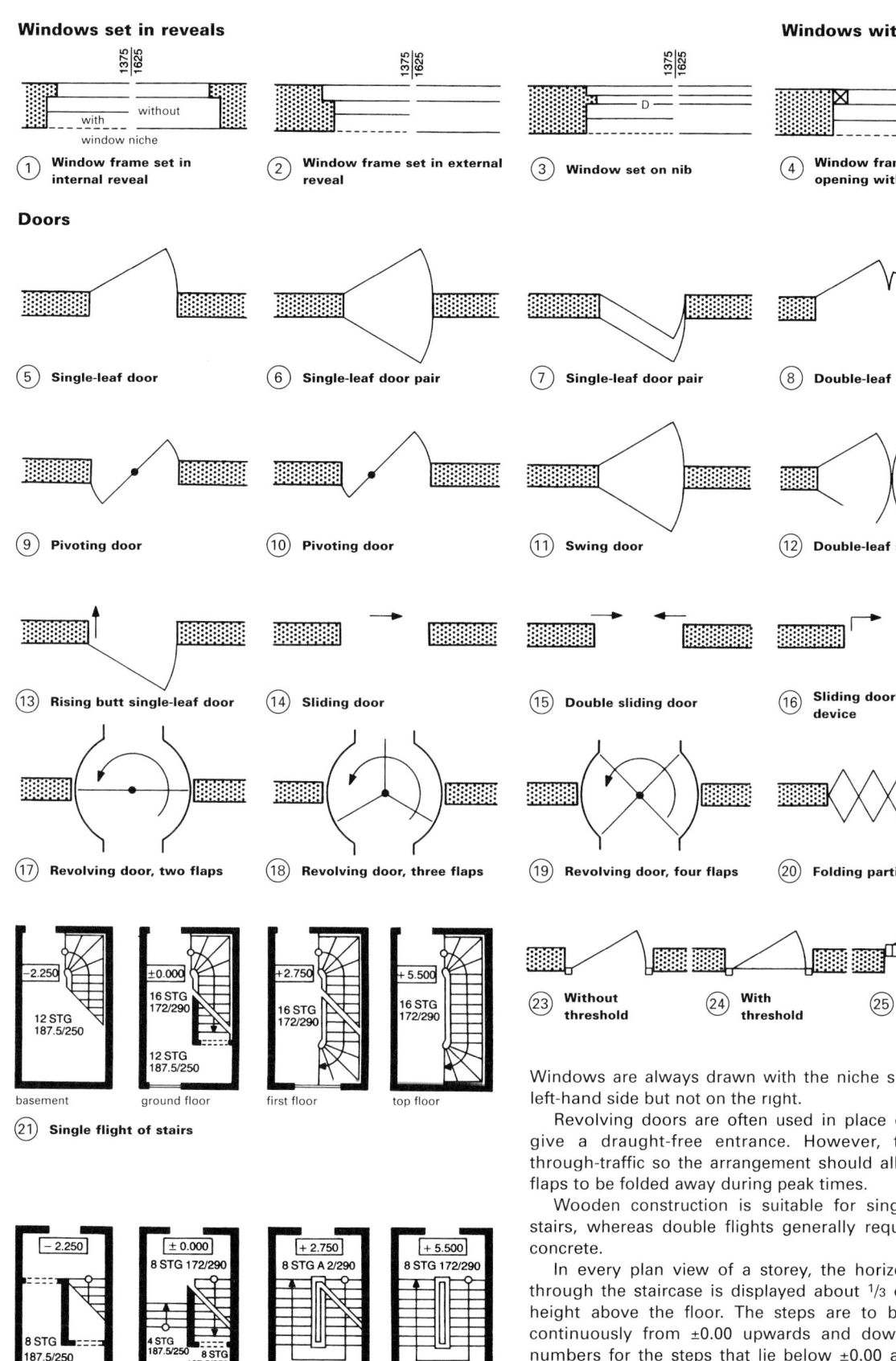

Windows without reveals

① **Window frame set in internal reveal**

② **Window frame set in external reveal**

③ **Window set on nib**

④ **Window frame set in opening without reveals**

Doors

⑤ **Single-leaf door**

⑥ **Single-leaf door pair**

⑦ **Single-leaf door pair**

⑧ **Double-leaf door**

⑨ **Pivoting door**

⑩ **Pivoting door**

⑪ **Swing door**

⑫ **Double-leaf swing door**

⑬ **Rising butt single-leaf door**

⑭ **Sliding door**

⑮ **Double sliding door**

⑯ **Sliding door with a lifting device**

⑰ **Revolving door, two flaps**

⑱ **Revolving door, three flaps**

⑲ **Revolving door, four flaps**

⑳ **Folding partition**

㉓ **Without threshold**

㉔ **With threshold**

㉕ **Threshold both sides**

㉑ **Single flight of stairs**

basement   ground floor   first floor   top floor

㉒ **Double flight of stairs**

basement   ground floor   first floor   top floor

Windows are always drawn with the niche shown on the left-hand side but not on the right.

Revolving doors are often used in place of lobbies to give a draught-free entrance. However, they restrict through-traffic so the arrangement should allow the door flaps to be folded away during peak times.

Wooden construction is suitable for single flights of stairs, whereas double flights generally require stone or concrete.

In every plan view of a storey, the horizontal section through the staircase is displayed about 1/3 of the storey height above the floor. The steps are to be numbered continuously from ±0.00 upwards and downwards. The numbers for the steps that lie below ±0.00 are given the prefix – (minus). The numbers start on the first step and finish on the landing. The centre-line begins at the start with a circle and ends at the exit with an arrow (including for the basement).

CONSTRUCTION DRAWINGS: SYMBOLS

monochrome display	coloured display	to be used for
	light green	grass
	sepia	ground peat
	burnt sienna	natural ground
	black/white	infilled earth
	red brown	brick walling with lime mortar
	red brown	brick walling with cement mortar
	red brown	brick walling with lime cement mortar
	red brown	porous brick walling with cement mortar
	red brown	hollow pot brick walling with lime cement mortar
	red brown	clinker block walling with cement mortar
	red brown	calcium-silicate brick walling with lime mortar
	red brown	alluvial stone walling with lime mortar
	red brown	walling of . . . stone with . . . mortar
	red brown	natural stone walling with cement mortar
	sepia	gravel
	grey/black	slag
	zinc yellow	sand
	ochre	floor screed
	white	render
	violet	pre-cast concrete units
	blue green	reinforced concrete
	olive green	non-reinforced concrete
	black	steel in a section
	brown	wood in section
	blue grey	sound insulation layer
	black and white	barrier against damp, heat or cold
	grey	old building components

(1) **Symbols and colours in plan views and sections**

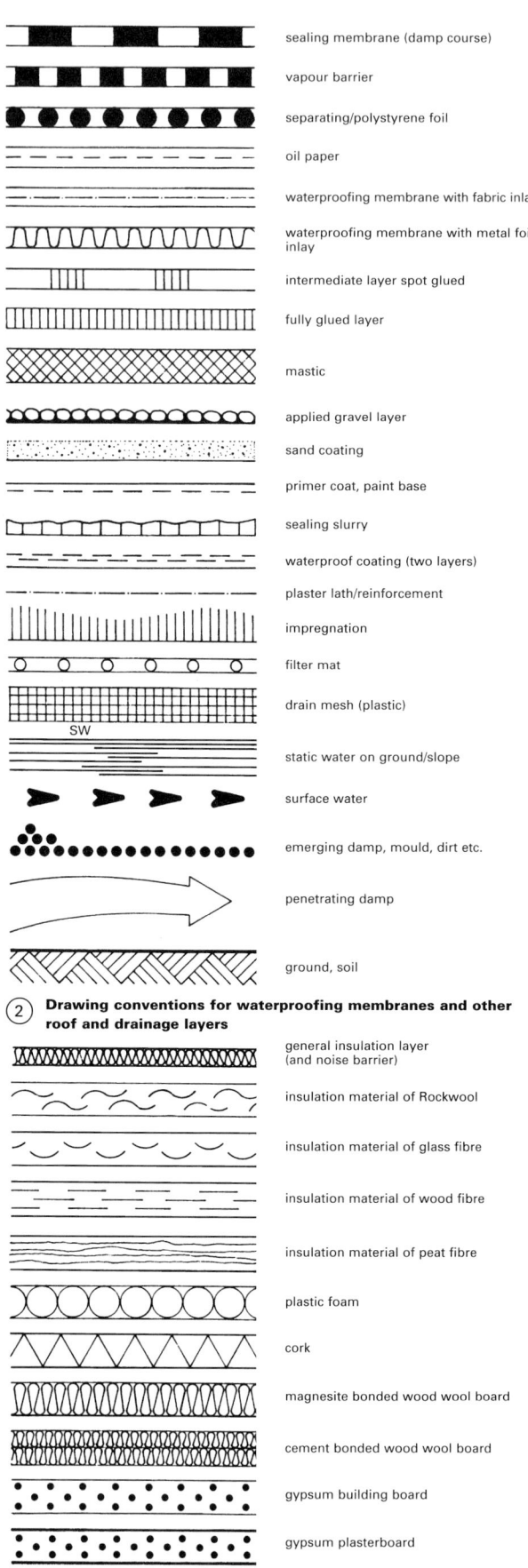

sealing membrane (damp course)

vapour barrier

separating/polystyrene foil

oil paper

waterproofing membrane with fabric inlay

waterproofing membrane with metal foil inlay

intermediate layer spot glued

fully glued layer

mastic

applied gravel layer

sand coating

primer coat, paint base

sealing slurry

waterproof coating (two layers)

plaster lath/reinforcement

impregnation

filter mat

drain mesh (plastic)

static water on ground/slope

surface water

emerging damp, mould, dirt etc.

penetrating damp

ground, soil

(2) **Drawing conventions for waterproofing membranes and other roof and drainage layers**

general insulation layer (and noise barrier)

insulation material of Rockwool

insulation material of glass fibre

insulation material of wood fibre

insulation material of peat fibre

plastic foam

cork

magnesite bonded wood wool board

cement bonded wood wool board

gypsum building board

gypsum plasterboard

(3) **Drawing conventions for thermal insulation**

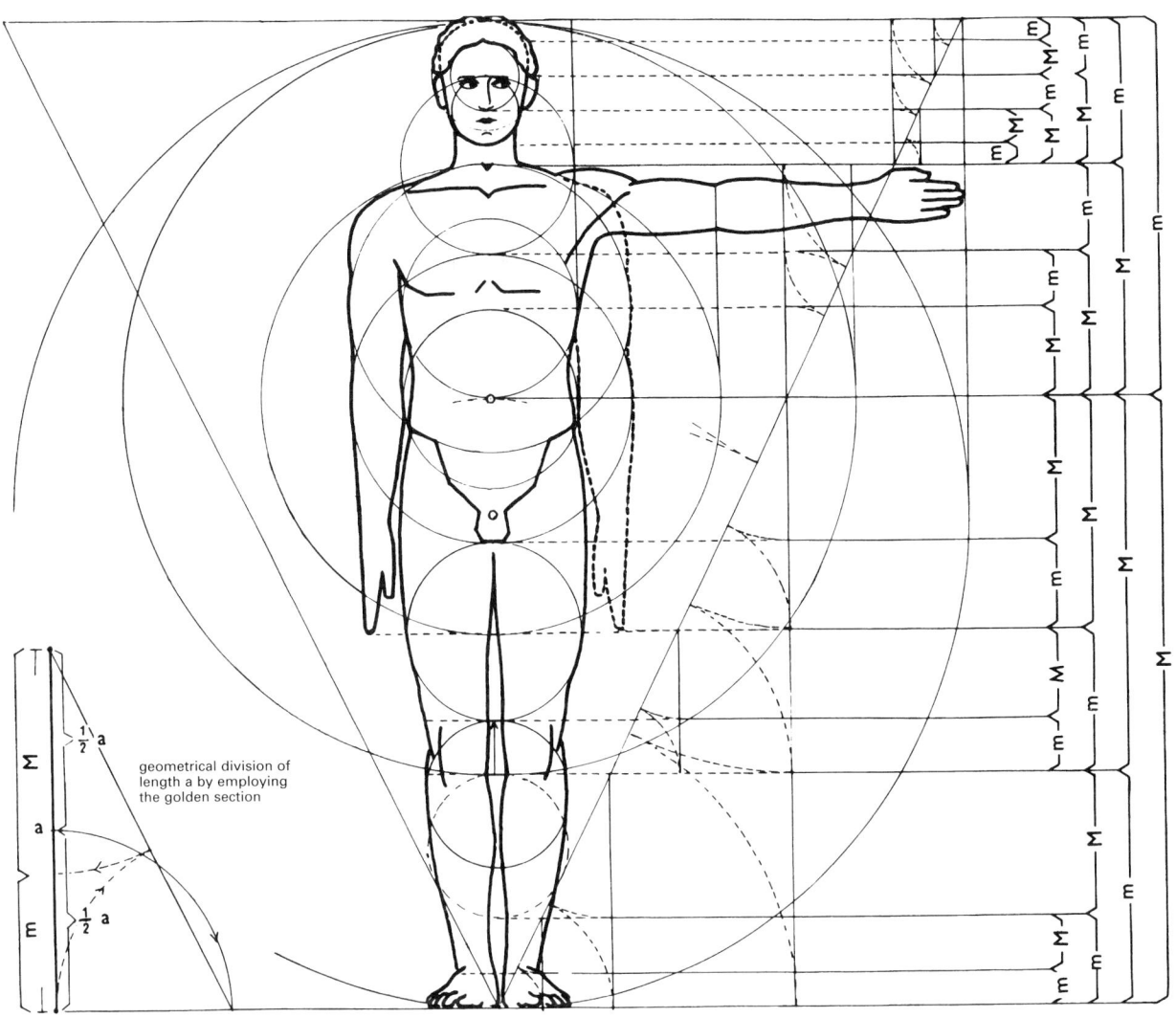

geometrical division of length a by employing the golden section

Man's dimensional relationships

The oldest known code of dimensional relationships of man was found in a burial chamber of the pyramids near Memphis and are estimated to date back to roughly 3000 BC. Certainly since then, scientists and artists have been trying hard to refine human proportional relationships.

We know about the proportional systems of the Empire of the Pharaohs, of the time of Ptolemy, the Greeks and the Romans, and even the system of Polycletes, which for a long time was applied as the standard, the details given by Alberti, Leonardo da Vinci, Michelangelo and the people of the Middle Ages. In particular, the work of Dürer is known throughout the world. In all of these works, the calculations for a man's body were based on the lengths of heads, faces or feet. These were then subdivided and brought into relationship with each other, so that they were applicable throughout general life. Even within our own lifetimes, feet and ells have been in common use as measurements.

The details worked out by Dürer became a common standard and were used extensively. He started with the height of man and expressed the subdivisions as fractions:

$1/2$ h = the whole of the top half of the body, from the crotch upwards
$1/4$ h = leg length from the ankle to the knee and from the chin to the navel
$1/6$ h = length of foot
$1/8$ h = head length from the hair parting to the bottom of the chin, distance between the nipples
$1/10$ h = face height and width (including the ears), hand length to the wrist
$1/12$ h = face width at the level of the bottom of the nose, leg width (above the ankle) and so on.

The sub-divisions go up to $1/40$ h.

During the last century, A. Zeising, brought greater clarity with his investigations of the dimensional relationship of man's proportions. He made exact measurements and comparisons on the basis of the golden section. Unfortunately, this work did not receive the attention it deserved until recently, when a significant researcher in this field, E. Moessel, endorsed Zeising's work by making thorough tests carried out following his methods. From 1945 onwards, Le Corbusier used for all his projects the sectional relationships in accordance with the golden section, which he called 'Le Modulor' → p. 30.

MAN: DIMENSIONS AND SPACE REQUIREMENTS

Body measurements

In accordance with normal measurements and energy consumption

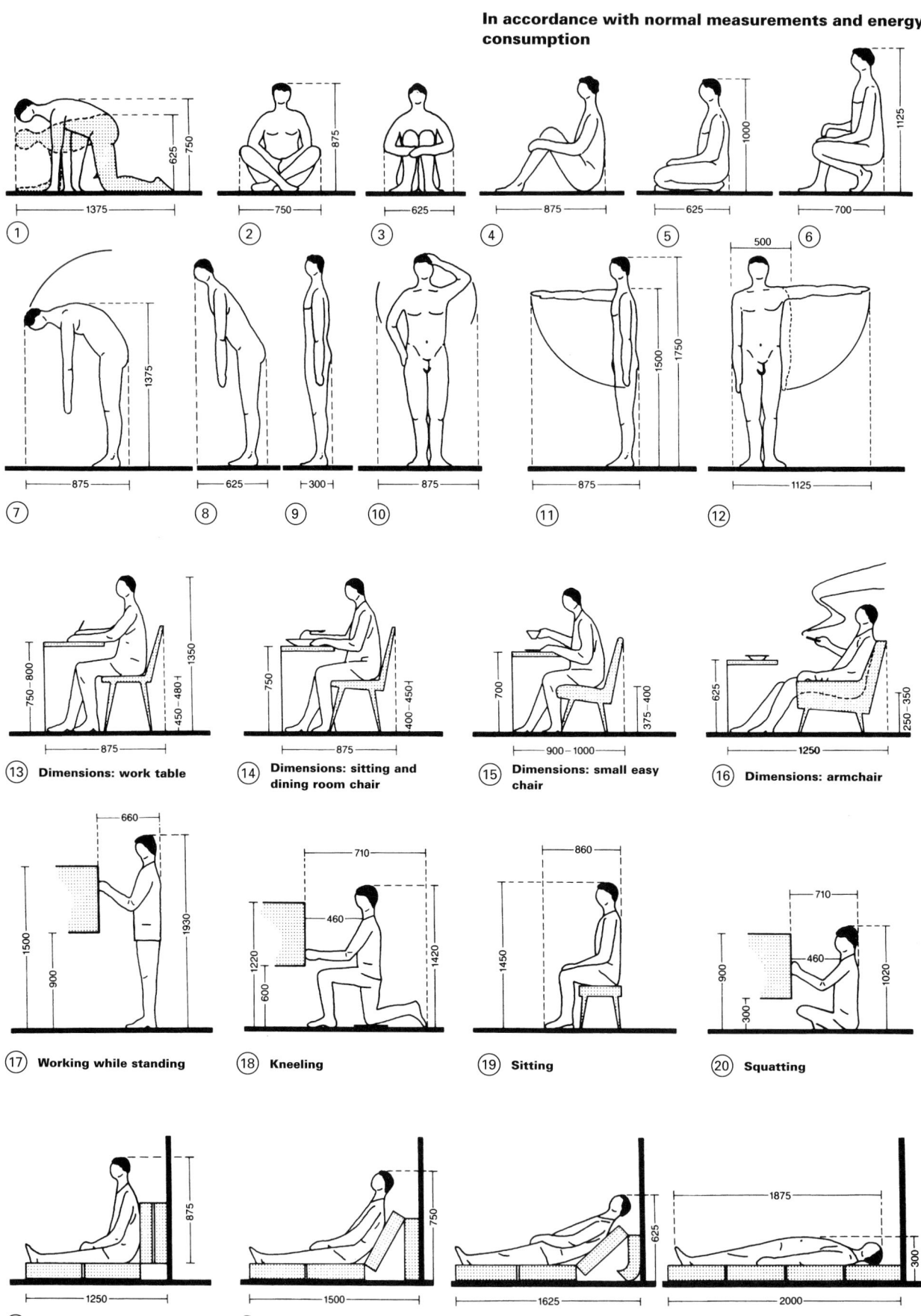

① ② ③ ④ ⑤ ⑥

⑦ ⑧ ⑨ ⑩ ⑪ ⑫

⑬ Dimensions: work table

⑭ Dimensions: sitting and dining room chair

⑮ Dimensions: small easy chair

⑯ Dimensions: armchair

⑰ Working while standing

⑱ Kneeling

⑲ Sitting

⑳ Squatting

㉑ ㉒ ㉓ ㉔

MAN: DIMENSIONS AND SPACE REQUIREMENTS

Space Requirements

SPACE REQUIREMENTS BETWEEN WALLS

for moving people, add ≥10% to widths

In accordance with normal measurements and energy consumption

 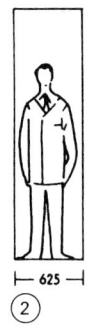    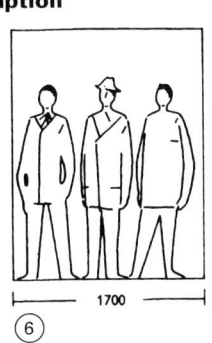 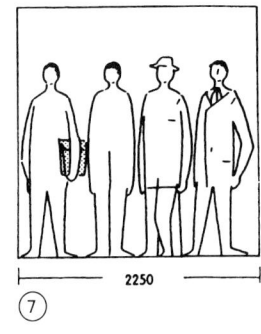

|375| |625| |875| |1000| |1150| |1700| |2250|
① ② ③ ④ ⑤ ⑥ ⑦

SPACE REQUIREMENTS OF GROUPS

   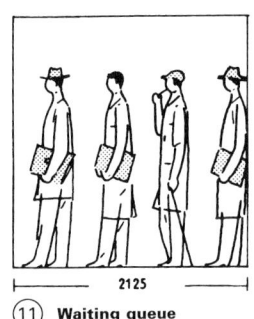 

|1250| |1875| |2000| |2125| |2250|
⑧ Closely packed ⑨ Normal spacing ⑩ Choir ⑪ Waiting queue ⑫ With back packs

STEP MEASUREMENTS

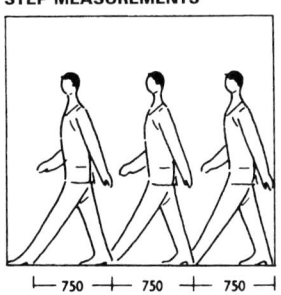  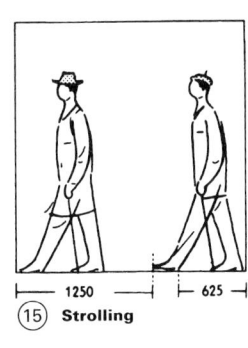 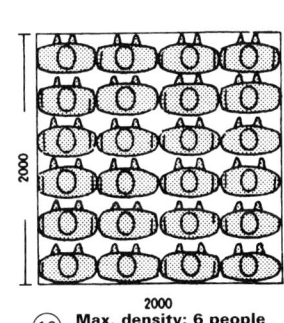

|750| |750| |750| — ⑬ Walking in step

|875| |875| |875| — ⑭ Marching

|1250| |625| — ⑮ Strolling

2000 / 2000 — ⑯ Max. density: 6 people per m² (e.g. cable railway)

SPACE REQUIREMENTS OF VARIOUS BODY POSTURES

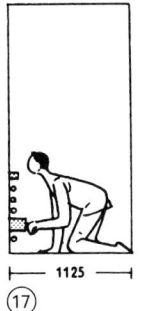 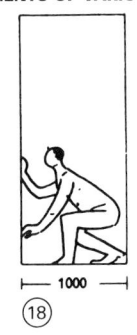 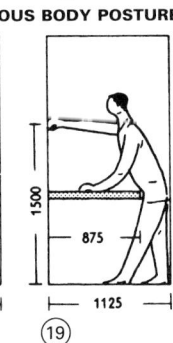 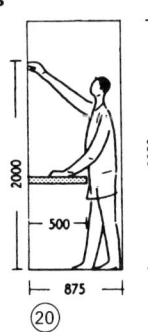 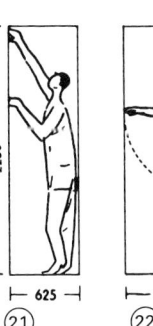 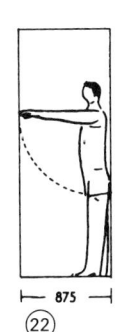 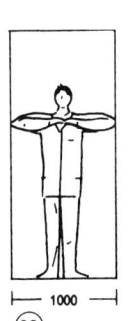 

|1125| |1000| 1500 / |1125| 2000 / |875| 2250 / |625| |875| |1000| |1750|
⑰ ⑱ ⑲ ⑳ ㉑ ㉒ ㉓ ㉔

SPACE REQUIREMENTS WITH LUGGAGE

SPACE REQUIREMENTS WITH STICKS AND UMBRELLAS

  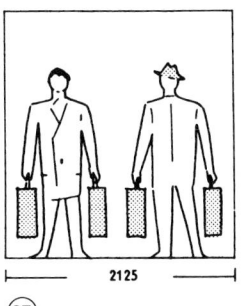  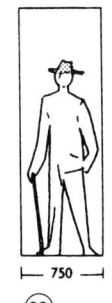  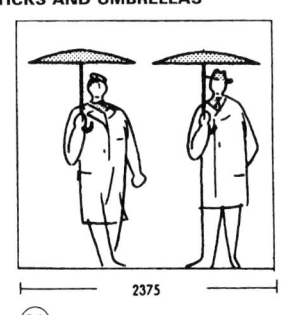

|800| |1000| |2125| |875| |750| |1125| |2375|
㉕ ㉖ ㉗ ㉘ ㉙ ㉚ ㉛

DIMENSIONS FOR RAILWAY CARRIAGES

① **Local passenger train carriage, plan view**

68 seats, 0.45 m per seat; overall length 19.66 m, compartment carriage length 12.75 m; luggage van length 12.62 m, step height 28–30 cm

cross-section through ①

old and new rolling stock as an example of minimum space requirements for passenger transport

② **Intercity express carriage, plan view**

48 seats; overall length 20.42 m, luggage van 18.38 m

first class

(second class) 1.05 m per seat
door height 2.0 m
door width 60–70 cm

second class

first class

longitudinal section through ②

③ **Top deck: 4-axle double decker carriage**

longitudinal section

④ **Lower deck: 4-axle double decker carriage**

100 seats; 18 folding seats

⑤ **Top deck: 4-axle double decker carriage**

top deck   restaurant

buffet area

restaurant car with 32 seats

⑥ **Lower deck: 4-axle double decker carriage with catering compartment, restaurant and luggage van**

longitudinal section
luggage area

lower deck

kitchen counter   kitchen

28 seats, second class

18

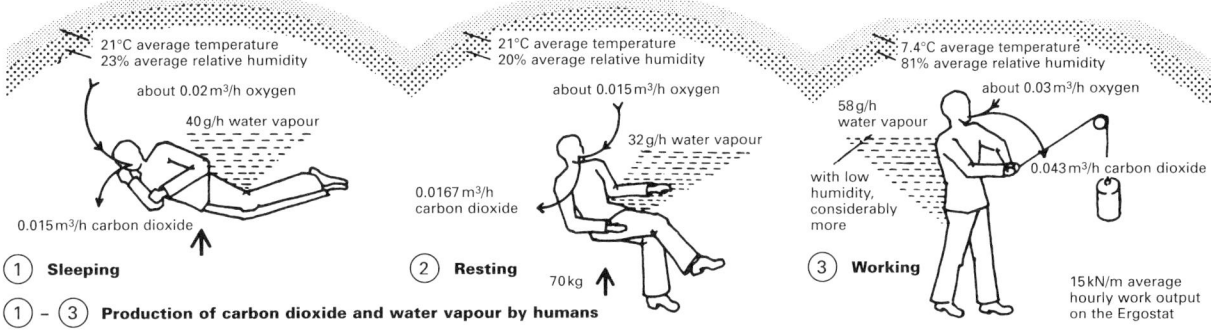

① Sleeping **②** Resting 70 kg **③** Working

15 kN/m average hourly work output on the Ergostat

①–③ Production of carbon dioxide and water vapour by humans

The function of housing is to protect man against the weather and to provide an environment that maintains his well-being. The required inside atmosphere comprises gently moving (i.e. not draughty), well oxygenated air, pleasant warmth and air humidity and sufficient light. To provide these conditions, important factors are the location and orientation of the housing in the landscape (→ p. 272) as well as the arrangement of spaces in the house and its type of construction.

The prime requirements for promoting a lasting feeling of well-being are an insulated construction, with appropriately sized windows placed correctly in relation to the room furnishings, sufficient heating and corresponding draught-free ventilation.

The need for air
Man breathes in oxygen with the air and expels carbon dioxide and water vapour when he exhales. These vary in quantity depending on the individual's weight, food intake, activity and surrounding environment → ①–③.

It has been calculated that on average human beings produce 0.020 m³/h of carbon dioxide and 40 g/h of water vapour.

A carbon dioxide content between 1 and 3‰ can stimulate deeper breathing, so the air in the dwelling should not, as far as possible, contain more than 1‰. This means, with a single change of air per hour, a requirement for an air space of 32 m³ per adult and 15 m³ for each child. However, because the natural rate of air exchange in free-standing buildings, even with closed windows, reaches 1¹/₂ to 2 times this amount, 16–24 m³ is sufficient (depending on the design) as a normal air space for adults and 8–12 m³ for children. Expressed another way, with a room height ≥2.5 m, a room floor area of 6.4–9.6 m² for each adult is adequate and 3.2–4.8 m² for each child. With a greater rate of air exchange, (e.g. sleeping with a window open, or ventilation via ducting), the volume of space per person for living rooms can be reduced to 7.5 m³ and for bedrooms to 10 m³ per bed.

Where air quality is likely to deteriorate because of naked lights, vapours and other pollutants (as in hospitals or factories) and in enclosed spaces (such as you in an auditorium), rate of exchange of air must be artificially boosted in order to provide the lacking oxygen and remove the harmful substances.

Space heating
The room temperature for humans at rest is at its most pleasant between 18° and 20°C, and for work between 15° and 18°C, depending on the level of activity. A human being produces about 1.5 kcal/h per kg of body weight. An adult weighing 70 kg therefore generates 2520 kcal of heat energy per day, although the quantity produced varies according to the circumstances. For instance it increases with a drop in room temperature just as it does with exercise.

When heating a room, care must be taken to ensure that low temperature heat is used to warm the room air on the cold side of the room. With surface temperatures above 70–80°C decomposition can take place, which may irritate the mucous membrane, mouth and pharynx and make the air feel too dry. Because of this, steam heating and iron stoves, with their high surface temperatures, are not suitable for use in blocks of flats.

Room humidity
Room air is most pleasant with a relative air humidity of 50–60%; it should be maintained between limits 40% and 70%. Room air which is too moist promotes germs, mould, cold bridging, rot and condensation. → ⑥. The production of water vapour in human beings varies in accordance with the prevailing conditions and performs an important cooling function. Production increases with rising warmth of the room, particularly when the temperature goes above 37°C (blood temperature).

	tolerable for several hours (‰)	tolerable for up to 1h (‰)	immediately dangerous (‰)
iodine vapour	0.0005	0.003	0.05
chlorine vapour	0.001	0.004	0.05
bromine vapour	0.001	0.004	0.05
hydrochloric acid	0.01	0.05	1.5
sulphuric acid	–	0.05	0.5
hydrogen sulphide	–	0.2	0.6
ammonia	0.1	0.3	3.5
carbon monoxide	0.2	0.5	2.0
carbon disulphide	–	1.5*	10.0*
carbon dioxide	10	80	300

*mg per litre

④ Harmful accumulation of industrial gases

activity	energy expenditure (kJ/h)
at rest in bed (basal metabolic rate)	250
sitting and writing	475
dressing, washing, shaving	885
walking at 5 km/h	2050
climbing 15 cm stairs	2590
running at 8 km/h	3550
rowing at 33 strokes/min	4765

note that this expenditure in part contributes to heating air in a room

⑤ Human expenditure of energy

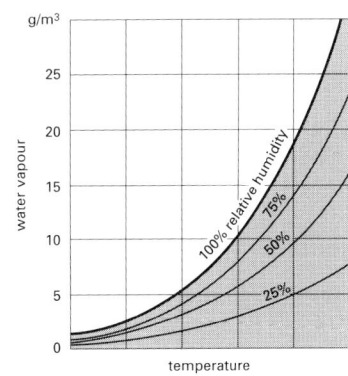

⑥ Room humidity

temperature (°C)	water content (g/m³)
50	82.63
49	78.86
48	75.22
47	71.73
46	68.36
45	65.14
44	62.05
43	59.09
42	56.25
41	53.52
40	50.91
39	48.40
38	46.00
37	43.71
36	41.51
35	39.41
34	37.40
33	35.48
32	33.64
31	31.89
30	30.21
29	28.62
28	27.09
27	25.64
26	24.24
25	22.93
24	21.68
23	20.48
22	19.33
21	18.25
20	17.22
19	16.25
18	15.31
17	14.43
16	13.59
15	12.82
14	12.03
13	11.32
12	10.64
11	10.01
10	9.39
9	8.82
8	8.28
7	7.76
6	7.28
5	6.82
4	6.39
3	5.98
2	5.60
+ 1	5.23
0	4.89
− 1	4.55
2	4.22
3	3.92
4	3.64
5	3.37
6	3.13
7	2.90
8	2.69
9	2.49
10	2.31
11	2.14
12	1.98
13	1.83
14	1.70
15	1.58
16	1.46
17	1.35
18	1.25
19	1.15
20	1.05
21	0.95
22	0.86
23	0.78
24	0.71
25	0.64

maximum water content of one cubic metre of air (g)

physical conditions
air movement (draughts)
relative humidity
ambient surface temperature
air temperature
atmospheric charge
air composition and pressure
room occupancy
optical/acoustic influences
clothing

physiological conditions
sex
age
ethnic influences
food intake
level of activity
adaptation and acclimatisation
natural body rhythms
state of health
psycho-sociological factors

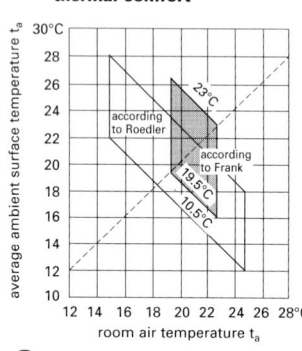

① **Factors that affect thermal comfort**

② **Heated walls**

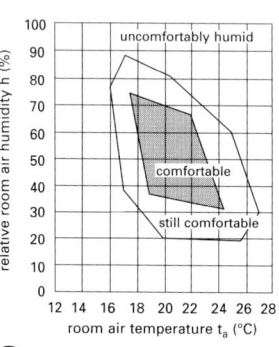

③ **Field of comfort**   ④ **Field of comfort**

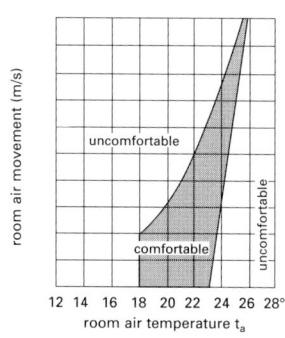

⑤ **Field of comfort**

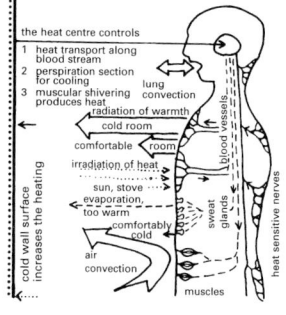

⑥ **Human heat flows**

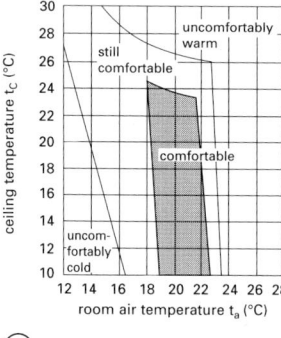

⑦ **Field of comfort**

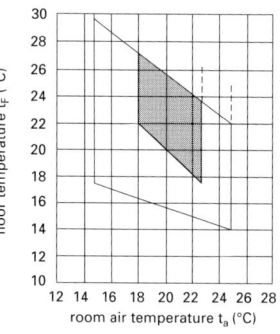

⑧ **Field of comfort**

water content of the air (g/kg)	suitability for breathing	sensation
0 to 5	very good	light, fresh
5 to 8	good	normal
8 to 10	satisfactory	still bearable
10 to 25	increasingly bad	heavy, muggy
over 25	becoming dangerous	very humid
41	water content of the air breathed out 37°C (100%)	
over 41	water condenses in pulmonary alveoli	

⑨ **Humidity values for air we breathe**

In the same way as the earth has a climate, the insides of buildings also have a climate, with measurable values for air pressure, humidity, temperature, velocity of air circulation and 'internal sunshine' in the form of radiated heat. Efficient control of these factors leads to optimum room comfort and contributes to man's overall health and ability to perform whatever tasks he is engaged in. Thermal comfort is experienced when the thermal processes within the body are in balance (i.e. when the body manages its thermal regulation with the minimum of effort and the heat dissipated from the body corresponds with the equilibrium loss of heat to the surrounding area).

Temperature regulation and heat loss from the body

The human body can raise or lower the rate at which it loses heat using several mechanisms: increasing blood circulation in the skin, increasing the blood circulation speed, vascular dilation and secreting sweat. When cold, the body uses muscular shivering to generate additional heat.

Heat is lost from the body in three main ways: conduction, convection and radiation. Conduction is the process of heat transfer from one surface to another surface when they are in contact (e.g. feet in contact with the floor). The rate of heat transfer depends on the surface area in contact, the temperature differential and the thermal conductivities of the materials involved. Copper, for example, has a high thermal conductivity while that of air is low, making it a porous insulating material. Convection is the process of body heat being lost as the skin warms the surrounding air. This process is governed by the velocity of the circulating air in the room and the temperature differential between the clothed and unclothed areas of the body. Air circulation is also driven by convection: air warms itself by contact with hot objects (e.g. radiators), rises, cools off on the ceiling and sinks again. As it circulates the air carries dust and floating particles with it. The quicker the heating medium flows (e.g. water in a radiator), the quicker is the development of circulation. All objects, including the human body, emit heat radiation in accordance to temperature difference between the body surface and that of the ambient area. It is proportional to the power of 4 of the body's absolute temperature and therefore 16 times as high if the temperature doubles. The wavelength of the radiation also changes with temperature: the higher the surface temperature, the shorter the wavelength. Above 500°C, heat becomes visible as light. The radiation below this limit is called infra-red/heat radiation. It radiates in all directions, penetrates the air without heating it, and is absorbed by (or reflected off) other solid bodies. In absorbing the radiation, these solid bodies (including human bodies) are warmed. This radiant heat absorption by the body (e.g. from tile stoves) is the most pleasant sensation for humans for physiological reasons and also the most healthy.

Other heat exchange mechanisms used by the human body are evaporation of moisture from the sweat glands and breathing. The body surface and vapour pressure differential between the skin and surrounding areas are key factors here.

Recommendations for internal climate

An air temperature of 20–24°C is comfortable both in summer and in winter. The surrounding surface areas should not differ by more than 2–3°C from the air temperature. A change in the air temperature can be compensated for by changing the surface temperature (e.g. with decreasing air temperature, increase the surface temperature). If there is too great a difference between the air and surface temperatures, excessive movement of air takes place. The main critical surfaces are those of the windows.

For comfort, heat conduction to the floor via the feet must be avoided (i.e. the floor temperature should be 17°C or more). The surface temperature of the ceiling depends upon the height of the room. The temperature sensed by humans is somewhere near the average between room air temperature and that of surrounding surfaces.

It is important to control air movement and humidity as far as possible. The movement can be sensed as draughts and this has the effect of local cooling of the body. A relative air humidity of 40–50% is comfortable. With a lower humidity (e.g. 30%) dust particles are liable to fly around.

To maintain the quality of the air, controlled ventilation is ideal. The CO_2 content of the air must be replaced by oxygen. A CO_2 content of 0.10% by volume should not be exceeded, and therefore in living rooms and bedrooms provide for two to three air changes per hour. The fresh air requirement of humans comes to about 32.0 m³/h so the air change in living rooms should be 0.4–0.8 times the room volume per person/h.

absolute water content (g/kg)	relative humidity (%)	temperature (°C)	description
2	50	0	fine winter's day, healthy climate for lungs
5	100	4	fine autumnal day
5	40	18	very good room climate
8	50	21	good room climate
10	70	20	room climate too humid
28	100	30	tropical rain forest

⑩ **Comparative relative humidity values**

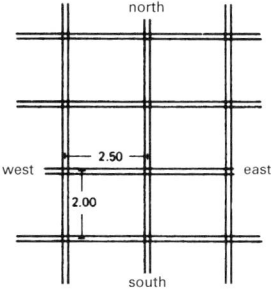

① Global net, magnetically ordered, with pathogenic intersection points

② Left bed on an intersection point; right bed is crossed by edge zone; the hatched edge strips are not deleterious

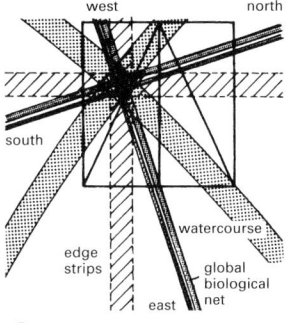

③ Left bed is particularly at risk – crossed by net intersection and a watercourse, which intensifies the bad effects

④ Disturbance-free zone between net strips 1.80×2.30 m

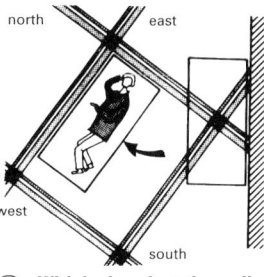

⑤ With bed against the wall, health suffered; moving it as shown resulted in a speedy recovery

⑥ Global net at centres of 4×5 m, with dashed half-distance lines 2×2.5 m centres → ①

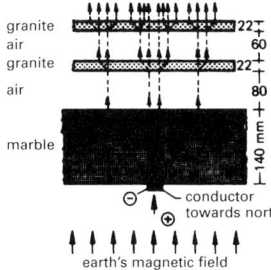

⑦ Experimental model showing how quadrant lines of force split/multiply to vertical lines at surfaces

⑧ Electrical field lines from an underground watercourse bundle to cause the pathogenic zones

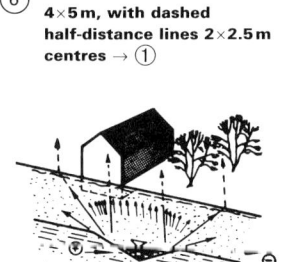

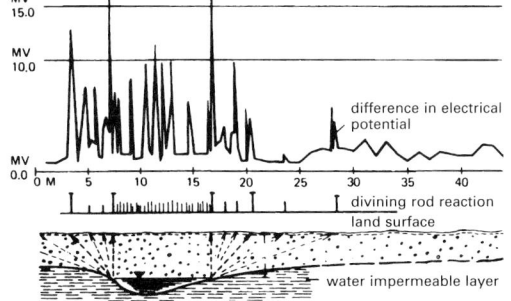

⑨ Measured differences in electrical potential and divining rod reactions above an underground watercourse

For over a decade, medical doctors such as Dr Palm and Dr Hartmann at the Research Forum for Geobiology, Eberbach-Woldbrunn-Waldkatzenbach, among others, have been researching the effects that the environment has on people: in particular the effects of the ground, buildings, rooms, building materials and installations.

Geological effects

Stretched across the whole of the earth is a so-called 'global net' → ① consisting of stationary waves, thought to be induced by the sun. However, its regularity, according to Hartmann, is such that it suggests an earthly radiation which emanates from inside the earth and is effected by crystalline structures in the earth's crust, which orders it in such a network. The network is orientated magnetically, in strips of about 200 mm width, from the magnetic north to south poles. In the central European area these appear at a spacing of about 2.50 m. At right angles to these are other strips running in an east/west direction at a spacing of about 2 m → ①.

These strips have been revealed, through experience, to have psychologically detrimental effects, particularly when one is repeatedly at rest over a point of intersection for long periods (e.g. when in bed) → ②. In addition to this, rooms which correspond to the right angles of the net do not display the same pathogenic influences.

These intersection points only become really pathogenic when they coincide with geological disturbances, such as faults or joints in the ground, or watercourses. The latter, in particular, are the most influential → ③. Hence, there is a cumulative effect involved so the best situation is to make use of the undisturbed zone or area of 1.80×2.30 m between the global strips → ④. According to Hartmann, the most effective action is to move the bed out of the disturbance area, particularly away from the intersection points → ⑤.

According to Palm, the apparent global net of about 2×2.50 m is made up of half-distance lines. The actual network would be, as a result, a global net with strips at 4–5 m and 5–6 m centres, running dead straight in the east/west direction all round the earth. Every 7th one of these net strips is reported to be of a so-called 2nd order and have an influence many times greater than the others. Also based on sevenths, an even stronger disturbance zone has been identified as a so-called 3rd order. This is at a spacing of about 250 and 300 m respectively. The intersection points here are also felt particularly strongly.

Also according to Palm, in Europe there are deviations from the above norm of up to 15% from the north/south and the east/west directions. Americans have observed such strips with the aid of very sensitive cameras from aeroplanes flying at a height of several thousand meters. In addition to this, the diagonals also form their own global net, running north-east to south-west and from north-west to south-east → ⑥. This, too, has its own pattern of strong sevenths, which are about one quarter as strong again in their effect.

It is stated that locating of the global strips depends on the reliability of the compass, and that modern building construction can influence the needle of the compass. Thus variations of 1–2° already result in faulty location and this is significant because the edges of the strips are particularly pathogenic. Careful detection of all the relationships requires much time and experience, and often needs several investigations to cross-check the results. The disturbance zones are located with divining rods or radio equipment. Just as the radiation pattern is broken vertically at the intersection between ground and air (i.e. at the earth's surface), Endros has demonstrated with models that these breaks are also detectable on the solid floors of multistorey buildings → ⑦. He has shown a clear illustration of these breaks caused by an underground stream → ⑧ and measured the strength of the disturbances above a watercourse → ⑨.

The main detrimental effect of such pathogenic zones is that of 'devitalisation': for example, tiredness, disturbances of the heart, kidneys, circulation, breathing, stomach and metabolism, and could extend as far as serious chronic diseases such as cancer. In most cases, moving the bed to a disturbance-free zone gives relief within a short space of time → ⑤. The effect of so-called neutralising apparatus is debatable, many of them having been discovered to be a source of disturbance. Disturbance does not occur, it seems, in rooms proportioned to the golden section (e.g. height 3 m, width 4 m, length 5 m) and round houses or hexagonal plans (honeycomb) are also praised.

BUILDING BIOLOGY

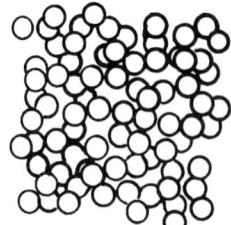

(1) Arrangement of atoms: metal in solid phase

(2) Arrangement of atoms: metal in liquid phase

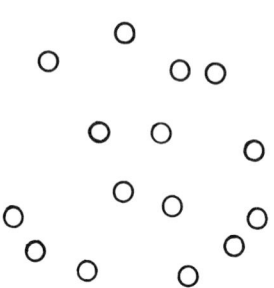

(3) Arrangement of atoms: metal in gaseous phase

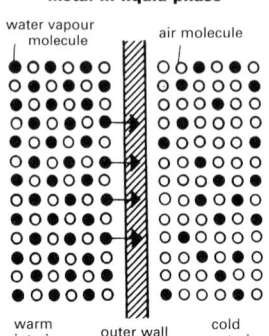

water vapour molecule · · · · air molecule

warm interior · · · outer wall · · · cold exterior

(4) Water vapour moves from warm interior of a building, hindered by outer wall, to cooler outside air; air molecules move inside in exchange

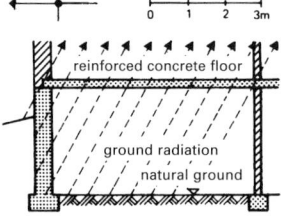

N

0 1 2 3m

reinforced concrete floor

ground radiation

natural ground

(5) Radiation from the ground passes unhindered through concrete floors

(6) Atomic structure of calcite

● = carbon
● = calcium
○ = oxygen

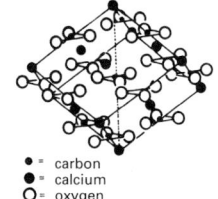

N

0 1 2 3m

asphalt sheet (2–2.5mm)

reinforced concrete floor

ground radiation

natural ground

(7) Asphalt sheeting diverts the southerly inclined radiation away but emanations at the beginning of the next room are concentrated, resulting in increased potential harm

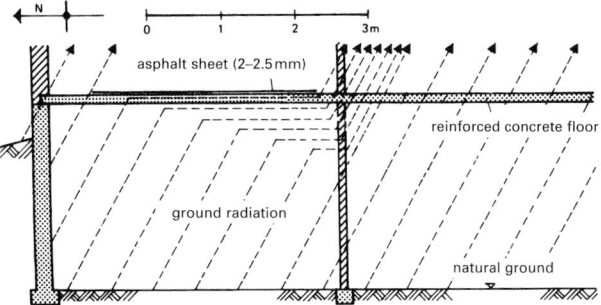

N

0 1 2 3m

cork granules

reinforced concrete floor

ground radiation

natural ground

(8) Cork granules or tongue and grooved cork sheets ≥25–30mm thick (not compressed and sealed; bitumen coated) absorb the harmful radiation

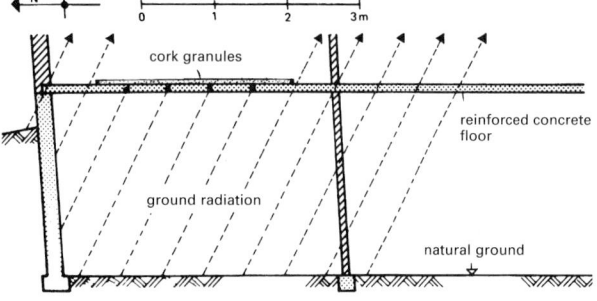

Physicists recognise that matter exists in three 'phases', depending on its temperature and external pressure: (a) solid, (b) liquid and (c) gaseous. For example, with water, when under 0°C it exists as a solid (a), namely ice; at normal temperature = (b) = water; when over 100° = (c) = steam. Other materials change phase at different temperatures.

The atoms or molecules that make up the material are in constant motion. In solid metals, for example, the atoms vibrate around fixed points in a crystalline structure → (1). When heated, the movement becomes increasingly agitated until the melting point is reached. At this temperature, the bonds holding specific atoms together are broken down and metal liquefaction occurs, enabling the atoms to move more freely → (2). Further heating causes more excitation of the atoms until the boiling point is reached. Here, the motion is so energetic that the atoms can escape all inter-atom forces of attraction and disperse to form the gaseous state → (3). On the reverse side, all atomic or molecular movement stops completely at absolute zero, 0 kelvin (0K = –273.15°)C).

These transitions in metals are, however, not typical of all materials. The atomic or molecular arrangement of each material gives it its own properties and dictates how it reacts to and affects its surroundings. In the case of glass, for example, although it is apparently solid at room temperature, it does not have a crystalline structure, the atoms being in a random, amorphous state. It is, therefore, technically, a supercooled liquid. The density of vapour molecules in air depends on the temperature, so the water molecules diffuse to the cooler side (where the density is lower). To replace them, air molecules diffuse to the inside, both movements being hindered by the diffusion resistance of the wall construction → (4).

Many years of research on building materials by Schröder-Speck suggests that organic materials absorb or break up radiation of mineral origin. For instance, asphalt matting, with 100mm strip edge overlaps all round, placed on concrete floors diverted the previously penetrating radiation. The adjacent room, however, received bundled diverted rays. → (5) – (7). In an alternative experiment, a granulated cork floor showed a capacity to absorb the radiation. Cork sheets 25–30mm thick (not compressed and sealed), tongued and grooved all round are also suitable → (8).

Clay is regarded as a 'healthy earth' and bricks and roofing tiles fired at about 950°C give the optimum living conditions. For bricklaying, sulphur-free white lime is recommended, produced by slaking burnt lime in a slaking pit and where fatty lime is produced through maturation. Hydraulic lime should, however, be used in walls subject to damp. Lime has well known antiseptic qualities and is commonly used as a lime wash in stables and cow sheds.

Plaster is considered best when it is fired as far below 200°C as possible, preferably with a constant humidity similar to animal textiles (leather, silk etc.). Sandstone as a natural lime-sandstone is acceptable but should not be used for complete walls.

Timber is light and warm and is the most vital of building materials. Timber preservation treatments should be derived from the distillation of wood itself (e.g. as wood vinegar, wood oil or wood tar). Timber reacts well to odours and it is therefore recommended that genuine timber be used for interior cladding, if necessary as plywood using natural glues. Ideally, the 'old rules' should be followed: timber felled only in winter, during the waning moon, then watered for one year in a clay pit before it is sawn. However, this is very expensive.

For insulation, natural building materials such as cork granules and cork sheets (including those with bitumen coating) are recommended, as well as all plant-based matting (e.g. sea grass, coconut fibre etc.), together with expanded clay and diatomaceous earth (fossil meal). Plastics, mineral fibres, mineral wool, glass fibre, aerated concrete, foamed concrete and corrugated aluminium foil are not considered to be satisfactory.

Normal glass for glazing or crystal glass counts as neutral. Better still is quartz glass (or bio-glass), which transmits 70–80% of the ultra-violet light. Doubts exist about coloured glass. Glazing units with glass welded edges are preferable to those with metal or plastic sealed edges. One is sceptical about coloured glass.

Metal is rejected by Palm for exterior walls, as well as for use on large areas. This includes copper for roofs on dwellings (but not on churches). Generally the advice is to avoid the extensive use of metal. Copper is tolerated the best. Iron is rejected (radiators, allegedly, cause disturbance in a radius of 4m). Zinc is also tolerated, as is lead. Bronze, too, is acceptable (≥75% copper) and aluminium is regarded as having a future. Asbestos should not be used. With painting it is recommended that a careful study is made of the contents and method of manufacture of the paint in order to prevent the introduction of damaging radiation. Plastics are generally regarded as having no harmful side effects. Concrete, particularly reinforced concrete, is rejected in slabs and arches but is, however, permitted in foundations and cellars.

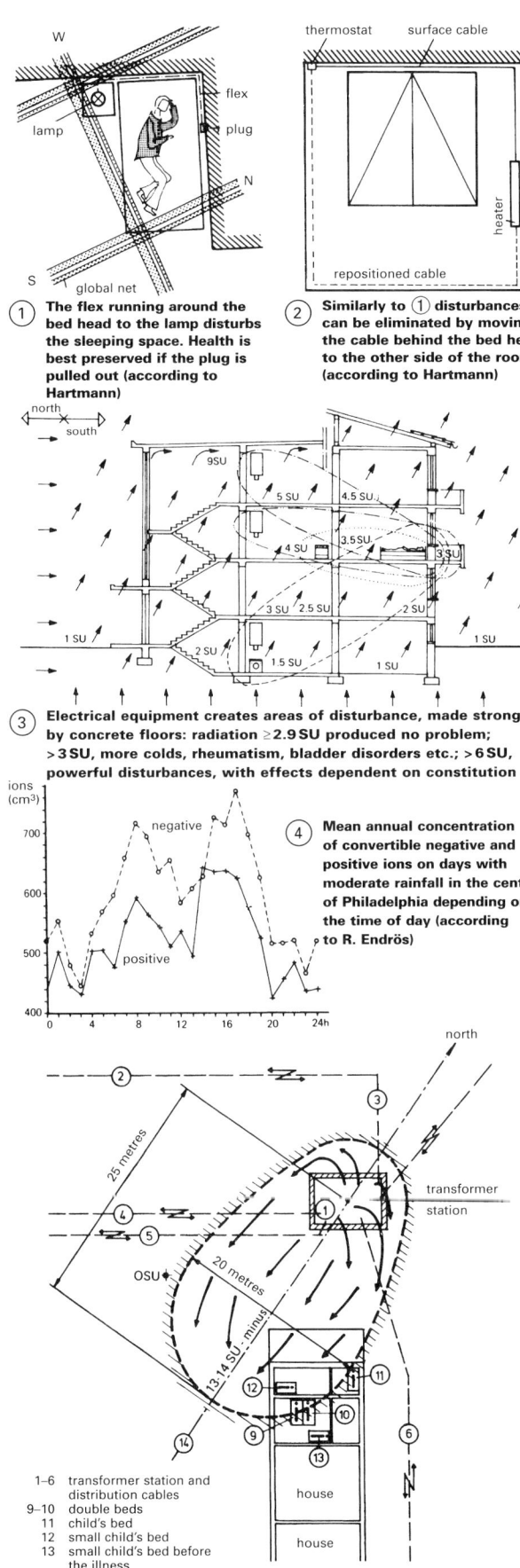

① **The flex running around the bed head to the lamp disturbs the sleeping space. Health is best preserved if the plug is pulled out (according to Hartmann)**

② **Similarly to ① disturbances can be eliminated by moving the cable behind the bed head to the other side of the room (according to Hartmann)**

③ **Electrical equipment creates areas of disturbance, made stronger by concrete floors: radiation ≥2.9 SU produced no problem; >3 SU, more colds, rheumatism, bladder disorders etc.; >6 SU, powerful disturbances, with effects dependent on constitution**

④ **Mean annual concentration of convertible negative and positive ions on days with moderate rainfall in the centre of Philadelphia depending on the time of day (according to R. Endrös)**

1–6 transformer station and distribution cables
9–10 double beds
11 child's bed
12 small child's bed
13 small child's bed before the illness
14 north–south axis of the disturbance area

⑤ **Disturbance area around a transformer station, with harmful effects on people in beds 9 to 12 (according to K.E. Lotz)**

A differentiation should be made between concrete with clinker aggregate and man-made plaster (which have extremely high radiation values) and 'natural' cement and plaster. Lightweight concrete with expanded clay aggregate is tolerable.

All pipes for water (cold or hot), sewage or gas radiate to their surroundings and can influence the organs of living creatures as well as plants. Therefore, rooms that are occupied by humans and animals for long periods of time (e.g. bedrooms and living rooms) should be as far away as possible from pipework. Consequently, it is recommended that all installations are concentrated in the centre of the dwelling, in the kitchen or bathroom, or collected together in a service wall (→ p. 277 ⑤).

There is a similar problem with electrical wiring carrying alternating current. Even if current does not flow, electrical fields with pathogenic effects are formed, and when current is being drawn, the electromagnetic fields created are reputed to be even more harmful. Dr Hartmann found an immediate cure in one case of disturbed well-being by getting the patient to pull out the plug and therefore eliminate the current in the flex which went around the head of his bed → ①. In another case similar symptoms were cured by moving a cable running between an electric heater and the thermostat from behind the head of the double bed to the other side of the room → ②. Loose cables are particularly troublesome, as they produce a 50 Hz alternating field syndrome. In addition, electrical equipment, such as heaters, washing machines, dish washer, boilers and, particularly, microwave ovens with defective seals, situated next to or beneath bedrooms send out pathogenic radiation through the walls and floors, so that the inhabitants are often in an area of several influences → ③. Radiation can largely be avoided in new buildings by using wiring with appropriate insulating sheathing. In existing structures the only solution is to re-lay the cables or switch off the current at the meter. For this purpose it is now possible to obtain automatic shut-off switches when no current is being consumed. In this case, a separate circuit is required for appliances that run constantly (e.g. freezers, refrigerators, boilers etc.).

Additionally, harmful radiation covers large areas around transformer stations (Schröder-Speck measured radiation from a 10–20 000 V station as far away as 30–50 m to the north and 120–150 m to the south), electric railways and high-voltage power lines. Even the power earthing of many closely spaced houses can give rise to pathogenic effects.

The human metabolism is influenced by ions (electrically charged particles). A person in the open air is subjected to an electrical voltage of about 180 V, although under very slight current due to the lack of a charge carrier. There can be up to several thousand ions in one cubic metre of air, depending on geographical location and local conditions → ④. They vary in size and it is the medium and small ions that have a biological effect. A strong electrical force field is produced between the mostly negatively charged surface of the earth and the positively charged air and this affects the body. The research of Tschishewskij in the 1920s revealed the beneficial influence of negative ions on animals and humans, and showed a progressive reduction in the electrical potential of humans with increasing age. In addition, the more negative ions there are in the air, the slower the rate at which humans age. Research in the last 50 years has also confirmed the beneficial effects of negative ions in the treatment of high blood pressure, asthma, circulation problems and rheumatism. The positive ions are predominant in closed rooms, particularly if they are dusty, rooms; but only negatively charged oxygenated air is biologically valuable. There is a large choice of devices which can be placed in work and utility rooms to artificially produce the negative ions (i.e. which produce the desirable steady field). Such steady fields (continuous current fields) change the polarisation of undesirably charged ions to create improved room air conditions. The devices are available in the form of ceiling electrodes and table or floor mounted units.

(SU is a measurement value; derived from Suhr, the home town of Schröder-Speck)

MEASUREMENT BASIS

THE EYE: PERCEPTION

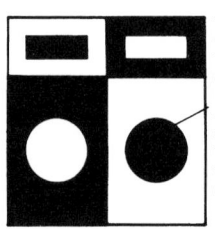

from a distance the black circle looks about 30% smaller than the white circle

(1) Black areas and objects appear smaller than those of the same size which are white: the same applies to parts of buildings

same size / same effect

(2) To make black and white areas look equal in size, the latter must be drawn smaller

(3) These vertical rules are actually parallel but appear to converge because of the oblique hatching

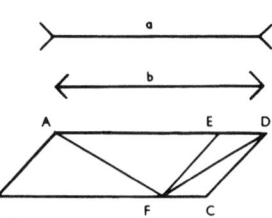

(4) Lengths a and b are equal, as are A–F and F–D, but arrowheads and dissimilar surrounds make them appear different

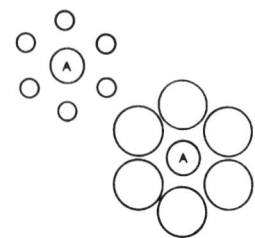

(5) Although both are equal in diameter, circle A looks larger when surrounded by circles that have a smaller relative size

(6) Two identical people seem different in height if the rules of perspective are not observed

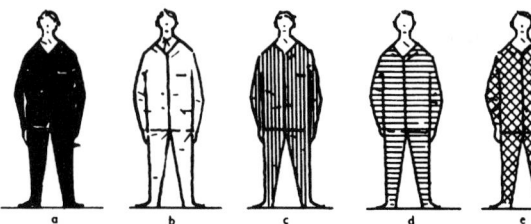

(7) The colour and pattern of clothing can change people's appearance: (a) thinner in black (black absorbs light); (b) more portly in white (white spreads light); (c) taller in vertical stripes; (d) broader in horizontal stripes; (e) taller and broader in checked patterns

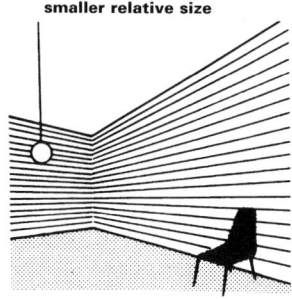

with different divisions, identical rooms can appear to differ in size and form

(8) Dynamic effect

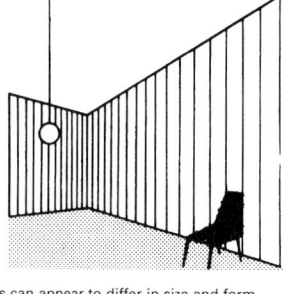

(9) Static effect

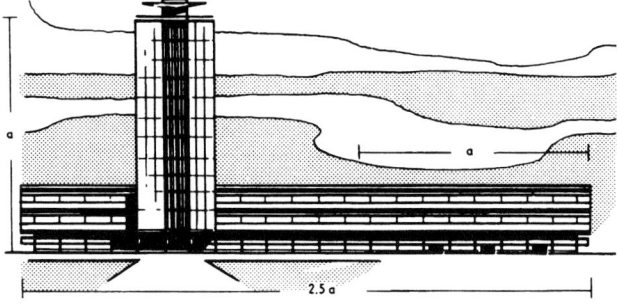

(10) Vertical dimensions appear disproportionately more impressive to the eye than horizontal ones of the same size

(11)–(14) The perception of scale is changed by the ratio of the window area to the remaining area of wall as well as by architectural articulation (i.e. vertical, horizontal or mixed → (10)); glazing bars can contribute substantially to this

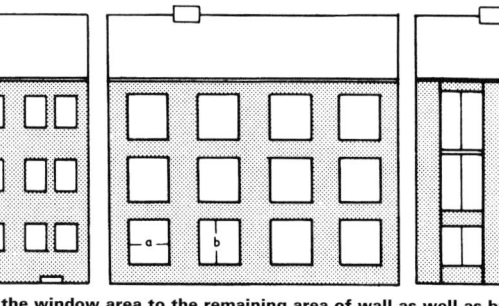

(15)–(17) The positioning of windows, doors and furnishings can give a room different spatial appearances: (15) long and narrow; (16) seems shorter with the bed across the room, or the table below the window; (17) with windows opposite the door and appropriate furniture, the room seems more wide than deep

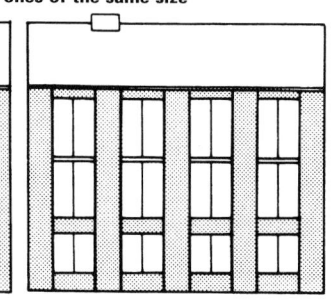

(18) A structure can appear taller if viewed from above; there is a greater feeling of certainty when looking up

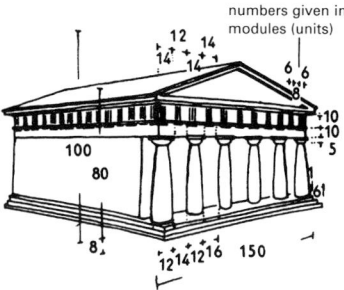

numbers given in modules (units)

(19) The walls slanting suitably inward seem vertical; steps, cornices and friezes when bowed correctly upwards look horizontal

24

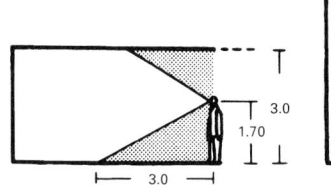

① The perception of a low room is gained 'at a glance' (i.e. still picture)

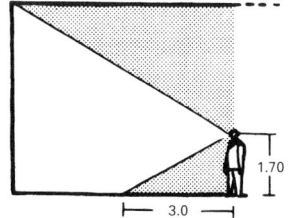

② In higher rooms, the eyes must scan upwards (i.e. scan picture)

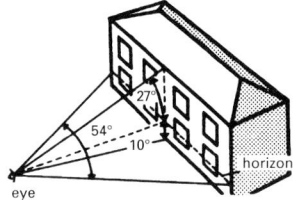

③ The human field of vision (head still, moving the eyes only) is 54° horizontally, 27° upwards and 10° downwards

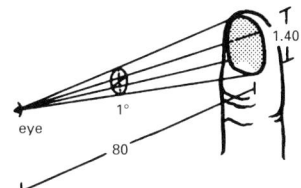

④ The field of view of the normal fixed eye takes in a perimeter of 1° (approx. the area of a thumbnail of an outstretched hand)

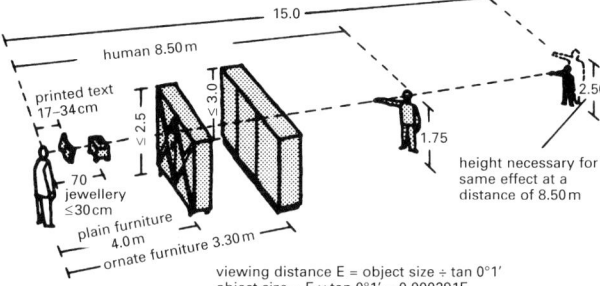

viewing distance E = object size ÷ tan 0°1'
object size = E × tan 0°1' = 0.000291E

⑤ The eye can resolve detail within a perimeter of only 0°1' (the field of reading), thus limiting the distances at which objects and shapes can be distinguished accurately → ⑥

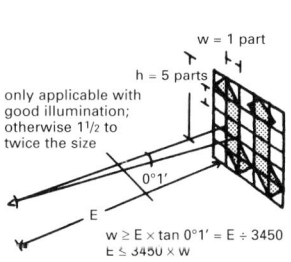

$w \geq E \times \tan 0°1' = E \div 3450$
$E \leq 3450 \times w$

⑥ To be readable at a distance of, say, 700 m the width w of the letters must be:
$\geq 700 \times 0.000291 = 0.204$;
height h is usually 5w:
$5 \times 0.204 = 1.020$ m

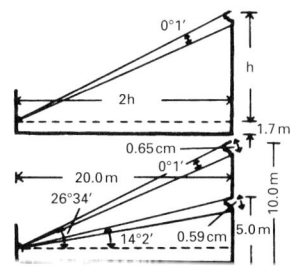

⑦ As in the previous examples, the size of structural parts which are differentiable can be calculated using the viewing distance and trigonometry

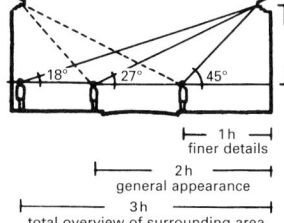

⑧ Street widths play an important role in the level of detail which is perceived from ground level

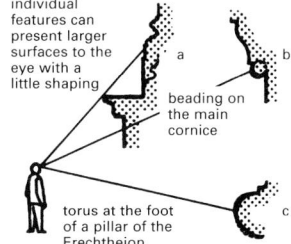

individual features can present larger surfaces to the eye with a little shaping

beading on the main cornice

torus at the foot of a pillar of the Erechtheion

⑨ Parts of buildings meant to be seen but sited above projections must be placed sufficiently high up (see a)

The activity of the eye is divided into seeing and observing. Seeing first of all serves our physical safety but observing takes over where seeing finishes; it leads to enjoyment of the 'pictures' registered through seeing. One can differentiate between a still and a scanned picture by the way that the eye stays on an object or scans along it. The still picture is displayed in a segment of the area of a circle, whose diameter is the same as the distance of the eye from the object. Inside this field of view the objects appear to the eye 'at a glance' → ③. The ideal still picture is displayed in balance. Balance is the first characteristic of architectural beauty. (Physiologists are working on a theory of the sixth sense – the sense of balance or static sense – that underpins the sense of beauty we feel with regard to symmetrical, harmonious things and proportions (→ pp. 27–30) or when we are faced with elements that are in balance.)

Outside this framework, the eye receives its impressions by scanning the picture. The scanning eye works forward along the obstacles of resistance which it meets as it directs itself away from us in width or depth. Obstacles of the same or recurring distances are detected by the eye as a 'beat' or a 'rhythm', which has the same appeal as the sounds received by the ear from music. 'Architecture is Frozen Music. This effect occurs even when regarding a still or scanned picture of an enclosed area → ① and ②.

A room whose top demarcation (the ceiling) we recognise in the still picture gives a feeling of security, but on the other hand in long rooms it gives a feeling of depression. With a high ceiling, which the eye can only recognise at first by scanning, the room appears free and sublime, provided that the distance between the walls, and hence the general proportions, are in harmony. Designers must be careful with this because the eye is susceptible to optical illusions. It estimates the extent of width more exactly than depths or heights, the latter always appearing larger. Thus a tower seems much higher when seen from above rather than from below → p. 24 ⑩ and ⑱. Vertical edges have the effect of overhanging at the top and horizontal ones of curving up in the middle → p. 24 ① – ⑨, ⑲. When taking these things into account, the designer should not resort to the other extreme (Baroque) and, for example, reinforce the effect of perspective by inclined windows and cornices (St Peter's in Rome) or even by cornices and vaulting painted in perspective and the like. The decisive factor for the measurement of size is the size of the field of view → ③ and, if applicable, the field of vision → ④ and, for the exact differentiation of details, the size of the field of reading → ⑤ and ⑥. The distance of the latter determines the size of the details to be differentiated.

The Greeks complied exactly with this rule. The size of the smallest moulding under the cornice of the individual temples of varying height is so dimensioned that, at an angular distance of 27° → ⑦, it complies with the reading field of 0°1'. From this also results the reading distances for books (which varies with the size of the letters) and the seating plans for auditoriums etc.

MAN AND COLOUR

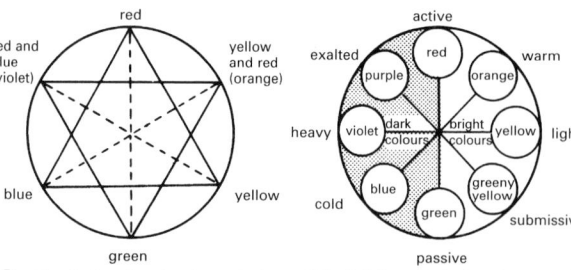

① Goethe's natural colour circle: red–blue–yellow triangle are basic colours (from which all colours can be mixed); green–orange–violet triangle shows colour mixtures of the first rank

② Bright and dark colours and their effect on humans

③ Light and heavy colours (not the same as bright and dark colours → ②): create a 'heavy' feeling

④ The colour circle's twelve segments

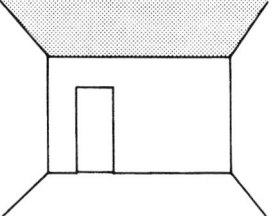

⑤ Dark colours make a room heavy: rooms seem to be lower, if ceilings are heavily coloured

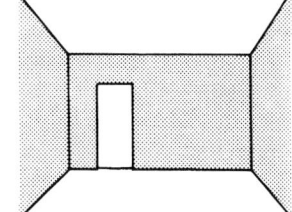

⑥ Bright colours give a lift: rooms seem higher with emphasis on walls and light ceilings

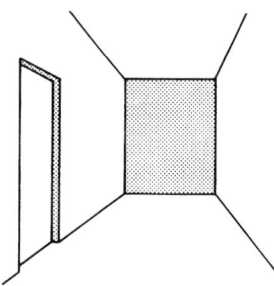

⑦ Long rooms seem shorter if end cross walls stand out heavily

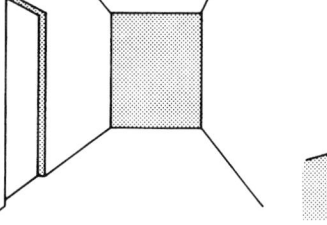

⑧ White as a dominant colour, e.g. in laboratories, factories etc.

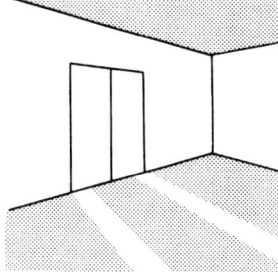

⑨ Dark elements in front of a bright wall give a powerful effect

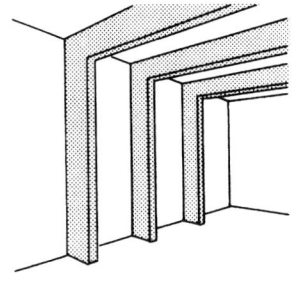

⑩ Bright elements in front of a dark background seem lighter, particularly when over-dimensioned

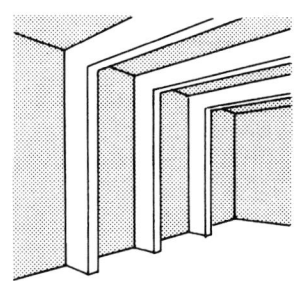

Colours have a power over humans. They can create feelings of well-being, unease, activity or passivity, for instance. Colouring in factories, offices or schools can enhance or reduce performance; in hospitals it can have a positive influence on patients' health. This influence works indirectly through making rooms appear wider or narrower, thereby giving an impression of space, which promotes a feeling of restriction or freedom → ⑤ – ⑦. It also works directly through the physical reactions or impulses evoked by the individual colours → ② and ③. The strongest impulse effect comes from orange; then follow yellow, red, green, and purple. The weakest impulse effect comes from blue, greeny blue and violet (i.e. cold and passive colours).

Strong impulse colours are suitable only for small areas in a room. Conversely, low impulse colours can be used for large areas. Warm colours have an active and stimulating effect, which in certain circumstances can be exciting. Cold colours have a passive effect – calming and spiritual. Green causes nervous tension. The effects produced by colour also depend on brightness and location.

Warm and bright colours viewed overhead have a spiritually stimulating effect; viewed from the side, a warming, drawing closer effect; and, seen below, a lightening, elevating effect.

Warm and dark colours viewed above are enclosing or dignified; seen from the side, embracing; and, seen below, suggest safe to grip and to tread on.

Cold and bright colours above brighten things up and are relaxing; from the side they seem to lead away; and, seen below, look smooth and stimulating for walking on.

Cold and dark colours are threatening when above; cold and sad from the side; and burdensome, dragging down, when below.

White is the colour of total purity, cleanliness and order. White plays a leading role in the colour design of rooms, breaking up and neutralising other groups of colours, and thereby create an invigorating brightness. As the colour of order, white is used as the characteristic surface for warehouses and storage places, for road lines and traffic markings → ⑧.

Brightness of surfaces

Values between theoretical white (100%) and absolute black (0%)

white paper	84	light brown	approx. 25	grass green	approx. 20	asphalt, dry	approx. 20
chalky white	80	pure beige	approx. 25	lime green, pastel	approx. 50	asphalt, wet	approx. 5
citron yellow	70	mid brown	approx. 15	silver grey	approx. 35	oak, dark	approx. 18
ivory	approx. 70	salmon pink	approx. 40	grey lime plaster	approx. 42	oak, light	approx. 33
cream	approx. 70	full scarlet	16	dry concrete, grey	approx. 32	walnut	approx. 18
gold yellow, pure	60	carmine	10	plywood	approx. 38	light spruce	approx. 50
straw yellow	60	deep violet	approx. 5	yellow brick	approx. 32	aluminium foil	83
light ochre	approx. 60	light blue	40–50	red brick	approx. 18	galvanised iron sheet	16
pure chrome yellow	50	deep sky blue	30	dark clinker approx.	10		
pure orange	25–30	turquoise blue, pure	15	mid stone colour	35		

DIMENSIONAL RELATIONSHIPS

Basis

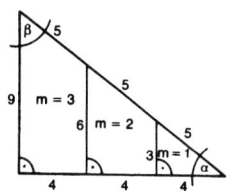

fourth 3/4
octave 1/2   third 4/5
sixth 3/5
fifth 2/3   prime 1/1
minor third 5/6

(1) **Pythagoras's rectangle includes all interval proportions and excludes the disharmonious second and seventh**

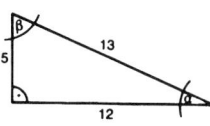

(2) **Pythagoras's triangle**

α	a	b	c	β	m	x	y
36°87'	3	4	5	53°13'	1	1	2
22°62'	5	12	13	67°38'	1	2	3
16°26'	7	24	25	73°74'	1	3	4
28°07'	8	15	17	61°93'	0.5	3	5
12°68'	9	40	41	77°32'	1	4	5
18°92'	12	35	37	71°08'	0.5	5	7
43°60'	20	21	29	46°40'	0.5	3	7
31°89'	28	45	53	58°11'	0.5	5	9

(3) **Some numerical relationships from Pythagoras's equations**

(4) **Example**

There have been agreements on the dimensioning of buildings since early times. Essential specific data originated in the time of Pythagoras. He started from the basis that the numerical proportions found in acoustics must also be optically harmonious. From this, Pythagoras developed his right-angled triangle → ①. It contains all the harmonious interval proportions, but excludes both the disharmonious intervals (i.e. the second and seventh).

Space measurements are supposed to have been derived from these numerical proportions. Pythagoras or diophantine equations resulted in groups of numerals → ② – ④ that should be used for the width, height and length of rooms. These groups can be calculated using the formula $a^2 + b^2 = c^2$.

$$a^2 + b^2 = c^2$$
$$a = m(y^2 - x^2)$$
$$b = m \cdot 2 \cdot x \cdot y$$
$$c = m(y^2 + x^2)$$

In this x and y are all whole numbers, x is smaller than y, and m is the magnification or reduction factor.

The geometric shapes named by Plato and Vitruvius are also of critical importance (i.e. circle, triangle → ⑤ and square → ⑥ from which polygonal traverses can be constructed). The respective bisection then results in further polygonal traverses. Other polygonal traverses (e.g. heptagon → ⑨, nonagon → ⑩) can only be formed by approximation or by superimposition. So we can construct a fifteen-sided figure → ⑧ by superimposing the equilateral triangle on the pentagon.

The pentagon or pentagram has a natural relationship with the golden section, just like the decagon which is derived from it ⑪, ⑫ and → p. 30. However, in earlier times its particular dimensional relationships found hardly any application. Polygonal traverses are necessary for the design and construction of so-called 'round' structures. The determination of the most important measurements (radius r, chord c, and height of a triangle h) are shown in → ⑬ and ⑭.

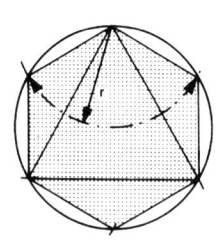

(5) **Equilateral triangle, hexagon**

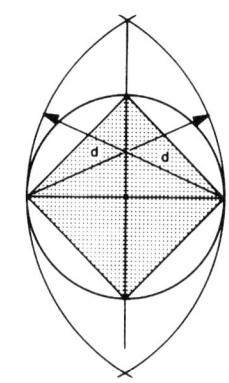

(6) **Square**

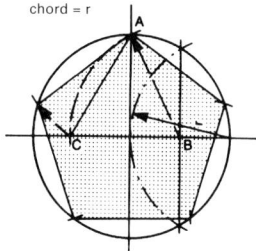

chord = r

bisection of the radius △ B;
arc at B with AB △ C
A–C △ side of a pentagon

(7) **Pentagon**

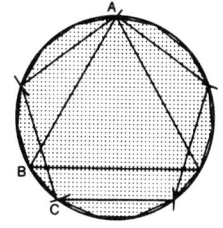

(8) **Fifteen angle BC = $\frac{2}{5} - \frac{1}{3} = \frac{1}{15}$**

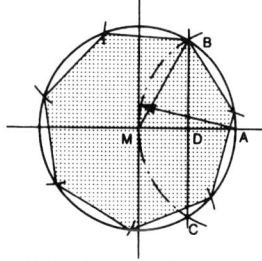

straight BC bisects AM at D;
BD is approx. 1/7 of the circumference of the circle

(9) **Approximated heptagon**

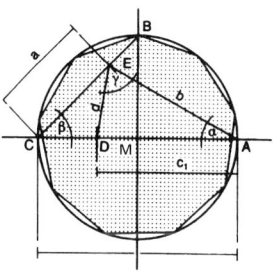

arc of the circle at A with AB results in point D on AC = c_1;
arc of the circle at C with CM results in point E on arc of BD = a;
segment DE approximately corresponds with 1/9 of the circle's circumference △ D

(10) **Approximated nonagon**

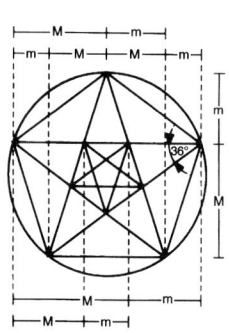

(11) **Pentagon and golden section**

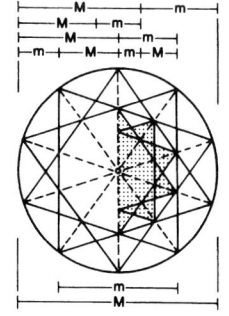

(12) **Decagon and the golden section**

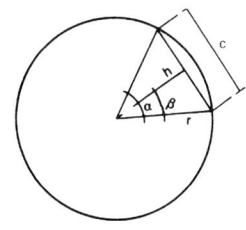

$$h = r \cdot \cos\beta$$
$$\frac{c}{2} = r \cdot \sin\beta$$
$$c = 2 \cdot r \cdot \sin\beta$$
$$h = \frac{c}{2} \cdot \cotan\beta$$

(13) **Measurement calculation in polygonal traverse → p. 28**

(14) **→ ⑬ formula**

DIMENSIONAL RELATIONSHIPS

Basis

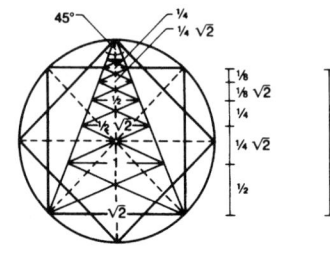

(1) π/4 triangle
(according to A. V. Drach)

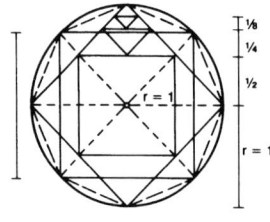

(2) Squares developed from the octagon → ② − ④

A right-angled isosceles (i.e. having two equal sides) triangle with a base-to-height ratio of 1:2 is the triangle of quadrature.

An isosceles triangle with a base and sides that can be contained by a square was successfully used by Knauth, the master of cathedral construction, for the determination of the dimensional relationships for the Strasbourg Cathedral.

Drach's π/4 triangle → ① is somewhat more pointed than the previous one described, as its height is determined by the point of a slewed square. It, too, was successfully used for details and components.

Apart from these figures, the dimensional proportions of the octagon can be detected on a whole range of old structures. The so-called diagonal triangle serves as a basis here. The triangle's height is the diagonal of the square built on half the base → ② − ④.

The sides of the rectangle depicted in ⑤ have a ratio of 1:√2. In accordance with this, all halvings or doublings of the rectangle have the same ratio of 1: √2. The 'step ladders' within an octagon make available the geometric ranges in ② − ④. The steps of square roots from 1–7 are shown in ⑥. The connection between square roots of whole numbers is shown in ⑦.

The process of factoring makes possible the application of square roots for building in non-rectangular components. By building up approximated values for square figures, Mengeringhausen developed the MERO space frames. The principle is the so-called 'snail' → ⑧ − ⑩. The inaccuracies of the right angle are compensated for by the screw connections of the rods at the joints. A subtly differentiated approximated calculation of square roots of whole numbers √n for non-rectangular components is available from the use of continued fractions (→ p. 30) in the formula expressed as G =

$$\sqrt{n} = 1 + \frac{n-1}{1+G} \to ⑪$$

(3) ③ → ②

(4) ④ → ②

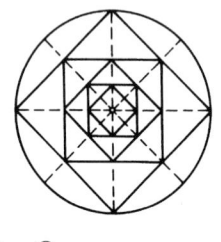

(5) 1:√2 rectangle

(6) Step ladder of square roots

√7 = 2.646
√6 = 2.450
√5 = 2.236
√4 = 2.000 (double square)
√3 = 1.732
√2 = 1.414
1 (square)

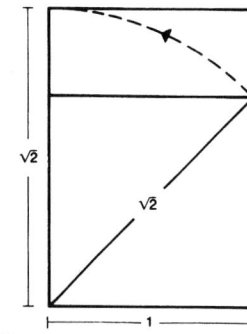

(7) Connection between square roots

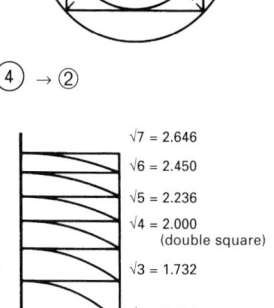

(8) The 'Snail'

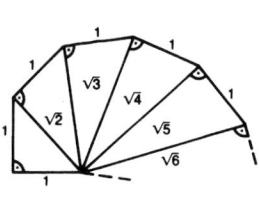

(9) Non-rectangular co-ordination – MERO space frames: building on √2 and √3 → pp. 90–91

(10) √3

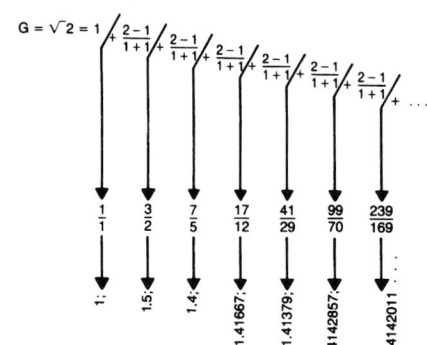

$$G = \sqrt{2} = 1 + \frac{2-1}{1+1} + \frac{2-1}{1+1} + \frac{2-1}{1+1} + \frac{2-1}{1+1} + \frac{2-1}{1+1} + \frac{2-1}{1+1} + \frac{2-1}{1+1} + \ldots$$

$\frac{1}{1}$ $\frac{3}{2}$ $\frac{7}{5}$ $\frac{17}{12}$ $\frac{41}{29}$ $\frac{99}{70}$ $\frac{239}{169}$ . . .

1:   1.5;   1.4;   1.41667;   1.41379;   1.4142857;   1.4142011

√2 = 1.4142135

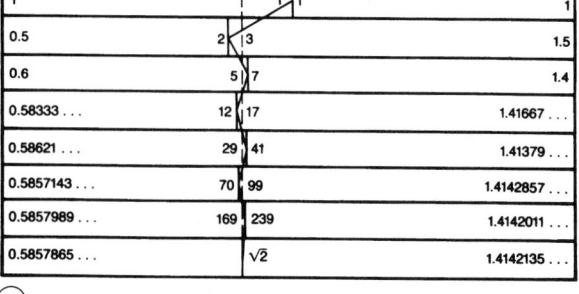

1	1 / 1	1
0.5	2 / 3	1.5
0.6	5 / 7	1.4
0.58333 . . .	12 / 17	1.41667 . . .
0.58621 . . .	29 / 41	1.41379 . . .
0.5857143 . . .	70 / 99	1.4142857 . . .
0.5857989 . . .	169 / 239	1.4142011 . . .
0.5857865 . . .	√2	1.4142135 . . .

(11) Continued fraction √2

Application

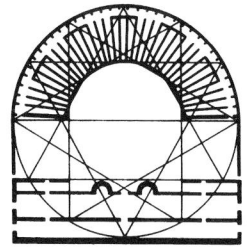

① **Roman theatre (according to Vitruvius)**

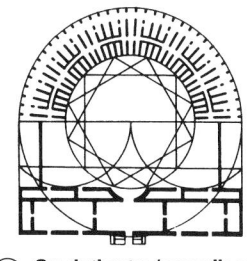

② **Greek theatre (according to Vitruvius)**

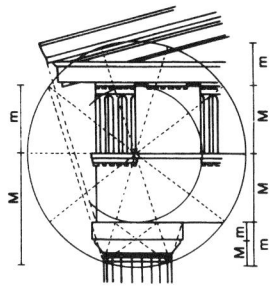

③ **Dimensional proportions of the gable corner of a Doric temple on the basis of the golden section (according to Moessel)**

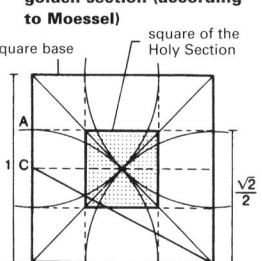

④ **Theatre at Epidaurus**

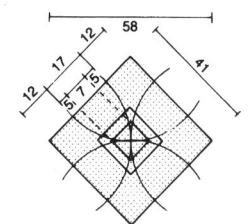

1 newest cavea
2 oldest cavea
3 orchestra
4 scenery storage
5 side gangway
6 retaining wall

⑤ **Holy Section, building in Antica-Ostia**

x	x	y/x (√2 = 1.4142...)
1	1	1
2	3	1.5
5	7	1.4
12	17	1.4/66...
24	41	1.4/37...

⑥ **Geometrical principle**

The application of geometrical and dimensional relationships on the basis of the details given earlier was described by Vitruvius. According to his investigations, the Roman theatre, for example, is built on the triangle turned four times → ① the Greek theatre on a square turned three times → ②. Both designs result in a dodecagon. This is recognisable on the stairs. Moessel has tried to detect the use of proportional relationships in accordance with the golden section → ③, although this is not obvious. The only Greek theatre whose plan view is based on a pentagon stands in Epidaurus → ④.

In a housing estate recently uncovered in Antica-Ostia, the old harbour of Rome, the golden section is recognised as being the design principle. This principle consists of a bisection of the diagonal of a square. If the points at which the arc of the circle cuts the sides of the square are joined with √2/2, a nine-part grid is obtained. The square in the middle is called the square of the Holy Section. The arc AB has up to a 0.6% deviation and the same length as the diagonal CD of the base square. Thus the Holy Section shows an approximate method for squaring the circle → ⑤ – ⑧. The whole building complex, from site plan to the general arrangement details, is built with these dimensional proportions.

In his four books on architecture, Palladio gives a geometrical key, which is based on the details given by Pythagoras. He uses the same space relationships (circle, triangle, square, etc.) and harmonies for his structures (→ ⑨ and ⑩).

Such laws of proportion can be found formulated in absolutely clear rules by the cultures of the ancient peoples of the Far East → ⑪. The Indians with their 'Manasara', the Chinese with their modulation in accordance with the 'Toukou' and, particularly, the Japanese with their 'Kiwariho' method have created structural systematics, which guarantee traditional development and offer immense economic advantages.

In the 18th century and later, it was not a harmonic but an additive arrangement of dimensions which was preferred → ⑫. The Octameter system developed from this. It was only with the introduction of the modular ordering system that the understanding of harmonic and proportional dimensional relationships returned → ⑬ and ⑭. Details of the coordination system and coordination dimensions are given on pp. 34–5.

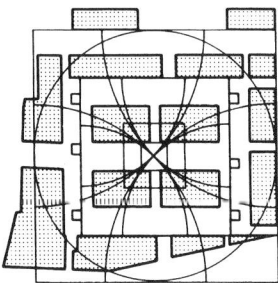

⑦ **Plan view of the whole installation**

⑧ **Floor mosaic in a house at Antica-Ostia**

⑨ **Geometric key to Palladio's villas**

⑩ **Palladio, Villa Pisani at Bagodo**

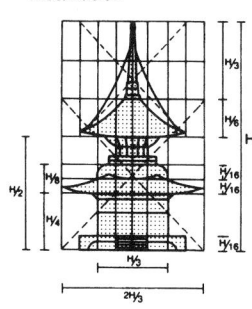

⑪ **Japanese treasury building**

⑫ **Guildhouse Rügen in Zurich**

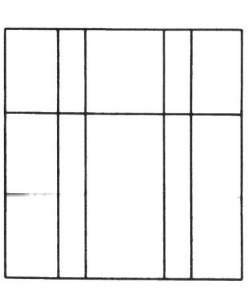

⑬ **Plan view of the BMW Administration Building in Munich**

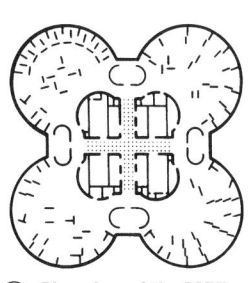

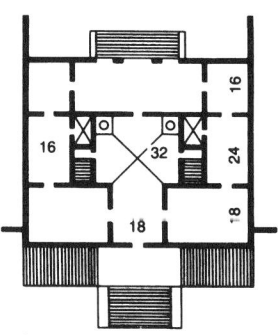

⑭ **Octagonal coordination system for columns made of squares, each subdivided into six façade elements, 48 angles developed from a triangle → ⑬**

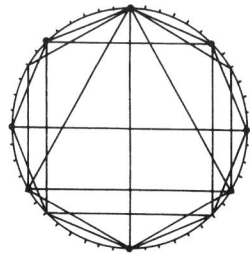

DIMENSIONAL RELATIONSHIPS

Application of Le Modulor

The architect Le Corbusier developed a theory of proportion, which is based on the golden section and the dimensions of the human body. The golden section of a segment of a line can be determined either geometrically or by formulae. It means that a line segment can be divided so that the whole of the line segment can be related to a bigger dividing segment, just as the larger is to the smaller → ①.

That is: $\dfrac{1}{\text{major}} = \dfrac{\text{major}}{\text{minor}}$

and shows the connection of proportional relationships between the square, the circle and the triangle → ②.

The golden section of a line segment can also be determined by a continued fraction

$$G = 1 + \frac{1}{G}$$

This is the simplest unending regular continued fraction. Le Corbusier marked out three intervals in the human body, which form a known golden section series according to Fibonacci. These are between the foot, the solar plexus, the head, the finger of the raised hand. First of all Le Corbusier started out from the known average height for Europeans (1.75 m → pp. 16–17), which he divided up in accordance with the golden section into 108.2 – 66.8 – 41.45 – 25.4 cm → ④.

As this last dimension was almost exactly equal to 10 inches, he found in this way a connection with the English inch, although not for the larger dimensions. For this reason, Le Corbusier changed over in 1947 to 6 English feet (1.828 m) as the height of the body. By golden section division he built the red row up and down → ⑤. As the steps in this row are much too big for practical use, he also built up a blue row, starting from 2.26 m (i.e. the finger tips of the raised hand), which gave double the values expressed in the red row → ⑤. The values of the red and blue rows were converted by Le Corbusier into dimensions which were practically applicable.

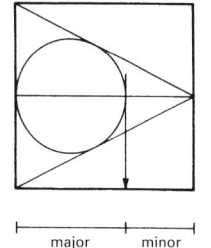

① Geometric design of the golden section

② Connection between square, circle, and triangle

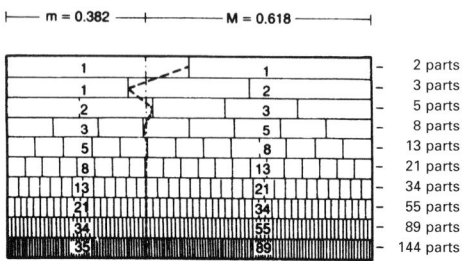

representation of the Lamesch Row from Neufert 'Bauordnungslehre'

③ Continued fraction: golden section

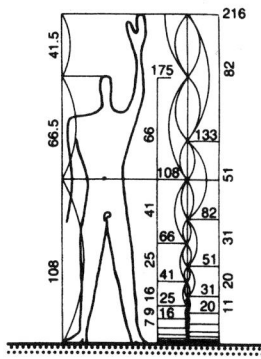

④ Proportional figure

$$G = 1 + \frac{1}{G}$$

$$G = 1 + \cfrac{1}{1 + \cfrac{1}{1 + \cfrac{1}{1 + \cfrac{1}{1 + \cfrac{1}{1 + \cfrac{1}{1\dots}}}}}}$$

values expressed in the metric system			
red row: re		blue row: bl	
centimetre	metre	centimetre	metre
95 280.7	952.8		
58 886.87	588.86	117 773.5	1 177.73
36 394.0	363.94	72 788.0	727.88
22 492.7	224.92	44 985.5	449.85
13 901.3	139.01	27 802.5	278.02
8 591.4	85.91	17 182.9	171.83
5 309.8	53.10	10 619.6	106.19
3 281.6	32.81	6 563.3	65.63
2 028.2	20.28	4 056.3	40.56
1 253.5	12.53	2 506.9	25.07
774.7	7.74	1 549.4	15.49
478.8	4.79	957.6	9.57
295.9	2.96	591.8	5.92
182.9	1.83	365.8	3.66
113.0	1.13	226.0	2.26
69.8	0.70	139.7	1.40
43.2	0.43	86.3	0.86
26.7	0.27	53.4	0.53
16.5	0.16	33.0	0.33
10.2	0.10	20.4	0.20
6.3	0.06	7.8	0.08
2.4	0.02	4.8	0.04
1.5	0.01	3.0	0.03
0.9		1.8	0.01
0.6		1.1	

⑤ Explanation of the values and sets of the Le Modulor according to Le Corbusier

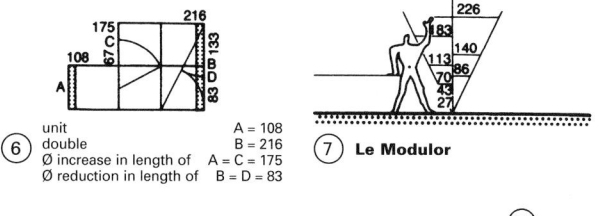

⑥ unit A = 108
double B = 216
Ø increase in length of A = C = 175
Ø reduction in length of B = D = 83

⑦ Le Modulor

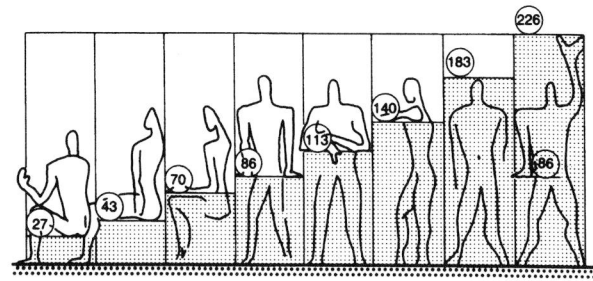

⑧ The limitless values of figures

For any construction project, completed standard description forms give the most valuable and clearest information, and are ideal for estimating, for the construction supervisor and as a permanent reference in the site office. Any time-consuming queries based on false information are virtually eliminated; the time gained more than compensating the effort involved in completing the record book. At the top of the form, there are columns for entering relevant room dimensions, in a way easily referred to. The inputs are most simply made using key words. The column 'size' should be used merely for entry of the necessary dimensions of the items, e.g., the height of the skirting board or the frieze, the width of the window sill, etc. Finally, several spaces are provided for special components. A space should be left free under each heading, so that the form can easily be extended for special cases. The reverse side of the form is best left free so that drawings may be added to elaborate on the room description on the next sheet. The A4 format pages are duplicated, each position containing exactly the same text; the sheets are kept up to date and eventually bound together. At the conclusion of the building work, the record book is the basis for the settlement of claims, using the dimensions at the head of the room pages. Later, the record book provides an objective record of progress, and is available for those with specialist knowledge.

① A sheet from the room record book

BASIC MEASUREMENT

② Representation of the Standard Number Series (base series 10)

Standard Numbering System

Metric units of linear measurement were first defined in France in 1790, although official recognition did not take place until 1840. The metre was established as the new decimal unit of length on a scientific basis, defined as the length of a simple pendulum having a swing of one second at sea level on latitude 45°. A standard numbering system was devised in Germany, shortly after World War I, to achieve uniformity and standardisation in the measurement of machines and technical equipment – a system also used in France and the USA. The starting point for measurement is the Continental unit of measurement: the metre. In the Imperial system (used in the UK, USA and elsewhere), 40 inches = 1.016 m ≈ 1.00 m.

The requirement of building technology for geometrical subdivisions precluded the use of the purely decimal subdivision of the metre, so the Standard Numbering System, based on the structure of 2s, was introduced into the decimal structure: 1, 2, 4, 8, 16, 31.5, 63, 125, 250, 500, 1000 → ②. (The coarser 5-part division and the finer 20- and 40-part division series are inserted appropriately with their intermediate values.) The geometrical 10-part division of the standard number series was formed from the halving series (1000, 500, 250, 125, ...) and from the doubling series (1, 2, 4, 8, 16, ...). Because π = 3.14 and √10 ≈ 3.16, the number 32, following 16 in the series, was rounded down to 31.5. Similarly, in the halving sequence, 62.5 was rounded up to 63.

Standard numbers offer many advantages in calculations:
1 the product and quotient of any two standard numbers are standard numbers
2 integer powers of standard numbers are standard numbers, and
3 double (or half) a standard number is a standard number.

Building measurements

In contrast to engineering, in building construction, there is little requirement for a geometric division as opposed to the prevailing arithmetic addition of identical structural components (e.g. blocks, beams, joists, girders, columns and windows). Routine measurements for standard components must, therefore, comply with these requirements. However, they should also conform to concepts of technical standardisation and the standard numbering system. A standard system of measurement for building construction was based on the standard numbering system, and this is the basis for many further building standards and of measurement for design and construction, particularly in building construction above ground.

Standard measurements

The controlling dimensions are dimensions between key reference planes (e.g. floor-to-floor height); they provide not only a framework for design but also a basis which components and assemblies may refer to → ③.

Standard dimensions are theoretical but, in practice, they provide the basis for individual, basic structural and finished measurements; thus all building components are linked in an organised way (e.g. standard building brick length = 250 mm (225 mm in UK), in situ concrete wall thickness = 250 mm.)

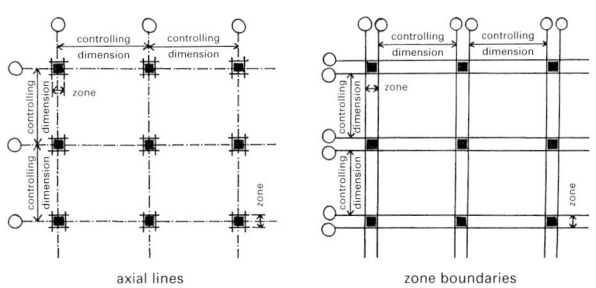

axial lines   zone boundaries

③ Horizontal controlling dimension

BASIC MEASUREMENTS

preferred series for basic construction		preferred series for individual measurements				preferred series for finishing		
a	b	c	d	e	f	g	h	i
25	$\frac{25}{2}$	$\frac{25}{3}$	$\frac{25}{4}$	$\frac{25}{10} = \frac{5}{2}$	5	2 × 5	4 × 5	5 × 5
				2.5				
				5				
			6¼	7.5				
		8⅓		10	10	10		
	12½			12.5				
			12½	15	15			
		16⅔		17.5				
			18¾	20	20	20	20	
				22.5				
25	25	25	25	25	25			25
				27.5				
			31¼	30	30	30		
		33⅓		32.5				
				35	35			
	37½		37½	37.5				
		41⅔		40	40	40	40	
			43¾	42.5				
				45	45			
50	50	50	50	50	50	50		50
				52.5				
			56¼	55	55			
		58⅓		57.5				
				60	60	60	60	
	62½		62½	62.5				
				65	65			
		66⅔	68¾	67.5				
				70	70	70		
				72.5				
75	75	75	75	75	75			75
				77.5				
			81¼	80	80	80	80	
		83⅓		82.5				
				85	85			
	87½		87½	87.5				
		91⅔		90	90	90		
			93¾	92.5				
				95	95			
				97.5				
100	100	100	100	100	100	100	100	100

(4) **Standard building dimensions**

Individual (mostly small) dimensions are used for details of basic construction/ finishing (e.g., thickness of joints/ plaster, dimensions of rebates, wall fixings/tolerances). Basic structural measurements relate, for example, to masonry (excluding plaster thicknesses), structural floor thicknesses, unplastered doors and window openings. Finished measurements refer to the finished building (e.g. net measurements of surface finished rooms and openings, net areas and finished floor levels). For building construction without joints, nominal dimensions equal the standard dimensions; with joints, the allowance for the joint is subtracted: e.g. building brick nominal length = standard length (250 mm) – thickness of intermediate joint (10 mm) = 240 mm; nominal thickness of in-situ concrete walls = standard thickness = 250 mm. In accordance with the standard number and measurement systems, small dimensions (≤25 mm), are chosen (in mm) as: 25, 20, 16,12.5, 10, 8, 6.3, 5, 3.2, 2.5, 2, 1.6, 1.25, 1. In many European countries, even small structural components conform with the standard building numbering system, e.g. standardised building bricks. A nominal brick dimension of 240×115 mm reconciles the old non-metric format (250×120 mm or 260×130 mm with joints) with the new standard (250×125 mm with joints). With the appropriate height, with joint, of 62.5 mm (nominal brick dimension = 52 mm), this gives an aspect ratio of 250×125×62.5 – 4:2:1. → (4)

Other basic construction component dimensions (e.g. concrete blocks → p. 63, window and door openings → p. 176–87 and floor levels) are similarly aligned, so these numerical values reoccur. The UK brickwork dimensions differ: in the past, large variations in the size of ordinary fired clay products often led to critical problems when bonding clay bricks; now, BS 3921: 1895 provides one standard for dimensioning (→ (5)): coordinating size (225×112.5×75 mm, including 10 mm in each direction for joints and tolerances), and the relating work size (215 (2 headers plus 1 joint) × 102.5 × 65 mm).

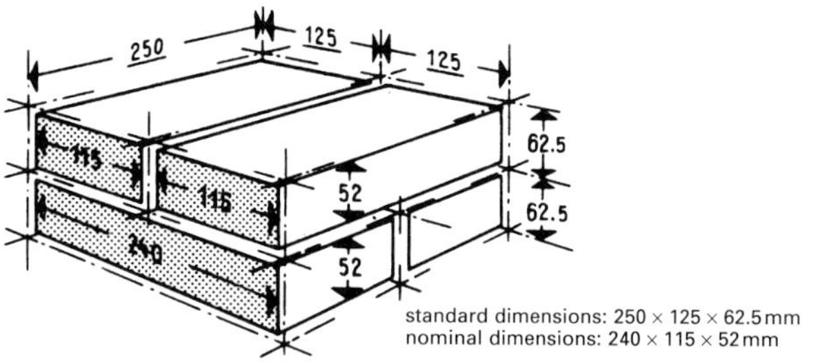
250
125
125
115
115
240
52
52
62.5
62.5
standard dimensions: 250 × 125 × 62.5 mm
nominal dimensions: 240 × 115 × 52 mm

(5) **Nominal and standard dimensions for continental European wall bricks**

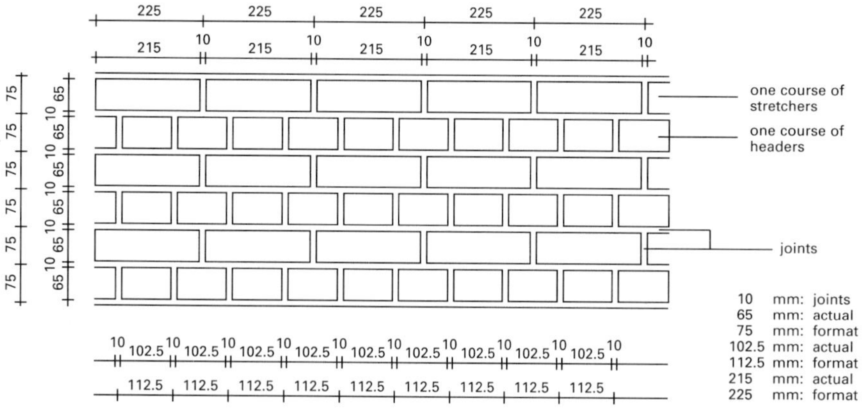
225
215
10
75
65
102.5
112.5
one course of stretchers
one course of headers
joints
10 mm: joints
65 mm: actual
75 mm: format
102.5 mm: actual
112.5 mm: format
215 mm: actual
225 mm: format

(6) **A wall elevation illustrating brick sizes in the UK**

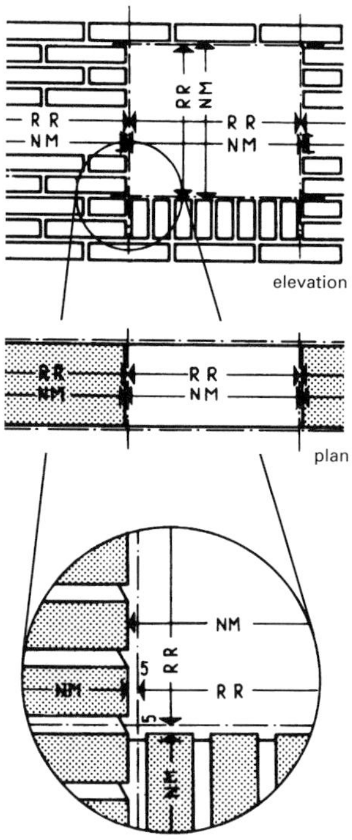
RR
NM
elevation
plan
5

(7) **Standard dimensions for basic construction (RR) and nominal dimensions (NM) for brickwork**
For openings: NM = RR + 2 × 1/2 joint = RR + 2.5 mm

Japan has the oldest building size regulations where, following the great fire in Tokyo in 1657, the style and size of houses were laid down on the basis of systematic measurement according to the 'Kiwariho method'. The basic dimension was the Ken = 6 Japanese feet = 1.818 m. The distances between the wall axes were measured in half or whole Ken, windows doors and even mat sizes were determined on this basis, which considerably simplified house building in Japan, making it quicker and cheaper. Examples → BOL.

In Germany, a similar system was developed in the area of half-timbered construction, prior to the introduction of the metre. The determining unit was the Prussian foot, which was most widely propagated and corresponded to the Rhenish and Danish foot.

The dimension between the axes of uprights was mostly 1 Gefach = 2 Ellen = 4 feet → ①. The Prussian, Rhenish and Danish foot, still in use in building practice in Denmark, is translated as 312.5 mm, the Elle as 625 mm and the Gefach as 1.25 m, in the metric system. Private construction firms had adopted a similar system of 1.25 m, for their system buildings, particularly for wood panel construction.

The UK and USA adopted a system of measurement based on 4 feet, which is close to 1.25 m, with 4 English feet = 1.219 m. Building panels (e.g. hardboard) manufactured on US machines are therefore 1.25 m wide in countries using the metric system. German pumice boards for roofs also have the standard dimension of 2 × 1.25 = 2.50 m, the same as plaster boards. Finally, 125 is the preferred number in the standard number system. The series of measurements resulting from 1.25 m was standardised in Germany in 1942 with the corresponding roof slopes → ②. In the meantime, thousands of types of structural components have been produced to this system of measurement. The distance between the axes of beams in finished ceilings today is, accordingly, usually 125/2 = 625 mm = the length of the stride of a human adult → p. 17.

Unified distances between axes for factory and industrial premises and accommodation

Industrial structures and structures for accommodation are mostly subdivided in plan into a series of axes at right angles. The line of measurement for these axes is always the axis of the structural system of the construction. The separations between axes are dimensional components of the plan, which determine the position of columns, supports, the centres of walls, etc. In the case of rigid frames, the centre axes of the bearing points of the foundations are decisive. The measurements are always referenced to the horizontal plan and vertical projection plane, even in the case of sloping roofs.

In industrial structures, a basic measurement of 2.5 m applies to the spacing of axes. Multiples of this give axis spacing of 5.0, 7.5 and 10.0 m, etc. In special cases

(accommodation or slab structures), a basic measurement of 2.50/2 = 1.25 m, or a multiple thereof, can be used. This results in intermediate dimensions of 1.25, 3.75, 6.25, 8.75 m. However, so far as possible, these sub-dimensions should not be used above 10 m.

Appropriate geometric steps over 10 m are recommended as follows: 12.50 m, 15.00 m, 20.00 m, 25.00 m, 30.00 m, 40.00 m, 50.00 m, 60.00 m, (62.50 m), 80.00 m, 100.00 m.

Roof slopes depend on the type of roofing and the sub-construction employed. The following roof slopes have been established to correspond with practical requirements:

1:20   for boarded roofing on steel and reinforced concrete structures and wood cement roofs, with the exception of special designs such as shell and saw-tooth roofs, etc.

1:12.5 for boarded roofing on wooden structures

1:4   for corrugated cement roofing, ridged zinc roofing, corrugated sheet roofing, steel roofs on lattice work or casings, ribbed steel roofs of galvanised, double folded sheet and roofing in waterproof paper-based materials for accommodation premises

1:2   for flat roofs, etc.

The systematic unification of industrial and accommodation structures has been a gradual process of type development.

The cited axis spacings influence the individual structural components: columns, walls, ceilings, trusses, purlins, rafters, roof planking, windows, glazing, doors, gates, crane runways and other elements. The establishment of a specified basic measurement for the spacing of axes creates the prerequisites for a hierarchical system of measurement standardisation for individual structural components and their matching interconnection. The spacings between axes are simply added together, without intermediate measurements. However, masonry, glass panes, reinforced concrete panels etc., must include an element for the jointing arrangements.

The points of support for a travelling crane can be unified on the basis of the standardised axis spacings.

The matched, standardised components and assemblies are interchangeable, can be prepared off-site and used in a versatile manner. Mass production, interchangeability of components/assemblies and the availability of standardised components and assemblies in store result in savings in work, materials, costs and time. The arrangement of the structural axes brings considerable simplification to building supervision.

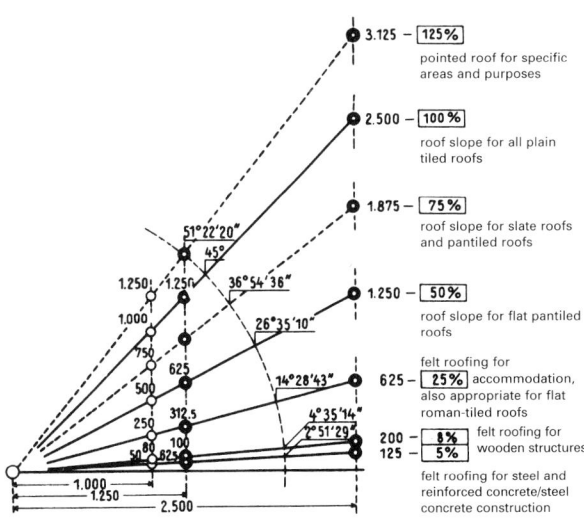

②   **Roof slopes at regular intervals appropriate to specified types of roof construction**

①   **Old Danish framed building with 1 'Gefach' separation between the axes of the uprights**

MODULAR SYSTEM

International agreements on the planning and execution of building work and for the design and manufacture of building components and semi-finished products are incorporated into national standards. The modular system is a means of coordinating the dimensions applicable to building work.

The term 'coordination' is the key, indicating that the modular layout involves an arrangement of dimensions and the spatial coordination of structural components. Therefore, the standards deal with geometrical and dimensional requirements. The modular system develops a method of design and construction which uses a coordinate system as a means of planning and executing building projects. A coordinate system is always related to specific objects.

Geometric considerations

By means of the system of coordinates, buildings and components are arranged and their exact positions and sizes specified. The nominal dimensions of components as well as the dimensions of joints and interconnections can thereby be derived. → ① – ⑥, ⑬

A coordinate system consists of planes at right angles to each other, spaced according to the coordinate measurements. Depending on the system, the planes can be different in size and in all three dimensions.

As a rule, components are arranged in one dimension between parallel coordinate planes so that they fill up the coordinate dimension, including the allowance allocated to the joints and also taking the tolerances into account. Hence a component can be specified in one dimension in terms of its size and position. This is referred to as boundary reference. → ⑦ → ⑫

In other cases, it can be advantageous not to arrange a component between two planes, but rather to make the central axis coincide with one plane of the coordinate system. The component is initially specified in one dimension with reference to its axis, but in terms of position only. → ⑦ → ⑫

A coordinate system can be divided into sub-systems for different component groups, e.g. load-bearing structure, component demarcating space, etc. → ⑧

It has been established that individual components need not be modularised, e.g. individual steps on stairways, windows, doors, etc. → ⑭

For non-modular components which run along or across the whole building, a so-called 'non-modular' zone can be introduced, which divides the coordinate system into two-sub systems. The assumption is that the dimension of the component in the non-modular zone is already known at the time of setting out the coordinate system, since the non-modular zone can only have completely specified dimensions. → ⑨

Further possible arrangements of non-modular components are the so-called centre position and edge position within modular zones. → ⑩ – ⑪

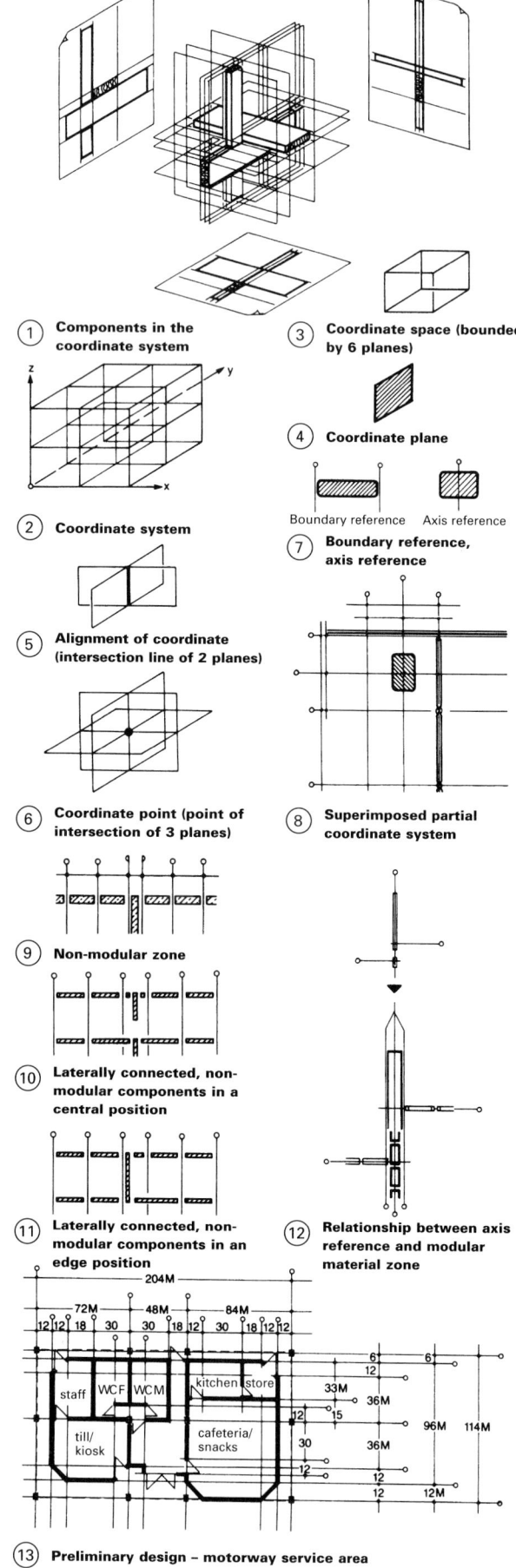

① Components in the coordinate system

② Coordinate system

③ Coordinate space (bounded by 6 planes)

④ Coordinate plane

Boundary reference   Axis reference

⑤ Alignment of coordinate (intersection line of 2 planes)

⑥ Coordinate point (point of intersection of 3 planes)

⑦ Boundary reference, axis reference

⑧ Superimposed partial coordinate system

⑨ Non-modular zone

⑩ Laterally connected, non-modular components in a central position

⑪ Laterally connected, non-modular components in an edge position

⑫ Relationship between axis reference and modular material zone

⑬ Preliminary design – motorway service area

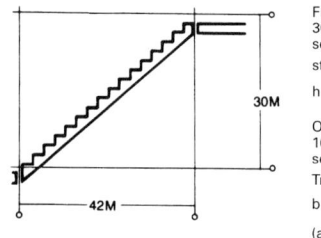

Floor-to-floor height:
30M = 300:19 = 15.8
select 16 steps

step rise:

$h = \frac{300}{16} = 18.75 \text{ cm}$

Overall length:
16.26 = 416cm
select 420 = 42M

Tread going:

$b = \frac{419}{16} = 26.2 \text{ cm}$

(assuming joint dimension of 1cm)

⑭ Reinforced concrete staircase unit

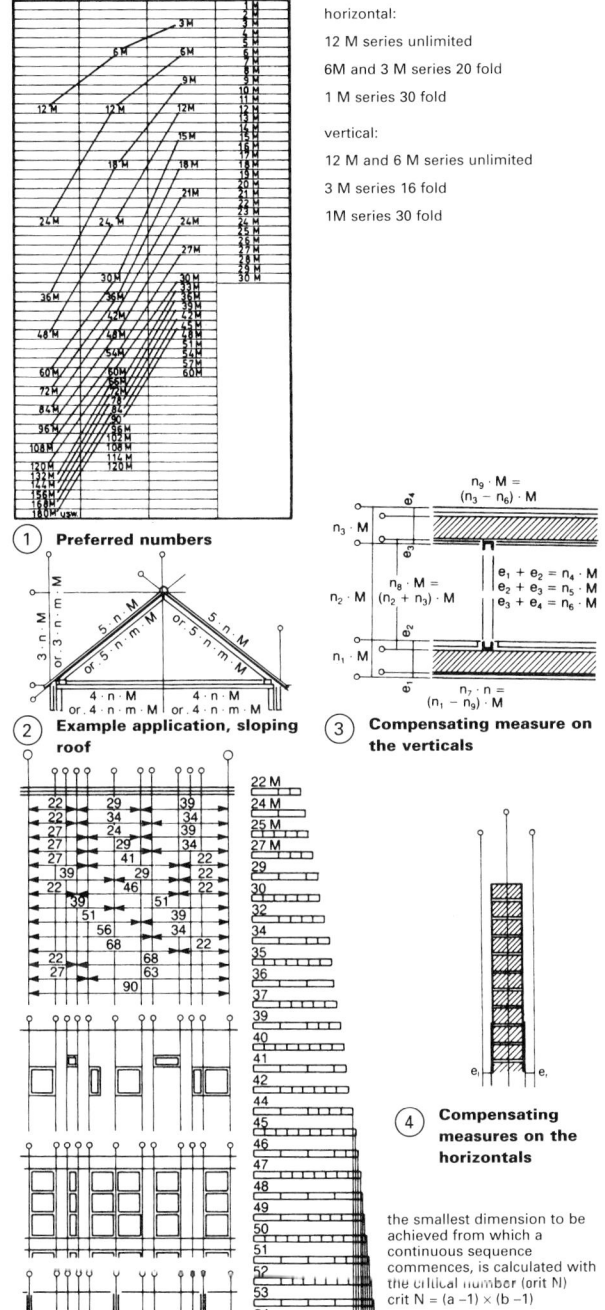

COORDINATE SYSTEM AND DIMENSIONING

Modular Arrangements in Building Practice

The units for the modular arrangement are M = 100 mm for the basic module and 3M = 300 mm, 6M = 600 mm, and 12 M = 1200 mm, for the multi-modules. The limited multiples of the preferred numerical series are generated in this way. The coordinate dimensions – theoretical standard dimensions – are, ideally, generated from these. These limitations are the result of functional, constructional and economic factors. → ①

In addition, there are standardised, non-modular extending dimensions, l = 25 mm, 50 mm and 75 mm, e.g., for matching and overlapping connection of components. → ③

The coordinate system in practical usage

Using rules of combination, different sizes of components can also be arranged within a modular coordinate system. → ⑤

With the help of calculations with numerical groups (e.g. Pythagoras) or by factorisation (e.g. continued fractions), non-rectangular components can also be arranged within a modular coordinate system. → ② + ⑥

By constructing polygonal traverses (e.g. triangular, rectangular, pentagonal and the halves of the same), the so-called 'round' building structures can be devised. → ⑦ – ⑧ Using modular arrangements, technical areas such as those for structural engineering, electrotechnology, transportation, which are dependent on each other from a geometrical and dimensional viewpoint, can be combined. → ⑨

limitation:

horizontal:

12 M series unlimited

6M and 3 M series 20 fold

1 M series 30 fold

vertical:

12 M and 6 M series unlimited

3 M series 16 fold

1M series 30 fold

① **Preferred numbers**

② **Example application, sloping roof**

③ **Compensating measure on the verticals**

④ **Compensating measures on the horizontals**

the smallest dimension to be achieved from which a continuous sequence commences, is calculated with the critical number (crit N)
crit N = (a −1) × (b −1)

crit N = (12−1) • (5−1) = 44

⑤ **Combination of component dimensions without a common divisor**

⑥ **Application of rotation about 45° using 12 M in the plan view**

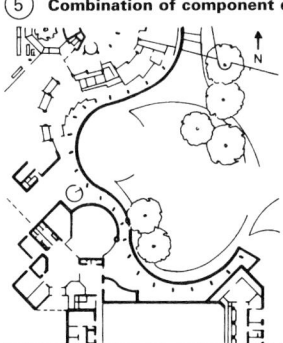

⑦ **Construction of a curving roof edge from regular polygonal traverses (site plan)**

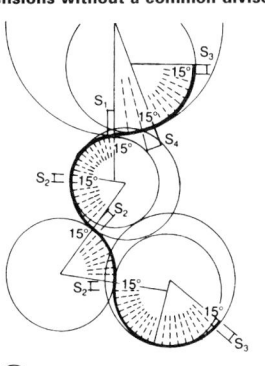

⑧ **Modular polygonal traverse**

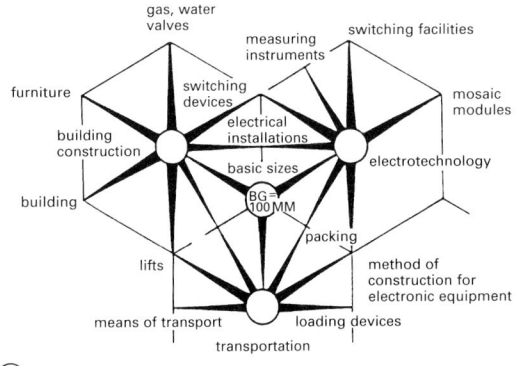

⑨ **Example of the linkage of technical areas using modular arrangements**

Functional Use of Materials

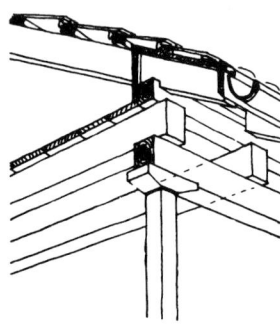

triglyphs
(three grooves)
metopes
(interspaces
→ ③)

① **Original timber construction used as a basis for the design of the Greek temple**

② **Stone construction developed by the Greeks and based on ①**

In the earliest civilisations, building form was dictated by the techniques of binding, knotting, tying, plaiting and weaving. Building in timber followed later, and in nearly all civilisations became the basis for architectural form (see the example of the Greek temple → ① and ②).

Recognition of this is relatively recent, but there is an increasing number of examples which support the accuracy of this theory. Uhde researched this matter at length and established that Moorish architectural skills originate from timber construction, in particular the Alhambra at Granada. The internal surface decor of Moorish buildings has its source in weaving techniques (like the ribbons and beaded astragals on Greek buildings), although it was actually pressed into the gypsum by moulds or inlaid as 'Azujelos' (glazed strips of clay). In several rooms of the Alcazar in Seville one can clearly see in the corners of the rooms the knotting together of the walls in the gypsum finish exactly in the way that the wall carpets of the tents were knotted at the corners in earlier centuries. Here the form derived from tent construction was simply transferred to the gypsum mould.

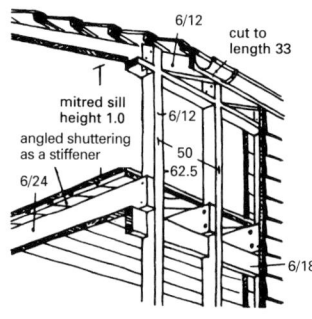

sprocket

render

wall plate

rendered rubble

dressed stone

③ **Timber construction (similar to ①) still used in many countries**

④ **Rubble walls need framing with dressed stones → p. 37**

Under the same conditions, forms which result from the material, construction and functional requirements are similar or even identical in every country and time.

The 'eternal form' was traced by V. Wersin with convincing examples. He showed that utensils used in the Far East and in Europe in 3000 BC are strikingly similar to those in use today. With new material, new technology and changing use, a different form inevitably evolves, even though embellishments can obscure or conceal the true form, or even give the impression of something quite different (baroque). The spirit of the age tends to decide the form of the building.

Today, in the buildings of other periods, we study not so much the result as the origin of the art. Each style arrives at its 'eternal form', its true culmination, after which it is developed and refined. We still strive after a true expression with our use of concrete, steel and glass. We have achieved success in finding some new and convincing solutions for factories and monumental buildings, in which the need for extensive window areas determines and expresses the structure.

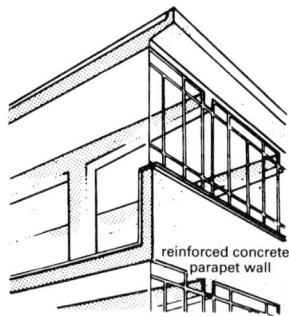

6/12

cut to length 33

mitred sill height 1.0

angled shuttering as a stiffener

6/12

6/24

50

62.5

6/18

drainage (internal)

stone coping

hollow pot slab

hollow blocks

facing brick

⑤ **Nailed timber frame. Practical and economical but without character; best hidden behind cladding**

⑥ **Reinforced concrete building with supports in external wall, fronted by outer leaf of parapet wall supported by the cantilevered floor**

The plain and distinct representation of the building parts, in conformity with their technical functions, provides possibilities for new forms in the details and the outward expression of buildings. Herein lies the new challenge for architects today. It is wrong to believe that our age needs only to develop clean technological solutions and leave it to the next period to cultivate a new form emanating from these structures → ②. On the contrary, every architect has the duty to harness contemporary technical possibilities extensively and to exploit their artistic potential to create buildings that express the ethos of the modern world (→ p. 39). This requires tact, restraint, respect for the surroundings, organic unity of building, space and construction, and a harmonious relationship between the articulation of interior spaces and the exterior form, in addition to fulfilling technological, organisational and economic demands. Even major artists with true creative drive ('those who have something to say') are subject to these restrictions and are influenced by the spirit of the age.

The clearer the artistic vision or the view of life of the artist, the more mature and rich the content of his work, and the longer it will endure as a beautiful object of true art for all time.

reinforced concrete parapet wall

light stone wall

⑦ **Reinforced concrete structure with internal columns, cantilevered floor and continuous ribbon windows**

⑧ **Reinforced concrete mushroom structure with light steel supports in outer wall between windows → p. 38**

VAULTING

The Result of Construction

1. **Primitives build circular huts with local materials: stones, poles and woven lianas are clad with leaves, straw, reeds, hides etc.**

2. **Similarly, Eskimos build summer houses of skin-clad whale ribs with windows made from seals' intestines, akin to the wigwam; winter houses are made of snow blocks**

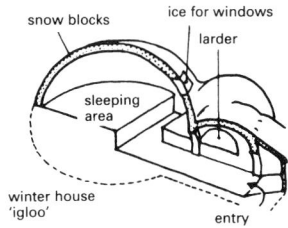

3. **The Romans built the first stone domes on a circular plan (e.g., in its purest form, Pantheon, Rome)**

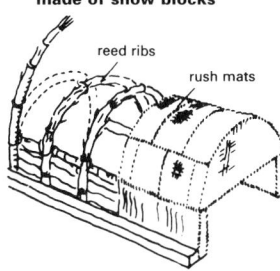

4. **The Sassanians in Persia (6th century AD) constructed their first domes on a square plan; transition from square to circle via squinch arches**

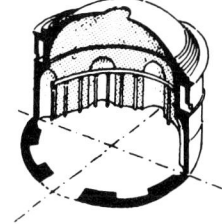

5. **1400 years ago, Byzantine architects created domes on the square plan of the Hagia Sophia, using the pendentive. Construction obscured inside (i.e. dematerialisation)**

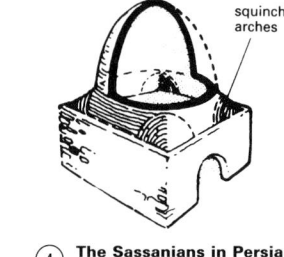

6. **As well as circular domes, barrel vaulting was widely used (e.g. Mesopotamia: reed ribs were covered with rush mats)**

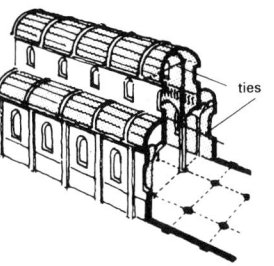

7. **Barrel vaulting in masonry was first used by the Romans and later appeared in Romanesque architecture (e.g. Šibenik church, Yugoslavia)**

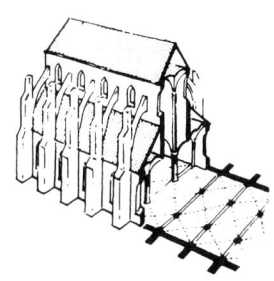

8. **Gothic architecture evolved from cross-vaulting, allowing the vaulting of oblong bays by using the pointed arch (characteristic buttresses and flying buttresses)**

TIMBER

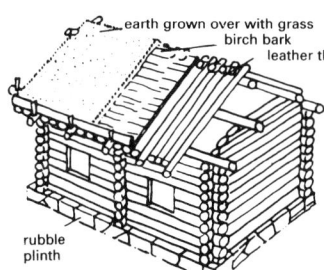

9. **Block-houses in wooded countries have a universal form dictated by the nature of their construction**

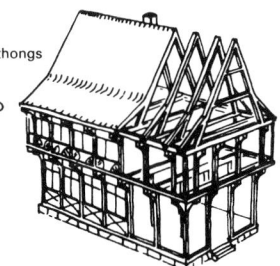

10. **In areas short of timber, buildings used wood posts; posts have windows between them and there are braces in the window breasts**

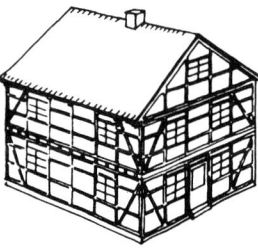

11. **In contrast, this framed building has isolated windows and corner struts; the panels are interlaced wickerwork with mud or clay rendering (wattle and daub)**

12. **Panel construction uses large prefabricated wall panels, which are quick and inexpensive to erect**

STONE

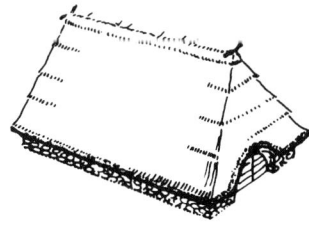

13. **Buildings of field stones without mortar (uncoursed random rubble) must have a low plinth; the structure consists almost entirely of roof, with a low entrance**

14. **Cut and dressed stones allow the construction of higher walls; with mortar joints, gables in stone with arched or vaulted openings become practicable**

15. **From a later period: framed openings and corners with carefully formed, dressed stones; the rest of the walls in rubble masonry which was then rendered**

16. **The desire for larger windows in town buildings led to a stone pillar construction style similar to the earlier timber post method → 10**

To begin with, it is always construction that is the basis of form. Later it develops onto a pure, and often abstract form, which is initially adopted when new building materials are introduced. Numerous examples of this can be found in history, from ancient stone tombs, in which even the lay observer can discern the basic timber form, to the automobile of 1900 that imitated the horse-drawn carriage (even down to the provision of a whip holder).

STEEL

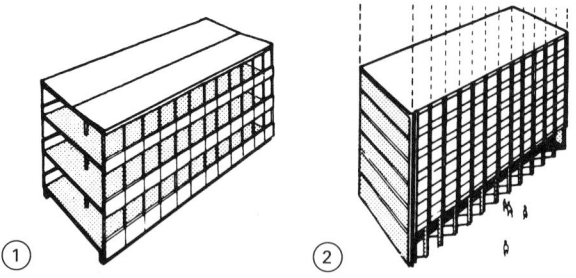

①   ②

Slender supports give steel-framed construction the lightest possible appearance → ①. However, this form is not permitted everywhere. Exterior unenclosed supports are rarely allowed → ② but, if combined with externally visible

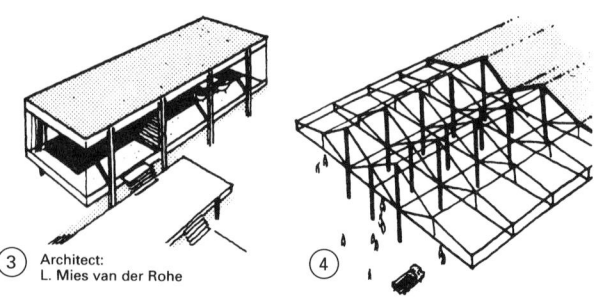

③ Architect:
L. Mies van der Rohe   ④

horizontal girders, can create an especially light but solid appearance of unobstructed space → ③. Steel and aluminium structures are particularly suitable for light open halls with few supports and cantilevered roofs → ④.

REINFORCED CONCRETE

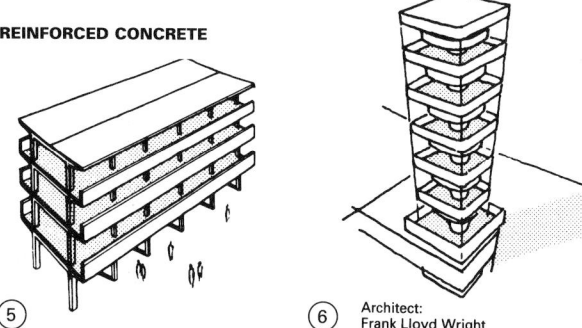

⑤   ⑥ Architect:
Frank Lloyd Wright

For many building types, building regulations require fire resistant or even fire proof construction and encased steel members consequently resemble reinforced concrete.

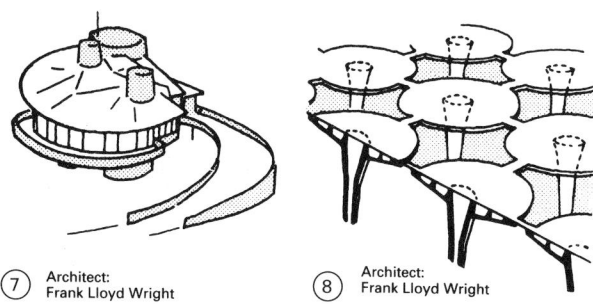

⑦ Architect:
Frank Lloyd Wright   ⑧ Architect:
Frank Lloyd Wright

Typical characteristics are cantilevered floors on beams → ⑤ from tower cores → ⑥, or house core supports → ⑦, or as mushroom structures → ⑧.

SHELL ROOFS

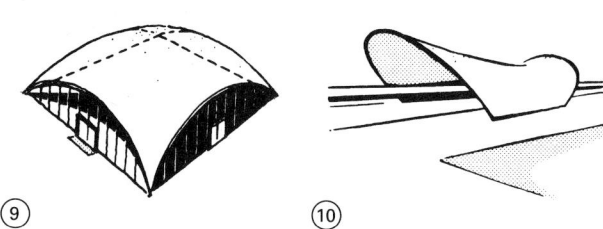

⑨   ⑩

In shell structures, forces are distributed uniformly in all directions. Types include: cupola with segments → ⑨, oblong

CABLE STRUCTURES

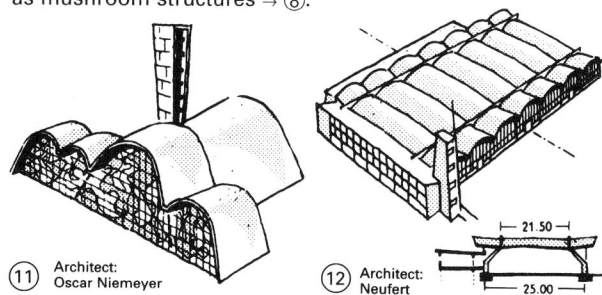

⑪ Architect:
Oscar Niemeyer   ⑫ Architect:
Neufert

shell → ⑩, rhythmically arranged transverse shells → ⑪, rows of shells with inclined supports at neutral points → ⑫.

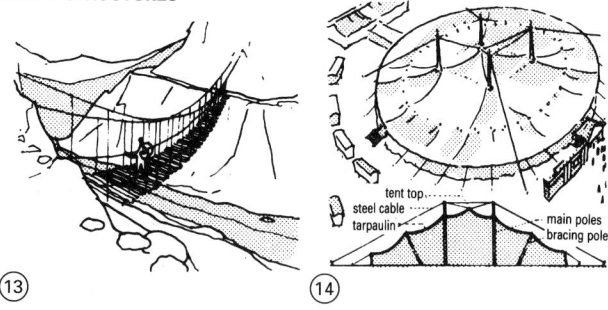

tent top
steel cable
tarpaulin
main poles
bracing pole

⑬   ⑭

Cable structures for long spans have been in use since early times → ⑬. Circus tents are the best-known lightweight suspended diaphragm structure → ⑭. Modern reinforced

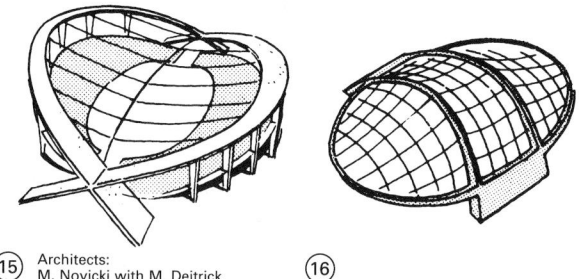

⑮ Architects:
M. Novicki with M. Deitrick   ⑯

concrete suspended diaphragms with rigid edge beams can create economical and impressive buildings → ⑮, and may be used as basis for cantilever constructions → ⑯.

The challenge for architects is to create form based on a fusion of architectural expression and knowledge of the technological principles of modern construction techniques. This unity was lost in the wake of the Industrial Revolution, before which available forms were used on a 'decorative' basis in any construction type, whether in stone, wood or plaster.

The latest fire protection techniques can obviate the need for concrete encasement altogether. Intumescent coatings are often used for protecting structural steelwork against fire (especially the visually expressed elements). These look like normal paint but, in the event of fire, they foam, thus creating a protective layer around the steel.

ACCESS

① Around AD 1500, houses and towns were protected by high walls and heavy gates

② By 1700 walls and gates were only symbolic, giving glimpses of the garden

③ In the 1800s, detached houses were built in open surroundings with low fences

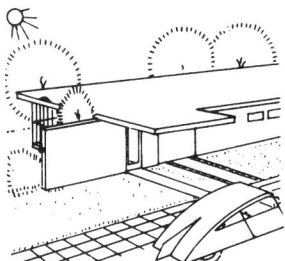

④ Twentieth century houses have no enclosure (in the US, particularly) and stand unobtrusively among trees in large communal parks

ENTRANCES

⑤ AD 1000: log cabins had low doors, high thresholds; no windows; lit through an opening in the roof

⑥ By 1500: heavy, studded doors with knocker, and windows with bars and bull's eye panes

⑦ Around 1700, doors had clear glass panes with decorative glazing bars (also, a bell-pull)

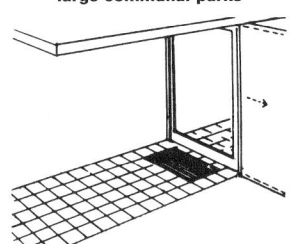

⑧ Twentieth century: covered walkway leads from car to door (wired plate glass), which slides open when an electric eye is activated

ROOM CONNECTIONS

⑨ AD 1500: low, heavy doors, sparse daylighting, and floors of short, wide boards

⑩ In the 1700s, wide double doors led into suites of rooms with parquet flooring

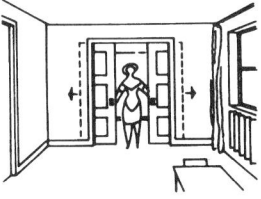

⑪ By 1900, sliding doors were fitted between rooms, linoleum flooring, sliding windows, and draw curtains

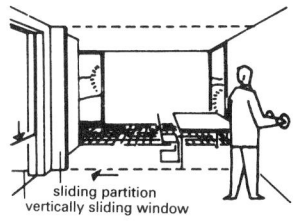

⑫ Twentieth century rooms are flexible: sliding walls and plate glass windows; venetian blinds/shutters as protection from the sun

HOUSES

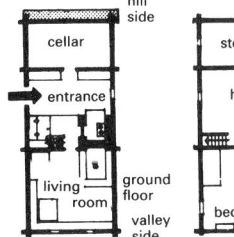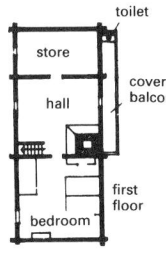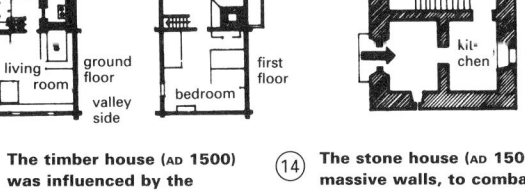

⑬ The timber house (AD 1500) was influenced by the environment, method of construction and the way of life; e.g. Walser house

⑭ The stone house (AD 1500): massive walls, to combat enemies/cold, required the same area as the rooms themselves

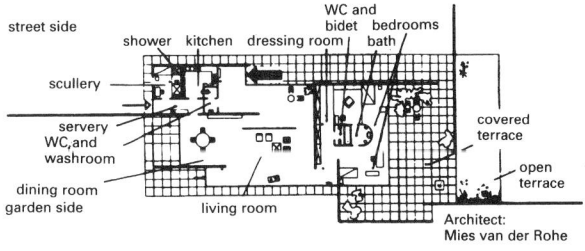

⑮ The house of the 2000s will have slender steel supports and slim non-load-bearing curtain walling, the composition of which affords full protection against the weather, and maximum noise and heat insulation. Open plan, with dividing screens between living area, dining room and hall (no doors)

In the time between the beginning of the 16th century (the period of witch-hunts, superstition, leaded lights and fort-like houses, a form which is still occasionally in demand) and the present day, astonishing advances have been made in science, technology and industry. As a result the outlook of society has changed radically. In the intervening centuries it is clearly evident from buildings and their details, as well as other aspects of life, that people have become freer and more self-aware, and their buildings lighter and brighter. The house today is no longer perceived as a fortress offering protection against enemies, robbers or 'demons' but rather as a complementary framework for our way of life – open to nature and yet in every respect protected against its inclemency.

People generally see and feel things differently. Designers must therefore use their creativity as far as possible to translate our shared experience into reality and express it through the materials at their disposal. The attitude of the client is of the greatest significance in this issue. In some ways, many clients and architects are still living in the 15th century while few of each have arrived in the new millennium. If the 'centuries' meet in the right way, then a happy marriage between client and architect is assured.

DESIGN METHOD

Working Process

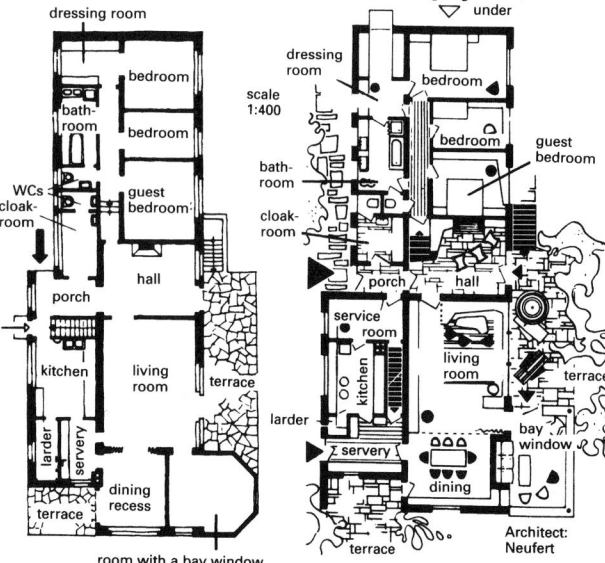

M. 1:2000

main road
main road
entrance drive
adjacent plot
58.5
59.04
59.5
north
bedroom
service room
living room
rose garden
north lawns
side road
side road
60.0
neighbouring site

① Four site layout proposals for development of a 3000 m² plot with a NE slope: proposal 4 planned by the client; proposal 1 accepted → ②

② This development, with a SE slope in front of the house, uses the contours correctly; yard to the west; entry from road to the north

dressing room
bedroom
bedroom
bathroom
WCs cloakroom
guest bedroom
hall
porch
kitchen
living room
terrace
larder
servery
dining recess
terrace

room with a bay window

garage access under
dressing room
scale 1:400
bedroom
bathroom
bedroom
cloakroom
guest bedroom
porch
hall
service room
kitchen
living room
terrace
larder
bay window
servery
dining
terrace
Architect: Neufert

③ House sketch design with faults: cloakroom and porch are too big; bathroom and servery are too narrow; the steps in the corridor are dangerous; restricted view from kitchen

④ Improved design for ③: better room plans; bedrooms 2.5 m above ground, using the site's natural slope; garage at ground level

The sketch scheme is begun by drawing up individual rooms of the required areas as simple rectangles drawn to scale and put provisionally into groups. After studying the movements of the people and goods (horizontally and vertically), analyse circulation and the relationships of rooms to each other and the sun → p. 272. During this stage the designer will progressively obtain a clearer understanding of the design problems involved. Instead of starting to design at this stage they should, on the basis of their previous work to establish the building area, determine the position of the building on the site, by exploring the various means of access, the prevailing wind, tree growth, contours, aspect, and neighbourhood. Try out several solutions to explore all possibilities → ① and use their pros and cons for a searching examination – unless of course a single obvious solution presents itself. Based on the foregoing, decision-making is normally fairly quick, and the 'idea' becomes clearer; then the real picture of the building emerges → ②.

Now the first design stage can begin, firstly as an organisational and spiritual impression in the mind. From this, a schematic representation of the general configuration of the building and its spatial atmosphere is built up, from which the designer can develop the real proposal, in the form of plans and elevations. Depending upon temperament and drawing ability a quick charcoal sketch, or a spidery doodle, forms the first tangible result of this 'birth'.

The first impetus may become lost if the efforts of assistants are clumsy. With growing experience and maturity, the clarity of the mental image improves, allowing it to be communicated more easily. Older, mature architects are often able to draw up a final design in freehand, correctly dimensioned and detailed. Some refined mature works are created this way, but the verve of their earlier work is often lacking.

After completion of the preliminary design, → ③, a pause of 3–14 days is recommended, because it provides a distancing from the design and lets shortcomings reveal themselves more clearly. It also often disposes of assumptions, because in the intervening time preconceived ideas are put aside, not least as a result of discussions with staff and clients. Then the detailed design of the project is begun with the assistance of various consultants (e.g. a structural engineer, service engineers for heating, water and electricity) firmly establishing the construction and installations.

Following this, but usually before, the plans are submitted to the relevant authorities for examination and permission (which might take about 3–6 months). During this time the costs are estimated and specification and Bill of Quantities produced, and the tendering procedure is undertaken, so that as soon as the permission to proceed is received, contracts can be granted and the work on site commenced.

All these activities, from receiving the commission to the start of building operations for a medium-sized family house, takes on average 2–3 months of the architect's time; for larger projects (hospitals, etc.) 6–12 months should be allowed. It is not advisable to try to make savings at this juncture; the extra time spent is soon recovered during building operations if the preparation has been thoroughly carried out. The client thus saves money and mortgage interest payments. The questionnaire (→ pp. 41 and 42) and the room specification folder (→ p. 31) will be important aids.

Building programme

The work begins with the drawing-up of a detailed brief, with the help of an experienced architect and guided by the questionnaire shown on the following pages. Before planning starts, the following must be known:

1 Site: location, size, site and access levels, location of services, building and planning regulations and conditions. This information should be sought from the local authority, service providers and legal representatives, and a layout plan to comply with this should be developed.

2 Space requirements with regard to areas, heights, positioning and their particular relationship with one another.

3 Dimensions of existing furniture.

4 Finance: site acquisition, legal fees, mortgages etc. → pp. 43–50.

5 Proposed method of construction (brick, frame construction, sloping roof, flat roof etc.).

Preparatory Work: Collaboration with Client

Preparatory work is often done in a rush, resulting in an insufficiently detailed scheme being put out to tender and commenced on site. This is how 'final' drawings and costs only become available when the building is nearly complete. Explanations are of no help to the client. The only way of solving the problem is faster and better organised work by the architect and sufficient preparation in the design office and on the construction site.

Similar information is required for most building projects, so detailed questionnaires and pro formas, available when the commission is received, can be used to speed things up. Certainly there will be some variations, but many factors are common and make questionnaires useful to all those involved in the project, even if they are only used as checklists.

The following questionnaire is only one of the labour saving pro formas which an efficient and well-run architect's office should have available, along with pro formas for costing purposes, etc.

Briefing Questionnaire

Commission No.:

....

Employer:

....

Project Description:

....

Information collected by:

....

Copies to:

....

I Information on the client
1 What is their financial status?
   Business outlook? Total capital employed? ⎫ confidential
   Where was the information obtained? ⎭
2 How does the business seem to be conducted?
3 Who is our main contact? Who is our contact is his absence? Who has the final authority?
4 Has the client any special requests regarding design?
5 Have they any special interest in art? (In particular with regard to our attitude and design method.)
6 What personal views of the client need to be taken into account?
7 Who is liable to cause us difficulties and why? What could be the effects?
8 Is the customer interested in publication of his building later on?
9 Do the drawings have to be capable of being understood by laymen?
10 Who was the client's architect previously?
11 For what reason did he or she not receive this commission?
12 Is the client thinking of further buildings? If so, when, what type, how large? Have they already been designed? Is there the possibility that we might obtain this commission? What steps have been taken in this direction? With what success?

II Agreements on fees
1 On what agreement with the client are the conditions of engagement and scale of professional charges based?
2 What stages of the work are included in the commission?
3 Is the estimated project cost the basis for the fee calculation?
4 What is the estimated project cost?
5 Are we commissioned to carry out the interior design?
6 Has a form of agreement between employer and architect been signed and exchanged?

III Persons and firms involved in the project
1 With whom do we have to conduct preliminary discussions?
2 Who is responsible for what special areas of activity?
3 Who is responsible for checking the invoices?
4 Which system of ordering and checking will be used?
5 Will we have authority to grant contracts in the name of the client? If so, to what value? Do we have written confirmation for this? Who does the client recommend as contractor or sub-contractor? (Trade; Name; Address;

Telephone)
6 Is a clerk of works essential or merely desirable, and should he or she be experienced or junior? When is he or she required, and for how long (duration of job or only part)?
7 Have we explained duties and position of clerk of works to client?
8 Is accommodation available for site offices and material storage? What about furniture, telephone, computers, fax, heating, lighting, WC and water?

IV General
1 Is hoarding required? Can it be let for advertising? Is signboard required and, if so, what will be on it?
2 Exact address of the new building and name after completion?
3 Nearest railway station?
4 Postal district/town?
5 Is there a telephone on site, and if not when will one be available? Alternatively is there a telephone in the vicinity?
6 Have we obtained a local edition of the national working rules for the building industry? Are there any additional clauses?

V The project
1 Who has drawn up the building programme? Is it exhaustive or has it to be supplemented by us or others? Has the client to agree again before the design work starts?
2 Has the new building to be related to existing and future buildings?
3 Which local regulations have to be observed? Who is building inspector or district surveyor? Who is town planning officer?
4 What special literature is available on this type of building? What do we have in our files?
5 Where have similar buildings been built?
6 Have we taken steps to view them?

VI Basic design factors
1 What are the surroundings like? Are landscaping and trees to be considered? What about climate, aspect, access, and prevailing wind?
2 What is the architecture of existing buildings? What materials were employed?
3 Do we have photographs of neighbourhood with viewpoints marked on plan? If not, have they been ordered?
4 What other factors have to be considered in our design?
5 What are the existing floor-to-floor heights and heights of buildings? What is the situation with regard to roads, building lines, future roads, trees (types and sizes)?
6 What future development has to be considered?
7 Is it desirable to plan an area layout?
8 Are there regulations or restrictions concerning elevational treatment in district?
9 What is known of attitude of town planning officer or committee towards architecture? Is it advisable to discuss initial sketches with town planning officer before proceeding?
10 In case of appeal, is anything known of the time taken and the ministry's decision in similar cases in this district?

VII Technical fact finding

1 What sort of subsoil is common to this area?
2 Has the site been explored? Where have trial holes been sunk? What were the results?
3 What is load-bearing capacity of subsoil?
4 Average ground water level? High water level?
5 Has the site been built on previously? Type of buildings? How many storeys? Was there a basement and, if so, how deep?
6 What type of foundation appears to be suitable?
7 What type of construction is envisaged?
   In detail:
   Basement floor: Type? Applied load? Type of load? Floor finish? Insulation? Tanking?
   Ground floor: Type? Applied load? Type of load? Finishes?
   Other floors: Type? Applied load? Type of load? Finishes?
   Roof: Structure? Loading? Type of loading? Roof cladding? Protective finishes and coatings? Gutters? Internal or external downpipes?
8 What insulation materials are to be employed? Sound insulation: horizontal/vertical? Impact sound: horizontal/vertical? Heat insulation: horizontal/vertical?
9 Type of supports? Outer walls? Partitions?
10 Staircase structure? Applied load?
11 Windows: steel/timber/plastic/wood/aluminium? Type and weight of glass? Internal or external seating? Single, double or combination windows? Double glazing?
12 Doors: steel frames? Plywood? Steel? Lining? Fire grading? Furniture? With an automatic door closing device?
13 Type of heating: solid fuel/gas/electricity/oil? Fuel storage?
14 Domestic hot water: amount required and at what times? Where? Water softener required?
15 Ventilation: air conditioning? Type? Air change? In which rooms? Fume extraction? Smoke extraction?
16 Cooling plant? Ice making?
17 Water supply? Nominal diameter of supply pipe and pressure? Is pressure constant? Water price per cubic metre or water rate? Stand pipes required? Where and how many?
18 Drainage and sewerage? Existing? Connection points? Nominal bore of main sewer? Invert levels? Where does the sewage flow to? Soak pits? Possible, advisable, permitted? Septic tank or other sewage treatment necessary?
19 Nominal bore of the gas supply pipe? Pressure? Price per cubic metre? Reduction for large consumption? Special regulations concerning installation of pipes? Ventilation?
20 Electricity? A.C. or D.C.? Voltage? Connection point? Voltage drop limit? Price per kW? Off-peak? Price reduction for large consumption? Transformer? High-voltage transformer station? Own generator? Diesel, steam turbine, windmill?
21 Telephone? Where? ISTD? Telephone box? Where? Cable duct required?
22 Intercom? Bells? Lights? Burglar alarm?
23 What type of lift? Maximum load? Speed? Motor at top or bottom?
24 Conveyor systems? Dimensions? Direction of operation? Power consumption? Pneumatic tube conveyor?
25 Waste chutes or sink destructor disposal units? Where? Size? For what type of refuse? Waste incineration? Paper baling press?
26 Any additional requirements?

VIII Records and preliminary investigations

1 Have deeds been investigated? Copy obtained? Anything relevant with regard to the project planning?
2 Map of the locality available? Ordered? Transport details?
3 Does site plan exist? Ordered?
4 Does contour map exist? Ordered?
5 Water supply indicated on plan?
6 Mains drainage drawing checked out and cleared?
7 Gas supply shown on the drawing?
8 Is electricity supply agreed with Board and shown on plan? Underground cable or overhead line?
9 Telephone: underground cable or overhead wires?
10 Have front elevations of the neighbouring houses been measured or photographed? Has their construction been investigated?
11 Has datum level been ascertained and fixed?
12 Is site organisation plan required?
13 Where does the application for planning permission have to be submitted? How many copies? In what form? Paper size? With drawings? Prints? On linen? Do drawings have to be coloured? Are regulations for signs and symbols on drawings understood?
14 Requirements for submission of the structural calculations? Building inspector? (Normally decided by council planning department)

IX Preliminaries

1 How far is the construction site from the nearest rail freight depot?
2 Is there a siding for unloading materials? What gauge? What are the off-loading facilities?
3 What are access roads like, in general? Are temporary access roads necessary?
4 What storage space facilities are available for materials? Available area open/under cover? What is their level in relation to site? Can several contractors work alongside one another without any problems?
5 Will the employer undertake some of the work himself; supply some material? If so what: landscaping, site cleaning/security services?
6 Method of payment, interim certificates, etc.? Otherwise what terms and conditions of payment are to be expected?
7 What local materials are available? Are they particularly inexpensive in the area? Price?

X Deadlines for:

1 Preliminary sketches for discussion with staff and consultants?
2 Preliminary sketches for meetings with the client, town planning officer, district surveyor or building inspector?
3 Sketch design (to scale) with rough estimates?
4 Design (to scale)?
5 Estimate? Specification? Bill of Quantities?
6 Submission of the application for planning permission and building regulations approval with structural calculations, etc.?
7 Anticipated time for gaining permits? Official channels? Possibilities for speeding things up?
8 Pre-production drawings, working drawings?
9 Selection of contractors? Letters of invitation? Despatching of tender documents?
10 Closing date for tenders? Bill of Quantities?
11 Acceptance of tender? Progress chart? Date for completion?
12 Possession of site? Commencement of work?
13 Practical completion?
14 Final completion?
15 Final account?

DESIGN

Organisation

The range of topics discussed in this section are listed below:

A Definition of terms
  1.0 Building design
  2.0 Building construction
B Duties and outputs for construction management
  1.0 Construction planning
  1.1 Definition of duties and outputs/contents
  1.2 Aims/risks of construction planning
  1.3 Means and tools for construction management
   * Construction drawings
   * Sectional drawings (component drawings, junction drawings)
   * Special drawings
   * Specifications
   * Area/room/component schedules, specifications, bills of quantities
  2.0 Tender action and letting of contracts
  2.1 Definition of duties and outputs/contents
  2.2 Aims/risks of tender action and letting of contracts
  2.3 Means and tools of tender action and letting of contracts
   * Contract laws and regulations
   * Contract conditions and articles of agreement
   * Technical conditions and preambles
   * Standard specifications, manufacturers' specifications and performance specifications
  3.0 Construction supervision
  3.1 Definition of duties and outputs/contents
  3.2 Aims/risks of construction supervision
  3.3 Means and tools of construction supervision
   * Standard procedures
   * Techniques of project management/time management

A Definition of terms

Definition of duties describing the necessary architectural services and the relevant fees are contained in the respective guidelines for each country or professional body, e.g. the RIBA Architects' Plan of Work in the UK, or the HOAI [Honorarordnung für Architekten und Ingenieure] in Germany.

1.0 Building design

The briefing and design stages (A–D in RIBA Plan of Work, 1–4 in HOAI) include inception/feasibility (3%), outline proposals (7%), scheme design (11%) and approvals planning (6%). Design services typically represent 27% of the total fee.

2.0 Building construction

The production drawings and information stages (E–H in RIBA Plan of Work, 5–9 in HOAI) include detail design, production information, bill of quantities (if applicable) (25%), preparing tender documents (10%), tender action (4%), site supervision (31%), project administration and documentation (3%). Construction management duties typically represent 73% of the total fee.

B Duties and outputs for construction management
1.0 Construction planning

1.1 Definition of duties and outputs/contents

Basic services

 * Working through the results of stages 2 and 4 (stage by stage processing information and presenting solutions) – taking into account the urban context, design parameters, and functional, technical, structural, economic, energy (e.g. rational energy use) biological, and economical requirements – and co-operating with other building professionals, to bring the design to the stage where it can be constructed
 * Presenting the design in a full set of drawings with all the necessary documentation including detail and construction drawings, 1:50 to 1:1, and accompanying specifications in text

 * In schemes which include interior fittings and design, preparing detailed drawings of the rooms and fittings to scales 1:25 to 1:1, together with the necessary specifications of materials and workmanship
 * Coordination of the input of the other members of the design team and integrating their information to produce a viable solution
 * Preparation and co-ordination of the production drawings during the building stage

Additional services

These additional services can be included as basic services if they are specifically listed in a schedule of services. This will negate some of the limitations in the standard list of basic services.

 * Setting up a detailed area-by-area specification in the form of a room schedule to serve as a basis for a description of materials, areas and volumes, duties and programme of works
 * Setting up a detailed specification in the form of a bill of quantities to serve as a basis for a description of materials, duties and programme of works
 * Inspection of the contractors' and sub-contractors' specialist design input developed on the basis of the specification and programme of works, to check that it accords with the overall design planning
 * Production of scale models of details and prototypes
 * Inspection and approval of design drawings produced by organisations outside the design team, testing that they accord with the overall design planning (e.g., fabrication drawings from specialist manufacturers and contractors, setting-up and foundation drawings from machine manufacturers), insomuch as their contracts do not form a part of the main contract sum (upon which the professional fees have been calculated)

1.2 Aims/risks of construction planning

Construction planning aims to ensure a trouble- and fault-free execution of the works. This requires a complete and detailed establishment of the formal and technical requirements, and their compliance with formal, legal, technical and economic matters.

 * *Legal basis:* planning and building regulations, and other regulations such as safety guidelines, e.g. for places of assembly
 * *Technical basis:* established standards and techniques of construction and materials, e.g. building standards, consultation/agreement with specialists and specialist contractors
 * *Economic basis:* cost control techniques, e.g. cost estimates/calculations, and consultation/agreement with specialists in this field

Insufficient construction planning results in – among other things – wastage of materials (correction of errors, breakages and decay), waste of productive time (time wasting, duplicated work), and persistent loss of value (planning mistakes/construction faults).

1.3 Means and tools for construction management

Construction drawings contain all the necessary information and dimensions for construction purposes; normal scale is 1:50.

Sectional drawings (component drawings, junction drawings), expand on the construction drawings with additional information on parts of the building works; normal scale is 1:20 , 1:10 , 1:5 or 1:1.

Special drawings are tailored to the specific requirements of elements of the work (e.g. reinforced concrete work, steelwork or timber structural work) and show only the essential aspects of the other building features which relate to that particular specific element of work; normal scale is 1:50, depending on the particular needs. National standards and conventions govern the

43

drawing modes which, ideally, should be compatible with CAD (computer aided design) and the standard methods of specification and measurement of quantities and pricing. Suitable software packages are available.

Area/room/component schedules, specifications, bills of quantities, contain full information – in the form of lists and tables – about the sizes (e.g. length, width, height, area and volume), the materials (e.g. wall coverings and floor finishes), and equipment (e.g. heating, ventilation, sanitary, electrics, windows and doors) of which make up the building, building elements, rooms or other areas. They serve as a basis for a full specification of materials and workmanship. Bills of quantities are commonly used in the UK and for large contracts in other countries.

2.0 Tender action and letting of contracts i.e. the preparation/co-operation during tender action and letting of contracts

2.1 Definition of duties and outputs/contents i.e. stages G + H in RIBA Plan of Work, and 6 + 7 in HOAI
Basic services
* Production and collation of quantities as a basis for setting up specifications, using information from other members of the design team
* Preparation of specifications with schedules according to trades
* Co-ordination and harmonisation of specifications prepared by other members of the design team
* Compiling the preambles of the specifications for all the trades
* Issuing the tender documents and receiving tenders
* Inspection and evaluation of the tenders, including preparation of a cost breakdown by element, in co-operation with the rest of the design team engaged in these stages
* Harmonisation and collation of the services of the design team engaged in tender action
* Negotiation with tenderers
* Setting up of cost predictions, including the fixed price and variable price elements of the tenders
* Co-operation during the granting of contracts
Additional services
* Setting up specifications and bills on the basis of area schedules and building schedules
* Setting up alternative specifications for additional or specific works
* Compiling comparative cost estimates for the evaluation and/or appraisal of the contributions of other members of the design team
* Inspection and evaluation of the tenders based on specifications of materials and workmanship, including a cost breakdown
* Setting up, inspecting and valuing cost breakdowns according to special conditions

2.2 Aims/risks of tender action and letting of contracts
The tender action aims to formulate contract documents which will enable the construction work of a project to be carried out within the civil legal framework, thus affording the relevant structure of regulation and guarantees. Tenders can be sought when all the relevant information is available for costing. Tender documents consist of: schedule of conditions (e.g. specifications and contractual obligations) plus clauses with descriptions (e.g. possibilities for inspecting the details of the conditions / location, date of the project commencement and completion / limits to time and additional costs).

Tender documents that include the price of the work and signature of the contractor (or his rightful representative) become an *offer*, which can be negotiated or accepted unchanged, resulting in the formulation of a contract, governing everything necessary for the carrying out of the works (e.g. type and extent of the work, amount and manner of payment, timetable and deadlines, and responsibilities).

To prevent, from the outset, differences of understanding and opinion between the members of the contract – and to make clear their mutual responsibilities – contract documents (and hence also the tender documents) must be comprehensive and complete.

Unclear, incomplete tender documents lead to poor building contracts, which provoke conflict, time overruns, defects, loss of value and additional costs.

2.3 Means and tools of tender action and letting of contracts
Contract laws and regulations depend on the country and local situation, and regulate, through the building contract, the legal relationship between the client and the contractor. They generally determine what constitutes a valid contract, how long the liabilities of the contract are valid, recourse to damages, dispute settlement, professional responsibilities and liabilities, and other aspects with regard to contractual relationships.

Contract conditions and articles of agreement are specific to the particular form of contract being used. Because there are many types of standard contract document, it is important that a suitable contract type is chosen to meet the needs of the particular project. Typical headings of clauses of a contract for larger works are listed here:
* Identification of the different members mentioned in the contract, and a description of their role and duties, e.g. employer, contractor, sub-contractors or architect
* Interpretation, definitions, etc.
* Contractor's obligations
* The contract sum, additions or deductions, adjustments and interim certificates for partial completion of work
* Architect's instructions, form and timing of instructions during the contract
* Contract and other documents, and issues of certificates for completions
* Statutory obligations, notices, fees and charges
* Levels and setting out of the works
* Materials, goods and workmanship to conform to description, testing and inspection
* Royalties and patent rights
* Identification of the person in charge of the works
* Access for architect to the works
* Clerk of works or client's representative on site
* Details and procedure in the event of variations and provisional sums
* Definition of the contract sum
* Value added tax (VAT) and other taxes
* Materials and goods unfixed off or on site, ownership, responsibilities incurred
* Practical completion of the contract and liability in the case of defects
* Partial possession by employer
* Assignment of sub-contracts and fair wages
* Insurance against injury to persons and property, and employer's indemnity
* Insurance of the works against perils
* Date of possession, completion and postponement
* Damages for non-completion
* Extension of time
* Loss and expenses cause by matters materially affecting regular progress of the works
* Determination (pulling out of contract) by contractor or employer
* Works by employer or persons employed or engaged by employer, part of, or not part of, the contract
* Measurement of work and certificates for completed work and payment

* Tax obligations
* Unusual eventualities, e.g. outbreak of hostilities, war damage, discovery of antiquities
* Fluctuations in labour and material costs and taxes, and the use of price adjustment formulae

Technical conditions and preambles relate directly to the work to be undertaken and are formulated as general specifications, schedules of duties, general quality of workmanship, programmes of work, etc. and are often divided into the various trades. Typical headings under this section are listed below:

* Scope of work and supply of goods, e.g. includes provision of all necessary tools, purchase, delivery, unloading, storage and installation of all goods
* Quality of goods and components, national or international standards which must be adhered to
* Quality of workmanship, national or international standards of workmanship which must be achieved
* Additional and special duties, specification of the types and range of additional works included within the price, and those special duties which are to be charged in addition
* Method of calculating the amount to be paid to the contractor, and determination of the means of measurement of the work done, e.g. quantitative units, boundaries between different sections of work, measuring techniques, and types of pay calculations (on a time basis, piece work, fixed rates, fluctuating rates, etc.)
* Preambles, more specific and general items of agreement not covered in detail in the main contract conditions can be classed under three headings: *necessary items* are prescriptive (e.g. methods of handover), *recommended items* are advisory (e.g. sequence of work and programming) and *possible items* are suggested (e.g. feedback protocols, meetings, etc.) – taking care that there is no conflict between the preambles and the main contract

Specifications, manufacturers' specifications, performance specifications are detailed descriptions for every part of the work which needs to be carried out. The extent and sophistication of these specifications vary, depending on the size and complexity of the project: for small, simple projects, drawings and specifications will suffice; larger projects need, in addition, schedules (e.g. door and window ironmongery) and bills of quantities (listing the extent of the various elements of the work and giving a basis for the pricing of the work) together with a variety of additional specialist drawings, specifications and schedules (e.g. reinforced concrete work, steelwork, mechanical and electrical equipment, etc.).

To help in the production of specifications and bills of quantities, various systems of standardised texts, split into units or paragraphs, can be included or omitted as required. The suitability and acceptability of the various systems depends on the regulations of each country and profession (e.g. National Building Specification and Standard Measurement of Works in the UK, and the Standardleistungsbuch and LV-Muster in Germany).

Manufacturer's information in relation to materials and equipment, offers additional, useful information in application and installation techniques, constructional details and necessary safety precautions.

In general, in relation to tender action, the use of suitable computer software which links CAD drawings with specifications and bills of quantities is recommended.

3.0 Construction supervision (inspection and supervision of the building works and necessary documentation)

3.1 Definition of duties and outputs/contents i.e. stages J–L in RIBA Plan of Work, and 8 + 9 in HOAI

Basic services will vary according to the conditions of appointment agreed by the architect with the client, and the type of contract agreed between the employer and contractor. The list of basic services will also vary from country to country, depending on the local professional norms. Typical services are listed below.

* Inspection during the progress of the building works to check compliance with the planning approval, the contract drawings and the specifications, as well as with generally accepted qualities of workmanship and adherence to safety regulations and other relevant standards
* Inspection and correction of details of prefabricated components
* Setting up and supervision of a time plan (bar chart)
* Writing of a contract diary
* Combined measuring up of work with the building contractor
* Measuring up and calculating the value of completed work with the co-operation of other members of the design and supervision team while establishing defects and shortcomings, and issuing of certificates
* Inspection of invoices
* Establishing final cost estimates according to the local or regulated method of calculation
* Application to the authorities for grants or subventions according to local and specific circumstances
* Handing over of the building, together with compiling and issuing the necessary documents, e.g. equipment instruction manuals
* Testing protocol
* Listing the guarantee periods
* Supervising the making good of defects listed at handing over
* Ongoing cost control
* Inspection of the project for defects before the end of the guarantee periods of the various sub-contractors and contractor
* Supervision of the making good of defects detected in the inspections before the end of the guarantee periods
* Depending on local laws, inspections for up to five years after completion
* Systematic compilation of the drawings and calculations related to the project

Additional services

* Setting up, supervision and implementation of a payment plan
* Setting up, supervision and implementation of comparative time, cost or capacity plans
* Acting as the agent responsible for the works, as far as these duties go beyond the responsibilities listed as basic services
* Setting up of progress plans
* Setting up of equipment and material inventories
* Setting up of security and care instructions
* Site security duties
* Site organisation duties
* Patrol of the project after handover
* Supervision of the security and care tasks
* Preparation of the measurement data for an object inventory
* Enquiries and calculation of costs for standard cost evaluations
* Checking the building and business cost-use analysis

3.2 Aims/risks of construction supervision

Construction supervision consists of two major elements:

Control, measurement, accounting in relation to the contract conditions and plan of work, and *building programme planning* through the use of project management techniques (availability of people, machines, material at the right time, in the right amount, at the right place). Important aids include operation planning techniques and time planning techniques using various recognised methods.

Poor building supervision and insufficient control lead, among other things, to unsatisfactory execution of the works, faults (obvious or hidden), faulty measurements and payments for work, additional costs, and danger to operatives (accidents) and materials. Unsatisfactory project management and poor co-ordination normally lead to building delays and extra costs.

3.3 Means and tools of construction supervision

Standard procedures vary according to the country and profession, together with techniques/instruments for project management. Supervision of the works, measurement of works and accounting is based on the drawings (production drawings, detail drawings, special drawings), specifications, schedules, possibly a bill of quantities, and the contract conditions.

The techniques of operation and time planning make use of various common methods: bar charts, line diagrams and networks.

Bar charts (according to Gantt, bar drawings), show the work stages/trade duties on the vertical (Y) axis, and the accompanying building duration or time duration (estimated by experience or calculation) on the horizontal (X) axis. The duration of the various stages/duties are shown by the length of the particular bars (shown running horizontally).

Building stages which follow on from another should be depicted as such on the chart. The description of the building stages and trade categories help in the setting up of the bar chart, and make possible the comparison of the planned programme and the actual progress of the work.

* Advantages: provides a good overall view; clarity; ease of interpretation (type of presentation shows time scales)
* Disadvantages: strict separation of work tasks; no identification of sub-tasks; difficult to show connections and dependence relationships of the work stages (thus critical and non-critical sequences are not identified, and if altering the time duration of one stage will result in the alteration of the duration of the whole project)
* Context of use: illustration of straightforward, self-contained building projects which have a simple sequence of tasks and no directional element (e.g. as in road construction), planning of individual tasks, resource planning (staffing programme/equipment and plant planning) → ① p. 49

Line diagrams – speed–time distance–time (or quantities–time diagrams) – show measures of time (selected) on the one axis (which ones depending on the building task), and measures of length (or, less frequently, building quantities) on the other axis. The speed of the production process (the slope of the line), and the division (in terms of time and space between tasks) are clearly portrayed.

* *Advantages*: clear presentation of speed of progress and critical separations
* *Disadvantages*: poor portrayal of parallel and layered task sequences (spacing and timing of tasks which have no directional element)
* *Context of use*: illustration of building projects with a strong directional element, e.g. length, height,(roads or tunnels) or (towers or chimneys) → ② p. 49

Networks resulting from network planning techniques (as part of operational research) → ③ p. 49 help in the analysis, presentation, planning, directing and control of tasks. The relationships between different operations show how they are influenced by many possible factors (e.g. time, costs and resources).

To calculate the overall project duration, assume a project starting point at time PT_0 and show (calculating

forward) the earliest point in time ET (earliest time of start event EST/ earliest time of finish event EFT) for each task (D = duration, time span, beginning/finish of the task). The overall project duration is the duration of project path (critical path)/project finish time ET_n. Incorporating estimated float (buffer time) elements (added together) produces the given project finish time point PT_n. To determine the latest project start time, perform a backward pass (from right to left), taking the latest time point LT (latest time of start event LST, latest time of finish event LFT) for each task (calculating backwards), and hence the latest project start time for the project PT_0, respectively the total float TF of the individual tasks = (latest time point LT – latest start/finish LST/LFT) – (earliest time point – earliest start/finish EST/EFT) → ④ p. 49

The critical path method (CPM) puts task arrows into order. Nodes show the start or finish events of the tasks. The fundamental arrangement of relationships (= dependence between tasks, quantifiable) in CPM is the normal sequence (order relationship from the finish of the previous to the beginning of the following; finish event of task A = start event of task B). The time frame is determined (i.e. the task is allotted a definite estimated duration time). Tasks which are running parallel and are dependent on each other, dependencies of parts of tasks with each other which are a condition for the progress of a further task, are displayed as dummies (dummy arrows, order relationships in the network with time interval of 0). → ① + ② p. 50

The content of the critical path chart mirrors the list of tasks (list of individual activities together with timing estimates). → ③ p. 50

The metra-potential method (MPM) orders the task nodes. Arrows display the order relationships. The fundamental arrangement of relationships with MPM is the order of starts (order relationship between the start of the previous task to the start of the following task; start event of task A = start event of task B). The time frame is determined (as with CPM). The content of the task node network mirrors the list of tasks (compare with CPM). → ②, ③, ④ p. 50

The programme evaluation and review technique (PERT) orders the task nodes. Arrows display the order relationships. The time model is normally stochastic (i.e. the determination of the time intervals between the events is by probability calculations). Geometric models of PERT + CPM can be combined in a mixed presentation (tasks as arrows, and events as nodes). Theoretically, an event arrow-network plan is feasible; however, no practical method is available.

Advantages/disadvantages/appropriate applications of the various network planning methods:

* Pre-organised networks with deterministic time model (CPM/MPM) are the most suitable for detailed direction/control of building operations (emphasis on individual tasks).
* Event-orientated networks (PERT) are more suitable for strategic planning and overview of the project (events = milestones).
* Task node networks (MPM) are easier to set up and alter (consistent separation of tasks planning/time planning), and reproduce a greater number of conditions than task arrow networks (CPM; however, CPM is more widely used in practice, being older, more developed, and because 70–80% of ordering relationships which occur in network plans are standard sequences).

Networks are primarily very detailed but are difficult to read, so additional presentation of the results as a barchart/diagram is necessary. Computers are predestined to be an aid, particularly in setting up large networks (resulting from entries of relevant data from the list of tasks). Suitable software is available (the majority being for CPM).

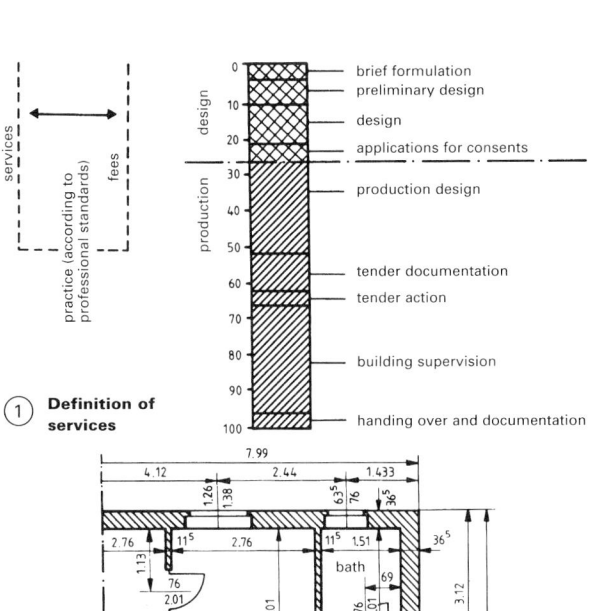

(1) **Definition of services**

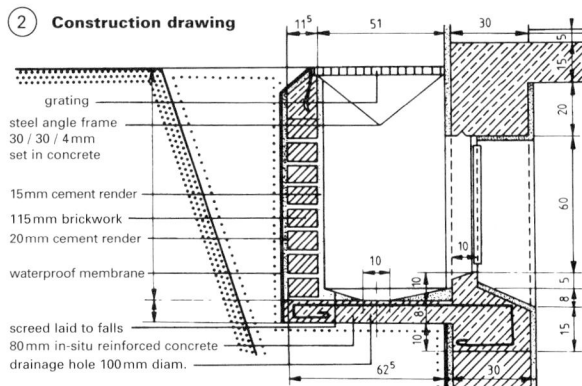

(2) **Construction drawing**

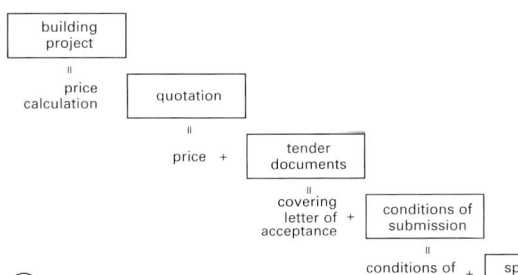

grating
steel angle frame
30 / 30 / 4 mm
set in concrete

15 mm cement render
115 mm brickwork
20 mm cement render
waterproof membrane

screed laid to falls
80 mm in-situ reinforced concrete
drainage hole 100 mm diam.

(3) **Detailed drawing**

building project
=
price calculation   quotation
=
price + tender documents
=
covering letter of acceptance + conditions of submission
=
conditions of contract + specification of work

(4) **Building contract**

ARTICLES OF AGREEMENT
1 contractor's obligations
2 contract sum
3 architect
4 quantity surveyor
5 settlement of disputes

Conditions: Part 1: General
1 interpretation, definitions, etc.
2 contractor's obligations
3 contract sum – additions or deductions – adjustment – interim certificates
4 architect's instructions
5 contract documents – other documents – issue of certificates
6 statutory obligations, notices, fees and charges
7 levels and setting out of works
8 materials, goods and workmanship to conform to description, testing and inspection
9 royalties and patent rights
10 person-in-charge
11 access for architect to the works
12 clerk of works
13 variations and provisional sums
14 contract sum
15 VAT – supplemental provisions
16 materials and goods unfixed or off-site
17 practical completion and defects liability
18 partial possession by employer
19 assignment and subcontracts, fair wages
20 injury to persons and property, and employer's indemnity
21 insurance against injury to persons and property

22 insurance of the works against perils
23 date of possession, completion and postponement
24 damages for non-completion
25 extension of time
26 loss and expense caused by matters materially affecting regular progress of the works
27 determination by employer
28 determination by contractor
29 works by employer or persons employed by employer
30 certificates and payment
31 finance – statutory tax deduction scheme
32 outbreak of hostilities
33 war damage
34 antiquities

Conditions: Part 2: Nominated subcontractors and nominated suppliers
35 nominated subcontractors – general, procedure for nomination, payment, extension of period for completion of works, failure to complete works, practical completion, final payment, position of employer in relation to subcontractor, etc.
36 nominated suppliers

Conditions: Part 3: Fluctuations
37 choice of fluctuations conditions
38 contribution, levy and tax fluctuations
39 labour and material cost, and tax fluctuations
40 use of price adjustment formulae

(6) **Typical headings for contract clauses**

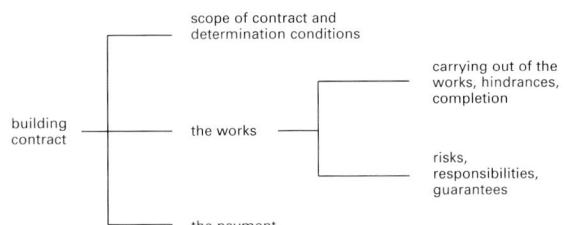

building contract
the works — carrying out of the works, hindrances, completion
scope of contract and determination conditions
risks, responsibilities, guarantees
the payment

(7) **General contract conditions**

groundworks
excavations
boreholes
diversion of springs
retaining walls
bored piling
water retention works
land drainage
underground gas and water mains
underground drainage
consolidation
retaining works on water courses, ditches and embankments
underwater excavation, dredging
underpinning
sheet piling
sprayed concrete work

construction work
brickwork
concrete and reinforced concrete work
stonework
blockwork
carpentry work
steelwork
waterproofing work
roofing and tiling work
plumbing work

finishing work
plastering and rendering
floor and wall tiling, and paving work
screeding work
asphalt laying
joinery work
floor laying and finishing work

(8) **Typical division of the work into sections**

A2 room description			B2 room dimensions						B4 service connections for						B5 values			
1	2	3	1		2		3		1	2	3	4	5	6	1	3	6	
prov. room number	use	user	type	area	type	height	type	volume	heating	ventilation	sanitation	elec. supply	other wiring	mech. conv.	temp.	vent.	light	notes
A	B	C		m²		m		m³							°C	per h	lux	(key)
	W	104	hall	N	6.92	L	2.47	N	14.87	–	–	–	SW CL FB	TS SI		20	1		AS aerial socket
	W	204	bath/WC	N	3.47	L	2.475	N	8.588	CH	MV	BA WB WC	WB SO TF	–	–	24	7		CL ceiling light SSO spurred socket outlet TF transformer
	W	304	kitchen	N	6.09	L	2.47	N	15.04	CH	MV	SI	SW SO SWL SSO CL	–	–	20	4		SW switch SI sink IC intercom SO socket outlet TS telephone socket
	W	404	loggia	N	1.69	L	2.363	N	4.000	CH	MV		SW	AS	–	21	1		BA bath WB wash basin WL wall light (without switch)
	W	504	liv./din.	N	19.77	L	2.47	N	48.63	CH	MV		SO CL	–	–	–			SWL wall light (with switch) WC WC FB fuseboard
	W	604	service rm	F		L	2.475	N	0.891				–						CH central heating MV mechanical ventilation

(5) **Example of a room schedule (Raumbücher in Germany) (abbreviated version)**

Information on this page was provided by the Stanley Partnership, Cheltenham.

CONSTRUCTION MANAGEMENT

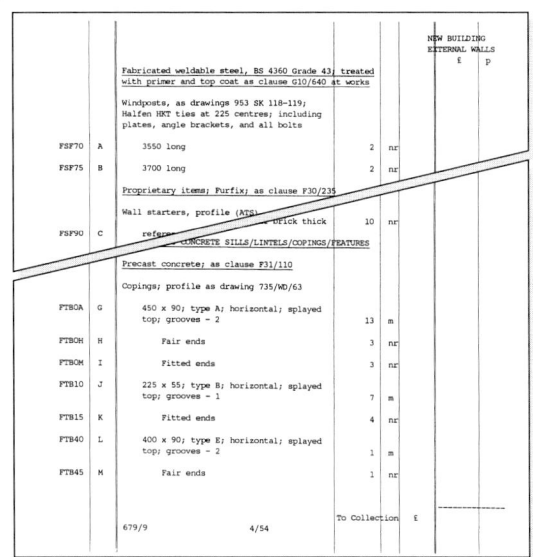

(1) **An interim certificate according to RIBA**

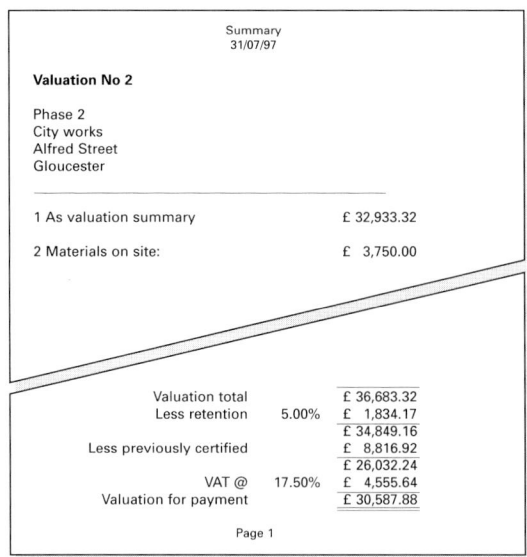

(3) **Extract from a bill of quantities**

Summary
31/07/97

Valuation No 2

Phase 2
City works
Alfred Street
Gloucester

1 As valuation summary	£ 32,933.32	
2 Materials on site:	£ 3,750.00	

Valuation total		£ 36,683.32
Less retention	5.00%	£ 1,834.17
		£ 34,849.16
Less previously certified		£ 8,816.92
		£ 26,032.24
VAT @	17.50%	£ 4,555.64
Valuation for payment		£ 30,587.88

Page 1

(5) **Example of architect's valuation**

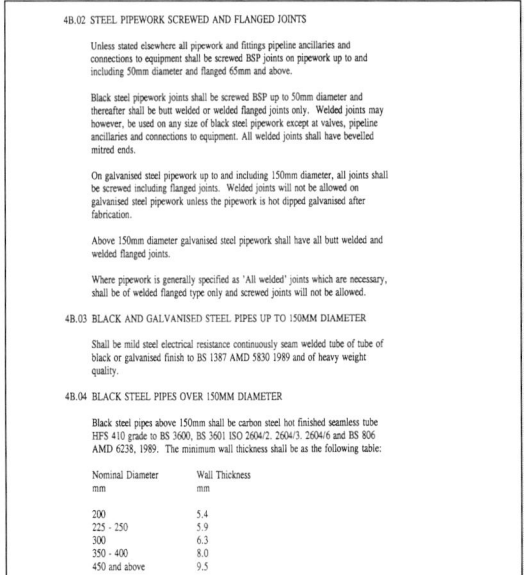

4B.02 STEEL PIPEWORK SCREWED AND FLANGED JOINTS

Unless stated elsewhere all pipework and fittings pipeline ancillaries and connections to equipment shall be screwed BSP joints on pipework up to and including 50mm diameter and flanged 65mm and above.

Black steel pipework joints shall be screwed BSP up to 50mm diameter and thereafter shall be but welded or welded flanged joints only. Welded joints may however, be used on any size of black steel pipework except at valves, pipeline ancillaries and connections to equipment. All welded joints shall have bevelled mitred ends.

On galvanised steel pipework up to and including 150mm diameter, all joints shall be screwed including flanged joints. Welded joints will not be allowed on galvanised steel pipework unless the pipework is hot dipped galvanised after fabrication.

Above 150mm diameter galvanised steel pipework shall have all butt welded and welded flanged joints.

Where pipework is generally specified as 'All welded' joints which are necessary, shall be of welded flanged type only and screwed joints will not be allowed.

4B.03 BLACK AND GALVANISED STEEL PIPES UP TO 150MM DIAMETER

Shall be mild steel electrical resistance continuously seam welded tube of tube of black or galvanised finish to BS 1387 AMD 5830 1989 and of heavy weight quality.

4B.04 BLACK STEEL PIPES OVER 150MM DIAMETER

Black steel pipes above 150mm shall be carbon steel hot finished seamless tube HFS 410 grade to BS 3600, BS 3601 ISO 2604/2. 2604/3. 2604/6 and BS 806 AMD 6238, 1989. The minimum wall thickness shall be as the following table:

Nominal Diameter mm	Wall Thickness mm
200	5.4
225 - 250	5.9
300	6.3
350 - 400	8.0
450 and above	9.5

(2) **Extract from a specification of piped services**

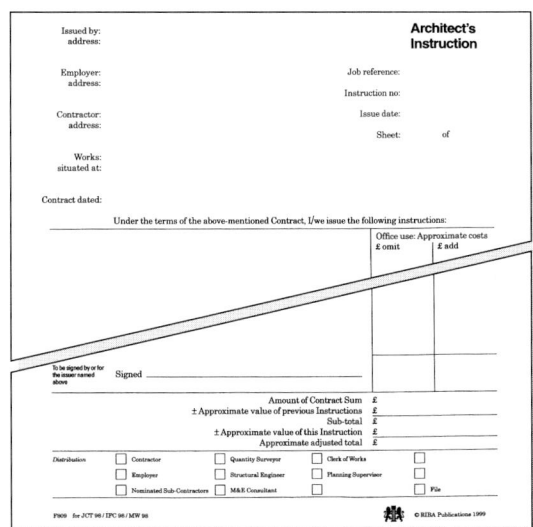

(4) **An architect's instruction according to RIBA form**

(6) **Architect's record of a communication**

CONSTRUCTION MANAGEMENT

48

building programme

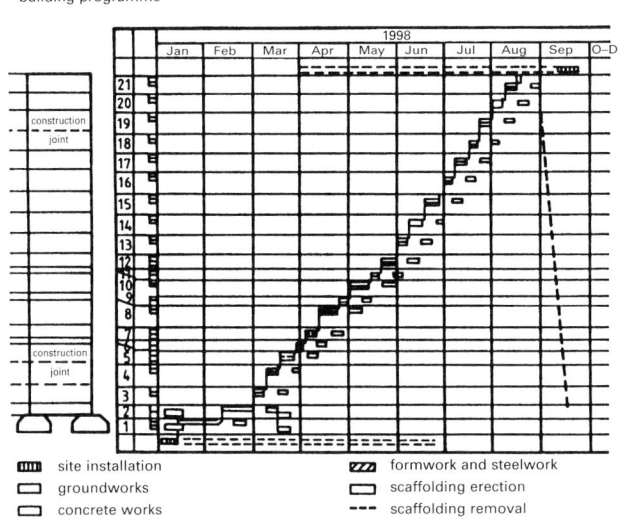

site installation | formwork and steelwork
groundworks | scaffolding erection
concrete works | scaffolding removal

timetable bar diagram, divided into separate trades

plant and equipment programme

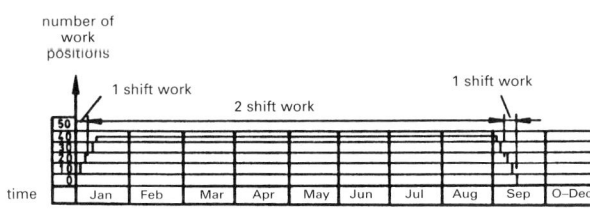

number of work positions

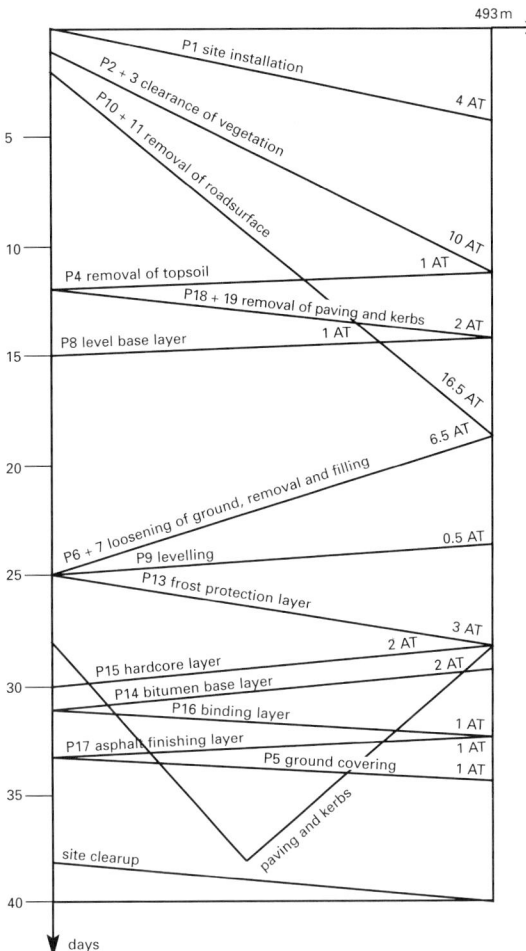

sequence of works:
site installation and clearing
demolition and earthworks
construction of road profile
metalling, paving and kerbs

$\tan a = v = \dfrac{d_s}{d_t}$

(2) **Building time plan**

(3) **Network**

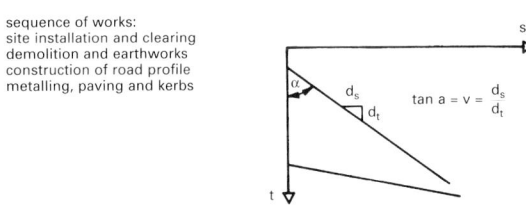

latest project commencement time point

latest time points
LST = latest start time point
LFT = latest finish time point

$PT_0 \leftarrow LT_1 \leftarrow LT_2 \leftarrow \cdots \leftarrow PT_{(n)}$ calculating backwards

$PT_1 \to ET_1 \to ET_2 \to \cdots \to ET_{(n)} + float = PT_{(n)}$

calculating forwards

project commencement date

critical path earliest time points

project finish time point

given project finish time point

EST = earliest start time point
EFT = earliest finish time point

(4) **Network calculation**

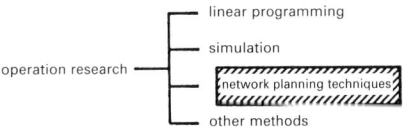

operation research — linear programming
— simulation
— network planning techniques
— other methods

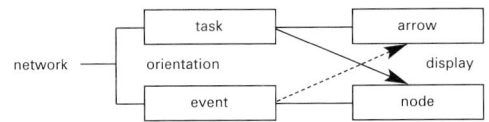

network — task — arrow
— orientation — display
— event — node

(5) **Network orientation and precedence**

(1) **Check list for measured work**

list no.	building section	job description	unit	amount	consumption h/E	Σh	duration h/time unit (day, week, month)	comparison	
								should be	
								is	
								should be	
								is	
								should be	
								is	

finish-start-relationship (dummy arrow) · normal sequence · normal sequence with dummy arrow · time-dependent dummy arrow

nodes

LS	ES
LF	EF
TF	NPN

TN — task number
TD — task duration
NPN — network plan number
ES — earliest start
EF — earliest finish
LS — latest start
LF — latest finish
TF — total float
——— task (arrow)
- - - dummy arrow
······ critical path

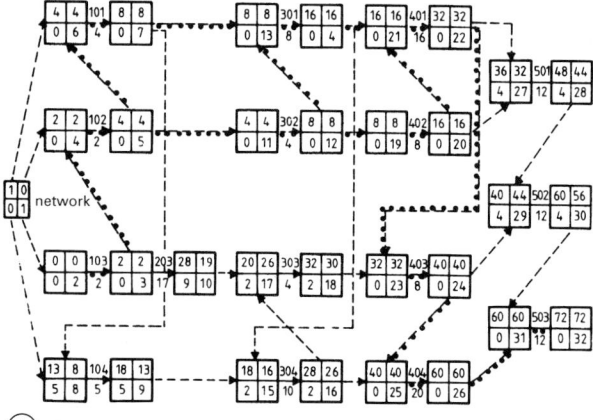

① **Task-arrow network planning method**

Comparison of the display forms of different process diagrams

standard methods		network planning methods		
line diagrams	bar charts	order labelling	CPM arrow-orientated	MPM node-orientated
				→ i →
		normal sequence (NS) = 0		$Z = D_1$
		normal sequence (NS) = 1		$Z = D_1 + 1$
		start sequence (SS) = 0		$Z = D_0$
		start sequence (SS) = 1		$Z = D_1$
		normal sequence (NS) = 1 or 2		$Z = D_i + 2$ / $Z = D_i + 2$ / $Z = D_i + 2$

② **Comparison of the display forms of different process diagrams**

tasks		point of time		dummy		earliest		latest		total float time [1]
pos. no.	short description	duration	from (task number)	to (task number)	from (task number)	to (task number)	begin	finish	begin	finish	
103	excavation P2	2	2	3	1	2	0	2	0	2	0
102	excavation P1	2	4	5	1 or 3	4	2	4	2	4	0
101	excavation W1	4	6	7	1 or 5	6	4	8	4	8	0
104	excavation W2	5	8	9	1 or 7	8	8	13	13	18	5
203	piling	17	3	10			2	19	11	28	9
302	foundations P1	4	11	12	5	11	4	8	4	8	0
301	foundations W1	8	13	14	7 or 12	13	8	16	8	16	0
304	foundations W2	10	15	16	9 or 14	15	16	26	18	28	2
303	foundations P2	4	17	18	10 or 16	17	26	30	28	32	2
402	concrete columns P1	8	19	20	12	19	8	16	8	16	0
401	concrete columns W1	16	21	22	14 or 20	21	16	32	16	32	0
403	concrete columns P2	8	23	24	18 or 22	23	32	40	32	40	0

[1] added up

③ **Task list (CPM) cf. → ①**

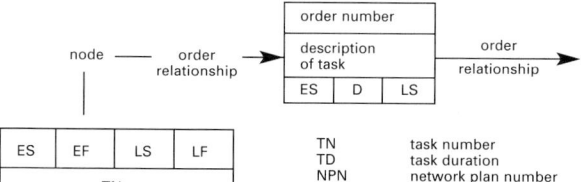

node — order relationship →

order number
description of task
| ES | D | LS |

node box:

ES	EF	LS	LF
	TN		
NPN	TD	TF	

TN — task number
TD — task duration
NPN — network plan number
ES — earliest start
EF — earliest finish
LS — latest start
LF — latest finish
TF — total float
→ arrow (relationship)
······ critical path

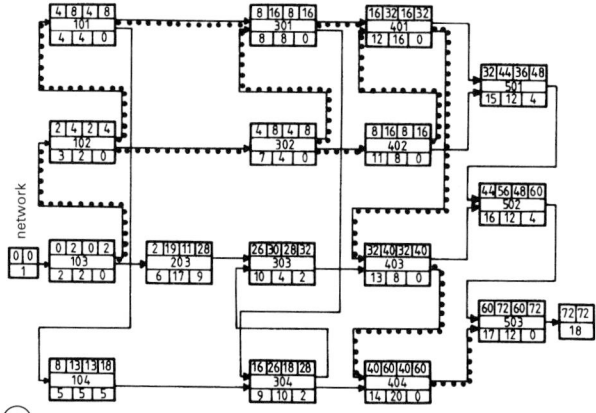

④ **Network plan (CPM)**

pos. no.	description of task	duration	previous task	earliest		latest		total float time [1]
				begin	finish	begin	finish	
103	excavation P2	2		0	2	0	2	0
102	excavation P1	2	103	2	4	2	4	0
101	excavation W1	4	102	4	8	4	8	0
104	excavation W2	5	101	8	13	13	18	5
203	piling	17	103	2	19	11	28	9
302	foundations P1	4	102	4	8	4	8	0
301	foundations W1	8	101, 302	8	16	8	16	0
304	foundations W2	10	104, 301	16	26	18	18	2
303	foundations P2	4	203, 304	26	30	28	32	2
402	concrete columns P1	8	302	8	16	8	16	0
401	concrete columns W1	16	301, 402	16	32	16	32	0
403	concrete columns P2	8	303, 403	40	60	40	60	0
501	beams P1–W1	12	401, 402	32	44	36	48	4
502	beams P1–W2	12	403, 501	44	56	48	60	4
503	beams P2–W2	12	404, 502	60	72	60	72	0

[1] added up

⑤ **Process list (MPM) cf. → ④**

Foundations, Excavation, Trenches

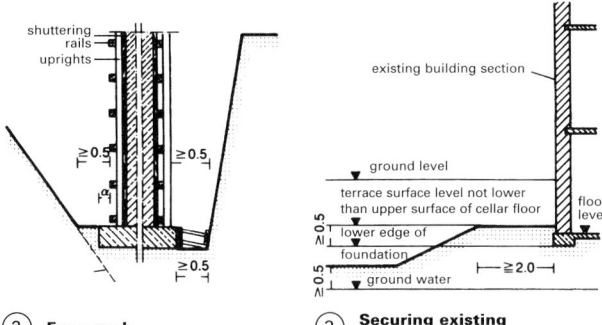

① **Banked excavation with terrace for the collection of precipitating material**

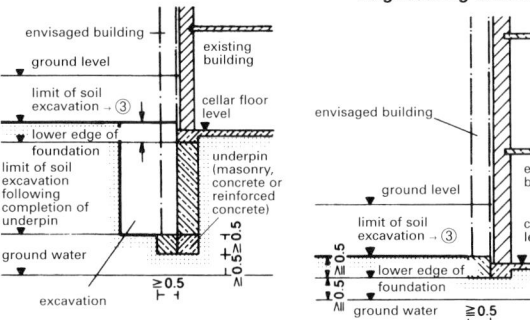

② **Formwork**

③ **Securing existing neighbouring buildings**

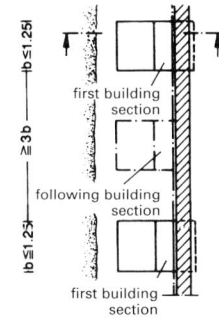

④ **Section through underpinning** → ⑤

⑥ **Section through foundations** → ⑦

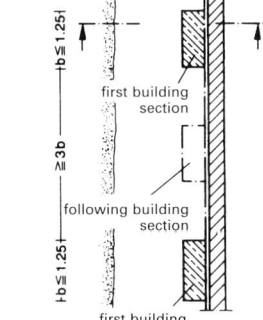

⑤ **Plan view** → ④

⑦ **Plan view** → ⑥

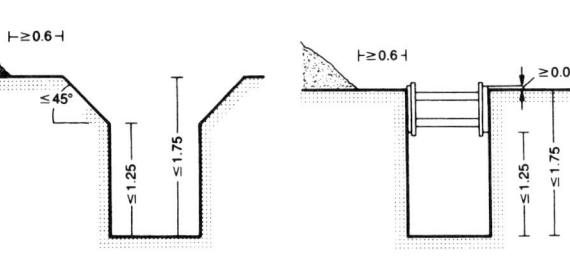

⑧ **Excavation with banked edges**

⑨ **Partly secured excavation**

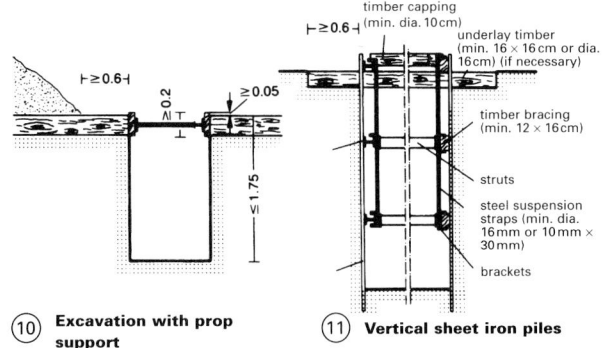

⑩ **Excavation with prop support**

⑪ **Vertical sheet iron piles**

Surveying, site investigation, appraisal

Failure to accurately assess the building site and water table conditions and to specify the correct foundations generally leads to irreparable structural damage and serious cost overruns.

Lateral ground displacement due to the load on the foundations causes the foundations to sink into the ground or become laterally displaced. This leads to total failure of the foundations.

Settlement due to compression of the building site under the foundations due to the load on the foundations and/or loads caused by neighbouring structures leads to deformations and damage (cracks) in the superstructure.

Where there is adequate local knowledge of the nature, mechanical properties, stratification and bearing strength of the sub-soil layers, calculations can be made which determine the dimensions of shallow foundations (individual and strip foundations; foundation pads and rafts) and deep foundations (pile foundations). If such knowledge is not available, timely investigation of the ground is required, if possible in consultation with an appropriate expert. This involves examination of the strata by excavation (manual or mechanical excavator), borings (auger/rotary bit or core drilling) with the extraction of samples and probes. The number and depth of inspections required depends on the topography, type of building and information available.

The depth of the ground water table can be investigated by inserting measuring pipes into boreholes and taking regular measurements (water table fluctuations). The ground water samples should also be tested to assess whether it is aggressive towards concrete (i.e. presence of sulphates, etc.).

Ground probes (and sample cores) are used to investigate granular composition, water content, consistency, density, compressibility, shear strength and permeability. Probes provide continuous information on soil strength and density as they penetrate the various sub-soil layers.

All test results and the opinion of an expert site investigator should be brought to the attention of the building supervisors.

Consult local and national standards for ground (rock) descriptions, classification of earthworks, sub-soil characteristics, stratification, ground water conditions, necessary foundation/excavation depths, calculation of excavation material quantities, and construction and safety of excavations.

51

EXCAVATIONS

Site and Building Measurements

The building site must be surveyed and the plan of the proposed house entered on the official site plan → ① – ②. When the requirements of the planning and building regulations have been met and planning permission granted, the foundations are pegged out as shown by wooden pegs and horizontal site boards → ④ – ⑧. The excavation must exceed the cross-sectional area of the house to provide adequate working space ≥500 mm → ④ – ⑤. The slope of the sides of the excavation depends on the ground type; the sandier the soil, the flatter the slope → ④.

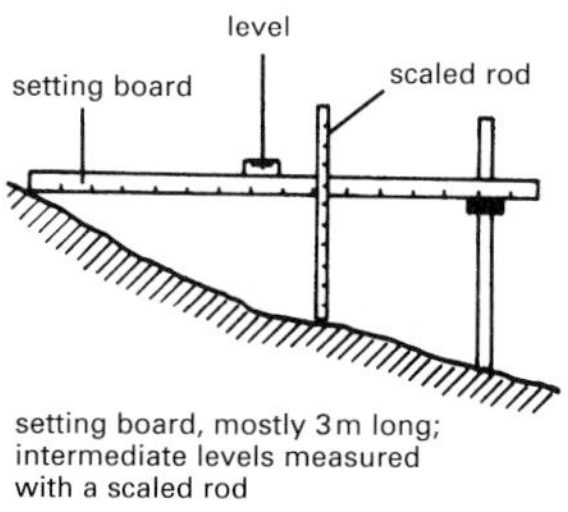

After excavation, string lines are tightly stretched between the site boards → ⑧ to mark out the external dimensions of the building. The outside corners of the house are given at the crossing points of the lines by plumb bobs. The correct level must be measured → ⑦. Dimensions are orientated by fixed points in the surroundings. Setting boards → ⑩, of wood or aluminium, 3m long, with a level built-in or fixed on top, are installed horizontally with the ends supported on posts. Intermediate contour heights are measured with a scaled rod.

A water-filled, transparent, flexible hose 20–30m long, with glass tube sections at each end marked out in mm, when held vertically, is used to read water levels. After calibrating by holding both glass tubes together, levels between points on the site can be compared accurately to the mm, without the need for visual contact (e.g. in different rooms).

---

① **Official site plan**

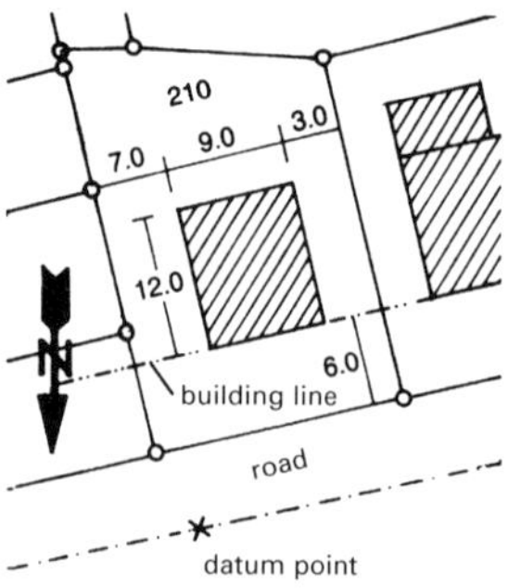

② **Site plan with the building dimensions drawn in**

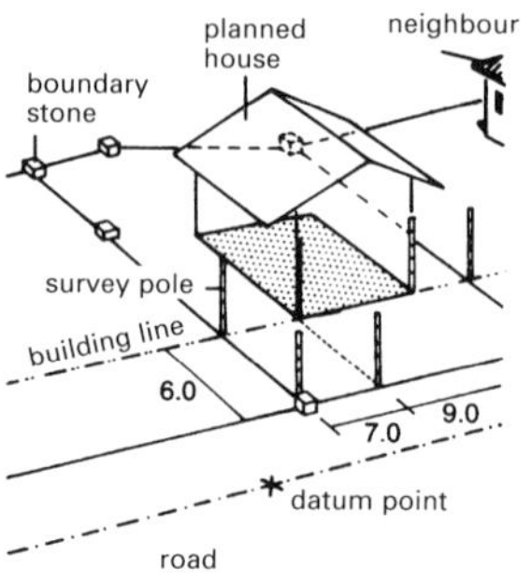

③ **The planned house in relation to the site**

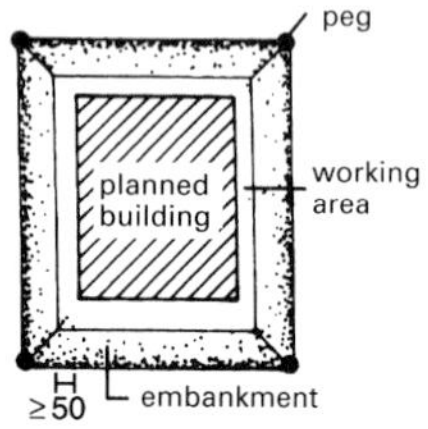

type of ground	embankment angle
loose soil	40°
medium loose soil	40°
firm soil	60°
loose and firm rock	80°

④ **Excavation**

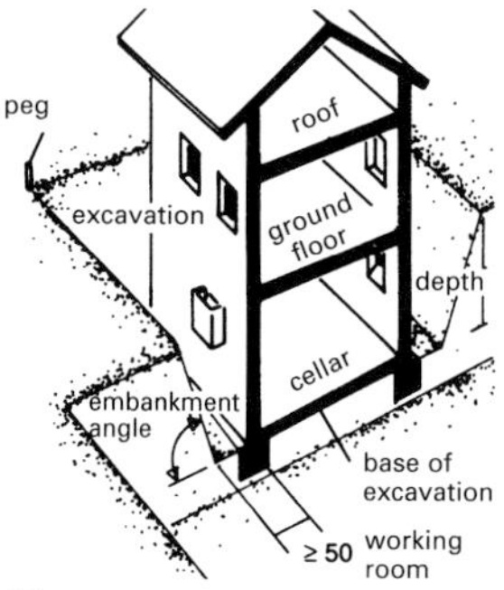

⑤ **The house in the excavation**

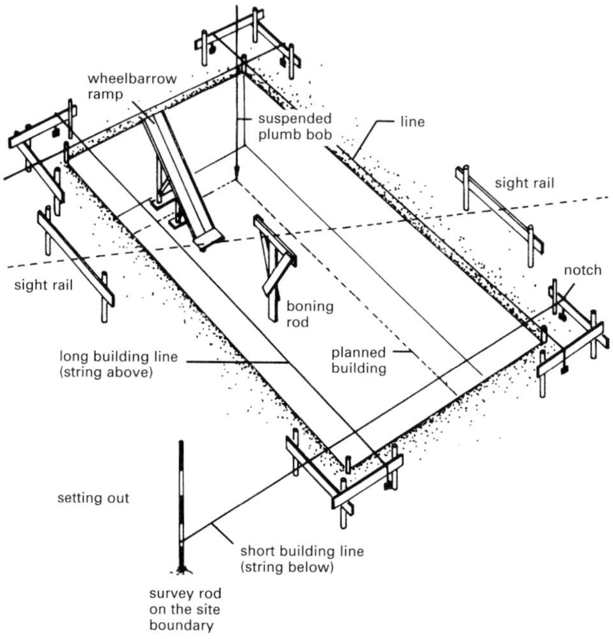

⑥ **Boning rods**

⑧ **Setting out: how the building is measured into place → ⑨**

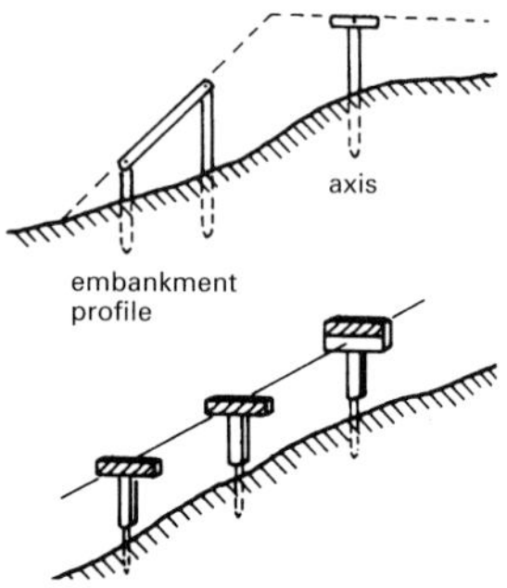

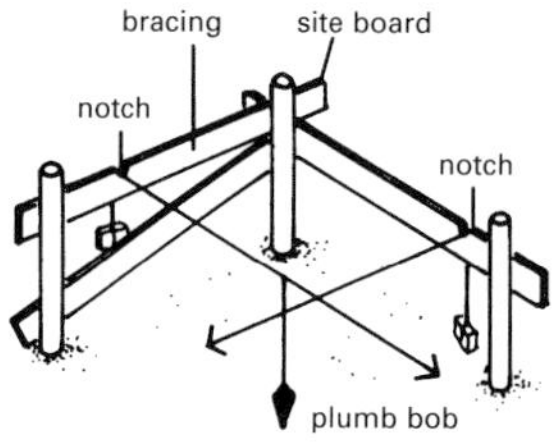

⑨ **Corner site boards**

⑩ **Setting board**

setting board, mostly 3m long; intermediate levels measured with a scaled rod

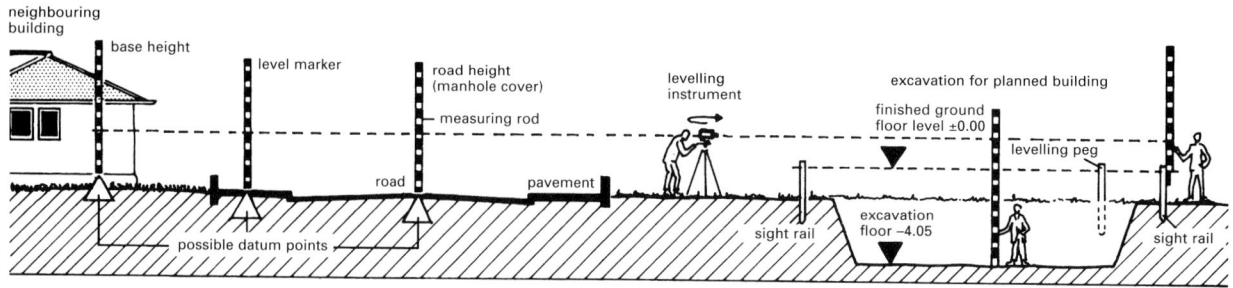

⑦ **Measuring levels for the building**

52

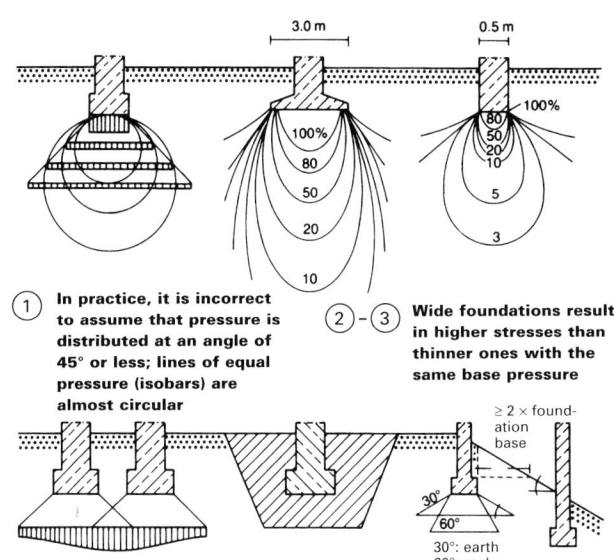

① In practice, it is incorrect to assume that pressure is distributed at an angle of 45° or less; lines of equal pressure (isobars) are almost circular

②–③ Wide foundations result in higher stresses than thinner ones with the same base pressure

④ Intersection of foundation influence lines causes danger of settlement and crack formation (important when new building is adjacent to old building)

⑤ Foundations on a sand filling of 0.8–1.20 m high, applied in layers of 15 cm in a slurry; the load is distributed over a larger area of the site

⑥ Foundations on a hillside: lines of pressure distribution = angle of slope of the ground

EARTHWORKS AND FOUNDATION STRUCTURES

Technical investigations of the ground should provide sufficient data for efficient construction planning and execution of the building work. Depending on the construction type, the ground is evaluated either as building (for foundations), or as building material (for earth works). Building structures are planned (if legally possible and with local approval), according to expert assessment (i.e. avoiding marshy areas, landfill, etc.). The building construction type and the prevailing ground conditions affect the design of the foundations, e.g. individual footings → ⑦, strip foundations → ⑧, raft foundations → ⑨, or if the ground strata are only able to carry the load structure at greater depth, pile foundations → ⑩. Pressure distribution must not extend over 45° in masonry, or 60° in concrete. Masonry foundations are seldom used, due to high cost. Unreinforced concrete foundations are used when the load spreading area is relatively small, e.g. for smaller building structures. Steel reinforced concrete foundations are used for larger spans and at higher ground compression; they contain reinforcement to withstand the tensile loads → ⑪ + ⑫. Reinforced, instead of mass, concrete is used to reduce foundation height, weight and excavation depth. For flexible joints and near to existing structures or boundaries → ⑬. For cross-sections of raft foundations → ⑭ – used when load-bearing capacity is lower, or if individual footings or strip foundations are inadequate for the imposed load. Frost-free depth for base ≥ 0.80 m, for engineering structures 1.0–1.5 m deep.

Methods to improve the load-bearing capacity of the site
Vibratory pressure process, with vibrator, compact in a radius of 2.3–3 m; separation of the vibration cores approx. 1.5 m; the area is thus filled; improvement depends on the granulation and original strata. Ground compression piles: core is filled up with aggregate of varied grain size without bonding agent. Solidification and compression of the ground: pressure injection of cement grout; not applicable to cohesive ground and ground which is aggressive to cement; only applicable in quartzous ground (gravel, sand and loose stone); injection of chemicals (silicic acid solution, calcium chloride); immediate and lasting petrifaction.

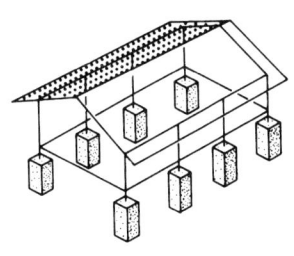

⑦ Individual foundations for light buildings without cellars

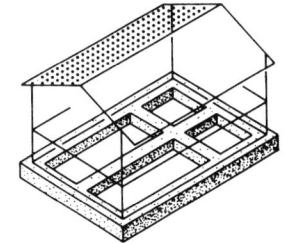

⑧ Strip foundations are most frequently used for building

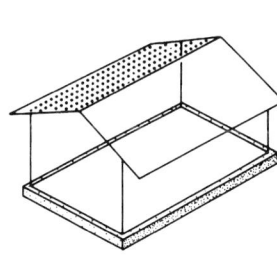

⑨ Raft foundation reinforced with structural steel

⑩ Grid pile and sinking caisson arrangement for deep foundations

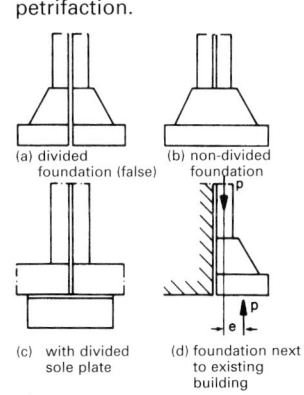

⑬ Application of foundations on dividing lines and movement joints

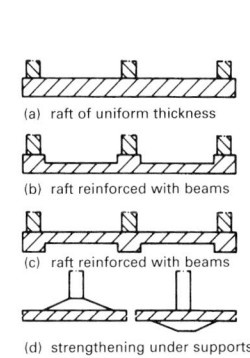

⑭ Cross-sections of raft foundations

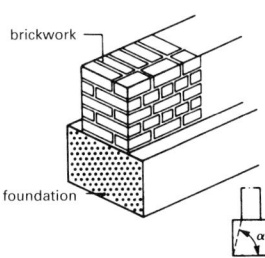

⑪ Simple strip foundation on lean concrete

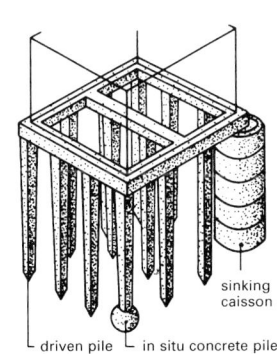

⑫ Widened, stepped foundation in unreinforced concrete

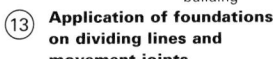
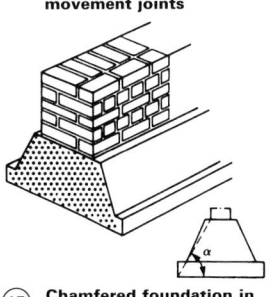

⑮ Chamfered foundation in unreinforced concrete

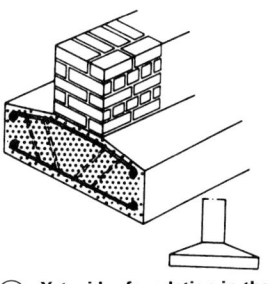

⑯ Yet wider foundation in the form of a steel reinforced concrete plate

53

EARTHWORKS AND FOUNDATION STRUCTURES

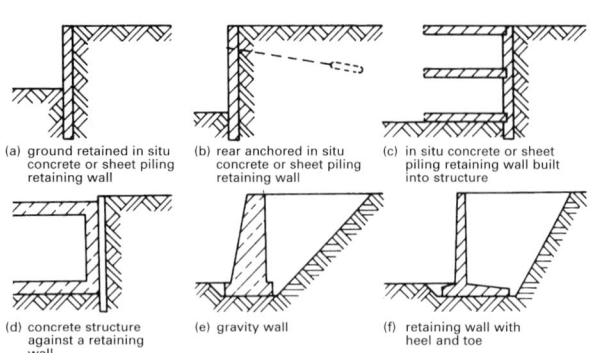

(a) ground retained in situ concrete or sheet piling retaining wall

(b) rear anchored in situ concrete or sheet piling retaining wall

(c) in situ concrete or sheet piling retaining wall built into structure

(d) concrete structure against a retaining wall

(e) gravity wall

(f) retaining wall with heel and toe

(1) **Building structures rated for the retention of soil pressure**

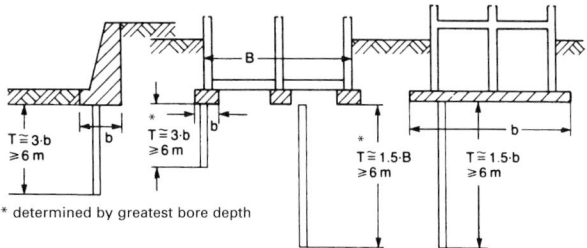

* determined by greatest bore depth

(2) **Minimum depths for trial bores**

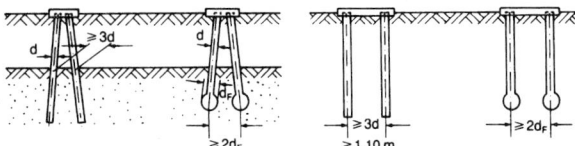

(3) **Requisite pile separations for bored piles**

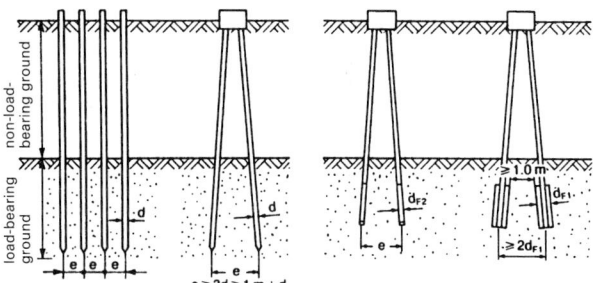

(4) **Requisite pile separations for driven piles**

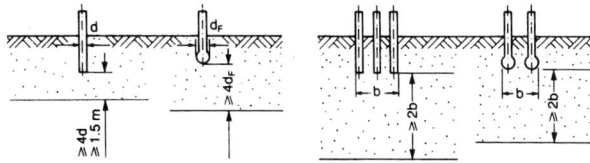

(5) **Requisite depth of load supporting ground under bored piles**

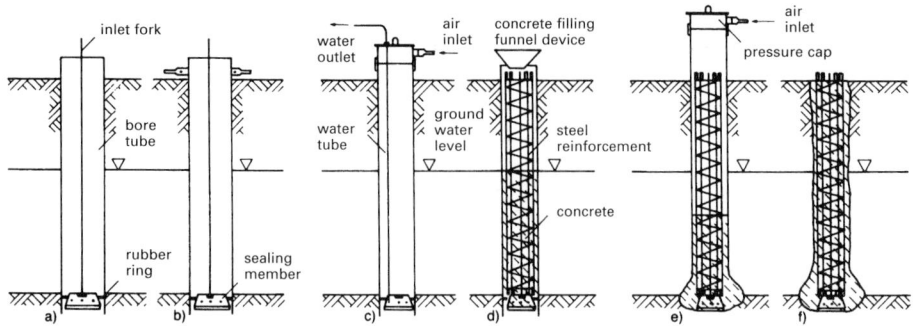

(6) **Compressed concrete bore pile (Brechtel System)**

To calculate the active soil pressure on retaining walls → (1) and the permissible loading sub-soil, the type, composition, extent, stratification and strength of the ground strata must be known. Where local knowledge is inadequate, trial excavation and boreholes are necessary (separation of the bore holes ≤ 25 m). For pile foundations, the bore depths should extend to the foot of the piles → (2). According to the method of measurement, these depths can be reduced by a third (T = 1.0 B or 2 × pile diameter, but ≥ 6.0 m). For the required pile separations for bored piles → (3); for driven piles → (4). The stated values do not apply to load-bearing plugged and bored pile walls. For the requisite depth of the load-bearing ground under bored piles → (5); for compressed concrete bored piles, Brechtel System → (6).

Pile foundations: Loads can be transmitted by the piles to the load-bearing ground by surface friction, end bearing or both bearings; the type of load transfer depends on the building site and the nature of the piling. Bearing pile foundations: load transmission takes place at ends of the piles onto the load-bearing ground and/or through skin friction. Suspended pile foundations: the piles do not extend downwards until the ends are on the load-bearing region. Weak load-bearing layers are compacted by pile driving.

Type of load transfer: Friction piles essentially transfer the load through surface friction via the load bearing region around the circumference of the pile. End bearing piles: the load is principally transmitted by the pile end on to the bearing stratum; in this case, surface friction is not significant. The permissible end pressure is significantly increased in some types of pile by widening the bases of the piles.

Position of the piles in the ground: Foundation piles are in the ground over their whole length. Retaining and projecting piles are free standing piles, whose lower portions only are below ground; the tops of these piles are exposed and therefore subject to buckling stresses.

Materials: wood, steel, concrete, reinforced concrete and prestressed concrete piles.

Method of insertion in the ground: Driven piles are rammed into the ground by pile driving hammers. Jacked piles are inserted by pressure. Bored piles are inserted by way of a bore hole. Screwed piles are inserted by rotation. With driven tube piles, a steel tube former is driven into the ground and withdrawn as the concrete pile is cast in situ. A distinction is made between piles which compact the ground, pierce it, or pass through a hole in it.

Type of loading: Axially loaded piles. Bearing piles are subject to compressive stresses – the load being transmitted through point pressure and surface friction. Tensile piles are subjected to tensile stress with loads transmitted through surface friction. Horizontally loaded piles. Retaining or projecting piles are subject to bending stresses, e.g., horizontally loaded large bore piles, sheet piles.

Manufacture and installation: Prefabricated piles are made in finished sections and delivered to the point of use, and driven into the ground by hammering, pressing, vibrating, screwing or by inserting in ready-prepared bore holes. In situ piles are created in a hollowed-out chamber in the ground, such as bored piles, tube piles, auger piles and cylinder piles. Mixed foundation piles are assembled from in situ and prefabricated parts. In situ piles provide the advantage that their length is not critical pre construction, and can be designed on the basis of compaction results, and examination of cores of the ground strata obtained during the boring process.

material	internal connecting drains	stacks	internal collection drains	u/ground drains inaccessible: in building	u/ground drains in earth	vent pipes	rainwater drains within buildings	rainwater drains in the open	condensation pipes from boilers	fire resistance
clay pipes with sleeves	–	–	+	+	+	–	+	–	+	A1 non-combustible
clay pipes with straight ends	–	+	+	+	+	–	+	–	+	A1
thin-walled clay pipes with straight ends	+	+	+	+	+	+	+	–	+	A1
concrete pipes with rebate	–	–	–	–	+	–	–	–	–	A1
concrete pipe with sleeve	–	–	+	+	+	–	–	–	–	A1
reinforced concrete pipe	–	–	+	+	+	–	–	–	–	A1
glass pipe	+	+	+	–	–	+	+	–	+	A1
cement fibre pipe	+	+	+	+	+	+	+	+	–	A1 non-combustible
cement fibre pipe	–	–	+	+	+	–	–	–	–	A2
metal pipe (zinc, copper, aluminium, steels)	–	–	–	–	–	–	–	+	–	A1
cast iron pipe without sleeve	+	+	+	+	+	+	+	+	–	A1
steel pipe	+	+	+	+	+	+	+	+	–	A1
stainless steel pipe	+	+	+	+	+	+	+	+	+	A1
PVC-U pipe	–	–	–	+	+	–	–	–	+	B1 low combustibility
PVC-U pipe, corrugated outer surface	–	–	–	+	+	–	–	–	+	–
PVC-U pipe, profiled	–	–	–	+	+	–	–	–	+	–
PVC-U foam-core pipe	–	–	–	+	+	–	–	–	+	–
PVC-C pipe	+	+	+	+	–	+	+	+	+	B1
PE-HD pipe	+	+	+	+	–	+	+	+	+	B2 combustible
	–	–	–	+	+	–	–	–	+	–
PE-HD pipe, with profiled walling	–	–	–	–	+	–	–	–	+	–
PP pipe	+	+	+	+	–	+	+	–	+	B1
PP pipe, mineral reinforced	+	+	+	+	–	+	+	–	+	B2
ABS/ASA/PVC pipe	+	+	+	+	–	+	+	–	+	B2
ABS/ASA/PVC pipe, mineral reinforced outer layer	+	+	+	+	–	+	+	–	+	B2
UP/GF pipe	–	–	–	+	+	–	–	–	+	–

key: + use permitted, – use not permitted or inappropriate

(1) **Types of use for drainage pipes of different materials**

BUILDING AND SITE DRAINAGE

External underground drains are understood to be those which are laid outside the plan area of the building. Drains underneath cellar areas are taken as interior drains. Depending on topography, the depths required are 0.80 m, 1.00 m and 1.20 m. In severe climates, measures must be taken to protect against frost.

Changes in direction of main drains must be constructed only with prefabricated bend fittings and no individual bend should be greater than 45°. If a junction of drains cannot be formed with prefabricated fittings, then a manhole must be constructed. Inaccessible double junctions are not permitted and a drain must not be reduced by connection into a narrower pipe in the direction of flow (with the exception of rainwater drainage outside buildings).

nominal dimensions, DN (mm)		minimum falls for:				
		foul water drains within buildings	rainwater drains within buildings	combined drains within buildings	foul water drains outside buildings	rainwater and combined drains outside buildings
up to	100	1:50	1:100	1:50	1:DN	1:DN
	125	1:66.7	1:100	1:66.7	1:DN	1:DN
	150	1:66.7	1:100	1:66.7	1:DN	1:DN
from	200	$1:\frac{DN}{2}$	$1:\frac{DN}{2}$	$1:\frac{DN}{2}$	1:DN	1:DN
fill level h/d		0.5	0.7	0.7	0.5*	0.7**

*   for ground drains greater than 150 mm dia.; also 0.7
** for ground drains greater than 150 mm dia. connected to a manhole with open throughflow; also 1.0

(2) **Minimum falls for drains**

term	symbol	unit	explanation
rainfall value	$r_{T(n)}$	l/(s·ha)	rainfall value, calculated according to the building section of the drainage system, with accompanying rain duration (T) and rain frequency (n)
rainfall area	A	m²	the area subjected to rainfall measured in horizonal plane (A) from which the rain water flows to the drainage system
discharge coefficient	Ψ	1	in the meaning of this standard, the relationship between the rainwater flowing into the drainage system and the total amount of rainwater in the relevant rainfall area
water flow	V_e	l/s	effective volume of water flow, not taking into account simultaneity
rainwater discharge	V_r	l/s	discharge of rainwater from a connected rainfall area by a given rainfall value
foul water discharge	V_s	l/s	discharge in the drainage pipe, resulting from the number of connected sanitary units taking into account simultaneity
combined water discharge	V_m	l/s	sum of the foul water discharge and rainwater discharge $V_m = V_s + V_r$
pumping flow	V_p	l/s	calculated volume flow of a pump etc.
connection value	AW_s	1	the value given to a sanitary fitting to calculate the following drainage pipe ($1 AW_s \approx 1$ l/s)
drainage discharge factor	K	l/s	amount depending on the type of building; results from the characteristics of the discharge
discharge capacity	V_v	l/s	calculated discharge through a drainage pipe when full, without positive or negative static pressure
partial fill discharge	V_T	l/s	discharge through a drainage pipe while partly full
degree of fill	h/d_i	1	relationship between the filling height h and the diameter d_i of a horizontal drainage pipe
fall	l	cm/m	difference in level (in cm) of the base of a pipe over 1 m of its length or its relative proportion (e.g. 1:50 = 2cm/m)
functional roughness	k_b	mm	roughness value, which takes into account all the loss in flow in drainage pipes
nominal bore	DN	–	this is the nominal size, which is used for all compatible fittings (e.g. pipes, pipe connectors and bends); it should be similar to the actual bore; it may only be used instead of the actual bore in hydraulic calculations when the cross-sectional area calculated from the smallest actual bore is not more than 5% less than that calculated from the nominal bore (in relation to a circular cross-section this represents about 2.5%)
actual bore	DS	mm	internal dimension (diameter) of pipes, fittings, manhole covers etc., with specified permitted tolerances* (used as production specification to maintain the necessary cross-sectional properties (area, circumference etc.)
minimum bore	DS_{min}	mm	according to the regulations the smallest permissible bore, given by the smallest tolerated actual bore dimension
minimum inner diameter	$d_{i\,min}$	mm	the minimum inner diameter of drainage pipes, related to the 5% tolerance allowed from the dimension of the nominal bore
flooding	–	–	the situation when foul and/or rainwater escapes from a drainage system or cannot enter into it, irrespective of whether this happens in the open or inside a building
overloading	–	–	the situation when foul and/or rainwater runs under pressure in a drainage system, but does not leak to the surface and therefore causes no flooding
drainage section	T_S	m	a section of the drainage system in which the volume of effluent, the diameter d_i and/or the fall l of the drainage pipe does not alter

*now: lower dimensional limit

① **Terminology for building and site drainage**

BUILDING AND SITE DRAINAGE

Calculation of foul water flow

The deciding factor in calculating the size of the nominal bore is the maximum expected foul water discharge $\dot{V}_s$, which is given by the sum of the connection values and/or, if appropriate, the effective water consumption, while taking into account the simultaneous use of the various sanitary fittings.

$$\dot{V}_s = K \cdot \sqrt{\Sigma AW_s} + \dot{V}_e$$

Guide values for the drainage discharge factor K are shown in ② and example connection values AW_s are given in ③.

If the foul water discharge $\dot{V}_s$ is smaller than the largest connection value of an individual sanitary fitting, then the latter value is to be taken. For drainage systems that do not fit into the categories of building listed in ②, K values should be calculated according to individual specific uses.

type of building, drainage system	K (l/s)
apartment buildings, pubs/restaurants, guest houses, hostels, office buildings, schools	0.5
hospitals (wards), large pubs/restaurants, hotels	0.7
launderettes, rows of showers	1.0*
laboratory installations in industrial organisations	1.2*

*in the cases when the total water flow $\dot{V}_e$ is not relevant

② **Factors for drainage discharge**

sanitary fitting or type of drainage pipe	connection value AW_s	DN of the single connecting drain
hand basins, vanity units, bidets, row of wash basins	0.5	50
kitchen waste run-off (single/double sink), including dishwasher for up to 12 covers, floor gully, washing machine (with trapped drain) for up to 6kg dry laundry	1	50
washing machines for 6–12kg dry laundry	1.5*	70*
commercial dishwashers	2*	100*
floor gullies: nominal bore 50	1	50
nominal bore 70	1.5	70
nominal bore 100	2	100
WC, basin type dishwasher	2.5	100
shower tray/unit, foot bath	1	50
bath tub with direct connection	1	50
bath tub with direct connection, (up to 1m length) above floor level, connected to a drain DN ≥70	1	40
bath tub or shower tray with an indirect connection, connection from the bath outlet less than 2m length	1	50
bath tub or shower tray with an indirect connection, connection from the bath outlet longer than 2m length	1	70
connecting pipe between bath overflow and bath outlet	–	≥40
laboratory sink	1	50
outlet from dentists' treatment equipment (with amalgam trap)	0.5*	40*
urinal (bowl)*	0.5	50
		nominal bore of internal collecting drain
number of urinals: up to 2	0.5	70
up to 4	1	70
up to 6	1.5	70
over 6	2	100

* using these given estimated values, the actual values should be calculated

③ **Connection values of sanitary fittings and basic values for nominal bores of individual drainage connections (branch drains)**

type of unit		ΣAW_s
(a)	**multi-room flat** for drainage from all sanitary rooms and kitchen	5
(b)	**multi-room flat** for drainage from all sanitary rooms, but without the kitchen	4
studio flat for drainage from all sanitary fittings		4
hotel rooms and similar for drainage from all sanitary fittings		4

(1) **Connection values for specific units (for stacks, above- and underground drainage)**

In the calculation of water flows for load types listed in (2), no conversion of the connection value AW_s needs to be carried out.

type of load	flow measurement
launderettes, rows of showers	water flow $\dot{V}_e$
laboratory installations	water flow $\dot{V}_e$
sundry separators (e.g. oil)	water flow $\dot{V}_e$
drainage pumps, sewage pumps and large washing and dishwashing machines, connected to the mains water and to the drains	pumped flow $\dot{V}_p$
rainwater share in a combined drainage system	rainwater discharge $\dot{V}_r$

(2) **Load types**

sanitary units	nominal bore (DN) basis	length L (m[1])	height H (m[1])	number of bends[2]	DN (unventilated)	DN (ventilated)
sink unit, washbasin, bidet	40	up to 3	up to 1	up to 3	40	40
		up to 3	up to 1	over 3	50	40
	40	over 3 or	over 1 up to 3	over 3	70	50
bath tubs – connection to a stack above floor level – DN of the stack ≥70	40	up to 1	up to 0.25	without limit	40	40
bath tub with direct connection	50	up to 3	up to 0.25	without limit	50	50
		over 3 or	over 1 up to 3		70	50
bath tub with connection to floor gulley	≥40	up to 3	up to 0.25	without limit	40	40
floor gully (bath drain) with connection to bath tub or shower tray	70	up to 5	up to 1	without limit	70	70
		over 5 or up to 10	over 1 up to 3		100	70
single connection pipes	50	over 3	over 1 up to 3	without limit	70	50
single connection pipes	70	over 5 or	over 1 up to 3		100	70
single connection pipe without WC	100	up to 10	up to 1	without limit	100	100
		over 10 or	over 1 up to 3		125	100
WC	100	up to 5	up to 1		100	100
WC max. 1m horizontal distance to stack	100	up to 5	over 1 up to 4	without limit	100	100
single connection pipes	all		over 3		ventilation essential	

[1]

H difference in height between the connection to a ventilated pipe and the trap of a sanitary unit
L straightened out length of pipe up to the trap

(maximum permitted lengths and height differences of single connection pipes)

[2] number of bends including exit bend of trap

(3) **Nominal bores of above-ground drainage in connection with the layout criteria of the pipe runs**

BUILDING AND SITE DRAINAGE

Dimensioning of drainage systems following the connection of a pump installation

Non-pressurised drainage following a pump installation is to be calculated as follows.

(a) With rainwater drainage, the pumped flow from the pump $\dot{V}_p$ is to be added to the rainwater discharge $\dot{V}_r$.

(b) With foul water and combined drainage, the relevant highest value (pumped flow or the remaining effluent flow) is to be taken, under the condition that the addition of $\dot{V}_p$ and $\dot{V}_m$ or $\dot{V}_s$ does not result in a complete filling of the underground or above-ground drainage pipework. The calculated testing of the complete filling of pipes is only to be carried out on pipes for which there is a filling level of $h/d_i = 0.7$. If there are several foul water pump installations in a combined underground/above-ground drainage system, then the total pumped flow of the pumps can be reduced (e.g. for every additional pump add 0.4 $\dot{V}_p$).

Dimensioning of foul drain pipes: connecting pipes → (3)

Single connecting pipes from hand basins, sink units and bidets, which do not have more than three changes of direction (including the exit bend of the trap) can be constructed from nominal bore 40 pipes. If there are more than three changes of direction, then a nominal bore 50 pipe is necessary.

Internal collecting drainage

With unventilated internal collection drains, the drain length L, including the individual connection furthest away, should not exceed 3m for nominal bore 50 pipe, 5m for nominal bore 70, and 10m for pipes with a nominal bore of 100 (without WC connection). Where greater lengths are required, wider bores or the use of ventilated pipework should be considered. Internal collection drain pipes over 5m in length with a nominal bore of 100, WC connections and falls H of 1m or more must be ventilated.

ΣAW_s unventilated	ΣAW_s ventilated	DN	length L m[1]	height H m[1]	unventilated DN	ventilated DN
1	–	50	up to 3	up to 1	50	–
1	1.5	50	up to 6	over 1 up to 3	70 from stack	50
3	–	70	up to 5	up to 1	70	–
3	4.5	70	up to 10	over 1 up to 3	100 from stack	70
16	–	100 without WC	up to 10	up to 1	100	–
				over 1 up to 3	–	100
	1.5	50	over 6 or	over 3	ventilation essential	
–	4.5	70	over 10 or	over 3		
–	25	100 without WC	over 10 or	over 3		
16	–	100 with WC	up to 5	up to 1	100	
–	25	100 with WC	over 5	over 1	ventilation essential	
–	>16	all			ventilation essential	
3	–	100	WC with 1 sink unit on the ground floor – H at least 4m above the horiz. drain pipe – distance of WC from stack max. 1m			

[1]

diagram 1   diagram 2

H difference in height from the connection to a ventilated pipe (stack, above-ground, underground) to the highest situated trap
L straightened out pipe length to the furthest situated trap

(4) **Nominal bores of above-ground drainage in connection with the layout criteria of the pipe runs**

DN	$d_{i\,min}$ (mm) *)	upper limit $\dot{V}_s$ (l/s)	$K = 0.5$ l/s		$K = 0.7$ l/s		$K = 1.0$ l/s	
			ΣAW_s	max number of WCs	ΣAW_s	max number of WCs	ΣAW_s	max number of WCs
70**)	68.2	1.5	9	–	5	–	2	–
100	97.5	4.0	64	13	33	8	16	4
125	115.0	5.3	112	22	57	14	28	7
	121.9	6.2	154	31	78	20	38	10
150	146.3	10.1	408	82	208	52	102	25

*) see explanations → p. 56
**) it is not permitted to connect more than four kitchen sanitary units to one separate stack (kitchen stack)

(1) **Foul water stack drains with top ventilation**

DN	$d_{i\,min}$ (mm) *)	upper limit $\dot{V}_s$ (l/s)	$K = 0.5$ l/s		$K = 0.7$ l/s		$K = 1.0$ l/s	
			ΣAW_s	max number of WCs	ΣAW_s	max number of WCs	ΣAW_s	max number of WCs
70**)	68.2	2.1	18	–	9	–	4	–
100	97.5	5.6	125	25	64	16	31	8
125	115.0	7.4	219	44	112	28	55	14
	121.9	8.7	303	61	154	39	76	20
150	146.3	14.1	795	159	406	102	199	50

*) see explanations → p. 56
**) it is not permitted to connect more than four kitchen sanitary units to one separate stack (kitchen stack)

(2) **Foul water stack drains with direct or indirect additional ventilation**

DN	$d_{i\,min}$ (mm) *)	upper limit $\dot{V}_s$ (l/s)	$K = 0.5$ l/s		$K = 0.7$ l/s		$K = 1.0$ l/s	
			ΣAW_s	max number of WCs	ΣAW_s	max number of WCs	ΣAW_s	max number of WCs
70**)	68.2	2.6	27	–	14	–	7	–
100	97.5	6.8	185	37	94	24	46	12
125	115.0	9.0	324	65	165	41	81	20
	121.9	10.5	441	88	225	56	101	28
150	146.3	17.2	1183	237	604	151	296	74

*) see explanations → p. 56
**) it is not permitted to connect more than four kitchen sanitary units to one separate stack (kitchen stack)

(3) **Foul water stack drains with secondary ventilation**

type of surface	coefficient
waterproof surfaces, e.g.	
– roof areas >3° falls	
– concrete surfaces, ramps	
– stabilised areas with sealed joints	1.0
– asphalt roofs	
– paving with sealed joints	
– roof area ≤3° falls	0.8
– grassed roof areas [1]	
– intensive planting	0.3
– extensive planting above 100 mm built-up thickness	0.3
– extensive planting less than 100 mm built-up thickness	0.5
partially permeable and surfaces with slight run-off, e.g.	
– concrete paving laid on sand or slag, areas with paving	0.7
– areas with paving, with joint proportion >15% (e.g. 100 × 100 mm and smaller)	0.6
– water consolidated areas	0.5
– children's play area, partly stabilised	0.3
– sports areas with land drainage	
– artificial surfaces	0.6
– gravelled areas	0.4
– grassed areas	0.3
water permeable surfaces with insignificant or no water run-off, e.g.	
– park and planted areas	
– hardcore, slag and coarse gravelled areas, even with partly consolidated areas such as:	
– garden paths with water consolidated surface or	0.0
– drives and parking areas with grassed concrete grid	
[1] according to guidelines for the planning, construction and maintenance of roof planting	

(4) **Discharge coefficient (ψ) to calculate the rainwater discharge ($\dot{V}_r$)**

BUILDING AND SITE DRAINAGE

Foul water stacks

The nominal bore of all foul water stacks must be at least DN 70. For foul water stacks with top ventilation the figures given in (1) should be used for design calculations. The nominal bores shown for the stacks considered are associated with the maximum sum of the connection values with which the stack can be loaded. It should be noted that to avoid functional disruptions a limit is put upon the number of WCs (i.e. sanitary units that introduce quantities of large solid objects and surges of water) that may be connected to the various stacks. In addition to foul water flows, tables (1) – (3) also show examples of sums of connection values (see p. 56).

Foul water stacks with secondary ventilation can be loaded with 70% more foul water flow than stacks with top ventilation. They can be estimated in accordance with → (3).

Calculations governing underground and above-ground collection pipes (horizontal foul water drains) should be made based on the ratio $h/d_i = 0.5$ although for under-ground pipes outside the building over DN 150 can use $h/d_i = 0.7$. The values for the partial fill discharge flow of the pipes with minimum falls l_{min} are identified in relation to whether the pipes are laid inside or outside the building. Values below the given size steps are allowed for pipe calculations only in individually justified cases.

Calculations for rainwater pipes: rainwater discharge and rainfall value

The discharge from a rainfall area is calculated using the following relationship:

$$\text{(5)} \qquad \dot{V}_r = \psi \cdot A \cdot \frac{r_{T(n)}}{10\,000} \quad \text{in l/s}$$

where
$\dot{V}_r$ = rainwater discharge in l/s
A = connected rainfall area in m^2
$r_{T(n)}$ = rainfall value in l/(s·ha)
ψ = discharge coefficient according to → (4)

Rainwater drainage pipes inside and outside buildings are fundamentally to be calculated with a minimum rainfall value of at least 300 l/(s·ha). It is also important to ensure that there are enough emergency overflows for large internal rainwater drainage systems. The requirements can be checked using the following standard figures for the location:

$r_{15(1)}$ Fifteen minute rainfall value, statistically exceeded once per year. This rainfall value should only be used in exceptionally well reasoned cases for the calculation of rainwater drainage pipe sizes.

$r_{5(0.5)}$ Five minute rainfall value, statistically exceeded once every two years.

$r_{5(0.05)}$ Five minute rainfall value, statistically seen is exceeded once every twenty years.

For above- and underground drains within a building, subject to agreement with local guidelines, a rainfall value of less than 300 can be employed, though it must be at least as great as the five minute rainfall value in two years ($r_{5(0.5)}$). Across Germany, $r_{5(0.5)}$ varies from around 165 up to as much as 445 l/(s·ha) so it is important to check the figures with the local authority.

If smaller rainfall values are proposed and there are large roof drainage areas (e.g. above 5000 m^2), it is necessary to carry out an overloading calculation on the basis of what can be expected in the case of rainfall equivalent at least to a five minute rainfall value in 20 years ($r_{5(0.05)}$). These rainfall values can be as high as 950 l/(s·ha). Within the overload sector, take into account the resistances due to the layout of the pipes. If a special roof form is proposed (e.g. those with areas of planned flooding) they must be waterproofed to above the flood level and the additional loads must be taken into consideration.

Underground rainwater drainage pipes should have a nominal bore of DN 100 or more. If the pipe is outside the building and for mixed drainage (i.e. will also carry foul water), and connects to a manhole with open access, the nominal bore should be DN 150 or above.

DAMP-PROOFING AND TANKING

Cellars are used less these days as storage rooms and more as places for leisure or as additional rooms for accommodation and domestic purposes. So, people want greater comfort and a better internal climate in the cellar. A prerequisite for this is proofing against dampness from outside. For buildings without cellars, the external and internal walls have to be protected from rising damp by the provision of horizontal damp-proof courses → ③ – ⑥. On external walls, the damp-proofing is 150–300 mm above ground level → ③ – ⑥. For buildings with brick cellar walls, a minimum of 2 horizontal damp-proof courses should be provided in the external walls → ⑦ – ⑧. The upper layer may be omitted on internal walls. Bituminous damp-proof membranes, asphalt, or specifically designed high-grade plastic sheet should be used for the vertical tanking in walls. Depending on the type of back filling used in the working area and the type of tanking used, protective layers should be provided for the wall surfaces → ⑫ – ⑭. Rubble, gravel chippings or loose stones should not be deposited directly against the tanking membrane.

① Cellar level protected horizontally and vertically against rising damp → ⑦ – ⑭

② Good protection required on hill side of building; hillside water conducted away by drainage → ⑤ – ⑥

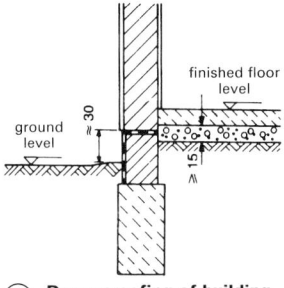

③ Damp-proofing of building with no cellar and with non-habitable room use; hardcore at the level of the damp-proof course

④ Damp-proofing of building with no cellar and with non-habitable room use; floor at ground level

water occurs as	proofing required against	type of proofing
rising damp	capillary effect on vertical building elements	protective layers against ground dampness (damp proofing)
precipitation, running water	seepage of water not under pressure on sloping surfaces of building elements	proofing against seepage (tanking)
ground water	hydrostatic pressure	pressure retaining proofing (tanking)

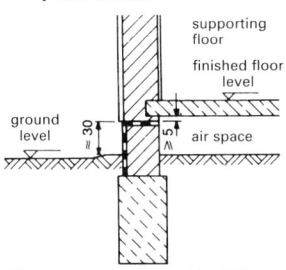

⑤ Damp-proofing of building with no cellar; floor with ventilated air gap between floor and ground level

⑥ Damp-proofing of building with no cellar; low lying floor at ground level

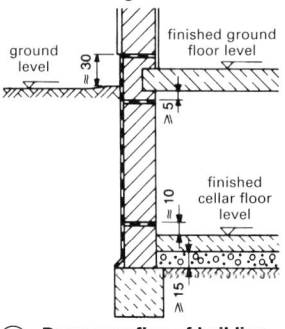
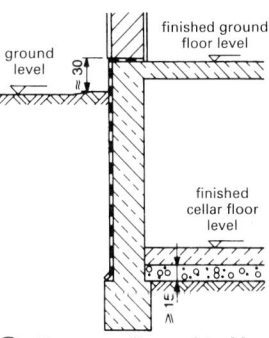
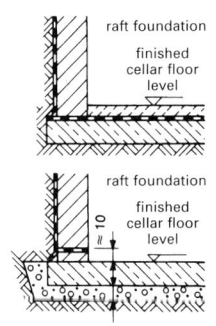

⑦ Damp-proofing of building with cellar with non-habitable room use (masonry walls on strip foundation)

⑧ Damp-proofing of building with cellar; masonry walls on strip foundations

⑨ Damp-proofing and tanking of building with cellar; walls of concrete

⑩ Damp-proofing and tanking of building with cellar; masonry walls on a raft foundation

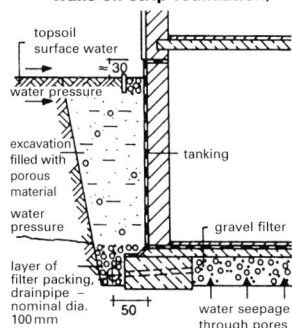
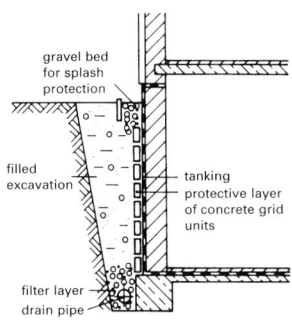
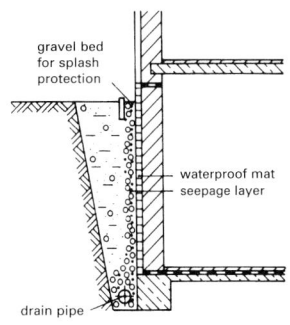
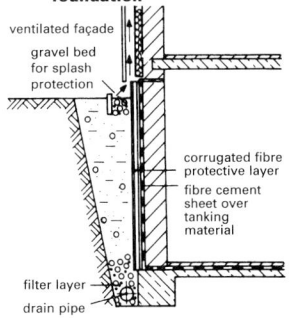

⑪ Drainage and tanking

⑫ Protective wall of concrete grid units

⑬ Waterproof mat

⑭ Protective layer of fibre cement boards

DAMP-PROOFING AND TANKING

Ground Water Drainage

Ground water drainage involves the removal of water from the building site area through drainage layers and drainpipes to prevent the build-up of water pressure. This process should prevent blocking by soil particles (fixed filter drainage). A drainage facility consists of perforated drains, inspection and cleaning devices, and drainage pipes for water disposal. Drainage is the collective term for drain pipes and drainage layers. If drainage at the wall is necessary, reference should be made to the cases → ① – ③. → ① is relevant if ground dampness only occurs in very porous ground. → ② is relevant if the accumulation of water can be avoided by means of a drain, so that water under pressure does not occur. → ③ is relevant if water is present under pressure, as a rule in the form of ground water, or when removal of the water via a drain is not possible.

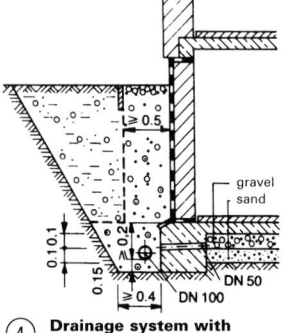

① **Ground dampness in very porous ground**

② **Non-pressurised water in slightly porous ground**

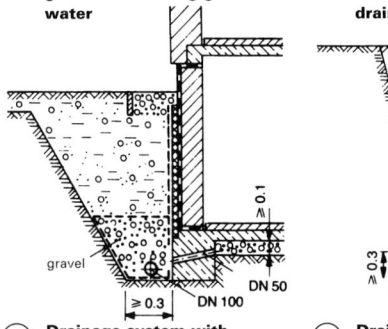

③ **Water under pressure in ground containing ground water**

④ **Drainage system with rubble trench fill (French drain)**

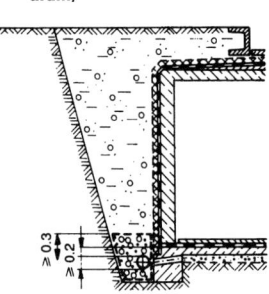

⑤ **Drainage system with granular material around the pipe (tile drain)**

⑥ **Drainage system for deep building work**

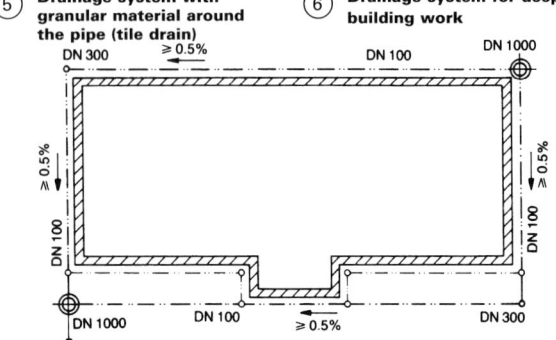

⑦ **Example of an arrangement of drainpipes, inspection and cleaning access in a ring drainage system**

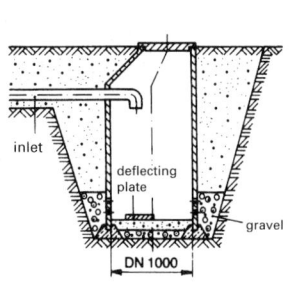

⑧ **Soakaway for low drainage requirement**

representation	component	material
	filter layer	sand geotextile (filter fleece)
	drainage layer	gravel individual/ composite elements (drainage units, boards) (drainage mat)
	protective, separating	membrane, render
	d/proofing	
	drainpipe washout/ inspection pipe	
⊕	washout/ inspection/ collecting shaft	

⑨ **Key to diagrammatic representation**

position	material	thickness (m)
in front of walls	sand/gravel	≥0.50
	filter layer coarseness 0–4 mm	≥0.10
	seepage layer coarseness 4–32 mm	≥0.20
	gravel coarseness 4–32 mm and geotextile	≥0.20
on roof slabs	gravel coarseness 4–32 mm and geotextile	≥0.50
under floor slabs	filter layer coarseness 0.4 mm seepage layer coarseness 4–32 mm gravel coarseness 4–32 mm and geotextile	≥0.10
around land drains	sand/gravel	≥0.15
	seepage layer coarseness 4–32 mm and filter layer coarseness 0–4 mm	≥0.10
	gravel coarseness 4–32 mm and geotextile	≥0.10

drainpipe: nominal diameter 100 mm, 0.5% fall
washout and inspection pipe: nominal diameter 300 mm
washout, inspection and collecting shaft: nominal diameter 1000 mm

⑩ **Specifications and depths of granular materials for drainage layers**

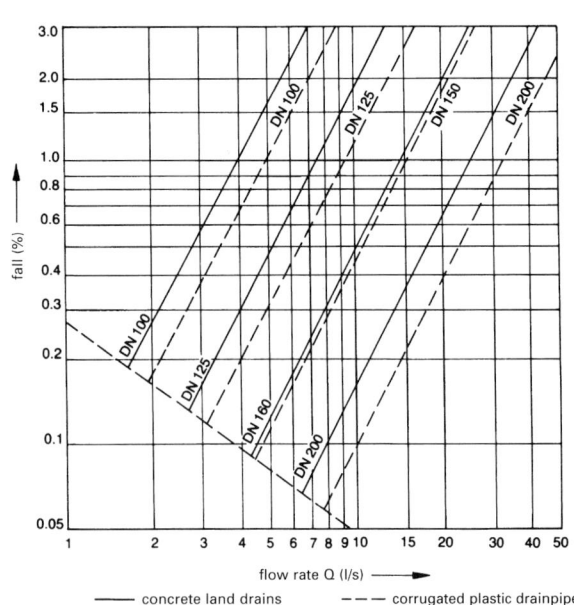

fall (%) / flow rate Q (l/s)

——— concrete land drains   – – – corrugated plastic drainpipe

⑪ **Measurement nomogram for drainage pipework**

DAMP-PROOFING AND TANKING

If the precipitation on the site is not absorbed quickly, a build-up of water pressure can occur and tanking against the water pressure is needed, with drainage to conduct water away. For these measures → ① – ③; for tanking methods → ④ – ⑬.

Water pressure

If parts of buildings are immersed in ground water, a water pressure retaining barrier layer (tanking) must be positioned over the base and side walls. To plan this design, the type of subsoil, the maximum ground water level and the chemical content of the water must be known. The tanking should extend to 300 mm above the maximum ground water level. The materials can be 3-layer asphalt or specially designed plastic membranes, with metal fittings if necessary.

When the water level has sunk below the cellar floor level, the protective walls are constructed on the concrete base layer and rendered ready to receive the tanking. After the tanking is applied, the reinforced floor slab and structural cellar walls are completed hard against the tanking. NB the rounding of the corners → ⑥ – ⑦. The tanking must be in the form of a complete vessel or enclose the building structure on all sides. Normally, it lies on the water side of the building structure → ⑥ – ⑦. For internal tanking, the cladding construction must be able to withstand the full water pressure → ⑫.

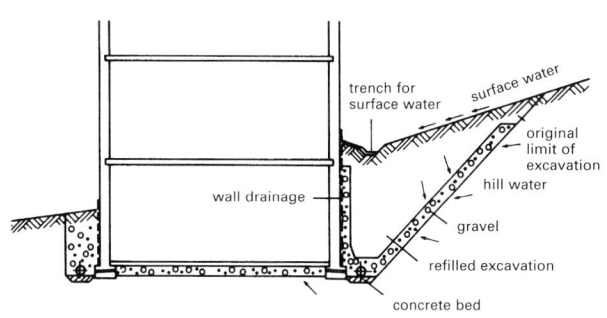

① **Building walls on hillside must be well drained**

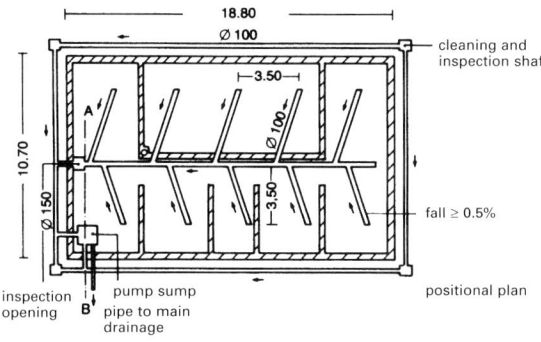

② **Surface drainage with perforated land drains and ring drainage pumped to main drain**

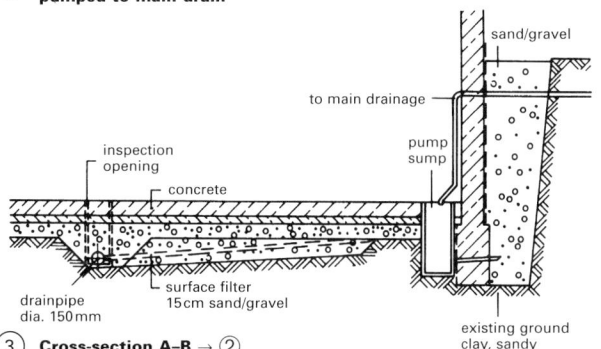

③ **Cross-section A–B → ②**

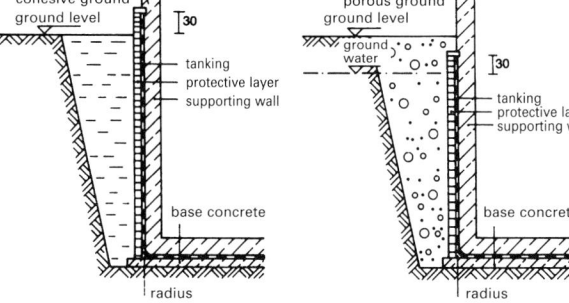

④ **Pipe drainage with mixed infill (French drain)**

⑤ **Pipe drainage with layered infill (tile drain)**

⑥ **Continuous water pressure resistant tanking**

⑦ **Continuous water pressure resistant tanking**

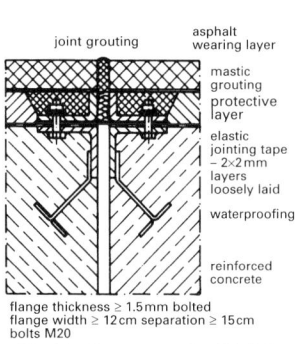

⑧ **Tanking over a flexible joint in reinforced concrete slab**

⑩ **Tanking over expansion joint in reinforced concrete slab; thermal insulating screed**

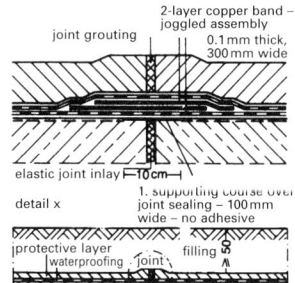

⑫ **Subsequently constructed tanking**

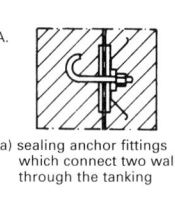

⑨ **Details: tanking between two walls**

(a) sealing anchor fittings which connect two walls through the tanking

(b) sealing a pipe penetration of the tanking with flanges

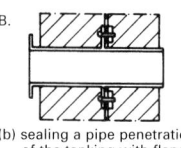

⑪ **Tanking at connections to windows and access openings**

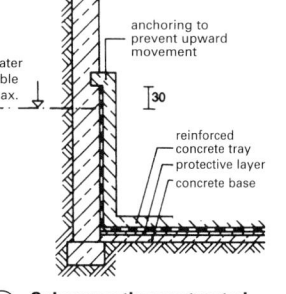

⑬ **Tanking at junctions of slab bearing on retaining wall**

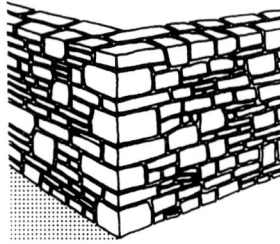

① **Dry stone walling**

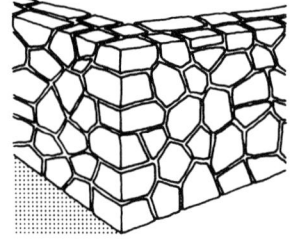

② **Rough hewn uncoursed random rubble walling**

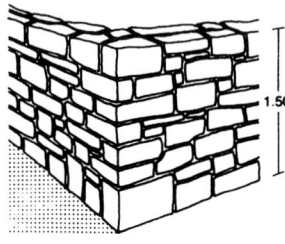

③ **Squared random rubble uncoursed walling**

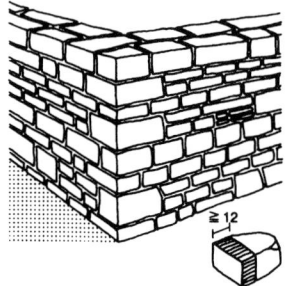

④ **Hammer-faced squared random rubble irregularly coursed walling**

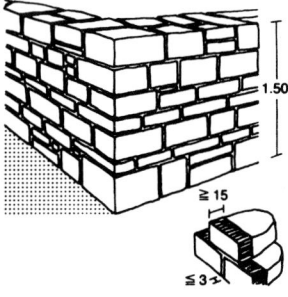

⑤ **Irregular masonry courses**

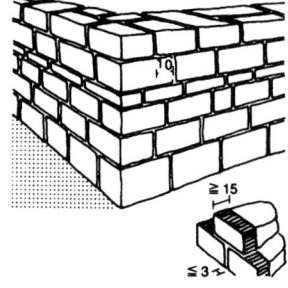

⑥ **Regular masonry courses**

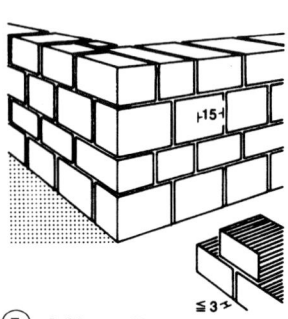

⑦ **Ashlar walling**

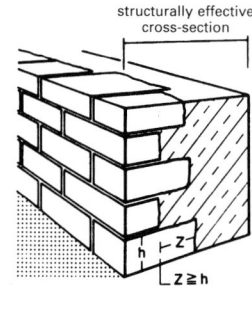

⑧ **Ashlar faced mixed masonry walling**

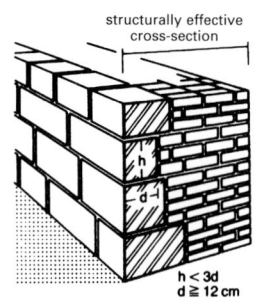

⑨ **Mixed masonry with structurally effective cross-section**

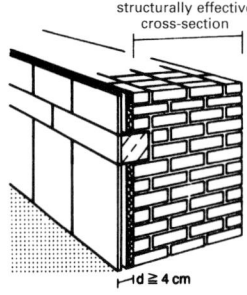

⑩ **Stone cladding: structurally ineffective**

MASONRY

Natural Stone

Masonry in natural stone is referred to as random rubble, squared, dressed, ashlar, uncoursed, coursed, etc. → ① – ⑩. Stone quarried from natural deposits should be laid in the orientation as found in the quarry → ①, ③, ④, to give an attractive and natural appearance; this is also better from a structural viewpoint, as the loading is mainly vertical in pressure between the courses. Igneous stone is suitable for random, uncoursed masonry → ②. The length of the stones should be four or five times their height, no more, and certainly no less than the stone height. The stones' size is of great significance to the scaling of a building. Attention must be paid to good bonding on both sides. In natural masonry, the bonding should show good craftsmanship across the whole cross-section.
The following guidelines should be observed:
(a) Nowhere on the front and rear faces should more than three joints run into each other.
(b) No butt joint should run through more than two courses.
(c) There must be a minimum of one header on two-stretcher courses, or the header and stretcher courses should alternate with one another.
(d) The depth of the header must be approx. 1.5 times the height of a course and not less than 300 mm.
(e) The stretcher depth must be approx. equal to the course height.
(f) The overlap of the butt joints must be ≥100 mm (masonry courses) and 150 mm on ashlar walling → ⑤ – ⑦.
(g) The largest stones should be built in at the corners → ① – ⑥. The visible surfaces should be subsequently pointed.

The masonry should be levelled and trued for structural bearing every 1.5–2.0 m (scaffold height). The mortar joints should be ≤30 mm thick, depending on coarseness and finish. Lime or lime cement mortar should be used, since pure cement mortar discolours certain types of stone. In the case of mixed masonry, the facing layer can be included in the load-bearing cross-section if the thickness ≥120 mm → ⑨. Front facing (cladding) of 25–50 mm thickness (Travertine, limestone, granite, etc.) is not included in the cross-section and the facing is anchored to the masonry with non-corroding tie-rods, with a 2 mm separation from it → ⑩.

group	type of stone	min. compressive strength in kp/cm^2 (MN/m^2)
A	limestone, travertine, volcanic tufa	200 (20)
B	soft sandstone (with argillaceous binding agent)	300 (30)
C	dense (solid) limestone and dolomite (inc. marble) basalt lava and similar	500 (50)
D	quartzitic sandstone (with silica binding agent), greywacke and similar	800 (80)
E	granite, synite, diorite, quartz porphyry, melaphyre, diabase and similar	1200 (120)

⑪ **Minimum compressive strengths of types of stone**

	masonry type	mortar group	group as in ⑪				
			A	B	C	D	E
1	quarry stone	I	2 (0.2)	2 (0.2)	3 (0.3)	4 (0.4)	6 (0.6)
2		II/IIa	2 (0.2)	3 (0.3)	5 (0.5)	7 (0.7)	9 (0.9)
3		III	3 (0.3)	5 (0.5)	6 (0.6)	10 (1.0)	12 (1.2)
4	hammer finished	I	3 (0.3)	5 (0.5)	6 (0.6)	8 (0.8)	10 (1.0)
5	masonry courses	II/IIa	5 (0.5)	7 (0.7)	9 (0.9)	12 (1.2)	16 (1.6)
6		III	6 (0.6)	10 (1.0)	12 (1.2)	16 (1.6)	22 (2.2)
7	irregular and	I	4 (0.4)	6 (0.6)	8 (0.8)	10 (1.0)	16 (1.6)
8	regular masonry	II/IIa	7 (0.7)	9 (0.9)	12 (1.2)	16 (1.6)	22 (2.2)
9	courses	III	10 (1.0)	12 (1.2)	16 (1.6)	22 (2.2)	30 (3.0)
10	ashlar walling	I	8 (0.8)	10 (1.0)	16 (1.6)	22 (2.2)	30 (3.0)
11		II/IIa	12 (1.2)	16 (1.6)	22 (2.2)	30 (3.0)	40 (0.4)
12		III	16 (1.6)	22 (2.2)	30 (3.0)	40 (4.0)	50 (5.0)

⑫ **Basic values – permissible compressive stress on natural stone masonry in kp/cm^2 (MN/m^2)**

	slenderness ratio or eff. sl. ratio	8 (0.8)	10 (1.0)	12 (1.2)	16 (1.6)	22 (2.2)	30 (3.0)	40 (4.0)	50 (5.0)
1	10	8 (0.8)	10 (1.0)	12 (1.2)	16 (1.6)	22 (2.2)	30 (3.0)	40 (4.0)	50 (5.0)
2	12	6 (0.6)	7 (0.7)	8 (0.8)	11 (1.1)	15 (1.5)	22 (2.2)	30 (3.0)	40 (4.0)
3	14	4 (0.4)	5 (0.5)	6 (0.6)	8 (0.8)	10 (1.0)	14 (1.4)	22 (2.2)	30 (3.0)
4	16	3 (0.3)	3 (0.3)	4 (0.4)	6 (0.6)	7 (0.7)	10 (1.0)	14 (1.4)	22 (2.2)
5	18			3 (0.3)	4 (0.4)	5 (0.5)	7 (0.7)	10 (1.0)	14 (1.4)
6	20					3 (0.3)	5 (0.5)	7 (0.7)	10 (1.0)

⑬ **Permissible compressive stresses on natural stone masonry in kp/cm^2 (MN/m^2)**

MASONRY

Bricks and Blocks

As per BS 6100: Section 5.3: 1984, masonry units include several terms: unit (special, shaped, standard shaped, cant, plinth, bullnose, squint, solid, cellular, hollow, perforated, common, facing, split-faced, lintel, fixing, concrete, calcium silicate, sandlime, flintlime, fired-clay, terracotta, faience), header, stretcher, closer (king, queen) and air brick. Brick: a masonry unit not over 338mm in length, 225mm in width or 113mm in height. The term 'brick' includes engineering, frogged, hand-made, stock, wire-cut, rusticated, rubber, tile and damp proof course bricks. Block: a masonry unit exceeding the size of any dimension of brick, including dense concrete, lightweight concrete, lightweight aggregate concrete, aerated concrete, autoclaved aerated concrete, thermal insulation, foam-filled concrete, clinker, dry walling, cavity closer and quoin blocks. All masonry work must be horizontally and vertically true, and properly aligned in accordance with regulations. On double leafed masonry → ⑦ + ⑨, floors and roof must be supported only by the inner leaf. Masonry leafs should be joined with a min. of 5 stainless steel wire ties, 3mm in diameter, per sq. m. The ties are separated 250mm vertically and 750mm horizontally.

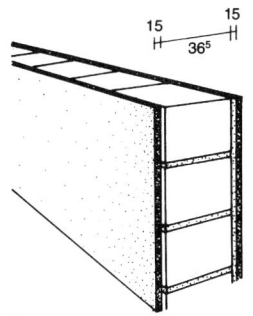

① **Single leaf plastered**

② **Single leaf fairfaced**

③ **Double leaf with brick facing**

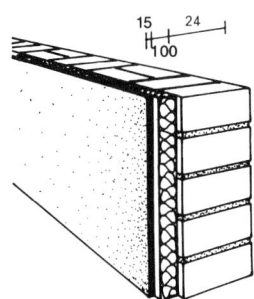

④ **Single leaf with thermal insulated facing**

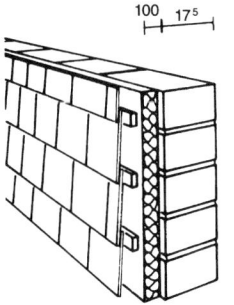

⑤ **Single leaf with tile hanging**

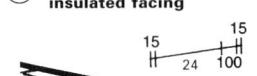
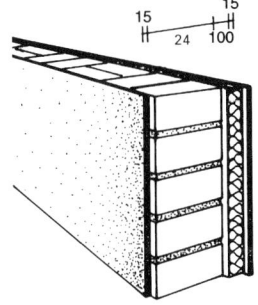

⑥ **Single leaf with internal insulation**

⑦ **Double leaf cavity wall with partial fill cavity insulation**

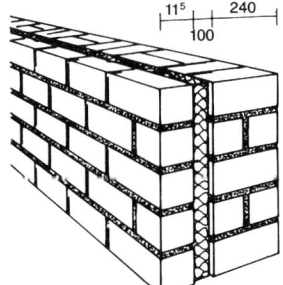

⑧ **Double cavity wall with full fill insulation**

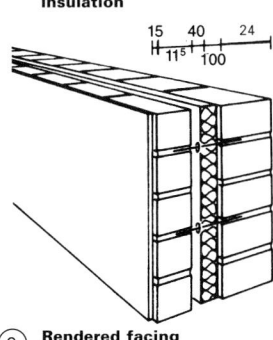

⑨ **Rendered facing with/without air cavity**

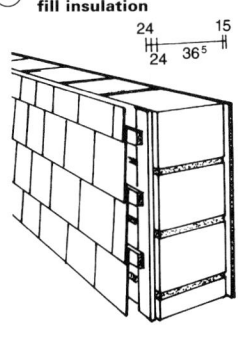

⑩ **Tile hanging on insulating blockwork**

designation		length (cm)	breadth (cm)	height (cm)
thin format	TF	24	11.5	5.2
standard format	SF	24	11.5	7.1
1½ standard format	1½ SF	24	11.5	11.3
2½ standard format	2½ SF	24	17.5	11.3

⑪ **Masonry formats**

⑫ **Interrelationship between brick/block height dimensions → ⑪**

cellar wall thickness, d (cm)	height h (m) of ground above cellar floor with vertical wall loading (dead load) of	
	≥ 50 kN/m	< 50 kN/m
36.5	2.50	2.00
30	1.75	1.40
24	1.35	1.00

⑬ **Minimum thickness of cellar walls**

thickness of the supporting wall to be braced	height of storey (m)	bracing wall in the 1st to 4th and 5th and 6th full storey levels from top		spacing (m)	length
11.5 ≤ d < 17.5 17.5 ≤ d < 24	≤ 3.25	thickness (cm)		≤ 4.50 ≤ 6.00	≥ 1/5 of the height
24 ≤ d < 30 30 ≤ d	≤ 3.50 ≤ 5.00	≥ 11.5	≥ 17.5	≤ 8.00	

⑭ **Thickness, spacing and length of bracing walls**

dimensions (cm)		thickness of wall (cm)				
		11.5	17.5	24	30	≥ 36.5
recesses in masonry bonding	breadth	–	≤ 51		≤ 63.5	≤ 76
	residual wall thickness	–	≥ 11.5		≥ 17.5	≥ 24
sawn out slots	breadth	≤ wall thickness				
	depth	≤ 2	≤ 3	≤ 4	≤ 5	≤ 6
min. spacing between recesses and slots distance from openings distance from wall junctions		199 ≥ 36.5 ≥ 24				

⑮ **Permissible vertical recesses and slots in braced and bracing walls**

BUILDING COMPONENTS

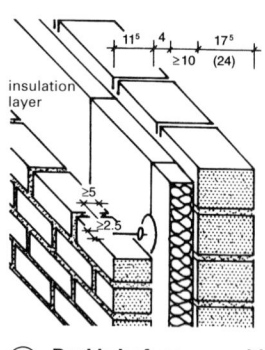

(1) Double leaf masonry with full fill cavity insulation

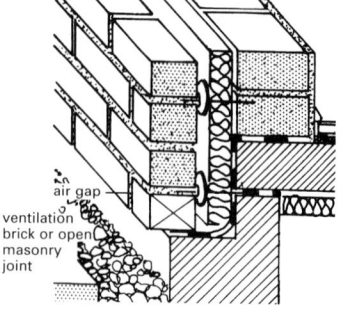

(2) Detail at base

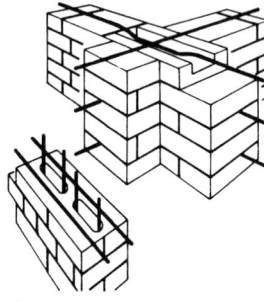

(3) Crossover with reinforced light concrete masonry blocks

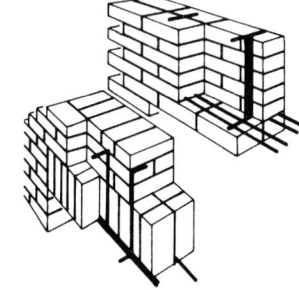

(4) Reinforced masonry for door or window lintel

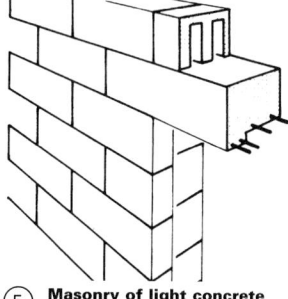

(5) Masonry of light concrete blocks (hollow blocks) with reinforced pumice concrete lintel

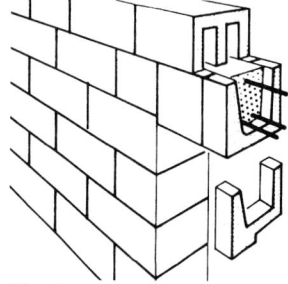

(6) Masonry in hollow blocks with in situ reinforced trough lintel

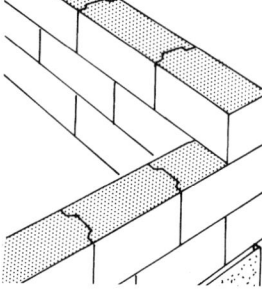

(7) Aerated concrete blocks with cemented joints: 1 mm

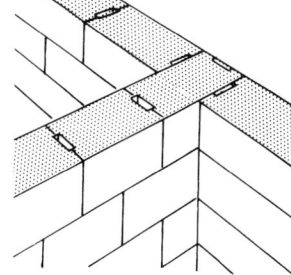

(8) Poroton blocks with mortar filling

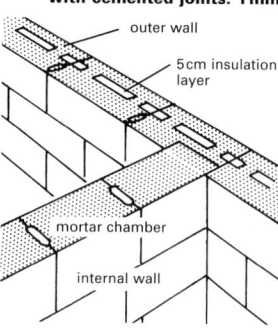

(9) Building blocks with 5 cm insulation layer and mortar filled cavities

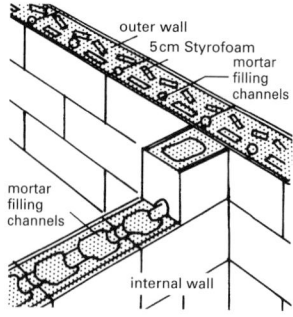

(10) Special wall blocks with insulation and mortar filling channels

Masonry walling has to be braced with lateral walls and the tops restrained by upper floors (cellular principle). Bracing walls are plate-like components which stiffen the structure against buckling → p. 63 (14). They are rated as supporting walls if they carry more than their own weight from one storey. Non-supporting walls are plate-like components which are stressed only by their own weight and do not provide buckling support. Recesses and slots have to be cut out or positioned in the masonry bonds. Horizontal and slanting recesses are permitted, but with a slenderness ratio of ≤ 140 mm and thickness ≥ 240 mm under special requirements → p. 63 (15). Ties should be provided for connection between external walls and partition walls acting as bracing walls that transmit horizontal loads. Horizontal reinforcement is required in structures of more than two complete storeys or which are more than 18[t]m long, if the site conditions demand it, or where there are walls with many or large openings (if the sum of the opening widths is more than 60% of the wall length, or where the window width is over 2/3 of the storey height or more than 40% of the wall length).

heading number	lengthwise dimension* (m)			number of courses	height dimension (m), with block thickness (mm)					
	OD	OS	OL		52	71	113	155	175	238
1	0.115	0.135	0.125	1	0.0625	0.0833	0.125	0.1666	0.1875	0.25
2	0.240	0.260	0.250	2	0.1250	0.1667	0.250	0.3334	0.3750	0.50
3	0.365	0.385	0.375	3	0.1875	0.2500	0.375	0.5000	0.5625	0.75
4	0.490	0.510	0.500	4	0.2500	0.3333	0.500	0.6666	0.7500	1.00
5	0.615	0.635	0.625	5	0.3125	0.4167	0.625	0.8334	0.9375	1.25
6	0.740	0.760	0.750	6	0.3750	0.5000	0.750	1.0000	1.1250	1.50
7	0.865	0.885	0.875	7	0.4375	0.5833	0.875	1.1666	1.3125	1.75
8	0.990	1.010	1.000	8	0.5000	0.6667	1.000	1.3334	1.5000	2.00
9	1.115	1.135	1.125	9	0.5625	0.7500	1.125	1.5000	1.6875	2.25
10	1.240	1.260	1.250	10	0.6240	0.8333	1.250	1.6666	1.8750	2.50
11	1.365	1.385	1.375	11	0.6875	0.9175	1.375	1.8334	2.0625	2.75
12	1.490	1.510	1.50	12	0.7500	1.0000	1.500	2.0000	2.2500	3.00
13	1.615	1.635	1.625	13	0.8125	1.0833	1.625	2.1666	2.4375	3.25
14	1.740	1.760	1.750	14	0.8750	1.1667	1.750	2.3334	2.6250	3.50
15	1.865	1.885	1.875	15	0.9375	1.2500	1.875	2.5000	2.8125	3.75
16	1.990	2.010	2.000	16	1.0000	1.3333	2.000	2.6666	3.0000	4.00
17	2.115	2.135	2.125	17	1.0625	1.4167	2.125	2.8334	3.1875	4.25
18	2.240	2.260	2.250	18	1.1250	1.5000	2.250	3.0000	3.3750	4.50
19	2.365	2.385	2.375	19	1.1875	1.5833	2.375	3.1666	3.5625	4.75
20	2.490	2.510	2.500	20	1.2500	1.6667	2.500	3.3334	3.7500	5.00

* OD = outer dimension, OS = opening size, OL = overlap

(11) Setting out dimensions for masonry work

block format	block format	dimension (cm)	number of courses per 1 m height	wall thickness (cm)	per m² of wall		per m³ of masonry	
					no. of blocks	mortar (litre)	no. of blocks	mortar (litre)
perforated blocks (up to 10% less mortar for solid blocks)	DF	24 × 11.5 × 5.2	16	11.5	66	29	573	242
					132	68	550	284
				36.5	198	109	541	300
	NF	24 × 11.5 × 7.1	12	11.5	50	26	428	225
				24	99	64	412	265
				36.5	148	101	406	276
	2 DF	24 × 11.5 × 11.3	8	11.5	33	19	286	163
				24	66	49	275	204
				36.5	99	80	271	220
	3 DF	24 × 17.5 × 11.3	8	17.5	33	28	188	160
				24	45	42	185	175
	4 DF	24 × 24 × 11.3	8	24	33	39	137	164
	8 DF	24 × 24 × 23.8	4	24	16	20	69	99
blocks and hollow blocks	blocks and hollow blocks	49.5 × 17.5 × 23.8	4	17.5	8	16	46	84
		49.5 × 24 × 23.8	4	24	8	22	33	86
		49.5 × 30 × 23.8	4	30	8	26	27	88
		37 × 24 × 23.8	4	24	12	26	50	110
		37 × 30 × 23.8	4	30	12	32	42	105
		24.5 × 36.5 × 23.8	4	36.5	16	36	45	100

(12) Building material requirements for masonry work

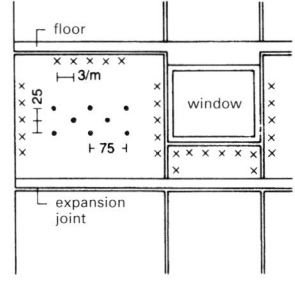

(1) **Wire ties for external double leaf cavity walls**

(2) **Anchoring of the outer leaf → pp. 63–4**

wall thickness (cm)	17.5	11.5
storey height (m)	≤ 3.25	
live load (kN/m²) including addition for light dividing walls	≤ 2.75	
number of complete storeys above	4[1][2]	2[2]

Only permissible as intermediate support for one way spanning floors of span ≤4.5 m; while for two way spanning floors, the smaller span is to be taken [3].
Between the bracing walls, only one opening is permitted with a width of ≤1.25 m.
[1] Including any storeys with walls 11.5 cm thick
[2] If the floors continuously span in both directions, then the values for the direction which results in the lower loading of the walls from the floor should be multiplied by 2.
[3] Individual loads from the roof construction imposed centrally are permissible if the transference of the loads on to the walls can be proved. These individual loads must be ≤30 kN for 11.5 cm thick walls and ≤50 kN for walls which are 17.5 cm thick.

(3) **Supporting internal walls with d < 24 cm; conditions of use**

wall thickness (cm)	permissible maximum value for openings (m²) at a height above ground level of					
	0–8 m		8–20 m		20–100 m	
	ε = 1.0	ε ≥ 2.0	ε = 1.0	ε ≥ 2.0	ε = 1.0	ε ≥ 2.0
11.5	12	8	5	5	6	4
17.5	20	14	13	9	9	6
≥ 24	36	25	23	16	16	12

(4) **Areas of openings in non-supporting walls (only mortar IIa or III)**

description	gross density (kg/m³)	outer walls	party and staircase walls
light hollow concrete blocks two and three chambers	1000	300	300
	1200	365	240
	1400	490	240
light solid concrete blocks	800	240	300
	1000	300	300
	1200	300	240
	1400	365	240
	1600	490	240
aerated concrete blocks	600	240	365
	800	240	365
autoclaved aerated concrete	800	175	312.5
large format components with expanded clay, expanded shale, natural pumice, lava crust without quartz sand	800	175	312.5
	1000	200	312.5
	1200	275	250
	1400	350	250
light concrete with porous debris structure with non-porous additions such as gravel	1600	450	250
	1800	625	250
	2000	775	250
as above, but with porous additions	1200	275	250
	1400	325	250
	1600	425	250

(5) **Minimum thicknesses of external party and staircase walls plastered on both sides**

Solid masonry walling comprises a single leaf, where the facing work is attached to the background masonry by a masonry bond. Each course must be at least two bricks/blocks in depth, between which there is a continuous, cavity-free longitudinal mortar joint of 20 mm thickness. The facing leaf is included in the load-bearing cross-section → p. 63.

In double leaf walling without cavity, for load considerations, only the thickness of the inner leaf is taken into account. For calculating the slenderness ratio and spacing of the bracing components, the thickness of the inner shell plus half the thickness of the outer is used. If regulations allow it the cavity can be completely filled (double leaf cavity walling with insulating cavity fill).

Double leaf cavity walling without cavity fill: min. thickness of inner leaf → (6); outer leaf ≥ 115 mm; the air gap should be 60 mm wide; the leafs are connected by ties → (1) – (2). The outer leaf must be supported over the whole area and attached at least every 12 m. The air gap is to extend from 100 mm above the ground to the roof, without interruption. The outer leafs are to be provided with ventilation openings top and bottom, on every 1500 mm² wall area (including openings). Vertical movement joints are to be provided in the outer leaf, at least at the corners of the building, and horizontal movement joints should be provided at the foundation level → (2).

Reinforced masonry: wall thickness ≥115 mm; block/brick strength classification ≥12, mortar III; joints with ≤20 mm reinforcement; steel diameter ≤ 8 mm, ≤ 5 mm at crossover points.

Wall types, wall thicknesses: Evidence must be provided of required structural wall thicknesses. This is not necessary where the selected wall thickness is clearly adequate. When selecting the wall thickness, particular attention should be paid to the function of the walls with regard to thermal and sound insulation, fire protection and damp-proofing. Where external walls are not built of frost resistant brick or stone, an outer rendering, or other weather protection should be provided.

Supporting walls are predominantly subjected to compressive stresses. These panel type structural elements are provided for the acceptance of vertical loads (e.g. floor and roof loads) and horizontal loads (e.g. wind loads).

number of permissible full storeys including the finished roof structure	2	≥ 3
for ceilings that only load single leaf transverse walls (partitioned type of construction) and on heavy ceilings with adequate lateral distribution of the loads	11.5[1]	17.5
for all other ceilings	24	24

[1] highest permissible vertical live load including addition for light dividing walls: p = 2.75 kN/m²

(6) **Minimum thickness (in cm) of the internal leaf in double leaf masonry external walls**

thickness of the supporting wall to be braced (cm)	storey height (m)	bracing wall		spacing (m)
		1st and 4th storeys from the top, thickness (cm)	5th and 6th storeys from the top, thickness (cm)	
≥ 11.5 < 17.5 ≥ 17.5 < 24	≤ 3.25	≥ 11.5	≥ 17.5	≥ 4.50 ≥ 6.00
≥ 24 < 30 ≥ 30	≥ 3.50 ≤ 5.00			≤ 8.00

(7) **Thickness and spacing of bracing walls**

EXTERNAL WALLS

Low-energy Building Construction

The thermal insulation characteristics of external walls is an important element in the saving of thermal energy. The insulation provided by low energy building construction is greatly affected by the connections between the various building components. Significant heat losses can occur in these locations. Standard cross-sections depicting various types of building materials indicate the insulation values which can be achieved. A large range of building materials are available, such as concrete, masonry, timber, insulation materials, plaster, cork, reeds and clay. Clay has proved itself as a building material for thousands of years. It is the most common and most tested material in the world and, biologically and ecologically, is an exemplary material. Finished clay insulation products are now available and are well suited to today's level of technology → ⑩ – ⑪.

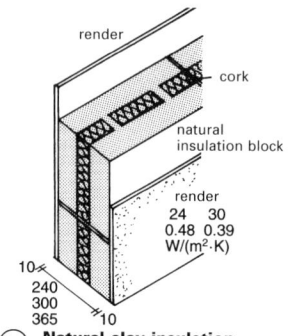

synthetic resin render
insulation
masonry plaster
10
120–150
175+240
10
0.17–0.27 W/(m²·K)

① **Masonry with bonded insulation panels**

synthetic resin render
insulation
concrete
plaster
10
120+150
150
10
0.22–0.30 W/(m²·K)

② **Concrete with bonded insulation panels**

render
cork
natural insulation block
render
24 30
0.48 0.39
W/(m²·K)
10
240
300
365
10

③ **Natural clay insulation blocks (Bioton)**

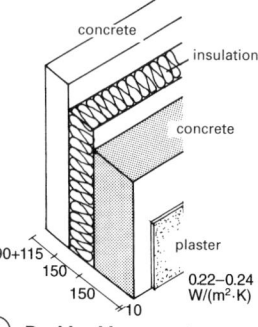

external leaf
insulation
blockwork
plaster
115
40
40
175
10
0.37 W/(m²·K)

④ **Cavity walling**

concrete
insulation
concrete
plaster
90+115
150
150
10
0.22–0.24 W/(m²·K)

⑤ **Double skin concrete**

facing leaf
insulation
masonry
plaster
115
150
175+240
10
0.15–0.24 W/(m²·K)

⑥ **Aerated concrete cavity wall**

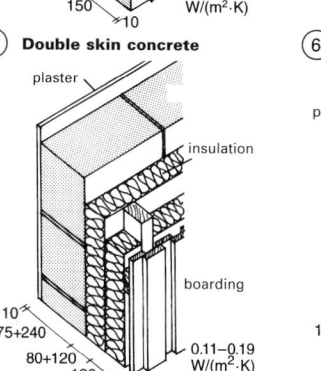 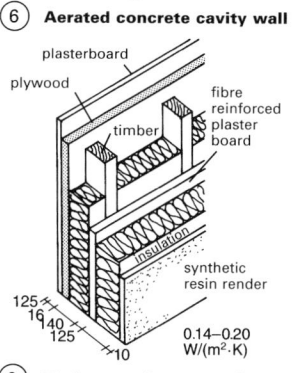

fibre reinforced plaster board
plywood sheet
cellulose insulation
timber
fibre-board insulation
timber boarding
376
0.23 W/(m²·K)

⑦ **Low energy wall (Heckmann Ecohouse)**

plaster
insulation
boarding
10
175+240
80+120
120
0.11–0.19 W/(m²·K)

⑧ **Walling with applied sheathing**

plasterboard
plywood
fibre reinforced plaster board
timber
synthetic resin render
insulation
125
16
40
125
10
0.14–0.20 W/(m²·K)

⑨ **Timber panel construction**

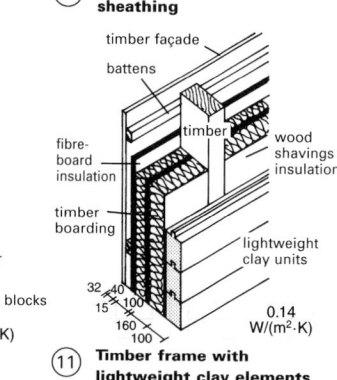 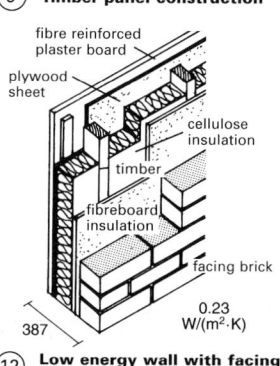 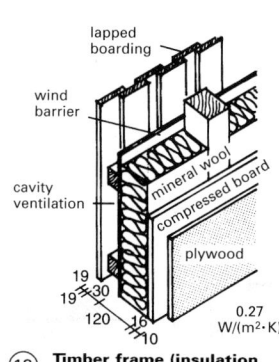

reed insulation board
timber boarding
timber
clay render
lightweight clay blocks
50–100
115–365
0.24 W/(m²·K)

⑩ **Balloon frame with lightweight clay blocks**

timber façade
battens
fibre-board insulation
timber boarding
timber
wood shavings insulation
lightweight clay units
32 40
15 100
160
100
0.14 W/(m²·K)

⑪ **Timber frame with lightweight clay elements**

fibre reinforced plaster board
plywood sheet
cellulose insulation
timber
fibreboard insulation
facing brick
387
0.23 W/(m²·K)

⑫ **Low energy wall with facing brick**

lapped boarding
wind barrier
cavity ventilation
mineral wool
compressed board
plywood
19
19 30
120
10
0.27 W/(m²·K)

⑬ **Timber frame (insulation between the posts)**

render
insulating fibreboard
wind barrier
timber wall unit
plasterboard
18.6–28.6
0.27
0.392–0.238 W/(m²·K)

⑭ **Timber unit wall (Lignotrend)**

façade
bitumen coated insulating fibreboard
insulating fibreboard
wind barrier
timber wall unit
plaster-board
22.5–30.5
22.5–30.5
0.332–0.209 W/(m²·K)

⑮ **Variation of →⑭**

outer leaf
Poroton
plaster
115
40
300
10
0.56 W/(m²·K)

⑫ **Poroton (clay insulating block) cavity wall**

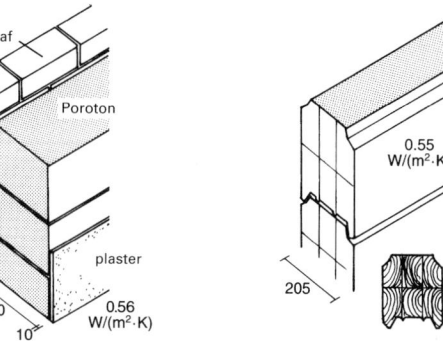

0.55 W/(m²·K)
205

⑬ **Profiled laminated timber log construction**

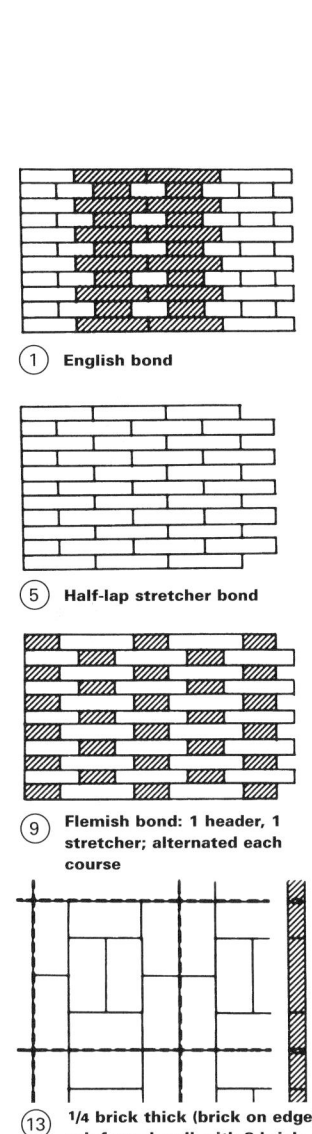

(1) **English bond**

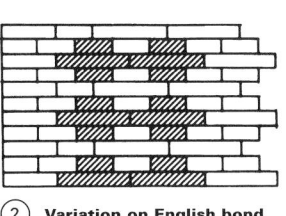

(2) **Variation on English bond**

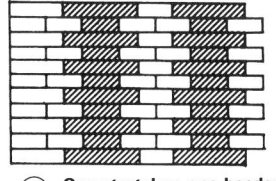

(3) **One stretcher, one header; alternating with course of headers**

(4) **Two stretchers, one header; alternating with course of headers**

(5) **Half-lap stretcher bond**

(6) **Quarter-lap stretcher bond**

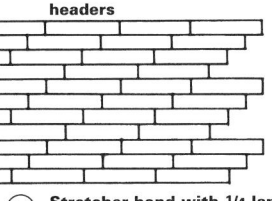

(7) **Stretcher bond with 1/4 lap rising right**

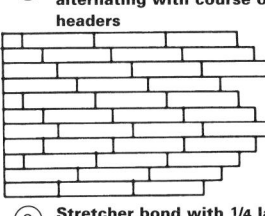

(8) **Stretcher bond with 1/4 lap rising right and left**

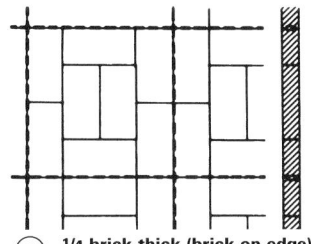

(9) **Flemish bond: 1 header, 1 stretcher; alternated each course**

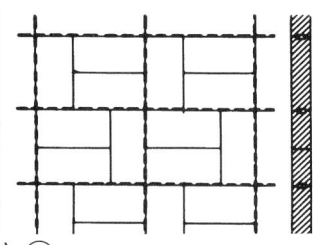

(10) **1 header; 2 stretchers alternating coursewise**

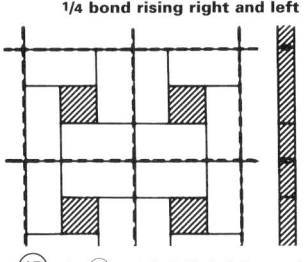

(11) **1 header; 1 stretcher alternating coursewise with 1/4 bond rising right and left**

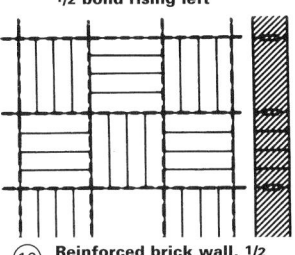

(12) **1 header; 1 stretcher alternating coursewise with 1/2 bond rising left**

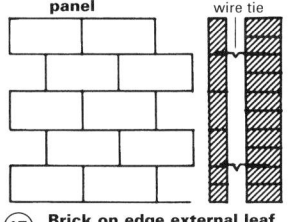

(13) **1/4 brick thick (brick on edge) reinforced wall with 8 brick panel**

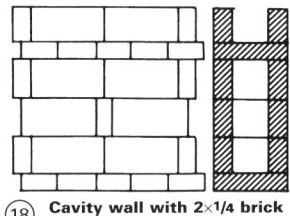

(14) **As (13), with 3 brick panel**

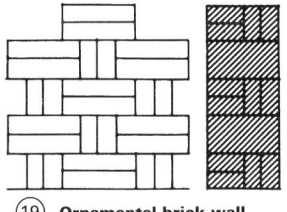

(15) **As (13), with 4 1/2 brick panel**

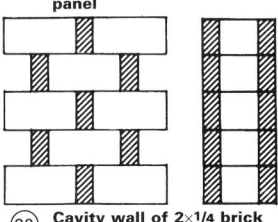

(16) **Reinforced brick wall, 1/2 brick thick with 4 brick panel**

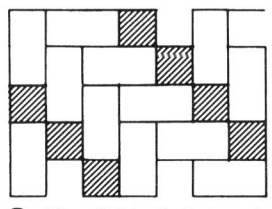

wire tie

(17) **Brick on edge external leaf linked by ties to internal leaf**

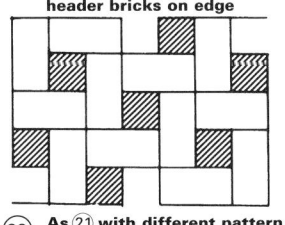

(18) **Cavity wall with 2×1/4 brick leafs, tied by a connecting header course, and alternate header bricks on edge**

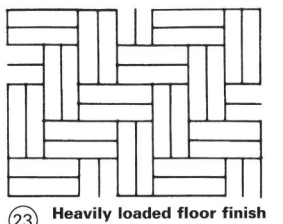

(19) **Ornamental brick wall**

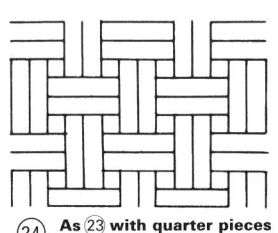

(20) **Cavity wall of 2×1/4 brick leafs bonded by header bricks on edge**

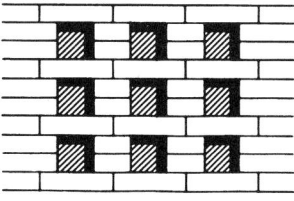

(21) **Floor finish of whole and half bricks**

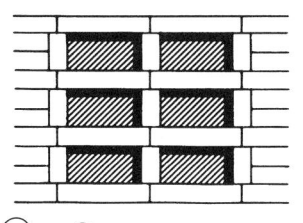

(22) **As (21) with different pattern (other versions possible)**

(23) **Heavily loaded floor finish with bricks on edge (herringbone pattern as in parquet)**

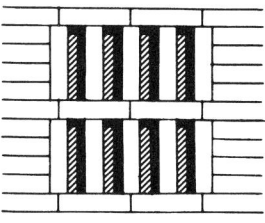

(24) **As (23) with quarter pieces (weave pattern)**

(25) **Brickwork with gaps (honeycomb) for light or air admission (holes 1/2 × 1/2 brick)**

(26) **As (25) (holes 1/2 × 3/4 brick)**

(27) **As (25) (holes 1/4 × 1/2 brick)**

(28) **As (25) (holes 1 × 1/4 brick)**

67

FIREPLACES

Every open fire must be connected to its own separate flue and should be immediately adjacent to the next → ① – ④. Flue cross-sections must be matched to the size of the open fire → ⑧. The effective height of the flue from the smoke hood to the chimney mouth should be ≥ 4.5 m. The angle of a connecting flue to the main flue should be 45° → ⑨ – ⑩. Open fires must not be sited in rooms with less than 12 m² floor area. Only wood with a low resin content, and beech, oak, birch or fruit tree timber with few knots, should be used for burning. In the case of the use of gas appliances, reference should be made to the relevant regulations.

Air for combustion must come from outside and needs to be able to enter even if the doors and windows are airtight. Air admission openings can usefully be sited in the base of the fire, or at the front, and ducts that introduce air to a position close to the fireplace opening should be provided → ⑦.

The fireplace opening must be separated from combustible materials and built-in furniture by at least 800[t]mm to the front, above and to the sides → ⑥ – ⑦. Open fires must be constructed from non-combustible materials that satisfy local regulations and must be of stable construction. The floor, walls and grate and the smoke hood should be made from fire clay bricks/slabs, fire resistant concrete or cast iron (although the grate and hood are often metal). Any bricks or stones used must be of suitable type for chimney construction. Smoke hoods can be made from 2 mm steel brass, or copper sheet.

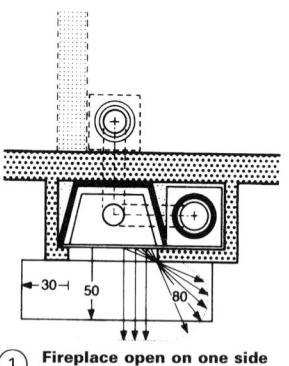

① Fireplace open on one side with safety area

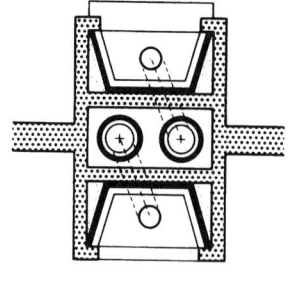

② Fireplaces open on one side in separate rooms

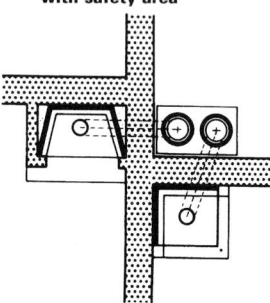

③ Fireplaces open on one/two sides in separate rooms

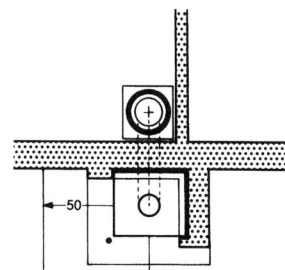

④ Fireplace open on two sides with safety area

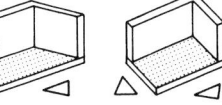
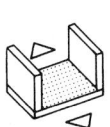
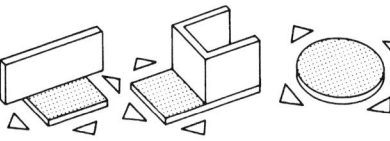

⑤ Heat radiation surfaces and directions

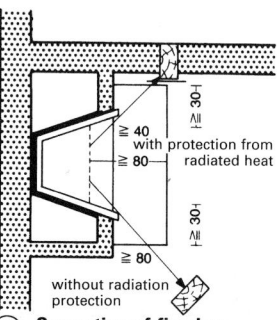

⑥ Separation of fireplace opening from combustible materials

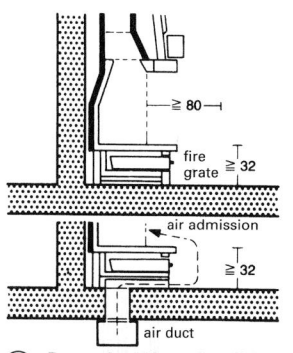

⑦ Protection of combustible floor from the fireplace opening/air admission

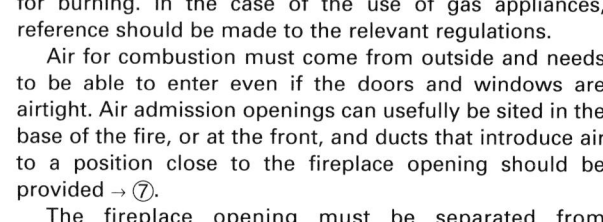

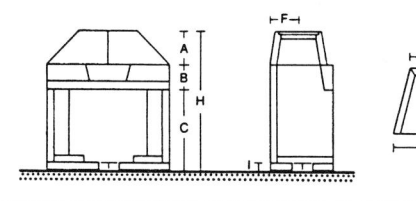

type	open on 1 side					open on 2 sides			open on 3 sides		
	1	2	3	4	5	6	7	8	9	10	11
room area (m²)	small rooms	16–22	22–30	30–35	33–40	25–35	35–45	over 48	35–45	45–55	over 55
room volume (m³)	small rooms	40–60	60–90	90–105	105–120	90–105	105–150	over 150	35–150	45–150	over 200
size of fire opening (cm²)	2750	3650	4550	5750	7100	5000	6900	9500	7200	9800	13500
dimension fire opening (cm)	60/46	70/52	80/58	90/64	100/71						
diameter (cm) of associated flue	20	22	25	30	30	25	30	35	25	30	35
all dimensions (cm) A	22.5	24	25.5	28	30	30	30	30	30	30	30
B	13.5	15	15	21	21	–	–	–	–	–	–
C	52	58	64	71	78	50	58	65	50	58	65
D	72	84	94	105	115	77	–	108	77	90	114
E	50	60	65	76	93	77	90	108	77	90	114
F	19.5	19.5	22.5	26	26	27.5	30	32.5	27.5	30	32.5
G	42	47	51	55	59	64	71	82	64	71	82
H	88	97	104.5	120	129	80	88	95	80	88	95
I	6	6	6	7	7	6.4	6.4	6.4	6.4	6.4	
weight	165	80	310	385	470	225	300	405	190	255	360

⑧ Dimensions and sizes of open fires

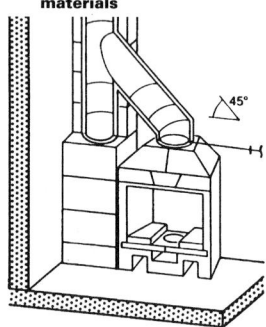

⑨ Fireplace open on one side

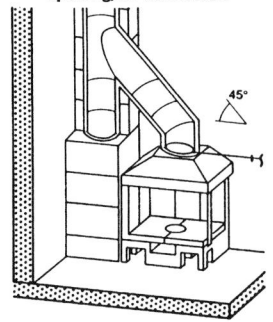

⑩ Fireplace open on two sides

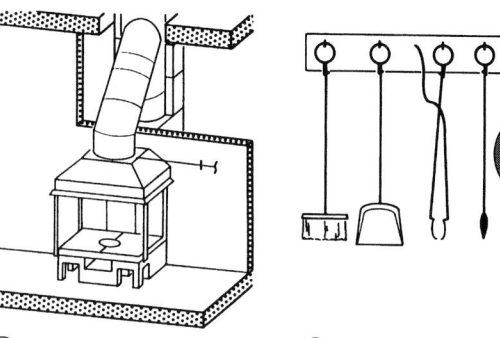

⑪ Fireplace open on three sides

⑫ Fireplace tools

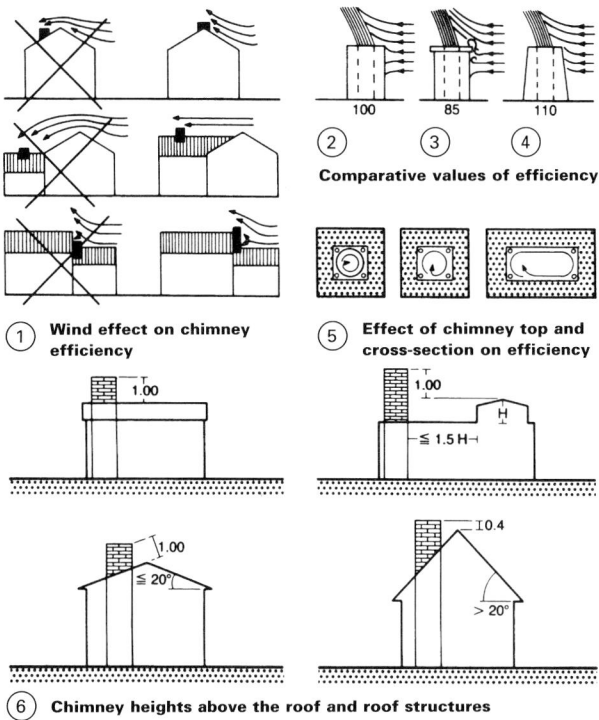

① **Wind effect on chimney efficiency**

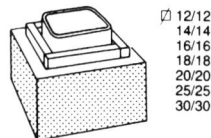

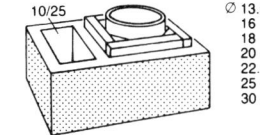

② ③ ④

Comparative values of efficiency

⑤ **Effect of chimney top and cross-section on efficiency**

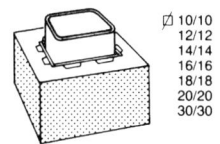

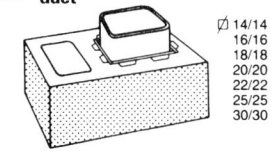

⑥ **Chimney heights above the roof and roof structures**

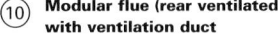

⑦ **Modular flue**
Ø 12/12
14/14
16/16
18/18
20/20
25/25
30/30

⑧ **Modular flue with ventilation duct**
10/25
Ø 13.5
16
18
20
22.5
25
30

⑨ **Modular flue (rear ventilated)**
Ø 10/10
12/12
14/14
16/16
18/18
20/20
30/30

⑩ **Modular flue (rear ventilated) with ventilation duct**
Ø 14/14
16/16
18/18
20/20
22/22
25/25
30/30

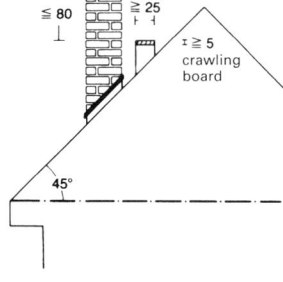

⑪ **Access opening with ladder and platform**

chimney cleaning opening on roof
steel rods
≦ 80
access opening
exit platform
wooden ladder with inset, square treads
≧ 30

⑫ **A crawling board is necessary for roof slopes above 15°**

≦ 80
≧ 25
ɪ ≧ 5 crawling board
45°

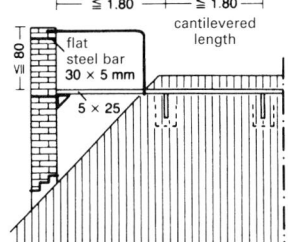

⑬ **Length and attachment of the crawling board**

≦ 1.80 — ≦ 1.80
cantilevered length
flat steel bar 30 × 5 mm
5 × 25

⑭ **Crawling boards are fixed more firmly to rafters than to the tile battens**

≧ 25
≧ 5
screws 4 × 6

Flues and chimneys are ducts in and on buildings, which are intended exclusively to convey the gases from fireplaces to the outside over the roof. The following should be connected to a flue: fireplaces with a nominal heat output of more than 20 kW; gas fire places with more than 30 kW; every fireplace in buildings with more than five full storeys; every open fire and forge fire; fireplaces with a means of opening and every fireplace with a burner and fan.

Provision should be made in the foundation plans to support the weight of the fireplace, flue and chimney. Flues must have circular or rectangular internal cross-sections. The cross-section must be ≥ 100 cm^2, with a shortest side of 100 mm. Brick flues must have a shortest internal side of length ≥ 135 mm, the longer side must not exceed 1.5 times the length of the shorter. The shortest effective flue height ≥ 4 m; for gaseous fuels ≥ 4 m. The mouth of the chimney should be ≥ 400 mm above the apex of the roof, where the roof slope is greater than 20° and for roof slopes less than 20° this dimension is ≥ 1 m → ⑥. Where chimneys are closer to structures on the roof than between 1.5 and 3 times the height of the structure, it must be ensured that they clear the structure by at least 1 m. Where the mouth of a chimney is above a roof which has a parapet which is not closed on all four sides, it must be at least 1 m above the parapet. Every flue must have a ≥ 100 mm wide by ≥ 180 mm high cleaning opening which is at least 200 mm lower than the lowest fireplace connection. Chimneys which cannot be cleaned from the mouth opening, must have an additional cleaning opening in the flue in the roof space or in the chimney above the roof. The following materials may be used for single skin flues: light concrete blocks, clay bricks, lime sandstone –solid bricks, foundry bricks.

Materials for treble-skinned chimneys, with outer casing, insulation layer and moveable inner lining can be formed components in light concrete or fireclay for the inner lining; for the outer casing, formed components in light concrete, masonry stone, bricks with vertical perforations, lime sandstone, foundry bricks, or aerated concrete blocks. For the insulating layer, non-combustible insulating material must be used. Exposed outer surfaces of the chimney in the roof space should be provided with a rough cast finish of at least 5–10 mm thickness. Flue walls must not be loadbearing. The chimney can be clad with slates, shingle slates or cement fibre sheets. Zinc or copper sheet can be fixed to the chimney on to the sub-structure using dowels (not wooden dowels). Prefabricated claddings are recommended.

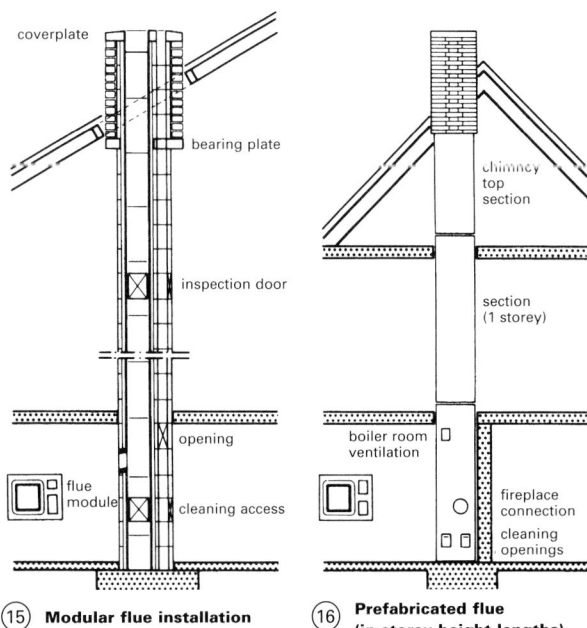

coverplate
bearing plate
inspection door
opening
flue module
cleaning access

chimney top section
section (1 storey)
boiler room ventilation
fireplace connection
cleaning openings

⑮ **Modular flue installation**

⑯ **Prefabricated flue (in storey height lengths)**

VENTILATION DUCTING

Extract fan units should meet the ventilation requirements of bathrooms and lavatories in residential and non-residential buildings (such as schools, hotels and guest houses) and extract air from one or several rooms into an extract duct → ① – ②. Ventilation systems should be sized for a minimum of 4 complete changes of air in the rooms which need to be ventilated. A flow of 60 m³/h is adequate for bathrooms with a toilet and a flow of 30 m³/h is adequate for one toilet. Every internally sited room to be ventilated must have a non-closable ventilation opening. The size of the area through which air flows must be 100 mm² for every m³ of room volume. Gaps around the door may be taken as equivalent to 250 mm². In bathrooms, the temperature must not fall below 22°C, due to the flow of air.

The velocity of flow in the living area should be ≥ 0.2 m/s. The exhausted air must be led outside. Each individual ventilation system must have its own main duct → ③ – ⑤.

Central ventilation systems have common main ducting for a number of living areas → ④ – ⑥.

The effective functioning of branching duct convection ventilation systems depends essentially on the available cross-section area of duct available per connection → ⑨. The cross-section of the ventilation shaft for single-duct systems without mechanical extract → ⑦ in bathrooms and WCs without open windows (up to 8 storeys) should be 1500 mm² per room.

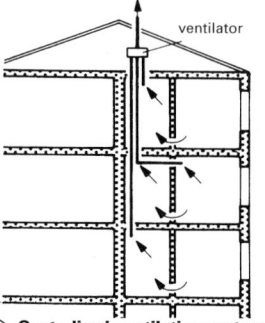

① Single-room extract fan unit for concealed installation

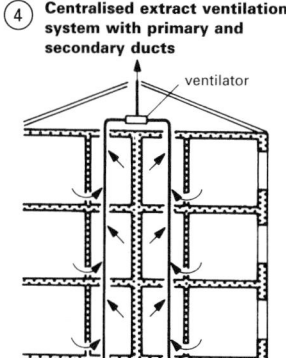

② Extract fan unit for two rooms: concealed installation

③ Centralised extract ventilation system with exhaust ducted via roof

④ Centralised extract ventilation system with primary and secondary ducts

⑤ Centralised ventilation system with separate primary ducts

⑥ Centralised ventilation system with a number of primary ducts without secondary ducts

⑦ Single duct convection ventilation system

⑧ Supply and extract convection ventilation system

clear cross-section of the main duct cm²	permissible no. of adjacent duct connections with average effective total height			internal dimensions	
	up to 10 m	10–15 m	over 15 m	main duct (cm)	auxiliary duct (cm)
340	5	6	7	20 × 17	9 × 17
400	6	7	8	20 × 20	12 × 20
500	8	9	10	25 × 20	12 × 20
340	5	6	7	20 × 17	2 × 9/17
400	6	7	8	20 × 20	2 × 12/20
500	8	9	10	25 × 20	2 ×12 × 20
340	5	6	7	2 × 12/17	9 × 17
400	6	7	8	2 × 20/20	12 × 20
500	8	9	10	2 × 25/20	12 × 20

⑨ Table of dimensions for branching duct convection systems

1 x 15/10   2 x 15/10   3 x 15/10
4 x 15/10   5 x 15/10   6 x 15/10
7 x 15/10   8 x 15/10

thin walled – lengthwise; web thickness 5 cm

⑩ Single duct ventilation

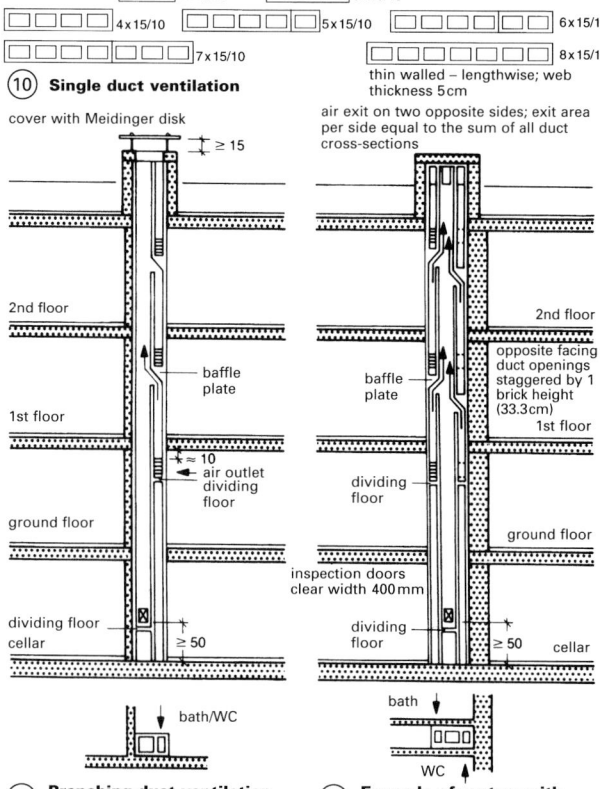

⑪ Branching duct ventilation system with one main and one auxiliary duct

⑫ Example of system with one main duct and two auxiliary ducts

SERVICES: CONNECTIONS

In houses for one and two families there is no necessity for a mains connection room.

Mains connections rooms should be planned in collaboration with the mains service providers. They must be in locations which can be accessed easily by all (e.g. off the staircase or cellar corridor, or reached directly from outside) and they must not be used for through passage. They have to be on an outside wall, through which the connections can be routed → ①–②. Walls should have a fire resistance of at least F30 (minutes). Doors should be at least 650/1950 mm. With district heating schemes, the door must be lockable. A floor gully must be provided where there is connection to water or district heating mains. Mains connections rooms must be ventilated to the open air. The room temperature must not exceed 30°C, the temperature of the drinking water should not exceed 25°C, and the room must not be susceptible to frost.

For up to 30 dwellings, or with district heating for about ten dwellings, allow the following room size: clear width >1.80 m, length 2.00 m, height 2.00 m → ①. For up to approximately 60 dwellings or where there is district heating for 30 dwellings: 1.80 m wide, 3.5 m long, 2.0 m high.

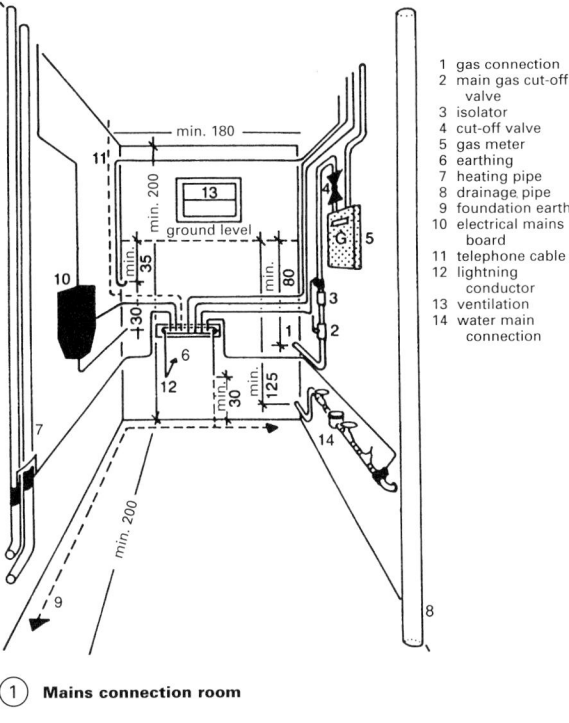

1 gas connection
2 main gas cut-off valve
3 isolator
4 cut-off valve
5 gas meter
6 earthing
7 heating pipe
8 drainage pipe
9 foundation earth
10 electrical mains board
11 telephone cable
12 lightning conductor
13 ventilation
14 water main connection

① **Mains connection room**

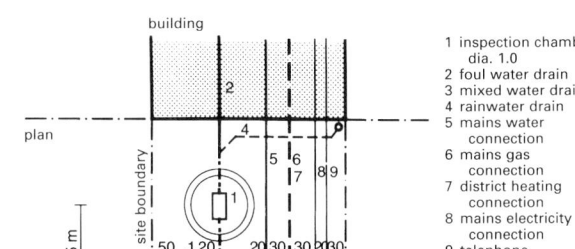

1 inspection chamber dia. 1.0
2 foul water drain
3 mixed water drain
4 rainwater drain
5 mains water connection
6 mains gas connection
7 district heating connection
8 mains electricity connection
9 telephone connection

② **Mains connections**

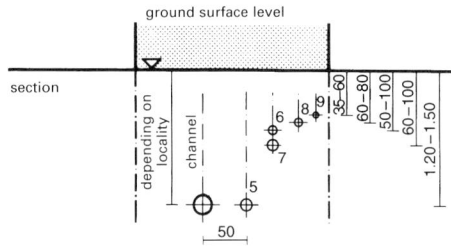

section through manhole	clear width of manholes in m for a manhole depth of	
	> 0.4 to ≤0.8 (min.)	> 0.8 (min.)
○	0.8	1*)
□	–	0.9 × 0.9
▭	0.6 × 0.8	0.8 × 1
	no rungs	with rungs

*) shafts above a working height of 2 m calculated from the invert level can be reduced to a diameter of 0.8 m

③ **Sizes of manholes**   **Inspection and cleaning manhole**

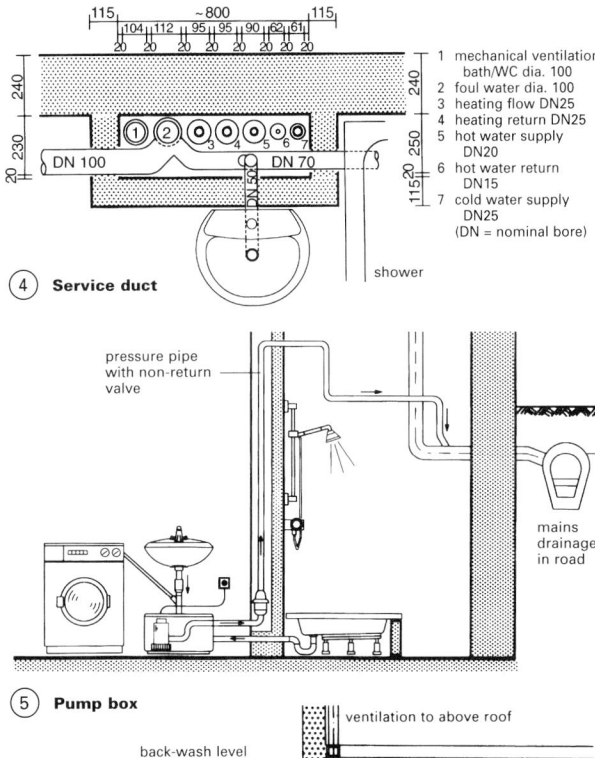

④ **Service duct**

1 mechanical ventilation bath/WC dia. 100
2 foul water dia. 100
3 heating flow DN25
4 heating return DN25
5 hot water supply DN20
6 hot water return DN15
7 cold water supply DN25
(DN = nominal bore)

⑤ **Pump box**

⑥ **Pump installation**

	capacity	lift (m)			dimensions (mm)			DN$_Z$ (mm)
		3	7	14	A	B	Z	
family house	m³/h	47	12	–	1000	1000	450–500	100
multi-family home	m³/h	64	22	–	1800	1300	700–850	125
large complex	m³/h	144	100	18	2600	1950	800–900	150

ROOF STRUCTURES

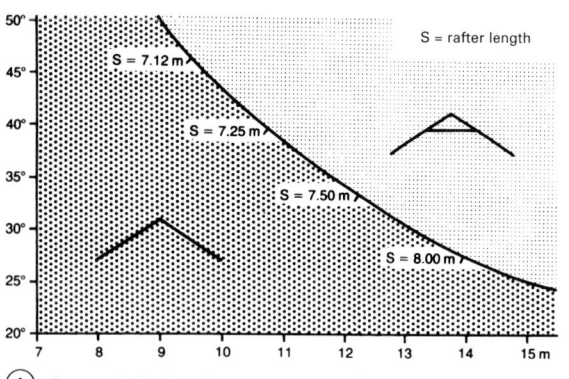

(1) **Economic limits, slope v. span: couple/collar roofs**

Couple roofs represent the most economical solution for low building widths.

Collar roofs are never the cheapest for slopes under 45°, but are suitable for large free span roofs.

Simply supported roofs are always more expensive than couple roofs and are only used in exceptional cases.

Roofs with two hangers (vertical posts) almost always are the most economical construction.

Purlin roofs with three hangers are only considered for very wide buildings.

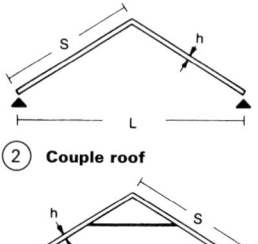

(2) **Couple roof**

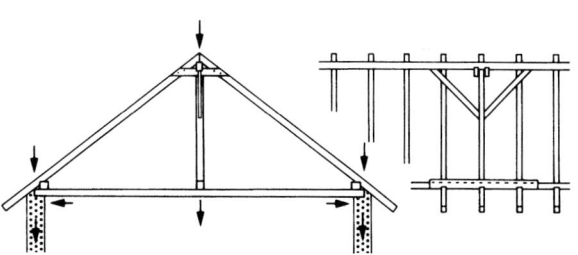

(3) **Collar roof**

roof slope (degrees)	span L (m)	height of structural component h
15–40	10–20	$h \sim \frac{1}{25} \cdot S$
30–60	10–20	$h \sim \frac{1}{30} \cdot S$

Roofs form the upper enclosure of buildings, protecting them from precipitation and atmospheric effects (wind, cold, heat). They comprise a supporting structure and a roof cover. The supporting components depend on the materials used (wood, steel, reinforced concrete), roof slope, type and weight of roof covering, loading, etc. Loading assumptions must comply with current regulations (dead-weight, live loads, wind and snow loadings). A distinction is made between roofs with and without purlins, because of their different structural system, and of the different functions of the supporting components. However, these two types of construction may be combined. The different types of load transfer also have consequences for the internal planning of the building.

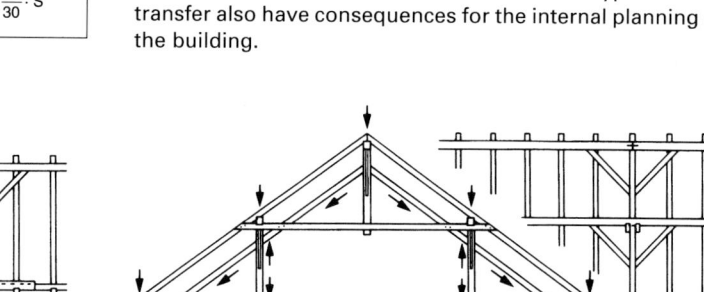

(4) **Strutless purlin roof with centre hanger**

(5) **Strutted purlin roof**

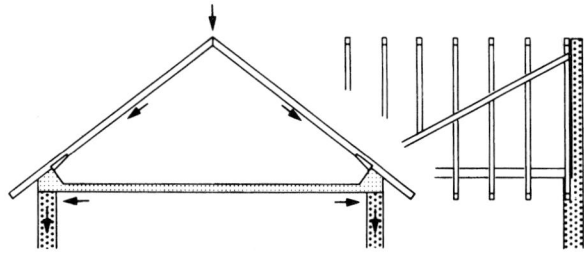

(6) **Couple roof**

(7) **Couple roof with hangers**

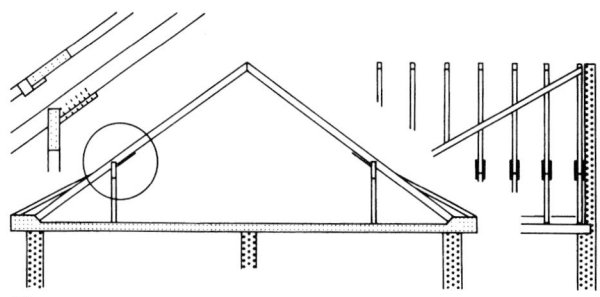

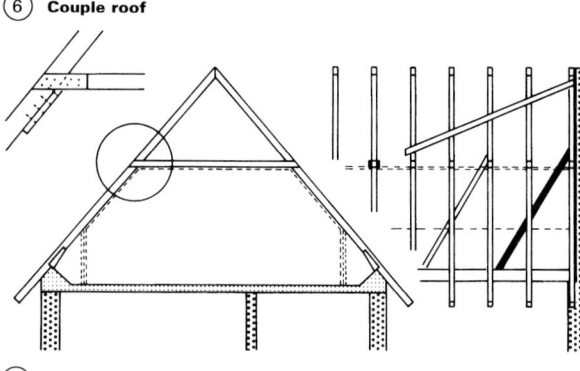

(8) **Collar roof with loft room**

(9) **Close couple roof with collar and purlins**

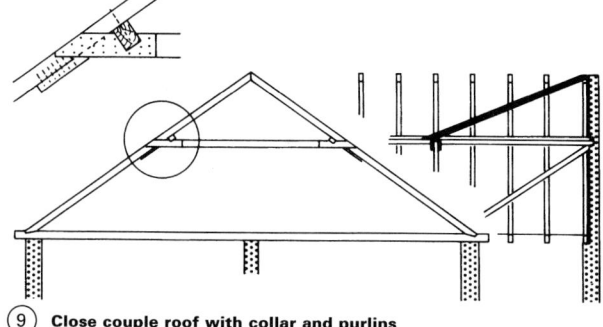

In a purlin roof, rafters have a subordinate function (round section timber spars also possible for small spans). Purlins are load-bearing beams, conducting loads away from the rafters to the supports. Regular supports are required for the purlins (trusses or cross-walls). Early type: ridge purlin with hanger. Double pitch purlin roofs have at least one hanger, situated in the centre of the roof. Suitable when the length of the rafters ≤ 4.5 m; on wider house structures, with rafter length > 4.5 m, then two or more purlins with suitable vertical hangers are required. A rafter roof (rigid triangle principle) is possible in simple form, with short rafters up to 4.5 m. If the rafters' length exceeds 4.5 m, intermediate support is required in the form of collars. This regular, strong system of construction provides a support-free internal roof space. Couple close roofs require a strong tensile connection between the feet of the rafters and the ceiling beams. Sprocketed eaves are a common feature, giving a change of angle in the roof slope. Simple couple and collar roof construction is unsuitable for large roofs. Collar roofs are suitable for building widths to approx. 12.0 m, rafter lengths up to 7.5 m, collar lengths up to 4 m. The collar roof is a three-link frame with a tension member. Prefabricated roof trusses are a very common form of structure for pitched roofs. While economical in the use of timber and light and easy to erect, they have the disadvantage of totally obstructing the roof space.

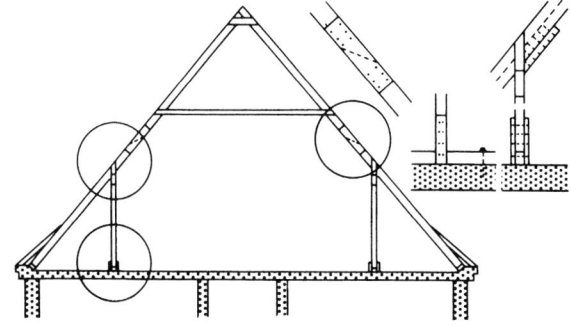

12.50

(1) **Restrained couple roof with hangers and jointed rafters**

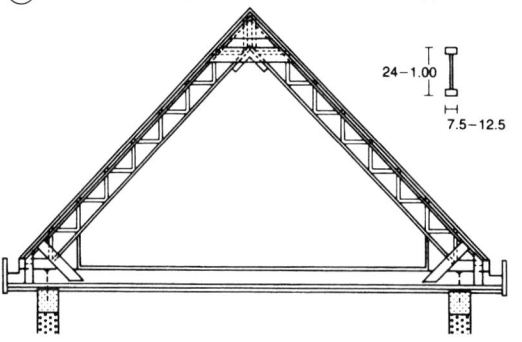

(2) **Collar roof with jointed rafters, with three types of stiffening**

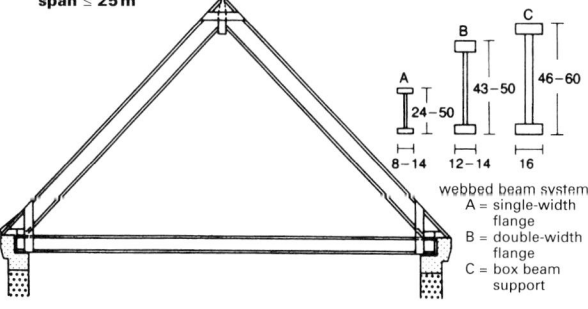

24 – 1.00

7.5 – 12.5

(3) **Couple close roof in timber framing with lifetime guaranteed glued joints with 45° inclined struts as twinned supports over span ≤ 25 m**

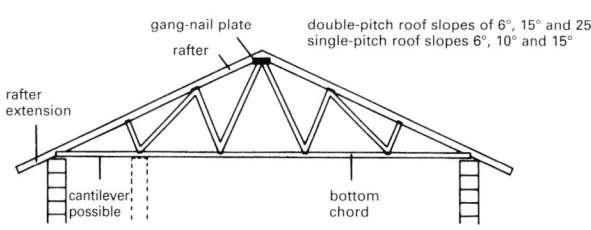

A 24 – 50
8 – 14

B 43 – 50
12 – 14

C 46 – 60
16

webbed beam system
A = single-width flange
B = double-width flange
C = box beam support

(4) **Couple close roof with webbed rafters, glued timber construction; ratio of profile height to supported span = 1:15–1:20**

gang-nail plate
rafter
rafter extension
cantilever possible
bottom chord

double-pitch roof slopes of 6°, 15° and 25°
single-pitch roof slopes 6°, 10° and 15°

(5) **Trussed rafter with 'gang nail' system for flat roof, lean-to roof and ridge roof**

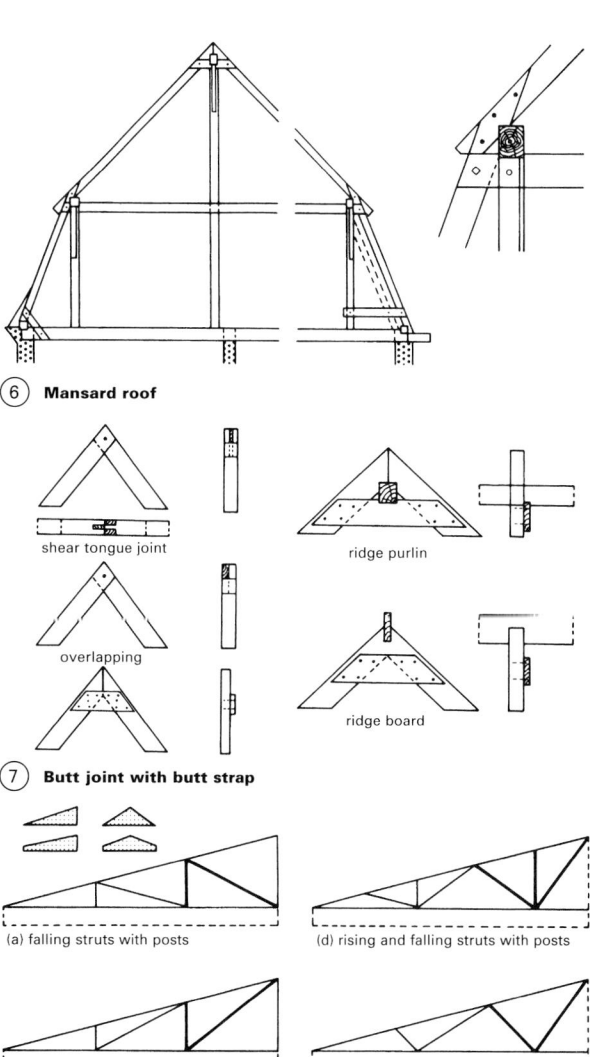

(6) **Mansard roof**

shear tongue joint

overlapping

ridge purlin

ridge board

(7) **Butt joint with butt strap**

(a) falling struts with posts

(b) rising struts with posts

(c) rising and falling struts

(d) rising and falling struts with posts

(8) **Timber construction forms and reinforcings**

73

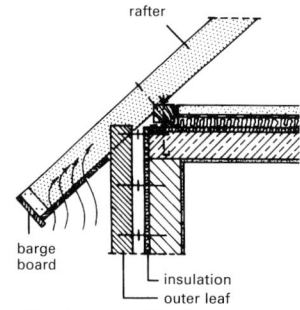

rafter

barge
board

masonry

4/6

① **Eaves detail, purlin roof**

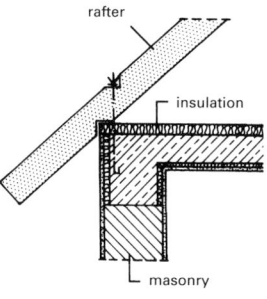

rafter

barge
board

insulation
outer leaf

② **Eaves detail with cavity
walling**

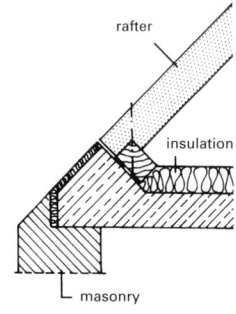

rafter

insulation

masonry

③ **Rafter ends fixed with
bolts into downstand beam**

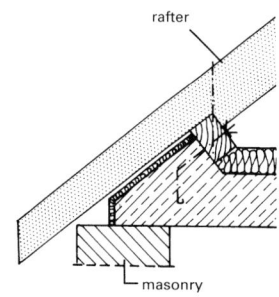

rafter

insulation

masonry

④ **Curb support, sole plate,
rafter nailing**

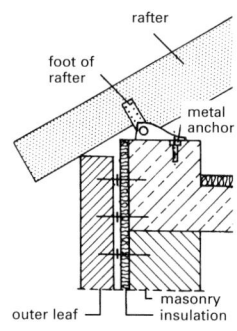

rafter

masonry

⑤ **Rafter continued to the eaves**

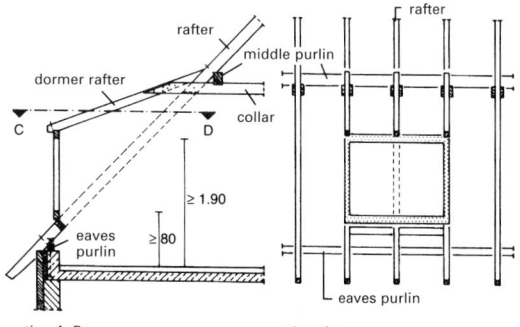

rafter

foot of
rafter

metal
anchor

outer leaf

masonry
insulation

⑥ **Steel rafter connection**

rafter

dormer rafter

middle purlin

collar

C

D

≥ 1.90

≥ 80

eaves
purlin

section A–B

elevation

rafter

eaves purlin

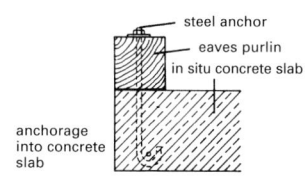

steel anchor
eaves purlin
in situ concrete slab

anchorage
into concrete
slab

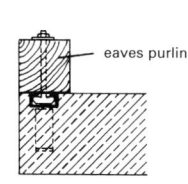

eaves purlin

⑧ **Anchorage to solid slab**

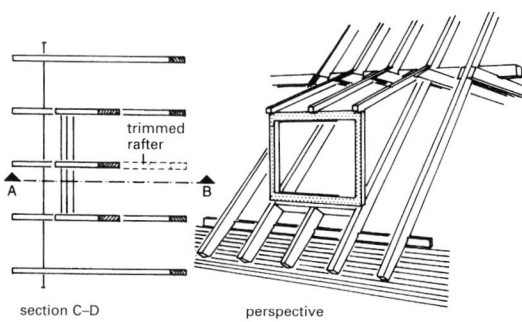

trimmed
rafter

A

B

section C–D

perspective

⑦ **Dormer window in a purlin roof**

rafter

nail plate

timber beam

rafter end
fixing with nail plate

rafter

bolt

timber beam

⑨ **Rafter end fixing with bolts**

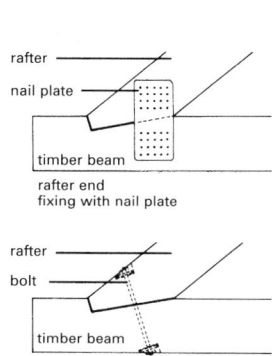

rafter

eaves purlin

rafter transmits its load directly

rafter

insert

eaves purlin

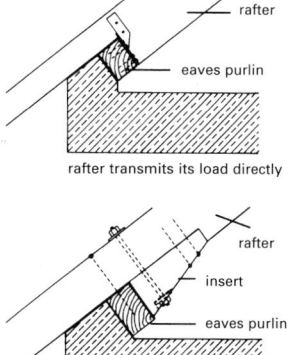

⑩ **Detail at foot of roof
allowing rafters to overhang**

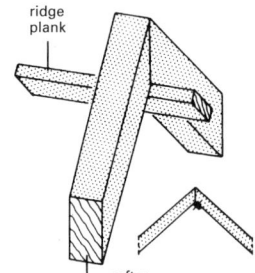

ridge
plank

rafter

⑪ **Ridge details of purlin roof;
ridge plank to align the
ridge**

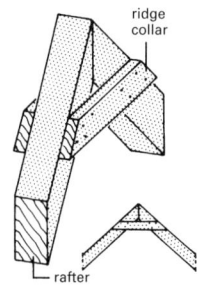

ridge
collar

rafter

⑫ **Ridge collar connecting two
rafters**

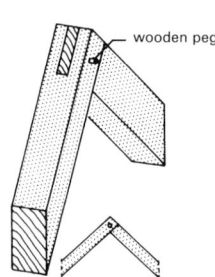

wooden peg

⑬ **Simple tenon joint
connecting two rafters**

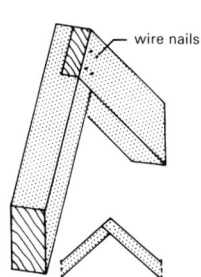

wire nails

⑭ **Scarf joint connecting two
rafters**

ROOF FORMS

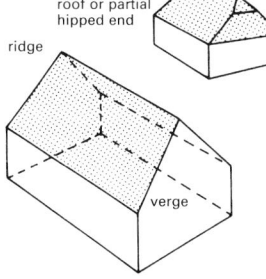

① **Mono-pitch roof**

② **Ridge roof**

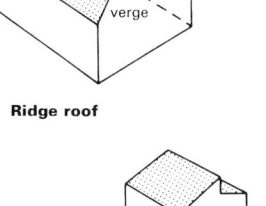

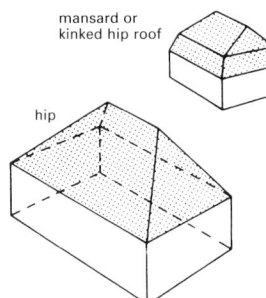

③ **Hipped roof**

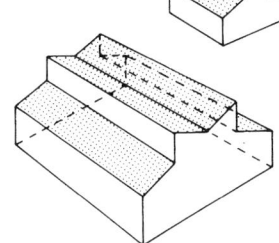

④ **Combination roof**

⑤ **Pyramid roof**

⑥ **Pyramid roof, polygonal planform**

⑦ **Roof house**

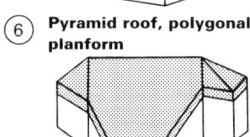

⑧ **Mansard roof, polygonal planform**

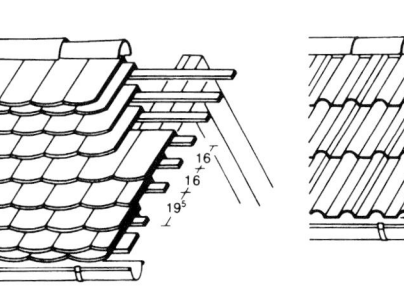

⑩ **Thatched roof of rye straw or reed, 0.7 kN/m²**

⑪ **Shingle roof, 0.25 kN/m²**

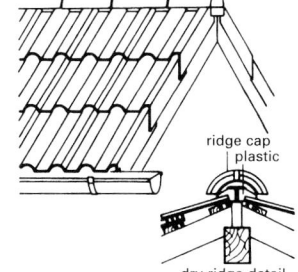

⑭ **Double roof (plain tiles) heavy roofing, 0.6 kN/m², 34–44 tiles/m²**

⑮ **Concrete roof tiles, 0.6–0.8 ≥ slope 18° kN/m²**

ROOF COVERINGS

Thatched roofs are of rye straw or reeds, hand-threshed 1.2–1.4 m long on battens, 300 mm apart with the thatching material laid butt-end upwards and built up to a thickness of 180–200 mm. The life of such a roof is 60–70 years in a sunny climate, but barely half that in damp conditions. Shingle roofs use oak, pine, larch, and, rarely, spruce. Slate roofs are laid on ≥ 25 mm thick sheathing of ≥ 160 mm wide planks, protected by 200 gauge felt against dust and wind. Overlap is 80 mm, preferably 100 mm. The most natural effect is given by 'German slating' → ⑫. Rectangular patterns are more suitable for artificial slates (cement fibre tiles) → ⑬. Tiles: choice of plain tiled, interlocking tiled, or pantiled roof → ⑭, ⑯ – ⑰ or concrete roof tiles with ridge capping → ⑮. Special shaped tiles are available to match standard roof tiles → ⑨:

1 mono-pitch: edge tile, corner tile right
2 eaves tile
3 mono-pitch roof tile
4 wall connecting tile
5 eaves: wall connecting, corner tile right
6 wall connecting tile right
7 wall connecting tile left
8 lean-to roof: wall connecting, corner tile left
9 ridge end tile left
10 ridge and hip tile
11 edge tile left
12 eaves edge tile left
13 ridge connecting edge tile, corner tile left
14 ridge starting tile right
15 ridge edge connecting tile corner tile right
16 ridge connecting tile
17 edge tile right
18 eaves edge corner tile right

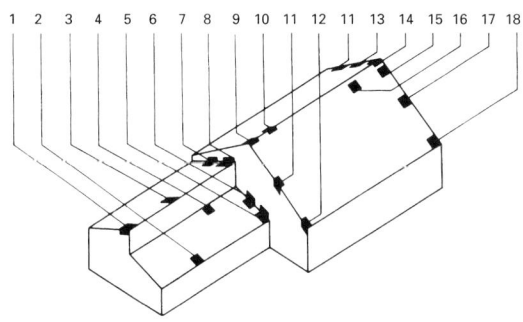

⑨ **Shaped tiles**

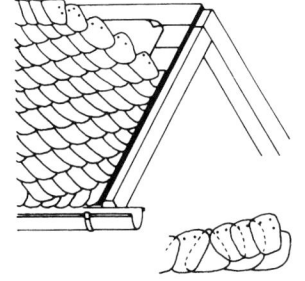

⑫ **German slate roof, 0.45–0.6 kN/m²**

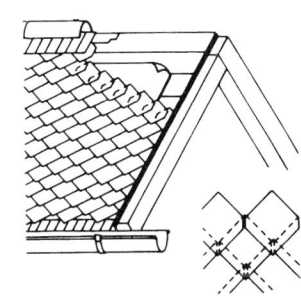

⑬ **English slate roof with cement fibre boards, 0.45–0.55 kN/m²**

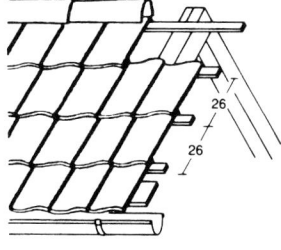

⑯ **Pantile roof, lighter, 0.5 kN/m²**

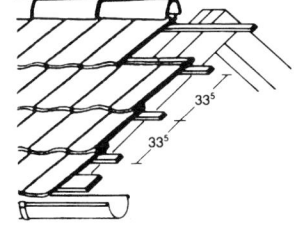

⑰ **Interlocking tile roof, 0.55 kN/m²**

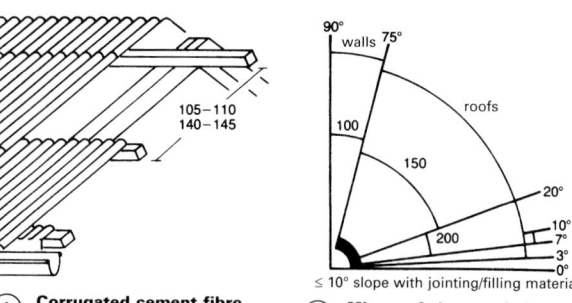

① Corrugated cement fibre board with ridge and eaves components 0.2 kN/m²

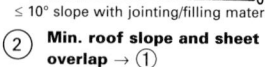

② Min. roof slope and sheet overlap → ①

| length (mm) | 2500 | 2000 | 1600 | 1250 | thickness 6.5 |
| width (mm) | 920 | 920 | 920 | 920 | weight 16–32 kg |

effective width 873
roofing width — exposed width
profile

| length (mm) | 2500 | 2000 | 1600 | 1250 | thickness 6.0 |
| width (mm) | 1000 | 1000 | 1000 | 1000 | weight 15.8–31.5 |

effective width 910
roofing width — exposed width
profile

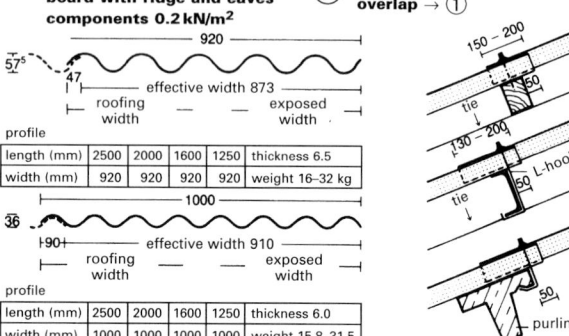

③ Corrugated fibre cement sheets

④ Fixing arrangements

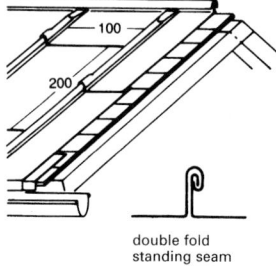

double fold standing seam

⑤ Sheet roofing; welted joint construction 0.25 kN/m²

1° (2%)   3° (5%)

| length (mm) | 9000 | 7500 | 4000 | thickness 8.0 |
| width (mm) | 1000 | 1000 | 1000 | weight 19 kg/m |

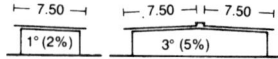

panel width 100
effective width 91⁵
fixing

⑦ Large elements for roof and wall (Canaleta)

roof drainage

semicircular   rectangular

lying

hanging

vertical

⑨ Shape and position of the guttering

⑥ Steel pantile roofing 0.15 kN/m²

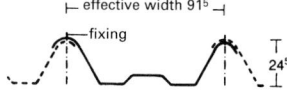

½ corrugation standard

1 corrugation

1½ corrugations

roof depth eaves/ridge	profile ht 18–25mm	26–50mm
up to 6m	10° (17.4%)	5° (8.7%)
6–10m	13° (22.5%)	8° (13.9%)
10–15m	15° (25.9%)	10° (17.4%)
over 15m	17° (29.2%)	12° (20.8%)

8–10°	200mm with sealing of overlap
10–15°	150mm without sealing of overlap
over 15°	100mm without sealing of overlap

⑧ Min. slope: corrugated sheet roof, side overlap

supplied form	rolls	panels
length (m)	30–40	2.0
max. width (m)	0.6 (0.66)	1.0
thickness (mm)	0.1–2.0	0.2–2.0
specific wt (kg/dm³)	8.93	8.93

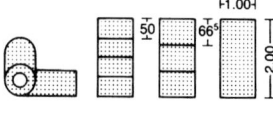

⑩ Form and dimensions of rolled copper for strip and sheet roofing

Cement fibre sheet roofs have corrugated sheets with purlins 700–1450 mm apart with 1.6 m long sheets, or 1150–1175 mm with 2.50 m long sheets. Overlap: 150–200 mm → ① – ②. Metal sheet roofs are covered in zinc, titanium-coated zinc, copper, aluminium, galvanised steel sheet, etc. → ⑤ + ⑥. Many shapes are available for ridge, eaves, edge, etc. Copper sheet comes in commercially produced sizes → ⑩. Copper has the highest ductility of all metal roofings, so it is suitable for metal forming operations, pressing, stretching and rolling. The characteristic patina of copper is popular. Combinations involving aluminium, titanium-coated zinc and galvanised steel should be avoided, combinations with lead and high grade steel are quite safe. Copper roofs are impervious to water vapour and are therefore particularly suitable for cold roofs → p. 81.

Roof load: calculation in kN per m² of roof surface. Roof coverings are per 1m² of inclined roof surface without rafters, purlins and ties. Roofing of roof tiles and concrete roof tiles: the loadings do not include mortar jointings – add 0.1kN/m² for the joints.

Plain tiles and plain concrete tiles	
for split tiled roof including slips	0.60
for plain tiled roof or double roof	0.80
Continuous interlocking tiles	0.60
Interlocking tiles, reformed pantiles, interlocking pantiles, flat roof tiles	0.55
Interlocking tiles	0.55
Flanged tiles, hollowed tiles	0.50
Pantiles	0.50
Large format pantiles (up to 10 per m²)	0.50
Roman tiles without mortar jointing	0.70
with mortar jointing	0.90
Metal roofing aluminium roofing (aluminium 0.7mm thick)	
including roof boards	0.25
Copper roof with double folded joints (copper sheet 0.6mm thick)	
including roof boards	0.30
Double interlocking roofing of galvanised sheets (0.63mm thick)	
including roofing felt and roof boards	0.30
Slate roofing – German slate roof on roof boards including roof felting	
and roof boards with large panels (360mm × 280mm)	0.50
with small panels approx. (200mm × 150mm)	0.45
English slate roof including battens on battens in double planking	0.45
on roof boards and roofing felt, including roof boards	0.55
Old German slate roof on roof boards and roofing felt	0.50
double planking	0.60
Steel pantile roof (galvanised steel sheet)	
on battens – including battens	0.15
on roof boards, including roofing felt and roof boards	0.30
Corrugated sheet roof (galvanised steel sheet) including fixing materials	0.25
Zinc roof with batten boards – in zinc sheet no. 13, including roof boards	0.30

roof area to be drained: semicircular guttering (m²)	guttering diameter (mm)	drain channel section width (mm)
up to 25	70	200
25–40	80	200 (10 parts)
40–60	80	250 (8 parts)
60–90	125	285 (7 parts)
90–125	180	333 (6 parts)
125–175	180	400 (5 parts)
175–275	200	500 (4 parts)

roof area to be drained: round drain pipe (m²)	diameter of drainpipe (mm)	section width of sheet metal pipes (mm)
up to 20	50	167 (12 parts)
20–50	60	200 (10 parts)
50–90	70	250 (8 parts)
60–100	80	285 (7 parts)
90–120	100	333 (6 parts)
100–180	125	400 (5 parts)
180–250	150	500 (4 parts)
250–375	175	
325–500	200	

General rule: guttering should be provided with a fall to achieve greater flow velocities to combat blockages, corrosion and icing. Guttering supports are usually of flat galvanised steel in widths from 20 to 50mm and 4–6mm thick.

⑪ Standard sizes: guttering v. surface area to be drained

Fixing by means of pipe brackets (corrosion protected) whose internal diameter corresponds to that of the drain pipe; minimum distance of drain pipe from wall = 20mm; pipe brackets separated by 2.0m

⑫ Standard sizes: drain pipes v. surface area to be drained

DORMERS

When gable windows do not allow sufficient light into the attic then roof windows or dormer windows are required. The size, form and arrangement of dormers depend on the type of roof, its size and the light requirement.

Dormers should all be of the same size and shape if possible. The shape, materials used and the consistent use of details ensure harmonious integration into the roof slope. Normally, to avoid expensive trimming of rafters, the width of the dormers should conform to the rafter spacing.

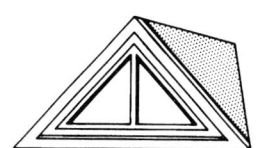

① Triangular dormer 45°

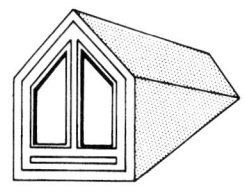

② Gabled dormer 45°

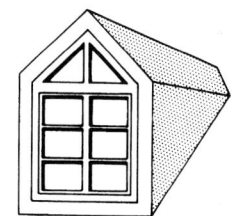

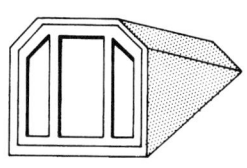

③ Trapeze shaped dormer

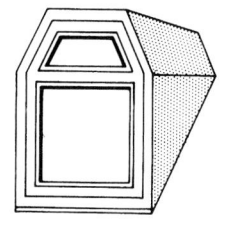

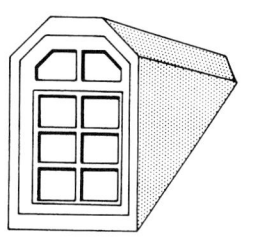

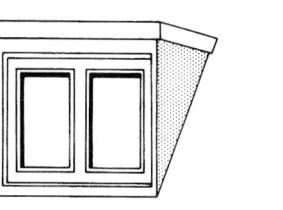

④ Flat roofed dormer

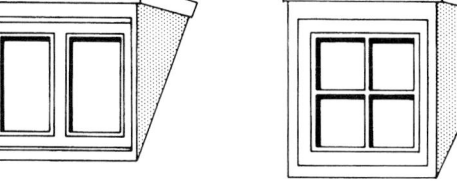

⑤ Sloped dormer

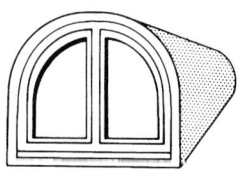

⑥ Round roof dormer

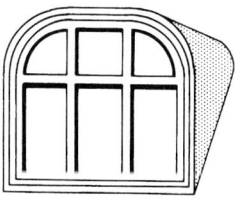

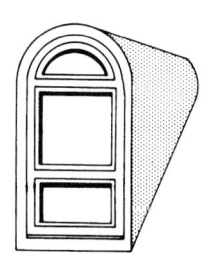

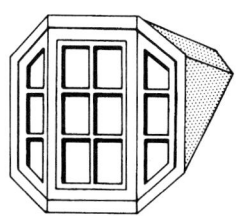

⑦ Bay dormer

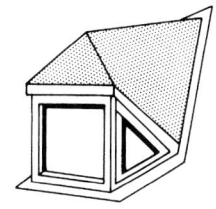

⑧ Hip roofed bay dormer

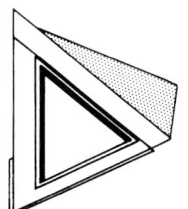

⑨ Triangular dormer

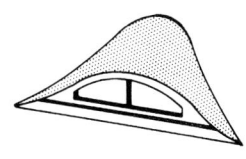

⑩ Ox-eye dormer

Unoccupied roof space in old Alpine farmhouses served as 'stores' for the preservation of harvested crops (hay, straw, etc.). They were open at the eaves, so that cold external air circulated around the roof area, the temperature being little different from the outside → ①, so that snow would lie uniformly distributed on the roof. The living rooms below were protected from the cold by the goods stored in the roof space. If the roof space was heated, without adequate thermal insulation, the snow would melt and ice would build up on the roof → ②. The installation of thermal insulation material under the ventilated roof alleviates the situation. Openings are arranged on two opposite sides of the ventilated roof space, each equivalent to at least 2% of the roof area which is to be ventilated. So that dampness can be removed, this corresponds on average to a slot height of 20 mm/m → ⑤ – ⑩.

① Cross-section through an alpine farmhouse with a storage room

② Ice blockage sequence

③ Examples of ventilated roofs: roof sloping at ≥ 10° (schematic)

④ Examples of ventilated roofs – roof sloping at < 10° (schematic)

⑤ Ventilation of the roof space through joints in the wood facia

⑥ Eave design: double layer cold roof with counter battens and air paths

⑦ Concrete roof

⑧ Wooden roof construction

⑨ Wooden roof with suspended ceiling

⑩ Double layer cold roof: exhaust of both air flows through slots in the facia board

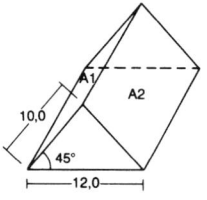

⑪ Dimensions of double pitch roof

calculation

Example:

eaves

Condition:
≥ 2‰ of the associated inclined roof surface A1 or A2
However, at least 200 cm²/m
A_L = ventilation cross-section
A_L eaves ≥ $^2/_{1000}$ × 9.0 = 0.018 m²/m
= 180 cm²/m
Since, however, 180 cm²/m is less than the required minimum cross-section of 200 cm²/m, the minimum value must be taken.

Measurement:
A_L eaves ≥ 200 cm²/m

Application:
Determination of the height of the ventilation slot of the unrestricted air space to be ventilated, allowing for the 8 cm wide rafters, with A_L – 200 cm²/m:
Height:
Ventilation slot $H_L = \dfrac{\text{required } A_L}{100 - (8+8)}$
$H_L = \dfrac{200}{100 - 16}$
$H_L ≥ 2.4$ cm

On a double pitch roof with a rafter length < 10 m, the value of ≥ 200 cm²/m applies, for the eaves (A_L eaves)
On double pitch roofs with rafter length ≥ 10 m
A_L eaves ≥ $^2/_{1000}$ × A1 or A2 cm²/m

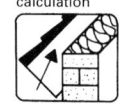

Example:
ridge

Condition:
≥ 0.5‰ of the associated sloping roof surface A1+ A2

Calculation:
A_L ridge = $^{0.5}/_{1000}$ × (9.0+9.0) = 0.0009 m²/m
= 9 cm²/m

Measurement:
A_L ridge = 9 cm²/m

Application:
Ridge elements with ventilation cross-section and/or vent tiles according to manufacturer's data.

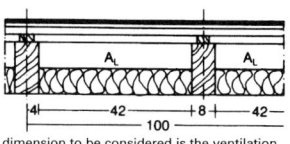

dimension to be considered is the ventilation cross-section between the thermal insulation and the underside of the roof assembly

⑫ Roof construction: insulation between the rafters

calculation

Example:

remaining roof surface

Free ventilation cross-section A_L ≥ 200 cm²
Free height ≥ 2 cm

Calculation:
Height of the ventilation area = $\dfrac{\text{required } A_L}{100 - (8 + 8)}$
= $\dfrac{200}{100 - 16}$
= 2.4 cm

The space under the sarking felt must be taken into account, i.e. with a 2 cm height, the distance from the upper edge of the thermal insulation to the upper edge of the rafter must be at least 4.4 cm.

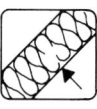

Example:
equivalent air layer diffusion thickness

Condition:
a = length of rafters
s_d = equivalent air layer diffusion thickness
a ≤ 10 m: $s_d ≥ 2$ m
a ≤ 15 m: $s_d ≥ 5$ m
a > 15 m: $s_d ≥ 10$ m
with $s_d = \mu \cdot s$ (m)
μ = water vapour
Coefficient of diffusion resistance
s = material thickness (m)

Application:
(a) Rigid polyurethane foam (8 cm thick)
s = 8 cm = 0.08 m
μ = 30/100
s_d = 30 × 0.08 = 2.4 m
s_d required = 2 m

(b) Mineral fibre insulating mat with laminated aluminium foil (by enquiry to manufacturer)
s = 8 cm
s_d = 100 m > s_d required = 2 m

By using a suitable insulation, the requirement s_d = 2 m can be easily met. The equivalent thickness s_d of the insulation system is best obtained by enquiry to the manufacturer.

⑬ Example: calculation of the ventilation cross-section of a ridge roof

paved roof for walking on	2°	– 4°	usually	3°	– 4°
wood cement roof	2.5°	– 4°	usually	3°	– 4°
roof with roof felting, gravelled	3°	– 30°	usually	4°	– 10°
roof with roof felting, double	4°	– 50°	usually	6°	– 12°
zinc, double upright folded joints (standing seams)	3°	– 90°	usually	5°	– 30°
felted roof, single	8°	– 15°	usually	10°	– 12°
plain steel sheeted roof	12°	– 18°	usually	15°	
interlocking tiled roof, 4 segment	18°	– 50°	usually	22°	– 45°
shingle roof (shingle canopy 90°)	18°	– 21°	usually	19°	– 20°
interlocking tiled roof, standard	20°	– 33°	usually	22°	
zinc and steel corrugated sheet roof	18°	– 35°	usually	25°	
corrugated fibre cement sheet roof	5°	– 90°	usually	30°	
artificial slate roof	20°	– 90°	usually	25°	– 45°
slate roof, double decked	25°	– 90°	usually	30°	– 50°
slate roof, standard	30°	– 90°	usually	45°	
glass roof	30°	– 45°	usually	33°	
tiled roof, double	30°	– 60°	usually	45°	
tiled roof, plain tiled	35°	– 60°	usually	45°	
tiled roof, pantiled roof	40°	– 60°	usually	45°	
split stone tiled roof	45°	– 50°	usually	45°	
roofs thatched with reed or straw	45°	– 80°	usually	60°	– 70°

(1) **Roof slopes**

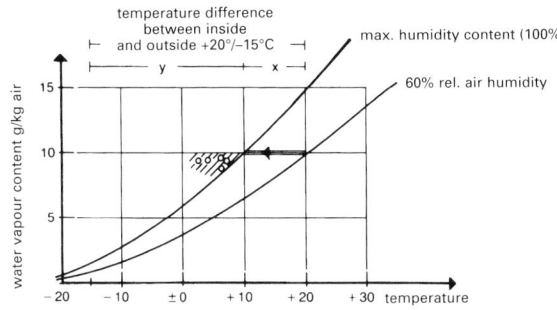

(2)
(1) water precipitates out from air if the air is cooled below the dew point; the temperature difference between the room air and the dew point (dependent on the water vapour content of the room air) can be expressed as a percentage 'x' of the temperature difference between inside and outside (3)
(2) the temperature difference between inside and outside depends on the structural layers and air, in accordance with their contribution to the thermal insulation
(3) if the fraction by which the layers on the inside of the condensation barrier contribute to the thermal insulation 'x and y' remains less than the percentage 'x', then the temperature of the condensation barrier remains above the dew point and no condensation can occur.

	living rooms 20°C, 60% rel. humidity			swimming bath 30°C, 70% rel. humidity		
outside temperature	−12	−15	−18	−12	−15	−18
(%)	25	23	21	15	14	13

(3) **Maximum contribution 'x' to the thermal insulation of a building component, which the layers on the inside of the condensation barrier, including the air boundary layer, can have so as to avoid condensation.**

example:
living room 20°/60% rel. humidity
outside temperature   −15°C, x = 23%
concrete layer 20cm 1/C   = 0.095 m²K/W
air boundary layer inside 1/α   = 0.120 m²K/W
layers up to the vapour barrier   = 0.215 m²K/W
0.215 ≈ 23%; 100%   = 0.94 m²K/W
outer insulation of ≥ 0.94−0.215 ≥ 0.725 ≥ 3cm Styrofoam on the vapour barrier = no condensation

- 5cm washed gravel 7/53 on double hot applied coating
- glass mesh, bitumen paper 3kg/m²
- glass wool layer No. 5 in 3kg/m² filled bitumen (pouring and rolling process)
- 500 jute felt, bitumen roof felting in 1.5kg/m² bitumen 85/25 (fold-over process)
- balancing layer (ribbed felting) against bubble formation
- thermal insulation (≥ 20kg/m³)
- 1.5kg/m² bitumen 82/25 applied to vapour barrier, this in 3.5kg/m² filled bitumen (pouring and rolling process)
- glass wool porous layer (loosely laid)
- bitumen prior application 0.3kg/m²
- concrete deck, possibly to falls

(4) **Ideal layout of a warm roof**

roof weight	required thermal resistance
100kg/m²	0.80 m² · K/W
50kg/m²	1.10 m² · K/W
20kg/m²	1.40 m² · K/W

(5) **Insulation values for flat roofs**

ROOF SLOPES AND FLAT ROOFS

Cold roof → p. 81: constructed with ventilation under roof covering; critical in respect of through flow of air if the slope is less than 10%, therefore, now only used with vapour barrier. Warm roof in conventional form → (4): (construction including a vapour barrier) from beneath is roof structure – vapour barrier – insulation – weatherproofing – protective layer. Warm roof in upside-down format → p. 81: construction from beneath is roof structure – weatherproofing – insulation using proven material – protective layer as applied load. Warm roof with concrete weatherproofing → p. 81: built from underneath: insulation – concrete panels as roof structure and waterproofing (risky). Solid slab structure – must be arranged to provide room for expansion due to heat; consequently, flexible joints arrangement over supporting walls → p. 80 (5) – (8) and separation of internal walls and roof slab (Styrofoam strips are first attached by adhesive to the underside of the slab). Prerequisites for correct functioning: built-in slope ≥ 1.5%, and preferably 3% (or a build-up of surface water can result).

Vapour barrier: if possible, as a 2mm roof felt incorporating aluminium foil on a loosely laid slip layer of perforated glass fibre mat on top of the concrete roof slab, treated with an application of bitumen solution as a dust seal. The vapour barrier is laid as far beneath the roof build-up as required to exclude condensation → (2) + (3).

Insulation of non-rotting material (foam); see dimensions in → (4); two-layer arrangement or single layer with rebated joints: ideally, interlocking rebates all round.

Roof membrane on vapour permeable membrane (corrugated felting or insulating layer to combat bubble formation), triple layer using the pouring and rolling technique with two layers of glass fibre based roofing felt with a layer of glass fibre mat in between, or two layers of felt using the welding method with thick bitumen course (d ≥ 5mm). A single layer of sheeting is permissible, but due to risk of mechanical damage caused by the thinness of the layer and possible faulty seams, two layers offer additional safety.

Protective layer should consist, if possible, of a 50mm ballast layer with 15–30mm grain size on a doubled hot brush applied layer on a separating membrane; prevents bubble formation, temperature shocks, mechanical stresses, and damage from UV radiation. Additional protection with 8-mm layer of rubber shred sheeting under the ballast layer. The joints should be hot sealed (a basic prerequisite for terraces and roof gardens).

Essential detail points

Outlets → p. 80 → (1) – (4) always thermally insulated, two draining levels, with connection also at the vapour barrier, to form an outlet then sealed against the drain pipe. For thermally insulated discharge pipe with condensation layer → p. 80 (4) for prevention of damage due to condensation. The surface slope to the intakes should exceed 3%. A 'ventilator' for the expansion layer is not required. The flexible joint should be continued to the edge of the roof → p. 80 → (5) – (8). The edge details must be flexible, using aluminium or concrete profiles → p. 80 → (5) – (8); zinc connections are contrary to technical regulations (cracking of roof covering). Wall connection should be ≥ 150mm above the drainage level and fixed mechanically, not by adhesive only. If steel roof decking is used as a load-bearing surface, the roof skin may crack due to vibration; precautions are required to increase the stiffness by using a thicker sheet or a covering of 15mm woodwool building board (mechanically fixed), to reduce the vibrations (gravel ballast layer) and crack resistant roof sheeting! The vapour barrier on the decking should always be hot fused (due to thermal conduction).

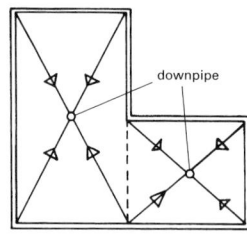

(1) **Roof drainage – at least 2 outlets – slope 3%**

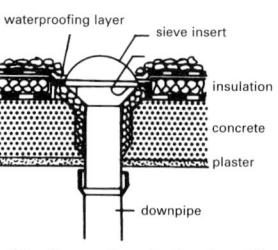

(2) **Flat roof outlet in glass-fibre reinforced polyester with prefabricated insulation; better: two stage → (3)**

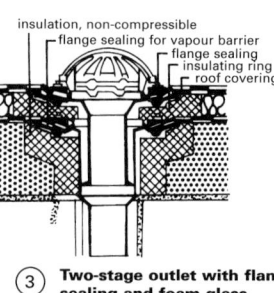

(3) **Two-stage outlet with flange sealing and foam glass insulation material, underside embedded in concrete ('Passavant') scale 1:10**

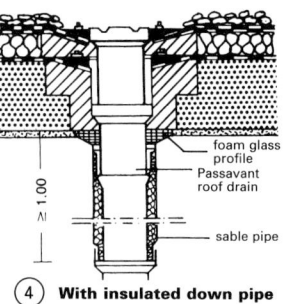

(4) **With insulated down pipe**

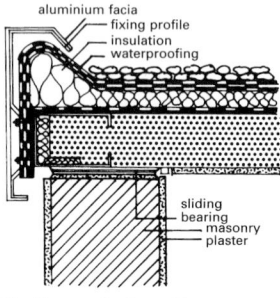

(5) **Flat roof edge with open sliding joint**

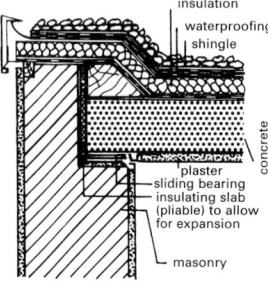

(6) **Flat roof edge with concealed sliding joint (slide track)**

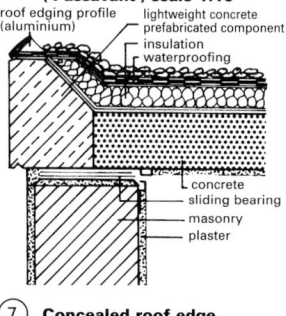

(7) **Concealed roof edge**

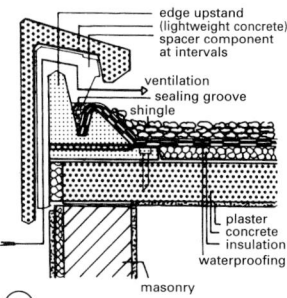

(8) **Concrete edge profile**

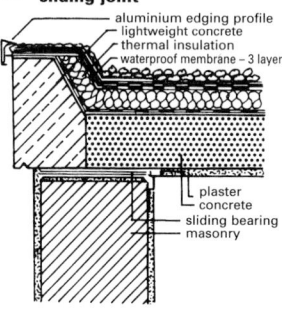

(9) **Protective layer – double layer gravel bedding; better: ballasting**

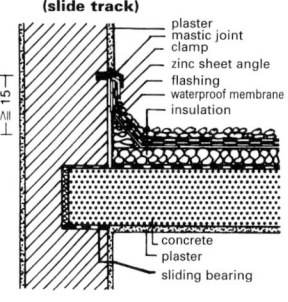

(10) **Wall connection zinc sheet angle and flashing**

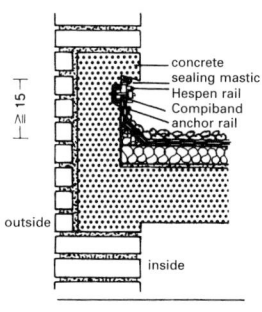

(11) **Wall connection: flanged connection with anchorage and Hespen rail**

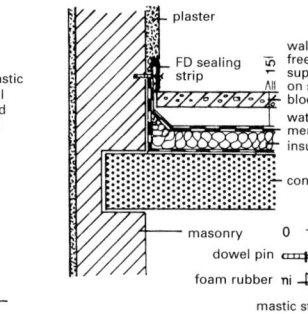

(12) **Wall connection with FD sealing strip (walkway)**

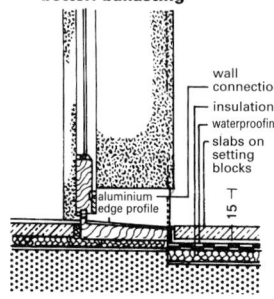

(13) **Wall connection in the vicinity of a terrace door**

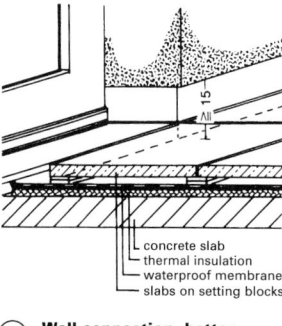

(14) **Wall connection, better with door threshold at the level of the upstand**

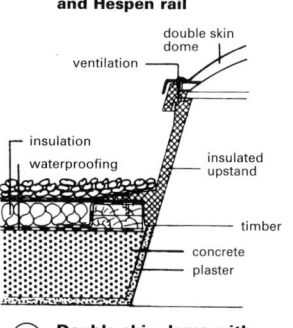

(15) **Double skin dome with ventilation gap → p. 159**

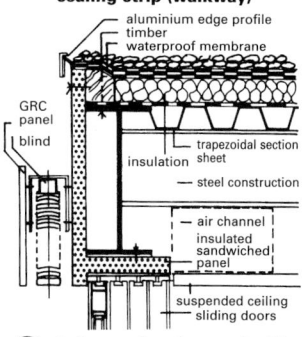

(16) **Indoor swimming pool with insulated sandwiched panel fascia**

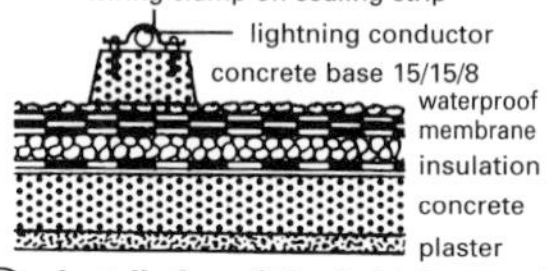

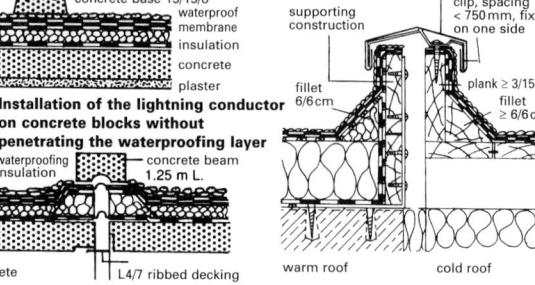

(17) **Installation of the lightning conductor on concrete blocks without penetrating the waterproofing layer**

(18) **Raised expansion joint with additional protection**

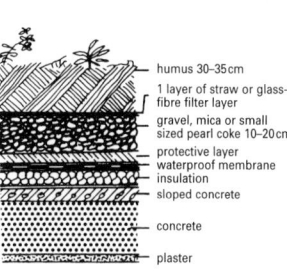

(19) **Movement joint with supporting construction and capping**

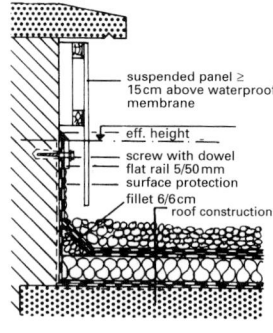

(20) **Roof garden on a warm roof – protective layer could be replaced by shredded rubber sheet**

(21) **Chimney connection with suspended facia panel**

Cold Roof Construction

Roof terrace surfaces are loose laid in a bed of shingle or on block supports. Advantage: water level is below surface; no severe freezing. Roof garden has surface drainage through drainage layers, ballasting of shingle or similar, with a filter layer on top → p. 80 ⑳.

Roofs over swimming pools, etc. are suspended ceilings with ventilated or heated void; see Table ③ → p. 79. Usually, the contribution of all layers up to the vapour barrier, including the air boundary layer, gives a max. 13.5% of the resistance to heat 1/k.

On wood → ⑤ is a simple solution, and good value for money. NB: insulation above the vapour barrier should be thicker than with a concrete roof, not only due to the low surface weight, but also because the contribution of the layers up to the vapour barrier (air boundary layer + wood thickness) would otherwise be too high.

An inverted roof → ② is an unusual solution with long-term durability (up to now, however, only achievable with various polystyrene foam materials). Shingle alone as the upper roof layering is insufficient in certain cases; it is better to have a paved surface. Advantage: quickly waterproof, examination for defects is easy, no limit to use. Insulation 10–20% thicker than for a normal warm roof.

With a concrete roof → ①, due to the position of the insulation, condensation occurs in certain conditions, which always dry out in the summer; unsuitable for humid rooms. The risk is dependent on the care taken by the manufacturer to avoid cracks due to the geometry (shrinkage) and solving the problem of connections to, and penetrations of, the concrete.

A completely flat cold roof → ⑥ – ⑧ is only allowable with vapour barrier: diffusion resistance → pp. 111–14 of the inner skin ≥ 10 m; the air layer here is only for vapour pressure balance, analogous to the warm roof, as it does not function properly as a ventilation system unless the slope is at least 10%. Layer sequence → ⑥ and ⑧. NB: inner skin must be airtight; tongue and groove panelling is not. Insulation → p. 79. Waterproofing as for warm roof → p. 80. Slope ≥ 1.5%, preferably 3% – important for drainage. Inlets should be insulated in the air cavity region; use insulated inlet pipes → ⑨. It is necessary for the vapour barrier to be unbroken (tight overlapping and wall connections, particularly for swimming pools; unavoidable through-nailing is permissible).

On light constructions, the internal temperature range should be improved by additional heavy layers (heat storage) under the insulation. Unfavourable internal temperature range: temperature fluctuations almost the same as those outside implies an internal climate similar to that of an unheated army hut; this cannot be improved by thermal insulation alone. A quick response heating system and/or additional thermal mass is required. For the artificial ventilation of rooms under cold roofs, always maintain a negative pressure; otherwise, room air will be forced into the roof cavity.

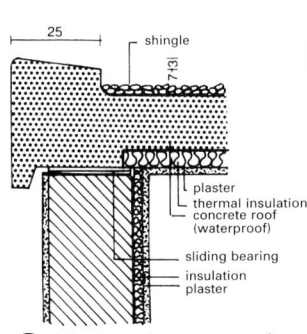

① **Waterproof concrete roof (Woermann roof)**

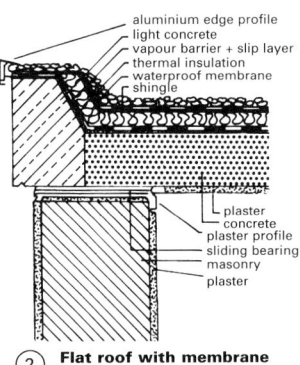

② **Flat roof with membrane waterproofing**

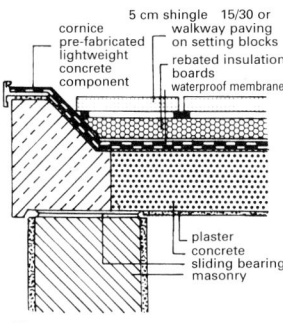

③ **Flat roof construction**

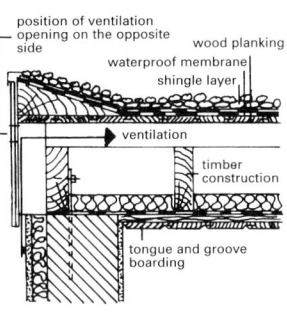

④ **Cold roof in timber construction**

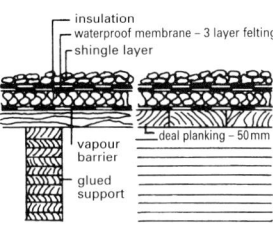

⑤ **Warm roof with glue-laminated beams and sheathing of planed planks**

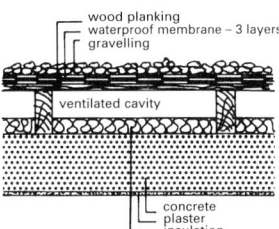

⑥ **Cold roof – heavy construction**

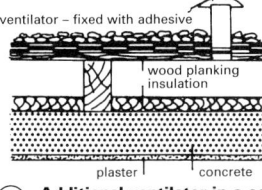

⑦ **Additional ventilator in a cold roof for oversized roof areas and for ventilation at the connection to taller structural components**

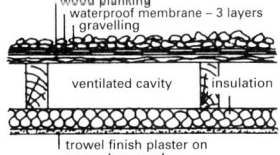

⑧ **Cold roof – light construction**

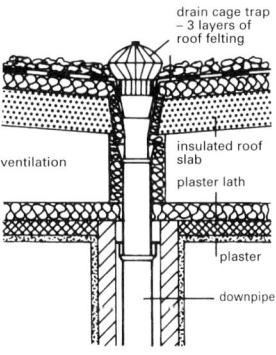

⑨ **Cold roof – flat roof outlet, insulated in void**

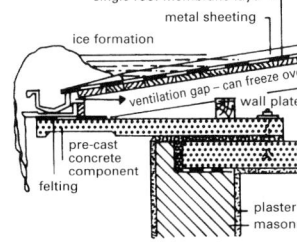

⑩ **Cornice of pre-fabricated components; if the ventilation opening is too large a projection, it may freeze over**

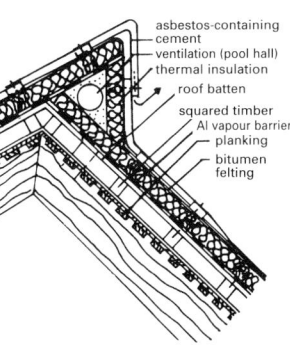

⑪ **Ridge ventilation on a sloping cold roof (indoor swimming pool)**

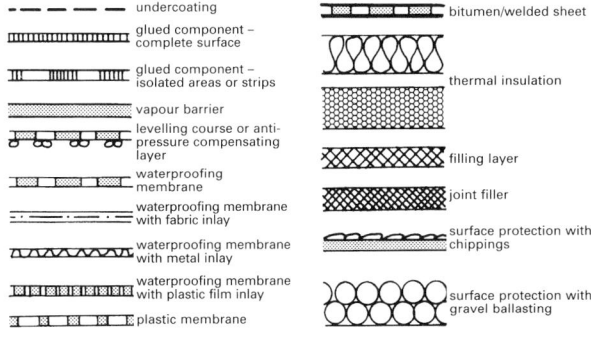

– – – – – undercoating	bitumen/welded sheet
glued component – complete surface	thermal insulation
glued component – isolated areas or strips	thermal insulation
vapour barrier	filling layer
levelling course or anti-pressure compensating layer	joint filler
waterproofing membrane	surface protection with chippings
waterproofing membrane with fabric inlay	surface protection with gravel ballasting
waterproofing membrane with metal inlay	
waterproofing membrane with plastic film inlay	
plastic membrane	

⑫ **Key to representation of roof covering components**

ROOF GARDENS

History

The concept of roof gardens and roof cultivation had already been exploited by the Babylonians in biblical times by 600 BC. In Berlin, in 1890, farm house roofs were covered with a layer of soil as a means of fire protection, in which vegetation seeded itself. Le Corbusier was the first in our century to rediscover the almost forgotten green roof.

The characteristics of roof cultivation

1. Insulation by virtue of the layer of air between blades of grass and through the layer of soil, with its root mass containing microbial life processes (process heat).
2. Sound insulation and heat storage potential.
3. Improvement of air quality in densely populated areas
4. Improvements in microclimate
5. Improves town drainage and the water balance of the countryside
6. Advantageous effects for building structures: UV radiation and strong temperature fluctuations are prevented due to the insulating grass and soil layers
7. Binds dust
8. Part of building design and improves quality of life
9. Reclamation of green areas

(1) Roof garden on rented housing: 'Pointer towards a new form of architecture'

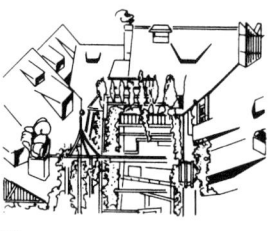

(2) Roof garden in the form of a collection of plant containers on balconies and roof terraces

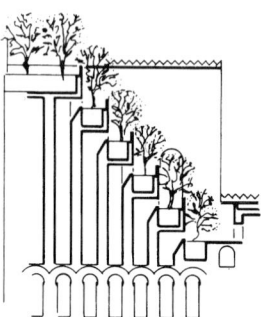

(3) The hanging gardens of Semiramis in Babylon (600 BC)

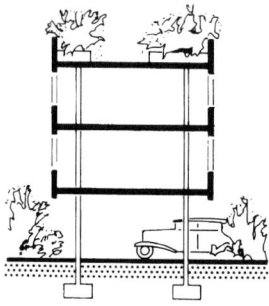

(4) 'Lost' areas of greenery are reclaimed by roof planting

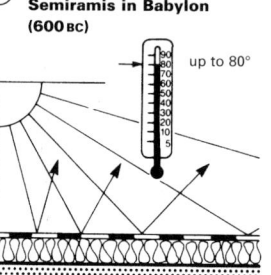

(5) Overheated, dry town air → (6)

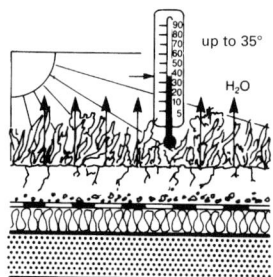

(6) Cooler and moister air due to energy consuming plant transpiration

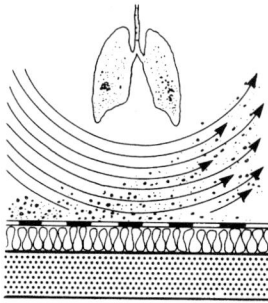

(7) Production of dust and dust swirling → (8)

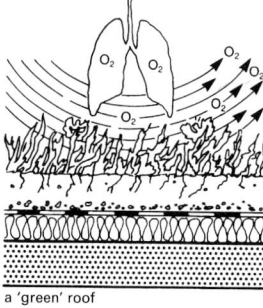

(8) Improvement of city air due to filtering out and absorption of dust and due to oxygen production by plants

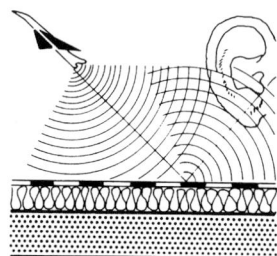

(9) Sound reflection on 'hard surfaces' → (10)

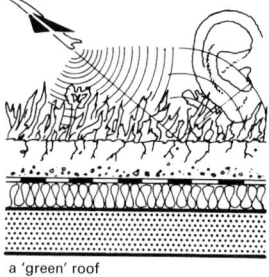

(10) Sound absorption due to the soft planted surface

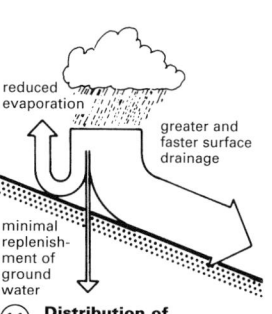

(11) Distribution of precipitation – consolidated surfaces → (12)

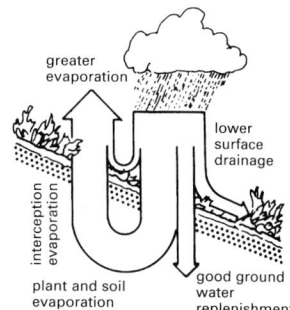

(12) Distribution of precipitation – natural surfaces

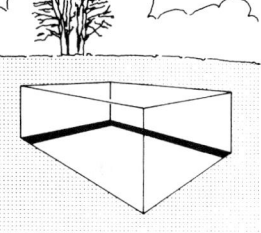

(13) With the construction of every house, a part of the countryside is lost → (14)

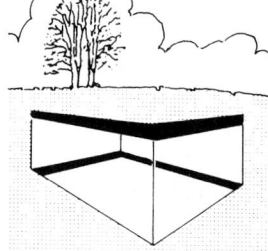

(14) A major proportion of the lost ground area can be regained by cultivating the roof

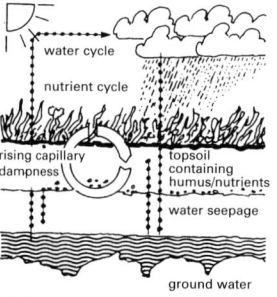

(15) Natural cycle of water and nutrients

(16) Psycho-physiological value of cultivated areas (the feeling of well being is positively influenced by the areas of greenery)

① **Intensive cultivation**

② **Extensive cultivation**

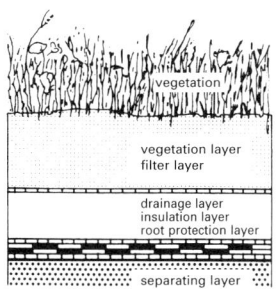

③ **Layer construction of a cultivated roof**

vegetation
vegetation layer
filter layer
drainage layer
insulation layer
root protection layer
separating layer

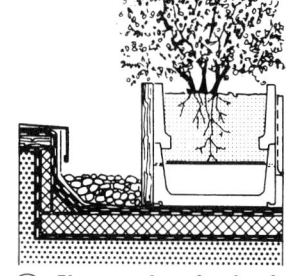

④ **Plant containers forming the boundary of a cultivated area**

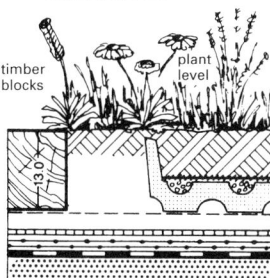

timber blocks
plant level

insulating mat
two root protection/
waterproof membranes

⑤ **Zinco Floraterra roof cultivation system**

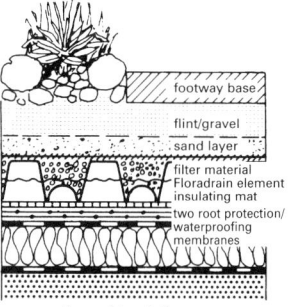

footway base
flint/gravel
sand layer
filter material
Floradrain element
insulating mat
two root protection/
waterproofing
membranes

thermal insulation
vapour barrier

⑥ **Zinco Floradrain roof cultivation system**

Roof slope

The slope of a double pitch roof should not be greater than 25°. Flat roofs should have a minimum slope of 2–3%.

Types of roof cultivation

Intensive cultivation: the roof is fitted out as a domestic garden, with equipment such as pergolas and loggias; continual attention and upkeep are necessary; planting – grass, shrubs and trees. Extensive cultivation: the cultivation requires a thin layer of soil and requires a minimum of attention; planting – moss, grass, herbs, herbaceous plants and shrubs. Mobile cultivation: plants in tubs, and other plant containers serve for the cultivation of roof terraces, balustrades and balconies.

Watering

Natural watering by rain water: water is trapped in the drainage layer and in the vegetation layer. Accumulated water: rain water is trapped in the drainage layer and is mechanically replenished if natural watering is inadequate. Drip watering: a water drip pipe is placed in the vegetation or drainage layer to water the plants during dry periods. Sprinkling system: sprinkling system over the vegetation layer.

Fertiliser

Fertiliser can be spread on the vegetation layer or mixed with the water during artificial watering.

botanical name	English name (colour of the flower)	height	flowering season
Saxifraga aizoon	encrusted saxifrage (white-pink)	5 cm	VI
Sedum acre	biting stonecrop (yellow)	8 cm	VI--VII
Sedum album	white stonecrop (white)	8 cm	VI-VII
Sedum album 'Coral Carpet'	white variety	5 cm	VI
Sedum album 'Laconicum'	white variety	10 cm	VI
Sedum album 'Micranthum'	white variety	5 cm	VI-VII
Sedum album 'Murale'	white variety	8 cm	VI-VII
Sedum album 'Cloroticum'	(light green)	5 cm	VI-VII
Sedum hybr.	(yellow)	8 cm	VI-VII
Sedum floriferum	(gold)	10 cm	VIII-IX
Sedum albumreflexum 'Elegant'	rock stonecrop (yellow)	12 cm	VI-VII
Sedum album sexamgulare	(yellow)	5 cm	VI
Sedum album 'Weiße Tatra'	bright yellow variety	5 cm	VI
Sempervivum arachnoideum	cobweb houseleek (pink)	6 cm	VI-VII
Sempervivum hybr.	selected seedlings (pink)	6 cm	VI-VII
Sempervivum tectorum	houseleek (pink)	8 cm	VI-VII
Pelosperma	(yellow) not fully winter hardy	8 cm	VI-VII
Frestuc glauca	blue fescu (blue)	25 cm	VI
Festuca ovina	sheep's fescu (blue)	25 cm	VI
Koeleria glauca	opalescent grass (green/silver)	25 cm	VI
Melicia ciliatx	pearl grass (light green)	30 cm	V-VI

⑧ **Proven categories and varieties of plants for roof cultivation (extensive)**

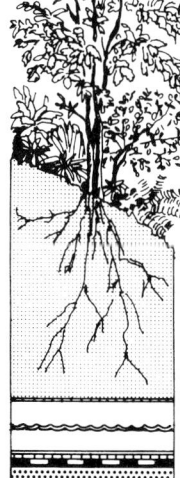

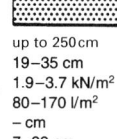

growth height > 250 cm	up to 250 cm	5–25 cm	5–20 cm	5–20 cm	5–10 cm	1 mulch layer
build-up height from 35 cm	19–35 cm	14 cm	12 cm	12 cm	10 cm	2 soil mixture
surface loading 3.7 kN/m²	1.9–3.7 kN/m²	1.4 kN/m²	1.1 kN/m²	1.15 kN/m²	0.9 kN/m²	3 filter mat
water supply 170 l/m²	80–170 l/m²	60 l/m²	45 l/m²	40 l/m²	30 l/m²	4 drainage layer
mulch layer – cm	– cm	– cm	1 cm	– cm	1 cm	5 root protection membrane
soil mixture 23 cm	7–23 cm	5 cm	4 cm	7 cm	4 cm	6 separation and protection layers
drainage layer 12 cm	12 cm	9 cm	7 cm	5 cm	5 cm	7 roof sealing
watering, by hand or automatic	by hand or automatic	by hand or automatic	by hand	by hand	by hand	8 supporting construction

⑦ **Various types of roof cultivation**

ROOF GARDENS

Roof Construction

For the vegetation layer, expanded clay and expanded slate are used, these materials offering structural stability, soil aeration, water storage potential and lending themselves to landscaping. Problems to be solved: storage of nutrients, soil reaction (pH value), through-ventilation, water storage. The filter layer, comprising filter material, prevents clogging of the drainage layer. The drainage layer prevents excessive watering of the plants and consists of: mesh fibre mats, foam drainage courses, plastic panels and protective structural materials. The protective layer provides protection during the construction phase and against point loading. The root protection layer of plants, etc., are retained by PVC/ECB and EPDM sheeting. The separating layer separates supporting structure from the roof cultivation. Examples → ① – ⑧ illustrate a range of customary flat roof structures and variations incorporating roof cultivation. Before roof cultivation is applied, the integrity of the roof and of the individual layers must be established. The technical condition of the roof surface must be carefully checked. Attention should be paid to: construction of the layers (condition); correct roof slope; no unevenness; no roof sagging; no waterproofing membrane faults (bubbles, cracking); expansion joints; edge attachments; penetrating elements (light shafts, roof lights, ventilating pipes); and drainage. Double pitch roofs can also be cultivated, but much preparatory construction work is needed when inclined roofs are cultivated (danger of slippage, soil drying out) → ⑨ – ⑫.

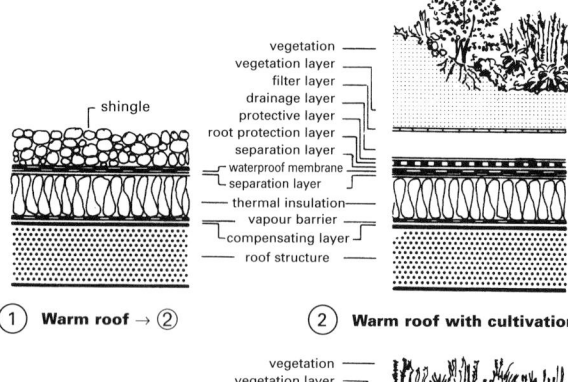

vegetation
vegetation layer
filter layer
drainage layer
protective layer
root protection layer
separation layer
waterproof membrane
separation layer
thermal insulation
vapour barrier
compensating layer
roof structure

shingle

① **Warm roof** → ②   ② **Warm roof with cultivation**

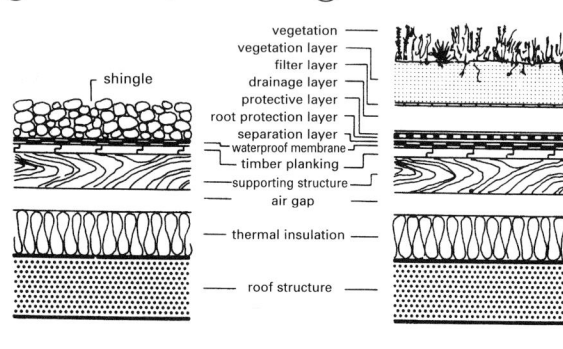

vegetation
vegetation layer
filter layer
drainage layer
protective layer
root protection layer
separation layer
waterproof membrane
timber planking
supporting structure
air gap
thermal insulation
roof structure

shingle

③ **Cold roof** → ④   ④ **Cold roof with cultivation**

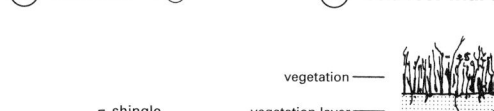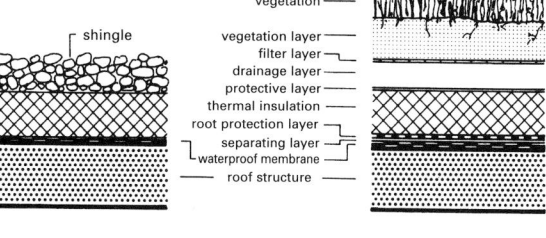

vegetation
vegetation layer
filter layer
drainage layer
protective layer
thermal insulation
root protection layer
separating layer
waterproof membrane
roof structure

shingle

⑤ **Inverted roof** → ⑥   ⑥ **Inverted roof with cultivation**

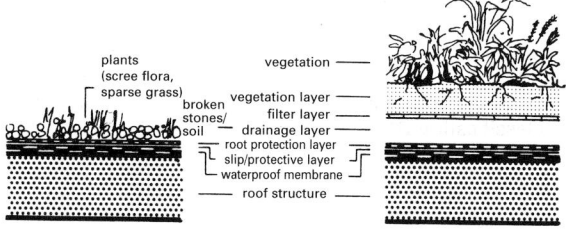

plants
(scree flora,
sparse grass)
broken
stones/
soil

vegetation
vegetation layer
filter layer
drainage layer
root protection layer
slip/protective layer
waterproof membrane
roof structure

⑦ **Retrospective roof cultivation at low expense**   ⑧ **Retrospective roof cultivation (if constructionally and structurally possible)**

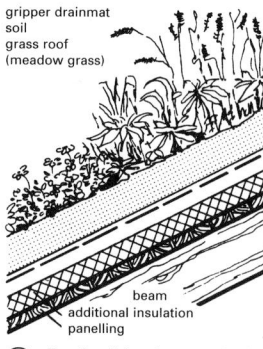

gripper drainmat
soil
grass roof
(meadow grass)

beam
additional insulation
panelling

⑨ **Roof cultivation on sloping roof**

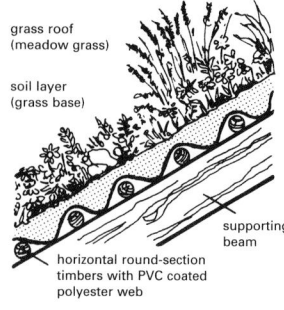

grass roof
(meadow grass)

soil layer
(grass base)

supporting
beam

horizontal round-section
timbers with PVC coated
polyester web

⑩ **Roof cultivation on a steep roof**

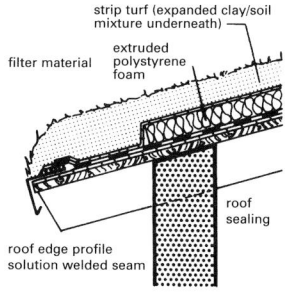

strip turf (expanded clay/soil
mixture underneath)
filter material
extruded
polystyrene
foam
roof
sealing
roof edge profile
solution welded seam

⑪ **Detail of the eaves on a sloping 'green' roof**

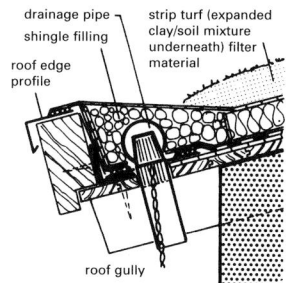

drainage pipe
shingle filling
roof edge
profile
strip turf (expanded
clay/soil mixture
underneath) filter
material
roof gully

⑫ **Eaves detail** → ⑪

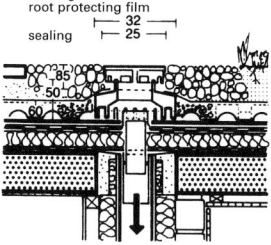

flag stones on sand bed
filter material
drainage element
root protecting film
sealing
32
25

⑬ **Drainage inspection shaft**

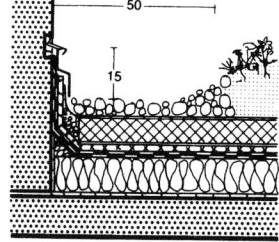

50
15

⑭ **Wall connection with shingle edging strip**

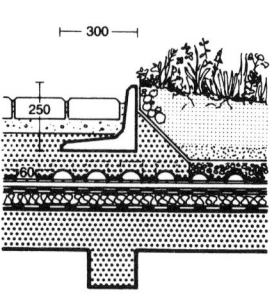

300
250

⑮ **Transition from road surface to intensive roof cultivation**

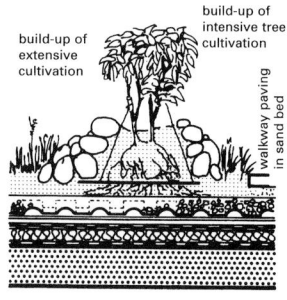

build-up of
intensive tree
cultivation
build-up of
extensive
cultivation
walkway paving
in sand bed

⑯ **Transition from footpath to intensive or extensive cultivation**

ROOF CULTIVATION

Definitions

(1) Extensive roof cultivation implies a protective covering that needs upkeep, replacing the customary gravel covering.

(2) To a large extent, the planted level is self-replenishing and the upkeep, i.e., maintenance, is reduced to a minimum.

Scope

These guidelines apply to areas of vegetation without natural connection to the ground, particularly on building roofs, and roofs of underground garages, shelters, or similar structures.

Principles of constructive planning and execution

(1) In extensive roof cultivation, the cultivated area acts as a protective covering – see the recommendations for flat roofs.

(2) Roof construction and structure: the relevant structural and constructional principles of the building and its roof must be carefully interrelated with the technical requirements imposed by the vegetation and its supporting elements.

(3) The surface loading required to secure the waterproof membrane is the minimum weight per unit area of the operative layers in accordance with the table below, taken from the Roof Garden Association recommendations for planting on the flat roofs.

(4)

Height of the eaves above ground level (m)		Load on the edge region (kg/m²)	Inner region (kg/m²)
up to 8	at least	80	40
8–20	at least	130	65
over 20	at least	160	60

(5) The type of construction employed in the roof and the degree of surface loading are dependent on the wind loading, the height of the building and the surface area of the roof.

(6) High suction loads can occur around the edges and corners of the roof over a width $b/8 \geq 1\,m \leq 2\,m$.

(7) 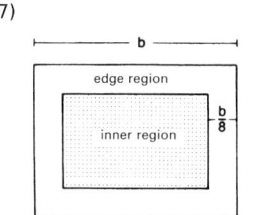   (8)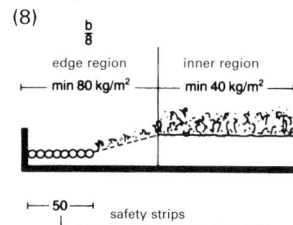

(9) Cultivated roofs should be designed to be easily maintained, i.e. areas which need regular attention (such as roof drainage inlets, structures which protrude from the cultivated area, expansion joints and wall junctions) should be easily accessible.

(10) In these areas, the protective layer should comprise of inorganic materials such as shingle or loose stones.

(11) These areas should be linked with the roof drainage inlets, so that any overflow from the planted areas can drain away.

(12) Large surface areas should be subdivided into separate drainage zones.

Requirements, functions, constructive precautions

(1) The waterproofing membrane should be designed in accordance with the recommended specifications for flat roofs.

(2) The development of the cultivated area should not impair the function of the roof waterproofing membrane.

Extract from Guidelines of the Roof Garden Association

(3) It should be possible to separate the waterproofing layers from the cultivation layers, i.e. it must be possible to inspect the waterproof membrane of the roof.

(4) The root protection layer must provide durable protection to the roof waterproofing layers.

(5) High polymer waterproofing membranes should, because of their physical and chemical makeup, be able to satisfy the demands of the root protection layer.

(6) If a bituminous roof waterproofing system is applied, then bitumen-compatible root protection layers should be employed.

(7) The root protection layer should be protected from mechanical damage by a covering; non-rotting fibre mats should be used since these can store nutrients and additional water.

(8) The vegetation layer must have a high structural stability and must exhibit good cushioning capability and resistance to rotting.

(9) The pH value should not exceed 6.0 in the acidic range.

(10) The construction of the layers must be capable of accepting a daily precipitation level of at least 30/m².

(11) There should be a volume of air of at least 20% in the layer structure in the water saturated condition.

Maintenance at the plant level

(1) Wild herbaceous plants and grasses from the dry grassland, steppe and rock crevice species should be used in the planted areas. All plants used should be perennial.

(2) The plants used should be young plants, sown as seed or propagated by cuttings.

(3) Maintenance: at least one routine per year, when the roof inlets, security strips, roof connections and terminations are inspected and cleaned as necessary.

(4) Plants, mosses and lichen which settle are not considered as weeds.

(5) All undesirable weeds should be removed.

(6) Woody plants, in particular willow, birch, poplar, maple and the like, are considered to be weeds.

(7) Regular mowing and fertilising should be carried out.

(8) Changes at the plant level may occur through environmental effects.

Fire prevention

(1) All fire precaution recommendations should be observed.

(2) The requirements are fulfilled if the flammability of the structure is classed as flame resistant (material classification B1)

Characteristics of a satisfactory roof cultivation

An extensive planted area has planting out, sowing, setting of cuttings, pre-cultivated plants (plant containers, mats and panels). The vegetation layer provides stability for the plants, contains water and nutrients and allows material and gas exchange and water retention. The vegetation layer must have a large pore volume for gas exchange and water retention. The filter layer prevents the flushing out of nutrients and small components of the vegetation layer and silting up of the drainage layer. It also ensures that water drains away gradually. The drainage layer provides safe removal of overflow water, aeration of the vegetation layer, the storage and, if necessary, a water supply. Root protection protects the roof waterproofing membrane from chemical and mechanical contact with the roots of the plants which, in searching for water and nutrients, can be destructive. Roof construction must be durably waterproof, both on the surface and in all connections with other components. The formation of condensation water in the roof structure must be effectively and permanently prevented.

TENSILE AND INFLATABLE STRUCTURES

The construction of awnings and tensile roofs is becoming more widespread. These constructions vary from simple awnings and roofs, to technically very complicated tensile structures of the most diverse types.

Materials: artificial fibre material (polyester) is used as the base fabric, with corrosion resistant and weather proof protective layers of PVC on both sides.

Characteristics: high strength (can resist snow and wind loads); non-rotting; resistant to aggressive substances; water and dirt repellent, and fire resistant.

Weight: 800–1200 g/m².

Permeability to light: from 'impermeable' up to 50% permeability.

Life: 15–20 years; all popular colour shades; good colour fastness

Workability: manufactured in rolls; widths 1–3 m, usually 1.5 m; length up to 2000 running metres; cut to shape to suit structure; can be joined by stitching, welding, with adhesives, combinations of these, or by clamp connectors.

Add-on standard systems ①
Standard units allow the structure to be extended indefinitely, often on all sides. They embrace most planforms: square, rectangular, triangular, circular, polyhedra. *Application:* connecting passageways, rest area pavilions, shade awnings, etc.

Framed structures
A supporting frame is made from wood, steel or aluminium, over which the membrane is stretched as a protective covering. *Application:* exhibition halls, storage and industrial areas.

Air supported structures → ④
The structural membrane is supported by compressed air at low pressure, and air locks prevent the rapid release of the supporting air. The system can be combined with heating, and additional insulation can be provided by an inner shell (air mattress). Maximum width is 45 m, with length unlimited. *Application:* exhibition, storage, industrial and sport halls; also as roofing over swimming pools and construction sites in winter.

Tensioned structures → ⑤
The membrane is supported at selected points by means of cables and masts, and tensioned around the edges. To improve thermal insulation, the structure may be provided with additional membranes. Span can be up to more than 100 m. *Application:* exhibition, industrial and sports halls, meeting and sports areas, phantom roofs.

edge cable

① **Standard add-on systems**

ventilation

② **Domed construction**   ③ **Canopies**

max. 45 m

④ **Air supported structures, pneumatic roofing**

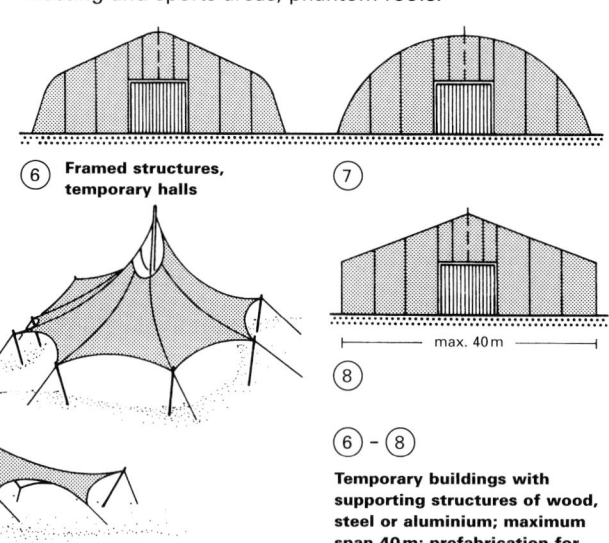

⑥ **Framed structures, temporary halls**   ⑦

⑧   max. 40 m

⑥ – ⑧

Temporary buildings with supporting structures of wood, steel or aluminium; maximum span 40 m; prefabrication for rapid assembly and low cost

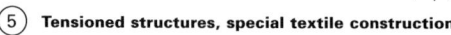

⑤ **Tensioned structures, special textile constructions**

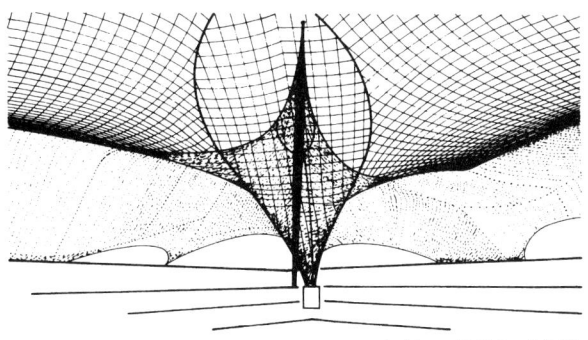

(1) **German Pavilion, Expo Montreal 1967**

Architects: R. Gutbrod, F. Otto

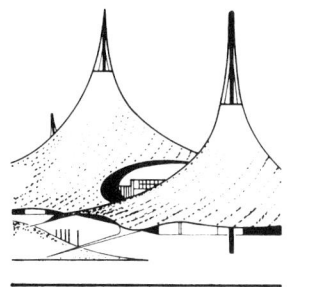

(2) **Montreal 1967**

stadium

sports hall

sports hall

(3) **Olympic park, Munich 1972**

Cable net structures offer the possibility of covering large unsupported spans with considerable ease. The German pavilion at the World Exhibition in Montreal in 1976 was constructed in this fashion → (1) + (2), the Olympic Stadium in Munich, 1972 → (3) – (8) and the ice rink in the Olympic Park in Munich → (10) – (13). An interesting example is also provided by the design for the students club for the University and College of Technology in Dortmund → (9).

As a rule, the constructional elements are steel pylons, steel cable networks, steel or wooden grids, and roof coverings of acrylic glass or translucent, plastic-reinforced sheeting.

Cables are fastened into the edges of the steel network, the eaves, etc., and are laid over pin-jointed and usually obliquely positioned steel supports, and then anchored.

'Aerial supports', cable supporting elements which are stayed from beneath, divide up the load of the main supporting cable to reduce the cable cross-sections.

The transfer of load of the tension cables usually takes place via cast components – bolt fixings, housings, cable fixings, etc. The cable fixings can be secured by self-locking nuts or by the use of pressure clamps.

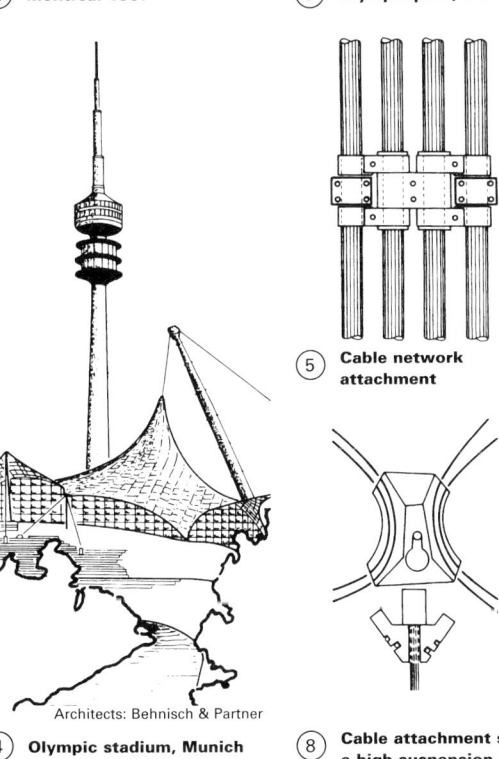

Architects: Behnisch & Partner

(4) **Olympic stadium, Munich 1972**

(5) **Cable network attachment**

(8) **Cable attachment saddle at a high suspension point**

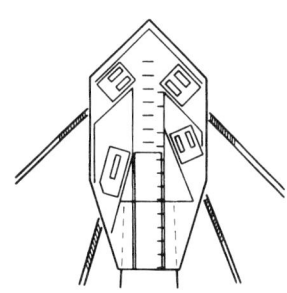

(6) **Transfer of loads from the cables to the cross-beams on a mast head**

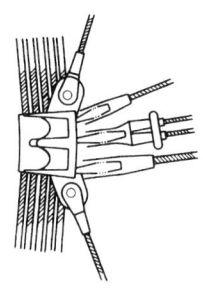

(7) **Support cable attachment point to the edge cables**

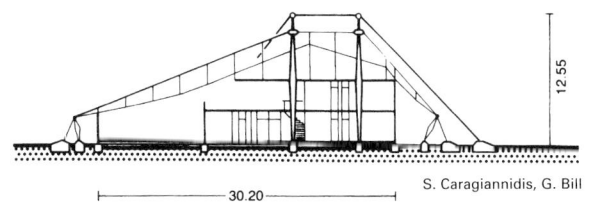

S. Caragiannidis, G. Bill

30.20

12.55

(9) **Student design**

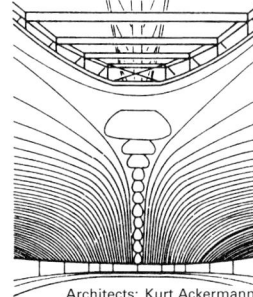

Architects: Kurt Ackermann and Partner, 1983

(10) **Ice rink, Olympic park, Munich**

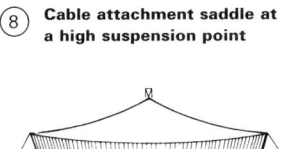

cross-section

longitudinal section

(11) **Canopies → (10)**

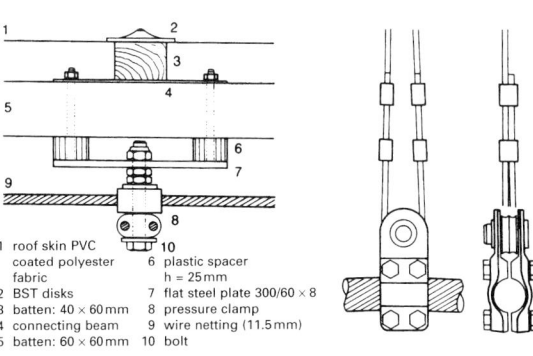

1 roof skin PVC coated polyester fabric
2 BST disks
3 batten: 40 × 60mm
4 connecting beam
5 batten: 60 × 60mm
6 plastic spacer h = 25mm
7 flat steel plate 300/60 × 8
8 pressure clamp
9 wire netting (11.5mm)
10 bolt

(12) **Cable clamp, showing roof construction**

(13) **Cable network; edge cable clamp**

SUSPENDED AND TENSIONED STRUCTURES

The suspension or support of load-bearing structures provides a means of reducing the cross-sections of the structural members, thus enabling delicate and filigree designs to be developed. As a rule, this is only possible in steel and timber skeletal structures. The tensioning cables are of steel and can usually be tensioned on completion of the structure. The cables support tensile forces only.

Suspended structures have the purpose of reducing the span of supporting beams or eliminating cantilevered structures. Tensioned structures, likewise, reduce the span of beams and, hence, also the section modulus which has to be considered in determining their cross-section → ⑫. In similar fashion to cable network structures, aerial supports are required on trussed structures. They have to accept buckling (compressive) stresses.

Significant contributions to the architecture of suspended structures have been made by Günter Behnisch → ⑤, Norman Foster → ①–④, Richard Rogers → ⑥–⑦ and Michael Hopkins → ⑧–⑨. The Renault building in Swindon, by Norman Foster, consists of arched steel supports, which are suspended from round, pre-stressed hollow steel masts from a point in the upper quarter of the gable → ①–④. The design enabled the ground area to be extended by approximately 67%. The suspended construction offers connection points which make it possible to execute the construction work without interfering with other work.

The new Fleetguard factory in Quimper, for an automobile concern in the USA, had to be designed for changing requirements and operations. For this, Richard Rogers chose a suspended construction so to keep the inside free of any supporting structure → ⑥–⑦. The same design ideas form the basis of the sports halls of Günter Behnisch → ⑤ and the Schlumberger Research Centre in Cambridge, by Michael Hopkins → ⑧ – ⑨. An airport administration building (proposed design for Paderborn/Lippstadt) → ⑩ and a concert hall (proposed design for the Dortmund Fair) → ⑪ may also be built in this fashion.

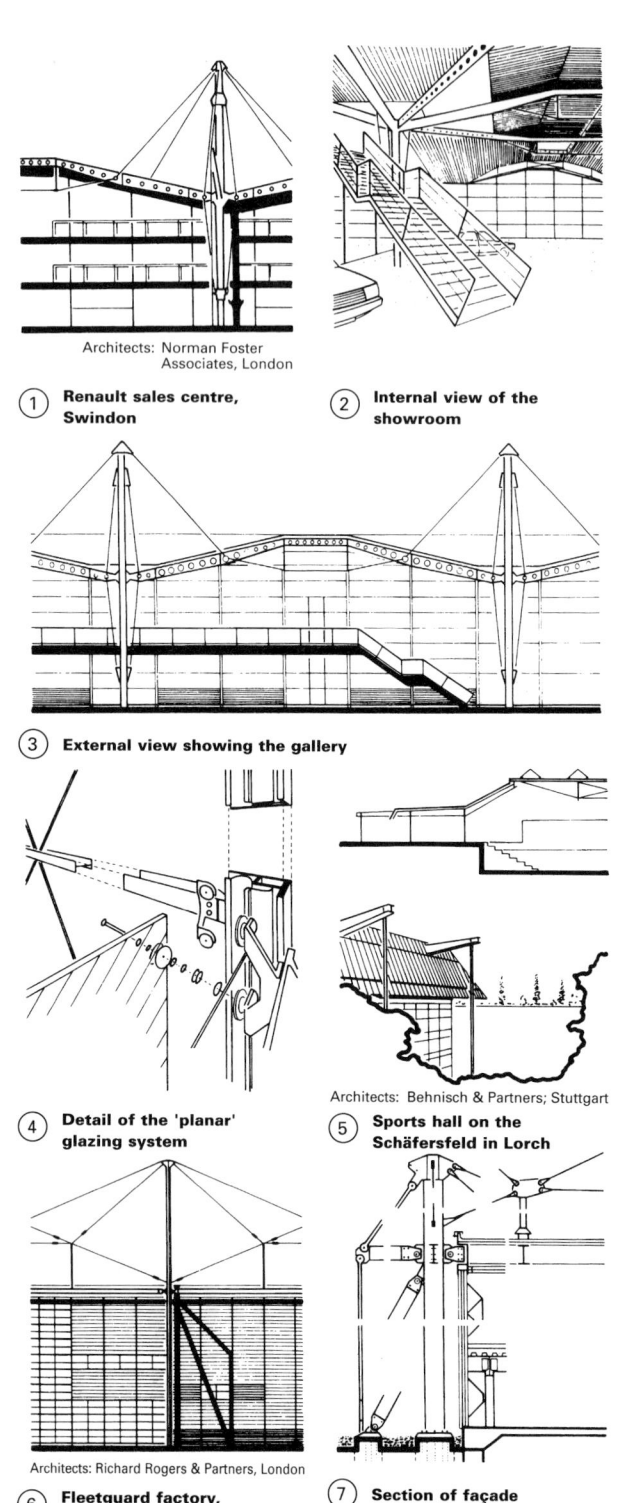

Architects: Norman Foster Associates, London

① **Renault sales centre, Swindon**
② **Internal view of the showroom**

③ **External view showing the gallery**

Architects: Behnisch & Partners; Stuttgart

④ **Detail of the 'planar' glazing system**
⑤ **Sports hall on the Schäfersfeld in Lorch**

Architects: Richard Rogers & Partners, London

⑥ **Fleetguard factory, Quimper, France**
⑦ **Section of façade**

Architects: Michael Hopkins & Partners; London

⑧ **Schlumberger Research Centre, Cambridge/GB**
⑨ **Winter garden: internal perspective**

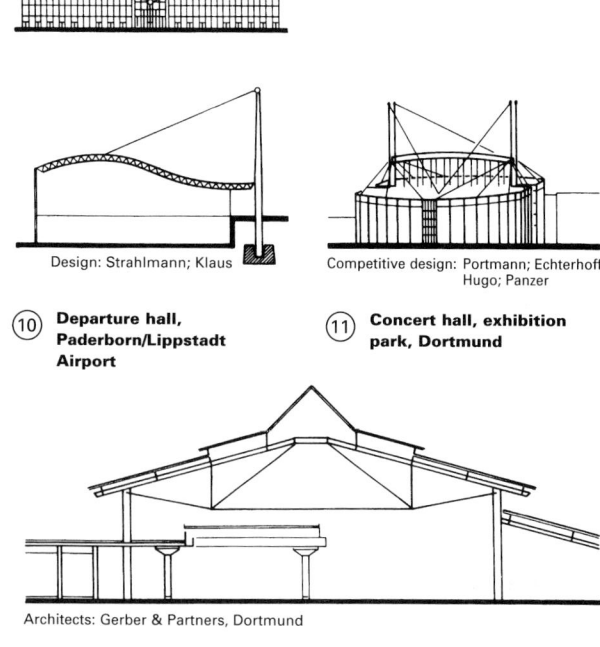

Design: Strahlmann; Klaus

Competitive design: Portmann; Echterhoff; Hugo; Panzer

⑩ **Departure hall, Paderborn/Lippstadt Airport**
⑪ **Concert hall, exhibition park, Dortmund**

Architects: Gerber & Partners, Dortmund

⑫ **Underground station, Stadtgarten, Dortmund**

SPACE FRAMES: PRINCIPLES

Ideally, space frames should be constructed from equal sided and/or isosceles right-angled triangles, so that regular polyhedrons are formed. In plane infinite networks, there are exactly three geometric structures; in spherical finite structures, there are exactly five regular polyhedron networks, which are comprised of only one type of joint, member, and hence also, surface. Regular plane networks are triangular, square and hexagonal.

Of the five platonic bodies used, the space frame formula decrees that only those three-dimensional joint-member space frames whose members form a closed triangular network are kinematically stable, i.e. the tetrahedron, the octahedron and the icosahedron. The cube requires an additional 6, and the dodecahedron, an additional 24 members, to become stable. If a spherical, triangular network is not closed over the whole surface, the basic polygon must be prevented from moving by an appropriate alternative method.

The lengths of the members of a body for a space frame form a geometric series with the factor 2. One joint with a maximum of 18 connections at angles of 45°, 60° and 90° is sufficient for the construction of a regular framework. As with plane structures, it must be accepted that the members are connected with flexible joints.

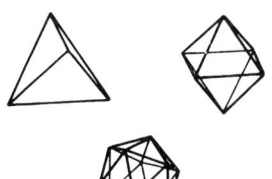

tetrahedron (4 faces)
cube (6 faces)
octahedron (8 faces)
dodecahedron (12 faces)
icosahedron (20 faces)

→ spherical network

(1) **Five platonic bodies**

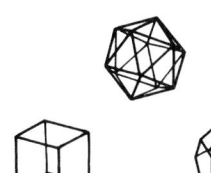

each joint in the three-dimensional space must be fixed by three members to make the three-dimensional frame rigid so, to achieve kinematic stability:
no. of members =
3 × number of joints − (1 + 2 + 3)

(2) **Föppl framework formula**

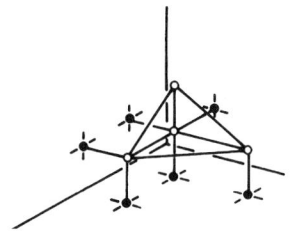

(3) **Space structure grid of octahedrons and tetrahedrons with regular cut-outs in the lower section**

(4) **Space structure grid of octahedrons and tetrahedrons in compressed format**

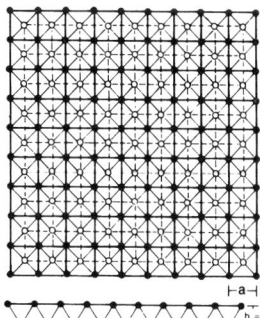

(5) **Space structure grid of semi-octahedrons and tetrahedrons parallel to the edges**

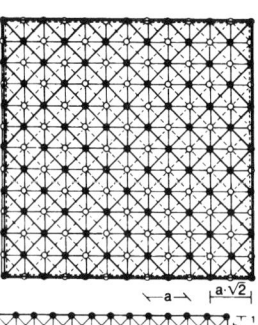

(6) **Space structure grid of semi-octahedrons and tetrahedrons in a rotated position (45°)**

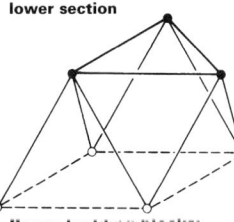

(7) **Space building blocks: octahedron and tetrahedron**

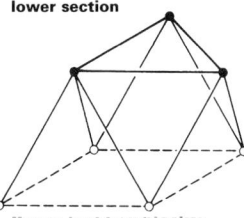

(8) **Space building blocks: octahedron and tetrahedron (large cube corners) in compressed format**

(9) **Space building blocks: semi-octahedron and tetrahedron**

(10) **Space building blocks: semi-octahedron and tetrahedron**

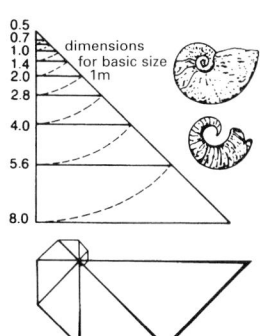

dimensions for basic size 1m

0.5
0.7
1.0
1.4
2.0
2.8
4.0
5.6
8.0

(11) **The geometric series for the length of members with the factor √2 and the natural pattern for the geometric series: shells of Ammonites**

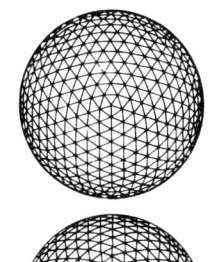

(12) **Spherical dome featuring an icosahedron structure**

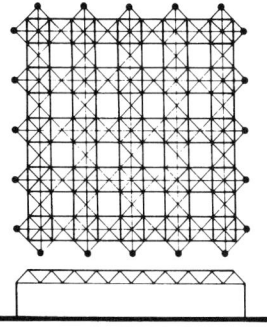

(13) **Space frame structure**

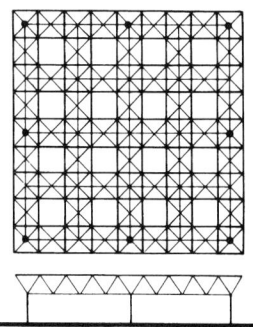

(14) **Space frame structure**

the standard 18-surface joint permits connection angles of 45°, 60°, 90° and multiples of these to be achieved; only one standard jointing device is in mass production

the regular, usually 10-surface, joint contains only sufficient holes as are required for closed, regular continuous surface framework structures

on the other hand, the special jointing fittings can be freely arranged as required, both in respect of the size of connection and the angle between two threaded holes

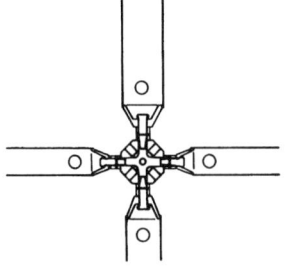

(1) **MERO joint connections**

(2) **Arrangement of members at a joint**

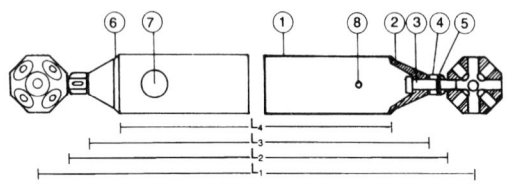

L₁ = system axial dimension
L₂ = nominal dimension of member
L₃ = finished dimension of member
L₄ = net length of tube

1 hollow section profile (tube)
2 cone
3 threaded bolts
4 keyed sleeve
5 slotted pin
6 weld seam
7 drainage hole
8 bolt insertion hole

(3) **Construction of a MERO frame member**

SPACE FRAMES: APPLICATION

The MERO space frame developed by Mengeringhausen consists of joints and members → ① – ③. The underlying principle is that joints and members are selected from the frame systems as are appropriate for the loads which are to be carried. In the MERO structural elements, the joint/member links do not act as 'ideal pin-joints', but are able to transmit flexural moments in addition to the normal forces in the members → ④ – ⑦. This three-dimensional format permits a free selection of a basic grid unit, then, with the factors √2 and √3 to size the lengths of the members, to develop a structure to provide the required load-bearing surfaces → ⑫ – ⑭ The unlimited flexibility is expressed in the fact that curved space frames are also possible. The Globe Arena in Stockholm → ⑬ is, at present, the largest hemispherical building in the world. The assembly methods involve elements of prefabrication, sectional installation or the slab-lift method. All the components are hot galvanised for corrosion protection. As a consequence of the high level of static redundancy of space frames, the failure of a single member as a result of fire will not lead to the collapse of the structure. Starting from spherical joints, that allow 18 different points of attachment for tubular members, a large variety of other joint systems between nodes and members have been developed so as to optimise the solution to load-bearing and spanning requirements → ⑧ – ⑪.

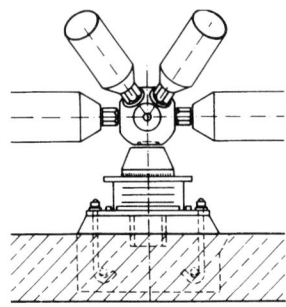

(4) **Frame support**

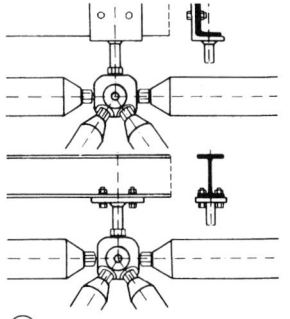

(5) **Purlin support**

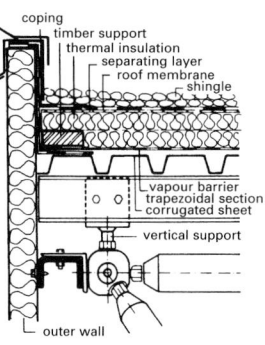

coping
timber support
thermal insulation
separating layer
roof membrane
shingle
vapour barrier
trapezoidal section
corrugated sheet
vertical support
outer wall

(6) **Structural connections to wall and roof**

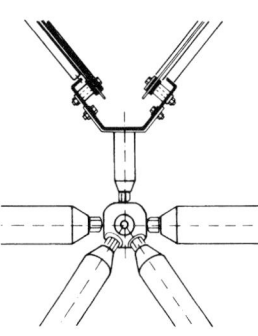

(7) **Structural connections – central channel**

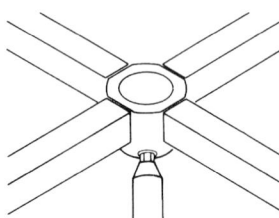

direct support of the roof skin on upper beam members, two layer supporting structure, screwed connections not resistant to bending, interlocked transition from frame member to joint in the upper beam, lower beam in the KK system

(8) **NK System (cup joint)**

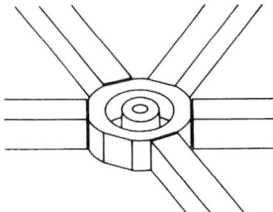

direct support of the roof skin, single-layered structure in triangular grid, screwed connections not resistant to bending, interlocked transition from structure member to joint

(9) **TK System (plate joint)**

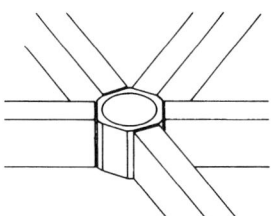

direct support of the roof skin, single layered structure, also in trapezoidal surface geometry, multi-screwed connections resistant to bending, interlocked transition from structure member to joint

(10) **ZK System (cylindrical joint)**

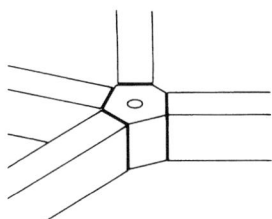

direct support of the roof skin, single and multi-layered structures, single and multi-screwed connections; member-integrated nodal optical points

(11) **BK System (block joint)**

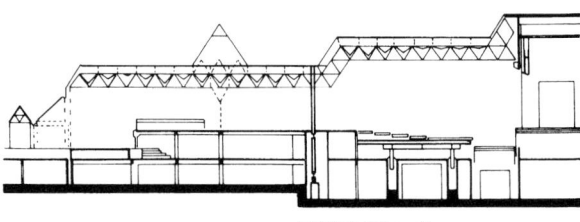

Architect: Strizewski

(12) **Partial section through the city hall in Hilden**

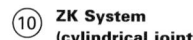

ca. 110m

Architect: Berg

(13) **Section through the Globe Arena in Stockholm**

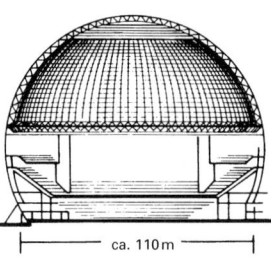
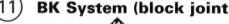
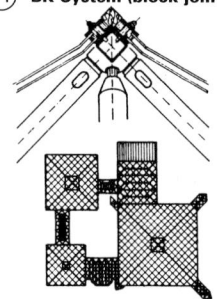

(14) **Detail of the roof ridge; roof plan of the plant exhibition hall, Gruga, Essen (NK System)**

The Krupp–Montal® space frame was developed by E. Rüter, Dortmund-Hörde. The members are bolted to the forged steel sphere with bolts inside the tubes. The bolts have hexagonal recesses in their heads and are inserted into a guide tube through a hole in the tubing of the structural member. In general, all members are hot galvanised. A coloured coating may also be applied to them. On the Krupp–Montal® System, the bolts can be examined without being removed from the frame members; if required, it is possible to replace framework members without destroying the framework. The Krupp–Montal® System is illustrated in → ① – ⑤, with points of detail in → ⑥ – ⑧.

The KEBA tube and joint connection has been designed for the transmission of tensile and compressive forces. It does not require bolts and can be dismantled without problems → ⑨ – ⑬. The KEBA joint consists of the jaw fitting, the interlocking flange, the tapered wedge and the caging ring with locking pin.

The Scane space frame has been developed by Kaj Thomsen. Bolts provide the means of connection, which are inserted in the ends of the members using a special method and are then screwed into the threaded bores of the spherical joint fittings → ⑭ – ⑮.

In the case of all space frames, an unsupported span of at least 80–100 m is possible.

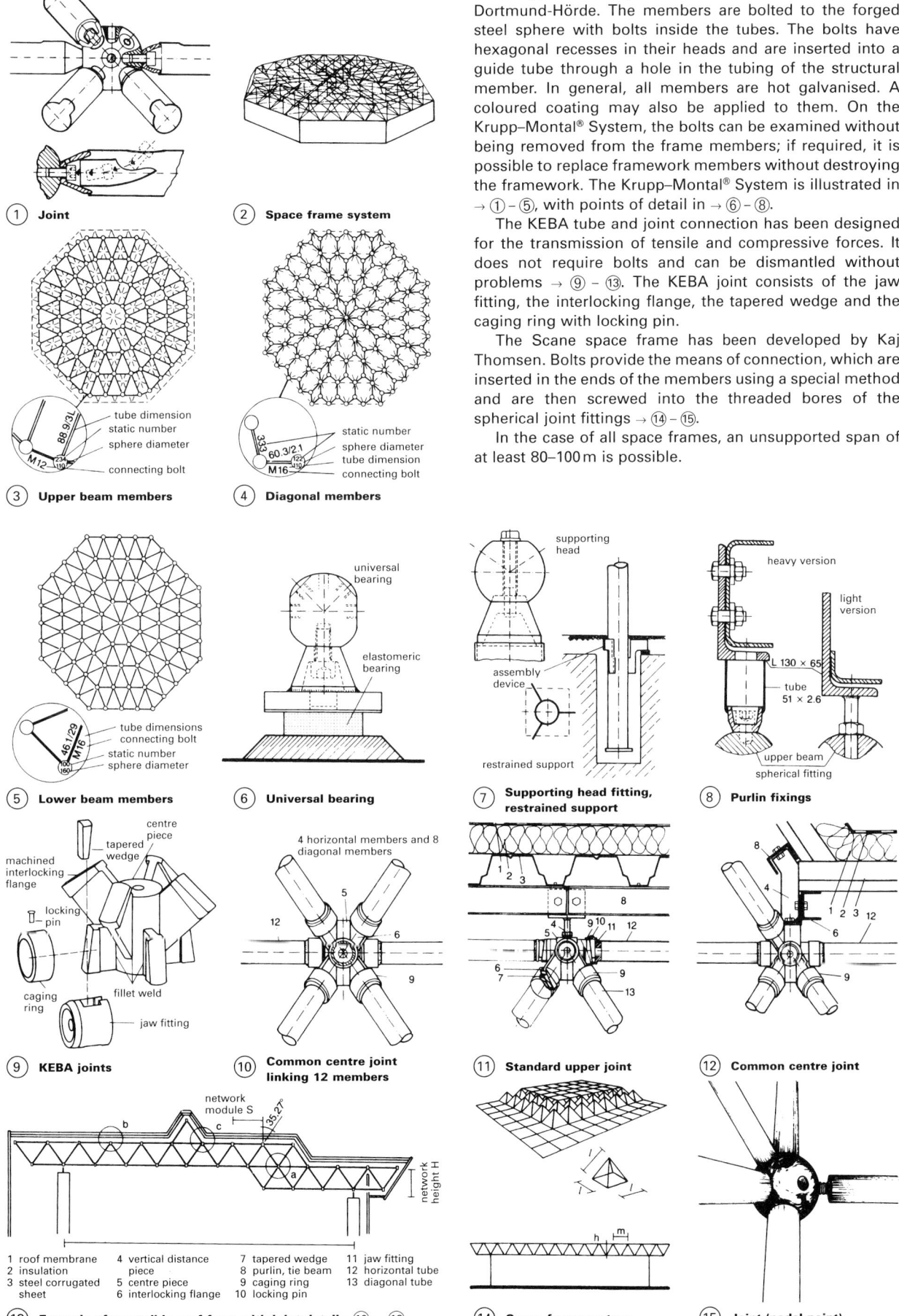

① **Joint**

② **Space frame system**

③ **Upper beam members**
- tube dimension
- static number
- sphere diameter
- connecting bolt
- 88.9/3
- M 12

④ **Diagonal members**
- static number
- sphere diameter
- tube dimension
- connecting bolt
- 333
- 60.3/2.1
- M 16

⑤ **Lower beam members**
- tube dimensions
- connecting bolt
- static number
- sphere diameter
- 46.1/29
- M16

⑥ **Universal bearing**
- universal bearing
- elastomeric bearing

⑦ **Supporting head fitting, restrained support**
- supporting head
- assembly device
- restrained support

⑧ **Purlin fixings**
- heavy version
- light version
- L 130 × 65
- tube 51 × 2.6
- upper beam
- spherical fitting

⑨ **KEBA joints**
- centre piece
- tapered wedge
- machined interlocking flange
- locking pin
- caging ring
- fillet weld
- jaw fitting

⑩ **Common centre joint linking 12 members**
- 4 horizontal members and 8 diagonal members

⑪ **Standard upper joint**

⑫ **Common centre joint**

⑬ **Example of a possible roof form with joint details ⑩ – ⑫**
- network module S
- 35.2°
- network height H

1 roof membrane
2 insulation
3 steel corrugated sheet
4 vertical distance piece
5 centre piece
6 interlocking flange
7 tapered wedge
8 purlin, tie beam
9 caging ring
10 locking pin
11 jaw fitting
12 horizontal tube
13 diagonal tube

⑭ **Space frame system**

⑮ **Joint (nodal point)**

MULTISTOREY STRUCTURES

The main choice is of in situ or prefabricated manufacture in the form of slab or frame construction. The selection of the materials is according to type of construction and local conditions.

As in all areas of building construction, the number of storeys is limited by the load-bearing capacity and weight of the building materials. Construction consists of a vertical, space enclosing supporting structure made from structural materials with or without tensile strength. Vertical and lateral stiffening is necessary through connected transverse walls and ceiling structures. Frame construction, as a non-space enclosing supporting structure, permits an open planform and choice of outer wall formation (cantilevered or suspended construction). A large number of floor levels is possible with various types of prefabrication.

Structural frame materials: reinforced concrete – which provides a choice of in situ and prefabricated, steel, aluminium and timber.

Types of structure: frames with main beams on hinged joints, or rigid frame units in longitudinal and/or transverse directions. *Construction systems:* columns and main beams (uprights and ties) determine the frame structure with rigid or articulated joints (connecting points of columns and beams). *Fully stiffened frames:* columns and beams with rigid joints are connected to rigid frame units. *Articulated frame units* one above the other: columns and beams are rigidly connected into rigid frame units and arranged one above the other with articulated joints. *Pure articulated frames:* nodal points are designed to articulate, with diagonal bracing structures (struts and trusses) and solid diaphragms (intermediate walls, gable walls, stairwell walls); mixed systems are possible. *Rigid joints* are easily achieved with in situ and prefabricated reinforced concrete; however, prefabricated components are usually designed with articulated joints and braced by rigid building cores.

Construction

Framed structures with continuous vertical supports → ① – ②; ties beams rest on visible brackets or conceal bearings. *Skeleton structures* with sectional vertical supports → ③ – ⑤; the height of the verticals can possibly extend over more than two storeys; the supporting brackets can be staggered from frame to frame; hinged supports with stiffened building cores. *Framed structures* with frame units → ⑥ – ⑧: H-shaped frame units, if required, with suspended ties at the centre connection (articulated storey height frames); U-shaped frame units, with separate ties in the centre, or with ties rigidly connected to frames (articulated storey height frames). *Flat head mushroom unit frame construction* → ⑨: columns with four-sided cantilevered slabs (slabs and columns rigidly connected together, articulated connection of the cantilevered slab edges). *Floor support structures* directly accept the vertical loads and transmits them horizontally onto the points of support; concrete floor slabs of solid, hollow, ribbed or coffered construction are very heavy if the span is large, and prove difficult in service installation; use of the lift-slab method is possible, suitable principally for rectangular planforms → ⑩ – ⑫.

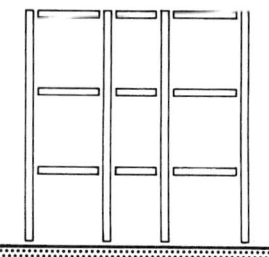

① **Continuous verticals, ties on concealed brackets**

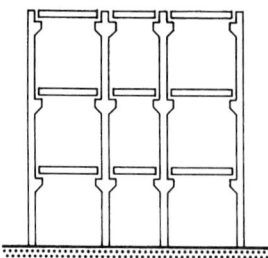

② **Continuous verticals, ties on brackets**

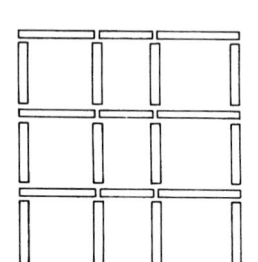

③ **Sectional verticals, individual vertical supports with ties**

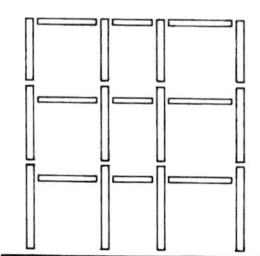

④ **Sectional verticals, ties on brackets**

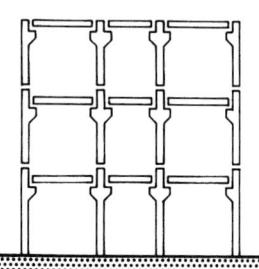

⑤ **Sectional verticals, ties on brackets**

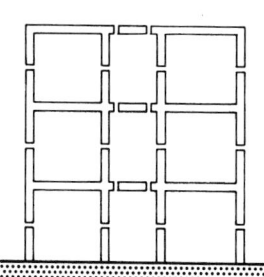

⑥ **H-shaped rigid frame units**

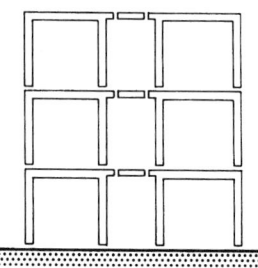

⑦ **U-shaped linked frame units**

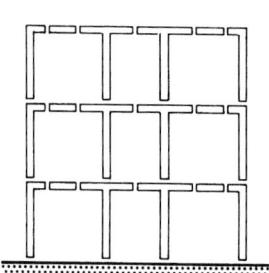

⑧ **T- and L-shaped vertical supports**

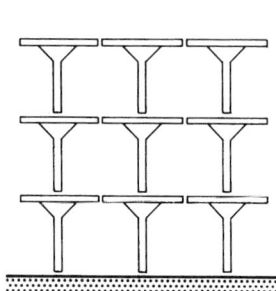

⑨ **Square headed mushroom frame unit**

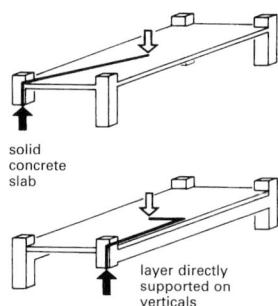

solid concrete slab

layer directly supported on verticals

⑩ **Floor support structure with a single load-bearing layer**

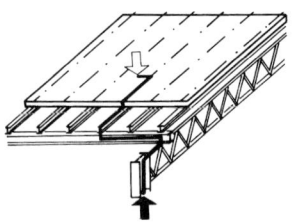

loads on the decking are transmitted via the beams to the points of vertical support

⑪ **Floor support structure with two layers**

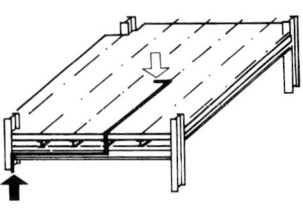

loads on the beams are taken to the main supports

⑫ **Floor support structure with three layers (for very large supported spans)**

SUSPENDED FLOORS

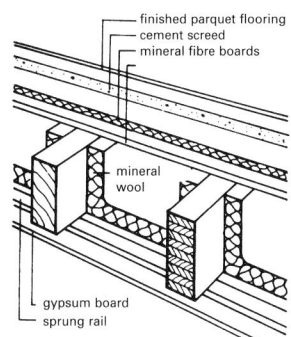

① **Timber joist/laminated beam floor construction with ceiling**

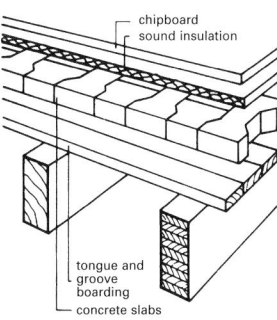

② **Timber joist/laminated beam floor construction with exposed floor underside**

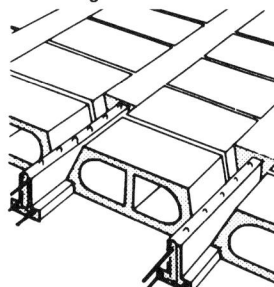

③ **Prefabricated reinforced concrete component floor with non-load-carrying filling blocks**

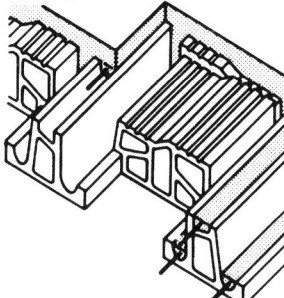

④ **Floor assembled from reinforced concrete ribs with cellular clay infill components**

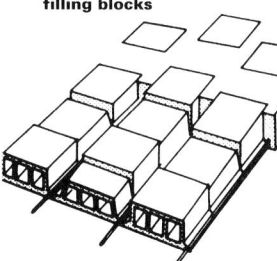

⑤ **In situ reinforced hollow pot concrete floor**

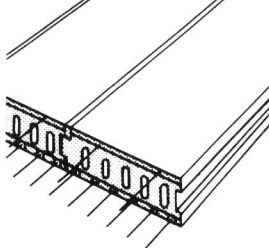

⑥ **Hollow core, pre-cast concrete flooring units with twisted, pre-stressed steel wires**

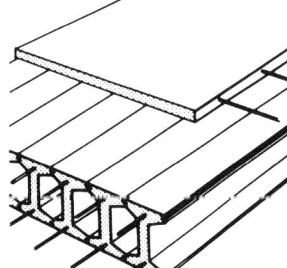

⑦ **Prefabricated reinforced concrete I-beam floor**

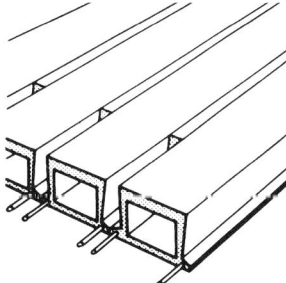

⑧ **Prefabricated reinforced concrete hollow beam floor**

⑨ **In situ reinforced concrete ribbed floor, rib separation ≤ 70 cm, rib width ≥ 5 cm**

⑩ **U-section reinforced concrete beams bolted to provide lateral stiffness**

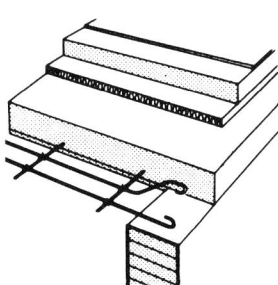

⑪ **Reinforced concrete slab floor, reinforced in one or two directions**

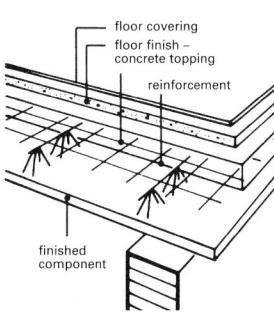

⑫ **Pre-cast concrete reinforcing shuttering for in situ floor**

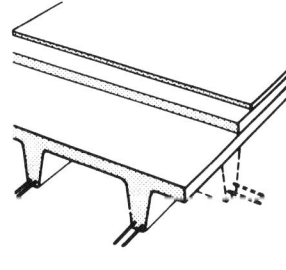

⑬ **Composite steel/concrete floor**

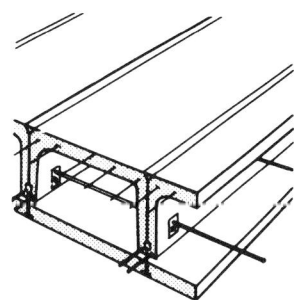

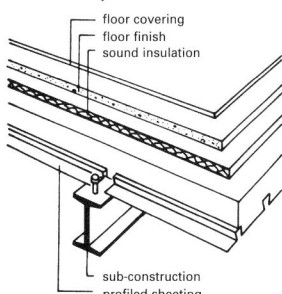

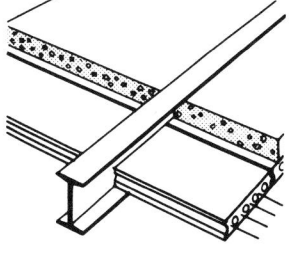

⑭ **Steel supported floor with pre-cast reinforced pumice concrete infill units**

Wooden beam floors with solid timber joist or laminated beam supports → ① – ② in open or closed construction. Sound insulation is increased by laying additional 60 mm thick concrete paving slabs → ②. Part or full assembled floors are laid dry, for immediate use → ③ – ⑧. *Ribbed floors:* space the axes of the beams as follows: 250–375–500–625–750–1000–1250 mm. *Heavy floors* use in situ concrete on shuttering → ⑪. They can support only when cured and add moisture to the construction. *Reinforced concrete slab floors* span both ways; the span ratio 1:1.5 should not be exceeded. Thickness ≥ 70 mm – economic to approx. 150 mm. Pre-cast concrete reinforcing shuttering, of large format finished concrete slabs of a least 40 mm thickness which have integrated exposed steel reinforcing mesh, are completed with in situ concrete to form the structural slab → ⑫. The floor thickness is from 100–260 mm. This method combines the special features of pre-finished with those of conventional construction. Maximum slab width is 2.20 m. When the joints have been smoothed, the ceiling is ready for painting; finishing plaster is unnecessary. *Hollow pot floors* → ⑤ also as prefabricated floor panels. Floor thickness is 190–215 mm max., with supported spans of 6.48 m. *Prefabricated floor panels* are 1.00 m wide; concrete covering layer is not required. *Pre-stressed concrete – hollow slab floor* → ⑥, consists of self-supporting pre-stressed units with longitudinal cavities, so they have a low unit weight. They are joined together using jointing mastic. Slab width: 150 and 180 mm, 1.20 m wide. The elements can be max. 7.35 m long. *Composite steel floors* → ⑬. Trapezoidal and composite floor profiles, made of galvanised steel strip sheet, form the basic element for shuttering and ceilings.

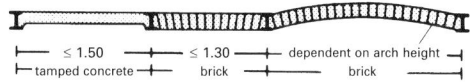

≤ 1.50 — tamped concrete

≤ 1.30 — brick

dependent on arch height — brick

tamped concrete with axis spacing ≤ 150 cm
brick with axis spacing ≤ 130 cm
cambered (Prussian cap): axis spacing depending on structural calculations ≈ 3 m
steel supported floor with infills → ⑭

FLOORING

Flooring has a decisive effect on the overall impression created by rooms, the quality of accommodation and maintenance costs.

Natural stone floors: Limestone, slate or sandstone slabs can be laid rough hewn, in natural state, or with some or all edges cut smooth or polished → ①–②. The surfaces of sawn tiles, limestone (marble), sandstone and all igneous rocks can be finished in any manner desired. They can be laid in a bed of mortar or glued with adhesive to the floor sub-layer.

Mosaic floors: Various coloured stones: (glass, ceramics or natural stone) are laid in cement mortar or applied with adhesives → ③–⑧.

Ceramic floor tiles: Stoneware, floor, mosaic and sintered tiles are shapes of coloured clay which are sintered in the burning process, so that they absorb hardly any water. They are, therefore, resistant to frost, have some resistance to acids and high resistance to mechanical wear, though they are not always oil resistant.

Parquet flooring is made from wood in the form of parquet strips, tiles, blocks or boards → ⑰–㉒. The upper layer of the finished parquet elements consists of oak or other parquet wood, in three different styles → ⑰–⑱.

Pine or spruce are used for floor boarding. Tongue and groove planks are made from Scandinavian pine/spruce, American red pine, pitch pine.

Wood block paving (end grained wood) is rectangular or round, and laid on concrete → ㉓–㉔.

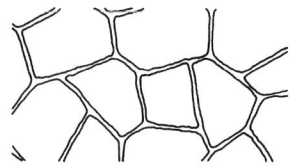

① Natural, irregularly laid stone floor

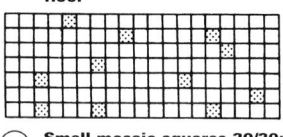

② Small mosaic squares 20/20; 33/33 mm

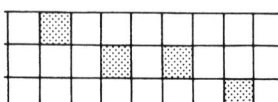

③ Square mosaic: 50/50; 69/69; 75/75 mm

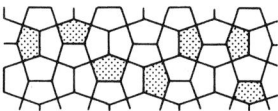

④ Small mosaic: five-sided 45/32 mm

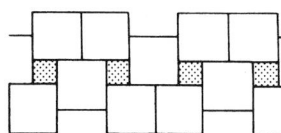

⑤ Square, with an inlay of smaller tiles

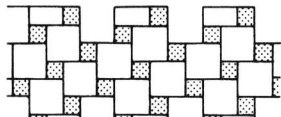

⑥ Square, with displaced inlay of smaller tiles

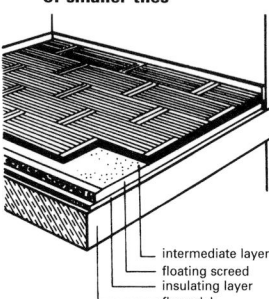

⑰ Finished parquet elements on floor screed

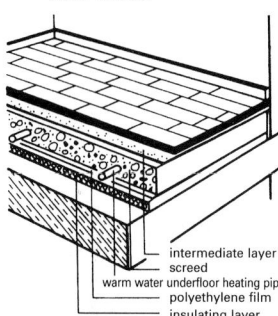

㉑ Finished parquet flooring elements on underfloor heating

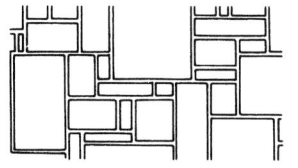

② Natural stone floor in Roman style

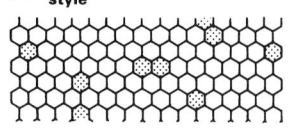

④ Small mosaic: hexagonal 25/39; 50/60 mm

⑥ Small mosaic: intersecting circle pattern 35/35; 48/48 mm

⑧ Small mosaic in Essen pattern: 57/80 mm

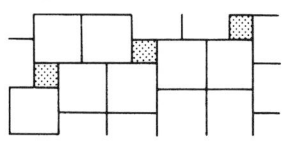

⑩ Square, with inlay 100/100; 50/50 mm

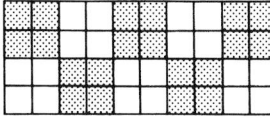

⑫ Square, incorporating doubled chessboard pattern

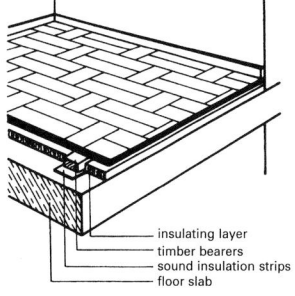

⑱ Finished parquet elements on timber battens

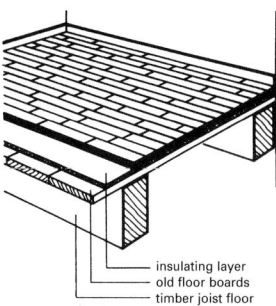

㉒ Finished parquet flooring elements on old wooden floor

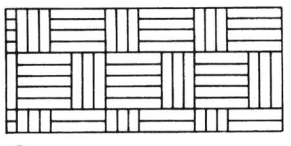

⑬ Open basket

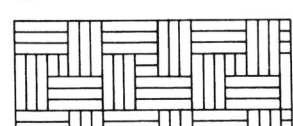

⑮ Open basket

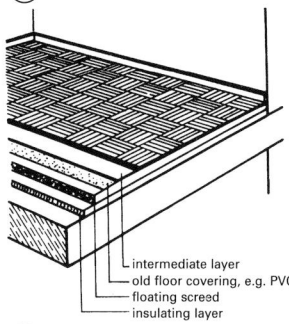

⑲ Finished parquet elements on old floor covering

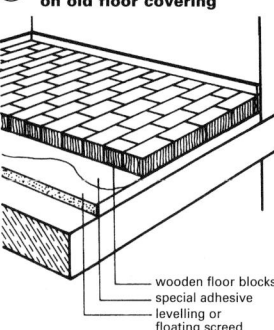

㉓ Wooden floor blocks, glued down, with surface treatment (living area)

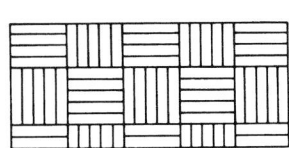

⑭ Square basket

⑯ Herring bone pattern

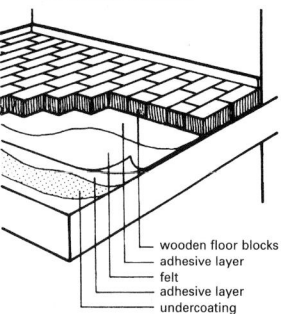

㉔ Wooden floor blocks, glued down on even, smoothed concrete underlayer (specialised finish)

94

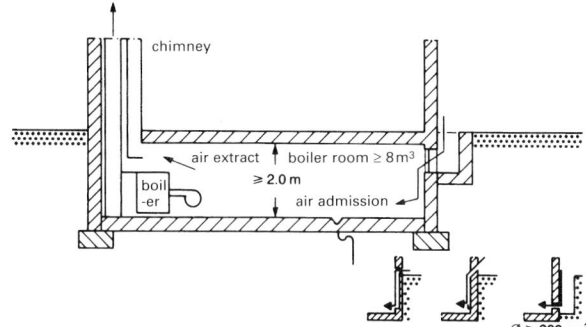

130 W/m²	385 m²	2700 m²
90 W/m²	550 m²	3900 m²
50 W/m²	1000 m²	7000 m²

① **Central heating boilers with a heat output > than 50 kW require individual boiler rooms**

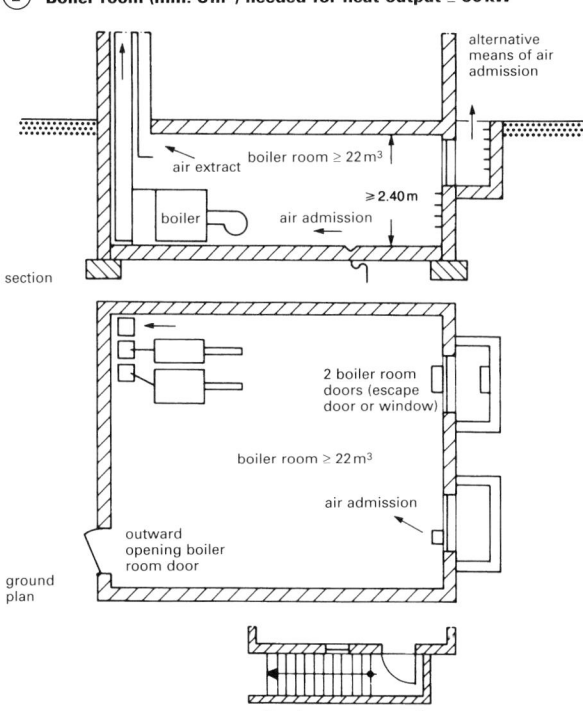

② **Boiler room (min. 8 m³) needed for heat output ≥ 50 kW**

③ **Boiler room with 2 doors (min. 22 m³) needed for heat output > 350 kW**

Heating systems are distinguished by the type of energy source and type of heating surface.

Oil firing: nowadays, light. *Advantages:* low fuel costs (relative to gas, approx. 10–25%); not dependent on public supply networks fuel oil is the most widespread source of heating energy; easy to regulate. *Disadvantages:* high costs of storage and tank facilities; in rented housing, space required for oil storage reduces rent revenue; where water protection measures apply or there is a danger of flooding, this form of heating is only possible if strict regulations are observed; fuel paid for prior to use; high environmental cost.

Gas firing: natural gas is increasingly being used for heating purposes. *Advantages:* no storage costs; minimal maintenance costs; payment made after usage; can be used in areas where water protection regulations apply; easy to regulate; high annual efficiency; may be used for individual flats or rooms; minimal environmental effects. *Disadvantages:* dependent on supply networks; higher energy costs; concern about gas explosions; when converting from oil to gas; chimney modifications are required.

Solid fuels such as coal (anthracite), lignite or wood, are rarely used to heat buildings. District heating stations are the exception, since this type of heating is only economical above a certain level of power output. Also, depending on the type of fuel used, large quantities of environmentally damaging substances are emitted, so that stringent requirements are laid down for the use of these fuels (protection of the environment). *Advantages:* not dependent on energy imports; low fuel costs. *Disadvantages:* high operating costs; large storage space necessary; high emission of environmentally unfriendly substances; poor controllability.

Regenerative forms of energy include solar radiation, wind power, water power, biomass (plants) and refuse (biogas). Since amortisation of the installation costs is not achieved within the lifetime of the plant required, the demand for this type of energy is correspondingly low.

Remote heating systems are indirect forms of energy supply, as opposed to the primary forms of energy discussed above. Heat is generated in district heating stations or power stations by a combined heat/power system. *Advantages:* boiler room and chimney not required; no storage costs; energy is paid for after consumption; can be used where water protection regulations apply; environmentally friendly association of power/energy coupling. *Disadvantages:* high energy costs; dependency on supply network; if the heating source is changed, a chimney must be fitted.

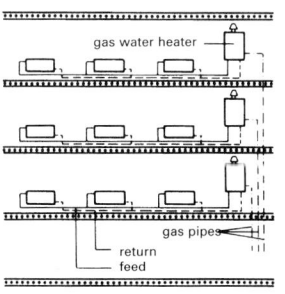

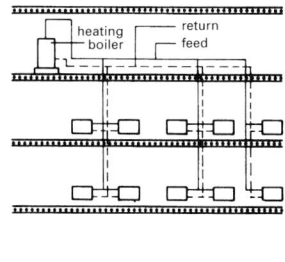

④ **Twin-pipe system with distribution from below and vertical rising branches**

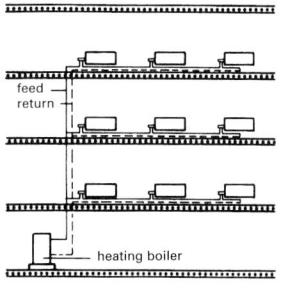

⑤ **Twin-pipe system with distribution from above and vertical branches**

⑥ **Single-pipe system with special valves and horizontal distribution**

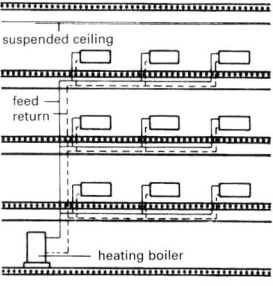

⑦ **Twin-pipe system with horizontal distribution (standard construction for office buildings)**

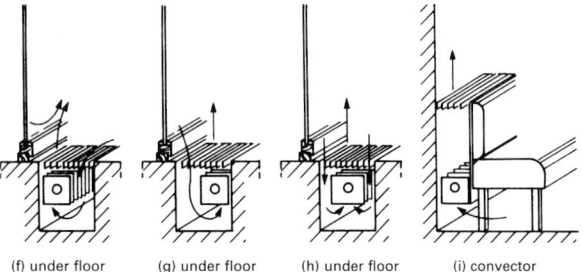

(a) under window   (b) in front of smooth wall   (c) free standing (for heating of 2 rooms)   (d) built into wall   (e) built into wall

(f) under floor convector with room air intake   (g) under floor convector with cold air intake   (h) under floor convector with intake on both sides   (i) convector behind bench seat

(1) Various installation options for convectors

Electrical heating: Apart from night storage heating, the continuous heating of rooms by electrical current is only possible in special cases, due to the high costs of electricity. Electrical heating of rooms in temporary use may be advantageous, e.g. garages, gate keepers' lodges and churches. *Main advantages*: short heating-up period; clean operation; no fuel storage; constant availability; low initial costs.

Night storage heating is used for electrical floor heating, electrical storage heaters or for electrically heated boilers. Off-peak electricity is used to run the heaters. For electrical floor heating, the floor screed is heated overnight to provide heat during the day to the room air. Correspondingly, for electrical storage heaters and electrically heated boilers, the energy storage elements are heated during the off-peak period. However, by contrast to the floor heating system, the latter two devices can be regulated. *Advantages*: neither a boiler room nor chimney is required; no gases are generated; minimal space requirement; low servicing costs; no need to store fuel.

Convectors: Heat is not transferred by radiation, but by direct transmission to the air molecules. For this reason, convectors can be covered or built in, without reducing the heat output. *Disadvantages*: strong movement of air and the dust swirling effect; performance of convector depends on the height of the duct above the heated body; cross-sections of air flowing into and away from the convector must be of sufficient size. → ① For under-floor convectors → ① f – ① h, the same prerequisites apply as for above-floor convectors. The disposition of the under-floor convectors depends on the proportion of heating requirement for the windows as a fraction of the total heating requirement of the room. Arrangement → ① f should be adopted if this proportion is greater than 70%; arrangement → ① h for 20–70%; if the proportion is less than 20%, then arrangement → ① g is favoured. Convectors without fans are not suitable for low-temperature heating, since their output depends on the throughput of air and, hence, on the temperature difference between the heated body and the room. The performance of convectors with too low a duct height (e.g. floor convectors) can be increased by the incorporation of a blower. Blower convectors are of limited use in living-room areas, due to the build-up of noise. Heaters can be covered in various ways. Losses in efficiency can be considerable, and attention should be paid to adequate cleaning. For metal cladding, the radiative heat contribution is almost entirely given to the room air. For material coverings with a lower thermal conductivity, the radiative heat is damped considerably. → ① p.98 A representation is shown of the movement of air within a heated room. The air is heated by the heater, flows to the window and then to the ceiling and is cooled on the external and internal walls. The cooled air flows over the floor and back to the heater. → ② p.98 A different situation arises if the heater is on a wall which is away from the window: air cools on the window, then flows cold over the floor to the heater, where it is heated up.

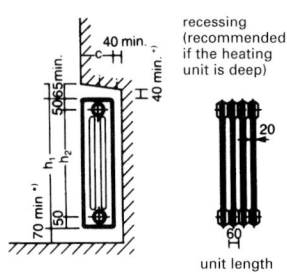

recessing (recommended if the heating unit is deep)

height h1 (mm)	distance between connections h2 (mm)	depth c (mm)	surface area per element (m²)
280	200	250	0.185
430	350	70	0.09
		110	0.128
		160	0.185
		220	0.255
580	500	70	0.12
		110	0.18
		160	0.252
		220	0.345
680	600	160	0.306
980	900	70	0.205
		160	0.41
		220	0.58

unit length

(2) Dimensions of cast radiators

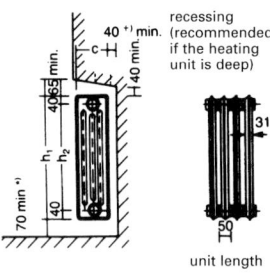

recessing (recommended if the heating unit is deep)

height h1 (mm)	distance between connections h2 (mm)	depth c (mm)	surface area per element (m²)
300	200	250	0.16
450	350	160	0.155
		220	0.21
600	500	110	0.14
		160	0.205
		220	0.285
1000	900	110	0.24
		160	0.345
		220	0.48

unit length

(3) Dimensions of steel radiators

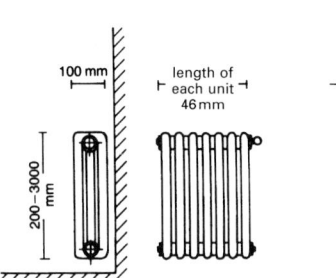

length of each unit 46mm

(4) Tube radiator (3 tubes)

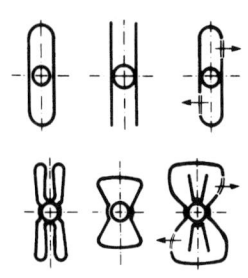

(5) Various rib shapes for the down tubes in tube radiators

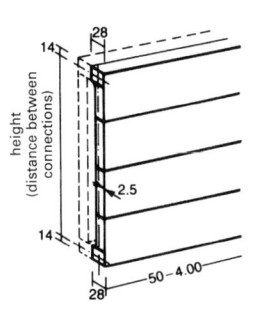

height (distance between connections)

(6) Section through a flat panel radiator

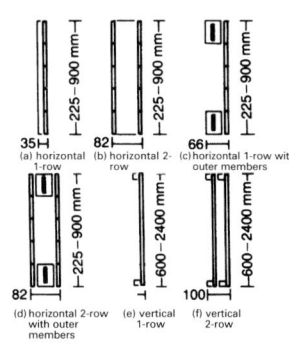

(a) horizontal 1-row   (b) horizontal 2-row   (c) horizontal 1-row with outer members

(d) horizontal 2-row with outer members   (e) vertical 1-row   (f) vertical 2-row

(7) Summary of different panel radiators

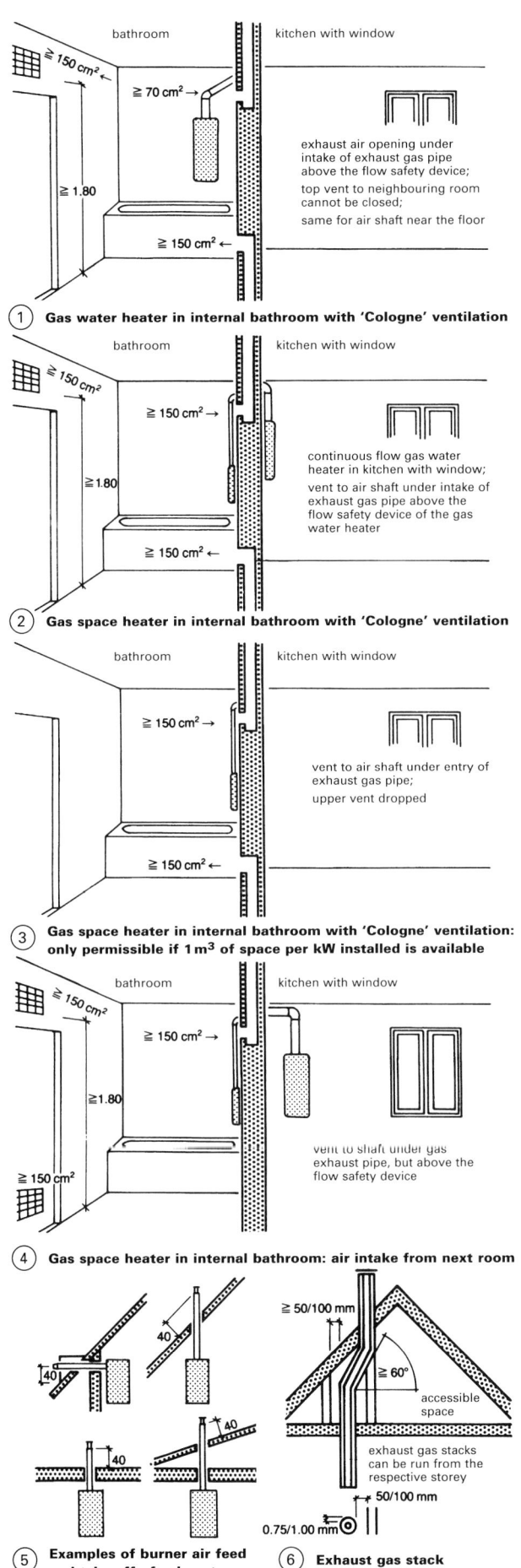

(1) **Gas water heater in internal bathroom with 'Cologne' ventilation**

exhaust air opening under intake of exhaust gas pipe above the flow safety device;
top vent to neighbouring room cannot be closed;
same for air shaft near the floor

(2) **Gas space heater in internal bathroom with 'Cologne' ventilation**

continuous flow gas water heater in kitchen with window;
vent to air shaft under intake of exhaust gas pipe above the flow safety device of the gas water heater

(3) **Gas space heater in internal bathroom with 'Cologne' ventilation: only permissible if 1 m³ of space per kW installed is available**

vent to air shaft under entry of exhaust gas pipe;
upper vent dropped

(4) **Gas space heater in internal bathroom: air intake from next room**

vent to shaft under gas exhaust pipe, but above the flow safety device

(5) **Examples of burner air feed and take-off of exhaust gas to above roof height**

(6) **Exhaust gas stack**

exhaust gas stacks can be run from the respective storey

(7) **Connections to the exhaust gas stack**

efficient stack height ≥4m otherwise special stack necessary

offset of the junctions

building materials v. distance of combustible building blocks

exhaust pipe through fitted cupboard

Gas heating systems

Regulations and legislation (UK): the provision of gas supply into a building in England, Wales and Scotland is controlled by the Gas Safety (Installation and Use) Regulations, 1998, which revoke and replace the 1994 and 1996 (amendment) regulations. They make provision for the installation and use of gas fittings for the purpose of protecting the public from the dangers arising from the distribution, supply or use of gas.

One of the major tasks of the architect is to make sure that the design provisions, such as locations of meters and pipe routes, do as much as possible to make it easy for the installer to comply with the regulations.

Gas fired appliances must be of an approved type and can only be installed in those spaces where no danger can arise from position, size, or construction quality of the surrounding building. Distances between components made of combustible materials and external heated parts of a gas appliance, or from any radiation protection fitted in between, must be sufficient to exclude any possibility of fire (i.e. ≥5 cm). In addition, spaces between components made of combustible materials and other external heated parts, as well as between radiation protection and gas appliances or radiation protection, must not be enclosed in such a way that a dangerous build-up of heat can occur. Heaters with an enclosed combustion chamber fitted against external walls and housed in a box-like enclosure must be vented to the room, with bottom and top vents each having ≥600 cm² free cross-section. Air vents must be arranged in accordance with details and drawings of the appliance manufacturer. The casing must have a clear space of ≥10 cm in front and at the side of the heater cladding. Heaters not mounted on external walls must be fitted as close as possible to the chimney stack.

The minimum size and ventilation of rooms containing heating appliances is determined by the output or sum of outputs of the heating appliances. For ventilated enclosed internal areas, the volume must be calculated from the internal finished measurements (i.e. measured to finished surfaces and apertures).

All gas appliances, apart from portable units and small water heaters, must be fitted with a flue. Flues promote air circulation and help remove the bulk of gas in case the appliance is left with the gas unlit. Cookers should be fitted with cowls and vents which should considerably help to remove fumes and reduce condensation on walls. Bathrooms equipped with gas heaters must be fitted with adequate ventilation and a flue for the heater. Flues for water heaters must include a baffle or draught diverter to prevent down-draughts.

HEATING AND VENTILATION

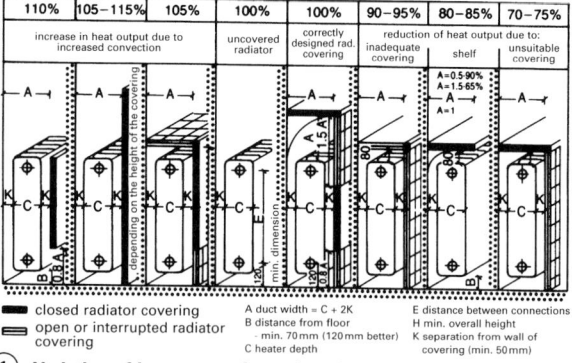

110%	105–115%	105%	100%	100%	90–95%	80–85%	70–75%
increase in heat output due to increased convection			uncovered radiator	correctly designed rad. covering	reduction of heat output due to: inadequate covering	shelf	unsuitable covering

■ closed radiator covering
▨ open or interrupted radiator covering

A duct width = C + 2K
B distance from floor - min. 70 mm (120 mm better)
C heater depth

E distance between connections
H min. overall height
K separation from wall of covering (min. 50 mm)

(1) **Variation of heat output for various heater/covering combinations**

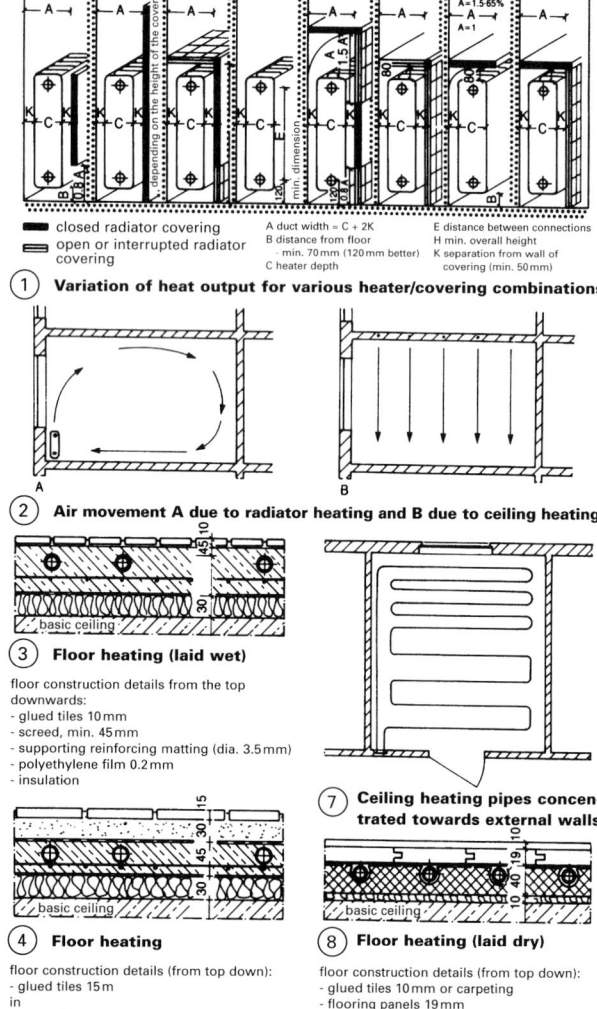

(2) **Air movement A due to radiator heating and B due to ceiling heating**

(3) **Floor heating (laid wet)**

floor construction details from the top downwards:
- glued tiles 10 mm
- screed, min. 45 mm
- supporting reinforcing matting (dia. 3.5 mm)
- polyethylene film 0.2 mm
- insulation

(7) **Ceiling heating pipes concentrated towards external walls**

(4) **Floor heating**

floor construction details (from top down):
- glued tiles 15 m
in
- mortar bed 30 mm
- slip membrane 0.3 mm
- floor covering 45 mm
- supporting mat for heating tubes
- polyethylene film 0.2 mm
- insulation

(8) **Floor heating (laid dry)**

floor construction details (from top down):
- glued tiles 10 mm or carpeting
- flooring panels 19 mm
- polyethylene film 0.2 mm
- aluminium conducting fins
- polystyrene layer with grooves for heating tubes 40 mm
- mineral fibre matting 13/10 for footfall insulation, if required

(5) **Floor heating (heat module)**

floor construction details (from top down):
- floor finish with supporting layer (depth variable)
- polyethylene film
- heat module with insulating shell

(6) **Ceiling heating using aluminium panels**

(10) **Fan heater**

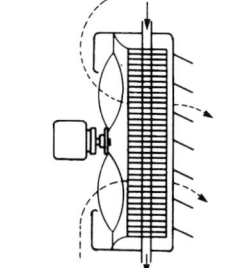

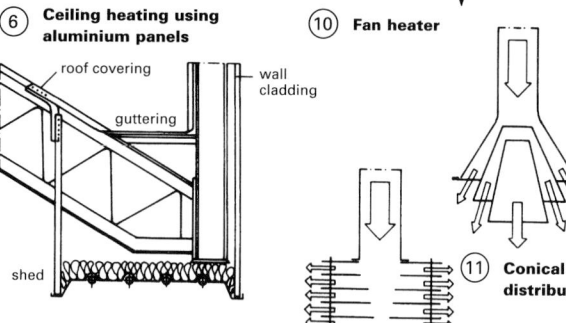

(9) **Sunstrip**

roof covering
wall cladding
guttering
shed

(11) **Conical distributor**

(12) **Air distribution fins**

For uniform heating of the room air, convector heaters can be replaced by a floor heating system. Problems arise only where large window areas are involved, but this can be overcome by the installation of additional heating – such as floor convectors.

In general, surface heating includes large areas of surface surrounding a room and involves relatively low temperatures. Types of surface heating include floor heating, ceiling heating and wall heating. With floor heating, the heat from the floor surface is not only imparted to the room air, but also to the walls and ceiling. Heat transfer to the air occurs by convection, i. e. by air movement over the floor surface. The heat given to the walls and ceiling takes place due to radiation. The heat output can vary between 70 and 110 W/m², depending on the floor finish and system employed. Almost any usual type of floor finish can be used – ceramics, wood or textiles. However, the diathermic resistance should not exceed 0.15 m²k/W.

House dust allergies can be a problem in heated rooms. Previously, precautions against house dust or dust mite allergy paid no attention to the effects of heating units. Heaters cause swirling of house dust containing allergens, which can then rapidly come into contact with the mucous membranes. In addition to this, there are insoluble difficulties in cleaning heaters which have convection fins. It is therefore advantageous if heaters are designed to embody the smallest possible number of convection elements and to have straightforward cleaning procedures. These requirements are fulfilled by single-layer panels without convection fins and by radiators of unit construction.

Storage of heating oil: The quantity of heating oil stored should be sufficient for a minimum of 3 months and a maximum of one heating period. A rough estimate of the annual requirement for heating fuel is 6–10 l/m³ of room volume to be heated. A maximum volume of 5 m³ may be stored in a boiler house. The container must be within a storage tank capable of accepting the total quantity. Storage containers in the ground must be protected from leakage, e.g. through the use of double-walled tanks, or plastic inner shells. Maximum capacities and additional safety measures are prescribed for areas where water protection regulations are in force. Within buildings, either plastic battery tanks with a capacity per tank of 500–2000 litres may be installed, or steel tanks which are welded together in situ, whose capacities may be freely chosen. The tank room must be accessible.

The tanks must be inspected for oil-tightness at regular intervals. In the event of an emergency, the tank room must be able to retain the full amount of oil. Tank facilities must have filling and ventilation pipe lines. Additionally, overfilling prevention must be incorporated and, depending on the type of storage, a leak warning system may be prescribed (e.g. in the case of underground tanks).

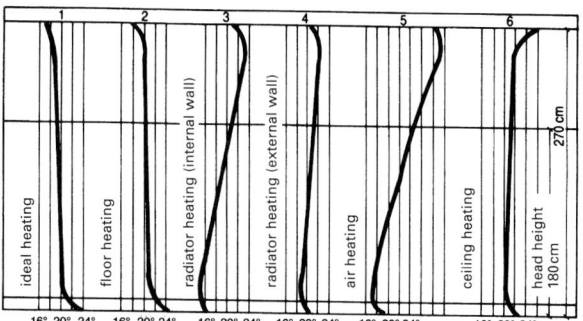

(13) **Room temperature curves for physiological evaluation of a heating system**

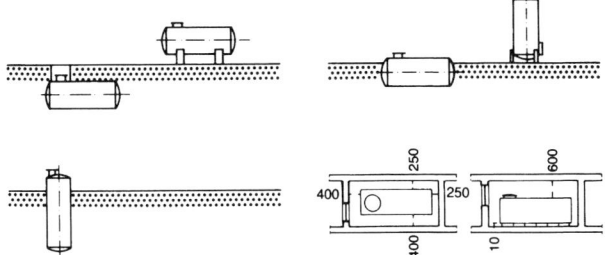

(1) **Alternative installations of standard heating oil storage tanks**

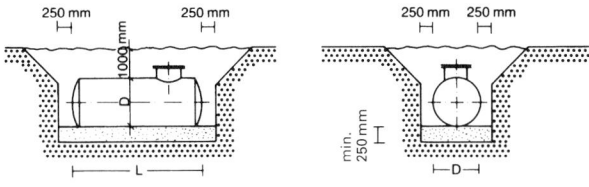

(2) **Underground installation of heating oil storage tanks**

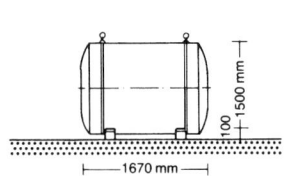

(3) **Nylon unit containers (polyamide) – side view**

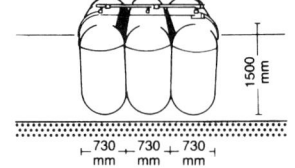
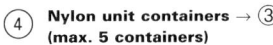

(4) **Nylon unit containers → (3) (max. 5 containers)**

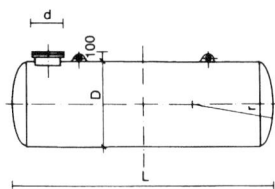

(5) **Storage tank for heating oil (side view)**

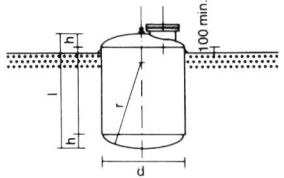
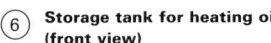

(6) **Storage tank for heating oil (front view)**

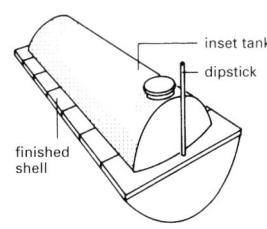

(7) **Inset tank**

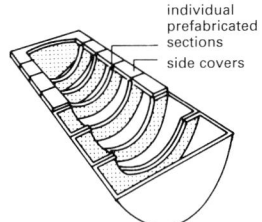

(8) **Prefabricated protective concrete hull for oil tank**

HEATING

The floor screed for floor heating systems must satisfy local regulations. The thickness of the screed depends on the type of covering used, its preparation and the anticipated loading. A minimum covering over the heating pipes of 45 mm is prescribed when using cement floor screed and heating pipes which are directly above the thermal insulation. If there is no finish over the basic floor, then a minimum total depth of 75 mm is required. The floor screed expands during use, and a temperature difference arises between the top and bottom surfaces of the screed.

Due to the differential expansion, tensile stresses occur in the upper region of the layer. In the case of ceramic floor coverings, this can only be countered by top reinforcement. On carpeted floors or parquet floors, the reinforcement can be avoided, since the temperature drop between the upper and lower surfaces of the floor covering is less than in the case of a ceramic finish. Special requirements are contained in the thermal insulation regulations with respect to the limitation of heat transfer from surface heating, irrespective of the choice of type of insulation method: 'In surface heating, the heat transfer coefficient of the component layer between the hot surface and the external air, the ground, or building section having an essentially lower internal temperature, must not exceed a value of 0.45 W/m^2'.

The maximum permissible floor surface temperature for a permanently occupied area is 29°C. For the boundary zone it is 35°C, where the boundary zone is not to be wider than 1 m. For bathrooms, the maximum permissible floor temperature is 9°C above normal room temperature.

Under normal conditions, floor heating is possible, since the heating requirement seldom lies above 90 W/m^2. In only a few exceptions (e.g. when there are large window areas, or when the room has more than two external walls) is there a greater heating requirement, and then additional static heating surfaces or air heating must be installed in addition to the floor heating.

nom. contents V in litres (dm³)	max. dimensions (mm) length	depth	weight incl. accessories (kg)
1000 (1100)	1100 (1100)	720	≈ 30–50 kg
1500 (1600)	1650 (1720)	720	≈ 40–60 kg

(9) **Dimensions of plastic battery tanks (battery containers)**

min. contents V (m³)	min. dimensions (mm) external diameter d₁	length l	sheet thickness 1 wall	sheet thickness 2 walls	filler cap diameter	weight (kg) 1,1 1 wall	1,2 A/C	B
1	1000	1510	5	3	–	265	–	–
3	1250	2740	5	3	–	325	–	–
5	1600	2820	5	3	500	700	–	–
7	1600	3740	5	3	500	885	930	980
10	1600	5350	5	3	500	1200	1250	1300
16	1600	8570	5	3	500	1800	1850	1900
20	2000	6969	6	3	600	2300	2400	2450
25	2000	8540	6	3	600	2750	2850	2900
30	2000	10120	6	3	600	3300	3450	3450
40	2500	8800	7	4(5)	600	4200	4400	4450
50	2500	10800	7	4	600	5100	5300	5350
60	2500	12800	7	4	600	6100	6300	6350

min. contents V (m³)	external diameter d₁	length l	sheet thickness 1 wall	sheet thickness 2 walls	filler cap diameter	weight (kg) 1,3 A	B	2,1	2,2B
1.7	1250	1590	5	–	500	–	–	–	390
2.8	1600	1670	5	–	500	–	–	–	390
3.8	1600	2130	5	–	500	–	–	–	600
5	1600	2820	5	3	500	700	745	–	740
6	2000	2220	5	–	500	–	–	–	930
7	1600	3740	5	3	500	885	930	935	–
10	1600	5350	5	3	500	1250	1250	1250	–
16	1600	8570	5	3	500	1800	1950	1850	–
20	2000	6960	6	3	600	2300	2350	2350	–
25	2000	8540	6	3	600	2750	2800	2800	–
30	2000	10120	6	3	600	3300	3350	–	–
	2500	6665	7	–	600	–	–	3350	–
40	2500	8800	7	4	600	4200	4250	4250	–
50	2500	10800	7	4	600	5100	5150	–	–
	2900	8400	9	–	600	–	–	6150	–
60	2500	12800	7	4	600	6100	6150	–	–
	2900	9585	9	–	600	–	–	6900	–

(10) **Dimensions of cylindrical oil tanks (containers)**

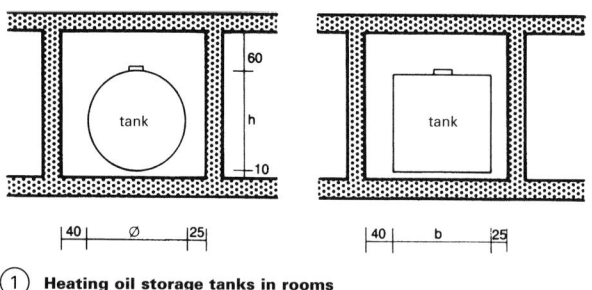

① **Heating oil storage tanks in rooms**

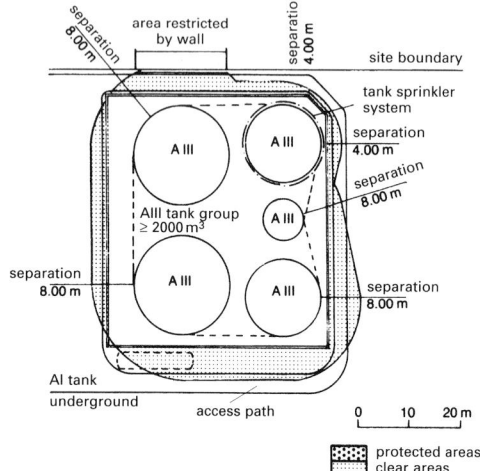

② **Small tank store**

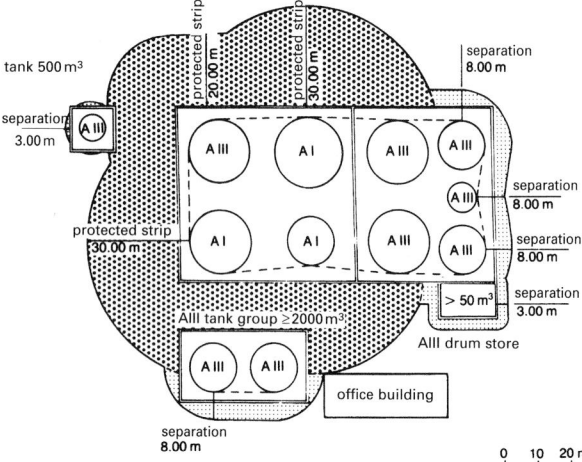

③ **Large tank store**

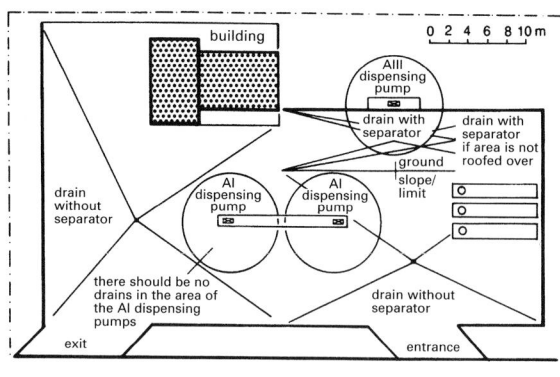

④ **Tank facility**

HEATING: OIL STORAGE TANKS

→ pp. 98–9

The fuel containment enclosures must be designed so that, if fluid escapes from a storage device, it is prevented from spreading beyond the enclosure area. The enclosures must be able to safely contain at least one-tenth of the volume of all the tanks it contains, and at least the full volume of the largest tank.

Tanks in rooms: containment enclosures are required if the storage volume is ≥ 450 l, unless the storage tanks are of steel with a double wall. Tanks can have a capacity of up to 100000 l, with leakage indicator devices, or manufactured from glass fibre reinforced plastics of an approved type of construction, or they can be metal tanks with plastic inner linings of an approved form of construction. Containment enclosures must be constructed from non-flammable fire-resistant materials of adequate strength, leakproof and stability, and must not contain any outlets. The tanks must have access on at least two sides with a minimum clearance of 400 mm from the wall, or 250 mm in other cases, and at least 100 mm from the floor and 600 mm from the ceiling → ①.

Classifications:

A	Flash point	< 100°C
AI	Flash point	< 21°C
AII	Flash point	21–55°C
AIII	Flash point	55–100°C
B	Flash point	< 21°C with water solubility at 15°C

Outside tanks, above ground: containment enclosures are required for capacity ≥ 1000 l. Otherwise, conditions are as for tanks in rooms. Storage areas can be ramparts. For tanks > 100 m³ capacity, clearance to the ramparts, walls or ringed enclosures must be at least 1.5 m. For vertical cylindrical tanks of capacity < 2000 m³ in square or rectangular catchment areas, clearance may be reduced to 1 m. Arrangements must be made for the removal of water and these must be capable of closure. If water can discharge by itself, then separators must be built in. Above ground facilities require protected access. A distance of at least 3 m from neighbouring facilities is required if there is a storage capacity > 500 m³ and correspondingly more as capacity increases, to a clearance of 8 m for a storage capacity of 2000 m³. Access routes are required for fire-fighting appliances and equipment → ② – ③.

Underground tanks: > 0.4 m clearance of tanks from boundaries; > 1 m from buildings. Underground anchorage of the tanks is required to prevent movement of empty tanks in the presence of ground water or flooding. Backfilling is required to a depth of 0.3–1 m above the tanks. Also, 600 mm diameter access openings into the tanks are needed, serviced by a watertight shaft with a clear width of at least 1 m, and 0.2 m wider than the tank access opening lid. The shaft cover must be able to withstand a test proof loading of 100 kN where vehicular access is to take place. Filling points are subject to approval for combustible fluids in hazard classes AI, AII or B. They must be immediately accessible, with protected access. The ground surface must be impermeable and constructed of bitumen, concrete or paving with sealed joints. Drainage outlets with separators, overfilling protection, and emptying and washing facilities for tanker vehicles are required.

Tankage facilities for the fuelling of all vehicles with combustible fluids in hazard classes AIII (e.g. heating oil and diesel fuel) must not be stored together with those in hazard classes AI, AII or B. Neither must the effective regions of separators and operating surfaces of such storage areas overlap → ④.

Requirements for all tanks: Ventilation and venting facilities must be sited at least 500 mm above the access cap, or above ground level in the case of underground tanks, and be protected from the ingress of rain water. Devices must be provided to determine the filling levels in the tanks. Access openings must have a clearance diameter of at least 600 mm and visual inspection openings, 120 mm diameter. Protection must be provided against lightning and electrostatic discharge. Additional provisions cover flame spread resistance, internal and external corrosion, and fire extinguishers of the appropriate type. Tanks for diesel fuel or heating oil EL with a capacity over 1000 l, must have fill meters and overfill protection.

SOLAR ARCHITECTURE

Components

Essentially, economic considerations led architects and building developers to seek alternatives to the conventional fossil fuel sources of energy. Today, equal emphasis is placed on the ecological necessity for change. By means of energy conscious construction, the energy requirements of living accommodation can be reduced by around 50% in comparison to older buildings.

Energy balance of buildings

Solar energy is available free of charge to every building. Unfortunately, in many climatic areas, solar radiation is very low, so that other forms of energy must be used for room heating, hot water, lighting and for the operation of electrical appliances.

The greatest energy losses from a building arise due to the conduction of heat through windows, walls, ceilings and roofs.

Considerations of energy conscious construction

There are three fundamental points which lead to a considerable reduction in the energy requirement of a domestic building:

(1) Reduction of heat losses
(2) Increase in energy saving through the use of solar radiation
(3) Conscious efforts by users to improve the energy balance

The choice of building location itself can reduce the heat losses from a building. Within a small area in a region, conditions will vary; e.g. wind and temperature conditions vary with the altitude of a building site.

Relatively favourable microclimatic conditions result on south-facing slopes when the area of ground is situated on the upper third of the slope but away from the crest of the hill.

The shape of the building plays an important role in terms of energy conscious construction. The outer surface of the building is in direct contact with the external climate and gives up valuable energy to the outside air. The design of the building should ensure that the smallest possible external surface is presented to the outside air in relation to the volume of the building. The shape to be aimed for is a cube, although a hemisphere in the ideal case. However, this ideal assumption applies only to a detached house.

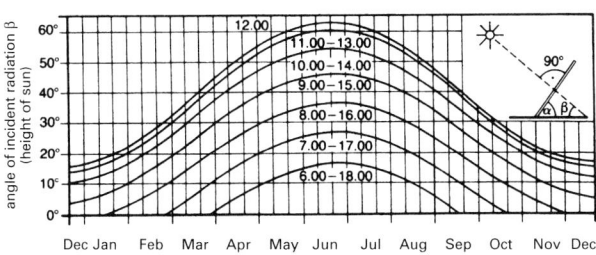

(1) Average daily totals of solar radiation (MJ/m²)

(2) Incident radiation angle β (height of sun at the geographical latitude 50°N at various times, over the course of a year)

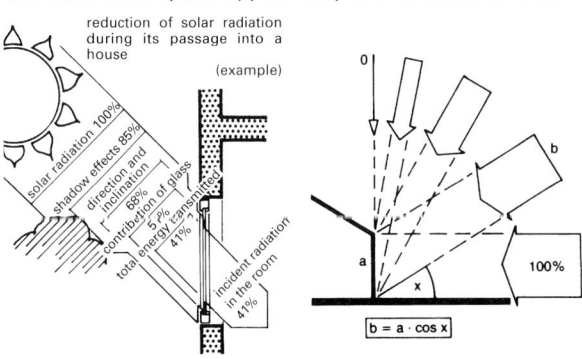

(3) To keep the reduction in radiation as small as possible, each individual influencing factor should be carefully considered

(4) The dependency of the level of incident radiation on a surface on the angle of incidence

$$b = a \cdot \cos x$$

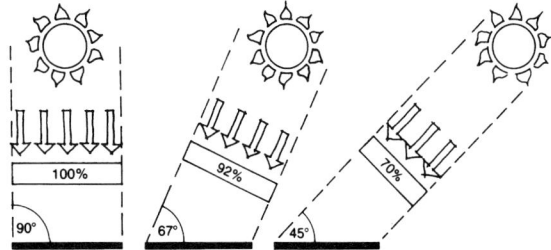

(5) Both effects act simultaneously in two dimensions – height and azimuth angle variation

101

SOLAR ARCHITECTURE

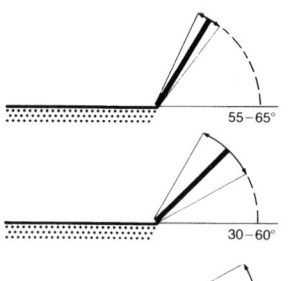

South-facing surfaces inclined at an angle of 55–65° provide optimum utilisation of solar energy during the cold winter months

55–65°

South-facing surfaces inclined at 30–60° are suited to good solar energy usage during the transition periods (these periods of the year are decisive for solar house optimisation)

30–60°

South-facing surfaces inclined at 0–30° are typical for summer use (e.g. for solar panels for domestic water heating), this being the optimum range for the collection of diffuse radiation

0–30°

(1) **Solar energy usage as a function of the inclination**

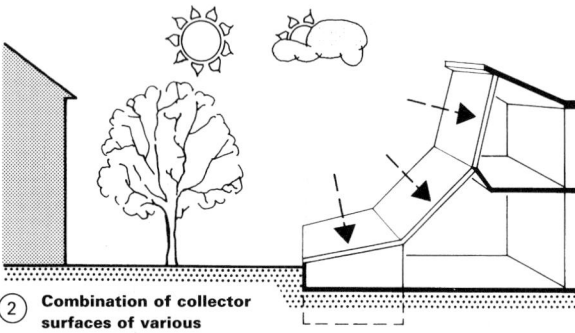

(2) **Combination of collector surfaces of various inclinations**

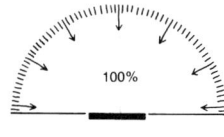 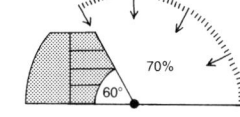

100%   70%   60%

50%   90%   40%   105%

(3) **Flat horizontal and inclined surfaces are well suited for the collection of diffuse radiation**

(4) **Vertical windows receive only up to 50% of the diffuse radiation when the sky is clouded**

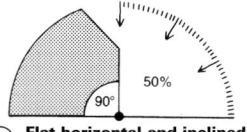 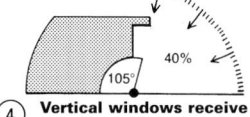

(5) **Cross-section of a house planned only for the gain of direct radiation (cloudless sky)**

(6) **Cross-section of a house planned only for the receipt of diffuse radiation (cloudy sky)**

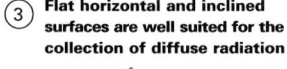

100% ± 0°   125% – 3°   83% – 2°   110% – 1°

(7) **Heat losses and temperature differences as a function of position on the terrain**

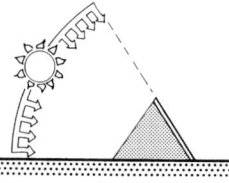 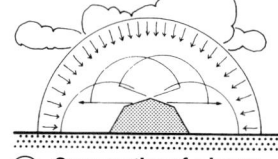

81%   92%   98%   105%
hemisphere   cylinder   pyramid   cube

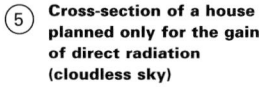 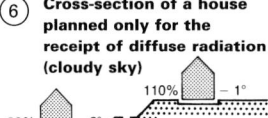

100%   117%   167%   142%

half cube with 4 compact units   row of units   separated units   stacked units

(8) **Surface optimisation – the heat loss reduces in proportion to the reduction in surface area**

Organisation of the ground plan

In the passive utilisation of solar energy, the heat is utilised through direct incident radiation and heat storage in specific structural components such as walls and floors.

Because of the conditions under which solar energy is used passively, the arrangement of the ground plan necessarily follows a particular logical layout. The continuously used living and sleeping accommodation should be south-facing and provided with large window areas. It is useful to provide glazed structures in these living and sleeping areas. There are three important reasons for this:

(1) Extension of the living area
(2) Gain in solar energy
(3) Provision of a thermal buffer zone

The little-used low-temperature unheated rooms, with low natural light requirements should be north-facing. They act as a buffer zone between the warm living area and the cold outside climate.

Use of solar energy

In the use of solar energy, a distinction is drawn between the active and passive use of solar energy.

The active use of solar energy necessitates the application of equipment such as solar collectors, pipework, collector vessels circulation pumps for the transfer of the solar energy. This system entails large investment and maintenance costs which must be recovered solely by saving in the cost of energy. As a result, such systems cannot be operated economically in single family houses.

The passive use of solar energy necessitates the use of specific structural components as heat stores, such as walls, ceilings and glazed units. The efficiency of this system depends on specific factors:

(1) Climatic conditions – mean monthly temperature, solar geometry and incident solar radiation, hours of sunshine and level of incident energy radiation
(2) Method of using the solar energy – indirect usage, direct usage
(3) Choice of materials – absorption capability of the surface and heat storage capability of the materials

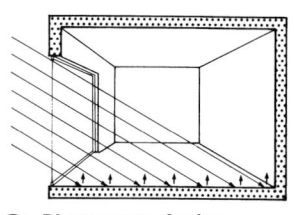 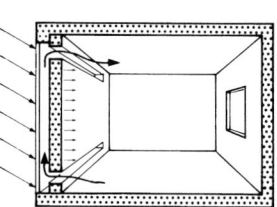

(9) **Direct usage of solar energy through glazed surfaces**

(10) **Indirect use of solar energy through a Trombé wall**

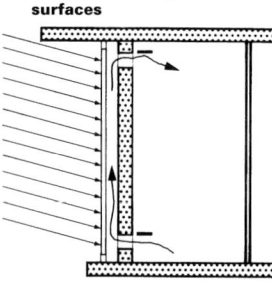 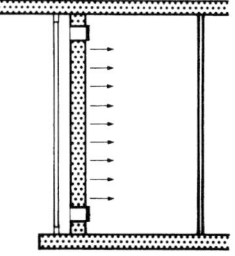

(11) **Winter day: incident solar radiation heats the air between the pane and the Trombé wall; room air is circulated through the lower and upper flaps and thus heated**

(12) **Winter night: thoroughly warmed wall acts as a radiant heat surface in the room; with the upper and lower flaps closed, the stationary layer of air between the external glazing and the Trombé wall helps to reduce the heat loss**

SOLAR ARCHITECTURE

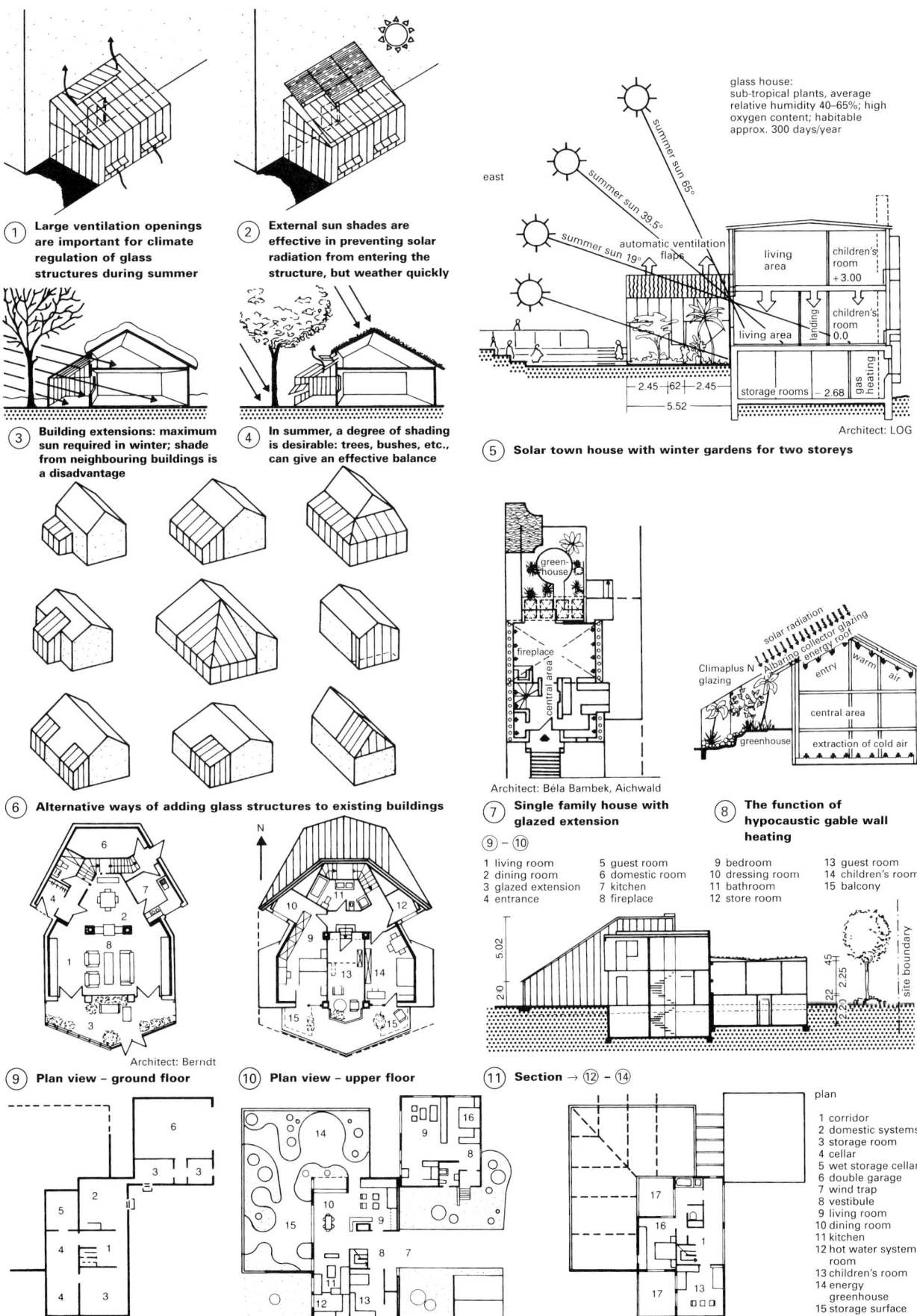

① **Large ventilation openings are important for climate regulation of glass structures during summer**

② **External sun shades are effective in preventing solar radiation from entering the structure, but weather quickly**

③ **Building extensions: maximum sun required in winter; shade from neighbouring buildings is a disadvantage**

④ **In summer, a degree of shading is desirable: trees, bushes, etc., can give an effective balance**

glass house:
sub-tropical plants, average relative humidity 40–65%; high oxygen content; habitable approx. 300 days/year

east

summer sun 65°
summer sun 39.5°
summer sun 19°

automatic ventilation flaps

living area

children's room +3.00

living area

landing

children's room 0.0

storage rooms − 2.68

gas heating

2.45 | 62 | 2.45
5.52

Architect: LOG

⑤ **Solar town house with winter gardens for two storeys**

⑥ **Alternative ways of adding glass structures to existing buildings**

green-house

fireplace

central area

Architect: Béla Bambek, Aichwald

⑦ **Single family house with glazed extension**

solar radiation

Albarino collector glazing
Climaplus N glazing
energy roof
entry
warm air
central area
greenhouse
extraction of cold air

⑧ **The function of hypocaustic gable wall heating**

⑨ **Plan view – ground floor**

⑩ **Plan view – upper floor**

⑨ – ⑩

1 living room	5 guest room
2 dining room	6 domestic room
3 glazed extension	7 kitchen
4 entrance	8 fireplace

9 bedroom	13 guest room
10 dressing room	14 children's room
11 bathroom	15 balcony
12 store room	

Architect: Berndt

N

⑪ **Section → ⑫ – ⑭**

5.02

2.0

45
2.25
22
2.20

site boundary

⑫ **Basement → ⑪**

⑬ **Ground floor**

⑭ **Upper floor**

Architect: Planning team LOG

plan

1 corridor
2 domestic systems
3 storage room
4 cellar
5 wet storage cellar
6 double garage
7 wind trap
8 vestibule
9 living room
10 dining room
11 kitchen
12 hot water system room
13 children's room
14 energy greenhouse
15 storage surface
16 bedroom
17 balcony

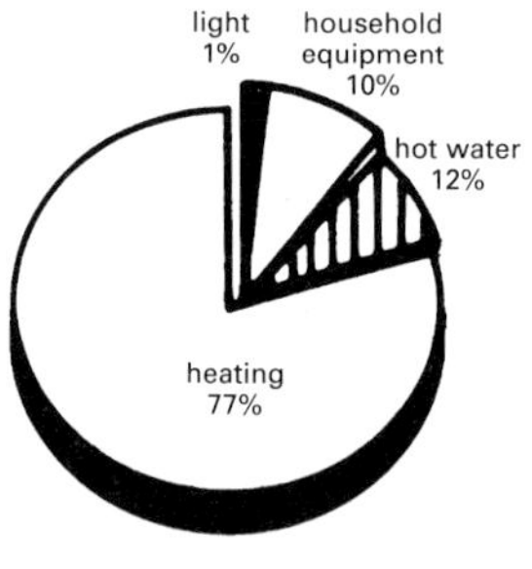

SOLAR ENERGY

About 1.5 m² of collector area and about 100 l volume of water in the storage tank is needed per person in the household. → ① A 30-pipe solar collector with an absorption surface of 3 m² is needed to produce hot water for a 4-person household. The collector will produce about 8.5–14.0 kWh solar heat per day, depending on the amount of sunshine, i.e. enough to heat 200–280 l of water. → ⑤ Within the foreseeable future, the sun cannot provide enough power for heating, so solar heating installations still require a conventional heating system.

There are two different technologies. Solar heat: thermal collection of solar energy using collectors (equipment which catches and accumulates solar thermal energy). Thermal energy is used to heat water. Solar electricity: photovoltaics is the direct conversion of the sun's rays into electrical energy (direct current) with the help of solar cells.

① Energy use in a household
light 1%, household equipment 10%, hot water 12%, heating 77%

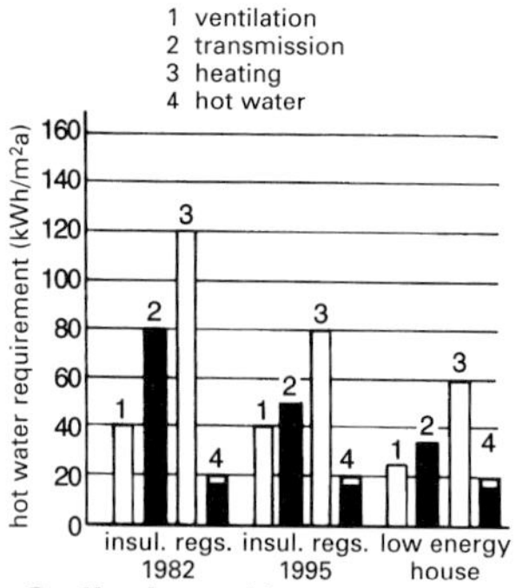

② Heating and hot water requirements of a single family house
1 ventilation
2 transmission
3 heating
4 hot water

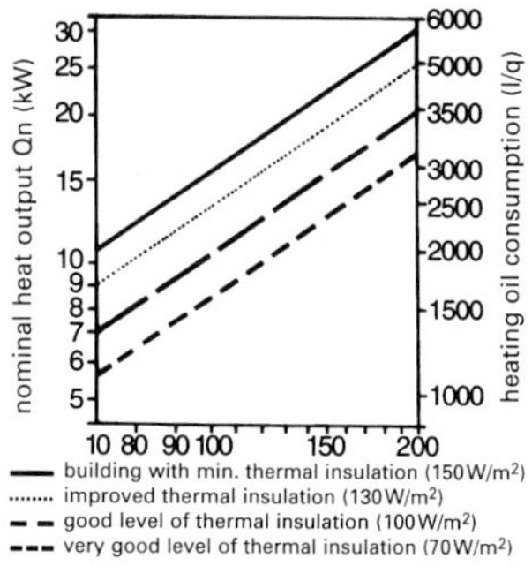

③ Heating and fuel requirements of houses in relation to insulation levels

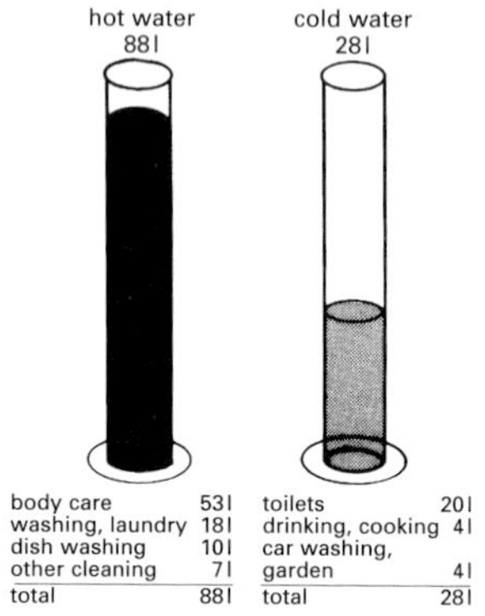

— building with min. thermal insulation (150 W/m²)
...... improved thermal insulation (130 W/m²)
– – good level of thermal insulation (100 W/m²)
–––– very good level of thermal insulation (70 W/m²)

④ Use of water in a household

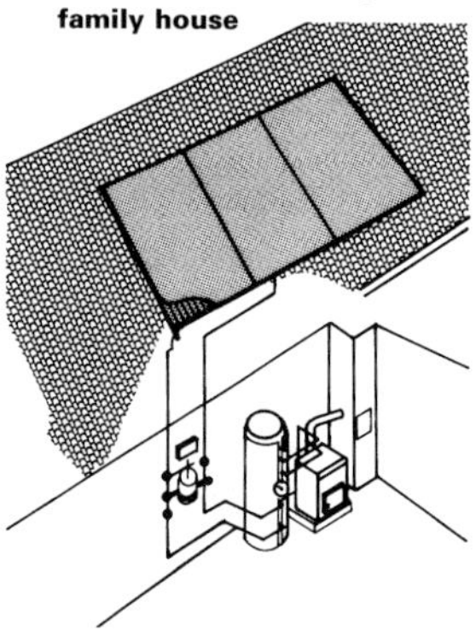

hot water 88 l		cold water 28 l	
body care	53 l	toilets	20 l
washing, laundry	18 l	drinking, cooking	4 l
dish washing	10 l	car washing, garden	4 l
other cleaning	7 l		
total	88 l	total	28 l

⑤ Hot water production

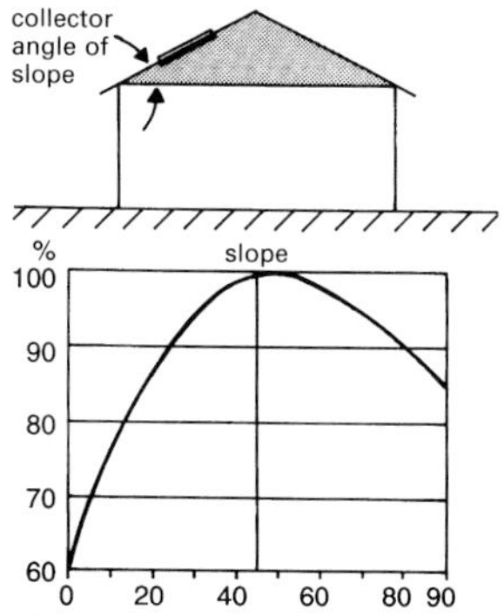

⑥ Angle of slope of collector

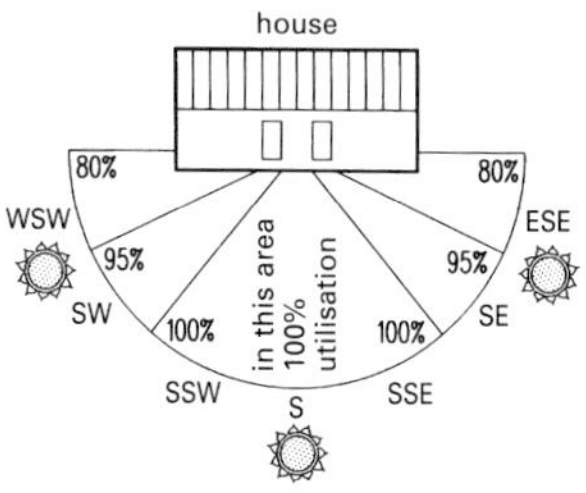

⑦ Use of sun's radiation

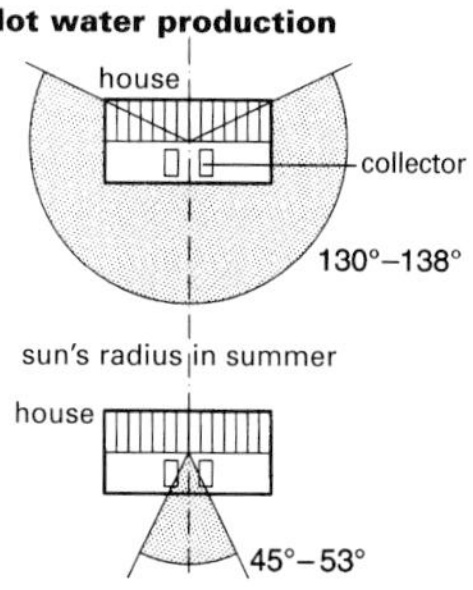

⑧ Sun's radius in winter

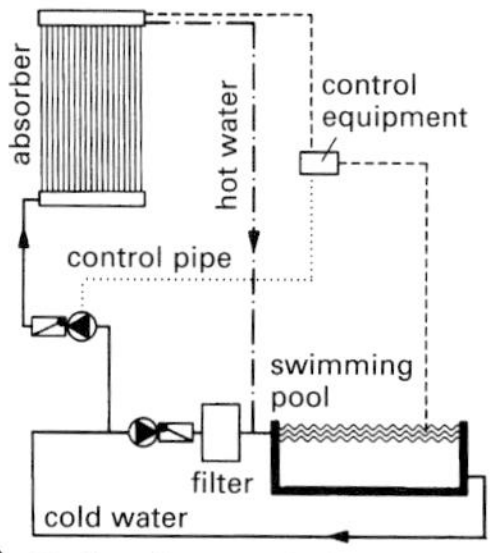

⑨ Swimming pool absorber

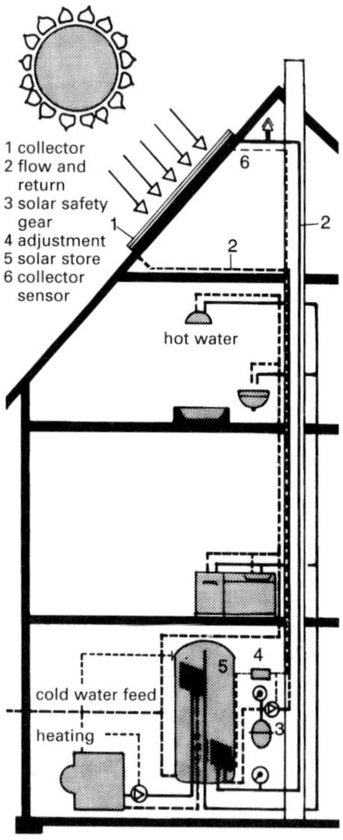

1 collector
2 flow and return
3 solar safety gear
4 adjustment
5 solar store
6 collector sensor

⑩ Hot water supply solar installation

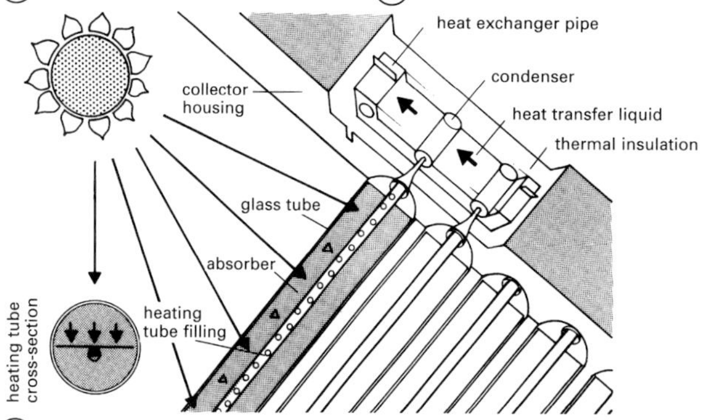

⑪ Vacuum tube collector

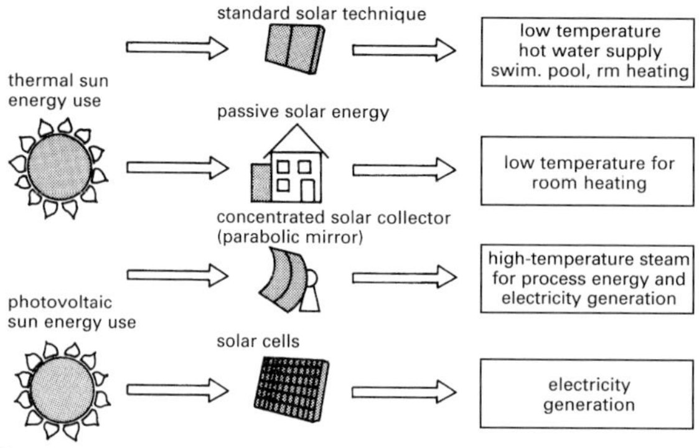

⑫ Solar techniques (diagrammatic representation)

Air movement is caused by pressure differences, i.e., disturbances to the state of equilibrium, resulting from:
(1) temperature differences
(2) natural wind
(3) ventilators.

'natural ventilation' – windows, doors, ventilation shafts
'mechanical ventilation' – admission and discharge of air brought about by heating and ventilation systems

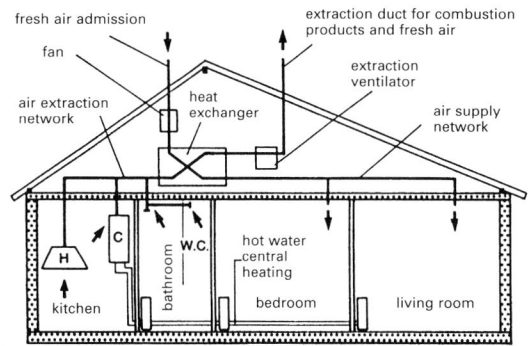

① **Arrangement of ventilation and air conditioning systems**

Room ventilation systems are used to guarantee a specific room climate. In fulfilling this objective, the following requirements must be satisfied, depending on the application:
(a) Removal from rooms of impurities in the air including smoke and other harmful substances, and suspended particles
(b) Removal of perceptible heat from rooms: unwanted quantities of both hot and cold air
(c) Removal of latent heat from rooms: enthalpy flows of humidifying air and dehumidifying air
(d) Protective pressure maintenance: pressure maintenance in buildings for protection against unwanted air exchange.

Most of the requirements under (a) are solved through continuous replacement of air (ventilation) and/or suitable air treatment (filtering). Requirements of type (b) and (c) are usually met by appropriate thermodynamic treatment of the air, and, to a limited degree, by air replacement. Requirements of type (d) are solved by various types of mechanical control of supply and extraction air.

Natural ventilation
Uncontrolled air is admitted through joints and gaps in window frames, doors and shutters (as a result of the effects of wind) rather than through the walls. However, the increased use of thermal insulation measures in buildings means that the natural sources of ventilation through gaps in windows and doors may no longer be adequate. It may therefore be necessary to provide controlled ventilation in living accommodation, using mechanical ventilation systems and, if necessary, to replace the heat lost as a consequence.

Window ventilation → ⑤ – ⑧ p.179 is generally adequate for living rooms. Sash windows are favourable, where the outside air is admitted at the bottom and internal air flows out above.

Intensive ventilation is brought about by mechanical ventilation systems. In accordance with the building regulations, this is a requirement for windowless bathrooms and WCs, with the removal of air to the outside via ducting. Allowance should be made for the requirement of a flow of replenishment air through ventilator grills, windows and/or gaps in the fabric of the building. Furthermore, as far as is possible, draught-free admission of the outside air must be provided.

The installation of simple ventilator grills in outside walls for inflow and outflow of air leads to the danger of draughts in the winter. Mechanical ventilation systems are better.

VENTILATION AND AIR CONDITIONING

Humidity of room air
For comfort, the upper limit for the moisture content of the air is 11.5 kg of water per kg of dry air. A relative humidity of 65% should not be exceeded. The minimum flow of fresh air per person for cinemas, banqueting halls, reading rooms, exhibition halls, sale rooms, museums and sports halls is 20 m³/h. The value for individual offices, canteens, conference rooms, rest rooms, lecture halls and hotel rooms is 30 m³/h; it is 40 m³/h for restaurants, and 50 m³/h for open plan offices.

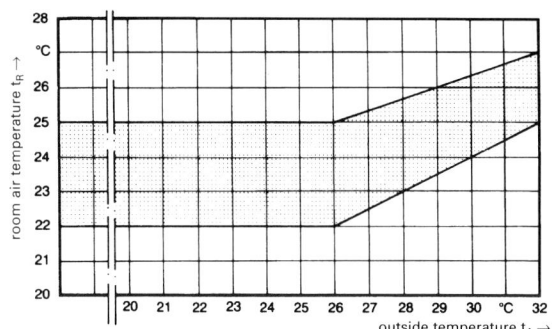

② **Scheme for an installation incorporating a 'twin-flow gas system'**

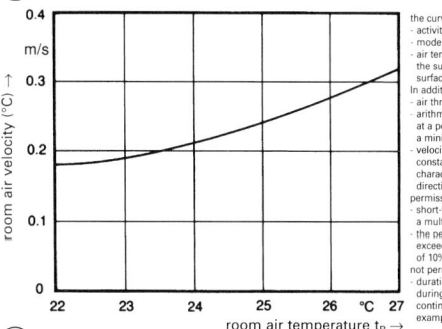

③ **Comfortable room air temperature range**

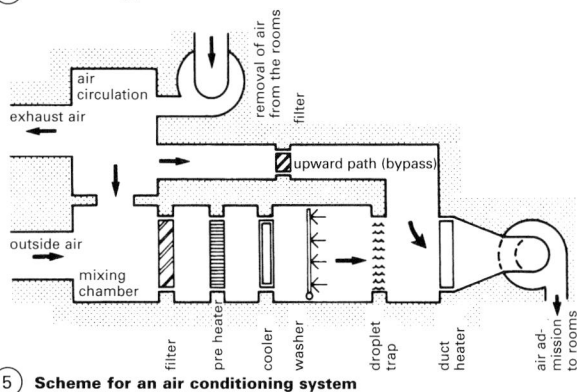

the curve applies to:
- activity grade 1
- moderate clothing
- air temperature approximately equal to the surface temperature of the enclosing surfaces.
In addition, the following is assumed:
- air throughput with turbulent mixing
- arithmetic mean value of the air velocity at a point, during a measuring period of a minimum of 200s
- velocity measuring sensor with a time constant of 2s max. and cosine characteristic in both incident flow directions
permissible:
- short-term velocity peaks, which can be a multiple of the arithmetic mean value
- the permissible air velocities may be exceeded by up to 10% at a maximum of 10% of the measuring stations
not permissible:
- durations of longer than 1 minute during which the permissible velocity is continuously exceeded, caused for example by unsteady control inputs

④ **Curve of upper limit for comfortable room air velocities**

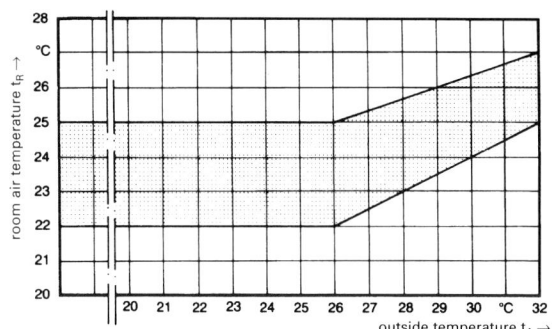

⑤ **Scheme for an air conditioning system**

Several handling stages are usually involved in ventilation and air conditioning. Filtering; air heating; air cooling; and washing, humidifying and evaporative cooling are discussed on this page. For ventilation and damping → p. 107.

Filtering

Air cleaning to eliminate coarse dust particles:
- (a) Oiled metal filter plates in air filter chambers or automatic circulation filters; used particularly for the ventilation of industrial premises. Disadvantage: entrainment of oil mist.
- (b) Dry layer filter mats made of textile or glass fibre in metal frames; not recoverable; also as roll tape filter with automatic cleaning.

Fine cleaning and separation of fine soot
- (c) Electrostatic air filter; the dust is ionised and deposited on negatively charged metal plates. Very low air resistance. Disadvantages: large filter chambers; cleaning with warm water.
- (d) Fine filtering through filter media of paper, or glass fibre. Advantages: cheap to manufacture; no corrosion from air containing harmful substances; high operating safety. Disadvantage: greater air resistance than electro filters, which increases as the filter is soiled, leading to disruption of the air flow.
- (e) Air washing: removes dust or aerosols and acid fumes, but not soot, and therefore should not be used in areas with many oil-fired heating installations.

filter class	mean level of particle separation A_m relative to synthetic dust (%)	mean efficiency E_m relative to atmospheric dust (%)
EU 1	$A_m < 65$	–
EU 2	$65 \leq A_m < 80$	–
EU 3	$80 \leq A_m < 90$	–
EU 4	$90 \leq A_m <$	–
EU 5	–	$40 \leq E_m < 60$
EU 6	–	$60 \leq E_m < 80$
EU 7	–	$80 \leq E_m < 90$
EU 8	–	$90 \leq E_m < 95$
EU 9[1]	–	$95 \leq E_m$

[1] air filters having a high mean efficiency may already satisfy the classification requirements for suspended material filter class

① **Air filter classes**

Air heating
- (a) Controllability is limited with simple gravity-circulation solid-fuel heating installations.
- (b) Controllability is good with natural gas and heating oil, and with electrically heated equipment.
- (c) Heating with low-pressure steam, warm and hot water, using finned tube radiators made from galvanised steel or copper tube with copper or aluminium fins. Good, simple controllability. No need for local chimneys and flues.

Air cooling

Used principally for industry when constant temperature and humidity must be maintained over the whole year, also for commercial buildings and office blocks, theatres and cinemas in summer.
- (a) Cooling of the air with mains water or spring water. At a temperature of 13°C, spring water should be allowed to drain back again as much as possible on account of the ground water table level. In most towns, the use of mains water for cooling is not permitted and is uneconomical anyway, due to the high price of water. Spring water systems require the approval of the water authorities.

VENTILATION AND AIR CONDITIONING

- (b) Compression cooling systems for room air conditioning must accord with strict regulations and must use non-poisonous refrigerants such as Freon 12 or Freon 22 (F12, F22), etc. If the cooling plant is in the direct vicinity of the central air conditioning area, direct evaporation of the refrigerant should take place in the cooling radiators of the air conditioning plant. Since 1995, substances containing CFCs are prohibited.
- (c) In large installations, cooling of the water takes place within a closed circuit, with distribution by pumps. Advantages: the central cooling plant can be in an area where noise and vibration are not troublesome; very safe in operation. Today, compact cold water systems and prefabricated air conditioning/cooling units are available.

For large cooling installations
- (d) Compression of the refrigerant in a sealed unit turbo compressor (complete machine installation with compressor, water-cooler and condenser), low vibration and very low noise levels.
- (e) Absorption cooling facility with lithium bromide and water. Due to the vaporisation of the water, heat is extracted from the water to be cooled; water vapour is absorbed by the lithium bromide and continuously evaporated in the cyclic process, then condensed again and passed to the first vaporisation process. Very low noise levels; vibration-free system requiring little space.
- (f) Steam jet cooling: A high velocity steam jet induces a negative pressure in a vessel. Circulating cooling water becomes atomised and vaporised, with simultaneous cooling. The cold water is transferred to the air coolers of the air conditioning plant. This method of cooling is employed in industrial applications.

The condenser heat must be disposed of in all mechanical cooling systems. Various means are employed for this purpose, e.g. water cooled condensers, which are cooled by spring water or circulating water, and air cooled condensers. On water-cooled condensers, the spring water installation requires approval by the local water authorities. Also, careful checks should be made as to whether the spring water contains any aggressive substances which would damage the condensers in the cooling installation. If appropriate, sea water resistant condensers must be used (cost factors).

A return cooling system is necessary on circulating water installations (cooling tower). In the cooling tower, circulating water is sprayed by jets. The water then flows over layers of granular material and is blown through with air (evaporative cooling). The cooling towers should be sited away from buildings or, better still, be sited on the roofs of buildings, due to the level of noise generated. The same applies to air cooled condensers.

Washing, humidifying, evaporative cooling

Air washers provide humidification for dry air (when correctly set) and, to a certain degree, they can also provide air cleaning. By means of saturation, i.e. increasing the absolute water content of the air in the washer, 'evaporative cooling' can take place at the same time; this provides the possibility of cheap cooling for industrial air conditioning facilities in areas where the outside air is of low humidity. The water is very finely atomised in the air washer, through the use of pumps and jet sprays. The sprays are housed in galvanised steel sheeting or watertight masonry or concrete. An air rectifier or water-control sheeting prevents the escape of water into the conditioning chamber.

Other humidifying devices
- (a) Evaporation vessels on heating elements or atomisers.
- (b) Centralised device with steam or electrically heated evaporation vessels (disadvantage is scaling).
- (c) Rotating atomisers (aerosol apparatus) – only usable where low volumes of air are involved

The efficiency of a good ventilation design can be 80–90%, depending on the application. Both radial and axial fans produce the same noise levels up to a total delivery pressure of approx. 40 mm head of water. Above this level, axial fans are louder and they are used particularly in industrial construction. Special foundations are provided with damping elements to isolate vibration levels.

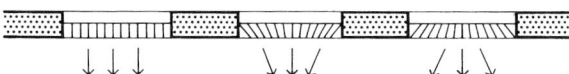

(1) **Air admission grilles showing flow directions**

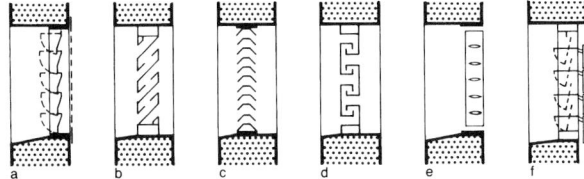

(2) **Ventilation openings: a = self opening; b,c,d,e = non-moving; d = for dark rooms; f = manually operated**

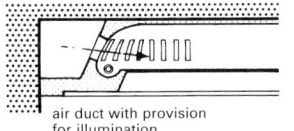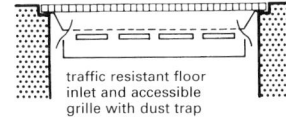

air duct with provision for illumination

traffic resistant floor inlet and accessible grille with dust trap

(3) **Air inlet and outlet grilles**

Sound damping

Sound dampers are provided in air ducts to reduce noise from installed machinery into the air-conditioned rooms. The length of these in the direction of air flow is 1.5–3 m, depending on the damping to be achieved. The design may embody baffles made from non-combustible material, e.g. moulded fibre boards or from sheeting with a rockwool filling. The requirements for sound insulation in building construction should be observed.

Ducts and air outlets and inlets are in galvanised steel sheet, high-grade steel or fire-resistant fibre board or similar. Ideally, the cross-section should be square or round, or rectangular with an aspect ratio of 1:3. Regular servicing is necessary, and the requirements for fire protection of ventilation systems must be observed.

Masonry or concrete built ducts are more economical than sheet construction for large floor or rising ducts. Masonry ducts dampen noise better than concrete. The insides should be smoothly plastered and have a washable surface coating. Air entry ducts should be provided with lightweight insulation only, so that heat retention is avoided. The duct cross-sections should be large enough for cleaning (soiling impairs the condition of the air). So, the floor air-exhaust ducts should be equipped with drainage pipes or channels with sealed screwed connections and the air ducting should have adequate access openings for cleaning purposes.

Cement fibre ducts (asbestos-free) are suitable for moist, non-acid containing air and plastic ducts for aggressive, gaseous media. Inlet and outlet gratings should not be sited in accessible floor areas (except in industrial construction and electronic data processing rooms). Air outlets are crucial for the distribution of air in rooms; the flow should be directed horizontally and vertically. Grilles for air inlets and outlets should be designed from an air conditioning standpoint, but should also be easy to clean – ideally made from stove enamelled sheet. → (1) – (3)

The introduction of air into offices should, when possible, be at a window (point of most pronounced passage of cold and heat). Air removal should be on the corridor side. For theatres, cinemas and lecture rooms, admit air under the seats, and remove through the ceiling. This method depends on the shape and usage of the room.

VENTILATION AND AIR CONDITIONING

Plant rooms

Air conditioning and ventilation systems should be considered during preliminary planning, as they have a major influence on building design and construction. Plant rooms should be as near as possible to the rooms to be air-conditioned, provided this is acoustically acceptable, and have good accessibility. The walls should be of masonry, plastered, with a washable coating, preferably tiled.

Floor drainage should be provided in all compartments, and have traps and airtight removable covers. Where plant rooms are above other rooms, watertight floors should be provided. External walls need insulation and vapour barriers, to avoid damage by condensation. The extra floor loading for machinery in a plant room can be 750–1500 kg/m², plus the weight of the walling of the air ducting. In situations where there are extremely high requirements for noise and vibration reduction, consideration should be given to flexible mounting and isolating a plant room as a 'room within a room'.

Space requirements for air conditioning equipment are very much dependent on the demand for air filtering and sound damping. In narrow, long floor shapes, the compartments can be arranged in sequence, one after the other.

- Simple industrial conditioning systems: approx. 12 m long
- For full air conditioning systems: approx. 16–22 m long
- For air extract systems: approx. 4–6 m long.

Width and height (clear space) for industrial and full air conditioning system plant rooms:

air supply m³/h	width (m)	height (m)	
< 20 000	3.0	3.0	
20–40 000	4.0	3.5	} room centre
40–70 000	4.75	4.0	

An additional 1.5–2 m should be allowed for assembly and maintenance access. In the case of large installations, for heating and air conditioning distribution systems, allowance should be made for common maintenance access and space for the control panel.

Air conditioning systems for large offices

It is useful to use several conditioning systems for large and open planned rooms. An isolated conditioning zone can be installed in the façade area (high-velocity systems) and a separate area for the internal zone, with low pressure or high velocity systems → (4).

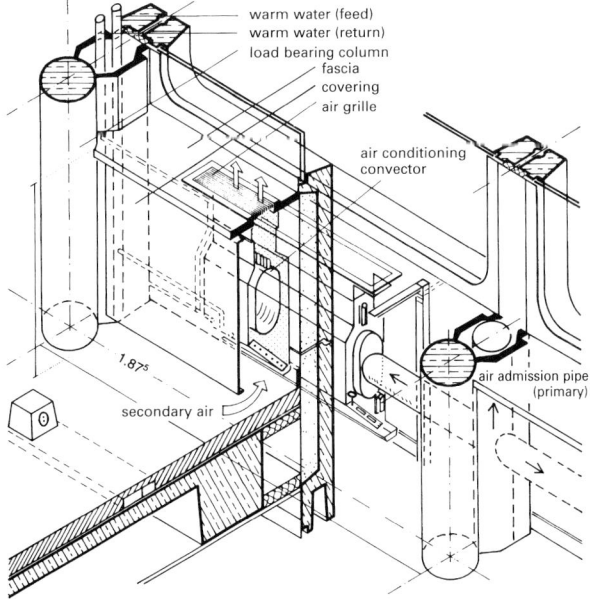

warm water (feed)
warm water (return)
load bearing column
fascia
covering
air grille

air conditioning convector

air admission pipe (primary)

secondary air

1.875

Construction management: Dyckerhoff Zement AG

(4) **Example of a high pressure air conditioning system (System LTG).**

VENTILATION AND AIR CONDITIONING

High-pressure air conditioning systems

To meet the demand for heat in winter and cooling in summer, large cross-sections of low-pressure air conditioning systems are needed – it is not for ventilation. High-pressure air conditioning systems require only approx. $1/3$ of the usual air quantities; they use external air for ventilation while transporting heat and cold through water pipes (1 m³ of water can transport approx. 3450 times more heat than 1 m³ of air). An air conditioning convector unit (with special air outlet jets and a heat exchanger) installed under every window is supplied with conditioned air and cooled or heated water. Regulation takes place only at the heat exchanger. Smaller quantities of air enable smaller control rooms to be used and with acceptable air conditioning. The external air is cleaned using a pre-filter and a fine filter. The whole building is at a slight positive pressure with respect to the outside, so that any air gaps in the building fabric have virtually no effect.

Air conditioning convectors

General requirements: noise intensity ≤ 30–33 phon; air filter for cleaning the secondary air; heat exchanger must be able to ensure full heating to room temperature in any weather, even without the ventilation air system; cold water temperature in summer must be 15–16°C, or the cooling operation will be uneconomical and condensation will form on window systems (soiling of cooling surfaces). For ideal flow conditions without vibration, high-pressure air ductwork should be of round section where possible. With a vertical arrangement of supply lines and window spacings of 1.5–2 m, alternate the structural columns with vertical service ducts containing the air ductwork and water pipes. Rising air ductwork for buildings with 7 storeys are 175–255 mm diameter. For taller buildings, separate

supplies lines are needed for each 7–10 storeys and a storey devoted to the installation of heating and ventilation plant. A more expensive arrangement involves a main air shaft, with horizontal distribution along the corridors and branching ductwork directed outwards into the ceiling voids above rooms, to terminate directly behind the facade above the windows, or, at floor level, in the rooms above through holes in the floor structure. Max. office depth for high-pressure installations: 6 m, beyond which air cooling requires an additional central conditioning system. Max. building depth without a central system: (2 × 6 =) 12 m plus the corridor. Air can be removed through ducts over corridor wall storage cupboards or in ducting above the corridors and through WCs. In high-pressure systems, air is not recirculated (the air mass has already been reduced to that required for acceptable ventilation). For limited operation, the primary air flow can be reduced in the plant room.

Ventilation systems for kitchens

For large kitchens (height 3–5 m), render the upper sections (walls and ceilings) in porous plaster (no oil painting); provide 15–30 air changes, pressure below atmospheric, creating air flow from adjacent rooms into the kitchen; use larger radiators as appropriate; group boilers, cookers and fryers together; provide air extraction with a fat filter; clean ducting annually; filter and heat the air inlet flow in winter. No air circulation system is needed; local heating and insulating glazing are needed.

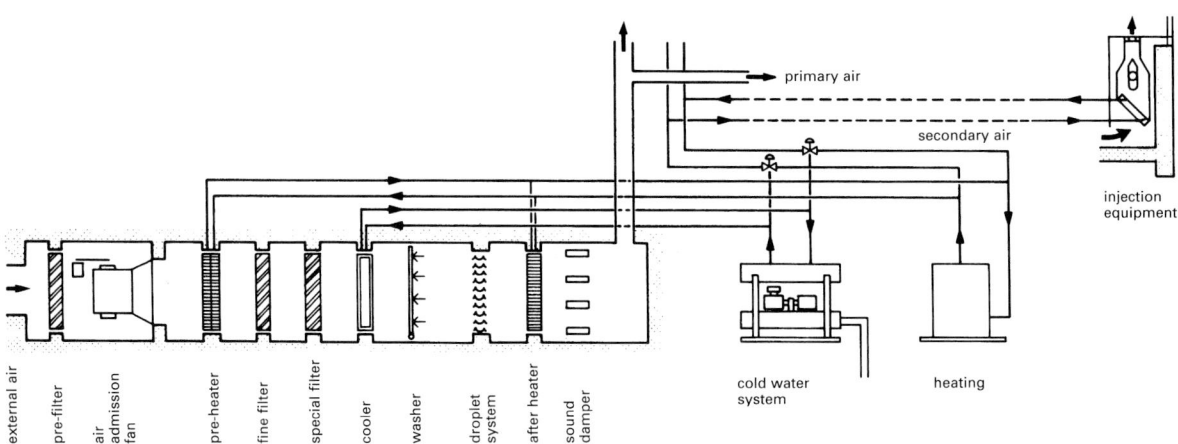

(1) **High-pressure air conditioning system (System LTG)**

component	maximum heat exchange coefficient W/(m²K)[1]	required minimum thickness of insulating material without certificate[2]
external walls	0.60	50mm
windows	double windows or double glazing	
ceilings under uninsulated roof space, and ceilings (including sloping roofs) and floors that form a boundary between rooms and the outside air above or below	0.45	80mm
cellar floors and other floors which separate the building from the surrounding ground; walls/floors which form boundaries to an unheated room	0.70	40mm

[1] heat transfer coefficients can be determined taking account of existing structural components

[2] thickness data relates to a thermal conductivity (–0.04 W/(mK); where the insulating material has to be built in, or in the case of materials with other thermal conductivity values, the insulation material thicknesses must be balanced accordingly; existing mineral fibre or foam plastic materials can be assumed to have a thermal conductivity of 0.04 W/(mK).

(1) **Limitation of heat transfer on initial construction, replacement and on renewal of structural components**

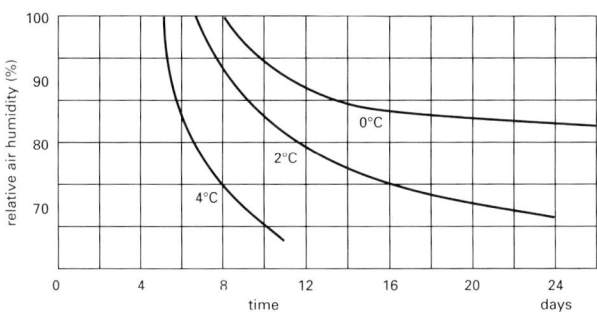

(2) **Maximum storage duration at various temperatures and degrees of humidity (0 K = –273.15°C)**

type of meat	storage temperature	storage duration (months)
beef	– 18	15
	– 12	4
	– 9.5	3
pork	– 18	12
	– 12	2 up to 4
	– 9.5	1
loin of pork	– 18	5 1/2
	– 10	4
chicken	– 22	up to 18
	– 18	up to 10
	– 12	4
	– 9.5	2
turkey	– 35	over 12
	– 23	12
	– 18	6
	– 12	3

(3) **Storage temperature and duration of storage**

COLD STORAGE ROOMS

To determine the cooling requirements for cold rooms, attention must be paid to the requirements of the commodities stored; humidity content, air changes, cooling or freezing duration, type of storage, etc. Also, consider the specific heat of the goods, internal environment, method of manufacture, position, heat from lighting and movements within the cold store. Calculation of the cooling requirement takes the following form (→ pp. 111–16):

(1) Cooling/refrigeration of the goods (cooling to the freezing point – freezing – supercooling) ($Q = m \times cp \times \Delta t$); if goods are to be frozen solid, the necessary heat must be removed at the freezing point, and, subsequently, the specific heat of the frozen goods is lower; the humidity extraction is approximately 5%

(2) Cooling and drying of the extracted air

(3) Heating effects through walls, ceiling, floor

(4) Losses: movements in and out of storage (door opening), natural and electric lighting, pump and ventilator operation

(5) Condensation of water vapour on walls

The cold storage of freshly slaughtered meat is cooled from 303.15K to a temperature of 288.15K. This is achieved by placing it in a temperature of 280.15–281.15K at a relative humidity of 85–90% in the pre-cooling room for 8–10 hours, and then storing it at 275.15K–281.15K at a relative humidity of 75% for up to 28–30 hours in the cool room. Cooling and storage takes place separately. Weight loss over 7 days is 4–5%. Today, rapid cooling is used increasingly, no pre-cooling stage, meat is cooled from a slaughter temp. of 303.15K to a storage temp. of 274.15K, with 60–80 circulations of the air per hour and at a relative humidity of 90–95%.

Meat cooling and refrigeration

The freezing process changes the condition and distribution of the water in meat, while the meat composition remains unchanged.

Beef is frozen to 261.15K and pork to 258.15K, at a relative humidity of 90%. Duration of freezing: mutton, veal, pork, 2–4 days; beef, hindquarters 4 days, forequarters, 3 days. Correct thawing period: 3–5 days to 278.15–281.15K, restores the meat to a fresh condition.

Recently, mainly in the USA, rapid freezing methods have been employed, at temperatures of 248.15–243.15K, involving 120–150 air circulations per hour. The advantages are: lower weight loss, increase in tenderness, replacement of the curing process, lower liquid loss, good consistency and preservability after thawing.

Storage duration is dependent on the storage temperature; for example, for beef the storage duration is 15 months at 255.15K, 4 months at 261.15K and 3 months at 263.65K.

Cold room volume: 1m³ is suitable for the storage of 400–500kg of mutton, 350–500kg of pork, 400–500kg of beef, with a standard stacking height of 2.5m.

Refrigeration of fish

Fresh fish can be maintained in this condition on ice at 272.15K and at a relative humidity of 90–100% for a period of 7 days. Longer storage times can be achieved through the use of bactericidal ice (calcium hypochlorite or caporite). For even longer storage, rapid freezing to 248.15 –233.15K is required, if necessary use glazing with fresh water to keep air out and prevent drying up. Fish crates are 90 × 50 × 34, giving a weight of approx. 150kg.

Refrigeration of butter

Butter refrigerated to 265.15K has a storage duration of 3–4 months and a duration of 6–8 months at a temperature of 258.15–252.15K. Lower temperatures can provide a period of up to 12 months. The relative humidity should be 85–90%. Butter drums are 600mm high with a diameter of 350–450mm, resulting in a weight of 50–60kg.

Refrigeration of fruit and vegetables

Immediate cooling is required, since a reduction of temperature to 281.15K delays ripening by 50%. Storage duration depends on air quality (temperature, relative humidity, movement), variety, maturity, soil quality, fertilising, climate, transportation, pre-cooling, etc.

Cooling of eggs

Cold storage eggs are those stored in rooms whose temperature has been artificially controlled to a value lower than 8°C. Such eggs must be identified as 'cold storage eggs'. To avoid sweating, if the temperature outside the cold storage room is more than 5°C greater than inside, the eggs must be warmed in a defrosting room with controlled air conditioning on removal from cold storage. The area of the defrosting room is approx.12% of that of the cold storage room. The warming-up time for quarter crates is approx. 10 hours; 18–24 hours for complete and half crates. Stacking of the quarter crates in the defrosting room: around 5000–6000 eggs (approx. 400 kg gross) per m². Crates of 500 eggs are 920 mm long, 480 mm wide and 180 mm high; for 122 dozen (= 1440) eggs, 1750 × 530 × 250 mm. A basis for calculation is 10–13 crates for 30 dozen, occupying 1 m³ in the storage room; since one egg weighs 50–60 grams, there is a weight of between 180–220 kg of eggs in the 1 m³. A net volume of 2.8 m³ cold room capacity is required for 10,000 eggs. Two million eggs fill 15 freight wagons. For export, the eggs are packed in crates of 1440 items; wood shavings are used as packing between the eggs, giving a gross weight of 80–105 kg. For Egyptian eggs, this weight is 70–87 kg, tare, i.e. the empty crate and shavings weigh 16–18 kg. One wagon contains 100 half export crates holding 144,000 eggs or 400 'lost' crates with 360 items each. Standard crates for 360 eggs are 660 mm long, 316 mm wide and 361 mm high (the so-called 'lost' crates). They can be divided into two by a central partition. Cardboard inserts are used. The crates are made from dry spruce; pine is unsuitable. Stacked 7 crates high, 10,000–11,000 eggs can be stored on a net area of 1 m². Dry air, at 75% humidity and air-tight packaging is used, with cube-shaped crates with 360 eggs in each, in protective cardboard pockets. If the eggs are exposed to the ingress of air, the air humidity can be 83–85%. The air humidity in the store is controlled by first supercooling then heating it within the ventilation system. The weight loss during the first months in cold storage is severer than later months; a weight loss of 3–4.5% occurs after 7 months. Eggs can also be conserved in a gaseous atmosphere of 88% CO_2 and 12% N, after Lescardé-Everaert, in gas-filled autoclaves at around 0°C. This preserves the eggs in their natural state. Uniformity of temperature and air humidity are important factors. Ozone is frequently introduced into egg cold storage rooms. The cooling requirement during storage is 3300–5000 kJ/day per m² of floor surface – higher during the period when eggs are introduced. The storage periods run from Apr/May to Oct/Nov.

Cooling and refrigeration of poultry and game

Large game (red deer, roe deer, wild boar) must be drawn before freezing, but this is not necessary for small game (hare, rabbit, game birds). Freezing takes place before plucking, with the game free-hanging; storage being in stacks on gridded floor panels. There should be plenty of air movement during freezing, but little during storage. These numbers of game can be stored per square metre of floor area (3[t]m high): approx. 100 hares, or 20 roe deer, or 7–10 red deer. The air humidity should be approx. 85% at −12°C.

Domestic poultry should not be frozen and stored with game, as the fat content of the former requires a lower temp. and is sensitive to the smell of game. The cooling of poultry takes place at 0°C and at 80–85% relative humidity, with the birds suspended on frames, or alternatively, in iced water; storage at 0°C and 85% relative humidity, with a storage duration of approx. 7 days. Freezing at approx. −30−−35°C, storage at around −25°C and 85–90% relative humidity. The freezing time for a chicken is approx. 4 hours at an air velocity of 2–3 m/sec. Deep freezing, using the cryovac method, takes place in vacuum latex bags. Young chickens will freeze through in 2–3 hours. Storage duration is approx. 8 months at −18°C. To prevent rancidity, the poultry is protected by wrapping in water vapour tight polyethylene film.

Brewery products

Malt floors: 8–0°C
Cooling requirement per m² of floor area: 5000–6300 kJ/day
Fermentation cellars: duration is 8–10 days at 3.5–6°C
Cooling requirement: 4200–5000 kJ/day per m² of floor area
Cooling requirement for the fermentation vat cooling: 500–630 kJ per hl fermented wort per day
Storage cellar: −1.0°C to +1.5°C; cooling requirement approx. 20–25 Wm³, related to the empty room, or 2.5–3 kcal/h per hl of storage capacity
Installed cooling power: approx. 2.1–2.3 Whl yearly output

Room cooling, general

From the viewpoint of reserves and safety, the cooling system is designed to have a higher performance than the calculated cooling requirement. It is assumed that the cooling system will operate for 16–20 hours per day in cooling and freezing rooms; in individual cases, e.g. for efficient utilisation of electrical tariffs, the period may be even shorter. In meat cold storage rooms, the cooling power should not be too high, so that during periods of reduced cooling requirements, adequate operating durations and the required throughput of air in the room will still be guaranteed.

In small commercial cold storage rooms with a temperature of approx. 2–4°C and a product throughput of 50 kg/m² per day, the following table serves as a reference to determine the cooling requirement and the requisite power of the cooling system.

cold storage room floor area requirement m²	cooling power (kJ/day)	cooling system (W)
5	50 000	870
10	82 000	1400
15	111 300	1900
20	138 600	2400
25	163 800	2850
30	187 000	3250

The following figures can be used for further calculations:
Cold storage rooms with multi-storey construction: 5000–8400 kJ/day/m²
Cold stores of single-storey construction: 1050–1700 kJ/day/m²
Storage capacity per m² of floor area – hanging storage – after reduction of approx. 15–20% for gangways: mutton 150–200 kg (5–6 items), pork 250–300 kg (3–3.5 whole, 6–7 sides), beef 350 kg (4–5 quarters of beef)
Per running metre – low hanging rail: 5 halves of pork or 3 quarters of beef or 2–3 calves
Distance from centre to centre of rails (low rail): approx. 0.65 m, height to centre of rail: 2.3–2.5 m
Distance from rail to rail (high rail): 1.20–1.50 m with free passage way; height with tubular track: 3.3–3.5 m
Per running metre of high rail: 1–1 5 m (2–3 sides of beef), depending on size

Estimate of cooling requirements for meat: rapid cold storage room, 21000–31500 kJ/m²/day; most rapid cold storage room, 4200 kJ/m²/hour

Storage room for frozen meat – storage capacity per m³ of room volume: frozen mutton, 400–500 kg; frozen pork, 350–500 kg; frozen beef, 400–500 kg

Standard stacking height: 2.5 m

Fats become rancid with the passage of time under the effects of light and oxygen, so that the storage duration is limited.

Meat curing room: temperature 6–8°C
Cooling requirement per m² of floor area: 4200–5000 kJ/day

Brine in curing vats absorbs moisture from the air.

One railway goods wagon of 15000 kg loaded weight can accept approx. 170 hanging sides of pork over a floor area of 21.8 m².

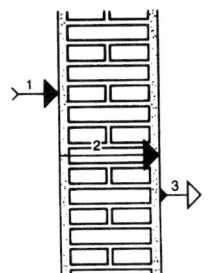

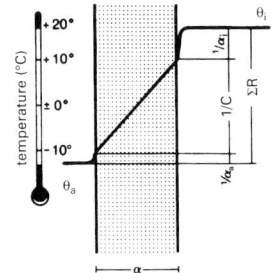

(1) Principle of heat transfer through a component

(2) Temperature variation in a single-layer component

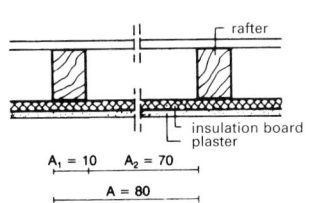

internal plaster

outside rendering

wall

	thickness l (m)		k (W/mK)		R (=l/k)
internal plaster	0.015	:	0.7	=	0.02
wall	0.30	:	0.22	=	1.36
outside rendering	0.025	:	0.87	=	0.03
1/C					1.41
$1/\alpha_i$					0.12
$1/\alpha_a$					0.04
ΣR					1.57
$U = \dfrac{1}{\Sigma R}$					0.64 (W/m²K)

example: wall made from aerated concrete, 500 kg/m³, 300 mm thick, plastered and rendered

(3) Calculation of the U value of a multilayer component

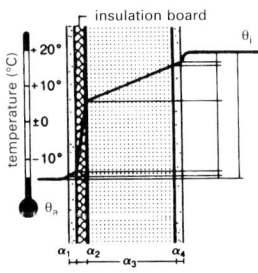

rafter

insulation board
plaster

A₁ = 10   A₂ = 70

A = 80

example: section through an attic area

$$U_m = \frac{A_1}{A}\cdot U_1 + \frac{A_2}{A}\cdot U_2 + \dots + \frac{A_n}{A}\cdot U_n$$

U, rafter area = 0.45

U, rafter field = 0.95

$$U_m = \frac{10}{80}\cdot 0.45 + \frac{70}{80}\cdot 0.95$$

$$= 0.056 + 0.83 = 0.89 \; (W/m^2K)$$

(4) Calculation of the mean thermal insulation value for combined components

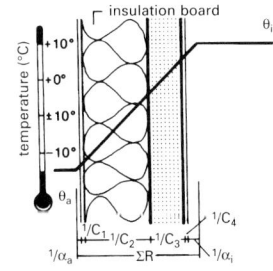

temperature drop corresponds to ΣR

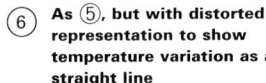

layers shown in proportion to their individual thermal insulation values

(5) Temperature variation in a multilayer component

(6) As (5), but with distorted representation to show temperature variation as a straight line

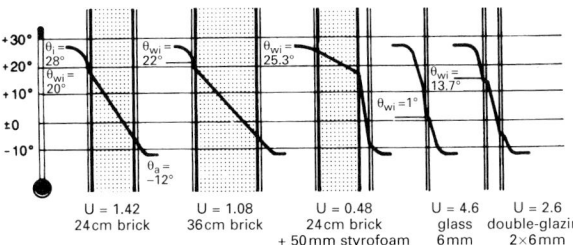

U = 1.42 24 cm brick	U = 1.08 36 cm brick	U = 0.48 24 cm brick + 50 mm styrofoam	U = 4.6 glass 6 mm	U = 2.6 double-glazing 2×6 mm

temperature of the inner surface of the wall θ_{wi} increases as the thermal insulation is improved

(7) Temperature variation across variously insulated components for an internal temperature $\theta_i = 28°$ and outside air temperature $\theta_a = -12°$

THERMAL INSULATION

Terminology and Mechanisms

Thermal insulation should minimise heat loss (or gain) allowing energy savings to be made, provide a comfortable environment for occupants, and protect a building from damage that might be caused by sharp temperature fluctuations (in particular, condensation). Heat exchange – by thermal convection, conduction, radiation and water vapour diffusion – cannot be prevented, but its rate can be reduced by efficient thermal insulation.

Terms used in calculating thermal insulation values

Although temperature is often given in degrees Celsius (°C), kelvin (K) is also used (0 K = −273.15°C).

Quantity of heat is expressed in watt hours (Wh). (1 Wh = 3.6 kJ.)

Thermal capacity, the heat necessary to raise the temperature of 1 kg of material by 1 K, is a measure of the readiness to respond to internal heat or to changing external conditions. 1 kcal (= 1.16 Wh) is the heat required to increase the temperature of 1 kg of water by 1 K.

Thermal conductance (C-value), in W/m²K, measures the rate at which a given thickness of material allows heat conduction, based on temperature differences between hot and cold faces; no account is taken of surface resistance. Thermal conductivity (k-value or λ specific to a given material), in W/mK (or kcal/mhK), measures the rate at which homogenous material conducts heat: the smaller the value, the lower the thermal conductivity. Thermal resistance (R-value = thickness/k), the reciprocal of thermal conductance (1/C), measures the resistance of material or structure with a particular thickness to heat transfer by conduction. Thermal resistivity (r-value), is the reciprocal of conductivity (1/k).

UK thermal insulation standards have risen since 1990, under the new Building Regulations, in which the thermal insulation value is used to evaluate temperature variation in, and possibility of damage to, a structural component due to condensation.

The thermal boundary layer resistance, 1/α, is the thermal resistance of the air 'boundary' layer on a structural component: $1/\alpha_a$ on the outside and $1/\alpha_i$ on the inside of the component. The lower the velocity of the air, the higher is the value of 1/α. Total resistance to heat flow ΣR is the sum of the resistances of a component against heat conductance: $\Sigma R = 1/\alpha_i + 1/C + 1/\alpha_a$.

The coefficient of thermal transmittance (U-value) – like thermal conductance – measures the rate at which material of a particular thickness allows heat conduction, i.e. the heat loss, and thus provides a basis for heating calculations, but the calculation is based on temperature difference between ambient temperatures on either side; account is taken of surface resistances of the structure. As the most important coefficient in calculating the level of thermal insulation, its value is specified in the Building Regulations, and is used by the heating systems manufacturer as a basis of measurement.

The mean U-value of window (w) and wall (W) is calculated as $U_{m(w+W)} = (U_w \times F_w + U_W \times F_W) \div (F_w + F_W)$, F being the surface area. Similarly, U_m, the coefficient of a building cell is calculated from the F and U values of the components making up the cell – window (w), wall (W), ceiling (c), floor surface (f) and roof area in contact with air (r) – taking account of minimum factors for roof and ground areas:

$$U_m = \frac{U_w \times F_w + U_W \times F_W + U_r \times F_r + 0.8 U_c \times F_c + 0.5 U_f \times F_f}{F_w + F_W + F_r + F_c + F_f}$$

Heat transfer through a component: a quantity of heat is conducted through the internal air boundary layer and then the inner surface of the component; some of this heat overcomes the thermal insulation value of the component to reach the outer surface, overcomes the outer air boundary layer and reaches the outside air → (1). Changes in temperature through the individual layers are in proportion to the percentage each contributes to the resistance to heat flow ΣR → (3).

Example: If $1/\alpha_i + 1/C + 1/\alpha_a = 0.13 + 0.83 + 0.04 = 1.00$, then $1/\alpha_i : 1/C : 1/\alpha_a$ = 13%:83%:4%. For a temperature difference of 40 K between inside and outside, then: temperature difference across inner boundary layer = 13% of 40 K = 5.2 K; temperature across material = 83% of 40 K = 33.2 K; and temperature across outer boundary layer = 4% of 40 K = 1.6 K.

The lower the thermal insulation of the component, the lower is the temperature of the inner surface of the component → (7), and the easier it is for condensation to occur. Since the temperature varies linearly through each individual layer, this appears as a straight line if the component is represented to scale in proportion to the thermal insulation of the individual layers → (5) – (6); the interrelationships are then more easily seen. The variation of temperature is particularly important in considering the expansion of the component due to heat, in addition to the question of condensation → p. 112.

111

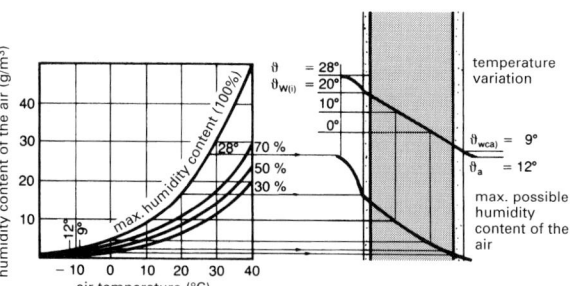

(1) **Water vapour content of the air at various relative air humidities**

(2) **Curve of max. water vapour content of air diffusing through the component is given by the temperature variation in the component – saturation partial pressure curve**

(3) **Relative vapour pressure difference between the sides of the components**

(4) **Absolute vapour pressure difference (air pressure difference) between the sides of the component**

temp. (°C)	max. vapour pressure of the air (kp/m²)
– 10	26.9
– 5	40.9
0	62.3
+ 5	88.9
+ 10	125.2
+ 15	173.9
+ 20	238.1
+ 25	323.0

(5) **Vapour pressure of the air**

outside temp. (°C)	relative air humidity		
	50	60	70
– 12	33.5%	25%	17.8%
– 15	30.8%	23%	16.2%
– 18	28.4%	21%	15.0%

(6) **Max. contribution of air boundary layer or the condensation barrier ('X')**

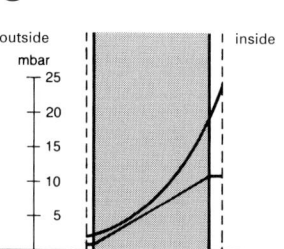

(7) **The vapour pressure remains less than the maximum possible, no condensation**

(8) **Excess contribution by air boundary layer: condensation in and on component**

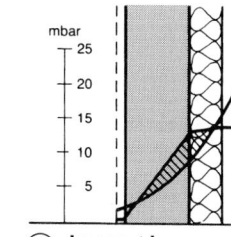

(9) **The storage factor = slope of curve; falls towards the outside: good**

(10) **Incorrect layer sequence: the storage factor = slope of the curve; increases towards the outside: condensation occurs inside**

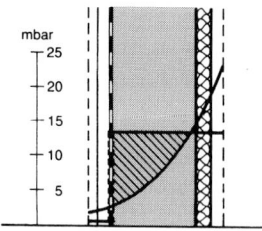

(11) **Condensation barrier on cold side: condensation in component**

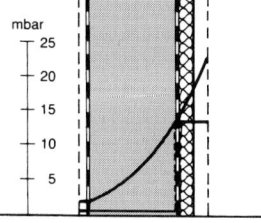

(12) **Extra condensation barrier on warm side prevents condensation**

THERMAL INSULATION

Water Vapour Diffusion

Water vapour, the gaseous form of water, arises through steaming (at boiling point) and evaporation (at any temperature); the heat required for conversion to the gaseous form (approx. 700 Wh) is extracted from the surroundings. Water vapour is invisible in the air; 'clouds of steam' are water droplets suspended in the air. Air can only contain a certain amount of water vapour: the warmer the air, the greater the possible water vapour content. The relative humidity of the air is given by the percentage value of this maximum quantity actually contained in the air. If the temperature of the air falls, then for a given water vapour content, the relative air humidity increases.

Example: Water vapour content of air at 12.3 mbar
Air 20°C; 12.3 mbar / 23.4 mbar = 52%
Air 15°C; 12.3 mbar / 17.5 mbar = 72%
Air 10°C; 12.3 mbar / 12.3 mbar = 100%

If, in this example, the air temperature fell even lower, then the water vapour would condense to become water – as seen in early morning 'dew'. The temperature at which the relative air humidity reaches 100%, is called the dew point of the prevailing water vapour/air mixture.

The atmospheric air pressure is of the order of 1 bar or 1000 mbar (also referred to as a HectoPascal). In a water vapour/air mixture, a part of this pressure is created by the water vapour, referred to as the vapour pressure. In practice, this quantity is used to quantify the water vapour content of the air → (5), since the consideration of diffusion is then more clearly seen (0.6 mbar corresponds to 1 g water/kg air).

Differences in vapour pressure → (3) are thus only different contents of water vapour molecules at the same total (air) pressure. (Note, by contrast: the absolute pressure difference in the sense of a steam boiler → (4), and for example in roof sheeting blisters → p. 79.)

Also, different vapour pressures always tend to equalise through diffusion, by feeding through the components and their layers. The component layers oppose this process through the diffusion resistance μd. This product gives the thickness of the air layer which would have the same diffusion resistance; it is calculated as the product of the layer thickness d and the diffusion resistance coefficient μ (→ pp. 115–16).

Due to the diffusion, a vapour pressure drop occurs within the components; this drop is distributed through the individual layers in accordance with their contribution to the total diffusion resistance of the component – analogous to the temperature variation in the components. The air boundary layers can be neglected due to their small thicknesses (05 mm outside, 20 mm inside).

Example: inside 20°/50% = 11.7 mbar, outside 15°/80% = 1.3 mbar
difference 119 – 14 = 10.4 mbar
wall 240 mm brick; μ×d 4.5×24 = 1080 mm 94.7% ×105 = 9.8 mbar
internal plaster 15 mm; μ×d 6×1.0 = 60 mm 5.3% ×105 = 0.6 mbar
1140 mm 100%

Diffusion examples

To avoid damage to buildings, condensation in the components should be avoided. Condensation occurs where the actual water vapour content threatens to become greater than that possible for the temperature. In examples → (7) – (12), the component, including its air boundary layers, is represented to scale in terms of the thermal insulation; the curved line represents the maximum vapour pressure – as given by the linear variation in temperature. The following points are important in avoiding damage:

- Sufficient thermal insulation
  In example (7), the single-layer component has no condensation; however, in (8) condensation occurs on the inner surface of the component, since, clearly, the contribution of the air boundary is too large. The air boundary layer must not exceed a specific contribution X to the resistance to heat ΣR → (6).

- Correct layering
  The slope of the diffusion curve should be as steep as possible inside, but flat on the outside → (9); otherwise, condensation will occur → (10). This slope is given by the layer factor μλ: inside, high diffusion resistance coefficient (μ) and good thermal conduction (λ) gives a high layer factor μλ: outside, low diffusion resistance coefficient, poor thermal conduction gives a low layer factor μλ.

- Vapour barrier in the right place
  If a vapour barrier layer is on the outside, then the total vapour pressure drop takes place there; the result is condensation → (11); if this is to be avoided, there must be a vapour barrier on the inside and the layers up to the vapour barrier must not exceed a specific contribution X of the total thermal resistance ΣR → (6).

Types of Construction

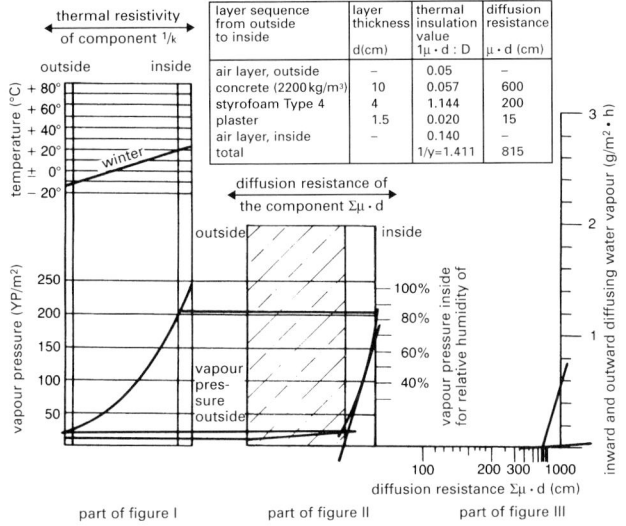

① **Solid wall without insulation**

② **Solid roof with vapour-proof outer skin**

layer sequence from outside to inside	layer thickness d(cm)	thermal insulation value $1\mu \cdot d : D$	diffusion resistance $\mu \cdot d$ (cm)
air layer, outside	–	0.05	–
concrete (2200 kg/m³)	10	0.057	600
styrofoam Type 4	4	1.144	200
plaster	1.5	0.020	15
air layer, inside	–	0.140	–
total	–	$1/y = 1.411$	815

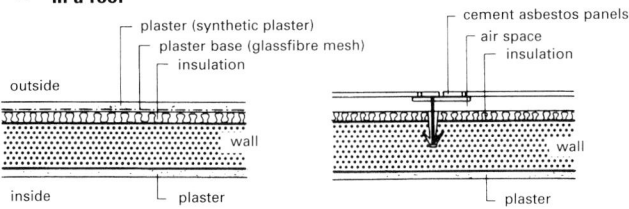

③ **Investigation of the production of water through condensation in a roof**

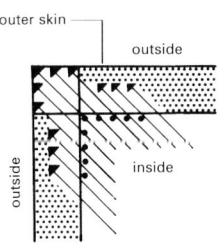

④ **Solid wall with vapour-proof outer skin**

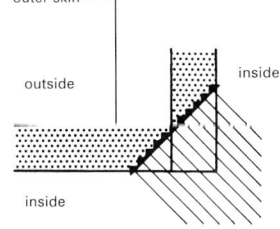

⑤ **Solid wall with rear-ventilated outer skin**

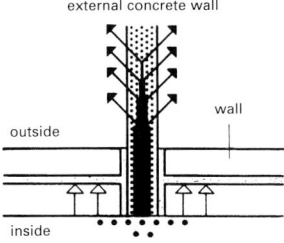

⑥ **Water from condensation occurs on inside surface of the outside corner**

⑦ **No water due to condensation occurs on the inside corner**

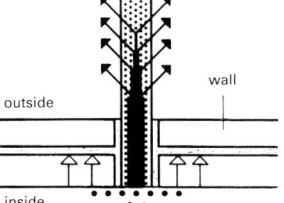

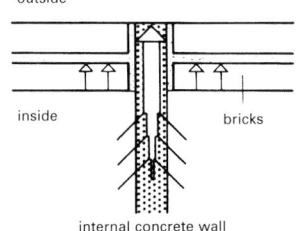

⑧ **Water from condensation occurs on large outer surface of the cold bridge (high heat extraction per unit area)**

⑨ **The heat extraction per unit area is significantly less on the large inside surface of the cold bridge**

Construction without vapour barrier → ①
Conventional construction contains no vapour retarding layers. Layers should be provided so that no condensation occurs: for sufficient thermal insulation, the layer factor λ should fall from inside to outside. In the case of very damp rooms (e.g. swimming pools), the vapour pressure variation should be checked either graphically or by calculation.

Note: on the outside of thermal insulation layers with normal plastering, there is a danger of cracking due to the build up of heat and low shear strength of the base material; therefore, glass fibre reinforced finishing plaster should be applied (but not in the case of swimming pools – see pp. 242–3).

Construction with vapour barrier → ②
In more recent building construction ('warm roof', 'warm façade'), there is a vapour impermeable outside layer, resulting in the necessity for an internal vapour barrier (→ p. 112). On vertical components, this is difficult to accomplish; a better form of construction is to provide a rear-ventilated outer skin (except for prefabricated walls). Note: the thermal insulation, including the air boundary layer on the layers up to the condensation barrier, must not exceed a specific level of contribution to the resistance to heat (p. 112). In solid constructions, protection of the vapour barrier against mechanical damage can be achieved by means of a protective layer. Since no high pressure – in the sense of a steam boiler – occurs on the inside of the vapour barrier, only vapour pressure (→ p. 112), the frequently recommended 'pressure compensation' provided by this layer, is not in fact required.

Construction with rear ventilated outer skin → ⑤
Rear ventilation avoids the vapour barrier effect of relatively vapour tight outer layers. It works by exploiting height difference (min. fall 10% between air inlet and air outlet). If there is only a small difference, then a vapour-retarding layer or vapour barrier is required (arrangement → construction with a vapour barrier), otherwise there will be excessive vapour transmission and condensation at the outer skin. The layering on the inner skin should be as for construction without a vapour barrier. However, the inner skin must always be airtight.

Cold bridges are places in the structure with low thermal insulation relative to their surroundings. At these places, the contribution of the air boundary layer to the resistance flow to heat increases, such that the surface temperature of the inner surface of the cold bridge reduces and condensation can occur there. The increase in heating costs due to the cold bridge, on the other hand, is insignificant, so long as the cold bridge is relatively small; this is not the case, however, for single-glazed windows which, in reality, are also cold bridges → ⑦ p. 111.

To avoid condensation on the surface of the component and its unwelcome consequences (mould growth, etc.), the temperature of the inner surface of the cold bridge, must be increased. This can be achieved by either reducing the heat extraction through the cold bridge by means of an insulating layer against the 'outer cold' (increasing the thermal insulation reduces the percentage contribution of the air boundary layer to the resistance to heat flow ΣR), or increasing the heat input to the cold bridge by increasing the inner surface of the cold bridge, e.g. good conducting surroundings to the cold bridge, and/or blowing with warm air. This will result in an actual reduction in the inner surface resistance $1/\alpha_i$ in relation to the cold bridge and hence also the contribution of the air boundary layer to the resistance to heat flow ΣR. Typical examples are shown in ⑧. However, a normal outer corner in a building → ⑥, forms a cold bridge, since, at such a point, the opposite to that shown in ⑨ occurs; a large heat transmitting outer surface is in combination with a small heat inputting inner surface, so that the insulation of the air boundary layer in the corners is appreciably higher than that on the surface.

For this reason, condensation and mould are often seen in the corners of walls with minimal thermal insulation.

description and illustration	thickness S (mm)	thermal resistance 1/Λ m²K/W in the centre	in the worst position
1. reinforced concrete			
reinforced concrete ribbed floor (without plaster)	120	0.20	0.06
	140	0.21	0.07
	160	0.22	0.08
	180	0.23	0.09
	200	0.24	0.10
	220	0.25	0.11
	250	0.26	0.12
reinforced concrete beamed floor (without plaster)	120	0.16	0.06
	140	0.18	0.07
	160	0.20	0.08
	180	0.22	0.09
	200	0.24	0.10
	220	0.26	0.11
	240	0.28	0.12
2. reinforced concrete ribbed/beamed floors with hollow clay blocks			
hollow clay blocks as intermediate components without cross webs (without plaster)	115	0.15	0.06
	140	0.16	0.07
	165	0.18	0.08
hollow clay blocks as intermediate components with cross webs (without plaster)	190	0.24	0.09
	225	0.26	0.10
	240	0.28	0.11
	265	0.30	0.12
	290	0.32	0.13
3. reinforced concrete floors with hollow clay blocks			
hollow clay blocks for partly grouted butt joints	115	0.15	0.06
	140	0.18	0.07
	165	0.21	0.08
	190	0.24	0.09
	225	0.27	0.10
	240	0.30	0.11
	265	0.33	0.12
	290	0.36	0.13
hollow clay blocks for fully grouted butt joints	115	0.13	0.06
	140	0.16	0.07
	165	0.19	0.08
	190	0.22	0.09
	225	0.25	0.10
	240	0.28	0.11
	265	0.31	0.12
	290	0.34	0.13
4. reinforced concrete hollow beams			
(without plaster)	65	0.13	0.03
	80	0.14	0.04
	100	0.15	0.05

(1) **Thermal resistance (thermal insulation values) 1/Λ m²K/W)**

type of concrete	raw weight of concrete (kg/m²)	thickness (cm) 12.5	18.75	25.0	31.25	37.5
aerated concrete, foam concrete, lightweight concrete, autoclaved aerated concrete	400	0.89[3]	1.34[3]	1.79[2]	2.23[2]	2.68[2]
	500	0.78[3]	1.17[2]	1.56[2]	1.95[1]	2.34[1]
	600	0.66[3]	0.99[2]	1.32[1]	1.64[1]	1.97
	800	0.54[2]	0.82[1]	1.09	1.36	1.63
lightweight reinforced concrete in closed structure, using expanded clay, expanded slate, etc., without quartz sand	800	0.41[2]	0.63[1]	0.83[1]	1.04	1.29
	1000	0.33[2]	0.49[1]	0.66	0.82	0.99
	1200	0.25	0.38	0.50	0.63	0.79
	1400	0.20	0.30	0.40	0.50	0.60
	1600	0.17	0.26	0.34	0.43	0.51
lightweight concrete with porous additions, without quartz sand	600	0.57[3]	0.85[2]	1.14[1]	1.42[1]	1.70
	1000	0.35	0.52	0.69	0.87	1.04
	1400	0.22	0.33	0.44	0.55	0.66
	1800	0.14	0.20	0.27	0.34	0.41
reinforced concrete	(2400)	0.06	0.09	0.12	0.15	0.18

[1] weight per unit surface area, including plaster ≥ 200 kg/m²
[2] weight per unit surface area, including plaster ≥ 150 kg/m²
[3] weight per unit surface area, including plaster ≥ 100 kg/m²

(2) **Thermal resistance 1/Λ (thermal insulation value; m²K/W) large format concrete components: the use of light reinforced concrete (e.g. for balconies) provides an improvement in thermal insulation of up to 68.3%**

Exterior Walls and Roofs

Mineral plaster should not be used with outer insulation; instead, a rear-ventilated type should be used → (5) or synthetic plaster (reinforced glassfibre), if necessary, with a mineral finishing plaster.

Critical detail points: Movement joint at flat roof junction → pp. 80–1 et seq.; radiator alcove → (6). Thermal insulation is essential to reduce costs (thin wall, higher temperature) for the window junctions → (6).

Special case of damp rooms (e.g. swimming baths): Greater insulation; max. contribution X of the inner layers (air boundary layer, layers up to the vapour barrier, → p. 113 is smaller. Synthetic plaster is used here, so a rear-ventilated cladding is a better barrier to condensation → (5); or use a construction incorporating a vapour barrier → (4).

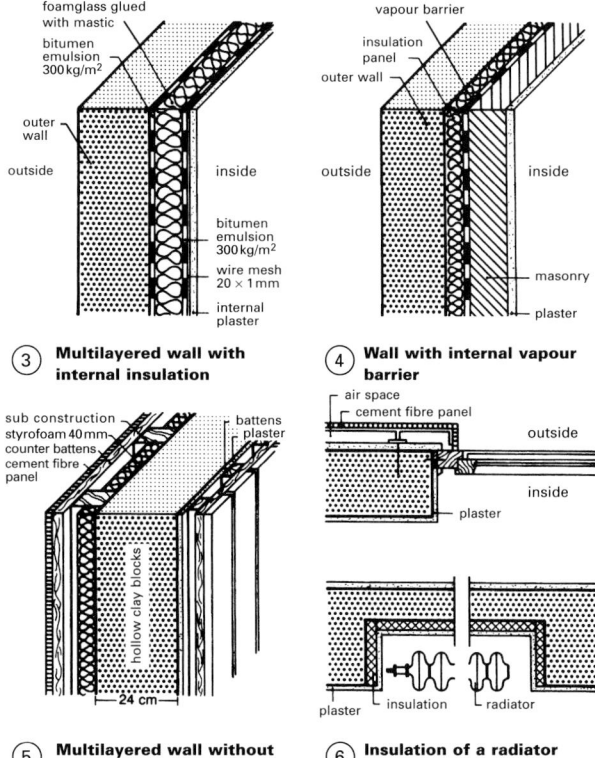

(3) **Multilayered wall with internal insulation**

(4) **Wall with internal vapour barrier**

(5) **Multilayered wall without vapour barrier**

(6) **Insulation of a radiator recess**

Thermal insulation details: Roof

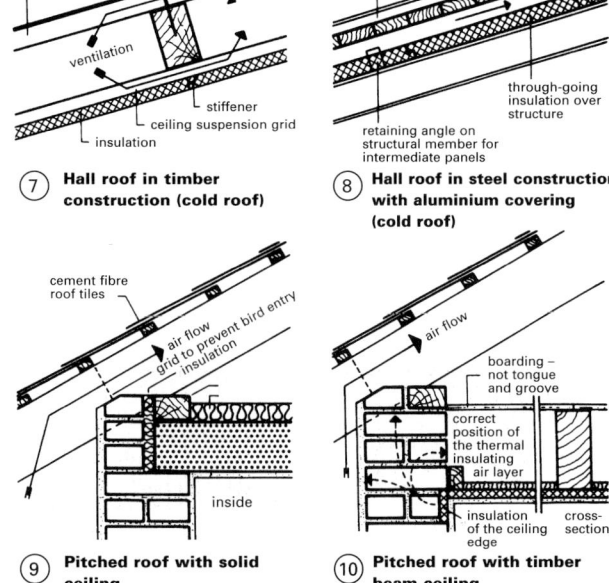

(7) **Hall roof in timber construction (cold roof)**

(8) **Hall roof in steel construction with aluminium covering (cold roof)**

(9) **Pitched roof with solid ceiling**

(10) **Pitched roof with timber beam ceiling**

item	material	gross density or gross density classification [1] [2] kg/m³	calculated value of thermal conductivity λ_R [2] W/(m·K)	standard value of water vapour diffusion resistance coefficient μ [4]
1 render, screed and other mortar layers				
1.1	lime mortar, lime cement mortar, mortar from hydraulic lime	(1800)	0.87	15/35
1.2	cement mortar	(2000)	1.4	15/35
1.3	lime plaster, plaster, anhydrous mortar, anhydrous lime mortar	(1400)	0.70	10
1.4	stucco without additives	(1200)	0.35	10
1.5	anhydrous screed	(2100)	1.2	
1.6	cement screed	(2000)	1.4	15/35
1.7	magnesia screed			
1.7.1	sub-floors and underlayers of two-layer floors	(1400)	0.47	
1.7.2	industrial floors and walkways	(2300)	0.70	
1.8	poured asphalt floor covering, thickness ≥ 15 mm	(2300)	0.90	[5]
2 large format components				
2.1	standard concrete (gravel or broken concrete with closed structure; also reinforced)	(2400)	2.1	70/150
2.2	light concrete and reinforced concrete with closed structure manufactured with the use of additions with porous surface with no quartz sand additions	800 900 1000 1100 1200 1300 1400 1500 1600 1800 2000	0.39 0.44 0.49 0.55 0.62 0.70 0.79 0.89 1.0 1.3 1.6	70/150
2.3	steam hardened aerated concrete	400 500 600 700 800	0.14 0.16 0.19 0.21 0.23	5/10
2.4	lightweight concrete with porous structure			
2.4.1	with non-porous additions e.g. gravel	1600 1800 2000	0.81 1.1 1.4	3/10 5/10
2.4.2	with porous additions with no quartz sand additions	600 700 800 1000 1200 1400 1600 1800 2000	0.22 0.26 0.28 0.36 0.46 0.57 0.75 0.92 1.2	5/15
2.4.2.1	using exclusively natural pumice	500 600 700 800 900 1000 1200	0.15 0.18 0.20 0.24 0.27 0.32 0.44	5/15
2.4.2.2	using exclusively expanded clay	500 600 700 800 900 1000 1200	0.18 0.20 0.23 0.26 0.30 0.35 0.40	5/15
3 construction panels				
3.1	asbestos cement panels	(2000)	0.58	20/50
3.2	aerated concrete building panels, unreinforced			
3.2.1	with standard joint thickness and wall mortar	500 600 700 800	0.22 0.24 0.27 0.29	
3.2.2	with thin joints	500 600 700 800	0.19 0.22 0.24 0.27	5/10
3.3	wall construction panels in lightweight concrete	800 900 1000 1200 1400	0.29 0.32 0.37 0.47 0.58	5/10
3.4	wall construction panels from gypsum, also with pores, cavities, filling materials or additions	600 750 900 1000 1200	0.29 0.35 0.41 0.47 0.58	5/10
3.5	gypsum board panels	(900)	0.21	8

4 masonry work, including mortar joints				
4.1	masonry work in wall bricks			
4.1.1	solid facing brick, vertically perforated facing brick, ceramic facing brick	1800 2000 2200	0.81 0.96 1.2	50/100
4.1.2	solid brick, vertically perforated brick	1200 1400 1600 1800 2000	0.50 0.58 0.68 0.81 0.96	5/10
4.1.3	hollow clay blocks	700 800 900 1000	0.36 0.39 0.42 0.45	5/10
4.1.4	light hollow clay blocks	700 800 900 1000	0.30 0.33 0.36 0.39	5/10
4.2	masonry work in limy sandstone	1000 1200 1400 1600 1800 2000 2200	0.50 0.56 0.70 0.79 0.99 1.1 1.3	5/10 15/25
4.3	masonry work in foundry stone	1000 1200 1400 1600 1800 2000	0.47 0.52 0.58 0.64 0.70 0.76	70/100
4.4	masonry work in aerated concrete blocks	500 600 700 800	0.22 0.24 0.27 0.29	5/10
4.5	masonry work in concrete blocks			
4.5.1	hollow blocks of lightweight concrete, with porous additions without quartz sand addition			
4.5.1.1	2-K block, width ≤ 240 mm 3-K block, width ≤ 300 mm 4-K block, width ≤ 365 mm	500 600 700 800 900 1000 1200 1400	0.29 0.32 0.35 0.39 0.44 0.49 0.60 0.73	5/10
4.5.1.2	2-K block, width = 300 mm 3-K block, width = 365 mm	500 600 700 800 900 1000 1200 1400	0.29 0.34 0.39 0.46 0.55 0.64 0.76 0.90	5/10
4.5.2	solid blocks in lightweight concrete			
4.5.2.1	solid blocks	500 600 700 800 900 1000 1200 1400 1600 1800 2000	0.32 0.34 0.37 0.40 0.43 0.46 0.54 0.63 0.74 0.87 0.99	5/10 10/15
4.5.2.2	solid blocks (apart from solid blocks S-W of natural pumice as for item 4.5.2.3 and of expanded clay, as for item 4.5.2.4)	500 600 700 800 900 1000 1200 1400 1600 1800 2000	0.29 0.32 0.35 0.39 0.43 0.46 0.54 0.63 0.74 0.87 0.99	5/10 10/15
4.5.2.3	solid blocks S-W of natural pumice	500 600 700 800	0.20 0.22 0.25 0.28	5/10
4.5.2.4	solid blocks S-W of expanded clay	500 600 700 800	0.22 0.24 0.27 0.31	5/10

① **Characteristic values for use in heat and humidity protection estimates**

item	material	gross density or gross density classification [1] [2] kg/m³	calculated value of thermal conductivity λ_R [2] W/(m·K)	standard value of water vapour diffusion resistance coefficient μ [4]
4.5.3	hollow blocks and T hollow bricks of standard concrete with a closed structure			
4.5.3.1	2-K block, width ≤ 240 mm 3-K block, width ≤ 300 mm 4-K block, width ≤ 365 mm	(≤1800)	0.92	
4.5.3.2	2-K block, width = 300 mm 3-K block, width = 365 mm	(≤1800)	1.3	
5 thermal insulation materials				
5.1	light wood fibre board panels panel thickness ≤ 25 mm = 15 mm	(360–480) (570)	0.093 0.15	2/5
5.2	multilayer light building panels of plastic foam sheets with coverings of mineral bound wood fibre plastic foam panels wood fibre layers (individual layers) 10 mm ≤ thickness < 25 mm ≥ 25 mm wood fibre layers (individual layers) with thickness < 10 mm must not be considered when calculating the thermal resistance 1/Λ	(≥15) (460–650) (360–460) (800)	0.040 0.15 0.093	20/70
5.3	foam plastic manufactured on the construction site			
5.3.1	polyurethane (PUR) foam	(≥37)	0.030	30/100
5.3.2	urea formaldehyde resin (UF) – foam	(≥10)	0.041	1/3
5.4	cork insulation material cork sheets thermal conductivity group 045 050 055	(80–500)	0.045 0.050 0.055	5/10
5.5	foam plastic			
5.5.1	polystyrene (PS) rigid foam thermal conductivity group 025 030 035 040 polystyrene particle foam polystyrene extruded foam	 (≥15) (≥20) (≥30) (≥25)	0.025 0.030 0.035 0.040	 20/50 30/70 40/100 80/300
5.5.2	polyurethane (PUR) rigid foam thermal conductivity group 020 025 030 035	(≥30)	0.020 0.025 0.30 0.035	30/100
5.5.3	phenolic resin (PF) – rigid foam thermal conductivity group 030 035 040 045	(≥30)	0.030 0.035 0.040 0.045	30/50
5.6	mineral and vegetable fibre insulation materials thermal conductivity group 035 040 045 050	(8–500)	0.035 0.040 0.045 0.050	1
5.7	foam glass thermal conductivity group 045 050 055 060	(100 to 105)	0.045 0.050 0.055 0.060	5)
6 wood and wood materials				
6.1	wood			
6.1.1	pine, spruce, fir	(600)	0.13	40
6.1.2	beech, oak	(800)	0.20	
6.2	timber materials			
6.2.1	plywood	(800)	0.15	50/400
6.2.2	chip board			
6.2.2.1	flat compressed panels	(700)	0.13	50/100
6.2.2.2	extruded panels (full panels not planking)	(700)	0.17	20
6.2.3	particleboard			
6.2.3.1	dense particleboard	(1000)	0.17	70
6.2.3.2	porous particleboard and bitumen wood particleboard	200 300	0.045 0.056	5
7 coverings, sealing materials and sealing rolls				
7.1	floor coverings			
7.1.1	linoleum	(1000)	0.17	
7.1.2	cork linoleum	(700)	0.081	
7.1.3	linoleum composite coverings	(100)	0.12	

item	material	gross density	calc. value	standard value
7.1.4	plastic coverings, e.g. including PVC	(1500)	0.23	
7.2	sealing materials, sealing rolls			
7.2.1	asphalt mastic, thickness ≥ 7 mm	(2000)	0.70	5)
7.2.2	bitumen	(1100)	0.17	
7.2.3	roofing strip, roof sealing rolls			
7.2.3.1	bitumen roof rolls	(1200)	0.17	10 000/ 80 000
7.2.3.2	bare bitumen roof rolls	(1200)	0.17	2000/ 20 000
7.2.3.3	glass fibre – bitumen roof rolls			20 000/ 60 000
7.2.4	plastic roof rolls			
7.2.4.1	PVC soft			10 000/ 25 000
7.2.4.2	PIB			400 000/ 1 750 000
7.2.4.3	ECB 2.0K			50 000/ 75 000
7.2.4.4	ECB 2.0			
7.2.5	sheets			
7.2.5.1	PVC sheets, thickness ≥ 0.1 mm			20 000/ 50 000
7.2.5.2	polyethylene sheets, thickness ≥ 0.1 mm			100 000
7.2.5.3	aluminium sheets, thickness ≥ 0.05 mm			5)
7.2.5.4	other metal sheets, thickness ≥ 0.1 mm			5)
8 other useful materials				
8.1	loose ballasting, covered			
8.1.1	of porous materials: expanded perlite expanded mica cork scrap, expanded blast furnace slag expanded clay, expanded slate pumice grit lava crust	(≤100) (≤100) (≤200) (≤600) (≤400) (≤1000) ≤1200 ≤1500	0.060 0.070 0.050 0.13 0.16 0.19 0.22 0.27	
8.1.2	of polystyrene plastic foam particles	(15)	0.045	
8.1.3	of sand, gravel, chippings (dry)	(1800)	0.70	
8.2	flagstones	(2000)	1.0	
8.3	glass	(2500)	0.80	
8.4	natural stone			
8.4.1	crystalline metamorphous rock (granite, basalt, marble)	(2800)	3.5	
8.4.2	sedimentary rock (sandstone, metamorphic, conglomerate)	(2600)	2.3	
8.4.3	natural porous ignous rock	(1600)	0.55	
8.5	soil (naturally damp)			
8.5.1	sand, sand and gravel		1.4	
8.5.2	cohesive soil		2.1	
8.6	ceramic and glass mosaic	(2000)	1.2	100/300
8.7	thermal insulating plaster	(600)	0.20	5/20
8.8	synthetic resin plaster	(1100)	0.70	50/200
8.9	metals			
8.9.1	steel		60	
8.9.2	copper		380	
8.9.3	aluminium		200	
8.10	rubber (solid)	(1000)	0.20	

[1] the gross density values given in brackets are only used to determine the surface area related quantities, e.g. to demonstrate heat protection in summer

[2] the gross density values relating to stone are descriptions of class corresponding to the related material standards

[3] the given calculated values of thermal conductivity λ_R of masonry work may be reduced by around 0.06 W/(mK) when factory standard light masonry mortar from additions with a porous structure, without quartz sand additions are used – with a solid mortar gross density ≤ 1000 kg/m³, however, the reduced values for aerated concrete blocks – item 4.4 and the solid blocks S-W of natural pumice and expanded clay – items 4.5.2.3 and 4.5.2.4 – must not be less than the corresponding items 2.3 and 2.4.2.1 and 2.4.2.2

[4] the respective, least favourable values, should be used for building construction

[5] in practice, vapour tight s_i ≥ 1500 m

[6] in the case of quartz sand additions, the calculated values of thermal conductivity increase by 20%

[7] the calculated values of thermal conductivity should be increased in the case of hollow blocks with quartz sand additions, by 20% for 2-K blocks and by 15% for 3-K blocks and 4-K blocks

[8] panels of thickness < 15 mm must not be taken account of in thermal insulation considerations

[9] in the case of footstep sound insulation panels in plastic foam materials or fibrous insulation materials, the thermal resistivity 1/Λ is stated on the packaging in all cases

[10] the given calculated values of thermal conductivity λ_R apply to cross grain application in wood and at right angles to the plane of the panel in the case of timber materials. In the case of wood in the direction of the grain and for timber materials in the plane of the panel, approx. 2.2 times the values should be taken, if more accurate information is unavailable

[11] these materials have not been standardised in terms of their thermal insulation values; the given values of thermal conductivity represent upper limiting values

[12] the densities are given as bulk densities in the case of loose ballasting

(1) **Characteristic values for use in heat and humidity protection estimates**

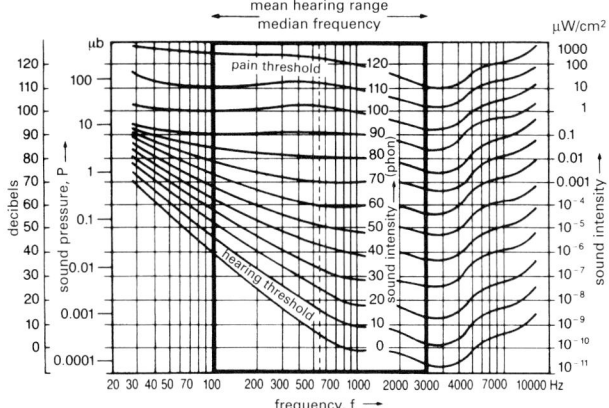

① **Relationship between loudness intensity (phon), acoustic pressure (µb), sound level (dB) and acoustic intensity (µW/cm²)**

0–10	hearing sensitivity commences
20	soft rustle of leaves
30	lower limit of noises of everyday activities
40	mean level of noises of everyday activities, low level of conversation; quiet residential road
50	normal level of conversation, radio music at normal room level in closed rooms
60	noise of a quiet vacuum cleaner; normal road noise in commercial areas
70	a single typewriter; or a telephone ringing at a distance of 1m
80	road with very busy traffic; room full of typewriters
90	noisy factory
100	motor horns at a distance of 7m; motor cycle
100–130	very noisy work (boilermakers' workshop, etc.)

② **Scale of sound intensities**

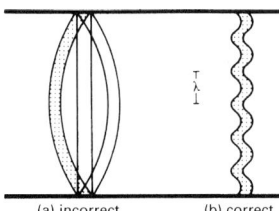

(a) incorrect   (b) correct

the wall (a) does not oscillate as a whole, but rather (b) in parts which vibrate in opposition to one another

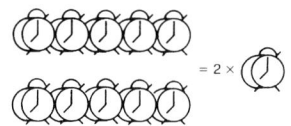

= 2 × ①

in general, humans hear a sound as having increased in intensity only twofold when, in fact, it has increased tenfold

③ **Representation of transverse waves on a wall at normal frequencies**

④ **Sensitivity to sound intensity**

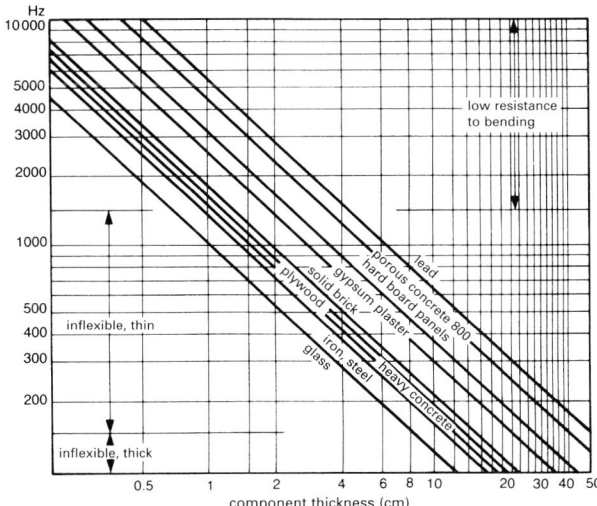

⑤ **Boundary frequency of panels in various building materials**

Even if propagation of sound is avoided, complete elimination of a noise is impossible. If the sound source and the hearer are located in the same room, then some reduction takes place through sound absorptivity → p. 120. If they are in separate rooms, then sound insulation is the main remedy.

A distinction is made between sound insulation of airborne sound and sound insulation of structure-borne sound: airborne sound sources initially disturb the surrounding air, e.g. radio, shouting or loud music; with structure-borne sound, the sound source is propagated directly through a structure, e.g. movement of people on foot, noise from plant and machinery. Sound from a piano is an example of both airborne sound and structure-borne sound.

Sound is propagated by mechanical vibration and pressure waves – very small increases and decreases in pressure relative to atmospheric pressure of the order of a few microbars (µb). (The pressure fluctuation generated by speaking in a loud voice is about one millionth of atmospheric pressure.) Sounds and vibrations audible to humans lie in the frequency range 20Hz–20000Hz (1Hz = 1 cycle per second). However, as far as construction is concerned, the significant range is 100–3200Hz, to which the human ear is particularly sensitive. In the human audible range, sound pressures extend from the hearing threshold to the pain threshold → ①. This hearing range is divided into 12 parts, called bels (after A. G. Bell, inventor of the telephone). Since 0.1 bel (or 1 decibel = 1dB) is the smallest difference in sound pressure perceptible to the human ear at the normal frequency of 1000Hz, decibels are a physical measure of the intensity of sound, related to unit surface area → ①. Usually, noise levels of up to 60dB are expressed in dB(A); those of more than 60dB in dB(B), a unit which is approximately equivalent to the former unit, the phon.

For airborne sound, the sound level difference (between the original sound level and the insulated sound level) serves to indicate the degree of sound insulation. For body-propagated sound, a maximum level is given, which must remain from a standard noise level. Sound insulation, principally due to mass, is provided by the use of heavy, thick components in which the airborne sound energy is initially dissipated through transfer of the airborne sound into the component, then through excitation of the mass of the component itself and then, finally, by transfer back into the air. If the component is directly excited (body sound), then its insulation is naturally lower.

Light sound-damping construction → ⑥ makes use of multiple transfer (air to component to air to component to air) in providing sound insulation; better insulation, relative to that expected due to component mass, only occurs above the resonant frequency, however, which consequently should be below 100Hz. (This is comparable to the resonant frequency of the oscillation of a swinging door which is already swinging due to light impacts. It is simple to slow the motion of the door by braking; to make it move more quickly is more difficult and requires force.) The intermediate space in double-shell construction is filled with sound-absorbing material, to avoid reflection of the sound backwards and forwards. The sound propagates in the air as a longitudinal wave → ③, but as a transverse wave in solid materials. The speed of propagation of longitudinal waves is 340m/sec but, within materials, this depends on the type of material, layer thickness and frequency. The frequency at which the velocity of propagation of a transverse wave in a structural component is 340m/sec, is called the boundary frequency. At this frequency, the transfer of sound from the air into the component and vice versa, is very good; therefore, the sound insulation of the component is particularly poor, poorer than would be expected from the weight of the wall. For heavy, quite inflexible building components, the boundary frequency is close to the frequency range of interest and therefore exhibits reduced sound insulation properties; for thin, flexible components, the boundary frequency is below this frequency range → ⑤.

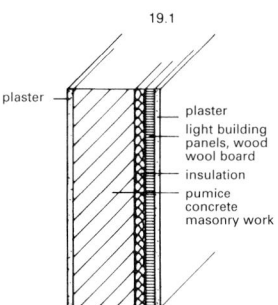

facing panel of plastered wood fibre board; light construction panels 15mm plaster; 115mm pumice concrete masonry; 16mm expanded styrofoam; 25mm light wood wool building panels – nailed, with large separation between nails; 20mm gypsum-sand-plaster

⑥ **Light sound-damping construction**

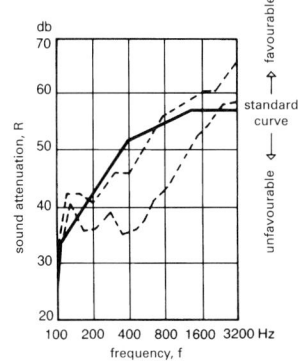

⑦ **Airborne sound insulation of the wall → ① from measurements by Prof. Gäsele: sound insulation without covering –7dB; with covering +2dB**

SOUND INSULATION

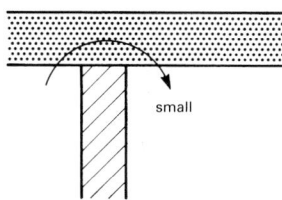

① **Airborne sound**

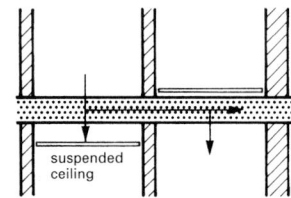

② **Standard curve for airborne sound**

③ **Secondary path via bordering single layer component**

④ **Diagonal transmission**

Thickness (cm) at given weight/unit surface area

heavy concrete* (2200 kg/m³): 6.25 | 12.5 | 25

solid brick*, limy sandstone* (1800 kg/m³): 5.25 | 11.5 | 24

hollow clay blocks* (1400 kg/m³): 5.25 | 11.5 | 24 | 36.5

lightweight concrete* (800 kg/m³): 6.25 | 12.5 | 25 | 37.5

*walls plastered on both sides (overall dimension)

brick (1900 kg/m³): 5.25 | 11.5 | 24

glass (2600 kg/m³): 0.3 | 0.5 | 1 | 1.5 | 2

compressed asbestos cement (2000 kg/m³): 0.3 | 0.5 | 1 | 1.5 | 2.5

gypsum (1000 kg/m³): 1 | 1.5 | 2 | 3 | 4 | 5 | 10 | 15 | 20 | 25

plywood (600 kg/m³): 0.3 | 0.5 | 1 | 1.5 | 2 | 3

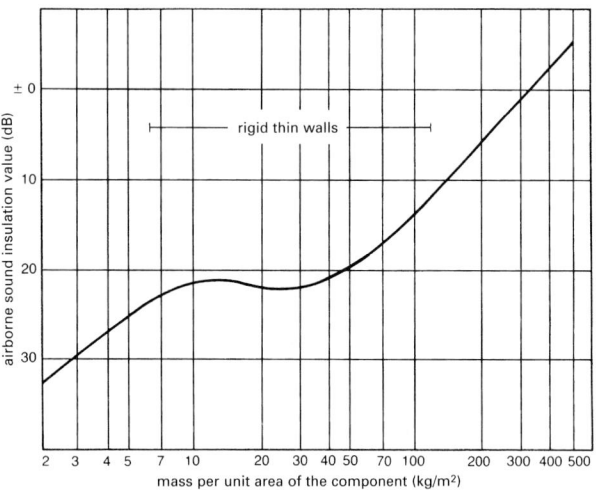

⑤ **Airborne sound insulation, weight/unit surface area and component thickness (Gäsele)**

1	simple door with threshold, without special sealing	up to	20 db
2	heavy door with threshold and good sealing	up to	30 db
3	double doors with threshold, without special sealing, opening individually	up to	30 db
4	heavy double doors, with threshold and sealing	up to	40 db
5	simple window, without additional sealing	up to	15 db
6	simple window, with good sealing	up to	25 db
7	double window, without special sealing	up to	25 db
8	double window, with good sealing	up to	30 db

⑥ **Sound insulation of doors and windows**

With airborne sound, the aerial sound wave excites the component → ①; hence, the effect of the boundary frequency on the sound insulation increases → ⑤.

The standard curve shows how large the sound level difference must be at the individual frequencies, as a minimum, so as to achieve a level of sound insulation of ±0 dB. Prescribed values → ②; required wall thicknesses → ⑦.

However, the effect of sound transmitted by 'secondary paths' (e.g. sound from foot steps) can be more disruptive than that from impact, so these must be taken into account in the sound insulation calculations. (For this reason, test results should always be drawn up for sound insulating walls with due consideration of the usual secondary paths.) Components which are stiff in bending, with weights per unit surface area of 10–160 kg/m², are particularly likely to provide secondary paths. Therefore, living room dividing walls – which are contacted by such components in the form of lateral walls – should have a weight of at least 400 kg/m². (Where the contacting walls have a surface weight of over 250 kg/m², this value can be 350 kg/m².)

Doors and windows, with their low sound insulation properties → ⑥, have a particularly adverse effect on insulation against airborne sound; the small proportion of the surface occupied by the openings is usually subject to a sound insulation value which is less than the arithmetic mean of the sound damping of wall and opening. Therefore, the sound insulation of the door or window should always be improved where possible. Walls which have insufficient sound insulation can be improved through the addition of a non-rigid facing panel → ⑥ p. 117. Double walls can be particularly well soundproofed if they contain soft, springy insulating material and are relatively flexible → ⑥ p. 117, or if the two wall panels are completely separately supported. Flexible panels are relatively insensitive to small sound bridges (by contrast to rigid panels). Type testing methods of construction should always be employed on sound insulating double walls. Covering layers of plaster on insulation materials of standard hardness (e.g. on standard styrofoam) considerably reduces the sound insulation.

item	description	gross density (kg/dm³)	wall weight >400 kg/m²		wall weight >350 kg/m² <400 kg/m²	
			mm	kp/m²	mm	kp/m²
	masonry work in solid, perforated and hollow blocks, plastered on both sides to a thickness of 15 mm					
1	perforated brick, solid brick	1	365	450	300	380
2		1.2	300	445	240	360
3		1.4	240	405	–	–
4	solid engineering brick	1.8	240	485	–	–
5		1.9	240	505	–	–
6	hollow sand lime bricks	–	–	–	300	380
7		1.2	300	440	240	360
8	sand lime perforated bricks	1.2	300	445	240	360
9		1.4	240	405	–	–
10		1.6	240	440	–	–
11	solid sand lime bricks	1.6	240	440	–	–
12		1.8	240	485	–	–
13		2	240	530	–	–
14	foundry stone	1.8	240	485	–	–
15	hard foundry stone	1.9	240	505	–	–
16	2- or 3-chambered hollow concrete blocks / reversed laid, with cavities filled with sand	1	300	420	–	–
17		1.2	300	460	–	–
18		1.4	240	410	–	–
19		1.6	240	440	–	–
20		1	365	400	–	–
21	without sand filling	1.2	–	–	–	–
22		1.4	–	–	300	355
23		1.6	300	430	240	380
24	lightweight concrete solid blocks	0.8	365	405	–	–
25		1	365	450	300	380
26		1.2	300	445	240	360
27		1.4	240	405	–	–
28		1.6	240	440	–	–
29	aerated/foamed concrete blocks	0.6	–	–	490	390
30		0.8	490	485	365	380
	lightweight concrete and concrete in unjointed walls and storey-depth panels, 15 mm plaster on both sides					
31	aerated/foamed concrete blocks	0.6	–	–	500	350
32		0.8	437.5	400	375	350
33	pumice/bituminous coal slag,	0.8	437.5	400	375	350
34	concrete with brick debris,	1	375	425	312.5	360
35	or similar	1.2	312.5	425	250	–
36		1.4	250	400	–	350
37		1.6	250	450	187.5	350
38		1.7	250	475	187.5	370
39	concrete with porous debris,	1.5	250	425	–	–
40	with non-porous additions,	1.7	250	475	187.5	370
41	e.g. gravel	1.9	187.5	405	–	–
42	gravel or broken concrete with closed structure	2.2	187.5	460	150	380

⑦ **Minimum thicknesses of single-layer walls for airborne sound insulation ≥ 0dB**

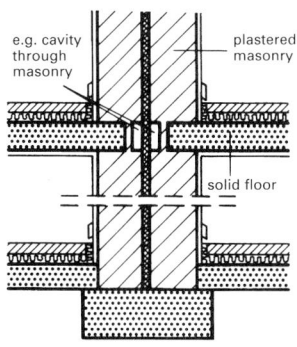

(1) **Double skin dividing wall with continuous cavity**

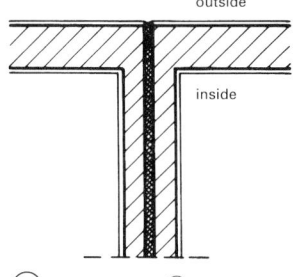

(2) **Plan view → (1)**

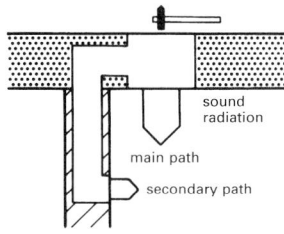

(3) **Sound conduction through solid structure**

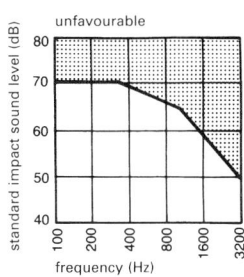

(4) **Standard curve for impact sound**

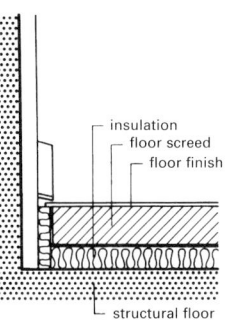

(5) **Plaster applied down to floor level before floor screed; prescribed for porous walls**

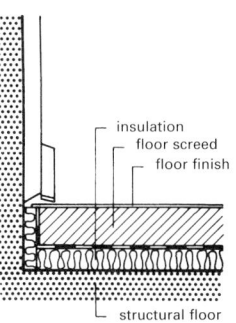

(6) **Plaster applied after floor screed, on solid walls**

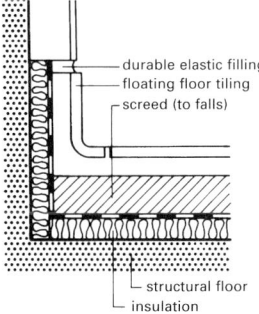

(7) **Floating tiled floor (baths)**

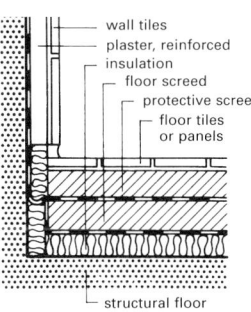

(8) **Floor construction with ceiling for bathrooms with shower**

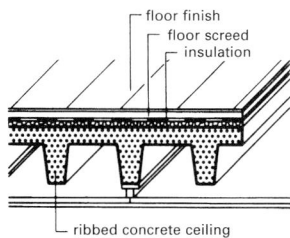

(9) **Soft, pliable suspended ceiling**

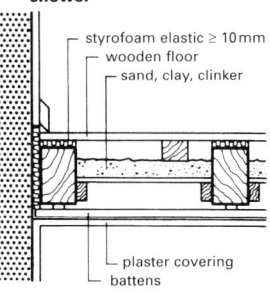

(10) **Possible solution for impact sound insulation on a timber joist ceiling**

House dividing walls

House dividing walls constructed from wall leafs with leaf weights per unit surface area < 350 kg/m² must be separated by a cavity over the entire depth of the house; their mass should be ≥150 kg/m² (200 kg/m² in multi-storey residences). If the dividing wall commences at the foundations, no additional precautions are necessary; if it commences at the ground level (as for dividing walls between separate residential accommodation), the floor above the cellar must have a suspended floor or a soft springy covering. The cavity should be provided with filling material (foam panels, etc.) preferably with staggered joints; small jointing areas can reduce the sound insulation, because the structure is resistant to bending.

Composite walls

In this case (including any walls with areas of different sound insulation properties, e.g. with a door), the total insulation value D_g is obtained after deducting the insulation reduction R from the overall insulation value → (11).

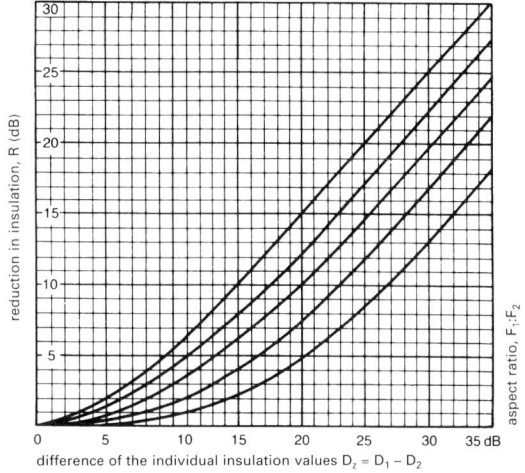

(11) **Determination of reduction in insulation**

calculation procedure:
1 establish the difference of the individual insulation values $D_z = D_1 - D_2$ (where $D_1 > D_2$)
2 determine aspect ratio of the insulating wall components
3 reduction in insulation R is given by the point of intersection of aspect ratio with the vertical ordinate D_z

Impact sound insulation

In the case of impact sound (e.g. noise due to footsteps), the ceiling is directly excited into vibration → (3). The standard curve → (4) gives a standardised impact sound level, i.e., the maximum that should be heard in the room below when a standard 'tramper' is in action above. To allow for ageing, the values achieved immediately after construction must be 3 dB better than the values shown.

The usual form of impact sound insulation is provided by 'floating' screed, i.e. a jointless, soft, springy insulating layer, covered with a protective layer and, then, a screed of cement concrete, anhydrous gypsum or poured asphalt. This simultaneously provides protection against airborne sound and is therefore suitable for all types of floors (floor groups I and II). The edge should be free to move, and mastic joint filler with enduring elasticity should always be used, particularly with tiled floors → (7), since the screed is thin and stiff, and is therefore extremely sensitive to sound bridges. With floors whose airborne sound insulation is already adequate (floor group II), impact insulation can also be provided by using a soft, springy floor finish → (8). Floors in floor group I can be upgraded to group II by the provision of a soft, springy suspended floor → (9). The degree to which this floor finish improves the impact sound insulation is judged from the improvement in dB attenuation.

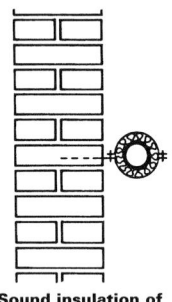

SOUND INSULATION

(1) **Sound insulation of pipework**

construction:
concrete B25   12 cm
bitumen felt   500 g/m²
cork sheet   5 cm
bitumen felt   500 g/m²
concrete B25   12 cm

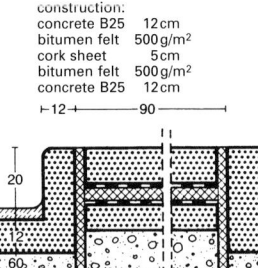

(2) **Sound insulated boiler foundation 90 cm wide**

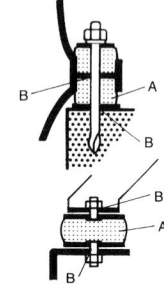

A = sound insulating material, e.g. rubber
B = air space – if necessary, filled with sound insulating material

(3) **Metal/rubber element**

(4) **Duct packed with sound absorbing material (transmitted sound damper)**

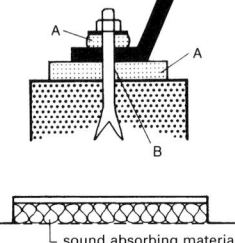

└ sound absorbing material

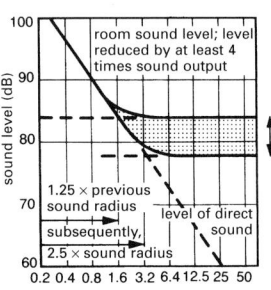

(5) **The level of reflected sound can be reduced by sound absorption measures; the sound radius increases but, at the same time, the noise level reduces outside the previous sound radius**

(6) **Sound radius and sound absorbing capability of a room**

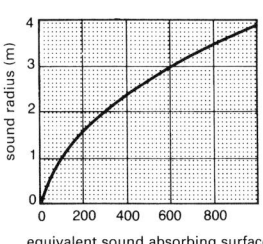

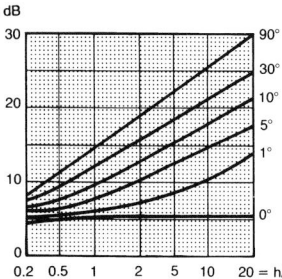

read off the shielding ordinate as a function of angle α → (8), and height (m)/sound wavelength
example: α = 30°, h = 2.50 m: at 500 Hz (med. freq. range) ≈ 340/500 = 0.68, wavelength is h/λ = 2.5/0.68 = 3.68, hence shielding effect = 17 dB

Q = sound source
B = hearer

(7) **Sound proofing due to outside barriers**

(8) **Diagram → (7)**

Noise from services

Noise from services can occur as plumbing fixture noise, pipework noise and/or filling/emptying noises:

- For plumbing fixture noise, the remedy is provided by sound-insulated valves with inspection symbols (test group I with at most 20 dB(A) overall noise level, test group II with at most 30 dB(A) only permissible for internal house walls and adjoining service rooms). All installations are improved, among other measures, by sound dampers.
- For pipework noise due to the formation of vortices in the pipework, the remedy is to use radiused fittings instead of sharp angles, adequate dimensioning, and sound damping suspensions → (1).
- For filling noise caused by water on the walls of baths, etc. the remedy is to muffle the objects, fit aerator spouts on the taps, and to sit baths on sound damping feet (and use elastic joints around the edges).
- For emptying noise (gurgling noises), the remedy is correct dimensioning and ventilation of drain pipes.

The maximum permissible sound level due to services in adjoining accommodation is 35 dB(A). Sound generating components of domestic services and machinery (e.g. water pipes, drain pipes, gas supply pipes, waste discharge pipes, lifts) must not be installed in rooms intended for quiet everyday activities (e.g. living rooms, bedrooms).

Sound insulation for boilers can be effected by sound-damped installation (isolated foundation → (2), sound-absorbing sub-construction), sound-damping hood for the burner, connection to chimney with sound-damping entry, and connection to hot pipework by means of rubber compensators.

In ventilation ducts of air conditioning systems, noise from sound transmission is reduced by means of so-called telephonic sound dampers; these comprise sound-absorbing packings, between which the air flows. The thicker the packing, the lower the frequencies which are covered. The ventilation ducts themselves should also be sound insulated.

Sound absorption

In contrast to sound insulation, sound absorption does not usually reduce the passage of sound through a component. It has no effect on the sound which reaches the ear directly from the source; it merely reduces the reflected sound.

Although the direct sound diminishes with distance from the source, the reflected sound is just as loud, or louder than the direct sound, at a distance greater than the 'sound' radius about the sound source → (5). If the reflection of sound is reduced, then the level of the reflected sound is reduced outside the original 'sound' radius, while the sound radius itself increases. Nothing changes within the original sound radius.

The sound absorption capability of a room is expressed in m² equivalent sound absorption, i.e. the ideal sound absorbing surface that has the same absorption capability as the room itself. For a reverberation time of 1.5 sec. – ideal for private swimming baths, etc. – the equivalent sound absorption surface A must be 0.1 m² for every m³ of room volume v (the sound radius would then be only 1.1 m in a room 6 × 10 × 2.5 m) and twice as large to achieve half the reverberation time.

Example: Swimming bath

40 m² water × 0.05		=	2.00 m²
100 m² walls and floor × 0.03		=	3.00 m²
60 m² acoustic ceiling × 0.4		=	24.00 m²
			29.00 m²

$A = \dfrac{29}{150} \approx 0.2\,V$; reverberation time is thus 0.75 seconds.

Protection against external noise

Precautions can be taken against external noise (traffic, etc.):

- Appropriate planning of the building, e.g. living/recreation rooms away from sources of noise
- Sound insulation of outer walls, particularly window and outer door insulation; fixed glazed installations with ventilation systems
- Installation of sound insulation shields in facades
- Sound protection through landscaping, e.g. embankments, walls or planted areas

In the case of embankments, walls and other screens, the sizing of the protective device can be obtained → (7) for the various wavelengths (wavelength is approx. 340 m/frequency). It can be seen how important dimension h is, as given by angle α.

THERMAL AND SOUND INSULATION

VIBRATION DAMPING

Sound Conduction Through Structures

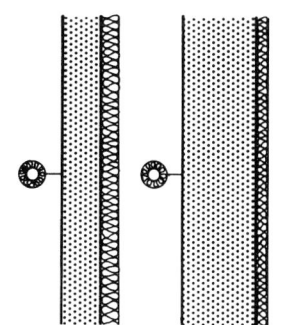

① Light wall – high excitation Heavy wall – less excitation

② Causes of structure-borne sound

airborne sound

sound transmitted through structure

③ Separate lift shaft with ≥30 mm mineral fibre lining

mineral fibre

lift

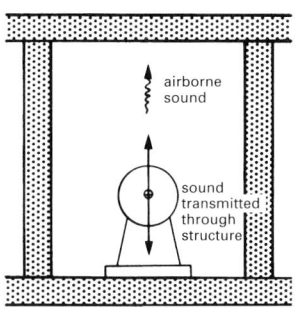

④ Top of shaft with Neoprene bearing layer

Neoprene

lift

⑤ Equipment installation with elastic insert in foundation

compensators with longitudinal limits

pipeline fixing point

concrete foundation bedplate

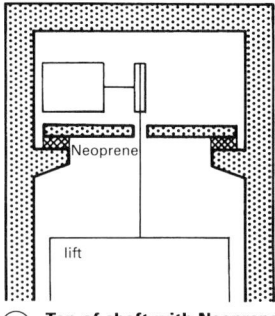

⑥ Example of individual spring element

after assembly

∅ d
vibration mounting

machine foot

height with no load

nickel-steel spring

⑦ Alignment of spring with centre of gravity

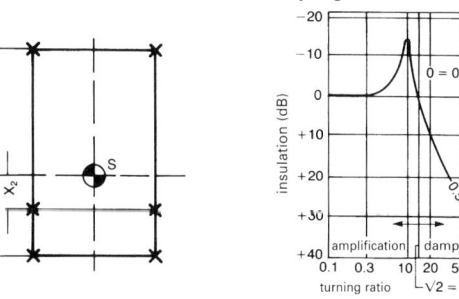

⑧ Effect of elastic bearing

insulation (dB)

amplification — damping

turning ratio   √2 = 1.41

⑨ Double elastic suspension for ventilator

spring

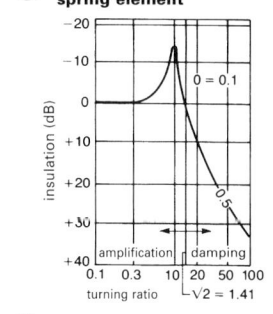

⑩ Example of vibration mounting ceiling element

splined pin
ceiling suspension
anchoring suspension
mineral fibre

min. 140

angle anchorage
gypsum board panels

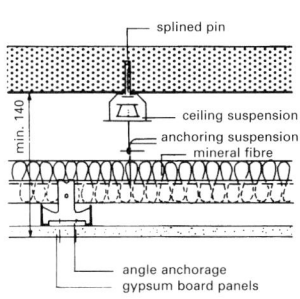

Vibrations in solid bodies, 'structure-borne sounds', are created either by sound in air, or directly, by mechanical excitation → ① + ②.

Since the alternating mechanical forces are usually higher than any produced by fluctuating air pressure, the audible radiation is usually greater in the case of direct excitation. Frequently, resonance phenomena occur, which lead to higher audible radiation in narrow frequency ranges.

If the radiated sound remains monotonic, the cause is usually the result of direct excitation of the structure. Anti 'structure-borne sound' measures must therefore seek to reduce this direct excitation and its further propagation.

Precautions to combat structure-borne sound transmission
In the case of water installations, only valves carrying inspection symbols in accordance with group I or II should be used. The water pressure should be as low as possible.

The water velocity plays a subordinate role.

Pipework should be attached to walls in accordance with good practice, with surface loading $m'' \geq 250 \, kg/m^2$.

Baths and tanks should be installed on floating screed and separated from walls. Walled enclosures should be flexibly jointed to the primary walls. Wall-suspended WC fittings cause direct excitation of the structure; however, rigid fixing is unavoidable, so if necessary, elastic layers should be introduced.

Water and drainage pipes must be fixed using elastic materials and should not be in direct contact with the structural wall.

Lifts should be installed in separate shafts → ③ and joints filled with at least 30 mm mineral fibre, or the top of the shaft provided with Neoprene bearing strips → ④.

Pumps and equipment must be installed on structure-borne sound insulated foundations and elastically connected.

Compensators are subject to tensile stresses, since the internal pressure also acts on the longitudinal axis of the assembly → ⑤.

Rubber granulate panels are particularly suitable as insulating material for foundations, due to their high compressive strength. If required, impact sound insulating materials of mineral fibre and plastic foam can be built in. Cork and solid rubber are unsuitable, since these materials are too stiff. The more the insulating materials are compressed together under load, without being overloaded, the better is the insulating effect.

With flat insulating materials, the loading must usually be greater than $0.5 \, N/mm^2$. If this cannot be guaranteed, then individual elements are required, effectively to add to the weight of the equipment.

The insulating effect is also greatest here if the elements are loaded to a maximum, without becoming overloaded. The individual elements can be of Neoprene or steel → ⑥.

Steel springs provide the best structural sound insulation, due to their low stiffness. In special cases, air springs can be used. In the case of individual springs, attention must be paid to the centre of gravity, to ensure the elements are uniformly loaded → ⑦.

In the case of periodic excitation (e.g. due to oscillating or rotating masses), the frequency of excitation must not coincide with the natural frequency of the elastically suspended system. Large motions result from the reverberation which, in the case of elements with low damping, can lead to structural failure → ⑧. Particularly high insulating properties may be obtained by using doubled elastic suspensions → ⑨. Unfavourable interaction between foundations on floating layers can lead to a reduction in insulation.

121

ROOM ACOUSTICS

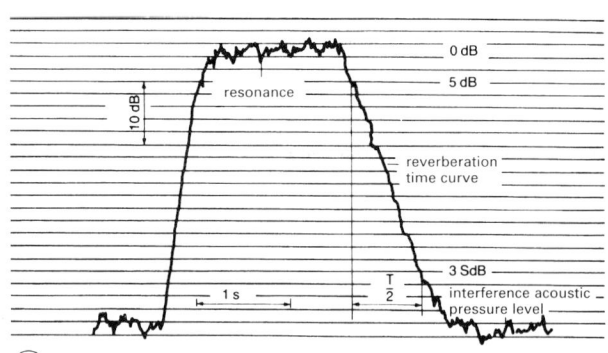

① **Measurement of reverberation time**

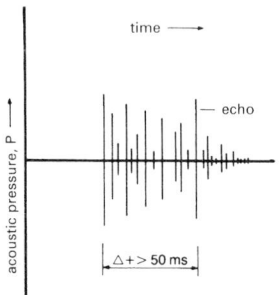

② **Echo criterion**

room function	reverberation time (s)	
speech	cabaret	0.8
	drama	1.0
	lecture	
music	chamber music	1.0...1.5
	opera	1.3...1.6
	concert	1.7...2.1
	organ music	2.5...3.0

③ **Reverberation times: optimum range**

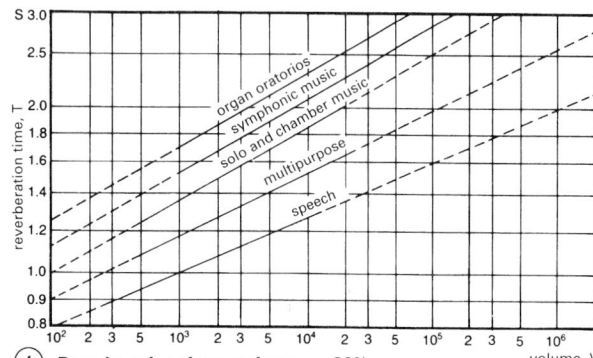

④ **Reverberation times: tolerance ±20%**

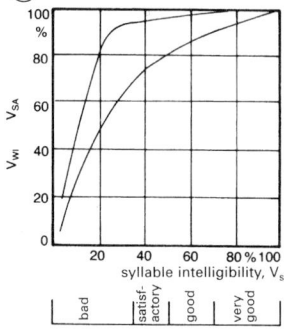

⑤ **Speech intelligibility**

purpose	characteristic volume (m³ per seat)	max. volume (m³)
spoken theatrical work	3...5	5000
multipurpose: speech and music	4...7	8000
musical theatre (opera, operetta)	5...8	15000
chamber music concert hall	6...10	10000
symphony music concert hall	8...12	25000
rooms for oratorios and organ music	10...14	30000

⑥ **Table of specific volumes**

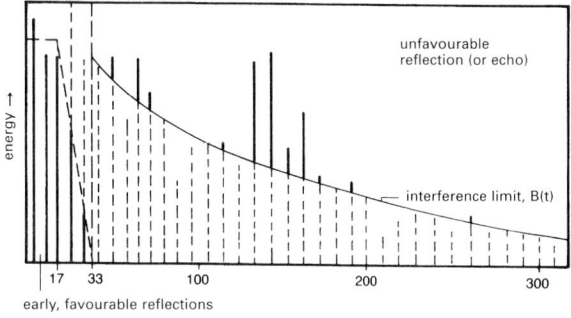

⑦ **Reflection sequence in the room**

Room acoustic planning should ensure that optimum audible conditions are created for listeners in rooms where speech and music are to be carried out. Various factors should be considered, of which the two most important are reverberation time, and reflections (as a consequence of the primary and secondary structure of the room).

(1) Reverberation time

This is the time taken for the decay of a noise level of 60 dB after the sound source has been switched off → ①. Evaluation is carried out over the range –5 to –35 dB.

(2) Absorption surface

The absorption surface is determined by the amount of absorbing material, expressed as an area having complete absorption (open window):

$A = \alpha_s \times S$

where α_s is the degree of sound absorption from echo chamber measurements, and S is the area of surface portion.

The reverberation time is calculated from the absorption surface from:

$t = 0.163 \times V \div \alpha_s \times S$ (after Sabine)

(3) Echoes

When individual, subjectively recognisable peaks are superimposed on a smoothly falling reverberation time curve → ①, these are described as echoes → ②. Various values of time and intensity apply as the echo criterion for speech and music. Rooms devoted to music should have a longer reverberation time, but are usually regarded as less critical from the point of view of echoes.

Requirements for rooms

(1) Reverberation time

The optimum value for reverberation time is dependent on the particular use and room volume → ③. In general, reverberation time is frequency-dependent (longer at low frequencies, shorter at high frequencies.) For f = 500 Hz, surveys have shown that approximations may provide optimum values → ④.

(2) Speech intelligibility

This is used to judge the degree of audibility of the spoken word → ⑤. It is not standardised, so various terms – sentence intelligibility, syllable intelligibility, evaluation with logatomes – are usual. In determining the intelligibility of speech, a number of collectively heard individual syllables of no significance (logatomes such as lin and ter) are noted; the correctness is used to make an assessment – a score of more than 70% implies excellent speech intelligibility. Newer, objective, methods make use of modulated noise signals (RASTI method) and lead to reproducible results at low expense.

(3) Impression of space

This is determined by the reception of reflections with respect to time and direction. For music, diffuse reflections are favourable for sound volume, while early reflections with delays of up to 80 ms (corresponding to 27 m path difference) with respect to the direct sound promote clarity → ⑥. Speech requires shorter delays (up to 50 ms) so as not to degrade the intelligibility.

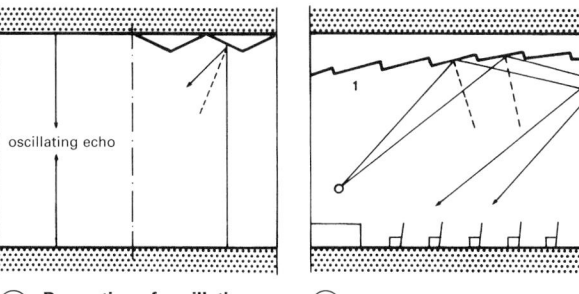

(1) Prevention of oscillating echoes

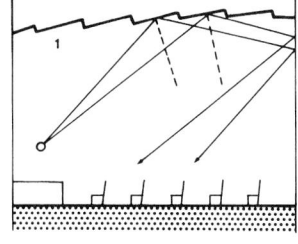

(2) Unfavourable ceiling shape

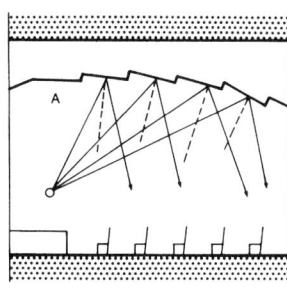

(3) In one plane for music; inclined downward towards the back for speech

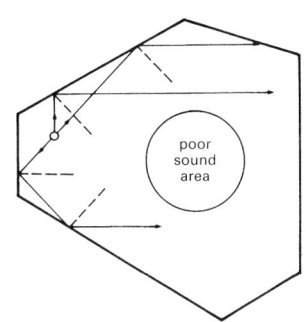

(4) Less favourable platform

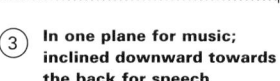

(5) Berlin Philharmonic – staggering the auditorium

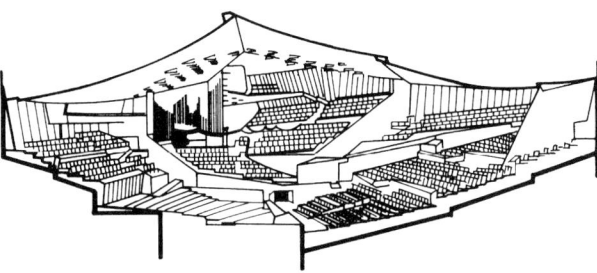

(6) Podium with small chamber music hall – Beethoven Archive, Bonn

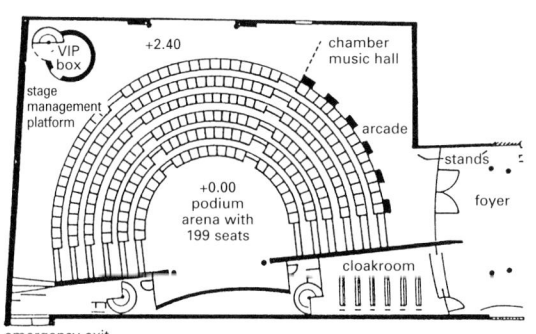

(7) Seats on ascending logarithmic curve

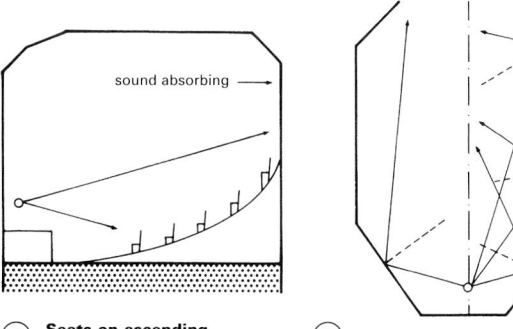

(8) Folding wall surface

For the music listener, early sideways reflections are better than ceiling reflections, even at very low delay times (asymmetry of the acoustic impression), since each ear receives a different signal. Narrow, high rooms with geometrically reflecting walls with multiple angles and diffusely reflecting ceilings are the simplest from the point of view of room acoustics.

Primary structure of rooms

Volume is application dependent → (6) p. 122: 4 m³/person for speech, 18 m³/person for concerts; too small a volume results in insufficient reverberation time. Narrow, high rooms with walls with multiple angles (early sideways reflections) are particularly suitable for music. For early initial reflections and balance of the orchestra, reflection surfaces are needed in the vicinity of the podium. The rear wall of the room should not cause any reflections in the direction of the podium, since these can have the effect of echoes. Parallel, planar surfaces should be avoided, to prevent directionally oscillating echoes due to multiple reflections → (1). Providing projections in the walls, at angles greater than 5°, avoids parallel surfaces and allows diffuse reflection to occur. The ceiling serves to conduct the sound into the back part of the room and must be shaped accordingly → (3). If the ceiling shape is unfavourable, large differences in sound intensity occur due to sound concentrations. Rooms where the walls are further apart at the back than at the front of the room produce unfavourable effects, since the reflections from the sides can be too weak → (4); this disadvantage can be compensated by the using additional reflection surfaces (Weinberg steps) – as in the Berlin and Cologne Philharmonics → (5) – or the walls may be provided with pronounced folding to guide the sound.

Wherever possible, the podium should be on the narrow side of the room; in the case of the spoken word or in small rooms (chamber music), it may even be arranged on a long wall (Beethoven Archive → (6)). Multipurpose rooms with variably arranged podia and plain parquet floors are frequently problematic for music. The podium must be raised in relation to the parquet, so as to support the direct propagation of the sound; otherwise, the level of the sound propagation would fall too quickly → (9). Providing an upward inclination of the seating levels, to obtain a uniform level of direct sound at all seats gives better visibility and acoustics → (7); the slope of the seating levels should follow a logarithmic curve.

Secondary structure

Reflection surfaces can compensate for an unfavourable primary structure: projections on the surface of walls which diverge, ceiling shapes produced by hanging sails or the use of individual elements → p. 124.

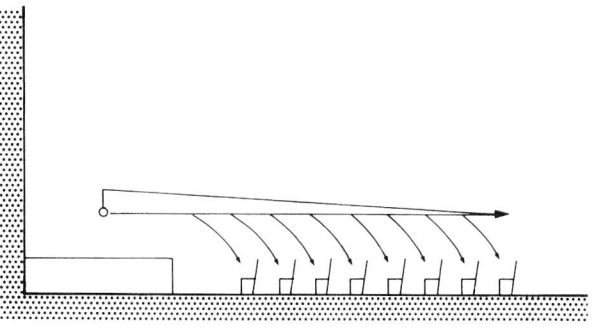

(9) Drop in sound level over absorbing surface

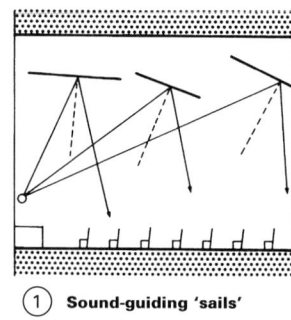

(1) Sound-guiding 'sails'

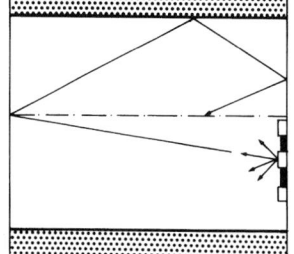

(2) Splitting unfavourable reflecting surfaces into elements

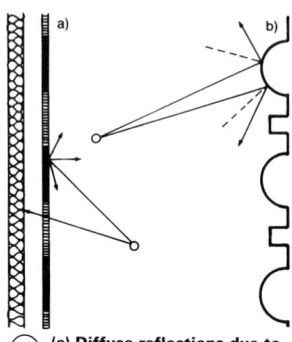

(3) (a) Diffuse reflections due to alternating material surface
(b) Diffusely reflecting surface

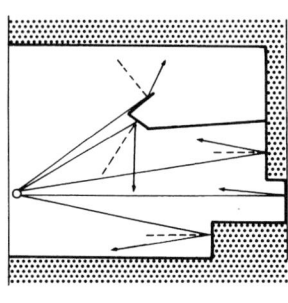

(4) Diffusion from reflections which occur at different times

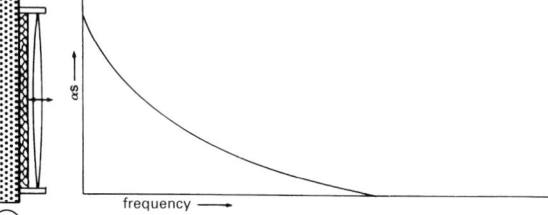

(5) Absorption of low frequencies due to surface oscillation

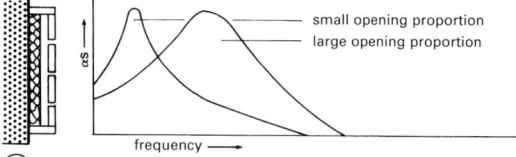

small opening proportion
large opening proportion

(6) Absorption behaviour of resonators

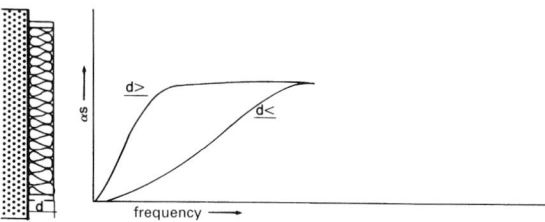

(7) Absorption by porous materials

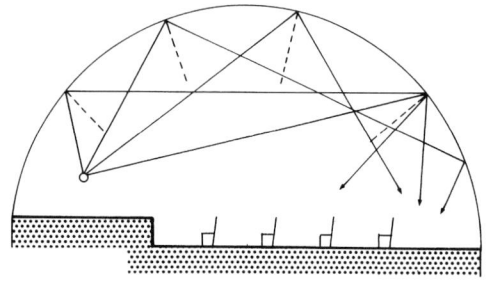

(8) Formation of focal point due to curved surface

Absorbing surfaces avoid sound concentrations, and allow the reverberation time to be matched to the required value. A suitable alternately reflecting and absorbing surface has the same reflecting effect as that produced by making the surfaces highly uneven, at strongly contrasting angles → ③. Curved surfaces can cause a focal point to develop (dome). Semi-circular rooms are particularly unsuitable due to a 3D concentration of the sound, if the centre of the circle is at the same height as the podium → ⑧; however, this can be avoided by shaping the ceiling curvature so as to achieve a very good sound reflection characteristic → ⑨. Surfaces from which echoes are anticipated must produce diffuse reflections, i.e. they must scatter the incident sound → ③. Diffuse reflections lead to smooth, uniform reverberation time curves due to the uniform distribution of the resulting sound. Subdivision of the surface with folds at angles greater than 5° is needed. Strong surface features, such as breastings or recesses, are equally effective, due to the division of the sound waves or non-simultaneous reflections → ④.

Reverberation time (based on the formula after Sabine) is given by:

$$t = \frac{0.163 \times V}{\alpha_s \times S}$$

In halls, the degree of sound absorption, α_s, determined using standard methods has a value between 0 and 1. Reverberation time is calculated for frequencies f of 125 Hz, 250 Hz, 500 Hz, 1000 Hz, 2000 Hz and 4000 Hz, but assessments of the mean reverberation time refer mostly to a value at 500 Hz. The calculation allows for all the specific values for individual surfaces, persons, seating and decoration. Frequently, the attainable reverberation time is determined solely from the absorption of the number of persons and of the seating. To make the reverberation time more independent of the number of persons, the type of seating material must exhibit the greatest possible absorption, both on the seat and the back of the seat, so that the absorption characteristics of the seating are the same when unoccupied as when occupied. Additional absorption surfaces for high frequencies are then required only if the specific volume → ⑥ p.122 is considerably exceeded. If the room volume and the seating are correctly determined, it is usually then only necessary to correct the reverberation time at low frequencies; adjustment is achieved through combining surfaces with different characteristics, and these are determined from their structure:

- Resonant surfaces absorb low frequencies. Surface area, separation and the level of filling of cavities are varied for fine tuning → ⑤.
- Surfaces with openings in front of cavities mainly absorb medium frequencies (Helmholtz Resonator). The proportion of the surface occupied by the hole, the volume of the cavity and the attenuation of the cavity determine the frequency, level and form of the maximum absorption → ⑥.
- Porous materials are used for the absorption of higher frequencies. Thickness and porosity of finishing layers influence the absorption of lower frequencies → ⑦.

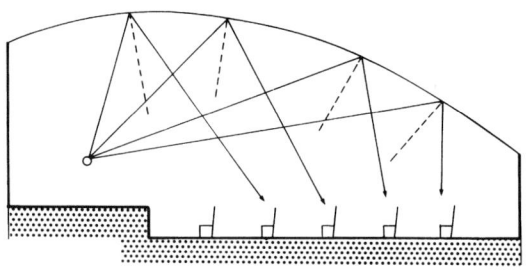

(9) Favourably directed sound from suitable curvature

Building regulations require that due consideration must be given in buildings to:

- the flammability of building materials
- the duration of fire resistance of the components expressed in terms of fire resistance classifications
- the integrity of the sealing of openings
- the arrangement of escape routes.

The aim is to prevent the start and spread of a fire, stem the spread of smoke and facilitate the escape or rescue of persons and animals. In addition consideration must be given to effective extinguishing of a fire. Active and passive precautions must be taken to satisfy these requirements. Active precautions are those systems that are automatically deployed in the event of fire; passive precautions are the construction solutions in the building and its components.

Active precautions include smoke and fire alarm systems, sprinkler systems, water spray extinguisher plant, CO_2 extinguishing installations, powder and foam extinguisher plant, and automatic smoke and heat venting systems. Passive precautions relate mainly to minimum structural sections, casings and coatings. In addition to these, other important measures are the layout of rising mains, installation of fire doors and fire windows, construction of supporting floors, water cooling of hollow steel profiles and the dimensioning of casings and coatings for steel profiles.

Fire detectors

A fire detector is a part of the fire alarm system and can trigger a transmitting device that raises the alarm in a remote control centre. There are automatic and non-automatic fire detectors. The latter are those which can be activated manually. Automatic fire detectors are parts of the overall fire alarm system that sense changes in specific physical and/or chemical parameters (either continuously or sequentially in set time intervals) to detect a fire within the monitored area. They must be:

- installed in sufficient numbers and be suited to the general arrangement of the area to be monitored
- selected according to the fire risk
- mounted in such a way that whatever parameter change triggers the alarm can be easily sensed by the detector.

Typical applications for different types of fire detectors

(1) Smoke detectors
These are used in rooms containing materials that would give off large volumes of smoke in the event of a fire.

- Optical smoke detectors: triggered by visible smoke.
- Ionisation smoke detectors: triggered by small amounts of smoke which have not been detected by optical means. These detectors provide earlier warning than optical smoke detectors and are suitable for houses, offices, storage and sales rooms.

(2) Flame detectors
These are activated by radiation emanating from flames and are used in rooms containing materials that burn without smoke, or produce very little.

(3) Heat detectors
These are useful for rooms in which smoke that could wrongly set off other early warning systems is generated under normal working conditions (e.g. in workshops where welding work is carried out).

- Maximum detectors: triggered when a maximum temperature is exceeded (e.g. 70°C).
- Differential detectors: triggered by a specified rise in temperature within a fixed period of time (e.g. a rise of 5°C in 1 minute).

The planning and installation of fire detection systems must be designed to suit the area to be monitored, room height and the type of ceiling and roofing.

Typical extracts from building regulations and guidelines produced by fire and insurance specialists

Fire development If the initial phase of a fire is likely to be of a type characterised by smouldering (i.e. considerable smoke generation, very little heat and little or no flame propagation), then smoke detectors should be used. If rapid development of fire is anticipated in the initial phase (severe heat generation, strong flame propagation and smoke development), then smoke, heat and flame detectors can be used, or combinations of the various types.

Fire detection areas The total area to be monitored must be divided into detection areas. The establishment of these detection areas should be carried out in such a way that rapid and decisive pinpointing of the source of the fire is possible. A detection area must only extend over one floor level (the exceptions to this being stairwells, ventilation and elevator shafts and tower type structures, which must have their own detection areas). A detection area must not overlap into another fire compartment and typically should not be larger than 1600 m².

Fire detection systems for data processing facilities The monitoring of electronic data processing facilities places special additional requirements on the planning and execution of fire alarm systems.

Factors influencing detector positions and numbers

(1) Room height
The greater the distance between the fire source and the ceiling, the greater the zone of evenly distributed smoke concentration will be. The ceiling height effects the suitability of the various types of smoke and fire detectors. Generally, higher ceiling sections whose area is less than 10% of the total ceiling area are not considered, so long as these sections of ceiling are not greater in area than the maximum monitoring area of a detector.

(2) Monitoring areas and distribution of the detectors
The number of fire detectors should be selected such that the recommended maximum monitoring areas for each detector are not exceeded. Some standards specify the maximum distance between detectors and the maximum distance allowed between any point on the ceiling and the nearest detector. Within certain limits there may be a departure from the ideal square grid pattern of the detectors.

(3) Arrangement of detectors on ceilings with downstanding beams
Depending on the room size, beams above a specified depth must be taken into account in the arrangement of the fire detectors. Typically, if the area of ceiling between the downstanding beams is equal to or greater than 0.6 of the permissible monitoring area of the detector, then each of these soffit areas must be fitted with detectors. If the portions of soffit area are larger than the permissible monitoring area, then the individual portions of soffit must be considered as individual rooms. If the depth of the downstanding beam is greater than 800 mm, then a fire detector must be provided for each soffit area.

(4) For spaces with multi-bay type roofs
Generally in this case, each bay must be provided with a row of detectors. Heat detectors are always to be fitted directly to the ceiling. In the case of smoke detectors, the distances required between the detector and the ceiling, or the roof, depend on the structure of the ceiling or roof and on the height of the rooms to be monitored. In the case of flame detectors, the distances should be determined for each individual case.

Internal fire spread (surface)

The linings of walls and ceilings can be an important factor in the spread of a fire and its gaining hold. This can be particularly dangerous in circulation areas, where it might prevent people escaping. Two factors relating to the property of materials need to be taken into account: the resistance to flame spread over the surface and the rate of heat release once ignited. Various testing methods are used to establish these qualities. In the UK, a numbered system categorises the levels of surface flame spread and combustibility: 0, with the highest performance (non-combustible throughout), followed by classes 1, 2, 3 and 4.

There are a series of standards that must be complied with relating to allowable class of linings in various locations. For example, for small rooms in residential buildings (4 m²) and non-residential buildings (30 m²), class 3 materials are acceptable; for other rooms and circulation spaces within dwellings, use class 1 materials; and for busy public circulation spaces, class 0 materials should be used. Rooflights and lighting diffusers that form an integral part of the ceiling should be considered a part of the linings. There are limitations on the use of class 3 plastic roof-lights and diffusers.

Internal fire spread (structure)

There are three factors to be considered under this heading:

(1) Fire resistance and structural stability

It is necessary to protect the structure of a building from the effects of fire in order to allow people to escape, to make it safe for firefighters to enter the building to rescue victims and tackle the fire, and also to protect nearby people and adjacent buildings from the effects of a collapse. The level of fire resistance required depends on a range of factors: an estimation of the potential fire severity (depending on the use and content of the building); the height of the building; type of building occupancy; the number of floors and the presence of basements. Fire resistance has three aspects: resistance to collapse, resistance to fire penetration and resistance to heat penetration. Building regulations provide tables that set out specific provisions and minimum requirements of these aspects for different structural elements in different classes of buildings.

(2) Compartmentation within buildings

It is often necessary to divide a large complicated building into separate fire-resisting compartments in order to prevent the rapid spread of fire throughout the building. The factors to be considered are the same as those for fire resistance. Regulations stipulate maximum sizes of compartments for different building types. In general, floors in multistorey buildings form a compartment division, as do walls that divide different parts of multi-use buildings. The use of sprinklers can allow an increase in the compartment size in non-residential buildings.

Careful attention should be paid to construction details of compartment walls and floors, particularly the junction details between walls, floors and roofs, such that the integrity of fire resistance is maintained. Strict rules apply to openings permitted in compartment walls and floors, these being restricted to automatic self-closing doors with the appropriate fire resistance, shafts and chutes with the requisite non-combustible properties and openings for pipes and services, carefully sealed to prevent fire spread.

There is a wide range of constructions, each of which offers a specific duration of resistance. For example, a floor of 21 mm of tongue and groove timber boards (or sheets) on 37 mm wide joists with a ceiling of 12.5 mm plasterboard with joints taped and filled, will provide 30 minutes of fire resistance. For 60 minutes' resistance the joists need to be 50 mm wide and the ceiling plasterboard 30 mm with joints staggered. This period is also achieved with a 95 mm thick reinforced concrete floor, as long as the lowest reinforcement has at least 20 mm cover.

An internal load-bearing wall fire resistance of 30 minutes can be achieved by a timber stud wall with 44 mm wide studs at 600 mm centres, boarded both sides with 12.5 mm plasterboard with joints taped and filled. The same will be achieved by a 100 mm reinforced concrete wall with 24 mm cover to the reinforcement. A resistance of 60 minutes is achieved by doubling the thickness of plasterboard on the stud wall to 25 mm, and increasing the thickness of the concrete wall to 120 mm. A 90 mm thick masonry wall will achieve the same 60 minutes resistance (only 75 mm is required for non-loadbearing partitions).

(3) Fire and smoke in concealed spaces

With modern construction methods there can be many hidden voids and cavities within the walls, floors and roofs. These can provide a route along which fire can spread rapidly, sometimes even bypassing compartment walls and floors. This unseen spread of fire and smoke is a particularly dangerous hazard. Steps must therefore be taken to break down large or extensive cavities into smaller ones and to provide 'cavity barriers', fire-resistant barriers across cavities at compartment divisions.

Regulations stipulate the maximum permitted dimensions for cavities depending on the location of the cavity and the class of exposed surface within it. Further stipulations dictate where cavity barriers must be installed (e.g. within roof spaces, above corridors and within walls). Generally the minimum standard of fire resistance of cavity barriers should be 30 minutes with regard to integrity and 15 minutes with regard to insulation. Fire stops must also be considered. These are seals that prevent fire spreading through cracks at junctions between materials that are required to act as a barrier to fire, and seals around perforations made for the passage of pipes, conduits, cables etc.

External fire spread

The spread of fire from one building to another is prevented by the fire resistant qualities of external walls and roofs. They must provide a barrier to fire and resist the surface spread of flame. The distance between buildings (or between the building and the boundary) is obviously an important factor, as is the likely severity of the fire, which is determined by the fire load of a building (i.e. the amount of combustible material contained within). Regulations therefore stipulate the required fire resistant qualities of external walls and the proportion and size of allowable unprotected areas (e.g. windows, doors, combustible cladding, etc.) depending on the type of building and the distance of the façade from the boundary.

For example, the façade of a residential, office, assembly or recreation building at a distance of 1 m from the boundary is allowed only 8% of unprotected area; at 5 m, 40%; and at 12.5 m, 100%. In contrast, the figures for shops, commercial, industrial and storage buildings are: at 1 m, 4%; at 5 m, 20%; and at 12.5 m 50%; and only at 25 m, 100%. More complex calculations are required when the façade is not parallel with the boundary, or is not flat.

Generally, roofs do not need to be resistant to fire from inside the building, but should be resistant to fire from outside, and also resist surface flame spread. Again, the type of roof construction permitted depends on the type of building, its size and its distance from the boundary. Different roof coverings are rated as to their resistance to fire: on pitched roofs; slates, tiles, profiled metal sheet are in the highest category, bitumen strip slates in the lowest. Sheet metal flat roof coverings perform the best, whilst the performance of various bitumen felt roof coverings depend on the types of layers, underlayers and supporting structure.

Smoke and heat venting systems

Smoke and heat venting systems comprise one or more of the following elements, together with the associated activation and control devices, power supplies and accessories:

- smoke vents
- heat vents
- mechanical smoke extractors.

Given that they have the task of removing smoke and heat in the event of fire, these systems contribute to:

- preserving escape and access routes
- facilitating the work of the firefighters
- the prevention of flash-over, hence retarding or avoiding a full fire
- the protection of equipment
- the reduction of fire damage caused by burning gases and hot ash
- reducing the risk of fire encroaching on structural elements.

The main function of smoke venting is to create and maintain smoke-free zones in which people and animals can escape from a fire. These zones also ensure firefighters are unimpeded by smoke when tackling the fire and give the contents better protection from damage. In addition, smoke vents contribute to heat venting.

The task of heat vents is to conduct away hot burning gases during the development of a fire. There are two main intentions:

- to delay or retard the flash-over
- to reduce the risk of the fire encroaching on structural elements.

In the same way as smoke vents contribute to heat venting, heat vents contribute to smoke venting.

The working principle of smoke and heat venting systems lies in the property of hot gases to rise. The effectiveness of the system depends on:

- the aerodynamic efficiency of the air venting
- the effect of wind
- the size of the air vents
- the activation of air vents
- the location of the installation relative to the general arrangement and size of the building.

Mechanical smoke extractors

Mechanical smoke extractors perform the same task as smoke vents but use forced ventilation (e.g. fans) to achieve the extraction of smoke. These smoke extractors are particularly useful where smoke vents are neither appropriate nor feasible for technical reasons.

Appropriately sized smoke vents or mechanical smoke extractors can, in principle, be used in the place of heat vents.

In view of their function and how they work, mechanical smoke extractors should be provided:

- for single storey buildings with very large areas and volumes
- for buildings with long escape routes which cannot be kept smoke-free for a sufficient period by other means
- for buildings subject to particular regulations, in which special protection is necessary
- for buildings housing particularly valuable articles or equipment, or materials that are susceptible to smoke damage and therefore require extra protection.

Arrangement and sizing of smoke and heat vents

Smoke and heat vents should be arranged as uniformly as possible within the roof sections. Special attention should be given to ensuring that, in the event of fire, the smoke and heat vents do not increase the danger of the fire spreading from building to building, or jumping between fire compartments within the building. In this respect, the boundary wall should be considered as a fire wall, for which there are increased requirements.

To conduct the smoke and combustion gases directly to the outside, it is more effective to have a large number of smoke and heat vents with small openings than to provide a smaller number with larger openings. Typically, the spacing between smoke and heat vents and the distance from the lower edge of the structure (eaves) should not be greater than 20 m and not less than the minimum distance from the walls, which is 5 m. The distance of smoke and heat vent openings from structures on the surface of the roof must be large enough to ensure that their operation is not impaired by wind effects.

A possible increase in wind loading should be noted when smoke and heat vents are located at the perimeter of flat roofs.

As a general guideline, in roofs having a slope of from 12° to 30°, the smoke and heat vents should be arranged as high as possible and there must be a minimum of one smoke and heat vent per 400 m² of plan surface area (projected roof area). For roof slopes >30°, the required efficiency of the smoke and heat venting should be considered on an individual project basis. In roof areas with a slope of <12°, one smoke and heat vent should serve not more than 200 m². Where, due to the building structure, there are further subdivisions of the roof, there must be a minimum of one smoke and heat vent per subdivision.

Smoke and heat venting system efficiency

To ensure the smoke and heat venting system operates at full aerodynamic efficiency, care must be taken to ensure that there is an adequate volume of air in the lower region of the building. The cross-sectional area of the intake vents should therefore be at least twice as large as the cross-sectional area of the smoke and heat vents in the roof.

Sprinkler systems

Wet sprinkler systems are systems in which the pipeline network behind the wet alarm valve station is permanently filled with water. When a sprinkler responds, water emerges from it immediately.

In dry sprinkler systems, on the other hand, the pipeline network behind the dry sprinkler valve station is filled with compressed air, which prevents water from flowing into the sprinkler network. When the sprinkler system is triggered, the retaining air pressure is released and water flows to the sprinkler heads. Dry sprinkler systems are used where there is a risk of frost damage to the pipework.

Normal sprinklers deliver a spherical water distribution towards the ceiling and the floor whereas the water from umbrella sprinklers falls in a parabolic pattern towards the floor. Both kinds can take the form of self-supporting or hanging devices. → ② + ③

Automatic fire extinguisher systems commonly employ fixed pipelines to which closed nozzles (sprinklers) are connected at regular intervals. When the system is activated, water is released only from those sprinklers where the sealing devices have reached the set response temperatures required to open them. These types of arrangements are also known as selectively operated extinguishing systems.

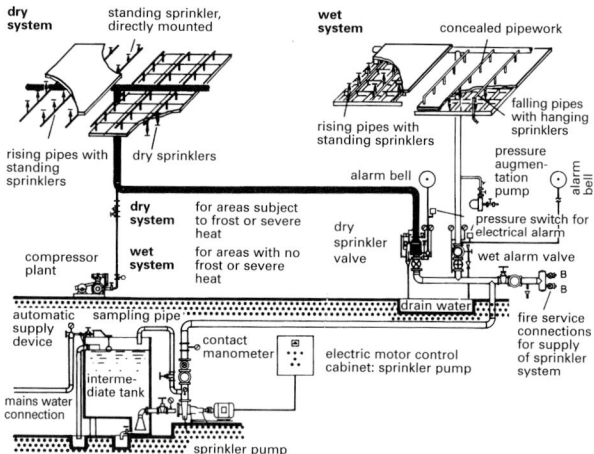

① **General arrangement of a sprinkler system**

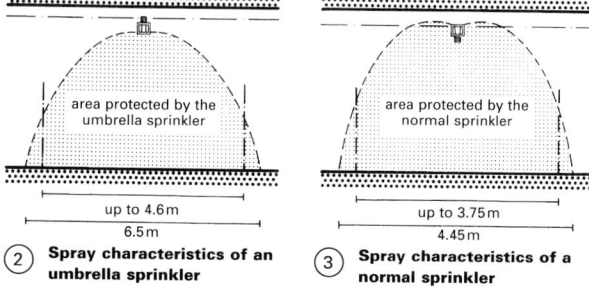

② **Spray characteristics of an umbrella sprinkler** ③ **Spray characteristics of a normal sprinkler**

up to 4.6 m — 6.5 m   up to 3.75 m — 4.45 m

Sprinkler distribution

A choice can be made between a normal or staggered distribution of sprinklers but where a staggered distribution is proposed the sprinklers should be arranged in as uniform a way as possible.

Spacing between sprinklers; distance from walls and ceilings

The spacing between sprinklers must be at least 1.5 m. The maximum spacing is determined as a function of the area the sprinkler is protecting, the distribution of the sprinklers and the fire hazard. This rule does not apply to sprinklers in stacking systems.

EXTINGUISHER SYSTEMS

The permissible spacing between sprinklers and flat ceilings/roofs varies according to the type of sprinkler and the flammability of the inside of the ceiling or roof. It also depends on the insulating layer of profiled cladding roofs. For trapezoidal section cladding roofs, the minimum spacing of the sprinkler from the ceiling is measured from the lowest point of the corrugation and the maximum spacing is measured from the mean point between the lowest and highest points of the corrugations.

Spacing of sprinklers relative to supporting beams or other structural components

If supporting beams, joists or other obstructions (e.g. air conditioning ducts) run below the ceiling, then the minimum spacings must be maintained between these components and the sprinklers. The exceptions here are side wall sprinklers, installation of which is only permitted for flat ceilings.

Open nozzle systems

Systems with open nozzles are water distribution systems with fixed pipelines, to which open nozzles are attached at regular intervals. When on standby, the pipe network is not filled with water. When the system is activated, the peak flow pressure passes immediately from the water supply into the network of pipes and nozzles.

The water pressure is directed according to the size and shape of the room which is to be protected and the type and quantity of the contents. Depending on the height and type of storage facility, and any wind effects, the system must deliver between 5 and 60 litres per minute per square metre → ④. For room protection systems which are subdivided into groups, the area protected by a group should generally lie between 100 m² (high fire risk) and 400 m² (low fire risk).

Water spray extinguisher systems are used, for example, in aircraft hangars, refuse bunkers and incinerator facilities, arenas, facilities for containers and combustible fluids, cable ducting, chipwood silos and factories, power stations, and factories making fireworks or munitions.

Extinguisher water pipelines

Extinguisher water pipelines are fixed pipes in structures. They make available the water supply for fire extinguisher hoses, which are connected by valve couplings that can be closed. There are two main types: (1) wet risers, which are extinguisher water pipelines that are continually under pressure, and (2) dry risers, which are pipelines to which extinguisher water is supplied by the fire service when it is required. Wet/dry risers are extinguisher water pipelines which, on the remote activation of valves, are supplied with mains water when required. (→ p. 130.)

The following are typical nominal pipe bore sizes for extinguisher pipes and wall hydrants:
- where there are two interconnected access points: 50 mm minimum
- where there are three interconnected access points: 65 mm minimum
- where there are four or more interconnected access points: 80 mm minimum.

With wet risers, wall hydrants can be accommodated in built-in recesses or in wall cavities. The lower edge of the wall hydrant should be between 800 and 1000 mm above floor level.

Dry risers have a nominal diameter of 80 mm and have a drainage facility. The couplings of the supply valve should be 800 mm above the surface level of the surroundings and the hose connector valve should be 1200 mm above floor level.

protected area	minimum water flow l/(min.m²)	extngshng time, min. (min)	group area (m²)	number
stages/arenas				
up to 350 m², height ≤10 m	5	10	–	1
up to 350 m², height >10 m	7	10	–	1
over 350 m², height ≤10 m	5	10	–	3
over 350 m², height >10 m	7	10	–	3
woodchip silos				
height of layer ≤3 m	7.5	30	–	1
height of layer >3 m ≤5 m	10	30	–	1
height of layer >5 m	12.5	30	–	1
refuse bunkers				
height of layer ≤2 m	5	30		–
height of layer >2 m ≤3 m	7.5	30	–	–
height of layer >3 m ≤5 m	12.5	30	100–400	–
height of layer > 5 m	20	30		–
foam stores				
storage height ≤2 m	10	30	150 min.	
storage height >2 m ≤3 m	15	45	150 min.	
storage height >3 m ≤4 m	22.5	60	200 min.	
storage height >4 m ≤5 m	30	60	200 min.	

(4) **Protected area and water flow rates**

CO₂ FIRE EXTINGUISHER SYSTEMS

Carbon dioxide works as an extinguishant by reducing the oxygen content in the air to a value at which the burning process can no longer be sustained. Being gaseous, it can flood the threatened area rapidly and uniformly to provide very effective protection.

CO_2 is suitable for extinguishing systems in buildings containing the following substances and installations:
- flammable fluids and other substances that react as flammable fluids when burning
- flammable gases, provided that precautions are taken to ensure that following successful extinguishing, no combustible gas/air mixture forms
- electrical and electronic equipment
- flammable solids susceptible to water damage, such as paper and textiles, although fires involving these materials require high concentrations of CO_2 and prolonged exposure to put them out.

Fixed CO_2 systems are frequently used in areas given over to:
- machines that contain flammable fluids, or in which such fluids are used
- paint manufacture, spray painting, printing, rolling mills, electrical switch rooms and data processing rooms.

Typically, where these systems are to be used for the protection of rooms, one nozzle must not safeguard an area greater than 30 m². Where rooms are over 5 m high, the nozzles used for general spraying of CO_2 must not only be installed in the upper portion of the room, under the ceiling, but also at a level approximately equal to one third of the room height.

The function of CO_2 systems is to extinguish fires during the initial phase and to maintain a high CO_2 concentration until the danger of re-ignition has abated. These systems consist essentially of CO_2 containers, back-up supplies of extinguishant, the necessary valves and a fixed pipe network with a suitable distribution of open nozzles and devices for fire detection, activation, alarm and extinguisher operation.

Powder extinguisher systems

Extinguishing powders are homogeneous mixtures of chemicals that act as fire suppressants. Their base constituents are, for example, as follows:
- sodium/potassium bicarbonate
- potassium sulphate
- potassium/sodium chloride
- ammonium phosphate/sulphate.

Since the powder is ready for use under normal conditions at temperatures of –20°C to +60°C, it is used for buildings, in closed rooms and also for outdoor industrial applications. Powder extinguishants are suitable, for example, where the following substances and installations are involved:

EXTINGUISHER SYSTEMS

- solid flammable substances such as wood, paper and textiles, where a suitable powder is required in all cases
- flammable fluids and other substances which, when burning, react as flammable fluids
- flammable gases
- flammable metals, such as aluminium, magnesium and their alloys, for which only special extinguishant powders are employed.

Examples of industrial areas where fixed powder systems are frequently used include chemical plant and associated process plant, underground oil storage facilities, filling stations, compressor and pumping stations, and transfer stations for oil and gas. There are also some installations in which powder extinguishants should not be used. These include areas housing, for example:
- dust sensitive equipment and low-voltage electrical installations (e.g. telephone systems, information processing facilities, measurement and control facilities, distribution boxes with fuses and relays, etc.)
- materials which are chemically incompatible with the extinguishant (i.e. there is the danger of chemical reaction).

Halon room protection systems

Halon is a halogenated hydrocarbon, usually bromotri-fluoromethane. Its extinguishing effect is based on the principle that it supresses the reaction between the burning material and oxygen. Halon systems can only be used in extinguishing areas where the room temperature will remain between –20°C and +450°C and neither should there be any equipment with an operating temperature above 450°C in the extinguishing area.

Halon 1301, for example, is suitable for fires in areas containing:
- fluids and other substances that react as flammable fluids when burning
- gases, provided that no combustible gas/air mixture can form after the fire has been extinguished
- electrical and electronic equipment and plant.

Examples of activities and areas for which halon systems are suitable include:
- paint manufacture, spray paint shops, powder coating plant
- electrical equipment rooms
- electronic data processing and archiving rooms.

The possibility of environmental damage cannot be excluded and should be considered where halon systems are proposed.

Foam extinguishing systems

Foam systems are used for extinguishing fires in buildings, rooms and outdoors, and they can also be used to form a protective layer over flammable liquids. The foam extinguishant is generated through the action of a water/foaming agent mixture with air. The foaming agents are liquid additives that consist of water-soluble products of protein synthesis and, if required, may contain additional fluorinated active ingredients.

The key characteristics of foam extinguisher systems to be considered are the water application rate, the requisite amount of foaming agent and the minimum operating time (e.g. between 60 and 120 minutes, depending on the type of foam). The system should be sized so that, in the event of a fire, sufficient foam enters the protected area to provide an effective cover. Precautions must be taken to prevent the escape of flammable fluids from the protected area (e.g. upstands). Account must also be taken of flow and spraying distances, possible obstructions, and the spacing and type of objects to be protected.

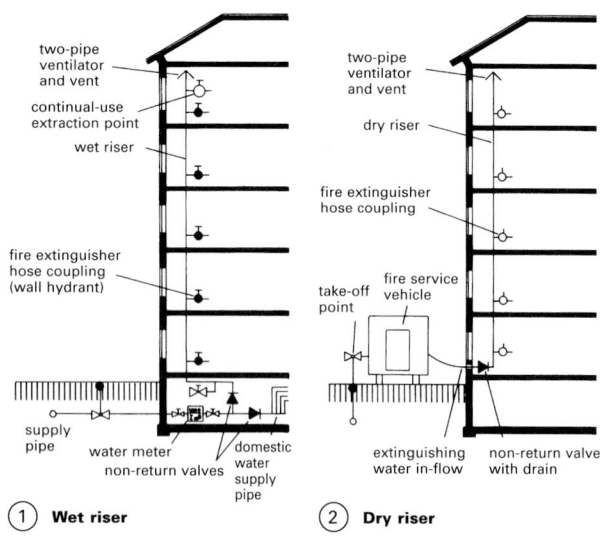

① **Wet riser**

② **Dry riser**

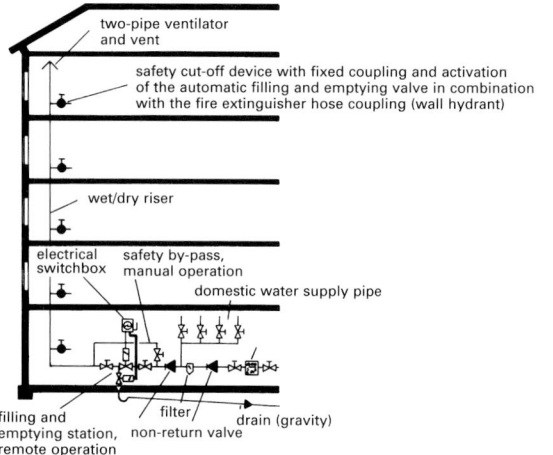

③ **Wet/dry risers**

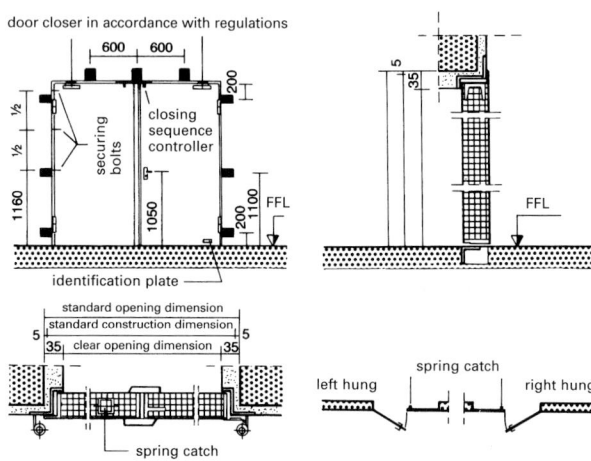

④ **Example of a 30 minute double door**

FIRE PROTECTION: CLOSURES AND GLAZING

Fire protection closures

Fire protection closures are units comprising:
- a door, or doors, with associated frames and fixings for the frame
- a self-closing device (either a flat spring or door closer with hydraulic damping)
- a closing sequence regulator (on double doors)
- relevant mechanisms required if sliding, roller or vertical lift doors are fitted
- a door lock
- a locking system with release devices for closures, which, during normal usage, must be held open and closed only in the event of fire.

If a fire takes hold, considerable distortion can occur between the wall and the door. Fire protection doors should therefore be considered in conjunction with the method of construction of the wall (i.e. solid walls or stud construction) to ensure that the combination is effective and permissible.

The level of fire resistance is dependent to a large degree on:
- the size of the door and opening
- the precision of manufacture
- the standard of workmanship during installation.

Smoke protection doors

Smoke protection doors are suitable for the limitation of smoke propagation in buildings but they are not fire protection enclosures in accordance with fire regulations. These doors are self-closing doors that are intended, when closed, to stop smoke passing from one part of the building into another.

Closures in walls of lift shafts

Closures in lift shaft walls, particularly the doors, must be constructed to prevent fire and smoke being transmitted to other floor levels. The effectiveness of the closure is then only assured, if suitable lift shaft ventilation is available and the lift cage consists predominantly of fire resistant construction materials. The size of the ventilation openings will be given in the local building regulations. In general, a cross-section of at least 2.5% of the plan area of the lift shaft is required, but this must be at least $0.1\,m^2$.

Fire protection glazing

Fire protection glazing is a component consisting of a frame with one or more light transparent elements (e.g. panes of fire protective glazing), mountings, seals and means of fixing. It will resist fire, in accordance with the classification, for 30, 60, 90, or even 120 minutes.

Heat radiation resisting glazing These are light transparent components that can be arranged vertically, horizontally or be inclined. They are suitable as fire protection glazing to impede the propagation of fire and smoke and the passage of heat radiation, according to their fire resistance period. Their stability will have been demonstrated in a strength test.

Heat radiation resistant glazing loses its transparency in the event of fire and provides wall-like fire protection. This implies that thermal insulation must be preserved during the whole of the fire resistance period.

This type of glazing is predominantly used internally, although recent developments have rendered it suitable for external use.

Heat radiation resistant glass consists of two pre-stressed panes 6 mm apart which are prefabricated as a type of double glazing unit. During manufacture, the air between the panes is replaced by an organic, water-containing substance (gel). In the event of fire, the individual pane exposed to the fire cracks and the gel then compensates for the heating by evaporation. Due to the scalding on the surface of the fire protective layer, the glass becomes discoloured and is then non-transparent to light.

Alternatively, this type of glazing may also consist of three or four silicate glass panes, laminated with fire protection layers of gel containing an inorganic compound. These layers provide the fire retarding effect. The gel itself is formed from a polymer, in which the inorganic salt solution is embedded, which is highly water-retentive.

In the event of fire, a thermal insulation layer forms and considerable amounts of energy are absorbed through the vaporisation of the water. This process repeats itself, layer by layer, until the gel in the intermediate layers between all of the panes has been dissipated. In this way, fire resistance times of 30, 60, 90 minutes and longer are achieved.

The gel layers in this heat radiation resisting glazing can only tolerate temperatures between −15°C and +60°C. With regard to temperatures above the permitted upper limit of +60°C, application in individual cases must be decided on the basis of the orientation of the façade to the sun and whether the absorption of radiation by the gel might result in the temperature limit being exceeded. If necessary, the intensity of radiation from the sun must be reduced through the use of protective glass or by other shading precautions. However, as a rule, such precautions are not necessary.

These glazing systems usually have special steel glazing bars, which are thermally isolated, and the surfaces of the frames can be faced with aluminium, if required.

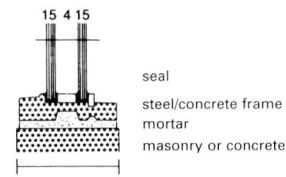

15 4 15

seal
steel/concrete frame
mortar
masonry or concrete

two composite glass panes
(Pyrostop 30 minutes)

(1) 60 minute fire resistance, heat radiation resistant

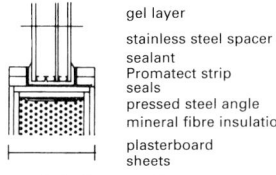

gel layer
stainless steel spacer
sealant
Promatect strip
seals
pressed steel angle
mineral fibre insulation
plasterboard
sheets

two pre-stressed, single pane safety
glass panels on the outside, one float
glass between the gel layers

(2) 90 minute fire resistance, heat radiation resistant

The typical maximum height is 3.50 m, with a maximum individual pane size of 1.20 × 2.00 m. There is also the possibility of replacing individual panes of glass with non-load bearing panels.

Fire resistant glazing without heat radiation resistance These are light transparent components that can be arranged vertically, horizontally or be inclined. They are suitable as fire protection glazing to impede the propagation of fire and smoke according to their fire resistance period. They do not, however, prevent the passage of radiated heat. This type of glazing remains transparent in the event of fire and is as effective as glass for fire protection.

Glazing without heat radiation resistance reduces the temperature of the radiating heat by about one half as it passes through the pane.

This grade of fire resistance can be achieved by three different types of glass:
(1) Wire reinforced glass with spot welded mesh such that in the event of breakage the glass pane is retained by the wire mesh. Maximum resistance up to 90 minutes.
(2) Specially manufactured double glazing units. Maximum resistance up to 60 minutes.
(3) Pre-stressed borosilicate glass (for example, Pyran). Maximum resistance up to 120 minutes resistance as a single pane.

The installation of this type of glazing in the façades of high buildings can prevent the spread of fire from one level to another. This applies especially to high-rise buildings which are subdivided into horizontal fire compartments. On buildings with inside corners, an unimpeded spread of fire can occur in the region of windows but this can also be avoided by using this type of glazing.

Generally, glazing without resistance to heat radiation should only be installed in places which do not serve as an escape route (for example, as light openings in partition panels). If used adjacent to escape routes, the lower edge of the glass should be at least 1.80 m above floor level. The permitted use of this glazing must be decided on an individual basis by the relevant local building authority.

Door glazing
The frames for fire protection glazing, together with the light transparent elements (glass), ensure integrity according to grade of fire resistance in the event of fire. The following materials (and material combinations) have proved to be suitable for the construction of frames:
 – steel tube sections with an intumescent protective coating
 – plasterboard and wood with, for example, light metal (LM) facings
 – light metal sections with fire resistant concrete cores
 – heat radiation protected LM laminated sections
 – combined sections: concrete outside (paintable), inside of LM, sections of pre-cast concrete (paintable), hardwood sections, heat insulated profiles with steam relieved interstitial air gaps and light metal with fire resistant and penetration resistant concrete cores.

Water cooled structures in steel-framed buildings

A closed circuit cooling system is created by connecting the upper column ends to header pipes from an overhead reservoir. The cooling medium flows to the lower column ends, which are connected to distributor pipes that lead to a riser pipe back to the overhead reservoir. Two circuit systems must be provided following the general structural arrangement of the building. In some cases, building regulations demand that, in the event of the destruction of a structural member, for example, as a consequence of an explosion, the overall structure must remain stable ③. For this kind of catastrophic loading case (i.e. for the failure of every second support), a design stress of 90% of the yield point value is used as a basis for structural calculations.

Typically, four $3\,m^3$ overhead tanks (i.e. $12\,m^3$ of water), are sufficient to counteract a normal fire of 90 minutes duration, involving a spread of fire to two floor levels. On the basis of expert opinion, this also gives a safety margin of almost a third in respect of the available water.

Where the structural columns are outside the building, freezing of the cooling water is prevented by the addition of potassium carbonate in a 33% solution, lowering the freezing point to −25°C. Internal corrosion of the columns of the circulation pipework and of the tanks is prevented by the addition of sodium nitrite to the cooling liquid.

A good example of the use of water cooling is the ten-storey building in Karlsruhe for the Landesanstalt für Umweltschutz (Federal Institute for Environmental Protection). It has (12 + 12) × 2 = 48 steel columns, which are supplied with cooling water circulation such that the 12 + 12 columns are alternately connected to separate water circuits. The two circulatory systems of the front and rear elevations are separate.

Very high temperatures have also been measured on the steel structural elements due to normal warming by the sun in summer. In one instance, following an increase of 30°C, the approximately 33 m long outer columns of the building expanded vertically by about 12 mm, resulting in displacements of the supports for the continuous, multi-span structural frame. This factor had to be taken into account in the design. Since differences in density of the cooling medium occur due to warming, not only by fire but also through solar radiation, a natural circulation of the coolant takes place and the columns which are heated by the sun are cooled. A favourable effect here is that each of the four cooling systems has columns on both the north and south side of the building, so that a temperature equalisation can take place. Column temperatures of −15°C and +50°C were therefore taken as the basis for calculation. Without the equalisation through the cooling medium, values of around −25°C and +80°C would have had to be assumed in demonstrating structural integrity.

Fire resistance of steel structural elements

The fire resistance duration of structural steel elements for a prescribed level of fire intensity is dependent on the rate of heat increase and the respective critical temperature of the element. The temperature of a steel member increases more rapidly as the ratio of the surface exposed to the fire increases in relation to the steel cross-section. Large steel cross-sections heat up at a slower rate given the same depth of coating, the same material and equal fire surface coverage, and therefore have a greater resistance to fire than smaller cross-sections.

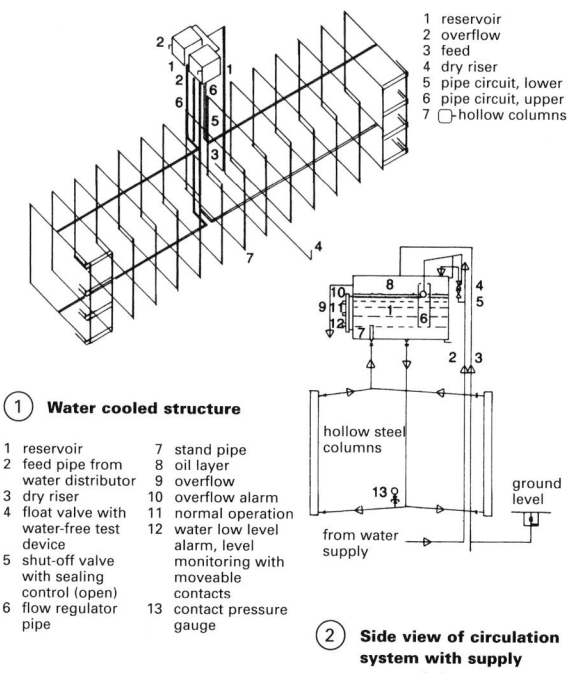

1 reservoir
2 overflow
3 feed
4 dry riser
5 pipe circuit, lower
6 pipe circuit, upper
7 ⬡-hollow columns

① Water cooled structure

1 reservoir	7 stand pipe
2 feed pipe from water distributor	8 oil layer
3 dry riser	9 overflow
4 float valve with water-free test device	10 overflow alarm
5 shut-off valve with sealing control (open)	11 normal operation
	12 water low level alarm, level monitoring with moveable contacts
6 flow regulator pipe	13 contact pressure gauge

② Side view of circulation system with supply reservoir (not to scale)

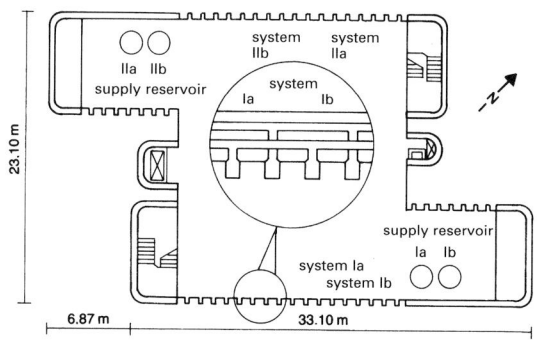

③ Water cooling scheme

An important influencing parameter for the heating up process is therefore the section factor Hp/A (i.e the ratio of the heated perimeter to nominal cross-sectional area. The characteristics of the coating material are also decisive to this heating up process, as is the adhesion of the coating to the steel surface. The heating up period can be calculated or obtained from fire tests in accordance with relevant standards.

Steel components can fail if the 'critical steel temperature' is reached on critical cross-sections. The fire resistance period is therefore dictated by the time taken for the component to be heated up to this critical steel temperature.

The relationship between section factor, depth of coating and the duration of fire resistance of steel columns and steel girders has been investigated for various types of covering. The results are widely available and should be considered in the light of the possible fire risks associated with the proposed building.

Building regulations stipulate what measures must be taken to ensure that occupants of buildings can escape if there is a fire. If there are spaces in the building which have no direct access to the outside, then a route protected from fire that leads to safety must be provided. Different standards apply to different building types as follows:

(1) dwellings, including flats
(2) residential (institutional) buildings, namely those that have people sleeping in them overnight (e.g. hotels, hospitals, old people's homes)
(3) offices, shops and commercial premises
(4) places of assembly and recreation, such as cinemas, theatres, stadiums, law courts, museums and the like
(5) industrial buildings (e.g. factories and workshops)
(6) storage buildings, such as warehouses and car-parks.

Special provisions must be made for escape from very tall buildings.

Factors to be taken into account when designing means of escape from buildings are:

- the activities of the users
- the form of the building
- the degree to which it is likely that a fire will occur
- the potential fire sources
- the potential for fire spread throughout the building.

There are some assumptions made in order to achieve a safe and economic design:

(1) Occupants should be able to escape safely without outside help. In certain cases this is not possible (e.g. hospitals) so special provisions need to be made.
(2) Fire normally breaks out in one part of the building.
(3) Fires are most likely to break out in the furnishings and fittings rather than in the parts of the building covered by the building regulations.
(4) Fires are least likely to break out in the structure of the building and in the circulation areas due to the restriction on the use of combustible materials.
(5) Fires are initially a local occurrence, with a restricted area exposed to the hazard. The fire hazard can then spread with time, usually along circulation spaces.
(6) Smoke and noxious gases are the greatest danger during early stages of the fire, obscuring escape routes. Smoke and fume control is therefore an important design consideration.
(7) Management has an important role in maintaining the safety of public, institutional and commercial buildings.

GENERAL PRINCIPLES

The general principle applied in relation to means of escape is that it should be possible for building occupants to turn away from the fire and escape to a place of safety. This usually implies that alternative escape routes should be supplied. The first part of the route will usually be unprotected (e.g. within a room or office). Consequently, this must be of limited length, to minimise the time that occupants are exposed to the fire hazard. Even protected horizontal routes should be of limited length due to the risk of premature failure. The second part of the escape route is generally in a protected stairway designed to be non-combustible, and resistant to the ingress of flames and smoke. Once inside, the occupants can proceed without rushing directly, or via a protected corridor, to a place of safety. This is generally in the open, away from the effects of the fire.

In certain cases, escape in only one direction (a dead end) is permissible, depending on the use of the building, the risk of fire, the size and height of the building, the length of the dead end and the number of people using it.

Mechanical installations such as lifts and escalators cannot be included as means of escape from fire. Nor are temporary devices and fold-down ladders acceptable. Stairs within accommodation are normally ignored.

Due regard must be given to security arrangements so that conflicts with access and egress in an emergency are resolved.

RULES FOR MEASUREMENT

The rules for measurement relate to three factors: occupant capacity, travel distance and width of escape route.

Occupant capacity is calculated according to the design capacities of rooms, storeys and hence that of the total building. If the actual number of people is not known, then they can be calculated according to standard floor space factors, giving the allotted metre area per person depending on the type of accommodation.

Travel distance is calculated according to the shortest route, taking a central line between obstructions (such as along gangways between seating) and down stairs.

Width is calculated according to the narrowest section of the escape route, usually the doorways but could be other fixed obstructions.

MEANS OF ESCAPE FROM DWELLINGS

The complexity of escape provisions increases with the height of the building and the number of storeys above and below the ground. However, there are recommendations that refer to all dwellings:

Smoke alarms These should be of approved design and manufacture and installed in circulation areas near to potential sources of fire (e.g. kitchens and living rooms) and close to bedroom doors. Installation should be in accordance with the details of the manufacturer and the building regulations. The number of alarms depends on the size and complexity of the building, but at least one alarm should be installed in each storey of the dwelling, and several interlinked alarms may be needed in long corridors > 15 m). Consideration must be given to ensure the easy maintenance and cleaning of the alarms.

Inner rooms Escape from these might be particularly hazardous if the fire is in the room used for access. Inner rooms should therefore be restricted for use as kitchens or utility rooms, dressing rooms, showers or bathrooms, unless there is a suitable escape window at basement, ground or first floor levels.

Basements Gases and smoke at the top of internal stairs makes escape from basements hazardous. Therefore basement bedrooms and inner rooms should have an alternate means of escape via a suitable external door or window. Regulations stipulate detailed dimensions for windows and doors used for escape purposes.

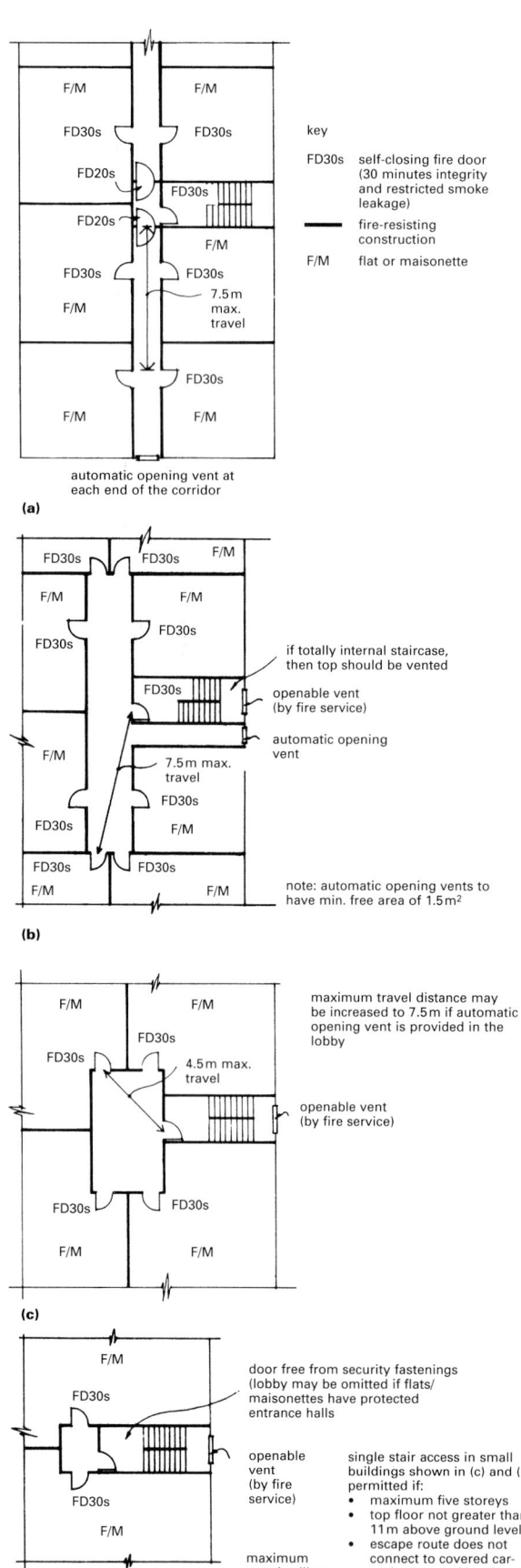

(a) key

FD30s self-closing fire door (30 minutes integrity and restricted smoke leakage)

fire-resisting construction

F/M flat or maisonette

7.5 m max. travel

automatic opening vent at each end of the corridor

(b)

if totally internal staircase, then top should be vented

openable vent (by fire service)

automatic opening vent

7.5 m max. travel

note: automatic opening vents to have min. free area of 1.5m²

(c)

maximum travel distance may be increased to 7.5 m if automatic opening vent is provided in the lobby

4.5 m max. travel

openable vent (by fire service)

(d)

door free from security fastenings (lobby may be omitted if flats/ maisonettes have protected entrance halls)

openable vent (by fire service)

maximum two dwellings per floor

single stair access in small buildings shown in (c) and (d) permitted if:
- maximum five storeys
- top floor not greater than 11m above ground level
- escape route does not connect to covered car-park at ground level (unless open sided)

① Typical arrangements for flats or maisonettes with single common stairs according to the Building Regulations for England and Wales: (a) corridor access, (b) lobby access, (c) and (d) single stair access in small buildings

MEANS OF ESCAPE FROM FIRE

Generally, single dwellings of three or more storeys (or, according to the UK Building Regulations, with one or more floors over 4.5 m above the ground) require protected stairways of 30 minutes fire-resistant construction, furnished with self-closing fire doors.

Dwellings divided into flats or maisonettes should have fire protected access corridors leading to protected common escape stairs. The provision of two stairs giving alternative escape routes is necessary in all but the smallest buildings. It is essential to provide for ventilation of escape corridors and stairs in order to dissipate smoke.

Each flat or maisonette is regarded as a separate fire compartment so only the unit on fire needs to be initially evacuated. Hence, entrance doors to flats and maisonettes must be self-closing fire doors (30 minutes) and open into a protected internal lobby with self closing fire doors which give access to the rooms. (→ ① + ②)

MEANS OF ESCAPE FROM BUILDINGS OTHER THAN DWELLINGS

General guidelines cover the following features.

Construction and protection of escape routes These cover the fire resistance of the enclosures including any glazed panels and doors (varying according to situation), headroom (2 m minimum), safety of floor finish (non-slip), and ramps (not steeper than 1:12).

Provision of doors These should open at least 90 degrees in the direction of travel and be easily opened (use simple or no fastenings if possible). They should not obstruct the passageway or landing when open (use a recess if necessary) and be of the required fire/smoke resistance depending on the particular situation. Vision panels are required when the door may be approached from both sides or swings two ways.

Construction of escape stairs Escape stairs should be constructed of materials of limited combustibility in high-risk situations (e.g. when it is the only stair, a stair from a basement, one serving a storey more than 20 m above ground level, an external stair or one for use by the fire services. Single steps should be avoided on escape routes, though they are permitted in a doorway. Special provisions apply to spiral and helical stairs. Fixed ladders are not suitable as means of escape for the public.

Final exits These should be very obvious to users and positioned so as to allow the rapid dispersion of escaping people in a place of safety, away from fire hazards such as openings to boiler rooms, basements, refuse stores etc.

Lighting and signing Escape routes should be well lit with artificial lighting, and generally equipped with emergency escape lighting in the event of a power failure. Stairs should be on an independent circuit. In crucial areas, the wiring should be fire resistant. The exits must be well signposted with illuminated signs.

Lift installations and mechanical services, etc. Lifts cannot be used as a means of escape. Because they connect storeys and compartments, the shafts must be of fire resisting construction. The lift doors should be approached through protected lobbies unless they are in a protected stairway enclosure. The lift machine room should be situated over the lift shaft if possible. Special recommendations cover the installation of wall-climber and feature lifts. Mechanical services should either close down in the event of a fire, or draw air away from the protected escape routes. Refuse chutes and refuse storage must be sited away from escape routes and separated from the rest of the building by fire resistant construction and lobbies.

Horizontal escape routes

The number of escape routes and exits required depends on the maximum travel distance that is permitted to the nearest exit and the number of occupants in the room, area or storey under consideration.

Generally, alternative escape routes should be provided from every part of the building, particularly in multistorey and mixed-use buildings. Areas of different use classes (e.g. residential, assembly and recreation, commercial, etc.) should have completely separate escape routes.

Below are examples of typical maximum permitted travel distances in various types of premises. If, at the design stage, the layout of the room or storey in not known (for instance, in a speculative office building) then the direct distance measured in a straight line should be taken. Maximum direct distances are two thirds of the maximum travel distance.

- institutional buildings: 9m in one direction, 18m in more than one
- office and commercial buildings, shops, storage and other non-residential buildings: 18m in one direction, 45m in more than one
- industrial buildings: 25m in one direction, 45m in more than one.

There are more stringent and detailed requirements for places of special fire risk and plant rooms.

Note how the travel distances are much reduced where escape is possible in only one direction. However, this is only suitable where the storey or room contains few people (e.g. less than 50). Rooms at the beginning of an escape route may only have one exit into the corridor; in this case

the single directional travel distance should apply within the room and the two directional travel distance should apply to the distance between the furthest point in the room and the storey exit.

The layout of the exits from a room or storey may be such that from certain parts of the room they do not offer alternative escape routes. Figure ③ shows regulations as applied to two types of room configuration. If the angle of 45 degrees cannot be achieved, then alternative escape routes separated by a fire-resisting construction should be provided, or the maximum travel distance will be that allowed for one direction of travel.

The number of exits and escape routes required depends also on the maximum number of people in the area under consideration. Below are typical requirements:

500 people	2 exits
1000	3
2000	4
4000	5
7000	6
1100	7
1600	8
1600+	8 plus 1 per extra 500 persons

The minimum width of horizontal escape routes is also determined by the number of people using them. Typical values are:

50 people	800mm
110	900mm
220	1100mm
220+	extra 5mm per person

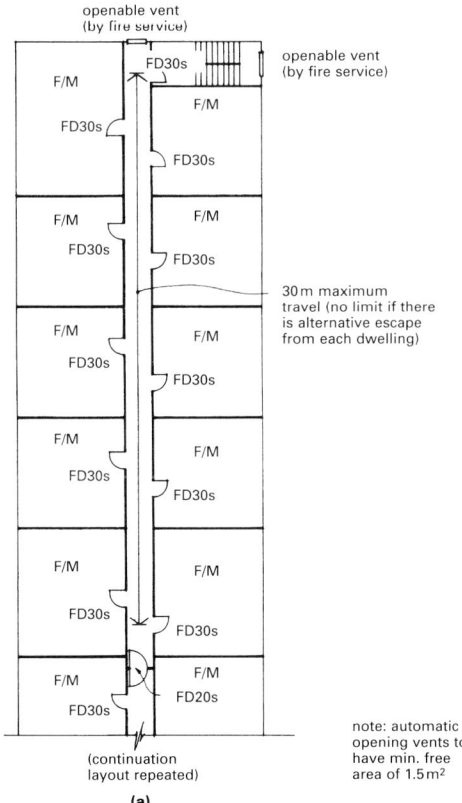

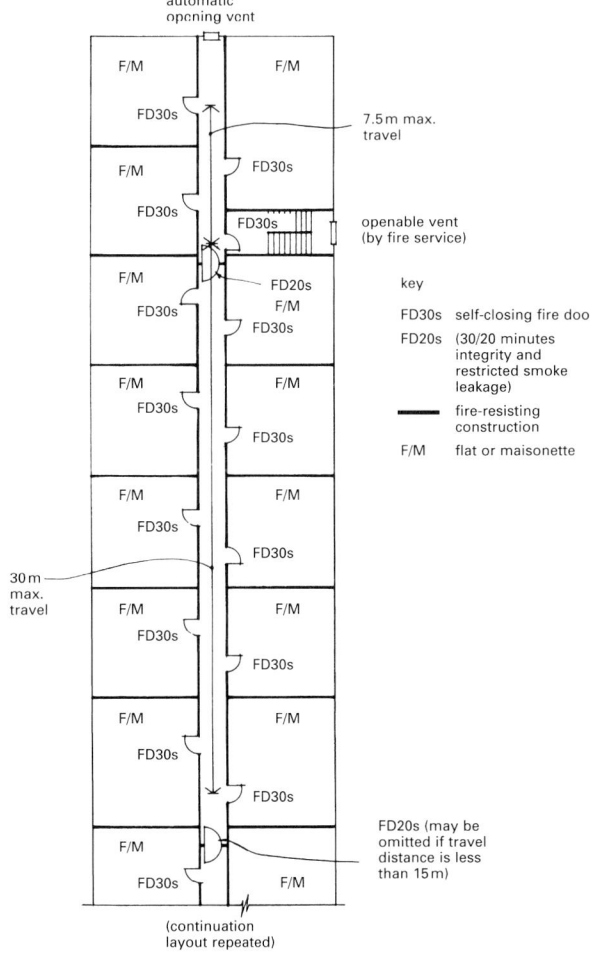

② **Typical arrangements for flats or maisonettes with more than one common stair according to the Building Regulations for England and Wales: (a) corridor access, (b) corridor access with dead ends**

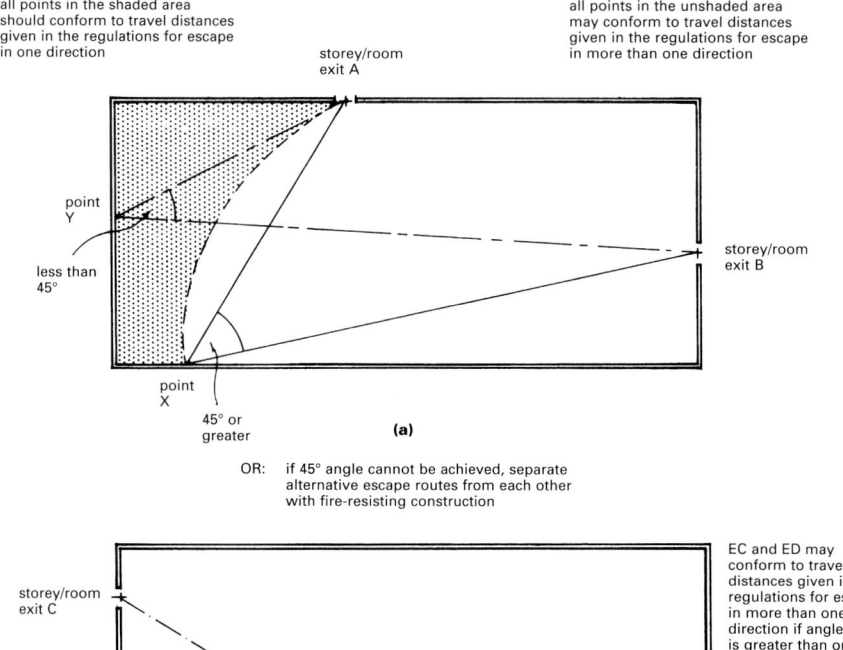

all points in the shaded area should conform to travel distances given in the regulations for escape in one direction

all points in the unshaded area may conform to travel distances given in the regulations for escape in more than one direction

storey/room exit A

storey/room exit B

point Y

less than 45°

point X

45° or greater

(a)

OR: if 45° angle cannot be achieved, separate alternative escape routes from each other with fire-resisting construction

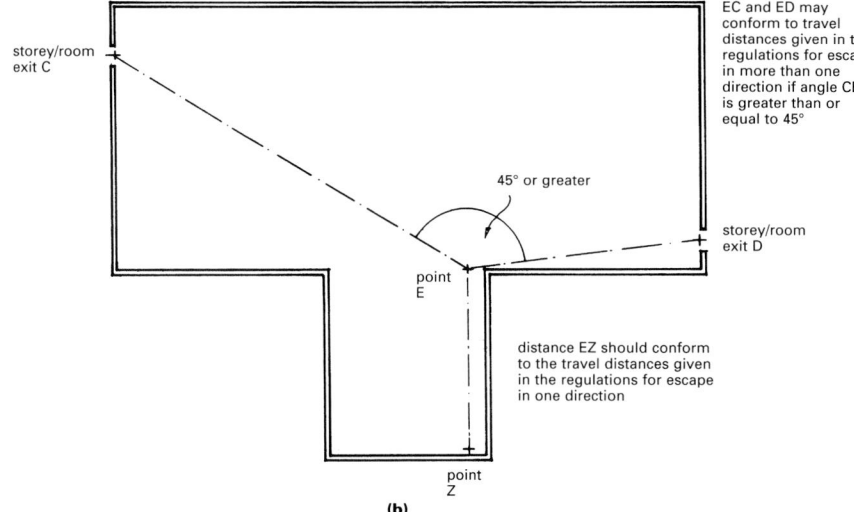

storey/room exit C

EC and ED may conform to travel distances given in the regulations for escape in more than one direction if angle CED is greater than or equal to 45°

45° or greater

storey/room exit D

point E

distance EZ should conform to the travel distances given in the regulations for escape in one direction

point Z

(b)

③ **Alternative escape routes in buildings other than dwellings according to the Building Regulations for England and Wales**

The design of escape routes must take into account planning considerations such as:

Inner rooms More stringent rules apply to these than in dwellings, such as reduced travel distances, restrictions on use and occupancy as well as construction and the provision of fire detection equipment.

Relationships between horizontal escape routes and stairways It is important to avoid: the need to pass through one stairway to reach another; the inclusion of a stairway enclosure as the normal route to various parts of the same floor; linking separate escape routes in a common hall or lobby at ground floor.

Common escape routes by different occupancies These should be fire protected or fitted with fire detection and alarm systems. Escape from one occupancy should not be via another.

Escape routes, design factors Fire protection to escape corridors should be provided for in all residential accommodation, dead ends and common escape routes. Other escape corridors should provide defence against the spread of smoke in the early stages of the fire. To prevent blockage by smoke, long corridors (>12m) connecting two or more storey exits should be divided by self-closing fire doors. Fire doors should also be used to divide dead-end corridors from corridors giving two directions of escape. See ④ for typical arrangements.

Vertical escape routes

These are provided by protected escape stairs of sufficient number and adequate size. Generally, the rules requiring alternative means of escape mean that more than one stairway is required. The width of the stairs should allow the total number of people in the storey or building subjected to fire to escape safely. Wide stairways must be divided by a central handrail. The width should be at least that of the exits serving it, and it should not reduce in width as it approaches the final exit. Typical minimum escape stair widths, depending on the type of building and the number of people they serve, are as follows: 1000mm for institutional buildings serving up to 150 people; 1100mm for assembly buildings serving up to 220 people; between 1100mm and 1800mm for any other building serving more than 220 people, depending on the number of people and number of floors.

Each internal escape stair should be contained in its own fire-resisting enclosure and should discharge either directly, or by means of a protected passageway, to a final exit. As protected stairways must be maintained as a place of relative safety, they should not contain potentially hazardous equipment or materials. These restrictions do however allow the inclusion of sanitary facilities, a lift well, a small enquiry office or reception desk, fire protected cupboards and gas meters.

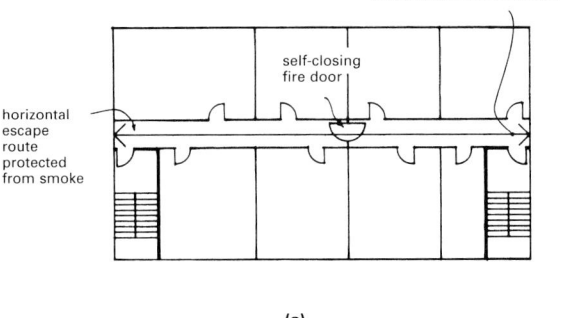

subdivide corridor if exceeding 12 m in length and giving access to alternative escape routes

self-closing fire door

horizontal escape route protected from smoke

(a)

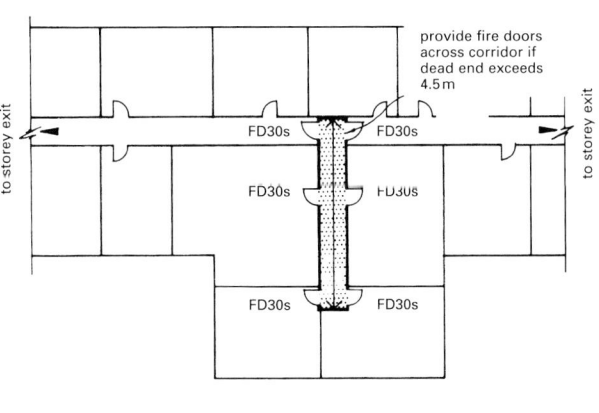

provide fire door across corridor if dead end exceeds 4.5 m

FD30s   FD30s

FD30s

FD30s   FD30s

key

▨ protected corridor with fire-resisting construction

FD30s   self-closing fire door (30 minutes integrity and restricted smoke leakage)

(b)

provide fire doors across corridor if dead end exceeds 4.5 m

to storey exit

FD30s   FD30s

FD30s   FD30s

to storey exit

FD30s   FD30s

(c)

④ **Typical arrangements of escape corridors in buildings other than dwellings according to the Building Regulations for England and Wales**

MEANS OF ESCAPE FROM FIRE

Reductions in the level of fire resistance are allowed on the outside wall of a staircase, depending on the proximity to other openings in the façade.

Basement stairs need special attention. The danger of hot gases and smoke entering the stair and endangering upper storeys means that at least one stair from the upper storeys should not continue down to the basement. In continuous stairs, a ventilated lobby should separate the basement section from the section serving the upper floors.

External escape stairs are usually permissible as an alternative means of escape, but should be adequately protected from the weather and fire from the building. They are not suitable for use by members of the public in assembly and recreation buildings.

ACCESS FOR FIREFIGHTERS

Provision should be made in design to allow firefighters good access to the building in the event of a fire, and to provide facilities to assist them in protecting life and property.

Sufficient access to the site for vehicles must be provided to allow fire appliances to approach the building. Principal appliances are ladders, hydraulic platforms and pumping appliances. Access roads for fire appliances should be at least 3.7 m wide with gates no less than 3.1 m. Headroom of 3.7 m for pumps and 4.0 m for high-reach appliances is required. The respective turning circles of these appliances are 17 m and 26 m between curbs. Allow 5.5 m wide hardstanding adjacent to the building, as level as possible (not more than 1:12), with a clearance zone of 2.2 m to allow for the swing of the hydraulic platform.

Firefighters must be able to gain access to the building. The normal escape routes are sufficient in small and low buildings, but in high buildings and those with deep basements additional facilities such as firefighting lifts, stairs and lobbies, contained within protected shafts, will be required.

Fire mains in multistorey buildings must be provided. These may be wet or dry risers (fallers in basements). → p. 128.

A means of venting basements to disperse heat and smoke must be provided. In basements, flames, gases and smoke tend to escape via stairways, making it difficult for firefighters to gain access to the fire. Smoke vents (or outlets) are needed to provide an alternative escape route for these emissions directly to the outside air and allow the ingress of cooler air. Regulations stipulate the positions and sizes of vents. Either natural venting or mechanical venting in association with a sprinkler system may be used.

① **Single pitch roof**

② **Flat roof**

③ **Double pitch roof**

④ **Hipped roof**

⑤ **Pyramid roof**

⑥ **Sawtooth roof**

PROTECTION FROM LIGHTNING

Around a latitude of 50°, lightning strikes the ground approximately 60 times (and cloud 200–250 times) per hour of storms. Within a radius of 30 m from the point of strike (trees, masonry work, etc.), persons in the open air are in danger from stepped voltages and, consequently, should stand still with their feet together.

The damage liable to be inflicted on building constructions is due to the development of heat. Ground strikes heat and vaporise the water content to such a degree that walls, posts, trees, etc., can explode due to the overpressure generated wherever dampness has collected. Roof structures, dormer windows, chimneys and ventilators should receive particular attention in lightning protection systems and should be connected into the system.

A lightning protection system consists of lightning rods, down conductors and earthing devices. In essence, a lightning protection system represents a 'Faraday cage', except that the mesh width is enlarged. Also, initial contact points (or lightning rods) are fitted, so that the point of impact of the strike can be fixed. Thus, the lightning protection system has the function of fixing the point of lightning strike by means of the air terminals and ensuring that the structure lies within a protected zone.

The air terminals or lightning conductors are metal rods, roof wires, surfaces, roof components or other bodies. No point on the roof surface should be further than 15 m from an air terminal device.

On thatched roofs, due to the danger of ignition resulting from the corona effect, metal bands (600 mm wide) should be laid over the ridge on wooden supports → ⑧. When flowing, a lightning current can reach 100 000 A and, due to the earthing resistance, a voltage drop of 500 000 V occurs. In the instant of the strike, the entire lightning protection system, and all components which are connected to it by metal parts, are subjected to this high potential.

Equipotential bonding is the very effective precaution of connecting all large metal components and cables to the lightning protection system.

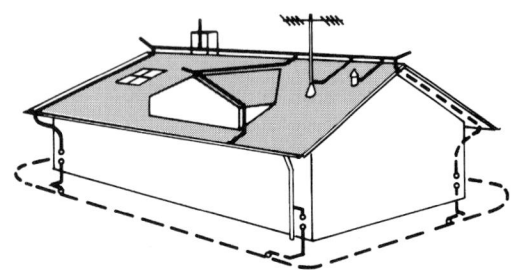

⑦ **Typical modern lightning protection system**

ridge wire on wooden props 600 mm above the ridge

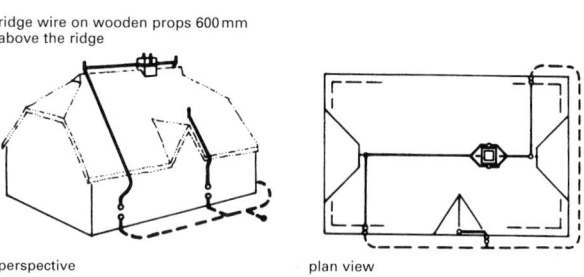

perspective   plan view

⑧ **Thatched building conductor is 400 mm from roof surface and connected to collective earthing**

PROTECTION FROM LIGHTNING

The earthing system is required to conduct the lightning current rapidly and uniformly to earth; this is achieved by using uninsulated metal bands, tubes and plates, pushed so deep into the ground that a low resistance to ground dissipation is attained → ⑫ – ⑬. The level of earthing resistance depends on the type of ground and the dampness → ⑪. A distinction is made between deep earthing electrodes and surface earthing electrodes. Surface earthing electrodes are designed either in a ring shape or in a straight line; preferably, they are embedded in the concrete of the foundations → ⑫ – ⑬. Rod earthing electrodes (round rods or rods with an open profile) are contained in a tube driven into the ground. Earthing electrodes inserted to a depth of more than 6 m are called 'buried earth electrodes'. A star type earth electrode is one consisting of individual strips which radiate out from a point or from an earthing strip. On roofs, walls, etc., clad in aluminium, zinc or galvanised steel → ① – ⑥, bare or galvanised copper conductors are not permissible; instead bare aluminium conductors or galvanised steel conductors should be used.

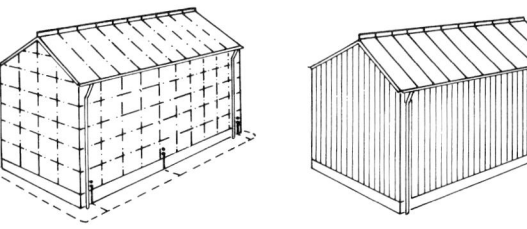

① **Steel frame construction: frame connected to the roof conductor and to the earthing conductor**

② **Sheeted roof with wooden walls: roof connected to ridge conductor and the conductor to earth**

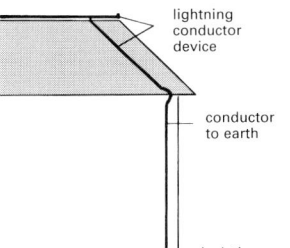

③ **The main components of a lightning protection system**

④ **Aluminium roof decking used as a lightning conductor**

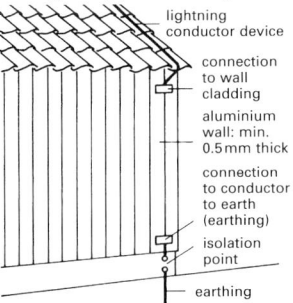

⑤ **Aluminium wall cladding used as a conductor to earth**

⑥ **Aluminium roof and wall**

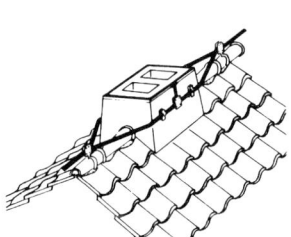

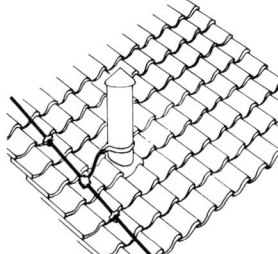

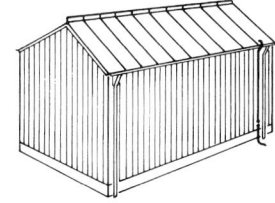

⑦ **Chimney on ridge with angled steel strips as lightning conductor**

⑧ **Chimneys with lightning conductor connected to the ridge conductor**

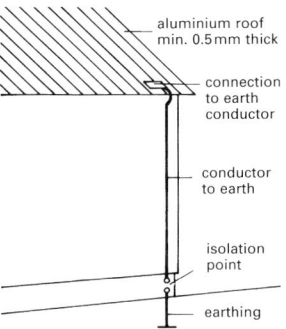

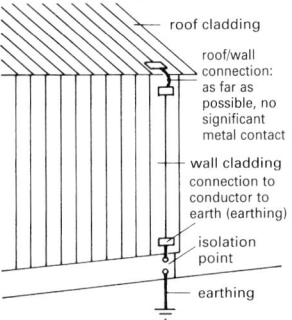

earthing type	marshy soil	loam, clay, arable soil	damp sand	damp gravel	dry sand and gravel	stony ground	ground resistance (Ω)
earth strip length (m)	12	40	80	200	400	1200	
earth pipe depth (m)	6	20	40	100	200	600	5
earth strip length (m)	6	20	40	100	200	600	
earth pipe depth (m)	3	10	20	50	100	300	10
earth strip length (m)	4	13	27	67	133	400	
earth pipe depth (m)	2	7	14	34	70	200	15
earth strip length (m)	2	7	13	33	67	200	
earth pipe depth (m)	1	3	7	17	33	100	30

→ economic ← no longer economic

⑪ **Ground resistance of strip and pipe earthing electrodes**

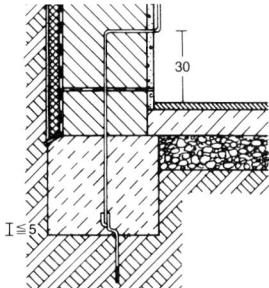

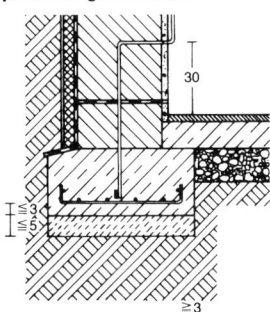

⑫ **Earthing electrode in a foundation of unreinforced concrete**

⑬ **Earthing electrode in a reinforced concrete foundation**

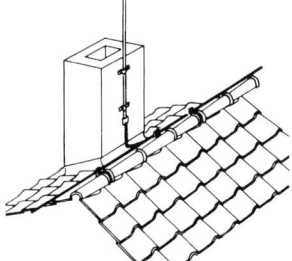

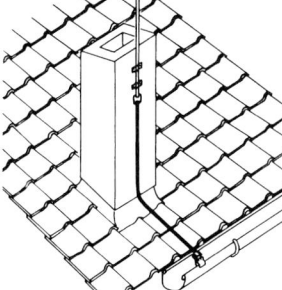

⑨ **Metal roof structures and ventilation pipes connected to the lightning protection system**

⑩ **Lightning conductors on chimneys close to the eaves connected to the roof guttering**

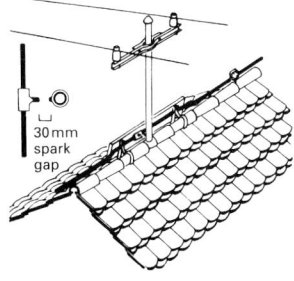

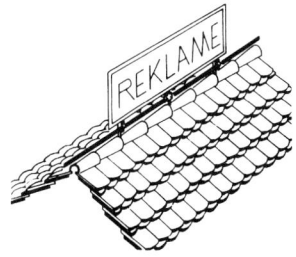

⑭ **The high voltage cable is not directly connected to the roof, and is therefore on a support; a spark gap of 30 mm is provided**

⑮ **Steel components for electrical sign equipment incorporate a voltage surge protection device**

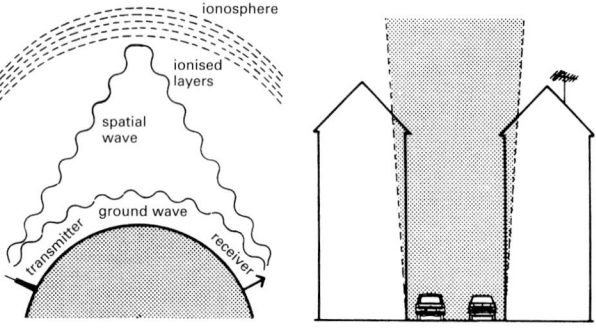

① **The propagation of electromagnetic waves obeys the principles of wave optics**

warm, damp air
boundary layer
cold, dry air
reception due to curvature

prescribed polarisation direction | reception of a reflection | direct reception | no reception due to interruption | excess range due to refraction

② **Propagation of radio waves**

ionosphere
ionised layers
spatial wave
ground wave
transmitter — receiver

③ **Choose location to avoid zones of maximum interference**

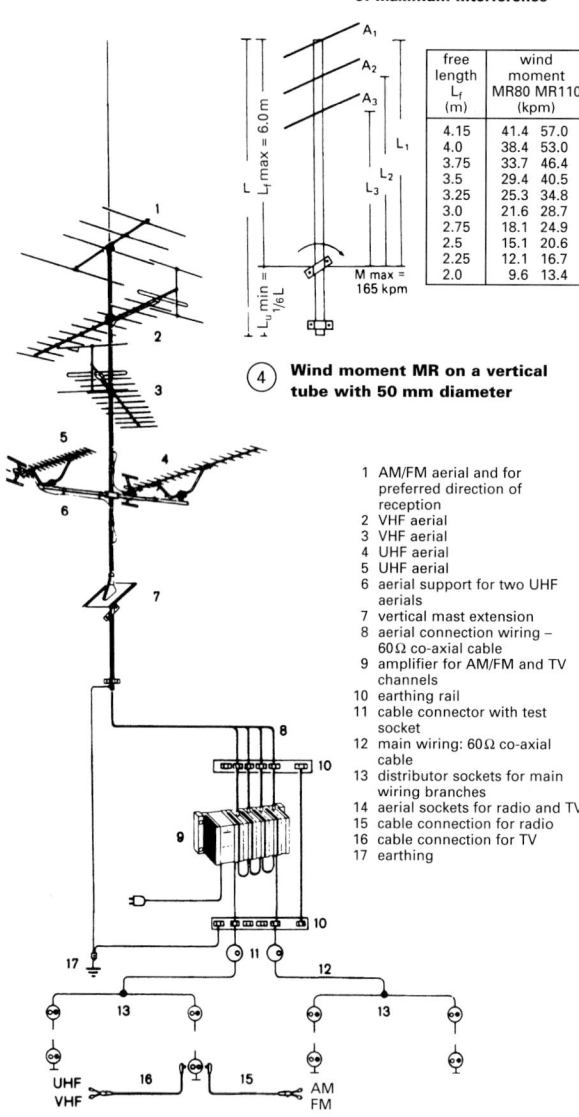

free length L_f (m)	wind moment MR80	MR110 (kpm)
4.15	41.4	57.0
4.0	38.4	53.0
3.75	33.7	46.4
3.5	29.4	40.5
3.25	25.3	34.8
3.0	21.6	28.7
2.75	18.1	24.9
2.5	15.1	20.6
2.25	12.1	16.7
2.0	9.6	13.4

L_f max = 6.0 m
L_u min = $\frac{1}{6}L$
M max = 165 kpm

④ **Wind moment MR on a vertical tube with 50 mm diameter**

1 AM/FM aerial and for preferred direction of reception
2 VHF aerial
3 VHF aerial
4 UHF aerial
5 UHF aerial
6 aerial support for two UHF aerials
7 vertical mast extension
8 aerial connection wiring – 60 Ω co-axial cable
9 amplifier for AM/FM and TV channels
10 earthing rail
11 cable connector with test socket
12 main wiring: 60 Ω co-axial cable
13 distributor sockets for main wiring branches
14 aerial sockets for radio and TV
15 cable connection for radio
16 cable connection for TV
17 earthing

⑤ **Scheme for communal aerial facility**

Aerials affect the appearance of cities, and, when close together and in the same line of sight to the transmitter, they are subject to mutual interference. Communal aerials can solve these problems, but planning of these is needed at the initial stage of construction. Provision should be made in the basic construction of buildings for the space requirement and installation of facilities for amplifiers to oppose the current drop in the cabling and to provide adequate earthing → ⑤ – ⑥ plus the additional equipment needed to earth the lightning protection system → p.138. For connections to water pipes, care is needed to avoid short circuiting water meters → ⑥. Aerial performance is strongly influenced by the surroundings → ① e.g. trees extending above the aerial height -- evergreens, in particular – and overhead high voltage power lines. Good reception requires alignment (polarisation) with the nearest transmitter – the best position being when the aerial is in line of sight with the transmitter. Short waves do not follow the curvature of the Earth and ultra short waves only partially – a portion reaching the troposphere is reflected, so that TV reception may be possible even when the transmitter would not normally be of sufficient strength to reach the receiver. Various aerial shapes are available. Basic fundamentals should be observed → ③. Aerials under the roof, intended for the UHF range, provide low-quality reception. In the VHF range, the drop in reception relative to outside aerials is only about half as great. Room aerials (auxiliary aerials) are many times weaker. One aerial should serve for the reception of long, medium, short, ultrashort waves and for a number of TV channels – with corrosion protection for long life. For aerial mast systems, reference should be made to the appropriate regulations → ④. Normally, the aerial mast is inserted into the roof framework, on a support member with a span of at least 0.75 m. On flat roofs, attachment to an outer wall is a practical proposition. Attachment to a chimney which is in use is disadvantageous due to the danger of corrosion. Aerials must not be mounted on roofs made from easily combustible roofing materials, e.g. straw or reeds; instead, mast or window-mounted aerials should be provided. Aerials are not required for wide band cable systems. In addition to the point of connection (to household), space should be provided in the cellar for the amplifier with mains connection.

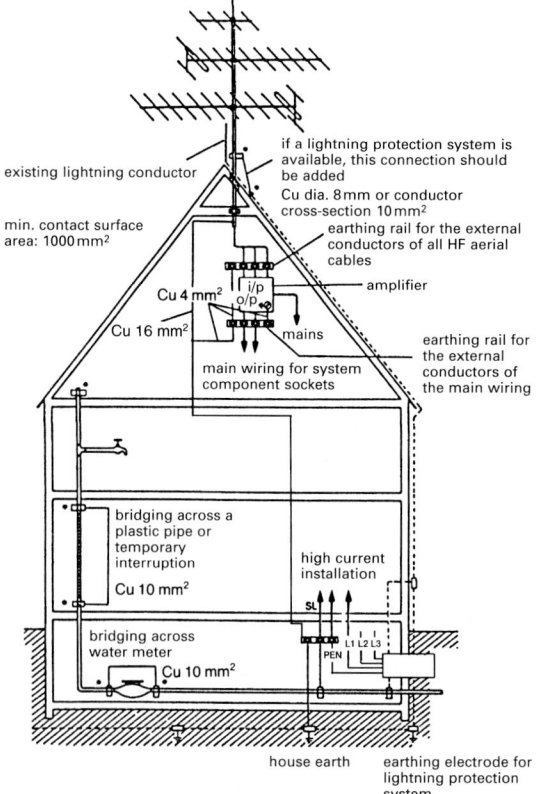

if a lightning protection system is available, this connection should be added
Cu dia. 8mm or conductor cross-section 10 mm²
earthing rail for the external conductors of all HF aerial cables
existing lightning conductor
amplifier
min. contact surface area: 1000 mm²
earthing rail for the external conductors of the main wiring
Cu 4 mm²
i/p o/p
Cu 16 mm²
mains
main wiring for system component sockets
bridging across a plastic pipe or temporary interruption
Cu 10 mm²
high current installation
SL
bridging across water meter
Cu 10 mm²
PEN L1 L2 L3
house earth
earthing electrode for lightning protection system

⑥ **Scheme for lightning protection earthing**

radiation physics quantity	lighting technology quantity and symbol		lighting technology unit and abbreviation	
radiation flux	luminous flux	Φ	lumen	(lm)
radiant intensity	light intensity	I	candela	(cd)
irradiance	illuminance	E	lux	(lx)
radiance	lighting density	L		(cd/m²)
radiant energy	quantity of light	Q		(lm · h)
irradiation	light exposure	H		(lx · h)

(1) **Quantities relating to radiation physics and lighting technology**

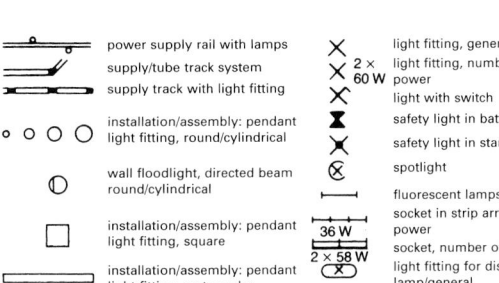

(2) **General lighting symbols for architectural plans**

(3) **Standard lighting symbols for architectural plans**

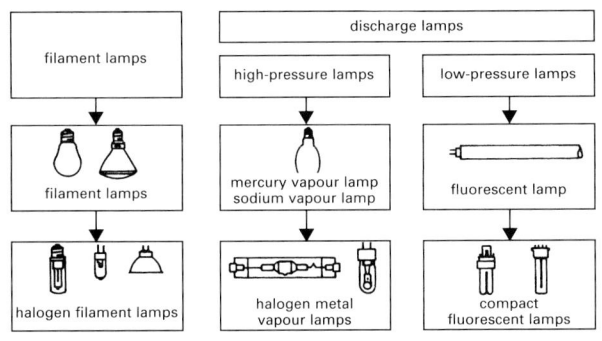

(4) **Diagrams of lamp types**

filament lamps

A — P(W): 60–200 general purpose lamp (bulb)

PAR 38 — P(W): 60–120 reflector lamp

PAR 56 — P(W): 300 reflector lamp

R — P(W): 60–150 reflector lamp

A — P(W): 25–100 soft-tone lamp

A — P(W): 25–100 krypton lamp

A — P(W): 15–60 candle lamp

A — P(W): 35–120 strip light

halogen filament lamps

QT — P(W): 75–250

QT-DE — P(W): 200–500

QT — P(W): 300 500 750 1000

PAR 38 (QR 122) — P(W): 75–250 parabolic reflector lamp

low-voltage halogen lamps

QT — P(W): 20–100

GR-48 — P(W): 20 reflector lamp

QR-CB — P(W): 20–75 cold light reflector

QR-111 — P(W): 35–100 reflector lamp

(5) **Table of lamp types**

LIGHTING: LAMPS AND FITTINGS

Significant lighting parameters

The radiated power of light, as perceived by the eyes, is measured in terms of the luminous flux Φ. The luminous flux radiated per solid angle in a defined direction is referred to as the light intensity I. The intensity of a light source in all directions of radiation is given by the light intensity distribution, generally represented as a light intensity distribution curve (see following page). The light intensity distribution curve characterises the radiation of a light source as being narrow, medium or wide, and as symmetrical or asymmetrical.

The luminous flux per unit area is the lighting intensity or illuminance E. Typical values:

global radiation (clear sky)	max. 100 000 lx
global radiation (cloudy sky)	max. 20 000 lx
optimum sight	2000 lx
minimum in the workplace	200 lx
lighting orientation	20 lx
street lighting	10 lx
moonlight	0.2 lx

The lighting density L is a measure of the perceived brightness. For lamps it is relatively high and results in glare, which necessitates shielding for lights in indoor areas. The lighting density of room surfaces is calculated using the lighting intensity E and the degree of reflection.

Lamps

Lamps convert electrical power (W) into luminous power (lumen, lm). The light yield (lm/W) is a measure of efficiency.

For internal room lighting, filament and discharge lamps are used → (4).

Filament lamps typically provide warm white light that is flicker-free, can be dimmed without restriction and give very good colour rendering. They offer high lighting intensity, particularly in the case of halogen bulbs, and their compact size allows small lighting outlines and very good focusing characteristics (e.g. spotlights). However, filament lamps also have a low lighting efficiency (lm/W) and a relatively short bulb life of between 1000 and 3000 hours.

Discharge lamps usually operate with a ballast device, and sometimes an ignition system, and offer high lighting efficiency with relatively long life (between 5000 and 15000 hours). The colour of the light depends on the type of lamp: warm white, neutral white or daylight white. Colour rendering is moderate to very good, but it is only possible to dim the lamps to a limited extent. Flicker-free operation can only be achieved by the use of an electronic ballast device.

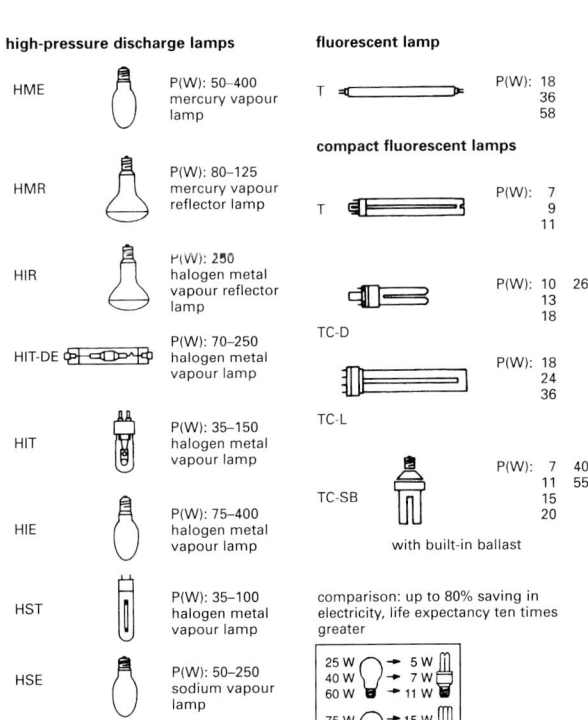

high-pressure discharge lamps

HME — P(W): 50–400 mercury vapour lamp

HMR — P(W): 80–125 mercury vapour reflector lamp

HIR — P(W): 250 halogen metal vapour reflector lamp

HIT-DE — P(W): 70–250 halogen metal vapour lamp

HIT — P(W): 35–150 halogen metal vapour lamp

HIE — P(W): 75–400 halogen metal vapour lamp

HST — P(W): 35–100 halogen metal vapour lamp

HSE — P(W): 50–250 sodium vapour lamp

fluorescent lamp

T — P(W): 18 36 58

compact fluorescent lamps

T — P(W): 7 9 11

TC-D — P(W): 10 26 13 18

TC-L — P(W): 18 24 36

TC-SB — P(W): 7 40 11 55 15 20

with built-in ballast

comparison: up to 80% saving in electricity, life expectancy ten times greater

25 W	→ 5 W
40 W	→ 7 W
60 W	→ 11 W
75 W	→ 15 W
100 W	→ 20 W
120 W	→ 23 W

ARTIFICIAL LIGHTING AND DAYLIGHT

lighting type		flood lighting	spotlights	uplights	downlights	grid lighting square grids	grid lighting rectangular grids
A	general purpose lamp 60–200 W		○		○		
PAR, R	parabolic reflector lamp reflector lamp 60–300 W		○		○		
QT	halogen filament lamp 75–250 W	○	○	○	○		
QT–DE	halogen filament lamp, sockets both sides 100–500 W	○		○			
QT–LV	low-voltage halogen lamp 20–100 W		○		○		
QR–LV	low-voltage halogen reflector lamp 20–100 W		○		○		
T	fluorescent lamp 18–58 W	○		○		○	○
TC TC–D TC–L	compact fluorescent lamp 7–55 W	○	○	○	○	○	○
HME	mercury vapour lamp 50–400 W				○		
HSE/ HST	sodium vapour lamp 50–250 W				○		
HIT HIT-DE	halogen metal vapour lamp 35–250 W	○	○	○	○		

(1) **Allocation of lamp types and lighting types**

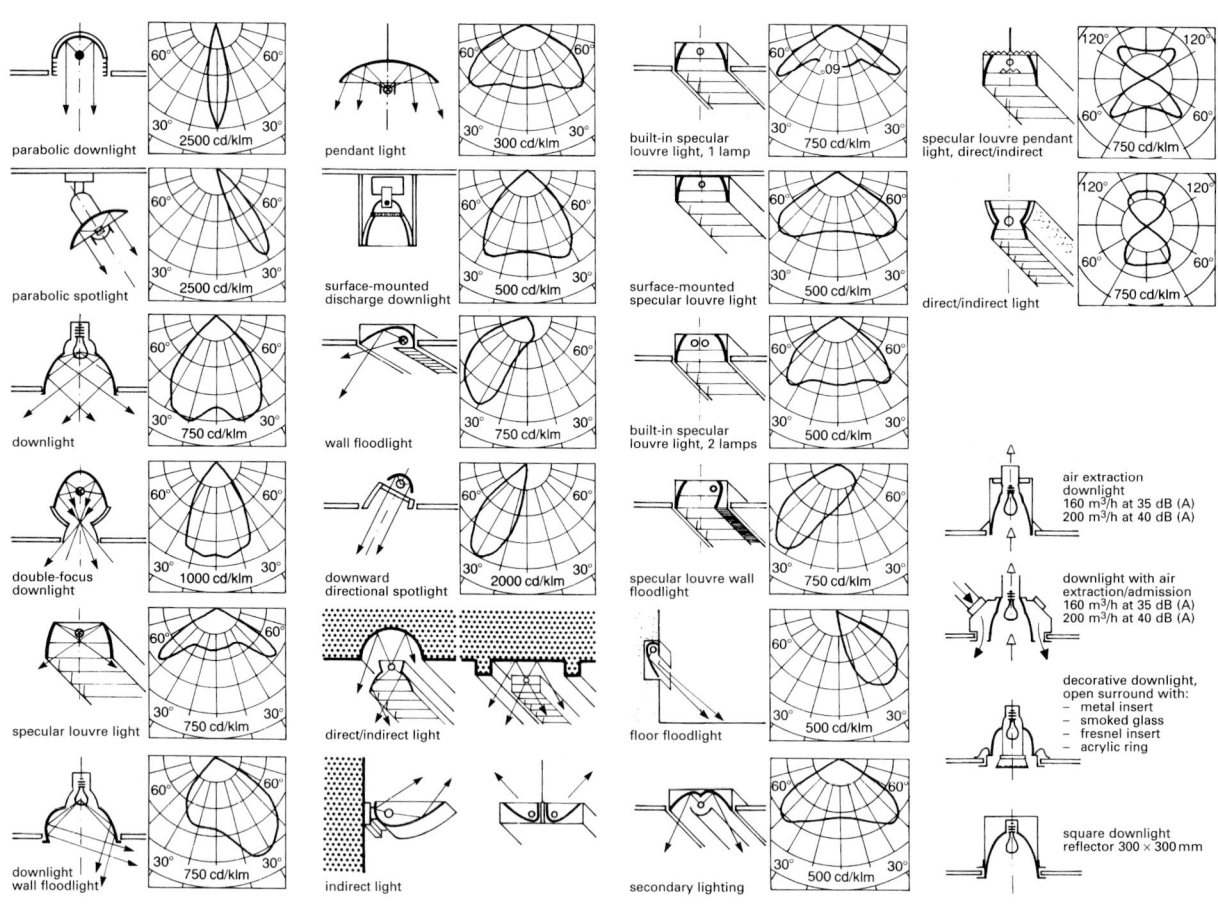

parabolic downlight — 2500 cd/klm
parabolic spotlight — 2500 cd/klm
downlight — 750 cd/klm
double-focus downlight — 1000 cd/klm
specular louvre light — 750 cd/klm
downlight wall floodlight — 750 cd/klm

pendant light — 300 cd/klm
surface-mounted discharge downlight — 500 cd/klm
wall floodlight — 750 cd/klm
downward directional spotlight — 2000 cd/klm
direct/indirect light
indirect light

built-in specular louvre light, 1 lamp — 750 cd/klm
surface-mounted specular louvre light — 500 cd/klm
built-in specular louvre light, 2 lamps — 500 cd/klm
specular louvre wall floodlight — 750 cd/klm
floor floodlight — 500 cd/klm
secondary lighting — 500 cd/klm

specular louvre pendant light, direct/indirect — 750 cd/klm
direct/indirect light — 750 cd/klm

air extraction downlight 160 m³/h at 35 dB (A) 200 m³/h at 40 dB (A)
downlight with air extraction/admission 160 m³/h at 35 dB (A) 200 m³/h at 40 dB (A)
decorative downlight, open surround with:
– metal insert
– smoked glass
– fresnel insert
– acrylic ring
square downlight reflector 300 × 300 mm

(2) **Light fittings and light distribution**

142

room height	nominal illuminance	area	A ≤ 100 W	A > 100 W	PAR 38	PAR 56	R	QT ≤ 250 W	QT – DE	QT > 250 W	QT – LV	QR – CB – LV	QR – LV	T	TC	TC – D	TC – L	HME ≤ 80 W	HME > 80 W	HSE	HST	HIT – DE ≤ 70 W	HIT – DE > 70 W	HIT ≤ 70 W	HIT > 70 W	HIE
up to 3 m	up to 200 Lux	garage car parks, packing rooms												●					●	●	●					
		service rooms												●	●	●	●			●	●					
		workshops												●												
		restaurants	●				●				●	●	●													
		foyers	●	●	●						●	●		●		●										
	up to 500 Lux	standard offices, classrooms/lecture rooms, counters and cash desks												●	●	●	●									
		sitting rooms	●	●							●	●		●	●	●	●									
		workshops												●				●	●							
		libraries									●			●												
		sale rooms									●	●		●	●	●	●					●		●		
		exhibition rooms				●					●			●	●	●	●					●		●		
		museums, galleries, banqueting rooms	●	●	●	●	●	●		●	●	●	●	●	●	●	●									
		entrance halls	●	●							●			●	●	●	●									
	up to 750 Lux	data processing, standard offices with higher visibility requirements												●			●									
		workshops												●					●					●	●	
		shops												●		●	●									
		supermarkets												●												
		shop windows						●	●	●	●	●	●									●	●	●	●	
		hotel kitchens												●												
		concert stages				●				●	●															
		drawing offices, large offices												●												
3 m up to 5 m	up to 200 Lux	storage rooms												●		●	●	●	●							
		workshops												●		●										
		industrial workshops												●					●	●	●		●			
		foyers	●	●	●						●				●	●										
		restaurants	●				●				●	●	●		●	●										
		churches	●	●	●		●																			
		concert halls, theatres	●	●			●																			
	up to 500 Lux	workshops												●					●					●	●	
		industrial workshops												●					●					●	●	
		lecture halls, meeting rooms		●							●			●			●									
		sale rooms												●	●	●	●							●	●	
		exhibition rooms, museums, art galleries	●	●	●	●	●	●	●	●				●	●	●										
		entrance halls	●	●	●						●			●	●	●								●	●	
		restaurants													●	●										
		sports halls, multipurpose halls and gymnasiums									●			●					●					●	●	●
	up to 750 Lux	workshops												●				●	●					●	●	
		art rooms												●		●										
		laboratories												●												
		libraries, reading rooms									●			●		●										
		exhibition rooms												●		●		●						●	●	●
		exhibition halls																●								●
		shops												●		●								●	●	
		supermarkets												●												
		large kitchens												●												
		concert stages			●	●				●	●															
over 5 m	up to 200 Lux	industrial workshops, machine rooms, switchgear installations												●					●	●	●				●	
		rooms for racked storage systems												●					●							
		churches			●	●	●																			
		concert halls, theatres			●	●	●																			
	up to 500 Lux	industrial workshops												●					●					●		●
		museums, art galleries			●		●							●			●									
		airports, railway stations, circulation zones												●					●	●	●			●		●
		banqueting halls				●	●							●												
		sports and multipurpose halls					●							●										●	●	
	up to 750 Lux	industrial workshops																●	●	●					●	●
		auditoriums, lecture halls									●			●		●										
		exhibition rooms										●		●		●								●	●	●
		exhibition halls																	●					●	●	●
		supermarkets												●											●	●

A	= general purpose lamps	QT – LV	= low-voltage halogen lamps	TC – D	= compact fluorescent lamps, 4 tubes
PAR	= parabolic reflector lamps	QR – LV	= low-voltage reflector lamps	TC – L	= compact fluorescent lamps, long
R	= reflector lamps	QR – CB – LV	= low-voltage reflector lamps, cold light	HME	= mercury vapour lamps
QT	= halogen filament lamps	T	= fluorescent lamps	HSE	= sodium vapour lamps
QT – DE	= halogen filament lamps, 2 sockets	TC	= compact fluorescent lamps	HST	= sodium vapour lamps, tubular
				HIT	= halogen metal vapour lamps
				HIE	= halogen metal vapour lamps, elliptical

(1) **Provision of lighting for internal areas**

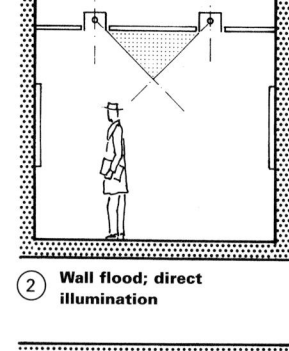

① Direct symmetrical illumination

② Wall flood; direct illumination

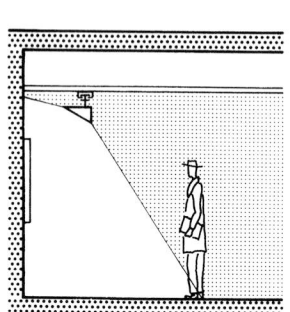

③ Wall flood on a power supply rail; partial room illumination

④ Wall floodlight

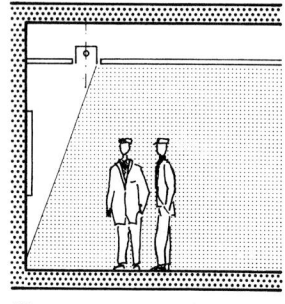

⑤ Directional spotlights

⑥ Indirect lighting

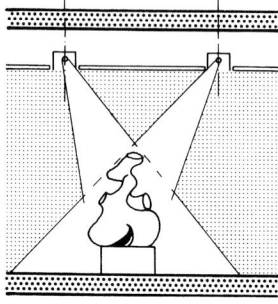

⑦ Direct/indirect lighting

⑧ Ceiling floodlighting

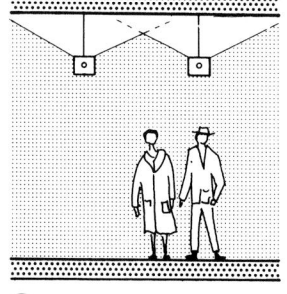

⑨ Floor floodlighting

⑩ Wall light; direct/indirect lighting

⑪ Wall flood on power supply rail

⑫ Spotlight on power supply rail

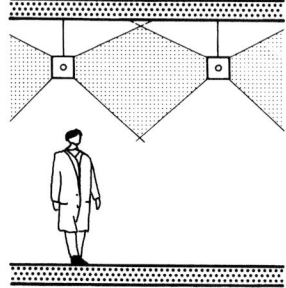
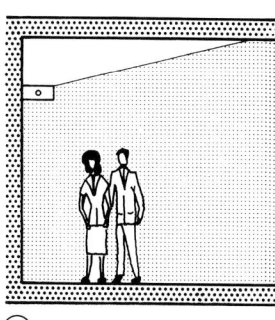
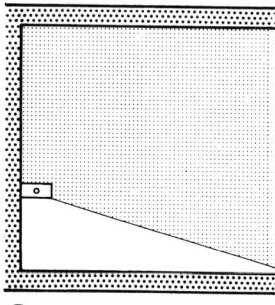
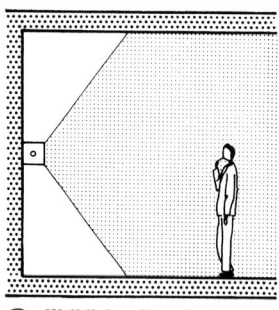
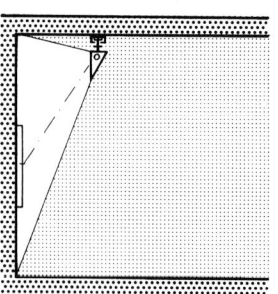
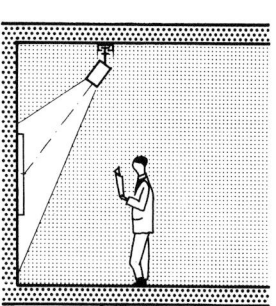

LIGHTING: ARRANGEMENT

Forms of Lighting for Internal Areas

Direct, symmetrical lighting → ① is preferred for all general illumination of work rooms, meeting rooms, rooms in public use and circulation zones. The required level of illumination can be achieved with relatively little electrical power: standard values for specific loadings are given on p. 147. When designing a lighting system, an angle of illumination between 70° and 90° should be tried first.

Downlights (wall floods, louvre lighting) → ② can provide uniform wall illumination while the effect on the rest of the room is that of direct lighting. Wall floods on a power supply rail → ③ can also give uniform wall illumination over the required area, depending on the separation between the lamp and the wall; up to 500 lx can be achieved. Fluorescent lamps and halogen filament lamps can also be used.

Wall floods for ceiling installation → ④ can be sited so as to provide low room light or illumination of one wall. These can also make use of halogen filament lamps and fluorescent lamps.

Downlighting with directed spotlights → ⑤ using a regular arrangement of lamps on the ceiling and swivelling reflectors can give different lighting levels in the room. Halogen filament lamps are most suitable, in particular those with low-voltage bulbs.

Indirect lighting → ⑥ can give an impression of a bright room free of glare even at low lighting levels, although the room must be sufficiently high and careful ceiling design is needed to give the required luminance. Energy consumption in this form of lighting is up to three times higher than for direct lighting so combinations are often used (e.g. 70% direct, 30% indirect) providing the room height is adequate (h≥3m) → ⑦. Fluorescent lamps are usually used in direct/indirect lighting, but they may also be combined with filament lamps.

Ceiling and floor floods → ⑧ – ⑨ are employed to illuminate ceiling and floor surfaces. They usually use halogen filament or fluorescent lamps, although high-pressure discharge lamps are also a possibility.

Wall lights → ⑩ are principally used for decorative wall lighting and can also incorporate special effects (e.g. using colour filters or prisms). To a limited extent, they can also be used for the illumination of ceilings or floors.

Wall floodlights and spotlights on power supply rails → ⑪ – ⑫ are particularly useful in sale rooms, exhibitions, museums and galleries. With wall floodlights, typical requirements are for vertical illumination levels of 50 lx, 150 lx or 300 lx; filament and fluorescent lamps are usually preferred. For spotlights, the basic light emission angles are 10° ('spot'), 30° ('highlight') and 90° ('flood'). The angle of the light cone can be varied by passing the light through lenses (sculptured lenses, Fresnel lenses), and the spectrum of the light can be varied using UV and IR filters and colour filters. Shading can be arranged by means of louvres and anti-glare flaps.

Geometry of Lighting Arrangements

The spacing between light fittings and between the light fittings and the walls depends on the height of the room → ① – ④.

The preferred incidence at which light strikes objects and wall areas is between 30° (optimum) and 40° → ⑤ – ⑨.

The shading angle of downward lighting lies between 30° (wide-angle lighting, adequate glare control) and 50° (narrow-angle lighting, high glare control) → ⑩, and between 30° and 40° in the case of louvred lighting.

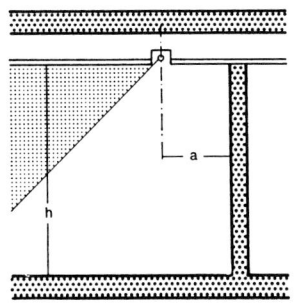

① Downlight/wall floodlight, distance from wall: a ≈ ¹/₃h

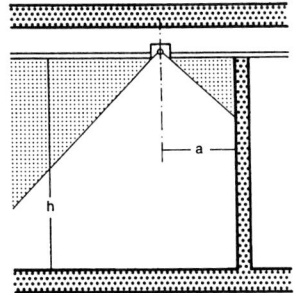

② Downlight, distance from wall: a ≈ ¹/₃h

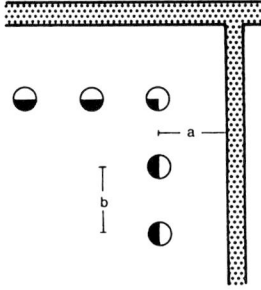

③ Downlight/wall floodlight, separation between lights: b = 1–1.5a

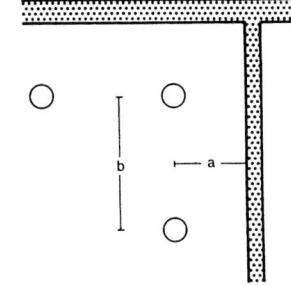

④ Downlight, separation between lights: b ≈ 2a

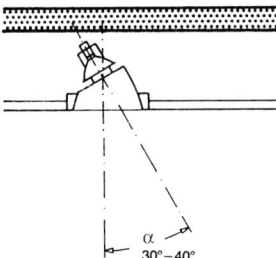

⑤ Angle of inclination of directional spotlights and floodlights: α = 30°–40° (optimum)

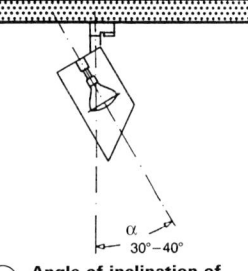

⑥ Angle of inclination of spotlights illuminating objects and walls: α = 30°–40° (optimum)

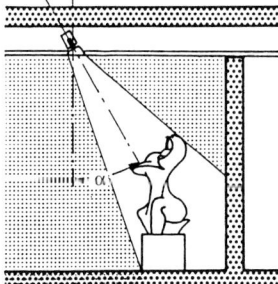

⑦ Illumination of objects

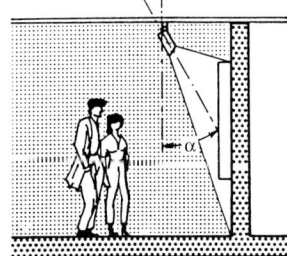

⑧ Wall illumination, spotlight

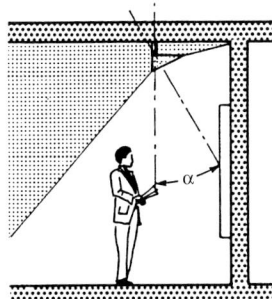

⑨ Wall illumination, floodlight

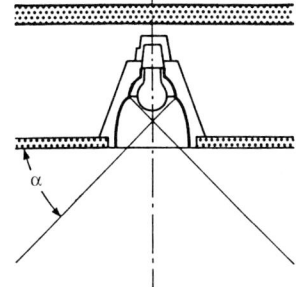

⑩ Shading angle (= 30°/40°/50°)

20 lx	necessary for the recognition of critical features. 20 lx is the minimum value of horizontal illuminance for internal areas, except work areas
200 lx	work areas appear dull with illuminance E < 200 lx, therefore 200 lx is the minimum value of illuminance for continually occupied work areas
2000 lx	2000 lx is recommended as the optimum illuminance for work areas
	the lowest perceptible change in illuminance is by factor of 1.5; therefore, the gradation of nominal illuminance levels for internal areas is: 20, 30, 50, 75, 100, 150, 200, 300, 500, 750, 1000, 1500, 2000 etc.

⑪ Range of illuminance values for internal areas

recommended illuminance			area/activity
20	30	50	paths and work areas in the open air
50	100	150	for orientation in rooms for short-stay periods
100	150	200	for work areas not in constant use
200	300	500	for visual tasks of little difficulty
300	500	750	for visual tasks of moderate difficulty
500	750	1000	for visual tasks with higher demands, e.g. office work
750	1000	1500	for visual tasks of great difficulty, e.g. fine assembly work
1000	1500	2000	for visual tasks of considerable difficulty, e.g. inspection
over 2000			additional lighting for difficult and special visual tasks

⑫ Recommended illuminance values in accordance with CIE (Commission International de l'Eclairage)

identifying letters: IP	example IP 44
first identifying digit 0 – 6	degree of protection against contact and foreign bodies
second identifying digit 0 – 8	degree of protection against ingress of water

first digit	area of protection	first digit	area of protection
0	no protection	0	no protection
1	protection against large foreign bodies (>50 m)	1	protection against vertical drops of water
2	against medium-sized foreign bodies (>12 mm)	2	against drops of water at an incidence of up to 15°
3	against small foreign bodies (<2.5 mm)	3	against water splashing
4	against granular foreign bodies (<1 mm)	4	against water spraying
5	against dust deposits	5	against water jets
6	against entry of dust	6	against ingress of water due to flooding
		7	against dipping in water
		8	against immersion in water

⑬ Types of protection required for lighting

stage	index Ra	typical areas of application
1A	> 90	paint sampling, art galleries
1B	90 > RA > 80	living accommodation, hotels, restaurants, offices, schools, hospitals, printing and textile industry
2A	80 > RA > 70	industry
2B	70 > RA > 60	
3	60 > RA > 40	industrial and other areas with low demands for colour rendering
4	40 > RA > 20	ditto

⑭ Colour reproduction of lamps

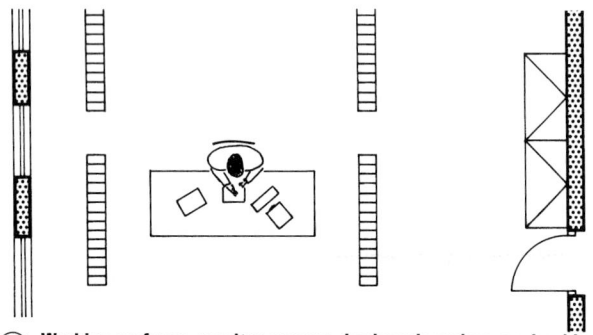

(1) **Correct arrangement of lights in relation to work position: light from the side**

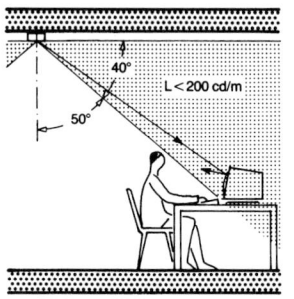

(2) **Working surfaces, monitor screens, keyboards and paper should have matt surfaces**

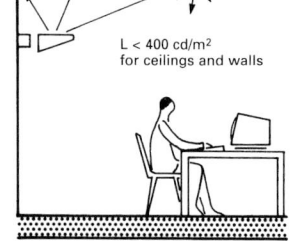

(3) **Lights which can generate reflections should have low luminance levels in the critical incidence range**

(4) **Luminance of indirect lighting**

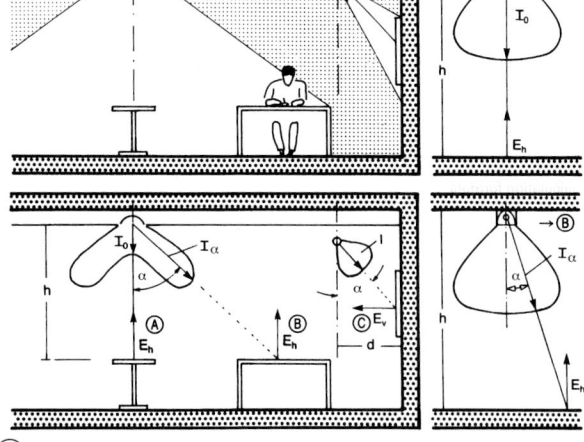

(5) **Illuminance at a point**

Ⓐ $E_h = \dfrac{I_0}{h^2}$

Ⓑ $E_h = \dfrac{I_\alpha}{h^2} \cdot \cos^3 \alpha$

Ⓒ $E_v = \dfrac{I_\alpha}{d^2} \cdot \cos^3 (90 - \alpha)$

(6) **Photometric distance principle**

LIGHTING: ARRANGEMENT

Lighting Quality Characteristics

Any good lighting design must meet functional and ergonomic requirements while taking cost-effectiveness into account. In addition to the following quantitative quality criteria, there are qualitative, in particular architectural, criteria which must be observed.

Level of illumination

A mean level of between 300 lx (individual offices with daylight) and 750 lx (large rooms) is required in work areas. Higher illumination levels can be achieved in uniform general lighting through the addition of lighting at workplace positions.

Light direction → (1)

Ideally, light should fall on a working position from the side. The prerequisite for this is a wing-shaped light distribution curve (p. 142).

Limitation of glare → (2) – (3)

Direct glare, reflected glare and reflections from monitor screens should all be limited. Limiting direct glare is achieved by using lights with shading angles $\geq 30°$.

Limiting reflected glare is achieved by directing light from the side onto the working position, in conjunction with the use of matt surfaces on the surrounding areas. → (2).

Limiting reflections from monitor screens requires the correct positioning of the screen. Lighting which nevertheless still reflects on a screen must have a luminance of ≤ 200 cd/m^2 in these areas.

Distribution of luminance

The harmonic distribution of luminance is the result of a careful balance of all the degrees of reflection in the room → (7). Luminance due to indirect lighting must not exceed 400 cd/m^2.

Colour of light and colour rendering

The colour of the light is determined by the choice of lamp. A distinction is made between three types: warm white light (colour temperature under 3300 K), neutral white light (3300–5000 K) and white daylight (over 5000 K). In offices, most light sources are chosen in the warm white or neutral white ranges. For colour rendering, which depends on the spectral composition of the light, stage 1 (very good colour rendering) should generally be sought.

Calculation of point illuminance levels → (6)

The illuminance levels (horizontal E_h, vertical E_v), which are generated by individual light sources, can be determined from the luminous intensity and the spatial geometry (height h, distance d and light incidence angle α) using the photometric distance principle.

	reflection factor (%)		reflection factor (%)
lighting materials			
aluminium, pure, highly polished	80 to 87	plaster, light	40 to 45
aluminium, anodised, matt	80 to 85	plaster, dark	15 to 25
aluminium, polished	65 to 75	sandstone	20 to 40
aluminium, matt	55 to 76	plywood, rough	25 to 40
aluminium coatings, matt	55 to 56	cement, concrete, rough	20 to 30
chrome, polished	60 to 70	brick, red, new	10 to 15
vitreous enamel, white	65 to 75	**paints**	
lacquer, pure white	80 to 85	white	75 to 85
copper, highly polished	60 to 70	light grey	40 to 60
brass, highly polished	70 to 75	medium grey	25 to 35
nickel, highly polished	50 to 60	dark grey	10 to 15
paper, white	70 to 80	light blue	40 to 50
silvered mirror, behind glass	80 to 88	dark blue	15 to 20
silver, highly polished	90 to 92	light green	45 to 55
other materials		dark green	15 to 20
oak, light, polished	25 to 35	light yellow	60 to 70
oak, dark, polished	10 to 15	brown	20 to 30
granite	20 to 25	light red	45 to 55
limestone	35 to 55	dark red	15 to 20
marble, polished	30 to 70		

(7) **Reflection factors for various materials**

specific connected load P* W/m² for 100lx for height 3 m, area ≥ 100 m² and reflection 0.7/0.5/0.2		
⊂◯ A		12 W/m²
◯ QT ◯		10 W/m²
⊂◯ HME		5 W/m²
▭ TC		5 W/m²
▭ TC-L		4 W/m²
▭ T26		3 W/m²

(1) **Specific connected load P* for various lamp types**

correction factor k				
height H	area A(m²)	reflection factor		
		070502	050201	000
		bright	medium	dark
up to 3m	20	0.75	0.65	0.60
	50	0.90	0.80	0.75
	≥ 100	1.00	0.90	0.85
3–5 m	20	0.55	0.45	0.40
	50	0.75	0.65	0.60
	≥ 100	0.90	0.80	0.75
5–7 m	50	0.55	0.45	0.40
	≥ 100	0.75	0.65	0.60

(2) **Table of correction factors**

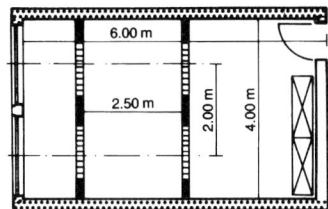

(3) **Calculation of illuminance for internal areas**

example
room area   A = 100 m²
room height   H = 3 m
reflection factor 0.5/0.2/0.1
         (medium reflection)
type of light
P^* = 4 W/m² · (compact fluorescent lamp)
P^* = 9 · 45 W = 405 W
type of light
P^* = 12 W/m² · (general purpose lamp)
P^* = 8 · 100 W = 800 W
type of light
P^* = 10 W/m² · (halogen filament lamp)
P^* = 16 · 20 W = 320 W
formula
$$E_n = \left(\frac{100 \cdot 405}{100 \cdot 4} + \frac{100 \cdot 800}{100 \cdot 12} + \frac{100 \cdot 320}{100 \cdot 10}\right) \cdot 0.9$$
E_n = 180 lx

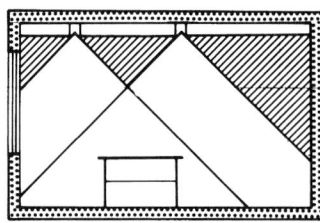

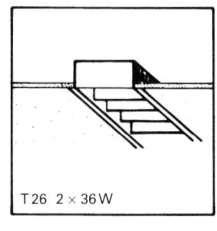

A = 24 m²
K = 0.75
   (bright reflection)
P = 4 · 90 W = 360 W
$$E_n = \frac{100 \cdot 4 \cdot 90}{24.3} \cdot 0.75$$
E_n = 375 lx

(4) **Calculation for offices**

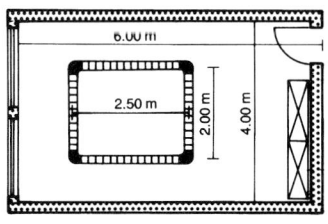

(5) **Built-in louvred lighting**

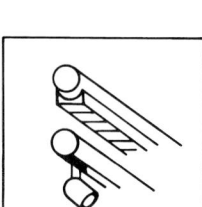

T26 2 × 36 W

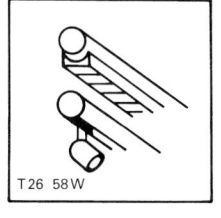

(6) **Structured lighting**

T26 58 W

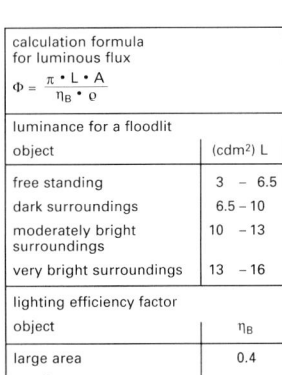

(7) **Built-in louvred lighting**

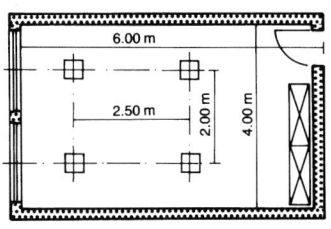

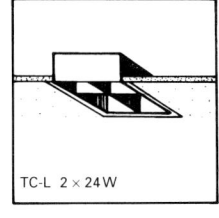

TC-L 2 × 24 W

LIGHTING: REQUIREMENTS

Calculation of mean illuminance

In practice, it is often necessary to obtain an estimate of the mean intensity of illuminance (E_n) for a given level of electrical power supplied, or the electrical power P required for a given level of illumination. E_n and P can be estimated from the formula in → ⑧. The specific power P* required for this calculation depends on the type of lamps used → ①, and relates to direct illumination. The correction factor k depends on the size of the room and the reflection levels of the walls, ceiling and floor → ②.

If the calculation is to be made for rooms with different types of lighting, the components are calculated individually and then added together → ③.

Calculation of the illumination using the specific power is also applicable to offices. In the example, a rectangular room with an area of 24 m² is equipped with 4 lights. From → ⑧, with 2 × 36 W lamps (connected value, including 90 W ballast), an illuminance of ca. 375 lx is achieved.

In offices, in addition to conventional louvred mirror lighting, square louvred lighting with compact fluorescent lamps → ⑦, or structured lighting → ⑥, are frequently installed. Lighting structures use a combination of power supply rails to carry spotlights.

Floodlighting buildings

The luminous flux required for lamps used to floodlight a building can be calculated from the formula in → ⑨. The luminance should be between 3 cd/m² (free-standing objects) and 16 cd/m² (objects in very bright surroundings).

$$E_n = \frac{100 \cdot P}{A \cdot P^*} \cdot k$$

$$P = \frac{E_n \cdot P \cdot P^*}{100} \cdot \frac{1}{k}$$

E_n nominal illuminance (lx)
P   connected load (W)
P^* specific connected load (W/m²) → ①
A   room floor area
k   correction factor → ②

(8) **Formula for mean illuminance E_n and connected load P**

calculation formula for luminous flux $\Phi = \frac{\pi \cdot L \cdot A}{\eta_B \cdot \varrho}$		
luminance for a floodlit object		(cdm²) L
free standing		3 – 6.5
dark surroundings		6.5 – 10
moderately bright surroundings		10 – 13
very bright surroundings		13 – 16
lighting efficiency factor object		η_B
large area small area		0.4
large distance		0.3
towers		0.2

Φ = luminous flux required L = mean luminance (cd/m²) A = surface to be floodlit η_B = lighting efficiency factor ϱ = reflection factor for the material	
level of reflection from illuminated materials	ϱ
brick, white vitrified	0.85
white marble	0.6
plaster, light	0.3–0.5
plaster, dark	0.2–0.3
light sandstone	0.3–0.4
dark sandstone	0.1–0.2
light brick	0.3–0.4
dark brick	0.1–0.2
light wood	0.3–0.5
granite	0.1–0.2

(9) **Luminous flux required for floodlighting**

147

ARTIFICIAL LIGHTING AND DAYLIGHT

light colours (Philips)	76	warm white					neutral white				daylight white			
		29	827	927	830	930	25	33	840	940	950	865	965	54
colour rendering level		3	1B	1A	1B	1A	2A	2B	1B	1A	1A	1B	1A	2A
sales areas														
foodstuffs			●						✕					
meat	✕													
textiles, leather goods				✕	●	✕			●					
furniture, carpets				✕	✕									
sports, games, paper goods					✕									
photography, watches, jewellery					✕	●			✕	●				
cosmetics, hairdressing			●	✕	●	✕			●	✕				
flowers	●								✕					✕
bakery goods			✕											
refrigerated counters, chests			✕											
cheese, fruit, vegetables			✕											
fish			✕											
department stores, supermarkets			✕		✕				✕					
trade and industry														
workshops							●		✕					
machinery, electrical manufacture							●		✕			✕		
textile manufacture									✕					
printing, graphic trades									●		✕	●		
paint shops											✕	✕		
varnishing shops											●	✕	●	
warehousing, dispatch								●	✕					
plant growing														✕
woodworking									✕		✕			
forging, rolling		●					●							
laboratories					✕						✕		✕	
colour testing											✕		✕	
offices and administration														
offices, corridors					✕				✕					
meeting rooms			✕		✕									
schools, places of education														
lecture theatres, classrms, play schools					✕				✕					
libraries, reading rooms			✕		✕									
social spaces														
restaurants, pubs, hotels			✕											
theatres, concert halls, foyers			✕											
event spaces														
exhibition halls			✕						✕					
sports and multipurpose halls					✕				✕					
galleries, museums					✕	✕								
clinics, medical practices														
diagnosis and treatment						●				●				
wards, waiting rooms			●		●									
domestic														
living room			✕		✕									
kitchen, bathroom, workroom, cellar			✕		✕				✕	✕				
external lighting														
roads, paths, pedestrian areas		✕					✕							
illumination of signs														✕

✕ = recommended   ● = possible

(1) **The correct use of fluorescent lamps**

recommended lighting levels for working areas

table of nominal levels of illuminance: standard values for working areas

type of area / type of activity	(lx)	type of area / type of activity	(lx)	type of area / type of activity	(lx)
general rooms:		**metal processing/working:**		**paper manufacture and processing, printing:**	
circulation zones in storage buildings	50	forging of small components	200		
storerooms	50	welding	300	pulp factory	200
storerooms with access requirements	100	large/medium machining operations	300	paper- and boardmaking machinery	300
storerooms with reading requirements	200	fine machining work	500	book-binding, wallpaper printing	300
gangways in storage racking systems	20	control stations	750	cutting, gilding, embossing, plate etching,	
operating platforms	200	cold rolling mills	200	work on blocks and plates, printing machines,	
dispatch areas	200	wire drawing	300	stencil manufacture	500
canteens	200	heavy sheet working	200	hand printing, paper sorting	750
break rooms	100	light sheet working	300	retouching, lithographics, hand and machine	
gymnasiums	300	tool manufacture	500	composition, finishing	1000
changing rooms	100	large assembly work	200	colour proofing in multicolour	
washrooms	100	medium assembly work	300	printing	1500
toilet areas	100	fine assembly work	500	steel- and copper-plate engraving	2000
first-aid areas	500	drop forging	200		
machinery rooms	100	foundries, cellars, etc.	50		
power supply installations	100	scaffolding, trestling	100	**leather industry:**	
postrooms	500	sanding	200		
telephone exchanges	300	cleaning castings	200	vat operations	200
		work positions at mixers	200	skin preparation	300
		casting houses	200	saddle making	500
circulation zones in buildings:		emptying positions	200	leather dyeing	750
		machine forming operations	200	quality control, moderate demands	750
for persons	50	manual forming operations	300	quality control, high demands	1000
for vehicles	100	core making	300	quality control, extreme demands	1500
stairs	100	model construction	500	colour inspection	1000
loading ramps	100	galvanising	300		
		painting	300		
		control stations	750	**textile manufacture and processing:**	
offices, administration rooms:		tool assembly, fine mechanics	1000		
		motor body operations	500	work in dyeing vats	200
offices with workstations near windows	300	lacquering	750	spinning	300
offices	500	night-shift lacquering	1000	dyeing	300
open-plan offices		upholstery	500	spinning, knitting, weaving	500
– high reflection	750	inspection	750	sewing, material printing	750
– moderate reflection	1000			millinery	750
technical drawing	750			trimming	1000
conference rooms	300	**power stations:**		quality control, colour check	1000
reception rooms	100				
rooms for public use	200	charging equipment	50		
data processing	500	boiler house	100	**foodstuffs industry:**	
		pressure equalising chambers	200		
		machine rooms	100	general work positions	200
chemical industry:		adjoining rooms	50	mixing, unpacking	300
		switchgear in buildings	100	butchery, dairy work, milling	300
facilities with remote controls	50	external switchgear	20	cutting and sorting	300
facilities with manual operations	100	control rooms	300	delicatessen, cigarette manufacture	500
continuously occupied technical processing		inspection work	500	quality control, decoration, sorting	500
facilities	200			laboratories	1000
maintenance facilities	300				
laboratories	300	**electrical industry:**			
work requiring a high degree of visual				**wholesale and retail trades:**	
acuity	500	manufacture of wire and cable, assembly			
colour testing	1000	work, winding thick wire	300	salerooms, continuously occupied	
		assembly of telephone equipment, winding		work positions	300
		medium-thick wire	500	cashier's positions	500
cement industry, ceramics, glass works:		assembly of fine components, adjustment			
		and testing	1000	**trades (general examples):**	
working positions or areas at furnaces,		assembly of fine electronic			
mixers, pulverising plant	200	components	1500	paint shops	200
rollers, presses, forming operations	300	repair work	1500	pre-assembly of heating and ventilation	
glass blowing, grinding, etching,				equipment	200
glass polishing, glass instrumentation				locksmiths	300
manufacture	500	**jewellery and watchmaking:**		garages	300
decorative work	500			joinery	300
hand grinding and engraving	750	manufacture of jewellery	1000	repair workshops	500
fine work	1000	preparation of precious stones	1500	radio and television workshops	500
		optical and watchmaking workshops	1500		
				service operations:	
iron and steel works, rolling mills, large foundries:		**wood preparation and woodworking:**			
				hotel and restaurant receptions	200
		steam treatment	100	kitchens	500
automated production facilities	50	saw mills	200	dining rooms	200
production facilities, manual work	100	assembly	200	buffet	300
continuously occupied work positions		selection of veneers, lacquers, model		lounges	300
in production facilities	200	woodworking	500	self-service restaurants	300
maintenance	300	woodworking machinery	500	laundries, washrooms	300
control stations	500	wood finishing	500	ironing machines	300
		defect control	750	hand ironing	300
				sorting	300
				inspection	1000
				hairdressers	500
				beauty salons	750

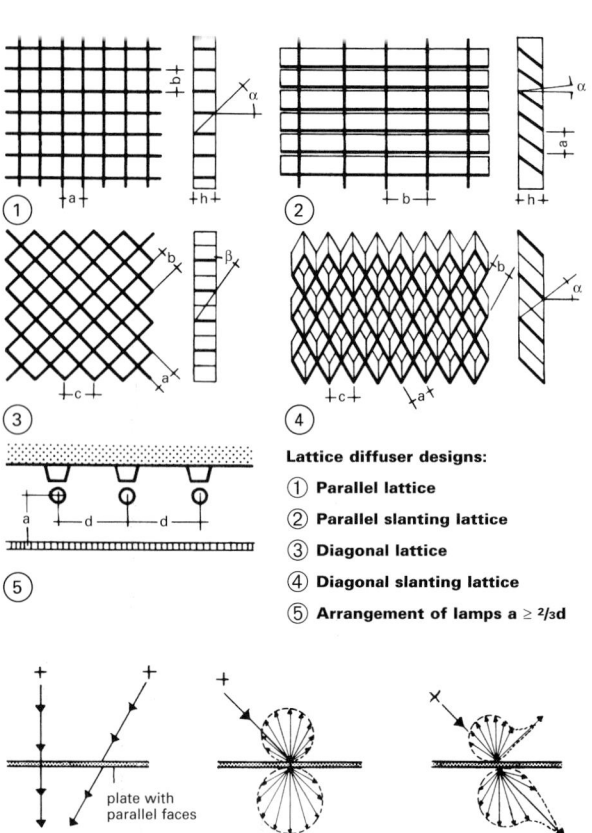

Lattice diffuser designs:

① **Parallel lattice**

② **Parallel slanting lattice**

③ **Diagonal lattice**

④ **Diagonal slanting lattice**

⑤ **Arrangement of lamps a ≥ ²/₃d**

⑥ **Directional permeability of clear glass, showing displacement of slanting radiation** — plate with parallel faces

⑦ **Scattered permeability of frosted glass, alabaster, etc.**

⑦ **Mixed permeability of ornamental glass, silk, light frosted glass, etc.**

material	scatter	thickness (mm)	reflection (%)	permeability (%)	absorption (%)
clear glass	none	2 – 4	6 – 8	90 – 92	2 – 4
ornamental glass	minimal	3.2 – 5.9	7 – 24	57 – 90	3 – 21
clear glass, frosted outside	minimal	1.75 – 3.1	7 – 20	63 – 87	4 – 17
clear glass, frosted inside	minimal	1.75 – 3.1	6 – 16	77 – 89	3 – 11
frosted glass: group 1	good	1.7 – 3.6	40 – 66	12 – 38	20 – 31
group 2	good	1.7 – 2.5	43 – 54	37 – 51	6 – 11
group 3	good	1.4 – 3.5	65 – 78	13 – 35	4 – 11
plated frosted glass: group 1	good	1.9 – 2.9	31 – 45	47 – 66	3 – 10
group 2	good	2.8 – 3.3	54 – 67	27 – 35	8 – 11
frosted glass, colour-plated					
red		2 – 3	64 – 69	2 – 4	29 – 34
orange		2 – 3	63 – 68	6 – 10	22 – 31
green		2 – 3	60 – 66	3 – 9	30 – 31
opaline glass	minimal	2.2 – 2.5	13 – 28	58 – 84	2 – 14
porcelain	good	3.0	72 – 77	2 – 8	2 – 21
marble, polished	good	7.3 – 10	30 – 71	3 – 8	24 – 65
marble, impregnated	good	3 – 5	27 – 54	12 – 40	11 – 49
alabaster	good	11.2 – 13.4	49 – 67	17 – 30	14 – 21
cardboard, impregnated	good		69	8	23
parchment, uncoloured	good		48	42	10
parchment, light yellow	good		37	41	22
parchment, dark yellow	good		36	14	50
silk, white	moderate		28 – 38	61 – 71	1
silk, coloured	moderate		5 – 24	13 – 54	27 – 80
cotton lining	good		rd.68	rd.28	rd.4
Formica, tinted	good	1.1 – 2.8	32 – 39	20 – 36	26 – 48
Pollopas, light colour	good	1.2 – 1.6	46 – 48	25 – 33	21 – 28
Perspex, white (frosted)	good	1.0	55	17	28
Perspex, yellow (frosted)	good	1.0	36	9	55
Perspex, blue (frosted)	good	1.0	12	4	84
Perspex, green (frosted)	good	1.0	12	4	84
mirror glass (plate)		6 – 8	8	88	4
wire-reinforced glass		6 – 8	9	74	17
crude glass		4 – 6	8	88	4
insulating glass (green)		2	6	38	56

⑨ **Relevant characteristics of materials permeable to light**

LIGHTING: REQUIREMENTS

Fluorescent Tubes for Advertising Displays

Every type of text and arbitrary line styles can be reproduced using fluorescent tubes, including ornamental and figured representations. Control is simple using rheostats or regulating transformers. Fluorescent tubes are commonly used for cinemas, theatres, sales advertising and publicity. In offices and businesses, louvred or gridded ceilings may be installed under fluorescent tubes to provide predominantly downward lighting → ① – ⑤.

Strip-lights and elongated lighting panels allow soft uniform lighting to be achieved, which approximates daylight and has shadow effects.

High-pressure mercury vapour lamps with fluorescent gas are used for the illumination of factories and workshops as well as for external lighting.

Mixed-light lamps with fluorescent gas produce light similar to daylight, with good colour reproduction. These lamps have standard fittings, without a ballast device (e.g. general-purpose lamps).

Transparent and Translucent Materials

In determining the size, colour, window dimensions and lighting of a room, a knowledge of the translucence, scatter and reflected radiation of the materials to be used in the room is required. This is particularly important for effective artistic and economic design.

A distinction is made between materials which reflect light → ⑨ with direct, totally scattered or partially scattered return radiation, and translucent materials with direct → ① – ⑥, scattered → ⑦ or mixed translucence → ⑧.

Note: Frosted glass with inside surface frosting (preferred owing to fewer soiling problems) absorbs less light than the same glass with external surface frosting → ⑨.

Coloured silk lampshades with white linings which minimally reduce translucence absorb around 20% less light than those without linings and with greater translucence.

Daylight glass which filters electric light to simulate sunlight absorbs approximately 35% of the total light. Glass which comes close to copying the scattered light of the sky must absorb 60–80%.

Clear window glass is translucent to between 65 and 95% of light. If poor-quality clear glass is used, particularly in the case of double or triple glazing, so much light is absorbed that it is necessary to increase the window size. This increase is not compensated for by the improved thermal insulation of the multi-paned window assembly.

Sheet glass is made mechanically, and is ready for use without further processing. It is a clear, transparent glass which is colourless and uniformly thick. Both sides have even plane surfaces, and its transparency to light is 91–93%.

Classification: Type 1: Best commercial quality product for rooms (living accommodation, offices).

Type 2: Structural glass for factories, storerooms, cellars and glass floors.

Glass of one type only should be used for glazed items which are sited next to each other. Such applications include window glazing, shop windows, doors, dividing walls, furniture construction, laminated safety glass and double-glazing units. Further processing might entail polishing, etching, frosting, stoving, silvering, painting, bending or arching. Special-purpose glass, such as silvered glass, dry plate glass, glass for automobiles and safety glass, is made in all thicknesses (→ pp. 166–173).

wavelength		frequency		
in metres (m)		in hertz (Hz)		
100 000	(10⁵)			
		10⁴		
10 000	(10⁴)			
		10⁵	long waves	
1 000	(10³)			
		10⁶	medium waves	
100	(10²)			
		10⁷	short waves	
10	(10¹)			
		10⁸	ultra-short waves	
1	(10⁰)			
		10⁹	television	
0.1	(10⁻¹)			
		10¹⁰		
0.01	(10⁻²)			
		10¹¹	radar waves	
0.001	(10⁻³)			
		10¹²		red
0.0001	(10⁻⁴)			
		10¹³	infra-red radiation	
0.00001	(10⁻⁵)			orange yellow
		10¹⁴		
0.000001	(10⁻⁶)			
		10¹⁵		green
0.0000001	(10⁻⁷)			
		10¹⁶	ultra-violet radiation	
0.00000001	(10⁻⁸)			blue
		10¹⁷		
0.000000001	(10⁻⁹)			violet
		10¹⁸	X-rays	
0.0000000001	(10⁻¹⁰)			
		10¹⁹		
0.00000000001	(10⁻¹¹)			
		10²⁰	gamma radiation	
0.000000000001	(10⁻¹²)			
		10²¹		
0.0000000000001	(10⁻¹³)			
		10²²		
0.00000000000001	(10⁻¹⁴)			
		10²³		
0.000000000000001	(10⁻¹⁵)			
		10²⁴		
		10²⁵		

(1 nanometre = 1 × 10⁻⁹ metres)

(1) **Spectrum of electromagnetic radiation**

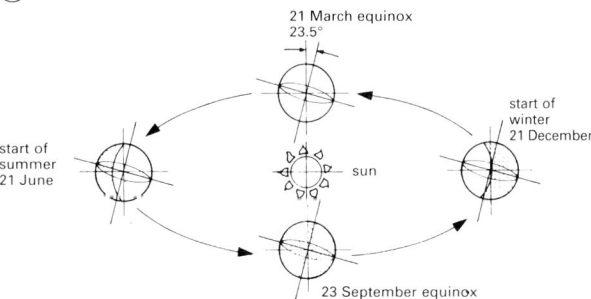

(2) **Seasons of the year, northern hemisphere**

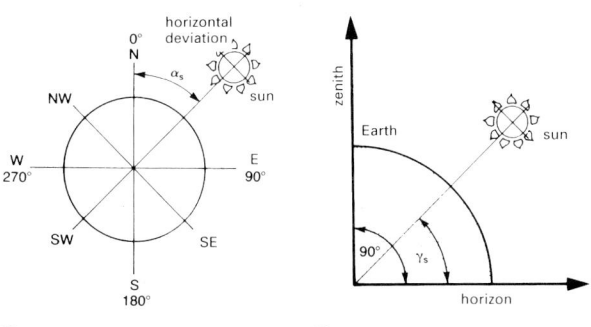

(3) **Azimuth (α_s)**   (4) **Angle of elevation (γ_s)**

General requirements for daylight illumination of internal areas

All rooms which are to be used for permanent occupation must be provided with adequate natural light. In addition, appropriate visual links with the outside world must be safeguarded.

Light, wavelength, light colour

Within the electromagnetic spectrum → ①, visible light occupies a relatively small band, namely 380–780 nm. Light (daylight and artificial light) is the visible band of electromagnetic radiation between ultra-violet and infra-red. The spectral colours which occur in this range each have corresponding wavelengths, e.g. violet is short wave and red is long wave. Sunlight contains relatively more short-wave radiation than a filament lamp, which has more long-wave radiation, i.e. a greater red light component. However, daylight is perceived by the human eye as being white, apart from at sunrise and sunset, when it appears red.

The unit of measurement for illuminance (particularly artificial light) is the lux (lx). The level of daylight in rooms is given as a percentage (see later).

Astronomical fundamentals: position of the sun

The radiation and light sources which give rise to daylight are not constant. The sun is the 'primary light source' of daylight → ② whatever the condition of the sky. The axis of inclination of the Earth (23.5°), the daily rotation of the Earth around its own axis and the rotation of the Earth around the sun over a period of 1 year determine the position of the sun as a function of the time of year and the day for each point on the surface of the Earth → ②.

The position of the Earth is defined by two angles: the azimuth, α_s, and the angle of elevation, γ_s. On a plan view → ③, the azimuth is the horizontal deviation of the position of the sun from 0°, where 0° = north, 90° = east, 180° = south and 270° = west as seen by the observer. On a vertical projection → ④, the angle of elevation is the position of the sun over the horizon as seen by the observer.

A number of measuring methods are used to determine the position of the sun at a given location, for example determination of the degree of latitude and the angle of elevation.

The declination of the sun during the annual cycle results in four main seasons in the year. The equinoxes are on 21 March and 23 September; this is when the declination of the sun is 0°. The winter solstice occurs on 21 December (the shortest day), when the declination of the sun is –23.5°; the summer solstice occurs on 21 June (the longest day), when the declination of the sun is +23.5° (see next page, → ⑤).

The position of the sun is given by the degree of latitude. On 21 March and 23 September, at 12.00 (α_s = 180°), the zenith angle of the sun at any latitude is of the same magnitude as the angle of latitude. For example, at 51° north (Brighton), the zenith angle at 12.00 (α_s = 180°) is 51° (see next page, → ⑥). The angle of elevation of the sun above the horizontal is 90° – 51° = 39°.

On 21 June, at midday, 12.00 (α_s = 180°), the sun is 23.5° higher than on 21 March and 23 September: 39° + 23.5° = 62.5°. On the other hand, on 21 December the sun is 23.5° lower than at the equinox: 39° – 23.5° = 15.5°. These deviations are the same for all degrees of latitude.

Thus, the angle of elevation of the sun, corresponding to the time of year, can be determined for all degrees of latitude.

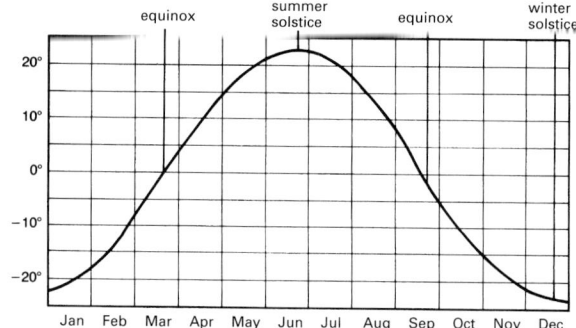

⑤ **Annual variation of the declination of the sun**

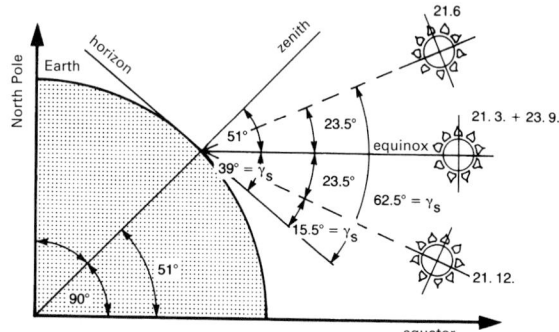

⑥ **Degree of latitude and angle of elevation γ_s**

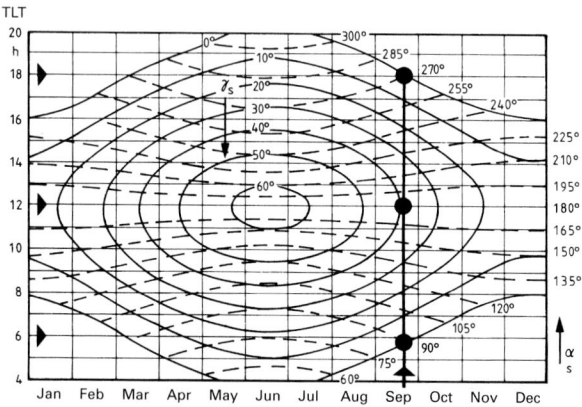

⑦ **Solar azimuth α_s and solar elevation γ_s at 51° latitude (English south coast: Southampton, Brighton) as a function of time of year and time of day**

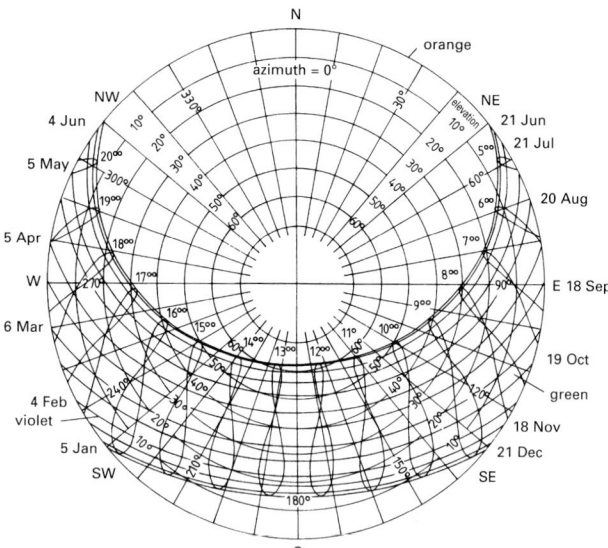

⑧ **Solar position chart for latitude 49°52´N, longitude 8°39´, time reference meridian: longitude 15°00´**

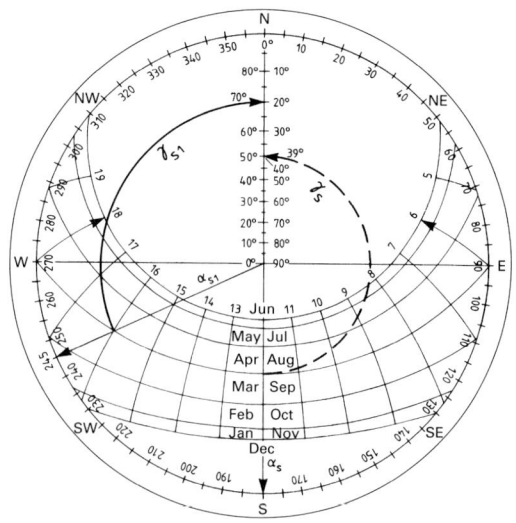

⑨ **Stereographic projection of the path of the sun, e.g. for latitude 51° on 21 March and on 23 September: sunrise at 6.00, sunset at 18.00, γ_s = 39° at 12.00**

DAYLIGHT

Solar position diagrams

An example is shown of a solar position diagram for 51°N → ⑦. The diagram shows the plan projection of the position of the sun, in terms of azimuth and elevation, at true local time, e.g. for Brighton on 23 September, sunrise is at 6.00 at α_s = 90° (east); on the same date at 12.00, α_s = 180° (south) and the elevation angle is 39°; sunset is at 18.00, α_s = 270°, on the same day.

To determine the local course of the sun, a coloured solar position chart is used → ⑧. The chart contains the plan projection of the azimuth α_s and the angle of elevation γ_s of the sun as a function of time of year and time of day for the appropriate angle of latitude and reference meridian.

In order to determine the position of the sun, loop-shaped curves are given for each hour of the day. In these, violet is used for the first half of the year and green for the second. The looped shape of the hourly curves is attributable to the elliptical path of the Earth and the inclination of the ecliptic. The times shown relate to the given time reference meridian, i.e. to the time zone of the location in question.

The intersection points of the daily curves with hourly curves of the same colour mark the position of the sun at any hour of the day. On the orange coloured polar diagram, the position of the sun can be read off as an angle of direction of the sun (azimuth) and angle of elevation of the sun (height) → ⑧.

Projection of the solar path

By using a stereographic projection → ⑨, the path of the sun can be determined for each degree of latitude (for the 21st day of each month) as a function of time of year and time of day.

Solar position, clock time and determination of time

The position of the sun determines the daylight conditions according to the time of day and time of year. The true local time (TLT) is the usual reference for time of day (e.g. in the solar position charts) in determining daylight. Each location is allocated to a time zone, within which the same time (zone time) applies. If the time zone input is of interest, then the TLT must be converted to the appropriate time zone.

152

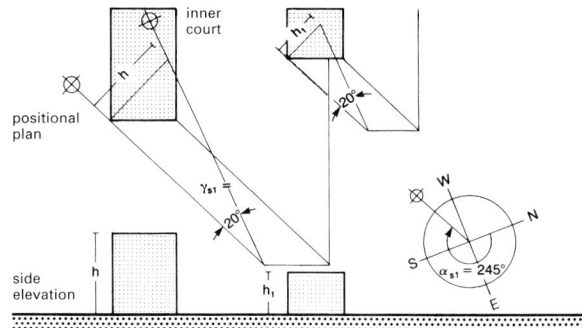

(10) **Graphical shadow construction**

(11) **Panorama mask (curved) in position**

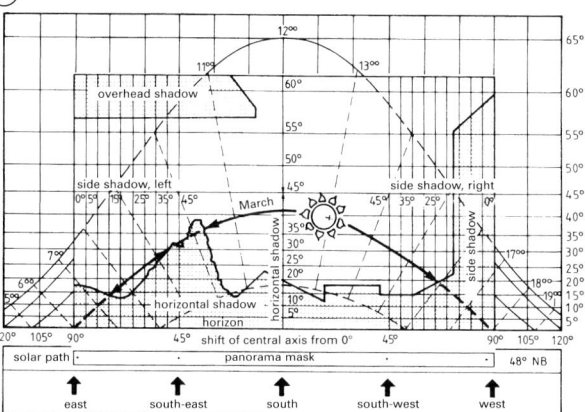

(12) **Possible course of shadows on the film**

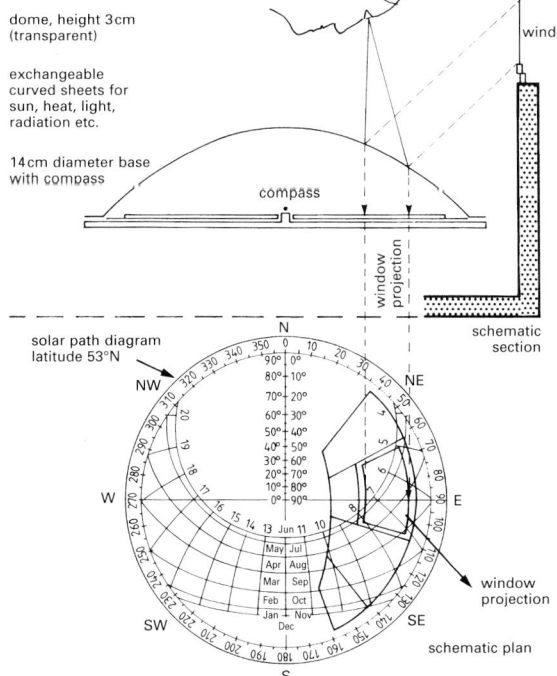

(13) **Horizontoscope with window projection, east side**

DAYLIGHT

Position of the sun: shadows, methods employed

The following methods are employed to determine and verify the actual solar radiation and shadow, both inside and outside buildings, as a function of geographical location, time of year and time of day, structural features and surrounding conditions.

Graphical construction of shadows. Determination of the shadows cast by a building can be accomplished using the projected (apparent) course of the sun, represented in → ⑨ (see previous page), by means of a plan and an elevation. As an example, the shadows in a courtyard in Brighton, latitude 51°N, will be constructed for 21 March, at 16.00. The sun appears at this time at an azimuth angle (α_{s1}) of 245° and an elevation (γ_{s1}) of 20° → ⑨ + ⑩. The positional plan is orientated with the north. The directions of the shadows are determined by the horizontal edges of the building, that is, a parallel shift of the direction of the sunshine (α_{s1} = 245°) due to the corners of the building. The length of the shadow is determined by the vertical edges of the building, that is, a rotation of the true height of the building (h) and application of the elevation angle of 20°. The point of intersection with the direction of the shadow gives the length of the shadow.

Panorama mask. In many countries, a representation of the path of the sun is available for various geographical areas. These representations are printed on clear film, and include data on azimuth and elevation angles, as well as time of year and time of day. In use, a copy of the relevant sheet is bent in a curve and positioned in the direction of the sun → ⑪. By looking through the panorama mask, any encroachment of shadows from the surroundings and from overhead shadows is transferred to the printed path of the sun, on a scale of 1:1 → ⑫. The film can then be used to analyse the occurrence of shadows and sunshine on façades and on sections of buildings to the correct scale.

Horizontoscope. The horizontoscope is an aid to determining the true conditions of sunshine and shadow on building sites and on and in buildings. The horizontoscope consists of a transparent dome, a compass, the base and exchangeable curved sheets which are placed on the base, according to the task in hand, to investigate light, radiation or heat, etc.

The purpose of the horizontoscope is to construct the light and shade conditions which exist in a room, e.g. → ⑬. At a particular point in the room, the opening for incident light can be assessed by means of a window cut-out projected on the dome and at the same time on the curved sheet underneath. It is therefore possible to determine both the radiation conditions and light effects in the room for each point in the room, and for any time of day and time of year, depending on the alignment of the building → ⑬.

Model simulation. In order to simulate and establish accurate annual shadow and solar radiation effects in and on a building, it is possible to construct a true-to-scale model and to test it under an artificial sun (parallel light) → ⑭.

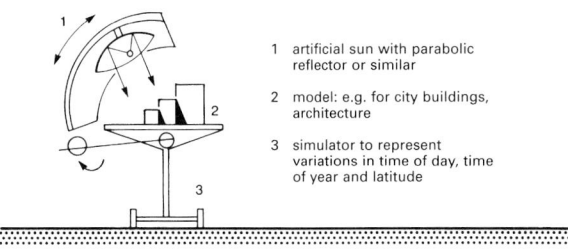

1 artificial sun with parabolic reflector or similar

2 model: e.g. for city buildings, architecture

3 simulator to represent variations in time of day, time of year and latitude

(14) **Artificial sun model**

153

DAYLIGHT

(15) **Mean daily solar radiation and hours of sunshine in the UK**

condition of sky, e.g. latitude 51°N	☀	⊙	░	
weather	clear, cloudless blue sky	misty, cloudy; sun visible as white disk	cloud-covered sky, dull day	
horizontal irradiance (W/m²)	600–800	200–400	50–150	
horizontal illuminance (lx)	60000–100000	19000–40000	5000–20000	
diffusion component, sky	10–20%	20–30%	80–100%	

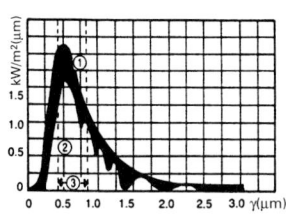

① intensity J of solar radiation at the limit of the Earth's atmosphere as a function of the wavelength ($\gamma_s = 90°$) the shaded region shows the losses from reflection, scatter and absorption of radiation due to the water vapour, carbon dioxide and ozone in the air, as well as dust particles
② intensity J of the solar radiation that reaches the Earth
③ range of visible light

(16) **Different intensities of radiation and varying quality of daylight in various weather conditions**

(17)

Meteorological features

The radiation of heat and the intensity of the sunlight on the surface of the Earth over the course of the year are determined by the geographical latitude, the weather and the varying conditions of the sky (clear, clouded, dull, partly clouded, etc.).

The facts given below are important with regard to our typical patterns of daylight and sunshine duration.

There are 8760 h in a year. The duration of 'bright daylight' during the course of a year amounts to around 4300 h on average.

The number of hours of sunshine per year varies from one country to another. Even within the same country it may vary from one location to another. The majority of these hours of sunshine usually occur during summer.

Over most of the year, that is, during ²/₃ of the daylight hours, the sunlight that reaches the Earth is scattered to a greater or lesser degree owing to the local weather conditions.

The direct and indirect solar radiation (global radiation) which reaches the surface of the Earth produces a locally varying climate on the surface and in its near vicinity (see → ⑮). The periods of sunshine are considered in units of tenths of hours. The data represent only the macro-climate; local variations in the micro-climate are not accounted for. Climatic data relating to a specific location (temperature, sunshine duration, sky conditions etc.) can be obtained, for example, from the Meteorological Office in Bracknell, UK.

During 'bright daylight hours', varying intensities of solar radiation are received on the surface, depending on the geographical latitude and the weather conditions, as are varying qualities of daylight → ⑯.

Physical basis of radiation

Solar radiation is a very inconstant source of heat. Only a small proportion of the solar energy radiated toward the Earth is transferred to the surface of the Earth as heat energy. This is because the Earth's atmosphere diminishes the solar radiation and does not permit a uniform intensity to penetrate to the surface.

This reduction essentially occurs because of various turbidity factors, such as scatter, reflection and absorption of the radiation by dust and haze (the cause of diffuse daylight), and also because of the water vapour, carbon dioxide and ozone in the air.

The total energy of solar radiation reaching the Earth is transmitted in the wavelength range 0.2–3.0 μm. Distribution of the total energy on the Earth's surface is as follows: approximately 3% ultra-violet radiation in the wavelength range 0.2–0.38 μm; approximately 44% visible radiation in the wavelength range 0.38–0.78 μm (the maximum lies at 0.5 μm in the visible light range); approximately 53% infra-red radiation in the wavelength range 0.78–3.0 μm.

The chart shown in → ⑰ represents the solar radiation which reaches the Earth. This is the solar constant, and has a value in our region of approximately 1000 W/m² on an illuminated vertical surface.

The radiation power is reduced by very thick cloud to approximately 200 W/m², and in the case of only diffuse radiation (a cloudy sky with the sun completely obscured) to approx. 50–200 W/m² (see → ⑯).

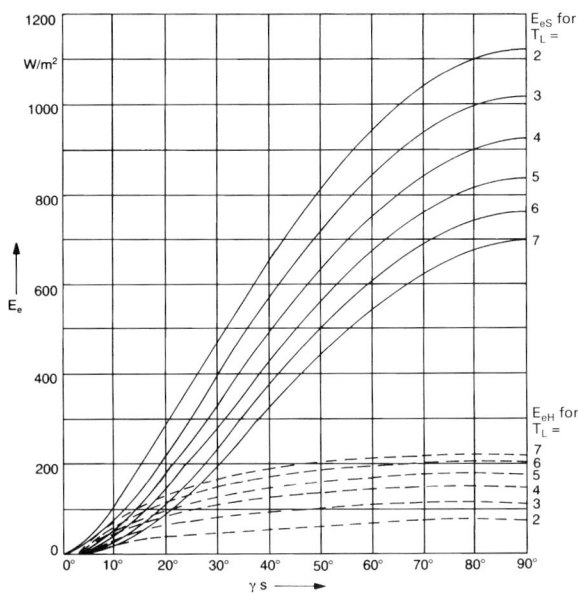

① internal building surfaces which can receive direct incident solar radiation from winter to summer

② optimum inclination of solar cells for global radiation used throughout the year → ㉒ – ㉔

⑱ **Optimum angles of inclination for south-facing surfaces**

⑲ **Horizontal irradiances due to the sun E_{eS} and the (cloudless) sky E_{SH}, with various turbidities T_L, as a function of the elevation of the sun γ_s**

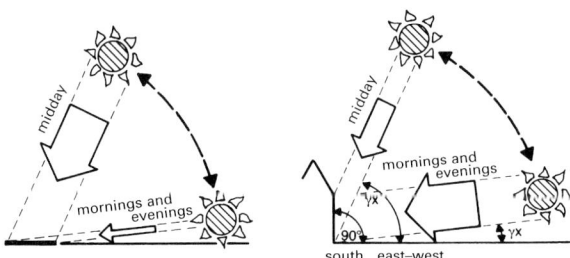

⑳ **Comparisons of the direct radiation on horizontal and vertical surfaces at various positions of the sun during the day. The level of incident radiation on a surface depends on the angle of that radiation (γ_x).**

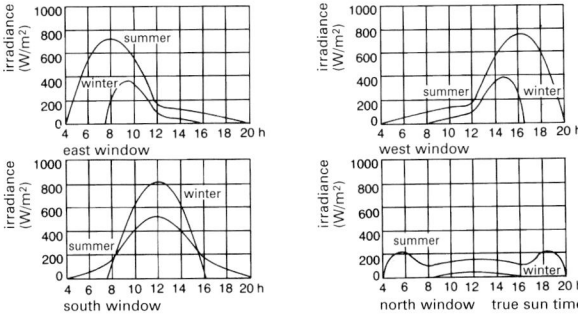

㉑ **Examples of radiation intensity on vertical surfaces facing in various directions on cloudless days in winter (Dec.) and summer (June)**

The effective solar radiation on a building (on the surfaces which are aligned with the direction of radiation at the time) is referred to as the global radiation E_{eg}. This is the sum of the 'direct' and 'diffuse' solar radiation (conditioned by the Earth's atmosphere and due to the scattered radiation caused by the varying conditions of the sky), given in W/m^2 or in Wh/m^2 per month or per day or per year. In the case of diffuse and direct radiation, the component of the radiation which is reflected from neighbouring buildings, roads and bordering surfaces, for example, must be taken into account (particularly when such reflections are strong).

Global radiation can be employed as a source of heat, directly for 'passive use' through structural measures (e.g. glass surfaces to utilise the greenhouse effect or internal heat storage walls) → ⑱, or indirectly by 'active use' (e.g. using collectors, solar cells) → ⑱ for the energy requirements of a building. Also, the proportion of global radiation received directly determines the effective heating influence of the sun on the cooling load, which has to be calculated in the layout of heating and ventilation systems for each type of building.

The necessary global radiation on buildings and collector surfaces for the utilisation of solar energy must be determined. This is related to the location of the building, and can be obtained as an energy parameter.

→ ⑲ shows the horizontal irradiance in W/m^2 due to the sun E_{eS} and the sky E_{eH} as a function of the elevation of the sun for clear skies. The horizontal global irradiance E_{eg} is the sum of the components generated by the sun E_{eS} and the sky E_{eH}.

Application: In order to be able to determine the actual amount of solar energy to be used, the contributions must be presented as functions of the inclination and, if necessary, the orientation of the surfaces of the building, corresponding to → ⑪. The horizontal irradiance can be obtained from → ⑲.

→ ⑳ shows the reduction of the incident level of solar radiation as a consequence of the different inclinations (0–90°) and orientations.

In the case of a vertical surface, only about 50% of the annual horizontal global irradiance can be utilised.

The quantity of radiation incident on a vertical, but differently orientated, surface under a cloudless sky can be read off the graphs in → ㉑, at least for the highest and lowest positions of the sun.

Passive and active solar systems

The energy requirement for a building in northern Europe during the 0-month period of heating in winter is relatively high in comparison to that required during the months from May to August. During the months of September and April, although the global radiation component is not very intensive (see → ㉒), part of the energy requirement of a building (heating, domestic water, ventilation etc.) can be covered by the use of the thermal energy of the surroundings, which again places emphasis on the problem of long-term storage.

In the application of solar energy, a distinction is made between two main systems according to their principle of operation: active or passive.

155

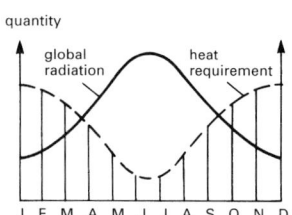

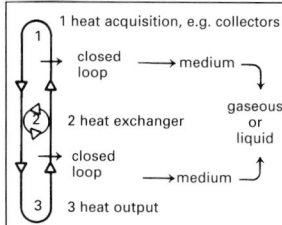

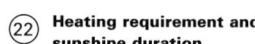

(22) **Heating requirement and sunshine duration**

(23) **Heat cascade, active system**

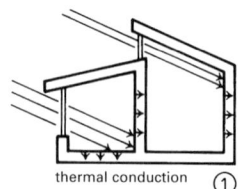

thermal conduction ①

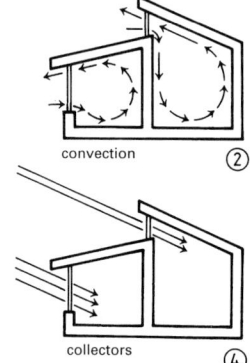

convection ②

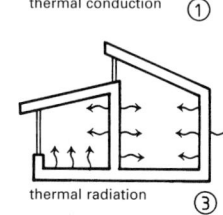

thermal radiation ③

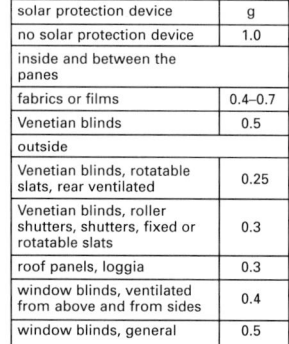

collectors ④

(24) **Passive system (principles)**

glazing	g
double glazing in clear glass	0.8
triple glazing in clear glass	0.7
glass blocks	0.6
multiple glazing with special glass (thermal insulating glass/solar control glass)	0.2–0.8

(25) **Total energy transmission factor g of various glazing types**

slot	1	2	3
item	internal construction type	recommended maximum value (gf × f)	
		increased natural ventilation not available	increased natural ventilation available
1	light	0.12	0.17
2	robust	0.14	0.25

(26) **Recommended maximum values (gf × f) as a function of natural ventilation alternatives**

solar protection device	g
no solar protection device	1.0
inside and between the panes	
fabrics or films	0.4–0.7
Venetian blinds	0.5
outside	
Venetian blinds, rotatable slats, rear ventilated	0.25
Venetian blinds, roller shutters, shutters, fixed or rotatable slats	0.3
roof panels, loggia	0.3
window blinds, ventilated from above and from sides	0.4
window blinds, general	0.5

(27) **Reduction factor z of solar protection devices in association with glazing types**

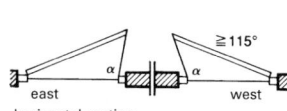

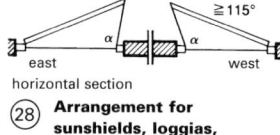

(28) **Arrangement for sunshields, loggias, window blinds or similar**

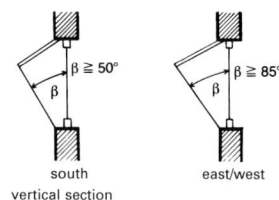

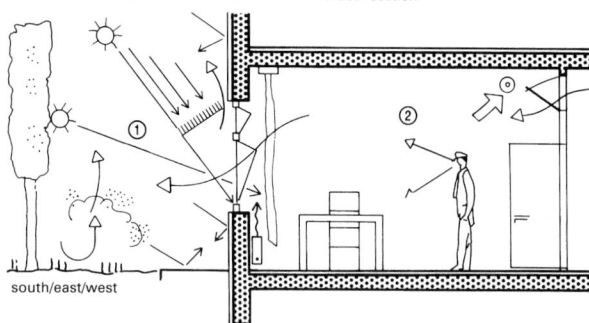

(29) **Heat reduction through solar protection with simultaneous cooling by means of passive precautions (e.g. office buildings without air conditioning)**

Active systems are those in which the heat gain and heat output processes are driven by equipment installed in the building. They are also referred to as indirect systems, since the heat output occurs after the conversion processes. The operating principle of an active system is represented in → (23) as a heat cascade. The heat gain can be achieved by means of solar collectors or something similar.

In passive systems, the solar energy is used 'directly'. This means that where the form of the building, the material, the type of construction and the individual components are suitable, the incident solar radiation is converted into heat energy, stored and then given out directly to the building.

Four physical processes which are important to the heat gain, conversion and output are described below.

(1) Thermal conduction → (24), ①

When a material absorbs solar radiation, this energy is converted into heat. Heat flow is caused by a temperature difference, and is also dependent on the specific thermal capacity of the material concerned. For example, if the temperature of the surroundings is lower than that of a heated wall, then the 'stored' heat energy is transferred to the surroundings.

(2) Convection → (24), ②

A wall or other material heated by solar radiation gives back the available energy to the surroundings, according to the temperature difference. The greater the temperature difference between wall and surroundings, the greater the amount of heat given up. Air that is heated in this process will rise.

(3) Thermal radiation → (24), ③

Short-wave solar radiation is converted into long-wave (infra-red) radiation on the surface of the material. The radiation is emitted in all directions, and is dependent on the surface temperature of the materials.

(4) Collectors → (24), ④

Sunlight penetrates glass surfaces which are orientated towards the south. Solar radiation converted inside the room (long-wave radiation) cannot pass back through the glass, and thus the inside of the room is heated (greenhouse effect) → (24), ④.

In any application of the systems described above, account must be taken of storage, controllability and distribution within the building.

Summertime thermal insulation

Summertime thermal insulation is recommended for transparent façades in buildings with natural ventilation in order to avoid the possibility of overheating. The recommendations are as follows: The product of the total energy transmission factor (g) (→ (25)) × the solar protection factor (z) (→ (27)) × the window surface component (f) on the façade, i.e. g × z × f, should have a value of 0.14–0.25 for strongly constructed buildings, and a value of 0.12–0.17 for those of lighter structure (see → (26)).

Extensive solar shading precautions → (28) should be critically evaluated, since wide-ranging visual effects may result and the view may be permanently impaired → (28).

The interplay of natural surroundings, physical laws and the development of constructional styles in specific materials means that each case requires accurate, individual analysis → (29).

Explanation of Figure (29)
Outside and façade → ①
* Shadows and cooling due to vegetation (trees, shrubbery, etc.)
* Light-coloured pathway (width approx. 1m), e.g. pebbles, in front of the house
* Sun or anti-glare protection (b = 35°) installed, extent approx. 900mm
* Façade in bright reflecting materials (pastel colours)
* Adequate window size (with insulating glass) for incident light and heat, with white internal frames

Inside → ②
* Consideration for house plants, if present
* Light- or medium-coloured floor covering
* Flexible heating system (a combination of air and hot water)
* Light-coloured curtains as anti-glare protection to diffuse direct solar radiation (particularly during transition periods)
* Light matt colours (pastel and natural colours for furniture) on surrounding areas, particularly the ceiling
* Cross-ventilation via tilting flaps
* Simple mechanical ventilation, if required

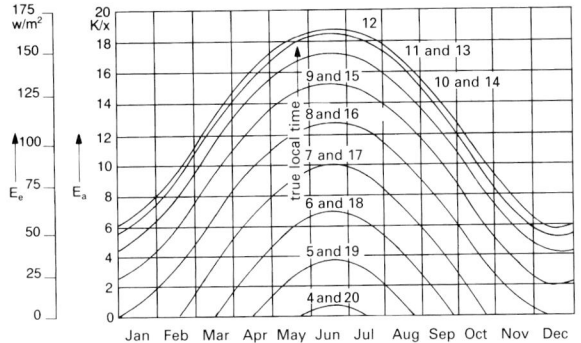

(30) Horizontal illuminance Ea for a clouded sky at latitude 51°N, as a function of time of year and time of day; E_e = horizontal irradiance

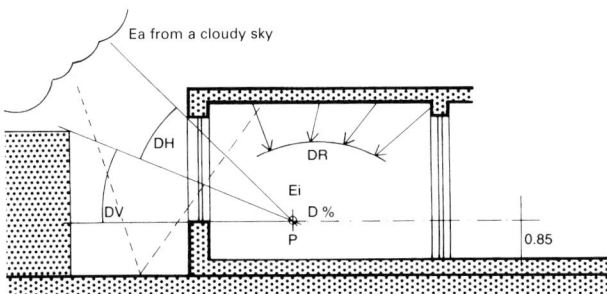

(31) Daylight and internal area illuminance at point P

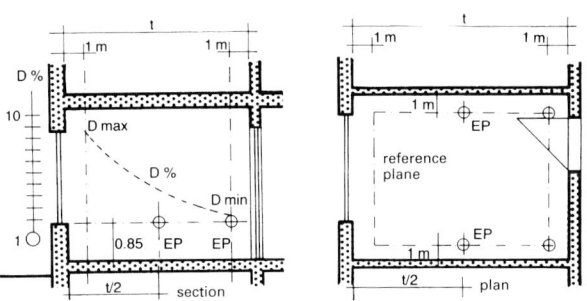

(32) Daylight ratio with side lighting, showing the reference plane and the variation in daylight in the internal area

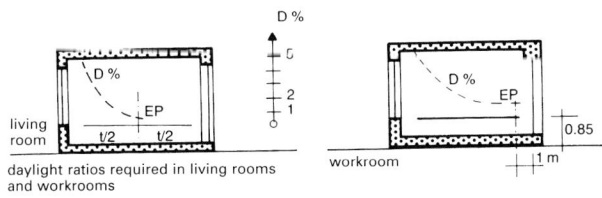

daylight ratios required in living rooms and workrooms

(33) Required daylight ratios in living and work rooms

internal illuminance Ei (lx)	external illuminance Ea (lx)	
	5000	10000
200	4.0%	2.0%
500	10.0%	5.0%
700	14%	7.0%

external illuminance Ea (lx)	internal illuminance Ei (lx)
5000	50
10000	100

1 Required daylight ratios for satisfactory internal area illuminance at various levels of illuminance from a clouded sky (D = Ei/Ea × 100%)

2 Anticipated internal area illuminance at EP, at various levels of illuminance from a clouded sky, with D = 1% (Ei = D × Ea/100%)

(34) Internal area illuminance

The measurement and evaluation of daylight in internal areas with light admission from the sides and above.

The daylight in internal areas can be evaluated according to the following quality criteria: illuminance and brightness; uniformity; glare; shadow.

Basis: In evaluating daylight in internal areas, the illuminance of a clouded sky (i.e. diffuse radiation) is taken as the basis. Daylight admitted to an internal area through a side window is measured by the daylight factor D. This is the ratio of the illuminance of the internal area (Ei) to the prevailing external illuminance (Ea), where D = Ei/(Ea × 100)%. Daylight in internal areas is always given as a percentage. For example, when the illuminance of the internal area is 500 lx and the external illuminance is 5000 lx, then D = 10%.

The daylight factor always remains constant. The illuminance of an internal area varies only in proportion to the external illuminance prevailing at the time. The external illuminance of a clouded sky varies from 5000 lx in winter to 20 000 lx in summer → (30), and depends on the time of year and the time of day.

The daylight factor at a point P → (31) is influenced by many factors. D = (DH + DV + DR) × t × k1 × k2 × k3, where DH is the component of light from the sky, DV is the effect due to neighbouring buildings, DR is the contribution from internal reflections, and the following reduction factors are taken into consideration: t, the light transmission factor for the glass; k1, the scatter effects due to the construction of the window; k2, the scatter effects due to the type of glazing; k3, the effects of the angle of incidence of the daylight.

The reference plane for the horizontal illuminance of daylight in an internal area is as shown in → (32). It can be taken as 0.85 m above floor level, and is separated from the walls of the room by 1 m. The points EP used for the horizontal illuminance are fixed on this reference plane. The corresponding (to be determined) daylight factors can then be represented in the form of a daylight factor curve → (32). The shape of the curve on the section provides information about the horizontal illuminance on the reference plane (at the corresponding points), and then Dmin and Dmax can be established (see also uniformity). The curve of the daylight factor also provides information on the variation of daylight in the room.

Required daylight factors D%. The relevant, currently valid requirements are laid down in regulations relating to daylight in internal areas and in the guidelines for work areas. Since no other relevant data are available at present, the required variation in daylight can be determined and checked from the uniformity (see later).

On the assumption that living rooms are comparable in terms of their dimensions with work rooms, the following values for the required daylight factors should be adhered to:

Dmin ≥ 1% in living rooms, reference point the centre of the room → (33);
Dmin ≥ 1% in workrooms, reference point the lowest position in the room → (33);
Dmin ≥ 2% in workrooms with windows on two sides;
Dmin ≥ 2% in workrooms with light coming from above, with the minimum mean daylight factor (Dm) ≥ 4%.

Note: With side windows, the associated maximum daylight factor should be at least six times greater than the minimum requirement, and in the case of light from above in workrooms, Dm should be twice as large as Dmin. Several examples for different internal area illuminance requirements as a function of external illuminance are shown in → (34).

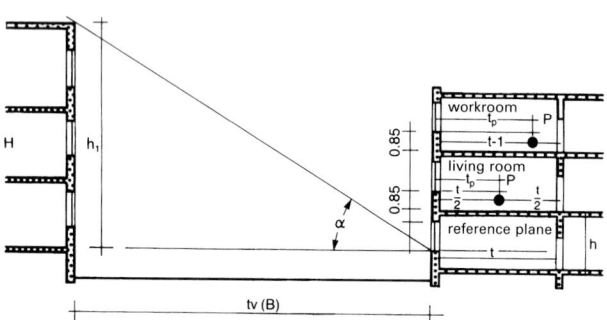

(35) **Various daylight patterns in an internal area with different vertical window positions**

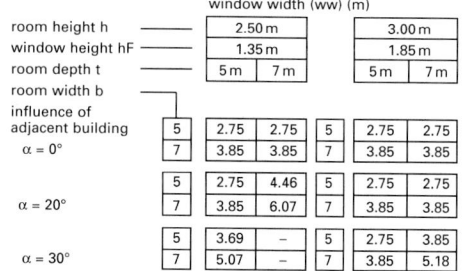

(36) **Diagram to determine the window widths required**

	window width (ww) (m)			
room height h	2.50 m		3.00 m	
window height hF	1.35 m		1.85 m	
room depth t	5 m	7 m	5 m	7 m
room width b influence of adjacent building				
α = 0°	5 → 2.75	2.75	5 → 2.75	2.75
	7 → 3.85	3.85	7 → 3.85	3.85
α = 20°	5 → 2.75	4.46	5 → 2.75	2.75
	7 → 3.85	6.07	7 → 3.85	3.85
α = 30°	5 → 3.69	–	5 → 2.75	3.85
	7 → 5.07	–	7 → 3.85	5.18

(37) **Determination of the required window widths (ww) with different room dimensions and interference from various adjacent building (extract)**

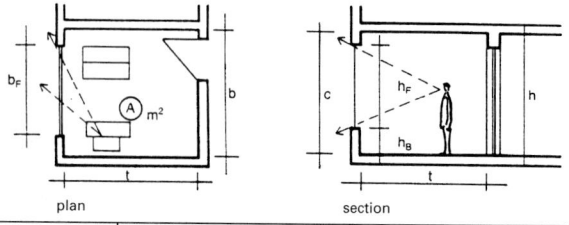

living rooms	workrooms		
c ≥ 2.20 m hB ≤ 0.90 m bF ≥ 0.55 · b minimum requirement	as for living rooms, if: h ≤ 2.50 m t ≤ 6.0 m A ≤ 50 m²	with h < 3.50 m window area > 30% of b × h	with h > 3.50 m c - hB ≥ 1.30 m hB ≤ 0.90 m bF ≥ 0.55 · b

(38) **Recommended visual links with outside**

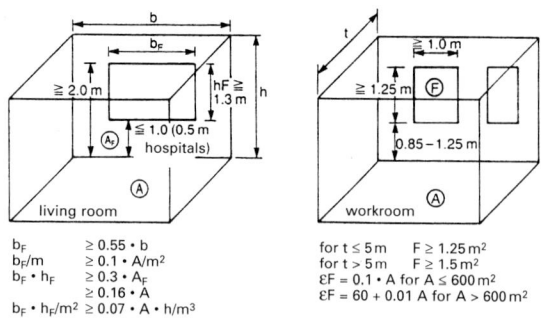

$b_F \geq 0.55 \cdot b$
$b_F/m \geq 0.1 \cdot A/m^2$
$b_F \cdot h_F \geq 0.3 \cdot A_F$
$\geq 0.16 \cdot A$
$b_F \cdot h_F/m^2 \geq 0.07 \cdot A \cdot h/m^3$

window requirements in living rooms

for t ≤ 5 m   F ≥ 1.25 m²
for t > 5 m   F ≥ 1.5 m²
$\varepsilon F = 0.1 \cdot A$ for A ≤ 600 m²
$\varepsilon F = 60 + 0.01 A$ for A > 600 m²

required window sizes in workrooms

(39) **Summary of visual links with outside and window sizes**

Brightness, window sizes and visual links

The position, size and type of windows essentially determine the pattern of daylight in an internal area → (35). The appropriate window sizes for living and work rooms of various dimensions are defined in → (38). The following conditions provide the basis for these calculations for living rooms:

- D% = 0.9 at the centre of a living room and at the lowest point in a workroom,
- width of window = 0.55 × room width,
- clouded sky,
- reflection from the wall = 0.6,
- reflection from the ceiling = 0.7,
- reflection from the floor = 0.2,
- light losses from the glass = 0.75,
- light losses from window-frame scatter k1 = 0.75,
- light losses from contamination k2 = 0.95,
- reflected light from neighbouring buildings Dv = 0.2,
- angle of light reflected from neighbouring buildings a = 0–50° (see → (36) + (37)).

Note: This applies by analogy to workrooms when their dimensions correspond to those of living rooms:

- room height (h) ≤ 3.50 m,
- room depth (t) ≤ 6 m,
- room area (A) ≤ 50 m².

Visual links with the outside also demand the requisite window dimensions for living rooms and workrooms. Minimum recommended requirements are summarised in → (38) and → (39). These recommendations contain the following points:

- limiting clearances and clearance areas for the relevant building heights must be maintained,
- visual link with the outside is a requirement for all accommodation;
- as a rule, a window size of approx. 1/8–1/10 of the usable room area must be provided for living rooms.

Among other factors in the town planning interpretation of building instructions and standards, incident light, building separation, the external aspects of neighbouring buildings and window design all have to be taken into account → (40). For example, a building separation of B = 2H (≥ 27°) is the desired value. This results in an aperture angle of ≥ 4° (limited by building geometry and neighbouring buildings) to achieve the minimum level of daylight in rooms.

Newly developed town planning schemes should be carefully checked for the quality of light in internal areas since, in general, the building regulations and standards only set minimum requirements.

It is advisable to carry out a visual inspection of the designs to check the expected appearance of internal and external areas, either in model form, under an artificial sun and artificial sky, or using an endoscope device.

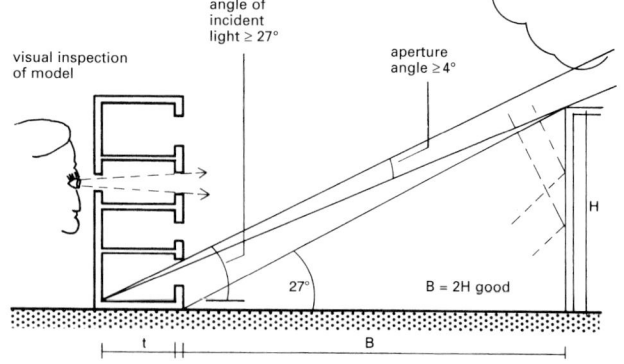

(40) **Incident light and building separation**

type of work	daylight, D%
coarse	1.33
moderately fine	2.66
very fine	5.00
fine	10.00
note: 10% is too high for the south side, but good on the north	

colour brightness		non-colour-treated materials		floor coverings, rolls and sheets	
(dark to bright)		(dark to bright)		(dark to bright)	
red	0.1 to 0.5	smooth concrete	0.25–0.5	dark	0.1–0.15
yellow	0.25–0.65	faced masonry		medium	0.15–0.25
green	0.15–0.55	red brick	0.15–0.3	bright	0.25–0.4
blue	0.1–0.3	yellow brick	0.3–0.45		
brown	0.1–0.4	lime sandstone	0.5–0.6		
white (medium)	0.7–0.75	wood			
grey	0.15–0.6	dark	0.1–0.2		
black	0.05–0.1	medium	0.2–0.4		
		bright	0.4–0.5		

(41) **Illuminance, D%** (42) **Reflection level (material colours, untreated)**

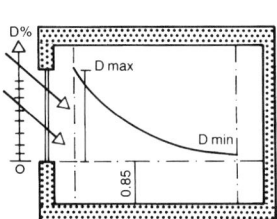
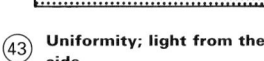

(43) **Uniformity; light from the side**

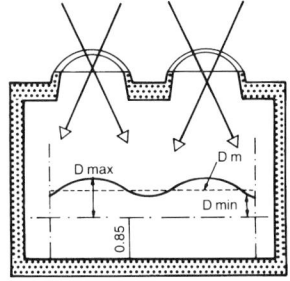

(44) **Uniformity; light from above**

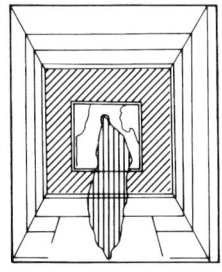

(45) **Glare**

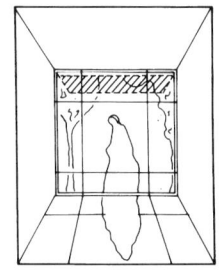

(46) **Low glare**

(1) D% curve
(2) Daylight-enhanced illumination (DEI)

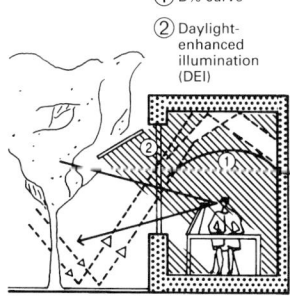

(47) **Shadows; light from the side**

● = (DEI)   ● = '(DEI)

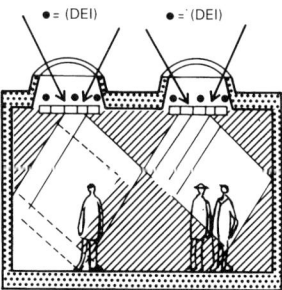

(48) **Shadows; light from above**

(49) **Light conditions in a Japanese house**

Illuminance, level of reflection, colour rendering and glare

The interplay of these characteristics of daylight has a great influence on the brightness in internal areas. To fulfil specific visual tasks, specific daylight illuminance levels are required, depending on the type of activity → (41). Therefore, the choice of reflection levels for the walls has to be coordinated with the requirements of the visual tasks which are to be performed. The varied structuring of the brightness in a room is dependent on the reflection levels of the surfaces and the choice of arrangement of the windows in the façade → (42) (and see also → (35)).

The uniformity G of the daylight illumination (defined as Dmin/Dmax) should be ≥ 1:6 in the case of light from the side → (43). In the case of light from above, G ≥ Dmin/Dmax 1:2 → (44). This, in principle, characterises the variation of daylight in internal areas. The uniformity is better in the case of overhead illumination, since the zenith luminance is three times greater than the luminance on the horizon.

Measures used to vary the uniformity can be influenced by:
- the level of reflection (if very high),
- the direction of any glare,
- the arrangement of the windows.

Glare is caused by direct and indirect reflection from the surfaces and by unfavourable luminance contrasts → (45), (46). Measures for the avoidance of glare include:
- solar shading outside,
- glare protection, inside and outside, in association with solar shading,
- matt surfaces,
- correct positioning of daylight-enhancing illumination.

Shadow is desirable to a certain degree, in order to be able to distinguish objects or other aspects of the room (→ (47), schematic). Measures required for a more three-dimensional shadow effect in the case of side lighting include:
- solar shading,
- glare protection (even in the north),
- balanced distribution of daylight,
- no direct glare,
- multi-layered or staggered façade.

Measures for appropriate shading with light from above include:
- incident daylight on the lower edge of the light opening, through translucent materials, light gratings or similar filters (→ (48), schematic),
- daylight-enhancing illumination,
- bright matt surfaces combined with coloured differentiation (e.g. a supporting structure).

Summary: Quality criteria, daylight coming from the side. In essence, the named quality criteria for daylight must be interpreted in such a way that spatial identity results. The variation of daylight in the internal area, combined with a good external view, are largely the result of the design of the façade, that is, the transition from inside to outside. A staggered, multi-layered and simultaneously transparent transition from inside to outside can satisfy the various requirements relating to daylight throughout the seasons of the year → (49).

ARTIFICIAL LIGHTING AND DAYLIGHT

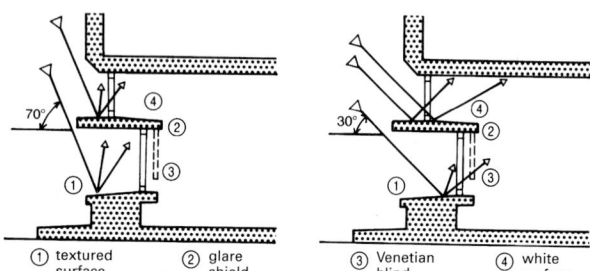

(50) **Principle of light redirection**

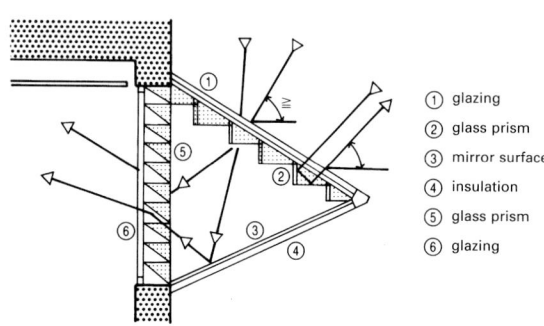

① textured surface ② glare shield ③ Venetian blind ④ white surface

(51) **Mount Airy Public Library, NC, USA**

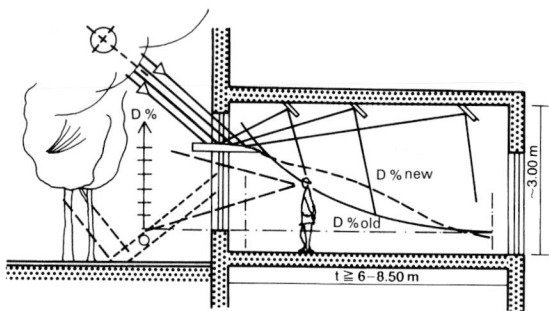

① glazing
② glass prism
③ mirror surface
④ insulation
⑤ glass prism
⑥ glazing

(52) **Prismatic redirection of light**

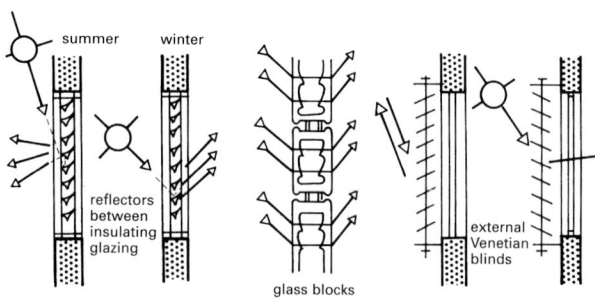

(53) **Ceiling design for light redirection**

summer winter

reflectors between insulating glazing

glass blocks

external Venetian blinds

(54) **Redirection of light**

Light redirection (light from the side)

As the depth of a room increases (normally 5–7 m), the intensity of the daylight in the room diminishes (see daylight factor curve). Redirecting the light allows rooms to be completely illuminated with daylight, even rooms of considerable depth.

The redirection of the light is based on the principle that the angle of incidence equals the angle of reflection. The aim of this redirection is (→ 50):

- to obtain a more uniform distribution of daylight;
- to obtain better daylight illumination in the depths of the room;
- to avoid glare when the sun is high, and to make use of winter sun;
- to mask out zenith luminance, or to make indirect use of it;
- to redirect particularly diffuse radiation;
- to eliminate the need for additional solar protection (possibly trees) by achieving glare protection on the inside.

Light shelves (reflectors). These can be placed inside or outside the window in the area of the abutment. Mirrored, polished or white surfaces can be used as the reflection plane. They improve the uniformity of the illumination, particularly if the ceiling is shaped to correspond with the redirected light. If necessary, glare protection can be provided in the region between the abutment and the ceiling → 51.

Prisms. Optical prisms can be used to achieve a desired selection of radiation and redirection → 52. Prism plates reflect the sunlight with less deviation, and only allow diffuse light from the sky to pass through. In order to prevent penetration of the sun's rays, the prism plates are mirrored. The prism plates guarantee adequate daylight illumination up to a room depth of approximately 8 m.

Outlook, light deflection and glare protection. The illumination in the depths of a room can be improved by redirecting the light and by providing reflecting surfaces on the ceiling → 53. The outlook remains the same, but the zenith illuminance is masked out. Glare protection is only required in winter, but if necessary, a means of enhancing daylight illumination may be provided on the abutment.

Solar control glass, glass bricks and Venetian blinds are used for radiation selection and redirection, and include the following systems (→ 54):

- solar control glass, i.e. mirror reflectors (rigid) between the glass panes cause the light to be reflected in summer and transmitted in winter;
- glass blocks, i.e. polished prisms to increase the uniformity of the light;
- Venetian blinds, i.e. adjustable bright outer blinds to deflect the daylight.

Examples of light redirection in ceiling areas in museums are shown in → 55.

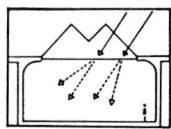

Neue Pinakothek, Munich

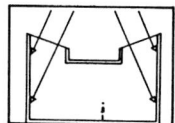

Art Gallery, Bremen

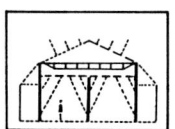

Brandywine River Museum, Chadds Ford, PA, USA

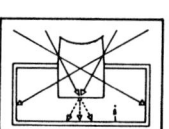

National Museum of Western Art, Tokyo

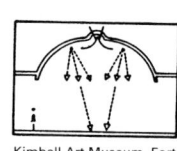

Kimbell Art Museum, Fort Worth, TX, USA

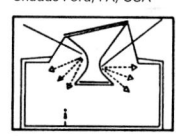

Nordjyllands Art Museum, Aalborg, Denmark

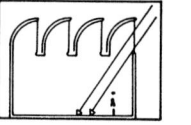

Bauhaus Archives, Berlin

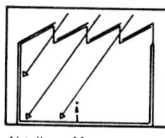

Abteiberg Museum, Mönchengladbach

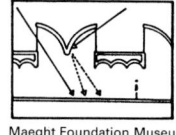

Maeght Foundation Museum, St. Paul-de-Vence, Paris

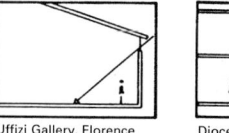

Uffizi Gallery, Florence

Diocese Museum, Paderborn

Guggenheim Museum, New York

(55) **Redirection of light; light from above (the examples shown here are museums)**

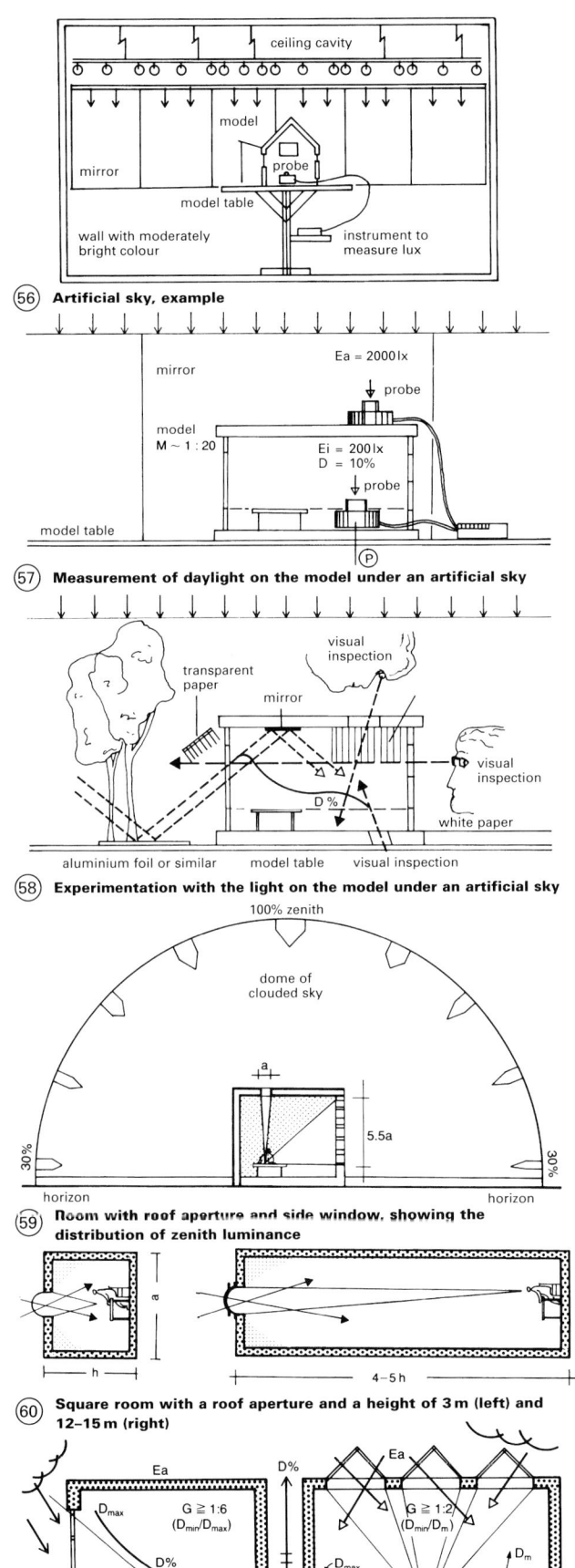

(56) **Artificial sky, example**

(57) **Measurement of daylight on the model under an artificial sky**

(58) **Experimentation with the light on the model under an artificial sky**

(59) **Room with roof aperture and side window, showing the distribution of zenith luminance**

(60) **Square room with a roof aperture and a height of 3 m (left) and 12–15 m (right)**

(61) **Daylight (D% and Dm%) and uniformity (G) with side and overhead light**

Methods and procedures for determining the level of daylight (D%) in internal areas (side and overhead light) with a clouded sky

A number of methods are available to determine the level of daylight, for example calculation, graphical methods, computer-supported methods and measurement techniques.

In order to arrive at a basis for a decision on the 'room to be built' or the 'building to be erected', an approximate simulation of the daylight levels is recommended. This can be accomplished using drawing methods or with a model.

However, the distribution of the daylight can only be determined and evaluated in three dimensions. Therefore a model of the room or building should be tested under simulated conditions so that the various effects of daylight can be examined.

Experimental method. A model room was built with a suspended bright, matt, translucent ceiling, artificial illumination above the ceiling and a mirrored surface rotating in a horizontal plane which mirrored the surrounding walls. This simulated the actual effect of a uniformly clouded sky → (56).

An illuminance of approx. 2000–3000 lx was adequate. The external illuminance of the artificial sky was measured (Ea = 2000 lx), using a special purpose-made device, on a 1:20 scale architectural model. The illuminance in the inner area of the model was measured by means of a probe (Ei = 200 lx). Thus the daylight factor in the internal area had a value of 10% at point P. The variation of daylight in the model was determined using this method → (57).

Different materials can be used to influence the variation in daylight, illuminance, colours effects, room dimensions, etc., but care should be taken that the quality criteria for daylight are maintained. The following materials can be used to experiment with the effects of light on the model: cardboard or paper of various colours, preferably pastels; transparent paper to prevent glare and to generate diffuse radiation; aluminium foil or glossy materials as reflective surfaces → (58).

Daylight in internal areas with light from above

The illumination of internal areas with daylight from 'above' is subject to the same prerequisites and conditions that apply to rooms with windows at the side, i.e. daylight illumination with a clouded sky. Whilst light from the side produces relatively poor uniformity of light distribution (and hence increased demand for D%), this is not the case with lighting from above. The quality of daylight in the latter case is significantly influenced by zenith luminance, room proportions, quality criteria, daylight from above and diminution factors.

The best place to work in the room shown (→ (59)) is at a distance from the side window which is equal to the height above the working position of the overhead light source. If the same level of illuminance that is produced by the overhead light on the reference plane (0.85 m above floor level) is to be generated by light from the side window, then the window must be 5.5 times larger in area than the roof light aperture. The reason for this is that the light from above is brighter, since the zenith luminance is roughly three times the horizontal luminance. This means the light from above represents 100% of the light from the sky, whereas only 50% of the light from the sky is admitted through a side window.

The illumination of a room from above is dependent on the proportions of the room, i.e. length, width and height (see → (60)). However, the possible occurrence of the 'dungeon effect' should be avoided.

Quality criteria for overhead light. The variation of daylight (D%) in an internal area with side windows is characterised by Dmin and Dmax → (61). A uniformity of G ≥ 1:2 (Dmin/Dm) and a Dmin of ≥ 2% is required for daylight illumination with overhead light in workrooms (Dm)min ≥ 4% → (61).

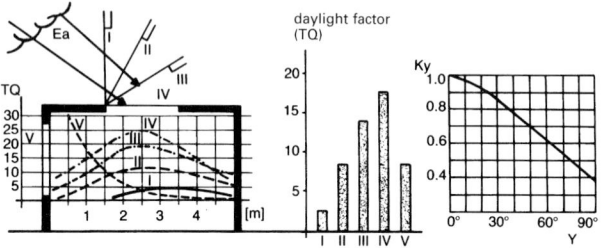

ratio Dmin:Dmax	recommendation	ke value = O/h 90°	ke value = O/h 60°	ke value = O/h 45°	O = h·ke
approx.1:1	target values	<1...1.1			
1:1.5		1.2	1.3	1.4	
1:2	tolerable	1.4	1.5	1.7	
1:2.5	critical	1.6	1.8	2.0	
1:3	avoid	1.7	2.0	2.2	

height of overhead illumination, room height and the uniformity of lighting which is sought, showing the corresponding overhead light arrangements in the roof area (ke factor)

62 **Recommended values for the ratio Dmin/Dmax**

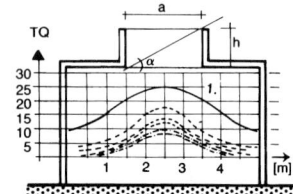

(a) Comparative variations in the daylight factor for side and overhead illumination with various inclinations of the rooflights

(b) Diminution factor ky as a function of the inclination y of the glazing in shed roofs

63

—— 1 with horizontal rooflight; no shaft, i.e. h = 0
- - - 2 with a light shaft; h = a
-·-·- 3 with a light shaft; h = 2a

64

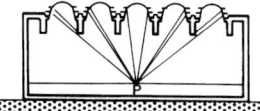

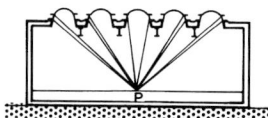

(a) Reduction in the quantity of daylight with overhead lighting with deep aperture shafts and bulky lower structures

(b) Uniform illumination in the internal area and hence better daylight conditions from rooflights with a lighter, filigree lower structure, with good reflection characteristics

65

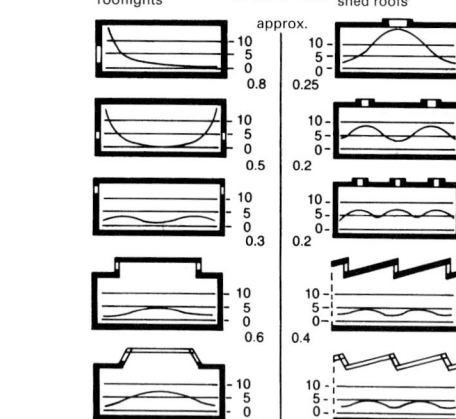

kF = window area/floor area = 1.6
values required for Dmin = 5% are shown for comparison

66 **Effects of different windows and rooflights on the variation in the daylight factor in a room with fixed principal dimensions**

DAYLIGHT

Rooflighting

Rooflights arranged at points on the ceiling area generate typical minimum and maximum brightnesses in the region where the light is required, the work plane. The mean value between these 'bright' and 'dark' areas is calculated, and this is termed the mean daylight factor Dm.

Thus, Dm is the arithmetic mean between Dmin and Dmax with respect to the reference or work plane (0.85 m above floor level). The required G ≥ 1:2 is not based on Dmax, but on Dmin, since unevenness in the daylight from above is sensed physiologically as 'stronger than contrast'. At this uniformity (Dmin = 1 and Dm = 2), Dmin must be ≥ 2% (compare → 61).

Furthermore, the quality criteria striven for in controlling the overhead daylight in the room are limited by the room height and the shape of the rooflight (ke factor).

An ideal uniformity is achieved when the spacing between the rooflights (O) is equivalent to the room height (h), i.e. a ratio of approximately 1:1.

In practice the rule is that the ratio of rooflight spacing to room height should be 1:1.5–1:2 (see → 62). This figure contains a table from which these ratios and their effects can be obtained. The figure also provides a recommendation for the light shafts which should be let into the roof.

Type of rooflight and construction

The inclination of the rooflights determines the percentage of the light component from the sky which is available. In → 63a, the quantity of incident light admitted through a side window is compared with the quantity of light provided by rooflights at various inclinations. The greatest quantity of light is received through a horizontal rooflight.

On the other hand, the maximum illuminance from a side window is achieved only in the vicinity of the window; for glazing which is vertically overhead, the lowest illuminance is on the reference plane.

Thus there is a diminution factor (ky) for the quantity of incident light which depends on the angle of inclination of the rooflight. The diminution factors corresponding to shed roofs of various inclinations are shown in → 63b.

The diffuse incident light which falls on the rooflight is affected by the construction and depth of the installation before it supplies the room with daylight. The various levels of incident light for shafts of different proportions beneath rooflights the are shown in → 64. Excessively high and massive shafts and built-in depths should be avoided → 65a, while a filigree, highly reflective construction is to be recommended → 65b.

The quality of daylight in an internal area with rooflights is not only dependent on the factors discussed above. Another significant factor is the ratio of the total area of the overhead lights to the floor area of the room (kF factor).

The diagrams in → 66 show the levels of daylight from side windows with various geometrical features and overhead illumination.

In order to increase the daylight factor Dmin by 5% for side windows or opposite-facing rooflights, the proportions of the windows must be increased significantly, typically up to a ratio of 1:1.5. By contrast, for the same demands from overhead lighting, particularly with shed roof-type lights, the area need only be increased by a relatively small amount. A ratio of rooflight area to floor area of from 1:4 to 1:5 is adequate.

Additional diminution factors for rooflights are given below.

- transmittance of the glazing, t
- scatter and constructional features, k1
- soiling of the glazing, k2
- diffuse illumination, k3.

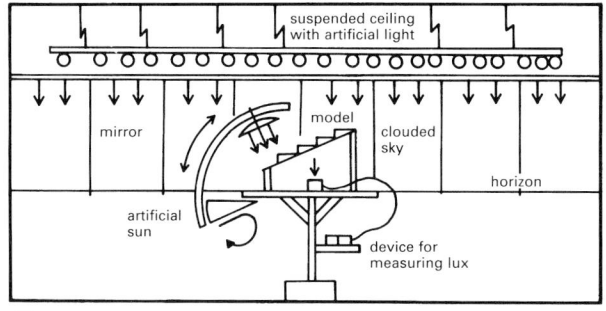

(67) **Artificial sky and artificial sun**

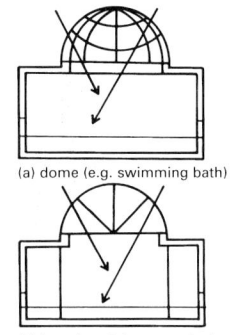

(a) dome (e.g. swimming bath)

(b) barrel vault (e.g. arcades)

(68) **Large individual rooflights**

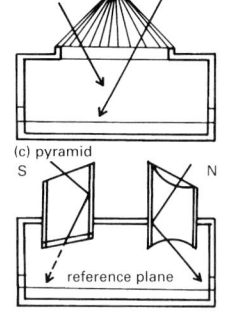

(c) pyramid

(d) light shafts for direct and indirect incident radiation

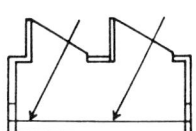

(a) monopitch rooflights

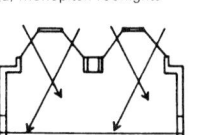

(b) inclined lantern lights

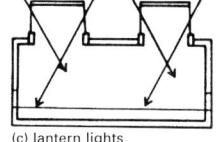

(c) lantern lights

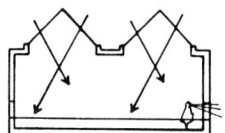

(d) ridgelights (also as individual pyramids)

(69) **Continuous rooflights**

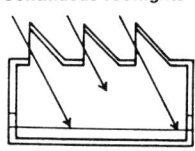

(a) 90° inclined

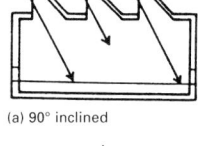

(b) 60° inclination (concave, convex)

(70) **Northlights (concave, convex)**

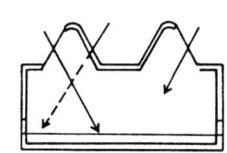

(c) opposed inclined surfaces (note corner illumination)

(d) rounded with white external surfaces

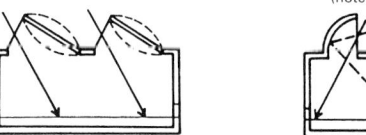

(a) intermeshed offset diagonal shells

(c) cornice rooflights

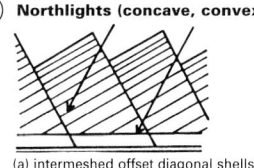

(b) butterfly rooflight with translucent ceiling

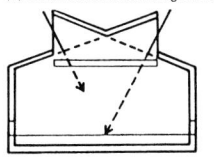

(d) glass roof with slats for diffuse and direct light

(71) **Special shapes**

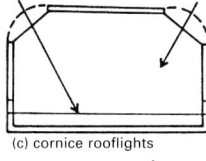

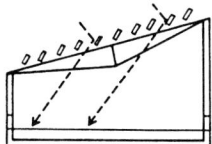

Empirical evaluation of the quality of daylight from overhead illumination

The definitive evaluation of daylight conditions should be performed against the background of a clouded sky. However, rooflights are not only recipients of diffuse radiation, they are also subject to direct solar radiation. These varying lighting conditions should be simulated, not only under an artificial sky, but also under an artificial sun. In this process, the quality criteria for the daylight on the model should be assessed by eye → (67).

Design parameters for overhead illumination are listed below (→ (68) – (72); see also → (55)).

- Rooflights should not be orientated toward the south.
- Convert solar radiation into diffuse light radiation.
- Maintain quality criteria for daylight.
- Avoid excessive contrasts in luminance levels.
- Pay attention to variation in Dm.
- Ensure illumination of all room corners and enclosing surfaces.
- Avoid glare by artificial shading.
- Treat room-enclosing surfaces according to their separate technical requirements.
- Ensure that it is possible to see outside.

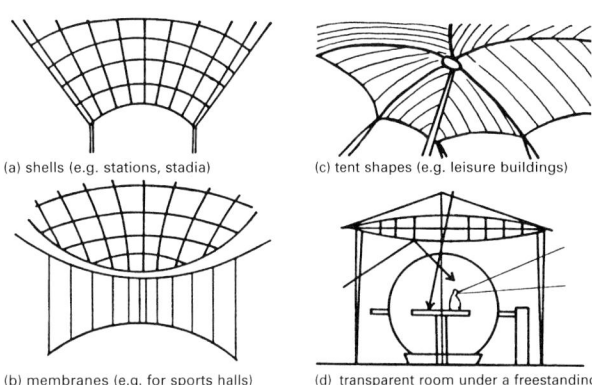

(a) shells (e.g. stations, stadia)

(b) membranes (e.g. for sports halls)

(c) tent shapes (e.g. leisure buildings)

(d) transparent room under a freestanding roof with directed outward vision and passage of light

(72) **Large rooflights with distinctive shapes**

Side and overhead lighting

The choice between side and overhead illumination depends on the use to which the building is to be put and also on the available external light sources, i.e. the geographical location. For example, where there are extreme light and climatic conditions, appropriate forms of construction must be developed and the shapes of buildings must be designed to match the prevailing light conditions at that latitude (i.e. to make optimum use of the diffuse and direct sunlight → (73) – (76).

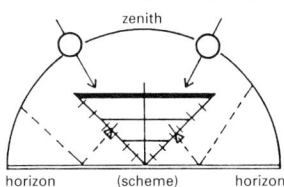

(73) **Constructional style suitable for southern regions (high direct solar radiation), side illumination**

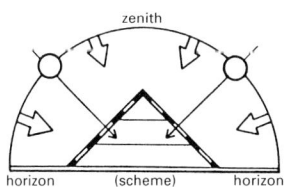

(74) **Constructional style suitable for northern regions (high proportion of diffuse light), side and overhead illumination**

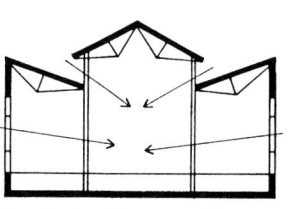

(75) **Style with potential for illumination from the side and overhead**

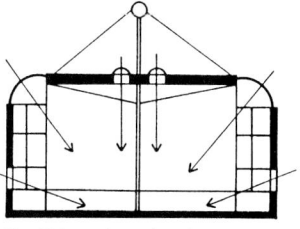

(76) **Side and overhead illumination, room-enclosing surfaces recessed**

DAYLIGHT: INSOLATION

Determination of the sunshine on structures

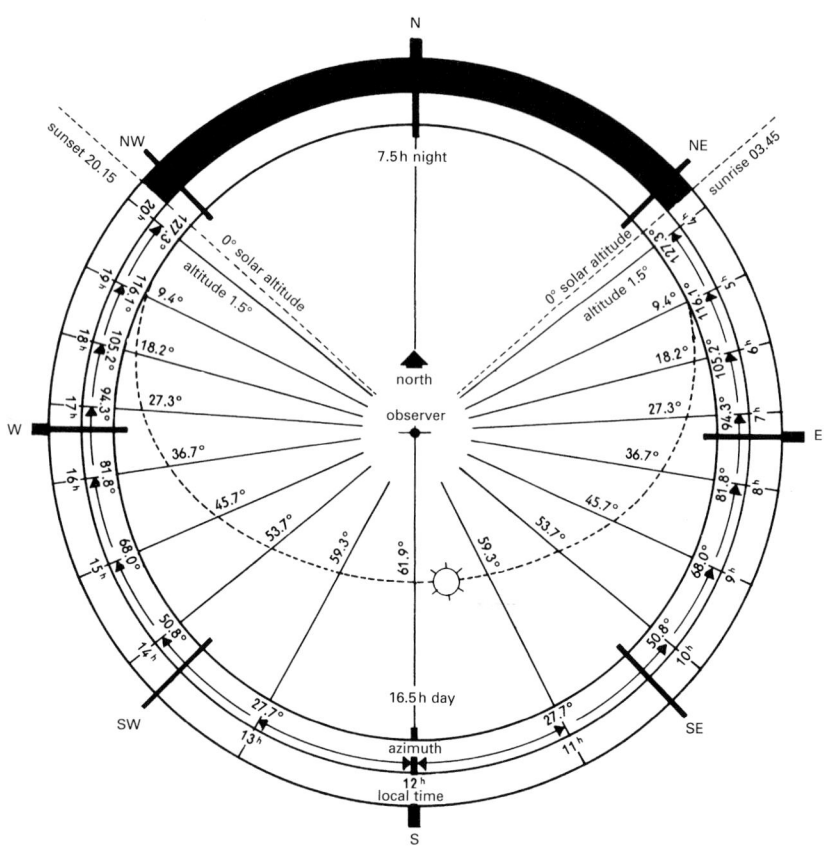

① **Solar path at the summer solstice (21 June)**
longest day of the year
51.5°N (London, Cardiff)

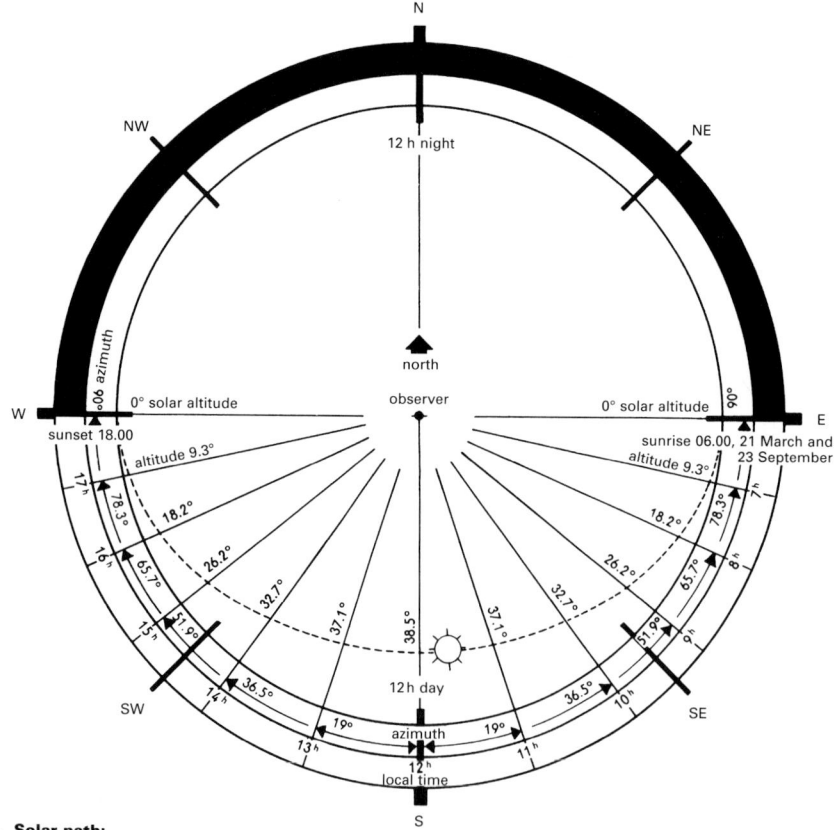

② **Solar path:**
spring equinox (21 March)
autumn equinox (23 September)

Application

The path of sunshine on a planned structure can be obtained directly from the following procedure if a plan of the structure, drawn on transparent paper, is laid in its correct celestial orientation over the appropriate solar path diagram. The following solar path data relate to the latitude region 51.5°N (London, Cardiff).

For more northern areas, e.g. at 55°N (Newcastle), 3.5° should be subtracted. The values in degrees given inside the outer ring relate to the 'azimuth', i.e. the angle by which the apparent east–west movement of the sun is measured in its projection on the horizontal plane. The local times given in the outer ring correspond to the standard time for longitude 0° (Greenwich, i.e. the meridian of Greenwich Mean Time).

At locations on degrees of longitude east of this, the local time is 4 min earlier, per degree of longitude, than the standard time. For every degree of longitude to the west of 0°, the local time is 4 min later than the standard time.

Duration of sunshine

The potential duration of sunshine per day is almost the same from 21 May to 21 July, i.e. 16–16¾h, and from 21 November to 21 January, i.e. 8¼–7½h. In the months outside these dates, the duration of sunshine varies monthly by almost 2h. The effective duration of sunshine is barely 40% of the figures given above, owing to mist and cloud formation. This degree of efficacy varies considerably depending on the location. Exact information is available from the regional observation centres of the areas in question.

Sun and heat

The natural heat in the open air depends on the position of the sun and the ability of the surface of the Earth to give out heat. For this reason, the heat curve lags approximately 1 month behind the curve of solar altitude, i.e. the warmest day is not 21 June, but in the last days of July, and the coldest day is not 21 December, but in the last days of January. Again, this phenomenon is such that local conditions are extraordinarily varied.

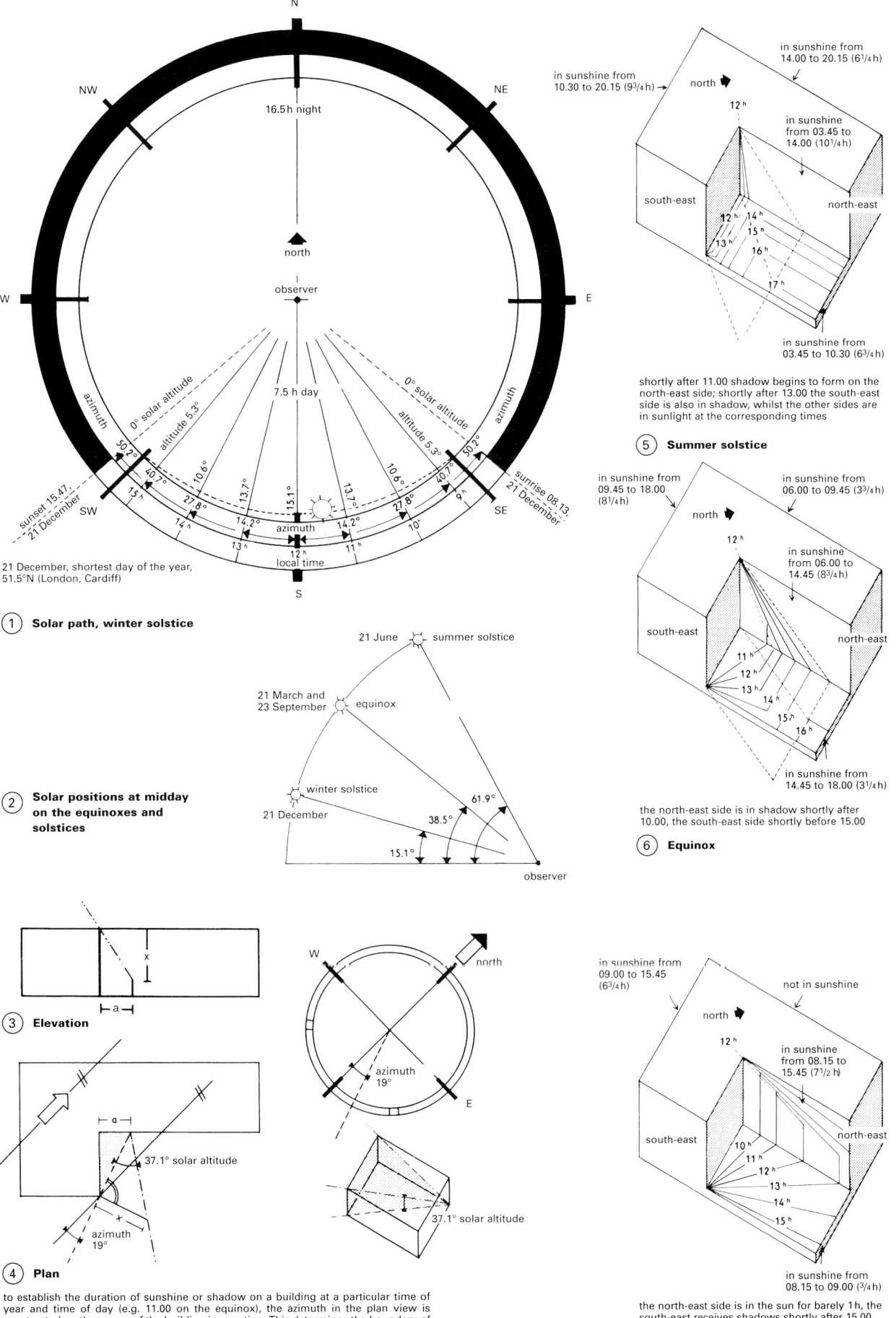

1 Solar path, winter solstice

21 December, shortest day of the year,
51.5°N (London, Cardiff)

2 Solar positions at midday on the equinoxes and solstices

3 Elevation

4 Plan

to establish the duration of sunshine or shadow on a building at a particular time of
year and time of day (e.g. 11.00 on the equinox), the azimuth in the plan view is
constructed on the corner of the building in question. This determines the boundary of
the shadow in the plan view upon which the solar altitude (effective light beam) is
constructed by rotation about the azimuth line. The intersection x at right angles to the
plan view shadow, translated to the elevation, provides the boundary of the shadow on
the front of the building as a distance below the upper edge of the building.

in sunshine from
10.30 to 20.15 (9¾ h)

in sunshine from
14.00 to 20.15 (6¼ h)

in sunshine
from 03.45 to
14.00 (10¼ h)

in sunshine from
03.45 to 10.30 (6¾ h)

shortly after 11.00 shadow begins to form on the
north-east side; shortly after 13.00 the south-east
side is also in shadow, whilst the other sides are
in sunlight at the corresponding times

5 Summer solstice

in sunshine from
09.45 to 18.00
(8¼ h)

in sunshine from
06.00 to 09.45 (3¾ h)

in sunshine
from 06.00 to
14.45 (8¾ h)

in sunshine from
14.45 to 18.00 (3¼ h)

the north-east side is in shadow shortly after
10.00, the south-east side shortly before 15.00

6 Equinox

in sunshine from
09.00 to 15.45
(6¾ h)

not in sunshine

in sunshine
from 08.15 to
15.45 (7½ h)

in sunshine from
08.15 to 09.00 (¾ h)

the north-east side is in the sun for barely 1 h, the
south-east receives shadows shortly after 15.00

7 Winter solstice

GLASS
Double/Triple Glazing

Multi-layered, insulating glazing units are manufactured out of two or more sheets of glass → ① (clear float glass, tinted and coated glass, rough cast and patterned glass) separated by one or more air- or gas-filled cavities. Multi-layered glazing units can, depending on the assembly, provide high thermal and/or sound insulation (e.g. sound-reducing units, solar protection units, heat-absorbing units, laminated glass with intermediate layers). There is dried air or a special gas in the spaces between the glass sheets. Different edge treatments define three types of units: full glass edge welding → ①A; edges welded together with inserts → ①B; glued organic edge sealing → ①C.

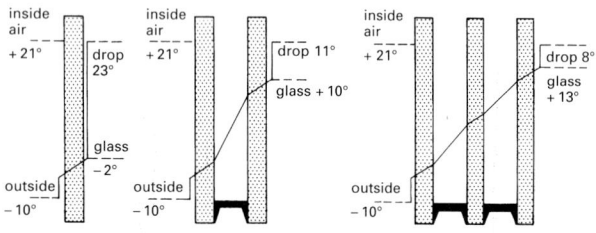

① **Multi-pane glazing units**

② **Heat transfer with single, double and triple glazing**

③ **Manufactured glazing units, possible shapes**

cavity width			double glazing with 2 × OPTIFLOAT float glass						k (W/m²K)
			4mm	5mm	6mm	8mm	10mm	12mm	
8	width	(cm)	141	185	185	300	300	300	3.2
	height	(cm)	240	300	500	500	500	500	
	surface area	(m²)	3.4	5.5	9.2	15.0	15.0	15.0	
	aspect ratio		1:6	1:10	1:10	1:10	1:10	1:10	
	overall thickness	(mm)	16	18	20	24	28	32	
10	width	(cm)	141	245	280	300	300	300	3.1
	height	(cm)	240	300	500	500	500	500	
	surface area	(m²)	3.4	7.3	14.0	15.0	15.0	15.0	
	aspect ratio		1:6	1:10	1:10	1:10	1:10	1:10	
	overall thickness	(mm)	18	20	22	26	30	34	
12	width	(cm)	141	245	280	300	300	300	3.0
	height	(cm)	141	245	280	300	300	300	
	surface area	(m²)	3.4	7.3	14.0	15.0	15.0	15.0	
	aspect ratio		1:6	1:10	1:10	1:10	1:10	1:10	
	overall thickness	(mm)	20	22	24	28	32	36	
thickness tolerance		(mm)	± 1.0	± 1.0	± 1.0	± 1.0	± 1.0	± 1.0	
size tolerance		(mm)	± 1.5	± 2.0	± 2.0	± 2.0	± 2.0	± 2.0	
weight		(kg/m²)	20	25	30	40	50	60	

⑤ **Double glazing**

build-up OPTIFLOAT (mm) cavity width (mm)	4 4 4 (8.5) (8.5)	5 5 5 (8.5) (8,.5)	4 4 4 (6) (6)	5 5 5 (6) (6)
k value (W/m²K)	1.9	1.9	2.0	2.0
light transmittance (%)	74	72	74	72
unit thickness (mm)	29	32	24	27
max. edge length (cm)	141 × 240	180 × 240	141 × 240	180 × 240
min. size (cm²)	24 × 24	24 × 24	24 × 24	24 × 24
aspect ratio	1:6	1:6	1:6	1:6
max. area (m²)	3.4	3.4	3.4	3.4
weight (kg/m²)	ca. 30	ca. 38	ca. 30	ca. 38
thickness tolerance:	−1mm +2mm			size tolerance: ±2.0 mm

⑥ **Triple glazing**

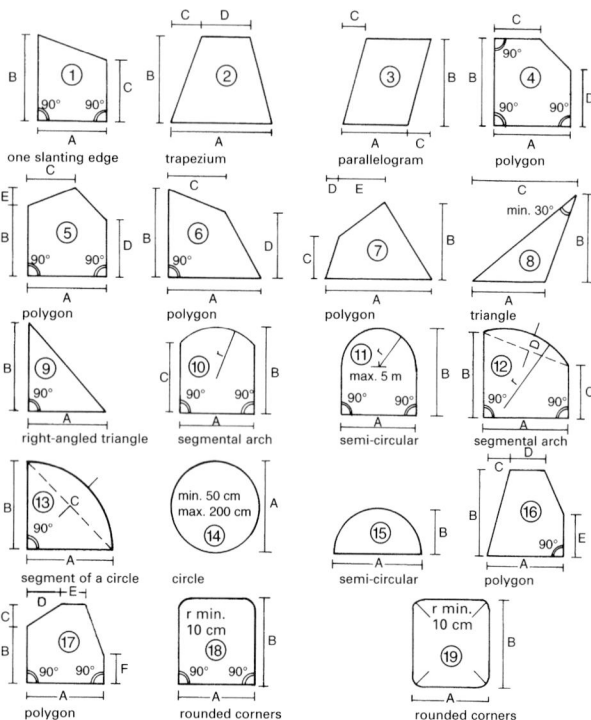

④ **Recommended thicknesses, 8 m high glass**

recommended glass thicknesses for inside and outside panes of double glazing up to 8.00 m installation height (wind load = 0.75 kN/m² or 750 Pa)

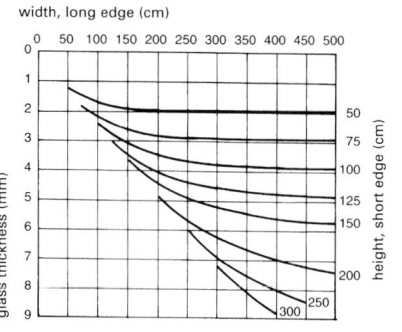

⑦ **Recommended thicknesses, 20 m high glass**

recommended glass thicknesses for inside and outside panes of double glazing up to 20.00 m installation height (wind load = 1.2 kN/m² or 1200 Pa)

166

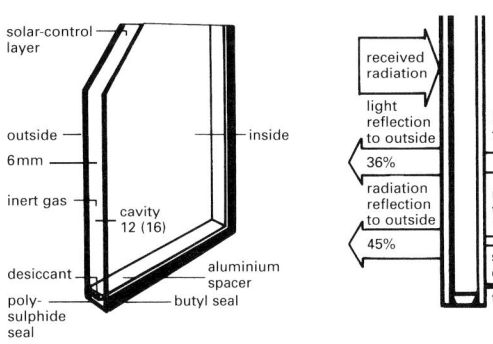

① **Solar control double glazing**

② **Solar control double glazing (gold 30/17)**

Labels in figure 1: solar-control layer; outside; 6 mm; inert gas; cavity 12 (16); desiccant; poly-sulphide seal; butyl seal; aluminium spacer; inside

Labels in figure 2: received radiation; light reflection to outside 36%; radiation reflection to outside 45%; light transmission 30%; radiation transmission 14%; secondary emissions to inside 3%

type	light transmittance, T_L (%)	light reflection outside/inside, R_L (%)	UV transmittance, T_{UV} (%)	k value (W/m²K)	total energy transmittance, g (%)	mean transmittance value, b	selectivity code, S	max. dimensions (cm × cm)
titanium 66/43	66	21	18	17	1.4	43	0.49	1.53	260×500
auresin 66/44	66	15	11	7	1.4	44	0.50	1.50	240×340
50/32	50	19	16	9	1.5	32	0.37	1.56	240×340
49/32	49	38	36	10	1.4	32	0.37	1.53	260×500
45/39	45	30	17	11	1.5	39	0.45	1.15	240×340
40/26	40	32	22	8	1.3	26	0.30	1.54	240×340
39/28	39	26	11	9	1.4	28	0.32	1.40	240×340
gold 40/26	40	25	36	11	1.4	26	0.30	1.54	240×340
30/23	30	18	40	11	1.4	23	0.26	1.30	240×340
silver 50/35	50	40	35	14	1.4	35	0.40	1.43	240×340
50/30	50	37	34	18	1.3	30	0.34	1.67	260×500
49/43	49	36	22	14	1.5	43	0.49	1.14	240×340
48/48	48	39	21	13	1.5	48	0.55	1.00	240×340
37/32	37	40	14	8	1.5	32	0.37	0.16	240×340
36/33	36	46	26	8	1.4	33	0.38	1.09	240×340
36/22	36	48	45	9	1.2	22	0.25	0.68	240×340
15/22	15	26	42	8	2.6	22	0.25	0.68	200×340
bronze 49/23	49	16	35	12	1.4	33	0.38	1.48	240×340
36/26	36	26	46	8	1.4	26	0.30	1.38	240×340
neutral 51/39	51	11	30	15	1.6	39	0.45	1.31	240×340
51/38	51	16	10	18	1.6	38	0.44	1.34	300×500
green 37/20	37	25	36	3	1.4	20	0.23	1.85	260×500
38/28	38	34	17	8	1.4	28	0.32	1.36	240×340
grey 47/51	47	6	22	27	2.9	51	0.59	0.92	240×340
43/39	43	7	17	18	1.5	39	0.45	1.09	240×340
clear glass (for comparison)	78	15	15	98	3.0	72	0.83	1.08	

③ **Solar control double glazing**

Solar Control Double Glazing

Solar control double glazing is characterised by a high light transmittance and an energy transmittance which is as low as possible. This is achieved by a very thin layer of precious metal deposited on the protected inside layer of one of the panes. Apart from its solar control qualities, solar control double glazing fulfils all the requirements of highly insulating double glazing, with k values up to 1.2 W/m²K. The choice of a wide range of colours and colourless tones, augmented by the availability of colour-matched single- and double-glazed façade panels, presents many design opportunities. Solar control glass can be combined with sound-reduction glass, armoured glass, laminated glass, safety glass or ornamental/cast glass as either internal or external sheets. A combination with wired glass is not possible.

Each glass type is identified by colour (as seen from the outside) as well as by a pair of values: the first is the light transmittance and the second the total energy transmittance, and both are given as percentages. Example: auresin (= blue) 40/26.

GLASS

Light transmittance T_L in the 380–780 nm (nanometres) wavelength band, based on the light sensitivity of the human eye (%).

Light reflection R_L from outside and inside (%).

Colour rendering index R_a:

$R_a > 90$ = very good colour rendering;

$R_a > 80$ = good colour rendering.

UV transmittance T_{UV} in the 320–2500 nm wavelength band is the sum of the direct energy transmission and the secondary heat emission (= radiation and convection) towards the inside.

The b value is the mean transmittance factor of the sun's energy based on an energy transmission of a 3 mm thick single pane of glass of 87%. Accordingly:

$$b = \frac{g\,(\%)}{87\%}$$

where g is the total energy transmittance.

Selectivity code S. $S = T_L/g$. A higher value for the selectivity code S shows a favourable relationship between light transmittance (T_L) and the total energy transmittance (g).

The thermal transmittance k of a glazing unit indicates how much energy is lost through the glass. The lower this value, the lower the heat loss. The k value of conventional double-glazing units is greatly dependent on the distance between the two sheets of glass and the contents of the cavity (air or inert gas). With solar-control glass, an improved k value is achieved because of the precious metal layer. Standard k values are based on a glass spacing of 12 mm.

Generally, colour rendering seems unaltered when looking through a glass window from inside a room. However, if a direct comparison is made between looking through the glass and through an open window, the slight toning produced by most glass is perceptible. Depending on the type of glass, this is usually grey or brown. This difference can also be seen when looking from outside a room through two panes set at a corner. The interior colour climate is only marginally effected by solar-control glazing since the spectral qualities of the daylight barely change. Colour rendering is expressed by the R index.

Multifunctional Double-Glazing Units

Owing to the increasing demands being placed on façade elements, glazing is required to provide a wide range of functions: thermal insulation, sound reduction, solar control, personal security, fire protection, aesthetic and design aspects, environmental protection and sustainability. These functions demand an increased protection element which cannot be provided by conventional double glazing.

Multifunctional double-glazing units can combine several protection properties, and it is technically possible to fulfil almost all of those listed above. However, a standard multifunctional double-glazing unit is not yet commercially available → ④.

build-up: glass/cavity/glass	unit thickness	thermal insulation, k_V value	sun control, g value	energy balance, k value	sound reduction, R_w	colour rendering, R_{aD}	security	aesthetics	environmental protection
mm	mm	W/m²K	%	W/m²K	dB	–	–	–	–
TG* 6/16/4	26	1.2	43	0.68	36	98	yes	yes	yes

*TG = toughened glass

④ **Examples of multifunctional glass**

167

TG combin-ations	glass thickness (mm)													
	float					TG					LG			
	4	5	6	8	10	4	5	6	8	10	6	8	10	12
4	100×200	100×200	100×200	100×200	100×200	100×200	100×200	100×200	100×200	100×200	100×200	100×200	100×200	100×200
5	120×240	120×300	120×300	120×300	120×300	100×300	120×300	120×300	120×300	120×300	120×300	120×300	120×300	120×300
6	141×240	210×300	210×360	210×360	210×360	100×360	210×360	210×360	210×360	210×360	210×360	210×360	210×360	210×360
8	141×240	210×300	210×360	210×360	210×360	100×360	210×360	210×360	210×360	210×360	210×360	210×360	210×360	210×360
10	141×240	210×300	210×360	210×360	210×360	100×360	210×360	210×360	210×360	210×360	210×360	210×360	210×360	210×360

TG = toughened glass, LG = laminated glass

① **Normal maximum sizes of glazing units using toughened glass (cm)**

LG combin-ations	glass thickness (mm)													
	float					TG					LG			
	4	5	6	8	10	4	5	6	8	10	6	8	10	12
6	141×240	225×300	225×321	225×321	225×321	100×200	120×300	210×321	210×321	210×321	225×321	225×321	225×321	225×321
8	141×240	225×300	225×400	225×400	225×400	100×200	120×300	210×360	210×360	210×360	225×321	225×400	225×400	225×400
10	141×240	225×300	225×400	225×400	225×400	100×200	120×300	210×360	210×360	210×360	225×321	225×400	225×400	225×400
12	141×240	225×300	225×400	225×400	225×400	100×200	120×300	210×360	210×360	210×360	225×321	225×400	225×400	225×400

TG = toughened glass, LG = laminated glass

② **Normal maximum sizes of glazing units using laminated glass (cm)**

Toughened (tempered) glass

Toughened safety glass is a pre-stressed glass. Pre-stressing is achieved by thermal treatment. The production method consists of rapid heating followed by rapid cooling with a blast of cold air. In comparison to float glass, which produces sharp, dagger-like glass splinters when broken, this glass breaks into small, mostly round-edged glass crumbs. The danger of injury is thus greatly reduced. Toughened glass has the further advantages of increased bending and impact-resistant qualities and tolerance to temperature change (150K temperature difference, and up to 300°C compared with 40°C for annealed material. It is also unaffected by sub-zero temperatures). Toughened glass also has enhanced mechanical strength (up to five times stronger than ordinary glass), so it can be used in structural glazing systems. Alterations to, and work on, toughened glass is not possible after production. Even slight damage to the surface results in destruction. However, tempered safety glass can be used in conventional double-glazing units → ①.

Areas of use: sports buildings (ball impact resistant); school and playschool buildings because of safety considerations; living and administration buildings for stairways, doors and partitions; near radiators to avoid thermal cracking; for fully glazed façades, and elements such as glazed parapets and balustrades on balconies and staircases to prevent falls.

Laminated glass

During the manufacture of laminated glass, two or more panes of float glass are firmly bonded together with one or more highly elastic polyvinylbutyral (PVB) films. Alternatively, resin can be poured between two sheets of glass which are separated by spacers, and the resin is then cured. This process is called cast-in-place (CIP). The normal transparency of the glass may be slightly reduced depending on the thickness of the glass. Laminated glass is a non-splintering glass as the plastic film(s) hold the fragments of glass in place when the glass is broken, thus reducing the possibility of personal injury to a minimum.

There are several categories of laminated glass: safety glass, anti-bandit glass, bullet-resistant glass, fire-resistant glass and sound-control glass. The thickness and the number of layers of glass, and the types of interlayer, are designed to produce the required properties.

Laminated safety glass

Laminated safety glass normally consists of two layers of glass bonded with polyvinylbutyral (PVB) foil. This is a standard product which is used to promote safety in areas where human contact and potential breakage are likely. The tear-resistant foil makes it difficult to penetrate the glass, thus giving enhanced security against breakage and break-in. Even when safety glass is broken, the security of the room is maintained. Laminated safety glass is always used for overhead glazing for safety and security reasons → ②. Building regulations insist on its use in certain situations.

Areas of use: glazed doors and patio doors; door side-lights; shops; all low-level glazing; balustrades; bathing and shower screens; anywhere that children play and may fall against the glass, or where there is a high traffic volume, e.g. entrance areas in community buildings, schools and playschools.

Laminated anti-bandit glass

Laminated anti-bandit glass is the most suitable material for providing complete security in protective glazing systems. Anti-bandit glass can be made with two glass layers of different thicknesses bonded with PVB foil, or with three or more glass layers of different glass thicknesses bonded with standard or reinforced PVB foil. Additional security can be provided by incorporating alarm bands, or wires connected to an alarm system.

One side of this glass will withstand repeated blows from heavy implements such as bricks, hammers, crowbars, pickaxes etc. There may be crazing in the area of impact, but the tough, resilient PVB interlayers absorb the shock waves, stop any collapse of the pane and prevent loose, flying fragments of glass. Even after a sustained attack, the glass continues to provide visibility and reassurance, as well as protection from the elements. Additional security can be achieved by bonding the glass to the framing members so that the frame and the glass cannot be separated during an attack. Normally, the side of the expected attack is the external side. Only in law courts should the side of the expected attack be on the inside. It is not permissible to change the orientation of the glazing without good reason.

Areas of use: shops; display cases; museums; kiosks and ticket offices; banks; post offices; building societies; wages and rent offices; etc.

Blast-resistant glass

Safety and anti-bandit glass can also be used to provide protection against bomb attack and blast. The glass performs in two ways. First, it repels any bomb which is thrown at it, causing it to bounce back at the attacker, and second, under the effects of a blast it will deform and crack, but the glass pieces remain attached, reducing the likelihood of flying splinters.

Bullet-resistant glass

For protection against gunshots, a build-up of multiple layers is required, the overall thickness (20–50 mm) depending on the classification required. This glass incorporates up to four layers of glass, some of different thicknesses, interlayered with PVB. When attacked, the outer layers on the side of the attack are broken by the bullet and absorb energy by becoming finely granulated. The inner layers absorb the shock waves. A special reduced-spalling grade of glass can be used to minimise the danger of glass fragments flying off from the rear face of the glass. Even after an attack, barrier protection is maintained and visibility (apart from the impact area) is unaffected. Bullet-resistant classifications are based on the type of weapon and calibre used, e.g. handgun, rifle or shotgun.

Areas of use: banks; post offices; building societies; betting offices; wages and rent offices; cash desks; security vehicles; embassies; royal households; political and government buildings; airports; etc.

ARTIFICIAL LIGHTING AND DAYLIGHT

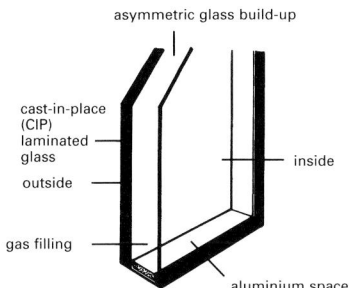

- weight of glass: the heavier the glass pane, normally the higher the acoustic insulation
- the more elastic the pane (e.g. resin-filled cast-in-place), normally the higher the acoustic insulation
- the thicknesses of the inner and outer panes must be different; the greater the difference, normally the higher the acoustic insulation

① **Sound-control double-glazing unit**

type	build-up outside, cavity inside	thickness	weight	k value, gas-filled	light transmittance	gen. colour rendering index	g value	sound reduction, R_w	max. edge length	max. area	max. side prop.	shading coeff.
	mm	mm	kg/m²	W/m²K	%	–	%	dB	cm	m²	–	–
37/22	6/12/4	22	25	2.9	82	97	75	37	300	4.0	1:6	0.86
39/24	6/14/4	24	25	2.9	82	97	75	39	300	4.0	1:6	0.86
40/26	8/14/4	26	30	2.9	81	97	72	40	300	4.0	1:6	0.83
43/34	10/20/4	34	35	3.0	80	96	69	43	300	4.0	1:6	0.79
44/38	10/24/4	38	35	3.0	80	96	69	44	300	4.0	1:6	0.79

② **Sound-control double-glazing units**

type	build-up outside, cavity inside	thickness	weight	k value, gas-filled	light transmittance	gen. colour rendering index	g value	sound reduction, R_w	max. edge length	max. area	max. side prop.	shading coeff.
	mm	mm	kg/m²	W/m²K	%	–	%	dB	cm	m²	–	–
45/30 CIP	CIP 9.5/15/6	30	40	3.0	78	97	64	45	200×300	6.0	1:10	0.74
47/36 CIP	CIP 10/20/6	36	40	3.0	78	97	64	47	200×300	6.0	1:10	0.74
50/40 CIP	CIP 10/20/10	40	50	3.0	77	95	62	50	200×300	6.0	1:10	0.71
53/42 CIP	CIP 12/20/10	42	55	3.0	75	95	60	53	200×300	6.0	1:10	0.69
55/50 CIP	CIP 20/20/10	50	75	3.0	72	93	54	55	200×300	6.0	1:10	0.62

③ **Super sound-control double-glazing units**

Fire-resistant glass

Fire resistance can be built up in two ways. One is a laminated combination of Georgian wired glass and float glass (or safety or security glass) with a PVB interlayer. The other way is to incorporate a transparent intumescent layer between the pre-stressed borsilicate glass sheets which, when heated, swells to form an opaque, fire-resistant barrier. Fire resistance of up to 2 h can be achieved. It must be remembered that in any given situation, the performance of the glazing depends on adequate support during the 'period of stability' prior to collapse.

Areas of use: fire doors; partitions; staircase enclosures; rooflights and windows in hospitals; public buildings; schools; banks; computer centres; etc. (→ pp. 130–31.)

Structural glazing

There is an increasing demand for large, uninterrupted areas of glass on façades and roofs, and it is now possible to use the structural properties of glass to support, suspend and stiffen large planar surfaces. Calculation of the required glass strengths, thicknesses, support systems and fittings to combat structural and wind stresses has become a very specialised area (consult the glass manufacturer). A wide variety of glass types may be used, e.g. toughened and laminated, single and double glazed, with solar control or with thermal recovery twin glass walls. Panels as large as 2 m × 4.2 m are possible. These are attached at only four, six or eight points and can be glazed in any plane, enabling flush glazing to sweep up walls and slopes and over roofs in one continuous surface. Various systems have been used to create stunning architectural effects on prestigious buildings throughout the world, even in areas which are prone to earthquakes, typhoons and hurricanes. Dimensional tolerances tend to be very small. For example, in a project for an art gallery in Bristol, UK, a tolerance of ±2 mm across an entire frameless glass façade 90 m long and 9 m high has been achieved. The 2.7 m × 1.7 m glass façade panels are entirely supported on 600 mm wide structural glass fins.

Sound-control glass → ① – ③

Compared with monolithic glass of the same total thickness, all laminated glass specifications provide an increased degree of sound control and a more consistent acoustic performance. The multiple construction dampens the coincident effect found in window glass, thus offering better sound reduction at higher frequencies, where the human ear is particularly sensitive. The cast-in-place type of lamination is particularly effective in reducing sound transmittance.

Sealed multiple-glazed insulating units and double windows, particularly when combining thick float glass (up to a maximum of 25 mm) and thinner glass, effectively help to dampen sound.

Areas of use: windows and partitions in offices; public buildings; concert halls; etc.

Other types of glass

There are other types of glass which have been developed especially for certain situations. Shielding glass has a special coating to provide electronic shielding. Ultra-violet light-control glass has a special interlayer which reflects up to 98% of UV rays in sunlight. Various mirror-type glasses are used in surveillance situations, e.g. one-way glass (which requires specific lighting conditions) or Venetian striped mirrors with strips of silvering (any lighting conditions).

glass pattern	colour	thickness (mm)	double-glazing unit structure direction	double-glazing unit structure side	max. aspect ratio with 12mm cavity	max. size (cm)
old German	yellow, clear	4	Δ	×	1:6	150 × 210
old German K, short side ≥250mm	clear, yellow, bronze, grey	4	×	×	1:6	150 × 210
ox-eye glass	yellow, clear	6	×	○	1:6	150 × 210
chinchilla	bronze, clear	4	Δ	×	1:6	156 × 213
Croco 129	clear	4	×	×	1:6	156 × 213
Delta	clear, bronze	4	×	×	1:6	156 × 213
Difulit 597	clear	4	×	×	1:6	150 × 210
wired Difulit 597	clear	7	×	×	1:10	150 × 245
wired glass[1]	clear	7	×	×	1:10	186 × 300
wired glass[1]	clear	9	×	×	1:10	150 × 245
wired optical	clear	9	×	○	1:10	150 × 300
wired ornamental 187 (Abstracto)	clear, bronze	7	□	○	1:10	180 × 245
wired ornamental 521, 523	clear	7	×	○	1:10	180 × 245
wired ornamental Flora 035 + Neolit	clear	7	Δ	×	1:10	180 × 245
Edelit 504, one or both sides	clear	4	Δ	×	1:6	150 × 210
Flora 035	bronze, clear	5	Δ	×	1:6	150 × 210
antique cast	yellow, grey, clear	4	×	×	1:6	150 × 210
antique cast 1074, 1082, 1086	grey	4	×	×	1:6	126 × 210
Karolit double-sided	clear	4	Δ	×	1:6	150 × 210
cathedral large and small hammered	clear	4	×	×	1:6	150 × 210
cathedral 102	yellow	4	×	×	1:6	150 × 200
cathedral 1074, 1082, 1086	grey	4	×	×	1:6	150 × 210
basket weave	clear, yellow	4	Δ	○	1:6	150 × 210
beaded 030	clear	5	Δ	×	1:6	150 × 210
Listral	clear	4	Δ	○	1:6	150 × 210
Maya	clear, bronze	5	×	○	1:6	156 × 213
Maya opaque	clear, bronze	5	×	○	1:6	156 × 213
Neolit	clear	4	Δ	×	1:6	150 × 210
Niagra	yellow, bronze, clear	5	Δ	○	1:10	156 × 213
Niagra opaque	clear	5	Δ	×	1:10	156 × 213
ornament 134 (Nucleo)	bronze, clear	4	Δ	×	1:6	150 × 210
ornament 178 (Silvit)	bronze, clear	4	Δ	×	1:6	150 × 210
ornament 187 (Abstracto)	yellow, bronze, clear	4	□	○	1:6	150 × 210
ornament 502, 504, 520	clear	4	×	×	1:6	150 × 210
ornament 521, 523	clear	4	×	○	1:6	150 × 210
ornament 523	yellow	4	×	×	1:6	150 × 210
ornament 528	clear	4	×	×	1:6	150 × 210
ornament 550, 552, 597	clear	4	×	×	1:6	150 × 210
patio	bronze, clear	5	Δ	○	1:10	156 × 213
hammered crude glass	clear	5	×	×	1:10	186 × 300
hammered crude glass	clear	7	×	×	1:10	186 × 450
Tigris 003	clear	5	Δ	×	1:6	150 × 210

□ = structured surface either way × = structured surface either side
Δ = structured surface vertical   ○ = structured surface outside only
[1] wired glass in rooflights, max. aspect ratio 1:3

(1) Cast glass combinations

The term cast glass is given to machine-produced glass which has been given a surface texture by rolling. It is not clearly transparent → ①. Cast glass is used where clear transparency in not desired (bathroom, WC) and where a decorative effect is required. The ornamental aspects of cast glass are classified as clear and coloured ornamental glass, clear crude glass, clear and coloured wired glass, and clear and coloured ornamental wired glass. Almost all commercially available cast glass can be used in double-glazing units → ①.

Normally, the structured side is placed outside in order to ensure a perfect edge seal. So that double-glazing units may be cleaned easily, the structured side is placed towards the cavity. This is possible only with lightly structured glass. Do not combine coloured cast glass with other coloured glasses such as float, armoured or laminated glass, or with coated, heat-absorbing or reflective glass.

glass type	nominal thickness (mm)	tolerance (mm)	max. dimensions (cm × cm)	
agricultural glass (standard sizes)	3	±0.2	48 × 120 / 46 × 144 / 60 × 174	73 × 143 / 73 × 165 / 60 × 200
	4	±0.3		

(2) Agricultural glass

Glass entrance screens consist of one or several glass doors, and the side and top panels. Other possibilities are sliding, folding, arched and half-round headed entrance screens. Various colours and glass structures are available. The dimensions of the doors are the same as those of the frame → ③ – ⑤. When violently smashed, the glass disintegrates into a network of small crumbs which loosely hang together. Normal glass thicknesses of 10 or 12mm are used, and stiffening ribs may be necessary, depending on the structural requirements.

(3) Single-leaf doors   **Double-leaf doors**

	size I	size II	size III
standard door leaf, overall dimensions	709 × 1972 mm²	834 × 1972 mm²	959 × 1972 mm²
frame rebate dimensions	716 × 1983 mm²	841 × 1983 mm²	966 × 1983 mm²
structural opening sizes	750 × 2000 mm²	875 × 2000 mm²	1000 × 2000 mm²

special sizes are possible up to dimensions of:

1000 × 2100 mm²
1150 × 2100 mm²

(4) Glass doors, standard sizes

glass type	glass thickness (mm)	maximum sizes (mm²)	thickness tolerances (mm)
clear, grey, bronze	10 / 12	2400 × 3430 / 2150 × 3500*	± 0.3
OPTIWHITE®	10 / 10	2400 × 3430 / 2150 × 3500*	± 0.3
structure 200	10 / 10	1860 × 3430 / 1860 × 3500*	± 0.5
bamboo, chinchilla clear/bronze	8 / 8	1700 × 2800 / 1700 × 3000*	± 0.5

(5) Glass entrance screens (side and top panels)

Glass Blocks

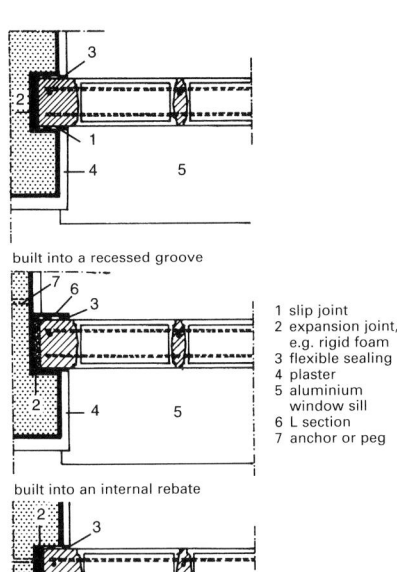

$$A = n_1 \cdot b + n_2 \cdot a$$
$$B = A + 2 \cdot c$$
$$H = A + c + d$$

n_1 = number of blocks (a)
n_2 = number of joints (b)
c = 8.5 cm
d = 6.5 cm

formula to calculate the minimum structural opening

(1) **Standard dimensions for glass block walls**

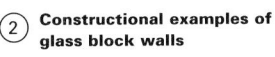

built into a recessed groove

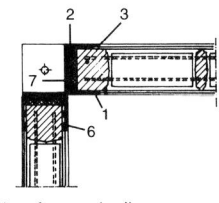

built into an internal rebate

1 slip joint
2 expansion joint,
e.g. rigid foam
3 flexible sealing
4 plaster
5 aluminium window sill
6 L section
7 anchor or peg

built onto a façade with angle anchoring
plan

(2) **Constructional examples of glass block walls**

1 slip joint
2 expansion joint,
e.g. rigid foam
3 flexible sealing
4 plaster
5 aluminium window sill
6 U section
7 L section
8 anchor or peg

plan of corner detail

(3) **Installation with U sections and external thermal insulation**

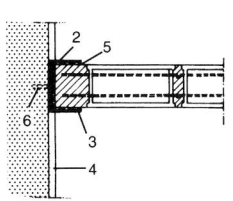

1 slip joint
2 expansion joint,
e.g. rigid foam
3 flexible sealing
4 plaster
5 U section
6 anchor or peg

plan

(4) **Internal wall junction using U sections**

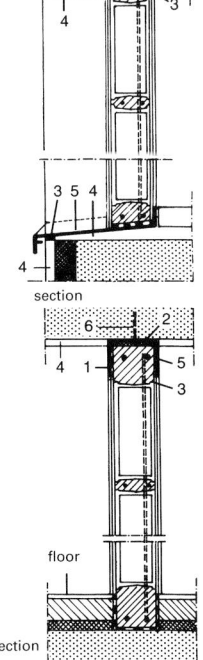

section

section

floor

section

Glass blocks are hollow units which consist of two sections melted and pressed together, thereby creating a sealed air cavity. Both surfaces can be made smooth and transparent, or very ornamental and almost opaque. Glass blocks can be obtained in different sizes, coated on the inside or outside, uncoated, or made of coloured glass. They can be used internally and externally, e.g. transparent screen walls and room dividers (also in gymnastic and sports halls), windows, lighting strips, balcony parapets and terrace walls. Glass blocks are fire-resistant up to G 60 or G 120 when used as a cavity wall with a maximum uninterrupted area of 3.5 m², and can be built either vertically or horizontally. Glass blocks cannot be used in a load-bearing capacity.

Properties: good sound and thermal insulation; high light transmittance (up to 82%), depending on the design; can have translucent, light scattering and low dazzle properties; can also have enhanced resistance to impact and breakage. A glass block wall has good insulation properties: with cement mortar, k = 3.2 W/m²K; with lightweight mortar, k = 2.9 W/m²K.

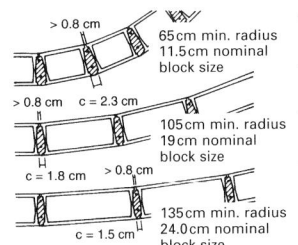

65 cm min. radius 11.5 cm nominal block size

105 cm min. radius 19 cm nominal block size

135 cm min. radius 24.0 cm nominal block size

smallest radius R with glass thickness 8 cm
joints must be < 1.0 cm wide

glass block nominal size	11.5 cm	19.0 cm	24.0 cm
joint width c = 1.5 cm	200.0 cm	295.0 cm	370.0 cm
joint width c = 1.8 cm	95.0 cm	180.0 cm	215.0 cm
joint width c = 2.3 cm	65.0 cm	105.0 cm	135.0 cm

(5) **Minimum radii of glass block walls**

	dimensions (mm)	weight (kg)	units (m²)	units, boxes	units, pallets
	115 × 115 × 80	1.0	64	10	1000
	146 × 146 × 98 6″ × 6″ × 4″	1.8	42	8	512
	190 × 190 × 50	2.0	25	14	504
	190 × 190 × 80	2.3	25	10	360
	190 × 190 × 100	2.8	25	8	288
	197 × 197 × 98 8″ × 8″ × 4″	3.0	25	8	288
	240 × 115 × 80	2.1	32	10	500
	240 × 240 × 80	3.9	16	5	250
	300 × 300 × 100	7.0	10	4	128

(6) **Dimensions of glass block walls**

arrangement of joints	thickness (mm)	wall dimensions shorter side (m)	longer side (m)	wind load (kN/m²)
vertical	≥80	≤1.5	≥1.5	≤0.8
offset (bonded)			≤6.0	

(7) **Permissible limits for unreinforced glass block walls**

GLASS

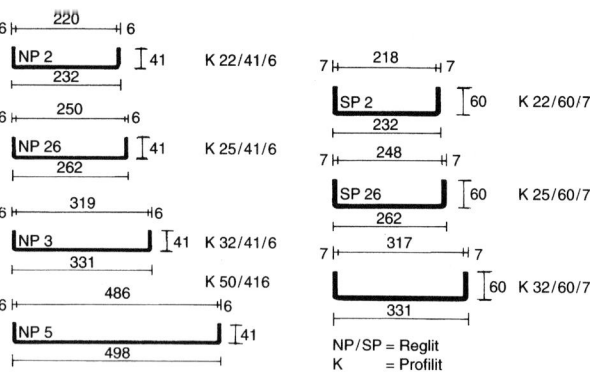

① **Profiled glass – sections**

NP/SP = Reglit
K = Profilit

Profiled glass is cast glass produced with a U-shaped profile. It is translucent, with an ornamentation on the outside surface of the profile, and conforms to the properties of cast glass.

Low maintenance requirements. Suitable for lift shafts and roof glazing. Rooms using this glass for fenestration are rendered dazzle-free.

Special types: Profilit-bronze, Cascade, Topas, Amethyst. Heat-absorbing glass Reglit and Profilit 'Plus 1.7' attain a k value of 1.8 W/m²K.

Solar-control glass (Type R, 'Bernstein'; Type P, 'Antisol'), which reflects and/or absorbs ultra-violet and infra-red radiation, can be used to protect delicate goods which are sensitive to UV radiation. The transmission of radiant energy into the room is reduced, as is the convection from the glazing, whilst the light transmission is maintained.

For glazing subject to impacts, e.g. in sports halls, Regulit SP2 or Profilit K22/60/7 without wire reinforcement should be used.

Regulit and Profilit are allowed as fire-resistant glass A 30. Normal and special profiles are also available reinforced with longitudinal wires.

Table ②

height from ground level to top of glazed opening	up to 8m	up to 20m	up to 100m	up to 8m	up to 20m	up to 100m	up to 8m	up to 20m	up to 100m
glass type → ①	L*	L*	L*	L*	L*	L*	L*	L*	L*
NP2 / K22/41/6	3.25	2.55	2.20	4.35	3.45	2.95	4.60	3.65	3.10
NP26 / K25/41/6	3.05	2.40	2.05	4.10	3.25	2.75	4.35	3.45	2.90
NP3 / K32/41/6	2.75	2.20	1.85	3.70	2.95	2.50	3.90	3.10	2.65
NP5 / K50/41/6	2.30	1.80	1.55	3.05	2.40	2.00	3.25	2.55	2.15
SP2 / K22/60/7	5.15	4.05	3.45	6.65	5.45	4.65	7.00	5.75	4.90
SP26 / K25/60/7	4.85	3.85	3.25	6.55	5.15	4.40	6.90	5.45	4.65
K32/60/7	4.40	3.45	2.95	5.85	4.55	3.90	6.20	4.90	4.15

② **Sheltered buildings (0.8 – 1.25 g)**

Table ③

height from ground level to top of glazed opening	h/a = 0.25; –(1.5·q)						H/a = 0.5; –(1.7·q)					
	up to 8m	up to 20m	up to 100m	up to 8m	up to 20m	up to 100m	up to 8m	up to 20m	up to 100m	up to 8m	up to 20m	up to 100m
glass type → ①	L*	L*	L*	L*	L*	L*	L*	L*	L*	L*	L*	L*
NP2 / K22/41/6	2.60	2.10	1.75	3.75	2.95	2.50	2.45	1.95	1.65	3.50	2.75	2.35
NP26 / K25/41/6	2.50	1.95	1.70	3.50	2.80	2.35	2.35	1.85	1.60	3.30	2.65	2.20
NP3 / K32/41/6	2.20	1.75	1.50	3.15	2.50	2.15	2.10	1.65	1.45	2.95	2.35	2.00
NP5 / K50/41/6	1.85	1.45	1.25	2.60	2.10	1.75	1.75	1.35	1.15	2.45	1.95	1.65
SP2 / K22/60/7	4.20	3.30	2.80	5.95	4.65	3.95	3.95	3.10	2.65	5.55	4.40	3.70
SP26 / K25/60/7	3.95	3.10	2.65	5.60	4.40	3.80	3.70	2.90	2.60	5.25	4.15	3.55
K32/60/7	3.60	2.80	2.40	5.00	4.00	3.40	3.35	2.65	2.25	4.75	3.75	3.20

③ **Exposed buildings**

L = length of glass units (m)

light transmittance	single-glazed	up to 89%
	double-glazed	up to 81%
sound reduction	single-glazed	up to 29 dB
	double-glazed	up to 41 dB
	triple-glazed	up to 55 dB
thermal insulation	single-glazed	k = 5.6 W/m²K
	double-glazed	NP k = 2.8 W/m²K
		SP k = 2.7 W/m²K

④ **Physical data**

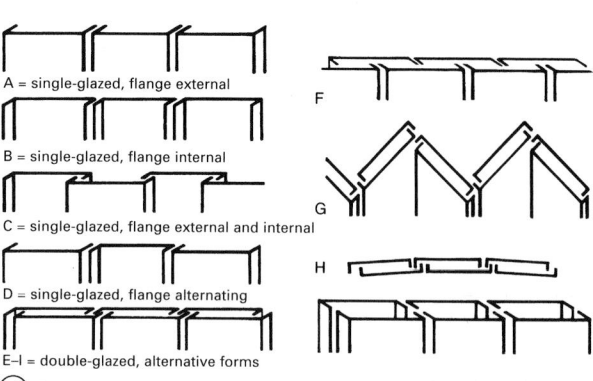

A = single-glazed, flange external
B = single-glazed, flange internal
C = single-glazed, flange external and internal
D = single-glazed, flange alternating
E–I = double-glazed, alternative forms

⑤ **Possible combinations**

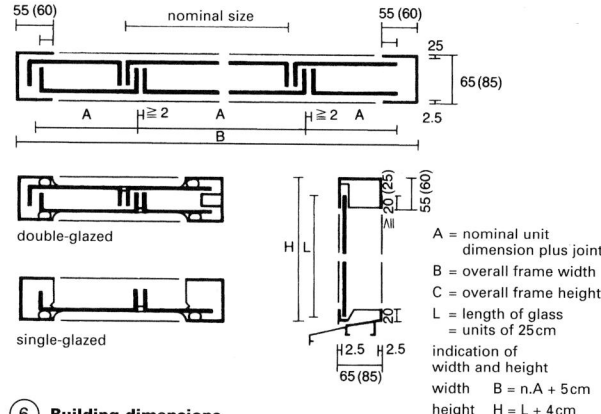

double-glazed

single-glazed

A = nominal unit dimension plus joint
B = overall frame width
C = overall frame height
L = length of glass unit
 = units of 25cm
indication of width and height
width   B = n.A + 5cm
height   H = L + 4cm

⑥ **Building dimensions**

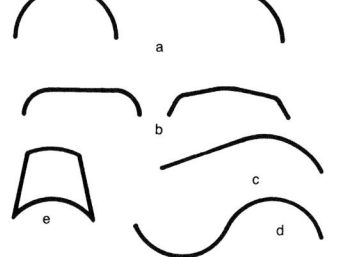

(a) single bends as sections of a circle with and without straight sections
(b) double or multiple bends with identical or different radii
(c) sine curve bends
(d) 'S' bends
(e) 'U' bends with or without straight sections

⑦ **Bent forms**

practical examples of possible bent forms using ornamental glass

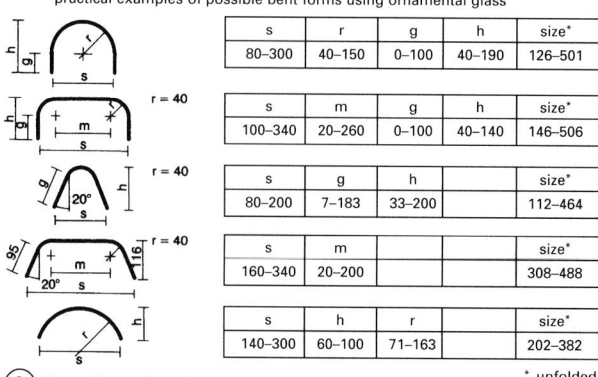

s	r	g	h	size*
80–300	40–150	0–100	40–190	126–501

s	m	g	h	size*
100–340	20–260	0–100	40–140	146–506

s	g	h		size*
80–200	7–183	33–200		112–464

s	m			size*
160–340	20–200			308–488

s	h	r		size*
140–300	60–100	71–163		202–382

⑧ **Bent forms (mm)**

* unfolded

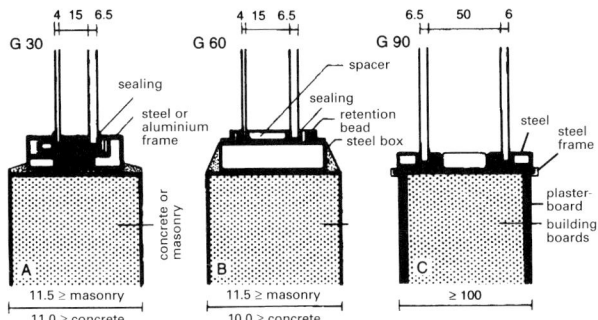

4 15 6.5   4 15 6.5   6.5   50   6

G 30   G 60   G 90

① Glazing with fire-protection class G

Fire-resistant glass

Normal glass is of only limited use for fire protection. In cases of fire, float glass cracks in a very short time due to the one-sided heating, and large pieces of glass fall out enabling the fire to spread. The increasing use of glass in multistorey buildings for façades, parapets and partitions has led to increased danger in the event of fire. In order to comply with building regulations, the fire resistance of potentially threatened glazing must be adequate. The level of fire resistance of a glass structure is classified by its resistance time: i.e. 30, 60, 90, 120 or 180 min. The fire resistance time is the number of minutes that the structure prevents the fire and combustion gasses from passing through. The construction must be officially tested, approved and certificated → ①.

Fire-resistant glass comes in four forms: wired glass with point-welded mesh, maximum resistance 60–90 min; special armoured glass in a laminated combination with double-glazing units; pre-stressed borosilicate glass, e.g. Pyran; multi-laminated panes of float glass with clear intumescent interlayers which turn opaque on exposure to fire, e.g. Pyrostop. (→ pp. 130–31)

Glass blocks with steel reinforcement

Fire-resistant, steel-reinforced glass blocks can, as with all other glass block walls, be fixed to the surrounds with or without U sections. All other types of fixing methods are also applicable. Because of the strongly linear spread of fire and the production of combustion gases, fire-resistant glass block walls should be lined all round with mineral fibre slabs (stonewool) → ③.

resistance class I	G 60	G 120	G 90	G 120	F 60	
glazing size (m²)	3.5 m²	2.5 m²	9.0 m²	4.4 m²	4.4 m²	
max. element height	1	3.5 m	3.5 m	3.5 m	3.5 m	3.5 m
max. element width	1	6.0 m	6.0 m	6.0 m	6.0 m	6.0 m
sill height needed	1.8 m	1.8 m	none	none	none	
type of glazing	single skin	double skin	single skin	double skin	double skin	
glass block format	190×190×80	190×190×80	190×190×80	190×190×80	190×190×80	

② Fire-protection classes for glass blocks

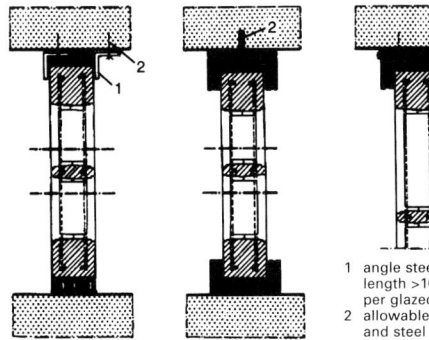

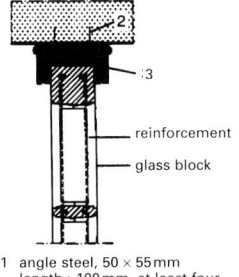

1 angle steel, 50 × 55 mm length >100 mm, at least four per glazed area
2 allowable fire-resistant pegs and steel screws M 10
3 flat steel strips to fix the glass block wall (welded)

reinforcement

glass block

③ Edge details, fire-protection glazing

Sound reduction

Because of its weight, a glass block wall has particularly good sound insulation properties:

  1.00 kN/m² with 80 mm glass blocks;
  1.25 kN/m² with 100 mm glass blocks;
  1.42 kN/m² with special BSH glass blocks.

To be effective, the surrounding building elements must have at least the same sound reduction characteristics. Glass block construction is the ideal solution in all cases where good sound insulation is required. In areas where a high level of sound reduction is necessary, economical solutions can be achieved by using glass block walls to provide the daylight while keeping ventilation openings and windows. These can serve as secondary escape routes if they conform to the minimum allowable size.

Follow the relevant regulations with regard to sound reduction where the standards required for particular areas can be found. The sound reduction rating (R'w) can be calculated from the formula R'w = LSM + 52 dB (where LSM is the reduction value of airborne sound) → ⑤. Single-skin glass block walls can meet the requirements of sound reduction level 5 → ⑥.

	type of room	permitted maximum sound levels in rooms from outside noise sources	
		mean levels*	mean max. levels
1	living rooms in apartments, bedrooms in hotels, wards in hospitals and sanatoriums	day 30–40 dB(A) night 20–30 dB(A)	day 40–50 dB(A) night 30–40 dB(A)
2	classrooms, quiet individual offices, scientific laboratories, libraries, conference and lecture rooms, doctors' practices and operating theatres, churches, assembly halls	30–40 dB(A)	40–50 dB(A)
3	offices for several people	35–45 dB(A)	45–55 dB(A)
4	open-plan offices, pubs/restaurants, shops, switchrooms	40–50 dB(A)	50–60 dB(A)
5	entrance halls, waiting rooms, check in/out halls	45–55 dB(A)	55–65 dB(A)
6	opera houses, theatres, cinemas	25 dB(A)	35 dB(A)
7	recording studios	take note of special requirements	

* equivalent maximum permitted constant level

④ Permitted maximum sound levels for different categories of room use

noise source	distance from window to centre of road	recommended standard sound reduction levels for standard categories of room use			
		1	2	3	4
motorways, average traffic	25 m	4	3	2	1
	80 m	3	2	1	0
	250 m	1	0	0	0
motorways, intensive traffic	25 m	5	4	3	2
	80 m	4	3	2	1
	250 m	2	1	0	0
main roads	8 m	3	2	1	0
	25 m	2	1	0	0
	80 m	1	0	0	0
secondary roads	8 m	2	1	0	0
	25 m	1	0	0	0
	80 m	0	0	0	0
main roads in city centres	small building intensive traffic	5	5	4	3
	large building average to intensive traffic	4	4	3	2

⑤ Recommended standard sound-reduction levels for standard categories of room use subjected to traffic noise

sound-reduction level	R_w	
6	≥ 50 dB	for double-skinned glass block walls/windows
5	45–49 dB	for single-skinned glass block areas
4	40–44 dB	for single-skinned glass block areas
3	35–39 dB	
2	30–34 dB	
1	25–29 dB	
0	≤25 dB	

⑥ Standard sound-reduction levels for windows

glass block format (mm)	airborne sound-reduction value (LSM)	sound-reduction rating (R'_w)
190 × 190 × 80	− 12 dB	40 dB
240 × 240 × 80	− 10 dB	42 dB
240 × 115 × 80	− 7 dB	45 dB
300 × 300 × 100	− 11 dB	41 dB
double-skinned wall with 240 × 240 × 80	− 2 dB	50 dB

⑦ Glass block areas

173

PLASTICS

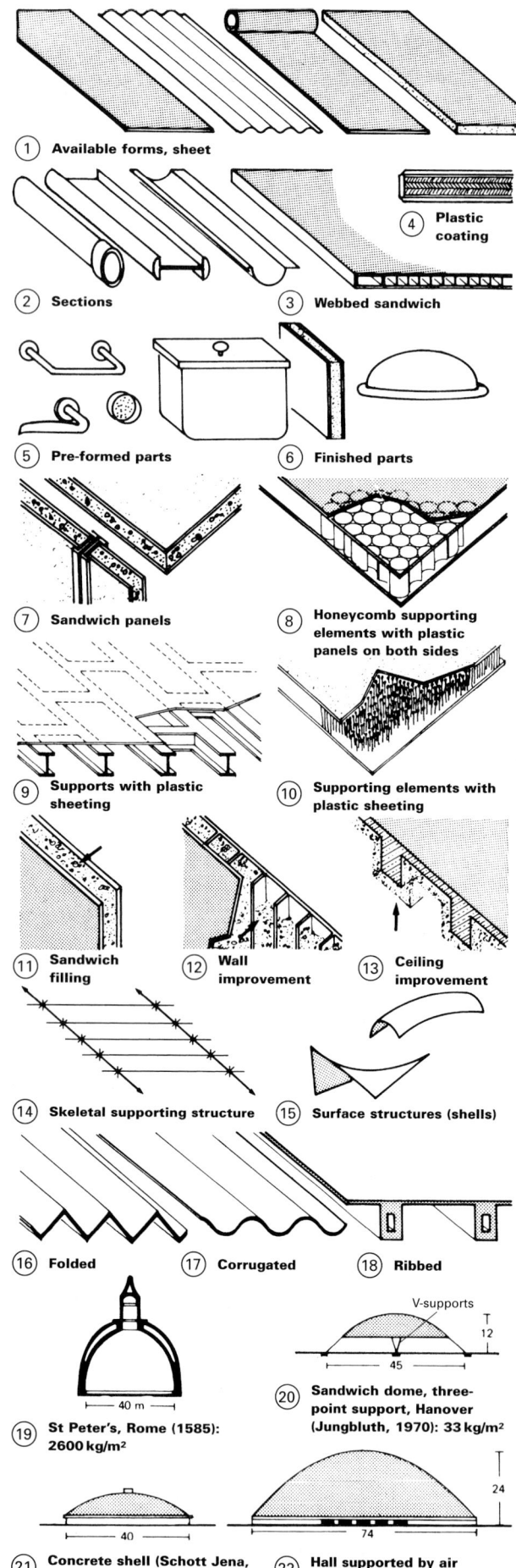

(1) Available forms, sheet

(2) Sections

(3) Webbed sandwich

(4) Plastic coating

(5) Pre-formed parts

(6) Finished parts

(7) Sandwich panels

(8) Honeycomb supporting elements with plastic panels on both sides

(9) Supports with plastic sheeting

(10) Supporting elements with plastic sheeting

(11) Sandwich filling

(12) Wall improvement

(13) Ceiling improvement

(14) Skeletal supporting structure

(15) Surface structures (shells)

(16) Folded

(17) Corrugated

(18) Ribbed

(19) St Peter's, Rome (1585): 2600 kg/m²

(20) Sandwich dome, three-point support, Hanover (Jungbluth, 1970): 33 kg/m²

(21) Concrete shell (Schott Jena, 1925): 450 kg/m²

(22) Hall supported by air pressure, Forossa, Finland (1972): 1.65 kg/m²

Plastics, as raw material (fluid, powdery or granular), are divided into three categories: (1) thermosetting plastics (which harden when heated); (2) thermoplastics (which become plastic when heated); (3) elastomers (which are permanently elastic). Plastics are processed industrially using chemical additives, fillers, glass fibres and colorants to produce semi-finished goods, building materials, finished products → (1) – (6).

The beneficial characteristics of plastics in construction include: water and corrosion resistance, low maintenance, low weight, colouring runs throughout the material, high resistance to light (depending on the type), applications providing a durable colour finish on other materials (e.g. as a film for covering steel and plywood → (4) etc.). They are also easy to work and process, can be formed almost without limits, and have low thermal conductivities.

Double-skinned webbed sections are available in a wide range of thicknesses, widths and lengths. Being translucent, these sections are suitable for roof or vertical glazing. These are permeable to light → (3).

The large number of trade names can be bewildering so designers must refer to the international chemical descriptions and symbols when selecting plastics, to ensure that their properties match those laid down in standards, test procedures and directives. The key plastics in construction, and their accepted abbreviations, are:

ABS	= acrylonitrile-butadiene-styrene	PC	= polycarbonate
CR	= chloroprene	PE	= polyethylene
EP	= epoxy resin	PIB	= polyisobutylene
EPS	= expanded polystyrene	PMMA	= polymethyl methacrylate (acrylic glass)
GRP	= glass fibre-reinforced plastic	PP	= polypropylene
GR-UP	= glass fibre-reinforced polyester	PS	= polystyrene
IIR	= butyl rubber	PVC	= polyvinyl chloride, hard or soft
MF	= melamine formaldehyde	UP	= unsaturated polyester resin
PA	= polyamide		

The plastics used to produce semi-finished materials and finished components contain, as a rule, up to 50% filling material, reinforcement and other additives. They are also significantly affected by temperature so an in-service temperature limit of between 80° and 120° should be observed. This in not a serious problem given that sustained heating to above 80° is found only in isolated spots in buildings (e.g., perhaps around hot water pipes and fires). Plastics, being organic materials, are flammable. Some are classed as a flame inhibiting structural material; most of them are normally flammable; however, a few are classed as readily flammable. The appropriate guidelines contained in the regional building regulations for the application of flammable structural materials in building structures must be followed.

Classification of plastic products for building construction

(1) Materials, semi-finished: 1.1 building boards and sheets; 1.2 rigid foam materials, core layers; 1.3 foam materials with mineral additions (rigid foam/light concrete); 1.4 films, rolls and flat sheets, fabrics, fleece materials; 1.5 floor coverings, artificial coverings for sports areas; 1.6 profiles (excluding windows); 1.7 pipes, tubes and accessories; 1.8 sealing materials, adhesives, bonding agents for mortar, etc.

(2) Structural components, applications: 2.1 external walls; 2.2 internal walls; 2.3 ceilings; 2.4 roofs and accessories; 2.5 windows, window shutters and accessories; 2.6 doors, gates and accessories; 2.7 supports.

(3) Auxiliary items, small parts, etc.: 3.1 casings and accessories; 3.2 sealing tapes, flexible foam rolls and sheets; 3.3 fixing devices; 3.4 fittings; 3.5 ventilation accessories (excluding pipes); 3.6 other small parts.

(4) Domestic engineering: 4.1 sanitary units; 4.2 sanitary objects; 4.3 valves and sanitary accessories; 4.4 electrical installation and accessories; 4.5 heating.

(5) Furniture and fittings: 5.1 furniture and accessories; 5.2 lighting systems and fittings.

(6) Structural applications; 6.1 roofs and supporting structures, illuminated ceilings; 6.2 pneumatic and tent structures; 6.3 heating oil tanks, vessels, silos; 6.4 swimming pools; 6.5 towers, chimneys, stairs; 6.6 room cells; 6.7 plastic houses.

Construction using plastics is best planned in the form of panel structures (shells). These have the advantage of very low weight, thus reducing loading on the substructure, and also offer the possibility of prefabricated construction → (14) – (17). Structures in plastics (without the use of other materials) at present only bear their own weight plus snow and wind loads, and possibly additional loads due to lighting. This allows large areas to be covered more easily → (19) – (22).

174

SKYLIGHTS AND DOME ROOFLIGHTS

Domes, skylights, coffers, smoke vents and louvres, as fixed or moving units, can be used for lighting and ventilation, and for clearing smoke from rooms, halls, stair wells etc. All these can be supplied in heat-reflecting Plexiglas if required.

By directing the dome towards the north (in the northern hemisphere), sunshine and glare are avoided → ④. The use of high curb skylights → ① will reduce glare because of the sharp angles of incidence of the sunlight. Dome rooflights used for ventilation should face into the prevailing wind in order to utilise the extraction capacity of the wind. The inlet aperture should be 20% smaller than the outlet aperture. Forced ventilation, with an air flow of 150–1000 m³/h, can be achieved by fitting a fan into the curb of a skylight → ②. Dome rooflights can also be used for access to the roof.

Attention should be given to the aerodynamic extraction surfaces of smoke exhaust systems. Orientating each extraction unit at an angle of 90° from the adjacent one will allow for wind coming from all directions. Position to leeward/windward if pairs of extraction fans are to be mounted in line with or against the direction of the prevailing wind.

Smoke extraction vents are required for stair wells more than four complete storeys high. Variable skylight aperture widths up to 5.50 m are available, as is a special version up to 7.50 m wide which does not need extra support.

Skylight systems offer diffuse room lighting which is free from glare → ⑭. North-facing skylights with spun glass fibre inlays guarantee all the technically important advantages of a workshop illuminated by a north light → ⑬. Traditional flat roofs can be modified to admit a north light by inserting skylights with curbs.

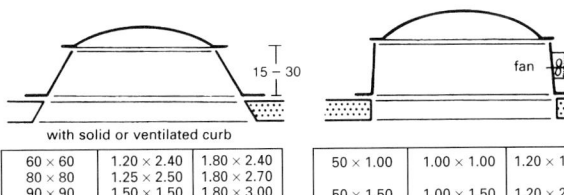

with solid or ventilated curb

60 × 60	1.20 × 2.40	1.80 × 2.40
80 × 80	1.25 × 2.50	1.80 × 2.70
90 × 90	1.50 × 1.50	1.80 × 3.00
1.00 × 1.00	1.50 × 1.80	2.20 × 2.20
1.00 × 2.00	1.50 × 2.40	2.50 × 2.50
1.20 × 1.20	1.80 × 1.80	
1.20 × 1.80		

round domes: 60, 90, 100, 120, 150, 180, 220, 250 cm dia.

① 'Normal' dome rooflight

50 × 1.00	1.00 × 1.00	1.20 × 1.50
50 × 1.50	1.00 × 1.50	1.20 × 2.40
60 × 60	1.00 × 2.00	1.50 × 1.50
60 × 90	1.00 × 2.50	1.50 × 3.00
90 × 90	1.00 × 3.00	1.80 × 2.70

② Dome rooflight with high curb

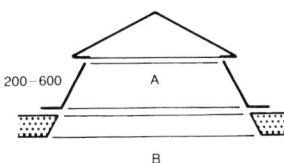

A	B	C	D
40	60 × 60	1.6	1.80 × 1.80
70	90 × 90	1.7	2.00 × 2.00
80	1.00 × 1.00	2.20	2.00 × 2.20
1.00	1.20 × 1.20	2.30	2.50 × 2.50
1.30	1.50 × 1.50	2.40	2.70 × 2.70

③ Pyramid rooflight

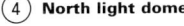

A = rooflight area	B = roof opening
72 × 1.20 × 1.08	1.25 × 1.25
72 × 2.45 × 2.30	1.25 × 2.50
75 × 1.16 × 76	1.50 × 1.50

④ North light dome

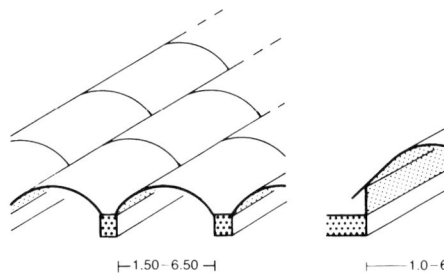

⑤ Continuous multiple barrel skylights

⑥ Continuous barrel skylight

⑦ Continuous double-pitched skylight

⑧ Continuous mono-pitched skylight

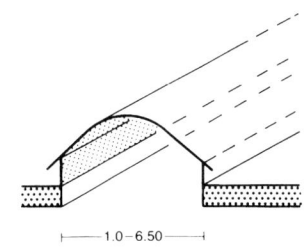

⑨ Monitor rooflight with inclined panes

⑩ Monitor rooflight with vertical panes

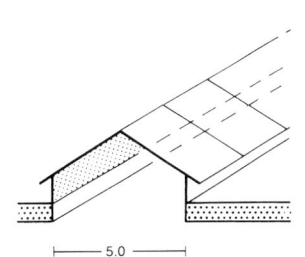

⑪ 60° saw-tooth north light

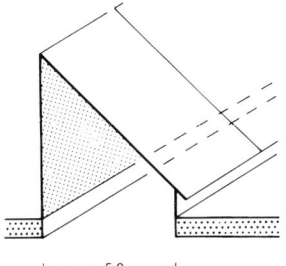

⑫ 90° vertical saw-tooth north light

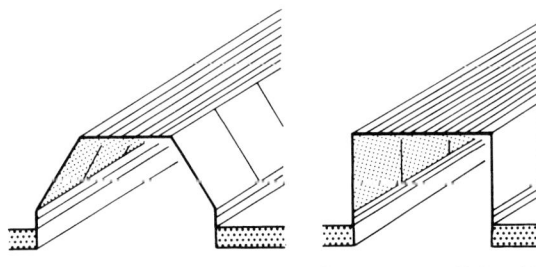

60° = angle of incidence of sun's rays

south

spun glass inlay

north

light transmission 76%

37°

30°

45°

96% 4%

heat insulation in area of shadow of spun glass inlay

up to 1.50	25 mm
1.51 – 2.50	30 mm
2.51 – 3.60	40 mm
3.61 – 4.50	70 mm
4.51 – 6.50	90 mm unit

⑬ Saw-tooth glass fibre-reinforced polyester skylight

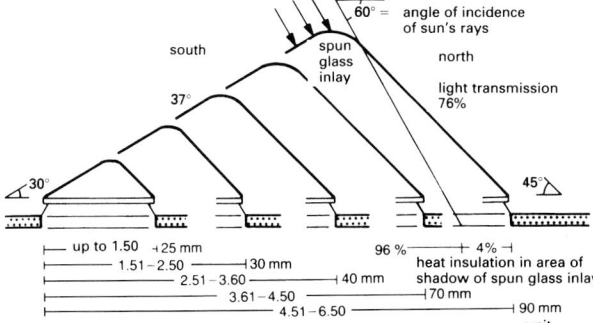

27°

≤ 1.50	25 mm
1.51 – 3.00	30 mm
3.01 – 4.00	40 mm
4.01 – 5.50	70 mm
5.51 – 7.50	90 mm unit

⑭ Double-skinned rooflight units

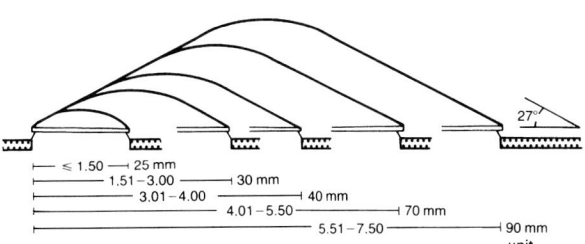

175

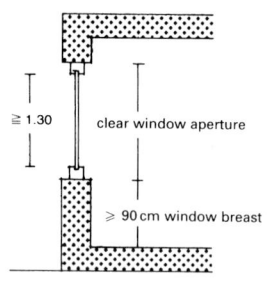

glass area = 1/20 of room area
window width = 1/10 (M + N + O + P)

① **Window sizes for industrial buildings**

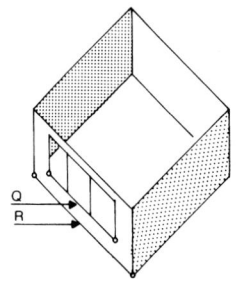

② **Window size ≥ 0.3 A × B**

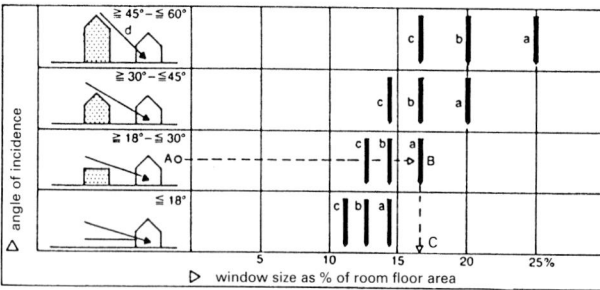

≧ 1.30

clear window aperture

≥ 90 cm window breast

③ **Section of façade**

④ **Width of the window aperture Q ≥ 0.5 R**

If daylight is considered to be essential for the use to which a room will be put, then windows are an unavoidable necessity. Simple apertures for daylight have developed into significant stylistic features, from Romanesque semi-circular arched windows to Baroque windows surrounded by rich, elaborate decoration. In the European cultural region lying north of the Alps, window forms reveal particularly strong features. In contrast to the climatically favoured cultural region of the Mediterranean, daily life here mainly had to be spent indoors. The people were thus dependent upon daylight because artificial light was expensive and good illumination of a room during the hours of darkness was beyond the means of most of the local population.

Every work area needs a window leading to the outside world. The window area which transmits light must be at least $1/20$ of the surface area of the floor in the work space. The total width of all the windows must amount to at least $1/10$ of the total width of all the walls, i.e. $1/10$ (M + N + O + P) → ①.

For workrooms which are 3.5m or more high, the light transmission surface of the window must be at least 30% of the outside wall surface, i.e. ≥ 0.3 A × B → ②.

For workrooms with dimensions similar to those of a living room, the following rules should be applied.

Minimum height of the glass surface, 1.3m → ③.

Height of the window breast from the ground, ≥ 0.9 m.

The total height of all windows must be 50% of the width of the workroom, i.e. Q = 0.5R → ④.

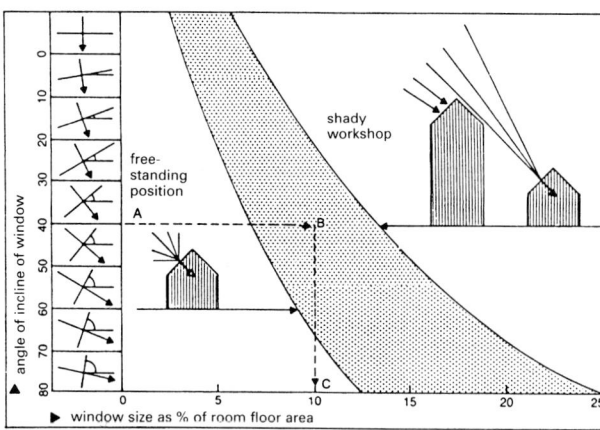

⑤ **Window sizes in domestic buildings**

angle of incidence (vertical axis)
≧ 45° – ≦ 60°
≧ 30° – ≦ 45°
≧ 18° – ≦ 30°
≦ 18°

window size as % of room floor area

⑥ **Window sizes**

angle of incline of window

window size as % of room floor area

free-standing position

shady workshop

Example → ⑤

A For a flat, angle of incidence of light 18°–30°
B Necessary window size for the living room
C 17% of the room floor surface area is sufficient for the size of the windows.

The slope of the roof surface is known. A skylight with a slope of 0° needs to be only 20% of the size of a vertical window to make the room equally bright – however, there is no view. Windows are generally the poorest point in terms of heat insulation. For this reason, it is convenient to fit the room with smaller windows, as long as the solar heat gain through the windows is discounted.

As well as the window size and the slope of the window surface, the siting of the house plays an important role. A free-standing house admits more light with the same surface area of windows than a house in the city centre.

Example → ⑥ – ⑦

A Slope of a roof window of 40°
B The house is not free standing, but is also not in heavy shadow.
C 10% of the room floor surface area is sufficient for the size of the windows.

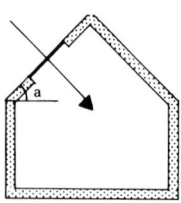

⑦ **Roof window**

When calculating the window size for a living room, both the floor area of the room and the angle of incidence of the light must be taken into account → ⑤. Here, 'a' is the minimum window size for a living room as a percentage of the floor area of the room, 'b' is the minimum size for a kitchen window and 'c' is the minimum size for all other rooms. The angle of incidence of the light is 'd'. The larger the angle of incidence, the larger the windows need to be. This is because the closer the neighbouring houses are, and the higher they are, the greater the angle of incidence and the smaller the amount of light penetrating into the house. Larger windows will compensate for this smaller quantity of light.

Dutch regulations stipulate the sizes of windows in relation to the angle of incidence of the light.

EFFECT ON WIDTH

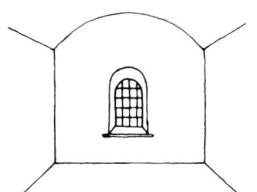

① **With stone walls**

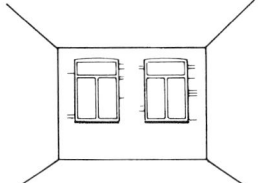

② **With brickwork**

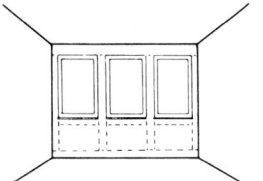

③ **With half-timbered construction**

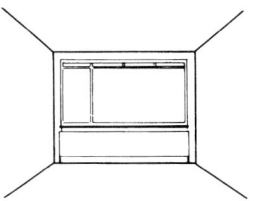

④ **With steel-frame structure With reinforced concrete**

EFFECT ON HEIGHT

⑤ **With scenic view and balcony**

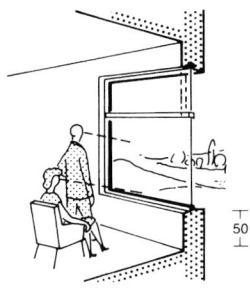

⑥ **Rooms with a view**

⑦ **Normal window height**

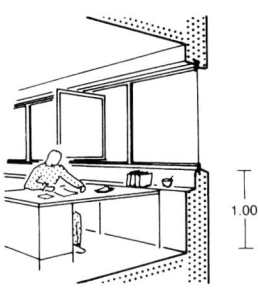

⑧ **Office**

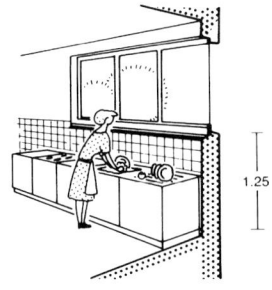

⑨ **Kitchen**

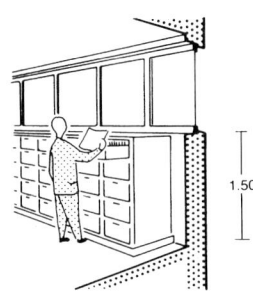

⑩ **Office (filing room)**

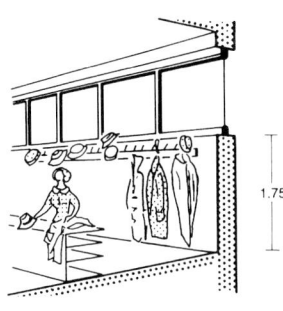

⑪ **Cloakroom**

⑫ **Skylight e.g. drawing office**

VENTILATION

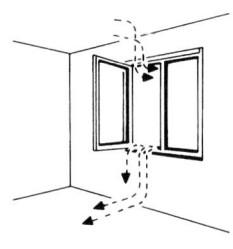

⑬ **Cool air drawn into room, warm air extracted**

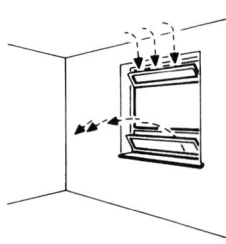

⑭ **Flap control: ventilation better**

HEATING

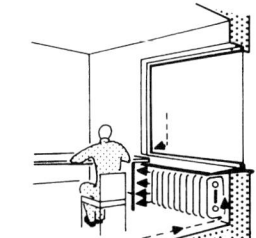

⑮ **Cold and warm air hitting the seated person (unhealthy)**

⑯ **Built-in radiators (convectors) require entry/exit for air**

BLINDS AND CURTAINS

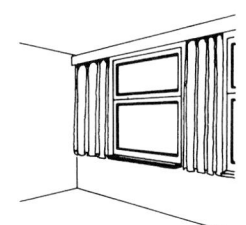

⑰ **Allow sufficient wall space in corners for curtains**

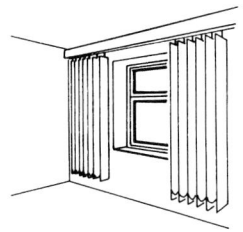

⑱ **Vertical blinds, slatted curtains**

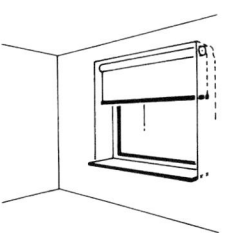

⑲ **Roller blinds of cloth or plastic**

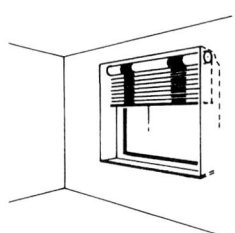

⑳ **Venetian blind**

PROTECTION FROM THE SUN

Protection measures must prevent glare and regulate the inflow of heat from sunlight. In temperate climates, large window apertures with a high but diffuse incidence of light are preferred, whereas in hot climates, small window apertures still allow sufficient light to enter.

Venetian blinds → ⑬ (with flat slats of wood, aluminium or plastic), roller shutters, roller blinds and partially angled sun blinds are all useful and can be adjusted as required. Fixed external devices are clearly less flexible than retractable or adjustable ones. Vertical panel blinds → ⑮ (either fixed or pivoting around the axis of the slat) are also suitable for tall or angled window surfaces.

Heat rising up the face of a building should be able to escape, and not be blocked by external sun screens or allowed to enter the building via open skylights.

Internal shades are less effective than external ones for reducing solar heat gain because the heat they absorb is released into the room.

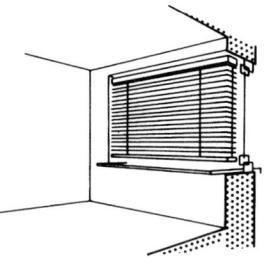
① **Internal venetian blind: sun comes through window (not good)**

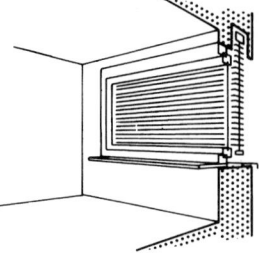
② **External louvred blind**

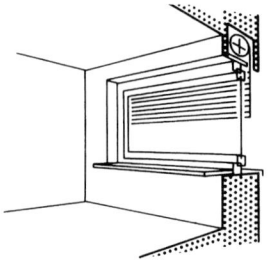
③ **Roller shutter**

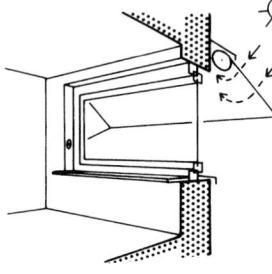
④ **Awning keeps sun's rays and heat at bay**

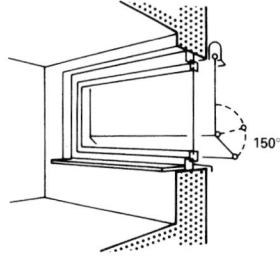
⑤ **Partly angled sun blind**

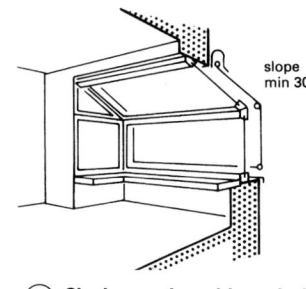
slope min 30°
⑥ **Sloping awning with vertical fringe**

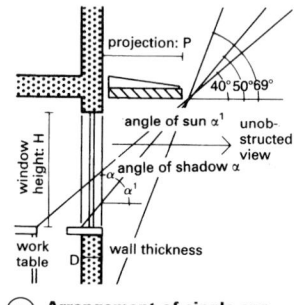
⑦ **Arrangement of single sun shades**

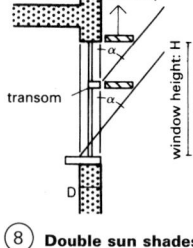
⑧ **Double sun shades**

angles of sun α^1 and angle of shadow α are given for a south wall at latitude 50° north → ⑦ – ⑧

21 June (summer solstice), midday
$\alpha^1 = 63°$; a = 27°

1 May and 31 July, midday
$\alpha^1 = 50°$; a = 40°

21 March and 23 Sept (equinox), midday
$\alpha^1 = 40°$; a = 50°

In general, projection P = tg angle of shadow α × height of window H; at the very smallest projection, P = (tg angle of shadow α × height of window H) – wall thickness D.

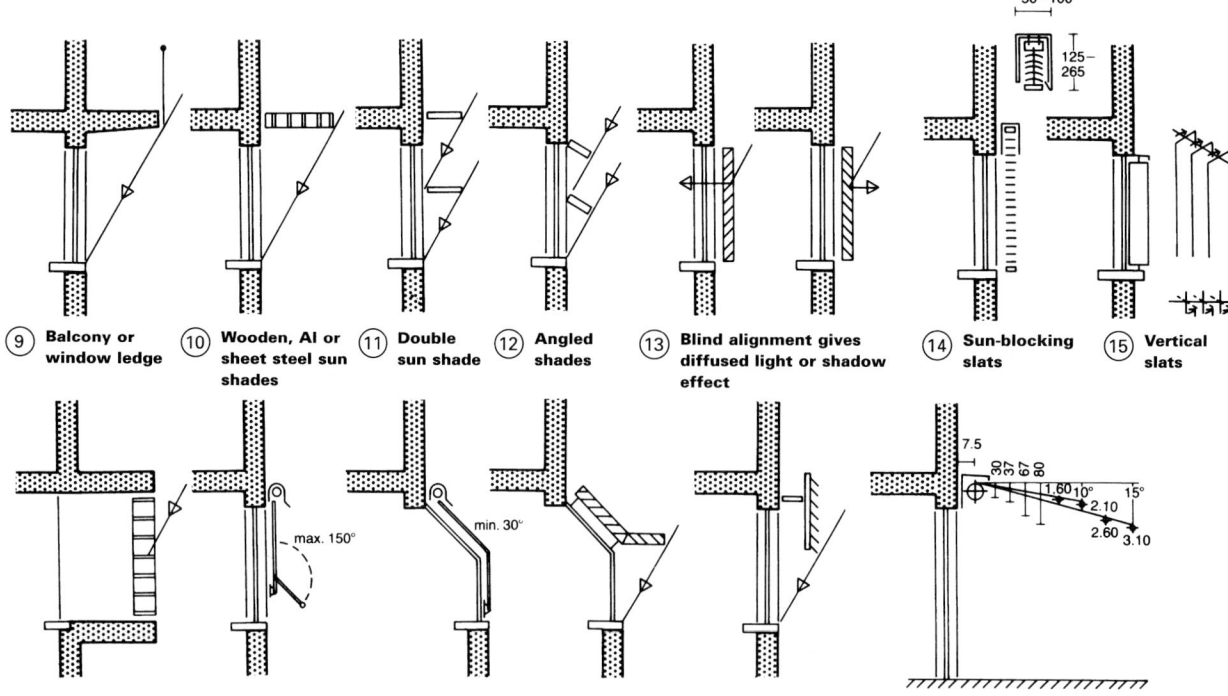

⑨ **Balcony or window ledge**
⑩ **Wooden, Al or sheet steel sun shades**
⑪ **Double sun shade**
⑫ **Angled shades**
⑬ **Blind alignment gives diffused light or shadow effect**
⑭ **Sun-blocking slats**
⑮ **Vertical slats**

⑯ **Sun screen**
⑰ **Partially angled blind**
⑱ **Sloping and vertical blind**
⑲ **Cantilevered screen**
⑳ **Projecting screen**
⑲ **Adjustable awning**

WINDOWS: TYPES AND DIMENSIONS

WAYS OF OPENING

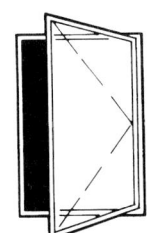

(1) **Fixed light**

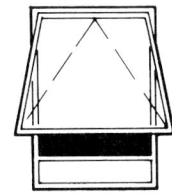

(2) **Casement, side hung**

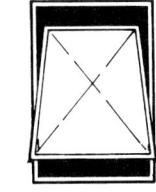

(3) **Casement, top hung**

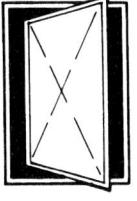

(4) **Casement, bottom hung**

(5) **Horizontally pivoted**

(6) **Vertically pivoted**

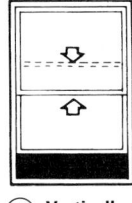

(7) **Vertically sliding**

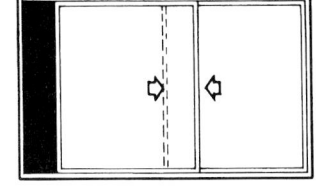

(8) **Horizontally sliding**

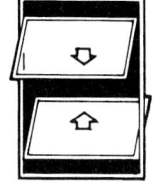

(9) **Linked hopper**

(10) **Projected, top hung**

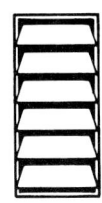

(11) **Louvred**

COORDINATING SIZES

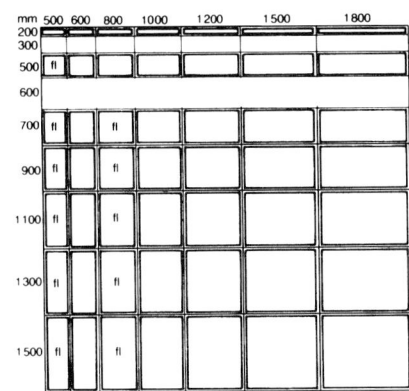

Note: BS and module 100 metric range includes doors & associated mixed lights (not shown); fl = fixed lights

(12) **Ranges of steel windows to BS 990: Part 2 and to 'Module 100 Metric Range' as given by Steel Window Association**

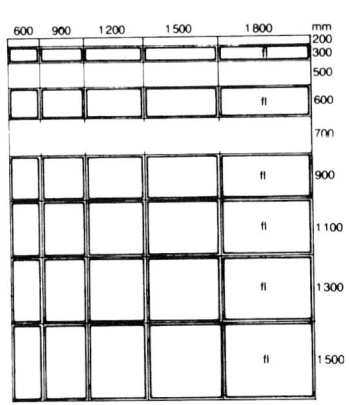

Note: This range also includes 1800 & 2100 h with fixed lights only; 2100 h include doors

(13) **Metric preferred range of W20 steel windows as specified by Steel Window Association**

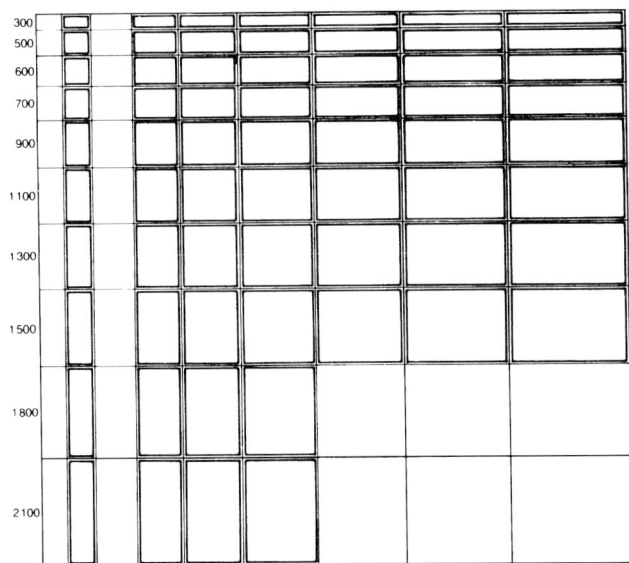

(14) **Ranges of aluminium windows to BS 4873 – wide range of windows including vertically and horizontally sliding types**

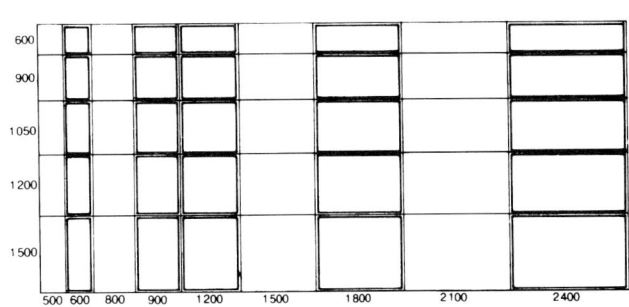

Note: Above diagrams intended for general guidance on overall sizes only; no distinction made between types of opening light; some sizes, fixed lights only (designated fl) obtainable in standard ranges

(15) **Dimensionally coordinated metric sizes for wood windows as recommended by British Wood-working Federation**

LOFT WINDOWS

In planning the size of windows, the optimum daylight level relative to the purpose of the room must be the deciding factor. For instance, building regulations require a minimum window area of $1/8$ of the floor surface area for living rooms → ⑪.

Large windows make living rooms more comfortable. The window width in secondary rooms can be chosen according to the distance between the rafters. Generously wide windows in living rooms can be achieved by the inclusion of rafter trimmers. Steeper roofs need shorter windows, while flatter roofs require longer windows. Roof windows can be joined using purpose-made prefabricated flashing, and can be arranged in rows or in combinations next to or above one another → ⑫ + ⑬

① **Pivoting windows**

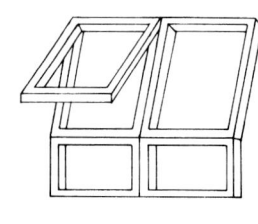

② **Top-hung windows; sliding**

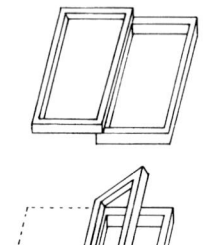

③ **Sliding windows; escape**

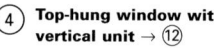

④ **Top-hung window with vertical unit** → ⑫

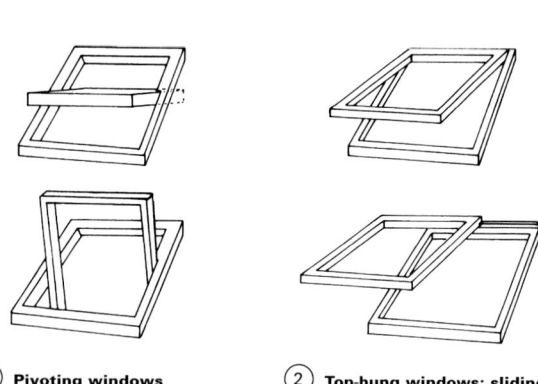

⑤ **Layout of roof windows**

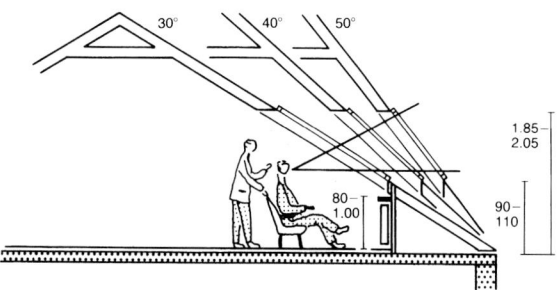

⑥ **At the eaves**

⑦ **With vertical unit**

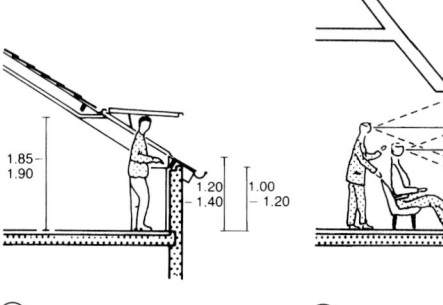

⑧ **Section of built-in options**

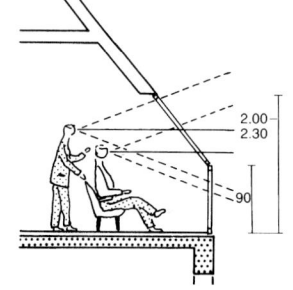

⑨ **Horizontal section**

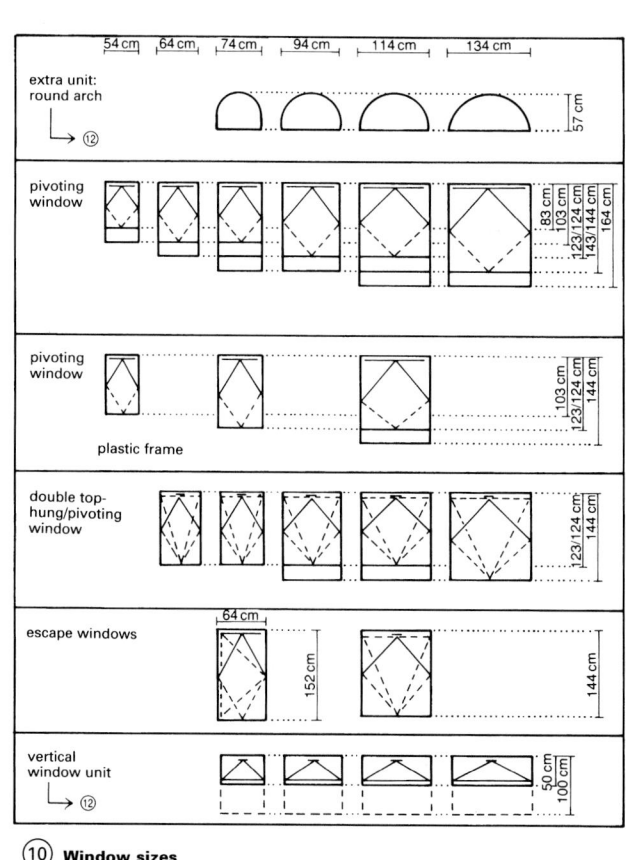

⑩ **Window sizes**

window size	54/83	54/103	64/103	74/103	74/123	74/144	114/123	114/144	134/144
surface area of light admission (m²)	0.21	0.28	0.36	0.44	0.55	0.66	0.93	1.12	1.36
room size (m²)	2	2–3	3–4	4–5	6–7	9	11	13	

⑪ **Calculation of window size, in relation to floor area**

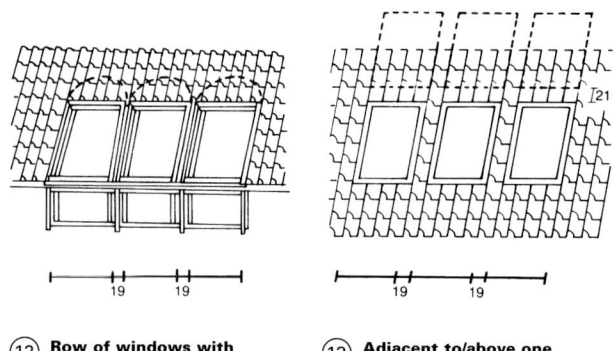

⑫ **Row of windows with vertical window units** → ⑩

⑬ **Adjacent to/above one another**

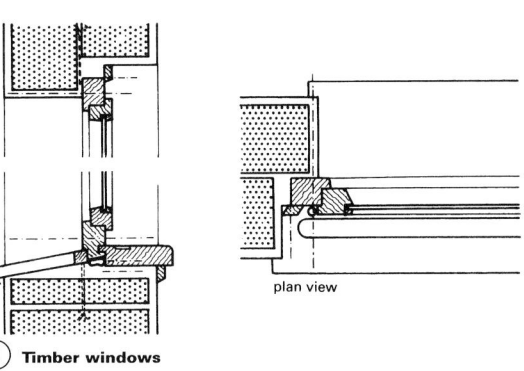

(1) **Timber windows**

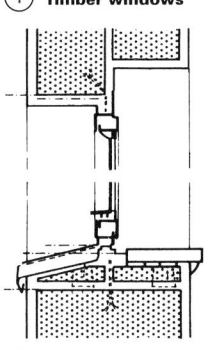
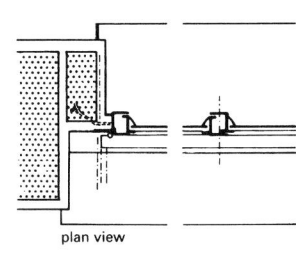

plan view

(2) **Steel windows**

(3) **Profiled steel tube windows**

plan view

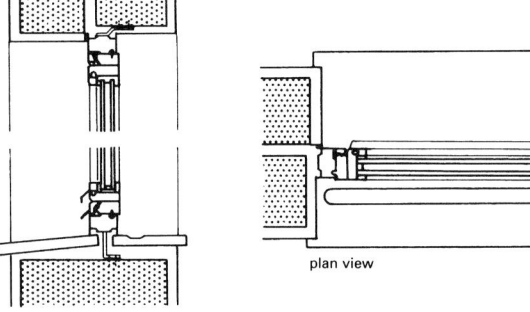

plan view

(4) **Plastic windows**

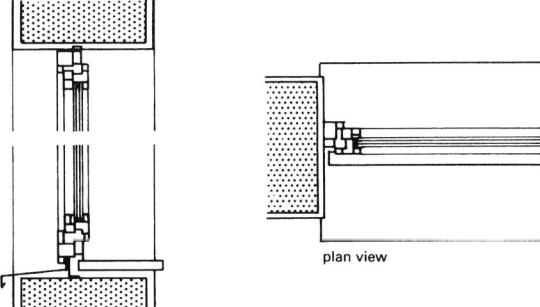

plan view

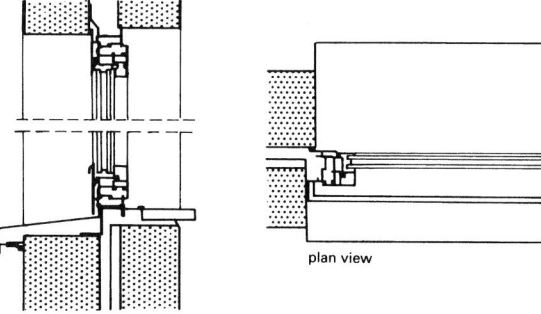

plan view

(5) **Aluminium windows**

WINDOWS AND DOORS

WINDOWS: CONSTRUCTION

Wooden sections for turning, turn and tilt, and tilting windows have been standardised. Windows are classified according to the type of casement → Ⓐ – Ⓓ or the type of frame → Ⓔ – Ⓗ. The many demands made on windows (e.g. protection against heat and noise) have resulted in a vast range of window shapes and designs → ① – ⑤. Externally mounted windows and French windows must at the very least be fitted with insulation or double glazing. The coefficient of heat transfer of a window must not exceed $3.1 W/m^2 K$.

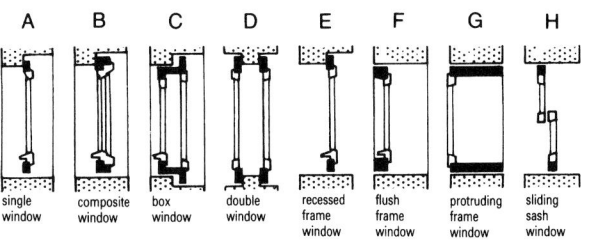

single window · composite window · box window · double window · recessed frame window · flush frame window · protruding frame window · sliding sash window

(6) **Window types**

1		2	3	4	5	6	7
description of glazing		glazing[1] C_G $Wm^{-2}K^{-1}$	C_W for windows and French doors, including frames of material group[2] $Wm^{-2}K^{-1}$				
			1	2.1	2.2	2.3	3
with use of normal glass							
1	single glazing	5.8	5.2				
2	double glazing: 6mm ≤ gap < 8mm	3.4	2.9	3.2	3.3	3.6	4.1
3	double glazing: 8mm ≤ gap < 10mm	3.2	2.8	3.0	3.2	3.4	4.0
4	double glazing: 10mm ≤ gap < 8mm	3.0	2.6	2.9	3.1	3.3	3.8
5	triple glazing: 6mm ≤ gap < 8mm (×2)	2.4	2.2	2.5	2.6	2.8	3.4
6	triple glazing: 8mm ≤ gap < 10mm (×2)	2.2	2.1	2.3	2.5	2.7	3.2
7	triple glazing: 10mm ≤ gap < 16mm (×2)	2.1	2.0	2.3	2.4	2.7	3.2
8	double glazing with 20 to 100mm between panes	2.8	2.6	2.7	2.9	3.2	3.7
9	double glazing with single glazing unit (normal glass; air gap 10 to 16mm) with 20 to 100mm between panes	2.0	1.9	2.2	2.4	2.6	3.1
10	double glazing with two double glazing units (air gap 10 to 15mm) with 20 to 100mm between the panes	1.4	1.5	1.8	1.9	2.2	2.7
11	glass brick wall with hollow glass bricks						3.5

[1] for windows in which the proportion of frame makes up no more than 5% of the total area (e.g. shop window installations) the coefficient of thermal conductance C_G can be substituted for the coefficient of thermal conductance C_W
[2] the classification of window frames into frame material groups 1 to 3 is to be done as outlined below

Group 1: Windows with frames of timber, plastic and timber combinations (e.g. timber frame with aluminium cladding) without any particular identification or if the coefficient of thermal conductance of the frame is proved with test certificates to be $C_W < 2.0 \ Wm^{-2}K^{-1}$
N.B. Sections for plastic windows are only to be classified under Group 1 when the plastic design profile is clearly defined and any possible metal inserts serve only decorative purposes

Group 2.1: Windows in frames of thermally insulated metal or concrete sections, if the coefficient of thermal conductance is proved with test certificates to be $C_F < 2.8 \ Wm^{-2}K^{-1}$

Group 2.2: Windows in frames of thermally insulated metal or concrete sections, if the coefficient of thermal conductance is proved with test certificates to be $2.8 < C_F < 3.6 \ Wm^{-2}K^{-1}$

(7) **Values of thermal conductance for glazing and for windows and French doors including the frames**

181

WINDOWS: CONSTRUCTION

Any window design must satisfy the technical requirements of the relevant parts of the building. The main considerations are the size, format, divisions, way of opening, frame material and surface treatment. Ventilation, thermal and sound insulation, fire resistance and general safety issues, including the use of security glazing, must also be taken into account. The design of the sections and the location and type of sealing are of great importance in guaranteeing a long-lasting water- and draught-proof seal. Built-in components such as roller shutter boxes, window sills and vents must match the noise insulation of the windows → ⑩ – ⑫ as well as other technical specifications.

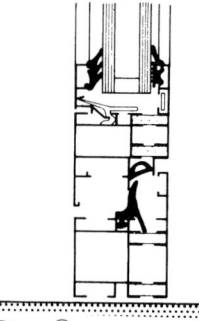

① Aluminium windows with flush mounted casements

② As ① but with thermally separated profile sections (up to 37 dB)

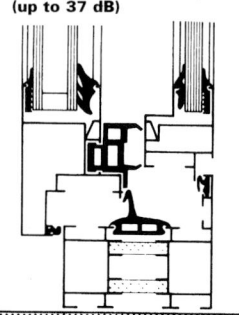

③ Universal aluminium window into which a sun screen can be fitted (up to 47 dB)

④ Aluminium thermally separated composite casement window (up to 47 dB)

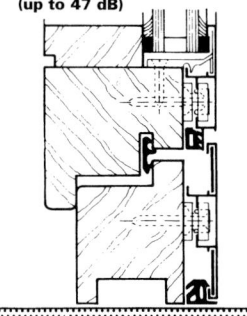

⑤ Aluminium thermally separated sliding window (up to 35 dB)

⑥ Aluminium/timber combination casement window (up to 40 dB)

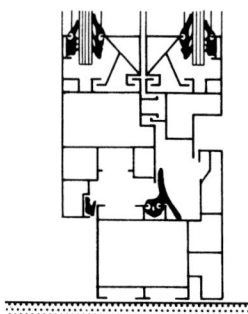

⑦ Plastic window with aluminium facing frame (up to 42 dB)

⑧ Plastic double glazed window, composite casement, intra-pane sun screen (up to 45 dB)

⑨ Coordinating sizes of (horizontally and vertically) aluminium sliding windows to BS 4873

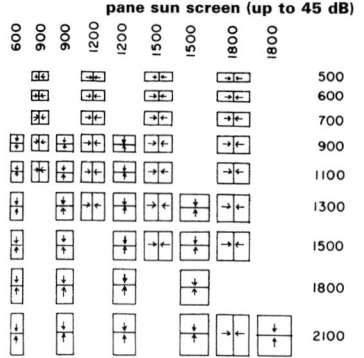

type of street	distance: window to middle of road (m)	daytime traffic density: vehicles per hour	noise band
residential street		< 10	0
two-lane	< 35		0
residential street	26–35	10–50	I
	11–25		II
	⩽ 10		III
residential main road (2 lane)	> 100		0
	36–100	50–200	II
	26–35		III
	11–25		III
	⩽ 10		IV
country road, built-up area[1] (2 lane)	101–300		I
	101–300		II
	36–100	200–1000	III
residential main road (2 lane)	11–35		IV
	⩽ 10		
urban main roads, industrial areas	101–300		III
	36–100	1000–3000	IV
	> 35		V
main roads 4 to 6 lanes	101–300		IV
motorway feeder roads and motorways	⩽ 100	3000–5000	V

[1] apply the next highest noise level band for surburban built-up areas and roads in commercial areas

⑩ How loud is it?

applicable noise level band	average external noise level (dB)	necessary window sound insulation R_w (dB) in residential habitable rooms of housing [1]
0	⩽ 50	25 (30)
I	51–55	25 (30)
II	56–60	30 (35)
III	61–65	35 (40)
IV	66–70	40 (45)
V	> 70	40 (45)

[2] values in brackets apply to outside walls and must also be used for windows if these form more than 60% of the outside wall surface

⑪ Selecting sound insulation

noise insulation class	noise insulation value (dB)	guiding remarks for design characteristics of windows and ventilation equipment
6	50	box windows with separate recessed frames specially sealed and very large gap between the panes; glazed with thick glass
5	45–49	box windows with special sealing, large gap between frames and glazed with thick glass; double glazed composite casement windows with isolated casement frames, special sealing, more than 100 mm between panes and glazed with thick glass
4	40–44	box windows with extra sealing and average density glazing; double glazed composite casement windows with special sealing, over 60 mm between panes and glazed with thick glass
3	35–39	box windows without extra sealing and with average density glass; double glazed composite casement windows with extra sealing, normal distance between panes and glazed with thick glass; sturdy double/triple glazing units; 12 mm glass in fixed or well-sealed opening windows
2	30–34	composite casement windows with extra sealing and average density glazing; thick double glazing units; in fixed or well-sealed opening windows; 6 mm glass, in fixed or well-sealed opening windows
1	25–29	double glazed composite casement windows with extra sealing and average density glazing; thin double glazing units in windows without extra sealing
0	20–24	unsealed windows with single glazing or double glazing unit

⑫ Noise insulation classification for windows

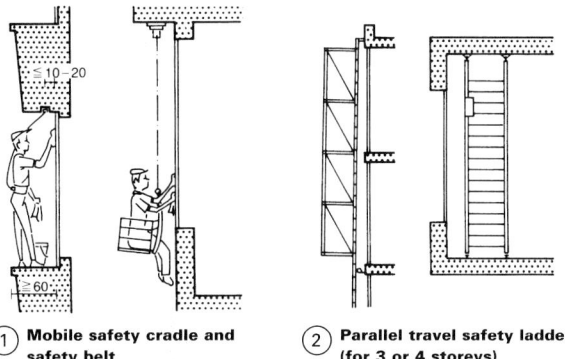

① Mobile safety cradle and safety belt

② Parallel travel safety ladders (for 3 or 4 storeys)

Safety belts with straps, safety cables or safety apparatus for working at heights should be used as a protection against falls → ①.

Façade hoists and mobile equipment (allowing access to fixed glazing) for cleaning windows and façades → ⑧ – ⑪ are available to carry out maintenance and repair work (thus saving the cost of scaffolding). If fitted at the right time, they can be used to carry out minor building work (such as fixing blinds, installing windows etc.). With slight modifications, façade hoists and access equipment can be used as rescue apparatus in the event of a fire. The options available include mobile suspended ladders mounted on rails, trackless roof gantry equipment with a cradle, and a rail-mounted roof gantry with a cradle and attached to the roof deck or the balustrade.

Suspended aluminium ladder equipment (for façade access) → ② consists of a suspended mobile ladder on rails. The width of the ladder is 724 mm or 840 mm, and the total overall length is 25 m maximum, depending on the shape of the building. The maximum safe working load (S.W.L.) is 200 kg (i.e. two men and the apparatus itself). Alternatives are available, such as maintenance gangways → ⑤ and cleaning balconies → ⑥.

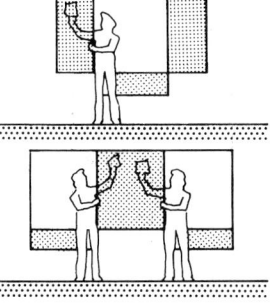

③ Adjacent window cleaning

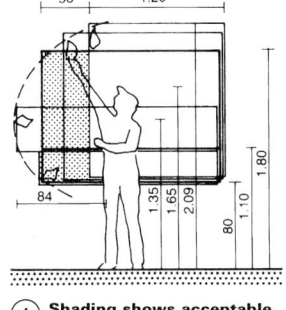

④ Shading shows acceptable cleaning surface area

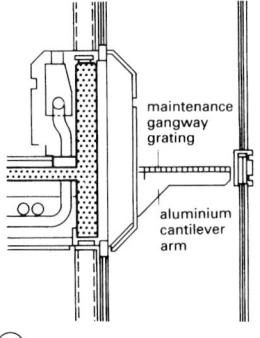

⑤ Maintenance gangway

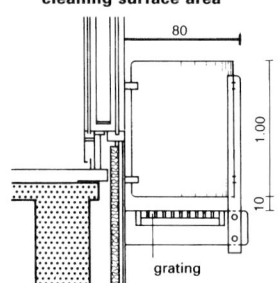

⑥ Cleaning platform

type of building	outside window	roof window
offices	every 3 months*	every 12 months
public offices	every 2 weeks	3 months
shops	every week (inside, 2 weeks)	6 months
shops (high street)	daily	3 months
hospitals	3 months	6 months
schools	3–4 months	12 months
hotels (first class)	2 weeks	3 months
factories (precision work)	4 weeks	3 months
factories (heavy industry)	2 months	6 months
private house	4–6 weeks	–

* ground floor windows must be cleaned more frequently

⑦ Intervals of time for window cleaning

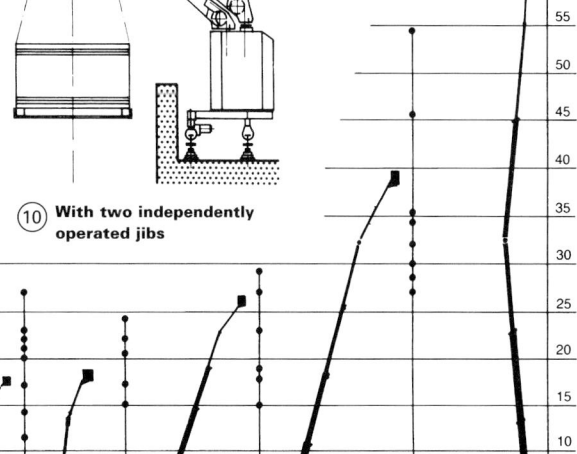

⑧ One person façade cradle hoist

⑨ Parallelogram jib action

⑩ With two independently operated jibs

Gardemann system

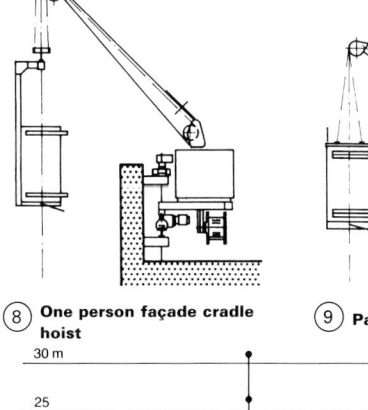

⑪ Work platform hoists

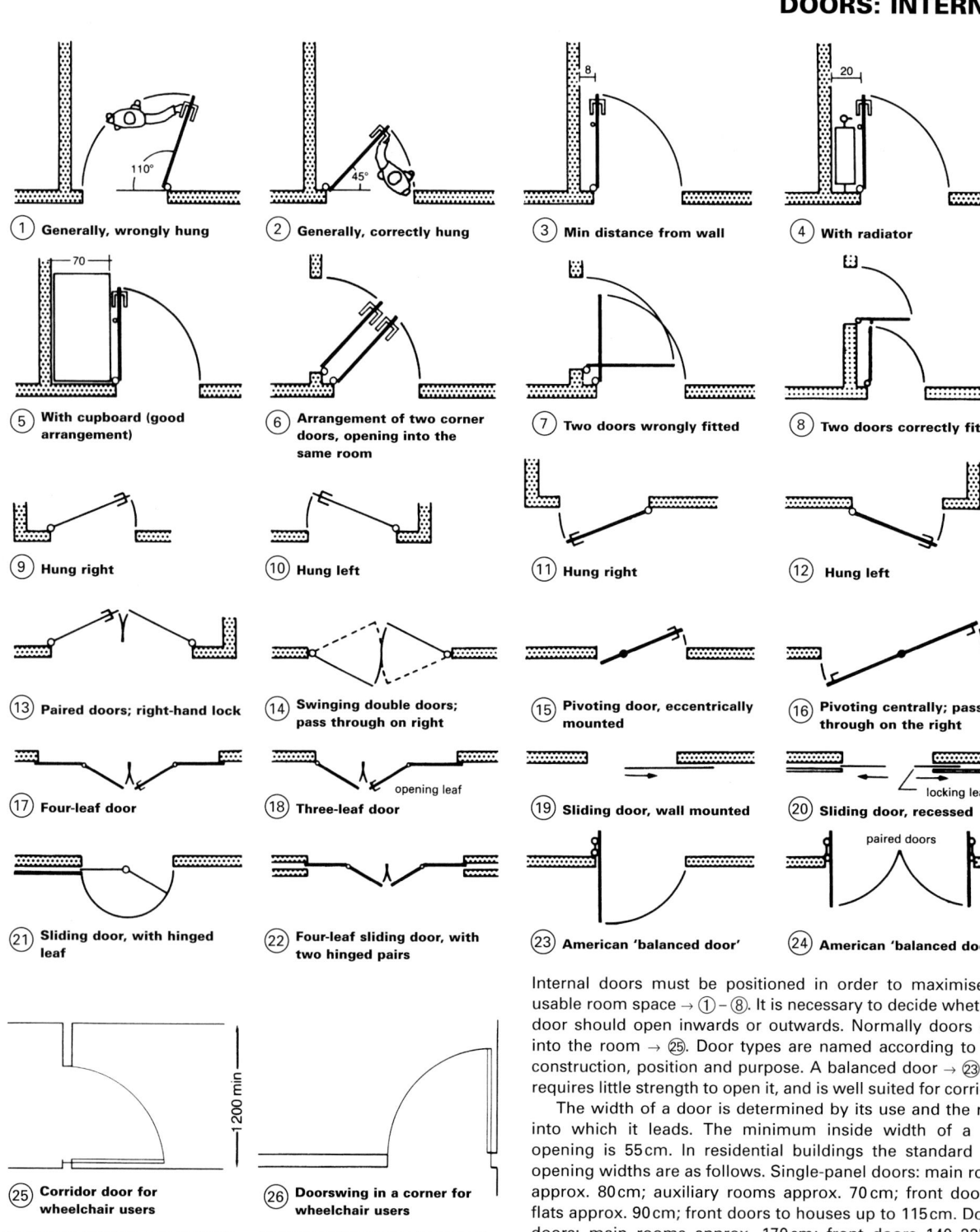

① **Generally, wrongly hung**

② **Generally, correctly hung**

③ **Min distance from wall**

④ **With radiator**

⑤ **With cupboard (good arrangement)**

⑥ **Arrangement of two corner doors, opening into the same room**

⑦ **Two doors wrongly fitted**

⑧ **Two doors correctly fitted**

⑨ **Hung right**

⑩ **Hung left**

⑪ **Hung right**

⑫ **Hung left**

⑬ **Paired doors; right-hand lock**

⑭ **Swinging double doors; pass through on right**

⑮ **Pivoting door, eccentrically mounted**

⑯ **Pivoting centrally; pass through on the right**

⑰ **Four-leaf door**

⑱ **Three-leaf door**

⑲ **Sliding door, wall mounted**

⑳ **Sliding door, recessed**

㉑ **Sliding door, with hinged leaf**

㉒ **Four-leaf sliding door, with two hinged pairs**

㉓ **American 'balanced door'**

㉔ **American 'balanced door'**

㉕ **Corridor door for wheelchair users**

㉖ **Doorswing in a corner for wheelchair users**

㉗ **Door panel shapes**

Internal doors must be positioned in order to maximise the usable room space → ① – ⑧. It is necessary to decide whether a door should open inwards or outwards. Normally doors open into the room → ㉕. Door types are named according to their construction, position and purpose. A balanced door → ㉓ + ㉔ requires little strength to open it, and is well suited for corridors.

The width of a door is determined by its use and the room into which it leads. The minimum inside width of a door opening is 55cm. In residential buildings the standard door opening widths are as follows. Single-panel doors: main rooms approx. 80cm; auxiliary rooms approx. 70cm; front doors to flats approx. 90cm; front doors to houses up to 115cm. Double doors: main rooms approx. 170cm; front doors 140–225cm. Door opening height at least 185cm, but normally 195–200cm. Sliding and revolving doors are not permitted for escape or exit doors, as they could block the route in an emergency.

Disabled persons have special requirements. The minimum convenient door width for the ambulant disabled is 80cm. This is too narrow for wheelchair users, but 90cm is usually adequate. There should be adequate space to position a wheelchair beside the door. Corridors should be not less than 120cm wide so that wheelchair users can position themselves to open a door in the end wall of a corridor or at the side. An end door should be offset to give maximum space beside the handle. Similarly, when a door is located in the corner of a room, it should be hinged at the side nearer the corner → ㉕, ㉕

DOORS: SIZES AND FRAMES

The sizes of wall apertures for doors → ① are nominal standard building sizes. If, in exceptional cases, other sizes are necessary, the building standard size for them must be whole number multiples of 125 mm (100 mm according to British Standards). Steel frames can be used as left- as well as right-hand frames → ⑩.

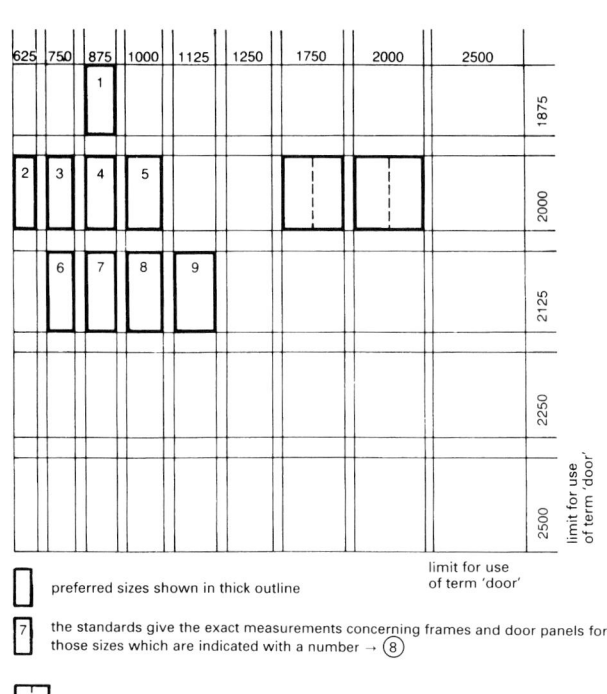

preferred sizes shown in thick outline

limit for use of term 'door'

7 the standards give the exact measurements concerning frames and door panels for those sizes which are indicated with a number → ⑧

structural openings for these preferred sizes are, as a rule, for double doors

① **Typical structural opening sizes to DIN 4172 → ⑧**

	nominal standard building size		size of door panel				size of door frame	
	standard structural opening sizes for doors		standard overall door dimensions		door rebate size, nominal dimensions		door opening width at the rebate	door opening height at the rebate
					tolerance ± 1	+ 2;– 0	tol. ± 1	tol. + 0; –2
1	875	1875	860	1880	834	1847	841	1858
2	625	2000	610	1985	584	1972	591	1983
3	750	2000	735	1985	709	1972	716	1983
4	875	2000	860	1985	834	1972	841	1983
5	1000	2000	985	1985	959	1972	966	1983
6	750	2125	735	2110	709	2097	716	2108
7	875	2125	860	2110	834	2097	841	2108
8	1000	2125	985	2110	959	2097	966	2108
9	1125	2125	1110	2110	1084	2097	1091	2108

⑧ **Standard rebated door panels and door frames**

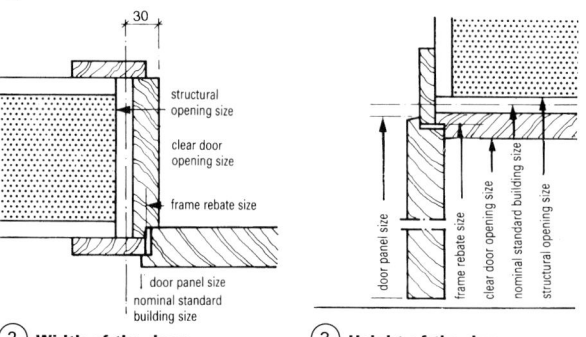

② **Width of the door**

③ **Height of the door**

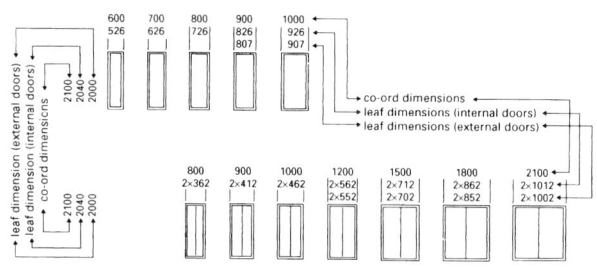

⑨ **Sizes of internal and external doors to BS 4787: Part 1**

④ **Width of the door (UK)**

⑤ **Height of the door (UK)**

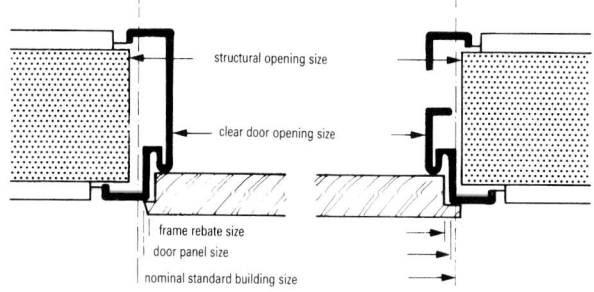

⑩ **Standard steel frame types**

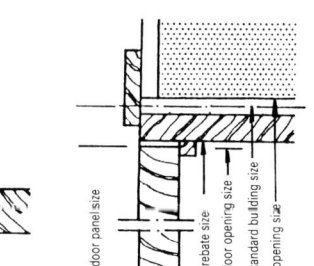

⑥ **Recessed door frame**

⑦ **Full lining door frame (UK)**

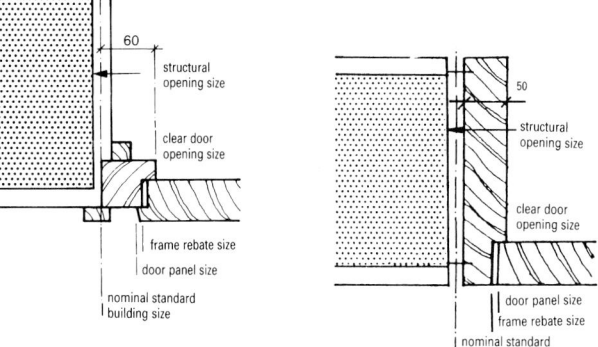

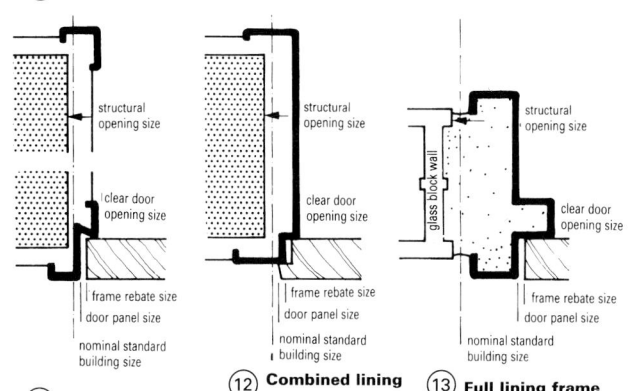

⑪ **Architrave frame**

⑫ **Combined lining and architrave frame**

⑬ **Full lining frame**

REVOLVING AND SLIDING DOORS

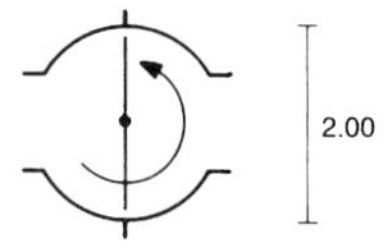

① **Revolving door, two panels**
2.00 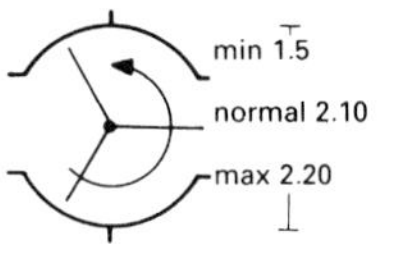

② **With three panels**
min 1.5
normal 2.10
max 2.20

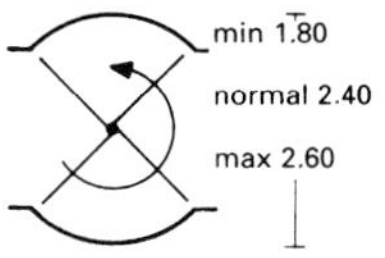

③ **With four panels**
min 1.80
normal 2.40
max 2.60

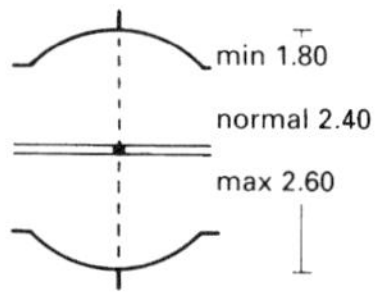

④ **Four panels, folded back**
min 1.80
normal 2.40
max 2.60

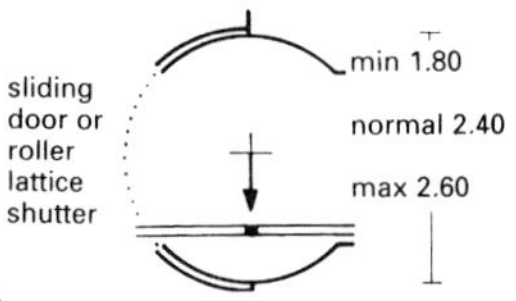

⑤ **Door assembly pushed to side**
sliding door or roller lattice shutter
min 1.80
normal 2.40
max 2.60

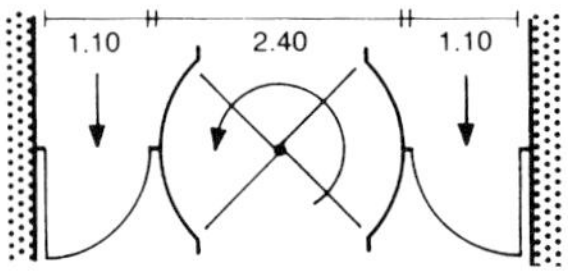

⑥ **Revolving door with extra emergency exits**
1.10   2.40   1.10

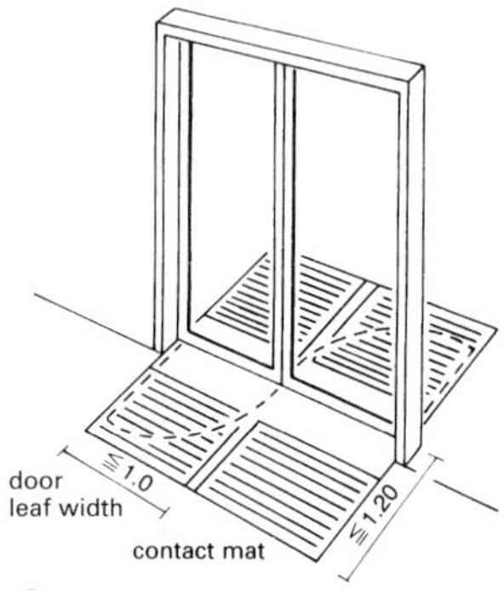

⑦ **Automatic hinged doors**
door leaf width ≦ 1.0
≦ 1.20
contact mat

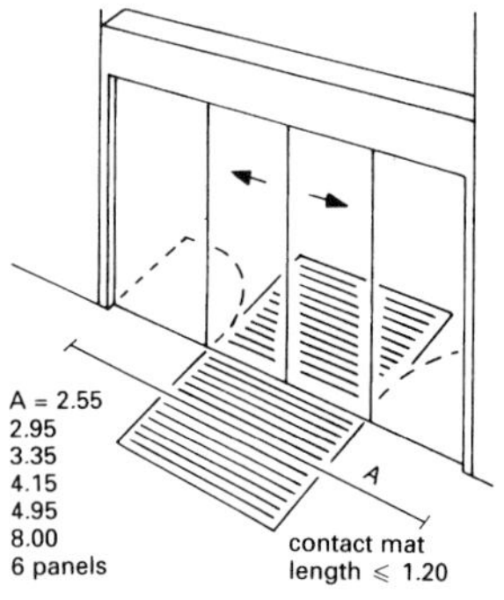

⑧ **Automatic sliding doors**
A = 2.55
2.95
3.35
4.15
4.95
8.00
6 panels
contact mat length ≦ 1.20

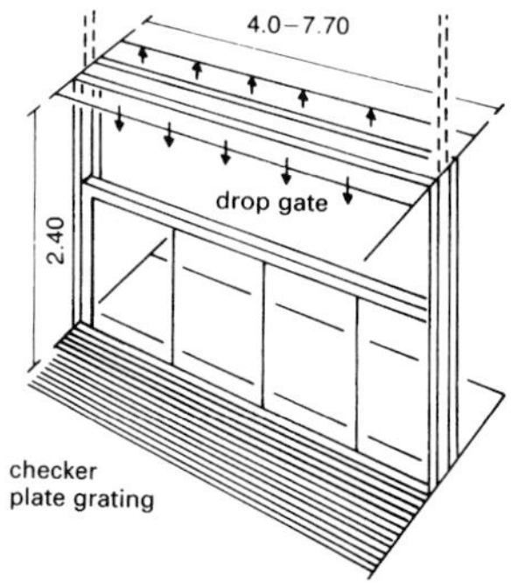

⑨ **Drop gate installation**
4.0 – 7.70
drop gate
2.40
checker plate grating

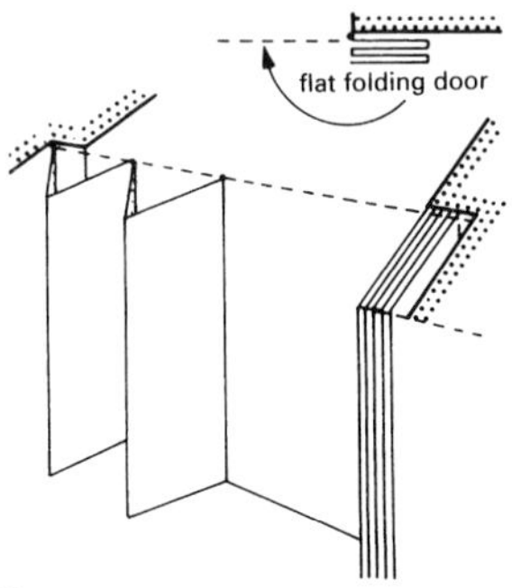

⑩ **Folding door with side guides**
flat folding door

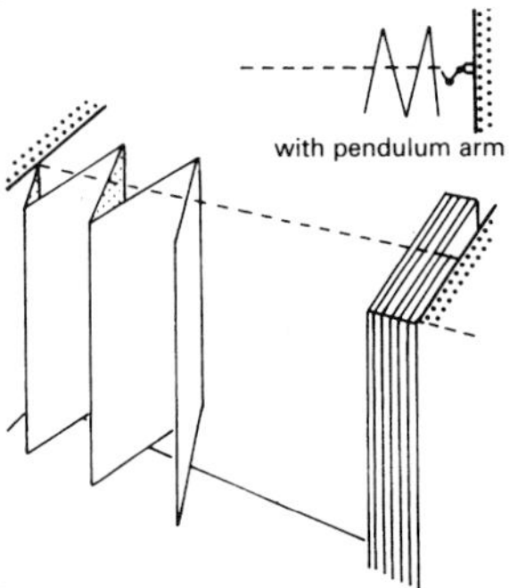

⑪ **Folding door with central guides (concertina door)**
with pendulum arm

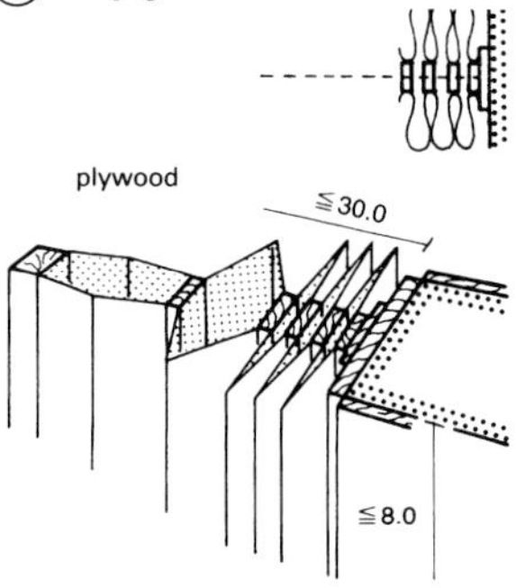

⑫ **Accordion door; wood panels or flexible material**
plywood
≦ 30.0
≦ 8.0

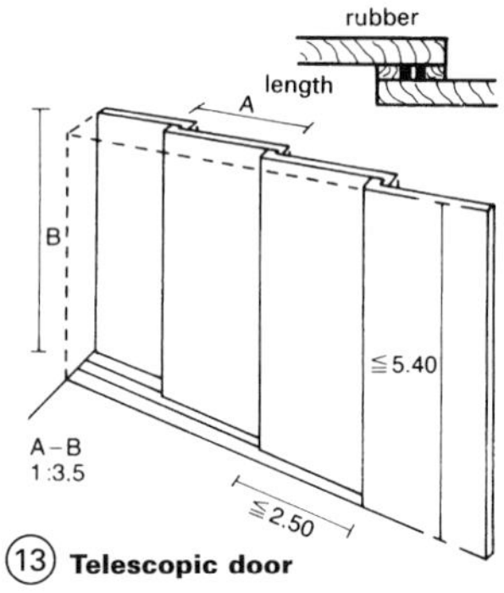

⑬ **Telescopic door**
rubber
length
A
B
≦ 5.40
A – B
1 : 3.5
≦ 2.50

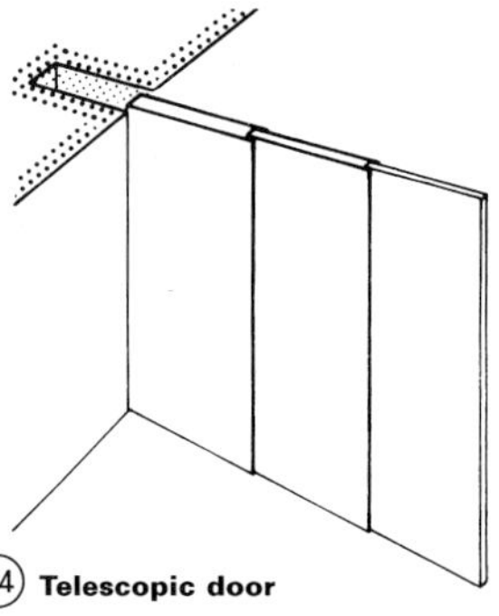

⑭ **Telescopic door**

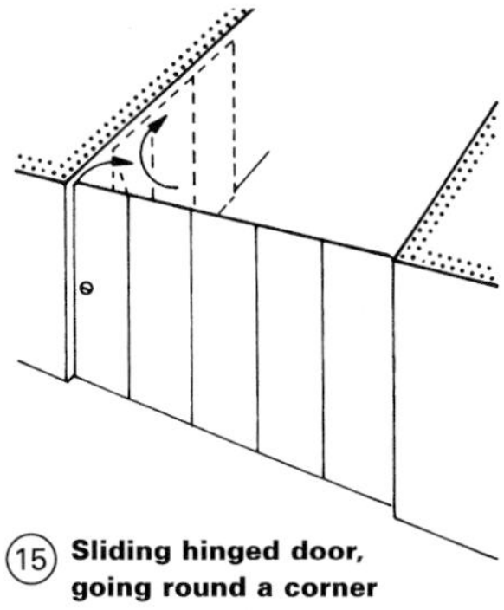

⑮ **Sliding hinged door, going round a corner**

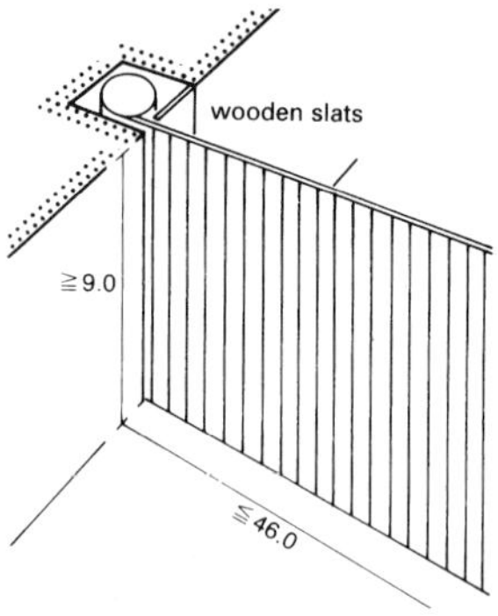

⑯ **Roller wall**
wooden slats
≧ 9.0
≦ 46.0

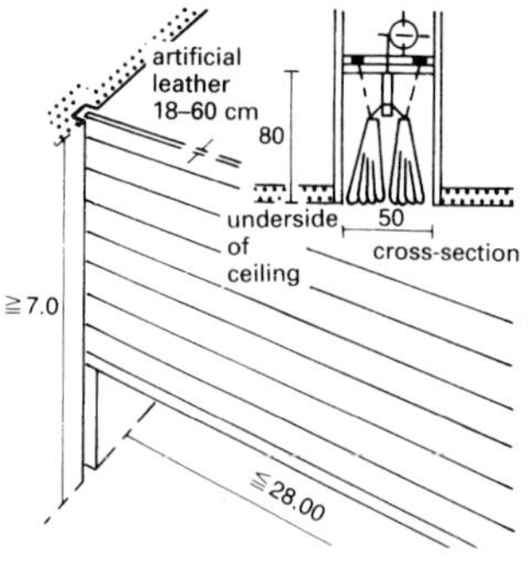

⑰ **Partition curtain**
artificial leather 18–60 cm
80
underside of ceiling
50
cross-section
≧ 7.0
≦ 28.00

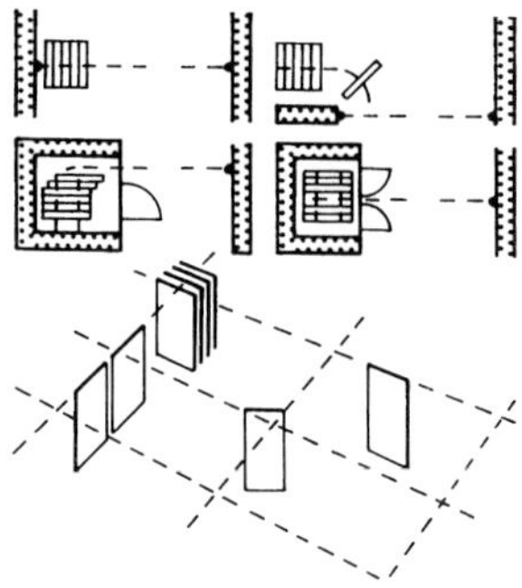

⑱ **Variable sliding doors**

⑲ **Air curtain installation → ⑨**

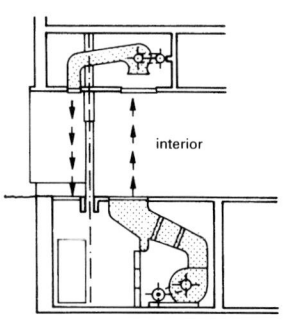
interior

Revolving doors are made in several different designs → ① – ⑥. Some are adjustable, e.g. when the number of users is large, particularly in the summer, the panels can be folded into the middle to allow people to go in on one side and out on the other at the same time. Some designs have panels which can be pushed to the side if traffic is only in one direction (e.g. when business closes for the day).

Actuating devices for *automatic doors* can be controlled by radar, electric contact mats → ⑦ – ⑧ or pneumatic floor contacts. Unidirectional or reflecting light barriers controlling automatic sliding doors with six panels up to 8 m wide are ideal for installation on emergency escape routes in office blocks, public buildings and supermarkets. Air curtain doors → ⑲ can be shut off at night by a raised door → ⑨.

Room dividers can be provided by the use of folding doors, guided from the side → ⑩. Concertina doors are centrally hung → ⑪ for closing off wide openings. A revolving movement can be combined with a sliding movement. Accordion doors can be made of plywood, artificial leather or cloth → ⑫.

Telescopic doors have several panels joined by engagers. Externally guided telescopic doors are single-skinned → ⑬; those with internal guides are double-skinned → ⑭. These doors can move alongside each other → ⑬ or retract inside each other → ⑭. Sliding wall doors, suspended from above, can be guided round corners → ⑮ or can be used as flexible enclosures → ⑱.

Curtain partitions can be folded down from above → ⑰, or can move horizontally with guides above → ⑯. They allow large rooms to be divided up into sections.

GARAGE/WAREHOUSE DOORS

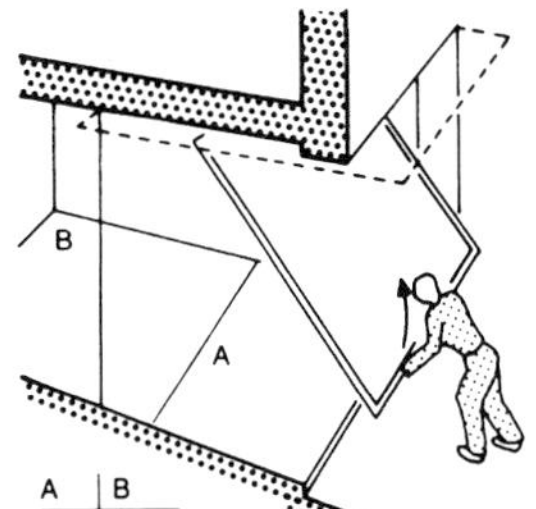

Up and over doors can be used for garages and similar installations → ①. They can be folding doors, or doors with a spring counterbalance or a counterbalance weight. They can have a single or a double skin, and be solid, partially glazed or fully glazed. They can have wooden panels, or be made of plastic, aluminium or galvanised sheet steel. The largest available dimensions for access purposes are 4.82 m × 1.96 m, and the maximum panel area is approx. 10 m². Up and over doors are also available in arched segments. They are easy to operate since the door drive is mounted on the ceiling and controlled by radio.

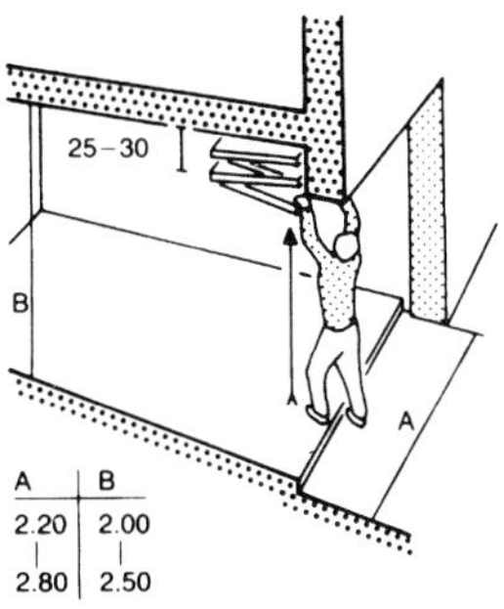

Also available are lifting folding doors → ②, sectional doors → ③, telescopic lifting doors → ④ and roller shutter doors made of aluminium → ⑤ which are completely out of the way when open. Single- or multiple-skin doors can be used for industrial, transport and workshop buildings. The maximum available size is 18 m wide and 6 m high. These doors can be activated by a ceiling pull switch, a light barrier, an induction loop or remote control (either electric or pneumatic), or contact pads.

Drive-through doors should be power-operated for speed → ⑧. Rubber swing doors → ⑨ and single-layer clear PVC are resistant to abrasion and impact, and PVC strip curtains are also available → ⑩. Rubber sections which serve as door seals and rubber cushion seals are available for loading and unloading from docks and in and out of heated storage depots. They give protection from the effects of the weather during these operations → ⑪, ⑫.

Fire protection doors T30–T90 can be single- or double-leaf → ⑬. Sliding fire protection doors are also available → ⑭. Any movable fire-resistant barrier, such as sliding, lifting or swing doors, must be able to operate independently of the mains electricity supply. In the event of fire, they must close automatically. (See also p. 130.)

A	B
2.25	190
2.50	201
3.00	212⁵
3.37	225
	237⁵

≤ 20 m² standard door

① **Up and over doors**

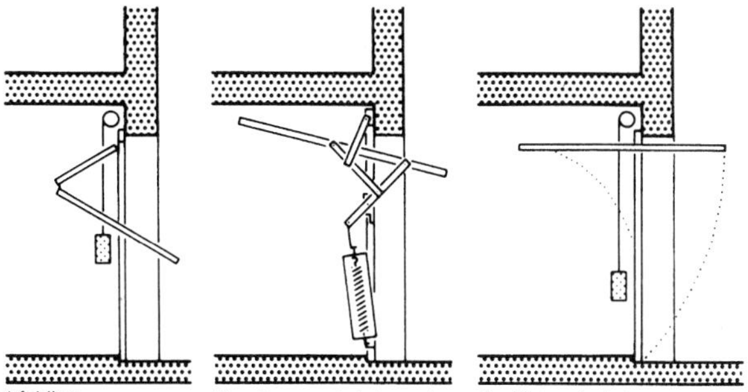

a) folding
b) spring counterbalanced, no rails, suspended from the ceiling
c) with counterbalance weight

25–30

A	B
2.20	2.00
2.80	2.50

② **Folding, lift door**

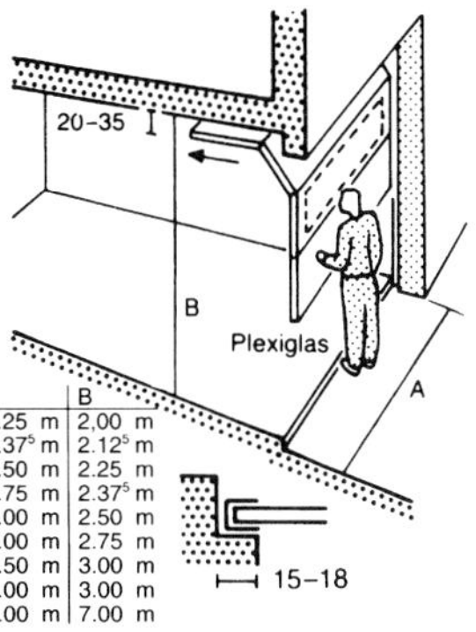

20–35

Plexiglas

A	B
2.25 m	2.00 m
2.37⁵ m	2.12⁵ m
2.50 m	2.25 m
2.75 m	2.37⁵ m
3.00 m	2.50 m
4.00 m	2.75 m
4.50 m	3.00 m
5.00 m	3.00 m
8.00 m	7.00 m

15–18

③ **Linked up and over door (sectional)**

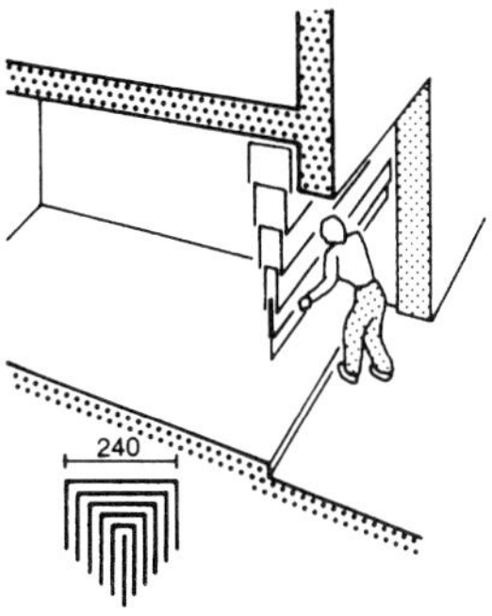

240

④ **Telescopic lifting door**

40–95

A	B
2.00	2.00
8.00	8.00

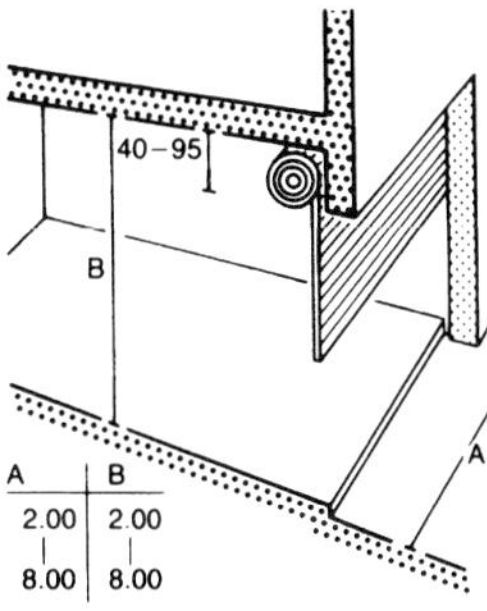

⑤ **Roller shutter door (in steel or aluminium)**

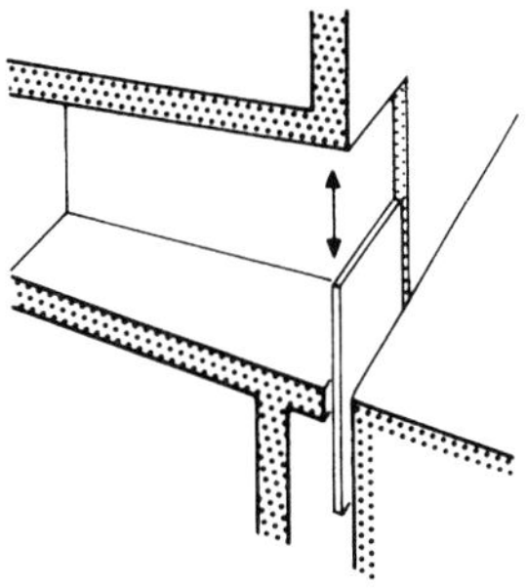

⑥ **Drop door**

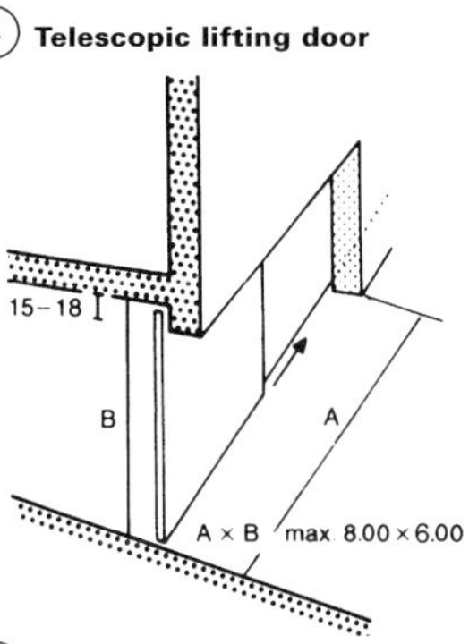

15–18

A × B max 8.00 × 6.00

⑦ **Sliding door (steel T30–T90)**

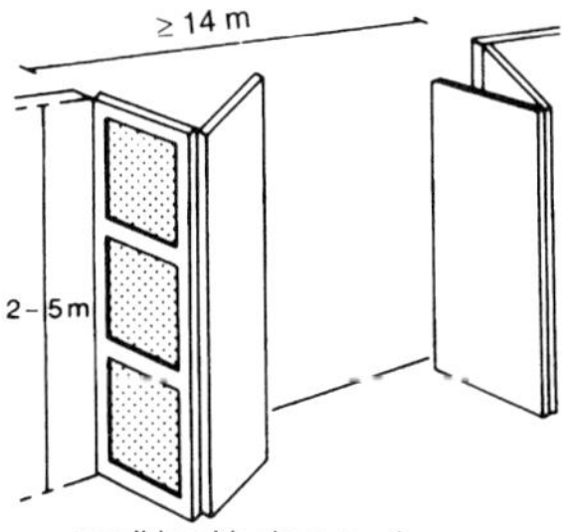

≥ 14 m

2–5 m

possibly with glass panels

⑧ **Power operated folding door (quick operation)**

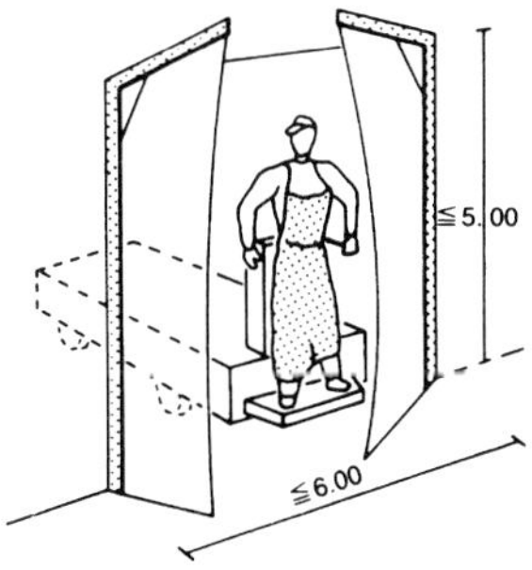

≤ 5.00

≤ 6.00

⑨ **Rubber swing door**

⑩ **PVC strip curtains for large drive-through passages**

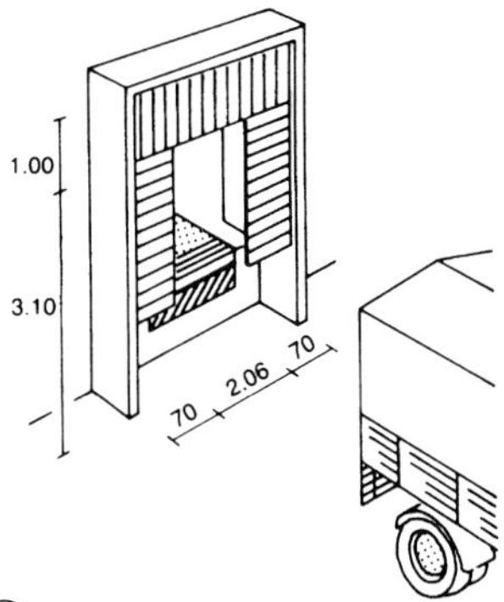

1.00

3.10

70 2.06 70

⑪ **Rubber segment door seal**

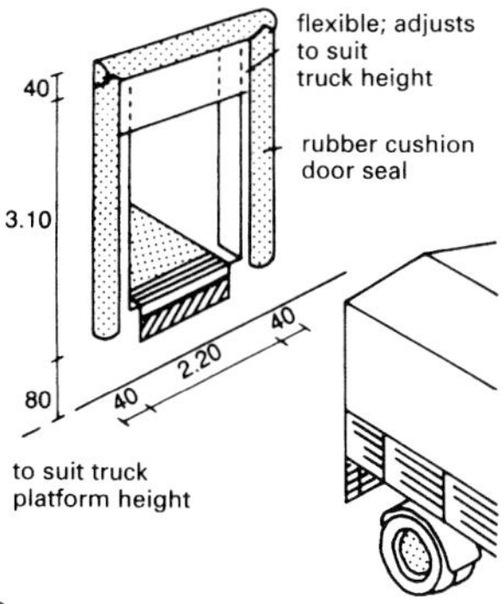

flexible; adjusts to suit truck height

rubber cushion door seal

40

3.10

80 40 2.20 40

to suit truck platform height

⑫ **Rubber cushion door seal**

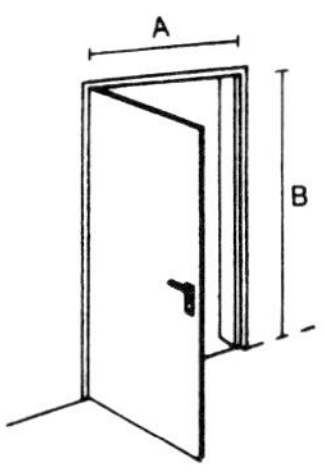

single leaf

A	B
75	1.75
75	1.875
75	2.00
80	1.80
80	1.875
80	2.00
875	1.875
875	2.00
1.00	1.875
1.00	2.00
1.00	2.125

double leaf

1.50	2.00
1.75	
2.00	
2.25	2.125

⑬ **Fire doors T30–T90**

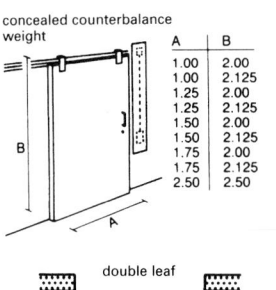

concealed counterbalance weight

A	B
1.00	2.00
1.00	2.125
1.25	2.00
1.25	2.125
1.50	2.00
1.50	2.125
1.75	2.00
1.75	2.125
2.50	2.50

double leaf

⑭ **Sliding fire doors T30–T90**

LOCKING SYSTEMS

Cylinder locks offer the greatest security, for it is virtually impossible to open them with tools. The cylinder lock developed by Linus Yale is very different from other locking systems. There are profile, oval, round and half cylinder locks. Cylinder locks are supplied with extensions as necessary on one or both sides, increasing in increments of 5 mm, to suit the thickness of the door → ⑥.

During the planning and ordering phase for a locking system, a locking plan is drawn up which includes a unique security certificate. Replacement keys are only supplied after production of this document.

Combination key systems

With a combination key system, the key of the entrance door to each flat also opens all doors to shared facilities as well as shared access doors, e.g. courtyard, basement or main front door. This is suitable for houses with multiple family occupancy or estate houses → ①.

Master key systems

In a master key system, a principal pass key opens all locks throughout the complete system. This is suitable for single family occupancy houses, schools and restaurants.

Central key systems

With a central key system, several combination key systems are combined. This is suitable for blocks of flats → ③. Separate keys unlock the front door to each flat and to all shared facilities. In addition, there is a master key which unlocks all the shared doors in the blocks.

General master key systems

A general master key system consists of multiple master key systems. The general master key allows one person access to all rooms. It is possible to subdivide areas by using main and group keys. Each cylinder has its own individual lock and, with the exception of the correct master (or pass) key, can only be opened with its own key.

This system is suitable for factories, commercial premises, airports and hotels → ④. Vulnerable points which should be taken into account during the planning stage are set out in → ⑤.

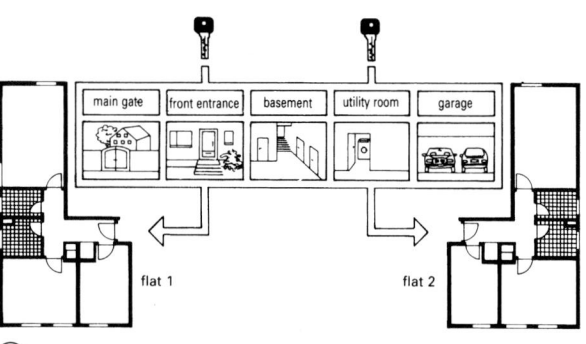

① Combination key system

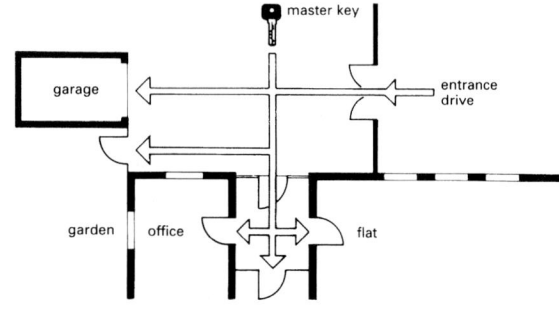

② Master key system

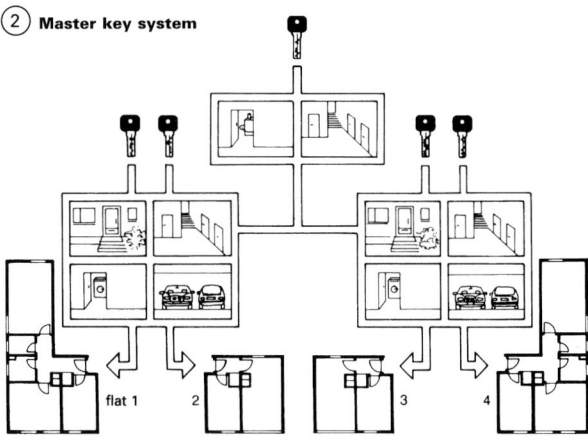

③ Combined combination key and master key system

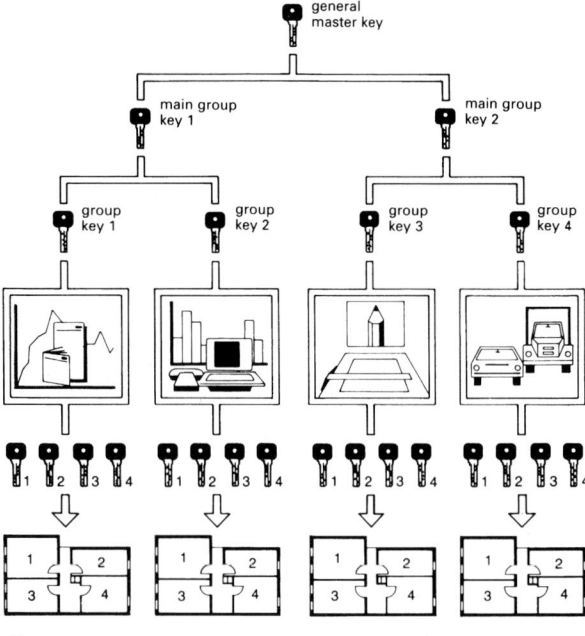

④ General master key system

filing cabinets, bath cubicles, letter boxes, access doors, emergency exit doors, cloakrooms, locks for boxes, cold stores, furniture doors, tubular framed doors, roller shutter doors, cupboard doors, writing desks, sliding bolts, changing cubicles	at risk
lift machinery room, lift switch box, electricity rooms, garage access doors, garage up and over doors, lattice gates, boiler room doors, basement doors, oil filler pipes, distribution boxes	strongly at risk
main office doors, skylights, tilt and turn windows, computer rooms, main entrance doors, gratings, front entrance doors to blocks of flats, trap doors, basement windows, fan lights, switch boxes	very strongly at risk

⑤ Check list

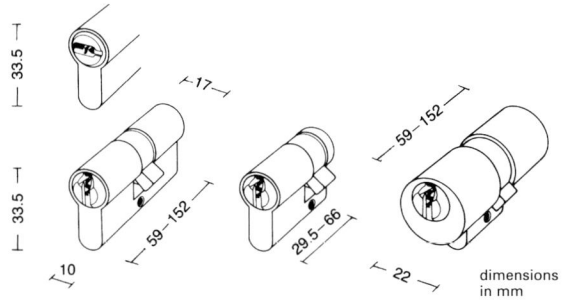

⑥ Cylinder lock: profile, half, round

SECURITY OF BUILDINGS AND GROUNDS

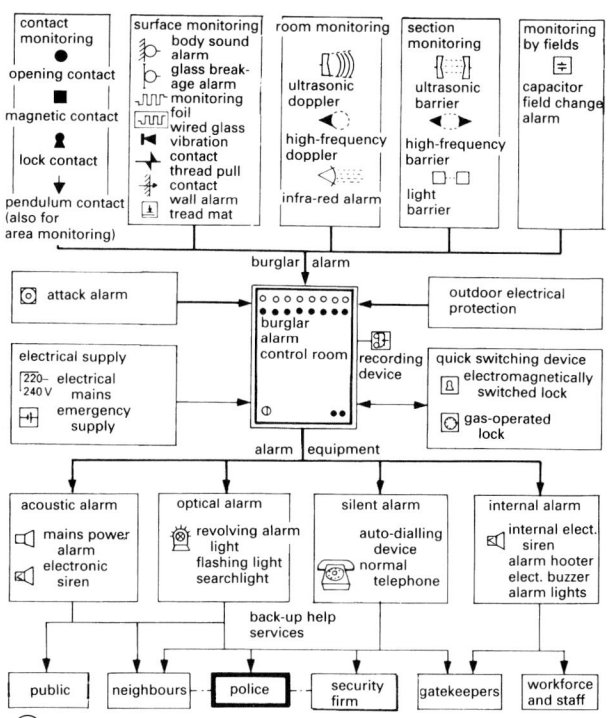

① **Burglar alarm systems (installation and working method)**

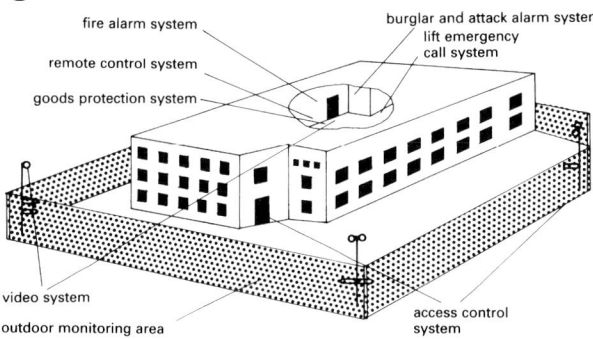

② **Security systems**

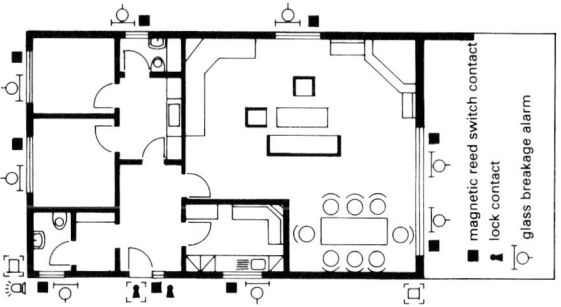

③ **Outer perimeter security on private premises**

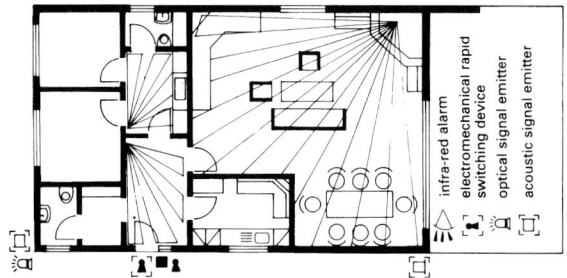

④ **Security in the industrial and community sectors**

The term 'security technology' is to be understood as covering all devices used for defence against criminal danger to the body, life or valuables. In reality, all parts of a building can be penetrated, even those made of steel and reinforced concrete. The need for security should be established by an in-depth study of vulnerable areas, with an estimate of costs and benefits. The police will advise on the choice of security and monitoring system equipment.

Mechanical protection devices are constructional measures which provide mechanical resistance to an intruder. These can only be overcome by the use of force, which will leave physical traces behind. An important consideration is the effectiveness of this resistance. Such measures are necessary for the main entrance doors, windows and basement entrances in blocks of flats, and display windows, entrances, other windows, skylights and fences in business premises. Mechanical protection devices include steel grilles, either fixed or as roller shutters, safety roller shutters, secure locks and chains. Wire-reinforced glass also has a deterrent effect, and acrylic or polycarbonate window panes offer enhanced protection.

Electrical security devices will automatically set off an alarm if any unauthorised entry to the protected premises is attempted. An important consideration is the time taken from when the alarm is triggered until the arrival of security staff or the police.

(1) Burglar and attack alarm systems help to monitor and protect people, property and goods. They cannot prevent intruders entering premises, but they should give the earliest possible warning of such an attempt. Optimum security can only be achieved by mechanical protection and the sensible installation of burglar alarm systems. Supervisory measures include monitoring the outside of the building, as well as each room and individual objects of value, security traps and emergency alarm calls.

Fire alarm systems give an early warning of smoke or fire, and may also alert the emergency services. Fire alarm systems are there to protect people and property.

(2) Outdoor supervision systems are used to monitor areas around the building. They increase security by recording all nearby activity, usually up to and including the property boundary. They consist of mechanical or constructional measures, electronic or other detection devices, and/or organisational or personnel action. Their objective is legal fencing, to deter or delay intruders, or to detect and give early warning about unauthorised people or vehicles. This also includes the detection and identification of possible sabotage attempts or espionage. Mechanical measures include construction work, fences, ditches, walls, barriers, gates, access control and lighting. Electrical measures can involve control centres, detectors, video/television sensors, an access control system, an alarm connected to higher communication systems, an automatic telephone dialling device and/or radio. Organisational actions include the briefing of personnel, observation, surveillance, security, task forces, technical staff, watchdogs and an emergency action plan.

(3) Goods protection systems, also called shoplifting protection systems, are electronic systems which serve to protect against theft and the illegal removal of goods from a controlled area during normal business hours.

WINDOWS AND DOORS

parts of building and equipment to be protected	lock contact	magnetic contact	surveillance contact	transitional contact	glass breakage alarm	monitoring foil	glass wired for alarm	body noise alarm	vibration contact	wallpaper alarm and wiring	tread mat	trip wire contact	pendulum alarm	special types
front doors, external doors	●2)	●	○											
internal security doors	●3)	●	●							○				●4)
room doors 12)	●3)	●	●							○		○5)		
internal sliding doors 12)	○3)	○	●	●						○		○5)		
garage up and over doors		●	○											●6)
windows with casements		●	○		●	○	●		○7)					
glass doors, lifting doors		●	○	○	●	○	●		○7)			○5)		
external glass sliding doors		○	●	●	●	○	●		○7)			○5)		
dome lights		○									●		○	●8)
roof windows		●			●		○9)		○7)					
glass block walls								○	●					
display windows, large fixed glazing					●	●	●		○7)					
heavy walls and ceilings								●	●	○				
light walls and ceilings									●					
loft ladder – retractable		○	○							●	○5)	●	○	
individual objects 12) – sculptures paintings		●												●10)
internal floor surfaces 12)											●			
safes 12)									●			○5)		●11)
cupboards for apparatus 12)		●	●									○5)		
conduits, ventilation shafts, service installations												●	●	

burglar alarm ● very suitable ○ still suitable

1) various alarms only to be used with reservations (e.g. not on wired, laminated or toughened glass)
2) principally as a security device
3) if there is rapid switching on this door
4) if only the internal security door is to be protected (cf. also door interlock with alarm)
5) designed for security traps
6) magnetic contact – special type for floor mounting
7) not to be used where it can be touched by hand, if panels are unstable or there are vibration sources near by
8) there are dome lights with built-in alarm protection
9) note reservations concerning the weight of glass
10) individual protection is recommended for very valuable furnishings or those with very valuable contents
11) capacitative field alarms are the recommended protection
12) and/or included in the room surveillance

(1) **Contact and surface monitoring -- appropriate use of burglar alarms**

comparative criteria	ultrasonic room protection	ultrasonic doppler	high-frequency doppler	infra-red alarm
monitoring features preferred, direction of movement registered				
monitoring range per unit - recommended values and range	when mounted on ceiling 90–110 m², wall mounted ≈ 40 m² up to 9 m	depending upon unit 30–50 m² up to 14 m	depending upon unit 150–200 m² up to 25 m	depending on unit 60–80 m² rooms up to 12 m corridors up to 60 m
surveillance of complete room (over 80% of the room monitored)	guaranteed	not guaranteed	not guaranteed	guaranteed
typical application	– small to large rooms – corridors – complete and part room monitoring	– small to large rooms – monitoring part of rooms – security traps	– long, large rooms – monitoring part of room – security traps in large spaces	– small to large rooms – complete and part room monitoring – security traps – at same time fire alarm
permissible ambient temperature: under 0°C / from 0°C to 50°C / over 50°C	conditionally permissible / permissible / not permissible	conditionally permissible / permissible / not permissible	permissible / permissible / permissible	permissible / permissible / not permissible
are several alarms possible in the same room?	no problem	with care	with care	no problem
influences from adjacent rooms or nearby road traffic	no problem	no problem	not recommended	no problem
possible cause of false alarms	– loud noises in ultrasonic frequency band – air heating near the alarm – strong air turbulence – unstable walls	– loud noises in ultrasonic frequency band – air heating – air turbulence – unstable walls – moving objects (e.g. small animals, fans) – disturbing influences near the alarm (sensitivity too great)	– deflection of beam by reflection from metal objects – beam penetrates walls and windows – unstable walls – moving objects (e.g. small animals, fans) – electromagnetic influences	– heat sources with rapid temperature changes (e.g. incandescent lamps, electric heating, open fire) – direct, strong and changing light effect on the alarm – moving objects (e.g. small animals, fans)

(2) **Room monitoring – the most important comparative criteria**

(4) Access control systems are devices which, in combination with a mechanical barrier, only allow free access to any area by means of an identity check. Access is only granted after electronic or personal authorisation. A combination of access control and a time-recording device is technically feasible.

(5) Remote control systems or data transfer/exchange over the public telephone network facilitate monitoring at a distance. Such systems can be used for measurement, control, diagnosis, adjustments, remote questioning, controlling the type of information, and assessing the position of one object in relation to another.

(6) Monitoring systems observe or control the sequence of events by means of a camera and a monitor which are operated either manually and/or automatically. They can be installed either inside or outside, and can operate both day and night throughout the year.

(7) Lift emergency systems are used in personnel lifts and goods lifts. Lift emergency call systems ensure the safety of the users. They are designed first and foremost to free people who are trapped inside. Anyone who is trapped can talk directly to someone in a control centre which is constantly manned, and who will alert the rescue services.

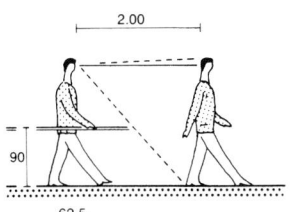

① **Standard stride of an adult on a horizontal plane**

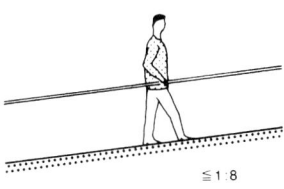

② **On a ramp the stride is reduced proportionately (desirable slope 1:10–1:8)**

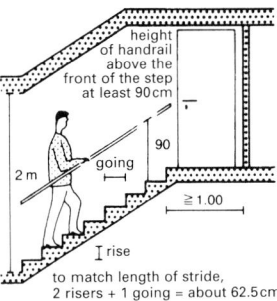

③ **Optimum rise-to-tread ratio 17/29**

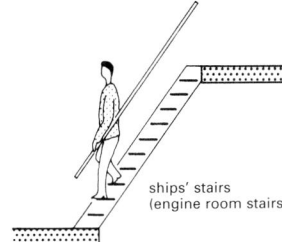

④ **Ladder stairs with a handrail**

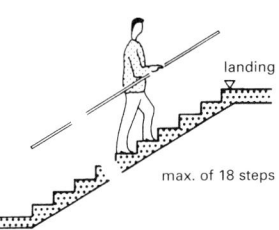

⑤ **Normal stairs 17/29; landing after a max. of 18 steps**

handrails and banisters are not needed for less than five steps

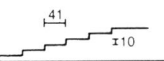

stairs with a rise of less than 1:4 do not require handrail

⑥ **Steps without a handrail**

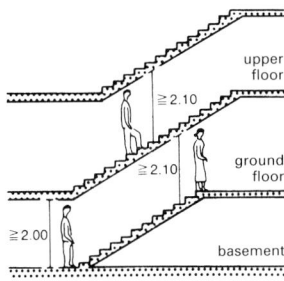

⑦ **Superimposed stairs save space**

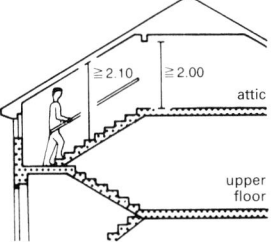

⑧ **Laying the rafters and beams parallel to the stairs saves space and avoids the need for expensive alterations**

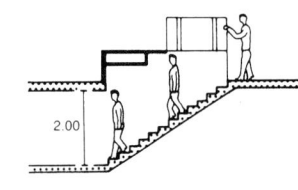

⑨ **Covered entrances to cellars and trapdoors should be avoided. However, this combination has advantages and is safe**

Calculations for the construction of stairs, ramps and guards are set out in various national building regulations. In the UK, British Standards and the Building Regulations should be consulted (see Approved Document K). The guidelines here are based on German standards.

Dwellings with no more than two flats must have an effective stair width of at least 0.80 m and 17/29 rise-to-tread ratio. Stairs which are not strictly covered by building regulations may be as little as 0.50 m wide and have a 21/21 ratio. Stairs governed by building regulations must have a width of 1.00 m and a ratio of 17/28. In high rise flats they must be 1.25 m wide. The length of stair runs from ≥3 steps up to ≤18 steps → ⑤. Landing length = n times the length of stride + 1 depth of step (e.g. with a rise-to-tread ratio of 17/29 = 1 × 63 + 29 = 92 cm or 2 × 63 + 29 = 1.55 m). Doors opening into the stairwell must not restrict the effective width.

The time required for complete evacuation must be calculated for stair widths in public buildings or theatres. Such staircases or front entrance steps are climbed slowly, so they can have a more gradual ascent. A staircase at a side entrance or emergency stairs should make a rapid descent easy.

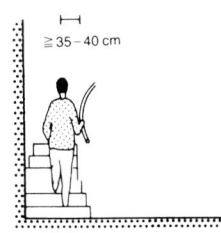

⑩ **If stairs are narrow or curved the distance of the line of walk to the outer string should be 35–40 cm**

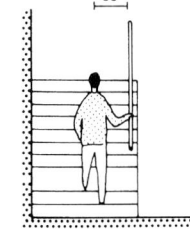

⑪ **If stairs are straight and wide the distance of the line of walk to the handrails should be 55 cm**

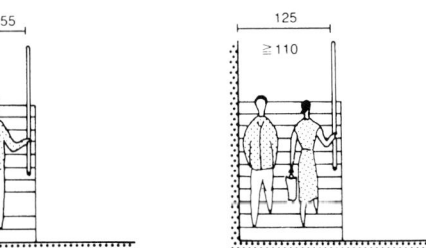

⑫ **Stair width allowing two people to pass**

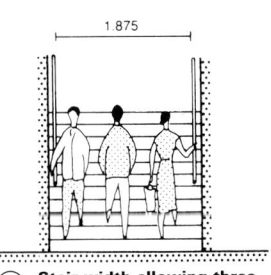

⑬ **Stair width allowing three people to meet and pass**

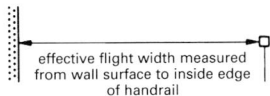

effective flight width measured from wall surface to inside edge of handrail

. . . or between the handrails

stairs must have a fixed handrail; if stair width is greater than 4 m, there must also be a central handrail; spiral staircases must have a handrail on the outside

⑭ **Minimum dimensions for stairs**

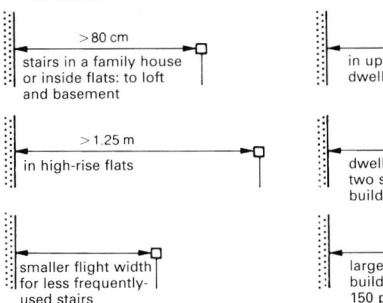

>80 cm
stairs in a family house or inside flats: to loft and basement

>1.25 m
in high-rise flats

smaller flight width for less frequently-used stairs

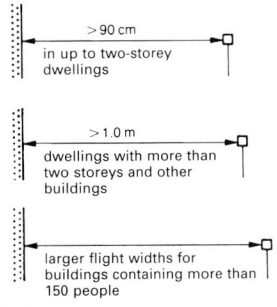

>90 cm
in up to two-storey dwellings

>1.0 m
dwellings with more than two storeys and other buildings

larger flight widths for buildings containing more than 150 people

⑮ **Measuring the effective flight width**

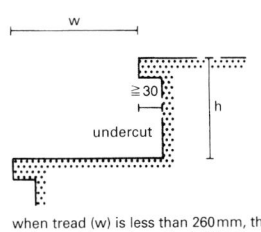

when tread (w) is less than 260 mm, the stairs must be undercut by ≥30 mm

⑯ **The proportions of the stair rises must not change as you go up**

STAIRS

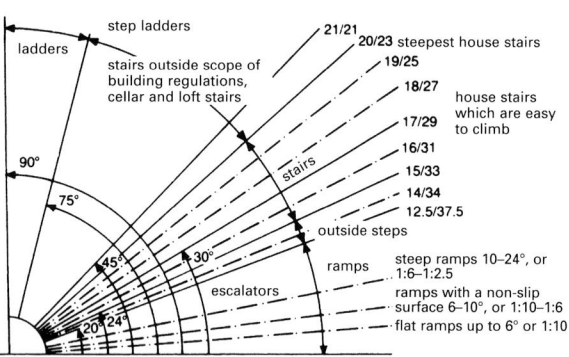

(1) Incline for ramps, outside stairs, house stairs, machinery access steps and ladders

height of storey	two-way stairs		single, triple width and stairs in buildings	
	easy rise		easy rise	
	steps, no.	steps, height	steps, no.	steps, height
a	b	c	f	g
2250	–	–	13	173.0
2500	14	178.5	15	166.6
2625	–	–	15	175.0
2750	16	171.8	–	–
3000	18	166.6	17	176.4

(2) Height of storey and step rise

type of building	type of stairs		effective width of stairs	rise, $r^{2)}$	going, $g^{3)}$
residential building with no more than two flats[1]	essential stairs (building regulations)	stairs leading to habitable rooms, cellar and loft steps which lead to non-habitable rooms	≥ 80	17 ± 3	28^{+9}_{-5}
			≥ 80	≤ 21	≥21
	stairs (additional) considered non-essential according to building regulations		≥ 50	≤ 21	≥21
stairs (additional) considered non-essential according to building regulations (flats)			≥ 50	no stipulations	
other buildings	essential stairs according to building regulations		≥ 100	17^{+2}_{-3}	28^{+9}_{-2}
	stairs (additional) considered non-essential according to building regulations		≥ 50	≤ 21	≥21

[1] Also includes maisonettes in buildings with more than two flats;
[2] but not <14 cm.; [3] but not >37 cm = stipulation of the ratio of rise r/g

(3) Stairs in buildings

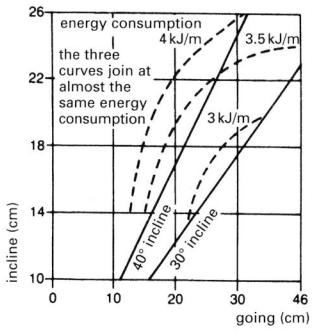

(4) Energy consumption of an adult climbing stairs

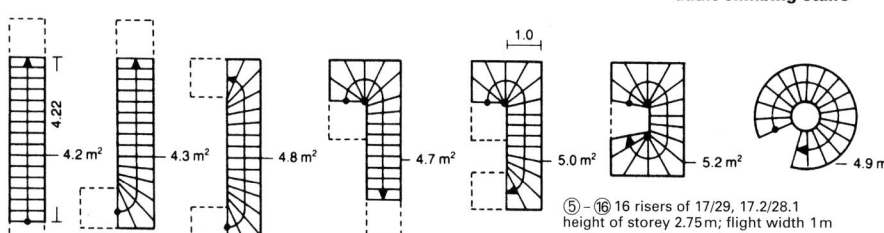

(5) – (16) 16 risers of 17/29, 17.2/28.1 height of storey 2.75 m; flight width 1 m

(5) – (11) All stairs without landings, whatever the type, take up almost the same surface area. However, the distance from the top of the lower floor stairs to the foot of the next staircase can be considerably reduced by curving the steps → (6) – (11). Therefore curved steps are preferred for multistorey buildings.

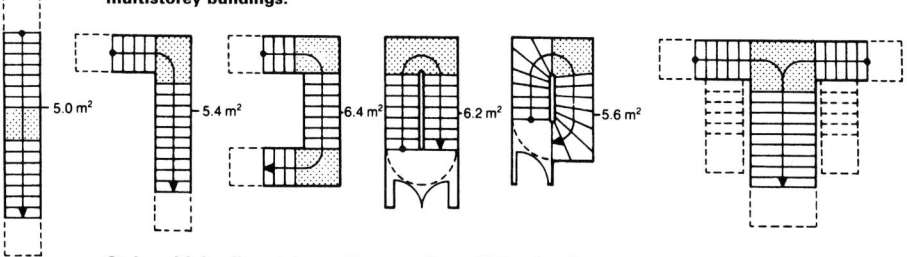

(12) – (16) Stairs with landings take up the area of one flight of stairs + the surface area of landing – surface area of one step. For a height per storey of ≥2.75 m, stairs with landings are necessary. Width of landing ≥ stair flight width.

(17) Three flight-width stairs are expensive and a waste of space

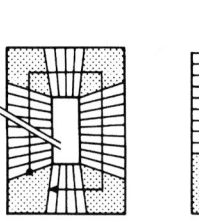

(18) Winders save space

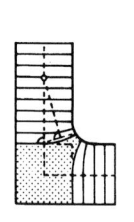

(19) Curved steps at the landing on a narrow stairway save landing space

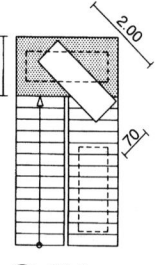

(20) Minimum space required for moving furniture

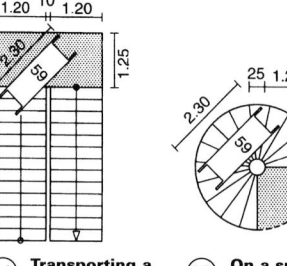

(21) Transporting a stretcher

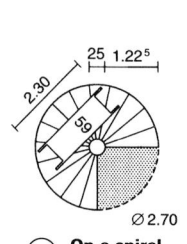

(22) On a spiral staircase

The experiences one has of ascending and descending stairs varies greatly with the stair design, for example there is a significant difference between an interior domestic design and a grand flight of entrance steps. Climbing stairs takes on average seven times as much energy as walking on the flat. From the physiological point of view, the best use of 'climbing effort' is with an angle of incline of 30° and a ratio of rise of:

$$\frac{\text{rise of step, } r}{\text{going of step, } g} = \frac{17}{29}$$

The angle of rise is determined by the length of an adult's stride (about 61–64 cm). To arrive at the optimum rise, which takes the least energy, the following formula can be applied:

$$2r + g = 63 \text{ cm (1 stride)}$$

In the dimensioning and design of flights of stairs, the function and purpose of the staircase is of primary importance, taking in the factors mentioned above.

Not only is the gaining of height important, but also the way that the height is gained. For front door steps in frequent use, low steps of 16 × 30 cm are preferable. However, stairs in a workplace, or emergency stairs, should enable height to be gained rapidly. Every main staircase must be set in its own continuous stairwell, which together with its access routes and exit to the open air, should be designed and arranged so as to ensure its safe use as an emergency exit. The width of the exit should be ≥ the width of the staircase.

The stairwell of at least one of the emergency staircases or fire exits must be ≤ 35 m from every part of a habitable room or basement. When several staircases are necessary, they must be placed so as to afford the shortest possible escape route. Stairwell openings to the basement, unconverted lofts, workshops, shops, storerooms and similar rooms must be fitted with self-closing fire doors with a fire rating of 30 minutes.

To avoid marking risers with shoe polish from heels, use recessed profiles which have longer goings → ①.

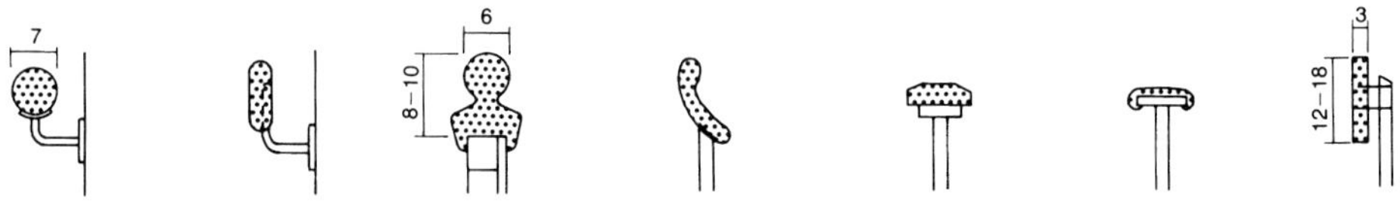

Maximum space is required at hip (handrail) level, but at foot level considerably less is needed so the width at string level can be reduced, allowing more space for the stairwell.

Staggering the handrail and string allows better structural fixing. A good string and handrail arrangement with a 12 cm space between stairwell strings is shown in ③. An additional handrail for children (height about 60 cm) is also shown, along with some less popular string and handrail positions.

Circles in theatres, choir lofts, galleries and balconies must have a protective guard rail (height *h*). This is compulsory wherever there is a height difference in levels of 1 m or more.

For a drop of <12 m, *h* = 0.90 m

For a drop of >12 m, *h* = 1.10 m

Loft ladders have an angle of 45–55°. However, if user requirements stipulate a stair-like access (e.g. where loads are carried and available length is too short for a flight of normal stairs), then alternating tread stairs may be designed → ⑪. There should be a minimum number of risers for this type of stair (riser ≤ 20 cm). Here 'the sum of the goings + twice the rise = 630 mm' is achieved by shaping the treads; goings are measured (staggered) at the axes a and b → ⑫, of the right and left foot.

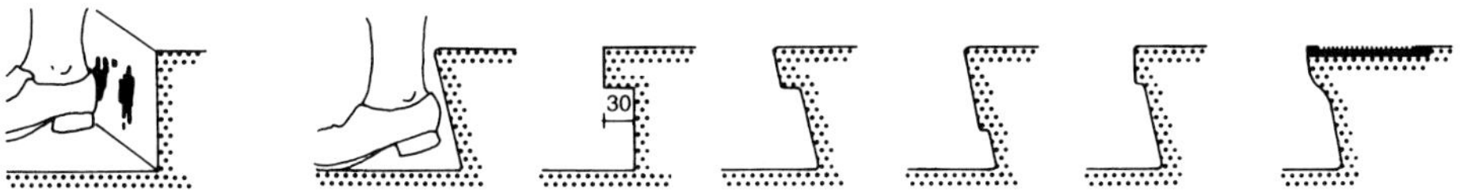

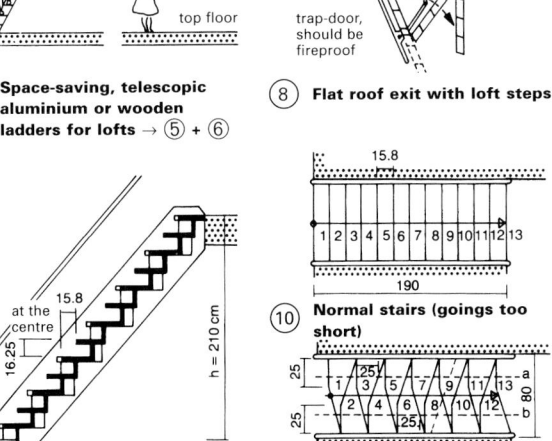

① **Step profiles**

② **Handrail profiles**

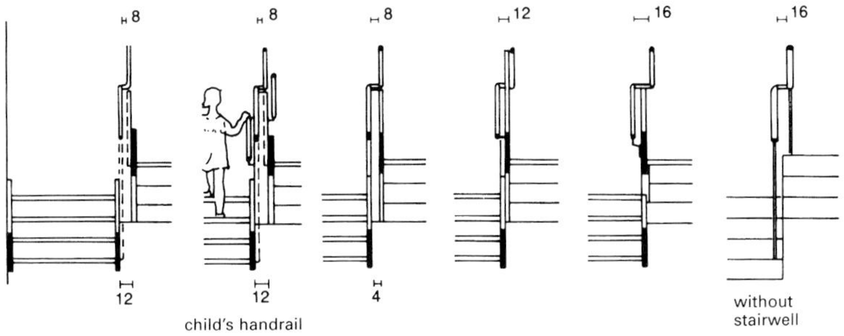

wood profiles   metal profile   plastic profile   Plexiglas

③ **Handrail and string details**

child's handrail   without stairwell

④ **Handrail on landing**

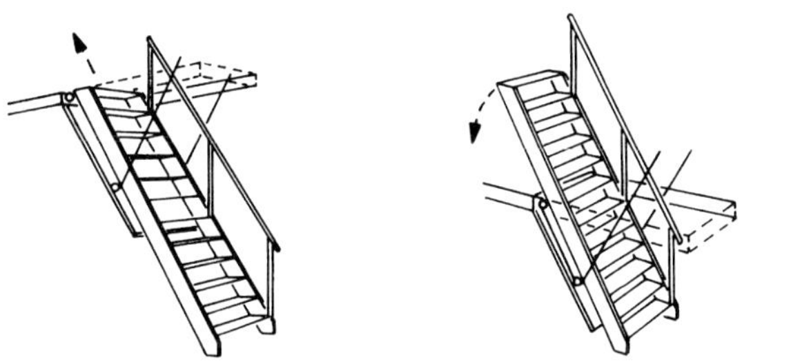

⑤ **Space-saving retractable stairs, in one, two or three sections → ⑦**

⑥ **Space-saving loft ladder (scissor frame) for rooms 2.0–3.8 m high**

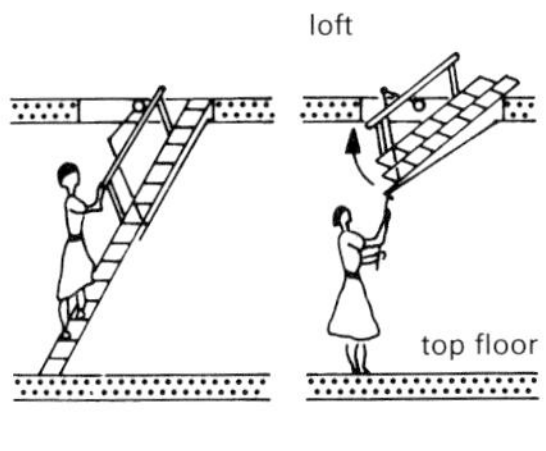

loft   top floor

⑦ **Space-saving, telescopic aluminium or wooden ladders for lofts → ⑤ + ⑥**

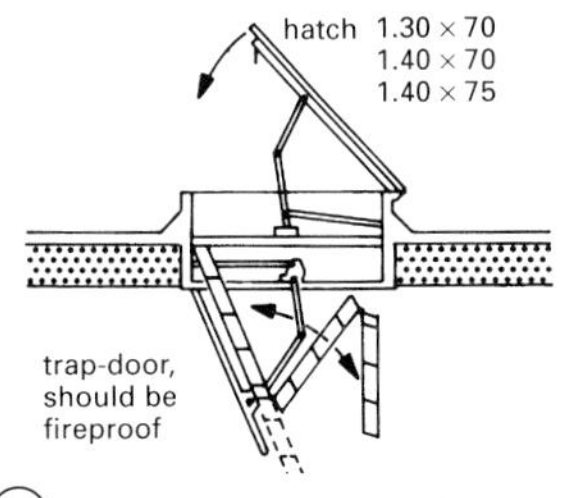

hatch 1.30 × 70
       1.40 × 70
       1.40 × 75

trap-door, should be fireproof

⑧ **Flat roof exit with loft steps**

⑨ **Wooden alternating tread stair, section through centre**

⑩ **Normal stairs (goings too short)**

⑪ **Plan: goings at lines a and b are ≥ 20 cm**

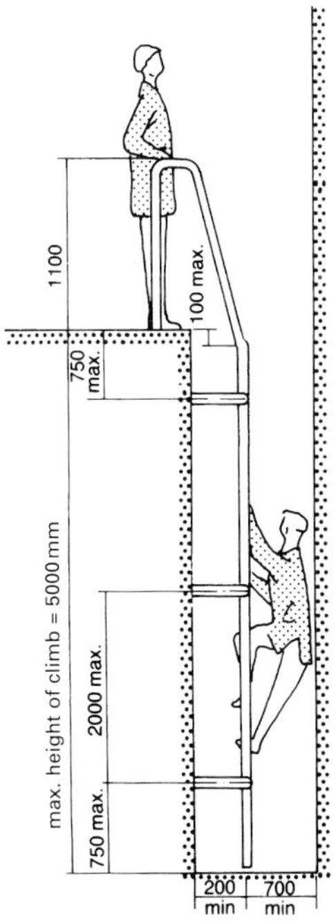

⑫ **Fixed catladder**

storey height, FFL to underside of ceiling (cm)	size of loft ladder (cm)
220–280	100 × 60(70)
220–300	120 × 60(70)
220–300	130 × 60(70,80)
240–300	140 × 60(70,80)

frame width:
W = 59, 69, 79 cm
frame length:
L = 120, 130, 140 cm
frame height:
H = 25 cm

⑬ **Telescopic loft ladders → ⑤ – ⑧**

RAMPS AND SPIRAL STAIRCASES

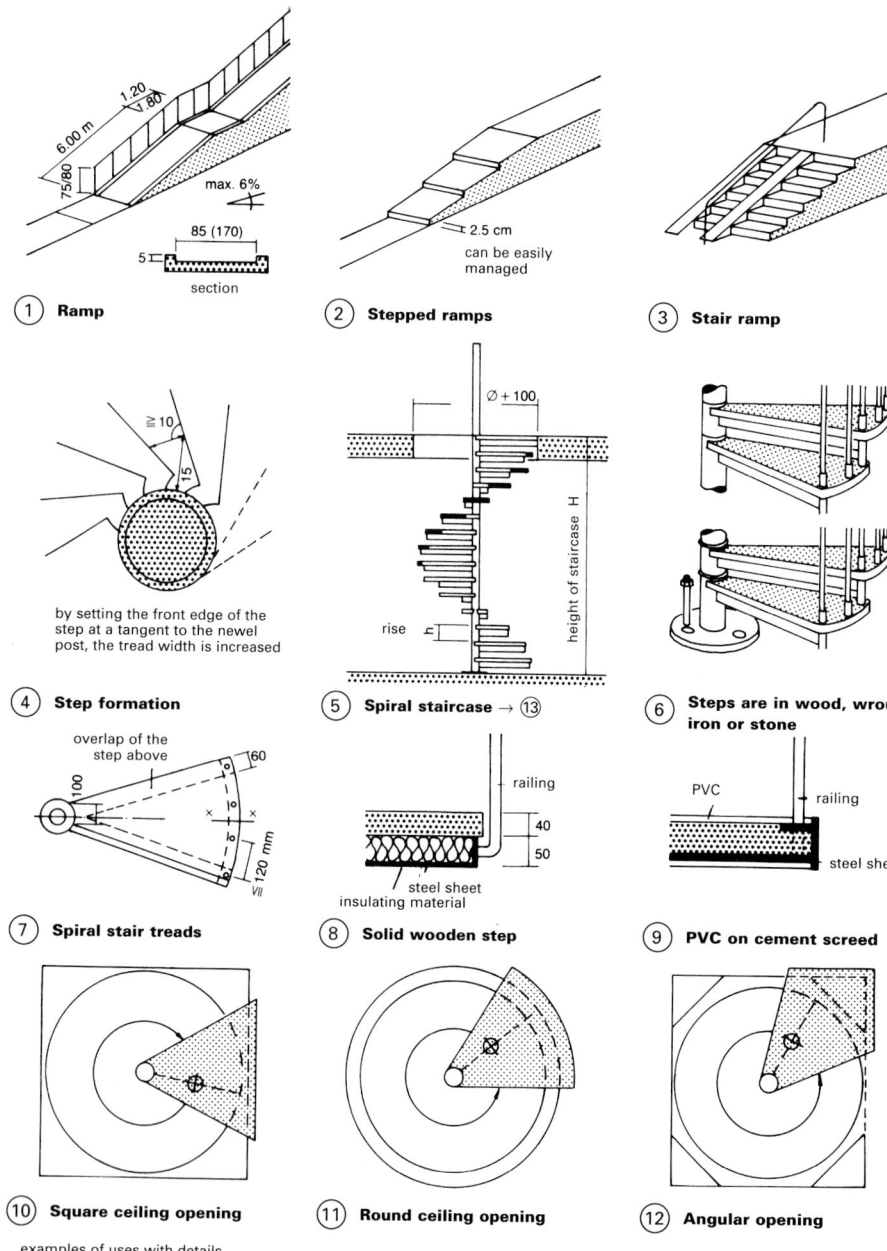

① **Ramp**

can be easily managed

② **Stepped ramps**

③ **Stair ramp**

by setting the front edge of the step at a tangent to the newel post, the tread width is increased

④ **Step formation**

⑤ **Spiral staircase → ⑬**

⑥ **Steps are in wood, wrought iron or stone**

⑦ **Spiral stair treads**

⑧ **Solid wooden step**

⑨ **PVC on cement screed**

⑩ **Square ceiling opening**

⑪ **Round ceiling opening**

⑫ **Angular opening**

examples of uses with details

Ramps should be provided to allow wheelchair users and those with prams or trolleys to move easily from one level to another → ① – ③.

Under building regulations, a main or 'essential' staircase with a ceiling aperture size of about 210 cm diameter (with a minimum 80 cm flight width) is permissible for family houses, and from 260 cm for other buildings (with a minimum 1.00 m flight width). Spiral stairs with less than 80 cm effective flight width are only permitted as 'non-essential' stairs. Material used can be metal plate (with a plastic or carpet overlay if needed), marble, wood, concrete or stone → ⑥ – ⑨. Stairs in pre-fabricated steel sections, aluminium castings or wood for installation on site, are suitable as service stairs, emergency stairs and stairs between floors → ⑬. Stair railings can be fitted in steel, wood or Plexiglas → ⑭. Spiral staircases are space-saving and, with a pillar in their central axis, are of sturdy design → ⑤ – ⑥. They can, however, also be designed without a central pillar, giving an open winding staircase with a stairwell → ⑭ – ⑮.

Spiral and helical stairs in the UK are usually designed in accordance with BS 5395: Part 2 to fulfil the recommendations of the Approved Document K (AD K).

use	two-way traffic impossible			two-way traffic possible		two-way traffic easy		
	still passable			easy to pass	easy to pass	passable with comfort		
				small furniture can pass through	dismantled furniture can pass through	furniture can pass through	for heavy traffic	
secondary rooms								
basements, lofts								
home bar, hobby room								
bedrooms, sauna								
swimming pool, laboratory								
workshop, garden								
gallery, small store								
salesroom								
maisonette, boutique								
office rooms, large storeroom								
consulting/shop room								
guest bedrooms								
emergency stairs								
main/'essential' domestic stairs								
stairs dia. (nominal dimension)	1200 1250 1300	to	1500 1550 1600 1650 1700 1750		1800 1850	to	2050 2100 2150 2200	to	2400
flight width (mm)	516 541 566		653 678 703 728 753 778		625 650		750 775 800 825		925
	between the newel post and handrail				from 10 cm depth of tread				

⑬ **Determination using minimum sizes for spiral stairs of all types**

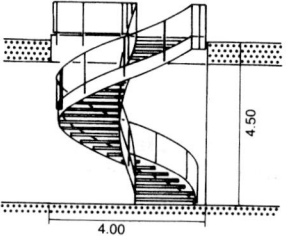

4.50

4.00

⑭ **Vertical section of spiral staircase**

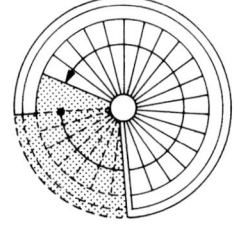

⑮ **Plan view of → ⑭**

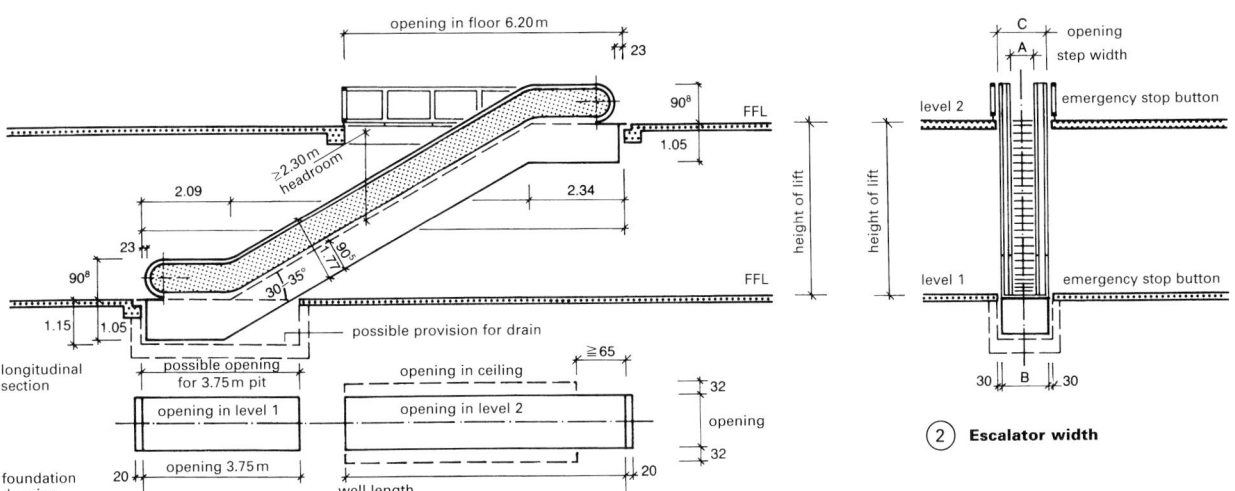

① **Cross-section/foundation diagram of an escalator**

② **Escalator width**

step width	600	800	1000
A	605–620	805–820	1005–1020
B	1170–1220	1320–1420	1570–1620
C	1280	1480	1680
transportation capacity/h	5000–6000 persons	7000–8000 persons	8000–10 000 persons

③ **Dimensions and performance for escalators with either 30° or 35° angle of ascent**

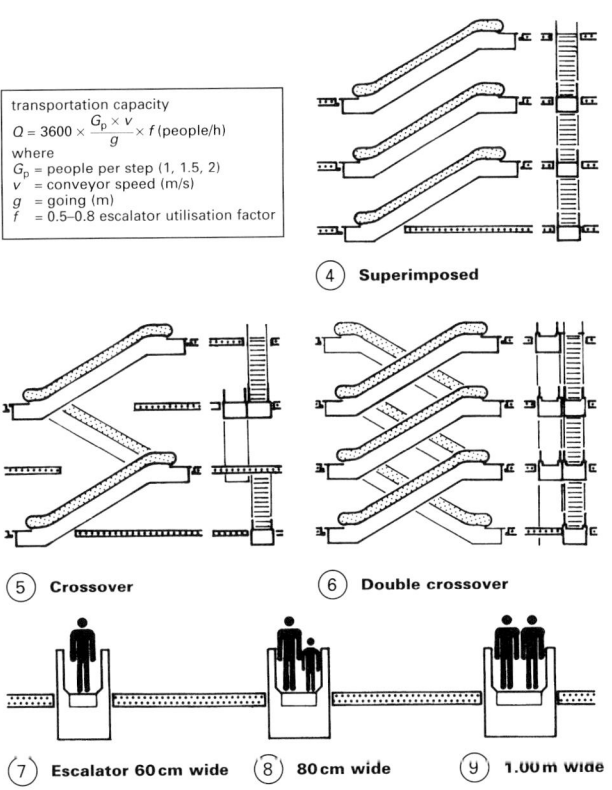

transportation capacity

$$Q = 3600 \times \frac{G_p \times v}{g} \times f \text{ (people/h)}$$

where
G_p = people per step (1, 1.5, 2)
v = conveyor speed (m/s)
g = going (m)
f = 0.5–0.8 escalator utilisation factor

④ **Superimposed**

⑤ **Crossover**   ⑥ **Double crossover**

⑦ **Escalator 60 cm wide**   ⑧ **80 cm wide**   ⑨ **1.00 m wide**

Length in plan → ①

with 30° escalator = 1.732 × storey height
with 35° escalator = 1.428 × storey height
Example: storey height 4.50 m and angle 30° (note that 35° angle is not allowed in some countries)
    length in plan: 1.732 × 4.5 = 7.794
Including landings top and bottom, total length is approximately 9 m, allowing for about 20 people to stand in a row on the escalator.

speed	time per person	width sufficient for :	
		1 person	2 persons
0.5 m/s	~ 18 s	4000	8000
0.65 m/s	~ 14 s	5000	10 000
		people/h can be transported	

⑩ **Performance data → ① – ③**

These guidelines are based on recommendations issued by the German Federations of Trade Associations. In the UK, reference is usually made to BS EN 115: 1995: *Safety rules for the construction and installation of escalators and passenger conveyors.*

Escalators → ① – ③ are required to provide continuous mass transport of people. (They are not designated as 'stairs' in the provision of emergency escape.) Escalators, for example, in department stores rise at an angle of between 30° and 35°. The 35° escalator is more economical, as it takes up less surface area if viewed in plan but for large ascents, the 30° escalator is preferred both on psychological as well as safety grounds. The transportation capacity is about the same with both.

Escalators in public transport installations are subject to stringent safety requirements (for function, design and safety) and should have angles of ascent of 27–28°. The angle of rise is the ratio 3/16, which is that of a gentle staircase.

In accordance with a worldwide standard, the width of the step to be used is 60 cm (for one-person width), 80 cm (for one- to two-people width) and 100 cm (for two-people width) → ⑦ – ⑨. A 100 cm step width provides ample space for people carrying loads.

A flat section with a depth of ≥2.50 m (minimum of two horizontal goings) should be provided at the access and exit points of the escalator.

In department stores, office and administration buildings, exhibition halls and airports the speed of travel should, as a rule, be no greater than 0.5 m/s, with a minimum of three horizontal exit goings. For underground stations and public transport facilities, 0.65 m/s is preferred.

The average split of traffic that goes upstairs in a large department store is:
    fixed stairs   2%
    lifts   8%
    escalators   90%
Coming down, about three-quarters of the traffic uses the escalators.

According to current assessments, on average one escalator is installed for every 1500 m² of sales area; but this average should be reduced to an optimum of 500–700 m².

TRAVELATORS

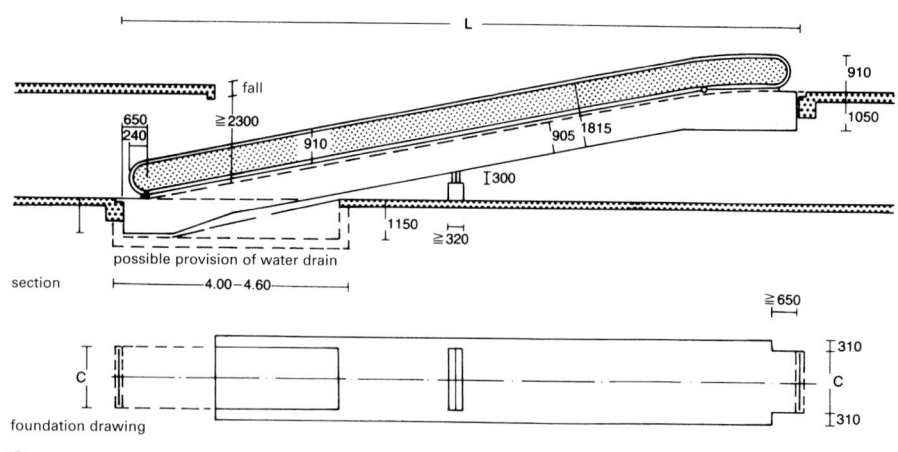

section ⊢——— 4.00–4.60 ———⊣

possible provision of water drain

foundation drawing

① **Travelator, cross-section and foundation diagram**

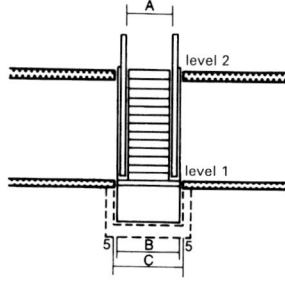

② **Cross-section → ①**

type	60	80	100
A	600	800	1000
B	1220	1420	1620
C	1300	1500	1700

③ **Dimensions → ① – ②**

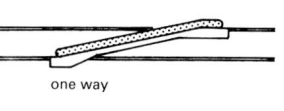

one way

superimposed

scissor arrangement

crossover arrangement

converging

④ **Arrangement of travelators**

The hourly capacity of a travelator is calculated according to the formula:

$$Q = \frac{3600\,K.w.v}{0.25}\ \text{(persons/h)}$$

where
w = transportation width (m)
v = speed (m/s)
K = load factor

The load factor varies between 0.5 and 0.9 (average 0.7) according to the use.
The 0.25 in the denominator represents a step area of $0.25\,\text{m}^2$/person.

⑤ **One person with 60 cm shopping trolley (width 80 cm)**

⑥ **Two people; 1 m width**

horizontal travelator	cleated belt	conveyor belt (rubber)	reversible travelator
effective width, S	800 + 1000	750 + 950	2 × 800 + 2 × 1000
overall width, B	1370 + 1570	1370 + 1570	3700 + 4200
design	flat construction with ≥4° incline		
length of a section	12–16 m		~ 10 m
inter-support distance	in accordance with structural requirements		
possible length, L	≥250 m		
capacity	40 m/min		11 000 people/h

⑪ **Dimensions and performance of horizontal travelator → ⑦ – ⑧**

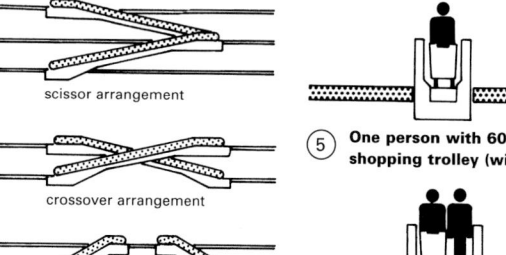

⑦ **Section of travelator with rubber conveyor belt**

rubber conveyor belt   with cleated belt

⑧ **Plan view → ⑦**

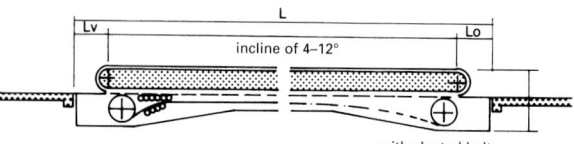

⑨ **Section of a reversible travelator → ⑩**

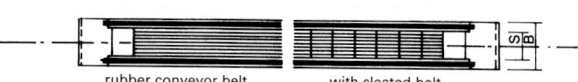

tensioning pulley   drive

⑩ **Plan view → ⑨**

Travelators (or moving pavements) are a means of conveying people horizontally or up a slightly inclined plane (up to a maximum angle of 12°, or 21%). The big advantage of the travelator lies in its ability to transport prams, invalid chairs, shopping trolleys, bicycles and unwieldy packages with only a slight risk of accident. At the planning stage the expected traffic must be carefully calculated, so that the installation provides the best conveying capacity possible. This capacity depends on the clear width available, the speed of travel and the load factor.

The number of people transported can be as high as 6000–12 000 people/h. The speed of travel on inclined travelators is normally 0.5–0.6 m/s although where the inclination angle is less than 4° they can sometimes be run a little faster, up to 0.75 m/s. Long travelators can be up to 250 m in length but shorter runs (e.g. about 30 m long) are better because they allow people to access and exit to and from the sides. It is therefore sensible to plan a series of smaller travelators.

The advantage of the reversible travelators is their ability to offer both horizontal directions of travel → ⑨ – ⑩, in contrast to → ⑦ – ⑧. The low height required for construction (this being only 180 mm) allows these travelators to be fitted into existing buildings.

The cotangents of the travelator gradient are:

Gradient W (°)	10°	11°	12°
cot W	5.6713	5.1446	4.7036

Horizontal length L = cotan W × conveyor lift
Example: conveyor lift, 5 m; gradient 12°
L = 4.7036 × 5 = 23.52 m
(to two decimal places).

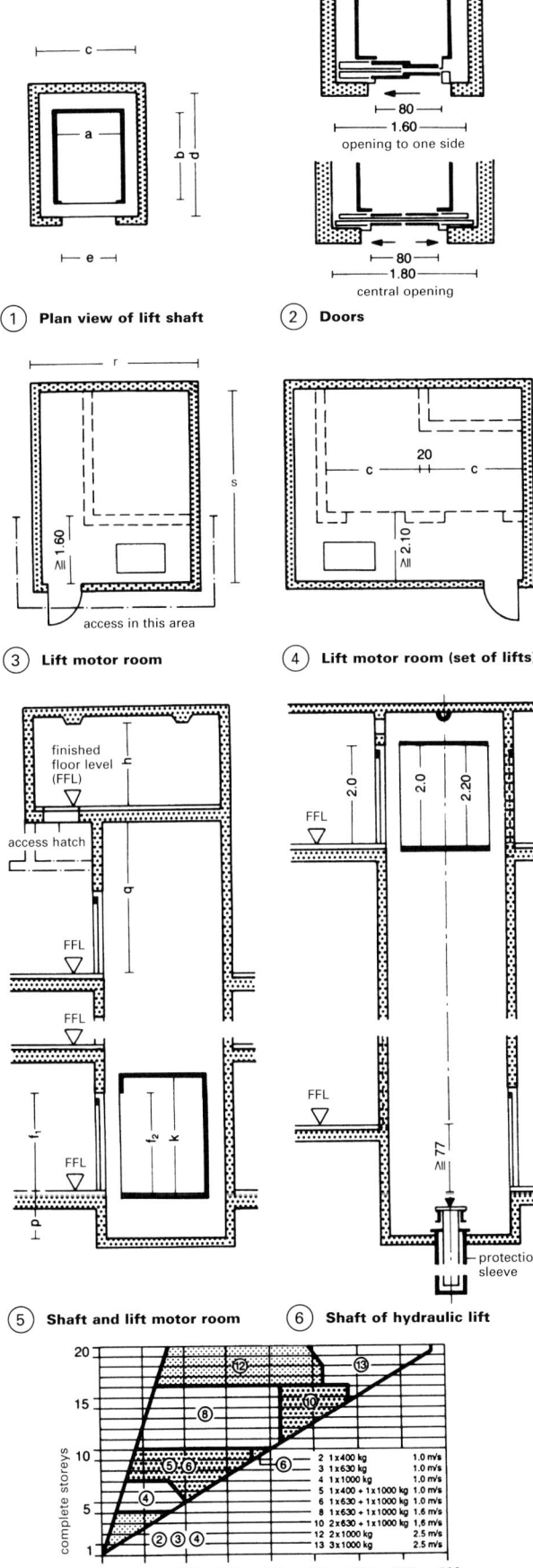

① **Plan view of lift shaft**

② **Doors**

— 80 —
— 1.60 —
opening to one side

— 80 —
— 1.80 —
central opening

③ **Lift motor room**

④ **Lift motor room (set of lifts)**

⑤ **Shaft and lift motor room**

⑥ **Shaft of hydraulic lift**

⑦ **Conveying capacity requirements for normal flats: finite elements method (FEM)**

The upward and downward movement of people in newly erected multistorey buildings is principally achieved by lifts. An architect will normally call in an expert engineer to plan lift installations. The guidelines given here are based on German standards. In the UK, lift installation is covered by BS 5655, which contains recommendations from CEN (Committee for European Normalisation) and the International Standards Organisation. It is anticipated that future standards relating to lifts will be fully international in their scope.

In larger, multistorey buildings it is usual to locate the lifts at a central pedestrian circulation point. Goods lifts should be kept separate from passenger lifts; though their use for carrying passengers at peak periods should be taken into account at the planning stage.

The following maximum loads are stipulated for passenger lifts in blocks of flats:

400 kg (small lift)	for use by passengers with hand baggage only
630 kg (medium lift)	for use by passengers with prams and wheelchairs
1000 kg (large lift)	can also accommodate stretchers, coffins, furniture and wheelchairs → ⑧

Lobbies in front of lift shaft entrances must be designed and arranged so that: (1) the users entering or exiting the lifts, even those carrying hand baggage, do not get in each other's way more than is absolutely necessary; and (2) the largest loads to be carried by the lift in question (e.g. prams, wheelchairs, stretchers, coffins and furniture) can be manoeuvred in and out without risk of injuring people or damaging the building and the lift itself. Other users should be not be obstructed by the loads more than is absolutely necessary.

For a lobby in front of a single lift: (1) the available minimum depth between the wall of the lift shaft door and the opposite wall, measured in the direction of the lift car, must be at least the same as the depth of the lift car itself; and (2) the minimum area available should be at least the same as the product of the depth of the lift car depth and the width of shaft.

For a lobby in front of lifts with adjacent doors the available minimum depth between the shaft door wall and the opposite wall, measured in the direction of the lift car depth, should be at least the same as the depth of the deepest lift car.

			400			630				1000			
load capacity	(kg)		400			630				1000			
operating speed	(≤m/s)		0.63	1.00	1.60	0.63	1.00	1.60	2.50	0.63	1.00	1.60	2.50
shaft	minimum width, c	(mm)	1800			1800				1800			
	minimum depth, d	(mm)	1500			2100				2600			
	min. shaft pit depth, p	(mm)	1400	1500	1700	1400	1500	1700	2800	1400	1500	1700	2800
	min. shaft head height, q	(mm)	3700	3000	4000	3700	3000	4000	5000	3700	3000	4000	5000
door	clear width lift door, c₂	(mm)	800			800				800			
	clear width shaft door, s₂	(mm)	2000			2000				2000			
lift motor room	minimum area	(m²)	8	10		10	12	14		12	14	15	
	minimum width, r	(mm)	2400	2400		2700	2700	3000		2700	2700	3000	
	minimum depth, s	(mm)	3200	3200		3700	3700	3700		4200	4200	4200	
	minimum height, h	(mm)	2000	2200		2000	2200	2600		2000	2200	2600	
lift car	clear width, a	(mm)	1100			1100				1100			
	clear depth, b	(mm)	950			1400				2100			
	clear height, k	(mm)	2200			2200				2200			
	clear access width, e₂	(mm)	800			800				800			
	clear access height, f₂	(mm)	2000			2000				2000			
	permitted no. passengers		5			8				13			

⑧ **Structural dimensions, dimensions of lift cars and doors**

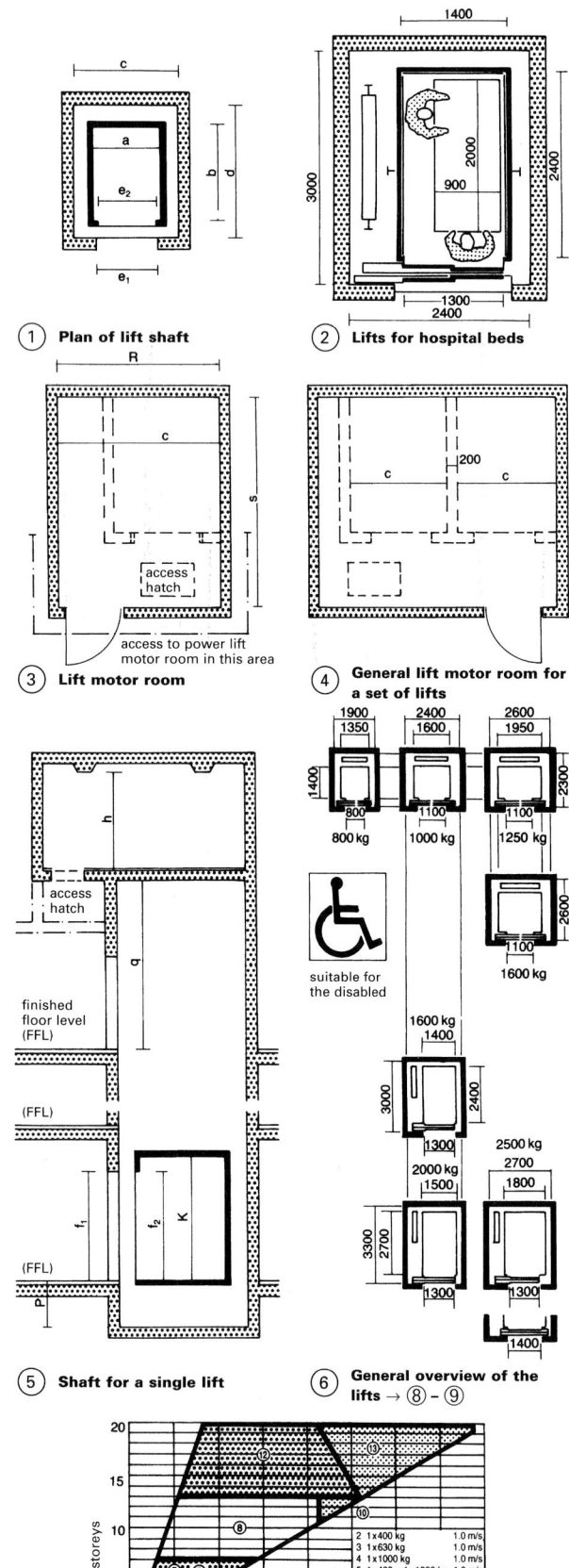

① **Plan of lift shaft**

② **Lifts for hospital beds**

③ **Lift motor room**

④ **General lift motor room for a set of lifts**

800 kg 1000 kg 1250 kg

1600 kg

suitable for the disabled

⑤ **Shaft for a single lift**

⑥ **General overview of the lifts → ⑧ – ⑨**

2 1×400 kg   1.0 m/s
3 1×630 kg   1.0 m/s
4 1×1000 kg   1.0 m/s
5 1×400 + 1×1000 kg   1.0 m/s
6 1×630 + 1×1000 kg   1.0 m/s
8 1×630 + 1×1000 kg   1.0 m/s
10 2×630 + 1×1000 kg   1.6 m/s
12 2×1000 kg   2.5 m/s
13 3×1000 kg   2.5 m/s

⑦ **Transportation capacity requirements for flats with and without floors of offices: finite elements method (FEM)**

LIFTS

For Offices, Banks, Hotels etc. and Hospital Bed Lifts

The building and its function dictate the basic type of lifts which need to be provided. They serve as a means of vertical transport for passengers and patients.

Lifts are mechanical installations which are required to have a long service life (anything from 25 to 40 years). They should therefore be planned in such a way that even after 10 years they are still capable of meeting the increased demand. Alterations to installations that have been badly or too-cheaply planned can be expensive or even completely impossible. During the planning stage the likely usage should be closely examined. Lift sets normally form part of the main stairwell.

Analysis of use: types and definitions

Turn-round time is a calculated value indicating the time which a lift requires to complete a cycle with a given type of traffic.

Average waiting time is the time between the button being pressed and the arrival of the lift car:

$$\text{average waiting time (s)} = \frac{\text{cycle time (s)}}{\text{number of lifts/set}}$$

Transportation capacity is the maximum achievable carrying capacity (in passengers) within a five minute (300 s) period:

$$\text{transportation capacity} = \frac{300\,(s) \times \text{car load (passengers)}}{\text{cycle time (s)} \times \text{no. of lifts}}$$

Transportation capacity expressed in percent:

$$\text{transportation capacity (\%)} = \frac{100 \times \text{transportation capacity}}{\text{number of occupants of building}}$$

carrying capacity	(kg)	800				1000 (1250)				1600			
nominal speed	(m/s)	0.63	1.0	1.6	2.5	0.63	1.0	1.6	2.5	0.63	1.0	1.6	2.5
min. shaft width,	c	1900				2400				2600			
min. shaft depth,	d	2300				2300				2600			
min. shaft pit depth,	p	1400	1500	1700	2800	1400	1700		2800	1400	1900		2800
min. shaft head height,	q	3800		4000	5000	4200			5200	4400			5400
shaft door width,	c_1	800				1100				1100			
shaft door height,	f_1	2000				2100				2100			
min. area of lift motor room	(m²)	15		18		20				25			
min. width of lift motor room,	r	2500		2800		3200				3200			
min. depth of lift motor room,	s	3700		4900		4900				5500			
min. height of lift motor room,	h	2200		2800		2400		2800		2800			
car width,	a	1350				1500				1950			
car depth,	b	1400				1400				1750			
car height,	k	2200				2300				2300			
car door width,	e_2	800				1100				1100			
car door height,	f_2	2000				2100				2100			
no. of people permitted		10				13				21			

⑧ **Structural dimensions (mm) → ① – ⑥: lifts allow wheelchair access**

carrying capacity	(kg)	1600				2000				2500			
nominal speed	(m/s)	0.63	1.0	1.6	2.5	0.63	1.0	1.6	2.5	0.63	1.0	1.6	2.5
min. shaft width,	c	2400								2700			
min. shaft depth,	d	3000								3300			
min. shaft pit depth,	p	1800	1700	1900	2800	1600	1700	1900	2800	1800	1900	2100	3000
min. shaft head height,	q	4400			5400	4400			5400	4800			5600
shaft door width,	c_1	1300								1300 (1400)			
shaft door height,	f_1	2100											
min. area of lift motor room	(m²)	26				27				29			
min. width of lift motor room,	r	3200								3500			
min. depth of lift motor room,	s	5500				5800							
min. height of lift motor room,	h	2800											
car width,	a	1400				1500				1800			
car depth,	b	2400				2700							
car height,	k	2300											
car door width,	e_2	1300								1300 (1400)			
car door height,	f_2	2100											
no. of people permitted		21				26				33			

⑨ **Structural dimensions of hospital bed lifts**

SMALL GOODS LIFTS

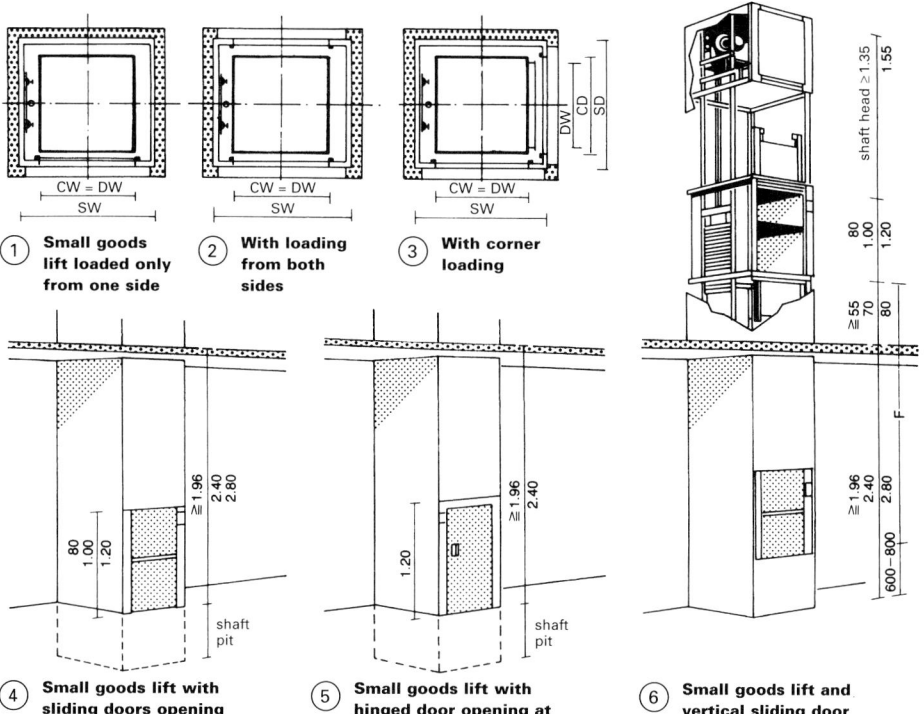

① Small goods lift loaded only from one side

② With loading from both sides

③ With corner loading

④ Small goods lift with sliding doors opening vertically at floor level

⑤ Small goods lift with hinged door opening at floor level

⑥ Small goods lift and vertical sliding door opening at waist level

Small goods lifts: payload ≥300 kg; car floor area ≤0.8 m²; for transporting small goods, documents, food etc.; not for use by passengers. The shaft framework is normally made of steel sections set in the shaft pit or on the floor, and clad on all sides by non-flammable building materials. → ① – ⑥ Dimensions and load-carrying capacity → ⑦.

The following formula is used to estimate the time, in seconds, of one transport cycle:

$$Z = \frac{2\,h}{v} + B_z + H\,(t_1 + t_2)$$

where

2 = constant factor for the round trip

h = height of the lift (m)

v = operating speed (m/s)

B_z = loading and unloading time (s)

H = number of stops

t_1 = time for acceleration and deceleration (s)

t_2 = time for opening and closing lift shaft doors (s)

With single doors t_2 = 6 s; with double doors, 10 s; with vertical sliding doors for small goods lifts, about 3 s.

The maximum transport-ation capacity in kg/min can be found from the time for one transport cycle, Z, and the maximum load the lift can carry:

$$\frac{\text{max. load (kg)} \times 60}{Z\ (\text{s})}$$

Under building regulations, the lift motor room must be lockable, have sufficient illumination and be of a size such that maintenance can be carried out safely. The height of the area for the lift motor must be ≥1.8 m.

For food lifts in hospitals, the lift shafts must have washable smooth internal walls.

An external push-button control must be provided for calling and despatching the lift to/from each stopping point.

Larger goods lifts may be designed to convey goods and carry passengers employed by the operator of the installation.

Accuracy of stopping: for goods lifts without deceler-ation = ±20–40 mm; for pas-senger and goods lifts with deceleration = ±10–30 mm

Speeds: 0.25, 0.4, 0.63 and 1.0 m/s.

loading arrangement		one side access and loading from both sides							corner access and loading				
payload,	Q (kg)	100						300	100				
speed,	v (m/s)	0.45						0.3	0.45				
car width = door width (CW = DW)		400	500	600	700	800	800	800	500	600	700	800	800
car depth	(CD)	400	500	600	700	800	1000	1000	500	600	700	800	1000
car height = door height (CH = DH)		800					1200	1200	800				1200
door width, corner loading (DW)		–	–	–	–	–	–	–	350	450	550	650	850
shaft width	(SW)	720	820	920	1020		1120	1120	820	920	1020	1120	1120
shaft depth	(SD)	580	680	780	880	980	1180	1180	680	780	880	980	1180
min. shaft head height (SHH)		1990					2590	2590	2145				2745
lift motor room door width		500	500	600	700	800	800	800	500	600	700	800	800
lift motor room door height		600							600				
loading point clearance		1930					2730	2730	1930				2730
loading point clearance		700						450	700				
min. sill height at		600					800	800	600				800
lowest stopping point,	B												

⑦ Dimensions of small goods lifts

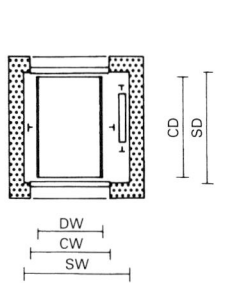

⑧ Goods lift with loading from both sides

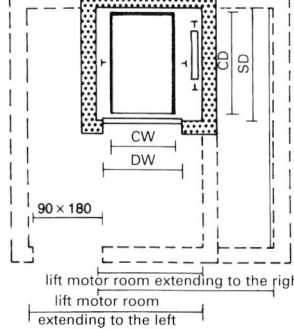

90 × 180

lift motor room extending to the right
lift motor room
extending to the left

⑨ Goods lift with loading only from one side, and the lift motor room

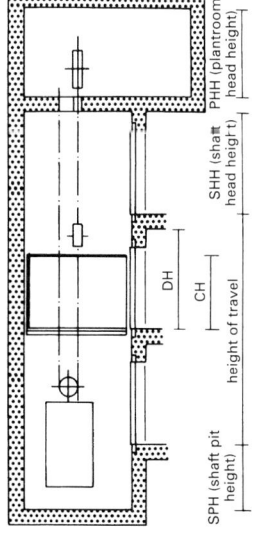

SD

⑪ Cross-section → ⑧ – ⑨

load carrying capacity (kg)		630	1000	1600	2000	2500	3200
nominal speed (m/s)		◄— 0.40 — 0.63 — 1.00 —►					
lift car dimensions (mm)							
	CW	1100	1300	1500	1500	1800	2000
	CD	1570	1870	2470	2870	2870	3070
	CH	2200	2200	2200	2200	2200	2200
door dimensions (mm)							
	DW	1100	1300	1500	1500	1800	2000
	DH	2200	2200	2200	2200	2200	2200
shaft dimensions (mm)							
	SW	1800	2000	2200	2300	2600	2900
	SD	1700	2000	2600	3000	3000	3200
SPH 0.4 and 0.63 (mm)		1200	1300	1300	1300	1300	1400
1.0 (mm)		1300	1300	1600	1600	1800	1900
SHH 0.4 and 0.63 (mm)		3700	3800	3900	4000	4100	4200
1.0 (mm)		3800	3900	4200	4200	4400	4400
PHH (mm)		1900	1900	1900	2100	1900	1900

⑩ Structural dimensions -- drive pulleys -- goods lifts → ⑧ – ⑨

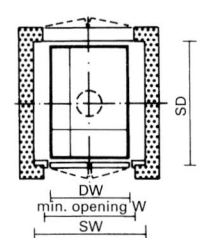

(1) **Plan view of shaft**

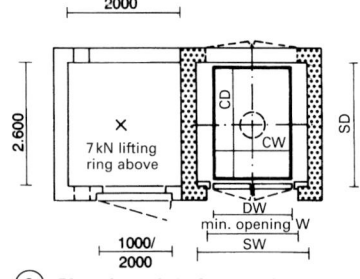

(2) **Plan view of shaft with lift motor room**

HYDRAULIC LIFTS

These meet the demand for transporting heavy loads economically up and down shorter lift heights and are best used for up to 12 m lift height. The lift motor room can be located remotely from the shaft itself.

Standard direct-acting piston lifts can be used to lift payloads of as much as 20 t up to a maximum height of 17 m → ① – ③, while standard indirect acting piston lifts can lift 7 t up to 34 m. The operating speed of hydraulic lifts is 0.2–0.8 m/s. A roof mounted lift motor room is not required. Several variations in hydraulics can be found → ⑥ – ⑨. The most commonly used is the centrally mounted ram → ① – ③.

The ram retraction control tolerance, regardless of load, has to be kept within ±3 mm, so that a completely level entry into the lift car is obtained. Height clearance of the lift doors should be 50–100 mm greater than other doors. Double swing doors or hinged sliding doors can be fitted – either hand-operated or fully automatic, with a central or side opening.

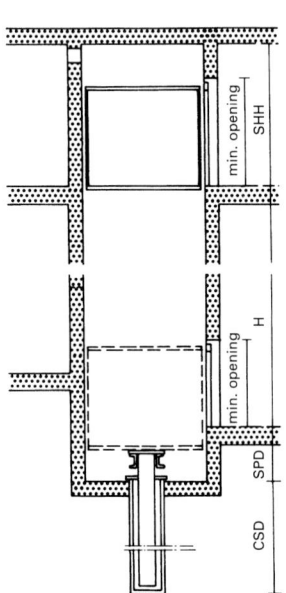

(3) **Vertical section of shaft**

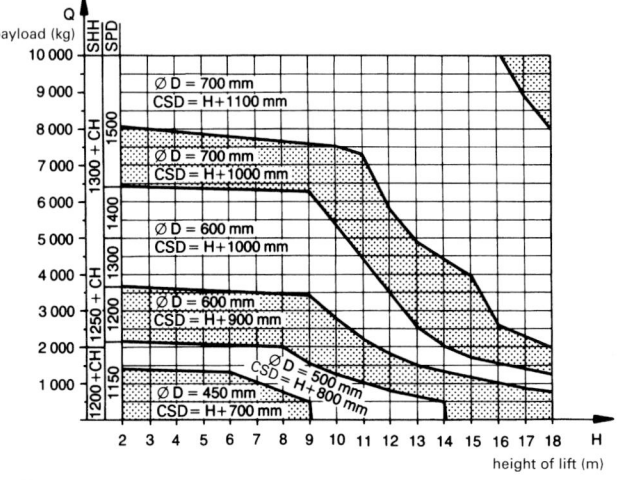

(4) **Graph to determine shaft head height SHH; shaft pit depth SPD; cylinder shaft depth CSD; cylinder shaft diameter D**

payload		Q ≠ 5000 kg	Q ≠ 10 000 kg
shaft width	SW	CW + 500	CW + 550
shaft depth	SD	CD + 150 with one door CD + 100 with opposite doors	
approx. measurements for lift motor room (lift motor room should be within 5 m of the shaft but may be further away if absolutely necessary)	width	2000	2200
	depth	2600	2800
	height	2200	2700

(5) **Technical data → ① – ③**

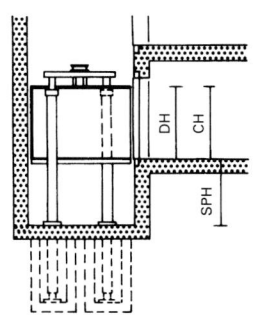

(6) **Rucksack arrangement 1:1**　　dimensions → ⑥

capacity	(kg)	630	1000	1600
speed	(m/s)	0.30	0.18	0.23
		0.47	0.28	0.39
max. lift height	(m)	6.0	7.0	7.0
car dimensions	(mm)			
	W	1100	1300	1500
	D	1500	1700	2200
	H	2200	2200	2200
door dimensions (mm)				
	W	1100	1300	1500
	H	2200	2200	2200
shaft dimensions (mm)				
	W	1650	1900	2150
	D	1600	1800	2300
	SPH min.	1200	1400	1600
	SHH min.	3200	3200	3200

(7) **Tandem arrangement 1:1**　　dimensions → ⑦

capacity	(kg)	1600	2000	2500	3200
speed	(m/s)	0.15	0.18	0.24	0.20
		0.24	0.30	0.38	0.30
max. lift height	(m)	6.0	7.0	7.0	7.0
car dimensions	(mm)				
	W	1500	1500	1800	2000
	D	2200	2200	2700	3500
	H	2200	2200	2200	2200
door dimensions (mm)					
	W	1500	1500	1800	2000
	H	2200	2200	2200	2200
shaft dimensions (mm)					
	W	2200	2200	2600	2800
	D	2300	2800	2800	3600
	SPH min.	1300	1300	1300	1300
	SHH min.	3450	3450	3450	3450

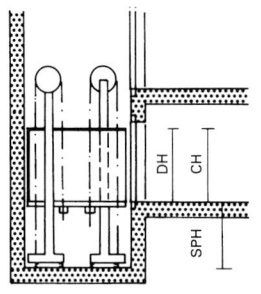

(8) **Rucksack arrangement 2:1**　　dimensions → ⑧

capacity	(kg)	630	1000	1600
speed	(m/s)	0.28	0.30	0.24
		0.46	0.50	0.42
		0.78	0.80	0.62
max. lift height	(m)	13.0	16.0	18.0
car dimensions	(mm)			
	W	1100	1300	1500
	D	1500	1900	2200
	H	2200	2200	2200
door dimensions (mm)				
	W	1100	1300	1500
	H	2200	2200	2200
shaft dimensions (mm)				
	W	1650	1900	2150
	D	1600	2000	2300
	SPH min.	1200	1400	1600
	SHH min.	3200	3200	3200

(9) **Tandem 2:1**　　dimensions → ⑨

capacity	(kg)	1600	2000	2500	3200
speed	(m/s)	0.23	0.19	0.25	0.21
		0.39	0.32	0.39	0.31
		0.61	0.50	0.64	0.51
max. lift height	(m)	13.0	14.0	16.0	18.0
car dimensions	(mm)				
	W	1500	1500	1800	2000
	D	2200	2200	2700	3500
	H	2200	2200	2200	2200
door dimensions (mm)					
	W	1500	1500	1800	2000
	H	2200	2200	2200	2200
shaft dimensions (mm)					
	W	2300	2300	2600	2900
	D	2300	2800	2800	3600
	SPH min.	1300	1300	1300	1300
	SHH min.	3400	3550	3650	3650

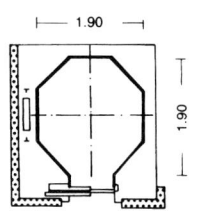

① Octagonal car shape

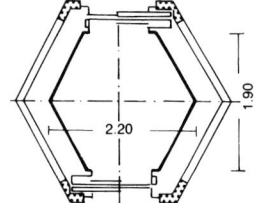

① Hexagonal shape

PANORAMIC GLASS LIFTS

Panoramic lifts are available in a variety of cabin shapes → ① – ⑥ and a carrying capacity of 400–1500 kg (5–20 passengers). There are several possible drive systems and nominal speeds, depending on the height of the building and requirements for comfort: 0.4, 0.63, 1.0 m/s with a three-phase a.c. drive; and 0.25–1.0 m/s with a hydraulic drive. Construction materials used are glass and steel – polished, brushed or with high gloss finish – brass and bronze.

The panoramic lift enjoys great popularity. This applies both to external lifts on the façades of imposing business premises from which passengers can enjoy the view, and internal lifts in department stores or in foyers of large hotels where they look out on to the sales floors and displays. → ⑩ – ⑪

Stairlifts

Stairlifts allow people with impaired mobility to move between floors with ease. They can be used on straight or curved stairways, and traverse landings. Aesthetics and maintenance of the rail mechanism must be given careful consideration during design and installation. In the UK, BS 5776: 1996 Powered stairlifts defines the requirements for such lift installations in domestic properties as well as in other buildings.

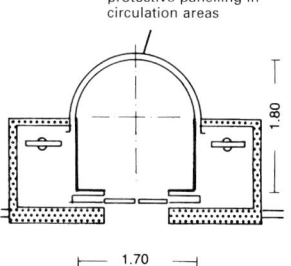

③ Semi-circular shape

protective panelling in circulation areas

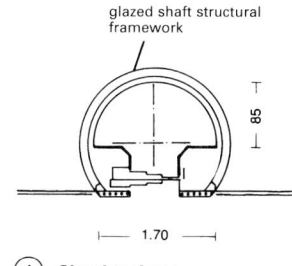

④ Circular shape

glazed shaft structural framework

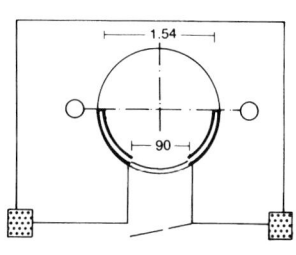

⑤ Circular car

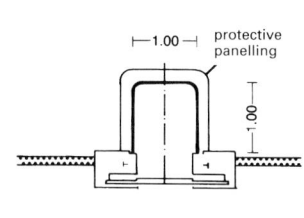

⑥ U-shape

protective panelling

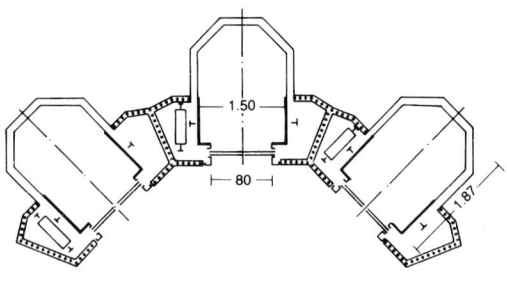

⑨ Group of panoramic glass lifts

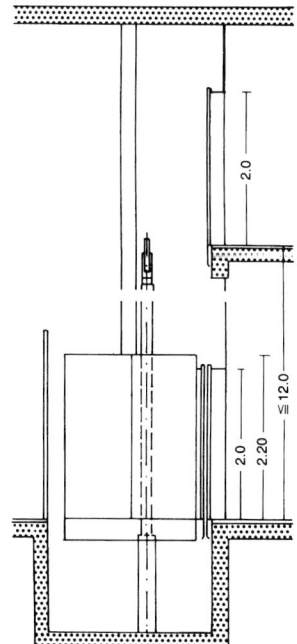

⑦ Cross-section of hydraulic lift → ③

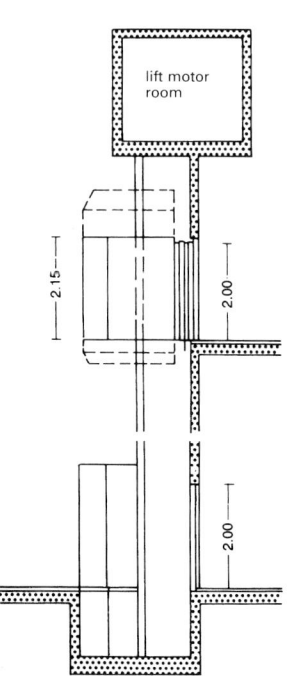

⑧ Cross-section of cable lift

lift motor room

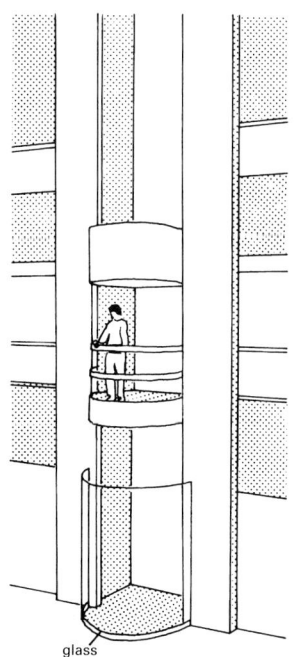

⑩ Lift on the inside of a building → ③

glass

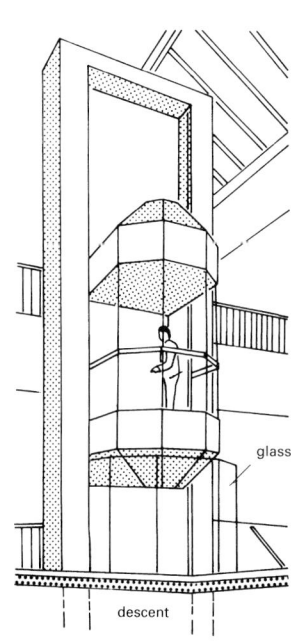

⑪ Panoramic lift → ⑨

glass

descent

(1) **Survey: measurement sketch**

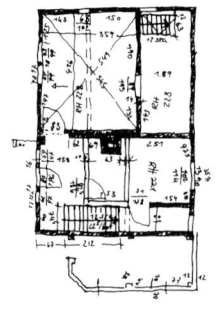

(2) **Survey: plan layout, sketch**

(3) **Survey: elevation drawing**

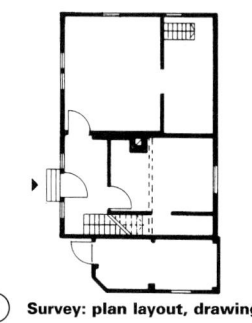

(4) **Survey: plan layout, drawing**

RENOVATION OF OLD BUILDINGS

Repairing, modernising, converting or adding structural extensions to an old building requires a different approach to the design process than for new buildings. It should be remembered that old buildings are often protected by law (e.g. listed buildings in the UK).

The first task in any renovation project is a thorough survey of the existing structure, in which every important component and detail has to be carefully inspected. The survey begins with a general description of the building (the plot, building specifications, applicable regulations or bylaws, the age of building and any historical design features, the use of the building (domestic or commercial) and any other features of interest) followed by a description of the building materials and the standard of the fittings, the technical building services, the framework and structural characteristics. Details about ownership, tenants and income from rental etc. should also be included. Sketches should be made and measurements taken so that plans of the building can be drawn → (1) – (4).

The survey must also describe the building's condition, with details of specific areas (façades, roof, stairs, cellar, and individual rooms), and all significant defective areas should be noted → (5). Typical problems include: cracked chimney tops, damaged and leaking roof structure, dry rot or woodworm in the timber (eaves, roof and wall connections, wooden joists in floors, doors, stairs etc.), cracks in the masonry and plaster, structural damage, leaking façades and guttering, no heat insulation and underlay, and cellar walls in need of damp-proofing. If structural steelwork is in place it should be checked for rust.

It is common to find that the existing heating and sanitation are unusable and that underground lines and house connections are damaged or possibly underdesigned.

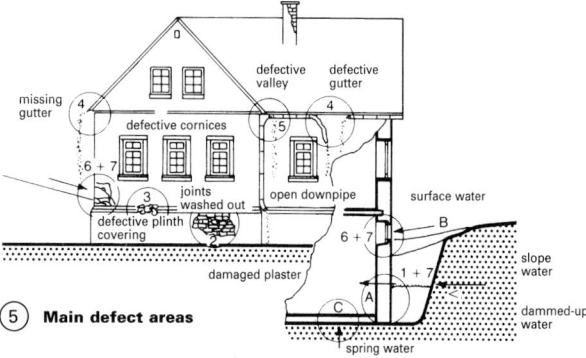

(5) **Main defect areas**

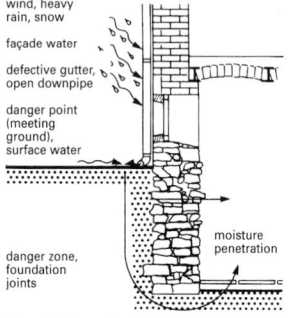

(6) **Main points of attack by non-pressurised water**

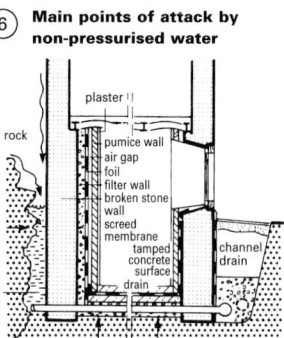

(7) **Main points of attack by pressurised water**

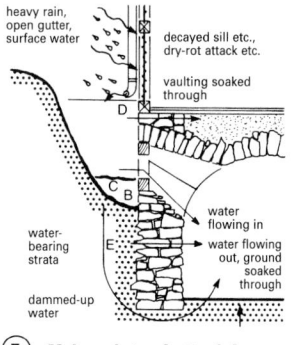

(8) **Retrofitted damp-proofing and drainage in cellar area**

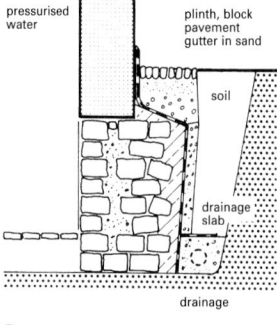

(9) **Injected damp-proofing**

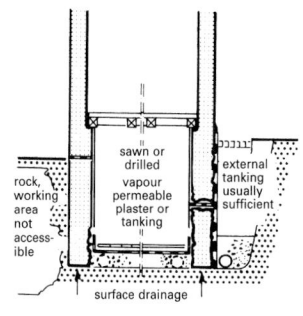

(10) **Damp-proofing from inside with partially inaccessible outer walls**

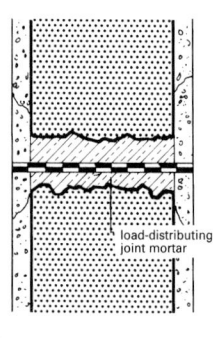

(11) **Repairs to soil side of masonry foundations**

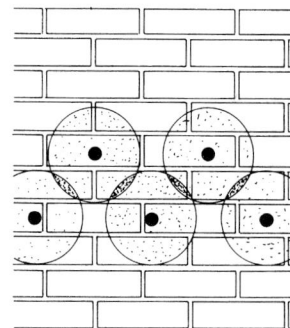

(12) **Retrofitted horizontal (damp-proof course)**

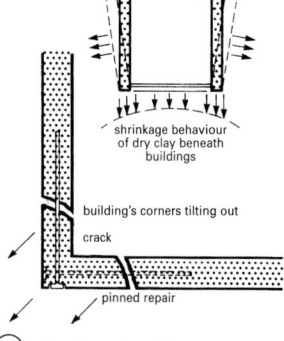

(13) **Pinning of a tilting corner**

202

RENOVATION OF OLD BUILDINGS

The early half-timbered houses contained no metal (nails, screws etc.) and repairs are possible using only parts made from wood if the intention is to preserve the house in its original state. The filling material used within the framework was traditionally earth or exposed masonry. There is no modern material that can be recommended as a substitute so these panels should be maintained and damaged ones repaired. Infilling with brickwork will stiffen the house and this is contrary to the structural principles of half-timbered structures.

The main defects encountered in half-timbered buildings appear in verges, eaves and roof connections, gutters and downpipes, connections on window plinths and other timber joints, where dry rot, fungal growth, mould, insects and water penetration can all cause problems → ①.

With old stone buildings, which may be either ashlar or 'rubble' construction, the main problems are with bulging/bowing of the walls, often accompanied by cracking, defective pointing, erosion and decay of the stones. As with conventional brick walls, there are effective restoration techniques to deal with these problems but it is important to understand the cause of the damage in order to make the repairs completely effective. If there are clearly major defects professional advice should be sought.

① **Main defect areas in half-timbered houses**

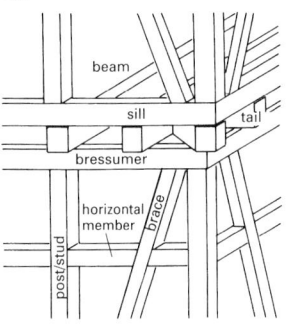

② **Framework construction**

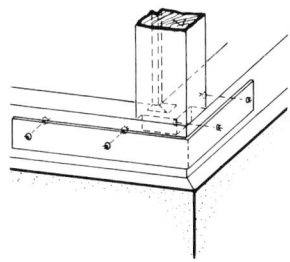

③ **Corner stiffening with metal anchor**

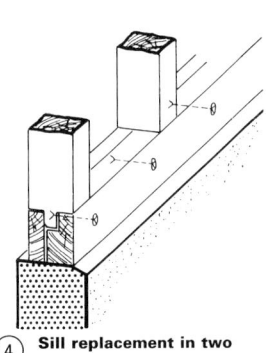

④ **Sill replacement in two operations**

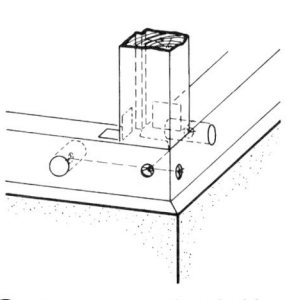

⑤ **Sill corner reanchored with cap screws**

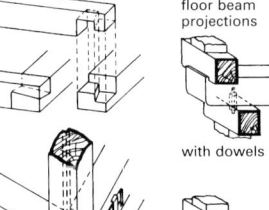

floor beam projections

with dowels

bracketed

⑥ **Corner connections for framework sills**

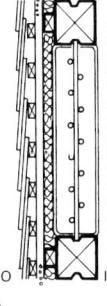

external insulation with highly vapour permeable insulating material under back-ventilated panelling: wood shingle, 24/48 mm battens, air gap, 40 mm heat insulation, old lime plaster, mud and straw with wooden supports made from oak canes and willow, inner plaster (lime)

⑦ **Exterior panelling**

construction with good heat insulation, internal frame panelled: external mineral plaster, 25 mm lightweight wood wool composite panel, 2 × 40 mm mineral fibre insulation boards, 24/48 mm battens, plasterboard or lightweight wood wool composite panels and reed mats, rendered

⑧ **New panel**

construction with framework visible from outside and inside: 15 mm silicate plaster, fabric, 20 mm lightweight wood wool composite panels, 80 mm mineral fibre insulating board, 25 mm lightweight wood wool composite panel, mesh (non-metallic), lime plaster

⑨ **New panel**

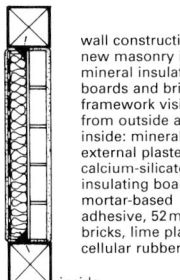

wall construction with new masonry infill, mineral insulation boards and bricks, and framework visible from outside and inside: mineral external plaster, 60 mm calcium-silicate insulating board, mortar-based adhesive, 52 mm solid bricks, lime plaster, cellular rubber strip

inside

⑩ **New panel**

⑪ **Panel built up with earth and wooden canes, filled in with building rubble, with klinker nogging**

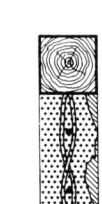

frame connection onto fresh wood

⑫ **Theoretically favourable panel formation**

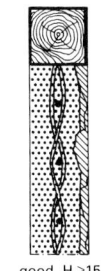

poor   good H ≥15

⑬ **Shallow repairs to earth panels**

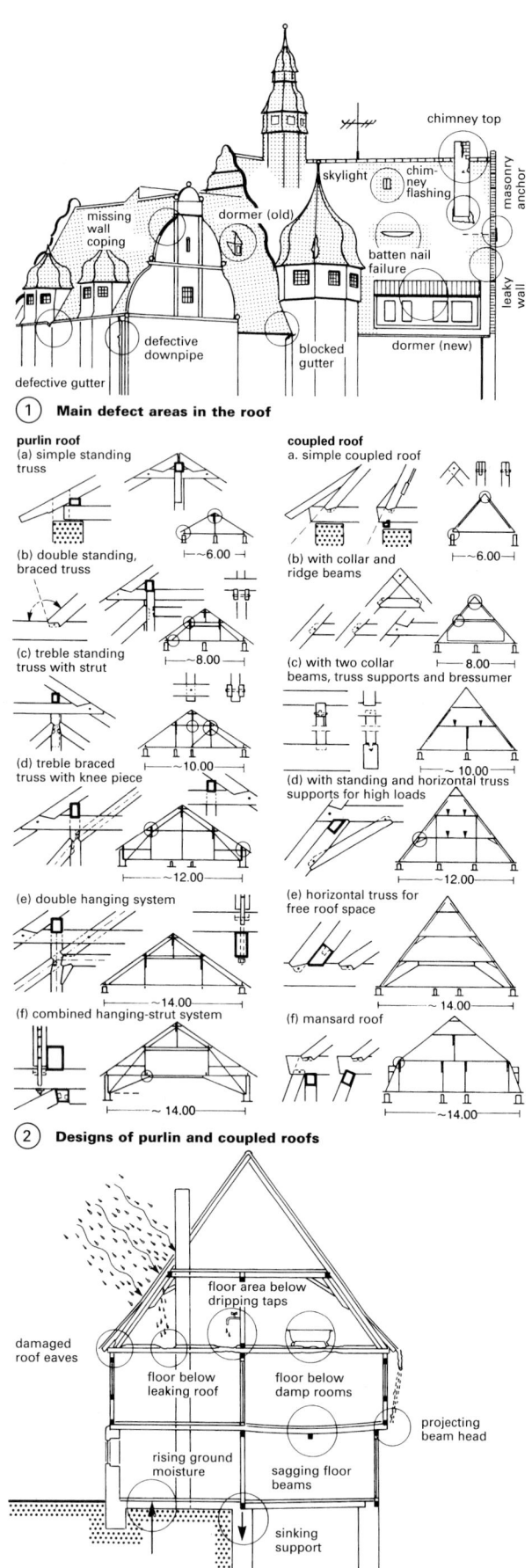

(1) **Main defect areas in the roof**

purlin roof
(a) simple standing truss
⊢~6.00⊣

(b) double standing, braced truss

(c) treble standing truss with strut
⊢~8.00⊣

(d) treble braced truss with knee piece
⊢~10.00⊣

(e) double hanging system
⊢~12.00⊣

(f) combined hanging-strut system
⊢~14.00⊣

coupled roof
a. simple coupled roof
⊢~6.00⊣

(b) with collar and ridge beams

(c) with two collar beams, truss supports and bressumer
⊢~8.00⊣

(d) with standing and horizontal truss supports for high loads
⊢~10.00⊣

(e) horizontal truss for free roof space
⊢~12.00⊣

⊢~14.00⊣

(f) mansard roof
⊢~14.00⊣

(2) **Designs of purlin and coupled roofs**

(5) **Key problems in floors and their causes**

labels: damaged roof eaves; floor area below dripping taps; floor below leaking roof; floor below damp rooms; projecting beam head; rising ground moisture; sagging floor beams; sinking support

RENOVATION OF OLD BUILDINGS

The roof is the part of a building that is subjected to the worst effects of the weather and roof maintenance is therefore crucial. Small defects, which may go unnoticed, can result in significant damage if left for a period of time. For a renovation project to be successful it is vital to have the roof framework and cover in perfect condition. → ① + ⑤

Historically, the material used for roof construction in most parts of the world has been wood and all forms of roof truss are still based on triangular bracing in many different designs → ② – ④.

To avoid later claims for damage, a thorough knowledge of the load distribution is required before carrying out roof renovation. Roof loads do not consist just of the dead weight of the roof and snow loading: rather, because roofs have a high surface area, loads are mainly imposed by wind. The condition and existence of wind bracing is therefore of great significance for the stability of the roof → ④.

Where there is no cellar below, it is recommended that existing floor coverings with no heat insulation or damp-proof membrane be renewed with a completely new structure → ⑤ + ⑦.

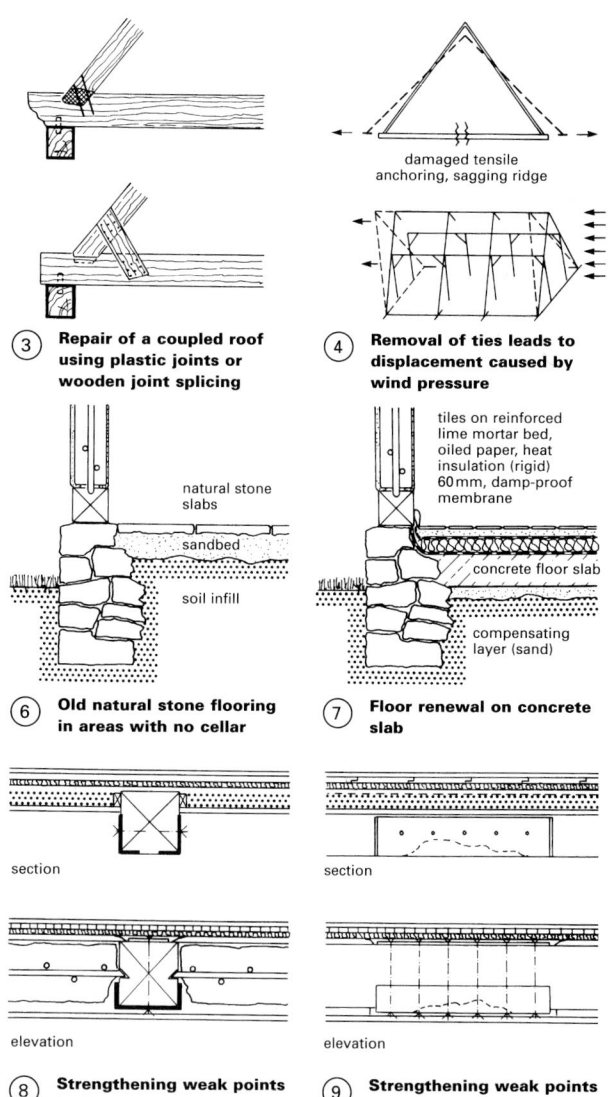

(3) **Repair of a coupled roof using plastic joints or wooden joint splicing**

(4) **Removal of ties leads to displacement caused by wind pressure**

damaged tensile anchoring, sagging ridge

(6) **Old natural stone flooring in areas with no cellar**

labels: natural stone slabs; sandbed; soil infill

(7) **Floor renewal on concrete slab**

labels: tiles on reinforced lime mortar bed, oiled paper, heat insulation (rigid) 60 mm, damp-proof membrane; concrete floor slab; compensating layer (sand)

(8) **Strengthening weak points in the span**

section

elevation

(9) **Strengthening weak points in the span**

section

elevation

RENOVATION OF OLD BUILDINGS

In early times the sizing of load-bearing floor beams in old buildings was calculated empirically by the carpenter. The loads are normally carried by cross-beams which are supported by one or more longitudinal joists.

An old building manual from 1900 gives a ratio of 5:7 for the height and the width of a beam as a starting point for the determination of the required beam strength. Another rule of thumb held that the beam height in cm should be approximately half the size of the room depth in decimetres. Because of these methods, old wooden beam floors often display significant sagging. However, this does not endanger the structural stability as long as the permitted tensions are not exceeded.

There are several options when carrying out renovation work: for example, joists can be strengthened by adding a second wooden beam and an improvement in load distribution can be achieved with the installation of additional floor beams or steel girders →①–④. In addition, the span can be shortened by installing one or more additional joists or a supporting cross-wall. However, structural changes of the framework must be preceded by an accurate analysis of all load-carrying and stiffening functions and the integrity of all connections must be checked thoroughly.

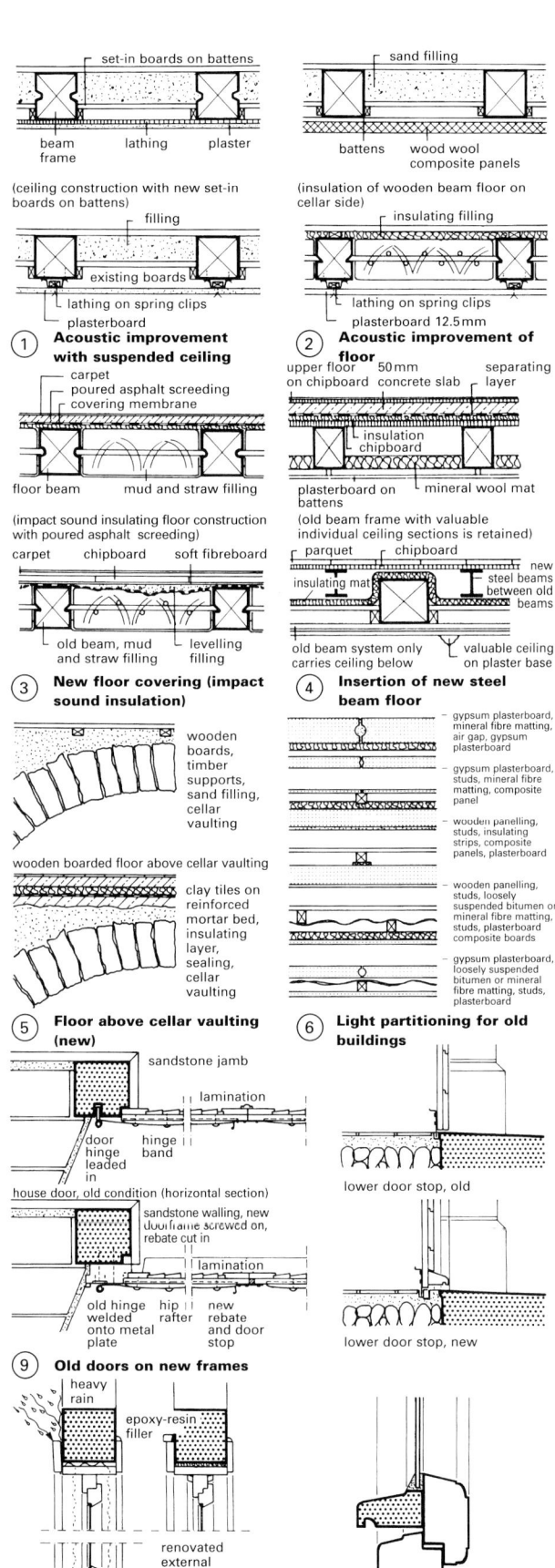

set-in boards on battens
beam / frame   lathing   plaster
(ceiling construction with new set-in boards on battens)

filling
existing boards
lathing on spring clips
plasterboard

① **Acoustic improvement with suspended ceiling**

carpet
poured asphalt screeding
covering membrane

floor beam   mud and straw filling
(impact sound insulating floor construction with poured asphalt screeding)

carpet   chipboard   soft fibreboard

old beam, mud and straw filling   levelling filling

③ **New floor covering (impact sound insulation)**

wooden boards, timber supports, sand filling, cellar vaulting

wooden boarded floor above cellar vaulting

clay tiles on reinforced mortar bed, insulating layer, sealing, cellar vaulting

⑤ **Floor above cellar vaulting (new)**

sand filling
battens   wood wool composite panels
(insulation of wooden beam floor on cellar side)

insulating filling
lathing on spring clips
plasterboard 12.5mm

② **Acoustic improvement of floor**

upper floor 50mm   separating
on chipboard concrete slab   layer
insulation
chipboard
plasterboard on battens   mineral wool mat
(old beam frame with valuable individual ceiling sections is retained)

parquet   chipboard
insulating mat   new steel beams between old beams
old beam system only carries ceiling below   valuable ceiling on plaster base

④ **Insertion of new steel beam floor**

gypsum plasterboard, mineral fibre matting, air gap, gypsum plasterboard

gypsum plasterboard, studs, mineral fibre matting, composite panel

wooden panelling, studs, insulating strips, composite panels, plasterboard

wooden panelling, studs, loosely suspended bitumen or mineral fibre matting, studs, plasterboard composite boards

gypsum plasterboard, loosely suspended bitumen or mineral fibre matting, studs, plasterboard

⑥ **Light partitioning for old buildings**

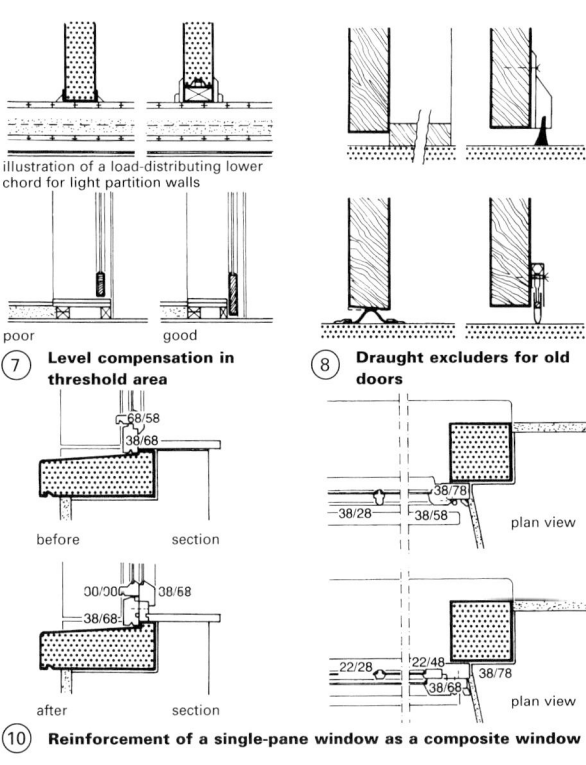

illustration of a load-distributing lower chord for light partition walls

poor   good

⑦ **Level compensation in threshold area**

before   section

after   section

⑧ **Draught excluders for old doors**

plan view

plan view

⑩ **Reinforcement of a single-pane window as a composite window**

sandstone jamb
lamination
door hinge leaded in   hinge band
house door, old condition (horizontal section)
sandstone walling, new doorframe screwed on, rebate cut in
lamination
old hinge welded onto metal plate   hip rafter   new rebate and door stop

⑨ **Old doors on new frames**

lower door stop, old

lower door stop, new

heavy rain
epoxy-resin filler

renovated external panelling

decayed sill beam

⑪ **Moisture damage to outer cladding**

⑫ **New oak door drip on old wooden frame**

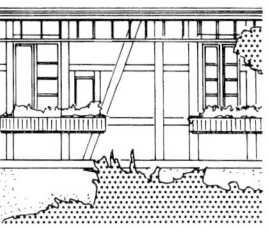

⑬ **Insertion of a prefabricated window**

⑭ **Timber-framed house**

worn steps
compensating layer (plastic or alternative material)
angle section (template for compensation)

step covered or coated

PVC edge-strip

(1) **Renovation of worn steps**

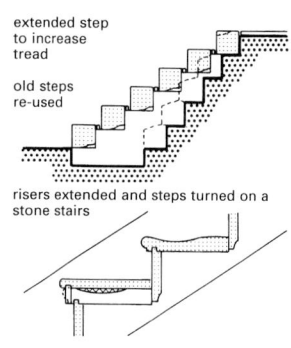

extended step to increase tread

old steps re-used

risers extended and steps turned on a stone stairs

(2) **Extension of worn stairs**

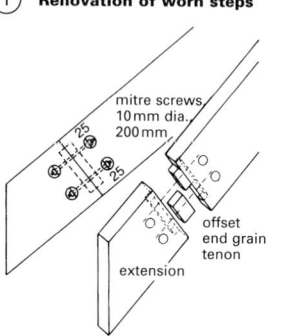

mitre screws, 10mm dia., 200mm.

25
25

offset end grain tenon

extension

(3) **Extension of stair strings**

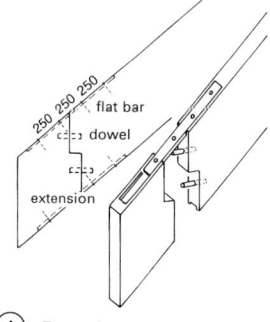

250 250 250

flat bar

dowel

extension

(4) **Extension of stair strings**

RENOVATION OF OLD BUILDINGS

Stairs

External and internal stairs are significant structural features in old buildings. If the stairs are in poor condition remember the most important rule for repairs is: repair only what can be repaired → (1) – (4).

External stairs are mostly made of natural stone and normally serve to reach floor levels on plinths → (2). Worn-down stone steps can sometimes be restored if they are reversed and dressed underneath.

There are many types of design and materials used for internal stairs although the most common material used is wood.

Wet rooms and bathrooms

Improvement in sanitary facilities is one of the most important modernisation tasks. Planning of the new solutions should be highly sympathetic to the existing layout and then coordinated with the technical necessities → (5) – (9).

Walls and floors must be planned and installed with care. The most serious damage to be avoided is that associated with leaks around showers and baths → (12) – (14). Faulty or missing vapour barriers mainly on outer walls with internal insulation can also lead to condensation forming in the structure. This is a major cause of rot and the incidence of mould.

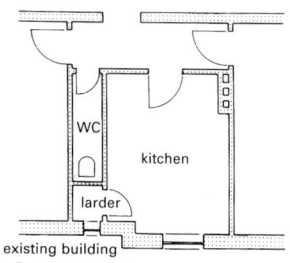

WC
kitchen
larder

existing building

(5) **New bathroom installations** → (6) – (8)

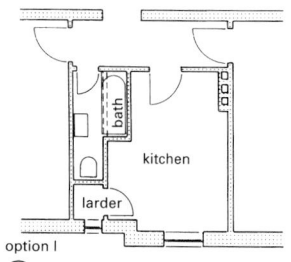

bath
kitchen
larder

option I

(6) **Increase around bath size**

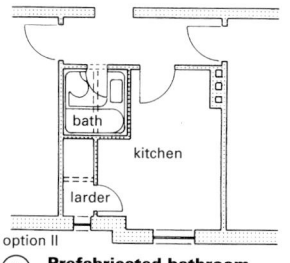

bath
kitchen
larder

option II

(7) **Prefabricated bathroom made of plastic**

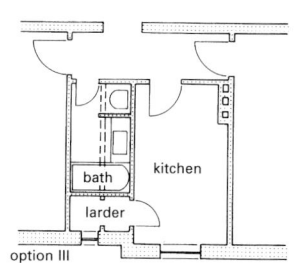

bath
kitchen
larder

option III

(8) **Widening to bath length**

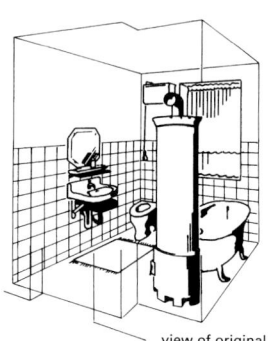

view of original

view of new arrangement

(9) **Pipes/lines laid in surface-mounted ducts**

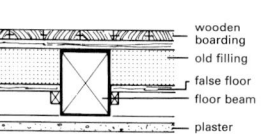
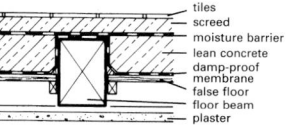

wooden boarding
old filling
false floor
floor beam
plaster

tiles
screed
moisture barrier
lean concrete
damp-proof membrane
false floor
floor beam
plaster

(10) **Sealing options for wooden beam floors**

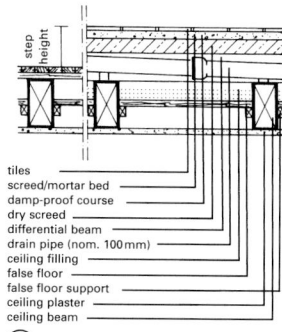

step height

tiles
screed/mortar bed
damp-proof course
dry screed
differential beam
drain pipe (nom. 100mm)
ceiling filling
false floor
false floor support
ceiling plaster
ceiling beam

(11) **Laying waste pipe below new floor**

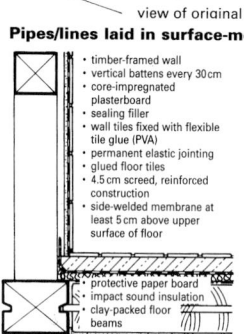

· timber-framed wall
· vertical battens every 30cm
· core-impregnated plasterboard
· sealing filler
· wall tiles fixed with flexible tile glue (PVA)
· permanent elastic jointing
· glued floor tiles
· 4.5cm screed, reinforced construction
· side-welded membrane at least 5cm above upper surface of floor

· protective paper board
· impact sound insulation
· clay-packed floor beams

(12) **Floor/wall structure in damp areas in a half-timbered building**

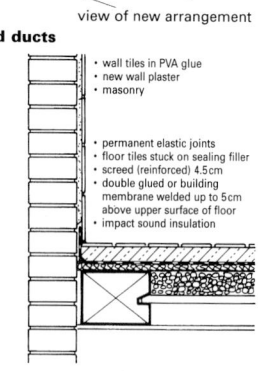

· wall tiles in PVA glue
· new wall plaster
· masonry

· permanent elastic joints
· floor tiles stuck on sealing filler
· screed (reinforced) 4.5cm
· double glued or building membrane welded up to 5cm above upper surface of floor
· impact sound insulation

(13) **Floor/wall structure in damp areas in a masonry building with wooden beam floors**

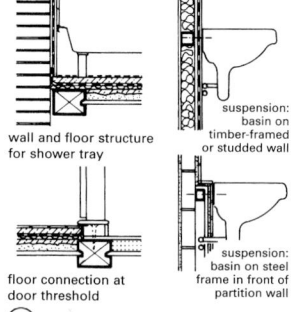

wall and floor structure for shower tray

suspension: basin on timber-framed or studded wall

floor connection at door threshold

suspension: basin on steel frame in front of partition wall

(14) **Important details in damp locations**

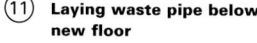

installation system in double-leaf partition wall

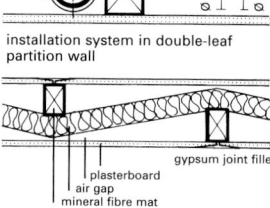

Ø pipeline
Ø connection

gypsum joint filler
plasterboard
air gap
mineral fibre mat
studs

(15) **Noise insulating double-leaf wall construction**

Drawings (left column)

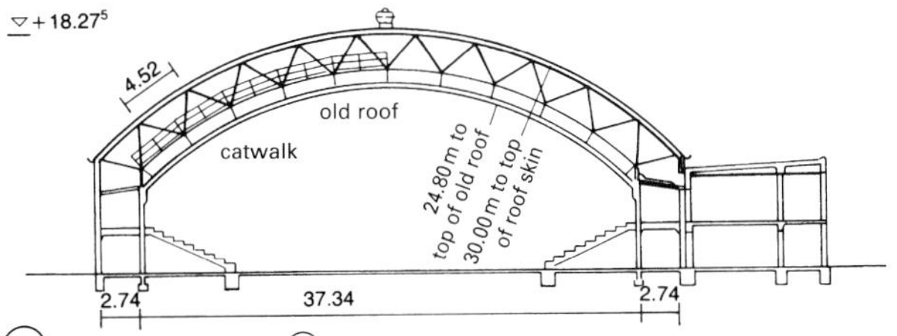

▽ +18.27⁵

4.52

old roof

catwalk

24.80 m to top of old roof
30.00 m to top of roof skin

2.74   37.34   2.74

① **Cross-section → ②**

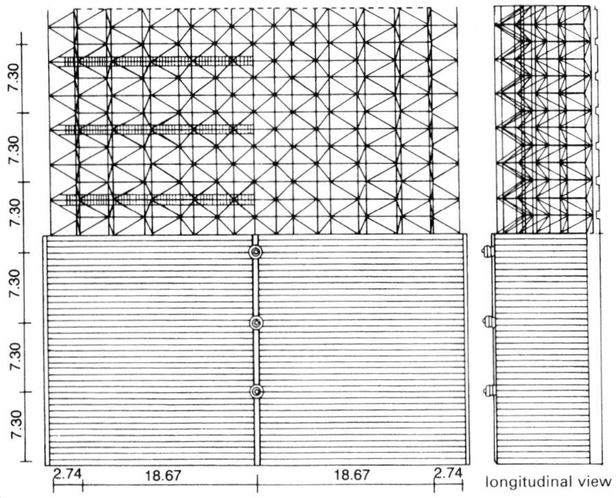

7.30 / 7.30 / 7.30 / 7.30 / 7.30 / 7.30

2.74   18.67   18.67   2.74

longitudinal view

② **Spaceframe/view of roof**

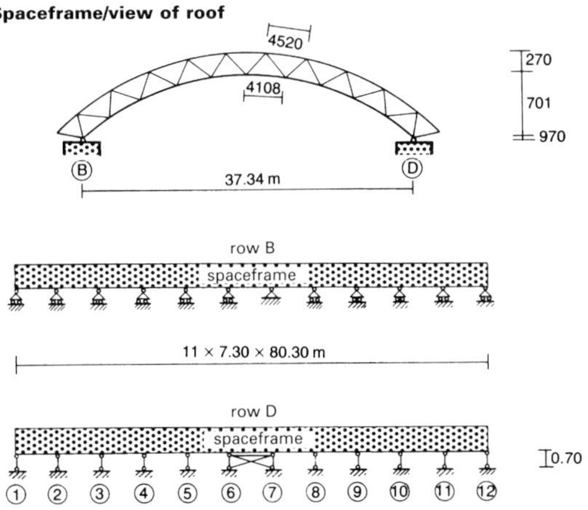

4520

4108

270
701
970

Ⓑ   37.34 m   Ⓓ

row B

spaceframe

11 × 7.30 × 80.30 m

row D

spaceframe

0.70

① ② ③ ④ ⑤ ⑥ ⑦ ⑧ ⑨ ⑩ ⑪ ⑫

③ **Static system to allow for movement**

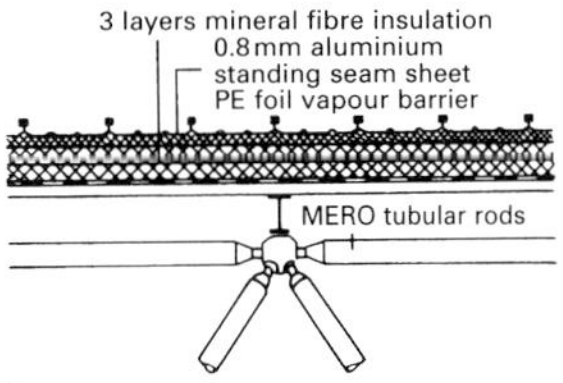

3 layers mineral fibre insulation
0.8 mm aluminium
standing seam sheet
PE foil vapour barrier

MERO tubular rods

fixing clip, galvanized
Z section

purlins

trapezoidal
sheet

④ **Roof skin structure, longitudinal view**

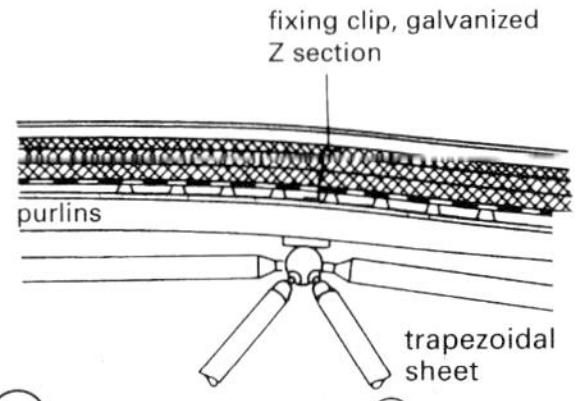

⑤ **Cross-section → ④**

⑥ **70 cm high support allowing one-way movement → ③**    ⑦

MAINTENANCE AND RESTORATION

Examples of solutions

In this example, the aim was to preserve an old wooden structure by covering it with an arched steel roof.

The multipurpose hall built in Münster in 1928 was covered over with a steel roof which was so badly damaged in the Second World War that it had to be completely renewed. However, after the war steel was too expensive to consider, so for 35 years the 37 × 80 m hall was covered only by a wooden network shell with no columns. The structure carried just its own weight, snow load or loads such as lighting platforms, and had no heat insulation.

Project requirements

The new roof skin must:
- meet heat insulation regulations;
- insulate the inside from external noises and keep internal reflected sound to a minimum.

The new structure should also:
- carry special loads, such as sporting equipment, backdrops, lighting bridges etc.;
- be sufficiently strong to be walked on;
- be able to be mounted on the existing foundations;
- allow the network construction to be maintained;
- offer planning and manufacturing times as short as possible.

Solution

A spaceframe structure made from circular-section tubes screwed into nodes gave the required minimisation of the total weight and the existing wooden structure was suspended from this → ①. Twenty-two of these spaceframe arches are cross-linked by expanding diagonals and bridge an area of 37.34 × 80.30 m. One of the two 70 cm high rows of supports has sliding bearings to allow movement and the second row is designed as a pin-jointed support system → ⑥. Ten transverse catwalks are installed in the spaceframe → ①.

Small cranes preassembled seven large-scale structural elements, weighing up to 32 t, which were then put in position in 2¹/₂ days with a 500 t crane → ⑦ – ⑧.

The structure is galvanized and painted with a PVC acrylic paint and a special insulation layer for corrosion and fire protection. The roof skin consists of purlins, steel trapezoidal sheets, a vapour barrier, heat insulation and aluminium standing seam sheeting to protect from rain → ④ – ⑤.

The parties involved were: Münsterlandhalle GmbH, Hochbauamt Münster, MERO spatial structures and numerous specialist engineers.

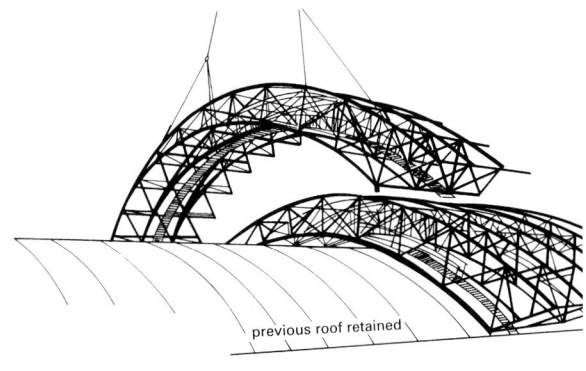

previous roof retained

⑧ **Lifting a space frame section into place → ⑦**

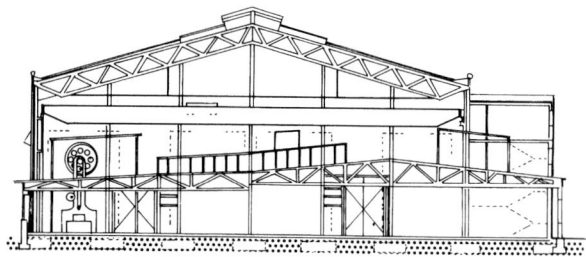

(1) **Old and new cross-section drawn over one another** → ② + ③

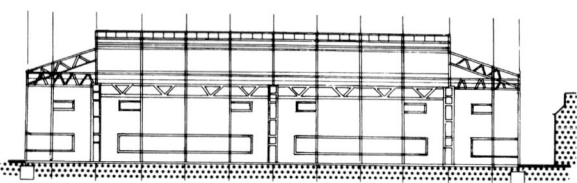

large machines remain in place during conversion

(2) **Longitudinal section** → ③

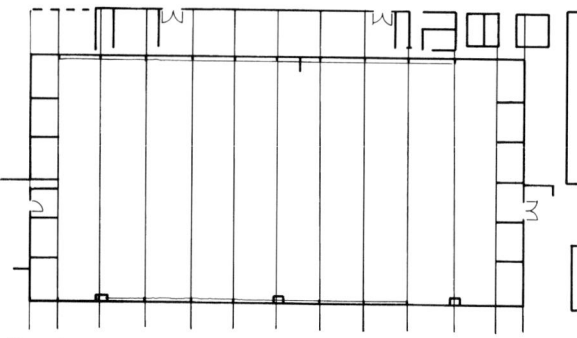

(3) **Plan view**

MAINTENANCE AND RESTORATION

In this example a renewal and extension was carried out by building a steel frame over the top of an existing building. On densely built-up land in Munich a light metal works had reached a stage at which it became necessary to renew and extend the forging shop. The old building had already been altered many times and with the installation of new machines had undergone many different roof reconstructions → ① – ③.

The requirements for the new shop were that it should:
- have substantially greater headroom;
- stand within the building lines of the old shop, because there was no possibility of pulling it down and rebuilding;
- not interrupt production for more than 2–3 weeks and keep disruption to the minimum;
- have an aesthetically attractive appearance that is in keeping with the adjacent listed administrative building;
- permit the addition of a second building phase.

Solution

The architects selected a steel structure to take advantage of:
- a column-free building → ② + ③;
- a large span with low dead weight
- opportunities for prefabrication and assembly in a short time with lightweight equipment, a decisive factor in the project.

The outer walls consist of suspended concrete-composite prefabricated panels. These provide the high noise insulation mass and robustness required for a forging shop as well as permitting dry assembly.

Conversion work was precisely planned: after assembly of the steel structure the old shell was dismantled with a new, in-house overhead travelling crane and at the same time the new roof covering was progressively fitted → ④ – ⑧.

The sloping roof with trussed rafters is hipped at one end of the building in order to match the hipped roof of the administrative building, to maintain the spacing heights and to permit natural ventilation. Air supply louvres are built into the outer walls and extract air openings are in the roof ridge → ⑨ + ⑩.

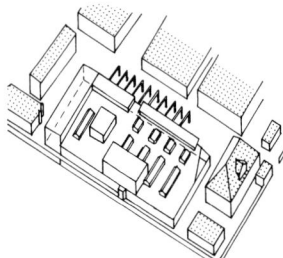

(4) **Existing situation when planning started**

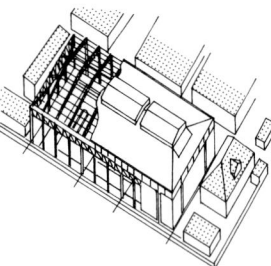

existing construction between forging shop and administrative building is removed

(5) **First demolition stage**

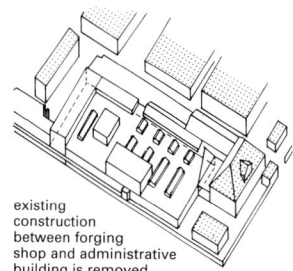

new steel structure is installed above existing roof of old shop

(6) **Installation of new steel structure begins**

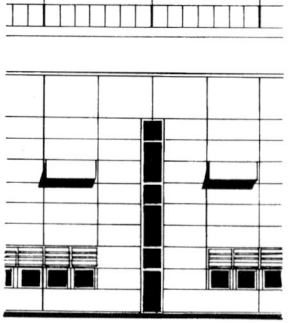

old walls dismantled after new steel structure is fully assembled

(7) **Dismantling of old walls begins**

new crane takes over dismantling old roof; parts removed through the still-open west gable; outer walls and roof are then closed up

(8) **Dismantling of old roof begins**

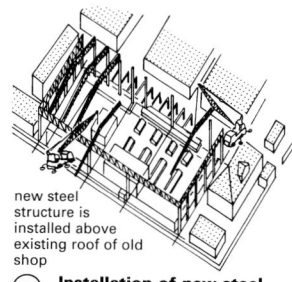

(9) **Section of façade with fresh air openings**

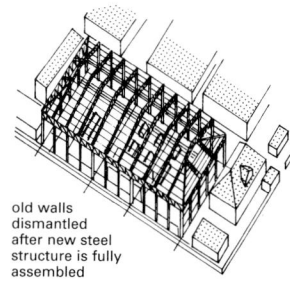

Architects: Henn and Henn

(10) **The new building is planned with regard to the old one**

208

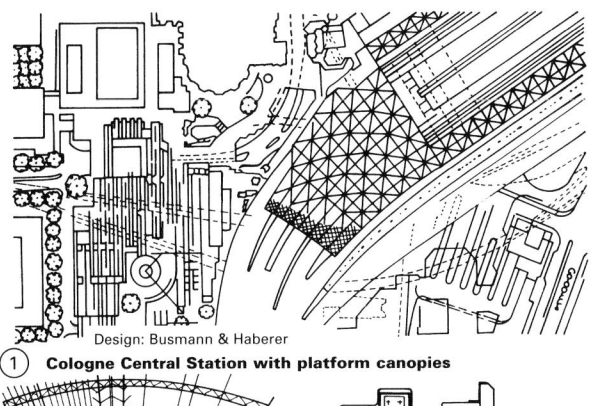

Design: Busmann & Haberer

① Cologne Central Station with platform canopies

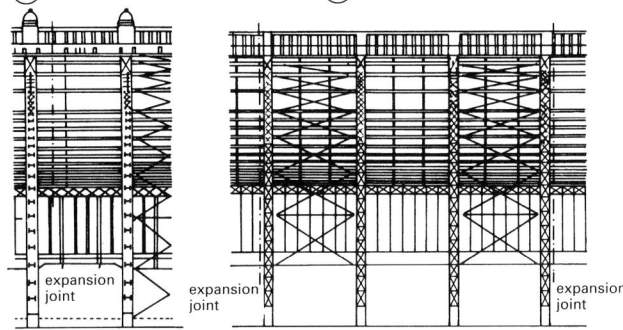

② Curved trusses span 62 m

A) old verge cornice
B) new verge cornice: reduced number of profiles; great attention paid to water run-off

③ Cornices

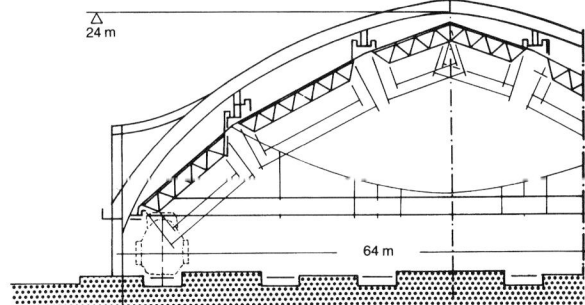

expansion joint   expansion joint   expansion joint

④ Old wind bracing installed right down to platform; new bracing with strengthened curved trusses in lower area

24 m

64 m

⑤ Section through main hall, with travelling internal scaffolding

MAINTENANCE AND RESTORATION

This example examines the refurbishment of the main platform hall of Cologne Central Station. All corrosion and residual war damage was to be removed from the beautiful 80-year-old steel structure, which has 30 main curved trusses. The multilayered roof skin and strip rooflights also had to be renewed. The historical shape had to be retained, despite the use of modern materials, and the building work could not significantly affect railway operations and traffic.

Solution

A travelling steel internal scaffolding unit was planned to give simultaneously a working platform and protect the railway operations below from falling tools or building components. It used the MERO nodal rod system, with 1400 nodes and 5000 rods, and consisted of five main components that were connected together to make one 50 tonne element of 38 m × 56 m. It was moved in sections on six tracks and in three-weekly cycles. The individual parts, which were pre-assembled in a goods yard, were mounted on wagons and put together under the main hall arch according to a time plan that had to be accurate to the minute → ⑤.

An illustration of how new technology was used in the restoration work is shown in the renewal of the transverse wind bracing. The old system connected two curved trusses respectively into one rigid unit and the round steel wind bracing extended right down to the luggage platform. In the new system, four curved trusses are respectively combined in the lower area to make a flexurally rigid frame and the expansion joints reduced → ④. Although the cornice details etc. have a lower number of profiles, they have also been designed to look almost identical to the old ones → ③.

Following completion of the restoration of the main hall it was planned to renew the vaulted roofs to the south east. Being close to the cathedral and a new museum, the requirements went far beyond simple functionalism and the awkward geometry of the tracks added further difficulty. Three proposals were made during an expert survey → ⑥ – ⑧. Two used intermediately suspended and differently curved shell construction. The third proposed a spatially effective bearer system, which spans the whole area, like crossed vaulting → ⑧. Because this system offered considerable advantages it was recommended for further development.

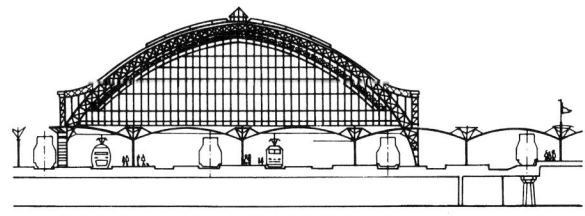

⑦ Design proposal: Neufert Planungs AG

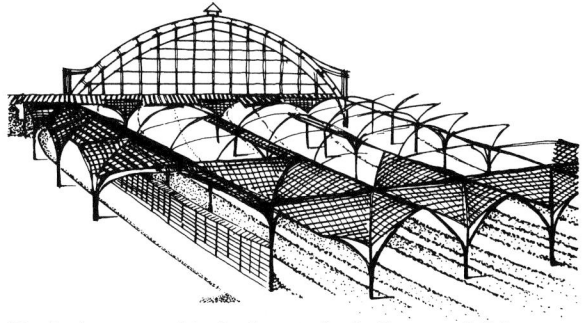

⑧ Design proposal for implementation by Busmann & Haberer with prof. Polónyi

⑥ Design proposal: Planteam West Köln-Aachen

CHANGE OF USE

There is currently enormous interest in converting structurally sound old buildings for new uses.

→ ① – ③ Previously a textile factory, the spinning hall was converted into a town hall and the textile mill was converted into dwellings and business premises. A hotel was created from the wool store.

→ ④ – ⑦ The old market halls at Covent Garden now house shops, restaurants and a pub. Offices have been installed on the upper floor.

→ ⑧ – ⑨ This silo plant is now an architect's office. Walls had to be taken out and bridge-type platforms installed to connect the silos at different levels.

→ ⑩ – ⑪ A waterworks that supplied Rotterdam with water until 1975 is now an arts centre, with workshops and dwellings too.

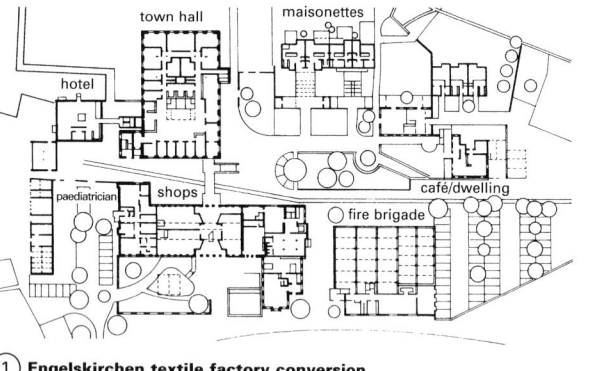

① **Engelskirchen textile factory conversion**

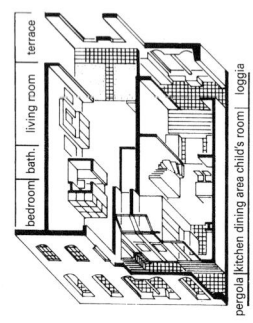

② **Maisonettes** → ①

③ **Town hall** → ①

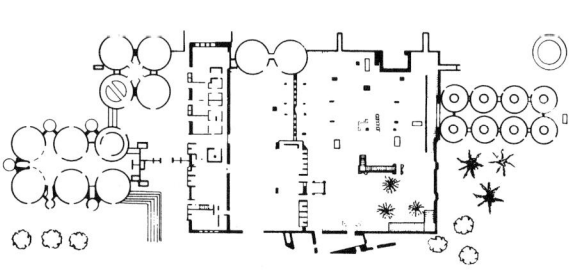

⑧ **Plan: a silo plant converted into an architect's office** → ⑨

④ **Covent Garden, London** → ⑤ – ⑦

⑤ **Covent Garden, plan**

⑨ **General view** → ⑧

Architect: R. Bofill

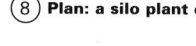

⑥ **Covent Garden, cross-section**

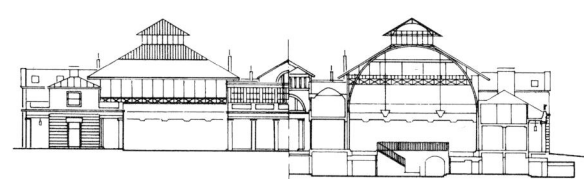

⑩ **Plan: conversion of Honingerdijk waterworks into an arts centre**

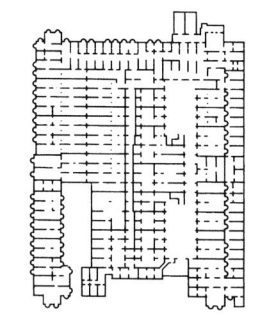

⑦ **Covent Garden: old market halls are now a complex of shops, restaurants and offices**

Utopia group, Rotterdam

⑪ **Section** → ⑩

Flats in Boston, USA

→ ① – ② This former piano factory has four wings surrounding an inner courtyard. The building is narrow and has many window openings, which made it highly suitable for flats.

Pavilion Baltard, Nogent-sur-Marne, France

→ ③ – ④ An old market hall is now a multipurpose hall suitable for events with up to 300 attendees. There are new parking facilities and function rooms in the basement.

Culture centre, Geneva

→ ⑤ – ⑦ This building, which had existed since 1848 and was previously a slaughterhouse, was converted into a culture centre with exhibition rooms, a theatre, music rehearsal room and a restaurant.

Flats, Nestbeth Housing, New York

→ ⑧ There are now 384 flats in this former telephone factory. In addition, shops, workshops, exhibition rooms, a cinema and rehearsal rooms were created on the available area of about 60000 m².

Schloß Gottorf, Schleswig

→ ⑨ – ⑪ This former riding hall was converted into a museum and now houses a collection of contemporary art. The building is the most significant cultural building in the region.

School building, San Francisco

→ ⑫ Originally a storehouse, this building is now a school. The fourth and fifth floors contain training laboratories, the second and third floors house the school and there are more laboratories on the first floor.

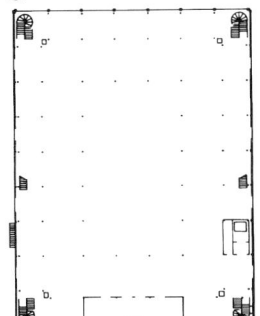

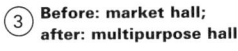

① **Typical plan**

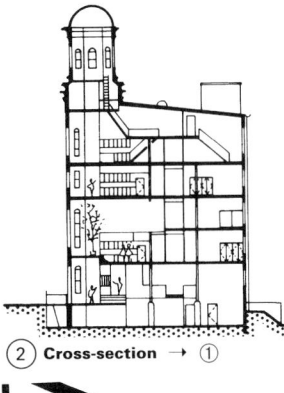

② **Cross-section** → ①

③ **Before: market hall; after: multipurpose hall**

④ **Inside view** → ③

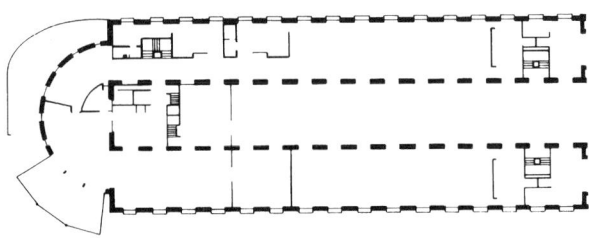

⑤ **Before: slaughterhouse; after: culture centre** → ⑥ – ⑦

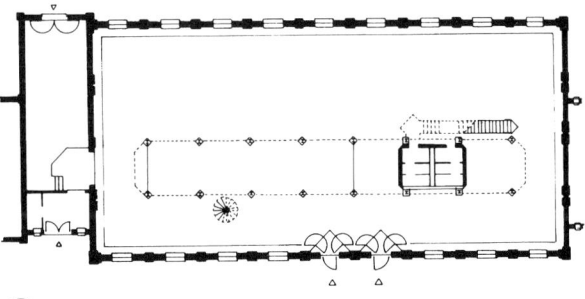

⑨ **Before: riding hall; after: museum** → ⑩ – ⑪

⑥ **Internal view** → ⑤

⑦ **General view** → ⑤

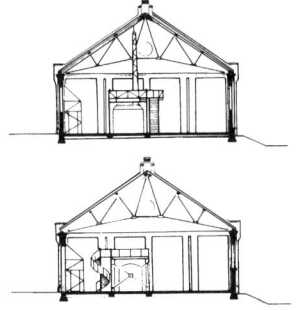

⑩ **Cross-section** → ⑨

⑪ **Internal view of hall** → ⑨

upper floor with dwellings

⑧ **Before: telephone factory; after: dwellings**

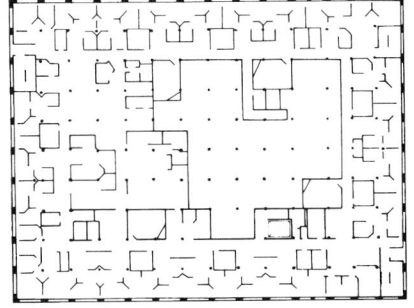

⑫ **Former storehouse is now a school**

ROAD DIMENSIONS

SPACE REQUIREMENT AT FULL SPEED (≥ 50 km/h)

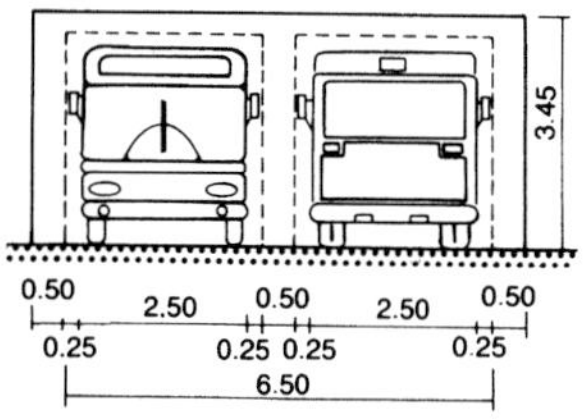

3.45
0.50 2.50 0.50 2.50 0.50
0.25 0.25 0.25 0.25
6.50

(1) **Bus/bus**

4.50
0.50 2.50 2.50 0.50
0.25 0.25 0.25 0.25
6.25

(2) **Lorry/lorry**

0.50 2.50 0.25 1.75 0.50
0.25 0.25 0.25 0.25
5.50

(3) **Lorry/car**

0.50 2.50 0.25 0.50
0.25 0.25
4.25

(4) **Lorry/bicycle**

2.70
0.50 2.10 0.25 2.10 0.50
0.25 0.25 0.25 0.25
5.45

(5) **Van/van**

0.50 2.10 0.25 1.75 0.50
0.25 0.25 0.25 0.25
5.10

(6) **Van/car**

0.50 2.10 0.25 0.50
0.25 0.25 1.00
3.85

(7) **Van/bicycle**

2.00
0.50 1.75 0.25 1.75 0.50
0.25 0.25 0.25 0.25
4.75

(8) **Car/car**

2.50
0.50 1.75 0.25 1.00 0.50
0.25 0.25
3.50

(9) **Car/bicycle**

SPACE REQUIREMENT AT LOWER SPEED (≤ 40 km/h)

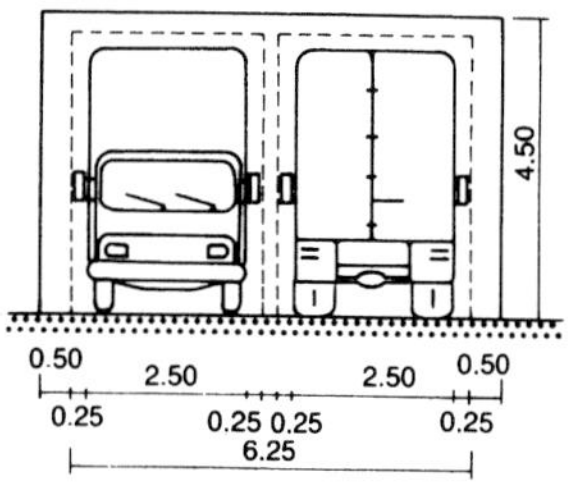

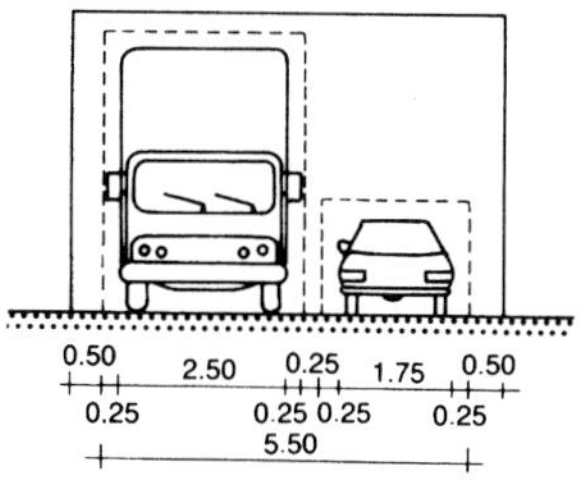

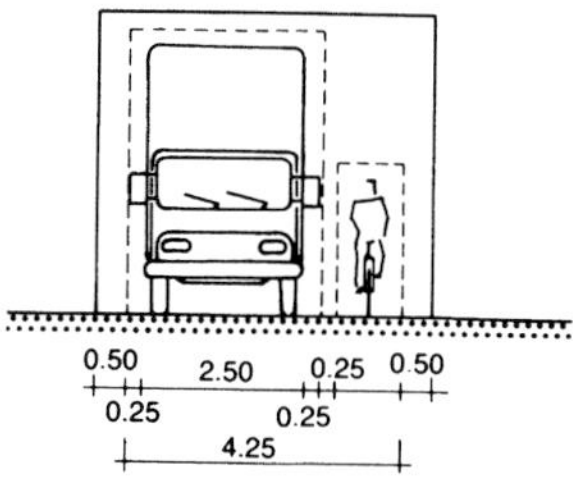

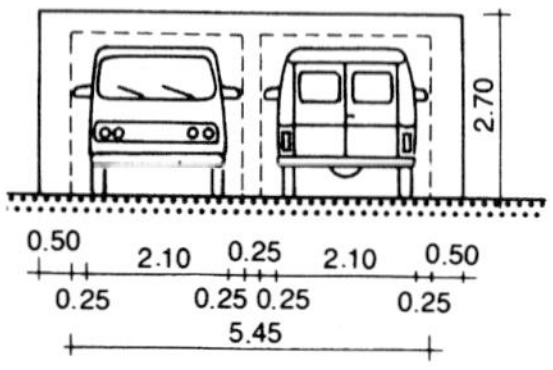

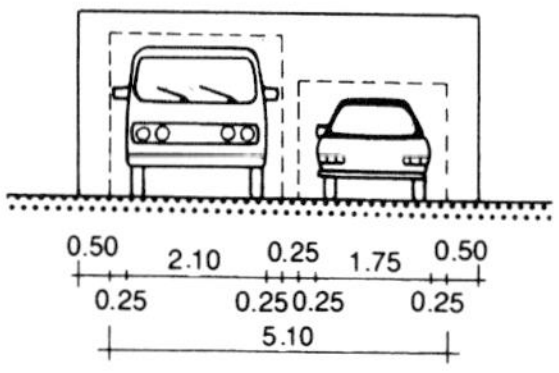

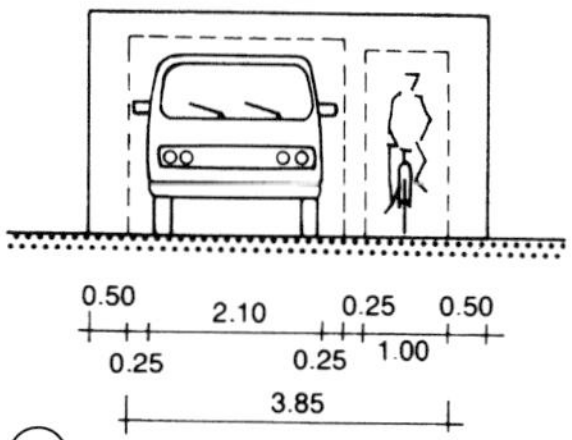

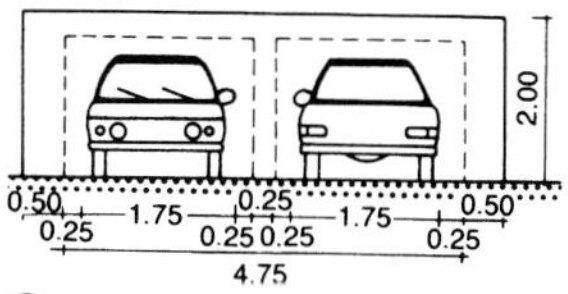

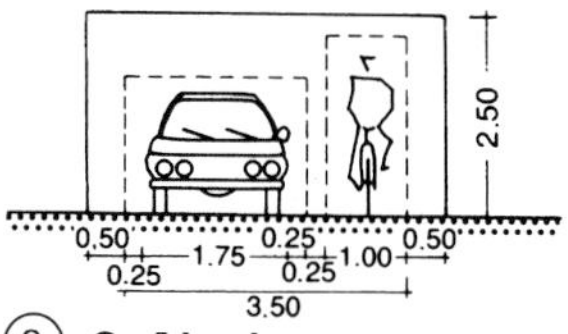

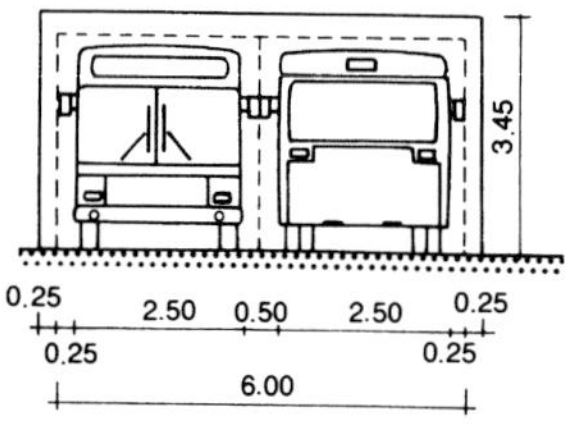

3.45
0.25 2.50 0.50 2.50 0.25
0.25 0.25
6.00

(10) **Bus/bus**

4.50
0.25 2.50 2.50 0.25
0.125 0.25 0.125
5.50

(11) **Lorry/lorry**

0.25 2.50 1.75 0.25
0.125 0.25 0.125
4.75

(12) **Lorry/car**

0.25 2.50 0.25 0.25
0.125 1.00 0.125
4.00

(13) **Lorry/bicycle**

2.70
0.25 2.10 2.10 0.25
0.125 0.25 0.125
4.70

(14) **Van/van**

0.25 2.10 0.125 1.00
0.125 0.25 0.25
3.60

(15) **Van/bicycle**

2.00
0.25 1.75 0.25 1.75 0.25
0.125 0.125
4.00

(16) **Car/car**

0.25 2.10 0.25 1.75 0.25
0.125 0.125
4.35

(17) **Van/car**

—— clearance limit
- - - - limit of space for traffic

Basic dimensions for traffic space and a selection of cases showing the clearance necessary for traffic passing in opposite directions both at full and lower speeds

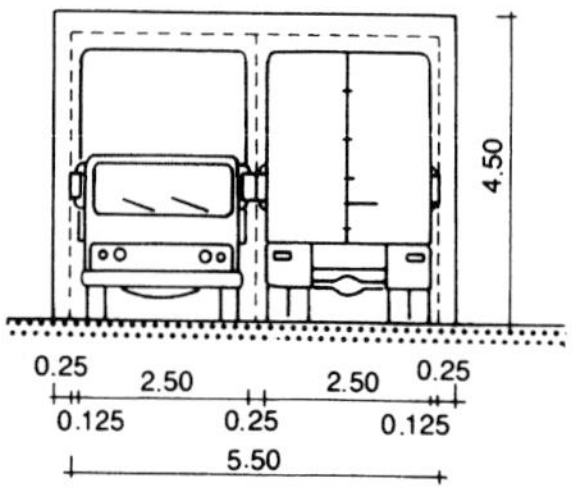

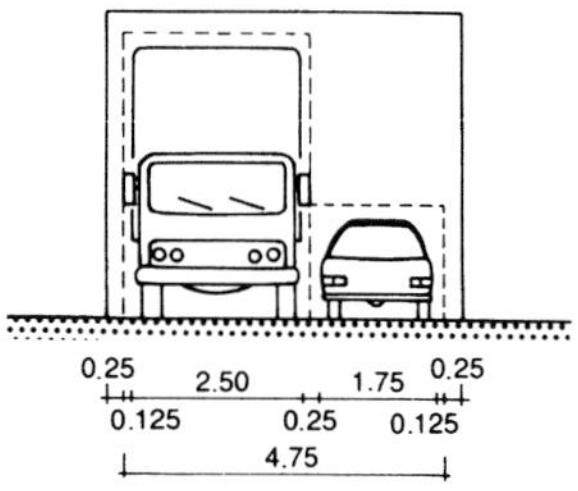

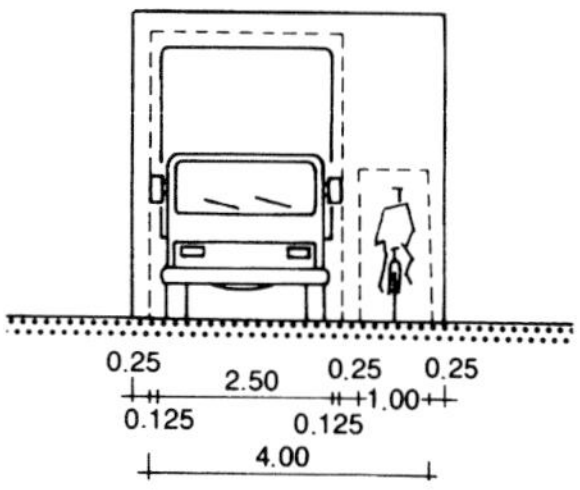

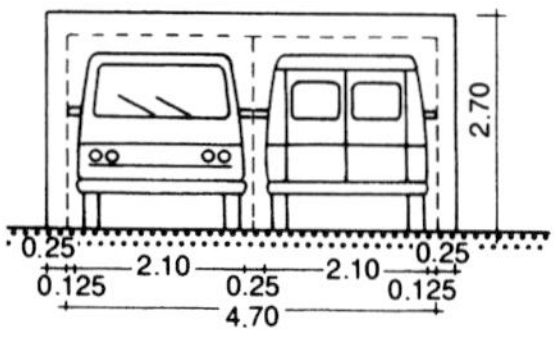

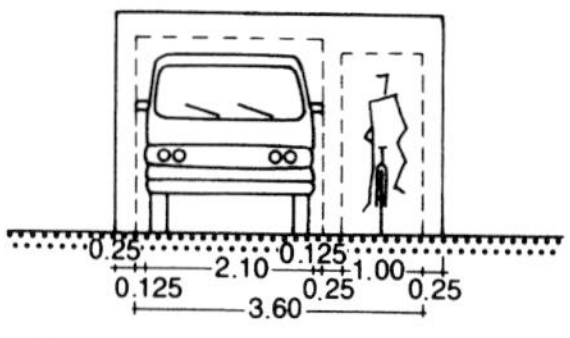

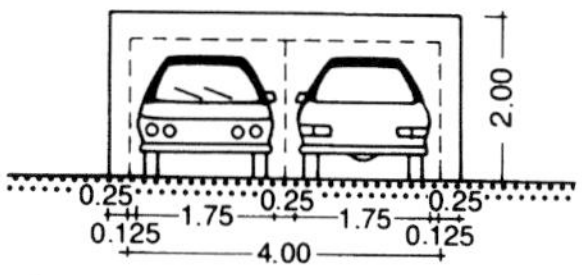

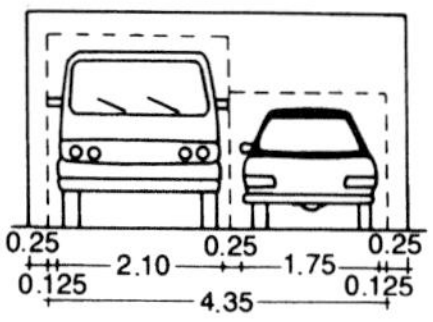

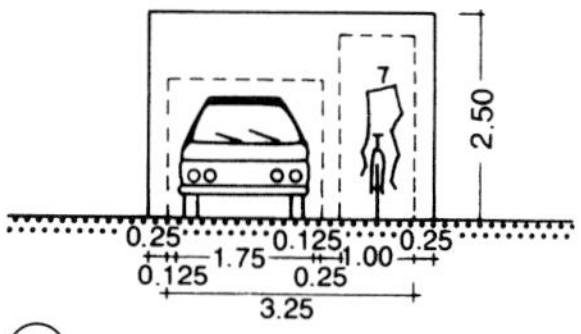

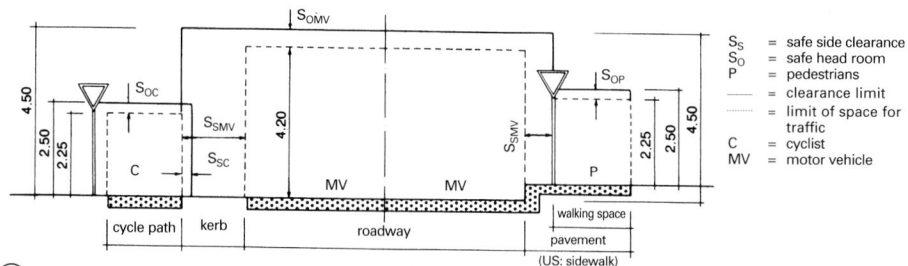

2.50
0.25 1.75 0.125 1.00 0.25
0.125 0.25
3.25

(18) **Car/bicycle**

S OMV
S OC
S OP
S SMV
S SC
4.50
2.50
2.25
4.20
C
MV
MV
P
cycle path
kerb
roadway
walking space
pavement
(US: sidewalk)

S_S = safe side clearance
S_O = safe head room
P = pedestrians
—— = clearance limit
······ = limit of space for traffic
C = cyclist
MV = motor vehicle

(19) **Clearance dimensions for motor vehicle traffic**

The road space necessary for the free movement of vehicles comprises vehicle size, → pp. 432–3, side and head clearances, an extra allowance for oncoming traffic, and space for verges, drainage gutters and hard shoulders. Based on a vehicle height of 4.20 m → (19), the safe clearance height is 4.50 m although it is better to allow 4.75 m to cater for repairs to the carriageway surface. The safe side clearance → (19) is dependent on the maximum speed limit for that area: ≥1.25 m for roads with ≥70 km/h limit; ≥0.75 m with a limit of ≤50 km/h.

The basic space required for cyclists is 1 m wide by 2.25 m high; for pedestrians it is 0.75 m by 2.25 m. For sufficient head clearance for foot- and cycle paths, 2.50 m should be allowed. The safe side clearance for cyclists is 0.25 m.

ROAD DESIGN

To harmonise the design, construction and operational use of roads, standard cross-sections should be strictly observed unless there are special reasons. The standard cross-sections for open roads are shown here → ① as are those for roads in built-up areas → ②.

Notation (e.g. 'c6ms'):

- a–f the cross-sectional group with the basic lane width being 3.00–3.75m
- 6 the number of lanes in both directions of travel
- m a central reservation (physical separation of the directions of travel)
- s a hard shoulder
- r path for cycle riders within the cross-section
- p parking bays or parking spaces on the edge of the road.

For application areas of these standard cross-sections → p. 214

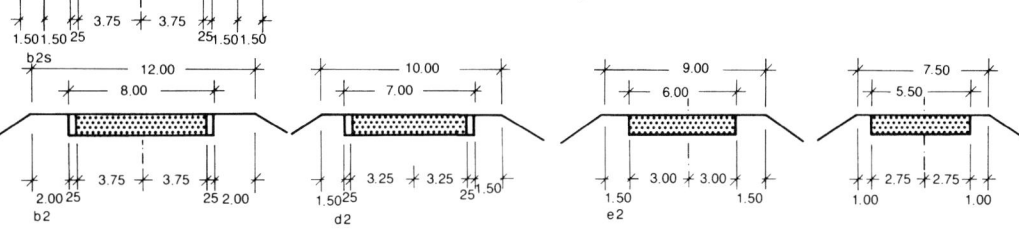

① **Standard cross-sections for open roads**

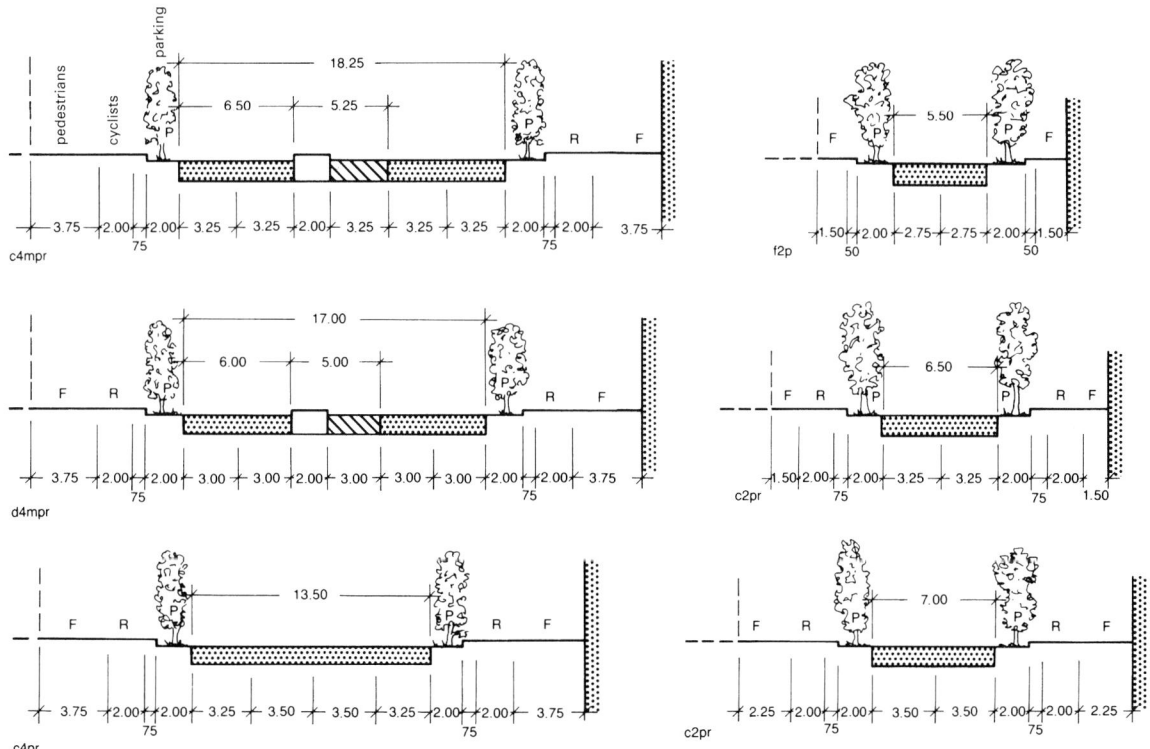

② **Standard cross-sections for roads in built-up areas**

A positive image of space on the road can be created by clear but subtle dimensional changes, varying the layout of the individual cross-sectional parts, and a rich variety of vegetation on the verges. The landscaping of the road should promote a feeling of well-being not only on the open road but also inside towns.

The verges on either side of the road have an influence on both the functional and visual shaping of space. The following items have to be co-ordinated: foot- and cycle paths alongside the roadway, areas for stationary vehicles, areas for public transport, residential areas and areas for manufacturing plants and commerce.

Road category	Field of application			Type of road				Design speed V_e (km/h)
	Traffic loading (vehicles/hr and speed)	Special criteria of application	Standard cross-section	Type of traffic	Speed limit V_{perm} (km/h)	Junctions		
1	2	3	4	5	6	7		8
A I	≤ 3800 with V = 90 km/h / ≤ 2800 with V = 110 km/h		a 6 ms	motor v	–	different level		120 100
	≤ 2400 with V = 90 km/h / ≤ 1800 with V = 110 km/h		a 4 ms	motor v	–	different level		120 100
	≤ 2200 with V = 90 km/h / ≤ 1800 with V = 100 km/h	With light lorry traffic or restricted conds.	b 4ms	motor v	–	different level		120 100
	≤ 1700 with V = 70 km/h / ≤ 900 with V = 90 km/h		b 2 s	motor v	≤ 100 (120)	(diff. level) same level		100 90
	≤ 1300 with V = 70 km/h / ≤ 900 with V = 80 km/h	With light lorry traffic	b 2	motor v	≤ 100	(diff. level) same level		100 90
A II	≤ 4100 with V = 70 km/h / ≤ 3400 with V = 110 km/h		b 6ms	motor v	–	same level		100 90
	≤ 2600 with V = 70 km/h / ≤ 2200 with V = 90 km/h		b 4ms	motor v	–	different level		100 90
	≤ 2300 with V = 70 km/h / ≤ 2100 with V = 80 km/h	With light lorry traffic or restricted conditions.	c 4m	motor v	≤ 100(80)	(diff. level) same level		100 90 (80)
	≤ 1700 with V = 70 km/h / ≤ 1400 with V = 80 km/h		b 2s	motor v	≤ 100	same level		100 90 80
	≤ 1600 with V = 60 km/h / ≤ 900 with V = 80 km/h	With light lorry traffic	b 2	motor v	≤ 100	same level		100 90 80
	≤ 1700 with V = 60 km/h / ≤ 900 with V = 80 km/h	With agricultural traffic > 10 veh/h	b 2s	general	≤ 100	same level		100 90 80
	≤ 1300 with V = 60 km/h / ≤ 900 with V = 70 km/h		b 2	general	≤ 100	same level		100 90 80
	≤ 1000 with V = 60 km/h / ≤ 700 with V = 70 km/h	With light lorry traffic	d 2	general	≤ 100	same level		100 90 80
A III	≤ 2600 with V = 60 km/h / ≤ 2100 with V = 80 km/h		c 4m	motor v	≤ 80(100)	(diff. level) same level		(100) (90) 80
	≤ 2300 with V = 60 km/h / ≤ 1800 with V = 80 km/h	With light lorry traffic or restricted conds.	d 4	motor v	≤ 80	same level		80 70
	≤ 1700 with V = 60 km/h / ≤ 900 with V = 70 km/h	With agricultural traffic > 20 veh/h	b 2s	general	≤ 100	same level		80 70
	≤ 1600 with V = 50 km/h / ≤ 900 with V = 70 km/h	With heavy lorry traffic	b 2	general	≤ 100	same level		80 70
	≤ 1300 with V = 50 km/h / ≤ 700 with V = 70 km/h	With light lorry traffic	d 2	general	≤ 100	same level		80 70 60
	≤ 800 with V = 50 km/h / ≤ 700 with V = 60 km/h		e 2	general	≤ 100	same level		80 70 60
A IV	≤ 1400 with V = 40 km/h / ≤ 1000 with V = 60 km/h	With heavy lorry traffic	d 2	general	≤ 100	same level		80 70 60
	≤ 900 with V = 40 km/h / ≤ 700 with V = 50 km/h		e 2	general	≤ 100	same level		80 70 60
	≤ 300	Measurement not tech. practical	f 2	general	≤ 100	same level		70 60
B II	≤ 2800 with V = 60 km/h / ≤ 2400 with V = 80 km/h	With heavy lorry traffic	b 4ms	motor v	≤ 80	different level		80 70
	≤ 2600 with V = 60 km/h / ≤ 2100 with V = 80 km/h		c 4m	motor v	≤ 80	diff. level (same level)		80 70 (60)
	≤ 2500 with V = 50 km/h / ≤ 2100 with V = 70 km/h	With light lorry traffic or restricted conds.	d 4	motor v	≤ 70	same level		70 (60)
B III	≤ 2500 with V = 50 km/h / ≤ 2100 with V = 60 km/h	With heavy lorry traffic	c 4m	general	≤ 70	same level		70 60
	≤ 2200 with V = 50 km/h / ≤ 1800 with V = 60 km/h		d 4	general	≤ 70	same level		70 60 (50)
	≤ 1400 with V = 40 km/h / ≤ 1000 with V = 50 km/h		d 2	general	≤70	same level		70 60 (50)
	≤ 900 with V = 40 km/h / ≤ 700 with V = 50 km/h	With light lorry and limited bus traffic	e 2	general	≤ 60	same level		60 (50)
B IV	≤ 1400 with V = 40 km/h / ≤ 1000 with V = 50 km/h		d 2	general	≤ 60	same level		60 50
	≤ 900 with V = 40 km/h / ≤ 700 with V = 50 km/h	With light lorry and limited bus traffic	e 2	general	≤ 60	same level		60 50
C III	≤ 2100		c 4mpr	general	≤ 50	same level		(70) (60) 50
	≤ 2000	With light lorry traffic	d 4mpr	general	≤ 50	same level		(70) (60) 50
	≤ 1900	Special case of the c4mpr with restricted conditions	c 4pr	general	≤ 50	same level		(70) (60) 50
	≤ 1800	Special case of the d4mpr with restricted conds.	d 4pr	general	≤ 50	same level		(70) (60) 50
	≤ 1700		c 2pr	general	≤ 50	same level		(60) 50 (40)
	≤ 1500	With light lorry traffic	d 2pr	general	≤ 50	same level		(60) 50 (40)
C IV	≤ 1000	With light lorry traffic	c 2pr	general	≤ 50	same level		(60) 50 (40)
	≤ 1000		d 2pr	general	≤ 50	same level		(60) 50 (40)
	≤ 600	limited bus traffic	f 2p	general	≤ 50	same level		50 (40)

(1) **Fields of application and standard cross-sections** → p. 213

Junctions are where one road flows into another (directly) → ①–②; crossroads are where two roads cross each other at their point of intersection → ⑤–⑧. Junctions on single carriageways are usually in the same plane (and can be with or without traffic lights).

Roundabouts → ⑭–⑮ are a form of intersection popular in some countries (e.g. UK). They offer several advantages: reduced risk of serious accidents; traffic lights are rarely necessary; there is less noise generated and energy is conserved. The diameter of the roundabout depends on the available space and the acceptable length of the tailbacks caused by high volumes of oncoming traffic. An offset crossroads makes more room available; road intersections are visible at a glance and the road ends can be spacious. They are suitable for slow flowing traffic, as is found in residential districts → ⑯.

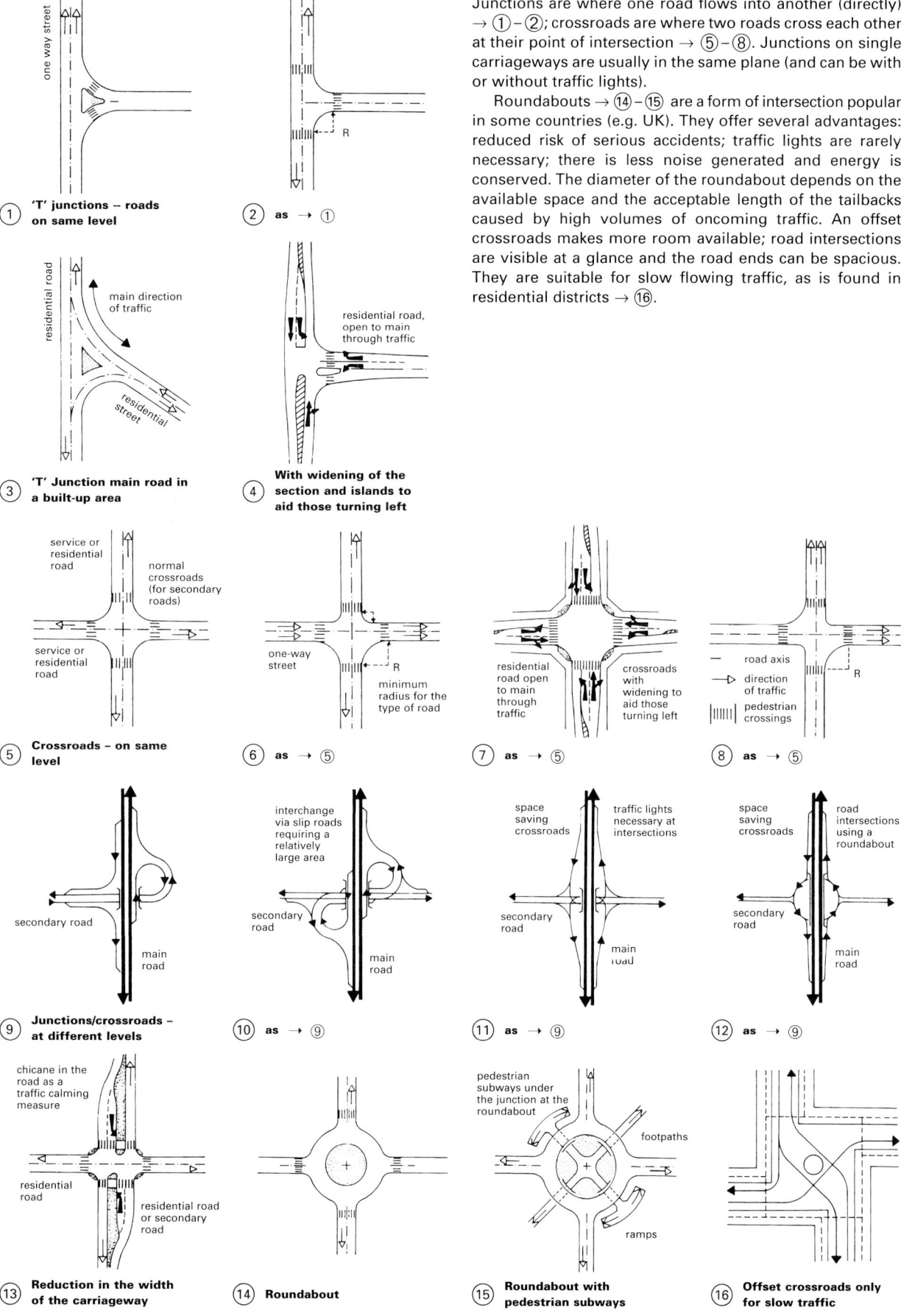

① 'T' junctions -- roads on same level

② as → ①

③ 'T' Junction main road in a built-up area

④ With widening of the section and islands to aid those turning left

⑤ Crossroads – on same level

⑥ as → ⑤

⑦ as → ⑤

⑧ as → ⑤

⑨ Junctions/crossroads – at different levels

⑩ as → ⑨

⑪ as → ⑨

⑫ as → ⑨

⑬ Reduction in the width of the carriageway

⑭ Roundabout

⑮ Roundabout with pedestrian subways

⑯ Offset crossroads only for slow traffic

215

ROADSIDE PATHS

Footpaths ≥2m wide (1.50m minimum clear width plus a 0.50m strip between the path and the road); ≥3m in the vicinity of schools, shopping centres, leisure facilities etc.

Cycle paths ≥1.00m wide for each lane, with 0.75m safety strips separating them from the road.

Combined use If the path is for both pedestrian and cycle riders' use, the width should be ≥2.50m.

cross-sections[1] (values in brackets are minimum dimensions in existing built-up area)	values for design details				
	R_1 min [m]	S[2] max %	R_B min [m]	R_S min [m]	clear height min [m]
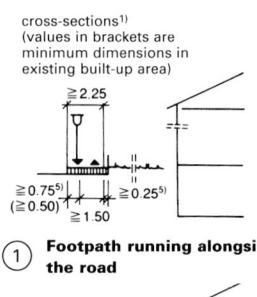 ① **Footpath running alongside the road**		6 (12)[8]			2.50
② **Cycle path running alongside the road**	10 (2)[7]	depending on type of street	30	10	2.50
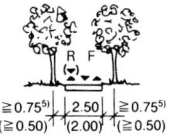 ③ **Common footpath and cycle path**	10 (2)[7]	3 (4 in <250m)[8] (8 in < 30m)[8]	30	10	2.50
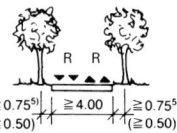 ④ **Cycle riding track**	10 (2)[7]	3 (4 in 250m)[8] (8 in < 30m)[8]	30	10	2.50
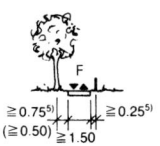 ⑤ **Separate footpath**		6 (12)[8]			2.50
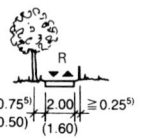 ⑥ **Separate cycle riders' path**	10 (2)[7]	3 (4 in <250m)[8] (8 in <30m)[8]	30	10	2.50
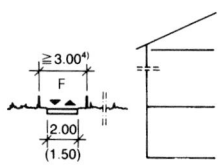 ⑦ **Path serving housing; not suitable for vehicles**		6 (12)[8]			3.50 (-2.50)

notes:
[1] Slight variances in the dimensions may be necessary due to the actual slab widths
[2] S_{min} = 0.5% (for drainage)
[3] Length of service paths unsuitable for vehicles
    1 – 2 storeys ≥ 80m
    3 storeys ≥ 60m
    4 storeys and more ≥ 50m
[4] With partitioning drain 4 - 4.50m
[5] Other additions to the width: continuous rows of trees require a strip of at least 2.50m width for planting
[6] Traffic in both directions only allowed in exceptional cases
[7] Radiused out at junctions
[8] In exceptional cases

abbreviations → ① – ⑦
F = footpath
R = cycle riding
R_1 = radius of bends
S = longitudinal slope
R_B = rounded out radius of brow
R_S = rounded out radius of dips

① – ⑦ **Pedestrian and cycle riders' paths**

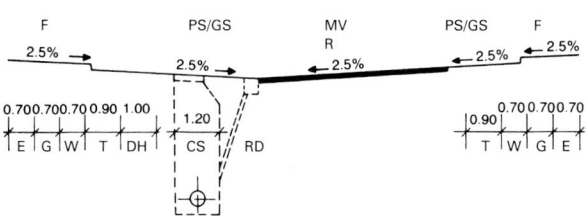

⑧ **Basic widths for the supply and drainage pipework layout in the road space**

⑨ → ⑧

E = electricity
G = gas
W = water
DH = district heating
T = telephone cable
CS = combined sewer
FW = foul water drain
RD = rainwater drain
F = footpath
R = cycle riding
MV = motor vehicle
PS/GS = parking or green strip

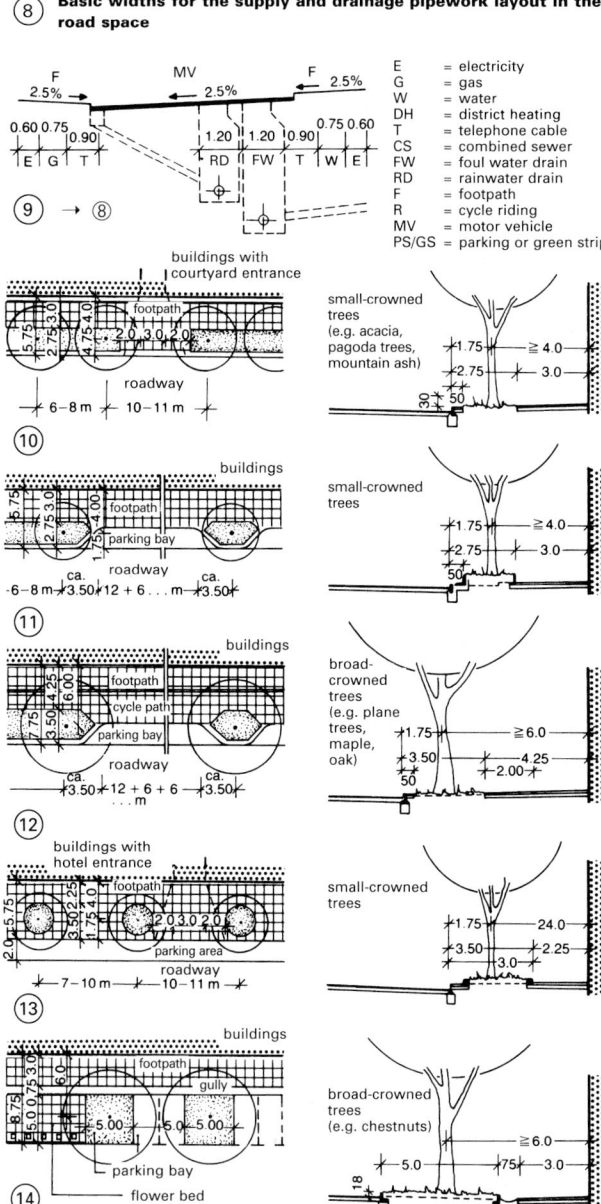

⑩ – ⑭ **Examples of lay-out of road space in built-up areas**

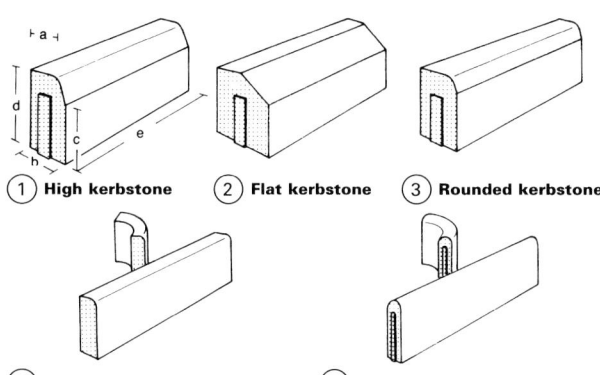

① **High kerbstone** ② **Flat kerbstone** ③ **Rounded kerbstone**

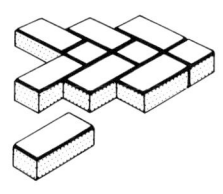

④ **Lawn kerbstone** ⑤ **Border kerbstone**

		a	b	c	d	e
high kerbstones	①	12	15	25	13	(100) (50)
flat kerbstones	②	7 15	12 18	20 19	15 13	100 50
round kerbstones	③	9	15	22	15	100 50
lawn kerbstones	④	– –	8 8	– –	20 25	(100) (50)
border kerbstones	⑤	–	6	–	30	100

In addition to pavements, interlocking block paving can be used for pedestrianised roads, parking areas, hall floors, paving between rail tracks and on the beds and side slopes of water courses.

The dimensions of paving blocks (length/width in cm) that match standard road building widths include: 22.5/11.25; 20/10; 10/10; 12/6 etc. Kerb heights of 6, 8 and 10 cm are commonly used.

The depth and material of the substructure (e.g. gravel, crushed stone with grain sizes 0.1–35 mm), which acts as a filter or bearing layer, should be adapted to the ground conditions and the expected traffic load. If the ground is load bearing the bearing layer should be 15–25 cm deep, compacted until it is sufficiently stable. Pavement beds can be 4 cm of sand or 2–8 mm of chippings. After vibrating the overlay the pavement bed can be compressed by about 3 cm.

Wedge-shaped curved blocks can be used for circular paved areas or curved edges → ⑬. For farm track paving, parking areas, fire-service access roads, spur roads, reinforcing slopes against erosion damage or access routes in areas liable to flooding, multi-sided lawn blocks are available → ⑪. These are also useful in heavily landscaped areas, allowing a fast covering of stable greenery to be provided.

Composite and round palisades made of concrete → ⑭ – ⑯ are suitable for bordering planted areas to compensate for height differences and for slope revetment → ⑰. These are also available in pressure-impregnated wood.

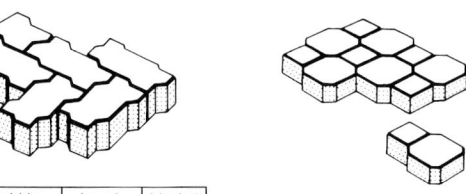

height (cm)	width (cm)	length (cm)	blocks/m²
6	11.25	22.5	39
8	11.25	22.5	39
10	11.25	22.5	39

⑥ **Interlocking blocks**

height (cm)	width (cm)	length (cm)	blocks/m²
6	14/9	23	38
8	14/9	23	38

⑦ **Ornamental interlocking blocks**

height (cm)	width (cm)	length (cm)	blocks/m²
6	10	10;20	48;96
8	10	10;20	48;96

⑧ **System paving blocks**

height (cm)	width (cm)	length (cm)	blocks/m²
8	7	21	68
8	14	14;21	51;34

⑨ **Rustic paving blocks**

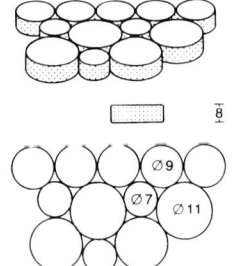

⑩ **Round paving blocks**

height (cm)	width (cm)	length (cm)	blocks/m²
10	33	16.5	18
10	33	33	12
solid block has same dimensions			

⑪ **Lawn blocks**

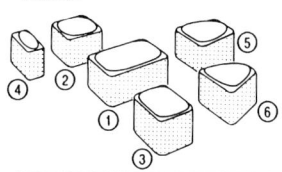

block	1½ ①	normal ②	¾ ③	½ ④	wedge –1 ⑤	wedge –2 ⑥
height	8	8	8	8	8	8
width	12	12	12	12	8/11	5/13
length	18	12	9	6	12	12
no./m²	46	69	92	139	87	92

⑫ **Concrete paving** → ⑬

fan 0.69 m²

Ø 11–204 cm

⑬ **Circle** → ⑫

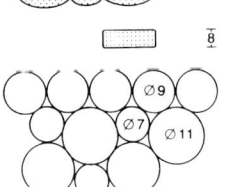

height (cm)	width (cm)	binder length (cm)	pieces/m²
40	9	12.5	8

⑭ **Palisades/concrete**

installation depth = one-third total height

height (cm)	40; 60; 80; 100;
	120; 150; 180; 200

⑮ **Composite palisades**

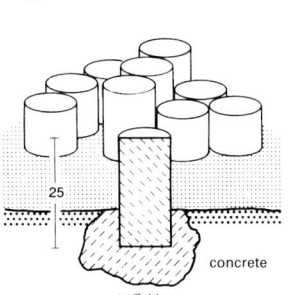

⑯ **Concrete border blocks**

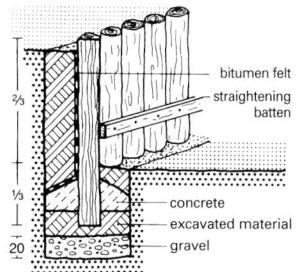

bitumen felt

straightening batten

concrete

excavated material

gravel

⑰ **Wooden palisades**

BICYCLE PARKING

Dimensions of bicycles → ①–②. Note allowances for baskets and children's seats. Include space for special types: recumbent bikes up to 2.35m long; tandems up to 2.60m; bicycle trailers (with shaft) approx. 1.60m long, 1.00m wide; bikes adapted for disabled people and for delivering goods.

Offer comfortable parking → ③ wherever possible: narrow parking can cause injury, soiling and damage during locking/loading. Double rows with overlapping front wheels can save space.

Cycle stands must give steady support, even when loading the bike. Locking should be possible using only one 'U' lock, securing the front wheel and the frame to the stand at the same time. Tubular stands are therefore suitable → ⑨. Provide an intermediate bar for children's bikes. Stands should be 1.20m apart with access lanes 1.50–1.80m wide → ⑦–⑨. Cycle stands which do not provide sensible locking opportunities only suitable for internal use in areas of restricted access.

General installation design should be clear and user-friendly: close to the destination, easy to find and approach. For long-term parking, consider roofing and lighting → p. 219. Supervision is advisable at railway stations, sports grounds, shopping centres etc.

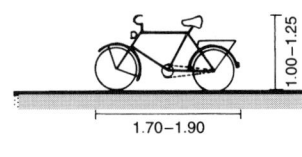

① **Basic bicycle dimensions**

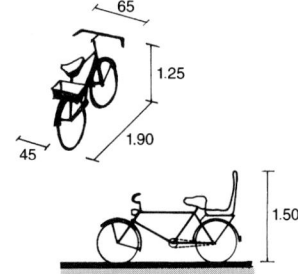

② **Bicycle with basket/child's seat**

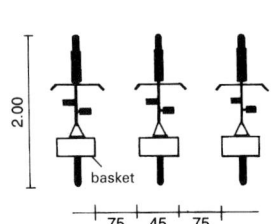

③ **Bicycle parking: ample space**

④ **Close packed**

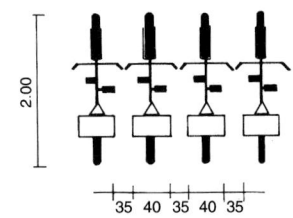
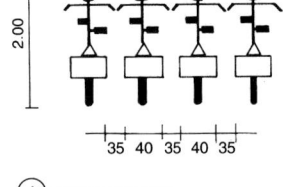

⑤ **Basic layout parallel in straight lines**

⑥ **Parallel, herringbone formation**

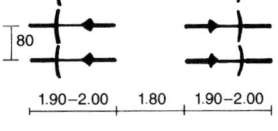
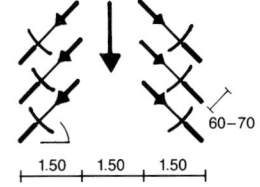

⑦ **Staggered, parallel straight formation**

⑧ **Staggered, herringbone formation**

apartments	1 per 30m² total living area
visitors to apartments	1 per 200m² total living area
student residential halls	1 per bed
secondary schools	0.7 per pupil place
colleges of further educ.	0.5 per student place
lecture theatres	0.7 per seat
libraries	1 per 40m
college canteens	0.3 per seat
places of work	0.3 per employee
shops for daily supplies	1 per 25m² sales area
shopping centres	1 per 80m² sales area
retail units for	1 per 35m² sales area
professional offices, doctors' practices	0.2 per client on premises
sports arenas, halls, indoor swimming pools	0.5 per clothes locker
regional gathering places	1 per 20 visitor places
other gathering places	1 per 7 visitor places
local restaurants	1 per 7 seats
beer gardens	1 per 2 seats

If several uses happen at the same time in a building, then the totals for the different uses should be added up.

⑪ **Guide values for capacity of cycle parking**

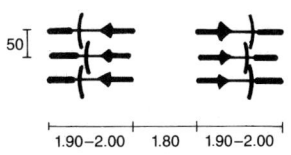
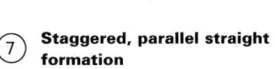

⑨ **With tubular stands**

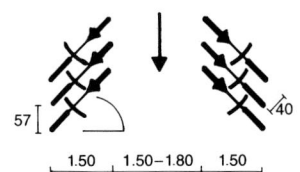

⑩ **Front wheel overlapping**

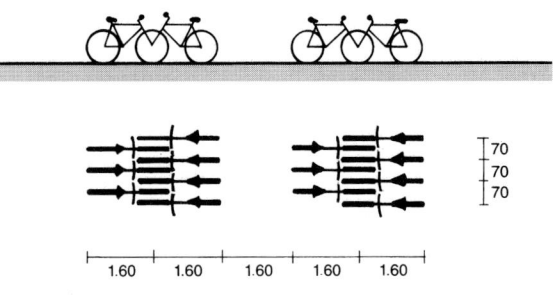

⑫ **Front wheel overlapping with central access**

BICYCLE PARKING AND CYCLE PATHS

Basic space requirements for cyclists are made up of the bicycle width (0.60 m) and the height allowed for the rider → ⑤ plus the necessary room for manoeuvre under various conditions. Although the minimum width of a single-lane cycle path is 1.00 m, it is preferable to increase this to 1.40–1.60 m, particularly where riders could be travelling at higher speeds. Where traffic is two way, an ideal width of 1.60–2.00 m allows oncoming cyclists to pass each other safely as well as making it easy to overtake slower riders.

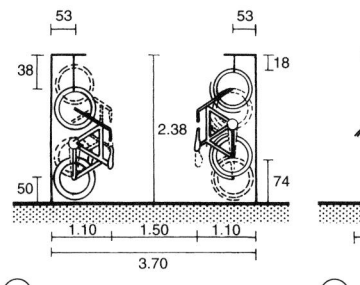

① **Cycle racks**

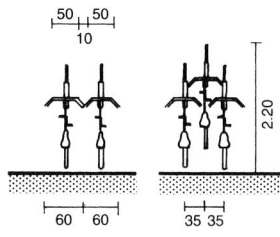

② **Parallel   Intermeshed**

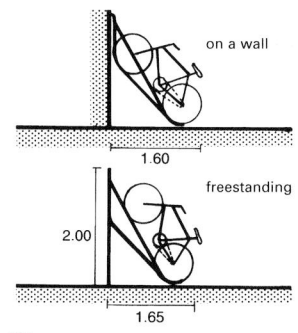

③ **Tilted racks**

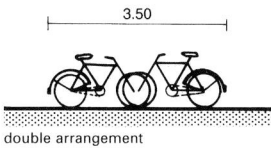

④ **With frame holder**

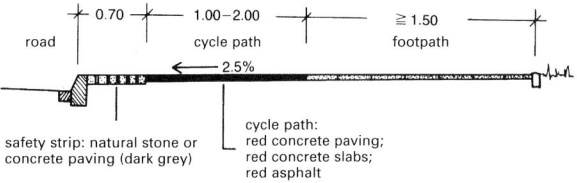

⑤ **Normal cross-section for cycle path width**

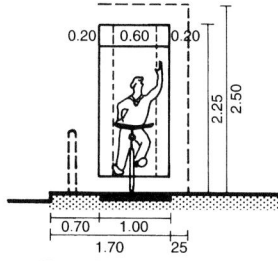

⑥ **Two lane**

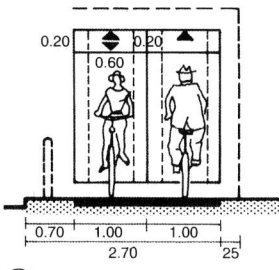

⑦ **Where space is limited**

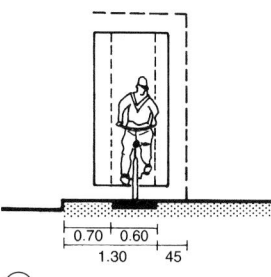

⑧ **Minimum cross-section**

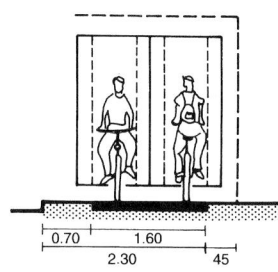

⑨ **Grass strips between them and the road are a good solution**

⑩ **Most suitable arrangement**

⑪ **Grass strips are necessary with two-way traffic**

⑫ **Cycle lanes avoiding drains and similar obstacles**

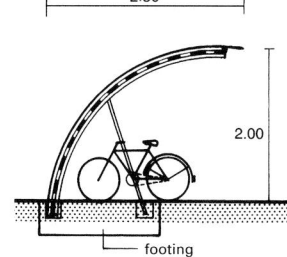

⑬ **Weather protection roof – curved roof**

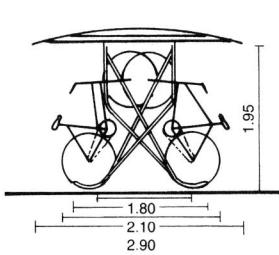

⑭ **Double racks with curved roof**

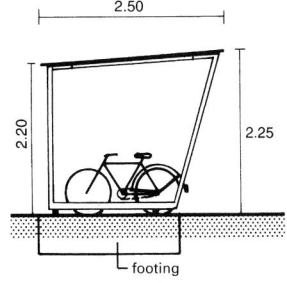

⑮ **Tubular framed cycle shed**

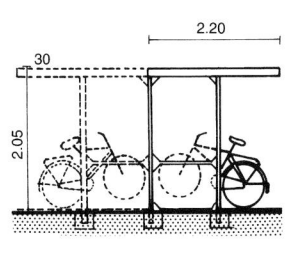

⑯ **Cycle sheds**

MOTORWAYS

Motorways are twin carriageway (each with two or more lanes and a hard shoulder, and separated by a central reservation) roads with no obstructions, designed for high-speed traffic → ①–③. They are the safest and most efficient roads. Environmental considerations have top priority in their planning and construction.

Motorway intersections are constructed using variations in levels of the carriageways → ④–⑨ with special entry and exit slip roads for junctions → ⑩–⑪.

Direction signs should be positioned at least 1000 m before an exit for connecting roads and 2000 m before motorway intersections → ⑫.

Building restrictions (i.e. a requirement for special planning permission) apply to the construction or major alteration of structures 40–100 m from the outside edge of motorway carriageways; construction of high buildings within 40 m of motorways is banned.

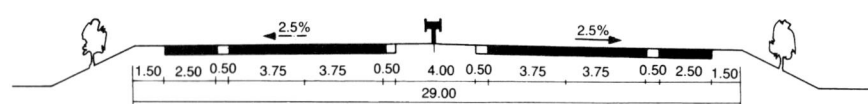

① **Standard cross-section for six-lane motorways 37.50 m wide**

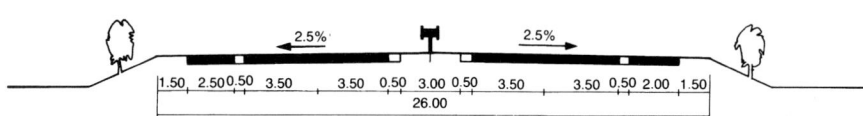

② **Standard cross-section for four-lane motorways 29 m wide**

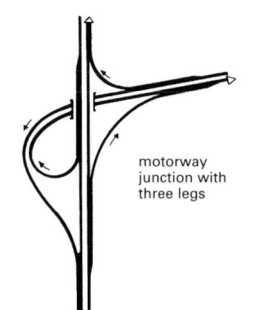

③ **As above but 26 m wide**

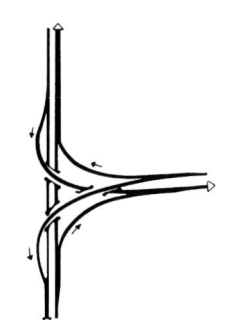

④ **Trumpet intersection**

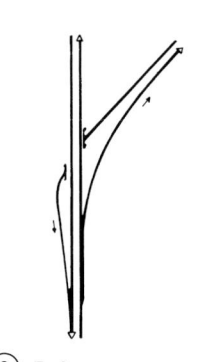

⑤ **Triangle**

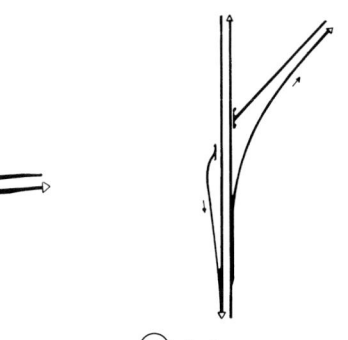

⑥ **Fork**

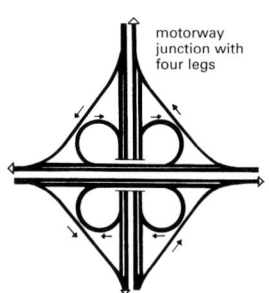

⑦ **Clover leaf**

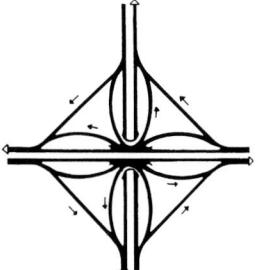

⑧ **Maltese cross**

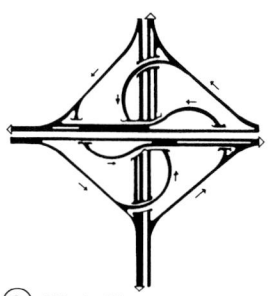

⑨ **Windmill**

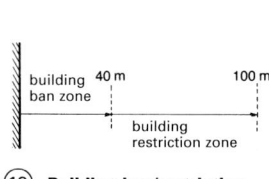

⑬ **Building ban/restriction**

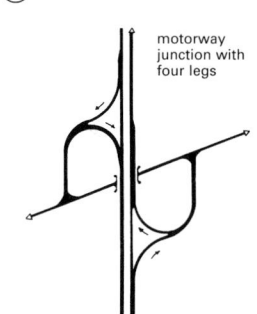

⑩ **Half-clover leaf**

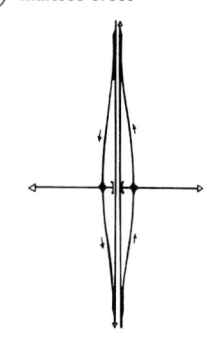

⑪ **Lozenge**

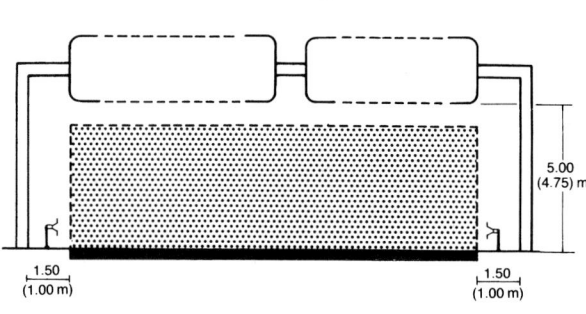

⑫ **Sign gantry over carriageway**

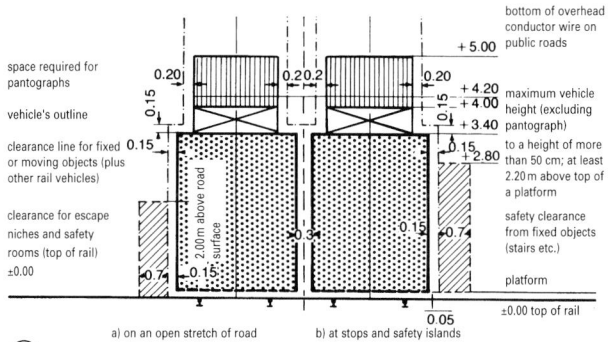

space required for pantographs

vehicle's outline

clearance line for fixed or moving objects (plus other rail vehicles)

clearance for escape niches and safety rooms (top of rail) ±0.00

0.20 0.20.2 0.20

0.15

+5.00 — bottom of overhead conductor wire on public roads

+4.20
+4.00 — maximum vehicle height (excluding pantograph)
+3.40

+2.80 — to a height of more than 50 cm; at least 2.20 m above top of a platform

+0.74 — safety clearance from fixed objects (stairs etc.)

platform

±0.00 top of rail

a) on an open stretch of road   b) at stops and safety islands

① **Minimum clearances for track laid in carriageway of public road**

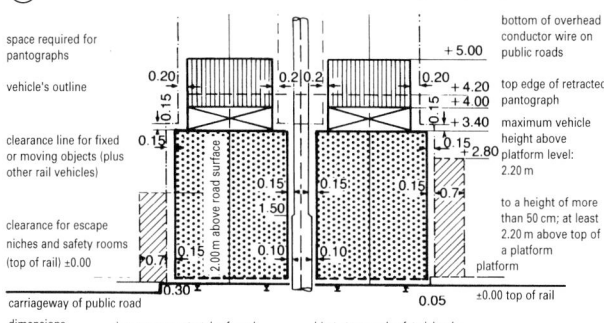

space required for pantographs

vehicle's outline

clearance line for fixed or moving objects (plus other rail vehicles)

clearance for escape niches and safety rooms (top of rail) ±0.00

carriageway of public road

dimensions in mm

+5.00 — bottom of overhead conductor wire on public roads

+4.20 — top edge of retracted pantograph
+4.00
+3.40 — maximum vehicle height above platform level: 2.20 m

+2.80 — to a height of more than 50 cm; at least 2.20 m above top of a platform

platform

±0.00 top of rail

a) on an open stretch of road   b) at stops and safety islands

② **Minimum clearances for track on special segregated sections on a public road**

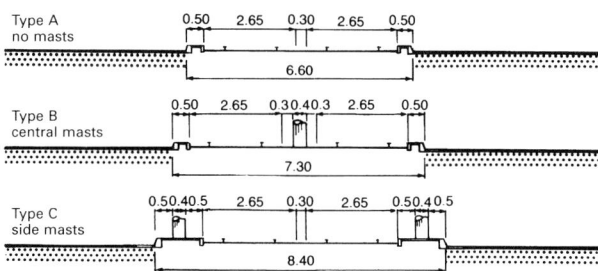

Type A no masts: 0.50 2.65 0.30 2.65 0.50 — 6.60

Type B central masts: 0.50 2.65 0.30 0.40 0.3 2.65 0.50 — 7.30

Type C side masts: 0.50 0.40.5 2.65 0.30 2.65 0.50 0.40.5 — 8.40

③ **Standard widths for segregated sections of track in secondary roads**

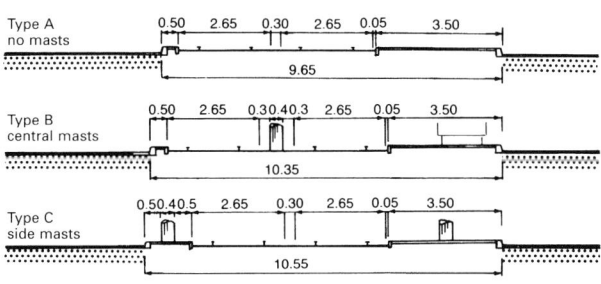

Type A no masts: 0.50 2.65 0.30 2.65 0.05 3.50 — 9.65

Type B central masts: 0.50 2.65 0.30 0.40 0.3 2.65 0.05 3.50 — 10.35

Type C side masts: 0.50 0.40.5 2.65 0.30 2.65 0.05 3.50 — 10.55

④ → ③ **Tram stops on one side**

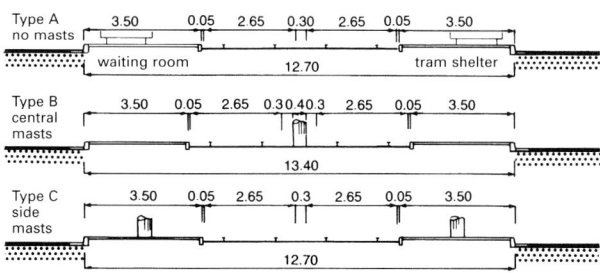

Type A no masts: 3.50 0.05 2.65 0.30 2.65 0.05 3.50 — waiting room — 12.70 — tram shelter

Type B central masts: 3.50 0.05 2.65 0.30 0.40 0.3 2.65 0.05 3.50 — 13.40

Type C side masts: 3.50 0.05 2.65 0.3 2.65 0.05 3.50 — 12.70

⑤ **Tram stops on both sides of road** → ③

TRAMWAYS/URBAN LIGHT RAILWAYS

A tramway is controlled entirely by sight and shares the road with other general traffic; an urban light railway travels over stretches of track with standard train safety equipment, just like the underground (US: subway) or main line railways, as well as alongside roads on special track bed. (The underground travels only on defined, independent track beds, with no crossings, and does not mix with urban traffic.)

- **Track gauge**   the standard gauge is 1.435 m, or a metric gauge of 1.000 m, and the clearance width is the carriage frame width (2.30–2.65 m) plus extra to compensate for deflectional movement on curves and an extra allowance for the width on cambers plus sway (at least 2 × 0.15 m)
- **Distance of kerbstone from carriage frame**   for special track beds 0.50 m; can be as little as 0.30 m in exceptional cases
- **Carriage heights**   the height of the carriage body should be ≤3.40 m; min. height allowance for safe passage under buildings is 4.20 m, and on roads should be 5.00 m
- **Safety clearance space**   0.85 m width from the outside limit of the vehicle outline on the door side of rail vehicles.

The width of street platforms should be at least 3.50 m (although 2 m can be regarded as an absolute minimum for platforms on the side of streets where space is limited). Where a waiting room is to be incorporated, the platform width should be at least 5.50 m. The platform length should exceed the train length by ≥5 m to allow for inaccurate braking.

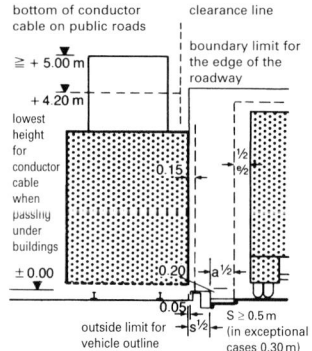

bottom of conductor cable on public roads

clearance line

boundary limit for the edge of the roadway

≧ +5.00 m
+4.20 m

lowest height for conductor cable when passing under buildings

±0.00

outside limit for vehicle outline

S ≥ 0.5 m (in exceptional cases 0.30 m)

⑥ **Clearance limits for the road and tramway**

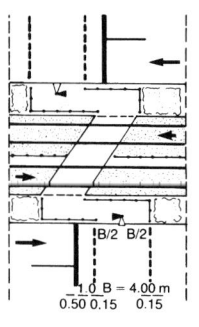

B/2 B/2
1.0 B = 4.00 m
0.50 0.15 0.15

⑦ **Permanent pedestrian crossing without signals**

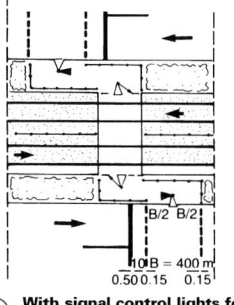

B/2 B/2
1.0 B = 400 m
0.50 0.15 0.15

⑧ **With signal control lights for crossing the track**

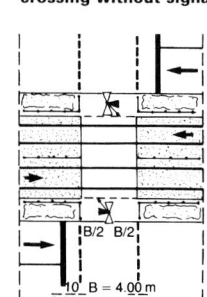

B/2 B/2
1.0 B = 4.00 m
0.50 0.15 0.15

⑨ → ⑧

The layouts for traffic must take all the associated circumstances into account. We need to differentiate between the following classifications:

I *Connecting traffic* – urban railways, motorways with ≤4 lanes

II *Main roads* with or without sections of tram tracks → ①

III *Secondary roads* with 2–4 lanes, some sections with parking at the side of the road → ②

IV *Residential roads* having ≤2 lanes, and parking spaces in the road → ③ + ④.

Residential roads must have large parking areas → ⑤ + ⑥; alternatively, where necessary, parking spaces between blocks of flats → ⑦. Class IV roads offer wide scope for good layout design, with footpaths, squares and open areas.

Local commuter rail traffic, where the urban railway is being extended, must be taken out of the road space and run on its own track bed → ① → p. 223 ① – ⑤.

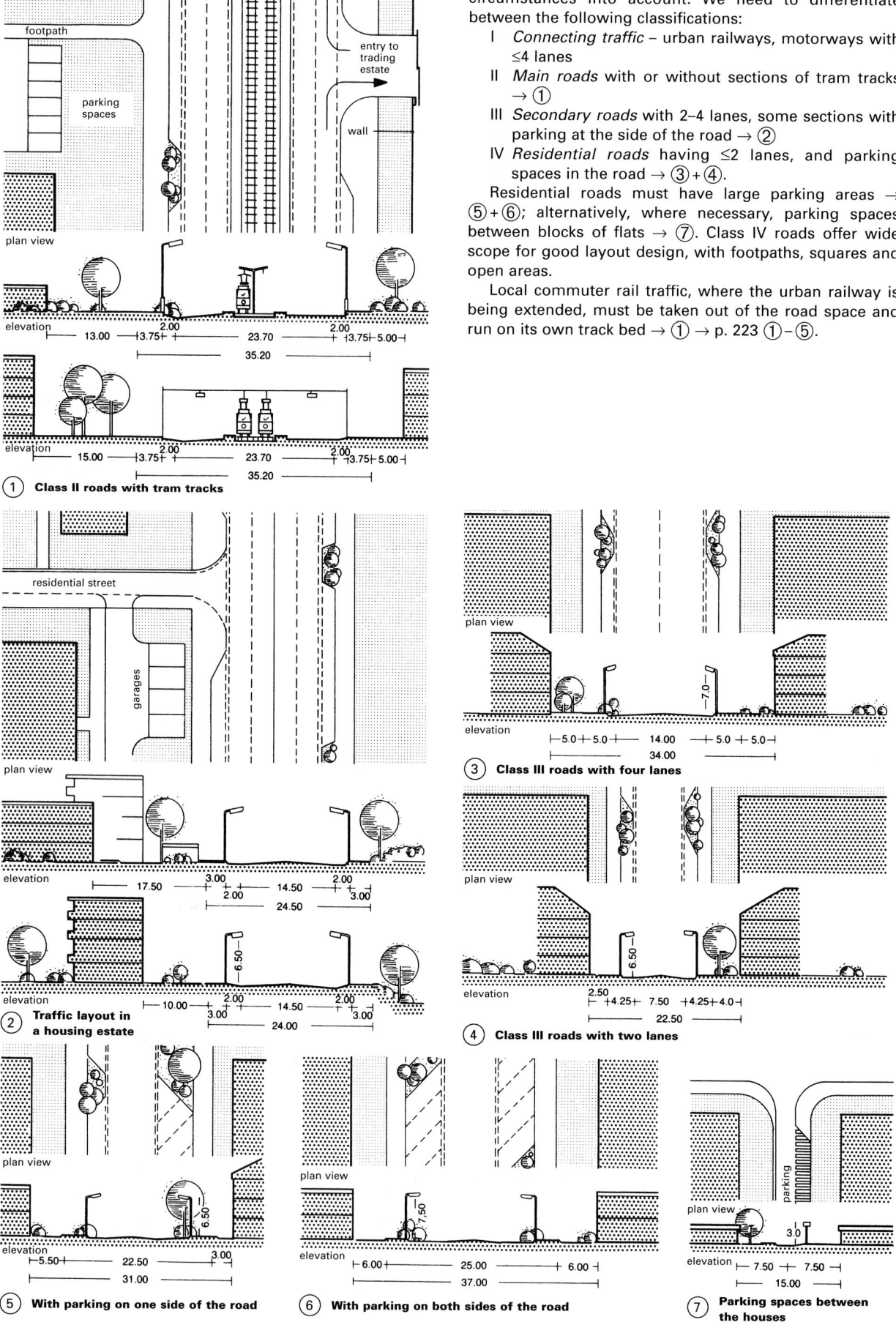

① **Class II roads with tram tracks**

② **Traffic layout in a housing estate**

③ **Class III roads with four lanes**

④ **Class III roads with two lanes**

⑤ **With parking on one side of the road**

⑥ **With parking on both sides of the road**

⑦ **Parking spaces between the houses**

TRAFFIC LAYOUT

Urban railways with overhead conductor cables – or, even better, with conductor rails – work efficiently on their own tracks and can be separated by railings or hedges from the road traffic → (1) + (2). Elevated railways (3) allow traffic to move freely below and improve rail traffic circulation because trains are not affected by road signals; however they increase noise for residents. A better solution is to run railways in shallow or deep cuttings, or even underground → (4) + (5) + (11).

Road noise in flat terrain is reduced by uninhabited buildings (e.g. garages), which provide sound insulation, by planting trees or by using backfilled earth embankments planted with trees. Even more effective are roads partly in cuttings with planted earth slopes or sunk completely in a cutting → (8) – (10).

In general, it is only possible to put in noise suppressing walls with new roads, particularly when planning the layout of new areas where high-speed traffic (100–120km/h) can be segregated from residential buildings and run in cuttings with slip roads leading to the residential areas. These would be flanked by rows of garages, with parking places in front of them, and linked by wide footpaths leading to the houses/flats. Plenty of lawns and evergreen trees (i.e. conifers), improve the quiet, homely environment.

Elevated roads are only convenient for commercial and industrial estates, where the road noise causes less disturbance.

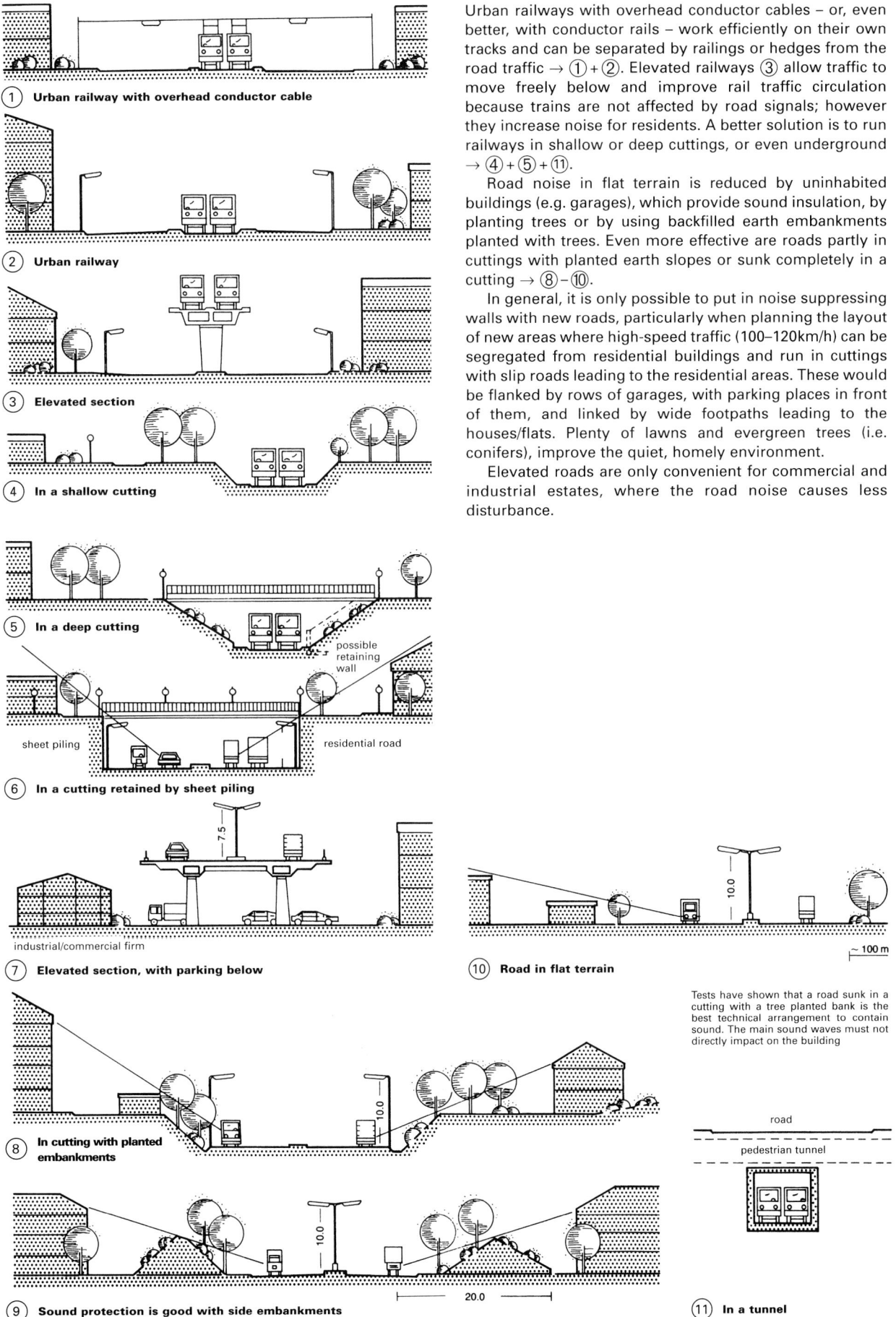

(1) **Urban railway with overhead conductor cable**

(2) **Urban railway**

(3) **Elevated section**

(4) **In a shallow cutting**

(5) **In a deep cutting**

possible retaining wall

sheet piling   residential road

(6) **In a cutting retained by sheet piling**

7.5

industrial/commercial firm

(7) **Elevated section, with parking below**

(8) **In cutting with planted embankments**

10.0

10.0

(9) **Sound protection is good with side embankments**

20.0

(10) **Road in flat terrain**

~ 100 m

10.0

Tests have shown that a road sunk in a cutting with a tree planted bank is the best technical arrangement to contain sound. The main sound waves must not directly impact on the building

road

pedestrian tunnel

(11) **In a tunnel**

223

no.	measures	suppression of outside traffic	speed reduction	emphasis on residential character	extra safety for pedestrians/children	extra space for pedestrian movement	reduction of traffic noise	enhanced consideration (positive motivation)	key to measures
A 1	blind alleys cul de sacs	●●	○		○		●		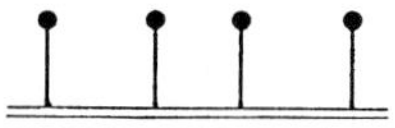
2	crescents	●						○	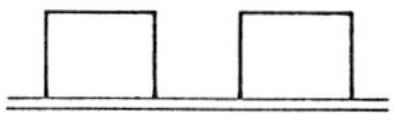
3	one way streets	●			○				
B 1	change of road surface material		●						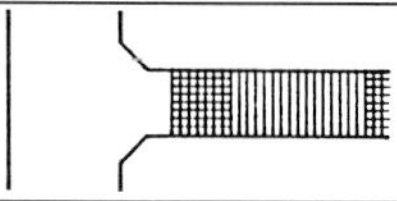
2	narrowing of road section	●	●●			●	●		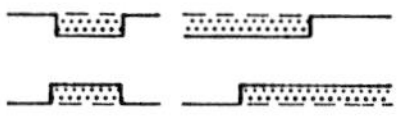
3	visual rearrangement of road space	●	●	●●	●		●	●	
4	dynamic obstacles (humps)	●	●●			●			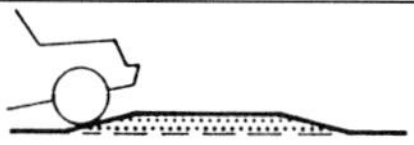
5	reorganisation of stationary traffic		●●			●			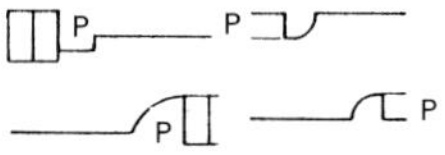
6	raised paving	●	●●	●●	●	●●	●	●●	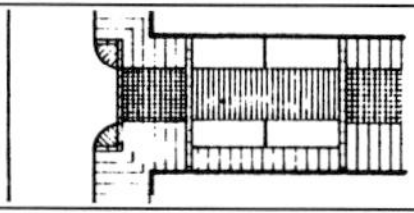
C 1	sign: 'Residential area'	●	●	●●	●●		●	●	 traffic signs
2	speed 30 km/h		●		●		●		
3	change of priority for drivers	○	●		○				

key to measures
A – traffic system
B – detailed layout
C – traffic control
●● desired effect
● probable effect
○ possible effect

① Traffic calming measures and effects in residential roads

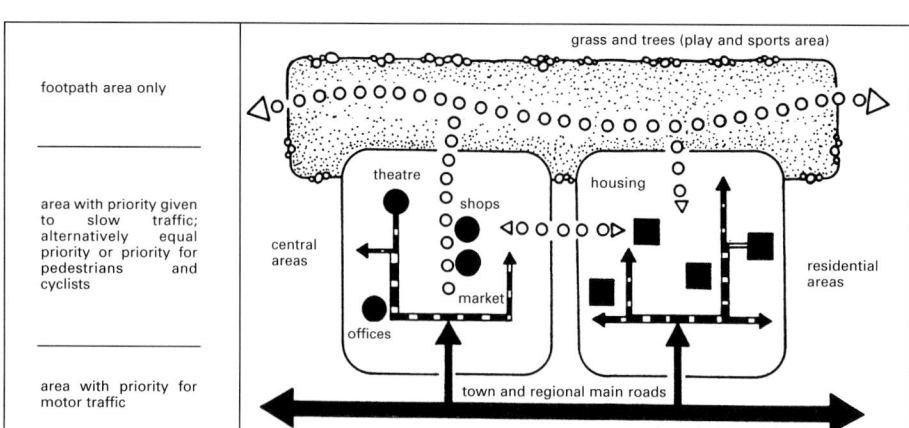

footpath area only

area with priority given to slow traffic; alternatively equal priority or priority for pedestrians and cyclists

area with priority for motor traffic

grass and trees (play and sports area)
theatre
shops
housing
central areas
market
offices
residential areas
town and regional main roads

② Outline diagram of the space allocation of traffic priorities

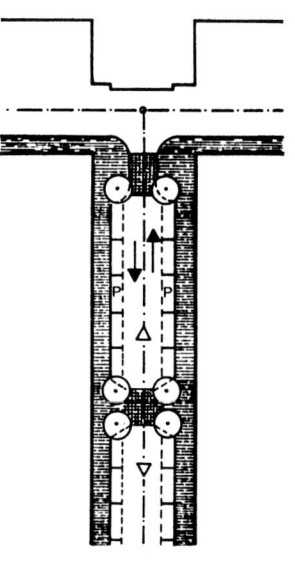

individual measures:
B1 + B2 + B3 +
(where appropriate, B4 + B6) + C1 + C2;
driving and pedestrian areas separated, reduction in road size in favour of wider pavements, speed reduction by narrowing the road and partial use of raised paving;
this gives more space and greater safety for pedestrians – improved layout through space subdivision

③ Road layout: proposal 1 → ①

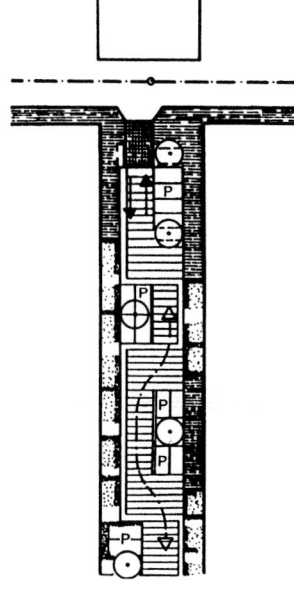

(A3) + B1 + B2 + B3 + B4 + B5 + B6 + C1;
layout for driving, parking and walking in a common (mixed) area so multiple use of the whole road area is possible;
speed is limited to 'walking pace' (or 20 km/h max.);
total reorganisation of the whole layout, taking into consideration the primarily residential needs

④ Road layout: proposal 2 → ①

TRAFFIC NOISE

Guidelines for Road Noise Shielding

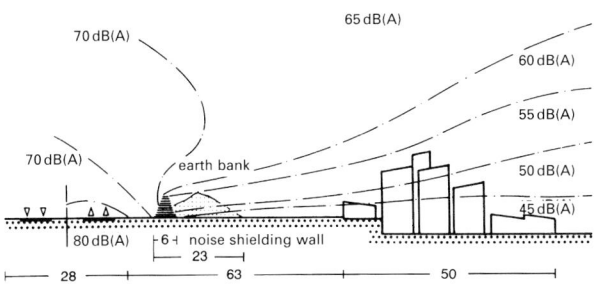

① **Isophonic map: effect of an earth bank or noise shielding wall on sound levels**

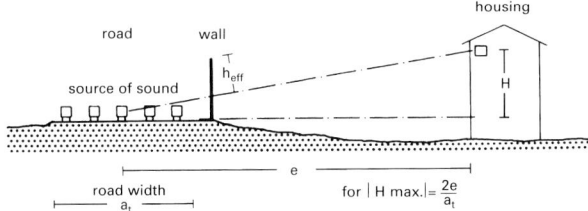

② **Determining the required height of a noise shielding wall**

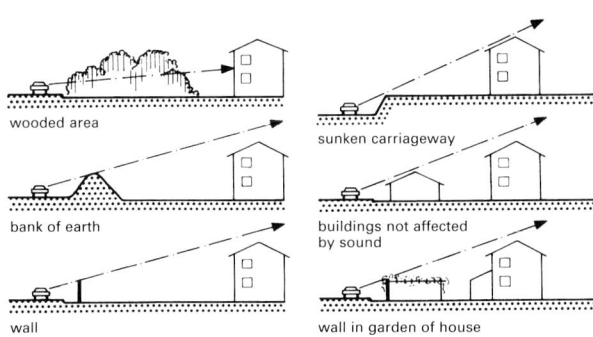

③ **Noise insulation measures on a main road**

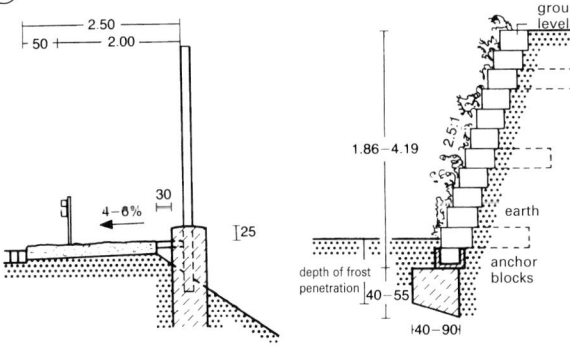

④ **Standard arrangement for noise shielding walls on roads**

⑤ **Noise insulating wall of concrete blocks**

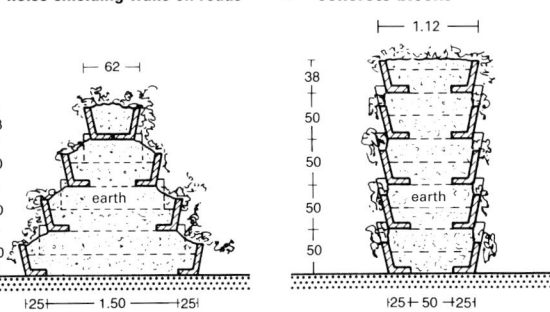

⑥ **Noise insulating pyramid (pre-cast concrete components)**

⑦ **Noise insulating modular wall**

Increased environmental concerns have made reduction of traffic noise a top priority. Effective measures include earth mounds and noise shielding walls and pyramids → ① – ⑦. There are many suitable pre-cast concrete products on the market today as well as sound insulating walls made from glass, wood and steel.

The sound level of road traffic can be reduced by ≥25 dB(A) after passing through a noise shielding wall. (With a reduction of 10 dB(A), the sound seems half as loud.)

The shielding effect is dependent on the wall material but far more so on its height. This is because refraction bends the path of the sound waves so a small part of the sound energy arrives in the shadow area. The higher the wall the lower the amount of sound penetration, and the longer the detour for the refracted sound.

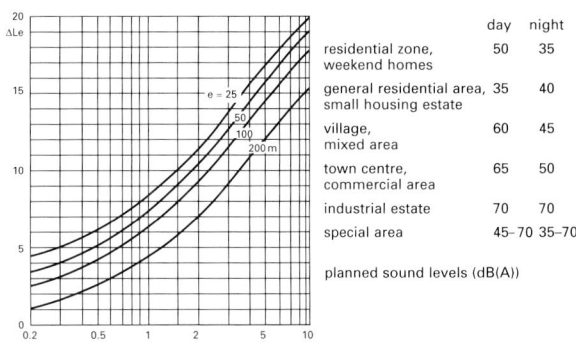

	day	night
residential zone, weekend homes	50	35
general residential area, small housing estate	35	40
village, mixed area	60	45
town centre, commercial area	65	50
industrial estate	70	70
special area	45–70	35–70

planned sound levels (dB(A))

⑧ **Reduction of sound level**

required reduction		10	15	20	25	30	35
necessary distance	meadows	75–125	125–250	225–400	375–555	–	–
	woods	50–75	75–100	100–125	125–175	175–225	200–250

⑨ **Sound reduction by distance**

wall or bank height (m)	1	2	3	4	5	6	7
reduction (dB(A))	6	10	14	16.5	18.5	20.5	23.5

⑩ **Rough estimate of anticipated traffic noise reduction**

traffic density, both directions (daytime vehicles/h)	classification of road types according to traffic density in urban areas	distance from noise emission point/centre of road (m)	noise level band
<10	residential road	–	0
10–50	residential road (2 lanes)	>35	0
		26–35	I
		11–25	II
		≤10	III
>50–200	residential main road (2 lanes)	>100	0
		36–100	I
		26–35	II
		11–25	III
		≤10	IV
>200–1000	country road within town area and main residential road (2 lanes)	101–300	I
		36–100	II
		11–35	III
		≤10	IV
	country road outside town and on trading estates (2 lanes)	101–300	II
		36–100	III
		11–35	IV
		≤10	V
>1000–3000	town high street and road on an industrial estate (2 lanes)	101–300	IV
		36–100	IV
		<35	V
>3000–5000	motorway feeder roads, main roads, motorway (4–6 lanes)	101–300	IV
		≤100	V

⑪ **Rough estimate of anticipated road traffic noise**

SECURING EMBANKMENTS

Long rounded banks with their faces planted as lawns or with shrubs and trees are aesthetically desirable but all steeply sloping surfaces must be secured. For a bank which is steeper than the natural angle of repose, turf, wattle, cobbles or retaining walls can be used for this purpose.

If the slope is more than 1:2 use grass turf fixed with wooden pegs or stepped turf for securing steeper slopes of 1:1.5 to 1:0.5 → p. 230. Wattle is suitable for fixing steep slopes on which it is difficult to establish plant growth → p. 230. It is necessary to distinguish between dead and live wattle: in the case of live wattle (willow cuttings) subsequent permanent planting with deciduous shrubs is called for because willow is only a pioneer plant.

Vegetation is not suitable for securing large bank cuttings, such as in road building or on sloping plots, so more expensive artificial forms of retention are necessary → ① – ⑥.

There are several types of anchored frameworks that can be used to create retaining walls. The simplest consists of horizontal, preanchored beams and vertical posts, with intermediate areas covered with reinforced sprayed concrete → ④. With planted supporting walls considerable height differences can be overcome to create ample space for roads or building plots in uneven terrain → ⑥ + ⑦. High walls can also be built with earth anchors, depending upon the system and the slope → ⑮.

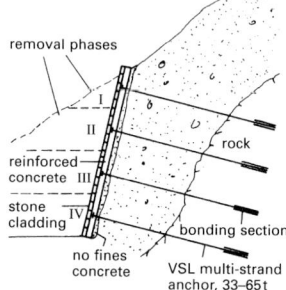

① **Lined wall for banks of loose stone**

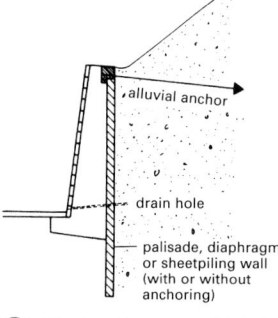

② **Lined wall; unconsolidated rock**

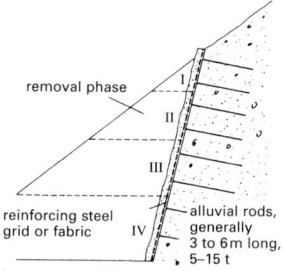

③ **Bank retention; unconsolidated rock**

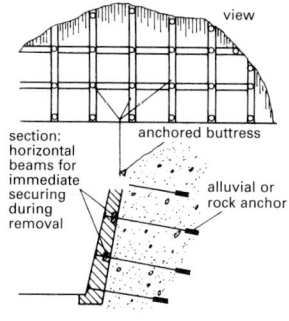

④ **Primary bank retention using anchored framework**

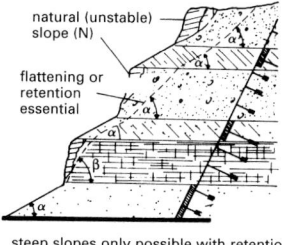

⑤ **Bank retention; unconsolidated rock**

⑥ **Lattice support wall (Krainer wall) made of concrete (Ebensee system)**

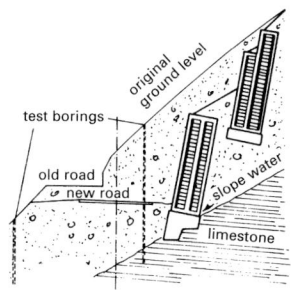

⑦ **Staggered 'Krainer' walls give space for new road**

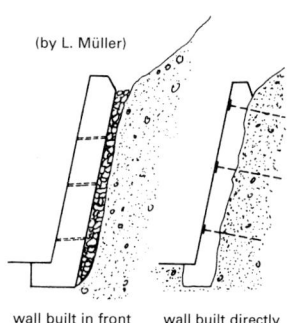

⑧ **Rock facing, either as filled or solid walling**

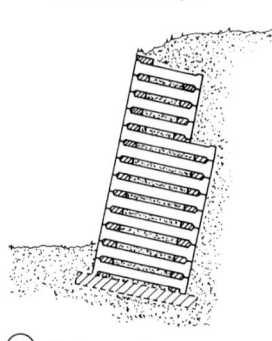

⑨ **Retention considerations: multi-strata slope**

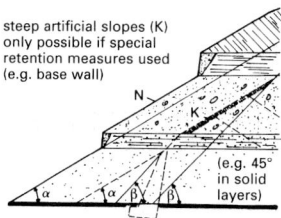

⑩ **Retention considerations: multi-strata slope**

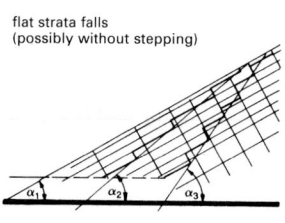

⑪ **Geological influence on slope retention**

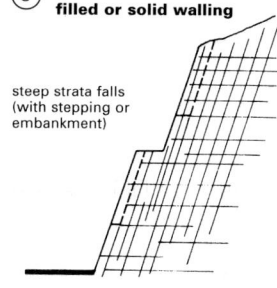

⑫ **Geological influence on slope retention**

⑬ **Krainer wall**

⑭ **RGS 80 wall**

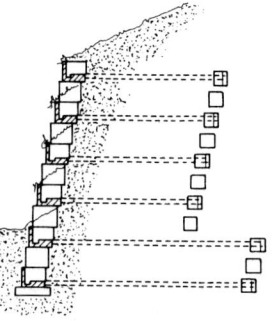

⑮ **Wall with land anchors (Lüdenscheid example)**

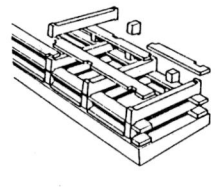

⑯ **The Ebensee Krainer wall** → ⑥ + ⑬

226

In most countries, neighbours have legal rights in relation to fencing. Within an area built as an integrated development, the owner of a building used for domestic or business purposes is obliged at the request of the owner of the neighbouring plot to enclose his plot along the common boundary. Local (or national) regulations may, if both plots are built on or used commercially, require both owners to erect a boundary fence/wall jointly and share the cost. Under English law, ownership of, and responsibility for, fences etc. is spelt out in the property owner's deeds.

A 'common fence' is located in the centre of the boundary whereas with an 'own fence' the foundation wall should be flush with the boundary.

The style of fence chosen should always suit the locality as far as possible → ⑤ – ㉑. Fencing that is intended to protect against wild animals should be sunk 10–20cm into the ground, particularly between hedges → ㉑.

Wooden fencing, posts, frames and palisades can last more than 30 years if they are first chemically impregnated in a tank.

Wooden louvre fences are best for privacy → ⑦ + ⑧ and can also provide some measure of sound insulation. Scissor or rustic fencing is also popular for plot enclosure → ⑨.

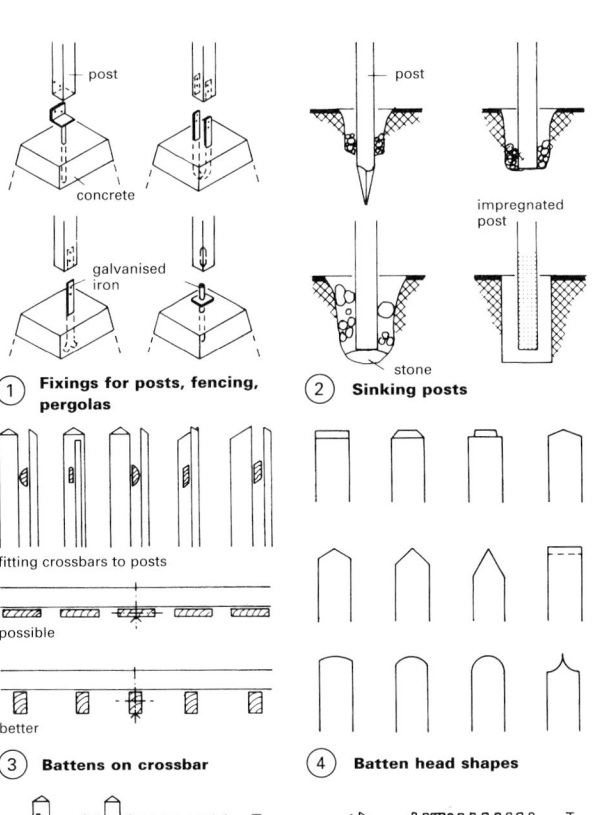

① Fixings for posts, fencing, pergolas

② Sinking posts

③ Battens on crossbar

④ Batten head shapes

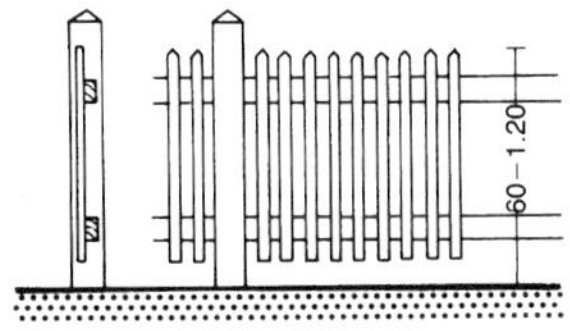

⑤ Fence with projecting posts

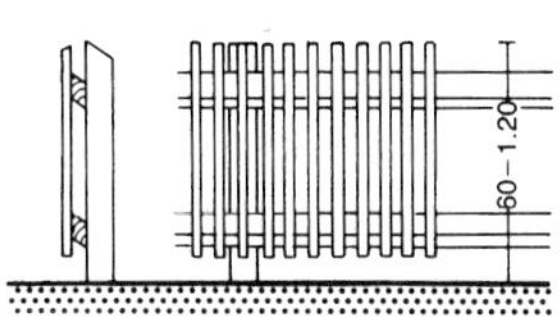

⑥ ...with continuous crossbars

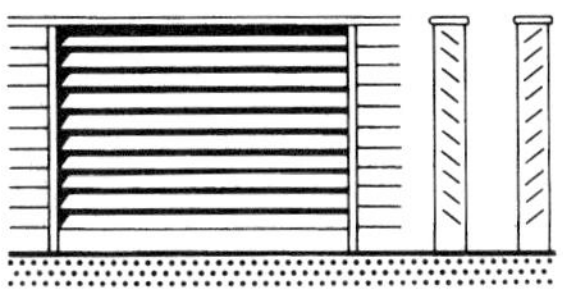

⑦ Horizontal louvres

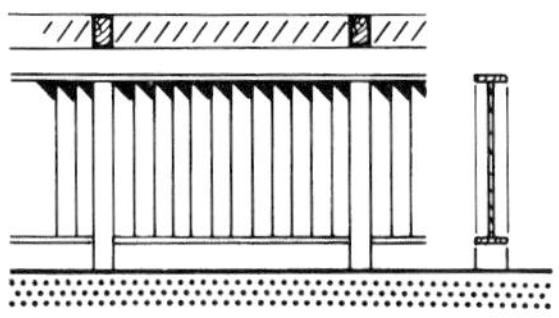

⑧ Vertical wooden louvres

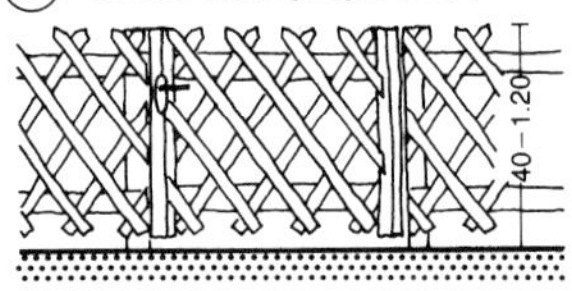

⑨ Rustic fence

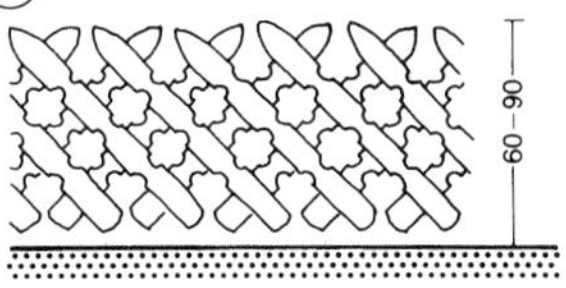

⑩ Ornamental fence

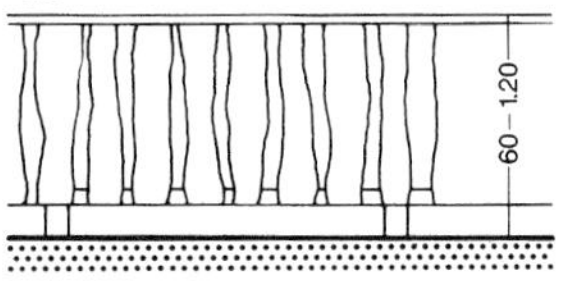

⑪ Rustic fence with frame

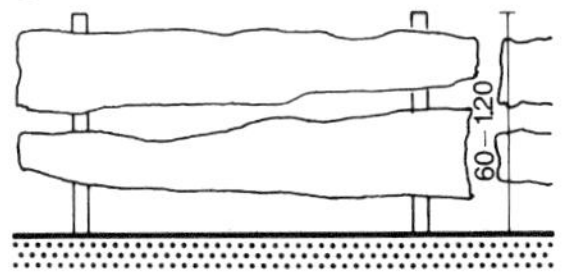

⑫ ...with rough-cut boarding

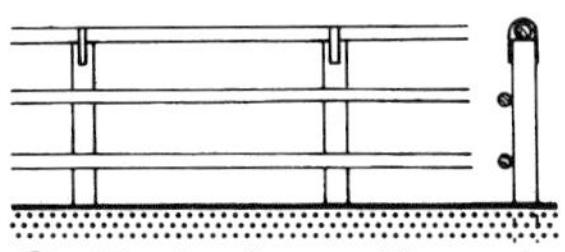

⑬ Meadow fence with round wood cap

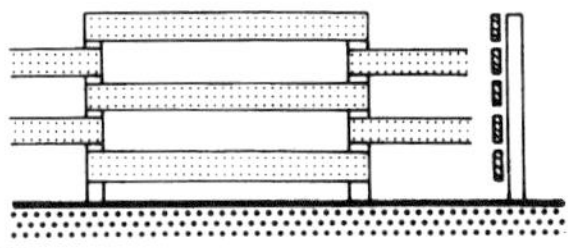

⑭ Alternating glued planks

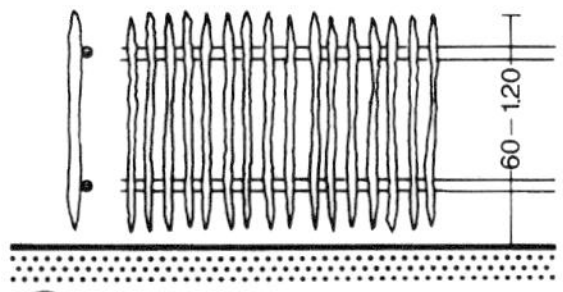

⑮ Simple wooden fence

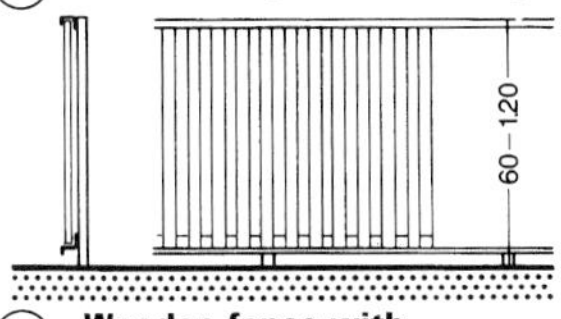

⑯ Wooden fence with aluminium plate fixings

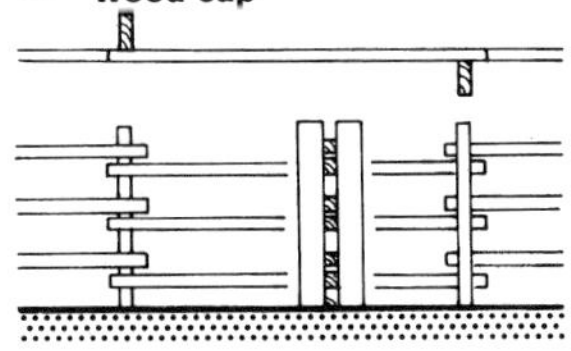

⑰ Meadow fence with offset posts and spars

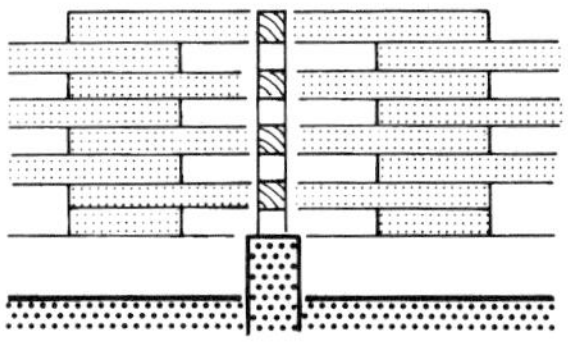

⑱ Square cross-section wood beam fence

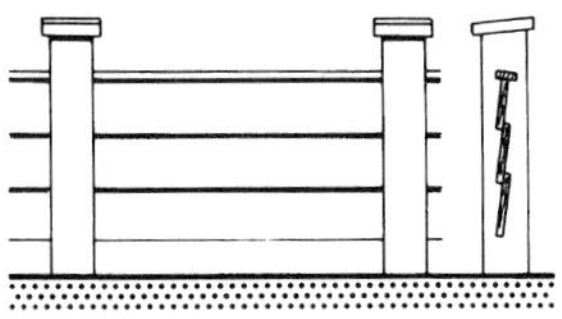

⑲ Rough-sawn boards nailed to posts

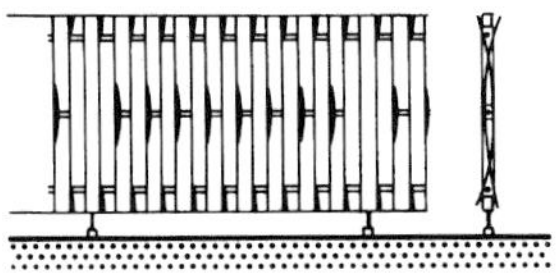

⑳ Bent wooden slats on tubular steel frame

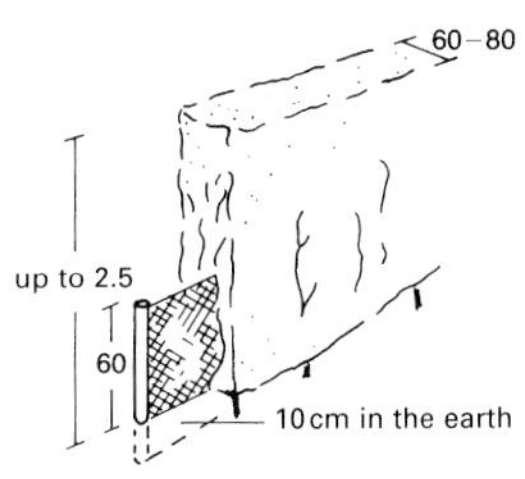

㉑ Hedge with wire netting

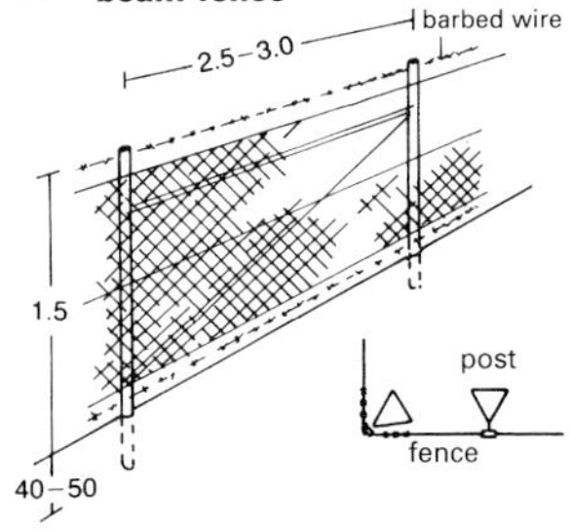

㉒ Wire netting: the bottom either has a small gap (with barbed wire) or is buried

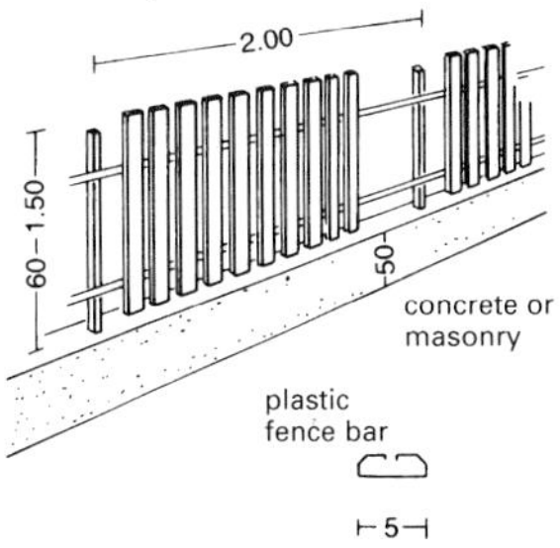

㉓ Steel profile fence (galvanised) with plastic fencing bars

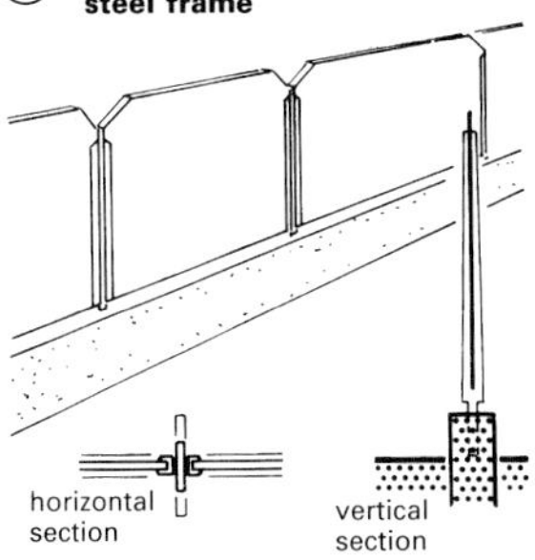

㉔ Partition fence of ornamental wired glass on concrete base

227

GARDEN ENCLOSURES

The owner of a plot usually erects fencing only on one long side since the neighbour on the other side puts up the fence on that long boundary.

Wire mesh fencing → ① can be obtained in many mesh sizes to cover a wide range of usage conditions and if the mesh is plastic coated and supported by galvanised posts the fence will require close to no maintenance. Mesh fences can be braced with wooden, concrete or steel posts which are anchored in the ground → ⑦ + ⑩. Ornamental wire or lattice fencing is usually spot-welded and galvanised → ③ + ④.

Wrought-iron fencing can be elaborate or simple in design and almost any shape is possible → ⑥.

Natural stone such as granite or quartz quarry stone can be used without any processing → ⑨ or cut to shape by a stonemason → ⑧. If possible, only one sort of stone should be used.

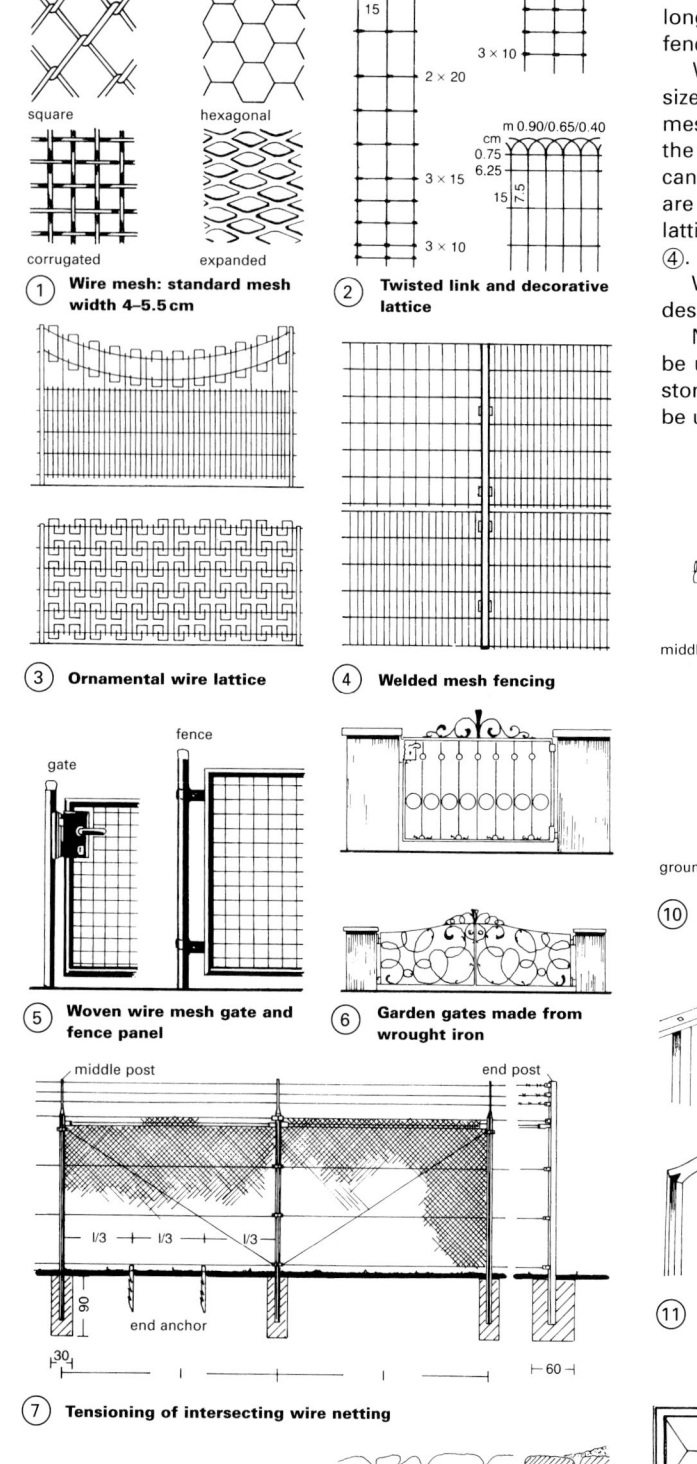

① **Wire mesh: standard mesh width 4–5.5 cm**

② **Twisted link and decorative lattice**

③ **Ornamental wire lattice**

④ **Welded mesh fencing**

⑤ **Woven wire mesh gate and fence panel**

⑥ **Garden gates made from wrought iron**

⑦ **Tensioning of intersecting wire netting**

⑧ **Layered walling with stone layers of different heights**

⑨ **Quarry and cast stone walls**

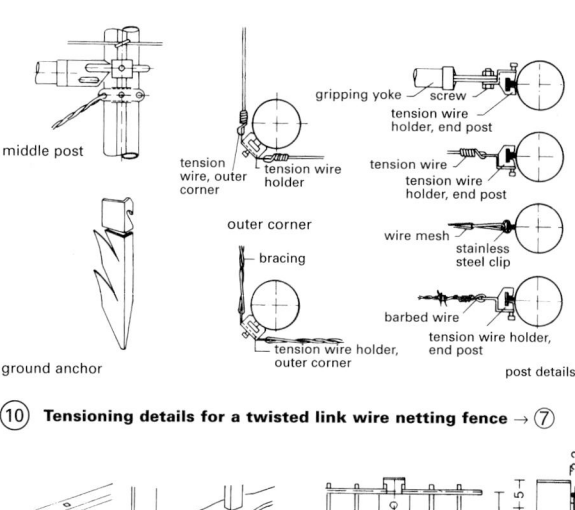

⑩ **Tensioning details for a twisted link wire netting fence → ⑦**

gripping yoke — screw
tension wire holder, end post
tension wire
tension wire holder, end post
tension wire, outer corner
tension wire holder
outer corner
wire mesh
stainless steel clip
bracing
barbed wire
tension wire holder, outer corner
tension wire holder, end post
middle post
ground anchor
post details

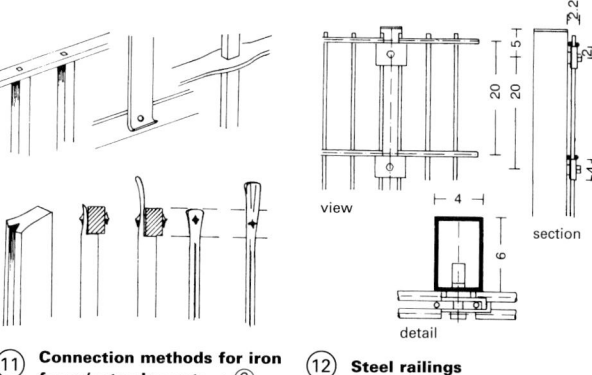

⑪ **Connection methods for iron fence/gate elements → ⑥**

⑫ **Steel railings**

view
section
detail

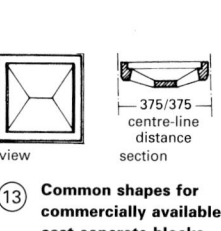

view
375/375 centre-line distance
section

⑬ **Common shapes for commercially available cast concrete blocks**

the table shows the dimensions according to the dimensional regulations for building construction: all centre-line distances are a multiple of 125 mm with 10 mm joints

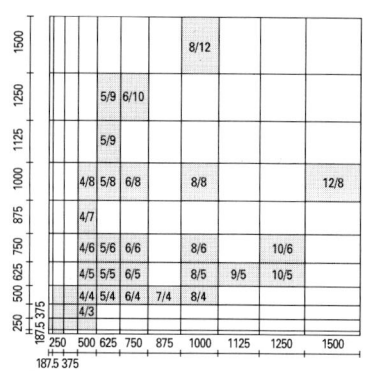

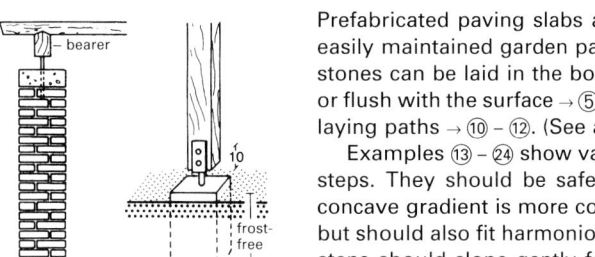

Prefabricated paving slabs are ideal for creating solid and easily maintained garden paths between beds → ④. Paving stones can be laid in the borders or the lawn, either raised or flush with the surface → ⑤ – ⑦. Allow for a gradient when laying paths → ⑩ – ⑫. (See also page 217.)

Examples ⑬ – ㉔ show various arrangements for garden steps. They should be safe and easy to use (note that a concave gradient is more comfortable to walk on → ⑧ + ⑨) but should also fit harmoniously into the surroundings. The steps should slope gently forwards to permit rainwater to run off. In gardens that are designed to be as close as possible to a natural state, log steps are a worthy solution → ⑬ + ⑲. Whatever type of garden steps are chosen, the same rules as apply to indoor stairs should be taken into account → pp. 191–4.

It is possible to incorporate ramps in the garden steps to facilitate movement of bicycles, prams and roller waste bins → ㉕. Wheelchairs being pushed by carers can also make use of such ramps.

Layered dry stone construction can be used for retaining walls up to 2m high in front of uncultivated earth, with an inclination to the slope of 5–20% → ㉖. However, concrete retaining walls → ㉗ are simpler and cheaper, and can be bought as ready-made sections → ㉘ in various sizes and shapes such as corner profiles, quarter segment profiles and round sections, making it possible to form bends with standard parts.

① **Climber supporting frame**

② **Pergola on brick pier** ③ **Raised timber frame (avoids rot)**

length (cm)	width (cm)	edge height (cm)
50	50	12
50	70	14

④ **Garden path blocks**

⑤ **Path raised above borders** ⑥ **Flush with lawn surface** ⑦ **Stepping stones**

easier to keep clean / no impediment to lawn mowers / slab spacing = stride length; thickness ≥ 3cm

⑧ **Good: concave slope (easiest to walk down)** ⑨ **Bad: convex slope**

⑩ **Paths beside house** ⑪ **Footpath on slope** ⑫ **Road on slope**

⑬ **Wooden posts** ⑭ **Vertical stone slabs** ⑮ **Stones smoothed on two edges** ⑯ **Gravel path** ⑰ **Small paving blocks, expensive but durable** ⑱ **Brick paving**

top layer / binding layer / fine layer / coarse layer

blocks (cobbles) / bedding sand

brick paving / sand / clinker or broken stone

⑲ **Steps made with wooden posts** ⑳ **Steps made with stone slabs** ㉑ **Block steps in natural or cast stone**

㉒ **Steps made with stone slabs on supporting blocks** ㉓ **Concrete steps on supporting blocks** ㉔ **Karlsruhe garden stones arranged as concrete steps**

sand / mortar / cobbles / crushed stone

㉕ **Concrete block steps with ramp**

㉖ **Dry wall, special drainage unnecessary**

earth (uncultivated) / bonded layers

㉗ **Concrete retaining wall (also available in ready-made sections) → ㉘**

filling / crushed stone / drainage

㉘ **Ready-made concrete sections for retaining walls**

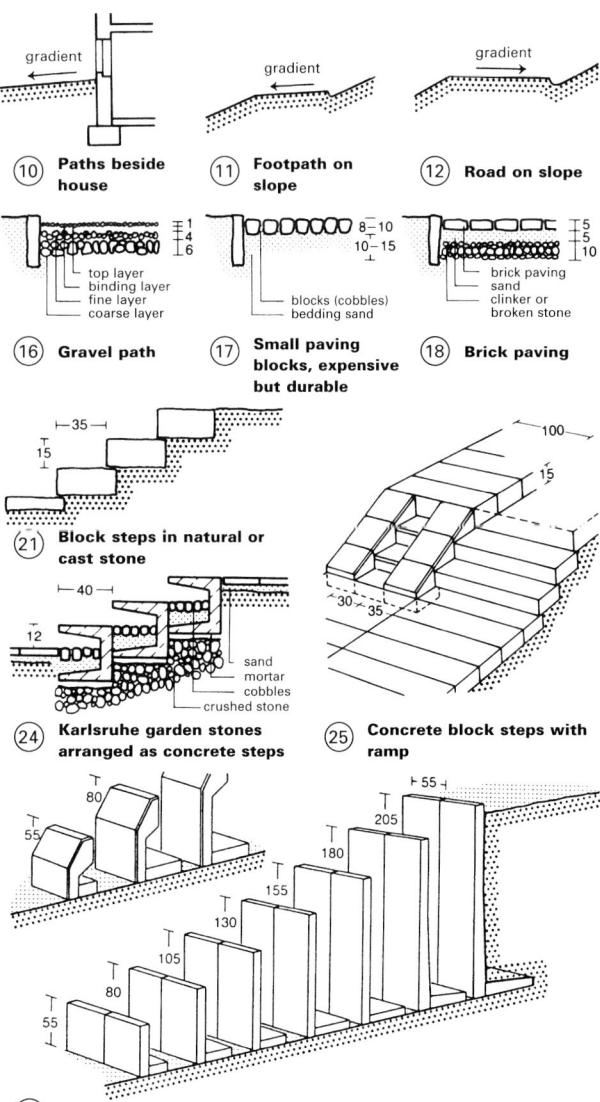

229

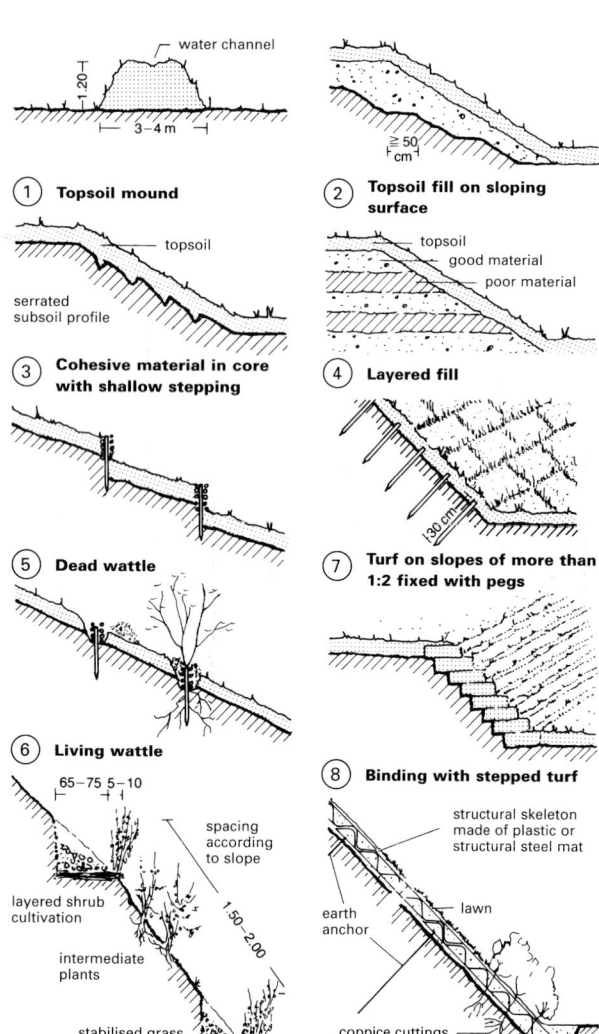

(1) **Topsoil mound**

(2) **Topsoil fill on sloping surface**

(3) **Cohesive material in core with shallow stepping**

(4) **Layered fill**

(5) **Dead wattle**

(7) **Turf on slopes of more than 1:2 fixed with pegs**

(6) **Living wattle**

(8) **Binding with stepped turf**

(9) **Preserving bank surface with shrubs and stabilised grass**

(10) **Preserving bank surface with structural skeleton**

(11) **Drainage and support of slope base**

(12) **Slope support using stone**

(13) **Stone ribs for drainage and support**

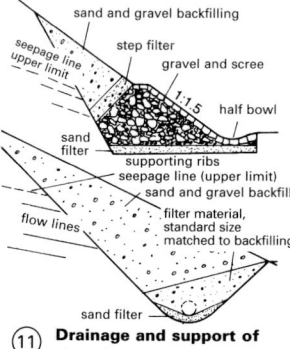

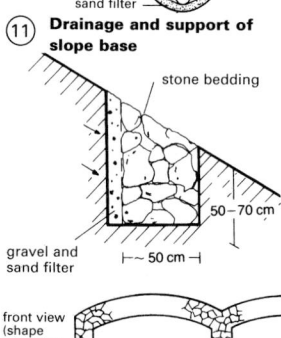

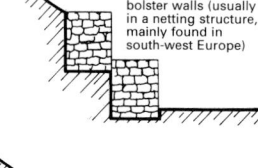

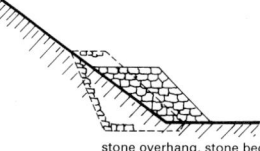

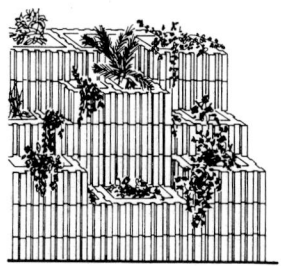

(14) **Open topped, stepped composite grid arrangement**

(15) **Densities and angles of repose for different soil types**

Topsoil can be stored on site by temporarily removing it and building soil mounds → (1). If it is not in the shade, the top of the mound should be protected (with turf, straw etc.) to prevent excessive drying out. Topsoil mounds should be turned over at least once per year, and 0.5kg of quicklime added per cubic metre. If the topsoil needs to be stored for very lengthy periods, consider sowing plants on the mound.

When making up the ground again after the earthworks are completed, compaction measures are necessary if landscaping, lawn laying or planting work is to be carried out immediately, and especially if the work involves laying paths and paved areas. The following techniques can be considered.

- Rolling using a tracked vehicle (e.g. bulldozer) usually provides sufficient compaction for each layer of fill.
- Soaking can be used, but only if the filling material is good (sand and gravel).
- Rolling with a drum roller to compact stable soil in layers (fill height 30–40cm per layer) is another option. Note that it is important always to roll from outside towards the centre (i.e. from the slope towards the centre of the built-up surface). Use rolling for broken stone hardcore when building roads and paths.
- Tamping or ramming is possible on all stable soils.
- Vibration can be used in the case of loose, non-binding materials.

All compaction should take account of subsequent work. For paths and paved areas compaction is needed up to and including the top layer while lawns require 10cm of loose topsoil, and planted areas 40cm.

Slope protection

To avoid slippage and erosion by wind, water run-off etc. the filling on slopes should be laid in layers. Serrated subsoil profiles → (2) prevent the loose infill mass from forming a slip plane on the base material. In the case of higher banks with steeper slopes → (3), stepping provides an effective means of preventing slippage (step width ≥50cm). If steps are inclined into the slope a longitudinal gradient must be created to allow any build up of water to run away.

soil type		density (kg/m³)	angle of repose (degrees)
earth	loose, dry	1400	35–40
	loose, naturally moist	1600	45
	loose, saturated with water	1800	27–30
	compacted, dry	1700	42
	compacted, naturally moist	1900	37
loam	loose, dry (average for light soil)	1500	40–45
	loose, naturally moist	1550	45
	loose, saturated with water (average for medium soil)	2000	20–25
	compacted, dry	1800	40
	compacted, naturally moist	1850	70
gravel	medium coarseness, dry	1800	30–45
	medium coarseness, moist	2000	25–30
	dry	1800	35–40
sand	fine, dry	1600	30–35
	fine, naturally moist	1800	40
	fine, saturated with water	2000	25
	coarse, dry	1900–2000	35
crushed stone, wet		2000–2200	30–40
clay	loose, dry	1600	40–50
	loose, very wet	2000	20–25
	solid, naturally moist (heavy soil)	2500	70
dry sand and rubble		1400	35

GARDENS: PLANTING METHODS

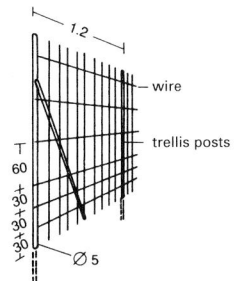

(1) **Trellis frame made of boiler pipes**

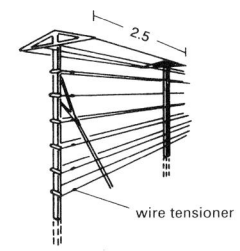

(2) **Frame for double trellis**

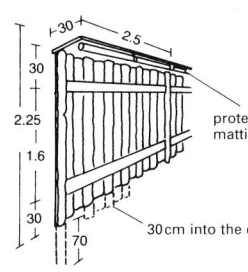

(3) **Trellis wall made of wood**

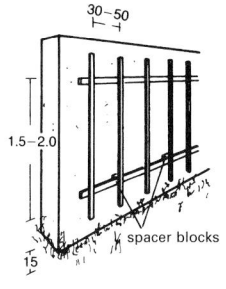

(4) **Trellis attached to wall**

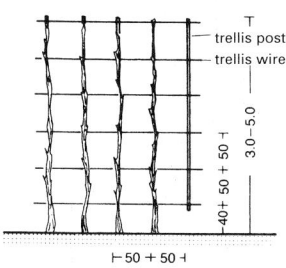

(5) **Vertical training**

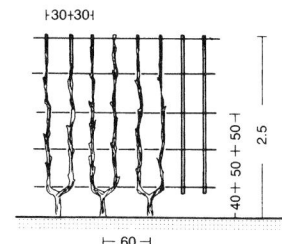

(6) **U-shaped training**

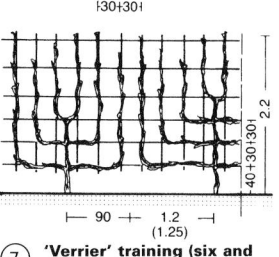

(7) **'Verrier' training (six and eight branches)**

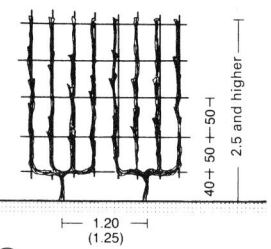

(8) **'Chandelier' training**

(9) **Two-armed horizontal training**

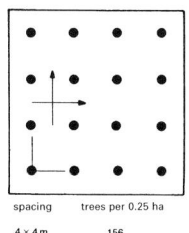

spacing	trees per 0.25 ha
4 × 4 m	156
6 × 6 m	69
10 × 10 m	25

(10) **Square planting system**

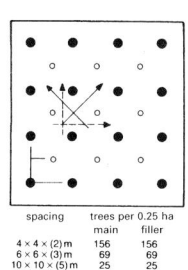

spacing	trees per 0.25 ha	
	main	filler
4 × 4 × (2) m	156	156
6 × 6 × (3) m	69	69
10 × 10 × (5) m	25	25

(11) **Square planting with infill**

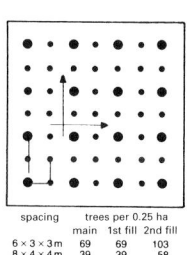

spacing	trees per 0.25 ha		
	main	1st fill	2nd fill
6 × 3 × 3 m	69	69	103
8 × 4 × 4 m	39	39	58
10 × 5 × 5 m	25	25	37

(12) **Square planting, double infill**

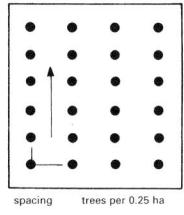

spacing	trees per 0.25 ha
2 × 4 m	312
6 × 6 m	69
4 × 10 m	42

(13) **Rectangular planting system**

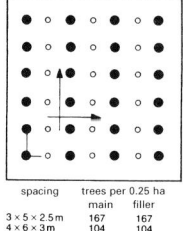

spacing	trees per 0.25 ha	
	main	filler
3 × 5 × 2.5 m	167	167
4 × 6 × 3 m	104	104
6 × 10 × 5 m	42	42

(14) **Rectangular planting with infill**

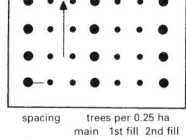

spacing	trees per 0.25 ha		
	main	1st fill	2nd fill
3 × 3 m	46	46	184
4 × 4 m	26	26	104

(15) **Rectangular planting, double infill**

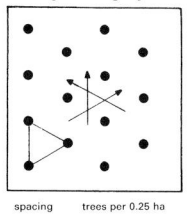

spacing	trees per 0.25 ha
3 × 3 × 3 m	320
4 × 4 × 4 m	178
6 × 6 × 6 m	80

(16) **Triangular planting system (equilateral)**

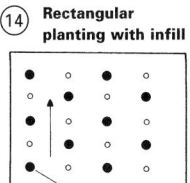

spacing	trees per 0.25 ha	
	main	filler
1.5 × 3 × 3 m	320	320
2 × 4 × 4 m	178	178
3 × 6 × 6 m	80	80

(17) **Triangular planting with infill**

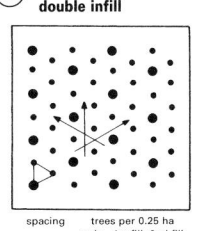

spacing	trees per 0.25 ha		
	main	1st fill	2nd fill
3 × 3 × 3 m	80	80	160
4 × 4 × 4 m	44	44	88

(18) **Triangular planting, double infill**

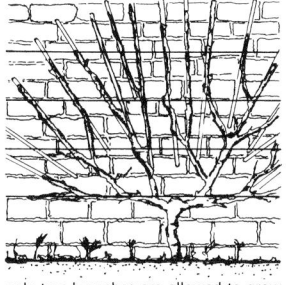

only two branches are allowed to grow at an angle to the ground; the shoots from these form the fan in early spring

(19) **Fan array**

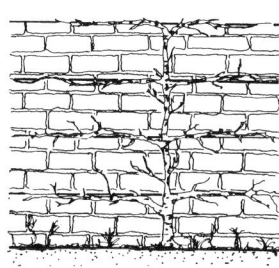

the central trunk of an espalier is grown vertically and the side branches are trained to each side at right angles

(20) **Espalier**

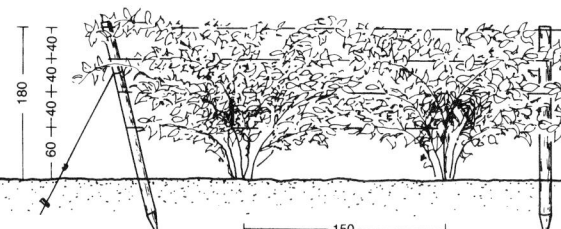

(21) **Wire framework for blackberry branches**

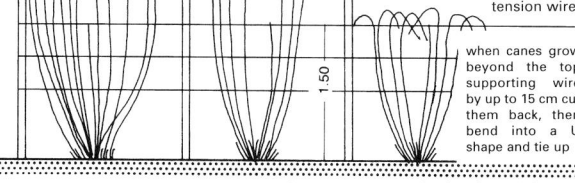

when canes grow beyond the top supporting wire by up to 15 cm cut them back, then bend into a U shape and tie up

after the harvest, cut back to leave 5–8 canes

(22) **Raspberries**

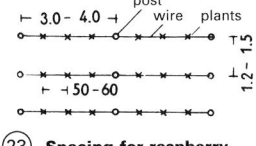

(23) **Spacing for raspberry plants**

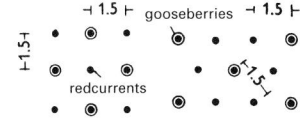

(24) **Gooseberries in square formation in combination with redcurrants**

GARDENS: PLANTING METHODS

Two important factors for the successful cultivation of climbing plants are the soil quality and the direction they face. In addition, the height to which they will grow must be taken into account → ①. Climbing aids are required for plants that are to grown up house walls → ② + ③.

In the case of beans each plant requires a climbing cane. The tent method is best used for two rows of plants → ⑦.

The wigwam method is ideal for growing plants in troughs and tubs → ⑥ and twigs gathered during coppicing can be used as a climbing aid for peas → ⑨, as can taut wire netting → ④ or a double wire mesh. Wire mesh is also useful to protect seeds and shoots from birds → ⑩ + ⑪.

Guidelines for the choosing the best conditions for perennial climbing and creeping plants are given in ⑫.

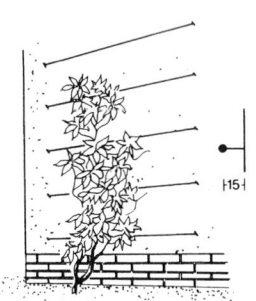

① **Climbing plants and their growth heights**

② **Horizontal climbing aids**

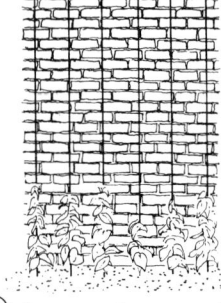

③ **Beans growing up a wall**

annuals	height (m)	growth	leaves
bell vine	4–6	fast	summer, green
ornamental gourd	2–5	fast	summer, green
Japanese hop	3–4	fast	summer, green
trumpet convulvulous	3–4	fast	summer, green
sweet pea	1–2	fast	summer, green
scarlet runner bean	2–4	fast	summer, green
nasturtium	2–3	fast	summer, green

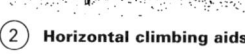

④ **Hexagonal wire mesh**

⑤ **Wooden fencing trellis**

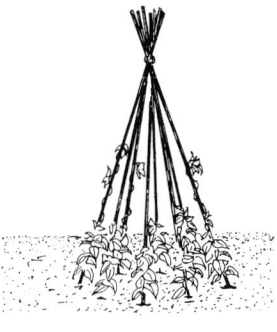

⑥ **Wigwam method for 8–11 plants**

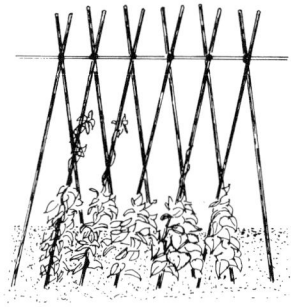

⑦ **Tent method**

distance apart: 70 × 60, maximum 50 × 100

⑧ **Twig frame**

⑨ **Double wire mesh frame**

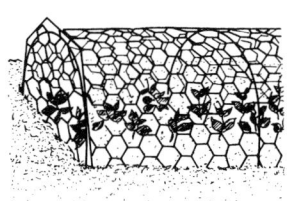

⑩ **Wire mesh to protect plants from birds**

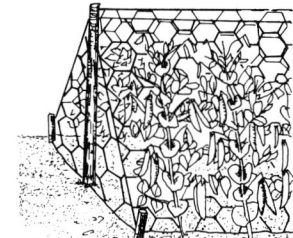

⑪ **Climbing mesh for peas made of wire netting**

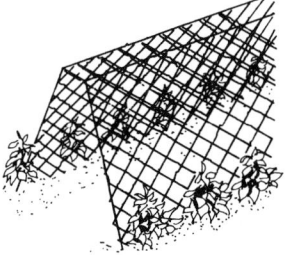

perennials	height	growth	climbing aid	leaves	watering	flowers/month	location
ivy (*Hedera helix*)	up to 25 m	slow		winter	–	9–10 greenish	○–●
knotgrass (*Polygonum aubertii*)	up to 15 m	fast	x necessary	summer	+	7–9 white	○–●
virginia creeper (*P. tricuspidata 'Veitchii'*)	up to 15 m	fast		summer	(+)	5–6 greenish	○◕
anemone (*Clematis montana*)	up to 8 m	fast	x	summer	+	5–6 white	○◕
wisteria (*Wisteria sinensis*)	up to 10 m	medium	x	summer	(+)	5–6 blue	○◕
common traveller's joy (*Clematis vitalba*)	up to 10 m	fast	x	summer	+	7–9 white	○◕
climbing hydrangea (*Hydrangea petiolaris*)	5 to 8 m	medium	(x) sensible	summer	–	6–7 white	◕●
dutchman's pipe (*Aristolochia macrophylla*)	up to 10 m	medium	x	summer	(+)	5–6 brown	◕●
trumpet vine (*Campsis radicans*)	up to 8 m	slow	(x) sensible	summer	+	7–8 orange	○
grapevine (*Vitis coignetiae*)	up to 10 m	medium	x	summer	(+)	5–6 greenish	○◕
grape (*Vitis vinifera*)	up to 10 m	medium	x	summer	+	5–6 greenish	○◕
red honeysuckle (*Lonicera heckrottii*)	3 to 4 m	medium	x	summer	(+)	6–9 yellow-red	◕
hop (*Humulus lupulus*)	4 to 6 m	fast	x	summer	–	5–6 greenish	◕
honeysuckle (*Lonicera caprifolium*)	up to 5 m	medium	x	summer	+	5–6 yellow-red	◕
climbing rose	up to 5 m	medium	x	summer	–	6–8 various	○◕
spindle shrub (*Euonymus fortunei*)	2 to 4 m	slow	(x) sensible	winter	(+)	6–8 greenish	◕●
traveller's joy (*Clematis hybriden*)	2 to 4 m	medium	x	summer	+	6–9 various	○◕
winter jasmine (*Jasminum nudiflorum*)	up to 3 m	slow	x	winter	+	1–4 yellow	○◕

⑫ **Summary of some climbing and creeping plants** → ①

○ = sunny location   ◕ = half shade, e.g. north wall   ● = shade

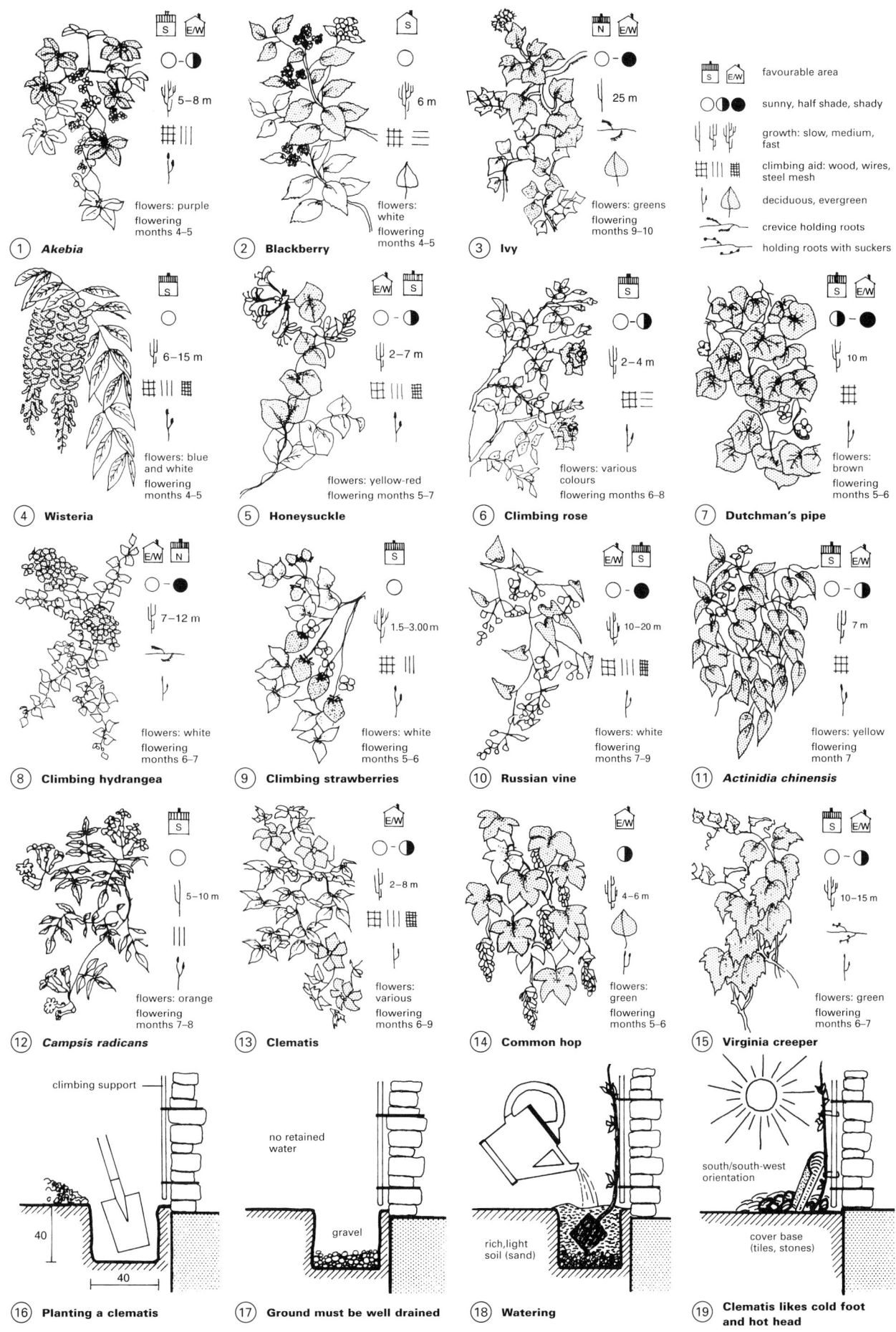

favourable area

sunny, half shade, shady

growth: slow, medium, fast

climbing aid: wood, wires, steel mesh

deciduous, evergreen

crevice holding roots

holding roots with suckers

① Akebia — flowers: purple; flowering months 4–5

② Blackberry — 6 m; flowers: white; flowering months 4–5

③ Ivy — 25 m; flowers: greens; flowering months 9–10

④ Wisteria — 6–15 m; flowers: blue and white; flowering months 4–5

⑤ Honeysuckle — 2–7 m; flowers: yellow-red; flowering months 5–7

⑥ Climbing rose — 2–4 m; flowers: various colours; flowering months 6–8

⑦ Dutchman's pipe — 10 m; flowers: brown; flowering months 5–6

⑧ Climbing hydrangea — 7–12 m; flowers: white; flowering months 6–7

⑨ Climbing strawberries — 1.5–3.00 m; flowers: white; flowering months 5–6

⑩ Russian vine — 10–20 m; flowers: white; flowering months 7–9

⑪ Actinidia chinensis — 7 m; flowers: yellow; flowering month 7

⑫ Campsis radicans — 5–10 m; flowers: orange; flowering months 7–8

⑬ Clematis — 2–8 m; flowers: various; flowering months 6–9

⑭ Common hop — 4–6 m; flowers: green; flowering months 5–6

⑮ Virginia creeper — 10–15 m; flowers: green; flowering months 6–7

⑯ Planting a clematis — climbing support; 40; 40

⑰ Ground must be well drained — no retained water; gravel

⑱ Watering — rich, light soil (sand)

⑲ Clematis likes cold foot and hot head — south/south-west orientation; cover base (tiles, stones)

233

BANKED AND RAISED BEDS

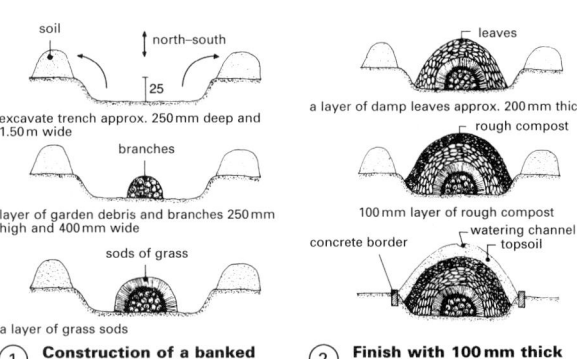

soil

↓ north–south

25

excavate trench approx. 250 mm deep and 1.50 m wide

branches

layer of garden debris and branches 250 mm high and 400 mm wide

sods of grass

a layer of grass sods

① **Construction of a banked bed → ② + ③**

leaves

a layer of damp leaves approx. 200 mm thick

rough compost

100 mm layer of rough compost

concrete border

watering channel

topsoil

② **Finish with 100 mm thick layer of topsoil**

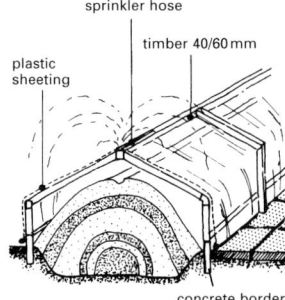

sprinkler hose

timber 40/60 mm

plastic sheeting

concrete border

③ **Bed covered with plastic sheeting**

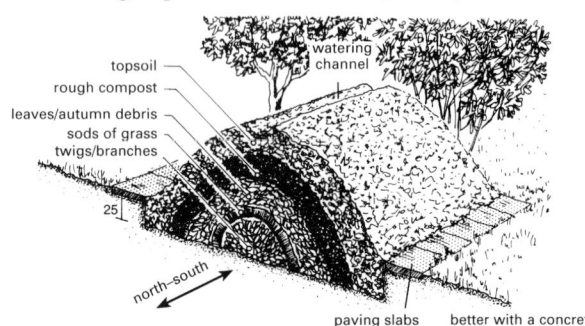

topsoil

watering channel

rough compost

leaves/autumn debris

sods of grass

twigs/branches

25

north–south

paving slabs

better with a concrete border finish → ② + ③

④ **Cross-section through a banked bed**

⑤ **Raised bed, ideal for terracing slopes**

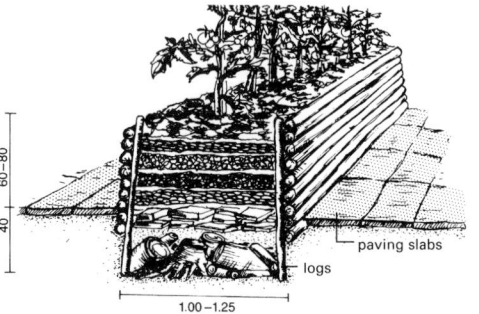

60–80

40

paving slabs

logs

1.00–1.25

⑥ **Raised bed: same layers as banked beds**

top-hinged widows

⑦ **Raised bed built against a south wall; covered with glass like small green house**

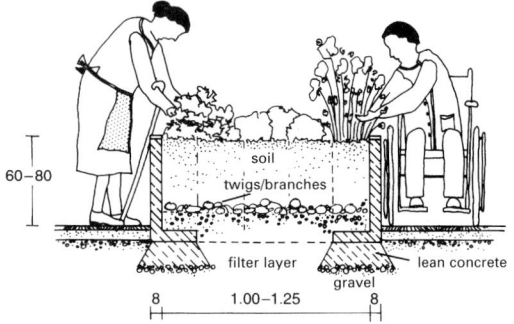

60–80

soil

twigs/branches

filter layer

gravel

lean concrete

8 1.00–1.25 8

⑧ **Raised bed made from prefabricated concrete units**

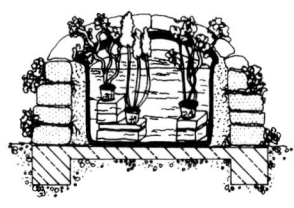

⑨ **Small pond in a raised bed made with stones**

Banked beds are ideal for growing vegetables in the garden. They offer the possibility of quick harvests and very high yields. The most important factors in constructing a banked bed are the correct build-up and a north–south orientation → ① – ③. Although they require some effort to build, banked beds can be used for several years. In general, a banked bed is approximately 1.50 m wide and 4 m long and watered with a sprinkler hose → ③ or trickle irrigation. It is best to carry out the construction process in the autumn when the most garden debris is available. Mixed planting has proved to be particularly effective in banked and raised beds.

The raised bed is a variation of the banked bed in that it has the same composition and is, in principle, a compost heap contained by a boarded frame → ⑥. Any rot-resistant material is suitable and can be used instead of wooden boards (e.g. impregnated logs, wood blocks, or stone walls). In addition to the advantages of the rich bedding material, the plants also benefit from the sunshine which impinges on the side walls.

If the beds are 600–800 mm high, it is no longer necessary to bend when planting seeds, bedding plants or harvesting → ⑥ + ⑧, which makes raised beds ideal for the elderly and wheelchair users. Raised beds give increased yields when they are filled with layers of organic materials, tree stumps at the bottom, then branches, then chopped twigs up to well rotted compost.

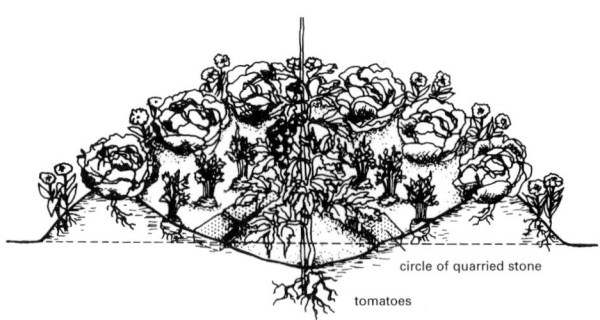

circle of quarried stone

tomatoes

⑩ **Crater bed 2 m diameter → ⑪**

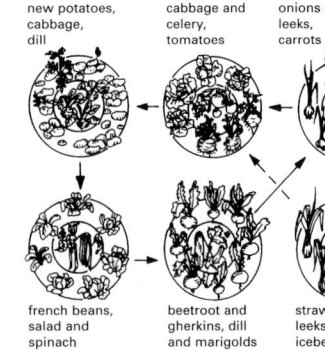

new potatoes, cabbage, dill

cabbage and celery, tomatoes

onions and leeks, carrots

french beans, salad and spinach

beetroot and gherkins, dill and marigolds

strawberries, leeks and iceberg lettuce

⑪ **Mixed planting in six crater beds → ⑩**

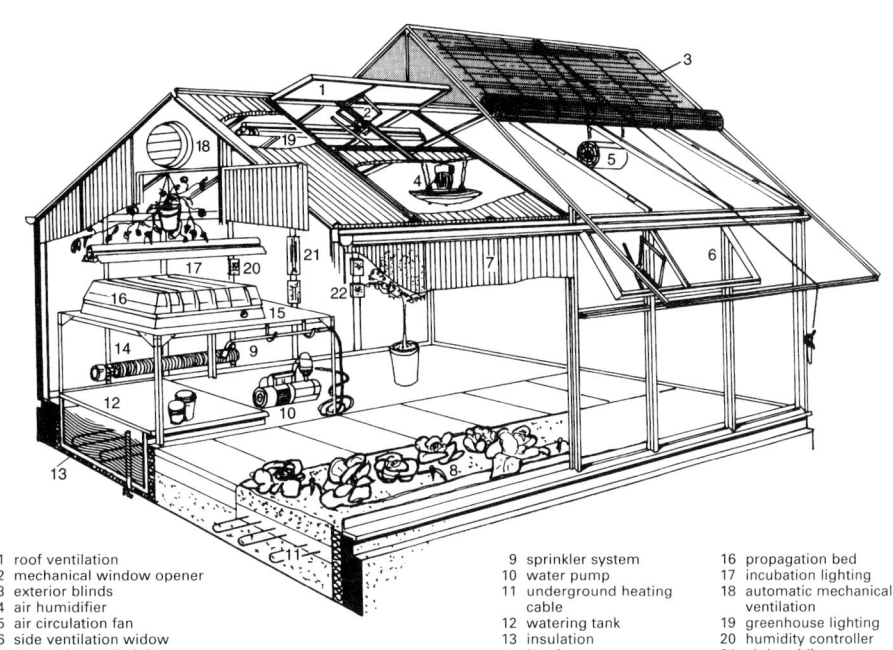

GREENHOUSES

The ventilation of green-houses should be calculated such that, when fully ventilated, the inside temperature can be held close to that outside. For this it is necessary that about 20% of the roof area consists of a ventilation strip or windows that can be opened individually. An adequate supply of fresh air must also be ensured.

Where there is insufficient natural shading from outside it may be necessary to install sun blinds in order to maintain temperate conditions during bright sunshine. Blinds can be installed on the inside or outside of the greenhouse. Although those inside are more economical, exterior blinds are more effective, particularly when there is a sufficient gap between the blinds and the glass → ⑩ + ⑪.

1 roof ventilation	9 sprinkler system	16 propagation bed
2 mechanical window opener	10 water pump	17 incubation lighting
3 exterior blinds	11 underground heating cable	18 automatic mechanical ventilation
4 air humidifier	12 watering tank	19 greenhouse lighting
5 air circulation fan	13 insulation	20 humidity controller
6 side ventilation widow	14 heating	21 air humidity sensor
7 double layer plexiglass	15 plant table	22 thermostat
8 trickle irrigation		

① **Greenhouse with practical climate control**

② **Banked bed with solar hood**
size 1.00/1.00 m and 1.00/2.00 m

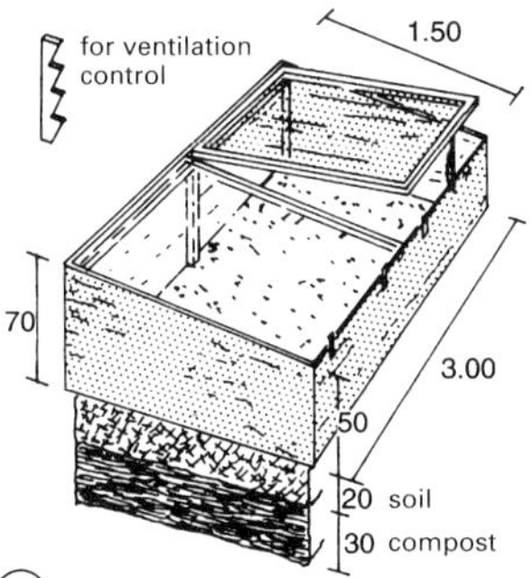

③ **Cold frame**
for ventilation control
1.50
70
3.00
50
20 soil
30 compost

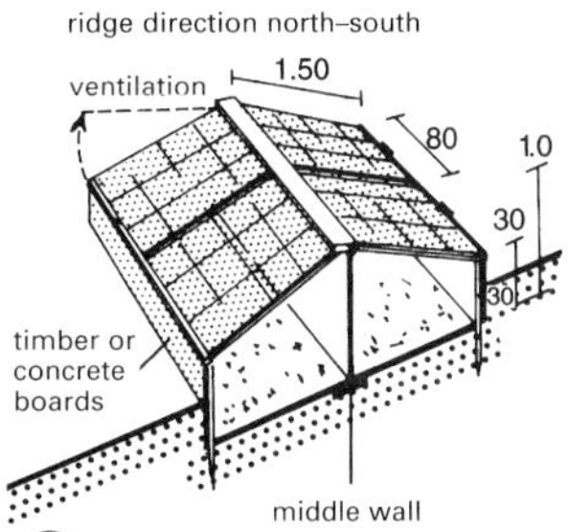

④ **Small greenhouse**
ridge direction north–south
ventilation
1.50
80
1.0
30
timber or concrete boards
middle wall

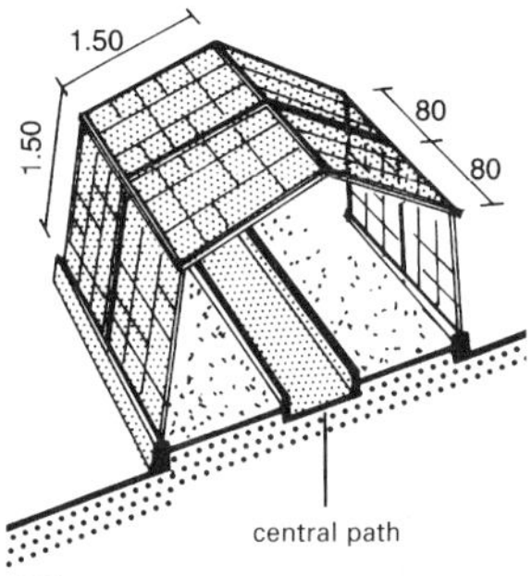

⑤ **Dutch greenhouse**
1.50
1.50
80
80
central path

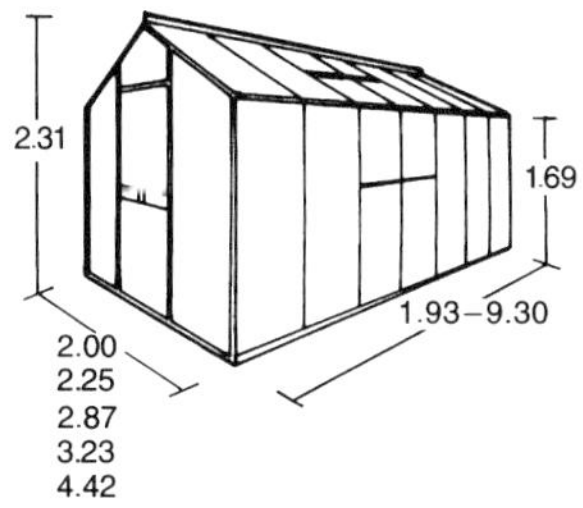

⑥ **Standard greenhouse**
2.31
1.69
1.93–9.30
2.00
2.25
2.87
3.23
4.42

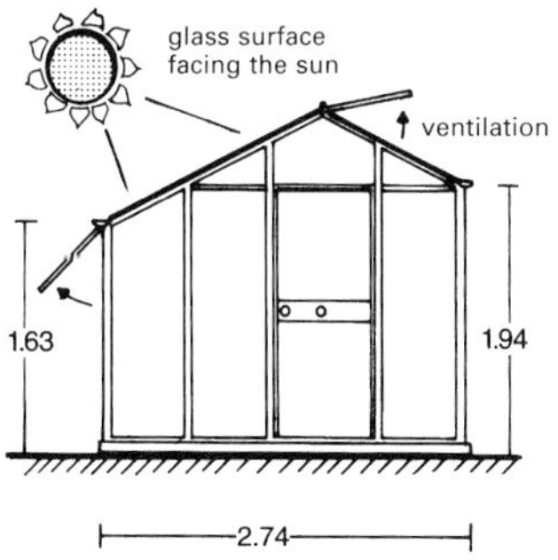

⑦ **Solar greenhouse**
glass surface facing the sun
ventilation
1.63
1.94
2.74

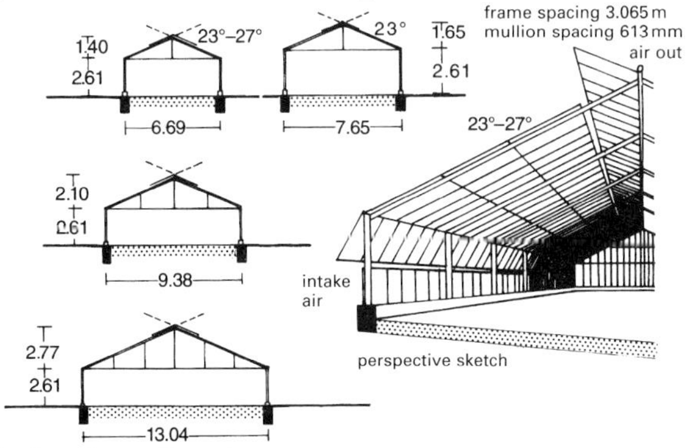

⑧ **Greenhouse dimensions and roof slopes**
1.40
23°–27°
23°
1.65
2.61
6.69
7.65
2.61
2.10
0.61
9.38
2.77
2.61
13.04
frame spacing 3.065 m
mullion spacing 613 mm
air out
23°–27°
intake air
perspective sketch

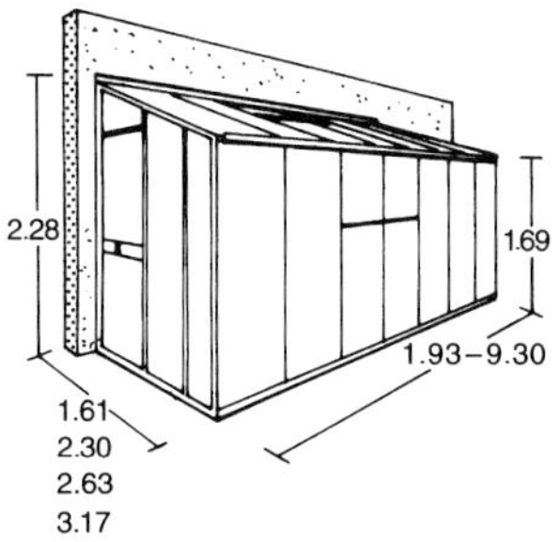

⑨ **Lean-to greenhouse**
2.28
1.69
1.93–9.30
1.61
2.30
2.63
3.17

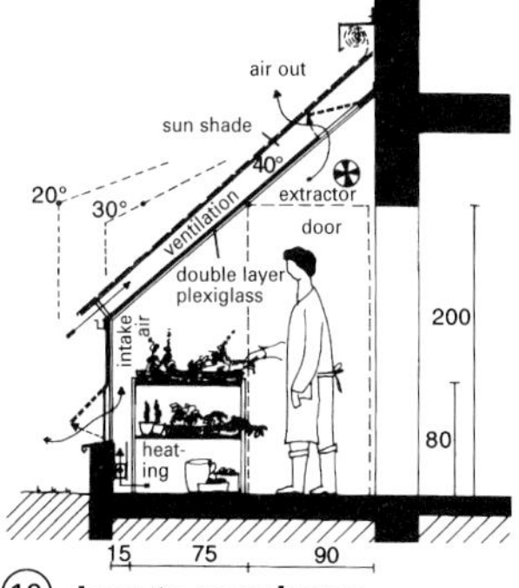

⑩ **Lean-to greenhouse**
air out
sun shade
20°
30°
40°
extractor
door
ventilation
double layer plexiglass
intake air
heating
200
80
15 75 90

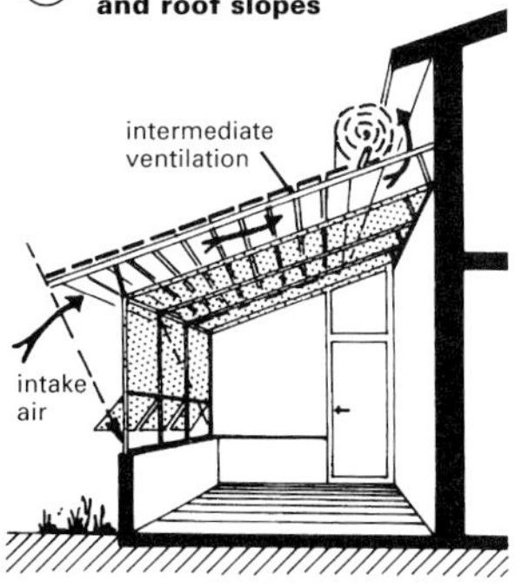

⑪ **Exterior blinds with full intermediate ventilation**
intermediate ventilation
intake air

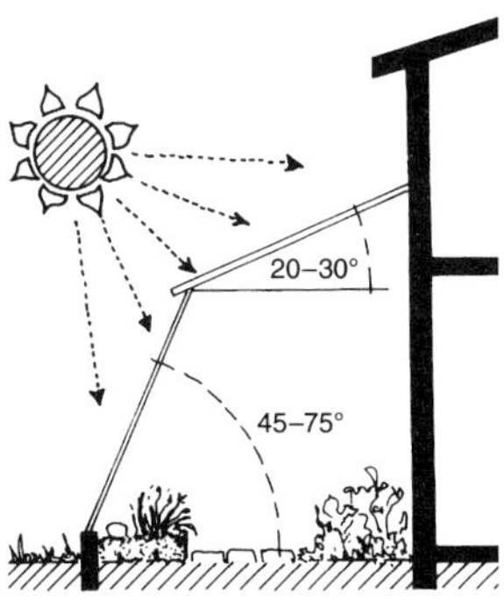

⑫ **Optimal angles for glass surfaces**
20–30°
45–75°

235

GARDENS: TREES AND HEDGES

Fertile soil contains an abundance of life, with the different layers being inhabited by different groups of species → ①. Tree roots can penetrate the soil down to rocky layers and the shape of the underground root network is usually a mirror image of the shape of the tree's crown → ②.

For cultivated trees the cup shape is preferred. These have open centres from which the branches are drawn outwards so that light can penetrate the treetops. Side branches are kept short so they will not break under the weight of fruit or snow.

The best time for planting fruit trees is late autumn (October in areas with early frost, November and in milder areas). Grafting points, which can be clearly recognised as a swelling on the end of the stem, must always be above the soil surface. Supporting posts must be a handbreadth away from the trunk and should be to the south to prevent sunburn. → ⑦

When planting hedges the correct distance from the neighbouring plot must be maintained: 0.25m for hedges up to 1.2m high, 0.5m for hedges up to 2m high and 0.75m for hedges over 2m. Hedges are ideal for providing privacy in one's own garden as well as protection from noise and dust. They also reduce wind speed, increase dew formation, regulate heat and prevent soil erosion. Banked hedges (so-called 'quick-set hedges' → ⑩) are used as windbreaks in coastal areas.

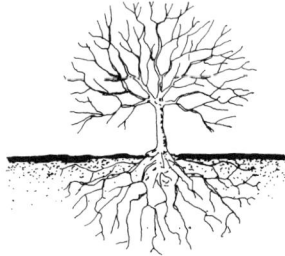

decomposition layer
synthesis layer
humus formation
main root area
soil's nutrients released
nutrient reservoir according to lower stratum

5cm soil cover (leaves, mulch)
digestion layer (bacteria, fungus, insects)
20–30cm humus layer (micro-organisms, nitrogen fixing bacteria, algae)
rainwater ducts through all layers
up to 2.50 mineral layer (decomposed rock water reservoir)
bedrock

① **Soil and humus layers are filled with life**

preferred to the 'Christmas tree', or pyramid, shape, is the cup shape: with branches grown outwards the tree has an open centre like a cup or goblet, which allows light into the fresh growth at the top; side branches are kept short so that they can withstand the weight of fruit or snow

② **The root network mirrors the natural top of the tree**

③ **Tree shapes**

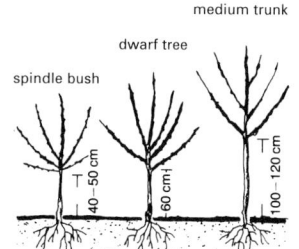

leave trunk and two or three branches to retain the desired shape

④ **High trunk on a sapling**

medium trunk
dwarf tree
spindle bush
40–50 cm
60 cm
100–120 cm

⑤ **Tree shapes for small gardens**

⑧ **Trim a hornbeam hedge in the 1st, 3rd and 5th year after planting (left summer, right winter)**

supporting post set at an angle

⑥ **When planting a conifer the root ball must be loosened**

good   bad   good

⑨ **Hedge heights**

1.20–1.50
0.60–1.20
0.60–0.80
0.50–1.00
trench

⑩ **'Quick-set hedge' (North Germany)**

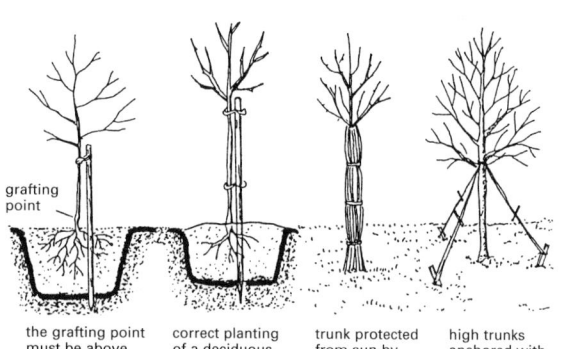

grafting point

the grafting point must be above the soil

correct planting of a deciduous tree

trunk protected from sun by straw matting

high trunks anchored with tensioning wires

⑦ **Planting garden trees**

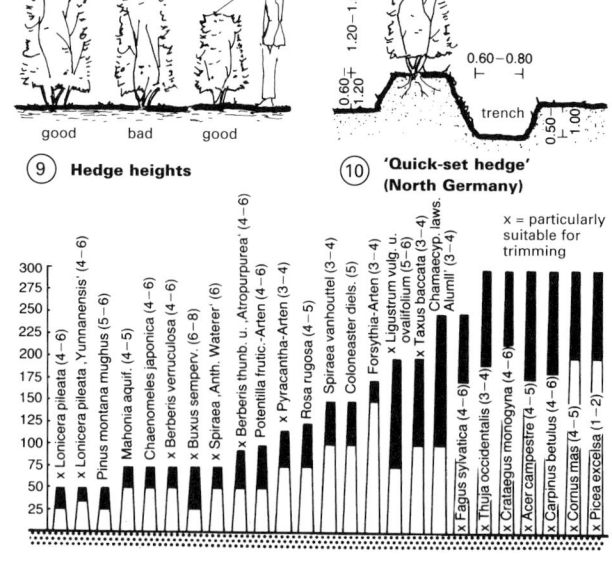

x = particularly suitable for trimming

x Lonicera pileata (4 – 6)
x Lonicera pileata 'Yunnanensis' (4 – 6)
Pinus montana mughus (5 – 6)
Mahonia aquif. (4 – 5)
Chaenomeles japonica (4 – 6)
x Berberis verruculosa (4 – 6)
x Buxus semperv. (6 – 8)
x Spiraea 'Anth. Waterer' (6)
x Berberis thunb. u. 'Atropurpurea' (4 – 6)
Potentilla frutic.-Arten (4 – 6)
x Pyracantha-Arten (3 – 4)
x Rosa rugosa (4 – 5)
Spiraea vanhouttei (3 – 4)
Cotoneaster diels. (5)
Forsythia-Arten (3 – 4)
x Ligustrum vulg. u. ovalifolium (5 – 6)
x Taxus baccata (3 – 4)
Chamaecyp.laws. Alumii (3 – 4)
x Fagus sylvatica (4 – 6)
x Thuja occidentalis (3 – 4)
x Crataegus monogyna (4 – 6)
x Acer campestre (4 – 5)
x Carpinus betulus (4 – 6)
x Cornus mas (4 – 5)
x Picea excelsa (1 – 2)

⑪ **Heights for trimmed and free-growing hedges (number of plants required per metre run in parentheses)**

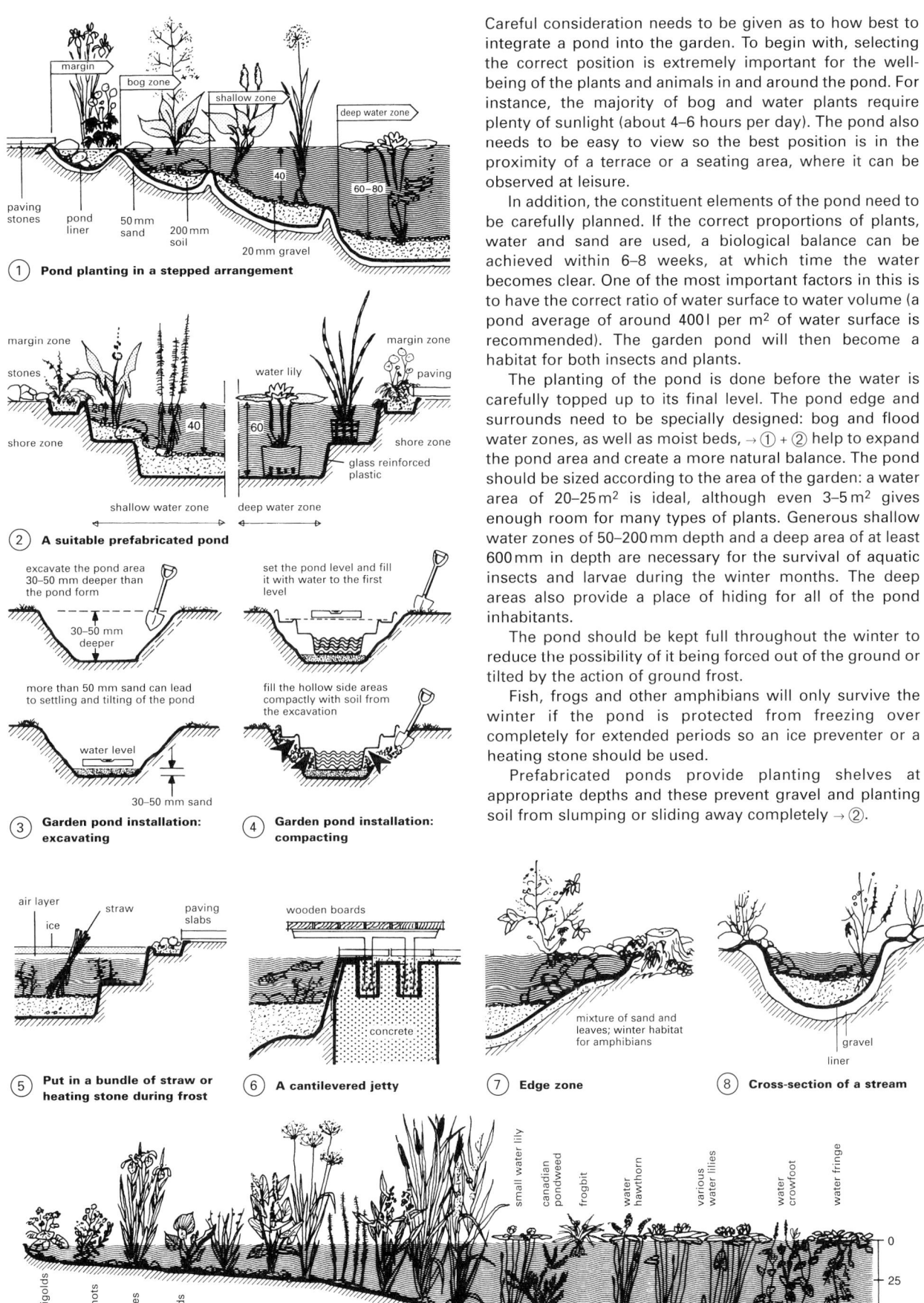

① **Pond planting in a stepped arrangement**

margin

bog zone

shallow zone

deep water zone

paving stones | pond liner | 50 mm sand | 200 mm soil | 20 mm gravel

40 | 60–80

② **A suitable prefabricated pond**

margin zone

stones

shore zone

water lily | paving

margin zone

shore zone

glass reinforced plastic

shallow water zone | deep water zone

40 | 60

③ **Garden pond installation: excavating**

excavate the pond area 30–50 mm deeper than the pond form

30–50 mm deeper

more than 50 mm sand can lead to settling and tilting of the pond

water level

30–50 mm sand

④ **Garden pond installation: compacting**

set the pond level and fill it with water to the first level

fill the hollow side areas compactly with soil from the excavation

⑤ **Put in a bundle of straw or heating stone during frost**

air layer | straw | paving slabs

ice

⑥ **A cantilevered jetty**

wooden boards

concrete

⑦ **Edge zone**

mixture of sand and leaves; winter habitat for amphibians

⑧ **Cross-section of a stream**

gravel

liner

⑨ **Aquatic plants**

marsh marigolds | water forget-me-nots | aquatic irises | monkshoods | dwarf rush | pickerel weed | flowering rush | fir frond | porcupine quill | wide-leaved bull rushes | zebra rush | small water lily | canadian pondweed | frogbit | water hawthorn | various water lilies | water crowfoot | water fringe

0 | 25 | 50 | 80

Careful consideration needs to be given as to how best to integrate a pond into the garden. To begin with, selecting the correct position is extremely important for the well-being of the plants and animals in and around the pond. For instance, the majority of bog and water plants require plenty of sunlight (about 4–6 hours per day). The pond also needs to be easy to view so the best position is in the proximity of a terrace or a seating area, where it can be observed at leisure.

In addition, the constituent elements of the pond need to be carefully planned. If the correct proportions of plants, water and sand are used, a biological balance can be achieved within 6–8 weeks, at which time the water becomes clear. One of the most important factors in this is to have the correct ratio of water surface to water volume (a pond average of around 400l per m² of water surface is recommended). The garden pond will then become a habitat for both insects and plants.

The planting of the pond is done before the water is carefully topped up to its final level. The pond edge and surrounds need to be specially designed: bog and flood water zones, as well as moist beds, → ① + ② help to expand the pond area and create a more natural balance. The pond should be sized according to the area of the garden: a water area of 20–25 m² is ideal, although even 3–5 m² gives enough room for many types of plants. Generous shallow water zones of 50–200 mm depth and a deep area of at least 600 mm in depth are necessary for the survival of aquatic insects and larvae during the winter months. The deep areas also provide a place of hiding for all of the pond inhabitants.

The pond should be kept full throughout the winter to reduce the possibility of it being forced out of the ground or tilted by the action of ground frost.

Fish, frogs and other amphibians will only survive the winter if the pond is protected from freezing over completely for extended periods so an ice preventer or a heating stone should be used.

Prefabricated ponds provide planting shelves at appropriate depths and these prevent gravel and planting soil from slumping or sliding away completely → ②.

GARDENS: USE OF RAINWATER

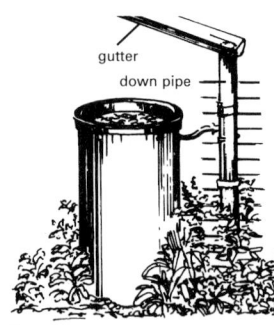

① **Constant storage for watering (rainwater butt)**

gutter
down pipe

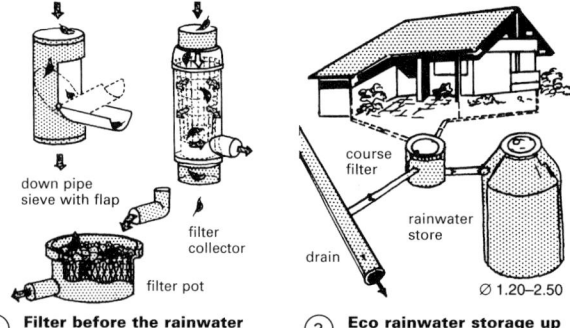

② **Filter before the rainwater store**

down pipe sieve with flap
filter collector
filter pot

③ **Eco rainwater storage up to 12500 l**

course filter
rainwater store
drain
Ø 1.20–2.50

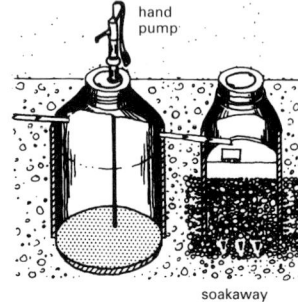

④ **Rainwater storage with eco soakaway**

hand pump
soakaway

1 domestic water supply
2 non-return valve
3 drinking water supply
4 storage tank
5 overflow
6 down pipe
7 drain
8 filter pot
9 trap

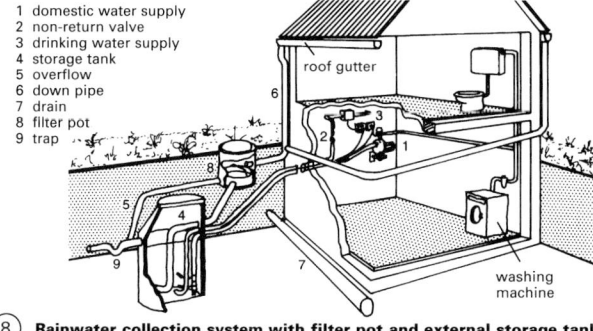

⑧ **Rainwater collection system with filter pot and external storage tank**

roof gutter
washing machine

capacity	length	width	height	weight
1100 l	1.45	72	1.33⁵	53 kg
1500 l	1.52	72	1.60⁵	81 kg
2000 l	2.05	72	1.64	130 kg

⑤ **Storage containers**

1 down pipe/gutter
2 filter collector
3 supply pipe
4 storage tank
5 trapped overflow
6 suction pipe
7 domestic water supply
8 empty running protection
9 rainwater supply pipework
10 drinking water supply
11 magnetic valve
12 floating switch

inspection chamber
to main drains

⑨ **Rainwater system**

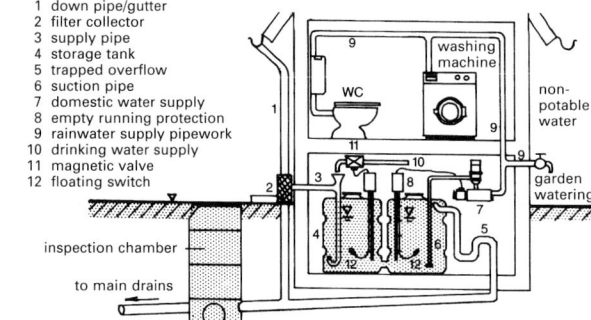

washing machine
WC
non-potable water
garden watering

⑥ **Distribution system**

roof gutter
1100 l   1500 l   2000 l

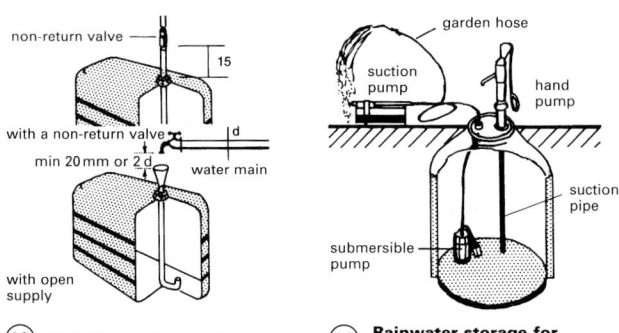

non-return valve
15
with a non-return valve
d
min 20 mm or 2 d
water main
with open supply

⑩ **Drinking water supply**

garden hose
suction pump
hand pump
suction pipe
submersible pump

⑪ **Rainwater storage for garden watering**

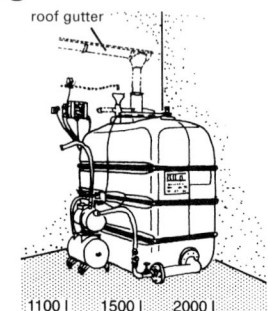

house
down pipe
ring-shaped filter inserts
overflow
filter plate
large filter area, flush-back effect
cistern

⑦ **In-flow filter**

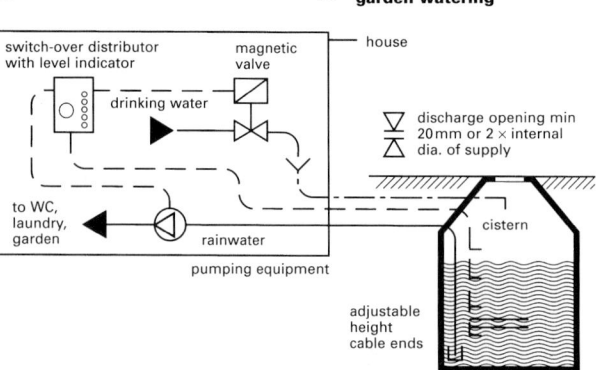

switch-over distributor with level indicator
magnetic valve
house
drinking water
discharge opening min 20 mm or 2 × internal dia. of supply
to WC, laundry, garden
rainwater
cistern
pumping equipment
adjustable height cable ends

⑫ **Drinking water supplementary supply**

In the design of new buildings it is desirable to include means for collecting and storing rainwater. Rainwater systems can also be installed in existing houses or gardens. The storage volume should be generous because the greater the volume, the more the potential economies. The average storage required for garden watering (given 40–60 l/m² as a typical annual usage) for a single family house is about 5000 l (it depends on the area of garden, annual rainfall, roof area and run-off value). To calculate domestic water needs, use the following figures for average water consumption per person per day: 15 l drinking/cooking, 10 l washing, 40 l bathing/showering (total: 65 l potable water); 18 l clothes washing, 4 l cleaning, 45 l WC flushing (18 l with economy flush), 8 l sundries (total: 75 l rainwater or 48 l with economy flushing).

Example

Annual rainfall 800 mm = 800 l/m²
Pitched roof run-off value f = 0.75
Net roof area = 120 m²
Rainwater production = net roof area (m²) × annual rainfall (l/m²) × run-off value (f)
= 800 × 120 × 0.75
= 72000 l/year

Number of persons = 4
Usage per day = 45 l per person (WC with economy flush)
Garden area = 200 m²
Annual garden watering = 50 l/m²
Rainwater requirement = persons × usage per day (l) × 365 days) + (garden area (m²) × usage per year (l/m²))
(4 × 45 × 365) + (200 × 50)
= 75700 l/year

Factor g = (1 – [rainwater production ÷ rainwater requirement]) x 100%
= (1 – [72000/75700]) × 100 = 4.9%
(this is less than 20% so use g = 0.05)
Storage requirement = rainwater production (l) × g
= 72[t]000 × 0.05
= 3600 l
Recommendation: 4500 l rainwater storage tank

Explanations

Net area: the plan area of the roof connected to the gutters (equivalent to the plan area of the house).

Annual rainfall: mean annual rainfall (e.g. typical values are 740–900 mm = 740–900 l/m²) as read from appropriate rainfall maps or information from a local weather station.

Run-off value (f): f = 0.75 for pitched and flat roofs.

Factor g: when the difference between rainwater production and rainwater requirement is less than 20%, use g = 0.05.

g = 0.03 when the difference between rainwater production and rainwater requirement is more than 20%.

g = 0.20–0.40 when the water is used mainly for garden watering and when there are large seasonal rainfall variations.

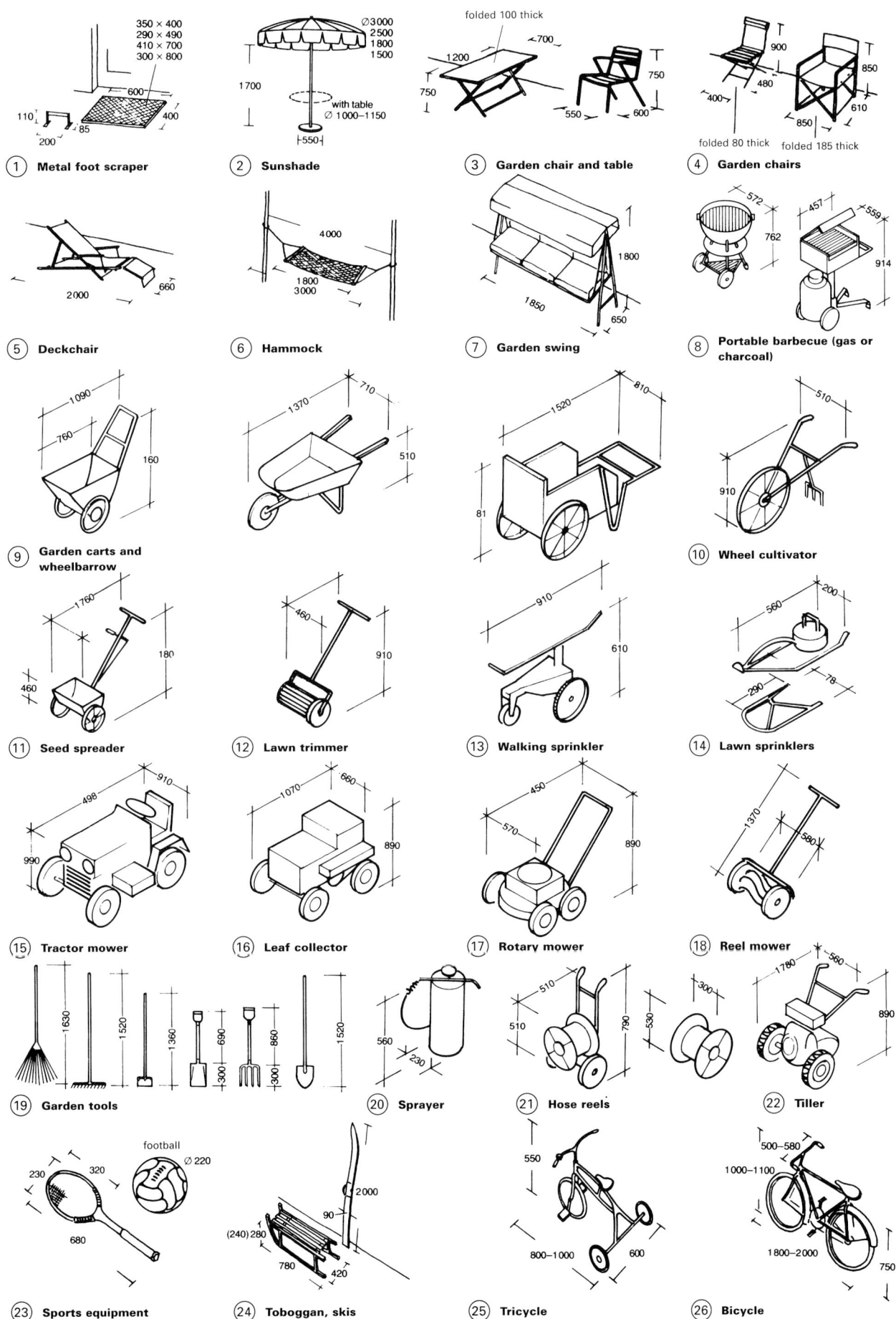

① **Metal foot scraper**
350 × 400
290 × 490
410 × 700
300 × 800
600 · 400 · 110 · 85 · 200

② **Sunshade**
Ø3000 · 2500 · 1800 · 1500 · 1700 · with table Ø 1000–1150 · 550

③ **Garden chair and table**
folded 100 thick · 1200 · 700 · 750 · 750 · 550 · 600

④ **Garden chairs**
900 · 480 · 850 · 400 · 610 · 850 · folded 80 thick · folded 185 thick

⑤ **Deckchair**
2000 · 660

⑥ **Hammock**
4000 · 1800 · 3000

⑦ **Garden swing**
1800 · 1850 · 650

⑧ **Portable barbecue (gas or charcoal)**
572 · 762 · 457 · 559 · 914

⑨ **Garden carts and wheelbarrow**
1090 · 760 · 160 · 1370 · 710 · 510 · 1520 · 810 · 81

⑩ **Wheel cultivator**
510 · 910

⑪ **Seed spreader**
1760 · 180 · 460

⑫ **Lawn trimmer**
460 · 910

⑬ **Walking sprinkler**
910 · 610

⑭ **Lawn sprinklers**
200 · 560 · 78 · 290

⑮ **Tractor mower**
910 · 498 · 990

⑯ **Leaf collector**
1070 · 660 · 890

⑰ **Rotary mower**
450 · 570 · 890

⑱ **Reel mower**
1370 · 580 · 1780 · 560 · 890

⑲ **Garden tools**
1630 · 1520 · 1360 · 690 · 860 · 1520 · 300 · 300

⑳ **Sprayer**
560 · 230

㉑ **Hose reels**
510 · 510 · 790 · 530 · 300

㉒ **Tiller**

㉓ **Sports equipment**
football Ø 220 · 230 · 320 · 680

㉔ **Toboggan, skis**
2000 · 90 · (240) 280 · 780 · 420

㉕ **Tricycle**
550 · 800–1000 · 600

㉖ **Bicycle**
500–580 · 1000–1100 · 1800–2000 · 750

239

GARDEN SWIMMING POOLS

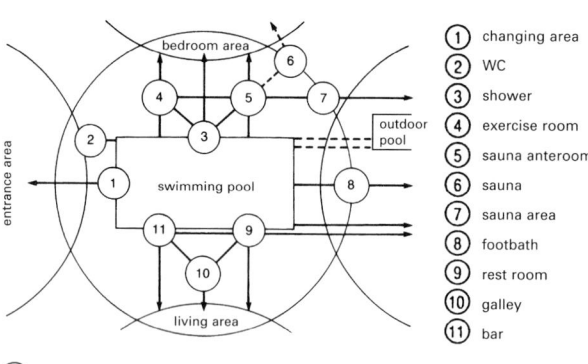

(1) changing area
(2) WC
(3) shower
(4) exercise room
(5) sauna anteroom
(6) sauna
(7) sauna area
(8) footbath
(9) rest room
(10) galley
(11) bar

(1) **Layout of an integrated swimming pool in a single family house**

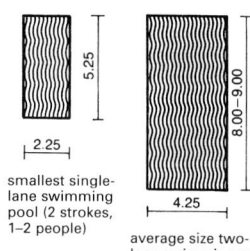

smallest single-lane swimming pool (2 strokes, 1–2 people)

average size two-lane swimming pool (3–4 strokes, 4–5 people); minimum size for racing dive from deep end

(2) **Pool sizes**

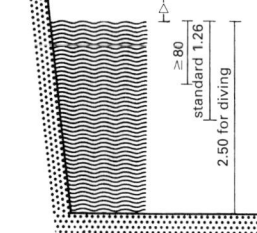

flat shallow pool for adults

(3) **Normal depths of garden swimming pools**

(4) **Pool depths**

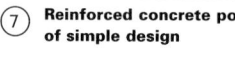
edge strip
concrete slab
squared timber 10/10
seal
soil

(5) **Pool with sloping sides, liner and squared timber edge surround**

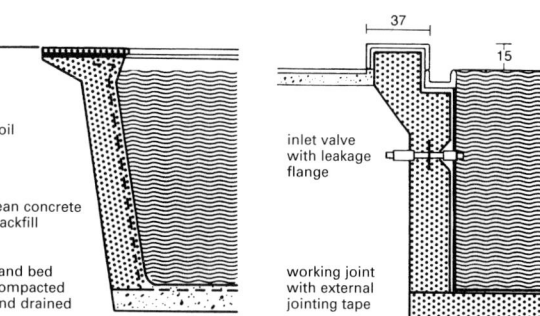

soil

lean concrete backfill

sand bed compacted and drained

(6) **Single-shell precast polyester pool**

inlet valve with leakage flange

working joint with external jointing tape

(7) **Reinforced concrete pool of simple design**

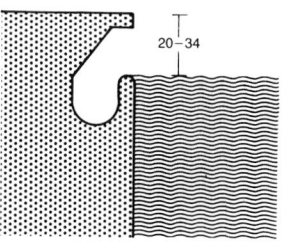
plastic sealing strip
aluminium section edge strip
slabs
mortar
coarse gravel filter
concrete blocks, cement plaster on both sides
drainage pipe

(8) **Masonry pool with drainage**

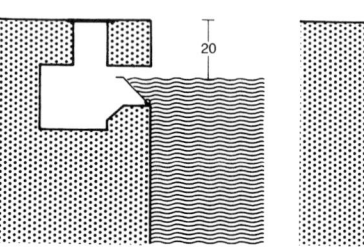

(9) **Skimmer**

(10) **Pool with 'Wiesbaden' overflow channel**

(11) **'Zürich' channel in surrounding walkway**

The ideal position for a garden pool is sheltered from the wind and visible from the kitchen and living room (to allow supervision of children). There should be no deciduous trees or shrubs immediately next to the pool and a surrounding walkway ought to be provided to prevent grass etc. from falling into the water.

Realistically, the pool should no less than 2.25 m wide and the length worked out on the basis of a swimming stroke length of approximately 1.50 m plus body length (e.g. four swimming strokes equates to 8 m). The standard water depth is usually based on the average height to the chin of an adult. The difference between the overall pool depth and the water depth depends on the type of water extraction system → (9) – (11).

For reasons of cost and the water circulation system (see below), the shape of the pool should be kept as simple as possible.

The standard type of pool design uses a sealed surface on a supporting structure made of masonry → (8), concrete, steel (particularly for above ground pools) or dug out of the earth → (5). Polyester pools (which are rarely made on site, being mostly made up from prefabricated parts) are generally not self-supporting so lean concrete backfill necessary → (6). Cast or sprayed concrete pools → (7) must be watertight. The surface is usually ceramic tiles or glass mosaic, although they are sometimes painted (chlorine rubber, cement paints).

The water needs to be kept clean and this is normally done by water circulation systems and filters. The process is improved with a good surface cleaning system using a skimmer → (8) or channel → (10) + (11). Adding a regulated countercurrent plant or through-flow heater can extend the swimming season considerably without prohibitive costs.

Other factors to consider are child-proofing measures and frost protection.

water	season			additional months	
ϑw	4 months	5 months	6 months	5th month	6th month
22°C	1.25/6.5	1.33/7.2	1.55/7.8	1.65/7.2	2.65/7.8
23°C	1.50/7.2	1.70/7.9	2.00/8.5	2.50/7.9	3.50/8.5
24°C	2.08/7.9	2.26/8.6	2.66/9.2	2.98/8.6	4.66/9.2
25°C	2.60/8.5	2.80/9.3	3.20/9.8	3.60/9.5	5.25/9.8
26°C	3.50/9.2	3.75/10.0	4.00/10.5	4.75/10.0	5.25/10.5

figures are in kWh/m²/d; special influences are not included, such as the considerable heat losses in public or hotel pools through the use of heated pool water for filter back-flushing (up to 1.5 kWh/m²/d or 1300 kcal/m²/d)

(12) **Heat losses in open-air pools (average/maximum)**

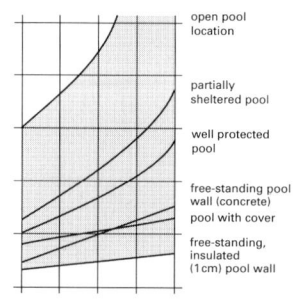
open pool location
partially sheltered pool
well protected pool
free-standing pool wall (concrete)
pool with cover
free-standing, insulated (1 cm) pool wall

(13) **Relative heat losses in a 5 month season (averages)**

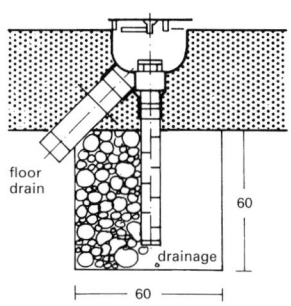
floor drain
drainage

(14) **Floor drain with groundwater pressure balance**

Example → ① – ④: house on a slope with an outdoor swimming pool reached from the lower floor or exterior steps.

Example → ⑥ – ⑧: the pool is a short distance from the sauna and bedrooms and on the same level in front of the living room.

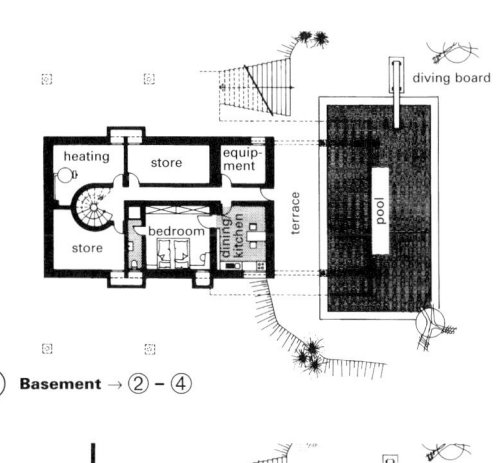

① Basement → ② – ④

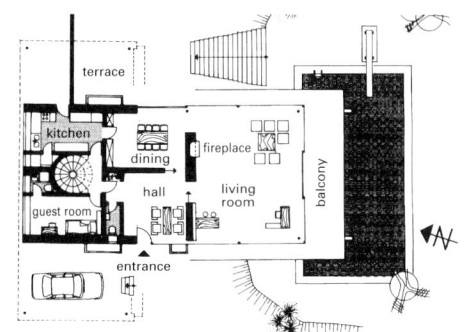

② Ground floor

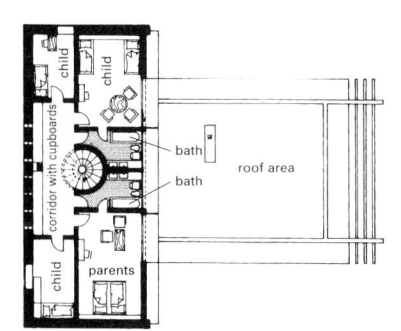

③ Upper floor

④ Section → ① – ③

Architect: P. Neufert

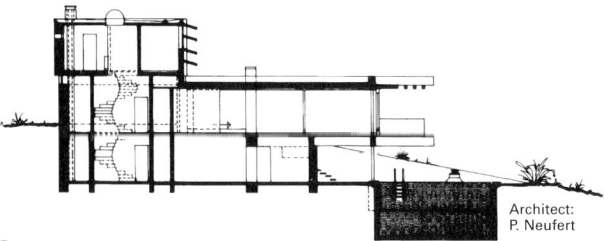

⑤ Circular swimming pool on a slope

Architect: P. Neufert

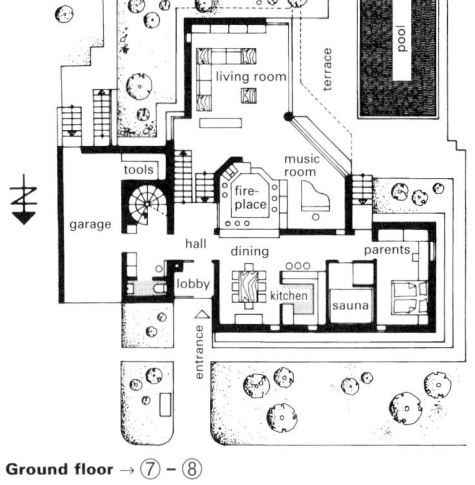

⑥ Ground floor → ⑦ – ⑧

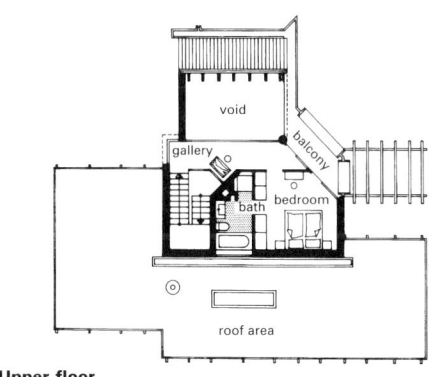

⑦ Upper floor

⑧ Section → ⑥ – ⑦

Architect: K. Richter

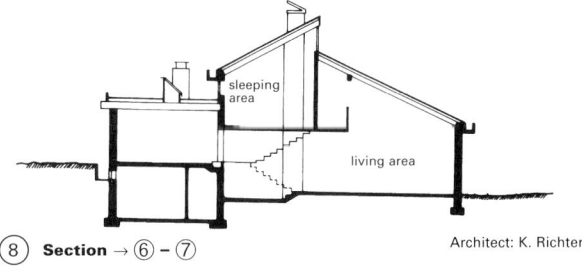

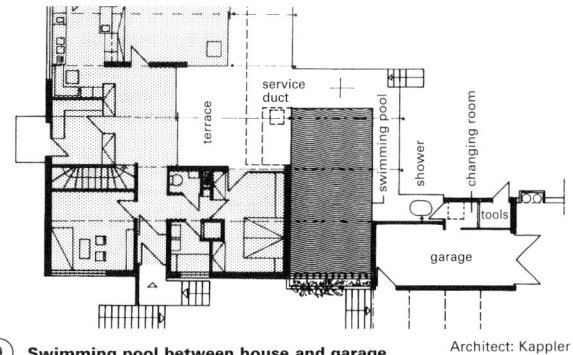

⑨ Swimming pool between house and garage

Architect: Kappler

241

PRIVATE SWIMMING POOLS

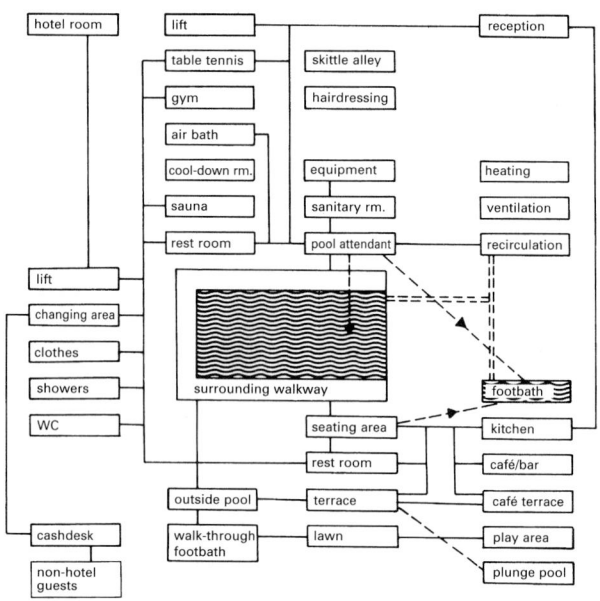

① **Arrangements relating to indoor pools**

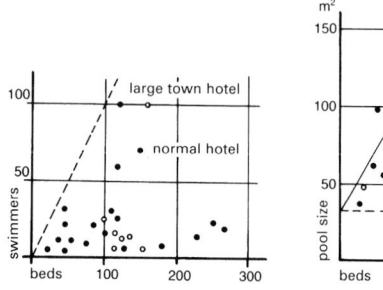

② **Maximum number of swimmers present at one time**

③ **Rough guide to hotel pool sizes**

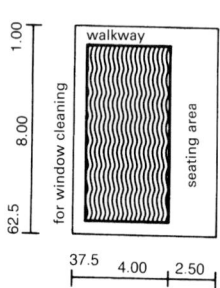

④ **Common size of private indoor pool**

⑤ **Indoor pool in a single-family house**

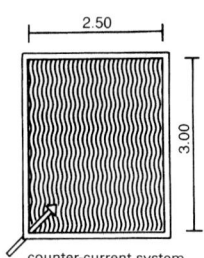

⑥ **Smallest pool**

⑦ **Splash distance from point of origin**

Atmosphere is a very important factor in the enjoyment of indoor pools so they should be well lit with natural daylight. An ideal location for the pool is at the rear of the house, overlooking the garden. With removable or sliding wall and ceiling panels it is possible to give the feel of being in an outdoor pool when the weather permits. Although this is the ideal it does introduce problems with heat bridges. Access to the pool can be through the living room or the master bedroom (allowing an en suite bathroom to be used for showering and changing) and should include a walk-through footbath to combat infections.

The standard conditions for indoor pools are: water 26–27°C, air 30–31°C and 60–70% relative humidity; maximum air circulation speed 0.25 m/s.

Construction considerations

The main problem with indoor pools is controlling the air humidity. Water evaporates from the pool at rates from 16 g/m²/h (when still) up to a maximum of 204 g/m²/h (when in use) and the process continues until the saturation point is reached → p. 243 ⑪ + ⑮. Evaporation loss approaches zero when the pool is still if a vapour-saturated 'boundary layer' develops just above the pool surface. Therefore, the water should not be disturbed by strong air currents from the ventilation system.

Removing moisture from the pool area is very expensive using ventilation systems but it is indispensable. If the air humidity is above 70% every small heat bridge can lead to structural damage within a short time. Ventilation equipment may be fresh air or a mixed air system → p. 243, with ducts in the ceiling and floor, or ventilation box and extractor (with the air flow kept low to avoid draughts).

The most common structural design is a fully insulated all-weather pool with glazed panel roof and walls. Less common are non-insulated 'summer' pools (which can also be of a kind that can be dismantled). The materials used should be corrosion-proof (galvanised steel, aluminium, plastics and varnished woods): avoid plasterboard.

The pool area in most cases should include a WC and shower, and a deck for at least two reclining chairs. The layout must allow 10 m² for a plant/boiler room. When considering the width of the surrounding walkway take into account the wall surface and the likely extent of splashes → ⑦. It is essential to provide an accessible below-ground passage around the pool to contain pipework and ventilation ducts as well as to check for leaks. Space permitting, the design could also include a gym area, a sauna, a hot whirlpool, a solarium and a bar.

Equipment

The equipment needed for a pool includes: water treatment and filtration plant, steriliser dosing system, overflow water trap (approx. 3 m³), water softener (from water hardness 7° dH) and foot disinfecting unit (particularly if carpeting is laid around the pool). Heating can be with radiators, convectors or air heating, combined with the ventilation system, or possibly a solar energy collection unit. Under-floor heating adds additional comfort but is only worth while with floor insulation k over 0.7 or hall air temperature below 29°C. Energy savings are possible using heat pumps (cost depends on electricity price) and/or recovery heat exchanger in the ventilation system, or covering the pool (roller shutters or covering stage, but only where hall air is below 29°C) or by increasing air temperature (controlled by hygrostat) when the pool is not in use. Savings of up to 30% are possible.

Other considerations are underwater floodlighting (safety element), slide, diving boards (if the pool depth and hall height are sufficient), shade from the sun, counter-current systems (which make small pool sizes practicable → ⑥) and acoustic qualities/noise insulation.

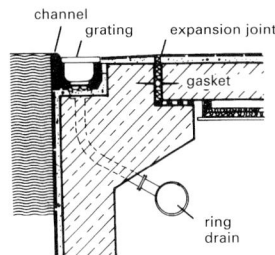

① 'Weisbaden' type pool rim overflow channel

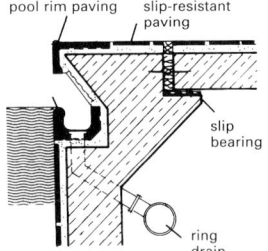

② 'Weisbaden' type poolside overflow channel

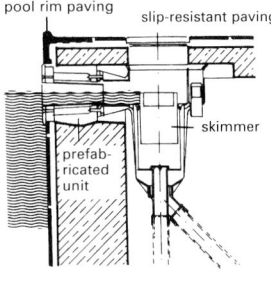

③ Surface skimmer system

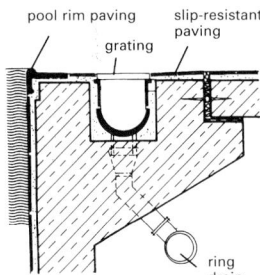

④ Overflowing pool with rim paving and channel

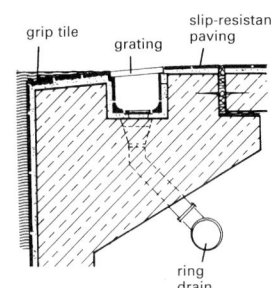

⑤ Finnish type rim and channel

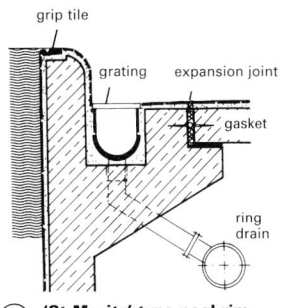

⑥ 'St Moritz' type pool rim overflow channel

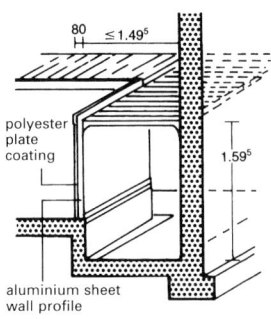

⑦ Aluminium pool with polyester lining

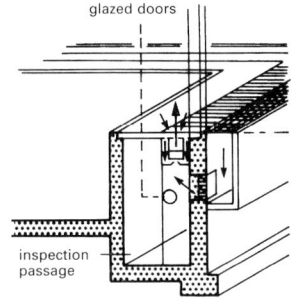

⑧ Ventilation with motor-controlled air supply valve (simple solution)

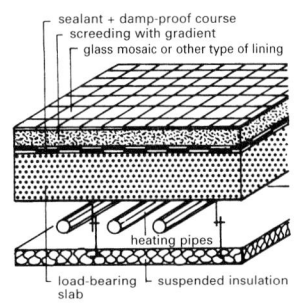

⑨ Suspended underfloor heating: simple, cheap and can be easily inspected

Pools that are within the fabric of residential properties or hotel buildings are generally constructed from reinforced concrete and supported separately. It is essential that they have groundwater compensating valves to avoid damage to the pool although expansion joints are unnecessary for pools under 12 m long. Plastic pools are used only in exceptional cases because of the requirement for a surrounding inspection and services passage → ⑦. Their use is only possible with a special reinforcing support structure.

Pool linings can be ceramic tiles, glass mosaic or a simple painted layer (so long as waterproof cement has been used). Another possibility is to use a polyester or PVC film at least 1.5mm thick to seal the pool.

The edge of the pool requires at least a surface skimmer arrangement or, better still, an overflow channel to feed the filtration and recirculation system. There are several types that can be considered → ① – ⑥.

Plan for a drainage grille at the deepest point and, possibly, a counter-current swimming system and underwater floodlights. All such fittings must be installed with sealed flanges.

The surrounding floor finish is normally slip-resistant ceramic tiles or natural stone and must be inclined towards the pool or overflow channel on all sides. It is also possible to use water-permeable carpet flooring on a damp-proof base. This improves both comfort and the hall acoustics.

For indoor hotel pools, it is important to have large surrounding lounge areas with chairs and lockers. A separate connection between hotel rooms and the pool area is essential.

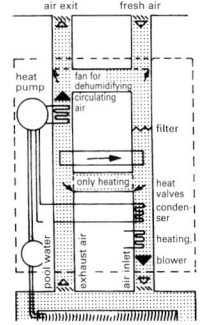

⑩ Underground swimming pool

water temp.	relative air humidity				
	50%	60%			70%
	air temperature				
	28°C	26°C	28°C	30°C	28°C
24°C R M	21 / 219	13 / 193	0 / 143	– / –	0 / 67
26°C R M	48 / 294	53 / 269	21 / 218	2 / 263	0 / 243
28°C R M	96 / 378	104 / 353	66 / 302	31 / 247	36 / 227
30°C R M	157 / 471	145 / 446	123 / 395	81 / 339	89 / 320

¹⁾ temperature difference 4k water/air cannot be maintained permanently

at rest (R) and during maximum use (M)

⑪ Evaporation rates for indoor pools (g/m²/h)

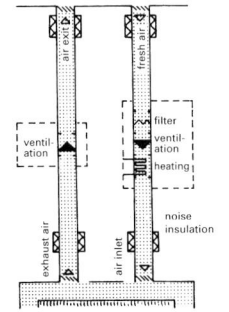

⑫ Hybrid heat pump and dehumidification plant

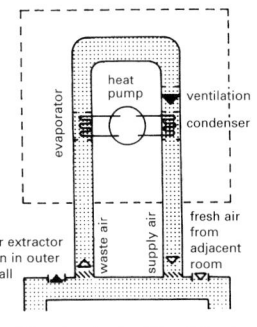

⑬ Layout of a fresh-air ventilation plant

⑭ Simple plant without fresh air supply (cheaper to operate and install)

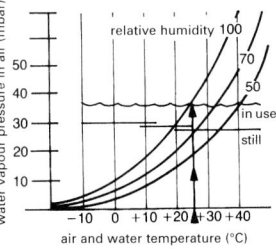

e.g. water temperature t_w 27°C: evaporation limit in use 36mbar (30°C/84% humidity) and 28mbar when still (30°C/65% humidity)

⑮ Evaporation limit for indoor pool

PRIVATE SWIMMING POOLS

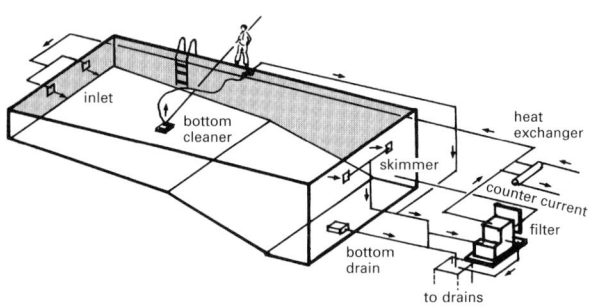

① Classic filter system with skimmer and supply

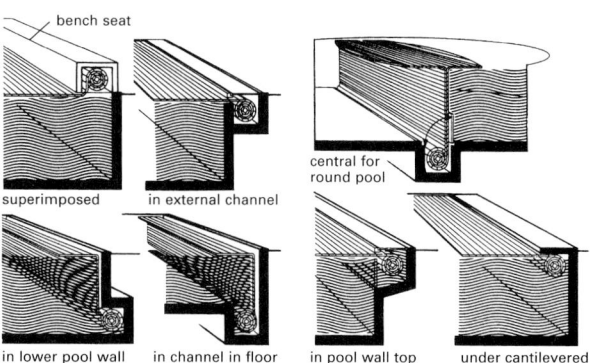

② Pool covers: built-in options

superimposed · in external channel · central for round pool

in lower pool wall · in channel in floor · in pool wall top · under cantilevered edge

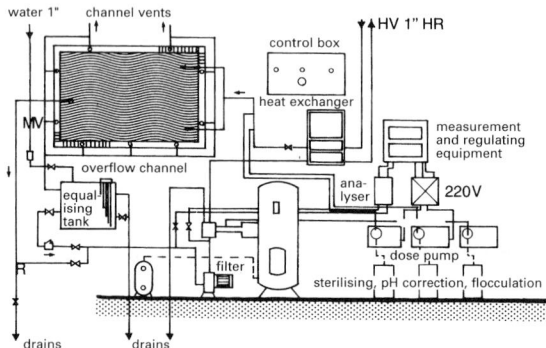

③ Servicing diagram for pool with overflow channel

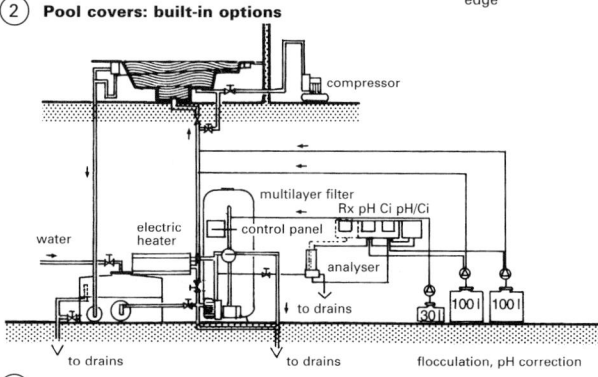

④ Whirlpool servicing diagram

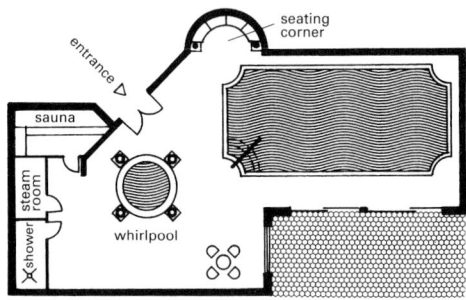

⑤ Swimming pool, whirlpool and sauna

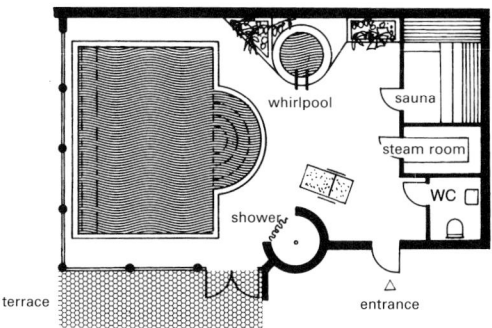

⑥ Whirlpool, sauna and pool with roman steps

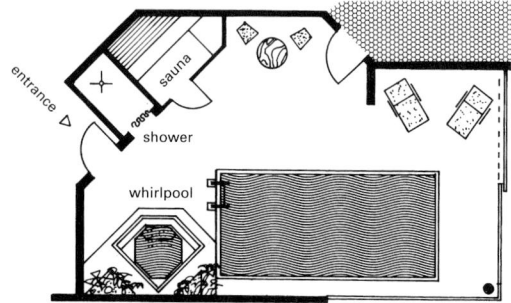

⑦ Swimming pool, whirlpool and sauna

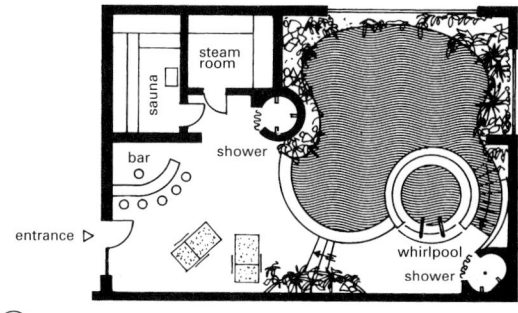

⑧ Round pool with integrated whirlpool

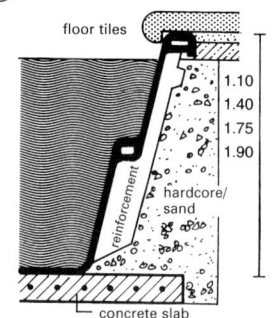

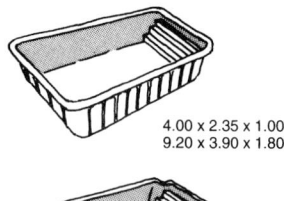

4.00 x 2.35 x 1.00
9.20 x 3.90 x 1.80

6.80 x 3.40 x 1.50
8.40 x 3.90 x 1.50

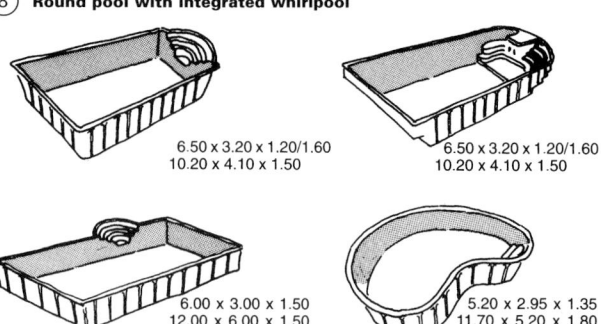

6.50 x 3.20 x 1.20/1.60
10.20 x 4.10 x 1.50

6.50 x 3.20 x 1.20/1.60
10.20 x 4.10 x 1.50

6.00 x 3.00 x 1.50
12.00 x 6.00 x 1.50

5.20 x 2.95 x 1.35
11.70 x 5.20 x 1.80

⑨ Polyester prefabricated pool → ⑩

⑩ Prefabricated pools

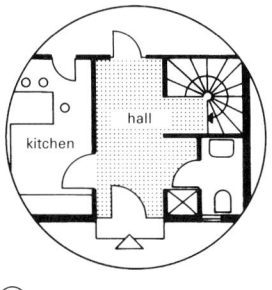

HOUSES: PORCHES AND ENTRANCE HALLS

Porches play a crucial part in sheltering the entrance hall from inclement weather conditions. They should be designed as far as possible with the prevailing local wind direction taken into account. In addition, they should be visible from the street or garden gate.

The key rooms with the highest levels of circulation, and, in particular, stairways, should be immediately accessible from the hall → ② – ④. For instance, an effective design could have the hall providing a direct connection between the kitchen, stairs and WC → ⑧.

① **Relationships between rooms**

② **Central entrance**

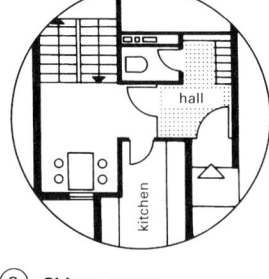

③ **Side entrance**

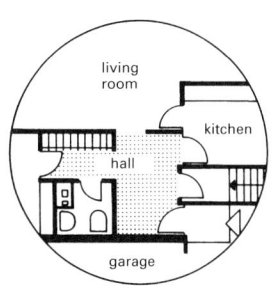

④ **Entrance adjacent to cellar steps**

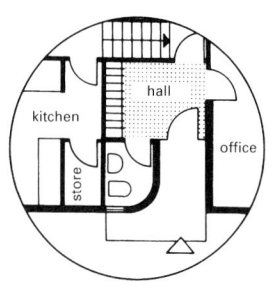

⑤ **Hall adjacent to office room**

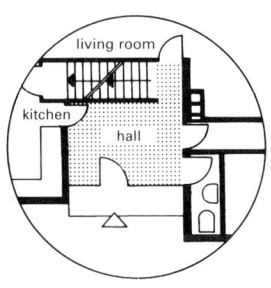

⑥ **adjacent to cellar steps**

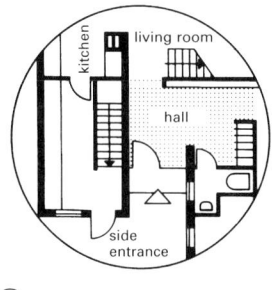

⑦ **adjacent to living room**

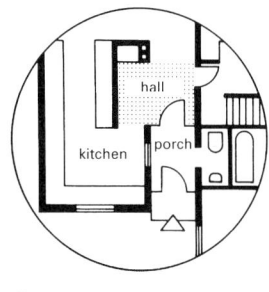

⑧ **adjacent to porch**

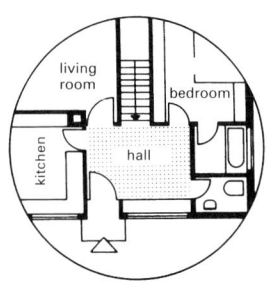

⑨ **adjacent to kitchen, WC, cellar steps, bathroom and bedroom**

CORRIDORS

Where a long corridor is necessary, the width is established according to its position, whether the doors are on one or both sides, the arrangement of the doors, and the anticipated volume of circulation. Appropriate corridor widths are shown in → ⑩ + ⑪.

If possible all doors should open into the rooms.

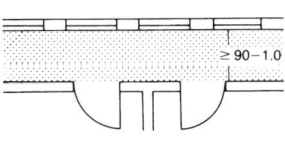

doors on one side and low level of traffic: minimum width of 0.9m required (1.0m is better)

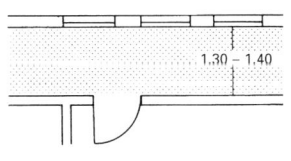

doors on one side, and wide enough for two people to pass one another unhindered: width 1.30 to 1.40m

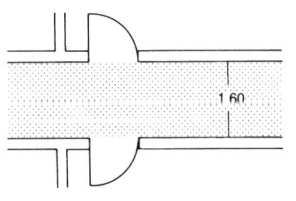

doors on both sides, large volume of traffic: 1.6m width to allow two (2.0m or more for three) people to pass each other comfortably

⑩ **Corridor with doors opening into the rooms**

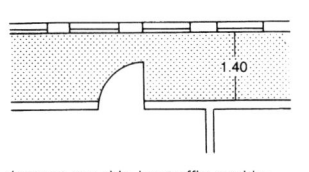

doors on one side, low traffic: corridor width = door width plus 50 cm

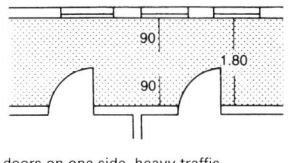

doors on one side, heavy traffic

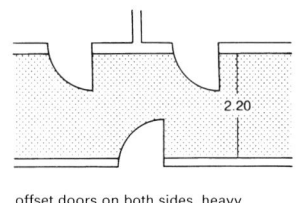

offset doors on both sides, heavy traffic

doors opposite one another on both sides

⑪ **Doors open into these corridors**

245

LANDINGS AND HALLWAYS

Floor areas required for different numbers of rooms

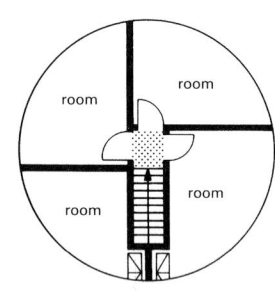

① 1 m² landing serving three large rooms at end of stairway, no continuation

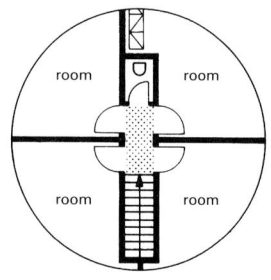

② 2 m² landing serving four large rooms and WC (best use of space, good layout)

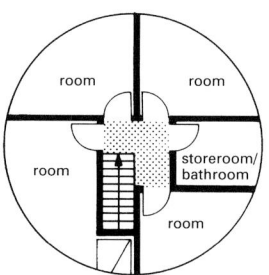

③ 3 m² landing, as ④, with store/bathroom but no WC (open stairway gives appearance of 4 m² landing)

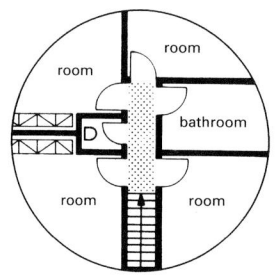

④ 3 m² landing serving four large rooms, a small one (e.g. bathroom) and a WC

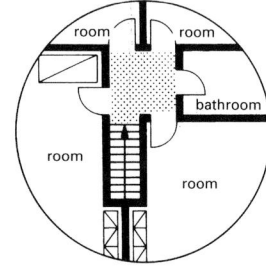

⑤ 4 m² landing, similar to ③ + ④, serving no more rooms but with better plan

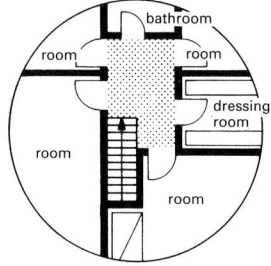

⑥ 5 m² landing serving four large and two small rooms

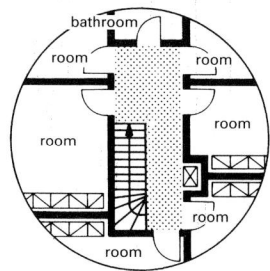

⑦ 7 m² landing serving six large rooms and one small one

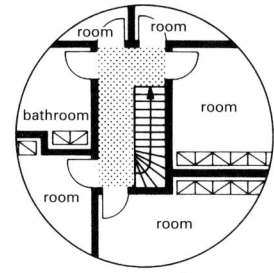

⑧ 5 m² landing serving five rooms and a bathroom

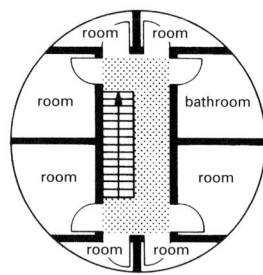

⑨ 7 m² landing serving eight rooms

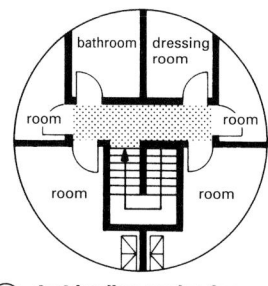

⑩ 4 m² landing serving four rooms, a bathroom and a dressing room

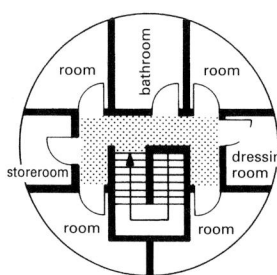

⑪ 6 m² landing serving four rooms, a bathroom, dressing room and storeroom

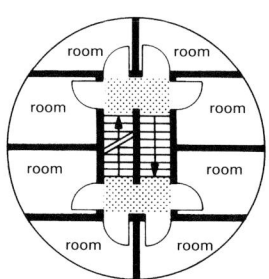

⑫ 4 m² landing serving eight rooms, with split-level floors (best use of staircase areas)

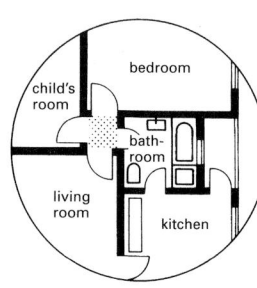

⑬ 1 m² hallway serving four rooms, separating the bedroom, children's room, bathroom and living room

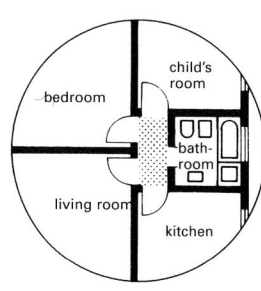

⑭ 2 m² hallway serving three rooms; otherwise like ⑬

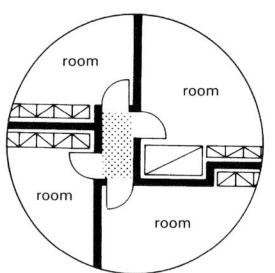

⑮ 2 m² hallway serving four rooms with fitted wardrobes and cupboards

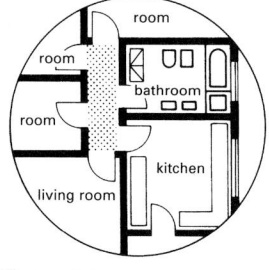

⑯ 3 m² hallway serving six rooms: kitchen, bathroom, three bedrooms and a living room

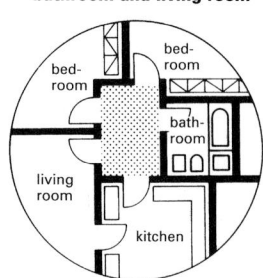

⑰ 4 m² hallway serving five rooms, some with fitted wardrobes

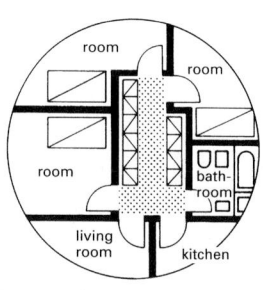

⑱ 5.2 m² hallway with built-in cupboards serving six rooms

These figures show the arrangement and number of doors to rooms that are 2 m wide or more for different sizes and shapes of landing and hallway. The layouts giving the most economical use of space are shown in ④, ⑧, ⑫ and ⑯. The majority of these examples are based on an aisle width of 1 m, which is suitable as a minimum because two members of a family can still pass one another. This width does not, however, leave enough space for built-it cupboards, which are often desirable → ⑱. Enlargement of a landing or hallway at the expense of room size can allow better door arrangements and not make the rooms feel any less spacious → ⑰.

STORAGE SPACE

Corners behind doors and spaces under stairs and sloping roofs can all be used to provide storage space.

The easiest space to exploit is under the staircase, where there is often room for large sliding cupboards → ⑥ or even a work space → ⑧.

Where cupboards are built into spaces under roof slopes it is important to ensure good insulation must be provided behind the units. Such cupboards should also have air holes at the top and bottom, or have louvre doors → ⑬ – ⑮, so that there is constant ventilation.

① **Corner cupboards next to side door**

corner cupboards → ①

② **Cupboard in the WC** → ③

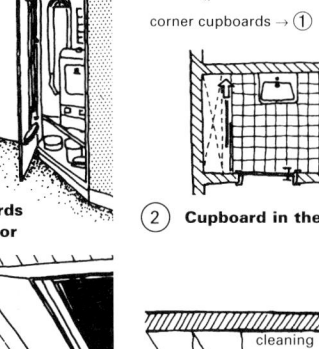

③ **Cupboard in the WC** → ②

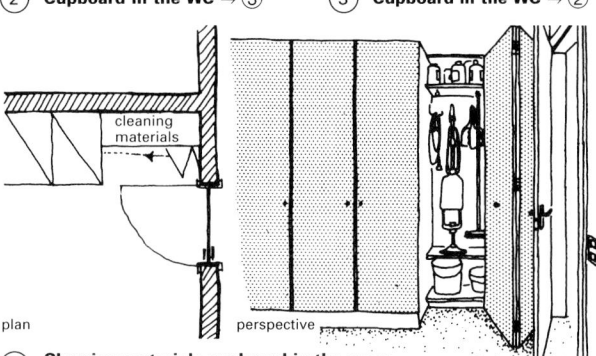

④ **Equipment storage in the roof space**

⑤ **Cleaning materials cupboard in the spare space next to a fitted wardrobe**

⑥ **Sliding cupboards under the stairs**

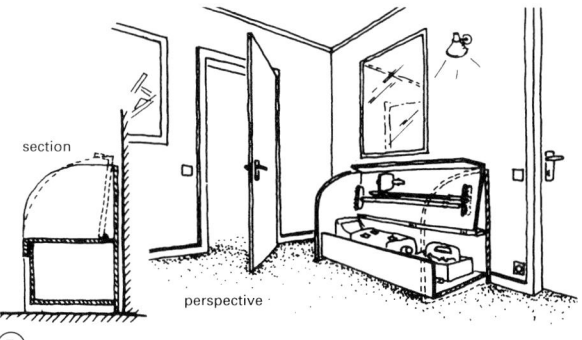

⑦ **Box bench for cleaning materials and equipment**

⑧ **Work space under the stairs**

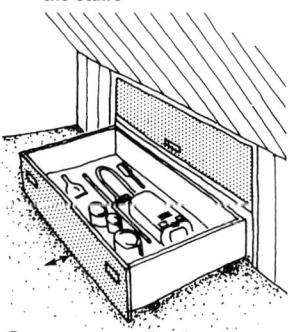

⑨ **Drawers in the roof space**

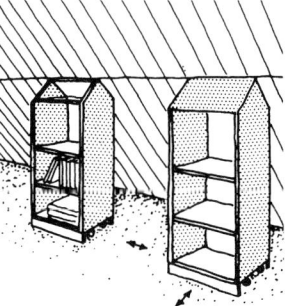

⑩ **Shelves on rollers under the roof slope**

⑪ **Extended drawers can be used under the roof slope**

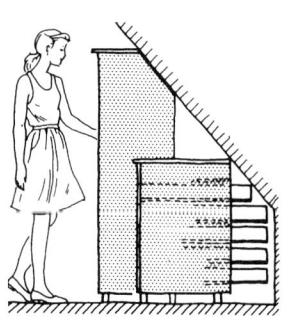

⑫ **Sliding bed stored in roof space**

⑬ **Sliding cupboards in the eaves**

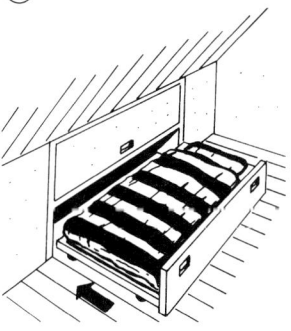

⑭ **Roof-space cupboards with louvre doors**

⑮ **Roof-space cupboards next to the dormer**

⑯ **Folding bed under a steep roof slope**

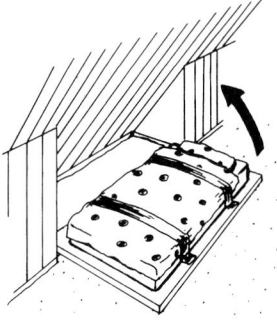

247

UTILITY ROOMS

In utility rooms there must be adequate cupboard space for storing cleaning materials and equipment, tools and ladders → ① – ⑥. Each cupboard should, if possible, be no less than 60 cm wide.

In some circumstances, and particularly in multistorey housing units, chutes made of stainless steel or galvanised steel sheet can be used for discharging household waste or collecting laundry → ⑪ – ⑬. They will require a ventilation shaft with a cross-sectional area of 30–35% of the waste chute. For safety, chute insertion points can have electrical doors so that only one load at a time can be dropped.

Linen chutes are most likely to be worth considering in houses on sloping sites with utility rooms in the basement.

Household waste should ideally be collected and transported in portable containers → ⑬ + ⑮, the dimensions of which need to be taken into account when planning the standing and movement areas required. These intermediate waste containers are made of steel sheet or polyethylene and have capacities up to 110 m^3 (1100 l). More common household dustbins of polyethylene or galvanised sheet steel are free-standing and have no wheels → ⑭. They range from 50 to 110 l capacity and can be contained in a purpose-built outhouse → ⑨.

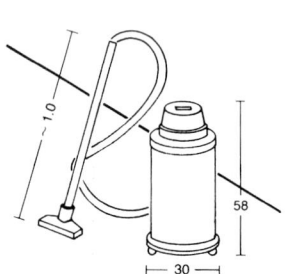

① **Dimensions: bucket and long-handled brush/mop**

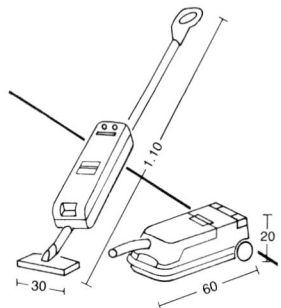

② **Dimensions: waste bin, broom, dustpan and brush**

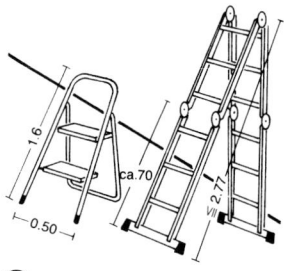

③ **Multipurpose vacuum cleaner**

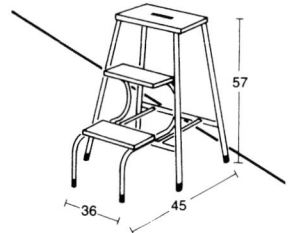

④ **Vacuum cleaners**

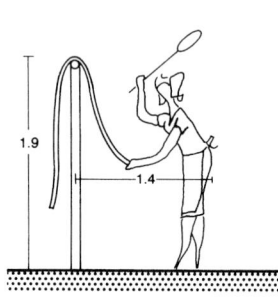

⑤ **Folding step-ladders → ⑩**

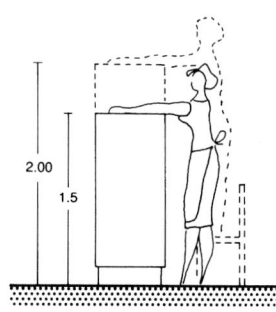

⑥ **Stepping stool**

rungs	for room height (mm)	side rail length (mm)	rungs	for room height (mm)	side rail length (mm)
3	2400	1350	12	3630	1710
4	2600	1580	16	4750	2250
up to 8	3500	2540	20	5870	2770

⑩ **Ladders**

	shaft dia. (cm) chute	air vent	a	b	c	d	e
loose household waste	40+45	25	55	55	24	95	
waste in bags (110 l)	50	30	60	60	24	130	
paper (office waste)	55	30	65	65	24	110	fire-resistant
linen (family house)	30	15	35	35	11.5	110	
linen (larger units such as	40	25	45	45	11.5	110	
flats, hostels, hotels	45	25	50	50	11.5	110	
or hospitals)	50	30	55	55	11.5	110	

⑪ **Waste disposal and laundry collection systems → ⑫ + ⑬**

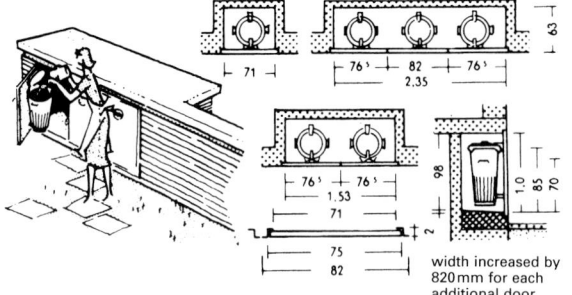

⑦ **Carpet-beating bar**

⑧ **Useful cupboard height**

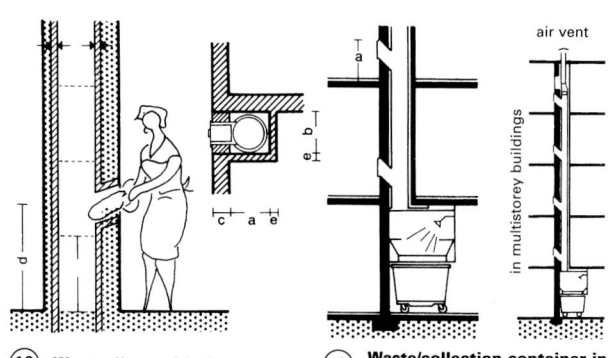

⑫ **Waste disposal in bags**

⑬ **Waste/collection container in cellar**

⑨ **Space requirement for enclosed external waste bins**

width increased by 820 mm for each additional door

⑭ **Dustbins**

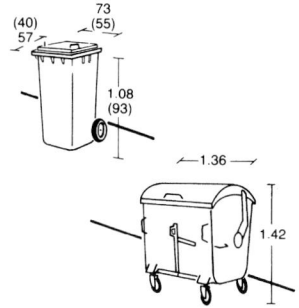

⑮ **Large bins (intermediate waste containers)**

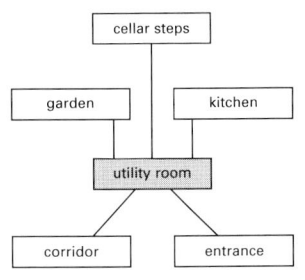

1 Arrangement for utility rooms

fittings/equipment	width, min (cm)	better
automatic washing machine and dryer (upright unit)	60	60
wash-basin with water heater	60	60
dirty laundry container	50	60
worktop for folded linen	60	1.20
ironing surface	ca. 100	1.00
storage cupboard	50	60
total	ca. 380	4.60

2 Standing space required for equipment

The best position for utility rooms is facing north. They should ideally be near the side or rear door and be adjacent to or accessible from the kitchen → ⑦ – ⑩.

Utility rooms are used for a variety of purposes, including storage, laundry and ironing, sewing and possibly also for hobby activities. To be of real value, the length available for standing space or work surface should be a minimum of 3.80 m (preferably 4.60 m) → ②.

The arrangement of the equipment should allow safe and convenient use: for example, an ironing board when used standing needs to be at a different height than when seated → ⑫ – ⑬.

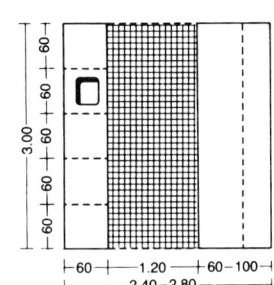

3 Single-sided domestic utility room (L shape)

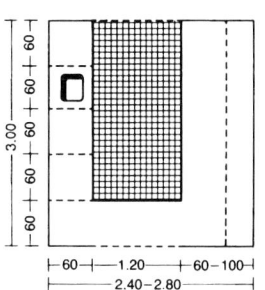

4 Double sided

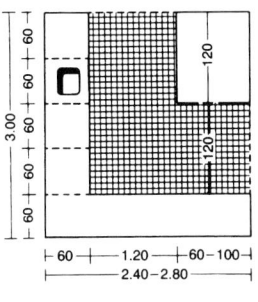

5 U shape

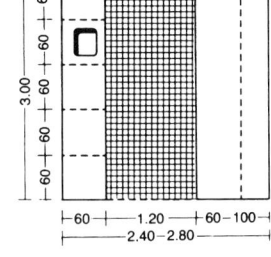

6 L shape

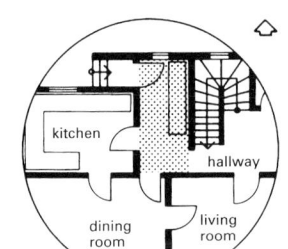

7 Utility room at side entrance

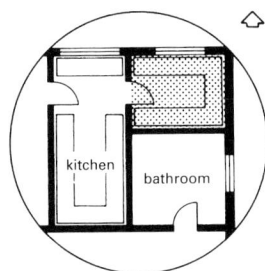

8 Accessible from kitchen

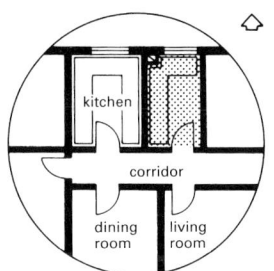

9 Beside kitchen, accessible from corridor

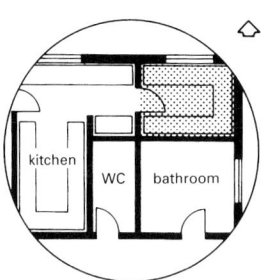

10 Behind kitchen and bathroom

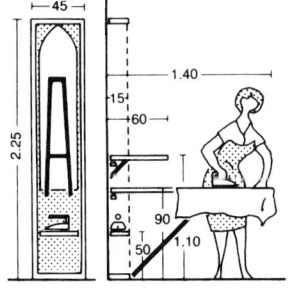

11 Hinged ironing boards on wall or in cupboard

12 Space requirement when ironing seated

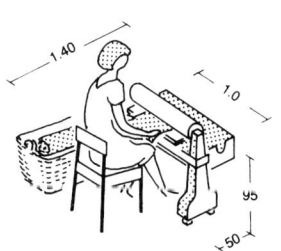

13 Electrical clothes press

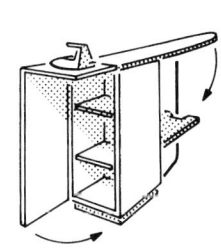

14 Ironing combination, collapsible

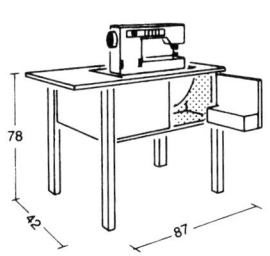

15 Sewing machine

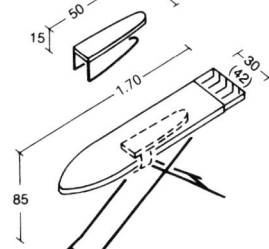

16 Ironing and sleeve pressing board

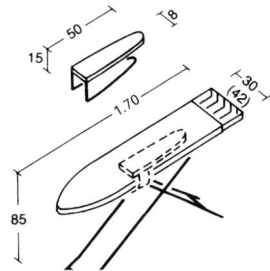

17 Electrical ironing machine

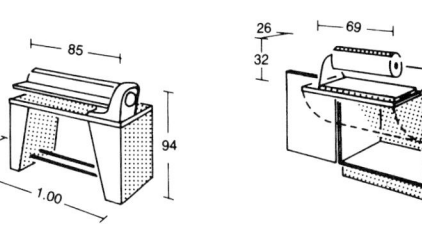

18 Ironing machine built into cupboard

PANTRIES, LARDERS

When planning houses or flats, space should be allocated for rooms such as larders, pantries or cold stores. The most practical solution is to have a larder in or beside the kitchen → ② – ⑧. It must be cool, well-ventilated and shaded from the sun. Connections for a freezer unit and a drinks cooler should also be provided if the larder is of sufficient size and storage shelves are best arranged right up to the ceiling.

In very large households, there may be a need for a cold store. These are supplied in modular form in a range of sizes → ⑨ and include separate cooling and freezer sections.

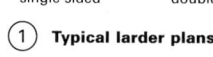

single sided · double sided · U shape · L shape

① **Typical larder plans**

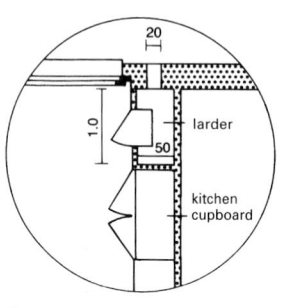

② **Larder and cupboard**

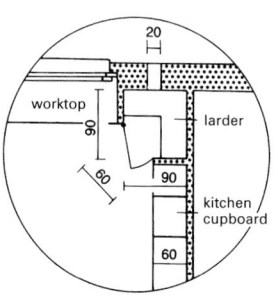

③ **Corner larder**

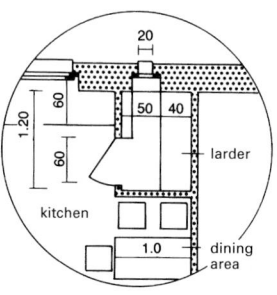

④ **Larder behind dining area**

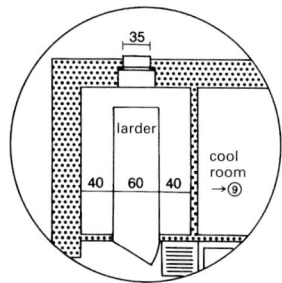

⑤ **Spacious larder**

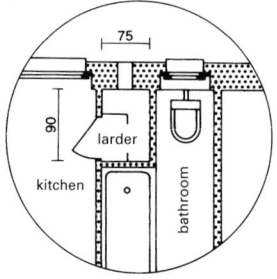

⑥ **Space-saving larder adjacent to bathtub recess**

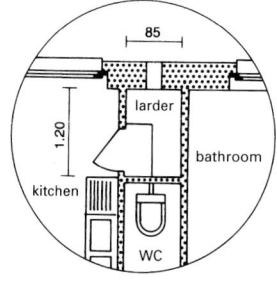

⑦ **As ⑥ but adjacent to WC**

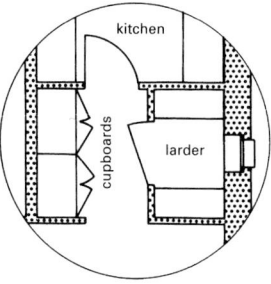

⑧ **Larder by kitchen entrance**

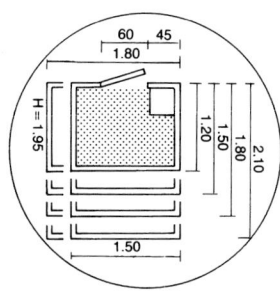

⑨ **Sizes of cold stores (useful area 1.23–3.06 m²)**

STORAGE

Apart from the cellar and attic rooms there should be at least one storeroom (1 m² or more, with a minimum internal width of 75 cm and good ventilation) in the house. For larger dwellings at least 2% of the living area should be planned as storage room. The space is needed for storing cleaning equipment and materials, tools, ironing board, shopping baskets and bags, cases, stepladder etc. Doors should open outwards to give more space and internal lighting must be provided, perhaps by a contact switch on the door. A recess close to kitchen for built-in cupboards is desirable → ⑬.

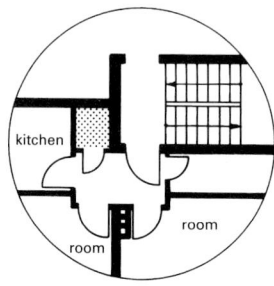

⑩ **Storeroom in hallway**

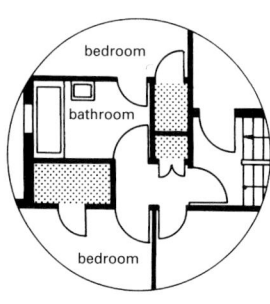

⑪ **Storerooms in bedrooms and hallway**

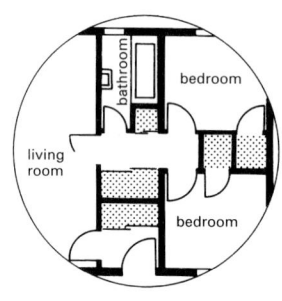

⑫ **Storerooms and cupboards**

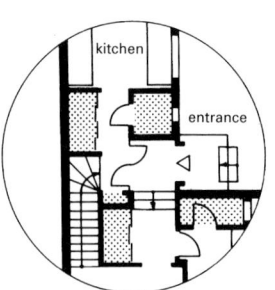

⑬ **Storerooms in entrance area**

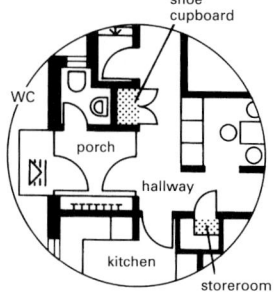

⑭ **Storeroom and shoe cupboard in entrance area**

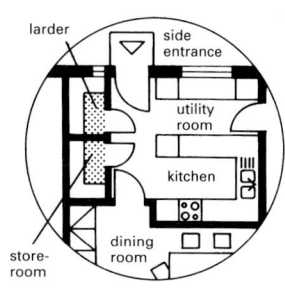

⑮ **Larder and storeroom in kitchen area**

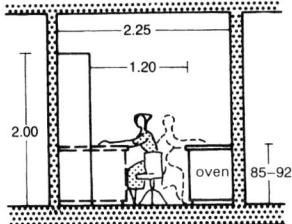

① Section through kitchen with two worktops

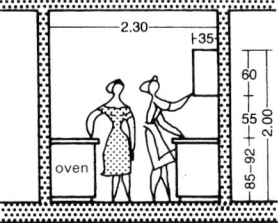

② Section through kitchen; space for two people

③ Low-level oven requires adequate space in front; extractor hood above cooker

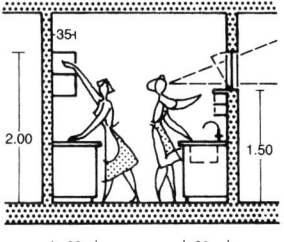

④ Worktops and storage 60 cm deep

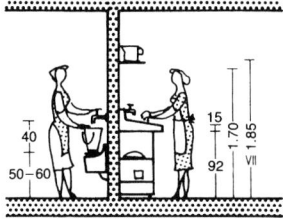

⑤ Household sink heights and high shelving

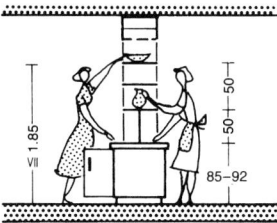

crockery storage cupboards, accessible from both sides

⑥ Hatch between kitchen and dining room

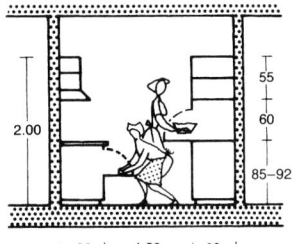

⑦ Side-by-side working

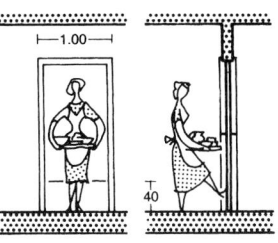

⑧ Self-closing doors with kick-plate between pantry and dining room

⑨ Correct/incorrect kitchen lighting

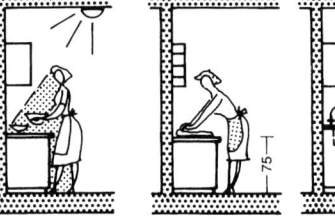

⑩ Normal table height of 85 cm lies between the best heights for baking and dish-washing

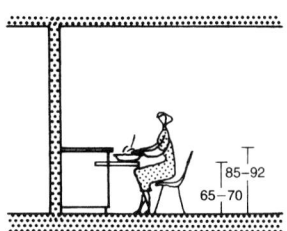

⑪ Pull-out worktop for use when seated

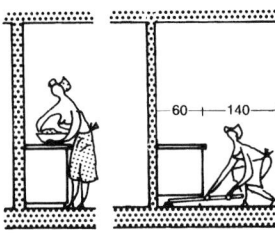

⑫ Correct design of cabinet bases for convenient cleaning and working (≥8 cm)

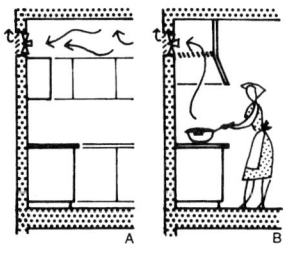

⑬ Extractor fan on outer wall (A), better if directly above cooker (B)

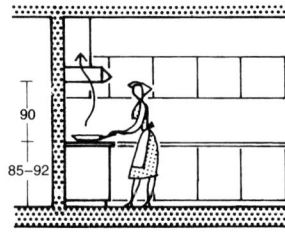

⑭ Extractor hood: better than just a fan

⑮ Pull-out/swivelling table

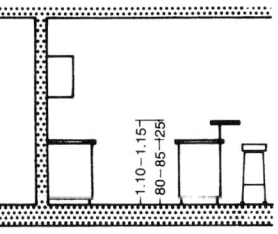

⑯ A breakfast bar arrangement

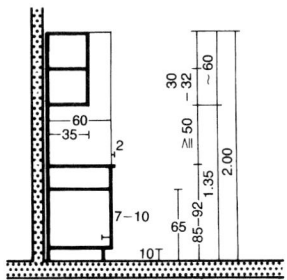

⑰ Section through kitchen units: preferred measurements

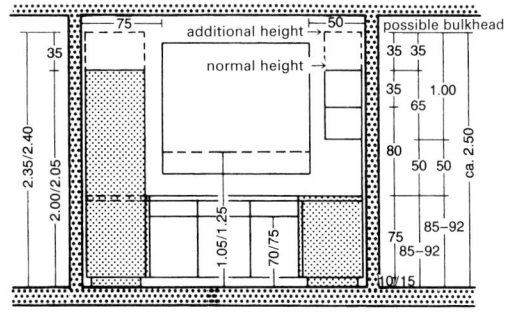

⑱ Kitchen fittings and standing areas required

recommended maximum height is 92 cm

⑲ Plinth depth varies height of work surface

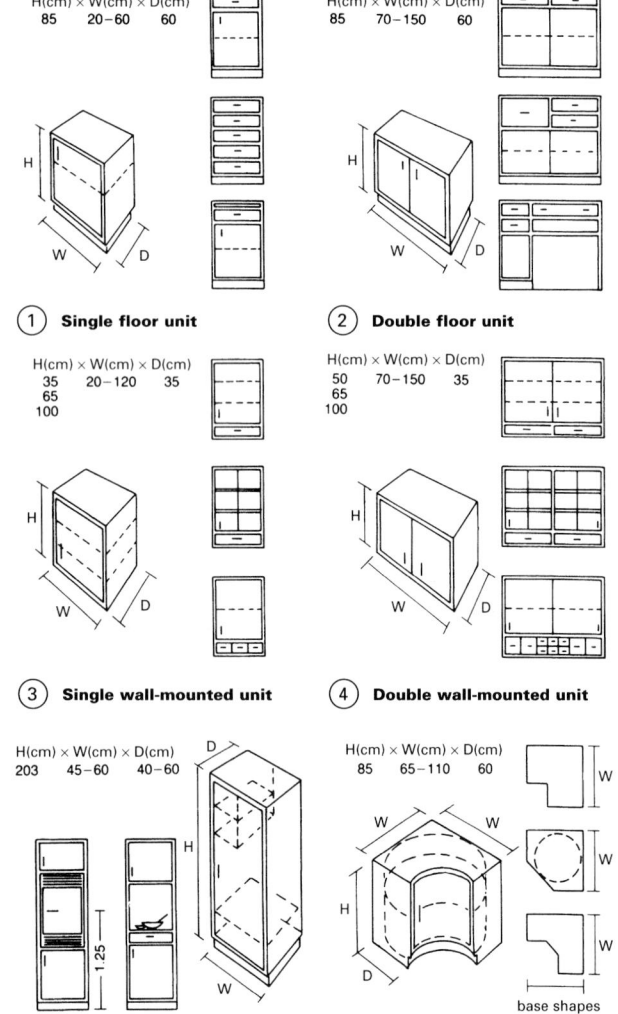

H(cm) × W(cm) × D(cm)
85   20–60   60

① **Single floor unit**

H(cm) × W(cm) × D(cm)
85   70–150   60

② **Double floor unit**

H(cm) × W(cm) × D(cm)
35   20–120   35
65
100

③ **Single wall-mounted unit**

H(cm) × W(cm) × D(cm)
50   70–150   35
65
100

④ **Double wall-mounted unit**

H(cm) × W(cm) × D(cm)
203   45–60   40–60

⑤ **Full-height cupboards**

H(cm) × W(cm) × D(cm)
85   65–110   60

base shapes

⑥ **Corner units**

KITCHENS

Built-in and Fitted Units

Despite increasing standardisation, the dimensions and manufacturing ranges of kitchen fittings still vary considerably. Built-in units are generally available from 20–120 cm (in 5 cm steps), usually with a height of 85 cm.

In an architect-designed kitchen, the various elements are assembled in a way that cannot be altered, with worktops and storage surfaces, possibly including an electric oven (with cut-outs for hotplates) and a continuous cover plate.

The materials used in kitchen units include, wood, plywood, chipboard and plastic. Exposed wood surfaces are varnished or laminated with plastic. Shelves are of wood or plastic-coated chipboard; metal shelves are best for pots and pans. Sliding or folding doors are useful if space is restricted because they require no additional space when opened.

Floor units → ① + ② are for storing large, heavy or seldom-used kitchen equipment. Wall-mounted cabinets → ③ + ④ have a small depth so that the worktops beneath them can be used without hindrance. They allow crockery to be reached without bending.

Full-height cupboards → ⑤ can be used for storing cleaning materials, brooms etc. but are are also suitable for housing refrigerators, ovens, or microwaves at a convenient height.

Sinks and draining boards should be fitted into floor units, which may also include a waste bin, dishwasher and disposal units (and, if necessary, an electric water heater).

Special equipment, such as retractable breadbins with universal cutting board, equipment cupboards with special pull-out or hinged compartments, retractable kitchen scales, spice drawers, pull-out towel rails etc., save time and effort.

An extractor above the cooker is recommended → ⑫ and extractor hoods are most suitable for this task. There is a differentiation to be made between air extraction and recirculation systems. Extractor systems require a vent to the outside but are more effective than recirculation systems and so are the preferred type.

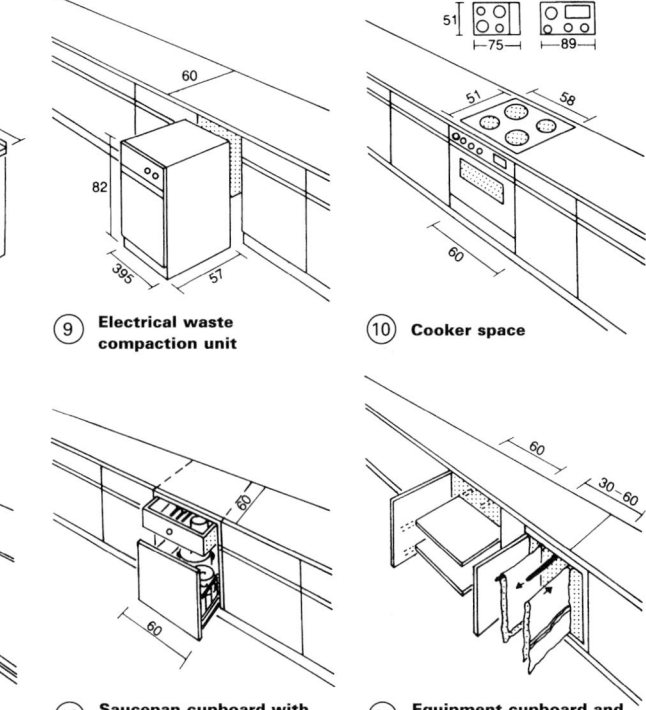

⑦ **Built-in cooker**

⑧ **Kitchen centre**

floor unit
dishwasher
electric cooker

⑨ **Electrical waste compaction unit**

⑩ **Cooker space**

⑪ **Dishwasher**

⑫ **Extractor hood**

⑬ **Saucepan cupboard with drawers**

⑭ **Equipment cupboard and towel cupboard**

The dimensions of built-in units and equipment must be taken into consideration when designing the layout and storage areas of a space-efficient kitchen. Modern electrical and gas units as well as kitchen furniture are made such that they can usually be fitted together and built in, giving combinations that ensure a smooth flow of work. Provide sufficient shock-proof sockets: a minimum of one double socket for each working and preparation area.

A double sink unit is usually required → ⑦ – ⑨, ideally with a draining surface on one side and a standing surface on the other. Dishwashers should be fitted to the right or left of the sink. Where the kitchen is very small, compact kitchens → ⑩ offer a solution. They require little space and can be fitted with many useful features.

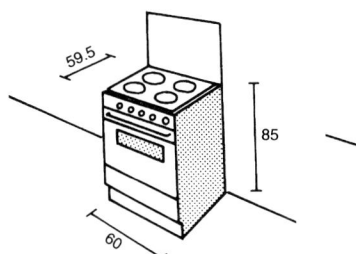

① **Electric cooker**

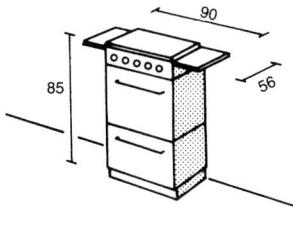

② **Large gas cooker**

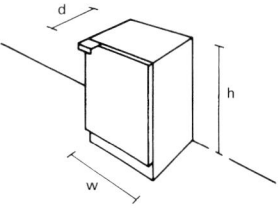

③ **Refrigerator**

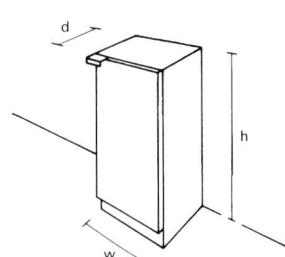

④ **Upright freezer**

⑤ **Dimensions: refrigerators and freezers → ③ + ④**

size (l)	w (cm)	d (cm)	h (cm)
50	55	55–60	80–85
75	55	60–65	85
100	55–60	60–65	85
125	55–60	65–70	90–100
150	60–65	65–70	120–130
200	65–70	70–75	130–140
250	70–80	70–75	140–150

⑥ **Dimensions: built-in refrigerators**

size (l)	w (cm)	d (cm)	h (cm)
50	55	55–60	80–85
75	55	60–65	85–90
100	55	60–65	90

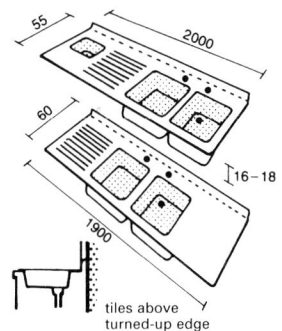

⑦ **Dimensions: built-in sinks**

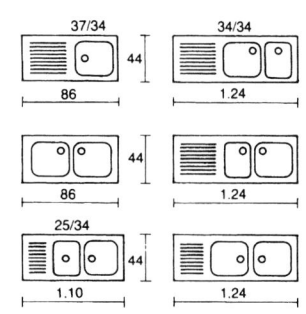

⑧ **Types of built-in sinks**

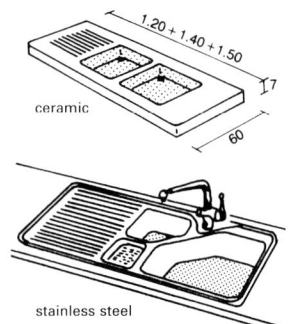

⑨ **Sink units**

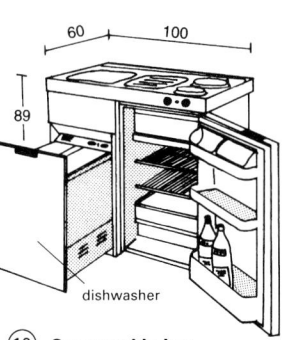

⑩ **Compact kitchen**

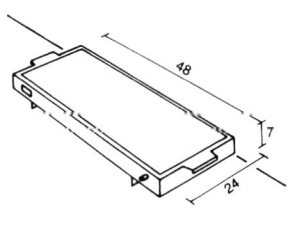

⑪ **Cooking plates**

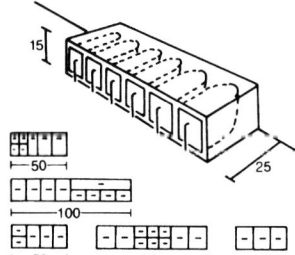

⑫ **Hotplate**

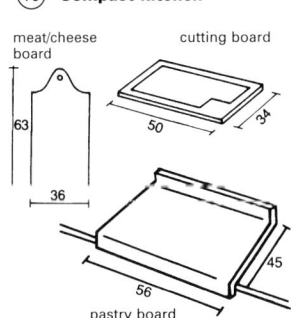

⑬ **Glass or plastic storage canisters**

⑭ **Kitchen boards**

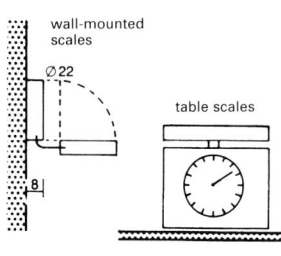

⑮ **Kitchen scales**

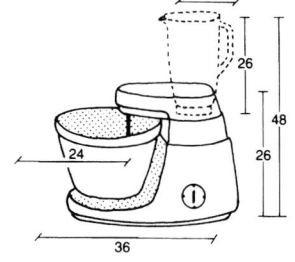

⑯ **Food processor**

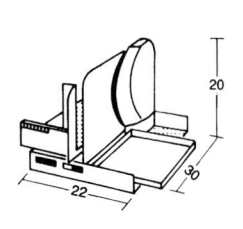

⑰ **Multipurpose slicer**

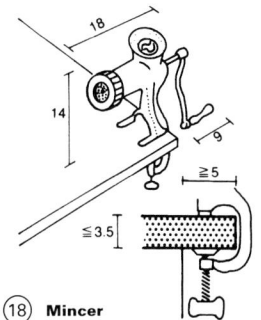

⑱ **Mincer**

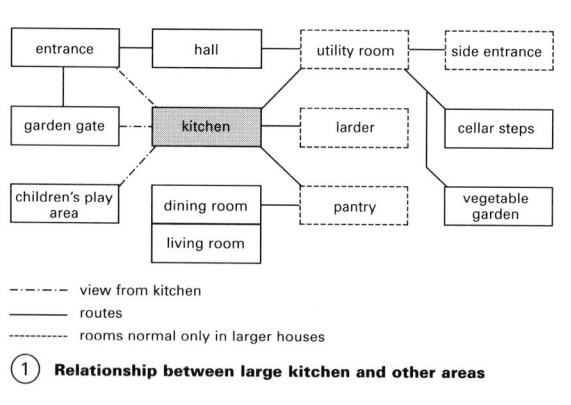

-·-·-·- view from kitchen
——— routes
---------- rooms normal only in larger houses

(1) **Relationship between large kitchen and other areas**

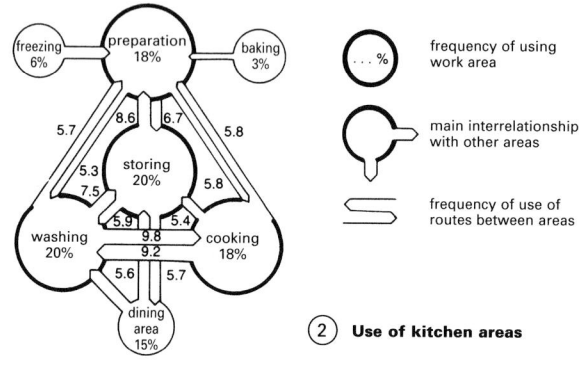

⬤ ... %   frequency of using work area

main interrelationships with other areas

frequency of use of routes between areas

(2) **Use of kitchen areas**

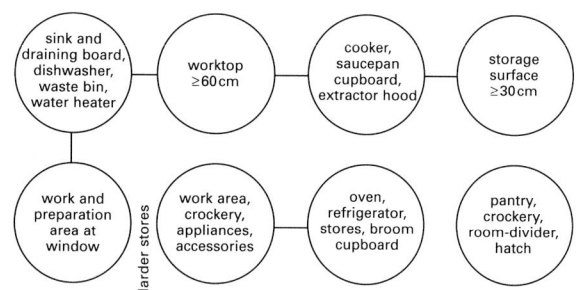

(3) **Effective kitchen workplace arrangement**

Kitchens should face north-east or north-west and be adjacent to any vegetable/herb garden and cellar. Ideally the kitchen should look out on the garden gate, house door, children's play area and the patio → ①. They should be well located internally with respect to the pantry, dining room and utility room.

Although the kitchen is primarily a workplace within the house, it is a room in which the householder may spend long periods so careful design is important. The kitchen is also often a meeting point for the family if it contains a dining or snack area → ⑦.

When fitting out the kitchen arrange the units in a way that follows the sequence of tasks to reduce the amount of walking required, and ensure there is sufficient room for free movement. Where possible, seek to reduce the amount of work done standing and ensure no activity requires an unfavourable body posture by matching working heights to body sizes. Good lighting of the work surfaces is another essential provision (→ p. 251).

An appropriate arrangement to ease work in the kitchen would be, from right to left: storage surface, cooker, preparation area, sink, draining surface → ③ – ④. (Note that left-handed people often prefer to work from left to right.) A width of 1.20 m between the sides is essential for free movement and using appliances and fittings. With a depth of 60 cm on each side this gives a minimum kitchen width of 2.40 m → ⑤.

The minimum area for a cooking recess is 5–6 m²; for normal kitchens it is 8–10 m², and 12–14 m² for normal kitchens with dining or snack areas → ④ – ⑦.

For planning purposes, the following width requirements for fittings and equipment may be used: cooker 60 cm, twin sinks and draining surface (including dishwasher) 150 cm, refrigerator 60 cm, freezer 60 cm, cupboards (provisions, cleaning materials, crockery and appliances) 170 cm. With a worktop surface width of 200 cm, this gives a total requirement of 700 cm of standing area.

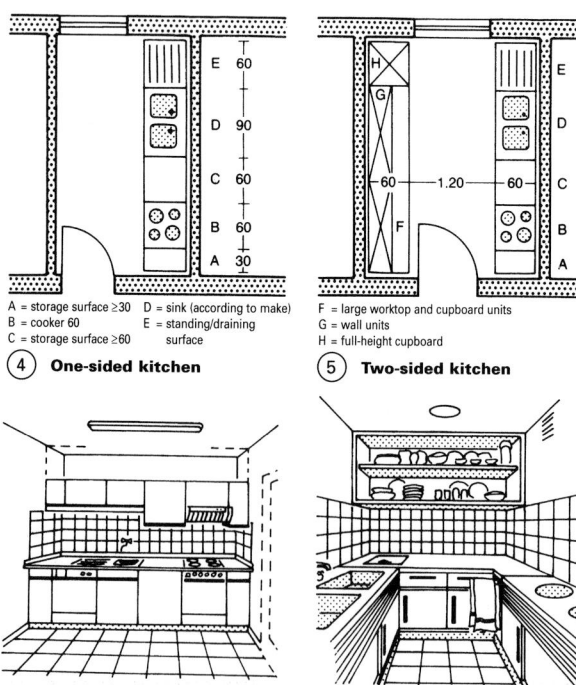

A = storage surface ≥30   D = sink (according to make)
B = cooker 60   E = standing/draining surface
C = storage surface ≥60

F = large worktop and cupboard units
G = wall units
H = full-height cupboard

(4) **One-sided kitchen**

(5) **Two-sided kitchen**

(6) **U-shaped kitchen**

(7) **L-shaped kitchen with dining area**
(Haas & Sohn)

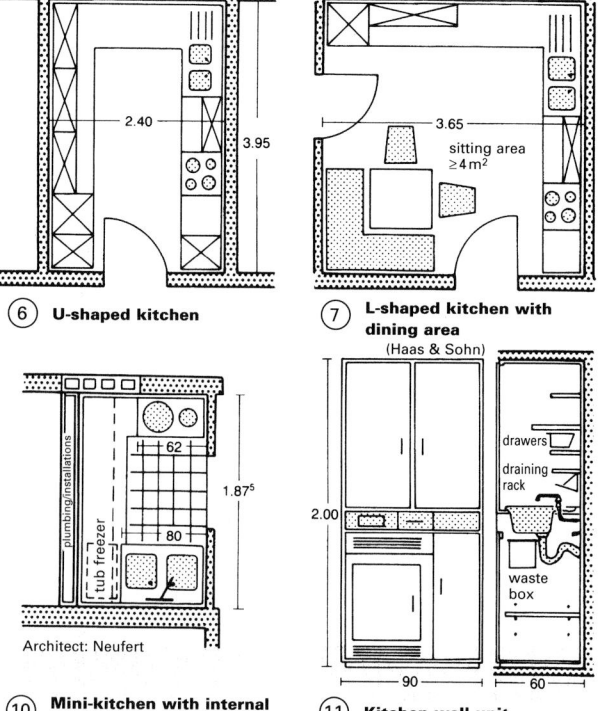

(8) **Perspective view of one-sided kitchen → ④**

(9) **General view → ①**

(10) **Mini-kitchen with internal ventilation**
Architect: Neufert

(11) **Kitchen wall unit**

① **Glasses**

labels: red wine glass, small; Burgundy glass; champagne flute; sherry goblet; white wine glass; beer tulip; balloon glass

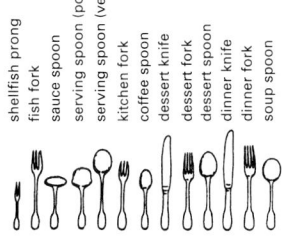

② **Dining cutlery**

labels: shellfish prong; fish fork; sauce spoon; serving spoon (potatoes); serving spoon (vegetables); kitchen fork; coffee spoon; dessert knife; dessert fork; dessert spoon; dinner knife; dinner fork; soup spoon

③ **Serving cutlery**

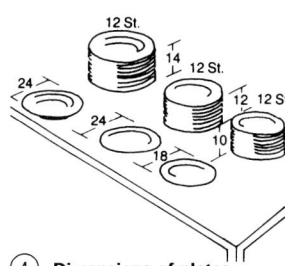

④ **Dimensions of plates**

⑤ **Menu: soup, meat course, dessert, drink**

⑥ **Menu: soup, fish and meat course, dessert, white and red wine**

⑦ **Menu: soup, fish and meat course, ice cream, white, red and sparkling wine**

⑧ **Menu: starter, fish and meat course, dessert, white, red and sparkling wine**

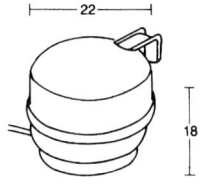

⑨ **Egg boiler**

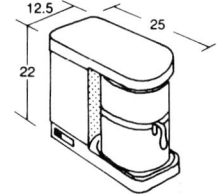

⑩ **Coffee machine**

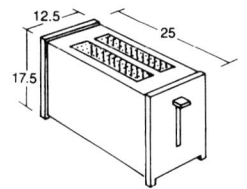

⑪ **Toaster**

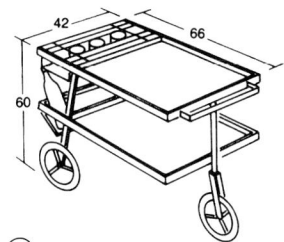

⑫ **Tea-trolley**

⑬ **Serving table**

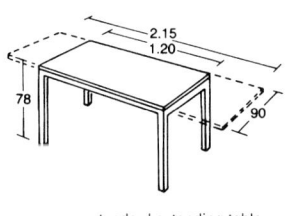

standard extending table

⑭ **Dining table**

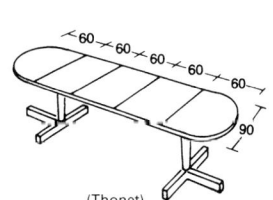

(Thonet)

⑮ **Large extending table**

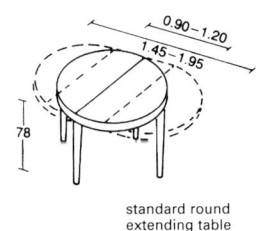

standard round extending table

⑯ **Dining table**

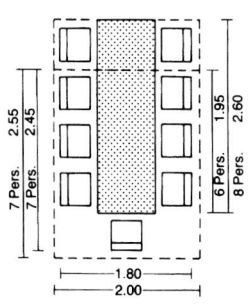

⑰ **Minimum area requirements**

⑱ **Minimum area requirements**

number of diners	width (cm)	depth (cm) (cm)	space required (m²)
four people		≥ 130	2.6
five people		≥ 180	3.8
six people	≥ 180	≥ 195	3.9
seven people		≥ 245	5.1
eight people		≥ 260	5.2

$$\varnothing \text{ round table} = \frac{(\text{seat width (m)} \times \text{number of people})}{3.142}$$

e.g. for 0.60 m seat width and six people $= \frac{(0.60 \times 6)}{3.142} = 1.15\,m^2$

⑲ **Minimum area requirements** → ⑰ + ⑱

DINING AREAS

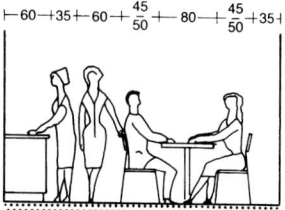

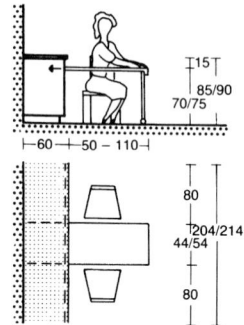

① Minimum table-to-wall distance depends on how food will be served

② Allow space between sideboard and table for walkway

③ Allow for drawers and doors

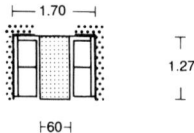

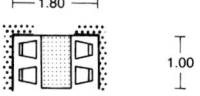

④ Retractable table

⑤ Fitted table

⑥ Breakfast bar

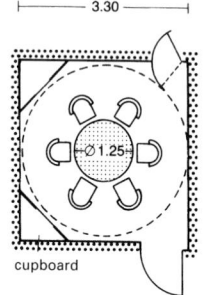

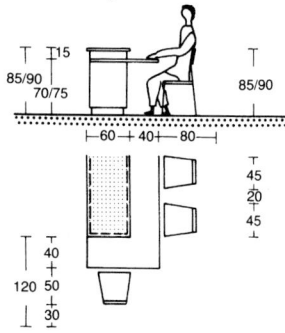

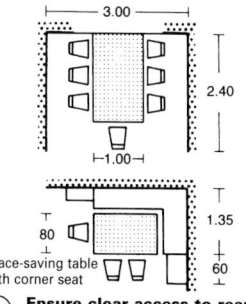

similar space to railway restaurant cars

space-saving table with corner seat

⑦ Smallest space for dining table and recess

⑧ Ensure clear access to rear seats with more than five diners

⑨ Round table, four to six people

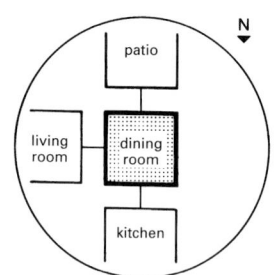

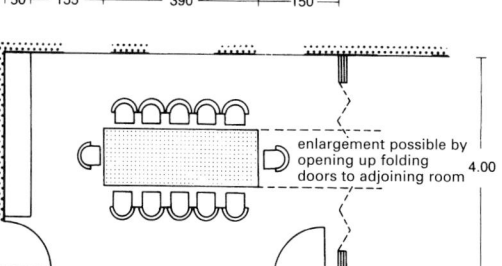

cupboard

enlargement possible by opening up folding doors to adjoining room

⑩ Minimum size for six diners with round table

⑪ Most comfortable seating arrangement in dining room for 12 people (with sideboard)

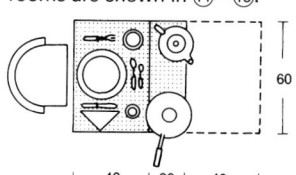

⑫ Typical table cover

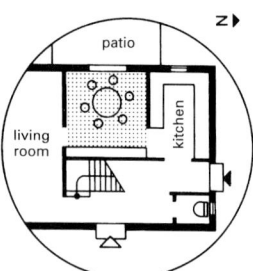

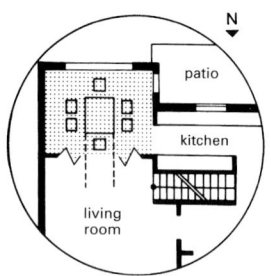

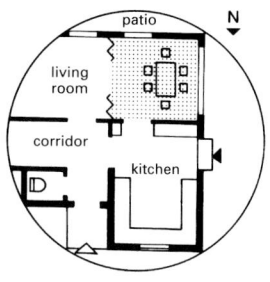

⑬ Dining room layout scheme

⑭ Self-contained dining room between kitchen and living room (undisturbed dining area)

⑮ Dining room between patio and living room: folding doors allow combination with the living room

⑯ Dining room and living room, as ⑮, on common patio giving good natural lighting

It is often desirable to have space in the kitchen for eating snacks, breakfast etc. and use the dining room for main meals only. This can be provided by including a retractable table, with a height of 70–75cm, which is pulled out of a base unit → ④. A movement area of at least 80cm is needed to the left and right of the table. If sufficient space is available a fixed table against a free-standing unit can be used → ⑤. Another alternative is the breakfast bar arrangement → ⑥. This requires less depth than the fixed table, even though the surface is also 40cm deep, because of its elevation but this also means that special stools are required. Depending on their design, full dining areas require far more space but they can obviate the need for an additional dining room → ⑦ + ⑧. A corner seat and dining table take up the least amount of space → ⑧.

It is useful to be able to extend the dining room through wide doors or a folding wall for special occasions → ⑪ + ⑮. To eat comfortably an individual needs a table area of 60 × 40cm. A strip of 20cm is needed in the centre of the table for dishes, pots and bowls → ①. Lighting should not be dazzling: the ideal distance from lower edge of the light to the table top is around 60 cm → ①.

Suitable locations for dining rooms are shown in ⑭ – ⑯.

256

To ensure comfort while sleeping, the bed length should be 250mm longer than the individual's height. Based on average heights, beds are produced in a range of standard sizes: 900 × 1900 mm, 1000 × 1900 mm, 1000 × 2000 mm, 1600 × 2000 mm and 2000 × 2000 mm. The bedroom layout should give at least 600mm, preferably 750mm, around the bed → ①. This is important to allow the bed to be made easily and also, if there is a cupboard standing parallel to the bed, to give enough space for movement even if the cupboard doors are open.

There should always be a bedside cabinet to the left and right of double beds and a headboard, onto which one can fix clip lights for reading, is also useful → ②. Bedside lamps should be provided in addition to general lighting.

About 1m of cupboard length should be planned per person. If there is not enough room in the bedroom, then space can be found in the corridor → ⑩. At least one mirror, in which one can see oneself from head to toe, should be fitted in a bedroom: mirrored cupboard fronts are even better.

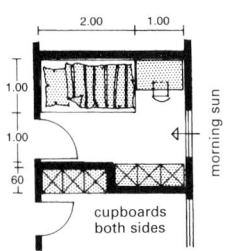

① Allow 750 mm around beds

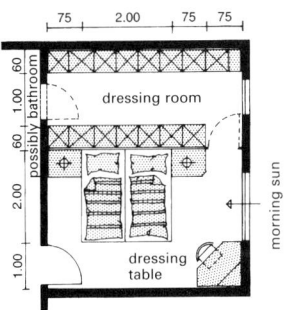

② Storage: bedside table

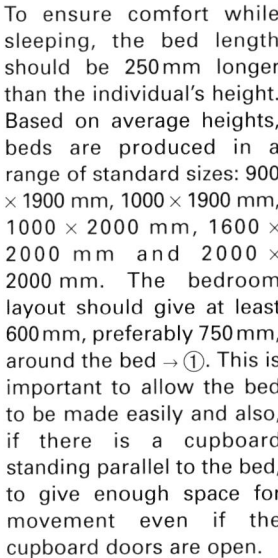

③ Walk-in cupboard with folding doors

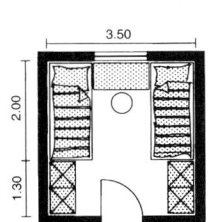

④ Small bedroom for a child

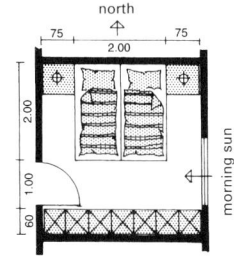

⑤ Standard bedroom layout

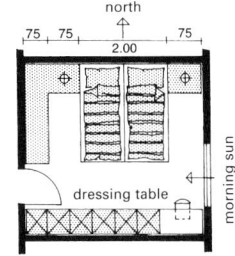

⑥ Bedroom with space for dressing table and side cupboard

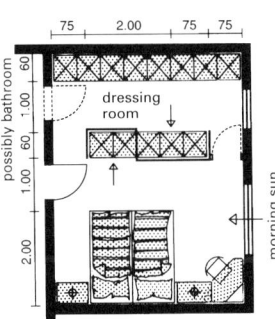

⑦ Bedroom with dressing room

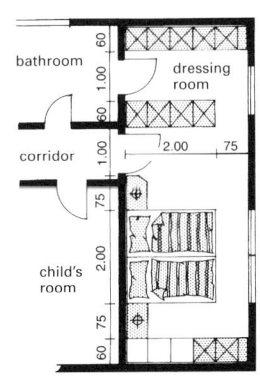

⑧ Bedroom with dressing room

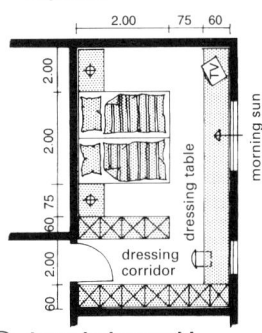

⑨ Large bedroom with dressing corridor

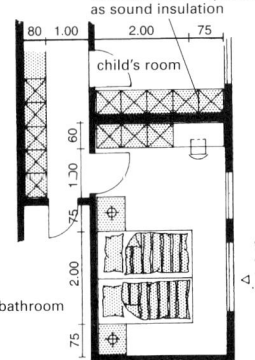

⑩ Bedroom with adjacent cupboard corridor

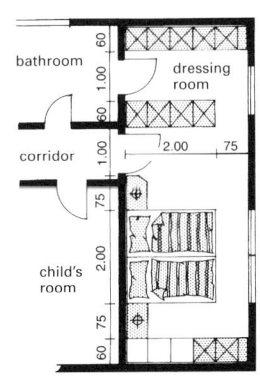

⑪ Bedroom with dressing room and access to bathroom

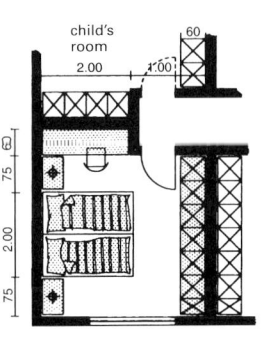

⑫ Bedroom with adjacent child's room

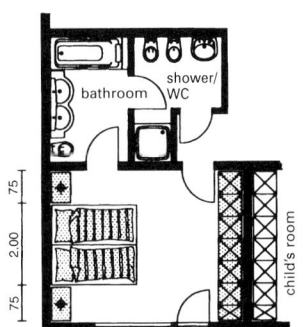

⑬ Bedroom with shower/bathroom

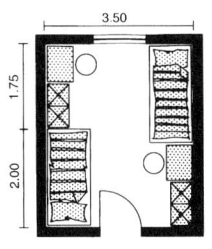

⑭ Two-bed room for children/guests

⑮ → ⑭

⑯ Two-bed room

⑬ Dividable → ⑯

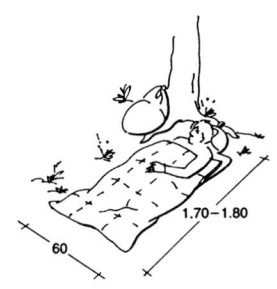

① **Sleeping bag**

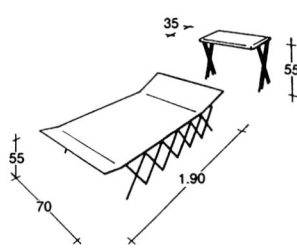

② **Canvas bed; folds to give a stool**

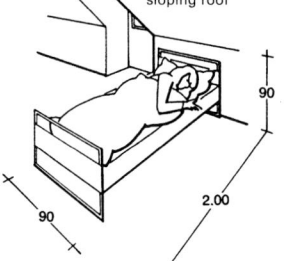

③ **Low steel tubular bed**

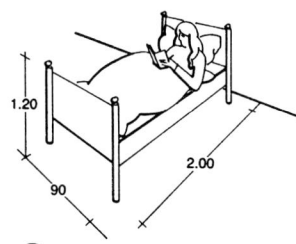

④ **Grandmother's feather bed**

Couch/bed conversions

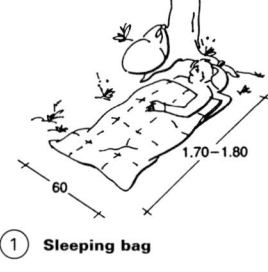

⑤ **Sofa-bed: bedding rolls up in zipped covers**

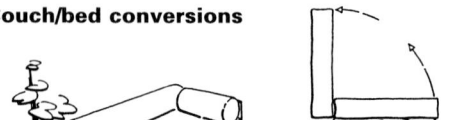

⑥ **Sofa-bed: bedding stored in drawers under the mattress**

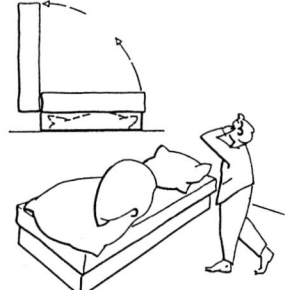

⑦ **Sofa-bed: bedding stored behind backrests**

⑧ **Sofa-bed: pull-out mattress**

Bunk beds and units

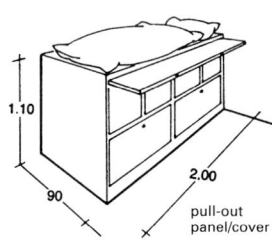

⑨ **Bed on cupboard unit**

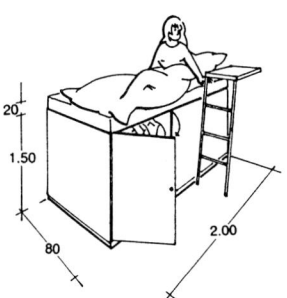

⑩ **Bed on cupboard for small rooms, ships' cabins etc.**

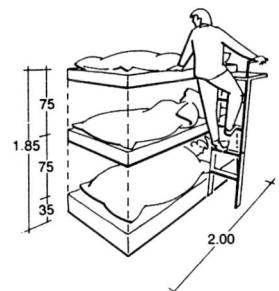

⑪ **Bunk for railway sleeping cars, holiday homes etc.**

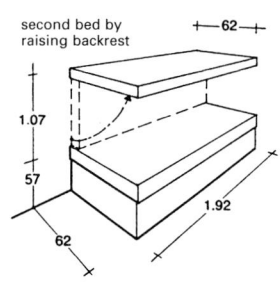

⑫ **Pullman bed for caravans and railway sleeping cars**

Fold-up beds

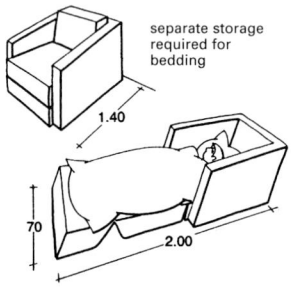

⑬ **Bed/chair (fold-out)**

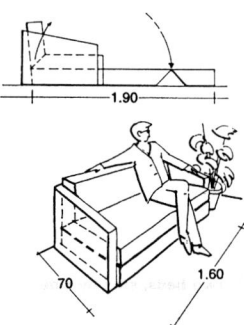

⑭ **Sofa-bed (fold-out)**

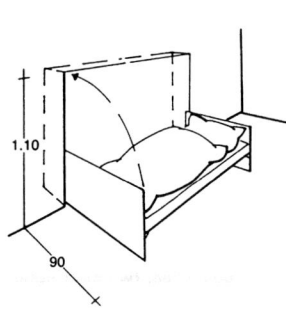

⑮ **Side-hinged folding bed**

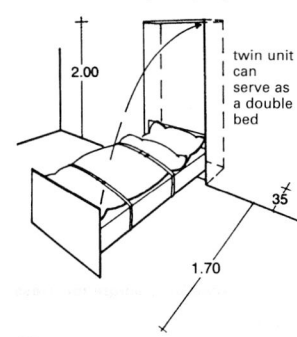

⑯ **Top-hinged folding bed**

Castor-mounted folding and wall beds

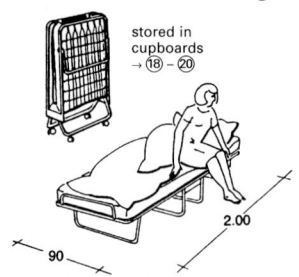

⑰ **Folding bed on castors**

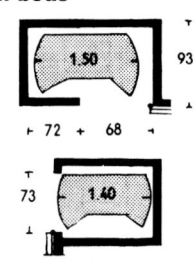

⑱ **Wall cupboards for folding beds**

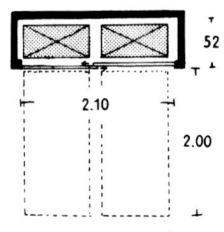

⑲ **Beds unfolded in front of cupboard doors**

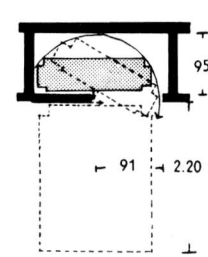

⑳ **Hinged/swinging folding beds**

Bed Positions

The position of the bed within a room can have a significant effect on a person's feelings of well-being:

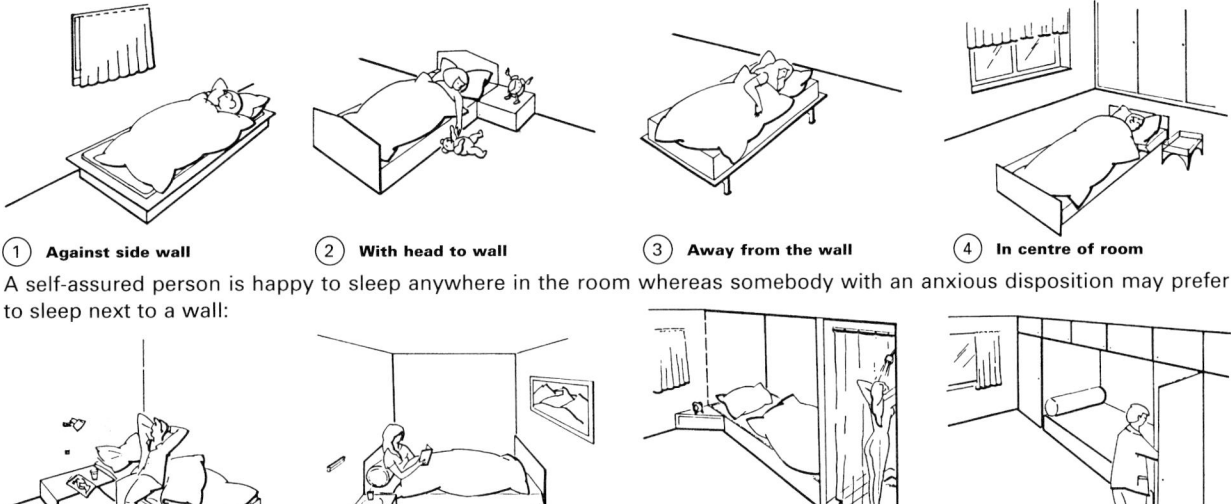

① **Against side wall** ② **With head to wall** ③ **Away from the wall** ④ **In centre of room**

A self-assured person is happy to sleep anywhere in the room whereas somebody with an anxious disposition may prefer to sleep next to a wall:

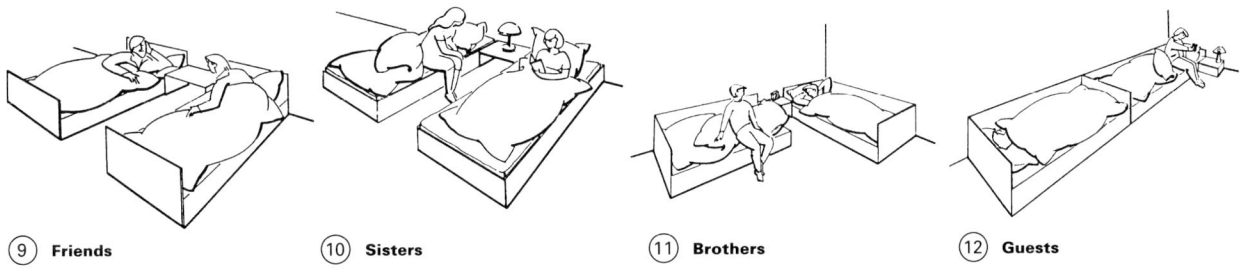

⑤ **In corner of room** ⑥ **End of room** ⑦ **In wall alcove** ⑧ **In cupboard alcove**

In addition to room decoration and furnishings, a restful atmosphere also depends on the orientation of the bed (head best towards north), position with respect to the light (looking away from window) and the door (looking towards door). Where there is more than one bed their position with respect to each other is important:

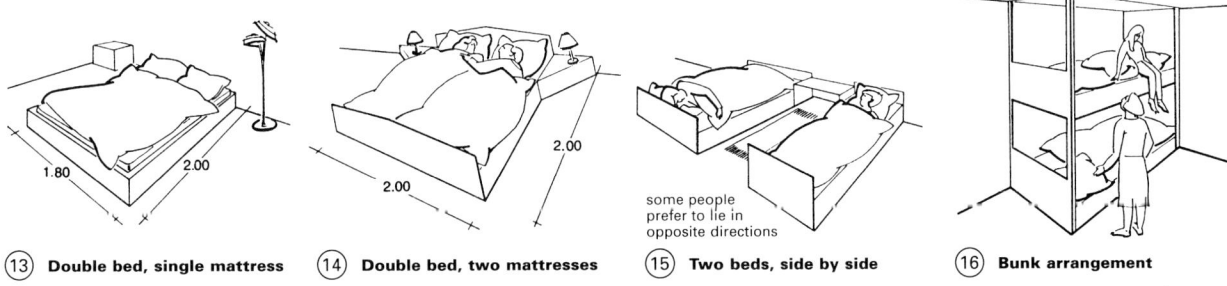

⑨ **Friends** ⑩ **Sisters** ⑪ **Brothers** ⑫ **Guests**

Different arrangements of beds may be desirable if friends, sisters, brothers or guests sleep in one room:

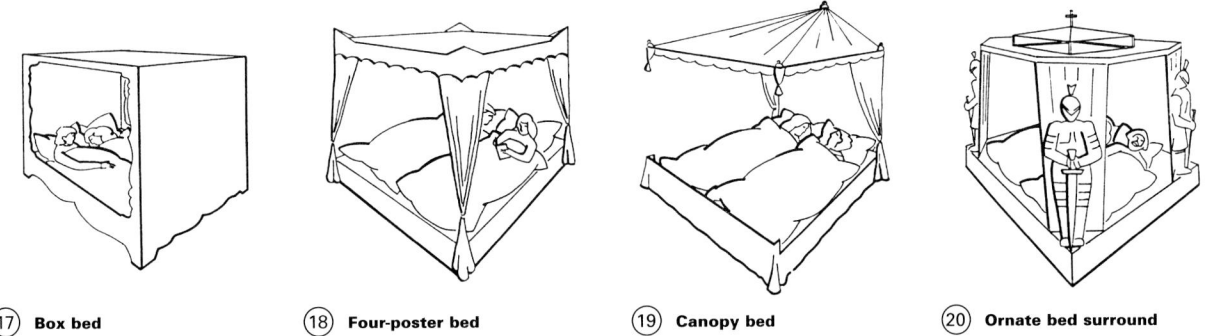

⑬ **Double bed, single mattress** ⑭ **Double bed, two mattresses** ⑮ **Two beds, side by side** ⑯ **Bunk arrangement**

The arrangement of double beds (and single beds placed side by side or as bunks) has more to do with personal preference than space. Separate beds have now become common for couples whereas an enclosed double bed was customary in the past:

⑰ **Box bed** ⑱ **Four-poster bed** ⑲ **Canopy bed** ⑳ **Ornate bed surround**

The last example is formed like a basilica and lit by a special ceiling light when the curtains are closed. These last four examples show how the room and furniture decoration has depended strongly on the customs of the era.

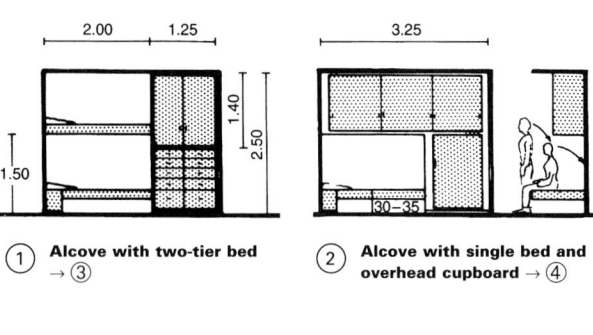

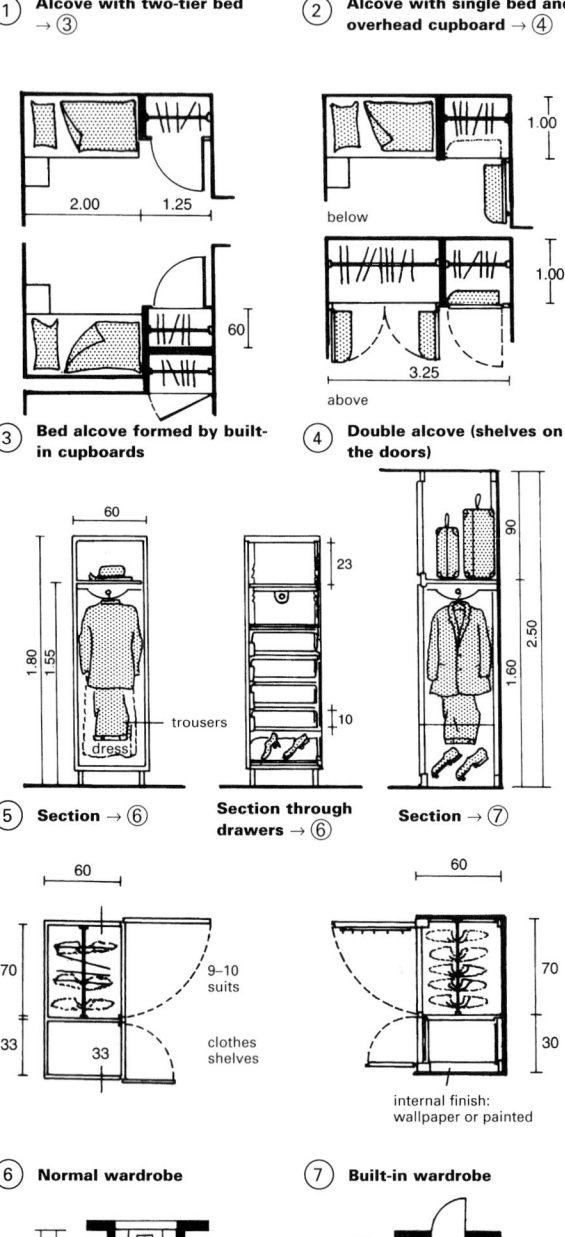

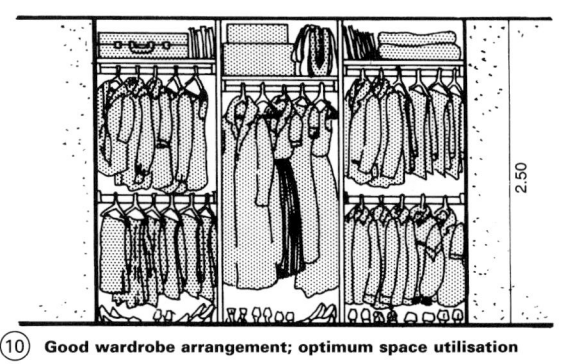

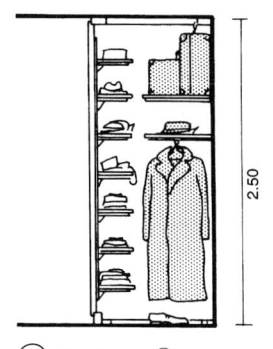

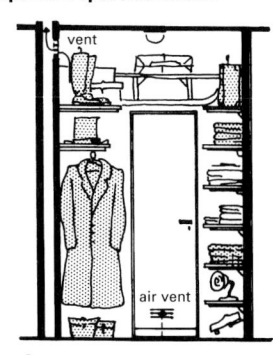

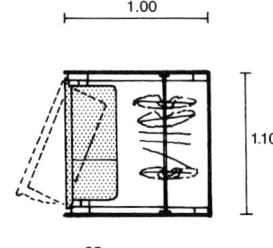

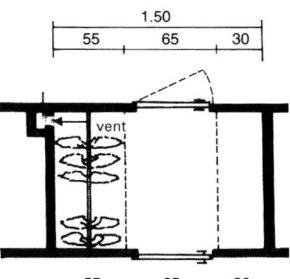

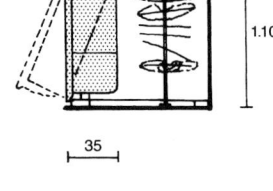

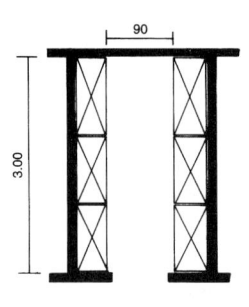

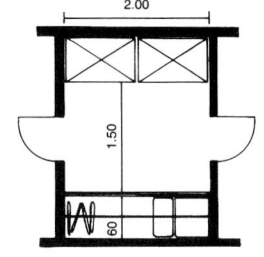

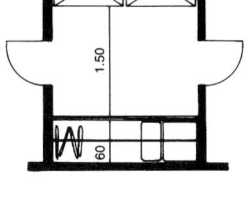

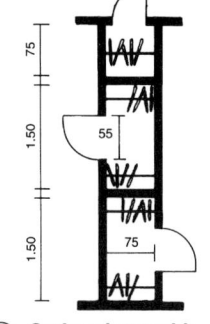

BEDROOMS

Bed Alcoves and Wardrobes

Built-in cupboards and fitted wardrobes are ideal for owner-occupied houses, whereas free-standing units are better for rented housing. With small rooms it is necessary to make use of every space and this need can be satisfied effectively by creative use of built-in cupboards. Highly suitable are complete fitted wardrobes or cupboard rooms in walls between the bedrooms.

Care must be taken to avoid condensation in cupboards on exterior walls. This is achieved by providing insulation and good ventilation. Ventilation is also necessary for cupboard rooms → (14).

(1) Alcove with two-tier bed → (3)

(2) Alcove with single bed and overhead cupboard → (4)

(3) Bed alcove formed by built-in cupboards

(4) Double alcove (shelves on the doors)

(5) Section → (6)

Section through drawers → (6)

Section → (7)

(6) Normal wardrobe

(7) Built-in wardrobe

(8) Cupboard space and shower between two child's bedrooms

(9) Cupboard area with separate accesses

(10) Good wardrobe arrangement; optimum space utilisation

(11) Section → (13)

(12) Section → (14)

(13) Built-in double wardrobe; economical and compact

(14) Cupboard room between two bedrooms

(15) Cupboard room with cupboards on both sides

(16) Cupboard room with space for dressing

260

Storage requirements

When planning storage areas in bedrooms the following numbers may be used to work out an approximate minimum volume.

For men	For women
8 suits	6 suits
6 coats	10 coats
8 jackets	5 jackets
12 pairs trousers	20 dresses
20 shirts	15 skirts
15 tee-shirts	15 blouses
12 jumpers	20 tops
4 pairs pyjamas	15 jumpers
8 pairs shoes	15 pairs leggings/trousers
2 hats	6 pyjamas/nightdresses
	10 pairs shoes
	4 hats

Sundry items
6 sheets
6 duvet covers
12 pillows and cases
8 bath towels
8 hand towels

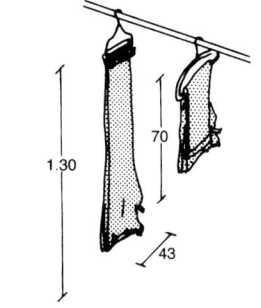

5–10 = 50–70 cm
5–10 = 45–65 cm
1.35–1.45
1.25–1.35
women's coats
men's coats

① **Coats**

5–10 = 35 cm min
1.45–1.60
50

② **Women's dresses**

5–10 = 90 cm
85
55

③ **Jackets**

1.30
70
43

④ **Trousers**

50
5–10 shirts 12 cm high
17
48
12
30
55

⑤ **Men's clothes**

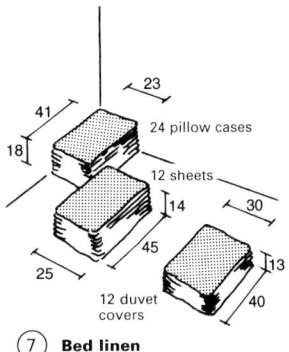

45
6
30
12 men's handkerchiefs 14 × 14 × 7
12 women's handkerchiefs 11 × 8 × 3

⑥ **Pyjamas and handkerchiefs**

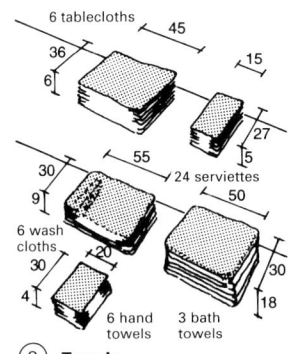

41
18
23
24 pillow cases
12 sheets
14
30
45
25
40
13
12 duvet covers

⑦ **Bed linen**

6 tablecloths   45
36
6
15
55
24 serviettes
30
9
50
6 wash cloths
30
4
20
27
5
6 hand towels
3 bath towels
30
18

⑧ **Towels**

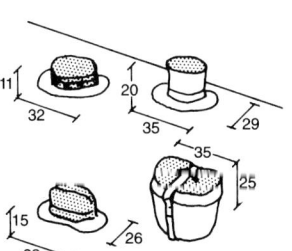

11
32
20
35
29
35
25
15
32
26

⑨ **Men's hats**

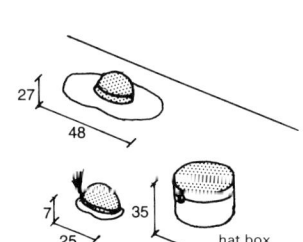

27
48
7
25
35
20
hat box

⑩ **Women's hats**

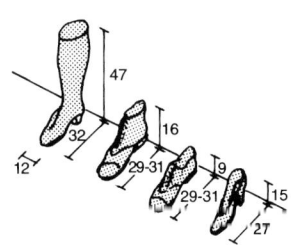

47
32
12
16
29–31
9
29–31
15
27

⑪ **Boots and shoes**

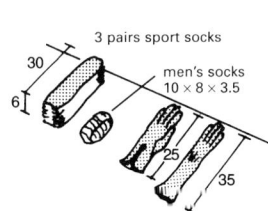

3 pairs sport socks
30
6
men's socks 10 × 8 × 3.5
25
35

⑫ **Socks and gloves**

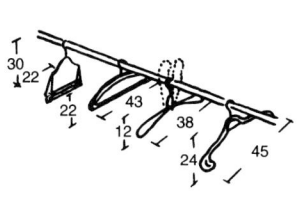

30
22
22
43
12
38
24
45

⑬ **Clothes hangers**

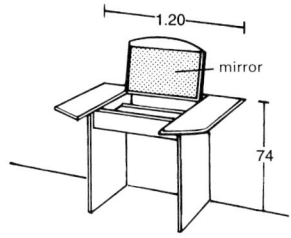

1.20
mirror
74

⑭ **Dressing table**

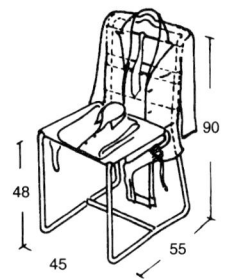

90
48
45
55

⑮ **Clothes chair (back in the form of a hanger)**

⑯ **Built-in clothes cupboard using the doors for storage**

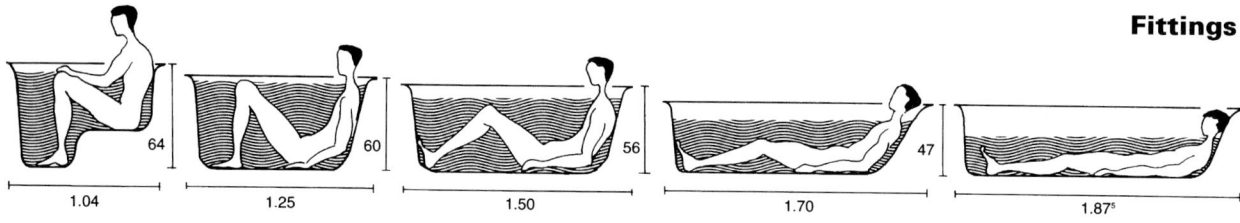

① Deeper water required for shorter baths

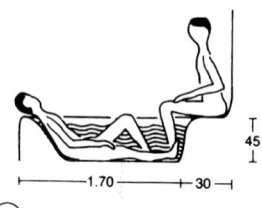

② Bathing and sitting

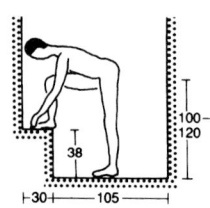

③ In the shower

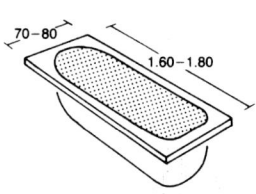

④ Bath unit

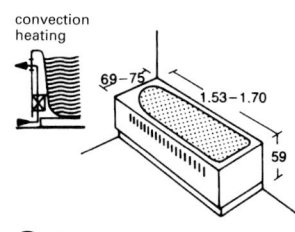

⑤ Bath panelled on one or two sides with convection heating

⑥ Wall-mounted bidet

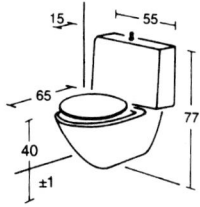

⑦ Wall-mounted deep-flush toilet bowl and cistern

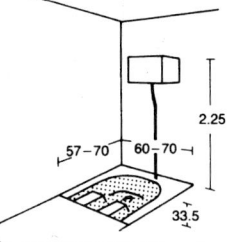

⑧ Squatting WC (French style)

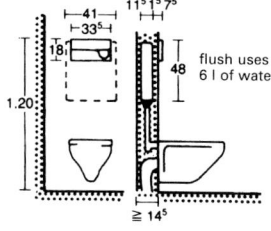

⑨ Deep-flush toilet bowl; built-in cistern

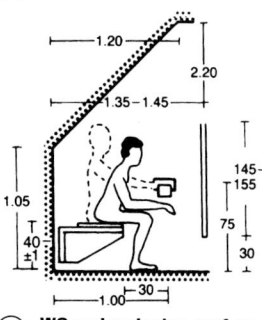

⑩ WC under sloping roof or stairs

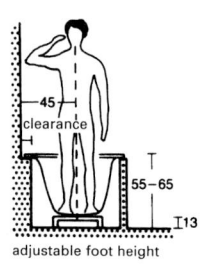

⑪ Necessary minimum wall clearance for washing

⑫ Minimum space between bath and wall

⑬ Recommended clearance

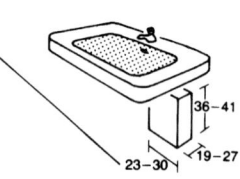

⑭ Hot water storage tank beneath wash-basin

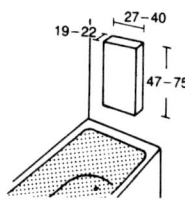

⑮ Gas heater: requires a flue

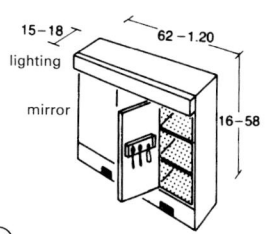

⑯ Bathroom cupboard

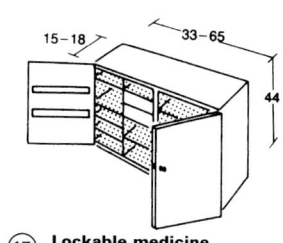

⑰ Lockable medicine cupboard

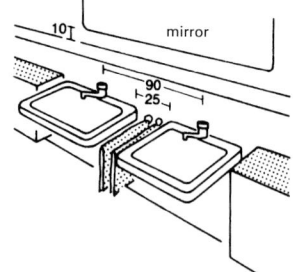

⑱ Two wash-basins, towel rails between

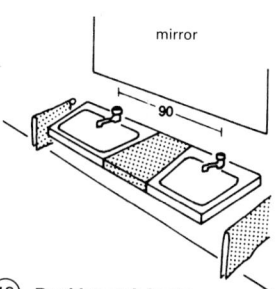

⑲ Double wash-basin

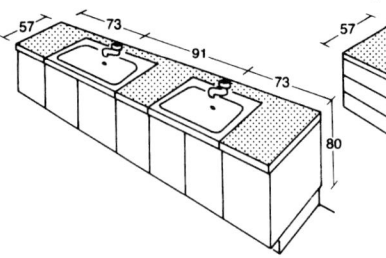

⑳ Double vanity unit, cupboards below

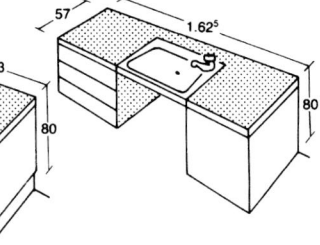

㉑ Single vanity unit

HOUSES AND RESIDENTIAL BUILDINGS

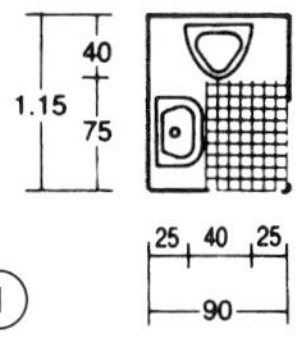

<... >
</>

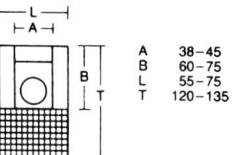
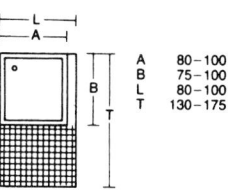
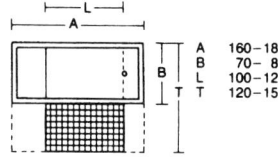
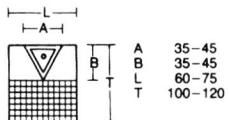
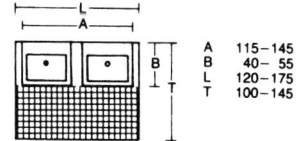

BATHROOMS

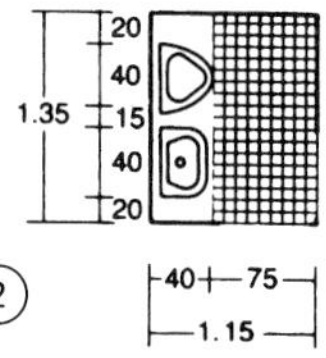

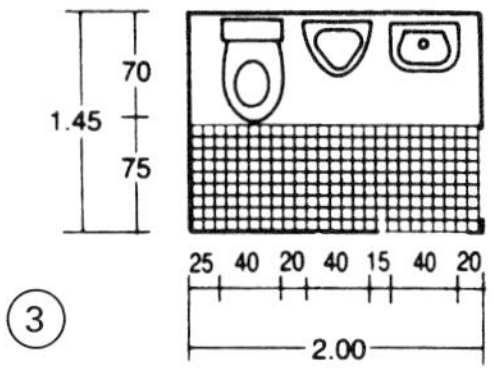

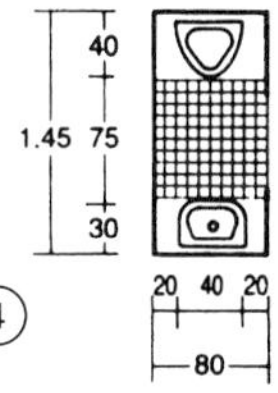

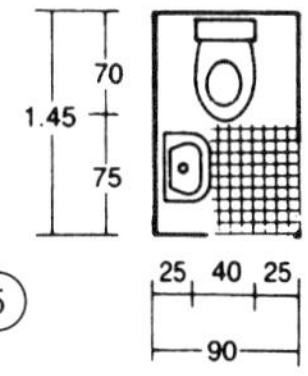

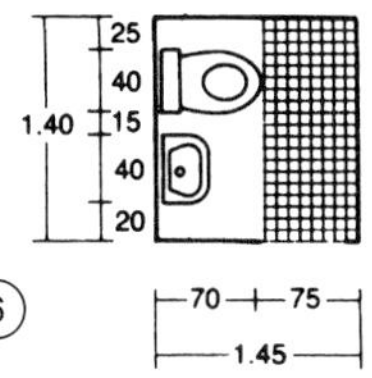

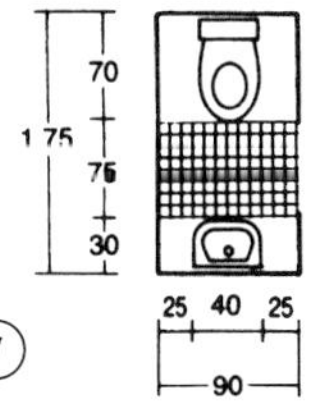

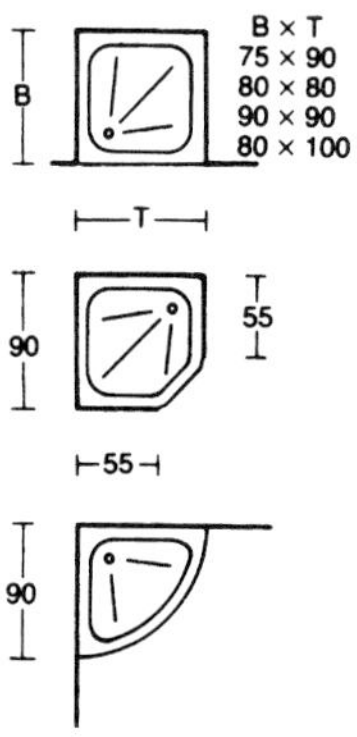

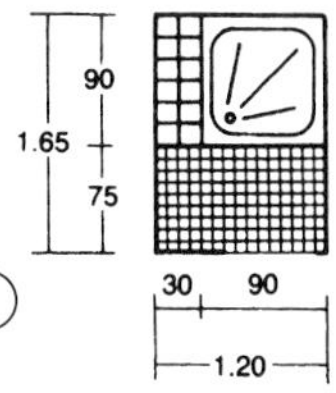

1. Wall-mounted units are preferable for hygiene reasons and for ease of cleaning. Deep-flush WCs reduce odours.

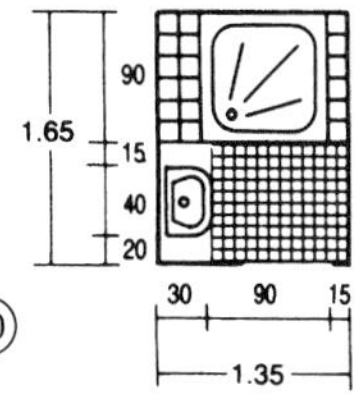

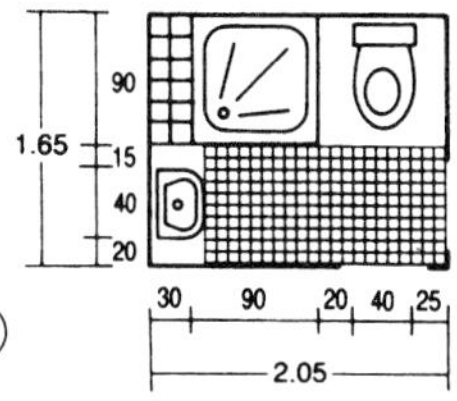

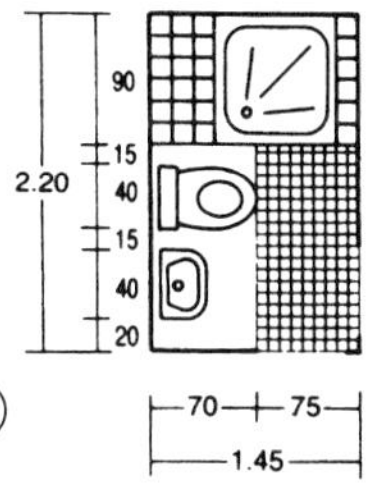

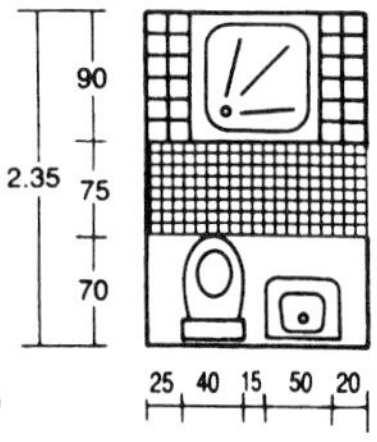

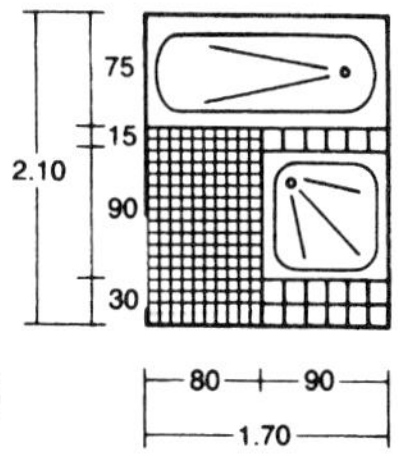

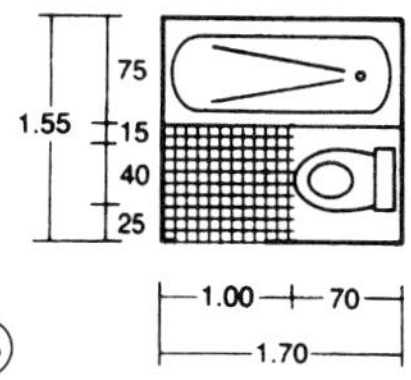

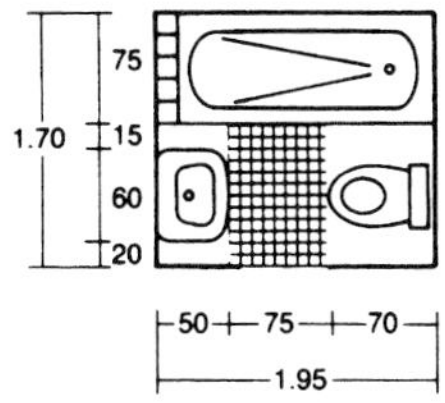

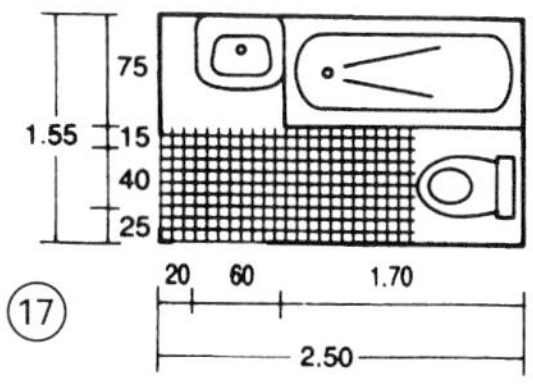

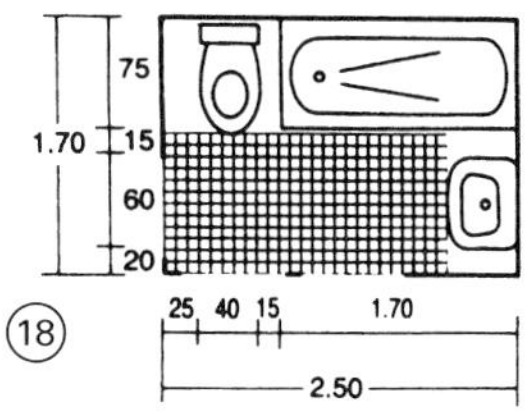

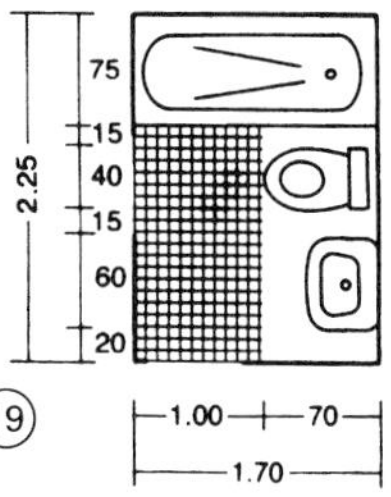

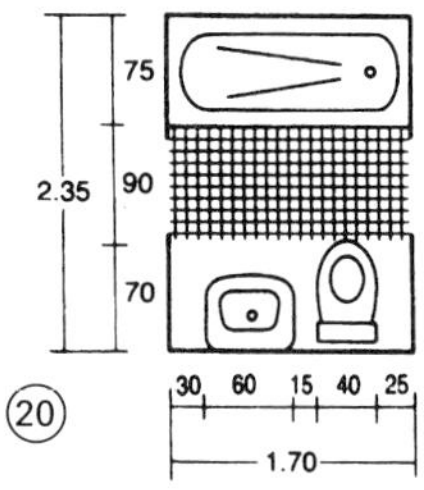

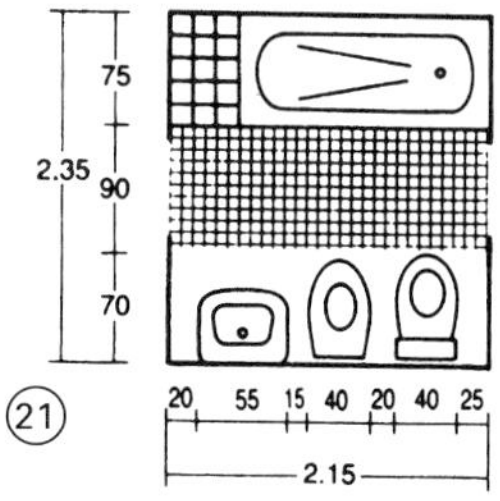

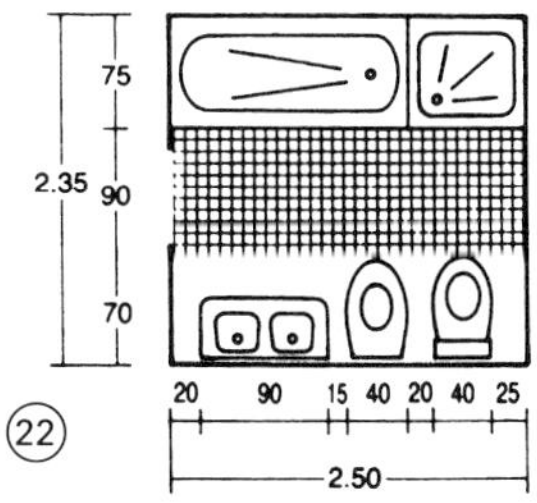

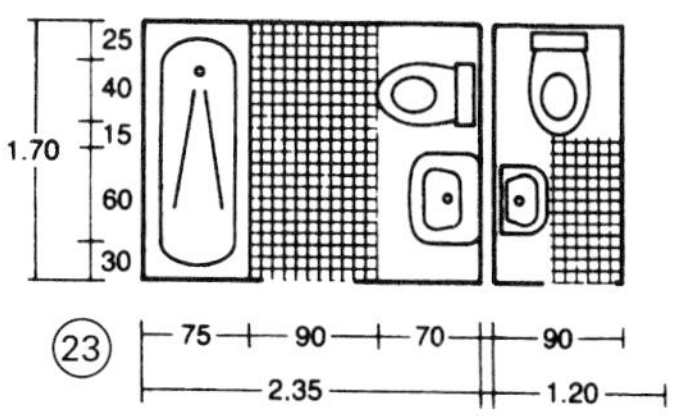

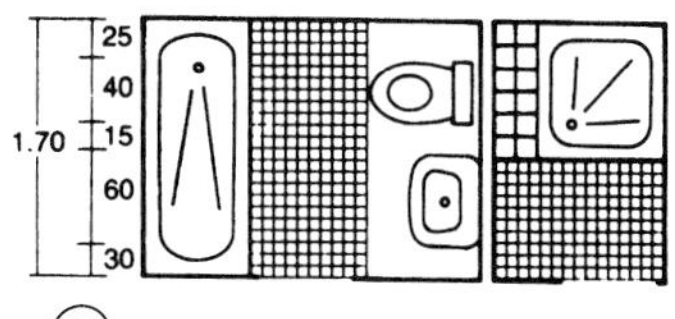

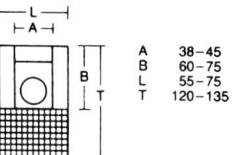

A	38–45	
B	60–75	
L	55–75	
T	120–135	

2. In contrast to showers, baths may be used medicinally (e.g. muscle relaxation) as well as for washing.

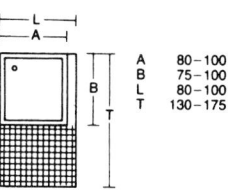

A	80–100
B	75–100
L	80–100
T	130–175

3. Bath tubs are usually installed as built-in units and may have convection heating inside.

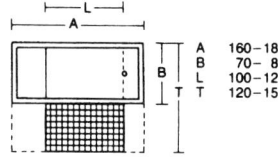

A	160–18
B	70– 8
L	100–12
T	120–15

4. Urinals → ① – ④ are often found in today's households.

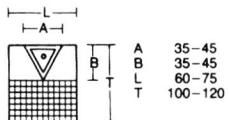

A	35–45
B	35–45
L	60–75
T	100–120

5. Wash-basins:

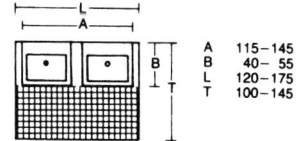

A	115–145
B	40– 55
L	120–175
T	100–145

Should be of a suitable size and have ample surrounding flat storage surfaces. Flush-mounted fittings save space and are easy to clean. Mixer taps save water and energy. Note that 1.20 m wide double wash-basins do not really provide enough free arm movement when washing: better is a layout with two basins, towel rails in between and storage to the sides → p. 262 ⑱.

BATHROOM

Cubicles

Traditional wet room installations usually involve substantial expenditure and a lot of time. Because the requirements are largely standardised, prefabrication is desirable, especially for terraced and multi-family housing projects, holiday homes, apartments, hotel facilities and for old building restoration work. Sanitary blocks can be prefabricated → ① – ③, as well as utility walls or complete cubicles → ④ – ⑬, with premounted piping as well as units with accessories. Prefabricated compact cubicles are supplied in a range of fixed dimensions.

Prefabricated cubicles are mostly sandwich construction, with wooden frame and chipboard or fibre-cement panels. They use aluminium, moulded stainless steel or glass-fibre reinforced plastic to match the units and accessories.

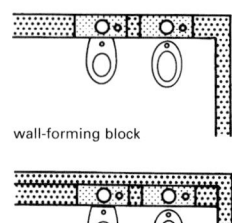

wall-forming block

block placed against wall

① **WC sanitary elements**

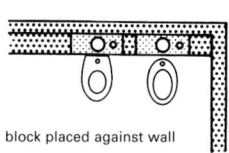

wall-forming block

block placed against wall

② **Bathroom sanitary elements**

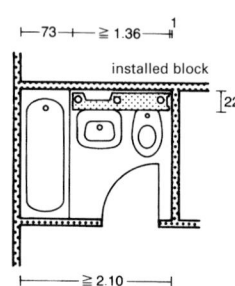

③ **Sanitary block in front of wall**

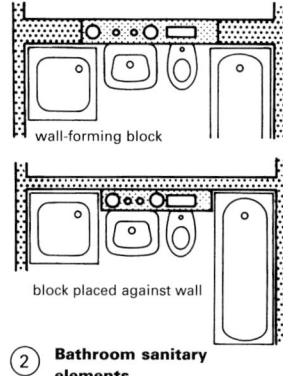

④ **Utility wall**

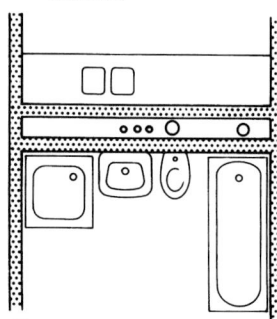

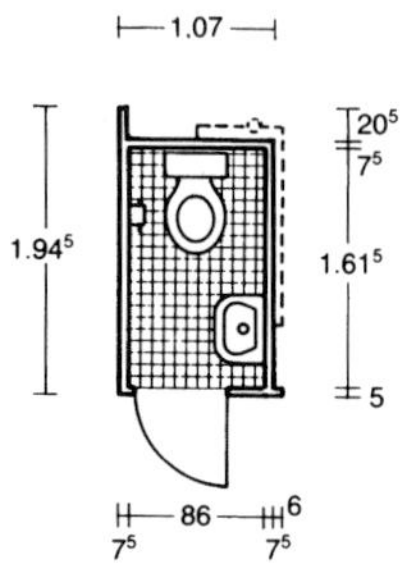

⑤ **Compact WC cubicle with units**

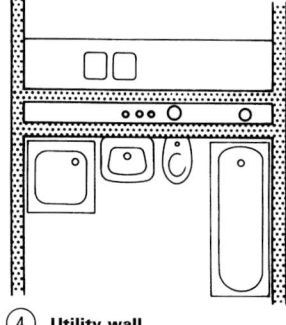

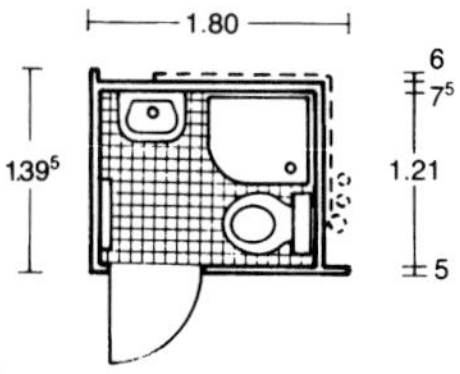

⑥ **As ⑤ with shower**

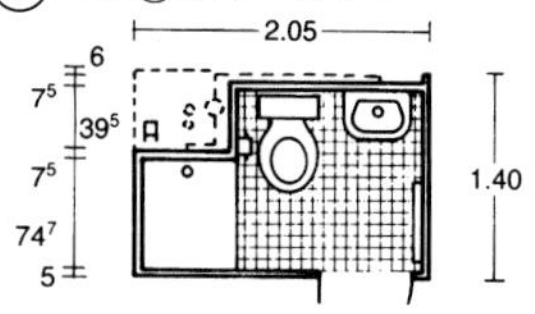

⑦ **Shower cubicle with service duct**

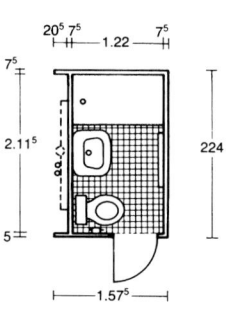

⑧ **Larger WC cubicle with shower**

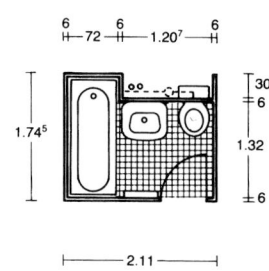

⑨ **Bathroom cubicle**

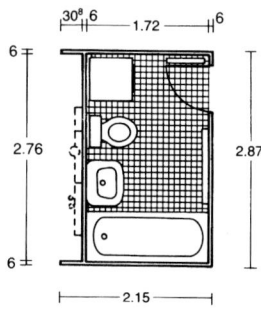

⑩ **Bathroom cubicle with washing machine**

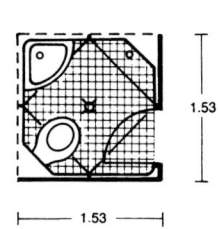

⑪ **Compact WC cubicle**

⑫ **As → ⑪ but with shower to one side**

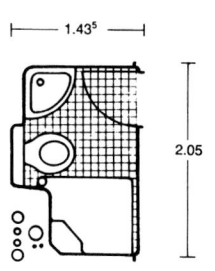

⑬ **Compact cubicle with shower**

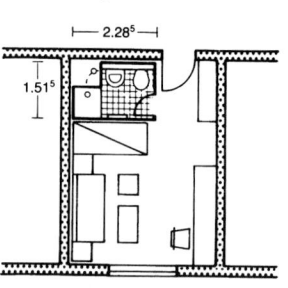

⑭ **Hotel-style shower cubicle**

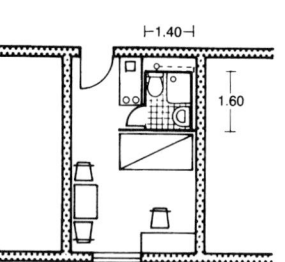

⑮ **Shower cubicle in the smallest flat**

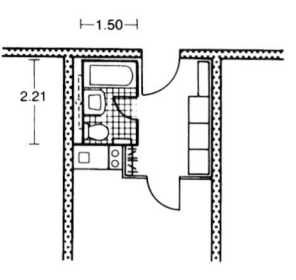

⑯ **Prefabricated bathroom with kitchen utility wall**

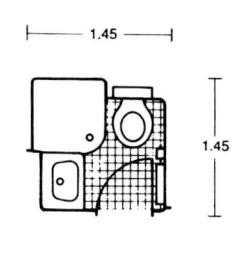

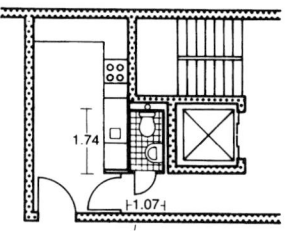

⑬ **Hospital-style WC cubicle**

BATHROOMS

Location

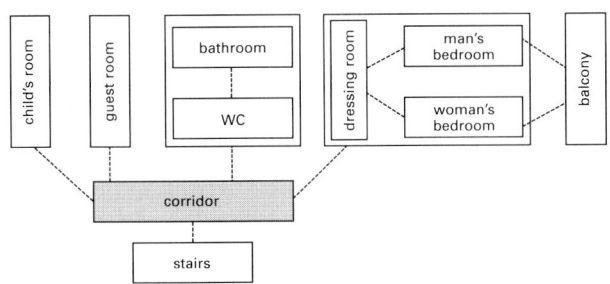

① **Spatial relationships with the bathroom**

The most convenient location for the bathroom is adjacent to the bedrooms (and the WC if it is not incorporated in the bathroom itself). Although showers are compact and often preferred by younger people, baths are generally more suitable for the elderly.

If the house has no utility room and a small kitchen, spaces and connections can be provided in the bathroom for washing machines and laundry baskets.

② **Bathroom between bedrooms, WC accessible from corridor**

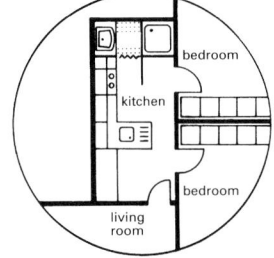

③ **Bathroom built into kitchen**

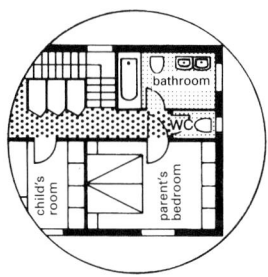

④ **Swing doors to bathroom and WC from parents' bedroom**

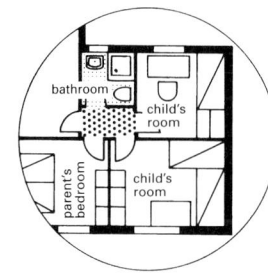

⑤ **Bathroom on landing between bedrooms**

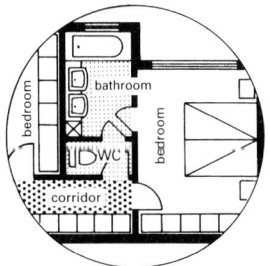

⑥ **Bathroom accessible from corridor and bedroom**

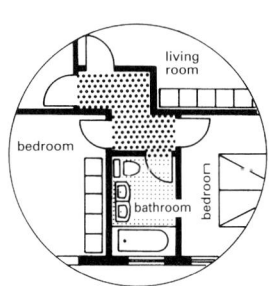

⑦ **Bathroom between bedrooms**

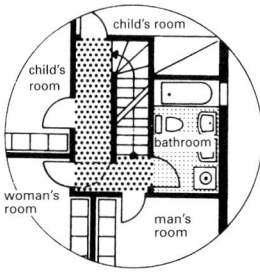

⑧ **Bedrooms and bathroom can be closed off using swing doors**

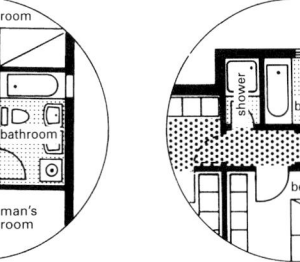

⑨ **Bathroom and separate shower**

bathroom unit/equipment	floor area	
	width (cm)	depth (cm)
built-in wash-basins and bidets		
1 single built-in wash-basin	> 60	> 55
2 double built-in wash-basin	> 120	> 55
3 built-in single wash-basin with cupboard below	> 70	> 60
4 built-in double wash-basin with cupboard below	> 140	> 60
5 hand wash-basin	> 50	> 40
6 bidet (floor-standing or wall-mounted)	40	60
tubs/trays		
7 bathtub	> 170	> 75
8 shower tray	> 80	> 80*
WC and urinals		
9 WC with wall unit or pressure cistern	40	75
10 WC with built-in wall cistern	40	60
11 urinal	40	40
washing equipment		
12 washing machine	40 to 60	60
13 clothes drier	60	60
bathroom furniture		
14 low cupboards, high cupboards, wall-hung cupboards	according to make	40
* in the case of shower trays with w = 90 this can also be 75cm		

⑩ **Space requirements for bathroom and WC units**

water consumption for:	water consumption (l)	water temperature (°C)	approximate time (mins)
washing:			
hands	5	37	2
face	5	37	2
teeth	0.5		3
feet/legs	25	37	4
whole body	40	38	15
hair washing	20	38	10
children's bath	30	40	5
bathing:			
full bath	140–160	40	15
sitz bath	40	40	8
shower bath	40–75	40	6
grooming:			
wet shave	1	37	4

⑪ **Hot water requirements: temperature and usage time for domestic water heaters**

BATHROOMS

Location

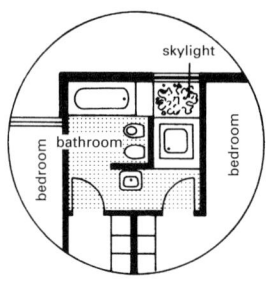

① Bathroom under roof with skylight

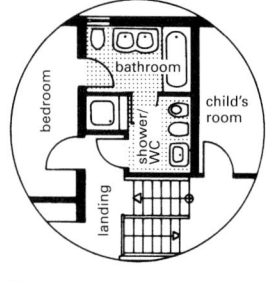

② Bathroom accessible from bedroom and via shower/WC

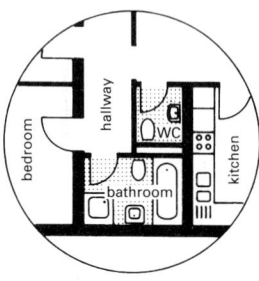

③ Bathroom accessed from corridor

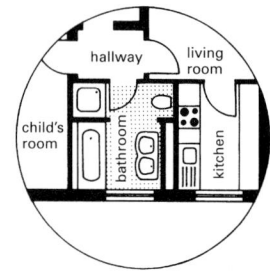

④ Kitchen and bathroom with common utility wall

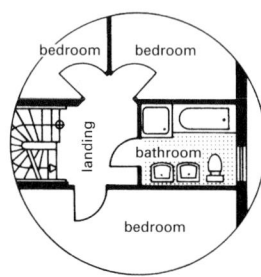

⑤ Typical bathroom in terraced house

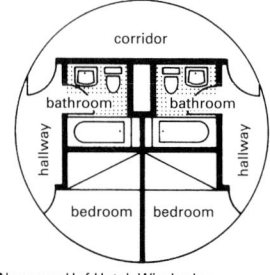

Nassauer Hof Hotel, Wiesbaden

⑥ Typical hotel layout

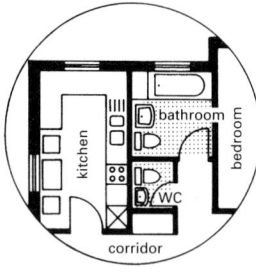

⑦ Kitchen, bathroom and WC on one utility wall

⑧ Kitchen, utility room, bathroom and WC centrally grouped

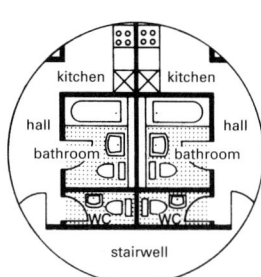

⑨ Kitchen, bathroom and WC on one utility wall

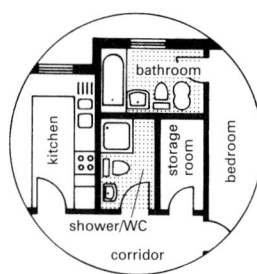

⑩ *En suite* bathroom and separate shower room

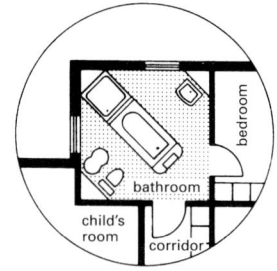

⑪ Spacious bathroom

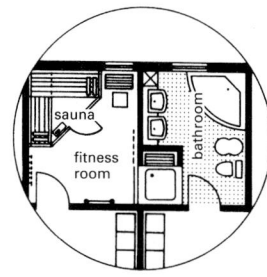

⑫ Bathroom and sauna (linked via shower)

Bathrooms with WCs are self-contained rooms which are equipped with all of the fittings necessary to meet all the sanitary needs of the occupants. However, the plan should ideally include two separate lockable rooms for the bathroom and WC and this is essential in dwellings for more than five people. A bathroom with WC can be directly accessible from the bedroom as long as another WC can be reached from the corridor → ② + ⑩.

A bathtub and/or shower tray plus a wash-basin are installed in the bathroom, while a flushing toilet, bidet and hand washing basin are installed in the WC.

For cost efficiency and technical reasons the bathroom, WC and kitchen should be planned such that they can share the same service ducts → ③ + ④, ⑦ – ⑩. In multistorey homes, an arrangement such that the utility walls for the bathrooms and WCs are directly above one another helps to keep installation costs and the necessary sound insulation measures as low as possible. However, adjacent bathrooms in two different flats must not be connected to a single supply or discharge pipe system.

The bathroom and WC should be orientated towards the north, and should normally be naturally lit and ventilated. At least four air changes per hour are required for internal rooms. For comfort, a bathroom temperature of 22 to 24°C is about right. A temperature of 20°C is suitable for WCs in homes. This is higher than that encountered in office buildings, where 15 to 17°C is the common norm.

Bathrooms are particularly susceptible to damp so appropriate sealing must be provided. Surfaces must be easy to clean because of high air humidity and condensation, and the wall and ceiling plaster must be able to withstand the conditions. Choose slip resistant floor coverings.

Consider the required noise insulation: the noise levels from domestic systems and appliances heard in neighbouring flats or adjoining rooms must not exceed 35 dB(A).

At least one sealed electrical socket should be provided at a height of 1.30 m beside the mirror for electrical equipment. It is also necessary to consider the following for the bathroom/WC: cupboards for towels, cleaning items, medicines and toiletries (possibly lockable), mirror and lighting, hot water supply, supplementary heater, towel rails, drier, handles above the bathtub, toilet paper holder within easy reach, toothbrush holder, soap container and storage surfaces.

BATHROOMS

Planning Examples

Specially designed polyester baths (wide shoulder and narrow foot sections) and shower units offer space savings that make small rooms appear more spacious → ① – ③.

Baths with chamfered corners can be useful in renovation projects → ⑲.

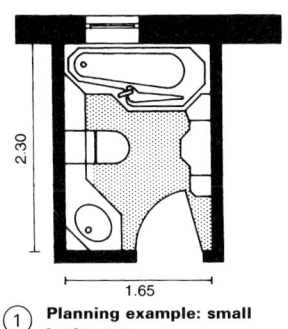

① **Planning example: small bathroom**

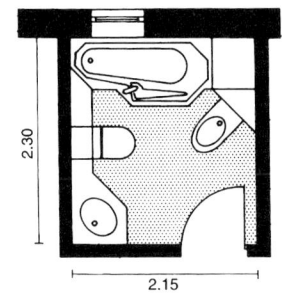

② **As → ①, but 2.15 m wide**

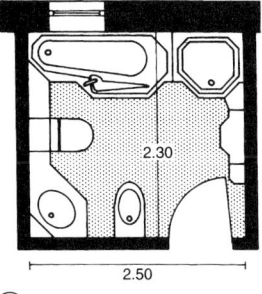
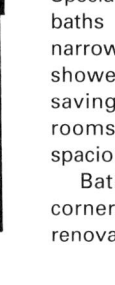

③ **As → ①, but 2.50 m wide**

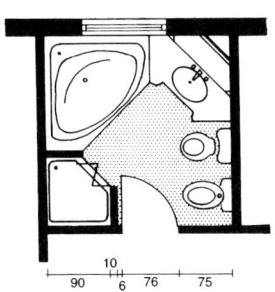

④ **Small bathroom with corner bath**

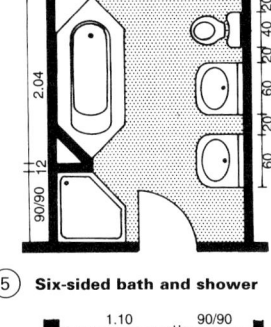

⑤ **Six-sided bath and shower**

⑥ **Corner bath**

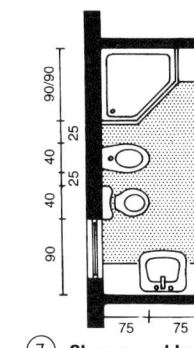

⑦ **Shower and bath on 7 m²**

⑧ **Corner bath and shower**

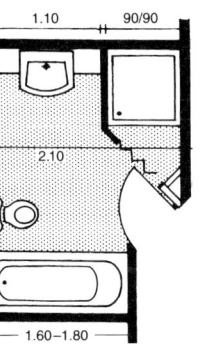

⑨ **Bathroom with separate shower**

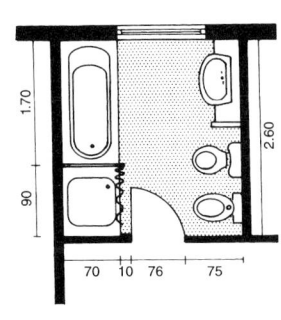

⑩ **Double-sided arrangement**

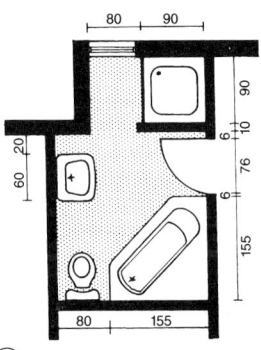

⑪ **Separate shower area**

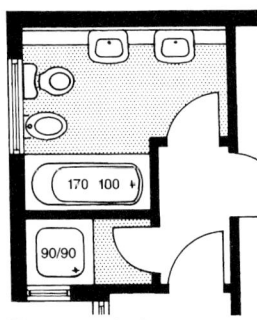
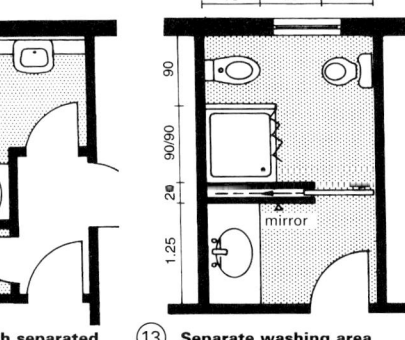

⑫ **Shower and bath separated**

⑬ **Separate washing area**

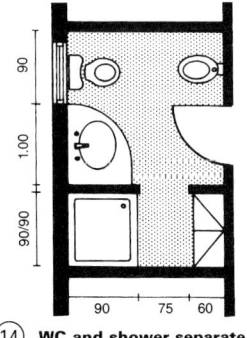

⑭ **WC and shower separate**

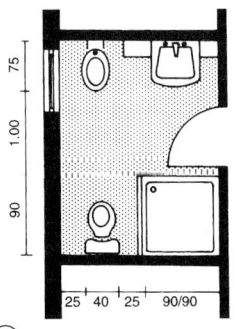

⑮ **Shower, WC, bidet, basin**

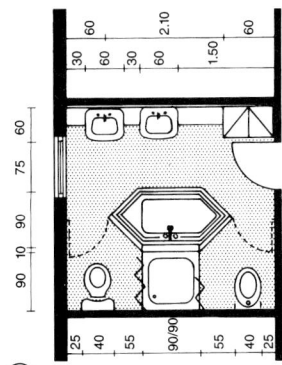

⑯ **Spacious bathroom**

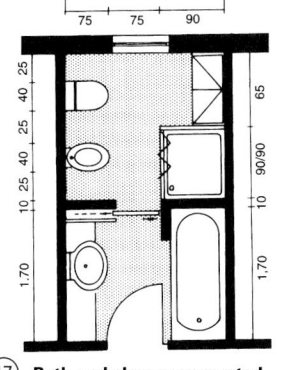

⑰ **Bath and shower separated**

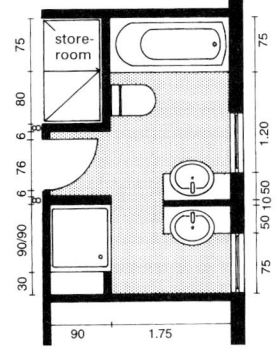

⑱ **Bath and shower with separate washing area**

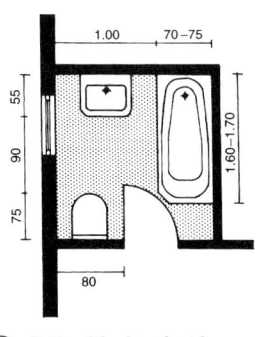

⑲ **Bath with chamfered corner (necessitated by limited space)**

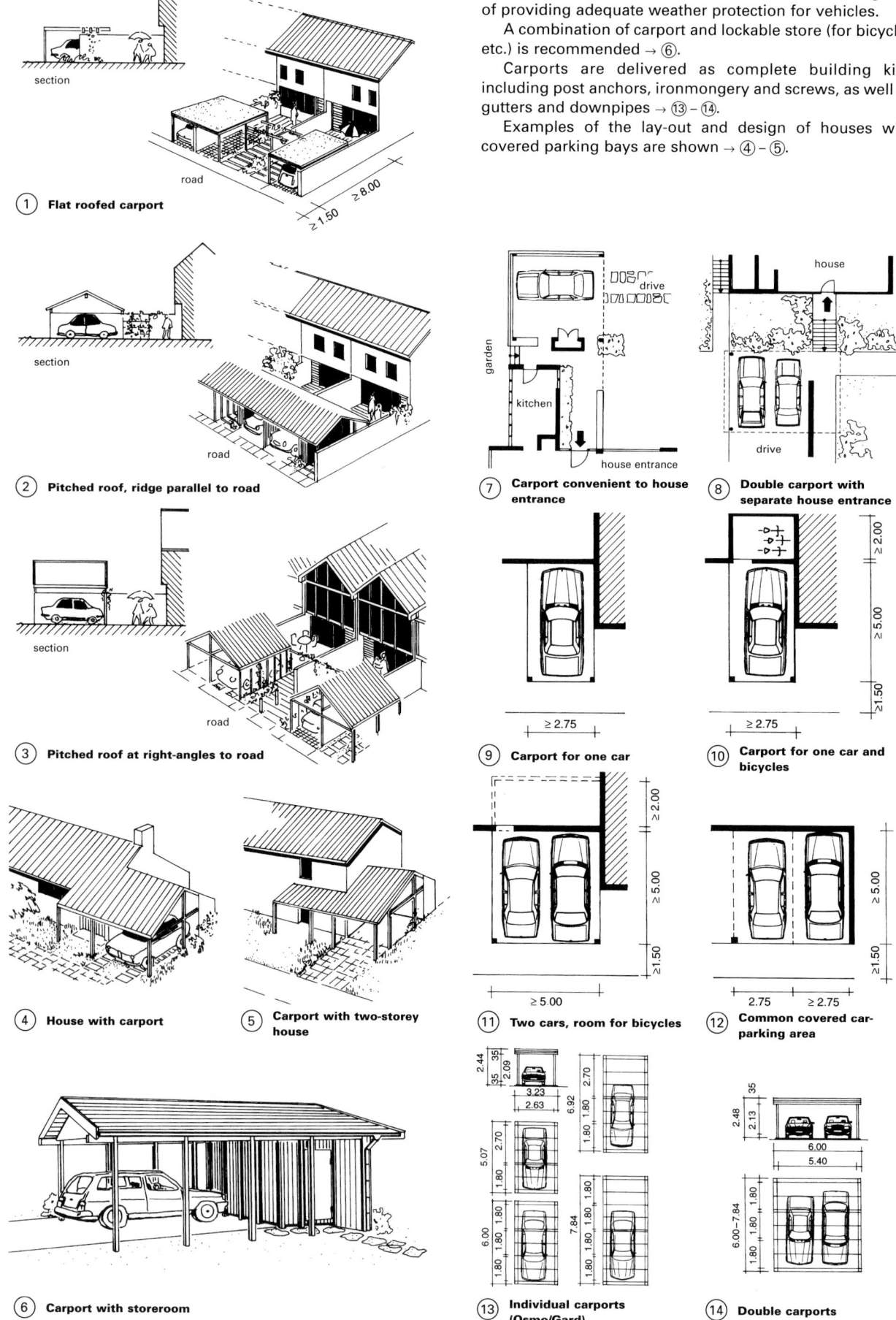

CARPORTS

Covered parking spaces (preferably with a solid wall on the weather side) provide an economical and space-saving way of providing adequate weather protection for vehicles.

A combination of carport and lockable store (for bicycles etc.) is recommended → ⑥.

Carports are delivered as complete building kits, including post anchors, ironmongery and screws, as well as gutters and downpipes → ⑬ – ⑭.

Examples of the lay-out and design of houses with covered parking bays are shown → ④ – ⑤.

① Flat roofed carport

② Pitched roof, ridge parallel to road

③ Pitched roof at right-angles to road

④ House with carport

⑤ Carport with two-storey house

⑥ Carport with storeroom

⑦ Carport convenient to house entrance

⑧ Double carport with separate house entrance

⑨ Carport for one car

⑩ Carport for one car and bicycles

⑪ Two cars, room for bicycles

⑫ Common covered car-parking area

⑬ Individual carports (Osmo/Gard)

⑭ Double carports

HOUSES AND RESIDENTIAL BUILDINGS

268

Tents

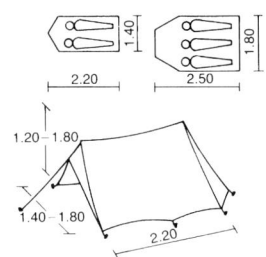

① **Small tent with apse**

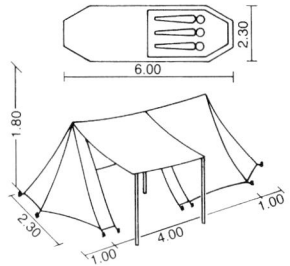

② **With inner tent, two apses and canopy**

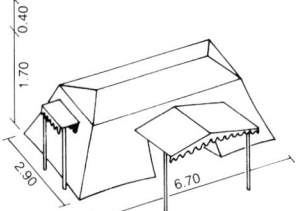

③ **Large family tent with high lateral walls, inner tent, canopy and window**

Caravans and campers

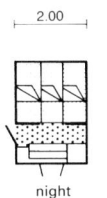

④ **Caravan with three beds and built-in kitchen**

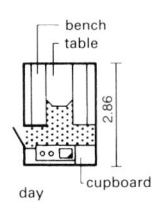

⑤ **Caravan with five beds**

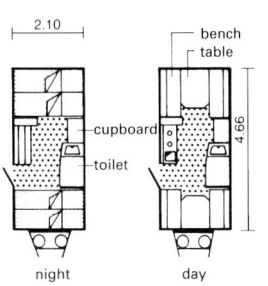

⑥ **Caravan with four beds and toilet**

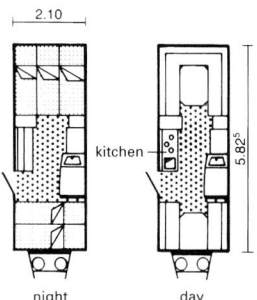

⑦ **Caravan with five beds, toilet and kitchen**

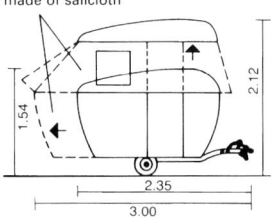

view of vehicle when open: front and back sections made of sailcloth

⑧ **Fold-out caravan**

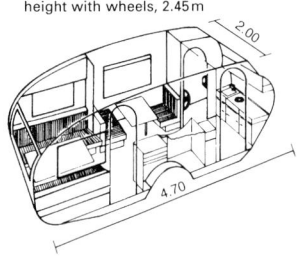

at night, table becomes sleeping area for three people

⑨ **Perspective view of ⑧**

height with wheels, 2.45 m

⑩ **Caravan with areas for cooking and eating**

⑪ **As ⑩, equipped for sleeping (for five people)**

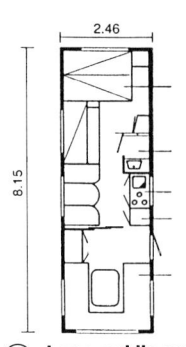

⑫ **Large mobile caravan: sleeps eight to nine**

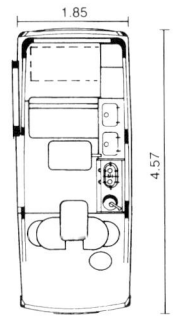

⑬ **Camper: Westfalia Joker 1/Club Joker 1**

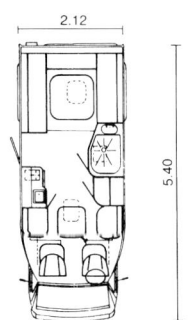

⑭ **Camper: Tischer XL65**

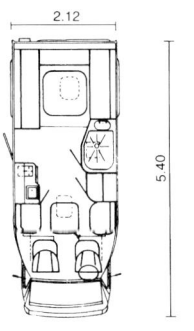

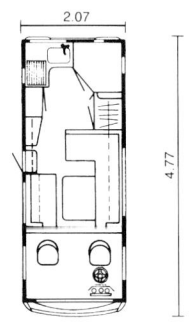

⑮ **Camper: Lyding ROG2**

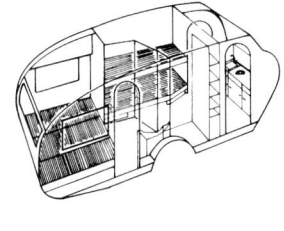

Ships' cabins

⑯ **With a double bed and bath/toilet**

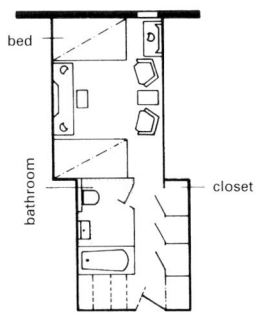

⑰ **With two beds and bath/toilet**

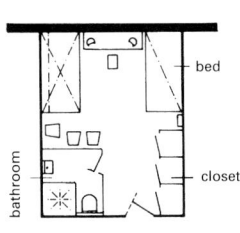

⑱ **With one single and one bunk bed, shower/toilet**

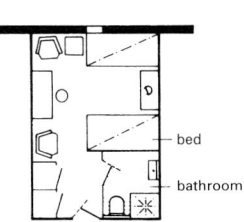

⑲ **Twin cabin with shower/toilet**

SHEDS/SUMMER HOUSES

Factors to take into account when assessing a plot are: prevailing wind direction, groundwater, drinking water supply, drainage, heating, access and parking space for cars. Whenever possible, construction should be from natural local materials (stone or wood). For security reasons, furnishings should be secured and entrances fitted with lockable shutters to protect against theft.

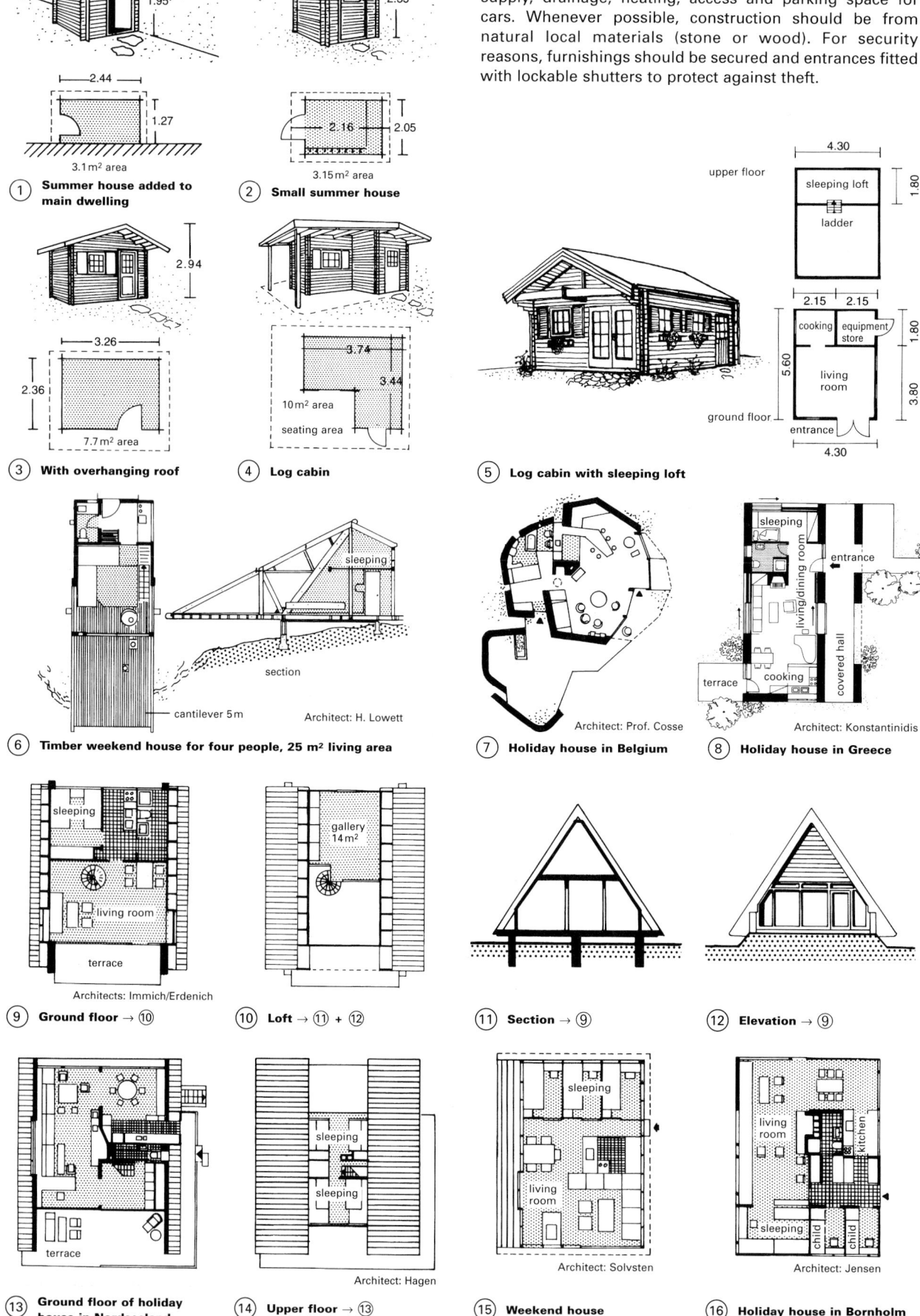

(1) **Summer house added to main dwelling** — 1.95, 2.44, 1.27, 3.1 m² area

(2) **Small summer house** — 2.35, 2.16, 2.05, 3.15 m² area

(3) **With overhanging roof** — 2.94, 3.26, 2.36, 7.7 m² area

(4) **Log cabin** — 3.74, 3.44, 10 m² area, seating area

(5) **Log cabin with sleeping loft** — upper floor: sleeping loft, ladder, 4.30, 1.80; ground floor: cooking, equipment store, living room, entrance, 2.15, 2.15, 1.80, 3.80, 5.60, 4.30

(6) **Timber weekend house for four people, 25 m² living area** — sleeping, section, cantilever 5m, Architect: H. Lowett

(7) **Holiday house in Belgium** — Architect: Prof. Cosse

(8) **Holiday house in Greece** — sleeping, entrance, living/dining room, terrace, cooking, covered hall, Architect: Konstantinidis

(9) **Ground floor → 10** — sleeping, living room, terrace, Architects: Immich/Erdenich

(10) **Loft → 11 + 12** — gallery 14 m²

(11) **Section → 9**

(12) **Elevation → 9**

(13) **Ground floor of holiday house in Nordseeland** — terrace

(14) **Upper floor → 13** — sleeping, sleeping, Architect: Hagen

(15) **Weekend house** — sleeping, living room, Architect: Solvsten

(16) **Holiday house in Bornholm** — living room, kitchen, sleeping, child, child, Architect: Jensen

270

TIMBER HOUSES

The oldest form of timber housing consisted of prepared logs or blocks placed one upon the other and structurally connected by rebated corner joints. Today, the most common form is timber framed housing (also balloon framed or half-timbered construction). Vertical loads are transmitted to the ground through structural posts giving an economic form of construction that fulfils all the requirements in relation to building physics, quality, structure and comfort. The most important precaution is to protect the façade cladding to prevent water from penetrating the timber. Plan the cladding so that the rain flows off quickly and, where splashing occurs, design for the replacement of parts. Also plan for sufficient roof overhang.

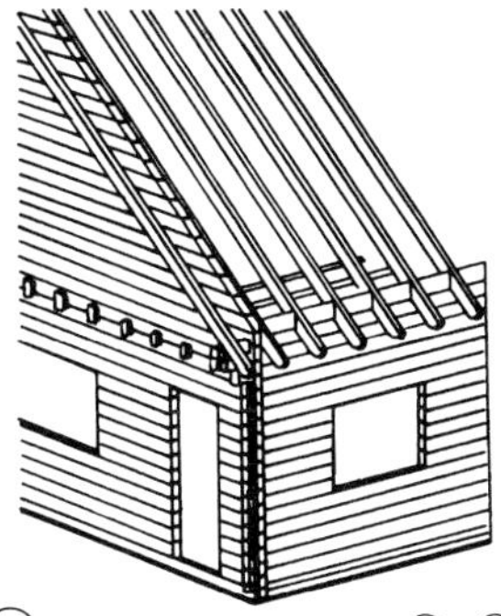

① Timber construction → ② + ③

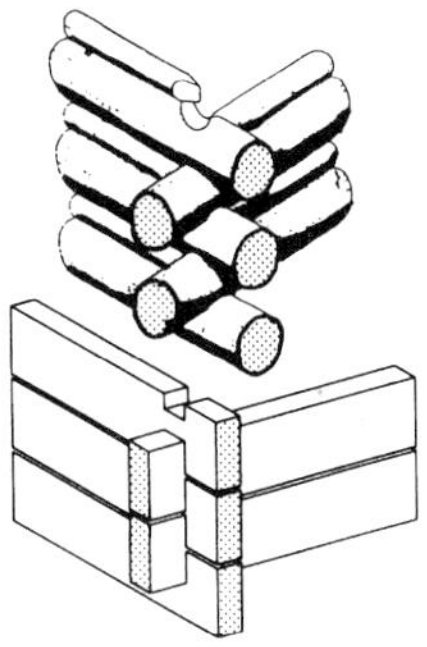

② Log and block construction methods

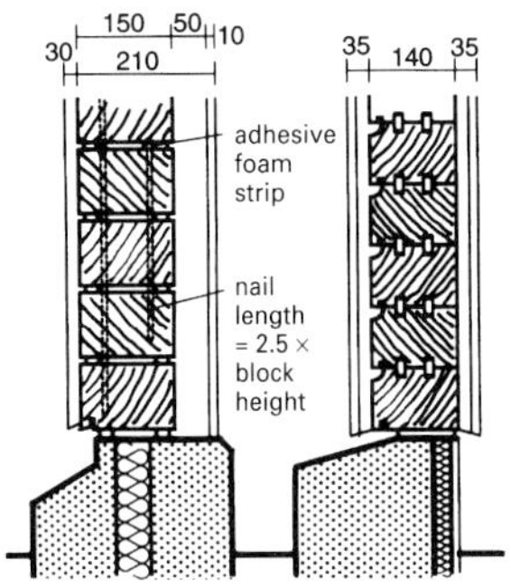

③ Solid timber walls

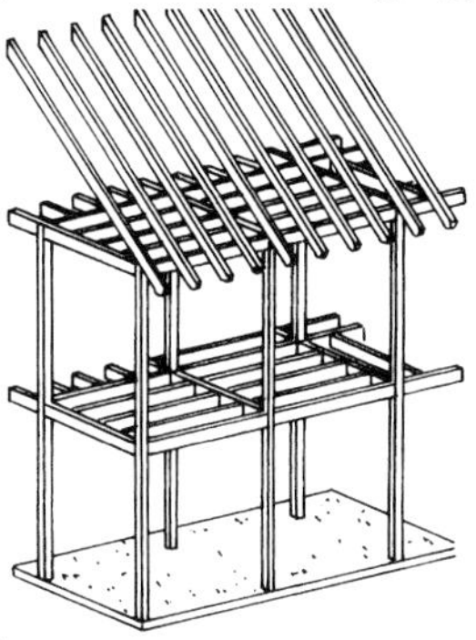

④ Timber frame

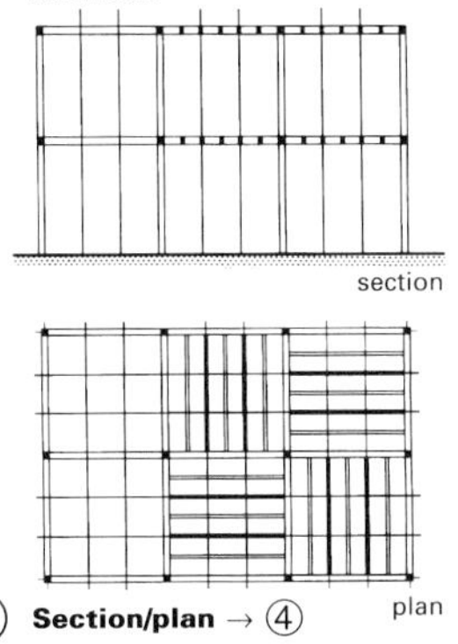

⑤ Section/plan → ④

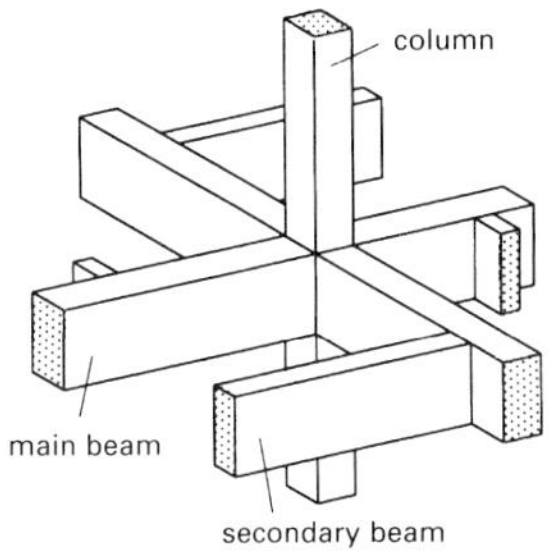

⑥ Node: continuous column

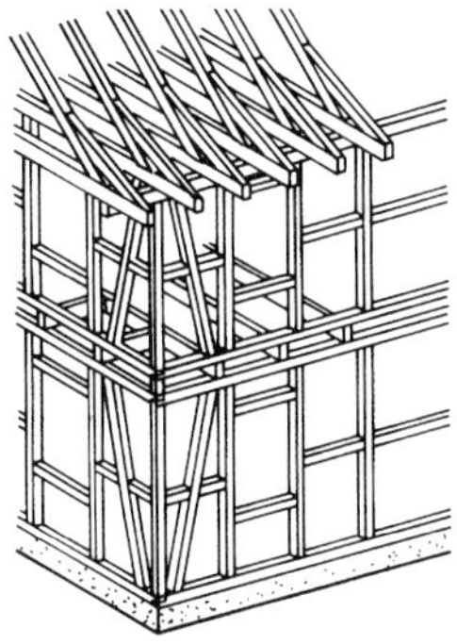

⑦ Visible frame

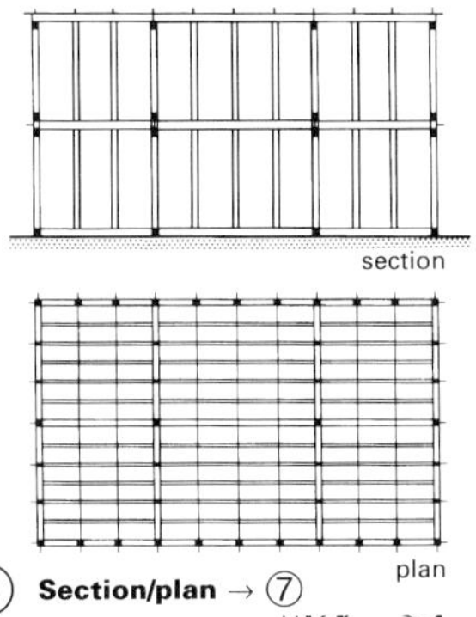

⑧ Section/plan → ⑦

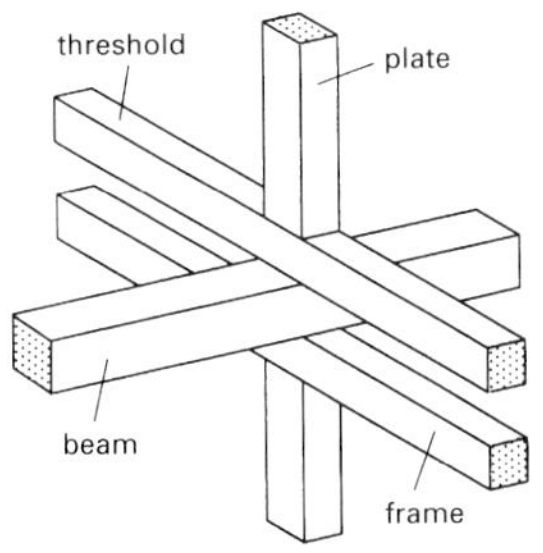

⑨ Joints in half-timbered frame

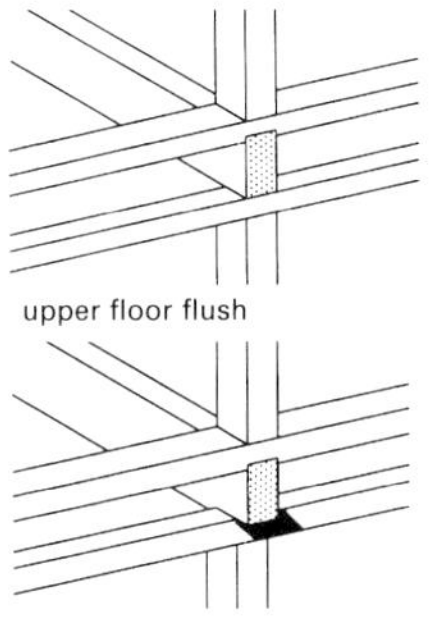

⑩ Projecting upper floors

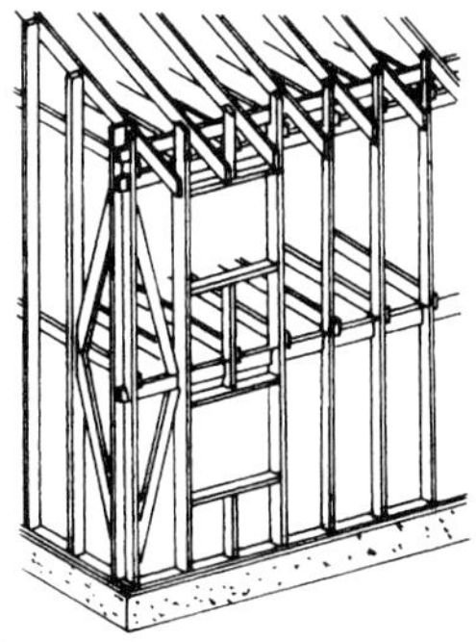

⑪ Balloon frame made with studs

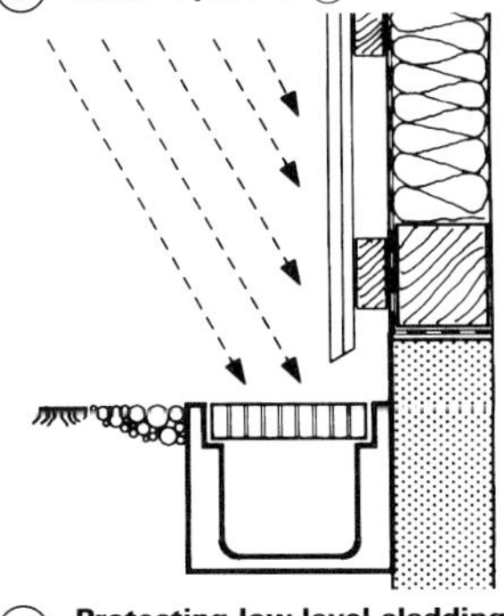

⑫ Protecting low-level cladding against water splashes

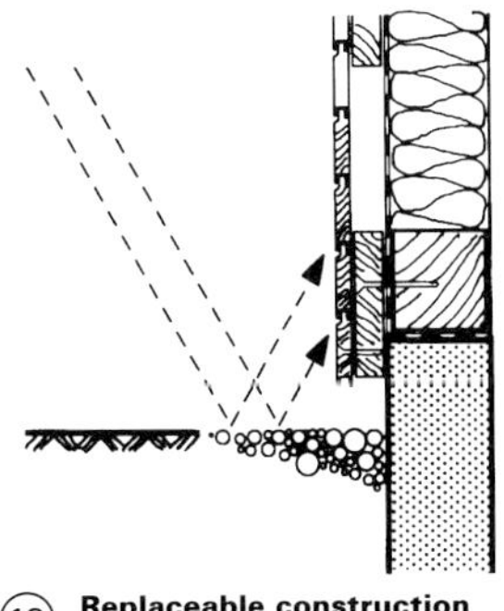

⑬ Replaceable construction of heavily weathered cladding

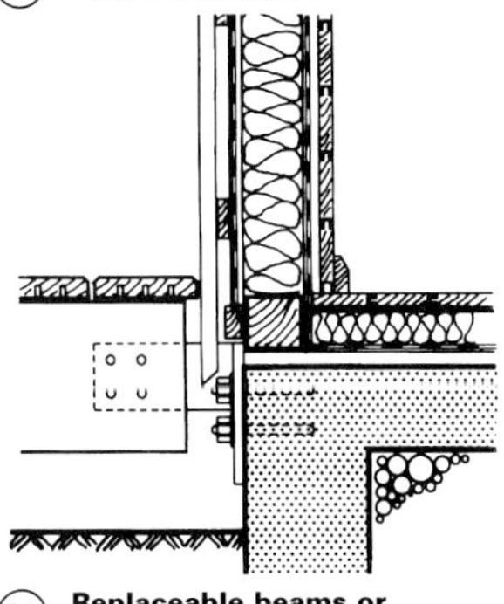

⑭ Replaceable beams or terrace supports

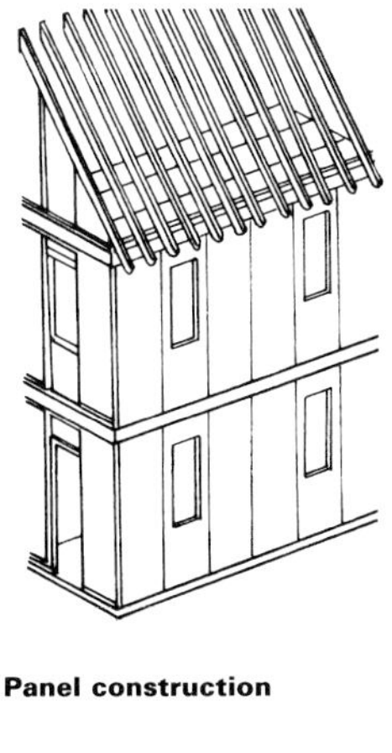

⑮ Panel construction

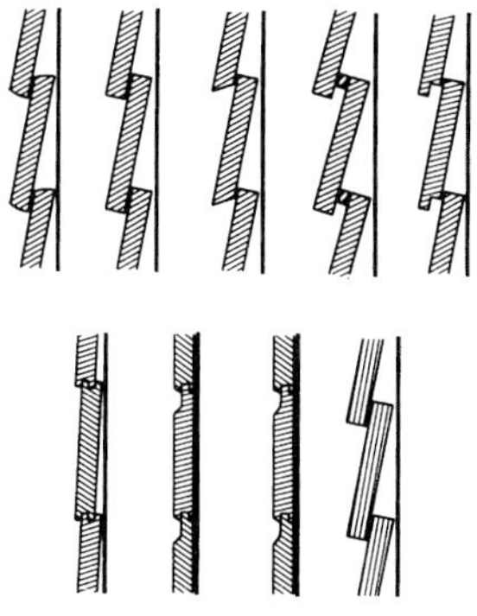

⑯ Horizontal cladding

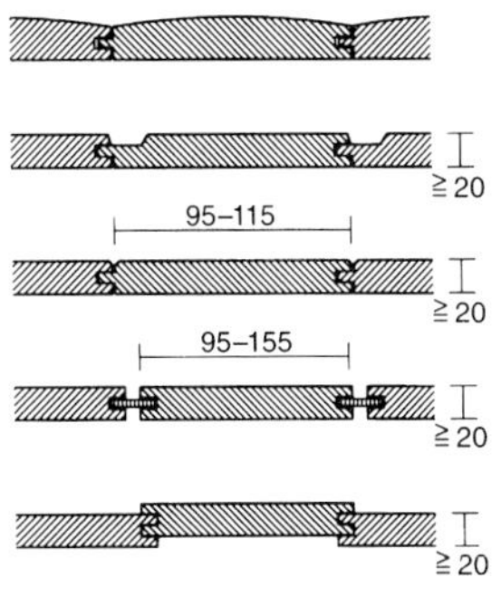

⑰ Vertical cladding

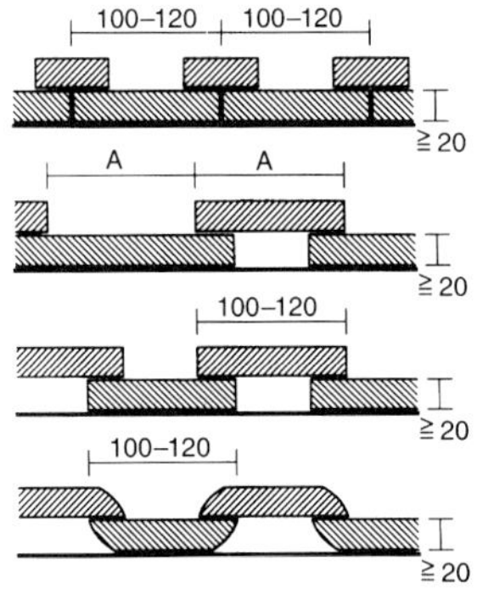

⑱ → as ⑰

271

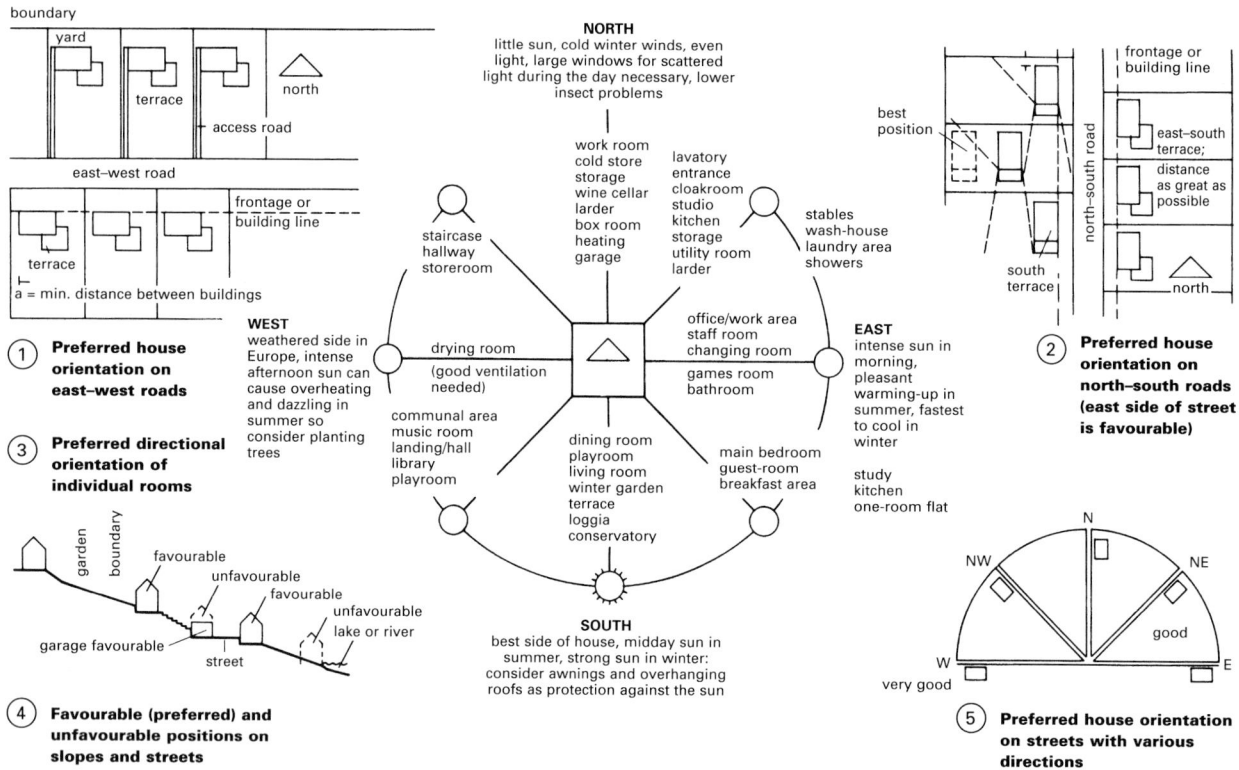

① **Preferred house orientation on east–west roads**

③ **Preferred directional orientation of individual rooms**

④ **Favourable (preferred) and unfavourable positions on slopes and streets**

② **Preferred house orientation on north–south roads (east side of street is favourable)**

⑤ **Preferred house orientation on streets with various directions**

Optimal residential sites

As a rule, sites to the west and south of towns and cities are preferred for residential development in areas where the prevailing winds are generally southerlies or westerlies (e.g. many parts of western Europe). This means the houses receive fresh air from the countryside while urban pollution is dissipated to the north and east. These latter areas, therefore, are not desirable for housing and should instead be considered for industrial buildings. Note that in mountainous areas or by lakes the wind behaviour described above may be different. For example, sunny southern and eastern slopes in the north and west of a city located in a valley basin could be sought-after locations for the construction of private homes.

Plots located on mountain slopes

Plots located on the lower side of mountain roads are particularly favourable because they offer the possibility of driving directly up to the house, where a garage can be located, and leave a tranquil rear garden with an uninterrupted view and sun. On the upper side of the street, this is far harder to provide and walls and concrete ditches are usually necessary behind the house to guard against falling rocks and collect rainwater running off the mountain.

Plots located by water

The potential nuisance from mosquitoes and foggy conditions make it inadvisable to build too close to rivers and lakes.

Orientation relative to the street

For separate houses with boundary walls, the most favourable plots are usually situated south of the street so that all auxiliary rooms, together with the entrance, are then automatically positioned facing the street. This solves any privacy problems because it leaves the main living and sleeping areas located on the quiet, sunny side (east--south--west), facing away from the street and overlooking the garden. If the plot has sufficient width, large French windows, terraces and balconies can be used to good effect. → ①

Plots are generally narrow and deep in order to keep the street side as short as possible. If the plot is situated to the north of the street, the building should be located towards the rear, despite the extra costs of a longer access. This is in order to take advantage of the sunny front garden area. Buildings on such plots can be impressive when seen from the street. → ①

Plots on the east of streets running north–south → ② are the most favourable in areas with westerly prevailing winds because gardens and living areas then face east, which is the most sheltered. Additionally, it is less likely that there will be neighbouring buildings close enough to obstruct low sun in the east. To take advantage of winter sun (low in the southern sky), the buildings must be situated close to the northern boundary so a large area of terrace can be south-facing. Plots on the west of a north–south street should be planned in a way that maximises the amount of southern sunlight received and gives an unobstructed view from the terrace. This might require the house to be built on the rear boundary → ②. The most favourable plots for houses in streets running in other directions are shown in → ⑤.

Plots adjacent to existing houses built on the sunny side have the advantage that the position and ground-plan of the new house can be designed in a way that ensures the sun will not be obstructed at any time in the future.

Room orientation

Whenever possible, all living and sleeping areas should face towards the garden on the sunny side of the house, with the utility areas on the opposite side → ③. This allows rooms that are occupied for the most time to take advantage of natural solar heating. Use of a local sun diagram (pp. 164 and 165) will indicate when the sun will shine into a room, or a part thereof, at a particular hour for any season. This information may also be used to decide which way the building should be orientated and where it should be placed to avoid being shaded by neighbouring buildings, trees and the like.

house type, buildings with attached plot	detached single family home		semi-detached house		linked houses (with yard)		terraced house		
characteristics									
1 minimum front width (m)	20	20	15	13	13.5	15 (13.5)*	5.5	5.5	7.5
2 plot depth, minimum (m) / plot depth (preferred value)	22 (25)	20 (25)	20 (25)	20 (25)	18.5 (25)	17.5 (20)	24 (26)	30	25
3 minimum size of plot (m²)	440 (500)	400 (500)	300 (375)	260 (325)	250 (338)	262 (236) (300)	130 (143)	165	188
4 additional area for separate garage or parking space (m²)	–	–	–	–	–	(30)	30	–	–
5 plot area = net land for construction (3 + 4) (m²)	440 (500)	400 (500)	300 (375)	260 (325)	250 (338)	262 (266) (330)	160 (173)	165	188
6 normal number of storeys	1	1 1/2	1 1/2	2	(1)–2	1	2		
7 average gross floor area/house (m²)	150	160	150	160	150	150	130	130	150
8 floor area index (calculated)	0.34 (0.3)	0.4 (0.32)	0.5 (0.4)	0.62 (0.5)	0.6 (0.45)	0.57 (0.45)	0.8 (0.75)	0.78	0.79
9 maximum permitted floor area index**	0.5		0.5	0.8	(0.5)–0.8	0.6	0.8		
maximum permitted land use ratio**	0.4		0.4		0.4	0.6	0.4		
10 average occupancy (occupants/dwelling)	3.5		3.5		3.5		3.5		
11 net residential density (dwellings/hectare) maximal	22	25	33	38	40	38	62	60	53
variance	20–25		26–38		29–40		50–62		
12 net residential density (occupants/hectare) maximal	77	88	116	133	140	133	217	210	186
variance	70–90		90–130		100–140		170–210		

* without garage on the property
** village and residential areas

(1) **Summary of typical housing densities**

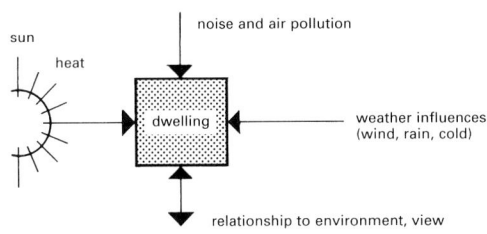

(2) **The relationship between dwellings and surroundings**

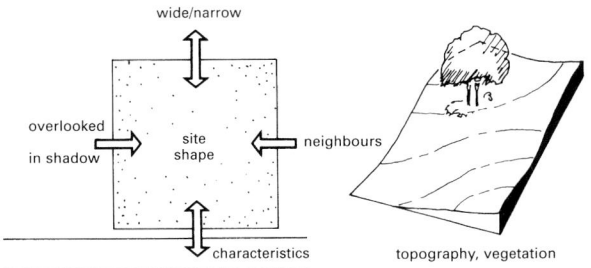

(3) **Relationship between dwelling and plot**

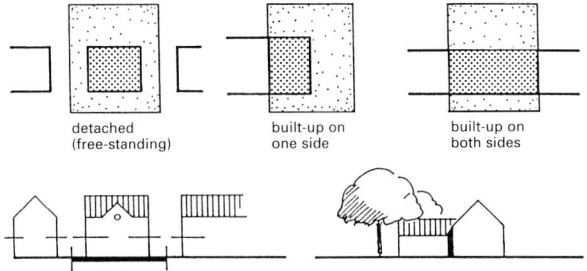

design-related integration with regard to architecture and vegetation

(4) **Positioning of the house on the plot and integration in the neighbourhood**

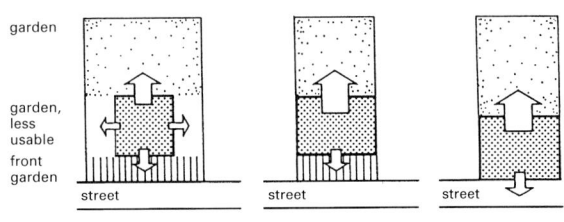

(5) **Plot zones and the impact on the design of the dwelling plan (the arrangement of rooms, functional areas)**

273

HOUSING TYPES

In addition to complimenting the overall features of the site and satisfying the requirements of access and spatial relationships between buildings the arrangement of the houses on the site plan should have an orientation based on the path of the sun. This allows the architect to produce a design that gives the optimum levels of sunlight in specific parts of the dwelling at certain times of the day.

principal use of space	principal period of use; desired orientation of the sun	
living area	afternoon to evening	
eating area/dining room	morning to evening	
children's room	afternoon to evening	
bedroom	night: morning sun desired	

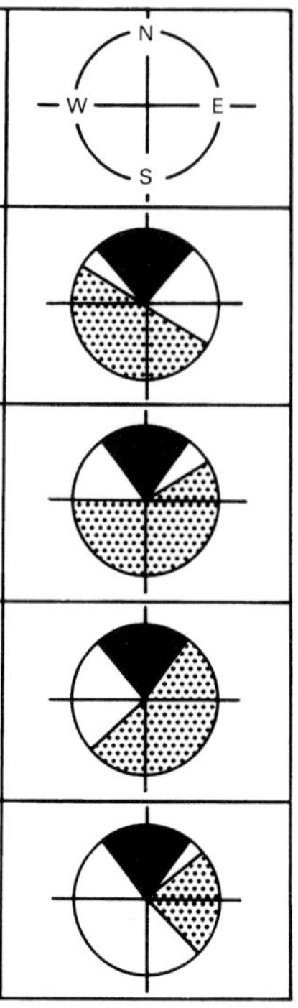

① **Orientation of living spaces**

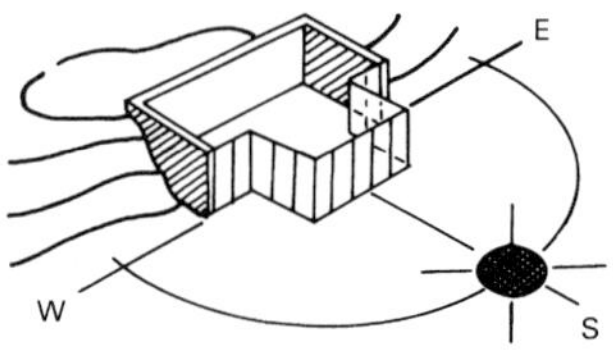

② **Orientation of living space**

③ **Annual insolation (solar orientation)**

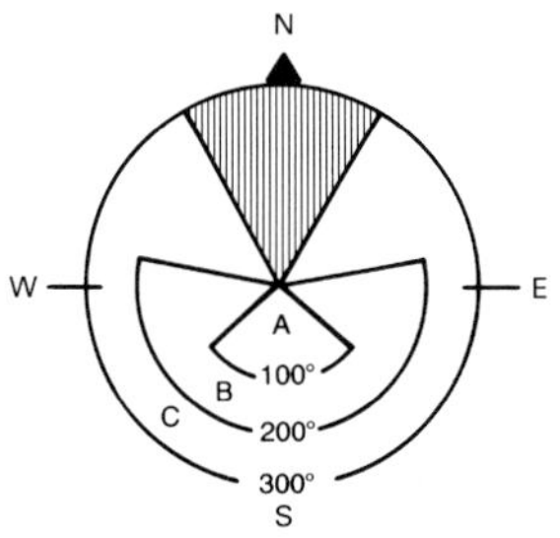

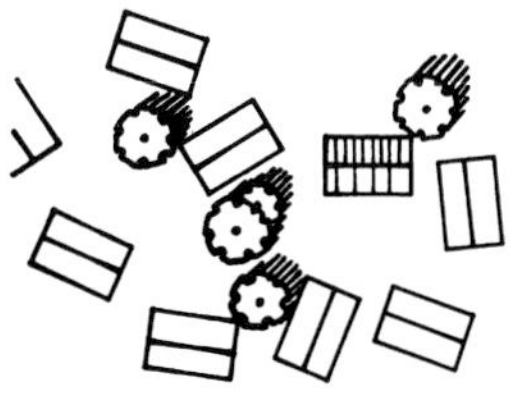

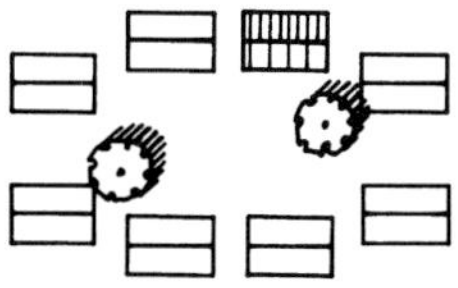

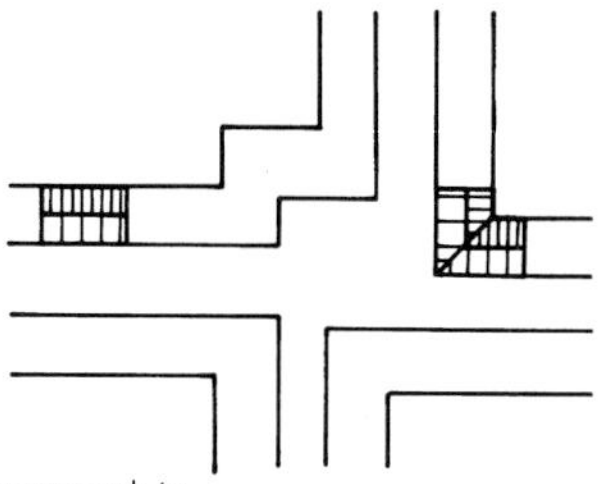

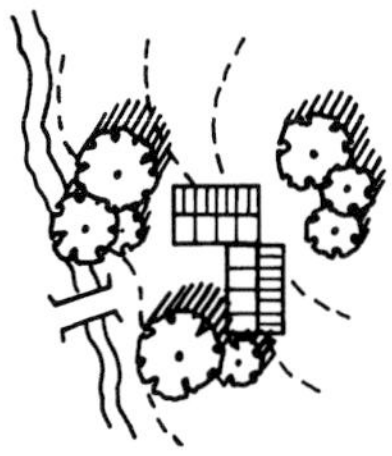

A: 100° sun on the shortest winter's day

B: 200° sun from the beginning of spring to the end of autumn

C: 300° sun on the longest summer's day

successful integration of houses into urban and country environments demands a flexible approach to designing the dwelling plan and must take into account the site-specific features (other houses in the vicinity, streets, plazas or the natural terrain) to create housing that is compatible with the surroundings

④ **In a village setting**   ⑤ **On a housing estate**   ⑥ **In an 'urban' plan**   ⑦ **In the country**

adaptability of dwellings to topography

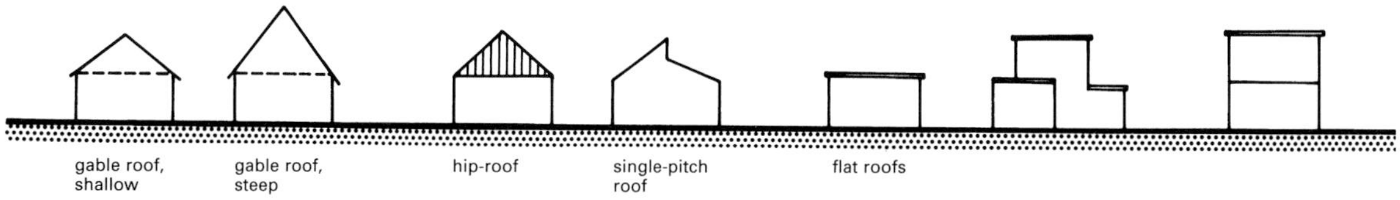

gable roof, shallow | gable roof, steep | hip-roof | single-pitch roof | flat roofs

⑧ **Level building ground**

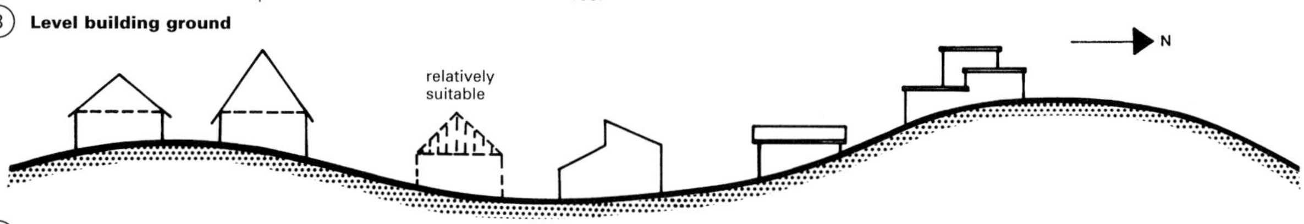

relatively suitable

⑨ **Undulating ground; building on slopes**

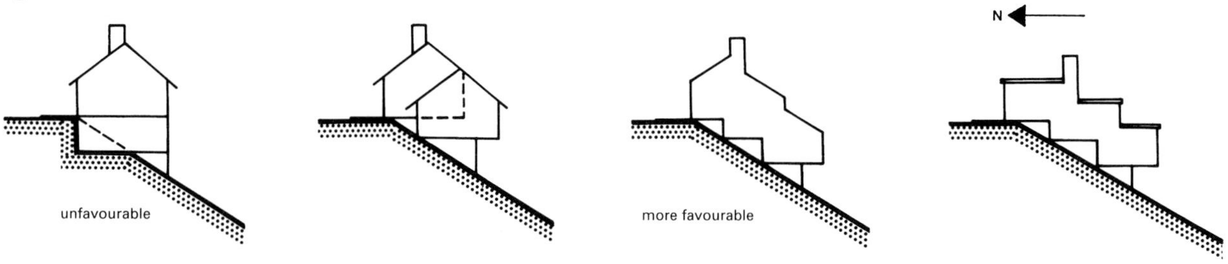

unfavourable   more favourable

⑩ **Steeply inclined slopes**

274

Examples of Typical Designs

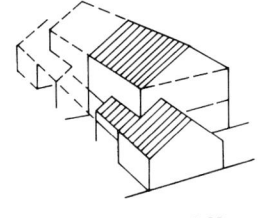

1½ GR

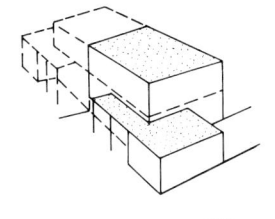

2 GR

2 FR

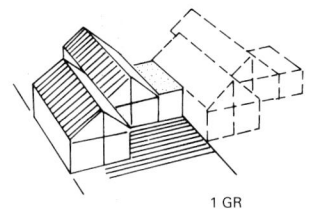

1 GR

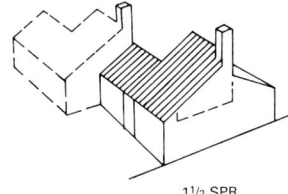

1½ SPR

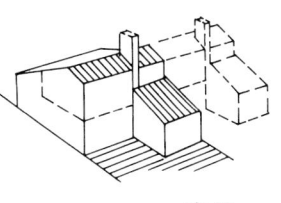

1½ GR

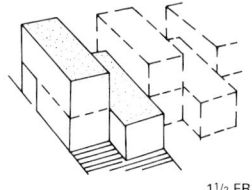

1½ FR

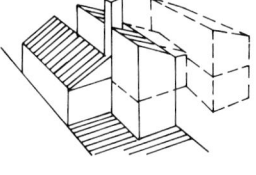

1½ SPR

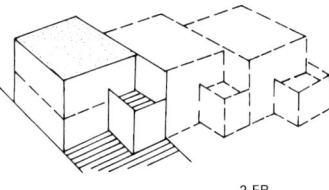

2 FR

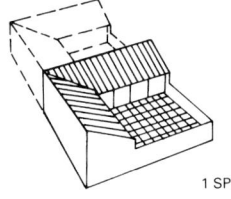

1 SPR

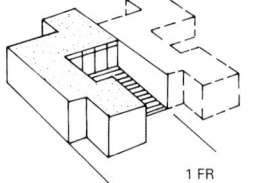

1 FR

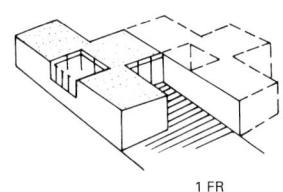

1 FR

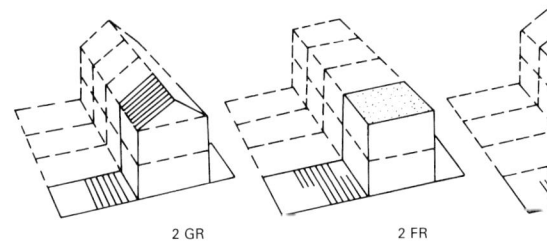

2 GR   2 FR   2 GR (staggered storeys)   3 FR

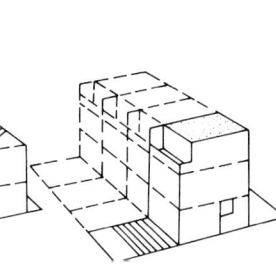

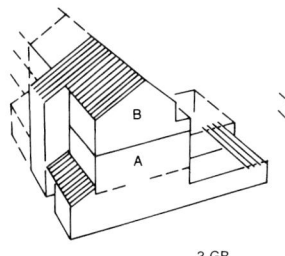

3 GR

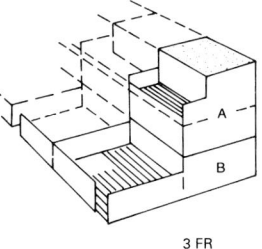

3 FR

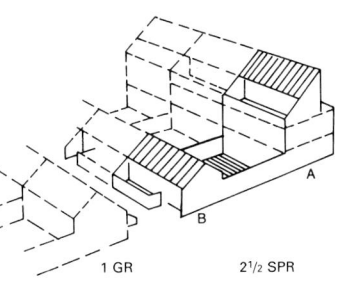

1 GR   2½ SPR

A: main residence   B: separate residence

key
1, 1½: number of storeys
GR: gable roof
SPR: single-pitch roof
FR: flat roof

HOUSING TYPES

① Semi-detached housing

Frequently employed by developers and based on the use of identical designs. Also used on single-plot projects but rarely are the two halves individually designed. Garages or car ports are often included on the side boundaries.

② Linked housing

Usually used only by developers undertaking large-scale residential projects. The groups of houses are built with uniform plans and designs and can be layed out in compact or spacious configurations. Garages or parking spaces can be incorporated in the individual plots or a separate parking area provided.

③ Houses with courtyard gardens

Can be planned as individual buildings or as groups with coordinated design. Groups are usually considered only for large developments. Include individual garages or a communal parking area.

④ Terraced houses

A shared building form that gives rows of identical (or slightly varied) houses. Parking is usually on-street or in communal car parks.

⑤ Town houses

Another shared building form resulting in rows of houses that are identical or contain a matching variety of designs. Parking space may be on the plot, on-street, or in communal car parks. As with all these examples, design coordination and regulatory agreements are necessary.

HOUSING TYPES

① Semi-detached housing

Offers wide planning freedom and solar orientation potential. Minimum size of individual plot: 375 m².

35–45°

flat roof

18–22°

section

② Linked housing

This type is economical and has space-saving benefits as well as adequate solar orientation potential. Offering high-density housing with good quality living standards, this building form is recommended. Minimum size of individual plot: 225 m².

flat roof

12–18°

section

③ Houses with courtyard gardens

Offers high-density housing and agreeable living quality combined with wide planning freedom. Minimum size of individual plot: 270 m².

flat roof

12–18°

18–22°

section

④ Terraced houses

Although they have reduced adaptability for solar orientation (unless the ground plan has been appropriately conceived), this is the most economical residential form. High-density developments that offer occupants a good living standard are possible with uniform plans.

35–40°

flat roof

section

⑤ Town houses

High density housing for urban developments using standard or individual designs.

First row (Semi-detached)

street
N
ground floor

≧ 18.00 — 13.00 — 8.0 — 7.5

ground floor   upper floor

Second row (Linked)

street
ground floor
N

18.00 — 10.00 — ≧ 25.00

ground floor   upper floor

Third row (Houses with courtyard gardens)

street
N

16.00 — 12.50 — 20.00 — 13.50

ground floor   upper floor

Fourth row (Terraced)

street
N   street

11.50 — 24.00 — ≧ 10.00
A 6.00   B 6.00   AI   BI

ground floor   upper floor

Fifth row (Town houses)

≧ 25.00
≧ 8.00   ≧ 8.00
3–4 storeys

development plan

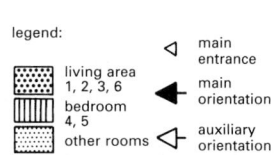

legend:

living area 1, 2, 3, 6
bedroom 4, 5
other rooms

◁ main entrance
◀ main orientation
◁ auxiliary orientation

276

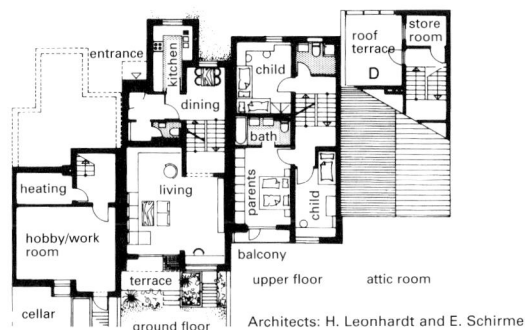

Architects: H. Leonhardt and E. Schirmer

(1) **Row of terraced houses with offset levels**

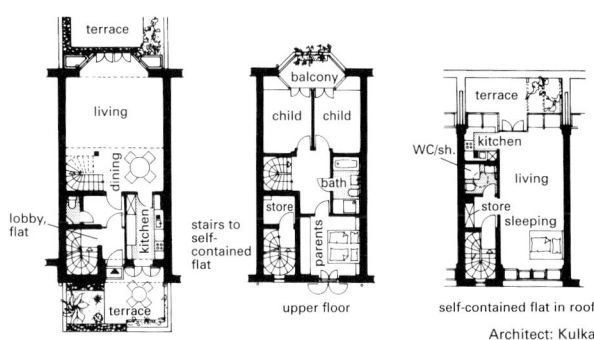

Architect: Kulka

(2) **Terraced houses with a self-contained flat in the roof**

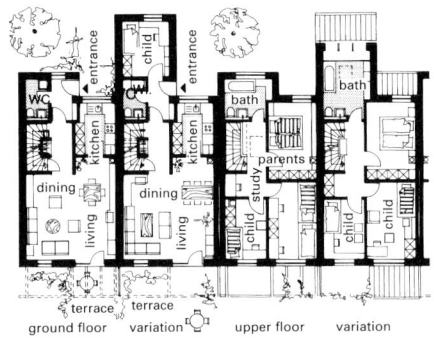

Architects: K. and B. Woicke

(3) **Terraced houses with varying depths**

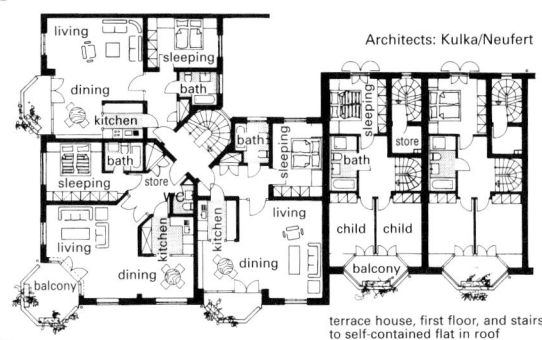

Architects: Kulka/Neufert

terrace house, first floor, and stairs to self-contained flat in roof

(4) **Corner solution for terraced houses**

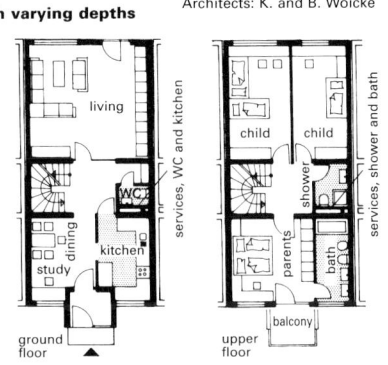

(5) **Terraced houses: all services contained in one duct**

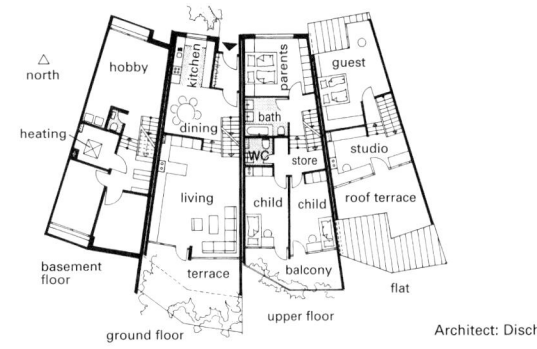

Architect: Disch

(6) **Terraced houses orientated for favourable lighting and sunshine**

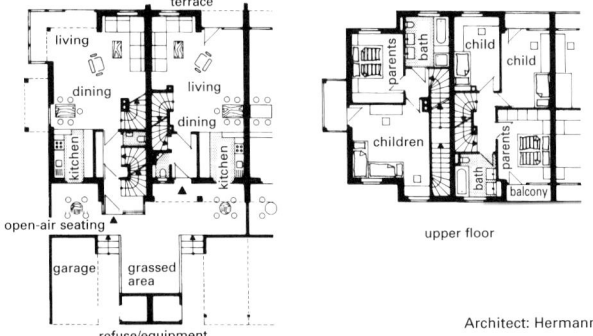

Architect: Hermann

(7) **Ground floor → (8)**

(8) **Basement and top floor → (7)**

(9) **Terraced houses with transverse stairs**

(10) **Terraced houses with garage space**

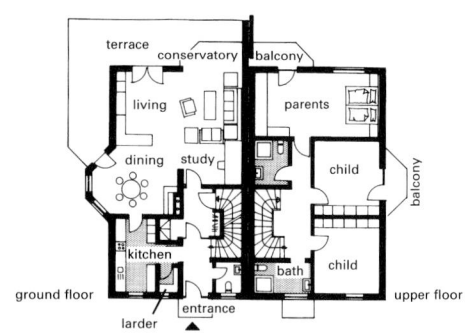

① Semi-detached houses with dining room and surrounding terrace

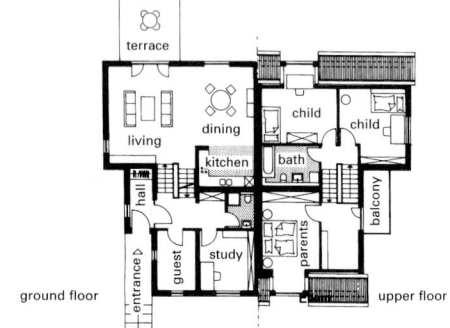

② Semi-detached houses with off-set levels

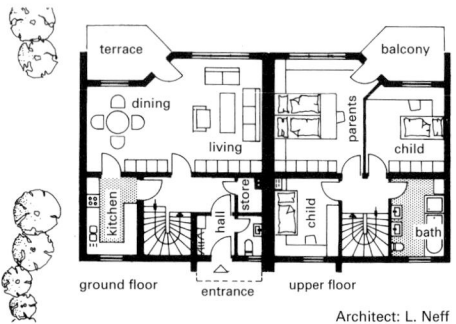

Architect: L. Neff

③ Semi-detached houses with square plan

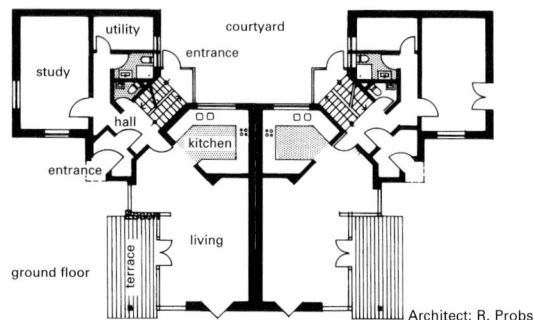

Architect: R. Probst

④ L-shaped semi-detached houses with courtyard

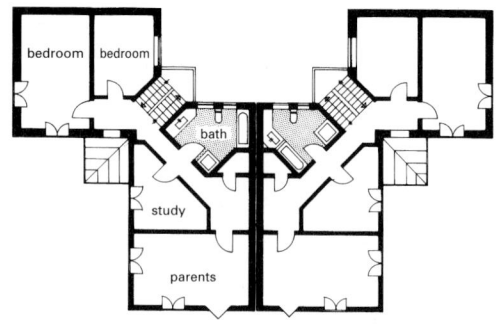

⑤ Upper floor → ④

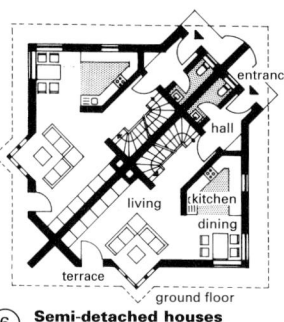

⑥ Semi-detached houses divided diagonally

⑦ Upper floor → ⑥

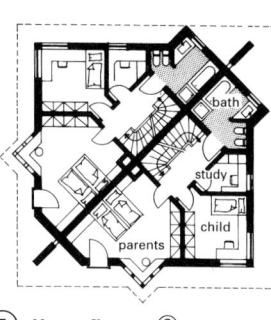

⑧ Semi-detached houses with front entrance

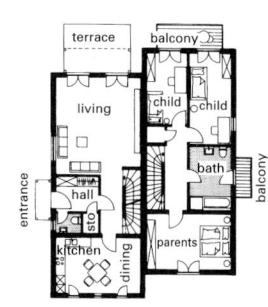

⑨ Semi-detached houses with side entrance

⑩ L-shaped semi-detached houses with two terraces

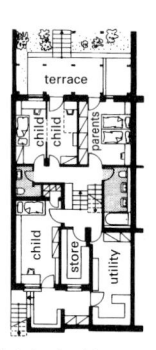

⑪ Semi-detached house basement

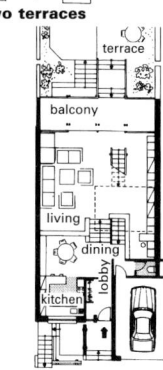

⑫ Ground floor

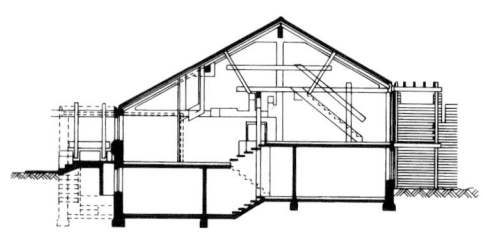

Architects: Höyng, Nettels, Sandfort

⑬ Cross-section → ⑪ + ⑫

278

COURTYARD HOUSES

By using courtyards it is possible to provide additional living space that is both sheltered and private. In contrast to detached housing, courtyard developments allow a high quality of life to be offered to occupants using only a comparatively small amount of land area.

Enclosed courtyards can be as small as a living room but might need to be artificially lit if the surrounding walls are all higher than one storey. If, however, a garden courtyard is required much larger areas are desirable to take full advantage of the sunlight and allow a full range of plants to be considered.

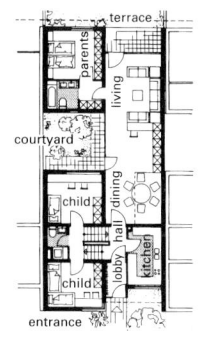

① **Ground floor → ②**

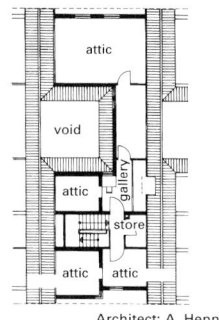

Architect: A. Hennig

② **Upper floor**

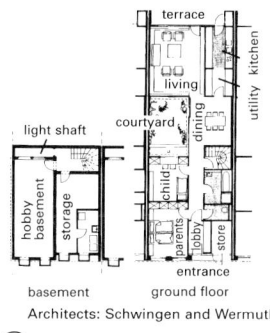

Architects: Schwingen and Wermuth

③ **180 m² living area**

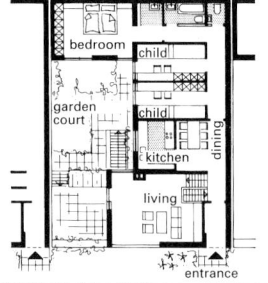

Architects: Kuhn, Boskamp and Partners

④ **Courtyard house with directly accessible open area**

Architects: Latty and Tucker

⑤ **House with garden and service court**

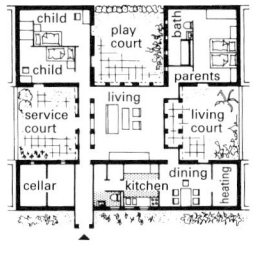

Architect: Ungers

⑥ **Differentiated courtyards**

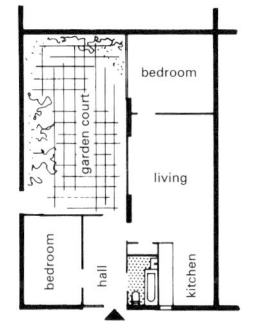

⑦ **Ground floor and courtyard**

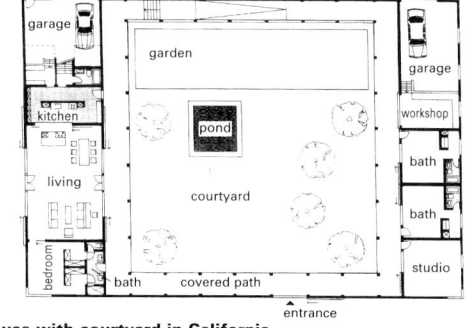

⑧ **House with courtyard in California**

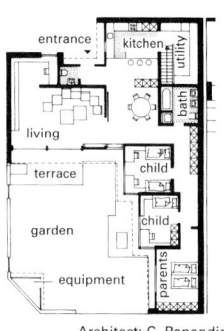

Architect: C. Papendick

⑨ **Courtyard house, ground floor**

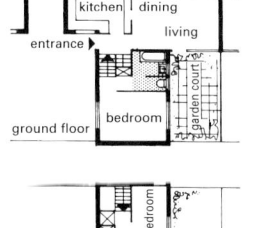

Architect: Chamberlin

⑩ **Courtyard house on two floors**

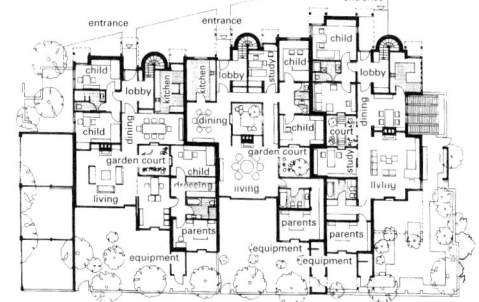

Architect: Bahlo, Köhnke, Stosberg and Partners

⑪ **Single-family courtyard houses**

Architect: Butler

⑫ **Two-storey patio house**

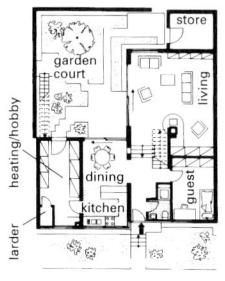

⑬ **Ground floor**

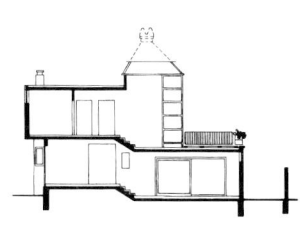

⑭ **Upper floor**

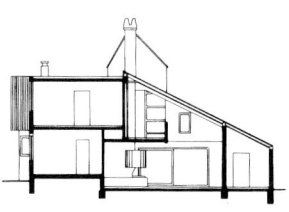

Architects: Jacobs and Wiedemann

⑮ **Section → ⑬ + ⑭**

⑯ **Section**

Architect: L. Neff

Architect: R. Gray

① Ground floor → ② ② Upper floor ③ Upper floor → ④ ④ Ground floor

⑤ Ground floor → ⑥ ⑥ Upper floor ⑦ Ground floor → ⑧ ⑧ Upper floor

Architect: Brons

⑨ Ground floor → ⑩ – ⑫ ⑩ Upper floor ⑪ Attic floor ⑫ Section

Architects: Tissi and Pötz

⑬ Ground floor → ⑭ – ⑯ ⑭ Upper floor ⑮ Section ⑯ Section

Architect: Heckrott

⑰ Ground floor → ⑱ – ⑳ ⑱ Upper floor ⑲ Attic floor ⑳ Section

HOUSES WITH CONSERVATORIES

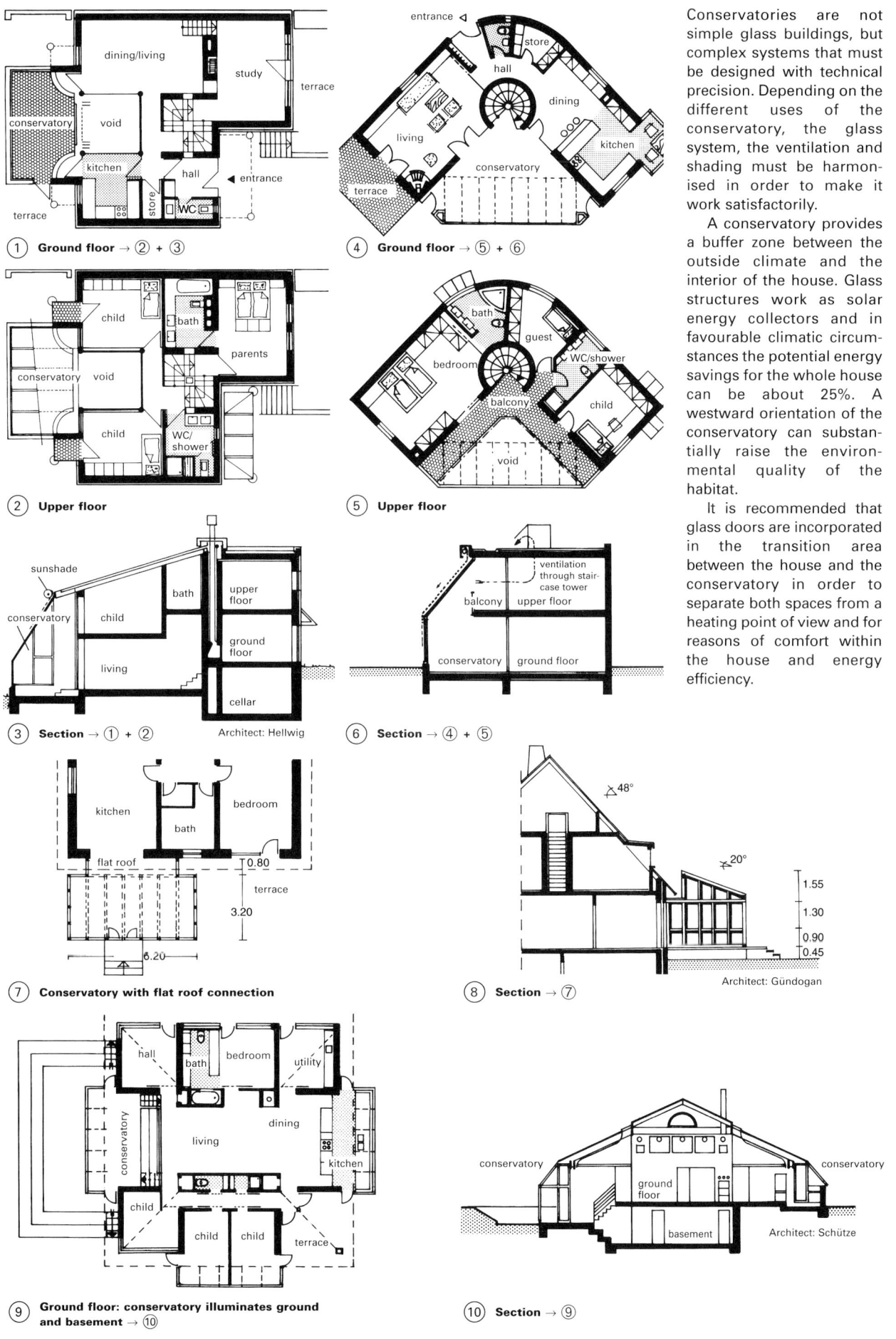

① **Ground floor** → ② + ③

② **Upper floor**

③ **Section** → ① + ②   Architect: Hellwig

④ **Ground floor** → ⑤ + ⑥

⑤ **Upper floor**

⑥ **Section** → ④ + ⑤

⑦ **Conservatory with flat roof connection**

⑧ **Section** → ⑦   Architect: Gündogan

⑨ **Ground floor: conservatory illuminates ground and basement** → ⑩

⑩ **Section** → ⑨   Architect: Schütze

Conservatories are not simple glass buildings, but complex systems that must be designed with technical precision. Depending on the different uses of the conservatory, the glass system, the ventilation and shading must be harmonised in order to make it work satisfactorily.

A conservatory provides a buffer zone between the outside climate and the interior of the house. Glass structures work as solar energy collectors and in favourable climatic circumstances the potential energy savings for the whole house can be about 25%. A westward orientation of the conservatory can substantially raise the environmental quality of the habitat.

It is recommended that glass doors are incorporated in the transition area between the house and the conservatory in order to separate both spaces from a heating point of view and for reasons of comfort within the house and energy efficiency.

HOUSES AND RESIDENTIAL BUILDINGS

281

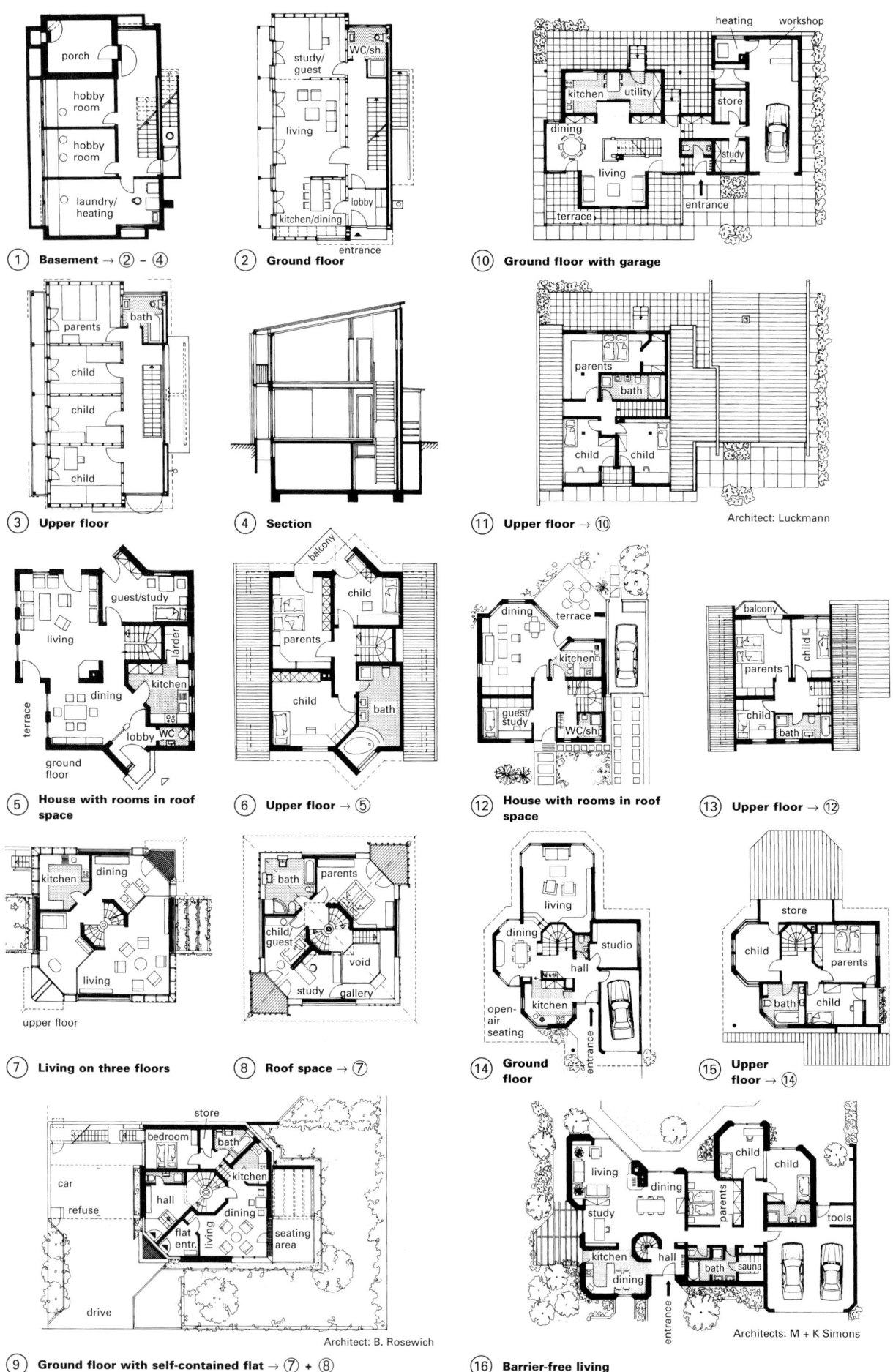

HOUSES AND RESIDENTIAL BUILDINGS

① **Basement → ② – ④**

② **Ground floor**

⑩ **Ground floor with garage**

③ **Upper floor**

④ **Section**

⑪ **Upper floor → ⑩**

Architect: Luckmann

⑤ **House with rooms in roof space**

⑥ **Upper floor → ⑤**

⑫ **House with rooms in roof space**

⑬ **Upper floor → ⑫**

⑦ **Living on three floors**

⑧ **Roof space → ⑦**

⑭ **Ground floor**

⑮ **Upper floor → ⑭**

Architect: B. Rosewich

⑨ **Ground floor with self-contained flat → ⑦ + ⑧**

Architects: M + K Simons

⑯ **Barrier-free living**

SQUARE, CUBIC AND TENT-SHAPE FORMS

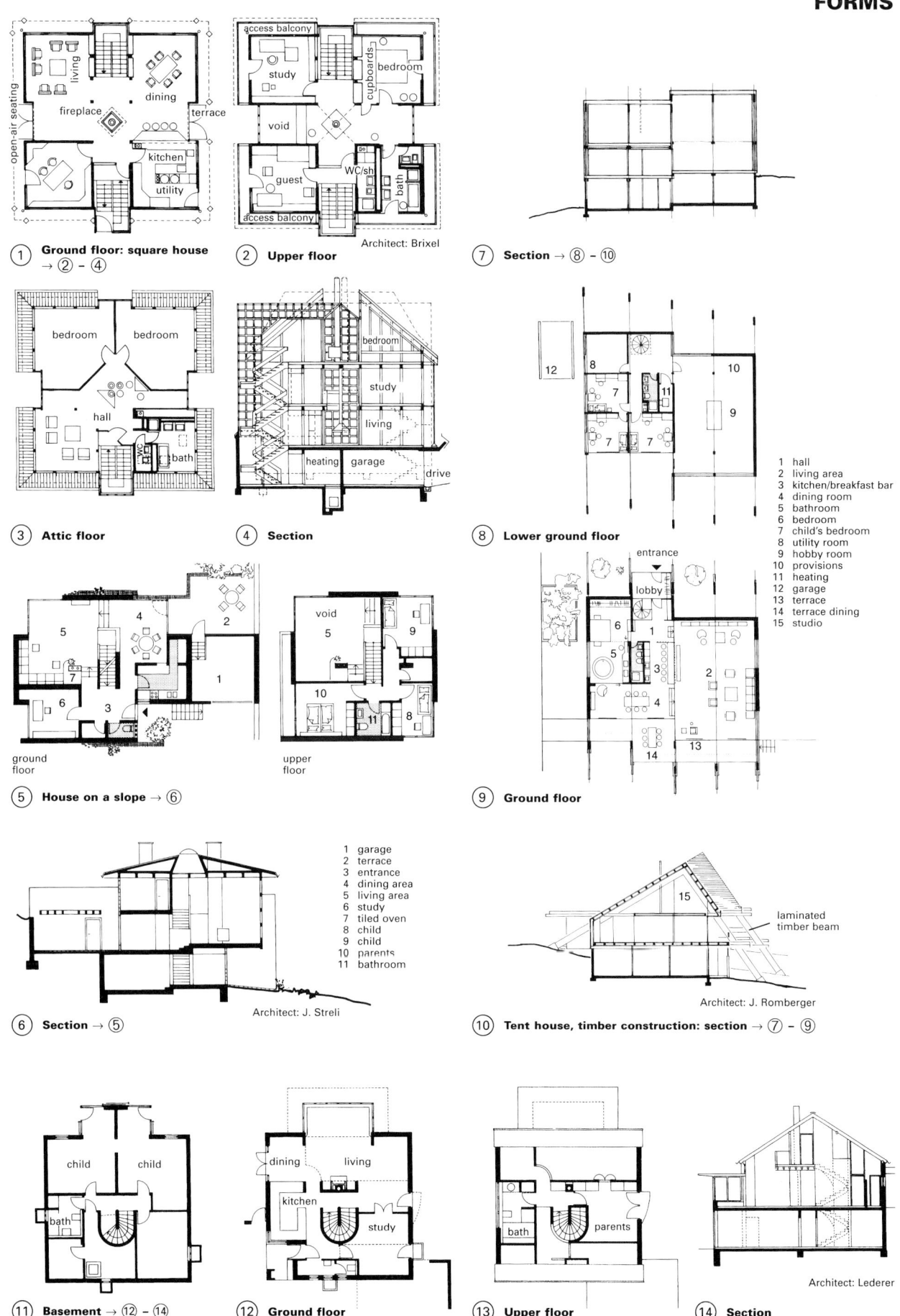

(1) **Ground floor: square house** → (2) – (4)

(2) **Upper floor**

Architect: Brixel

(3) **Attic floor**

(4) **Section**

(5) **House on a slope** → (6)

(6) **Section** → (5)

Architect: J. Streli

1 garage
2 terrace
3 entrance
4 dining area
5 living area
6 study
7 tiled oven
8 child
9 child
10 parents
11 bathroom

(7) **Section** → (8) – (10)

(8) **Lower ground floor**

(9) **Ground floor**

1 hall
2 living area
3 kitchen/breakfast bar
4 dining room
5 bathroom
6 bedroom
7 child's bedroom
8 utility room
9 hobby room
10 provisions
11 heating
12 garage
13 terrace
14 terrace dining
15 studio

(10) **Tent house, timber construction: section** → (7) – (9)

Architect: J. Romberger

(11) **Basement** → (12) – (14)

(12) **Ground floor**

(13) **Upper floor**

(14) **Section**

Architect: Lederer

283

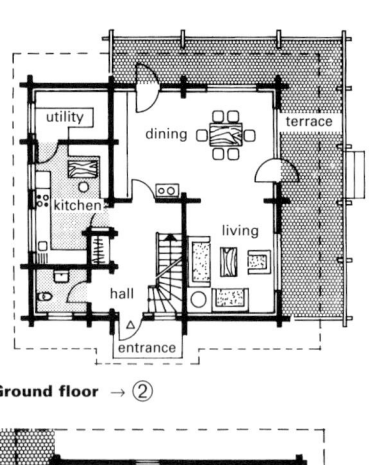

① **Ground floor** → ②

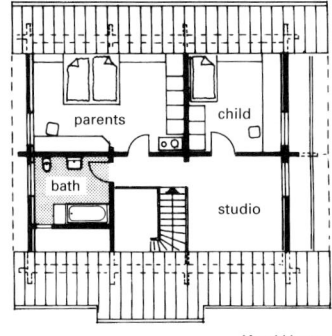

② **Upper floor**   Kemi Haus

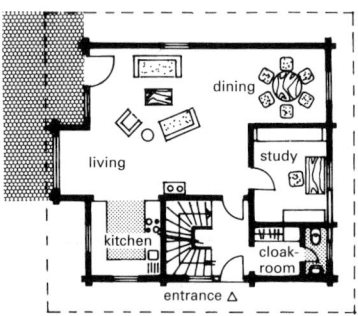

③ **Ground floor** → ④

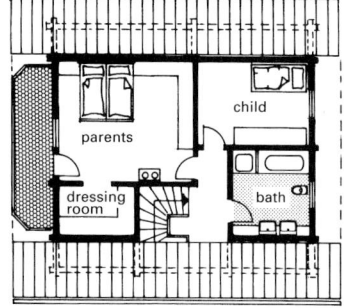

④ **Upper floor**   Gruber Holzhaus

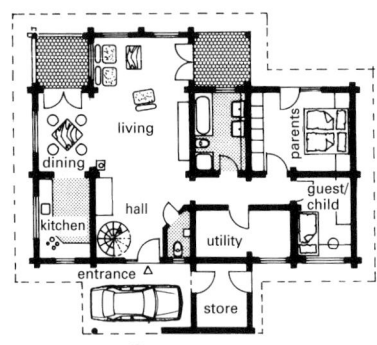

⑤ **Ground floor** → ⑥

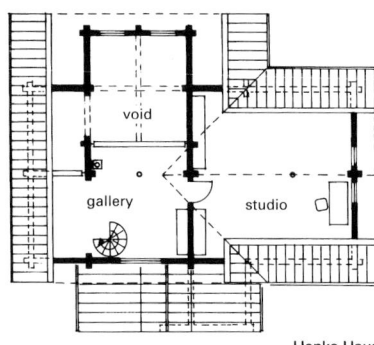

⑥ **Upper floor**   Honka Haus

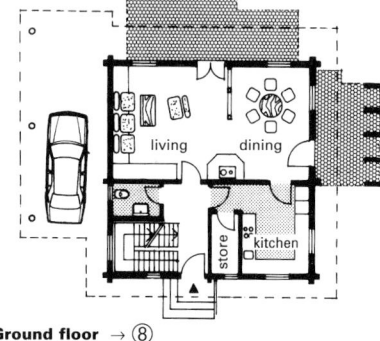

⑦ **Ground floor** → ⑧

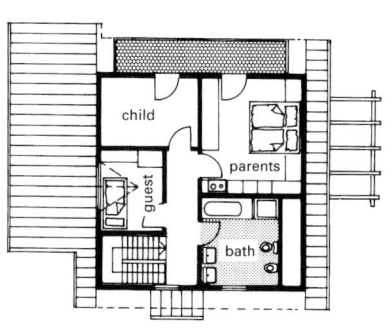

⑧ **Attic floor**   Iller Haus

ECOLOGICAL BUILDING

The timber house is the epitome of natural, traditional and healthy living. This form of construction conforms to many clients' ecological, biological and, not least, economical, requirements. It uses selected solid timbers, natural insulation materials (e.g. cotton, wool or cork), natural materials for the roofing (e.g. clay tiles), and plant-based paints for decoration, all leading to a high standard of eco-friendliness.

Usually, only the slow growing timbers from northern countries are used for this type of construction. Unlimited life and low maintenance are the rule: for example, red cedar, as it is commonly known, contains a tannin which acts as a natural wood preservative, making impregnation unnecessary. Deeply overhanging roofs are used to shelter the façades. Manufacturers offer several types of external wall construction. Double-block construction consists usually of two identical leafs containing an insulation layer between. Single-leaf log walls produce the typical traditional atmosphere of the log cabin. The purchaser has the choice of round logs or squared blocks.

Many timber houses can be freely planned to meet the client's requirements. The client also has a choice of which type of timber to use (spruce, larch, cedar). Many suppliers offer self-build options together with assistance from the firm's construction specialists.

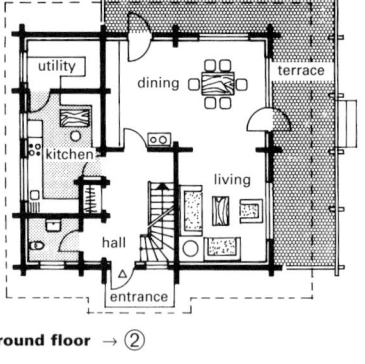

Architects: Baker-Brown & McKay

⑨ **Ground floor**

1 bathroom extractor
2 ventilation/windows
3 stepped ventilation to under-floor cavity
4 cavity
5 solid-fuel heater flue
6 boiler flue
7 air intake to heating
8 kitchen extractor
9 boiler
10 air supply
11 solid-fuel heater flue taken down to floor level for cleaning access
12 extractor, bath and WC
13 solid-fuel heater
14 air supply to open windows
15 fresh air intake to house

16 automatic vent to prevent overheating
17 solar energy pre-heats conservatory
18 conservatory

19 ventilation duct from cavity to conservatory
20 floor stores heat pre-heats the air ducted to the conservatory

⑩ **Diagram of energy system** → ⑨

HOUSE TYPES: EXAMPLES

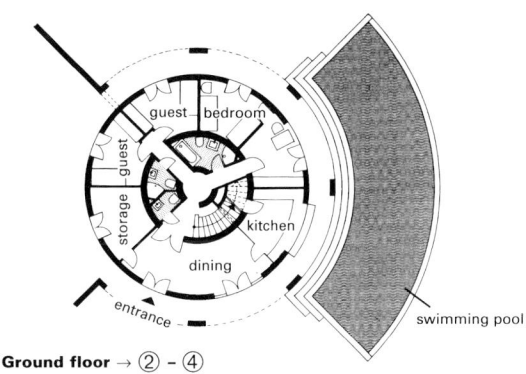

① **Ground floor → ② – ④**

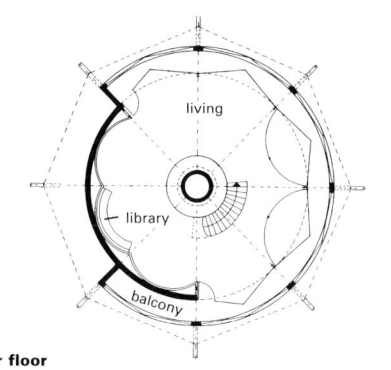

② **Upper floor**

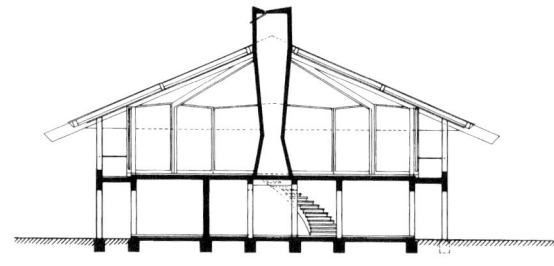

③ **Section**

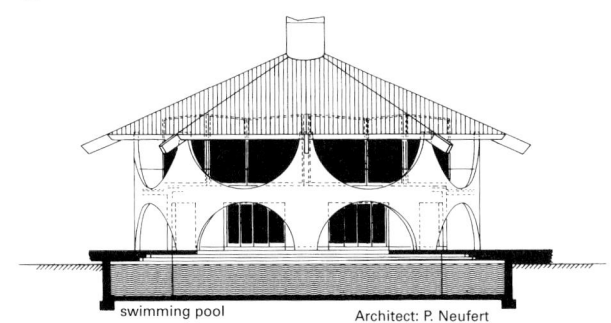

④ **View from south and section through swimming pool**

Architect: P. Neufert

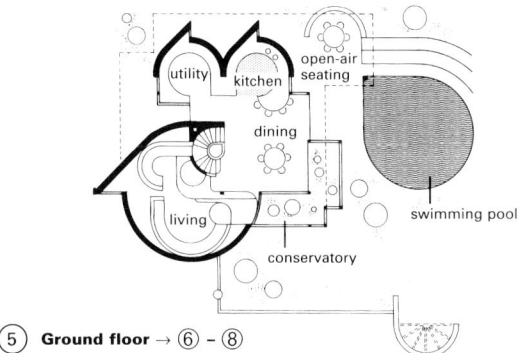

⑤ **Ground floor → ⑥ – ⑧**

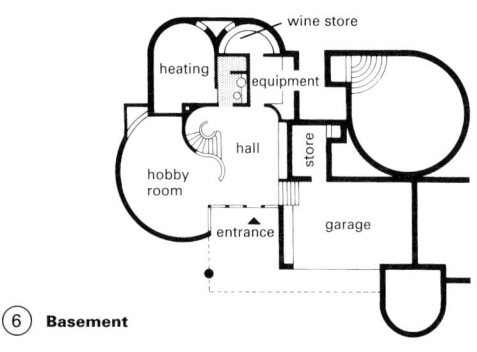

⑥ **Basement**

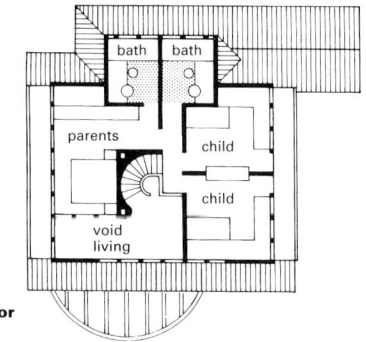

⑦ **Upper floor**

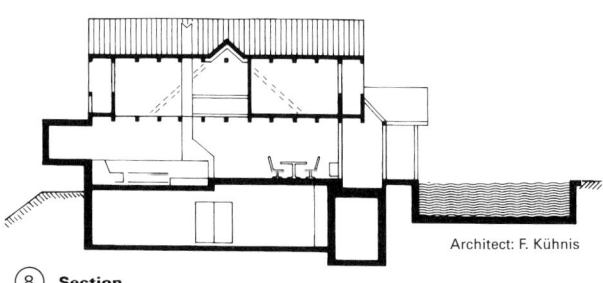

⑧ **Section**

Architect: F. Kühnis

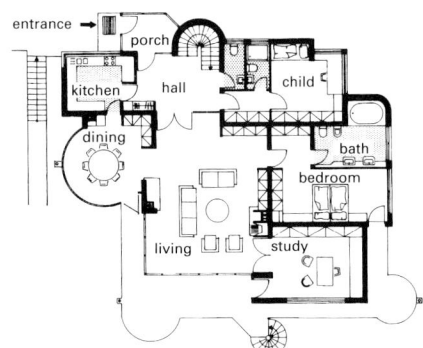

⑨ **Ground floor**

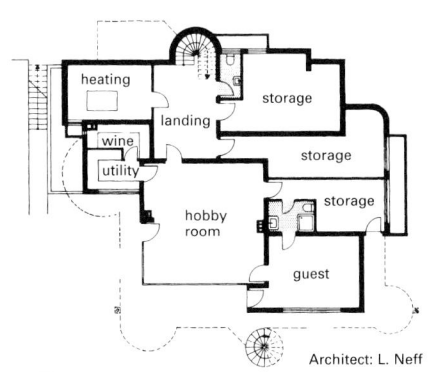

⑩ **Lower floor**

Architect: L. Neff

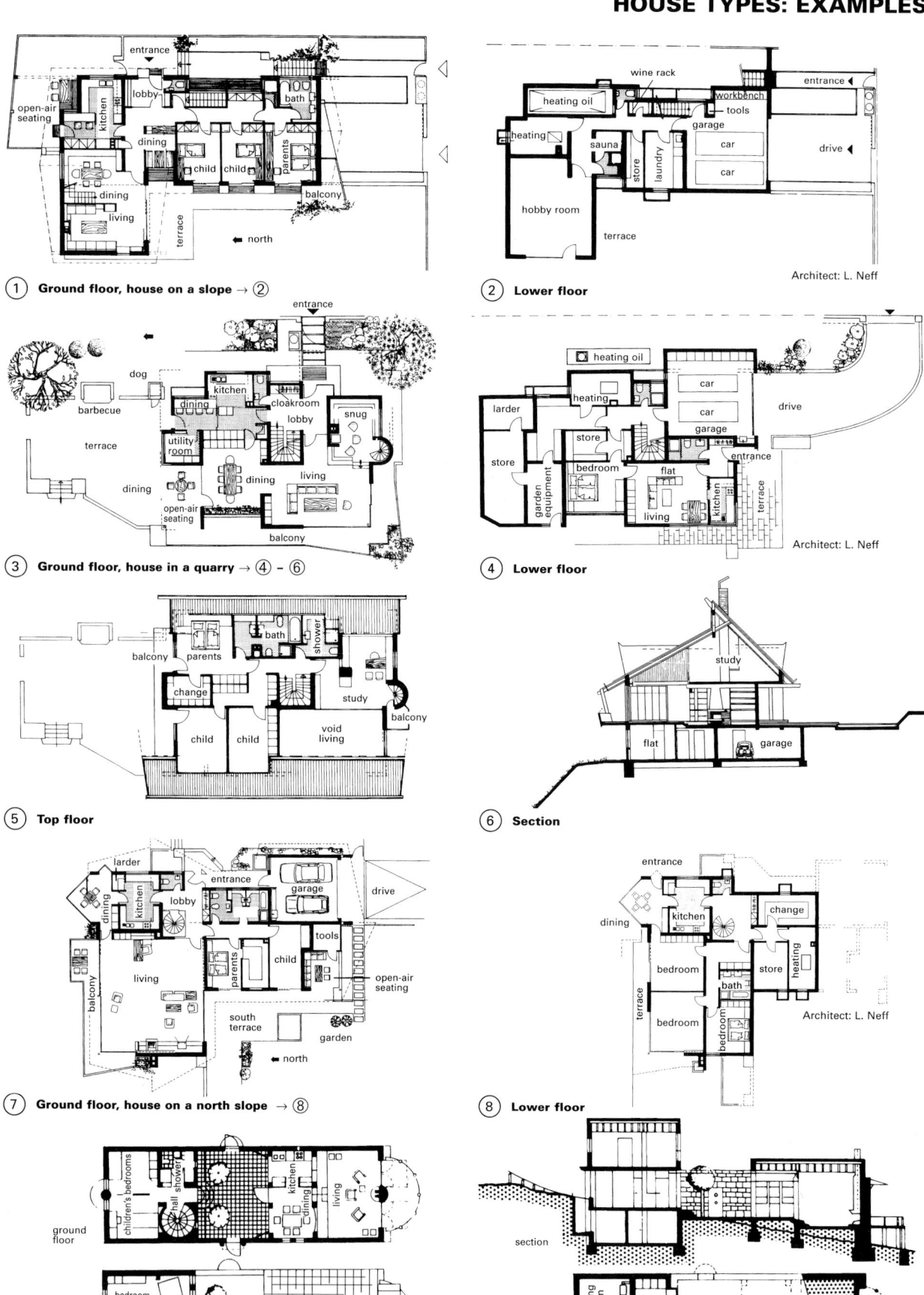

① **Ground floor, house on a slope** → ②

② **Lower floor**
Architect: L. Neff

③ **Ground floor, house in a quarry** → ④ – ⑥

④ **Lower floor**
Architect: L. Neff

⑤ **Top floor**

⑥ **Section**

⑦ **Ground floor, house on a north slope** → ⑧

⑧ **Lower floor**
Architect: L. Neff

⑨ **Ground and upper floors** → ⑩

⑩ **Section and cellar**
Architect: V.D. Valentyn

(1) **Basement, house on a north slope** → (2) + (3)

(2) **Ground floor**

(3) **Upper floor**

Architect: L. Neff

(4) **Basement** → (5) + (6)

(5) **Ground floor**

(6) **Upper floor**

(7) **Section, small house without basement** → (8) + (9)

(8) **Ground floor**

(9) **Upper floor**

(10) **Basement** → (11) – (13)

(11) **Top floor**

(12) **Ground floor**

(13) **Section**

Architects: Kaplan and Könnemund

287

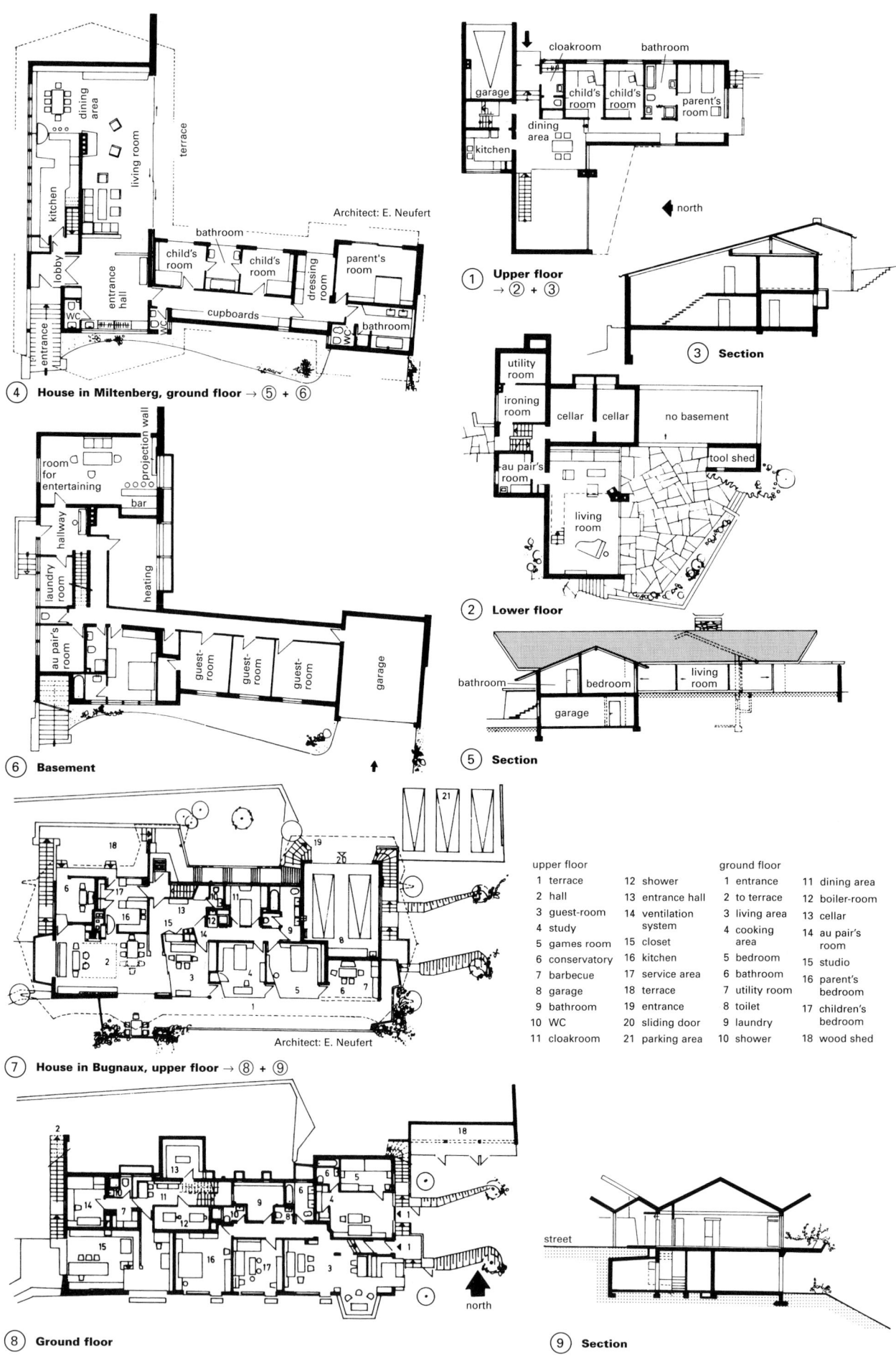

HOUSES ON SLOPES

HOUSES AND RESIDENTIAL BUILDINGS

(4) **House in Miltenberg, ground floor** → (5) + (6)

Architect: E. Neufert

(6) **Basement**

(1) **Upper floor** → (2) + (3)

(3) **Section**

(2) **Lower floor**

(5) **Section**

(7) **House in Bugnaux, upper floor** → (8) + (9)

Architect: E. Neufert

upper floor
1 terrace
2 hall
3 guest-room
4 study
5 games room
6 conservatory
7 barbecue
8 garage
9 bathroom
10 WC
11 cloakroom
12 shower
13 entrance hall
14 ventilation system
15 closet
16 kitchen
17 service area
18 terrace
19 entrance
20 sliding door
21 parking area

ground floor
1 entrance
2 to terrace
3 living area
4 cooking area
5 bedroom
6 bathroom
7 utility room
8 toilet
9 laundry
10 shower
11 dining area
12 boiler-room
13 cellar
14 au pair's room
15 studio
16 parent's bedroom
17 children's bedroom
18 wood shed

(8) **Ground floor**

(9) **Section**

288

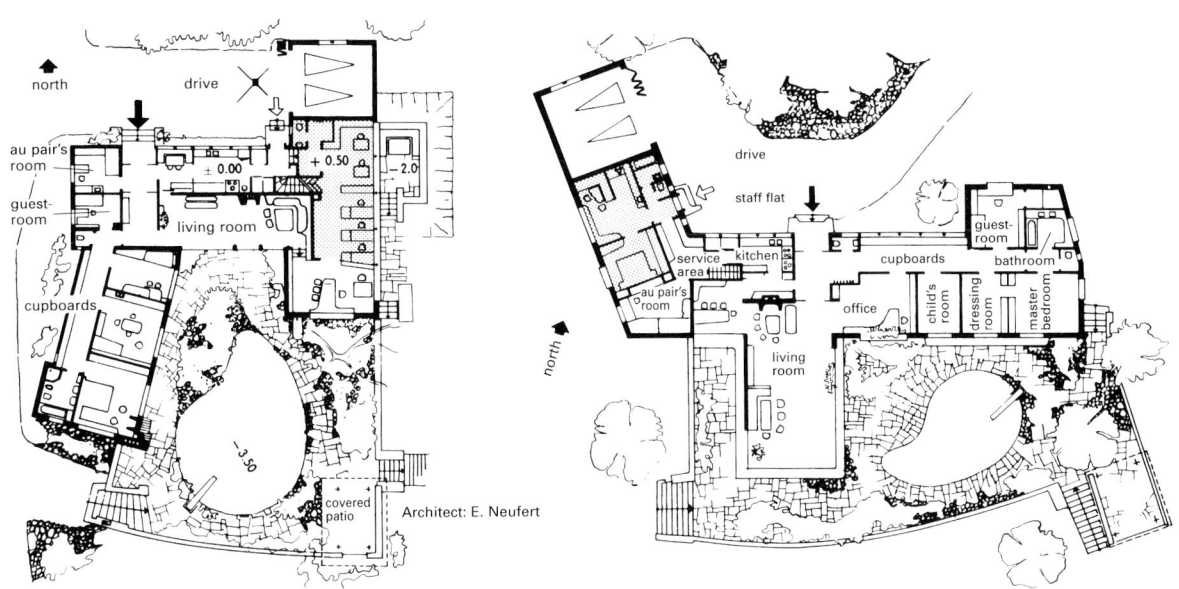

Architect: E. Neufert

Architect: E. Neufert

studio and service rooms are near the side entrance, with the office between studio and living room;
further draughting rooms with north light are situated above the kitchen;
the bedrooms are on the east side, sheltering the residential area (located to the north) from the wind and preserving the view;
the covered outdoor patio gets western sun

(1) **Architect's house: scale 1:500**

(2) **Single-storey house with separate accommodation (chauffeur): scale 1:500**

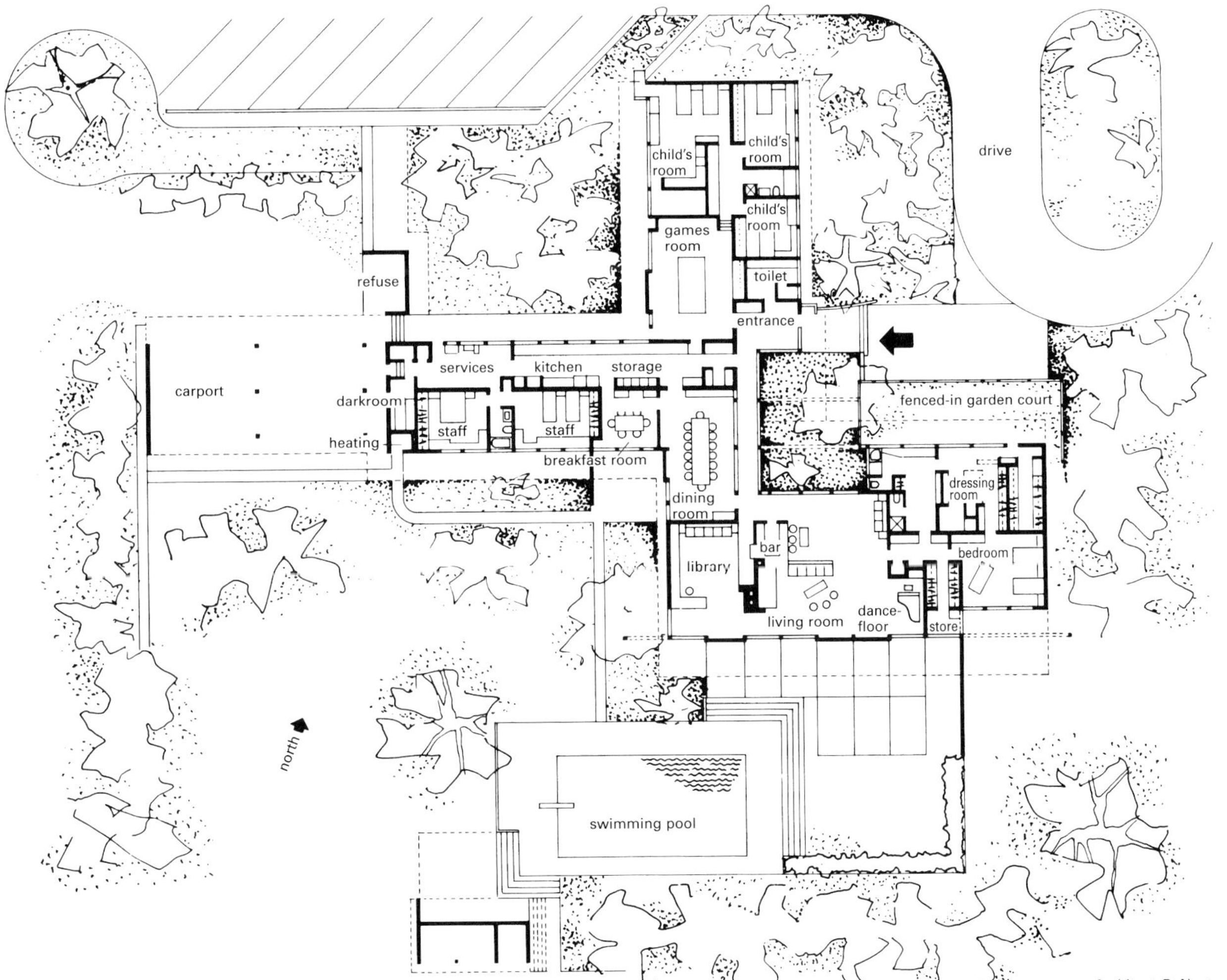

Architect: R. Neutra

(3) **House in Beverly Hills, California: scale 1:500**

INTERNATIONAL EXAMPLES

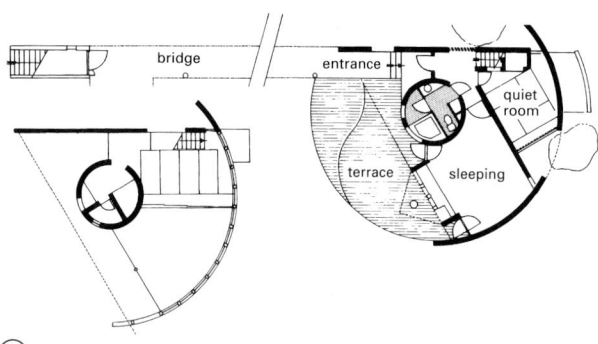

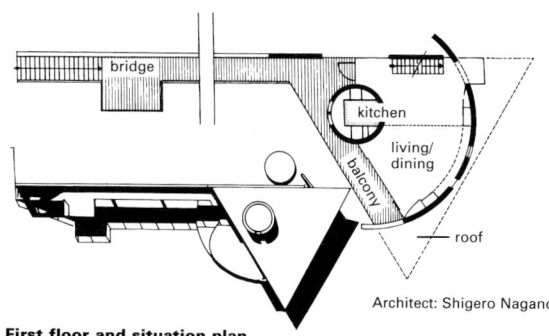

Architect: Shigero Nagano

(1) **Second floor and ground floor → ②**

(2) **First floor and situation plan**

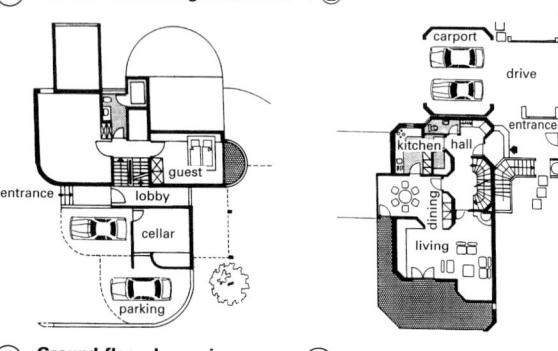

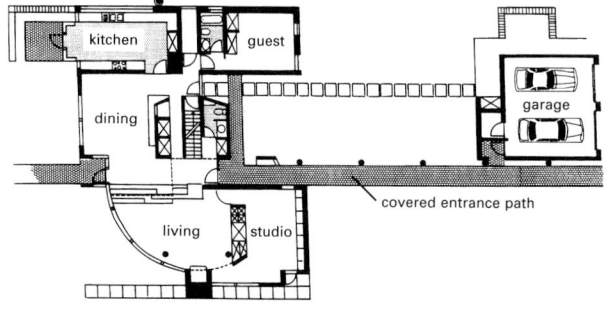

(3) **Ground floor, house in California → ④ + ⑤**

(6) **Ground floor → ⑦ + ⑧**

(10) **Ground floor, house in the USA → ⑪**

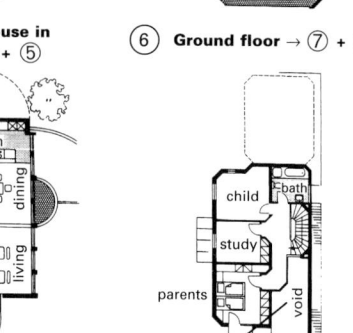

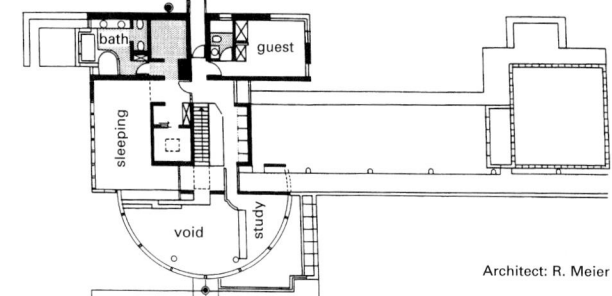

Architect: R. Meier

(4) **First floor**

(7) **Upper floor**

(11) **Upper floor**

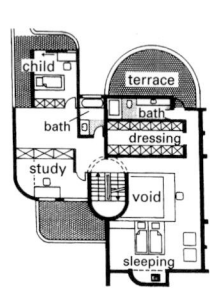

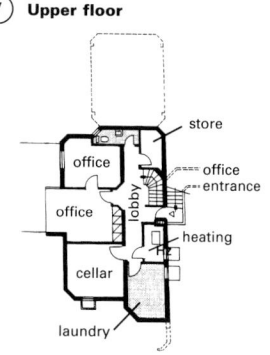

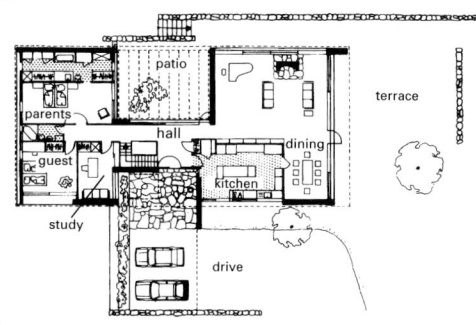

Architect: R. Kappe, Los Angeles

Architect: L. Neff

(5) **Second floor**

(8) **Basement**

(12) **Ground floor, house in the USA → ⑬**

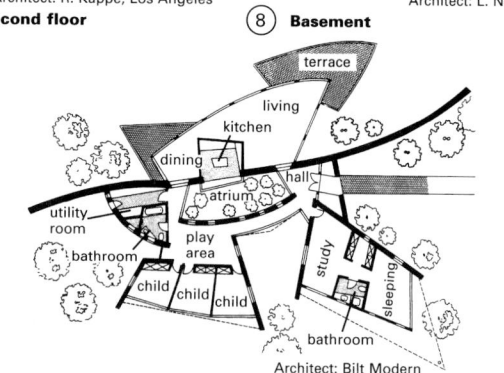

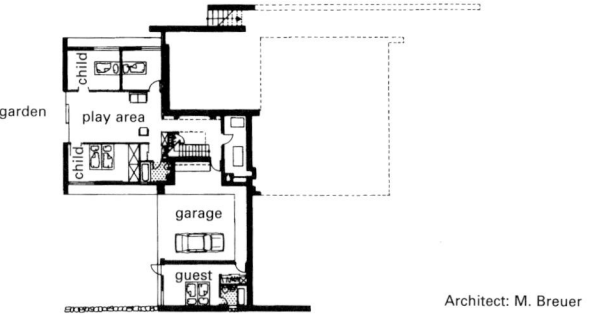

Architect: Bilt Modern

Architect: M. Breuer

(9) **One storey house in Victoria, Australia**

(13) **Lower floor**

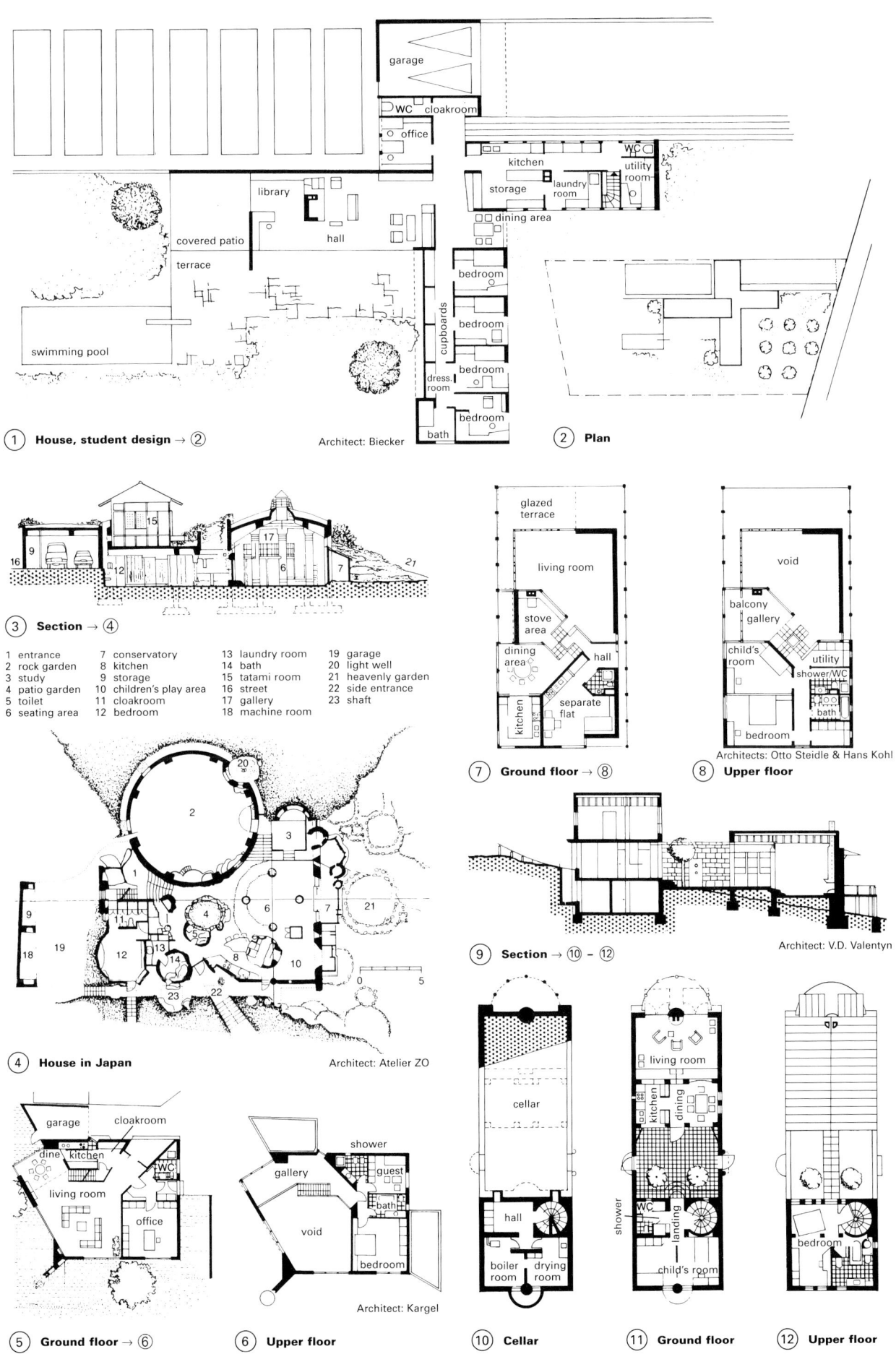

garage

WC cloakroom

office

kitchen

WC

utility room

storage

laundry room

library

dining area

covered patio

hall

terrace

bedroom

cupboards

bedroom

swimming pool

bedroom

dress. room

bedroom

bath

① House, student design → ②

Architect: Biecker

② Plan

15

16 9

12

17

6

7

21

③ Section → ④

1 entrance	7 conservatory	13 laundry room	19 garage
2 rock garden	8 kitchen	14 bath	20 light well
3 study	9 storage	15 tatami room	21 heavenly garden
4 patio garden	10 children's play area	16 street	22 side entrance
5 toilet	11 cloakroom	17 gallery	23 shaft
6 seating area	12 bedroom	18 machine room	

20

2

3

1

9

11

6

7

21

18   19

12

13

4

14

8

10

23   22

0   5

④ House in Japan

Architect: Atelier ZO

---

glazed terrace

living room

void

stove area

balcony

gallery

dining area

hall

child's room

utility

kitchen

separate flat

shower/WC

bedroom

bath

Architects: Otto Steidle & Hans Kohl

⑦ Ground floor → ⑧

⑧ Upper floor

---

⑨ Section → ⑩ – ⑫

Architect: V.D. Valentyn

---

garage

cloakroom

dine kitchen

WC

shower

gallery

guest

living room

bath

office

void

bedroom

Architect: Kargel

⑤ Ground floor → ⑥

⑥ Upper floor

---

cellar

living room

kitchen

dining

hall

shower

WC

landing

boiler room

drying room

child's room

bedroom

⑩ Cellar

⑪ Ground floor

⑫ Upper floor

MULTISTOREY HOUSING

(1) Blocks
A compact, layered building form (either single buildings or in groups) that gives high occupancy densities. The external spaces within and around the building are clearly differentiated in relation to form and function.

(2) Linear arrangement
A spacious building configuration: either groups of identical block types or of buildings of completely different designs. There is little or no differentiation of the external spaces around the buildings.

(3) Slab-blocks
This building form is often used in an isolated configuration. It can be extended both in length and height but allows little scope for variety among the room layouts. Differentiation of the surrounding areas is difficult.

(4) Large-scale developments
By expanding and interconnecting slab buildings to create large forms stretching out over a wide area it is possible to develop large tracts. Differentiation between spaces defined by the buildings is almost impossible to achieve.

(5) Point-blocks
These are distinctive individual buildings, often standing isolated in open spaces. A 'dominant element' in town planning, this building type is frequently designed in combination with low-rise developments.

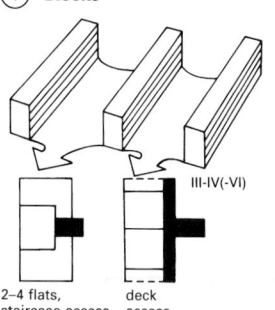

III-IV (-VI)

2–4 flats, staircase access | deck access

(1) **Blocks**

III-IV(-VI)

2–4 flats, staircase access | deck access

(2) **Linear arrangement**

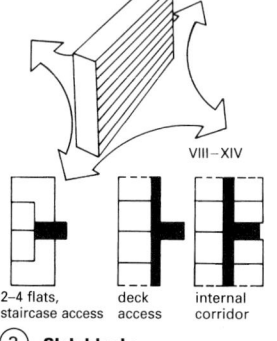

VIII–XIV

2–4 flats, staircase access | deck access | internal corridor

(3) **Slab-blocks**

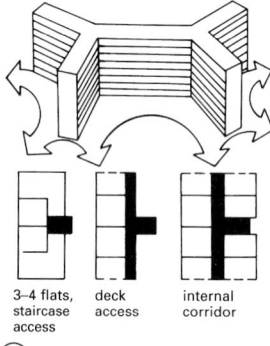

3–4 flats, staircase access | deck access | internal corridor

(4) **Large-scale developments**

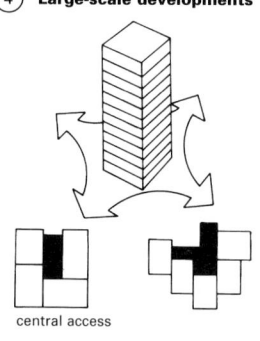

central access

(5) **Point-blocks**

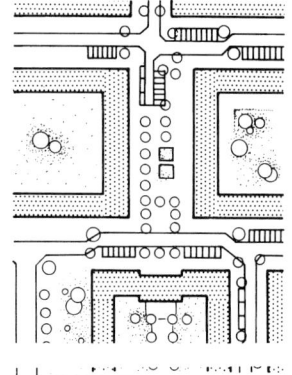
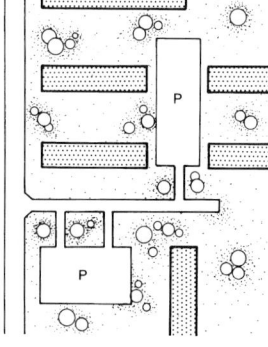
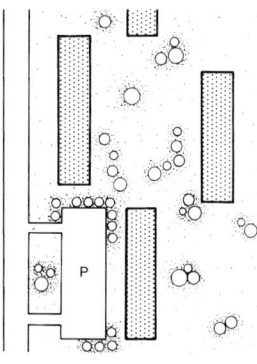
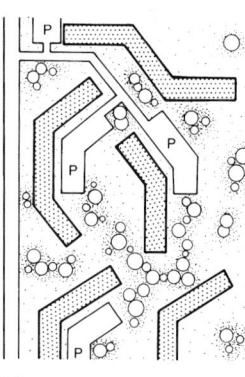
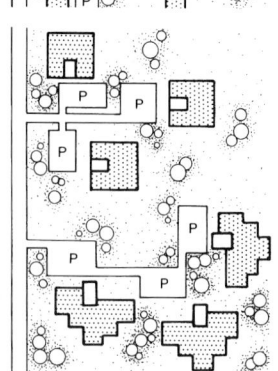

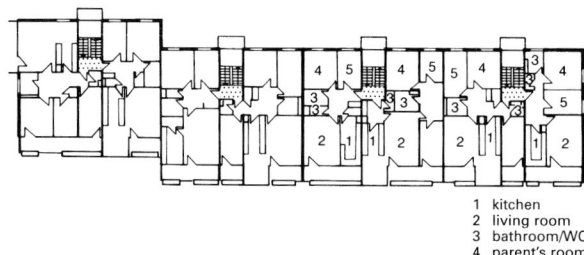

1 kitchen
2 living room
3 bathroom/WC
4 parent's room
5 child's room

(6) **Building layout in Augsburg** Architect: E.C. Müller

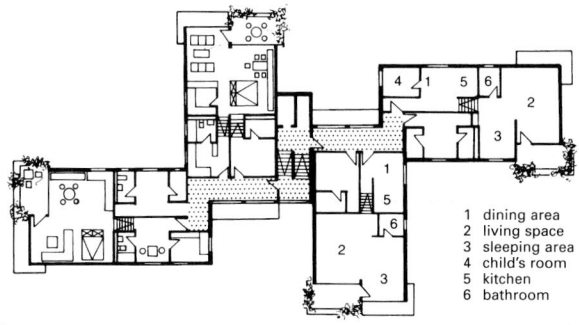

1 dining area
2 living space
3 sleeping area
4 child's room
5 kitchen
6 bathroom

(7) **Flats off a corridor**

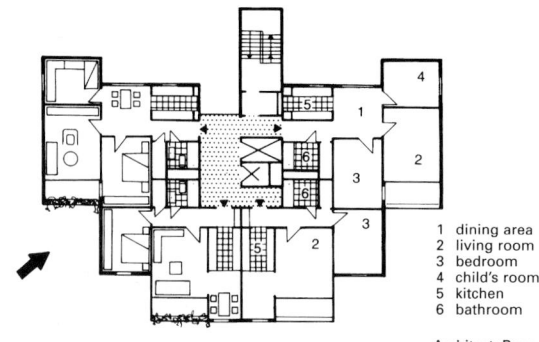

1 dining area
2 living room
3 bedroom
4 child's room
5 kitchen
6 bathroom

Architect: Pogadl

(8) **Plan of building with four flats per floor and staircase access**

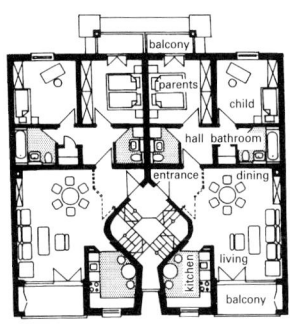

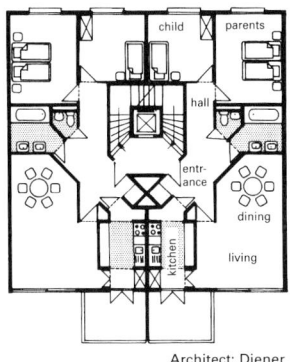

Architect: Diener

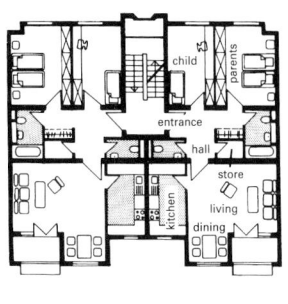

Architects: HPP and LKT

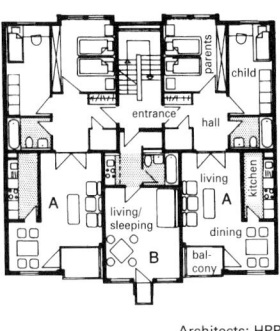

Architects: HPP

(1) **Two dwellings per floor, staircase on outside wall**

(2) **Two dwellings per floor, internal staircase**

(3) **Two dwellings per floor**

(4) **Three dwellings per floor: 2 apartments and one studio flat**

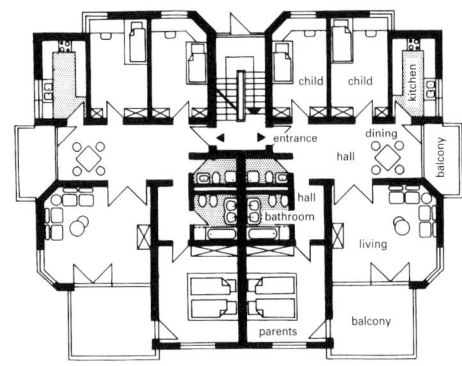

(5) **Two 60 m² apartments per floor**

(6) **Two dwellings per floor with lift**

(7) **Two dwellings per floor**

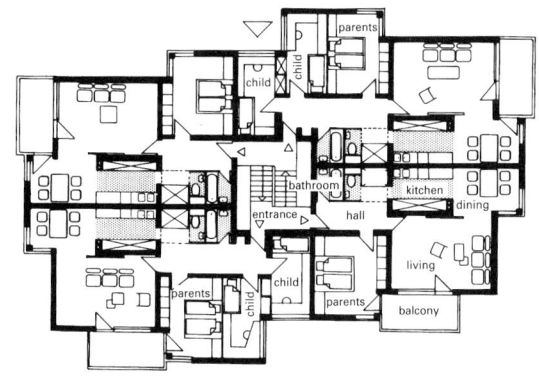

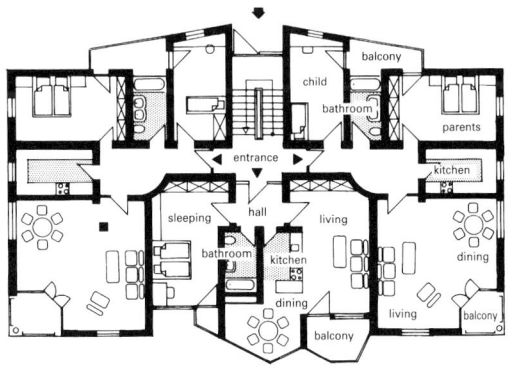

Architect: L. Neff

(8) **Four dwellings per floor: two two-room apartments, two four-room apartments**

(9) **Three dwellings per floor**

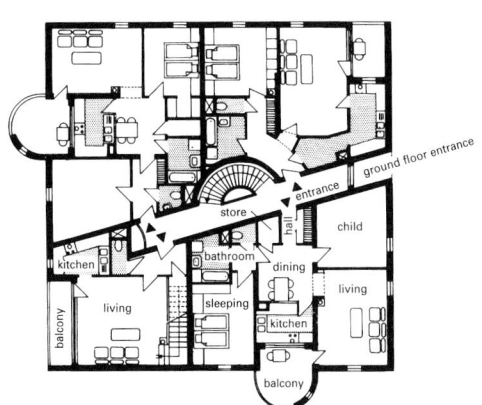

Architect: Peichl

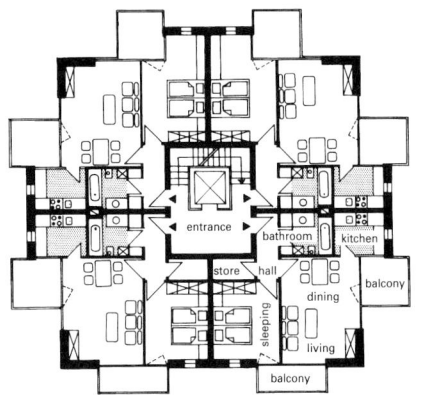

(10) **Four dwellings per floor**

(11) **Four dwellings per floor**

Architect: Neufert/Meittmann/Graf

293

MULTISTOREY HOUSING

Developments with only one dwelling per floor → ① (the basic form for town houses) are often uneconomical. Four-storey buildings without lifts are the usual form.

Housing with two dwellings per floor around a central core → ② provides a good balance between living quality and economy, allowing a variety of plans with satisfactory solar orientation and flats with different numbers of rooms. Buildings up to four storeys can have stairs only whereas those with five or more require a lift. For flats over a height of 22 m, high-rise building conditions apply.

Having three dwellings per floor and a central staircase → ③ again offers a good mix of economy and living quality, and this form is suitable for building corner units. Two-, three- and four-roomed dwellings can be considered. Housing with four dwellings per floor and a shared staircase → ④ requires appropriate planning to provide a satisfactory relationship between economy and living quality. Different types of flat on each floor are possible.

With point-blocks → ⑤ the three-dimensional design is determined by the plan form.

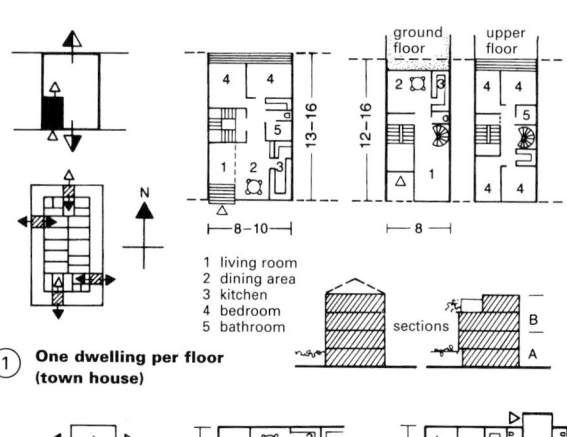

1 living room
2 dining area
3 kitchen
4 bedroom
5 bathroom

① One dwelling per floor (town house)

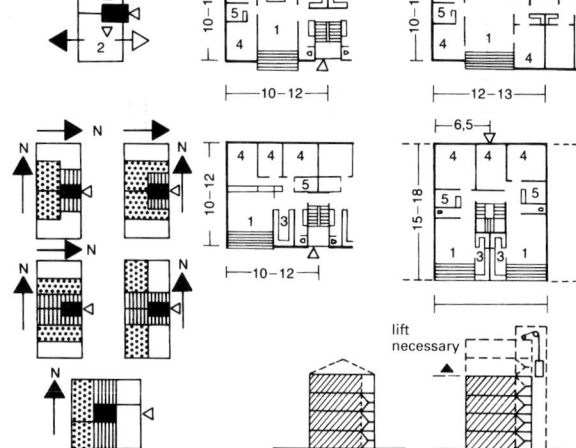

② Two dwellings around a central staircase

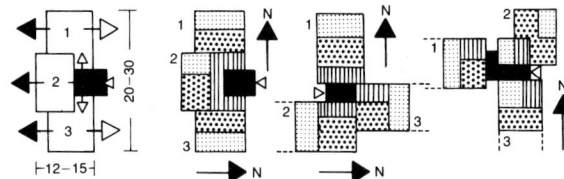

③ Three dwellings per floor, staircase access

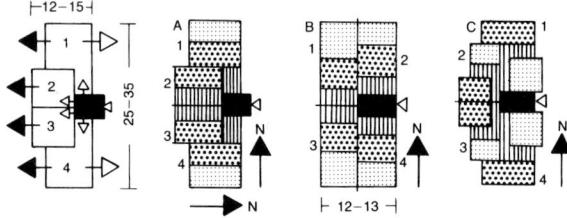

④ Four dwellings per floor, staircase access

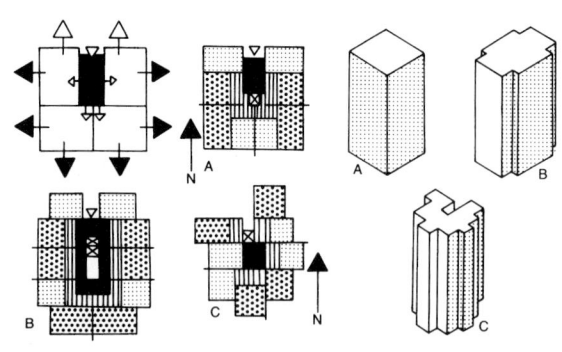

⑤ Point-block

key:

- living area ◁ entrance
- sleeping area ◀ main orientation
- other rooms ◁ secondary orientation

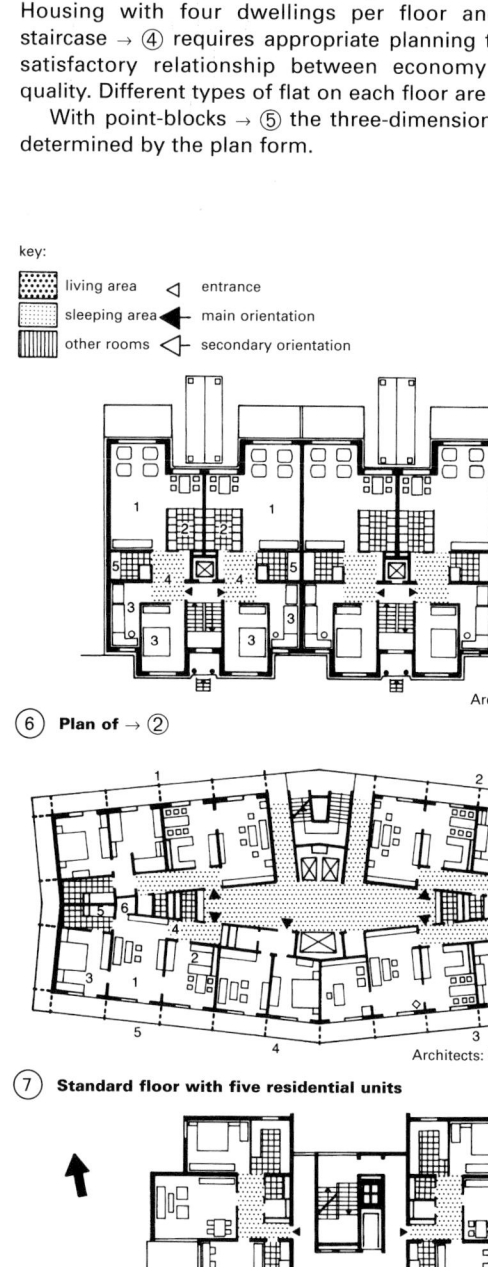

1 living room
2 kitchen
3 bedroom
4 hall
5 bathroom

Architect: W. Dörink

⑥ Plan of → ②

Architects: Schmitt & Heene

⑦ Standard floor with five residential units

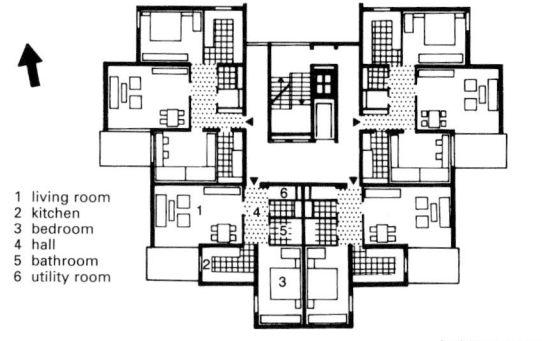

1 living room
2 kitchen
3 bedroom
4 hall
5 bathroom
6 utility room

Architect: W. Iron

⑧ High-rise block of flats

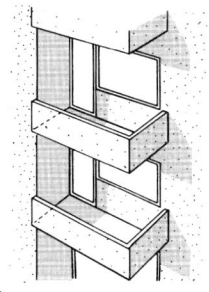

(1) **Corner balcony**

(2) **Open balcony with screen**

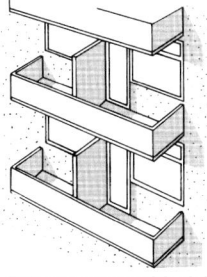

(3) **Balcony group with sight and wind screens**

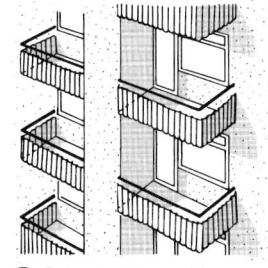

(4) **Balcony group with intermediate storage space for balcony furniture**

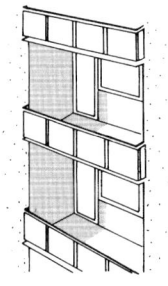

(5) **Inset balconies (loggia)**

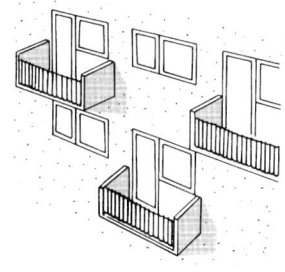

(6) **Offset balconies**

Balconies offer an effective means of improving the attractiveness of domestic accommodation units. They also give an extended work space as well as an easily supervised outdoor children's play area. Typical uses include relaxation, sunbathing, sleeping, reading, eating etc.

In addition to the required functional living space an area for plant boxes should be provided wherever possible → (8) + (14).

Corner balconies → (1) offer privacy and good shelter and are therefore preferable to open balconies. Open balconies require a protective screen on the side facing the prevailing wind → (2).

Where there are groups of balconies (as in blocks of flats), screens should be used to ensure privacy and give shelter from the wind → (3). Even better is to separate the balconies with part of the structure because this makes it possible to include some storage space (e.g. for balcony furniture, sunshade etc.) → (4) + (12).

Loggias are justifiable in hot climates but are inappropriate in cooler countries. They only get the sunshine for a short time and cause an increase in the external wall areas of the adjacent rooms, which increases heat loss → (5). Balconies which are offset in their elevation can make façades less severe but it is difficult to provide privacy and protection from the weather and sun → (6). Balconies which are offset in their plan layout on the other hand offer excellent privacy and shelter → (7).

During planning specify:
- good orientation in relation to the the path of the sun and the view;
- appropriate location with respect to neighbouring flats and houses;
- effective spatial location with respect to adjacent living rooms, studios or bedrooms;
- sufficient size, privacy, protection from noise and the weather (wind, rain and direct sunshine);
- suitable materials for parapets (e.g. opaque glass, plastic or wooden balusters within a frame).

The balcony frame is best made from light steel profiles or tubes with a good anchorage in the masonry. Balcony balusters made from vertical steel rods (note that horizontal rods can be climbed by children) can be considered but are not desirable because they do not offer shelter from the wind and lack privacy. Where they are used, they are often covered by the tenants themselves with all sorts of different materials.

Draughts can occur in the intermediate spaces between parapets and the concrete slab → (8), so it is better to extend the parapet down in front of the balcony slab or to have a solid parapet. This must be kept low to avoid a trough-like character and there must be a steel rail above it at the regulation height (≥900 mm). Allow space for flower boxes if possible → (8).

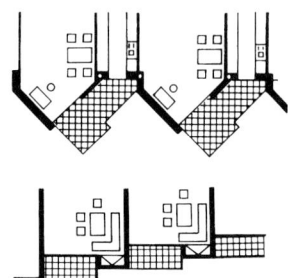

(7) **Offset balconies making use of angles and staggering**

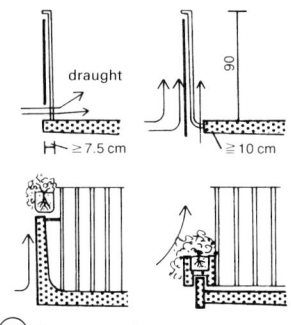

(8) **Parapet variants**

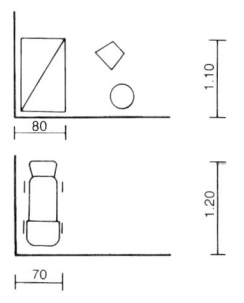

(11) **Child's cot and pram**

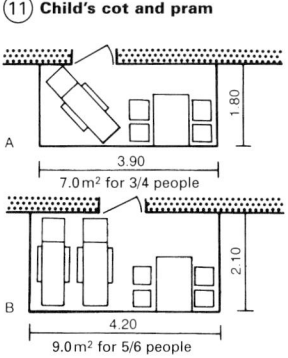

(12) **Balcony with storage space for balcony furniture**

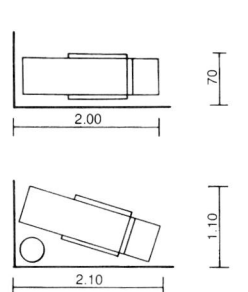

(9) **Reclining chairs**

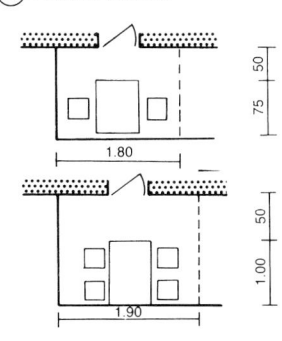

(10) **Seating around tables**

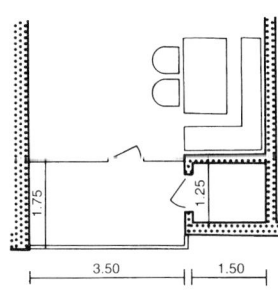

(13) **Balcony layouts**

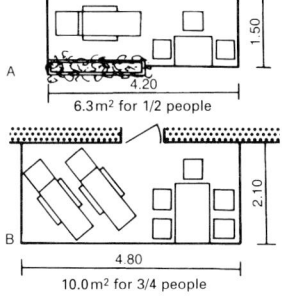

(14) **Balcony layouts**

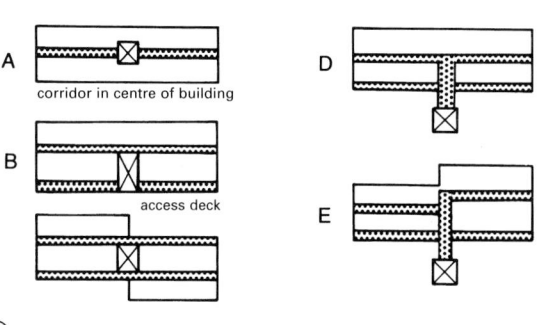

A corridor in centre of building

B access deck

D

E

① **Vertical connections**

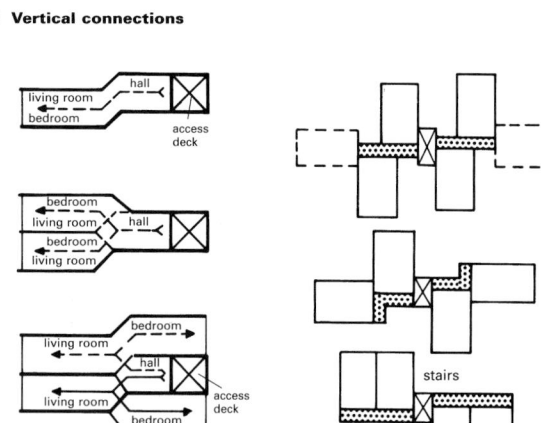

living room / hall / bedroom — access deck

bedroom / living room / hall / bedroom / living room

living room / bedroom / hall / living room / bedroom — access deck

stairs

② **Possible corridor arrangements**

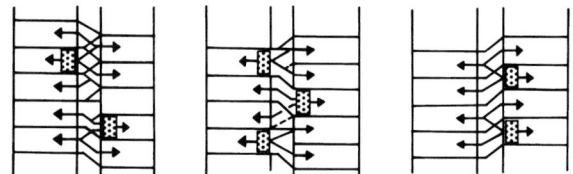

③ **Section showing possible arrangement of corridors in the core of the building**

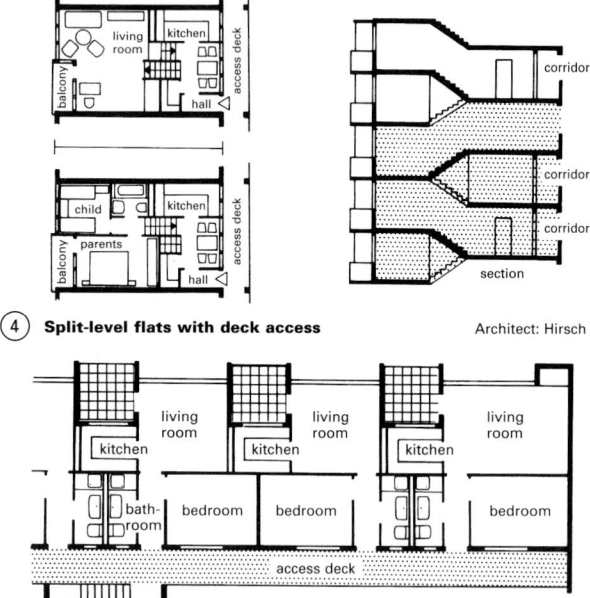

living room, kitchen, balcony, hall, access deck

child, kitchen, balcony, parents, hall, access deck

corridor, corridor, corridor, section

④ **Split-level flats with deck access** Architect: Hirsch

living room, kitchen, bath-room, bedroom, bedroom, living room, kitchen, bedroom, living room, kitchen, bedroom

access deck

Architect: Seitz

⑤ **Stairway installed in front of the access deck: kitchens are lit and ventilated via an inset balcony**

ACCESS CORRIDORS/DECKS

An alternative to the centralised layout (i.e. buildings with dwellings on each floor around a central staircase or lift) is to have the dwellings accessed from an internal corridor or a covered external walkway. This is more economical in large housing projects. Each level is served by one or more vertical connection points (lifts and/or stairs) which also lead to the main entrance to the building. In addition to stairways and lifts, vertical systems of service shafts are needed and there should be a clear differentiation of built-in, added and free-standing constructions. → ①

Dwellings on either side of an interior corridor have a single orientation and this makes it desirable to employ a design that uses two or more levels → ③. A similar arrangement can be exploited in buildings with an access deck running along the exterior → ⑥ + ⑦. Note that open access decks can cause problems in harsh climates.

It is considerably better if the dwelling is on two or more levels because it allows the functional requirements to be met more satisfactorily and half-storey split levels, for example, can be stacked easily → ②. Dwellings on only one level are particularly suitable as studio flats → ⑤.

To improve the realtionship between circulation and dwelling areas the goal should be to minimise the length of horizontal access routes. Planning corridors on alternate floors provides the best arrangement for larger multi-level dwellings and good solutions can be attained by siting the deck access on alternate sides. The number of corridors can also be reduced with a mirrored staggering of maisonettes or a similar arrangement of split-level dwellings.

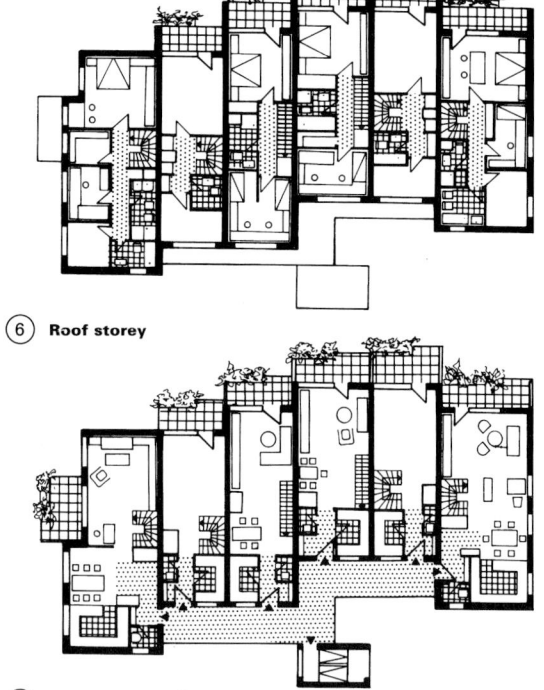

⑥ **Roof storey**

⑦ **Floor beneath ⑥**

STEPPED HOUSING

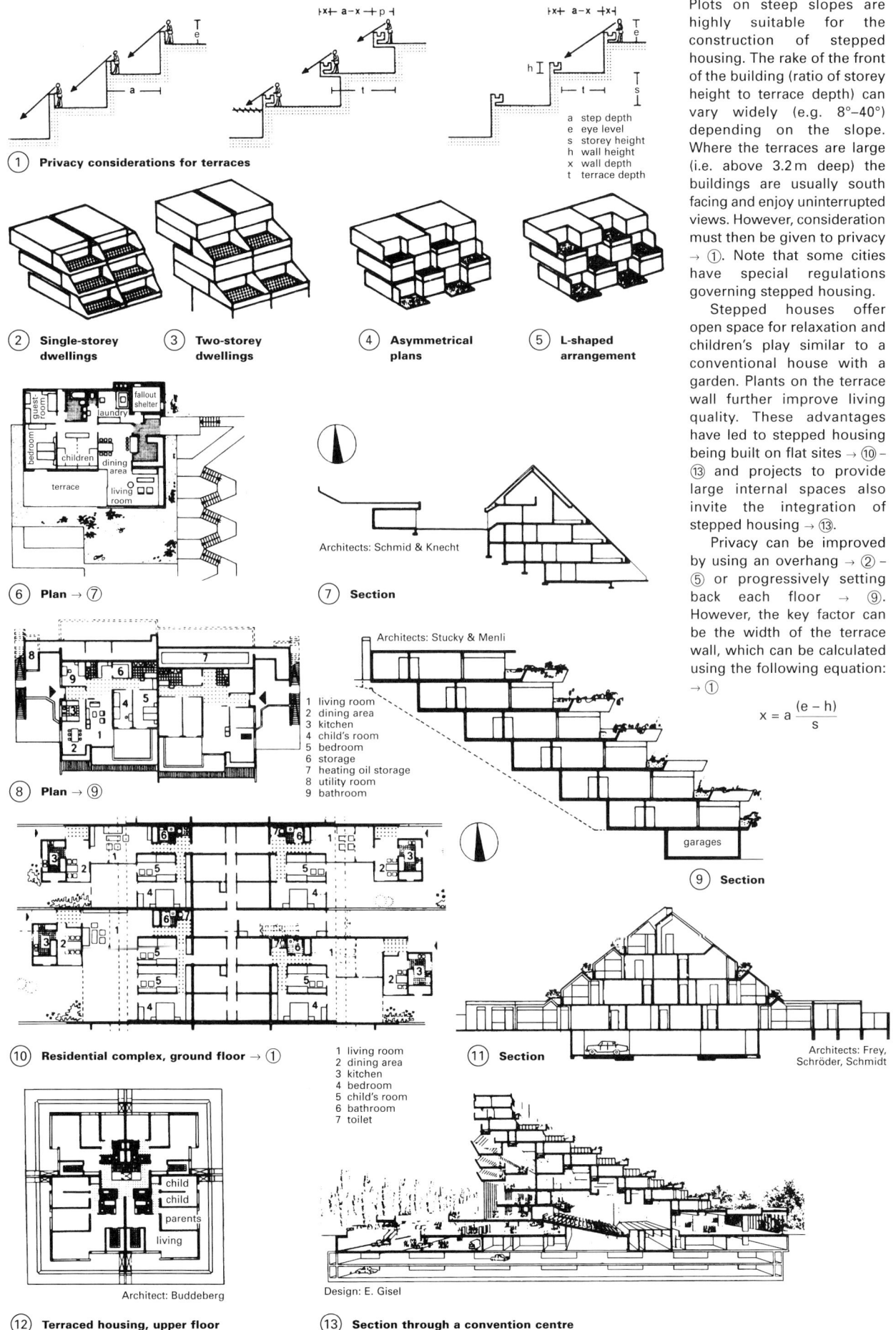

① **Privacy considerations for terraces**

a step depth
e eye level
s storey height
h wall height
x wall depth
t terrace depth

② **Single-storey dwellings**

③ **Two-storey dwellings**

④ **Asymmetrical plans**

⑤ **L-shaped arrangement**

⑥ **Plan → ⑦**

fallout shelter
laundry
guest room
bedroom
children
dining area
terrace
living room

Architects: Schmid & Knecht

⑦ **Section**

⑧ **Plan → ⑨**

8
9
7
6
5
4
3
2
1

1 living room
2 dining area
3 kitchen
4 child's room
5 bedroom
6 storage
7 heating oil storage
8 utility room
9 bathroom

Architects: Stucky & Menli

garages

⑨ **Section**

⑩ **Residential complex, ground floor → ①**

1 living room
2 dining area
3 kitchen
4 bedroom
5 child's room
6 bathroom
7 toilet

⑪ **Section**

Architects: Frey, Schröder, Schmidt

⑫ **Terraced housing, upper floor**

child
child
parents
living

Architect: Buddeberg

⑬ **Section through a convention centre**

Design: E. Gisel

Plots on steep slopes are highly suitable for the construction of stepped housing. The rake of the front of the building (ratio of storey height to terrace depth) can vary widely (e.g. 8°–40°) depending on the slope. Where the terraces are large (i.e. above 3.2 m deep) the buildings are usually south facing and enjoy uninterrupted views. However, consideration must then be given to privacy → ①. Note that some cities have special regulations governing stepped housing.

Stepped houses offer open space for relaxation and children's play similar to a conventional house with a garden. Plants on the terrace wall further improve living quality. These advantages have led to stepped housing being built on flat sites → ⑩ – ⑬ and projects to provide large internal spaces also invite the integration of stepped housing → ⑬.

Privacy can be improved by using an overhang → ② – ⑤ or progressively setting back each floor → ⑨. However, the key factor can be the width of the terrace wall, which can be calculated using the following equation: → ①

$$x = a\,\frac{(e - h)}{s}$$

297

BUILDING FOR DISABLED PEOPLE

An environment for disabled people needs to be designed to accommodate wheelchairs and allow sufficient space for moving around in safety (see ①–④ and ⑨–⑫ for dimensions and area requirements). Example door and corridor widths are given in ⑬–⑯. All switches, handles, window fittings, telephone points, paper roll or towel holders, lift controls, etc. must be within reach of an outstretched arm ⑨–⑫. The layout of the WC, in particular, requires careful planning: assess how many doors, light switches etc. are needed. Consider technical aids (e.g. magnetic catches on doors and remote controls).

Access paths to the building should be 1.20–2.00 m wide and be as short as possible. Ramps should ideally be straight, with a maximum incline of 5–7%, and should be no longer than 6 m ⑤. The ramp width between the handrails should be 1.20 m. Corridors should be at least 1.30 m (preferably 2.00 m) wide; clear opening of doors, 0.95 m; height of light switches and electrical sockets, 1.00–1.05 m (use switches and control devices which have large buttons or surfaces).

During urban planning, consideration should also be given to providing wheelchair users with easy access to general amenities such as supermarkets, restaurants, post offices, pharmacies, doctors' surgeries, car parks, public transport etc.

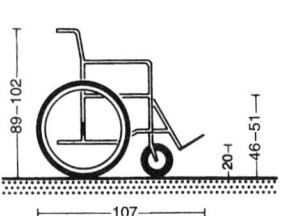

① Side view of standard wheelchair

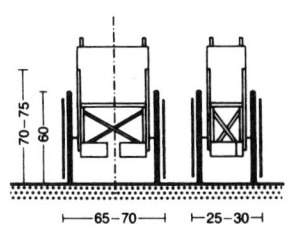

② Front view (and folded)

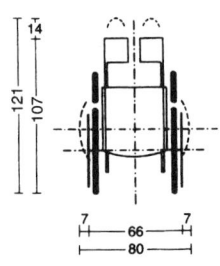

③ Plan view

④ Turning circle

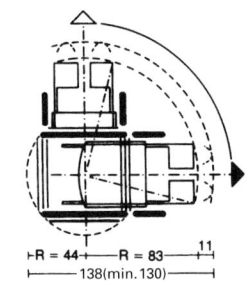

⑤ Wheelchair on a slope

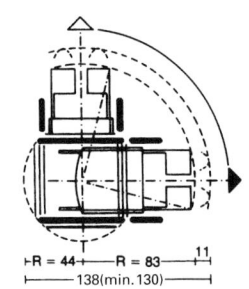

⑥ On stairs

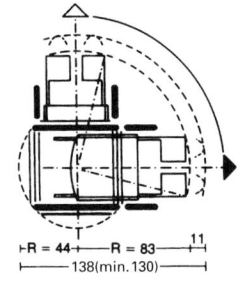

⑦ VDU workstation

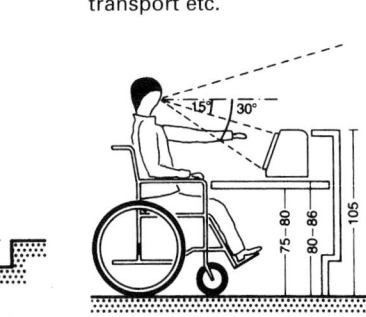

⑧ At a window

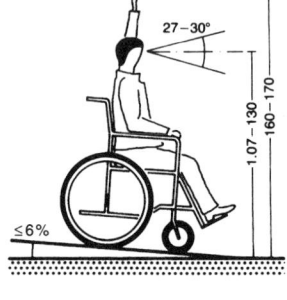

⑨ Plan view

⑩ Side elevation

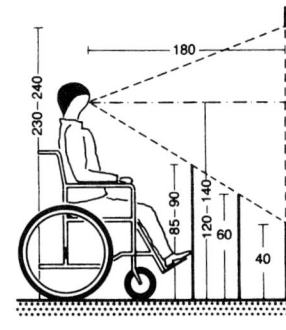

⑪ Rear elevation

⑫ Minimum turning circle

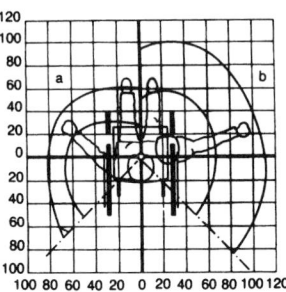

⑬ Door access with one door

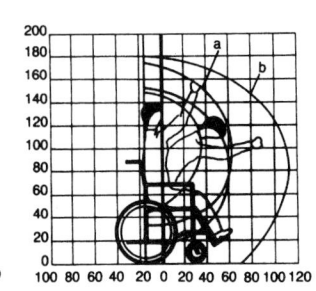

⑭ with 2 doors

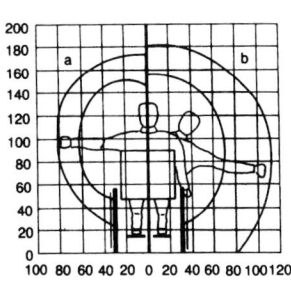

⑮ with three doors

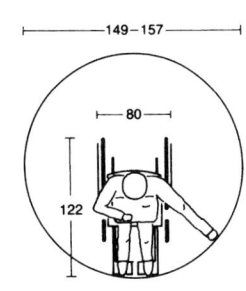

⑯ with four doors

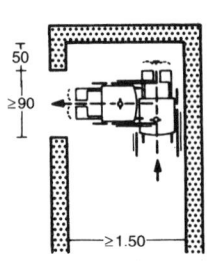
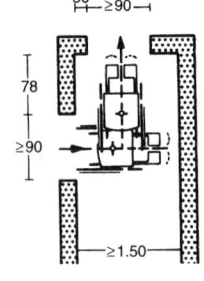
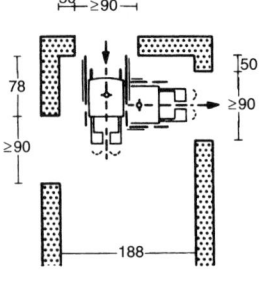
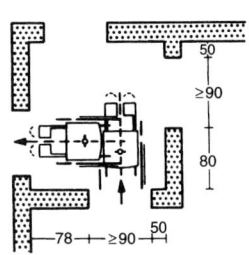

BUILDING FOR DISABLED PEOPLE

Houses and Apartments

Accessibility: In the rented residential sector, access via corridors is the most common layout. This enables large numbers of angles and corners to be avoided; a straight main corridor is preferable. The entrance area should be of an appropriate size, with shelves and coat hooks planned in. The minimum area of entrance halls is 1.50×1.50 m, and 1.70×1.60 m for a porch with a single-leaf door. (It should be noted, however, that minimum recommended dimensions are often not very generous and in practice can prove to be too small.) For blind residents it is important to have an intercom system at the apartment door and the building's main entrance.

Living area: Living rooms should allow adequate free movement for wheelchair users and have sufficient space for two or three more visitors' wheelchairs. For blind people, additional space should be provided for their literature and tape equipment: Braille books and newspapers are roughly three times bulkier than their printed equivalents. Single disabled people need more space than those in shared households. In apartments, recommended minimum areas for living rooms with a dining area are: 22 m² for one person; 24 m² for two to four people; 26 m² for five; and 28 m² for six. The minimum room width is 3.75 m for a one- or two-person home → ⑤.

If an additional study area is to be incorporated, the floor area must be increased by at least 2 m².

Kitchen: Ergonomic planning is of great importance in the kitchen to allow disabled people to utilise their capabilities to the full. The arrangement of the storage, preparation, cooking and washing areas should be convenient and streamlined. The cooker, main worksurface and taps should be placed as close together as possible. Storage spaces must be accessible to wheelchair users (i.e. no high cupboards). The reach of the arm is roughly 600 mm horizontally and between 400 and 1400 mm vertically. The optimal working height must be adapted to suit each disabled person, within the range 750–900 mm, so it is desirable to have a simple adjustment mechanism.

Single-family houses: The single-storey family house with garden is often the preferred form of residence for disabled people. Their requirements can be satisfied easily in this type of accommodation: i.e. no steps at the entrance and no difference in level between the individual rooms and the garden; rooms can be connected without doors and custom designed to best suit the residents. However, two-storey family houses can also be suitable, even for wheelchair users, if a suitable means of moving between floors (vertical elevator or stair lift) is incorporated.

Multi-apartment dwellings: The grouping of apartments in multiple occupancy dwellings is a housing solution that offers disabled people an environment which is both sociable and supportive. In economic terms, it is rarely possible to convert ordinary apartments into adequate homes for the severely disabled, so they need to be included at the preliminary planning stage. It is once again preferable to situate apartments for disabled people at ground-floor level to avoid the necessity of installing lifts/elevators.

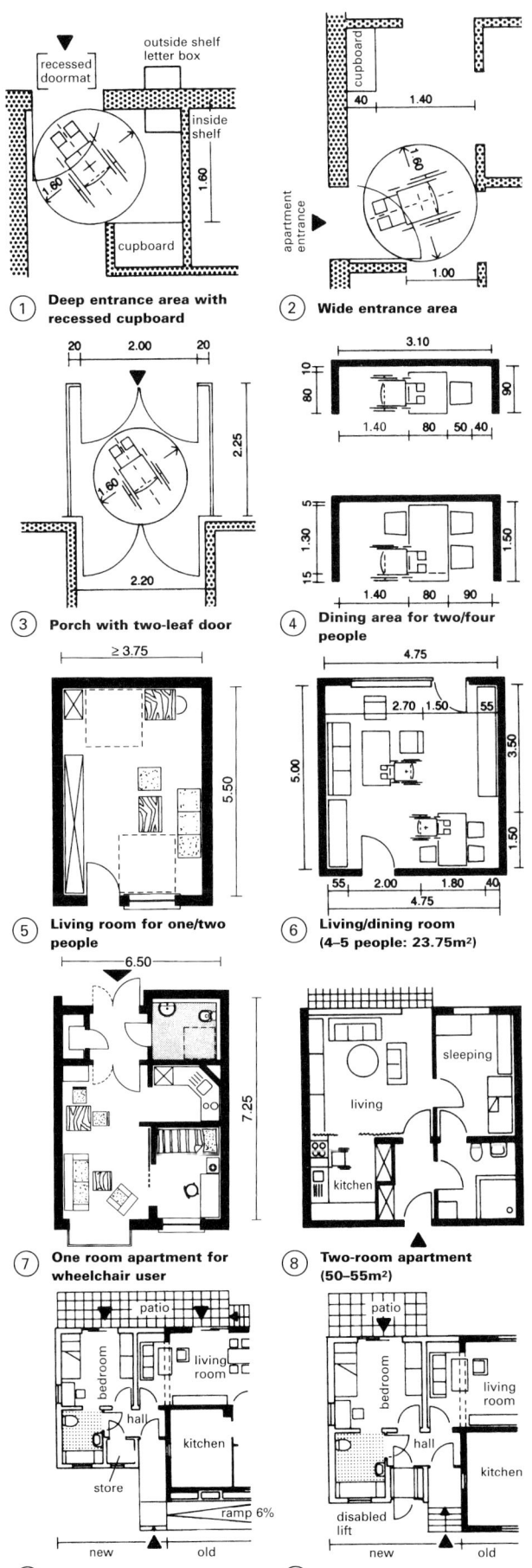

① **Deep entrance area with recessed cupboard**

② **Wide entrance area**

③ **Porch with two-leaf door**

④ **Dining area for two/four people**

⑤ **Living room for one/two people**

⑥ **Living/dining room (4–5 people: 23.75m²)**

⑦ **One room apartment for wheelchair user**

⑧ **Two-room apartment (50–55m²)**

⑨ **Annex for disabled person built onto existing house; ramps compensate for height differences**

⑩ **Installation of an elevator**

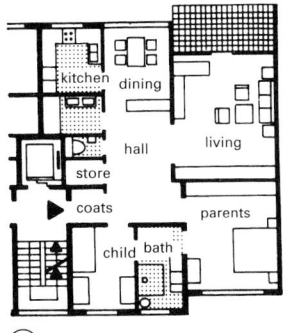

⑪ **Three-person appartment including one disabled, two apartments per floor**

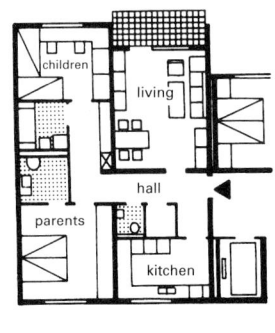

⑫ **Four-person appartment including one disabled, three apartments per floor**

299

BUILDING FOR DISABLED PEOPLE

Conversions

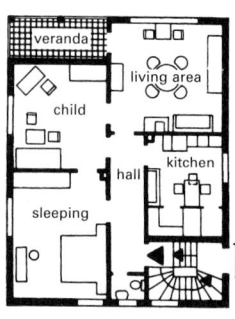

(1) **Family house before conversion → (2)**

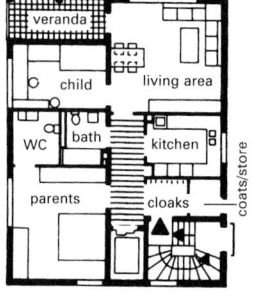

(2) **Converted to an apartment for severely disabled**

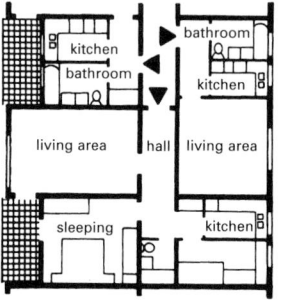

(3) **One and two-room apartment prior to conversion (visually impaired, child) → (4)**

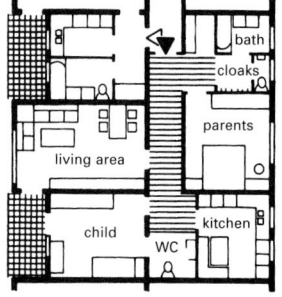

(4) **After conversion**

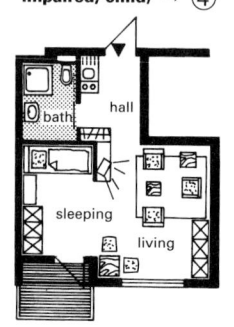

(5) **Studio apartment (40 m²)**

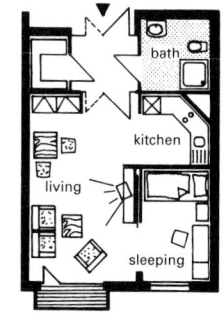

(6) **Studio apartment (45 m²)**

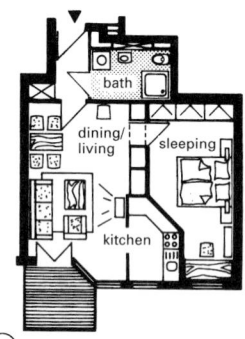

(7) **Two-room apartment (54 m²)**

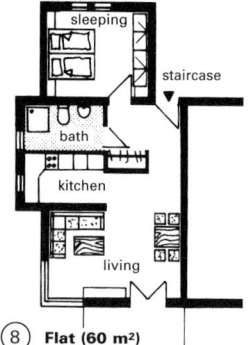

(8) **Flat (60 m²)**

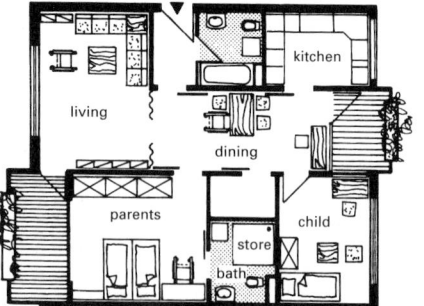

(9) **Three-room apartment (95 m²)**

The needs of disabled people are often not taken into account sufficiently in new building projects, so it is frequently necessary to convert existing residential units into appropriate apartments. Suitable buildings have a generous floor area and offer simple opportunities for alteration in accordance with the occupant's needs. The conversion measures required can include: alterations to the plan, including building work (which is limited by structural considerations, the type of construction and floor area); alterations to services, bathroom and kitchen fittings etc.; and supplementary measures, such as the installation of ramps, lifts and additional electrical equipment. Attention should also be paid to access from the street, any floor coverings which require changing and the creation of a car parking space with ample allowances for wheelchair users. The extent of the alterations depends on the degree of disability of the residents and the specific activity within the apartment. As a result, the conversion measures will often be specified in conjunction with the disabled person and tailored to his or her needs.

Prior to commencing conversion work, the plan and structure of the existing apartment should be examined carefully. Ground floor apartments of an adequate size are particularly suitable because additional services (passing through the basement) can be installed more cheaply and entrance modifications are easier.

Extent of the conversion work: Three groups of disabled people can be identified, each with corresponding requirements:
- Disabled members of a family (husbands, wives, children) who go to work or school outside the home. Alterations in such cases relate to access to the house/apartment, furnishings and provision of sufficient freedom of movement in the living and sleeping areas, and specially adapted facilities in the bathroom/WC.
- Disabled persons who carry out household tasks. Here, additional alterations must be made to the kitchen and elsewhere to simplify work in the home.
- Severely disabled persons who are only partially independent, if at all, and thus require permanent care. Extra space must be provided for manoeuvring wheelchairs and facilities to aid the work of carers should be added. Note that self-propelled wheelchairs require most space.

Comparison of sizes of living area: While apartments for the elderly are no larger in area than standard apartments (any changes consisting only of adjusting door widths and tailoring the functional areas), living areas for disabled people need to be increased appropriately, particularly for wheelchair users and the visually impaired. Regulations often require additional rooms in these apartments as well as a modified bathroom with WC for wheelchair users.

Recommended values for habitable areas are: 45–50 m² for a one-person household; 50–55 m² for two people.

apartment	for disabled (m²)	standard (m²)
1 person studio	49.99	40.46
2 person apartment	67.69	56.47
3 person apartment	94.80	79.74
4 person apartment	95.26	80.50
1 person apartment	53.70	43.93
3 person apartment	101.17	86.38
4 person apartment	103.23	88.33

(11) **Example apartment areas before/after conversion**

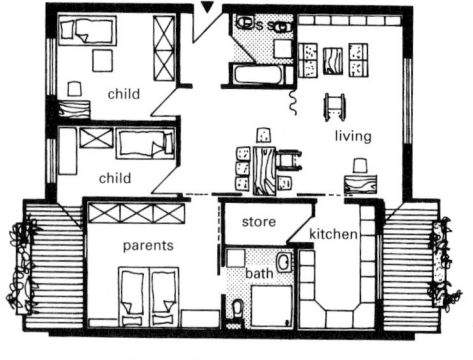

(10) **Four-room apartment (110 m²)**

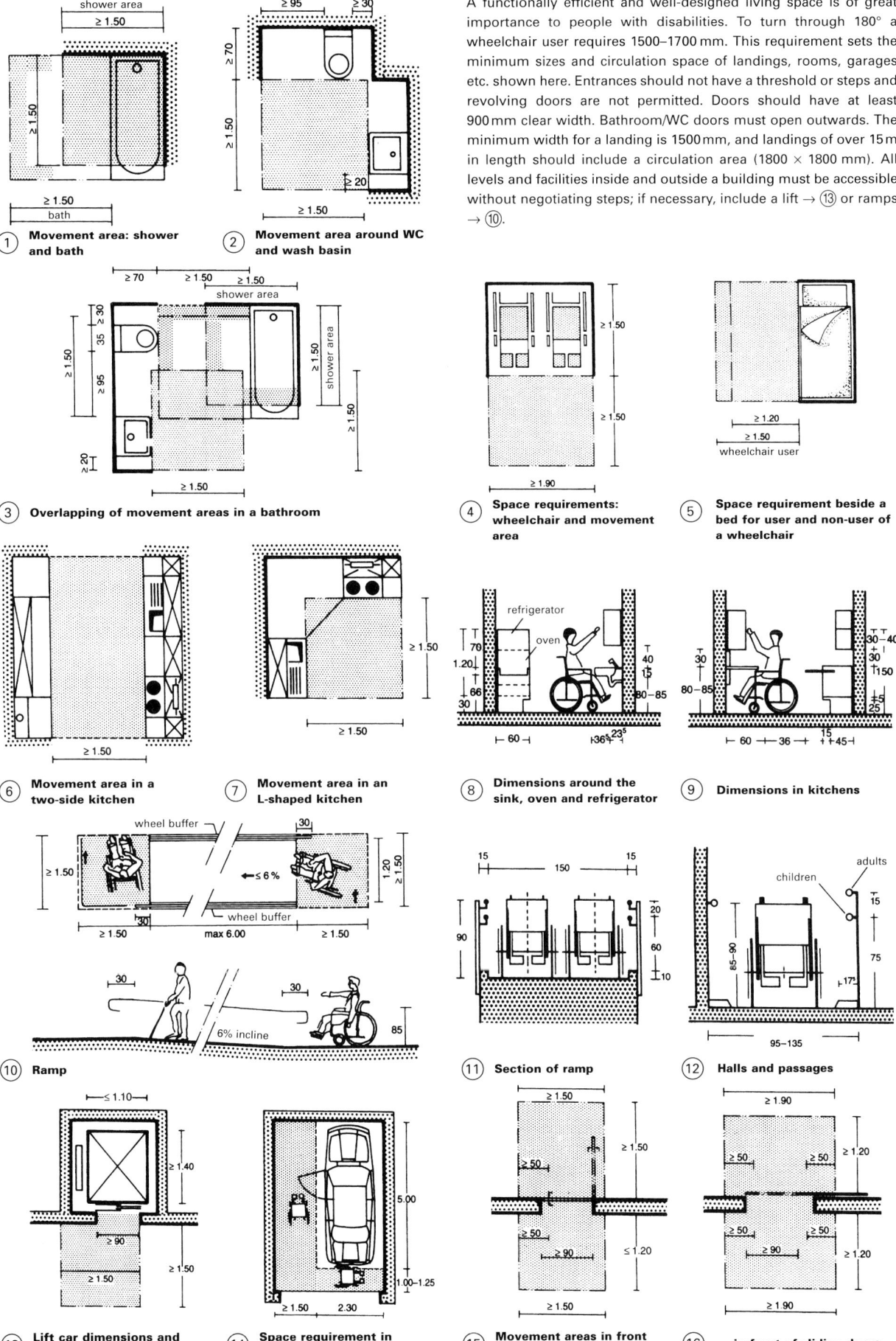

BARRIER-FREE LIVING

A functionally efficient and well-designed living space is of great importance to people with disabilities. To turn through 180° a wheelchair user requires 1500–1700 mm. This requirement sets the minimum sizes and circulation space of landings, rooms, garages etc. shown here. Entrances should not have a threshold or steps and revolving doors are not permitted. Doors should have at least 900 mm clear width. Bathroom/WC doors must open outwards. The minimum width for a landing is 1500 mm, and landings of over 15 m in length should include a circulation area (1800 × 1800 mm). All levels and facilities inside and outside a building must be accessible without negotiating steps; if necessary, include a lift → ⑬ or ramps → ⑩.

① Movement area: shower and bath

② Movement area around WC and wash basin

③ Overlapping of movement areas in a bathroom

④ Space requirements: wheelchair and movement area

⑤ Space requirement beside a bed for user and non-user of a wheelchair

⑥ Movement area in a two-side kitchen

⑦ Movement area in an L-shaped kitchen

⑧ Dimensions around the sink, oven and refrigerator

⑨ Dimensions in kitchens

⑩ Ramp

⑪ Section of ramp

⑫ Halls and passages

⑬ Lift car dimensions and movement area in front of the lift door

⑭ Space requirement in garages

⑮ Movement areas in front of hinged doors and ...

⑯ ... in front of sliding doors

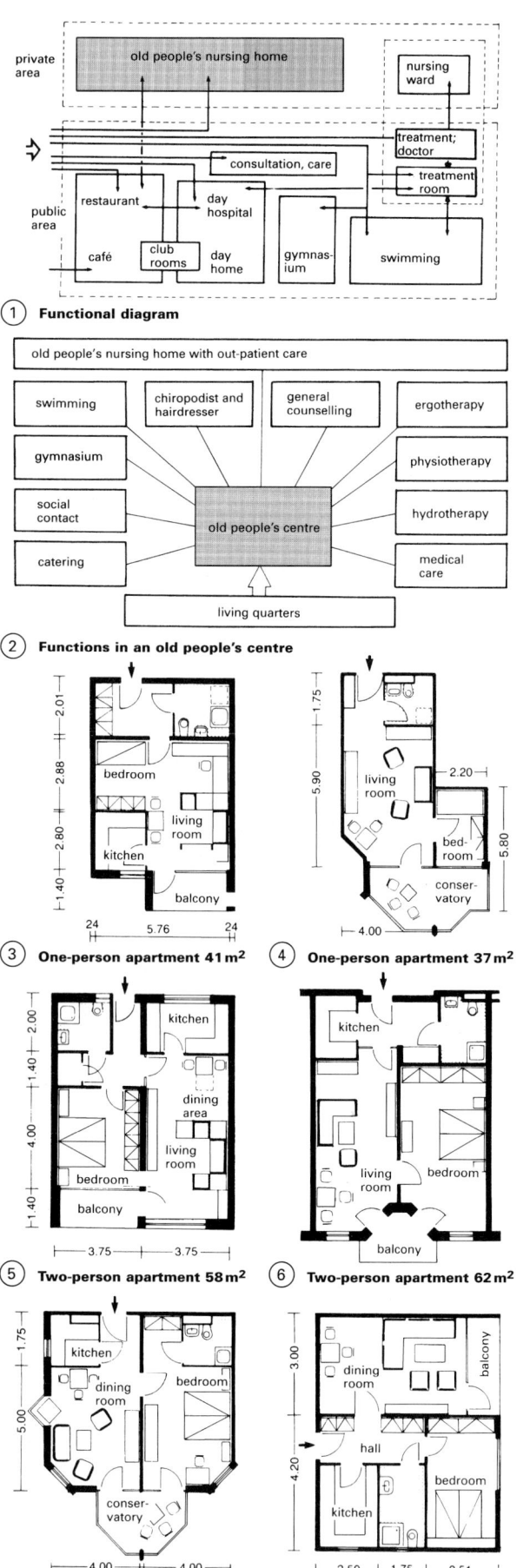

① **Functional diagram**

② **Functions in an old people's centre**

③ **One-person apartment 41 m²**

④ **One-person apartment 37 m²**

⑤ **Two-person apartment 58 m²**

⑥ **Two-person apartment 62 m²**

⑦ **Two-person apartment 56 m²**
with conservatory 9 m²

⑧ **Two-person apartment 55.5 m²**

OLD PEOPLE'S ACCOMMODATION

Depending on the degree of support required, there are three main types of accommodation and care for the elderly: (1) old people's housing, (2) old people's homes and (3) nursing homes.

In the United Kingdom, depending, inter alia, on type of dwelling and facilities provided, housing for elderly people can be classified into: category one housing, category two housing, sheltered housing, very sheltered housing, retirement housing, extra-care housing, residential care homes, nursing care homes, and dual registration homes. In the United States, although similar building types have been developed, the terminology differs. The building types that house elderly people in the United States can be described as independent retirement housing units, congregate housing, personal care housing, skilled nursing home, and life care communities.

Old people's housing → ③ – ⑧ consists of self-contained flats or apartments which cater for the needs of the elderly so that they can avoid moving into an old people's home for as long as possible. Such housing is usually scattered around residential areas, with a density of 2–10%. Flats for one person are 25–35 m²; for two people 45–55 m². Sheltered balconies ≥3 m².

Sheltered housing is generally a group of flats (each ≥20 m²) in one building, with common rooms and a tea kitchen. A good solution is to build these facilities close to a nursing home for the elderly which offers meals, leisure, recreation and various therapies. Provide one car parking space per 5–8 residents. Note that heating costs will be 2% higher than normal.

Old people's homes offer residential care facilities and must conform to regulations on planning, licensing. The large amount of ancillary space required means the most economic size is about 120 places. Meals, entertainment and therapies are provided and an integrated nursing section for short-term care. General design features: stairs 16/30 cm without open riser; edges of steps defined with a colour; handrails on both sides of stairs and in corridors; where necessary, lifts for moving patients on stretchers or in folding chairs. The buildings should all be adapted for the disabled and have open spaces with benches.

Homes should be sited close to the infrastructure of a town or village and to public transport. The inclusion of a daycare centre should be considered to provide opportunities for people living independently to make contact and receive non-residential care (approximately one daycare centre is needed per 1600 elderly people).

Architects: Turk/Richter/Bordurs

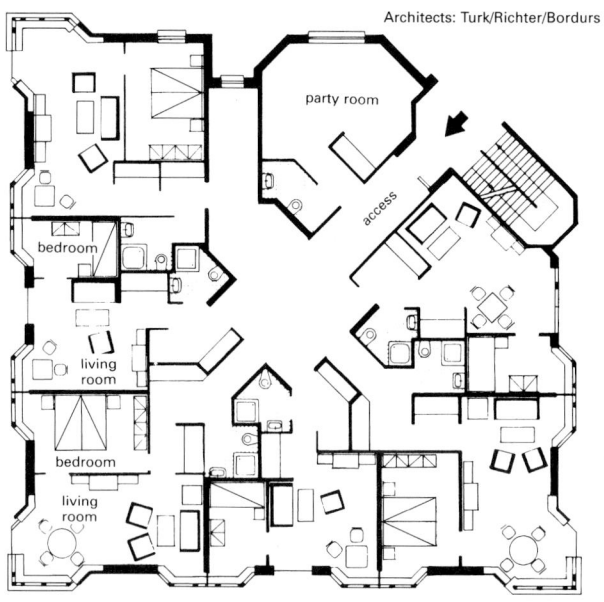

⑨ **Ground floor of residential wing, old people's home and nursing home**

OLD PEOPLE'S ACCOMMODATION

Nursing homes for the elderly provide care for people who are chronically ill and in need of medical attention. The residential area consists of a 50:50 split of single and double rooms → ① – ④. It must be clearly separated from the administration and office areas → ⑥. Residents are frequently split into groups consisting of 8–10 people, with a shared lounge and possibly a tea kitchen where meals may also be eaten → ⑤. Provide one treatment room per two groups.

Central facilities are best grouped together on ground floor. Rooms are required for administration, consultation, occupational therapy, physiotherapy, chiropody. In addition, rooms for entertainment, common rooms, cafeteria and hairdressing should be provided.

Some key issues affecting design

When considering building layout, measures will be required to reduce the risk of cross-infection. Changes in level are best avoided but if this is not possible, ramps must be provided inside and outside building. Circulation distances for residents should be kept to a minimum and all main routes will need handrails. Corridors must be wide enough to allow two people in wheelchairs or walking with frames to pass each other comfortably.

Careful interior design is necessary. Doors must not restrict the residents' ability to get around; automatic opening may be required. Furniture and fittings must be suitable for older people.

Consistent temperatures are required and contingency plans for providing heating in the event of power failures should be considered. The ability to control temperature and sunlight penetration, particularly in bedrooms and sitting rooms, is important to residents. Hot pipes and heaters must be protected: the maximum acceptable surface temperature is around 43°C.

Hot water systems must be designed to resist infection such as that causing Legionnaire's disease.

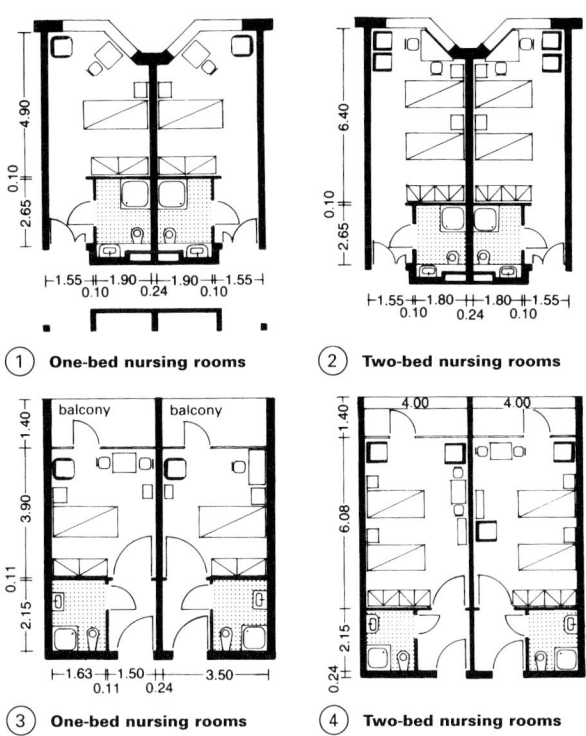

① **One-bed nursing rooms**

② **Two-bed nursing rooms**

③ **One-bed nursing rooms**

④ **Two-bed nursing rooms**

⑤ **Part of a pilot project** Architect: Pfleiderer

living/group room

two residents

one resident

bathroom

gymnasium

integrated nursing home for 36 residents

entrance

⑥ **Ground floor, old people's home and nursing home**

deliveries

hair-dresser

admin.

kiosk

hall

club room

kitchen

terrace

staff apartments

Architect: K.H. Muth

OLD PEOPLE'S ACCOMMODATION

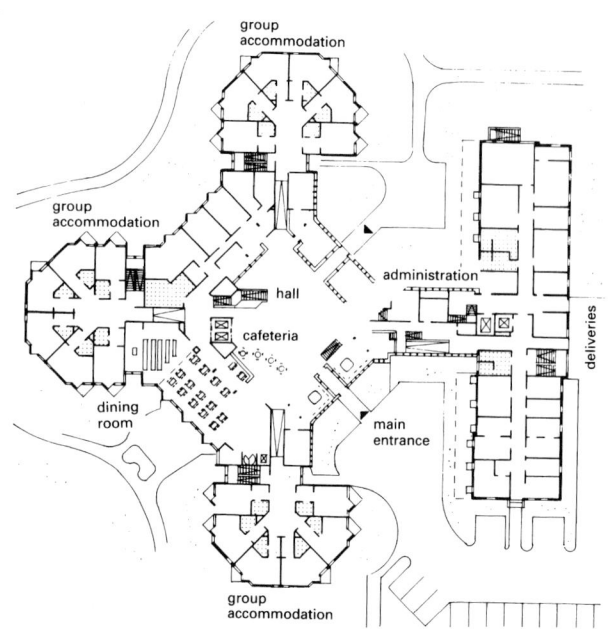

group accommodation

group accommodation

hall

cafeteria

administration

dining room

main entrance

deliveries

group accommodation

① **Ground floor, old people's centre in Viersen**

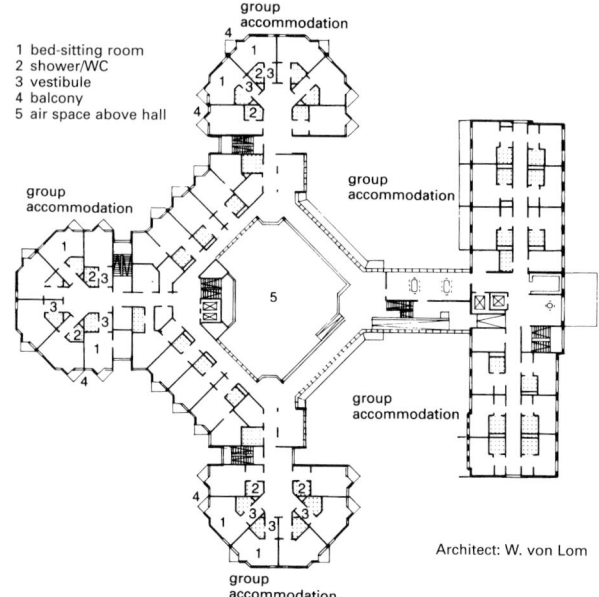

1 bed-sitting room
2 shower/WC
3 vestibule
4 balcony
5 air space above hall

group accommodation

group accommodation

group accommodation

group accommodation

group accommodation

Architect: W. von Lom

② **First floor → ①**

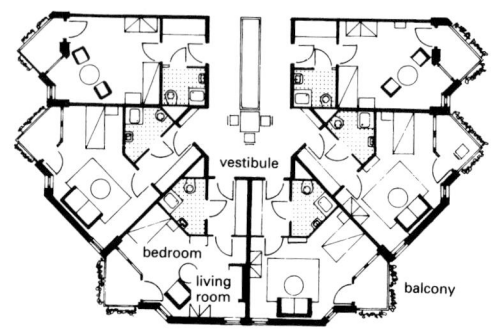

vestibule

bedroom

living room

balcony

③ **Part of floor plan → ①, ②**

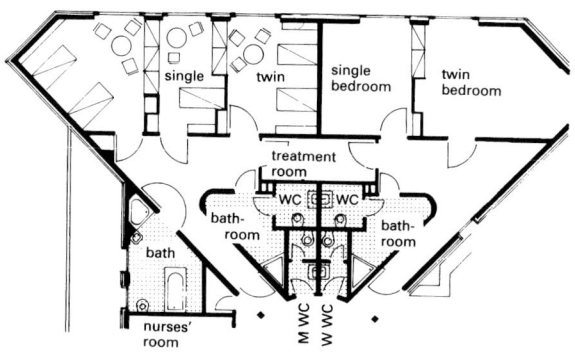

single

twin

single bedroom

twin bedroom

treatment room

WC   WC

bath-room

bath-room

bath

nurses' room

M WC   W WC

④ **Typical nursing unit → ⑤, ⑥**

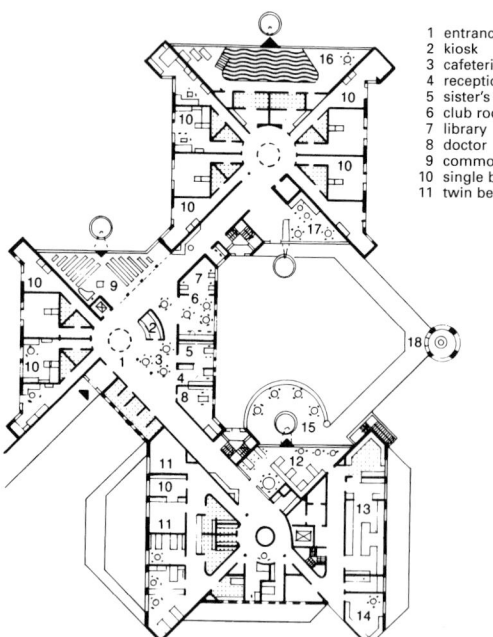

1 entrance hall
2 kiosk
3 cafeteria
4 reception
5 sister's office
6 club room
7 library
8 doctor
9 common room
10 single bedroom
11 twin bedroom
12 dining room
13 kitchen
14 staff dining room
15 dining terrace
16 physiotherapy pool
17 lounge area
18 pavilion with fountain
19 gallery
20 ventilation for physiotherapy pool
21 veranda with beds
22 dining room gallery

⑤ **Ground floor, old people's home in Mühlheim**

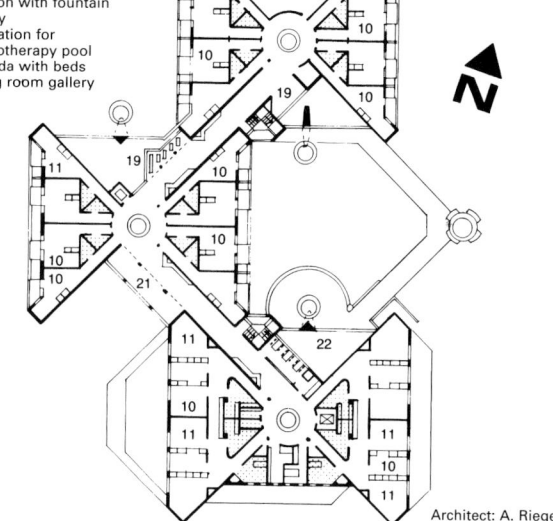

Architect: A. Riege

⑥ **First floor → ⑤**

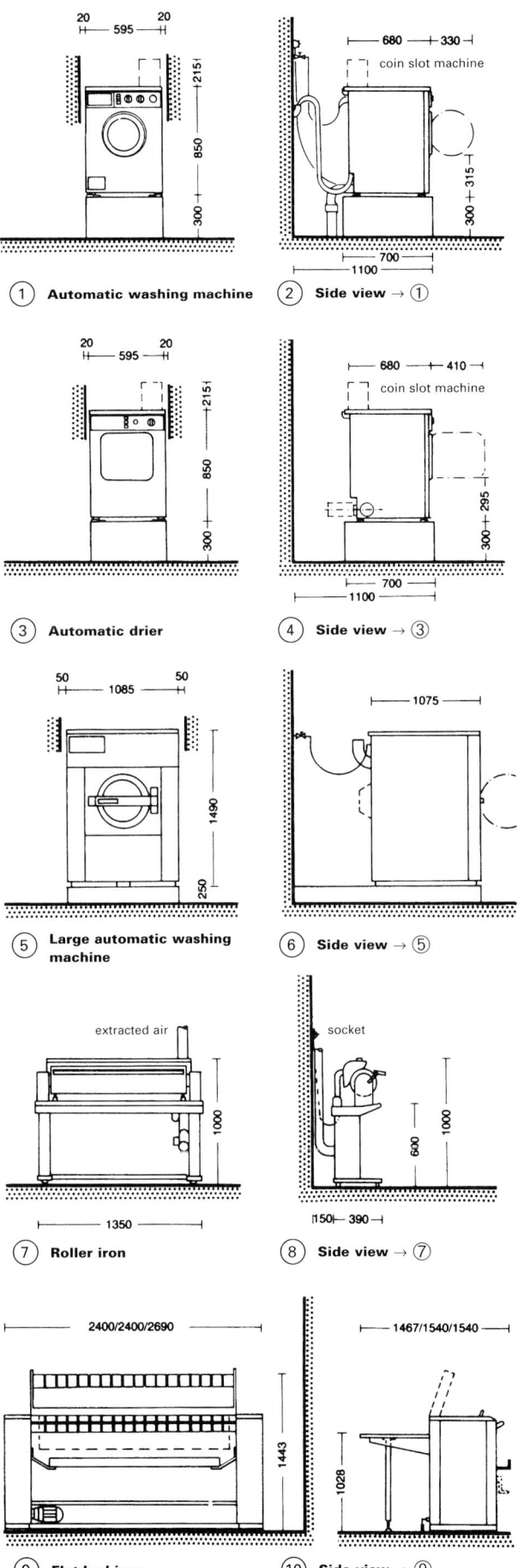

(1) **Automatic washing machine**

(2) **Side view → (1)**

coin slot machine

(3) **Automatic drier**

(4) **Side view → (3)**

coin slot machine

(5) **Large automatic washing machine**

(6) **Side view → (5)**

extracted air

socket

(7) **Roller iron**

(8) **Side view → (7)**

(9) **Flat-bed iron**

(10) **Side view → (9)**

LAUNDRIES

The following figures may be used to estimate the amount of washing arising per week in kg of dry laundry:

Domestic: approx. 3 kg/person
(proportion for ironing approx. 40%)

Hotels: approx. 20 kg/bed
(bedclothes and hand towels changed daily)
approx. 12–15 kg/bed
(change of bedclothes 4 times/week)
approx. 8–10 kg/bed
(change of bedclothes 2–3 times/week)
approx. 5 kg/bed
(tourist hotel, change of bedclothes once/week)

The values given include restaurants.

Guest-houses: approx. 8 kg/bed
Restaurants: approx. 1.5–3.0 kg/seat

The proportion of ironing is about 75% for hotels, guest-houses and restaurants.

Old peoples' homes: Residential: approx. 3 kg/bed
Nursing home: approx 8 kg/bed
Incontinent: approx. 25 kg/bed

Children's home: approx. 4 kg/bed
for babies: approx. 10–12 kg/bed

Medical nursing
homes: approx. 4 kg/bed

Incontinent: approx. 25 kg/bed

The proportion of ironing is about 60% for the above homes.

Hospitals and clinics (up to about 200 beds):

General hospital: 12–15 kg/bed

Gynaecological/
maternity unit: approx. 16 kg/bed

Children's clinic: approx. 18 kg/bed

The proportion of ironing is about 70% for hospitals.

Nursing staff: approx. 3.5 kg/person

$$\text{Required washing capacity} = \frac{\text{Amount of washing/week}}{\text{Washing days/week} \times \text{number of washes/day}}$$

Example calculations:

1) Hotel with 80 beds; utilisation 60% = 48 beds
Four changes of bedclothes/week and daily change of hand towels = approx. 12 kg/bed

48 beds at 12 kg laundry	= 576 kg/week
Table and kitchen washing, approx.	74 kg/week
	650 kg/week

Required washing capacity $= \dfrac{650}{3 \times 7} = 18.6$ kg per wash

2) Hotel with 150 beds; utilisation 60% = 90 beds
Daily changes of bedclothes and hand towels = 20 kg/bed

90 beds at 20 kg laundry	= 1800 kg/week
Table and kitchen washing, approx.	200 kg/week
	2000 kg/week

Required washing capacity $= \dfrac{2000}{3 \times 7} = 57.1$ kg per wash

3) Old people's and nursing home: 50 residential beds, 70 nursing beds

70 nursing beds at 12 kg clothes	= 840 kg/week
	(suspected of being infected)

Required washing capacity $= \dfrac{840}{5 \times 5} = 33.6$ kg per wash

50 old people's beds at 3 kg laundry	= 150 kg/week
Table and kitchen washing, approx.	100 kg/week
	250 kg/week
	(not suspected of being infected)

Required washing capacity $= \dfrac{250}{3 \times 6} = 8.3$ kg per wash

LAUNDRIES

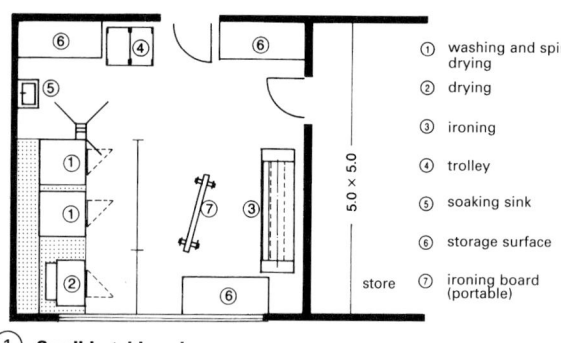

① washing and spin drying
② drying
③ ironing
④ trolley
⑤ soaking sink
⑥ storage surface
⑦ ironing board (portable)

store

① **Small hotel laundry**

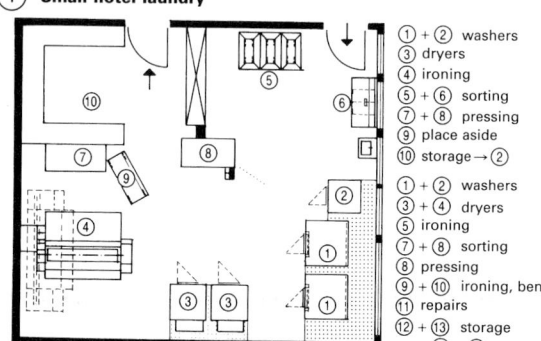

① + ② washers
③ dryers
④ ironing
⑤ + ⑥ sorting
⑦ + ⑧ pressing
⑨ place aside
⑩ storage → ②

① + ② washers
③ + ④ dryers
⑤ ironing
⑦ + ⑧ sorting
⑧ pressing
⑨ + ⑩ ironing, bench
⑪ repairs
⑫ + ⑬ storage → ③ + ④

② **Laundry of average size**

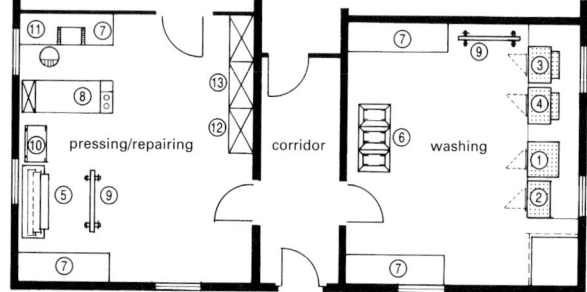

pressing/repairing   corridor   washing

③ **Laundry in two separate rooms**

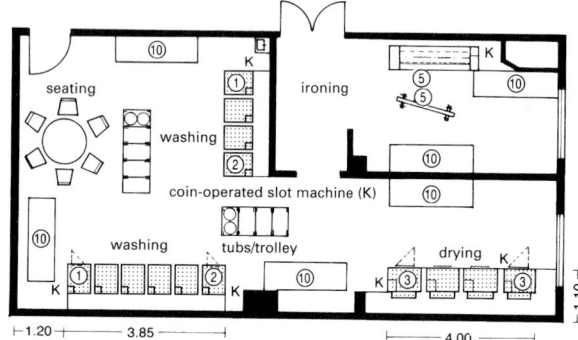

seating   ironing

washing

coin-operated slot machine (K)

washing   tubs/trolley   drying

④ **Self-service laundry/launderette**

1.20   3.85   4.00   1.10

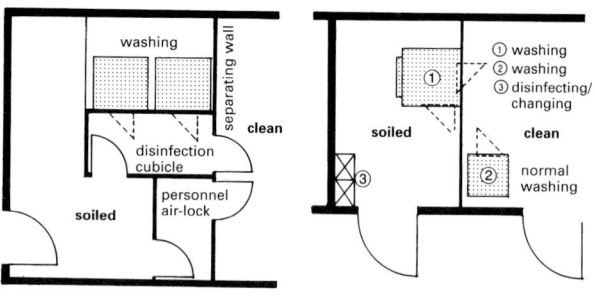

washing

separating wall

clean

disinfection cubicle

personnel air-lock

soiled

⑤ **Single-door washing machines in disinfection cubicle**

soiled   clean

① washing
② washing
③ disinfecting/changing

normal washing

⑥ **Clean and soiled laundry separated**

Some laundries may have to be separated into 'clean' and 'soiled' sections (e.g. in hospitals), each with its own entry point → ⑤ – ⑥ + ⑧.

On the soiled side, the floors, walls and surfaces of all installed equipment must be suitable for wet cleaning and disinfection.

Walkways between the soiled and clean areas should be designed as personnel air-lock systems with facilities for hand disinfection and space for protective clothing. The doors in the air-lock system must be linked such that only one door can be opened at a time.

		weight g
men's clothing		
shirt		170
vest	light	100
	heavy	150
underwear	briefs	75
	boxer	180
pyjamas		450
handkerchief		20
socks (pair)		70
women's clothing		
blouse		140
underwear sets		140
petticoat		75
pyjamas		350
nightdress		170
handkerchief		10
apron		170
smock		130
children's clothing		
dress		110
underwear		80
jacket, pullover		75
bib		25
handkerchief		15
socks (pair)		70
tights		100

		weight g
for swimming		
beach/bathrobe		900
bath towel	100 × 200	800
beach towel	67 × 140	400
hand towel	50 × 100	200
swimming trunks		100
swimming costume 1-piece		260
	2-piece	200
bedclothes		
duvet cover	160 × 200	850
sheet	150 × 250	670
top sheet	140 × 230	600
pillow case	80 × 80	200
table and kitchen linen		
tablecloth	125 × 160	370
table cover	125 × 400	1000
serviette	70 × 70	80
hand towel	40 × 60	100
dish towel	60 × 60	100
working clothes		
working suit		1200
dungarees		800
apron		200
men's overalls		500
women's overalls		400

⑦ **Average weight of clothes items**

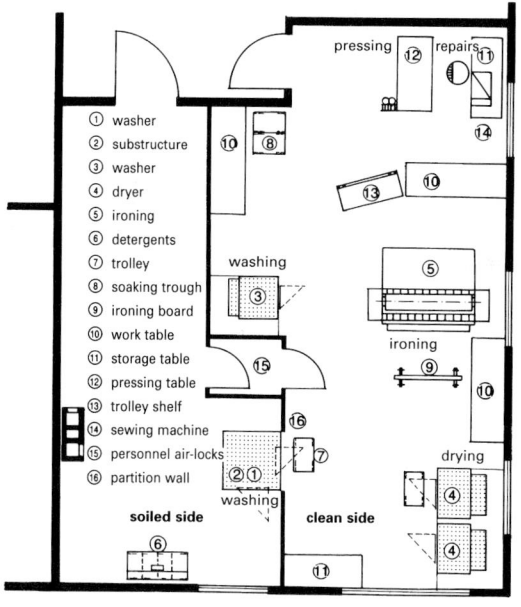

① washer
② substructure
③ washer
④ dryer
⑤ ironing
⑥ detergents
⑦ trolley
⑧ soaking trough
⑨ ironing board
⑩ work table
⑪ storage table
⑫ pressing table
⑬ trolley shelf
⑭ sewing machine
⑮ personnel air-locks
⑯ partition wall

pressing   repairs

washing

ironing

drying

washing

soiled side   **clean side**

⑧ **Laundry in an old people's home**

General guidelines

Secondary schools (with no 6th form)

e.g. 2 or 3 classes per year

10 (12) or 15 (18) classrooms	each 65–70 m²
1 extra-large classroom (can be divided)	85 m²
3 classrooms for special courses	40–45 m²

Science rooms

1 or 2 for demonstrations & practicals, or	each 70–75 m²
1 for physics demonstrations & practicals	70–75 m²
1 for chemistry and biology demonstrations & practicals, or	70–75 m²
1 for chemistry demonstrations & practicals	70–75 m²
1 for biology demonstrations & practicals	70–75 m²
1 or 2 preparation rooms, plus rooms for collections and materials, or	each 40 m²
1 preparation room for physics and chemistry (also used for collections and materials), or	30–35 m²
1 physics preparation room	30–35 m²
1 chemistry preparation room	20 m²
1 biology preparation room	30–35 m²
1 or 2 science rooms	each 30–35 m²
1 room for photography	20–25 m²

Domestic science

1 kitchen	70–75 m²
1 classroom/dining room	30–40 m²
rooms for provisions, materials and household appliances	30–40 m²
1 washroom/changing room	15–20 m²

Art, crafts and textiles

1 drawing studio (arts and crafts)	
1 or 2 rooms for technical crafts	
1 or 2 rooms for materials	
1 washroom/changing room total of approx.	180–220 m²
1 room for textile design	70–75 m²
3 rooms for teaching materials	each 10–15 m²
1 music room	65–70 m²
1 storeroom (instruments, music, stands)	15–20 m²

Language lab

1 room for language teaching system	80–85 m²
1 room for materials and equipment	10–15 m²
1 room for library and magazines	60–65 m² or 70–75 m²
1 room for pupils' committee	15–20 m²
1 recreation room (to accommodate a maximum of half the total no. of pupils at 1 m²/pupil)	

Administration

1 staffroom (meeting room)	80–85 m²
1 staff study (staff library) (or can be combined)	100–105 m²
1 office for headteacher	20/25 m²
1 office for deputy head	20–25 m²
1 office	15–20 m²
1 room for meeting parents, doubles as sickroom	20–25 m²
1 caretaker's room (also for milk distribution)	20–25 m²

Sport

Gymnasium (per 10–15 classes)
1 exercise area of 15 × 27 m
Sports grounds according to requirements

Secondary school (with 6th form)

e.g. 2 classes per year

18 classrooms:

12 classrooms	65–70 m²
6 classrooms (upper level)	50 m²

5 classrooms:

2 supplementary classrooms	65–70 m²
3 supplementary classrooms	50 m²
1 extra-large classroom (history, geography)	
1 room for social sciences	50 m²

Science rooms

Physics and biology

1 classroom	each 55–60 m²
1 room each for collections and materials	30–35 m²
1 room each for preparation	30–35 m²
1 room each for demonstrations & practicals	70–75 m²

Chemistry

1 room for theory and practical work	80–85 m²
1 room for preparation	30–35 m²
1 room for collections and materials	30–35 m²
2 rooms for science groups	each 30–35 m²
1 room for photography	20–25 m²

Domestic science

1 kitchen	70–75 m²
1 classroom/dining room	30–40 m²
Rooms for provisions, materials and household appliances	30–40 m²
1 washroom/changing room	15–20 m²

Art

1 drawing studio	80–85 m²
2 rooms for crafts	60–65 m²
2 rooms for materials	each 20–25 m²
1 washroom/changing room	15–20 m²
1 room for textile design	70–75 m²
1 music room	65–70 m²
1 storeroom	15–20 m²

Language lab

1 room for language teaching system	80–85 m²
1 room for materials and equipment	10–15 m²
3 rooms for teaching materials	each 10–15 m²
1 room for school library	70–75 m²
1 room for pupils' committee	15–20 m²
1 recreation room to accommodate a maximum of half the total no. of pupils at 1 m²/pupil)	

Administration

1 staffroom (meeting room)	80–85 m²
1 staff study (staff library) (or can be combined)	100–105 m²
1 office for headteacher	20–25 m²
1 office for deputy head	20–25 m²
1 office	15–20 m²
1 room for meeting parents (doubles as sickroom)	20–25 m²
1 caretaker's room (also for milk distribution)	20–25 m²

Sport

Gymnasium (per 10–15 classes or part of)
1 exercise area of 15 × 27 m
Sports ground according to requirements

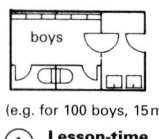

(e.g. for 100 boys, 15 m²)

(1) **Lesson-time WCs**

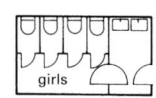

girls

(e.g. for 100 girls, 15 m²)

(2) **Lesson-time WCs**

(e.g. for 250 girls, 40 m² and 250 boys, 40 m²)

(3) **Break-time WC facilities**

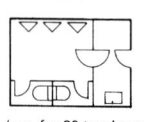

(e.g. for 30 teachers, 15 m²)

(4) **WCs for male staff**

(e.g. for 20 teachers, 10 m²)

(5) **WCs for female staff**

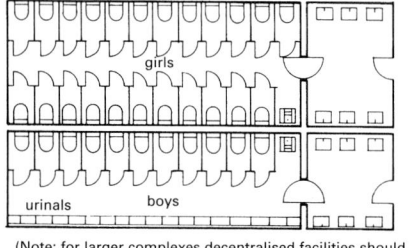

urinals   boys

(Note: for larger complexes decentralised facilities should be provided.)

(6) **Double-range facilities for 500 girls, 65 m²; for 500 boys, 40 m²**

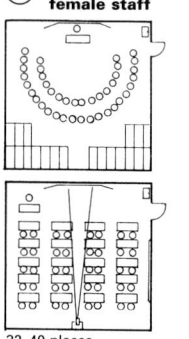

32–40 places

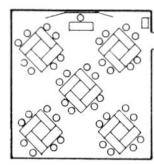

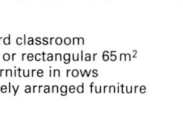

standard classroom square or rectangular 65 m² with furniture in rows and freely arranged furniture

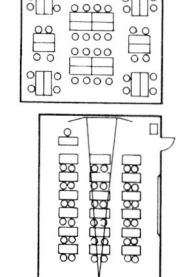

30–36 places

(7) **Rooms and areas for general-purpose teaching**

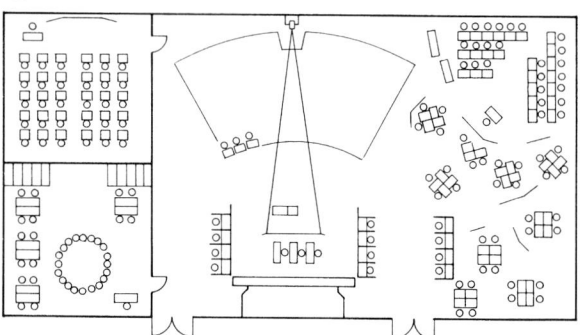

option: either divided into 6 standard classrooms and staffroom or as open-plan teaching space

(8) **Teaching area with desks for 180 pupils 550 m²**

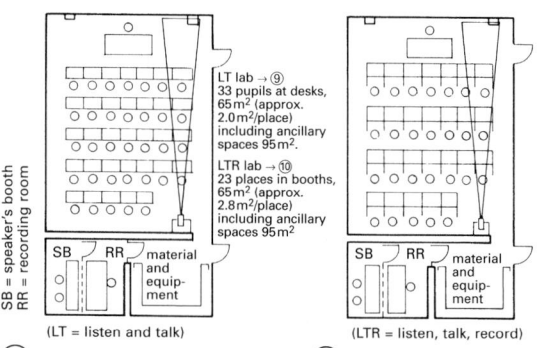

SB = speaker's booth
RR = recording room

LT lab → (9)
33 pupils at desks, 65 m² (approx. 2.0 m²/place) including ancillary spaces 95 m².

LTR lab → (10)
23 places in booths, 65 m² (approx. 2.8 m²/place) including ancillary spaces 95 m².

SB   RR   material and equipment

(LT = listen and talk)

(9) **Language lab**

SB   RR   material and equipment

(LTR = listen, talk, record)

(10) **Language lab**

308

Cloakroom facilities can be decentralised by allocating space outside the classrooms but directly linked to them. The number of toilets, urinals and wash-basins required, based on total number of pupils and separated according to sex, should be as set out in the local school building guidelines (e.g. → (11)). Sanitary installations with direct daylight and ventilation are preferable, and there must be separate entrances for boys and girls. Examples of different toilet facilities for schools are shown in (1) – (6).

Horizontal and vertical circulation usually doubles as an emergency escape route. Escape routes must have a clear width of min. 1 m/150 people, but min. width of corridors in classroom areas is 2.00 m or 1.25 m for less than 180 people. Stairs in classroom areas must be 1.25 m, other escape routes 1.00 m. Max. length of escape routes: 25 m measured in a straight line from the stairwell door to the furthest workplace, or 30 m in an indirect line to the centre of the room. Capacity of stairs is dependent on number of users, average occupancy, etc. Width of stairs: 0.80 m/100 people (minimum 1.25 m, max. 2.50 m). Alternatively: 0.10 m/15 people. (Only the top floor is calculated at 100% occupancy, remaining floors at 50%.)

General-purpose teaching area includes standard classrooms, supplementary classrooms, extra-large classrooms, rooms for special courses, rooms for teaching languages and social studies, language labs, rooms for teaching material, maps and other ancillary rooms.

Space requirements: classroom for traditional teaching 2.00 m²/pupil; for teaching in sets 3.00 m²/pupil, for open plan teaching 4.50 m²/place including ancillary areas needed for each subject.

Standard room shape: rectangular or square (12×20, 12×16, 12×12, 12×10); with a max. room depth of 7.20 m it is possible to have windows on one side only. → (7)

Floor areas are: traditional classroom, 1.80–2.00 m²/pupil; open plan 3.00–5.00 m²/pupil. The clear height should be 2.70–3.40 m.

Language labs should be within or directly related to the general-purpose teaching area, and close to media centre and library. Approximately 30 language lab. places per 1000 pupils will be needed → (9) – (11). The size of LT (listen/talk) and LSR (listen/talk/record) labs is approx. 80 m²: booths 1×2 m, number of places/lab. 24–30, i.e. 48–60 m², plus ancillary spaces (e.g. studio, recording room, archive for teachers' and pupils' tapes). Artificially-lit internal language labs with an environmental control system are also possible.

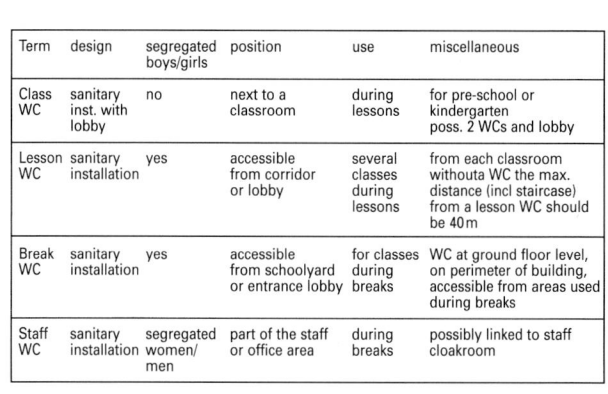

Term	design	segregated boys/girls	position	use	miscellaneous
Class WC	sanitary inst. with lobby	no	next to a classroom	during lessons	for pre-school or kindergarten poss. 2 WCs and lobby
Lesson WC	sanitary installation	yes	accessible from corridor or lobby	several classes during lessons	from each classroom withouta WC the max. distance (incl staircase) from a lesson WC should be 40 m
Break WC	sanitary installation	yes	accessible from schoolyard or entrance lobby	for classes during breaks	WC at ground floor level, on perimeter of building, accessible from areas used during breaks
Staff WC	sanitary installation	segregated women/men	part of the staff or office area	during breaks	possibly linked to staff cloakroom

(11) **Recommended WC facilities**

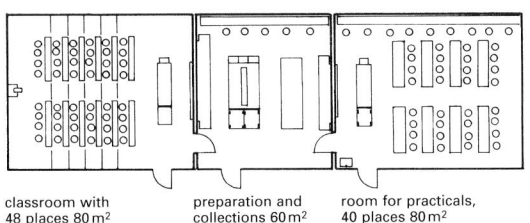

classroom with 48 places 80 m²　　preparation and collections 60 m²　　room for practicals, 40 places 80 m²

① **Rooms and areas for science teaching**

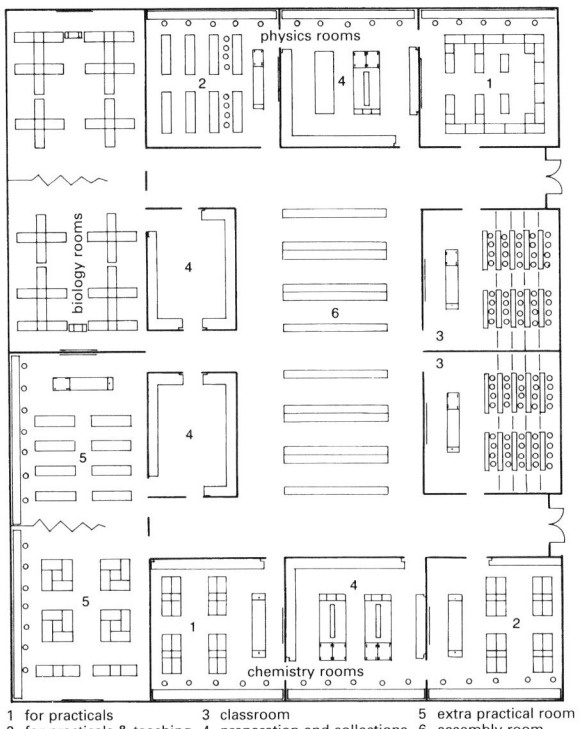

1 for practicals　　3 classroom　　5 extra practical room
2 for practicals & teaching　　4 preparation and collections　　6 assembly room

② **Science area with 400 places 1400 m²**

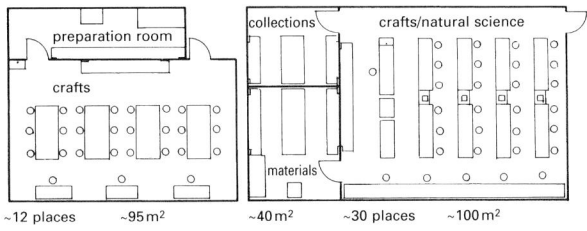

preparation room
crafts
collections
crafts/natural science
materials
~12 places　　~95 m²　　~40 m²　　~30 places　　~100 m²

③ **Rooms and areas for technical subjects, economics, music and art → ④ – ⑥**

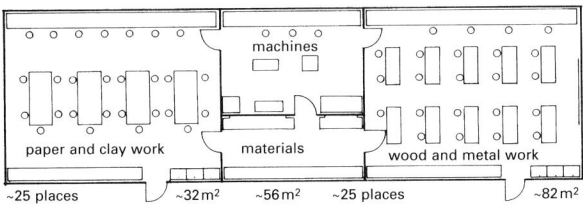

paper and clay work　　machines　　materials　　wood and metal work
~25 places　　~32 m²　　~56 m²　　~25 places　　~82 m²

④ **Areas for technical subjects**

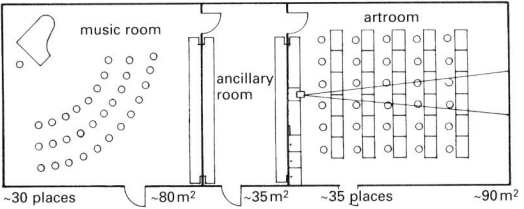

music room　　artroom　　ancillary room
~30 places　　~80 m²　　~35 m²　　~35 places　　~90 m²

⑤ **Music and art**

Science area includes rooms for teaching of theory and practice, practicals, preparation and collections, photographic studios and labs. Classrooms for biology, physics and chemistry 2.50 m²/place. For lectures and demonstrations in practical work 4.50 m²/place including special-purpose ancillary space but not including ancillary rooms.

Room sizes for demonstrations and practicals in chemistry and biology, physics, or combinations should be 70–80 m² → ①. Ideally, for physics, biology and chemistry lectures (possibly including demonstrations) 60 m² is needed, with fixed raked seating. Second entrance/exit. Possibility of internal classroom with artificial lighting.

Room for practical work, group work in biology and physics and as well as interdisciplinary work, space divisible into smaller units. 80 m² per individual room or space.

Rooms for preparation, collections and materials for individual subjects or combinations of subjects. Total of 30–40 or 70 m² depending on the size of the school and the science area. Internal rooms with artificial light allowable.

Rooms for photographic work and photographic labs are best associated with the science rooms. Ideally, they should be in the form of a studio, with a lobby between the lab and teaching area. Dark room with areas for printing (1 enlarging table for 2–3 pupils, combined with wet-processing places), for developing negatives and rooms or area for loading film.

Position of rooms: best north-facing with constant room temperature. Space required depends on number of pupils, generally 6–14 pupils per group, at least 3–4 m² per workplace. Type of photo lab depends on areas and sizes:

- one-room lab 20–30 m², minimum size with separate bay of 1.50–2.0 m² for loading film.
- two-room lab 30–40 m², consisting of lit room, light lock and dark room (positive and negative work), film-loading room 2 m².
- three-room lab, printing room, lit room with necessary light locks, light locks 1–2 m² without furniture, dark room lamps only.

For exhibitions, etc. shared use of other rooms is possible.

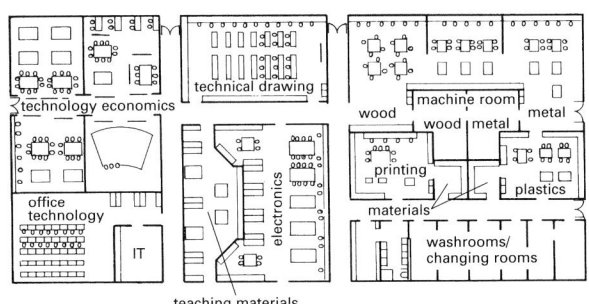

⑥ **Areas for economics of technology, office technology, technical drawing and crafts, total of 350 places, 1600 m²**

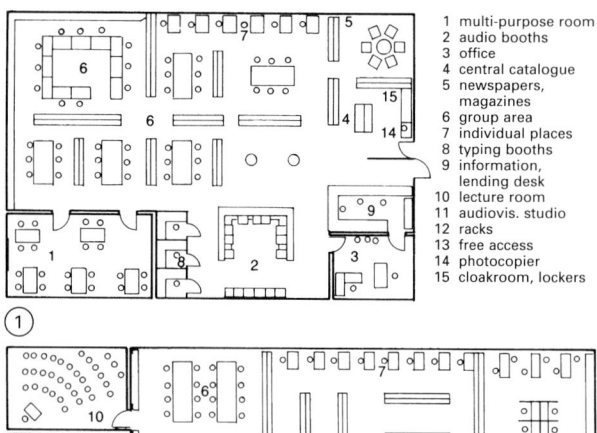

1 multi-purpose room
2 audio booths
3 office
4 central catalogue
5 newspapers, magazines
6 group area
7 individual places
8 typing booths
9 information, lending desk
10 lecture room
11 audiovis. studio
12 racks
13 free access
14 photocopier
15 cloakroom, lockers

①

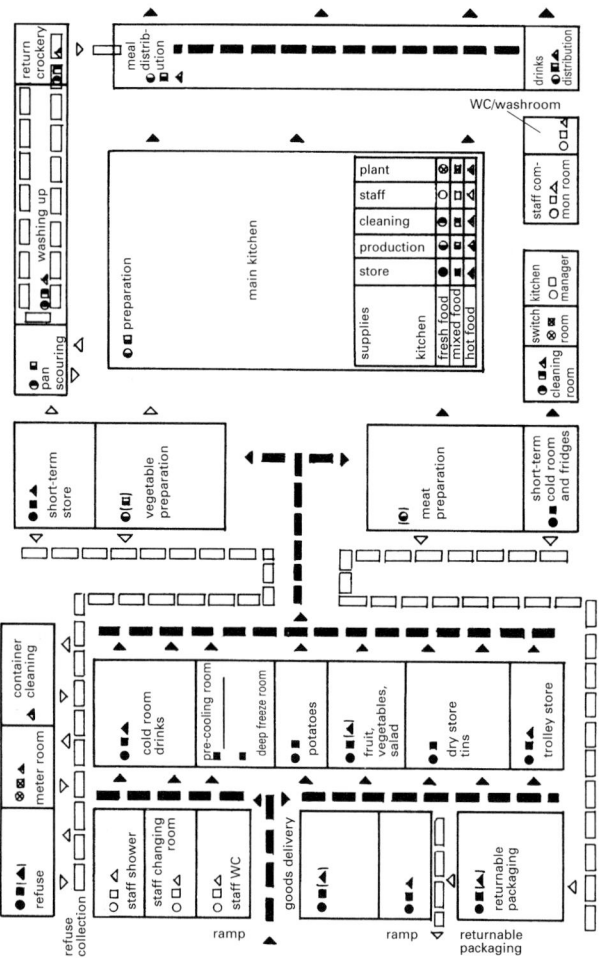

② **Example of school library/media centre**

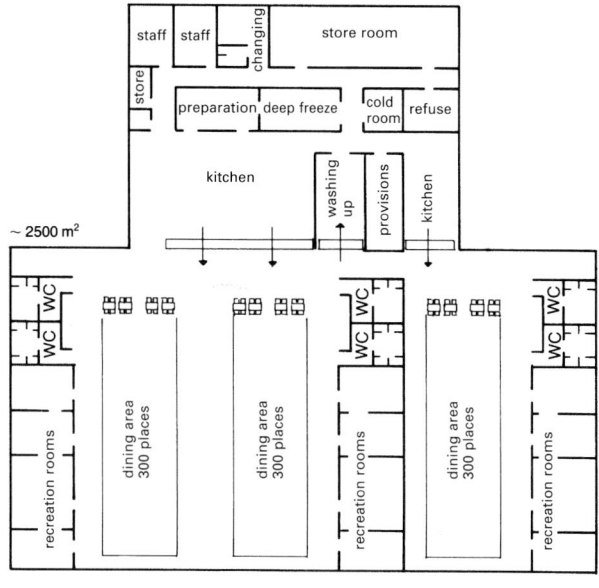

③ **Organisation of space and functions in school kitchen**

Library, media centre and central amenities:

Purpose: information centre for classwork, further education and leisure and may be used by pupils, teachers and non-school users.

Library includes a conventional school library for pupils and teachers with books and magazines, lending facilities, reading and work places. The media centre is an extension of the library with recording and playback facilities for radio, film, TV, i.e. audio-visual equipment and a corresponding stock of software, microfilm and microfiche facilities.

Standard space requirement overall: library/media centre 0.35–0.55 m^2/pupil. Broken down into:

- book issues and returns, 5 m^2 per workplace, and catalogue space of 20–40 m^2
- information: librarian, media advisor, media technician, etc. 10–20 m^2 per person

Compact book storage in 1000 volume stacks at 20–30 volumes/metre run of shelving. Free access bookcase approx. 4 m^2 including circulation space, reading places and catalogues. For 1000 volumes reference books 20–40 m^2, study area generally per 1000 volumes reference books 25 m^2 for 5% of the pupils/teachers, but at least 30 study spaces at 2 m^2 each, i.e. 60 m^2 carrels 2.5–3.0 m^2. Room for work in groups of 8–10, 20 m^2 → ① – ②.

For kitchen and ancillary rooms, the size and equipment specification depends on the catering system. Table service for food and table clearing for young children (portions possibly served by teacher), otherwise self-service (e.g. from conveyer belt, counter, cafeteria line or free-flow system). Distribution capacity of 5–15 meals/minute or 250–1000/ hour, variable staffing levels. Space required for distribution systems 40–60 m^2. Dining room size depends on number of pupils and number of sittings, min. of 1.20–1.40 m^2 per place. Larger spaces should be divided up. For every 40 places, 1 wash-basin in the entrance area → ③ – ④.

④ **Meal and crockery distribution and dining area**

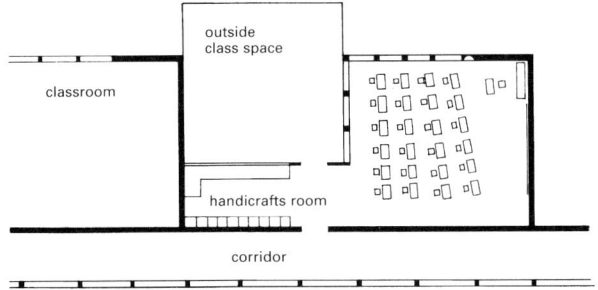

1. Example of school library/media centre. Classroom lit and ventilated from two sides via cloakroom and corridor. Corridor opens out every second classroom with a room for teaching materials
Architect: Yorke, Rosenberg, Mardall

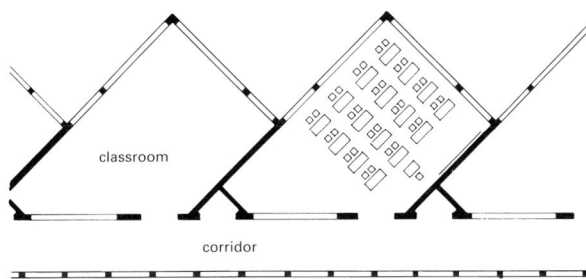

2. Example of joining classroom, outside classroom space and hobby room
Architect: Neutra

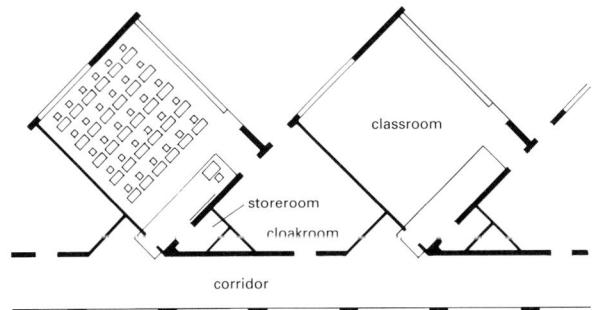

3. Saw-tooth layout, risk of disturbance between rooms
Architect: Carbonara

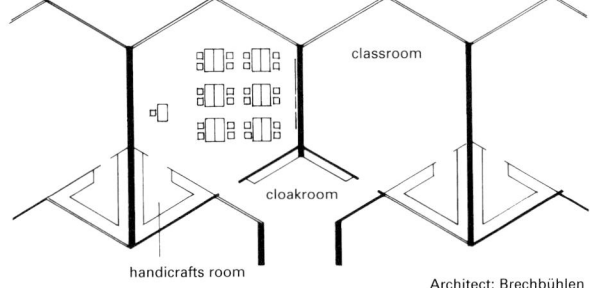

4. Classroom with daylight from high window, but no window at the back. Corridor opens out in front of each classroom with cloakroom and store room
Architect: Carbonara

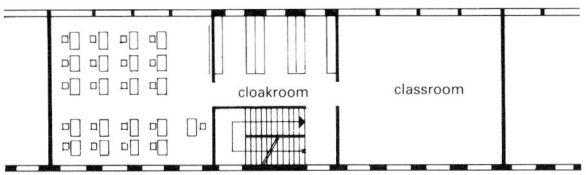

5. Hexagonal classrooms and internal triangular handicrafts room with no windows
Architect: Brechbühlen

Classrooms: one classroom per class, square if possible, in exceptional cases rectangular, max. 32 pupils, min. of 65–70 m^2 (approx. 2.00 m^2 × 2.20 m^2 per pupil) if possible daylit on two sides → ③ + ⑥. Furniture either in rows or informally arranged.

Front of class: chalkboard with sliding panels, projection space, socket for TV, radio, tape recorder, etc., wash-basin near entrance. Provision for hanging maps. Facility to black out windows. Group rooms divided into separate workspaces to accommodate mixed ability classes only in special cases.

Alternatives to individual classes and group rooms: 2–3 classrooms joined together to make teaching spaces for discussions between pupils and teachers, or lessons in larger groups; can also be divided by partitions. Draught-excluding lobbies and entrance areas also connect to horizontal and vertical circulation (corridors, stairs, ramps) and can be used during breaks (0.50 m^2/pupil). Multi-use area for parties, play or exhibitions.

Room for teaching materials 12–15 m^2: centrally positioned, part of the staff area or in a multi-purpose room.

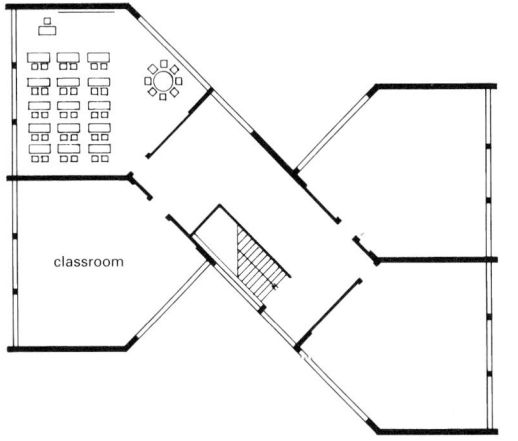

6. Multistorey building, two classes around a staircase, daylight from two sides
Architect: Schuster

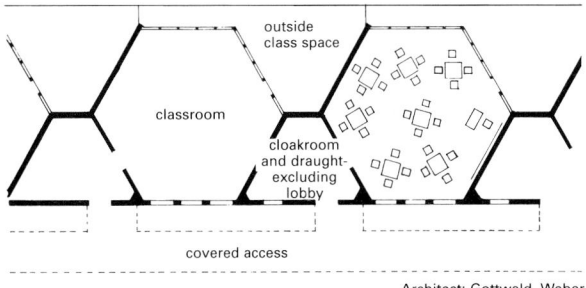

7. Four classrooms/floor with daylight from two sides, extended on one side for group teaching
Architect: Haefeli, Moser, Steiger

8. Hexagonal classrooms with no corridor, access through cloakroom, lobby
Architect: Gottwald, Weber

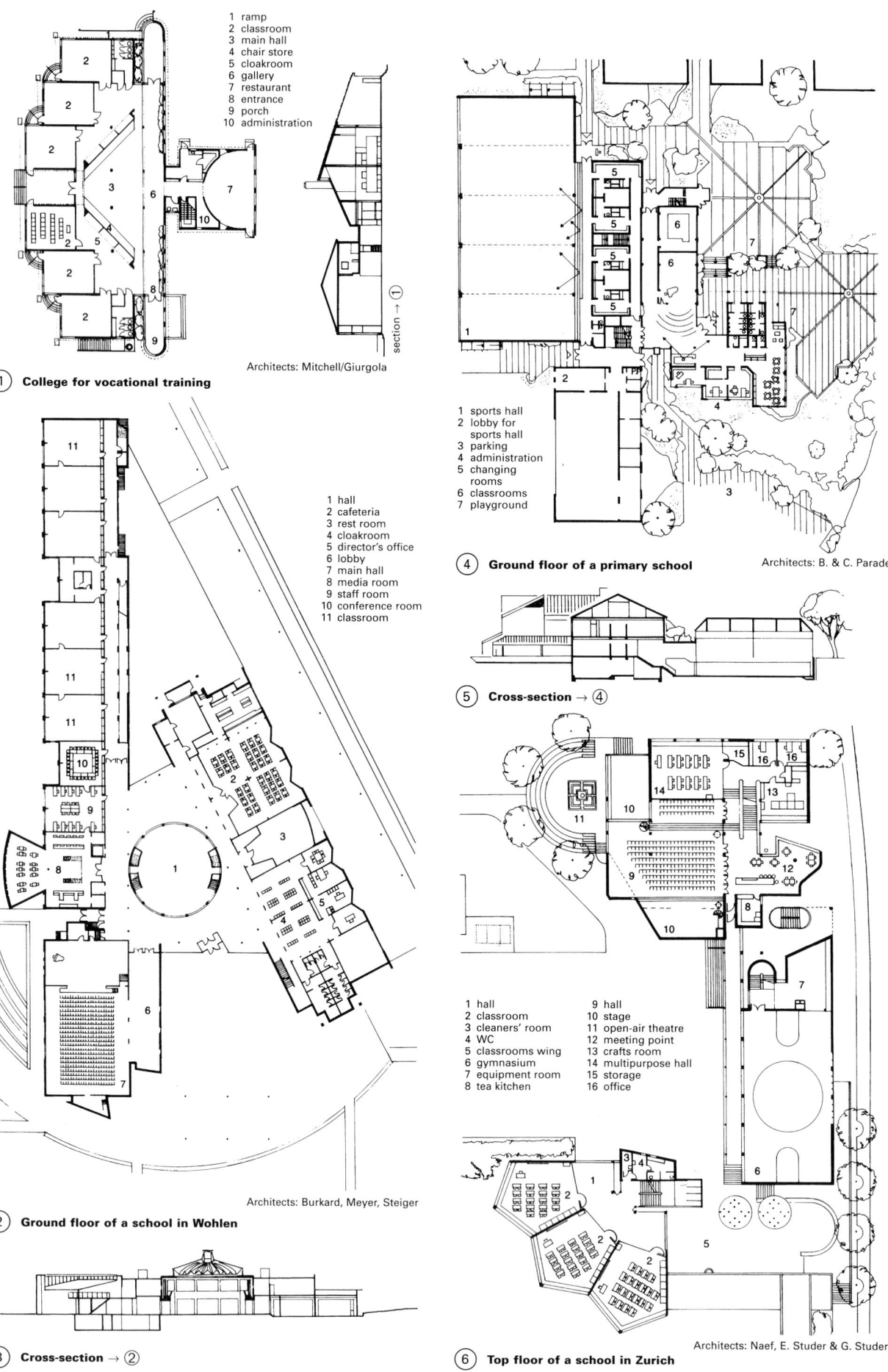

1 ramp
2 classroom
3 main hall
4 chair store
5 cloakroom
6 gallery
7 restaurant
8 entrance
9 porch
10 administration

section → (1)

Architects: Mitchell/Giurgola

(1) **College for vocational training**

1 sports hall
2 lobby for sports hall
3 parking
4 administration
5 changing rooms
6 classrooms
7 playground

(4) **Ground floor of a primary school**　　　　Architects: B. & C. Parade

(5) **Cross-section → (4)**

1 hall
2 cafeteria
3 rest room
4 cloakroom
5 director's office
6 lobby
7 main hall
8 media room
9 staff room
10 conference room
11 classroom

Architects: Burkard, Meyer, Steiger

(2) **Ground floor of a school in Wohlen**

(3) **Cross-section → (2)**

1 hall   9 hall
2 classroom   10 stage
3 cleaners' room 11 open-air theatre
4 WC   12 meeting point
5 classrooms wing 13 crafts room
6 gymnasium   14 multipurpose hall
7 equipment room 15 storage
8 tea kitchen   16 office

Architects: Naef, E. Studer & G. Studer

(6) **Top floor of a school in Zurich**

Open-plan

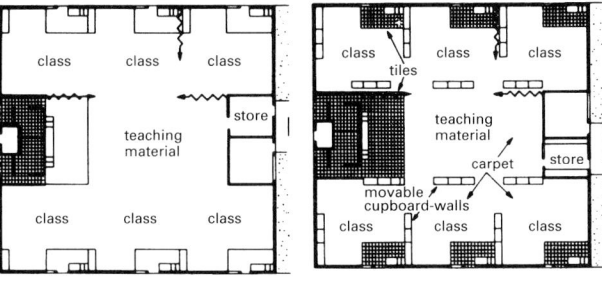

① **Schoolroom without walls**

② **Divided by movable cupboard-walls**

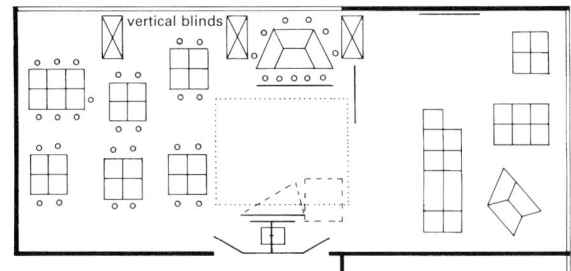

③ **Tannenberg School in Seeheim, practising team teaching**

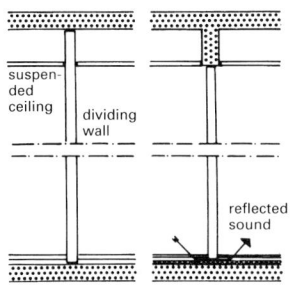

④ **Floor and ceiling connections for partitions**

⑤ **Ceiling void for services**

Nowadays, it is often considered normal for offices to be open plan. This sometimes influences school architecture. The two have similar requirements regarding size of room, lighting, ventilation, acoustics, floor and ceiling finishes, furniture, and colour.

Main advantage: flexibility → ① + ②. Team teaching in groups of up to 100 pupils. Space per pupil (not incl. core) 3.4 m²–4 m².

The later addition of partitions should be possible → ④. There are many US examples. German model example: Tannenberg School, Seeheim → ③. However, vertical drainpipes and service ducts, etc. are a problem because of the need to fix sound-insulating partitions → ④. Ceiling panels should be removable so that services in the ceiling void are accessible → ⑤.

Large groups of 40–50 pupils, divided into medium-sized groups of 25–26 pupils, small groups of 10 pupils → ③.

Planning grid 1.20 × 1.20 m throughout; clear room height 3 m. Movable partitions which can be taken down provide a solution for the transition from old fixed classrooms to open plan → ④. Also, building forms which create small spaces → ① + ② and → ⑥ – ⑧. Examples of seating arrangement for watching films, slides etc → ⑨ – ⑩.

Educational experts maintain that, during conscious learning, people best retain information that they have obtained themselves, more precisely:

10% of what they read;
20% of what they hear;
30% of what they see;
50% of what they hear and see;
70% of what they say themselves; and
90% of what they do themselves involving their own actions.

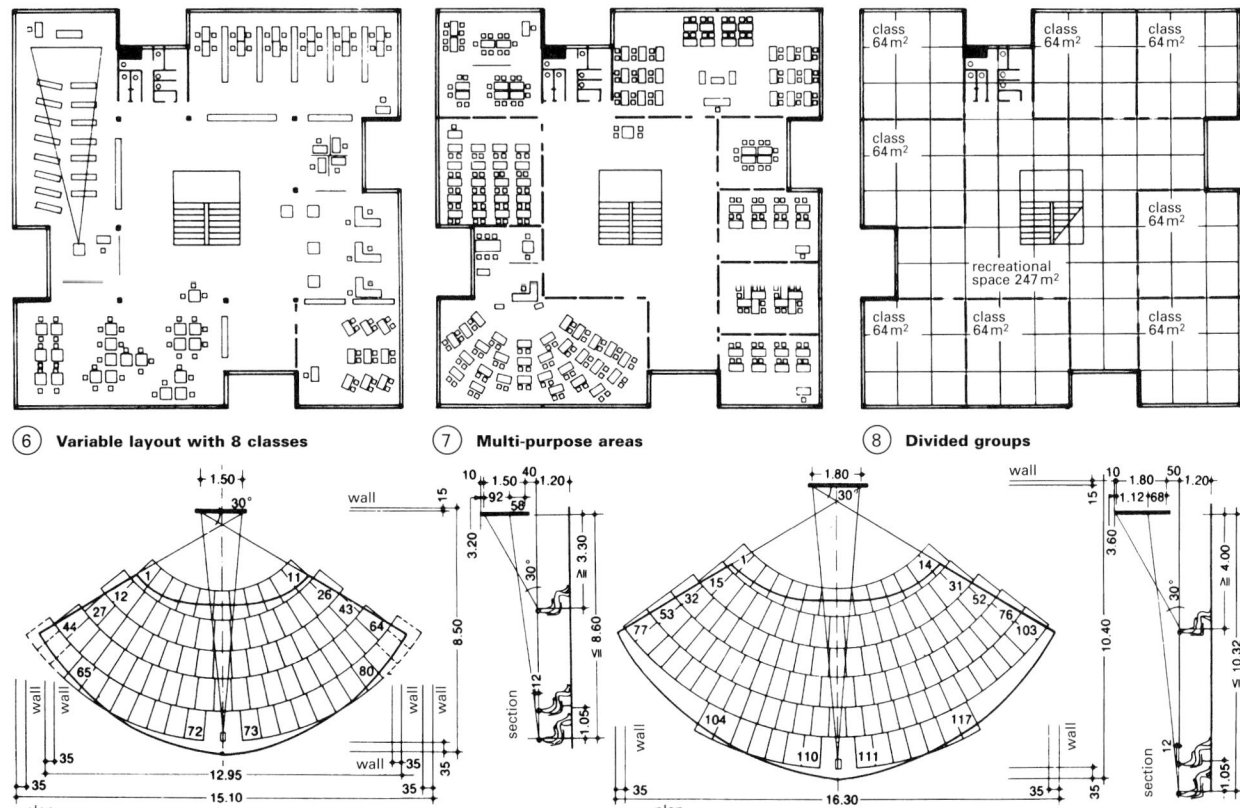

⑥ **Variable layout with 8 classes**

⑦ **Multi-purpose areas**

⑧ **Divided groups**

⑨ **Seating arrangement for 80 pupils (over 10 years old) for film, slide and overhead projection**

⑩ **for 117 pupils over 10 years old**

FURTHER EDUCATION COLLEGES

Technical colleges and colleges of further education

The type of college depends on regional and local factors, so that it is not really possible to give absolute sizes for systems. The figures cover both part-time and full-time students; as an approximate guidelines, and depending on the area served, there are 2000–6000 pupils per 60000–150000 inhabitants. Owing to the large catchment areas, the schools should be well served by public transport. Site: at least 10 m² per part-time student and at least 25 m² per full-time student of college site area, as far as possible free of pollution from noise, smoke, odour and dust. Ensure a good-shaped site and the possibility for extension. Arrangement on the site, type of construction and building design depend on the sizes of the spaces that can be accommodated on several levels (classrooms for general subjects, specialist subjects, administration) and those which cannot - areas for non-academic work, e.g. workshops or sports areas. College buildings are, as a rule, 2–3 storeys, higher only in exceptional cases. Workshop buildings with heavy machines or frequent deliveries are single storey only.

Access: entrance area and foyer with central facilities used as circulation space connecting horizontal and vertical movement as in general school centres or comprehensive schools. Teaching areas divided according to type of teaching and their space requirements. General-purpose teaching areas occupy 10–20% of the space. General classrooms as normal with 50–60 m², small classrooms 45–50 m², oversize classrooms 85 m², possibly open-plan classrooms doubling as a film or lecture hall of 100–200 m².

Building requirements, furnishings and fittings basically the same as for general school centres and comprehensive schools. An assembly room of 20 m² per 5 normal classes.

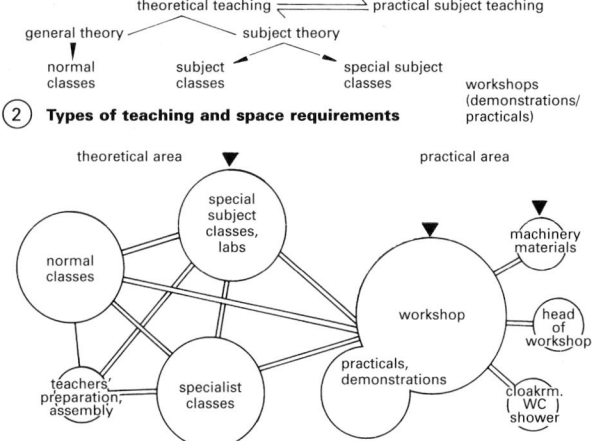

1 used by all depts
2 technical dept.
3 business studies dept.
4 young workers' dept.
5 elec. dept.
6 administration
7 caretaker's flat
8 parking (teachers, pupils, visitors)

(1) **Space allocation scheme: college of further education**

(2) **Types of teaching and space requirements**

theoretical teaching ⇌ practical subject teaching
general theory — subject theory
normal classes — subject classes — special subject classes
workshops (demonstrations/practicals)

(3) **Organisation of areas**

theoretical area — practical area
normal classes, special subject classes, labs, machinery materials, workshop, head of workshop, teachers' preparation, assembly, specialist classes, practicals, demonstrations, cloakrm. WC shower

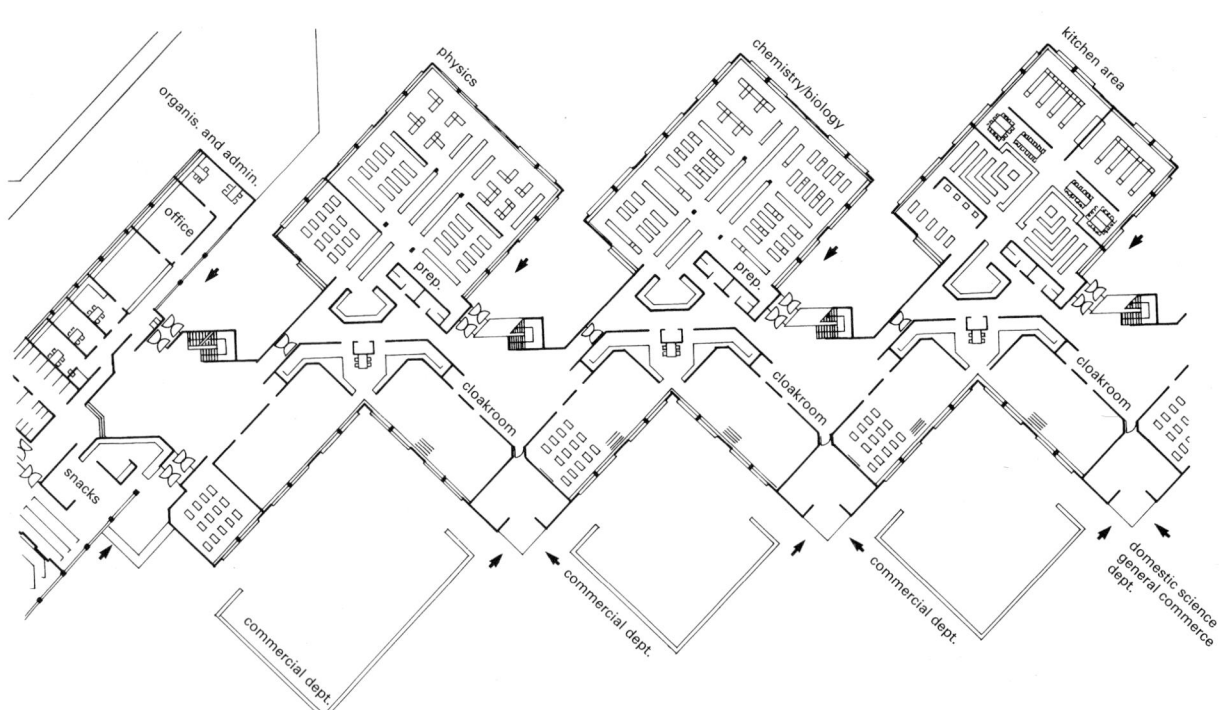

(4) **Part of the college of further education in the district of Viersen**

314

Lecture Theatres

Central facilities

Main lecture theatre, ceremonial hall, administration, dean's office, students' union building. Also libraries, refectories, sports facilities, halls of residence, parking.

Technical facilities for central services supply.

Boiler room, services supply.

Subject-specific teaching and research facilities.

Basic facilities for all subjects:

Lecture theatres for basic and special lectures, seminar and group rooms (some with PC workstations) for in-depth work. Departmental libraries, study rooms for academic staff, meeting rooms, exam rooms, etc. → ①.

Subject-specific room requirements:

Humanities: no particular requirements.

Technical/artistic subjects, e.g. architecture, art, music, etc.: rooms for drawing, studios, workshops, rehearsal and assembly rooms of all kinds.

Technical/scientific subjects, e.g. civil engineering, physics, mechanical engineering, electrical engineering: drawing studios, labs, workshops, industrial halls and labs.

Scientific and medical subjects, e.g. chemistry, biology, anatomy, physiology, hygiene, pathology, etc.: labs with adjoining function rooms, workshops, rooms for keeping animals and for long-term experiments.

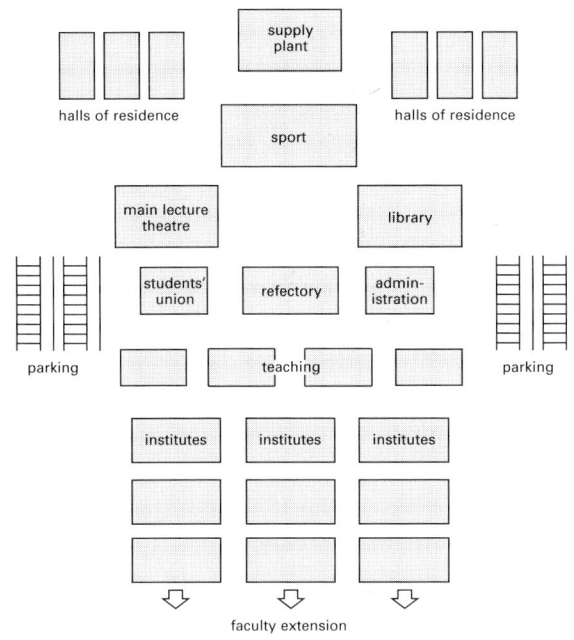

① **Schematic layout of university facilities**

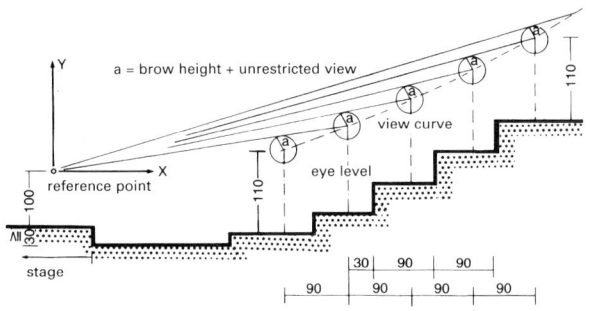

② **Drawing for calculating view curve**

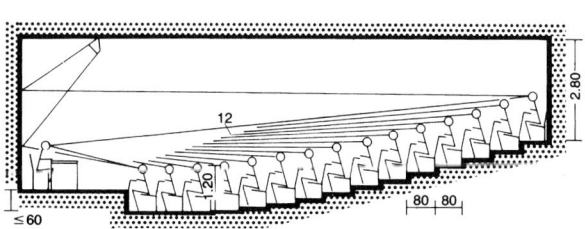

③ **Long section of a lecture theatre**

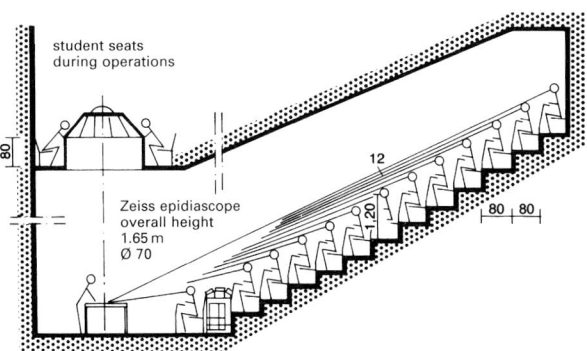

④ **Standard lecture theatre shape**

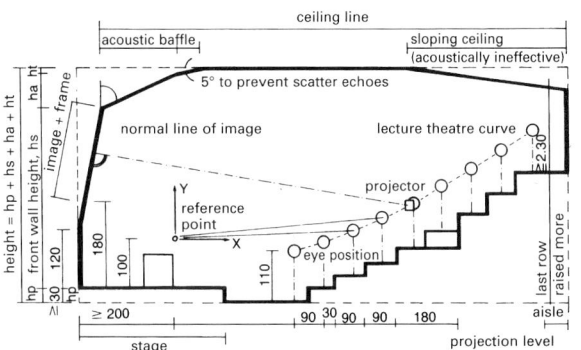

⑤ **More steeply raked lecture theatre**

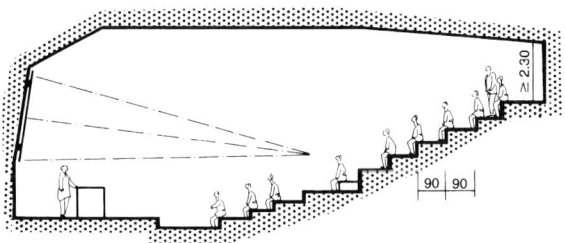

⑥ **Lecture theatre with demonstration table (medical)**

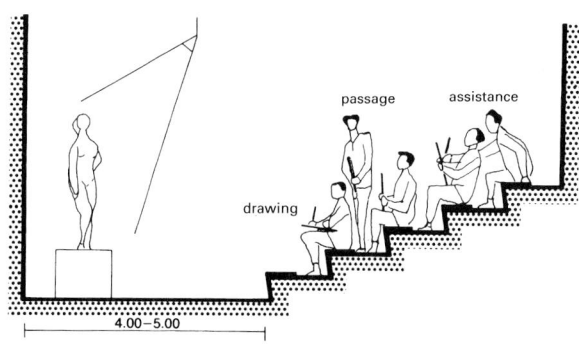

⑦ **Tiers in life drawing studio: 0.65 m² seating space per student**

COLLEGES AND UNIVERSITIES

Lecture Theatres

It is preferable to group larger lecture theatres for central lectures in separate complexes. Smaller lecture theatres for lectures on specialist subjects are better in the individual department and institute buildings. Access to the lecture theatre is separated from the research facilities, with short routes and entrances from outside at the back of the lecture hall; for raked seating entrances can be behind the top row and larger theatres can also have them in the centre on each side → ③ + ⑥. Lecturers enter at the front, from the preparation room, from where equipment carrying the experimental animals can also be trollied into the lecture theatre.

Usual sizes for lecture theatres: 100, 150, 200, 300, 400, 600, 800 seats. Theatres with up to 200 seats have a ceiling height of 3.50m and are integrated into the departmental buildings, if larger they are better in a separate building.

- Lecture theatres for subjects involving writing on chalkboards and projection have seating on shallow rake → p. 315 ④
- Demonstration lecture theatres for science subjects have experiment benches and seating steeply raked → p. 315 ⑤
- Medical demonstration lecture theatres, 'anatomy theatres', have steeply raked seating → p. 315 ⑥

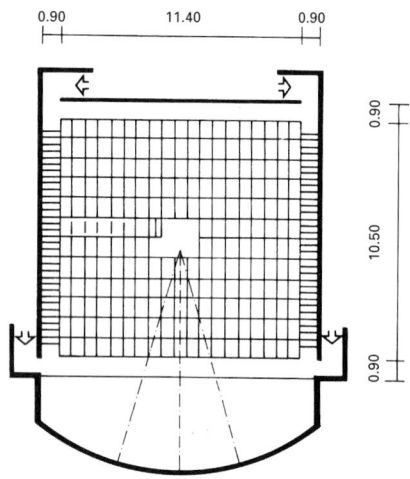

① 200-seat, rectangular lecture theatre

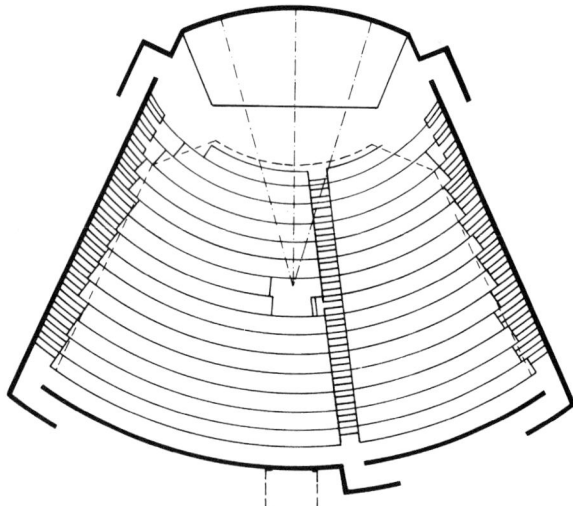

② 400-seat, trapezoidal lecture theatre

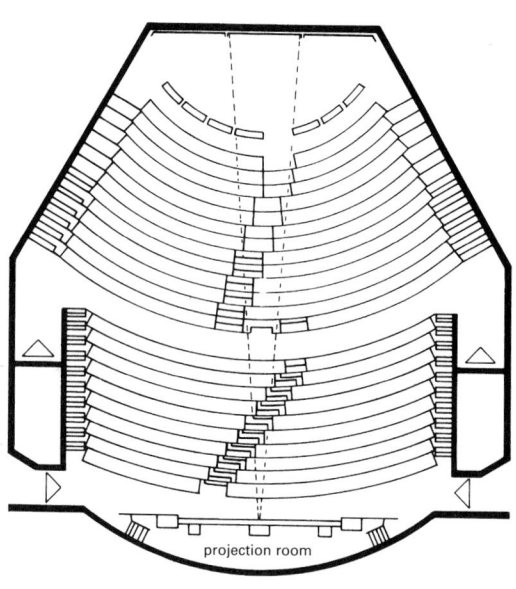

③ 800-seat lecture theatre

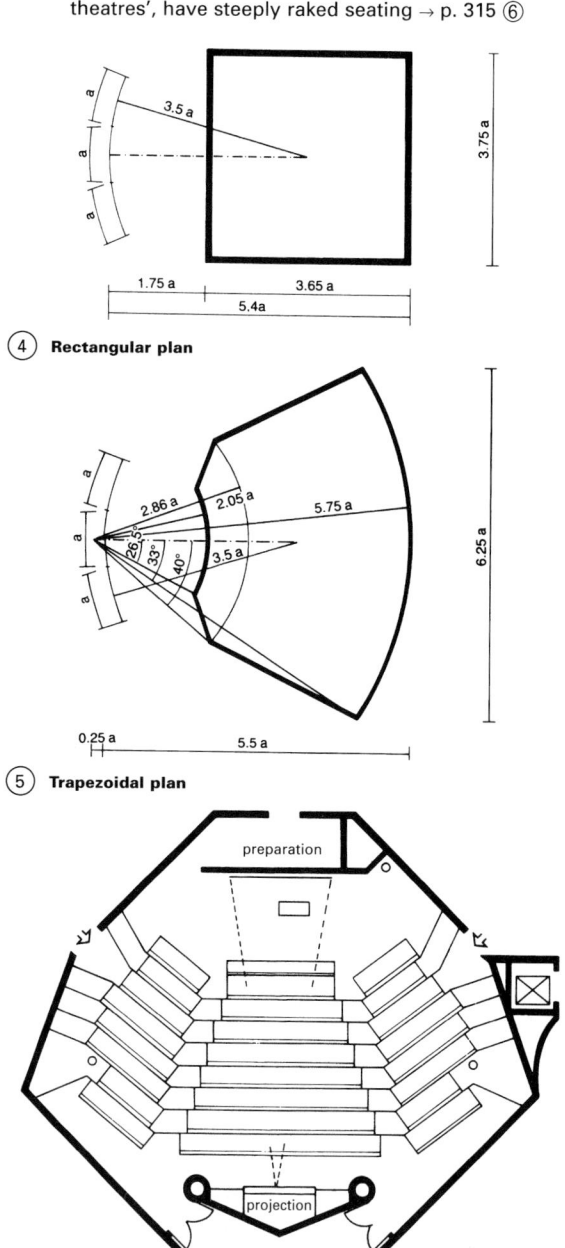

④ Rectangular plan

⑤ Trapezoidal plan

⑥ 200-seat theology lecture theatre at the University of Tübingen

① **Section** → ②

② **Physics lecture theatre with double walling to prevent sound and vibration travelling**

TH Darmstadt

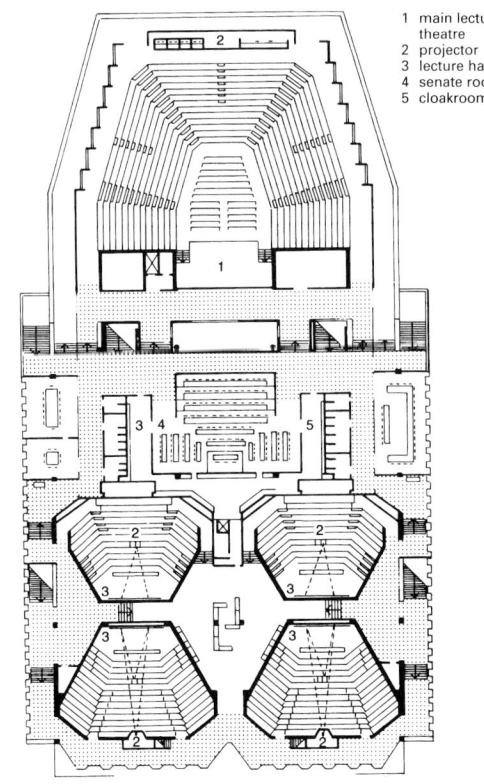

1 main lecture theatre
2 projector
3 lecture hall
4 senate room
5 cloakroom

Architect: Brdek + Bakema

③ **Lecture theatre at the TH Delft**

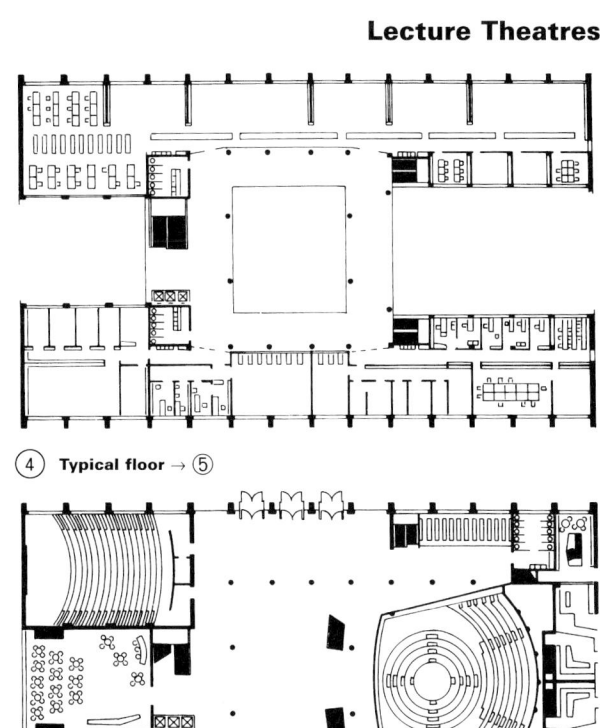

④ **Typical floor** → ⑤

entrance hall and two-storey main lecture theatre;
typical floor with seminar rooms and administration offices

Architect: O.E. Schweizer

⑤ **Ground floor of the theological college at the University of Freiburg**

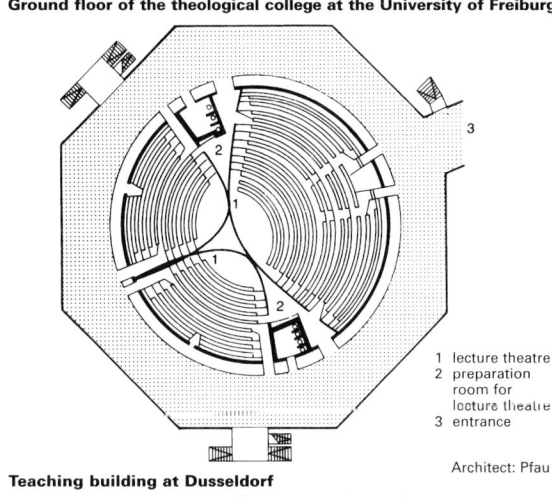

1 lecture theatre
2 preparation room for lecture theatre
3 entrance

Architect: Pfau

⑥ **Teaching building at Dusseldorf**

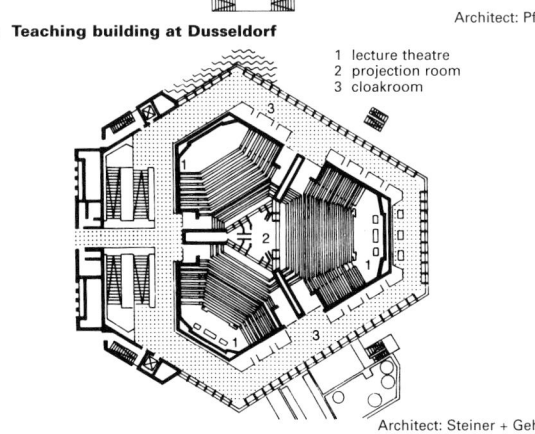

1 lecture theatre
2 projection room
3 cloakroom

Architect: Steiner + Gehry

⑦ **Lecture theatre at the ETH Honggerberg in Zurich**

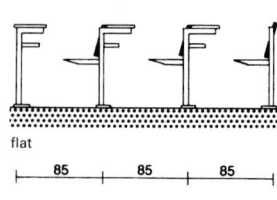

flat

| 85 | 85 | 85 |

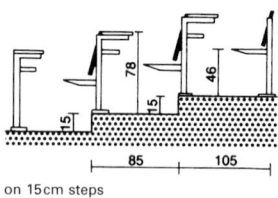

on 15cm steps

| 85 | 105 |

78 46

15 15

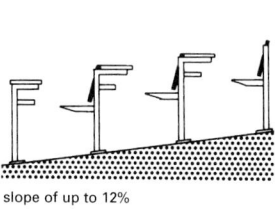

slope of up to 12%

(1) **Seating for lecture theatre**

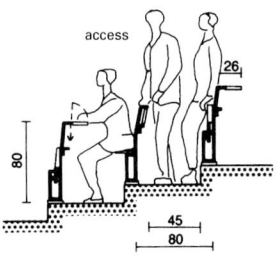

access

26

80

| 45 |
| 80 |

(2) **Seating arrangement with tip-up seats and writing shelves**

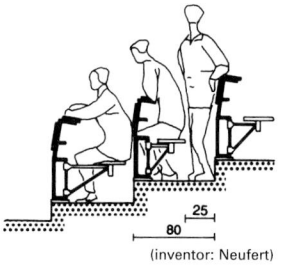

| 25 |
| 80 |

(inventor: Neufert)

(3) **Arrangement with fixed writing shelves and swing seats**

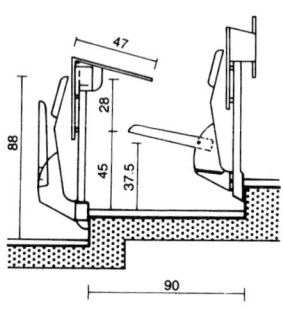

47
28
45 37.5
88

90

(4) **Lecture theatre seating**

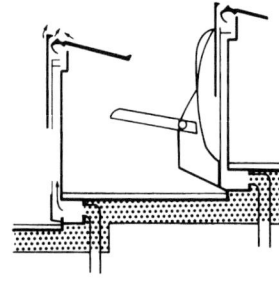

section

105 ~75 1.20 1.70

>35

(1) large projector
(2) 8-mm film projector
(3) slide projector
(4) working projector

(5) **Ventilation via desks/air circulation**

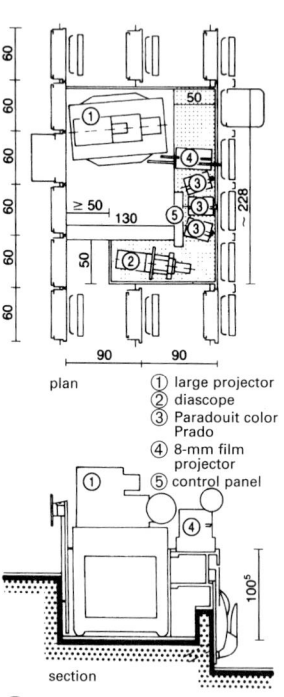

60 60 60 60 60

50
≥ 50 130 ~228
50

| 90 | 90 |

plan

(1) large projector
(2) diascope
(3) Paradouit color Prado
(4) 8-mm film projector
(5) control panel

100⁵

section

(6) **Projection stand**

field of vision

≥ 1.80 - 2.00
≥ 50
2.50

(2)
(3)
(3)
(1)
(3)
(4)

plan

(7) **Projector room**

COLLEGES AND UNIVERSITIES

Lecture Theatres

Seating in lecture theatres: combined units of tip-up or swing seats, backrest and writing ledge (with shelf or hook for folders), usually fixed → (1) – (3).

Seating arrangement depending on subject, number of students and teaching method: slide lectures, electro-acoustic systems on a gentle rake; surgery, internal medicine, physics on a steep rake. View curve calculated using graphic or analytic methods → (4) – (5).

Amount of space per student depends on the type of seat, depth of writing shelf and rake of floor.

Amount of space per student: for seating in comfort 70×65 cm; and on average $60 \times 80 = 55 \times 75$ cm. $0.60 \, m^2$ needed per student including all spaces in larger lecture theatres under the most cramped conditions; in smaller lecture theatres and in average comfort $0.80-0.95 \, m^2$. (Cont. next page)

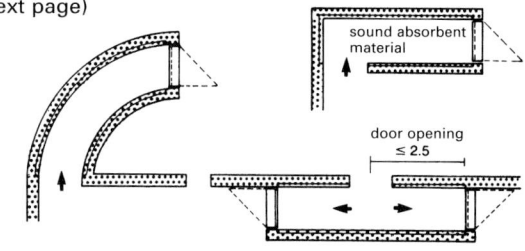

sound absorbent material

door opening
≤ 2.5

(8) **Plan of light and sound locks**

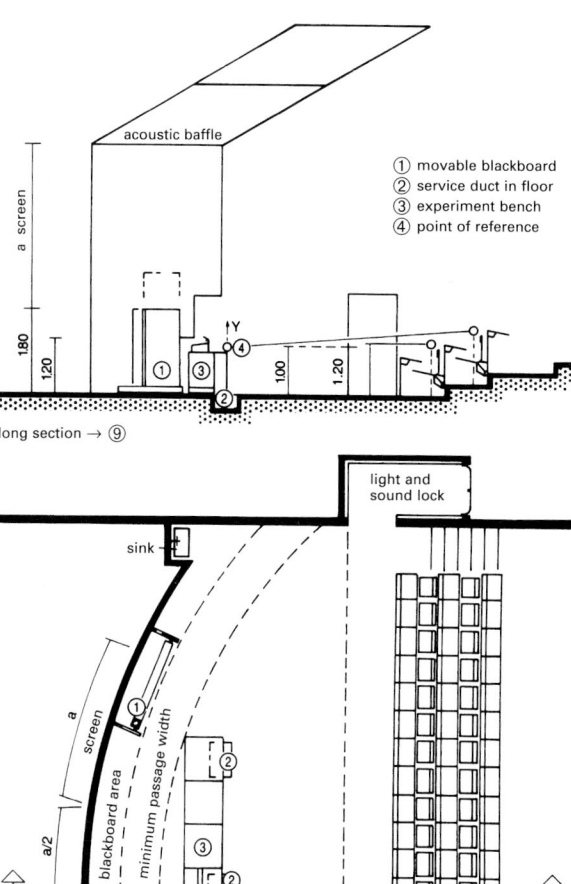

acoustic baffle

a screen

(1) movable blackboard
(2) service duct in floor
(3) experiment bench
(4) point of reference

180 120 Y 1.00 1.20

long section → (9)

light and sound lock

sink

a Screen
a/2
blackboard area
minimum passage width

(1)
(2)
(3)
(2)

stage area

| 75 | 90 | | 90 |
| 300 | X1 | 30 |

(9) **Plan of stage area**

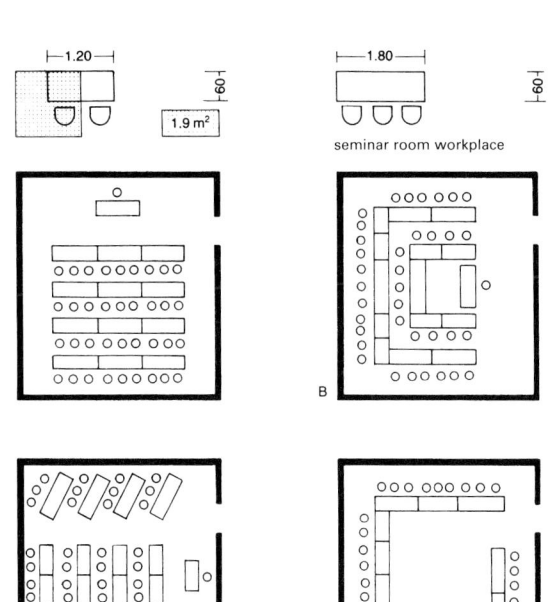

1 **Seminar rooms, variable seating arrangements**

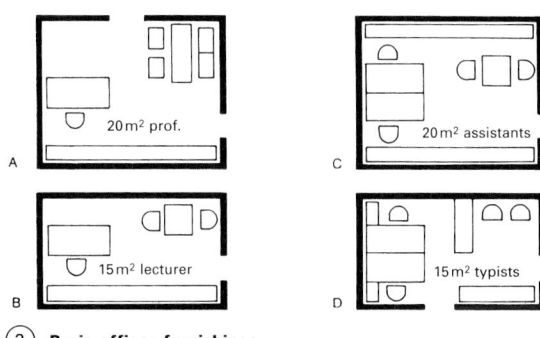

2 **Basic offices furnishings**

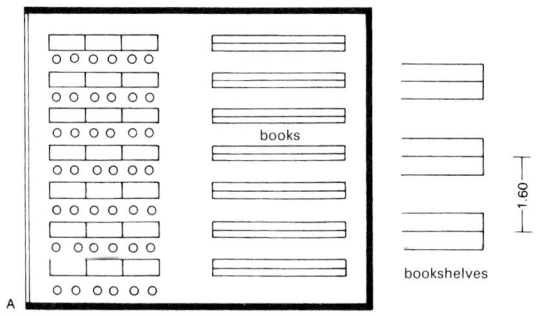

3 **Arrangement of reading places and bookshelves**

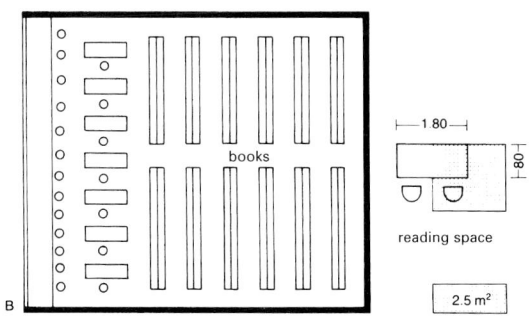

4 **Arrangement of reading places and bookshelves**

COLLEGES AND UNIVERSITIES

Experiment benches suitable for laboratory work should, if possible, be interchangeable units on castors and must be provided with a power point.

Projection screens and boards can be designed as a segmented, curved wall or simply fixed to a flat end-wall. Wall blackboards are usually made up of several sections which can be moved up and down manually or mechanically. They can be designed to drop down beneath the projection area. Blackboards on wheels can also be considered.

Acoustics and lighting
Sound should reach each member of the audience with equal amplitude without any echo. Suspended ceilings for reflection and absorption. Rear walls lined with sound-absorbent material, other walls smooth. Light level in a windowless lecture theatre: 600 lx.

Related additional spaces
Each lecture theatre should have an ancillary room, with no fixed function which can also be used for storage. In lecture theatres where animal experiments are performed sufficient space for preparation should be provided. It should be on the same level and close to the stage. Standard minimum size for a rectangular shaped lecture theatre: 0.2–0.25 m²/seat; for trapezoidal shape: 0.15–0.18 m²/seat. For scientific and pre-clinical lectures: 0.2–0.3 m²/seat.

Spaces for storage and service rooms are essential for the proper running of a lecture theatre complex: a service room for the technical staff servicing the equipment in the lecture theatres, a service room for cleaners, storeroom for spare parts, light bulbs, fluorescent-light tubes, chalkboards, clothes, etc. Minimum room size 15 m², overall space requirement for ancillary rooms at least 50–60 m².

Clothes lockers and WCs: rough estimate for both together 0.15–0.16 m²/seat as a guideline.

Basic room requirement for all subjects
General-purpose seminar rooms usually have 20, 40, 50 or 60 seats, with movable double desks (width 1.20, depth 0.60); space required per student 1.90–2.00 m → ①.

Different arrangements of desks for lectures, group work, colloquiums, language labs, PCs, labs and meeting rooms have the same space requirements → ①.

Offices for academic staff:
Professor 20–24 m² → ② A
Lecturer 15 m² → ② B
Assistants 20 m² → ② C
Typists 15 m² (if shared by two typists 20 m²) → ② D
Departmental (open shelf) libraries:
Capacity for 30 000–200 000 books on open shelves

Book space: → ③
Bookcases with 6–7 shelves, 2 m high (reach height)
Distance between bookcases 1.50–1.60 m
Space required 1.0–1.2 m²/200 books

Reading spaces: → ④
Width 0.9–1.0 m/depth 0.8 m
Space required 2.4–2.5 m² per space

Control counter at entrance with locker for personal property, catalogue and photocopying rooms.

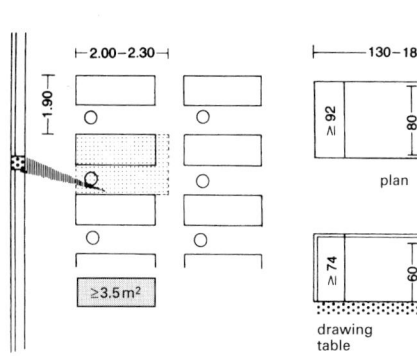

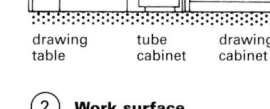

① **Workplace in drawing room**

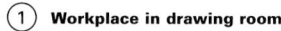

② **Work surface**

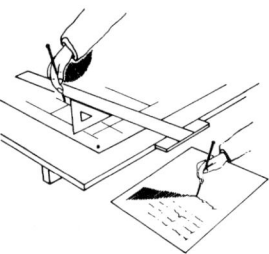

③ **Light for writing coming from behind left, and for drawing from the front left**

A0 92 × 127
A1 65 × 90
A2 47 × 63
A3 37 × 44

④ **Drawing board sizes**

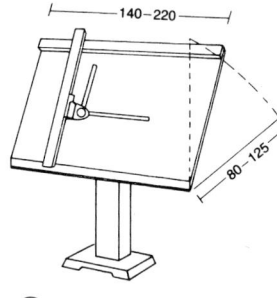

⑤ **Adjustable drawing table**

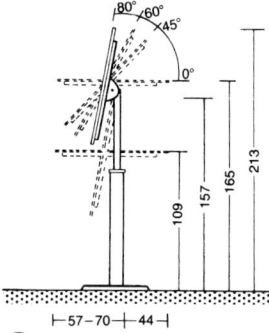

⑥ **Section → ⑤**

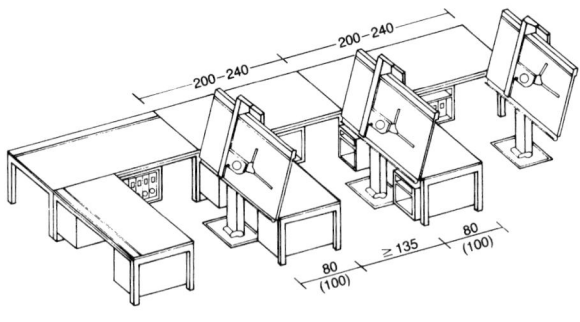

⑦ **Work space plan → ⑧**

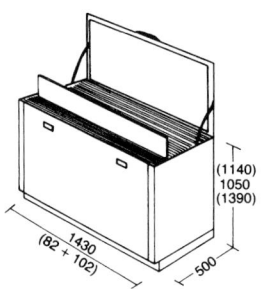

⑧ **Drawing office**

DRAWING STUDIOS

Various space requirements for technical subjects, including architecture, and art academies (painting and modelling rooms).→ ① – ②

Basic equipment

Drawing table of dimensions suitable for A0 size (92×127 cm); fixed or adjustable board → ②, ⑤ – ⑦. Drawings cabinet for storing drawings flat, of same height as drawing table, surface can also be used to put things on → ②. A small cupboard on castors for drawing materials, possibly with filing cabinet, is desirable → ② + ⑪ – ⑫. Adjustable-height swivel chair on castors. Drawing tables, upright board, adjustable height or usable as flat board when folded down → ⑤ – ⑪. Further accessories: table top for putting things on, drawing cabinets for hanging drawings or storing flat, suitable for A0 at least → ⑨ – ⑩. Each workplace should have a locker.

Drawing studios

Each space requires 3.5–4.5 m², depending on size of drawing table → ①.

Natural lighting is preferable and so a north-facing studio is best to receive even daylight. For right-handed people it is best if illumination comes from the left → ③. Artificial light should be at 500 lx, with 1000 lx (from mounted drawing lamps or linear lamps hung in variable positions above the long axis of the table) at the drawing surface.

Rooms for life drawing, painting and modelling:

Accommodated if possible in the attic facing north with large windows (1/3–1/4 of floor space) and, if necessary, additional top lights.

Rooms for sculptors and potters

Large space for technical equipment such as potters' wheels, kilns and pieces of work, also storeroom, plaster room, damp room, etc.

⑨ **Drawings stored upright**

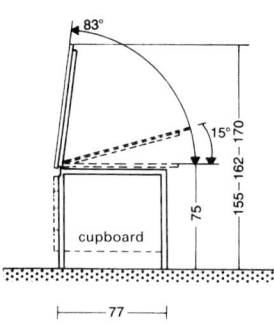

⑩ **Sheet steel drawings cabinet**

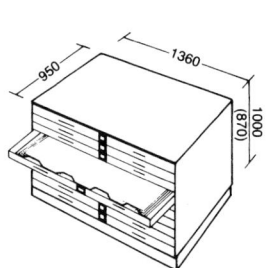

⑪ **Section → ⑫**

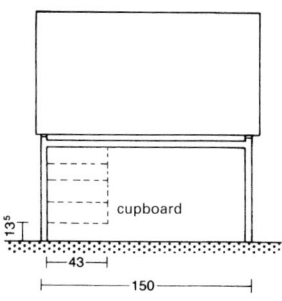

⑫ **Adjustable angle desk and drawing table**

LABORATORIES

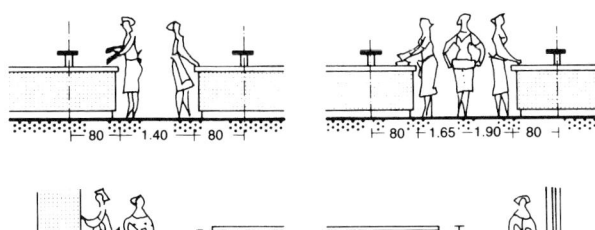

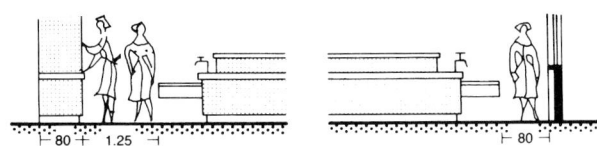

(1) **Minimum passage width between workstations**

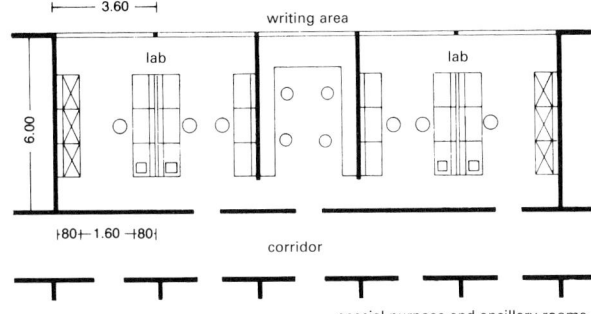

(2) **Research lab**

Laboratories differ according to type of use and discipline.

According to use:
Laboratories for teaching and practicals, comprising a large number of workstations, usually with simple basic equipment. → ③ Research labs are usually in smaller spaces with special equipment and additional rooms for activities such as weighing and measuring, centrifuges and autoclaves, washing up, climatised and cold storage rooms with constant temperature, photographic rooms/dark rooms, etc. → ②.

According to subject:
Chemistry and biology labs with fixed benches. Rooms have frequent air exchange, often additional fume cupboards (digestors) for work which produces gas or smoke. Digestors often in separate rooms. Physics labs mainly with movable benches and a range of electrical installations in trunking in the wall or suspended from the ceiling; few air changes. Special labs for specific requirements, e.g. isotope labs for work with radioactive substance in differing safety categories. Clean-room labs → ④ for work needing dust-free filtered air, e.g. in the field of microelectronics or for particularly dangerous substances, which should be prevented from entering surrounding rooms by separate air circulation and filtering systems (microbiology, genetic engineering, safety levels L1–L4).

(3) **Lab for teaching and practicals**

Lab safety level 3
1 warning sign
2 double-door safety lobby, self-closing doors
3 outdoor clothing
4 protective clothing
5 floor trough (pos. disinfectant mat) in front of shower
6 hand wash basin with disinfectant dispenser
7 workbench (clean bench) with separate special filter
8 extractor
9 autoclave (in lab or building)
11 flat panel radiator (7.5 cm from wall)
12 control and monitoring cupboard: electricity box, emergency mains off-switch, error board
13 pressure difference display readable from inside and out with acoustic alarm
14 emergency telephone, telephone
15 two-way intercom, electric door-opener
16 windows: gas-tight, non-combustible, leaded
17 pass-door: fireproof

Lab safety level 4
2 three-chamber safety lobby. Doors self-closing and gas-tight
5 personal shower (L-3 system can be upgraded*). Collect and disinfect waste water
7 gas-tight, enclosed workbench, separate air supply and extraction, additional special filter
9 autoclave with lockable doors on both sides, disinfect condensation
10 flood lock
18 autoclavable container for used protective clothing

*) Only required if upgrading to L-4 lab.

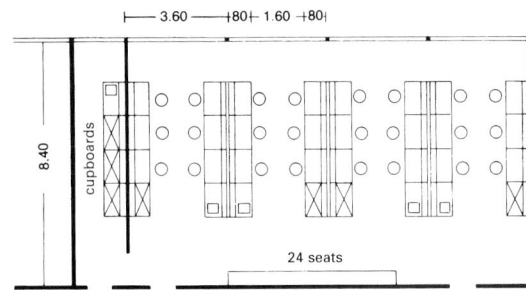

(4) **Example of clean-room lab**

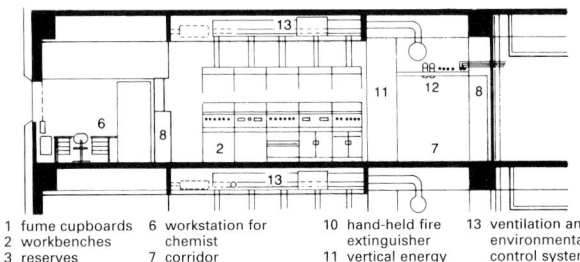

1 fume cupboards
2 workbenches
3 reserves
4 dry work places
5 weighing tables
6 workstation for chemist
7 corridor
8 materials cupboards
9 eye douche
10 hand-held fire extinguisher
11 vertical energy supply
12 overhead pipes
13 ventilation and environmental control system

(5) **BASF plastics laboratory: section**

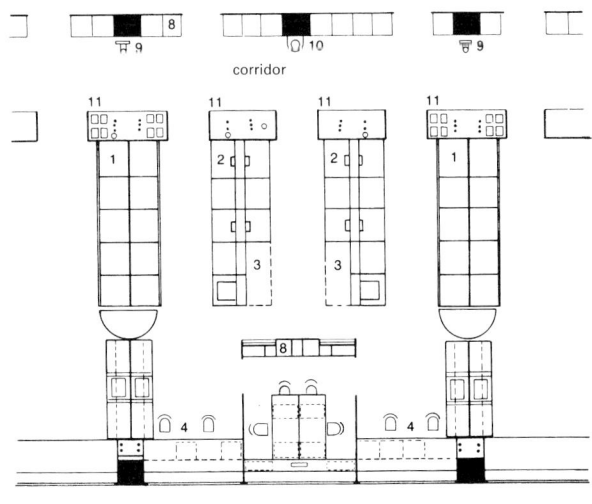

(6) **Plan → ⑤**

LABORATORIES

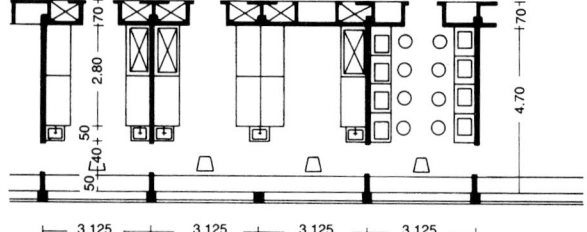

(1) Room dimensions derive from bench size (size of workstation). Services and cupboards in corridor wall. Separate weighing room.

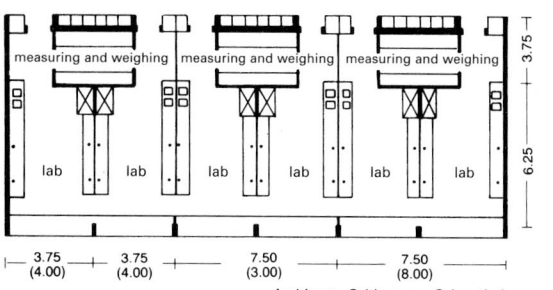

3.75 (4.00)   3.75 (4.00)   7.50 (3.00)   7.50 (8.00)

Architects. Schlempp + Schwethelm

(2) Uniform labs with measuring and weighing rooms in front of them (University clinic in Frankfurt/Main)

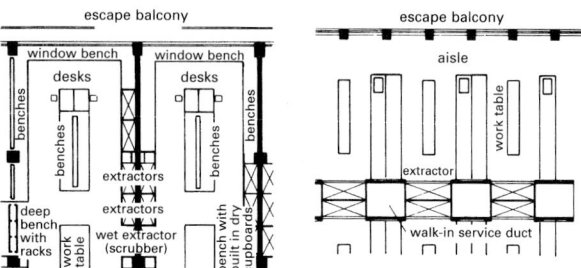

(3) Laboratory equipment in main science lab (Bayer AG dye factory)

(4) Arrangement of walk-in ducts (BASF)

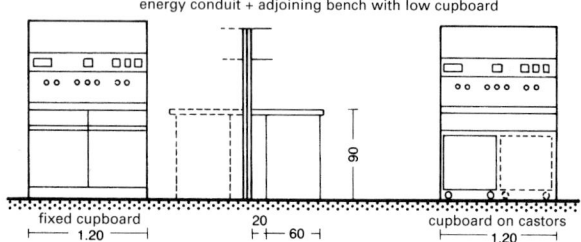

energy conduit + adjoining bench with low cupboard

fixed cupboard 1.20   20   60   cupboard on castors 1.20

(5) Chemistry bench

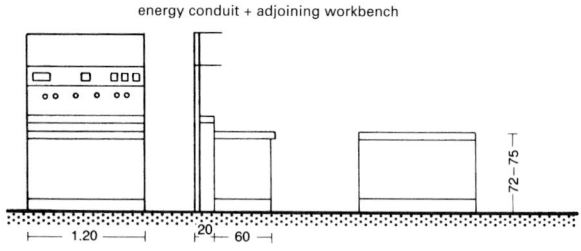

energy conduit + adjoining workbench

1.20   20   60

(6) Physics bench

Unserviced work rooms are also part of the lab area:

Study cells, service rooms for lab. personnel. Also central rooms such as general storerooms, chemicals stores and supplies with special protective equipment, isotope stores with cooling containers, etc. Experimental animals are kept in a special location. Particular kinds of equipment are needed, depending on the type of animal and they have differing requirements for separate air circulation.

Lab workstation

The bench, fixed or movable, is the module which determines the lab workstation; its measurements, including work space and passage space, form the so-called lab axis, the basic spatial unit. Normal measurements for standard workbench: 120cm width for practicals, several times this for a research lab, 80cm depth of work surface including energy conduit → (5) – (6).

Benches and fume cupboards are usually part of a modular system, width of elements 120cm, fume cupboards 120 and 180cm → (7). The conduit carries all the supply systems; benches and low cupboard are placed in front of it → (5) – (7).

Benches are made of steel tubing, with work-surfaces of stoneware panels without joints, less frequently tiles, or chemical-resistant plastic panels. Low cupboards are of wood or chipboard with plastic laminate. Supply services are from above from the ceiling void, or from below through the floor structure.

Ventilation:

Low-pressure or high-pressure systems, the latter are recommended particularly in multi-storey buildings for institutes with higher air requirement in order to reduce the cross-sections of the ducts. Cooling and humidification as required. Ventilation systems have the highest space requirement of all services.

Labs where chemicals are used must have artificial air supply and extraction. Air changes per hour:

chem. labs 8
biology labs 4
physics labs 3–4 (in extraction area)

Electrical services:

Where a high number of connections and special supplies of electricity are required, a separate transformer in the building is essential. Electrical plant must be in a fireproof enclosure without any other cables running through it.

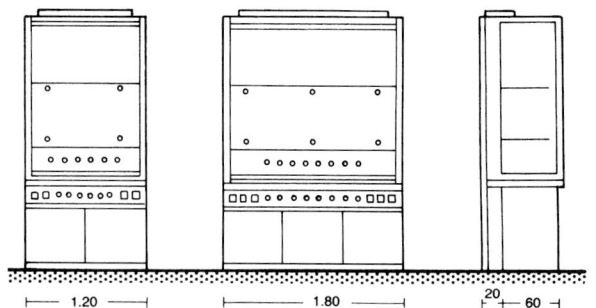

1.20   1.80   20   60

(7) Digestors (fume cupboards)

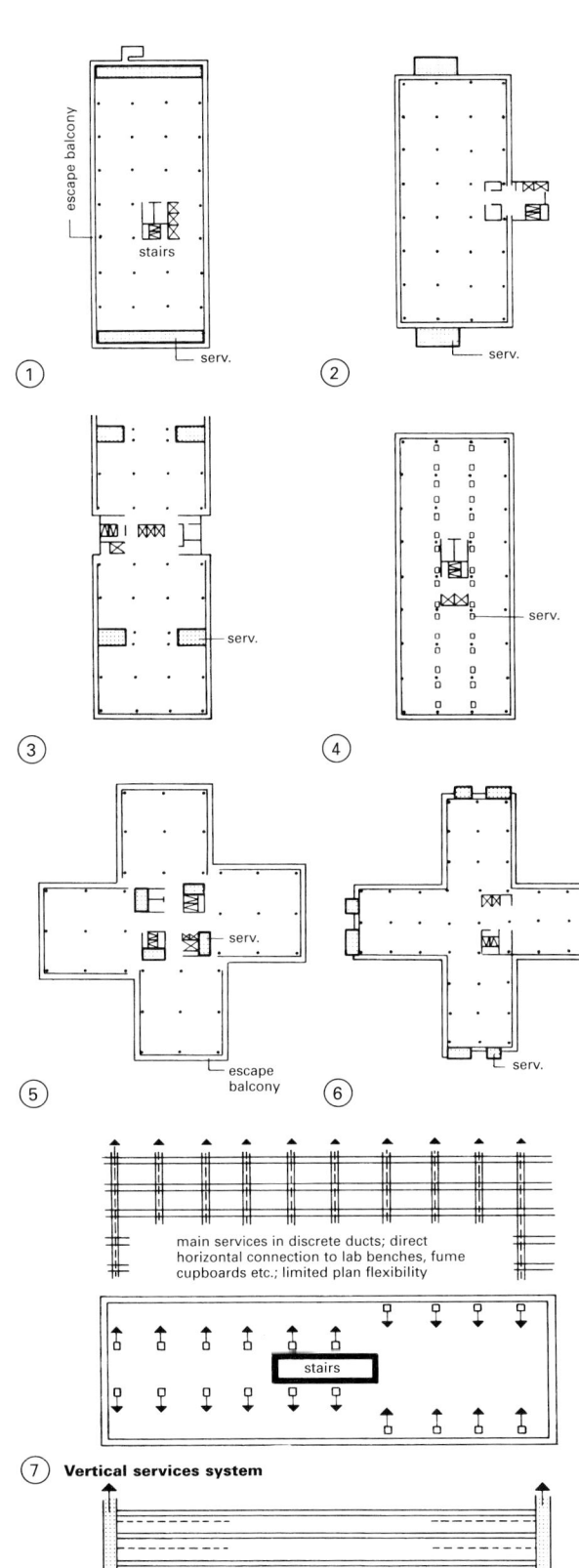

LABORATORIES

There are various possible arrangements of service ducts, columns and vertical circulation cores:

① Services concentrated in internal main shafts at each end of the building, vertical circulation core inside

② Services concentrated in external shafts at each end of the building, vertical circulation core outside

③ Services concentrated in main shafts centrally in each part, circulation core as link element

④ Services distributed in discrete duct installations, vertical circulation core inside

⑤ Main services inside linked to vertical circulation core

⑥ Service shaft outside, vertical circulation core off-centre.

Vertical services system

There are many vertical service ducts inside the building or on the façade, taking the services directly into the labs in separate ducts: decentrally distributed air supply and exhaust air to fume cupboards, separate ventilators on the roof.

Advantages:
Maximum supply to individual workplaces. Short, horizontal connections to the bench.

Disadvantages:
Plan flexibility limited, more space needed on services plant floor → ⑦.

Horizontal services system

Vertical main services concentrated in shafts and distributed from there horizontally via the service plant floors to the bench by connections from above or below.

Advantages:
Fewer conduits and less space needed for the services ducts, greater flexibility of plan, easier maintenance, central ventilation plants, later installation easier → ⑧. High density of services requires more space. Vertical mains ducts with concentrated services are more manageable, access is easier and they can be installed later. Conduits insulated from heat, cold, condensation and noise → ⑨ – ⑩.

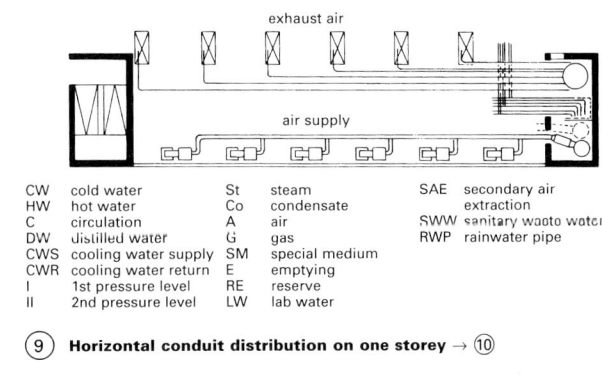

CW	cold water	St	steam	SAE	secondary air extraction
HW	hot water	Co	condensate		
C	circulation	A	air	SWW	sanitary waste water
DW	distilled water	G	gas	RWP	rainwater pipe
CWS	cooling water supply	SM	special medium		
CWR	cooling water return	E	emptying		
I	1st pressure level	RE	reserve		
II	2nd pressure level	LW	lab water		

⑨ **Horizontal conduit distribution on one storey** → ⑩

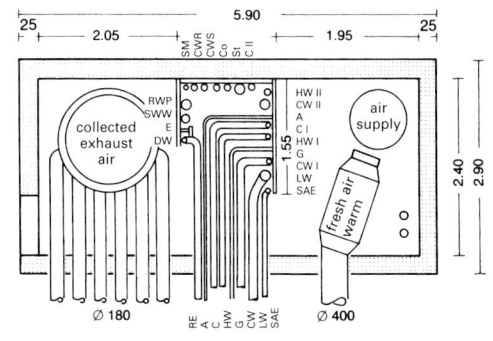

⑩ **Main services concentrated in shaft: plan** → ⑨

⑦ **Vertical services system**

⑧ **Horizontal services system**

LABORATORIES

Rooms are used according to a schedule of accommodation and plan. Rooms with natural or artificial light and ventilation, with high or low servicing, allow the creation of zones of differing use and technical qualities. For this reason laboratory buildings often have large internal areas (with two corridors) → ① + ③. The building length depends on the longest reasonable horizontal run of wet services.

Services floors for plant in the basement or at roof level.

Grid for structure and fittings:

For adaptability of use, a reinforced concrete frame structure, pre-cast or poured in-situ, is preferable. The main structural grid is a multiple of the typical planning grid of 120 × 120 cm (decimal system). A convenient structural grid for a large proportion of rooms without columns is: 7.20 × 7.20 m, 7.20 × 8.40 m, 8.40 × 8.40 m. Storey height normally 4 m, clear room height up to 3.0 m.

Columns stands on the grid off-set from the planning grid to increase the flexibility of the servicing. Separation is by a system of partitions and suspended ceilings which enclose the rooms. Movable dividing walls should be easy to assemble and have chemical-resistant surfaces. Ceilings should be designed to be disassembled and should absorb sound. Floor coverings should be water- and chemical-resistant, without joints and be poor electrical conductors: as a rule welded plastic sheet or tiles.

Provide viewing windows into the labs from the corridor or in the doors.

Isotope labs have smooth surfaced walls and ceilings without pores, rounded corners, shielded in lead or concrete, waste water monitoring, with shower cubicles between the lab and exits. Concrete container for active waste and refuse, concrete safe with lead doors, etc.

A weighing table is part of every lab, usually in a separate balance room. Benches lie along the wall in front of vibration-free walls.

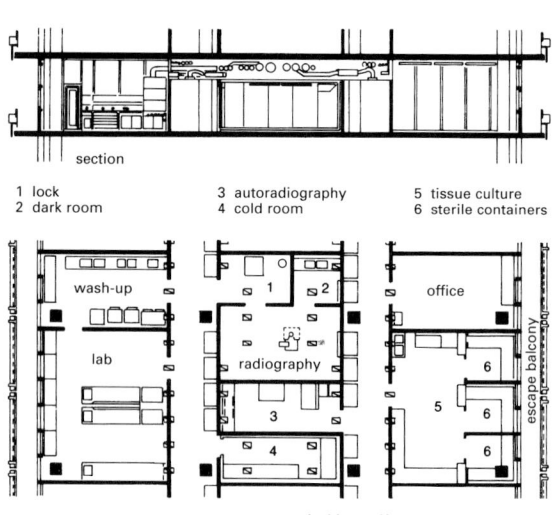

1 lock   3 autoradiography   5 tissue culture
2 dark room   4 cold room   6 sterile containers

Architects: Heine, Wischer & Partner

① **Part of plan of cancer research centre in Heidelberg**

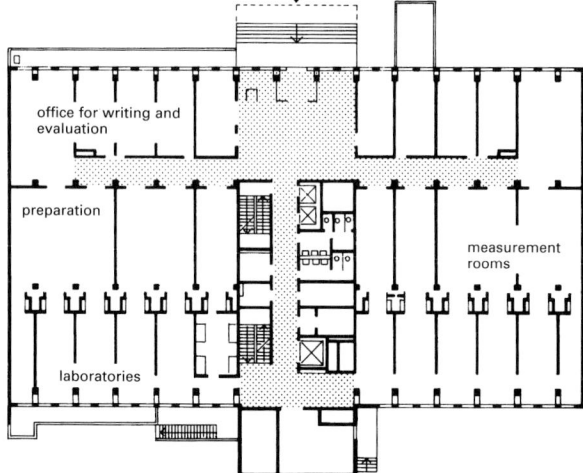

② **Analytical physics lab (BASF, Ludwigshafen)**

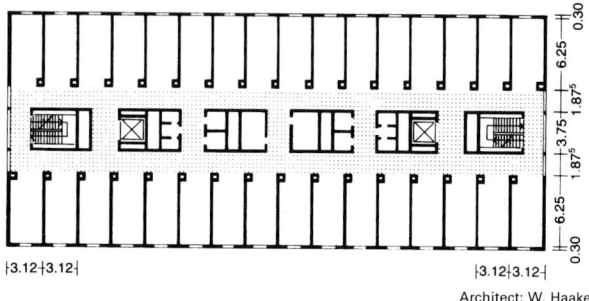

Architect: W. Haake

③ **Typical plan of a variable multi-purpose institute**

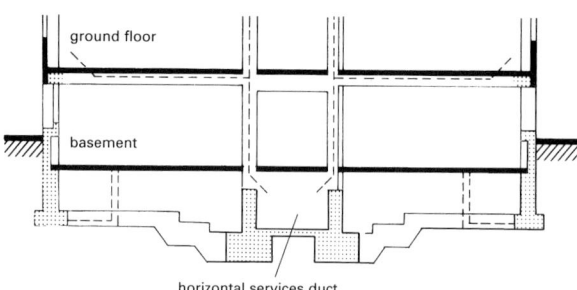

④ **Cross-section of lab with well-positioned central corridor**

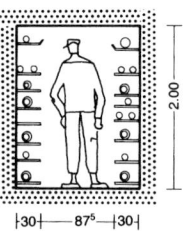
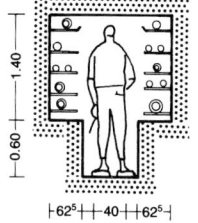

⑤ **Section of main service route (walk-in) varies according to number of ducts it is carrying**

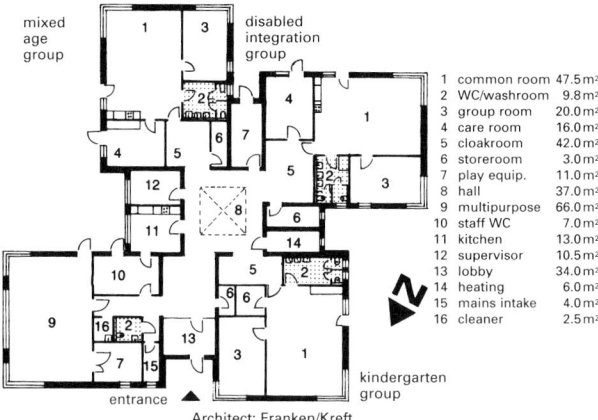

1	terrace	
2	common room	45–48 m²
3	dining	
4	kitchen	
5	entrance	
6	role-play	4 m²
7	building	4 m²
8	bonding	4 m²
9	group room	18 m²
10	washroom/WC	

Architect: Franken/Kreft

① **Kindergarten: typical plan**

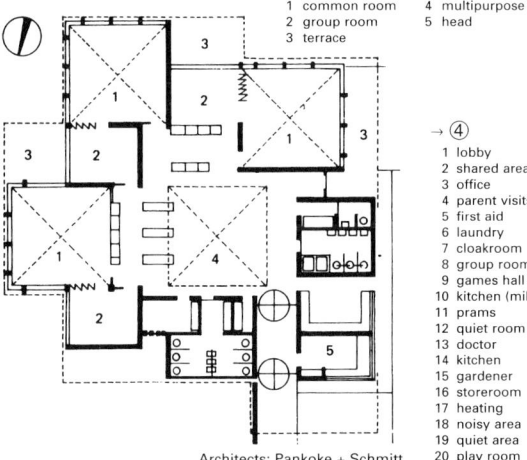

1	common room	47.5 m²
2	WC/washroom	9.8 m²
3	group room	20.0 m²
4	care room	16.0 m²
5	cloakroom	42.0 m²
6	storeroom	3.0 m²
7	play equip.	11.0 m²
8	hall	37.0 m²
9	multipurpose	66.0 m²
10	staff WC	7.0 m²
11	kitchen	13.0 m²
12	supervisor	10.5 m²
13	lobby	34.0 m²
14	heating	6.0 m²
15	mains intake	4.0 m²
16	cleaner	2.5 m²

Architect: Franken/Kreft

② **'Robin Hood' daycare centre: ground floor**

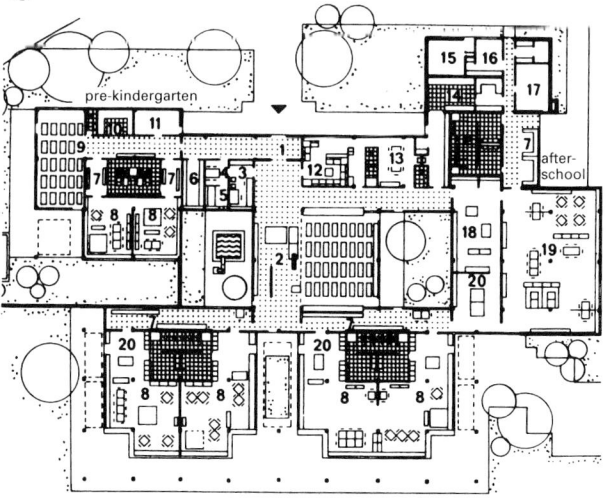

1	common room	4	multipurpose
2	group room	5	head
3	terrace		

→ ④

1 lobby
2 shared area
3 office
4 parent visits
5 first aid
6 laundry
7 cloakroom
8 group room
9 games hall
10 kitchen (milk)
11 prams
12 quiet room
13 doctor
14 kitchen
15 gardener
16 storeroom
17 heating
18 noisy area
19 quiet area
20 play room

Architects: Pankoke + Schmitt

③ **Kindergarten with central multipurpose room**

④ **Child daycare centre**

Architects: J. + W. Lippert

CHILD DAYCARE CENTRES

Child daycare centres provide social and educational facilities for daytime care of pre-school children and school children up to the age of 15. Children's needs should be taken into consideration in the planning. Division according to age groups:

Creche from 8 months to 3 years, groups of 6–8 children; kindergarten from 3 years to school age groups of 25–30 children; children's after-school care centre from 6–15 years, groups of 25–30 children. If possible, provision should be made for age groups to be combined. The centre should be near housing and traffic-free.

Size of rooms, schedule of accommodation and details → ① + ②.

Creche 2–3 m² floor space/child (babies, crawlers and toddlers) plus spaces for: nappy changing table, playpens, cupboards, toy racks, child-size tables and chairs.

Kindergarten 1.5–3 m² floor space/child. 15–30 children/room plus spaces for cupboards, toy racks, child-size tables and chairs, chalkboards, etc.

After-school care centre 1.5–4 m² floor space/child. 20 children/room plus spaces for cupboards, toy racks, child-size tables and chairs, chalkboards, storage facilities, homework room with cupboard for teaching material, shelves, desks and chairs. Arts and crafts room with cupboard for tools and materials, workbench, carpentry bench, etc.

With more than two group rooms a multipurpose room is required, preferably next to the group rooms and with a view of them. Good sound insulation, so as to help concentration in group learning processes, e.g. play rehearsals, etc.

If the room is large enough (min. 60 m²) it can also be used as a gymnasium and for afternoon naps. Apparatus store.

There is a trend towards two-storey buildings with staircases and emergency stairs, especially in high-density urban areas; and child daycare centres with longer opening hours for working or single parents (07.30 – 17.00). Facilities for disabled children, WCs and washrooms accessible to wheelchairs, therapy room. Min. 6 parking spaces and space for bicycles and prams.

Driveway and parking for staff and people collecting children, playground.

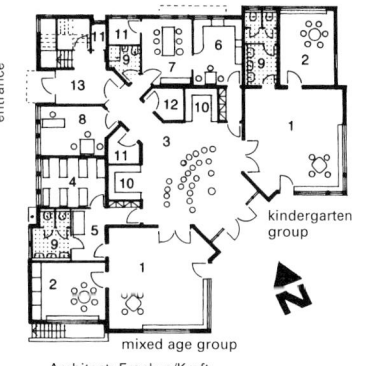

1 common room
2 group room
3 play hall
4 quiet room
5 babies' changing
6 kitchen
7 staff
8 head
9 WC/washroom
10 cloakroom
11 storeroom
12 cleaning materials
13 lobby

Architect: Franken/Kreft

⑤ **'Pusteblume' child daycare centre: ground floor**

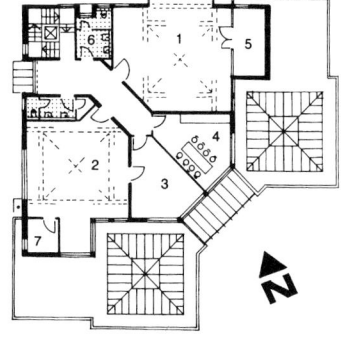

1 multipurpose room
2 common room
3 homework
4 handicrafts
5 apparatus
6 WC
7 storeroom

⑥ **First floor → ⑤**

PLAYGROUNDS

Play makes a fundamental contribution to the development of a child's personality. It is mainly through play that small children adapt to their environment. Play areas must be varied, changing and changeable. They must meet children's needs. Play is a social experience, through it children learn to understand the consequences of their behaviour.

Requirements of play areas: traffic safety, no pollution, adequate sunshine, ground water level not too high.

Play areas should be focal points within residential areas and should be connected to residential and other areas by simple networks of paths. They should not be pushed out on to the periphery but planned in connection with communication systems. Guidelines for planning playgrounds take into account the following data: age group, usable space per person, play area size, distance from dwellings, etc.

age group	area (m²)	distance from home	
		(m)	(minutes)
0 – 6	0.6	110 – 230	2
6 – 12	0.5	350 – 450	5
12 – 18	0.9	700 – 1000	15

When building housing, private outdoor playgrounds in the grounds of the housing complex should be provided for younger children up to the age of 6, for children from 6–12 and for adults. A basis for calculating the size of all public playgrounds can often be found in planning regulations. For example, 5 m² play area per housing unit, minimum size of playground 40 m². Open spaces for play must be enclosed by a barrier at least 1 m high (dense hedge, fences, etc.) to protect them from roads, parked cars, railway lines, deep water, precipices and other sources of danger.

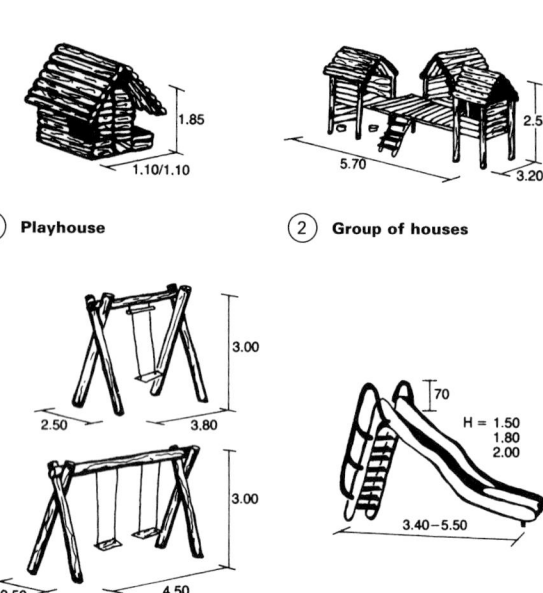

① **Playhouse**   ② **Group of houses**

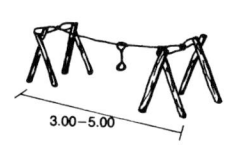

③ **Swings**

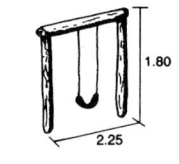

④ **Slides**

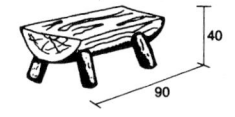

⑤ **Aerial runway**

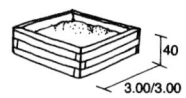

⑥ **Toddler's swing**

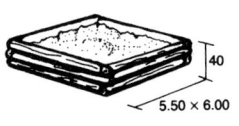

⑦ **Dough table**   ⑧ **Sandpit (planks)**

⑨ **Sandpit (logs)**   ⑩ **Exercise bars**

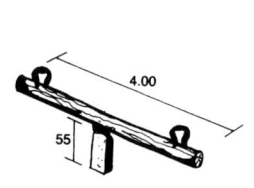

⑪ **See-saw**

D/W/H 7.30/3.80/3.40

⑫ **Slide and climbing frame**

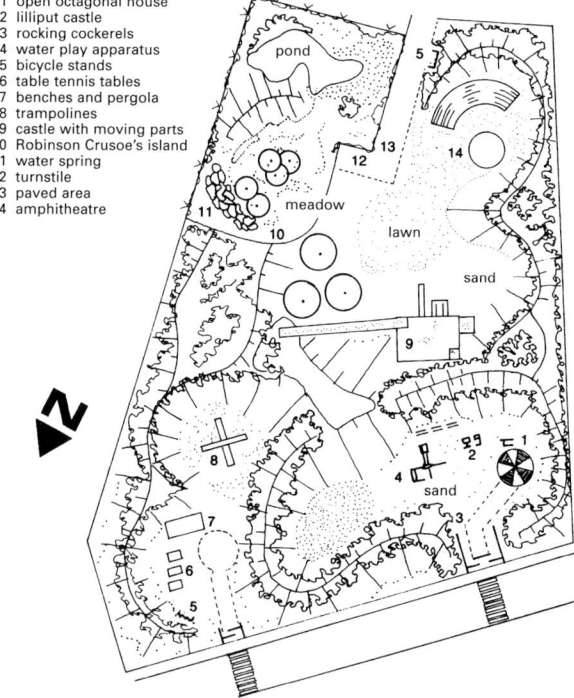

1 open octagonal house
2 lilliput castle
3 rocking cockerels
4 water play apparatus
5 bicycle stands
6 table tennis tables
7 benches and pergola
8 trampolines
9 castle with moving parts
10 Robinson Crusoe's island
11 water spring
12 turnstile
13 paved area
14 amphitheatre

⑬ **'Karnacksweg' playground**

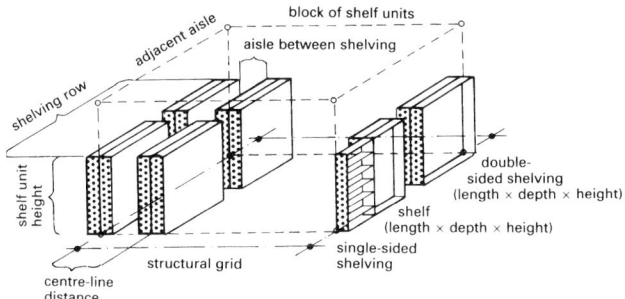

(1) **Drawing to explain terms used in calculating floor area for shelving (not to scale)**

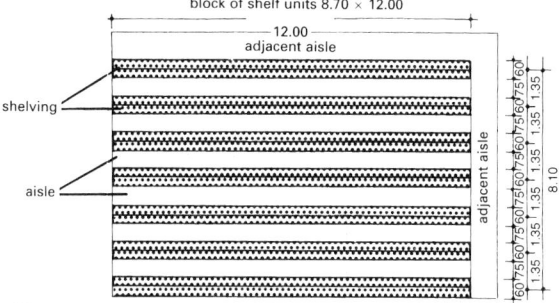

(2) **Floor space for bookshelves in areas closed to the public**

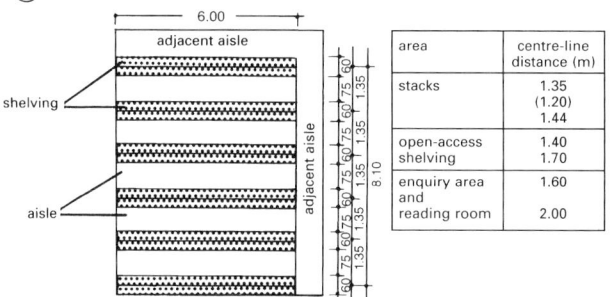

(3) **Floor area for open-access bookshelves 8.70 × 6.00 m per block of shelf units**

area	centre-line distance (m)
stacks	1.35 (1.20) 1.44
open-access shelving	1.40 1.70
enquiry area and reading room	1.60 2.00

structural grid	7.20 m × 7.20 m	7.50 m × 7.50 m	7.80 m × 7.80 m	8.40 m × 8.40 m
n × centre-line distance	6 × 1.20	6 × 1.25	6 × 1.30	6 × 1.20
	5 × 1.44	5 × 1.50	5 × 1.56	5 × 1.40
	4 × 1.80	4 × 1.87	4 × 1.95	4 × 1.68

(4) **Example distances between shelf unit centre-lines; common grids**

area	volumes per shelf
stacks	25–30
open-access shelving	20–25
enquiry area and reading room	20

(5) **Volumes per shelf**

	structural grid							
	3.60	4.20	4.80	5.40	6.00	7.20	8.40	
stacks		1.05		1.08		1.10		1.05
open-access shelving	1.20	1.20	1.20	1.10	1.20	1.20	1.20	1.12/1.2
								1.29
open-access shelving			1.40	1.37	1.35	1.33	1.32	1.31	1.40
	1.44				1.50	1.47	1.44	
			1.60	1.54			1.60	1.53
		1.68				1.65		1.68
reading room	1.80			1.80	1.71		1.80	
			1.92		2.00			
		2.10					2.07	2.10
work spaces (2.25)	2.40	2.10	2.40	2.10	2.40	2.20	2.40	2.10
group work spaces	3.60	4.20	4.80	3.60	4.00	4.40	3.60	4.20

(6) **Suitability of common structural grids for fundamental library functions**

shelves above one another	7	6	5	on the basis of a book size distribution of
maximum book height (cm)	25	30	35	up to 25 cm 65% 25 up to 30 cm 25% 30 up to 35 cm 10%
average book depth (cm)	18	20	22	an assumed floor load of 7.5 kN/m² results
load per shelf	0.38	0.51	0.55	

(7) **Loadings for 7.5 kN/m² book stack floors**

Libraries perform a range of functions in society. Academic libraries, for example, obtain, collect and store literature for education and research purposes, and are usually open to the general public. Public libraries provide communities with a wide choice of more general literature and other information media, with as much as possible displayed on open shelves. The functions of academic and public libraries are often combined in a single library in larger towns. National libraries, for example, may house collections of literature and historical documentation produced in one country or region (deposit copies) and are open to the public, whereas specialist libraries for the collection of literature and media in limited subject areas often have limited access.

In academic libraries, reference rooms are provided. There may also be counters for loans from the closed stacks, and free access to the open shelves of magazines, books or separately presented educational material in reading rooms. Apart from books and journals, almost all the different information media forms are collected and presented for use in an accessible way. The number of reading places depends on the number of students in the various subjects. The information is arranged in a systematic way, i.e. by subject. The services offered include inter-library loans as well as photocopying, and reading and printing from microforms (microfiche and microfilm). In addition, an on-line literature search and a literature search on data bases stored on CD-ROM are available.

University libraries are organised in either one or two layers. The one-layer system is administered centrally (book processing and services) and normally has very few separate branch or subject libraries. The two-layer system includes a central library and usually a large number of faculty, subject and institute libraries. The stock is held on open shelves in reading rooms, or in accessible book stacks (with the same shelf spacing as in closed stacks), as well as in restricted-access closed stacks. Arrangements such as these are found in various proportions in almost all academic libraries. The proportions of loan (open and closed access) and reference stocks depend on the type of organisation, i.e. the aims of the library and the form of the buildings often have a significant effect. The number of book shelves depends on the type of organisation, accessibility for users, type of shelving (fixed or mobile), the system of subject ordering in use and its method of installation, the separation of different formats and also the structural grid of the building → (4) – (7).

Reading room areas, with space for reading and working, should be easily accessible and therefore situated on as few levels as possible. This also aids book transport. There should be a clear directional system with easily read signs giving directions to services and book shelves. Avoid offset levels. Access to the operational areas and reading rooms on different floors should be by staircase, but lifts must also be provided for the use of disabled people and for book transport. Floor loadings in the operational and reading areas should be ≥ 5.0 kN/m².

Circulation routes should be >1.2 m wide, and clear spaces between shelves at least 1.3–1.4 m wide (or in accordance with local regulations). Avoid crossings and overlapping of routes for users, staff and book transport. Access to reading rooms can be through control gates equipped with book security equipment and, if possible, only one entrance and exit. For functional reasons, the control gates should be near the lending desk/central information desk.

distance between centre lines of shelving (m)	volumes per metre of single shelf	number of stacked shelves	volumes per metre of shelving	space needed for 1000 volumes (m²)	volumes per m²
1.20	30	6	360	3.99	250.6
	30	6.5	390	3.68	271.7
	25	6.5	325	4.43	225.7
	30	7	420	3.42	292.3
	25	6	300	4.80	208.3
1.25	30	6	360	4.16	240.3
	30	6.5	390	3.84	260.4
	25	6.5	325	4.61	216.9
	30	7	420	3.56	280.8
	25	6	300	4.99	200.4
1.30	30	6	360	4.33	230.9
	30	6.5	390	3.99	250.6
	25	6.5	325	4.80	208.3
	30	7	420	3.70	270.2
	25	6	300	5.19	192.6
1.35	30	6	360	4.50	222.2
	30	6.5	390	4.15	240.9
	25	6.5	325	4.98	200.8
	30	7	420	3.85	259.7
	25	6	300	5.40	185.1
1.40	30	6	360	4.85	206.1
	30	6.5	390	4.47	223.7
	25	6.5	325	5.17	193.4
	30	7	420	4.16	240.3
	25	6	300	5.82	171.8
	20	5.5	220	7.63	131.0
1.44	25	6	300	6.00	166.6
	25	5.5	275	6.53	153.1
	20	6	240	7.50	133.3
	20	5.5	220	8.17	122.3
1.50	25	6	300	6.25	160.0
	25	5.5	275	6.81	146.8
	20	6	240	7.81	128.0
	20	5.5	220	8.51	117.5
1.68	25	6	300	7.00	142.8
	25	5.5	275	7.62	131.2
	20	6	240	8.75	114.2
	20	5.5	220	9.53	104.9
1.80	20	5.5	220	10.22	97.8
	20	5	200	11.25	88.8
1.87	20	5.5	220	10.62	94.1
	20	5	200	11.68	85.6
2.10	20	5.5	220	11.92	83.8
	20	5	200	13.12	76.2
	20	4	160	16.40	60.9

Row groups (left axis): closed stacks (additional area 20%) — 1.20 to 1.35; open stacks (additional area 25%) — 1.40 to 1.50; reading room (additional area 25%) — 1.68 to 2.10

Source: Schweigler

(1) **Floor area calculation for double-sided shelving**

library area/ floor type	closed and open stacks	compact storage systems	reading room and open-access shelving	administration
on floors with lateral distribution	7.5	12.5	5.0	5.0
on floors without lateral distribution	8.5	15.0	5.0	5.0

(2) **Assumed floor loads (kN/m²)**

number of shelves	distance between centre-lines of shelf units (m)							
	1.10	1.20	1.30	1.40	1.50	1.60	1.70	1.80
4	3.83	3.72	3.62	3.54	3.46	3.39	3.33	3.27
5	4.38	4.24	4.11	4.00	3.90	3.81	3.73	3.65
6	4.93	4.75	4.60	4.46	4.34	4.23	4.13	4.03
7	5.48	5.27	5.09	4.93	4.78	4.65	4.53	4.42
8	6.03	5.79	5.58	5.39	5.22	5.07	4.93	4.80
9	6.58	6.31	6.07	5.85	5.66	5.49	5.33	5.18

(3) **Live floor loadings for different numbers of shelves and centre-line distances**

Facilities inside the controlled area should include reading room information, bibliographies, on-line catalogue terminals, the issue and return of books which can only be used in the reading room, copying equipment (in separate rooms), open-access book shelves, work spaces and, if necessary, the open-access book stacks.

Facilities outside the controlled area should include cloakrooms or briefcase and coat lockers, toilets, a cafeteria, a newspaper reading area, an exhibition room, lecture and conference rooms (possibly for use outside library opening hours), an information desk (central enquiries), card and microfiche indexes, on-line catalogue terminals, book return and a collection area for ordered/reserved books.

The provision of work spaces in college libraries depends on the number of students and the distribution of individual subject groups. Special work places are required for people with disabilities (wheelchair users and the visually impaired) and for special operations (microform reading and enlarging equipment, PCs, terminals, use of CD-ROMs etc; take note of the relevant guidelines), as well as for individual study (cubicles, carrels, individual work rooms). Work spaces should preferably be in daylight areas. The area required for a simple reading/work place is 2.5 m²; for a PC or individual work place, $\geq 4.0\,m^2$ is needed.

Security is vitally important in user areas. Fire precautions must comply with national and local building regulations and procedures. The installation of a book security system will prevent theft, and the optimal security of unsupervised escape exits is achieved with automatic electronic lock-up when an alarm is triggered. Securing emergency doors mechanically with acoustic and/or visual alarms is less effective.

The archive store is best situated in the basement because of the high floor loads and the more even climate. 'Book towers' are not convenient because of the increased need for climate control, transport and staff, as well as limited flexibility. The most efficient method is to have linked areas which are as large as possible without changes in level. The divisions between fixed stacks and those of mobile (compact) systems are dependent on the structural grid of the columns. Capacity can be increased by approx. 100% by using mobile stacks. The floor loading with fixed stacks is at least 7.5 kN/m²; with mobile stacks it is at least 12.5 kN/m².

The internal climate in user areas should be 20° ±2°C, with approx. 50 ±5% relative air humidity and air changes (fresh replacement air) of 20 m³ per hour per person. These values can be increased or reduced depending on the weather conditions. Avoid direct sunlight, since UV and heat radiation destroy paper and bindings. Because of the high energy consumption, and therefore high running costs, air conditioning should be introduced only where absolutely necessary. Natural ventilation is possible with narrow buildings.

The internal climate in archive stores should be 18° ±2°C, with 50 ±5% relative air humidity and air changes (fresh replacement air) of $\geq 3\,m^3h^{-1}m^{-1}$. Air filtration is necessary to eliminate any harmful substances in the atmosphere (e.g. dust, SO_2, NO_x etc.). By using wall materials with good moisture- and heat-retaining properties, it is possible to reduce the necessity for air conditioning. Slight air circulation is necessary to prevent the growth of mould, particularly with mobile stacks (use open ends). Special collections and materials (e.g. photographic slides, film, and sound and data media, as well as cards, plans and graphics) require a special internal climate. The internal environment should be appropriate to each area of the library, rather than being uniform throughout, and no open-plan offices should be sited in administrative areas. However, full environmental control is needed in stacks, because the building structure alone cannot provide suitable conditions

Floor loading in administration and book-processing areas should be >5.0 kN/m². In technical areas (workshops), individual structural requirements will depend on the types of machinery and equipment. Reinforced concrete and steel-frame buildings with a structural grid of >7.20 m × 7.20 m have been found to be suitable owing to the flexibility they allow in fitting out. Room heights should be ≥3.00 m.

Transport books horizontally in book trolleys (avoid thresholds; changes of level should have ramps ≤6% or platform lifts) and/or on conveyer belts. Transport books vertically in lifts, on conveyer belts (the route must be planned very carefully, with sloping inclines; very low maintenance costs), by a container transport system (mechanically programmable, a combination of horizontal stretches and paternoster lifts) or by an automatic container transport system (routes can be horizontal and/or vertical as desired, fully automatic, generally computer-controlled; high investment cost, rather high running costs).

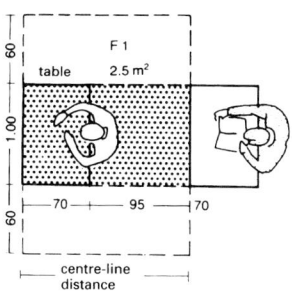

① **Floor area for an individual workstation**

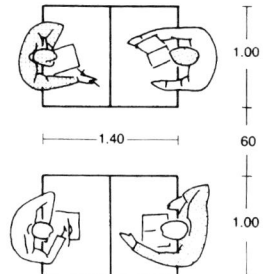

② **Minimum distances between tables**

$$F_1 = b \cdot e \cdot (1 + \frac{N\%}{100}) \quad \text{formula 1}$$

F1   floor area required for an open workstation for library user
b   width of table
e   distance between centre-lines of tables arranged one behind the other
N%   percentage of area allowed for adjacent aisles providing access to individual workstations

Under the conditions listed above, the floor area required for an individual workstation is approx. 2.50 m². Example:
$F_1 = 1.00 \text{ m} \cdot (0.70 + 0.95) \cdot (1 + \frac{50}{100})$
$F_1 = 2.48 \text{ m}^2$

③ **Floor area calculation (m²)** → ①

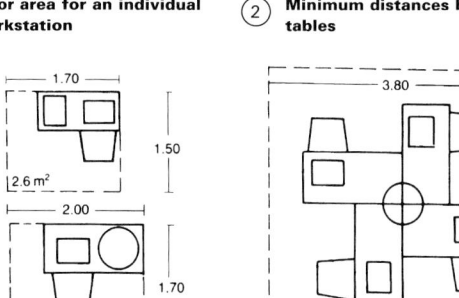

A │ 2.6 m²
B │ 3.4 m²

④ **Microfiche reading workstation**

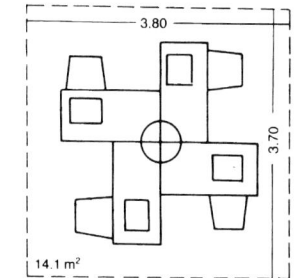

14.1 m²

⑤ **Four-seat microfiche station**

Workstation for microfiche reader: 60 × 120 cm table with rotating table stand (having maximum 10 vertical hanging storage units) → ④ A

Workstation for microfiche reader: 75 × 150 cm table with table stand (for maximum 15 storage units) or rotating stand (having maximum 50 hanging storage units → ④ B

Four-seat microfiche reading workstation: 75 × 150 cm tables for one (or two) rotating stands with maximum 50 (or 100) hanging storage units (3.70 × 3.80 m) → ⑤

⑥ **Dimensions ④ – ⑤**

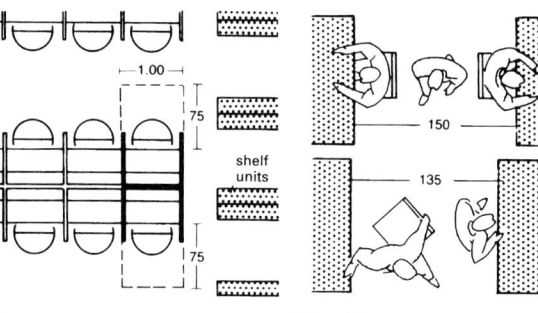

shelf units

⑦ **Individual study booths**

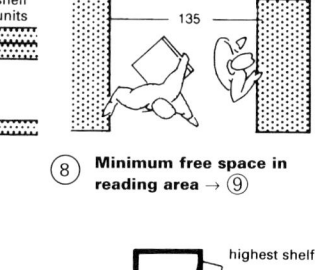

⑧ **Minimum free space in reading area** → ⑨

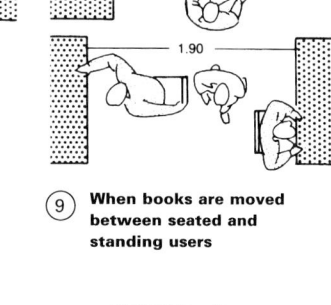

⑨ **When books are moved between seated and standing users**

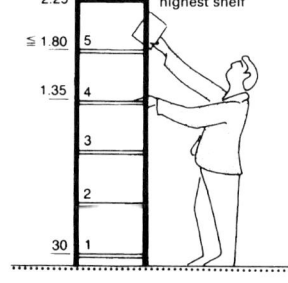

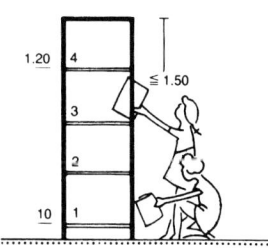

⑩ **Height of five-shelf unit**

⑪ **Bookshelf for schoolchildren**

⑫ **Height of four-shelf unit for small children**

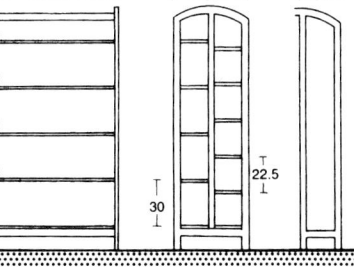

double-sided   single-sided

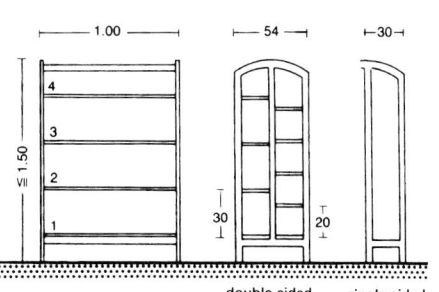

double-sided   single-sided

⑭ **Shelf units: for adults, 5--6 shelves; for children 4--5 shelves** → ⑫

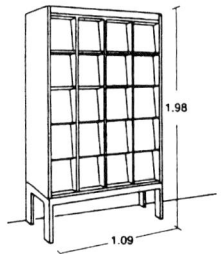

1.98
1.09

⑬ **Periodical rack**

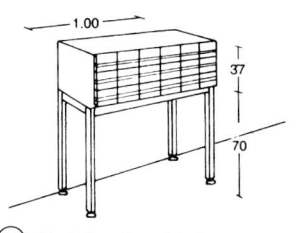

1.00
37
70

⑪ **Traditional card index**

A pneumatic tube system can convey information such as lending tickets. Modern systems tend to use plastic conveyors, running in plastic tubes, with comparatively small plants. Other methods of sending call-slip information to the stack as part of retrieval communication are faxes, gravity tubes and document carriers. A computer link between the request counter and the stack is also possible. Ideally, all material should be moved directly to where it is required. The return of books to their correct place on the shelf is very important.

Lighting should be appropriate to the use to which the area is put. Bookshelves should be protected from daylight. Sensitive materials should not be exposed to a level >50 lx. Artificial light is preferable in an exhibition area since it is easier to control. The best illuminance distribution ratio at workstations is 10:3:1 (book:surface:background). Non-work rooms need 100–300 lx, stacks need 150–300 lx, office and administration blocks need 250–500 lx, and reading rooms without individual lights and catalogue rooms need 300–850 lx. Lighting should have separate switches in each area and be individually adjustable at each work station.

Building design should be based on climate, and internal environmental control should be based on the building. The recommended temperature for reading rooms and open access areas is 22°C in summer and 20°C in winter, with 50–60% relative humidity and six or seven air changes per hour. Stacks should be kept at 17–22°C in summer and 17°C in winter, with 50–60% relative humidity and six to seven air changes per hour. The recommended humidity level in libraries is between 45% and 55%. Special measures should be taken for unusual and sensitive materials; humidity which is too low or too high can damage films. The air should be changed at least three times per hour, depending on the area of the library and time of year. The air intake per cycle should preferably be 25%, but is often reduced to 15% for economic reasons.

LIBRARIES

Public libraries offer general literature and other information media which are directly accessible on open shelves. Systematic collections and subject searches of material in print and in other media are limited to the larger public libraries. Public libraries have no academic collection obligations or archiving functions, and are usually without, or with only very small, archive stores. They are freely accessible to the public, and are used by children, adolescents and adults. Public libraries orientate their level and choice of stock and services to the needs of their users. As a communication 'market-place' for all population groups, in addition to the traditional provision of books, the library may have browsing areas, a citizens' advice/enquiries desk, a cafeteria, music listening facilities, recreation and meeting rooms, and study seating for groups and individuals. It may also include a music library, an art lending library and a mobile lending service. In addition to books and newspapers, the collection may include periodicals, brochures, games, or new media (CDs, videos, PC software) to be used in the library or borrowed.

The room design should encourage adults, children and young people to spend time in separate open-plan spaces where activities take place. The floor area depends on the size of the collection. There should be 300 m² of usable floor area for every 10000 units of media in the collection → ②. The objective is to have a minimum of two media units per occupant.

Ideally, the design should include large, open, extendible multipurpose areas, which are roughly square, and organised horizontally rather than vertically, and an inviting entrance. Areas for adult users can have five or six shelf levels (maximum reach 1.80 m → ③); in the children's area there should be four shelf levels with a reach height of around 1.20 m. Shelf aisles should not be more than 3 m long, and can also be used to produce niches and exhibition stands. Book transport should be with book trolleys 920 mm × 990 mm × 500 mm (D×H×W). The goods elevator should be at the service entrance, and larger libraries should also have book conveyors.

Floor loadings in public libraries should not exceed 5.0 kN/m², in archive storage and similar open access areas with closely spaced stacks they should be 7.5 kN/m² maximum, and with compact storage (mobile shelving) 12.5 or 15.0 kN/m².

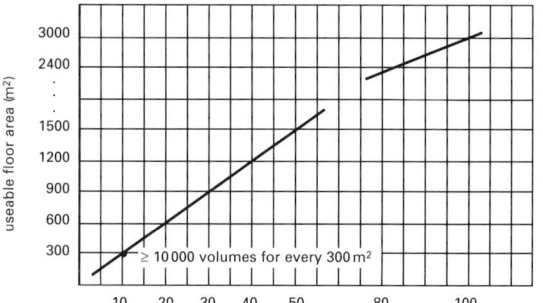

① **Functional diagram of medium-sized library**

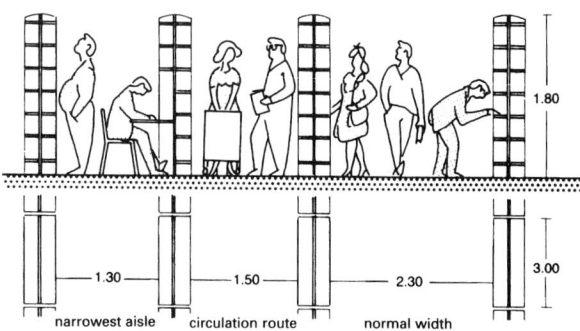

② **Public library floor area as a function of collection size**

≥ 10 000 volumes for every 300 m²

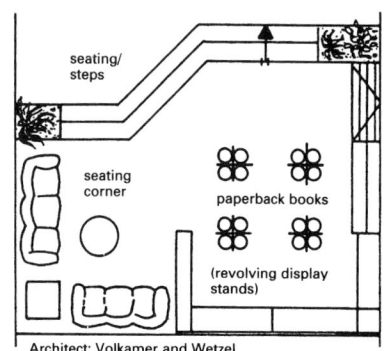

③ **Minimum distances**

narrowest aisle — 1.30
circulation route — 1.50
normal width — 2.30
3.00

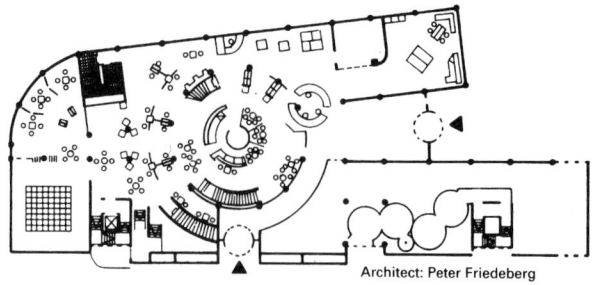

seating/ steps
seating corner
paperback books
(revolving display stands)
Architect: Volkamer and Wetzel

④ **Small browsing area**

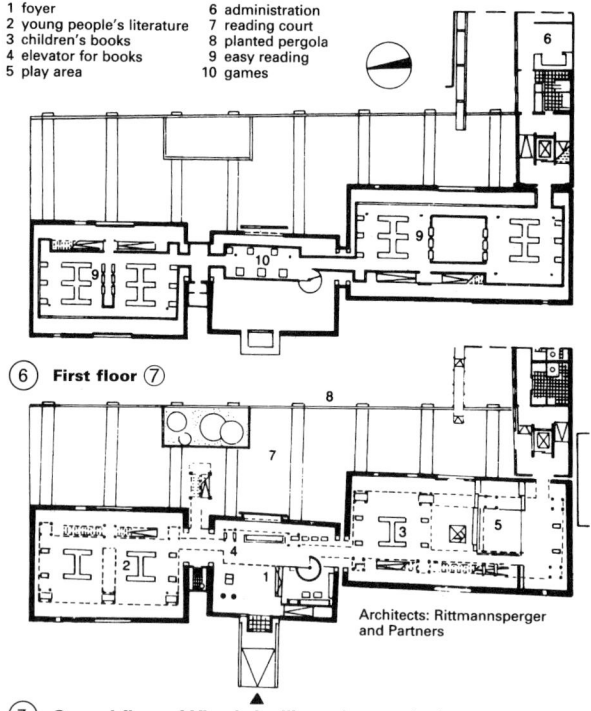

1 foyer
2 young people's literature
3 children's books
4 elevator for books
5 play area
6 administration
7 reading court
8 planted pergola
9 easy reading
10 games

⑥ **First floor** ⑦

Architects: Rittmannsperger and Partners

⑦ **Ground floor of Viernheim library (conversion)**

Architect: Peter Friedeberg

⑤ **Library in Gütersloh**

Science Libraries

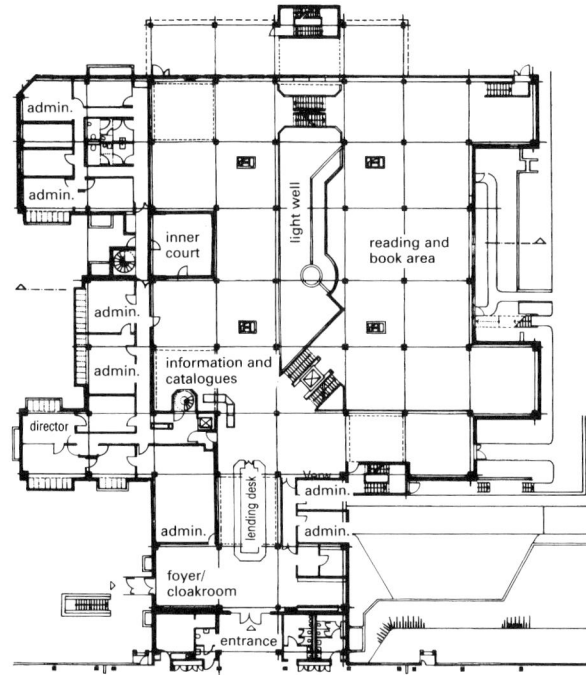

① **Section through Bereichsbibliothek Berlin** → ② ③ ⑥

Science libraries have always had a central position in science and the life of universities. They are not only locations to store books, but also places to work with books. Important and decisive contributions to world literature have been produced in libraries. The erection of libraries is one of the most notable building duties of society. Important architectural examples from the 19th century (such as the Biblioteca Laurenziana, Florence, and the Bibliothèque Nationale, Paris) show how these demands were met. The Bereichsbibliothek, Berlin → ①, has a gross area of 3800 m² containing 200000 books in the reading rooms, 300000 volumes in the open stacks and 8500 journals.

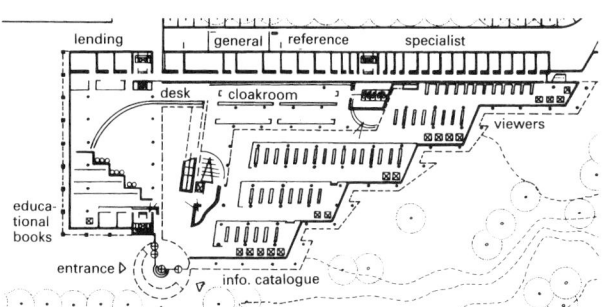

④ **State and University Library, Göttingen: ground floor**

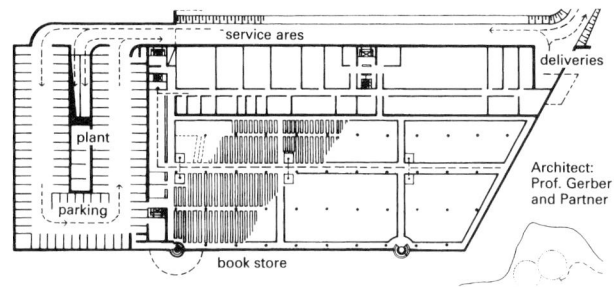

Architect: Prof. Gerber and Partner

⑤ **Basement** → ④

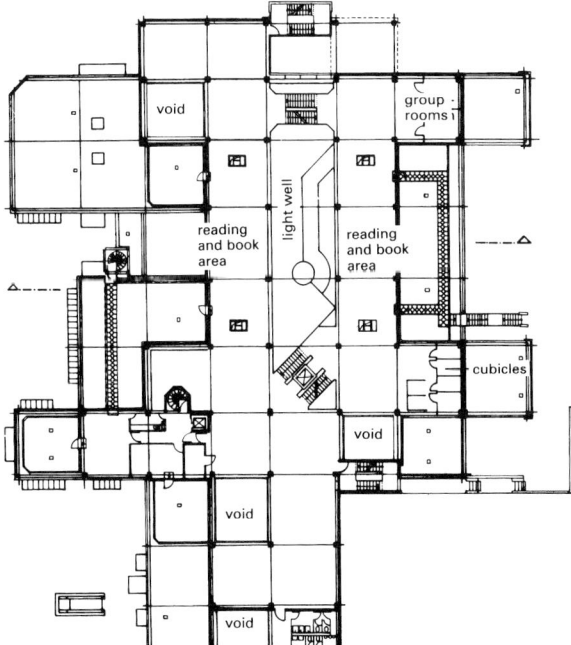

Architect: M. Shiedheim

② **Ground floor**

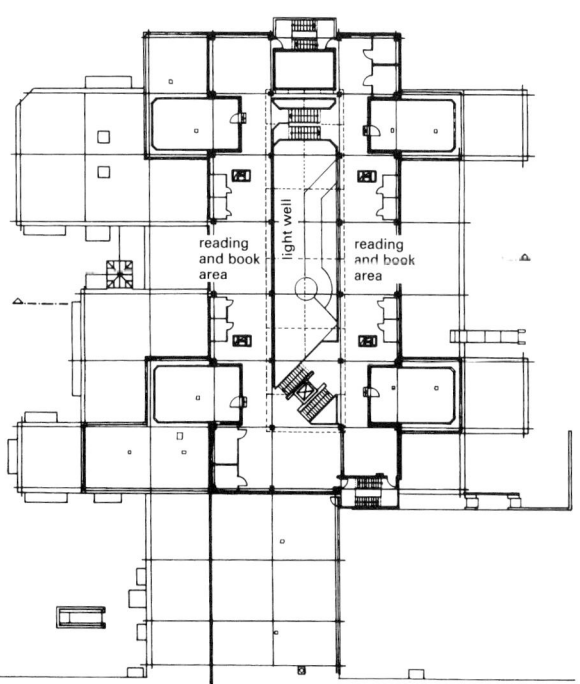

③ **First floor**

⑥ **Second floor**

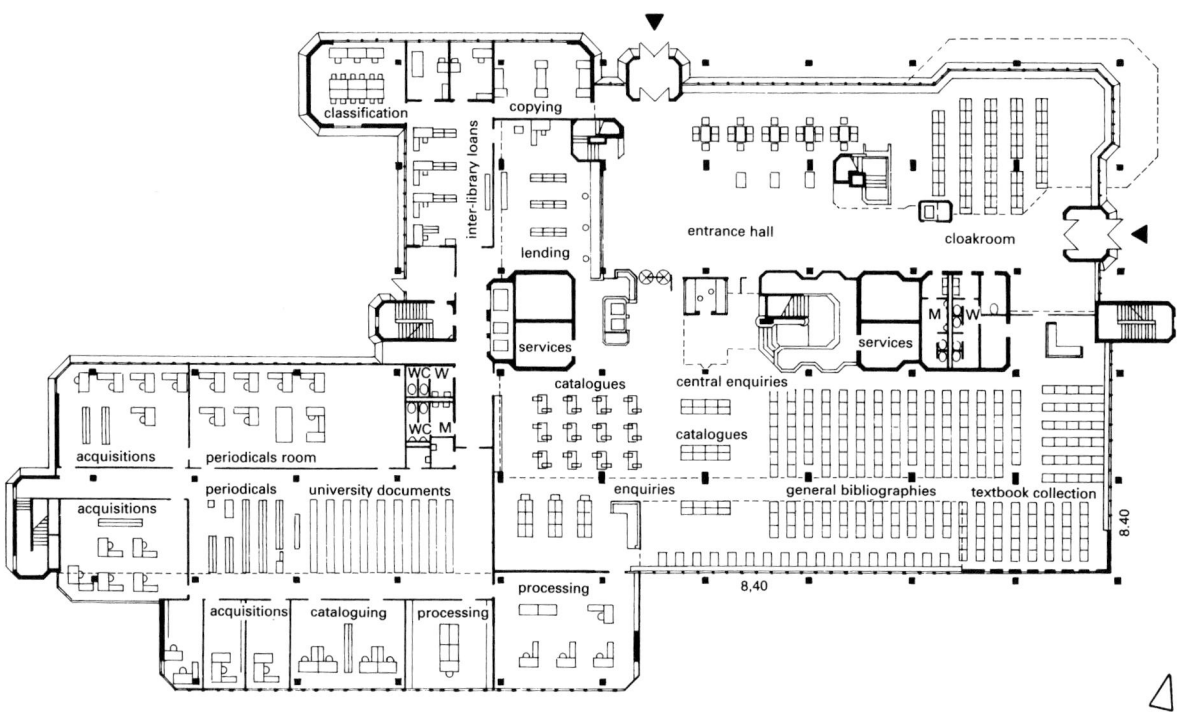

classification

copying

inter-library loans

entrance hall

cloakroom

lending

services

catalogues

central enquiries

services

M W

acquisitions

periodicals room

WC W

WC M

catalogues

periodicals

university documents

enquiries

general bibliographies

textbook collection

acquisitions

8,40

acquisitions

cataloguing

processing

processing

8,40

① **Ground floor of Düsseldorf University Library**

Designed by: Düsseldorf Architects Department

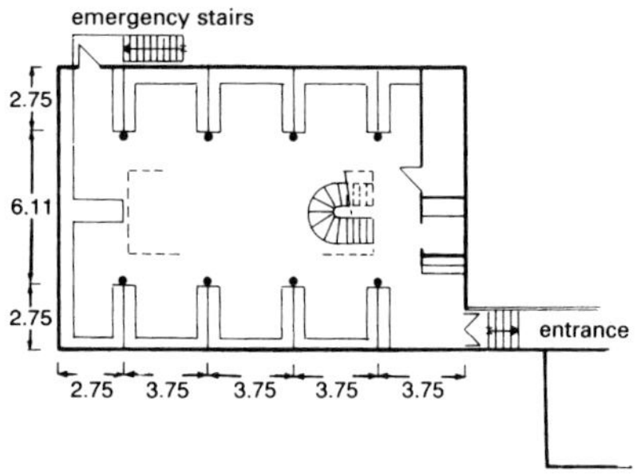

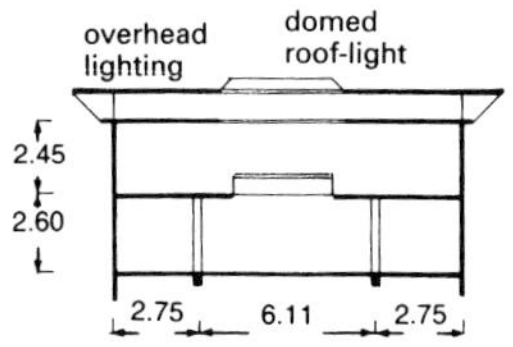

emergency stairs

2.75

6.11

2.75

2.75   3.75   3.75   3.75   3.75

entrance

overhead lighting

domed roof-light

2.45

2.60

2.75   6.11   2.75

③ **Cross-section → ② – ④**

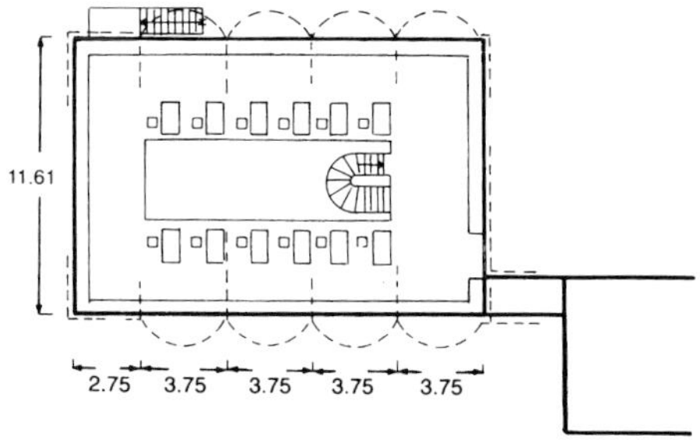

11.61

2.75   3.75   3.75   3.75   3.75

② **Ground floor of institute library**

Architect: author

④ **Upper floor**

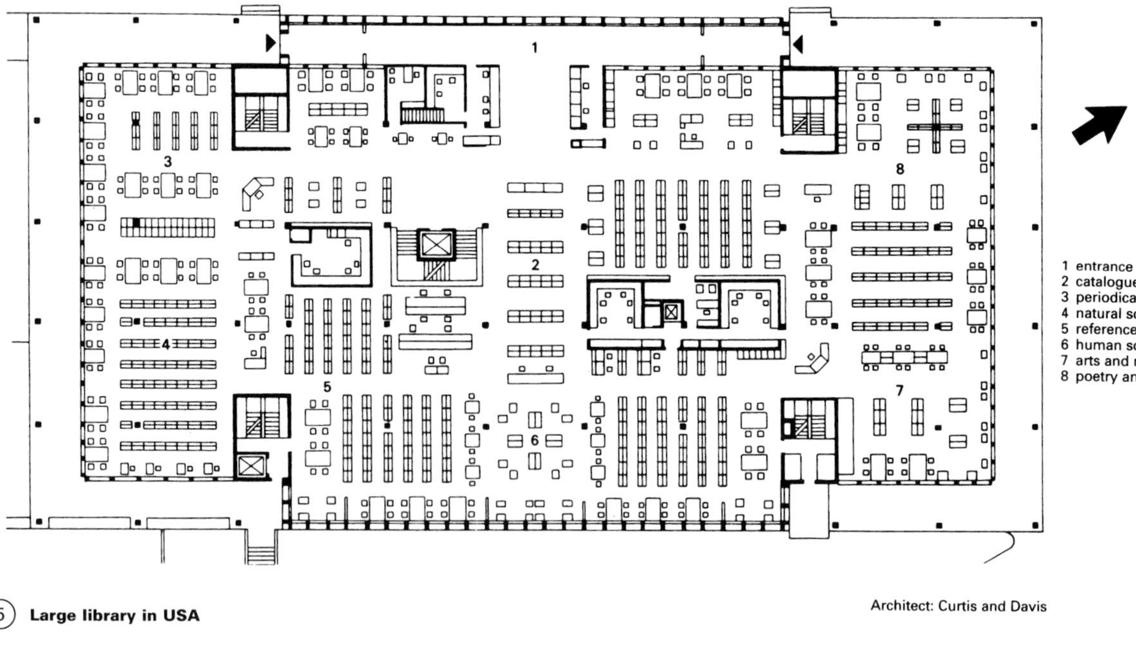

1
3
8
2
4
5
6
7

1 entrance hall
2 catalogues hall
3 periodicals
4 natural sciences
5 reference section
6 human sciences
7 arts and music
8 poetry and fiction

⑤ **Large library in USA**

Architect: Curtis and Davis

MUSEUMS AND ART GALLERIES

Museums and art galleries tend to have several of the same concerns, and as building types they tend to share many of same features. In general, the main concerns of museums and art galleries are collecting, documenting, preserving, researching, interpreting and exhibiting some form of material evidence. For this purpose, many people with varied skills are required. There are, however, important distinctions not only between museums and art galleries, but also between the different types of museum and art gallery. There are institutions such as heritage centres, exploratoria and some cultural institutes which are considered to be types of museums.

To show works of art and objects of cultural and scientific interest, the institution should provide protection against damage, theft, damp, aridity, sunlight and dust, and also show the works in the best light (in both senses of the term). This is normally achieved by dividing the collection into (a) objects for study, and (b) objects for display. Exhibits should be displayed in a way which allows the public to view them without effort. This calls for a variety of carefully selected, spacious arrangements, in rooms of a suitable shape and, especially in museums, in an interesting and logical sequence.

As far as possible, each group of pictures in an art gallery should have a separate room and each picture a wall to itself, which means small rooms. This option also provides more wall space in relation to floor area than large rooms, which are nevertheless necessary for big pictures. The normal human angle of vision starts 27° up from eye level. For a standing viewer, this means that well-lit pictures should be hung 10 m away with the top not more than 4.90 m above eye level and the bottom about 70 cm below → ⑥. The best hanging position for smaller pictures is with the point of emphasis (the level of the horizon in the picture) at eye level → ⑨.

It is necessary to allow 3–5 m² hanging surface per picture, 6–10 m² ground surface per sculpture, and 1 m² cabinet space per 400 coins.

Calculations for museum and art gallery lighting are highly theoretical; the quality of light is decisive. Experiments carried out in America can be useful. Recently there has been a steady increase in the use of artificial lighting instead of daylight, which constantly changes even if north light is used.

According to experiments carried out in Boston, a favourable viewing space is between 30° and 60° up, measured from a point in the middle of the floor. This means a sill height of 2.13 m for pictures and a viewing range of 3.00–3.65 m for sculpture → ⑩.

In art galleries there is generally no continuous circular route, just separate wings. Both museums and art galleries need side rooms for packing, dispatch, administration, a slide section, conservation workshops and lecture theatres. Disused castles, palaces and monasteries are usually suitable for housing museums. They are particularly suitable for historical objects, for which they provide a more appropriate setting than some modern museums.

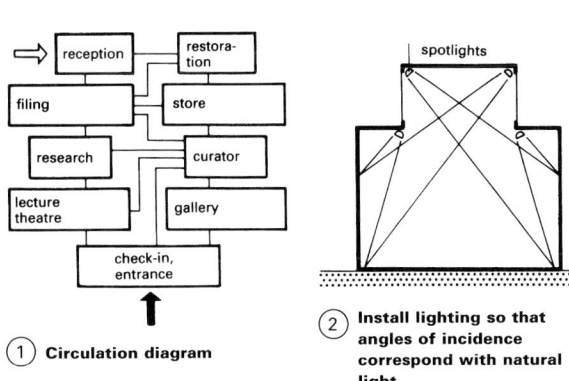

① Circulation diagram

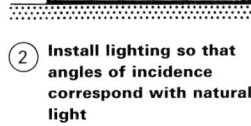

② Install lighting so that angles of incidence correspond with natural light

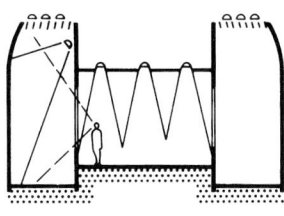

③ Typical cross-section for museum of natural history

④ Gallery passage, lit from one side only, lower part with indirect, attenuated lighting

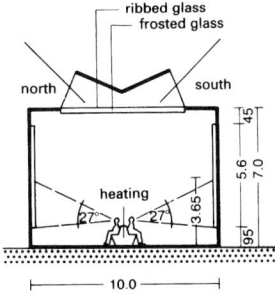

⑤ Well-lit exhibition hall based on Boston experiments

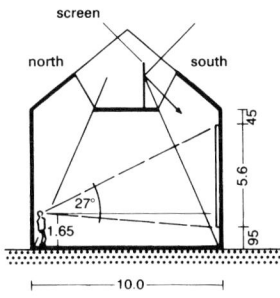

⑥ Ideal uniform lighting from both sides (following S. Hurst Seager)

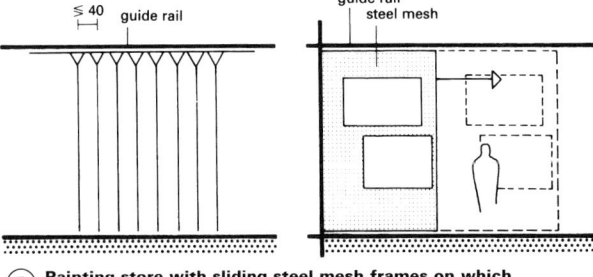

⑦ Painting store with sliding steel mesh frames on which pictures can be hung as desired and be available for study

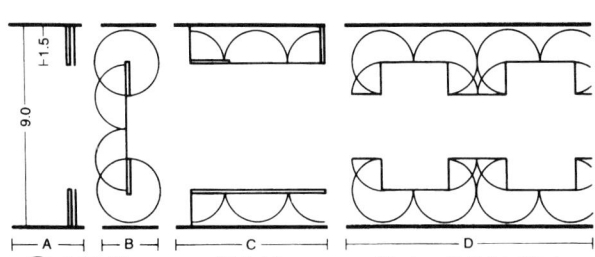

⑧ Exhibition room with folding screens (design: K. Schneider) allows great variety of room arrangements

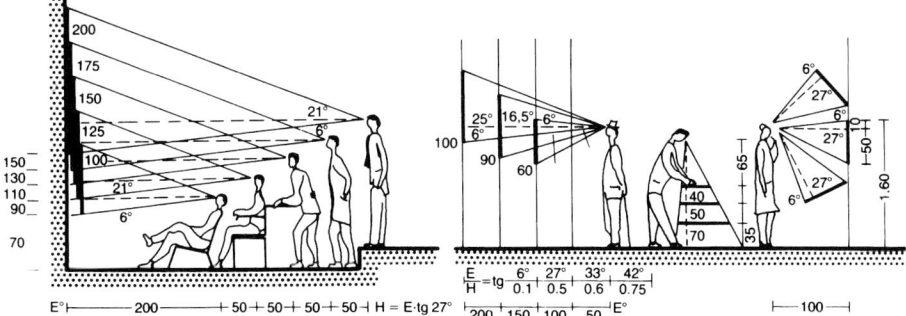

⑨ Field of vision: height/size and distance

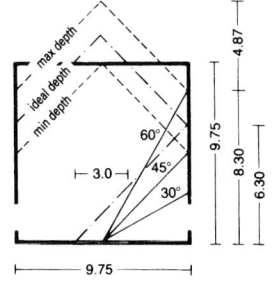

⑩ Exhibition room with side lighting

333

MUSEUMS: EXAMPLES

Nowadays, many museum buildings are also used as culture centres, and this possibility must be included in the planning stage. Spaces must be available for permanent and temporary exhibitions, libraries, media rooms and lecture theatres. There should also be places for relaxation and refreshments, as well as space for transport, storage, conservation, workshops and administration.

Technological innovations are having a big effect not only on museum function, but also on the design of exhibits. Two examples are the computerisation of collection records and design documentation, and lamp miniaturisation and fibre optics and their effect on lighting design.

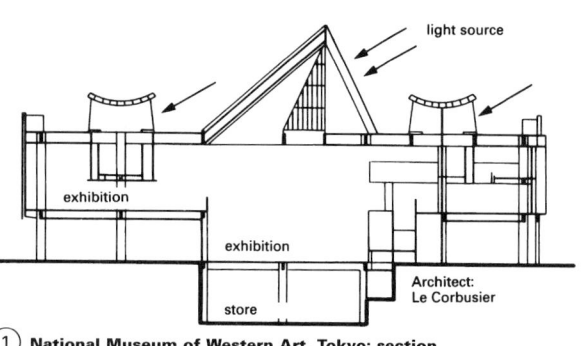

① **National Museum of Western Art, Tokyo: section**

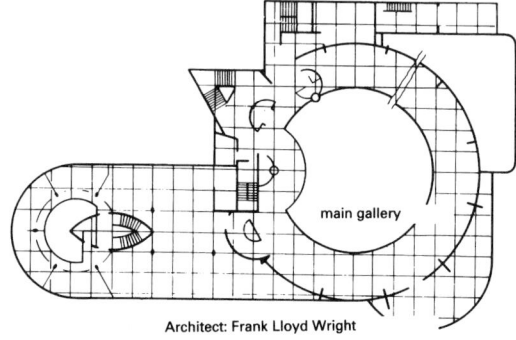

② **Guggenheim Museum, New York: plan → ③④⑤**

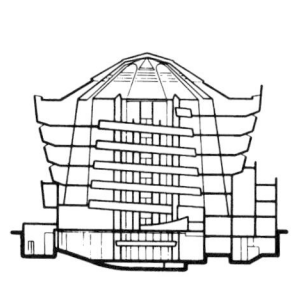

③ **Section → ②**

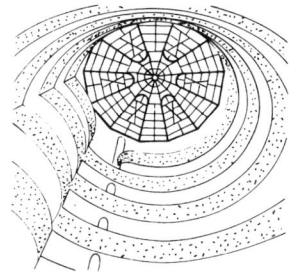

④ **Interior → ② - ③**

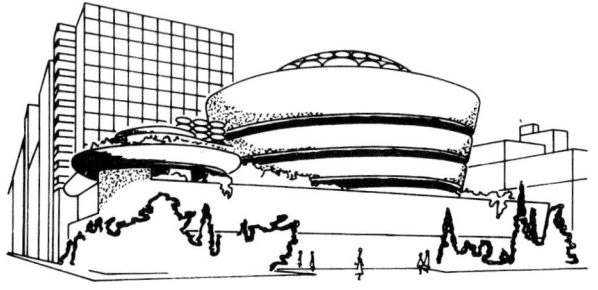

⑤ **Elevation → ② - ④**

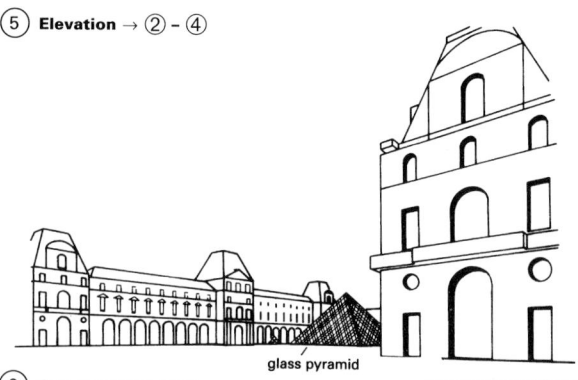

⑥ **Grand Louvre, Paris** — Architect: Pei and Partners

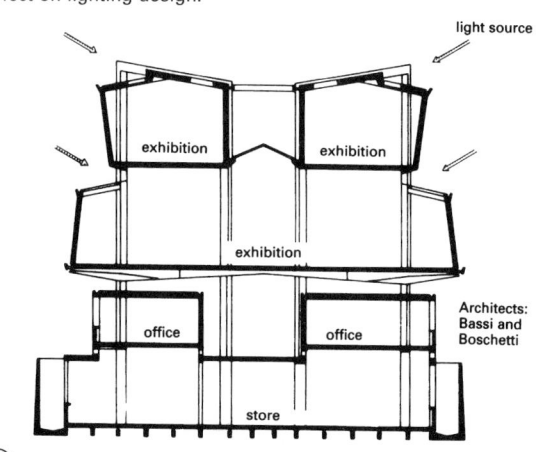

⑦ **Section and light sources Museo Civico, Turin**

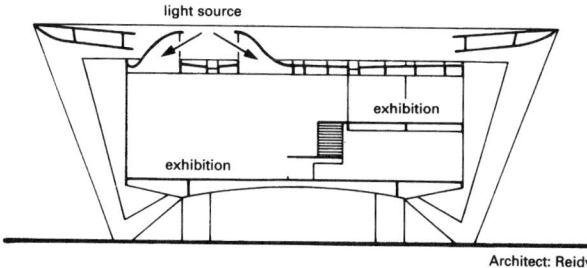

⑧ **Section and light sources Museum of Modern Art, Rio de Janeiro**

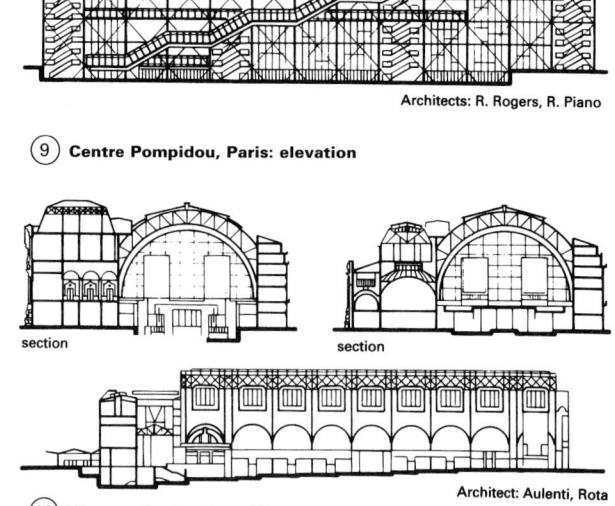

⑨ **Centre Pompidou, Paris: elevation** — Architects: R. Rogers, R. Piano

⑩ **Museum in the Gare d'Orsay** — Architect: Aulenti, Rota

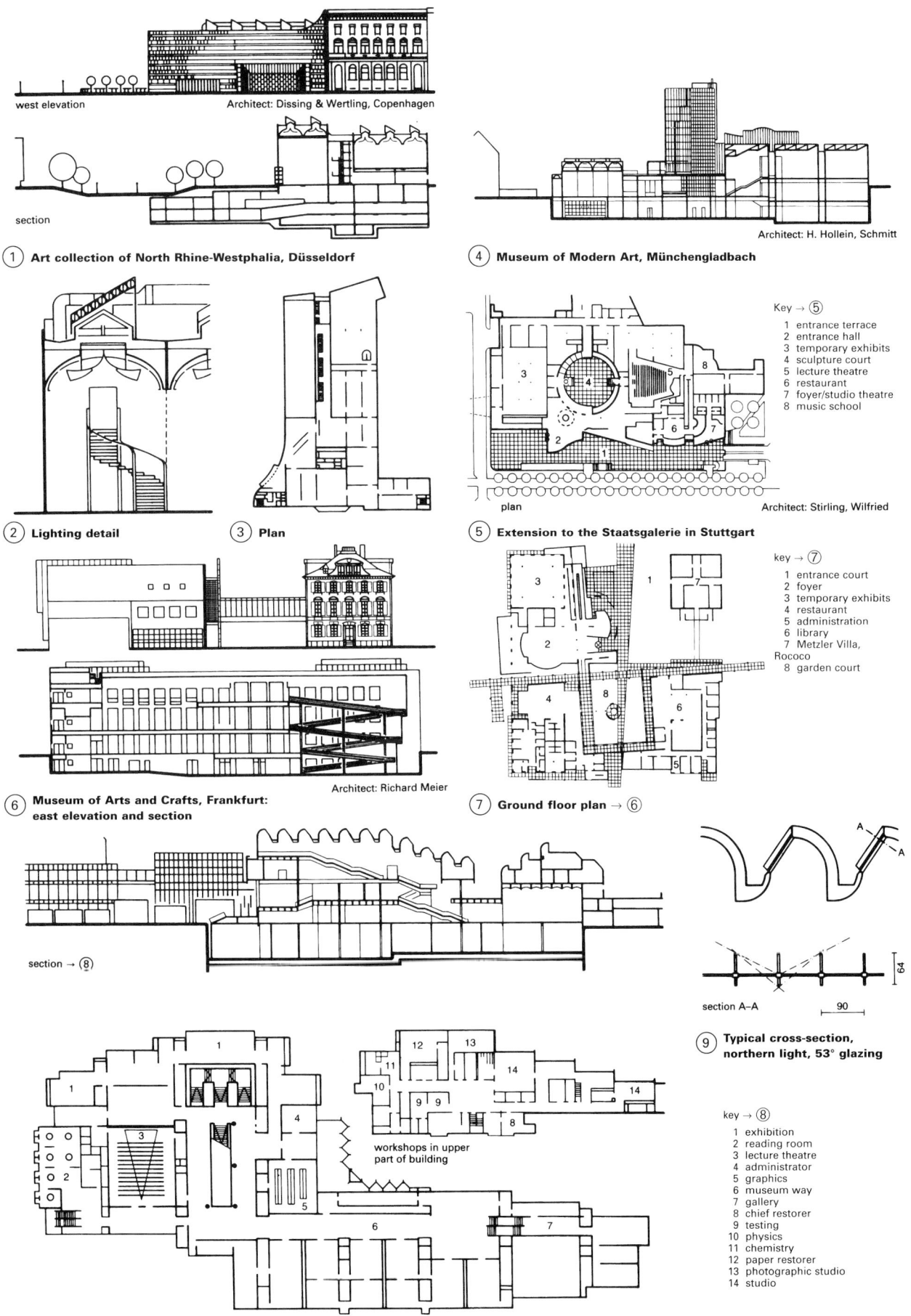

west elevation — Architect: Dissing & Wertling, Copenhagen

section

(1) **Art collection of North Rhine-Westphalia, Düsseldorf**

(2) **Lighting detail**

(3) **Plan**

(6) **Museum of Arts and Crafts, Frankfurt: east elevation and section**

Architect: Richard Meier

section → (8)

(4) **Museum of Modern Art, Münchengladbach**

Architect: H. Hollein, Schmitt

Key → (5)
1 entrance terrace
2 entrance hall
3 temporary exhibits
4 sculpture court
5 lecture theatre
6 restaurant
7 foyer/studio theatre
8 music school

plan — Architect: Stirling, Wilfried

(5) **Extension to the Staatsgalerie in Stuttgart**

key → (7)
1 entrance court
2 foyer
3 temporary exhibits
4 restaurant
5 administration
6 library
7 Metzler Villa, Rococo
8 garden court

(7) **Ground floor plan → (6)**

section A–A

(9) **Typical cross-section, northern light, 53° glazing**

key → (8)
1 exhibition
2 reading room
3 lecture theatre
4 administrator
5 graphics
6 museum way
7 gallery
8 chief restorer
9 testing
10 physics
11 chemistry
12 paper restorer
13 photographic studio
14 studio

workshops in upper part of building

(8) **Wallraf Richards Museum, Ludwig Museum, Cologne**

Architect: Busmann, Haberer

Diagram 1

work evaluation → work analysis → formation of groups

tests, observation → selection: suitability

preventive measures → rest → meals

holiday → leisure time → break

production capability

maintaining efficiency

education → instruction → training

artists, design → emotional factors

colour → light → visual characteristics

noise → acoustics

air quality → temperature → climate

performance requirements

environmental influences

work psychology — the person — work psychology

dynamics office

statics office

work duties

task specification → work guidance

supervision of duties → review → organisation

work flow

timing of work flow → times → speeds → deadlines

quantitative work flow → quantity → sizes → weights

geographical work flows → stations → routes

paper-work

documents → raw materials → document movement → filing department → current filing dept.

file index → raw materials → current file index → non-current file index → archive

documentation → books → periodicals → storage: non-current

equipment

tools → chairs → tables → file indexing → document writing

machines → for documents → for calculations → for duplication → for conveyance

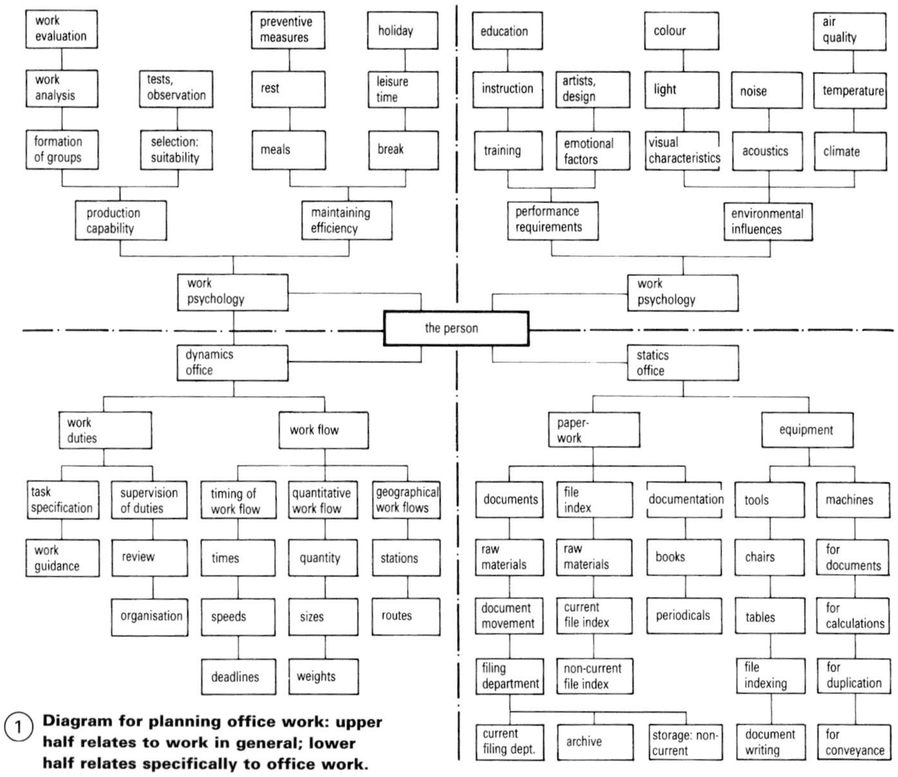

(1) **Diagram for planning office work: upper half relates to work in general; lower half relates specifically to office work. Problems in the left half can be solved by preventive measures and training; those on the right require technical and organisational solutions**

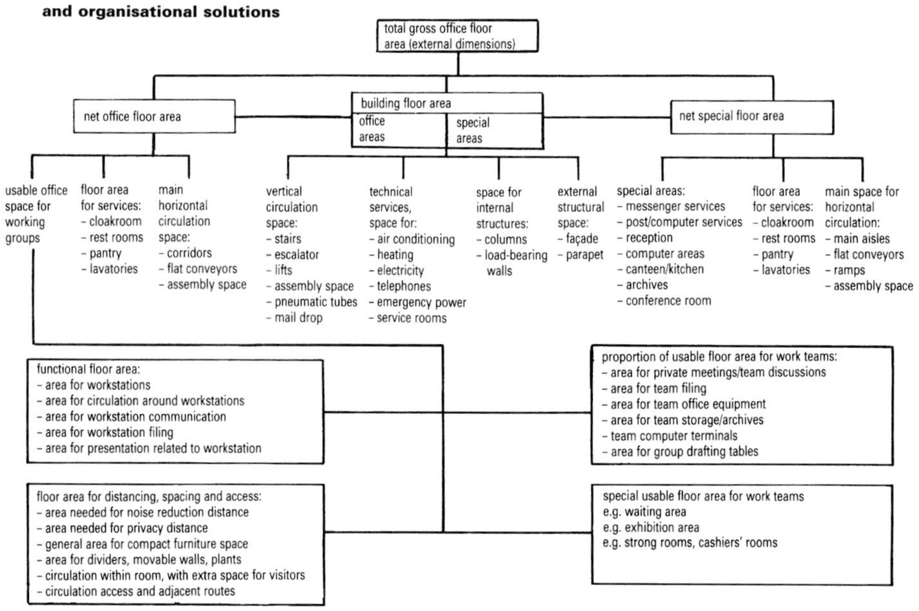

Diagram 2

total gross office floor area (external dimensions)

net office floor area

building floor area — office areas — special areas

net special floor area

usable office space for working groups

floor area for services:
– cloakroom
– rest rooms
– pantry
– lavatories

main horizontal circulation space:
– corridors
– flat conveyors
– assembly space

vertical circulation space:
– stairs
– escalator
– lifts
– assembly space
– pneumatic tubes
– mail drop

technical services, space for:
– air conditioning
– heating
– electricity
– telephones
– emergency power
– service rooms

space for internal structures:
– columns
– load-bearing walls

external structural space:
– façade
– parapet

special areas:
– messenger services
– post/computer services
– reception
– computer areas
– canteen/kitchen
– archives
– conference room

floor area for services:
– cloakroom
– rest rooms
– pantry
– lavatories

main space for horizontal circulation:
– main aisles
– flat conveyors
– ramps
– assembly space

functional floor area:
– area for workstations
– area for circulation around workstations
– area for workstation communication
– area for workstation filing
– area for presentation related to workstation

proportion of usable floor area for work teams:
– area for private meetings/team discussions
– area for team filing
– area for team office equipment
– area for team storage/archives
– team computer terminals
– area for group drafting tables

floor area for distancing, spacing and access:
– area needed for noise reduction distance
– area needed for privacy distance
– general area for compact furniture space
– area for dividers, movable walls, plants
– circulation within room, with extra space for visitors
– circulation access and adjacent routes

special usable floor area for work teams
e.g. waiting area
e.g. exhibition area
e.g. strong rooms, cashiers' rooms

(2) **Organisational arrangement of floor areas in office buildings**

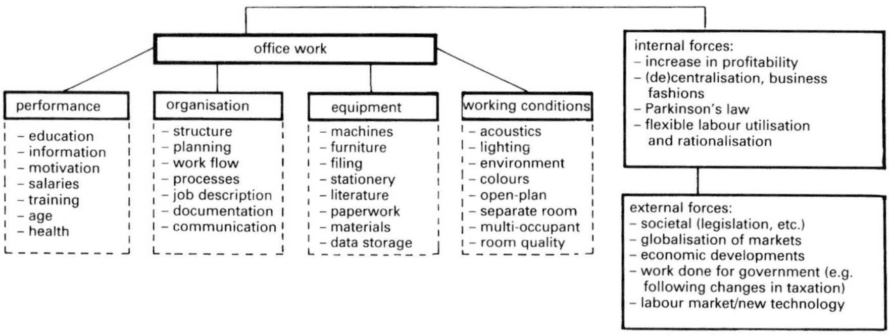

Diagram 3

office work

performance
– education
– information
– motivation
– salaries
– training
– age
– health

organisation
– structure
– planning
– work flow
– processes
– job description
– documentation
– communication

equipment
– machines
– furniture
– filing
– stationery
– literature
– paperwork
– materials
– data storage

working conditions
– acoustics
– lighting
– environment
– colours
– open-plan
– separate room
– multi-occupant
– room quality

internal forces:
– increase in profitability
– (de)centralisation, business fashions
– Parkinson's law
– flexible labour utilisation and rationalisation

external forces:
– societal (legislation, etc.)
– globalisation of markets
– economic developments
– work done for government (e.g. following changes in taxation)
– labour market/new technology

(3) **Factors affecting office work**

PRINCIPLES

Office Work

The way in which office work is organised and roles are defined (office structure, customer management, office technology) affects the requirements for office space.

Building types develop and change over time. In addition to innovative prototypes, there are types of buildings which are representative of the forces and influences around when they were built → ③. The organisation of office work increasingly focuses on human relationships and communications → ①. As office work continues to change (from the introduction of new technologies), a clear understanding of the task required becomes a significant motivating force. Designers can influence all aspects of the working environment. Good design is extremely important, and has a strong influence on job satisfaction.

The space allocated to a person to execute a task is referred to as a workstation. This can be a private office with full-height partitions and a door, an open-plan 'cubicle' configured from systems furniture or low-height partitions, or an individual desk in an undivided space.

A large office building will consist of several different types of space → ②. (1) Office areas will have separate offices for one to three people with workstations for trainees, group offices for up to 20 people, also with workstations for trainees, and open-plan offices for up to 200 people on a single level. Some offices may combine individual workstations with areas used by groups. In an open-plan office, all spaces are multipurpose for individual or team work, except for a separate secretarial department. (2) Records areas are for the storage of files, drawings, microfilm and electronic media, filing and recording equipment, document reproduction, play-back and shredding. (3) Central clerical services areas contain dictating, duplicating, printing and photocopying equipment, and personal computers. (4) The post room handles all incoming and outgoing post. (5) Corporate display areas contain board rooms with moveable walls, exhibition areas, conference rooms and meeting rooms. (6) Social facilities should include cloakrooms, a kitchen for each floor or area, toilets, a rest area for employees, refreshment rooms, sports facilities and a dining room with a kitchen. (7) Additional spaces and extensions may be needed for training on audio-visual equipment. (8) It may also be necessary to have an entrance drive, parking spaces (possibly underground) and delivery bays. (9) Circulation spaces include corridors, stairways, lifts, and internal and external emergency exits. (10) Central services are responsible for technical equipment, air conditioning, ventilation, heating, electric power, the water supply, data processing, the computer centre, telecommunications, and cleaning and maintenance.

A detailed description of the company and its organisational structure, including company-specific functions and relationships, will help produce a suitable analysis of its requirements.

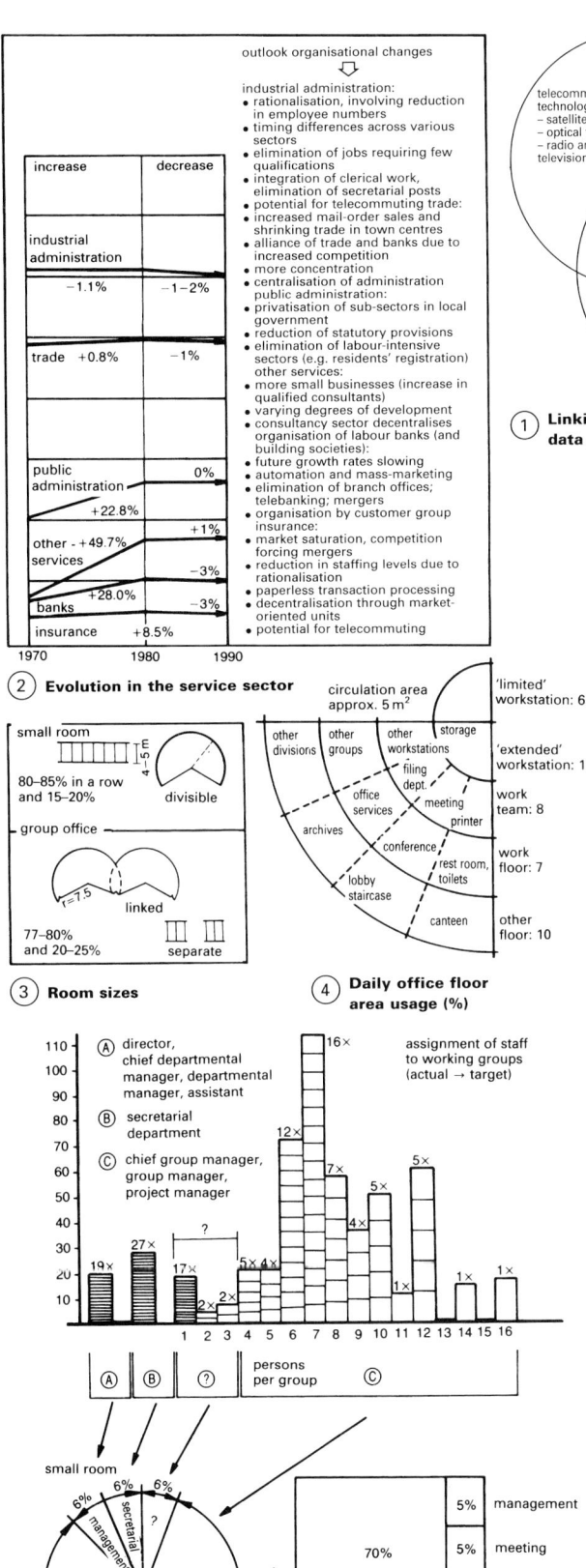

(3) **Room sizes**

(4) **Daily office floor area usage (%)**

(5) **Principles of use for distribution of space**

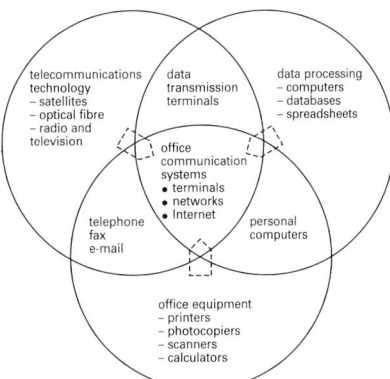

(1) **Linking telecommunications technology, data processing, and office equipment**

Effects of information technology and office automation

Developments in information and communication technologies have contributed greatly to the changing working conditions in offices. Multipurpose terminals are replacing individual data-, word- and image-processing equipment, and individual systems are being networked to form integrated office communication systems → ①. Video display stations, which also require computer terminals and additional equipment, have increased the floor area needed in offices by approx. 2–3 m^2 to approx. 15–18 m^2. The effects of office automation on workstations and layout have created needs which existing office buildings can no longer fulfil. These include the greater importance given to the quality of the individual workstation, which improves flexibility, minimises operating costs, and results in working environments that are ecologically acceptable. Reorganisation of space and the modernisation of furniture and fittings are just as important as new buildings → ②.

Streamlining working procedures can potentially reduce the time spent on administrative activities (filing, sorting, copying, searching, acquisition of material etc.) and communication (conferences and meetings) by approx. 25%. Good design can minimise interruptions to the workflow. More telecommuting (work at home) compensates for the increased floor area requirement described above, but some activities (meetings, etc.) must still take place in the office building. There are also limits to the usefulness of telecommuting.

There are other forces which tend to work against potential decentralisation, and which may be very important. A centralised location may have a prestige advantage, a company's presence in a city is a symbol of continuity, and employees often prefer a communal working atmosphere and shared leisure activities. Video-conferencing, however, could reduce job-related travel by approx. 50%.

Changes in the workplace

Increased efficiency due to information technology and changes in work requirements (processes and organisational patterns) are changing office structures. Staffing levels are dropping, and working groups are getting smaller. The former hierarchical division of labour amongst staff, such as manager, secretary, senior clerk etc., often develops into an integrated working group. This in turn may change floor space allocations. A greater awareness of the immediate working environment is closely linked to current societal values. These are reflected in attitudes toward workplace quality (daylight, use of environmentally friendly products, energy conservation) and daily activities (ecological aspects, consumption of materials, waste disposal). From the employee's viewpoint, the workplace is a vital forum for social interaction. This is increasingly important because of the stress caused by new technology and formalised work structures. Rising levels of physical and psychological stress have resulted in greater attention being paid to the work environment. Office workers need sufficient space, the freedom to arrange their own furniture, good ventilation and lighting, and protection against external or unnecessary disruptions. Approximately 65% of the working day is spent in limited work areas and 10% in extended work areas → ④. Work contacts and shared equipment are becoming more important, resulting in the need for individual and shared offices and workstations → ③ + ⑤.

In addition to reorganisation of existing buildings, new concepts for individual and group offices are taking shape, e.g. the interconnecting group office partially divided into zones, the combined office, or the multiple or multivalent workstation, although the latter does not appear to be popular.

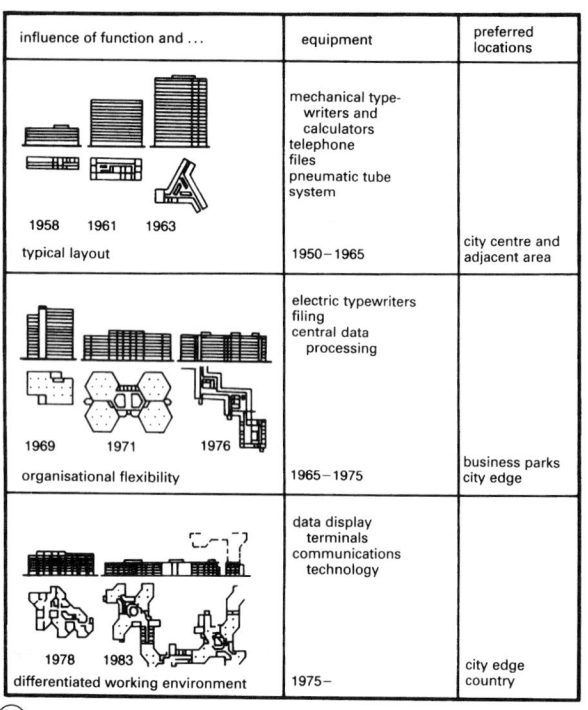

influence of function and ...	equipment	preferred locations
1958 1961 1963 typical layout	mechanical type-writers and calculators telephone files pneumatic tube system	city centre and adjacent area 1950–1965
1969 1971 1976 organisational flexibility	electric typewriters filing central data processing	business parks city edge 1965–1975
1978 1983 differentiated working environment	data display terminals communications technology	city edge country 1975–

① Floor plans since 1950

time	type	equipment	process diagram
from 1950	small room: in rows, stacked	mechanical office machines telephone files	linear
from 1965	open-plan office: transparent, flexible	electric typewriters photocopier central data processing	networked
from 1980	group office: connected, articulated	decentralised data processing word processing data display terminals computers	sequential

② Building type and working arrangement

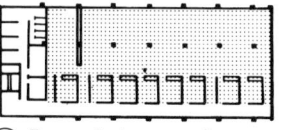
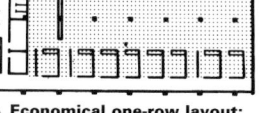

③ Economical one-row layout; very deep offices

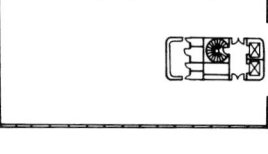

④ Double row layout

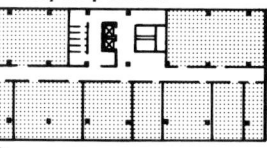
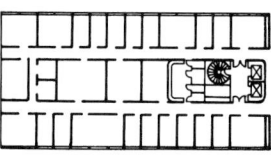

⑤ Three-row layout

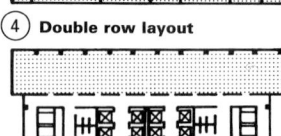
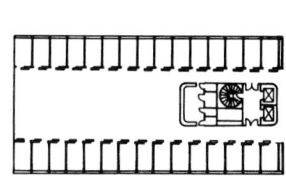

⑥ Layout without corridor

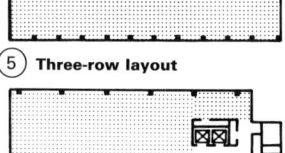
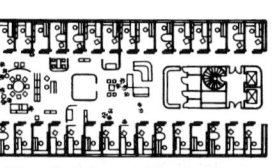

⑦ First design, combined office: ESAB HQ, Tenbom Arkitekter AB, Stockholm. Various internal arrangements: open-plan, group, separate and combined offices

Types of office space

The layout of office space has changed dramatically since the 1950s → ①. Working methods are always closely linked to available technology → ②, and the working structure of earlier years is being expanded by modern information technology and office automation. As a result, new forms of floor plan are being generated.

After changing from separate offices in the 1950s, to open-plan concepts after the mid-1960s, and group office principles in the 1970s and 1980s, it seems that a combined office design is becoming established in the 1990s. The first examples appeared in Denmark in 1976, where new space dividers and combinations of all known basic forms were being used.

The orientation of a new office building will depend on location. Where possible, the building should be orientated to admit useful daylight while avoiding glare and solar heat gain. In the USA, the principal axis of 90% of office buildings runs east–west, since deep penetration by morning and evening sun is unpleasant. It is easy to use canopies to block the sun from the south. However, if the primary axis runs north–south, the sunlight can reach every room. In the northern hemisphere, north-facing rooms are justifiable only when the building does not have a corridor.

Systems

A single row of rooms is generally uneconomical, and is only justified for deep office spaces where daylight is a problem → ③. A double row of individual small rooms, all with daylight, was previously used in most office buildings → ④. A three-part arrangement is typical of high-rise office buildings → ⑤. In city centres in the USA, designs without corridors evolved. In some, all rooms (with either natural or artificial lighting) were grouped around a circulation core containing elevators, staircases, ventilation ducts etc.; in others, services were located on the periphery → ⑥.

Outside the city centre, another US system had a large work space in the centre, with sound insulation, ventilation and lighting in the ceiling; small offices with daylight were placed around the edge. These combined offices were used in Scandinavia after the mid-1970s. As in the US system, the floor plan was normally 16–18 m deep. They were also built as a large open-plan office or as separate offices divided into three rows → ⑦.

Daylight can usually be used up to a distance of 7.00 m from the window. New daylight technology systems (see section on daylight) which convey and change the direction of the light (prisms and reflectors) can make more efficient use of daylight.

A schedule of accommodation is shown → ⑧ which compares five alternatives in order to obtain quantifiable information about floor area requirements. (1) A standard separate office, 1.25 m grid module, three module spaces only. (2) Deluxe separate office, grid module 1.50 m, various widths. (3) Open-plan office, room depth 20–30 m, floor area up to 1000 m². (4) Group offices for 15–20 employees, workstations no more than 7.50 m from the façade. (5) Combined office, all single rooms approx. 10 m² with a common area 6–8 m deep.

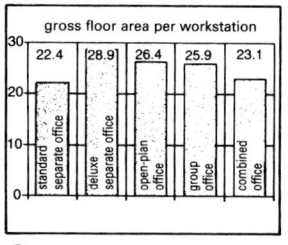

gross floor area per workstation

22.4	28.9	26.4	25.9	23.1
standard separate office	deluxe separate office	open-plan office	group office	combined office

⑧ Types of offices and comparison of floor area requirements

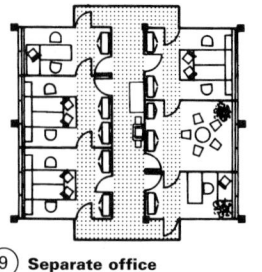

⑨ Separate office

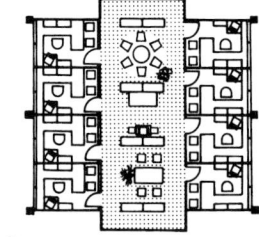

⑩ Combined office

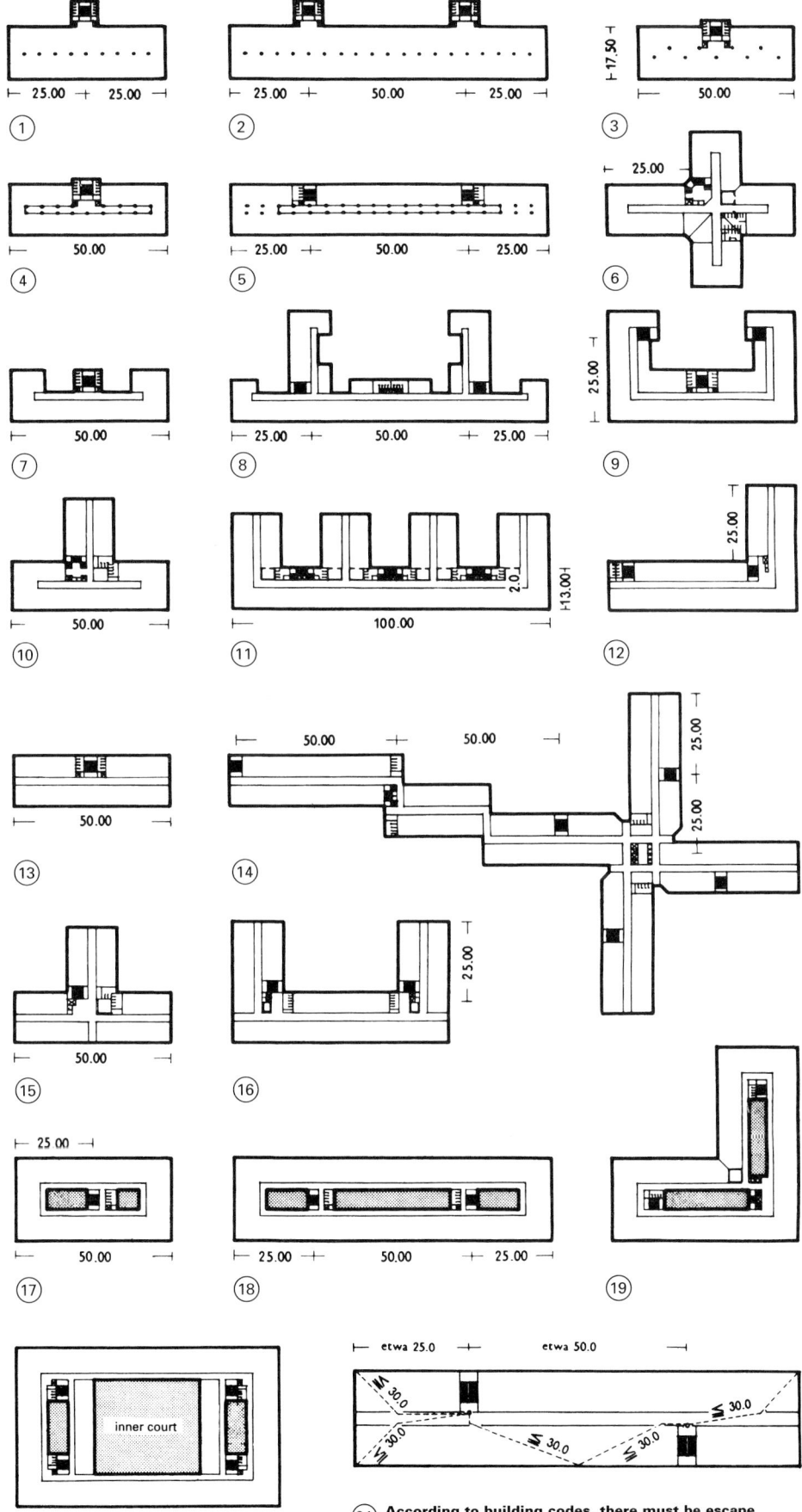

PRINCIPLES

Typology

Large office buildings are usually multistorey structures with moveable internal walls → (p. 92). Service cores, containing plumbing, staircases, elevators etc., are generally located at the maximum distances specified by the building regulations. Service cores can be placed at the front of the building → ① + ②, to one side within the building → ③ – ⑤, at interior corners → ⑥ + ⑩ – ⑫ + ⑮ + ⑯, at the end of a passage → ⑧,⑨,⑪,⑫,⑭ or between corridors next to a light shaft → ⑰ – ㉑, in order to maintain the greatest possible length and continuity in working spaces. A simple central rows of columns → ① + ② allows for a corridor on one side or the other according to space requirements. A double row of columns allows for offices of equal depth → ③ – ⑤. In such cases the corridors may be lit directly by high-level windows and/or by glass doors in the corridor wall. Daylight in the corridor may be provided economically by overhead skylights in buildings with wings → ⑩ + ⑪, and those that are short → ⑬, angled → ⑫, T-shaped → ⑮ or U-shaped → ⑯.

Lateral illumination of corridors by recesses is less economical → ⑦ + ⑧. On deep, expensive sites it is best to locate corridors, service rooms, archives, toilets and cloakrooms on interior courts or atria → ⑰ – ⑳. Elevators and toilets can be located at the interior corners of stairwells. Dark rooms, strong rooms and storage rooms should be in dark areas → ⑩ + ⑪ + ⑲.

The area required to connect functional spaces in office buildings is the circulation area. In a closed plan, this is the corridors between rooms; in an open plan, it is the paths through the workstations. Path widths need careful consideration, especially when they are part of an escape route. Disability access considerations include the width of doors and circulation routes, wheelchair turnaround clearances, and the slope and length of ramps, etc.

Fire safety is a primary consideration in the planning of circulation routes, and should be considered at an early stage. The main considerations are the width of escape routes, the distance to be travelled, provision of alternative escape routes and the avoidance of dead-end corridors. The plan must comply with local statutory safety requirements → ㉑.

㉑ **According to building codes, there must be escape stairs no more than 30 m from any point in a non-work room. It is best to calculate the distance of the staircases as 25 m from the site boundary and the distance between staircases as 50 m → ① – ㉑**

PRINCIPLES OF TYPOLOGY

1950s–1960s

Building concepts I

The relationships between office organisation and spatial design have been classified in a field study in the USA which provided a benchmark for changes in office structures as a result of office automation.

Open-plan offices are suitable for large groups of employees with a high degree of division of labour, performing routine activities with a low level of concentration. Nowadays, open plan is more the exception than the rule. The concept was developed in the 1960s to provide efficiently organised, multipurpose areas, based on arguments such as transparency and clarity of working processes, and the development of a group spirit. Data processing equipment was kept in separate rooms and was not available at each workstation. Extremely deep offices (from 20 to 30 m) resulted in the use of expensive services technology that became unsuitable when the building use changed. Modern requirements, such as windows which open, lighting and environmental control, and electric power suitable for partitioned spaces all limit potential flexibility.

Sociologists have attested to the implicit coercive nature of open-plan offices, which is caused by social control, reliance on technical equipment, and visual and acoustic disruptions. This has led to a rejection of this type of office by employees.

Separate offices are suitable for independent work requiring concentration, and also for multi-occupant offices for very small groups constantly exchanging information. They are still used for certain workstation requirements, and in multistorey office buildings where the structural form of the building is so dominant that it determines the spatial and organisational features of the workstations.

(1) **Separate office, Garrick Building, Chicago**

Architects: Dankmar Adler and Louis H. Sulliran, 1892

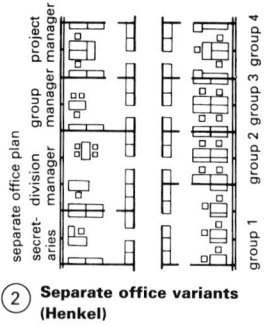

(2) **Separate office variants (Henkel)**

separate office plan · secret-aries · division manager · group manager · project manager · group 1 · group 2 · group 3 · group 4

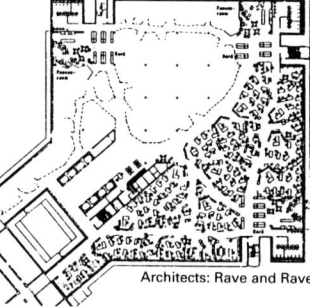

(3) **Open-plan office, Leiter Building I, Chicago**

Architect: William LeBaron Jenney, 1879

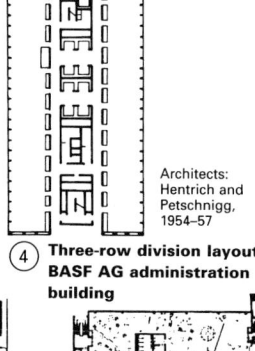

(4) **Three-row division layout: BASF AG administration building**

Architects: Hentrich and Petschnigg, 1954–57

(5) **German Federal Employment Office HQ, Berlin**

Architects: Rave and Rave

(6) **First open-plan office with 270 workstations in Germany (5th floor, former warehouse)**

Architect: Walter Henn, 1962

(7) **Open-plan office, Hamm (upper floor)**

Architect: author

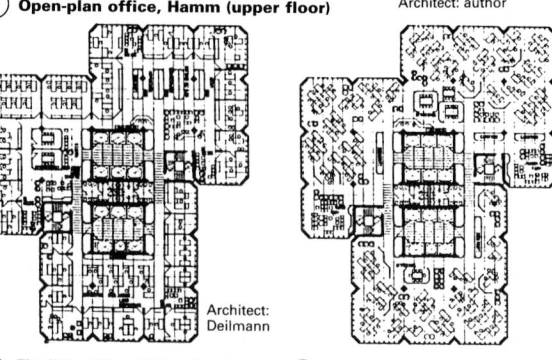

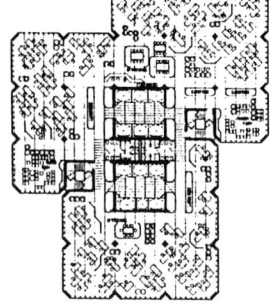

(8) **Flexible office. Rhine Province Regional Insurance Institution HQ, Düsseldorf**

Architect: Deilmann

(9) → (8)

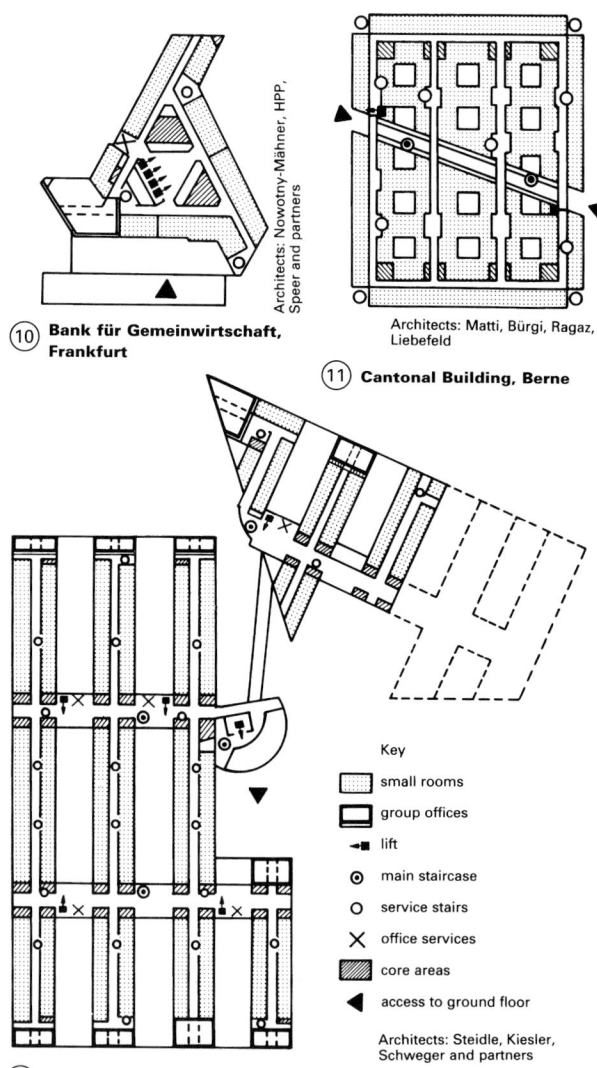

(10) **Bank für Gemeinwirtschaft, Frankfurt**

Architects: Nowotny-Mähner, HPP, Speer and partners

(11) **Cantonal Building, Berne**

Architects: Matti, Bürgi, Ragaz, Liebefeld

Key

▢ small rooms
▭ group offices
→■ lift
⊙ main staircase
○ service stairs
✕ office services
▨ core areas
◀ access to ground floor

Architects: Steidle, Kiesler, Schweger and partners

(12) **G+J Publishing Company, Hamburg**

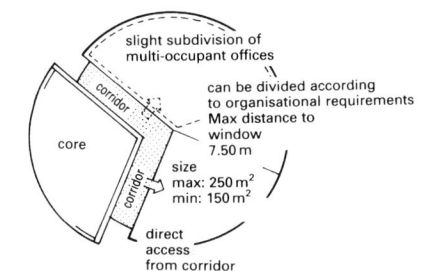

Architect: Striffler, 1977

(13) **Group office, ÖVA insurance, Mannheim**

(14) **Requirements for group office**

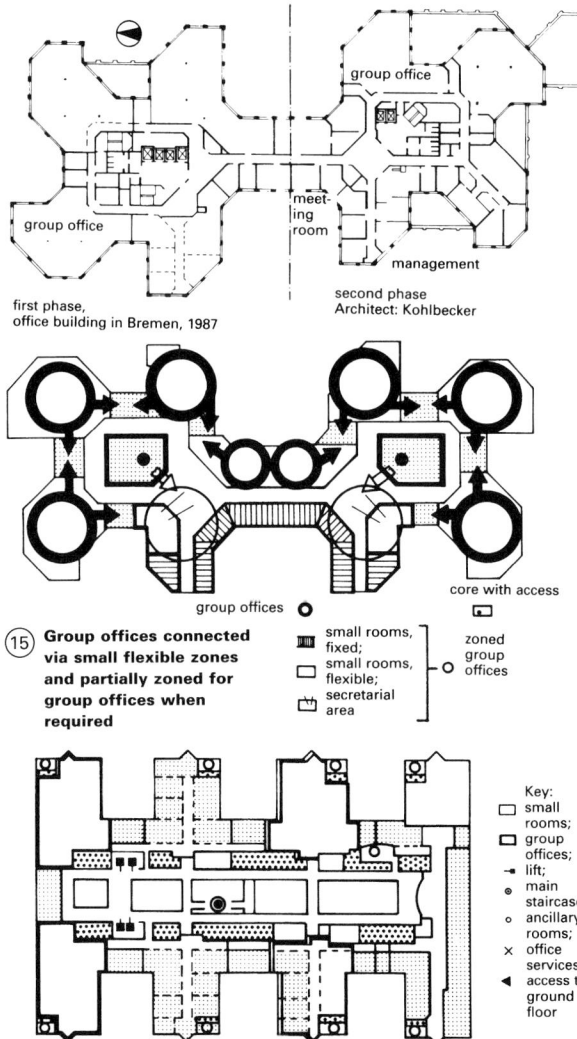

first phase,
office building in Bremen, 1987

second phase
Architect: Kohlbecker

(15) **Group offices connected via small flexible zones and partially zoned for group offices when required**

- small rooms, fixed;
- small rooms, flexible;
- secretarial area
- zoned group offices

Key:
- □ small rooms;
- □ group offices;
- → lift;
- ● main staircase;
- ○ ancillary rooms;
- × office services;
- ◄ access to ground floor

Architects: Jourdan, Müller, et al., 1988

(16) **Provincial State Central Bank of Hesse, Frankfurt am Main**

Building concepts II

The reversible office was an attempt to improve the open-plan office system, which was felt to have many drawbacks for users. These included no individual environmental or daylight control, and visual and acoustic disturbances. Larger areas were subdivided into separate offices, which are better for work requiring great concentration, and this began a move toward greater flexibility. In addition, skyrocketing energy prices also cast doubt on the desirability of open-plan offices.

Changes in working structures as a result of new technologies (such as personal computers) made it possible to organise work in small groups. Group offices (small open-plan offices) are suitable for teams of clerical workers who constantly exchange information. They also allow greater flexibility for individual decisions about the working environment because of their smaller size (max. 7.50m to window) (see earlier notes on changes in the workplace). Fully localised environmental control is not necessary; back-up control methods can be used, in addition to ventilation fins on façades and heating surfaces.

Methods of reorganisation include remodelling the building, providing daylight through courtyards, clear subdivisions in the floor plan to create workstations with uniform standards of light, ventilation and noise protection, or the use of office equipment that can quickly be adapted to fulfil new technical functions that entail more electrical cables and complex connections, as well as dividing the space. Raised floors and movable partitions often provide an easy way to adapt a building in terms of services, communication and space division. An example of space reorganisation after employee dissatisfaction is provided on the next page (→ 26 – 28). Although it is still a popular trend, the open-plan office appears to be useful for very few organisational forms or types of work. The prime objectives at Bertelsmann were to improve the quality of the workplace while retaining the flexibility to adapt to new office technologies and group reorganisation, and to use the working space economically and reduce operating costs.

Building concepts III

Recent trends aim to provide a spatial design that is appropriate for all the individual office requirements of an organisation. That means providing a space that is flexible when required, allows for group work, and includes individual rooms for work requiring concentration. It should also provide equipment that can be used both separately and collectively by groups, and which is particularly well-suited for high-quality independent work while allowing workstations to change according to daily requirements.

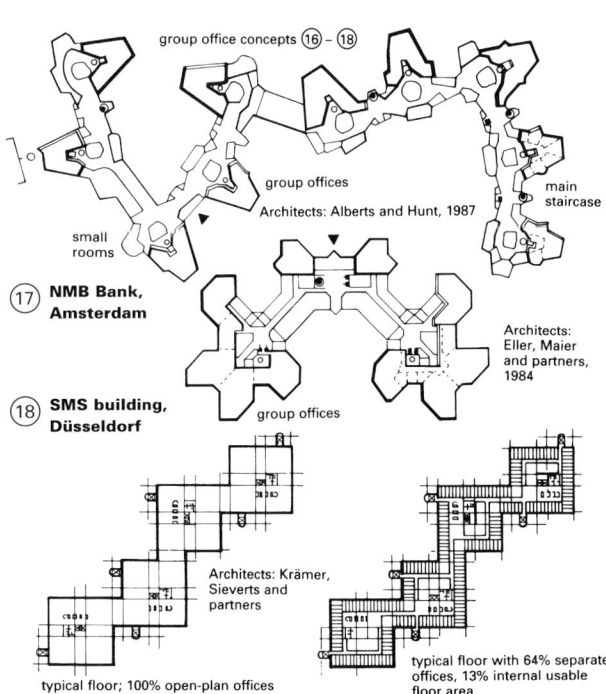

group office concepts (16) – (28)

group offices

main staircase

small rooms

Architects: Alberts and Hunt, 1987

(17) **NMB Bank, Amsterdam**

Architects: Eller, Maier and partners, 1984

(18) **SMS building, Düsseldorf**

group offices

Architects: Krämer, Sieverts and partners

typical floor; 100% open-plan offices

typical floor with 64% separate offices, 13% internal usable floor area

(19) **Flexible office, Dortmund City Administration**

PRINCIPLES OF TYPOLOGY

1980s–1990s

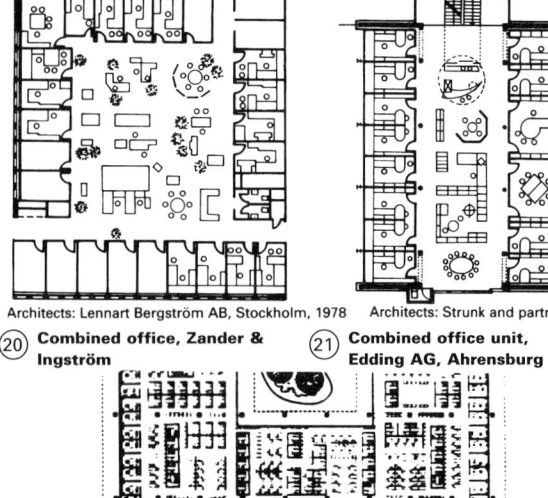

Architects: Lennart Bergström AB, Stockholm, 1978

(20) **Combined office, Zander & Ingström**

Architects: Strunk and partners

(21) **Combined office unit, Edding AG, Ahrensburg**

In general, modern office buildings tend to fall into three categories: closed plan, open plan, and modified open plan. Selection criteria include:

- the amount of planning flexibility required;
- the amount of visual and acoustic privacy required;
- initial and life-cycle costs.

Closed-plan offices have full-height walls or partitions dividing the space into offices with doors. Private offices are typically located along the window wall. Administrative support is housed in workstations along corridors or in shared rooms. The advantages include a controlled environment, security, visual privacy, physical separation, external views, and traditional and systems furniture applications. Disadvantages include lower efficiency than in an open-plan office, lack of flexibility, especially in responding to changes in office technology, the high cost of relocation, restricted individual and group interaction, and the fact that more extensive mechanical systems are required.

In open-plan offices, all workstations are located in an open space with no ceiling-height divisions or doors. Administrative support is located in rooms with floor-to-ceiling partitions and doors. The advantages include efficient space utilisation, greater planning flexibility, ease of communication and lower life-cycle costs. Disadvantages include higher initial costs, no visual privacy, no external views and less environmental control.

Modified open-plan offices combine elements of both the others by positioning certain workstations in an open plan with systems furniture, and others in private offices. Administrative support is also located in enclosed rooms.

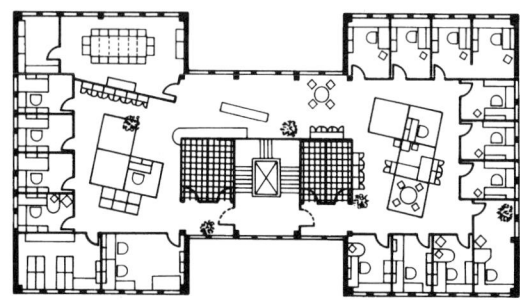

Architects: Skidmore, Owings & Merrill

(22) **American Can Company HQ, Greenwich, Connecticut**

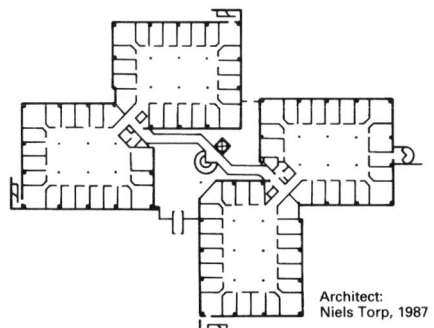

Architect: Niels Torp, 1987

(24) **Combined office, Nafslund Nycomed A/S, Oslo**

Architects: Bernhard Steiner and Bernhard von Wallis, 1991

(23) **Combined sales office of PPC Hellige, Stuttgart**

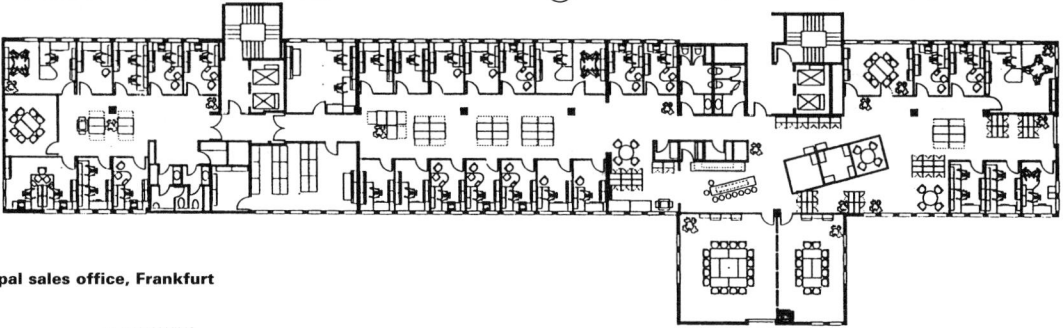

(25) **Principal sales office, Frankfurt**

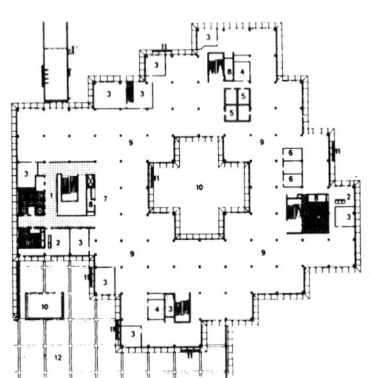

1 lobby
2 lounge
3 office
4 meeting room
5 recording studio
6 storage
7 document conveyor
8 air conditioning shaft
9 open-plan office
10 central courtyard
11 escape ladder
12 roof terrace

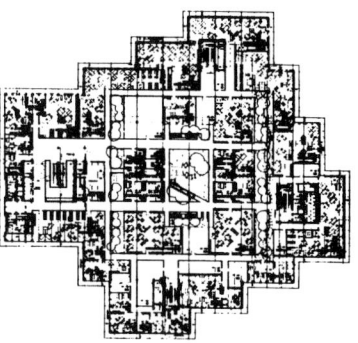

(26) **1976: completion of phase one of the administration building (V1) for Bertelsmann → (27) – (28)**

(27) **Complete re-arrangement of workstations, 1985**

(28) **Reorganisation: mixture of individual and group offices**

CALCULATIONS: CONSTRUCTION

The structural members of the building have a strong influence on the possible ways in which an office area can be divided → ① – ④. A clear floor-to-ceiling height of 2.75m permits the later installation of raised floors or suspended ceilings. Ceilings can be 25cm lower if most activities are carried out while seated, but the clear height should not be less than 2.50m. Corridors and toilets can be 2.30m high, but must have space for ducts and pipes. The economic efficiency of load-bearing members depends far less on the optimisation of individual components than on their integration into a functionally efficient building

Beam systems may be longitudinal or transverse → ① – ④. This example of the range of design approaches is based on a reinforced concrete floor with a span of 6.50m. The cost and weight of the span affects the choice of supporting structure and foundation. A greater floor thickness has advantages because the optimum rigidity of the structure will be maintained if the loadings vary.

A ribbed floor is economical only for larger spans. Although it is light weight, it costs more for sound insulation. It is not possible to cut through ribs, and openings cannot be introduced owing to the limited space between ribs. Double-T or Pi-shaped slabs or beans are structurally better for large spans. Transverse service ducts should be located in the floor in corridor areas → ① – ⑤. The facade plane may be located either behind, between or in front of the structural plane. The maximum flexibility of space is achieved if the external skin is independent of the structure of the building.

With interior columns, cantilever floors (with curtain walls) can even up the loads on the columns. Rigidity is provided by the use of wall plates, multistage bracing, and solid access cores with secondary zones on the ends.

Solid dividing walls can replace columns and main beams in some parts of the structure, and the inclusion of panels helps to improve rigidity → ⑥ – ⑧. Fixed openings should be specified in advance to prevent later problems. Lightweight partitions have the advantage of being movable and also permit later decisions concerning the division of space.

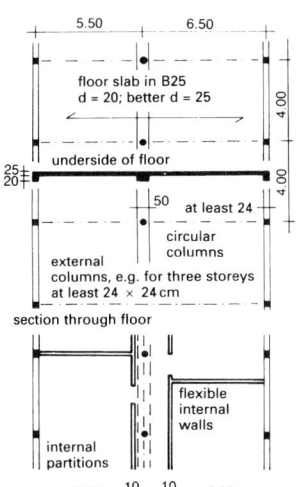

① Structural system: asymmetrical double-span beams

Floor spans building. Main beams run longitudinally in centre, with columns at side within corridor area, separated from corridor wall.
– Unlimited flexibility; reversibility.
– Sufficient corridor width required for clear passage between columns and wall.
– Suitable for structures without suspended ceilings or on top of carparks with access lanes running the length of building.

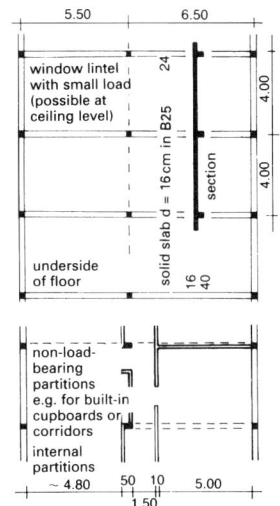

② Structural system: multi-span beams

Floor stressed the length of building. Main beams run across building from external columns over centre columns to external columns.
– Unlimited flexibility; reversibility.
– Additional sound insulation required due to low floor density (suspended ceiling, floating composite floor).
– Suitable for structures above carparking with access lanes running the length of building.

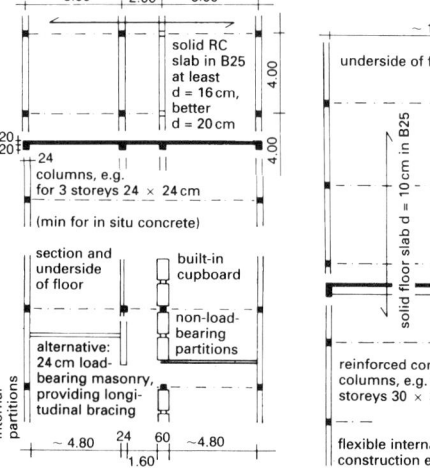

③ Structural system: triple-span beams

Floor spans building. Main beams run length of building in centre span on both sides of the corridor. Corridor wall can also act as bearing/stiffening panel to increase longitudinal rigidity.
– Masonry corridor wall cannot be changed; limited flexibility of depth of space.
– Min floor thickness 20cm (impact noise insulation) if suspended ceiling or floating composite floor not used.
– Not suitable above car parking.
– Economical to use corridor wall as bearing panel.
– Increasingly economical for greater building depths and distances between columns in the length of the building.

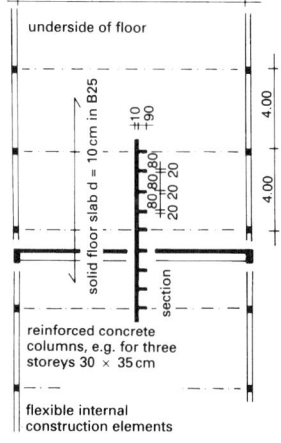

④ Structural system: T-beam ceiling

Main beams: uninterrupted span, without central columns, between external columns.
– Unlimited flexibility; reversibility.
– Suspended ceiling required.
– Services run across building between webs. Longitudinal installation through holes in beams almost impossible.
– Uneconomical overall structure, high main beams (also in steel structure), large building volumes, only for superstructures without columns. Reduced main beam height of 60cm, structure sensitive to vibration with high degree of deflection.

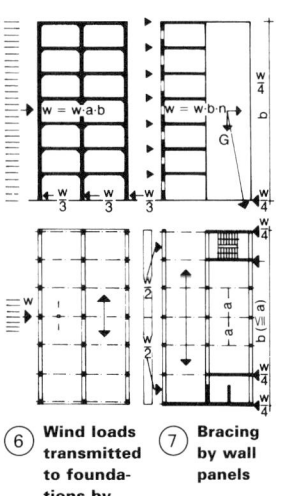
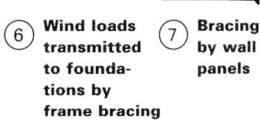

⑥ Wind loads transmitted to foundations by frame bracing

⑦ Bracing by wall panels

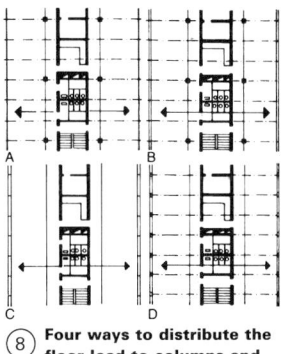
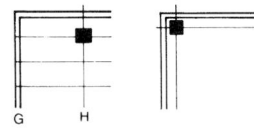

⑧ Four ways to distribute the floor load to columns and the core zone for three-part structures

A–H: influence of design on ability to subdivide office space with movable partitions. A–B: external columns; C–E: columns within or immediately behind façade; E–F: internal columns (possibility to create corners G–H)

⑤ Structural connections and division of office floor space

CALCULATIONS: BUILDING TECHNOLOGY

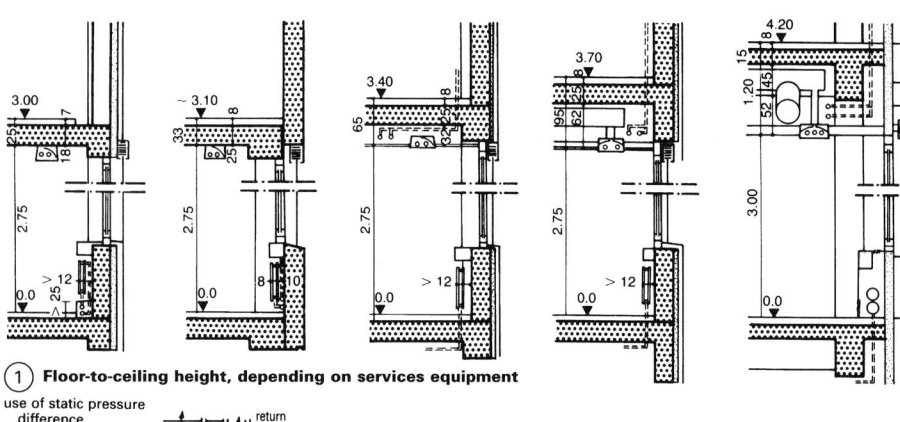

① Floor-to-ceiling height, depending on services equipment

② Air conditioning technology, heating and cooling

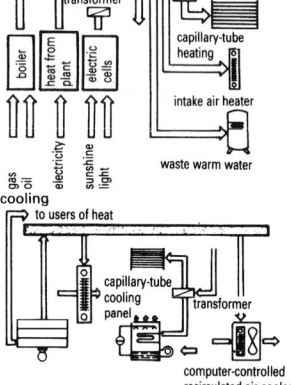

⑤ Air movement due to temperature gradient

⑥ Heating panel; capillary mat

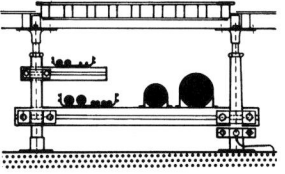

⑦ False floor with cable runs

⑧ Floor/wall section: dividing wall

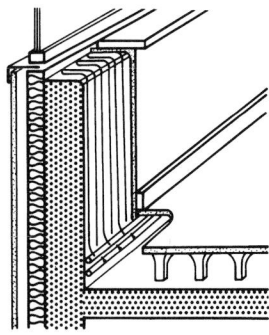

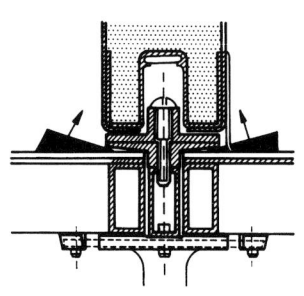

③ Air conditioning with localised element cooling

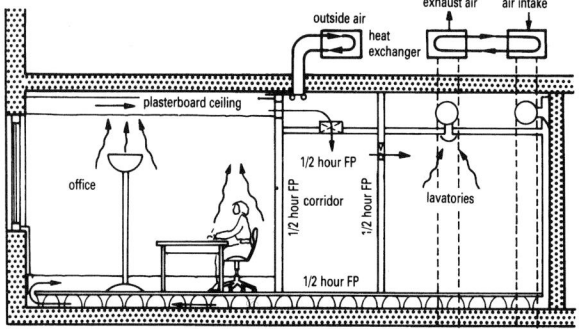

④ System section for Klimadrant® Control of air to individual desks

	average (%)	range (%)
lighting	40	± 10
elevator and conveyors	6	± 2
low voltage equipment	1	± 0.5
heating, cooling and ventilation systems	47	± 15
lavatories	2	± 1
kitchen facilities (electric)	2	± 1
cleaning and waste disposal	2	± 1
total	100	

⑨ Energy costs of service plant in an office building

The gross volume of space needed and the total construction cost mean that fully air-conditioned buildings are 1.3–1.5 times more expensive than non-air-conditioned buildings, i.e. those which are naturally ventilated → ①.

A ceiling height of 3.0–3.10 m is suitable for buildings with little service equipment, no suspended ceilings and heating pipes on an exterior wall. Electric power should be supplied through ducts in window sills or floors, and the power supply for ceiling lights through conduits or partitions. Corridor areas should also be used for ducts and pipes.

A ceiling height of 3.4 m is suitable for a building with some service equipment, but without ventilation equipment. Ducts under the floor in corridor areas (h = 32 cm) should be used for heat, electricity and water.

A ceiling height of 3.70 m is suitable for office buildings using ventilation equipment. A duct height of at least 50 cm is needed for air-conditioned offices, with long ducts in the corridor area.

Open-plan offices need a clear ceiling height of only 3.00 m. However, the ceiling height should be 4.20 m if ventilation ducts are to be installed. All height-related building components affect the cost of the building in relation to its usable office floor area.

Air-conditioning systems with capillary tube mats use water and the principle of localised cooling → ② + ③. The air intake is equivalent to the minimum air-change rate. Comfortable cooling is achieved by radiant protection and displacement ventilation without turbulence (expanding-air ventilation). This creates a flow of fresh air (with outlets near the floor and at the base of furniture), a cushion of warm air at the ceiling, and an air-flow through the room → ⑤ caused by the temperature gradient (main surfaces 32°C at the ceiling, 20°C at each wall).

Radiant heating from panels in combination with an air intake system may be sufficient for heating → ⑥. Such a system uses less equipment and thus increases the usable floor area. The cost of air conditioning with localised cooling compares favourably with the cost of conventional air conditioning. The advantages include no draughts, quiet, lower investment and operating costs (the volume of water that has to be conveyed is 1000 times less than the volume of air for a closed system with the same output and heat recovery), a reduction of the space required for services (water instead of air) and a smaller energy plant. Raised floors are required to achieve the necessary room ventilation and for installing services to areas with a large amount of equipment. There is an increased demand for space for services (cables, office automation), and a need to guarantee flexibility when functional processes change → ⑦ + ⑧.

The selection of a heating, ventilation and air conditioning (HVAC) system is usually based on performance characteristics, system capacity and the availability of space to accommodate the equipment.

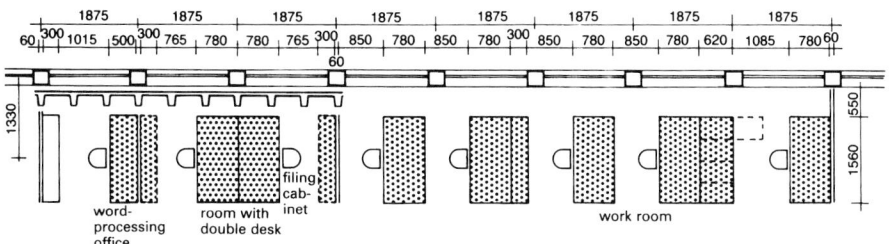

① With standard desks (size 0.78 × 1.56 m), a division of 187.5 is suitable for a ribbed/slab-and-beam floor having a 62.5 grid module (Koenen floor) with normal formwork. Better for movable partitions

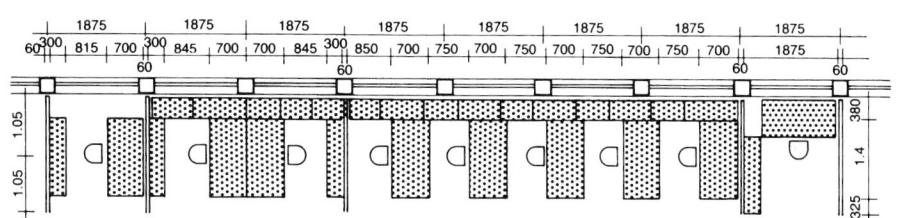

② Modular desks (size 0.70 × 1.40 m, Velox system). By combining modular desks with Velox continuous table with filing units below windows instead of filing cabinets (→ ①), one grid module in every five was saved. Desk clearance of 75 cm is possible only when swivel chairs on casters are used.

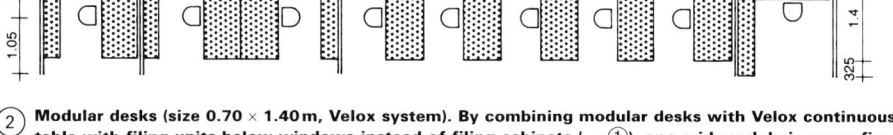

③ Division of space using modular desks. Various office spaces in open-plan office system: a) manager, with small meeting or conference room; b) assistant or departmental head; c) secretary, receptionist; d) senior clerk dealing with public; e) work rooms (working groups)

⑥ Individual office within a combined office

⑦ Division of combined office, with outer individual offices and related common areas

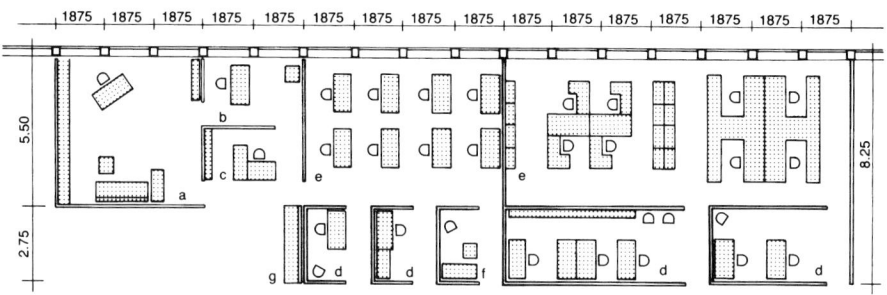

④ Section through office space

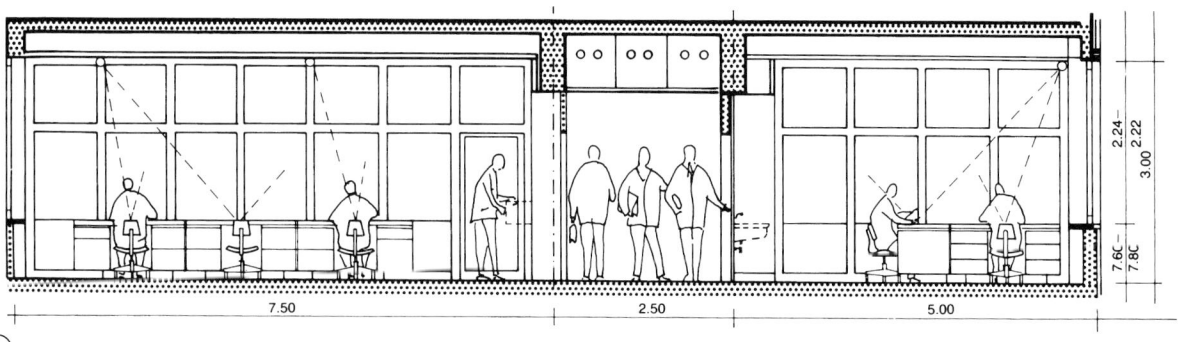

⑤ Section through individual and shared rooms in a combined office

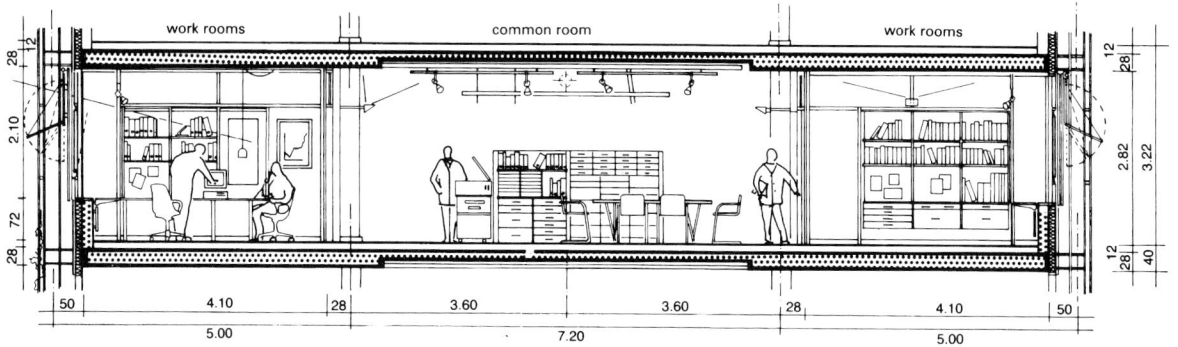

Architects: Struhk and partners

345

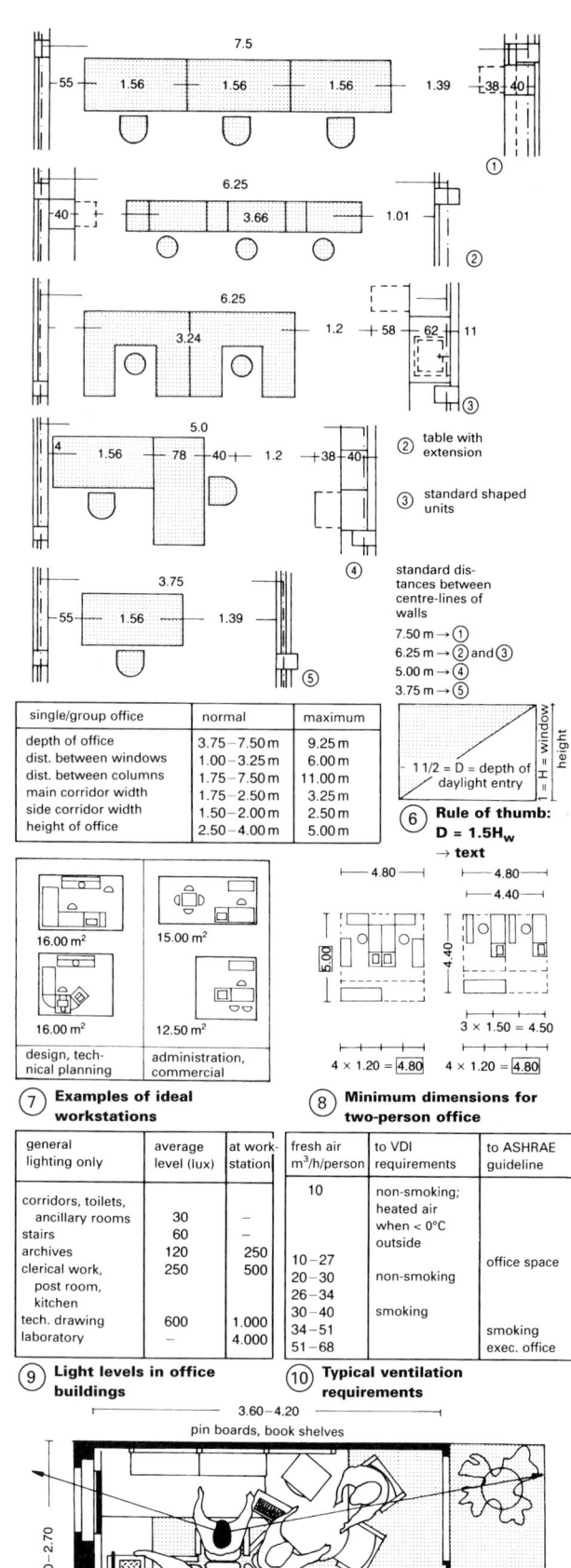

single/group office	normal	maximum
depth of office	3.75–7.50 m	9.25 m
dist. between windows	1.00–3.25 m	6.00 m
dist. between columns	1.75–7.50 m	11.00 m
main corridor width	1.75–2.50 m	3.25 m
side corridor width	1.50–2.00 m	2.50 m
height of office	2.50–4.00 m	5.00 m

② table with extension
③ standard shaped units
④ standard distances between centre-lines of walls
7.50 m → ①
6.25 m → ② and ③
5.00 m → ④
3.75 m → ⑤

$1\tfrac{1}{2} = D$ = depth of daylight entry
H = window height
⑥ **Rule of thumb:** $D = 1.5H_w$ → text

16.00 m² | 15.00 m²
16.00 m² | 12.50 m²
design, technical planning | administration, commercial
⑦ **Examples of ideal workstations**

4.80   4.80   4.40
5.00   4.40
3 × 1.50 = 4.50
4 × 1.20 = 4.80   4 × 1.20 = 4.80
⑧ **Minimum dimensions for two-person office**

general lighting only	average level (lux)	at workstation
corridors, toilets, ancillary rooms	30	–
stairs	60	–
archives	120	250
clerical work, post room, kitchen	250	500
tech. drawing	600	1.000
laboratory	–	4.000

⑨ **Light levels in office buildings**

fresh air m³/h/person	to VDI requirements	to ASHRAE guideline
10	non-smoking; heated air when < 0°C outside	
10–27		office space
20–30	non-smoking	
26–34		
30–40	smoking	
34–51		smoking exec. office
51–68		

⑩ **Typical ventilation requirements**

3.60–4.20
pin boards, book shelves
2.40–2.70
pin boards, book shelves, pull-out shelves, suspended files   wardrobe
⑪ **Possible layout of a small room in a combined office (perhaps, home-based)**

CALCULATIONS: FLOOR AREA REQUIREMENTS

Office area requirements are calculated in two parts.
(1) People space is calculated as (standard individual space × number of people) + allowances for immediate ancillary needs + a factor (usually 15%) for primary circulation.
(2) Non-people space (e.g. machine rooms, and libraries and the like for which fittings and equipment sizes are more important than staff numbers in setting the area requirement) should be calculated by informed estimates based on existing good practice or comparable examples + an additional factor for primary circulation.

Figures for the average floor area requirement for each workstation and employee in an organisation (including office equipment and space to operate it), not including management, have roughly the following distribution:

30%	3.60–4.60 m²
55% (average 8.5 m²)	7.00–9.00 m²
15%	>9.00–15.00 m²

The space requirement per employee clearly depends on a number of factors, e.g. type of work, use of equipment and machinery, degree of privacy, level of visits made by outsiders and storage needs. The average workstation floor area requirement until 1985 was 8–10 m²; in future it will be 12–15 m². Although a minimum floor area requirement for office workstations has not been defined, the following guidelines should be followed: separate offices, minimum 8–10 m² (according to the grid module); open-plan offices, minimum 12–15 m².

A representative calculation of the space requirement for a workstation is as follows:
work room, min. 8.00 m² floor area;
free circulation space, min. 1.5 m² per employee, but min. 1 m wide;
surrounding volume of air, min. 12 m³ when most work is done while seated, min 15 m³ when most work is done while not seated.

The following floor-to-ceiling heights are recommended for floor areas of:

up to 50 m²	2.50 m
over 50 m²	2.75 m
over 100 m²	3.00 m
over 250 and up to 2000 m²	3.25 m

An American study (Connecticut Life Insurance) indicates the following requirements for floor area and space to operate office equipment (personal floor area + an additional 50 cm on all sides):

office employee	4.50 m²
secretary	6.70 m²
departmental manager	9.30 m²
director	13.40 m²
assistant vice president	18.50 m²
vice president	28.00 m²

The depth of a room depends on the space required for an individual in a multi-occupant, open-plan, group or office room. The average depth of office space is 4.50–6.00 m. Daylight illumination reaches work workstations to a depth of approx. 4.50 m from the window (depending on the location of the office building, e.g. in a narrow street or in an open area). Rule of thumb: $D = 1.5H_w$, where D is the depth of light penetration and H_w is the height of the window head (e.g. $H_w = 3.00$ m, D = 4.50 m). Workstations located in the deepest third of the room require artificial light. Working groups often have to do without daylight penetration, since they may be allocated to deeper rooms if that is required by the building layout.

The width of corridors depends on the occupation of the space and the area required to move equipment. Generally speaking, it should be possible for two people to pass each other.

CALCULATIONS: FLOOR AREA REQUIREMENTS

Usable floor area is based on the principle of office units arranged in a row along the façade or some variant thereof, with office size determined by rank or function.

user	usable floor area in office
One senior staff member with a need for discretion regarding personnel or social services, or needing to be able to concentrate	approx. 12 m²
Two senior staff members (perhaps with seating provided for a trainee) or one employee with a conference table for about four people	approx. 18 m²
Manager with a conference table for about six people, or three senior staff members or secretaries, or two senior staff members with additional equipment or a workstation, or a room in front of the Director's office with a waiting area	24–30 m²
Section leader's office or functional room containing a great deal of equipment	larger than 30 m²

③ Number of occupants for various office sizes

1.20 m grid module

The standard room size of 18 m² (3 × 1.20 m less 0.10 m for the partition) corresponds to a 3.50 m room width, which is too narrow for standard furnishings for two employees (2 × 1.00 m clearance plus 2 × 0.80 m depth of desk = 3.60 m). The two-grid-module room, 2.30 m wide, is too narrow for one senior staff member with seating for a visitor. Deeper workstations with video display units and other special equipment require the next largest room (4.70 m).

1.30 m grid module

A room 3.80 m wide, corresponding to 18 m² usable floor area, allows for an additional filing cabinet, two video display stations 0.90 m deep, one drawing table or drawing machine and one desk, and one desk and conference table for four people. Such an office is very flexible, and will accommodate workstations of all standard office sizes without any need to move the walls.

1.40 grid module

A room 4.10 m wide, i.e. 3 × 1.40 m less 0.10 m for a partition, provides excellent possibilities for furnishing and more flexible use. A room depth of 4.40 m, providing 18 m² floor area (i.e. 4.10 m × 4.40 m), is normally sufficient for special uses or greater demands on space. Increasing the room depth to 4.75 m increases the usable floor area of a three-grid-module standard room to 19.5 m² (i.e. 4.10 m × 4.75 m).

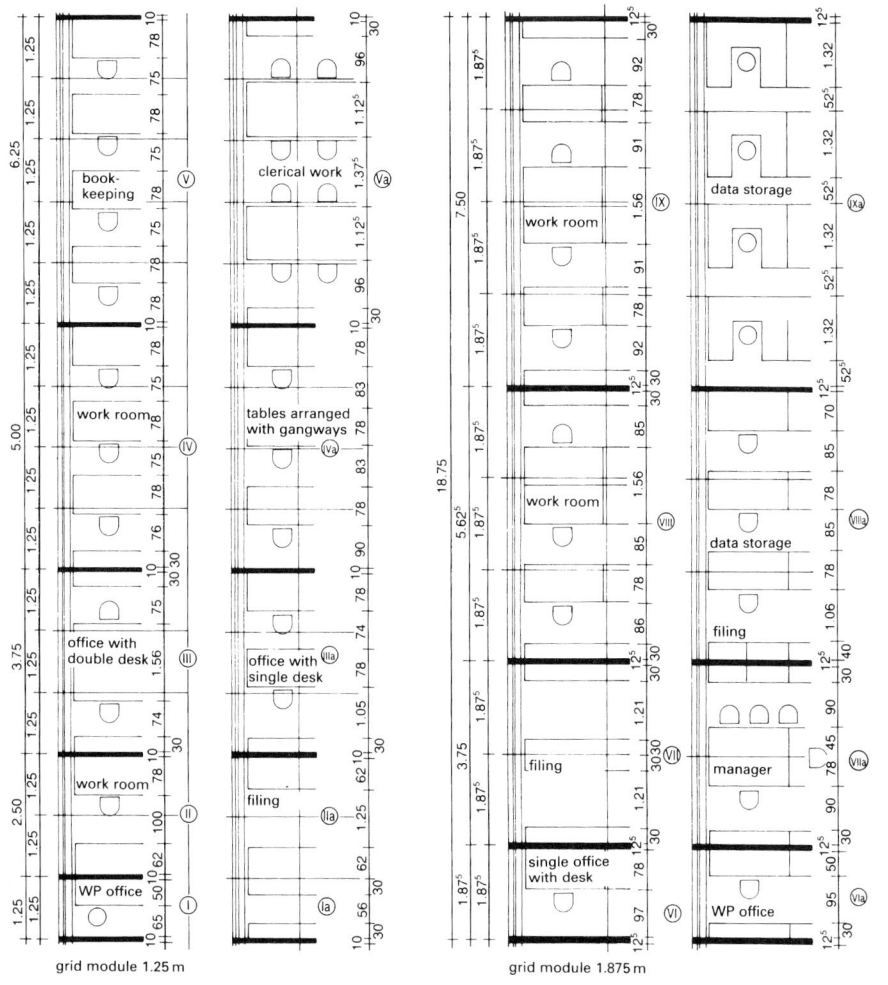

grid module 1.25 m   grid module 1.875 m

① Minimum room width according to window grid modules

According to standard dimensions relating to the varied space requirements in office buildings, the minimum distance between the centre lines of windows or window columns is 1.25 m. The resulting distances between the centre lines of partitions are 2.50 m, 3.75 m, 5.00 m etc. → ① – ⑤. These offer considerable choice in positioning furniture, and are flexible enough to fulfil almost every requirement. If a larger module is needed, the spacing shown in ⑪ should be selected.

The largest grid module for office buildings is 1.875 m; the figure → ⑥ – ⑩ₐ shows some examples of the many efficient ways to position furniture. Beam spacing according to the standard dimensions of 625 mm or 1.25 m is also suitable for this centre distance, and every third beam will coincide with a façade column.

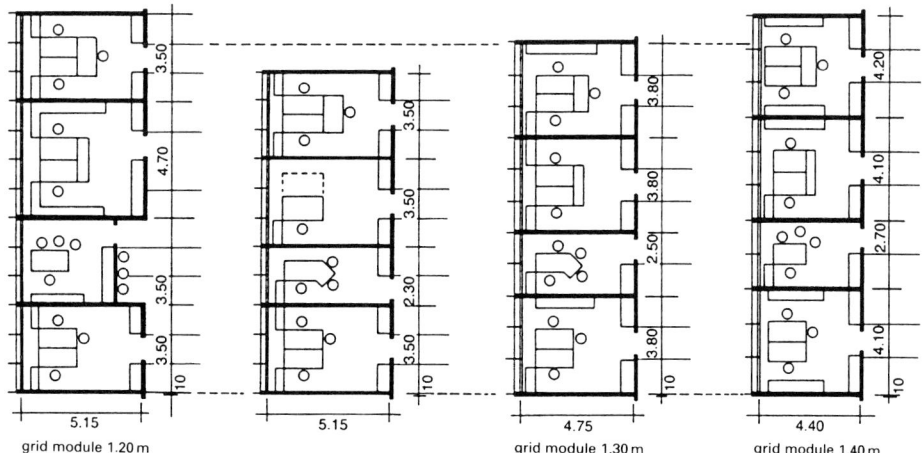

grid module 1.20 m   grid module 1.30 m   grid module 1,40 m

② Possible arrangement for different window grid modules

CALCULATIONS: SPACE FOR FURNITURE

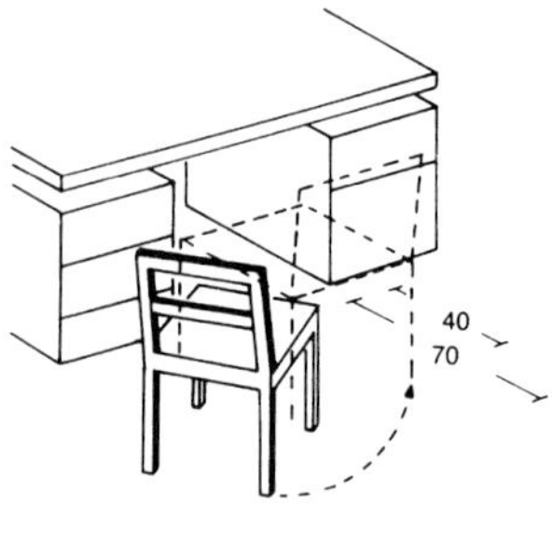

(1) **Traditional chair**
40
70

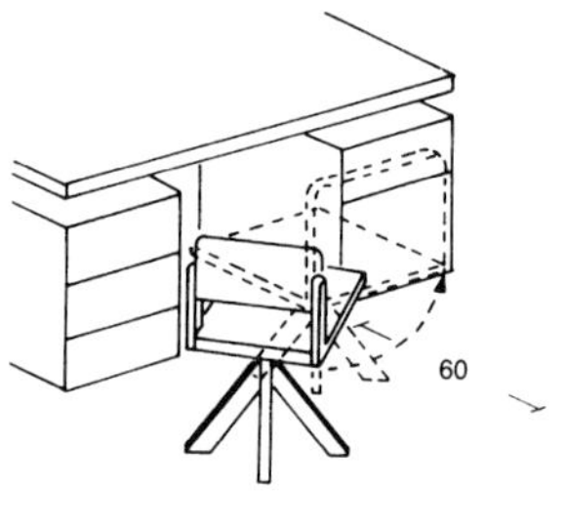

(2) **Swivel chair**
60

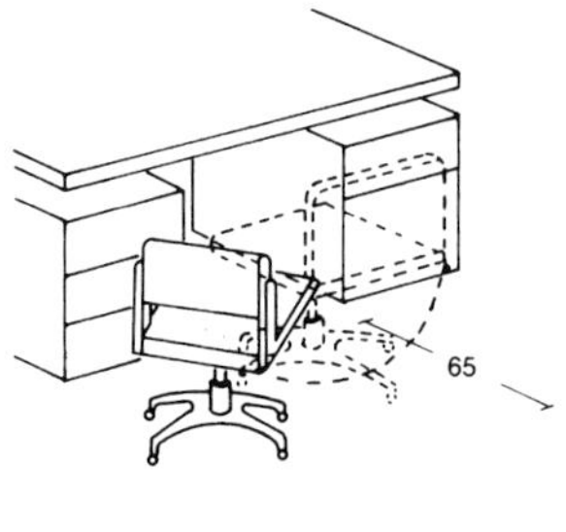

(3) **Swivel chair on casters**
65

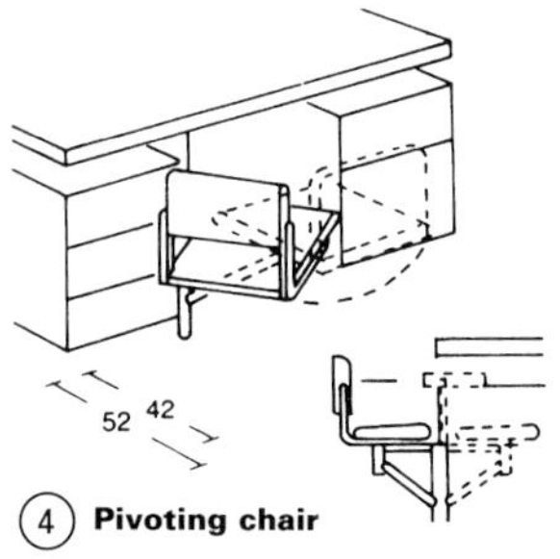

(4) **Pivoting chair**
52 42

(5) **High desk**
80

(6) **Individual tables**
75
70

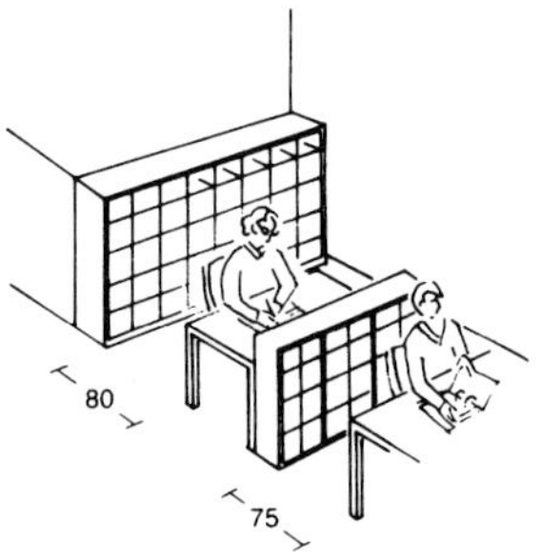

(7) **Individual tables with filing racks to rear**
80
75

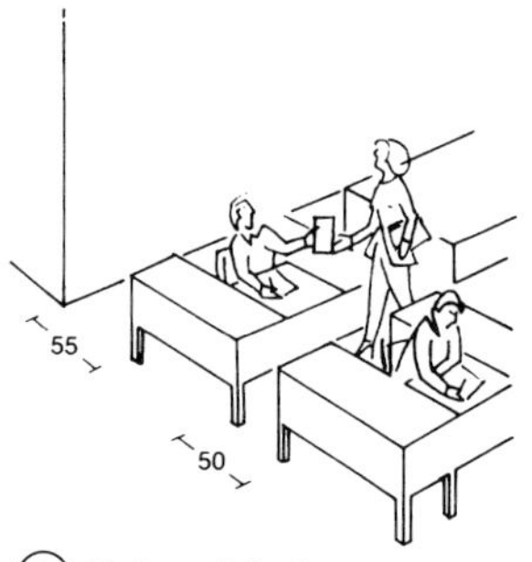

(8) **U-shaped desk**
55
50

(9) **Rows of tables with circulation behind**
95
85

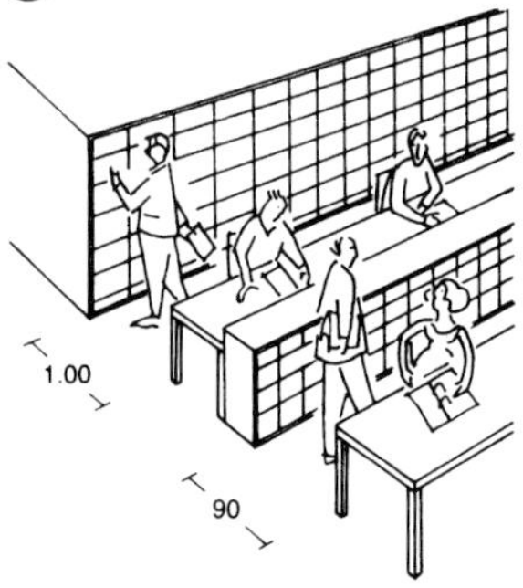

(10) **Rows of tables with filing racks to rear**
1.00
90

(11) **Rows of tables in blocks with staggered seating**
1.00

(12) **Blocks with in-line seating**
1.40

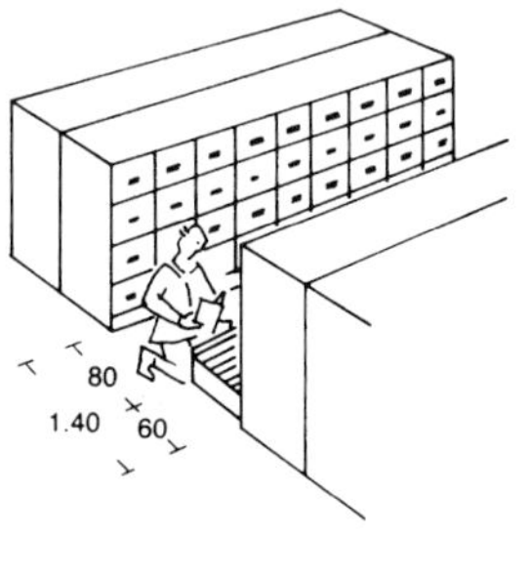

(13) **Filing cabinets**
80
1.40   60

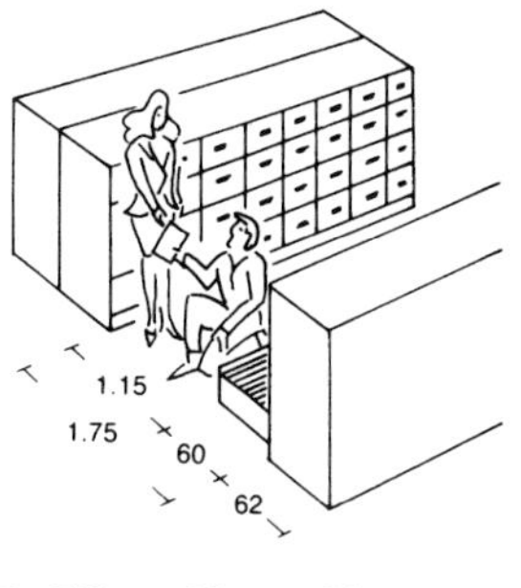

(14) **Filing cabinets with passageway**
1.15
1.75   60
62

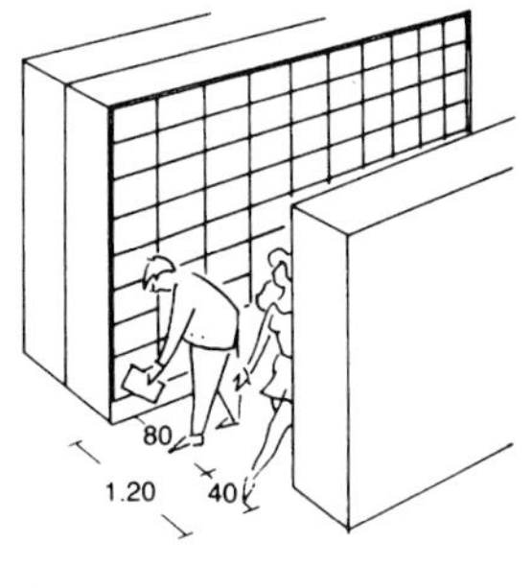

(15) **Pigeon-holes**
80
1.20   40

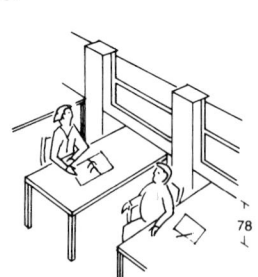

(16) **Tables connected directly to window sills**
78

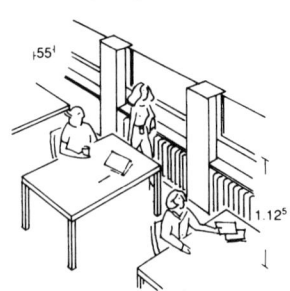

(17) **Circulation between tables and windows**
55
1.12⁵

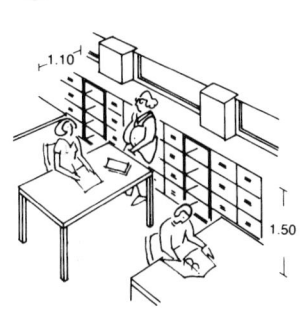

(18) **Filing cabinets beneath window sills**
1.10
1.50

A wide range of office furniture is available. The suitability of furniture for any office is influenced by its flexibility, adjustability, durability, IT compatibility, storage space, ergonomics, aesthetics and cable handling.

The space required while seated and standing is used to calculate the minimum clearance between individual desks or tables (preferably a minimum of 1m), depending on whether they are placed against walls or other tables, or in front of filing cabinets.

Windows placed high in the wall provide satisfactory illumination deep into the room, which allows efficient use of space and access to the window ledge → (18).

CALCULATIONS: SPACE FOR FURNITURE

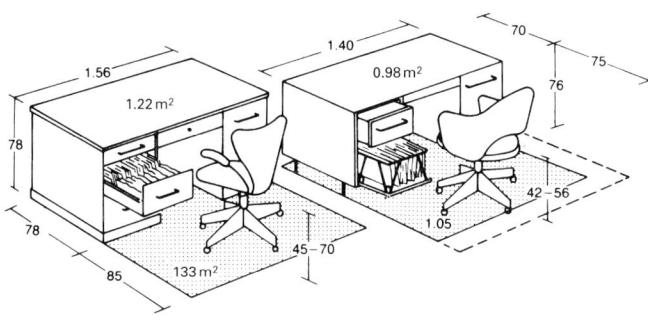

① **Standard writing desk with drawers**

② **Office desk; 0.5 m² less floor space than** ①

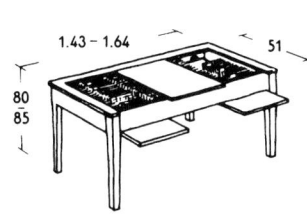

③ **High desk for card index; 1500 cards in each box**

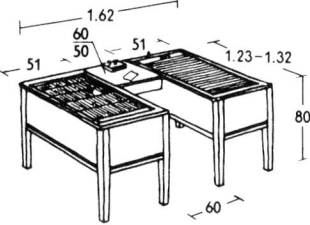

④ **Double unit →** ③

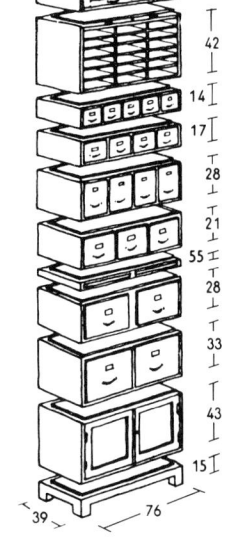

⑤ **Cabinet for storage of various standard size cards and diskettes**

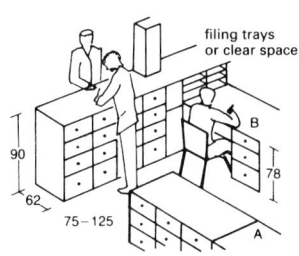

⑥ **Service counter
A: with passage behind it
B: with adjoining desk**

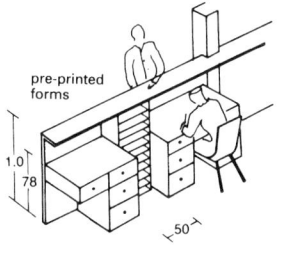

⑦ **Service counter with desk facing clients (Swedish style)**

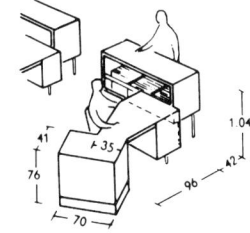

⑧ **Individual counter units; can be separated**

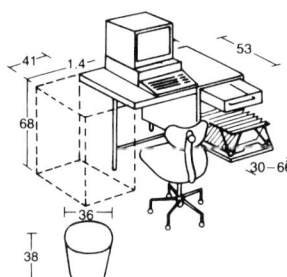

⑨ **Computer desk with double retractable trays (Velox)**

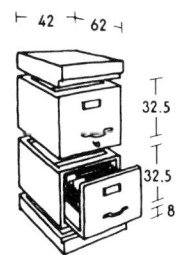

⑩ **Stackable filing cabinets**

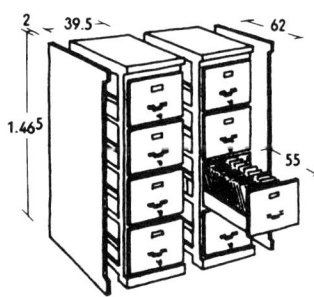

⑪ **Filing cabinets that can be combined in rows**

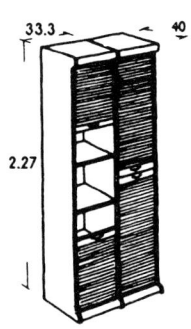

⑫ **Cabinet for vertical filing**

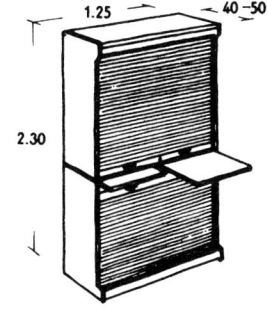

⑬ **Roll-front cabinet**

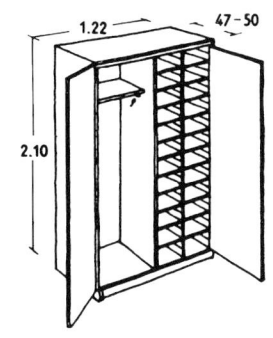

⑭ **Cupboard with space to hang clothing**

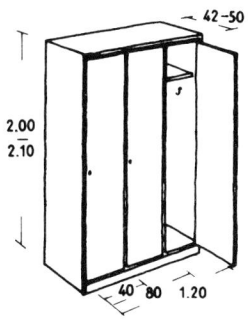

⑮ **Cupboard for employees' clothing**

Many furniture systems in contemporary offices are still designed according to standards in use since 1980. In addition, furniture units such as simple work tables and desks that incorporate filing systems are still used. Because of the increasing use of VDUs and keyboards, European standards for workstations specify a surface height of 72cm high. A new desk measuring 140cm x 70cm x 74cm → ② has been introduced, together with the standard desk whose dimensions are 156cm x 78cm x 78cm. The requirements include adjustable workstation height, protection against vibrations, a sound-absorbent surface and foot rests with ergonomically correct height, preferably adjustable.

Chairs should be adjustable, with castors and upholstered seats and backs. Properly contoured back support for the lumbar curve is essential in an office chair. It should also provide firm support for the lower part of the back and the upper thighs. Many combinations of typewriter stand and desk are available, ranging from space-saving units to built-in systems.

Filing, archives and card indexes may use cabinets without sides, usually in steel units of standard dimensions.

Counters for transactions with a person standing on the other side are generally long, and should be 62cm wide and approx. 90cm high → ⑥. If a counter is only 30cm wide, its height should be approx. 100cm → ⑦. In public areas of a building where high security is required, this makes it difficult for any person in front of the counter to reach anything behind it → ⑦. Clearance to stand and deal with members of the public should be provided behind the counter → p. 362 ②–⑥. Individual counters are easier to reorganise since the floor space is more flexible → ⑧.

Some counters and switchboards, e.g. in reception areas, hold VDU terminals and probably keyboards. Their design should take account of this.

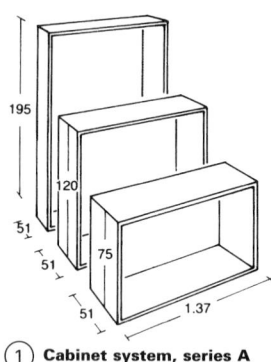

(1) **Cabinet system, series A**

(2) **Series B → ③ – ⑩**

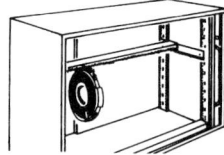

(3) **Shelves: usable depth 42 cm; 1.37 m wide**

(4) **Pull-out shelf with telescopic runners**

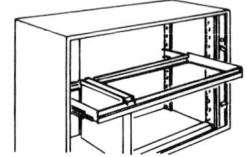

(5) **Rack for magnetic tapes or film (49 separate holders)**

(6) **Pull-out shelf for microfilm cassettes (164 capacity)**

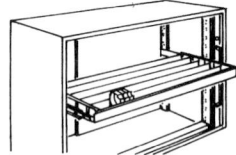

(7) **Pull-out rack for suspended files**

(8) **Rack to hold suspended files parallel to front**

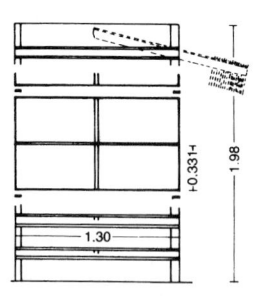
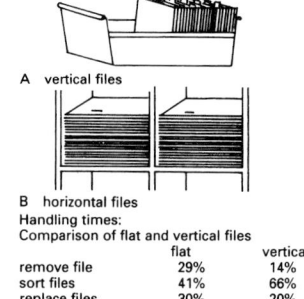

(9) **Pull-out shelf for diskettes**

(10) **Supporting rail for centre-mounted suspended files**

(11) **Circulation/furniture areas for various filing systems**

(12) **Large Velox archival shelf (section and plan)**

(13) **Filing systems**

A vertical files

B horizontal files
Handling times:
Comparison of flat and vertical files

	flat	vertical
remove file	29%	14%
sort files	41%	66%
replace files	30%	20%
	100%	100%

CALCULATIONS: ARCHIVE SPACE

In spite of new office technologies, the use of paper as the main storage medium for information has increased. Paper consumption doubled every 4 years until 1980. Computer memory has now become a more common way of storing information in office communication systems, but the need for what is known as uncoded information (printed letters, texts, periodicals etc.) means that paper will continue to be used.

It is necessary to arrange stored documents in a clearly labelled system, with short circulation routes and efficient use of space. Space should also be available for archives → ①. As cabinet widths increase, the aisle between cabinets should also get wider.

$$L \times W \text{ (filing equipment)} = \text{space for furniture}$$
$$+ \tfrac{1}{2}L \times W + 0.5 = \text{aisle space}$$
Total requirement = space for furniture + aisle space

Deep filing cabinets are more economical. The diagram in → ⑪ shows the relationship between furniture floor area and aisle space required for a vertical filing system using large archival shelves (Velox system) or a flat filing system. The floor area needed for a vertical filing system is 5.2 m² (100:90). For flat filing systems, the floor area is 3.2 m² and the aisle space 3.6 m² (90:100, ratio reversed). Flat filing systems cannot hold as much as vertical ones, and high shelf units are hard to organise. Vertical files may reduce staffing levels in the filing section by 40%. Hanging files use wall space 87% better than box files → ⑮. An efficient way to move files is by paternoster elevator. Workstations should include shelves for sorting, a small table and a chair on castors.

The filing room should be centrally located, and the best window grid module is between 2.25 m and 2.50 m. Since a clear height of only 2.10 m is required, three storeys of filing could be fitted into a space which would only take two storeys in normal offices. Dry storage rooms are essential, and therefore attics and basements are unsuitable.

Narrow shelves → ⑯ and ⑰ with hanging files and a writing surface can provide a functional connection between workstations. Trolleys can be used either as writing surfaces or for card-index boxes. Movable filing systems give substantial space saving (100–120%) by eliminating intermediate passages → ⑱B. There are no fixed standards for filing systems. They are usually adapted to suit individual requirements, such as registries, archives, libraries and storage areas. The increase in load for each square metre of floor space must be taken into account. File shelving may be moved by hand or by mechanical means. In some designs, the entire filing system, or only parts of it, can be locked by one handle.

10000 files approx. 2mm thick (without holders); approx. 25 sheets each		flat filing in loose-leaf binder on open shelves 35 × 200	library: storage in letter organiser in roll-front cupboard 40 × 125 × 220	combined vertical and suspended filing in folders, units 65 × 78 × 200
	1) continuous cabinet or wall length	7.25 m	11.00 m	2.4 m
	2) floor area (m²) including operation but excluding side passages	5.92 m²	8.25 m²	3.6 m²

(14) **Space required by different filing systems**

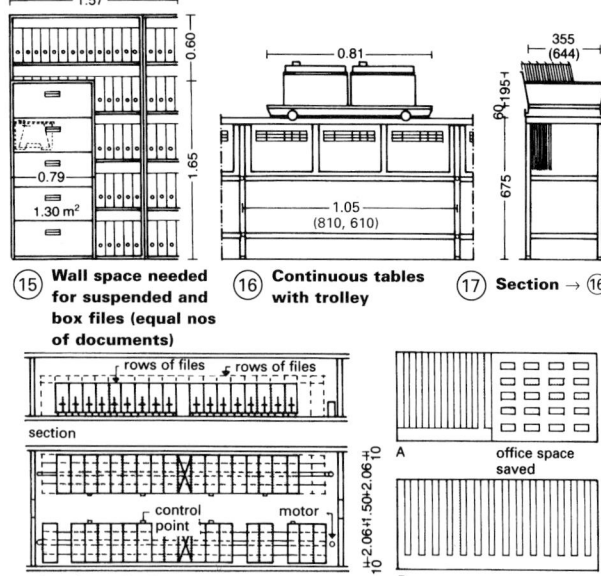

(15) **Wall space needed for suspended and box files (equal nos of documents)**

(16) **Continuous tables with trolley**

(17) **Section → ⑯**

A office space saved

(18) **A = movable filing; B = comparison with space for normal filing**

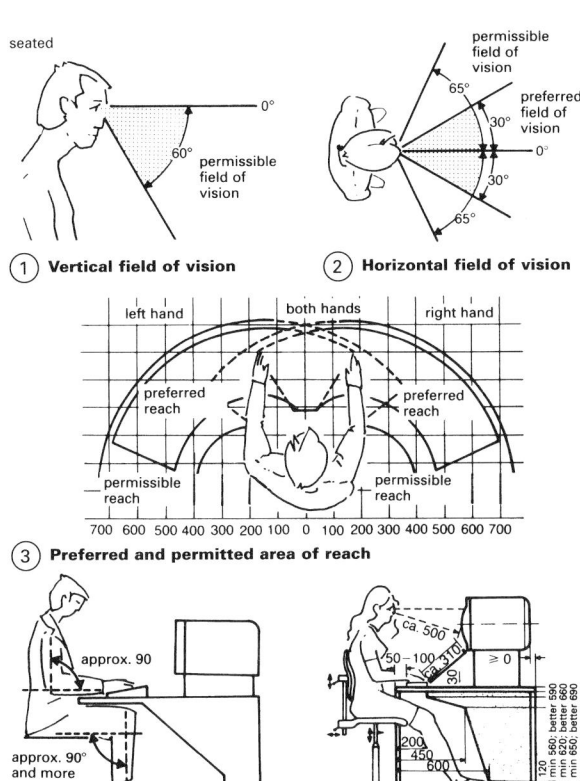

① **Vertical field of vision**

② **Horizontal field of vision**

③ **Preferred and permitted area of reach**

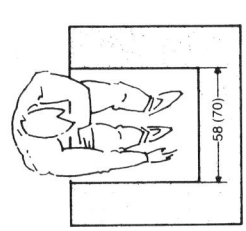

④ **Correct ergonomic position**

⑤ **Ergonomic VDU workstation with fixed-height table**

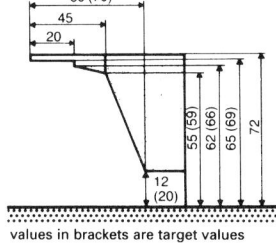

⑥ **Leg space**

values in brackets are target values

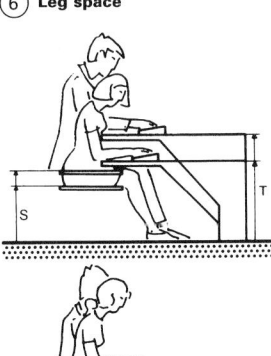

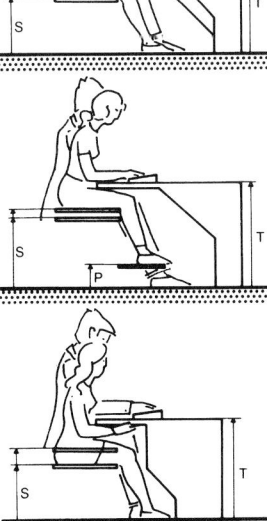

⑦ **Dimensions of workstation furniture**

Type 1 workstation
adjustable-height table
adjustable-height seat

	women	men and women
T	(630 – kb) – (730 – kb)	(630 – kb) – (780 – kb)
S	420 – 460	420 – 500

Type 2 workstation
fixed height table
adjustable-height seat
adjustable-height footrest

	women	men and women
T	(700 – kb) – (730 – kb)	(750 – kb) – (780 – kb)
S	460 – 500	500 – 550
P	0 – 100	0 – 150

Type 3 workstation
fixed-height table
adjustable-height seat

	women	men and women
T	(640 – kb) – (800 – kb)	(680 – kb) – (800 – kb)
S	420 – 460	420 – 500

T = table height
S = seat height
P = footrest height
kb = height of keyboard above table top

CALCULATIONS: WORKSTATIONS WITH COMPUTERS

Workstations equipped with a computer must accommodate at least a visual display unit (VDU) and an alphanumeric keyboard. There is no standard for such workstations because the requirements vary widely depending on individual work processes (e.g. from a simple networked terminal for enquiries to stand-alone systems for data entry and manipulation, which in addition to the VDU and keyboard may also have disk drives, scanners, printers and other peripherals). These workstations should be designed according to national safety requirements and generally accepted technical standards for good practice based on an understanding of ergonomics.

Workstation design

Items that are used frequently should be placed within the preferred field of vision and reach area → ① – ③.

The best working position is when the person is seated with the upper arm perpendicular to the floor and the forearm at a 90° angle. The thighs should be parallel to the floor with the lower leg at a 90° angle → ④. The table and chair must be adjustable to allow proper positioning for users of different heights. Two ergonomic systems are equally acceptable.

A: Type 1 workstation
Adjustable-height table	60–78 cm
Adjustable-height chair	42–54 cm

B: Types 2 and 3 workstations
Fixed-height table	72 cm
Adjustable-height chair	42–50 cm
Adjustable foot rest	0–15 cm

Sufficient leg clearance should be provided → ⑥.

In work areas, all items of equipment close to the user (on the desk top, etc.) should have a 20–25% reflection factor. Illumination should be between 300 and 500 Lx, and glare from lights must be limited (e.g. by providing specular louvred ceilings above VDU stations). Arrange lighting strips parallel to the window. Matt surfaces in the room should have the recommended reflection factors (ceiling approx. 70%, walls approx. 50%, movable partitions approx. 20–50%).

The worker's line of sight to the monitor should be parallel to the windows and to any lighting tubes; the monitor should be between these if possible. It is necessary to install blinds to control daylight at visual display workstations.

Follow local recommendations for environmental control and noise protection. The increased use of heat-generating electronic equipment in offices tends to result in the need for additional cooling to maintain a comfortable temperature.

The impact of information technology

Employment usually required attendance at a place of work because the materials and tools were there, and the work needed to be supervised. However, advances in information technology mean that the 'material' for most office work (information) can be transmitted electronically. The tools of office work are increasingly a telephone and a workstation, both of which can be installed at home. Innovations in communication technology are gradually having a major impact on how the work environment is defined. It is also freeing many workers from geographical constraints. The free-address workstation is becoming a technical reality, with portable voice and data links to anywhere in the world. However, the free-address workstation has implications for both people and organisations, such as the need for increased social interaction and new management techniques which are able to cope with a widespread workforce.

OFFICE BUILDINGS

Examples

Organisation of plan

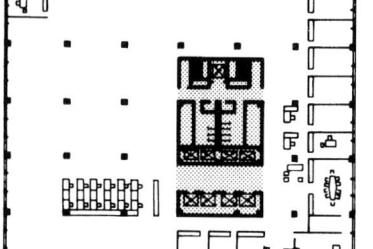

Architects: I.M. Pei & Associates

① Rental offices; 93% rentable floor area. Public circulation vertically. Asymmetrical design allows small rooms and large open offices

Architects: Skidmore, Owings & Merrill

③ Typical floor-plan for open offices; lavatories separated. External columns allow furniture to be positioned anywhere. 17.50 m free span

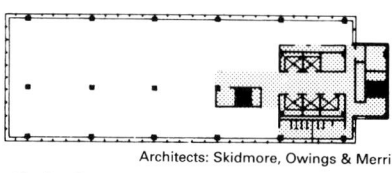

Architects: Skidmore, Owings & Merrill

④ Design without corridor, service core at one end. Manager's office accessible from open office

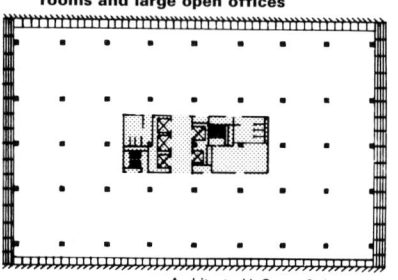

Architects: V. Gruen & Associates

② Steel skeleton acts as rigid load-bearing structure; no need for bracing with wall panels. Vertical fins, east and west; horizontal sun shades, south

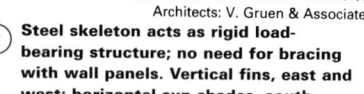

Architect: H. Kosaka

⑤ Open offices with closest possible direct access to fireproof strong rooms. Service core in centre minimises circulation space

Architect: Phil Johnson

⑥ Single-storey building with offices on periphery. Conference room and secretarial open onto garden court

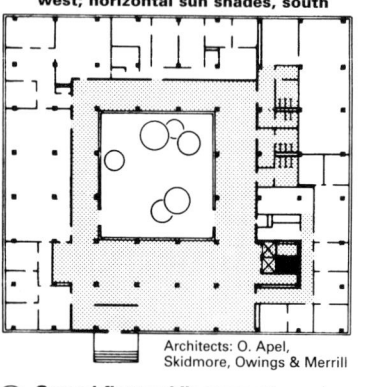

Architects: O. Apel, Skidmore, Owings & Merrill

⑦ Ground floor public space; three-storey north wing for offices

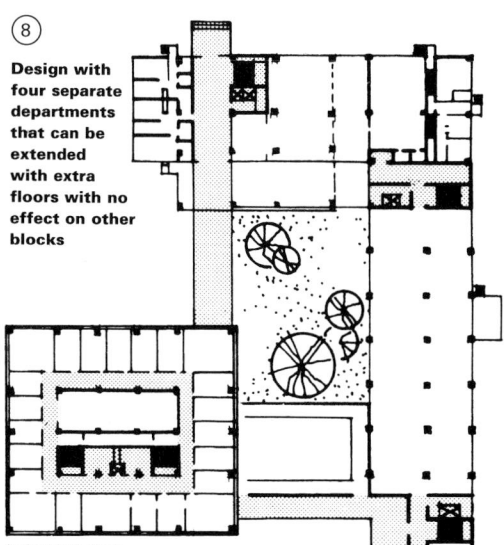

⑧

Design with four separate departments that can be extended with extra floors with no effect on other blocks

Architect: O. Apel

Architect: A. Jacobsen

The placement of general expansion joints depends on the type of structure, foundations, ground conditions, etc. They are usually between 30 and 60 m apart. Joints are generally required to accommodate movement safely. e.g. structural movement, or thermal expansion and contraction.

- The simplest design uses reinforced concrete to erect paired columns that are covered to protect against weather.
- Cantilevered floors and expansion joints between the two cantilevers are subject to the greatest stress.
- Complex designs, e.g. with connected buildings and parapets, usually create enormous stresses.

⑪ Wind force on high-rise buildings causes areas of high or low pressure that can force rainwater in through window joints or cracks in walls

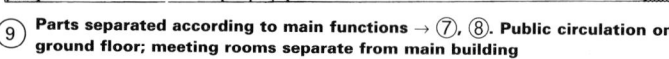

⑨ Parts separated according to main functions → ⑦, ⑧. Public circulation on ground floor; meeting rooms separate from main building

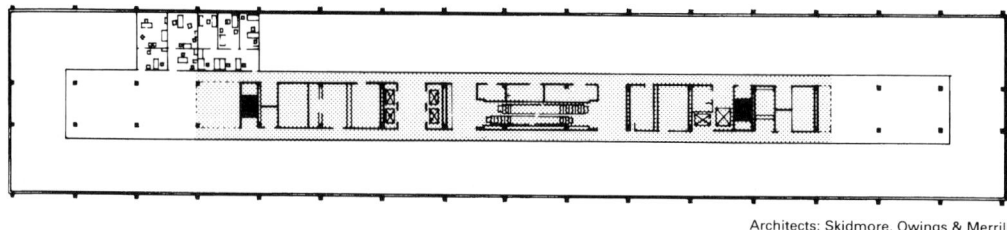

Architects: Skidmore, Owings & Merrill

⑩ Very deep, subdivided offices. Secretary or receptionist and senior clerks have open or enclosed workstations with access to corridor. Artificial ventilation and lighting

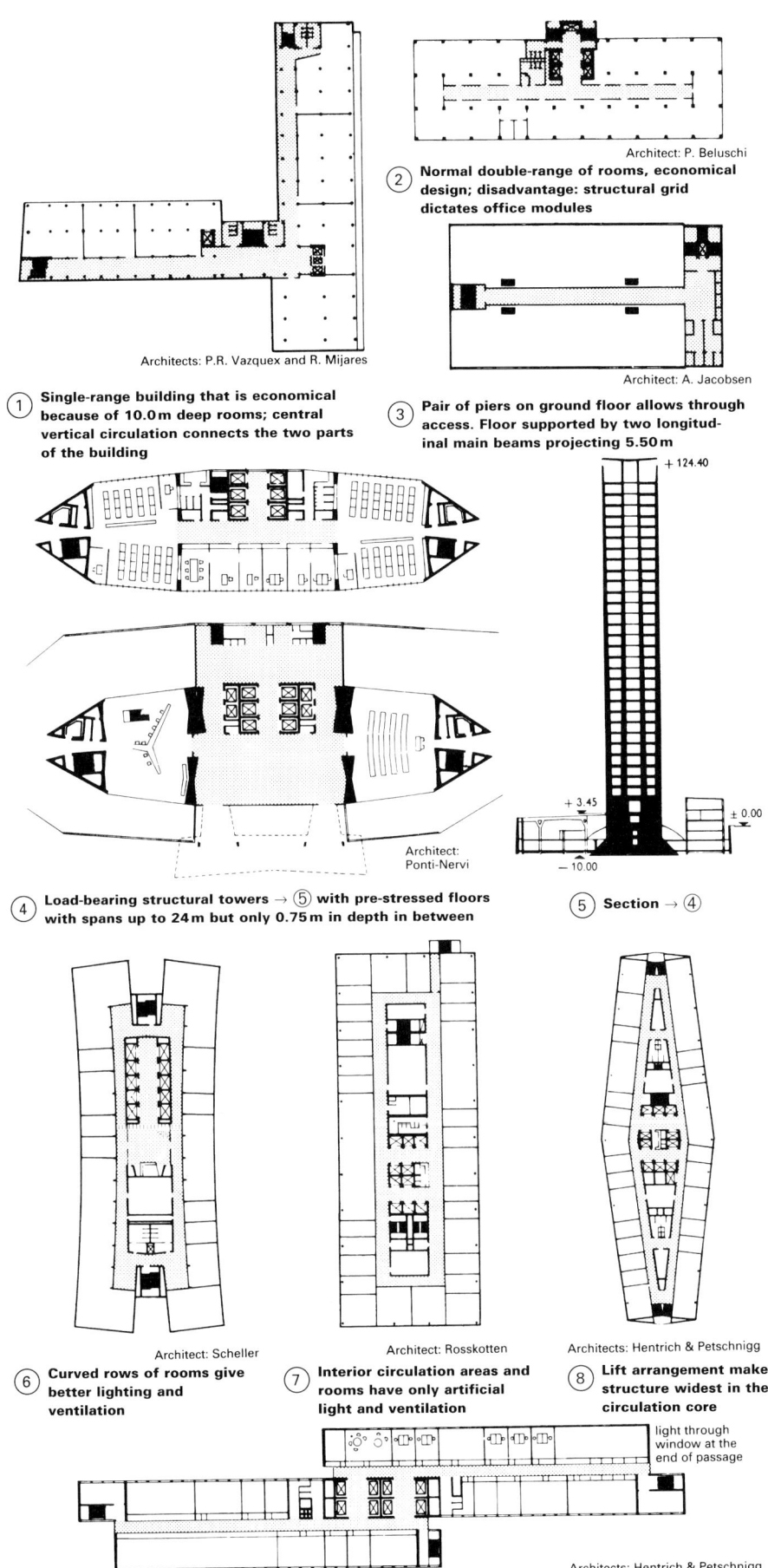

OFFICE BUILDINGS

Examples

High-rise buildings

The first high-rise buildings were office blocks. Lower floors usually contained shops and stores with sales areas throughout and no atria. Office areas were located above, and were often set off by a different scale and choice of materials. Vertical circulation components, lifts, stairs and service rooms in a central location had only artificial ventilation and lighting. New possibilities were provided by stepped buildings with stairway and lift towers situated immediately to one side.

High-rise buildings are intended for continuous human occupation, and have a floor on the top storey on at least one side of the building that is more than 22 m above ground level. Window sills must be at a height of at least 0.90 m above floor level and be fire resistant. Window surfaces that cannot safely be cleaned from inside the building must be cleaned by experts, using exterior equipment. High-rise buildings should be divided into fire compartments that are 30 m long and enclosed by fire-resistant walls. Escape routes from each room on each storey must be provided via at least two independent staircases. Alternative escape routes within limited travel distance must be accessible from the fire to a protected zone. One stairway must have external windows on each floor. In high-rise buildings, some staircases should be constructed as fire-fighting staircases with smoke outlets, vents and fire-resistant, self-closing doors. The effective width of stairways and landings depends on the function of the building, but must be at least 1.25 m. Emergency stairs must have an effective width of at least 0.80 m.

A frame construction of steel or reinforced concrete is the standard structure for high-rise buildings. The need for flexible spaces with large spans is making masonry construction obsolete. However, the size of span depends on material and design. A solid reinforced concrete floor can have a span of 2.5–5.5 m, and a ribbed floor 5.0–7.5 m, both with a maximum 12.5 m between main beams. The effective span of pre-stressed concrete is 25.0 m, but only with 0.75 m structural depth. The exterior wall should be a curtain wall in front of set-back external columns. In both steel construction and assembly units, steel main and secondary beam systems make assembly easier but shorten the possible spans. A mixed design with a steel frame and concrete floors is often used.

Architect: P. Beluschi

② Normal double-range of rooms, economical design; disadvantage: structural grid dictates office modules

Architect: A. Jacobsen

③ Pair of piers on ground floor allows through access. Floor supported by two longitudinal main beams projecting 5.50 m

Architects: P.R. Vazquex and R. Mijares

① Single-range building that is economical because of 10.0 m deep rooms; central vertical circulation connects the two parts of the building

Architect: Ponti-Nervi

④ Load-bearing structural towers → ⑤ with pre-stressed floors with spans up to 24 m but only 0.75 m in depth in between

⑤ Section → ④

Architect: Scheller

⑥ Curved rows of rooms give better lighting and ventilation

Architect: Rosskotten

⑦ Interior circulation areas and rooms have only artificial light and ventilation

Architects: Hentrich & Petschnigg

⑧ Lift arrangement makes structure widest in the circulation core

light through window at the end of passage

Architects: Hentrich & Petschnigg

⑨ Two double-range buildings connecting at a single vertical circulation core → p. 339 ⑭

OFFICE BUILDINGS

Examples

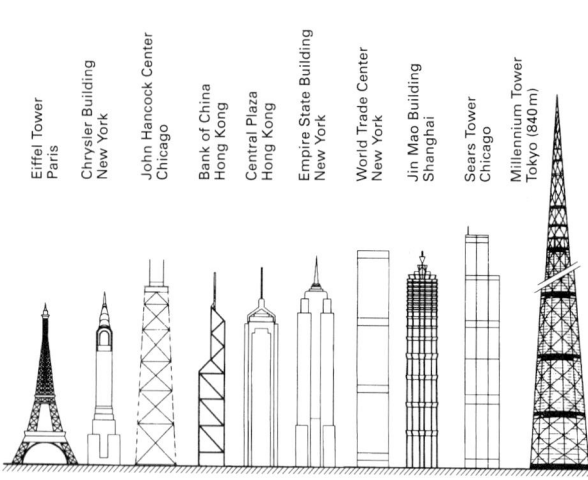

Eiffel Tower Paris — Chrysler Building New York — John Hancock Center Chicago — Bank of China Hong Kong — Central Plaza Hong Kong — Empire State Building New York — World Trade Center New York — Jin Mao Building Shanghai — Sears Tower Chicago — Millennium Tower Tokyo (840 m)

(1) **Some of the world's tallest structures**

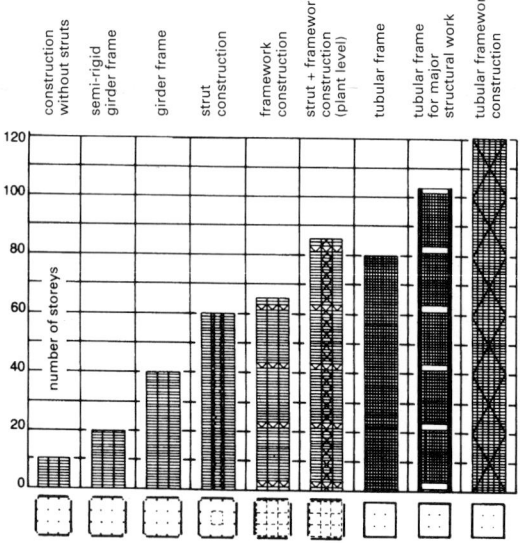

construction without struts — semi-rigid girder frame — girder frame — strut construction — framework construction — strut + framework construction (plant level) — tubular frame — tubular frame for major structural work — tubular framework construction

number of storeys

(2) **Economic efficiency range of structural systems**

Skyscrapers

New York City passed a new planning law in 1982 to regulate skyscraper construction. Its provisions represented an attempt to come to grips with dense traffic, 3 million commuters daily, and town-planning aspects such as maintenance of street spaces, expansion of public sidewalks and subway entrances, pedestrian traffic, availability of daylight and micro-climates → (3).

Structural engineering for skyscrapers

Structural systems and vertical-access elements are of decisive importance when designing skyscrapers. The ratio of usable floor area to construction costs worsens as building height increases. Structural areas and circulation spaces occupy more of the building. Dividing skyscrapers into sections with 'sky lobbies', served by express elevators where passengers can change to local elevators, minimises the space required for shafts and reduces travel time.

Economic efficiency depends on the 'sway factor', i.e. the ratio of the maximum allowable horizontal deformation at the top to the total height of the building (max. 1:600). Horizontal forces (wind) are much more important than vertical loads when making calculations for very tall buildings. Ninety percent of horizontal deformations result from shifting of the frame ('shear sway'), while 10% come from the leaning of the building as a whole. Frame construction with special wind bracing is impracticable beyond ten storeys. Conventional framework systems result in uneconomical dimensions above the 20th storey. Reinforced concrete framework structures are limited to ten storeys without bracing walls and 20–30 storeys with them. Higher buildings require concrete pipe or double-pipe construction.

Factors determining whether a building is economic include use of materials, appropriate design and efficient structural engineering methods → (2). The John Hancock Center, Chicago, 1965 → (1), was the result of an economical structural approach by Skidmore, Owings & Merrill. The visible structural components were part of the design concept. Use of the pipe principle significantly reduced the use of steel. Its efficiency of operation is due to its multiple uses: floors 1–5 have shops, floors 6–12 are parking spaces, floors 13–41 are flexible-use offices, floors 42–45 have technical facilities and a sky lobby, floors 46–93 are residences, floors 94–96 are for visitors and restaurants, and floors 97 and 98 house television transmission equipment.

New York's Department of City Planning has issued a brochure that contains examples of how statutory requirements attempt to guarantee sufficient daylight and circulation space in spite of the increasing volume of construction.

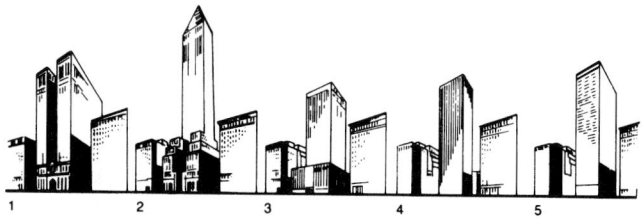

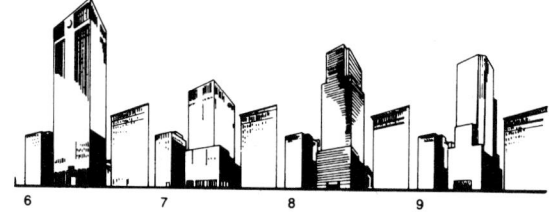

1 Equitable Building, 120 Broadway, built in 1916 before the first zoning regulation
2 The 1916 regulation required a specific ratio of street width to building height. That led to the typical 'wedding cake' skyscraper
3 The plot ratio as a regulatory instrument was introduced in 1961. The initial limit was 15
4 At the same time more street space was required, resulting in the tower over a plaza. The Seagram Building is shown here
5 Plazas received a bonus that increased the plot ratio to 18

6 The use of plazas would have meant the destruction of avenues in some cases, so the system of running public roads through buildings was developed. The plot ratio was increased to 21.6
7 More recent regulations once again deal with daylight, with one alternative involving a daylight curve for a plot ratio of 15
8 Another alternative depends on the dimensions of the unobstructed skyline (plot ratio of 18)
9 The most recent daylight chart may also be used (plot ratio of 18)

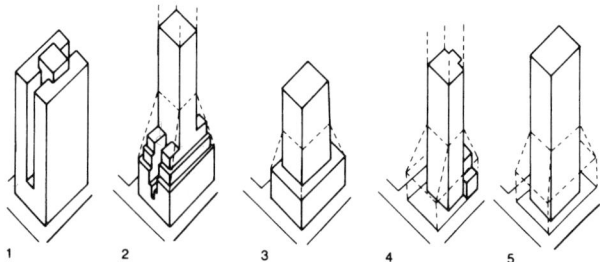

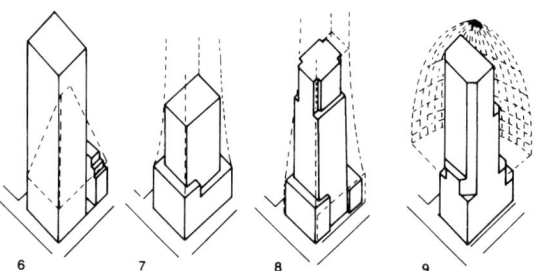

(3) (1) – (9) **Zoning laws indicate permissible building volumes**

Examples

① and ② Curved surfaces reduced wind load by up to 25%, and also saved 10% in structural steel.

③ and ④ Office tower taking the geometry of its plan from the triangular shape of the site on which it is built.

⑤ and ⑥ Part of site transferred to public use in return for a planning gain increasing the number of storeys.

⑦ and ⑧ Recessed façade in the arc of a circle creating a new plaza. The rotunda is an enclosed atrium.

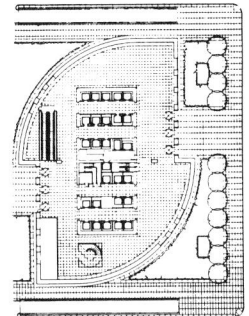

① **Ground floor, Allied Bank Plaza, Houston (71 storeys)**

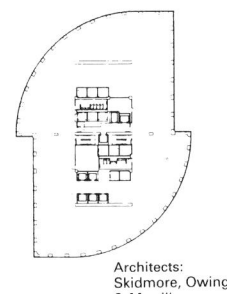

Architects: Skidmore, Owings & Merrill

② **Typical floor**

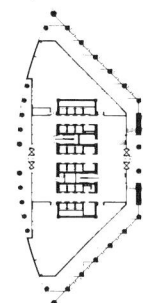

③ **Ground floor, 333 Wacker Drive, Chicago (37 storeys)**

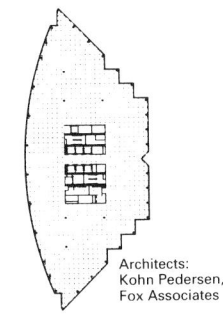

Architects: Kohn Pedersen, Fox Associates

④ **Typical floor**

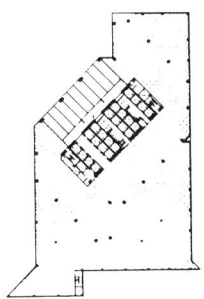

⑤ **Typical floor, plinth area, 101 Park Avenue, New York City (48 storeys)**

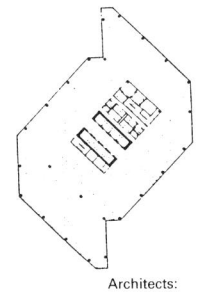

Architects: Eli Attia Associates

⑥ **Typical floor, tower portion**

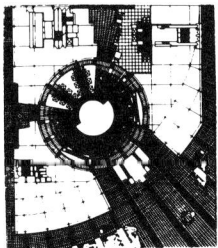

⑦ **Ground floor, 1985. State of Illinois Center, Chicago (17 storeys)**

Architects: Murphy/Jahn, Lester B. Knight and Associates

⑧ **Office floor**

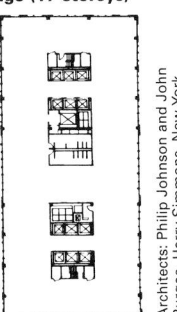

Architects: Philip Johnson and John Burgee, Harry Simmons, New York

⑨ **AT&T headquarters, New York. Typical floor, 1984**

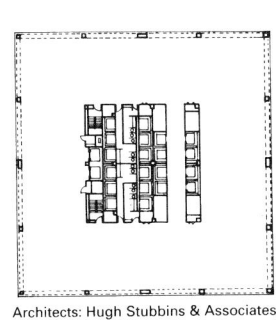

Architects: Hugh Stubbins & Associates, Cambridge, Massachusetts

⑩ **Typical floor, Citycorp Center, New York**

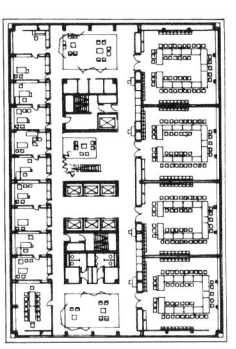

Architects: E. Eiermann in conjunction with the BBD (Federal Department of Building)

⑪ **Floors 2–17 of 'Abgeordnetenhaus' in Bonn contain offices for German MPs, 1969**

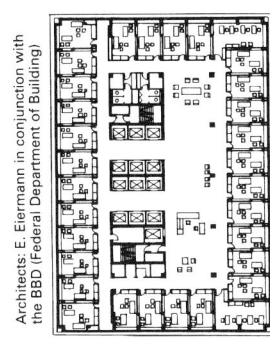

⑫ **Floors 19–28 contain meeting rooms**

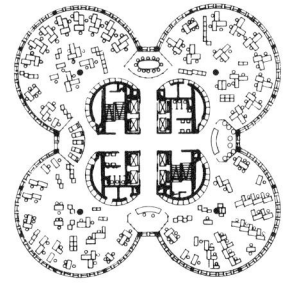

Architect: Karl Schwanzer

⑬ **Typical floor used for open-plan office, BMW headquarters, Munich, 1972**

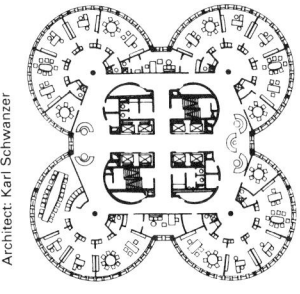

⑭ **Floor plan showing individual offices**

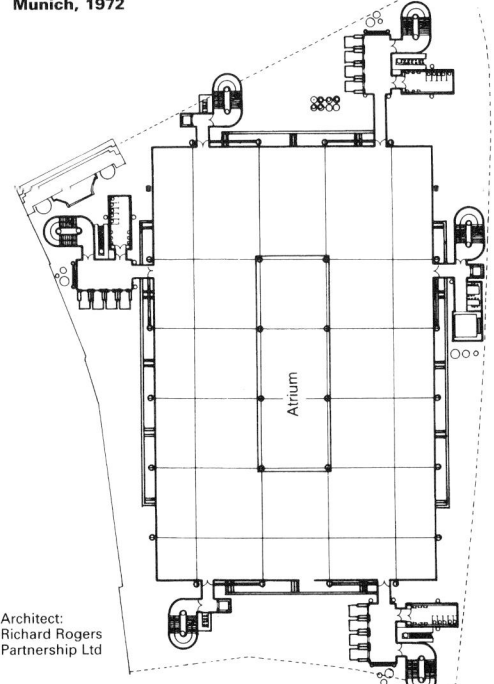

Atrium

Architect: Richard Rogers Partnership Ltd

⑮ **Lloyd's of London, floors 4–7/ complete floors, 1986**

OFFICE BUILDINGS

Examples

Vertical components

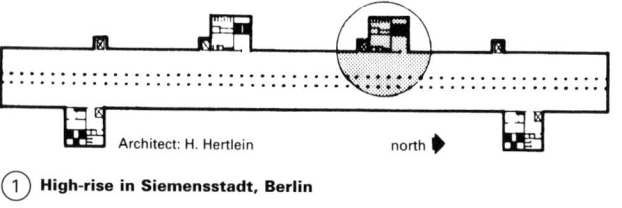

Architect: H. Hertlein   north ►

① **High-rise in Siemensstadt, Berlin**

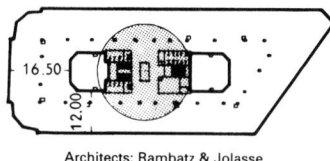

16.50
12.00

Architects: Rambatz & Jolasse

② **Bieberhaus, Hamburg**

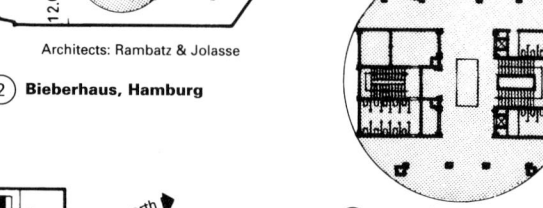

② a   service core in Bieberhaus

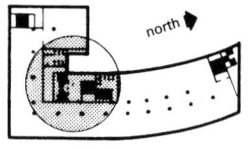

north ►

Architect: E. Mendelsohn

④ **Columbushaus, Berlin**

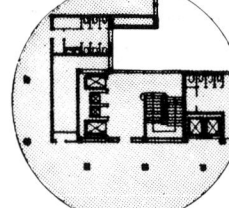

④ a   service core in Columbushaus

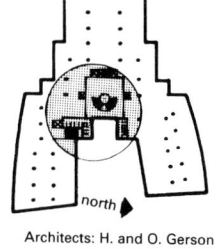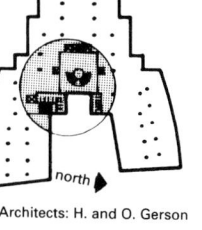

north ►

Architects: H. and O. Gerson

③ **Ballinhaus, Hamburg**

Architect: H. Hertlein

⑤ **Siemenshaus, Essen**

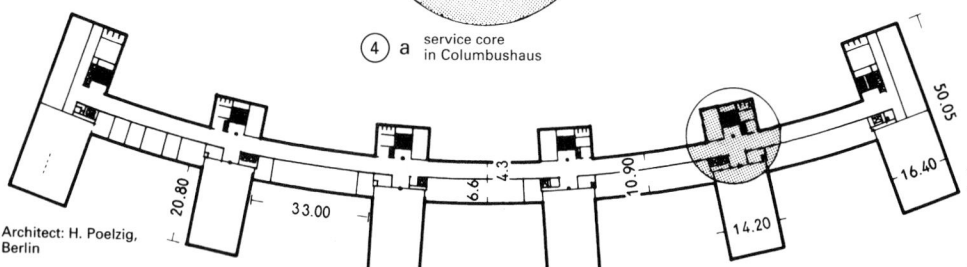

20.80   33.00   6.6   4.3   10.90   14.20   50.05   16.40

Architect: H. Poelzig, Berlin

⑥ **I.G. Farben headquarters, Frankfurt am Main**

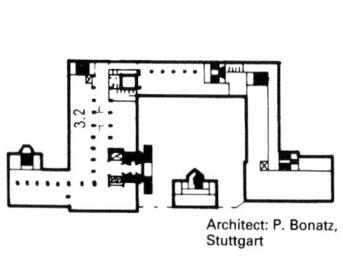

84.00   16.48   99.99   53.98   56.46   north ◄

Architect: P. Bonatz, Stuttgart

⑦ **Stummhaus, Dusseldorf**

Architect: H. Hertlein

⑧ **Wernerwerke HQ in Siemensstadt, Berlin**

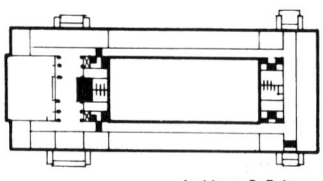

Architect: G. Epitanse

⑨ **International Labour Organisation, Geneva**

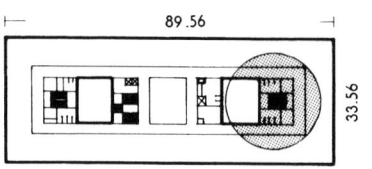

89.56   33.56

Architect: Blecken

⑩ **Headquarters of Vereinigten Stahlwerke, Duisburg-Ruhrort**

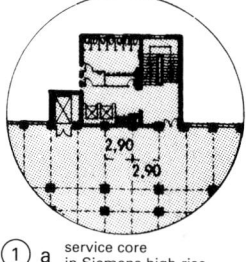

2.90   2.90

① a   service core in Siemens high-rise

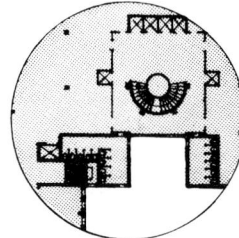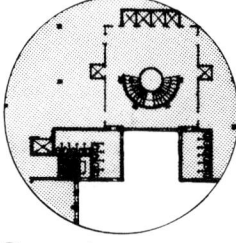

③ a   service core in Ballinhaus

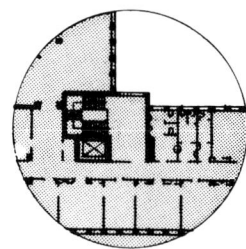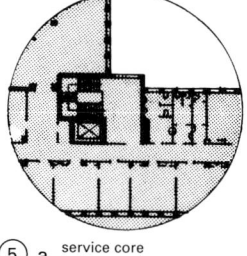

⑤ a   service core in Siemenshaus

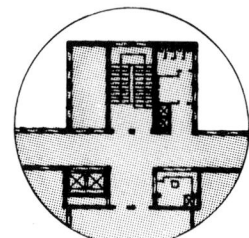

⑥ a   service core in I.G. Farben headquarters

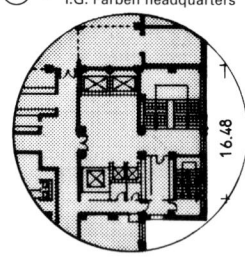

16.48

⑧ a   service core in Wernerwerke headquarters

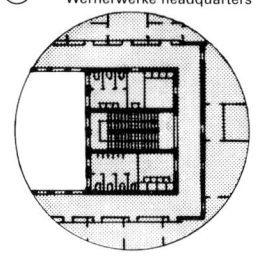

⑩ a   service core in Vereinigten Stahlwerke

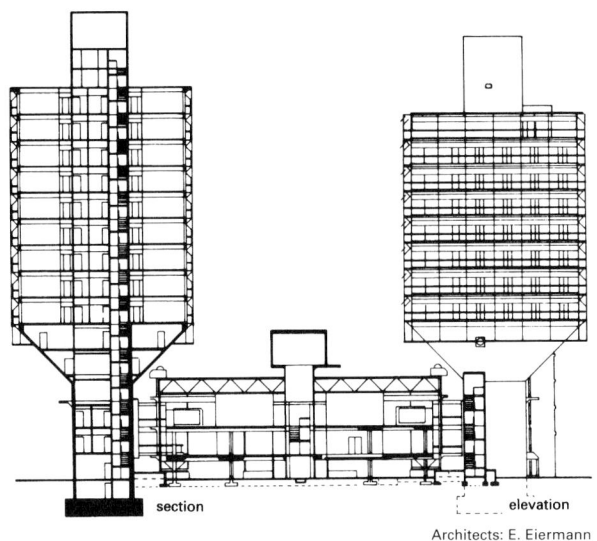

section elevation

Architects: E. Eiermann

Section of high-rise office building and training centre, including high-rise accommodation for trainees. Centre includes secretarial department, classrooms, computer suite, sales offices, service areas, and underground level with outdoor parking places for cars. Administration high-rise has office space, technical facilities and access to archives and environmental control (cooling and re-cooling plant) → ②

① **Deutsche Olivetti, Frankfurt am Main, 1972**

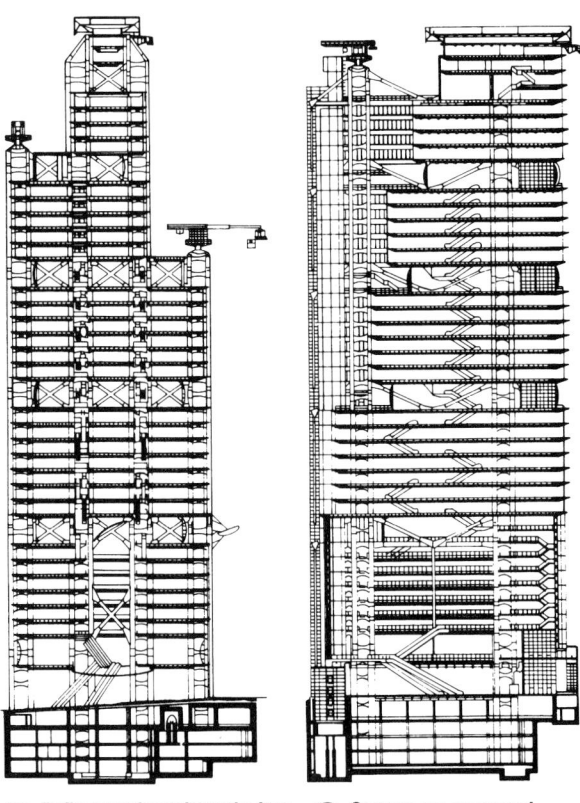

③ **Reflectors throughout the low levels reflect daylight into the atrium hall → ④ – ⑥**

④ **Storeys are staggered within the office spaces**

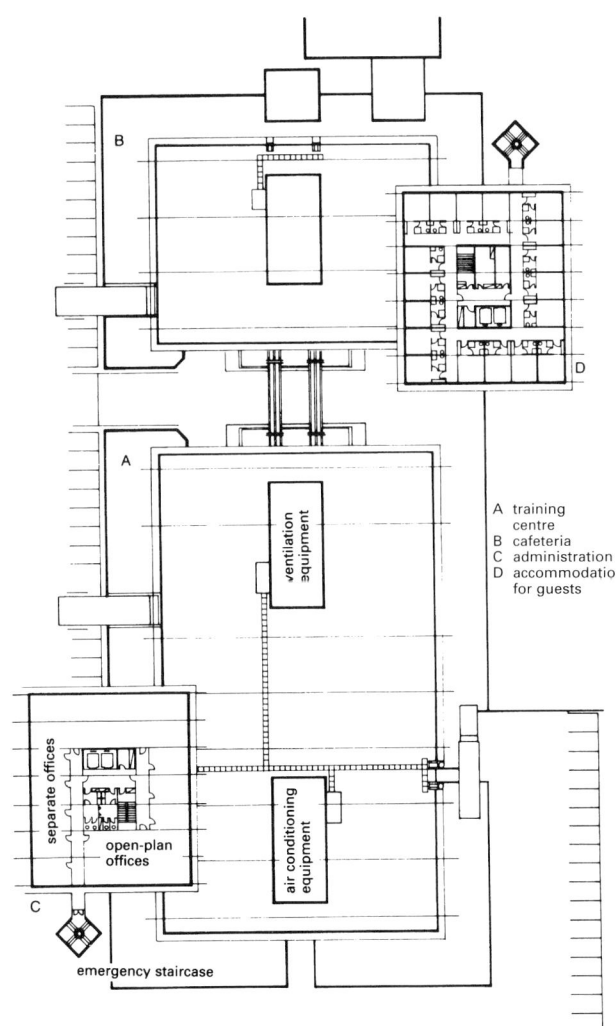

B

A

ventilation equipment

separate offices

open-plan offices

air conditioning equipment

C

emergency staircase

A training centre
B cafeteria
C administration
D accommodation for guests

② **Typical floors in towers. Space is suitable for both separate and open-plan offices → ①**

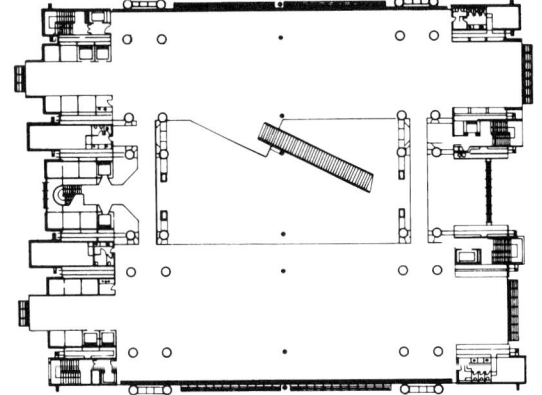

⑤ **Upper floor, upper banking hall**

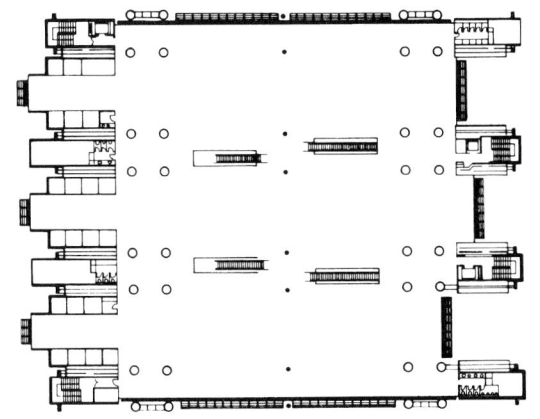

Architects: Foster Associates

⑥ **Typical three-bay floor, Hong Kong & Shanghai Bank, 1986**

OFFICE BUILDINGS

Examples

A high-rise office block project in Frankfurt am Main, 1990, was the outcome of a competition. The offices were to be let. Most of the ground floor area was kept open, and the plinth floors recall the requirements of New York City's zoning laws. A striking effect in the urban space was an important criterion in appraising the entries to the competition. The building has 51 storeys, including 45 floors of offices, and is over 200 m high. Gross usable floor area is 66081 m² → ① – ⑩.

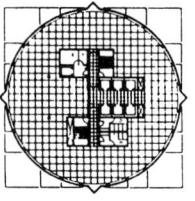

① Offices on floors 41–47 (core 231 m²)

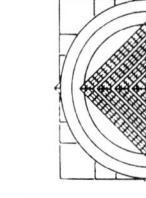

② Roof plan

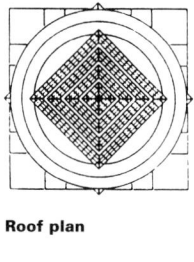

③ Offices on floors 5–25 (core 309 m²)

④ Offices on floors 26–40 (core 231 m²)

⑤ Sky lobby, second floor

⑥ Offices on third and fourth floors (core 307 m²)

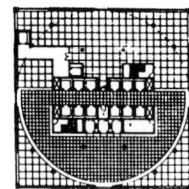

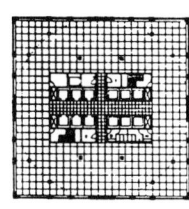

⑦ Lobby on ground floor

⑧ Technical plant, first floor

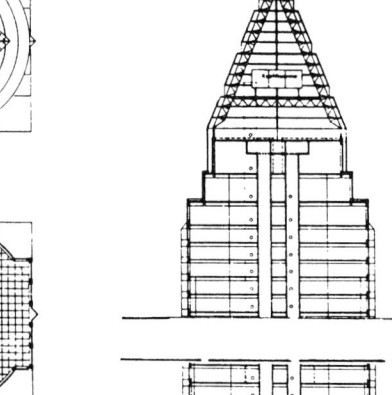

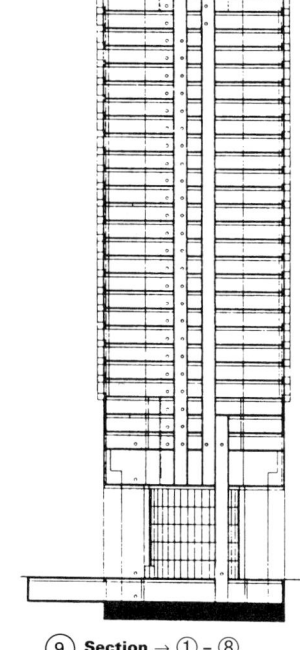

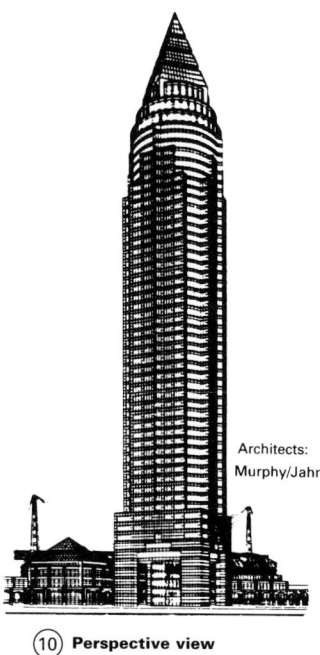

Architects: Murphy/Jahn

⑨ Section → ① – ⑧

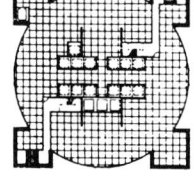

⑩ Perspective view

Millennium Tower, Tokyo: study commissioned by Ohbayashi company. Anchored in the sea, 2 km outside Tokyo, on an artificial atoll 400 m in diameter. Usable floor area designed to accommodate 50000 people. Office space is included in part of the tower at a height of 600 m. Building diameter at ground level is 130 m. Lifts for 160 passengers provide express transport to the five 'sky centres' where passengers can change lifts to gain access to 30 other storeys. The pipe-like construction, involving multiple concentric rings, has foundations 80 m deep in the sea. A dynamic balance regulation system that uses weights and water tanks, automatically controlled according to wind measurements, has been designed to counterbalance movements of the building caused by wind pressure. The result is a slimmer structure using less material → ⑪, ⑫ and ⑭.

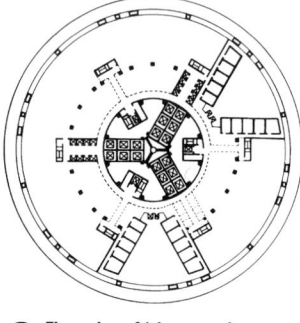

⑪ Floor-plan of 'sky center' on thirty-third floor (diameter 106.8 m)

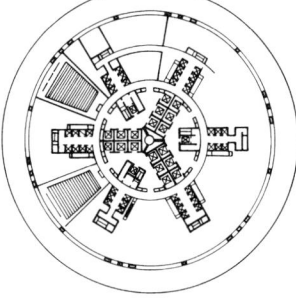

⑫ Office floor-plan, seventeenth floor. (diameter 116.4 m)

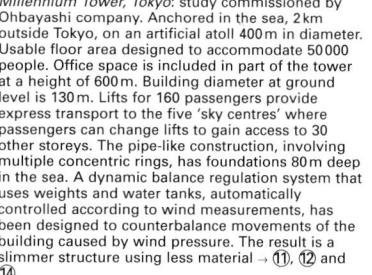

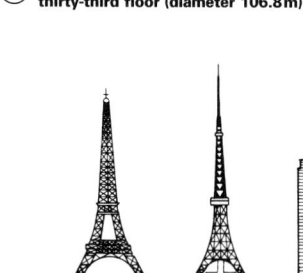

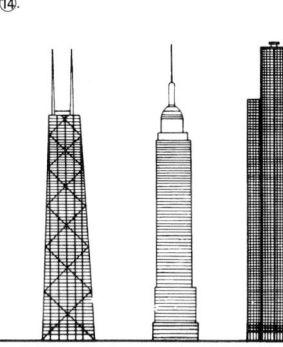

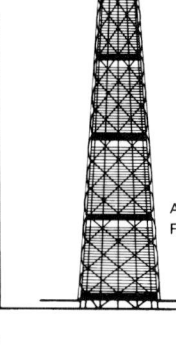

Architect: Foster, London

Eiffel Tower | Tokyo Tower | HSBC Building | Bank of China | Chrysler Building | Standard Oil | Hancock Tower | Empire State Building | Sears Tower

⑬ Comparative heights of well-known buildings

⑭ Millennium Tower, Tokyo

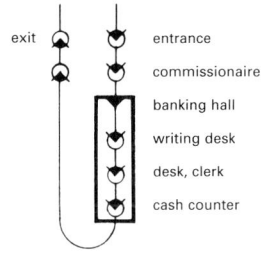

(1) **Customer circulation in large banks**

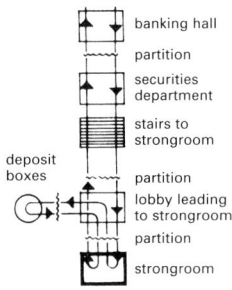

(2) **Routes to strongroom**

The requirements for the construction of a bank vary and depend on the nature of the bank's business (e.g. a high street bank with a large number of customers or an institution that handles large-scale investments and corporate work). In general the function of a high street bank is to allow money, whether in cash or some other form, to be paid in and withdrawn. Procedures must be transacted as quickly, securely and simply as possible.

Customers enter from the street outside, and then pass through a lobby, if appropriate, into the banking hall. The latter is often fitted with bench seats or chairs for waiting customers and small writing desks for customers, and has various positions for conducting transactions.

Desks for accounts and bookkeeping staff are usually behind the service counters, where transactions are verified and related operations are dealt with → (1). Cashiers nowadays have individual terminals that display the the customers' account details. Other areas serving customers, such as managers' offices, credit and auditing departments, are usually in the rooms leading off the main banking hall, often with separate anterooms, or on an upper floor → (3).

If the bank has safety deposit boxes, access from the banking hall should be via a partition, usually past the securities department and safe custody department, often one flight down, to a protective grille in front of the lobby leading to the strongroom containing the boxes. In smaller banks the strongroom may be divided behind the door into two, one part for bank use the other for customers → p. 361 (9). Larger banks normally have a separate bank strongroom next to that for customers. Offices of safe custody departments are in front of the entrance to the bank strongroom and have a separate staircase to the banking hall or secure lifts. → (3) Other basement areas must be accessed by a separate staircase. They can provide space for cloakrooms, storage, heating and ventilation plant, communications equipment and so on.

Building societies have existed in the UK since the end of the 18th century. They are societies of investors that accept investments, paying interest on the deposits, and lend to people building or buying properties. The investors are either member-shareholders or simply depositors. They supply the funds from which the house purchase loans are made. The operating basis of an incorporated and permanent Building Society resembles that of a bank so both have similar requirements in terms of building design.

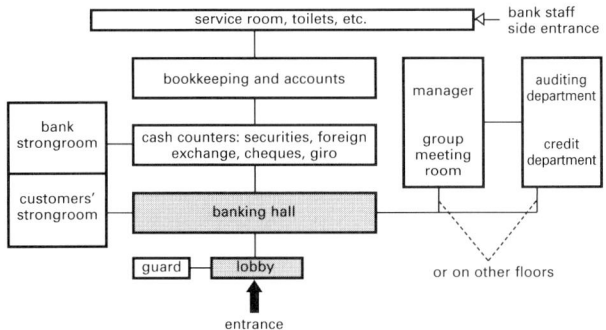

(3) **Relationships of rooms in large banks**

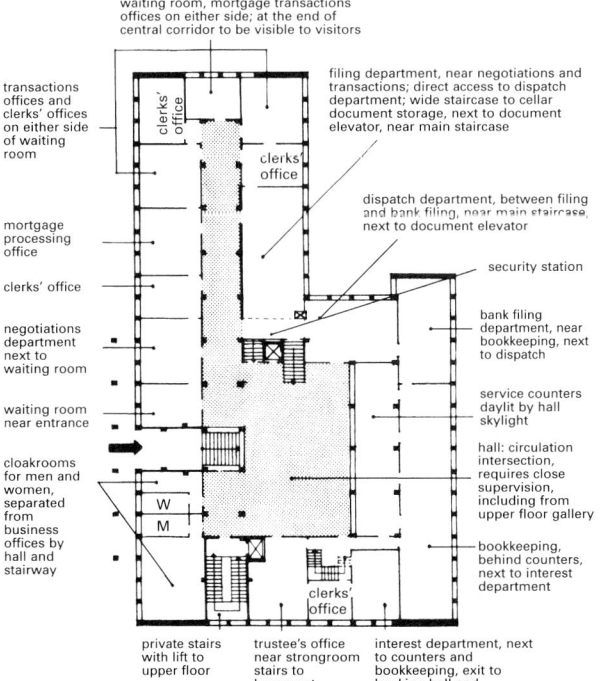

(designed by author for the Mitteldeutsche Hypothekenbank in Weimar)

(4) **Practical relationships of rooms in a large building society/mortgage bank, ground floor**

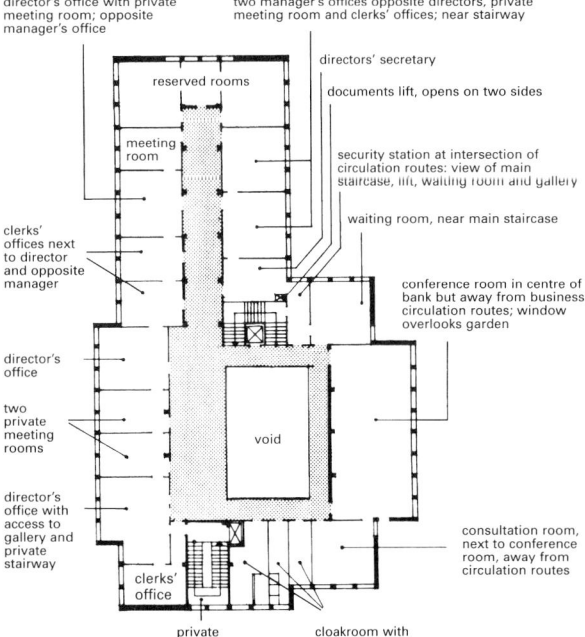

(5) **Upper floor → (4)**

BANKS AND BUILDING SOCIETIES

Open-plan Layout

There is a trend towards open-plan layouts in modern banks and building societies. This is intended to provide more room for the customers, making them feel comfortable and welcome. Since bulky protective screens are now almost unnecessary, large additional areas can be opened up for customer use.

Over recent years bank design has evolved to accommodate the following ideals:

- A 'shop-like' retail environment.
- Fully glazed or open frontages to create a more inviting image.
- Services that are dealt with as products to be 'sold' by staff trained to deal with customers in a friendly, attractive environment.
- More space given over to the customer and designs with better use of light and colour, prominent merchandising and designated sales, comfortable waiting areas and private interview rooms.

Open-plan principles

The idea of open planning is to bring staff and customers much closer together and build up customer loyalty. The aim is to generate an environment for improved service and with it enhanced business for the bank. Pugh Martin, an architect working with Barclays Bank, listed the following guiding principles relating to a high street open-plan bank.

- Maximise space given over to customer: move service counters as close to perimeter walls as possible; reduce space for support staff and equipment.
- Minimise space for processes and secure areas ('back office' functions are increasingly being moved from branches and centralised).

- Maximise potential for 'selling' financial products: by re-locating counters and non-sales functions, wall and floor space is released for displaying product literature and advertising material. This makes it possible to deliver coordinated marketing campaigns easily seen by the customers.
- Create personal contact space for dealing with financial products: allow for specialised, sometimes purpose-built, self-contained desks at which trained staff can deal face-to-face with customers.
- Achieve an open, inviting and customer-friendly environment that brings the customer in easily, makes each service easy to find and enables the customer to circulate throughout the bank comfortably.

Cash dispensers

Cash dispensers (or automatic teller machines, ATMs) are now a universal feature of modern high street banks and building societies. They can sit inside the bank or face into the street, the latter allowing customers access to their account details and funds 24 hours per day.

Cash dispensers are usually built into the bank façade and they need to: (1) be at or near ground level to allow for easy public access, (2) allow access from the rear to bank staff, (3) not disrupt window frames, sills or horizontal banding, and (4) correspond to the rhythm and scale of the fenestration above. Sometimes, cash dispensers are placed at the side of the building, which helps to solve the problems of disabled access and of obstruction of the pavement if queues form at busy times when the bank is closed. In larger banks, a number of cash dispensers can be set in an adjoining lobby that is open to customers at all times.

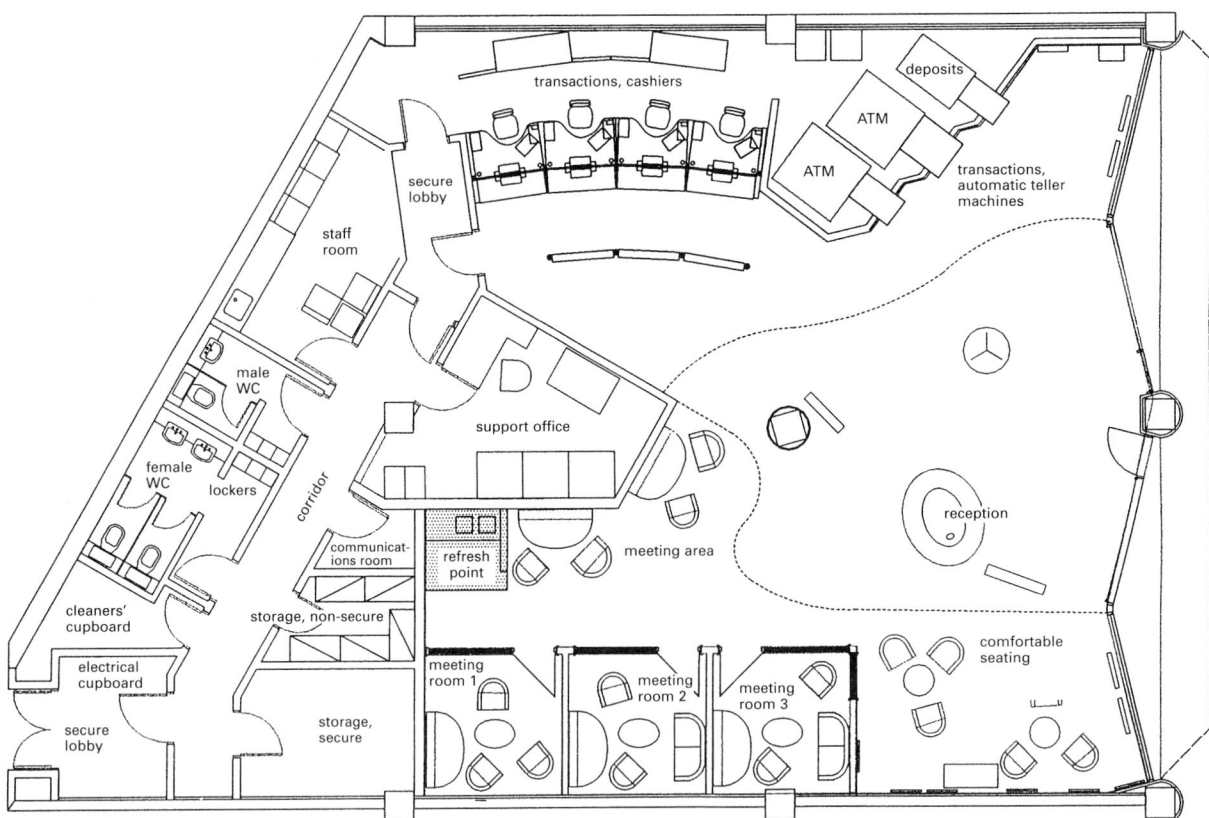

(the floor plan of a building which does not exist, but which might be in 'Anytown', conceived by Peter J. Clement)

(1) **Floor plan of a financial outlet: the layout incorporates all the likely features needed to develop a solution for a high street location**

Safes and Strongrooms

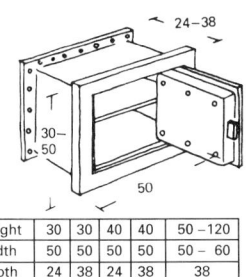

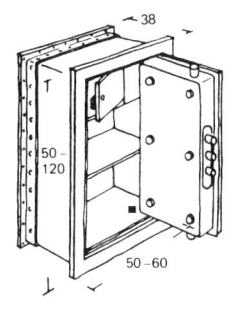

		24–38			38

	height	30	30	40	40	50 –120
exterior	width	50	50	50	50	50 – 60
	depth	24	38	24	38	38
interior	height	17	17	27	27	37 –107
	width	37	37	37	37	37 – 47
	depth	16	30	16	30	30

① + ② **Sizes of typical wall safes**

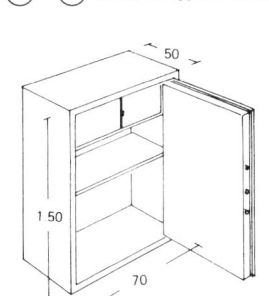

size	exterior			interior		
	H	W	D	H	W	D
1 door	150	70	50	137	57	41
2 doors	195	95	50	182	82	41

③ **Document cabinet with internal safe**

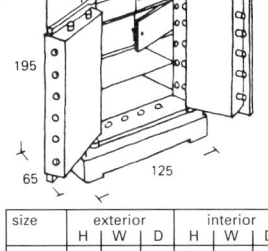

size	exterior			interior		
	H	W	D	H	W	D
1 door	80	60	60	50	37	36
	100	60	60	70	37	36
	125	80	60	95	57	36
	150	80	60	120	57	36
	175	80	65	145	57	41
2 doors	195	125	65	165	102	41

④ **Floor safe for bookkeeping documents and cash**

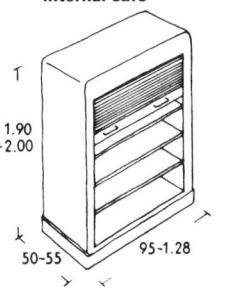

⑤ **Roll-front cabinet for valuables**

⑥ **Bank deposit boxes rented out**

savings bank
strongboxes
6 × 20 × 36
strongboxes
8 × 30 × 50
strongboxes
12 × 30 × 50
strongboxes
22 × 30 × 50
strongboxes
at base
40 × 45 × 50

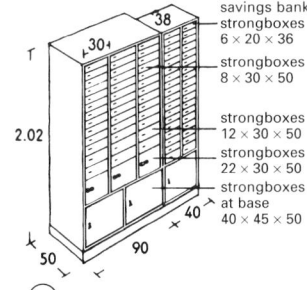

⑦ **Steel window for strongroom**

⑧ **Ventilation ducts in strongroom wall**

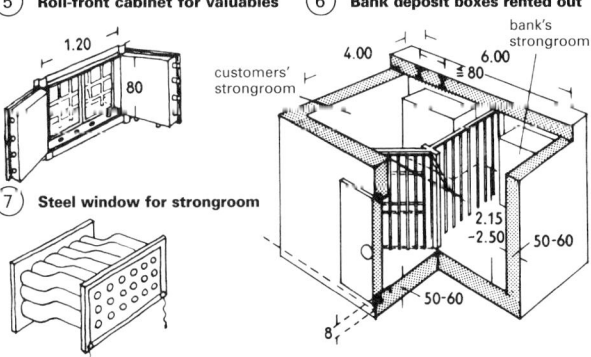

⑨ **Strongroom for smaller bank branch**

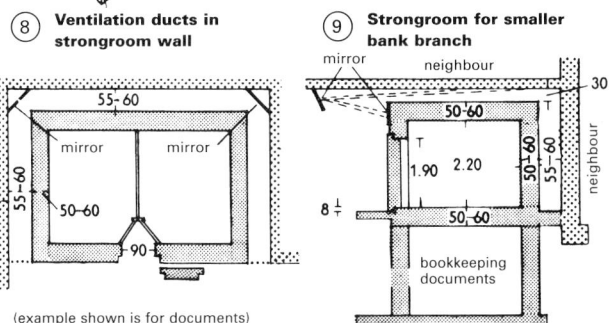

(example shown is for documents)

⑩ + ⑪ **Strongroom surrounded by neighbouring walls**

external dimensions			internal dimensions			number of shelves
height	width	depth	height	width	depth	
50	50	45	35	35	33	1
60	50	45	45	35	33	1
80	60	45	65	45	33	2
100	60	45	85	45	33	2
120	60	45	105	45	33	2

⑫ **Small money cabinets: typical sizes**

external dimensions			internal dimensions			number of shelves
height	width	depth	height	width	depth	
120	70	60	97	55	39	2
155	70	55	125	50	34	3
195	95	60	172	80	39	4

⑬ **Fireproof document cabinets: typical sizes**

In general, wall safes are metal boxes built into the walls and hidden behind wallpaper or a painting. They are used to protect valuables in both domestic properties and business premises. → ① + ②

To store valuable and confidential paperwork securely, businesses make use of steel document cabinets → ③, many of which also contain a safe and are fireproof. Floor safes are used for secure storage of petty cash and documents → ④. Valuables that are rarely used are best kept in a rented safety deposit box in the strongroom of a bank → ⑥.

Bank strongrooms should be designed to prevent criminals from breaking in forceably. The enclosing structure and door must be able to resist penetration for sufficient time to thwart potential intruders. Structures enclosing strongrooms should, therefore, neither adjoin neighbouring spaces (i.e. no party walls) nor be built in seldom-used areas of the bank, and must not have earth below. Experience has shown that intruders otherwise have ample time to work in the unsupervised location and reduce the wall to a thin layer that can then be quickly broken through. Therefore, if a strongroom is not surrounded on all sides, including above and below, by parts of the bank that are in constant use, it must be an independent structure that is surrounded by a free space allowing full supervision.

Tests have shown that a 1:3 mix concrete with specific mineral additives offers better protection than masonry. A proficient mason equipped with sharp chisels would need over 12 hours to break through a 40cm thick wall of that type, compared with only 9 hours for a hard-fired brick wall with 1:3 mortar. Iron reinforcement barely slows down a thief (hardened rods can be broken with a hammer and normal rods can be cut out) so the added cost is not justified.

The most economical way to enclose a strongroom is by 50cm of 1:4 concrete, which would require 20 hours to break through. Assuming an 8 hour working day, a thief would have only 16 hours available. However, in the worst case, with a Sunday and two holidays, thieves could have 88 hours and since modern electric and pneumatic drills are increasingly powerful, strongrooms are always vulnerable. Therefore, they should be inspected frequently outside of official business hours and this can be done using electronic listening devices that can notify the watchman's station at the bank, or the closest police station, of the slightest noise occurring outside of business hours.

BANKS AND BUILDING SOCIETIES

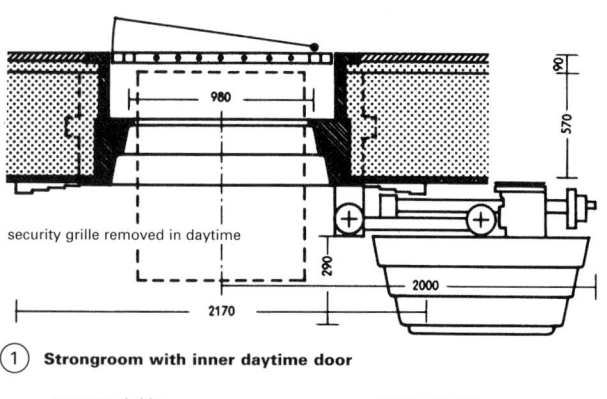

(1) **Strongroom with inner daytime door**

security grille removed in daytime

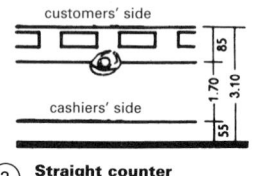

(2) **Straight counter arrangement**

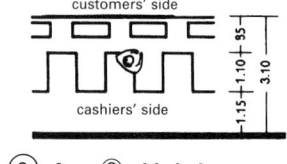

(3) **As → (2) with desks**

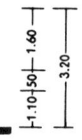

(4) **Sawtooth counter arrangement with desks at sides**

Strongroom doors

To withstand any attack, strongroom doors are made from toughened steel plate with fireproof and non-melting reinforcement, and are typically 27–30 cm thick. The armoured doors pivot smoothly on steel hinges and the edges are machined to fit exactly into the reinforced door surround. They do not have keyholes, instead using elaborate remote-controlled locking devices, and are usually protected by electrically operated alarm systems that are triggered by the slightest vibration of door.

Cashier positions

The cashiers' counter is provided with an electric alarm system operated by foot or knee to guard against potential attack. Money is held securely in standard steel cabinets, usually underneath the counter.

Drive-in banks

To save time, customers do not go into bank but drive up to an external cash point that may either be manned or automated. This avoids parking problems. The cash points can be integrated in bank building or built separately on islands. Each cash point can serve up to 250 customers per day; transactions can take as little as 60 seconds. However, a normal banking hall is also needed for lengthier business transactions.

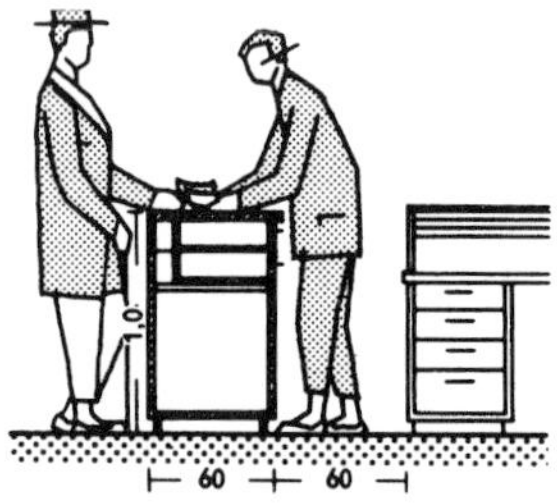

(5) **German cash desks**

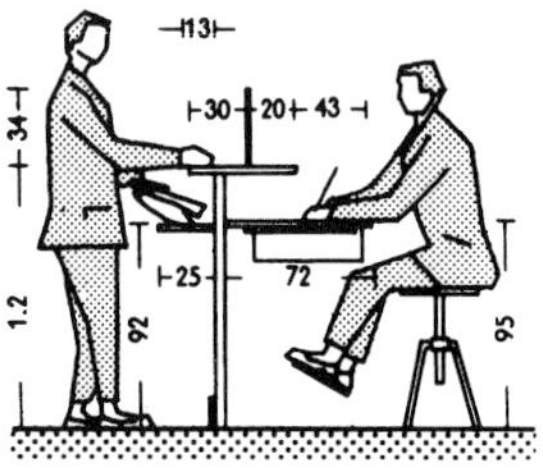

(6) **Swedish type cash desk**

cashier positions are usually completely protected with bulletproof reinforced glass (≥ 25 mm thick) to prevent criminals jumping over the counter; similar protection over sunken drawers → (8)

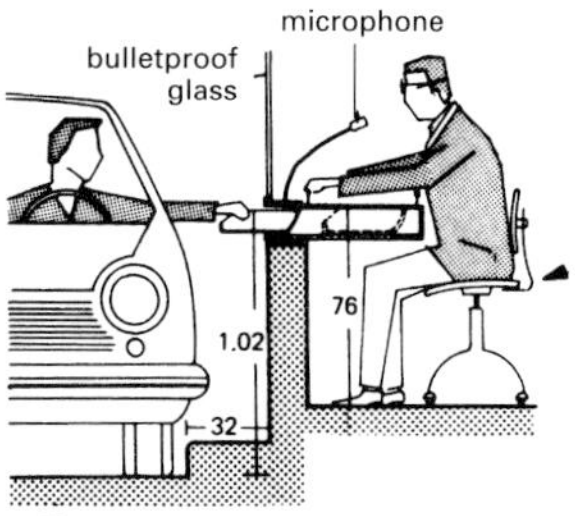

(8) **Drive-up cash point, no parking**

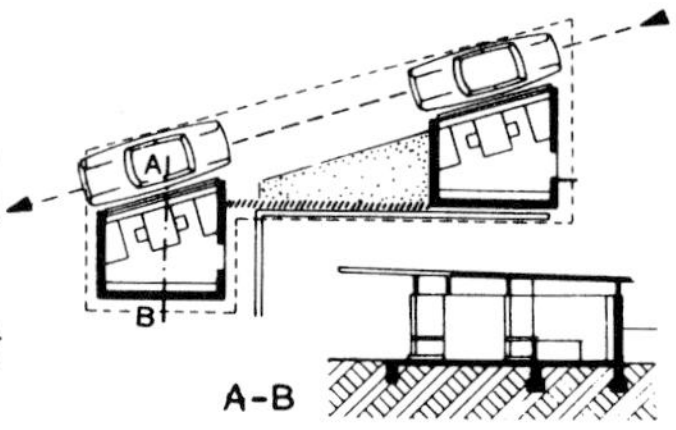

(9) **Drive-up cash point kiosk**

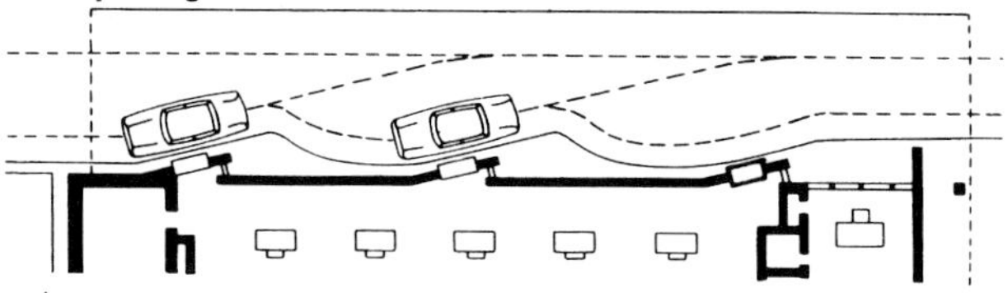

A–B

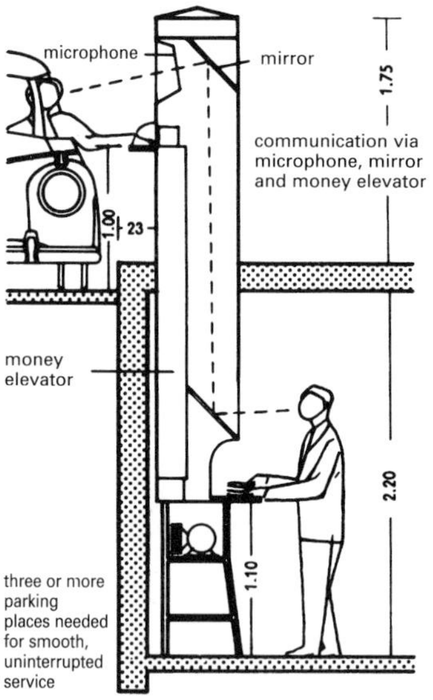

(7) **Cash point below pavement with customer service shaft (snorkel bank)**

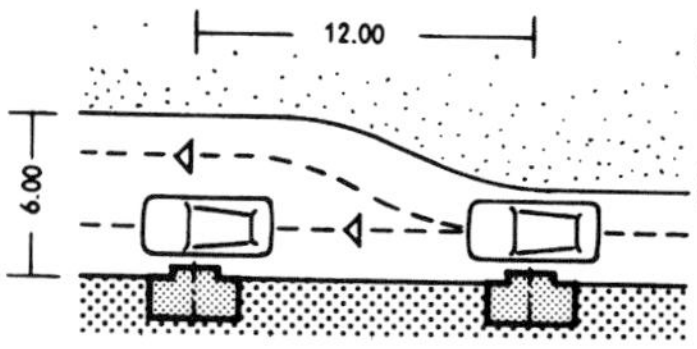

microphone   mirror

communication via microphone, mirror and money elevator

money elevator

three or more parking places needed for smooth, uninterrupted service

(10) **Drive-up cash points**

(11) **Cash points integrated with bank building**

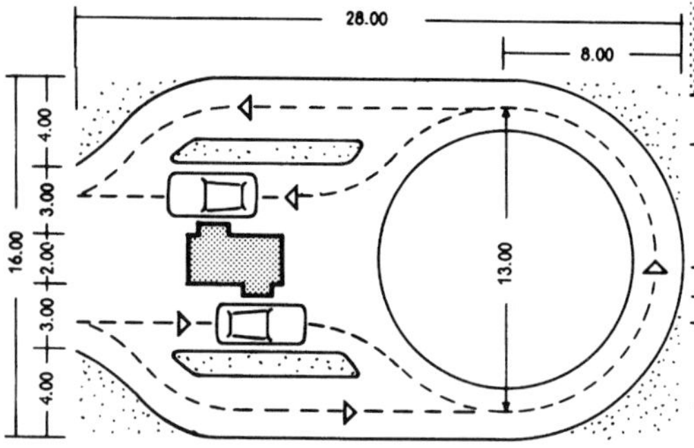

(12) **Twin cash points; islands to ease traffic flow**

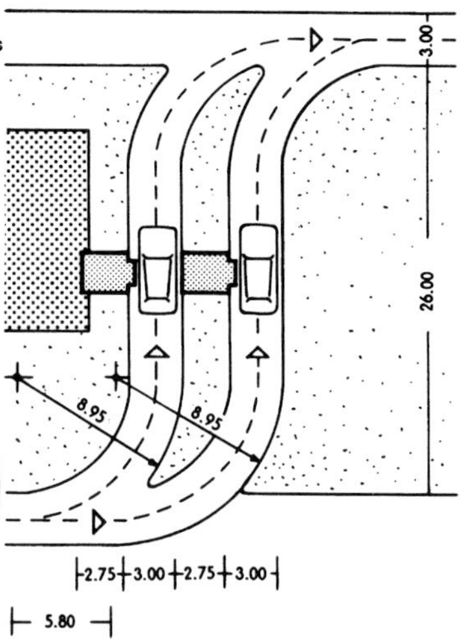

(13) **Cash points as → (8) + (9) for through traffic**

Typology

The glazed arcade is a building type which is both interesting and popular in contemporary architecture. Arcades may be on a single level, slope gently to follow the contours of the site, or have a split-level arrangement to change levels. Arcades are through routes intended exclusively for pedestrians. They should be accessible around the clock as semi-public routes. Arcades can have a multiplicity of uses (retail sales, mixed sectors, etc.). Therefore facilities that will attract customers outside normal business hours should be encouraged. Glass structures are supported by steel, aluminium or laminated wood beams.

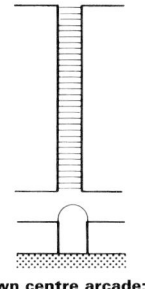

(1) **Town centre arcade: glass-covered connecting corridor (for daylight); much longer than its width or height**

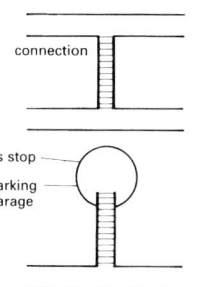

(2) **Arcades should be integrated into main pedestrian flows in the town centre → (3)**

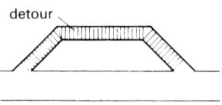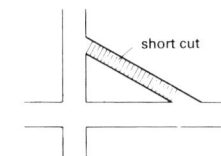

(4) **Position of arcades**

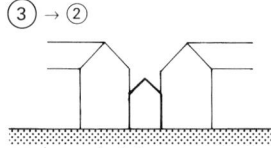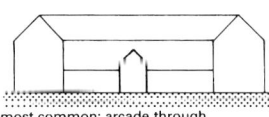

(5) **Plan of routes followed by arcades**

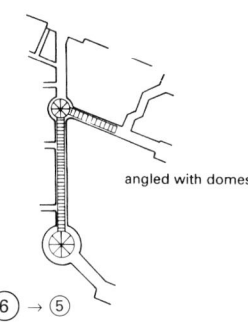

(6) → (5)

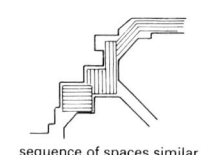

sequence of spaces similar to town squares

(7) → (5)

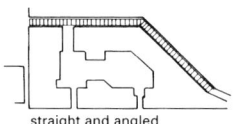

straight and angled

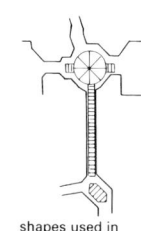

(8) → (5)

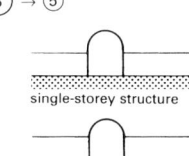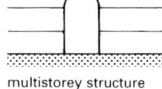

(9) **Main pedestrian level is usually the ground floor**

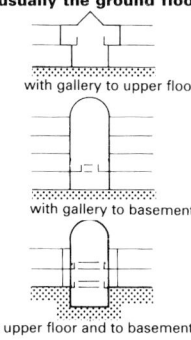

(10) **Multistorey structures**

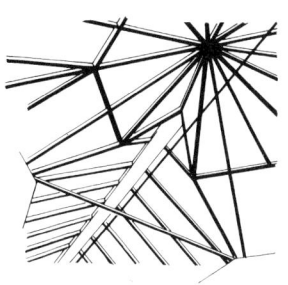

Architect: Gottfried Böhm, Cologne

(11) **Arcade of department store in Dudweiler**

(12) **Possible coverings**

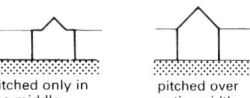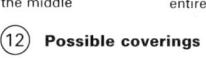

(13) **Support structure position**

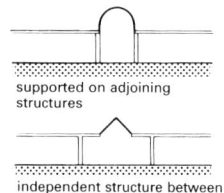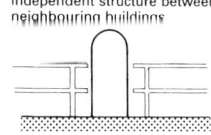

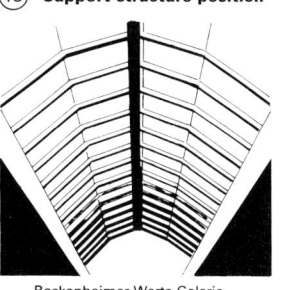

Bockenheimer Warte Galerie (Architects: Speerplan GmbH)

(14) **Structure made of load-bearing glazing bars that span the space**

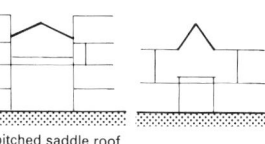

pitched saddle roof

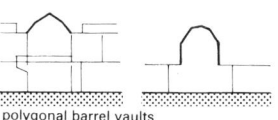

polygonal barrel vaults

(15) **Glass roof shapes**

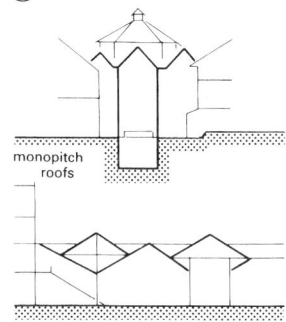

(16) → (15)

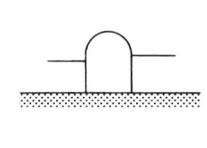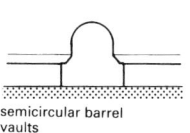

(17) → (15)

(18) → (15)

GLAZED ARCADES

Historic Examples

Passage du Caire → ①,⑤ is the oldest surviving glazed arcade in the world, and at 370 m is the longest in Paris. This low-key, two-storey arcade is on average only 2.70 m wide. It houses two storeys of shops, as well as apartments above the glass roof. Galerie Vivienne → ②,⑨, by architect François Jacques Delannoy (1755–1835), was built at nearly the same time as Galerie Colbert, which is located in the same block of buildings. Passage du Grand Cerf → ③,⑩ is only 4 m wide, but is three storeys high and 120 m long. It runs straight through a block of buildings. There are shops on the ground floor, offices and workshops on the first floor, and apartments on the second floor. More than most other arcades in Paris, the 190 m long Passage Choiseul → ④ is a roofed-over street. There is separate access to each building by a spiral staircase. Passages Joufroy and Verdeau → ⑥ is a combined, roofed pedestrian system which is 400 m long. Galleria Mazzini → ⑦+⑧ is one of the monumental arcades. Leeds Thornton's Arcade → ⑪ has houses in front and an arcade area occupying three storeys. Galleria Umberto I → ⑬,⑭ is an ideal embodiment of a cross-shaped design with four entrances. The crossing is crowned with a giant dome. Morgan Arcade → ⑮,⑯ was built in 1897 by the architect Edwin Seward for David Morgan. It was altered by the later addition of department store buildings on the Hayes.

① Passage du Caire, Paris, in 1952

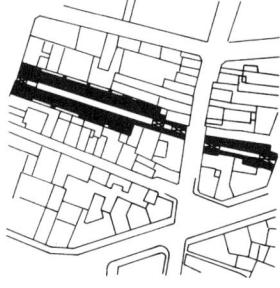

② Galerie Vivienne and Galerie Colbert, Paris, in 1966

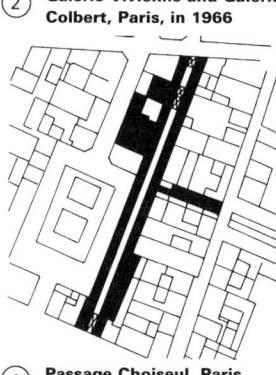

③ Passage du Grand Cerf, Paris

④ Passage Choiseul, Paris, around 1966

⑤ Passage du Caire, Paris, around 1798

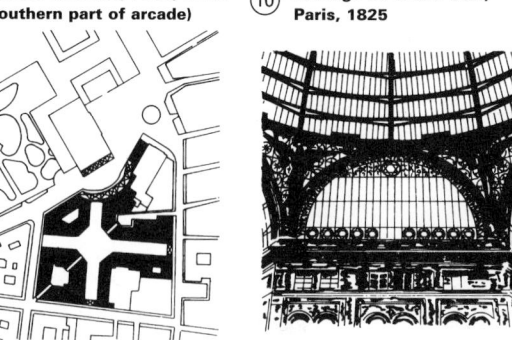

⑥ Passage Joufroy, Paris, 1845

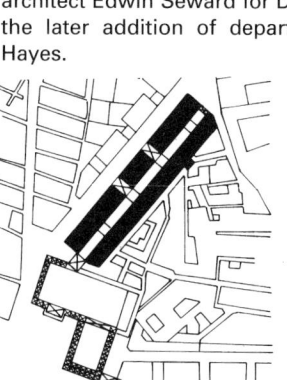

⑦ Galleria Mazzini, Genoa, around 1930

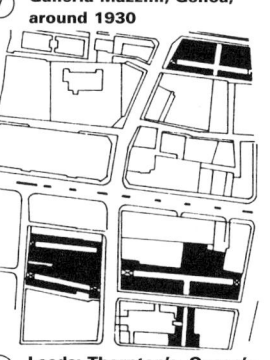

⑧ Galleria Mazzini

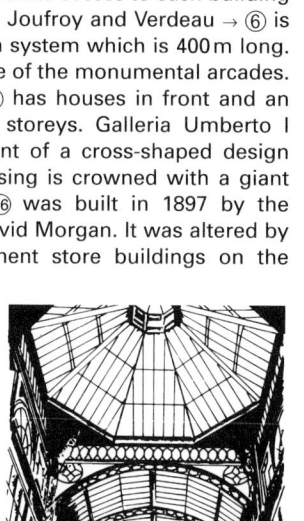

⑨ Galerie Vivienne, Paris, 1823 (southern part of arcade)

⑩ Passage du Grand Cerf, Paris, 1825

⑪ Leeds: Thornton's, Queen's, Grand, Country, Cross (1961)

⑫ Queen's Arcade, Leeds, 1889

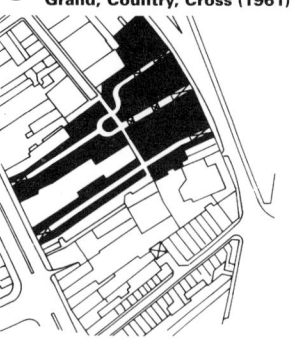

⑬ Galleria Umberto I, Naples in 1960

⑭ Galleria Umberto I, Naples

⑮ Morgan Arcade, Cardiff → ⑯   ⑯ Morgan Arcade, Cardiff

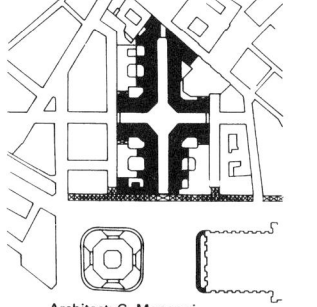

Architect: G. Mengoni

(1) **Milan: Cathedral Square and Galleria Vittorio Emanuele II in 1900**

(6) **The arcade through fish-eye lens** → (1)

(2) **The glass dome** → (1)

(7) **View out of the dome** → (1)

Galleria Vittorio Emanuele II in Milan represents the developmental zenith of arcade architecture. It is the culmination of a process that began with the 'passages' in Paris and reached an intermediate stage with the Galeries St. Hubert in Brussels. The plan of the Galleria is in the shape of a Latin cross with its centre expanded into an octagon. The main dimensions are: longitudinal arm 196.62 m; diameter of octagon 36.60 m; height to top of lantern 47.08 m → (1) + (2), and (6) + (7). Those dimensions are exceeded only in some details of later arcades, e.g. the height of the Galleria Umberto I in Naples, and the length of the GUM department store in Moscow → (3). Significant references to the urban façades of Palladio can be seen in the design of its interior.

The GUM department store building in Moscow → (3) + (4) and (8) + (9) is in approximately the shape of a parallelogram, with sides measuring 90 m × 250 m on average. The polygonal extension in the centre of the intersecting central aisles is reminiscent of the arcade in Milan, although the tranverse arm does not extend up to the roof.

Galeries St. Hubert → (11) + (13) is the first example of a monumental arcade. Its volume has rarely been exceeded by later examples. The Galeries St. Hubert were also the first to be publicly funded.

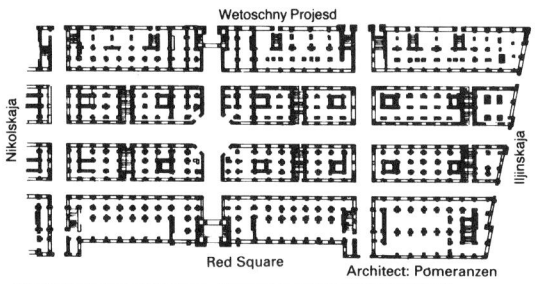

Wetoschny Projesd

Nikolskaja

Iljinskaja

Red Square

Architect: Pomeranzen

(3) **GUM department store, Moscow (ground floor plan)** → (4) + (5) and (8) + (9)

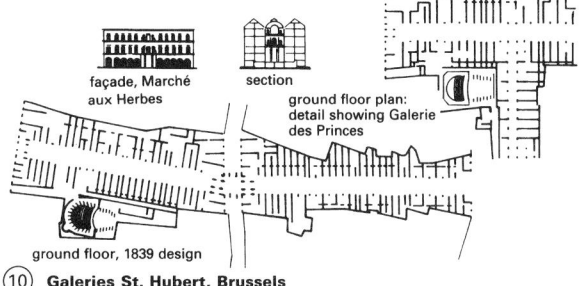

façade, Marché aux Herbes

section

ground floor plan: detail showing Galerie des Princes

ground floor, 1839 design

(10) **Galeries St. Hubert, Brussels**

(4) **Central arcade** → (3)

(8) **Lateral arcade space** → (3)

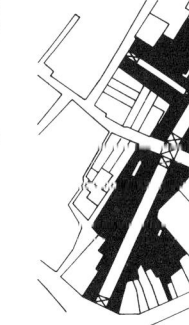

(11) **Galeries St. Hubert, in 1866**

(13) **Arcade** → (11)

(5) **View of Petrówskij Arcade**

(9) **Central arcade space** → (3)

(12) **Arcade in Budapest**

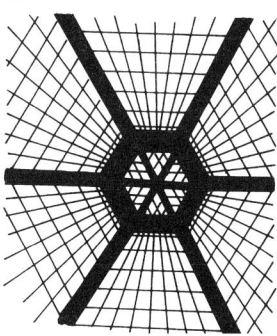

(14) **Glass dome** → (12)

GLAZED ARCADES

Applied Examples

Galleries and arcades are design elements that have been re-discovered by architects. Their transparent roofs span roads, paths and squares, and connect buildings, shops and stores. Galleries and arcades have been used to expand pedestrian zones, protect against bad weather, and provide a meeting place.

A shopping arcade in Hamburg → ① – ③ has a site area of 11 000 m² . There is shopping space of 9400 m² over three levels, and roof parking for 180 cars.

Kaiserpassage in Bonn → ⑥ – ⑧ is based on 19th century arcades and galleries. Bringing together specialised shops, boutiques, kiosks, cafés, restaurants and cinemas is intended to encourage passers-by to linger without regard to the weather.

Calwer Passage in Stuttgart is covered by a huge vaulted glass roof → ④ + ⑤ + ⑩.

Wilhelm-Arcade in Wiesbaden → ⑪ – ⑬ connects the Marktplatz (market square) and Wilhelmstrasse. The ground floor has shops, and the upper floor accommodates a restaurant and the personnel and service rooms needed by the businesses.

'Galerie Kleiner Markt' in Saarlouis → ⑭ – ⑯ has escalator access to three storeys. Inclusion of the basement floor area gives the arcade the appearance of a gallery.

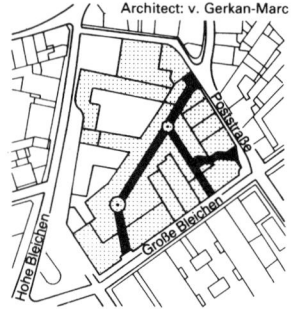

Architect: v. Gerkan-Marc

① **Hanse quarter, Hamburg: layout → ② – ③**

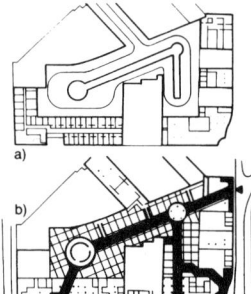

② **Arcade plans: a) parking deck, b) ground floor**

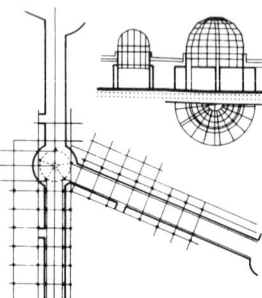

③ **Section of small dome; plan and section → ①**

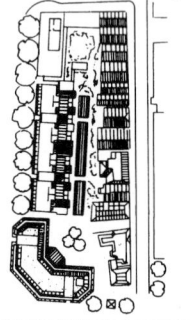

Architect: Kammerer and Belz

④ **Calwer Passage, Stuttgart: layout**

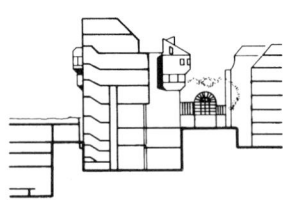

⑤ **Calwer Passage: section → ⑩**

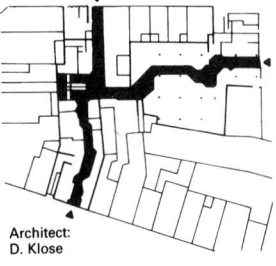

Architect: D. Klose

⑥ **Shopping arcade, Bonn, 'Kaiserpassagen': ground floor plan → ⑦ + ⑧**

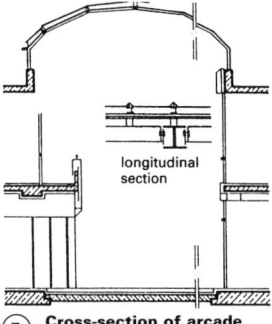

⑦ **Cross-section of arcade with glass roof → ⑥**

⑧ **Plan and general view → ⑥ and ⑦**

⑨ **Plan, elevation and detail of barrel roof → ⑫**

⑩ **Detailed section → ⑤**

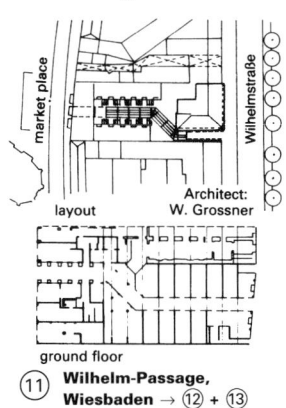

Architect: W. Grossner

⑪ **Wilhelm-Passage, Wiesbaden → ⑫ ⑬**

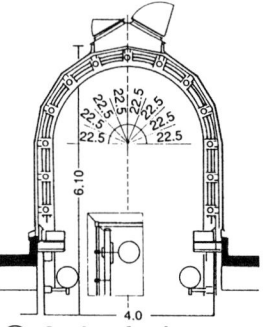

⑫ **Section of arch structure → ⑪ and ⑬**

⑬ **Arcade in Wilhelmstrasse, Wiesbaden → ⑪**

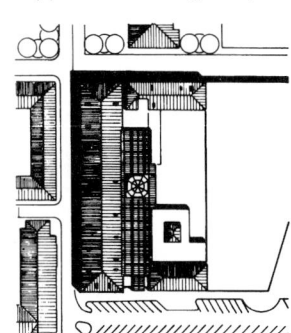

⑭ **'Galerie Kleiner Markt' shopping mall, Saarlouis: layout → ⑮ + ⑯**

⑮ **Entrance area → ⑭ and ⑯**

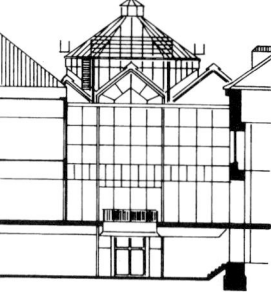

⑯ **'Galerie Kleiner Markt' shopping mall: section of building**

TRANSPARENT ROOFS AND CANOPIES

To make life more agreeable for city inhabitants and visitors, large transparent canopies are playing an increasing role in the architectural concepts of modern town planning. The transparent canopies not only protect against wind and weather, but also add decorative accents to the appearance of our cities. Transparent roofs improve the quality of life of city residents. They increase the quality of leisure time, for example, by protecting window shoppers on commercial streets and in pedestrian zones. Transparent roofs are also used for outdoor theatres, swimming pools, or sports facilities to provide shelter from inclement weather.

It is obviously essential that fire rescue services are still able reach the buildings, and that the micro-climate in the street, shops, restaurants and offices is not adversely affected. The following materials are used for transparent roofs:

- silicate glass panes/pyramids;
- acrylic glass domes;
- vaults made of acrylic glass or polycarbonate;
- intersecting skins containing synthetic fibres and the like;
- fire-resistant glass (→ pp. 130–31, 169, 173);
- curved glass (3–8 mm; radii 50–230 mm).

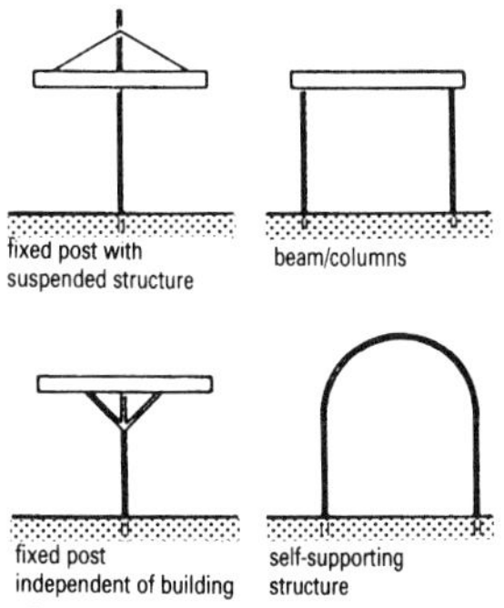

fixed post with suspended structure

beam/columns

fixed post supporting cantilevered structure

suspended from building

fixed post independent of building

self-supporting structure

supported by building and post

cantilever from building

① **Possible canopies**

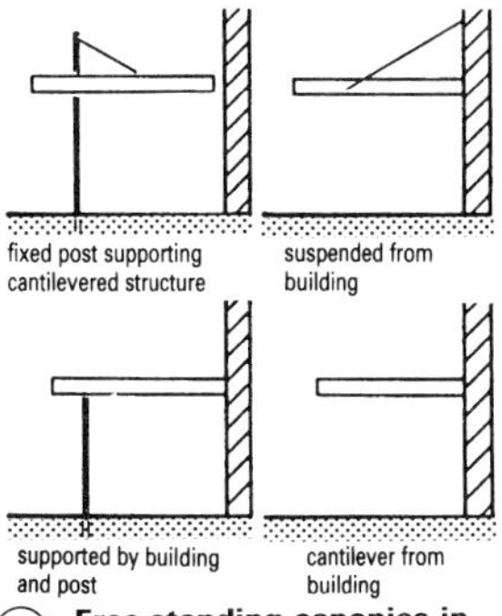

② **Free-standing canopies in streets**

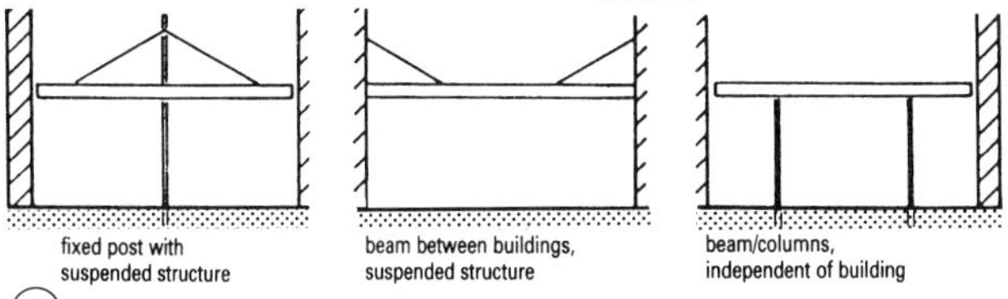

fixed post with suspended structure

beam between buildings, suspended structure

beam/columns, independent of building

③ **Canopies providing complete coverage**

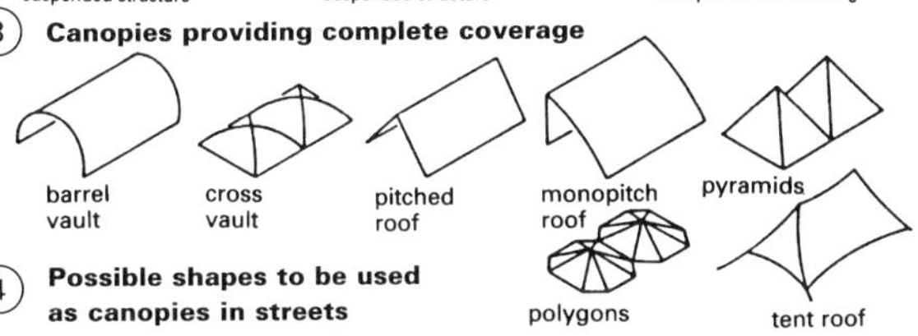

barrel vault

cross vault

pitched roof

monopitch roof

pyramids

polygons

tent roof

④ **Possible shapes to be used as canopies in streets**

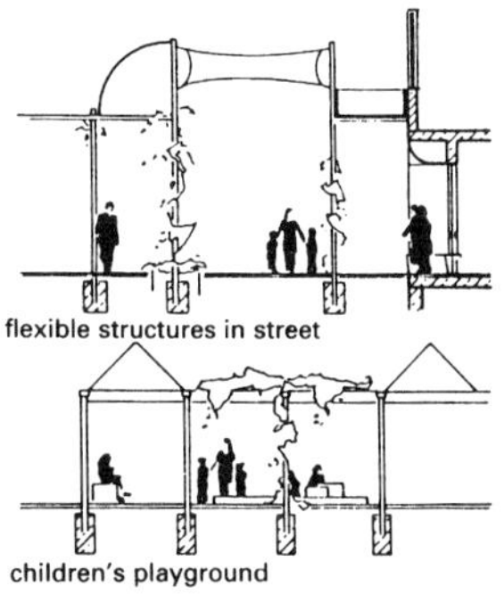

flexible structures in street

children's playground

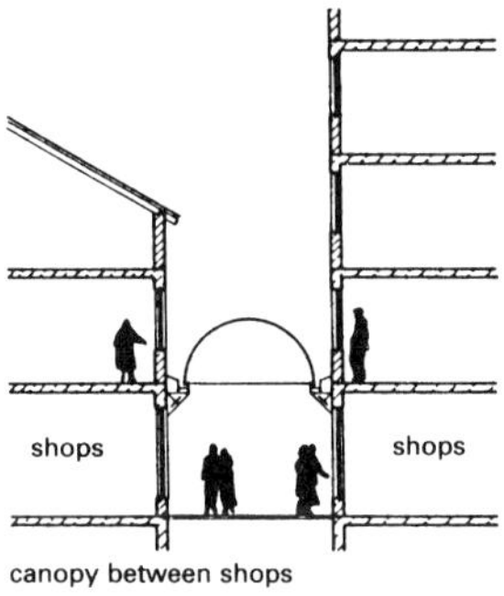

shops

shops

canopy between shops

⑤ **Transparent street canopies**

⑥ → ⑤

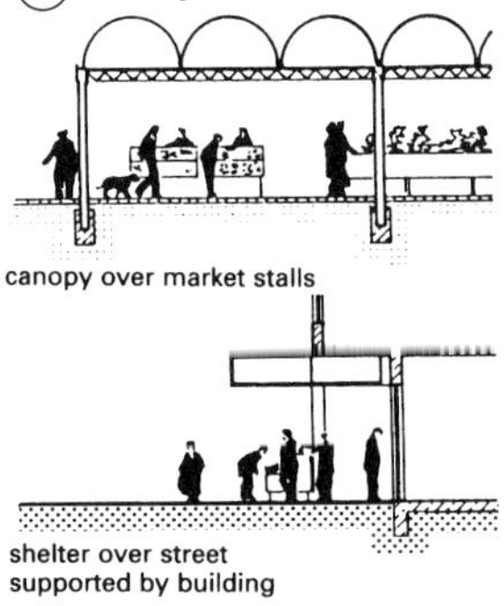

canopy over market stalls

two storey café, glazed roof

shelter over street supported by building

bus station, glazed canopy

⑦ → ⑤

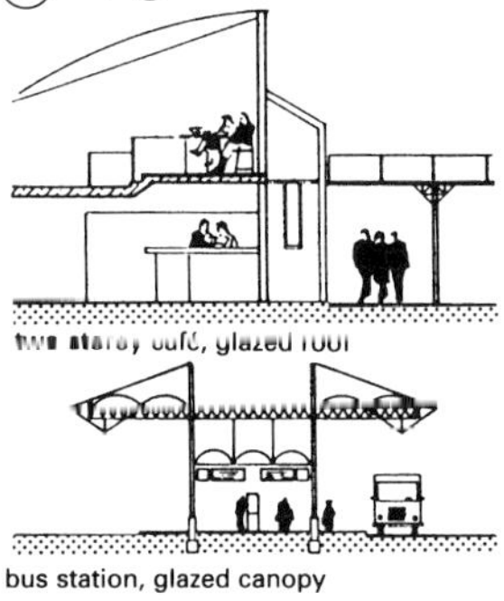

⑧ → ⑤

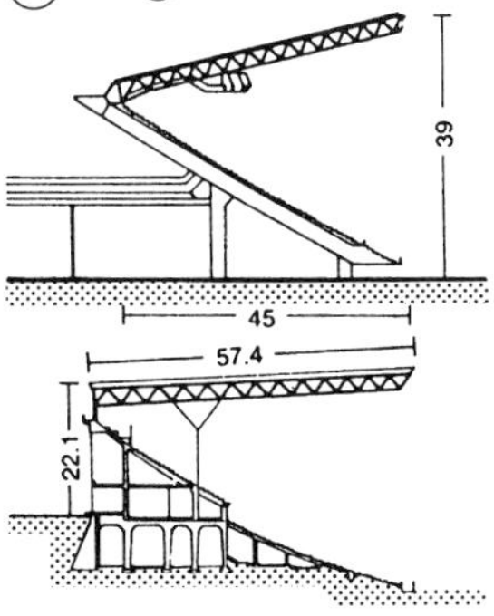

⑨ **Light canopies for stadiums**

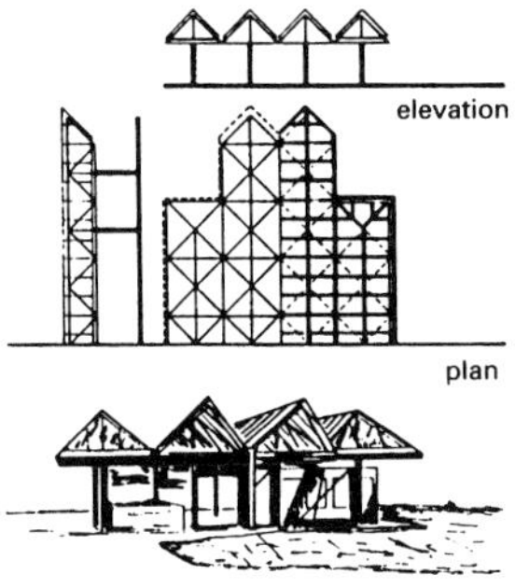

⑩ **Access stairs with gabled roofs**

elevation

plan

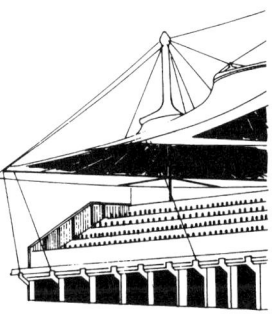

⑪ **Suspended tent-like canopy over stand at Lords Cricket Ground, London**

⑭ **Spa at Bad Krozingen; roof over entrance**

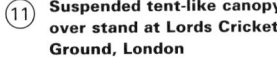

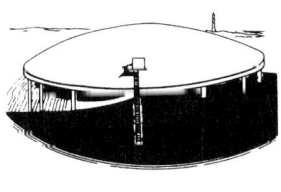

⑫ **Nîmes, France: inflated light cushion roof anchored to a ring resting on the steel supports of the top row of arena seating**

⑮ **Canopies over schoolyard at Römerschule, Stuttgart**

Design: Architects Graaf-Schweger and Partners, Hamburg

⑬ **Porch-roof, Hamburg main railway station**

⑯ **Rheingarten in Cologne**

367

Shelf units in shops → ① – ⑥ from which customers pick their own goods should be no higher than 1.8m and no lower than 0.3m above floor level.

Attention must be paid to circulation routes in larger shops → ⑩ + ⑪. They should begin at the trolley/basket pick-up and end at the check-outs.

All shops require some provision for the handling of goods. These needs may vary from off-pavement deliveries for small units to the complex operations carried out by large retail businesses.

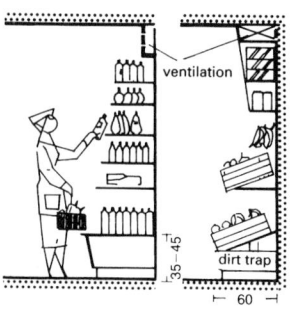

① Shelves for bottles   Shelves for fruit, vegetables and loose goods

② Partition allowing replacement of containers from refilling aisle

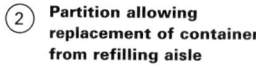

③ Bread display

④ Shelf display unit

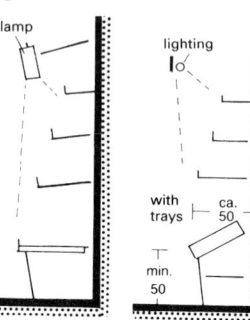

⑤ Self-service shelves

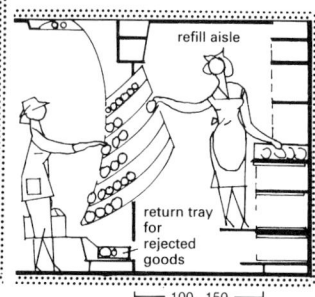

⑥ Shelf unit with refill aisle and return tray

⑦ Minimum width of a shop ≥ 4.0 m, preferably 5.0 m

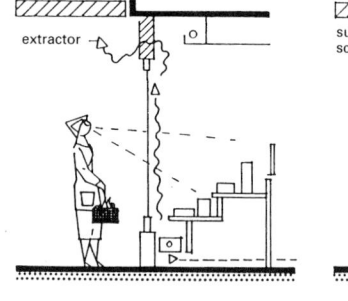

⑧ Stepped window display, with protective glass behind

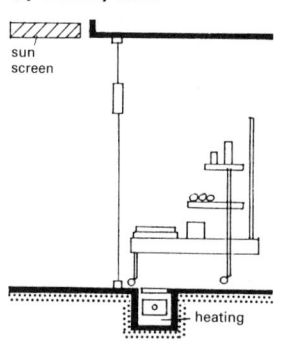

⑨ Mobile window carousel, protective screen behind

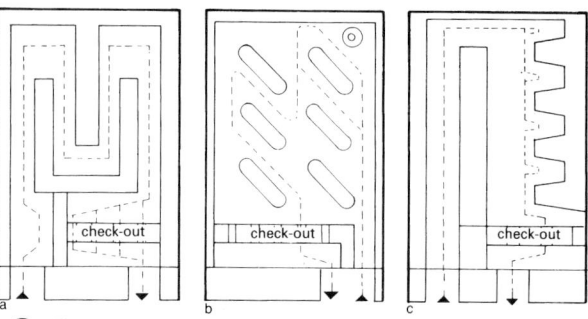

⑩ Circulation routes must account for corners (a and c, entrance and exit separate; b, together)

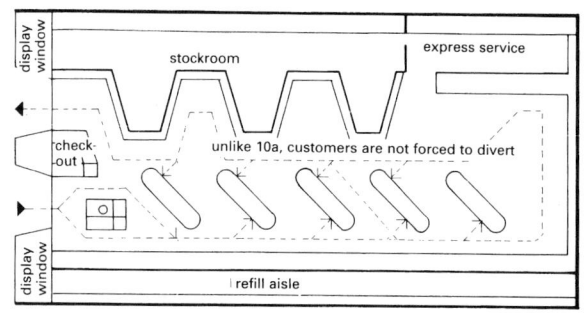

⑪ Good view of the whole shop from check-outs is essential for customer convenience and security

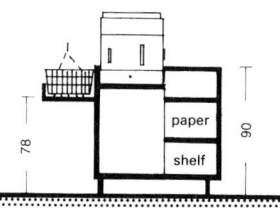

⑫ Section through small check-out position

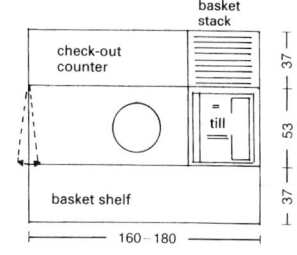

⑬ Plan of a check-out position giving minimum dimensions

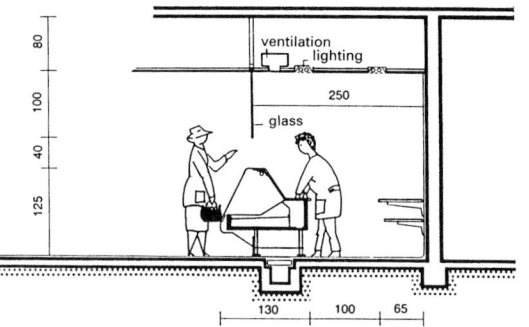

⑭ Section through counter in a self-service shop

The walls, floors, counter tops and work surfaces in fishmongers, game and poultry shops and butchers must be washable. Suitable materials therefore include marble, ceramic tiles, glass and plastics.

Fish perishes quickly and so must be kept chilled. It also smells strongly so fishmongers' shops should be surrounded by air-locks or air-curtains. Note that smoked fish, unlike fresh fish, must be stored in dry conditions and provision must be made for this. The possibility of large bulk deliveries should be taken into consideration. There may also be a need for an aquarium to attract the eye. → ① + ②

Game and poultry shops are sometimes part of fish shops and often stock only one day's supply of goods. They require a separate work room with facilities for plucking and scraping. As poultry absorbs smells, it must be stored separately both in the cold room and shop. Large refrigerated compartments and display cases are needed. → ③ + ④

Butchers' shops → ⑩ + ⑪ should preferably be on one level and have trucks on rails or castors to allow carcasses (which can weigh up to 200 kg) to be moved easily. Work rooms and cold rooms should be one and a half to two times the size of the shop.

All fittings in cold stores must be adequately protected against corrosion, due to the high humidity level in these spaces.

The conflict in fishmongers' and butchers' shops between balancing the requirements of temperature for staff comfort (around 16°C) and the display of provisions (–2°C to 0°C), can be dealt with by using directional fan heaters, which blow warm air towards staff and away from food, radiant heaters placed high on the walls or under-floor heating.

In addition, adequate ventilation is required for the removal of smells.

Fruit and vegetables need to be kept cool but not refrigerated. Potatoes should be kept in dark rooms. Sales are mostly from delivery containers (baskets, crates, boxes etc.) and dirt traps and refuse collectors should provided below storage racks. → ⑦ + ⑧

In general, the planning and design of greengrocers' shops should consider the requirements for delivery and unpacking of goods, washing, preparing, weighing, wrapping, waste collection and disposal. Flower shops can be combined with fruit and vegetable shops.

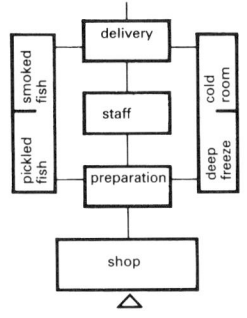

① **Functional diagram for fishmonger's**

② **Fish counter with cooling compartment and drain**

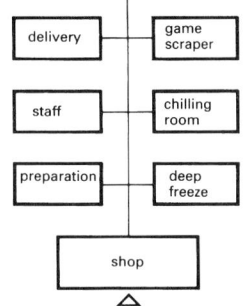

③ **Functional diagram for poultry and game shop**

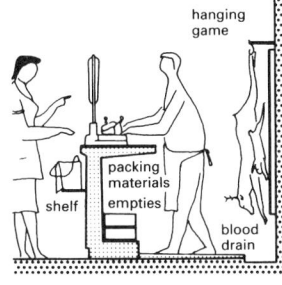

④ **Solid counter with marble or tile facing**

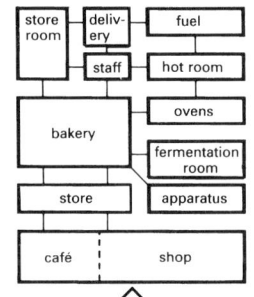

⑤ **Functional diagram for a bakery: good ventilation needed, possibly dehumidify**

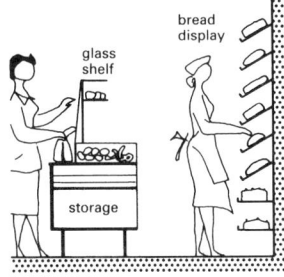

⑥ **Sales counter with screen**

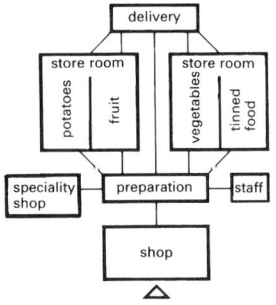

⑦ **Functional diagram for fruit and vegetable shop: little storage provision as most goods delivered daily**

⑧ **Counter with stands for boxes and baskets, drip pan and dirt trap**

⑨ **Pavement sales from trolleys or shop-front displays**

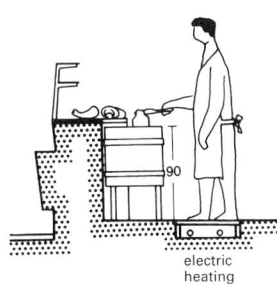

⑩ **Butcher's counter with chopping block**

⑪ **Normal butcher's counter (also for fishmonger's → ②)**

Food courts are large halls that house groups of small outlets selling a wide variety of specialist food products. Customers can either sit and eat on the premises or take the food away. With attractive displays and a market-style environment, food courts offer a pleasant shopping environment and can be added to supermarkets beyond the check-outs → ①.

The produce is predominantly fresh or cooked on the premises so storage space for one day's trade is adequate. Deliveries are usually made early in the morning.

A typical food court might include a bakery, a butcher, cafés and bars, a delicatessen snack bar, an ice-cream parlour plus shops and counters selling sea food, fruit, vegetables, flowers, beers and wines, pizza, wholefood, local specialities etc.

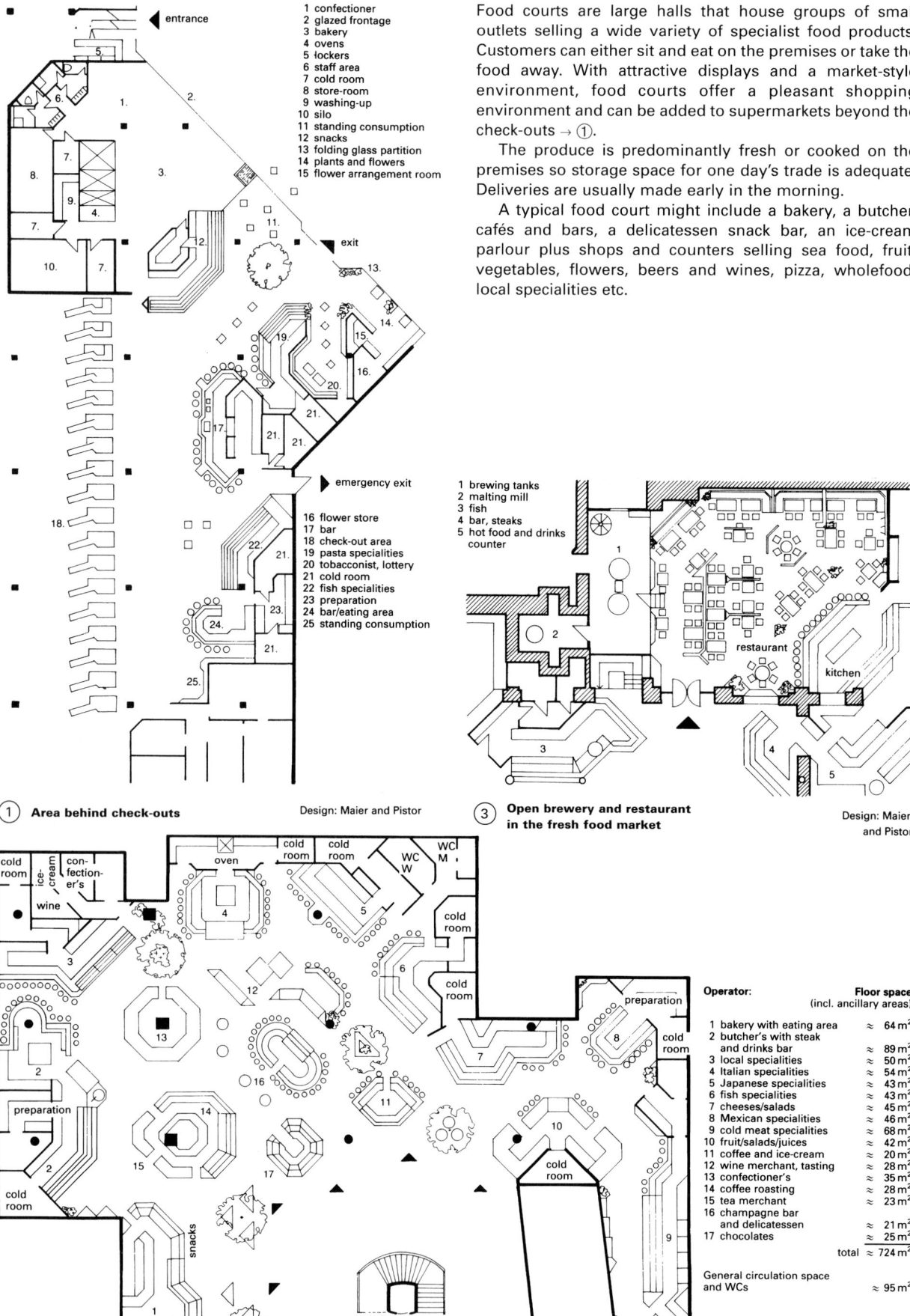

Key for ①:
1 confectioner
2 glazed frontage
3 bakery
4 ovens
5 lockers
6 staff area
7 cold room
8 store-room
9 washing-up
10 silo
11 standing consumption
12 snacks
13 folding glass partition
14 plants and flowers
15 flower arrangement room

16 flower store
17 bar
18 check-out area
19 pasta specialities
20 tobacconist, lottery
21 cold room
22 fish specialities
23 preparation
24 bar/eating area
25 standing consumption

① **Area behind check-outs** — Design: Maier and Pistor

Key for ③:
1 brewing tanks
2 malting mill
3 fish
4 bar, steaks
5 hot food and drinks counter

③ **Open brewery and restaurant in the fresh food market** — Design: Maier and Pistor

② **Fresh food market at Hamburg Central Station**

Operator:	Floor space (incl. ancillary areas)
1 bakery with eating area	≈ 64 m²
2 butcher's with steak and drinks bar	≈ 89 m²
3 local specialities	≈ 50 m²
4 Italian specialities	≈ 54 m²
5 Japanese specialities	≈ 43 m²
6 fish specialities	≈ 43 m²
7 cheeses/salads	≈ 45 m²
8 Mexican specialities	≈ 46 m²
9 cold meat specialities	≈ 68 m²
10 fruit/salads/juices	≈ 42 m²
11 coffee and ice-cream	≈ 20 m²
12 wine merchant, tasting	≈ 28 m²
13 confectioner's	≈ 35 m²
14 coffee roasting	≈ 28 m²
15 tea merchant	≈ 23 m²
16 champagne bar and delicatessen	≈ 21 m²
17 chocolates	≈ 25 m²
total	≈ 724 m²
General circulation space and WCs	≈ 95 m²

Design: Maier and Pistor

DEPARTMENT STORES AND SUPERMARKETS

When designing retail outlets all national regulations (building and planning, fire, health and safety at work etc.) should be observed.

Basic dimensional guidelines give the minimum heights of spaces in shops and storage facilities as:

up to 400 m² retail floor space	3.00 m
over 400 m² retail floor space	3.30 m
over 1500 m² retail floor space	3.50 m

Ventilation ducts or other structures should not reduce the required clear room heights. If possible rooms up to 25 metres wide should be free of columns. The load-bearing capacity of floors should be designed to take additional loads such as light fittings, suspended ceilings, decoration, ducts, sprinkler systems etc. (approximately 20 kp/m²). In the shopping areas and store-rooms it should be 750–1000 kp/m², and 2000 kp/m² for ramps. The floors connecting sales areas, stores, and delivery ramps should be at the same level. Note that delivery ramps or platforms are 1.10–1.20 m above ground level.

Shelf arrangements are developed from considerations of how best to lead customers past all the different ranges of goods. → ① + ②

① Dimensions of counters and shelf units (grid 10 × 10 m)

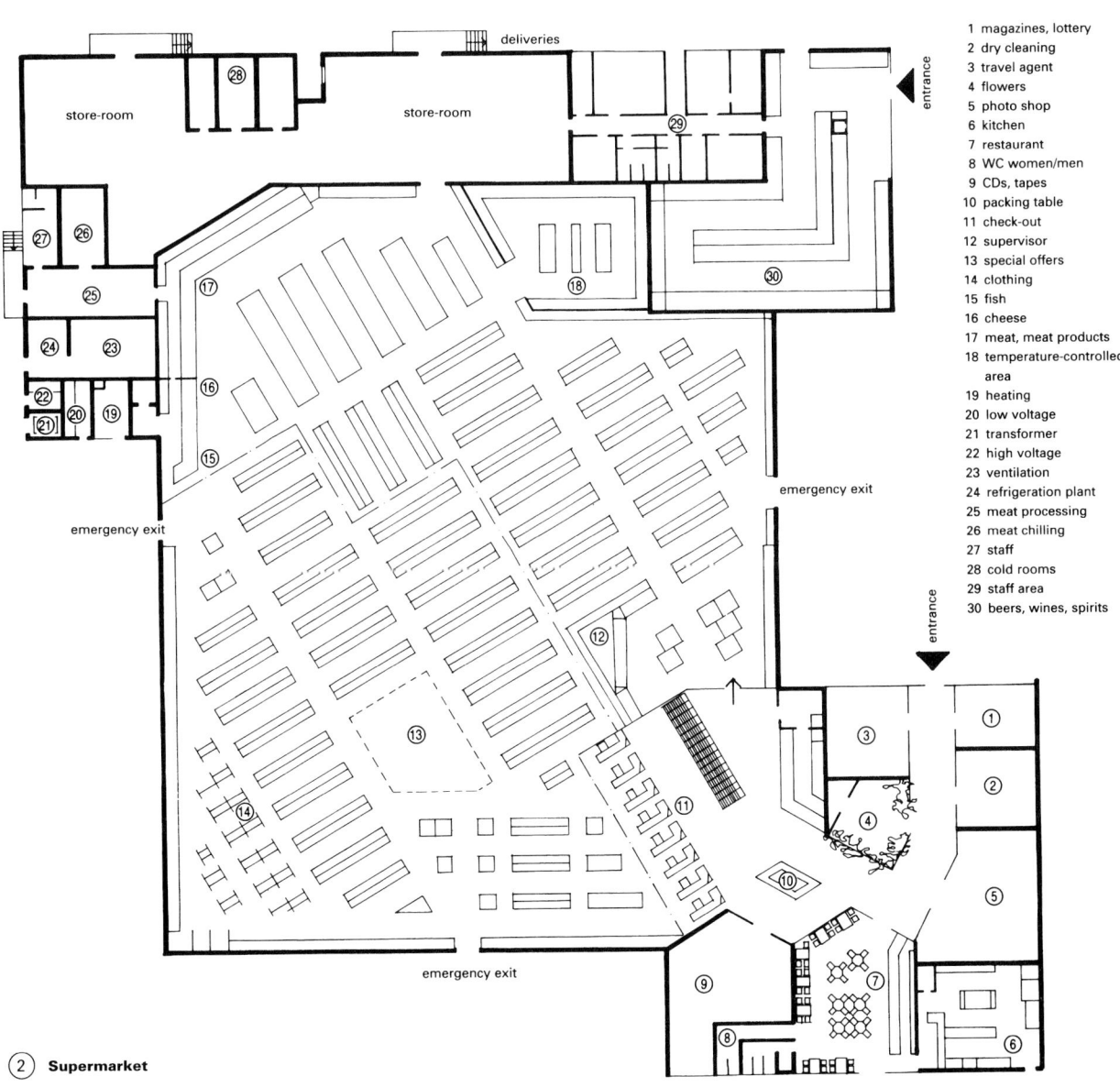

1 magazines, lottery
2 dry cleaning
3 travel agent
4 flowers
5 photo shop
6 kitchen
7 restaurant
8 WC women/men
9 CDs, tapes
10 packing table
11 check-out
12 supervisor
13 special offers
14 clothing
15 fish
16 cheese
17 meat, meat products
18 temperature-controlled area
19 heating
20 low voltage
21 transformer
22 high voltage
23 ventilation
24 refrigeration plant
25 meat processing
26 meat chilling
27 staff
28 cold rooms
29 staff area
30 beers, wines, spirits

② Supermarket

DEPARTMENT STORES AND SUPERMARKETS

The department store is essentially a very large shop, generally on several floors, selling a wide variety of goods, including clothes, household goods and food. Their design should provide maximum flexibility to permit frequent adjustments required for the seasonal sales patterns. The food department is the only one purpose designed. A main structural grid between 5.4 and 6m is commonly used, with 5.4m being considered optimum.

The increasing requirement for car-parking space has led to the growth of purpose-built out-of-town shopping centres. These in turn have encouraged the development of huge DIY warehouses, discount markets and 'hypermarkets', which are modelled along supermarket lines.

The largest hypermarkets are about 250000 m². Shoppers generally purchase a greater quantity of goods in hypermarkets than in supermarkets and therefore larger size trolleys are used. This needs to be considered in the design. The 'superstore' is a further development of the hypermarket.

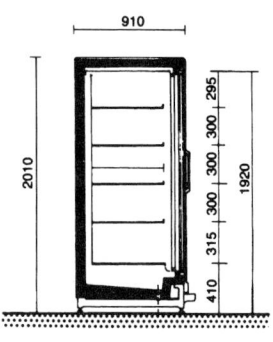

(1) **Chest freezer, shelves above** (2) **Chest freezer, without shelves**

(3) **Combined chest/upright freezer** (4) **Refrigerator**

Requirements	up to 399 m²	400 – 499 m²	500 – 599 m²	600 – 799 m²	800 – 899 m²	1000 – 1499 m²
1. Staffing levels in terms of full-time staff	10.6 7 – 14	12.9 10 – 16	15.3 12 – 18	17.7 16 – 20	22.1 18 – 25	30.2 25 – 33
2. Raw and processed meat section a) proportion of turnover (%) b) length of counter (m) c) preparation room (m³) d) chilling room (m³)	22 19 – 28 6.50 6.0 – 7.0 14 8 – 20 11 7 – 15	21 20 – 32 7.60 7.0 – 8.2 19 13 – 25 13.5 9 – 18	20 20 – 28 8.75 7.5 – 9.0 24 18 – 30 15 10 – 20	19 17 – 25 9.08 1.5 – 10.5 26 20 – 32 15 10 – 20	18 16 – 24 9.75 9.0 – 10.5 30 23 – 38 22 14 – 30	17 14.5 – 24 11.75 10.0 – 13.5 36 23 – 50 25 16 – 35
3. Dairy products and fats a) refrigerated shelves (m) b) cold room (m²)	6.75 6.3 – 7.3 6.0 4.0 – 8.0	8.0 6.5 – 9.5 7.6 5.0 – 10.5	8.75 7.5 – 11 10.0 8.0 – 12.0	10.25 9 – 12 12.0 8.0 – 15.5	11.25 10 – 13.5 13.0 8.0 – 18.0	15.7 12 – 18.5 15.0 10.0 – 20.0
4. Frozen foods (not ice-cream) a) normal island unit (m) b) extra-wide island unit (m) c) shelf units (m) d) deep freeze room (m²)	5.5 5.0 – 6.0 3.85 2.6 – 4.6 2.4 2.3 – 2.5 2.4 2.0 – 2.8	6.1 5.5 – 7.0 4.1 3.0 – 5.0 2.75 2.3 – 3.2 3.25 2.0 – 4.5	7.5 6.5 – 8.5 5.5 4.0 – 7.0 3.6 3.2 – 4.0 5.0 4.0 – 6.0	8.75 7.5 – 10.0 6.75 4.0 – 7.5 4.4 4.0 – 4.8 5.75 4.0 – 7.5	10.1 7.5 – 12.0 7.75 5.5 – 10.0 5.8 5.0 – 6.5 8.25 6.0 – 10.5	13.5 12.0 – 15.0 8.75 6.0 – 10.0 6.6 5.5 – 8.0 8.5 6.0 – 11.0
5. Wall unit for fruit and vegetables (with two shelves) (m)	6.5 5.0 – 8.0	7.5 6.5 – 8.5	7.5 7.0 – 8.0	8.75 7.0 – 10.5	10.0 8.0 – 12.0	10.75 9.0 – 12.5
6. Number of cash desks – at the check-out – in the sections	2.5 2 – 3 0.2 0 – 1	2.9 2 – 3 0.3 0 – 1	3.4 3 – 4 0.4 0 – 1	3.9 3 – 4 0.5 0 – 1	4.9 4 – 5 1.3 1 – 2	6.3 6 – 7 1.3 1 – 2
7. Number of shopping trolleys needed	85 70 – 100	105 85 – 130	120 100 – 160	150 100 – 200	180 150 – 220	240 200 – 300

(5) **Planning data for fitting shops and supermarkets**

NB: first row = average values
second row = range of variation

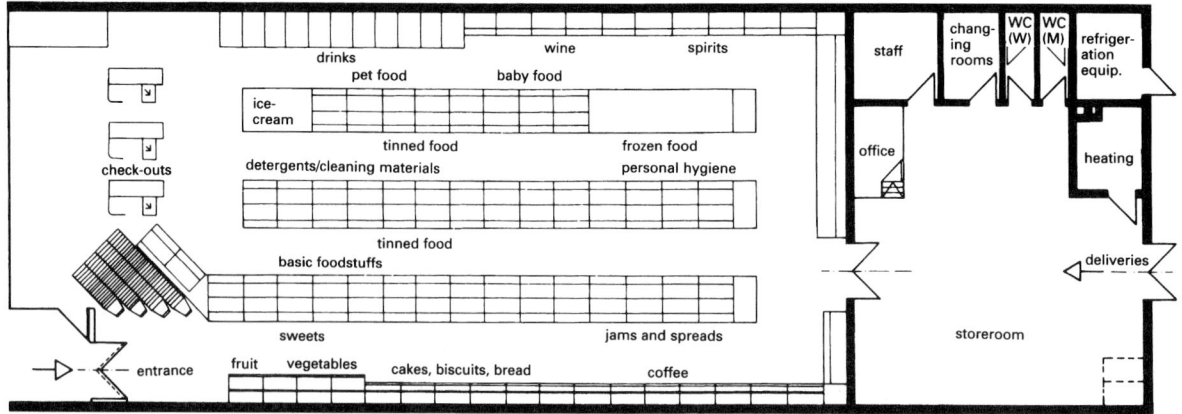

(6) **Discount market, 300–500 m² sales area**

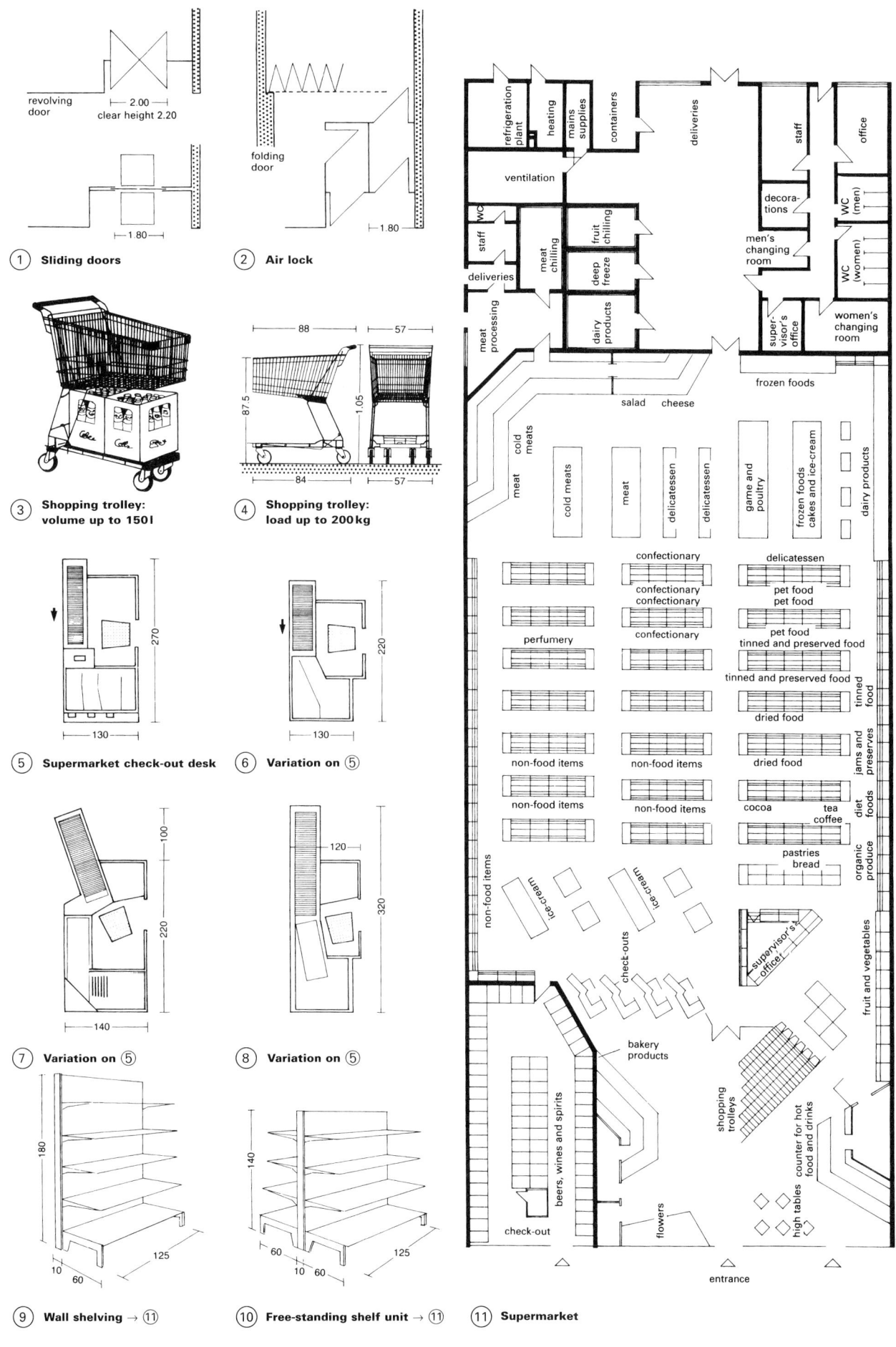

① **Sliding doors**

② **Air lock**

③ **Shopping trolley: volume up to 150 l**

④ **Shopping trolley: load up to 200 kg**

⑤ **Supermarket check-out desk**

⑥ **Variation on ⑤**

⑦ **Variation on ⑤**

⑧ **Variation on ⑤**

⑨ **Wall shelving → ⑪**

⑩ **Free-standing shelf unit → ⑪**

⑪ **Supermarket**

SUPERMARKETS/HYPERMARKETS

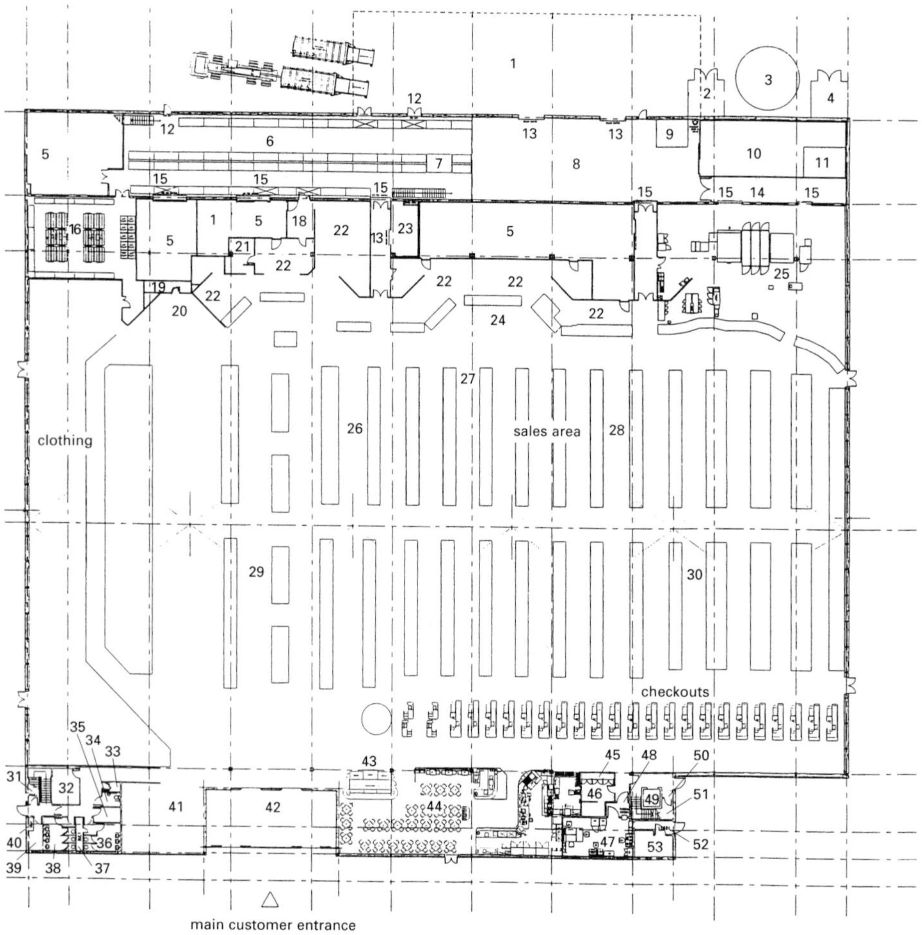

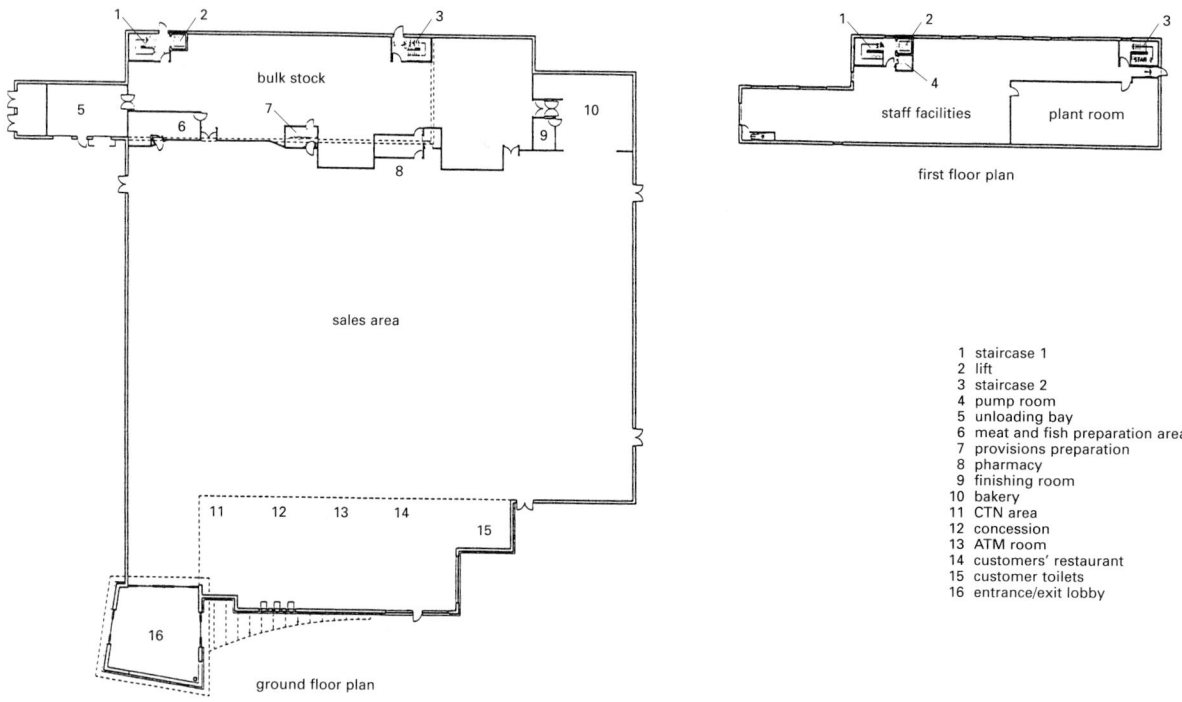

1 service area
2 space allocation
    sprinkler pump room
3 space allocation sprinkler tank
4 high-voltage switchroom in wire
    cage or disclosure 4 m × 4 m
5 cold room
6 warehouse area
7 goods hoist
8 marshalling area
9 fork-lift recharge
10 frozen food store
11 bakery store
12 fire exit
13 roller shutter
14 bakery rack store
15 two-hour fire shutter
16 bulk store
17 sprinkler riser and valve
18 raw wash-up
19 store room
20 entertainments
21 cooked wash-up
22 preparation
23 cleaners
24 fresh food pizza
25 bakery
26 refrigerated
27 groceries
28 home and leisure
29 produce
30 drinks
31 panel
32 baby change
33 cleaners
34 disabled toilet
35 first aid
36 male toilets
37 duct
38 female toilets
39 switchroom
40 riser
41 concession
42 main lobby
43 kiosk
44 customer restaurant
45 electrical switches
46 office
47 cash office
48 window
49 lift shaft
50 disabled refuge
51 lift motor
52 lobby
53 ATMs

(1) **Floor plan of an Asda supermarket/hypermarket in the UK
(courtesy of Asda/WCEC Architects)**

1 staircase 1
2 lift
3 staircase 2
4 pump room
5 unloading bay
6 meat and fish preparation area
7 provisions preparation
8 pharmacy
9 finishing room
10 bakery
11 CTN area
12 concession
13 ATM room
14 customers' restaurant
15 customer toilets
16 entrance/exit lobby

(2) **Floor plan of a Sainsbury's supermarket in the UK (courtesy of Pick Everard)**

374

WORKSHOPS: WOODWORKING

Generally the change in plan form from long sheds to more compact developments → ② – ③ improves economy: the site is more efficiently used; routes are shorter in mixed production; service ducts are shorter. Multistorey buildings are not appropriate for production areas but are recommended for offices, ancillary rooms and store rooms for small and/or valuable articles. Predominant building types have steel frames with reinforced concrete and metal or timber cladding. Walls and roofs of large manufacturing units should have good heat and sound insulation. Windows of insulating glass are mostly fixed; natural lighting from above is possible; a smaller proportion of window area as required by regulations should serve for ventilation and view.

Space requirements (for examples shown): an average of 70–80 m² per employee (without open storerooms).

An extractor system is required in virtually all cases to remove wood chippings, sawdust and wheel dust, both for the sake of regulations on health and safety at work and on economic grounds. The arrangement of machines is determined according to the sequences of operations. Rubber bonding to metal mountings can reduce high levels of machine noise.

In small companies with up to ten employees, general production flow can be in a line or L-shaped. In medium-sized companies with more than ten employees, a U-shaped or circular (or square) arrangement gives a better flow. In the latter case functions are combined: gate, load and unload, ramp, supervision, checking, goods in, dispatch.

Work sequence: timber store, cutting area, drying room, machine room, bench workshop, surface treatment, store, packing. Machine room and bench workshop is divided by a wall with doors → ③. Office and foreman's room are glazed, with view of workshop. Workshop floor: wood, wood-block or composition flooring. All workstations should face the light. Continuous strip windows, high sills (1.00–1.35 m).

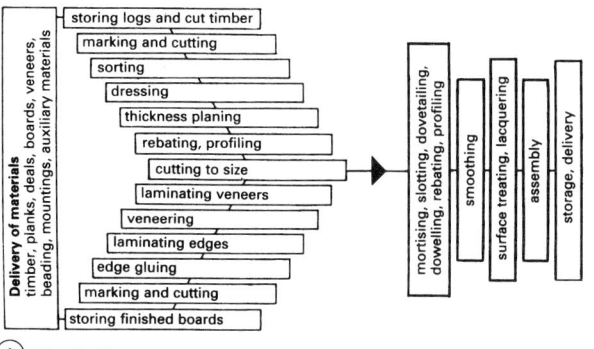

① Production sequence

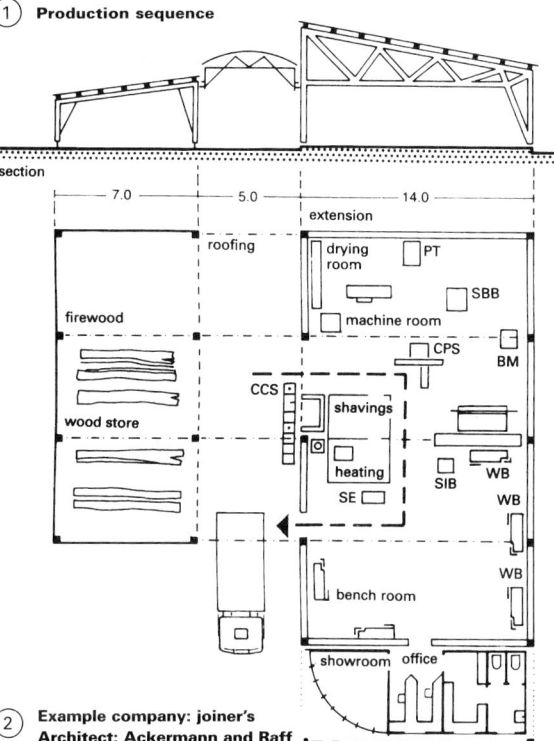

② Example company: joiner's
Architect: Ackermann and Raff

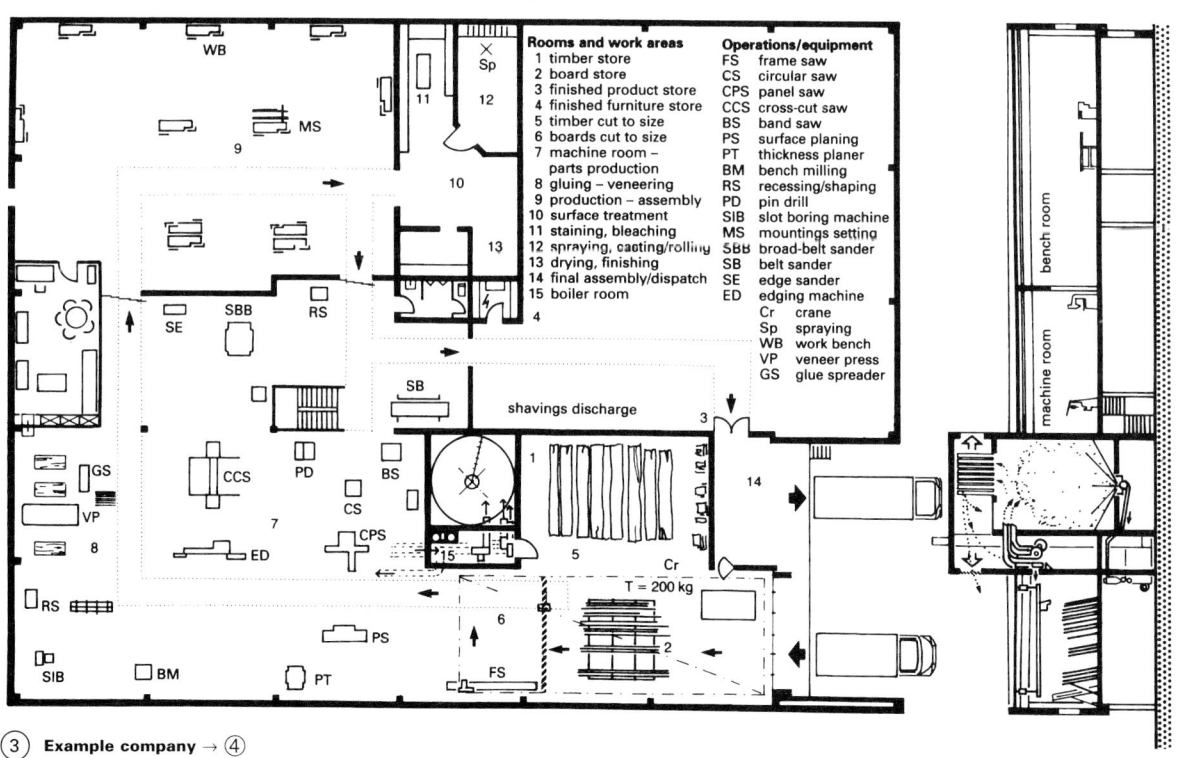

Rooms and work areas	Operations/equipment	
1 timber store	FS	frame saw
2 board store	CS	circular saw
3 finished product store	CPS	panel saw
4 finished furniture store	CCS	cross-cut saw
5 timber cut to size	BS	band saw
6 boards cut to size	PS	surface planing
7 machine room –	PT	thickness planer
parts production	BM	bench milling
8 gluing – veneering	RS	recessing/shaping
9 production – assembly	PD	pin drill
10 surface treatment	SIB	slot boring machine
11 staining, bleaching	MS	mountings setting
12 spraying, casting/rolling	SBB	broad-belt sander
13 drying, finishing	SB	belt sander
14 final assembly/dispatch	SE	edge sander
15 boiler room	ED	edging machine
	Cr	crane
	Sp	spraying
	WB	work bench
	VP	veneer press
	GS	glue spreader

③ Example company → ④

④ Section → ③

375

WORKSHOPS: WOODWORKING

In the workshop, there should be enough space to give each worker not only sufficient bench room, but also the required space to assemble the work. A large number of joiners' shops are mechanised; larger ones have separate assembly and machine shops, but in smaller shops machines may be grouped at one end of the work area.

Rooms and areas

Stores: for rough timber, boards, veneers, glass, plastics, auxiliary materials and fittings; temporary stores; stores for finished and partially finished products.

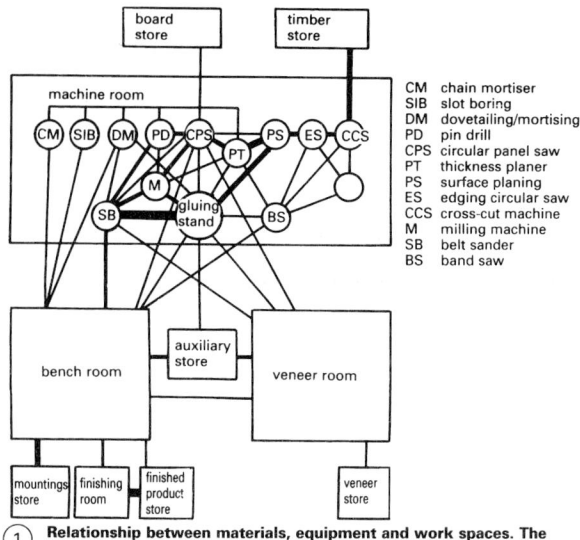

CM	chain mortiser
SIB	slot boring
DM	dovetailing/mortising
PD	pin drill
CPS	circular panel saw
PT	thickness planer
PS	surface planing
ES	edging circular saw
CCS	cross-cut machine
M	milling machine
SB	belt sander
BS	band saw

1 Relationship between materials, equipment and work spaces. The thickness of the lines is an indication of the level of in-house circulation

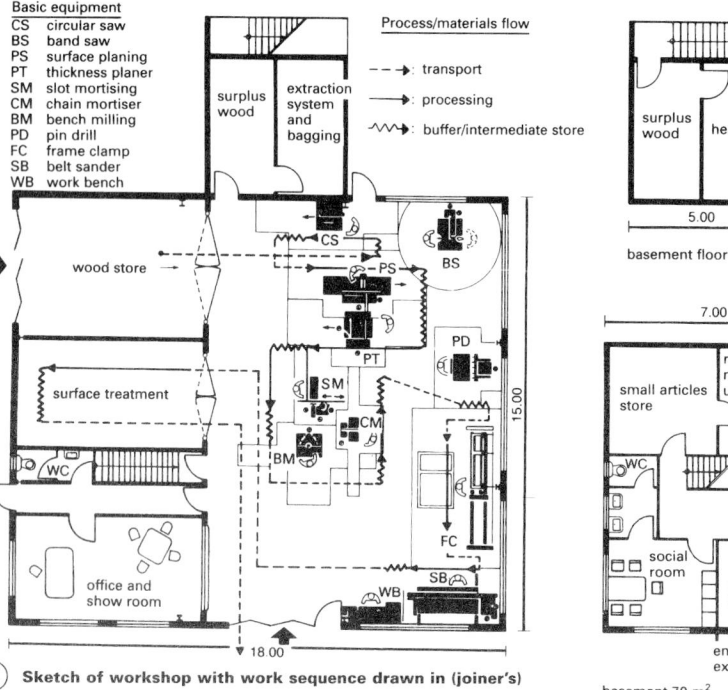

Basic equipment
CS circular saw
BS band saw
PS surface planing
PT thickness planer
SM slot mortising
CM chain mortiser
BM bench milling
PD pin drill
FC frame clamp
SB belt sander
WB work bench

Process/materials flow
- - → : transport
─→ : processing
〜〜→ : buffer/intermediate store

2 Sketch of workshop with work sequence drawn in (joiner's)

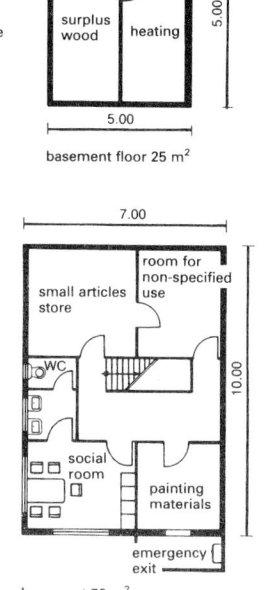

basement floor 25 m²

basement 70 m²

Workshops:
For drying wood, and cutting timber, boards and veneers. Machine shops for parts, processing timber, boards, gluing and veneering, production and assembly, bench work, bonding, surface treatment, final assembly and dispatch. Metal working facilities are often also required.

Administration and management: works office (foreman), technical offices, commercial offices, management and secretarial offices, meeting room, sales room.

Social and ancillary rooms should have wood-block or composition flooring, (not concrete).

Storage areas should be dust free (fine dust blunts tools).

Machines should be set up to match sequence of work. All workstations should face the light. Window area should be approximately 1/8 of floor space.

Basic equipment
CPS panel circular saw
PC combination planer
BM bench milling
BS band saw
SB belt sanding
GF gluing stands
WB work bench

Process/materials flow
- - → : transport
─→ : processing
〜〜→ : buffer/intermediate store

3 Sketch of workshop with work sequence drawn in (interior fitters)

first floor 84 m²

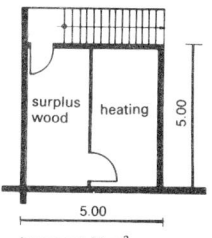

basement 25 m²

Operating design (planning): determine all factors relevant to the operational needs of the business. Machines: utilisation, costs and economic feasibility, power requirement, load-bearing capacity of floors, space requirement, costs. Production processes: production times, staffing levels, organisation of technical operations. Materials: types, quantities, weights, space requirement, storeroom dimensions. Energy supply: heat, electricity, compressed air. Waste materials: type, space requirement, waste management. Sequence of operations and tasks. Plan of operational utilisation of space (layout).

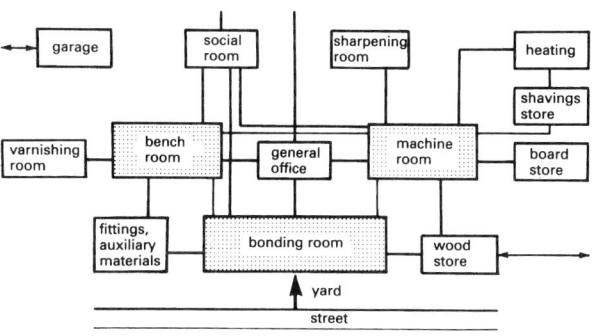

① **Functional diagram for carpentry and joinery business**

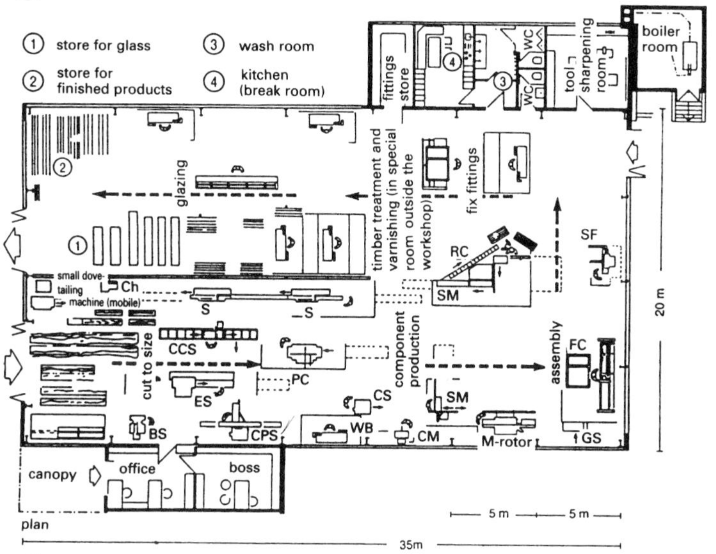

① store for glass ③ wash room
② store for finished products ④ kitchen (break room)

Tools and machines
CCS cross-cut saw
CS circular saw
ES edging circular saw
CPS panel circular saw
BS band saw
PC combination planing machine
PF fine planing machine
S shaping machine
M milling machine
CM chain mortiser
SM slot mortising machine
SF frame sanding machine
RC roller conveyor
GS glue-spreading machine
WB work bench
FC frame clamp
Ch chopper

shavings tower h = 15 m

② **Example of a carpenter and glazier's business → ③**

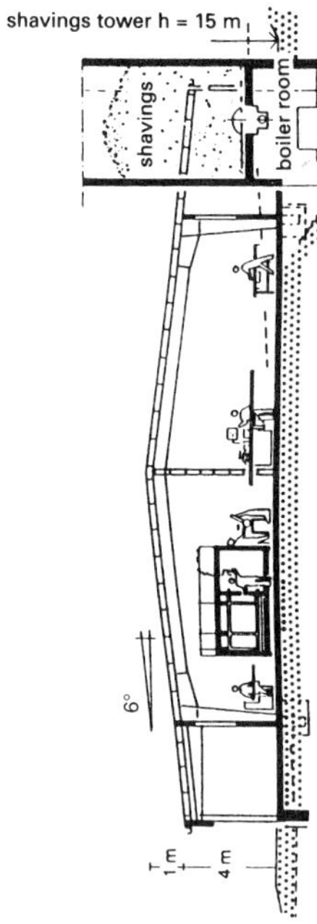

③ Cross-section → ②

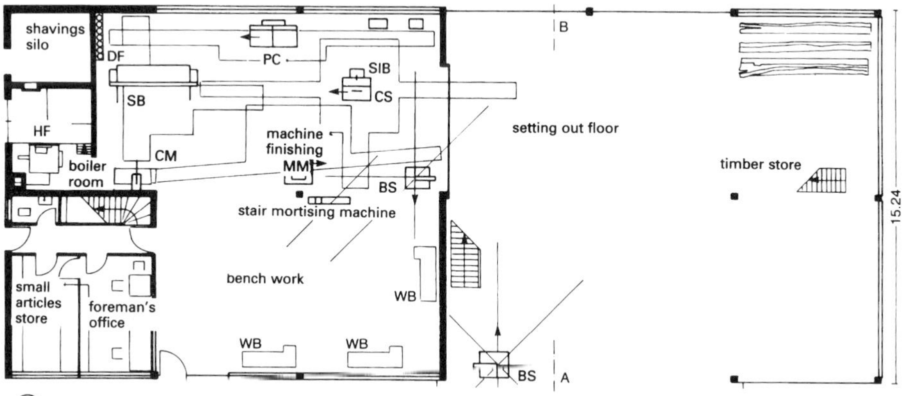

BS band saw
CS circular saw
SIB slot boring machine
PC combination surface planing machine
MM mortising machine
CM chain mortiser
SB belt sanding machine
WB work bench
HF combined heating furnace for oil and c
DF dust filter

④ **Example of a joiner's business – ground floor → ⑤ – ⑥**

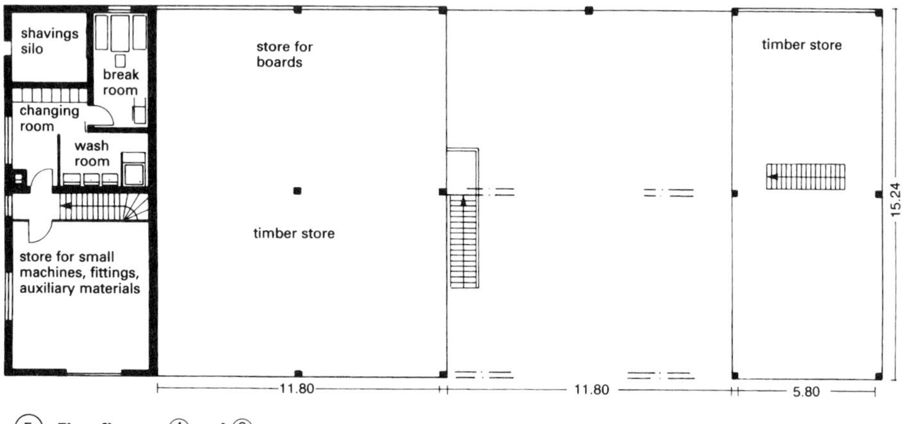

⑤ **First floor → ④ and ⑥**

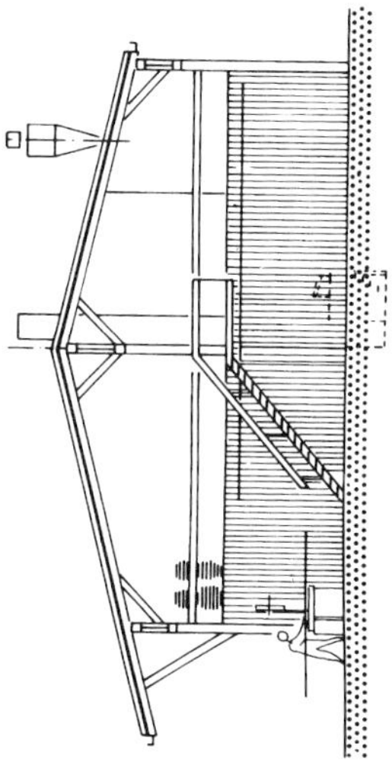

⑥ Section A–B → ④ – ⑤

WORKSHOPS: WOODWORKING

Recent advances in automation technology in production, storage and distribution will need to be taken into account, particularly for larger businesses.

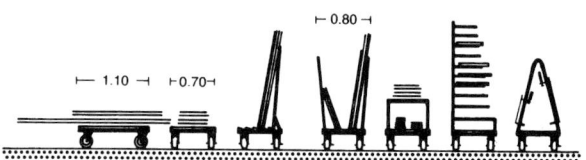

① **Types and dimensions of trolleys used for manual handling in a workshop environment**

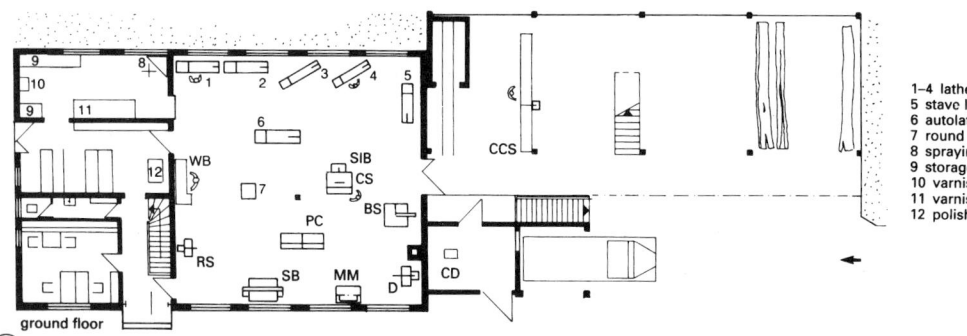

1–4 lathes
5 stave lathe
6 autolathe
7 round bar machine
8 spraying stand
9 storage bench
10 varnish dipping apparatus
11 varnish drying cupboard
12 polishing drum

ground floor

② **Example of a wood turner's shop**

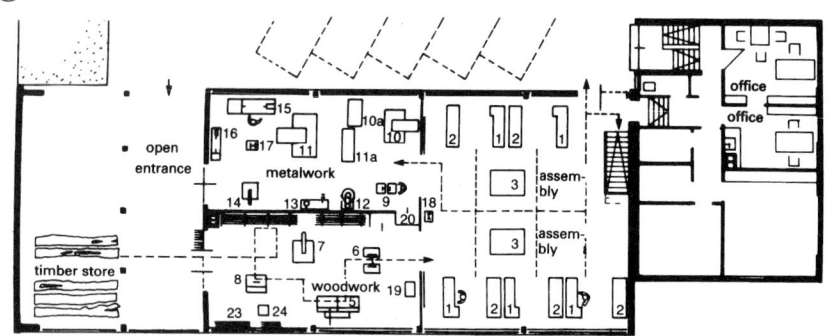

Assembly – bench room
1 carpenter's bench
2 tool bench
3 dressing plate
Woodwork
5 combined dressing and planing machine
6 disc sander
7 band saw
8 circular saw
Metalwork
9 disc grinder
10 milling machine 1 with tool bench
11 milling machine 2 with tool bench
12 post drill

13 work bench with vice and bench drill
14 band saw
15 lathe 1 (large)
16 lathe 2 (small)
17 grinding stand 1
18 grinding stand 2
19 tool sharpening machine
20/21 cupboards for auxiliary materials and tools
22 shelving for drying timber
23 board store
24 opening in the floor for ejecting wood waste

③ **Example of a model-maker's workshop (five employees)**

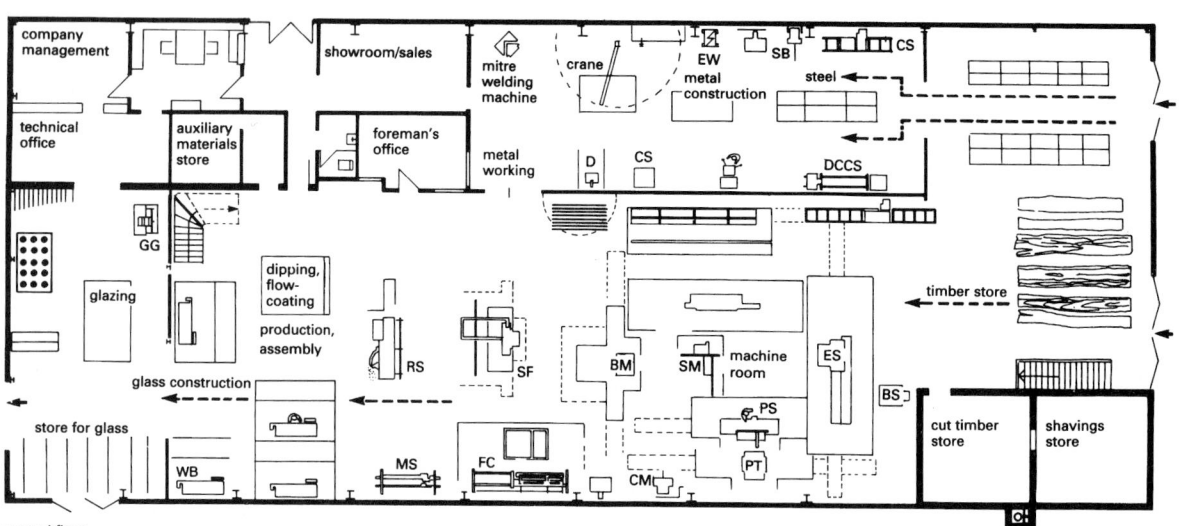

ground floor

④ **Example of a glazier's business**

CCS	cross-cut saw	BM	bench milling machine	RS	recessing/shaping machine
SIB	slot boring machine	CM	chain mortiser	WB	work bench
ES	edging circular saw	D	drill	MM	mortising machine
DCCS	double cross-cut saw	MS	mountings setting machine	EW	electric welder
BS	band saw	PD	post drill	SF	frame sanding machine
PS	surface planing machine	SM	slot mortising machine	FC	frame clamp
PT	thickness planer	CD	combination drill	SB	belt sander
GG	glass grinding machine	CS	circular saw		

378

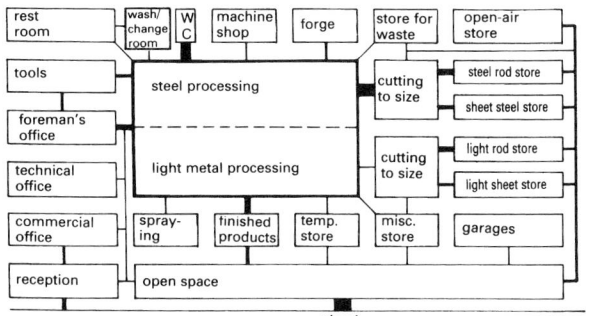

(1) **Space relationship diagram for a large metalworking company**

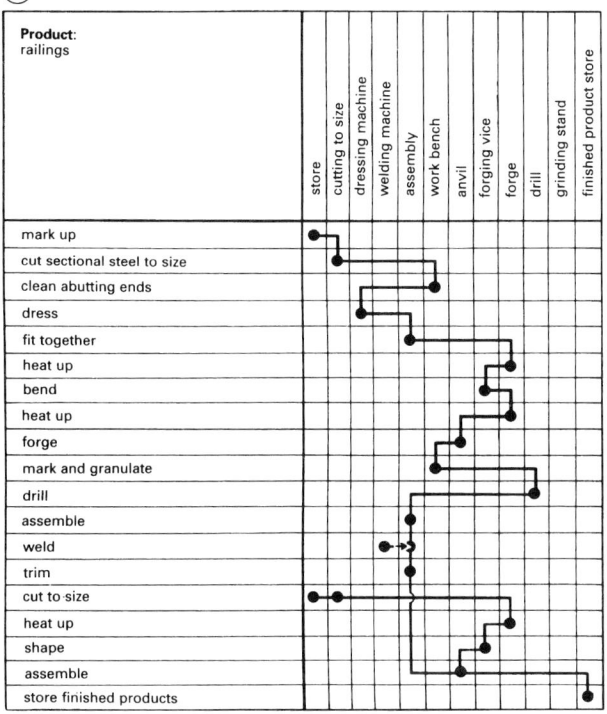

(2) **Production flowchart** → (3)

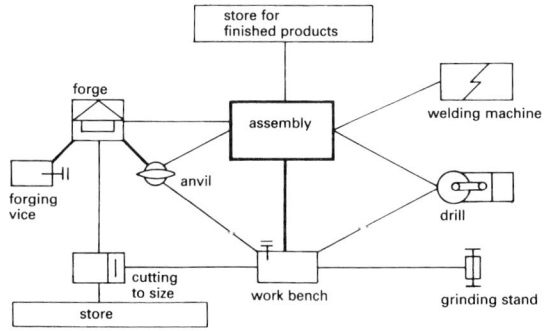

(3) **Example of sequence of work in an architectural ironmonger's shop** → (2)

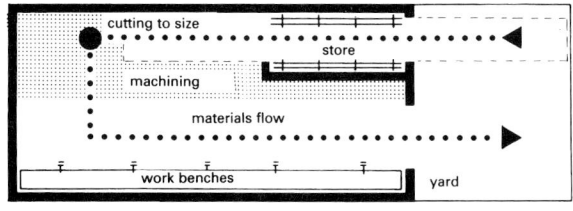

(4) **Relationship between rod store and material flow**

Capacity of storage systems: examples

Shelving with brackets

width w = 1.0 m; height h = 2.0 m; length l = 6.0 m

Enclosed shelving space

$V = b \times h \times l = 1.0 \times 2.0 \times 6.0 = 12.0 \, m^3$

If the density of material, r, is $0.8 t/m^3$, the total weight stored would be

$R = V \times r = 12.0 \times 0.8 = 10t$ (rounded up)

If the number of employees working in production is 8, and each uses 7.5t per year, the annual materials requirement is

$B = 8 \times 7.5 = 60t$

The store turnover frequency is then given by

$B \div R = 60 \div 10 = 6$ times

However, there is always lost space (space taken up by shelving itself, handling space, non-optimal storage) so a rack can never be fully (100%) used.

Compartments filled with objects of the same shape (homogeneous storage) – approx. 40% space usage

Compartments filled with a mixture of objects (heterogeneous storage) – approx. 20% space usage

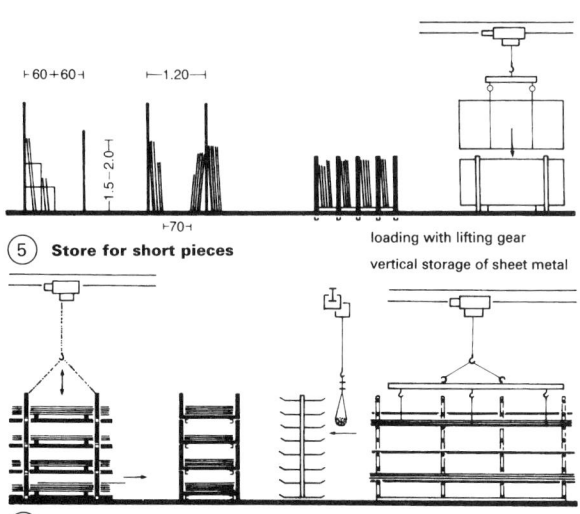

(5) **Store for short pieces**

loading with lifting gear

vertical storage of sheet metal

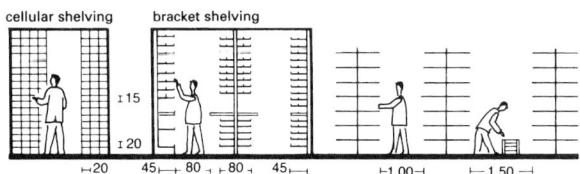

(6) **Horizontal storage and transport of sheet metal and rods**

(7) **Widths and lengths between shelving**

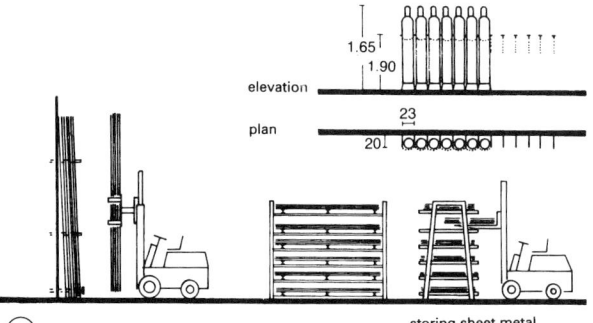

(8) **Upright storage of rods**

storing sheet metal on shelves

WORKSHOPS: METALWORKING

In larger metalworking businesses, the work areas are divided, as shown → ①.

Floor of concrete or, preferably, wood-block on concrete. Workshops are best lit from above and adequate lighting should be provided at each workstation. Individual control of machines is necessary (junction box in the floor).

Welding and forging shop Even in medium-sized work-shops, welding and forging areas should be sealed off by steel doors. Good ventilation should be provided. The welding bench surface should be made of firebricks. For cast iron and metal welding, charcoal pits are required for pre-warming, with small forge above that can also be used for soldering. Next to this, water and oil containers for quenching.

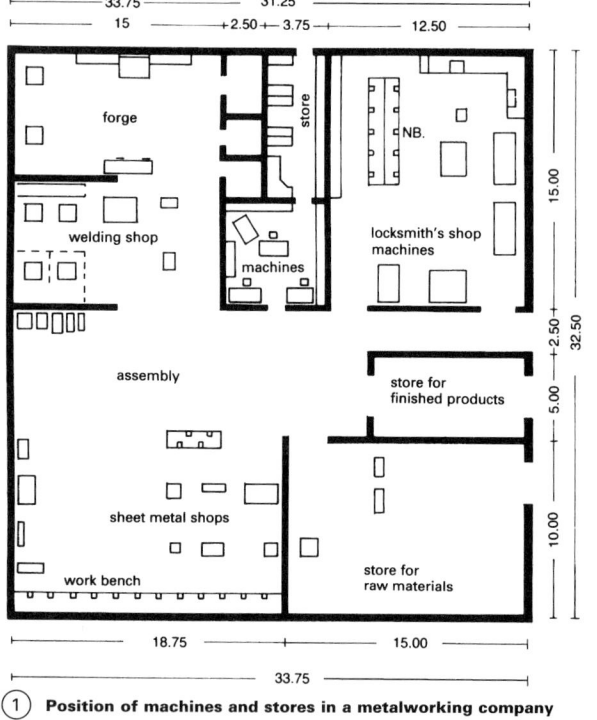

① **Position of machines and stores in a metalworking company**

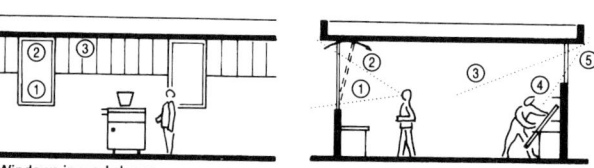

Windows in workshops:
① Workplace regulations (unrestricted view), low sill height
② Ventilation (high-level tilting windows)
③ Sufficient daylight into the middle of the shop (high windows)
④ Safety regulations (safe handling of glass sheets)
⑤ Sun can be shaded out on the southern side, e.g. using roof overhang

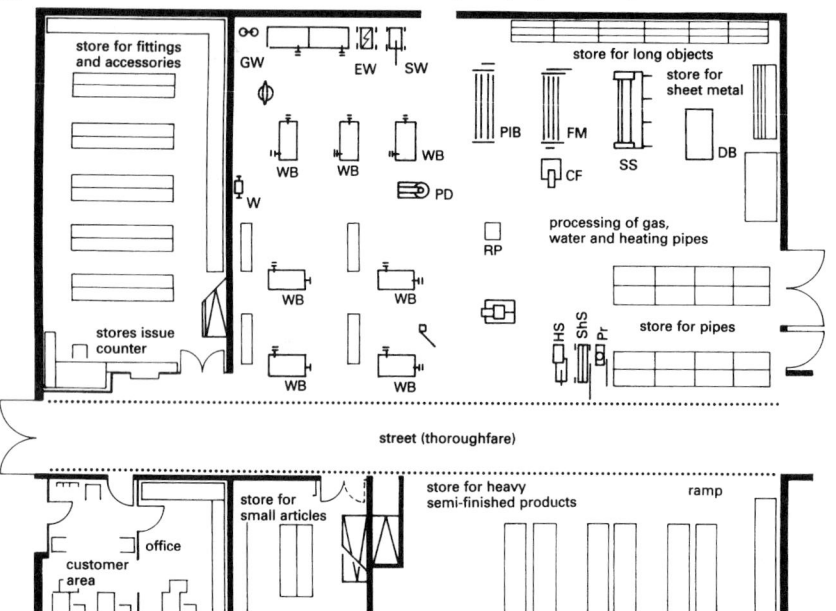

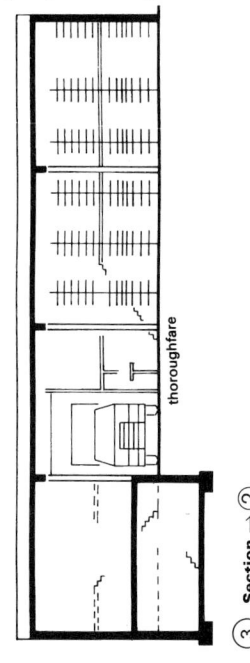

Tools and machines: FM folding machine; PD post drill; PIB plate-bending machine; DM dressing machine; DP dressing plate; HS hack-saw; XS bow-saw; SS sheet shears; ShS shaping shears; CF crimping and flanging machine; Pr press; W welding machines; GW gas welding machine; EW electrical welding machine; SW spot welding machine; DB drawing board; WB work bench

② **Sanitary and heating technology company**

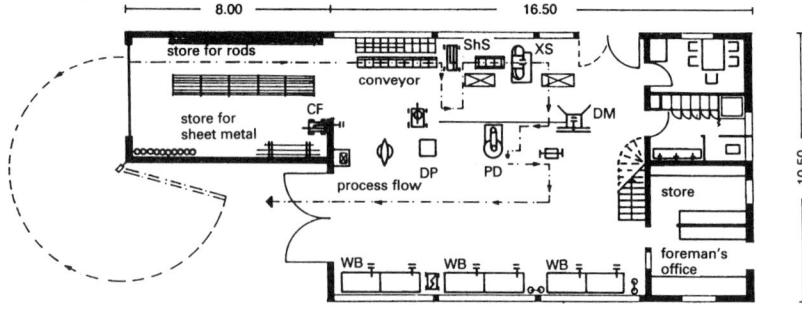

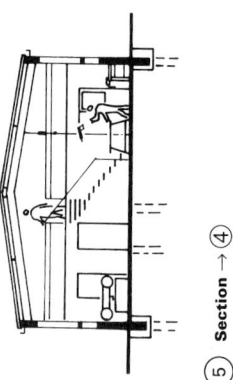

④ **Architectural ironmongery business and fine metal construction**

WORKSHOPS: SHOWROOMS AND VEHICLE REPAIRS

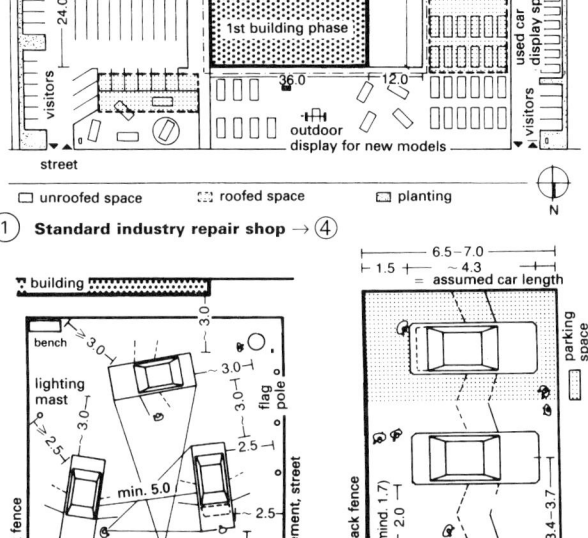

① Standard industry repair shop → ④

Site Ratio of built area to unbuilt area is approx. 1:3.5

Function/organisation Planning based on two versions of the 'three-point system' → ⑥

(1) works office, workshop, parts store
(2) service office, works office, parts store

Offices (depending on size of company): General manager's office 16–24 m², secretarial office 10–16 m², sales manager 16–20 m², after-sales service manager 12–15 m², stores manager 10–15 m², meeting room 12–24 m², accounts 12–20 m², sales personnel 9–12 m², computer room 9–16 m², works office 25–40 m². Storage space: 22–25 m² per workstation (in general repairs and body shop). Space per workstation: 4 × 7 m (general repairs, bodyshop, paint shop) for cars; 5 × 10 m for light commercial vehicles.

② Average space requirement for a car showroom

③ Average space requirement for a compact new car display

annual car sales	cars to be attended	size of site in m²	total built area in m²	space requirement per car sold	workshop area in m²	repair bays	inspection spaces	valeting bays	reception bays	car wash	polishing bays
50	150	2000	480	7.20	360	4	–	1	–	1	–
100	300	3000	835	6.25	625	7	1	1	–	1	–
200	600	4000	1420	5.70	1220	10	1	1	1	1	–
300	825	5000	2150	5.35	1610	16	3	1	1	2	–
400	1000	6000	2620	4.90	1960	19	4	2	1	2	1
500	1250	7000	2980	4.45	2230	23	5	2	2	2	2
750	1725	9000	4500	4.45	3375	32	6	3	2	X	–
1000	2000	10000	5770	4.30	4300	38	7	3	2	X	–

⑤ Repair shop space requirements

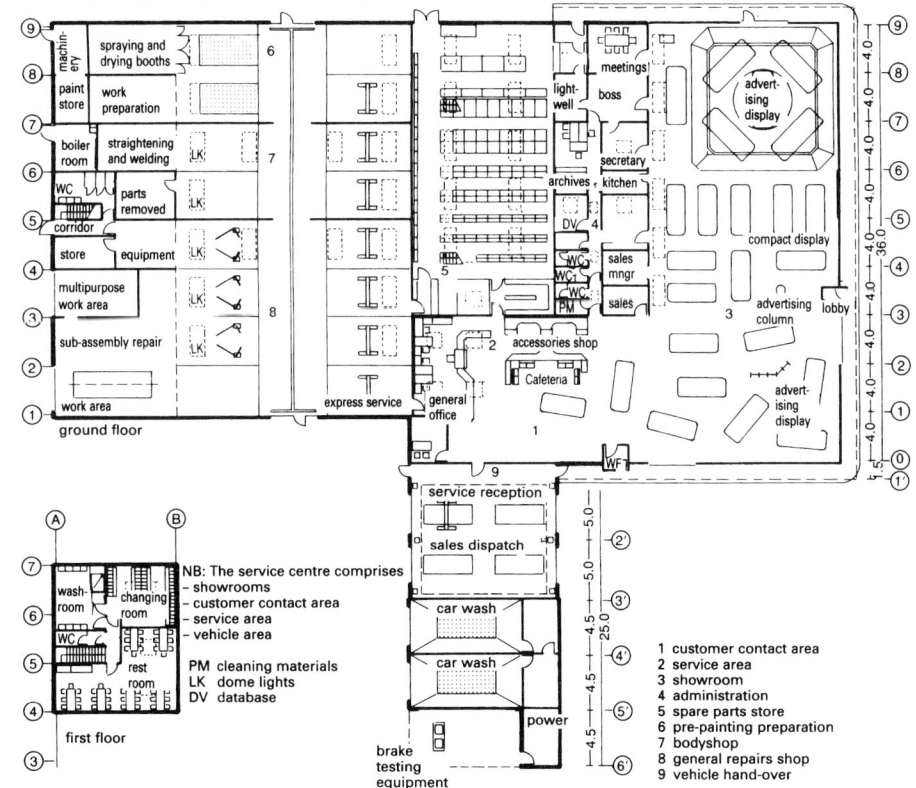

④ Example of a motor repair shop

NB: The service centre comprises
– showrooms
– customer contact area
– service area
– vehicle area

PM cleaning materials
LK dome lights
DV database

1 customer contact area
2 service area
3 showroom
4 administration
5 spare parts store
6 pre-painting preparation
7 bodyshop
8 general repairs shop
9 vehicle hand-over

Showroom: potential customers must be able to walk around the vehicle freely and to open the doors. Therefore, both the space per vehicle and the distance between them are important. To be able to see a vehicle properly the viewer ideally needs to be 5 m from it. → ② – ④

Guideline: for new cars, approximately 40–45 m² display area per car. Compact display, → ③: approximately 24 m² per car; distance between vehicles > 1.70 m.

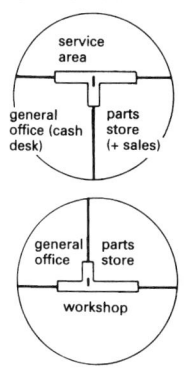

⑥ Interdepartmental relationships (three-point system)

VEHICLE REPAIR SHOPS

Usually single storey of light steel construction or prefabricated elements. Single-span shed without columns is preferable. Choose an appropriate module to allow extension.

Workshop floors should be sealed against grease and oil. Petrol and oil traps are essential. Provide extractor duct for exhaust fumes. Provide automatic doors with hot-air curtain → p. 185–6. Installation of ducts for electricity, compressed air, used oil and water is recommended. For companies with a service department choose a location with good transport links if possible, even if development and building costs are higher. If the site is on the edge of town provide appropriate advertising and transport for customers.

Basic rules: site built area $1/3$ to $2/3$ unbuilt area. Allow for possible extension. For larger companies the average area is $200\,m^2$ per workshop employee. Added to this are rooms for sales, works office, customers' waiting room, social rooms etc. Check mains services. For car washes high water consumption should be taken into account.

Large company workshop → ③ – ⑦ for lorries, towing vehicles, special vehicles, containers and trailers, cars, fork-lifts and electric vehicles.

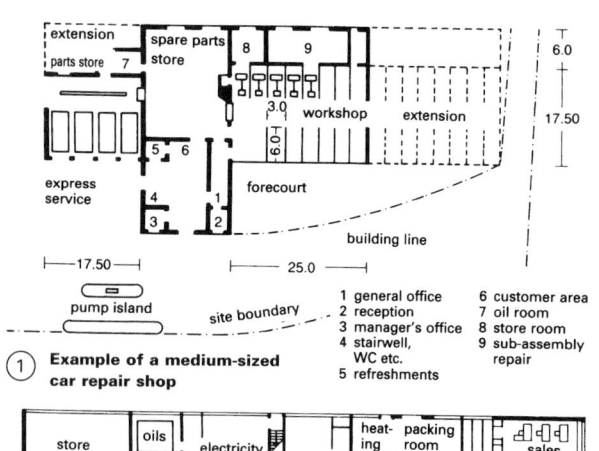

① **Example of a medium-sized car repair shop**

1 general office
2 reception
3 manager's office
4 stairwell, WC etc.
5 refreshments
6 customer area
7 oil room
8 store room
9 sub-assembly repair

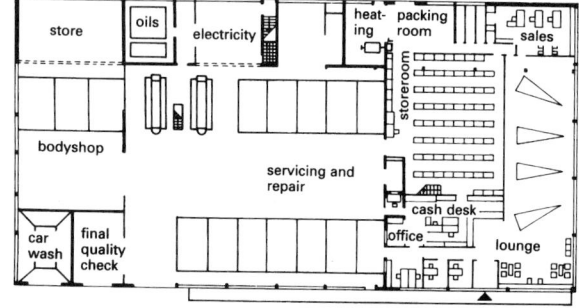

② **Car repair shop with administration and sales**

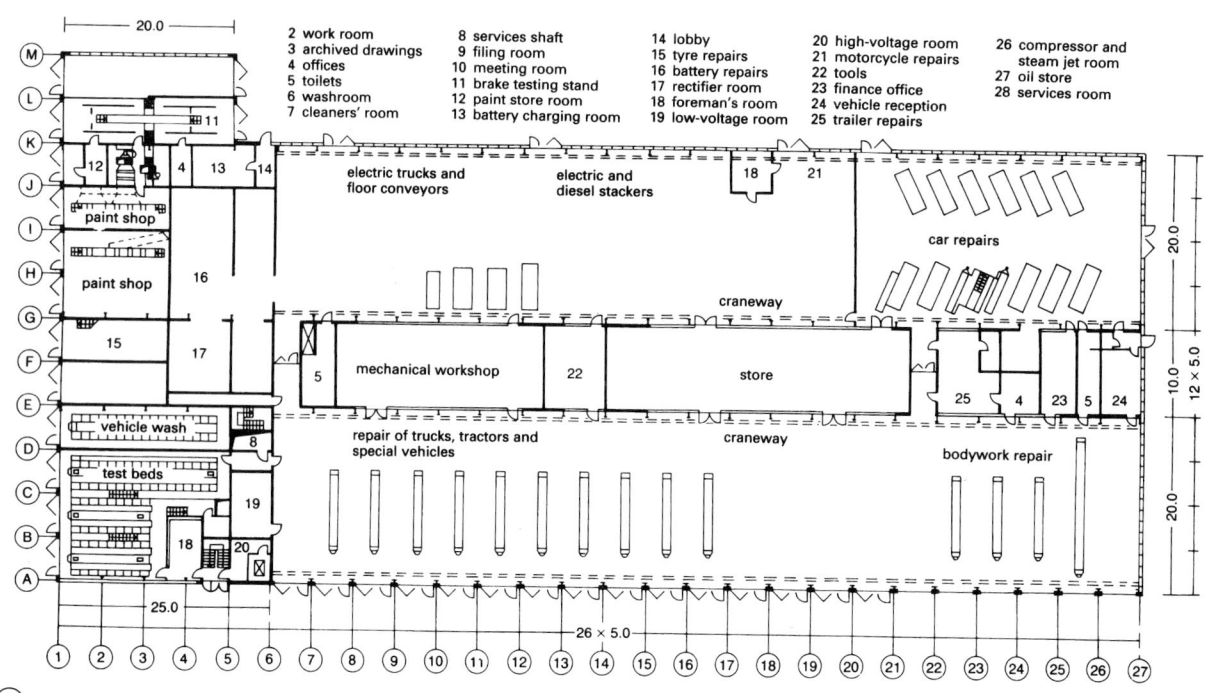

2 work room
3 archived drawings
4 offices
5 toilets
6 washroom
7 cleaners' room
8 services shaft
9 filing room
10 meeting room
11 brake testing stand
12 paint store room
13 battery charging room
14 lobby
15 tyre repairs
16 battery repairs
17 rectifier room
18 foreman's room
19 low-voltage room
20 high-voltage room
21 motorcycle repairs
22 tools
23 finance office
24 vehicle reception
25 trailer repairs
26 compressor and steam jet room
27 oil store
28 services room

③ **Workshop for transport vehicles, ground floor**

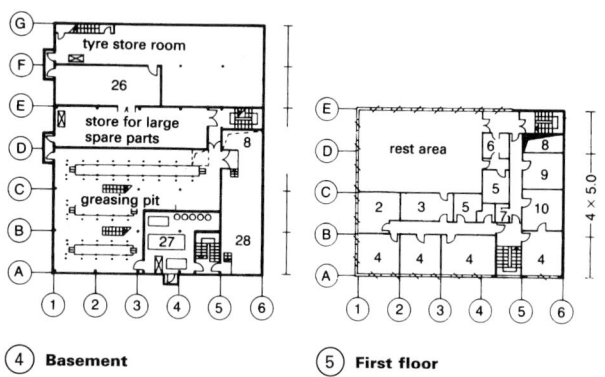

④ **Basement**   ⑤ **First floor**

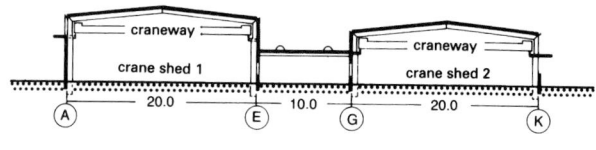

⑥ **Cross-section, axis 5**

⑦ **Cross-section, axis 16**

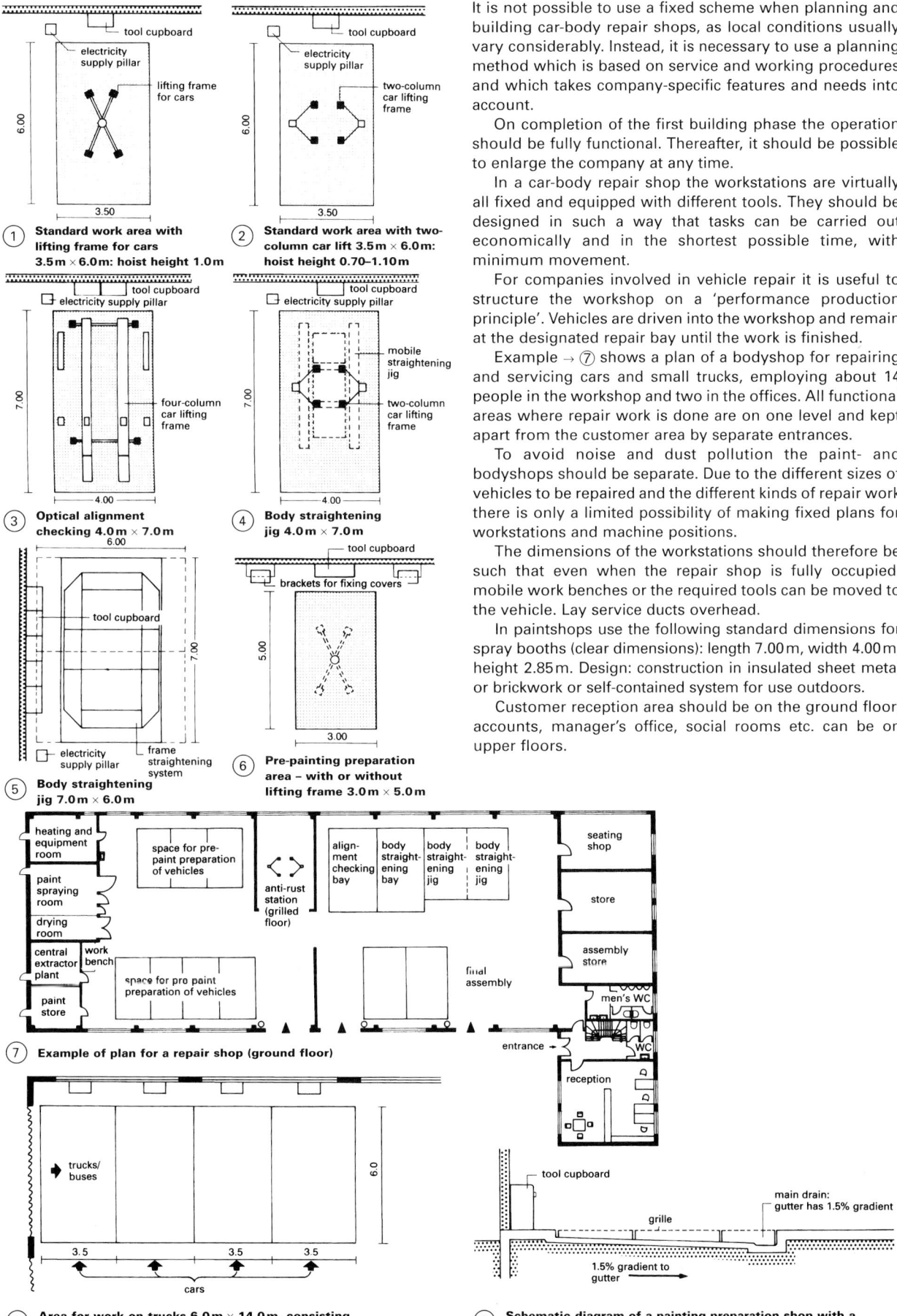

① **Standard work area with lifting frame for cars 3.5 m × 6.0 m: hoist height 1.0 m**

② **Standard work area with two-column car lift 3.5 m × 6.0 m: hoist height 0.70–1.10 m**

③ **Optical alignment checking 4.0 m × 7.0 m**

④ **Body straightening jig 4.0 m × 7.0 m**

⑤ **Body straightening jig 7.0 m × 6.0 m**

⑥ **Pre-painting preparation area – with or without lifting frame 3.0 m × 5.0 m**

⑦ **Example of plan for a repair shop (ground floor)**

⑧ **Area for work on trucks 6.0 m × 14.0 m, consisting of four standard work bays, 3.5 m × 6.0 m each**

⑨ **Schematic diagram of a painting preparation shop with a grilled floor → ⑥**

It is not possible to use a fixed scheme when planning and building car-body repair shops, as local conditions usually vary considerably. Instead, it is necessary to use a planning method which is based on service and working procedures and which takes company-specific features and needs into account.

On completion of the first building phase the operation should be fully functional. Thereafter, it should be possible to enlarge the company at any time.

In a car-body repair shop the workstations are virtually all fixed and equipped with different tools. They should be designed in such a way that tasks can be carried out economically and in the shortest possible time, with minimum movement.

For companies involved in vehicle repair it is useful to structure the workshop on a 'performance production principle'. Vehicles are driven into the workshop and remain at the designated repair bay until the work is finished.

Example → ⑦ shows a plan of a bodyshop for repairing and servicing cars and small trucks, employing about 14 people in the workshop and two in the offices. All functional areas where repair work is done are on one level and kept apart from the customer area by separate entrances.

To avoid noise and dust pollution the paint- and bodyshops should be separate. Due to the different sizes of vehicles to be repaired and the different kinds of repair work there is only a limited possibility of making fixed plans for workstations and machine positions.

The dimensions of the workstations should therefore be such that even when the repair shop is fully occupied, mobile work benches or the required tools can be moved to the vehicle. Lay service ducts overhead.

In paintshops use the following standard dimensions for spray booths (clear dimensions): length 7.00 m, width 4.00 m, height 2.85 m. Design: construction in insulated sheet metal or brickwork or self-contained system for use outdoors.

Customer reception area should be on the ground floor; accounts, manager's office, social rooms etc. can be on upper floors.

VEHICLE COMPANY WORKSHOPS

Design of premises: after space requirement has been established and a site chosen, planning the building can begin. The characteristics of the site, such as size, shape, vehicle access, road design etc., must be taken into consideration.

Planning example → ② Planning permits an efficient functioning design of all required spaces and facilities. The repair shop is designed to accommodate four 6.50 m × 3.50 m workstations, and equipped with a four-column car lifting frame and wheel balancing equipment; nearby spare parts store.

Planning example → ③ First construction phase includes three work bays in the repair shop and a car wash. The finished scheme has an extra five workstations in the repair shop and a showroom.

In a company working with commercial vehicles the choice of position for the gates depends primarily on the shape of the site. From both the fitters' and customers' points of view, the best design is one where entry to and exit from the repair bays are through separate gates, particularly for work on articulated vehicles.

Ideally, the site depth or width should be ≥ 80 m but repair shops for light commercial vehicles are possible on sites with little depth (minimum 40 m). → ④ – ⑤ for a company working with light commercial vehicles and buses.

Plan examples → ④ – ⑥ show the smallest unit of an independent commercial vehicle repair service. Offices and social rooms on the first floor → ④.

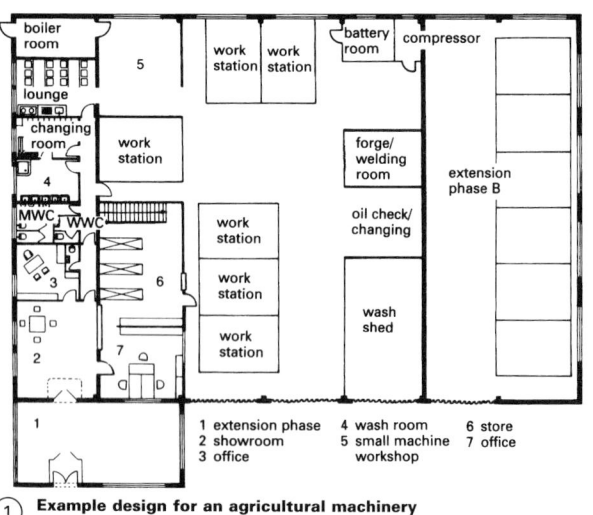

1 extension phase 4 wash room 6 store
2 showroom 5 small machine 7 office
3 office workshop

① Example design for an agricultural machinery company with 4–9 employees

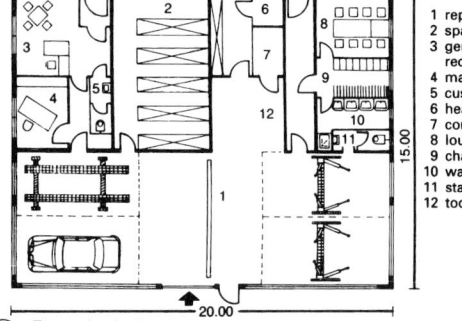

1 repair shop
2 spare parts store
3 general office, reception, cash desk
4 manager's office
5 customers' WC
6 heating
7 compressor
8 lounge
9 changing room
10 washroom
11 staff WC
12 tools

② Example design incorporating four work bays on a site with broad street frontage

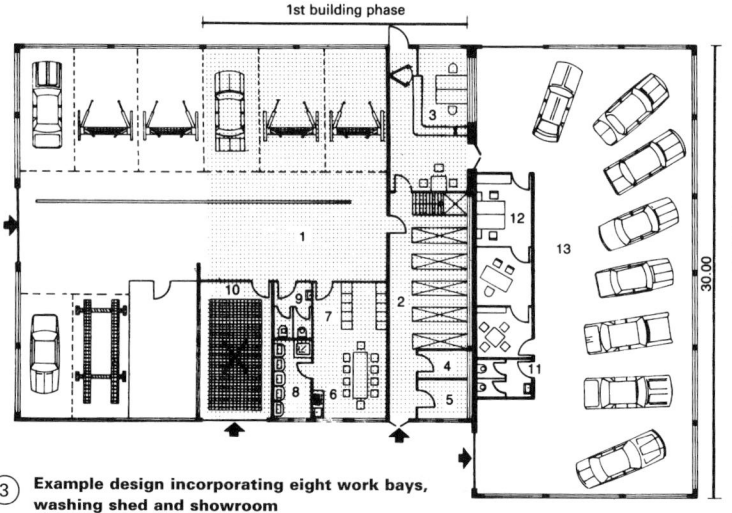

1st building phase

1 repair shop
2 spare parts store
3 general office, reception, cash desk
4 heating
5 compressor
6 lounge
7 changing room
8 washroom
9 staff WC
10 wash shed
11 customer's WC
12 meeting room
13 showroom

③ Example design incorporating eight work bays, washing shed and showroom

1 repair bay for trucks
2 reception for repairs
3 spare parts issue
4 foreman's office
5 spare parts in
6 compressor room
7 boiler room
8 manager's office
9 changing room
10 washroom
11 staff WC
12 general office
13 kitchen

④ → ⑥

④ First floor → ⑤   ⑤ Example plan for a truck company without thoroughfare   ⑥ With thoroughfare

384

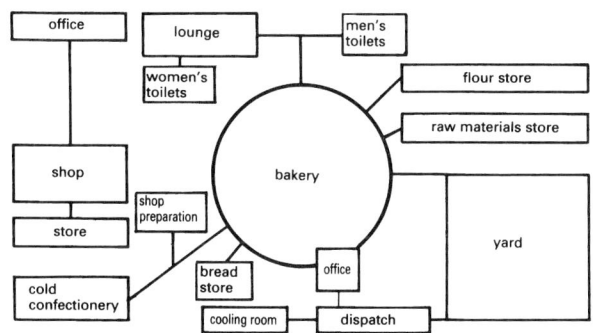

(1) Space relationship plan

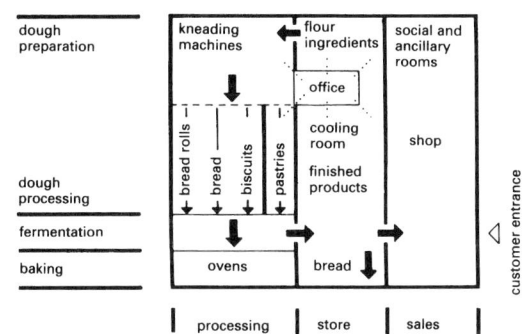

(2) Functional diagram

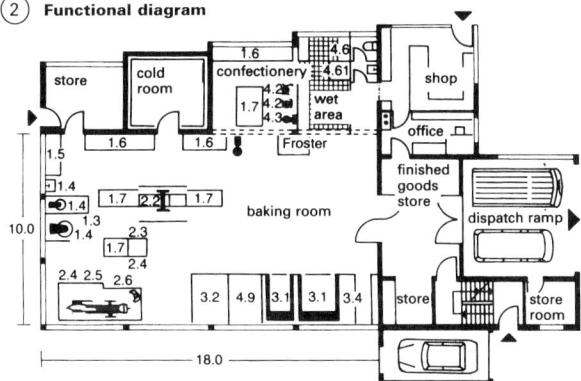

(3) Example plan layout

Systematic planning must anticipate possible future developments in technology and operating procedures to which building elements will have to adapt. The planning procedure must also always include a review of the location.

Schedule of accommodation and space requirements

There is a basic division into store areas, production areas, sales areas, building services areas, offices for administration and management, social rooms and ancillary rooms. → ①

Work processes in or between the individual areas → ②

Distinction should be made between store rooms for raw materials (coarse meal, sugar, salt, baking powder, dry goods in sacks, flour in silos or sacks), ingredients (fruit, garnishings, dried fruit, fats, eggs) and packaging. Daily supplies are stored at the workstations. Establish space requirement for containers (shelving, racks, cupboards), stacks, counters and circulation (corridors). Minimum area for stores is 15m²; roughly 8–10m² per employee for all store rooms. Routes between stores and work areas should be short.

Work areas for bakery and pastry should be separate. The bakery needs a warm and humid environment; pastry making needs a rather cooler environment. The bakery includes the following areas: dough preparation, working of dough, baking, storage of finished products. Pastry making is split: cold area (butter cream, cream, chocolate, fruit) and warm area (pastes, cake, pastries and biscuits).

The space requirement can be determined using a layout plan. In a work area space is needed for equipment, for handling and working, for intermediate storage (trolleys) and counters, and for circulation (lost space).

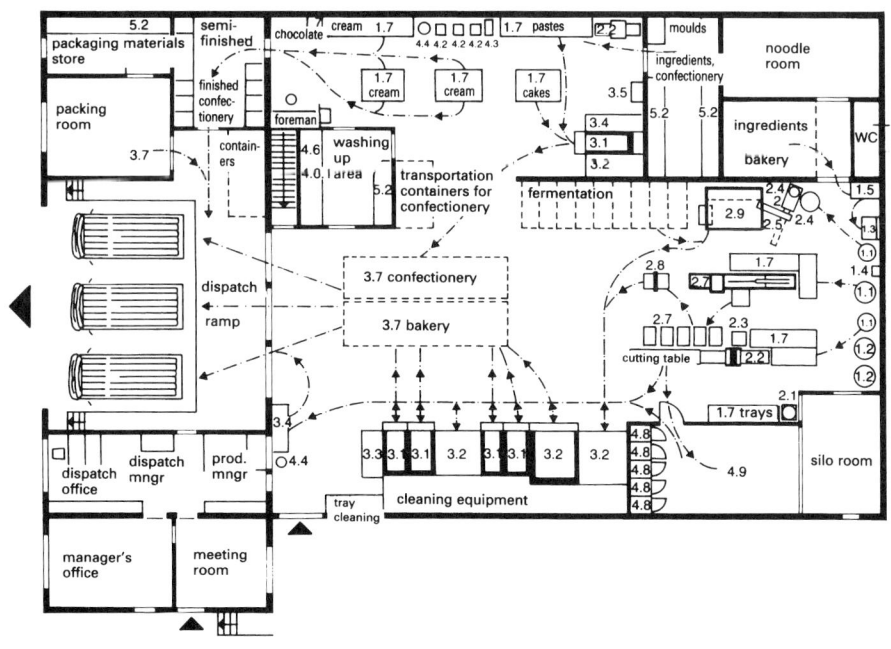

(4) Example plan layout

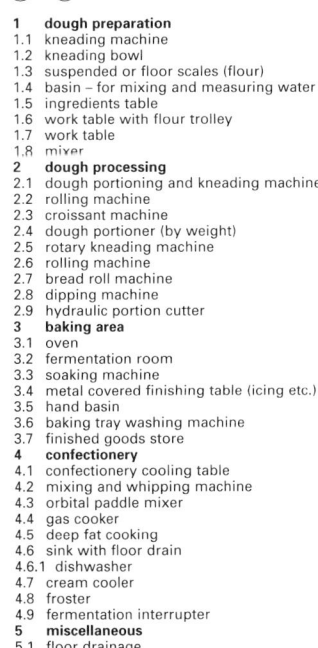

③ – ④ key

1 dough preparation
1.1 kneading machine
1.2 kneading bowl
1.3 suspended or floor scales (flour)
1.4 basin – for mixing and measuring water
1.5 ingredients table
1.6 work table with flour trolley
1.7 work table
1.8 mixer
2 dough processing
2.1 dough portioning and kneading machine
2.2 rolling machine
2.3 croissant machine
2.4 dough portioner (by weight)
2.5 rotary kneading machine
2.6 rolling machine
2.7 bread roll machine
2.8 dipping machine
2.9 hydraulic portion cutter
3 baking area
3.1 oven
3.2 fermentation room
3.3 soaking machine
3.4 metal covered finishing table (icing etc.)
3.5 hand basin
3.6 baking tray washing machine
3.7 finished goods store
4 confectionery
4.1 confectionery cooling table
4.2 mixing and whipping machine
4.3 orbital paddle mixer
4.4 gas cooker
4.5 deep fat cooking
4.6 sink with floor drain
4.6.1 dishwasher
4.7 cream cooler
4.8 froster
4.9 fermentation interrupter
5 miscellaneous
5.1 floor drainage
5.2 shelving

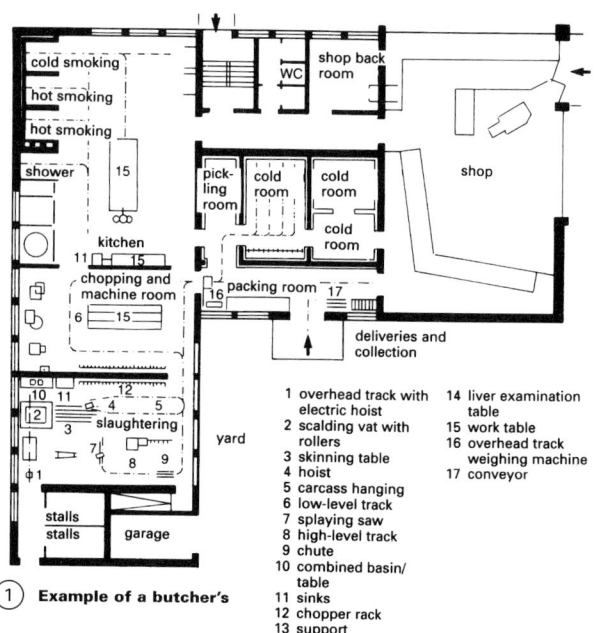

1 overhead track with electric hoist
2 scalding vat with rollers
3 skinning table
4 hoist
5 carcass hanging
6 low-level track
7 splaying saw
8 high-level track
9 chute
10 combined basin/ table
11 sinks
12 chopper rack
13 support
14 liver examination table
15 work table
16 overhead track weighing machine
17 conveyor

(1) **Example of a butcher's**

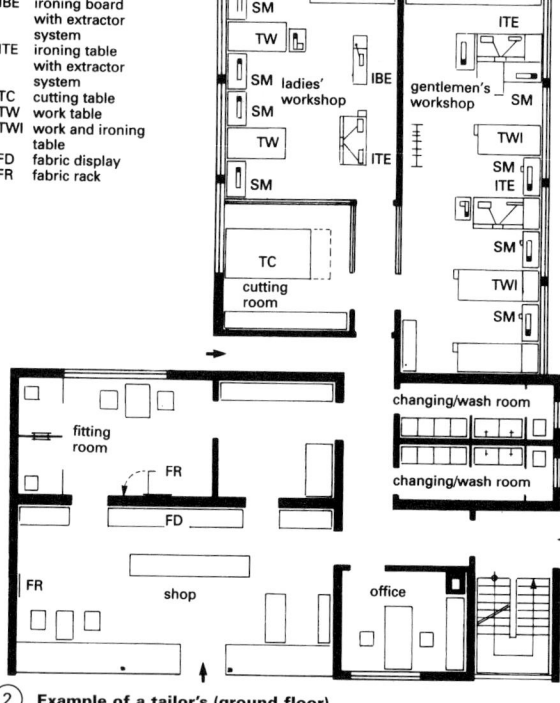

SM   sewing machine
IBE ironing board with extractor system
ITE ironing table with extractor system
TC   cutting table
TW   work table
TWI work and ironing table
FD   fabric display
FR   fabric rack

(2) **Example of a tailor's (ground floor)**

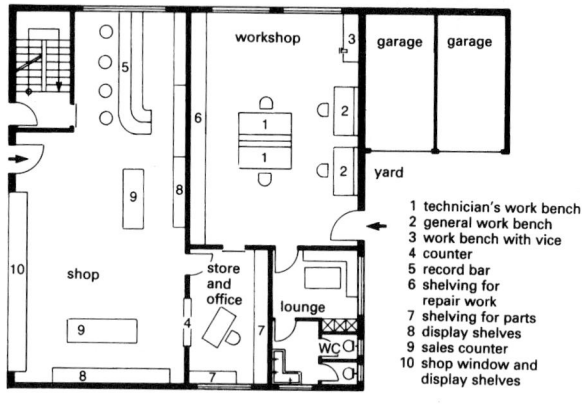

1 technician's work bench
2 general work bench
3 work bench with vice
4 counter
5 record bar
6 shelving for repair work
7 shelving for parts
8 display shelves
9 sales counter
10 shop window and display shelves

(3) **Example of an electrical repair (ground floor)**

Butcher's shop → ①

Model plan; 6–7 employees

Functional sequence within a sausage making company. Meat arrives in machine room for cutting and mincing, is taken into the smoking chamber and then into the boiler (kitchen). From there it is sent to the cooling area or shop.

Height of working areas (depending on size of company) ≥ 4.0 m. Width of circulation routes ≥ 2.0 m. Work space around cutter and mincer: 3 m² each.

Distance of machines from walls (for repairs) 40–50 cm. Cooling machines which work day and night must have good sound insulation. Water supply with hose connection should be provided in the kitchen, machine room and salting room. Floors should be non-slip and waterproof, preferably with corrugated tiles and drains. Walls should be tiled high. Good general lighting is needed, with 300 lx at workstations. Provide staff room, lockers, WC and shower for employees. Comply with relevant regulations on health and safety in the workplace, building regulations and accident insurance.

Ladies' and gentlemen's tailor → ②

Model layout for 10 employees

Electrical repair shop → ③

Work spaces should have a clear height of ≥ 3 m with 15 m³ air volume per employee. To minimise the risk of electrocution in the workshop, faultless insulating floor coverings should ideally be provided; at the very least the work benches for the technicians should be insulated. Recommended lighting level is 500 lx; 1500 lx for very fine assembly work.

Work benches must have a spacious worktop (1.0 m × 2.0 m if possible). Provide two under-desk units with shallow drawers for circuit diagrams, documentation and tools.

Example paint shop → ④

Includes extension possibilities.

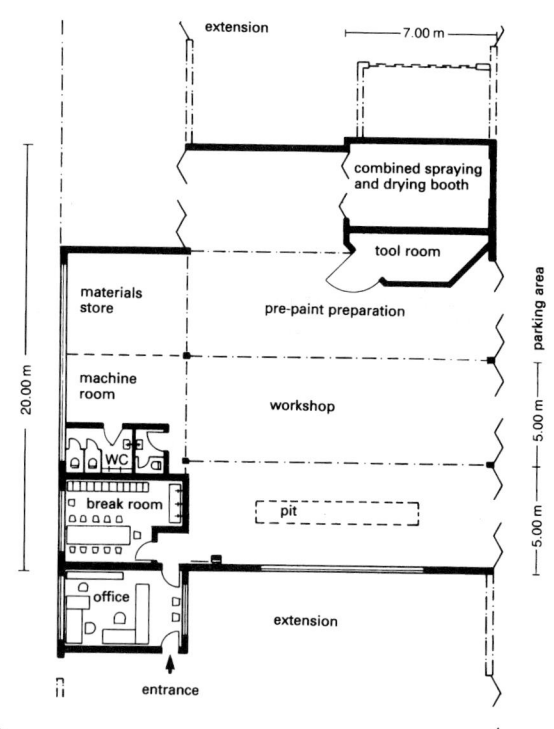

(4) **Example of a spray painting shop (ground floor)**

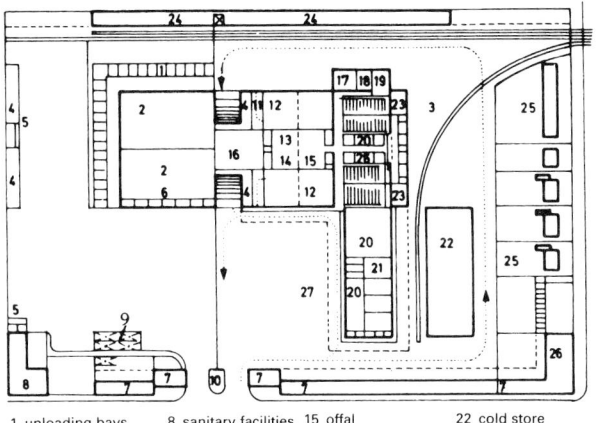

Layout of large abattoir and cattle yard ①

1 unloading bays	8 sanitary facilities	15 offal	22 cold store
2 market hall	9 disinfection	16 yard	23 staff
3 railway track	10 porter	17 heating plant	24 bone silos
4 stall	11 blood draining	18 workshop	25 works flats
5 hot fermentation	12 slaughter hall	19 plant room	26 garden restaurant
6 staff and equipment rooms	13 examination for diseases	20 cold room	27 collection area
7 administration	14 vets	21 freezer and storage room	

WHOLESALE BUTCHERS

Animals in abattoirs need to be provided with modern pens where they can be fed, watered and kept calm because this influences the quality of the meat, as does humane, painless anaesthetisation and slaughtering. This also allows a more complete draining of the blood and in turn ensures that the meat looks attractive and can be preserved for longer.

Following the BSE crisis many new practices have become compulsory so it is essential to consult the relevant guidelines at the start of the planning process.

The examples shown in ② – ⑤ are constructed on a grid of 15.50 × 15.50m. This evolved from the positioning of shelving in the central food store and allows for the width needed for fork-lift trucks (→ p. 392). Pallets are stacked in fives in racks, the two lower shelves containing pallets ready for dispatch, the top three shelves containing stocks.

This uniform grid is also used for other parts of the building such as the butchers' workshop (2 × 3 grid panels) and the offices. Extensions can be made using the same grid.

The butcher receives half-carcasses of pigs and cattle from the abattoir and processes them into ready-to-sell portions or cooked meat products and sausages. A deep freeze room is needed for imported poultry and a separate cold room for butter and margarine. A waste incinerator can be used alongside the oil heating system to heat the building, and in summer to air-condition the offices and run small cooling plants.

The required minimum height for processing is 3m → ③. The slaughter area for large animals, which includes a winch, should be 1.50m higher. The windows should be high enough to prevent children from looking in and walls should be tiled to a height of ≥2m.

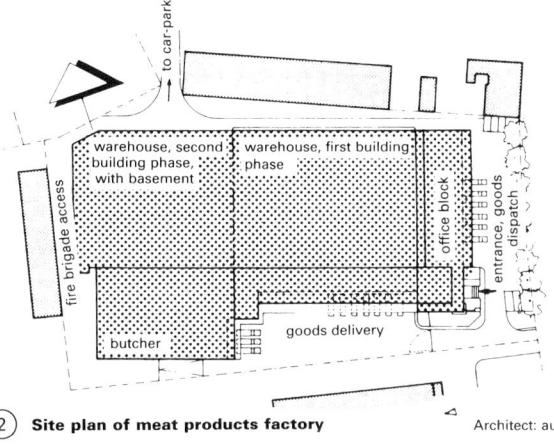

Site plan of meat products factory ②   Architect: author

Section along A axis → ⑤ ③

Section along B axis → ⑤ ④

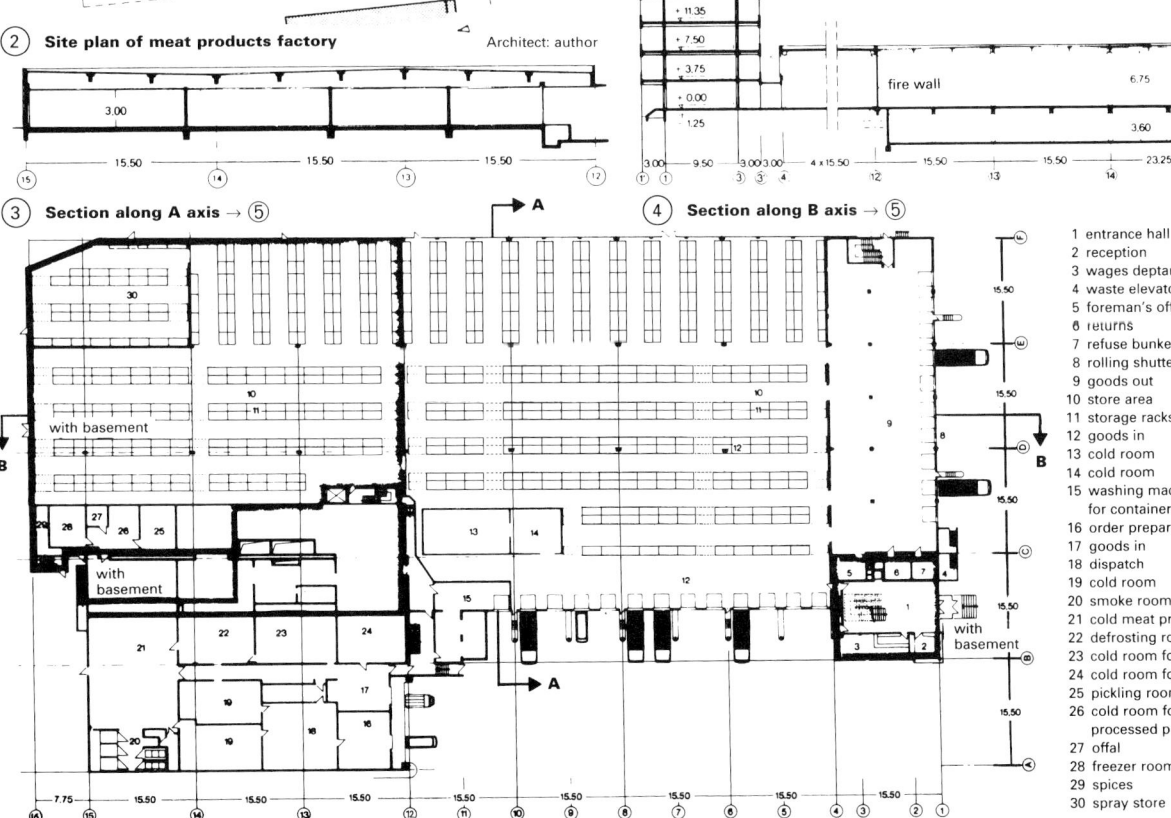

Ground floor of meat products factory ⑤

1 entrance hall
2 reception
3 wages deptartment
4 waste elevator
5 foreman's office
6 returns
7 refuse bunker
8 rolling shutter doors
9 goods out
10 store area
11 storage racks
12 goods in
13 cold room
14 cold room
15 washing machine for containers
16 order preparation
17 goods in
18 dispatch
19 cold room
20 smoke room
21 cold meat processing
22 defrosting room
23 cold room for meat
24 cold room for fats
25 pickling room
26 cold room for processed products
27 offal
28 freezer room
29 spices
30 spray store

MEAT PROCESSING CENTRE

On a ground floor area of 4500 m² → ③, cold meats, ham, sausages and delicatessen products are manufactured (approximately 25 tonnes per day). Offices, laboratories, canteen, kitchen, wash and changing rooms are on the first floor → ②. Different types of rooms require different temperatures: social rooms, offices, WC, 20°C; processing rooms, 18°C; air-conditioned rooms, 14–18°C; cool rooms 10–12°C; cold rooms, 0–8°C; deep-freeze rooms, –20°C.

A high standard of structure and materials is essential and all health regulations should be satisfied.

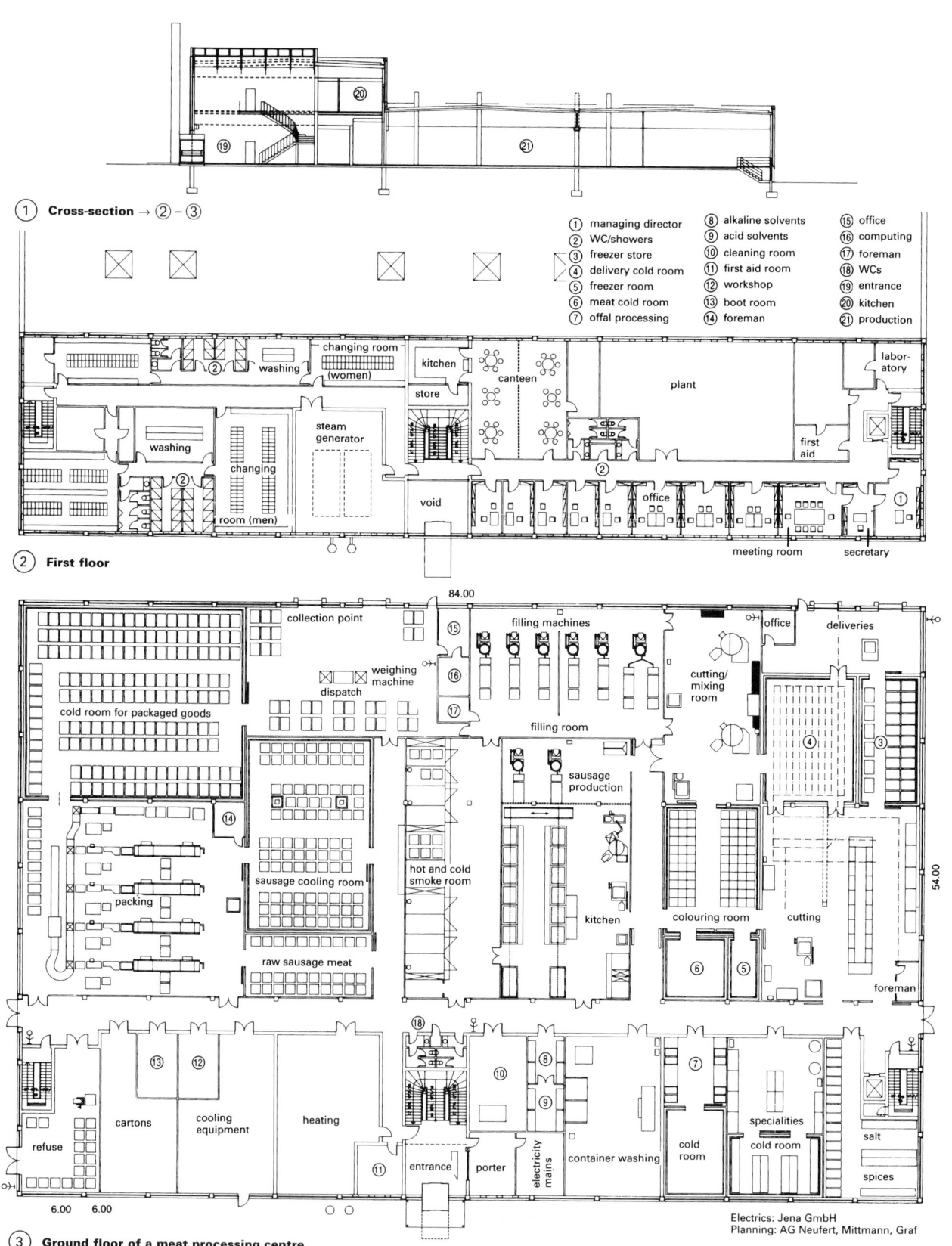

① **Cross-section** → ② – ③

① managing director	⑧ alkaline solvents	⑮ office
② WC/showers	⑨ acid solvents	⑯ computing
③ freezer store	⑩ cleaning room	⑰ foreman
④ delivery cold room	⑪ first aid room	⑱ WCs
⑤ freezer room	⑫ workshop	⑲ entrance
⑥ meat cold room	⑬ boot room	⑳ kitchen
⑦ offal processing	⑭ foreman	㉑ production

② **First floor**

③ **Ground floor of a meat processing centre**

Electrics: Jena GmbH
Planning: AG Neufert, Mittmann, Graf

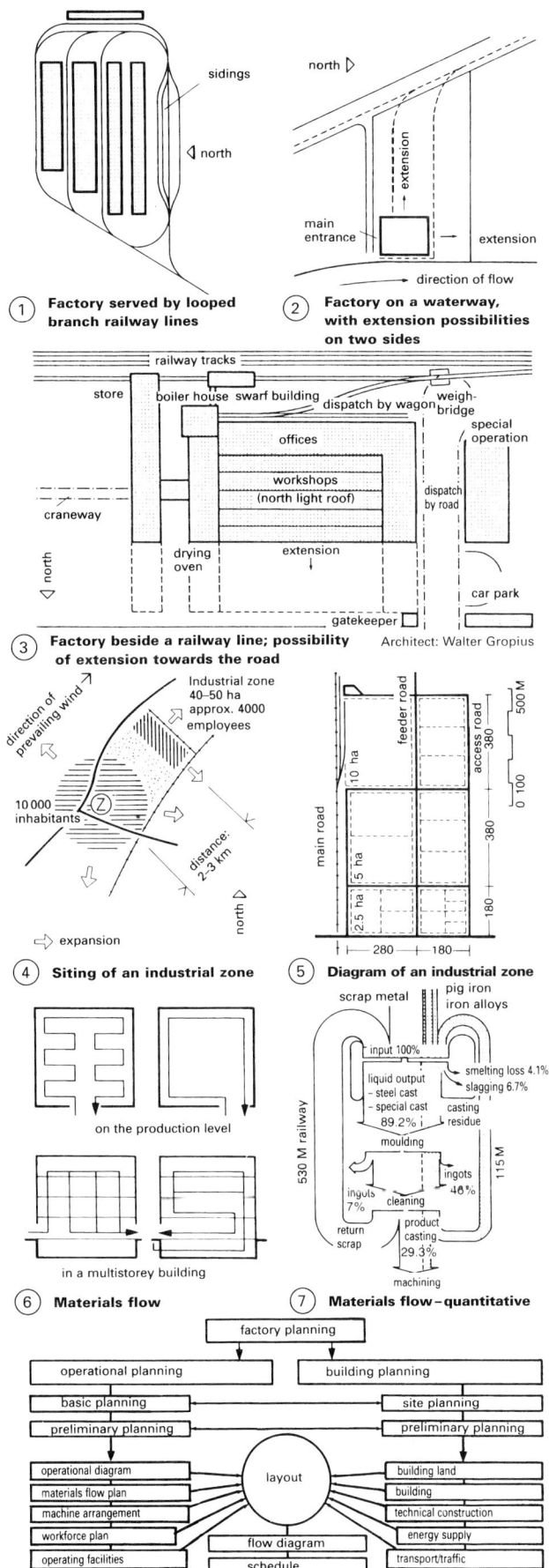

① **Factory served by looped branch railway lines**

② **Factory on a waterway, with extension possibilities on two sides**

north ▷

extension

main entrance

extension

→ direction of flow

---

③ **Factory beside a railway line; possibility of extension towards the road**

railway tracks

store   boiler house swarf building   weigh-bridge

dispatch by wagon

offices

special operation

workshops
(north light roof)

dispatch by road

craneway

◁ north

drying oven

extension

car park

gatekeeper ☐

Architect: Walter Gropius

---

④ **Siting of an industrial zone**

direction of prevailing wind ↗

Industrial zone 40–50 ha approx. 4000 employees

10 000 inhabitants

distance: 2–3 km

north △

⇨ expansion

⑤ **Diagram of an industrial zone**

feeder road

access road

380

500 M

10 ha

380

5 ha

2.5 ha

180

main road

├ 280 ┼ 180 ┤

---

⑥ **Materials flow**

on the production level

in a multistorey building

⑦ **Materials flow – quantitative**

scrap metal   pig iron iron alloys

530 M railway

input 100%

liquid output
– steel cast
– special cast
89.2%

smelting loss 4.1%
slagging 6.7%

casting residue

moulding

ingots 46%

ingots 7%

cleaning

return scrap

product casting 29.3%

115 M

machining

---

⑧ **Planning diagram for a factory**

factory planning

operational planning

building planning

basic planning

site planning

preliminary planning

preliminary planning

operational diagram

materials flow plan

machine arrangement

workforce plan

operating facilities

layout

building land

building

technical construction

energy supply

transport/traffic

flow diagram

schedule

construction

INDUSTRIAL BUILDINGS: PLANNING

(1) Siting

Location factors:
- raw materials
- markets
- workforce

The order of priority of these factors when selecting a location depends on the individual company's strategy in relation to the cost of raw materials, transport costs and labour costs.

(2) Site

Needs relating to site area are determined by the space required by the building, roads and rail track.

A rail track plan should be drawn up, since railway lines take up a lot of space due to wide turning circles. → ①

Suitable sites are those with railway lines running into the site diagonally. Otherwise the building can if necessary be positioned at an oblique angle.

In case of frequent rail traffic branch lines through site should be provided, which would allow a continuous flow. → ①

Sidings ending at the front of the shed are often sufficient for goods loaded by crane.

(3) Schedule of accommodation

The schedule of accommodation includes details about:
- type of use
- room sizes in square metres
- room sizes in clear dimensions
- number of employees, segregated according to gender (sanitary facilities)
- machine layout plan
- live (rolling, working) loads, single or point loads

Special requirements and other specifications include:
- noise and vibration countermeasures
- protection from fire, toxic and explosive substances
- energy mains supplies
- air conditioning
- escape routes
- intended or possible extension

(4) Operational planning

Careful operational planning is essential before work on planning the building begins. Process flows are depicted according to the type of production and estimated on the basis of annual production figures or number of employees.

If no empirical data are available, the works engineer will have to determine the usable space requirement on the basis of the machine layout plan and other company operating facilities.

The basis for the operational planning is taken from analysis of the following:
- operational diagram (of the production systems)
- materials flow diagram (essential criteria for evaluating economic efficiency and important basis for layout plan)
- machine location plan
- workforce plan
- schedule of accommodation
- list of buildings

Layout planning (i.e. allocation of employees, materials and machines designed to bring about the lowest production costs per unit) is the starting point for all industrial planning. From this, the basis for the factory design is derived – adaptability, extension possibilities, economic efficiency.

Note: the techniques of network planning and other methods are appropriate → ⑧

389

INDUSTRIAL BUILDINGS: PLANNING

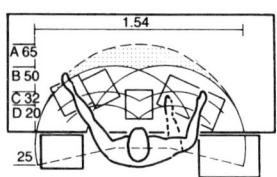

A maximum possible reach (≈65 cm)
B physiological limits of reach (≈50 cm)
C normal reach (≈32 cm)
D physiological inner limits of reach (16–20 cm)

(1) **Stier's guideline dimensions for optimum accessibility**

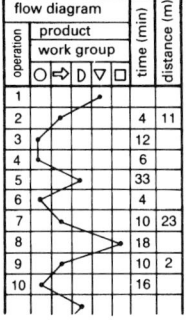

(2) **Production process flow**

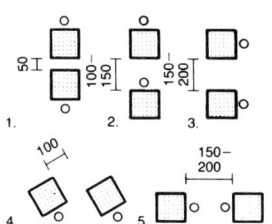

– work bench with small machinery (10–15 m²)
– regular machines (15–40 m²)
– add on space for: circulation; storage (30%)

(3) **Guidelines for space requirements in engineering factories**

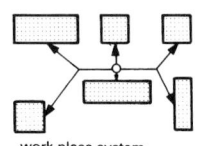

– work place system

– workshop system

(4) **Production systems**

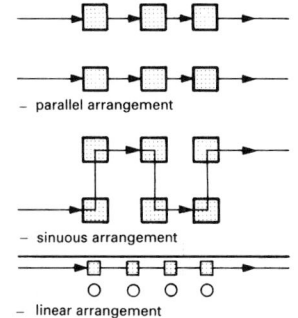

– parallel arrangement

– sinuous arrangement

– linear arrangement

(5) **Line/flow systems**

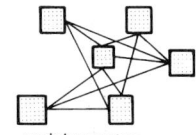

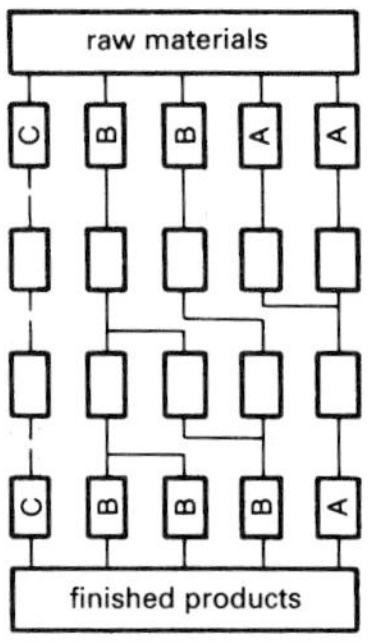

raw materials
finished products

(6) **Continuous production system**

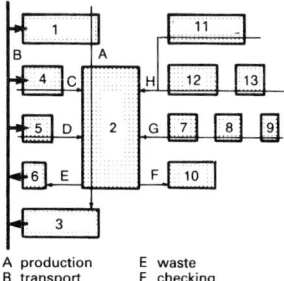

A production   E waste
B transport   F checking
C energy   G maintenance
D deliveries   H staff

(7) **Operational diagram showing main functions**

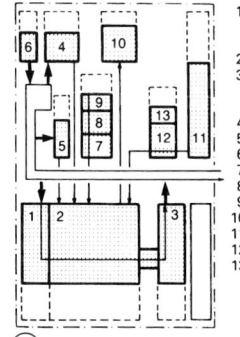

1 raw materials store and delivery
2 production
3 finished products store and delivery
4 energy supply
5 delivery
6 waste
7 workshop
8 maintenance
9 laboratory
10 test bed
11 administration
12 social rooms
13 training

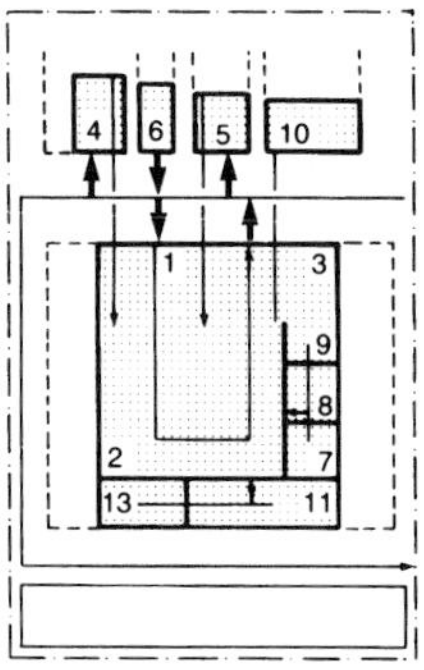

(8) **Open system**

(9) **Closed system**

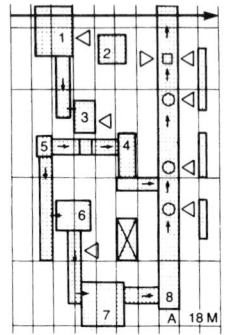

planning symbols			AMSE	VDI
No.	process			
1	processing		O	+
2	storage		▽	△
3	delay		D	D
4	checking		□	□
5	transport		⇨	>
6	handling			O
7	finishing/testing		◎	□

VDI symbols apply to Germany; those of the ASME are recommended for international use

(11) **Planning symbols**

No.	mains connections	
1	operating station	▼
2	electrics	Ẹ
3	water (hydraulics)	Ụ
4	air (pneumatics)	P̣
5	coolants	C̣
6	waste	Ẉ

common symbols denoting technical connection of mains services

(12) **Mains connections**

(13) **Extension at right angles to materials flow**

Space requirements for workshops and offices in precision engineering factories in multistorey buildings:

Useful floor space (m²/employee):
dense occupation   4.5–5.0
add on for:
ancillary spaces   2.0–2.5
                          6.0–7.5

Ancillary areas:
stairs   0.3–0.6
toilets   0.2–0.4
changing rooms   0.5–1.0

(14) **Example space requirement guidelines**

Corridors   0.5–1.5
lifts   0.0–0.2
walls/partitions   0.5–0.8
                          2.0–4.5

Total floor space
(m²/employee):   8.0–12.0
on average: 10.0

Generally valid guidelines for floor space requirements of industrial businesses cannot be provided because the continual advances in conditions and equipment change the basis of statistical data.

(15) **Example space requirement guidelines**

(5) Production

Production planning: work flow diagrams illustrate the steps within a production process and form a basis for the machine layout and material flow diagram.

Production systems vary according to the disposition of operating materials and the production process: workplace system; workshop system; line system; row system; flow system. The process can involve several production stages. The basic form is: delivery–raw materials store –production (preparation) –processing–intermediate storage–assembly–checking /testing –finished product store– delivery. → (4)–(6)

(6) Building design

Examples of design methods include: layout method, design using functional axes, design using grid axes.

Guidelines for work-station space requirements in factories with work benches and machines are as follows:
- small machines 10–15 m²
- standard machines 15–40 m²

Add on 30% for circulation space. → (3)

(7) Routes for two-way circulation

The calculation of the number of people moving to and from specific areas depends on the type of production system. Peak movement times (e.g. at shift changes) should be taken into account.

The width of corridors can in exceptional cases be as low as 0.60 m.

People (no.)	Width* (normal)
up to 5	0.875 m
up to 20	1.000 m
up to 100	1.250 m
up to 250	1.750 m
up to 400	2.250 m

* guideline dimension

Minimum clear height above the circulation routes should be 2.00 m.

A protective guard should be provided under overhead transport systems in circulation areas if there is any risk of falling objects. The clear height to the protective guard must be not less than 2.00 m.

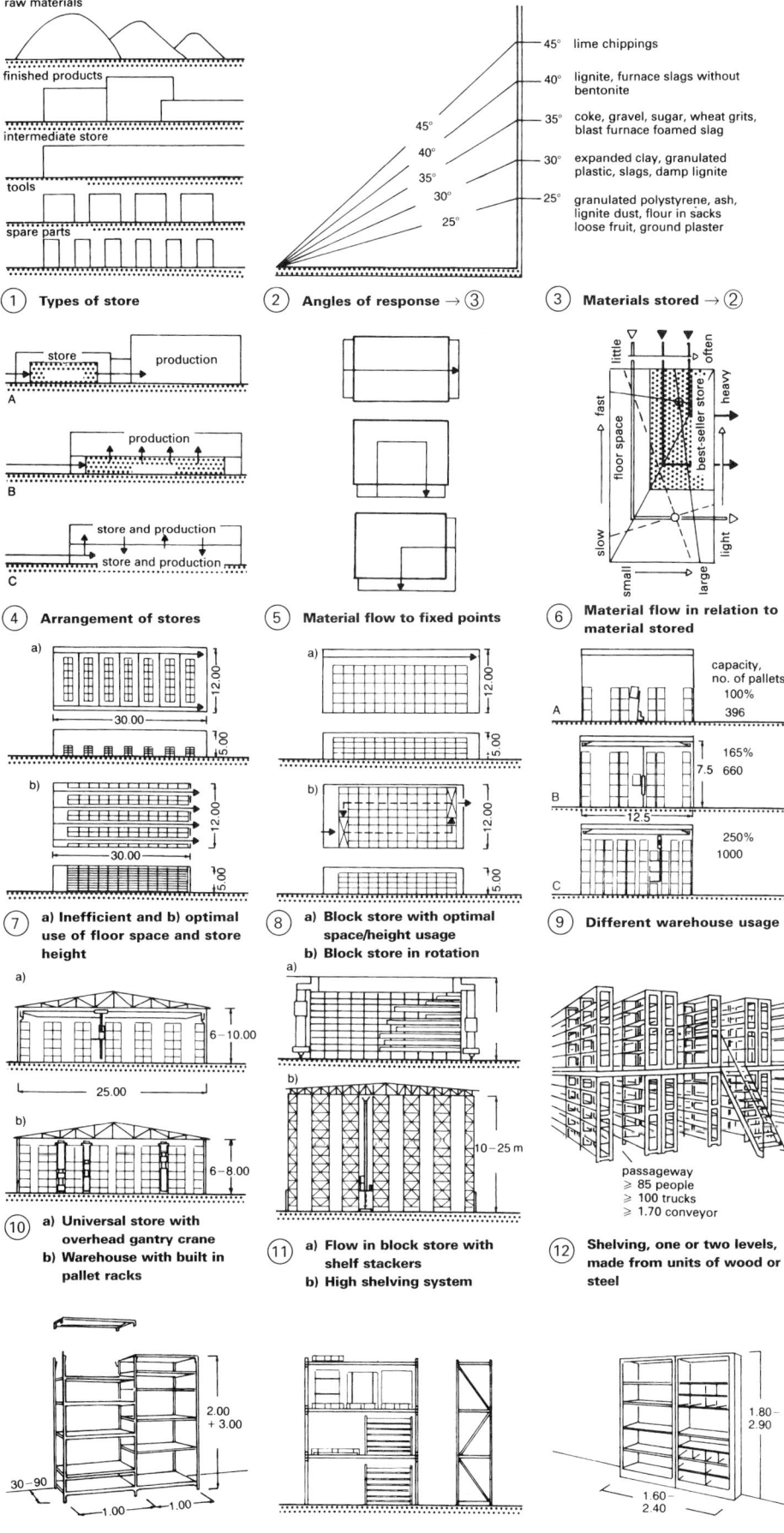

Warehouses are part of the production process and material flow. Store unit–transport unit–production unit–dispatch unit. Reduce 'non-production' elements as much as possible; integrate them (mobile stores) or avoid them entirely.

Articles stored: bulk goods stored according to quantities involved. → ⑤
Large quantities: silos, sheds, bunkers, stockpiles.
Small quantities: boxes, canisters, bins, dishes.

Options → ④
(A) Store and production on one level
(B) Store underneath production level
(C) Store and production, depending on use, on two or more levels

Determination of co-ordinates for the 'best-seller warehouse' with optimum 'playtime' for handling equipment (roughly $1/3$ of the total space of the store). → ⑥

Handling equipment in an existing store: a two-tonne fork-lift requires an aisle width of 3.45 m; stacker can stack three containers on top of each other. → ⑨ A Stacking crane permits stack height up to crane bridge. Five containers can be stacked. -→ ⑨ B Stacking crane with mechanised load lifting device, which grips the containers, requires only narrow aisles (storage volume 250%). → ⑨ C

Structure of high-bay stores
- Steel structure (roof and walls of the store, as well as guide rails of the handling equipment)
- Reinforced concrete structure (shelving is flexibly mounted on concrete walls as longitudinal and transverse cross-beams)

Advantages: greater stability; possibility of space segregation (fire compartments).
Control system: punch cards; off-line control; on-line system. → ⑩ – ⑪

① **Types of store**

② **Angles of response → ③**

45° lime chippings
40° lignite, furnace slags without bentonite
35° coke, gravel, sugar, wheat grits, blast furnace foamed slag
30° expanded clay, granulated plastic, slags, damp lignite
25° granulated polystyrene, ash, lignite dust, flour in sacks loose fruit, ground plaster

③ **Materials stored → ②**

④ **Arrangement of stores**

⑤ **Material flow to fixed points**

⑥ **Material flow in relation to material stored**

⑦ a) **Inefficient and** b) **optimal use of floor space and store height**

⑧ a) **Block store with optimal space/height usage**
b) **Block store in rotation**

⑨ **Different warehouse usage**

⑩ a) **Universal store with overhead gantry crane**
b) **Warehouse with built in pallet racks**

⑪ a) **Flow in block store with shelf stackers**
b) **High shelving system**

⑫ **Shelving, one or two levels, made from units of wood or steel**

⑬ **Self-assembly steel shelving**

⑭ **Pallet racks of prefabricated components (longitudinal transverse shelving)**

⑮ **Shelf/cupboard system manufacturer's dimensions**

HIGH-BAY WAREHOUSES

(1) **Pallet platform**

(2) **Flat pallet 80/120 100/120**

(3) - (5) **Stacking containers**

High-bay warehouses are changing modern warehousing techniques through the use of efficient stacking equipment or automatic computer-controlled systems. Handling equipment includes fork-lifts → (12), rack trucks, rack stacking equipment → (14) and stacker cranes → (13) which usually run in the storage area without an operator or supervision.

Many manufacturers of stackers or fork-lifts supply tailor-made systems to improve storage capacity and speed of dispatch.

Distributing warehouses throughout the field shortens transportation distances and allows rapid response to customer demand. Items can be picked and dispatched even on a daily basis.

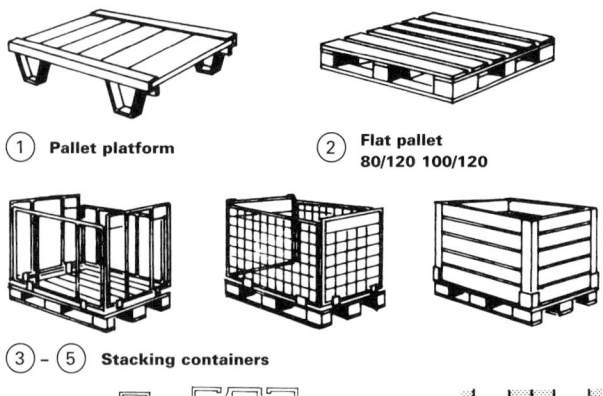

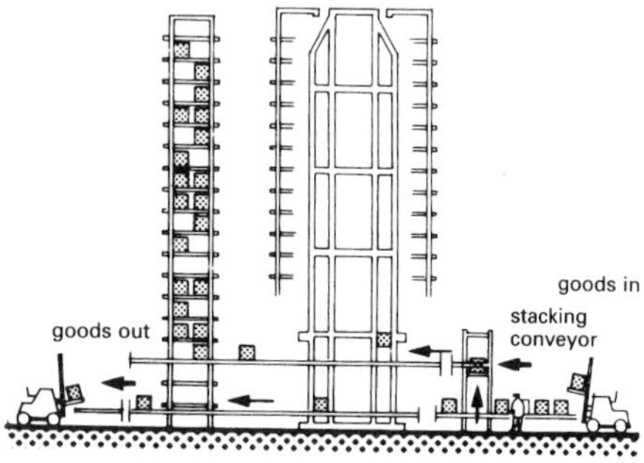

goods in
stacking conveyor
goods out

(6) **Computerised storage system**

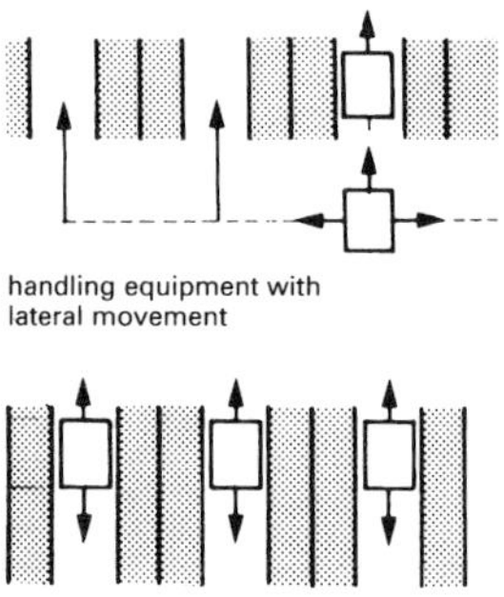

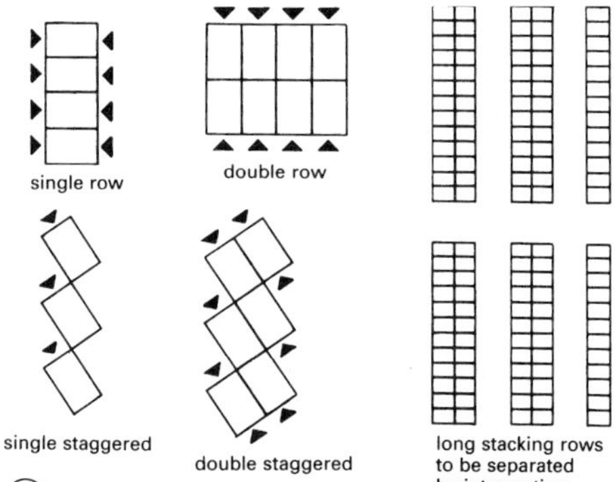

handling equipment with lateral movement

(7) separate handling machines for each aisle

single row
double row
single staggered
double staggered
long stacking rows to be separated by intersecting aisles

(8) **Ways of stacking pallets**

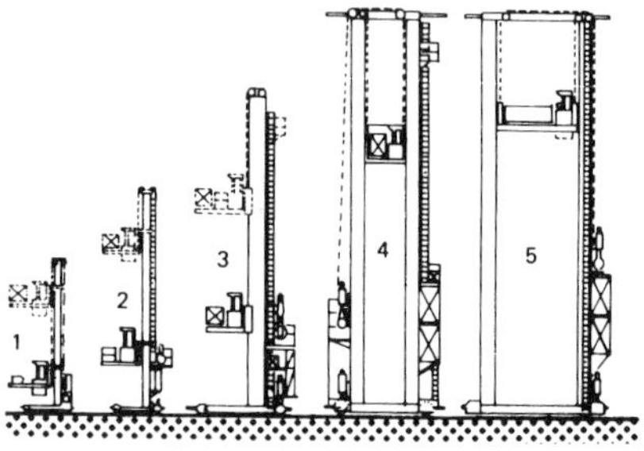

1
2
3
4
5

(9) **Handling machines**

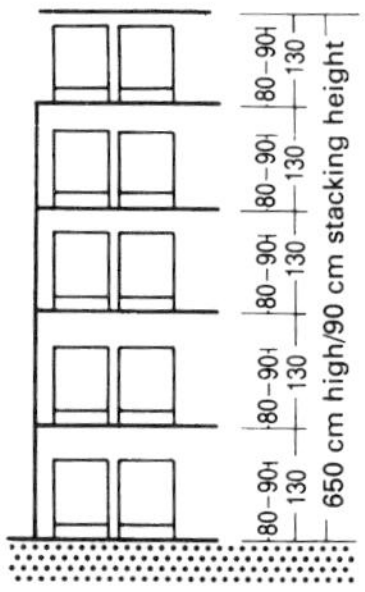

80–90
130
650 cm high/90 cm stacking height

(10) **Total stacking height**

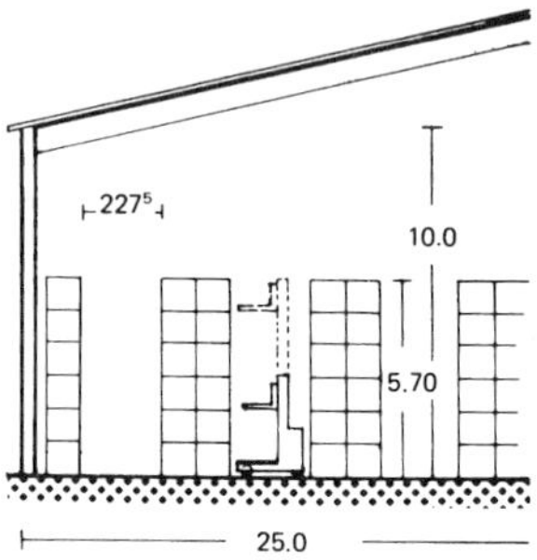

Type	1				2		3								4	5
standard height (m) / useful load (daN) (daN = kp): 1000 / 500 / 300 / 200	8 (300)	8 (200)	15 (300)	15 (200)	15 (500)	15 (500)	10 (1000)	10	15	15	20	20	30	30	40	40
max useful load (daN)	300	200	300	200	500	500	1500								1500	3000
width of aisle min–max (mm)	950–1200				1050–1400		1250–1800								1400–1800	1500–2000
driving speed max (m/min)	80				125		160								160	160
lifting speed max (m/min)	12				25		32								40	40
stacking speed max (m/min)		25		25		32	32								32	32
goods pallet		•		•		•	•	•	•	•	•	•	•	•	•	•
order assembly	•	•	•	•	•	•	•	•	•	•	•	•	•	•	•	•
automatic control						•	•	•	•	•	•	•	•	•	•	•
lateral stacker	•	•	•	•	•	•	•	•	•	•	•	•	•	•	•	•

(11) **Characteristics of handling machines** → (9)

227⁵
10.0
5.70
25.0

(12) **Use of storage space with fork-lift**

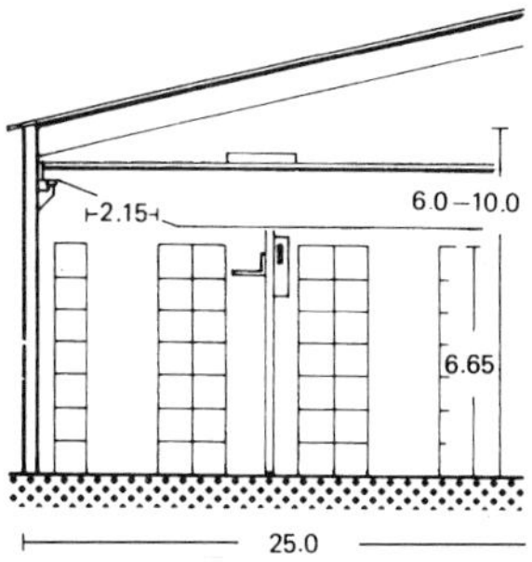

2.15
6.0–10.0
6.65
25.0

(13) **With stacker crane**

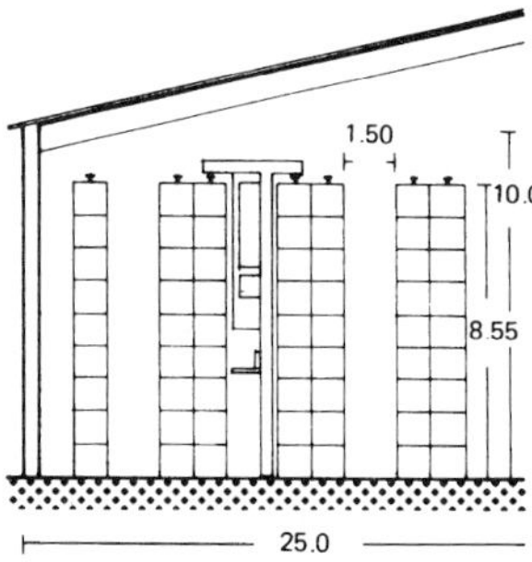

1.50
10.0
8.55
25.0

(14) **With stacker and extendable mast**

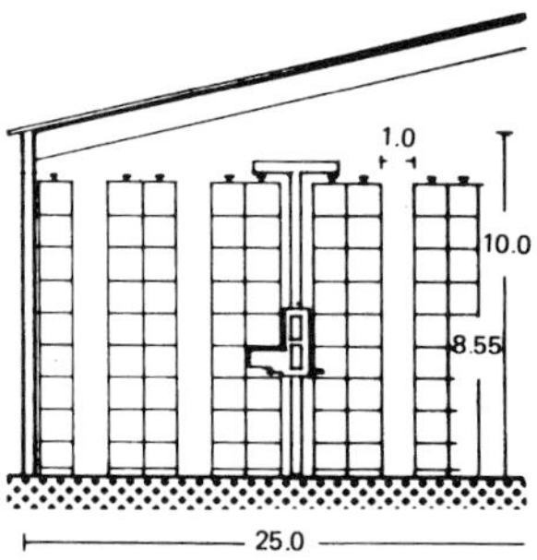

1.0
10.0
8.55
25.0

(15) **With stacker and reach fork-lift**

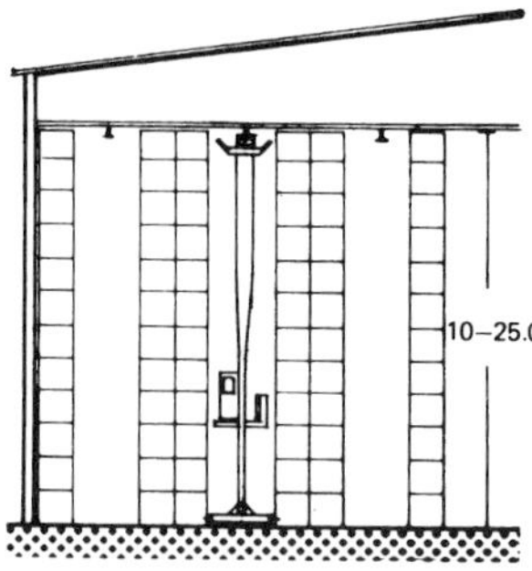

10–25.0

(16) **High-bay store (pallet silo)**

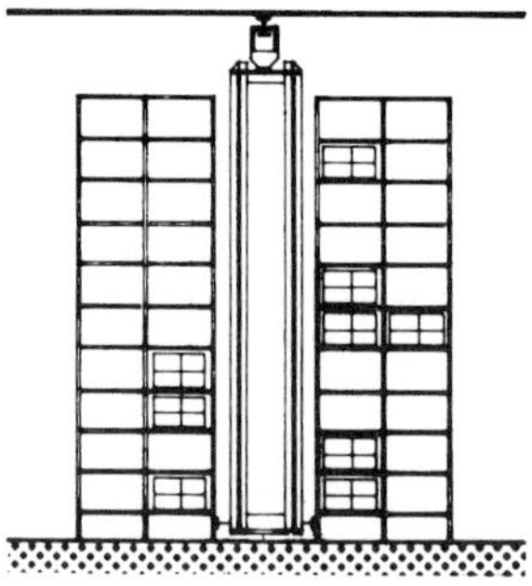

(17) **Possibilities for fixing guide rails: guide rails above**

(18) **Guide rails below**

(19) **Dual guide rails on racks**

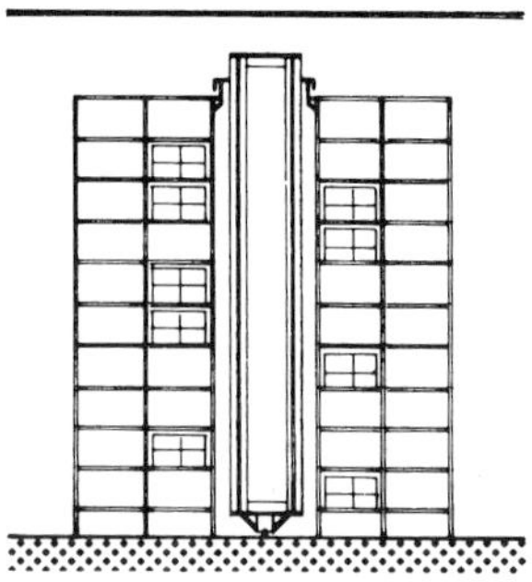

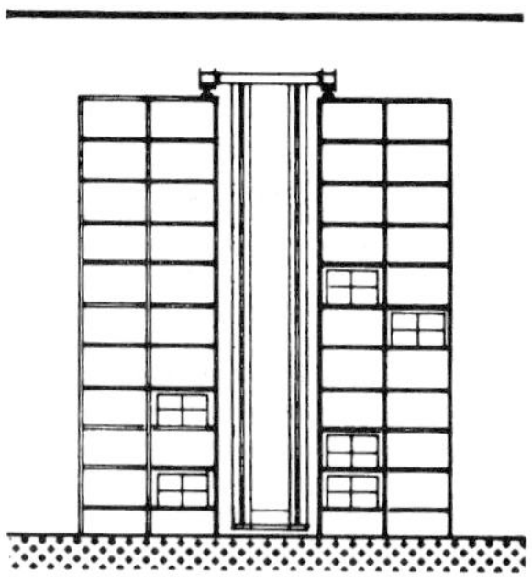

Planning/Logistics

Before planning a particular system of storage, various aspects concerning the logistics of materials and product flow must be considered. Co-operation between the commercial and design team is essential. Selection should be based on the following factors:

- Centralised or decentralised storage
- Throughput capacity of each system
- Internal storage organisation and operating method (which must be established with the long-term in view)
- Suitability of type of storage to handling method

In general, material storage considerations include the size, weight, condition, and stackability of the material; the required throughput; and the building constraints such as the floor loading, floor condition, column spacing, and clear height.

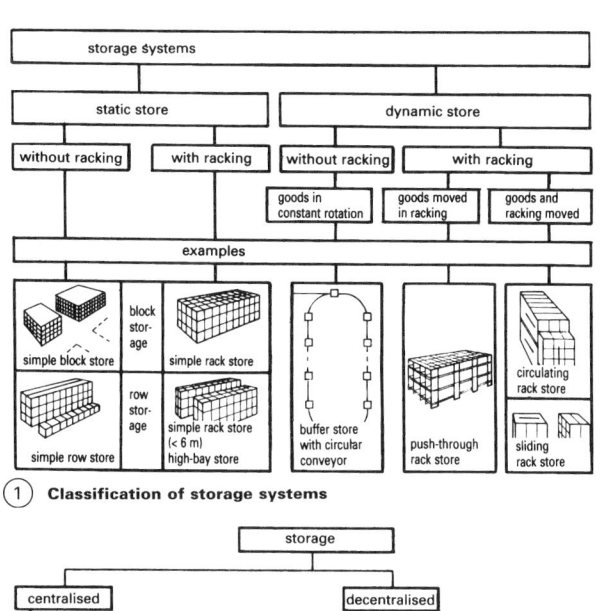

① Classification of storage systems

② Advantages of centralised and decentralised storage

centralised
- low capital outlay
- better stock control
- good use of floor space and cubage
- less complicated disposition
- better use of equipment capacity
- lower staff costs
- greater automation possibilities

decentralised
- lower transport costs
- shorter routes
- easily adapted to building
- use of special equipment
- faster order processing

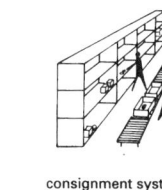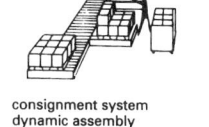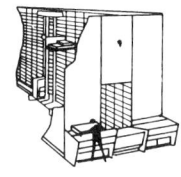

consignment system
static assembly
one-dimensional movement
manual picking
decentralised check-out

consignment system
dynamic assembly
one-dimensional movement
manual picking
centralised check-out

consignment system
dynamic assembly
two-dimensional movement
manual picking
decentralised check-out

③ Different order assembly systems

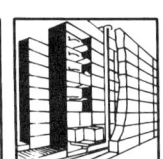

block store | high-bay store | high rack store | push-through rack store

	block store	high-bay store	high rack store	push-through rack store
Suitability	Large stocks of stackable goods; Interim store	High frequency of movement	Good sorting of large range of small stock items; Automatic operation	Small range of medium-size stock articles; Large stocks of each article; High throughput
Advantages	No fitting costs; High utilisation of floor space and cubage (80%)	Low medium-term capital outlay; Good access; Universal application	Good access to each article; Good use of floor space and cubage (60%); FIFO by organisation	FIFO ensured; Constant, good access to each article; High use of floor space and cubage (65%)
Disadvantages	No FIFO; No direct access to each pallet; Difficult to automate; Susceptible to changes in the structure of stock	Only limited FIFO; Low (45%) use of floor space and cubage; High staffing levels	Single purpose building; High capital outlay	High capital outlay; Complicated technology; Susceptible to changes in the nature of stock

④ Different storage systems

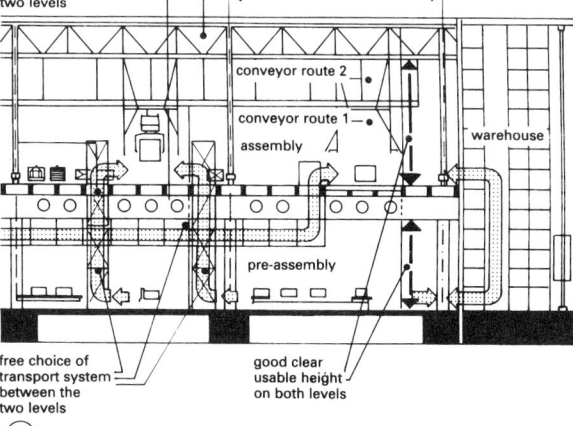

high-performance structure and service zones above the two levels

wide spans on both levels

conveyor route 2

conveyor route 1

assembly

warehouse

pre-assembly

free choice of transport system between the two levels

good clear usable height on both levels

⑤ Example of a production store integrated into the assembly

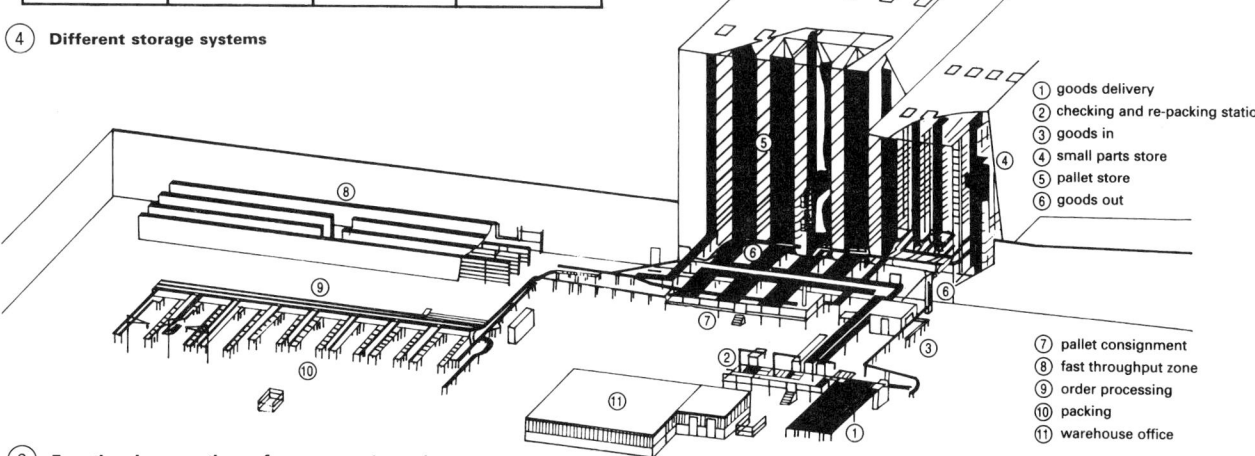

① goods delivery
② checking and re-packing station
③ goods in
④ small parts store
⑤ pallet store
⑥ goods out
⑦ pallet consignment
⑧ fast throughput zone
⑨ order processing
⑩ packing
⑪ warehouse office

⑥ Functional connections of a spare parts centre

WAREHOUSING TECHNOLOGY

Safety regulations

The choice of a high-bay store requires considerations about structure, assembly and internal work procedures. Material handling equipment and methods must concord with existing safety codes and regulations. Racks over 12 m high are subject to special approval procedures.

Fire precautions The building inspectorate imposes the following conditions for warehouses and other storage areas:

- Escape routes and exits must lead outside or to a protected stairwell, with a maximum length of 35 m
- Fire walls or compartments should be in place every 2000–3000 m²
- Extinguisher systems as well as smoke and heat vents must be provided
- Automatic sprinklers are required for combustible materials stored in high bays
- The structure itself must be fire resistant for an adequate length of time

Security Security of storage areas will be a problem if the layout is not specifically designed to secure the contents. Consider:

- Doors barred with heavy duty locks
- Constant casual observation, including security patrolling at night
- Good fencing around the site, with permanent lighting of the area between fence and building

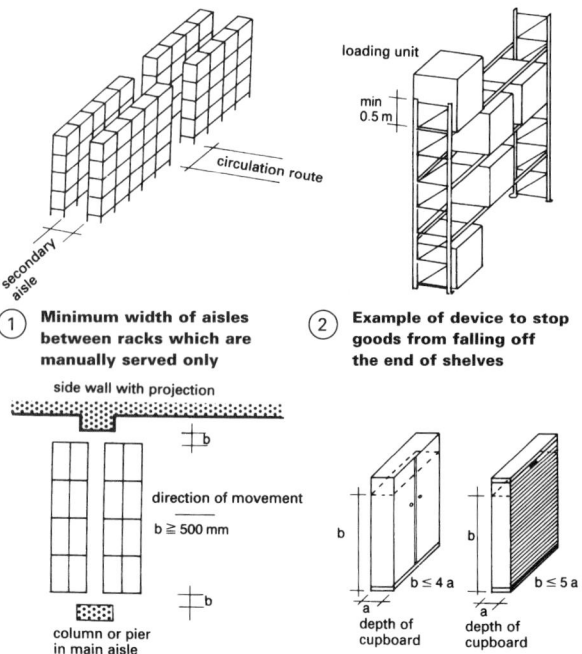

① Minimum width of aisles between racks which are manually served only

② Example of device to stop goods from falling off the end of shelves

③ Distance between walls of movable rack units and cupboards

④ Relationship between depth and height of cupboards

⑤ Assumed loads for storage equipment

Q_z = shelf load
H = horizontal force
H = $1/200\ Q_F$
HZ = additional horiz. force
HZ = min 500
Example
Q_F = 60 kg
H = 3 Ñ
HZ = min 50 N

⑥ Ground supports for wire-mesh pallets

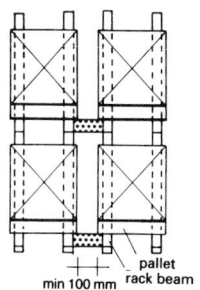

⑦ Device to stop pallet racks from sliding

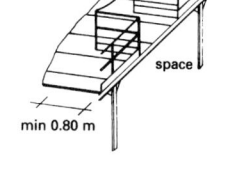

⑧ Example of an integrated storage space

⑨ Section through pallet rack for combined manual operation and operation by stacker (small articles)

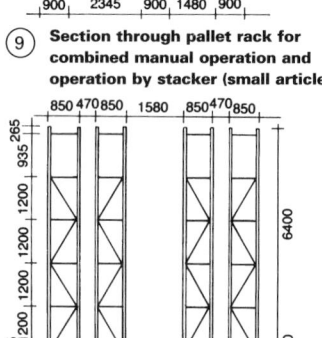

⑩ Section through pallet rack for stacker loading. U-section steel guide rails for stackers

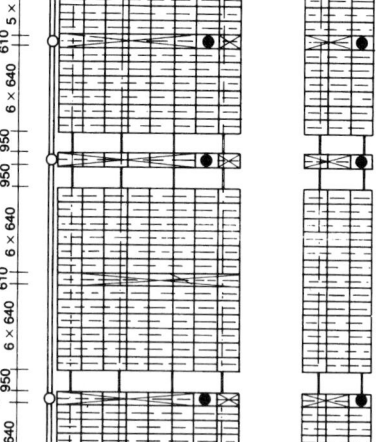

⑪ Detail of a sliding rack system for storing files

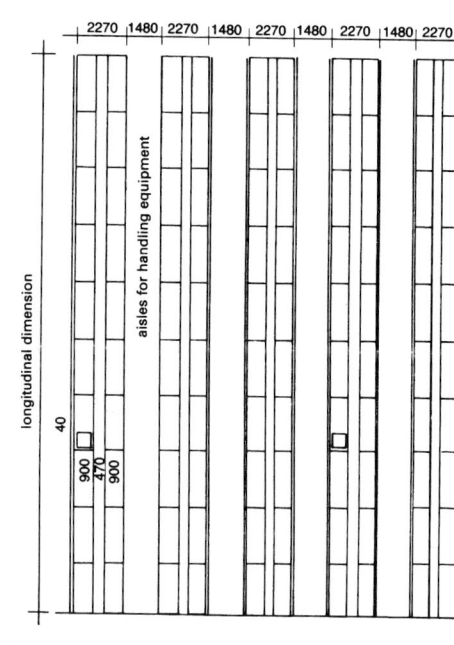

⑫ Detail of a plan for a pallet rack store for ball bearings (structural elements of shed concealed in shelving)

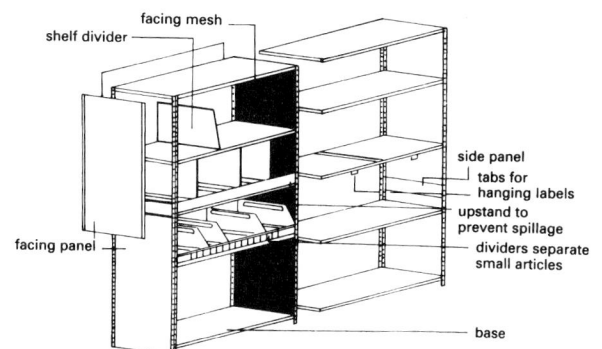

① **Angle-section bolted system for all-round use**

system: Hofe

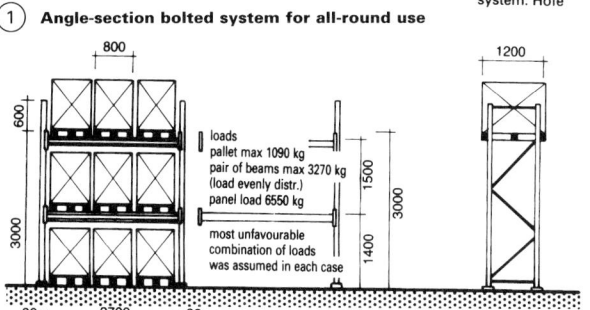

② **Pallet racking system for Euro pallets**

system: Händi/Opitz

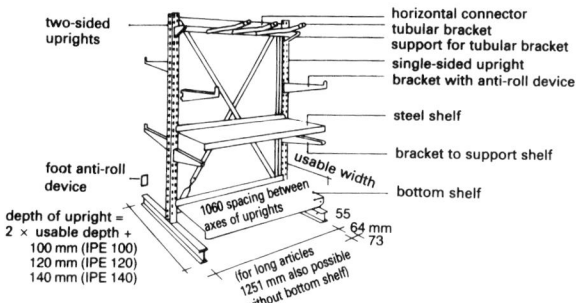

③ **Bracket rack system**

system: Hofe

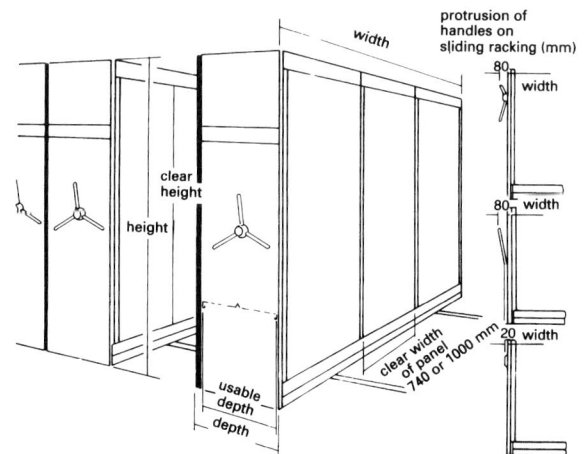

④ **Wide-span racking (depth 600–1100 mm)**

system: Hofe

WAREHOUSING TECHNOLOGY

Rack systems

The traditional storage system used in industrial buildings is shelving, either the screws and brackets type or the plug-in shelf system with prefabricated frames into which the steel shelves are slotted (the advantage of which is that it offers shorter assembly times). The latter type of shelving comes in different versions, in sheet metal, with or without perforations or wire netting.

Prefabricated systems are appropriate up to heights of about 4.5 m and for loads of up to 250 kg/shelf. For greater loads or heights, pallet racking is more suitable. Beams of IPE profiles with welded-in clips are hung in the prefabricated frames made of U-profiles into which grooves have been punched. Diagonal steel strips give vertical bracing. Racking systems at centres of 2.80 m have become standard (large enough to take three Euro pallets next to each other). They can be stacked to a height of 12.00 m. Intermediate platforms can be constructed for multistorey, self-supporting platforms with load bearing capacities of up to 500 kg/m².

Special types of racking such as barrel racks (2000 kg load per shelf), coil racks (coil weight per axis approx 1000 kg), comb racks, peg racks, tyre racks, wide-span racks and sliding racks are also available.

height of racking H	depth of frame b/B
3000	400 × 900
3300	400 × 950
3600	400 × 1000
3900	400 × 1050

number of barrels 2006	height of racking/ depth of roof (mm)
9	3600/1450
12	4800/1450

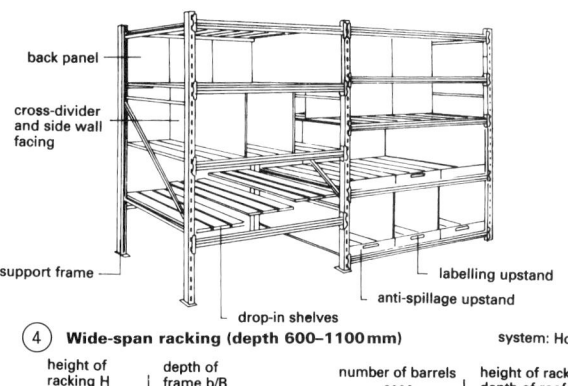

⑥ **Cable mast standard racking**

⑦ **Barrel racking for outdoor storage**

depths									heights	
depth sliding				640	760	840	940	1040	h.	clear h.
(mm) stationary	370	410	510	610	730	810	910	1010	(mm)	(mm)
useable depth	360	400	500	600	720	800	900	1000	2105	1850
									2405	2150
									2705	2450

system: Mauer

⑤ **Sliding racking (operated by hand or electric motor)**

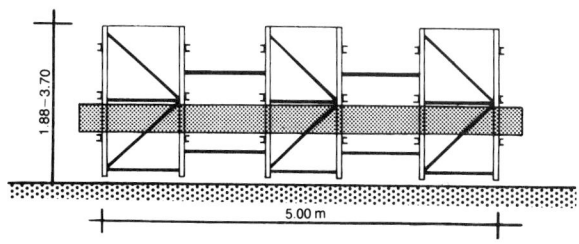

⑧ **Continuous bracket racking**

395

HANDLING

Basic dimensions of pallets according to European standards: 0.80 m × 1.20 m. Flat pallets (four-way pallets of wood), weight approx. 28–32 kg. → ① Lattice box pallets with fixed sides of structural steel mesh; max. stacking height five boxes.

Transport is part of the materials flow. Cost-savings are possible through simplification of handling method: choose uniform handling materials (e.g. pool pallets); adapt handling method to the tasks required and technical needs of the building.

Wheeled handling equipment has variable uses. → ④ – ⑤ Stacking heights up to 6 m are possible; in special cases up to 10 m using hub stacker trucks. Economically efficient owing to low capital cost and no re-loading if standard loading units are used (pallets). Flat routes with hard-wearing surface required.

Continuous conveying equipment allows easy handling of a range of goods (unit loads, boxes, bulk goods and liquids) → ⑦ – ⑨

Swivel cranes → ⑩ – ⑪ make it possible to move loads throughout a particular area.

Track-borne cranes are the simplest lifting device for vertical lifting. Simple travelling winches through to gantry cranes offer good horizontal mobility and can handle loads from 0.5–20 t → ⑫ – ⑭

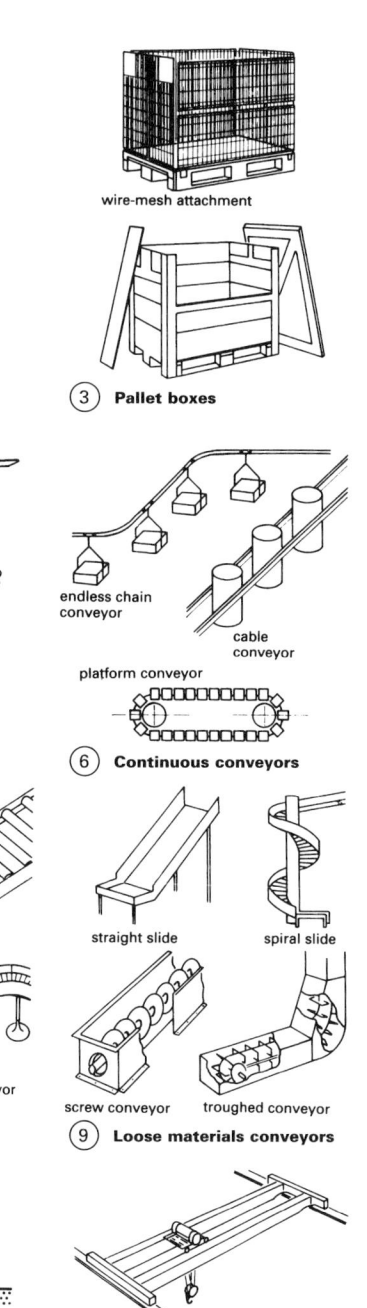

① **Pallets and attachments**
pallet
crate attachment

② **Attachments → ①**

③ **Pallet boxes**
wire-mesh attachment

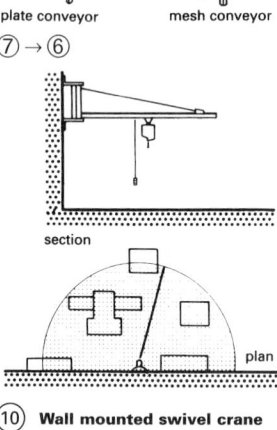

④ **Hand trolleys**

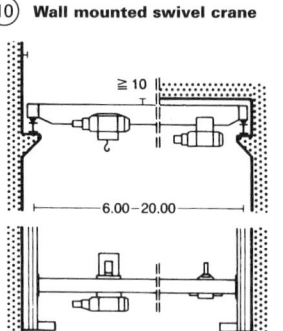

⑤ **Hand trucks**
electrically assisted fork-lift truck
manual fork-lift truck

⑥ **Continuous conveyors**
endless chain conveyor
cable conveyor
platform conveyor

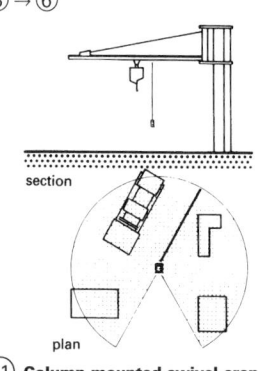

belt conveyor
steel belt conveyor
plate conveyor
mesh conveyor
⑦ → ⑥

chain conveyor
roller conveyor
incline 2–5%
skate wheel conveyor
hinged plate conveyor
⑧ → ⑥

straight slide
spiral slide
screw conveyor
troughed conveyor
⑨ **Loose materials conveyors**

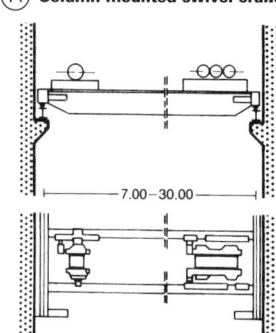

section
plan
⑩ **Wall mounted swivel crane**

section
plan
⑪ **Column mounted swivel crane**

fixed gantry crane
⑫ **Gantry cranes**

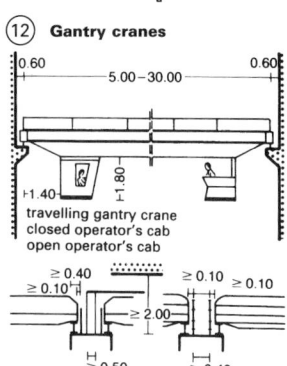

≥ 10
6.00 – 20.00
⑬ **Simple-girder gantry crane (capacity: 0.5–6.0 t)**

7.00 – 30.00
⑭ **Double-girder gantry crane (capacity: 2–20 t)**

0.60   5.00 – 30.00   0.60
travelling gantry crane
closed operator's cab
open operator's cab
1.40   1.80
≥ 0.40
≥ 0.10
≥ 0.40   ≥ 0.10   ≥ 0.10
≥ 2.00
≥ 0.50   ≥ 0.40
⑮ **Runway catwalks (safety dimensions)**

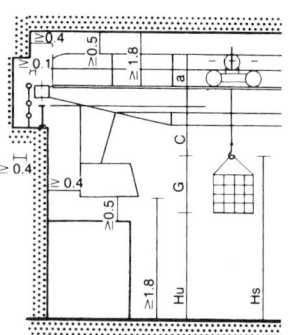

⑯ **Gantry crane (safety dimensions)**

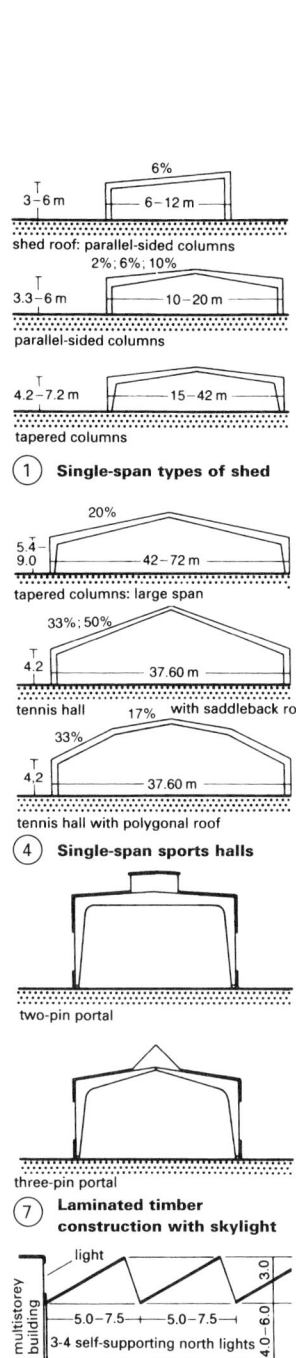

① **Single-span types of shed**
- shed roof: parallel-sided columns — 6%, 3–6 m, 6–12 m
- parallel-sided columns — 2%; 6%; 10%, 3.3–6 m, 10–20 m
- tapered columns — 2%; 6%; 10%, 4.2–7.2 m, 15–42 m

④ **Single-span sports halls**
- tapered columns: large span — 20%, 5.4–9.0, 42–72 m
- tennis hall with saddleback roof — 33%; 50%, 4.2, 37.60 m
- tennis hall with polygonal roof — 17%; 33%, 4.2, 37.60 m

⑦ **Laminated timber construction with skylight**
- two-pin portal
- three-pin portal

⑩ **Section through sawtooth roof with cross-bracing in glazing**
- section through north light roof (self-supporting) like lattice girder — light, 3.0, 5.0–7.5, 5.0–7.5, 4.0–6.0, multistorey building, 3–4 self-supporting north lights
- without support up to 50 m — light, 3.0, 4.0–6.0

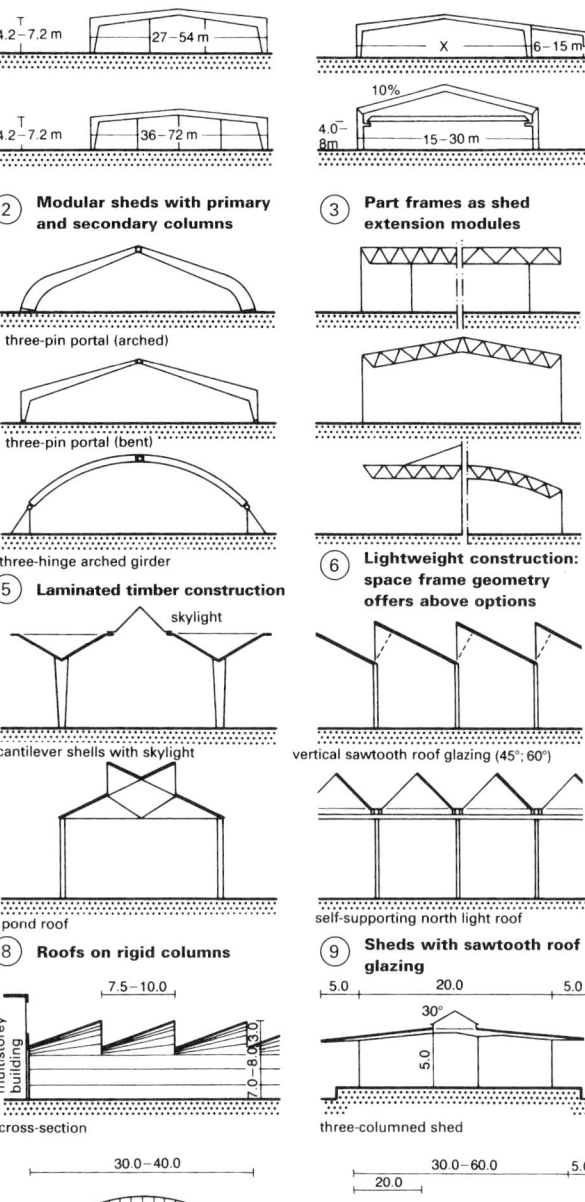

② **Modular sheds with primary and secondary columns**
- 2%; 6%; 10%, 4.2–7.2 m, 18–48 m
- 4.2–7.2 m, 27–54 m
- 4.2–7.2 m, 36–72 m

⑤ **Laminated timber construction**
- three-pin portal (arched)
- three-pin portal (bent)
- three-hinge arched girder

⑧ **Roofs on rigid columns**
- skylight
- cantilever shells with skylight
- pond roof

⑪ **Vaulted shed roof**
- cross-section — 7.5–10.0, 7.0–8.0
- longitudinal section — 30.0–40.0, tie rod, 7.0–8.0

③ **Part frames as shed extension modules**
- 2%; 6%; 10%, x, 6–15 m
- x, 6–15 m
- 10%, 4.0–8 m, 15–30 m

⑥ **Lightweight construction: space frame geometry offers above options**

⑨ **Sheds with sawtooth roof glazing**
- vertical sawtooth roof glazing (45°; 60°)
- self-supporting north light roof

⑫ **Shed with transverse roof lights; frame with cantilevered beams**
- three-columned shed — 5.0, 20.0, 5.0, 30°, 5.0
- 30.0–60.0, 20.0, 12.0, 5.0

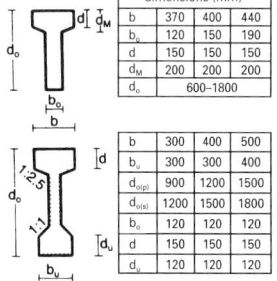

⑬ **Pre-cast concrete elements**
– roof beam: T section
I section

T section – dimensions (mm)

b	370	400	440
b_o	120	150	190
d	150	150	150
d_M	200	200	200
d_o	600–1800		

I section

b	300	400	500
b_o	300	300	400
$d_{o(p)}$	900	1200	1500
$d_{o(s)}$	1200	1500	1800
b_o	120	120	120
d	150	150	150
d_u	120	120	120

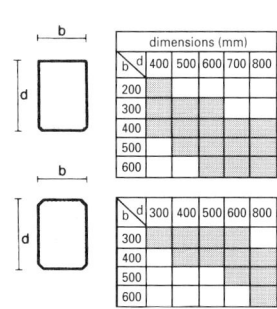

⑭ **Pre-cast concrete elements**
– joists/cross-members
lower corners chamfered
– pillars: all chamfered

dimensions (mm)

b \ d	400	500	600	700	800
200					
300					
400					
500					
600					

b \ d	300	400	500	600	800
300					
400					
500					
600					

⑮ **Pre-cast concrete elements**
– purlins
– joists (inverted T section)

d	b_o	b	fire resistance >450°C	350°–450°C
350	80	150	F-30-A	
	120	190	F-60-A	F-30-A
	160	230	F-90-A	F-60-A
500	80	180	F-30-A	
	120	220	F-60-A	F-30-A
	160	260	F-90-A	F-60-A

d_o \ b_o	500	600	700	800	900	1000
300						
400						
500						
600						

200 b_o 200

Shed designs satisfy the requirement for economy, standardisation, and the need for flexible non-specific or dumb space.

Advantages of single-storey: low building costs; even daylight; high floor loads possible; can be built on difficult sites; lower accident risk. Disadvantages: high heat loss (sky lights); high maintenance costs; large land requirement.

Wooden structures are suitable for lightweight buildings, and particularly for roofing in large buildings using modern truss systems with timber connectors. Construction using laminated timber beams is also a possibility. → ⑤

Steel structures are appropriate for industrial buildings because modifications or additions are easy to carry out in steel. Maintenance costs (painting) are higher than for masonry or concrete.

Reinforced concrete structures: constructed by casting in situ or using pre-cast elements; more resistant to chemical attack than steel and therefore necessary for certain industrial buildings. Normal (unstressed) reinforcement for small spans (heavy sections); for larger spans usually pre-stressed (often pre-cast elements). → ⑬ – ⑮ Dimensions: for lightweight buildings bay widths of 5–7.5 m; economically efficient for spans of 10–30 m. In cases where columns are a hindrance, spans of up to 50 m are possible. → ⑨ – ⑫

If possible, strutting which takes up space should be avoided and solid frames used instead → ① – ⑤ with tension members in the floor. When calculating the distance between columns take into account the arrangement of machines and access routes and turning circles of vehicles.

The shed height may have to be adapted to size of cranes. Usually no advantage in terms of ventilation with higher sheds; more important is an appropriate number of air changes, facilitated by ventilation elements (windows, ventilation hoods, air heaters) which are of the correct size and properly placed.

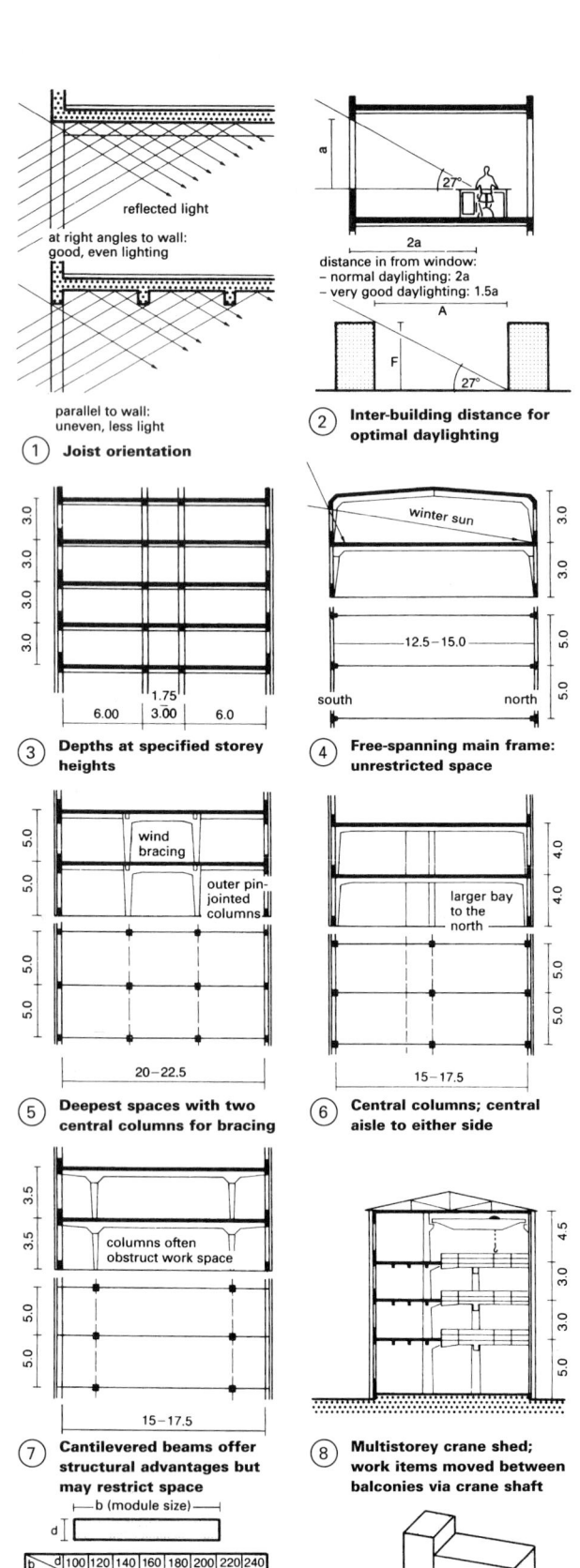

① **Joist orientation**

reflected light
at right angles to wall: good, even lighting
parallel to wall: uneven, less light

② **Inter-building distance for optimal daylighting**

distance in from window:
– normal daylighting: 2a
– very good daylighting: 1.5a

③ **Depths at specified storey heights**

④ **Free-spanning main frame: unrestricted space**

winter sun
south   north
12.5–15.0

⑤ **Deepest spaces with two central columns for bracing**

wind bracing
outer pin-jointed columns
20–22.5

⑥ **Central columns; central aisle to either side**

larger bay to the north
15–17.5

⑦ **Cantilevered beams offer structural advantages but may restrict space**

columns often obstruct work space
15–17.5

⑧ **Multistorey crane shed; work items moved between balconies via crane shaft**

⑨ **Double-T profile, pre-cast concrete floor slabs**

b (module size)

b \ d	100	120	140	160	180	200	220	240
2400	all dimensions adequate for F 90							

dR		300	400	500	600	700
b_o	$T_{crit} > 450°C$	190	180	170	160	150
	T_{crit} 350–450°C	230	220	210	200	190
d	≥ 60 pre-cast for				F 90-A	
	≥ 100 pre-cast for				F 90-A	
	≥ 50 cast in situ for					

⑩ **Joist/cross member support, rectangular cross-section**

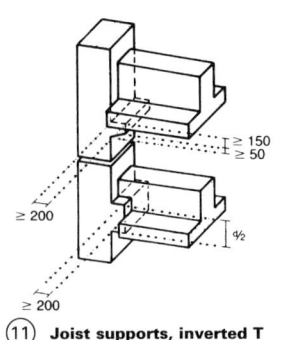

⑪ **Joist supports, inverted T**

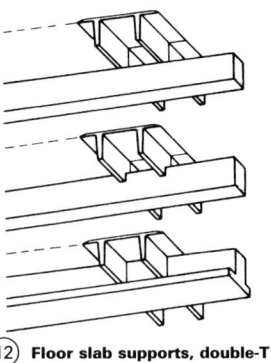

⑫ **Floor slab supports, double-T**

MULTISTOREY INDUSTRIAL BUILDINGS

Advantages over single-storey buildings

Smaller footprint, shorter routes between departments if the vertical connections are effective, shorter pipe runs, cheaper maintenance and heating, simpler ventilation. Suitable for breweries, paper mills, warehouses and other buildings where the materials are conveyed once to the upper floors and then move by gravity down onto the lower floors. Good side-lighting. Useful for optical, precision engineering and electronics firms, food processors and packagers, and textiles industries.

Siting

Depends on urban planning and operational considerations. If fenestration on one side only, building should face north-east; if, as is the norm, windows are on two sides, the building runs east–west with windows facing north and south. The summer sun then only shines a short distance into the rooms and can be easily controlled by awnings whilst in winter the sunlight penetrates even to the north side of the spaces. → ④ On the northern side: stairwell, WC (cool). Minimise distracting shadows in working areas.

On the free southern side it is possible to use motor-operated awnings. The best daylighting is achieved in free-standing high-rise buildings, which are twice their height apart (light incidence angle for the ground floor is 27 degrees). → ② Low buildings with roof lights can be positioned between them.

Dimensions: room height in accordance with building regulations for commercial buildings, ≥ 3.0 m and ≥ 2.5 m in basement and attic. Permitted depth of building depends on room height. Single room depth of free-standing multistorey factories is generally twice the height, with windows up to the ceiling. → ① Circulation routes in the middle of the building are not included in the calculation – see ③ for example with 3 m room height, giving total depth of 13.75 m–15.00 m. This is the most economic depth when roofing has no central supports. → ④ Rooms 4 m high are 15–17.5 m deep, usually with one or two central supports. Rooms 5 m high and 20–22.5 m deep with two columns are economically efficient. → ⑤ + ⑥

In special cases (courtyards etc.) the possible building depth can be calculated easily, taking into account the desired brightness, which differs according to the type of activity.

Approximate values for window areas:
ancillary and store rooms	10% of floor area
workshops for heavy work	12% of floor area
workshops for precision work	20% of floor area

At greater room depths, diffusion of the incoming light is desirable (pay attention to awnings, blinds, light refracting glass etc.). The direction of the joist span is also important. → ① Workstation to window distance should not be more than twice the height of the window head above the table surface. → ②

TOILET FACILITIES

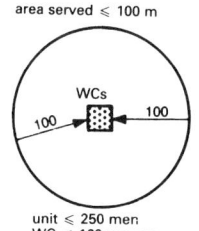

① **Area served**

area served ≤ 100 m

unit ≤ 250 men
WC ≤ 160 women

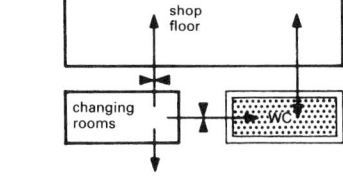

② **Arrangement of WCs**

shop floor

changing rooms

WC

To ensure a good working atmosphere it is essential to design sanitary facilities which are both functional and attractive.

Toilets should be approximately 100 m from each workstation; 75 m in the case of work at conveyor belts. In large companies it is useful to divide them into smaller units (e.g. on each floor next to the stairs on the landing). In companies with more than five employees separate toilets must be provided for men and women, as well as toilets for the exclusive use of employees where necessary. A lobby is not required if there is only one WC per toilet facility and no direct access to a work place or area used for breaks, for changing, washing or first aid. Toilet cubicles must be lockable. If ventilation is through windows on one side only, an area of 1700 cm² is required, or possibly 1000 cm² if space is restricted.

In toilet facilities for ≤250 men or ≤160 women a drainage point with smell seal and tap connection with stop cock and hose union must be provided, and a sink for cleaning purposes. Flooring should be non-slip, water-resistant and easy to clean. Walls should be washable to ≥2 m high. Room temperature 21°C. Well-ventilated lobbies are required in front of toilet facilities and should have one wash basin per five WCs minimum and the means for drying hands. If soap dispensers are fitted, one is sufficient for two wash basins. A minimum of one mirror for every two to three wash basins should be fitted. The minimum room height for toilets with four or fewer WCs can be 2.20 m.

Install washing facility for disabled people, according to regulations, recommendations and types of activities.

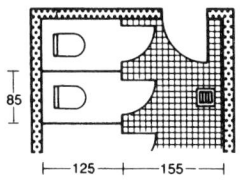

③ **Single row WCs, doors opening outwards**

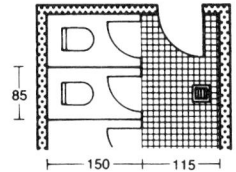

④ **Single row WCs, doors opening inwards**

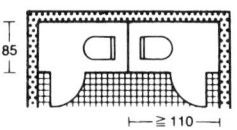

⑤ **Doors opening outwards; with urinal trough**

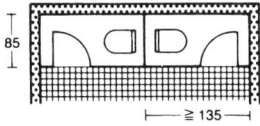

⑥ **Doors opening inwards; with urinal trough**

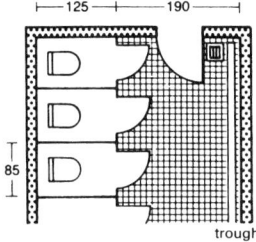

⑦ **With urinal bowls; doors opening outwards**

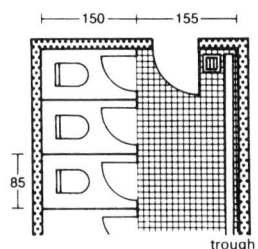

⑧ **As ⑦ but with doors opening inwards**

	Men						Women					
number of employees	flush toilets	urinals	troughs (m)[1]	hand basins[2]	additional flush toilets	additional urinals	number of employees	flush toilets	hand basins[2]	additional flush toilets	waste bins	sink
10[3]	1	1	0.6	1	1	1	10[3]	1	1	1	1	1
25	2	2	1.2	1	1	1	20	2	1	1	1	1
50	3	3	1.8	1	1	1	35	3	1	1	1	1
75	4	4	2.4	1	1	2	50	4	2	2	1	1
100	5	5	3.0	2	1	2	65	5	2	2	1	1
130	6	6	3.6	2	2	2	80	6	2	2	1	1
160	7	7	4.2	2	2	2	100	7	2	3	1	1
190	8	8	4.8	2	2	2	120	8	3	3	1	1
220	9	9	5.4	3	3	3	140	9	3	4	1	1
250[4]	10	10	6.0	3	3	4	160[4]	10	3	4	1	1

[1] an increase of up to 1.5 times is possible
[2] legislation stipulates that hot water taps must be situated above hand basins in the vestibules of toilet facilities in workplaces
[3] A shared facility is permissible for up to five employees
[4] WC facility should be no larger than for use by 250 men or 160 women

⑪ **Large WC facilities**

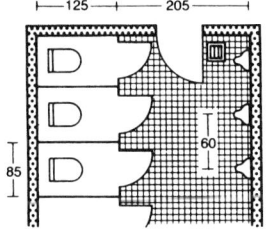

⑨ **Dual row WCs, doors opening outwards**

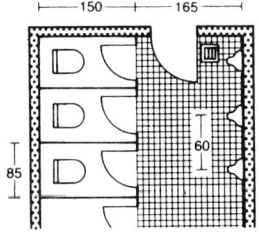

⑩ **As ⑨ but with doors opening inwards**

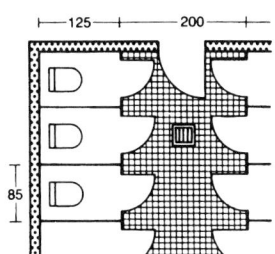

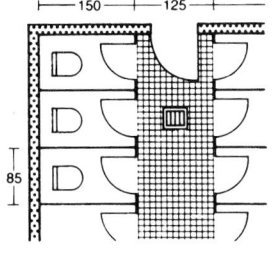

⑫ **Single row urinal bowls and trough**

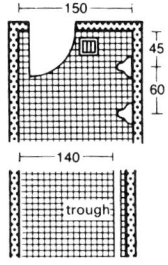

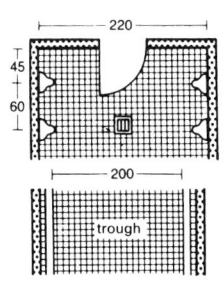

⑬ **Dual row urinal bowls and troughs**

WASHING FACILITIES

'Washing facilities' include all amenities and rooms which are used by staff for maintaining personal hygiene. They are divided into washrooms, shower rooms and bathrooms.

They should have a hot and cold water or mixed water supply. Each facility should have at least one drainage point with stop cock and hose union. During use the facilities should have adequate artificial ventilation.

The number of washing facilities depends on type of company. For 100 users: doing clean work, 15; doing moderately dirty work, 20; doing very dirty work, 25; doing hot, wet, dusty, smelly work, or handling toxic or germ-carrying substances, in sterile and pharmaceutical processes or the food industry, 25.

Depending on the type of company, the facilities should be divided into washing and showering facilities. Also depending on the type of company, drinking fountains should be provided close to work places. → ①

The temperature in changing and washing facilities should be 20–22°C. Water consumption per person per day is roughly 50 litres.

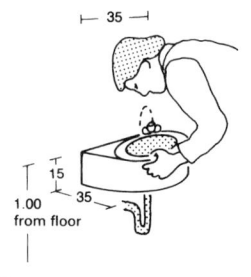

① Drinking fountain, operated by lever < 100 m from workstations

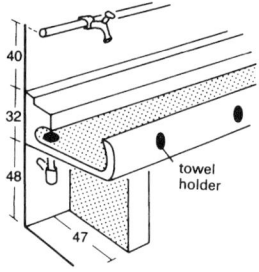

② Row washing trough (Rotter system)

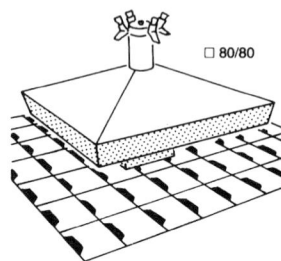

③ Foot-washing system

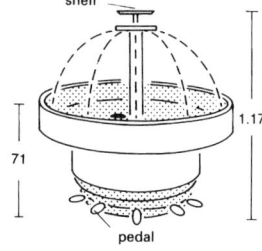

④ Washing fountain (gives 25% space saving over rows of wash-basins → ② + ⑪)

Washing spaces required

type of work	use per person	no. of users per space given a wash time of	
	min	15 min a	20 min b
slightly dirty	2	7	10
moderately dirty	3	5	6
very dirty	4	4	5

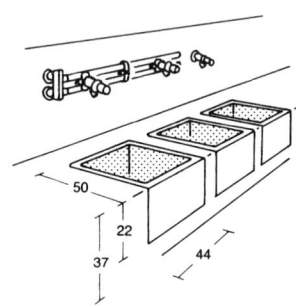

⑤ Foot baths

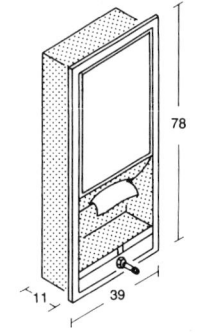

⑥ Paper towel dispenser, shelf and soap dispenser

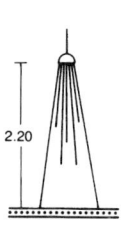

⑦ Clear height of shower heads

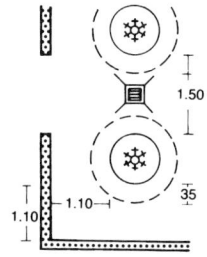

⑧ Space requirement for circular wash-basins

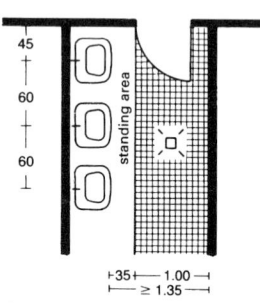

⑨ Washroom and hand basins

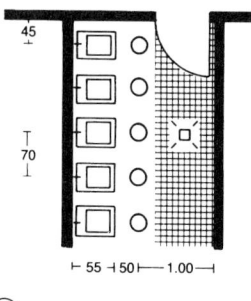

⑩ Washrooms with foot baths

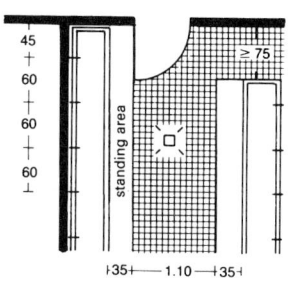

⑪ Washroom with washing trough

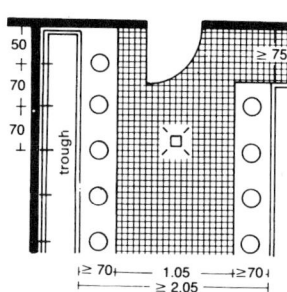

⑫ Washroom with foot washing trough

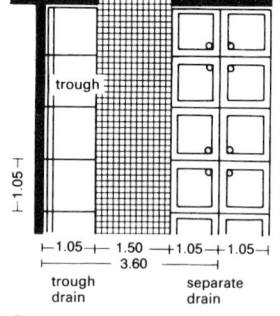

⑬ Semi-open showers

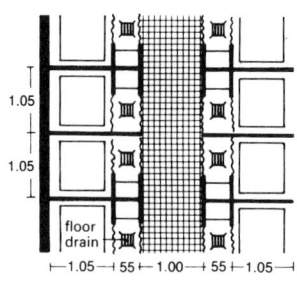

⑭ Individual showers with changing cubicle

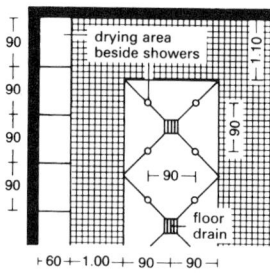

⑮ Open showers with drying area

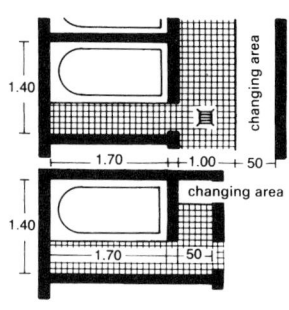

⑯ Bath cubicles

Type of space	Hygiene facilities
WCs[1] for women	1 cleaner's sink 1 toilet for every 3 to 10 women or 50 to 100 m² 1 wash-basin for maximum of 5 WCs
WCs[1] for men	1 cleaner's sink 1 toilet for every 10 to 15 men or 50 to 100 m² 1 to 3 urinal bowls for every 10 to 15 men or 50 to 100 m² 1 wash-basin for maximum of 5 WCs
Offices	1 wash-basin for every 8 to 10 people or 100 m² or at least 1 per office or 1 wash-basin for 3 to 7 people
Cleaner's room	1 cleaner's sink
Tea rooms	1 boiling water dispenser[2] 1 washing-up sink with draining board

[1] Maximum of 10 toilets per facility
[2] Average boiling water consumption per person per day is
0.75 litres (1 litre of water equals 5 to 6 cups)

(1) **Facilities for office buildings**

Women	WCs	Bidets	Wash- basins	Cleaner's sinks
8–10[1]	1	1	1	1
17–20	2	1	2	1
25–30	3	1–2	2–3	1
35–40	4	2	3	1
45–50	5	2	4	1
Men		**Urinals**		
10–13[1]	1	1	1	1
20–25	2	1–2	1	1
30–39	2–3	2–3	2	1
40–49	3	3	3	1
50–59	3–4	4	3	1

[1] When planning small offices it is advisable to double the [z1]number of wash-basins, WCs and urinals

(2) **Number of items per person**

Room	Type of work	Fittings	
Women's washroom/ toilets[1]	not very dirty	3 wash-basins 3 WCs 1 bidet 1 cleaner's sink	per 10–15 women
	moderately dirty	3 wash-basins 1 shower 1 foot bath 3 WCs 1 bidet 1 cleaner's sink	per 10–15 women
Men's washroom/ toilets[1]	not very dirty	3 wash-basins 2 WCs 2 urinals 1 cleaner's sink	per 10–15 men
	moderately dirty	3 wash-basins 1 shower 1 foot bath 2 WCs 2 urinals 1 cleaner's sink	per 10–15 men
	very dirty	as above, but add 1 shower per 10–15 people 1 bath per 2–3 people	
	with dirty or hot floor	as above, but add 1 foot bath per 10–15 people	
		1 disinfecting foot bath per 6–8 showers 1–2 drinking fountains per washroom	
Cleaner's room		1 cleaner's sink	
Tea room[2]		1 cleaner's sink 1 boiling water urn 1 double sink with draining board	
Work rooms[3]		1 drinking fountain per 100 people	

[1] Max 10 toilets per facility; 1 hand basin per 5 toilets
[2] Consumption of boiling water per person 0.75 l/day
(1 litre of water equals 5 or 6 cups)
[3] 100 m max between work spaces and drinking fountain

(3) **Facilities for industrial companies**

		Number of washing facilities per 100 employees	Wash-basins	Foot baths	Showers	Showers for the disabled (e.g. poliban bath)	Baths	Baths for the disabled	Drinking fountains
Normal working conditions	little dirt	office and administration							
		clothing, wood, light engineering	15	10	(10)	1	1	–	–	1
	moderately dirty	builder's yards, engineering works	20	10	(10)	8	2	–	–	1
Exceptional working conditions	very dirty	coal industry, limestone and cement industry, tar works	25	12	–	10	3	–	–	1
	hot	steel works, glass factories, work places using heat treatments	25	12	–	10	3	–	–	2
	dusty	aggregate crushers, quarries, parts of the ceramics industry	25	12	–	10	3	–	–	2
	humid	laundries, dyeworks	25	16	–	7	3	–	–	1
	humid and very dirty	coal and ore mines, coal washing, ore processing plants	25	12	–	10	3	–	–	1
	smelly	sewage plants, animal waste processing works	25	16	–	7	2	–	–	2
Dangerous working conditions	processing toxic, infectious or radio- active materials	plants processing lead, arsenic, mercury, phosphorous; animal waste processing (intestines and bones); biological research and isotope laboratories	25	12	–	5	2	5	–	1

(4) **Types of work and appropriate washing, shower and bath facilities**

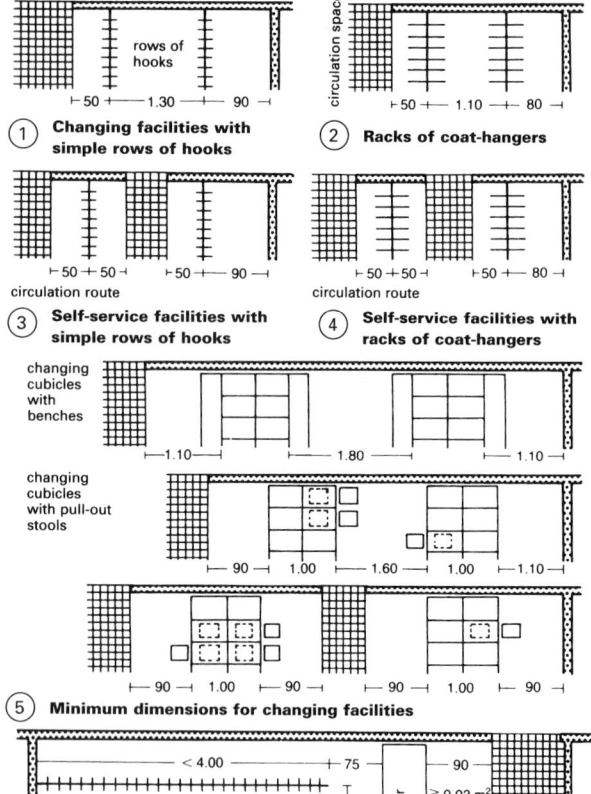

(1) **Changing facilities with simple rows of hooks**
rows of hooks
⊢50⊣ 1.30 ⊢ 90 ⊣

(2) **Racks of coat-hangers**
circulation space
⊢50⊣ 1.10 ⊣ 80 ⊣

(3) **Self-service facilities with simple rows of hooks**
circulation route
⊢50⊢50⊣ ⊢50⊢ 90 ⊣

(4) **Self-service facilities with racks of coat-hangers**
circulation route
⊢50⊢50⊣ ⊢50⊢ 80 ⊣

(5) **Minimum dimensions for changing facilities**
changing cubicles with benches
⊢1.10⊣ 1.80 ⊢ 1.10 ⊣
changing cubicles with pull-out stools
⊢90⊣ 1.00 ⊢1.60⊣ 1.00 ⊢1.10⊣
⊢90⊣ 1.00 ⊢ 90 ⊢ 1.00 ⊢ 90 ⊣

(6) **Supervised cloakroom, single rows of hooks**
< 4.00 ⊢ 75 ⊢ 90 ⊣ counter ≧ 0.03 m² per hook 1.00

(7) **Supervised cloakroom, with racks of coat-hangers**
< 4.00 ⊢ 75 ⊢ 90 ⊣ 90 ⊢ 75 ⊣ counter ≧ 0.03 m² per hook counter 60

CHANGING ROOMS, LOCKERS

Changing rooms are amenities used by staff to change from outdoor clothing into work clothes and store their belongings. They should be between the entrance to the factory and the working areas and be easily accessible. Changing rooms with a floor area of up to 30 m² must have a clear height of at least 2.30 m² and at least 2.50 m if the floor area exceeds 30 m². The basic floor area of a changing room should be at least 6 m². When changing rooms are not required provision should be made for hanging clothes and a locker provided for each employee. → (13) – (14)

It is best to place rows of cupboards and shelving at right angles to the windows. Window sills should if possible be at the height of the cupboards.

Changing rooms for men and women must be separate, sheltered from view and draughtproof. Washing and changing facilities must be in separate rooms that are directly linked.

Guidelines for widths of circulation routes: for companies with 20 people or less, routes should be between 0.875 and 1.00 m wide; for up to 100 people, min. 1.10 m and usually 1.20 m; for up to 250 people, min. 1.65 m and usually 1.80 m; for up to 400 people, min. 2.20 m and usually 2.40 m. → (1) – (7)

For open cloakrooms the following minimum distances between hooks or coat hangers must be adhered to: for street clothing, hooks 20 cm apart, coat hangers 10 cm; for dry work clothing, hooks 10 cm apart, coat hangers 6 cm; for wet work clothing, hooks 30 cm apart, coat hangers 20 cm. → (1) – (4)

Changing facilities: for normal work, one clothes locker per worker; for dirty work, one double locker (divided into compartments for work clothing and street clothing) per worker.

Changing space requirements per employee:
ideal working figure	0.50 m²
with locker and wash basin	0.50–0.60 m²
with locker but without wash basin	0.30–0.40 m²

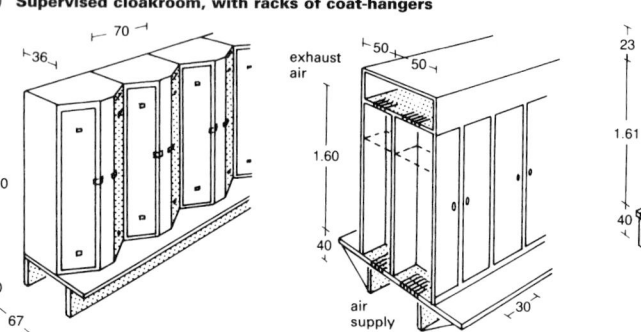

(8) **Trapezoid changing cubicles (Rotter system)**
⊢70⊣ ⊢36⊣ 1.70 30 67

(9) **Double rows of ventilated lockers and benches**
exhaust air ⊢50⊢50⊣ 1.60 40 air supply ⊢30⊣

(10) **Lockers with sloping roofs and ventilation pipe**
Ø 100 ventilation pipe ventilation slot 23 1.61 40

(11) **Narrow locker**
⊢18⊣ ⊢50⊣ 1.70

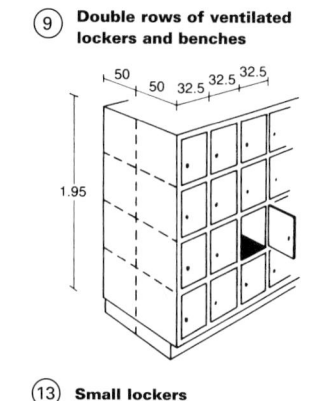

(12) **Two-level row of lockers**
⊢50⊣ 50 30 30 1.80 ventilation

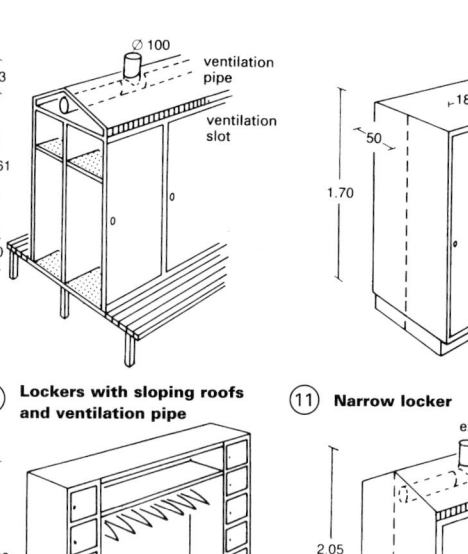

(13) **Small lockers**
⊢50⊣ 50 32.5 32.5 32.5 1.95

(14) **Lockers with open coat-hanging arrangement**
1.80 10 1.20 50 30

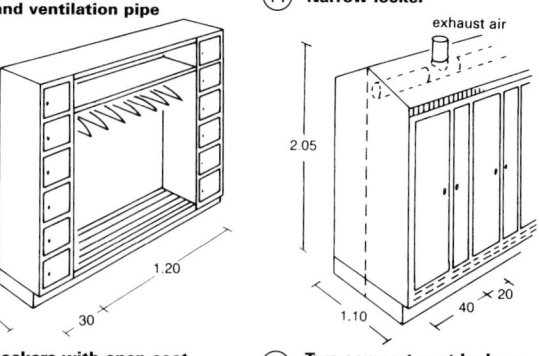

(15) **Two-compartment lockers (20 and 40 cm wide) for street and work clothes**
exhaust air 2.05 ⊢20⊣ 1.10 40

POWER STATIONS

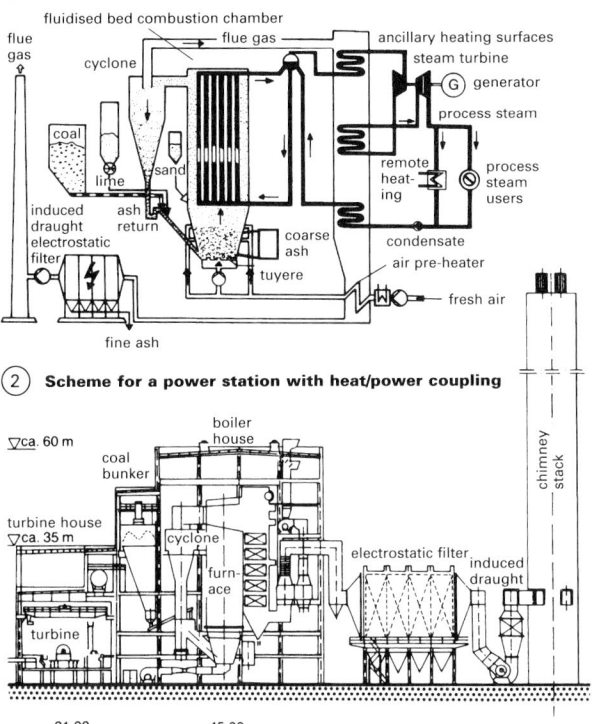

current generation   steam generation

extension

control rm

switch gear | turbine house | coal bunker | boiler house with 3 boilers | electro-static filter / induced draught | individual chimneys | alternative common chimney for a number of boilers

current | process steam | condensate | ancillary systems | coal | lime | sand | coarse ash | fine ash | flue gas

① **Power station schematic diagram**

flue gas | fluidised bed combustion chamber | flue gas | ancillary heating surfaces | cyclone | steam turbine | (G) generator | process steam | coal | lime | sand | remote heat-ing | process steam users | induced draught electrostatic filter | ash return | coarse ash | condensate | air pre-heater | tuyere | fresh air | fine ash

② **Scheme for a power station with heat/power coupling**

▽ca. 60 m | boiler house | coal bunker | chimney stack | turbine house ▽ca. 35 m | cyclone | furn-ace | electrostatic filter | induced draught | turbine

21.00 | 45.00

③ **Cross-section of the power station shown in the plan view ④**

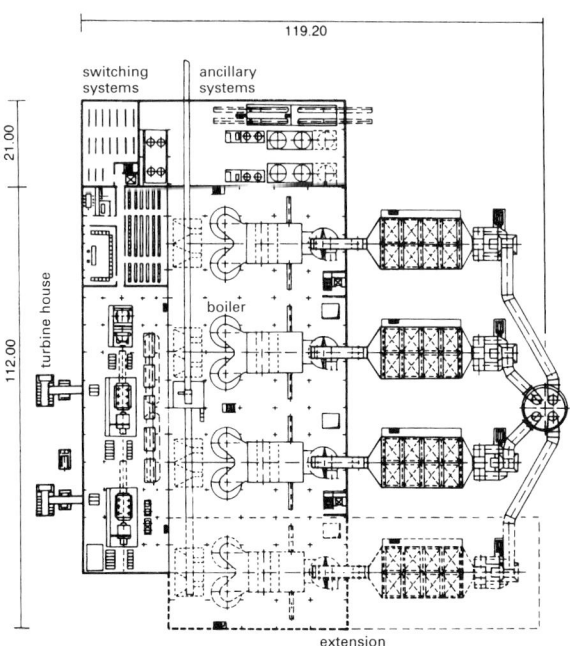

119.20 | switching systems | ancillary systems | 21.00 | turbine house | 112.00 | boiler | extension

④ **Plan of power station with fluidised bed firing**

Power station with fluidised bed firing

The function of a power station is to generate electrical current, steam or hot water in a safe and environmentally acceptable manner. In coal-fired power stations, fluidised bed firing became popular in the 1980s as an alternative to other means of firing, such as coal dust firing or grate firing. Various concepts and practical designs were developed: from stationary through to circulatory systems. Due to the increasing emphasis on protection of the environment, the trend is towards circulatory fluidised bed firing. Further developments are anticipated in the direction of pressurised fluidised bed firing.

The *essential system components* and the most important *process flows*. → ①

- Steam generation is a very significant part of the installation, consisting of the boiler house, with a number of boilers, the coal bunkers and small storage containers, auxiliary systems, electrostatic filters, induced draught plant and chimney stacks.
- There is a second complex for current generation, which contains the turbine house with turbines and steam distribution, switch gear with transformers, current distribution, electrical measuring, control and instrumentation equipment.
- The monitoring and control of all systems is carried out from a centralised control room.

The essential *material flows* are:
- inputs of coal, oil or gas, lime, sand and condensate
- output flows of electrical current, process steam, ash and flue gases
- internal flows such as cooling water.

The processing and storage of the solid and fluid substances take place centrally in the ancillary systems; the individual user equipment within the power station is supplied from this source.

The kind of application shown in the functional diagram of a power station with fluidised bed firing and heat/power coupling → ④ occurs in industry and heat generating stations.

The coal fuel is supplied by a mechanical conveyor to the hot ashes in the return ash circuit; it passes from there to the lower section of the furnace. In the case of dried types of coal, pneumatic conveyance direct into the furnace is preferred. Complete combustion takes place at 800–900°C. The air required for combustion is extracted from the boiler house or from the fresh air outside, warmed by an air pre-heater and fed via a pressurising blower through the base of the tuyere as primary air, and also on a number of levels, as secondary air. Hot flue gases arise during the combustion. The ash in the furnace, absorbing a portion of the heat of combustion due to intensive turbulence, is entrained by the flue gases and imparts heat to the heating surfaces in the furnace up to the point of entry into the cyclone.

The solid matter is mostly separated from the mixture of flue gas/solids in the cyclone and returns to the furnace via the ash return circuit – hence, a circulation of solid matter is achieved. The hot flue gases are cooled on the ancillary heating surfaces; depending on the temperature level, high pressure steam and medium pressure steam becomes superheated, then becomes a condensate, and combustion air is heated. The flue gases are cleaned at approximately 140°C in the electrofilter – or alternatively, in the gauze filter –and drawn off by the induced draught plant via either a single chimney stack or a collector chimney stack.

To maintain the sulphur emissions at an acceptable level, lime is fed into the furnace in metered quantities; sand and other materials are used on the first filling and, subsequently, provide a build-up of the circulating solid matter.

The generated high pressure steam is used to drive a steam turbine, and, then, following intermediate superheating as medium pressure steam, expanded to a condition suitable for process steam. The energy in the flow is converted to power in the turbine and thence to electrical current in the generator. The process steam is used, among other things, for the generation of hot water for remote heating systems, for drying processes and for chemical reactions. This steam gives up heat essentially through condensation and the condensate is collected, cleaned if necessary and returned to the boiler as feed water.

A cross-section → ③ and the plan of a power station → ④ give the dimensions of the salient parts. The dimensions apply to a medium industrial power station consisting of three boilers, each generating 200t/h of steam. An extension is shown with an additional boiler.

Stage-by-stage extension is possible by integrating new systems in existing power station complexes; new designs must also incorporate the facility for extension while existing systems are operated continuously and must reserve space for such developments.

403

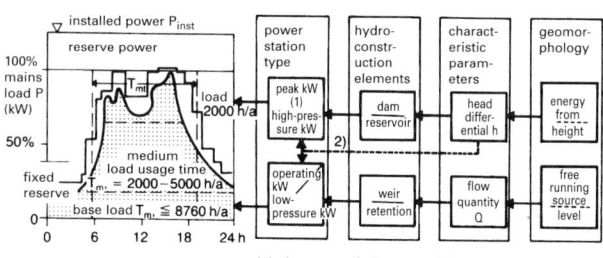

(1) also pump-fed power stations
(2) high-pressure power station (without reservoir)

① **Grid supply loading sequence and hydro-electric power station types**

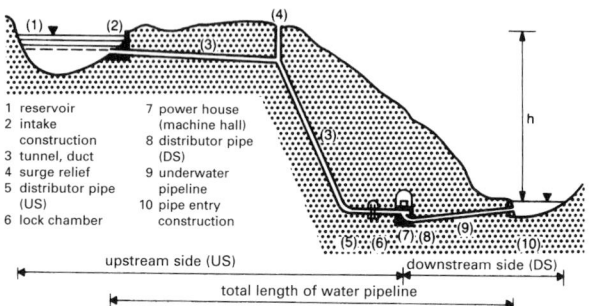

1	reservoir	7	power house (machine hall)
2	intake construction	8	distributor pipe (DS)
3	tunnel, duct	9	underwater pipeline
4	surge relief	10	pipe entry construction
5	distributor pipe (US)		
6	lock chamber		

② **Power station with high-level reservoir and long supply pipe line (underground)**

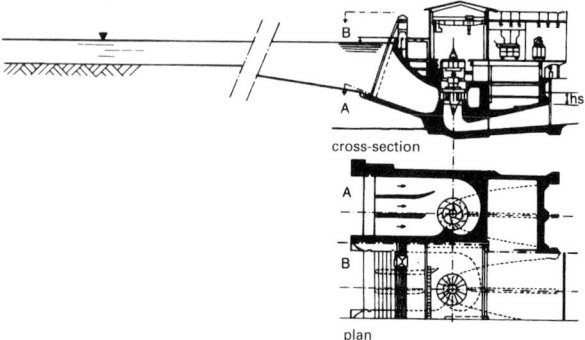

③ **Low-pressure power station with a vertical axis spiral turbine (above ground building)**

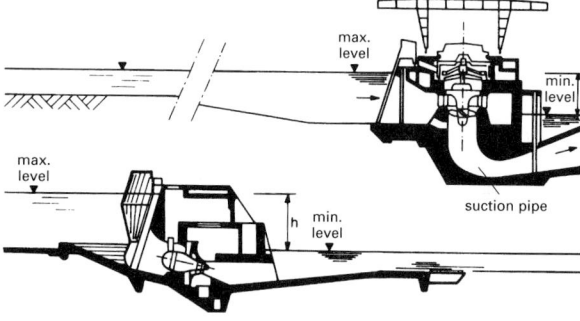

④ **Power house with inclined ducted turbine and spur**

⑤ **Power station with vertical Kaplan turbine (open air construction)**

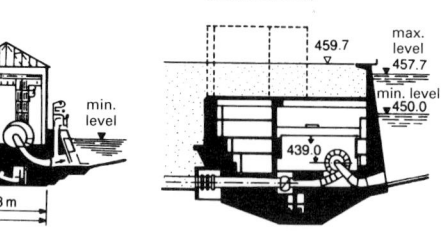

⑥ **Power house with free-standing machinery hall**

⑦ **Power house in trench infill installation**

HYDRO-ELECTRIC POWER STATIONS

The construction, shape and size of power stations in hydro-electric installations depend on the natural conditions and the type, housing shape, axial position and number of fluid power machines: the smaller the machine, the smaller the built elements.

Types of turbine are distinguished by their rotational speed. The different categories overlap with one another.

Turbine types	Applications
free jet (Pelton)-turbine	large heads (up to 1820m), low mass flows; multi-nozzled at high mass flows
Francis turbine	medium heads (670–50m) at high mass flows
Kaplan turbine	strongly fluctuating mass flows and low heads (max. 70m)
through flow (Ossberger) T	for power up to a max. 800kW with strongly fluctuating heads and mass flows

The pumps in pump-fed reservoir power stations, which store excess current as hydraulic energy, are centrifugal pumps of the Francis type. They may, however, be multi-staged when used to overcome greater supply heads. Pump turbines are reversible machines for pump and turbine operation.

In Francis and Kaplan turbines, as a rule, the water is fed to the turbine through a spiral housing, but at low powers and low-pressure heads the turbine assembly can be supplied from a duct. For Kaplan turbines of low to medium power, the ducted turbine has emerged, in which the ship's propeller type turbine wheel is installed in a tube. On free flow turbines, the housing acts as a spray protection for the water that has passed through the turbine. The axial direction of the machines can be vertical, horizontal, or even inclined, in the case of ducted turbines.

The output power is distributed by optimising the number of machines, each of which is of the same rating. Each set of machines is installed as a block, the 3D dimensions of which are directly dependent on the type and diameter of the turbine wheel. Correct vertical positioning of the turbines is crucial to construction costs and trouble-free operation; it is dependent on the type of turbine and on the height of the location relative to sea level.

The complete power station comprises the machine assemblies, the foundation blocks, which in plan view occupy about the same area, and the ancillary system housings, which are grouped around the main assemblies with the minimum demands on construction costs and space.

Methods of construction

With the exception of underground installations, the size and shape of the space occupied by the machines follows two trends: halls with gantry cranes, designed for the movement of the largest machine components (standard power station construction) or, alternatively, open air, low-lying construction, in which the largest machine components are lifted by means of an external mobile portal crane (or conventional mobile crane). Low-lying machine installations, which occur in high-pressure and pump storage power stations, are constructed in trench excavations with infill (horizontal machines), or using shaft construction (vertical machines). In underground installations, the turbine machinery is sited in mining industry type cavities, wherever possible in solid rock which requires little use of constructional concrete.

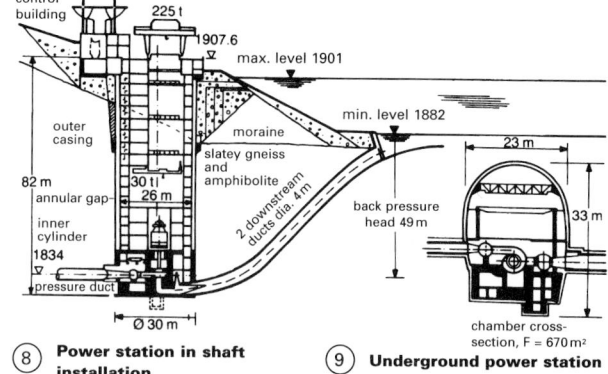

⑧ **Power station in shaft installation**

⑨ **Underground power station**

SMALL ANIMAL STALLS

Small stalls for use by hobbyists and smallholders require careful arrangement and construction if animals are to be kept successfully. They should be well ventilated but draught-free, dry, thermally insulated and easy to clean. Wooden construction with thermal insulation layers is preferred and the window area should be no more than 10% of the stall floor area. Discharge facilities must be provided for removing droppings. Adjacent rooms are needed for feed preparation and storage.

The design must consider the position of the sun: windows to the south, door to the east, laying nests in the darkest place. The stall is divided into a scratching area with a covering of straw and a droppings pit with perches fitted above → ⑩ + ⑪. Ideally, the outside run will be of an unlimited size but the essentials are a grassy surface with a tree for shade, a compost heap and a sandbath.

With an unlimited size of run, five birds may be kept per m² of stall area; two birds if the run is smaller than four times the stall area. Places for perches, droppings pit, feed and drink containers are included in the surface areas.

stall area per pair 0.15–0.20 m²
(more for purebred pigeons)
1 pair carrier pigeons 0.5 m³ airspace
1 pair purebred pigeons 1.0 m³ airspace
15–20 pairs of purebred pigeons in one stall
20–50 pairs of ordinary pigeons in one stall

① **Pigeons**

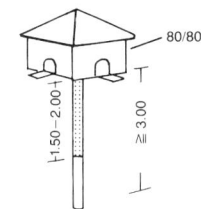

on 3–4 m high posts, fitted with 1.5 to 2.0 m of metal sheeting to thwart predators, or attached to the east or south side of a house

② **Dovecote**

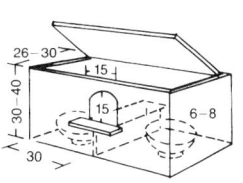

twin nesting box can be on the floor or on a special stand per pair of pigeons; feed using wooden boxes with small openings, drinking vessels with similar openings

③ **Nesting box (Fulton type)**

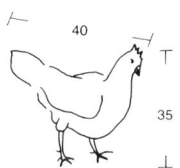

scratching area for 5 hens ≥3 m²
scratching area for 10 hens ≥5 m²
scratching area for 20 hens ≥10 m²
sleeping area for 5–6 lightweight hens or 4–5 heavy hens on 1 m of perch, 10–12 hens per 1 m²

④ **Chicken (Orpington hen)**

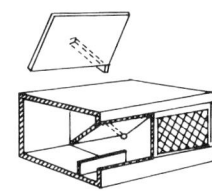

the laying nests are built into breeding stalls with a doorflap, which either hangs loosely from a hook or consists of two connected flaps; when the hen goes into the nest the flap is lifted and then

⑤ **Open laying nest**

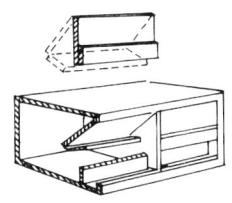

closes; the nest boxes can be on the floor or stacked three above each other; the nest size is 35 × 35 to 40 × 40 cm for the base area and 35 cm inside height

⑥ **Laying nest with flap**

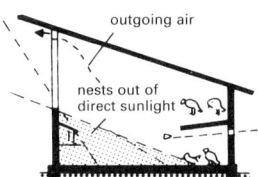

should be well ventilated but draught-free; closable ventilation flaps on the sunny side; laying nests facing away from the window; scratching area should be at outside temperatures, while the sleeping area must be warm and is, therefore, often separated by a curtain and built with special thermal insulation

⑦ **Henhouse (Peseda type)**

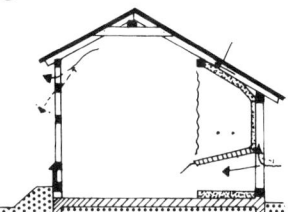

henhouse for 20 hens with separate, thermally insulated sleeping alcove, inclined droppings plate and wall ventilation; hen entrance/exit 18 × 20 to 20 × 30 cm, draught-proofed by side boarding and closed by a slider

⑧ **Section → ⑨**

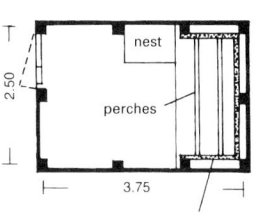

perches, according to the size of the hens, 4–7 cm wide, 5–6 cm high and 3.5 m unsupported length; they should be easy to remove, 4–6 hens per 1 m of perch

⑨ **Plan → ⑧**

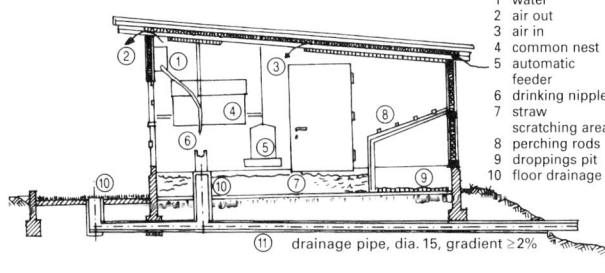

1 water
2 air out
3 air in
4 common nest
5 automatic feeder
6 drinking nipple
7 straw scratching area
8 perching rods
9 droppings pit
10 floor drainage

drainage pipe, dia. 15, gradient ≥2%

⑩ **Cross-section of henhouse → ⑪**

1 perches, droppings pit below
2 common nests
3 feed container
4 drinking nipple
5 outlet flap
6 sand bath (roofed)
7 compost heap
8 access to compost heap
9 wind break

fence 1.75–2.00 m high

gravel or slatted floor

run

tree

⑪ **Henhouse and run → ⑩**

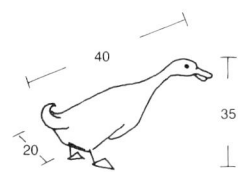

stall area (4–5 ducks) 1 m²
stall height 1.7–2 m
maximum stall occupancy: 1 drake and 20 ducks
base of stall should be solid, secure against rats, dry and airy, and have an outlet to water; ideal location is a marshy area

⑫ **Duck (Peking)**

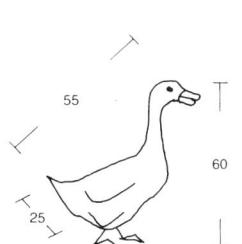

similar conditions as for ducks; for fattening purposes the animals are put in individual cells 40 cm long, 30 cm wide, with a droppings tray below and a feeding bowl at the front

⑬ **Goose (Pomeranian)**

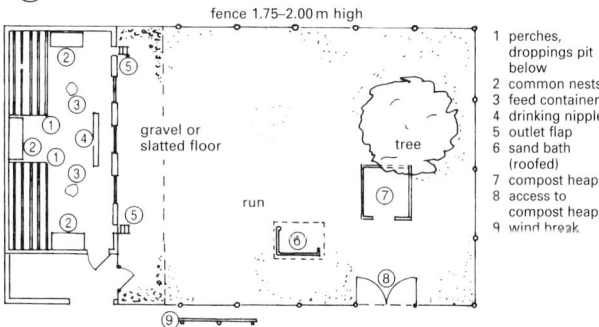

⑭ **Stall**

nests

⑮ **Plan of stall**

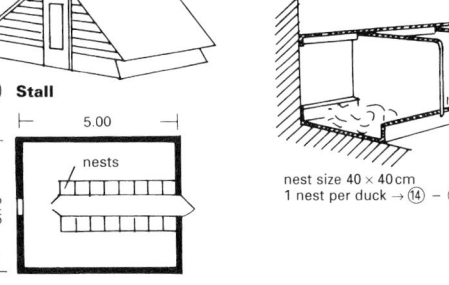

nest size 40 × 40 cm
1 nest per duck → ⑭ – ⑮

⑯ **Laying stall for 4–5 ducks**

SMALL ANIMAL STALLS

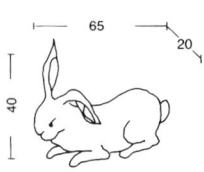

hutch area per animal 0.65–1.0 m²; should be well ventilated, dry and protected from sun and predators (rats); hutches usually made of wood with drainage → ②, 5% gradient

① **Rabbit (Belgian giant)**

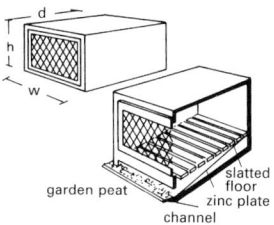

	w	d	h
small purebreds	80	80	55
medium purebreds	100	80	65
large purebreds	120	80	75

(depth is the same to ease subdivision)

② **Size of rabbit hutches (cm)**

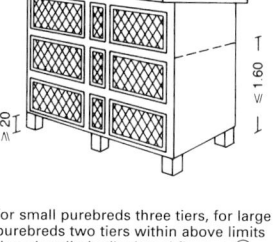

for small purebreds three tiers, for large purebreds two tiers within above limits (length unlimited); slatted floor → ② with drainage facilities and common urine collection channel below

③ **Three tier rabbit hutch**

Rabbit hutches → ② + ④ are usually free-standing and are positioned against the back of stalls or buildings so as to be sheltered from the wind. They must be protected against the weather, as well as rats and mice, and should be easy to clean, with good urine drainage → ②. They must also be well ventilated because rabbits are sensitive to poor air conditions, more so than pigs and chickens, for instance.

Thermally insulated hutches with forced-air ventilation are ideal for breeding and fattening. The temperature in the breeding hutch should be between 10 and 28°C, with an optimum of 18°C. In the fattening hutch, 20°C is desirable.

Goat sheds should be east or south facing. They need to be dry, with good ventilation and natural lighting (window area 5–7% of the floor area). For intensive accommodation of tethered goats (pens are preferred) the stalls should be 75–80 cm wide and 1.50–2.00 m deep, excluding the necessary aisles in front and behind. If possible, include a run on the south side, adjoining the shed.

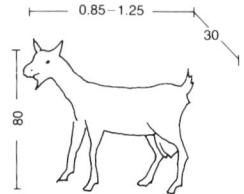

opening front or front section between two hutches → ③; front wall of galvanized wire netting; hutches for female hares with dark netting and 10cm high bed

④ **Feed trough in the hutch**

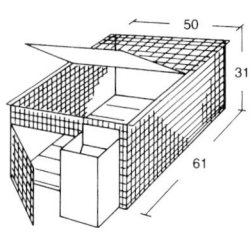

cage is made entirely from galvanised wire netting, mesh size 25 × 25 or 12 × 70 mm

⑤ **Wire cage with automatic feeding device**

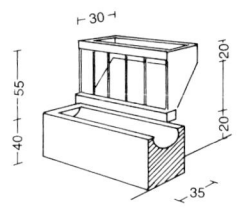

wooden or polyurethane nesting boxes for young animals; floor of nesting boxes at least 70 mm below base of cage

⑥ **Breeding cage with nesting box and automatic feeder**

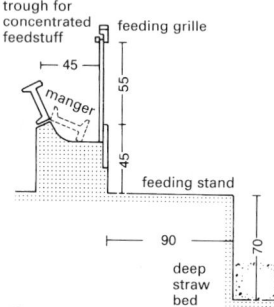

stall area per animal	1.5–2.0 m²
stall width per animal	0.75–1.00 m
stall depth, tethered	1.8 m
stall depth, free	2.5–2.8 m
stall height	1.7–2.5 m
stall temperature	10–20°C

⑦ **Goat (German Saanen goat)**

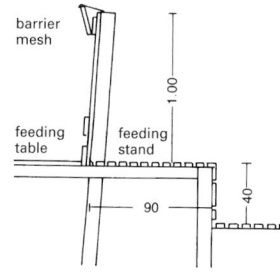

wire mesh above the rack level; tiled flooring at a gradient, with a channel for urine; feed rack and water trough serve both stalls

⑧ **Modern twin goat pen**

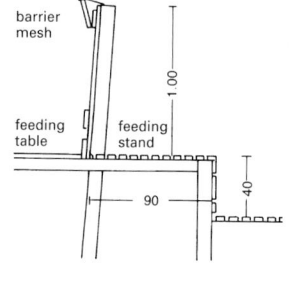

standard dimensions of a feeding rack and drinking trough in the feeding aisle (transverse aisle); daily requirements per goat: 1.2 kg hay, 2.3 kg of root crop, 2–3 l of water

⑨ **Feed rack and water trough for a goat pen**

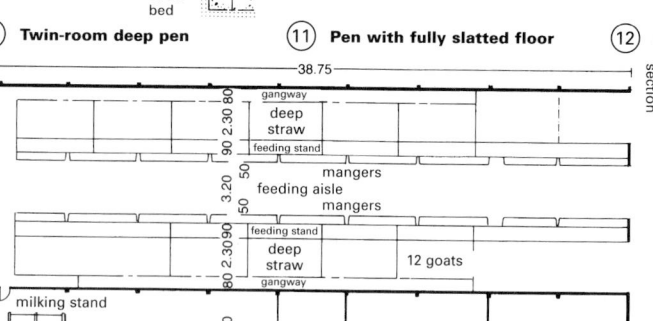

⑩ **Twin-room deep pen**

⑪ **Pen with fully slatted floor**

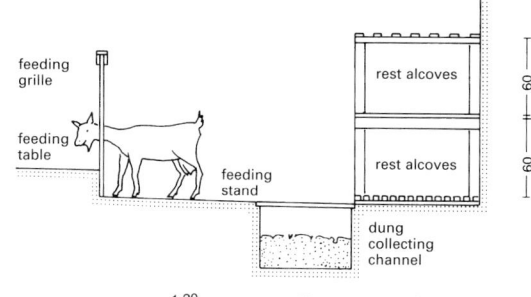

⑫ **Multi-room pen with free-standing rest alcoves**

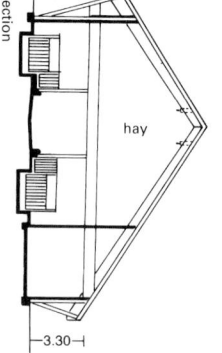

⑬ **Twin-room deep pen**

required sizes	pen (m²)	rack (cm)	tethered stall width (cm)	tethered stall length (m)
lamb	0.7–1.2	20–40	50	1.5
kid	1.5	40–50	50–70	1.5
billy goat	2.2–4.0	80	60	1.8

windows: 5–7% of stall area
stall height 1.70–2.50 m
drinking facilities: one trough for 30 animals
0.4 kg straw/day, 0.15 t per annum/animal
stall dung accumulation 0.7–1.5 t/goat

⑭ **Goat keeping**

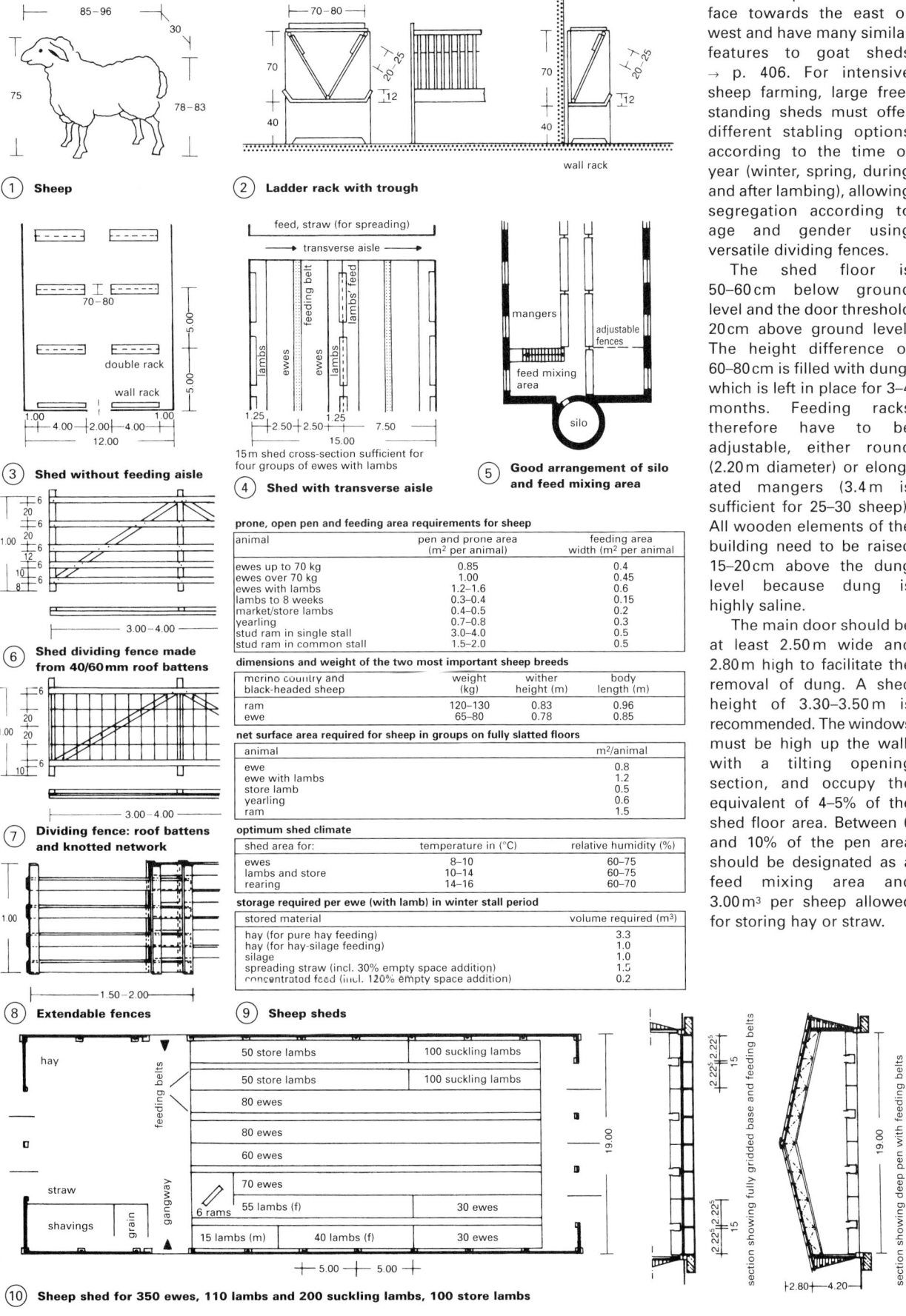

① **Sheep**

② **Ladder rack with trough**

wall rack

③ **Shed without feeding aisle**

double rack

wall rack

④ **Shed with transverse aisle**

feed, straw (for spreading)

transverse aisle

feeding belt

lambs' feed

lambs

ewes

ewes

lambs

15 m shed cross-section sufficient for four groups of ewes with lambs

⑤ **Good arrangement of silo and feed mixing area**

mangers

adjustable fences

feed mixing area

silo

⑥ **Shed dividing fence made from 40/60 mm roof battens**

⑦ **Dividing fence: roof battens and knotted network**

⑧ **Extendable fences**

⑨ **Sheep sheds**

prone, open pen and feeding area requirements for sheep

animal	pen and prone area (m² per animal)	feeding area width (m² per animal)
ewes up to 70 kg	0.85	0.4
ewes over 70 kg	1.00	0.45
ewes with lambs	1.2–1.6	0.6
lambs to 8 weeks	0.3–0.4	0.15
market/store lambs	0.4–0.5	0.2
yearling	0.7–0.8	0.3
stud ram in single stall	3.0–4.0	0.5
stud ram in common stall	1.5–2.0	0.5

dimensions and weight of the two most important sheep breeds

merino country and black-headed sheep	weight (kg)	wither height (m)	body length (m)
ram	120–130	0.83	0.96
ewe	65–80	0.78	0.85

net surface area required for sheep in groups on fully slatted floors

animal	m²/animal
ewe	0.8
ewe with lambs	1.2
store lamb	0.5
yearling	0.6
ram	1.5

optimum shed climate

shed area for:	temperature in (°C)	relative humidity (%)
ewes	8–10	60–75
lambs and store	10–14	60–75
rearing	14–16	60–70

storage required per ewe (with lamb) in winter stall period

stored material	volume required (m³)
hay (for pure hay feeding)	3.3
hay (for hay-silage feeding)	1.0
silage	1.0
spreading straw (incl. 30% empty space addition)	1.5
concentrated feed (incl. 120% empty space addition)	0.2

hay

feeding belts

straw

shavings

grain

gangway

50 store lambs	100 suckling lambs
50 store lambs	100 suckling lambs
80 ewes	
80 ewes	
60 ewes	
70 ewes	
6 rams	55 lambs (f)	30 ewes
15 lambs (m)	40 lambs (f)	30 ewes

section showing fully gridded base and feeding belts

section showing deep pen with feeding belts

⑩ **Sheep shed for 350 ewes, 110 lambs and 200 suckling lambs, 100 store lambs**

Small sheep sheds should face towards the east or west and have many similar features to goat sheds → p. 406. For intensive sheep farming, large free-standing sheds must offer different stabling options according to the time of year (winter, spring, during and after lambing), allowing segregation according to age and gender using versatile dividing fences.

The shed floor is 50–60 cm below ground level and the door threshold 20 cm above ground level. The height difference of 60–80 cm is filled with dung, which is left in place for 3–4 months. Feeding racks therefore have to be adjustable, either round (2.20 m diameter) or elongated mangers (3.4 m is sufficient for 25–30 sheep). All wooden elements of the building need to be raised 15–20 cm above the dung level because dung is highly saline.

The main door should be at least 2.50 m wide and 2.80 m high to facilitate the removal of dung. A shed height of 3.30–3.50 m is recommended. The windows must be high up the wall, with a tilting opening section, and occupy the equivalent of 4–5% of the shed floor area. Between 6 and 10% of the pen area should be designated as a feed mixing area and 3.00 m³ per sheep allowed for storing hay or straw.

Henhouses constructed as free-standing sheds have largely become the norm in all areas of poultry keeping. For intensive farming with hens kept on the floor, the smallest unit when building from new is based on a shed width of 7 m; if battery coops are used, the shed width is 6–15 m. The sheds must be thermally insulated, the optimum shed temperature, according to the application, being between 15 and 22°C.

During pre-planning it is necessary to decide on the method of removing droppings because the size of a cellar or droppings pit depends on this. Shed ventilation is another element that requires careful planning: fundamentally, they should be designed with ventilators for forced ventilation ① – ④.

Cellars for droppings below the battery coops need a longitudinal air extraction system under the service aisles.

Ventilation systems need to have the following capacity:
- air entry speed: 0.30 m/s (maximum 0.50 m/s)
- in summer, air circulation for laying hens reaches a maximum of 10 m³/h/kg bird;
- for young hens and broilers, it is 4.00 m³/h/kg bird.

Failure of the ventilation equipment can have a devastating effect in a very short time so it must have suitable warning mechanisms. A plan for emergency ventilation should also be drawn up.

An automated round drinking trough unit is sufficient for 75–100 hens; with channel troughs, allow 1.00 m for 80–100 hens. A tubular feeding unit is adequate for 25 hens per round trough (diameter 30 cm).

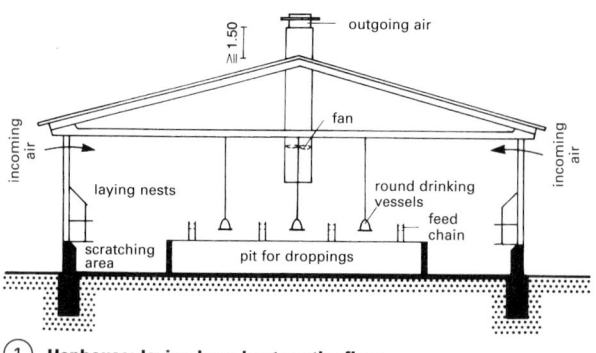

① **Henhouse: laying hens kept on the floor**

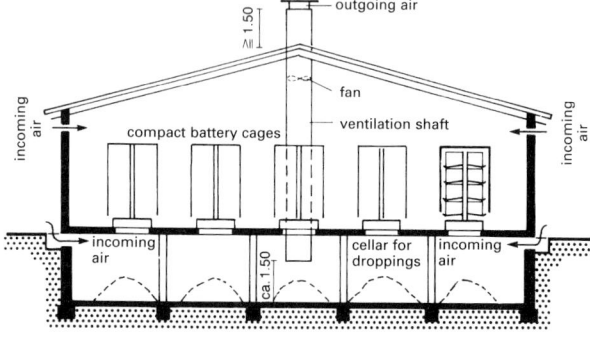

② **Battery henhouse with cellar for droppings**

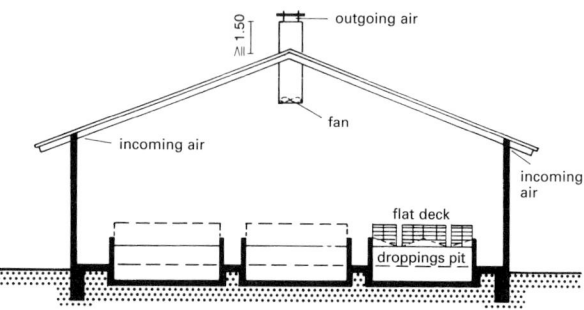

③ **Flat cage system (flat deck arrangement)**

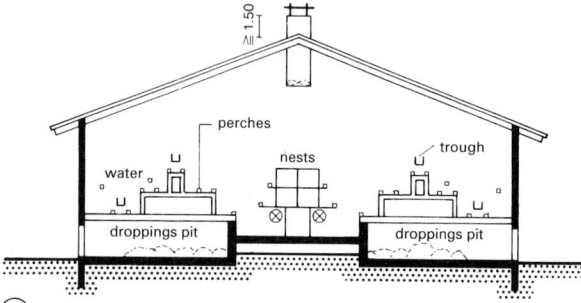

④ **Aviary system**

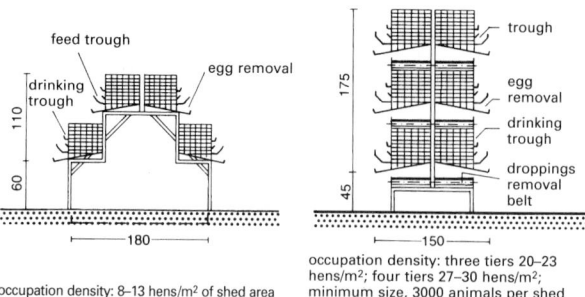

occupation density: 8–13 hens/m² of shed area

⑤ **Stepped cages**

occupation density: three tiers 20–23 hens/m²; four tiers 27–30 hens/m²; minimum size, 3000 animals per shed

⑥ **Tiered cages**

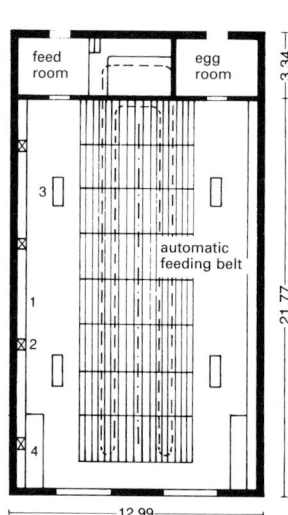

1 laying nests; 2 ventilation shaft; 3 feed trough; 4 dust bath

⑦ **Henhouse for 1600 laying hens on the floor**

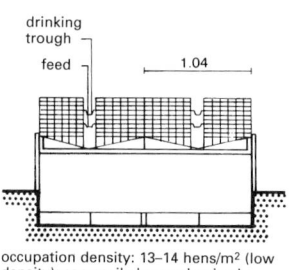

occupation density: 13–14 hens/m² (low density); can easily be mechanised

⑨ **Flat deck cages**

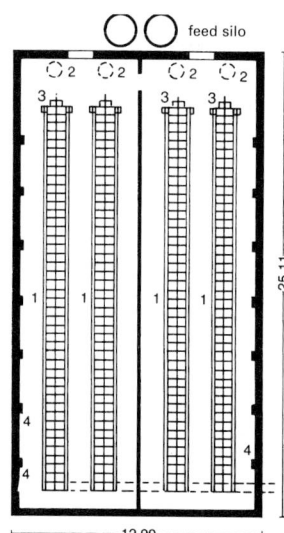

1 battery coops; 2 water storage containers; 3 feed trolleys; 4 ventilation and extraction

⑧ **Battery system, three tiers, about 4800 birds**

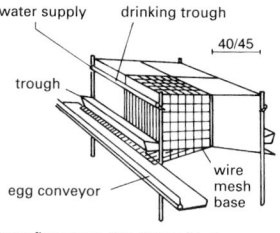

cage floor area: 430–450 cm²/hen
cage depth: 40–45 cm, sometimes more
cage height: front 50 cm, back 40 cm
trough length: 10–12 cm/hen

⑩ **Single cages**

PIG SHEDS: FATTENING

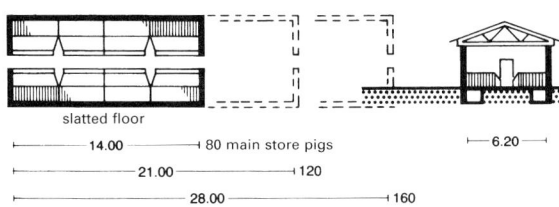

① Store pig shed: two rows, short stalls, longitudinal troughs (80–160 animals)

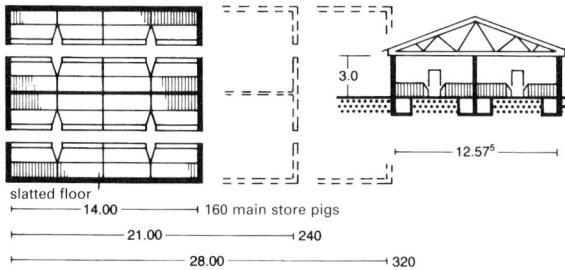

② Store pig shed: four rows, central wall (160–320 animals)

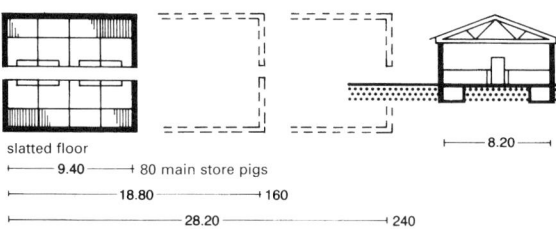

③ Store pig shed: two rows, long stalls, automatic feeding

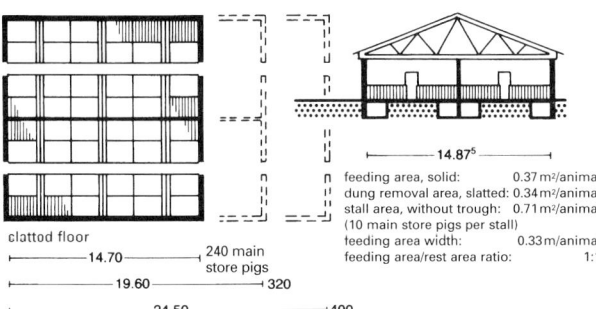

feeding area, solid: 0.37 m²/animal
dung removal area, slatted: 0.34 m²/animal
stall area, without trough: 0.71 m²/animal
(10 main store pigs per stall)
feeding area width: 0.33 m/animal
feeding area/rest area ratio: 1:1

④ Store pig shed: four rows, central wall, long stalls, transverse troughs

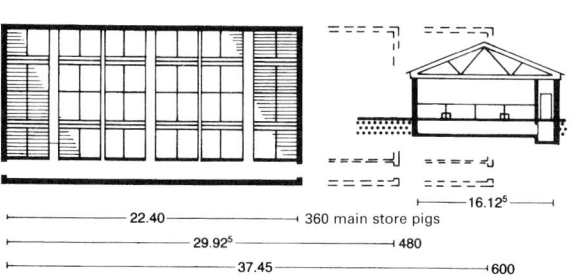

⑤ Store pig shed with rack stalls (120 animals per section)

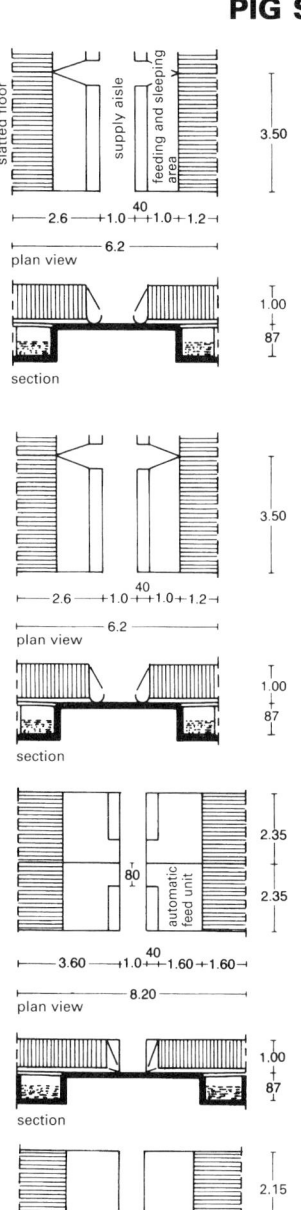

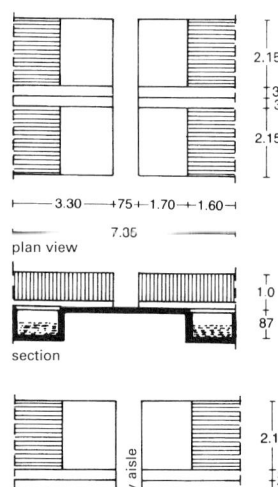

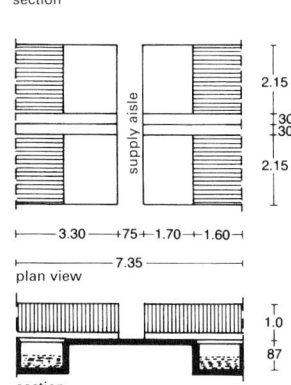

Roughly three-quarters of total farm turnover comes from animal products and about half is from the keeping of animals for milking and store pig production.

Good planning of agricultural buildings is a decisive factor in maintaining the livelihood of the farmer and this is particularly so for pig production. Specialisation and mechanisation of the production sequences will have the greatest influence on the plans. For instance, a vital factor in the planning process is to provide separate pig sheds for fattening and breeding operations. The considerations include:

- how the pigs will be kept, which could determine the number of shed changes needed during the fattening period of 150–160 days;
- feeding techniques – by hand or mechanical trough/ground feeding;
- removal of dung – dry dung/liquid dung (slurry).

Intensive fattening is divided into two periods (pre-fattening and main fattening) and should not involve changing sheds within each period. The shed stalls have partially or fully-slatted floors.

The two fattening periods can be distinguished as follows:

pre-fattening period:
approx. 50 days
weight in this period: 20–40kg
group size: 20 animals/stall
width of feeding spaces:
16.5cm/animal
main fattening period:
approx. 100 days
weight in this period: 40–100kg
group size: 10 animals/stall
width of feeding spaces:
33cm/animal
Dimensions for short-stall sheds → ① are:
feeding area, solid:
0.34 m²/animal
slatted dung area:
0.42 m²/animal
shed area, without trough:
0.76 m²/animal
(10 main store pigs per stall)
feeding area width:
0.32 m/animal
feeding/rest area ratio: 1:1

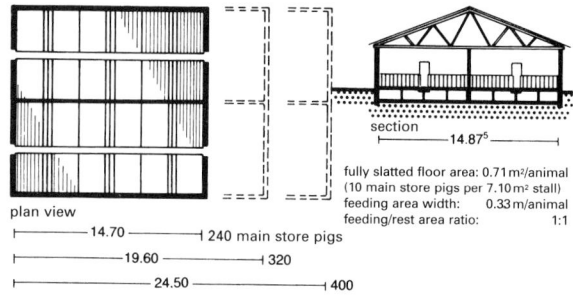

fully slatted floor area: 0.71 m²/animal
(10 main store pigs per 7.10 m² stall)
feeding area width: 0.33 m/animal
feeding/rest area ratio: 1:1

14.70 — 240 main store pigs
19.60 — 320
24.50 — 400

① **Store pig shed: longitudinally divided by centre wall, 2 × 2 rows, long stalls, transverse troughs, fully slatted floor**

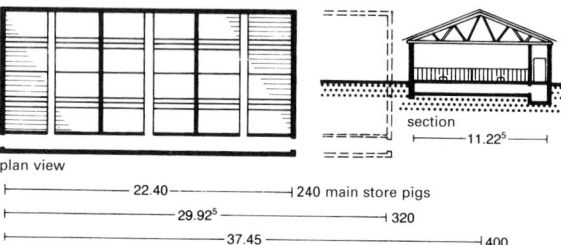

22.40 — 240 main store pigs
29.92⁵ — 320
37.45 — 400

② **Store pig shed: rack stalls, 80 pigs per section, long stalls, transverse troughs, fully slatted floor**

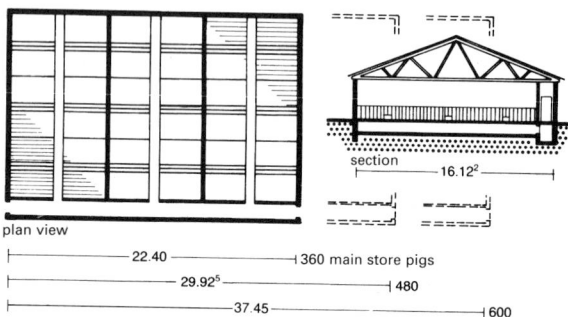

22.40 — 360 main store pigs
29.92⁵ — 480
37.45 — 600

③ **Store pig shed: rack stalls, 120 pigs per section, long stalls, transverse troughs, fully slatted floor**

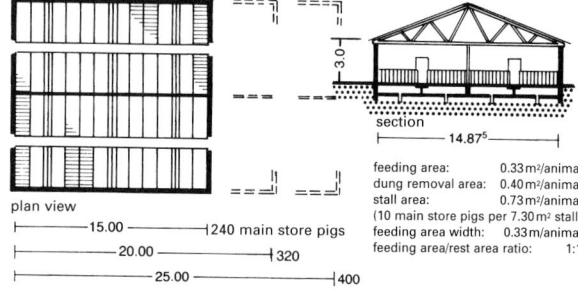

feeding area: 0.33 m²/animal
dung removal area: 0.40 m²/animal
stall area: 0.73 m²/animal
(10 main store pigs per 7.30 m² stall)
feeding area width: 0.33 m/animal
feeding area/rest area ratio: 1:1

15.00 — 240 main store pigs
20.00 — 320
25.00 — 400

④ **Store pig shed: longitudinally divided by centre wall, 2 × 2 rows, long stalls, transverse troughs, partially slatted floor, solid floors parallel to troughs**

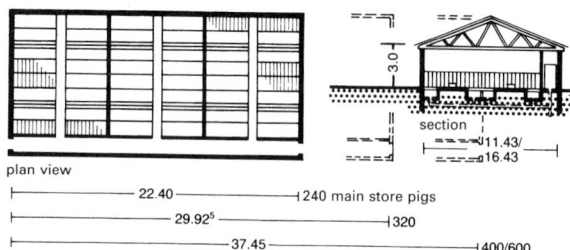

22.40 — 240 main store pigs
29.92⁵ — 320
37.45 — 400/600

⑤ **Store pig shed: rack stalls, 80 pigs per section, long stalls, transverse troughs, partially slatted floor, solid floors parallel to troughs**

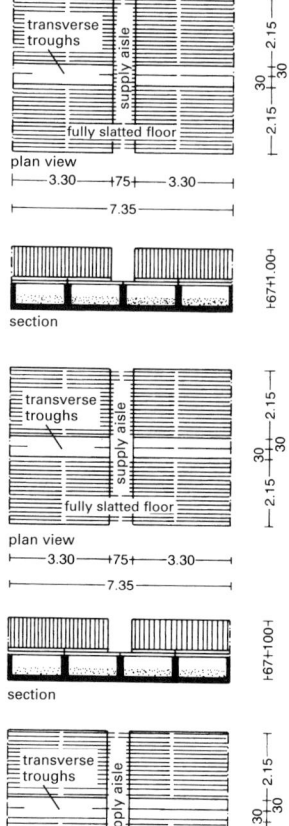

3.30 — 75 — 3.30
7.35

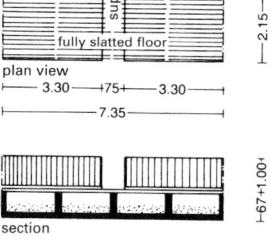

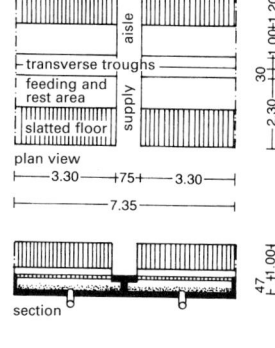

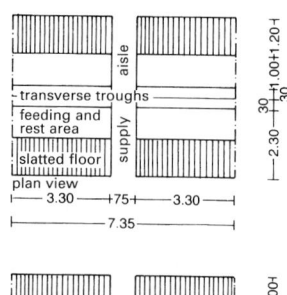

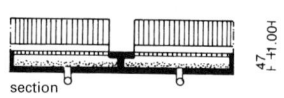

Fattening sheds for pigs must be of solid construction and have adequate thermal insulation to maintain the desired temperature. During the second, or main, fattening period, the store pigs are kept ten to a stall and fed dry or liquid feed from a trough. The quantity is rationed and feed apportionment can be partly or fully mechanised: this must be taken into consideration. The feeding area should have enough space for a double trough. Deep bowls or drinking nipples can be used to deliver drinking water.

Shed occupation during the main fattening phase can be an 'all in, all out' process or based on a batch system. The most important factor is that the pigs should not undergo shed changes during this 100-day period. By the end of this phase the animals achieve weights of up to 100 kg.

No straw is spread out on the slatted floors so liquid dung (slurry) can be removed via collection channels. It is stored for four, six or eight months in high or deep containers, or in plastic-lined reservoirs dug in the earth. The area in which the pigs lie down should ideally not have a slatted floor to make it more comfortable.

Sheds of the size shown have space for 20 animals in the pre-fattening phase. Pre-fattening spaces are normally installed in special shed sections, often in any available old buildings. Store pigs in the pre- and main fattening phases are kept in different conditions. The diagrams and information shown here refer only to the main fattening phase.

For aisle floors use 2.5 cm compound cement/sand screed on 10 cm of subconcrete and a 25 cm sand bed. The fully slatted floor surface should be finished with reinforced concrete sections.

For the outside walls use 24 cm lime-sand brick walling, flush jointed, with 6 cm of insulation, a 4 cm air gap and 11.5 cm fair-faced masonry (cavity wall). The windows should be double glazed, with plastic frames, and be around 75 × 100 cm in size.

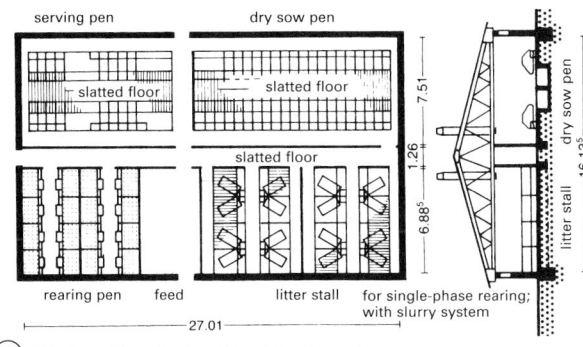

① **Pig breeding sheds without feeding aisles**

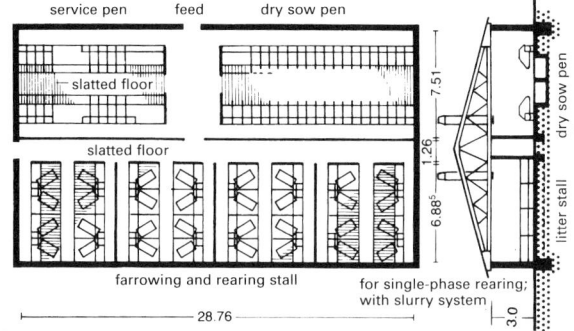

③ **Pig breeding sheds with feeding aisles**

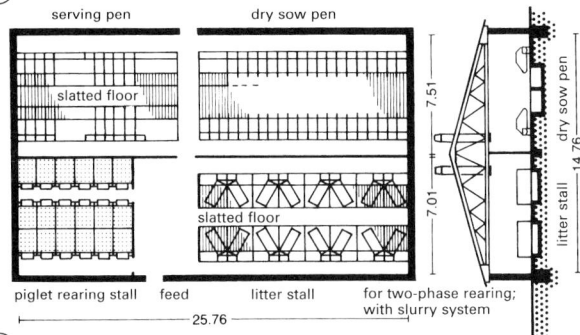

⑤ **Pig breeding sheds with feeding aisles**

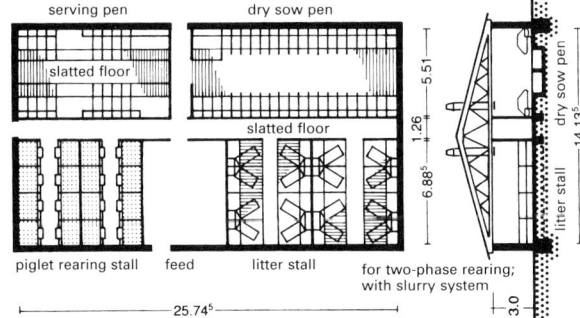

⑦ **Pig breeding sheds without feeding aisles**

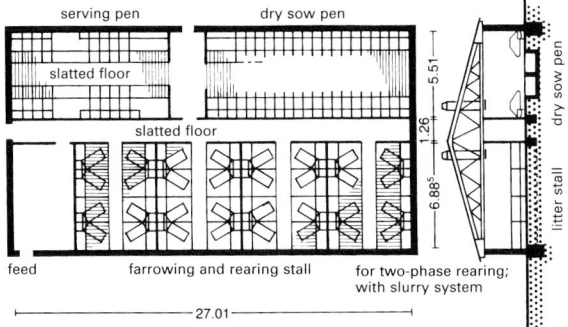

⑨ **Pig breeding sheds with feeding aisles**

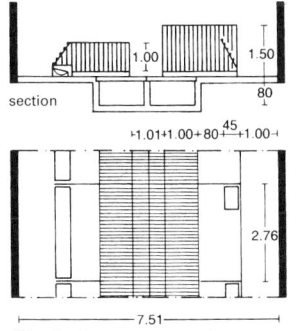

② **Stall arrangement in service pen → ③**

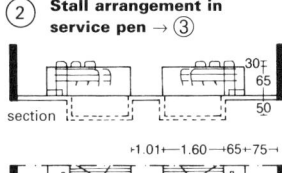

④ **Farrowing and rearing pen → ③**

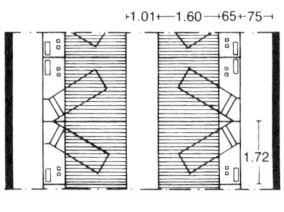

⑥ **Three-row piglet rearing pens → ⑤**

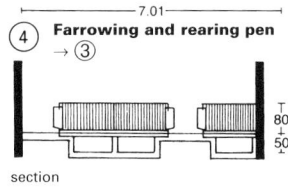

⑧ **Sow stalls with and without feeding aisles → ① + ②**

The breeding pens shown for 64 productive sows can be correspondingly extended to accommodate 96 or 128 sows. An allowance should also be made for gilts (young sows), corresponding to approximately 5% of the number of productive sows, and boars (one boar pen per 25 productive sows).

The breeding shed requires separate pen sections (serving pen, dry sow pen, farrowing pen and piglet rearing pen) and aisles to allow movement of the animals. Feeding aisles are often also included. No straw is spread on the partially or fully slatted stall floor and slurry is collected in channels.

With the all in, all out procedure and twin-phase piglet breeding, piglets can be weaned after 4–6 weeks. Piglets are ready for sale when they reach approximately 20 kg.

sows and boars

	temp. zone (°C)	air renewal rate (m³/h)	
animal weight (kg)		100	300
winter	−10	12.3	29.9
	−16	10.9	26.3
summer	≥26	109–146	271–361
	<26	73–88	180–216

piglets

	temp. zone (°C)	air renewal rate (m³/h)	
animal weight (kg)		10	20
winter	−10	3.0	3.6
	−16	2.8	3.4
summer	≥26	26–34	38–50
	<26	17–20	25–30

(individual site-related testing could be necessary)

⑪ **Ventilation data for sheds**

required storage capacity for 28 days' stock			
productive sows	64	96	128
sow feed (m³)	10.2	15.3	20.4
piglet feed (m³)	5.8	8.7	11.6

⑫ **Feed storage needs**

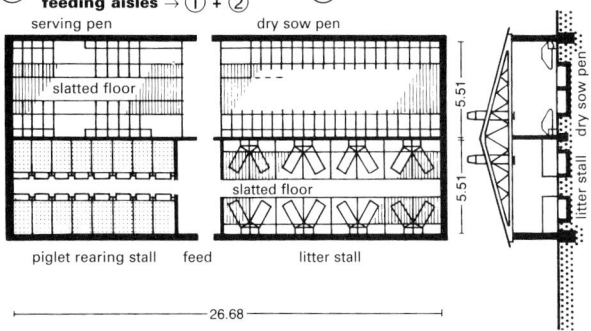

⑩ **Pig breeding sheds without feeding aisles for 40, 55 and 64 productive sows**

STABLES/HORSES

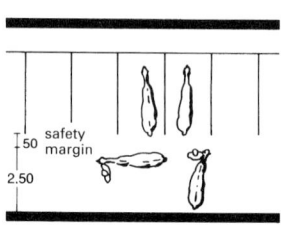

① **Pony, donkey, horse**

1.0–1.45 1.20 1.45–1.70

Stables in which the animals are tethered in stalls are not generally suitable for horses which are ridden → ② + ③: box stalls are preferable. Although there might be some breed-related behavioural features to be considered, the appropriate floor area of the box stall is usually based on the body length of the horse. However, because the length of horses is not measured, the wither, or stock, height is used as the reference dimension. As a rule of thumb, the box plan area is given by:

$$\text{stall area} = (2 \times W)^2$$

where W is the wither/stock height. A working value for the minimum length of the short sides of the stall is given by 1.5 × W. → ④ + ⑤ Common wither heights of horses that are ridden are 1.60–1.65 m, giving a stall floor area of approximately 10.5 m².

To turn a horse safely, a stable aisle width of at least 2.50 m is required → ② – ⑤. In stables with tethering stalls, provide an extra safety margin of 50 cm for each row → ② + ③.

In addition to the stalls or boxes, consideration needs to be given to a saddle room, forge, sick stall and feed storage rooms. The saddle room should be 15 m² or more, depending on the number of horses. For stables housing more than 20 horses a forge (5.0 × 3.6 m) and a stall for sick animals should be provided.

Although horses are insensitive to wind (indeed, they are reported to have physiological need for moving air), draughts should be avoided. This is achieved using artificial ventilation equipment and air ducting → ⑨ – ⑪. It is not practical to attempt to create an 'ideal' stable temperature. Nor is it crucial because, with appropriate preparation and expert care, any horse can withstand winter stable temperatures as low as a few degrees below zero.

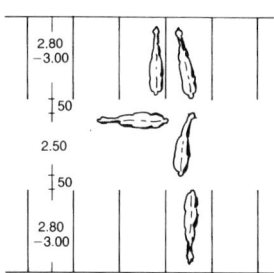

② **Stable: single row, tethered**

2.50, safety margin 50

③ **Stable: twin row, tethered**

2.80–3.00, 50, 2.50, 50, 2.80–3.00

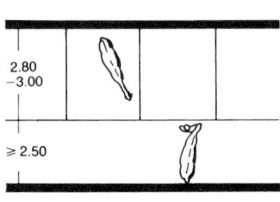

④ **Single-row box stable**

2.80–3.00, ≥ 2.50

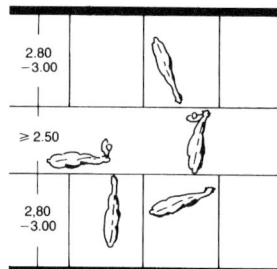

⑤ **Twin-row box stable**

2.80–3.00, ≥ 2.50, 2.80–3.00

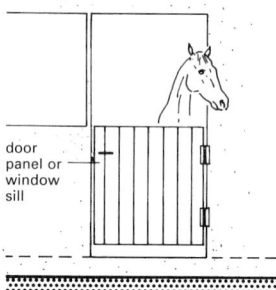

⑥ **Dimensions of stable doors**

door panel or window sill

B = 1.5W ≥1.35W normal dimension 2.50
A = 0.8W normal dimension 1.30
W

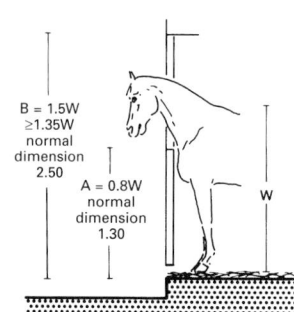

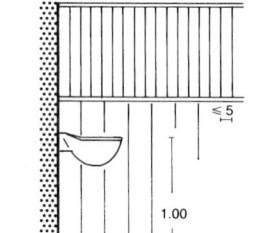

⑦ **Drinking bowl**

≤ 5, 1.00

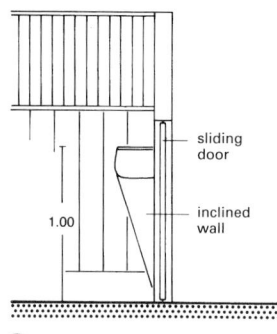

⑧ **Trough height**

sliding door, inclined wall, 1.00

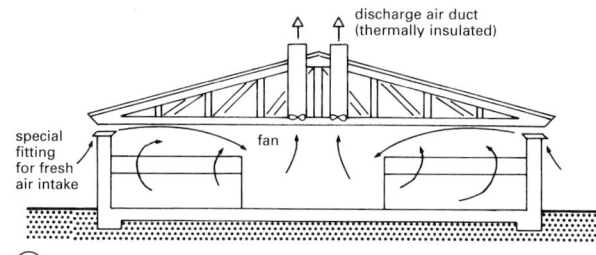

⑨ **Extract ventilation**

discharge air duct (thermally insulated), fan, special fitting for fresh air intake

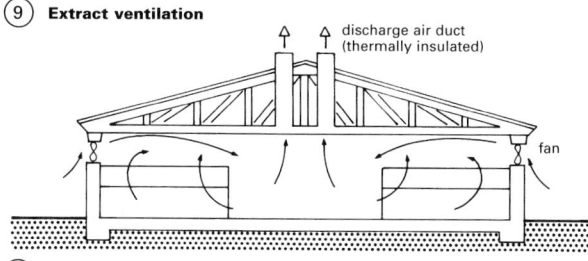

⑩ **Pressurised ventilation**

discharge air duct (thermally insulated), fan

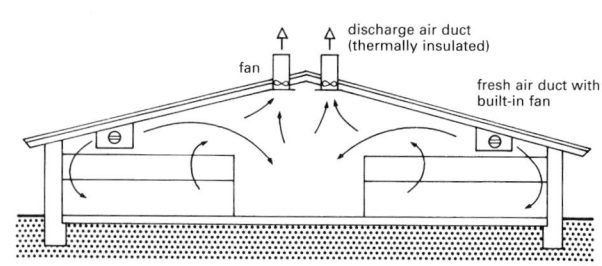

⑪ **Balanced pressure ventilation**

discharge air duct (thermally insulated), fan, fresh air duct with built-in fan

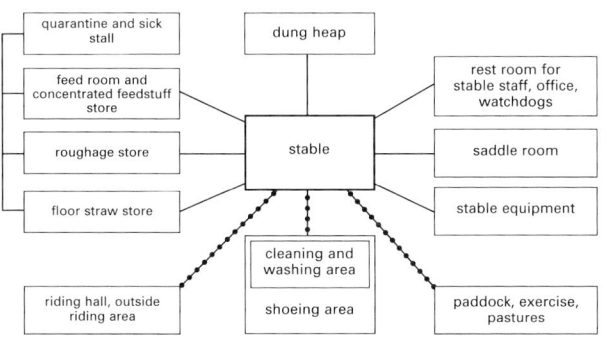

(1) **Function diagram of a horse stable**

The needs of the horses are paramount in designing stables and the methods of keeping them. Good design is a precondition not only for maintaining health, race competitiveness and longevity but also for ensuring the animals have an even temperament. Surprisingly, the requirements of horses today are not very different to those of the horses from the Asian plains which were first domesticated 5000 years ago.

material; storage; density (kg/m³)	required storage space with 20--30% empty space (m³)	
	200 days[1]	365 days[2]
Hay, long quality (75)	17–20	30–36
HD bales, non-stacked (150)	9–11	15–18
HD bales, stacked (180)	7–9	12–14

[1] corresponds to 1000–1200 kg
[2] corresponds to 1800–2200 kg

(9) **Space requirement for hay storage at 5–6 kg/horse/day**

material; storage; density (kg/m³)	required storage space with 20--30% empty space (m³)
	for 3 months[1]
straw, long quality (50)	22
HD bales, non-stacked (70)	15
HD bales, stacked (100)	11

[1] corresponds to 900 kg

(10) **Space requirement for straw storage at 10 kg/horse/day**

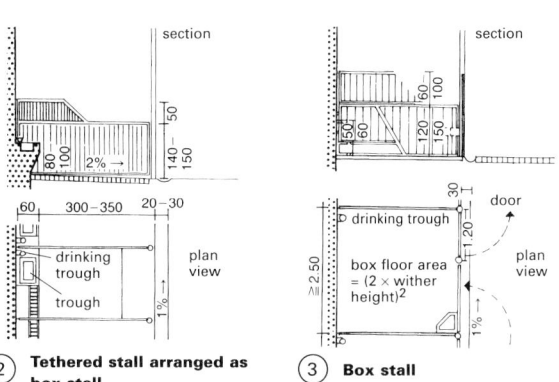

(2) **Tethered stall arranged as box stall**

(3) **Box stall**

	floor area (m²)	box size (m)	box height (m)
riding horses	10.00 / 12.00	3.30 × 3.30 / 3.50 × 3.50	2.60--2.80
dam and stallion	12.00 / 16.00	3.50 × 3.50 / 4.00 × 4.00	2.60--2.80
small horse (W ≤ 1.30 m)	4.00 / 5.00	2.00 × 2.00 / 2.25 × 2.25	1.50
small horse (W > 1.30 m)	6.00 / 9.00	2.45 × 2.45 / 3.00 × 3.00	1.50--2.00

W = height of horse at the withers

(11) **Dimensions of horse boxes**

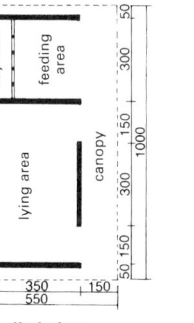

(4) **Small shelter**

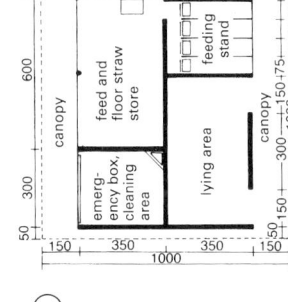

(5) **Large shelter**

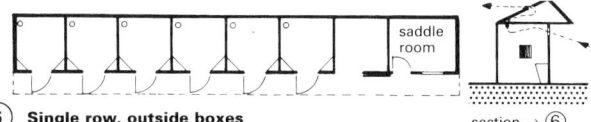

(6) **Single row, outside boxes**

section → (6)

(7) **Twin row, outside boxes**

section → (7)

(12) **Inside/outside boxes**

section → (12)

(13) **Inside boxes**

section → (13)

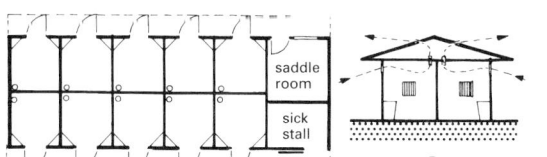

(8) **Example layout of associated rooms for a horse stable with 20--30 boxes**

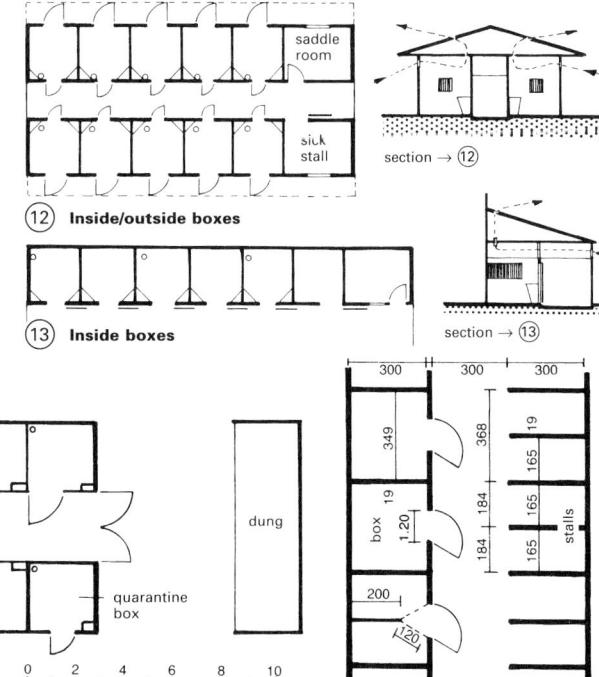

(14) **One box is as wide as two stalls**

413

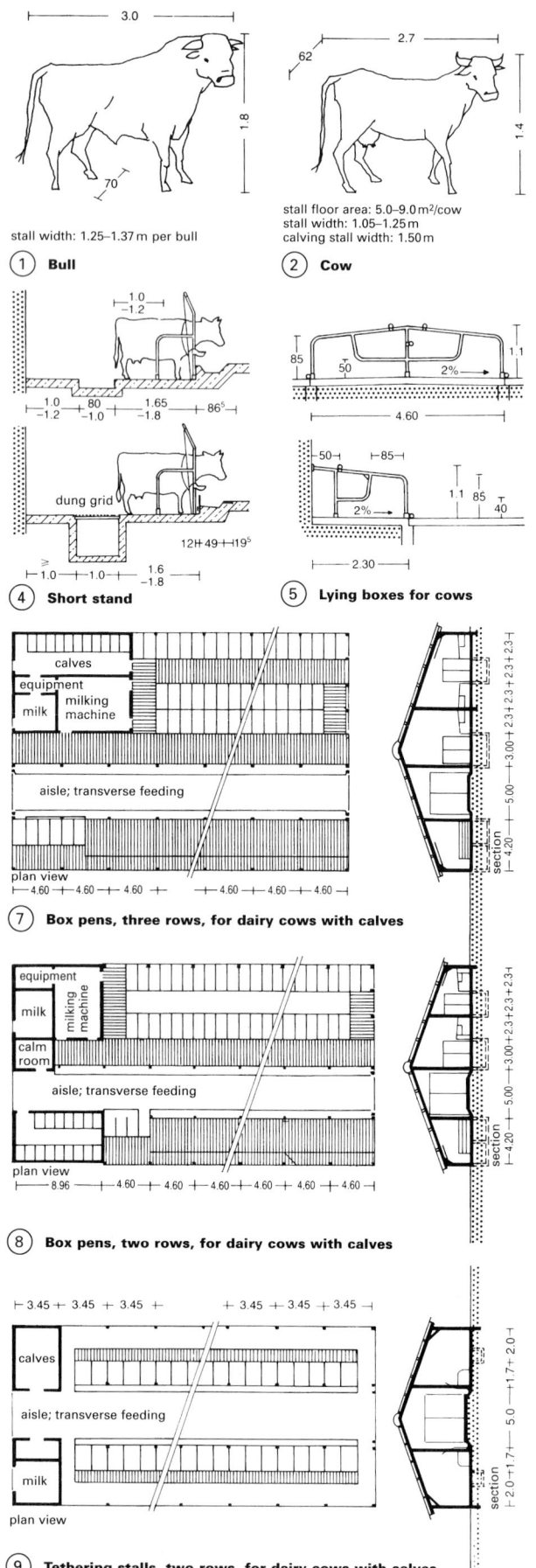

1 Bull

stall width: 1.25–1.37 m per bull

2 Cow

stall floor area: 5.0–9.0 m²/cow
stall width: 1.05–1.25 m
calving stall width: 1.50 m

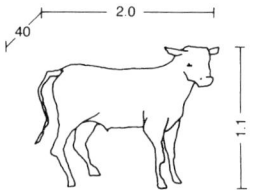

3 Young cattle

stall floor area:
under 1 year, 3.1–3.5 m²
1–2 years, 3.5–4.5 m²

4 Short stand

5 Lying boxes for cows

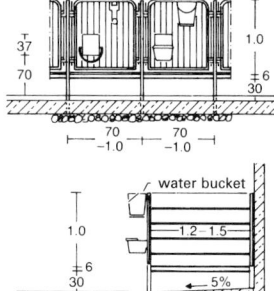

6 Single stalls for calves (14 days to 10 weeks)

7 Box pens, three rows, for dairy cows with calves

8 Box pens, two rows, for dairy cows with calves

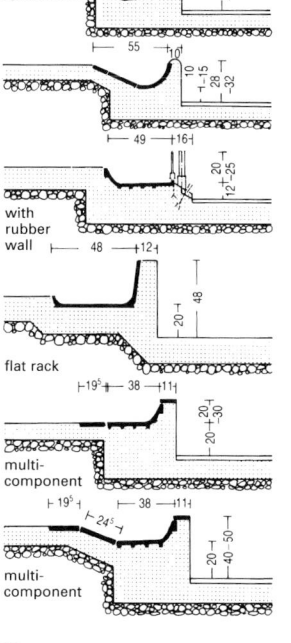

with rubber wall

flat rack

multi-component

multi-component

11 Shapes for milking cattle, tethered or pen stalls

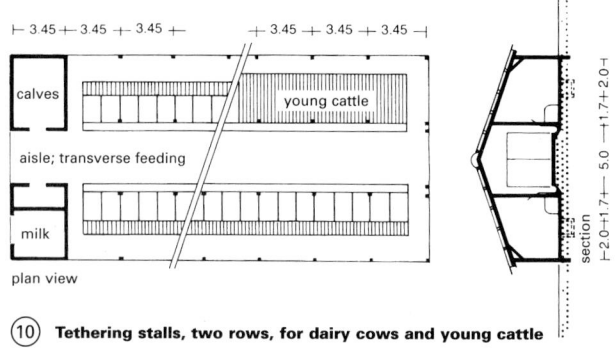

9 Tethering stalls, two rows, for dairy cows with calves

10 Tethering stalls, two rows, for dairy cows and young cattle

A differentiation is made here between tethering stalls and box pens, the latter being generally confined to dedicated milking sheds. In the tethering stall the cow is tied to one spot – here it stands, rests, drinks, urinates, defecates and can also be milked in some circumstances. The stall is 1.10–1.20 m wide and 1.40–1.80 m long, depending on the size of the animal (a factor of breed and age) as well as the type of stall → ⑨ + ⑩. For examples of box pen layouts → ⑦ + ⑧.

Illustration ④ shows short stalls with feeding stages 1.60–1.80 m long. These are often spread with straw, which gives a solid dung layer of 2–4 kg of straw/cow/day, but it is increasingly common to have low straw (0.5 kg straw/cow/day) or no straw sheds.

Even with small herds, it is desirable to mechanise the dung removal process. The dung removing equipment determines the height and width of the dung pit → ④. No straw should be used in short stalls with a droppings grid because it could limit the slurry removal system.

Single-row stall arrangements are not economical. The best use of space in a cow shed is made with a twin row of stalls, a central feeding aisle and outer dung collection channels.

The level of feeding mechanisation can have a bearing on shed widths and must be considered early in any new project. Minimum widths range from 10 m to 12 m.

To allow future longitudinal extension of the shed, one gable end should be left free. This means that storage areas, equipment and machinery, and associated rooms should be located at one gable end.

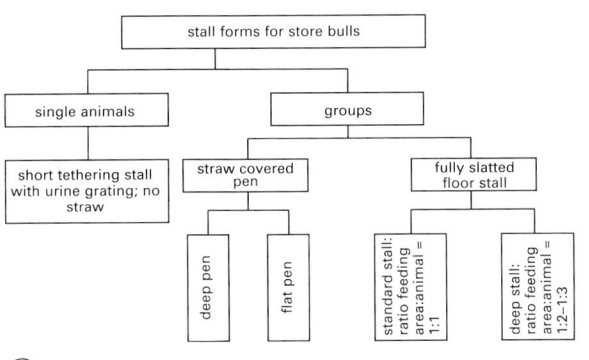

(1) **Stalls for store bulls**

There are two methods of keeping store bulls: they are either kept singly or in groups → ①. Keeping the animals singly requires constant adaptation of the stall to match the rapid growth of the bull and, therefore, a range of tethering stalls is necessary for the different age groups. Short stalls are recommended for this purpose → ② and it is important to ensure that the single pens have good drainage to remove urine from the lying area. The advantage of keeping the animals separately is that it eliminates herd behaviour.

An important precondition for keeping bulls in groups (6–15 animals of the same age and weight) is that they must have become accustomed to one other from the time they were calves.

A distinction can be made between deep and flat pens according to the straw quantities and dung removal system. In deep pens the whole stall serves as the movement and lying area and has a straw covering whereas in flat pens the lying and feeding areas are separated. The standard feed for special store bulls is maize silage.

When planning for store bulls, bear in mind that it must be possible to move single animals or whole groups into and out of the fattening stalls easily and in safety. Ventilation equipment such as convectors and extractor fans are recommended and these function best with a roof slope of around 20 degrees.

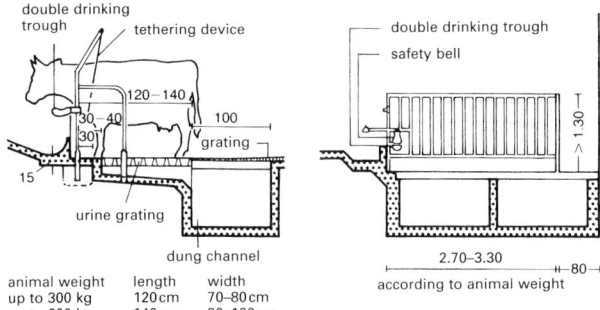

animal weight	length	width
up to 300 kg	120 cm	70–80 cm
up to 600 kg	140 cm	90–100 cm

(2) **Short stall without straw**　(3) **Stall with fully slatted floor**

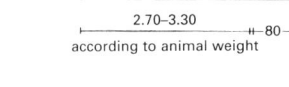

	maize silage			hay		
	(kg/day)	(kg/year)	storage req'd/year (m³)	(kg/day)	(kg/year)	storage req'd/year (m³)
first fattening section 125–350 kg	12	4380	6.15	0.5	180 (HD bales)	1.2
final fattening section 350–550 kg	22	8030	11.15		–	

(7) **Feeding requirements per animal**

weight section (kg)	stall area (m²)	feeding area width/animal (cm)	slatted floor dimensions: req'd widths (mm)	
			step	gap
125–150	1.20	40		
150–220	1.40	45		
220–300	1.50	50	1.20	
300–400	1.80	57	up to	35
400–500	2.00	63	1.60	
>500	2.20	70		

(8) **Space requirement and slatted floor dimensions for store bull sheds**

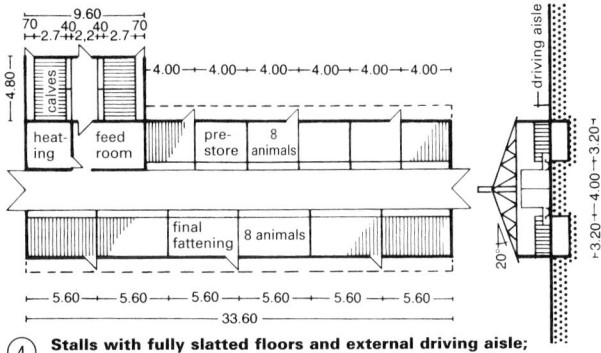

(4) **Stalls with fully slatted floors and external driving aisle; with stall changing (96 bulls)**

(5) **Stalls with fully slatted floors and driving aisle behind the stalls; with stall changing (96 bulls)**

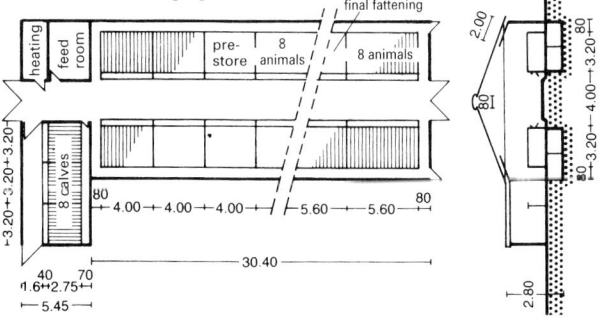

(9) **Fodder rack**　(10) **Fodder rack**

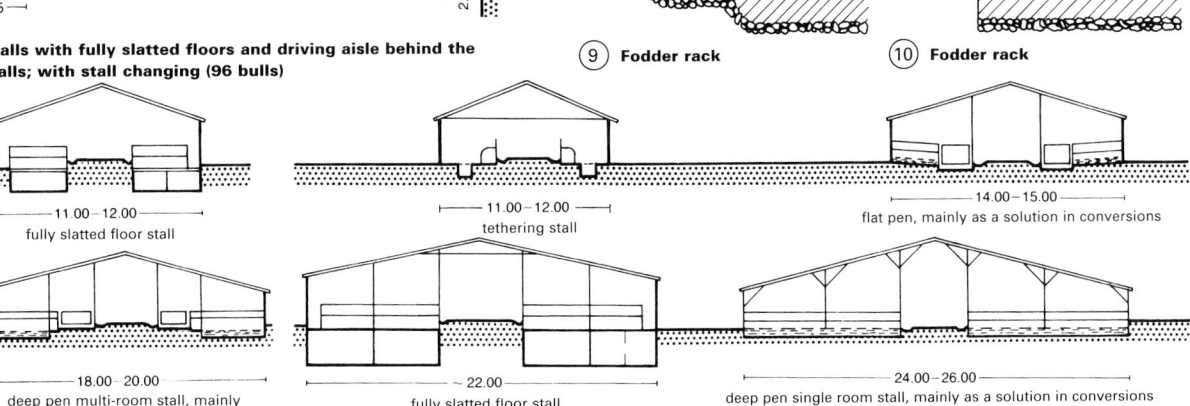

(6) **Shed cross-sections for various forms of stall**

BUILDINGS FOR FARM VEHICLES

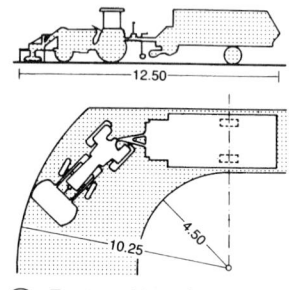

① Tractor with trailer

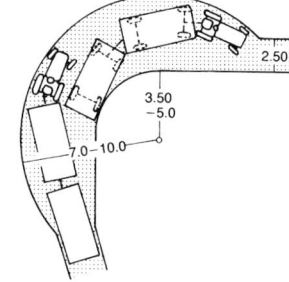

② Tractor with front loader

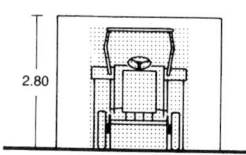

③ Tractor with push reaper and trailer

④ Minimum space required for traffic

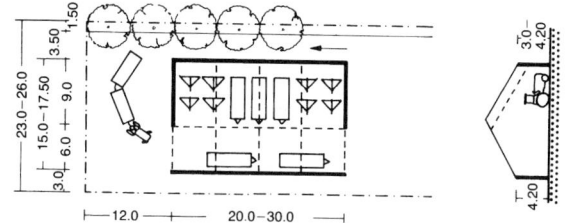

⑤ Minimum space for single standard tractor (base size of garage area)

trailer	(m³)	length	width	height
green fodder	12	6.95	2.35	2.26
dry fodder	19			2.94
green fodder	11	7.80	2.46	2.45
dry fodder	17			3.10
green fodder	12	7.25	2.25	2.30
dry fodder	18			3.25
green fodder	14	8.00	2.35	2.25
dry fodder	20			2.90
guide size for trailers	13–20	7.70	2.40	3.10
guide for shed areas		8.70	3.40	3.40

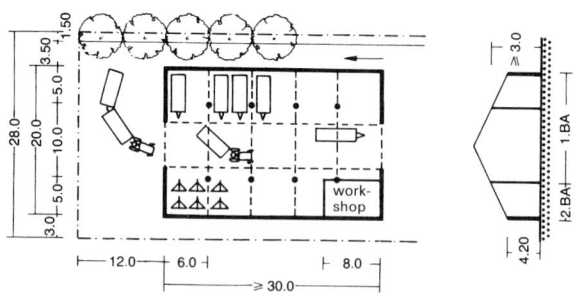

⑥ Small machine shed with side gangway

⑦ Large machine shed with central gangway: supported structure

Guideline space requirements for garages and sheds

building type: use/type of farm	reference dimension	farm size			
		10 ha	15 ha	20 ha	30 ha
garage for	floor area (m²)	26	43	44	62
tractors and	depth (m)	5.0	5.2	5.2	5.4
motor mower	height (m)	2.7	2.8	2.8	2.9
garage for	floor area (m²)	46			
mountain farm	depth (m)	7.3			
transporter with	height (m):				
loader;	transporter	2.9			
motor mower and	motor reaper	2.2			
belt reaper					
workshop	floor area (m²)	12	12	14	16
barns for	floor area (m²)	160	230	260	350
purely stock	depth (m)	7.6	8.7	8.7	9.5
farms	height (m)	3.3	3.4	3.4	3.5
barns for	floor area (m²)	180	310	370	520
mixed stock/	depth (m)	7.6	8.7	8.7	9.5
arable farms	height (m)	3.3	3.5	3.5	3.6
barns for	floor area (m²)		240	340	450
purely arable	room depth (m)		8.0	8.0	9.7
farm	height (m)		3.5	3.5	5.8
barns for	floor area (m²)		120		
mountain	depth (m)		8.3		
farms	height		3.2		

⑧ Guideline space requirements for garages and sheds

Unlike farms in other European countries, British farms tend to be larger than 30 ha. This might be partly due to differing inheritance practices.

machine		l (m)	w (m)	h (m)
tractors (with safety hooks)				
standard tractor	up to 60 hp	3.30–3.70	1.50–2.00	2.20–2.60
4-wheel drive tractor	60–100 hp	4.00–5.00	1.80–1.40	2.50–2.80
(incl. row-crop tractors)	120–200 hp	5.50–6.00	2.40–2.50	2.50–2.90
carrier:				
low-loader	up to 45 HP	4.50	1.70	2.50
transporter (with towing claw) twin-axle trailers				
flat-bed trailer	up to 3 t	ca. 6.00	1.80–1.90	ca 1.50
flat-bed trailers	3–5 t	ca. 6.50	1.90–2.10	ca 1.60
and tippers	5–8 t	ca. 7.00	2.10–2.20	ca 1.80
single axle trailers	up to 3 t	ca. 5.00¹⁾	1.90–2.10	ca 1.60
(with scraper floor)	3–5 t	5.00–5.50¹⁾	2.10	ca 1.60
or tippers	5–8 t	5.50–6.00	2.20–2.25	ca 2.00
slurry tank trailer	3–6 m³	5.50–6.50	1.80–2.00	1.80–2.20
earth tilling equipment (in transport mode)				
general purpose plough	2 blades	ca. 2.00	ca 1.20	ca 1.20
(mounted)	3 blades	2.70–3.30	1.30–1.50	ca 1.20
	5 blades	4.50–5.50	2.00–2.50	ca 1.20
reversible plough	2 blades	ca. 2.30	ca. 1.10	1.30–1.70
(mounted)	3 blades	2.90–3.00	1.40–1.60	1.30–1.70
	5 blades	4.50–5.50	2.00–2.50	1.30–1.70
grubber		1.50–3.00	2.30–3.00	0.60–1.10
disk harrow		3.20–3.50	1.70–3.50	0.70–1.10
combination device		2.70–3.00	1.10–1.30	
rotary hoe		1.10–1.40	2.00–3.00	1.10–1.20
vibrating harrow		0.80	up to 3m	1.00
rotary harrow		2.00–3.00	up to 3m	0.80
rollers	3-part	2.50	up to 3m	0.80
mineral fertilizer spreader				
box spreader		0.70–1.20	2.70–3.00	0.70–1.20
centrifugal spreader	(mounted)	1.00–1.50	1.40–1.50	0.90–1.40
large capacity spreader	(towed)	4.30–5.50	1.80–2.80	1.70–2.00

¹⁾ stable dung spreader approximately 0.5 m longer

⑨ Dimensions of agricultural equipment

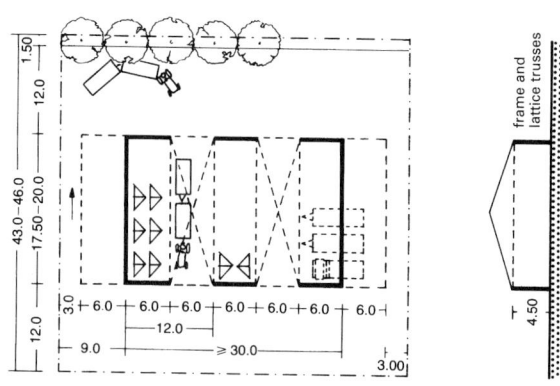

⑩ Large machine and equipment shed with through-gangways

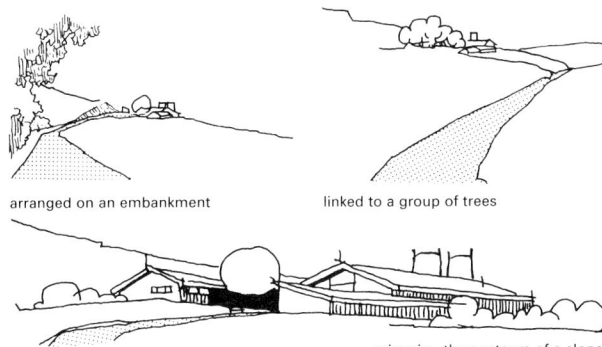

① **Using natural features, buildings can be blended into the landscape**

arranged on an embankment

linked to a group of trees

mirroring the contours of a slope

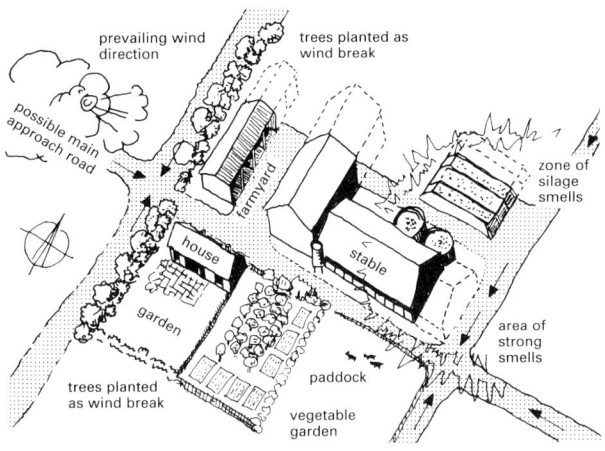

② **Schematic layout of the elements of a farm**

prevailing wind direction

trees planted as wind break

possible main approach road

farmyard

house

stable

zone of silage smells

garden

trees planted as wind break

paddock

area of strong smells

vegetable garden

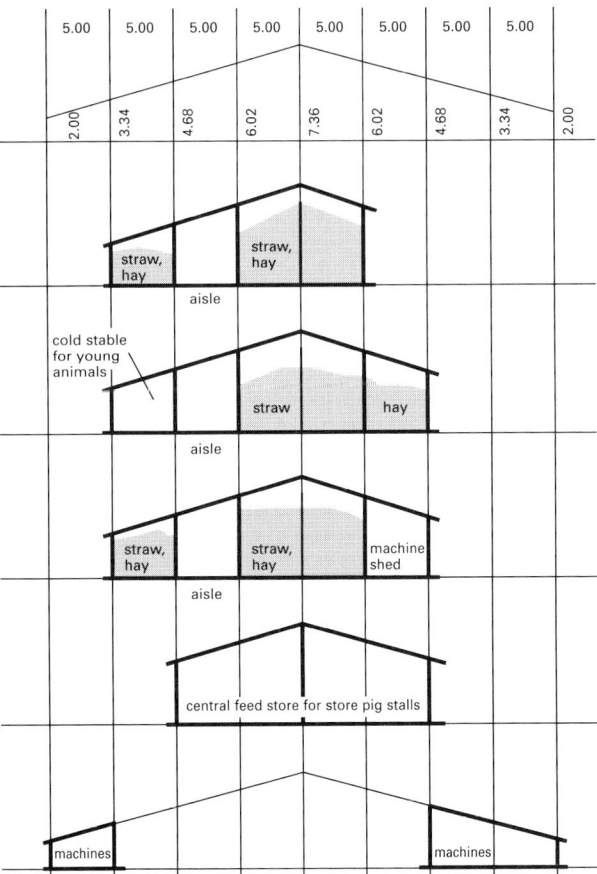

③ **Planning system for a flexible range of barns**

straw, hay

straw, hay

aisle

cold stable for young animals

straw

hay

aisle

straw, hay

straw, hay

machine shed

aisle

central feed store for store pig stalls

machines

machines

Design considerations

There are numerous factors that can influence the design of farm buildings. For individual buildings, it is necessary to consider the requirements of the following: Planning Authorities, Building Regulations, Water Authorities, Ministry of Agriculture, Health and Safety Executive, Milk Marketing Board, Dairy Husbandry Advisers, Welfare Codes, Farm Building Design Code and electricity, gas, telephone and water companies.

Planning considerations

In selecting the location a balance should be found between topographical and climatic conditions on the one hand and the business requirements on the other. For instance, stables require almost the same climatic conditions as domestic buildings so exposed areas prone to extreme weather should be avoided. The position of the buildings with respect to each other, and relative to any adjoining housing estates, and orientation to the prevailing wind direction must be carefully considered. Note that the prevailing wind direction in summer is more important than that in winter.

Vehicles should be able to move around the farm without needing to use public roads. However, an effective link to the public road network is obviously necessary to allow supplies to be brought in and produce to be shipped out. Commercially, this connection is more important than arranging the farm buildings so as to be close to the fields. The gradients of farm roads should not exceed the following maxima: 5% for manually operated vehicles, 10% for motorised vehicles, with an absolute maximum of 20% for short stretches.

In laying out the buildings the following minimum spacings should be maintained: at least 10m between all buildings and 15m between the farmhouse and stables or sheds → ②.

For a farmhouse and garden, about 1000 m² is required. The garden should be located to the south or west of the house if possible and can be used also for growing fruit and vegetables. Typical allowances are 50–60 m² of vegetable plot per person and approximately 100 m² of orchard per person.

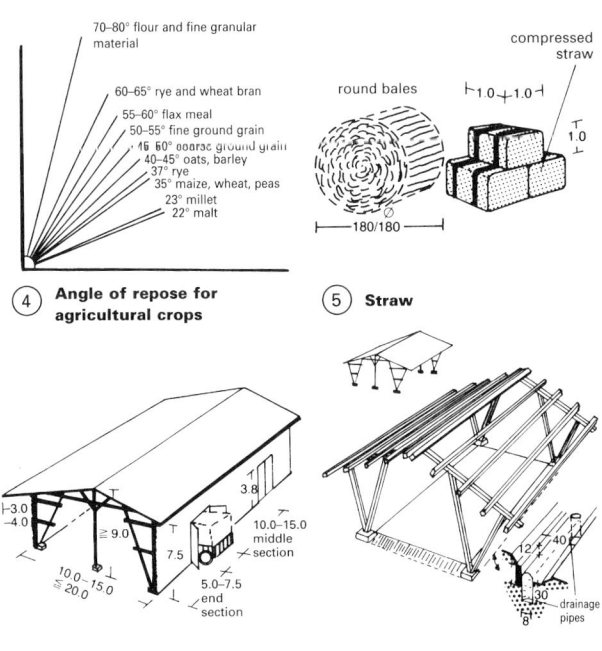

70–80° flour and fine granular material

60–65° rye and wheat bran

55–60° flax meal

50–55° fine ground grain

45–50° coarse ground grain

40–45° oats, barley

37° rye

35° maize, wheat, peas

23° millet

22° malt

④ **Angle of repose for agricultural crops**

round bales

compressed straw

180/180

⑤ **Straw**

⑥ **Barn with transverse aisles**

⑦ **Field barn**

drainage pipes

417

area requirement (m²)	tethering feeding/ lying stall for (no.) cows			box pen stall for (no.) cows			
	40	60	80	50	80	120	200
stalls	250	380	500	400	640	960	1600
milking area	10	20	30	50	80	120	200
low-level silo	200	300	400	250	400	600	1000
roughage	80	120	160	100	160	240	400
liquid manure store	160	240	320	200	320	480	800
roadways	400	600	720	500	720	960	1400
farmyard area	800	1050	1200	1250	1760	2400	3000
required total area (m²)	1900	2710	3330	2750	4080	5760	8400
required plot width (m)	33	33	33	45	45	45	45

(1) **Dairy cows without calves**

The tables presented here give guidance on the minimum required sizes of plot for different types of farming. Alternative values may be encountered depending on the assumptions. For example, the required plot area can be reduced by:

- using tower silos instead of flat silos
- the use of loft space instead of floor area for storage
- storing liquid manure under the slatted floor instead of in outside containers
- building up to the borders etc.

The plot sizes given in the tables do not take into account the area required for storage of farm machinery, workshops or dwelling areas because these do not have to be immediately beside the buildings involved directly in production.

area requirement (m²)	tethering feeding/ lying stall for (no.) cows			box stall for (no.) cows			
	40	60	80	50	80	120	200
stalls	320	470	630	440	700	1050	1750
milking area	20	20	30	60	80	80	80
low-level silo	250	380	500	310	500	750	1250
roughage	100	150	200	130	200	300	500
liquid manure store	200	300	400	260	400	600	1000
roadways	500	750	900	620	900	1200	1750
farmyard area	1000	1270	1500	1560	2200	3000	3750
required total area (m²)	2390	3340	4160	3380	4980	6980	10080
required plot width (m)	33	33	43	45	45	45	45

(2) **Dairy cows with calves**

area requirement (m²)	store calves: single boxes for (no.) calves				store bulls pen; fully slatted floor for (no.) animals			
	100	200	300	400	100	200	300	400
stalls	340	640	930	1200	400	940	1410	1880
roughage	–	–	–	–	50	100	150	200
low-level silo	–	–	–	–	560	1000	1250	1500
liquid manure store	50	100	150	200	120	200	300	400
roadways	200	200	200	200	650	560	750	850
farmyard area	1110	1600	2200	2640	1210	2100	3140	2170
required total area (m²)	1700	2540	3480	4240	2990	4900	7000	7000
required plot width (m)	45	45	45	45	35	35	50	50

(3) **Store cattle**

area requirement (m²)	sow stalls: for (no.) sows				sow stalls for S sows, with P store places for piglets		
	80	100	120	150	46S 400P	88S 800P	142S 1200P
stalls	720	850	1020	1200	880	1760	2640
liquid manure store	90	100	110	120	240	400	600
roadways	230	250	270	300	240	400	480
farmyard area (including run)	1600	1850	2100	2400	1480	2640	3120
required total area (m²)	2640	3050	3500	4020	2840	5200	6830
required plot width (m)	45	45	45	50	45	45	50

(4) **Piglet rearing (with stores)**

area requirement (m²)	store pig shed for (no.) animals			
	500	1000	1500	2000
stalls	850	1700	2500	3400
liquid manure store	250	400	600	800
roadways	240	400	440	400
farmyard area	1300	2300	2700	3000
required total area (m²)	2640	4800	6290	7600
required plot width (m)	35	35	55	55

(5) **Store pigs**

area requirement (m²)	laying hens, three-tier cages for (no.) animals			store chickens, cages for (no.) animals		
	10000	50000	100000	10000	50000	100000
stalls	630	3000	6000	400	2000	4000
egg sorting room	–	400	800	–	–	–
liquid manure store	110	550	1100	50	250	5000
roadways	200	1200	1800	100	500	1000
farmyard area	1260	5050	8000	1000	4000	7000
required total area (m²)	2200	10200	17700	1550	6750	12500
required plot width (m)	35	100	100	35	80	80

(6) **Hen keeping**

area requirement (m²)	root crop, cereal cultivation for (ha)			cereal feed cultivation on (ha)		
	60	80	100	80	100	120
machine hall	250	290	320	230	270	120
bulk storage area	250	250	250	250	250	250
roadways and machine storage	180	200	220	180	200	220
farmyard area	200	230	250	200	230	250
required total area (m²)	880	970	1040	860	950	1020
required plot width (m)	33	33	40	33	33	40

(7) **Market crop cultivation**

418

form of fodder		dimensions (cm)	fresh	wilted (35%)	hay	straw	handling method
long		ca. 25	170	120–150	50	30	in portions (grab)
cut		4–8	200	150–180	80	40	bulk material (dosing rollers)
short		4	350	250–300	60–100	50–80	bulk material (blower, cutter)
small bales		35 × 50 × 80	–	250–300	100–150	80–130	bulk material (manual)
large bales		Ø 180–150	–	300	80–180	60–130	bulk material (front loader)
		150 × 150 × 240 (160 × 120 × 70)	–		60–90	70–130	

(1) **Forms of harvested fodder (kg/m³)**

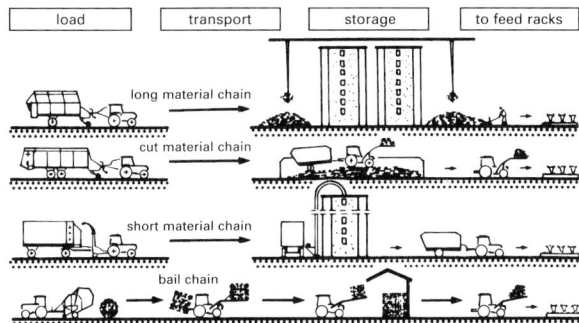

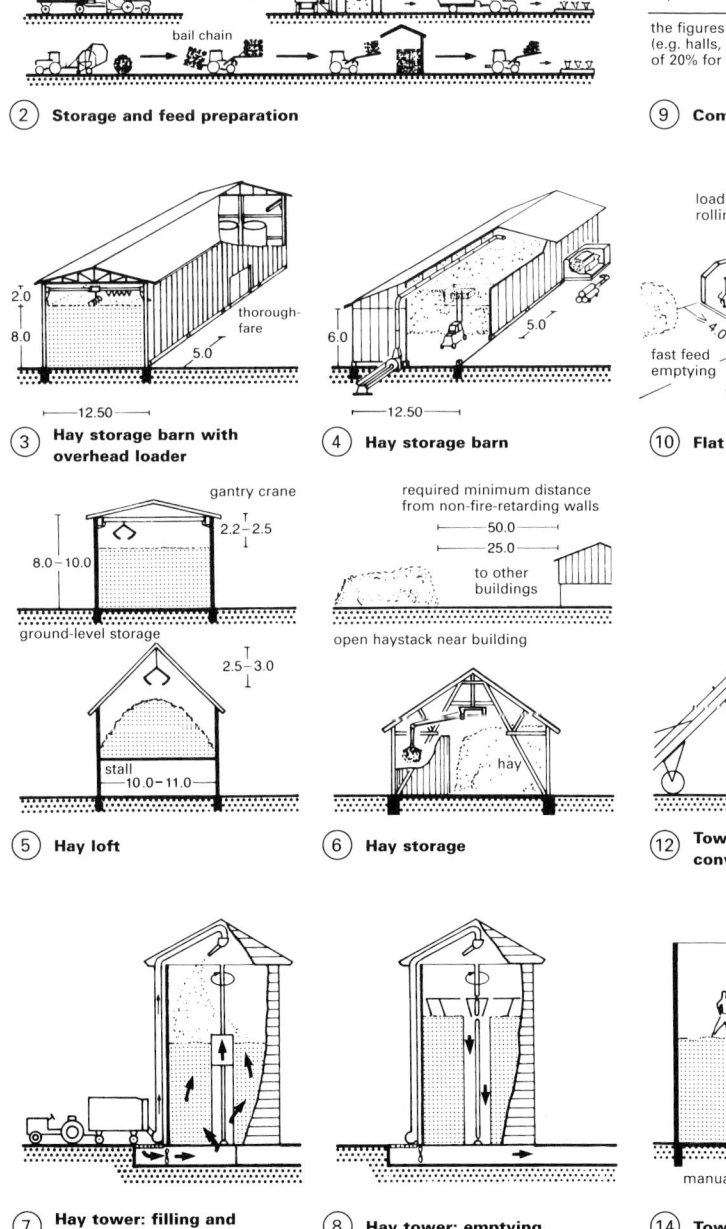

(2) **Storage and feed preparation**

Flat silos for storing silage require ducts to allow the liquor to drain off. The walls must be able to withstand the lateral pressure of silage depths ranging from 2.0 to 3.5 m so the detailed design work should be done by a structural engineer.

fodder		space required (when storing before setting (m³/t)
hay:	long material (quality good to very good; stack height 2–6 m)	17–10
	chaff material (5 cm; quality good to very good; stack height 2–6 m)	13–10
	HD bales, non-stacked	9–7
	HD bales, stacked	8–6
	aerated hay	10–7
	hay tower	8–7
	dry grass (cobs)	2–1.7
silage:	wilted silage (35–25% moisture content)	2–1.6
	maize silage (28–20% moisture content)	1.8–1.5
	turnip leaves	1.3–1.2
feed turnips		1.6–1.4
concentrated feed (coarse ground)		2.2–1.9
dry feedstuff		3.8–3.4

the figures above do not include space for getting material into and out of storage (e.g. halls, aisles, space for crane etc.); they do, however, include a filling supplement of 20% for hay and concentrated feedstuff and 10% for silages

(9) **Complete storage of animal feed**

(3) **Hay storage barn with overhead loader**

(4) **Hay storage barn**

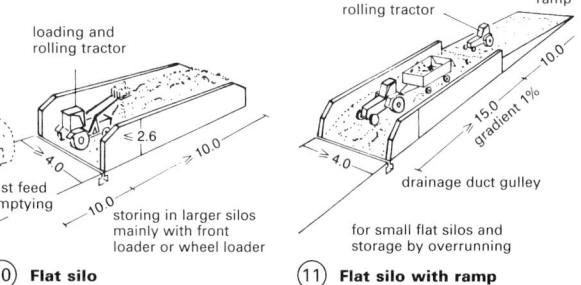

(10) **Flat silo**

(11) **Flat silo with ramp**

(5) **Hay loft**

(6) **Hay storage**

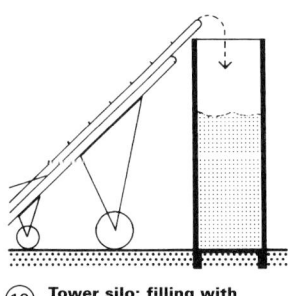

(12) **Tower silo: filling with conveyor belt**

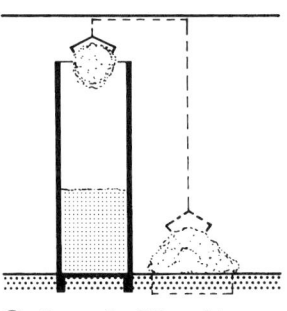

(13) **Tower silo: filling with overhead loader**

(7) **Hay tower: filling and ventilation**

(8) **Hay tower: emptying**

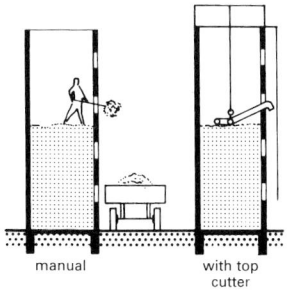

(14) **Tower silo: extraction**

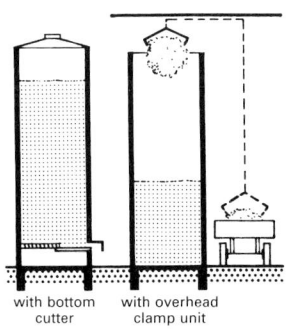

(15) **Tower silo: extraction**

419

Waste Water and Sewage

The amount of droppings and urine collected from farm animals depends upon the type of animal and its live weight (expressed in livestock units, 1LU = 500kg live weight), as well as the type and composition of the feed and drink. Because the composition of animal feed varies substantially throughout the year, the composition figures given here are averages.

With normal straw quantities of 1.5 to 2kg of straw per LU/day, a volume of 1.00–1.25 m³/LU/month is required for solid dung storage. With slurry (liquid manure), typical figures for dairy cattle are 1.4 m³/LU/month while for maize-fed store cattle the volume is reduced to 1.0 m³/LU/month.

Among the most frequent causes of pollution from farms are structural failure of slurry and effluent stores, mismanagement and lack of maintenance of slurry handling systems and problems with dirty water disposal. National regulations have been tightened to prevent such problems. In England and Wales the Control of Pollution (Silage, Slurry and Agricultural Fuel Oil) Regulations, 1991, set legal minimum standards of design and construction for silage, slurry and agricultural fuel installations. An important condition that affects the siting of any such installation is that it must not be constructed within 10 metres of watercourses (including land drains) into which silage effluent, slurry or oil could enter.

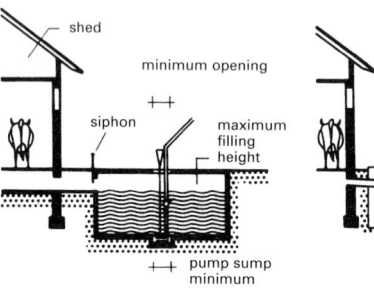

(1) **Summary of solid dung, slurry and liquid manure storage and removal**

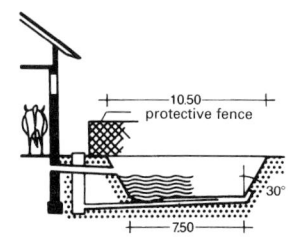

(2) **Underground tank (solid)**

(3) **Earth tank with plastic sealing layers**

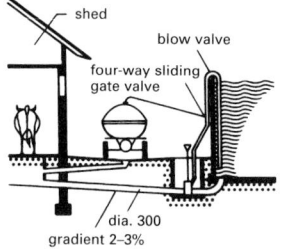

(4) **High container with pumping station**

(5) **High container with collection pit**

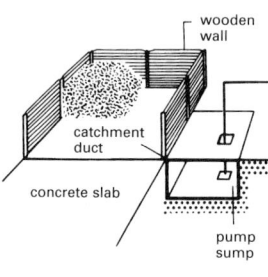

(6) **Solid dung store combined with liquid manure pit**

(7) **Solid dung stores with liquid manure pits**

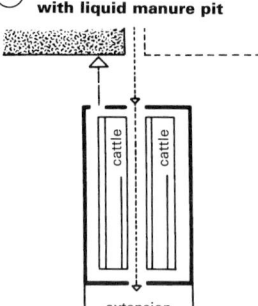

(8) **Solid dung store to front**

(9) **Solid dung store to front**

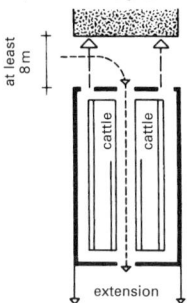

(12) **Solid dung store to side**

type of animal	solid dung		slurry	nutrients contained in solid dung (kg/LU/month)				
	(kg/LU/ month)	(m³/LU/ month)	(m³/LU/ month)	N	P₂O₅	K₂O	CaO	MgO
horse	750	1.0	0.1	4.5	2.1	4.0	1.8	1.05
cattle, in tethering stall	900	1.2	0.6	4.5	2.3	5.9	1.8	1.8
fattening bull, tethering stall	900	1.2	0.6					
fattening bull in deep straw	1500	2.0	1)					
sheep	650	0.9	1)	5.2	1.5	4.4	2.1	1.2
pig	500	0.6	0.6	2.8	3.8	2.5	2.0	1.0
pig in deep straw	1000	1.2	1)					
laying hens (dry droppings 80% total solids)	460	0.4		16.3	21.4	11.2	55.8	
laying hens (ground-kept, droppings 78% total solids)	550	0.7		14.3	18.7	10.5		
fattening hens (ground-kept, droppings)	590	0.8						
rabbit (dry droppings)	330	0.4		1.7	1.5	4.0	2.1	

1) bound in ground straw

(10) **Amount and average composition of solid dung**

type of animal	slurry arising (m³/LU/ month)	TS (total solids) content (%)	nutrients									
			N	P₂O₅	K₂O	CaO	MgO	N	P₂O₅	K₂O	CaO	MgO
			(kg/m³)					(kg/LU/month)				
cattle	1.4	10	4	2	6	2	1	5.6	2.8	8.4	2.8	1.5
pigs	1.4	7	6	4	3	3	1	8.4	5.6	4.2	4.2	1.4
laying hens	1.9	15	8	8	5	15	2	15.2	15.2	9.5	28.5	3.8

(11) **Amount and average composition of liquid manure**

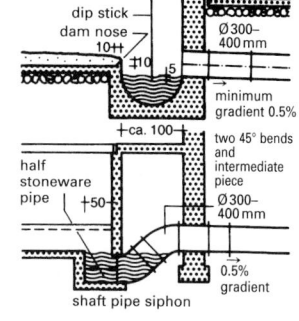

(13) **Gas traps and slurry channels for liquid manure pits**

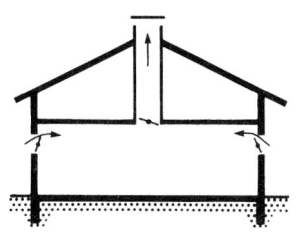

(1) **Classification of ventilation systems**

VENTILATION SYSTEMS

The stable climate (temperature, air composition and humidity) has a decisive role in maintaining the health of animals and ventilation is, therefore, one of the most important considerations in shed design. The objectives of ventilation in livestock buildings are to supply the oxygen needed by the stock, remove waste (mainly heat, water, carbon dioxide and ammonia) and keep down the level of airborne micro-organisms or pathogens. Ventilation systems may be natural, relying on convection and wind currents, or forced (mechanical), using fans to propel air through the building.

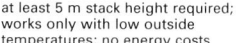

at least 5 m stack height required; works only with low outside temperatures; no energy costs

(2) **Stack ventilation**

precondition: roof = ceiling; difficulties with inverted weather conditions; the supply air must be regulatable

(3) **Eaves-ridge ventilation**

air temp. (°C)		recommended air speed (m/s)
under 18		0.15
	20	0.20
over	22	0.24
	24	0.35
	26	0.50

(9) **Recommended air speed depending on temperature**

	for animals l/m³	MWC* value
carbon dioxide	3.50	5.00
ammonia	0.05	0.05
hydrogen sulphide	0.01	0.01
* MWC = maximum workplace concentration		

(10) **Permissible concentrations in stable air**

Planning should start with a calculation of the size of the inlet and outlet air openings, as for mechanical ventilation. They should be calculated according to the summer air rates and in the case of no wind according to the following formula:

$$w = \frac{g \cdot H \cdot \Delta t/T1}{1 + F_1/F_2} \ (m/s) \qquad F_2 = \frac{Vi}{3600 \cdot w} \ (m^2)$$

w = speed of outgoing air in the ridge opening (m/s)
g = acceleration due to gravity (9.81 m/s²)
H = height from stable floor to ridge opening (m)
T_1 = external temperature (K) (add 273 to find temperature in °C)
Δt = temperature difference between internal and external air (K)
Vi = summer air renewal rate (m³/h)
F_1 = inlet air area (m²)
F_2 = outlet air area (m²)

(for simplicity $\frac{F_1}{F_2}$ can be set to 1)

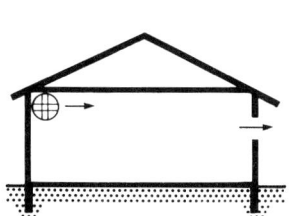

problems with wind direction; no specific outgoing air; good when used in connection with heating; energy requirement: 105–125 kWh/LU/year

(4) **Pressurised ventilation**

simple system; specific outgoing air (environmental protection); difficult to combine with heating; energy requirements: 98–105 kWh/LU/year

(5) **Extract ventilation**

axial fan

radial fan

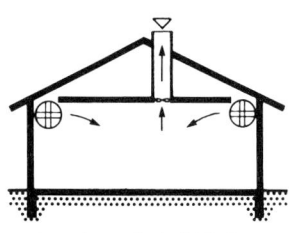

expensive system; safe air distribution; functions independently of weather; simple to combine with heating; high capital cost (1.5 to 2 times that of extract ventilation); energy requirement: 205 kWh/LU/year

(6) **Balanced pressure ventilation**

(7) **Types of fan**

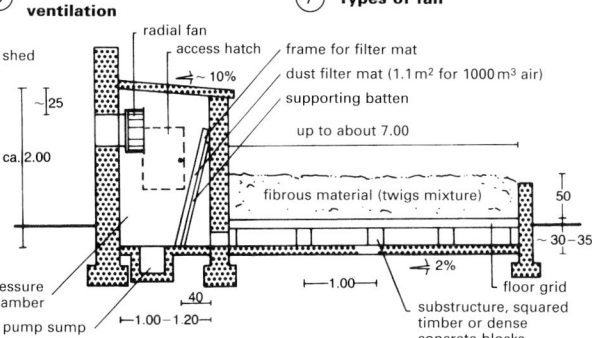

(8) **Earth filter system (design according to Zeisig)**

stable for:	optimal area for animals		recommended calculation value in winter	
	air temperature (°C)	relative humidity (%)	air temperature (°C)	relative humidity (%)
dairy cows, suckling calves, fattening bulls, young breeding cattle and calves	0–20	60–80	10	80
young store cattle, store bulls	12–20*	60–80	16	80
store calves	16–20*	60–80	18	70
gilts, dry and carrying sows, boars	5–15	60–80	12	80
store pigs	15–20*	60–80	17	80
sows and piglets:				
sows	12–16	60–80		
piglets at birth (when using zone heating)	30–32	40–60		
piglets up to 6 weeks	20–22	60–70		
market piglets and pre-store up to 30 kg	18–22*	60–80	20	60
cage-reared from about 5 kg to about 20 kg (2–8 weeks)	22–26*	40–60	26	60
hen chicks with zone heating; temperature in chick zone reduced by 3°C per week alive	32–18*	60–70	26	60
young and laying hens	15–22	60–80	18	70
turkey chicks with zone heating; temperature in chick zone reduced by 3°C per week alive	18–36*	60–80	22	60
store turkeys >7 weeks	10–18*	60–80	16	80
ducks	10–30*	60–80	20	60
workhorses	10–15	60–80	12	80
ridden horses	15–17	60–80	16	80
breeding sheep	6–14	60–80	10	80
store sheep	14–16*	60–80	16	80

* with increasing animal age the air temperature should be gradually reduced from the higher to the lower value

(11) **Air temperature and relative humidity in different stalls**

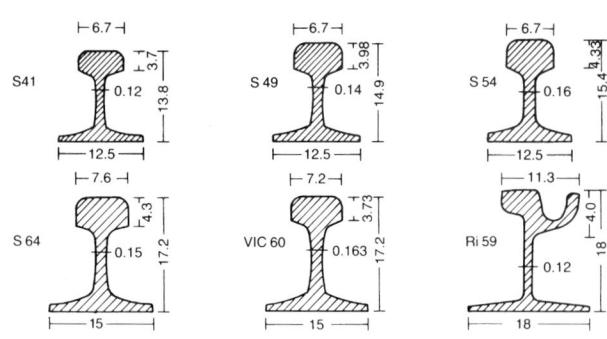

① **The common rail sections**

rail section	G (kg/m run)	A (cm²)	$W_{x\,head}$ (cm³)	$W_{x\,base}$ (cm³)	W_y (cm³)	I_x (cm⁴)	I_y (cm⁴)
S 41	40.95	52.2	196.0	200.5	41.7	1368	260
S 9	49.43	63.0	240.2	248.2	51.0	1819	320
S 54	54.54	69.4	262.4	276.4	57.0	2073	359
S64	64.92	82.4	355.9	403.5	80.5	3253	604
UIC 60	60.34	76.9	335.5	377.4	68.4	3055	513
Ri 59	58.96	75.1	372.6	351.8	81.0[*]	3257	781

[*] $W_{y1} = 118\,cm^3$ because of asymmetry

② **Rail dimensions → ①**

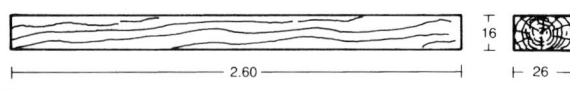

③ **Wooden sleeper**

④ **Steel sleeper**

⑤ **Concrete sleeper B70**

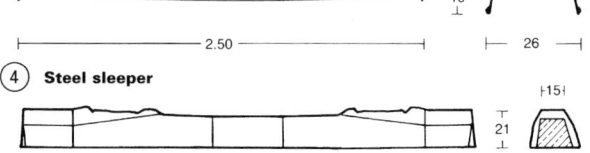

⑥ **Concrete sleeper B58**

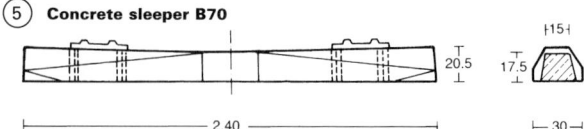

⑦ **Standard cross-section for a single track bed**

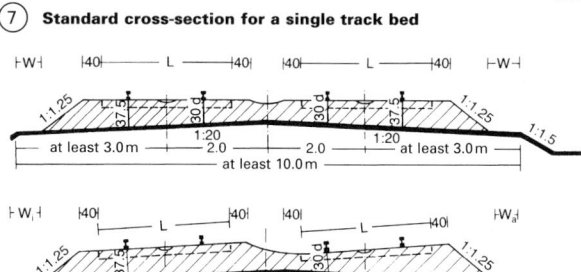

⑧ **Standard cross-section for a twin track bed**

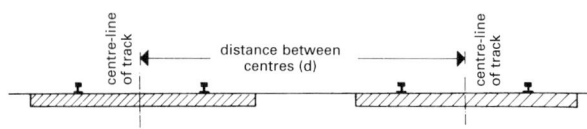

⑨ **Distance between centre-lines of tracks**

The key standard distances (d) between track centre-lines are as listed below:

- On open stretches of track — 4.00 m (3.5 m on older stretches)
  - where signals are installed — 4.50 m
  - as safety space after every second track — 5.40 m
  - on newly built stretches (V > 200 km/h) — 4.70 m
- In stations — 4.50 m (4.75 m)
  - main lines, straight through — 4.00 m
  - in sets of 5–6 lines — 6.00 m
  - for brake inspection/test tracks — 5.00 m
  - in sidings for carriage cleaning — 5.00 m

The standard gauge for the UK (and for 71% of all the railways in the world) is 1.435 m. Tolerances on the gauge width are, as follows:

-3/+30 mm on main lines
-3/+35 mm on branch lines

Gauges in other countries are: Russia 1.520 m, Spain and Portugal 1.668 m, South and Central Africa 1.067 m, Chile, Argentina and India 1.673 m.

Typically, the expected life of sleepers can be taken to be as follows:

- timber sleepers, impregnated with creosote 25–40 years
- timber sleepers, unimpregnated — 3–15 years
- steel sleepers — about 45 years
- concrete sleepers (estimated) — at least 60 years

The depth of trench in a cutting should be ≥0.4–0.6 m below grade and the slope of the trench 3–10%, depending on the type of consolidation of the trench floor.

Ground water in the case of retaining walls must be conducted away by pipes or drainage holes.

The longitudinal gradient for open stretches of main line should be ≤12.5‰, and ≤40‰ for branch lines. For lines in stations it should be ≤2.5‰. In exceptional circumstances, where special permission is granted, gradients up to 25‰ can be used on main lines.

When stationary, the permissible wheel load is 9 tonnes. On stretches with sufficiently strong track and supporting structures, a greater wheel loading is possible (up to 12.5 tonnes).

For further information on British railways contact Safety and Standards Directorate, Railtrack PLC, London.
For further information on European railways, contact the Union of European Railway Industries, Brussels.

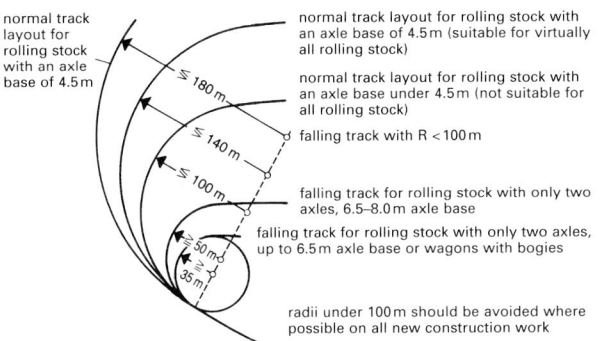

normal track layout for rolling stock with an axle base of 4.5 m

normal track layout for rolling stock with an axle base of 4.5 m (suitable for virtually all rolling stock)

normal track layout for rolling stock with an axle base under 4.5 m (not suitable for all rolling stock)

falling track with R < 100 m

falling track for rolling stock with only two axles, 6.5–8.0 m axle base

falling track for rolling stock with only two axles, up to 6.5 m axle base or wagons with bogies

radii under 100 m should be avoided where possible on all new construction work

(1) **Track radius (for turning round) in sidings**

Curved radii (to the centre-line of the track), R:

for direct main line fast track	≥300 m
for sidings in stations	≥180 m
for branch lines with main line rolling stock	≥180 m
without main line rolling stock	≥100 m
for sidings, used by main line engines	≥140 m
for sidings, not used by mainline engines possibly	≥100 m
minimum	≥35 m

Note that if 100 m > R ≥ 35 m carriages should only be pulled. In addition, R >130 m might not be suitable for all rolling stock so the types involved should be checked at an early stage.

Radii for narrow gauge railways

for 1.00 m gauge track	≥50 m
for 0.75 m gauge track	≥40 m
for 0.60 m gauge track	≥25 m

For track that will be used at speeds greater than shunting speed, a transitional section of curve must be laid between the straight section and the circular arc itself, giving a continuous curvature change from 1:∞ to 1:R → (2). Under certain circumstances the curves must be canted in order to keep the centrifugal force that arises during travel through the curve within reasonable limits. Canted curves and transition curves should be blended together. All details should satisfy the Service Regulations of the relevant Railway Authority.

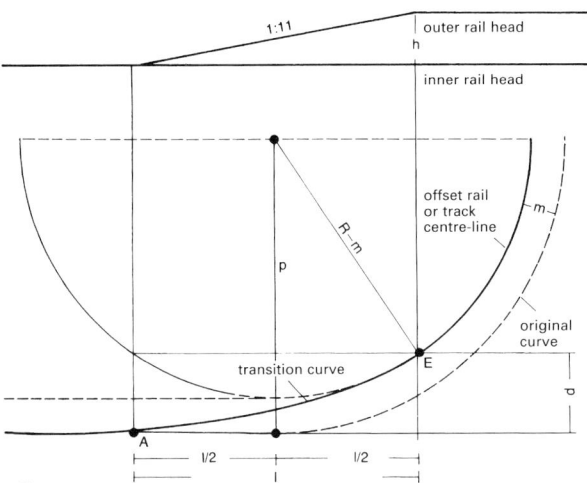

(2) **Canted curve and transition curve**

R	l	m	ramp gradient
180–200	40	0.370	1: 320
		0.333	1: 320
250–350	30	0.150	1: 300
		0.107	1: 400
400–2000	20	0.012	1: 310
		0.008	1:1300

(3) **Table for branch lines and normal sidings (m)**

Sets of points are designated in accordance with the rail shape, the branch line's radius and the pitch of the frog (e.g. 49–190–1:9). Below are example lengths of sets of points/switch rails:

49–190–1:7.5 = 25.222 m/12.611 m
49–190–1:9 = 27.138 m/10.523 m
49–300–1:9 = 33.230 m/16.615 m

Carriages must not stand beyond the marker sign, to prevent obstructing the set of points → (5). The distance between the track centre-lines at the marker sign should be ≥3.5 m.

The diameters, D, of normal turntables are: for axles, 2–3 m; for wagons, 3–10 m; and for engines, 12.5–23.0 m.

The sizes of transfer tables should be calculated as minimum axle base of the carriage to be transferred + 0.5 m.

Details for level crossings can be obtained from the Service Regulations of the relevant Authority.

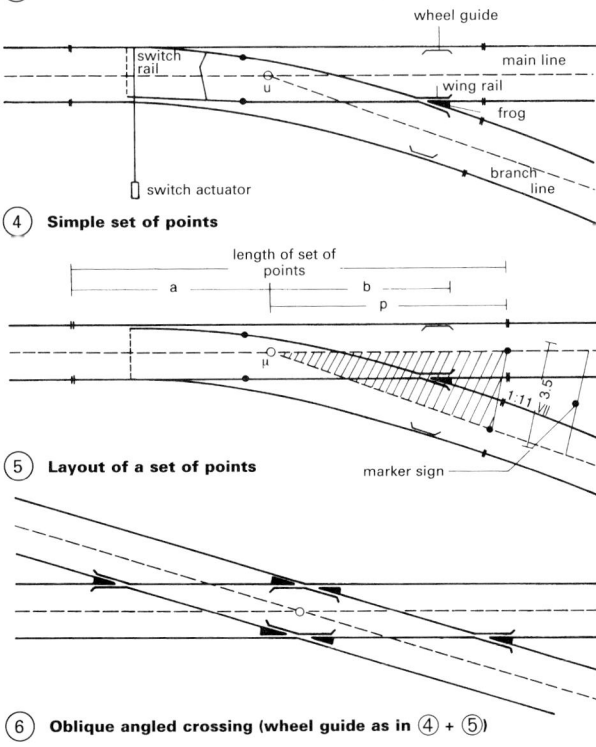

wheel guide

switch rail

main line

wing rail

frog

branch line

switch actuator

(4) **Simple set of points**

length of set of points

a, b, p

1:11

3.5

marker sign

(5) **Layout of a set of points**

(6) **Oblique angled crossing (wheel guide as in (4) + (5))**

buffers

loading gauge

track weighbridge

(7) **Display symbols**

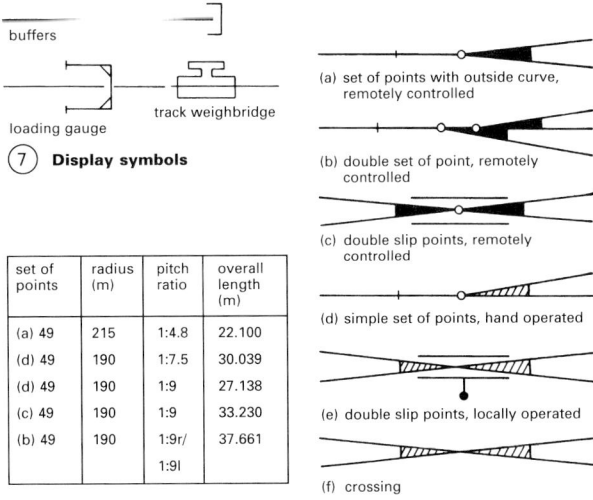

(a) set of points with outside curve, remotely controlled

(b) double set of point, remotely controlled

(c) double slip points, remotely controlled

(d) simple set of points, hand operated

(e) double slip points, locally operated

(f) crossing

set of points	radius (m)	pitch ratio	overall length (m)
(a) 49	215	1:4.8	22.100
(d) 49	190	1:7.5	30.039
(d) 49	190	1:9	27.138
(c) 49	190	1:9	33.230
(b) 49	190	1:9r/	37.661
		1:9l	

(8) **Dimensions for sets of points → (9)**

(9) **Display symbols**

standard gauge railways

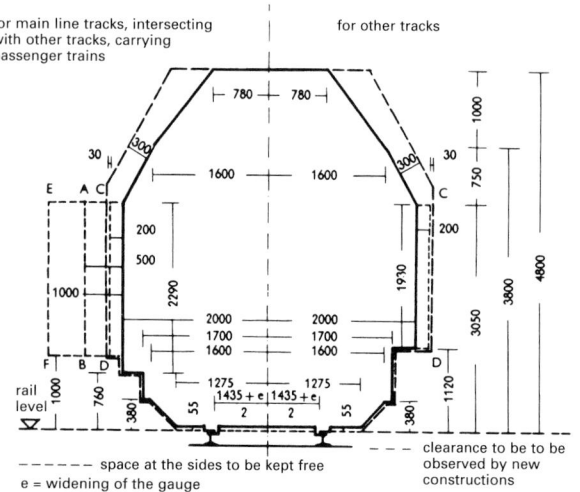

for main line tracks, intersecting with other tracks, carrying passenger trains

for other tracks

- - - - - space at the sides to be kept free
e = widening of the gauge

- - - - clearance to be to be observed by new constructions

A–B for main lines on open stretches for all objects with the exception of fabricated structures
C–D for station sidings and for open stretches of main lines with special structures and signals between the tracks
E–F for fixed objects on passenger platforms

(1) **Standard clearance profiles**
(straight track plus curves with radii ≥ 250 m)

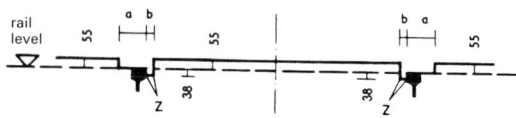

a ≥ 150 mm for immovable objects which are not firmly connected to the rail
a ≥ 135 mm for immovable objects which are firmly connected to the rail
b = 41 mm for devices guiding the wheel on the inside of the front surface
b ≥ 45 mm for level crossings
b ≥ 70 mm for all other cases
Z = corners which have to be radiused

(2) **Standard structure gauging and clearances at low level**

curve radius (m)	necessary increase in standard clearance on the	
	inside of the curve (mm)	outside of the curve (mm)
250	0	0
225	25	30
200	50	65
190	65	80
180	80	100
150	135	170
120	335	365
100	530	570

(3) **Necessary increase in the standard clearance for curves with radii < 250 m**

narrow gauge railways

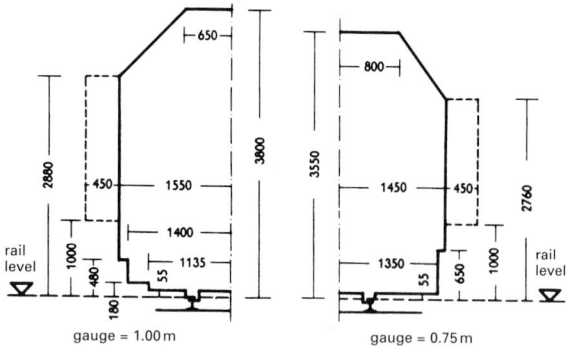

gauge = 1.00 m   gauge = 0.75 m

(7) **Standard clearance profiles, straight line track**

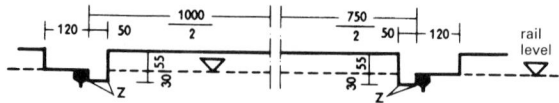

Z = corners which have to be radiused

(8) **Standard structure gauging and clearances at low level**

Typical Continental European Structure Gauging and Clearances

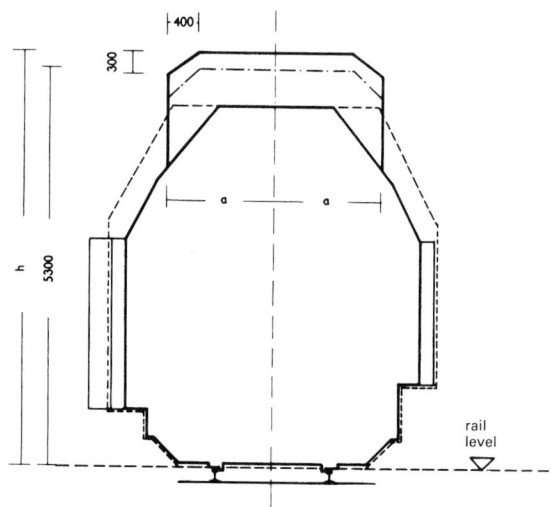

for existing superstructures, tunnels and engine shed doors when electrification takes place

(4) **Top limit of clearance for stretches with overhead conductor wire (15 kV)**

half the radius of the curve (m)	dimensions of half the width a (mm)
up to 250	1445
225	1455
200	1465
180	1475
150	1495
120	1525
100	1555

(5) **Dimensions for half the width of the upper limit of the clearance**

	h
heavy superstructures up to 15 m wide and in tunnels	5500 mm
heavy superstructures over 15 m wide	6000 mm
light superstructures, such as footbridges, sheds including doors	6000 mm
signal gantries and brackets	6300 mm

(6) **Minimum clearance under structures**

Other dimensions: European standards (Germany)

For entrance doorways the clear width should be ≥3.35 m and for new structures ≥4.00 m.

For tunnels, the extra clearance needed beyond the trains' kinematic envelope clearance to the wall for a single-track stretch of line is 0.40 m; for a double-track stretch of line it is 30 cm.

There are minimum distances required between buildings and railway tracks for new structures. These vary according to location. Typical examples are: a fire resistant structure with suitable cladding must be separated by ≥7.50 m from railway land; the corresponding distance for soft covered structures that are not fire resistant is ≥15 m. The latter also applies to structures in which combustible materials are stored.

Platform heights vary from country to country, and can be as small as 0.38 m. However, access to platforms must not involve passengers having to cross the track. This requires tunnels or bridges, which should have a width of 2.5–4.0 m. If there is circulation in both directions, 4.00–8.00 m is desirable. Steps on bridges or in tunnels should be the same width as the bridge or tunnel.

UK Structure Gauges and Clearances

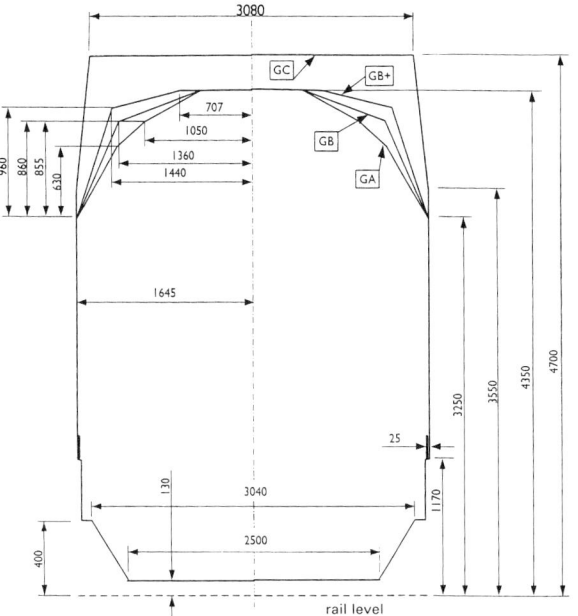

1 All dimensions are in mm.
2 The kinematic envelope is the cross-sectional profile of a vehicle at any position along its length, enlarged to include the effects of dynamic sway and vertical movement caused by speed, (dynamic effects of) track curvature and cant, track positional tolerances, rail wear, rail head/wheel flange clearances, vehicle wear and suspension performance for the particular track location under consideration. The determination of the kinematic envelope is the responsibility of the operator of the proposed vehicle and shall be in accordance with the Railway Group Standard.

(1) **UIC (International Union of Railways) reference profiles for kinematic gauges (GA,GB, GB+, GC)**

Further information: Safety and Standards Directorate, Railtrack PLC, London

This information is based on the Railway Group Standard which applied to all new design and new route clearances for railway vehicles and loads from 3 February 1996.

The purpose of this Railway Group Standard is to set down the engineering requirements for the safe passage of rail vehicles and their loads by reconciling their physical size and dynamic behaviour with the opportunities offered by the railway infrastructure.

This standard applies to infrastructure owned by Railtrack PLC and any other infrastructure interfacing with it and affecting its physical clearances (e.g. private sidings or works into which, or out of which, trains will work onto Railtrack lines).

It shall be complied with in the design, maintenance and alteration of the railway infrastructure, in the design and modification of traction and rolling stock and in the conveyance of out of gauge loads.

Standards are constantly evolving as faster trains are developed and heavier loads are transported. The national rail administration should, therefore, always be contacted for the latest standards and details.

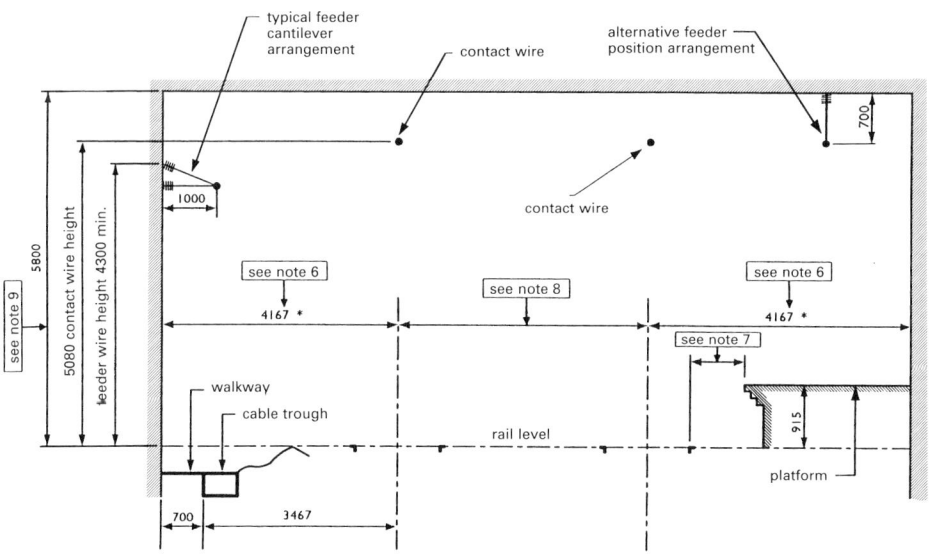

1 This drawing is not applicable to viaducts and tunnels.
2 All dimensions are in mm.
3 Track centres for a mixed traffic railway.
4 Applicable only to straight and level track.
5 Refer to GC/TW496 *Requirements for Constructional Work on or near Railway Operational Land for Non-Railtrack Contracts* for the design of supports for structures built over or close to railway lines.
6 It may be possible in tight situations to reduce the dimension marked with an asterisk, but only where alternative access is available, via a route in a petition of safety, connecting with the walkways each side of the structure or where the railway operates on a 'no person' basis, whereby staff are only allowed on the track when special protection measures are in place.

7 Platform clearances are subject to maintenance of HMRI stepping distances and specific requirement shall be calculated from the chosen kinematic envelope with an allowance made for structural clearance.
8 This dimension shall be calculated from the dimensions associated with the chosen kinematic envelope with an allowance made for passing clearance. At the time of calculating the required dimension an assessment shall be made of traffic proposed for the route such that aerodynamic effects can be taken into account.
9 This dimension accommodates full UIC GC reference profile and assumes train speeds up to 300 km/h. Commercial considerations will dictate whether it is necessary to amend this dimension and contact wire height for the actual type and speed of vehicles proposed for the route.

(2) **New construction gauge (derived from the UIC GC reference profile)**

UK Structure Gauges and Clearances

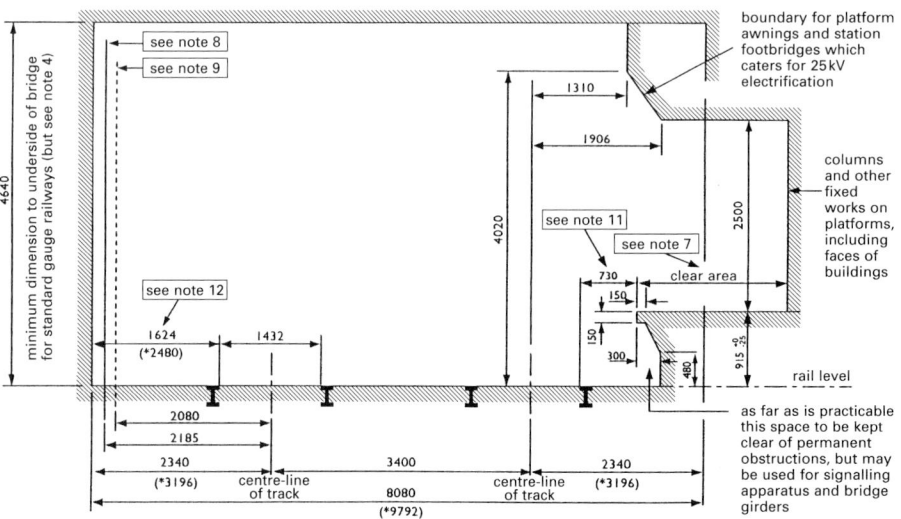

Railtrack shall give consideration to passenger safety by limiting the maximum stepping distance from the top edge of the platform to the top edge of the step board or floor of passenger rolling stock.

The following maximum dimensions for stepping distances, calculated from the centre of the bottom of the door opening, shall apply unless dispensation has been sought from HSVHMRI for site specific cases relating to identified rolling stock. All such cases must be recorded in writing and maintained for future reference.

horizontal	275 mm
vertical	250 mm
diagonal	350 mm

1 This diagram illustrates minimum lateral and overhead clearances to be adopted in construction or reconstruction and for alterations or additions to existing track and structures for line speeds up to 165 km/h (100 mph).
2 All dimensions are in mm.
3 * The dimension to be used when line speed exceeds 165 km/h (100 mph).
4 The clearance dimensions given are valid for straight and level track only and due allowance must be made for the effects of horizontal and vertical curvature, including super-elevation (cant).
5 The standard structure gauge allows for overhead electrification with voltages up to 25 kV. However, to permit some flexibility in the design of overhead equipment, the minimum dimension between rail level and the underside of the structures should be increased, preferably to 4780 mm or more if this can be achieved with reasonable economy. The proximity of track features such as level crossings or OHE sectioning may require greater than 4780 mm.
6 Permissible infringements in respect of conductor rail equipment, guard and check rails, train stops and structures in the space between adjacent tracks are not shown.
7 The minimum dimensions of a single face platform measured from the edge of the platform to the face of the nearest building structure or platform furniture

shall be 2500 mm for speeds up to 165 km/h and for speeds greater than 165 km/h the minimum dimension shall be 3000 mm. The minimum distance to the face of any column shall be 2000 mm.
8 Nearest face of all other structures including masts carrying overhead line equipment of electrified railways.
9 Nearest face of signal posts and other isolated structures less than 2 m in length but excluding masts carrying overhead line equipment on electrified railways.
10 Vertical clearances to the canopy above the platform shall be 2500 mm up to 2000 mm minimum from the platform edge or up to 3000 mm where the line speed exceeds 165 km/h. At distances beyond 2000 mm or 3000 mm from the platform edge, as applicable, the minimum headroom shall be 2300 mm.
11 Platform clearances are subject to the maintenance of HMRI stepping distances and specific requirements shall be calculated from the particular kinematic envelope with an allowance made for structural clearance. The minimum lateral dimension is 730 mm and is shown for guidance.
12 Where reasonably practicable these dimensions shall be increased by 300 mm to facilitate the provision of an access walkway in accordance with CC/RT5203 *Infrastructure Requirements for Personal Safety in Respect of Clearance and Access.*

(3) **Standard structure gauge**

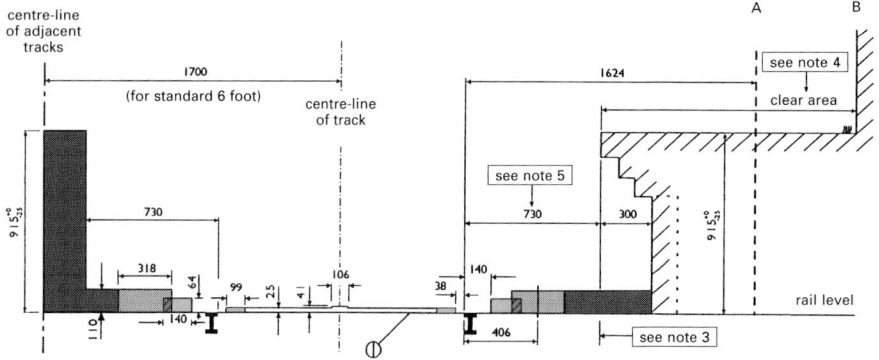

1 All dimensions are in mm.
2 The dimensions shown are for straight alignment and appropriate adjustments must be made for curvature. Except for dispensation which allows station platforms on curves with a radius greater than 360 m to be placed at standard dimensions (as shown), the amount of platform set-back for curves with a radius less than 360 m shall be determined by Railtrack.
3 Bridge girders, dwarf signals and other lineside equipment up to a height of 915 mm ARL may be positioned in the space available for platforms.

4 The minimum dimension of a single face platform shall be 2500 mm for speeds up to 165 km/h and for speeds greater than 165 km/h the minimum distance shall be increased to 3000 mm. The minimum distance to the face of any column shall be 2000 mm.
5 Platform clearances are subject to the maintenance of HMRI stepping distances and specific requirements shall be calculated from the particular kinematic envelope with an allowance made for structural clearance. The minimum lateral dimension is 730 mm and is shown for guidance.

key

A abutments, piers, stanchions etc. (clear of platform)
B columns and other works on platforms

▓ areas for conductor rails and guard boards

▒ areas for guard and check rails only

▒ areas available for dwarf signals, bridge girders and other lineside equipment

Ⓘ unhatched areas so marked are for permanent way, signal fittings and fourth rail electrification

(4) **Standard structure gauge applicable at and below 1089 mm above rail level (ARL)**

The freight yard is the traditional transfer point for goods being moved using a combination of rail and road transport.

Typical functional buildings and installations are: goods sheds, the freight office building and perhaps a customs hall. The loading yard will usually have end or side platforms and ramps. In addition, loading gauges, sidings for bulk offloading (e.g. coal and oil) and transfer terminals may also have to be installed. And, with the increasing use of standard containers, additional plant such as portal cranes will also be needed.

The effective depths for goods sheds are 10–18m or even 16–24m, depending on the freight to be handled, and they are usually 3.50–5.00m high. They can consist of any number of bays between structural frames, at 5m centres, up to a maximum of 400m.

The width of the platform on the track side of the shed should be at least 3.50m and for the loading dock on the service road side of the shed it is 2.50m. The height in both cases should be 1.20m above the rail level or, alternatively, the road surface of the freight yard. Both platform and loading dock should be covered by a canopy.

The area required for goods sheds → ① – ⑦ depends on the type and size of the goods and also the quantity of goods to be held in the store. To be able to determine the surface area required, the specific area needed for the types of goods involved (i.e. containers, pallets and goods which are not palletised) has to be known. A rule of thumb for values to be used in the calculation of the area requirement is as follows: for small containers with an area of $2m^2$, allow approximately $6.9m^2/t$; for pallets, each needing $1.2–1.4m^2$, allow $5.6–6.5m^2/t$; and for goods not on pallets and occupying $0.13–0.2m^2$ each, allow $6.5–10.0m^2/t$. The exact storage area requirement should only be calculated when planning a particular project. This is done by carrying out a physical count of the quantity of goods to be stored. Peak periods of traffic movements during the week (for instance Saturdays or Mondays) should be taken into account because they can be 25–30% higher than the daily average. Surface area requirements for traffic movements, and also adequate space between the goods in the store, must be determined at the very outset. For small containers this can be 80–100% of the actual space for storage, for pallets 180–210% and for goods not on pallets 100–160% of the storage area.

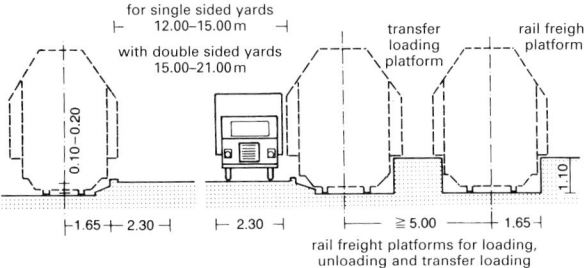

① End and side platforms

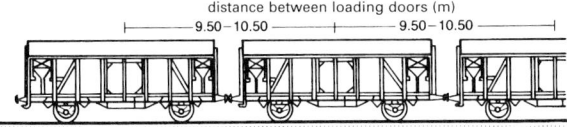

② Lay-out of yard for loading and unloading

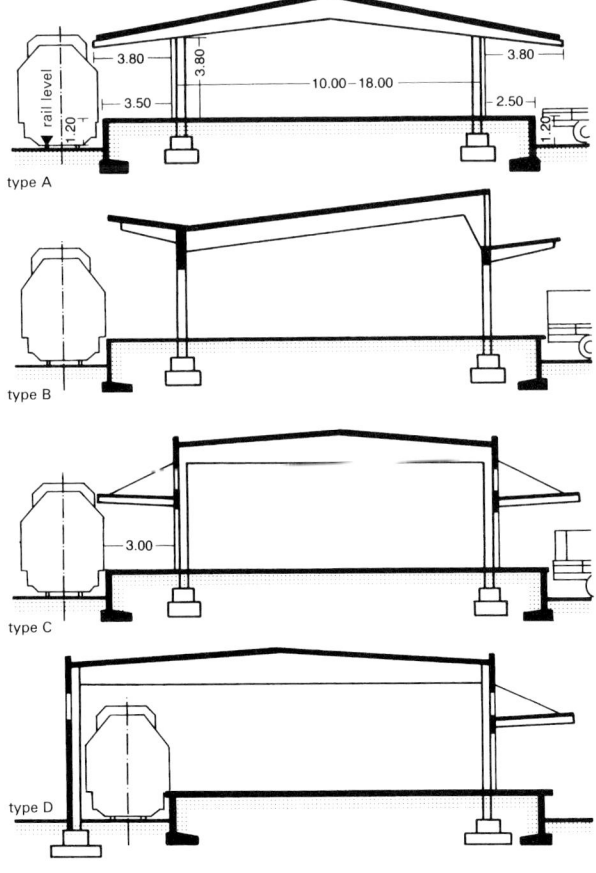

③ Common roofed goods truck

④ Examples of goods sheds: A, B, and C with siding outside, D with siding inside

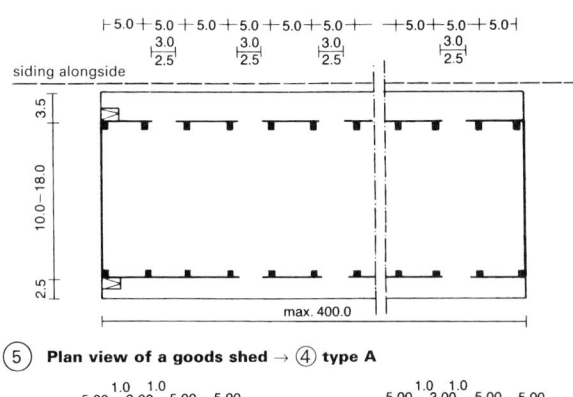

⑤ Plan view of a goods shed → ④ type A

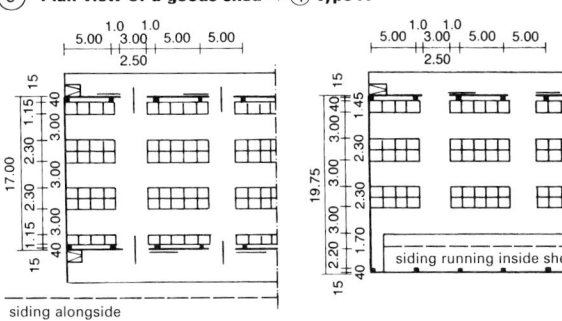

⑥ Plan view, cross-section → ④ type C

⑦ Plan view, cross-section → ④ type D

The layout of the rooms for push button signal controls should follow the schematic drawings set out below → ⑬ – ⑰. The control rooms do not have to have windows but all rooms should have a clear room height of ≥2.80 m, with the exception of those for the battery and electrical power. The clear widths for the doors should be ≥1.00 m.

The signal control manager's room should be near to the relay and telecommunications rooms and a full view out over the track layout must be ensured. The bottom edge of the lintel or window soffit should be 1.60–1.80 m above floor level, with the top of the window sill at a height of 0.40–0.50 m above the floor.

The relay room should have a minimum width calculated using the following formula: 0.23 m wall clearance + 0.66 m per rack + 1.25 m gangway.

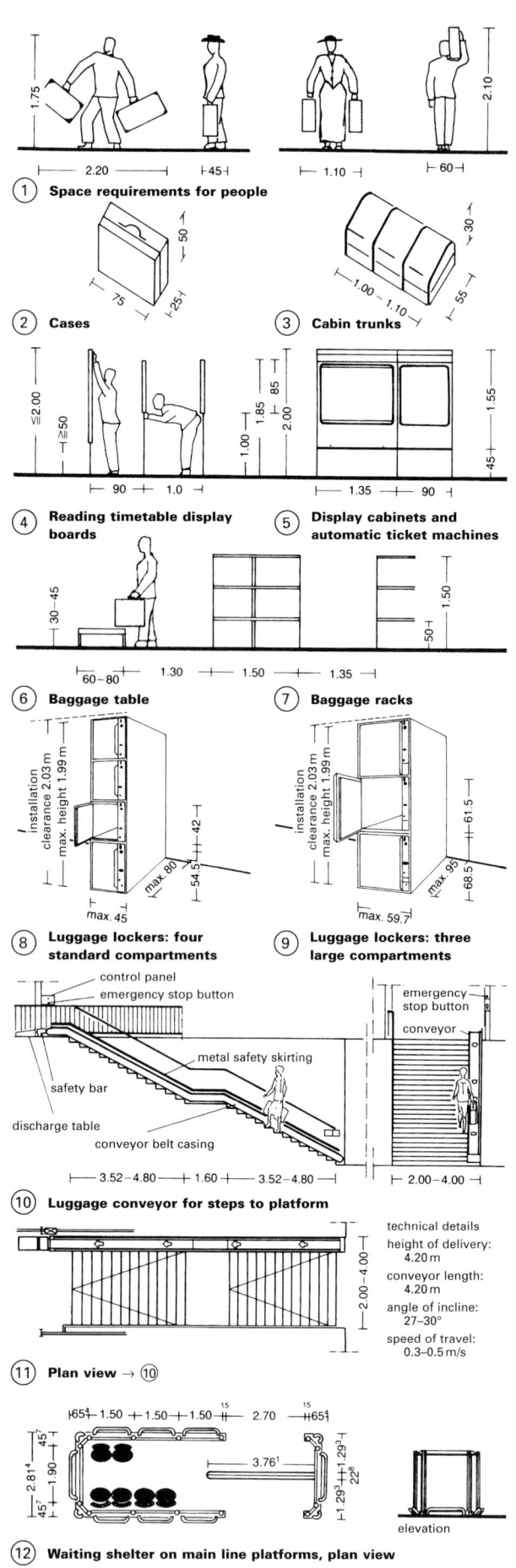

① Space requirements for people

② Cases

③ Cabin trunks

④ Reading timetable display boards

⑤ Display cabinets and automatic ticket machines

⑥ Baggage table

⑦ Baggage racks

⑧ Luggage lockers: four standard compartments

⑨ Luggage lockers: three large compartments

⑩ Luggage conveyor for steps to platform

⑪ Plan view → ⑩

technical details
height of delivery: 4.20 m
conveyor length: 4.20 m
angle of incline: 27–30°
speed of travel: 0.3–0.5 m/s

⑫ Waiting shelter on main line platforms, plan view

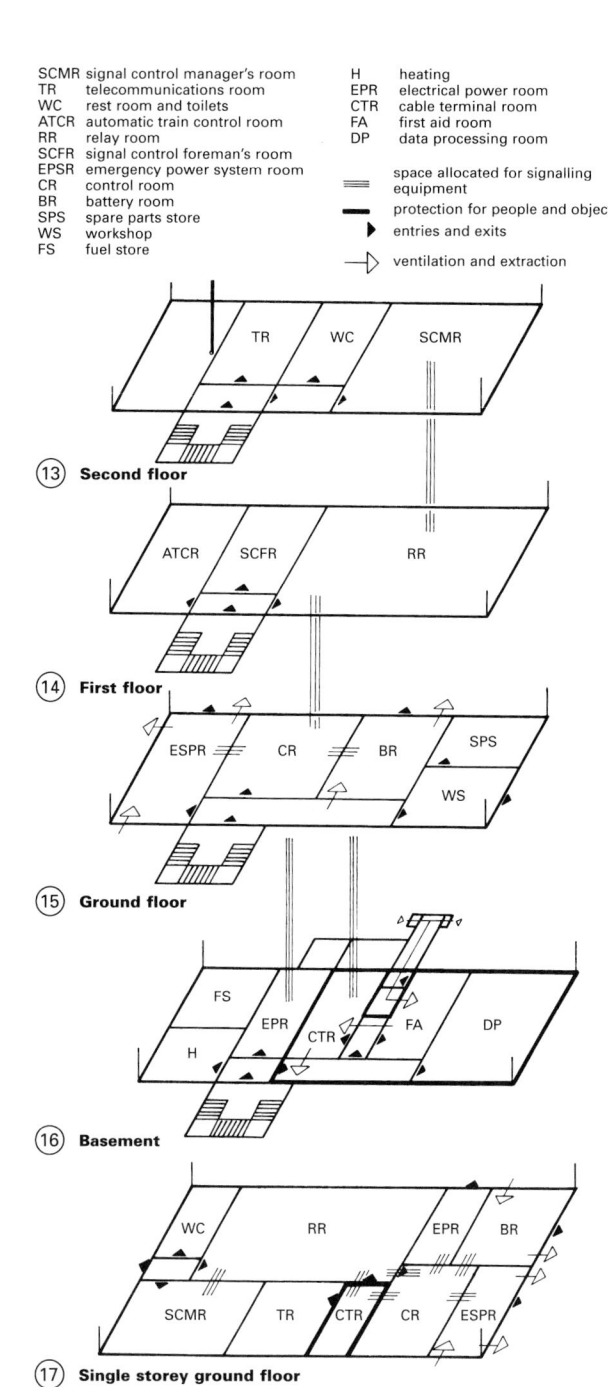

SCMR	signal control manager's room
TR	telecommunications room
WC	rest room and toilets
ATCR	automatic train control room
RR	relay room
SCFR	signal control foreman's room
EPSR	emergency power system room
CR	control room
BR	battery room
SPS	spare parts store
WS	workshop
FS	fuel store

H	heating
EPR	electrical power room
CTR	cable terminal room
FA	first aid room
DP	data processing room

space allocated for signalling equipment

protection for people and objects

entries and exits

ventilation and extraction

⑬ Second floor

⑭ First floor

⑮ Ground floor

⑯ Basement

⑰ Single storey ground floor

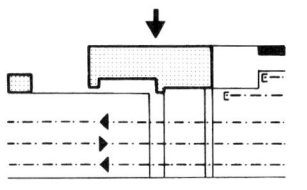

① **Station concourse on one side, at track level; passengers and luggage must cross the tracks (Only for small branch-line installations; not permitted in Britain)**

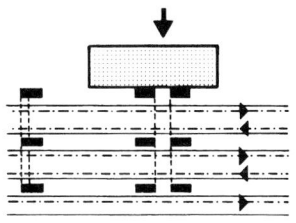

② **As ① but with tunnel for passengers, staircase access; luggage transported across the tracks (Only for medium-size installations)**

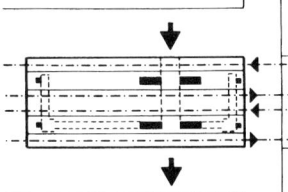

③ **Concourse on one side, below track level; tunnel for passengers and luggage; staircase and lift access to platforms (Typical, cost-effective solution)**

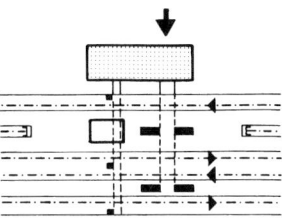

④ **Station concourse on one side, below track height; waiting room between the tracks (Suitable for interchange stations)**

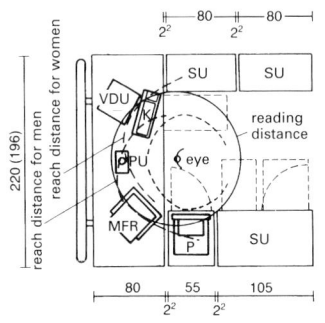

⑤ **Concourse in the middle, underneath the tracks: short walking distances and good natural lighting for the waiting room**

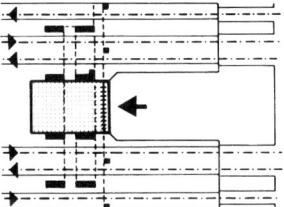

⑥ **Concourse in the middle, underneath the tracks: spacious access via forecourt and short walking distances**

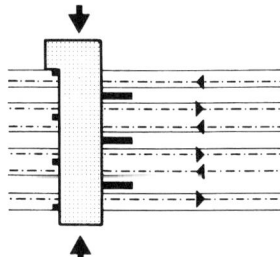

⑦ **Concourse over the tracks: acts as a bridge for passengers and baggage**

⑧ **Concourse at end of track, where possible at track height (Only suitable for terminal stations)**

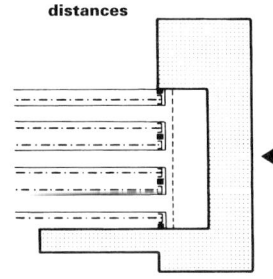

⑨ **Plan view: workstation layout for open counters → ⑩ – ⑪**

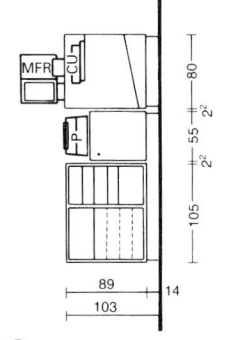

⑩ **Side view: side unit and printer → ⑨ – ⑪**

Further information: Railtrack PLC

Railway lines frequently pass through small and medium-size towns at street level, in which case the station buildings are on the same level as the tracks. At some small stations in continental Europe (e.g. Rüdesheim), access to the platforms for passengers and luggage → ① is achieved by crossing the tracks. Pedestrian tunnels are generally used for medium-size installations, such as Bonn → ②. In large terminals there are gently inclined tunnels for both pedestrians and luggage.

An improvement in layout can be achieved by raising the level of the track installation, as at Cologne and Hanover, or by lowering the level as in Darmstadt, Copenhagen and London → ③ – ⑦. This problem of access to the platforms does not arise in terminal stations → ⑧.

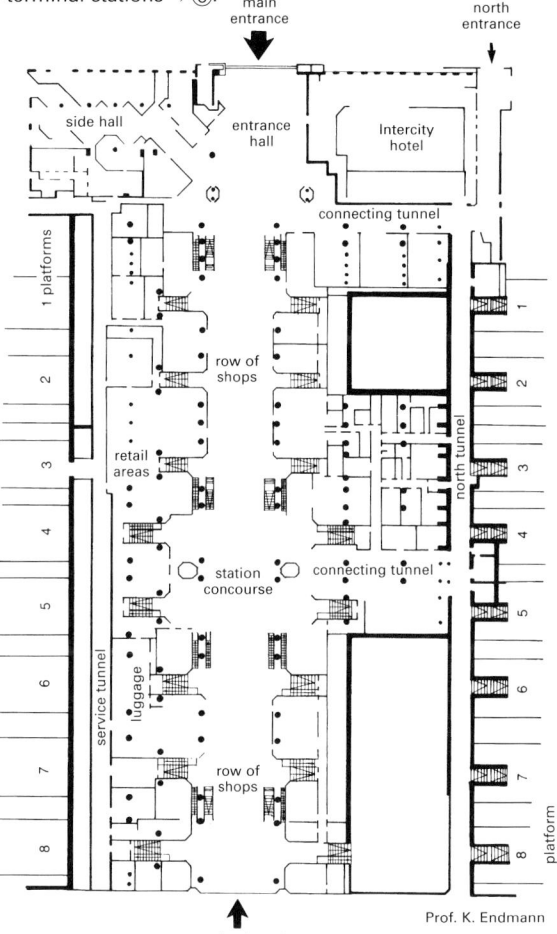

⑫ **Pedestrian arcade, Düsseldorf Main Station**

Prof. K. Endmann

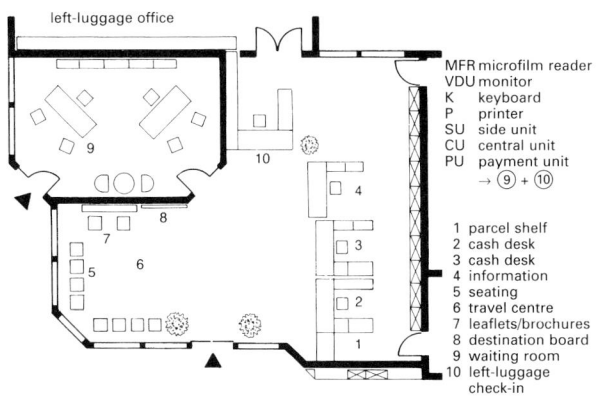

MFR microfilm reader
VDU monitor
K keyboard
P printer
SU side unit
CU central unit
PU payment unit → ⑨ + ⑩

1 parcel shelf
2 cash desk
3 cash desk
4 information
5 seating
6 travel centre
7 leaflets/brochures
8 destination board
9 waiting room
10 left-luggage check-in

⑪ **Plan view of a travel centre**

429

BUS STATIONS

Special provision has to be made for the widening of curves to match the turning circles of buses → ② – ⑮. Bus stops require shelters and special layouts (see also figures ① – ⑧ on the next page).

Ramps should be provided at the front to allow easy access up to a 30–40 cm high step → ⑪ – ⑫.

Short-stay car-parking space should be incorporated for passengers on the edge of towns (i.e. park and ride).

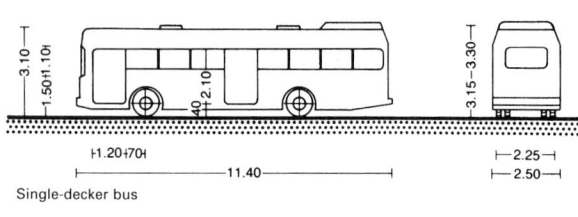

Single-decker bus

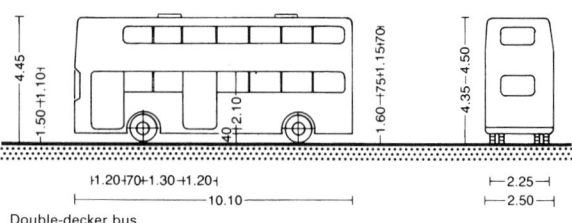

Double-decker bus

Articulated bus, common in Europe

① Bus dimensions

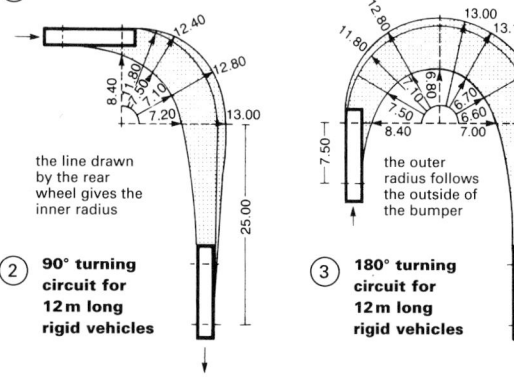

the line drawn by the rear wheel gives the inner radius

② 90° turning circuit for 12 m long rigid vehicles

the outer radius follows the outside of the bumper

③ 180° turning circuit for 12 m long rigid vehicles

the line drawn by the rear wheel of the trailer gives the inner radius

④ 180° turning circuit for 17 m long articulated vehicles

strengthened road surface

R = 7.0

R = 22.50

R = 22.50

unstrengthened surface

⑤ Turning circuit

	I	L	L'
bus	12.00	40.50	47.62 (49.05)
two buses	25.00	53.50	60.62 (62.05)
articulated bus	18.00	46.50	53.62 (55.05)

for 3 m wide bus stop bays
*) 25 m for bus stop bays for articulated buses

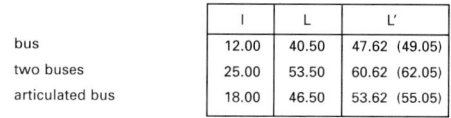

cycle racks
waiting room/shelter

⑧ Bus stop

platform shape	without passing lane			with passing lane			relation to line of arrival	parallel	at 45°	at 90°
	Aa	Ab	Ac	Ba	Bb	Bc				
layout of arrival line	parallel	at 45°	at 90°	parallel	at 45°	at 90°	length of parking space (m)	32	12 24	12 24
platform length (m)	24	24	24	36–60	36–60	36–69	parking options	1 artic. bus or 2 buses	1 bus / 1 artic. bus or 2 buses	1 bus / 1 artic. bus or 2 buses
platform width (m)	3	3	3	3.5–4	3.5–4	3.5–4				
number of loading points a) for buses	2	2	2	2–3	2–3	2–3	width of parking space (m)	3.5	3.5 3.5	3.5 3.5
b) artic. buses	1	1	1	1–2	1–2	1–2	width of arrival lane (m)	4.0	8.0 8.0	14 14
area of platform, roadway and arrival spur in m² a) for buses	138	176	189	293	296	313	parking area incl. roadway area in m² a) per bus	88	135 89	140 91
b) artic. buses	276	340	378	439	444	470	b) artic. bus	176	178	182

⑨ Space requirement for platforms

⑩ Space for parking spaces

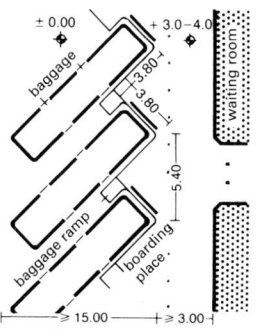

⑪ Standard interlocking layout

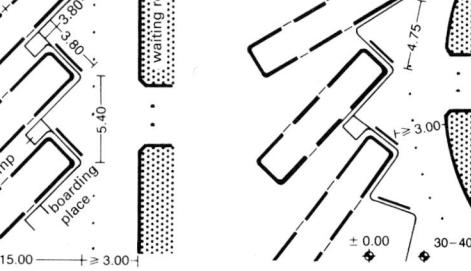

⑫ Radial layout providing more room at the front

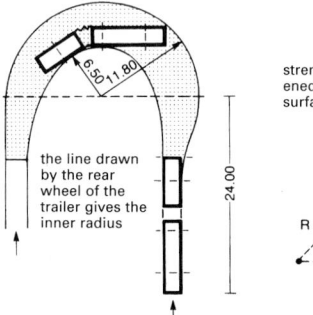

⑥ Small turn-around station

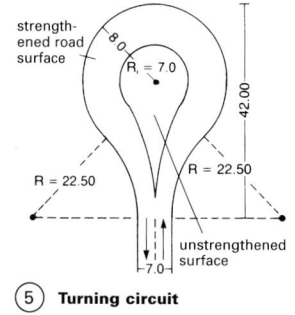

terminal building

platform

⑦ Platform on the outside of the turning loop

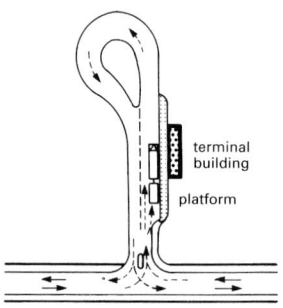

terminal building

pedestrians

⑬ Platform inside the turning loop

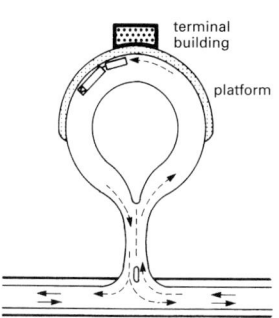

access

⑭ Semi-circular platform outside loop; no pedestrian crossing necessary

access

⑮ Semi-circular platform inside loop; accessible only by crossing the road

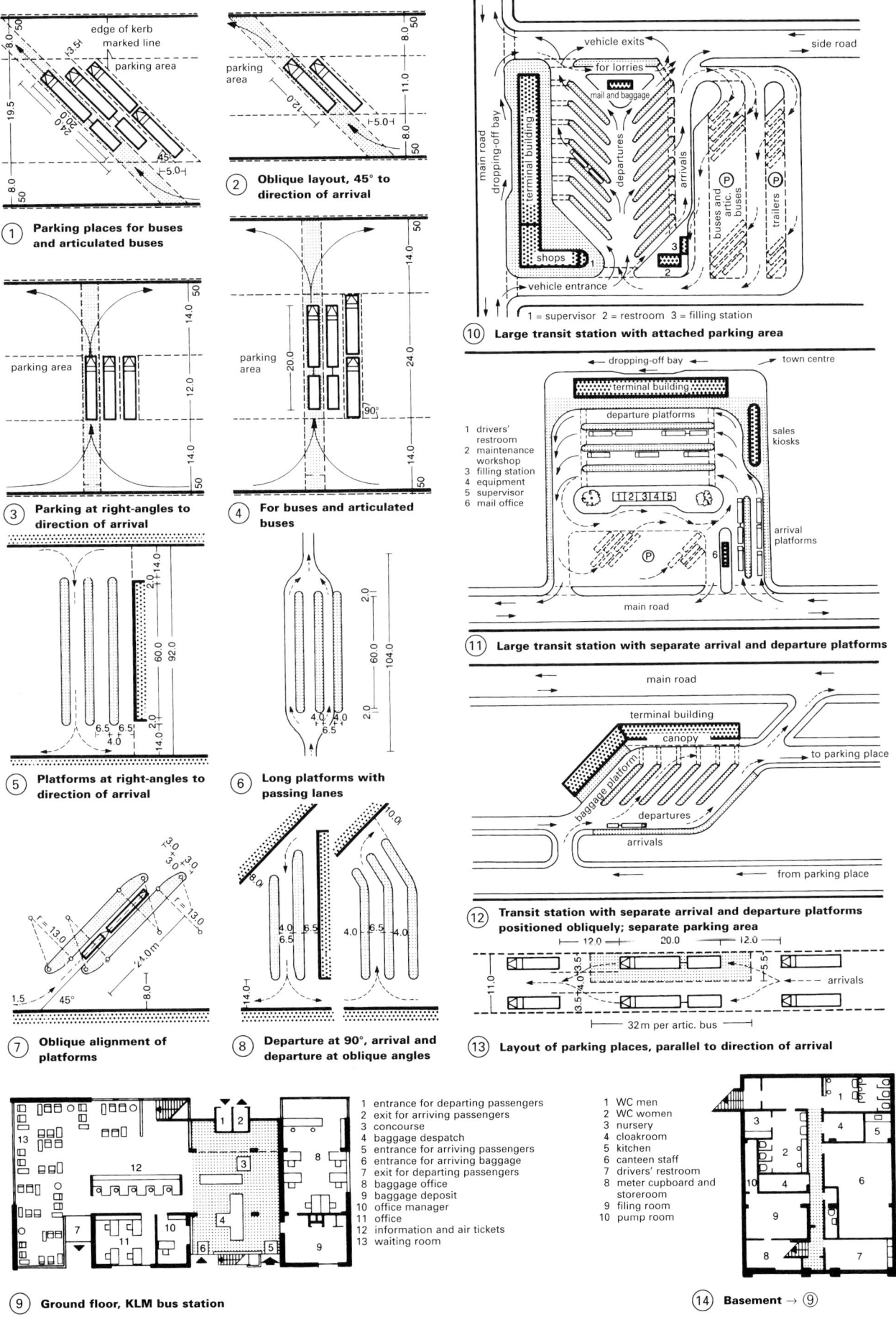

(1) **Parking places for buses and articulated buses**

(2) **Oblique layout, 45° to direction of arrival**

(3) **Parking at right-angles to direction of arrival**

(4) **For buses and articulated buses**

(5) **Platforms at right-angles to direction of arrival**

(6) **Long platforms with passing lanes**

(7) **Oblique alignment of platforms**

(8) **Departure at 90°, arrival and departure at oblique angles**

(10) **Large transit station with attached parking area**

1 = supervisor   2 = restroom   3 = filling station

(11) **Large transit station with separate arrival and departure platforms**

1 drivers' restroom
2 maintenance workshop
3 filling station
4 equipment
5 supervisor
6 mail office

(12) **Transit station with separate arrival and departure platforms positioned obliquely; separate parking area**

(13) **Layout of parking places, parallel to direction of arrival**

32 m per artic. bus

(9) **Ground floor, KLM bus station**

1 entrance for departing passengers
2 exit for arriving passengers
3 concourse
4 baggage despatch
5 entrance for arriving passengers
6 entrance for arriving baggage
7 exit for departing passengers
8 baggage office
9 baggage deposit
10 office manager
11 office
12 information and air tickets
13 waiting room

(14) **Basement → (9)**

1 WC men
2 WC women
3 nursery
4 cloakroom
5 kitchen
6 canteen staff
7 drivers' restroom
8 meter cupboard and storeroom
9 filing room
10 pump room

431

VEHICLE DIMENSIONS

The illustrations show dimensions, turning radii and weights of typical vehicles with particular reference to space requirements and regulations for garages, parking places, entrances and passages.

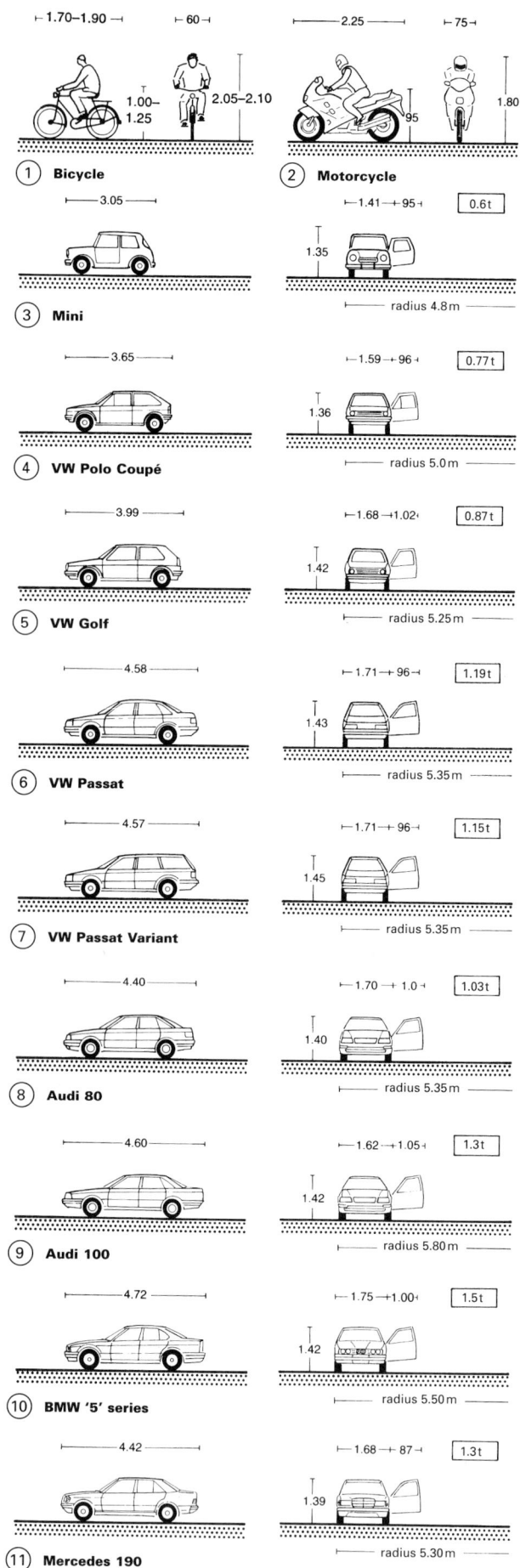

(1) Bicycle

(2) Motorcycle

(3) Mini

(4) VW Polo Coupé

(5) VW Golf

(6) VW Passat

(7) VW Passat Variant

(8) Audi 80

(9) Audi 100

(10) BMW '5' series

(11) Mercedes 190

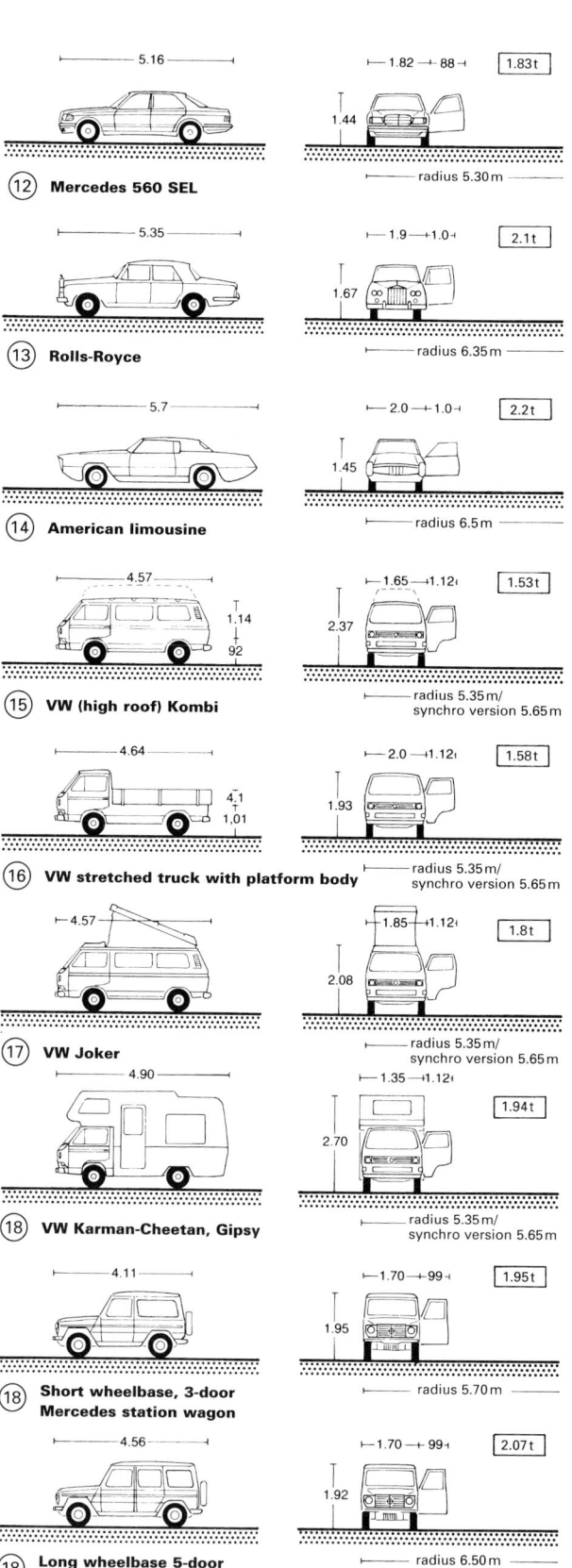

(12) Mercedes 560 SEL

(13) Rolls-Royce

(14) American limousine

(15) VW (high roof) Kombi

(16) VW stretched truck with platform body

(17) VW Joker

(18) VW Karman-Cheetan, Gipsy

(18) Short wheelbase, 3-door Mercedes station wagon

(18) Long wheelbase 5-door Mercedes station wagon

VEHICLE DIMENSIONS

Dimensions and Turning Circles of Typical Trucks and Buses

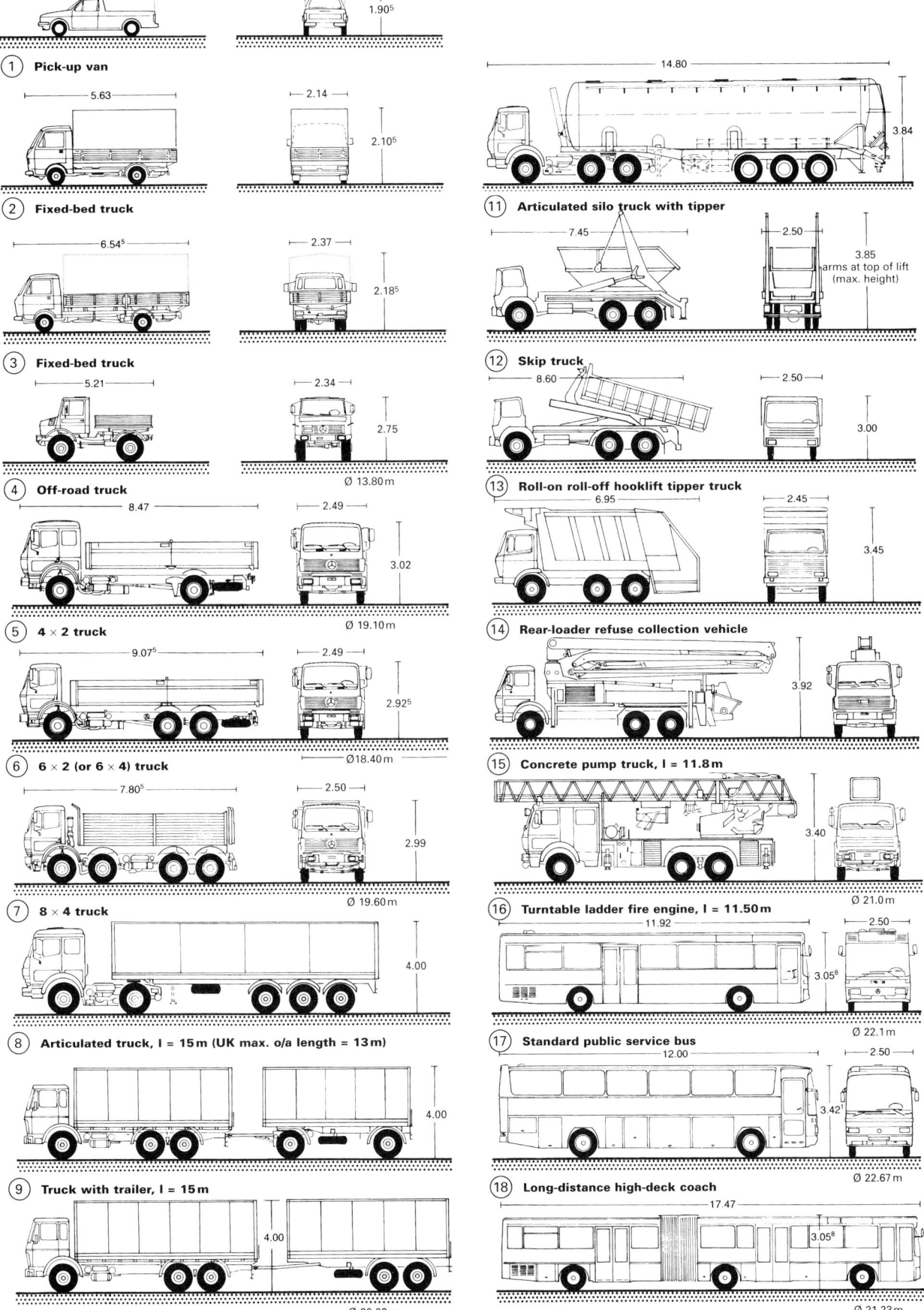

├─ 4.37 ─┤   ├─ 1.64 ─┤
                            1.90⁵

(1) **Pick-up van**

├─ 5.63 ─┤   ├─ 2.14 ─┤
                            2.10⁵

(2) **Fixed-bed truck**

├─ 6.54⁵ ─┤   ├─ 2.37 ─┤
                             2.18⁵

(3) **Fixed-bed truck**

├─ 5.21 ─┤   ├─ 2.34 ─┤
                            2.75

(4) **Off-road truck**
Ø 13.80 m

├─ 8.47 ─┤   ├─ 2.49 ─┤
                            3.02

(5) **4 × 2 truck**
Ø 19.10 m

├─ 9.07⁵ ─┤   ├─ 2.49 ─┤
                             2.92⁵

(6) **6 × 2 (or 6 × 4) truck**
Ø18.40 m

├─ 7.80⁵ ─┤   ├─ 2.50 ─┤
                             2.99

(7) **8 × 4 truck**
Ø 19.60 m

                            4.00

(8) **Articulated truck, l = 15 m (UK max. o/a length = 13 m)**

                            4.00

(9) **Truck with trailer, l = 15 m**

                            4.00

(10) **Truck with tandem trailer, l = 18 m, w = 2.50 m**
Ø 20.00 m

├──────── 14.80 ────────┤
                              3.84

(11) **Articulated silo truck with tipper**

├─ 7.45 ─┤   ├─ 2.50 ─┤
                            3.85
                            arms at top of lift
                            (max. height)

(12) **Skip truck**

├─ 8.60 ─┤   ├─ 2.50 ─┤
                            3.00

(13) **Roll-on roll-off hooklift tipper truck**

├─ 6.95 ─┤   ├─ 2.45 ─┤
                            3.45

(14) **Rear-loader refuse collection vehicle**

                            3.92

(15) **Concrete pump truck, l = 11.8 m**

                            3.40

(16) **Turntable ladder fire engine, l = 11.50 m**
Ø 21.0 m

├─ 11.92 ─┤   ├─ 2.50 ─┤
                             3.05⁸

(17) **Standard public service bus**
Ø 22.1 m

├─ 12.00 ─┤   ├─ 2.50 ─┤
                             3.42¹

(18) **Long-distance high-deck coach**
Ø 22.67 m

├──── 17.47 ────┤   3.05⁸

(19) **Standard articulated bus, w = 2.50 m**
Ø 21.23 m

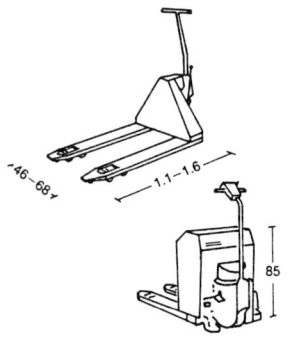

S.W.L. (t)	2.5	3.5	7	13
w (m)	1.0	1.0	1.2	1.5
l (m)	2.4	2.8	3.4	3.6

(1) **Pallet truck** (2) **Forklift truck**

Gaps between dock ramps and vehicles have to be safely bridged to allow loading and unloading operations to be carried out easily and smoothly.

Loading bridges should safely link a dock with any type of vehicle or railway truck. The loading platform of the vehicle can be either higher or lower than the ramp → ③ – ④ and aluminium wedge-shaped units are ideal for raising low vehicles into line with the height of the loading dock → ⑥. These can be mounted on rollers and easily moved to various work locations. Aluminium hinged loading platforms can be set at various levels → ⑨.

Portable loading bridges can be rolled and carried, and can also be used for loading on to railway trucks → ④. Loading platforms with projecting lips are also available with automatic hydraulic action → ⑩.

Hydraulic scissor lifts are used to adjust for differing levels between the yard and the vehicle platform → ⑧, between the vehicle and the dock ramp → ⑦ or between two dock ramps. Mobile lift platforms are also available.

Continuous height adjustment to any particular level during loading or unloading of the truck is best achieved using forklift trucks, which are available with electric, diesel, petrol and LPG engines → ②. The height of mobile drive-on ramps for loading containers, lorries and railway trucks can be automatically adjusted according to the suspension of the truck during loading and unloading.

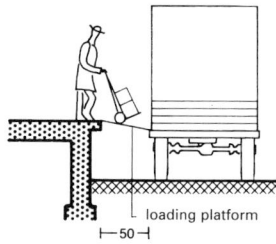

(3) **Portable loading platform**

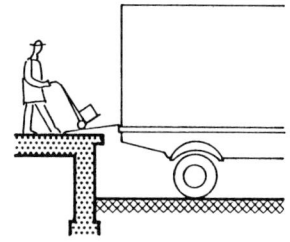

(4) **Flexible loading using a steel plate**

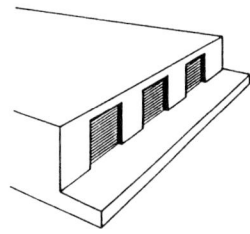

(11) **Loading bay** → ③ – ⑥

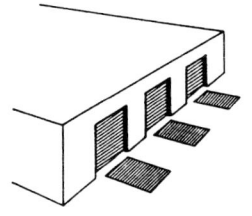

(12) **Ground level bay, loading with lifting tables or ramps** → ⑦

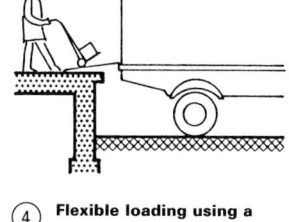

(5) **Close to the rear axle, using a jacking system**

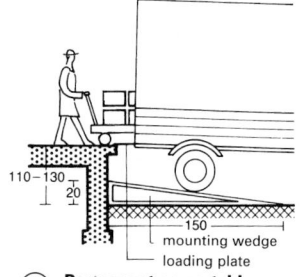

(6) **Permanent or portable dock leveller**

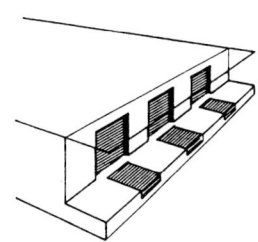

(13) **Loading bay with canopy and hydraulic dock loading ramps** → ⑩

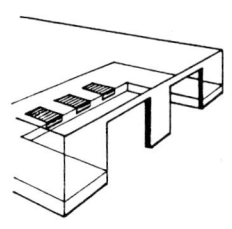

(14) **Indoor loading with hydraulic dock loading ramps** → ⑦

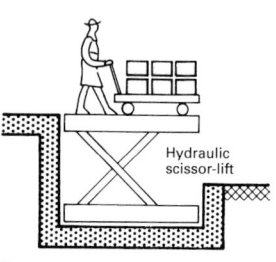

(7) **Lift platform from yard level to dock or vice-versa**

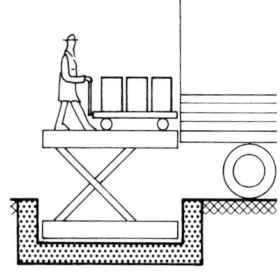

(8) **Dock to truck**

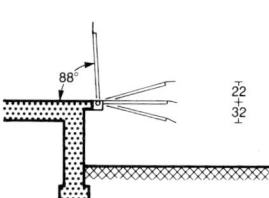

length (mm)	width (mm)	max. load (kg)
1500	1500	3000
1750	1500	3000
1750	1750	5000

(9) **Hinged loading platform, adjustable sideways**

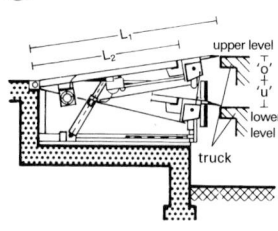

o	u	l₁	l₂	w	max load kp
290	300	2300	2000	1500	3000
360	300	2800	2500	1750	4000
430	300	3300	3000	2000	5000

(10) **Loading bridge**

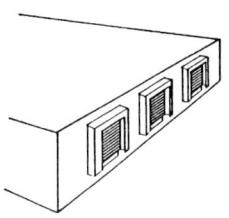

(15) **Dock loading ramps with weather-protection systems**

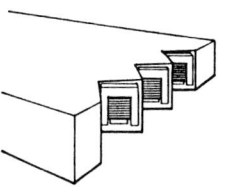

(16) **Saw-tooth bay ramps in a restricted area**

LOADING BAYS

An example of the ideal depth of yard for articulated trucks with overall lengths of 18 m is shown in → ①. Calculations based on experience show that under these conditions a length of 35 m is required for access. Even the longest articulated truck can then be driven swiftly in and out. This is an important factor in controlling the turn-round of the vehicles on scheduled runs. If the above-mentioned conditions cannot be met, the saw-toothed bay layout, with an angle of 10°–15° offers a practical solution.
→ ③, ⑤ + ⑥.

The largest turning radius for an articulated truck is about 12.00 m.

The safe distance to be allowed between two adjacent trucks is a minimum of:

- 1.50 m with the use of a loading dock;
- 3.00 m with the use of loading doors.

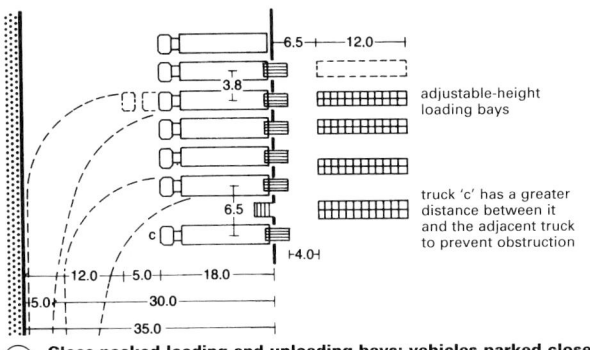

① Close-packed loading and unloading bays; vehicles parked close together must ease forward a little before they can drive off

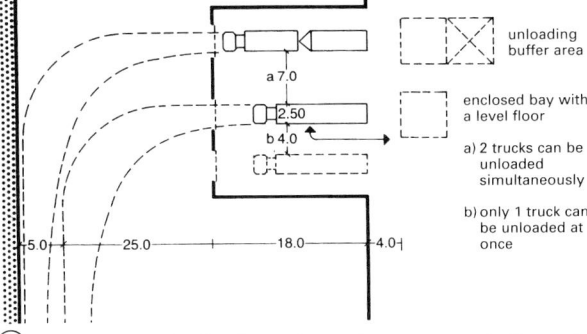

② Loading and unloading bays take up the most space in the yard

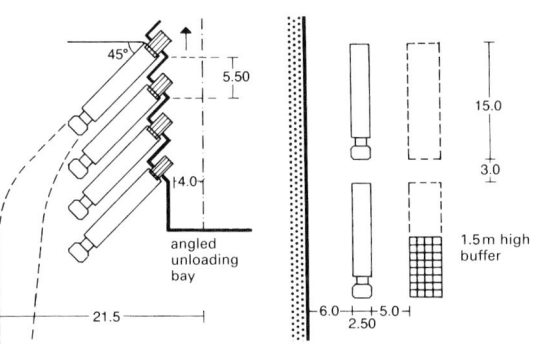

③ Loading and unloading bays ④ Loading and unloading bay

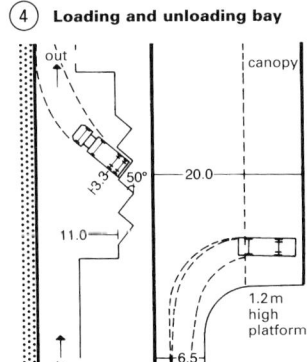
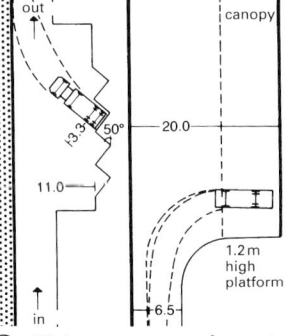

⑤ Loading and unloading bay with raised platform and side unloading

⑥ Minimum space requirement for loading bays

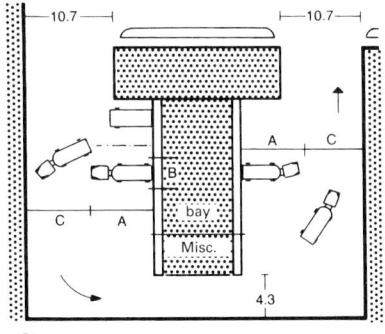

⑧ Normal turning circle dimensions for a 15 m long articulated truck

a: 4.7 m
b: 5.7 m
c: 7.3 m
d: 8.3 m
e: 8.8 m
f: 7.8 m
g: 27.0 m

⑨ Normal turning circle dimensions for a truck with a rigid chassis and long wheelbase

a: 2.8 m
b: 3.9 m
c: 4.7 m
d: 5.5 m
e: 5.1 m
f: 4.6 m
g: 26.8 m

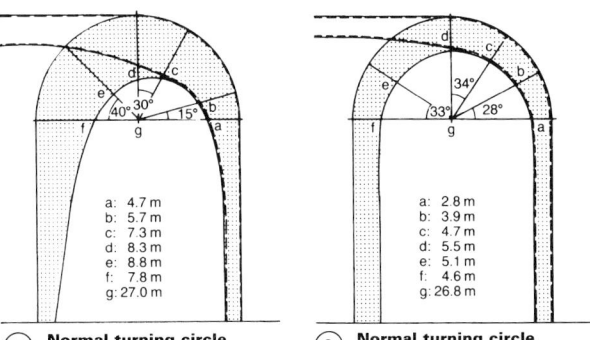
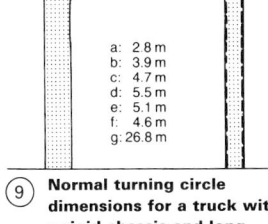

⑩ Loading and unloading in a courtyard

A articulated truck	B unloading position	C manoeuvring area
10.7	3.0	14.0
	3.7	13.1
	4.3	11.9
12.2	3.0	14.6
	3.7	13.4
	4.3	12.8
13.7	3.0	17.4
	3.7	14.9
	4.3	14.6

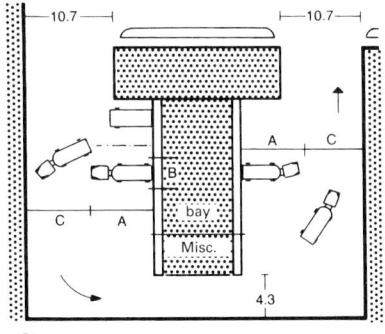

⑪ Traffic driving clockwise on the right-hand side of the road

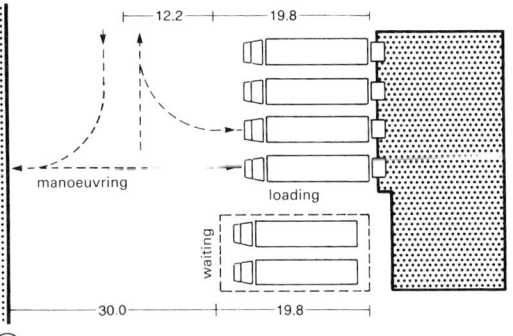

⑦ Section through a loading bay with an adjustable loading platform

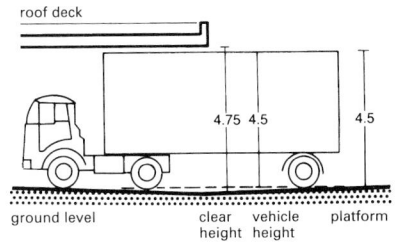

⑫ Dimensions for sheltered loading bays

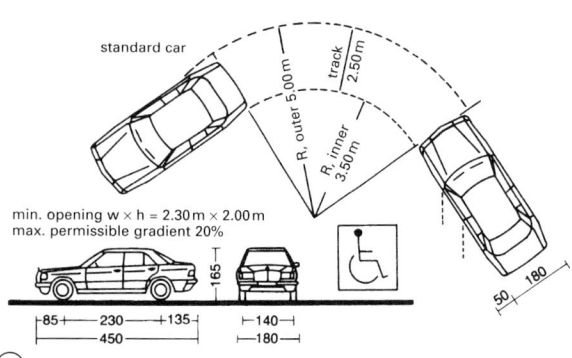

min. opening w × h = 2.30 m × 2.00 m
max. permissible gradient 20%

(1) **Standard car**

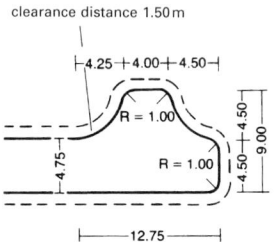

(2) **Car turning circle**

(3) **Car turning circle radius for an entrance drive ≥ 5–6.50 m**

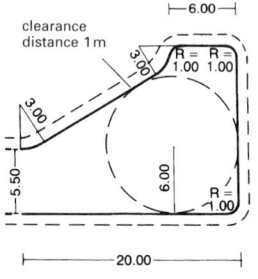

(4) **Hammerhead turning place for cars**

(5) **Hammerhead turning place for vehicles up to 8 m (refuse collection vehicles, fire tenders, trucks up to 6 t)**

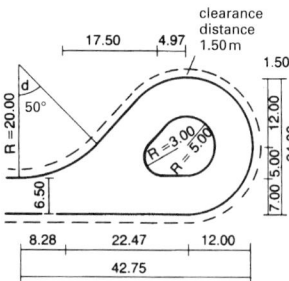

(6) **Turning area for trucks over 10 m long and 24 t 6 × 4 refuse collection vehicles**

(7) **As (6)**

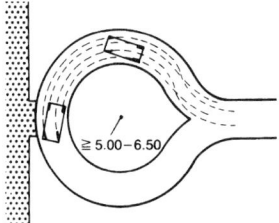

(8) **Turning loop for articulated trucks and buses**

(9) **Turning circle for 4 × 2 refuse collection vehicles and 6 m long delivery vans**

TURNING AND PARKING

The type, size and shape of a turning place in a road depends on the road use in that particular area. It also has to be suitable for the needs of the road users and must meet town planning requirements. It is difficult to make recommendations for a correct choice of road turning place which is valid in all cases.

The interests of the fire and refuse collection services have to be taken into account in deciding on road turning places. Many authorities refuse to service areas with dead-end roads or lanes, where refuse collection lorries can turn only by manoeuvring backwards and forwards or must reverse quite a long distance.

Road turning places can be designed as hammerheads → (4)–(5), turning circles or loops → (6)–(9). The hammerhead type turning place calls for backwards and forwards manoeuvring.

Turning circles and loops are preferable, as motor vehicles can drive straight round them without having to stop.

To facilitate steering, road turning places should be arranged asymmetrically on the left, or on the right in the case of those countries like the UK which drive on the left-hand side of the road → (6)–(9). Adequate clear areas should be left along the outside edges of the turning areas to safeguard fixed obstructions from the overhang of turning vehicles. In the case of turning loops, the central area to be driven around can be planted → (8).

Hammerhead turning places are really only suitable for cars. They are not required for carriageways over 6 m wide, if garage forecourts or footpath crossings are available for turning purposes.

type of vehicle	length (m)	width (m)	height (m)	turning circle radius (m)
motorcycle	2.20	0.70	1.00[2]	1.00
car				
- standard	4.70	1.75	1.50	5.75
- small	3.60	1.60	1.50	5.00
- large	5.00	1.90	1.50	6.00
truck				
- standard	6.00	2.10	2.20[1]	6.10
- 7.5 t	7.00	2.50	2.40[1]	7.00
- 16 t	8.00	2.50	3.00[1]	8.00
- 22 t (+16 t trailer)	10.00	2.50	3.00[1]	9.30
refuse collection vehicle				
- standard 2-axle vehicle (4 × 2)	7.64	2.50	3.30[1]	7.80
- standard 3-axle vehicle (6 × 2 or 6 × 4)	1.45	2.50	3.30[1]	9.25
fire engine	6.80	2.50	2.80[1]	9.25
furniture van	9.50	2.50	2.80[1]	9.25
(with trailer)	(18.00)			
standard bus I	11.00	2.50[3]	2.95	10.25
standard bus II	11.40	2.50[3]	3.05	11.00
standard vehicle - bus	11.00	2.50[3]	2.95	11.20
standard vehicle - articulated bus	17.26	2.50[3]	4.00	10.50–11.25
standard articulated truck	18.00	2.50[4]	4.00	12.00[5]
tractor		2.50[4]	4.00	
trailer		2.50[4]	4.00	
max. values of the road regulations				
2-axle vehicle (4 × 2)	12.00	2.50[4]	4.00	12.00
vehicle with more than 2 axles	12.00	2.50[4]	4.00	12.00
tractor with semi-trailer	15.00	2.50[4]	4.00	12.00
articulated bus	18.00	2.50[4]	4.00	12.00
trucks with trailer	18.00	2.50[4]	4.00	12.00

notes:
[1] height of driver's cab; [2] total height with driver, about 2 m; [3] with wing mirrors, 2.95 m; [4] without wing mirrors; [5] turning circle radius adjusted up to max. as per regulations

(10) **Basic vehicle data**

type of road	type of district	standard vehicle	R (m)	notes
accessible lightly used residential road	residential	car	6	turning circle for car
				special regulations for refuse collection vehicles (e.g. link road connection via lanes with limited traffic access)
residential road	mainly residential	cars, 2-axle (4 × 2) refuse collection vehicles	8	turning circle for small buses + most refuse collection vehicles
				room to turn by manoeuvring back and forth for all vehicles permitted under the regulations
residential road	residential area, heavily interspersed with business premises	cars , refuse collection vehicles, trucks with 3 axles (6 × 2 and 6 × 4), standard bus, articulated bus	10	adequate turning circle for most permitted trucks and buses
			11	turning circle for newer buses
			12	turning circle for articulated buses
	mainly for business premises	truck articulated truck articulated bus	12	turning circle for the largest vehicles permitted by the road regulations

1 m wide clearance on the outside of the turning areas is provided to allow for the rear overhang of vehicles

(11) **Recommendations for turning circle radius, R**

TURNING AND PARKING

Parking spaces are usually outlined by 12–20 mm wide yellow or white painted lines. When parking is facing a wall, these lines are often painted at a height of up to 1 m for better visibility. Guide rails in the floor along the side have also proved popular for demarcation of parking limits, and can be about 50–60 cm long, 20 cm wide and 10 cm high. Where vehicles are parked in lines facing walls or at the edge of the parking deck in a multi-storey car-park, it is common practice to provide buffers, restraining bars or railings up to axle height to prevent cars from going over the edge. Where cars are parked face to face, transverse barriers about 10 cm high can be used to act as frontal stops. Overhang on vehicles must be taken into account → ⑬. For lining up in front of a wall, a stop rail or rubber buffer will be sufficient → ⑬.

Garage parking spaces for cars should have an overall length of more than 5 m and a width of 2.30 m, but parking spaces for the disabled should be more than 3.50 m wide.

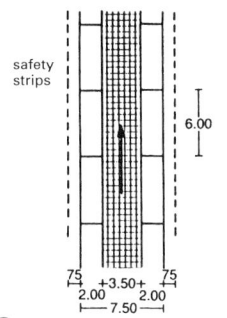

① **Parking parallel to the road**

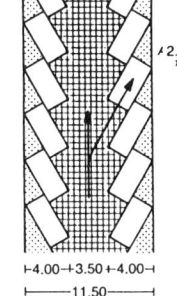

② **30° oblique spaces, easy entry and exit, but for use only with one-way traffic**

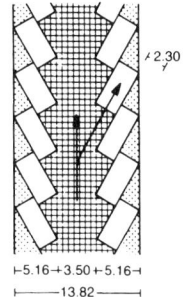

③ **45° oblique parking, one-way traffic only**

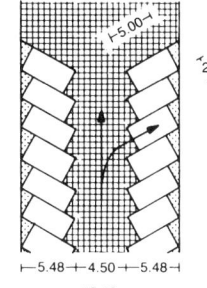

④ **60° oblique parking, one-way traffic only**

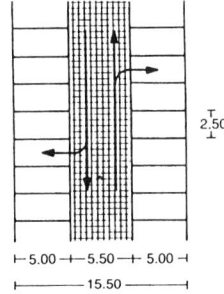

⑤ **90° entry/exit to parking spaces for two-way traffic Parking space 2.50 m wide**

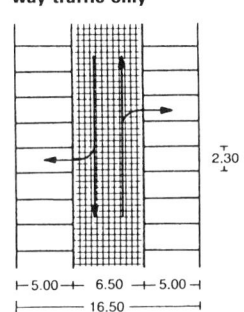

⑥ **90° entry/exit to parking spaces, for two-way traffic Parking space 2.30 m wide**

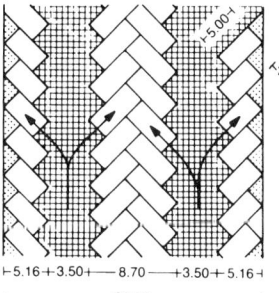

⑦ **45°-angled parking, one-way traffic only**

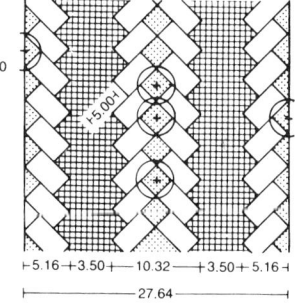

⑧ **Parking for one-way traffic (with spaces for plants)**

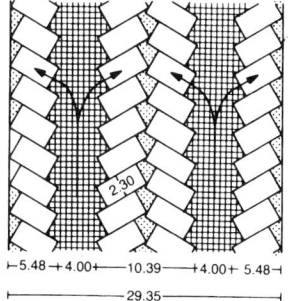

⑨ **60° angled parking, one-way traffic**

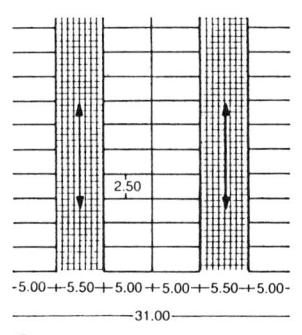

⑩ **90° parking, 5.5 m wide road Parking spaces 2.5 m wide**

parking space arrangement	area/space (inc. open doors)	possible no. of spaces/100 m² area	possible no. of spaces/100 m of road (one side only)
→ ① 0° - parallel to road. Entry and exit to parking bay difficult - suitable for narrow roads	2	4.4	17
→ ② 30° -angle to access road. Easy entry to parking bay and exit. Uses a large area.	26.3	3.8	21
→ ③ 45° -angle to access road. Good entry to parking bay and exit. Relatively small area/parking space. Normal type of layout	20.3	4.9	31
→ ④ 60° -angle to access road. Relatively good entry and exit to parking bay; small area/parking space. Arrangement often used	19.2	5.2	37
→ ⑤ Right-angles to road (parking spaces 2.50 m wide). Sharp turn needed for entry and exit	19.4	5.1	40
→ ⑥ Right-angles to road (parking spaces 2.30 m wide. Small area needed/parking space. Ideal for compact parking layouts, used frequently	19.2	5.2	37

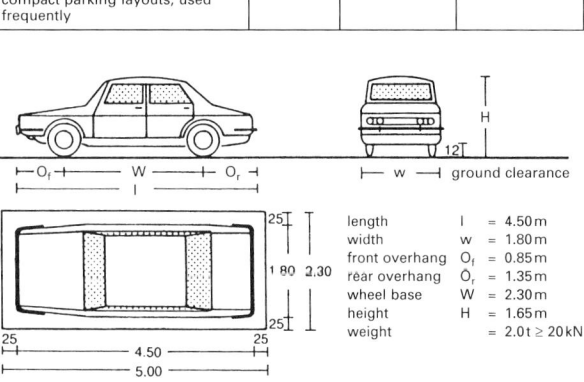

length   l = 4.50 m
width   w = 1.80 m
front overhang O_f = 0.85 m
rear overhang O_r = 1.35 m
wheel base   W = 2.30 m
height   H = 1.65 m
weight   = 2.0 t ≥ 20 kN

⑪ **Standard car**

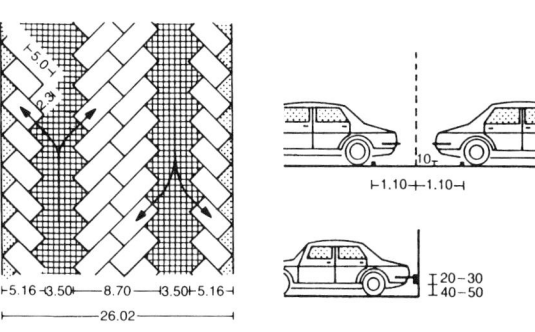

⑫ **Oblique parking layout**

⑬ **Stop rails and buffers**

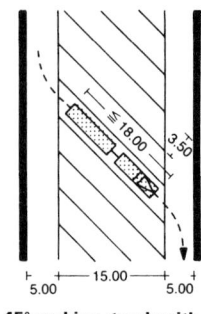

① **45° parking, truck with trailer**

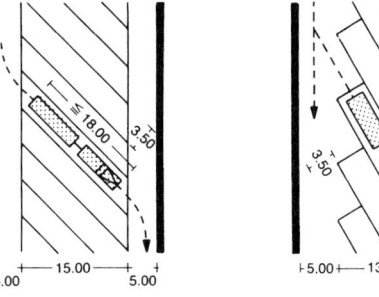

② **30° parking, truck with trailer**

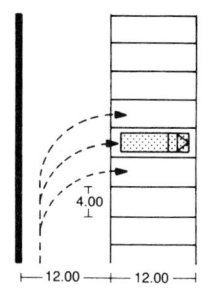

② **90° parking, a single truck**

Owing to the large variation in the size of trucks, it is not worth marking out permanent lanes or bays on the ground. The basic measurements for space and actual requirements for the manoeuvring and parking of trucks are taken from the vehicle dimensions whilst driving straight, cornering and entering into or driving out of the parking place. The line of the trailing inner rear wheels when cornering must be taken into account.

The turning circle for the largest vehicles permitted under the road traffic regulations is an outer turning circle radius of 12 m.

An outer turning circle radius of 10 m is nevertheless considered sufficient for the vast majority of trucks which come within the scope of the regulations (see 'Motor vehicles: turning').

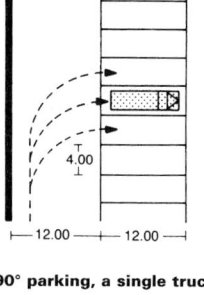

④ **90° parking, truck with trailer**

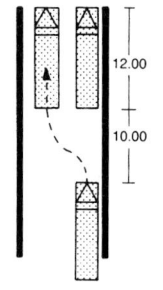

⑤ **Parking at less than 45°**

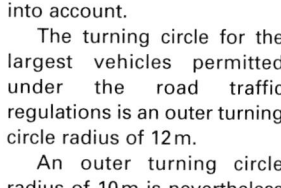

⑥ **Space loss, parking parallel to kerb**

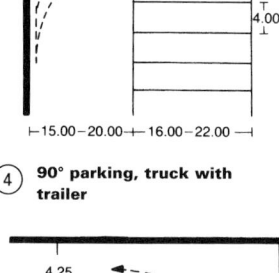

vehicle length	A
10.70 m	7.60
12.20 m	8.50
13.70 m	10.40

⑦ **Space needed at street corners**

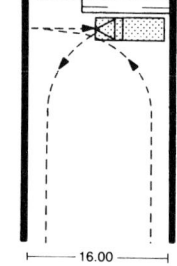

⑧ **Turning in restricted areas**

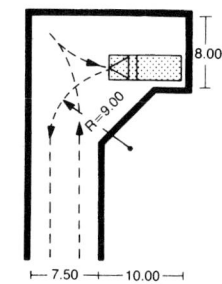

⑨ **Hammerhead turn in very tight space**

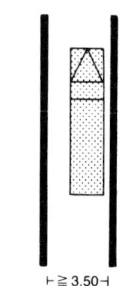

⑩ **Passage width**

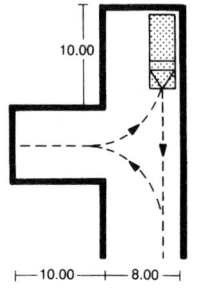

⑪ **Further turning options →** ⑫ – ⑭

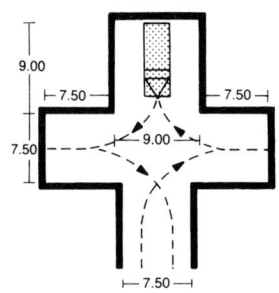

⑫

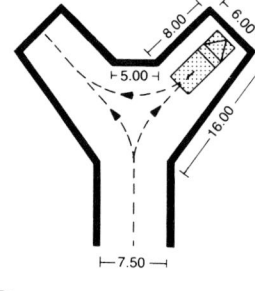

⑬

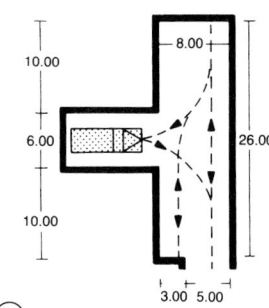

⑭

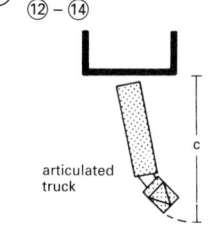

articulated truck

⑮ **Single parking**

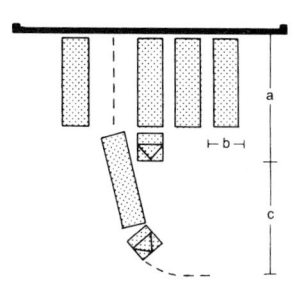

⑯ **Parking in a row**

area to be kept free for entry and exit of:		
vehicle length a	bay width b	area to be kept free c
22 t truck	3.00	14.00
10.00 m	3.65	13.10
	4.25	11.90
fixed bed truck	3.00	14.65
12.00 m	3.65	13.50
	4.25	12.80
	3.00	17.35
articulated truck	3.65	15.00
15 m	4.25	14.65

⑰ **Table for** ⑮ **and** ⑯

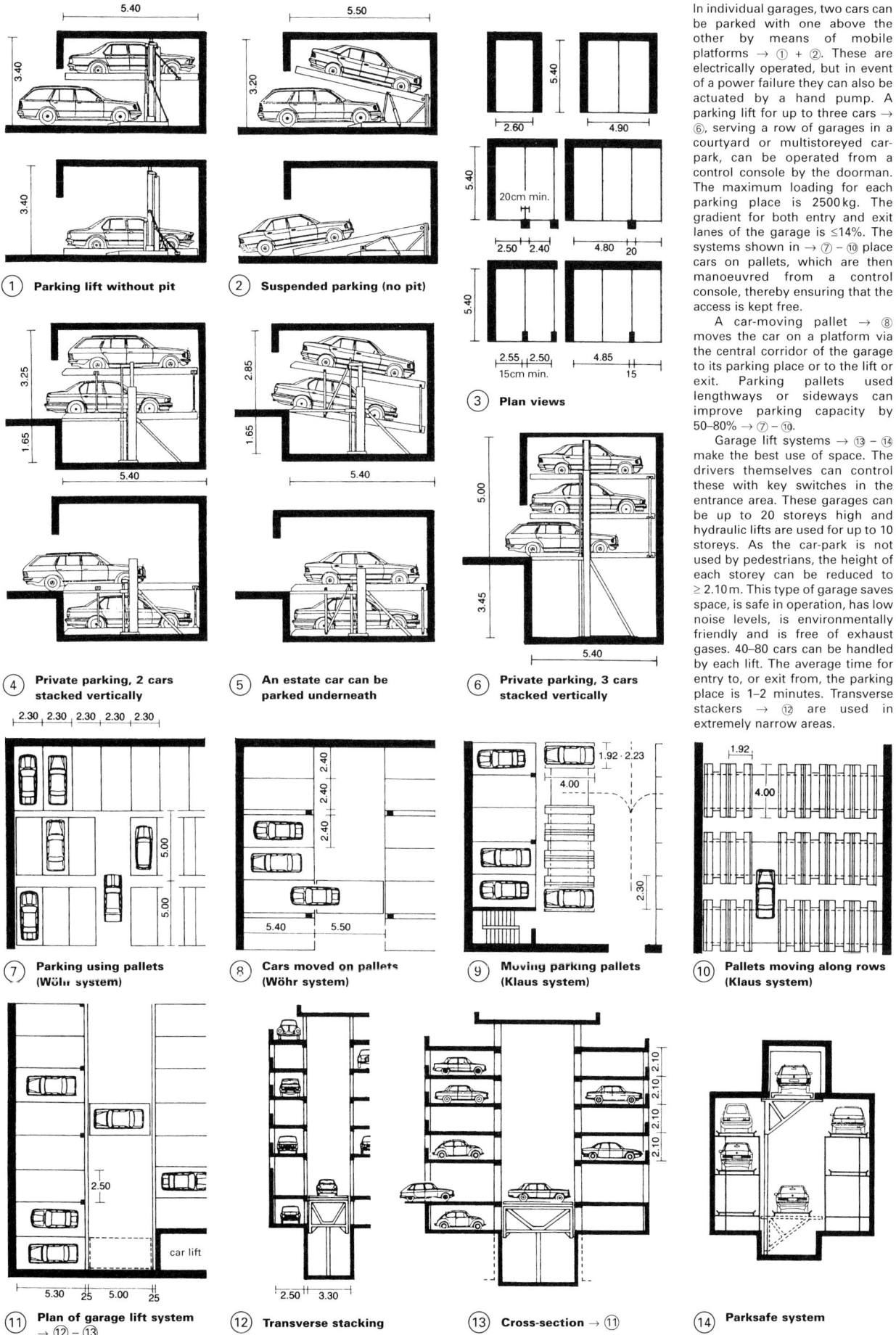

① **Parking lift without pit**

② **Suspended parking (no pit)**

③ **Plan views**

④ **Private parking, 2 cars stacked vertically**

⑤ **An estate car can be parked underneath**

⑥ **Private parking, 3 cars stacked vertically**

⑦ **Parking using pallets (Wöhr system)**

⑧ **Cars moved on pallets (Wöhr system)**

⑨ **Moving parking pallets (Klaus system)**

⑩ **Pallets moving along rows (Klaus system)**

⑪ **Plan of garage lift system → ⑫ – ⑬**

⑫ **Transverse stacking**

⑬ **Cross-section → ⑪**

⑭ **Parksafe system**

In individual garages, two cars can be parked with one above the other by means of mobile platforms → ① + ②. These are electrically operated, but in event of a power failure they can also be actuated by a hand pump. A parking lift for up to three cars → ⑥, serving a row of garages in a courtyard or multistoreyed car-park, can be operated from a control console by the doorman. The maximum loading for each parking place is 2500 kg. The gradient for both entry and exit lanes of the garage is ≤14%. The systems shown in → ⑦ – ⑩ place cars on pallets, which are then manoeuvred from a control console, thereby ensuring that the access is kept free.

A car-moving pallet → ⑧ moves the car on a platform via the central corridor of the garage to its parking place or to the lift or exit. Parking pallets used lengthways or sideways can improve parking capacity by 50–80% → ⑦ – ⑩.

Garage lift systems → ⑬ – ⑭ make the best use of space. The drivers themselves can control these with key switches in the entrance area. These garages can be up to 20 storeys high and hydraulic lifts are used for up to 10 storeys. As the car-park is not used by pedestrians, the height of each storey can be reduced to ≥ 2.10 m. This type of garage saves space, is safe in operation, has low noise levels, is environmentally friendly and is free of exhaust gases. 40–80 cars can be handled by each lift. The average time for entry to, or exit from, the parking place is 1–2 minutes. Transverse stackers → ⑫ are used in extremely narrow areas.

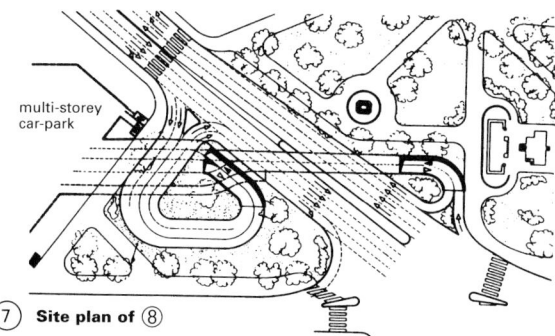

```
3.0
┌─┐
```

① **Large garage at Siemens**
Architect: H Hertlein

② **Longitudinal ramp**

③ **Transverse ramp**

④ **Section → ⑤**

| 2.80 |
| 2.80 |
| 3.50 |

⑤ **Plan view of multi-storey ramped car-park**

├─7.95─┼─7.95─┼─7.95─┼─5.00─┤

⑥ **Cross-section of ⑧**

high water 372.50
low water 370.85
374

| 0.55 |
| 2.20 |
| 2.20 |
| 2.20 |
| 2.20 |
| 0.85 |

| 5.32 | 6.50 | 10.25 | 6.50 | 10.25 | 6.50 | 10.25 | 6.50 | 5.32 | 1.00 |
| 4.38 | 8.38 | 8.37 | 8.38 | 8.37 | 8.38 | 8.37 | 8.38 | 5.53 | 15 |

68.54

⑦ **Site plan of ⑧**

multi-storey car-park

In accordance with the regulations applicable to garages:

- small garages are defined as those with ≤100 m² effective area;
- medium garages are those with 100–1000 m² effective area;
- large garages are those with ≥1000 m² effective area.

Underground garages are defined as those with the floor level on average ≥1.30 m below the surface of the ground.

Separate entrances and exits must be provided for large garages. These garages are normally located close to points of major traffic congestion such as railway stations, airports, shopping centres, theatres, cinemas, office and administration blocks and large residential buildings.

Medium and large garages must be located in easily accessible areas, have a clear headroom of 2.00 m, even below the main beams, ventilation ducts and other structural components. On the ground floor, this clear headroom is normally larger, as the space is often used for other purposes.

To accommodate small transport vehicles, this height should be 2.50 m. Floor loadings must be in accordance with local standards. Open garages have openings which cannot be closed (equal in size to one third of the total area of the outside walls) leading directly into the open air and divided in such a way that there is continuous through-ventilation, even in the presence of weather screening.

There is an ingenious example of a car-park in the centre of Geneva beneath the river Rhone. The entrance and exit points are on the approaches to the Rhone bridge → ⑦. Vehicles can easily filter in and out of the traffic flow by means of access ramps on both sides. All storeys are accessed by a right-hand drive up a central sloping ramp → ⑦ – ⑧. No staff are necessary as there are automatic parking ticket machines in use.

The criteria for the quality of multistorey car-parks are: safety in use, clear visibility, parking-space marking to enable drivers to remember the location of their vehicles, and integration into the context of town planning.

Other factors to be considered are: natural lighting and ventilation, clear views to the outside, plants and greenery and a simple system of collecting charges.

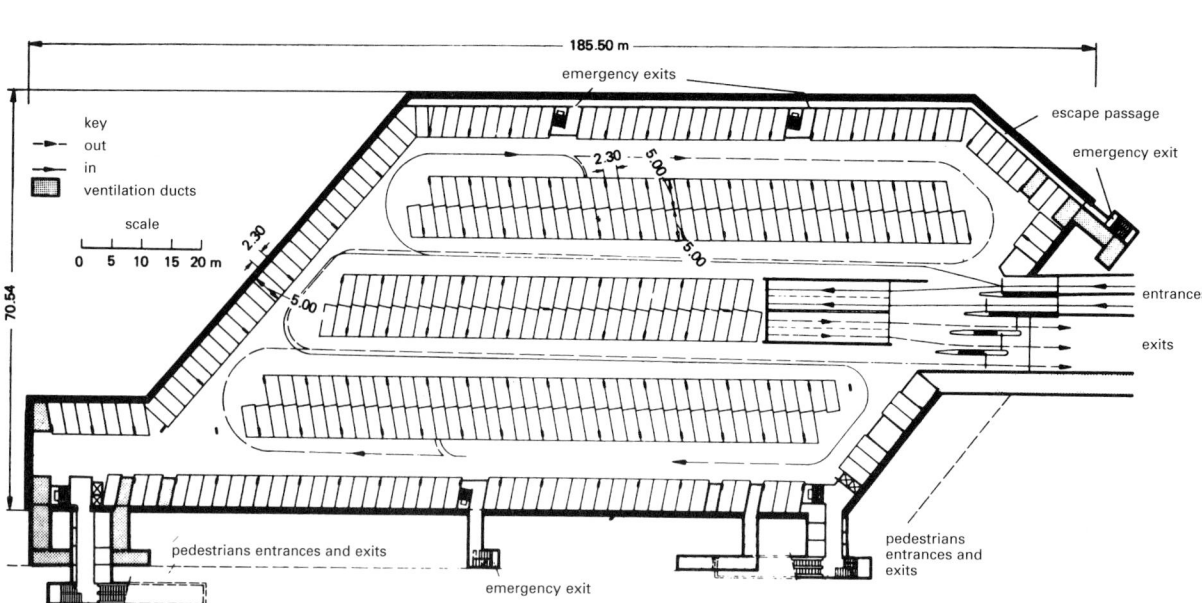

185.50 m

70.54

key
→ out
→ in
▓ ventilation ducts

scale
0 5 10 15 20 m

emergency exits
escape passage
emergency exit
entrances
exits
pedestrians entrances and exits
emergency exit
pedestrians entrances and exits

design and construction: C.Zschokke

⑧ **Under lake car-park in Geneva, Switzerland, Plan view of 1st floor. 372 parking spaces**

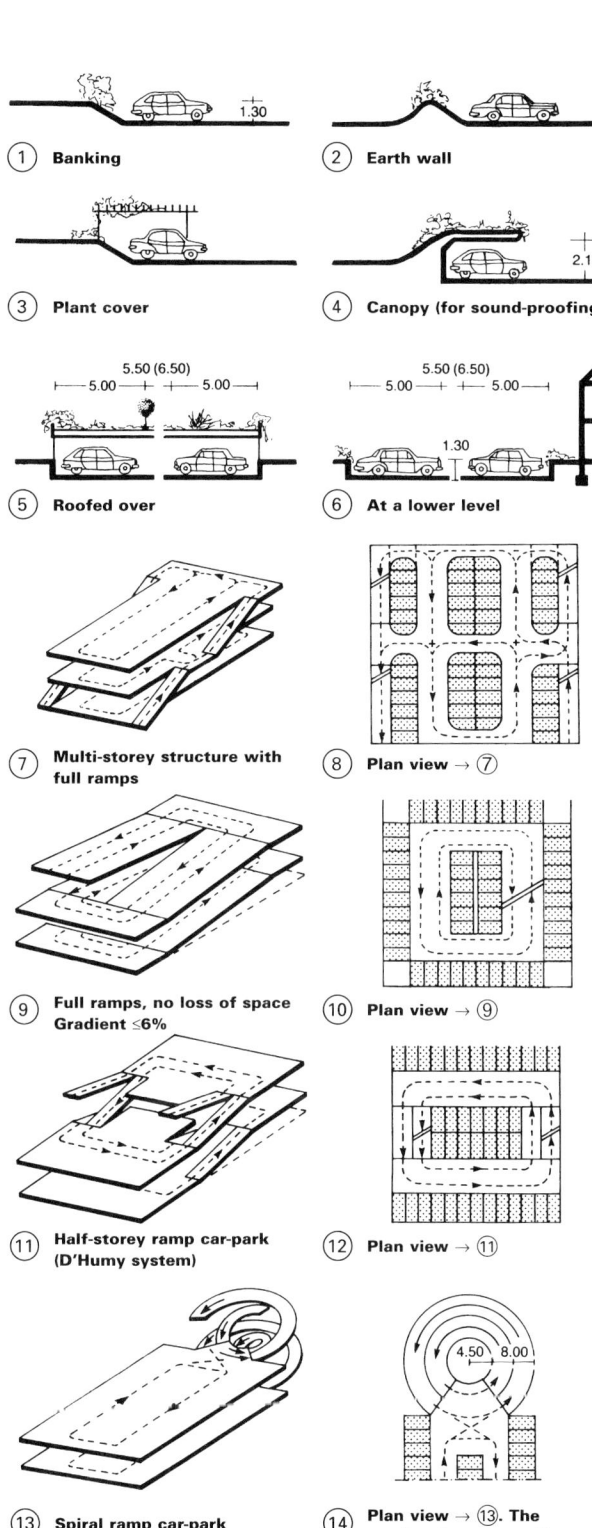

① Banking

② Earth wall

③ Plant cover

④ Canopy (for sound-proofing)

⑤ Roofed over

⑥ At a lower level

⑦ Multi-storey structure with full ramps

⑧ Plan view → ⑦

⑨ Full ramps, no loss of space Gradient ≤6%

⑩ Plan view → ⑨

⑪ Half-storey ramp car-park (D'Humy system)

⑫ Plan view → ⑪

⑬ Spiral ramp car-park

⑭ Plan view → ⑬. The smaller the ramp radius, the wider the lane

⑮ Separate circular towers for ramps at the corners

⑯ Plan view → ⑮

Examples → ① – ⑥ show how parking spaces can be creatively integrated into their surroundings without restricting their use. Parking spaces can be completely or partially sunken or provided with roof planting to increase the area of open space → ③ – ⑤. Planting not only enhances the look of the area, but also provides shade and improves the environment by absorbing dust.

There are various ramp systems for gaining access to upper and lower floors of car-parks. The gradients of the ramps should not exceed 15%, or in the case of small garages 20%. A horizontal run of more than 5 m must be included between an area carrying general traffic and ramps with more than 5% gradient. For car ramps the run must be more than 3 m long, with ramps that can be up to 10% gradient. The options available for the arrangement and design of ramps can be summarised under four main headings → ⑦ – ⑭:

(1) straight, parallel and continuous multi-storey ramps with intermediate landings, with separate ramps for up and down traffic located at opposite ends → ⑦ – ⑧;
(2) sloping floors, with a full width ramp with no loss of space. The entire car-park structure consists of sloping levels. A space-saving system is shown → ⑨ – ⑩ with a gradient of more than 6%;
(3) offset half storeys (D'Humy ramps); parking areas are offset half storeys, height is gained by the use of short ramps ⑪ – ⑫ and → ⑰ – ⑱;
(4) spiral ramps - a relatively expensive design which lacks good visibility. The circular shape makes poor use of remaining areas → ⑬ – ⑯ and → ⑲ and ⑳. Spiral ramps must have a transverse gradient of more than 3%. The radius of the edge of the inner lane must be more than 5 m. In large garages where special pedestrian routes are not provided, the ramps that are used by both vehicles and pedestrians must have a raised pavement at least 80 cm wide. Medium-sized and large garages must have the following minimum width of lanes at entrances and exits:
- 3 m when used by vehicles up to 2 m wide;
- 3.5 m when used by wider vehicles.

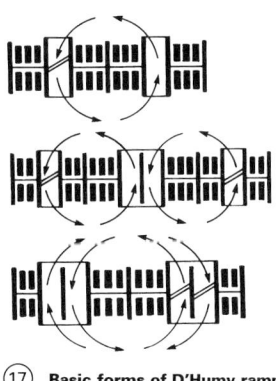
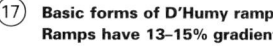

⑰ Basic forms of D'Humy ramp Ramps have 13–15% gradient

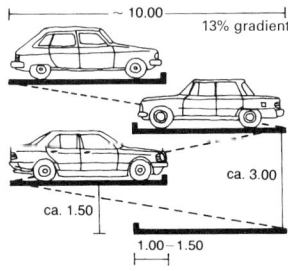

⑱ Dovetailing of storeys → ⑪ – ⑫

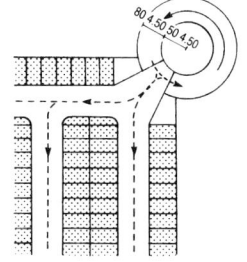

⑲ Spiral ramp, adjacent up and down lanes

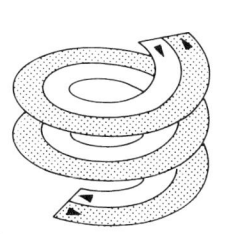

⑳ Double spiral ramps, superimposed up and down lanes

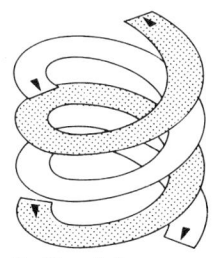

All the load bearing components of multistorey car-parks (floors, walls, support columns, bracing) must be fire-resistant. Garages open to the air must be of fire retardant design. The recommended clearance height in multistorey and basement garages is 2.20m. It is sensible to allow an extra 25cm for directional signs for drivers and pedestrians. A further 5cm is required for subsequent repair coats to the wearing surface, giving a total mean height of 2.50m, plus structures above the access lanes, which means a height per storey of 2.75–3.50m, depending upon the choice of design. A relatively narrow column grid pattern can, with careful planning and design, reduce building costs and height without any loss of function → ① + ②. Long span structures with no columns take up 7–12% less floor area than those with conventional support columns → ④.

Gradients and ramps must be appropriately shaped and designed → ③. Straight or spiral parking ramps are constructed by sloping the floor. With a spiral shape → ⑥, you can have vehicles on both sides of the ramp. In ⑧ it can be seen that the area required for a given number of cars to be parked, including the area required for manoeuvring, can be determined at the preliminary design stage. Layouts of multistoried garages and arrangements of ramps are shown → ⑦. These include two offset double rows of parked vehicles, four rows, six rows, parking in a corner, ramps in the direction of traffic, a multistorey car-park with ramps and finally one with parking on a continuous helical ramp.

Reinforced concrete structures (with concrete mixed on site, pre-cast sections or hybrid construction) best meet the requirements for fire protection. As a rule, steel structures provide the main and subsidiary support systems and must be protected from fire with concrete, fire resistant cladding or other fire-proofing coatings. In garages, high loads should be allowed for, in addition to permitted superimposed loads of motor vehicles of 3.5kN/m², and of ramps 5kN/m². Roofs with gardens on top have to be designed for a loading of 10kN/m².

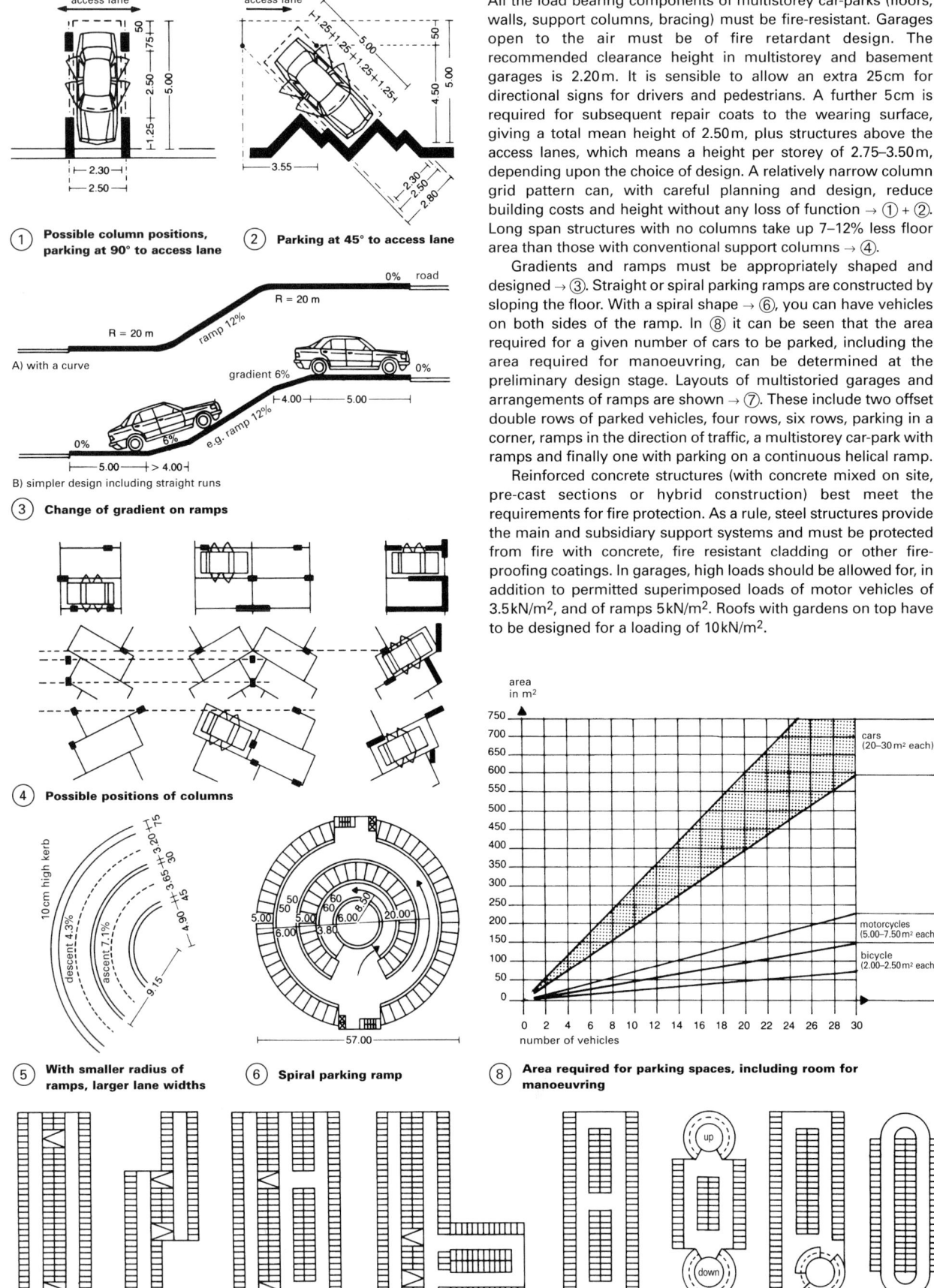

① Possible column positions, parking at 90° to access lane

② Parking at 45° to access lane

③ Change of gradient on ramps
A) with a curve
B) simpler design including straight runs

④ Possible positions of columns

⑤ With smaller radius of ramps, larger lane widths

⑥ Spiral parking ramp

⑦ Plan views and arrangement of ramps
four rows · two offset sets of two rows · six rows · right-angled layout ramps in direction of traffic · multistorey car-park with ramps · with spiral ramps

⑧ Area required for parking spaces, including room for manoeuvring
cars (20–30 m² each) · motorcycles (5.00–7.50 m² each) · bicycle (2.00–2.50 m² each)

Filling stations may be combined with other commercial services. The driver can therefore obtain fuel, oil, service and maintenance, repair work, car accessories and other goods all from one location.

If there are a number of filling stations on the same stretch of road, there should be ≥100 m between any two, or 250 m if the road carries heavy traffic.

On the open road, outside town limits, there should be one filling station for approximately every 25 km.

A plot size of about 800 m² is sufficient for a basic filling station, whereas one with service facilities will require about 1000 m² and a large installation usually needs up to 2000 m².

In the last 10 years the range of petrol available at filling stations has increased. Most stations now offer a variety of types petrol as well as diesel. The design of filling stations should be flexible enough to accommodate future requirements.

Filling stations should be easy to turn in to, easily visible, recognisable from a distance and located as near to the road as possible. They should almost never be built in the town centre, but rather on exit roads from the town, by-passes and trunk roads and not where queues build up before a set of traffic lights. It is not good practice to site filling stations at street corners. A better answer is to site them just before a corner, so that customers can drive out of the station into a side road.

Drivers should be able to refuel their cars, check and, where necessary, top up engine oil, cooling water, tyre pressure and battery fluid. Other services should be available, such as: checking the contents of the windscreen-washer bottle; cleaning the windscreen, headlights and hands; purchasing goods; using telephones and toilets and other facilities; as well as facilities for car washing, vacuum cleaning etc.

The building line and sight line, boundary distances etc., which are shown in the development plan, must be strictly observed, as well as those terms and conditions which form an integral part of the building regulations.

Typically, there are rules which govern the following:

- the size of short-term/long-term parking spaces (i.e. 2.50 m × 5.00 m = 12.50 m²);
- the number of parking spaces required (this is dependent upon the number of employees working at the station, in the workshops and on the pumps); and
- the space necessary for the queue at the automatic carwash (e.g. space required has to be sufficient for 50% of the hourly throughput of the carwash).

In accordance with the development plan, consideration must be given to the nominal dimensions laid down for motor vehicles, i.e.

turning circle:	car	12.50 m
turning circle:	truck	26.00 m
vehicle width:	car	1.85 m
vehicle width:	truck	2.50 m
vehicle length:	car	5.00 m
vehicle length:	articulated truck	18.00 m

Taking these figures as a basis, the appropriate dimensions of the pump islands and widths of the approach roads can be calculated.

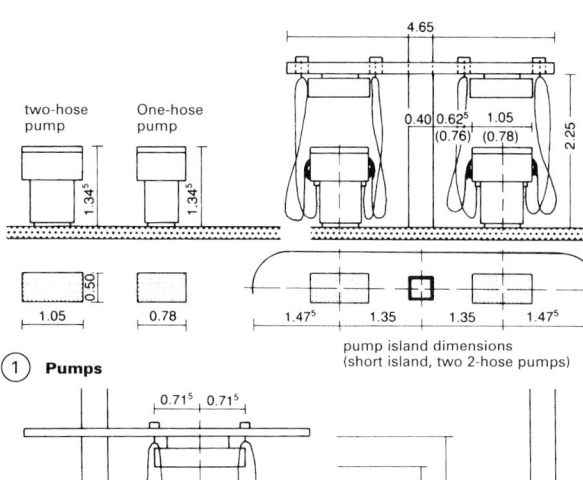

① **Pumps**

two-hose pump   One-hose pump

pump island dimensions (short island, two 2-hose pumps)

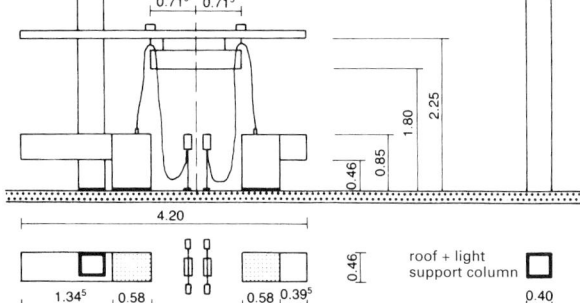

② **Single-fuel pump**

roof + light support column

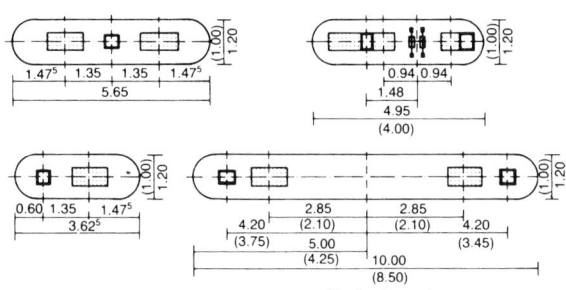

③ **Pump island dimensions**

( )min. dimensions

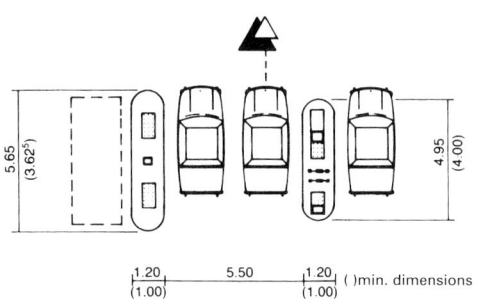

④ **2 short islands, parallel to the roadway**

( )min. dimensions

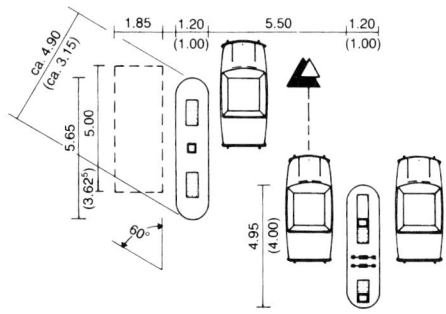

⑤ **2 short islands, <60° to the roadway**
( ) minimum dimensions

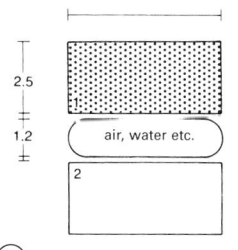

⑥ **Supply for air, water etc.**

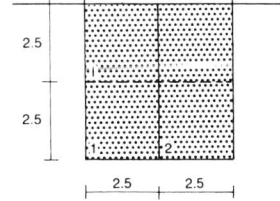

⑦ **Supply for air, water etc.**

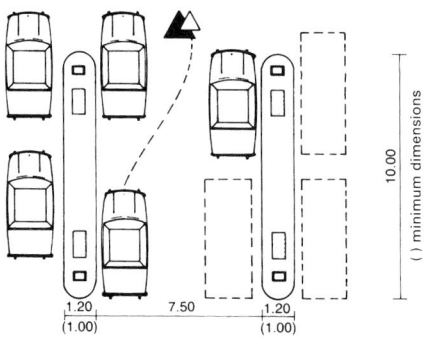

⑧ **2 long islands parallel to the roadway**
(this requires good driving skills)

( ) minimum dimensions

DESIGNING FOR VEHICLES

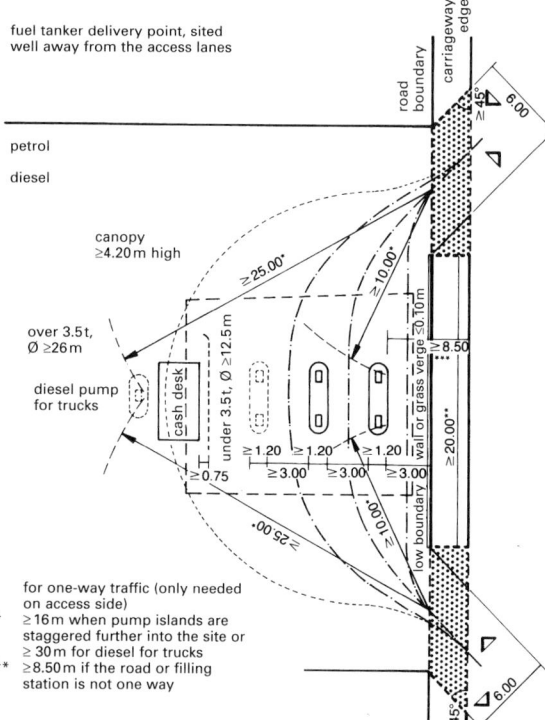

fuel tanker delivery point, sited well away from the access lanes

petrol

diesel

canopy ≥4.20 m high

over 3.5 t, Ø ≥26 m

diesel pump for trucks

cash desk

* for one-way traffic (only needed on access side)
** ≥16 m when pump islands are staggered further into the site or ≥ 30 m for diesel for trucks
*** ≥8.50 m if the road or filling station is not one way

(1) **Filling station for petrol and separate diesel fuel for trucks (≥3.5 t) on an enclosed site**

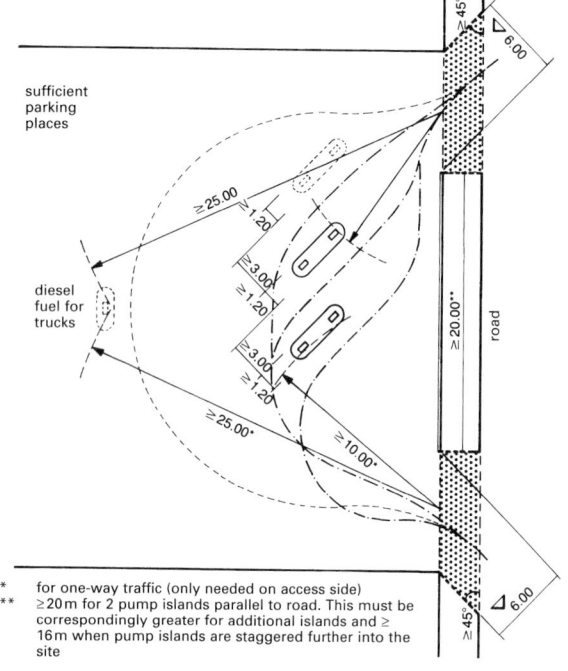

sufficient parking places

diesel fuel for trucks

* for one-way traffic (only needed on access side)
** ≥20 m for 2 pump islands parallel to road. This must be correspondingly greater for additional islands and ≥ 16 m when pump islands are staggered further into the site

(2) **Filling station with fuel pump islands obliquely angled in an enclosed site (mainly for one-way traffic)**

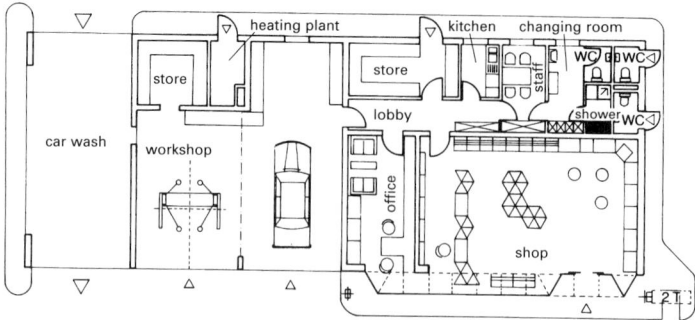

(3) **Plan of filling station with car wash and sales area**

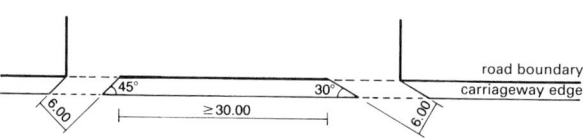

(4) **Without slip-roads in and out of traffic stream**

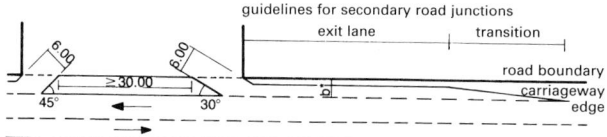

guidelines for secondary road junctions

exit lane · transition

(5) **Filling station entrance and exit off an open road**

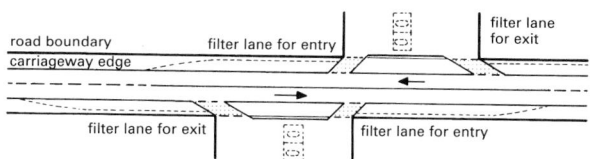

filter lane for entry · filter lane for exit

filter lane for exit · filter lane for entry

(6) **Filling stations on both sides of open road**

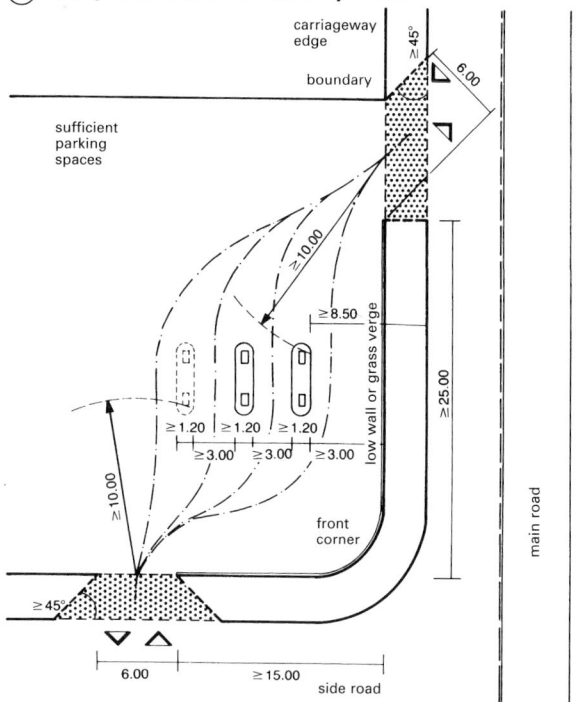

sufficient parking spaces

front corner

side road

(7) **Corner filling station on an enclosed site. This is used only in exceptional cases, and usually not suitable for trucks**

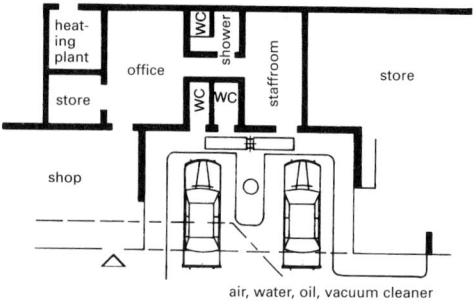

air, water, oil, vacuum cleaner

(8) **Fast-service station**

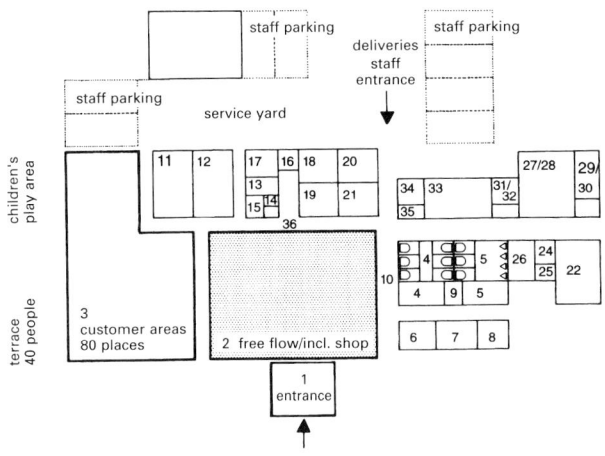

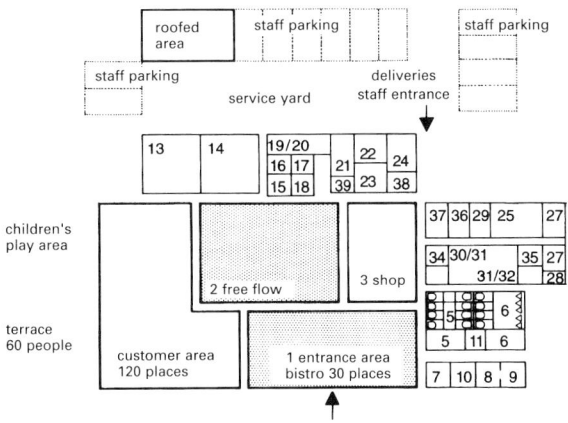

CUSTOMER AREA (80 people)

		approx. m²
	Sales area	**270.0**
1	entrance	20.0
2	free-flow incl. shop	120.0
3	customer area 80 places	130.0
	customer rooms	**70.2**
4	WC female	20.0
5	WC male	17.0
6	disabled toilets	6.0
7	shower room	5.0
8	baby changing room	4.0
9	cleaners' room 1 customer area	2.0
10	corridors of customer area, 30% of areas 4–9	16.2

SERVICE AREA

	Storage area	**68.0**
11	washing-up area	15.0
12	food preparation	15.0
13	chilled vegetable store	4.0
14	dairy and delicatessen refrigerators	1.0
15	meat cold store /or delicatessen refrigerators	2.0
16	chilling room	2.0
17	deep freeze rooms	5.0
18	drinks cold store	6.0
19/20/21	dry stores	18.0
	Services	**58.0**
22	services/heating	15.0
23	ventilation plant (or in roof space or on flat roof)	30.0
24	electrics	5.0
25	switchgear and meters	8.0
	Administration/staff	**134.7**
26	staff rest room	6.0
27/28	changing room male/female	22.0
29/30	staff wash room male/female	8.0
31/32	staff toilets male/female	3.0
33	office	30.0
34	files	4.0
35	cleaners' room 2 service area	1.5
36	corridors of service area, 30% of areas 11–35	60.2
	Net floor area	**600.9**
37	terrace 40 seating places	80.0

CUSTOMER AREA (150 people)

		approx. m²
	Sales area	**480.0**
1	entrance area, bistro 30 seating places	120.0
2	free flow	120.0
3	shop	60.0
4	customer area 120 places	180.0
	customer rooms	**99.1**
5	WC female	27.0
6	WC male	24.0
7	disabled toilets	6.0
8/9	shower room	10.0
10	baby changing room	4.0
11	cleaners' room 1 customer area	2.0
12	corridors of customer area, 22% of areas 5–11	18.1

SERVICE AREA

	Storage area	**121.0**
13	washing-up area	30.0
14	preparation	28.0
15	cold room	4.0
16/17	dairy/vegetable cold store	8.0
18	chilling room	3.0
19/20	meat cold store and deep freeze room	12.0
21	drinks cold store	10.0
22/23/24	dry stores	26.0
	Services	**84.0**
25	services/heating	20.0
26	ventilation plant (or in roof space or on flat roof)	40.0
27	air conditioning	10.0
27	electrics	6.0
28	switchgear and meters	8.0
	Administration/staff	**158.6**
29	staff rest room	10.0
30/31	changing room male/female	32.0
32/33	staff wash room male/female	8.0
34/35	staff toilets male/female	7.0
36/37	office	29.0
38	files	5.0
39	cleaners' room 2 service area	2.0
40	corridors of service area, 22% of areas 13–39	85.0
	Net floor area	**932.7**
41	terrace 60 seating places	120.0

(1) **Functional diagram of a service station for 80 people → (2)**

(3) **Functional diagram of a service station for 150 people → (4)**

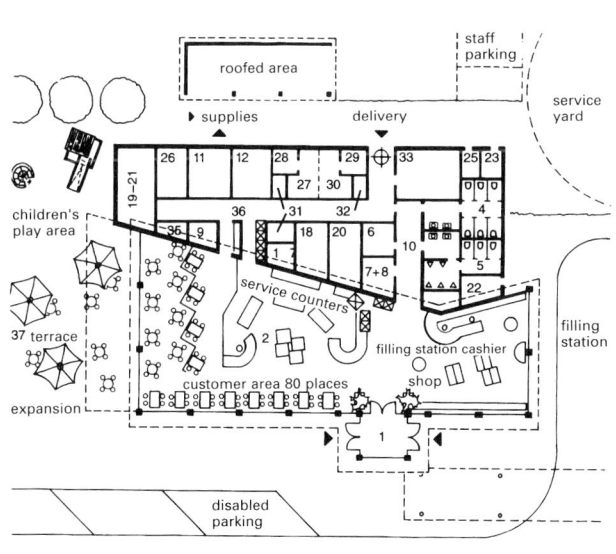

(2) **Petrol and service station for 80 people**

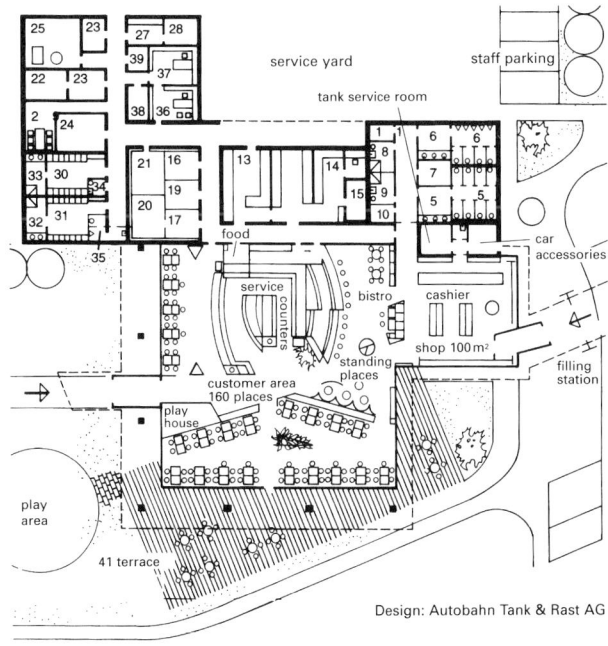

Design: Autobahn Tank & Rast AG

(4) **Petrol and service station for 150 people**

AIRPORTS: PLANNING

The term 'airport' can include not only the civil airports familiar to holidaymakers but also airfields (which may have few or no associated buildings) and heliports. They may be divided into those which are public (i.e. accessible to any air travellers) and those which are private (e.g. air-freight terminals, company airports, aeroclubs and airforce bases).

Location

The choice of location for an airport will depend on topographical, geological and meteorological conditions as well as the position of surrounding built-up areas. Sufficient land must be available for take-off and landing runways, taxiways, terminal buildings, maintenance areas, fuel storage, etc. and, ideally, for possible future expansion. Another important factor is proximity to existing and potential transport networks.

General expansion plan

For all airports, an expansion plan covering at least 20 years ahead should be drawn up, and revised at regular intervals in order to allow for changes in the volume and nature of air traffic, developments in aircraft technology and other innovations.

Traffic forecasts should include information about movements of aircraft, numbers of passengers and volume of freight. They should be checked and updated on a regular basis to account for the pace of modern change. For the calculations, and design of the airport facilities and installations, typical peak traffic values (i.e. those reached 30 times per year or 10 times within the peak month) should be chosen, not the absolute peak values.

① **Passenger arrival flow diagram**

② **Passenger check-in/ departure flow diagram**

— passenger flow
---- baggage flow

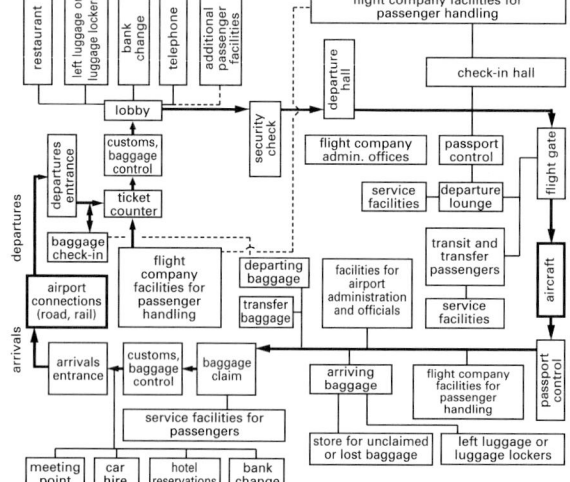

③ **Functional diagram of a terminal building**

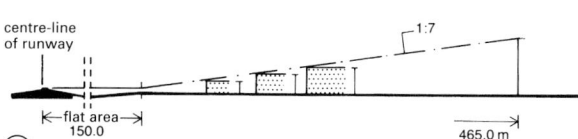

④ **Permissible building heights immediately beside runways**

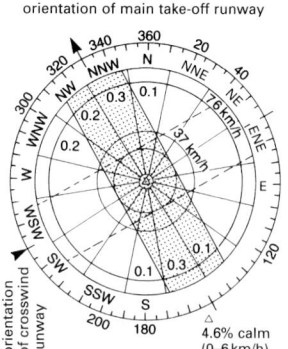

⑤ **Typical wind rose**

⑥ **Wind data**

direction	7–24 km/h	26–37 km/h	39–76 km/h	total
N	4.8	1.3	0.1	6.2
NNE	3.7	0.8	–	4.5
NE	1.5	0.1	–	1.6
ENE	2.3	0.3	–	2.6
E	2.4	0.4	–	2.8
ESE	5.0	1.1	–	6.1
SE	6.4	3.2	0.1	9.7
SSE	7.3	7.7	0.3	15.3
S	4.4	2.2	0.1	6.7
SSW	2.6	0.9	–	3.5
SW	1.6	0.1	–	1.7
WSW	3.1	0.4	–	3.5
W	1.9	0.3	–	2.2
WNW	5.8	2.6	0.2	8.6
NW	4.8	2.4	0.2	7.4
NNW	7.8	4.9	0.3	13.0
calm	(0–6 km/h)			4.6
total				100.0

breakdown of wind speeds and directions experienced

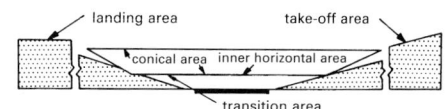

⑦ **Required obstruction-free area for take-off/landing, longitudinal section (A–A)**

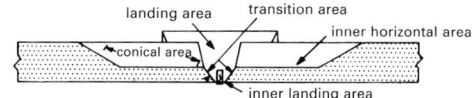

⑧ **Required obstruction-free area for take-off/landing, cross-section (B–B)**

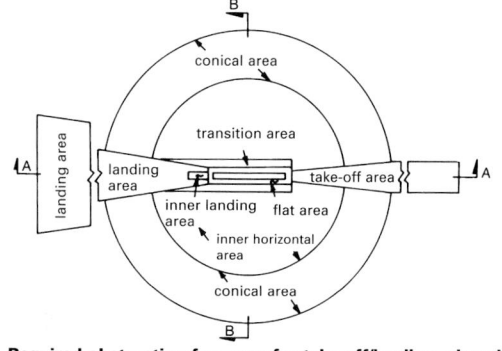

⑨ **Required obstruction-free area for take-off/landing, plan view**

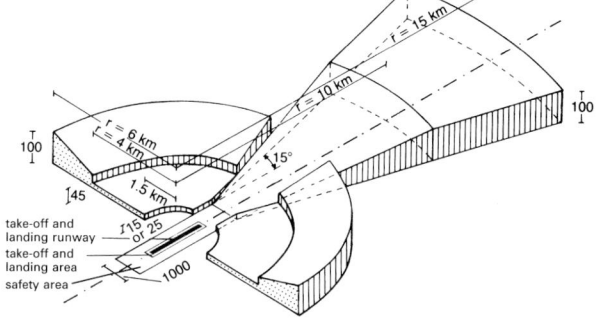

⑩ **Building protection areas for an airport with instrument landing**

Forward planning requires a traffic forecast based on the following data:

- average/peak passenger movements (overseas/domestic, arrivals/departures, transfers/transits, short-haul/long-haul);
- average/peak air-freight/mail take-offs and landings (overseas/domestic, import/export/transfer), proportion of standard dimensions (containers, pallets), average/peak total tonnage, number of items or volume of goods);
- average/peak movements of aircraft according to types of aircraft (passenger, freight, or mixed traffic).

Other factors important to planning are:

- choice of mode of transport by passengers (private car, taxi, public transport);
- average number of people accompanying each passenger, average number of pieces of luggage per passenger, number of visitors to airport (unconnected to passengers, employees).

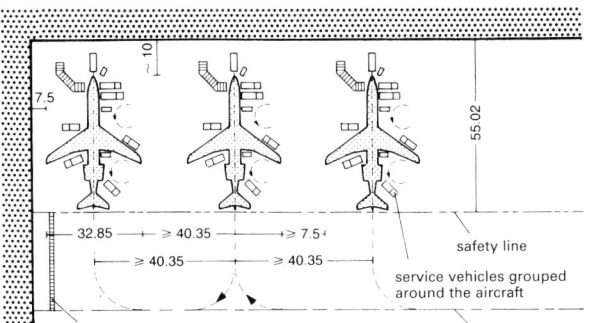

① **Nose-in parking position**

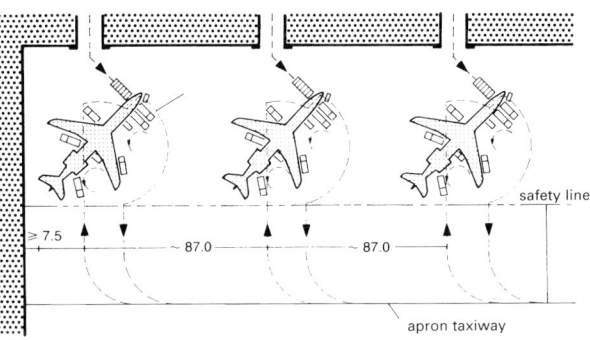

② **Diagonal nose-in parking position**

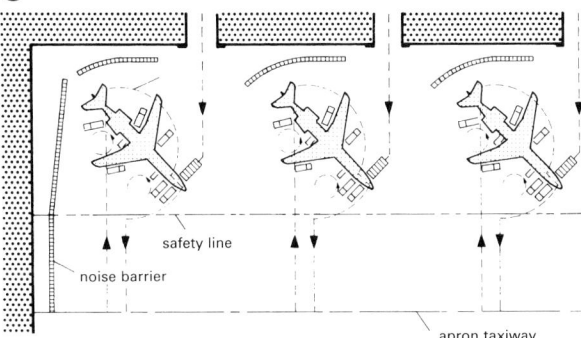

③ **Diagonal nose-out parking position**

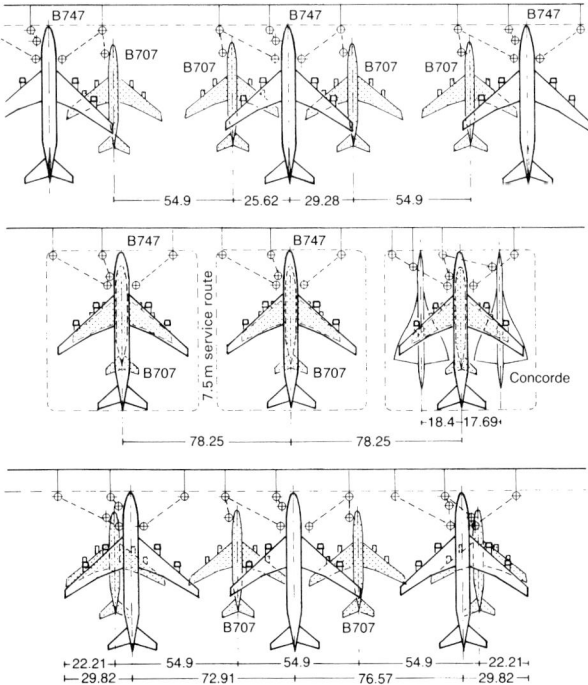

④ **Typical aircraft parking arrangements**

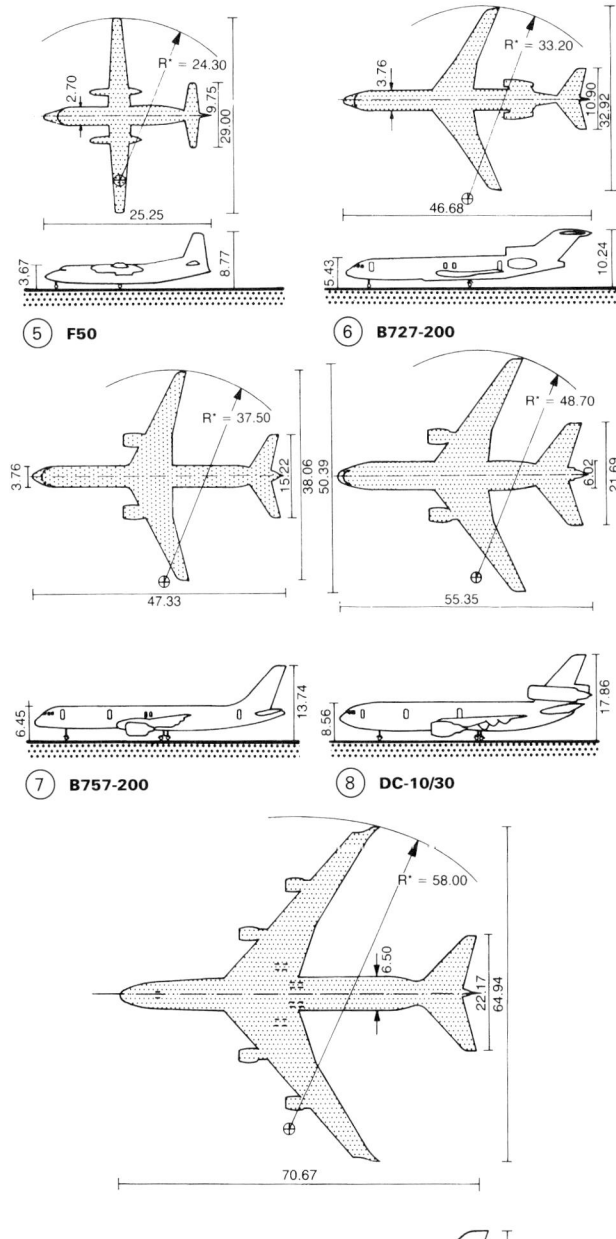

⑤ **F50**

⑥ **B727-200**

⑦ **B757-200**

⑧ **DC-10/30**

⑨ **B747-400**

AIRPORTS: TERMINALS

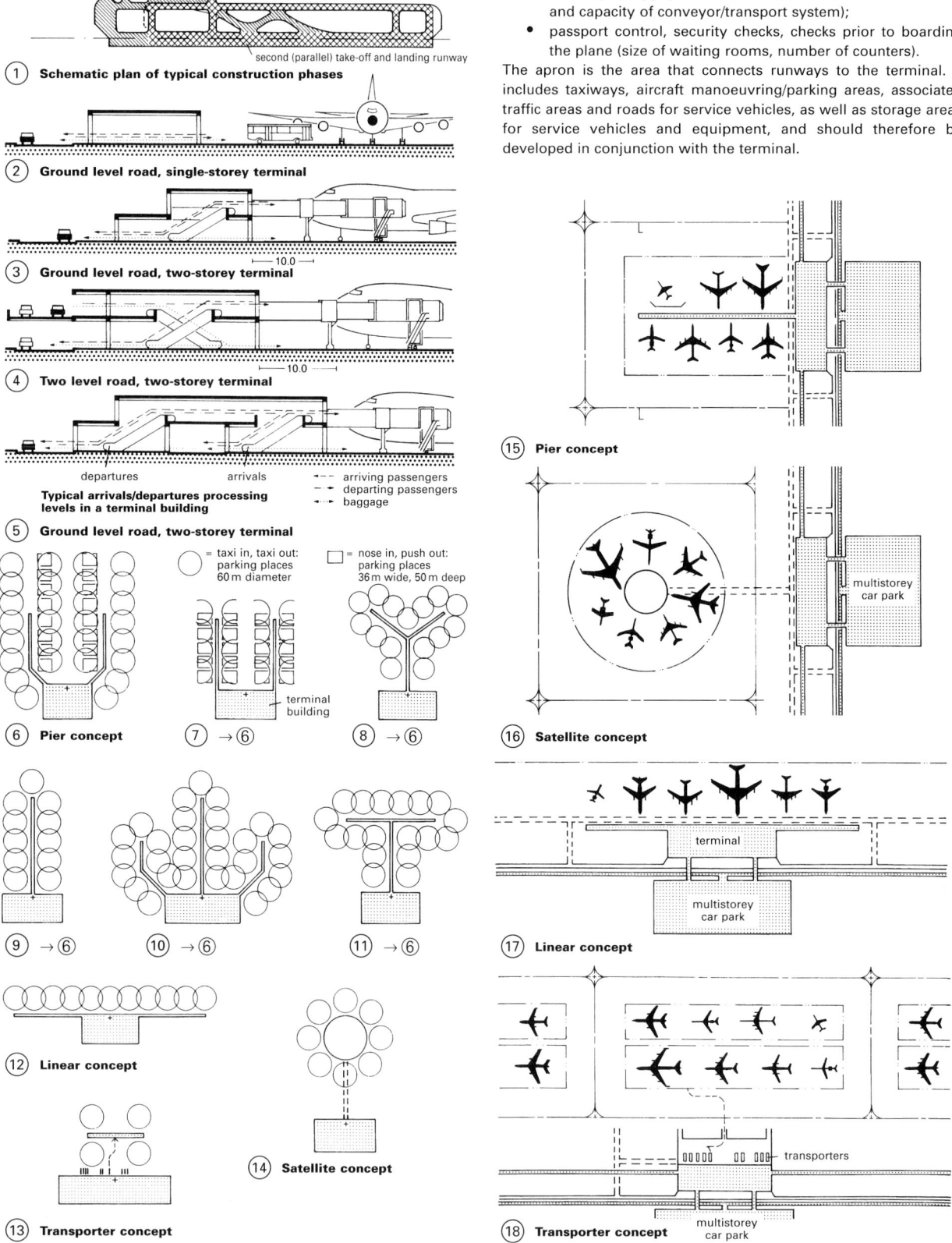

① **Schematic plan of typical construction phases**

turning circle · take-off and landing runway · link runway · (rapid) exit taxiway · turning area

parallel taxiway

waiting/overtaking area

	20000–30000 movements
	30000–60000 movements
	50000–99000 movements
	75000–150000 movements
	150000–250000 movements

second (parallel) take-off and landing runway

② **Ground level road, single-storey terminal**

③ **Ground level road, two-storey terminal** ← 10.0 →

④ **Two level road, two-storey terminal** ← 10.0 →

departures · arrivals · --- arriving passengers · – – departing passengers · ←·– baggage

Typical arrivals/departures processing levels in a terminal building

⑤ **Ground level road, two-storey terminal**

○ = taxi in, taxi out: parking places 60 m diameter

□ = nose in, push out: parking places 36 m wide, 50 m deep

terminal building

⑥ **Pier concept**

⑦ → ⑥

⑧ → ⑥

⑨ → ⑥

⑩ → ⑥

⑪ → ⑥

⑫ **Linear concept**

⑬ **Transporter concept**

⑭ **Satellite concept**

All parking places in adjacent building (linked by passenger bridges) are situated within 300 m of the centre of gravity (+) → ⑥ – ⑭

The following functional areas determine the airport capacity:
- take-off and landing runway system (possible movements of aircraft per unit time);
- taxiways and number of arrival/departure gates;
- passenger terminal buildings (possible movements of passengers, baggage and air-freight per unit time).

The capacity of the check-in system is determined by:
- the related road and rail systems (including parking provision, capacity of roads);
- passenger/baggage check-in clearance (number of counters and capacity of conveyor/transport system);
- passport control, security checks, checks prior to boarding the plane (size of waiting rooms, number of counters).

The apron is the area that connects runways to the terminal. It includes taxiways, aircraft manoeuvring/parking areas, associated traffic areas and roads for service vehicles, as well as storage areas for service vehicles and equipment, and should therefore be developed in conjunction with the terminal.

⑮ **Pier concept**

⑯ **Satellite concept**

multistorey car park

⑰ **Linear concept**

terminal

multistorey car park

⑱ **Transporter concept**

transporters

multistorey car park

take-off/landing runways	hourly capacity		annual traffic volume
	VFC	IFC	
	movements/hour		movements

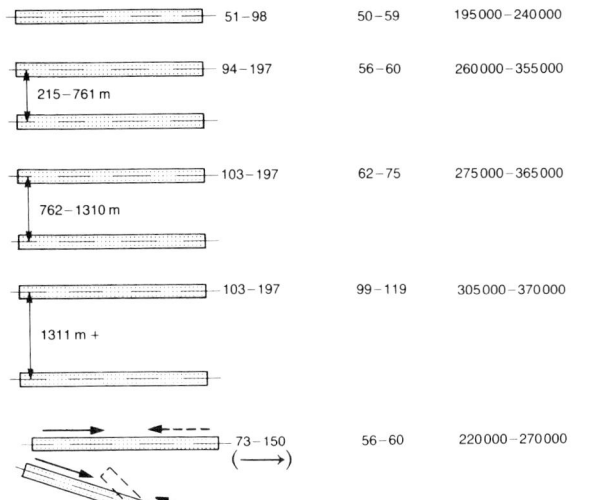

51–98	50–59		195 000–240 000
94–197 (215–761 m)	56–60		260 000–355 000
103–197 (762–1310 m)	62–75		275 000–365 000
103–197 (1311 m +)	99–119		305 000–370 000
73–150 (⟶)	56–60		220 000–270 000
73–132 (← − −)	56–60		215 000–265 000
72–98	56–60		200 000–265 000

VFC = visual flight conditions
IFC = instrument flight conditions

① **Capacity of different take-off/landing runway systems**

Passenger terminal concepts

Airports use different methods of accommodating aircraft and linking them with terminals and the main buildings. There are four main concepts.

(1) Pier concept (with central main terminal →p. 448, ⑥ – ⑪ + ⑮). Aircraft park on both sides of a pier connected to the terminal building. Where there are two or more piers, the space in between has to be sufficient for 1–2 apron taxiways each (allowing taxiing in and out at same time).

(2) Satellite concept (with central main terminal → p. 448, ⑭ + ⑯). One or more buildings, each surrounded radially with aircraft parking places, are connected to the main terminal, generally by large underground corridors.

(3) Linear concept (→ p. 448, ⑫ + ⑰). Aircraft are parked alongside the terminal building in a line next to one another in nose-in, parallel or diagonal positions. The parking position determines to a great extent the overall length of the terminal.

(4) Transporter concept (→ p. 448, ⑬ + ⑱). Aircraft parking is spatially separated from the terminal and the passengers are taken to and from their flights by specially designed transport vehicles.

Further mixed variations (hybrid concepts) can be developed from these basic layouts.

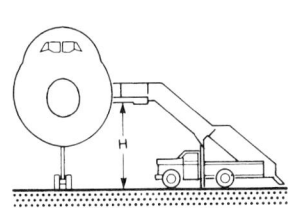

type	F50	B727	B757	DC-10	B747
H (m)	1.29	2.97	4.01	5.16	5.36

threshold height (H) of the integrated step to the cabin floor

② **Truck-mounted passenger steps**

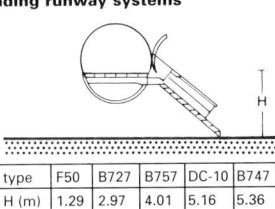

③ **Swivel landing bridge**

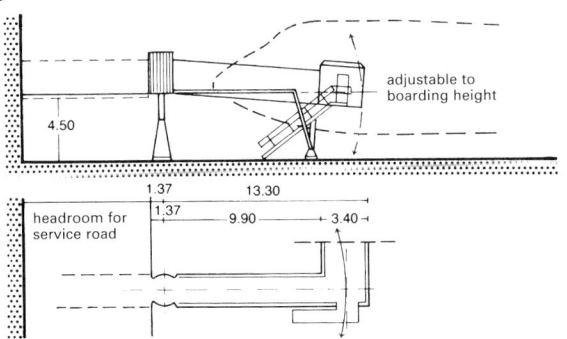

④ **Telescopic variable height landing bridge with support column**

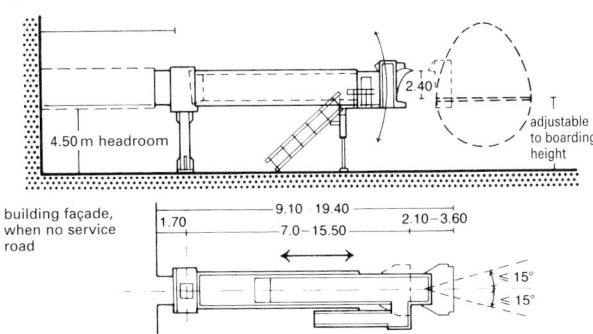

········· 6.00 – 10.00 hr
———— 10.00 – 18.00 hr
– – – – 18.00 – 24.00 hr

⑤ **Distribution of passenger arrival times ahead of scheduled take-off**

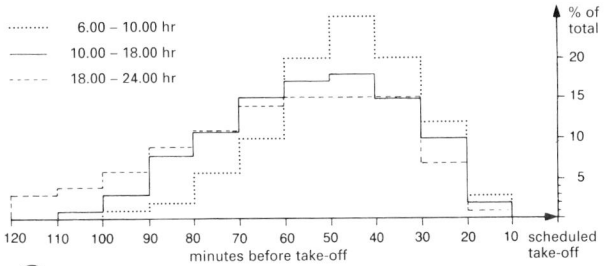

⑥ **Swivel and telescopic landing bridge**

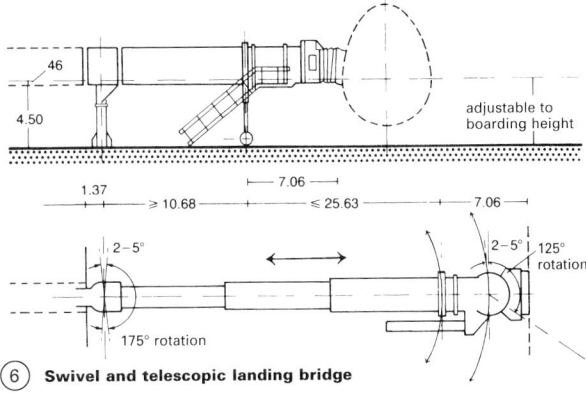

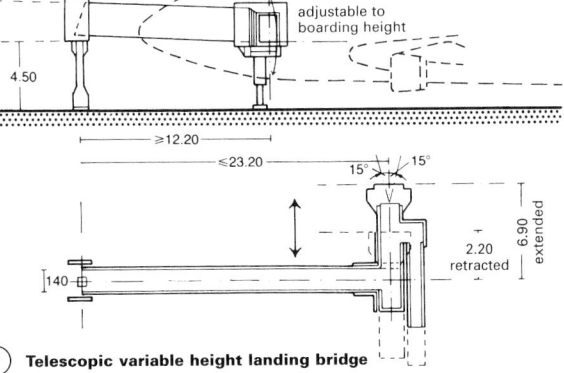

⑦ **Telescopic variable height landing bridge**

449

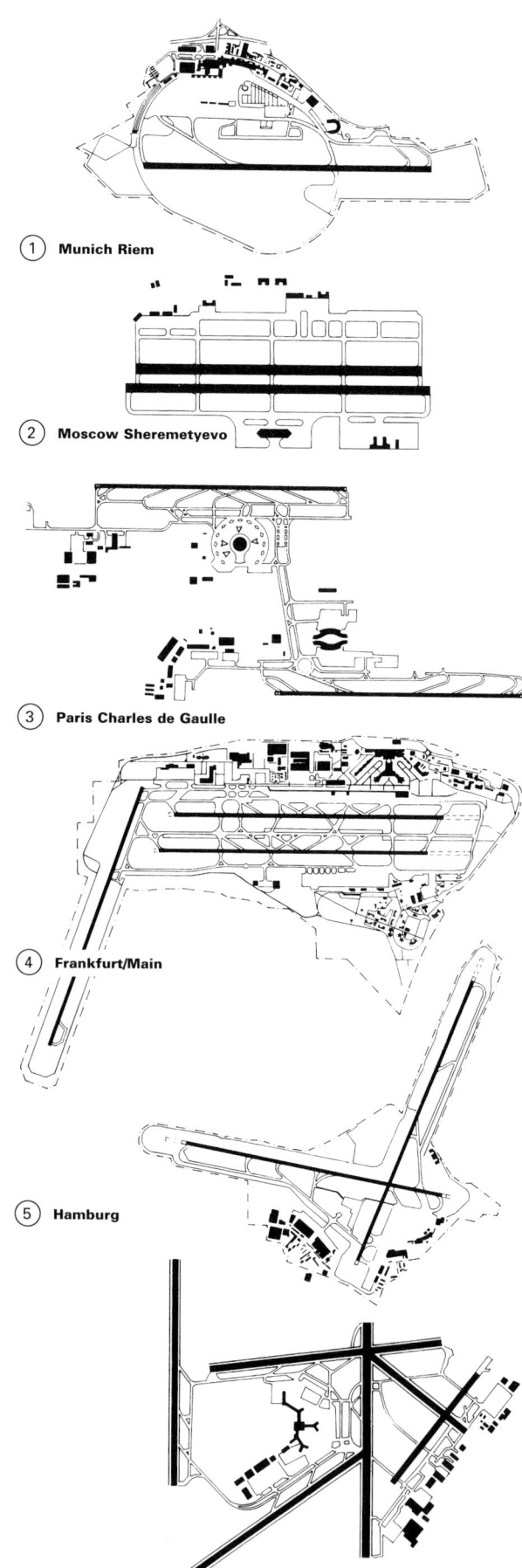

(1) **Munich Riem**

(2) **Moscow Sheremetyevo**

(3) **Paris Charles de Gaulle**

(4) **Frankfurt/Main**

(5) **Hamburg**

(6) **Amsterdam Schipol**

AIRPORTS: RUNWAYS AND APRONS

The orientations, lengths and numbers of take-off and landing runways are determined by a number of factors:

- Orientation is determined essentially by the prevailing local wind direction, the aim being to make it possible to approach the airport for 95% of the year (with a maximum side wind of 20 knots). Frequent strong crosswinds may make a corresponding second runway necessary → p. 446 (5) + (6).
- Length is determined by the type of aircraft, predominant climatic and topographic conditions, such as temperature, air pressure (related to height above sea level), land gradient etc.
- The number of runways is dependent upon the volume of traffic to be handled. A parallel arrangement (note that the minimum separation is 215 m) is particularly advantageous and, if the separation is more than 1310 m, simultaneous take-offs and landings are possible, which allows the highest theoretical capacity to be reached. → p. 449 (1).

The taxiing area is to be designed in such a way that the runways can be cleared as fast as possible after a landing ('fast exit taxiing runways') and parking positions can be reached by the shortest possible routes. In especially busy airports, provision of overtaking areas or by-pass runways can help to increase capacity.

Aircraft parking positions

The 'nose-in' position (→ p. 447 (1)) has the following advantages: small space requirements; few problems with exhaust streams for personnel, equipment and buildings; quick servicing times as the necessary equipment can be made available before arrival; and ease of connection to passenger bridges. However, this position requires a means of towing for manoeuvring purposes and this adds time and calls for trained personnel.

With 'taxi in/taxi out' parking (e.g. diagonal nose-in → p. 447 (2) and diagonal nose-out → p. 447 (3) towing is not necessary. However, such parking needs a larger space and creates more fumes and noise pollution directly in the vicinity of the terminal as the aircraft are taxiing, thus making it necessary to add protective measures such as blast barriers.

The parallel parking system offers the easiest manoeuvring for arriving and departing aircraft and there is no need for towing. The disadvantages are that parallel parking has the greatest overall space requirement and limits activity in neighbouring aircraft positions during taxiing.

Apron roadways and parking spaces

Signposting and positioning of service roadways on the apron are of great importance to the efficient and safe functioning of the airport. Apron roadways should be designed to give direct and safe connection of the apron to the other working areas of the airport. The points at which they cross aircraft taxiways or other service vehicle routes should be kept to the minimum. They can be run in front of or behind planes in the nose-in position, or between the wings → p. 447 (4).

Should the roadways run underneath passenger bridges, sufficient headroom for all service vehicles is required (usually 4.50 m minimum) → p. 449 (3) + (7). Because of the extensive mechanisation and containerisation of aircraft servicing, it is vital to provide enough space for loading and parking of service vehicles and equipment (including empty containers).

Terminals essentially facilitate the transfer of passengers from ground transport (public transport, taxis, private cars) to the aircraft. They must therefore be planned in such a way that the movement of passengers and their luggage takes place efficiently, comfortably and quickly, and at the same time with the lowest possible running cost. An important criterion is passenger travelling distance: the distances between the car park/drop-off point and the main functional areas should be kept as short as possible. Modification to accommodate any increases in traffic must also be possible without radical and costly alterations to the original terminal.

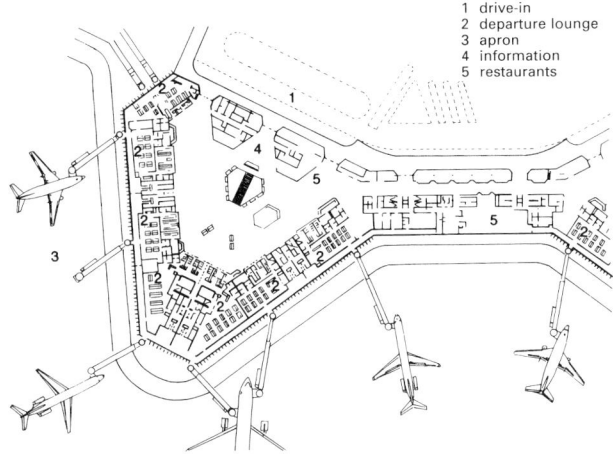

1 drive-in
2 departure lounge
3 apron
4 information
5 restaurants

(1) **Hannover airport (decentralised system), part of departures level**

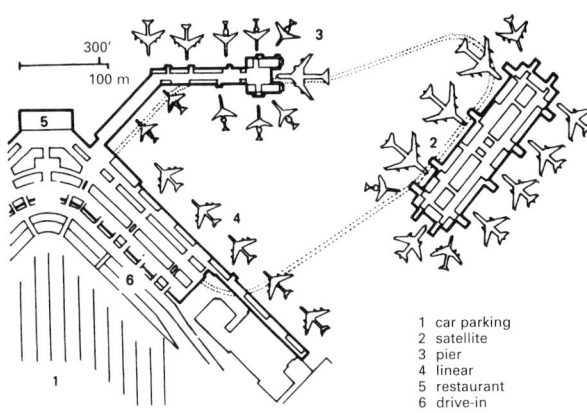

300'
100 m

1 car parking
2 satellite
3 pier
4 linear
5 restaurant
6 drive-in

(6) **Seattle Tacoma airport**
(combination of pier, linear and satellite system)

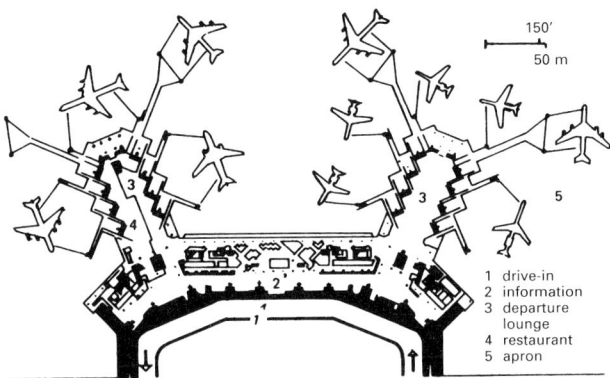

150'
50 m

1 drive-in
2 information
3 departure lounge
4 restaurant
5 apron

(2) **Orly West, upper floor (departures)**

1 arrivals
2 departures
3 baggage
4 passenger train

(7) **Section through satellite → (6)**

1 restaurant
2 transit passengers
3 offices

150'
50 m

(3) **Cologne-Bonn airport, second floor (satellite system)**

300'
100 m

1 departure lounge
2 travelator
3 customs
4 tunnel

(8) **Frankfurt/Main airport, part of ground floor**

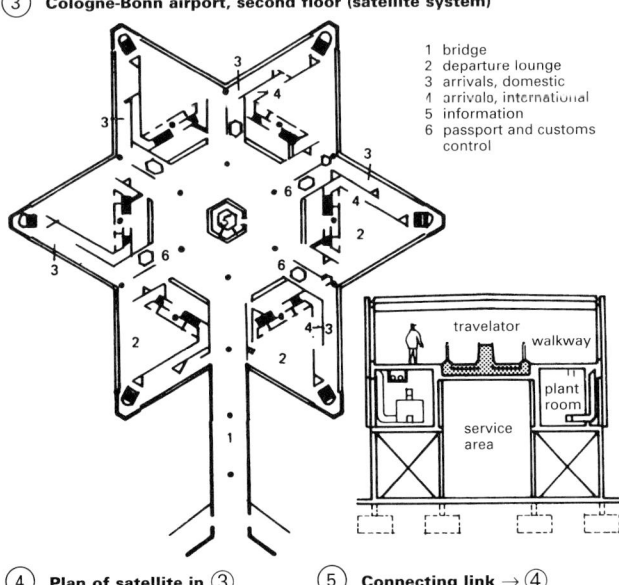

1 bridge
2 departure lounge
3 arrivals, domestic
4 arrivals, international
5 information
6 passport and customs control

travelator
walkway
plant room
service area

(4) **Plan of satellite in (3)**   (5) **Connecting link → (4)**

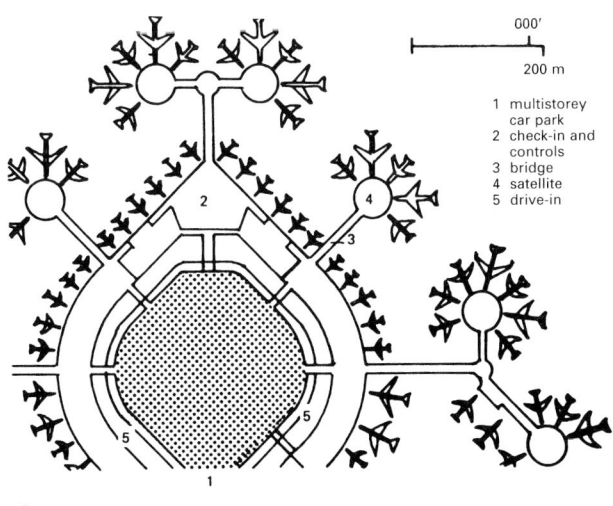

000'
200 m

1 multistorey car park
2 check-in and controls
3 bridge
4 satellite
5 drive-in

(9) **San Francisco airport, departures level**

451

FIRE STATIONS

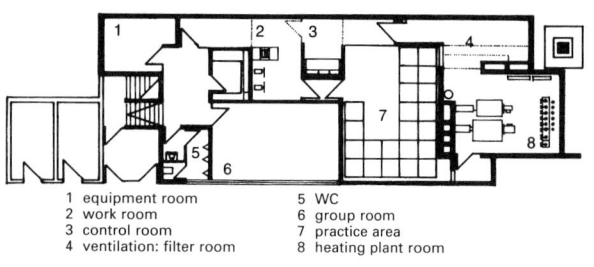

1 equipment room
2 work room
3 control room
4 ventilation: filter room
5 WC
6 group room
7 practice area
8 heating plant room

(1) **Basement** → (2) – (4)

Fire stations which serve districts, and are in contact with accident and emergency medical departments, can often usefully be linked to a motorway. They can also serve as education and training centres, and should be equipped with all the necessary maintenance, support and repair facilities for constant readiness. Hose storage and maintenance equipment should be provided as well as a drying tower which also serves as a practice tower with ladder access points.

Clear functional areas are necessary for preparing the fire engines for operation: all preparation rooms should be ranged along one axis leading towards the fire-engine hall.

Vehicles returning from incidents drive around the complex to the equipment, hose and tool return department, and retake their place in the fire-engine hall after being cleaned and prepared for operation.

A fire station can act as emergency medical communication centre as well as district or regional control centre in the event of a large-scale emergency → (1) – (5).

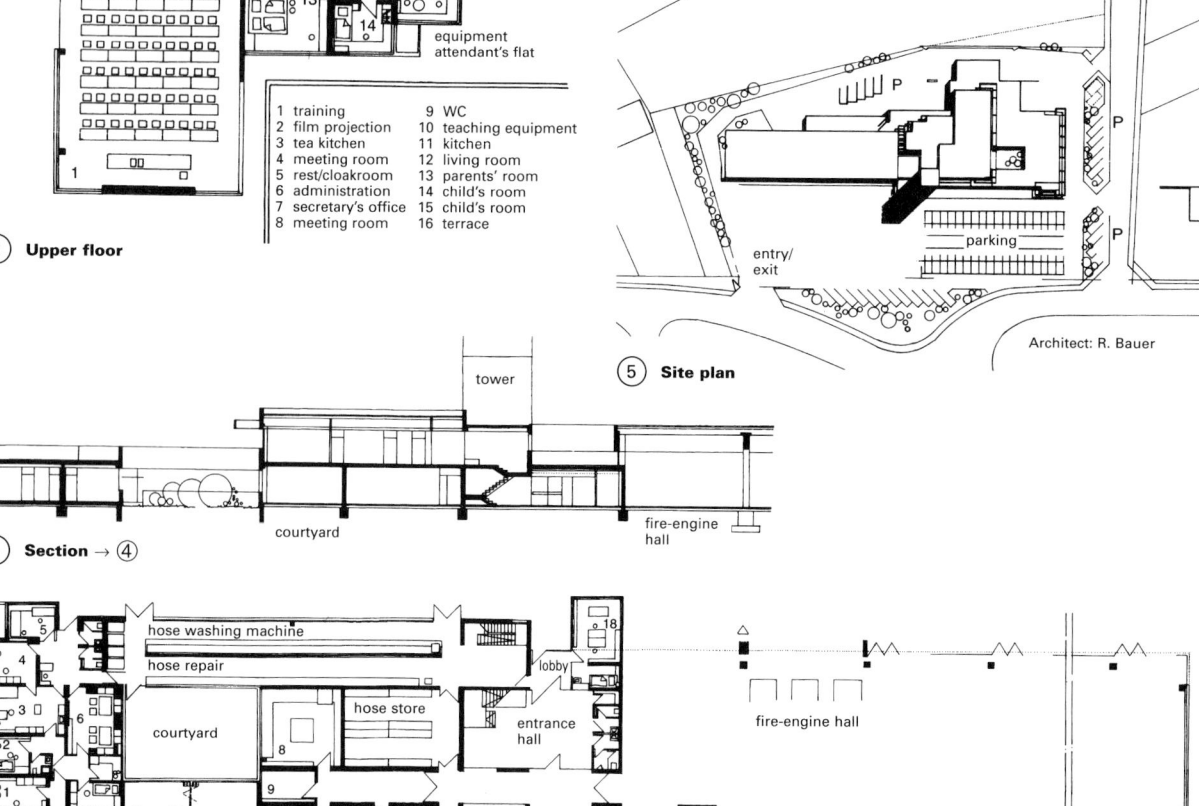

1 training
2 film projection
3 tea kitchen
4 meeting room
5 rest/cloakroom
6 administration
7 secretary's office
8 meeting room
9 WC
10 teaching equipment
11 kitchen
12 living room
13 parents' room
14 child's room
15 child's room
16 terrace

equipment attendant's flat

(2) **Upper floor**

Architect: R. Bauer

(5) **Site plan**

(3) **Section** → (4)

(4) **Ground floor, fire station**

1 backup service
2 restroom/doctor
3 treatment
4 waiting room
5 secretary's office
6 restroom/watch
7 quiet room
8 communications room
9 clothes store
10 clothes store
11 equipment/fittings
12 spare parts
13 oil store
14 restroom
15 quiet room
16 wash/shower room
17 changing room
18 operations centre
19 dirt sluice
20 chemical extinguishers
21 oil binders
22 equipment
23 emergency power

452

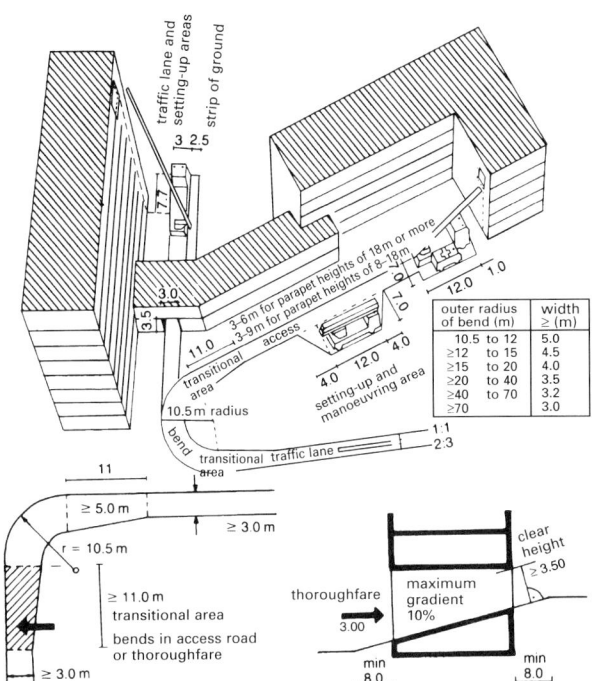

outer radius of bend (m)		width ≥ (m)
10.5	to 12	5.0
≥12	to 15	4.5
≥15	to 20	4.0
≥20	to 40	3.5
≥40	to 70	3.2
≥70		3.0

① Setting-up and manoeuvring areas

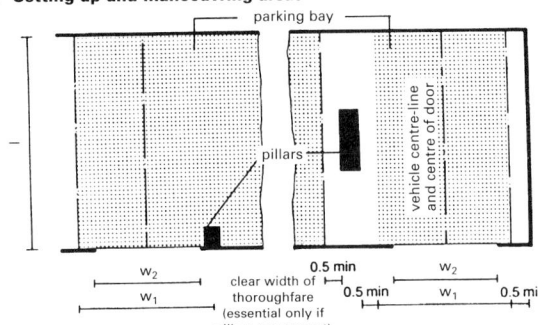

② Parking bays and doors

	parking bay			door (passage width w² × passage height)
size	width w¹ min.	length l min.		
1 to be avoided whenever possible	4.5	8		3.5 × 3.5
2	4.5	10		3.5 × 3.5
3	4.5	12.5		3.5 × 3.5
4	4.5	12.5		3.5 × 4

note: there are some very large new appliances in use: these might require larger bay areas and door widths

③ Dimensions of parking bay → ②

appliances	gross vehicle weight (kg)	wheelbase (mm)	turning circle Ø (mm)	length (mm)	width (mm)	max. height with loaded roof (mm)
fire tender LF 8	5450 (5800)	2600	11700 (S)	5650	2170	2800
fire tender LF 8	7490 (7490)	3200	15050 (F)	6400	2410	2950
fire tender LF 16	11300 (11500)	3750	16100 (F)	8000 with powered hose reel	2470	3090
fire tender LF 16-TS	10200 (11000)	3750	16100 (F)	7600	2470	3100
water tender + tank TLF 8/18	7490 (7490)	3200	14800 (F)	6250	2410	2850
water tender + tank TLF 16/25	10700 (11500)	3200	14400 (F)	6450	2470	2990
water tender + tank TLF 24/50	15900 (16000)	3500	15400 (F)	6700	2500	3270
foam tender with tank Tro TLF 16	11500 (12000)	3750	16100 (F)	7000	2470	2990
foam tender 1000	7300 (7490)	3200	14800 (F)	6100	2410	3250
foam tender 2000	10100 (11600)	3200	14400 (F)	6450	2410	3300
turntable ladder DL30	12550 (13000)	4400	18600 (S)	9800 with powered hose reel	2430	3250
turntable ladder LB30/5 with cradle	20200 (21000)	3800 × 1320	19900 (F)	9800	2490	3300
equipment truck RW1	7200 (7490)	3200	14800 (F)	6400	2420	2850
equipment truck RW2	10850 (11000)	3750	16100 (F)	7600	2480	3070
hose truck SW 2000	10200 (11000)	3200	14400 (F)	6500	2500	2980

④ Dimensions of current fire service appliances, from one of the largest German fire-equipment manufacturers (S = street vehicle, F = all-wheel drive)

A typical local fire station can be set out based on the following units (U):

- four bays for the fire tenders (4U)
- an appliance room and storeroom for special equipment (1U)
- a training room and a multipurpose room for
  - administration and control room staff (5U)
  - rest and recreation rooms (3U)
  - and a plant room (1U)

A fire station for both local and area support operations, providing, for example, fire prevention and technical services, central workshop, catering, training and practice facilities, can contain:

- up to 16 fire engine bays (16U)
  (with ambulance service, an additional 4U)
- an appliance room and storeroom for special equipment (4U)
- a training room (7U)
- rest and recreation rooms, including washroom, shower, WC, changing room and drying room (4U)
- rooms such as a duty room, restroom and small kitchen (3U)
- administration room and room for the station commander (1U)
- vehicle and equipment workshop and plant room (2U)
- an operations control room (4U)
- and a central workshop (as required).

Where no central hose servicing workshop is available, a hose servicing workshop (9U) should be included and, likewise, a workshop for servicing breathing apparatus (4U) will be needed if there is no centralised service. Where central workshops are available, additional suitable storage rooms are to be included.

Areas of the rooms → ③

The size of a fire station can be estimated using units (U) based on the largest parking bay (55m² or above). This gives an indication of the minimum sizes of the component rooms.

Appliance room	1U
Storage room for special equipment	1U
Training room	4U
ancillary space requirement	1U

Rest and recreation rooms:

washroom, shower, WC, changing and drying rooms	3U
watch room, restroom and mess room	3U
Administration	1U
station commander's room	1U
Control room	1U

Workshops:

hose service workshop, hose wash and test room (at least 26m long and 3m wide)	8U
hose store	1U
hose drying tower with practice wall [a] clear height inside tower, minimum 23m	1U

If a horizontal hose drying installation is provided in place of a hose drying tower, it must be housed in the hose wash and test room. The minimum area of this room must then be 9U and its clear height at least 3m.

Breathing apparatus workshop	4U

Service, repair, storage including that for radioactive protection gear and diving gear [b]

Room for breathing apparatus servicing	4U
Vehicle and appliance workshop, including battery charging point, linked to an existing parking bay	2U
Vehicle wash bay	4U

Services:

heating and fuel storage rooms	1U

[a] according to local fire regulations
[b] not for breathing apparatus training

FIRE STATIONS

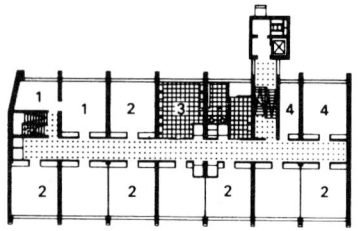

1 watch room
2 bedroom
3 washroom
4 station commander

① **First floor**

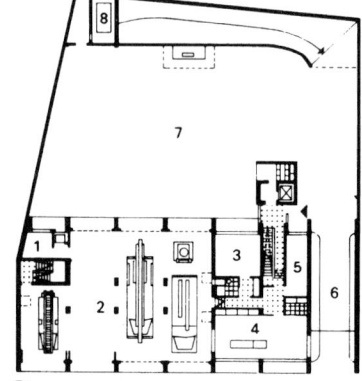

1 battery charging room
2 fire-appliance hall
3 bedroom
4 control centre
5 apparatus room
6 passage
7 yard
8 oil store

② **Ground floor**

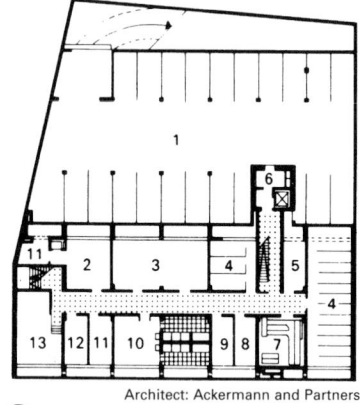

1 underground garage
2 day stores
3 hose room
4 cellar
5 ventilation
6 sluice
7 main control room
8 emergency power supply
9 pump room
10 changing room
11 store
12 gas and water supply
13 generator and central
heating room

Architect: Ackermann and Partners

③ **Basement at Fire Station No. 4, Munich**

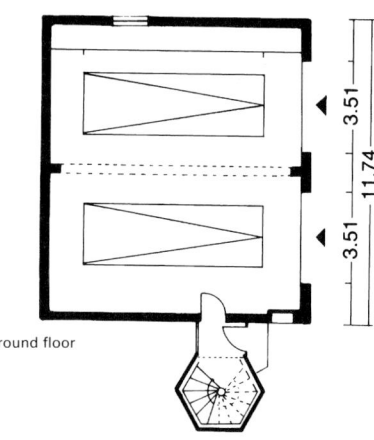

ground floor

④ **Fire station for two appliances**

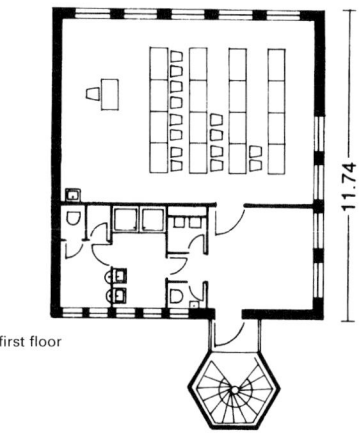

first floor

⑤ → ④ **Design by the Structural Engineering Dept., Cologne City Council**

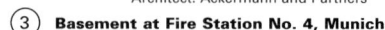

⑦ **First floor → ⑥**   ⑧ **Second floor → ⑥**

⑨ **Section → ⑥**

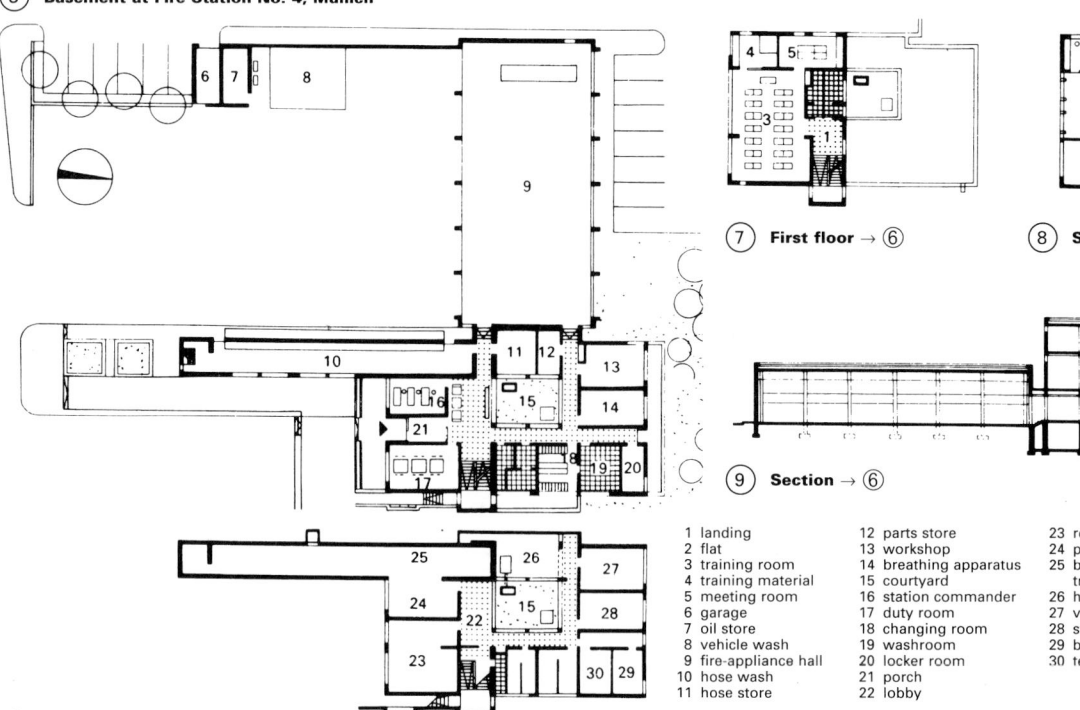

⑥ **Basement and ground floors, fire station**

1 landing	12 parts store	23 recreation room
2 flat	13 workshop	24 practice room
3 training room	14 breathing apparatus	25 breathing apparatus
4 training material	15 courtyard	training room
5 meeting room	16 station commander	26 heating plant
6 garage	17 duty room	27 ventilation plant
7 oil store	18 changing room	28 store
8 vehicle wash	19 washroom	29 battery room
9 fire-appliance hall	20 locker room	30 telephone/radio room
10 hose wash	21 porch	
11 hose store	22 lobby	

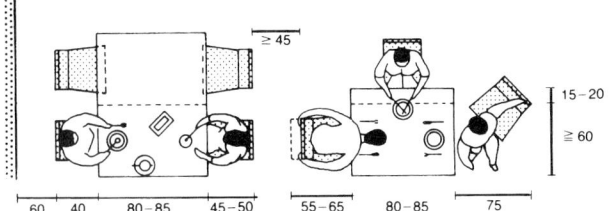

RESTAURANTS: SPACE REQUIREMENTS

(See also pp. 255–6)

To be able to eat comfortably, one person requires a table area of around 60cm wide by 40cm deep. This provides sufficient clearance between adjacent diners. Although an additional 20cm of space in the centre for dishes and tureens is sometimes desirable, an overall width of 80–85cm is suitable for a dining table. Round tables, or tables with six or eight sides, with a diameter of 90–120cm are ideal for four people and can also take one or two more diners.

The minimum spaces for thoroughfares, or between a table and a wall are shown in ①. Note that round tables require somewhat more floor area.

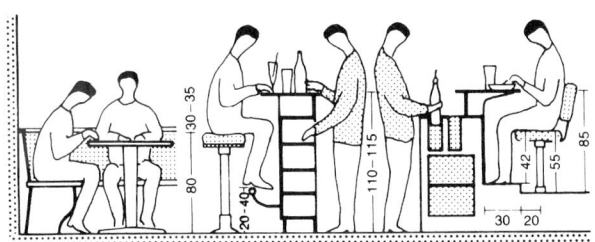

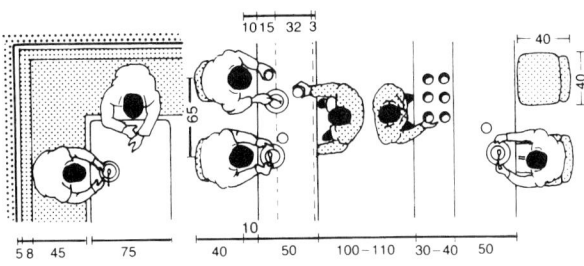

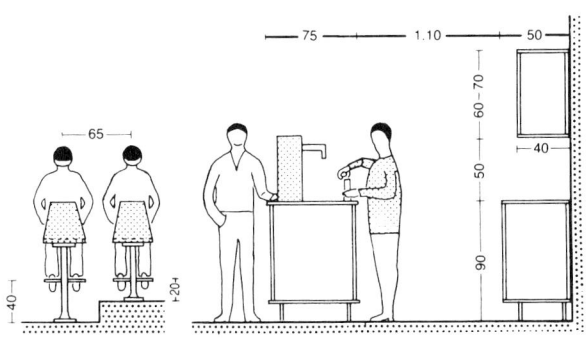

② **Breakfast setting** 1: tea or coffee pot; 2: milk jug; 3: jam or butter dish; 4: sugar basin; 5: fork; 6: knife; 7: teaspoon; 8: plate; 9: serviette; 10: saucer; 11: tea or coffee cup

③ **Simple lunch setting** 1: dinner fork; 2: dinner knife; 3: soup spoon; 4: dessert spoon; 5: tumbler; 6: wine glass; 7: soup dish; 8: dinner plate; 9: serviette

④ **Banquet setting** 1: entrée fork; 2: fish fork; 3: dinner fork; 4: soup spoon; 5: dessert spoon; 6: dinner knife; 7: fish knife; 8: entrée knife; 9: soup dish; 10: dinner plate; 11: serviette; 12: tumbler; 13: wine glass; 14: liqueurglass

② **Breakfast**   ③ **Luncheon**   ④ **Banquet**

① **Space requirements for server and diner**

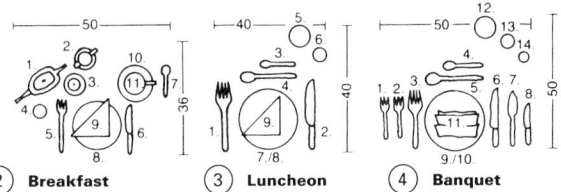

⑤ **Tables/seating plans**

RESTAURANTS: ARRANGEMENTS

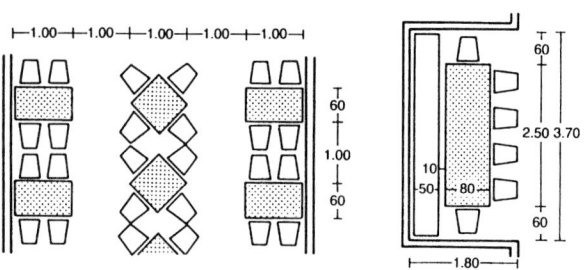

① **Minimal seating layout**

② **Alcoves arrangement**

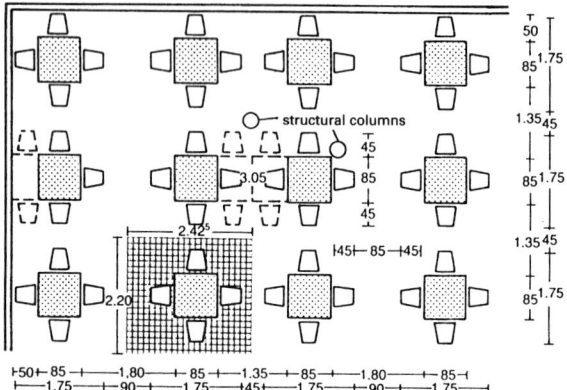

③ **Parallel table arrangement**

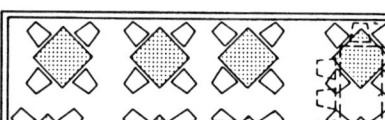

④ **Diagonal table arrangement**

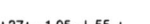

⑤ **Minimal table spacing**

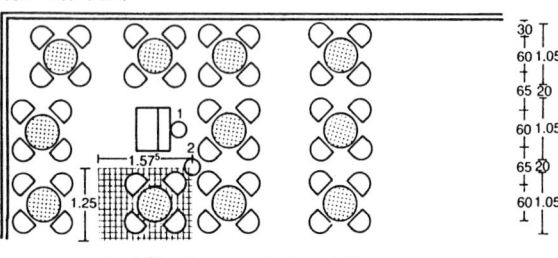

⑥ **Café table arrangement**

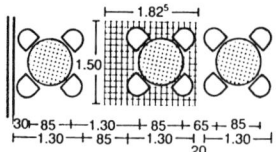

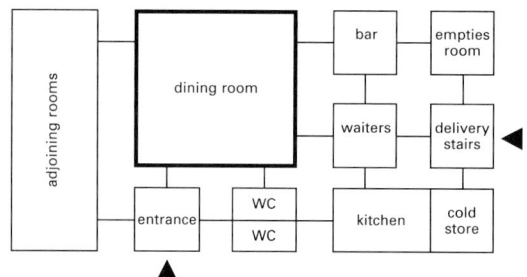

⑦ **Functional layout for a small restaurant**

Before any restaurant or inn is built, the organisational sequence should be carefully planned. It is essential to establish what meals will be offered, and at what quality and quantity. It is necessary to decide whether it will be à-la-carte with fixed or changing daily menus, plate or table service, self-service or a mixed system. Before deciding on the layout, it is important to know the anticipated numbers and type of clientele and the customer mix. Bring in planning specialists in kitchen and cold store design, as well as in electrical, heating and ventilation systems and washing/toilet facilities.

The position of the site will suggest what type of inn or restaurant is likely to be suitable.

The main room of a restaurant is the customers' dining room, and the facilities should correspond with the type of operation. A number of additional tables and chairs should be available for flexible table groupings. If appropriate, provide special tables for regular customers.

Any function or conference rooms should have movable furniture to allow flexibility of use. A food bar may be installed for customers who are in a hurry. Large dining rooms can be divided into zones. The kitchen, storerooms, delivery points, toilets and other service areas should be grouped around the dining room, although toilets can be on another floor → ⑦.

Structural columns in a dining room are best in the middle of a group of tables or at the corner of a table → ③. The ceiling height of a dining room should relate to the floor area: $\leq 50\,\text{m}^2$, 2.50 m; $>50\,\text{m}^2$, 2.75 m; $>100\,\text{m}^2$, $\geq 3.00\,\text{m}$; above or below galleries, $\geq 2.50\,\text{m}$.

Guidelines for toilet requirements in inns or restaurants are shown in → ⑨.

dining floor area	walkway width
up to 100 m²	≥ 1.10 m
up to 250 m²	≥ 1.30 m
up to 500 m²	≥ 1.65 m
up to 1000 m²	≥ 1.80 m
over 1000 m²	≥ 2.10 m

⑧ **Walkway widths**

customer places	toilets men	women	urinal bowls	urinals (m)
50	1	1	2	2
50–200	2	2	3	3
200–400	3	4	6	4
400	– determine in individual case -			

⑨ **Toilet facilities**

The minimum width of escape routes is 1.0 m per 150 people. General walkways should be at least 1.10 m → ⑧, with clearance heights $\geq 2.10\,\text{m}$. The window area should be $\geq 1/10$ of the room area of the restaurant.

type	chair occupancy per meal	kitchen area required (m²/cover)	dining area required (m²/seat)
exclusive restaurant	1	0.7	1.8–2.0
restaurant with high seat turnover	2–3	0.5–0.6	1.4–1.6
normal restaurant	1.5	0.4–0.5	1.6–1.8
inn/ guesthouse	1	0.3–0.4	1.6–1.8
approx. 80% supplement is added for storage rooms, personnel rooms etc. cover = seat × no. of seat changeovers			

⑩ **Floor area requirements**

tables	seats	waiter service (m²/seat)	self-service (m²/seat)
square	4	1.25	1.25
rectangular	4	1.10	1.20
rectangular	6	1.05	1.10
rectangular	8	1.05	1.05

⑪ **Total space requirements for dining rooms:** 1.4–1.6 m²/place

main aisles	min 2.00 m wide
intermediate aisles	min 0.90 m wide
side aisles	min 1.20 m wide

⑫ **Aisle widths**

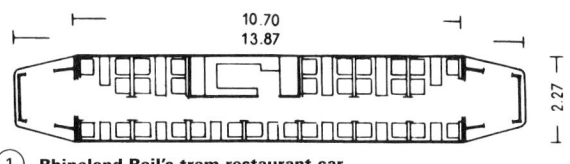

① Rhineland Rail's tram restaurant car

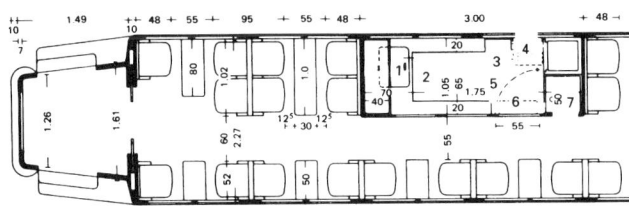

1: stores; 2: sink, warm water; 3: cold water sink; 4: folding seat; 5: kitchen
6: folding table; 7: crockery

② Details of ①

RESTAURANT CARS

The space needed for dining services in long-distance trams → ① + ② is small compared with train dining cars, and this is the result of many years' experience and numerous design changes.

The kitchen arrangements use most of the available space because of the need for wide doors and service hatches, and exceptionally large refrigeration units → ⑧.

All dishes have to be washed up in the kitchen between two meal services (main and snack lunch). Service in the dining car is made easier because the number of customers is limited to the number of places → ③ + ④.

RESTAURANTS

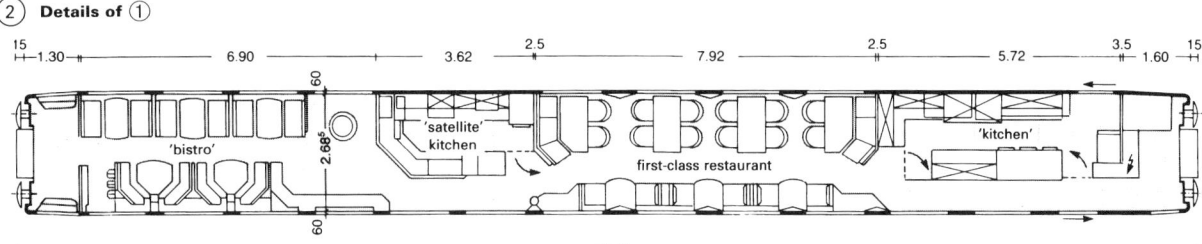

③ Floor plan of the Deutsche Bundesbahn 'Quick-Pick' restaurant car

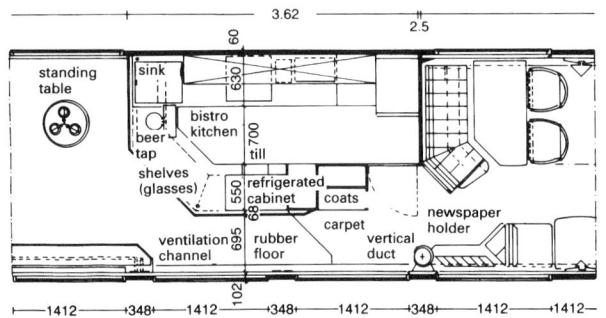

④ Floor plan of 'satellite kitchen' → ③

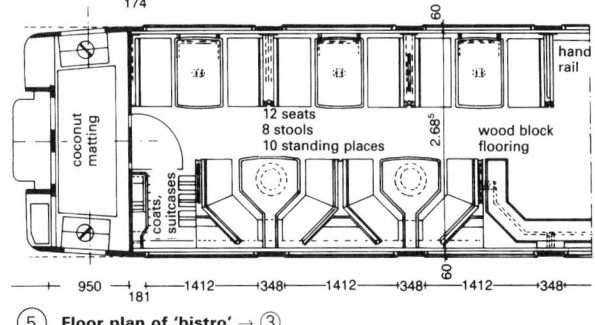

⑤ Floor plan of 'bistro' → ③

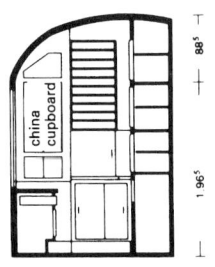

⑥ Cross-section of preparation area

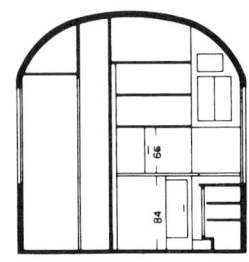

⑦ Cross-section of kitchen

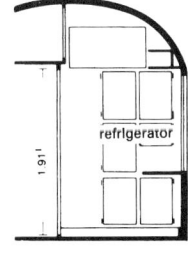

⑧ Cross-section of refrigerator area

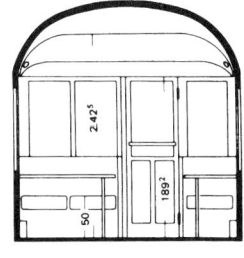

⑨ Cross-section of restaurant car

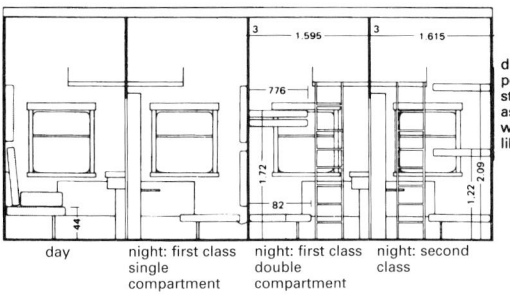

dimensions only possible with constant ventilation (e.g. as for dormitories with bunks and the like)

day   night: first class single compartment   night: first class double compartment   night: second class

⑩ Longitudinal section

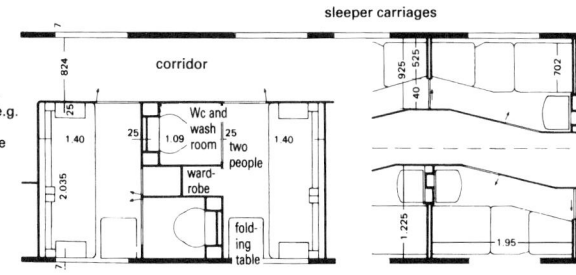

⑪ Double compartment

⑫ Compartment with berths along the train axis

457

RESTAURANT TYPES

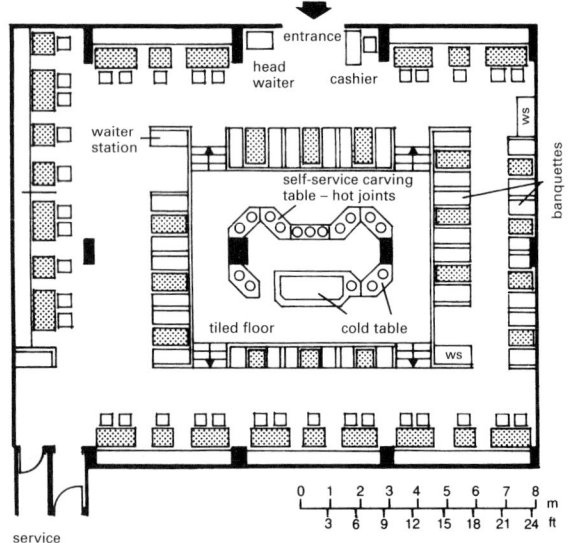

entrance

banquettes

service

head waiter's desk

food display with
refrigerated section

ws   ws

banquettes

waiter
stations

ws

decorative screen

ws

0 1 2 3 4 m
3 6 9 12 ft

① **Traditional restaurant: 110 seats**

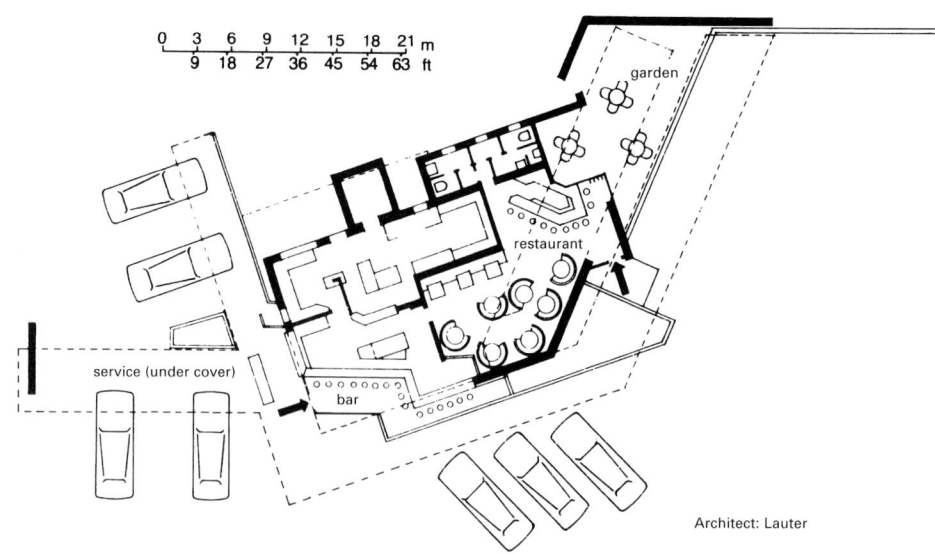

entrance

head
waiter   cashier

ws

waiter
station

banquettes

self-service carving
table – hot joints

tiled floor   cold table

ws

ws

0 1 2 3 4 5 6 7 8 m
3 6 9 12 15 18 21 24 ft

service

② **Restaurant seating 124, with self-service carving table**

Traditional restaurants → ① should ideally have space for a display table and flambé work. The tables should be arranged with generous spacing and seating.

In speciality restaurants the space requirements vary widely. Display cooking, a grill, a dance floor and special decorative effects may be required. A separate bar might also need to be included within the restaurant.

Ethnic restaurants are generally considered to specialise in non-European food, particularly Asian and Oriental. Depending on the market, traditional foods and methods of preparation may be modified to suit Western tastes. Character is often expressed in the design of the premises and rituals of food presentation and service.

Drive-in restaurants → ③ supply food and drinks direct to customers in their cars, allowing visitors to eat without leaving their vehicles if they so choose. One waiter can serve six cars. For access and service provide canopies and covered ways. There should also be a separate dining hall, with parking space close to the drive-in service.

Every public house has a different pattern of trade depending on location, catering facilities and time of year. Drinking is often concentrated at certain times, which are usually after 20.00 and particularly on Fridays and at weekends. Depending on its origin, a pub may emphasise its historical rustic character or the Victorian–Edwardian sophistication of later town houses. Pub designs often follow themes to recreate foreign characteristics (e.g. Irish pubs and Belgian or American bars).

0 3 6 9 12 15 18 21 m
9 18 27 36 45 54 63 ft

garden

restaurant

service (under cover)

bar

Architect: Lauter

③ **Drive-in restaurant, California**

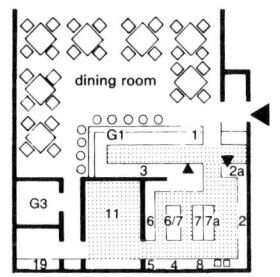

1	meals and drinks servery
2	dishwasher
2a	crockery returns
3	drinks bar with mixer, toaster, food containers etc.
4	oven for small pastry items
5	food storage
6	rotisserie
6/7	cooker rings
7a	water boiler and steam machine
8	pot and pan washer
11	stores/office; catering size refrigerators and freezers instead of cold store
19	staff toilets
G1	bar counter
G3	customer toilets

① **Snack-bar**

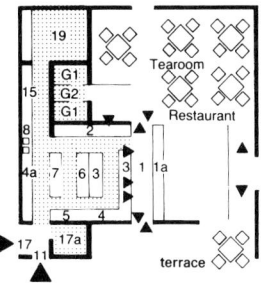

1	waiters' walkway
1a	service counter and cash tills
2	dishwasher
3	drinks bar with mixer, toaster, ice cream freezer etc.
4	pastry preparation
4a	pastry oven
5	sandwich preparation
6	reheating equipment (e.g. soup)
7	cooker rings
8	pot and pan washer
11	empties
15	linen store
17	deliveries and (a) store
19	staff toilets and cloakroom
G1	toilets
G2	telephone cubicle

② **Café restaurant**

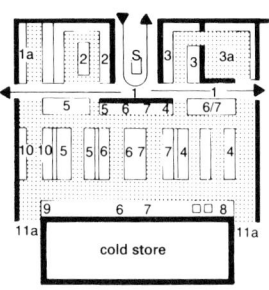

1	waiters' walkway
1a	garden service counter
2	dish-washing area
3	drinks counter
3a	drinks cellar
4	pastry counter
5	cold dishes
6	hot dishes and sauces
6/7	table with hot store
8	pot and pan washer
9	vegetable preparation
10	meat preparation
11a	deliveries, and access to stores, offices, staff cloakrooms and toilets
S	service accessories and tills

③ **Restaurant kitchen in large hotel**

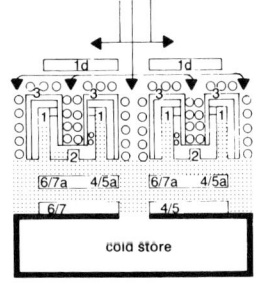

1	serving aisles in U-shaped counters
1d	vending machines
2	link between two counters with covered dishwashers, operated from both sides, each with two rinsing basins
4/5	cold meal preparation
4/5a	cold servery (salads, ices, desserts
6/7	griddle, soup heater, water boiler etc
6/7a	hot servery (bain-marie, hotplates)

④ **Restaurant with buffet and vending machines**

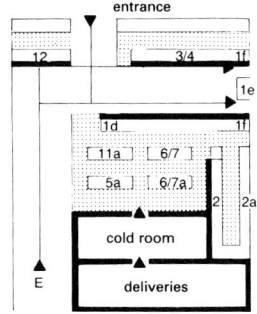

1d	self-service buffet with grill and chip fryer
1e	sauces, condiments, cutlery
1f	cash till
2	dishwasher
2a	crockery returns
3/4	food and drinks servery (service to street possible)
5a	cold meal preparation table
6/7	heating units, used from both sides
6/7a	hot meal preparation table
11a	refrigerators, used from both sides
12	sales kiosk (serving inside and to street)
E	entrance

⑤ **Self-service restaurant**

RESTAURANTS AND RESTAURANT KITCHENS

Snack-bar layouts → ① can be suitable for up to 60 seats in eating houses with fast turn-around times (five or six seating changes at lunchtime; two in the evenings). In between meal times, coffee, cakes and sandwiches can be served. The kitchen mainly makes use of ready-made items, and daily deliveries mean that stores do not need to be particularly large.

A café restaurant → ② with a tea room is usually a town-centre business located in a busy area. A café does not serve alcoholic drinks except for premium bottled beers, liqueurs etc., and specialises in hot and cold patisserie and snacks. Tea rooms serve alcohol-free drinks, patisserie and sandwiches, and have capacity for about 150 seats. They normally open from 11.00 to 17.30 p.m. They serve mainly pre-made meals, and therefore need little storage space.

A restaurant kitchen in a large hotel → ③ caters for one or more large restaurants with adjoining rooms, and sometimes supplies external locations or businesses. May have to feed 800–1000 people. The waiters' walkway may be in the centre, with special serving counters in the garden, or possibly of the bowling alley type with direct access to adjoining rooms. The kitchen is arranged in a cellular system, with large appliance blocks.

A restaurant with a buffet and vending machines → ④ provides a fast luncheon service for working people in restaurants, canteens, department stores and motorway service stations. Their capacity is about 500 people per hour. The kitchen only completes ready-prepared meals, except for salads and ice cream.

Self-service restaurants → ⑤ are suitable for department stores or in office blocks. Nothing is made on the premises. All supplies are ready-made and deep frozen.

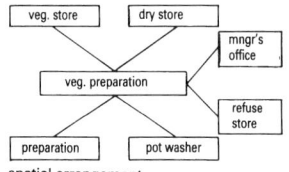

spatial arrangement

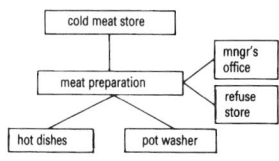

spatial arrangement

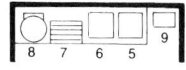

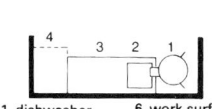

1	dishwasher
2	peelings catcher
3	cleaning table
4	storage surface
5	rinser
6	work surface/ cupboard below
7	cutting board (800 × 400 mm)
8	universal machine
9	hand basin

⑥ **Vegetable preparation**

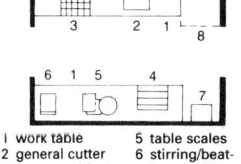

1	work table
2	general cutter
3	freezer cabinet
4	cutting board (800 × 400 mm)
5	table scales
6	stirring/beating machine
7	hand basin
8	storage surface

⑦ **Meat preparation**

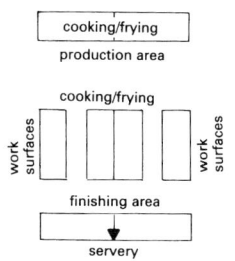

⑧ **French system for hotel kitchens; cooking area at right angles to the servery; split production/finishing**

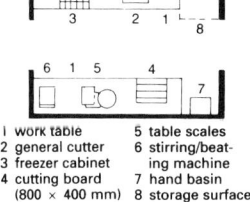

1 combined work area: adjacent production and finishing

cooking/frying

production

finishing

servery

2 split work area: production and finishing separated

cooking/frying

production

finishing

servery

⑨ **American system for hotel kitchens; cooking area in parallel with the servery**

RESTAURANT KITCHENS

The trend away from conventional restaurants to those offering a wide range of gastronomy not only affects the planning of dining rooms but also of kitchens. Small and medium-sized restaurant kitchens play a very important role here, and the following details are primarily aimed at such restaurants.

In the 'Gastronorm' system, the dimensions of containers, tables, shelves, equipment and crockery, as well as built-in units, are all based on a 530 mm × 325 mm module.

The function and organisation of the restaurant kitchen is summarised in ① + ②. The capacity of the kitchen is primarily dependent on the number of customer seats, customer expectations (type, extent and quality of the meals offered), and the proportion of raw materials which have to be freshly prepared (as opposed to ready-prepared food), as well as the frequency of customer changes over the whole day or at busy periods (consumer frequency).

In fast restaurants about three seat changes per hour can be expected; in conventional restaurants only about two. In speciality and evening restaurants customers stay on average 1.3–2 hours.

The percentage of the whole floor area required for each section → ④, and the detailed requirements for special purposes → ③, can be calculated in relation to small, medium and large kitchens.

Aisle widths in storage, preparation and production areas are different according to whether they are purely traffic routes, or if they also lead to service areas. Working aisle widths should be 0.90–1.20 m, local traffic routes with (occasional) additional usage 1.50–1.80 m and main traffic routes (transport and two-way through traffic) 2.10–3.30 m. Aisle widths of 1.00–1.50 m should be sufficient for small to medium-sized restaurant kitchen areas.

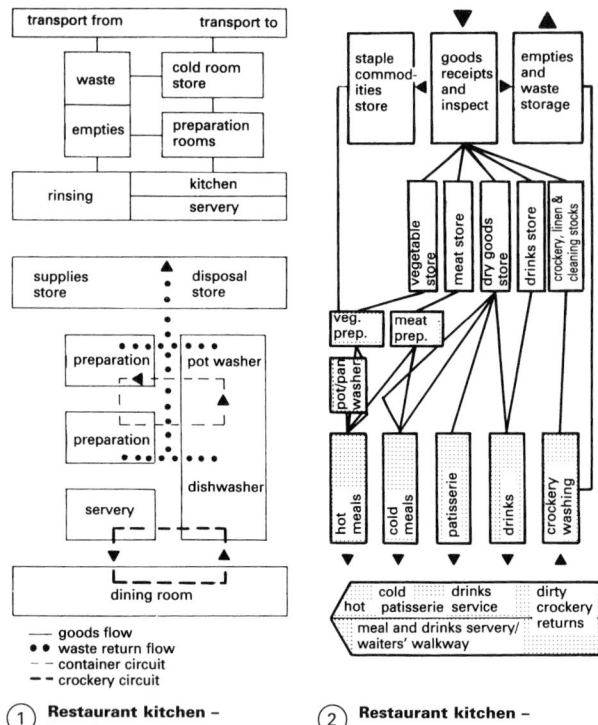

① Restaurant kitchen – function

— goods flow
• • waste return flow
- - container circuit
- - crockery circuit

② Restaurant kitchen – organisation

Bistros, snack-bars, small cafés, or speciality restaurants with 40–60 seats are classified as small operations. Small to medium units with 70–100 seats, on the other hand, require carefully zoned and fully fitted kitchen systems. Large restaurants (motorway service stations, fast restaurants, large hotel operations) often achieve considerably higher place numbers, frequently with integrated meal bar or self-service areas.

restaurant size/seats	small (up to 100)	medium (up to 250)	large (> 250)
goods receipts	0.06–0.08	0.05–0.07	0.04–0.06
empties	0.05–0.07	0.05–0.07	0.04–0.06
waste/refuse	0.04–0.06	0.04–0.06	0.03–0.05
office – stores manager	–	–	0.02–0.03
supplies/waste disposal	0.15–0.21	0.14–0.20	0.13–0.20
pre-cooling room	cupboards/	0.03–0.04	0.02–0.04
cold meat store	storage	0.05–0.06	0.03–0.05
dairy products store	surfaces	0.03–0.04	0.02–0.03
cold vegetable/fruit store	–	–	0.03–0.05
deep-freeze room	cupboards/	0.04–0.05	0.03–0.04
other cold stores	storage		
(patisserie/cold meals)	surfaces	0.03–0.04	0.02–0.03
chilled goods storage	0.04–0.31	0.21–0.26	0.16–0.21
dry goods/food store	0.13–0.15	0.12–0.14	0.10–0.12
vegetable store	0.08–0.10	0.06–0.08	0.04–0.06
daily supplies	0.04–0.06	0.03–0.04	0.02–0.03
ambient storage	0.25–0.31	0.21–0.26	0.16–0.21
vegetable preparation	0.08–0.10	0.05–0.08	0.04–0.06
meat preparation	0.06–0.09	0.04–0.07	0.03–0.05
hot meals	0.26–0.33	0.19–0.24	0.15–0.21
cold meals	0.13–0.15	0.09–0.12	0.07–0.11
patisserie	–	0.07–0.10	0.06–0.09
container washing	0.05–0.08	0.04–0.06	0.03–0.05
office – kitchen manager	0.03–0.05	0.02–0.03	0.02–0.03
kitchen area	0.60–0.80	0.50–0.70	0.40–0.60
dishwasher	0.10–0.12	0.09–0.11	0.08–0.10
servery/waiters' equipment	0.06–0.08	0.08–0.10	0.10–0.15
staff washing facilities and WC	0.40–0.50	0.30–0.40	0.28–0.30
= in total	1.60–2.10	1.50–2.00	1.30–1.80

③ Kitchen areas – space requirement (m²/seat)

area	proportion in %
goods deliveries, including inspection and waste storage	10
storage in deep freeze, cold and dry rooms	20
daily store	
vegetable and salad preparation kitchen	2
cold meals, desserts	8
cake shop	8
meat preparation	2
cooking area	8
washing area	10
walkways	17
staff rooms and office	15
	100

④ Basis for dimensions and space requirements

empties	lift	deliveries	waste	staff changing room
dry goods store	cold room	vege-tables	office	washroom / toilets
daily store	meat prep.	veg prep.	potato prep.	restroom
pot washer	hot dishes	cold dishes		cake shop
dishwasher	servery, waiter's walkway			coffee room
buffet		bar servery		

⑤ Kitchen areas – classification relationships

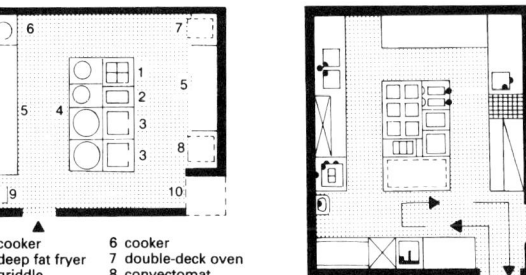

1 cooker
2 deep fat fryer
3 griddle
4 water boiler
5 work surface
6 cooker
7 double-deck oven
8 convectomat
9 hand basin
10 storage area

(1) **Basic organisation of kitchen → ② – ③**

1. production in block

(2) **Kitchen for restaurant with 60–100 seats**

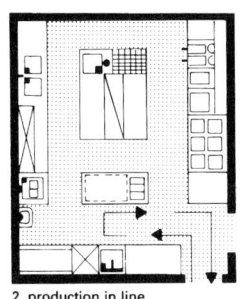

2. production in line

(3) **Kitchen for restaurant with 60–100 seats**

cooking: cooker, boiler (80 l), work surface, eight-ring hob, two ovens, bain-marie, hot cupboard
frying: griddle, work surface, twin deep fat fryer, frying pan, hot-air oven with table

(4) **Restaurant kitchen for 150–200 meals**

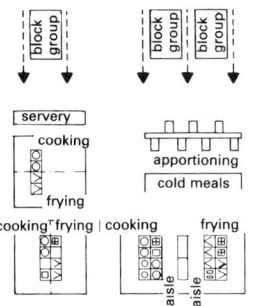

(5) **Function and organisation of kitchen**

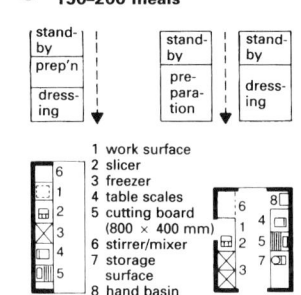

1 work surface
2 slicer
3 freezer
4 table scales
5 cutting board (800 × 400 mm)
6 stirrer/mixer
7 storage surface
8 hand basin

(6) **Organisation of cold meal kitchen**

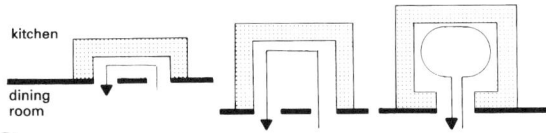

(7) **Servery, waiter's walkway**

(8) **Self-service restaurant**

(9) **Self-service restaurant**

(10) **Free-flow restaurant**

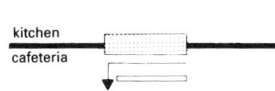

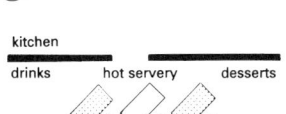

bar-counter servery (section system)

(11) **Self-service restaurant**

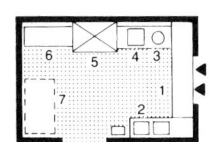

1: returns, sorting table; 2: sink; 3: waste clearance; 4: pre-wash; 5: dishwasher; 6: discharge table; 7: crockery area

(12) **Basic solution – dishwashing area**

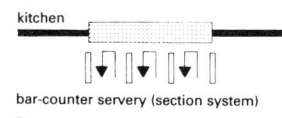

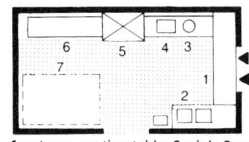

1: returns, sorting table; 2: sink; 3: wa clearance; 4: pre-wash; 5: dishwasher 6: discharge table; 7: crockery area

(13) **Basic solution – dishwashing area**

RESTAURANT KITCHENS

'Hot kitchens' contain finishing zones and some or all of the following equipment depending on their main function: cooker (two to eight rings), extractor hood, water boiler, automatic cooker, steamer, automatic steamer, pressurised steamer, convection ovens, water bath (bain-marie), baking and roasting oven, frying and grilling plates, frying pans, double-decker roasting oven, deep fryer, salamander, air circulation equipment (for deep-frozen goods), microwave oven and automatic through-flow frying and baking oven. Large automatic units are only found in very large kitchens. The main units should be arranged in a block in kitchens serving more than 100–200 meals or with more than 30 m² of space available. In even larger kitchens, over 50 m², finishing groups can be arranged as double blocks. Storage space and working surfaces should be conveniently placed between the units at the end of blocks → ① – ⑤.

In the 'cold kitchen', the layout should be logically planned in parallel with the hot kitchen and convenient for the (common) servery and bread area. The main fittings for a cold kitchen are a day refrigerator under/over the cold table, diverse cutting machines (bread, meats and cheese), mixing machine, scales, cutting boards, salad table with a lower cold cabinet, toaster or salamander, microwave, and sufficient working and storage surfaces → ⑥.

The meal servery for a restaurant kitchen with a counter or bar serving point is best located between the preparation area and the dining room. There should be an adequate storage surface, a hot cabinet with heated table plates, and a cool zone for cold meals. A crockery shelf or attachment, a cutlery container, and basket and plate dispensers are also necessary for large restaurants.

It is important to separate pot washers and dishwashers. With waiter service, crockery is returned via the servery in the waiter's own area → ⑫ – ⑮. There should be one or two rinsing sinks with draining surfaces, storage surfaces and shelves for pot washers. All other items should go into automatic dishwashers of suitable capacities fitted below the work surfaces. Rules should be laid down for loading and operating the dishwashers. Through-flow and circulation units are also necessary. Provide side storage and working surfaces for returns, and sorting, soaking and locating surfaces for crockery → ⑫ – ⑭.

About 10–15% of the kitchen area should be reserved for offices and staff rooms. Kitchen staff must be provided with changing rooms, a washroom and toilets. If more than ten staff are employed, rest and break rooms are required. Changing and social rooms should be close to the kitchen to avoid the staff having to cross unheated rooms or corridors (there is an increased risk of draughts in hot workplaces). More than 6 m² should be provided for the changing room, with four to six air changes per hour as well as visual screening. Provide a well-ventilated, lockable cupboard for each worker. In large kitchens there may be cupboards for street and working clothes. The minimum requirements of local workplace regulations should be used for the dimensions and fittings of the washing and toilet areas. Other guideline values for toilet systems are 5–6 m² per WC seat and wash basin unit, and about 5.5 m² per wash basin and shower unit, for five or more male or female workers.

Large kitchens must be equipped with a mechanical ventilation system according to current guidelines. Waste air must be extracted at each cooking point, with extraction pipes to the outside via a ducting system. Fresh air must be drawn in, i.e. recirculated air is not permitted.

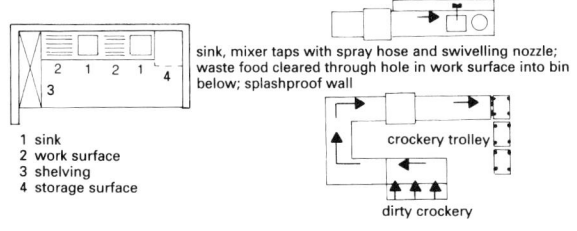

sink, mixer taps with spray hose and swivelling nozzle; waste food cleared through hole in work surface into bin below; splashproof wall

1 sink
2 work surface
3 shelving
4 storage surface

crockery trolley

dirty crockery

(14) **Basic solution – pot washing**

(15) **Functions and elements of the washing area**

461

Group-catering for large numbers of people in office blocks, hospitals, factories, etc., requires labour-saving mechanisation, electronic data processing (DP) and automatic units, i.e. the 'programmed kitchen' from the meals plan, through goods procurement to meal distribution and crockery cleaning → ② for more than 800–1000 table places and different dishes. Preparation tables and the meal servery are heated by steam or electricity. The surface temperature of table plates should be 60°C.

The advantage of such a system is that data about calorie content, nutritional value, vitamins and minerals, etc., are saved and are immediately available, and stores levels and order requirements are automatically updated. The preparation machinery is in continuous use, and the work sequence is controlled on a time basis. This covers the transport → ⑤ of unit containers → ③, an automatic through-flow roaster → ⑥ and cooker → ⑦, modern cooking processes for potatoes and vegetables, quick frying methods using little fat, fish cooked in a water bath, and thermal grilling. The automatic equipment is arranged in a flow system from loading to distribution → ④. Heating is by electricity or gas.

These serving systems are for pure catering operations such as hospitals, residential homes, canteens and cafeterias → ④,⑧,⑨.

Fully automatic crockery cleaning is also installed, using sorting and clearing equipment, and automatic removal of cutlery, dishes and cups. The cleaning and drying system should be suitable for the type of crockery, and automatic clearance of tray trolleys. Return transport of used crockery is via a transport conveyor to the washing kitch → ⑨.

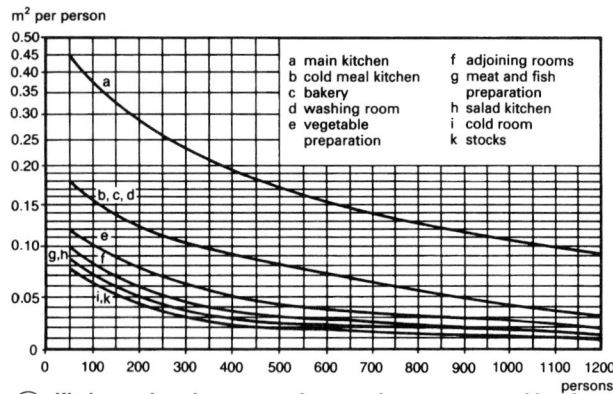

① Kitchen and work space requirements in restaurants and hotels (a–k = m² per person in single room group)

a main kitchen	f adjoining rooms
b cold meal kitchen	g meat and fish
c bakery	preparation
d washing room	h salad kitchen
e vegetable	i cold room
preparation	k stocks

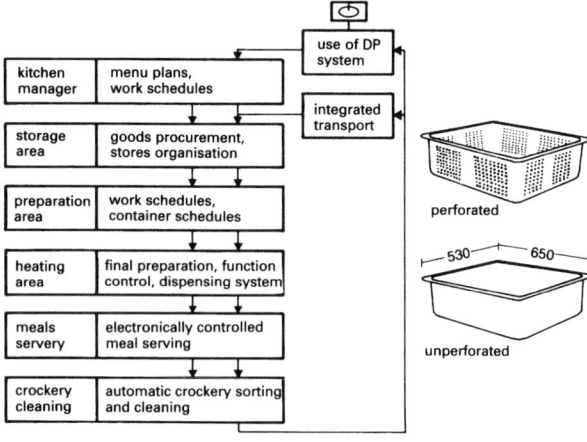

② Programmed kitchen function diagram

③ Serving trays

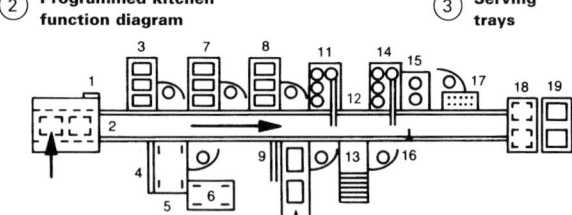

1 automatic crockery dispenser and tray unloader; dispensing from heated cabinet below; punched card reading device
2 meal distribution conveyor
3 electronically controlled serving trolley for potatoes
4 illuminated display for desserts and salads
5 rack trolley for desserts
6 rack trolley for salads
7 electronically controlled serving trolley for vegetables
8 electronically controlled serving trolley for meat
9 illuminated display for special diets
10 supplementary conveyor for special diets
11 automatic sauce dispenser
12 cutlery dispenser
13 soup plate dispenser
14 automatic soup dispenser
15 dispenser for heat-retaining container lids
16 automatic closing device for soup plate covers
17 control desk for diet assistant
18 automatic tray stacker
19 tray distribution trolley

④ Meal distribution system

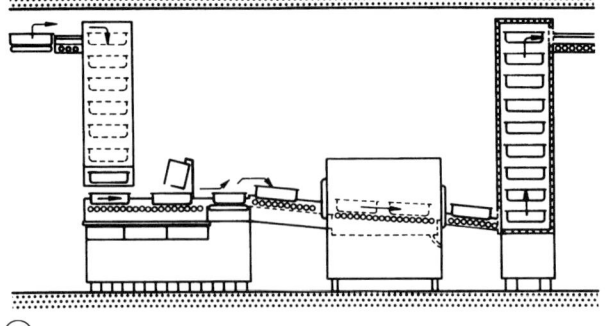

⑤ Container movement in the Contiport system

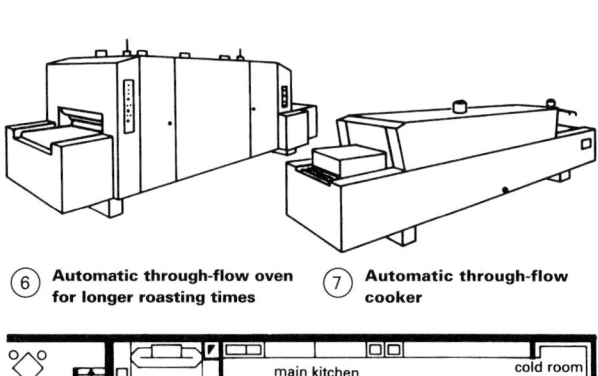

⑥ Automatic through-flow oven for longer roasting times

⑦ Automatic through-flow cooker

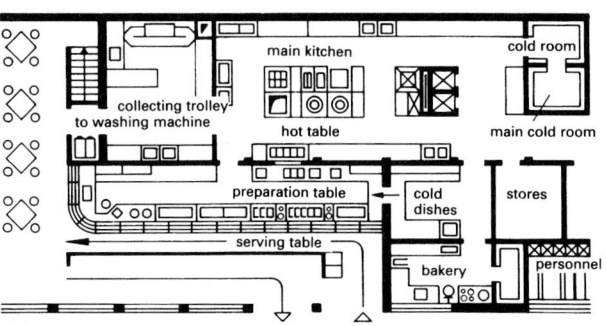

⑧ Cafeteria serving cold and hot meals → ⑨

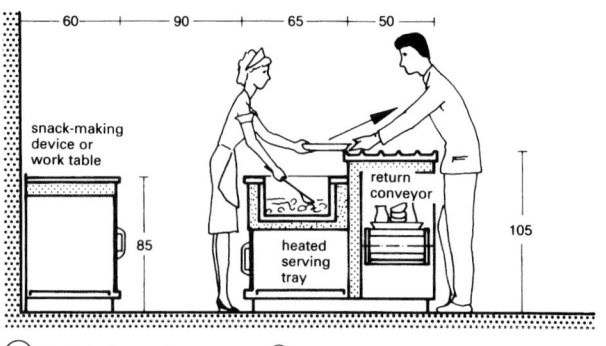

⑨ Cafeteria: meal servery → ⑧

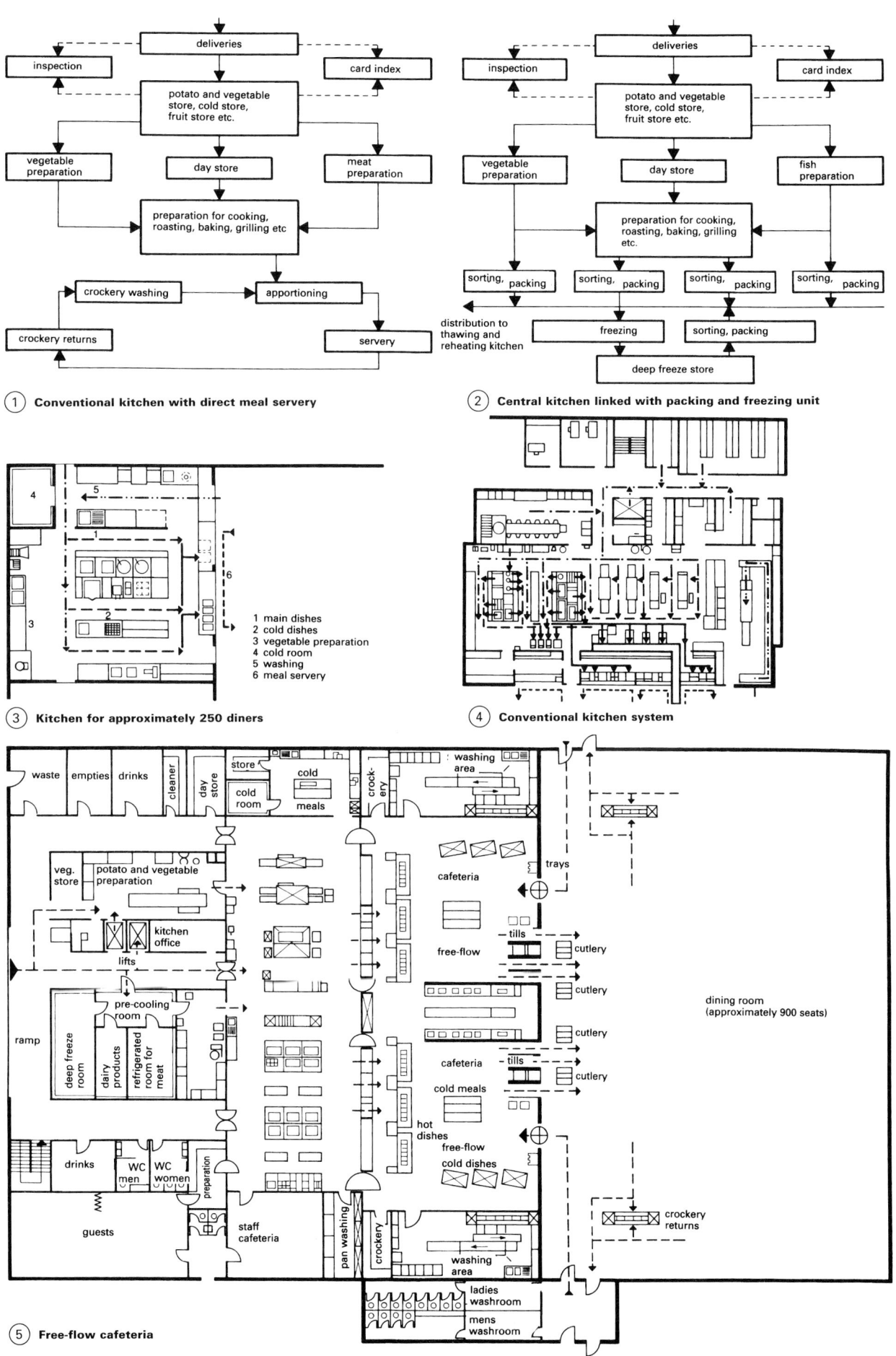

① **Conventional kitchen with direct meal servery**

② **Central kitchen linked with packing and freezing unit**

③ **Kitchen for approximately 250 diners**

1 main dishes
2 cold dishes
3 vegetable preparation
4 cold room
5 washing
6 meal servery

④ **Conventional kitchen system**

⑤ **Free-flow cafeteria**

Layout and area requirements

Different types of hotel offer varying standards of quality and facilities. Hotels may be part of a chain or independent. Where hotels do form part of a chain, special design requirements may be imposed. Hotel types include town hotels, holiday hotels, clubs, hotels with apartments and motels.

Accommodation facilities, including rooms, toilets, bathrooms, shower rooms, etc., hallways and floor service, should occupy 50–60% of the floor area. Public guest rooms, a reception area, hall and lounges require 4–7%, and hospitality areas, restaurants, and bars for guests and visitors 4–8%. A banqueting area with meeting and conference rooms needs 4–12%, domestic areas, kitchens, personnel rooms and stores

9–14%, administration, management and secretarial 1–2%, maintenance and repair 4–7%, and leisure, sport, shops and a hairdressing salon 2–10%.

Special areas for seminars, health centres and outdoor facilities, for which the space required can vary tremendously, may also be needed.

National systems of classification, compulsory or voluntary, vary in range of categories and method of designation (letters, figures, stars, crowns etc.). Over 100 classification systems are in use, most based on the World Tourism Organisation (WTO) model but customised to suit local conditions.

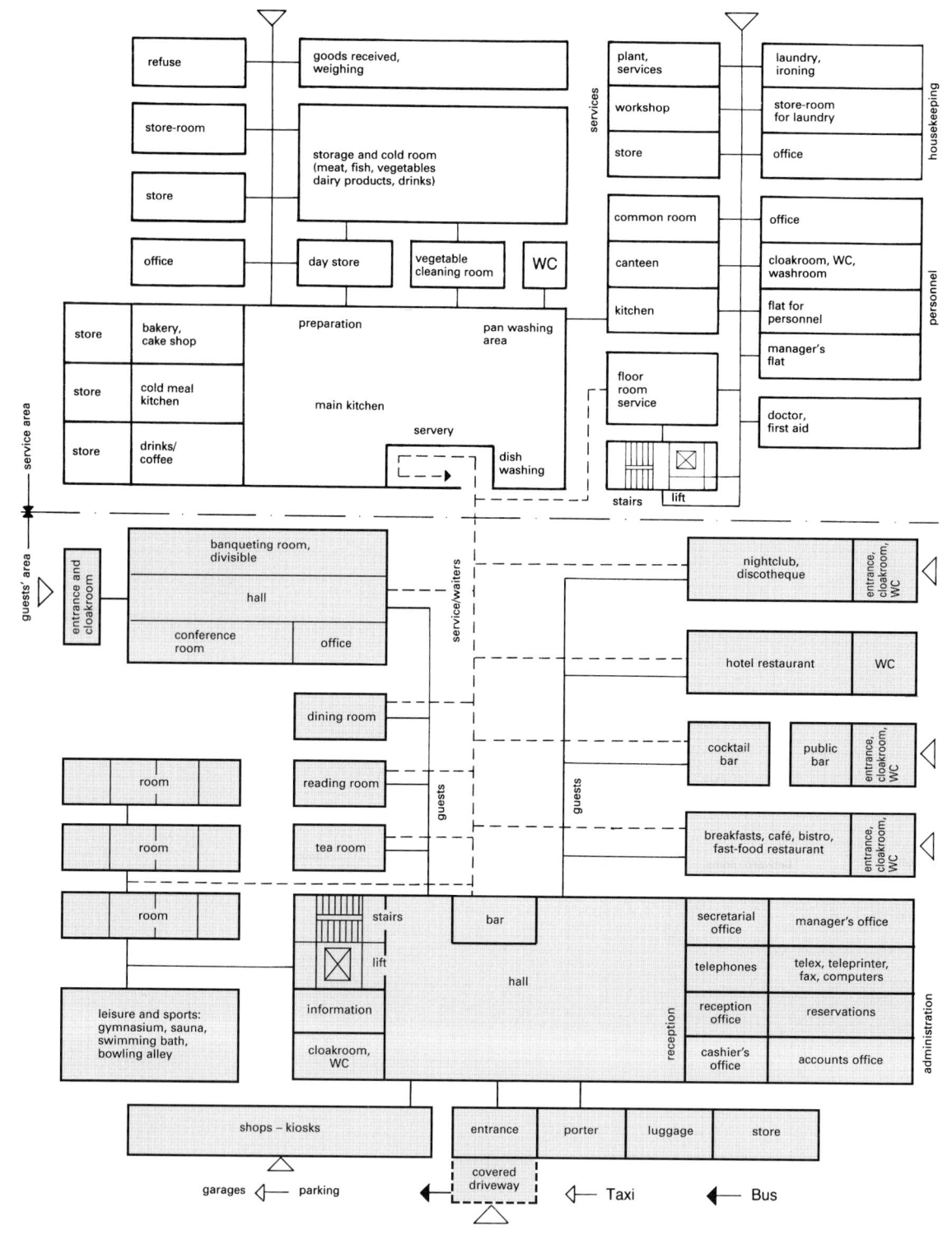

① **Typical interrelationships between rooms on hotel ground floor**

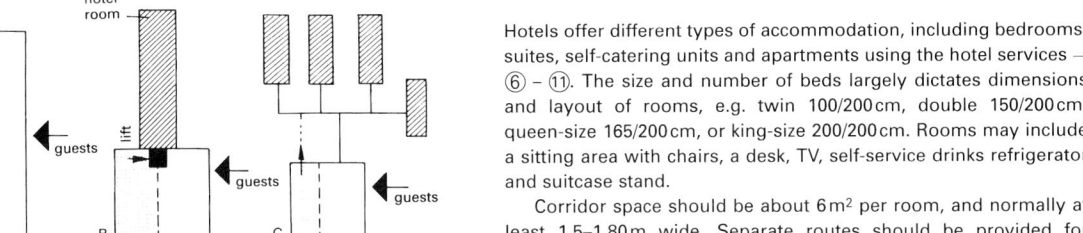

HOTEL LAYOUT AND AREA REQUIREMENTS

Hotels offer different types of accommodation, including bedrooms, suites, self-catering units and apartments using the hotel services → ⑥ – ⑪. The size and number of beds largely dictates dimensions and layout of rooms, e.g. twin 100/200cm, double 150/200cm, queen-size 165/200cm, or king-size 200/200cm. Rooms may include a sitting area with chairs, a desk, TV, self-service drinks refrigerator and suitcase stand.

Corridor space should be about 6m² per room, and normally at least 1.5–1.80m wide. Separate routes should be provided for guests, staff and goods → ① – ②.

There is always movement in and near a hotel. Customers move from parking areas, through the entrance and reception, and then to lifts, staircases or corridors leading to bedrooms or public rooms. In most hotels, customers are not allowed to go from bedrooms direct to the car park without passing through reception. Suitable fire escape routes must be provided to meet legislation. Staff move from staff housing, via their own entrance and changing rooms, to kitchens, service areas, bars, workshops, etc. All deliveries must be taken to the correct department or storage area, perhaps using special lifts. Disposals should be from special roofed-over areas (to limit night-time noise), with a clearance height of 4.35m.

Hotels usually have a restaurant and/or breakfast area and one or more bars. Hotels with conference facilities may include a multifunctional central hall, meeting rooms, exhibition areas and buffet facilities. Storage for extra furniture and additional parking space may be necessary. Specialist facilities may include audio-visual media rooms, projection equipment, simultaneous translation facilities, copying machines, fax machines and telephones.

Hotels should provide facilities for the handicapped and disabled in at least 1–2% of rooms, preferably on the ground floor, and with the following minimum criteria: ramps 1:20, corridors 915mm wide, doors 815mm clear opening, lobbies 460mm wider than the door on the latch side, closet doors either narrow or sliding, shelves 1.37m high. Bathrooms: central turning space 1.52m, width 2.75m, vanity tops 860mm high, 685mm knee space, mirrors extending down to 1.0m, compromise toilet seat height usually 430mm. Grab bars are needed on the headwall and sides of the bath and toilet. Standard bedrooms, 3.65m wide, can be adapted to the following criteria: switches 1.2m high, space between beds and furniture 910mm, beds 450–500mm high with toe space below. Eye level from a wheelchair is 1.07–1.37m; dressing tables should allow for this and have 685mm knee space. Low window sills are also preferable.

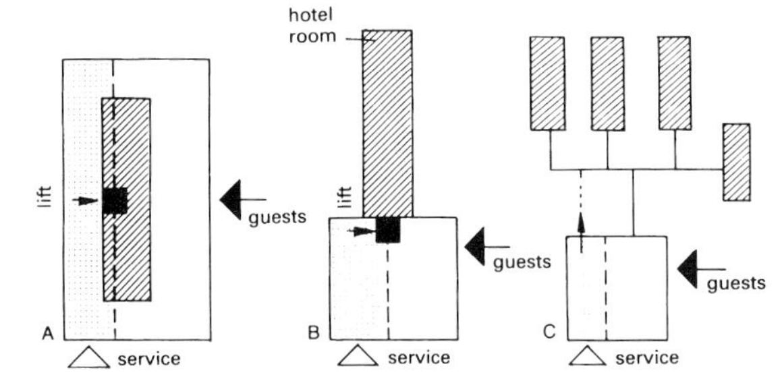

① **Relationship between services and guest rooms**

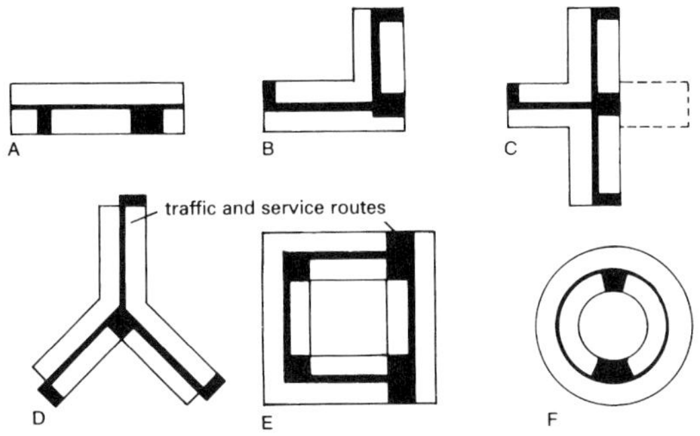

② **Plan views of hotels**

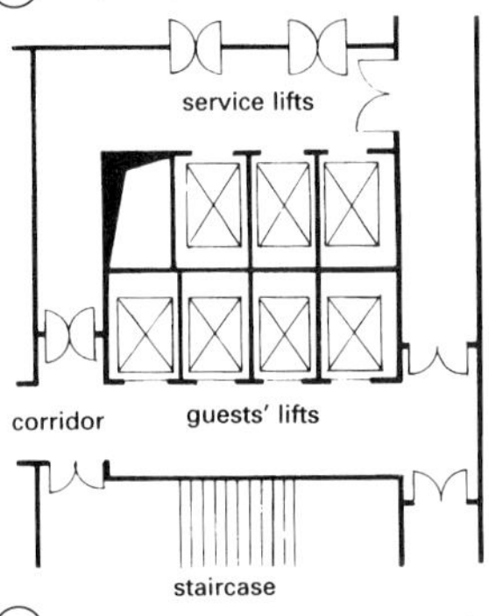

③ **Vertical circulation in hotel**

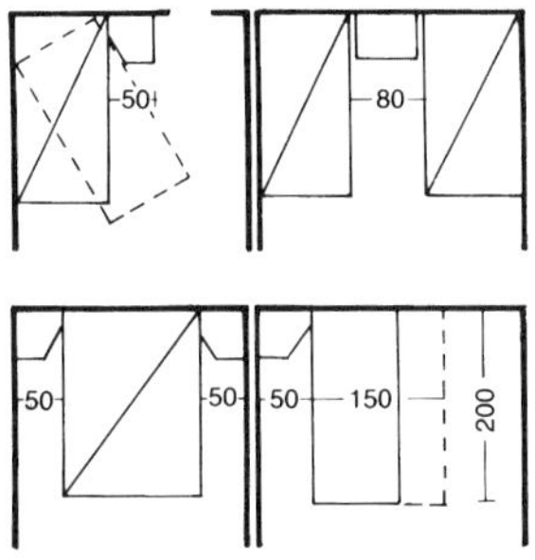

④ **Minimum spacing between hotel beds**

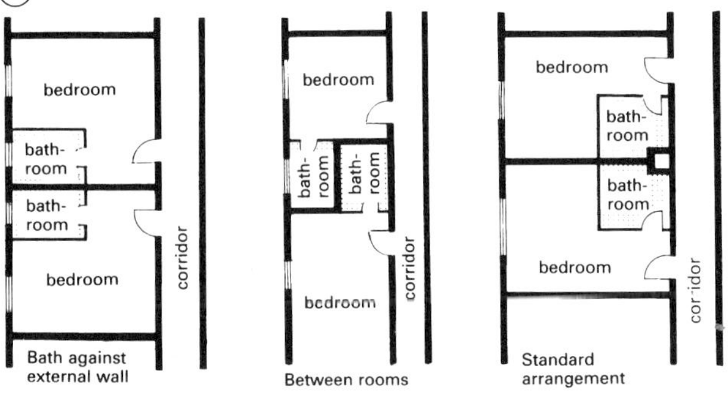

⑤ **Bathroom arrangement**

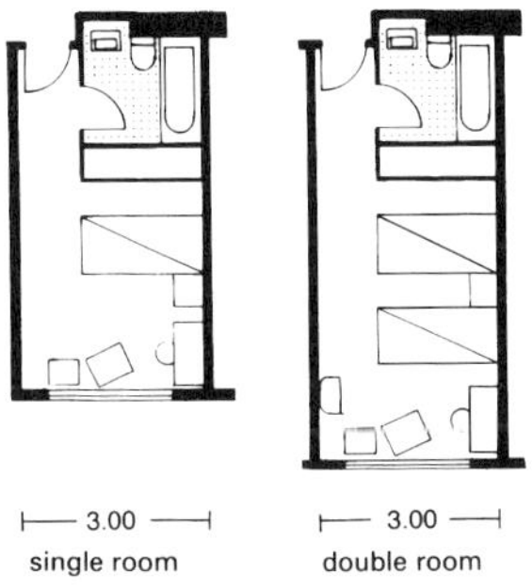

⑥ **Narrow hotel room**

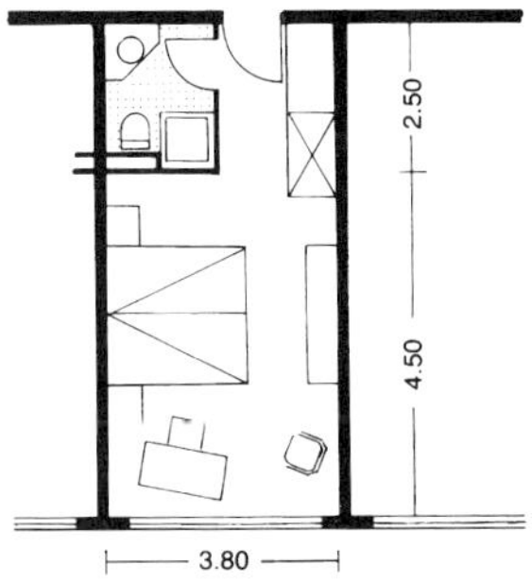

⑦ **Double bed in economy hotel**

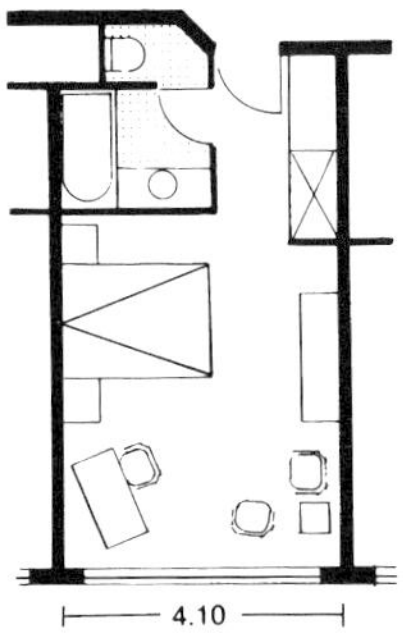

⑧ **Standard room**

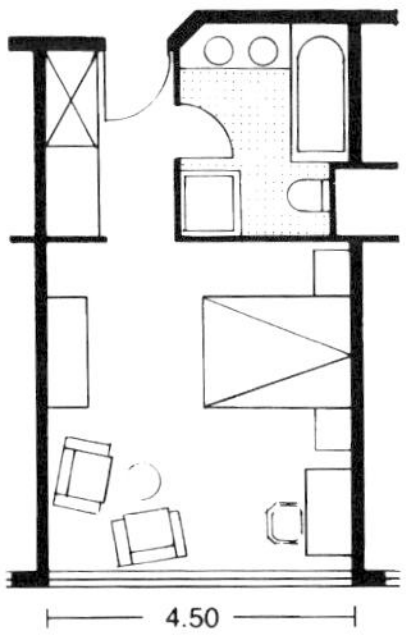

⑨ **Executive room**

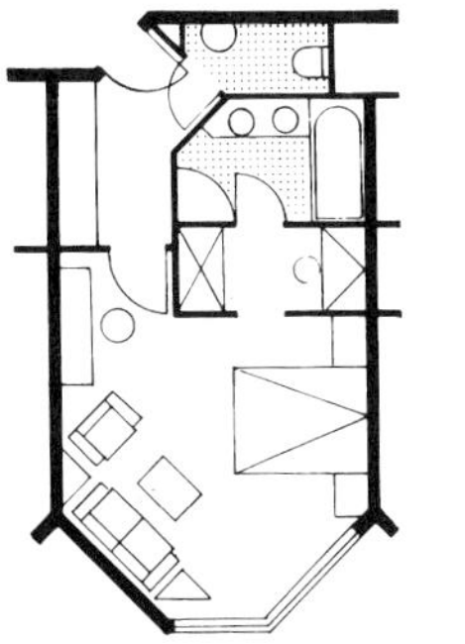

⑩ **Luxury room (> 5.0 m wide)**

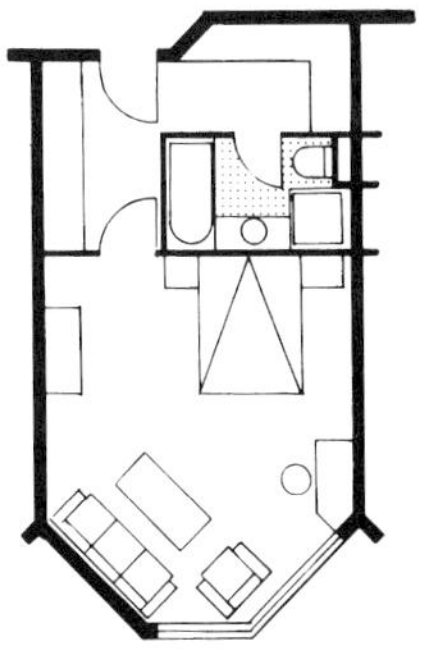

⑪ **A variant of** ⑩

465

HOTEL LAYOUT AND AREA REQUIREMENTS

Restaurants/catering

Care should be exercised when sizing restaurants on the basis of people per square metre since circulation requirements and table layouts, etc., vary considerably. The following table gives some basic guidelines.

hotel size (rooms)	coffee shop, café[a], brasserie (seats)	main or speciality restaurant (seats)	ethnic or gourmet restaurant (seats)
50	50–75	–	–
150	80	60	–
250	100	60	50
space provision/seat[b]	1.6 m²	2.0 m²	2.0 m²

[a] excluding poolside, café-bar and other club facilities; area also usable for breakfast meals with buffet or table service

[b] the area required per seat, dictated mainly by size and spacing of furniture, proportion of tables seating two persons and arrangements for food service (buffet, table service, etc.)

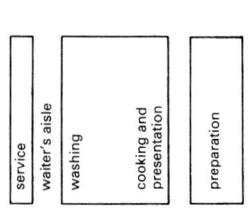

(1) **Layout for small business**

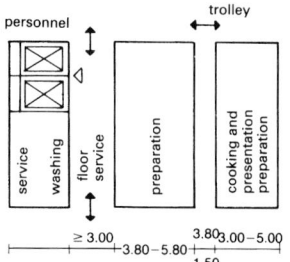

(2) **Layout for medium-size/large businesses**

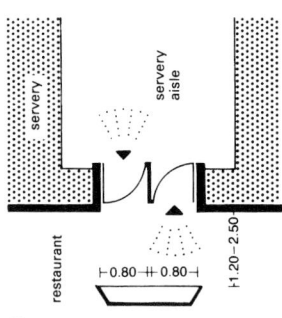

(3) **Waiters' door arrangement**

(4) **Service and tray trolleys**

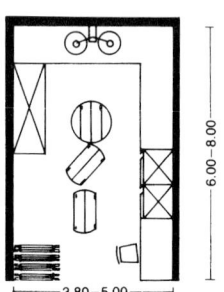

(5) **Floor servery**

(6) **Servery/dishwashing area**

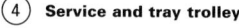

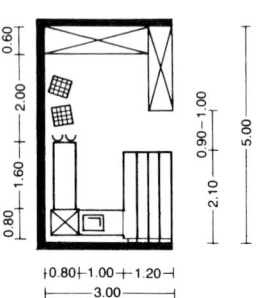

(7) **Dishwashing (1–2 people)**

(8) **Crockery and glasses**

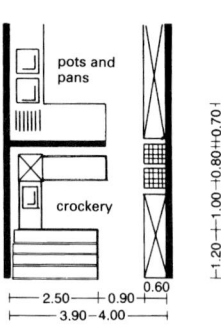

(9) **Crockery and pan washing**

(10) **Cold store Shelving   Metal trolleys**

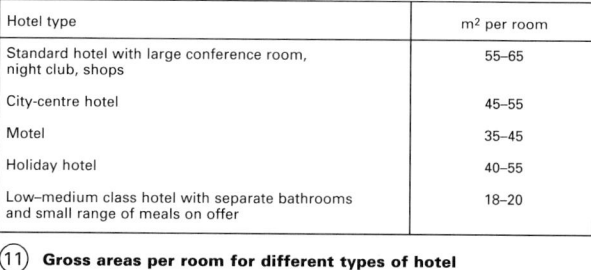

Hotel type	m² per room
Standard hotel with large conference room, night club, shops	55–65
City-centre hotel	45–55
Motel	35–45
Holiday hotel	40–55
Low–medium class hotel with separate bathrooms and small range of meals on offer	18–20

(11) **Gross areas per room for different types of hotel**

Area/department	200 rooms, in suburban setting m2 per room	500 rooms in central location m2 per room
Hotel room	24	26.5
Corridors, lifts, stairs	3.2	9.3
Service	0.6	0.7
Total per room	27.8	36.5
Entrance area including lifts for personnel and service	1.6	1.8
Reception, WC, reservations, telephones, luggage, cloakroom	0.4	0.4
Administration	0.3	0.4
Restaurant	1.1	0.6
Coffee bar	0.6	0.5
Bar 1, plus counter	0.9	0.4
Bar 2, plus counter	0.5	0.3
Lounge	0.5	0.3
Toilets	0.4	0.3
Conference/lecture rooms	1.1	1.3
Ancillary rooms		0.5
Furniture store	0.1	0.2
Private bedrooms and living rooms	0.4	0.9
Shops		0.2
Total entrance/guest area	7.8	8.2
Kitchen, provisions	3.8	2.5
General stores	0.9	0.9
Workshops, maintenance	0.8	0.4
Laundry, linen store	0.3	0.7
Staff dining room, WC, changing rooms	1.0	1.1
Personnel rooms, accounts, supervision, caretaker	0.3	0.5
Circulation areas, service lifts	0.8	0.9
Total rear hotel service area	7.9	7.7
Total area, without heating services or inside/outside parking facilities	43.5	51.7

(12) **Area requirement per hotel room → (11)**

HOTEL KITCHENS

Kitchen size is determined by the number of workstations, the space required for equipment, the range of meals and the extent of food preparation. Therefore number of covers or number of seats are not adequate guides. The following table provides an approximate basis for initial estimates of space requirements.

area per seat	high-grade hotels (m²)	mid-grade hotels (m²)	economy hotels (m²)
main kitchen and stores[a]	1.2	1.0	0.7[d]
satellite kitchen[b]	0.3		
banquet kitchens[c]	0.2		

[a] storage requirements depend on frequency of deliveries
[b] including local dish-washing
[c] 0.15 m² increase in main kitchen; 0.05 m² banquet pantry
[d] using some convenience foods

Kitchen planning requires four stages of development:
- determine a process plan covering all major areas;
- check maximum and minimum personnel needs per area;
- determine the equipment needed for each area;
- space allocation.

List the activities and functions of each of the three main areas: kitchen, stores and service. The central interface between guest, stores and service areas is the waiters' servery. Around this point are grouped the facilities for serving food and drinks as well as for disposal of soiled utensils and waste. Floor service is orientated toward the routes leading to the guests' rooms. However, for maximum efficiency it is important that routes between the kitchen, servery and restaurant are as short as possible.

Hotel food preparation and beverage services fall broadly into three groups. (1) A choice of restaurants and bars, including banqueting areas and room service. This needs a main kitchen and stores area, with satellite kitchens near each restaurant and banqueting room, and service pantries on each guest-room floor. (2) One or two restaurants and function rooms on the same floor. Needs one main kitchen serving restaurants and function rooms direct. (3) Minimal food service in the hotel, but separate restaurant(s) available (for budget hotels and holiday villages). Central vending machines and/or individual cooking facilities may be provided.

Laundry services for a hotel may be provided by:
- linen rental or contracts with outside laundries;
- centralised services operated by the hotel group;
- hotel-operated laundry on the premises.

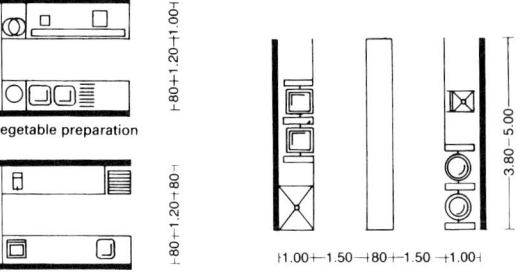

vegetable preparation

meat preparation

(1) **Vegetable/meat preparation**

(2) **Kitchen for banquets**

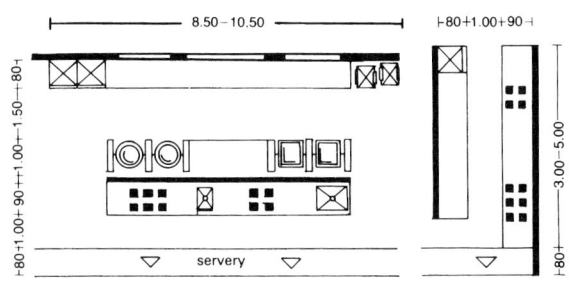

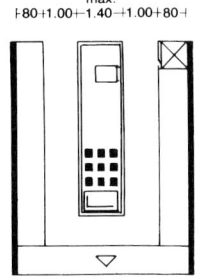

(3) **Hot meals kitchen (American line, 1–2 cooks)**

(4) **European line (1–2 cooks)**

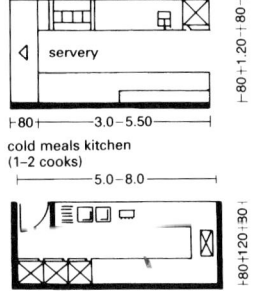

(5) **Hot meals kitchen (French block arrangement)**

(6) **Mixed meals kitchen (1–4 cooks)**

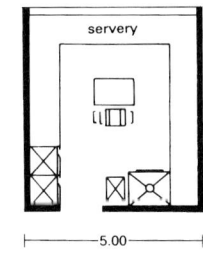

servery

cold meals kitchen (1–2 cooks)

(7) **Patisserie (1–3 pastry cooks)**

(8) **Drinks counter**

(9) **Meals/day: base kitchen size in m²**

equipment and cleaning

(10) **Meals/day: areas for different service types**

personnel, washing, serving, cooking, preparation, provisions

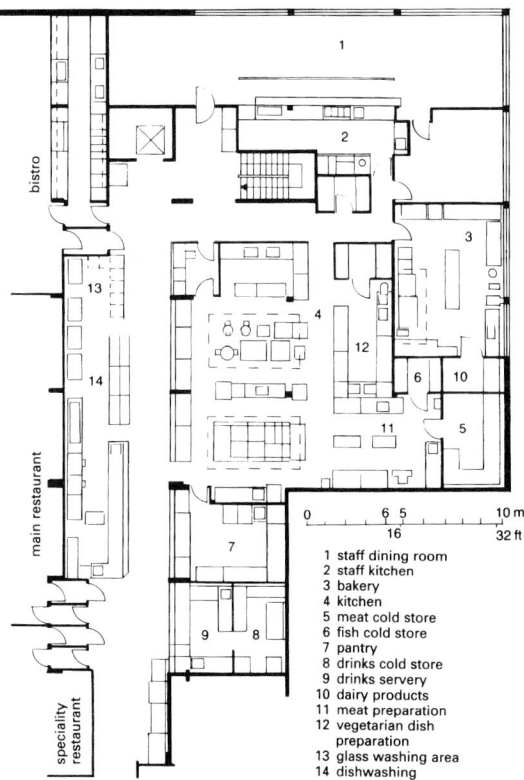

(11) **Kitchen for 100 standard meals, 100 speciality meals, 120 bistro covers and 80 staff meals**

1 staff dining room
2 staff kitchen
3 bakery
4 kitchen
5 meat cold store
6 fish cold store
7 pantry
8 drinks cold store
9 drinks servery
10 dairy products
11 meat preparation
12 vegetarian dish preparation
13 glass washing area
14 dishwashing

467

HOTELS: EXAMPLES

Nowadays, modern hotels often provide extra facilities such as swimming pools, fitness rooms, saunas etc. → ⑤.

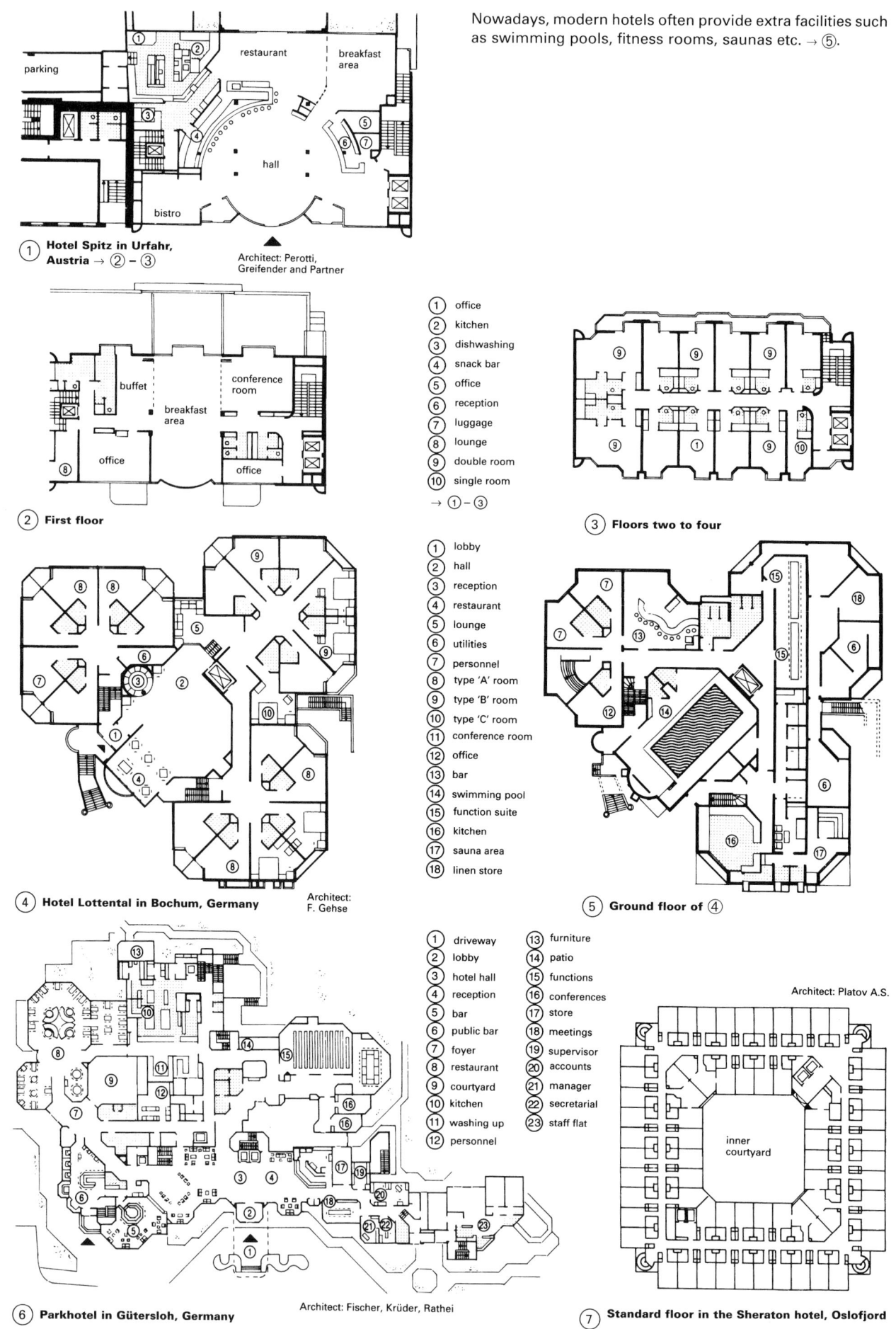

① **Hotel Spitz in Urfahr, Austria** → ② – ③

Architect: Perotti, Greifender and Partner

② **First floor**

① office
② kitchen
③ dishwashing
④ snack bar
⑤ office
⑥ reception
⑦ luggage
⑧ lounge
⑨ double room
⑩ single room
→ ① – ③

③ **Floors two to four**

① lobby
② hall
③ reception
④ restaurant
⑤ lounge
⑥ utilities
⑦ personnel
⑧ type 'A' room
⑨ type 'B' room
⑩ type 'C' room
⑪ conference room
⑫ office
⑬ bar
⑭ swimming pool
⑮ function suite
⑯ kitchen
⑰ sauna area
⑱ linen store

④ **Hotel Lottental in Bochum, Germany**

Architect: F. Gehse

⑤ **Ground floor of** ④

① driveway
② lobby
③ hotel hall
④ reception
⑤ bar
⑥ public bar
⑦ foyer
⑧ restaurant
⑨ courtyard
⑩ kitchen
⑪ washing up
⑫ personnel
⑬ furniture
⑭ patio
⑮ functions
⑯ conferences
⑰ store
⑱ meetings
⑲ supervisor
⑳ accounts
㉑ manager
㉒ secretarial
㉓ staff flat

⑥ **Parkhotel in Gütersloh, Germany**

Architect: Fischer, Krüder, Rathei

Architect: Platov A.S.

inner courtyard

⑦ **Standard floor in the Sheraton hotel, Oslofjord**

468

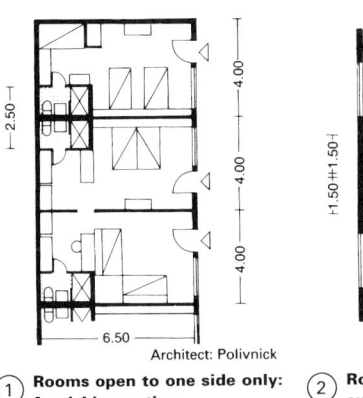

Architect: Polivnick

(1) **Rooms open to one side only: furnishing options**

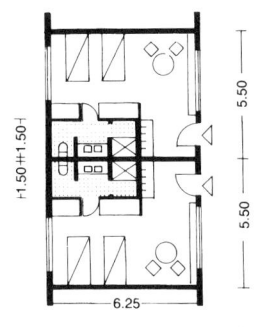

Architect: Roberto

(2) **Rooms lit from two sides: supervision more difficult**

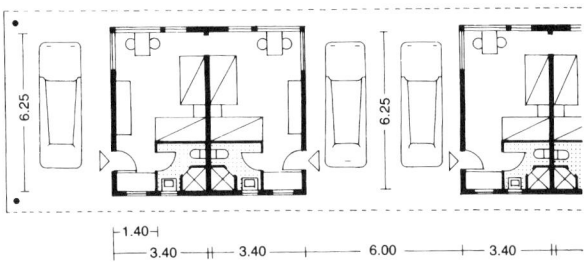

Architect: Duncan

(3) **Covered parking between units (3–6 units combined into one group)**

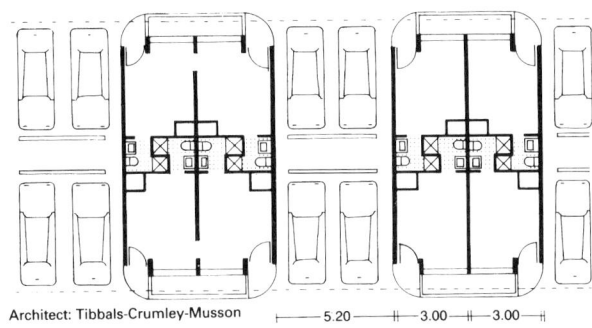

Architect: Tibbals-Crumley-Musson

(4) **Rooms with covered parking as in (3) but in blocks of four**

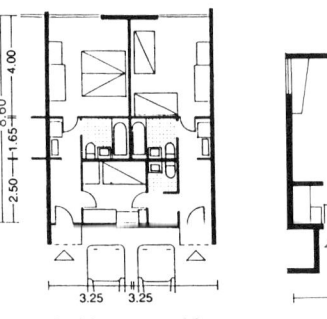

Architect: Thompson

(5) **Two double rooms with lobby, for cold climates, with sleeping cubicles in single and double layout**

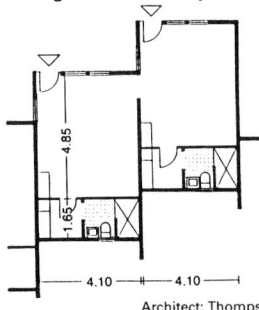

Architect: Hornbostel

(6) **Bathroom/WC between cars and bedrooms, for sound insulation**

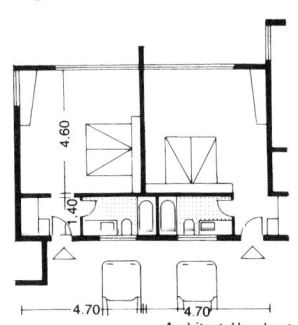

(7) **Staggered arrangement: access from one side only**

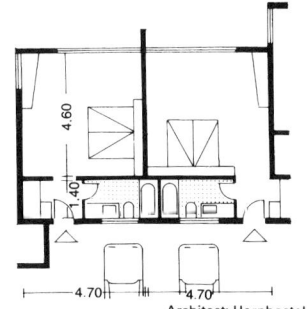

(8) **Staggered arrangement with reception and flat**

Motels are located on motorways and arterial roads near large towns, and tourist and holiday areas. Ideally, restaurants, petrol station(s) and car servicing should be available in the immediate locality. A motel should be positioned so that car headlights do not affect the residents.

The reception area should be close to the rooms, with short-term parking and one entry/exit point only.

Motels are generally one or two storeys and widely spaced out → (9), (10). Room sizes are between 4m × 4m and 5m × 5m, plus bathrooms and cooking facilities if provided → (8). Repetitive units may be arranged in pairs or clusters around a central service core, or in blocks with continuous or stepped facades, in courtyards or in other combinations to suit site contours, parking arrangements and boundaries. Parking is communal or immediately adjacent to the rooms. Motel units often provide convertible double/family rooms and sometimes self-catering kitchenettes. Access to rooms may be direct (ground floor) or via corridors or stairs.

Since about 90% of guests stay only one night, wardrobes often have no doors so that the contents can easily be seen and are less likely to be forgotten.

A well-equipped common room for guests is often provided, as well as a central laundry. Playgrounds should be well away from the motel so as not to disturb those wishing to sleep.

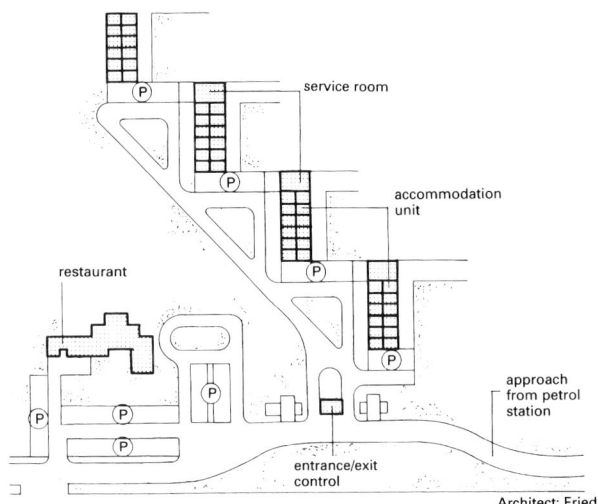

Architect: Fried

(9) **Motel layout with car-parks for each block and restaurant as separate business**

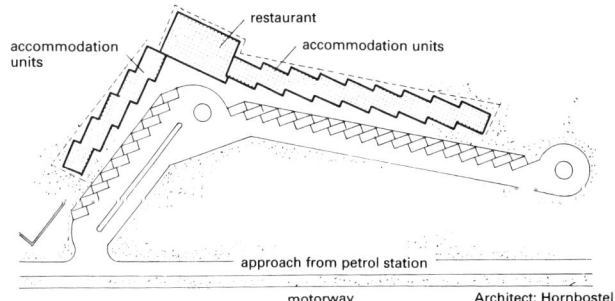

Architect: Hornbostel

(10) **Layout plan for (6) with restaurant**

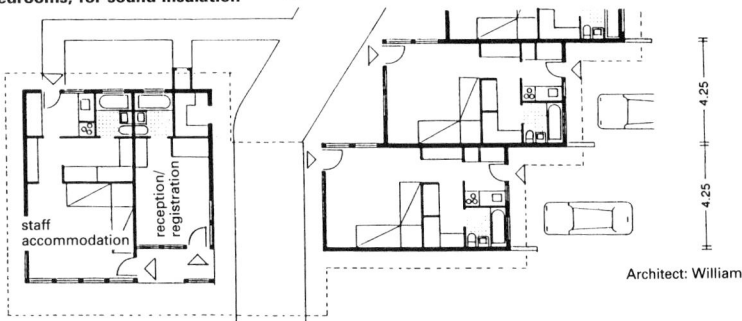

Architect: Williams

469

room	area (m²)	comments
entrance hall	14	with bench and shoe rack
office/reception/shop	11	hatch to entrance hall; close to warden's kitchen
drying room	14	preferably accessed via entrance hall without passing through principal rooms; with racks or hangers; heated
luggage room	14	if combined with drying room, laundry and WC, 14–18.5 m² each
common room	18.5–23	
dining room	46.5	or 0.7 m²/person
members' kitchen	16	direct access to dining room
warden's kitchen	16–23	if possible with combined door and hatch for direct service to dining room; sink in kitchen preferred to separate scullery; access to dustbins
larder	9.3	each
wash-up	11	with 1 or 2 sinks; table space for dirty crockery; easy access from dining room and to warden's kitchen (for crockery return) if possible
warden's lounge	14	layout of these will usually depend
warden's bedroom 1	11	on balance of convenience,
warden's bedroom 2	9.3	privacy, aspect
warden's bathroom	3.25	
dormitories	158–167	i.e. 3.16 m²/person
WCs		for hostellers not less than 5; 1 for warden
washing facilities		for each sex 1 washroom with bath (partitioned off) or shower, footbath and basins to DES standards
airing cupboard	1	for warden's use
blanket store	3.75	warmed
cycle store	28	for about 30 cycles, preferably in racks

note: floor areas are intended as minimum desirable but in alterations much will depend on the existing building

(1) **YHA schedule of accommodation for 50 bed hostel**

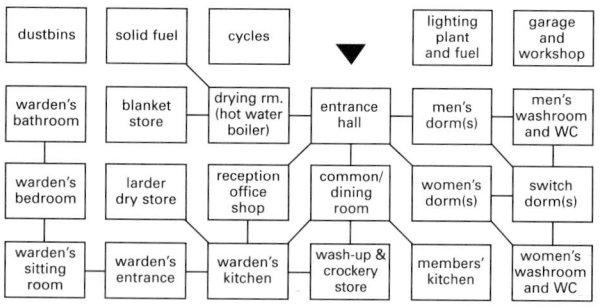

(2) **Schematic layout for single-storey youth hostel**

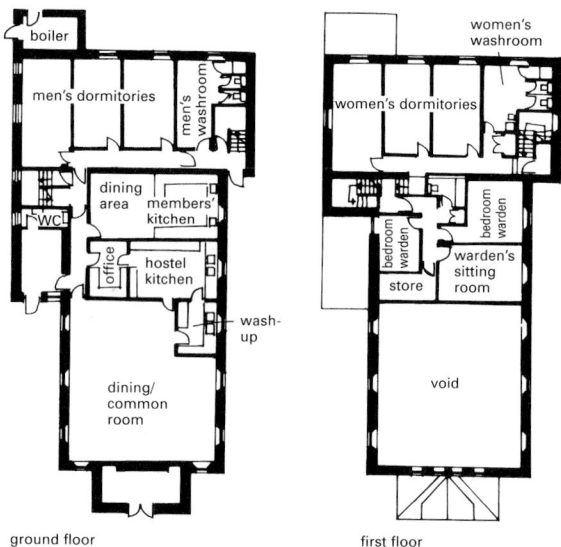

(3) **Youth hostel converted from existing house by YHA**

Youth hostels are often conversions of existing buildings partly because of a shortage of money and also because they are often located in aesthetically sensitive surroundings. The Youth Hostels Association (YHA) in the UK is therefore reluctant to lay down definitive plans for typical hostels. Nevertheless, there are specifications and requirements to be considered, particularly relating to fire safety, and the Department for Education and Employment (DFEE) in the UK also has requirements, governing space in particular, for the hostels to which it allocates funds.

Fire safety

The YHA is increasingly concerned with the application of more stringent standards of fire safety to both new and existing hostels. Principal sources of danger have been identified as interference with stoves or heaters, particularly in the drying room, electrical or gas faults and misuse of cooking stoves. Provision of means of escape in old buildings can be problematic and protected stairs are difficult to provide where there are timber floors. The distances to be covered on fire escape routes to reach safety are usually set out in fire regulations. Generally, 18 m to a place of safety is considered the maximum in buildings with timbered floors; where floors are non-combustible this distance is 30 m. In small hostels, akin to houses, the distances very rarely contravene the regulations. In larger hostels a minimum of two staircases are normally required in such positions that no person on any floor has to go further than the maximum travel distance to reach a point of safety.

Bed spaces

The following guidelines can be applied:

3.1 m² dormitory floor area per person
1 WC per 10 bed spaces
1 hand basin per 6 bed spaces
1 bath/shower per 20 bed spaces

For the purposes of calculating floor areas DFEE disallows any floor space over which the ceiling is less than 2.10 m.

The YHA has lower standards, depending on the grade of the hostel: simple or standard. For simple hostels (which need not have a resident warden) the minimum area per bed is 2.04 m²; for standard hostels (which must have a resident warden living within the curtilage of the hostel at all times when open to members) dormitories should have a minimum of 2.32 m² per bed space (2.78 m² is recommended). As double bunks are normally used this means 6.31 m² per bunk must be allowed if DFEE standards are to be met.

Dormitories

The YHA lays down that all hostels must have separate dormitories for men and women, with separate access, and the layout should allow them to be used by either sex as bookings demand. This means either sex must be able to reach the appropriate lavatory. The most compact solution is to have a block of interconnecting rooms and lock the appropriate doors to segregate the sexes. The YHA has been switching to the four-bed dormitory arrangement used in many Continental hostels, with sanitary facilities accessed via a common corridor, motel style. DFEE has been pressing for improved degrees of privacy for women's washing arrangements. This can be achieved by arranging wash basins in cubicles with curtained entrances.

Amenities

As hostels are generally closed during the day, a secure luggage room without access to the rest of the hostel must be provided so arriving members can store their gear. This could be part of the drying room, where hostellers remove their outer clothing before booking in at the reception desk.

To allow visitors to cook their own meals a members' kitchen should be provided in all hostels in addition to the kitchen for the warden, who will also cook for hostellers. These kitchens should be equipped with double cooking rings and grill units, fuelled by propane if no mains service is available. Lockers and washing-up space are also required.

Warden's quarters

Large hostels (40 beds or more) are often administered by married couples, possibly with children who will also need living quarters. The largest hostels can have assistant wardens, who could potentially need their own recreation rooms and a staff kitchen and dining room.

In large hostels, the chief warden's quarters should be in the form of self-contained houses or flats, with three bedrooms, a bathroom, kitchen, dining room and sitting room. In these circumstances hostellers' accommodation should never be above or below the warden's.

YOUTH HOSTELS

A distinction is made by the German Youth Hostel Association between youth hostels and youth hotels. The former are usually in the country and include children's hostels for children up to 13 and youth hostels for 13–17-year-olds, although there is usually an age overlap. Youth hotels are in towns and cities with tourist and cultural attractions, and there is an international trend towards a 3-star hotel standard with 120–160 beds.

Youth hostels and hotels have a variety of purposes: accommodation and meeting point for conferences, courses, seminars, educational courses for young people and adults, recreation, school trips, individual and family hiking.

The functional areas required include common rooms and dayrooms (one per 20–25 beds), several dining rooms (some of which can also be used for meetings and functions), multi-use circulation spaces with more secluded bays, cafeteria, lecture rooms, entrance hall/reception and office for youth hostel warden. The areas required are dependent on the number of bed spaces. Outside, there may be requirements for a camp site (with doors to sanitary facilities), sports and games pitches, parking for buses and cars, and a garden for the hostel warden.

There is a trend to reduce the numbers of beds in the hostel rooms to between four and six (eight maximum) and to have separate rooms for parents and children. In youth hotels there are usually two to four beds and single rooms are available for group leaders and visiting speakers.

Showers and washrooms must be near to all rooms and separate WCs provided. All should be accessible to the disabled. A lockable luggage store and cleaning rooms are desirable on each floor.

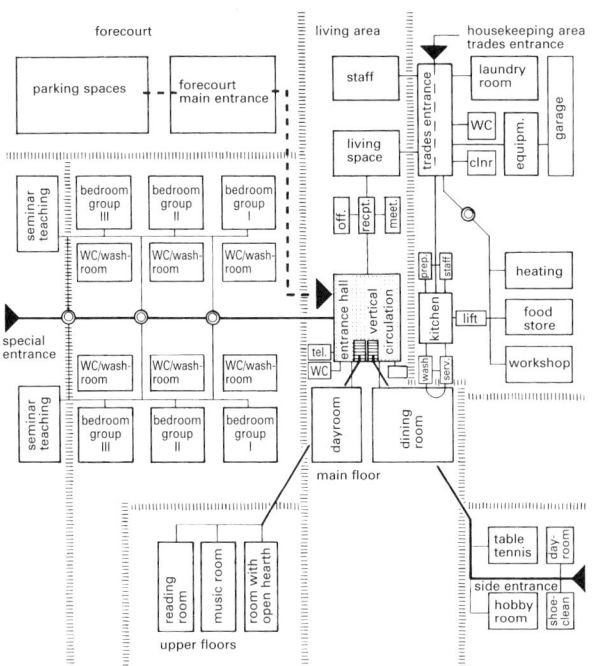

① **Schematic diagram of functions**

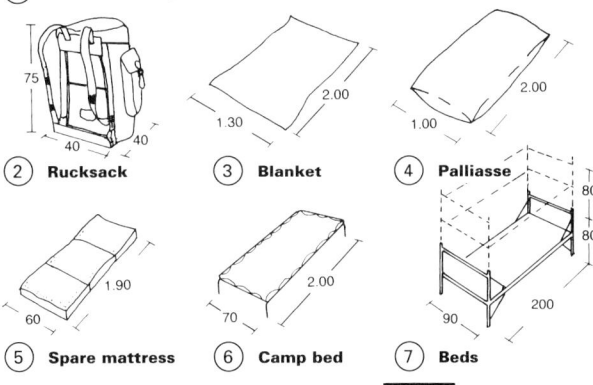

② **Rucksack** ③ **Blanket** ④ **Palliasse**

⑤ **Spare mattress** ⑥ **Camp bed** ⑦ **Beds**

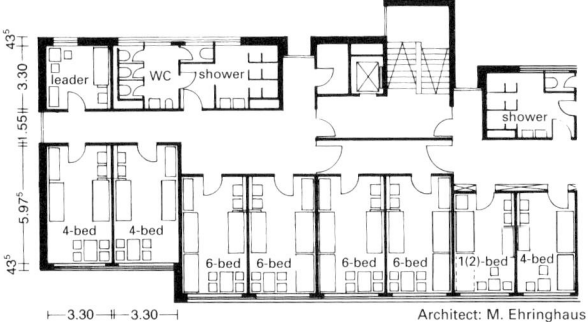

⑧ **Youth hotel with youth hostel in Cologne-Riehl; 4- and 6-bed rooms**

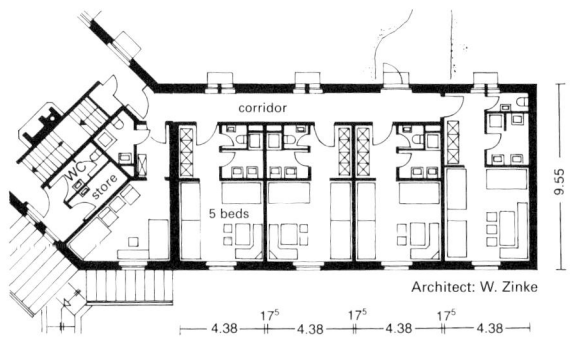

Architect: W. Zinke

⑩ **Habischried rural school hostel; 5-bed rooms**

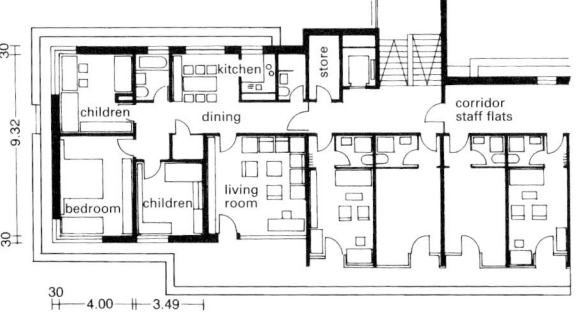

⑨ **Warden's flat and accommodation for other staff → ⑧**

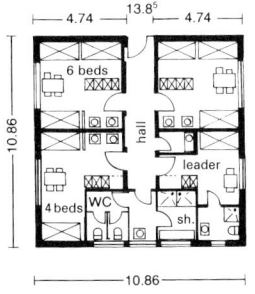

⑪ **Uslar youth hostel; pavilion with 18 beds**

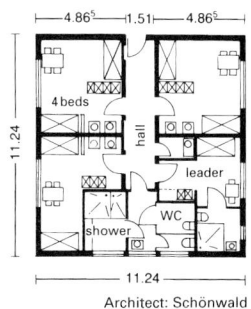

Architect: Schönwald

⑫ **Pavilion with 14 beds**

YOUTH HOSTELS

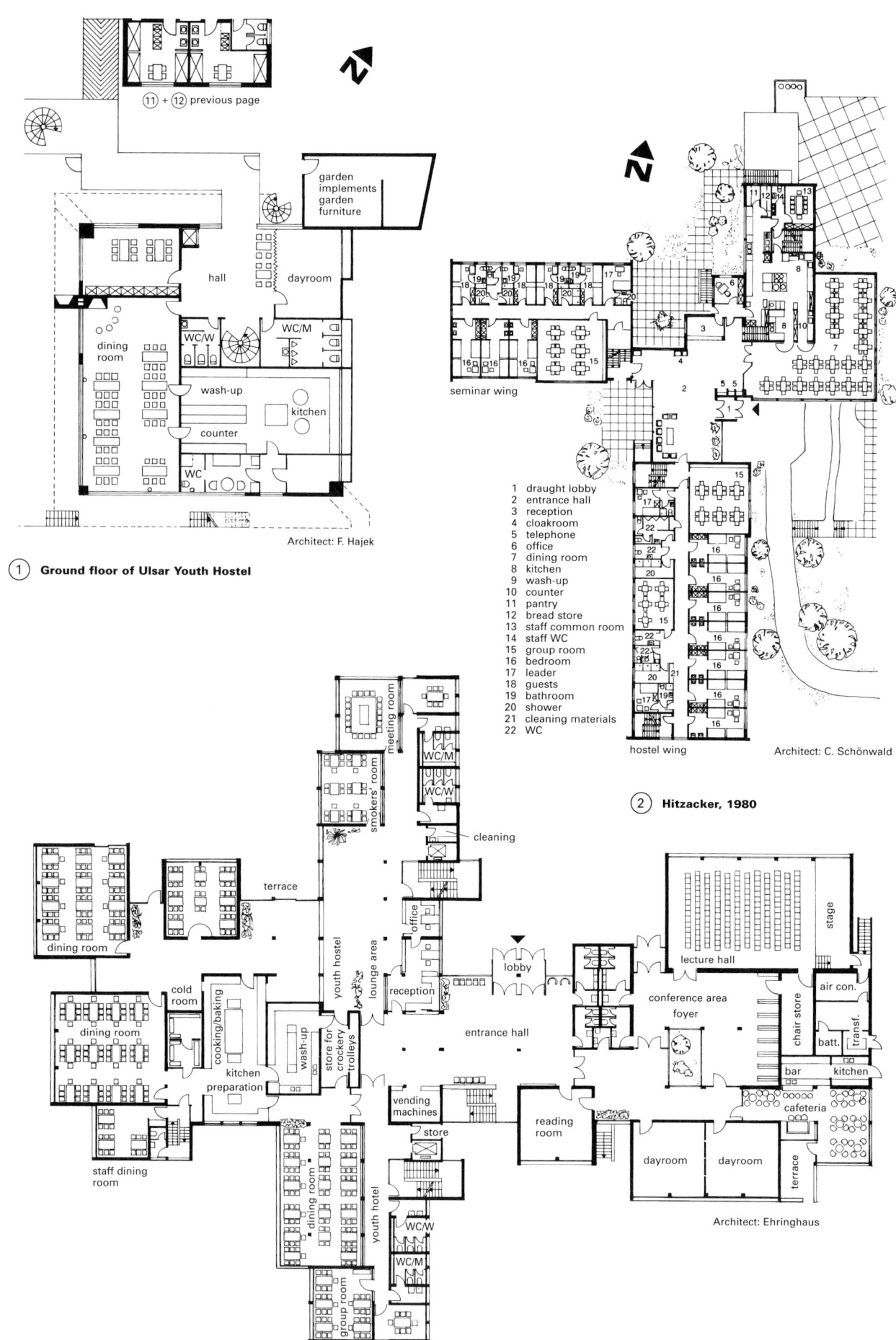

(11) + (12) previous page

garden implements
garden furniture

hall

dayroom

dining room

WC/W

WC/M

wash-up

counter

kitchen

WC

Architect: F. Hajek

① **Ground floor of Ulsar Youth Hostel**

seminar wing

1 draught lobby
2 entrance hall
3 reception
4 cloakroom
5 telephone
6 office
7 dining room
8 kitchen
9 wash-up
10 counter
11 pantry
12 bread store
13 staff common room
14 staff WC
15 group room
16 bedroom
17 leader
18 guests
19 bathroom
20 shower
21 cleaning materials
22 WC

hostel wing

Architect: C. Schönwald

② **Hitzacker, 1980**

meeting room

smokers' room

WC/M

WC/W

cleaning

terrace

office

youth hostel

lounge area

reception

lobby

dining room

cold room

cooking/baking

kitchen preparation

wash-up

store for crockery trolleys

entrance hall

vending machines

store

reading room

staff dining room

dining room

youth hotel

WC/W

WC/M

group room

lecture hall

stage

conference area foyer

air con.

chair store

transf.

batt.

bar

kitchen

cafeteria

dayroom

dayroom

terrace

Architect: Ehringhaus

③ **Youth hostel and youth hotel in Cologne-Riehl**

landscape typology

polar area
tundra
Arctic circle
taiga
European cultivated
wooded landscape
rocky area
semi-desert
tropic
steppes
savanna
jungle
equator
rainforest

Arctic regions

European

Africa

South America, Asia

Asia

① **Frankfurt Zoo**　　Architects: G + T. Hansjakob & K. Schmidthuber

② **Taiga**

③ **European cultivated landscape**

④ **Savanna, steppes**

⑤ **Rainforest**

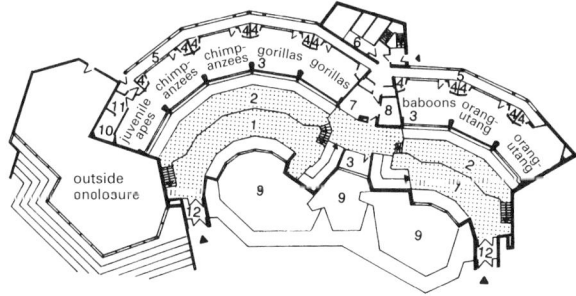

⑥ **Anthropoid enclosure, Wuppertal Zoo**

1 visitor level 1	7 feed kitchen
2 visitor level 2	8 keepers' room
3 inside enclosure	9 ponds
4 sleeping booths	10 juvenile apes' sleeping area
5 keepers' corridor	11 keepers' room
6 sick bay	12 porch

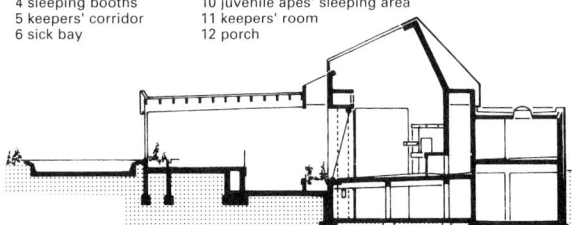

⑦ **Section →**⑥　　　　　Building Department, Wuppertal

ZOOS AND AQUARIUMS

The Zoological Society of London, founded in 1826, and its Zoological Gardens, opened in 1828, both had considerable influence on the development of animal research and collections throughout the world. The traditional role of zoological gardens (for education and scientific research) has become increasingly important because of the accelerating decimation of wildlife stocks. Zoos have expanded into breeding and preservation of different species as well as the return of animals to the wild. Many important specialist collections have recently been formed by private owners.

The following list shows examples of area requirements:

Cologne	20 ha	1860
Nuremberg	60 ha	1939
Sao Paulo	250 ha	1957
Healsville	175 ha	1964
Brazilia	2500 ha	1960
Abu Dhabi	1430 ha	1970
Berlin	34 ha	1983
Frankfurt	63 ha	in construction
Naples	300 ha	in construction

The main entrance of the zoo has: window displays; cash desks and information kiosks; WCs; large parking areas for cars and coaches; stops for public transport. It is also usually the location for: administration; all departments serving the public; function/lecture rooms plus a high-class restaurant overlooking the zoo area (all with separate entrances from outside for evening business). Other restaurants, self-service cafeteria, WCs and picnic areas can be sited within the zoo.

Operations departments should have separate entrances and be shielded from public view; they need large external areas for storage of feed, litter materials, hay, straw, sand, gravel, soil, building materials, etc. Within the buildings should be washing (plus disinfection) and changing facilities, cafeteria, training and quiet rooms (night watchmen). Provision should also be made for central and local feed preparation, water treatment, waste disposal, sheds for accommodating and servicing cleaning machines, transport units, low-loaders, transport cages and gardening equipment. Workshops are needed for carpenters, fitters and painters, including the necessary storage space. Other facilities include an animal hospital, quarantine stations, research laboratories, settling and rearing areas, carcass storage (cold stores) and disposal. Heating, air-conditioning and ventilation for all need to be planned.

Main paths, 5–6 m wide, for the public should form loops linking the main buildings and animal enclosures; secondary routes, 3–4 m wide, give access to the individual groups of animals. Paths and buildings should all be accessible to wheelchairs. It is important to create a feeling of seclusion by planting and sculpting the landscape. Service routes, for supplying and transporting animals to the enclosures, should cross the main routes as little as possible. Public transport systems: consider electric trolleys using the main paths, or miniature trains/cable railways with their own tracks or routes.

An important consideration is the means of separating the animals and the public: wire and steel netting (black), chains, water-filled and dry ditches, glass and plastic barriers, electrified fences.

The native climate/geography and social/territorial needs of the animals must always be taken into account, although some acclimatisation may be possible. The design should allow enclosures to be split (either in or out of public view) for reproduction and rearing. Equipment for catching and transporting animals must be accommodated. For open-air enclosures scents and wind direction are important criteria governing locations and fencing.

For mammals in buildings and outside enclosures or a

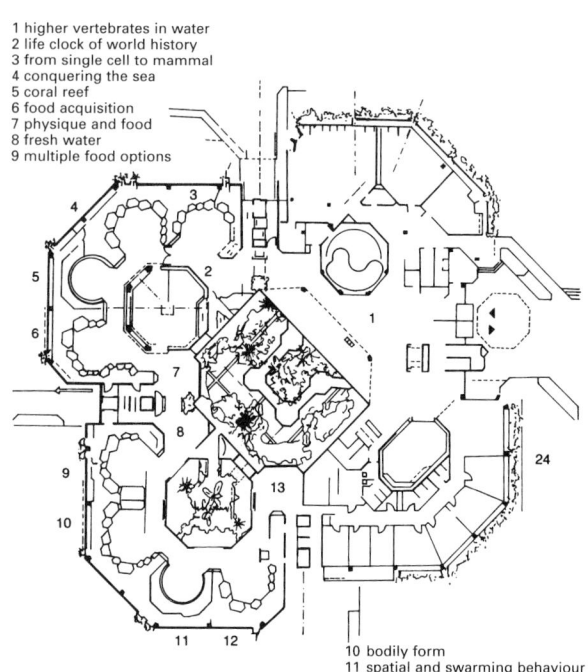

1 higher vertebrates in water
2 life clock of world history
3 from single cell to mammal
4 conquering the sea
5 coral reef
6 food acquisition
7 physique and food
8 fresh water
9 multiple food options

10 bodily form
11 spatial and swarming behaviour
12 native and foreign dwellers in our waters
13 tropical shores
14 mussels, snails and cuttlefish

(1) **Ground floor of the AQUAZOO in Düsseldorf**

Architects: Dansard, Kahlenborn etc.

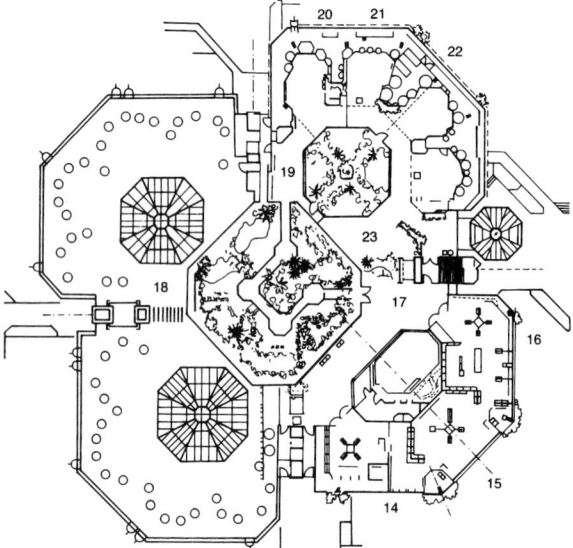

15 history of life, the story of mankind
16 changing exhibition
17 tropical house
18 adaptation of crustaceous form
19 amphibian form

20 reptile form
21 desert habitat
22 camouflage and warning
23 mankind and the environment
24 mineralogy

(2) **Upper floor**

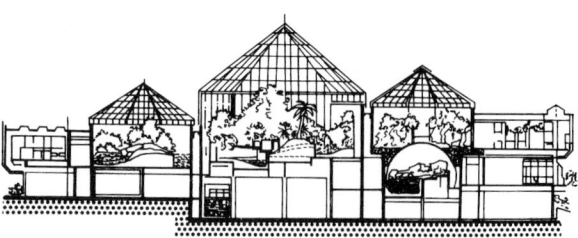

(3) **Section** → (1)—(2)

ZOOS AND AQUARIUMS

combination of these, with and without water, the height is often more important than the ground surface area.

Buildings to house birds must allow sunlight to enter, particularly for tropical birds; outside enclosures for waterfowl must give protection from predators.

Most reptiles and marine mammals require temperatures between 15 and 27°C. They should have an adequate volume of water and allow sufficient 'haul-out' space.

Fish and invertebrates must not come into contact with water containing metal particles. Mains water must first be filtered with carbon. A distinction is made between 'open systems' with single throughflow (1–2 water changes per hour) and 'closed systems' with filter and recirculation (6–20% water renewal in two weeks). Fresh and sea water reserves of 30–50% of the total volume should be held. Lighting of aquariums requires particular care to harmonise with the creatures' natural habitat and to avoid reflection in the display tank surfaces.

Terrestrial invertebrates (insects) in aquariums or terrariums require extensive safety precautions to avoid eggs or larvae being introduced into the local environment.

A children's zoo and play area gives urban families direct contact with animals and an understanding of their behaviour and eating habits.

Future trends will be improvements in meeting the natural needs of the animals being housed and giving the public an improved, more authentic view.

1 entrance
2 information
3 the successes of insects
4 eat and be eaten
5 defence and flight
6 insects in movement

7 four x life
8 how they live
9 distribution
10 mankind and insects
11 projection screen
12 special exhibitions

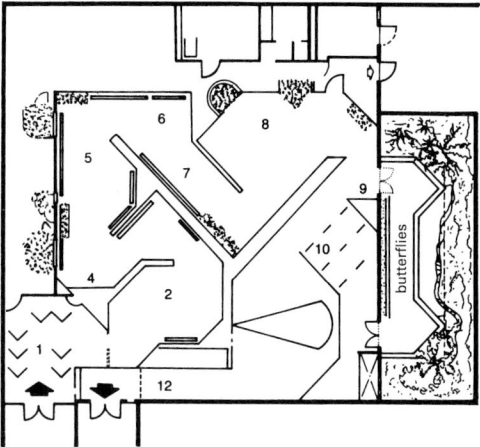

(4) **World of Insects**

Architect: Johnson

ZOOS AND AQUARIUMS

The preservation of animals, together with their renaturalisation, is a key concern. Peripheral zoo areas should also include exhibits which help to explain the interrelationships between humankind and nature, bordering on the educational function of natural science museums.

For the medical care of animals, plus research and reproductive support, zoos have developed clinics and hospitals not open the public → ④ – ⑤. External enclosures support the healing process, acclimatisation and quarantine. Elements include:

- padded stalls for recovery, acclimatisation and observation (inside and outside)
- separate access routes to the building, including isolated paths for transport cages
- quarantine rooms
- refrigerated rooms for animal carcasses; dissection room and carcass disposal; intensive care and operating rooms
- research laboratories and lecture theatres for teaching animal medicine
- food store and feed preparation
- special personnel rooms with disinfecting equipment
- air conditioning and ventilation with 12–15 air changes per hour (separate for quarantine rooms)
- water treatment facilities and filters
- cleaning equipment (often using steam).

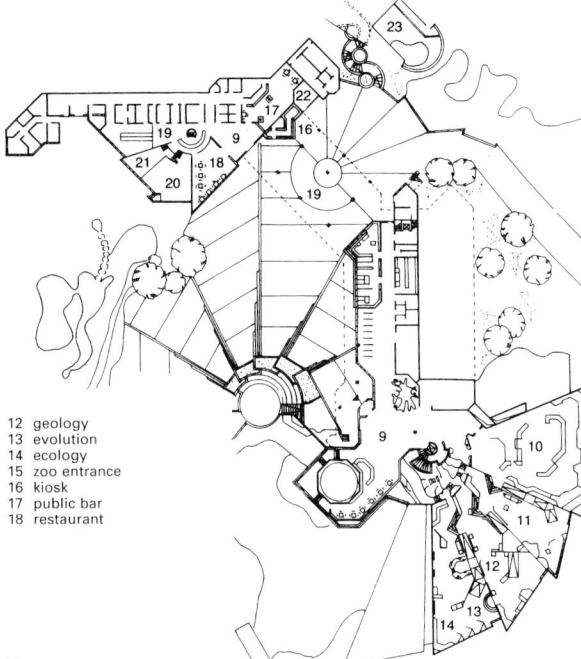

1 forum
2 waterfall
3 lake
4 island
5 sitting steps
6 swamp
7 regeneration source
8 planetarium
9 foyer
10 mineralogy
11 astronomy

12 geology
13 evolution
14 ecology
15 zoo entrance
16 kiosk
17 public bar
18 restaurant

① **Lower floor of the natural science museum/zoo entrance in Osnabrück**   Architects: C. + B. Parade

② **Ground floor**

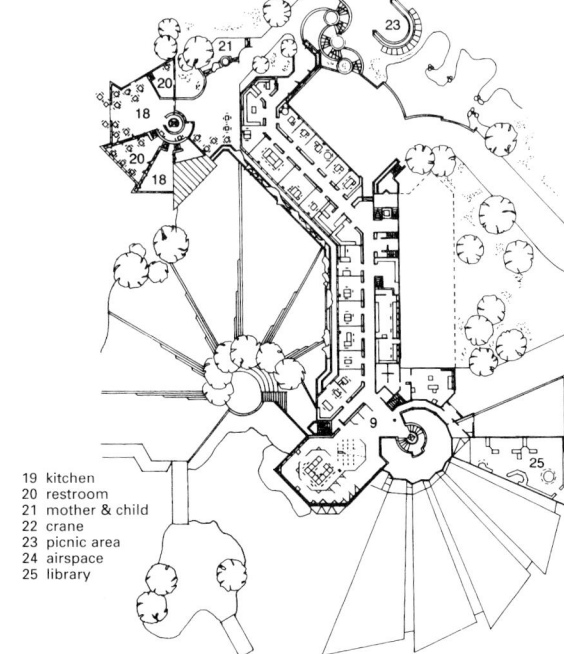

19 kitchen
20 restroom
21 mother & child
22 crane
23 picnic area
24 airspace
25 library

③ **Upper floor**

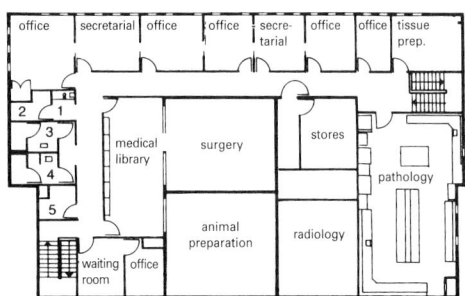

④ **Upper floor of the animal hospital zoo in San Diego**

1 kitchen	7 laundry	12 washroom
2 stores	8 sterilization	13 dark room
3-4 WC	9 deep freeze room	14 inspection
5 porter	10 porter	15 entrance store
6 stores	11 changing	16 entrance kitchen

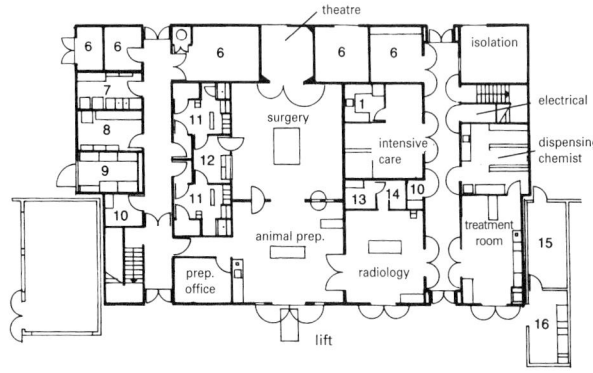

⑤ **Ground floor of → ④**

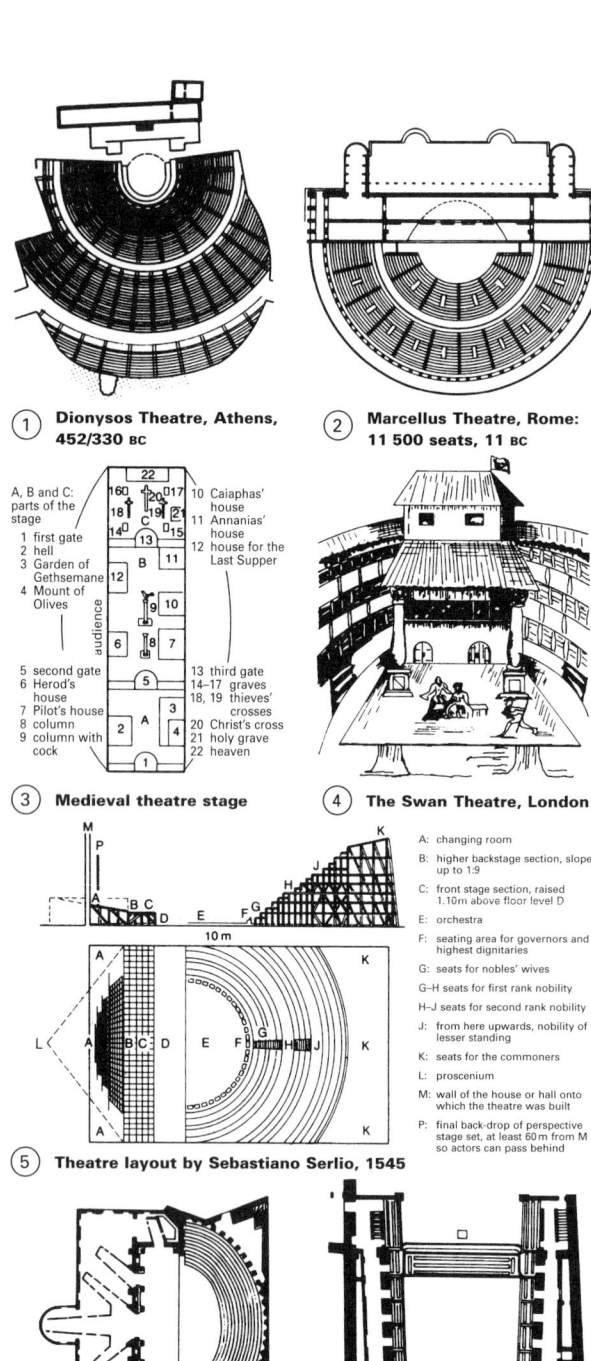

① **Dionysos Theatre, Athens, 452/330 BC**

② **Marcellus Theatre, Rome: 11 500 seats, 11 BC**

A, B and C: parts of the stage
1 first gate
2 hell
3 Garden of Gethsemane
4 Mount of Olives
5 second gate
6 Herod's house
7 Pilot's house
8 column
9 column with cock
10 Caiaphas' house
11 Annanias' house
12 house for the Last Supper
13 third gate
14–17 graves
18, 19 thieves' crosses
20 Christ's cross
21 holy grave
22 heaven

③ **Medieval theatre stage**

④ **The Swan Theatre, London**

A: changing room
B: higher backstage section, slope up to 1:9
C: front stage section, raised 1.10m above floor level D
E: orchestra
F: seating area for governors and highest dignitaries
G: seats for nobles' wives
G–H seats for first rank nobility
H–J seats for second rank nobility
J: from here upwards, nobility of lesser standing
K: seats for the commoners
L: proscenium
M: wall of the house or hall onto which the theatre was built
P: final back-drop of perspective stage set, at least 60m from M so actors can pass behind

⑤ **Theatre layout by Sebastiano Serlio, 1545**

⑥ **Teatro Olimpico, Vicenza, 1585**
Architects: Andrea Palladio & Vicenzo Scamozzi

⑦ **The old theatre of the Comédie Française, Paris 1687–1689**

⑧ **Teatro Farnese, Parma, 1618–1628**
Architect: Giovanni Battista Aleotti

THEATRES: HISTORICAL SUMMARY

Theatre planning requires an understanding of complex functional relationships which can, in part, be gained by examining the 2500-year-old history of theatre development. The examples shown here and on the following page give an insight into the tradition of theatre building, the principles of which are still in use today, although contemporary architects are increasingly injecting modern thinking into theatre design.

Dionysos Theatre, the start of European theatre building → ①. Marcellus Theatre, the first theatre in Rome built entirely of stone → ②. Medieval stage theatre, temporary platform and fittings → ③. Inner room of the Swan Theatre from a drawing by Van de Wit in 1596 → ④. Italian theatre from the start of the 16th century → ⑤. Early Renaissance theatres were temporary wooden structures in existing halls, e.g. Vasari developed a wooden reusable system for a theatre in the Salone dei Cinquencento Palazzo Vecchio in Florence. The Teatro Olimpico in Vicenza → ⑥. The first permanent theatre building of the Renaissance was the Comédie Française in Paris → ⑦. Boxes were first built in the mid-17th century. Teatro Farnese in Parma → ⑧ was the first building with a moving scenery system. Teatro 'San Carlo' in Naples → ⑨. Teatro alla Scala Milan → ⑩, the model for opera houses in the 18th and 19th centuries, but also the new Metropolitan Opera in New York, 1966. Grand Opéra House in Bordeaux → ⑪. The great foyer was the model for the Grand Opéra House in Paris, Garnier 1875.

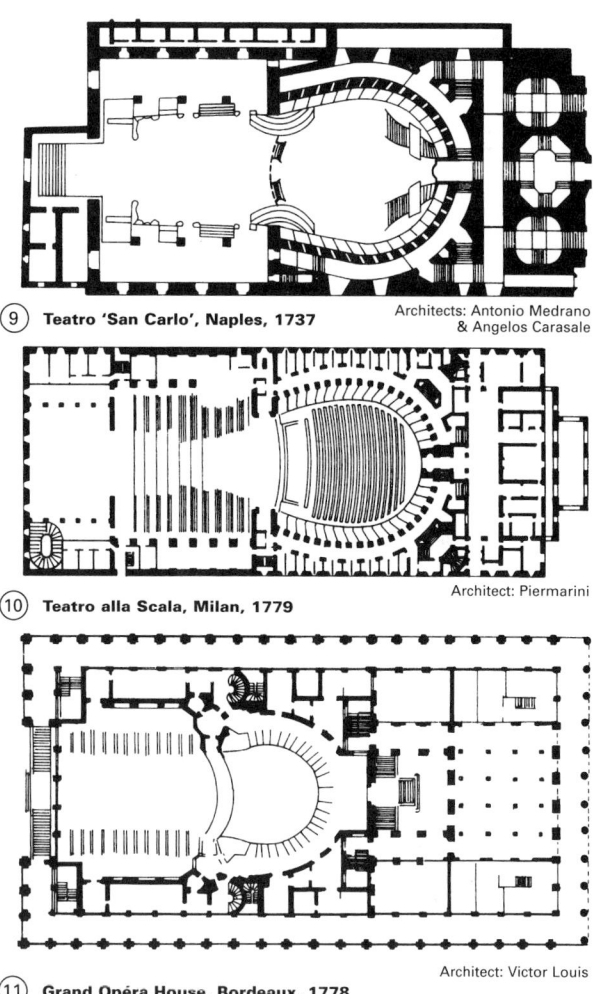

⑨ **Teatro 'San Carlo', Naples, 1737** Architects: Antonio Medrano & Angelos Carasale

⑩ **Teatro alla Scala, Milan, 1779** Architect: Piermarini

⑪ **Grand Opéra House, Bordeaux, 1778** Architect: Victor Louis

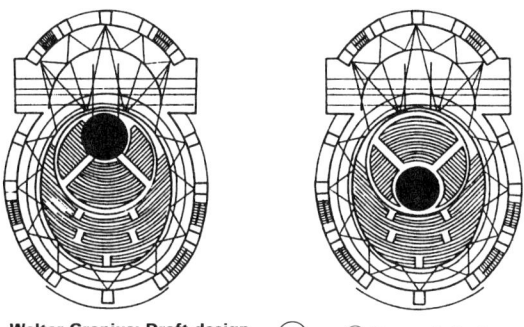

Architects: R. Wagner and O. Bruckwald

① **The Festival Theatre, Bayreuth 1876**

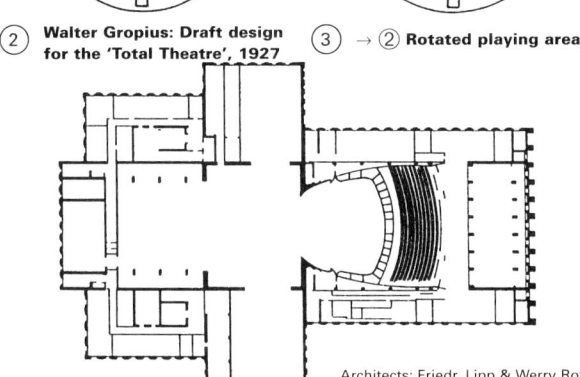

② **Walter Gropius: Draft design for the 'Total Theatre', 1927**

③ → ② **Rotated playing area**

Architects: Friedr. Lipp & Werry Roth

④ **Dessau Regional Theatre, 1938 (regional theatre), plan view of upper circle**

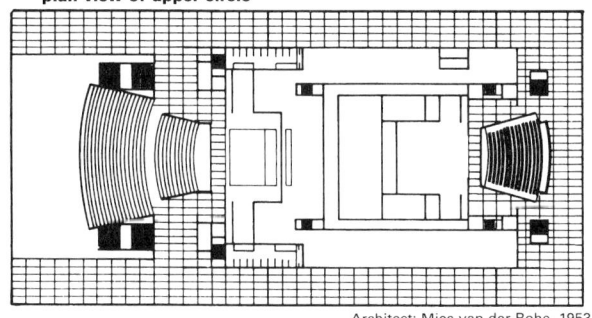

Architect: Mies van der Rohe, 1953

⑤ **Competition entry for the National Theatre, Mannheim**

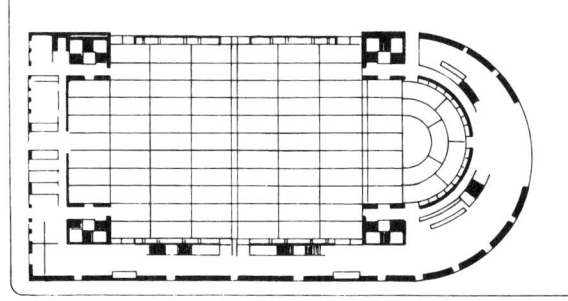

Architect: J. Savade

⑥ **Theatre on Lehniner Platz, Berlin 1982**

THEATRES: HISTORICAL SUMMARY

The Bayreuth Festival Theatre → ① With his theatre form, R. Wagner erected a counterpoint to the Grand Opéra House in Paris. Total theatre project by W. Gropius/E. Piscator. To note: rotating audience space, stage with paternoster system – projection options on walls and ceiling → ②–③. Dessau Regional Theatre → ④. Early example of a modern stage system with sufficient secondary stages. Draft for the National Theatre in Mannheim → ⑤. Theatre on Lehniner Platz, Berlin, the first large new building with a flexible theatre space (conversion of the Mendelsohn building 'Universum' from 1928) → ⑥. Opéra Bastille, Paris → ⑦, the previous largest stage system with ten secondary stages on two levels.

Trends in current theatre building

There are two trends today.

1. Preservation, restoration and modernisation of the previous theatres of the 19th and up to the middle of the 20th century.
2. New buildings with 'experimental' open space features, e.g. Theatre on Lehniner Platz, Berlin → ⑥. In a similar direction are the many conversions from previous rooms to theatre workshops with seats for about 80–160 onlookers.

Opera and theatre: There are two different expressions of theatre building: the opera and the theatre.

The *opera* is in the tradition of the Italian opera buildings of the 18th and 19th centuries → p. 476 ⑥ + ⑩. It is characterised by a clear spatial-architectural separation between the audience area and the stage by the orchestra pit, and through large seat numbers (1000 to almost 4000 seats), as well as the corresponding box system and the circles necessary for large numbers of spectators, e.g. Teatro allo Scala (Milan) with 3600 seats, Deutsche Oper (Berlin) with 1986 seats, Metropolitan Opera (New York) with 3788 seats, Opéra Bastille (Paris), 2700 seats → p. 476. As a counterpoint to the opera form as circle/box theatre is the The Festival Theatre, Bayreuth. This is conceived as a stalls theatre on the Greek/Roman principle and has only 1645 seats.

The *theatre* is structurally in the tradition of the German reform theatres of the 19th century. It is characterised by the stalls arrangement (i.e. the audience sit in a large ascending curved area) and by a distinctive, front acting stage (an acting area in front of the proscenium in the auditorium). Theatres, however, particularly seek the tradition of the English theatre → p. 476 ④, i.e. an acting area in the auditorium.

A modern example from the English speaking area is the Chichester Festival Theatre, England, by Powell & Moya, 1962. One example in Germany is the Mannheim National Theatre, small theatre, Weber, Hämer, Fischer 1957.

The variable open room form was intensified by the room experiments of the theatres in the 1970s, e.g., Concordia Theatre, Bremen, (conversion of a one-time cinema). Room variation options are shown in the Theatre on Lehniner Platz, Berlin → p. 476 ⑥.

A speciality in the German-speaking area is the multipurpose theatre (mixed form of opera house and theatre) which is characterised by the dominating requirements of the opera, e.g., Stadttheater Heilbronn, Biste & Gerling, 1982.

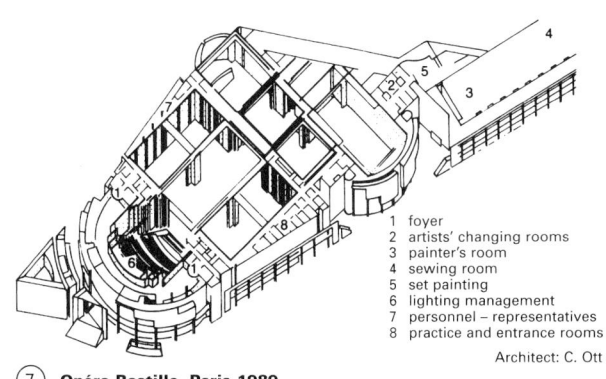

1 foyer
2 artists' changing rooms
3 painter's room
4 sewing room
5 set painting
6 lighting management
7 personnel – representatives
8 practice and entrance rooms

Architect: C. Ott

⑦ **Opéra Bastille, Paris 1989**

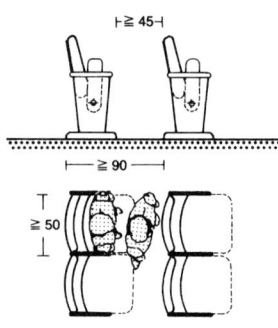

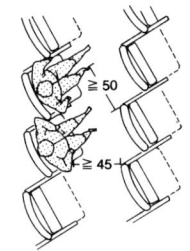

(1) **All seats apart from boxes must have fixed, self-operating folding seats with the above minimum dimensions**

(2) **Offset folding seats provide elbow space**

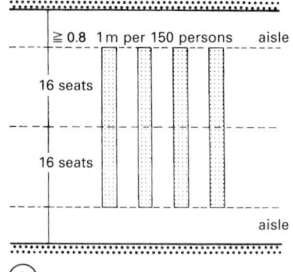

(3) **Row width: 16 seats**

(4) **Row width: 25 seats + necessary door**

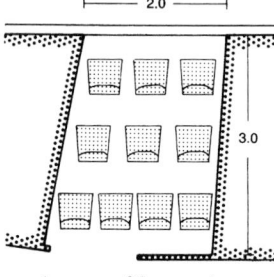

(5) **Boxes may have up to 10 loose chairs, else fixed chairs are necessary – area: minimum 0.65 m² per person**

(6) **Standing places should be arranged in rows, separated by fixed barriers according to the above minimum dimensions**

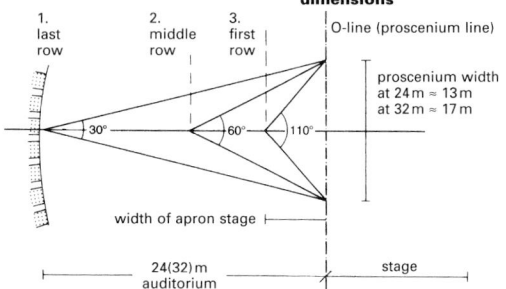

(7) **Proportions of the traditional auditorium (view)**

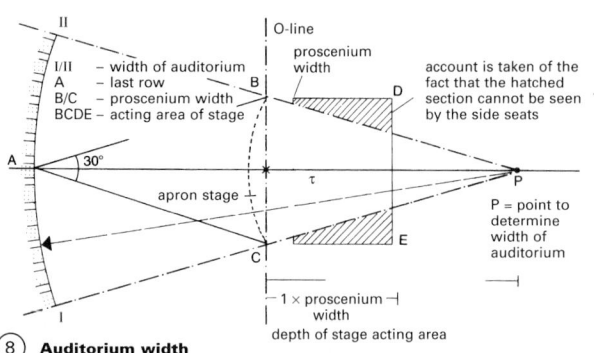

(8) **Auditorium width**

THEATRES: AUDITORIUMS

Audiences: assessing demand

An important element of a feasibility study is the assessment of demand for performing arts within the community that the facility is proposed to serve. The aim is to establish whether there are audiences for the proposed programme of use, and to define a catchment area from which audiences are to be drawn. Assessment of the area under consideration includes studies of:

- population characteristics
- transportation characteristics
- potential audiences
- local cultural traditions
- existing provision
- actual audiences
- pilot scheme.

Auditorium and stage/playing area

Seating capacity: In general, the maximum capacity of an auditorium depends on the format selected, and on aural and visual limitations set by the type of production. Other factors include levels, sightlines, acoustics, circulation and seating density, as well as size and shape of platform/stage.

Size of auditorium: An area of at least 0.5 m² per spectator is to be used for sitting spectators. This number is derived from a seat width × row spacing of at least 0.45 m² per seat, plus an additional minimum of 0.5 m × 0.9 m i.e. approximately 0.05 m² per seat → (1).

Length of rows: A maximum of 16 seats per aisle → (3). 25 seats per aisle is permissible if one side exit door of 1 m width is provided per 3–4 rows → (4).

Exits, escape routes: 1 m wide per 150 people (min. width 0.8 m) → (3) – (4).

Volume of room: This is obtained on the basis of acoustic requirements (reverberation) as follows: playhouses approx. 4–5 m³/spectator; opera approx. 6–8 m³/spectator of air volume. For technical ventilation reasons, the volumes should be no less than these figures so as to avoid air changes which are too pronounced (draughts).

Proportions of auditorium: These are obtained from the spectator's psychological perception and viewing angle, as well as the requirement for a good view from all seats.

- Good view without head movement, but slight eye movement of about 30°.
- Good view with slight head movement and slight eye movement approx. 60° → (7).
- Maximum perception angle without head movement is about 110°, i.e. in this field everything which takes place 'between the corners of the eyes' is perceived. There is uncertainty beyond this field because something may be missed from the field of vision.
- With full head and shoulder movement, a perception field of 360° is possible.

Proportions of the classical auditorium

(Opera, multipurpose theatre, traditional playhouse) → (7): Maximum distance of last row from the proscenium line ('start of stage'):

- for playhouse – 24 m (maximum distance from which it is still possible to recognise facial expressions)
- for opera – 32 m (important movements still recognisable).

Width of auditorium: This is derived from the fact that spectators sitting to one side should still be able to see the stage clearly → (7). Variants are possible. The comfortable proportions and often good acoustics of the classical theatres of the 18th and 19th century are based on special rules of proportion → (9) – (10).

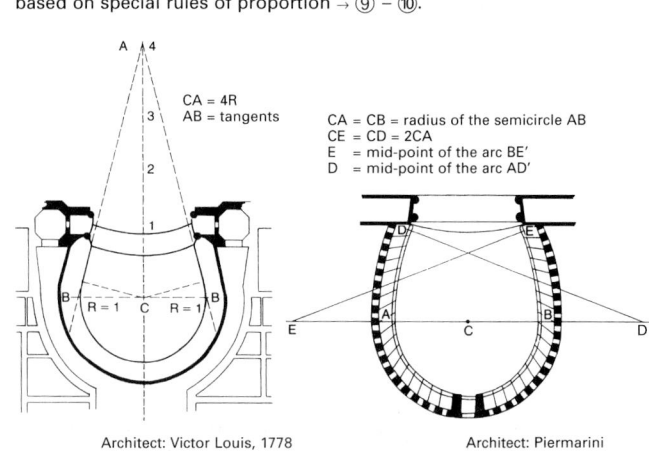

CA = 4R
AB = tangents

CA = CB = radius of the semicircle AB
CE = CD = 2CA
E = mid-point of the arc BE'
D = mid-point of the arc AD'

Architect: Victor Louis, 1778

Architect: Piermarini

(9) **Design of the contours of the auditorium in the Grand Theatre in Bordeaux**

(10) **Design of the curve of the auditorium in the Teatro alla Scala in Milan**

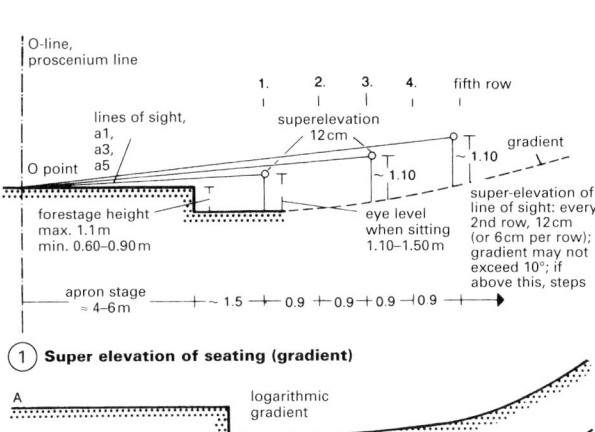

(1) **Super elevation of seating (gradient)**

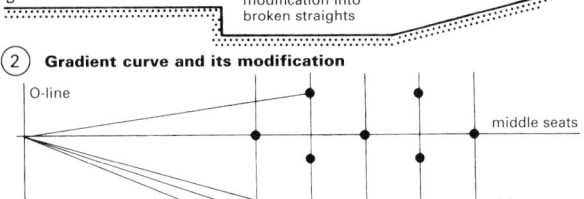

(2) **Gradient curve and its modification**

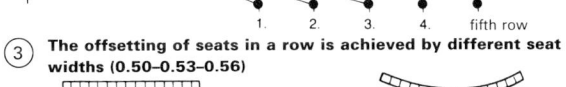

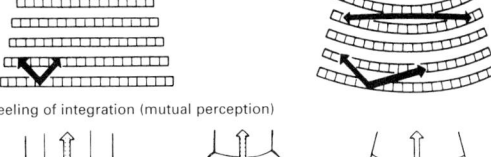

(3) **The offsetting of seats in a row is achieved by different seat widths (0.50–0.53–0.56)**

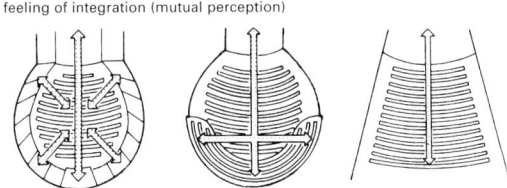

(4) **Contact relationships between public and stage and among one another**

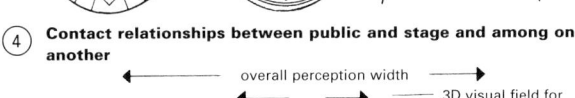

(5) **Perceptive field and proportions of proscenium arch**

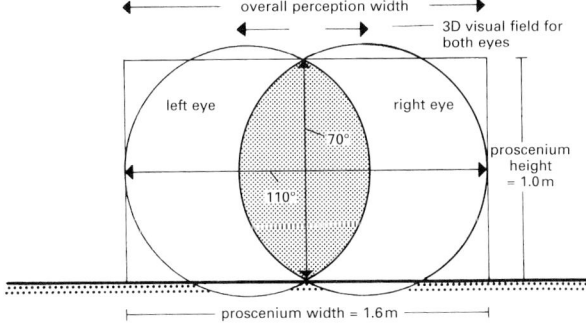

(6) **Ceiling shape and sound reflection**

Elevation of seating

Elevation of seating (gradient) in the auditorium is obtained from the lines of vision. Such lines are valid for all seats in the auditorium (stalls as well as circles) → (1). Since the spectators sit in 'gaps', only every second row requires full sight elevation (12cm). Special mathematical literature addresses the subject of sight problems in theatres in which the randomness of the distribution of different sizes of spectators is also taken into account. The rows of spectators should be formed in a circular segment with respect to the stage, not just for better alignment but also to achieve better mutual perception (feeling of integration) → (4).

Complete vertical section through auditorium

The proscenium height should first be determined. The ratio in a stalls theatre of proscenium height to width should be 1:6. The golden section, or the physiological perception field, is included in this → (5). After the proscenium height, the apron height, the banking of the stalls and the volume of the auditorium are determined; the lines of the ceiling are obtained from the acoustic requirements. The aim should be for the reflected sound from the stage or apron to be equally distributed throughout the auditorium. In the case of circles, it should be ensured that the full depth of the stage can be seen, even from the upper seats. This might require an increase in proscenium height.

The proportions of an experimental auditorium are shown on the following page.

Neutral or open theatre auditoriums permit different arrangements of spectator seating and stage areas. This variable arrangement is achieved in two ways:

(A) mobile staging and mobile spectator stands with a fixed auditorium floor

(B) movable floor consisting of lifting platforms.

Method A is technically more complicated and more expensive, and is therefore used only in larger auditoriums for at least 150–450+ people. Type B is especially suitable for smaller theatres and unused rooms which normally have insufficient subspace.

99 seats × 0.6m² needs a stage area of 60m² (2/3) + 30m² (1/3) i.e. 90–100m².

A room proportion of 1:1.6 is the best option for multiple use (see (1) – (3) on the following page).

Vertical room section

In simple auditoriums, the lighting rig is unnecessary → (2) – (3). Instead, manual hoists can be provided (bars which are pulled up to the ceiling with hand winches). Two examples are shown on the next page: a small theatre in Münster (Architect: v. Hansen, Rane, Ruhnau,1971), 170–380 seats, mid-section of floor is variable with lifting stage sections, acting stages (1) – (4) and Ulm podium (Architect: Schäfer, 1996), 150–2000 seats (4) – (7).

Larger type B has 450+ seats. It is designed like small type A, but with a mobile floor to simplify change in the floor topography. One problem is the size and lifting accuracy of the stage sections. Often, the rough topography of the stage sections has to be modified by manually arranging platforms to give fine topography → p. 480 (3). See Theatre on Lehniner Platz, Berlin → p. 477 (6).

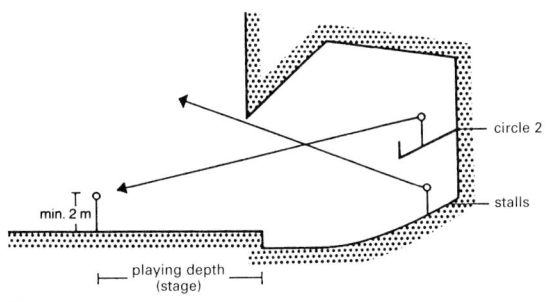

(7) **Circle theatre and view of stage**

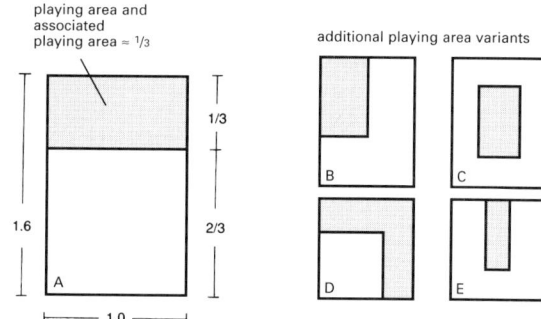

playing area and associated playing area ≈ 1/3

1/3

2/3

1.6

1.0

A

additional playing area variants

B

C

D

E

(1) **Playing area variants; smaller type A**

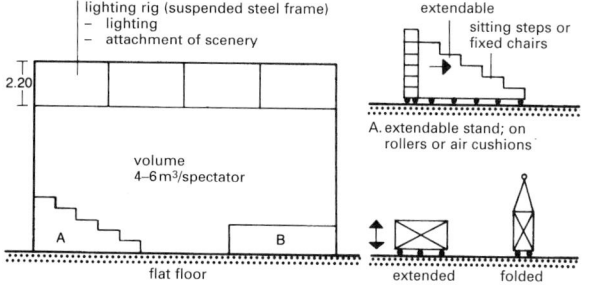

lighting rig (suspended steel frame)
- lighting
- attachment of scenery

extendable
sitting steps or fixed chairs

2.20

volume 4–6 m³/spectator

A

B

flat floor

A. extendable stand; on rollers or air cushions

extended   folded

B. travelling folding podium, height adjustable

(2) **Experimental theatre auditorium**

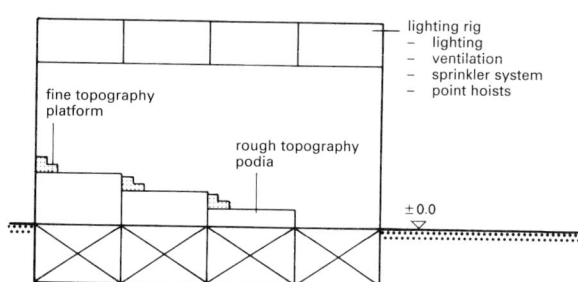

lighting rig
- lighting
- ventilation
- sprinkler system
- point hoists

fine topography platform

rough topography podia

± 0.0

(3) **Lifting stages – sketch showing principles**

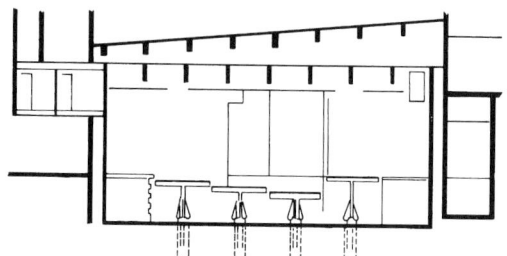

(4) **Podium in the theatre at Ulm (longitudinal section)**

Architect: Fr. Schäfer

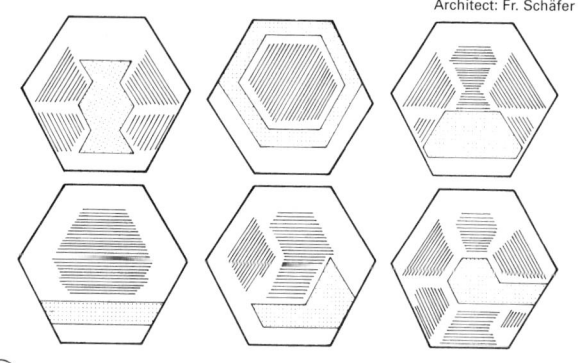

(5) **Ulm podium: six variants for arranging the action surfaces → (4)**

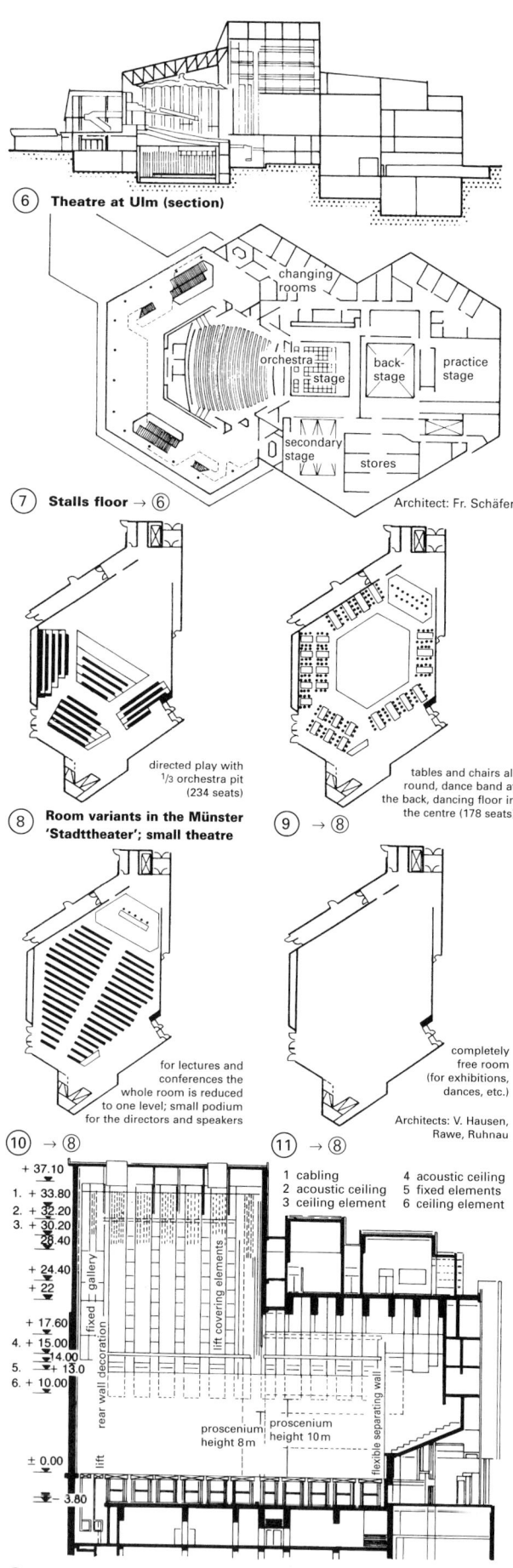

(6) **Theatre at Ulm (section)**

changing rooms

orchestra   back-   practice
stage   stage   stage

secondary
stage   stores

Architect: Fr. Schäfer

(7) **Stalls floor → (6)**

directed play with 1/3 orchestra pit (234 seats)

tables and chairs all round, dance band at the back, dancing floor in the centre (178 seats)

(8) **Room variants in the Münster 'Stadttheater'; small theatre**

(9) **→ (8)**

for lectures and conferences the whole room is reduced to one level; small podium for the directors and speakers

completely free room (for exhibitions, dances, etc.)

Architects: V. Hausen, Rawe, Ruhnau

(10) **→ (8)**

(11) **→ (8)**

1 cabling   4 acoustic ceiling
2 acoustic ceiling   5 fixed elements
3 ceiling element   6 ceiling element

+ 37.10
1. + 33.80
2. + 32.20
3. + 30.20
   28.40
+ 24.40
+ 22
+ 17.60
4. + 15.00
   14.00
5. + 13.0
6. + 10.00

± 0.00

3.80

proscenium height 8 m

proscenium height 10 m

(12) **Salle Modulable, Opéra Bastille, Paris (longitudinal section)**

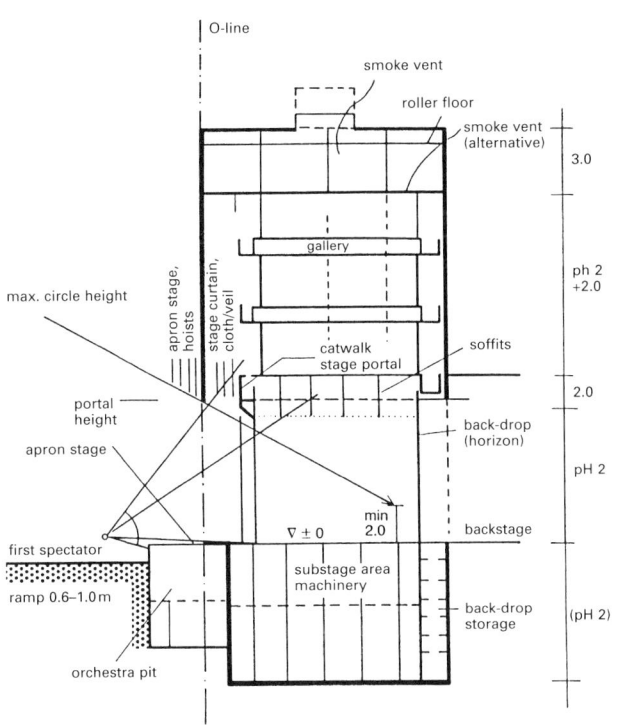

① **Cross-sectional proportions of a traditional stage (side view)**

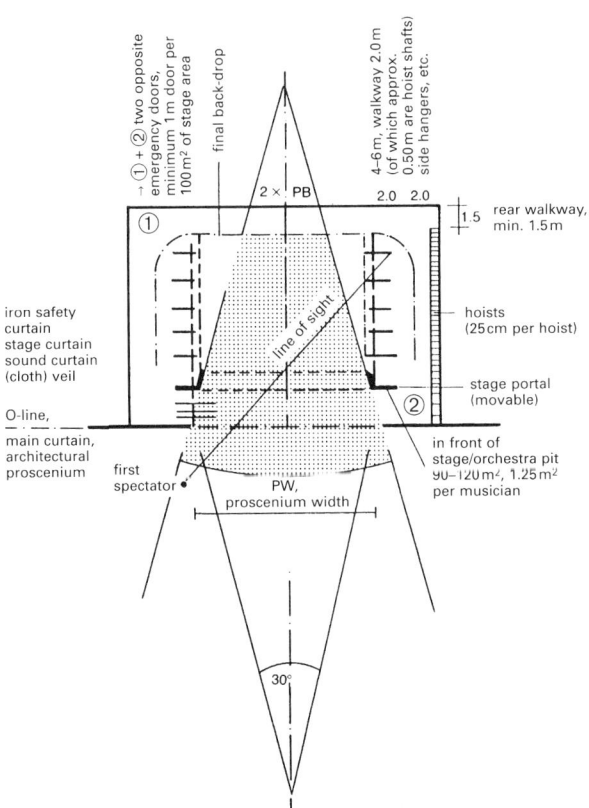

② **Proportions of a traditional stage (plan view)**

STAGES AND SECONDARY AREAS

Proportions of Stages, Secondary Stages and Stores

Stage forms

There are three stage forms: full stage, small stage and set areas.

Full stage: More than 100 m² of stage area. Stage ceiling more than 1 m above top of proscenium arch. An essential feature of a full stage is an iron safety curtain which separates the stage from the auditorium in the event of an emergency.

Small stage: Area no more than 100 m², no stage extension (secondary stages), stage ceiling not more than 1 m above top of proscenium. Small stages do not require an iron safety curtain.

Set areas: Raised acting areas in rooms without ceiling projection. The peculiarity with set areas is in the regulations with respect to curtains and scenery. They affect the operation, not the planning, of set areas. Experimental auditoria fall within the set area definitions.

Stage proportions

Stage proportions are developed from the lines of vision from the auditorium. The stage area is the playing area plus walkways (around the back of the stage) and working areas. The principle design of a traditional full stage → ① – ②.

Mobile set areas are formed from height-adjustable platforms or lifting podia. Variable shapes are achieved by splitting the area into individual elements. Basic dimensions 1 m × 2 m → ③ – ④.

Stage ventilation

Means should be provided for ventilating smoke and hot gases resulting from fire on the stage, e.g. provision of haystack lantern light or fire ventilator sited in highest point in roof over stage and as near to centre of stage as is reasonably practicable. An additional fresh air inlet may prove effective.

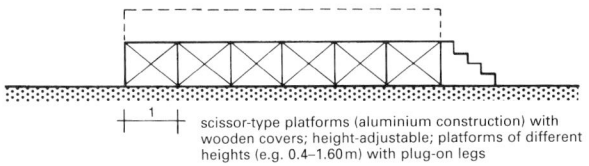

scissor-type platforms (aluminium construction) with wooden covers; height-adjustable; platforms of different heights (e.g. 0.4–1.60 m) with plug-on legs

③ **Set area**

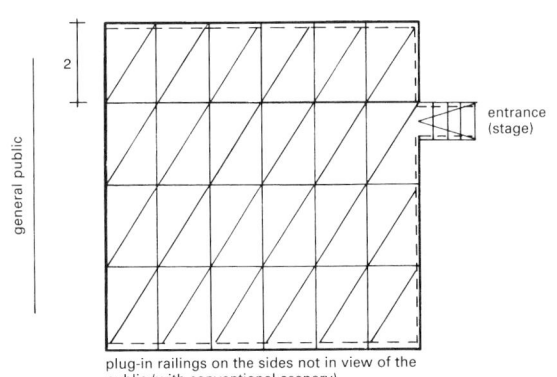

plug-in railings on the sides not in view of the public (with conventional scenery)

④ **Set area (plan view)**

The classical stage systems in the 18th and 19th centuries only recognised the main stage; scene-changing was done using minimum space and with astonishing speed with sliding scenery. A small backstage was used to provide space for deep stage perspectives → ①.

The modern stage has 3D stage structures (sets). Scene-changes require secondary stages to which the sets can be transported with flat stage trolleys. Apart from the removal of sets, there are additional scene-changing techniques → ② – ③.

Opera requires two side stages and one rear stage → ⑥ – ⑦.

The small three-section theatre only has one side stage and one rear stage → ④ – ⑤.

---

① Scene-changing technology, classical stage system of the 18th and 19th centuries

rear stage

store   store

set stage

audience

3-section theatre: 1 side stage, 1 rear stage

side stage

audience

rear stage

opera: 2 side stages, 1 rear stage

② Plan view

slow change 1890–1930/50

hoisting equipment

section

horizontal movement: trolley

lifting/lowering/turning podia turntable

turning: rotating stage

removal: hoisting equipment (bar/point)

turntable

lifting/lowering podia

tilting podia

③ Modern stage

---

④ Typical three-section theatre (section) → ⑤

1 removable floor structure and panels
2 side-stage trolleys with compensating podia
3 rear-stage trolleys with turntable, tilting
4 manual orchestra covers
5 portable lifting unit

---

⑤ Typical three-section theatre stage area (plan view)

store
rear stage
side stage
store

6 set transport/lifting stage
7 stage manager's lift
8 stairs
9 proscenium tower, fixed
10 proscenium frame, movable
11 steel safety curtain
12 border curtain, side stage
13 border curtain, rear stage
14 divisible main curtain

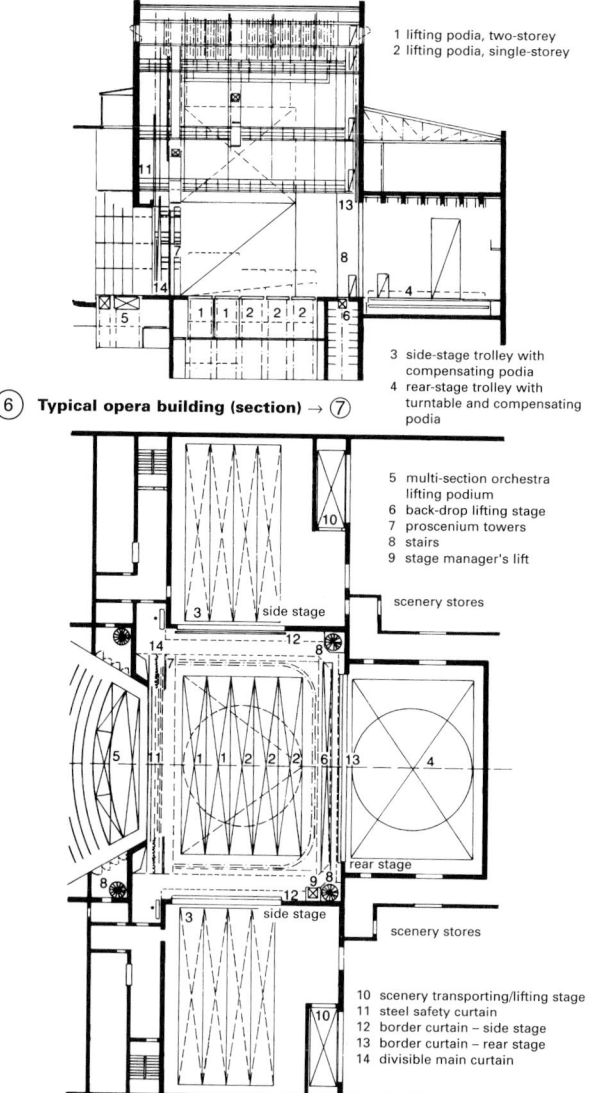

⑥ Typical opera building (section) → ⑦

1 lifting podia, two-storey
2 lifting podia, single-storey

3 side-stage trolley with compensating podia
4 rear-stage trolley with turntable and compensating podia

5 multi-section orchestra lifting podium
6 back-drop lifting stage
7 proscenium towers
8 stairs
9 stage manager's lift

scenery stores

⑦ Typical opera building (plan view)

side stage

rear stage

side stage

scenery stores

10 scenery transporting/lifting stage
11 steel safety curtain
12 border curtain – side stage
13 border curtain – rear stage
14 divisible main curtain

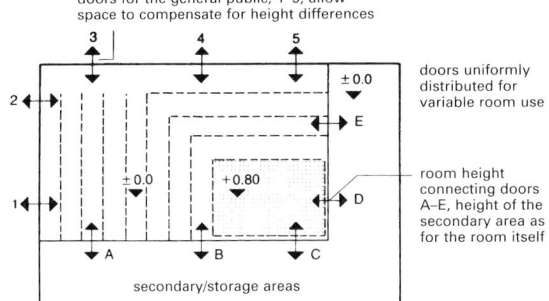

doors for the general public, 1–5, allow
space to compensate for height differences

doors uniformly distributed for variable room use

room height connecting doors A–E, height of the secondary area as for the room itself

secondary/storage areas

① **Secondary/storage areas**

traditional storage of back-drops
– on edge in boxes, manual transport, large proportion of area required, height: 9–12 m
– in boxes, manual transport, large proportion of area required for moving

② **Storage**

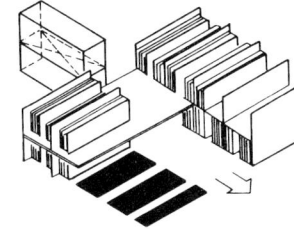

modern back-drop storage
– loading of containers by hand from secondary stage, or specific storage areas
– transport of container to external store
– computer-controlled storage of containers in multi-storey shelving

③ **Storage → ⑤**

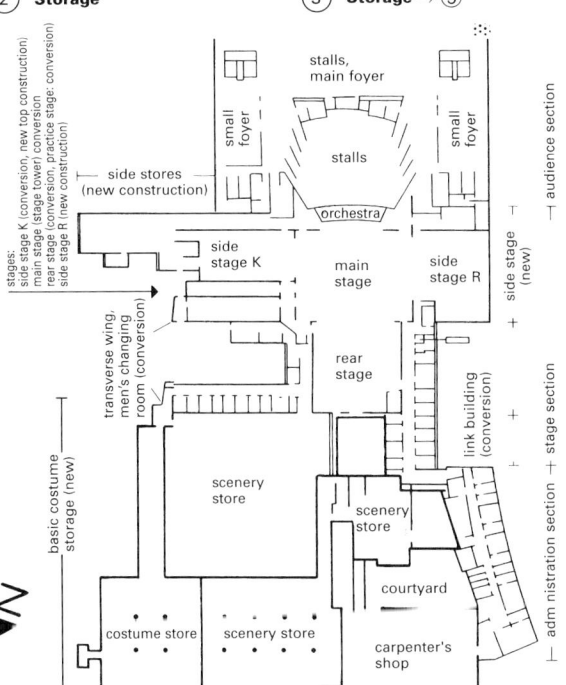

④ **Deutsche Oper, Berlin (plan view)**

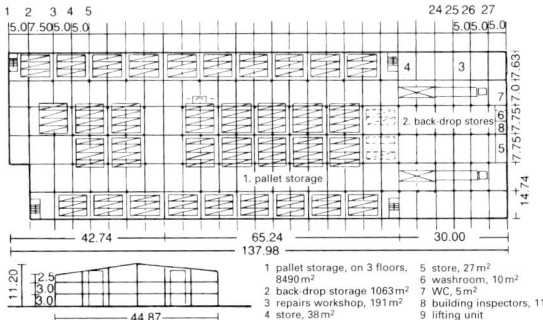

1 pallet storage, on 3 floors, 8490 m²
2 back-drop storage 1063 m²
3 repairs workshop, 191 m²
4 store, 38 m²
5 store, 27 m²
6 washroom, 10 m²
7 WC, 5 m²
8 building inspectors, 11 m²
9 lifting unit

Architect and Stage Technician: Biste & Gerling

⑤ **Ground floor of scenery store, National Theatre, Mannheim (plan view and section)**

STAGES AND SECONDARY AREAS
Secondary Areas

Open stages require secondary areas for the sets, and storage areas for platforms and stands – around 30% of the whole room. (The secondary areas should be the same size as the playing area; and the space required for storage areas can be calculated from the folded platforms and stands.)

Open stages require considerably less scenery than normal stages because the playing area is viewed from several sides.

Regulations limit the use of scenery for safety reasons → ①.

Storage rooms are used for the stage items and scenery. They can be subdivided into: sets, back-drop, furniture, props store, store for costumes, hats, shoes, masks, wigs, lighting, etc.

Scenery and costume stores need the greatest amount of space.

Scenery store: (particularly for heavy parts) at stage height and in the immediate vicinity of the stage. Rough values for the dimensions of scenery and costume stores can be obtained from the number of productions in the repertoire. For theatres and multipurpose theatres, this is normally 10–12; for opera, it is up to 50 productions and more.

Per play/production, around 20–25% of the playing area is required as storage area, i.e. for theatres about three times the playing area, and for opera, at least ten times. Practice has shown that, with time, the stores turn out to be too small; therefore, theatres and, especially, operas create storage areas outside the theatre.

The significant amount of transporting has inevitably led to the introduction of the most up-to-date transportation and storage technology: container systems with computer-controlled storage.

Around 2–4 containers are required per production (special operas may require up to 12 containers).

Examples: the Deutsche Oper (Berlin) stores are in direct connection with the stage → ④; the National Theatre (Mannheim) storage is outside the theatre, in containers → ⑤.

Surface area required for costumes is also calculated according to the number of productions in the repertoire and the size of the ensemble (e.g. opera) apart from the performers, the choir and ballet. Space requirement for costumes: 1–12 cm/costume or 1–15 costumes per rod → ⑥ – ⑦.

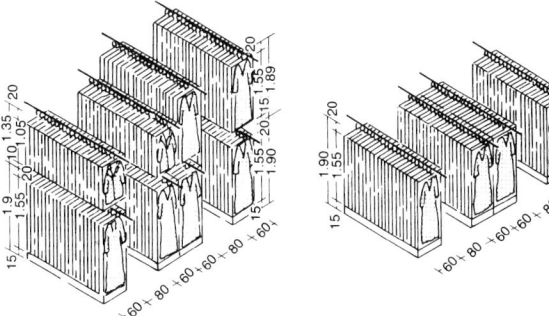

⑥ **Fixed two-storey clothes stands for the hanging and storage of costumes**

⑦ **Single-storey → ⑥**

STAGES AND SECONDARY AREAS

Workshops for making scenery

In his 1927 book *Stage technology today*, stage technician Kranich demanded that workshops should be excluded from the theatre. He gave two reasons: danger of fire, and limited space options.

In old theatres, the workshops were often installed in completely inaccessible places. Today, the demand is to have the workshops within the theatre with the aid of appropriate space planning so as to retain the specific, positive operating climate in the theatre (identification with the work). However, for space or economic reasons, in the case of large theatres, the workshops are often installed in separate buildings. Space required for scenery workshops in medium theatres (normal and multipurpose theatres) is 4–5 times the area of the main stage. In large opera houses or double theatres (opera and plays), ten times the area is required. Always install workshops on one level whether in or outside the theatre.

There are several classes of scenery workshop:

(a) The painting room area must be sufficient to allow two large back-drops or round horizons can be spread flat on the floor for painting. Average size of a round horizon is 10 m × 36 m. Due to spraying work, it is necessary to subdivide the room with a thick curtain. Floor heating is needed for drying the painted back-drops, and a wooden floor for spreading the canvases. A sewing room should be near the painting room for sewing together the canvas sections. Its size should be about 1/4 of the painting room.

(b) The carpenters' shop is subdivided into bench and machine rooms. It has wooden floors and a connected wood store for 3–10 productions.

(c) The upholstery room is about 1/10 the size of the painting room.

(d) Metalworking shop: size as for carpenters' shop, with a screed floor.

(e) Laminating shop: size as for (b) and (d).

(f) The workshops should be grouped around an assembly room, which serves for practice setting up of the scenery. The surface area should be as for the stage, and height according to proscenium height plus 2 m, 9–10 m across.

(g) Changing, washing and rest rooms (canteen) are required for technical personnel. Offices are needed for technical management personnel. Additional workshops are needed for sound, lighting, props and costumes. The size of these rooms should be according to requirements (i.e. production intensity, personnel numbers, etc.).

Personnel rooms

These are needed for artistic personnel, directors, and administration. From an historic perspective, the personnel rooms were placed on either side of the stage: women to the left and men to the right. However, this was unfavourable for the operation, so, nowadays, personnel rooms are built on one side, opposite the technical side, and on several floors. Here also are found the mask-making shops, frequently also the costume workshop, administration and directors.

Changing rooms: → ② – ⑨ typical plan views.

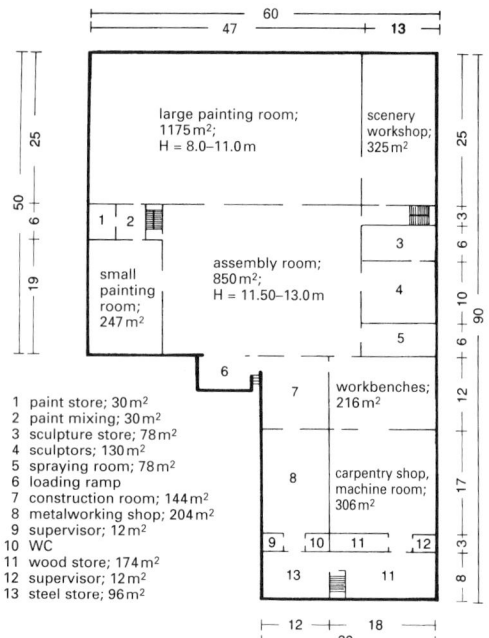

large painting room; 1175 m²; H = 8.0–11.0 m

scenery workshop; 325 m²

small painting room; 247 m²

assembly room; 850 m²; H = 11.50–13.0 m

workbenches; 216 m²

carpentry shop, machine room; 306 m²

1 paint store; 30 m²
2 paint mixing; 30 m²
3 sculpture store; 78 m²
4 sculptors; 130 m²
5 spraying room; 78 m²
6 loading ramp
7 construction room; 144 m²
8 metalworking shop; 204 m²
9 supervisor; 12 m²
10 WC
11 wood store; 174 m²
12 supervisor; 12 m²
13 steel store; 96 m²

Architect and Stage Technician: Biste & Gerling

① **Workshop building/ground floor**

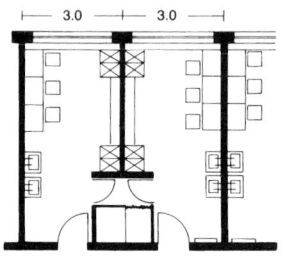

② **Soloists' changing rooms; min. 3.8–5 m²/person**

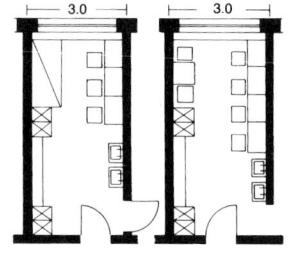

③ **Soloists' changing rooms; min. 5 m²/person**

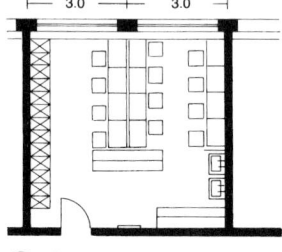

④ **Choir changing room; min. 2.75 m²/person**

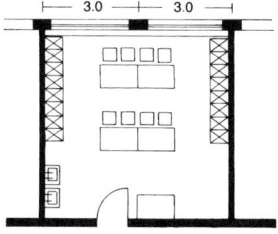

⑤ **Changing and tuning room (green room) for members of the orchestra; min. 2 m²/person**

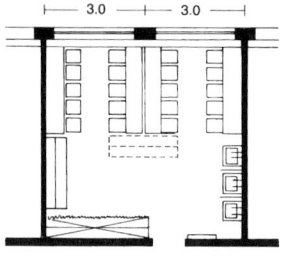

⑥ **Changing room for extra choir and/or minor players; min. 1.65 m²/person**

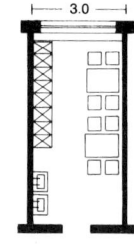

⑦ **Changing and rest room for technical personnel**

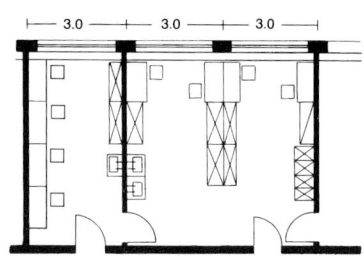

⑧ **Changing room for ballet group; min. 4 m²/person**

⑨ **Make up and work room for mask makers**

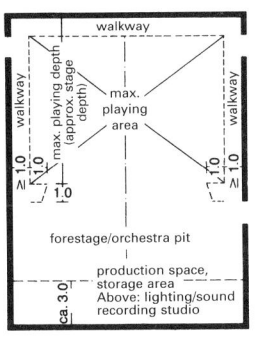

(1) **Typical large rehearsal stage (plan view)**

walkway
walkway
walkway
max. playing depth (approx. stage depth)
max. playing area
ca. 3.0
forestage/orchestra pit
production space, storage area
Above: lighting/sound recording studio

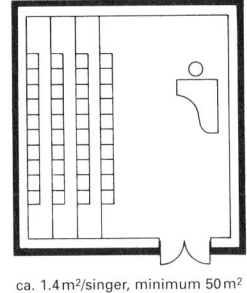

(2) **Typical choir rehearsal room (plan view)**

ca. 1.4 m²/singer, minimum 50 m²
ca. 7 m³/singer

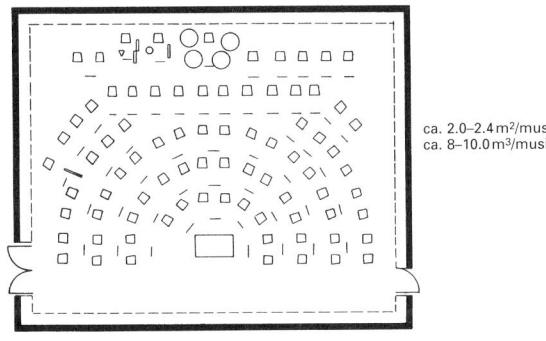

(3) **Typical large rehearsal stage (plan view)**

ca. 2.0–2.4 m²/musician
ca. 8–10.0 m³/musician

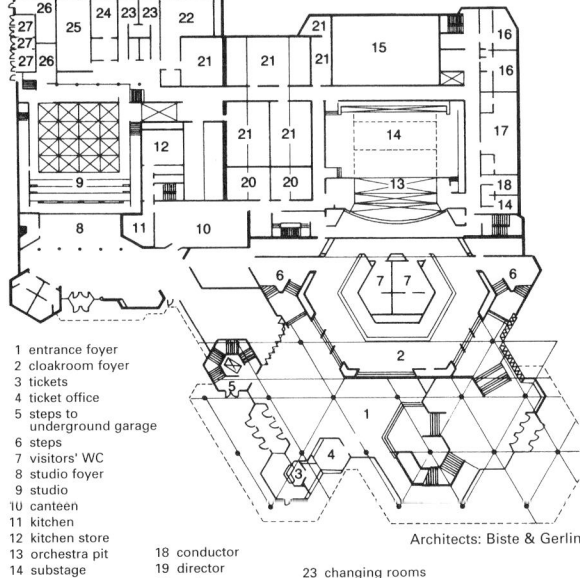

1 entrance foyer
2 cloakroom foyer
3 tickets
4 ticket office
5 steps to underground garage
6 steps
7 visitors' WC
8 studio foyer
9 studio
10 canteen
11 kitchen
12 kitchen store
13 orchestra pit
14 substage
15 rehearsal room
16 extras
17 choir
18 conductor
19 director
20 tuning room
21 stores
22 electrical shop
23 changing rooms
24 battery room
25 low-voltage switchroom
26 medium-voltage switchroom
27 transformer cells

Architects: Biste & Gerling

(4) **Entrance hall floor of Heilbronn Theatre**

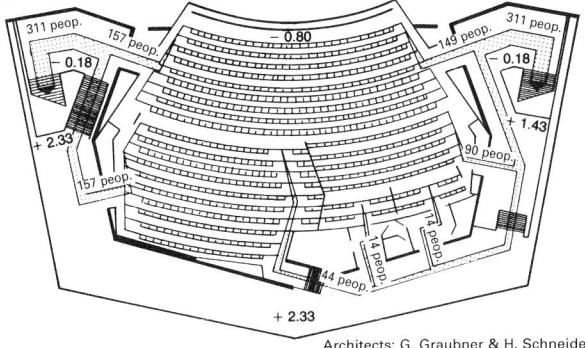

311 peop. 157 peop. 149 peop. 311 peop.
−0.80
0.18 0.18
+1.43
+2.33
157 peop. 90 peop.
+2.33
44 peop.

Architects: G. Graubner & H. Schneider
Stage Technician: A. Zotzmann, 1964

(5) **Evacuation plan: Trier Theatre (626 seats)**

STAGES AND SECONDARY AREAS

Rehearsal Rooms

To reduce the load on the main stage, every theatre must have at least one rehearsal stage e.g. in a small theatre, the scenery for the current piece is on the stage, with rehearsal on the rehearsal stage. Dimensions of the rehearsal room should be as per the main stage. Plan view of typical rehearsal stage for traditional theatre → ①. Orchestra rehearsal rooms → ③, choir rehearsal rooms → ②, soloist rehearsal rooms and ballet rooms are needed in multipurpose theatres or opera houses.

Experimental theatre

Personnel and rehearsal rooms, workshops and stores are also required in reduced form for continuous operation.

Technical utilities

Transformer room, medium- and low-voltage switchroom, emergency power batteries, air-conditioning and ventilation plant, water supply (sprinkler system) according to local requirements and specialist planning.

Public areas

The classical Italian opera houses had only narrow access doors and stairs – there was no actual foyer – whereas the huge public areas of the Grand Opéra House in Paris were impressive. The theatre fire in Vienna, in 1881, resulted in fundamental changes. Self-contained emergency stairs, separate for each level, were now required for the audience. Such a requirement in principle still applies today.

In the traditional theatre, the foyers are subdivided into the actual foyer, restaurant (buffet) and a smoking foyer. An area of foyer 0.8–2.0 m²/spectator and 0.6–0.8 m²/spectator, respectively, is realistic. The function of the foyer has changed today. It may be supplemented with displays, performances and other activities. Theatre performances must be taken into account during planning: room height, wall, ceiling and floor configuration.

Cloakrooms

Minimum: 4 m per 100 visitors. Nowadays, cloakrooms often have lockers: 1 locker per 4 visitors. The foyer is also the waiting and queuing area. WCs are installed with respect to the foyer in the normal ratio (i.e. 1 WC/100 people: 1/3 men, 2/3 women): there must be at least one men's and one ladies' toilet. The entrance hall (lobby) contains the day and evening ticket offices, which should be opposite each other.

External access and emergency routes

These are needed in accordance with local requirements and will depend on the location:
- prestigious location in an urban square
- location in a park or on a main street
- as part of a large building.

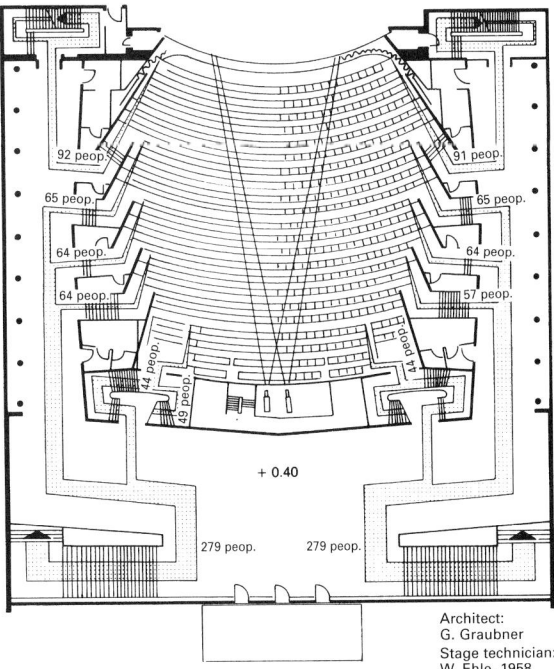

92 peop. 31 peop.
65 peop. 65 peop.
64 peop. 64 peop.
64 peop. 57 peop.
44 peop. 44 peop.
49 peop.
+0.40
279 peop. 279 peop.

Architect: G. Graubner
Stage technician: W. Ehle, 1958

(6) **Evacuation plan: Lünen Theatre (765 seats)**

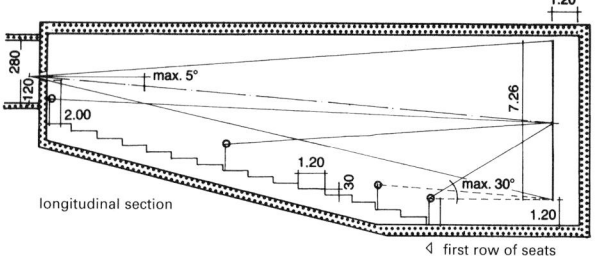

longitudinal section

◁ first row of seats

plan view

① **Optimum auditorium**

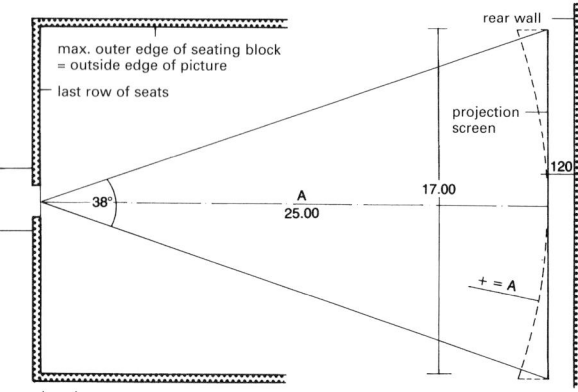

normal screen 1:1.37
wide screen 1:1.66
wide screen 1:1.85
'Kinoton' format 1:2
70mm
Cinemascope 1:2.34

② **Screen formats for the same screen height**

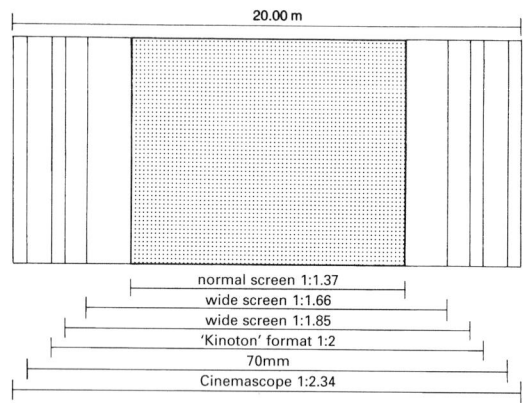

③ **Screen formats for the same screen width**

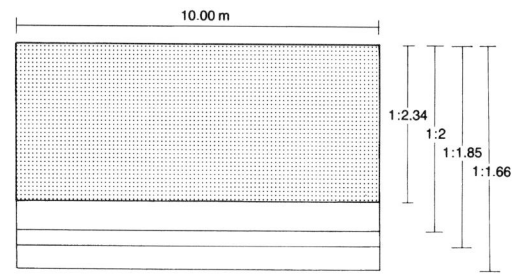

④ **Permitted noise level**

Before planning, bring in a cinema technology firm for advice.

Film projection: Fire separation materials are no longer required for the projection room with safety film. Projectionists operate several projectors; the projection room is no longer a continuously used workplace for staff. 1 m of space behind the projector and at the operating side, 2.80 m high, ventilation, noise insulation to the auditorium side. Projection rooms may be combined for several auditoriums.

Film widths of 16 mm, 35 mm and 70 mm. The centre of the projected beam should not deviate more than 5° horizontally or vertically from the centre of the screen, or it should be deflected via a deflection mirror. → ①

Conventional systems use two projectors in a superimposing operation. Nowadays, automatic operation with only one projector using horizontal film plates provides no-break film presentations with 4000 m spools. This system is sometimes used with several projection rooms and remote control from projection and control points. The film automatically gives control signals for all the functions of the projector, lens changes, auditorium lighting, stage lighting, curtain and picture cover.

Picture sizes depend on the distance of the projector from the screen; height/side ratio is 1:2.34 (Cinemascope) or 1:1.66 (wide screen) for smaller room widths. The angle from the middle of the last row of seats to the outer edge of the picture should be at most 38° for Cinemascope. The ratio of the spacing of the last row of seats to the projection screen should be 3:2 → ② – ③.

Projection screen: Minimum distance of projection screen from wall in the case of THX is 120 cm, according to theatre size and system reducible to 50 cm with respect to the sound system configuration.

The projection screen is perforated (sound-permeable). Movable blinds or curtains limit the projection screen to the side for the same picture height. Large projection screens are curved with a radius centred on the last row of seats. The lower edge of the projection screen should be at least 1.20 m above the floor → ①.

The auditorium should have no outside light other than emergency lighting. Walls and ceiling are made from non-reflective materials and in not too bright colours. Spectators should sit within the outside edge of the screen. The viewing angle from the first row of seats to the centre of the picture should not exceed 30°.

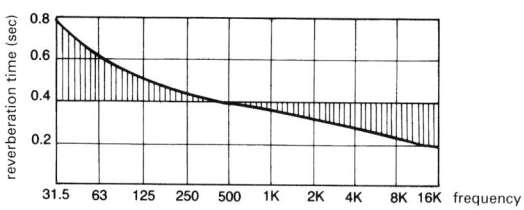

⑤ **Permitted reverberation time depending on frequency**

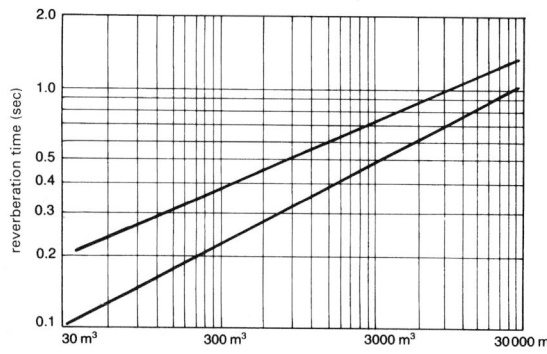

⑥ **Reverberation time with respect to room volume**

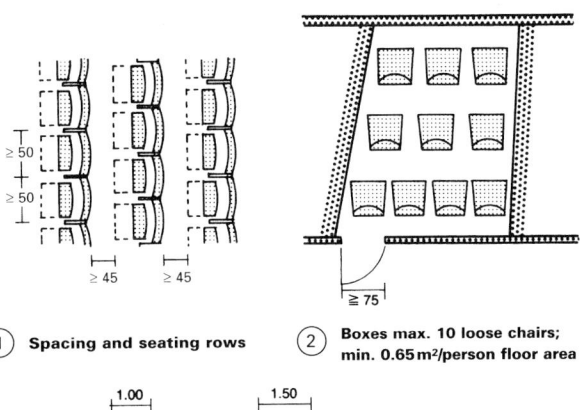

① **Spacing and seating rows**

② **Boxes max. 10 loose chairs; min. 0.65 m²/person floor area**

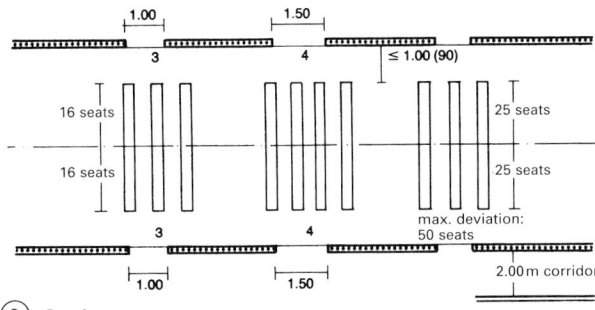

③ **Seating**

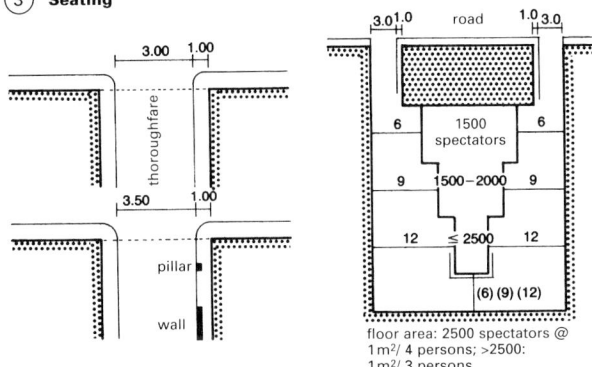

④ **Access roads and thoroughfares**

⑤ **Spacing within building boundaries**

floor area: 2500 spectators @ 1m²/ 4 persons; >2500: 1m²/ 3 persons

⑥ **Circarama: All-round film surface (360°) showing a connected film, projected by 11 synchronously running projectors, e.g. ExPo Brussels**

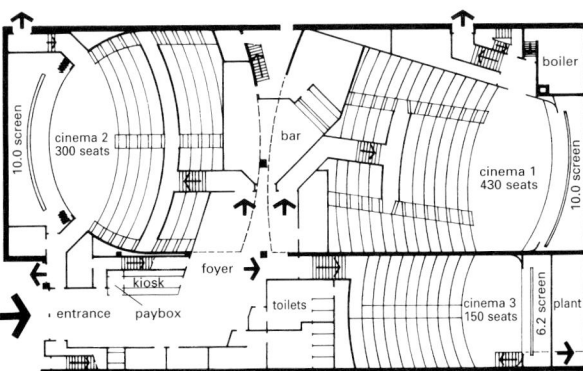

⑦ **Three-screen cinema in Putney, London**

The floor gradient is achieved by an inclination of up to 10% or by the use of steps with a maximum step height of 16 cm and with aisle widths of 1.20 m.

Acoustics

Neighbouring auditoriums should be separated with partitioning walls of approximately 85 dB 18–20 000 Hz.

Acoustic deflecting surfaces on the ceiling with low acoustic delay difference time. The reverberation time can increase with increasing room volume and decreases from 0.8–0.2 seconds from low to high frequencies → p. 486 ⑥.

The rear wall behind the last row of seats should be sound absorbent to prevent echo.

The loudspeakers should be distributed around the auditorium so that the volume difference between the first and last row of seats does not exceed 4 dB.

Sound reproduction

In future, apart from mono-optical sound reproduction, the Dolby stereo optical sound system in 4-channel technology is also necessary with three loudspeaker combinations behind the screen and the fourth channel with additional speakers to the side and rear.

For 70 mm film 6-channel magnetic sound, the additional speaker combination is behind the screen.

In the case of BTX, there is a sound absorption wall behind the screen according to the Lucas Film System into which the loudspeaker combination is built.

Ticket offices are now superseded by electronic booking and reservation systems.

Multi-screen complexes are now considered necessary to be commercially viable. Various theories are used to determine the total seats needed. A basic requirement is to give visitors a choice of programmes and to enable the operator to show each film in an auditorium with a capacity to match anticipated public demand. Thus, a film playing to half capacity audiences can be transferred to smaller auditorium or vice versa. Seating capacity varies between 100 and 600 chairs.

In larger units, there are boxes for smokers and families with children which have fire-resistant and sound-insulating partition walls and special sound reproduction systems.

Car parking space: normally one per 5–10 spectators. New larger cinemas with several projection rooms in combination with multi-level communications, leisure, sporting and shopping options provide entertainment for the whole family under one roof, and they can also be used for seminars and events.

Can be located in peripheral areas of towns with corresponding car parking spaces, e.g. Kinopolis in Brussels with an amusement park, 27 projection rooms with 7500 seats (150 and 700 per room) and screens from 12 m × 8 m up to 29 m × 10 m → ⑧.

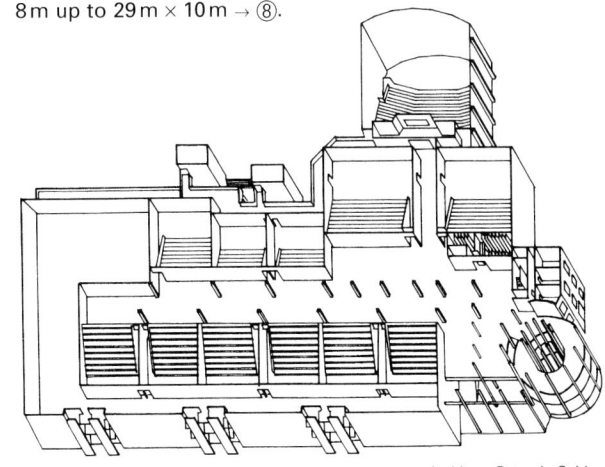

Architect: Peter de Gelder

⑧ **Kinopolis, Brussels**

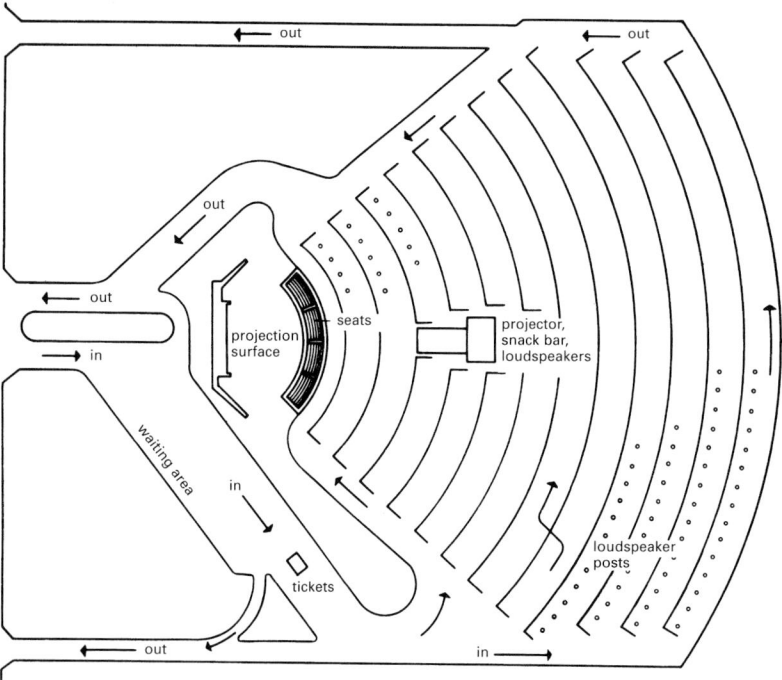

① Fan-shaped drive-in cinema with inclined ramps and low projection cabin which only takes up two rows

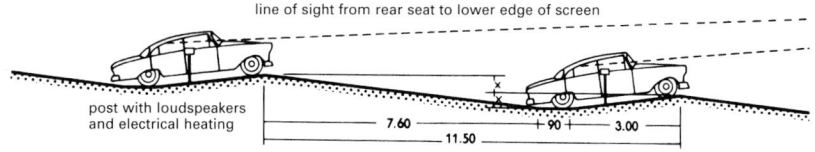

② Ramp arrangement and dimensions; elevations can be different according to screen picture height

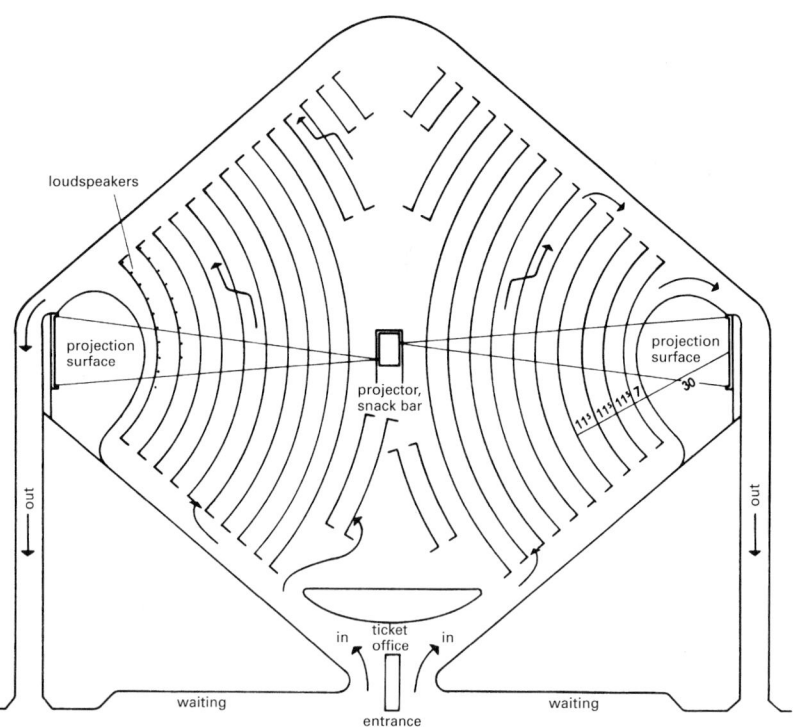

③ Double cinema (one projection room for both screens) creates the option of having half-time offset starting times; all other rooms (ticket offices, bar, toilets etc.) are shared.

DRIVE-IN CINEMAS

Drive-in cinema spectators do not leave their cars; they watch the film from their cars.

The size is limited by ramps and the number of cars (max. 1000–1300) which still permits a good view. Normal size is 450–500 cars → ①.

cars	no. of ramps	projection screen to rear edge of ramp (m)
500	10	155
586	11	170
670	12	180
778	13	195
886	14	210
1000	15	225

The location should be near to a motorway, petrol station or service area, and screened off so that light and noise from passing vehicles does not interfere.

An entrance with a waiting area will avoid traffic congestion on the road. A drive-past ticket office allows tickets to be obtained from the cars → ①.

Exiting is best done by leaving the ramp towards the front.

Ramps are inclined in curves so that the front of each vehicle is raised providing even the rear-seat passengers with a good view of the screen over the roofs of the front row of cars → ②.

The design of the whole ground area should be dust-free and not slippery when wet.

Ticket booths: one booth for 300 vehicles, two for 600, three for 800, and four for 1000 vehicles.

The screen size varies according to the number of vehicles, 14.50m × 11.30m for 650 cars; 17.0m ×13.0m for 950 cars. The screen is best facing east or north since this permits earlier performances and in areas with harsh climates the screen should be housed in a structure with solid walls.

The height above the ground depends on the ramp slope and angle of sight. A screen which is inclined towards the top reduces distortion. The framework and screen wall must be capable of withstanding the wind pressure.

Rows of seats should be included and a children's playground is desirable.

The projection building is usually centrally located at 100m from the screen. The projection room contains film projector(s), generator and sound amplification system.

Sound reproduction is best with loudspeakers inside the cars. These speakers (for two vehicles) are located on posts set 5.0m apart and are taken into the car by the cinema visitors.

Heating may be supplied on the loudspeaker posts with possible connections for internal car heating.

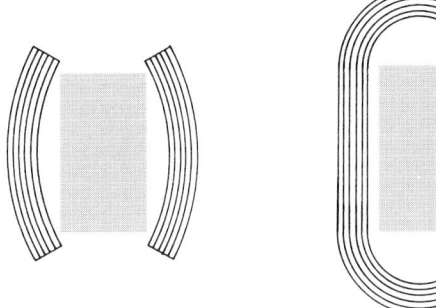

① **U-shaped stadium layout**

② **USA: segmented layout**

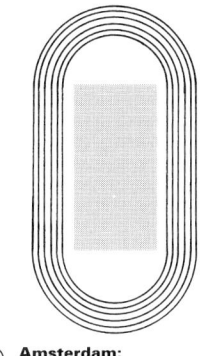

③ **Amsterdam: semicircular ends**

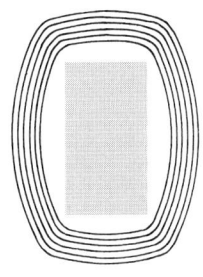

④ **Rotterdam: curved sides and corners**

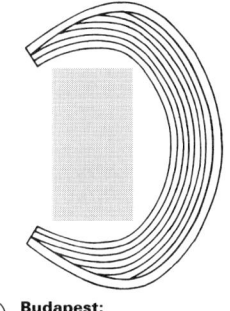

⑤ **Budapest: horseshoe around long axis**

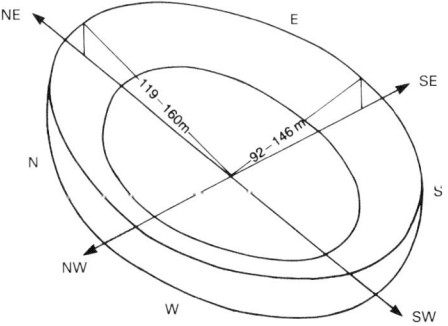

⑥ **Viewing distance determines the stadium size**

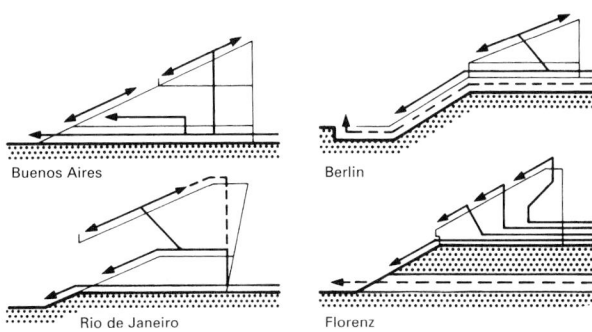

⑦ **Access arrangements in individual stadiums**

The stadiums of antiquity have never been matched for grandeur (the Circus Maximus in Rome, for instance, could hold 180000 spectators) but they form the basis for modern sports stadiums. The size of the inner sports field can be based loosely on the size of a football pitch, with measurements of 70×109m. For athletics stadiums there should be a running track surrounding the field (see page 500). The basic shape for the playing area is usually similar to the elliptical shape used in ancient stadiums. As a rule a stadium is partly below ground with the excavated earth heaped up around it. In relation to town planning, sports grounds must fit in well with the local topography and be designed with good transport links and supply facilities (train, bus and tram stations, large car parks etc.). They should not be sited close to industrial areas where smoke, odours and noise might create unpleasant conditions. Covered and open grounds for various sports can be combined and integrated into the town/district plan.

The orientations of ancient arenas were determined by the variable timing of the contests – axes ran west to east or south to north. In Europe today the main axis is usually north-east to south-west so that a maximum number of spectators have the sun at their backs → ⑥. Access gates are therefore situated to the east. The turnstiles are positioned so as to direct the stream of visitors to the various stadium entry points. Access into the stadium is often through the embankment formed from the excavated earth or via stairways leading halfway up the terraces to a point from which the rows above and below can be reached → ⑦.

To give spectators a clear view and ensure good acoustics, Vitruvius recommended a fixed gradient of 1:2 for both seating and standing areas. (If a public-address system is incorporated, then, of course, the view is the only determinant of the gradient.)

In staggered seating rows, spectators in every row should be able to see over the heads of those in the corresponding two rows in front. This results in a parabolic curve. The best viewing conditions are to be found on the 'long side' of the segment.

The arrival of spectators happens relatively slowly so the widths of entrances and stairways have to be calculated on the basis of the flow of spectators leaving the stadium. This is when the flow rate is at maximum. According to research in the Amsterdam stadium → ③, every 5000 spectators needs 7 minutes or 420 seconds to leave via the 9.5m wide steps. (In equivalent stadiums the times are: Los Angeles, 12 minutes; Turin, 9 minutes.) Therefore, one spectator uses 1m of staircase width in

$$\frac{9.5 \times 420}{5000} = 0.8 \text{ seconds}$$

Or, in 1 second a 1m wide staircase accommodates

$$\frac{5000}{9.5 \times 4.20} = 1.25 \text{ spectators}$$

The formula giving the staircase width necessary to allow a certain number of spectators to leave the stadium in a given time is:

$$\text{staircase width (m)} = \frac{\text{number of spectators}}{\text{emptying time (s)} \times 1.25}$$

First aid rooms for the spectators should be provided close to the spectator area. First aid treatment for 20000 or more spectators requires a suite of rooms: treatment and recovery rooms 15m², storeroom 2m² and two toilets with ventilation. For sports grounds with 30000 capacity or greater, provide an additional room of 15m² for the emergency services (police, fire brigade). Commentary boxes in the main stand must have a good view onto the field of play and each box should be at least 1.5m². Behind every five press boxes a control room of 4m² is necessary. One car parking space should be provided for every four spectators and spaces should be allocated for coaches and buses.

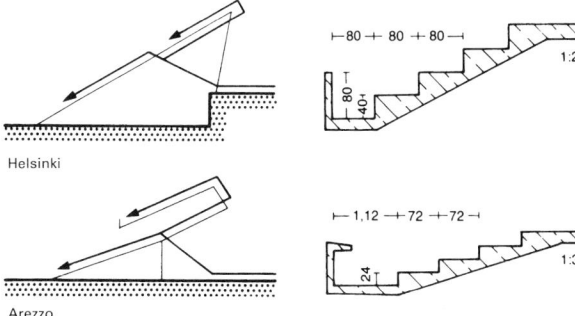

⑧ **Stand profiles**

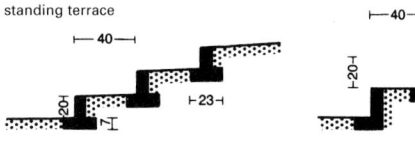

① **Construction of sightlines**

standing terrace

② **Movable concrete units**

③ **Angle steps**

④ **Angle steps**

⑤ **Reinforced concrete with drainage**

seating terrace

⑥ **Wooden bench with step board**

⑧ **Cantilevered seating**

⑦ **Raised seats on concrete uprights**

⑩ **Seating on precast concrete units**

⑨ **Sloping concrete floor with steps**

⑪ **Seats on metal brackets set in concrete**

SPECTATOR FACILITIES

All planning must be done in accordance with national 'regulations for the construction and management of meeting places', in which the requirements for access ways, stairways, ramps and spectator accommodation are set out.

Depending upon the planned capacity, seating is provided either along the long side of the ground (to take advantage of the shortest viewing distance) or, for capacities above 10000, around the whole ground. As most events take place in the afternoon, the best position for spectators is on the west side so that the sun is at their backs.

To improve viewing conditions in the multi-row layout, there has to be sufficient super-elevation. In smaller grounds with up to 20 rows of terracing or 10 rows of seats, a linear gradient of 1:2 can be taken as a basis. In all other grounds the linear gradient should ideally be replaced with one which is parabolic. In this case the gradient for seating and standing places is to be set using a construction based on the spectators' line of sight. In terracing stands the super-elevation should be 12cm and in rows of seating it should be 15cm → ①.

Seating Areas

The necessary space for seating areas is calculated as follows:

width of seat	0.5m
overall depth	0.8m
of which:	
seat depth	0.35m
circulation	0.45m

Rows of seats (benches) as well as single seats can be planned. Seats with back rests offer greater comfort. Depending on the arrangement of entrances and exits, each row can comprise:

on each side of a passage	
in shallow rising rows	48 places
in steeply rising rows	36 places

Seating and standing areas must be separated by fences. For every 750 seats an escape route (stairway, ramp, flat surface) with a minimum width of 1.00 m must be provided.

Standing Areas

The necessary space for standing spaces is calculated as follows:

width of standing space	0.5m
depth of standing space	0.4m

Again, for every 750 spaces an escape route (stairway, ramp, flat surface) with a minimum width of 1.00m must be provided. To allow standing areas to fill and empty evenly, and to prevent dangerous overcrowding, they should be divided into groups or blocks of around 2500 places. Each block should have its own entry/exit points and should be separated from the others by fences.

Inside the blocks of standing places, a staggered arrangement of crush barriers will be necessary to prevent diagonal crowd surges. It must also be ensured that there is a suitably strong barrier, with a height of around 1.10m, between every ten rows of standing spaces.

The building industry produces pre-cast concrete steps for the construction of spectator areas → ⑧ + ⑩.

Guests of honour: In larger stadiums an enclosed 'Royal box' with movable furniture may be needed.

Roofing of stands: Covering as many places as possible should be the aim. By designing overlapping stands the number of covered seats can be increased.

⑬ **Sketch of a partially sunken stadium with banking**

⑫ **Section through the Olympic Stadium, Berlin**

Architect: Professor Werner March

corridor for umpire/referee

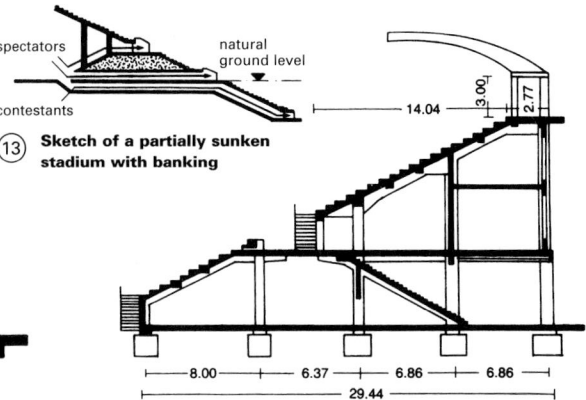

⑭ **Section through the Vienna Stadium**

Architect: O.E.Schweizer

SPORTS HALLS

The planning basics for multipurpose games halls should take into account the competition regulations of the individual sports organisations to give the best possible integration of all individual types of activity → ①. Note that a divisible hall offers more versatility than several separate dedicated halls.

The necessary size of the site depends on the area required for the desired sporting activities and administration rooms. As a rule of thumb, it can be estimated as follows: required sports area ×2 + necessary distance to site boundary + necessary parking area for vehicles.

The following ancillary rooms and spaces are required for sports events: an entrance area with ticket office, spectator cloakroom and cleaning equipment room (→ ② 0.1 m² per spectator); spaces for spectators (0.5 × 0.4–0.45 m per seat, including adjacent circulation area), and, as appropriate, for guests of honour, press, radio and television (including circulation areas: 0.75 × 0.8–0.85 m for each member of the press; 1.8 × 2.0 m per commentary box; 2.0 × 2.0 m per camera platform). A box office, cafeteria, emergency services room, administration office and meeting room will also be required.

① Hall dimensions

type of hall	dimensions (m)	useable sports area (m²)	indoor games¹⁾	number of training courts/pitches	number of competition courts/pitches²⁾
multifunctional halls					
single hall	15×27×5.5	405	badminton	4	
			basketball	1	
			volleyball	1	
triple hall	27×45×7³⁾⁴⁾ div. into 3 sections (15×27)⁵⁾	1,215	badminton	12	5⁶⁾
			basketball	3	1
			football		1
			handball		1
			volleyball	3	1
quadruple hall	27×60×7³⁾ div. into 4 sections (15×27)⁵⁾	1,620	badminton	16	7⁶⁾
			basketball	4	2
			football		1
			handball		1
			hockey		1
			volleyball	4	1
alternative: double hall	22×44×7³⁾⁴⁾ div. into 2 sections (22×28+22×16 or 22×16+22×18⁵⁾)	968	badminton	6	5⁶⁾
			basketball		1
			football		1
			handball		1
			hockey		1
			volleyball	3	1
games hall					
single hall	22×44×7³⁾⁴⁾	968	badminton	6	5
			basketball		1
			football		1
			handball		1
			hockey		1
			volleyball	3	1
triple hall	44×66×8³⁾ div. into 3 sections (22×44)⁵⁾	2,904	badminton	24	15
			basketball		4⁶⁾
			football 20 × 40		3
			30 × 60		1
			handball		3
			hockey		3
			volleyball	9	3
quadruple hall	44×88×9³⁾ div. into 4 sections (22×44)⁵⁾	3,872	badminton	32	25⁶⁾
			basketball	5⁶⁾	4
			football 20 × 40		4
			40 × 80		1
			handball		4
			hockey		4
			volleyball	12	4

¹⁾ normal hall games without regard to national or regional practices
²⁾ dimensions according to the regulations of the international sports organisations (can possibly be reduced for national events)
³⁾ the hall height may be reduced around the edges if in accordance with the functional requirements of the sport
⁴⁾ in the case of several halls on one site or in the same complex, it is feasible to reduce the height to 5.5 m in some halls, depending on the planned uses
⁵⁾ minus the relevant thickness of the divider
⁶⁾ maximum number without accounting for the dividers

③ Dimensions of additional activity rooms

room type	dimensions (m)	useable area (m²)
conditioning/weight training room	depending on the range of apparatus, minimum height 3.5 m	35 to 200
fitness room	depending on the range of apparatus, minimum height 2.5 m	20 to 50
gymnastics room	10 × 10 × 4 to 14 × 14 × 4	100 to 196

¹⁾ minimum room height generally 2.5 m
²⁾ space requirement per person is 0.7 to 1.0 m², based on allowances of 0.4 m bench length per person, 0.3 m sitting depth and minimum 1.5 m between benches or between bench and wall (1.8 m recommended)
³⁾ one shower per 6 persons (but a minimum of 8 showers and 4 wash-basins per facility), shower space including a minimum circulation area of 1.0 m² and circulation space at least 1.2 m wide
⁴⁾ training supervisors', umpire/referees' room, perhaps including first aid post (minimum 8 m² for separate first aid room), with changing cubicle and shower; can also be used as an administration room if correctly positioned, designed and of sufficient size
⁵⁾ because the range of apparatus provided varies according to location, it is likely that these minimum dimensions will have to be exceeded; no hall section in a multifunctional hall should have less than a 6 m length apparatus room
⁶⁾ divided into two sections, each with half of the apparatus;
⁷⁾ room depth normally 4.5 m, maximum 6.0 m;
⁸⁾ room depth normally 3 m, maximum 5.5 m;
⁹⁾ according to need;
¹⁰⁾ alternatively, two bigger rooms with proportionally more shower and washing facilities

② Sports hall ancillary rooms

type of hall	entrance area (m²)	changing room (at least 20 m²)²⁾ minimum number	shower room (at least 15 m²)³⁾ number	toilets for each changing room minimum number	toilets entrance area minimum number W	M	instructors' room⁴⁾ (12 m² min; with no first aid post, min 8 m²) minimum number	equipment room multifunctional hall m² minimum⁵⁾	equipment room games hall m² minimum⁵⁾	cleaning equipment room (min 5 m²) minimum number	caretaker's room (min 10 m²) number
single hall	15	2	1⁶⁾	1	1	1	1	60⁷⁾	20⁸⁾	1	1⁹⁾
double hall	30	2	2	1	1	1	1	90⁷⁾	–	1	1⁹⁾
triple hall	45	3¹⁰⁾	3¹⁰⁾	1	1	1	2	120⁷⁾	60⁸⁾	1	1
quadruple hall	60	4¹⁰⁾	4¹⁰⁾	1	1	1	3	150⁷⁾	80⁸⁾	1	1

491

SPORTS HALLS

type of sport	net useable area				additional obstruction-free zone		obstruction-free gross useable areas		clear height
	permissable dimensions		standard dimensions		long sides m	short sides m	length m	width m	
	length m	width m	length m	width m					
badminton	13.4	6.1	13.4	6.1	1.5	2.0	17.4	9.1	9[2]
basketball	24–28	13–15	28	15	1[3]	1[3]	30	17	7
boxing	4.9–6.1	4.9–6.1	6.1	6.1	0.5	0.5	7.1	7.1	4
cricket[7]	29.12–33.12	3.66–4.0	33.12	4.0	1	1	35	6	4.0– 4.5[8]
football	30–50	15–25	40	20	0.5	2	44	21	(5.5)
weightlifting	4	4	4	4	3	3	10	10	4
handball	40	20	40	20	1[4]	2	44	22	7[5]
hockey	36–44	18–22	40	20	0.5	2	44	21	(5.5)
judo	9–10	9–10	10	10	2	2	14	14	(4)
netball	28	15	28	15	1	1	30	17	(5.5)
body-building	12	12	12	12	1	1	14	14	(5.5)
gymnastics	52	27	52	27	–	–	52	27	8
bicycle polo/stunt cycling	12–14	9–11	14	11	1	2	18	13	(4)
rhythmic gymnastics	13[6]	13[6]	13[6]	13[6]	1	1	15	15	8[2]
wrestling	9–12	9–12	12	12	2	2	14	14	(4)
roller-skate hockey	34–40	17–20	40	20	–	–	40	20	(4)
roller-skating/dancing	40	20	40	20	–	–	40	20	(4)
dancing	15–16	12–14	16	14	–	–	16	14	(4)
tennis	23.77	10.97	23.77	10.97	3.65	6.4	36.57	18.27	(7)
table tennis	2.74	1.525	2.74	1.525	5.63	2.74	14	7	4
trampolining	4.57	2.74	4.57	2.74	4	4	12.57	10.74	7
volleyball	18	9	18	9	5	8	34	19	12.5[2]

[1] figures in brackets are recommended dimensions; [2] 7 m is sufficient for national events; [3] if possible, 2 m where there is a spectator area adjacent to the court; [4] additional space for the timers' table and reserves bench (possibly in sports apparatus room); [5] a uniform reduction to 5.5 m is permitted over a 3.3 m wide boundary zone around the net playing area; [6] 12 m for national competitions; [7] dimensions of a single practice net bay; [8] height of horizontal top net

(1) **Sizes of sports halls for competition use**

apparatus	obstruction-free total area[1] length × width × height (m)	safety distance[2] (m)			
		side	in front	behind	between each other
floor gymnastics	14 × 14 × 4.5	–	–	–	–
pommel horse	4 × 4 × 4.5	–	–	–	–
vaulting horse	36[3] × 2 × 5.5	–	–	–	–
suspended rings[4]	8 × 6 × 5.5	–	–	–	–
parallel bars	6 × 9.5 × 4.5	4.5[5][6]	4[5]	3[5]	4.5
horizontal bar	12 × 6 × 7.5[7]	1.5	6	6	–
asymmetric bars	12 × 6 × 5.5	1.5	6	6	–
beam	12 × 6 × 4.5	–	–	–	–
swinging rings[4]	18 × 4 × 5.5	1.5[5] (2) A	10.5[5] (7.5) A	7.5[5]	1.5[5]
climbing rope	–	1.5	4.5 (4) A	4.5 (4) A	1.5 (0.8) A
header hanging ball	–	4.5[5]	4.5[5]	4.5[5]	7
wall bars, freestanding	–	–	4.5[5][6]	4.5	4.5

[1] for competition standard; [2] for school and leisure standard (between fixed apparatus and wall or other fixed apparatus); [3] run-up length 25 m, apparatus length 2 m, run-out length 9 m; [4] distance between centres of ropes 0.5 m; [5] measured either from centres of apparatus posts, end of spar or centre of rope; [6] possible reduction to 4 m to walls or to 3.5 m to netting walls; [7] for national competitions 7 m height is sufficient; A = Austria

(2) **Obstruction-free areas and safety distances for fixed sports apparatus**

An area of 0.1 m² per vistor should be allowed for administration rooms adjacent to the entrance in multipurpose halls.

Cloakroom space of 0.05–0.1 m² should be allowed per visitor, with 1 m of counter for each 30 spaces.

The required number of toilets per visitor is 0.01, of which:

40% toilets for women
20% toilets for men
40% urinals

The storage space for tables and chairs per visitor works out at 0.05–0.06 m².

For cleaning/maintenance equipment stores, allow 0.04 m² per 100 m² (8 m² minimum) for hand tools and 0.06 m² per 100 m² (12 m² minimum) for machinery. If central services or outside contractors (who transport their own equipment) are used, this space can be dispensed with.

Stores for sports and maintenance equipment for adjacent outdoor facilities have to be included in the room programme of the sports hall if separate buildings are not provided. Allow 0.3 m² per 100 m² of useable sports area (minimum area of 15 m²).

If the centre is equipped with a small demountable stage (e.g. 100 m²), 0.12 m² of storage per m² of stage will be required. Changing facilities for actors also need to be considered.

The following dimensions apply to catering provision:

1.0 × 0.6 m standing area per vending machine;

12–15 m², with 6 m² storage, for a coffee shop;

8–12 m², with 10–12 m² storage, for a kiosk with bar;

1.5–2.7 m² per seat for a cafeteria/restaurant, of which 1.0–1.5 m² is for guests and 0.5–1.2 m² is for kitchen and storage;

1 m of service counter per 50 visitors for self-service and waiter service.

Rooms for lectures and a games room for board games, billiards etc., even a bowling alley, can also be considered.

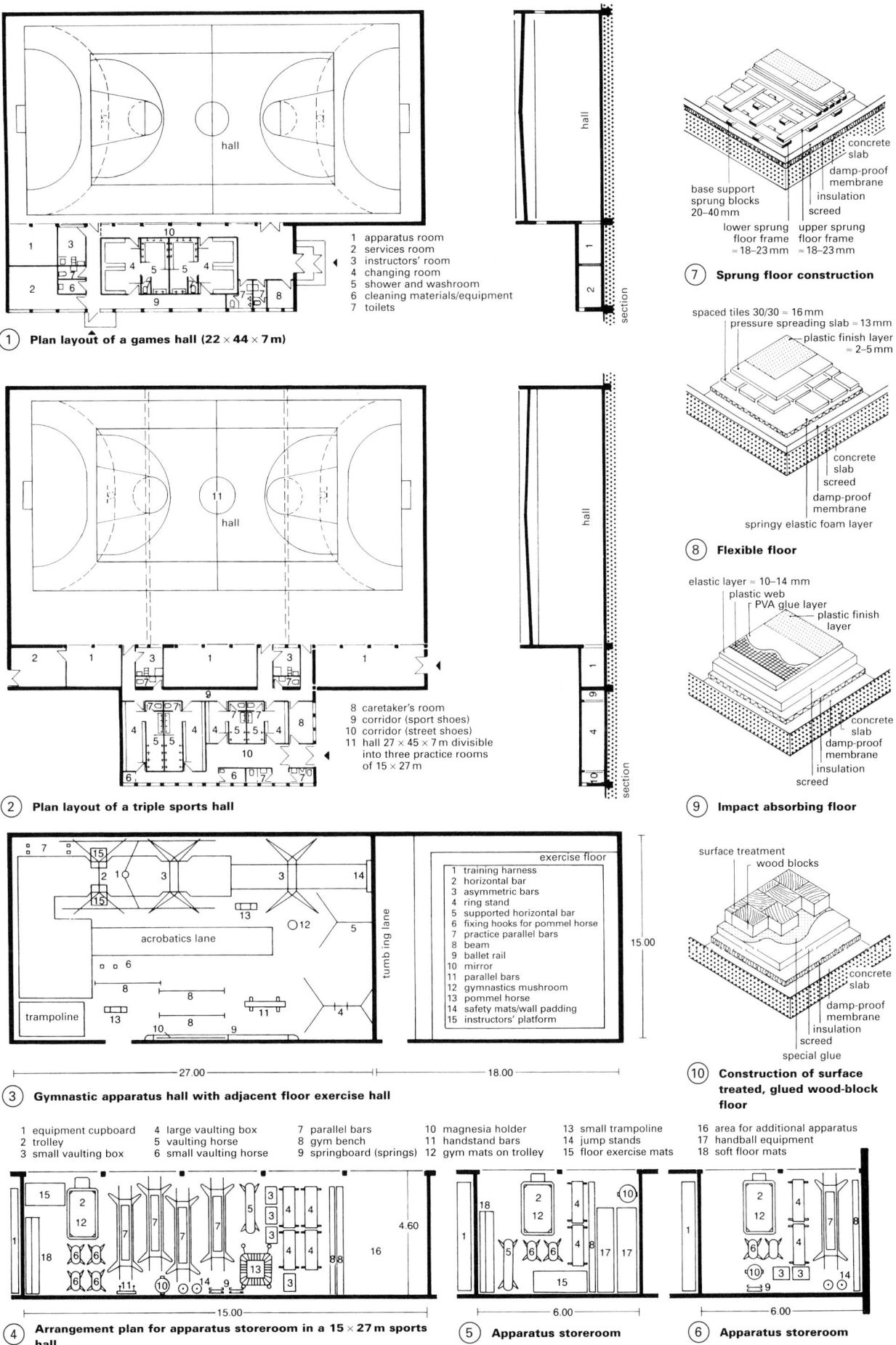

1 apparatus room
2 services room
3 instructors' room
4 changing room
5 shower and washroom
6 cleaning materials/equipment
7 toilets

① **Plan layout of a games hall (22 × 44 × 7 m)**

8 caretaker's room
9 corridor (sport shoes)
10 corridor (street shoes)
11 hall 27 × 45 × 7 m divisible into three practice rooms of 15 × 27 m

② **Plan layout of a triple sports hall**

⑦ **Sprung floor construction**

concrete slab
damp-proof membrane
insulation
screed
base support sprung blocks 20–40 mm
lower sprung floor frame ≈ 18–23 mm
upper sprung floor frame ≈ 18–23 mm

⑧ **Flexible floor**

spaced tiles 30/30 ≈ 16 mm
pressure spreading slab ≈ 13 mm
plastic finish layer ≈ 2–5 mm
concrete slab
screed
damp-proof membrane
springy elastic foam layer

⑨ **Impact absorbing floor**

elastic layer ≈ 10–14 mm
plastic web
PVA glue layer
plastic finish layer
concrete slab
damp-proof membrane
insulation
screed

exercise floor

1 training harness
2 horizontal bar
3 asymmetric bars
4 ring stand
5 supported horizontal bar
6 fixing hooks for pommel horse
7 practice parallel bars
8 beam
9 ballet rail
10 mirror
11 parallel bars
12 gymnastics mushroom
13 pommel horse
14 safety mats/wall padding
15 instructors' platform

tumbling lane
acrobatics lane
trampoline

③ **Gymnastic apparatus hall with adjacent floor exercise hall**

⑩ **Construction of surface treated, glued wood-block floor**

surface treatment
wood blocks
concrete slab
damp-proof membrane
insulation
screed
special glue

1 equipment cupboard
2 trolley
3 small vaulting box
4 large vaulting box
5 vaulting horse
6 small vaulting horse
7 parallel bars
8 gym bench
9 springboard (springs)
10 magnesia holder
11 handstand bars
12 gym mats on trolley
13 small trampoline
14 jump stands
15 floor exercise mats
16 area for additional apparatus
17 handball equipment
18 soft floor mats

④ **Arrangement plan for apparatus storeroom in a 15 × 27 m sports hall**

⑤ **Apparatus storeroom**

⑥ **Apparatus storeroom**

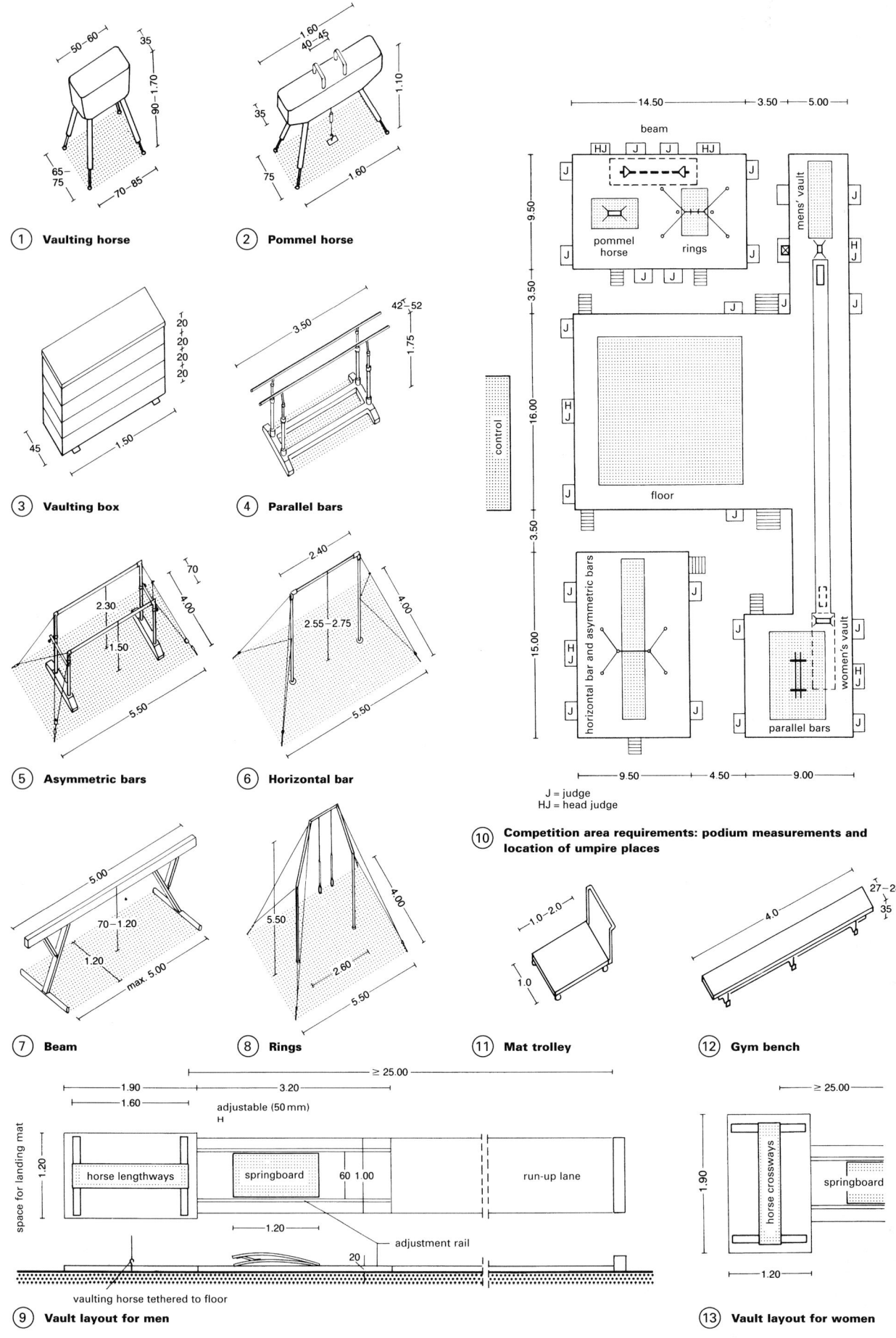

① **Vaulting horse**

② **Pommel horse**

③ **Vaulting box**

④ **Parallel bars**

⑤ **Asymmetric bars**

⑥ **Horizontal bar**

⑦ **Beam**

⑧ **Rings**

J = judge
HJ = head judge

⑩ **Competition area requirements: podium measurements and location of umpire places**

⑪ **Mat trolley**

⑫ **Gym bench**

⑨ **Vault layout for men**

⑬ **Vault layout for women**

494

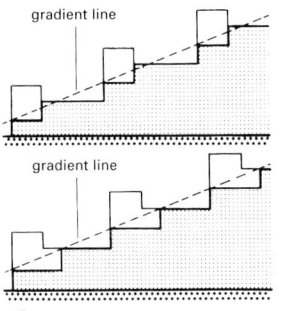

① Section through access steps

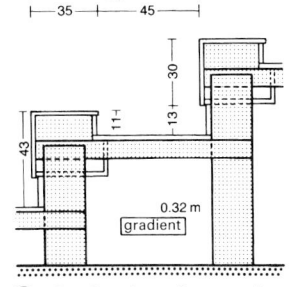

② Section through stepped seating; access steps behind

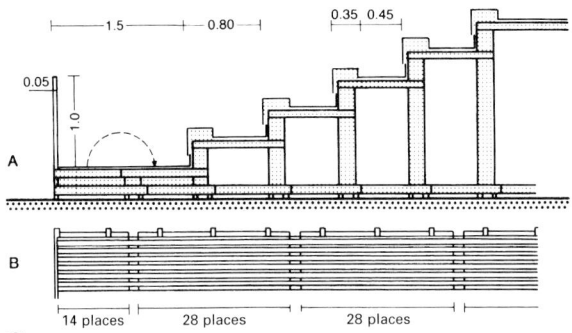

③ Spectator stand: access from below (A); access from above (B)

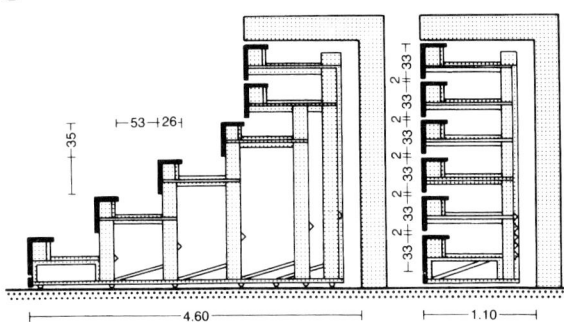

④ Retractable spectator stand (length up to 6 m)

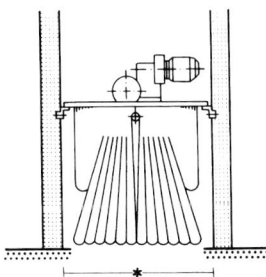

⑤ Partitioning curtain between two beams

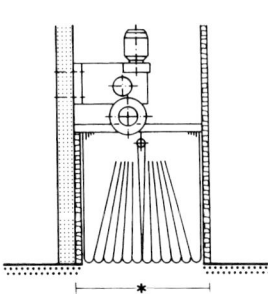

⑥ Partitioning curtain to one side of a beam; with sound absorbing recess

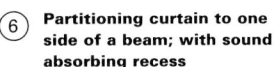

* – width, depending on height of hall and thickness of material

⑦ Partitioning curtains on both sides of a beam

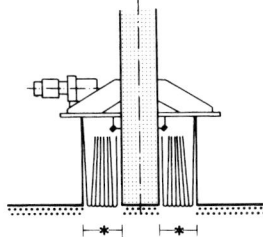

⑧ Partitioning curtain with pulley system mounted in a sound absorbing recess within a truss

Stands for spectators can be fixed or movable → ① – ④. For small stands with up to 10 steps of seating, the gradient of the rows can be linear (height 0.28–0.32 m). A parabolic slope should be planned for larger stands (height of eye level: 1.25 m seated, 1.65 m standing; height of sight-line: 0.15 m seated, 0.12 m standing). The distance between rows of seating should be 0.80–0.85 m → ② + ③ and for standing spaces 0.4–0.45 m. The point of reference for the sight-line is 0.5 m above the playing area boundary marking. Spectator areas behind goals should be protected with mobile safety nets.

Spectator stands can be accessed from above or below. Access from below is more cost-effective (saving on staircases and separate entrances) but has a disadvantage in that people arriving during an event will disturb the players and the spectators already present. Open sides need to have protective barriers at least 1 m high, measured from the surface of the circulation area → ③.

The design of ceiling and wall areas adjacent to partitioning curtains should ensure that sound bridging is minimised when the curtain is in the lowered position → ⑤ – ⑧.

It is recommended that walkways either side of the changing and shower rooms are segregated into those for street shoes and those for sports shoes only.

Showers have to be immediately accessible from the changing rooms and there needs to be a drying area in between. The shower rooms should be designed as two separable sections, both connected to the two neighbouring changing rooms in such a way that from each changing room either one or both sections can be accessed.

The first aid room should be on the same level as the playing area and could be integrated with the instructors'/referees' room, which should be near the changing rooms.

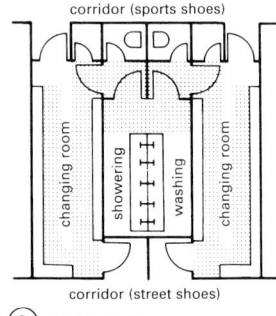

⑨ Example 1

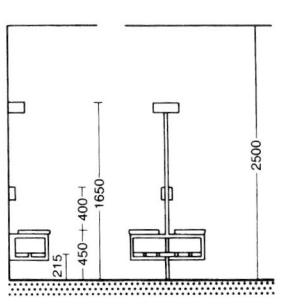

⑩ Wall-mounted and freestanding benches

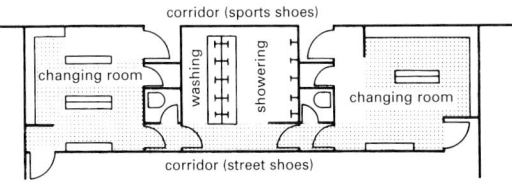

⑪ Example 2

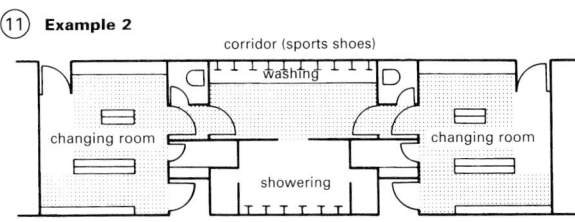

⑫ Example 3
Three suggested changing room layouts (shaded area: floor with PVC duckboard matting)

SPORTS HALLS

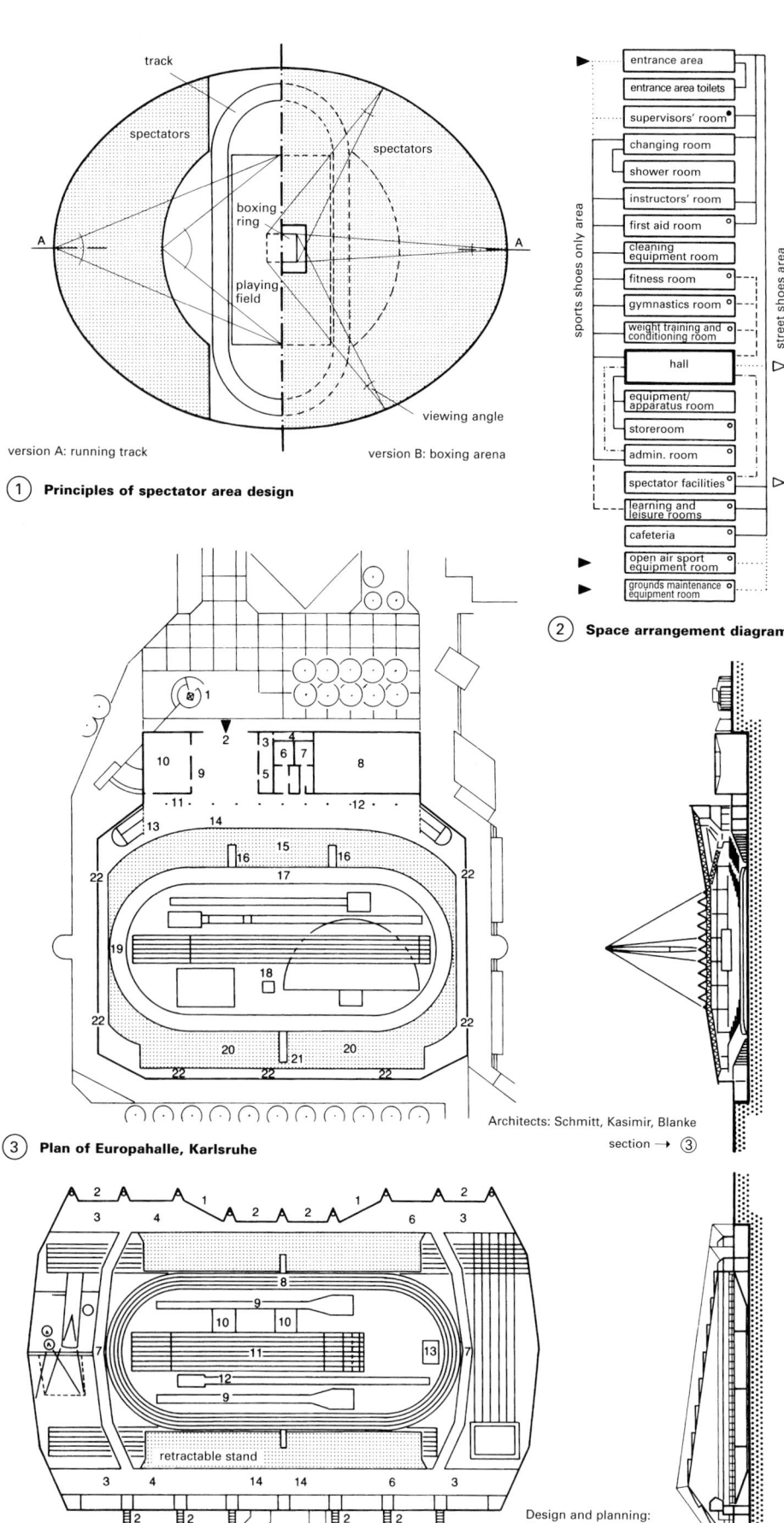

track

spectators

spectators

boxing ring

playing field

A — A

viewing angle

version A: running track

version B: boxing arena

(1) **Principles of spectator area design**

sports shoes only area

| entrance area |
| entrance area toilets |
| supervisors' room ● |
| changing room |
| shower room |
| instructors' room |
| first aid room ○ |
| cleaning equipment room |
| fitness room ○ |
| gymnastics room ○ |
| weight training and conditioning room ○ |
| **hall** |
| equipment/ apparatus room ○ |
| storeroom ○ |
| admin. room ○ |
| spectator facilities ○ |
| learning and leisure rooms ○ |
| cafeteria ○ |
| open air sport equipment room ○ |
| grounds maintenance equipment room ○ |

street shoes area

(2) **Space arrangement diagram**

► direct entrance
▷ alternative emergency exit
— principal connection
·—·— visual connection
– – – alternative connection
········· additional connection
● additional rooms with multipurpose halls
○ additional rooms and facilities depending on local situation and need
→ (2)

key → (3)

plan of entrance floor level
1 entrance on the competition level; 2 entrance and foyer for spectators; 3 administration; 4 ticket office; 5 cloakroom; 6 male toilets; 7 female toilets; 8 area above warm-up hall; 9 information; 10 teaching and leisure room; 11 access to lower floor; 12 drinks dispensary; 13 access to gallery; 14 control room with signboard and public address; 15 fixed spectator stand; 16 connection between changing area and hall; 17 200 m running track; 18 sports hall; 19 large sign board; 20 mobile spectator stand; 21 game signboard; 22 hall surround corridor with emergency exits

Flexible hall used for tennis, handball, athletics, boxing and school sports → (3). Partitioning curtains, with catching nets at the ends, allow the hall to be split into four parts, each the size of a school sports hall. With the warm-up hall and a training area below the retractable stand, a large sports hall such as this offers schools and clubs six practice areas. It is also large enough to stage top level sporting competitions.

Architects: Schmitt, Kasimir, Blanke

section → (3)

(3) **Plan of Europahalle, Karlsruhe**

key → (4)

plan of entrance level
1 entrance concourse with ticket offices; 2 exits/emergency exits; 3 foyer; 4 drinks dispensary; 5 telephone; 6 steps to the spectator toilets; 7 access as bridge over the sports level; 8 200 m running track; 9 pole vault facilities; 10 high jump facilities; 11 sprint competition track; 12 long jump facilities; 13 shot put facilities; 14 access to administration

The Dortmund athletics hall → (4) has a competition standard 200 m running track, a 130 m + 100 m straight sprinting track and facilities for shot put, discus and high jump.

retractable stand

Design and planning: Hochbauamt Dortmund

section → (4)

(4) **Plan of Dortmund Athletics Hall**

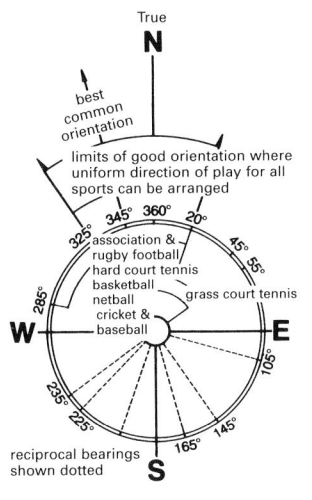

(1) **Orientation diagram, based on the following seasons (northern hemisphere): association football, August–May; hard court tennis, basketball, netball, all year round; cricket, baseball, grass court tennis, May–September. Pavilions should avoid SW–NW aspect (225°–315°)**

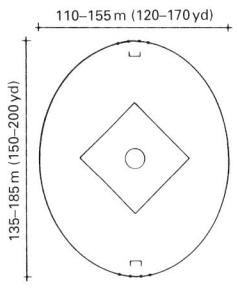

(8) **Football, Australian rules**

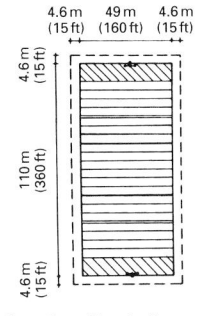

(9) **American Football**

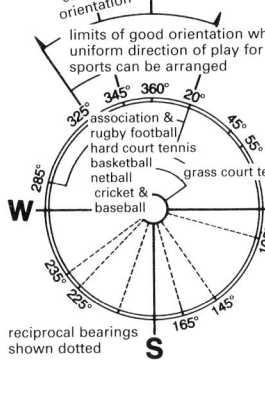

(2) **Archery, target**

(3) **Archery, clout**

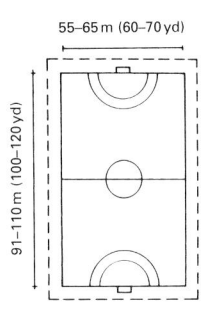

(10) **Gaelic football**

(11) **Rugby league**

(12) **Handball**

(13) **Hockey: 90 × 55 m (95 × 60 m overall space) recommended for county and club matches**

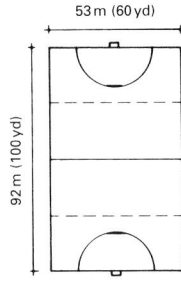

(4) **Baseball (little league two-thirds size)**

(5) **Bicycle polo**

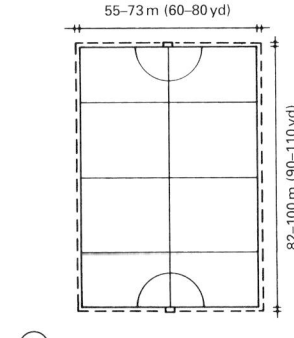

(14) **Rugby union**

(15) **Canadian football**

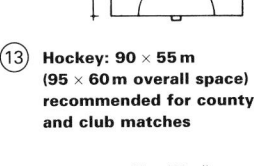

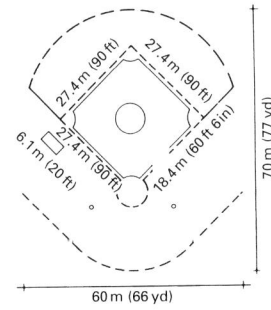

(6) **Camogie**

(7) **Association football: senior pitches 96–100 × 60–64 m; junior pitches 90 × 46–55 m; international 100–110 × 64–75 m**

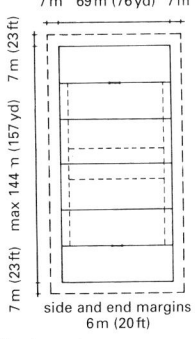

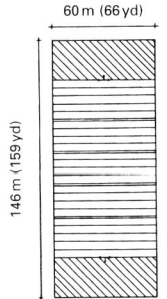

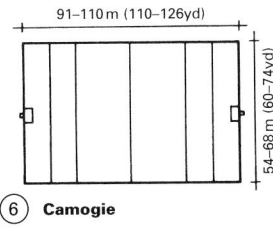

(16) **Hurling**

(17) **Korfball**

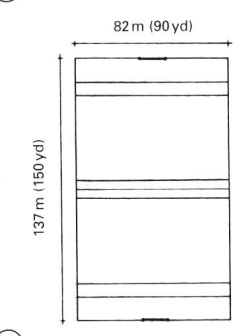

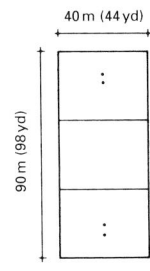

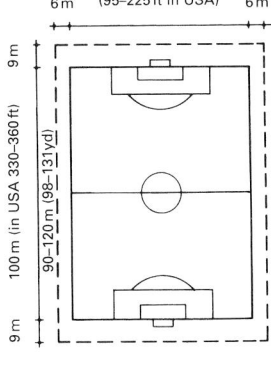

497

OUTDOOR PITCHES

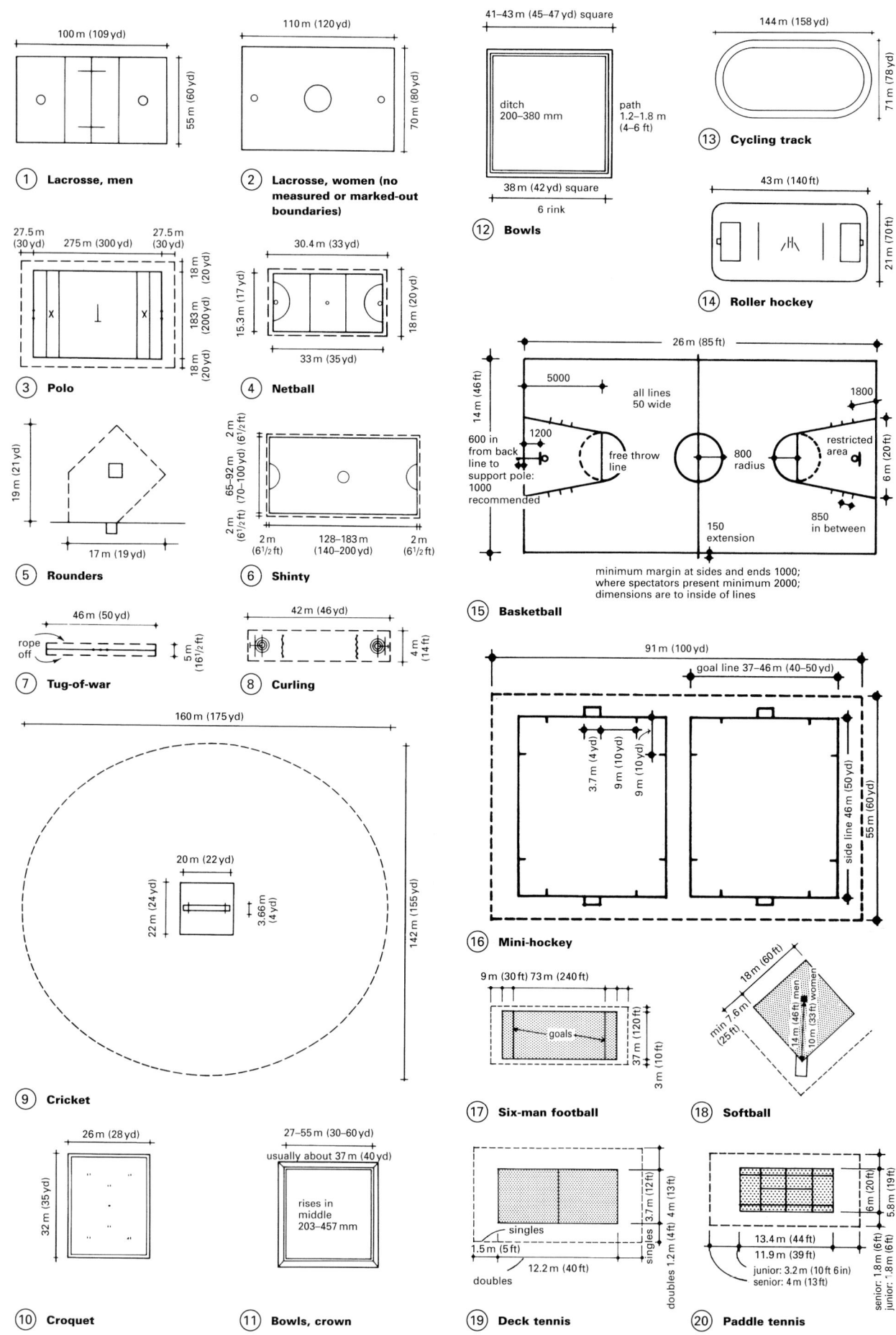

① Lacrosse, men

100 m (109 yd)
55 m (60 yd)

② Lacrosse, women (no measured or marked-out boundaries)

110 m (120 yd)
70 m (80 yd)

③ Polo

27.5 m (30 yd)   275 m (300 yd)   27.5 m (30 yd)
18 m (20 yd)
183 m (200 yd)
18 m (20 yd)

④ Netball

30.4 m (33 yd)
15.3 m (17 yd)   18 m (20 yd)
33 m (35 yd)

⑤ Rounders

19 m (21 yd)
17 m (19 yd)

⑥ Shinty

65–92 m (70–100 yd)
2 m (6½ ft)
2 m (6½ ft)
2 m (6½ ft)   128–183 m (140–200 yd)   2 m (6½ ft)

⑦ Tug-of-war

46 m (50 yd)
rope off
5 m (16½ ft)

⑧ Curling

42 m (46 yd)
4 m (14 ft)

⑨ Cricket

160 m (175 yd)
20 m (22 yd)
22 m (24 yd)
3.66 m (4 yd)
142 m (155 yd)

⑩ Croquet

26 m (28 yd)
32 m (35 yd)

⑪ Bowls, crown

27–55 m (30–60 yd)
usually about 37 m (40 yd)
rises in middle 203–457 mm

⑫ Bowls

41–43 m (45–47 yd) square
ditch 200–380 mm
path 1.2–1.8 m (4–6 ft)
38 m (42 yd) square
6 rink

⑬ Cycling track

144 m (158 yd)
71 m (78 yd)

⑭ Roller hockey

43 m (140 ft)
21 m (70 ft)

⑮ Basketball

26 m (85 ft)
14 m (46 ft)
5000
all lines 50 wide
1800
600 in from back line to support pole: 1000 recommended
1200
free throw line
800 radius
restricted area
6 m (20 ft)
150 extension
850 in between

minimum margin at sides and ends 1000; where spectators present minimum 2000; dimensions are to inside of lines

⑯ Mini-hockey

91 m (100 yd)
goal line 37–46 m (40–50 yd)
3.7 m (4 yd)
9 m (10 yd)
9 m (10 yd)
side line 46 m (50 yd)
55 m (60 yd)

⑰ Six-man football

9 m (30 ft) 73 m (240 ft)
goals
37 m (120 ft)
3 m (10 ft)

⑱ Softball

18 m (60 ft)
min 7.6 m (25 ft)
14 m (46 ft) men
10 m (33 ft) women

⑲ Deck tennis

singles
1.5 m (5 ft)
12.2 m (40 ft)
doubles
3.7 m (12 ft) 4 m (13 ft)
doubles 1.2 m (4 ft) singles

⑳ Paddle tennis

13.4 m (44 ft)
11.9 m (39 ft)
junior: 3.2 m (10 ft 6 in)
senior: 4 m (13 ft)
6 m (20 ft)
5.8 m (19 ft)
senior: 1.8 m (6 ft)
junior: 1.8 m (6 ft)

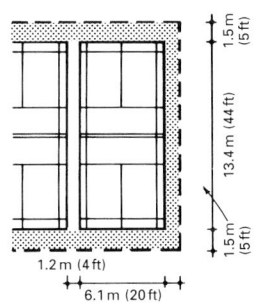

(1) **Badminton: minimum height 7.6 m**

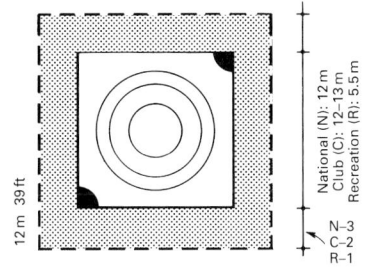

(6) **Wrestling**

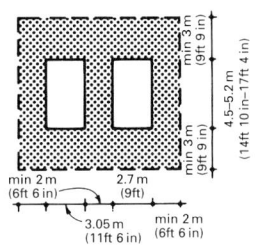

(11) **Trampoline**

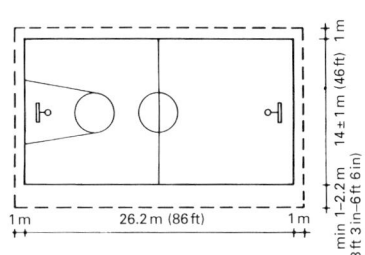

(2) **Basketball: minimum height 7.0 m (see also previous page)**

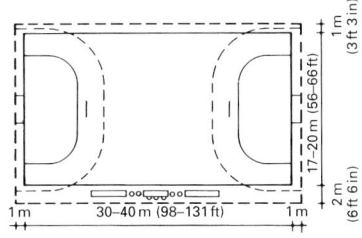

(7) **Handball (seven-a-side)**

Table tennis: minimum height 4.2 m

(12) **Table tennis: minimum height 4.2 m**

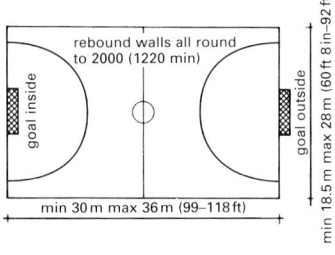

(3) **Five-a-side football**

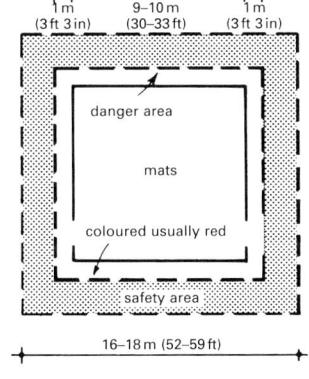

(8) **Judo**

(13) **Fencing pistes**

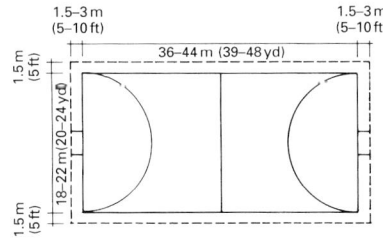

(4) **Hockey: team size according to pitch size**

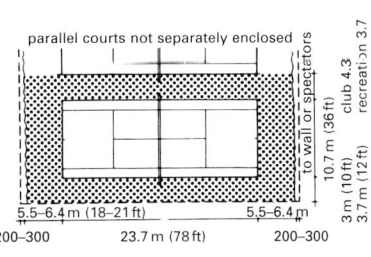

(9) **Tennis**

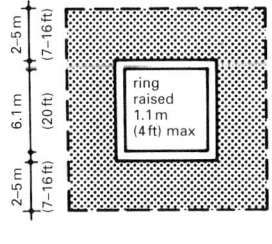

(14) **Boxing**

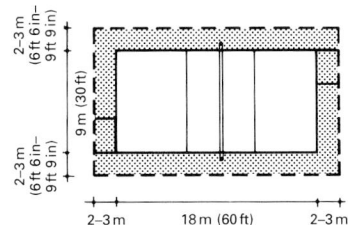

(5) **Volleyball**

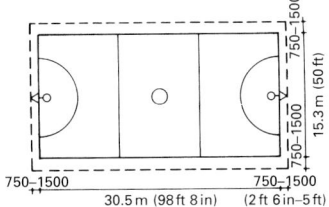

(10) **Netball**

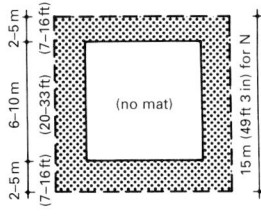

(15) **Karate**

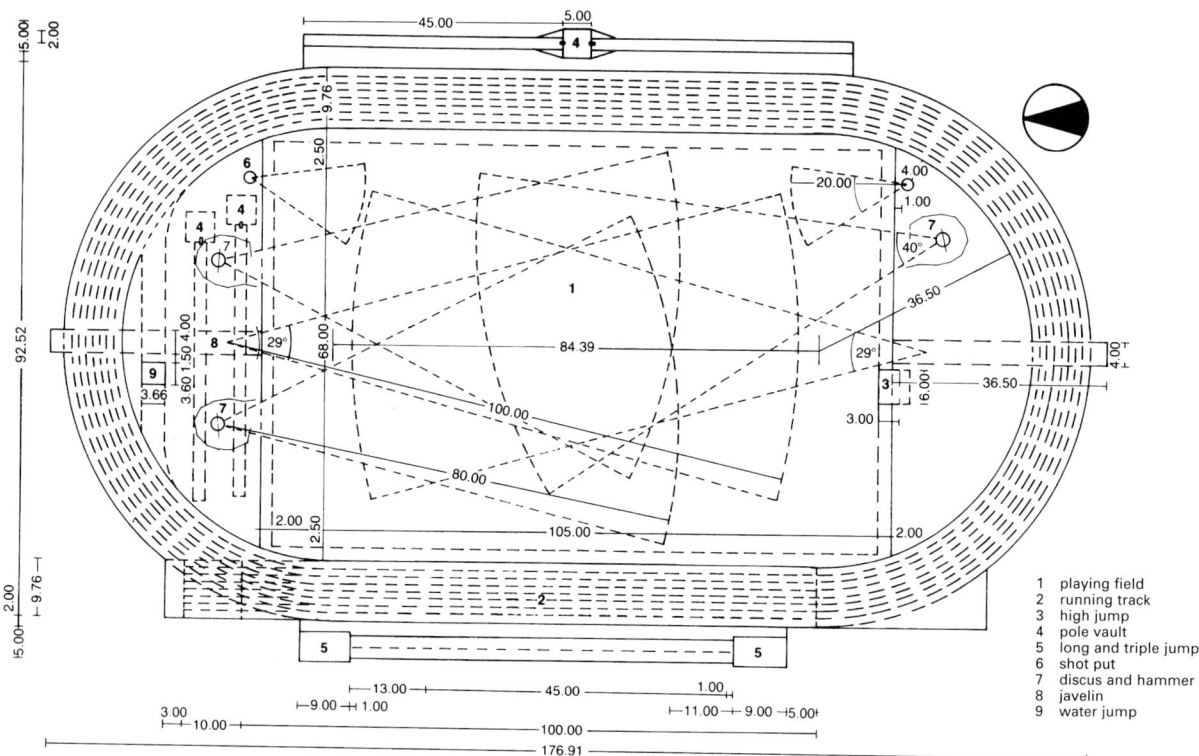

1 playing field
2 running track
3 high jump
4 pole vault
5 long and triple jump
6 shot put
7 discus and hammer
8 javelin
9 water jump

(1) Arena type A

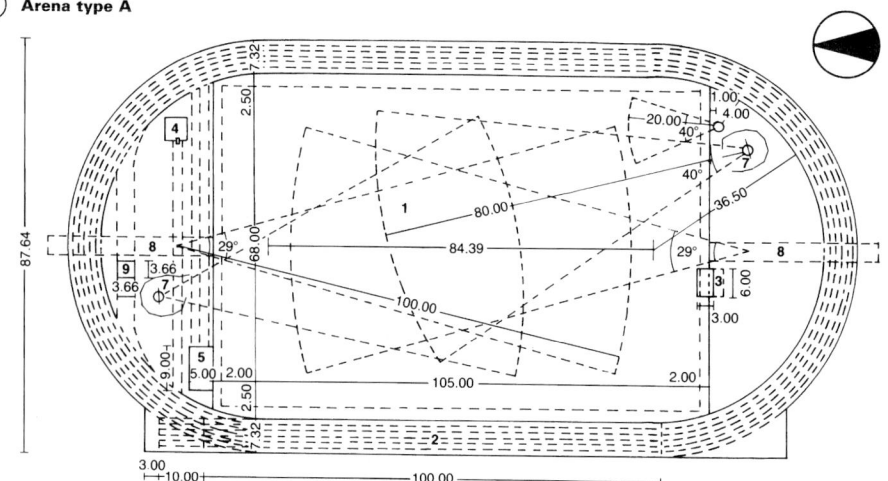

(2) Arena type B

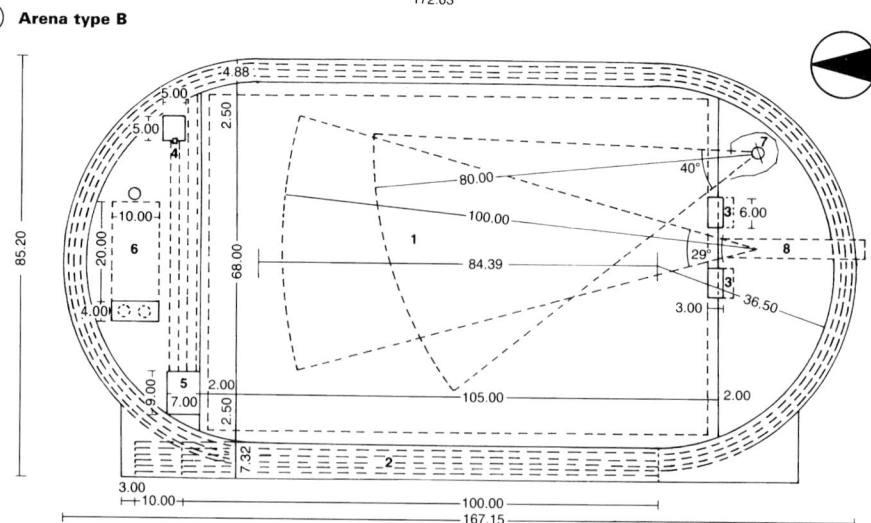

(3) Arena type C

Arena type A

These consist of an eight-lane running track around a central sports field. The field has areas for shot-putting, discus, hammer and javelin throwing. In the northern sector there is a water jump for the steeplechase; the high jump takes place in the southern sector. The pole-vaulting area is outside the running track, as are the pits for long and triple jumping. The former runs parallel to the easterly straight of the track while the latter are beside the straight to the west.

Arena type B

These consist of a six-lane running track around the interior field area. The layout is similar to type A arenas except that the pole vault, long jump and triple jump take place within the track, in the northern sector. However, these facilities can also be arranged outside of the running track.

Arena type C

These consist of a four-lane running track around a sports field. Areas for the discus, hammer and javelin are in the southern sector within the track, as is the high jump. The run-ups for pole-vaulting, long jump and triple jump are in the northerly segment, which also has an area for the shot put.

ATHLETICS FACILITIES

Arena type D

These consist of the following separate facilities → ①:

four- to six-lane sprint/hurdles track;

playing field 68 × 105 m (70 × 109 m with safety zones);

shot put training area, throwing south;

multipurpose area for long/triple jump, run-up west;

high-jump area, run-up north;

shot-putting ring, throwing north;

javelin/ball throwing area, throwing north.

Generally the running track surface in type D arenas is earth and cinders, but for very high usage it is advisable to use a synthetic finish.

Large combined playing fields include a straight running track and facilities for high/long/triple jump and shot-putting both next to and on the main playing field.

For training in field sports it is advisable for safety reasons to provide a 'throwing field'. This is simply a grassed target area of approximately the same size as an arena playing field → ③.

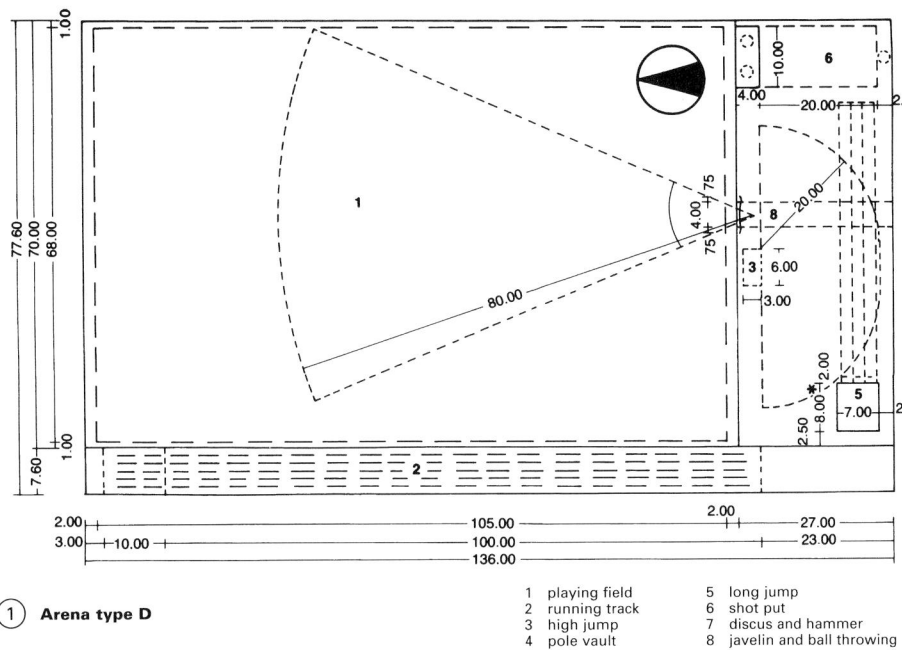

① Arena type D

1	playing field	5	long jump
2	running track	6	shot put
3	high jump	7	discus and hammer
4	pole vault	8	javelin and ball throwing

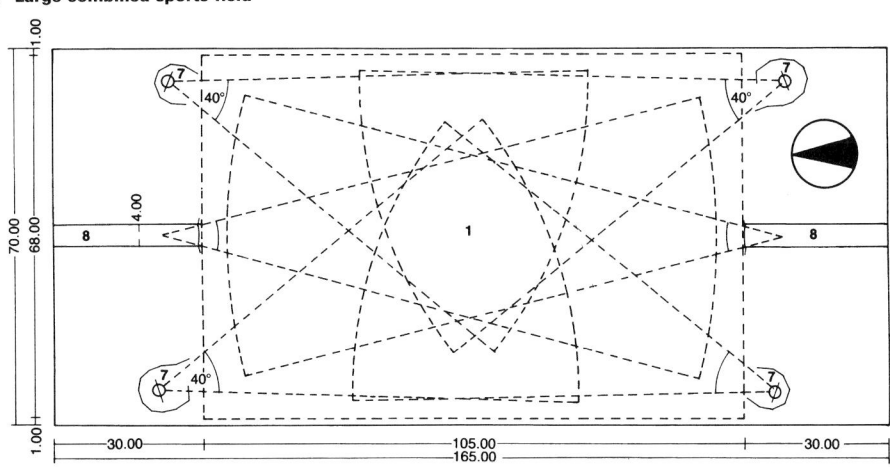

② Large combined sports field

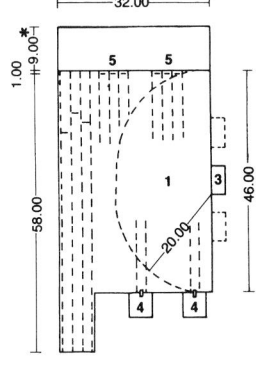

④ Central run-up area

③ Throwing field

• 9.00 m for competitions (take-off board offset 1.00 m)
  8.00 m for training (take-off board offset 2.00 m – see also the following page)

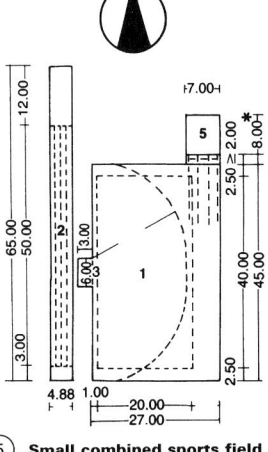

⑤ Small combined sports field

① **Hurdles with counterweight**

② **Jumps**

③ **Steeplechase track with 16 m transition curve and water jump**

④ **Steeplechase water jump: plan**

⑤ **Steeplechase water jump: section**

track type	length of start area (m)	track	run-out	lane widths[1]
sprint track	3	110[2]	17	1.22
elliptical track	—[3]	400	17	1.22

[1] an obstruction-free safety zone, 28 cm wide, is required for the outer lane; it need not be constructed as running track
[2] 110 m length is needed for the hurdle track; 100 m for sprints
[3] no additional starting area is required

⑧ **Running track dimensions → ①**

race distance	class	number of hurdles	height of hurdles	run-in	distance between hurdles	run-out
400 m	men/male youths A + B	10	0.914 m	45.00 m	35.00 m	40.00 m
400 m	women/female youths A	10	0.762 m	45.00 m	35.00 m	40.00 m
110 m	men	10	1.067 m	13.72 m	9.14 m	14.02 m
110 m	men/m. youths A	10	0.996 m	13.72 m	8.90 m	16.18 m
110 m	men/m. youths B	10	0.914 m	13.50 m	8.60 m	19.10 m
100 m	women/f. youths A	10	0.840 m	13.00 m	8.50 m	10.50 m
100 m	f. youths B (from 1984)	10	0.762 m	13.00 m	8.50 m	10.50 m
100 m	f. youths A (from 1983)	10	0.840 m	12.00 m	8.00 m	16.00 m
80 m	schoolboys A	10	0.840 m	12.00 m	8.00 m	12.00 m
80 m	schoolgirls A	8	0.762 m	12.00 m	8.00 m	12.00 m
60 m	schoolboys B schoolgirls B	8	0.762 m	11.50 m	7.50 m	11.00 m

note: permissible tolerance of ± 3 mm of the standard heights

⑨ **Hurdles track dimensions → ①**

type	run-up length (m)	width(m)	pit (P) or mat (M)	length (m)	width (m)
long jump	≥45[1]	1.22[2]	P	≥8	2.75
triple jump	≥45[3]	1.22[2]	P	≥8	2.75
pole vault	≥45	1.22	MP	≥5	5.00
high jump	radius ≥ 20 m		M	3	5 to 6

[1] take-off board at least 1 m in front of the pit; distance between take-off line and end of the pit at least 10 m; length of pit is 9 m
[2] for multipurpose facilities, the single lane width is 2 m
[3] take-off board 11 m in front of the pit (youths 9 m; top-level 13 m)

⑩ **Jump facilities dimensions → ⑥-⑦-⑬**

section through long jump pit
30 cm quartz sand
2 cm clean top layer
6–10 cm course slag
15–20 cm gravel layer
30 cm hardcore
drainage pipe

high jump: plan

plasticine
rubber
timber
metal container
section through take-off board

direction of run-up
mat
timber underframe
section A–B through mat and mat-frame

⑪ **Long and triple jump**

⑬ **High jump**

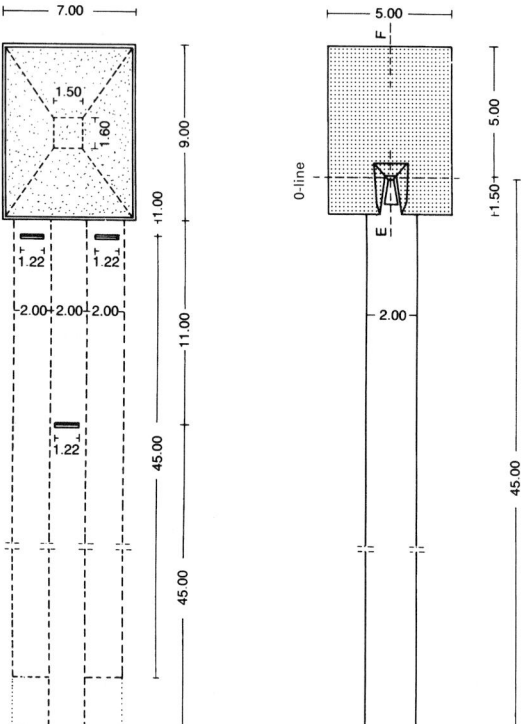

⑥ **Long and triple jump: plan**

⑦ **Pole vault: plan → ⑫-⑭**

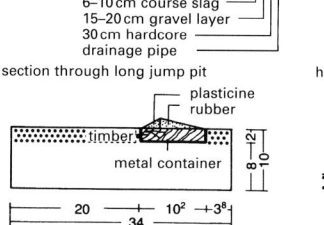

section C–D
section A–B
plan

⑫ **Pole vault → ⑦**

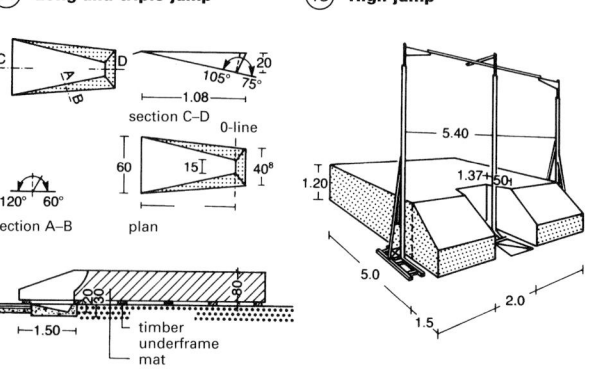

⑭ **Uprights and landing mat for pole vault → ⑦**

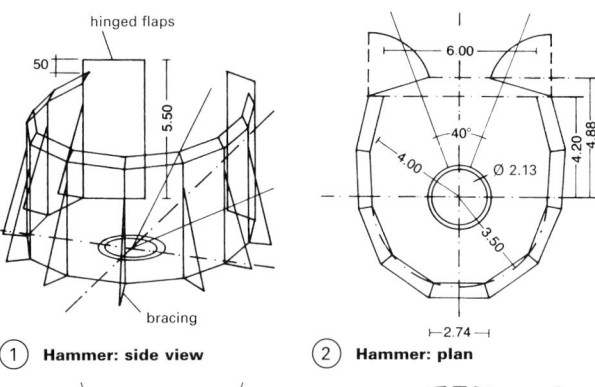

① **Hammer: side view**   ② **Hammer: plan**

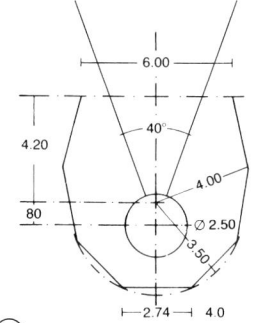

③ **Discus: plan**

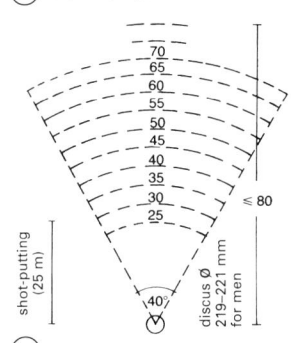

④ **Discus: field**

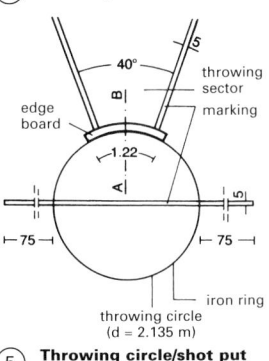

⑤ **Throwing circle/shot put** → ⑥

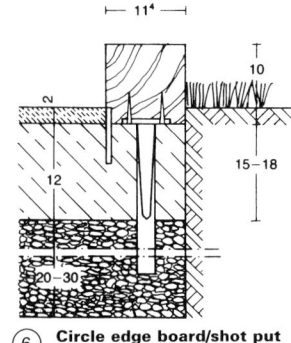

⑥ **Circle edge board/shot put section A–B**

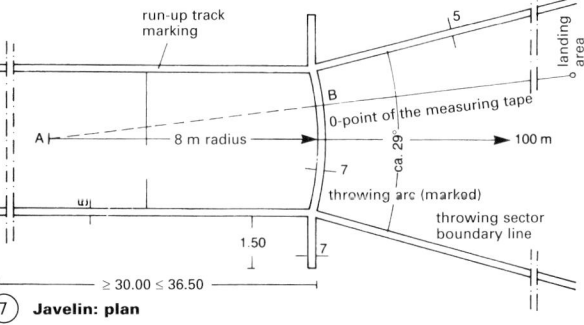

⑦ **Javelin: plan**

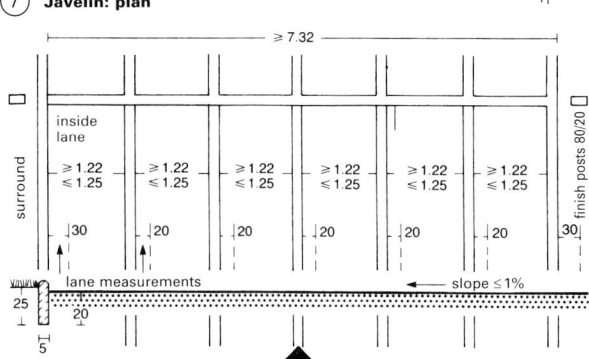

⑧ **Dimensions: running track type B**

In the table → ⑨, cited measurements correspond to the competition regulations and are to be strictly observed. Non-compliance is permitted in facilities for school sport, training and leisure.

The same facilities can be used for both hammer and discus throwing → ③ – ④ although the diameter of the throwing circle must be adjusted accordingly. Protective barriers → ① – ② are necessary only in competition events. Simpler constructions, such as netting or a protective grille, can be used for discus at other times → ③.

Javelin throwing facilities require a 4 m wide run-up track generally 36.5 m, but at least 30 m, in length and a landing area → ⑦. The end of the run-up track is permanently marked with a curved delivery line (arc).

For the shot put, a throwing circle and throwing sector are required → ⑤ – ⑥. The overall length required is normally 20 m; in top-level sport, 25 m.

type	throwing or putting area (m)	target area angle	target area length
discus	circle d = 2.50[1]	40°	80
hammer	circle d = 2.135	40°	80
javelin	run-up length = 36.5[2] run-up width = 4	ca. 29°	100
shot-putting	circle d = 2.135	40°	up to 25

[1] can also be used for hammer after insertion of a profile ring
[2] ≥ 30 m

⑨ **Dimensions: throwing and putting**

Planning examples I to V give a guide to the combination of useable areas (based on 4 m²/inhabitant) required by a variety of catchment areas

Example I: sports field for a catchment area of approximately 5000 inhabitants

1 running track type D	10 554 m²
2 small playing fields (27 × 45 m)	2430 m²
1 practice field	4500 m²
2 leisure playing fields	250 m²
1 playing and gymnastics lawn	1000 m²
1 fitness area	1400 m²
total useable area	ca. 20 000 m²

Example II: approximately 7000 inhabitants

1 running track type D	10 554 m²
1 large playing field (70 × 109 m)	7630 m²
2 small playing fields (27 × 45 m)	2430 m²
leisure area	3000 m²
1 playing and gymnastics lawn	1000 m²
1 fitness course	2300 m²
1 roller-skating rink	800 m²
total useable area	ca. 28 000 m²

Example III: approximately 7000 inhabitants

1 running track type B	14 000 m²
1 large playing field (70 × 109 m)	7630 m²
3 small playing fields (27 × 45 m)	3645 m²
1 playing and gymnastics lawn	1000 m²
1 fitness area	1400 m²
total useable area	ca. 28 000 m²

Example IV: approximately 15 000 inhabitants

1 running track type B	14 000 m²
3 large playing fields (70 × 109 m)	22 890 m²
7 small playing fields (27 × 45 m)	8505 m²
leisure area	6000 m²
1 fitness course	3300 m²
1 fitness area	1400 m²
1 fitness play area	1000 m²
2 playing and gymnastics lawns	2000 m²
total useable area	ca. 60 000 m²

Example V: approximately 20 000 inhabitants

1 running track type B	14 000 m²
1 multipurpose combined playing field	8400 m²
4 large playing fields (70 × 109 m)	30 520 m²
10 small playing fields (27 × 45 m)	12 150 m²
leisure area	6000 m²
1 fitness course	3300 m²
1 fitness area	1400 m²
1 fitness play area	1000 m²
2 playing and gymnastics lawns	2000 m²
total useable area	ca. 80 000 m²

⑩ **Planning examples for population centres of approximately 5000–20 000 inhabitants**

CONDITIONING AND FITNESS ROOMS

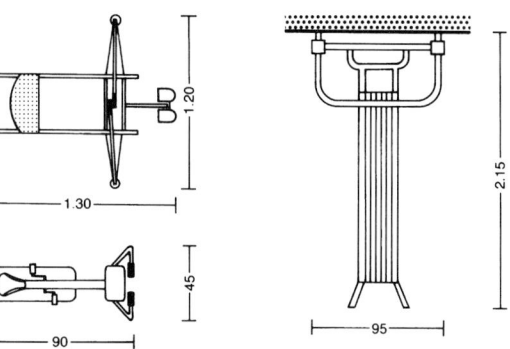

① **Rowing machine and exercise bike**

② **Stomach exercising bench with pull-up bar and wall bars**

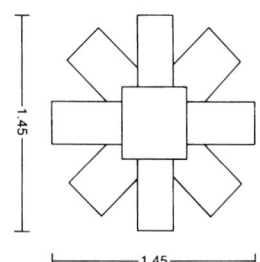

③ **Multi-exercise centre**

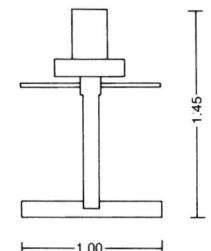

④ **Workout bench**

area	equipment	exercise	motor skills and/or strength	training aim
A	general training station	single-joint	strength/ mobility	fitness/ condition
B	special training station	multi-joint	strength/ speed	fitness/ condition
C	weightbench (with multipress or isometric extensions)	multi-joint	strength/ speed/ co-ordination	condition
D	usual small equipment	single- and multi-joint	strength/ mobility	fitness
E	special training equipment plus space for warming up (gymnastics etc.)	multi-joint	stamina/ co-ordination	fitness/ condition
		single- and multi-joint	mobility/ co-ordination	fitness/ condition

⑤ **Arrangement of equipment into categories**

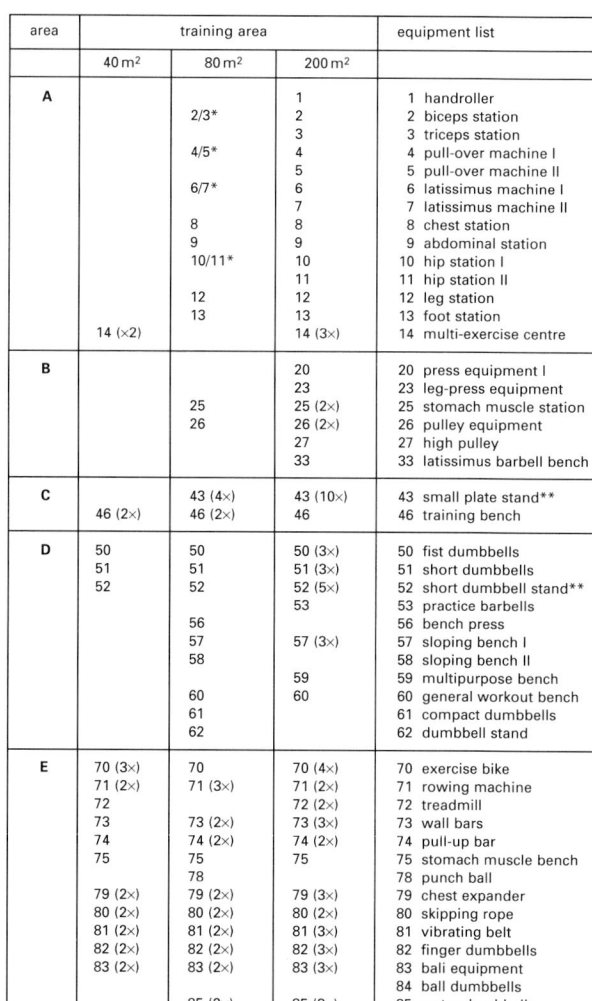

area	training area			equipment list	
	40 m²	80 m²	200 m²		
A			1	1	handroller
		2/3*	2	2	biceps station
			3	3	triceps station
		4/5*	4	4	pull-over machine I
			5	5	pull-over machine II
		6/7*	6	6	latissimus machine I
			7	7	latissimus machine II
		8	8	8	chest station
		9	9	9	abdominal station
		10/11*	10	10	hip station I
			11	11	hip station II
		12	12	12	leg station
		13	13	13	foot station
	14 (×2)		14 (3×)	14	multi-exercise centre
B			20	20	press equipment I
			23	23	leg-press equipment
		25	25 (2×)	25	stomach muscle station
		26	26 (2×)	26	pulley equipment
			27	27	high pulley
			33	33	latissimus barbell bench
C		43 (4×)	43 (10×)	43	small plate stand**
	46 (2×)	46 (2×)	46	46	training bench
D	50	50	50 (3×)	50	fist dumbbells
	51	51	51 (3×)	51	short dumbbells
	52	52	52 (5×)	52	short dumbbell stand**
			53	53	practice barbells
		56		56	bench press
		57	57 (3×)	57	sloping bench I
		58		58	sloping bench II
			59	59	multipurpose bench
		60	60	60	general workout bench
		61		61	compact dumbbells
		62		62	dumbbell stand
E	70 (3×)	70	70 (4×)	70	exercise bike
	71 (2×)	71 (3×)	71 (2×)	71	rowing machine
	72		72 (2×)	72	treadmill
	73	73 (2×)	73 (3×)	73	wall bars
	74	74 (2×)	74 (2×)	74	pull-up bar
	75	75	75	75	stomach muscle bench
		78		78	punch ball
	79 (2×)	79 (2×)	79 (3×)	79	chest expander
	80 (2×)	80 (2×)	80 (2×)	80	skipping rope
	81 (2×)	81 (2×)	81 (3×)	81	vibrating belt
	82 (2×)	82 (2×)	82 (3×)	82	finger dumbbells
	83 (2×)	83 (2×)	83 (3×)	83	bali equipment
				84	ball dumbbells
		85 (2×)	85 (3×)	85	water dumbbells
	89	89 (2×)	89 (2×)	89	equipment cupboard

* note that 2 and 3, 4 and 5, 6 and 7, and 10 and 11 are supplied by some manufacturers as dual-function machines

** note that 2–8 in the example illustrations are shown with the necessary stands for barbell plates, and fist, short and compact dumbbells: there are many different types of stands available and they must therefore be matched with the type and number of dumbbells, bars and plates to be stored

⑦ **Suggested equipment for fitness rooms**

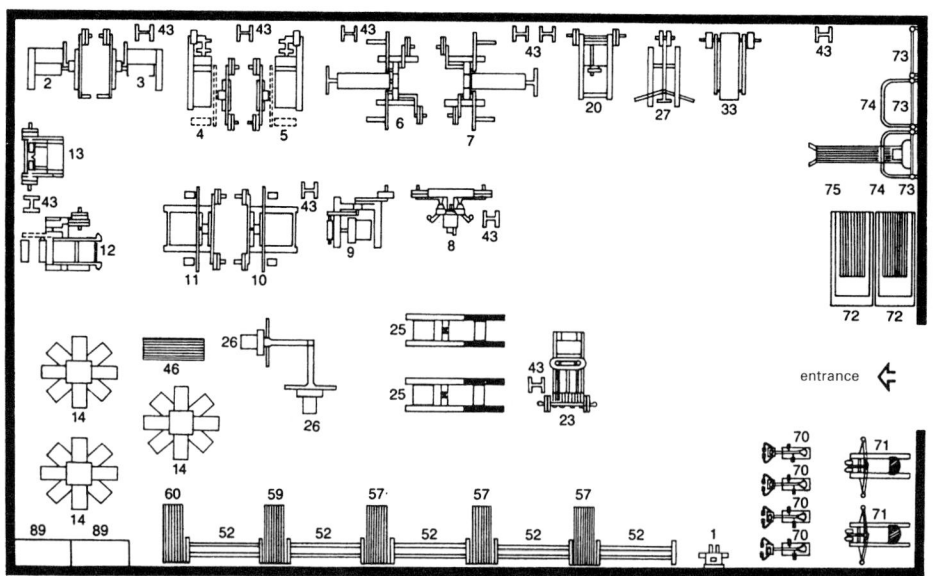

1 handroller
2 biceps station
3 triceps station
4 pull-over machine I
5 pull-over machine II
6 latissimus machine I
7 latissimus machine II
8 chest station
9 abdominal station
10 hip station I
11 hip station II
12 leg station
13 foot station
14 multi-exercise centre
20 press equipment I
23 leg-press equipment
25 stomach muscle station
26 pulley equipment
27 high pulley
33 latissimus barbell bench
43 small plate stand
46 training bench
52 short dumbbell stand
57 sloping bench I
59 multipurpose bench
60 general workout bench
70 exercise bike
71 rowing machine
72 treadmill
73 wall bars
74 pull-up bar
75 stomach muscle bench
89 equipment cupboard

entrance ⇐

⑥ **Example fitness room (approximately 200 m²)**

area	no.	description	movement	required space (cm)
A	1	handroller	bending/stretching hands	60/ 30
	2	biceps station	bending arms	135/135
	3	triceps station	stretching arms	135/135
	4	pull-over machine I	raising arms in front of the body	190/110
	5	pull-over machine II	lowering arms in front of the body	190/110
	6	latissimus machine I	raising and lowering arms to the sides	200/120
	7	latissimus machine II	moving arms together and apart	200/120
	8	chest station	moving bent arms together	165/100
	9	abdominal station	stretching and bending abdomen	135/125
	10	hip station I	lowering and lifting legs	175/125
	11	hip station II	lifting/pulling up legs	175/125
	12	leg station	stretching/bending legs	125/155
	13	foot station	stretching/bending feet	140/ 80
	14	multi-exercise centre	various leg and multi-joint movements	various
B	20	press equipment I	stretching arms horizontally (while standing)	120/140
	21	press equipment II	stretching arms vertically, and/or calf training while standing	70/160
	22	leg-stretch equipment	stretching legs on a sloping surface	90/140
	23	leg-press equipment	stretching legs horizontally (while seated)	120/160
	24	knee bending apparatus (with weights attachment)	stretching legs vertically (while standing)	200/ 90
	25	stomach muscle station	various exercises for stomach and back muscles	65/200
	26	pulley equipment	various single and multi-joint basic movements	100/140
	27	high pulley	bending and stretching arms vertically (hanging or stemmed)	120/155
	28	bench press I	stretching arms vertically (lying on bench)	200/120
	29	barbell equipment (multipress machine)	bench press, knee bending, standing pressing and pulling exercises (all exercises with controlled weights)	200/100
	30	bench press II (sloping bench for pull-ups)	press on sloping bench (while seated)	185/100
	31	curl bench	bending arms	150/ 70
	32	bench press III	bench press (lying on back sloping towards head)	160/170
	33	latissimus barbell bench	bending arms, pull-ups in stomach position	120/130
C	40	weightlifting mat with rubber sections	all exercises with free barbells (knee bending, press and push exercises)	300/300
	41	practice barbells bar		200
	42	large plate stand		50/100
	43	small plate stand		30/ 30
	44	magnesia holder		0/ 38
	45	kneebend stands (in pairs)		each 35/ 70
	46	training bench		40/120
	47	rubber plates (10, 15, 20, 25 kg)		
	48	plates with vulcanised rubber edges (15, 20, 25 kg)		
	49	cast iron plates (1.25, 2.50, 10, 25, 50 kg)		
D	50	fist dumbbells (1, 2, 3, 4, 5, 6, 7, 8, 10 kg)	various single and multi-joint exercises with fist and compact dumbbells, and barbells	
	51	short dumbbells (2.5, 5.0, 7.5 etc.–30 kg)		
	52	short dumbbell stand		140/130
	53	practice barbells		185
	54	knee bending bar (padded)		200
	55	curl bar		140
	56	bench press (adjustable)		40/120
	57	sloping bench I		40/120
	58	sloping bench II		40/120
	59	multi-purpose bench		40/120
	60	general workout bench (12 positions)		
	61	compact dumbbells (2–60 kg)		
	62	dumbbell stand		145/ 80

(1) **Equipment for workout and fitness rooms**

CONDITIONING AND FITNESS ROOMS

For 40–45 users a room size of at least 200 m² is needed → (2). Clear room height for all rooms should be 3.0 m. For an optimum double-row arrangement of machines, the room should be at least 6 m wide. To allow clear supervision of all training, the room length needs to be 15 m or less. The minimum room size of 40 m² is suitable for 12 users.

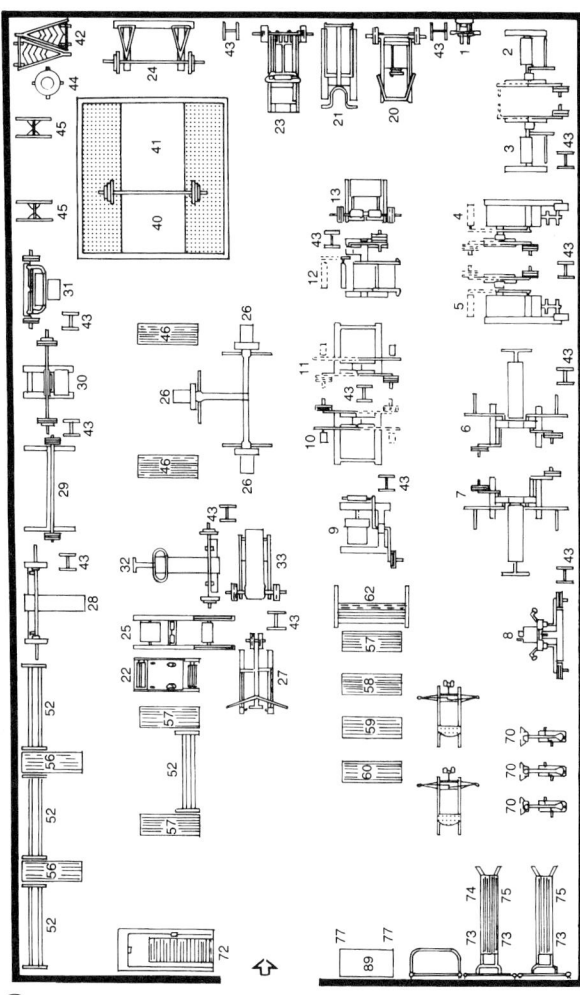

(2) **Example of a 200 m² workout room**

	no.	description	movement	required space
E	70	exercise bike	70–76: stamina, co-ordination (bending arms)	40/ 90
	71	rowing machine		120/140
	72	treadmill		80/190
	73	wall bars		100/ 15
	74	pull-up bar for wall bars		120/120
	75	stomach muscle bench for clipping in		100/180 70/150
	76	spine support equipment		
	77	power jump testing equipment	77–88: mobility, co-ordination	
	78	punch ball		
	79	chest expander		
	80	skipping rope		
	81	vibrating belt		
	82	finger dumbbells		
	83	bali equipment		
	84	ball dumbbells		
	85	water dumbbells		
	86	weighted vest		
	87	weight packs for arms/legs		
	88	mirror		
	89	equipment cupboard		50/110

TENNIS FACILITIES

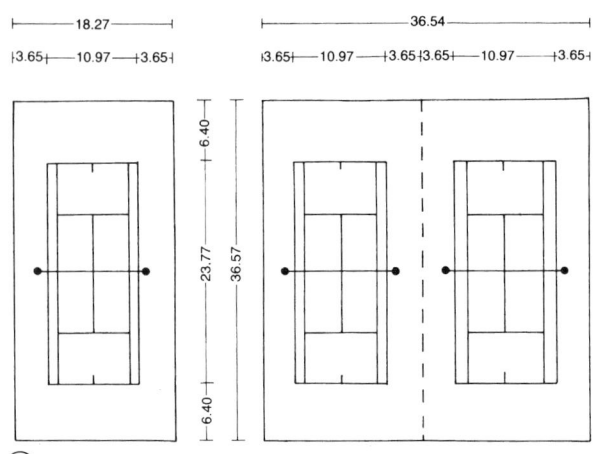

① Court dimensions

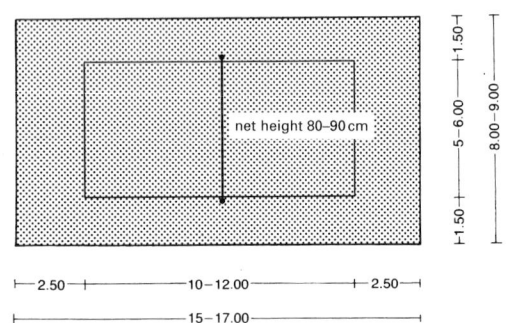

② Net

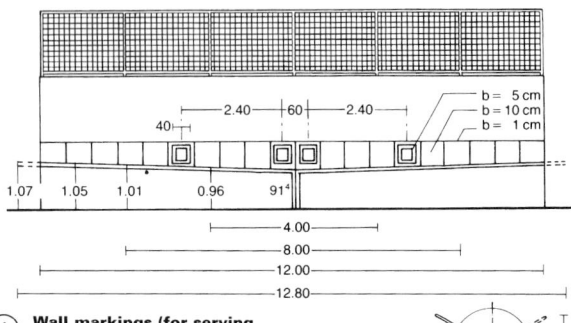

③ Children's tennis court

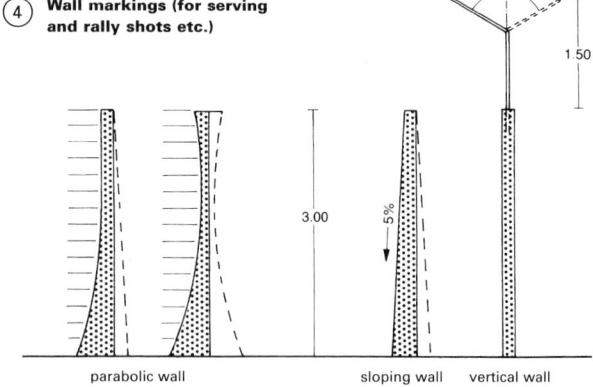

④ Wall markings (for serving and rally shots etc.)

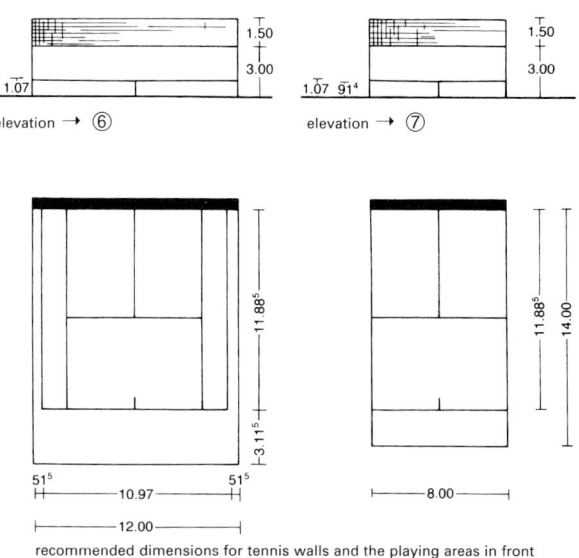

⑤ Forms of tennis walls

doubles court → ① – ②	10.97 × 23.77 m
singles court	8.23 × 23.77 m
side margin	≥3.65 m
side margin for competitions	4.00 m
end margin	≥6.40 m
end margin for competitions	8.00 m
between two courts	7.30 m
net height in the middle	0.915m
net height at the posts	1.07 m
height of surround netting	4.00 m

Use 2.5 mm thick wire net, with a 4 cm mesh width, for surround netting.

The number of active tennis players at present is between 1.6% and 3% of the total population. Use a 1:30 court:player ratio as a rule of thumb for the calculation of the number of courts needed in new developments.

$$\text{necessary courts (T)} = \frac{\text{population} \times 3}{100 \times 30}$$

The area needed for tennis courts in children's facilities is between 120 and 153 m² → ③.

For recreational tennis courts (i.e. where there are no spectators) four car parking spaces should be provided per court.

To calculate the size of plot required, add the net areas ('usable sports areas') needed for the planned number of tennis courts, training walls and children's facilities. To this add an additional 60–80% of the total net area to give the overall plot size.

Outdoor courts should, as near as possible, be orientated in the north–south direction. It is recommended that no more than two courts should be immediately next to one another and if they are behind each other a sight screen must be used to separate them. Artificial lighting should be at least 10 m high and along the sides of the court.

The layout should be designed so as to allow adaptation to meet future needs and planned so that any future building activity can take place without interrupting the playing activities. Potential future needs for accommodation (groundsman, trainer, tenant) and garages should be anticipated in the plans from the beginning. Tennis courts should not be 'foreign bodies' in the environment: they should fit in with their surroundings.

elevation → ⑥   elevation → ⑦

recommended dimensions for tennis walls and the playing areas in front

⑥ **Training wall: doubles**   ⑦ **Training wall: singles**

TENNIS FACILITIES

Ceiling heights of halls for indoor competition tennis courts are internationally fixed. A height of 10.67 m is required by the regulations of the Davis Cup. For leisure facilities, a height of 9–11 m is recommended; 9 m is generally sufficient → ①. In gymnasiums and sports centres, it is possible to play tennis with hall heights as low as 7 m. The applicable height of a hall is measured at the net from the floor to the underside of the roof truss. The same height is needed over the full 10.97 m width of the court. The height at the outer limit of the run-out area should be at least 3 m. For a summary of end- and side-section elevations of the different hall types see → ② – ④.

Halls may be permanent → ⑤ – ⑥, demountable or multipurpose. Based on the court and run-out measurements prescribed in the international regulations for competition-standard facilities, one court requires a hall size of 18.30 m × 36.60 m. Therefore, use the following hall areas:

two courts = (2 × 18.30) × (1 × 36.60) = 36.60 × 36.60
three courts = (3 × 18.30) × (1 × 36.60) = 54.90 × 36.60

These dimensions make the facilities suitable for both leisure and competition use. The possible uses are:

1. courts are competition-level 'singles'
2. courts are competition-level 'doubles'
3. courts are for training/leisure use, singles and/or doubles

If the tennis courts are for recreational use only, it is possible to use a reduced width to make space savings. The minimum size of hall for a two-court recreational facility is 32.40 m × 36.60 m.

The table below shows some of the possible options.

hall type	courts	S (single)	D (double)	width	length	use C*	use not C*
1	1	1	1	18.30	36.60	S/D	–
2	2	2	2	36.60	36.60	2S/2D	–
2 single span	2	2	2	33.90	36.60	2S/1 S/1D	2D or 2S
3	3	3	3	54.90	36.60	3S/3D	–
3 single span	3	3	3	49.50	36.60	3S/2D	3D or 3S
2a	2	1	1	33.90	36.60	1S/1D	–
2a single span	2	1	1	32.40	36.60	1S/1D	–
* competition level							

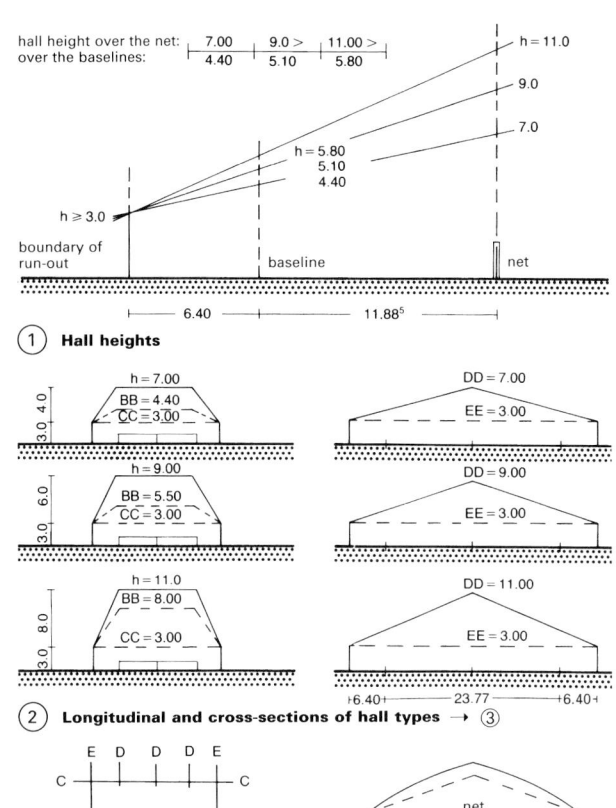

① Hall heights

② Longitudinal and cross-sections of hall types → ③

③ Schematic plans → ②

④ Hall dimensions and forms

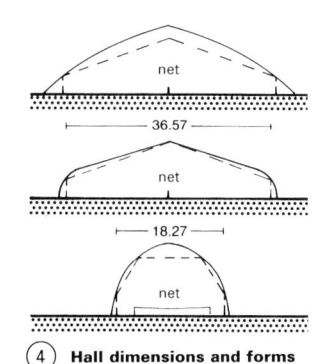

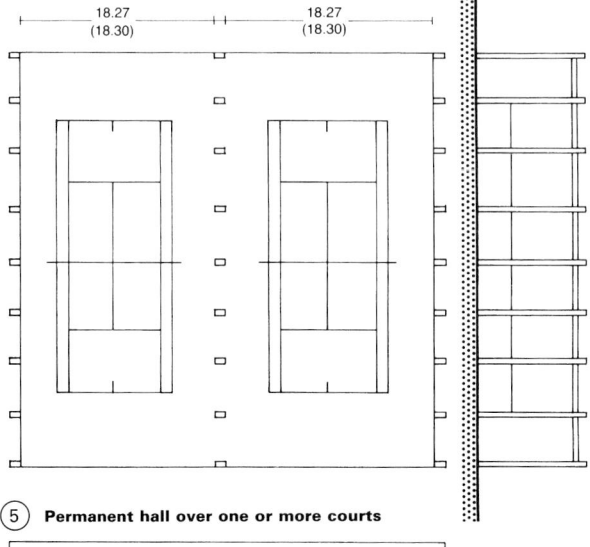

⑤ Permanent hall over one or more courts

section → ⑤

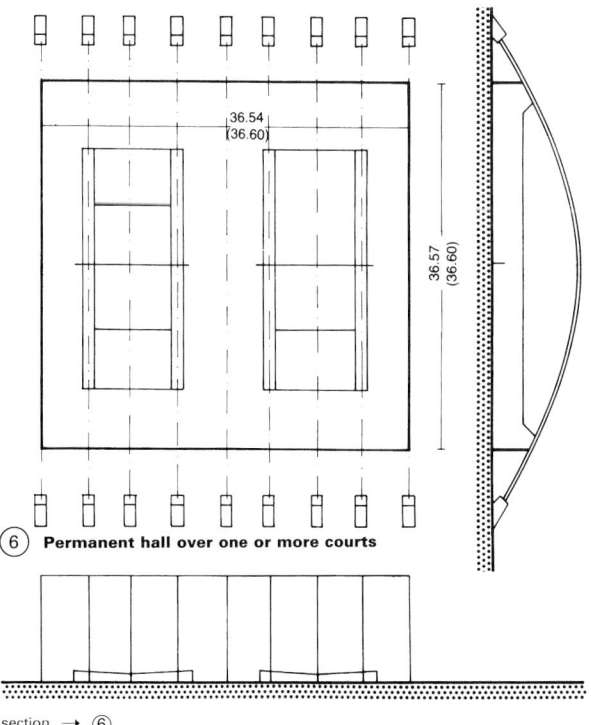

⑥ Permanent hall over one or more courts

section → ⑥

MINIATURE GOLF

A lane-golf course consists of 18 clearly separated lanes (with the exception of 'long shot') which have to be numbered and to accord with the relevant regulations. A course appropriate for tournaments comprises:

> lane separations (mostly ribbons or tapes)
> tee markings
> one or more hazards (can be omitted)
> borderline (can be omitted)
> setting-down markings (can be omitted)
> hole

Further specified details may need to be considered.

The lane playing area must have a minimum width of 80 cm and has to be at least 5.50 m long. Lanes designed for level playing must be completely flat, with a surface quality sufficient to guarantee a predictable path of travel of the balls. If lanes are not separated by fixed ribbons or tapes, they have to be marked in some other way (except long shot). Each lane has to have a tee marking and all markings should be standardised throughout the course (i.e. a specific system for all lanes). Hazards are usually fixed in position although, depending on their intended purpose and design, it is acceptable for some to be moveable. Those which are not fixed should be marked. All hazards must be robust in design and construction.

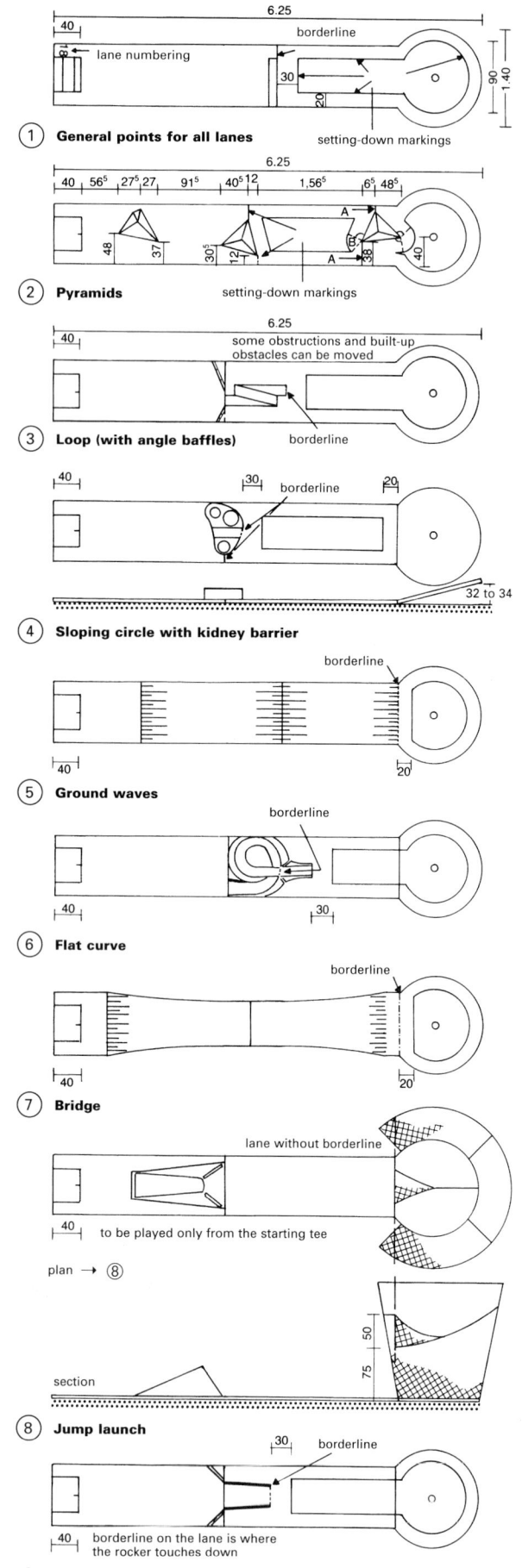

① General points for all lanes

② Pyramids

③ Loop (with angle baffles)

④ Sloping circle with kidney barrier

⑤ Ground waves

⑥ Flat curve

⑦ Bridge

⑧ Jump launch

⑨ Rocker with bracket

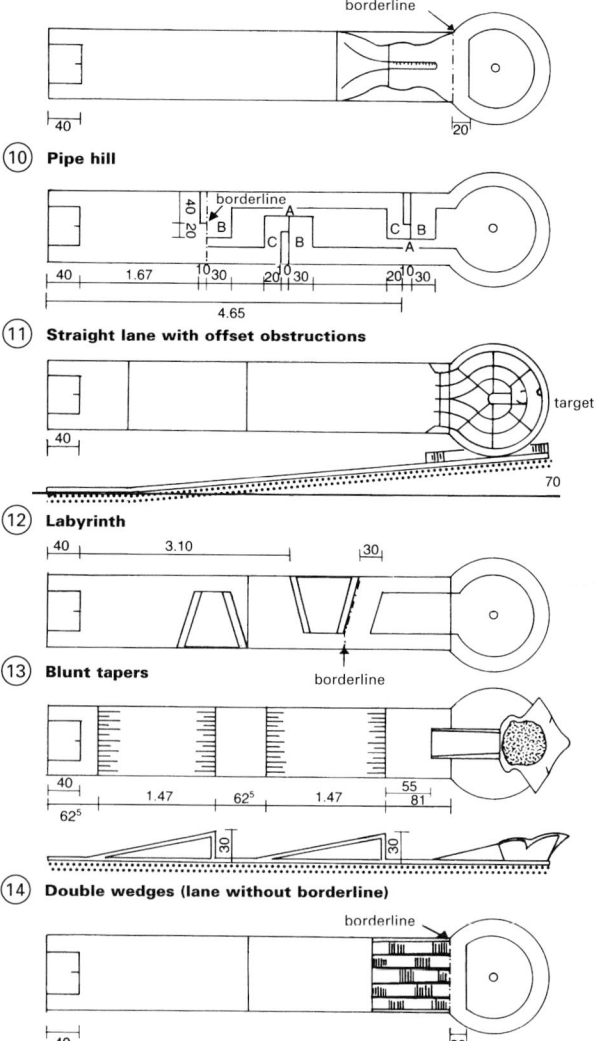

⑩ Pipe hill

⑪ Straight lane with offset obstructions

⑫ Labyrinth

⑬ Blunt tapers

⑭ Double wedges (lane without borderline)

⑮ Irregular passages

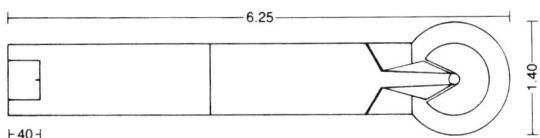

(16) **Central circle (lane without borderline)**

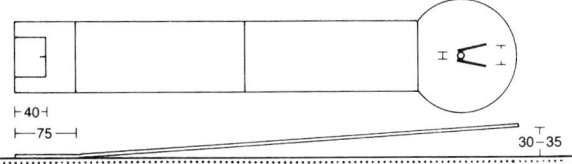

(17) **Volcano, to be played only from the tee (lane without borderline)**

(18) **Steep slope with V-shape hazard, to be played only from the starting tee (lane without borderline)**

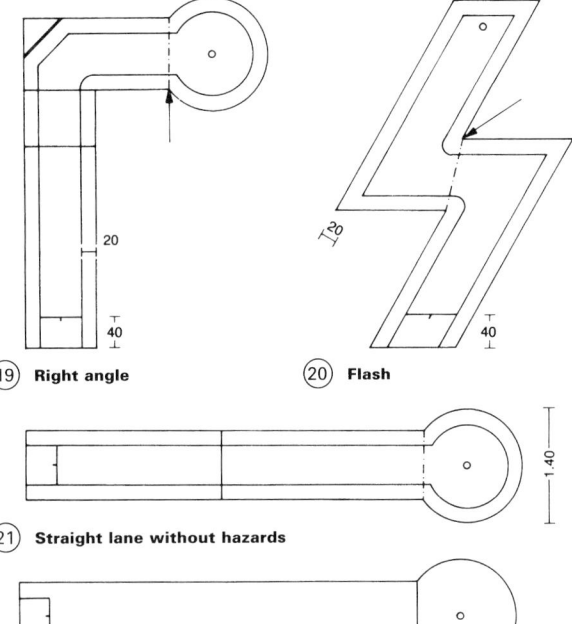

(19) **Right angle**　　(20) **Flash**

(21) **Straight lane without hazards**

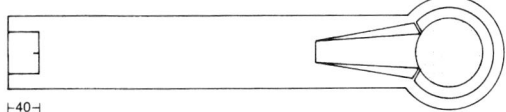

(22) **Sloping circle without hazards, to be played only from the tee (lane without borderline)**

(23) **Circle platform, to be played only from the tee (lane without borderline)**

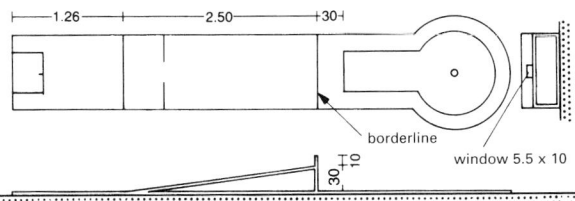

borderline

window 5.5 x 10

(24) **Rising wedge with central opening (window)**

MINIATURE GOLF

Each hazard has to be different from others on the same course, not just visually but also technically, and it should be possible for players to predict the effect it will have on the path of the ball.

The borderline marks the end of the first hazards. In lanes without built-in hazards, they show the minimum distance the ball has to travel to remain in the game. If the first hazard is the full width of the lane the borderline coincides with the end of the hazard.

Lanes that are only playable from the tee do not have a borderline.

Borderline markings have to be installed in such a way that the edge that marks the tee matches the end of hazard marking.

The setting-down markings indicate where a play-off or movement of the ball is allowed during the game. The markings show where the ball should be placed.

It must be possible to reach the target from the tee marking in one hit. Should the target be a hole, the diameter should not exceed 120 mm. For minigolf or star golf 100 mm is the limit.

The game does not require any special equipment: normal golf clubs, balls and accessories are permitted. However, the striking area of the club is not allowed to be more than 40 cm². All lane-golf and normal golf balls are permissible provided the diameter is between 37 mm and 43 mm. Balls made of wood, metal, glass, fibreglass, ivory or other materials are not accepted as lane-golf balls.

Miniature golf lanes are usually designed with the following standard sizes: lane length, 6.25 m; lane width, 0.90 m; diameter of end circle 1.40 m.

Minigolf

Developed at the beginning of the 50s, these courses consist of 17 concrete pistes (12 m long) and a long-range piste (approximate length, 25 m). The concrete pistes are set in a frame made from steel pipes and the hazards are made from natural stone.

Cobi Golf

This is one of the most difficult lane systems of golf to play. The special characteristics of Cobi golf are the small 'gates' placed in front of the hazards.

The courses again consist of 18 lanes but they can be in large format (12 to 14 m long) as well as in small format (length 6 to 7 m).

Stargolf

A stargolf course consists of 18 lanes with concrete pistes. The first 17 of these have a circular target area, but on the last lane the hole is in a star-shaped target area, hence the name of the system. The length of the lanes is 8 m; the width is 1 m; the diameter of the end circles is 2 m.

The concrete lanes are enclosed in pipe barriers. The tee marker is a circle with a diameter of 30 cm. The holes have a diameter of 10 cm.

In all miniature golf systems with lanes, the hazards are standardised and constructed according to the criteria dictated by the sport. The aim is to make it possible to play each lane of the course with a single stroke. With all holes being par 1, the golfers' ultimate goal is to complete the course with a total score of 18.

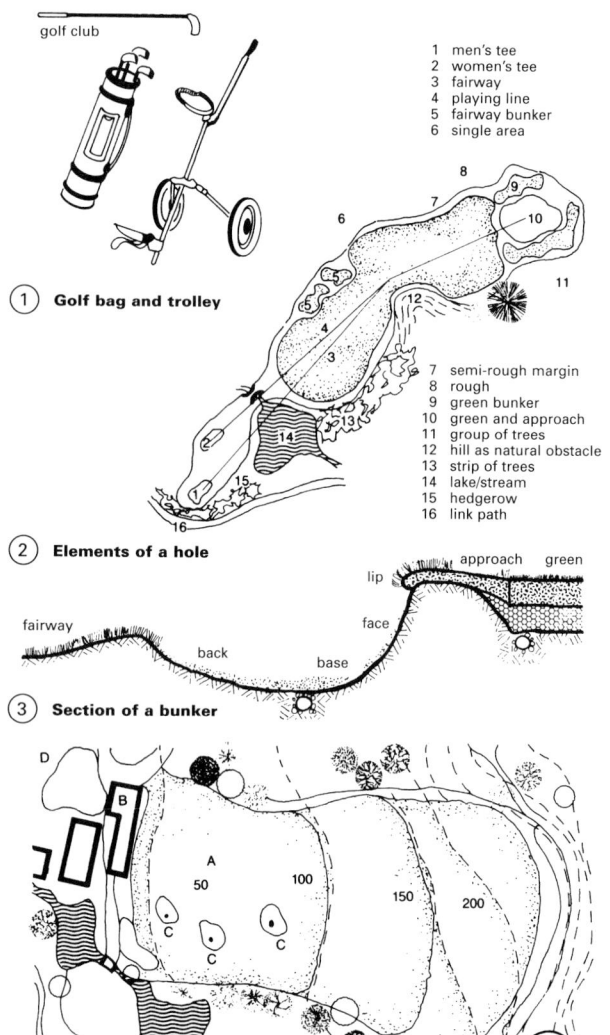

golf club

① **Golf bag and trolley**

1 men's tee
2 women's tee
3 fairway
4 playing line
5 fairway bunker
6 single area

7 semi-rough margin
8 rough
9 green bunker
10 green and approach
11 group of trees
12 hill as natural obstacle
13 strip of trees
14 lake/stream
15 hedgerow
16 link path

② **Elements of a hole**

③ **Section of a bunker**

④ **Basic design of a practice area** → ⑤

Golf courses are best situated in undulating terrain with gentle gradients, or in dunes if the site is on the coast. Ideally, the course should be surrounded by forest or light tree cover and have natural hazards (e.g. streams, lakes, etc.). The size of the course depends on the number of 'holes' and their length (i.e. the distance from tee to hole). Golf courses cannot be treated in the same way as other 'regulated' and standardised sports facilities.

Nowadays golf courses can be constructed almost only in rural areas, especially in areas previously used for farming or forestry. The planning of a golf course requires the direction of a widely experienced specialist who needs the knowledge of a landscape architect, golf player, landscape ecologist, soil scientist, agronomist, economist etc. Before any planning can commence, a detailed site investigation has to take place.

When considering a new course, a population of approximately 100 000 within an area less than 30 minutes away by car is needed for a nine hole course. This should ensure that membership will reach the necessary number for a viable golf club (around 300 members).

An important part of each golf course is the practice area, which comprises a driving range, a practice green and an approach green → ④. The driving range should be as even as possible and have a width of 80 m in order to allow 15 golfers to practice at once. The length should be at least 200 m, or 225 m ideally, and should be arranged in such a way that neighbouring holes are not disturbed. The approach green should have a size of at least 300 m². Sand hazards (bunkers) for practice shots should cover at least 200 m² and should be of various depths. The best place for the practice area is next to the club house.

The plan for a golf course should generally be based on the eventual provision of an 18 hole course, so an area of at least 55 ha, preferably 60 ha, should be available in the long term. To make it possible to play half a round (nine holes) on an 18 hole golf course, the first tee and the ninth green as well as the tenth tee and the eighteenth green should be as near the clubhouse as possible → ⑤.

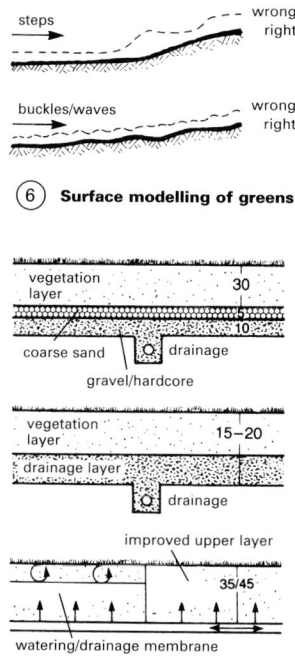

⑥ **Surface modelling of greens**

vegetation layer   30
coarse sand   drainage   10
gravel/hardcore

vegetation layer   15−20
drainage layer   drainage

improved upper layer   35/45
watering/drainage membrane

⑦ **Customary constructions for golf greens**

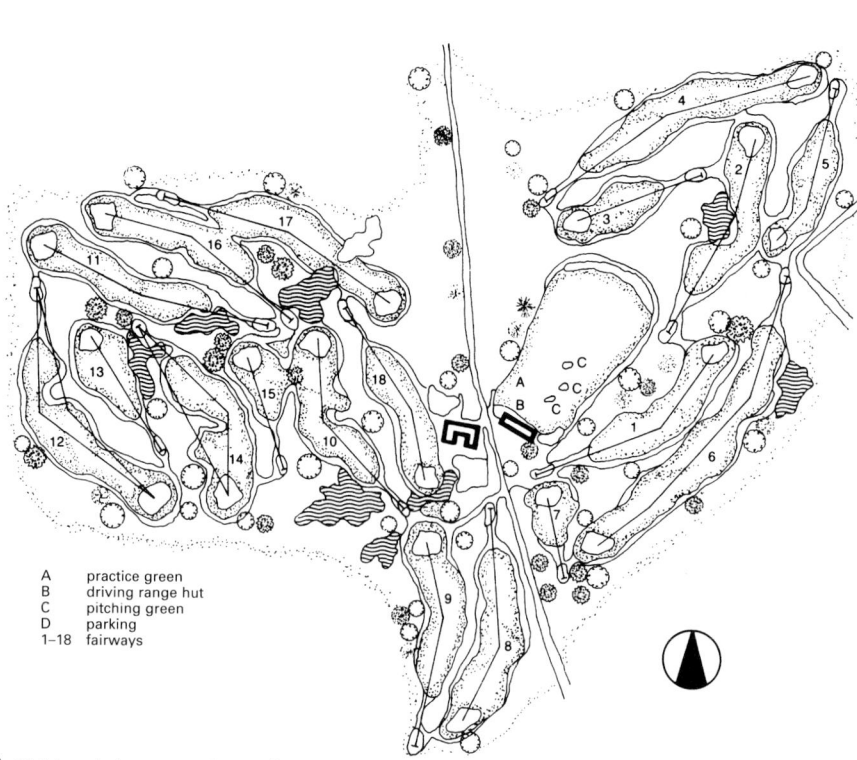

A   practice green
B   driving range hut
C   pitching green
D   parking
1–18   fairways

⑤ **Eighteen hole course of normal competition size**

GOLF COURSES

Practice areas can provide training either just for the short/approach game or offer instruction in all aspects of the game of golf. It is possible to establish independent golf centre in an area of 10 ha, or perhaps less. The centre should contain a driving range, an approach green, a practice green and a nine hole course (par 3) → ①.

The table below shows the lengths of the holes in relation to the par rating.

par	length of hole	
	for men	for women
3	up to 228 m	up to 201 m
4	229–434 m	202–382 m
5	from 435 m	from 383 m

Recognised standard lengths for golf courses range between standard 60 at a normal length of 3749 m and standard 74 at a normal length of 6492 m.

Elements of a golf course

At the start of each hole is the tee, which is not fixed in size but with sufficient width it should measure approximately 200 m². Fairways have a width of 30–50 m and vary in length from 100 m to up to more than 500 m. At the end of the fairway is the green, which should be at least 400 m² and is normally 500–600 m². 'Approach greens' are not found everywhere but where they are included they have a minimum width of 2.5 m. Rough areas with long grass and shrubs/trees border the edge of the course.

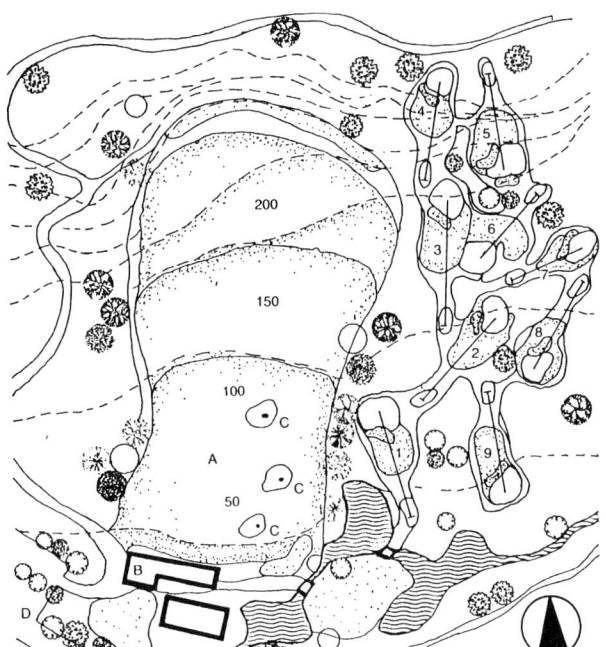

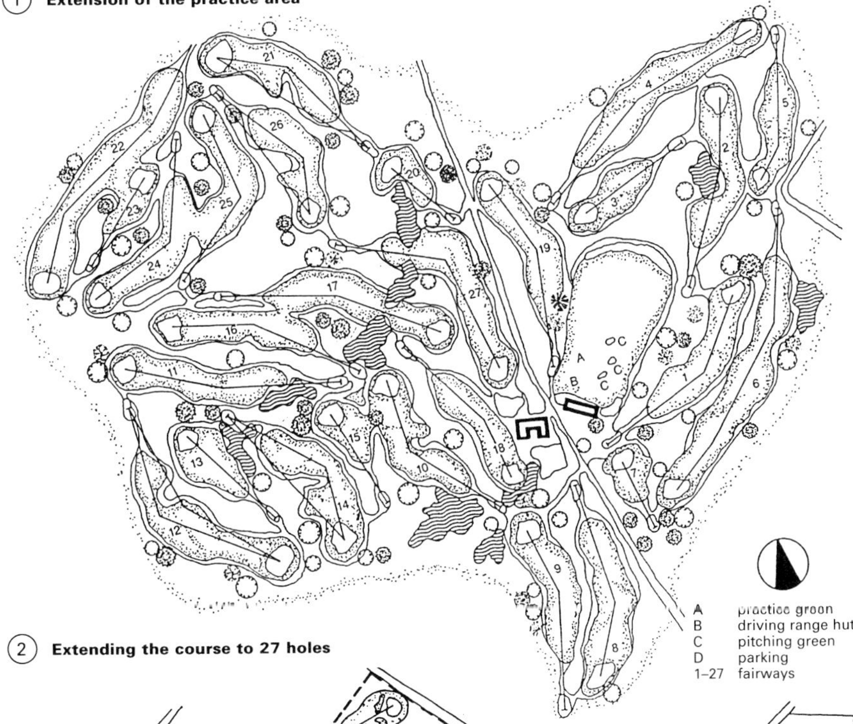

① **Extension of the practice area**

② **Extending the course to 27 holes**

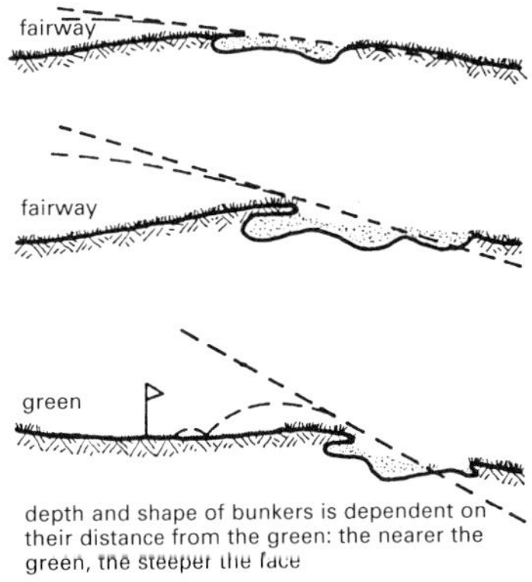

A practice green
B driving range hut
C pitching green
D parking
1–27 fairways

fairway

fairway

green

depth and shape of bunkers is dependent on their distance from the green: the nearer the green, the steeper the face

④ **Bunker design**

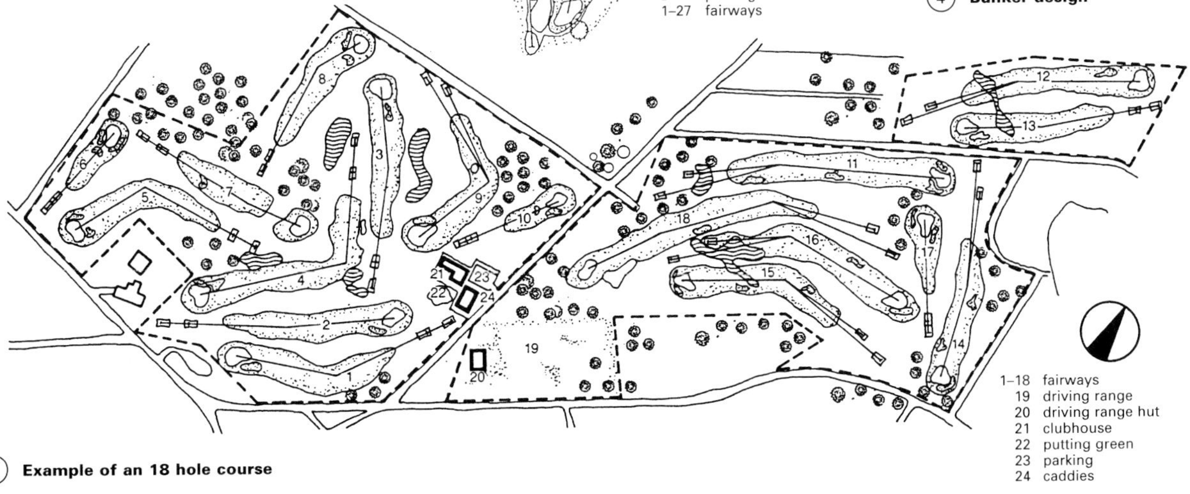

③ **Example of an 18 hole course**

1–18 fairways
19 driving range
20 driving range hut
21 clubhouse
22 putting green
23 parking
24 caddies

511

SAILING: YACHTS AND MARINAS

Mooring spaces for sailing and motor boats have to be planned carefully to make optimum use of the water area available. For reference, allocate 4–5 sailing boats or 6 motorboats per hectare of water area.

The necessary depth of water in harbours and marinas depends on the types of boats to be accommodated. Usually, dinghies and yachts with centre-boards require a depth of 1250 mm whereas fixed-keel boats need 4000–5000 mm. Constant water levels are obviously preferable for the safety of boats.

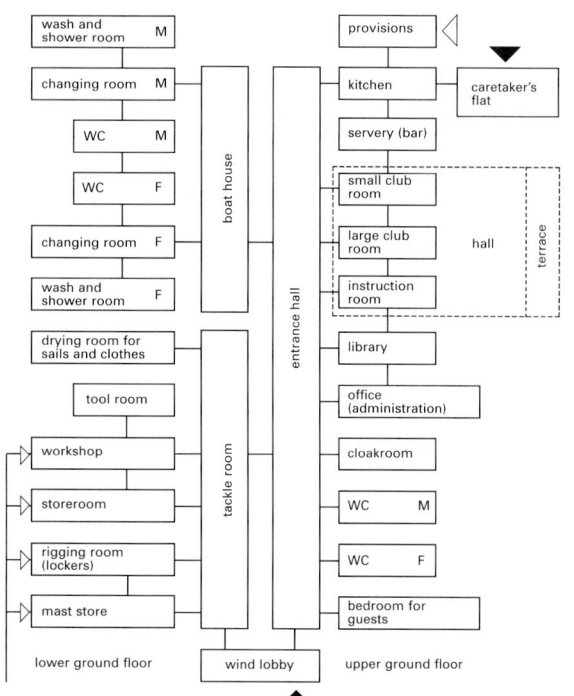

(1) Functional diagram of a clubhouse

(2) Types and classes of sailing boat: overview

boat type (crew: 1–3 persons)	class: std (S), consts. (C)	dimensions, length/width (m)	draft (m)	sail area 3 (spinnaker) (m²)	sail marking
Olympic classes:					
Finn dinghy[1] (1) Finn	S	4.50/1.51	0.85	10	two blue wavy lines, one above the other
Flying Dutchman	S	6.05/1.80	1.10	15 (s)	black letters FD
Star (2)	S	6.90/1.70	1.00	26	five pointed red star
Tempest	S	6.69/2.00	1.13	22.93 (s)	black letter T
Dragon[1] (3)	S	8.90/1.90	1.20	22 (s)	black letter D
Soling[1] (3)	S	8.15/1.90	1.30	24.3 (s)	black letter Ω (omega)
Tornado[1] (2)	S	6.25/3.05	0.80	22.5 (s)	black letter T with two parallel lines below
470[1] (2)	S	4.70/1.68	1.05	10.66 (s)	black number 470
5.50 m yacht	C	9.50/1.95	1.35	28.8	black number 5.5
Other international classes:					
Pirate (2)	S	5.00/1.62	0.85+	10 (s)	red axe
Optimist (1)	S	2.30/1.13	0.77+	3.33	black letter O
children/youth cadet (2)	S	3.32/1.27	0.74+	5.10 (s)	black letter G
OK dinghy (1)	S	4.00/1.42	0.95	8.50	black letters Ou.K
Olympia dinghy (1)	S	5.00/1.66	1.06+	10	red ring
420 dinghy (2)	S	4.20/1.50	0.95+	10 (s)	black number 420 set slanting

[1] Olympic classes 1980 in Moscow
+ with lowered centreboard

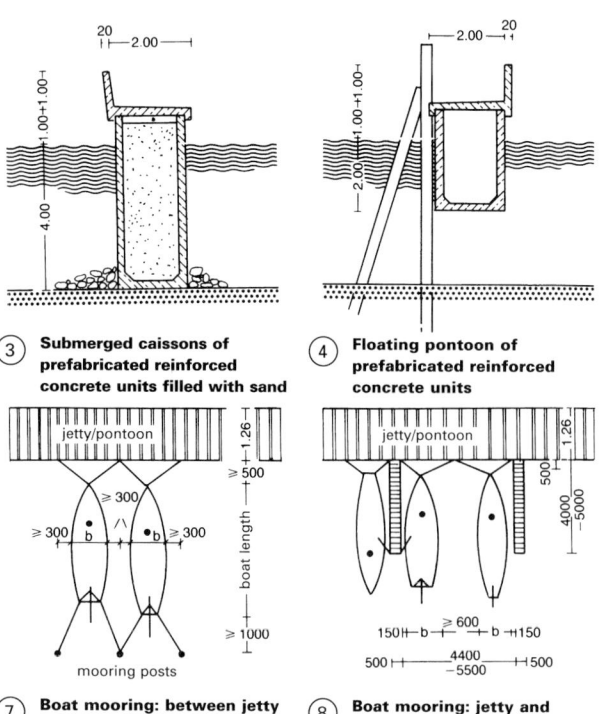

(3) Submerged caissons of prefabricated reinforced concrete units filled with sand

(4) Floating pontoon of prefabricated reinforced concrete units

(5) Submerged wall of prefabricated reinforced concrete units in the harbour of Insel Riems

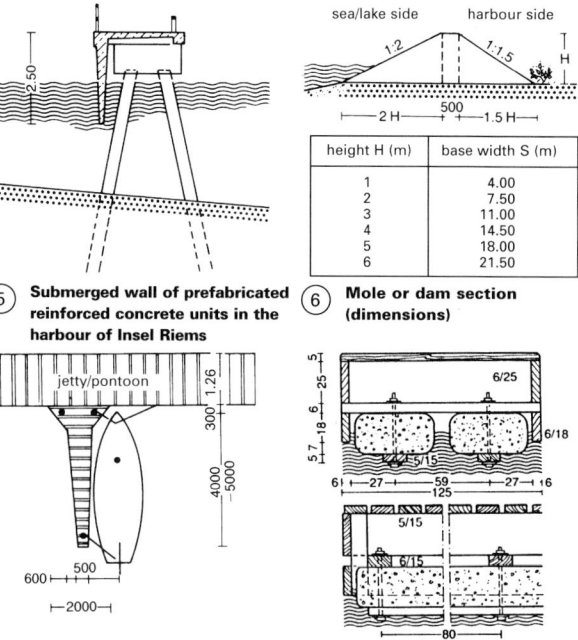

(6) Mole or dam section (dimensions)

height H (m)	base width S (m)
1	4.00
2	7.50
3	11.00
4	14.50
5	18.00
6	21.50

(7) Boat mooring: between jetty and mooring posts

(8) Boat mooring: jetty and finger piers

(9) Boat mooring: between jetty and Y-shaped finger pier

(10) Floating jetty; styrofoam floats: cross-/longitudinal section)

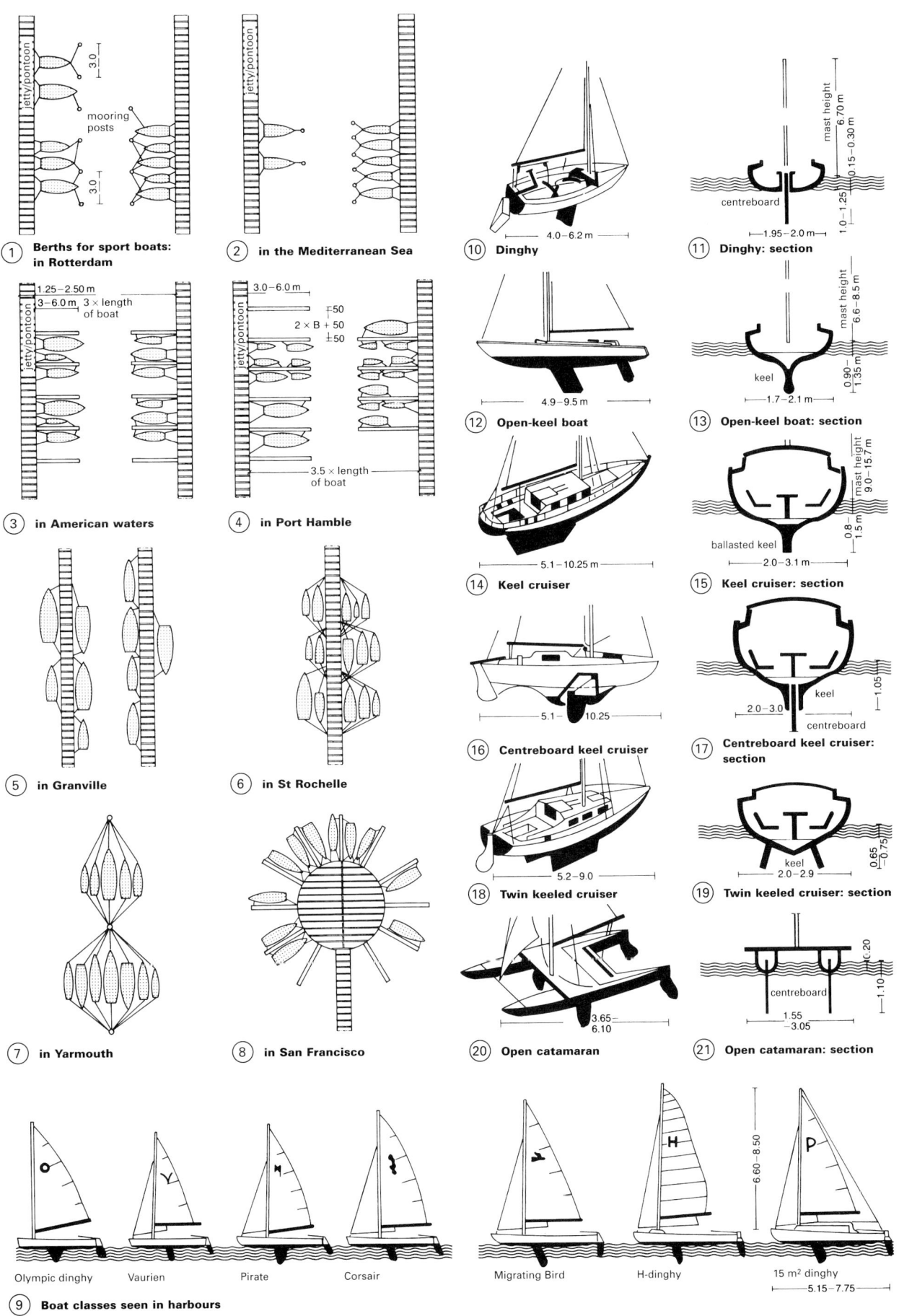

1 Berths for sport boats:
in Rotterdam

2 in the Mediterranean Sea

3 in American waters

4 in Port Hamble

5 in Granville

6 in St Rochelle

7 in Yarmouth

8 in San Francisco

9 Boat classes seen in harbours

Olympic dinghy   Vaurien   Pirate   Corsair

Migrating Bird   H-dinghy   15 m² dinghy

10 Dinghy

11 Dinghy: section

12 Open-keel boat

13 Open-keel boat: section

14 Keel cruiser

15 Keel cruiser: section

16 Centreboard keel cruiser

17 Centreboard keel cruiser:
section

18 Twin keeled cruiser

19 Twin keeled cruiser: section

20 Open catamaran

21 Open catamaran: section

SAILING: HARBOURS/MARINAS

The direction of the prevailing wind and waves is an important consideration in determining the position of the harbour entrance and also influences the the design of the breakwaters, which protect the interior of the harbour from waves → ① – ④. Entrances and exits have to be at least equal in width to the length of the mooring spaces for sailing boats or, preferably, one and a half times the maximum boat length.

It should be remembered that boats under sail will approach the harbour entrance from a variety of directions, depending on the prevailing wind on the day. Consequently, the harbour should have a turning area, with a diameter of 35–60 m, behind the entrance.

The construction of breakwaters, sea defences and landing stages, and the means of transport and storage for boats, have a fundamental influence on the type of use that can be made of the harbour or marina in different climatic conditions.

As well as offering protection from waves, breakwaters (also called moles) also prevent the harbour from filling up with silt carried by the sea currents. Stone breakwaters are built either from natural stone boulders or pre-cast concrete units in geometrical shapes (e.g. tetrahedron) that interconnect with each other when laid. As well as stone breakwaters, sheet-pile walls are also commonly used. These are made from framed steel sections and have a life expectancy of 20–30 years.

Each boat needs a berth appropriate to its use (e.g. training, weekend, holiday etc.). The options include water berths, land berths or hall/indoor berths and the areas required for boats and associated facilities are: water berths 90–160 m²; land berths 100–200 m². This gives a total area per boat of approximately 200–360 m². In addition, at least one family car parking space should be planned for every berth.

In choosing the layout of berths it may be necessary to consider the frequency and shape of ice formation. There may be a risk of damage through the expansion and thrust of pack-ice.

Floating pontoons of steel, reinforced concrete, inflated tubes and floating styrofoam pieces are used both as breakwaters and landing stages. Steel and reinforced concrete pontoons, which sink about 2 m, adapt to the particular water level and give the necessary calming of the water. Caissons are prefabricated reinforced concrete units which are sunk and filled with sand or gravel once in position. → Page 512.

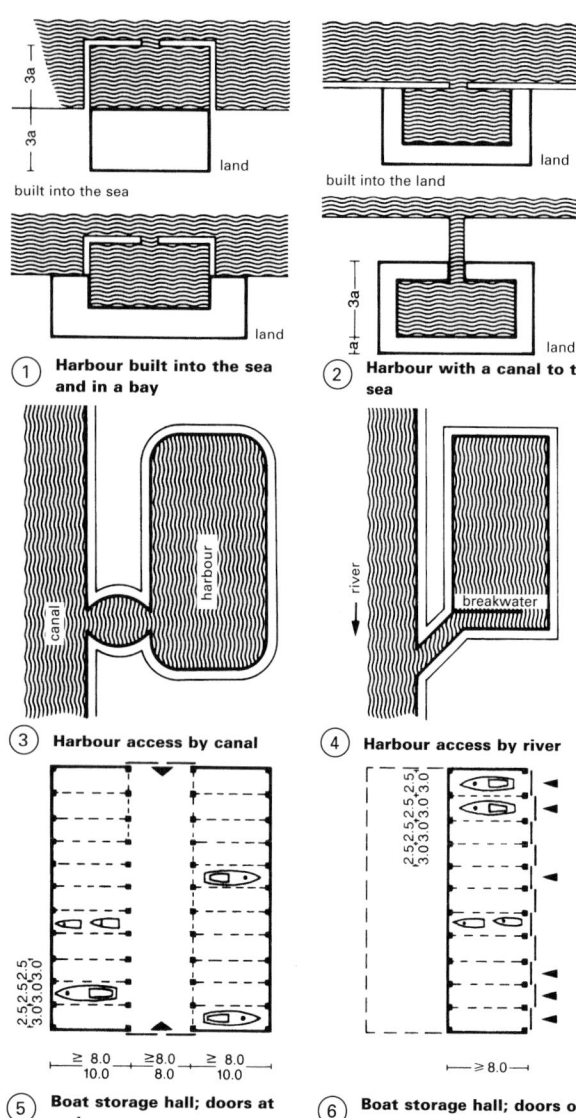

① Harbour built into the sea and in a bay

② Harbour with a canal to the sea

③ Harbour access by canal

④ Harbour access by river

⑤ Boat storage hall; doors at end

⑥ Boat storage hall; doors on one or two sides

⑦ Land berth size for Olympic sailing boat classes

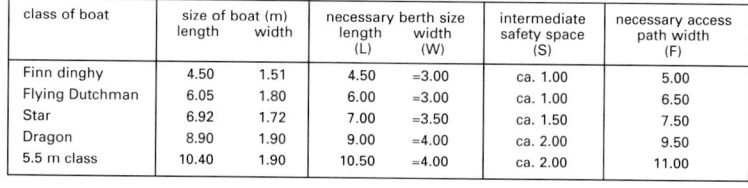

class of boat	size of boat (m) length	width	necessary berth size length (L)	width (W)	intermediate safety space (S)	necessary access path width (F)
Finn dinghy	4.50	1.51	4.50	=3.00	ca. 1.00	5.00
Flying Dutchman	6.05	1.80	6.00	=3.00	ca. 1.00	6.50
Star	6.92	1.72	7.00	=3.50	ca. 1.50	7.50
Dragon	8.90	1.90	9.00	=4.00	ca. 2.00	9.50
5.5 m class	10.40	1.90	10.50	=4.00	ca. 2.00	11.00

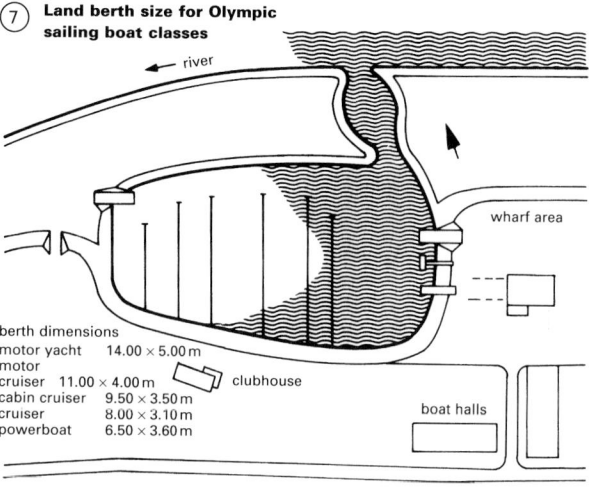

berth dimensions
motor yacht 14.00 × 5.00 m
motor cruiser 11.00 × 4.00 m
cabin cruiser 9.50 × 3.50 m
cruiser 8.00 × 3.10 m
powerboat 6.50 × 3.60 m

⑧ Example of a motorboat harbour

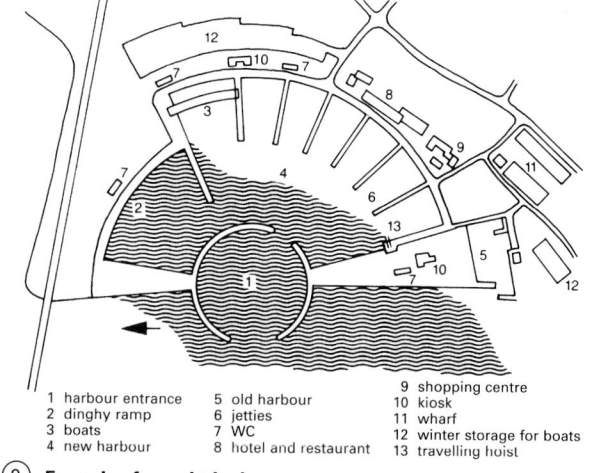

1 harbour entrance
2 dinghy ramp
3 boats
4 new harbour
5 old harbour
6 jetties
7 WC
8 hotel and restaurant
9 shopping centre
10 kiosk
11 wharf
12 winter storage for boats
13 travelling hoist

⑨ Example of a yacht harbour

Competition rowing boats are mostly team boats and usually belong to clubs situated on waterways that are flowing and obstacle-free, in pleasant natural settings. Such clubs may also use kayaks and Canadian canoes.

Boathouses with windows or roof-lights should be north facing to keep the sun out. The doors need to be at least 2.50 × 2.75 m to allow crews to carry in the boats held above their heads. The hall should have a width of at least 6.00 m and a length of 30 m or more. The height, if possible, should be 4.0 m → ⑭. Note that oars are 3.80 m long, with a blade width of 15–18 cm. They should be stored near the entrance, either horizontally on shelves or, preferably, suspended from pulleys above a pit (depending on the height of the hall). Between the boathouse and the landing stage, an area of bank with a width of 20–30 m is necessary for cleaning and preparing boats. A water pump and parking/storage space for boat trailers is also needed.

Single or double sided skulling pools for training with short oars → ⑯ might be required. For a full eight, a pool size of 12.60 × 7.60 m is necessary. The water circulation creates current conditions that are similar to open water.

Other facilities to consider in addition to changing rooms include a gymnasium and swimming pool.

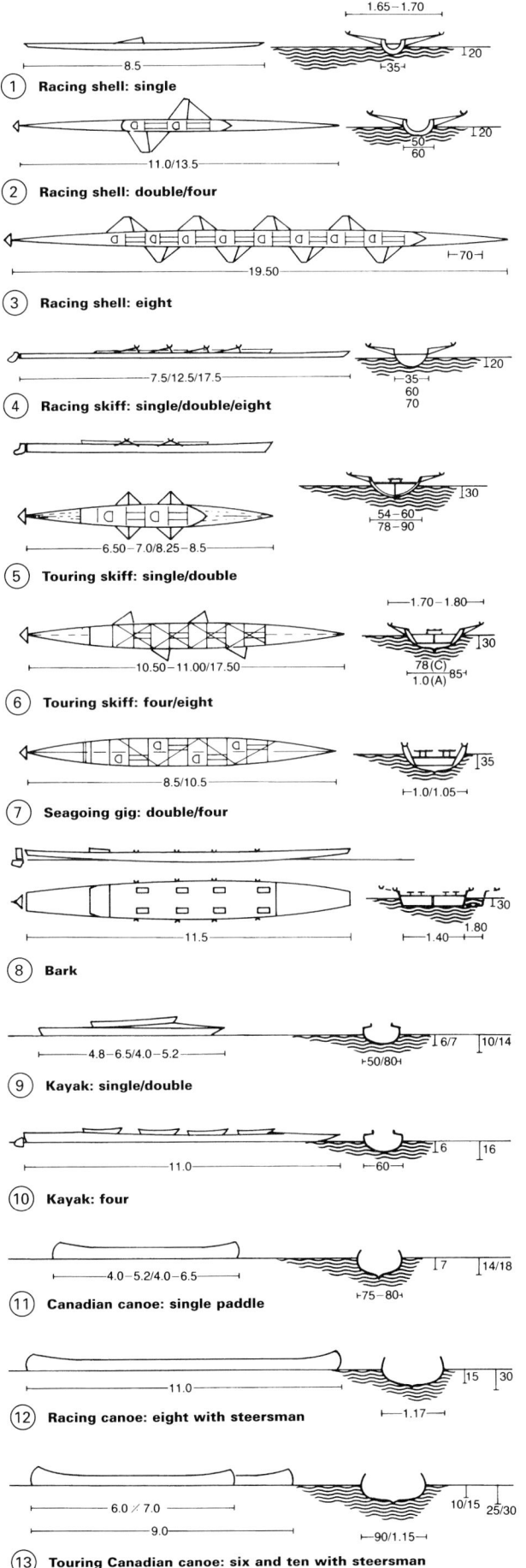

① Racing shell: single
② Racing shell: double/four
③ Racing shell: eight
④ Racing skiff: single/double/eight
⑤ Touring skiff: single/double
⑥ Touring skiff: four/eight
⑦ Seagoing gig: double/four
⑧ Bark
⑨ Kayak: single/double
⑩ Kayak: four
⑪ Canadian canoe: single paddle
⑫ Racing canoe: eight with steersman
⑬ Touring Canadian canoe: six and ten with steersman

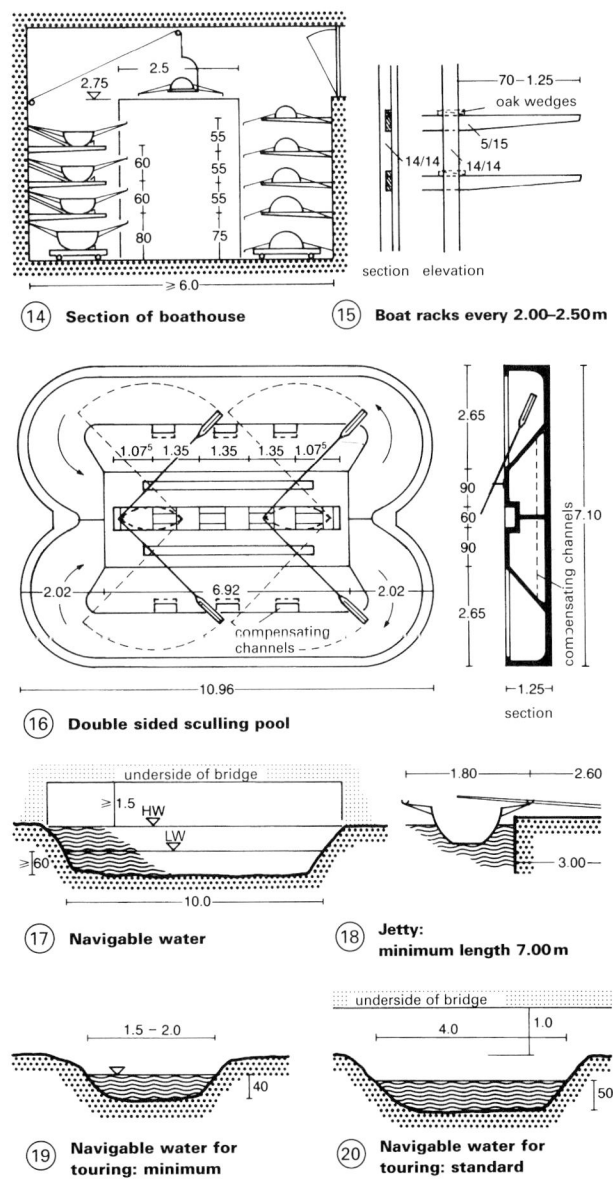

⑭ Section of boathouse
⑮ Boat racks every 2.00–2.50 m
⑯ Double sided sculling pool
⑰ Navigable water
⑱ Jetty: minimum length 7.00 m
⑲ Navigable water for touring: minimum
⑳ Navigable water for touring: standard

WATER SPORTS

Slalom courses can be established in natural settings or in artificial purpose-built facilities (e.g. the international regatta course in Munich → ⑤).

Natural courses require traffic-free stretches of river with a suitable gradient (1:100 or more) and flow rate, which may be natural or controlled by a weir upstream. If they are free of obstacles and at least 8m wide, mill or power station outflows can also be suitable. Artificial facilities are constructed from suitably inclined reinforced concrete channels with concrete stone obstacles. Consideration must be given to the installation of up to 32 gates → ③ for regattas.

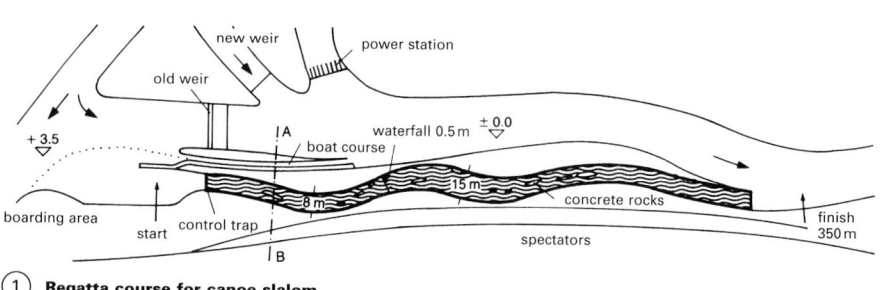

① **Regatta course for canoe slalom**

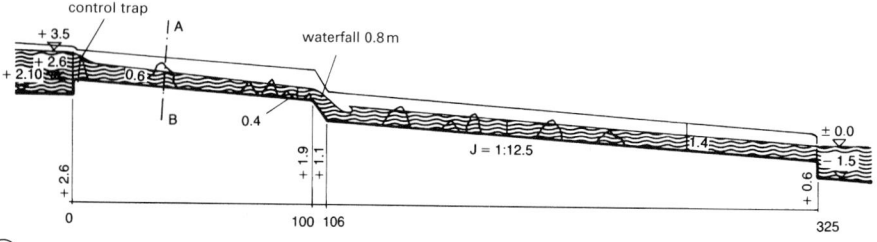

② **Horizontal section** → ①

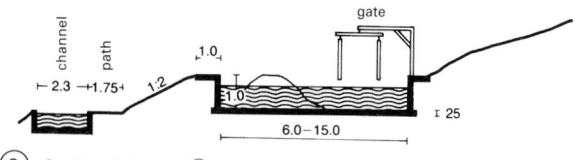

③ **Section A–B** → ①

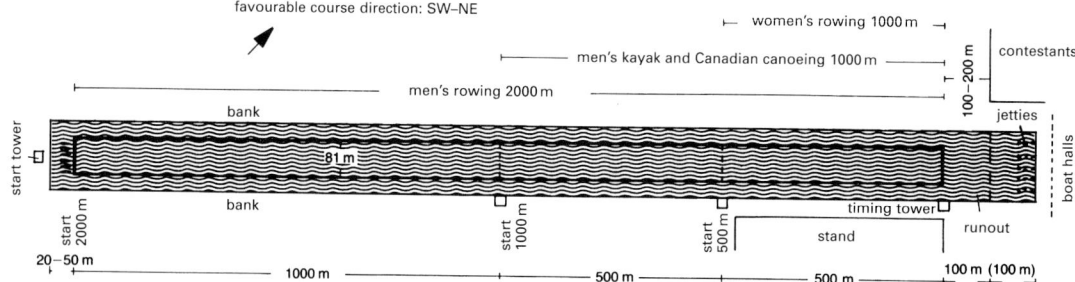

④ **Control trap with draining base**

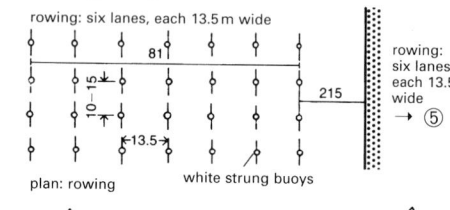

⑤ **Regatta course in Munich (international dimensions) for rowing and canoeing events**

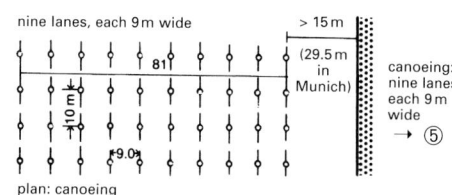

MOTOR BOATS

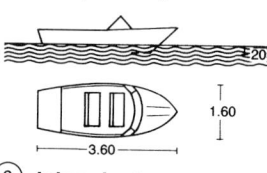

⑥ **Leisure boat**

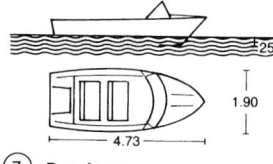

⑦ **Runabout**

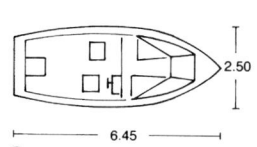

⑧ **Speedboat**

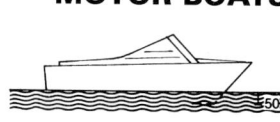

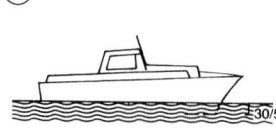

⑨ **Cruiser**

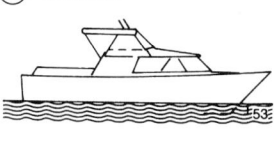

⑩ **Cabin cruiser**

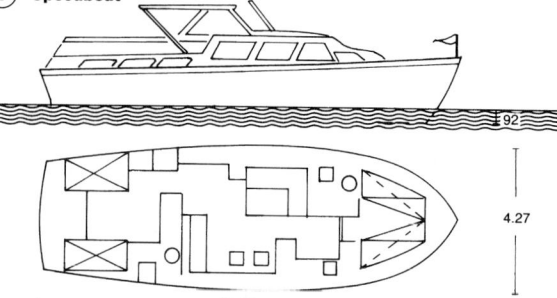

⑪ **Motor yacht**

516

RIDING FACILITIES

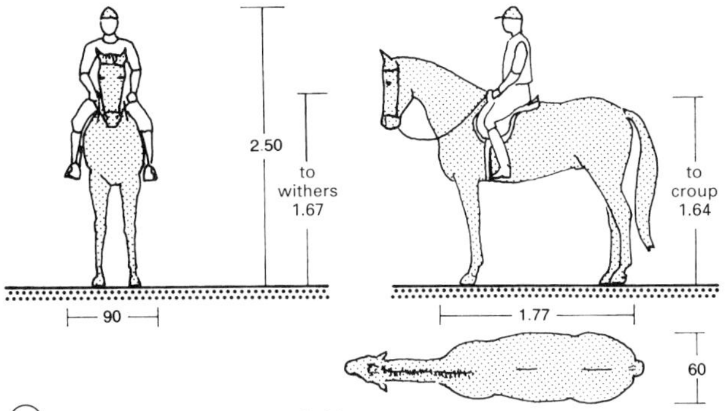

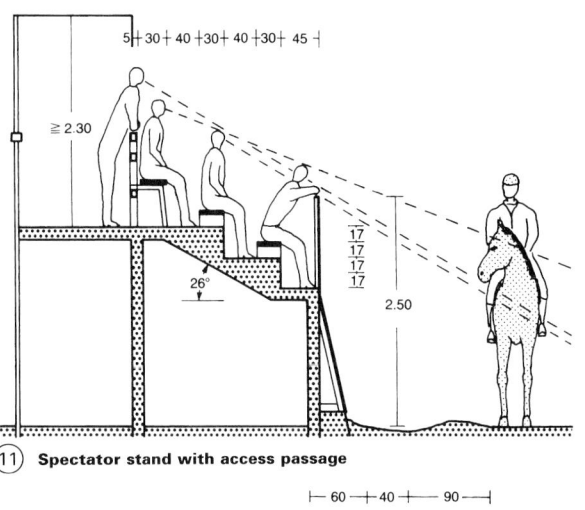

① Dimensions of horse and rider

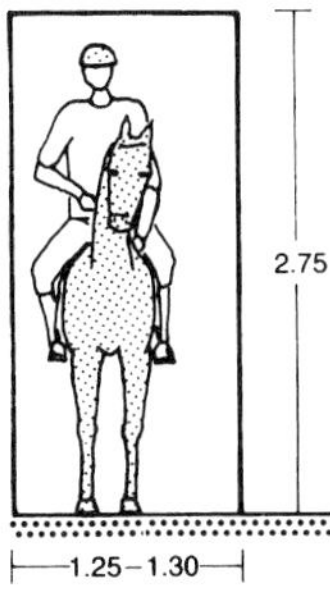

② Stable entrance, mounted

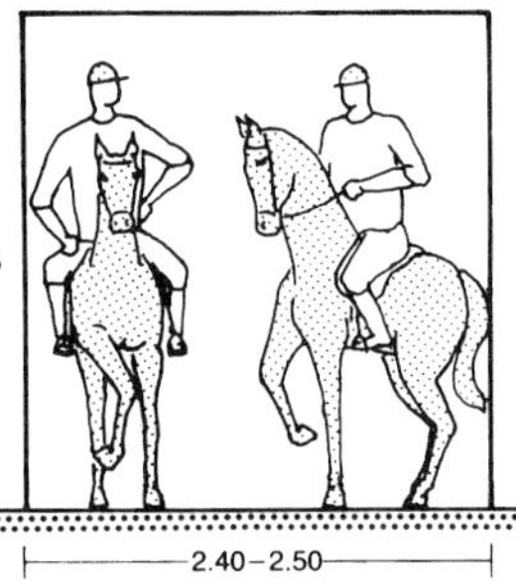

③ Door/stable passage

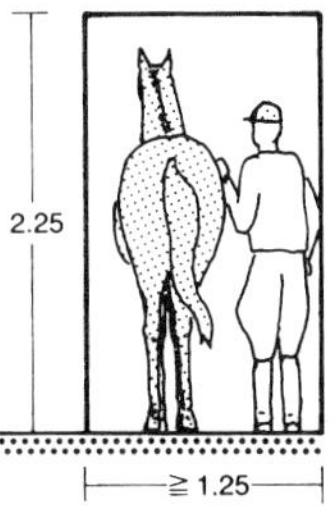

④ Entrance, dismounted

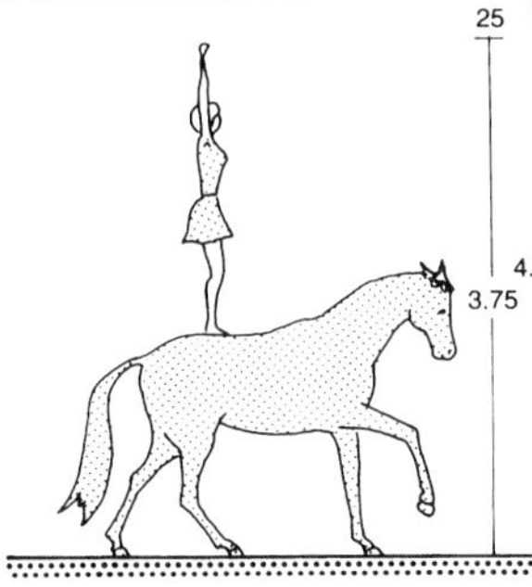

⑤ Space required for acrobatics on horseback

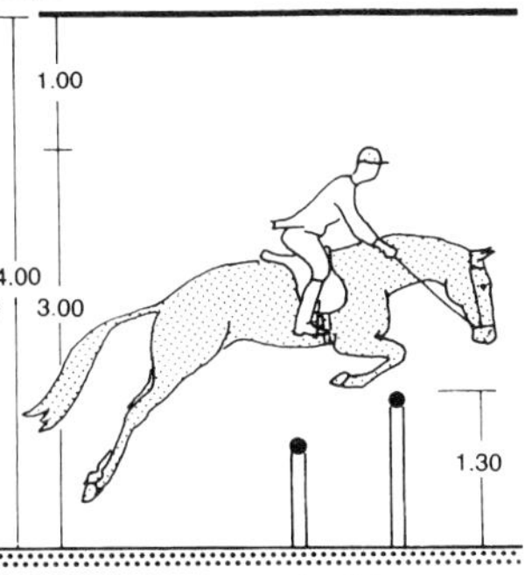

⑥ Space required for showjumping

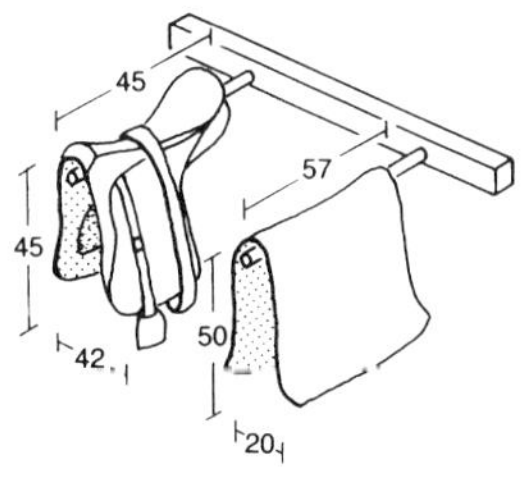

⑦ Saddle with blanket

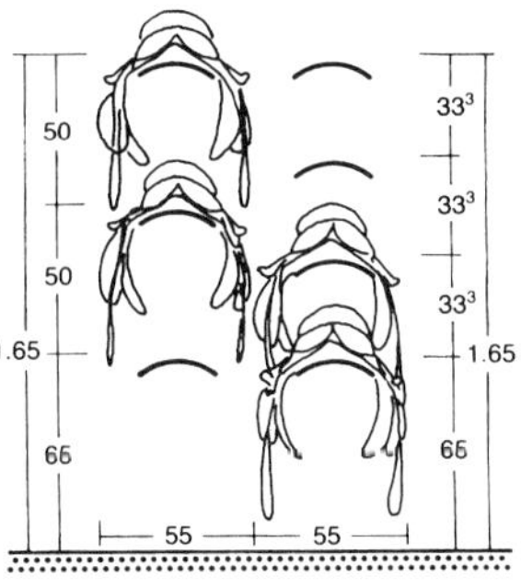

⑧ Saddle rack

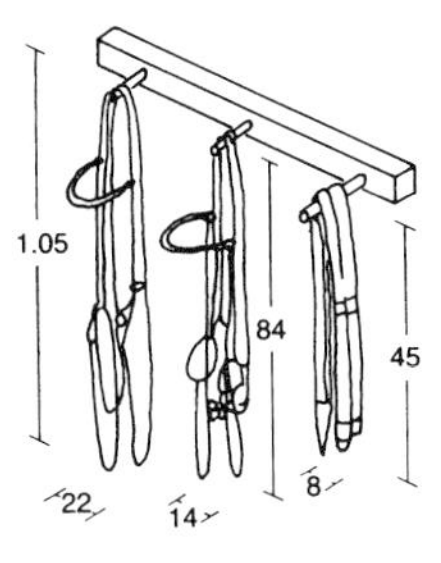

⑨ Tack rack

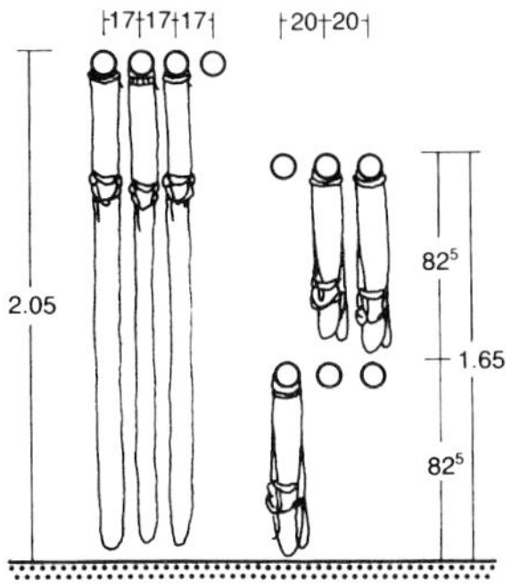

⑩ Bridle rack

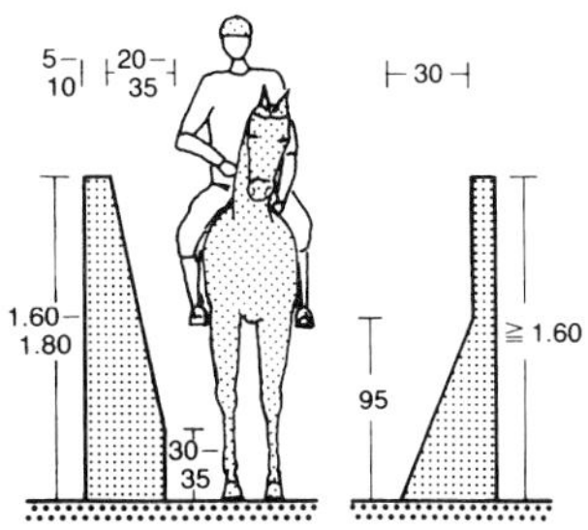

Riding facilities/stables should, if possible, be in the immediate vicinity of land suitable for riding. Areas with high ground and air humidity, as are often found in valleys, should be avoided, as should windless locations, where providing the desired ventilation may be difficult. Ideal sites are in hilly and windy areas. However, slope gradients for buildings and riding arenas should be less than 10%.

Saddle rooms, as far as possible, should be long and rectangular, with a large wall space and a width of 4.0–4.5 m. Saddles can be hung in rows staggered above each other → ⑧. Saddle rooms and grooming rooms should have heating and be well ventilated.

In riding arenas the minimum headroom for show jumping and horseback acrobatics is 4.00 m → ⑤ + ⑥.

No universal rule can be applied to the space allocated to spectators. In general, though, spectators should not look down too steeply on the horses. An effective solution can be to use a spectator gallery → ⑬, with the first row for seating and the second for standing. Behind this is room for two rows of circulating people. This arrangement will create 200 seated and standing places in a 20 × 40 m arena. The size of the main entrance has to be large enough to allow access for medium sized lorries (3.00 m wide, 3.80 high). Side entrances should be 1.20 m or more wide and a minimum of 2.80 m high. Doors have to open outwards.

Glass windows above the riding arena floor should be protected by a fine mesh grille.

An arena riding area of approximately 1000 m² is sufficient for ten horses.

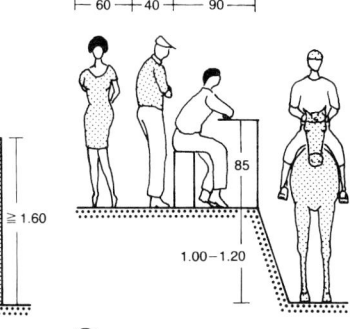

⑪ Spectator stand with access passage

⑫ Profile of barriers

⑬ Simple spectator stand

RIDING FACILITIES

Apart from variations due to organisational specialisms or local conditions, the operational functions of different riding schools are, basically, the same. Building specifications vary primarily in terms of the size of the organisation or number of stable users. This is vital for the organisation of the various rooms, and determines also whether various functions can be combined → ①. Generally, the elements in which the horses are housed and fed should be designed as a self-contained structure. A covered riding hall is indispensable for keeping stable activity going in adverse weather conditions. Accommodation for stable hands, grooms or instructors also needs to be planned.

For outdoor tournament facilities the long axis of the arena should be aligned in the north–south direction → ④. The judges' grandstand is positioned on the west side of the arena because most important competitions take place in the afternoon and so the sun will be at the judges' backs.

The minimum size of the riding area in a tournament arena is 20 × 40 m → ②. For dressage from class M and versatility exams a riding area of 20 × 60 m is required. In addition, 3.0 m side strips (5.0 m at the entrance) that can be ridden on should be provided, giving a gross arena size of 26 × 48 m → ⑤. The audience should be no further than 5 m from the riding area.

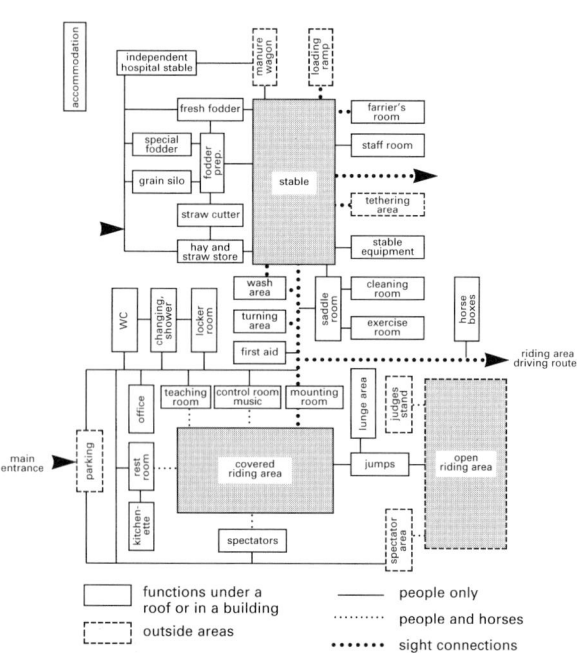

① **Internal connections for a riding establishment**

functions under a roof or in a building
outside areas
—— people only
········· people and horses
•••••• sight connections

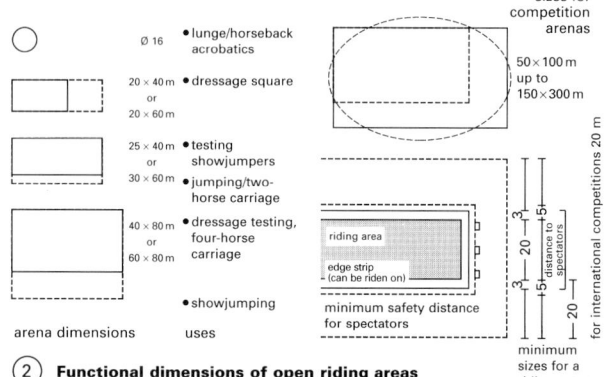

② **Functional dimensions of open riding areas**

arena dimensions	uses
Ø 16	lunge/horseback acrobatics
20 × 40 m or 20 × 60 m	dressage square
25 × 40 m or 30 × 60 m	testing showjumpers jumping/two-horse carriage
40 × 80 m or 60 × 80 m	dressage testing, four-horse carriage
	showjumping

sizes for competition arenas
50 × 100 m up to 150 × 300 m

minimum safety distance for spectators

minimum sizes for a riding arena

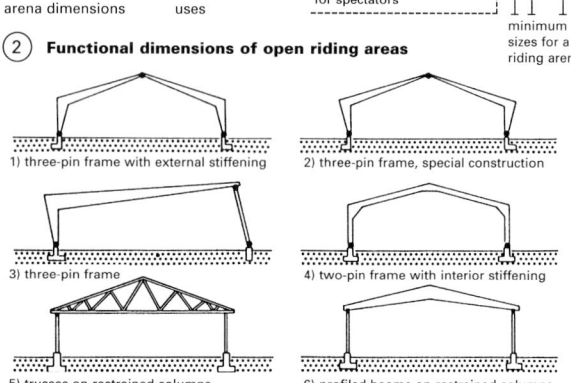

③ **Cross-sections of riding halls**

1) three-pin frame with external stiffening
2) three-pin frame, special construction
3) three-pin frame
4) two-pin frame with interior stiffening
5) trusses on restrained columns
6) profiled beams on restrained columns

④ **Dimensions of riding halls**

format of riding halls	arena dimensions	uses
	Ø 14.0 m	lunge/horseback acrobatics: alternative to a hall in the smallest clubs and private stables; used to relieve the main arena in larger establishments
	12.5 × 25.0 m	smallest arena: for private stables only and as an emergency solution for clubs; suitable as a second arena for larger establishments
	15.0 × 30.0 m	private stables and smaller club stables; second arena for larger establishments
	20.0 × 40/45 m	normal size for every type of establishment; dressage exams possible
	20.0 × 60.0 m	for larger establishments and institutions which specialise in dressage
	25.0 × 66.0 m	for large schools providing jumping and dressage training, and boarding establishments; hall dressage exams possible

material		volume of 100 kg (m³)	daily requirement per horse (kg)	required store provision per horse		
				number of months	kg	m³
oats (grain)		0.22	5	1	150	0.33
hay	long (stored compressed)	1.00–1.18	8	12	2.900	29–34
	wired bails	0.59				17
straw	long (stored compressed)	1.43–2.00	about 20 (with purely straw bedding in boxes)	3	1.825	29–34
	stringed bails	1.05–1.18				17
	wired bails	0.42–0.50				17
	chopped 100 mm long	2.22–3.33	about 15		1.375	31–16
useable store area per horse for feeding material						

⑤ **Store areas**

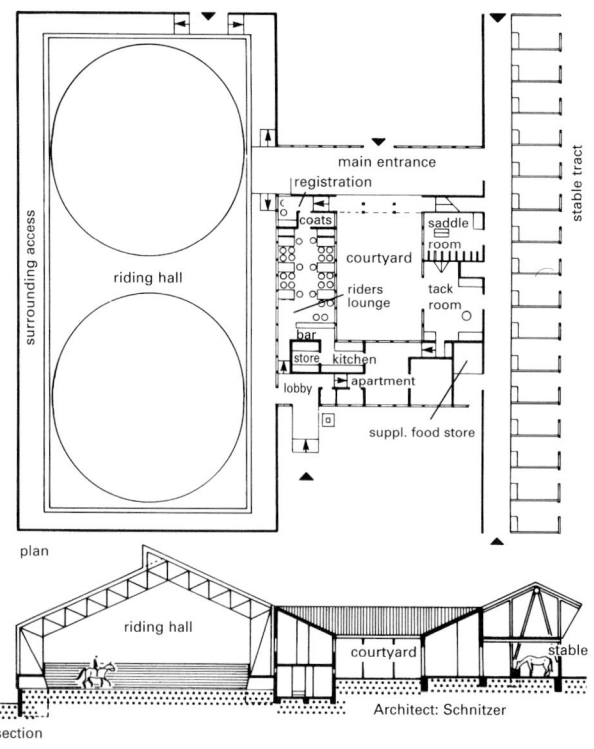

plan
section

main entrance
registration
coats
courtyard
saddle room
riders lounge
tack room
bar
store kitchen
lobby
apartment
suppl. food store
riding hall
surrounding access
stable tract

riding hall
courtyard
stable
Architect: Schnitzer

⑥ **Riding establishment in Gerolstein/Eifel**

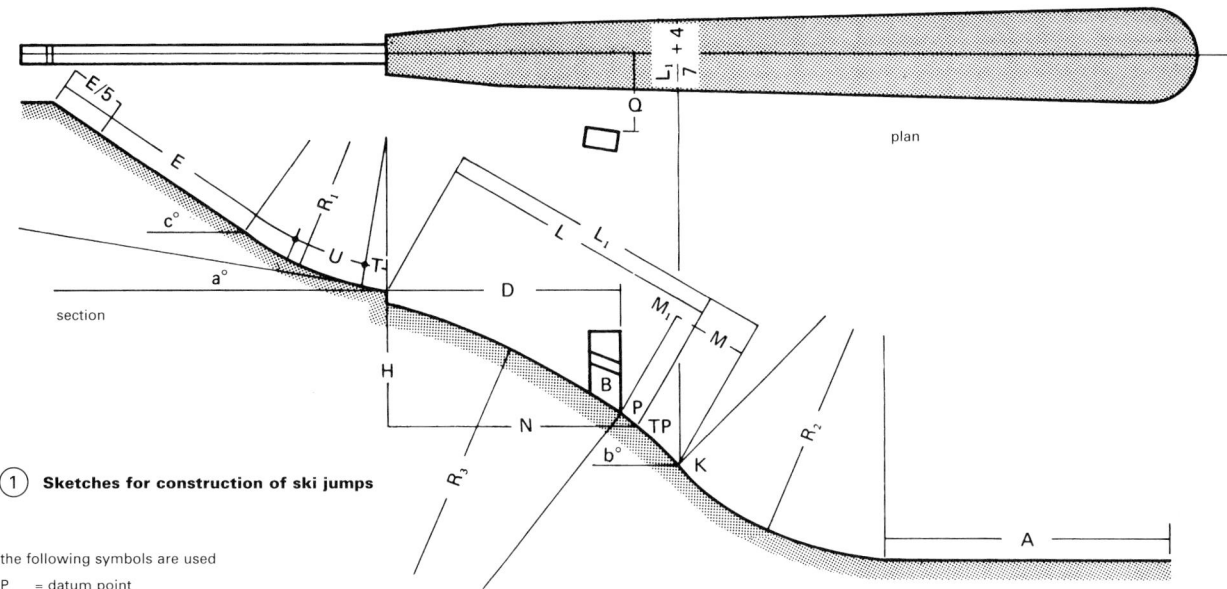

(1) Sketches for construction of ski jumps

the following symbols are used

P = datum point
TP = table point
K = critical point (end of the slowing down section and beginning of the run-out curve)
B = end of landing run curve
M = slowing down section (distance from P to K)
M_1 = distance from P to B
L = distance from edge of slope to P
L_1 = distance of edge of slope to K
H = vertical projection of L
N = horizontal projection of L
H:N = ratio of vertical to horizontal distance
a = slope of launch platform
b = slope of jump-off track at datum point (P) up to critical point (K)
c = run-up slope
R_1 = radius of curve from run-up to platform
R_2 = radius of curve from jump-off to run-out
R_3 = radius of curve from platform to jump-off track
T = length of platform
U = part of run-up in which speed no longer increases
E = part of run-up in which speed increases
F = overall length of run up (F = U + E + T)
A = length of run-out
V_o = speed at platform edge in m/s
D = horizontal distance from the platform edge to lower part of judges tower
Q = distance from landing track axis to front edge of judges tower

small jumps

E			L											
c	c	c				8–10°		7–9°		6–8°			a	
30°	35°	40°	U	T	Vo	$\frac{H}{N}$=0.50	0.48	0.46	0.44	0.42	0.40	0.38	b	↓
26	23	21	4.5	3.3	15	20.0	19.5	19.0	18.5	18.0	17.5	17.0	←30–34°
32	28	25	5.1	3.5	16	25.5	24.8	24.0	23.3	22.5	21.8	21.0	30–35°
39	32	28	5.8	3.7	17	31.0	30.0	29.0	28.0	27.0	26.0	25.0	33–36°
46	37	32	6.5	4.0	18	36.5	35.3	34.0	32.8	31.5	30.3	29.0	33–36°
52	43	37	7.2	4.2	19	42.0	40.5	39.0	37.5	36.0	34.5	33.0	34–37°
59	49	42	8.0	4.4	20	47.5	45.8	44.0	42.3	40.5	38.8	37.0	34–37°

(2) Measurements

standards for the most important parts of the ski jump

H:N = 0.48 to 0.56

datum point of jump can be determined:

P = L_1–M where standards of M are:
M = 0.5 to 0.8Vo for jumps up to P = 70 m
M = 0.7 to 1.1Vo for jumps up to P = 90 m
M_1 = 0 to 0.2Vo
R_1 = 0.12Vo² to 0.12Vo² = 8 m
R_2 = 0.14Vo² to 0.14Vo² = 20 m
R_3 = profile selected for front structure which best meets angle of flight
T = 0.22Vo
U = 0.02Vo²
A = 4 to 5Vo on horizontal run-out
D = 0.5 to 0.7L_1 to lower edge of tower
Q = 0.25 to 0.50L_1

example:
according to terrain, the following data apply to L_1 and H/N:
for example, H/N = 0.534, c = 35°, K = 87 m;
in the table you will find L = 87 for Vo = 26, and c = 35°, E = 90 m, U = 14, T = 5.7 at
the same level, then F = E + U + T = 90 + 14 + 5.7 = 109.7 m;
a ski jump with dimensions differing from the above may be approved by FIS, but in
such cases the designers must give detailed written reasons

medium and large jumps

E			L									
c	c	c				9–12°			8–10°		← a	
30°	35°	40°	U	T	Vo	$\frac{H}{N}$=0.56	0.54	0.52	0.50	0.48	b	↓
62	52	44	8.8	4.6	21				53.0	51.0	35–37°
71	58	49	9.7	4.8	22	65.3	63.0	60.8	58.5	56.2	
80	65	54	10.6	5.1	23	71.5	69.0	66.5	64.0	61.5	36–38°
89	72	60	11.4	5.3	24	77.7	75.0	72.2	69.5	66.7	
99	80	67	12.5	5.5	25	84.0	81.0	78.0	75.0	72.0	37–39°
111	90	74	14.0	5.7	26	90.2	87.0	83.7	80.5	77.2	
124	100	81	15.0	5.9	27	96.3	93.0	89.5	86.0	82.5	38–40°
137	110	88	16.0	6.2	28				91.5	87.7	

(3) Measurements

The judges' towers should be arranged in a stepped formation parallel to the line from the edge of the launch platform to the end of the landing run curve. Each tower should be skewed by 7° to 10° from the centre-line of the landing run so that the judges can observe the whole flight and the landing clearly. The parapet of the towers should be 1 to 1.20 m above the floor level.

In the run-up, as many starting positions as possible should be evenly distributed on a length E/5. Along this distance is a vertical fall of approximately 1 m. The lowest starting position is at E – E/5.

Note that the minimum width of the landing track at K = L_1/7 + 4 m.

General comments

All gradients are given in old divisions based on 360 degrees. Should the transition be parabolic, then R_1, R_2 and R_3 are the smallest radii of these parabolas.

With natural run-ups the most frequently used areas need to be marked at 2 m intervals in order to simplify the exact fixing of the starting position. The gradient of the launch platform as well as several points along the run-up curve should be indicated permanently on both sides with fixed built-in profiles so that even non-specialists can re-create the exact profile when preparing the ski jump.

It is recommended that profile markers are also installed alongside the landing track up to the run-out. This enables the snow profile to be established precisely, especially when the snow cover is deep.

As a rule, ski jumps with L greater than 50 m should not be built with a V_o of less than 21 m/s. Note that ski jumps with L above 90 m are not approved by the FIS.

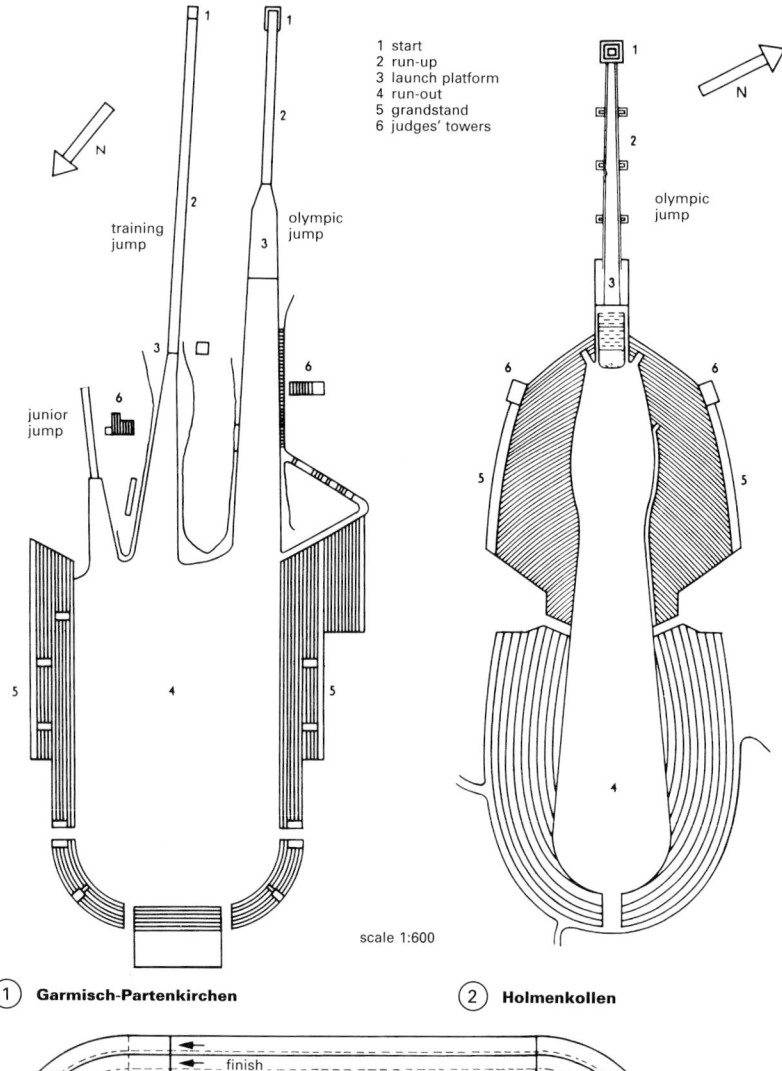

1 start
2 run-up
3 launch platform
4 run-out
5 grandstand
6 judges' towers

training jump

olympic jump

olympic jump

junior jump

scale 1:600

① **Garmisch-Partenkirchen**

② **Holmenkollen**

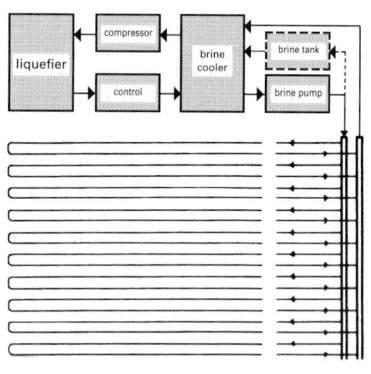

finish
11.95
100
start
500 m
25
111.94
20.97
70
20.97
1000 m
start
3000 m
4.18 5000 m
start: 1500 m
inner lane
7.95 7.76
outer lane
19.89
crossing straight

③ **Standard race track 400 m long**

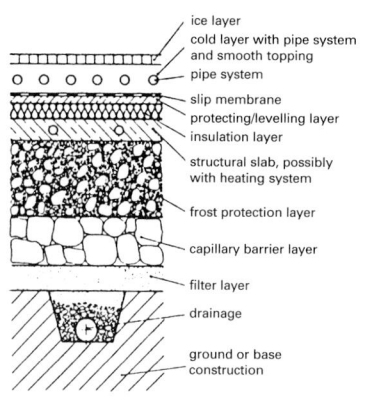

compressor
liquefier
brine cooler
brine tank
control
brine pump

④ **Artificial ice rink: layout of a refrigeration system (brine)**

ice layer
cold layer with pipe system and smooth topping
pipe system
slip membrane
protecting/levelling layer
insulation layer
structural slab, possibly with heating system
frost protection layer
capillary barrier layer
filter layer
drainage
ground or base construction

⑤ **Detail of surface pipes** → ④

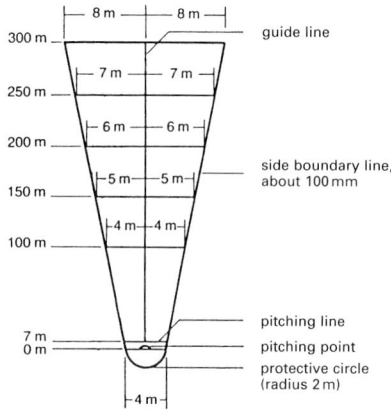

300 m
8 m — 8 m
guide line
250 m
7 m — 7 m
200 m
6 m — 6 m
side boundary line, about 100 mm
150 m
5 m — 5 m
100 m
4 m — 4 m
7 m
0 m
pitching line
pitching point
protective circle (radius 2 m)
4 m

⑥ **Long curling ground**

In cold climates, natural freezing of lakes and rivers provides suitable areas for ice skating, ice hockey and curling. Similarly, frozen lido pools (assuming the edges are strong enough to withstand the pressure of ice) may be used as temporary rinks.

By using 'sprayed ice', skating rinks can be created on tennis courts, roller skating rinks and other large flat spaces. A surrounding embankment or barrier approximately 100–150 mm high is needed and there must be suitable drainage for water run-off. Water is sprayed on to the surface to a depth of 20 mm.

In warm climates or for year-round use, artificial ice rinks are the solution. These consist of a cooling pipe system in a screed floor through which a deep frozen salt solution or cold air (usually a compressed ammonia system) is pumped. The pipes are roughly 25 mm below the screed surface. → ④ + ⑤

Standard race track: The track length is usually 400 m (although some can be 300 m or 333.5 m) and should be have two lanes → ③. The distance through the curves is measured 500 mm from the edge of the inside of the track. This gives the race distance of $(2 \times 111.94) + (25.5 \times 3.1416) + (35.5 \times 3.1416) + 0.18$ (extra through the crossing) = 400 m.

Bobsleigh and toboggan runs: Situated on north-facing slopes, these runs require tight curved embankments made from ice blocks. The lengths are 1500–2500 m, with slopes of 15–25% and a minimum run width of 2 m. Spectator places should, if possible, be on the inside of the curves or protected with mounds of snow or straw bales.

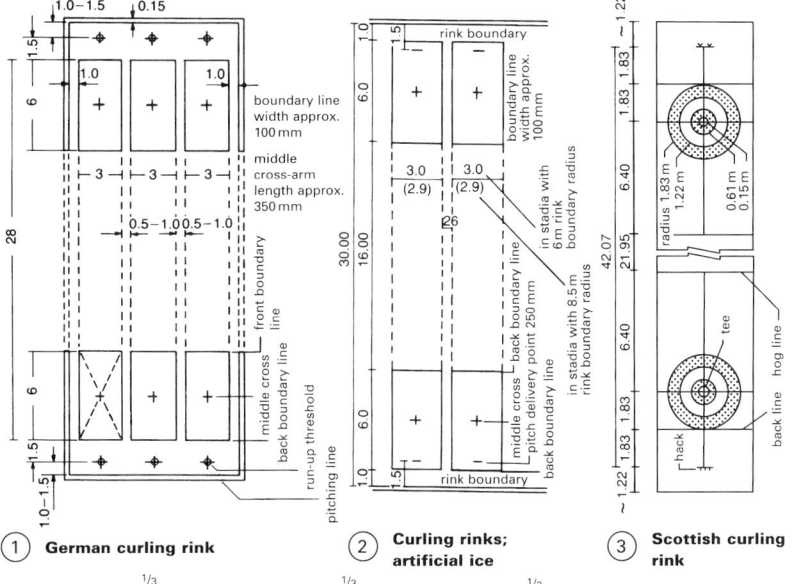

① **German curling rink**

② **Curling rinks; artificial ice**

③ **Scottish curling rink**

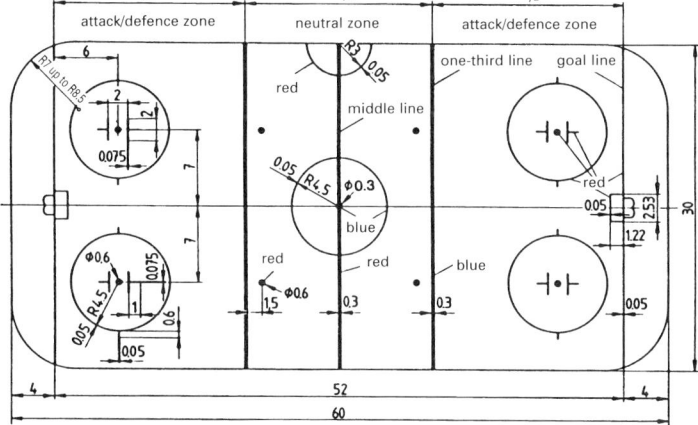

④ **Ice hockey**

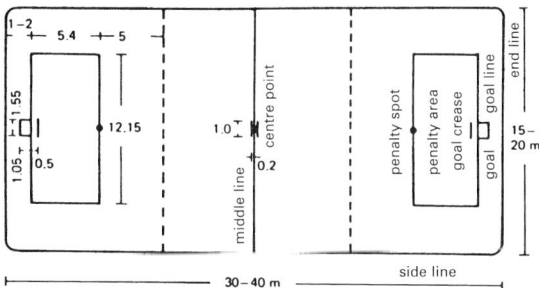

⑤ **Roller hockey**

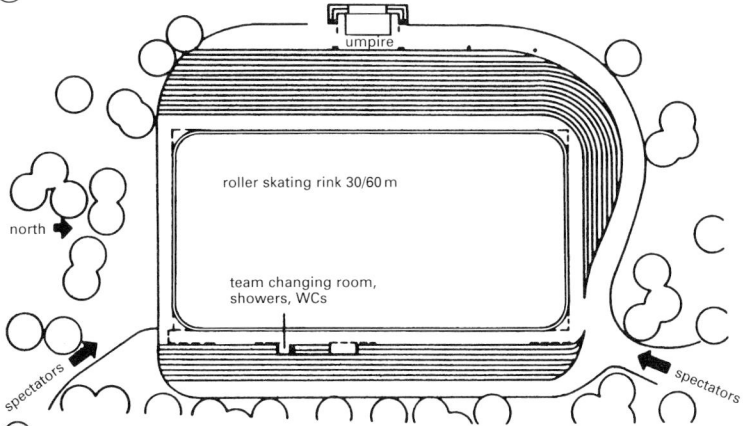

⑥ **Artificial ice and roller skating rink**

ICE RINKS

Curling: There are several types of curling and the lengths and widths of the track vary accordingly → ① – ③. See also ⑥ on page 496/497. In German curling the pitching and target areas require a low frame, which can easily be stepped over, on three sides. The track in Scottish curling is 42 m long, with 38.35 m between the target centres but this can be shortened to 29.26 m if the ice is in bad condition.

Ice hockey: The pitch area is 30 × 60 m and it has curved corners. The goals are 1.83 m wide, 1.22 m high, and are positioned such that players can skate around the back of them. The pitch needs to be fully surrounded by a wood or plastic barrier 1.15–1.22 m high → ④.

Figure skating: A rectangular ice rink between 56 × 26 m and 60 × 30 m in size is suitable for both figure skating and in-line skating, which is becoming increasingly popular. It is possible to create a multipurpose rink: roller skating from March to November and ice skating from December to February. This requires a cooling pipe system 25–50 mm below the rink surface (note that this is not possible in terrazzo) → ⑥.

ROLLER SKATING RINKS

(1) Sports rinks
   Roller hockey   15 × 30 to 20 × 40 m
   Figure roller skating   25 × 50 m
(2) Leisure rinks   10 × 10 to 20 × 20 m

An impact board 250 mm high, 30 mm above the rink surface, and an 800 mm solid barrier are required on all sides of the rink. Behind the short edges a 2 m high wire netting fence should be installed to catch stray balls. The rink should also have a surrounding walkway 1.2 m wide and a channel to collect and disperse surface water. The gradient of the rink surface should not be greater than 0.2%.

Construction
(1) Fibre reinforced cement sheets, 15 mm thick, laid on squared timber or on sand bedding.
(2) Concrete tracks, 100–150 mm depending on condition of subsoil, if possible jointless; if necessary cut in false joints 2–3 mm wide, space joints every 25–30 m with a gap width of 15 mm or more.
(3) Hard concrete screed, minimum of 8 mm thick on fresh concrete slab (20 mm of cement mortar is preferable to take up stress between the screed and the slab.
(4) Cement composite with additives 1–10 mm.
(5) Terrazzo, polished, 15 mm or more; joint rails made from brass, metal alloy or plastic should be used only for indoor rinks.
(6) Cast asphalt rinks on a fixed base.

ROLLER-SKATE RACING

For a standard racing circuit with an enclosed 20 × 40 m rink → ② the following room schedule gives guidance on the requirements.

- For competition use: four changing rooms, each with 8 m of benches, clothes hooks and lockers; additional lockers of 3 m² for roller hockey equipment; two shower rooms with four showers, two wash basins and separate toilets; and one referee/trainers' room of approximately 9 m².
- For public use: changing and equipment-fitting area with lockers and benches (20 m minimum length); ladies and gents toilets, with two WCs and a separate anteroom with showers and hand basins, connected to the changing area.
- General: entrance area with ticket machines and turnstile or staffed ticket office, approximately 40 m²; a 12 m² skate hire room (connected to the ticket office); an 8 m² supervision and management room (doubles as a control room for light and sound systems); staff changing rooms with shower, hand basins, toilet and lockers; a first aid room of 9 m²; equipment stores, 15 m² and 6 m²; cleaners' room, 12 m²; boiler room, 10 m²; services room, 4 m²; and a meter room, 3 m².

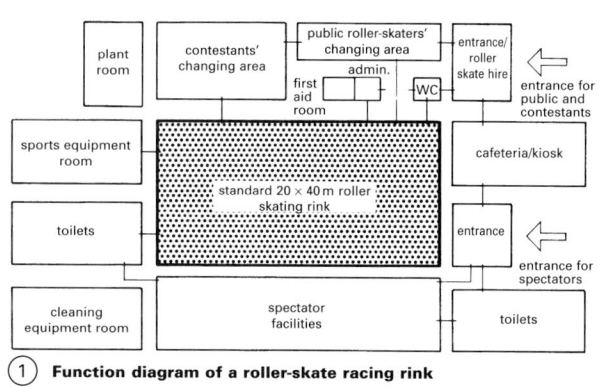

① **Function diagram of a roller-skate racing rink**

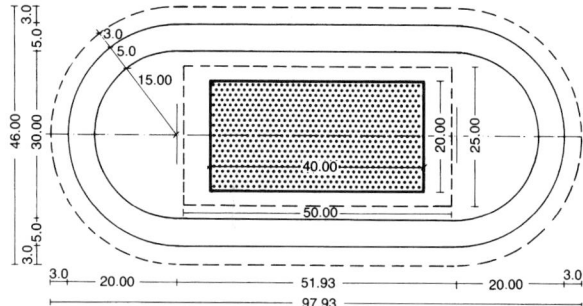

② **Dimensions of a 200 m roller-skate racing circuit with standard rink enclosed**

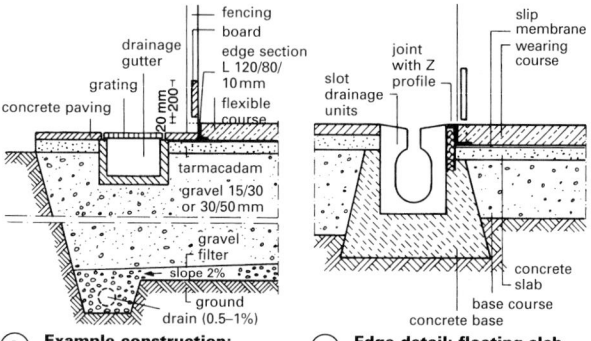

③ **Example construction; drainage suitable for cohesive ground**

④ **Edge detail: floating slab surface, no step down**

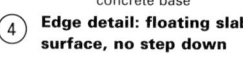

⑤ **Types of use and sizes of rinks**

possible uses	necessary skating area (m)	remarks
public roller skating rink, figure skating, roller dancing, roller hockey	20 × 40 m	**standard area** for roller hockey 17 × 34 m (min)
public roller skating rink, figure skating, roller dancing, and roller hockey	20 × 50 m	in special situations
public roller skating rink, figure skating, roller dancing, roller hockey, roller-skate racing and ice sports	30 × 60 m	generally only when used also as an ice rink; 110 m sprint track for roller-skate races possible on a rink area 30 × 60 m
roller-skate racing track length track width	200 m 333 1/2 m 400 m 5 m	**standard track** only when also used for cycle sports and/or ice-skate racing tracks

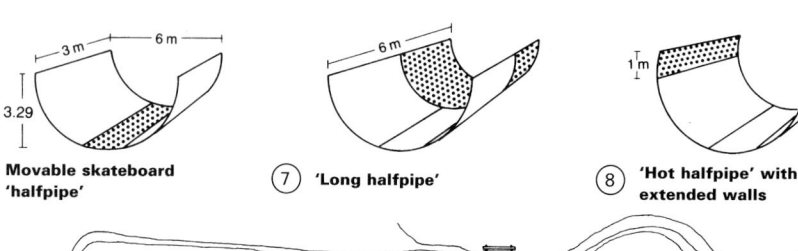

⑥ **Movable skateboard 'halfpipe'**

⑦ **'Long halfpipe'**

⑧ **'Hot halfpipe' with extended walls**

⑨ **'Divided halfpipe' with transition ramps**

SKATEBOARDING

Since arriving from America in the mid-1970s skateboarding has become popular throughout Europe. Although roller skating rinks of 200 m² or more are also suitable for skateboarding, as are playgrounds, car parks and pedestrianised areas in towns, custom-built facilities are preferable → ⑩.

Competition skateboarding makes extensive use of a variety of 'halfpipes' → ⑥ – ⑨.

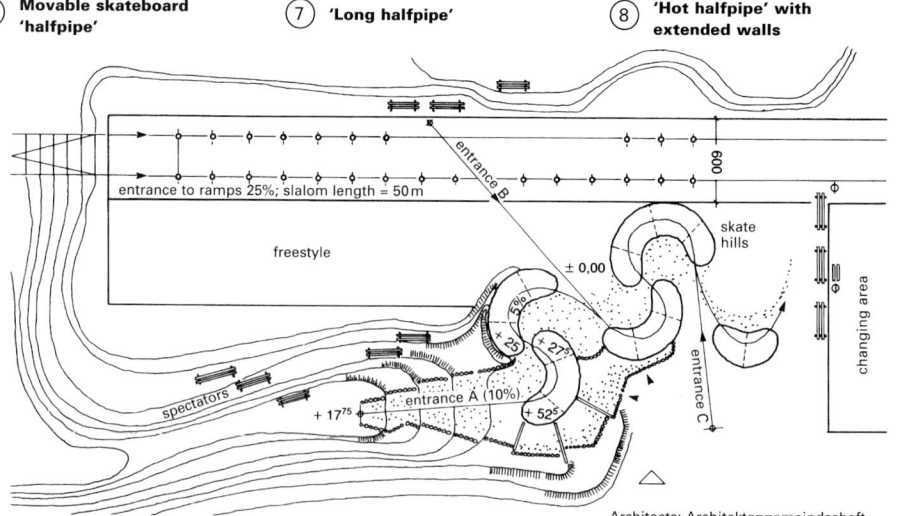

Architects: Architektengemeindschaft Franke/Mühlbauer/Schmidhuber, Munich

⑩ **Skateboard facilities in Ostpark, Munich**

CYCLECROSS/BMX

The minimum size of plot that can be used for BMX riding is 50 × 60 m whereas a large-scale competition track with ample space for spectators requires roughly 100 × 200 m. Depending on local conditions four varieties of BMX tracks are possible:

(1) C-track: length 200 m; 5 m wide starting hill with four start positions.
(2) B-track: length 250 m; 7 m wide starting hill with six start positions; minimum completion time 30 seconds.
(3) A-track/national: minimum length between 270 m and 320 m; 9 m wide starting hill with eight start positions; minimum completion time 35 seconds.
(4) A-track/international: minimum length 300 m; 9 m wide starting hill with eight start positions; minimum completion time 35 seconds.

The track can contain any types of curves and jumps, and in any order. For safety, solid materials (i.e. stone, concrete or wood) should not be used to mark the edge of the track; car tyres or straw bales are sufficient. Solid borders and barriers for the spectator areas should be a minimum of 1 m from the track. The length and gradient of downhill sections of the track should be such that the maximum attainable speed is 40 km/h and the overall completion time has to be within capabilities of an average rider of 15 years of age.

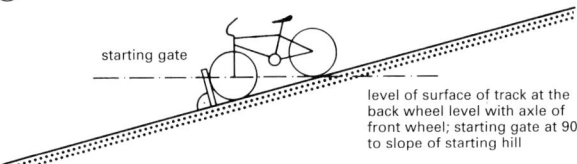

(1) **Starting hill**

(2) **Heights of starting hill**

(3) **Detail → (2)**

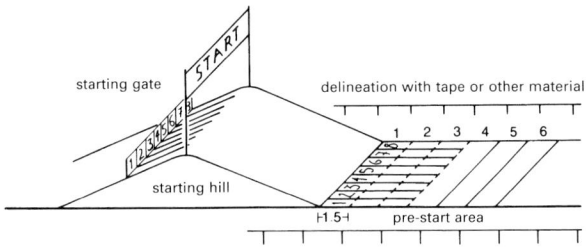

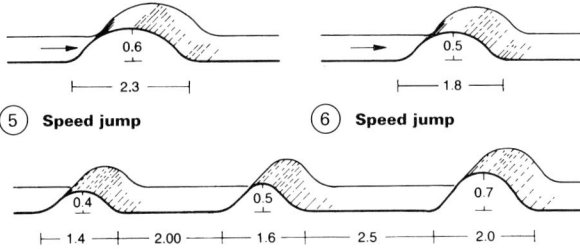

(4) **Starting hill with pre-start area**

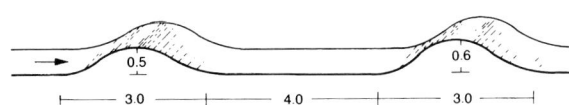

(5) **Speed jump**   (6) **Speed jump**

(7) **Triple jump**

(8) **Double speed jump**

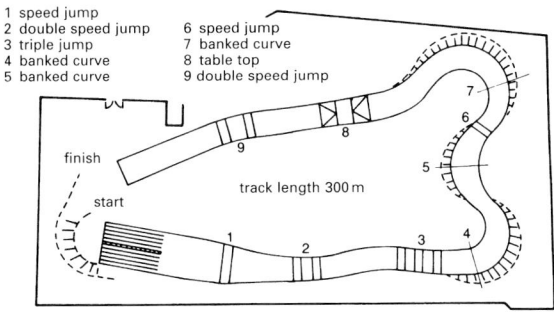

1 speed jump
2 double speed jump
3 triple jump
4 banked curve
5 banked curve
6 speed jump
7 banked curve
8 table top
9 double speed jump

finish

track length 300 m

start

(13) **Track for the '87 World Championship in Bordeaux**

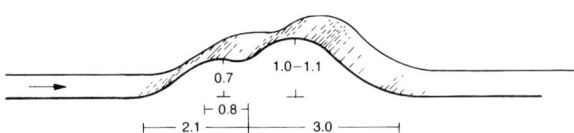

(9) **Step jump**

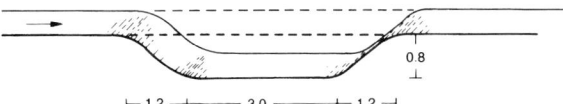

(10) **Canon jump**

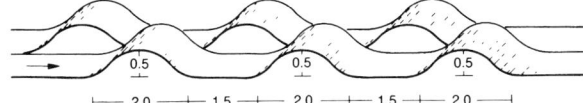

(11) **Mogul jump (moguls)**

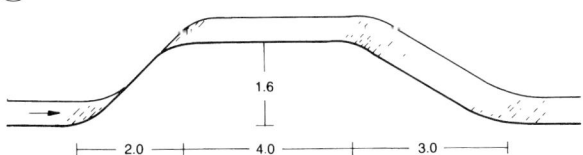

(12) **Table top**

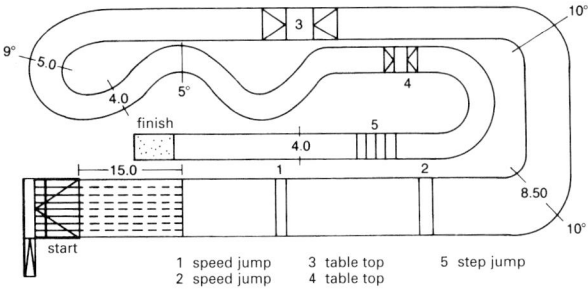

start

1 speed jump   3 table top   5 step jump
2 speed jump   4 table top

(14) **BMX track at the IFMA '84 in Cologne**

SHOOTING RANGES

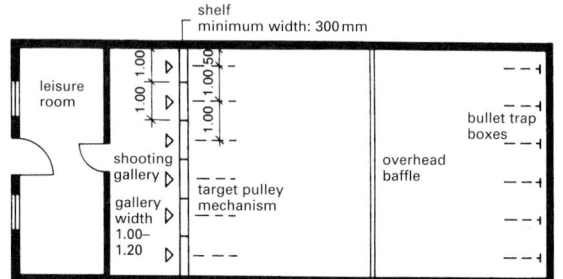

① **Section** → ②

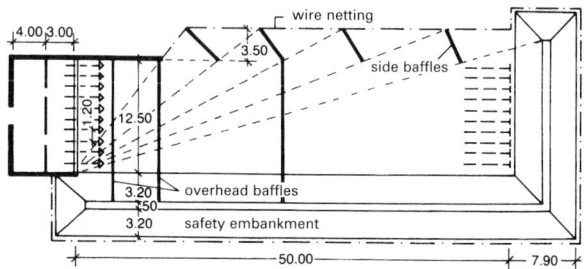

② **Shooting range for air and CO₂ guns: covered shooting gallery, range in the open**

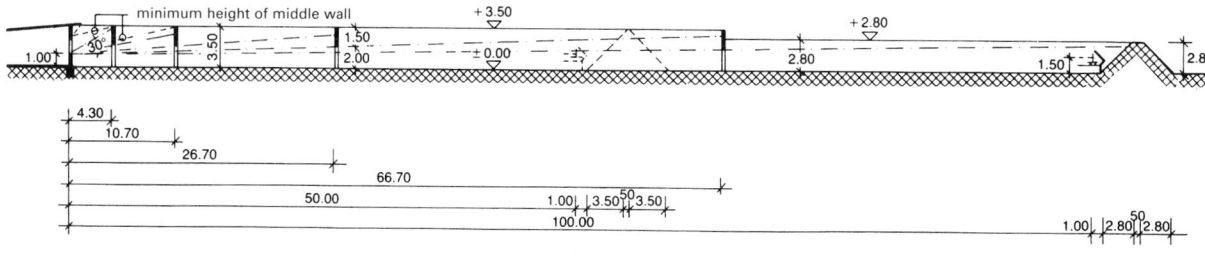

③ **Small calibre range with target pulleys**

Open shooting ranges should, if possible, be located in gulleys in forested areas, with the slope acting as a natural bullet trap. They must be well away from paths and areas open to the public. Indoor shooting ranges, which can be part of multipurpose sports facilities, provide a venue for air-rifle, pistol and small-bore rifle shooting → ① – ⑤.

In the UK, rifle and pistol ranges (but not air gun ranges) require not only planning permission and building regulation approval, but also the approval and safety certificate issued by the Ministry of Defence.

To gain the necessary approval from the National Small-Bore Rifle Association (NSRA) or the National Rifle Association (NRA), consultation should be made at the earliest stage of design. The local Environmental Health Department and the Health and Safety Executive ought to be consulted on current methods of combating lead pollution.

Safety devices like overhead and side baffles, safety walls and embankments must be built with approved building materials and certified by a specialist.

Objections by 'neighbours' concerned about noise are generally upheld.

Types of sport shooting

(Olympic competitions: x = for men, xx = for women and men, xxx = for women only.)

Rifle shooting: air rifle, 10 m xx; small-bore handguns, 15 m; small-bore rifles, 50 m x; small-bore standard rifles xxx; target rifle, 100 m, large-bore rifle, 300 m; large-bore standard rifle, 300 m.

Pistol shooting: air pistol, 10 m xx; olympic semi-automatic pistol, 25 m x; sports pistol, 25 m xx; standard pistol, 25 m; free pistol, 50 m x.

In the UK, handguns are no longer permitted in England, Wales and Scotland. They are, however, still permitted in Northern Ireland, the Channel Islands and the Isle of Man.

Clay pigeon shooting: trap shooting x; skeet shooting x.

Moving targets: 10 m and 50 m x.

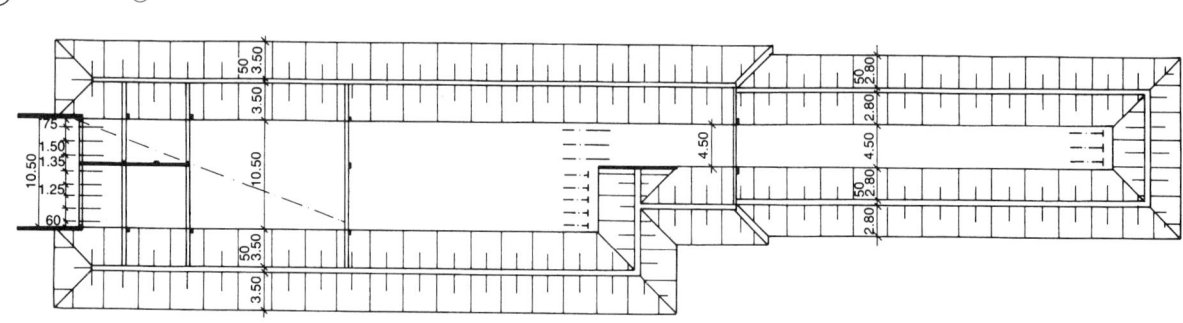

④ **Section** → ⑤

⑤ **Combined 100 m range for all calibers and a 50 m small calibre range** → ④

SHOOTING RANGES

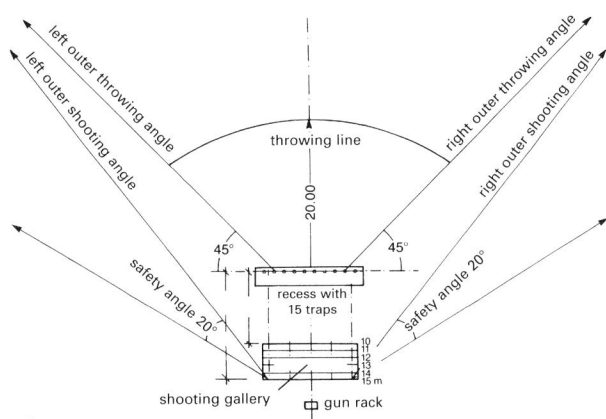

① **Clay pigeon shooting range**

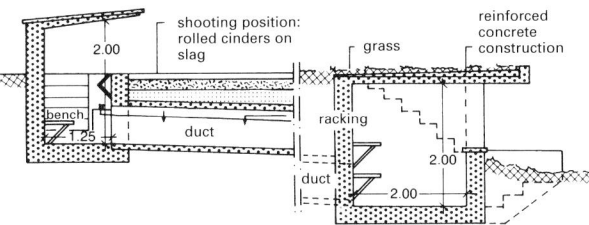

② **Section through clay pigeon shooting range**

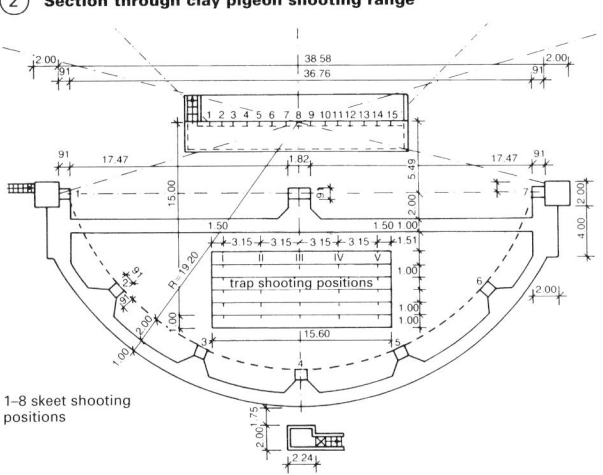

③ **Combined trap and skeet shooting range**

A shooting range has to arranged in such a way that it eliminates danger to people on the inside, i.e. those people who are shooting, as well as those in the surrounding area. Safety barriers are constructed to protect all directions within the overall potential firing spread. It has been found that for air and CO_2 guns, barriers must offer protection up to an angle of 20 degrees upwards from the firing point. For rifles and hand guns this angle is 30 degrees → ⑤.

Demands made by local regulations concerning the effects of air pollution, noise, noxious substances, radiation etc. also have to be fully satisfied.

For crossbow and archery ranges different regulations are in force. Areas adjacent to the line of fire need to be shielded through suitable safety constructions such as high baffles, walls or earth embankments along the sides and at the end of the range.

An assessment of the suitability of the chosen plot for the building of a shooting range is fundamental to the calculation of the projects costs. A shooting range specialist should always be consulted to provide the planner with the necessary specialist knowledge. Specific considerations are: distance to existing or planned building areas and to inhabited houses; planned shooting direction; soil conditions; supply arrangements and waste disposal facilities; situation in relation to road and rail links (including future developments), and parking spaces.

It is also important to assess whether it is possible or necessary to deviate from local guidelines. The control of noise pollution is a legal necessity and must be planned from the beginning. For open ranges, in particular, allowance should be made for additional noise reduction measures. These can be built-in in separate building phases. Approval and permission procedures are determined by national and local regulations.

The design and size of a shooting range should facilitate the economic construction of any necessary future additions and extension.

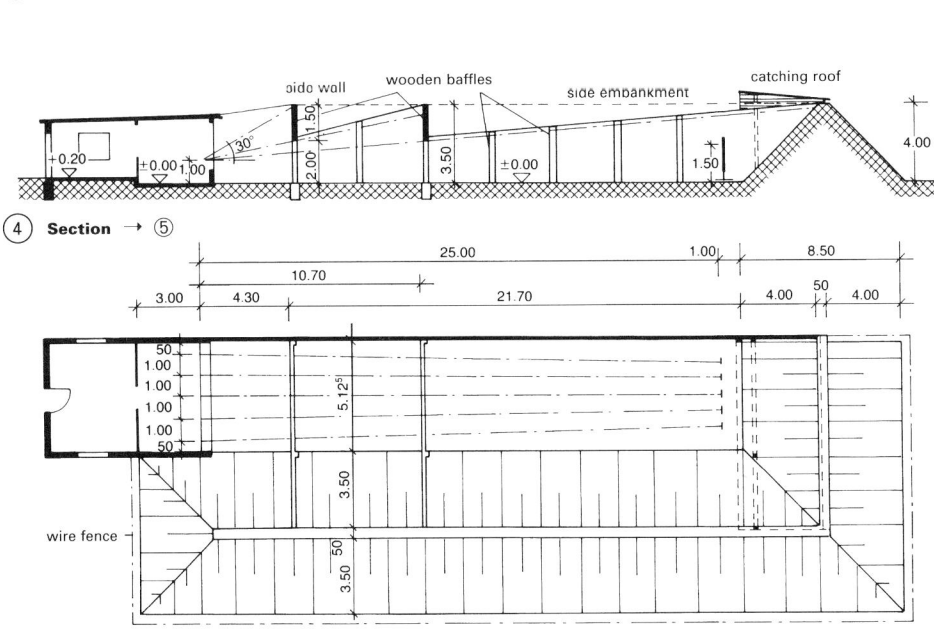

④ **Section** → ⑤

⑤ **25 m range for handguns (pistol and revolvers of all calibers): continuous side wall to left; continuous embankment to right (a wall or embankment can be chosen for both sides)**

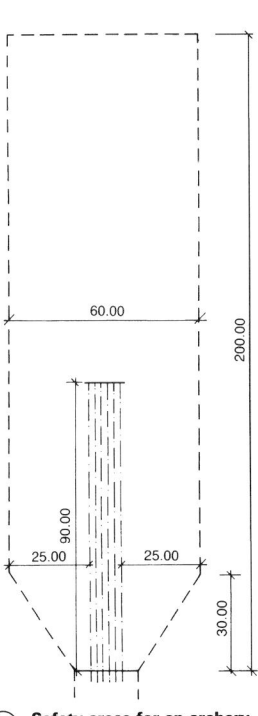

⑥ **Safety areas for an archery range with six targets**

525

Wrestling

The basic mat size for competitions is 5 × 5m; for German championships and international competitions it is 6 × 6m or greater, preferably 8 × 8m; and for international championships and the olympic games the size should be 8 × 8m. The middle of mat needs to be marked with a 1m diameter ring with 100mm wide edge strip. The thickness of the mat is 100mm and it has a soft covering. A protective edge strip, if possible, should be 2m wide; otherwise, bordering barriers with a slope of 45 degrees can be used. A 1.2m width of the protective strip should be equal in thickness to the mat and differentiated by use of colour. The protective strips in national bouts are 1m wide.

If the mat is on a platform the height should be no greater than 1.1m. There are no corner pillars or ropes.

Weight-lifting

The lifting area should be no smaller than 4 × 4m and on a strong wooden base, with markings in chalk. The floor must not be sprung because weight-lifters require a solid footing.

The largest diameter of weight plate is generally 450mm. The weight of plates for one-handed exercises range up to 15kg; for two-handed exercises, the plates are up to 20kg in weight.

Judo

The contest area ranges from 6 × 6m up to 10 × 10m or 6 × 12m and is covered with soft springy mat. Upholstered mats are not permitted. For international championship competitions, the contest area can be more than 10 × 10m.

Ideally, the mat should be raised about 15cm. The boundary between the contest area and the border has to be clearly visible → ①.

Boxing

The dimensions of boxing rings are set out in international regulations, and range from 4.9 × 4.9m up to 6.10 × 6.10m, although 5.5 × 5.5m is the size most commonly used. Rings are frequently raised on a podium that is 1m wider on each side than the ring, giving a total area of between 7.5 × 7.5m and 8 × 8m → ③.

Badminton

The standard size is that of a doubles court, although a singles court can be used where space is severely restricted. Outside the court area → ④ the appropriate measurements are:

safety strip (sides)	1.25m
safety strip (front and rear)	2.5m
side-to-side distance between courts	≥ 0.3m
ene-to-end distance between courts	≥ 1.3m
between court and walls	≥ 1.5m

Spectators must always be accommodated behind the safety strip. For international competitions, the minimum hall height is 8m, with at least 6m over the back line of the court. The height of the net at the posts is 1.55m and is 1.525m in the middle. The depth of the net is 760mm. The floor should be lightly sprung. The hall, if possible, should have no windows, the court being lit by roof lights, which should not be dazzling (i.e. 300 lux or less).

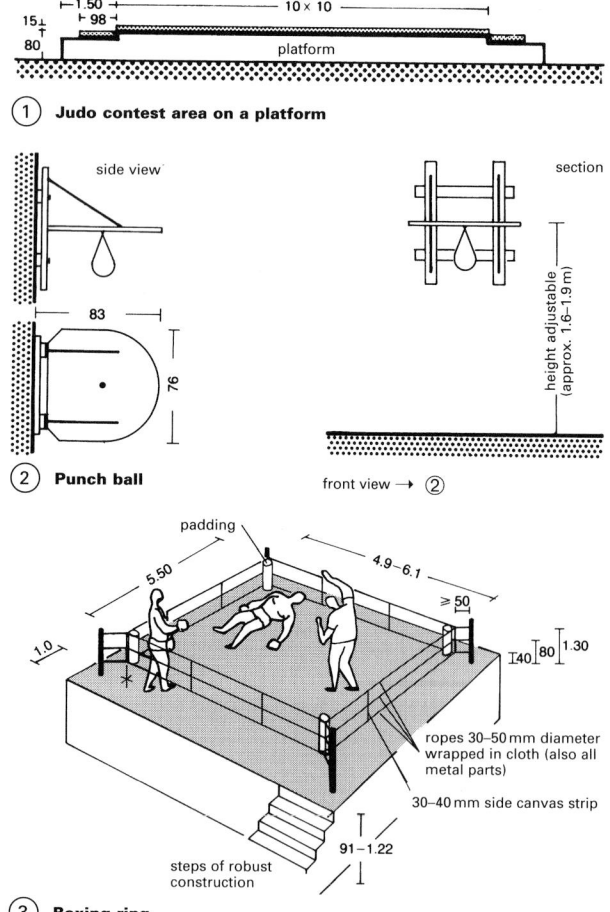

① **Judo contest area on a platform**

② **Punch ball**

front view → ②

③ **Boxing ring**

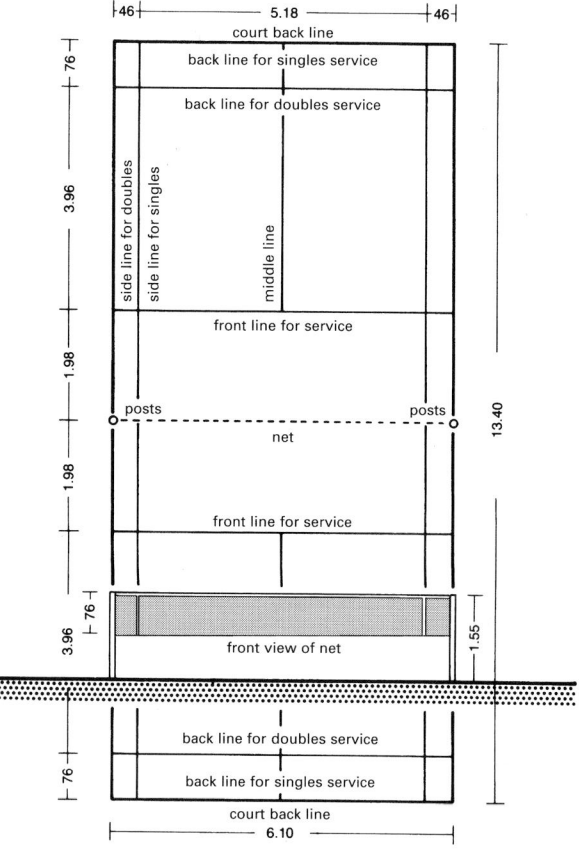

④ **Badminton court**

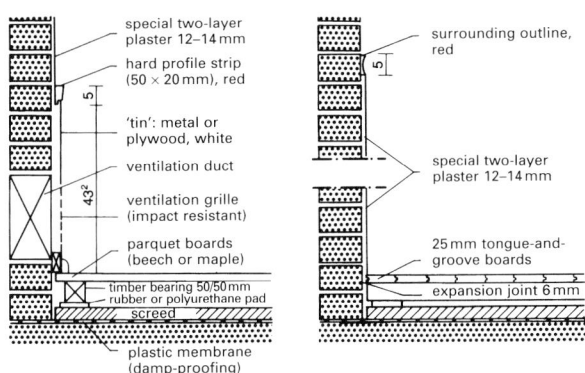

① **Squash court end wall**   ② **Squash court side wall**

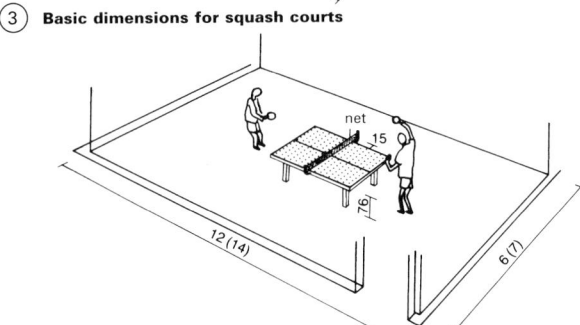

③ **Basic dimensions for squash courts**

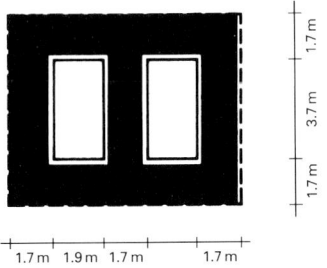

④ **Basic dimensions for table tennis**

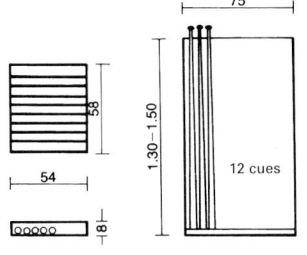

⑤ **Billiards and snooker, agreed standards table: 3.50 × 1.75 m playing area**

⑥ **Ball holder**   ⑦ **Cue rack**   ⑧ **Common billiards table dimensions**

Squash

Normal construction is used for the building of squash courts. Solid walls of precast concrete units or prefabricated panelled timber framed construction are finished with special white plaster. To improve the view for spectators it is advantageous to use transparent material for the back wall. The dimensions of the court are:

area	9.75 × 6.40 m
height	6.00 m

The floor needs to be slightly springy and have good surface grip. It is made of light coloured wood (maple or beech) boards running parallel to the side walls. Appropriate grade tongue-and-groove boards 25 mm thick and with a sealing coat should be used.

Across the foot of the front wall runs a strip (the 'tin') made of 2.5 mm thick sheet of metal or metal covered plywood painted white.

Table tennis

At championship level, table tennis is played only in halls. The table itself is matt green with white border lines and has the following dimensions:

area	1525 × 2740 mm
height	760 mm
thickness of table top	≥ 25 mm

The tops of tables used in the open should be made of 20 mm thick cement fibre board. The hardness of the table surface needs to be such that a normal table tennis ball will bounce approximately 230 mm when dropped from a height of 300 mm. A net with the following dimensions runs across the middle of the table:

length	1830 mm
height (over whole length)	152 mm

The playing area is cordoned off with 600–650 mm high canvas screens. The size is generally no less than 6 × 12 m, and 7 × 14 m for international competition. The spectators are seated beyond the screen. → ④

Billiards

Requirements for billiard rooms depend on the various billiard table sizes involved → ⑧. For normal private purposes, sizes IV, V and VI are used; in bars and clubs, sizes IV and V are most common, while in billiard halls sizes I, II and III will be required.

Billiard halls are usually on upper floors or in a bright basement, rarely on the ground floor. Where there is more than one table the distance between them should be at least 1.70 m for sizes I and II and 1.60 m or more for sizes III to V. The distance from walls should, if possible, be slightly more. A clear playing space is required all around the table and, if matches are to be televised, extra space must be provided for cameras.

A clear wall space is needed for cue-holders (1.50 × 0.75 m for 12 cues), score boards and rule sheets.

The smallest possible light fittings should be used to give full and even lighting of the playing surface. The normal height of the light above the table is 800 mm.

In the UK the Billiards and Snooker Control Council (B&SCC) introduced (with world agreement) the 'B&SCC 3.50 m standard table' and for the first time the actual playing area size (3.50 × 1.75 m) was specified within the cushion faces instead of the overall table size. However, these metric recommendations are still not often utilised, even in major competitions.

table sizes (cm)		I	II	III	IV	V	VI
playing surface area	A	285 × 142⁵	230 × 155	220 × 110	220 × 110	200 × 100	190 × 95
overall dimension	B	310 × 167⁵	255 × 140	245 × 145	225 × 125	225 × 125	215 × 120
space required		575 × 432⁵	520 × 405	510 × 400	500 × 395	490 × 390	480 × 385
weight (kg)		800	600	550	500	450	350

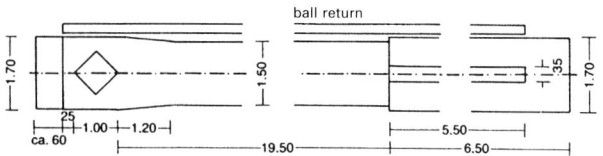

① **Skittle alley with boundary lines**

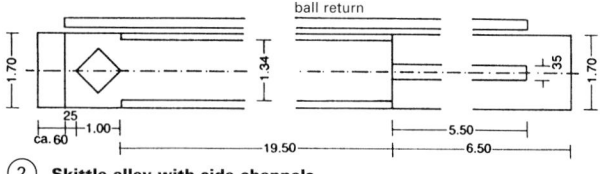

② **Skittle alley with side channels**

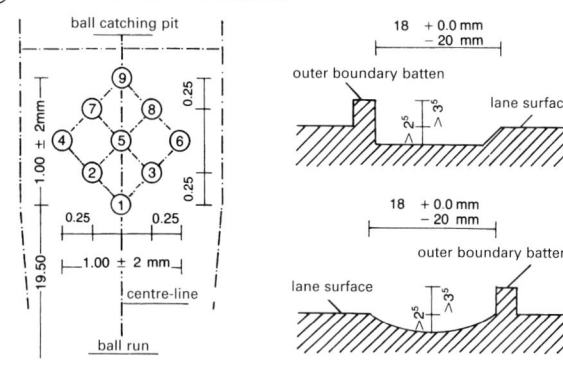

③ **Arrangement and numbering of skittles**

④ **Possible designs of side channels**

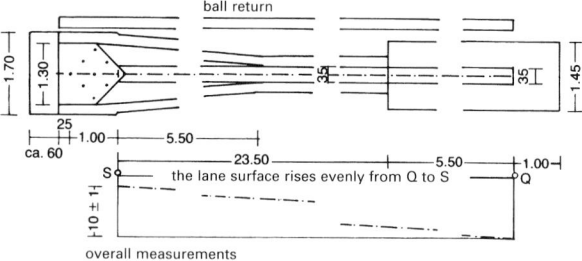

⑤ **Alternative skittle alley**

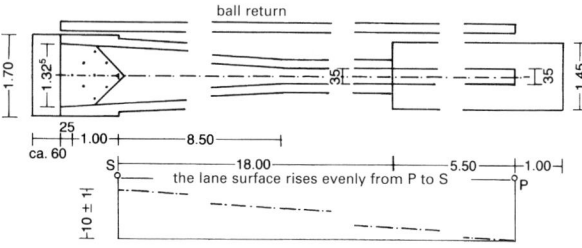

⑥ **Overall measurements of a scissor alley**

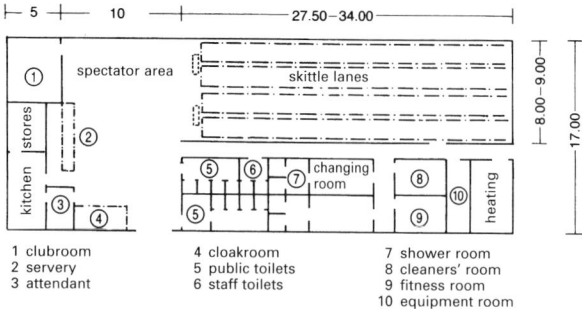

⑦ **Example of skittle alley premises**

1 clubroom
2 servery
3 attendant
4 cloakroom
5 public toilets
6 staff toilets
7 shower room
8 cleaners' room
9 fitness room
10 equipment room

SKITTLE AND BOWLING ALLEYS

Skittle and bowling alleys can be divided into the following areas:

(1) The run-up, in which the ball is bowled after a few approach steps;
(2) The lane, the surface along which the ball rolls;
(3) The catching pit, in which the fallen skittles/pins and balls are collected. (It is also where skittles/pins can be stored.)

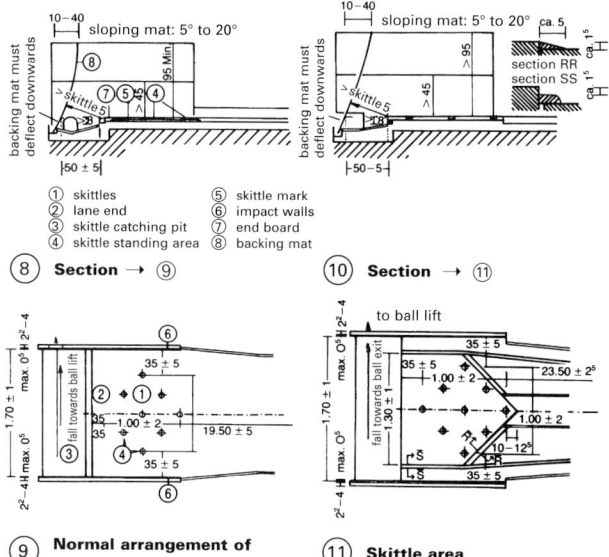

① skittles
② lane end
③ skittle catching pit
④ skittle standing area
⑤ skittle mark
⑥ impact walls
⑦ end board
⑧ backing mat

⑧ **Section → ⑨**

⑩ **Section → ⑪**

⑨ **Normal arrangement of skittle area**

⑪ **Skittle area**

An asphalt alley puts the highest demands on the skittle players. The lane is 19.50 m long and the width is 1.50 m (with side boundary batten) or 1.34 m (with side boundary channels). The lane surface is made from asphalt or plastic. → ① – ④

An important feature of some alternative wooden (or plastic) skittle alleys is the gradient of the lanes. From the edge of the run-up to the front pin of the skittle stand, a distance of 23.50 m, the lane rises through 100 mm. → ⑤

The scissor skittle alley also has wooden (or plastic) lanes. The lanes are 0.35 m wide until 9.5 m beyond the end of the run-up, after which they widen up to 1.25 m at the mid-point of the skittles. → ⑥

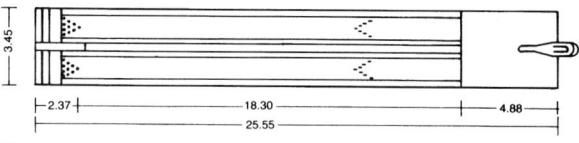

⑫ **Two-lane bowling alley**

In bowling alleys → ⑫ the run-up area is made from cleanly sanded parquet and the lanes are of polished or varnished parquet. In contrast to skittles the pins are arranged in a triangular formation and there are ten of them.

Bowling balls are 21.8 cm in diameter and have a range of weights up to 7257 g. They have three finger holes. For asphalt and scissor alleys, the balls have a diameter of 16 cm and weigh 2800–2900 g. Other balls in use are 16.5 cm in diameter, with weights between 3050 g and 3150 g. Most modern balls are made of a composite plastic mixture. Skittles are usually made from hardwood (white beechwood); pins are also made of wood but are covered with plastic. All pins and skittles have standardised dimensions.

INDOOR SWIMMING POOLS

Reference figures for estimating the required size of indoor swimming pools must take into account the demands made by the residents, schools and the sports clubs within the catchment area. As a rough guide, a pool area per inhabitant of between $0.025\,m^2$ (low population density) and $0.01\,m^2$ (high population density) may be used. $\rightarrow$ ②

Plot sizes (without car parks)

When estimating the plot size required for an indoor swimming pool, 6–$10\,m^2$ (excluding car parking; see below) should be allowed per square metre of planned pool area. The larger the pool area, the smaller the figure that will be sufficient. If an additional outdoor space (patios, sundecks, garden areas) is planned add 10–20% to the calculated plot size.

Flat and gently sloping (up to 15 degrees) sites simplify the planning of indoor pools on one level, a prerequisite for economically and functionally optimal design. Steeply sloping sites are usually associated with higher building costs and operational disadvantages.

Parking

The parking space to allow for each car is $25\,m^2$, and one space should be planned for every 5–10 changing room lockers in the pool complex. If spectator facilities are included, one additional car parking space per 10–15 spectator places should be added.

Bicycle parking spaces should be planned according to local needs, using an allowance of approximately $1.8\,m^2$ per bicycle.

Planning basics

A provision analysis should be done to determine whether additional sport and leisure facilities are to be included in the design. Using a needs analysis the types of use and total water area are determined in relation to the catchment area. The location should be chosen to give the best possible access.

room arrangement
expanded facilities

room arrangement
normal facilities

additional facilities | minimum facilities | direct access | possibly direct access

① **Indoor swimming pool: organisation of spaces**

catchment area (no. of inhabitants)	type of pool	planning unit						diving boards	factors for measuring the volume and area programmes		site area (without ancillary areas)
		basic unit		alternative 1		alternative 2		3)	standard unit value	training units	(m²)
		pool size (m/m²)	water area (m²)	pool size (m/m²)	water area (m²)	pool size (m/m²)	water area (m²)				
1	2	3		4		5		6	7	8	9
up to 5000	depending on local conditions										
5000 up to 10000	GP PP	10.00 × 25.00 up to 15	250 15 265					1B + 3B	150	2	2500
10000 up to 20000	GP TP PP	10.00 × 25.00 8.00 × 12.50 up to 20	250 100 20 370	12.50 × 25.00 10.00 × 12.50 up to 20	313 125 20 395	12.50 × 25.00 8.00 × 12.50 up to 20	313 100 20 433	1D + 3P	300 200	3	up to 3500
20000 up to 30000	GP TP or DP4) PP	12.50 × 25.00 8.00 × 12.50 up to 25	313 100 25 438	12.50 × 25.00 8.00 × 16.66 up to 25	313 133 25 471	12.50 × 25.00 8.00 × 12.50 10.60 × 12.50 up to 25	313 100 133 25 571	1B + 3P or 1P + 3P + 1P + 3P + 5P 1B + 1P combined + 3P + 3P combined 5P	250	3 or 4	3500 up to 4000
30000 up to 40000	GP TP DP4) PP	21.50 × 25.00 8.00 × 12.50 10.60 × 12.50 up to 30	313 100 133 30 576	12.50 × 25.00 8.00 × 16.66 10.60 × 12.50 up to 30	313 133 133 30 609	16.66 × 25.00 8.00 × 16.66 16.90 × 11.75 up to 35	417 133 147 30 727	1B + 1P combined + 3P + 3P combined 5P	300	4	4000 up to 4500
40000 up to 50000	GP TP DP4) PP	16.66 × 25.00 8.00 × 16.66 12.50 × 11.75 up to 35	417 133 147 35 732	16.66 × 25.00 8.00 × 16.66 16.90 × 11.75 up to 35	417 133 199 35 784			2 × 1B, 2 × 3B, 1P + 3P + 5P	400	4	4500
over 50000	further combinations of the above planning units in relationship to the size of the catchment area can be considered										

1) additional requirements may be needed for school use; 2) PP = paddling pool, TP = teaching pool, GP = general pool, DP = diving pool; 3) B = board, P = platform; 1–10 = diving height (m); 4) measurements with regard to safety dimensions should be pool size = pool width (diving end) × pool length (in the direction of diving)

② **Planning units for indoor swimming pools**

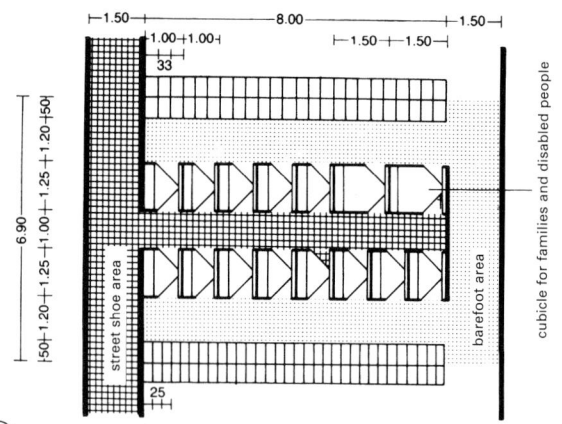

(1) **Changing area: changing cubicles with clothes lockers**

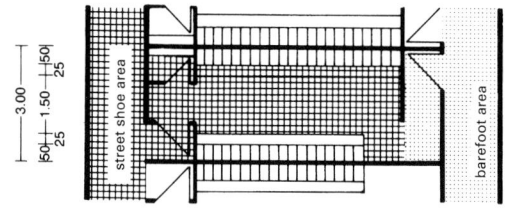

(2) **Communal changing without supplementary bench**

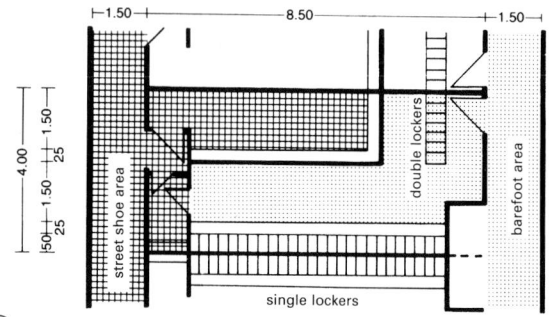

(3) **Communal changing with supplementary bench**

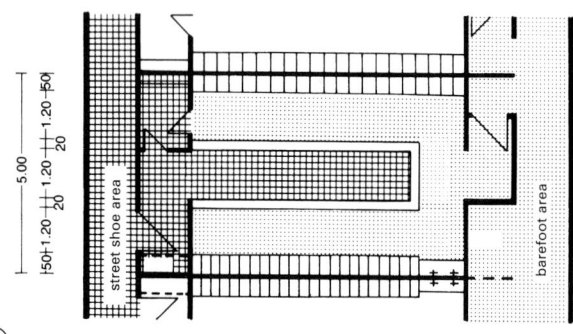

(4) **Communal changing with supplementary bench**

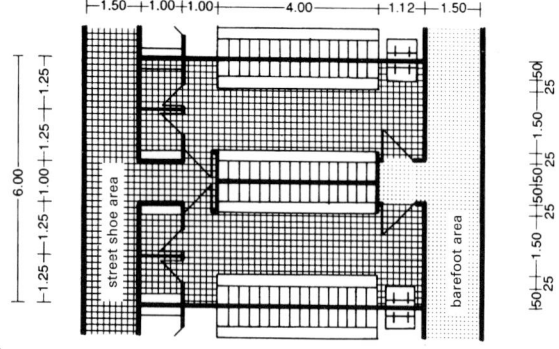

(5) **Changing area, mixed type**

INDOOR SWIMMING POOLS

To estimate the required size of the changing room area see the unit data values given in ②, column 7, page 529. All larger pools should contain at least two communal changing rooms. Allow a bathing time of 1.50 hours, except for peak periods.

For the purposes of estimation, the following figures can be used: locker spaces 0.6–0.8 of the standard unit value; number of changing spaces 0.15–0.2 of the standard unit value, of which 0.6–0.08 of the standard unit value are changing cubicles.

Of the changing cubicles available, 10% should be for families and disabled people. The ratio of cubicles to clothes lockers should be 1:4.

In a communal changing room at least 30 lockers are necessary and there should be no less than 7.50 m length of bench. The ratio of changing room spaces to lockers ranges up to 1:8. In holiday resorts it can become necessary to double the amount of locker spaces.

Other facilities per standard unit value are: hairstyling spaces with hairdryers 0.03, foot disinfection baths 0.015 and basins 0.015. A cleaning materials room of 1–2 m² must be planned within the changing room area. All rooms need a minimum clear height of 2.50 m. The minimum size of foot disinfection bath should be 0.75 m wide, 0.50 m deep.

In the changing room area, for built-in cubicles, the following minimum dimensions are valid: overall measurements 1.00 m wide, 1.25 m deep, 2.00 m high. Cubicles for families should be at least 1.50 m wide, 1.25 m deep, 2.00 m high. → ① Changing rooms for wheelchair users need overall measurements of 2.00 m wide, 1.00 m deep, 2.00 m high, and a clear door width of 0.8 m.

Lockers are 0.25 m or 0.33 m wide and 1.80 m or 0.90 m high, with a clear depth of 0.50 m. → ⑧

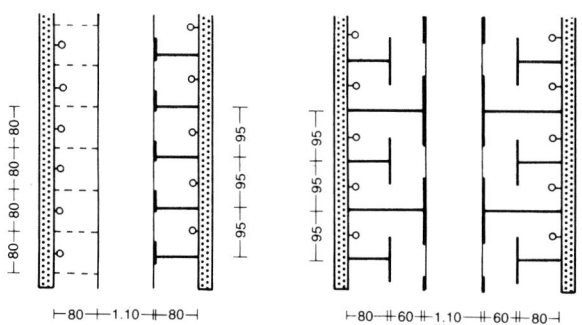

(6) **Open row of showers and showers with splash screens**

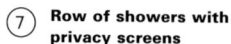

(7) **Row of showers with privacy screens**

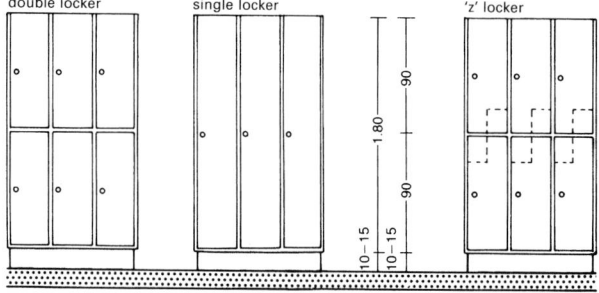

(8) **Clothes lockers**

INDOOR SWIMMING POOLS

Separate sanitary areas, containing shower rooms and toilets, must be provided for men and women. They should be positioned between the changing rooms and pool area. Toilets are usually positioned in such a way that the pool user has to re-enter the shower room before entering the pool area. Direct access to toilets from the pool area is not allowed. It is recommended that a direct route from the pool to the changing rooms be provided. → ① – ⑤

In swimming pools with 100–150 m² water area, one separable shower room with five showers each for women and men is sufficient → ②. For larger pools, there should be at least ten showers for each shower room. Basic toilet provision in the sanitary area is two toilets for women, one toilet and two urinals for men.

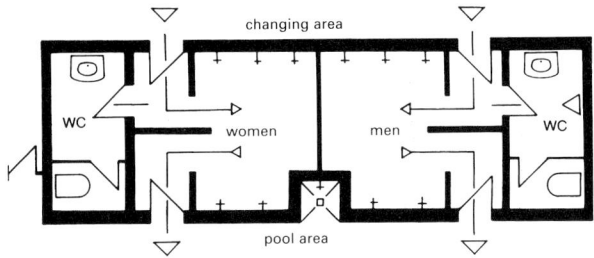

① **Shower and toilet area**

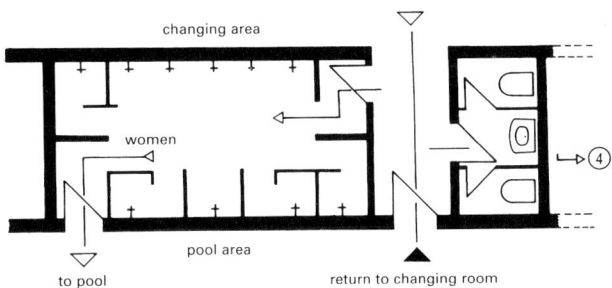

② **Shower and toilet area: divided shower room**

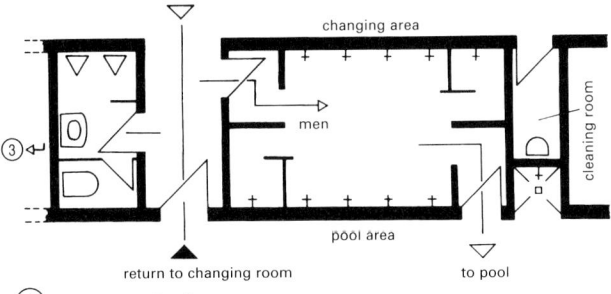

③ **Shower and toilet area: women**

④ **Shower and toilet area: men**

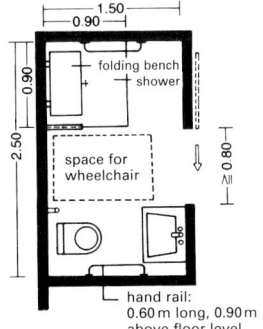

⑤ **Shower and toilet area for disabled people**

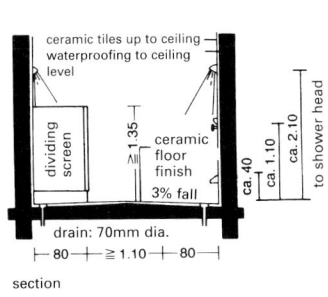

⑥ **Shower room**

Minimum recommended dimensions: → ① – ④

shower place without separating screens (open rows)	overall dimensions 0.80 m wide 0.80 m deep
shower place with separating screens (row showers with splash screens)	overall dimensions 0.95 m wide 0.80 m deep 1.45 m high
shower place with separating screens in double T-shape (with splash and privacy screens)	overall dimensions 0.80 or 0.90 m wide 1.40 m deep 1.45 m high
circulation space between shower rows	1.10 m
toilet cubicle with door: (opening inwards)	0.90 m wide 1.40 m deep 2.00 m high
toilet cubicle with door: (opening outwards)	0.90 m wide 1.20 m deep 2.00 m high
slab urinal: axis measurement	0.50 m wide 0.60 m deep
bowl urinal: axis measurement	0.75 m wide 0.80 m deep
installation height installation height for children	under 0.70 m under 0.45 m
hand basin	0.60 m wide 0.80 m deep
installation height	approx. 0.80 m
room height: clear height at least recommended height	2.50 m 2.75 m

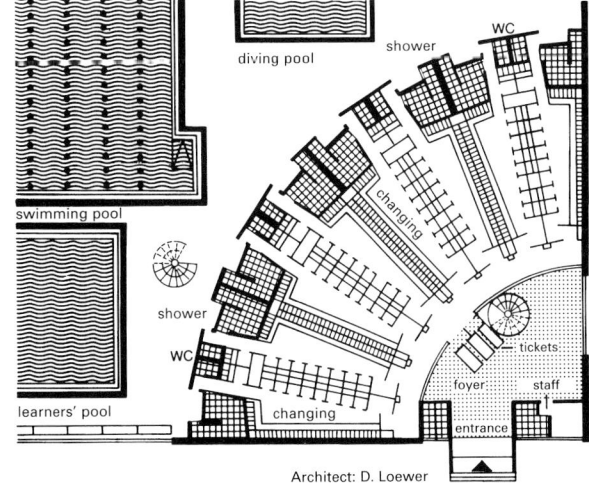

Architect: D. Loewer

⑦ **Changing area with WCs and automatic ticket machine**

531

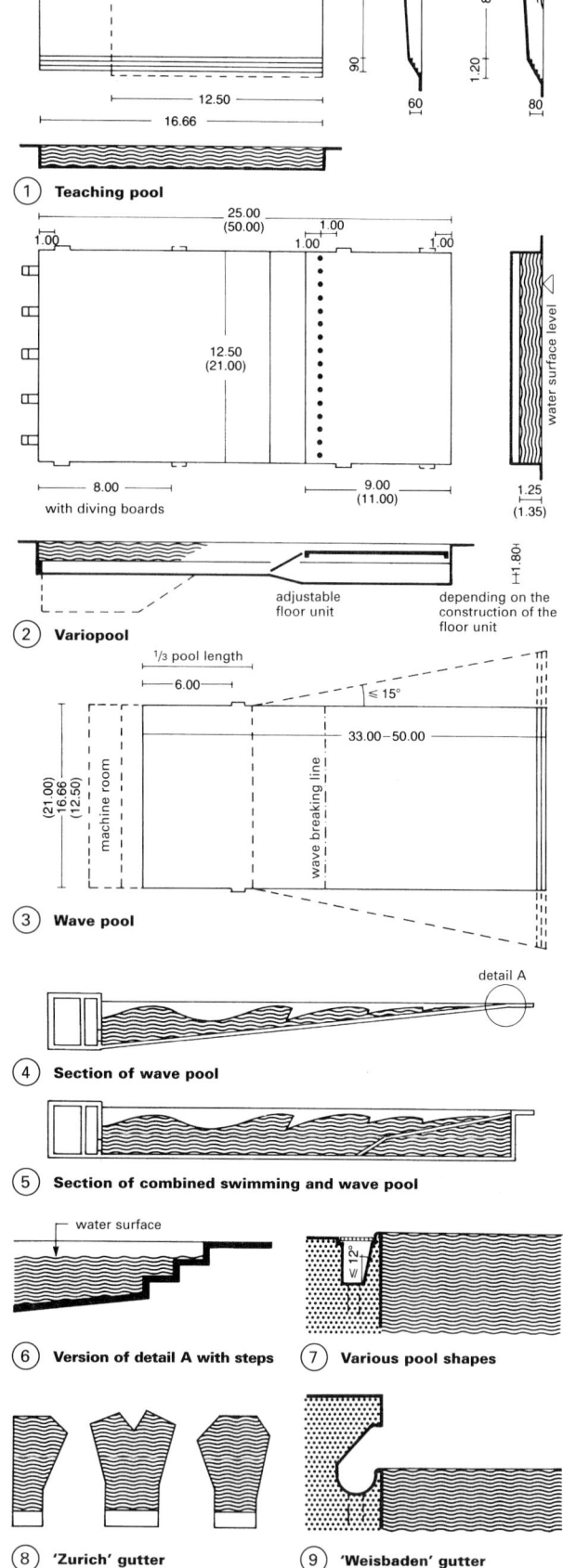

① **Teaching pool**

② **Variopool**

③ **Wave pool**

④ **Section of wave pool**

⑤ **Section of combined swimming and wave pool**

⑥ **Version of detail A with steps**   ⑦ **Various pool shapes**

⑧ **'Zurich' gutter**   ⑨ **'Weisbaden' gutter**

INDOOR SWIMMING POOLS

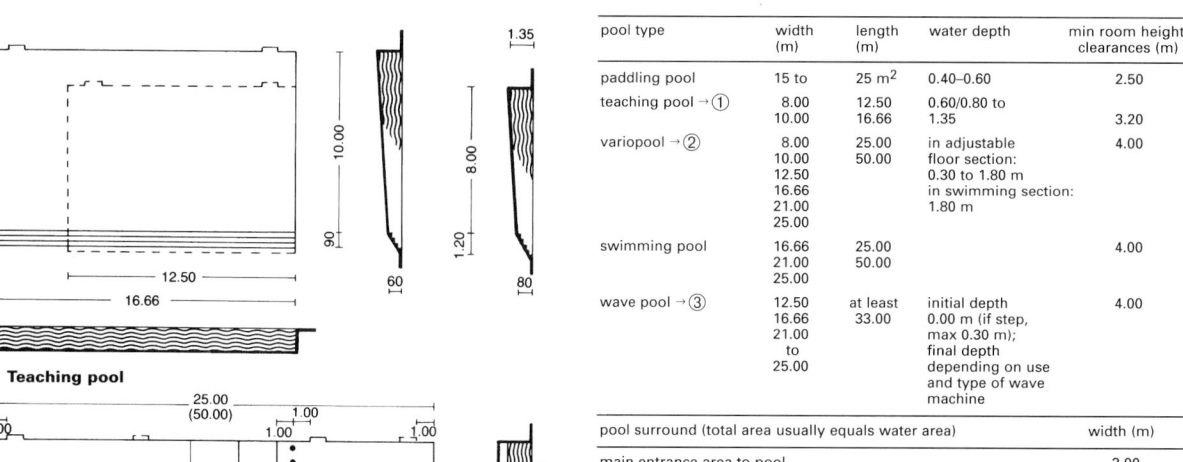

pool type	width (m)	length (m)	water depth	min room height, clearances (m)
paddling pool	15 to	25 m²	0.40–0.60	2.50
teaching pool → ①	8.00 10.00	12.50 16.66	0.60/0.80 to 1.35	3.20
variopool → ②	8.00 10.00 12.50 16.66 21.00 25.00	25.00 50.00	in adjustable floor section: 0.30 to 1.80 m in swimming section: 1.80 m	4.00
swimming pool	16.66 21.00 25.00	25.00 50.00		4.00
wave pool → ③	12.50 16.66 21.00 to 25.00	at least 33.00	initial depth 0.00 m (if step, max 0.30 m); final depth depending on use and type of wave machine	4.00

pool surround (total area usually equals water area)	width (m)
main entrance area to pool	3.00
main entrance area between pool steps and hall wall	2.50
area around starting blocks	3.00
area around diving boards (clear passageway at least 1.25 m wide behind 1 m boards)	4.50
access area to paddling pool	2.00
teaching pool (steps side)	2.50
teaching pool (narrow side)	2.50
between pools	3.00–4.00
(note: six swimming lanes = 30 m², eight = 50 m², ten = 70 m²	

rooms next to pool	height (m)
swimming instructor's/attendant's room area at least 6 m²	2.50
first aid room area at least 8 m²	2.50
accessory room up to 450 m² water area, at least 15 m² above 450 m² water area, at least 20 m²	2.50 2.50
waiting room for contestants	2.50
teaching and club room: 30–60 m²	2.50

spectator facilities

   stands: 0.5 seat space per square metre of water area used for sports
   space needed for one seat: 0.5 m² including surrounding circulation areas
   cloakroom: space required is 0.025 m² per square metre of water area used for sports

   toilets: in the entrance hall, two WCs for women and one WC plus one urinal for men will be sufficient for up to 200 spectators. For each further 100 spectators add one WC and urinal, preserving the ratio two WCs (women):one WC, two urinals (men)

working spaces for the press

   good lines of sight to the start and finish are needed (i.e. raised location); 5 to 20 spaces required, each space 0.75 × 1.20 m

for television

   four to six spaces are required, each space 1.20 × 1.50 m

catering

   space requirement for each vending machine, 0.5 to 0.8 m²

   seating area (café/restaurant): at least 50 seating spaces, each space 1–2 m²

   service and ancillary room area (in addition): for cafés, about 60% of the seating area, for restaurants about 100% of the seating area, of which 20–25% for stores and cold rooms, 15–20% for empties stores, and the remainder for kitchen, servery, office and staff

   toilets (at least): women, one WC; men, one WC, one urinal

plant area

   total plant area (without swell water storage, storerooms, transformer room and gas meter room): up to 1 m² per square metre of planned water area; in the case of large indoor swimming pools, a reduction to 30% is possible

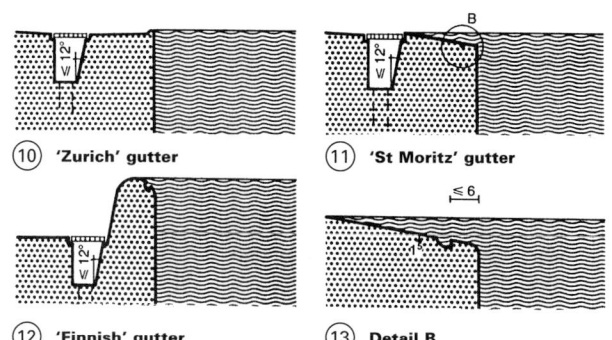

⑩ **'Zurich' gutter**   ⑪ **'St Moritz' gutter**

⑫ **'Finnish' gutter**   ⑬ **Detail B**

SPORT AND RECREATION

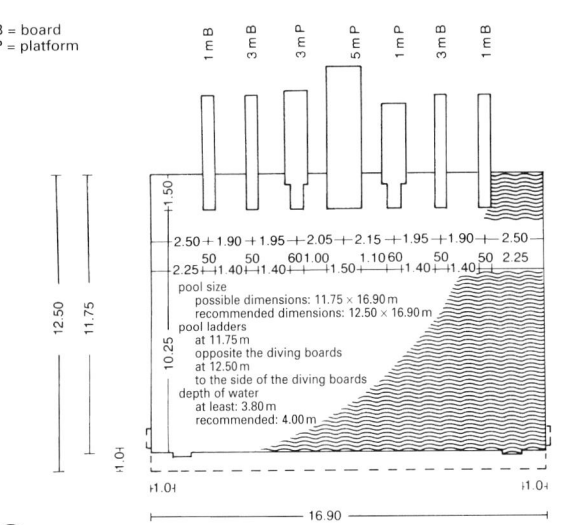
B = board
P = platform

1 m B 3 m B 3 m P 5 m P 1 m P 3 m B 1 m B

2.50 + 1.90 + 1.95 + 2.05 + 2.15 + 1.95 + 1.90 + 2.50
50   2.25 + 1.40 + 1.40 + 1.00   1.10 60 + 1.40 + 1.40 50 2.25
60 1.00   1.50
12.50   11.75   10.25

pool size
possible dimensions: 11.75 × 16.90 m
recommended dimensions: 12.50 × 16.90 m
pool ladders
at 11.75 m
opposite the diving boards
at 12.50 m
to the side of the diving boards
depth of water
at least: 3.80 m
recommended: 4.00 m

1.50
1.0   1.0   1.0

16.90

① **Diving facilities (complete): 1 to 5 m**

B = board
P = platform

1 m B 3 m B 7.5 m P 10 m P 5 m P 3 m P 1 m P 3 m B 1 m B

2.50 + 1.90 + 2.10 + 2.75 + 3.15 + 2.05 + 1.60 + 1.95 + 1.90 + 2.50
50   50   2.25 + 1.40 + 1.10 1.50 + 2.00 + 1.40 1.50 + 1.40 + 1.40 50 2.25
1.00   1.00   1.00
70 60   60 1.10
30 3030 30
40

size of pool
possible dimensions: 22.40 × 16.66 m
or 25.00 × 15.00 m
depth of water
at least: 4.50 m
recommended: 5.00 m
(competition standard)

15.00   13.50
1.50
1.0   1.0

22.40

② **Diving facilities (complete): 1 to 10 m**

Diving pits are usually equipped with two kinds of diving-off point: rigid platforms, which must be level, (1, 3, 5, and 10 m high) and springboards (1 and 3m high). The heights are measured from the water surface. Springboards are made of aluminium, wood or plastic. Both platforms and springboards must have non-slip surfaces. Ladders are usually used to reach platforms and boards, although lifts should be considered for large competition facilities. All boards and platforms are situated at one side of the pool → ① – ②. To allow divers to see the water surface better, water surface agitators or sprinklers are used.

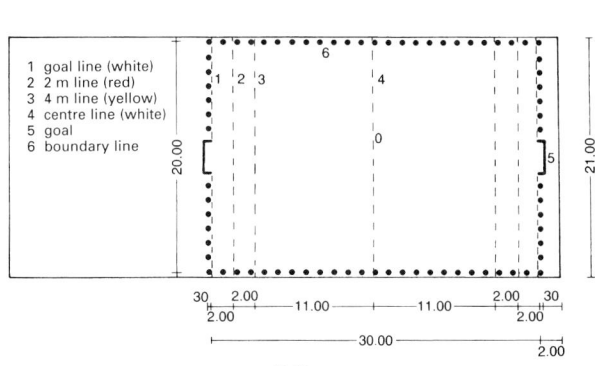

1 goal line (white)
2 2 m line (red)
3 4 m line (yellow)
4 centre line (white)
5 goal
6 boundary line

20.00   21.00

30 2.00 ⊢ 11.00 ⊣ 11.00 ⊢ 2.00 30
2.00   2.00

30.00

50.00   2.00

④ **Layout for water polo**

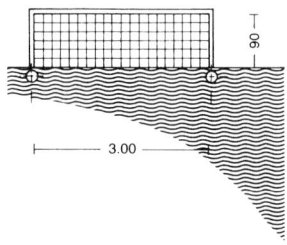

90   30

3.00   2.00

alternative: with a hook-in goal in a 25 m pool, at least 70 cm

⑤ **Water polo goal: front view**   ⑥ **Water polo goal: side view**

dimension → ⑦ – ⑧	length/width	1 m board 4.80/0.50		3 m board 4.80/0.50		1 m platform 4.50/0.60		3 m platform 5.00/0.60		5 m platform 6.00/1.50		7.5 m platform 6.00/1.50		10 m platform 6.00/2.00	
A: from front edge of board/platform back to pool side	see diagram minimum recommended	A-1 1.50 1.80	– – –	A-3 1.50 1.80	– – –	A-1 1.50 –	– – –	A-3 1.50 –	– – –	A-5 1.50 1.50	– – –	A-7.5 1.50 –	– – –	A-10 1.50 –	– – –
A–A: front edge back to lower platform	see diagram minimum recommended	– – –	– – –	– – –	– – –	– – –	– – –	– – –	– – –	A-A-5/1 1.25 –	– – –	A-A-7.5/3 1.25 –	– – –	A-A-10/5 1.25 –	– – –
B: board/platform edge to pool side	see diagram minimum recommended	B-1 2.50 3.00	– – –	B-3 3.50 –	– – –	B-1 2.30 –	– – –	B-3 2.80 –	– – –	B-5 4.25 –	– – –	B7.5 4.50 –	– – –	B10 5.25 –	– – –
C: between board/platform centres	see diagram minimum recommended	C-1 1.90 2.40/3.00	– – –	C-3 1.90 2.40/3.00	C-3/1 1.90 2.40/3.00	– – –	– – –	– – –	– – –	C-5/3B 2.10 –	C-5/1B 2.10 –	C-7.5/1P C-10/7.5 2.45 2.75		C-10/5 2.75 –	C-10/3B 2.65 –
D: front edge forward to edge of pool	see diagram minimum recommended	D-1 9.00 –	– – –	D-3 10.25 –	– – –	D-1 8.00 –	– – –	D-3 9.50 –	– – –	D-5 10.25 –	– – –	D-7.5 11.00 –	– – –	D-10 13.50 –	– – –
E: from board/platform to ceiling	see diagram minimum recommended	– – –	E-1 5.00 –	– – –	E-3 5.00 –	– – –	E-1 3.00 –	– – –	E-3 3.00 –	– – –	E-5 3.00 3.40	– – –	E-7.5 3.20 3.40	– – –	E-10 3.40 3.40
F: clear ceiling height behind and to each side of edge/centre	see diagram minimum recommended	F-1 2.50 –	E-1 5.00 –	F-3 2.50 –	E-3 5.00 –	F-1 2.75 –	E-1 3.00 –	F-3 2.75 –	E-3 3.00 –	F-5 2.75 –	E-5 3.00 3.40	F-7.5 2.75 –	E-7.5 3.20 3.40	F-10 – –	E-10 3.40 4.00/5.00
G: clear ceiling height ahead of front edge	see diagram minimum recommended	G-1 5.00 –	E-1 5.00 –	G-3 5.00 –	E-3 5.00 –	G-1 5.00 –	E-1 3.00 –	G-3 5.00 –	E-3 3.00 –	G-5 5.00 –	E-5 3.00 3.40	G-7.5 5.00 –	E-7.5 3.20 3.40	G-10 6.00 6.00	E-10 3.40 5.00
H: depth of water below board/platform edge	see diagram minimum recommended	– – –	H-1 3.40 3.80	– – –	H-3 3.80 4.00	– – –	H-1 3.40 3.80	– – –	H-3 3.40 3.80	– – –	H-5 3.80 4.00	– – –	H-7.5 4.10 4.50	– – –	H-10 4.50 5.00
J: safety zone (full depth of water)	see diagram minimum recommended	J-1 6.00 –	K-1 6.00 3.70	J-3 6.00 –	K-3 6.00 3.90	J-1 5.00 –	K-1 3.30 3.70	J-3 6.00 –	K-3 3.30 3.70	J-5 6.00 –	K-5 3.70 3.90	J-7.5 8.00 –	K-7.5 4.00 4.40	J-10 12.00 –	K-10 4.25 4.75
L: safety zone (full depth of water)	see diagram minimum recommended	L-1 2.25 –	- –	L-3 3.25 –	- –	L-1 2.05 –	- –	L-3 2.55 –	- –	L-5 3.75 –	- –	L-7.5 3.75 –	- –	L-10 4.50 –	- –
P: maximum angle of the ceiling slope															

note: if the platforms are built wider than the minimum recommended, then add half of the additional width to the axial spacing dimensions

③ **Dimensions of diving facilities** → ⑦ – ⑧

F   F
10.0 m
7.5 m   C-7.5-1   C-10/3
C-10/7.5
5.0 m   C-1   C-5/3   C-5/1 C-10/5   C-3
3.0 m   B-1   B-3
1.0 m
H   N
L   L

⑦ **Cross-section**

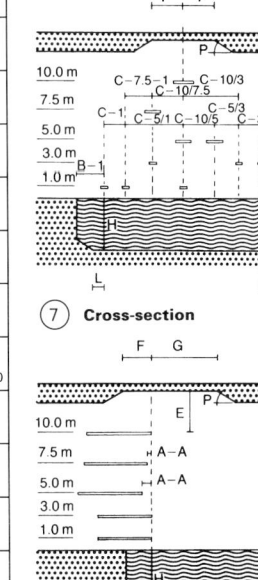

F   G
10.0 m   E   P
7.5 m   A-A
5.0 m   A-A
3.0 m
1.0 m
H   N
J
A   D

⑧ **Longitudinal section**

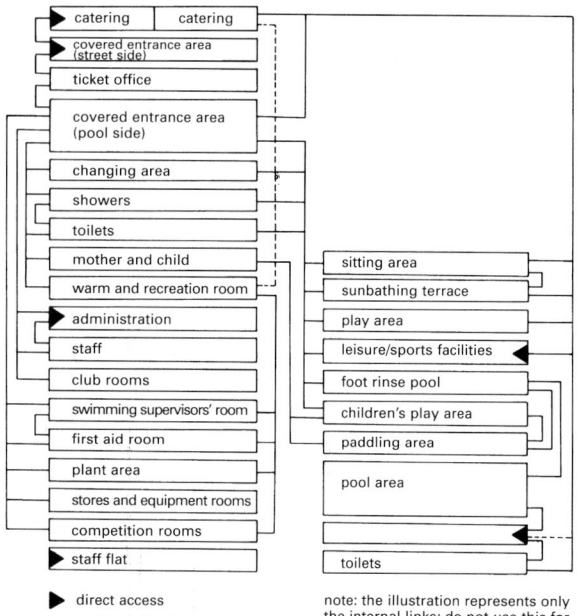

① **Space and area organisation diagram**

catering | catering
covered entrance area (street side)
ticket office
covered entrance area (pool side)
changing area
showers
toilets
mother and child | sitting area
warm and recreation room | sunbathing terrace
administration | play area
staff | leisure/sports facilities
club rooms | foot rinse pool
swimming supervisors' room | children's play area
first aid room | paddling area
plant area | pool area
stores and equipment rooms
competition rooms
staff flat | toilets

▶ direct access

◀ optional direct access

note: the illustration represents only the internal links; do not use this for room planning.

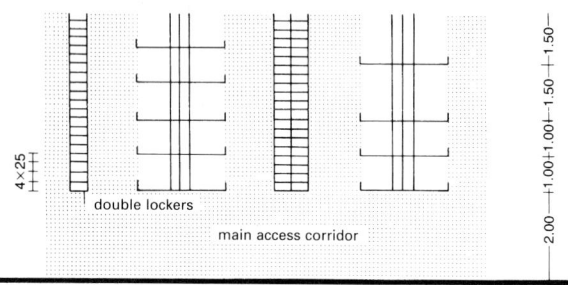

② **Changing area units (sketch)**

double lockers

main access corridor

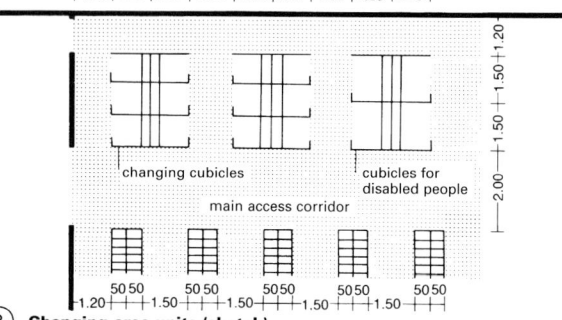

③ **Changing area units (sketch)**

changing cubicles

cubicles for disabled people

main access corridor

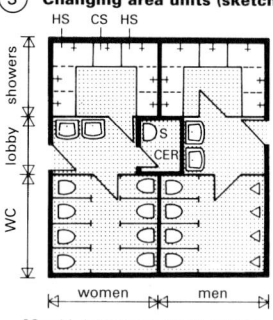

CS cold shower with splash screens
HS hot shower

④ **Shower/toilet area for 2000 m² water area (sketch)**

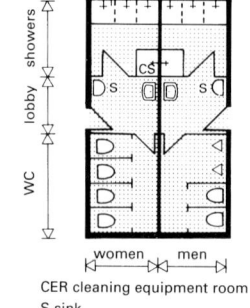

CER cleaning equipment room
S sink

⑤ **Shower/toilet area for 1000 m² water area (sketch)**

OPEN AIR SWIMMING POOLS

Open air pools are used almost exclusively for leisure activities. The required water area per inhabitant ranges from 0.15 m² in low population density catchment areas to 0.05 m² where the population density is high. This relationship between the number of inhabitants and the size of the water area ignores any element of tourism.

A site area of 8–16 m² per square metre of the planned water area should be planned. Allow parking space for one car and two bicycles for every 200–300 m² of the site area.

For the entry area, 200 m² should be allocated per 1000 m² water area, of which 50 m² will be for a covered entrance with a ticket office and some form of entry control.

An area of 10 m² should be planned for staff rooms in facilities with water areas up to 2000 m²; above this, 20 m² should be allowed for staff.

paddling pools

water area 100 to 400 m²; depth of water 0.00 to 0.50 m; above 200 m² the pool is divided into several sections with varying water depth

teaching pools

water area 500 to 1200 m²; depth of water 0.50/0.60 to 1.35 m; possibly divided into several pools of varying depths

swimming pools

water area 417 to 1250 m²; depth of water 1.80 m; pool sizes depend on the number of swimming lanes:

lanes	pool width	pool length
6	16.66 m	25.00 m
6	16.66 m	50.00 m
8	21.00 m	50.00 m
10	25.00 m	50.00 m

wave pool

width 16.66 m, 21.00 m or 25.00 m
length usually 50.00 m, but at least 33.00 m
water depth at the beginning 0.00 m
final water depth depends on pool use and the type of wave machine

catchment area (inhabitants)	type of pool	planning unit		diving boards	factor for volume and area calculation	site area (without ancillary areas)
		pool size	water area		standard unit value	
	[1]	(m or m²)	(m²)	[2]		(m²)
1	2	3		4	5	6
5000 up to 10000	SP DP[3] TP PP	16.66 × 25.00 12.50 × 11.75 500 100	417 147 500 100 1164	1B + 3B + 1P + 3P + 5P	1000	8000 up to 12000
10000 up to 20000	SP DP[3] TP PP	16.66 × 50.00 18.35 × 15.00 1050 150	833 275 1050 150 2308	1B + 3B + 1P + 3P + 5P + 7.5P + 10P	2000	20000 up to 25000
20000 up to 30000	SP DP[3] TP PP	21.00 × 50.00 22.40 × 15.00 1350 200	1050 336 1350 200 2936	2 × 1B + 2 × 3B + 1P + 3P + 5P + 7.5P + 10P	2500	30000 up to 35000
30000 up to 40000	SP DP[3] TP PP	21.00 × 50.00 22.40 × 15.00 1550 250	1050 336 1550 250 3186	2 × 1B + 2 × 3B + 1P + 3P + 5P + 7.5P + 10P	3000	40000 up to 45000
40000 up to 50000	SP DP[3] TP WP or 2 TP PP	21.00 × 50,00 22.40 × 15.00 1200 800 300	1050 336 1200 800 300 3686	2 × 1B + 2 × 3B + 1P + 3P + 5P + 7.5P + 10P	3500	50000 up to 55000
over 50000	consider further open air pools of the suggested above units at several sites in a catchment area of 50,000 or more					

[1] PP = paddling pool, TP = teaching pool, SP = swimming pool, DP = diving pool, WP = wave pool
[2] B = board, P = platform; 1–10 = diving height in m
[3] measurements with regard to safety dimensions: pool sizes = pool width (diving end) × pool length (in the direction of diving)

⑥ **Planning units for open air pools (example)**

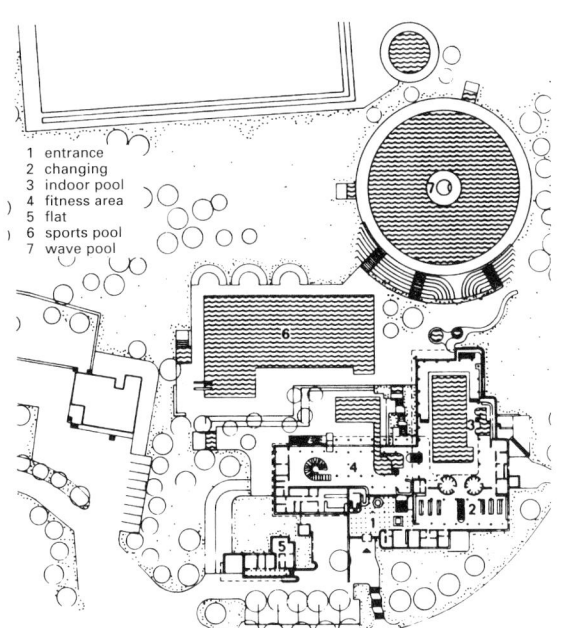

1 entrance
2 changing
3 indoor pool
4 fitness area
5 flat
6 sports pool
7 wave pool

1 **The Wellenberg Oberammergau**   Architect: P Seifert

INDOOR/OPEN AIR SWIMMING POOLS

General Planning Principles

Large complexes that combine indoor and open air swimming pools, depending on the type of design, offer more flexibility than separate facilities and are ideal centres for family leisure activities. However, the limitations imposed by the local seasonal weather patterns necessitate careful consideration of the allocation of indoor and outdoor water areas. The design must differentiate between the type of use during summer and winter times, as well as the transition periods in between.

The following types of use can be considered:
- inclusive use of all indoor and outdoor water areas at the same times, with unlimited bathing duration, for a standard admission charge;
- separate use of indoor and outdoor water areas during differing opening times, perhaps with unlimited bathing time only in the outdoor pool, and different admission charges;
- seasonal single use, for instance at times when one of the facilities (indoor or outdoor section) is closed.

Consider the following when deciding on the type of design:
- the area of the indoor and outdoor pools appropriate to the size of the catchment area;
- additional water area in one or both of the sections which may be required to meet increased demand resulting from tourism;
- additional water area in one or both sections necessitated by special circumstances (e.g. in spa resorts or for sporting competitions etc.).

Examples → ①–③.

1 sauna/leisure rooms
2 outdoor sauna
3 plunge pool
4 outdoor swimming pool
5 children's paddling pool
6 swimming pool
7 water grotto
8 changing
9 showers
10 sun beds
11 terrace
12 plant

2 **Heveney open air swimming pool**   Architects: Aichele, Fiedler, Heller

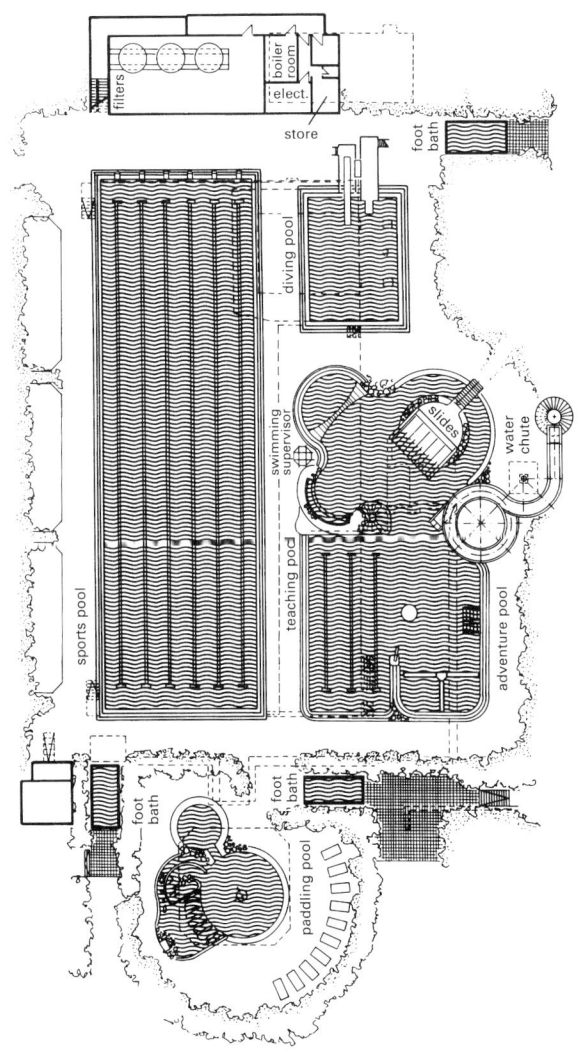

3 **Bad Driburg open air pool**   Architects: Geller + Müller

535

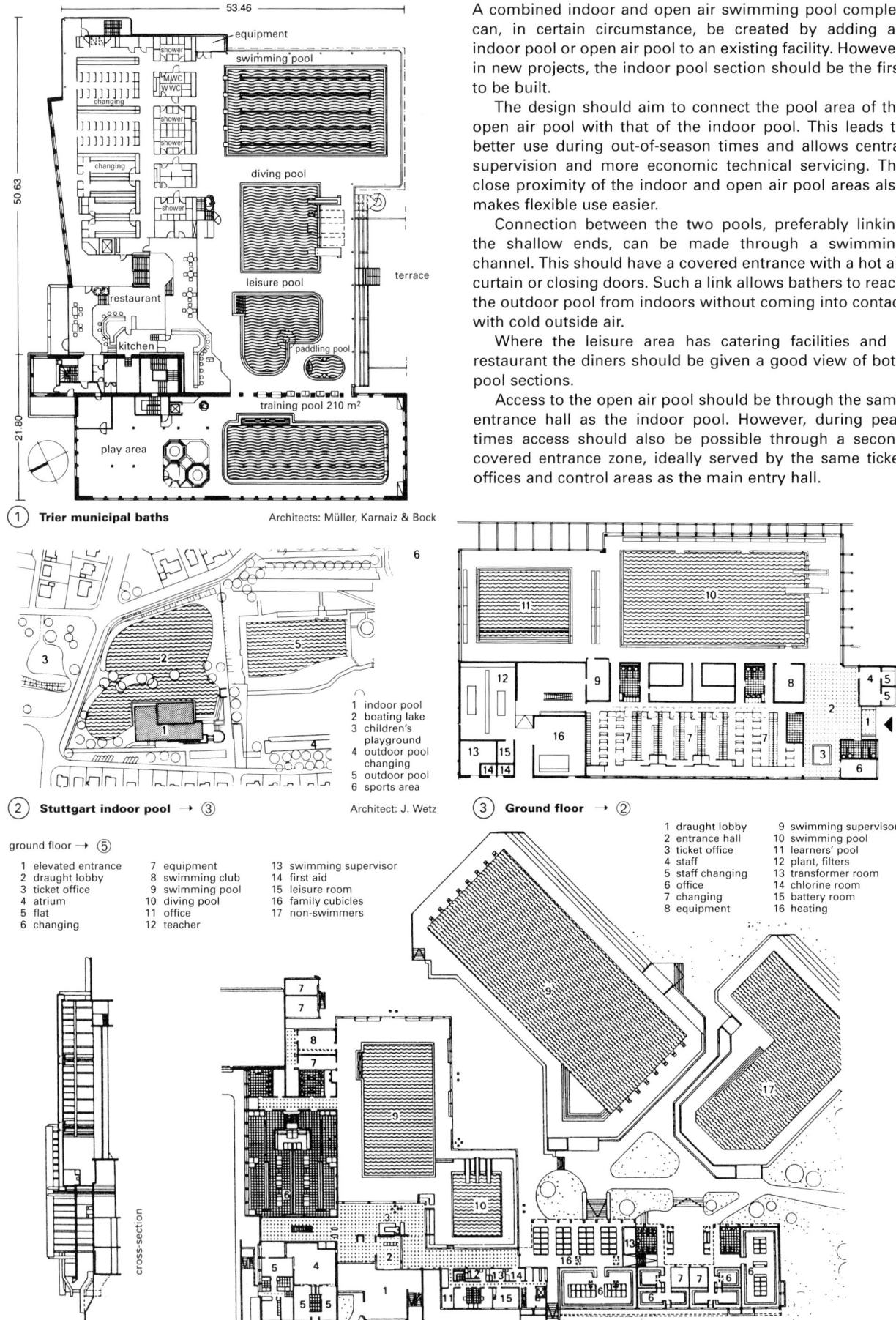

INDOOR/OPEN AIR SWIMMING POOLS

A combined indoor and open air swimming pool complex can, in certain circumstance, be created by adding an indoor pool or open air pool to an existing facility. However, in new projects, the indoor pool section should be the first to be built.

The design should aim to connect the pool area of the open air pool with that of the indoor pool. This leads to better use during out-of-season times and allows central supervision and more economic technical servicing. The close proximity of the indoor and open air pool areas also makes flexible use easier.

Connection between the two pools, preferably linking the shallow ends, can be made through a swimming channel. This should have a covered entrance with a hot air curtain or closing doors. Such a link allows bathers to reach the outdoor pool from indoors without coming into contact with cold outside air.

Where the leisure area has catering facilities and a restaurant the diners should be given a good view of both pool sections.

Access to the open air pool should be through the same entrance hall as the indoor pool. However, during peak times access should also be possible through a second covered entrance zone, ideally served by the same ticket offices and control areas as the main entry hall.

① **Trier municipal baths** Architects: Müller, Karnaiz & Bock

② **Stuttgart indoor pool** → ③ Architect: J. Wetz

1 indoor pool
2 boating lake
3 children's playground
4 outdoor pool changing
5 outdoor pool
6 sports area

③ **Ground floor** → ②

1 draught lobby
2 entrance hall
3 ticket office
4 staff
5 staff changing
6 office
7 changing
8 equipment
9 swimming supervisor
10 swimming pool
11 learners' pool
12 plant, filters
13 transformer room
14 chlorine room
15 battery room
16 heating

ground floor → ⑤

1 elevated entrance
2 draught lobby
3 ticket office
4 atrium
5 flat
6 changing
7 equipment
8 swimming club
9 swimming pool
10 diving pool
11 office
12 teacher
13 swimming supervisor
14 first aid
15 leisure room
16 family cubicles
17 non-swimmers

④ **Zollikon, indoor and outdoor pools** → ⑤

⑤ **Ground floor** Architects: E. Ulrich + C. Baum

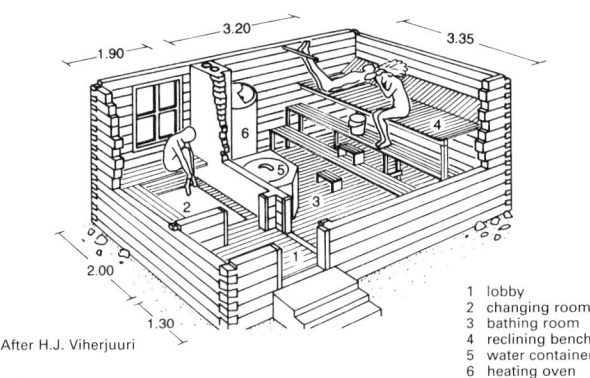

After H.J. Viherjuuri

1 lobby
2 changing room
3 bathing room
4 reclining bench
5 water container
6 heating oven

① **Basic sauna**

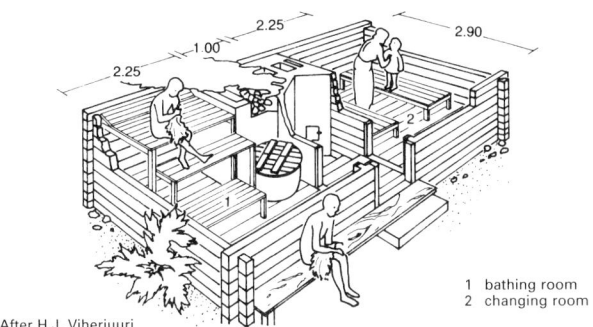

After H.J. Viherjuuri

1 bathing room
2 changing room

② **Sauna with central lobby**

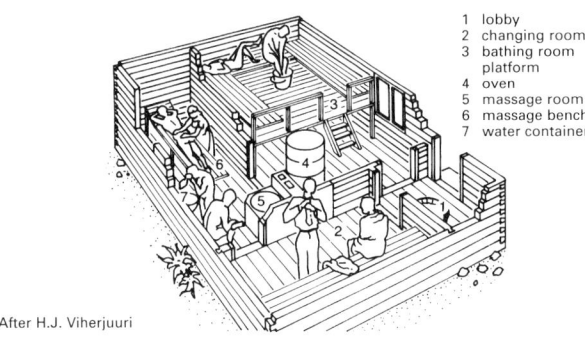

After H.J. Viherjuuri

1 lobby
2 changing room
3 bathing room platform
4 oven
5 massage room
6 massage bench
7 water container

③ **Larger sauna**

Architect: E. Sukonen

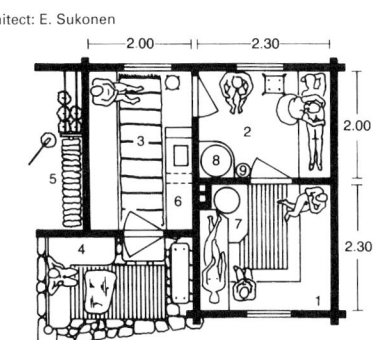

1 bathing room
2 massage and washing room
3 changing room
4 veranda
5 wood stack
6 cupboard
7 oven
8 water container
9 water scoop

④ **Sauna with a veranda**

The sauna is more than a method of bathing: for many it is a type of physical cleansing, almost a ritual, and it is now an essential part of all modern sports facilities. In Finland there is one sauna for every six people. They are built to a standard traditional design and used once a week, both communally within the family and also in public without segregation of the sexes.

The classic location for saunas is next to a clear lake with woods and meadows for air bathing between sweat baths.

Bathing sequence
The priciple involves alternating use of hot and cold air. Bathers sweat in dry hot air, and then in hot pure steam emissions, which are created every 5–7 minutes by pouring a quarter litre of water on to heated stones. The cycle between dry and damp results in a strong stimulation of the skin and strengthens resistance to illness. The effect is intensified by periodic cold water treatment, massage and rest.

Construction
Wood block or timber construction is by far the most common and good thermal insulation of the exterior is essential because the temperature difference between inside and outside can often be over 100°C in winter.

The bathing room should be as small as possible ($\leq 16\,m^2$, $\leq 2.5\,m$ high) and lined with dark coloured timber on the ceiling and walls to reduce heat radiation. Walls are solid softwood timber, with the exception of the oven area. The steps and benches are made of wood battens to give good air circulation and are at various heights, the top bench being about 1m beneath the ceiling. The benches are usually around 2m in length. All of the wood battens are nailed from below so that the body does not come into contact with hot nail heads. Benches should be easy to dismantle to allow easy cleaning. The floor must be made of non-slip material, not wood strips.

Smoke sauna
Large stones are piled up and strongly heated on a wood fire, the smoke escaping through the open door. When the stones are glowing the fire is removed and the last of the smoke is expelled by sprays of water. The door is then closed and, after a short time, the sauna is 'ripe' for bathing. Bathers can enjoy the wonderful smell of smoked wood and dependable steam quality. Roughly half of the old Finnish saunas are built in this way.

End smoke sauna
At the end of the heating period, when the stones have reached about 500°C, the oven flue is directed inwards. The combustion gases burn completely without any soot production. The top doors are then closed, even if there are still flames in the combustion chamber, and the temperature quickly rises by tens of degrees. Before bathing the last of the fumes are discharged by opening the door for a short period, and water is then poured over the hot stones.

Oven sauna
These use a ceramic or metal clad oven, heated by the flue gases from the combustion chamber. Heating takes place through a fire door from bathing room or lobby. Once the stones are hot, the fire door is closed and the doors at the top of the oven cladding are opened as required in order to let out hot air prior to pouring water on the stones.

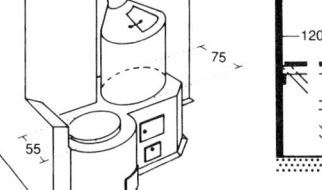

⑤ **Finnish sauna oven with water container (also useable for washing clothes)**

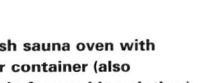

⑥ **Finnish standard reclining benches for sweat baths and saunas**

SAUNA

Bathing involves three periods of 8–12 minutes in the sauna followed by cooling off with pouring bowls, in showers or a plunge pool (although it is nicer to cool off in the natural water of a lake or the sea). The cooling process also includes the air bath, which entails the breathing in of fresh, cool air as a counterbalance to the hot air. The air bathing area should be screened off and seating provided → ① – ②.

In public saunas, adequate changing areas must be provided along with additional rest and massage rooms → ④.

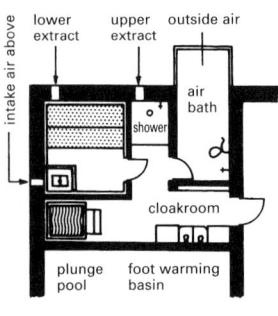

① Domestic sauna

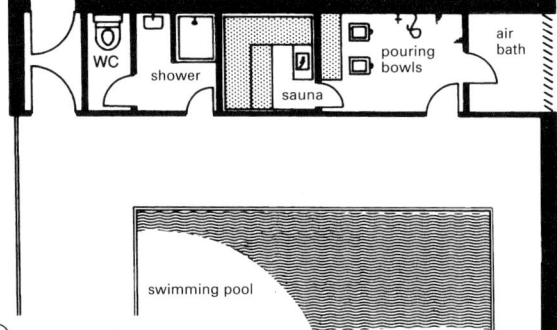

② Sauna and indoor swimming pool

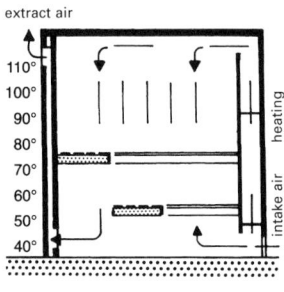

③ Section through a sauna with indirect heating (Bamberg)

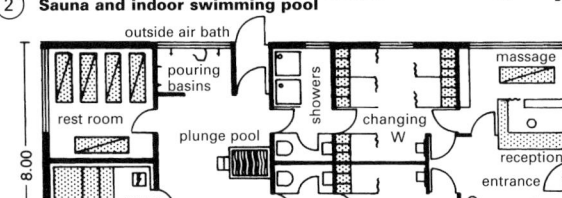

④ Plan of a sauna for 30 people

1 rest area
2 sauna
3 shower
4 plunge pool
5 foot bath
6 WC
7 bench
8 sunbed
9 wall bars
10 exercise bike

⑤ Attic sauna (35 m², 4–6 persons)

1 shower
2 steam bath
3 services
4 sauna
5 sunbed
6 shelf
7 rest area

⑥ Sauna in the basement (35 m², 4–6 persons)

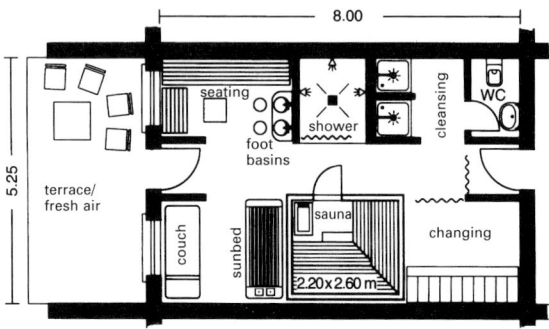

⑦ Hotel sauna 5.25 × 8.00 m

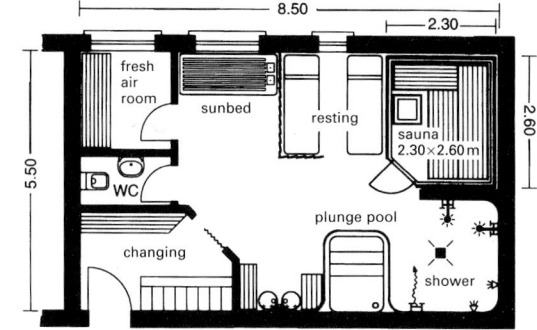

⑧ Hotel sauna 5.50 × 8.50 m

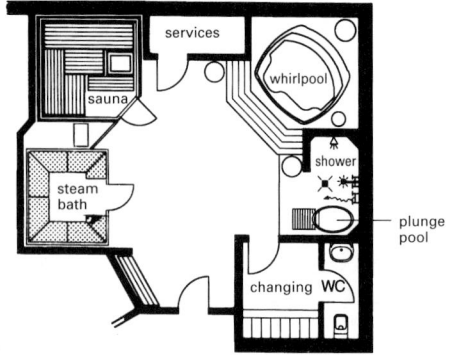

⑨ Sauna, steam bath, whirlpool

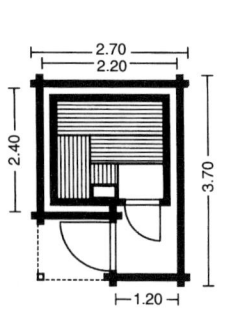

⑩ Garden sauna (log hut)

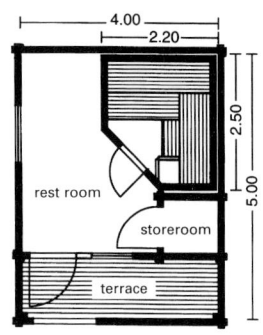

⑪ Log hut sauna

538

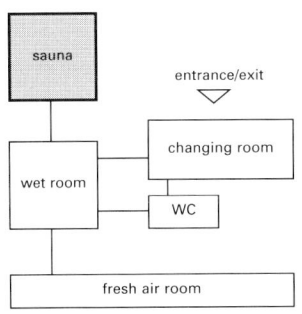

① **Functional diagram, private sauna**

area required per person	
changing room	0.8–1.0 m²
cleansing	0.3–0.5 m²
sauna room	0.5–0.8 m²
cooling room	1.0–1.8 m²
rest room	0.3–0.6 m²
fresh air room	> 0.5 m²
massage	6–8 m²/bench
room sizes (example 30 people)	
changing room	24–30 m²
cleansing	9–15 m²
sauna room	15–18 m²
cooling room	30–45 m²
rest room	9–18 m²
lobby, toilets	99–144 m²
corridors	+21–35 m²
air bath (20–50 m²)	120–179 m²

② **Area requirements and room sizes**

cap-acity	dimensions of heaters (cm)		cable cross-section	sauna room size
(kW)	1 (W D H)	2 (W D H)	(mm²)	(m³)
3	43 13 50		3 × 2.5	2–3
4.5	43 26 55	51 33 62	5 × 2.5	4–6
6	43 26 55	51 33 62	5 × 2.5	6–10
7.5	43 26 55	51 33 62	5 × 2.5	8–12
9	43 26 55	51 33 62	5 × 2.5	10–16
10.5		51 33 62	5 × 2.5	12–17
12	69 35 62		5 × 2.5	14–18
15	82 35 62		5 × 4	16–22
18	82 35 62		5 × 6	18–24
21	108 35 62		5 × 6	20–28
24	108 35 62		5 × 10	25–40

③ **Technical data for sauna equipment**

A plunge pool is provided for the necessary 'cooling off' after a sauna → ⑤. The warm footbath is another important component a of properly fitted out sauna bath → ⑥. A 19 mm hose, connected only to the cold water supply, should be included in the shower area, and provided with massage and fan shaped nozzles.

Space permitting, an exercise bike (or similar) and a set of wall bars can be included for fitness training. → ⑦ – ⑨

Saunas can be built to any size and shape according to individual wishes (e.g. triangular, round, six sided) → ⑭ – ⑰ and sauna roofs which are sloped to fit into attic spaces are readily available. Double glazed windows can be incorporated in front wall or door.

Room temperatures
Changing room 20–22°C, cleansing room ≥24–26°C, cooling down (cold water) room ≤18–20°C, rest room 20–22°C, massage room 20–22°C.

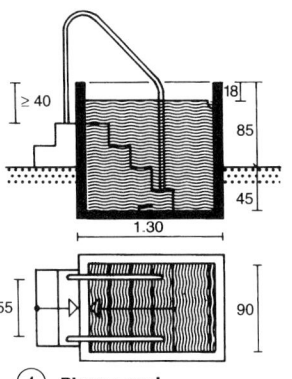

④ **Plunge pool**

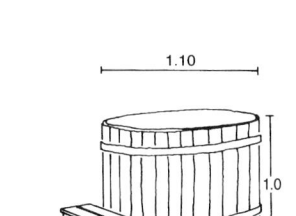

⑤ **Plunge tub**
capacity: approx. 650 l
filled: approx. 730 kg

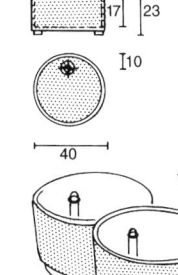

⑥ **Foot warming basins**
filled: 14 kg

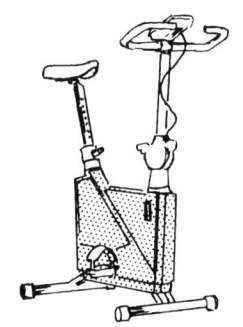

⑦ **Electric exercise bike for therapeutic use**

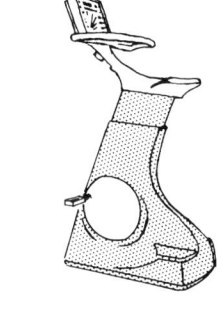

⑧ **Electric exercise bike for fitness training**

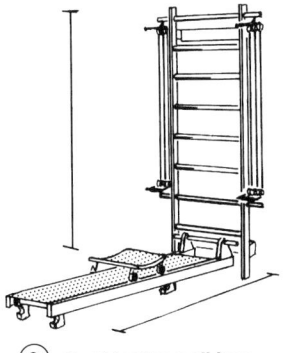

⑨ **Combination wall bars**

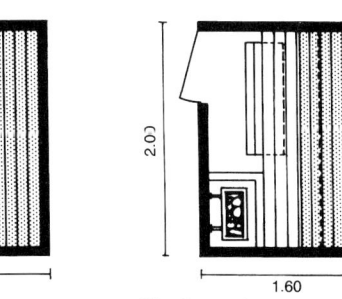

⑩ **Sauna: 1 person reclining, 2 sitting**

⑪ **Sauna: 2 persons reclining, 3 sitting**

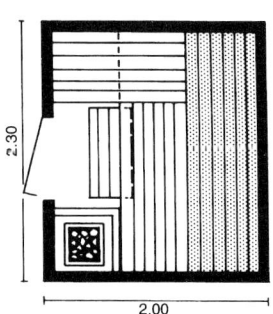

⑫ **Sauna: 3 persons reclining, 5 sitting**

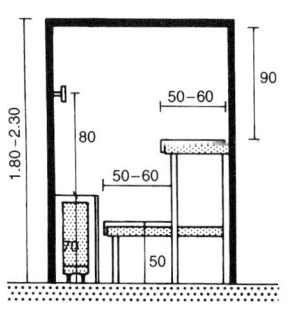

⑬ **Section**

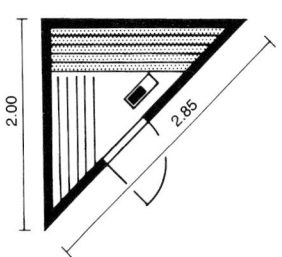

⑭ **Corner sauna**

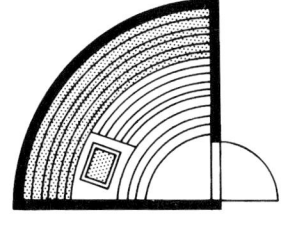

⑮ **Quarter circle**

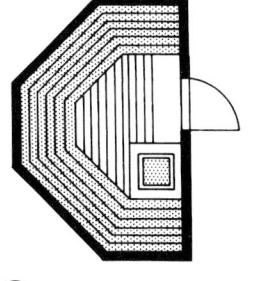

⑯ **Special shape**

⑰ **Circular**

AMUSEMENT ARCADES

The types of machines found in amusement arcades will vary from country to country given that the setting up of games for gambling is subject to regulations and licensing. It is therefore necessary to take into account the licensing policies if it is intended to provide games which produce winnings of money or goods in a games arcade or similar premises.

Where machines that provide winnings of goods or money are allowed in gaming halls, they must be separated from the machines which are designed for amusement only. It is permissible, however, for adjacent gaming and amusement arcades to share the same toilet facilities → ⑨.

The 'Pachinko' gaming halls, common in Japan → ⑩ + ⑪ are not permitted in some European countries. Balls won from the machines can be exchanged for goods at the service counter.

In the UK, gaming by means of machines is restricted and is governed by the Gaming Act 1968.

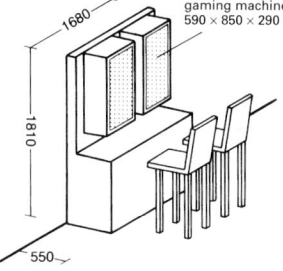

① **Video game**

② **Pinball machine**

③ **Gaming machine stand**

④ **Card games**

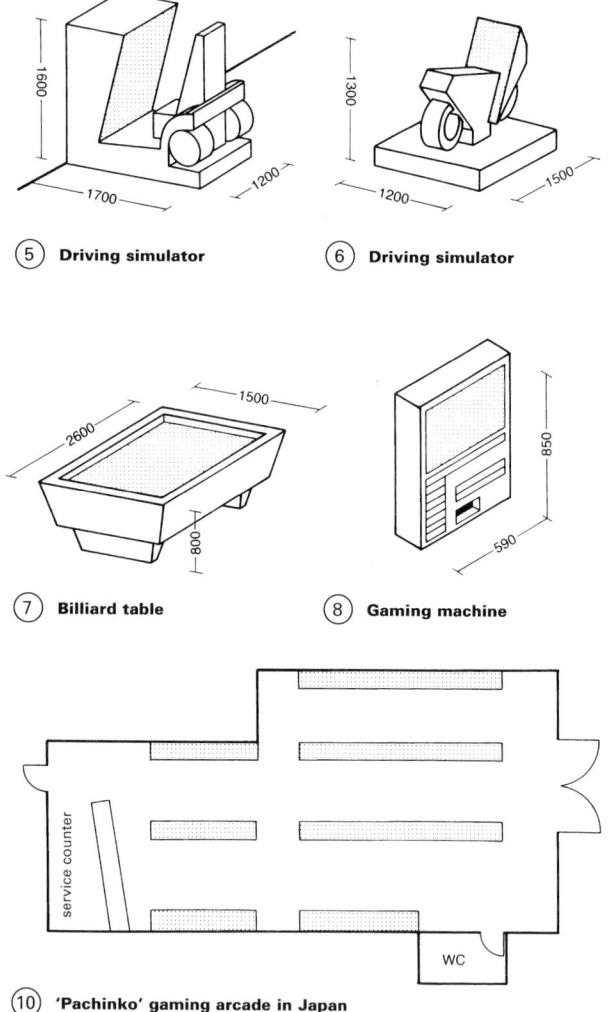

⑤ **Driving simulator**

⑥ **Driving simulator**

⑦ **Billiard table**

⑧ **Gaming machine**

⑩ **'Pachinko' gaming arcade in Japan**

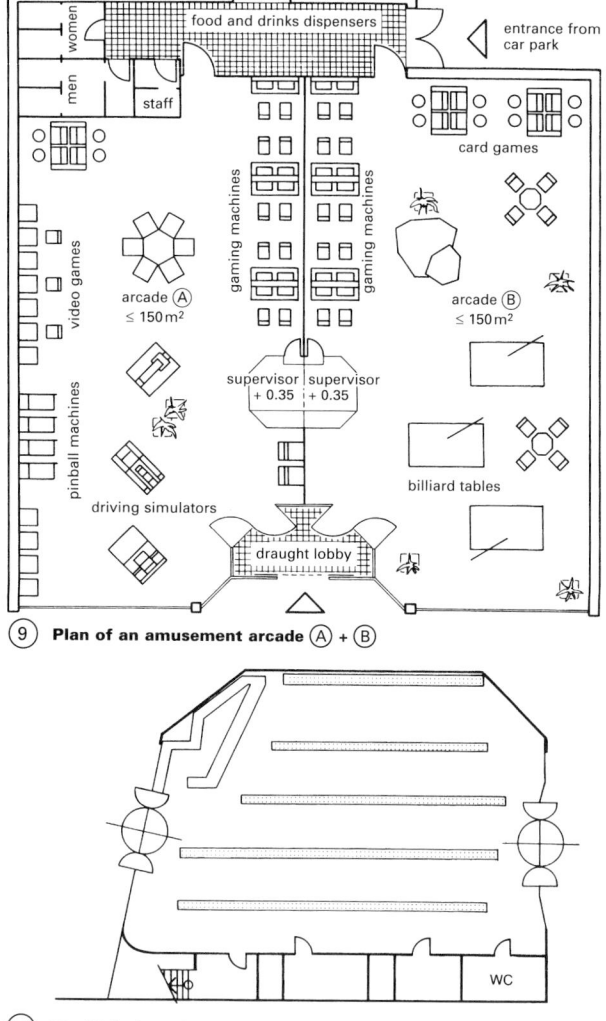

⑨ **Plan of an amusement arcade** Ⓐ + Ⓑ

⑪ **'Pachinko' gaming arcade in Japan**

GROUP PRACTICES AND HEALTHCARE CENTRES

Primary healthcare is delivered in the community at the first contact point between members of the public and health workers. In the past, people would see their general practitioners either at their homes or in the doctor's surgery. If necessary, they would be referred to specialists to receive care. However, the sustained trend towards specialisation amongst doctors starting out on their careers has produced a shift towards medical and diagnostic centres offering extensive medical services. The advantages for the patient are shorter waiting times and a greater possibility of being able to receive a diagnosis and treatment without having to be referred to another doctor. For the doctor, the advantages are the introduction of more regulated working hours and the ability to exchange and learn from the experiences of other doctors in the practice. The simplest form of care centre is the group practice. This is a combination of two or more practising doctors with shared staff and premises.

Although the main core of the primary care service is the general medical practice, with the emphasis on the general practitioner (GP), modern healthcare centres increasingly comprise nursing and other professional staff of primary and community healthcare teams whose roles are also important. There could be, for example, nursing and midwifery teams (practice nurse, health visitor, district nurse, midwife, community psychiatric nurse, school nurse, etc.) as well as visiting therapists and practitioners in specialist disciplines. The members of the team work interdependently, although each has his/her role clearly defined. There are also the administration staff who run the centre (e.g. practice manager, receptionist, records clerk and secretary). Social workers and dental practitioners might also use the facilities.

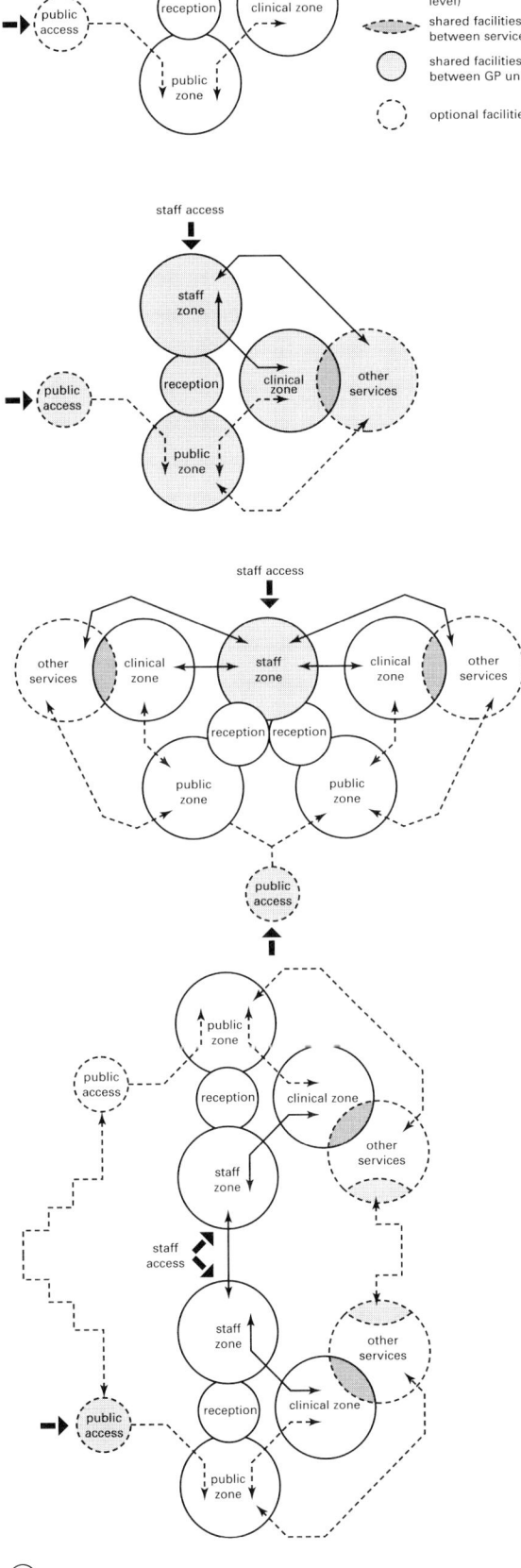

① General medical practice premises

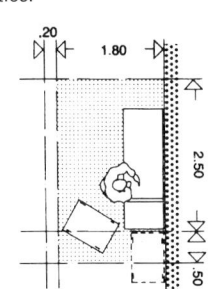

② Minimum area: doctor's consultation

③ Minimum area: examination of reclining patient

④ Minimum area: taking blood samples

⑤ Area for physiotherapy couches

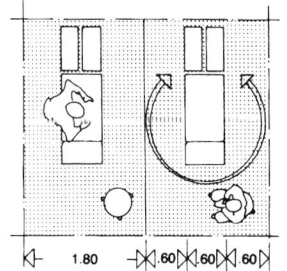

⑥ Minimum area: electrocardiogram (ECG)

⑦ Area requirements: ultrasound examination

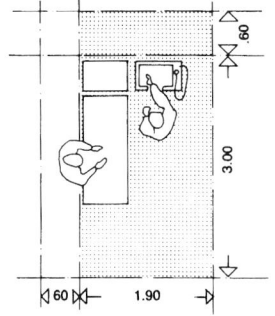

541

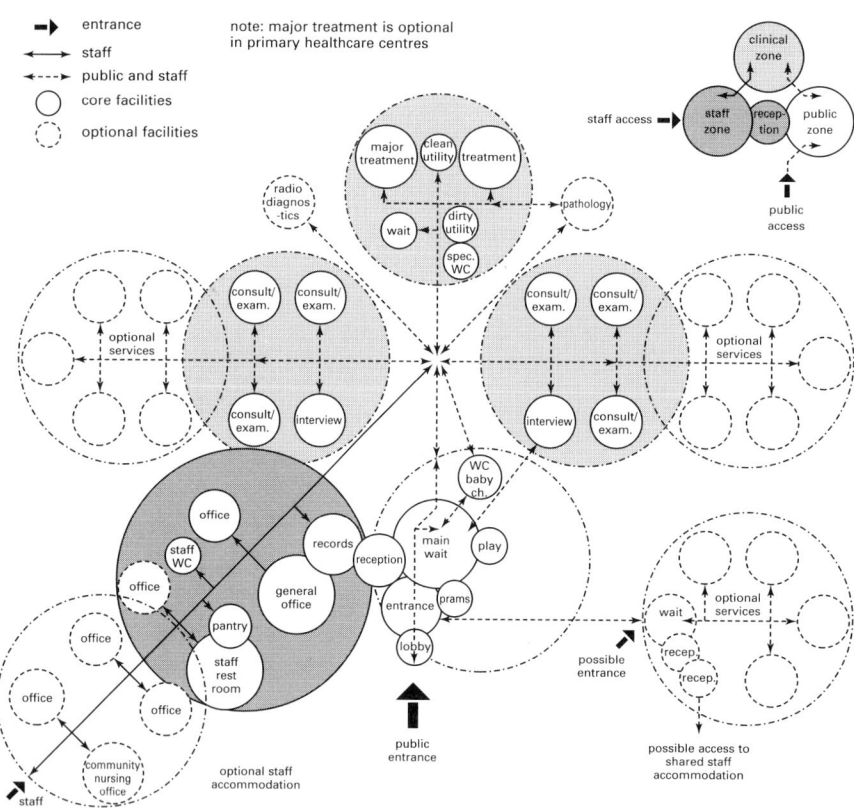

entrance
staff
public and staff
core facilities
optional facilities

note: major treatment is optional
in primary healthcare centres

(8) **Functional parts and relationships**

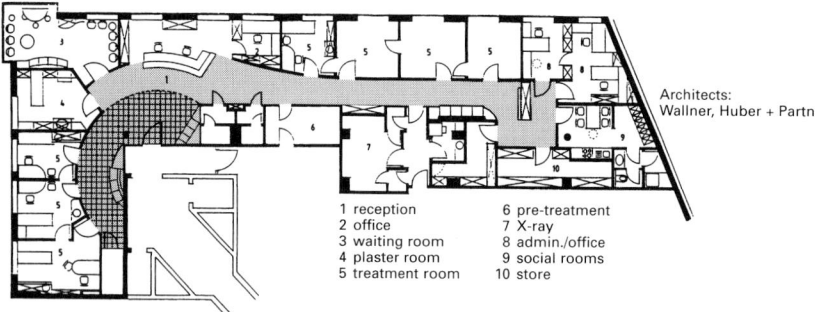

Architects:
Wallner, Huber + Partner

1 reception
2 office
3 waiting room
4 plaster room
5 treatment room
6 pre-treatment
7 X-ray
8 admin./office
9 social rooms
10 store

(9) **Group orthopaedic practice**

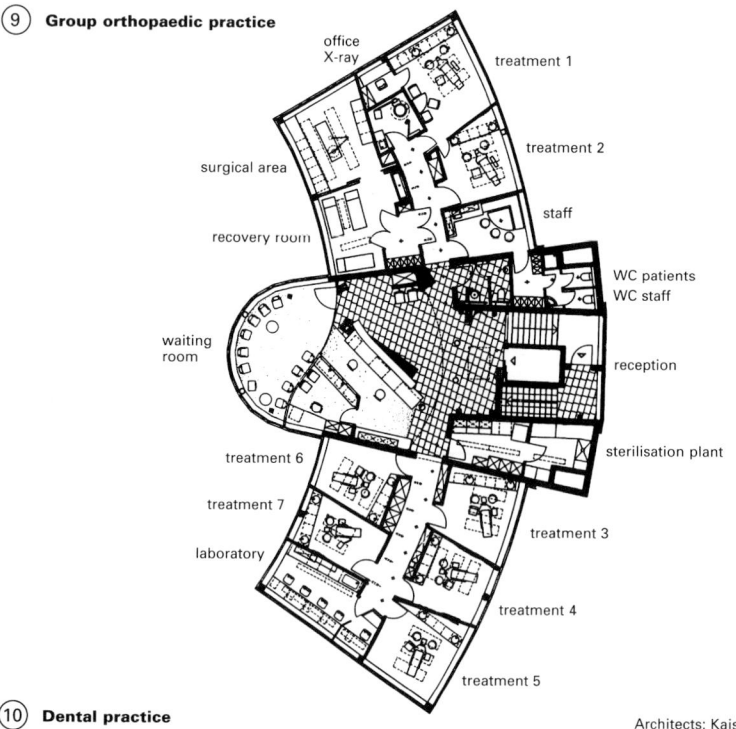

(10) **Dental practice**

Architects: Kaiser and Wildner

542

GROUP PRACTICES AND HEALTHCARE CENTRES

A primary healthcare centre therefore provides a range of medical services including: consultations, treatment/ diagnosis, minor surgery and health education. Sometimes it may also include day care for physiotherapy and occupational therapy, and outpatients' emergency treatment. In some cases there may be in-patient short-stay beds. These centres can offer great flexibility and tend to serve an average population of between 10 000 and 30 000 people.

Any of these building types may include general medical practitioners, dental, ophthalmic and pharmaceutical practitioners, community nursing services, such as chiropody, physiotherapy and speech therapy, non-acute beds, resource, educational facilities, out-of-hours facilities for GPs, 'drop-in treatment' and minor surgery facilities.

There are several factors that should be considered in the design of a primary healthcare building. These include:

- Location of the building: should be convenient in relation to the people it serves.
- Circulation: entrance and circulation within the building must consider wheelchair users, parents with small children and people with disabilities, etc.
- Effective zoning is required: public zone, clinical zone, and staff zone.
- Privacy and confidentiality are important, especially at the reception desk and clinical rooms during consultations and treatments.
- Security and supervision in the premises will be necessary, including staff protection against personal assault and equipment safeguarded against theft and vandalism.
- For running costs, efficient staffing, energy-efficiency, long-life and low-maintenance approaches should be adopted.
- Flexibility and growth should be catered for: flexibility in the use of some spaces, and potential for future extension of the building.

The following spaces should be considered. The design, number and areas (m²) of each of these spaces, should take account of several factors, including staff, the type and number of people to be served by the building, equipment and furniture, and with regard to functional content of the building, local circumstances, design guides: car parking spaces; main entrance; reception area; record storage; administration and office bases; waiting areas; consulting/ examination rooms; treatment rooms; minor surgery spaces; dental suites; multipurpose rooms; interview rooms; WCs for patients; WCs for staff; staff amenities; out-patient consulting and diagnostic facilities; beds; educational facilities; storage for each of the services; building services requirements; grouping of spaces.

The vocational regulations in individual countries must be observed because in some circumstances they may preclude some communal practices.

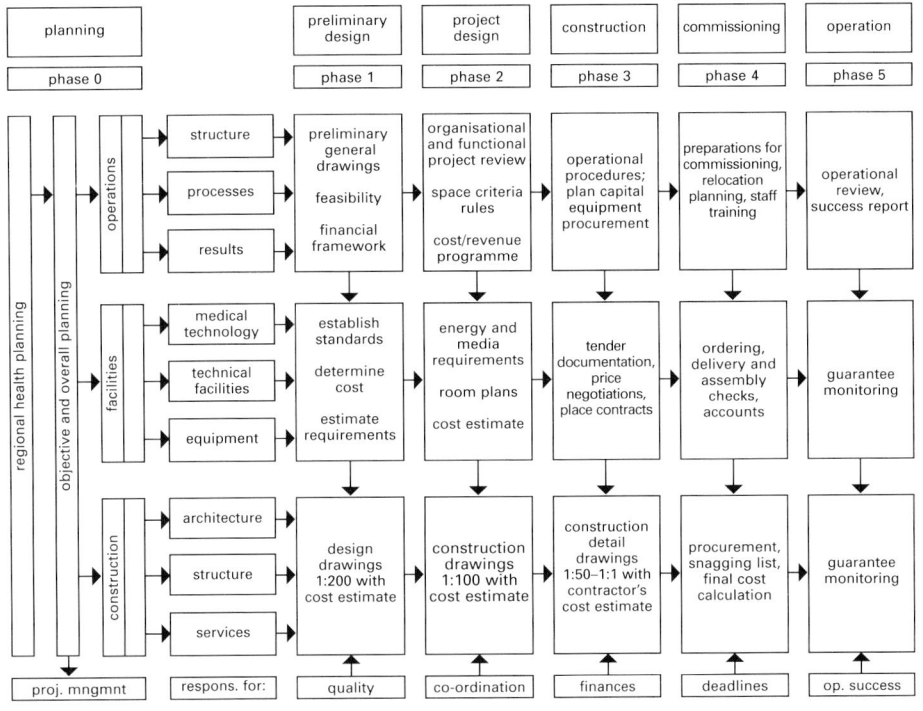

① **Planning areas and planning levels for hospital construction**

The costs involved in the construction of a hospital are extraordinarily high. Consequently, efficient project management and site planning is essential. The minimisation of project and staff costs must be made a priority.

Project planning must include intensive discussions with the client, doctors, architects, technical planners and hospital administrators during the preliminary stages to eliminate the risk of bad investment decisions and unfavourable growth in operating costs. The importance of co-operation between the architects, the administrators and technical experts cannot be overemphasised.

Following on from project planning, the building design stage will establish the structure and form of the hospital as well as the provision of services and engineering systems and details for fitting out with the required medical facilities and equipment.

General comments

Medical institutions provide treatment for and care of patients with a wide range of acute and chronic conditions. The objectives of the medical care may vary in nature and extent and so need to be identified accurately. Hospitals therefore differ in the number of specialisms they support and the size of the specialist departments and treatment facilities; in their provision of specialist curative medicine, preventive medicine (prophylactics) and aftercare (rehabilitation), examination (diagnostics) and treatment (therapy); in the intensity of care, the standard of accommodation and level of welfare, psychiatric care, training and research activity.

While early hospitals were consciously planned as medico-surgical institutions, nowadays a shift can be seen towards increasing humanisation of the facilities. Modern hospitals tend to be rather like hotels in nature; a residential atmosphere is considered to be more important than the uncompromising sanitary design of their predecessors. The length of stay of patients is getting progressively shorter, and there is a growing preference for rooms with one or two beds (particularly for private patients).

Demarcation

The general hospital is divided into operational areas of care provision, examination and treatment, supply and disposal, administration and technology. In addition, there are residential areas and possibly areas for teaching and research as well as support areas for service operations. All of these areas are precisely defined within the hospital. Opinions vary concerning the arrangement of the different areas but it is important to maintain the shortest practicable horizontal and vertical links while at the same time demarcating the individual departments as far as possible.

Types

Hospitals may be subdivided into the following categories: smallest (up to 50 beds), small (up to 150 beds), standard (up to 600 beds) and large hospitals. Very few of the smallest and large category hospitals have been built in recent times, the trend now seeming to be to create an even coverage of standard hospitals. In fact, modern health reforms have produced a noticeable reduction in the numbers of the smallest hospitals. The sponsors may be public, charitable or private or a mixture of these.

Hospitals are divided by function into general, specialist and university hospitals.

University hospitals

University hospitals with maximum provision are to be considered equal to the medical academies and some large general hospitals. They have at their disposal particularly extensive diagnostic and therapeutic facilities and systematically carry out research and teaching. Lecture theatres and demonstration rooms should be included in such a way that operations are not interrupted by the observers. Larger wards should be planned so as to accommodate both visitors and observers.

The amenities and special requirements of university hospitals frequently require a specially designed set of rooms.

Specialist hospitals

The number of specialist hospitals is growing fast because of the increasing focus on individual types of treatment or medical fields: casualty, rehabilitation, allergies, orthopaedics, gynaecology, etc. Also included in this category are special clinics dealing with, for example, cancers, skin problems, lung conditions, psychiatric disorders, and the like. In turn, these feed residential rehabilitation centres, nursing homes, special schools and old people's homes.

Bed requirements

The following are typical patient numbers per 1000 inhabitants per year in a typical developed country (here, Germany in 1996)

		acute hospitals	180.1
hospitals in total	183.7	special hospitals	3.6

At present there are typically the following numbers of beds per 1000 inhabitants:

		acute hospitals	6.9
hospitals in total	7.5	special hospitals	0.6

The average patient stay (in days) in 1996 was as follows:

		acute hospitals	11.4
hospitals in total	12.1	special hospitals	47.4

The number of beds available differs from one country to another. For example, in 1994/95, the total number of beds available in NHS hospitals in the UK was 4.8 per 1000 people; for acute beds the figure was 2.3 per 1000.

HOSPITALS
Construction Planning

Planning organisation in flux
Project management plays a central role in the timed planning and execution processes for a general hospital

① **Planning organisation today**

Building a hospital is a highly complex project and requires systematic planning to deliver the heterogeneity and flexibility required when such a large number of people are involved. The construction process must satisfy the needs of a number of functions: accommodation, research (in university hospitals), teaching, medical activity, storage and administration. A proper planning methodology enables this to be done by utilising a variety of room dimensions and installations.

The planning team, consisting of architects, doctors, nurses, specialist engineers and administrative staff, needs to co-operate closely throughout both the planning and construction stages because the design brief could, at any time before completion, be compromised by unforeseen developments which highlight inadequacies or errors.

It takes 8–10 years for a hospital construction project to move from initial planning discussions to commissioning. This is equivalent to the time required for the development of a whole new generation of medical technology, which puts the building at risk of being out of date when ready for use if conventional construction planning and construction methods are used.

To ensure the planning of the building is realistic, it is important to co-operate with related business and industrial concerns from an early stage. For example, because the size of equipment is constantly changing in parallel with advances in computer technology, it can have major consequences for the room arrangements. The size of individual departments (e.g. radiology, radiotherapy) has also changed considerably in recent years so consultation with the intended users is therefore important.

Health service reforms will have a substantial influence on hospital planning in the future as will the trend for individual medical specialisations to move out of general hospitals and set up separate clinical centres with their own administration (e.g. radiology, geriatric day clinics, ambulant treatment centres). In addition, ever greater influence is being exerted on planning by fire prevention and sound reduction requirements, as well as building regulations and the requirements of the related professional bodies.

Period of use
Building fabric, interior works and fitting out are subject to different periods of use.

As much as possible of the construction should be of frame type in order to allow flexibility in the fitting out.

Installations and interiors are, depending on the department and writing-off periods, changed about every 5–10 years, which can impose serious contraints on the spatial arrangements, particularly for large specialist equipment (e.g. linear accelerators). The installation and removal of such equipment must be taken into account during the planning stage such that the structure of the building does not have to be altered (which would, of course, have serious cost implications).

Economy
Possible changes in use, as well as the differing impact of wear, have an effect on construction planning and planning methodology. These criteria should be taken into account in economic assessments, together with short operational paths, appropriate work processes and general functional arrangements.

Construction costs
The building costs should conform to the relevant regulations and guidelines. Typical cost allocations are as follows:

- weather sealed structure — approx. 22%
- fitting out and services — approx. 40%
- installations and medical equipment — approx. 20%
- incidental costs — approx. 18%

In the planning of new buildings, about 70–100 m^2 must be allowed per sick bed, and roughly 200–280 m^3 per bed must be allowed for alterations (which includes all ancillary spaces such as environmental controls and storage spaces).

Design rules
Hospitals are often build in several phases or are added in stages to existing hospitals. Therefore, the design (circulation system, floor levels) and construction must be such as to allow a variety of extension possibilities.

Affinities
From the commencement of the first design activities, clarity must be achieved within the design team about the affinity between the individual operational spheres. The need for close co-operation between various hospital departments is facilitated by spatial proximity.

	nursing	operating	intensive care	sterilisation	maternity	emergency	laboratory	radiology	examination	X ray	out patients
nursing			□		□				□	◇	
operating			○	○	○	◇	◇				○
intensive care				◇		◇	◇			◇	
sterilisation											○
maternity						◇			□		
emergency								◇		○	○
laboratory									□		□
radiology											
examination										◇	◇
X ray											◇
out patients											

○ very good connection required   ◇ good connection sensible   □ connection desirable

② **Connections between areas**

Planning Conception

Location: The site should offer sufficient space for self-contained residential areas and hospital departments. It should be a quiet location with no possibility of future intrusive development not excluded by regulations on adjacent sites. No loss of amenity should result from fog, wind, dust, smoke, odours or insects. The land must not be contaminated and adequate open areas for later expansion must also be planned.

Orientation: The most suitable orientation for treatment and operating rooms is between north-west and north-east. For nursing ward façades, south to south-east is favourable: pleasant morning sun, minimal heat build-up, little requirement for sun shading, mild in the evenings. East and west facing rooms have comparatively deeper sun penetration, though less winter sun. The orientation of wards in hospitals with a short average stay is not so important. Some specialist disciplines might require rooms on the north side so that patients are not subjected to direct sunlight.

Concept: An existing hospital is to be expanded; the design includes four building phases. A large enclosed area containing a park will be created to allow windows to be opened without the need to tackle problems of noise protection.

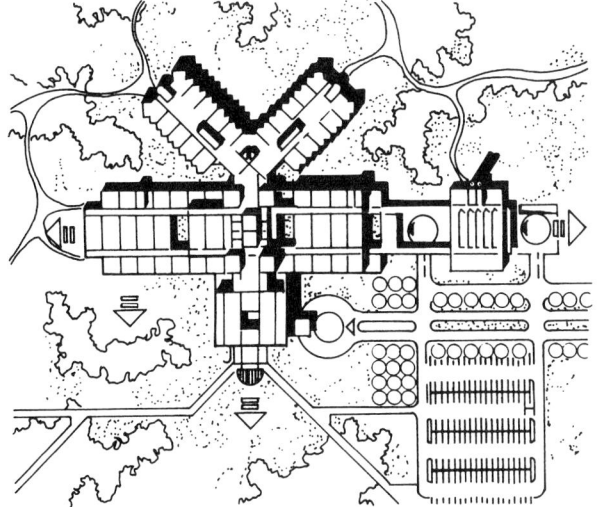

Proposal for a model clinic in co-operation with Hentrich Petschnigg & Partner and the German Hospitals Institute: the building can be expanded in three directions; pedestrian and emergency traffic are separated; supply and disposal separated from other hospital traffic

(1) **Model treatment clinic**

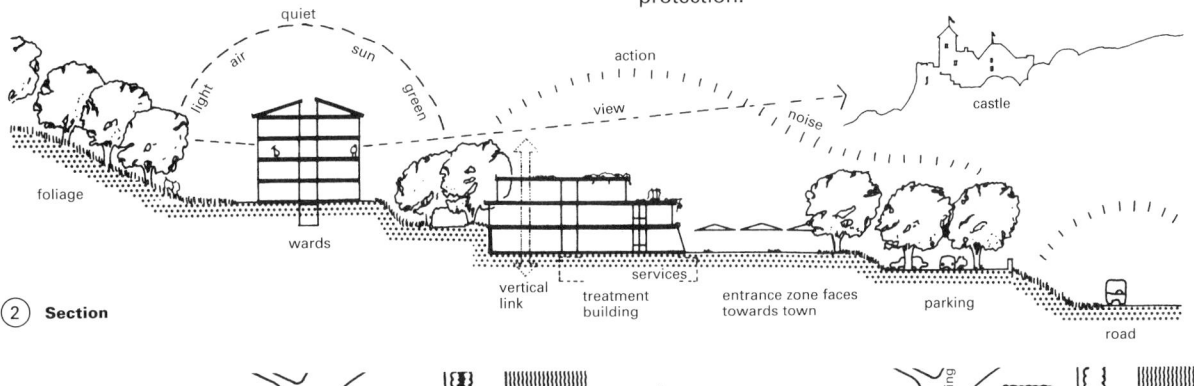

(2) **Section**

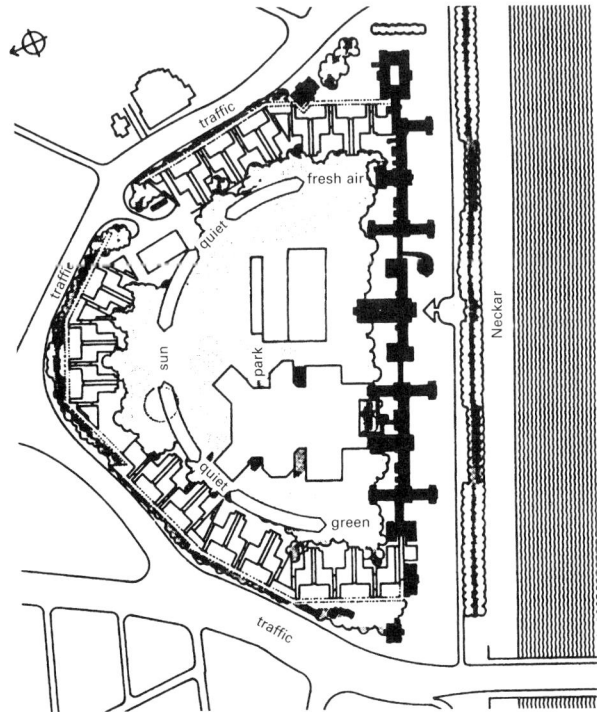

(3) **Rear of ward buildings along the periphery, blocking off traffic noise; all wards overlook the park**

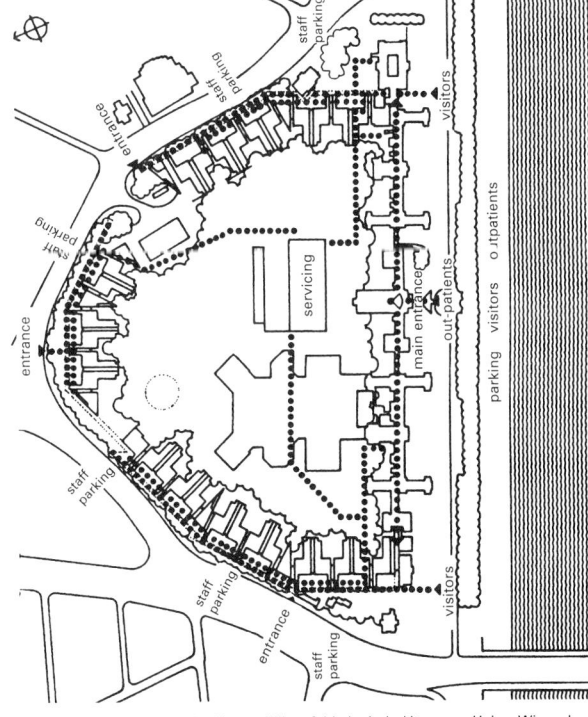

Architects: Eilingsfeld, Janisch, Utzmann, Heinz, Wissenbach

(4) **Free of car traffic; staff park at the rear of the ward buildings**

545

HOSPITALS

Forms of Building

The form of a building is strongly influenced by the choice of access and circulation routes. It is therefore necessary to decide early on whether to choose a spine form with branching sections (individual departments), or whether circulation will be radially outwards from a central core. Consideration must be given to future expansion: this is most easily carried out with an extended main tract. Self-contained circulation routes should be avoided as they make any extension work far more costly and disruptive.

The vertical arrangement within a hospital should be designed so that the functional areas – care, treatment, supply and disposal, access for bedridden patients, service yard, underground garage, stores, administration, medical services – can be connected and accessed most efficiently. An effective arrangement would be as follows:

top floor:	helipad, air-conditioning plant room, nursing school, laboratories
2nd/3rd floor:	wards
1st floor:	surgical area, central sterilisation, intensive care, maternity, children's hospital
ground floor:	entrance, radiology, medical services, ambulance, entrance for bedridden patients, emergency ward, information, administration, cafeteria
basement:	stores, physiotherapy, kitchen, heating and ventilation plant room, radio-therapy, linear accelerator
sub-basement:	underground garage, electricity supply

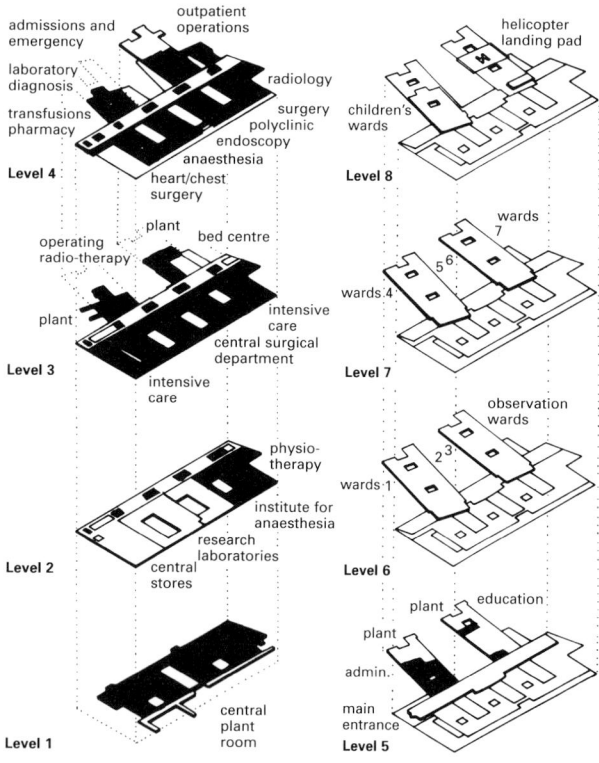

① **Functional areas/ vertical connections**   Architects: Schuster, Pechtold and Partners

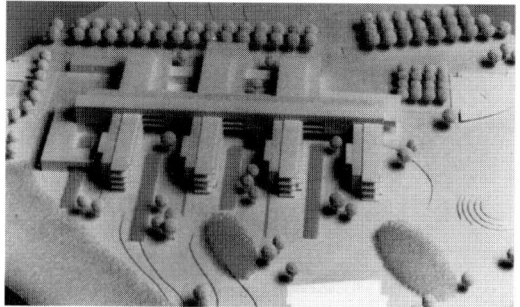

② **Hospital competition, Erfurt**   Architects: Prof. Rossmann and Partner

③   Architects: Prof. H. Nickl and Chris. Nicki-Weller

④   Architects: Hasek and Unterholzner

⑤   Architects: Thiede, Messhalter, Klösgen

⑥   Architects: Heinle, Wischer and Partner

⑦   Architects: Ondra and Heinzelmann

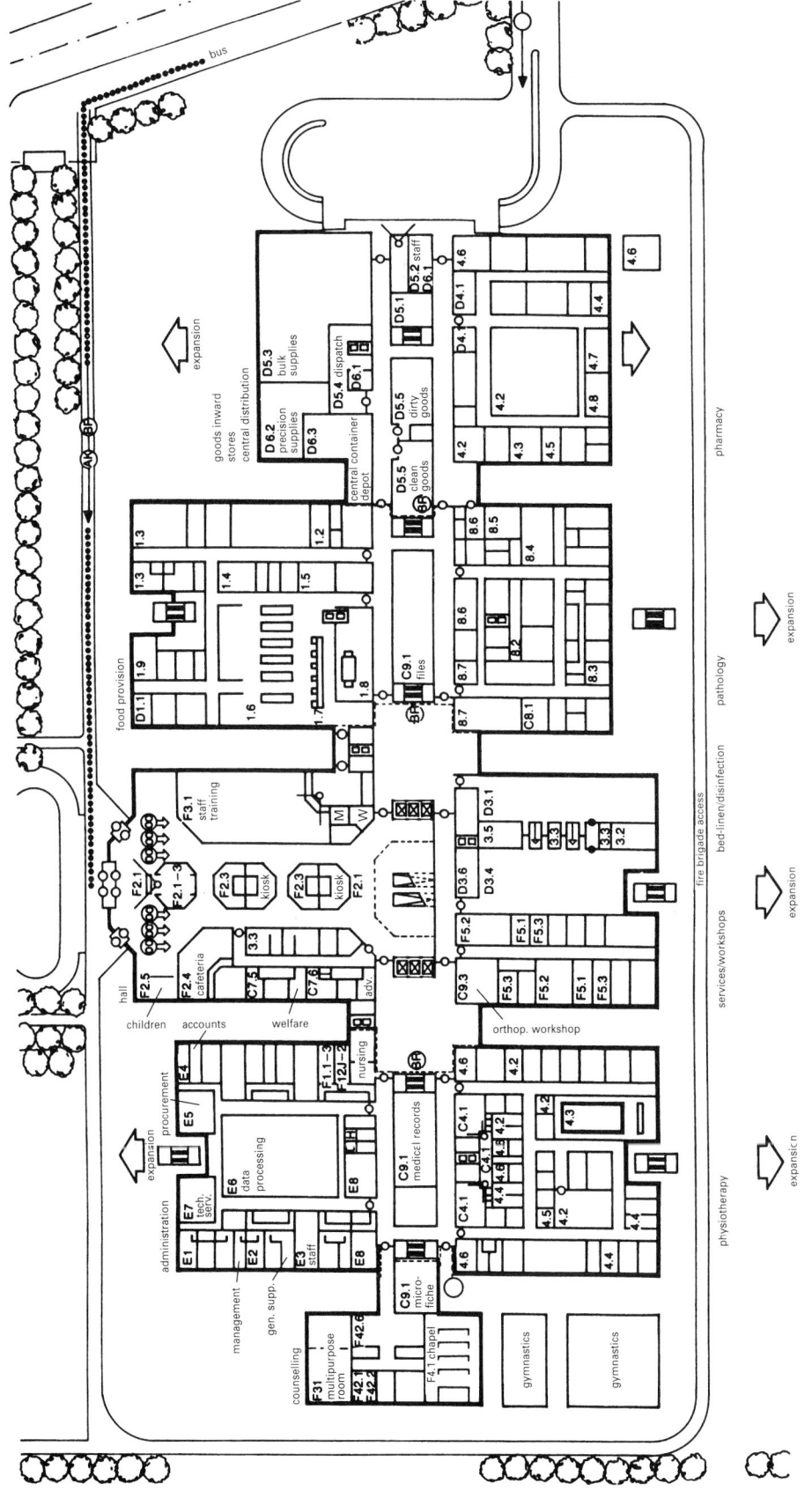

Forms of Building

Outpatients

The location of outpatient treatment rooms is of particular importance. Separation of the routes taken by outpatient emergencies and inpatients should be given consideration early in the planning process.

The number of patients concerned will depend on the overall size and technical facilities of the hospital. Where there is a consistently high number of outpatients a separate area can be created away from the other hospital operations. However, there must still be close links to the X-ray and surgical departments.

Outpatient operations are becoming increasingly important so larger waiting areas and more outpatient treatment rooms should be considered.

Design example

In a six-storey building, the vertical arrangement is designed with the nursing areas situated above the service, examination and treatment areas. On the ground floor are the accident and emergency, ambulance and X-ray departments; the surgical and intensive care departments occupy the first floor.

The constructional grid is 7.2×7.2 m.

The building is conceived in such a way that it can be erected in three building phases, resulting in a connection to an existing hospital. Vertical circulation is achieved via two lift blocks, each with four lifts and one staircase. In each corner of the building are emergency stair towers. Circulation on each floor centres on a main corridor (spine) 3.6 m wide. Note the use of different storey heights for treatment areas (4.5 m) and for nursing areas (3.4 m).

① **City Hospital Berlin-Reinickendorf: ground floor plan**   Architects: Mülberger, Schlenzig, Schneider

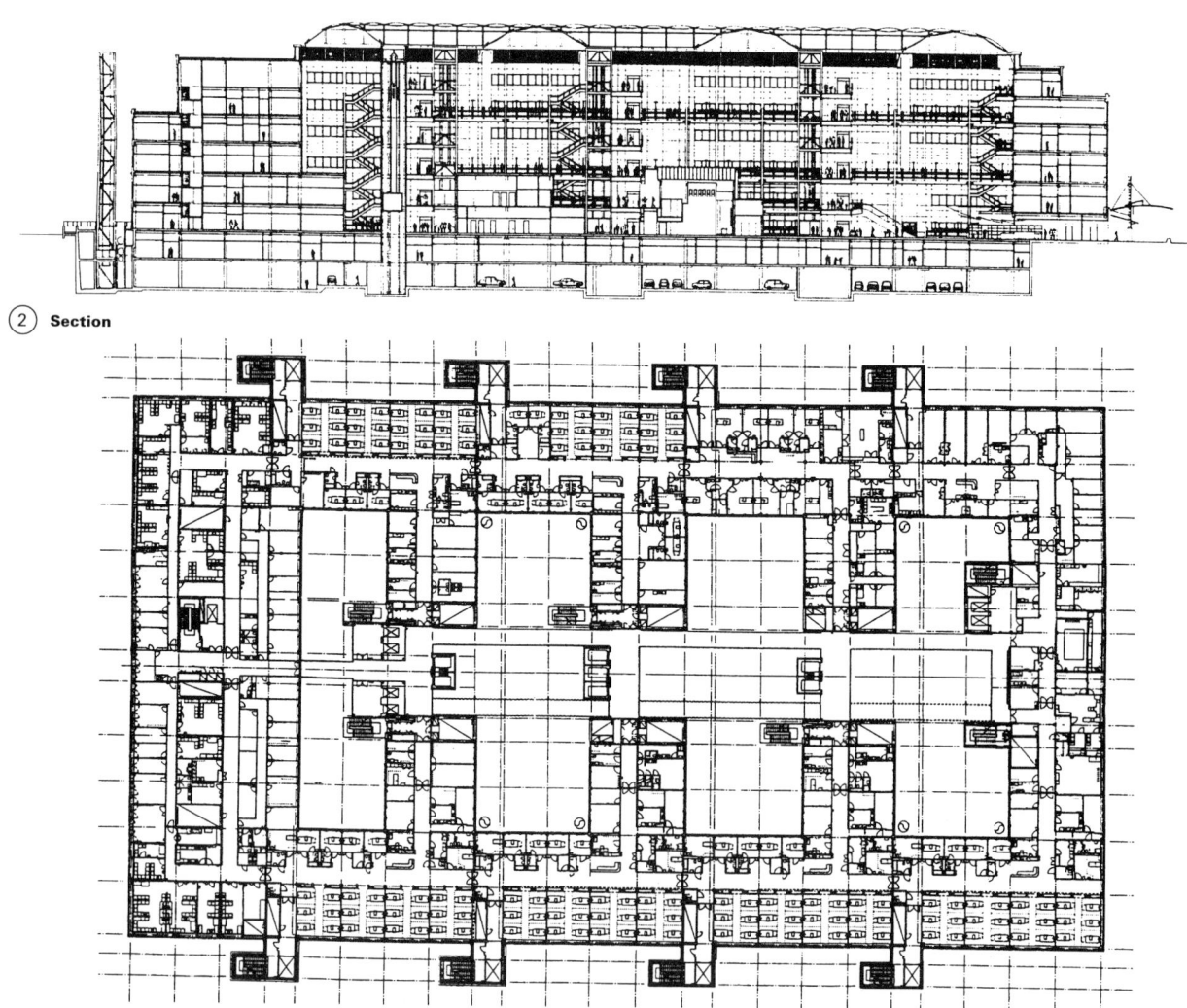

BM = basic module

(1) **Basle Cantonal Hospital: schematic ground floor plan**

HOSPITALS

Dimensional Co-ordination

Modules: Modular dimensional co-ordination is the best starting point for meeting strategic design requirements. Reference systems, basic modules and multiple modules for construction details, layout and dimensions of building parts are all to be considered. For hospital construction the preferred module dimensions 12M = 1.20m are recommended, or 6M or 3M if the increments are too numerous. In this system all the building components are co-ordinated with each other. The supporting structure can be drawn in by producing a horizontal and vertical basic grid.

An agreement on dimensions has considerable consequences for building construction, and the building systems available on the market must conform to this dimensional co-ordination. It is therefore helpful to prescribe a normal standard dimension in planning. The benefits of dimensional co-ordination are shorter construction periods and easier replacement of interior fittings, with less disruption of service. The schematic ground floor plan of the Cantonal Hospital for the City of Basle shows the structural grid, support dimensions, façade position and layout and dimensions of core zones and shafts.

Use of grids: The Chelsea and Westminster Hospital in London is one of the largest hospitals in Europe and demonstrates how a hospital of this size can be organised and planned around a simple grid. The large internal courtyards allow natural lighting into most of the rooms on all floors. The design grid, on which all subsequent divisions are based, measures about 7.2 × 2.2m. Both the examination rooms and wards (with centres at 3.6m) are designed to comply. The necessary escape stairs are situated in the internal courtyards or on the outside of the building.

(2) **Section**

(3) **Chelsea and Westminster Hospital, London: third floor**

Architect: Sheppard Robson

548

Dimensional Co-ordination

functional areas
intensive care special care normal care
functional area 1 – care
surgery recovery area rehabilitation physiotherapy X-ray diagnosis NMR diagnosis radiotherapy clinico-chemical laboratory clinico-physical laboratory clinico-neurophysical laboratory central reception and treatment delivery dialysis specialist anaesthesia department specialist eye department specialist surgical department specialist gynaecology department specialist obstetrics department specialist ENT department specialist internal medicine department specialist paediatric department specialist neurosurgery department specialist neurology department specialist psychiatry department specialist X-ray area department specialist urology department
functional area 2 – examination/treatment
functional area 3 – research
functional area 4 – pathology
functional area 5 – teaching/training
library files
functional area 6 – scientific information
emergency services blood bank
functional area 7 – special interdisciplinary facilities
central administration patient reception
functional area 8 – administration/management
staff changing room canteen shop other patient facilities
functional area 9 – housekeeping
food provision central store central sterilisation pharmacy laundry bed cleaning waste disposal transport service
functional area 10 – supply/disposal
foyer/entrance cleaning service maintenance
functional area 11 – other functions

(1) **Possible room schedule for a large hospital covering all specialist areas**

Structural grid
The constructional grid must provide a precise guide as well as allowing for differentiation of areas for the main functions, support functions and vehicular traffic.

A comparison of the individual operational areas and the rooms they require should result in a structural grid which is suitable for all functions.

The various operations centres can be planned most appropriately with a column grid spacing of 7.20m or 7.80m. Smaller construction grids are problematic because large rooms (e.g. operating theatres) which must be free from internal columns are more difficult to accommodate.

Room schedule
A room schedule showing the overall classifications and requirements of the hospital must be drawn up in order to generate an appropriate structural grid and ground plan. Depending on the type of hospital, this will not detail all of the possibilities but will cover only the key functional rooms. The specifics of the room schedule must be discussed with the users so it is therefore sensible to set up a detailed room-by-room specification procedure. Specialist areas within a hospital can affect the nature and size of other individual operations centres and close co-operation between planners and users will prevent possible problems arising later.

An overview of the size of the individual operations centres can be obtained using reference area values. However, these are only recommendations and depend on the orientation and services of the actual project in question.

areas for the overall hospital, including functional area for:	
supply/disposal	40 – 80 m² PA/planned bed-care area
nursing area	19 – 25 m² PA/planned bed
intensive therapy	30 – 40 m² PA/bed
surgical area	130 – 160 m² PA/surgical unit
rehabilitation	19 – 22 m² PA/treatment place
physiotherapy	68 – 75 m² PA/treatment place
X-ray	60 – 70 m² PA/diagnosis room
radiotherapy	300 – 350 m² PA/equipment
recovery area	25 – 30 m² PA/recovery bed
NMR diagnosis	100 – 150 m² PA/diagnosis room
clinical physiology	80 – 100 m² PA/diagnosis room
clinical neurophysiology	78 – 100 m² PA/diagnosis room
central reception	140 – 160 m² PA/examination/treatment room
delivery area	85 – 100 m² PA/delivery room
dialysis	70 – 80 m² PA/dialysis bed
specialist departments	55 – 75 m² PA/examination/treatment room
(PA = productive area)	

(2) **Guideline areas for a standard hospital**

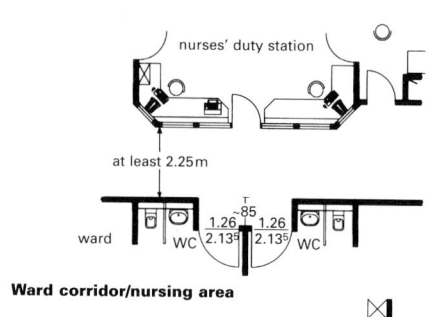

① **Ward corridor/nursing area**

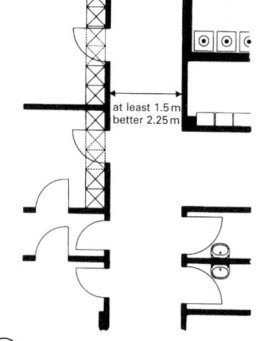

② **Main corridor (spine)**

③ **Medical services corridor**

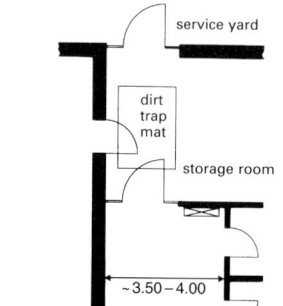

④ **Service corridor, deliveries, storage areas**

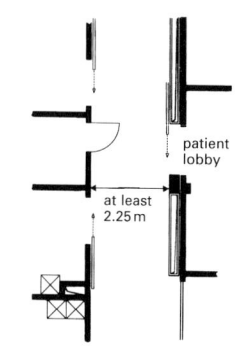

⑤ **Working corridor, surgical area**

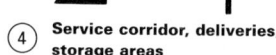

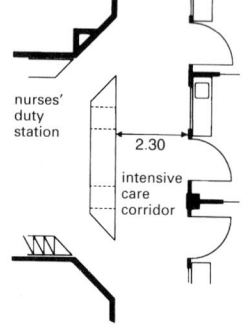

⑥ **Ward corridor, intensive care**

⑦ **Lift lobby**

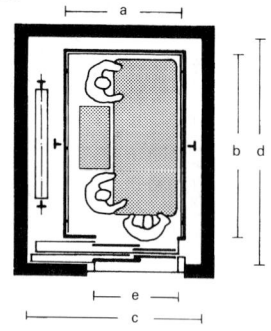

⑧ **Bed lift**

⑨ **Dimensions of bed lifts** → ⑧

capacity (kg)	1600	2000	2500
shaft width c	2400	2400	2700
shaft depth d	3000	3000	3300
car width a	1400	1500	1800
car depth b	2400	2700	2700
car door e	1300	1300	1300
car height	2300	2300	2300
car door height	2100	2100	2100
capacity (passengers)	21	26	33

Corridors → ① – ⑥

Corridors must be designed for the maximum expected circulation flow. Generally, access corridors must be at least 1.50m wide. Corridors in which patients will be transported on trolleys should have a minimum effective width of 2.25m. The suspended ceiling in corridors may be installed up to 2.40m. Windows for lighting and ventilation should not be further than 25m apart. The effective width of the corridors must not be constricted by projections, columns or other building elements. Smoke doors must be installed in ward corridors in accordance with local regulations.

Doors

When designing doors the hygiene requirements should be considered. The surface coating must withstand the long-term action of cleaning agents and disinfectants, and they must be designed to prevent the transmission of sound, odours and draughts. Doors must meet the same standard of noise insulation as the walls surrounding them. A double-skinned door leaf construction must meet a recommended minimum sound reduction requirement of 25 dB. The clear height of doors depends on their type and function:

normal doors	2.10–2.20m
vehicle entrances, oversized doors	2.50m
transport entrances	2.70–2.80m
minimum height on approach roads	3.50m

Stairs

For safety reasons stairs must be designed in such a way that if necessary they can accommodate all of the vertical circulation. The relevant national safety and building regulations will, of course, apply. Stairs must have handrails on both sides without projecting tips. Winding staircases cannot be included as part of the regulatory staircase provision. The effective width of the stairs and landings in essential staircases must be a minimum of 1.50 m and should not exceed 2.50 m. Doors must not constrict the useful width of the landings and, in accordance with hospital regulations, doors to the staircases must open in the direction of escape.

Step heights of 170 mm are permissible and the minimum required tread depth is 280 mm. It is better to have a rise/tread ratio of 150:300 mm.

Lifts → ⑧ ⑨

Lifts transport people, medicines, laundry, meals and hospital beds between floors, and for hygiene and aesthetic reasons separate lifts must be provided for some of these. In buildings in which care, examination or treatment areas are accommodated on upper floors, at least two lifts suitable for transporting beds must be provided. The elevator cars of these lifts must be of a size that allows adequate room for a bed and two accompanying people; the internal surfaces must be smooth, washable and easy to disinfect; the floor must be non-slip. Lift shafts must be fire-resistant.

One multipurpose lift should be provided per 100 beds, with a minimum of two for smaller hospitals. In addition there should be a minimum of two smaller lifts for portable equipment, staff and visitors:

clear dimensions of lift car:	0.90 × 1.20 m
clear dimensions of shaft:	1.25 × 1.50 m

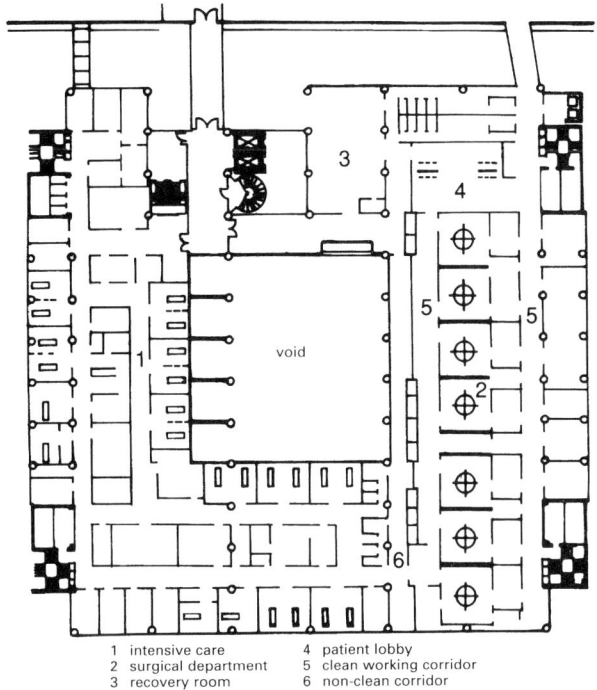

1 intensive care   4 patient lobby
2 surgical department   5 clean working corridor
3 recovery room   6 non-clean corridor

① **Surgical operations centre, Katharinen Hospital, Stuttgart: second floor**   Architects: Heinle, Wischer and Partners.

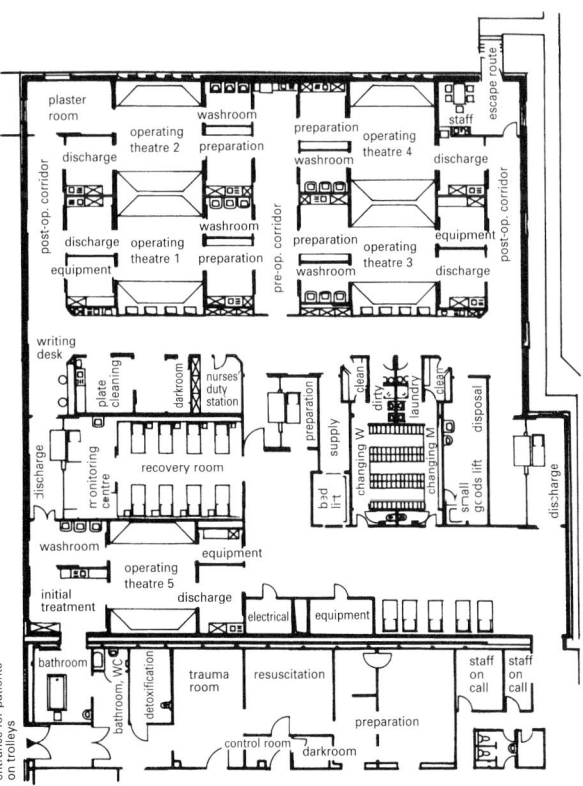

② **Ground plan of central surgical area**   Architects: Heinle, Wischer and Partners

Centralisation: advantages and disadvantages
In the past, surgical operations centres tended to be planned within the hospital as a centrally located examination and treatment unit for use by various specialist departments. The reasons for this were better utilisation of space, equipment and staff, better patient provision through centralised service functions under the management of specialists, and hygiene considerations. The possible disadvantages of particularly large centralised surgical departments are high organisational costs and an increased risk of infection because of the large numbers of people brought together. A further disadvantage is the combination of septic and aseptic operations in one centre. A plan for septic and aseptic surgical units must be discussed with surgeons and hygienists. Current designs for large hospitals have separate units for septic and aseptic operations as a rule. External surgical units can generally better meet the requirements. When deciding the location of the surgical department, service relationships with other operations centres must be checked. These include reception, the emergency service, casualty surgery, obstetrics, endoscopy and specialist clinics.

Function and layout
In the surgical department, treatment is given to the patients whose conditions have been diagnosed but cannot be cured solely with medication. It should be close to the intensive care department, the recovery room and the central sterilisation area because there is extensive interaction between these departments and so easy access must be assured. The hygiene precautions require the surgical unit to be isolated from the rest of the hospital operations. This is achieved by a demarcation system using lobbies.

Surgical departments are best located centrally in the core area of the hospital where they are easy to reach. The reception area for emergency cases (casualties) must be as close as possible to the surgical area since such patients often need to be moved into surgery immediately.

Organisation of the surgery department
Every surgical department requires the following rooms:

operating theatre	40–48 m²
entry room	15–20 m²
exit room	15–20 m²
washroom	12–15 m²
equipment room	10–15 m²

In new projects, it is permissible for two operating theatres to share the same exit room. Essential to surgical departments are a staff lobby, patient lobby, clean work corridor, anaesthetic workroom, waste lobby, supply lobby, standing area for two operating trolleys and, nearby, the recovery room.

The patient demarcation lobbies are also used for bed-to-bed transfer, preparation of operating tables and ward beds, and theatre stores. An appropriate size is around 35 m² and fittings should inlude wash-basins and an electric conveyor for bed-to-bed transfer.

→ ① Ideal floor plan of an external surgical area with a direct link to the main building. The corridor system is separated into staff corridors with links to the functional rooms and pre-operative and post-operative patient corridors. A requirement when planning a new building is that it must be expandable on at least one side.

→ ② Floor plan of the central operating area at the Northern Hospital Centre, Dortmund, with five operating theatres and additional rooms. Pre-operative and post-operative patients are separated and the staff circulate via the area accommodating non-anaesthetised patients area.

551

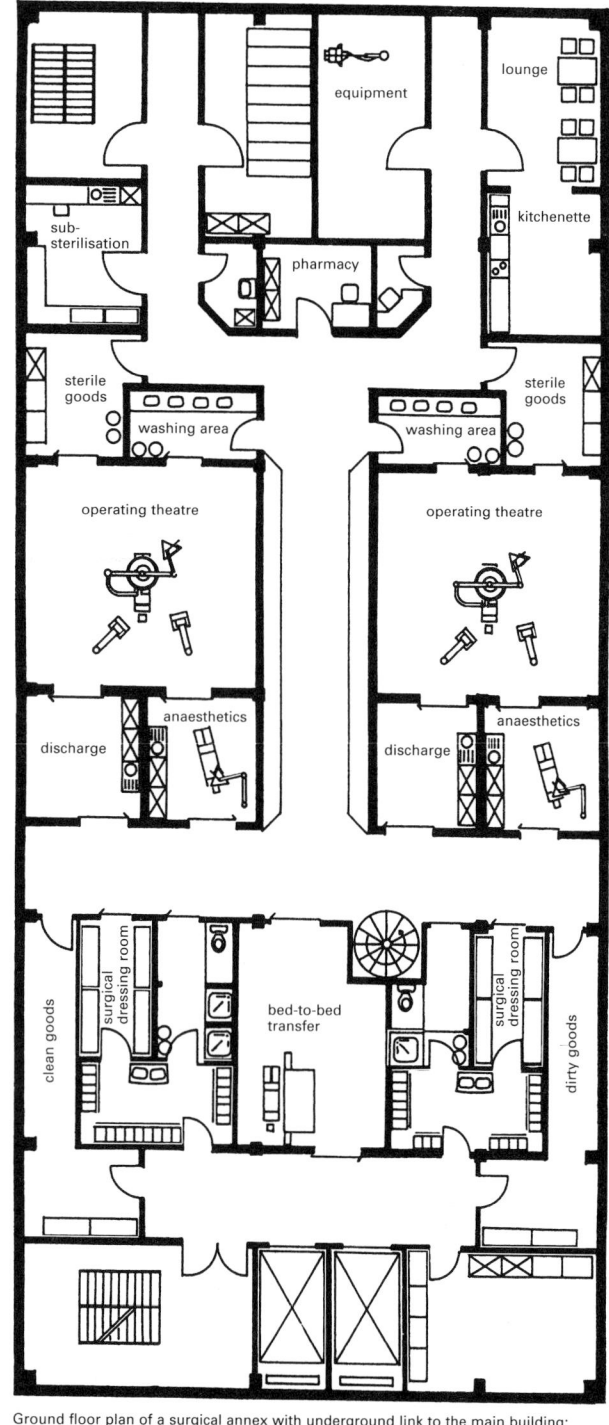

Ground floor plan of a surgical annex with underground link to the main building; recovery room one floor below

(1) **Main surgical rooms**   Architects: Köhler/Müller

A number of necessary supply and workrooms adjoin the operating theatre directly. The operating theatre should be designed to be as square as possible to allow working whatever direction the operating table is turned in. A suitable size would be 6.50 × 6.50 m, with a clear height of 3.00 m and an extra height allowance of roughly 0.70 m for air conditioning and other services. Operating theatres should be fitted out as uniformly as possible, in order to offer maximum flexibility, and centre on a transportable operating table system which is mounted on a fixed base in the middle of the room. Natural lighting in the operating theatre is psychologically advantageous but often cannot be provided because of the layout. Where it is, there must be the means to shut out the light completely (e.g. eye operations are carried out in very dark rooms). Nowadays service connections and technical supply facilities are generally supplied via suspended anaesthesia equipment. Otherwise, connections for vacuum lines, nitrous oxide and emergency power must be placed at least 1.20 m above floor level.

It is important to isolate the highly sterile areas to which sterile instruments are supplied. Division of the operating theatres into septic and aseptic zones is a matter of medical controversy, but is a sensible precaution. Floors and walls must be smooth throughout and easily washed; decorative or structural projections should be avoided.

Anaesthetics room
The anaesthetics room should be approximately 3.80 × 3.80 m in size and have electric sliding doors into the operating theatre (clear width 1.40 m). These doors must have windows to give a visual link with the operating theatre. The room should be equipped with a refrigerator, draining sink (sluice), rinsing line, cupboards for cannulas, connections for anaesthesia equipment and emergency power.

Anaesthetic discharge room
This is set out identically to the anaesthetics room. The door to the working corridor should be designed as a swing door with a clear width of 1.25 m.

Washroom
Division into clean and non-clean washrooms is ideal, but from a hygiene point of view a single large room is adequate. The minimum width of the room should be 1.80 m. For each operating theatre there should be three non-splash wash-basins with foot controls. Doors into the operating theatre must have an inspection window and, if they are electrical, be opened by foot controls. Swing doors can be used if cost saving is a priority.

Sterile goods room
The size of this room is more flexible but there must be sufficient shelf and cupboard space and it must be accessed directly from the operating theatre. One room of roughly 10 m^2 is required per operating theatre.

Equipment room
Although direct access to the operating theatre is preferable, it is not always feasible; where direct access cannot be provided, the equipment room must be located as close as possible to the theatre in order to reduce waiting times. A room size of approximately 20 m^2 should be allowed.

Substerilisation room
This room may or may not be connected directly to the operating theatre's sterile area. It contains an non-clean area for non-sterile material and a clean area for prepared sterile items. It should be equipped with a sink, storage surface, work surface and steam sterilisers. Linking a substerilisation room to several operating theatres causes hygiene problems and so should be avoided. Note that surgical instruments are prepared in the central sterilising unit, which lies outside the surgical area.

Plaster room
For hygiene reasons this is not located in the surgical zone but in the outpatient area. In emergencies the patient must be channelled through lobbies in order to get to the operating theatre.

Routeing
Different activities should be separated in order to reduce the transmission of germs through contact. The single corridor system, in which the pre-operative and post-operative patients, pre-operative and post-operative staff, clean and non-clean goods use a single working corridor without segregation, is no longer standard. It is better to have dual corridor systems in which patients and staff or patients and non-clean materials are separated. The best combination of the individual requirements has not been clarified and they are therefore dealt with individually. One effective strategy is to separate the flow of patients from the working areas used by the surgical staff.

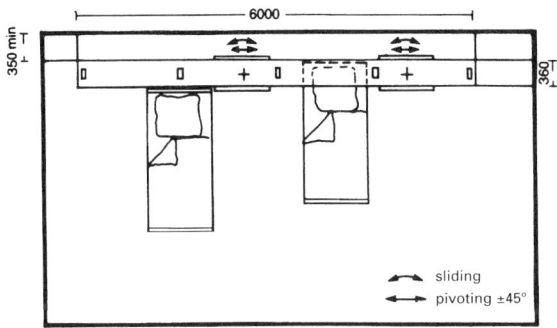

1 equipment trolley (e.g. for infusion)
2 equipment trolley (e.g. for respiration, monitoring, suction, etc.)
3 indirect lighting
4 service supply – high voltage, low voltage, gas

① **Ceiling service system (by Dräger)**

sliding
pivoting ±45°

② **Floor plan** → ①

→ ① Beds must not be too close together in the recovery room and allow enough space for the anaesthetist and his equipment to reach at least three sides. Awkward additional equipment, such as sublimation stands, also requires adequate space for ease of movement. The patient is supplied via mobile service bridges with connections for a vacuum line, nitrous oxide, oxygen, power and lighting. All the necessary equipment can be accommodated in a suspended equipment trolley.

The route between the recovery room, the operating theatre and the ward should contain several doors and be as short as possible so the anaesthetist can get to the patients quickly in case of emergency.

sterile goods store
sterile goods store
entry lobby
wash-room
exit lobby
corridor

③ **Arrangement of an operating theatre with adjacent rooms**   Architects: U + A Weicken

Recovery room requirements

The recovery room must accommodate the post-operative patients from more than one operating theatre. The number of beds required is calculated as 1.5 times the number of operating theatres. Adjoining is a small sluice room with drainage sinks. A nurse's monitoring position must be provided from which all the beds can be seen. Designs should allow in daylight to help the patients to orientate themselves.

Clean room technology and air conditioning

The air conditioning system is a vital part of clean room technology. A typical example uses a low-turbulence displacement with an even speed of moving air (0.45 m/sec) to produce a laminar flow, ahead of which any germs and particles released are propelled out of the room. An additional directed jet with the flow directed towards the operating area allows air turbulence to be minimised. The combination of contaminated air and fresh air (clean room air) can also then largely be avoided. To maintain the hygiene of the operating equipment an area of approximately 3.00×3.00 m should be allowed.

The air conditioning system also reduces the level of airborne germs by filtering, diluting and compressing the air before introducing the appropriately prepared air in the quantity required. For example, 15–20 air changes per hour are required to ensure adequate decontamination of the air between operations.

To create a zone which is as germ/particle-free as possible within the operating theatre, there must be no uncontrolled inward air flow from neighbouring rooms. This can be achieved by hermetic sealing of the operating theatre (all joints sealed as far as possible during construction) and/or by protective pressurising (i.e. highest pressure in the operating theatre, followed by the anaesthesia rooms, and the lowest pressure in the auxiliary rooms, thus creating a pressure gradient which moves air outwards from the theatre to the areas requiring less protection). Operating theatre windows must therefore be equipped with sealable ventilation grills. Specific regulations determine the flow of air between the rooms in the surgical area.

Auxiliary functions

The rooms for auxiliary functions do not need to be in the immediate area of the operating theatre. Separation by a corridor which is not intended for patient use is advisable.

Nurses' lounge

The dimensions of this room depend on the size of the surgical department. It should be assumed that there are eight members of staff per surgical team (doctors, theatre nurses, anaesthesia nurses). In the case of surgical units with more than two operating theatres, it is appropriate to separate smokers from non-smokers. The lounge must offer sufficient seating, cupboards and a sink.

Nurses' workstations

These should be located centrally and have large glass screens to allow the working corridor to be viewed. In addition to a desk they must have cupboards and walls on which organisational schedule planners can be mounted.

Dictation room

No larger than 5 m² in size, such rooms are where the doctors prepare reports following an operation. They are not absolutely necessary.

Pharmacy

A 20 m² pharmacy can supply a combination of anaesthetics and surgical medication and other materials, particularly if a space-saving rotating shelving system is installed.

Cleaning room

A size of 5 m² is sufficient for cleaning rooms. They should be close to the operating theatre since cleaning and disinfection are carried out after each operation.

Standing area for clean beds

Close to the patient demarcation lobby there should be sufficient space to stand beds which have been cleaned and prepared. The requirement is for one additional clean bed for each operating table.

WCs

For hygiene reasons, toilets should be located only within the lobbies and not in the surgical area.

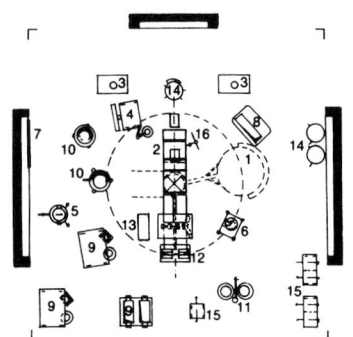

1 overhead operating lamp
2 operating table with fixed base
3 wall or ceiling pendulum
4 anaesthesia equipment
5 dish stand with heater
6 electric suction pump
7 X-ray display box
8 anaesthesia table
9 instrument table
10 waste bin, used instrument container
11 dish stand without heater
12 suturing materials table
13 operating steps
14 swivel stool for surgeon
15 drum stand
16 infusion stand

(1) **General arrangement of a surgical operating theatre**

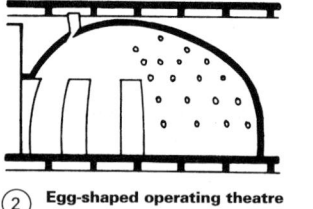

(2) **Egg-shaped operating theatre with built-in spotlights which can be switched on according to choice**

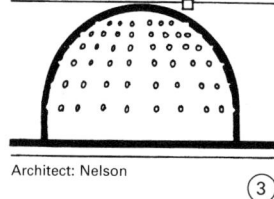

Architect: Nelson

(3)

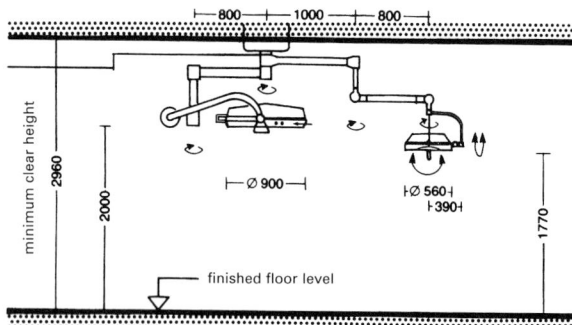

(4) **Surgical pendant lamp with satellite**

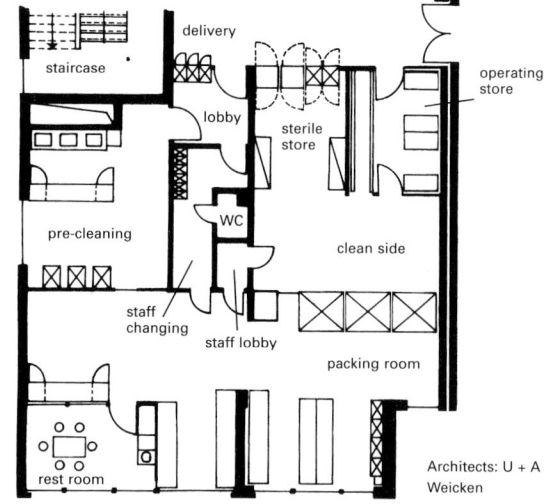

Architects: U + A Weicken

(5) **Central sterilisation unit, St Elisabeth, Halle/S**

SURGERY SAFETY REQUIREMENTS

The operating theatre should be connected to the anaesthetics room, discharge room, a wash room and sterile materials room via electric sliding doors, fitted on the outer side of the theatre so as not to constrict the space within. The opening mechanisms must be operated by foot switches for hygiene reasons. In the rooms for auxiliary functions, swing doors with a clear width of 1.00–1.25 m are sufficient.

It must be assumed that main anaesthetics rooms contain explosive mixtures of gases (vapours, oxygen or nitrous oxide). These may also pass into surgical areas, preparation rooms and plaster rooms. To counteract this accumulation of anaesthetic gases in the air, electrical and electro-medical connections are to be placed a minimum of 1.20 m above floor level. Explosion protection measures also relate to the avoidance of electrostatic charges.

Protective measures in the main anaesthetics rooms are:
- avoid materials which produce large electrostatic charges when rubbed or separated (e.g. plastic cloth)
- use conductive materials (e.g. conductive rubber)
- equalise charges through conducting floor
- maintain constant humidity between 60 and 65%

A back-up power supply is required for surgical equipment so that, in the event of a power cut, the operation can be continued and completed. Among other things, the following must continue to be operable:
- at least one operating lamp at each operating table, with a supply which will last for at least three hours
- equipment for maintaining vital bodily functions (e.g. for respiration, anaesthesia and resuscitation)

Specific regulations apply to operating rooms in which X-ray equipment is in operation. They define the lead thicknesses required in order to weaken the radiation sufficiently for maximum exposure not to be exceeded. Even the doors must have lead lining (e.g. 1 mm)

National standards provide conversion factors for usual building materials such as steel, concrete and masonry.

Rooms for storage of anaesthetic agents must be fire-resistant and not connected to operating theatres, delivery rooms or anaesthetics rooms.

Lighting
Lighting in the operating area must be adjustable in order to provide light at different angles according to the position of the surgical incision. The most frequently used lighting system is the mobile ceiling-pendant operating light. It consists of a main ceiling light which rotates and pivots and is generally equipped with an additional light on a secondary arm. The main light is made up of a large number of smaller lights in order to avoid heavy shadows. Occasionally nowadays egg-shaped operating theatres are being planned with integrated ceiling spotlights.

Guidelines for lighting in hospitals recommend the nominal lighting strength for operating theatres as 1000 lux and 500 lux for auxiliary surgical rooms.

Central sterilisation → (5)
This is where all hospital instruments are prepared. The majority of instruments are used by the surgical department (40%), surgical intensive and internal intensive care (15% each). For this reason central sterilisation should be installed close to these specialist areas. It is recommended that the sterilisation area be situated in areas with relatively low volumes of traffic (both people and materials).

The number of sterilisers is dependent on the size of the hospital and surgical department, and can occupy an area of approximately 40–120 m².

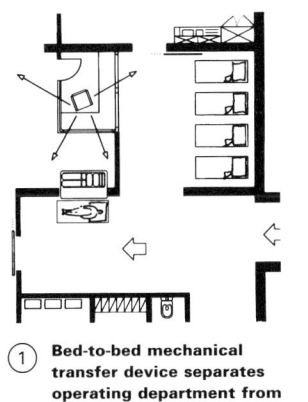

① **Bed-to-bed mechanical transfer device separates operating department from entrance area (by Maquet)**

② **Example of an enclosed patient transfer unit**

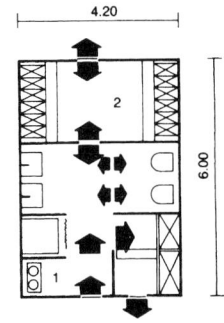

③ **Staff lobby**

④ **Staff lobby**

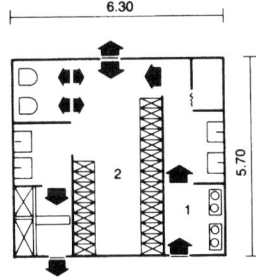

⑤ **Staff lobby**

⑥ **Staff and visitor lobby**

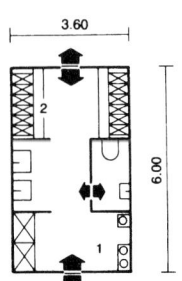

⑦ **Staff and visitor lobby**

⑧ **Staff and visitor lobby**

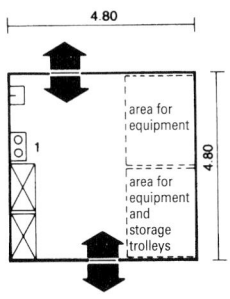

⑨ **Supplies lobby**

⑩ **Disposals lobby**

A 'demarcation area' is formed by the intermediate zone ('lobby') between the care area and the examination/treatment area.

Demarcation may be achieved in different ways depending on the required function and specialist area: patient lobby, staff lobby, combined staff and visitor lobby, supply and disposal lobby, gown lobby, lobbies before intensive care rooms. In addition, the lobbies differ according to their hygiene function (contact control, air control) and the constructional requirement (single-lobby control, multi-lobby control, air conditioned and non-air conditioned control).

The patient who is to undergo surgery is taken into the 'patient lobby' where he/she is placed on the operating table with the aid of a mechanical bed-to-bed transfer device.

Generally, regulations require separation into clean and non-clean areas. The boundary may be marked by a threshold which cannot be crossed. Direct access routes must be kept clear for emergencies.

Medical and nursing personnel pass through the 'staff lobby' into separate male and female treatment rooms. The demarcated operations centre is reached first via an non-clean outer room in which people wash and change and then via the clean inner room where surgical clothing is provided. On leaving the centre the used surgical clothing is left in the non-clean room and the demarcation lobby is exited via the outer room.

Shared 'staff and visitor lobbies' should be located in front of operations centres, from which infections requiring preferential treatment may emanate (isolation and intensive wards). Here single-chamber systems are sufficient, these taking up less space.

Highly sterile materials, equipment and laundry are channelled into the operations centre via 'supply and disposal lobbies'. These rooms frequently serve also as storage rooms.

The demarcation areas do not necessarily have to be rooms. They may instead be formed by segregating traffic areas. However, there must still be sufficient space in the operations centre for storage of sterile goods or waste.

The disposal demarcation lobby should not be overlooked because waste storage within the operations centre can be a source of hygiene risks.

'Gown demarcation lobbies' are found at the transition between areas with differing hygiene requirements (e.g. between the non-clean and clean sides of bed preparation) and before rooms which are to be protected from infection or from which infection may emanate (e.g. isolation wards).

Demarcation lobbies before intensive care rooms are required before approximately 30% of the operations centres and are to be agreed with the hospital hygienists. These lobby areas must contain a workstation for continual monitoring of the most seriously ill patients and also allow ample space for nursing work and disinfection of equipment.

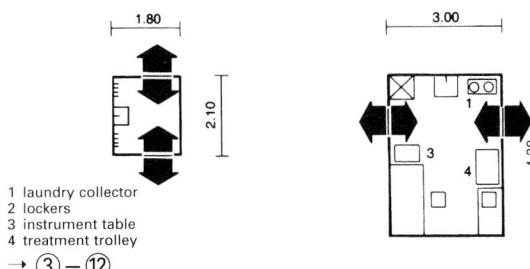

1 laundry collector
2 lockers
3 instrument table
4 treatment trolley

→ ③ – ⑫

⑪ **Gown lobby**

⑫ **Lobby before intensive care**

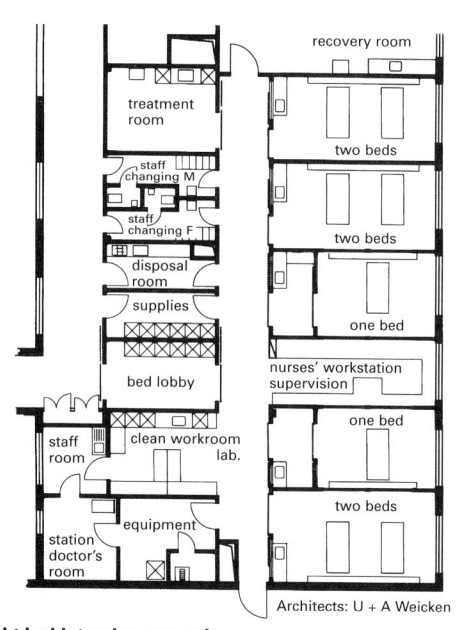

① **Eight-bed intensive care unit**

Architects: U + A Weicken

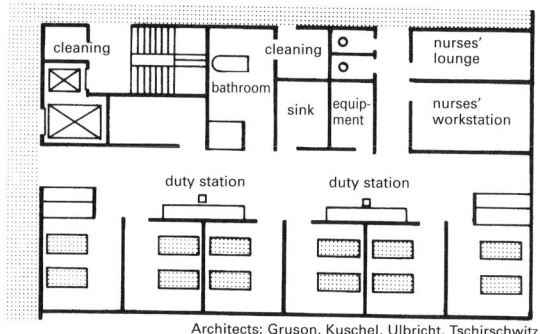

② **Intensive care group with 12 beds: St Vinzenzstift Hospital, Hanover**

Architects: Gruson, Kuschel, Ulbricht, Tschirschwitz

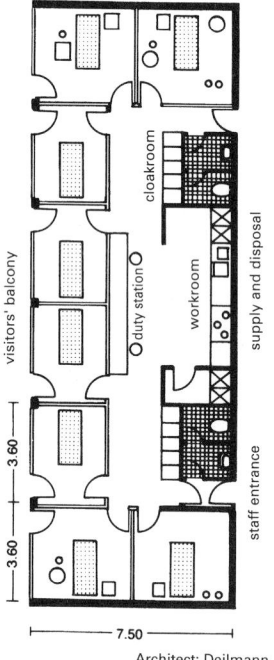

Architect: Deilmann

③ **Eight-bed intensive care subgroup; glazed individual rooms**

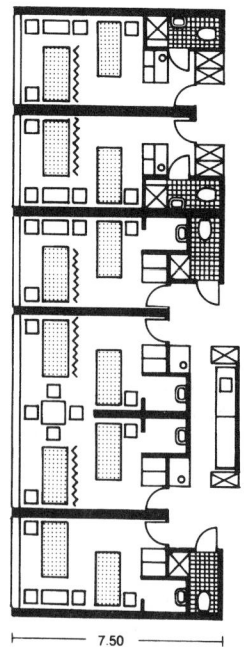

Architect: Deilmann

④ **Subgroup formed by combination of four two-bed rooms with WC/shower rooms and nurses' workstation**

HOSPITALS

Intensive Care Area

The task of intensive care is to prevent life-threatening disruption of the vital bodily functions: for instance, disruption of breathing, cardiovascular and metabolic disturbances, infections, severe pain and organ failures (e.g. liver, kidneys). The services of intensive care include monitoring and treatment as well as care of the patient. Special constructional and medical organisational measures are required for patients with paraplegia, burns and mental problems, which differ from usual intensive medicine.

The organisation of intensive medicine is oriented towards specialist disciplines such as neurosurgery, heart/thorax surgery, transplant surgery and neurology, or to interdisciplinary areas of surgery and internal medicine. In normal hospitals without a particular medical specialism, it is customary to divide intensive medicine into surgery and internal medicine.

Arrangement: The intensive care department must be a separate area, and only accessible through lobbies (for hygiene reasons). Note that according to hospital regulations, each intensive care unit must be a separate fire compartment. Apart from the patient and staff lobbies, visitors should only access the unit through a visitors' lobby (waiting room). The central point of an intensive care unit must be an open nurses' workstation from which it is possible to oversee every room. The recovery room of the operating department is often located in the intensive care unit so the patients can economically be cared for by the same staff.

The number of patients per unit should be between six and ten in order to avoid overloading the medical and nursing personnel and to provide the patient with the best possible care. One nurse's duty station, a sterile workstation (medication and infusion preparation), one materials room and one equipment room per unit (six to ten beds) should be included in the plan.

Arrangement of the bed spaces: The beds may be placed in an open, closed or combined arrangement. With an open arrangement a large floor area is required. All the beds must be in clear view of a central nurses' duty station and the patients are separated by moveable half-height partitions which should be lightweight and easy to move. With a closed arrangement the patients are accommodated in separate rooms which, again, must be in sight of a central nurses' workstation. Hygienically and psychologically the closed arrangement is preferable because the patients are extremely vulnerable. A compromise which is frequently adopted is to provide two or three beds in separate rooms.

The ideal plan is star shaped, with rooms radiating out from the nurses' workstation, but this is often not feasible because of space restrictions so more traditional arrangements are used.

Auxiliary functions: For auxiliary functions the following areas and rooms should be planned in: operating theatre for minor interventions (25–30 m²), laboratory space, kitchenette, substerilisation (20 m², clean material room, non-clean workroom, cleaning room, lounge for relatives, duty doctor's room, documentation room, possibly a consulting room, and sanitary facilities (co-ordinated with the hygiene department).

The operations centre must be self-sufficient in terms of medical facilities. Connection lines for oxygen, compressed air and vacuum suction must be available at all beds and, in addition to normal electrical sockets, low-voltage (for the nurse-call system) and high-voltage (e.g. for portable X-ray equipment) power must be provided.

The intensive surgical medicine ward should be close to and preferably on the same level as the surgical department and internal intensive medicine ward. It should also be close to reception and the emergency service operations centre. Intensive wards which are not associated with a specialist area should be close to the outpatients and surgical department. Short routes to the clinical laboratory and to the blood bank are preferable.

Areas for patient care should be enclosed and through-traffic kept to a minimum by careful planning of the circulation routes. Wards must have windows to give natural lighting whereas the service rooms (treatment areas, nurses' rooms, pharmacy etc.) can be located in the artificially lit inner area.

Care departments

The care departments are each assigned to a specialist discipline and subdivided into care groups. To maintain an adequate level of supervision each care area should contain no more than 16–24 beds. For economical use of staff, two workstations are often placed together and connected to a large central nurses' service area (caring for about 30–34

patients). The arrangement of the rooms is dependent upon the class, type and seriousness of the illness. The following nursing areas should be distinguished: normal nursing area, intensive care area, special care area.

There are fewer beds per care group in the intensive care and special care areas (6–12 beds, depending on the size of the hospital). The rooms must be arranged such that there is sufficient freedom of movement and that beds are accessible from both sides as well as the end. An adequate number of cupboards for patients' belongings must be provided as should space for care aids (trolleys, commodes) and equipment.

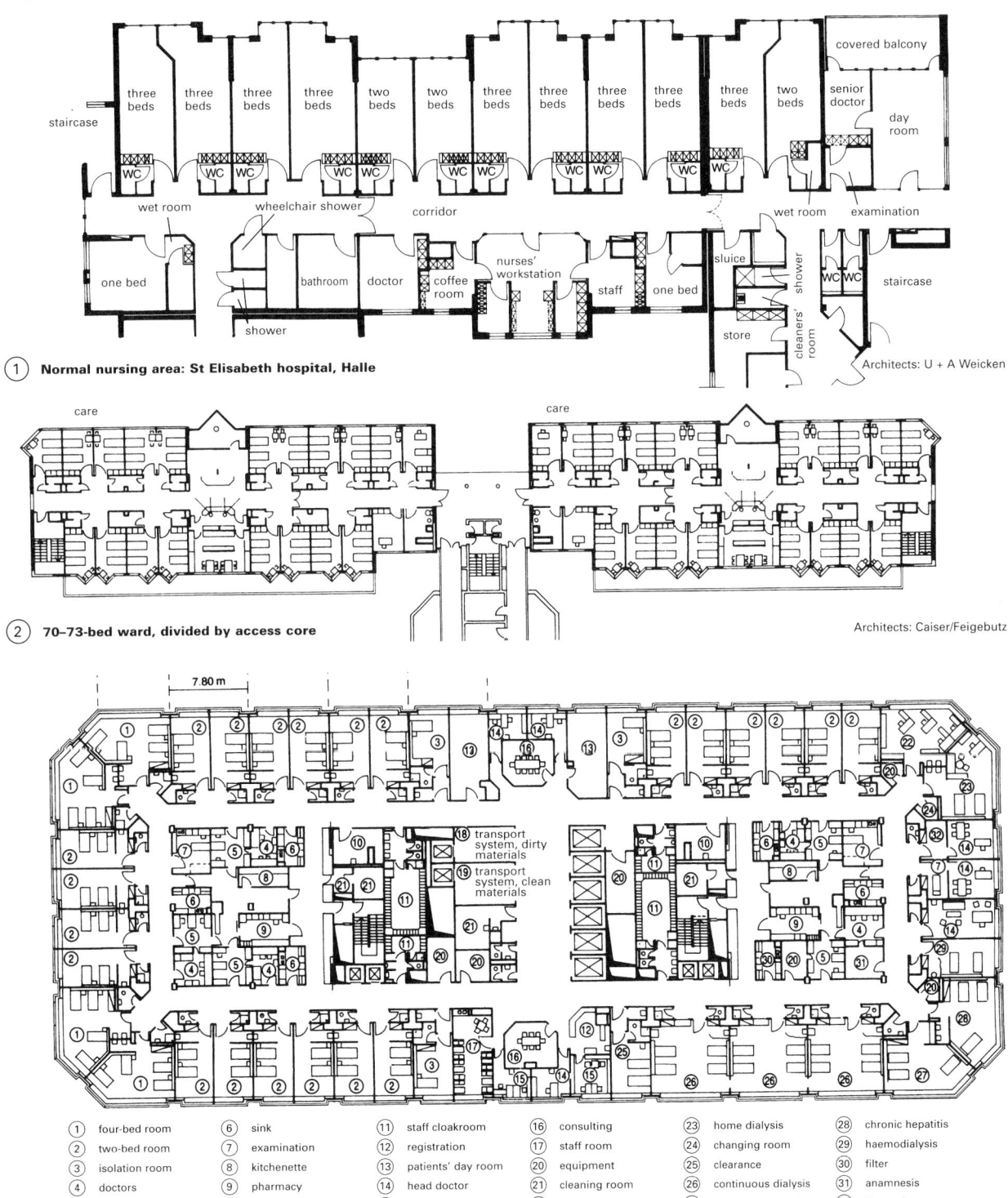

(1) **Normal nursing area: St Elisabeth hospital, Halle**   Architects: U + A Weicken

(2) **70–73-bed ward, divided by access core**   Architects: Caiser/Feigebutz

(1) four-bed room	(6) sink	(11) staff cloakroom	(16) consulting	(23) home dialysis	(28) chronic hepatitis
(2) two-bed room	(7) examination	(12) registration	(17) staff room	(24) changing room	(29) haemodialysis
(3) isolation room	(8) kitchenette	(13) patients' day room	(18) transport system, dirty materials	(25) clearance	(30) filter
(4) doctors	(9) pharmacy	(14) head doctor	(19) transport system, clean materials	(26) continuous dialysis	(31) anamnesis
(5) nurses	(10) bathroom	(15) sister	(20) equipment	(27) peritoneal dialysis	(32) X-ray pictures
				(21) cleaning room	
				(22) secretarial	

(3) **90–96-bed ward**   Architects: Suter & Suter

Care Areas

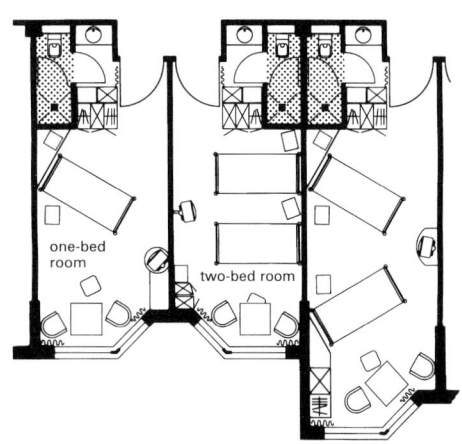

① **One- and two-bed private rooms: Unna Catholic Hospital**

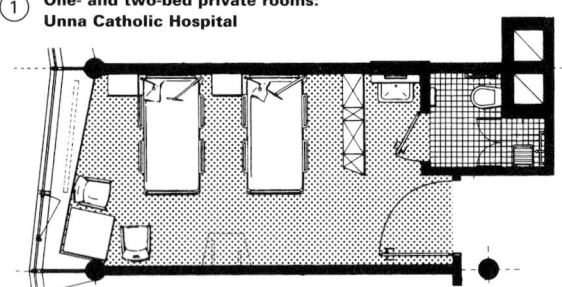

② **Two-bed room with shower**   Architects: Nickl + Partner

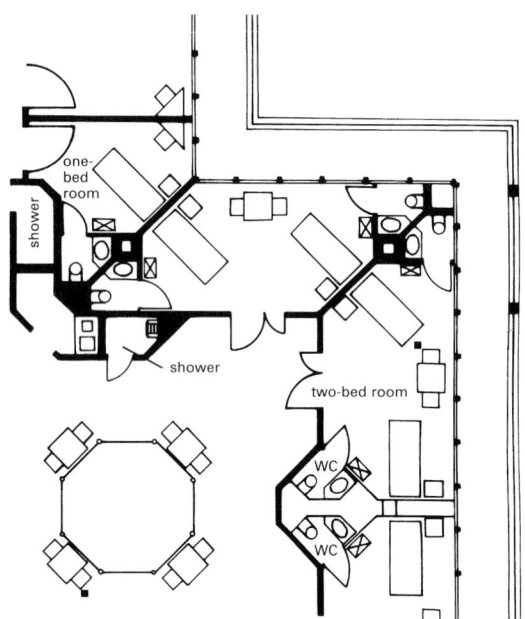

Architects: Joedicke and Partner

③ **One- and two-bed room; shower on the corridor: Clinic II, Munich**

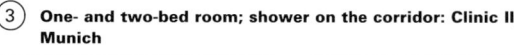

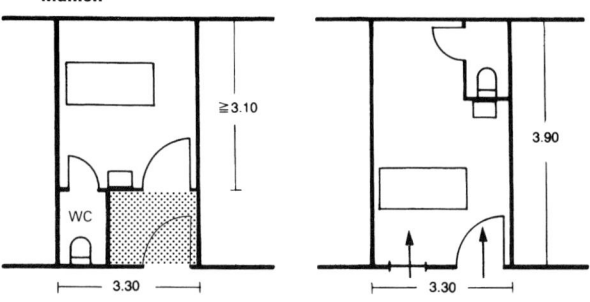

④ **Single-bed room with lobby**

⑤ **Single-bed room, no lobby; observation possible from corridor**

'Normal care units' are used for general inpatient care (the main function of general hospitals), particularly for short-term and acute illnesses, primarily with a short length of stay. These units can be stacked depending on the space requirement and organisational structure. Seriously ill patients are moved from normal care groups to intensive care groups.

'Intensive care groups' are for patients under constant observation and tend to be assigned to particular examination and treatment rooms. Generally, these rooms should be larger than normal care rooms because more instruments and equipment need to be accommodated.

Patients with special needs are placed in 'special care units'. These include newborn babies, people with infectious diseases, the chronically ill, rehabilitation patients, neurotics and hypochondriacs. The length of stay of these patients is frequently longer than average.

Function and structure
The individual care areas in a hospital are attached to the specific medical faculties (e.g. surgery, medical, accident and emergency etc,) and therefore need to be planned as separate units. Essentially, they cater for pre- and post-operative patients who must stay in the hospital for observation and recovery. The patients' basic bodily functions are routinely tested on the wards but more extensive examination is carried out in separate treatment rooms. Each station must have at least one assistant doctor's room and two doctor's rooms in which minor examination and treatment can be carried out.

The hierarchical hospital structure, in both medical and nursing domains, must be reflected in the planning (e.g. separate rooms for station supervisors, assistant doctors, senior doctors).

Layout of rooms
Medical rooms and washrooms should be accessed from the main station corridor which must be easily supervised from the glazed nurses' workstation to prevent unauthorised entry. The logistics of delivering patient care is an important factor in the cost-effectiveness of the department so it is desirable to plan the necessary supply and disposal rooms for medicines, linen, refuse, food etc. centrally in groups around the nurses' workstation.

Nursing teams
Each station (18–24 patients) is served by an independent nursing team which has full responsibility for patient care. As the nurses' workstation has to be constantly occupied, it is sensible to plan a direct connection to the nurses' kitchenette and rest room.

One-to-one nursing care is very much the exception nowadays and the rising costs of such provision mean that it is unlikely to be feasible in the future.

Wet cells
The strategy of combining one-, two- and three-bed rooms is specified by the financial department. The same constraints are also applied to the equipping of wet cells with WCs and showers or baths. If applicable, separate shower rooms are permitted.

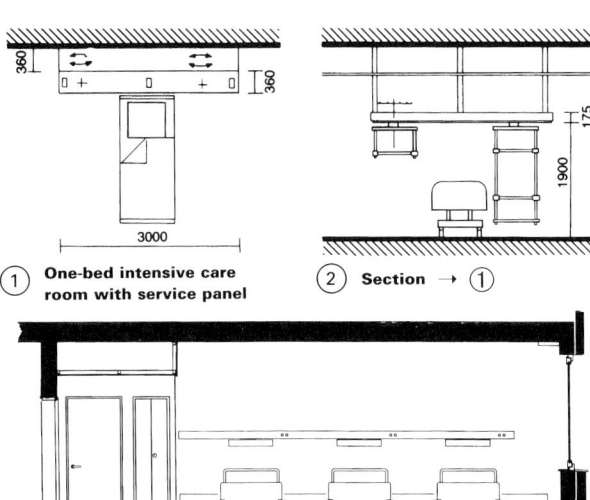

① One-bed intensive care room with service panel

② Section → ①

③ Section: three-bed room

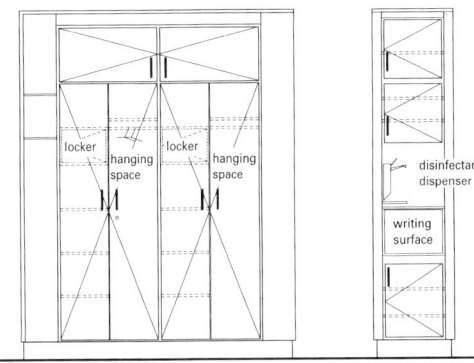

④ Patient's cupboard   side view

⑤ Wet cell   Architects: U + A Weicken

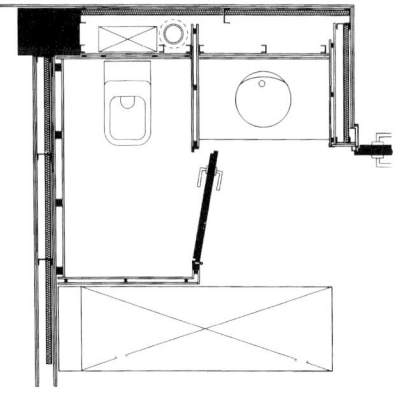

Size of the patient rooms

The patients' beds must be accessible from three sides and this sets the limits for the overall room sizes. The smallest size for a one-bed room is 10 m²; for a two- and three-bed room, a minimum of 8 m² per bed should be allowed (in accordance with hospital building regulations).

The room must be wide enough for a second bed to be wheeled out of the room without disturbing the first bed (minimum width 3.20 m).

Next to each bed must be a night table and, where appropriate, towards the window there should be a table (900 x 900 mm) with chairs (one chair per patient). The fitted cupboards (usually against the corridor wall) must be capable of being opened without moving the beds or night tables.

In new buildings, the wet cells should be located towards the inside, off the station corridor, because future renovations will most likely make use of the external walls as the means of extending the existing areas.

Equipping the patient room

Around the walls there should be a strip made of plastic or wood (at least 400–700 mm above floor level) to protect the wall from damage caused by the movement of beds, night tables and trolleys. Similar strips should be included in the station corridors.

The patients' cupboards must be large enough to store all of the belongings they have with them. It is best to have a suitcase locker over the cupboard and a lockable valuables section within the cupboard itself. A coin-operated locking system is recommended because keys often get lost. A lockable staff cupboard for medicines should also be planned for. Hinges which allow doors to open through 135 degrees should be fitted to all cupboards.

The room doors must be 1260 × 2130 mm in size and a design which gives a noise reduction of at least 32 dB should be considered (note that noise reduction seals are often necessary). The closing mechanisms must be overhead and the door furniture should be designed to suit the needs of patients and staff carrying trays.

The service supply duct runs behind the beds and supplies oxygen, a vacuum line and compressed air via special sockets. Power points, reading lights, telephone, nurse call and radio sockets are also housed in this duct.

Whether each patient room is equipped with a shower often depends on the financing of the project. However, a wash-basin and WC are today standard in new buildings. Attention must be paid to the heights of the wash-basin and the WC: the wash-basin needs to be roughly 860 mm from the floor to allow wheelchairs underneath and the WC for wheelchair users should have a seat height of about 490 mm. Each station must also have additional WCs for staff, visitors and wheelchair users.

activity	patient is restricted by bed rest and/or slight disability	patient is restricted by intensive bed rest and/or severe disability
1 bodily care	2 x daily/1 pers. help with washing	2 x daily/2 pers. carry out washing
2 help with excretion	4 x daily/1 pers.	4 x daily/1 pers.
3 beds	2 x daily/2 pers.	3 x daily/2 pers.
4 storage		3 x daily/2 pers.
5 mobilisation	1 x daily/1 pers.	3 x daily/1–2 pers.
6 preventive measures	2 x daily/1 pers.	3 x daily/1–2 pers.
7 provision of meals and help with eating	3 x daily/1 pers.	4 x daily/1 pers.
8 monitoring vital signs	2 x daily/1 pers.	3 x daily/1 pers.
9 patient observation	2 x daily/1 pers.	2 x daily/1 pers.
10 information and instruction	2 x daily/1 pers.	2 x daily/1 pers.
11 caring conversation	2 x daily/1 pers.	3 x daily/1 pers.
12 talking to relatives	2 x weekly/1 pers.	2 x weekly/1 pers.
13 counselling	2 x daily/min. 2 pers.	3 x daily/min. 2 pers.
14 care documentation	2 x daily/min. 2 pers.	3 x daily/min. 2 pers.
15 obtaining specialist help		
16 other assistance	3 x daily/1 pers.	6 x daily/1 pers.

⑥ Nursing categories

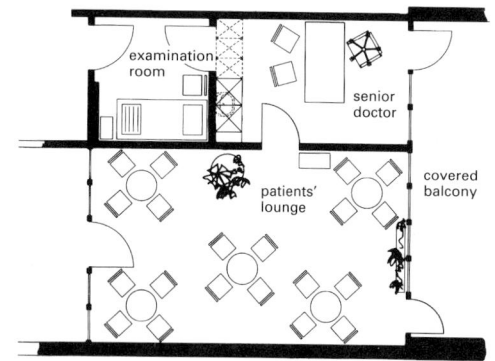

① **Nurses' work area**

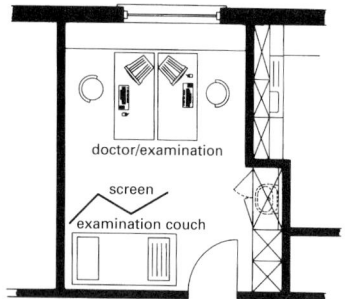

② **Senior doctor's office/patients' lounge**

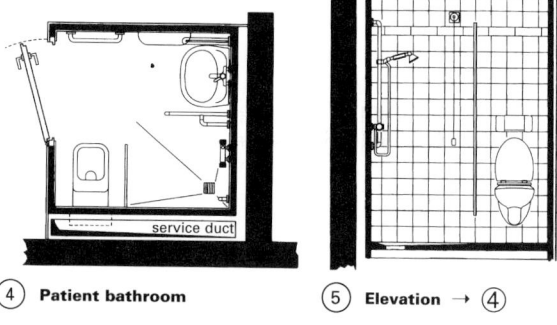

③ **Station doctor (room size 16–20 m²)**

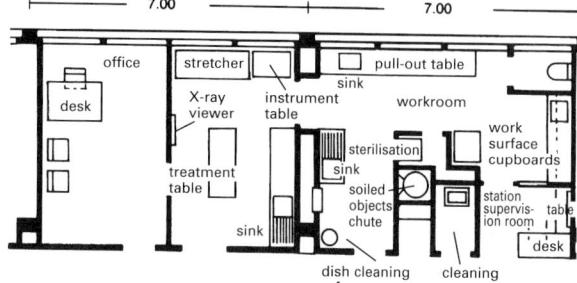

④ **Patient bathroom** ⑤ **Elevation → ④**

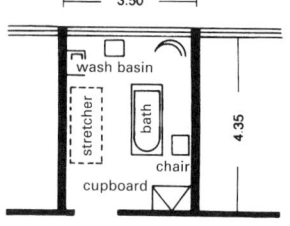

⑥ **Doctor's room, treatment room, nurses' workroom and station supervision room combined in one unit**   Architect: Rosenfield

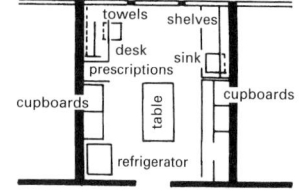

⑦ **Bathroom** ⑧ **Station pharmacy**

Non-clean workroom
Each care area station must have a workroom, approximately 10 m² in size, for handling soiled materials. The room will contain a sink and sluice, preferably in stainless steel, and fully tiled walls are recommended.

Nurses' work area → ①
The nurses' workstation should be situated in a central position and requires a size of about 25–30 m². The corridor wall must be glazed, but fireproofing is also a consideration so it is advisable to consult the fire officer and fireproofing specialists.

Rest rooms/kitchenette
Roughly 15 m² should be allocated for staff breaktime facilities. In larger hospitals consider the inclusion of a smoking area.

Station doctor
The station doctor must be provided with a 16–20 m² room in which to examine patients. In addition to a desk, there should be ample shelving and an examination couch on which the doctor can rest when on-call. → ③

Clean workroom
The clean workroom should have an area of about 10 m² and be equipped with fixed shelving (600 mm deep) or a flexible storage system consisting of modules which can be filled up in the central stores.

Patients' bathroom
Bathrooms are often equipped with a tub which is accessible from three sides to ease the lifting of patients. Showers are an option for more mobile patients and can also be suitable for wheelchair users provided enough space is allowed (1400 × 1400 mm). → ④

Plant room
Each station must have a small (approximately 8 m²) plant room equipped with a fuseboard.

Patients' lounge
A size of approximately 22–25 m² should be allocated to serve as a general meeting place for patients. The design should emulate a domestic environment.

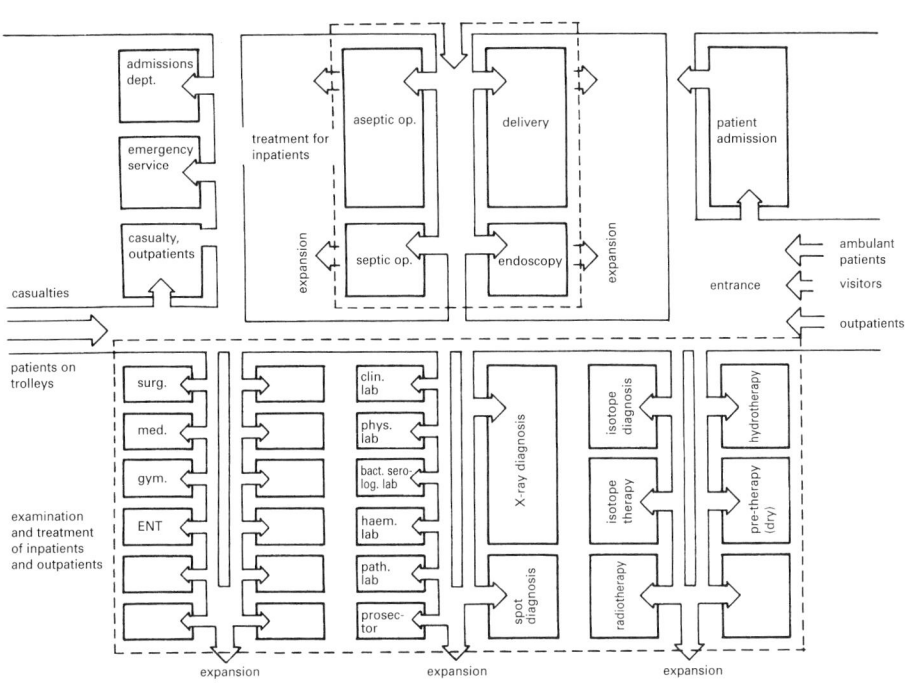

1. Access and assignment diagram of departments in the examination and treatment area

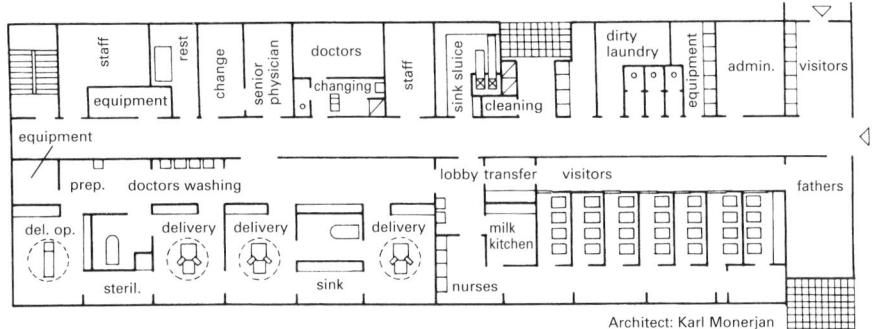

2. Waldbröl District Hospital: 448 beds; bath and sink directly accessible for every two places

Architect: Karl Monerjan

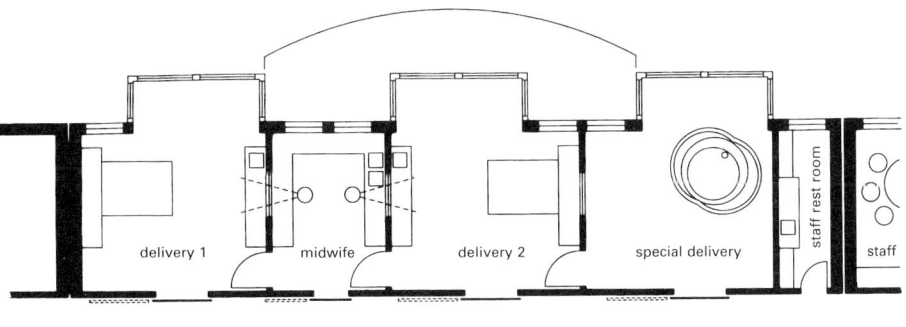

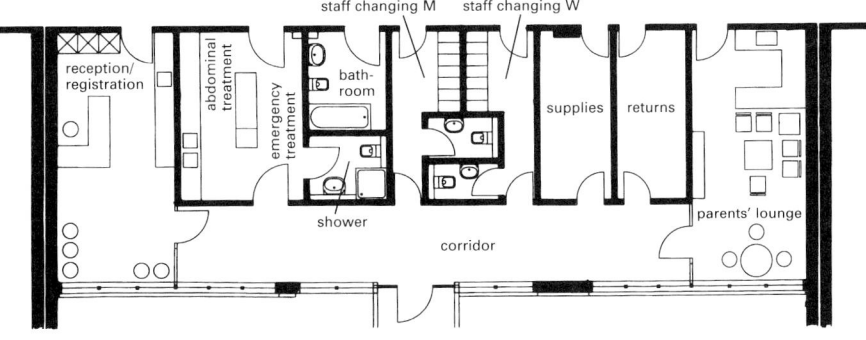

3. Delivery area/prenatal: St Elisabeth Hospital, Halle

Treatment Areas

Considerable changes have been seen in the functional area of hospitals in recent years. The proportion of bed-care space has decreased over 30 years from 70% to 40%, while the area for treatment has increased by 100%. This trend can be explained by the increasing demand for medical care, diagnosis and therapy. An important aspect here is to co-ordinate medical disciplines to ensure better co-operation and consultation.

The treatment areas should face north and have central access.

Obstetrics

In addition to looking after normal deliveries, the obstetrics department also has to handle complications during pregnancy and childbirth so it is therefore essential to have a treatment room next to the conventional delivery rooms. It is also sensible to position this near to the surgery and intensive care departments. The delivery area is separated from the maternity and baby care units, as these are connected more to the nursing areas.

Room planning

Among the central delivery rooms is an observation room with large glass windows as well as waiting and admission areas with 'contraction rooms'. In addition there should be a clean workroom ($12\,m^2$), a non-clean workroom ($12\,m^2$), a treatment room ($12\,m^2$), a midwives' workstation ($20\,m^2$), a staff rest room ($15\,m^2$), and staff and patient WCs.

The equipment in the delivery rooms will depend on the birthing method chosen but it should ideally also include a bath for patients.

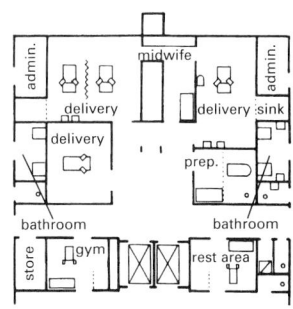

Architects: Bohne, Colling, Schneider

4. **Private hospital, Karlsruhe Durlach: 180 beds**

561

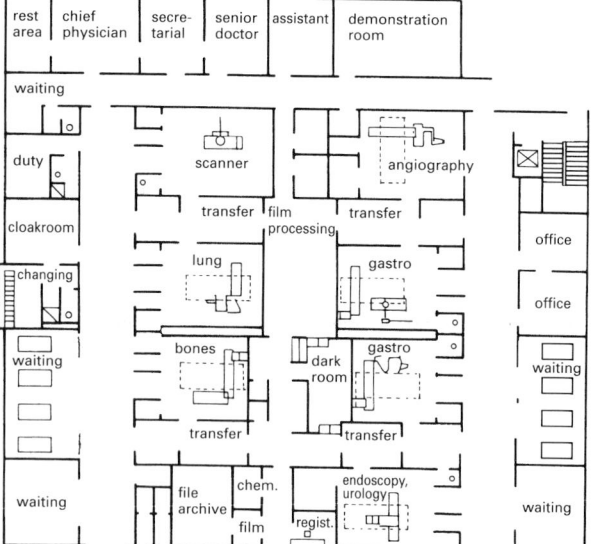

(1) **St Vinzenzstift Hospital, Kirschrode, Hanover: 430 beds**

Architects: Gruson, Kuschel, Tschirschwitz

(2) **Munich-Perlach Hospital: 687 beds**

Architects: Wichtendahl, Roennich

Internal medicine treatment area

This area brings together all the examination techniques and treatments associated with internal medicine which, depending on the size of the hospital, can encompass: cardiology, angiology, pulmonology, endocrinology and metabolism, and gastroenterology. The basic facilities comprise examination rooms (25 m²), a secretarial/administration office (20 m²) between the senior physician's room (15–20 m²) and the chief physician's room (20–25 m²), an archive room and patient waiting areas. Staff stand-by rooms (15 m²) should also be provided.

Radiology

Radiology includes the specialist areas which use ionising radiation for diagnostic and therapeutic purposes. This includes X-ray diagnosis, radiotherapy and nuclear medicine. The radiology department should always be close to the ambulance entrance and, because of the great weight of the equipment (up to 14 t), it is sensible to plan these areas on the ground or first basement floor.

The rooms of the individual diagnostic areas must be so arranged as to minimise the distance between them. A connecting corridor which can be used simultaneously as a store, dictating room and, possibly, a switchroom as well as for staff circulation, is desirable. The size of the rooms depends on their use and what they contain: for example, sonography, mammography and jaw X-ray require about 12–18 m² whereas standard X-ray and admission rooms need to be 20–30 m². The access route for patients should be through two changing cubicles, and a wide door (≥1250 mm) for beds is necessary. WCs should be installed in X-ray rooms used for stomach/intestinal inspection. Angiography rooms require an auxiliary room with a sink and built-in storage (e.g. medicine refrigerator); medical gases must be also available. The admission room for computertomography (CT) must be about 35 m² in area. The patients pass through lobbies or changing rooms in order to reach the admission room. The switchroom is connected by a door and a window. An additional room for switch cupboards and film developing is desirable. The walls, ceilings and floors must be shielded with lead sheeting, the thickness of which depends on the type of equipment to be used. Co-operation with the manufacturers of X-ray equipment is absolutely essential.

	max operating voltage (kV)	min thickness lead (mm)	concrete (mm)
transmitted light	75	1.0	120
X-ray photography	100	1.5	120
skin therapy	100	1.5	120
medium radiation	150	2.5	–
deep radiation	175	3.0	–
deep radiation	200	4.0	220
deep radiation	225	5.0	–
deep radiation	300	9.0	–
deep radiation	400	15.0	260

(3) **Minimum protection levels (according to Rendich and Braestrup)**

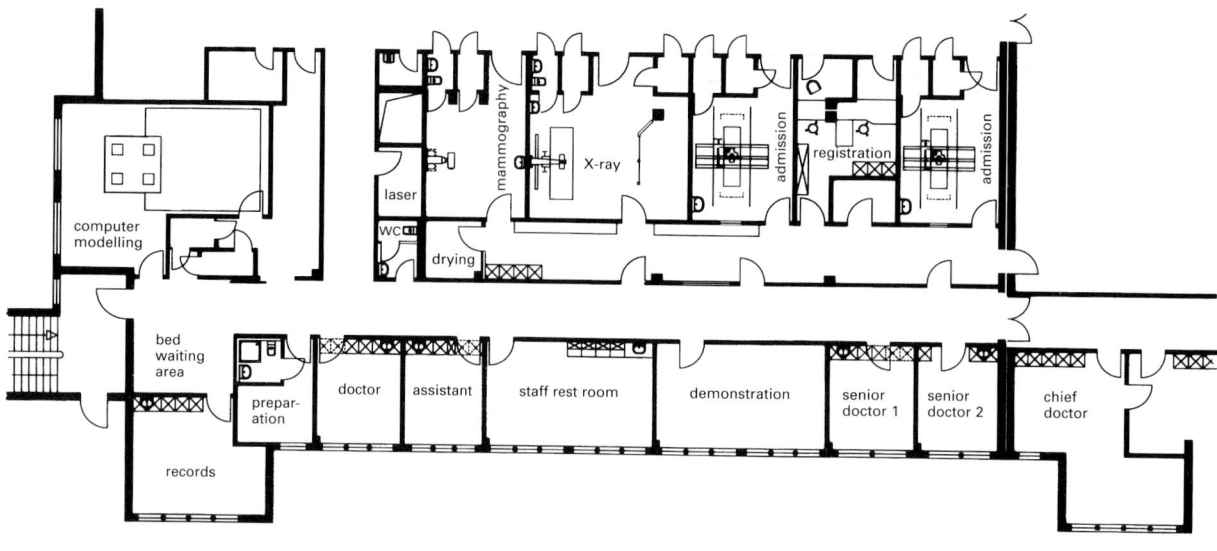

(4) **X-ray department, St Elisabeth, Halle/S**

Architects: U + A Weicken

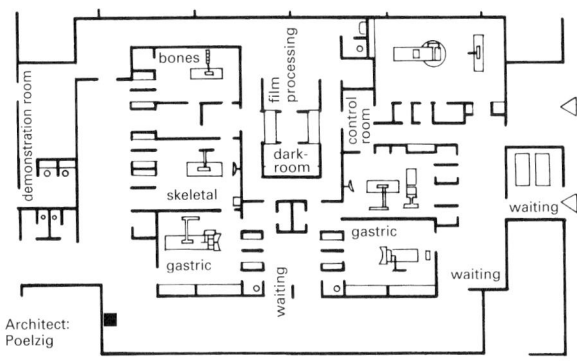

situated at the hub of the treatment area, in the immediate vicinity of functional diagnosis and diagnostic nuclear medicine

(1) **Fulda Municipal Hospital: 732 beds**

Architects: Köhler, Kässens

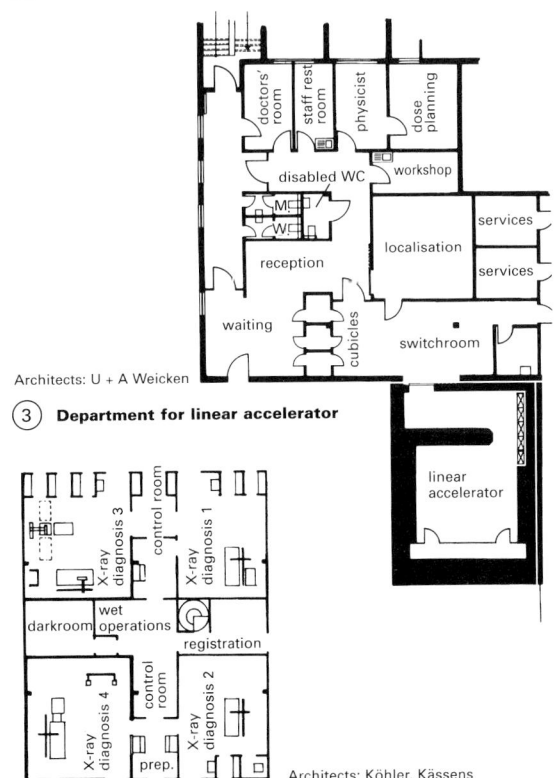

situated on one level with the central laboratory; diagnosis rooms using cystoscopy have adjoining waiting areas; double-sided access

Architect: Poelzig

(2) **Stade Hospital: 616 beds**

Architects: U + A Weicken

(3) **Department for linear accelerator**

Architects: Köhler, Kässens

X-ray diagnosis with layout known as an X-ray cross

(4) **University Hospital, Bonn**

Radiotherapy

In radiotherapy, conditions diagnosed in the radiography department (e.g. tumours) are treated. The radiotherapy department comprises a reception and waiting area, doctors' rooms (approximately $18\,m^2$), a switchroom ($15\,m^2$), possibly a localisation room ($20–25\,m^2$), a service room ($20\,m^2$), a film developing room ($10\,m^2$), stores and a cleaners' room. Each treatment room requires a changing cubicle for patients. If the department includes a linear accelerator a workshop ($15\,m^2$) and at least one physics laboratory ($15–18\,m^2$) will also be necessary. The clear height of the radiation rooms must be 4.30 m.

For hygiene reasons the patient waiting area, examination, localisation, preparation and radiation rooms must be well vented and well ventilated (at least five changes of air per hour).

The safety requirements are particularly strict for radiotherapy departments and must satisfy all applicable national and international regulations. Structural shielding from radiation can be achieved by using lead inserts or with thick concrete walls (e.g. barite concrete). The thickness of walls constructed in concrete only should be 3.00 m for treatment and examination rooms in the primary radiation area and 1.50 m for rooms in the secondary radiation area, according to the type of equipment.

The huge weight of the equipment and the required structural radiation protection measures make it necessary for radiotherapy departments to be located in the basement or on the ground floor.

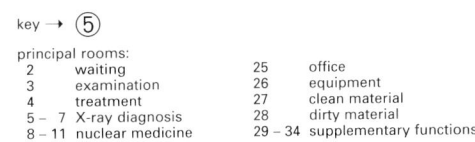

key → (5)

principal rooms:

2	waiting	25	office
3	examination	26	equipment
4	treatment	27	clean material
5 – 7	X-ray diagnosis	28	dirty material
8 – 11	nuclear medicine	29 – 34	supplementary functions
21 – 23	doctors' rooms		

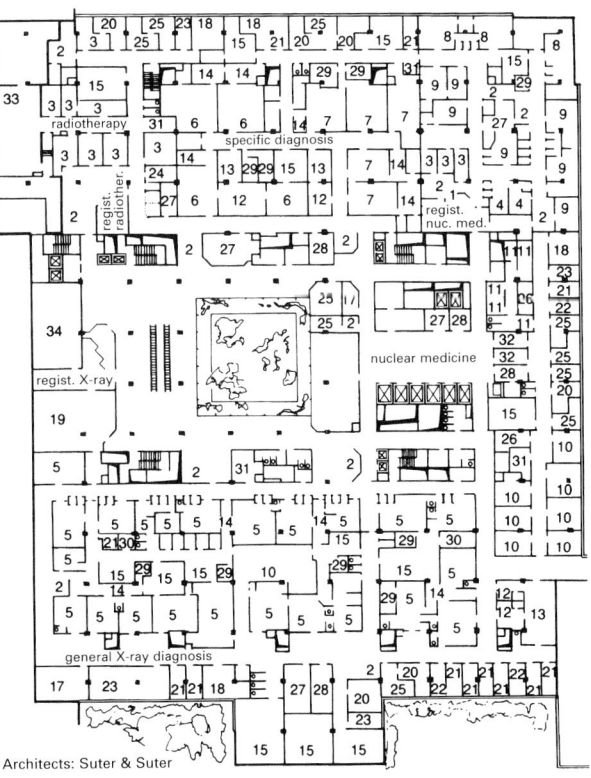

linking of the service area; radiotherapy, nuclear medicine and X-ray diagnosis are linked on one level; common access

Architects: Suter & Suter

(5) **Basel Cantonal Hospital**

Laboratories; Functional Diagnosis

Laboratory department

The laboratory department is concerned mostly with the preparation and processing of blood, urine and faecal samples. It is often separated from the treatment and nursing areas, the connection to the other departments being through a special pneumatic tube dispatch system.

The laboratory itself should be in a large room with built-in work surfaces (standing work places) to offer a high level of flexibility. Specialist laboratories are added on as separate rooms. Subsidiary rooms include rinsing rooms, sluice rooms, disinfection rooms, cool rooms, rest rooms and WCs for staff. The size of the department depends on the demands of the hospital.

Sometimes the laboratory departments are completely separate and serve a group of several hospitals.

Functional diagnosis

Functional diagnosis is playing an increasingly important role in hospitals due to advances in heart and thorax research and the rising number of patients with heart, lung and circulation problems. Flexibility in the design is absolutely essential to accommodate the wide range of techniques and equipment used in such departments. A direct connection with the laboratory department is beneficial, but not essential. A data link to the radiology, radiotherapy and surgical departments is necessary to allow combined monitoring (e.g. analysis of X-ray results together with ongoing assessment of the vital functions).

All examination rooms must be accessible through a patients' cubicle and, possibly, also a preparation room. Waiting rooms must be sympathetically designed because the patients are often extremely nervous.

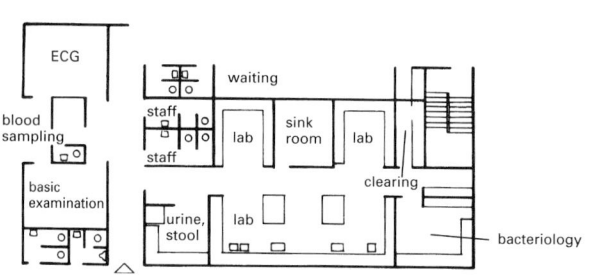

separation of rooms with and without patient traffic; routine laboratory segregated from clinical chemistry

(1) **Soltau District Hospital: 354 beds**   Architects: Poelzig/Biermann

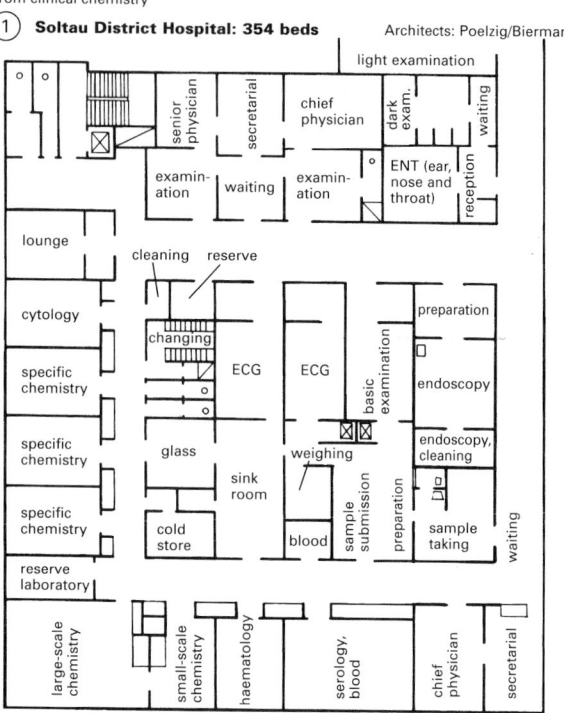

Architects: Wichtendahl & Roemmich

(2) **Laboratory area for large hospital, Munich-Perlach Municipal**

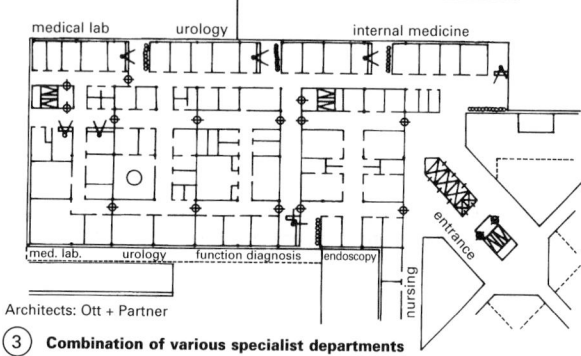

Architects: Ott + Partner

(3) **Combination of various specialist departments**

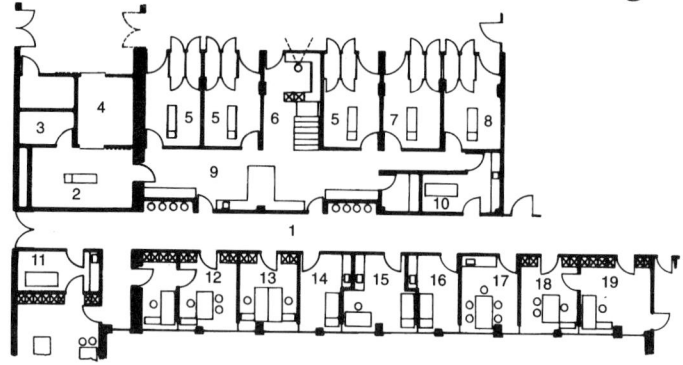

(4) **Functional diagnostics, St Elisabeth, Halle/S**

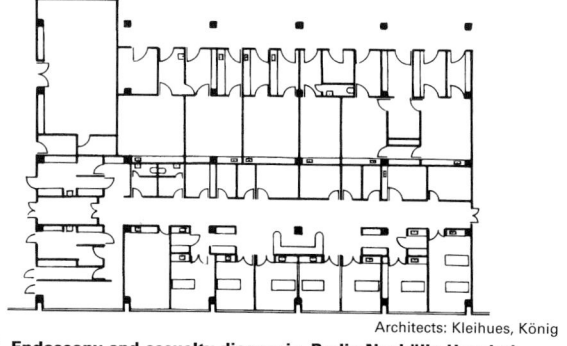

Architects: Kleihues, König

(5) **Endoscopy and casualty diagnosis, Berlin-Neukölln Hospital**

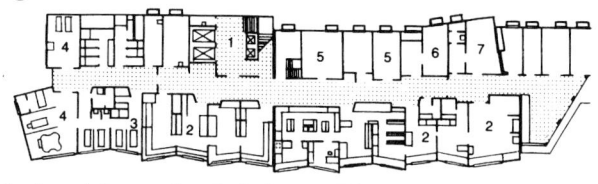

1 entrance hall	4 medical baths	7 linen	Architect: Bockemühl
2 laboratory	5 supplies		
3 massage	6 autopsy		

(6) **Laboratory/therapy departments, Herdecke Hospital, Ruhr**

1 functional diagnosis
2 heart monitoring
3 equipment
4 preparation
5 sonograph
6 current records
7 doppler
8 echocardiography
9 clean workroom
10 lung function testing
11 general examination room
12 senior doctor
13 assistant
14 electrocardiography
15 long-duration ECG
16 ECG
17 staff
18 senior doctor
19 secretary

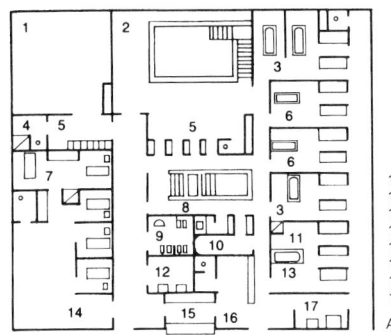

1 gymnastics
2 movement bath
3 medicinal bath
4 shower
5 changing room/cubicle
6 medicinal bath with solarium
7 fango (mud) bath
8 footbath
9 arm bath
10 spray shower
11 CO_2
12 inhalation
13 sudatorium
14 dry therapy
15 bathing supervisor
16 staff
17 wash room

Architect: Meckenig

(1) **St Marienwörth Hospital, Bad Kreuznach: 330 beds**

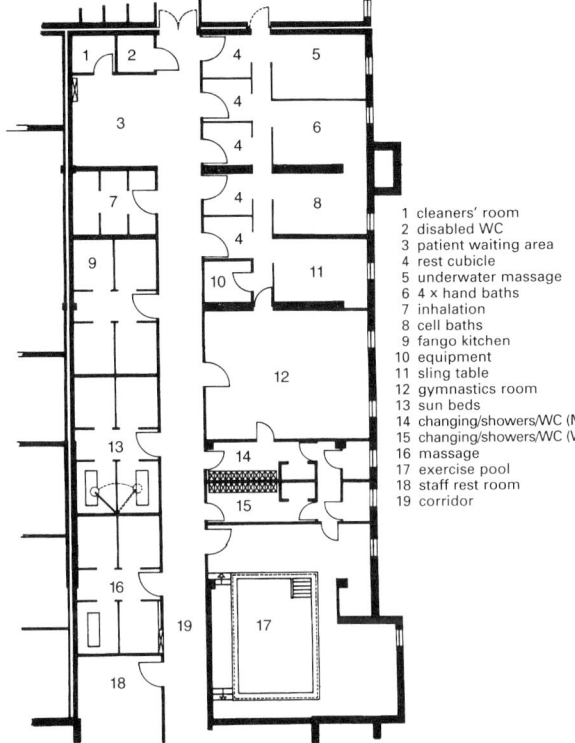

1 cleaners' room
2 disabled WC
3 patient waiting area
4 rest cubicle
5 underwater massage
6 4 × hand baths
7 inhalation
8 cell baths
9 fango kitchen
10 equipment
11 sling table
12 gymnastics room
13 sun beds
14 changing/showers/WC (M)
15 changing/showers/WC (W)
16 massage
17 exercise pool
18 staff rest room
19 corridor

(2) **Physical therapy department with gymnasium**

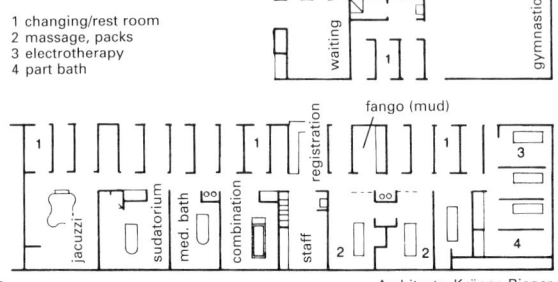

1 changing/rest room
2 massage, packs
3 electrotherapy
4 part bath

Architects: Kröger, Rieger

(3) **Velbert Hospital: 600 beds**

(4) **Munich-Perlach Municipal Hospital: 687 beds**

Architect: Wichtendahl

Supplementary Disciplines

Physiotherapy

The physiotherapy department contains a 'wet area' consisting of an exercise pool (approximately 4 × 6m), a 'four cell bath', a 'butterfly bath', inhalation rooms, a massage bath, hand and foot baths as well as the necessary subsidiary rooms. It is, obviously, important to use slip-resistant tiles in this area.

The department should be accessed through a main reception area and the division between wet and dry areas must be obvious. Additional rooms to be planned include changing rooms for men and women, wheelchair users' WC, staff and patient WCs, rest rooms, linen stores, waiting areas, cleaners' room and service rooms for the exercise pool.

A gymnasium is often included in the physiotherapy department. This will require a clear height of at least 3.00m, the provision of a sprung floor and the installation of impact resistant lighting. Because of the high internal temperatures (28–30°) construction physics problems should be anticipated.

Ideally, the physiotherapy rooms should be arranged on the basement floor where natural lighting can be admitted through roof lights and light shafts.

Urological treatment

This discipline is related to X-ray diagnosis. The treatment room should be 25–30m² in size and it must be close to the surgical department. The room should contain an examination and treatment table for endoscopic investigations and be equipped with a wash-basin, suspended irrigator, floor drainage, 4–6volt power points (cystoscopy), two changing cubicles and a WC. There should also be an instrument room adjoining (roughly 15m²), with sterilisers, sinks and a wash-basin, and a patient waiting area.

Eye treatment

Eye treatment can be carried out in a room approximately 25m² in size which can be darkened as required. The necessary equipment includes a treatment chair, examination and diagnostic instruments, an examination couch, a wash-basin and a writing desk. A patients' waiting room should be situated to the front of the treatment room.

Ear, nose and throat (ENT) treatment

ENT treatment is carried out for inpatients in their own care area. The treatment room (25–30m²), which can be darkened, should contain a treatment table for examinations, a treatment chair, a steriliser, a sink and wash-basin, storage spaces for portable equipment, 4–6volt power points and compressed air/suction lines. Adjoining the treatment room should be a rest room and a patients' waiting room.

Dental treatment

This specialist area of treatment should be provided primarily in special ENT and rheumatism clinics. The treatment room needs to be 25–30m² in size and contain a treatment chair with dental unit, a desk, a wash-basin, X-ray and anaesthetic equipment, a sink alcove with steriliser and, if possible, a darkroom.

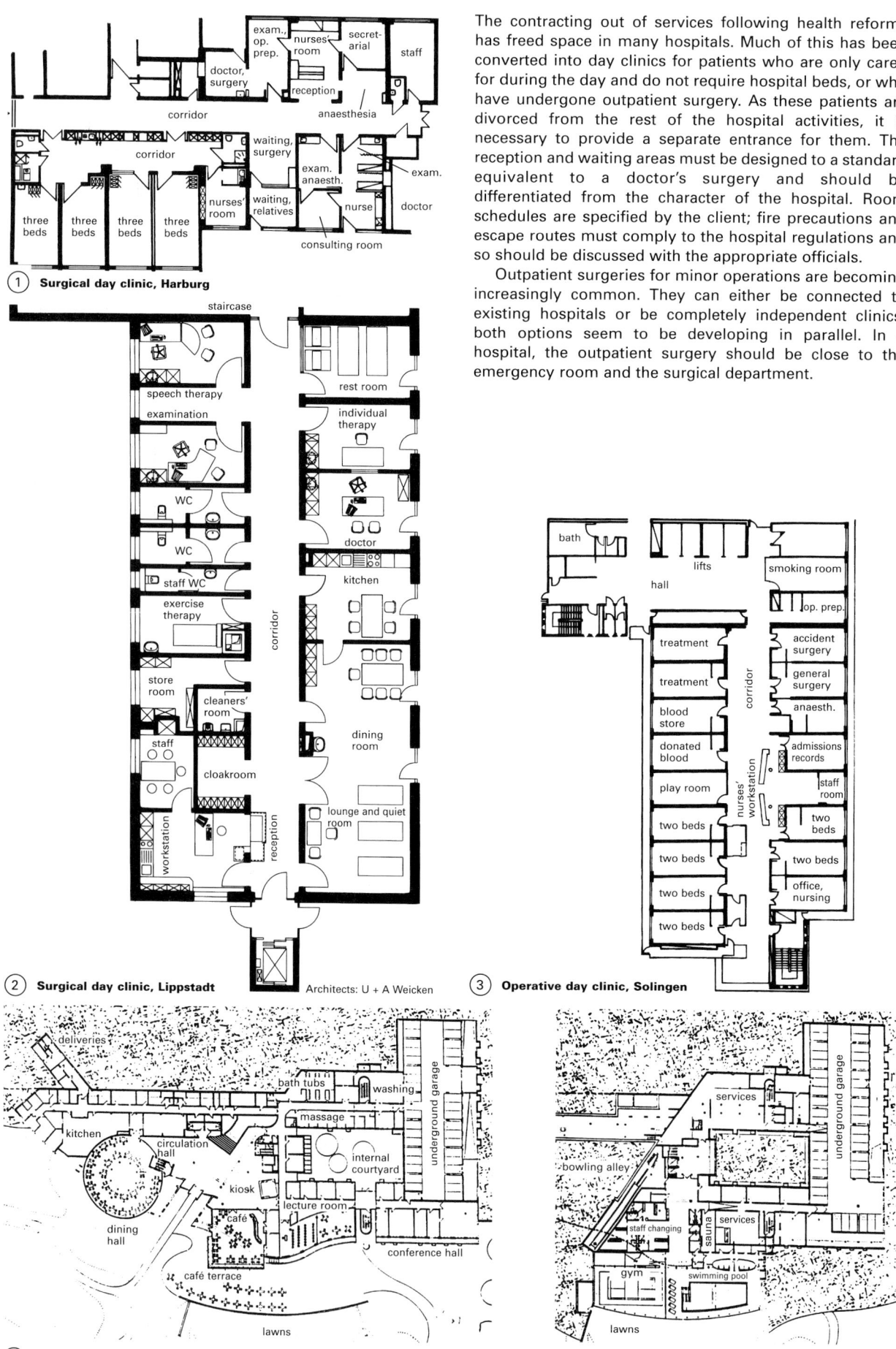

DAY CLINICS; OUTPATIENT SURGERY

The contracting out of services following health reforms has freed space in many hospitals. Much of this has been converted into day clinics for patients who are only cared for during the day and do not require hospital beds, or who have undergone outpatient surgery. As these patients are divorced from the rest of the hospital activities, it is necessary to provide a separate entrance for them. The reception and waiting areas must be designed to a standard equivalent to a doctor's surgery and should be differentiated from the character of the hospital. Room schedules are specified by the client; fire precautions and escape routes must comply to the hospital regulations and so should be discussed with the appropriate officials.

Outpatient surgeries for minor operations are becoming increasingly common. They can either be connected to existing hospitals or be completely independent clinics: both options seem to be developing in parallel. In a hospital, the outpatient surgery should be close to the emergency room and the surgical department.

(1) **Surgical day clinic, Harburg**

(2) **Surgical day clinic, Lippstadt**   Architects: U + A Weicken

(3) **Operative day clinic, Solingen**

(4) **Rehabilitation clinic, Constance**   Architect: Grüttner

(5) **Basement** → (4)

① **Supply and disposal area: route relationships**

For goods and materials which are required only by one department it is economic to provide a decentralised preparation/disposal unit (e.g. for surgical instruments and substerilisation, or for developing X-ray film in the X-ray diagnostic department).

Means of transport
In addition to the organisation of stores and the preparation of delivered and reused goods, there is the question of transportation. Multipurpose trolleys are frequently used for distributing the required items to each point of consumption and these can be used at the same time for storing equipment. In medium-size and large hospitals a vertical conveyor, with selective automated discharge, for distribution to the various storeys and return of used goods to the non-clean preparation zone is necessary in order to relieve personnel. A dispatch system using pneumatic tubes, for example, should be provided for sending small items such as drugs and notes.

The scale of the transport system depends on the size of the institution: the supply and disposal requirement per bed per day is 30–35 kg. For large or heavy items (e.g. beds, respiration equipment, heart and lung machines) conventional bed elevators are available. A fully automatic conveyor system can be used for transporting medium-size items (e.g. food, laundry, refuse, consumer goods) in large hospitals.

Central supply
The advantages of collecting together all of the supplies functions on one supply/disposal level are uniform overall management, common stock control and the utilisation of the same transport systems. Centralisation also means there is a single point to which goods are delivered; from here, distribution and storage of goods can be controlled efficiently.

For hygiene reasons it is important to separate clean and non-clean goods. This is a primary consideration when designing transport systems.

Staff rooms
In the supplies area, changing and washrooms, WCs, cleaning rooms, storage rooms (for cleaning equipment) and rest rooms must be provided in the immediate vicinity of the goods inward/collection point.

Sterilisation
Since it is primarily items for the surgical department which are prepared in the central sterilisation unit, the two should be situated close together. However, to meet immediate needs, the surgical department will have its own substerilisation facilities. The central store for drugs and instruments must be closely linked to the central sterilisation unit.

Dispensary
In institutions without a full pharmacy, medication requiring approval is distributed from the dispensary. This consists of a work and dispensing room (25 m²) which is accessed directly from the main circulation corridor. It is fitted out with a desk, washing facility, sink, weighing station and lockable cupboards. Adjoining are a dry store and proprietary medicines store (15 m²), a cold store (10 m²) for hazardous substances, a dressing materials room and a damp store in accordance with fire regulations. When planning new buildings, it is recommended that a full pharmacy be included in the design.

The clinical, nursing and technical supply centre is located either in a separate supplies building or at a neutral supplies and disposal level under the main building. It is best to have a goods yard which is separated from the main and ambulance entrances. A north-facing orientation for this entrance is ideal. External and internal circulation routes must be co-ordinated so that overlaps with the routes used by the care and treatment areas are avoided.

During the design stage, it must be remembered that this area of the hospital can create a great deal of noise (goods vehicles and machinery) and smells (refuse containers, kitchen waste etc.) and so should not be situated close to the nursing wing. The planning of the supplies area is arranged according to the medical departments of the hospitals. A detailed specification can only be devised after the detailed design of the nursing and treatment wings has been established. The increasing use of automation demands co-operation between the architects, specialist engineers and manufacturers in the design stages. A tendency towards greater centralisation is noticeable, the incentive being to keep investment at a minimum and to produce economies in staffing. As a result of this, in the case of small clinics, an in-house main kitchen and laundry can be dispensed with: meals are delivered from a central kitchen and the laundry is managed by an external service organisation.

HOSPITALS

Supplies Areas

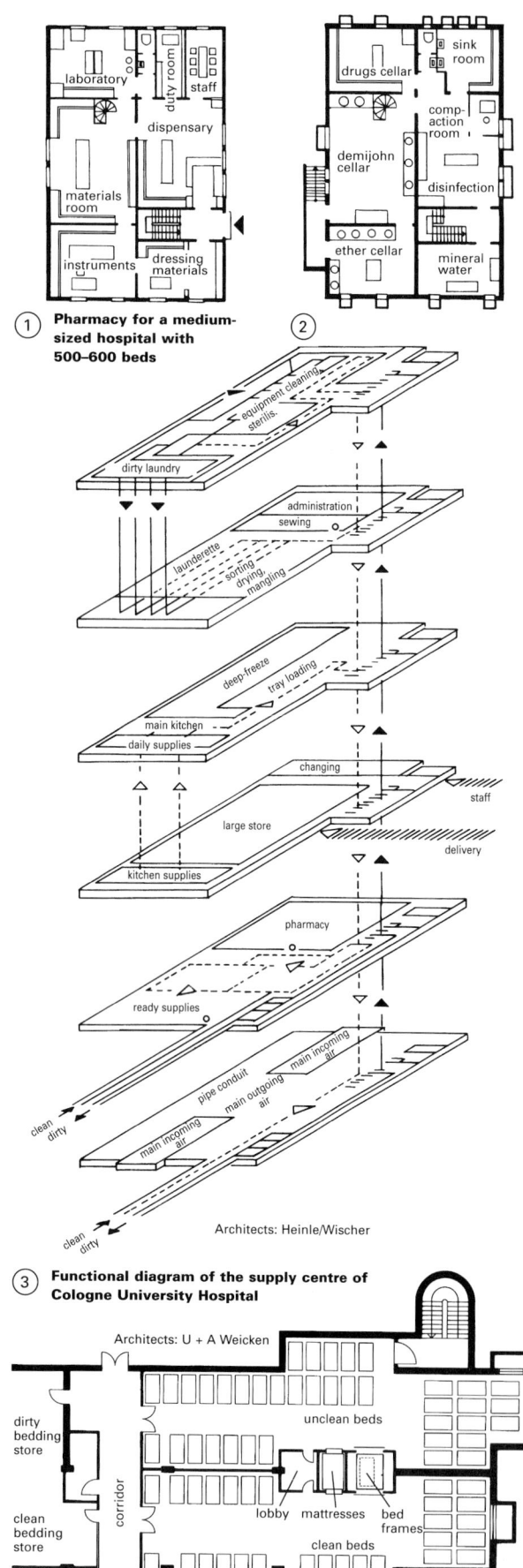

① **Pharmacy for a medium-sized hospital with 500–600 beds**

②

③ **Functional diagram of the supply centre of Cologne University Hospital**

Architects: Heinle/Wischer

Architects: U + A Weicken

④ **Central bed unit, St Elisabeth Hospital, Halle/S**

Pharmacy

In medium-size and large hospitals the pharmacy stocks prescriptions and carries out examinations under the management of an accredited pharmacist. In the design the following rooms are necessary: dispensary, materials room, drug store, laboratory and, possibly, an issue desk. If necessary, also include herb and dressing materials rooms, demijohn and acid cellar, and a room in which night duty personnel can sleep. The dispensary and laboratory should contain a prescription table, a work table, a packing table and a sink. The storage of inflammable liquids and acids, as well as various anaesthetics, means appropriate safety measures are stipulated for the walls, ceilings and doors.

The pharmacy must be close to lifts and the pneumatic tube dispatch system.

Central bed unit

From the point of view of hygiene and economy, every hospital should contain a bed unit, in which the appropriate staff strip down, clean, disinfect and make up the beds. A complete bed change is required for new admissions, patients after 14 days as an inpatient, after operations and deliveries, as well as after serious soiling. The size of the bed unit depends on the number of nursing beds in the hospital: for about 500 inpatients a bed unit for 70 beds should be provided. The functional demarcation requires a clean and non-clean side, separated by the bed cleaning room, mattress disinfecting room and staff lobby. For carrying out repairs, a special workshop, approximately 35 m², should be situated in the close vicinity, as should the laundry and store for clean bedding, mattresses etc. If machines are to be used to clean the bed frames and mattresses, the specific requirements of the equipment must be taken into account at an early stage (e.g. demands for floor recesses, clear heights).

Laundry provision

Figures for the amount of dirty dry washing generated per bed per day vary between 0.8 and 3.0 kg. The following sequence of work is preferred in the laundry: receipt, sorting, weighing, washing, spinning, beating out, mangling or drying (tumble dryer), pressing (if possible high pressure steam connection), ironing, sewing, storage, issue. The laundry hall consists of a sorting and weighing area (15 m²), laundry collection room under laundry chutes from the wards, wet working area (50 m²), dry working area (60 m²), detergent store (10 m²), sewing room (10 m²) and laundry store (15 m²).

Meal provision

Providing the patients with proper nutrition places high demands on food preparation since the required amounts of protein, fat, carbohydrates, vitamins, minerals, fibre and flavourings often vary. The dominant food provision systems are those which rationalise the individual phases of conventional food preparation (preparatory work, making up, transporting, distribution). Preparation of normal food and special diets takes place separately. After preparation and cooking the meals are put together on the portioning line. The portioned trays are transported with the supply trolleys to the various stations for distribution. The same trolleys are used to transport the used crockery back to the central washing up and trolley cleaning unit.

Staff catering consists of about 40% of the total catering demand. The staff dining room should be close to the central kitchen. A division into separate rooms for domestic staff, nurses, clerical staff and doctors could be considered in a large hospital but, again, for economic reasons, these rooms must be near to the main kitchen. For small and medium-size hospitals this type of division is not recommended.

Supplies Areas

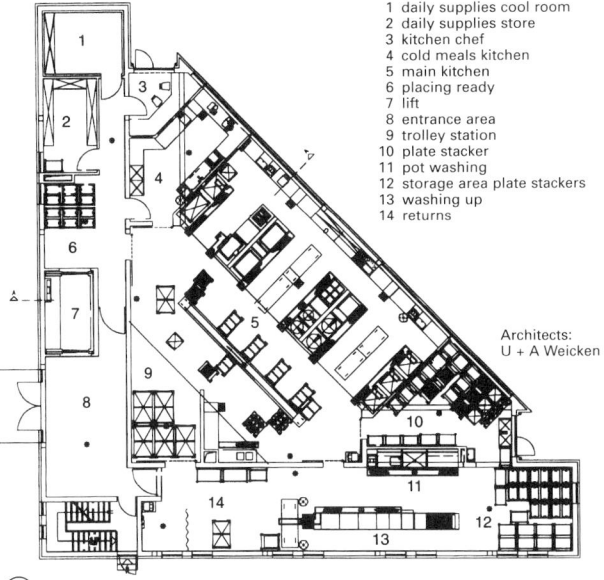

1 daily supplies cool room
2 daily supplies store
3 kitchen chef
4 cold meals kitchen
5 main kitchen
6 placing ready
7 lift
8 entrance area
9 trolley station
10 plate stacker
11 pot washing
12 storage area plate stackers
13 washing up
14 returns

Architects:
U + A Weicken

① **Kitchen building, ground floor**

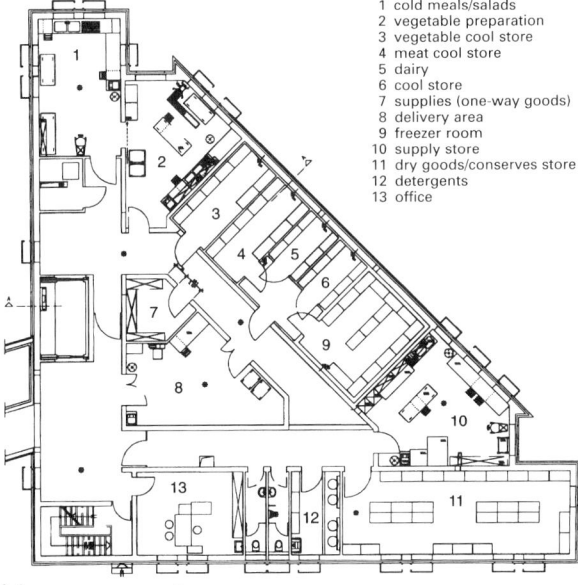

1 cold meals/salads
2 vegetable preparation
3 vegetable cool store
4 meat cool store
5 dairy
6 cool store
7 supplies (one-way goods)
8 delivery area
9 freezer room
10 supply store
11 dry goods/conserves store
12 detergents
13 office

② **Basement → ①**

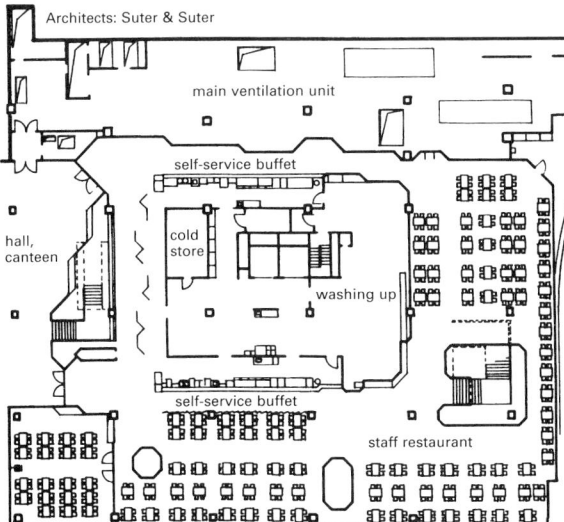

Architects: Suter & Suter

main ventilation unit

self-service buffet

hall,
canteen

cold
store

washing up

self-service buffet

staff restaurant

③ **Staff restaurant for 150 employees, Basel Cantonal Hospital**

Central kitchen: Historically, kitchens were on the top floor to reduce the smell and noise. Today they are positioned on the same level as supplies to give an efficient working process: delivery, storage, preparation, making up and dispatch. When deep-frozen food is used, the set-up of the kitchen changes. Here the architect and users must co-operate closely to optimise the meal preparation process and find an advantageous, space-saving solution. The clear height of the kitchen hall should be 4.00 m. The size of the kitchen depends on the requirements and number of patients in the hospital. In the main kitchen an area of 1.00 m^2 is needed per person. A special-diet kitchen (60 m^2 minimum) should also be planned, with a desk for the head chef, a 30 m^2 vegetable cleaning area and a 5 m^2 provision for waste disposal. In addition, the plan must include a daily supplies room (8 m^2), a cold store with compartments for meat, fish and dairy products (8 m^2 each) and a pre-cooling store (10 m^2) with a chest freezer and cooling unit. The goods delivery area should be connected to administration and have sufficient storage space (15–20 m^2). The main store should hold fruit and vegetables (20 m^2), dry goods (20 m^2) and tinned goods/preserves, and must be adjoining.

Central washing-up unit: The central washing-up unit, adjacent to the central kitchen, stores and cleans the staff and patients' dishes. The high level of automation makes it essential for the designer, at an early stage, to clarify and conform to the specific requirements of the individual pieces of equipment.

Technical supplies: The technical service is responsible for technical supplies and plays an increasingly important role as more automation is introduced. Tasks include building maintenance, domestic technology, medical technology, conveyor technology and administration.

It should be noted that sanitary installations are the subject of rapid technical development. It is advantageous to have ring circuits for the horizontal supplies on each storey and rising supplies in separate ducts for vertical connections. The horizontal supply pipes should be installed in the voids above suspended ceilings to make subsequent alterations easy. Water is treated centrally; only areas with higher quality requirements (pharmacy) have local water preparation (desalination, softening). Water consumption is calculated at 400–450 l of water per hospital bed per day, depending on the type and situation of the hospital. Note that waste water is subject to local regulations.

Ventilation and gases: The ventilation equipment is best situated near to the open air. During planning, the horizontal and vertical ventilation ducts should be tested against technical fire protection criteria.

It is necessary to provide medical gases for the surgical, intensive care and radiology departments, and special supply rooms are required. The pumps for oxygen, carbon dioxide, vacuum and compressed air should be duplicated so as to provide a backup in case of failure. An additional technical requirement is an emergency electrical supply system.

Central heating unit: Earlier systems, using a boiler room, required large basement areas (≥100 m^2), generally on two storeys. Current heating systems are less area-intensive and district heating is particularly advantageous. Note that the surgical and intensive care departments must have a continuous heat supply so emergency systems must therefore be planned. The heating system and medical services supply/emergency power unit may be accommodated in one large room. The layout requirements for services (water, electricity, gas etc.) and flues are laid down in regulations and these must be observed. Emergency escape doors must open outwards.

If possible, the 'heat store' (and entry to it) should be situated underground, outside the building. Note that there are building and heating room regulations which apply.

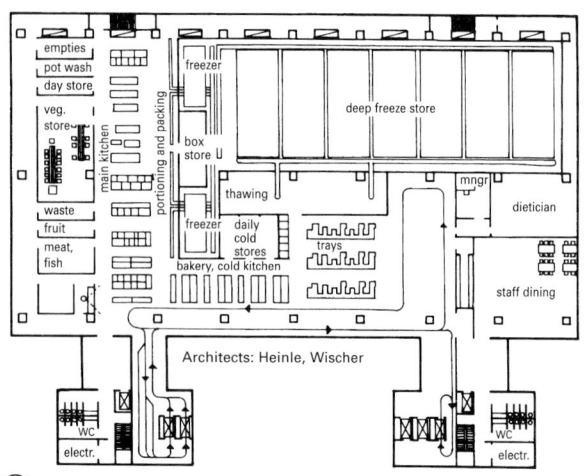

① **Kitchen area: Cologne University Hospital**

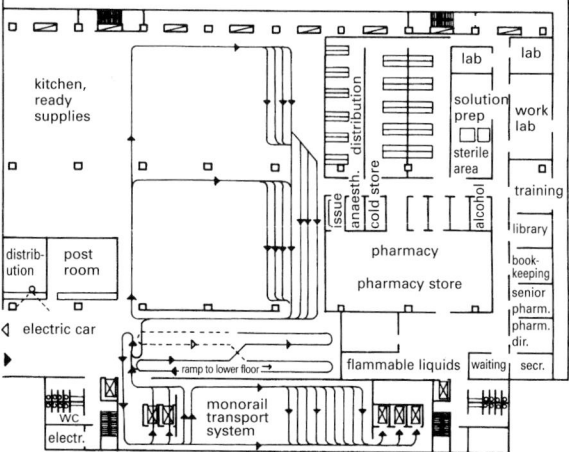

Architects: Heinle, Wischer

② **Supply centre: Cologne University Hospital**

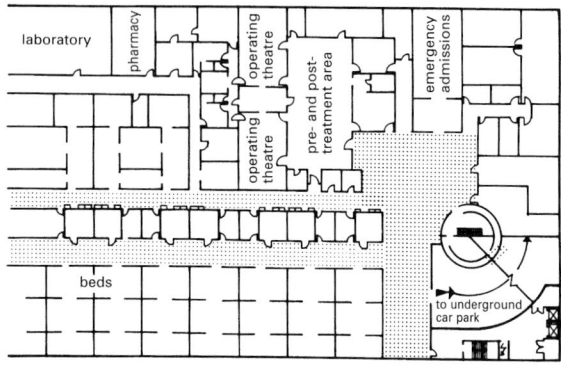

Architects: Suter & Suter

③ **Civil bunker with two operating theatres and recovery areas: Basel Cantonal Hospital**

HOSPITALS

Supplies Areas

In recent years increasing use has been made of modern organisational models. The central organisation of individual supply and disposal areas alleviates the problem of increasing staff shortages. Internal central supply routes are separated from the other traffic flows in the hospital and external disruption is avoided, allowing optimum use of the transport system's capacity. Computer simulation programs can show the architect efficient operational sequences (which can still be modified throughout the planning phase) and setting utilisation targets allows the space required in the supplies area to be minimised.

Electrical systems

The power supply is taken from the national grid: 220–240V standard voltage and 380V high voltage. The low voltage system is controlled from the distributor room which requires at least two free-standing transformer cell units. Sufficiently wide doors (at least 1.30m clear width) and good ventilation must be provided and all relevant VDE and professional association regulations must be complied with. The size and number of emergency power units depends on the size of the hospital and local plants for individual functional units (surgical/outpatients department, care areas, radiology) are preferable to a central emergency power system. Anti-vibration foundations should be used underneath these units to reduce noise. Additional batteries must be provided for lighting and emergency power in the surgical department.

Central gas supply

Oxygen and nitrogen lines are supplied from steel cylinders, alternating between operating and reserve batteries with an automatic changeover facility. To reduce the distance that these cylinders need to be transported, direct access to the goods yard is preferred. The cylinders may be stored with the medical services pumps (for vacuum and compressed air lines) at a central supply point (possibly computer-controlled). Gas cylinders are beginning to be replaced by 'cold gasifiers'. These must stand in the open air at least 5m from buildings.

Workshops

Connected to the goods yard are metalwork and electrical workshops (40m²), with a materials store, spare parts store (20m²), general store (60m²) and standing area for transport equipment (15m²). A water reservoir (emergency water tank) should be planned for, possibly at the elevator crossings over the top storey (40m³). Water treatment plant for the general hospital and the sterilisation area must be separated.

Communications centre

The following information and communications media could be needed in the hospital: telephones and faxes, intercom systems, nurse call system, clocks, pagers, a PA system for music and announcements, television, telex, radio. For a better overview, a central point should be set up for co-ordinating these media (in the entrance hall or in a room off reception). Pagers are to be provided in parallel with the telephone network where it is not feasible to reach a telephone for time or operational reasons (e.g. surgical area, radiology). The nurse intercom system allows a voice link between individual nurses' workrooms and the patients' rooms. Several hundred clocks with a second hand can be controlled from a quartz battery clock via the telephone network. Patients' rooms are to be equipped with telephone, telephone paging and television. In teaching and research hospitals it is important to have closed-circuit television (monitoring). All buildings must be monitored by an automatic fire alarm system, supplemented with manual alarm switches. In the event of fire, the ventilation system, transport systems and elevators are controlled via the fire alarm system. Consultation with specialist engineers is essential.

Bunkers

The requirements of structures providing protection from radioactive fall-out and air attack vary from country to country so the local guidelines must be followed. In Switzerland, for example, an auxiliary operating theatre, wards, sterile goods store and emergency technical systems must be provided.

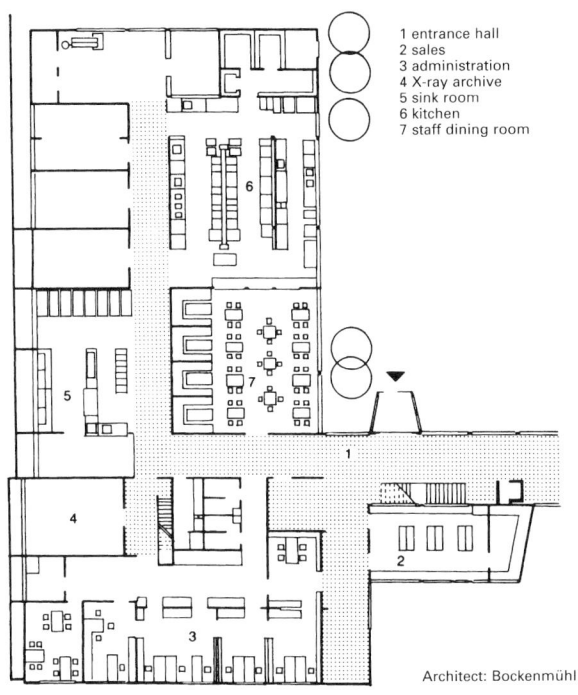

1 entrance hall
2 sales
3 administration
4 X-ray archive
5 sink room
6 kitchen
7 staff dining room

Architect: Bockenmühl

① Entrance hall and administrative area of Herdecke Community Hospital in the Ruhr: 192 beds

Archive and store rooms

A short route between archives and work areas is advantageous but generally difficult to provide. One possibility is to locate them in the basement and have a link by stairs. Distinctions should be made between store and archive rooms for files, documentation and film from administration, the X-ray department etc. and supplies (pharmacy, disinfection, kitchen etc.) and equipment (kitchen, administration, workshops etc.). The necessary depth of shelves and cupboards depends on the goods stored. For files, books and film, 250–400 mm is adequate; for equipment, china spare parts etc., 400–600 mm is needed. Mobile shelving systems are useful for reducing the floor area occupied. The high loads imposed by shelves (up to 1000 kg/m^2) must be taken into account from an early stage.

Communal rooms

Dining rooms and cafeteria are best situated on the ground floor, or on the top floor to give a good view, must have a direct connection to the servery. The connection to the central kitchen is by goods lift, which is not accessible to visitors. Consider whether it is sensible to separate visitors, staff and patients. Nowadays, the dining areas are often run by external caterers and the self-service system (servery 6–8 m) has become generally accepted. Salad counters should stand independently.

Prayer rooms

These should, preferably, occupy a central location, at the intersection of internal and external circulation routes, but outside the care, treatment and supply areas. This allows access for employees, visitors and inpatients. The size of devotional rooms and the facilities they offer will vary according to faith, place and person, but they are often not oriented towards a particular faith. At least 40 m^2 should be allocated.

In large hospitals, it might possibly be desirable to include a chapel, in which case the relevant church authorities should be consulted. (See the section entitled Places of Worship for details of the requirements.)

When planning rooms to cater for spiritual needs in hospitals, it is essential to consider space requirements for wheelchair users and those who are bedridden.

Administration rooms

Rooms for administration should be connected by corridor to the entrance hall and be close to the main circulation routes. A suitable route to the supplies area must also be planned.

Staffing per 100 occupied beds and 1000 patients (Germany, 1980–1995)

number per staff group	for each 100 beds					for each 1000 patients				
	1980 West Germany	1985 West Germany	1990 West Germany	1991 Unified Germany	1995 Unified Germany	1980 West Germany	1985 West Germany	1990 West Germany	1991 Unified Germany	1995 Unified Germany
1 medical	11.7	13.6	15.7	17.1	20.4	5.4	6.0	5.9	6.8	6.8
2 nursing	44.8	48.8	55.2	58.5	70.4	20.6	21.4	20.9	23.4	23.4
3 medical technical	14.1	15.8	17.5	21.9	25.0	6.5	7.0	6.6	8.8	8.3
4 operational	9.4	11.0	12.9	14.1	16.3	4.3	4.8	4.9	5.7	5.4
groups 1–4	80.1	89.2	101.2	111.5	132.2	36.8	39.2	38.4	44.7	43.9
5 clinical domestic	10.2	8.2	7.0	7.6	6.8	4.7	3.6	2.7	3.0	2.2
6 managerial and supplies	18.1	17.0	17.1	17.2	17.2	8.3	7.5	6.5	6.9	5.7
7 technical	1.3	2.3	3.3	4.4	4.5	0.6	1.0	1.3	1.5	1.8
8 administration	7.5	8.0	8.8	10.9	12.1	3.5	3.5	3.3	4.4	4.0
9 specialist	1.4	1.5	1.7	2.0	1.6	0.7	0.6	0.7	0.8	0.5
10 other staff	3.4	3.4	3.9	3.5	3.9	1.6	1.5	1.5	1.4	1.3
11 total staff	122.1	129.6	143.0	157.0	178.3	56.2	57.0	54.3	62.9	59.2
without 'other' (10)	118.6	126.2	139.1	153.5	174.4	54.6	55.4	52.8	61.5	57.9

source: German Hospital Association (DKG), issued 1997

The following requirements are based on a one hundred-bed occupancy level. In the administrative area, 7–12 m^2 per member of staff should be planned. Rooms for dealings with patients and relatives need to be connected to reception (entrance hall), admissions and accounts (25 m^2). Links to the casualty entrance are also important, and there should be at least two reception areas (each 5 m^2) for demarcation before the main reception, the cash-desk (12 m^2) and accounts (12 m^2).

Additional rooms needed include: an office for the administrative director (20 m^2), a secretarial room (10 m^2), an administrators' office (15 m^2, possibly in the supply area), a nurses' office (20 m^2), a personnel office (25 m^2) and central archives (40 m^2, possibly in the basement with a link to the administration department via stairs).

According to requirements, the plan should also provide: duty rooms for matron and welfare workers, a doctors' staff room and consulting rooms, a messenger room, a medical records archive, specialist and patients' libraries, and a hairdresser's room (with two seats).

The increasing rationalisation of accounts and the use of electronic systems and computers should be taken into consideration during planning (e.g. cableways in floors – possibly, raised floors – central desk with tube post link etc.).

Main entrance

General traffic goes only to the main entrance; for hygiene reasons (e.g. risk of infection), special entrances are to be shown separately. The entrance hall, on the basis of the open-door principle, should be designed as a waiting room for visitors. Today's layouts are more like that of a modern hotel foyer, having moved away from the typical hospital character. The size of the hall depends on bed capacity and the expected number of visitors. Circulation routes for visitors, patients and staff are separated from the hall onwards. The reception and telephone switchboard (12 m^2) are formed using counters, allowing staff to supervise more effectively. However, it must be possible to prevent public access from reception to inner areas and main staff circulation routes. The entrance hall should also contain pay phones and a kiosk selling tobacco, sweets, flowers and writing materials.

Casualty entrance

A covered access road or closed hall overlooked by the administration department, but not visible from the main entrance, is preferred for incoming casualty patients. Short routes to outpatients, the surgical/X-ray departments and the wards should be planned and these must be free of general traffic. An examination room for first aid (15 m^2), a washroom (15 m^2), an ante-room (10 m^2), standing room for at least two stretchers, and a laundry store should be included in an area where they are accessible directly beyond the entrance.

571

HOSPITALS

Teaching and Research

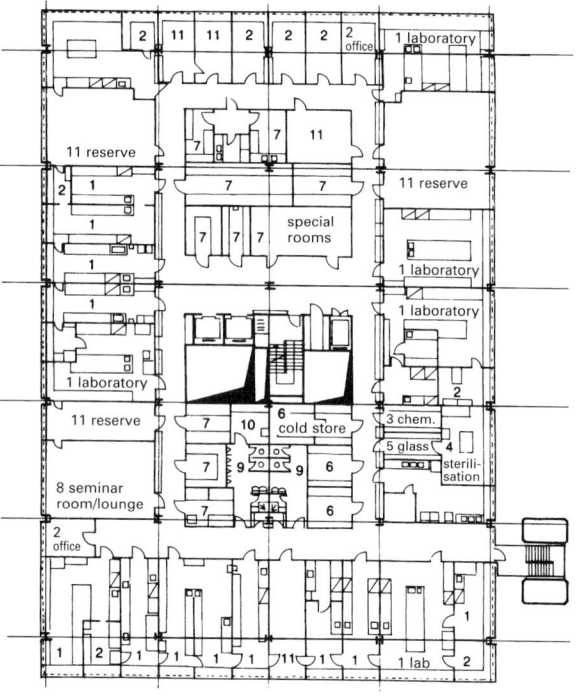

03 services
02 stores, laundry, pool
01 kitchen, workshops,
   experiment station

0 canteens, halls
1 cafeteria, lecture theatres
2 library

3 laboratories
4 training laboratory
5 plant

Architects: Suter & Suter

① **Teaching and research centre, Basel**

② **Level 3: research laboratory**

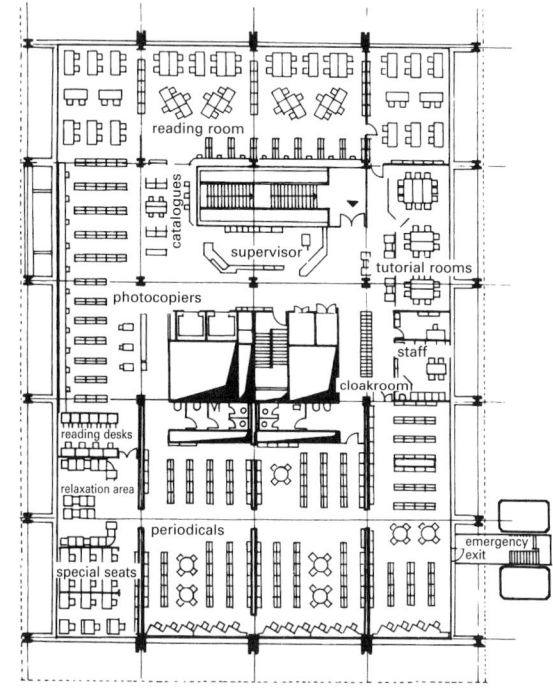

③ **Level 2: library**

Residential area

The residential areas are, without exception, separated from the main hospital but reached via the access road for the entire site. The area is divided into residential homes, apartments and training schools. There must be sufficient parking spaces for vehicles belonging to the employees.

In addition to nurses, residential homes for female employees should also accommodate female doctors, assistant physicians, auxiliary staff and students, if necessary. Bedsitting rooms should be designed uniformly as single rooms with a cupboard and wash-basin (16 m²) or, preferably, with a separate WC/shower area. The usual dimensions of the rooms are approximately 4.60–4.75 m × 3.00–3.50 m. The storey height of standard residential buildings is adequate.

Opinions on the arrangement of kitchen units vary. Previously, the norm was 10–12 bedsitting rooms in a residential group sharing a kitchen (6 m²), lounge (20 m²), possibly a balcony, and a cleaning room (10 m²). Today bedsitting rooms with an integrated cooking area and en-suite facilities are usual (see the section covering student halls of residence). Common rooms for all employees are one lounge (1.0 m² per bedsitting room; 20 m² minimum), connecting with a multipurpose room (20 m²), a cloakroom, WCs, a laundry room (10 m²), a drying room (15 m²) and a storage room (30 m²). Similar residential homes for male employees should be in the design unless the size of the hospital necessitates a common residential home.

Apartments

Doctors should be housed in two-room apartments (40 m²) in separate male and female residential blocks. Three- and four-room apartments (70–90 m²) away from these blocks should also be planned for doctors, hospital administrators and house masters. Communal rooms may be arranged for doctors if necessary: library and reading room (25 m²), club room (35 m²). The proportion of apartments for doctors is currently growing smaller.

Training schools

To provide practical experience, a specific area in close contact with the hospital is required for training medical students, teaching and research. Increasing student numbers are making greater demands on training schools. The following must be provided: stores, workshops, experimental stations (pharmacy), audiovisual facilities for video transmissions from the surgical department, possibly a separate cafeteria, lecture theatres (150–500 seats), a library, research and teaching laboratories, practice rooms and office space. The number and size of all rooms depend on the scale and location of the institution.

Experimental stations

This is where all laboratory animals are kept and is an area of particular importance in university hospitals. The experimental station is connected to other laboratory areas by passenger and goods lift. Large additional areas must be planned for the breeding and keeping of animals.

Library

Medical libraries should be designed as open-shelf libraries, with no closed stores and no requirement for issuing books. A large part of the literature will be made up of periodicals. It is important to have an adequate number of reading tables with reading lamps, workstations with microfiche readers, slide viewers and typewriters. It is advantageous if the library is connected to the small or medium-size transportation systems of the hospital.

A&E AND OUTPATIENTS DEPARTMENT

Accident and emergency (A&E)

The accident and emergency department is for ambulant and bedridden patients and is accessed via the emergency entrance (note that the minimum vehicle headroom is 3.50 m). Clear signposting to the drive-in entrance is of life-saving importance for ambulance drivers. It is convenient to site this entrance on the opposite side of the building to the main entrance to avoid contact with the visitors and other patients.

The accident and emergency department consists of emergency treatment rooms (20–25 m²) equipped with operating tables, small operating lights, cupboard units with sinks, and patient cubicles. In addition, a plaster room with plastering bench and equipment and a shock treatment and recovery room must be available.

Proximity to the surgical department is essential, even if a special intervention room for emergencies is included in the plan, and surgery and anaesthesia services should also be grouped nearby.

Casualty hospitals

These are generally found only in cities and often also serve rehabilitation purposes. Such auxiliary hospitals, with a well-trained surgical department, are often accommodated in old general hospitals which have been moved to new buildings.

Public health offices

In Germany these generally perform the functions of an outpatients clinic; they provide the outlet for preventive measures and follow-up treatment of ambulant patients who have been discharged.

Typical facilities in an outpatient clinic are as follows:

- examination and treatment rooms are needed for initial diagnosis, preliminary treatment, follow-up treatment and consultations, etc., all with separate waiting rooms
- office rooms should be provided for doctors co-ordinating, for example, strategies for combating epidemics and these should have ante-rooms (e.g. for records, inoculations etc.) as well as a separate waiting room
- venereal disease treatment requires examination rooms (with WCs), ante-rooms for patient records and medication etc., and waiting rooms
- infant welfare services should have a waiting room, a nursing room and ample space for prams (at the entrance), materials and records

In addition, plans must include medical-technical rooms, X-ray departments, rooms for administrators and personnel, and rooms for storage and archiving.

The size of all of these rooms varies and needs to be agreed between the planner and the users.

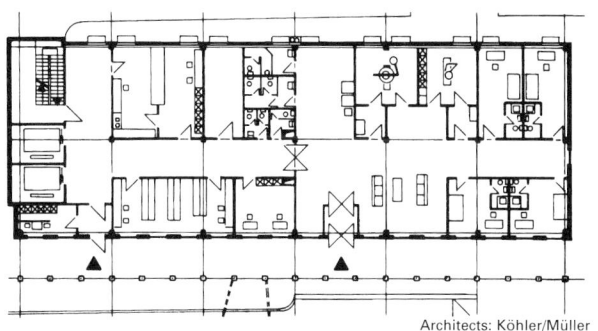

Architects: Köhler/Müller

(1) **Accident and emergency department: duty doctors' rooms; central sterilisation**

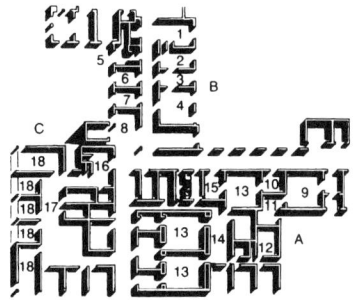

outpatients
1 admission/waiting
2 minor treatment
3 recovery room
4 multipurpose room (urology)
5 doctors' cloakroom
6 doctors' consulting room
7 doctor's room
8 free area for fresh beds ('bed waiting')

surgical area
9 septic surgery (endoscopy)
10 anaesthesia
11 equipment room
12 staff lounge
13 aseptic surgery
14 sterilisation, washing
15 discharge

intensive care ward
16 demarcation lobby to intensive care area
17 service corridor
18 intensive treatment rooms

(2) **Part-plan of the functional areas: A surgical, B outpatients, C intensive care**

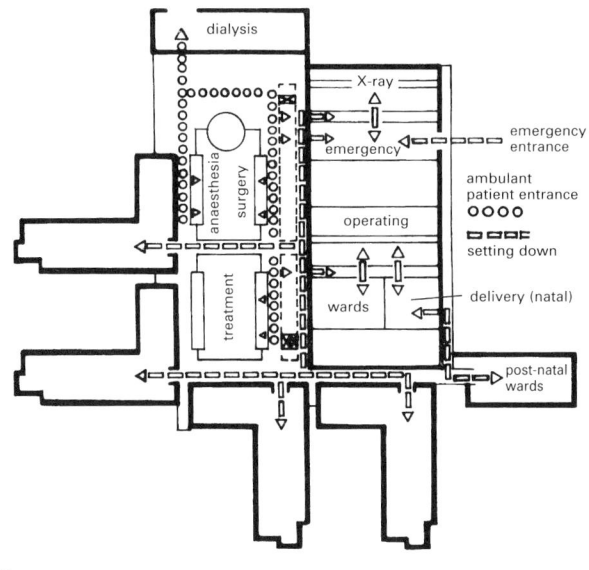

(3) **Internal connections, Prignitz Hospital**　　Architects: B + C Lambart

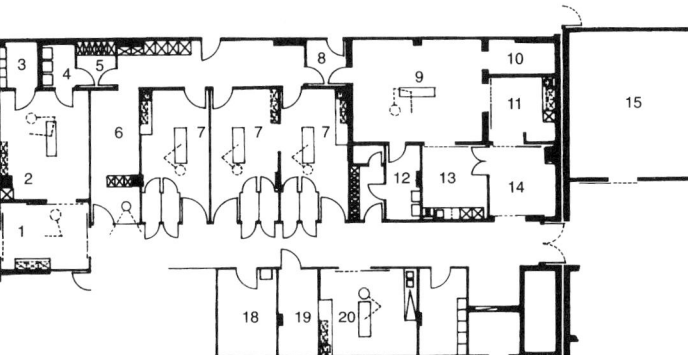

1 anaesthetics and discharge
2 septic intervention
3 equipment
4 waiting room
5 changing room
6 records
7 emergency treatment room
8 disposals
9 sterile operating theatre
10 equipment
11 anaesthetics
12 washroom
13 discharge
14 bed-to-bed transfer room
15 first aid
16 reception
17 admission
18 ultrasound
19 electrical switchgear
20 examination and treatment room

Architects: U + A Weicken

(4) **Accident and emergency, St Elisabeth Hospital, Halle**

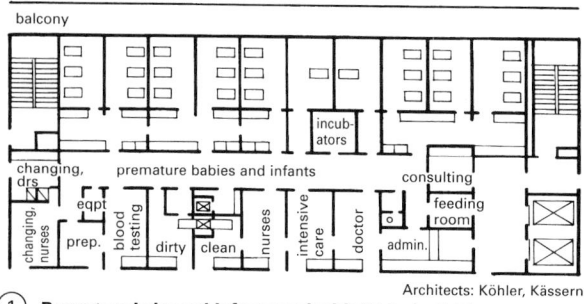

① **Premature baby and infant ward with 27 beds, Fulda**

Architects: Köhler, Kässern

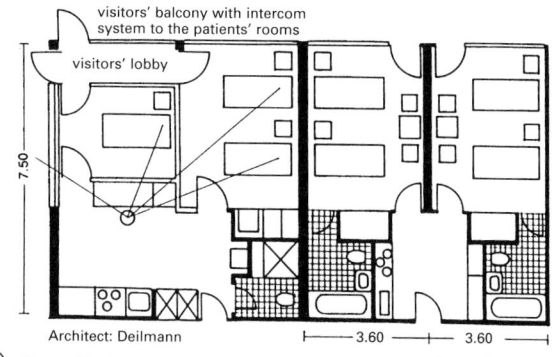

② **Care of infectious children: room variations** → ③ – ④

Architect: Deilmann

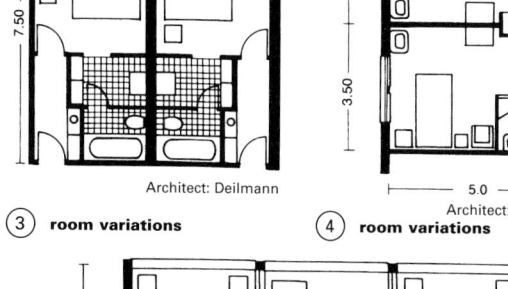

③ **room variations**

Architect: Deilmann

④ **room variations**

Architect: Deilmann

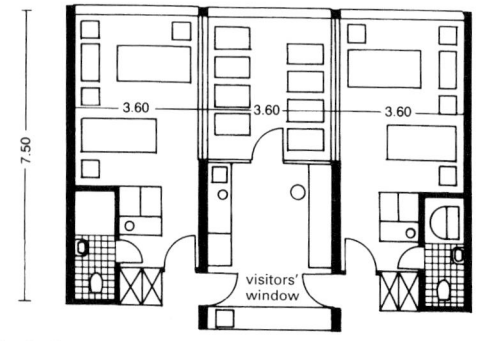

⑤ **One-bed room with separate infant room**

Architect: Mayhew

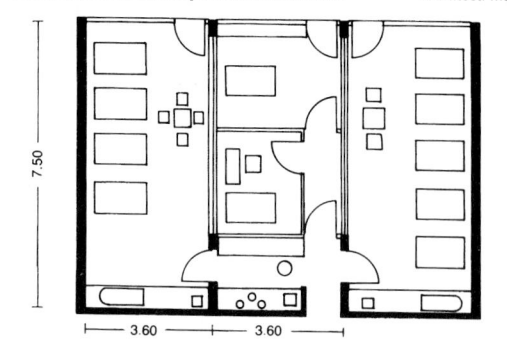

⑥ **Neonatal and maternity care**

Architect: Deilmann

HOSPITALS

Maternity and Neonatal Care

The maternity and neonatal department provides continual physical, medical, psychological and social care for mothers and new babies following a hospital delivery. After uncomplicated births, the care of new mothers can be considered part of normal care. However, new mothers with highly infectious diseases, such as typhoid, TB and hepatitis, need to be housed in an isolation care ward. Where vital functions are disrupted, provision should be made for easy transfer to the intensive care ward. Neonates with infections or respiratory difficulties (e.g. premature babies) have to be transferred to special departments or the nearest children's hospital.

The division of maternity care is the same as for normal care: basic care, treatment care, patient care, administration and supply. Organisation of the processes with the options of ward care, group care or individual care are also the same as for normal care. With centralised neonatal provision, the care unit for neonates is located at the side of or within the maternity care unit. To reduce infection, the area is divided into small rooms or compartments. Neonates are carried into the mother's room on trolleys or by hand for breast feeding. This achieves more frequent and more intensive contact between mother and child than in previous designs with central feeding rooms. Accommodating mothers and neonates in one room ('rooming in') means the infants do not need to be moved, which thus relieves the staff, but requires uneconomic local neonatal provision. Despite this, it has become standard practice in some hospitals.

Facilities and size of care units

They are generally smaller than the units in normal care areas. Smaller wards are preferable because they are easier to control in terms of hygiene (less movement of staff and visitors) so it is advisable to limit the size per care unit to 10–14 bed spaces. The functions may be divided into: care of healthy mothers, care of healthy neonates, care of special neonates (e.g. premature babies) and incidental functions. For hygiene reasons, higher demands are to be made on maternal and neonatal care than on normal care. Therefore, a visitors' lobby and cloakroom area must be provided in addition to the usual system of demarcation. The bed space can be planned as in normal care but the bed spacing must be increased to allow space for a baby's crib next to the beds. Sit-bath/shower combinations and showers must be provided in the sanitary zones where mothers should not take full baths in tubs.

The neonatal care units comprise: bed spaces for neonates, undressing/dressing areas, baby bathing, weighing point, children's nurses' duty station and, possibly, a trolley standing area. A special neonatal care unit with isolated beds and care points should be provided for babies with pathogenic conditions. The following elements or rooms are also to be included in an incidental function area: duty station for the ward sister, nurses' lounge, kitchenette, doctors' offices, examination and treatment room, clean workroom, patient bathroom, day-rooms for patients and visitors, storage space for equipment and cleaning materials, staff and visitors' WCs, linen cupboards and a room for consultation with relatives.

Environment

To minimise the transfer of airborne germs, the ventilation system must process eight changes of air per hour. The room temperatures must be between 24°C and 26°C.

Position

The transport route for new mothers and neonates after delivery should be as short as possible and not cross any other busy corridors. Obstetrics and maternity care should preferably be on one level to avoid the need to use lifts.

Mortuary, Pathology, Service Yard

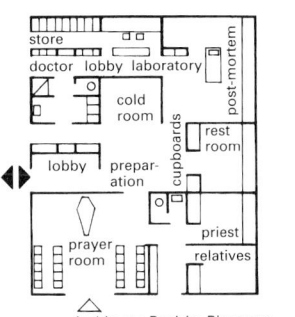

(1) **Soltau Hospital: 354 beds**
Architects: Poelzig, Biermann

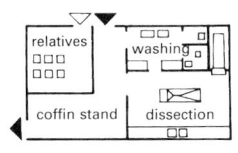

(2) **Mortuary, St Joseph's Hospital, Wipperfürth (372 beds)**
Architects: Köhler, Helfrich

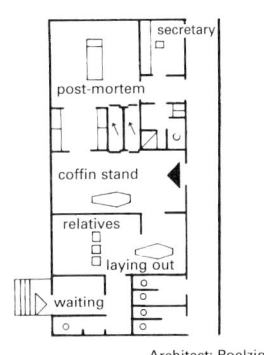

(3) **Mortuary, St Clemens Hospital, Geldern (480 beds)**
Architect: Poelzig

(4) **Mortuary, Municipal Hospital, Verbert (444 beds)**
Architects: Krüger, Krüger, Rieger

Mortuary, pathology

The mortuary of a hospital contains storage rooms and post-mortem rooms. Specifically, there must be a coffin store, refrigerated storage for corpses, an area for laying out and undertakers, and changing facilities for pathologists. As an independent hospital department it should be so planned as to have access by a short route to a group of lifts (to the nursing stations). The entrance must be clearly marked for the relatives and there should be a short drive-in entry point for the undertakers. Depending on the size of the hospital, this area can be extended with the addition of a laboratory and an archive.

Service yard

Hospital logistics should be centred in one place. A service yard, conveniently situated in a low-level supplies and disposal area, makes this possible. The supply and disposal of all hospital goods and materials is conducted via a separate road connection, segregated from the main and emergency entrances. During planning, consideration must be given not just to the parking and manoeuvring area for goods vehicles, but also to the wide variety of waste to be managed (kitchen, septic, metal, glass, paper, chemicals etc.) and the necessary storage requirements. In addition, service yard auxiliary rooms house emergency electricity generators, the sprinkler control room, the oxygen distribution system, and other services. As a result of the many different functions and the different types of supply vehicles which will have to be accommodated, it is not possible to specify the space needed for this area; at an early stage, the designer and users need to agree on the requirements. Given that the basement is the most suitable location for the service yard, it will only be accessible via a ramp; the slope must be less than 15°. Where the yard is built over, regulations regarding ventilation must be followed.

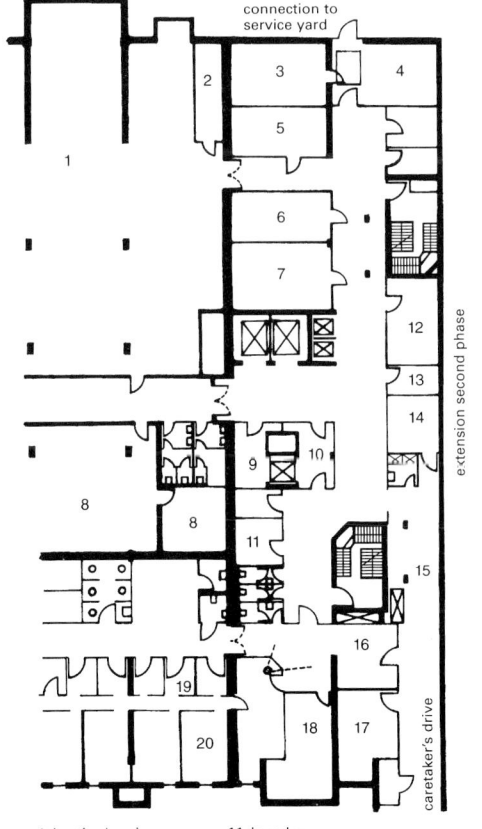

1 heating/services
2 electrical switchgear
3 water/gas feeds
4 store room
5 oxygen
6 electrical controls
7 data handling
8 store
9 supplies
10 disposals
11 laundry
12 store room
13 relatives
14 laying out
15 coffin standing
16 dissection
17 equipment
18 records
19 rest room
20 hydro-massage

Architects: U + A Weicken

(5) **Basement floor with supply and disposal provision, mortuary, physical therapy**

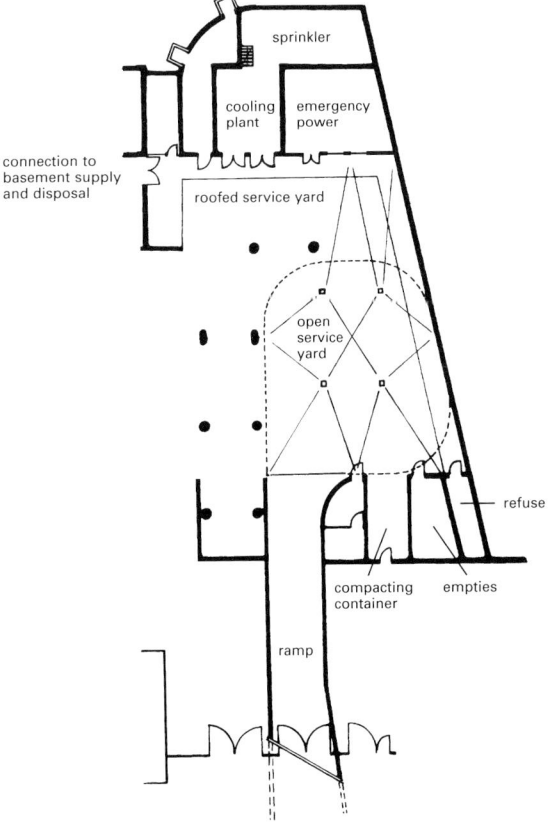

Architects: U + A Weicken

(6) **Service yard/ramp**

SPECIAL HOSPITALS

Hospitals specialising in specific medical fields are becoming increasingly important. They require a far more space-intensive general arrangement and this leaves the planner facing extra demands. It is vital to have ongoing co-operation between the architect, medical engineers and the doctors/nurses who will be working in the hospital.

Special hospitals cover medical disciplines such as specific surgical procedures, a range of therapies, psychiatry and paediatrics. There has been a proportionate increase in the number of clinics for treating allergies, skin complaints and lung diseases.

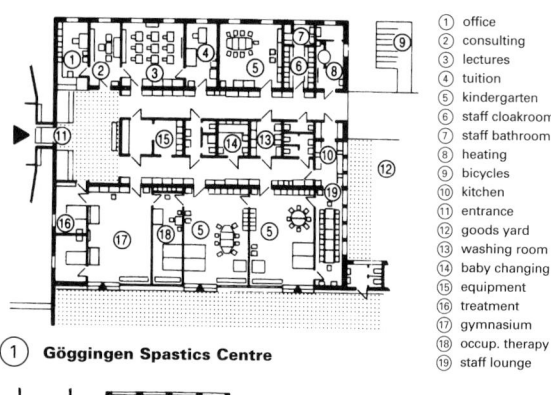

① office
② consulting
③ lectures
④ tuition
⑤ kindergarten
⑥ staff cloakroom
⑦ staff bathroom
⑧ heating
⑨ bicycles
⑩ kitchen
⑪ entrance
⑫ goods yard
⑬ washing room
⑭ baby changing
⑮ equipment
⑯ treatment
⑰ gymnasium
⑱ occup. therapy
⑲ staff lounge

① **Göggingen Spastics Centre**

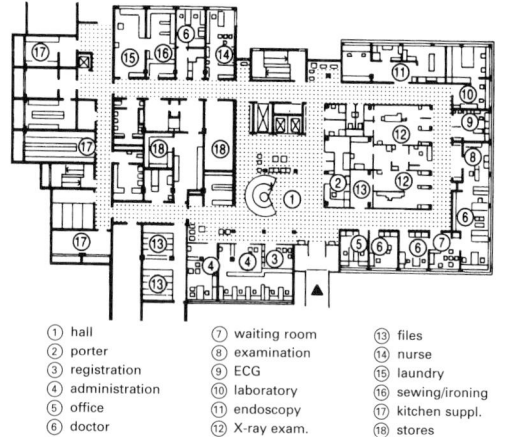

① hall
② porter
③ registration
④ administration
⑤ office
⑥ doctor
⑦ waiting room
⑧ examination
⑨ ECG
⑩ laboratory
⑪ endoscopy
⑫ X-ray exam.
⑬ files
⑭ nurse
⑮ laundry
⑯ sewing/ironing
⑰ kitchen suppl.
⑱ stores

② **Wildbad Rheumatism Hospital (100 beds): ground floor**

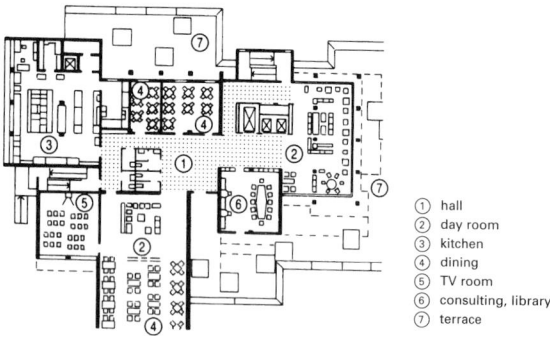

① hall
② day room
③ kitchen
④ dining
⑤ TV room
⑥ consulting, library
⑦ terrace

③ **Wildbad Rheumatism Hospital: first floor**

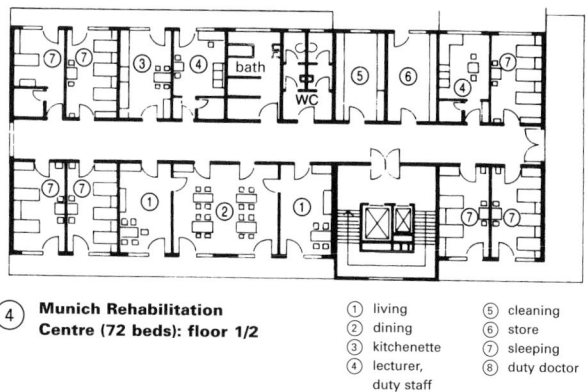

④ **Munich Rehabilitation Centre (72 beds): floor 1/2**

① living
② dining
③ kitchenette
④ lecturer, duty staff
⑤ cleaning
⑥ store
⑦ sleeping
⑧ duty doctor

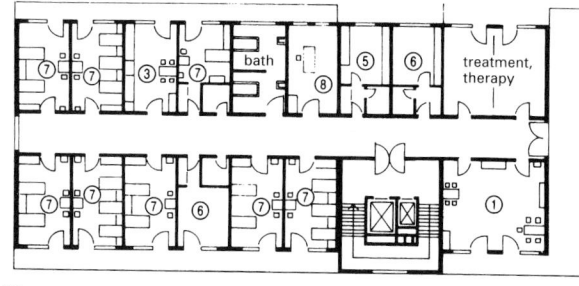

⑤ **Munich Rehabilitation Centre: fourth floor**

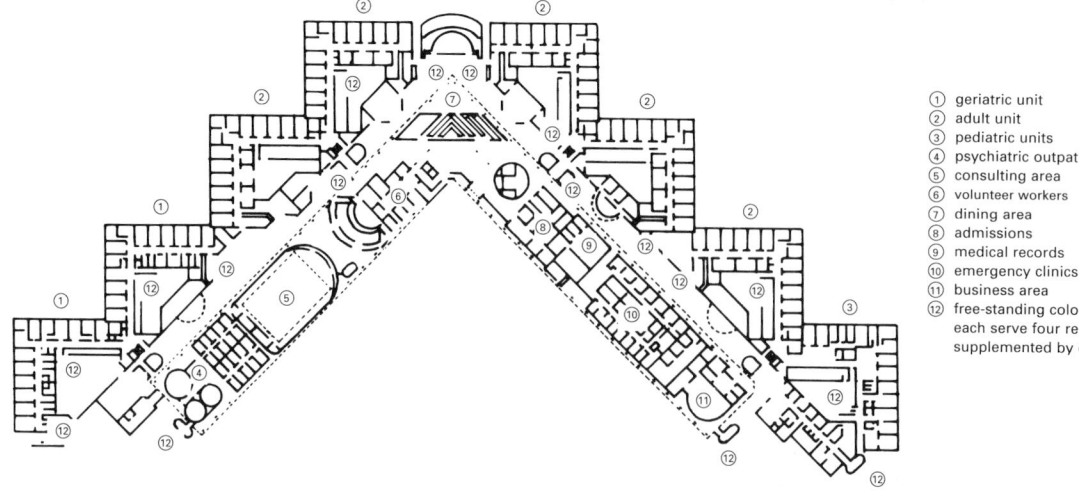

① geriatric unit
② adult unit
③ pediatric units
④ psychiatric outpatient clinics
⑤ consulting area
⑥ volunteer workers
⑦ dining area
⑧ admissions
⑨ medical records
⑩ emergency clinics
⑪ business area
⑫ free-standing colour-coded stairs in mall each serve four residential units; supplemented by elevators for disabled

Architects: Todd Wheeler & Perkins & Will Partnership

⑥ **Capital District Psychiatric Center, Albany, New York accommodates 400 inpatients in 16 residential units, each of which serves 25 day patients**

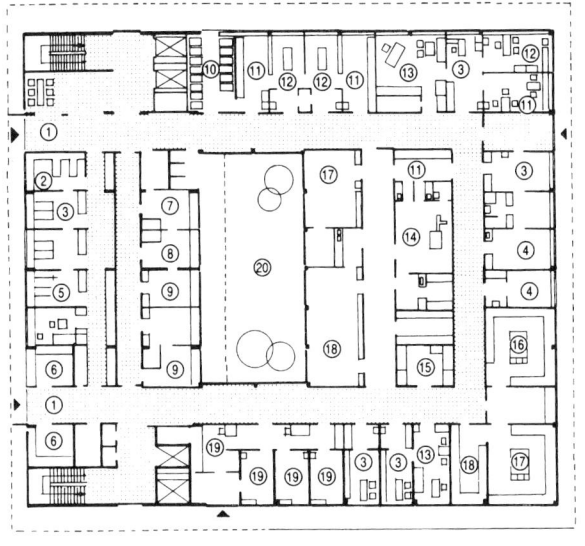

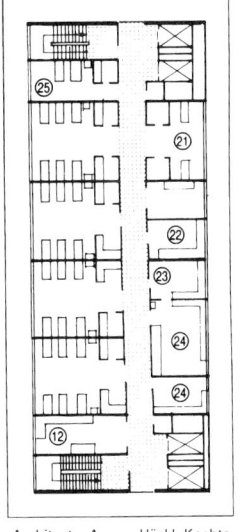

① entrance hall	⑭ X-ray
② porter	⑮ ECG
③ secretarial area	⑯ clinical lab
④ administration	⑰ serology lab
⑤ matron	⑱ bacteriology lab
⑥ admission	⑲ infection records
⑦ ENT	⑳ courtyard
⑧ eyes	㉑ isolation room
⑨ EEG	㉒ kitchen
⑩ pram	㉓ nurse
⑪ waiting room	㉔ care work
⑫ examination	㉕ parents
⑬ doctor	

Architects: Amon, Häckl, Kochta

① **200-bed Fürth Municipal Children's Hospital: ground floor**   ② **upper floor**

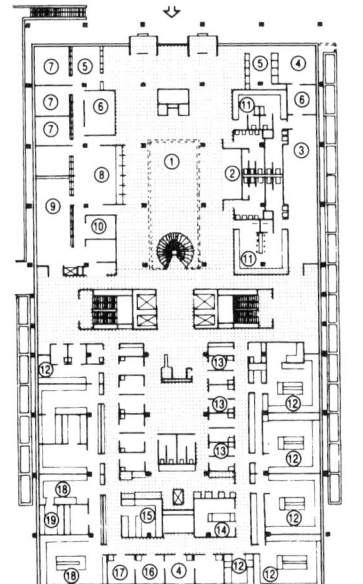

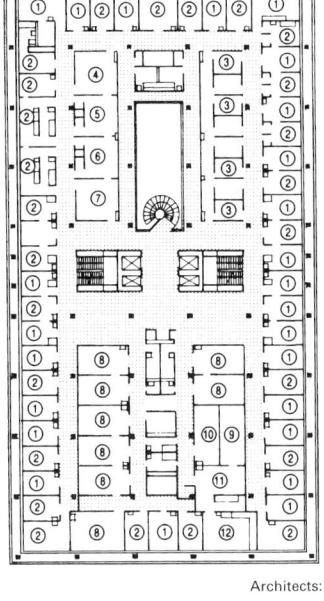

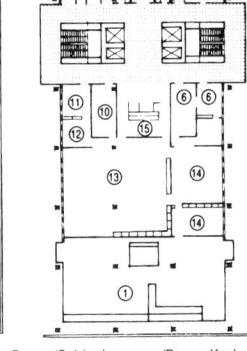

ground floor

① hall	⑥ files
② cloakroom	⑦ studio
③ lounge	⑧ gas sterilisation
④ doctor's room	⑨ central
⑤ anteroom	sterilisation
⑥ consultation	⑩ waiting
⑦ administration	⑪ manager
⑧ admissions	⑫ secretarial
⑨ main office	⑬ plant room
⑩ switchboard	⑭ programmer
⑪ changing	⑮ operator
⑫ laboratory	
⑬ blood sampling	**second floor**
⑭ sink room	① doctor's room
⑮ auto-analysis	② examination
⑯ secretarial	③ measuring centre
⑰ chemist	④ gas analyses
⑱ biochemistry	⑤ ergo-spirometry
⑲ physics/chemistry	⑥ ergometry
	⑦ dye testing
first floor	⑧ pathology
① ventilation centre	measuring
② doctor's room	⑨ strong room
③ nystagmography	⑩ dose admin.
④ myography	⑪ radioactivity lab
⑤ dark room	⑫ sample
	measuring

Architects: Braun/Schlockermann/Braun-Krebs

③ **Gorman Clinic for Diagnostics, Wiesbaden: ground floor**   ④ **first floor**   ⑤ **second floor**

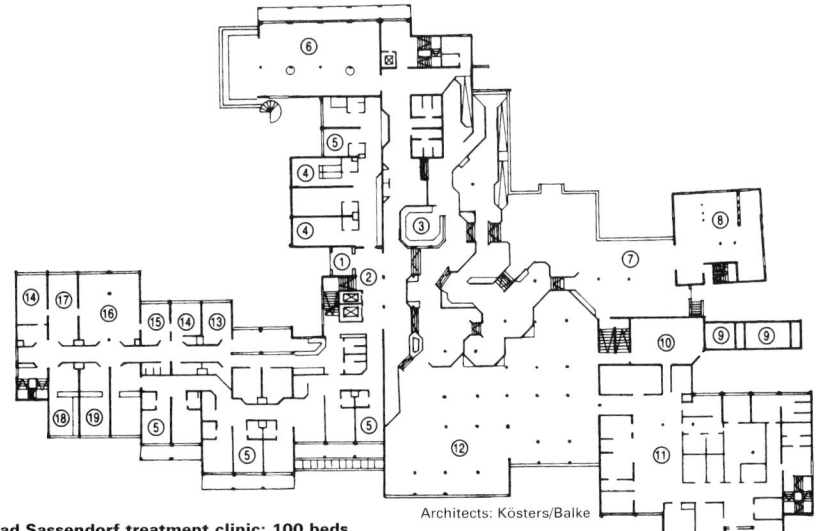

① porch	⑪ kitchen
② entrance hall	⑫ dining room
③ reception	⑬ laboratory
④ double room	⑭ senior physician
⑤ single room	⑮ examination
⑥ conference	⑯ chief physician
⑦ hall	⑰ secretarial area
⑧ lounge	⑱ staff nurse
⑨ electric plant	⑲ ECG
⑩ staff dining	

Architects: Kösters/Balke

⑥ **Bad Sassendorf treatment clinic: 100 beds**

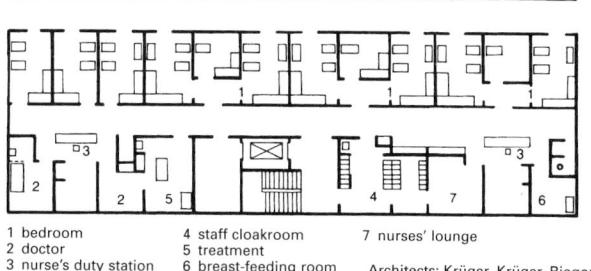

1 bedroom
2 doctor
3 nurse's duty station
4 staff cloakroom
5 treatment
6 breast-feeding room
7 nurses' lounge

Architects: Krüger, Krüger, Rieger

(1) **Children's ward with 28 beds, Velbert Municipal Hospital**

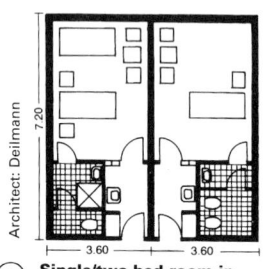
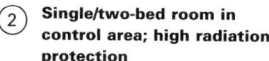

Architect: Deilmann
7.20
3.60 — 3.60

(2) **Single/two-bed room in control area; high radiation protection**

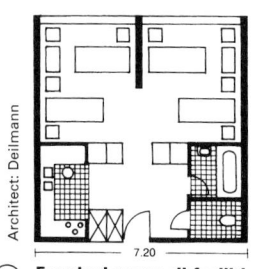

Architect: Deilmann
7.20

(3) **Four-bed room; all facilities for basic care (long-term patients)**

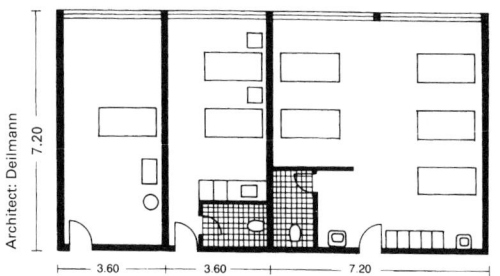

Architect: Deilmann
7.20
3.60 — 3.60 — 7.20

(4) **Room unit for people with slight mental illness and for those requiring care**

SPECIAL CARE AREA SAFETY

Infants and children

The patients generally found in special children's hospitals may be categorised as follows: infants (35%) and premature babies (13%), small children and schoolchildren up to the age of 14 (22%), and groups of all ages with infectious diseases (22%). In such areas, contact between the patients and other patients/staff should be avoided as far as possible.

Windows, heaters and electrical apparatus must be secured in such a way that children cannot be put at risk. Rooms for teaching, entertainment and play should be similarly fitted out.

Isolation wards must be provided for measles, chickenpox, diphtheria, scarlet fever and TB. The walls must withstand washing and disinfecting below a height of 1.50 m and the design should as far as possible resemble a kindergarten rather than a clinical area.

Care of patients receiving radiotherapy

When planning a care area using nuclear medicine for patients needing radiotherapy, the provisions of radiation protection regulations must be observed. The size of such care groups should be similar to that of a normal care group. The operations centre is divided into a control area and a supervision area. In this way, patients whose bodies have received the greatest radiation doses are separated from those who have received less. Patients should therefore be accommodated primarily in one-bed rooms.

Care of the mentally ill

The variable nature of mental illness results in a requirement for open and closed wards (for those in need of slight care and those who are seriously ill and possibly violent). The two types need to be accommodated when planning and setting up care units. Large areas are required for day-rooms, dining rooms and rooms for occupational and group therapy, because patients are not confined to bed. Small care units (up to 25 patients) should have short circulation routes and provide good observation points for nursing staff. A homely design should always be used to give patients a feeling of well-being. There is a trend towards integrating wards for the mentally ill into general hospitals to prevent these patients becoming institutionalised.

Architects: Köhler, Müller-Pauly

(5) **Closed psychiatric ward**

(6) **Open psychiatric ward**

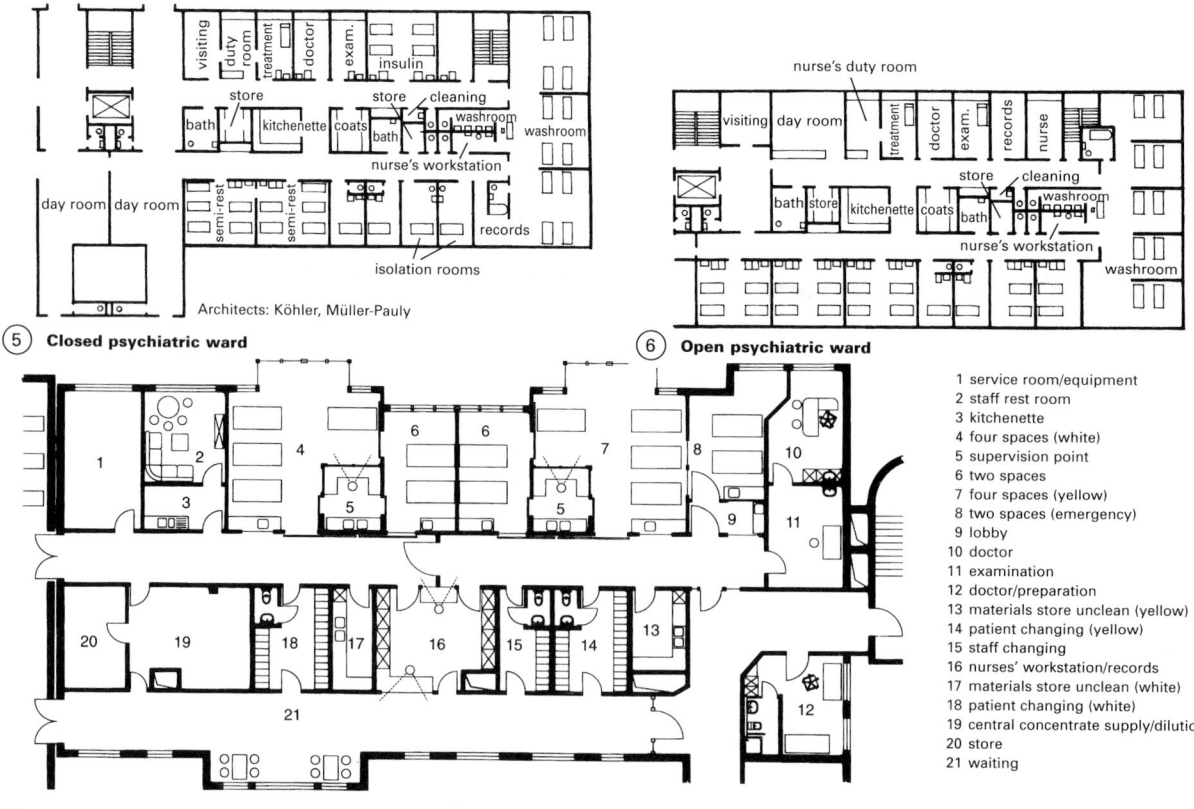

1 service room/equipment
2 staff rest room
3 kitchenette
4 four spaces (white)
5 supervision point
6 two spaces
7 four spaces (yellow)
8 two spaces (emergency)
9 lobby
10 doctor
11 examination
12 doctor/preparation
13 materials store unclean (yellow)
14 patient changing (yellow)
15 staff changing
16 nurses' workstation/records
17 materials store unclean (white)
18 patient changing (white)
19 central concentrate supply/dilution
20 store
21 waiting

(7) **Dialysis station for 12 places**

Architects: U + A Weicken

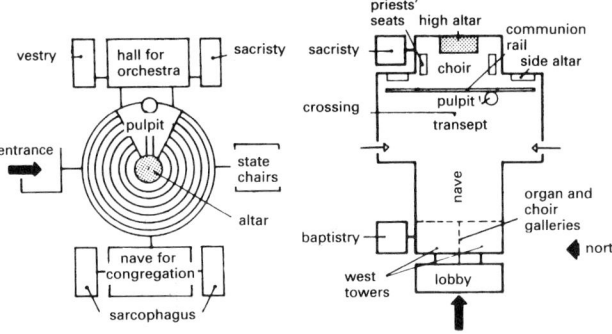

① **Layout of the Berlin Dom (Protestant cathedral) designed by Schinkel**

② **Layout of typical Roman Catholic church**

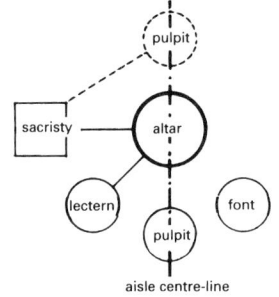

③ **Pulpit and altar on same axis**

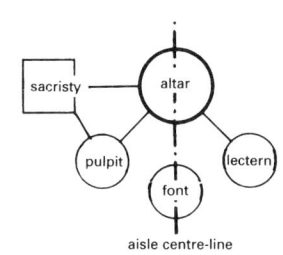

④ **Pulpit off the altar axis**

⑤ **Protestant altar table. Similar dimensions for side altars in Roman Catholic churches; main altars 3.00 length × 1.00 depth including tabernacle**

⑥ **Pulpit without sounding board (microphones have made sounding boards unnecessary)**

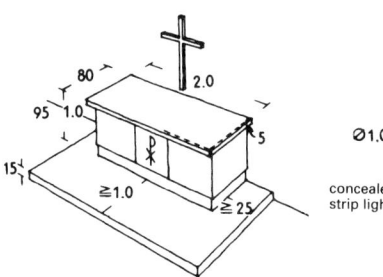

⑦ **Lectern (typical dimensions)** ⑧ **Font (typical dimensions)**

a = 80–90 (av. 85 cm)
seat width = 50–55 (norm. 50 cm)

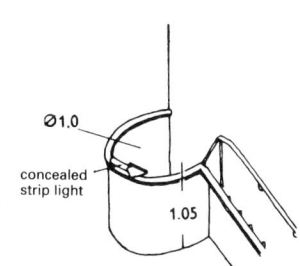

⑨ **Confessional for Roman Catholic church**

a = 85–95 (av. 90 cm)
b = 5–14 cm
seat width = 50–55 (norm. 50 cm)

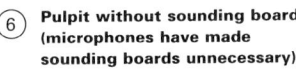

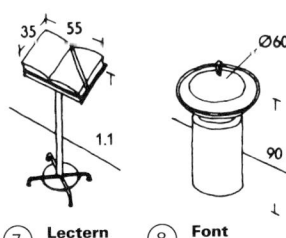

⑩ **Seating in Protestant church (without kneeler)**

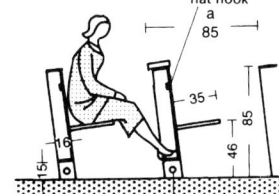

⑪ **Seating in Roman Catholic church (with kneeler)**

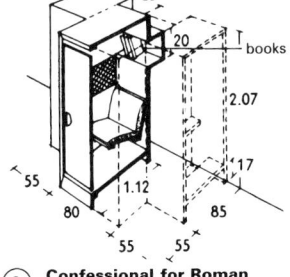

Since churches are places of worship, the form of the building should be derived from the worship and the liturgy. Each individual diocese or sect has guidelines for its own churches, but local regulations on places of assembly should also be observed.

Once, all Christian churches were Catholic. They were places for the 'servants of God' to worship. The common people often had to remain outside in the courtyard, in 'paradise'. The church was a sacred building, profoundly symbolic in its plan (cruciform), direction (choir in the east) and dimensions, and in all liturgical details. Later the whole congregation was admitted into the nave. The choir, with the high altar (a tomb with relics of saints), was separated by a grille, and in larger churches the central area, the 'heart of the church', was reserved for the clergy.

The space requirements are 0.4–0.5 m² per seat without a kneeler bench (Protestant) → ⑩, and 0.43–0.52 m² per seat with a kneeler bench (Catholic) → ⑪, not including aisles. The arrangement and form of seating is of great importance for the spatial effect, audibility and visibility. For smaller churches (or chapels), one side aisle, 1 m wide, with benches for six to ten people, is sufficient → ⑫, or one central aisle, 1.50 m wide, with seating on either side → ⑭. However, external walls can feel very cold, so two side aisles with benches between for 12–18 people are better → ⑬. Wider churches will need correspondingly more aisles → ⑮.

The total area required for standing room varies between 0.63 and 1 m². A large area of the aisle space, particularly along the back wall, is commonly used for standing. The width of the exit doors and stairs must comply with the same regulations as for other places of assembly (e.g. theatres and cinemas). The central aisle on the axis of the altar is useful for funerals, processions etc. → ③, but is a disadvantage to the preacher if the lectern is on the same axis, as is often required in Protestant churches.

Churches should always have a clergy house attached to them. Where appropriate, the advice of the Diocesan Commission should be sought for new buildings, conversions and refurbishments. In certain cases, approval must be given by the Bishop's representative. Vatican II has brought in a new orientation in Catholic church building.

The altar is the Lord's table (the communion table), the centre of the celebration of the Eucharist and often the focal point of the building. In churches, altars must have a top (mensa) of natural stone, but the support (stipes) can be of any material provided it is durable and worthy. In other places of worship, portable altars of a worthy material may be used. The altar should be 95 cm high, and free standing so that it is possible to walk around it easily → ⑤. The priest celebrates behind the altar facing the congregation. Relics of martyrs or saints may be set into the altar or sunk into the ground beneath it.

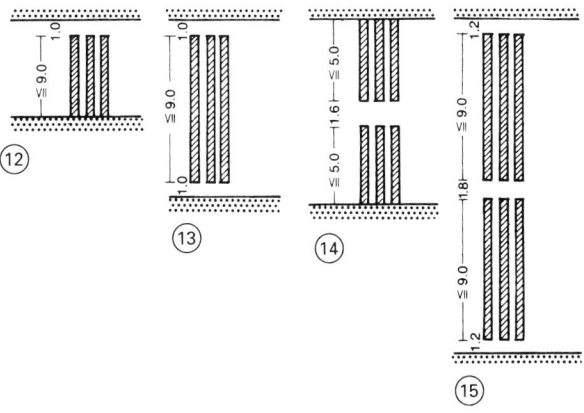

⑫ – ⑮ **Minimum width of churches depending on aisle arrangements**

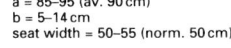
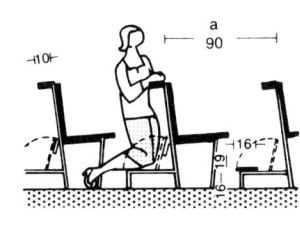

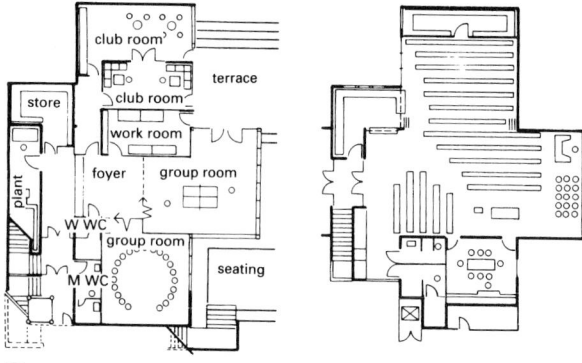

seating
meeting point
belfry
kitchen
parish hall
terrace (youth area)
foyer
worship room
M WC
W WC
sacristy
seating
storage
waste

Architect: Jochen Jakobs, 1986

① **Ground floor of parish centre in Widdersdorf, Cologne → ② – ③**

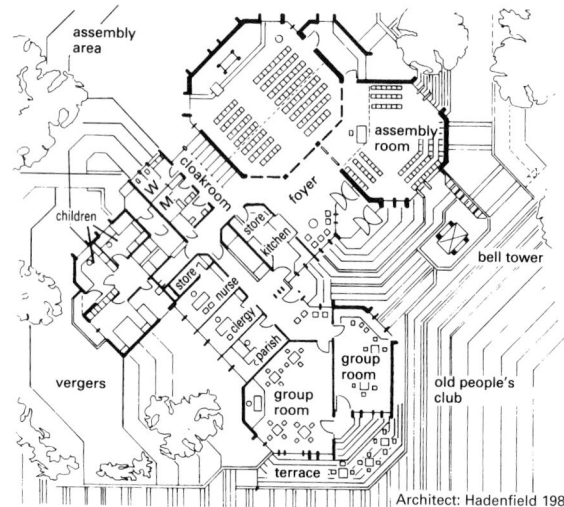

club room
store
club room
terrace
work room
plant
foyer
group room
W WC
group room
M WC
seating

② **First floor → ①**

③ **Ground floor: multi-use, 180 seats → ①**

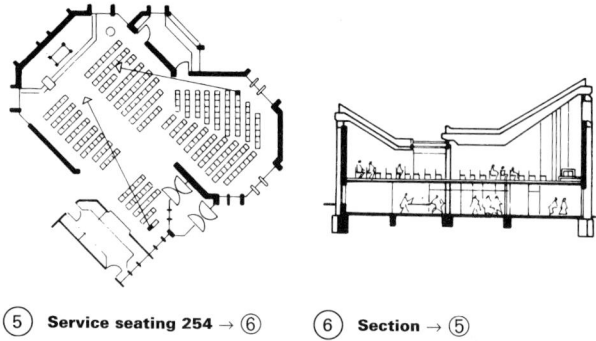

assembly area
cloakroom
W
M
children
store
kitchen
store
nurse
clergy
parish
vergers
group room
group room
terrace
foyer
assembly room
bell tower
old people's club

Architect: Hadenfield 1980

④ **Ground floor of the Hoffnungskirche in Porz, Cologne**

⑤ **Service seating 254 → ⑥**

⑥ **Section → ⑤**

In larger churches or cathedrals (the seat of the bishop), side chapels with ancillary altars may be built. The chancel should be slightly raised for good visibility, and suitably set off from other areas. As well as the altar, a table is required for the missal (Gospels) and the vessels, and also a seat for the priest and servers (not a throne), usually at the vertex of the altar facing the congregation. A fixed lectern (ambo) is also necessary. The sermon (homily) and intercessions should be given from the right as seen by the congregation. Communion benches are no longer obligatory. Side altars in Roman Catholic churches are movable or in lockable recesses ≥2.00m wide and 3m deep.

The nave should have benches for worshippers to sit and kneel (and in France, also low chairs with high backs). If absolutely necessary, install an amplifier system with microphones at the altar, the priest's chair and the lectern. Locate seats for the choir and musicians near the organist; galleries are not usually suitable. The organ loft needs expert acoustic and spatial planning in advance, as does the bell tower (see following pages). The Blessed Sacrament is kept in a secure tabernacle at a place marked by the sanctuary lamp. In front of the tabernacle place a table for the vessels and kneelers for private prayer. The 14 stations of the Way of the Cross, with symbolic, artistic depictions and the crosses of the 12 apostles, are distributed evenly for people to walk around. A baptistery with the font can be in the nave or in a side chapel. Confessionals in Roman Catholic churches are next to the choir or in the side aisles, and if possible can be entered from two sides.

The sacristy is used to keep robes and vessels and to prepare the services, and should be situated near the altar. Ventilation, heating, toilets, disabled access and seats for people with impaired hearing, as well as sufficient parking space, complete the brief.

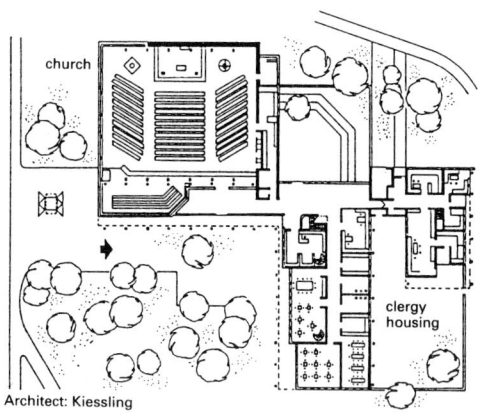

church
bell tower
clergy housing

Architect: Kiessling

⑦ **Catholic parish centre in Burglengfeld**

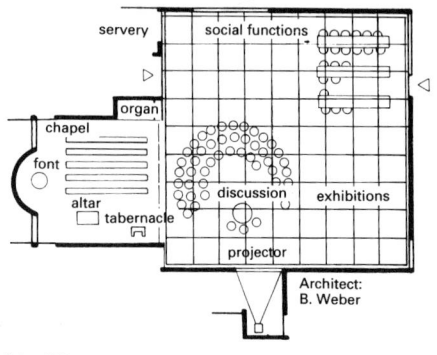

servery
social functions
organ
chapel
font
altar
tabernacle
discussion
exhibitions
projector

Architect: B. Weber

⑧ **Possible different usage of space**

CHURCH ORGANS

The organ in a church or concert hall is a work of art incorporating musical, architectural and technical aspects. There is no fixed form. The design is based on the technical requirements of the organ, and each organ is unique. The organ is an integral part of a space and of the architecture. The space and the organ must be planned together. At the beginning of the planning process, the architect and the organ builder should work together. The problems are complex and cannot be solved by the architect alone. The external appearance of the organ should match its inner structure. The factors affecting this are the volume of the space, the acoustics of the space, the position within the space, the number of seats and the musical requirements (solo instrument, accompaniment). The better the acoustics and the better the positioning of the organ, the smaller the organ needs to be. The optimum reverberation time is 3–4 seconds in a full space with high diffusion and good reflection from the rear wall, the side walls and the ceiling. The frequency range of an organ is between 16 Hz and over 10 000 Hz. The sound is better in front of, rather than behind, the organ. The sound in any space is best on the main/longitudinal axis. The units for determining musical capacity are register and number of stops → ⑫. In small spaces, one register requires 60 m³, medium-sized spaces require 100 m³ per register and larger spaces 150 m³. If the acoustics for the organ are not good (reverberation time under 3.5 seconds), 10% must be added to these figures. Organs actually consist of a number of different organs which are normally contained in a wooden frame or filled structure. Rough guidelines for the proportions are shallow rather than deep, and high rather than wide. Ensure that the space is sufficiently high. The casing is open at the front near the prospect pipes. These may only begin at head height (approx. 2 m). The rear wall has many doors to allow the organ to be tuned and maintained → ①. Tuning boards are 50–80 cm wide. The face of the organ is known as the prospect and holds the prospect pipes, which are made of a tin/lead alloy and are visible from the front. The prospect should preferably match the structure of the organ(s). The pipes produce the sound. Their shape (cylindrical, conical, open, covered), dimensions (narrow/wide) and material (tin/lead alloy, wood) determine the tone colour. For technical reasons, wind chests are always rectangular in plan. Organs with a round plan form should be large enough to house a rectangular wind chest.

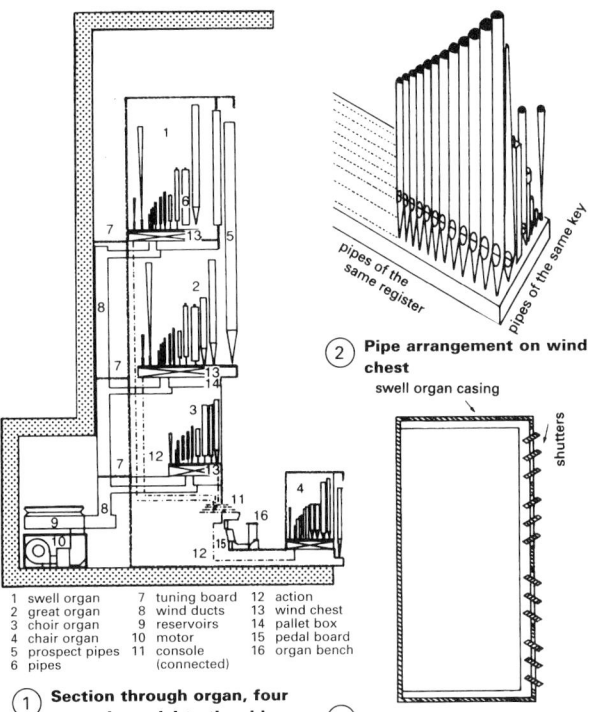

② Pipe arrangement on wind chest

③ Swell organ

① Section through organ, four manuals; pedal to the side (not shown)

1 swell organ	7 tuning board	12 action
2 great organ	8 wind ducts	13 wind chest
3 choir organ	9 reservoirs	14 pallet box
4 chair organ	10 motor	15 pedal board
5 prospect pipes	11 console	16 organ bench
6 pipes	(connected)	

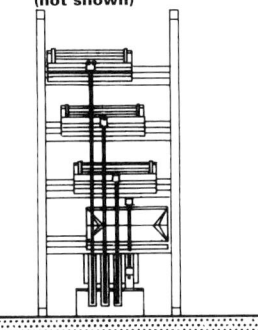

④ Wedge bellows

blower (incl. motor casing)				
registers (no.):	10	20	30	40
length (cm)	85	85	120	150
width (cm)	65	75	110	120
height (cm)	60	60	110	135

reservoirs: no. of organs					
	1	2	3	4	5
length (cm)	70	110	160	200	300
width (cm)	50	60	80	100	130
height (cm)	20	30	30	35	40

varying blown pressure may necessitate wedge bellows (to side/behind organ), in housing to following dimensions: length 300–400 cm width 110–150 cm height 130–390 cm

⑤ Dimensions of blower and reservoirs

a = body length, deepest note
b = body length, highest note
c = foot length, deepest note

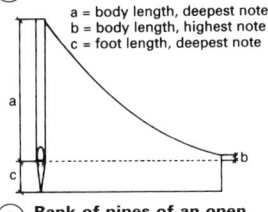

⑥ Rank of pipes of an open B flat register

	32′	16′	8′	4′
manual a	1000	488	240	119
56 notes b	38	19	9.5	4.8
C–9″ c	90	50	30	18
pedal a	1000	488	240	min
30 notes b	159	78	38.6	dimen-
C–9″ c	90	500	30	sions

⑦ Table with pipe bodies

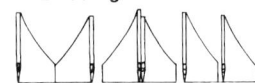

⑧ Diatonic pipe arrangement (C and C sharp side)

⑨ Tierce position

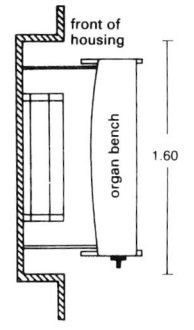

front of housing

organ bench

1.60

⑩ Plan of manual console

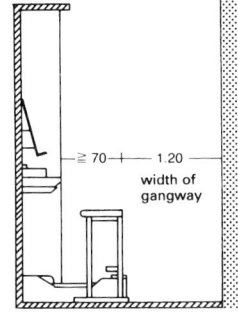

≥ 70 ⊢ 1.20
width of gangway

⑪ Section → ⑩

seats	registers	no. of organs incl. pedal boards	lowest main register		type of organ
			great organ	pedal board	
100	3–7	1	2′	none	A chest/positive
200	8–12	2	4′	8′	B positive
300	12–20	2	4′–8′	8′	C small
400	20–30	3	8′	8′	D
500	25–35	3–4	8′	16′	E
600	30–40	4	8′	16′	F
700	35–45	4	8′	16′	
800	40–50	4	8′–16′	16′	
900	45–55	4	16′	16′	G
1000	50–60	4–5	16′	16′	
1250	60–70	4–5	16′	16′–32′	H
1500	70–80	5	16′	16′–32′	
1750	75–85	6	16′	32′	I
2000	80–90	6	16′	32′	
2500	90–100	6	16′	32′	

⑫ Formula for determining number of registers (according to H.G. Klais)

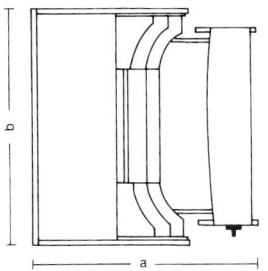

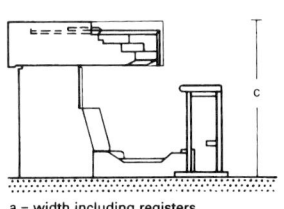

a = width including registers
b = depth including bench
c = height without music stand

⑬ Plan of free-standing console

⑭ Section → ⑬

CHURCH ORGANS

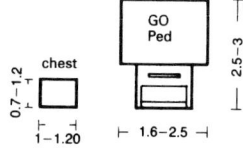

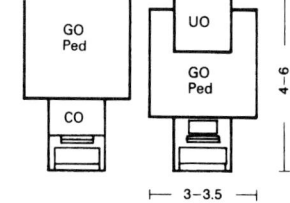

① **Plan of pedal towers on the parapet**

type	height (m)	width (m)	depth (flat prospect) (without tuning board)	
③ – ④	0.6 – 0.8	1 – 1.2	0.7 – 1.2	chest h = 0.6–0.8m
⑤	2.5 – 3	1.6 – 2.5	0.8 – 1.6	positive
⑥	4 – 6	3 – 3.5	1.2 – 1.8	small organ
⑦	6 – 7	5.5 – 6.5	1.2 – 2	II manuals/GO 8'/Ped 8'
⑧	6.5 – 9	4.5 – 7	1.5 – 2.5	II manuals/GO 8'/Ped 16'
⑨ – ⑩	7.5 –10	7 – 9	2 – 3	III man./GO 8'–16'/Ped 16'
⑪ – ⑫	9 –13	8 –12	2 – 4	IV–V man./GO 16'/Ped 16'–32'

dimensions given for the depth of the organ casing are meant
solely as a guideline; if the organs are arranged one behind the
other with a projecting prospect the organ will require more space

② **Summary of casing sizes → ③ – ⑫**

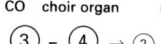

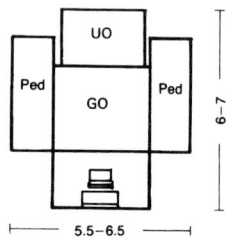

GO great organ
ChO chair organ
CO choir organ

SO swell organ
UO upper organ
Ped pedal organ

③ – ④ → ②

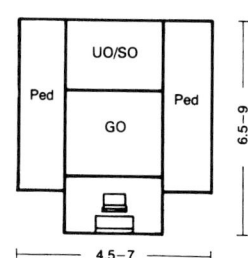

⑤ – ⑥ → ②

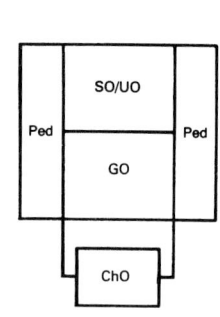

⑦ → ②

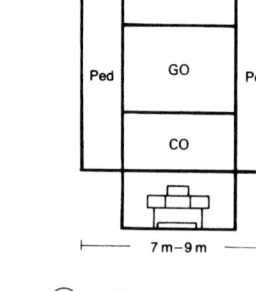

⑧ → ②

⑨ → ②

⑩ → ②

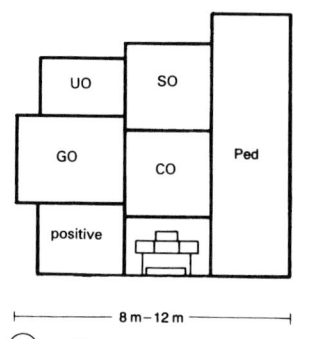

⑪ → ②

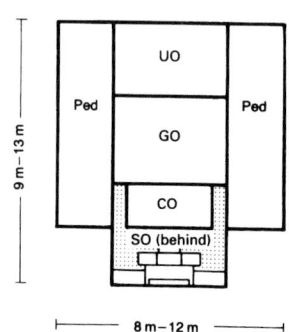

⑫ → ②

The console should be firmly connected to the organ when using a mechanical action. This is the only way to ensure short actions and an optimum touch. Electric actions (direct electric and electro-pneumatic) allow the console to be placed as far from the pipes as required, but normally the console is built into the front of the organ. In the case of a prospect organ, the console can be positioned to the side, but only rarely behind the organ.

A free-standing console must be in a central position in front of the organ, at a maximum distance of 2.00m. The organist should be facing the instrument (→ 570 ⑬ – ⑭). The mechanical devices connecting the console to the wind chest of the organ are called actions. They should be short and simple. The bellows consist of a blower, reservoirs and wind ducts leading from the bellows to the wind chests. Bellows are normally in the base of the organ, but can also be behind or to the side. Large bellows systems are in separate bellows chambers, particularly in concert halls.

Organs need not necessarily be housed in a gallery. They can also be located in the sanctuary or in a 'swallow's nest'. Avoid fitting them in towers, in deep recesses or in front of large windows (cooling surfaces). Do not impede the sound reflection with timbers or arches. In a concert hall, the organ should be positioned close to the stage.

In any building housing an organ, the humidity should be even throughout the year (optimum 60%) if possible. The limits are between 45% and 80% air humidity, with no draughts or rapid variations in temperature. Allow the organ 10 hours to warm up and to cool down. There should be no windows near the organ, and none behind it. If possible, install heat-insulated walls behind and to the sides of the organ, with hard, reflective surfaces. Do not place the display pipes in direct sunlight, and avoid floodlights.

Organs need regular maintenance. Leave tuning gangways behind the organ 50–80cm wide. Projecting organs should be accessible from below. Rostra for the choir and orchestra should be in front of organ.

The weight of an organ can range from 100kg per register for choir organs to 600kg per register for pedal organ bases, including frames and casework. Free-standing consoles with two keyboards weigh up to 250kg, and those with three manuals up to 300kg. The preponderance of point loads means that it may be necessary to fit load distributors.

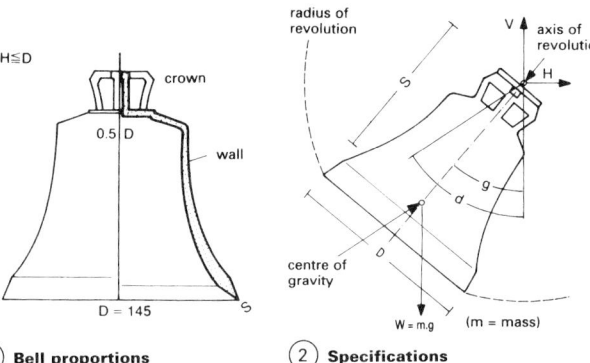

(1) **Bell proportions**

(2) **Specifications**

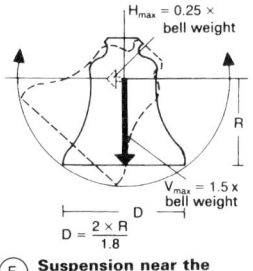

vertical thrust H_{max} = 1.55 × weight of bell

vertical thrust V_{max} = 3.1 × bell weight

$D = \dfrac{2 \times R}{2.5}$

(3) **Horizontal thrust**

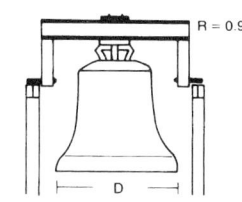

R = 1.25 D

(4) **Straight yoke**

H_{max} = 0.25 × bell weight

V_{max} = 1.5 × bell weight

$D = \dfrac{2 \times R}{1.8}$

(5) **Suspension near the centre of gravity**

R = 0.9 D

(6) **Returned steel yoke**

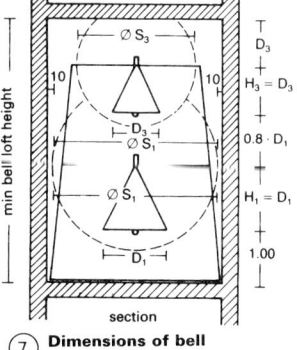

length of panels
∅ S_3 = swing diameter, bell 3 = 2.6 × D_3
∅ S_1 = of bell 1 = 2.6 × D_1
sound openings O in places where there is no clapper stroke

(7) **Dimensions of bell chamber (minimum)**

(8) **Plan** → (7)

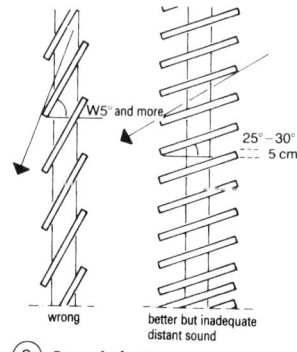

W5° and more

25°–30°

5 cm

wrong

better but inadequate distant sound

(9) **Sound shutters**

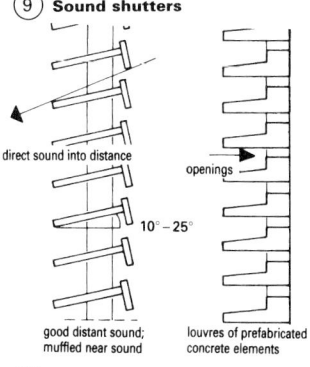

direct sound into distance

openings

10°–25°

good distant sound; muffled near sound

louvres of prefabricated concrete elements

(10) **Sound shutters**

Before planning, consult a bell specialist about the size and pitch of the bells, and their acoustics and weights. The foundryman designs the bell frame as the basis for the dimensions of the bell chamber and sound openings. He also provides the expected loads for the structural engineer. The structural engineer must take both static and dynamic loads into consideration. The inherent frequency of the tower must not resonate with the frequency of the bells.

The weight, alloy and thickness of the bell walls determine the volume of sound. Today, electric ringing machines are often used. Steel bells are about 15% larger in diameter and about 25% lighter than bronze bells, but are rarely manufactured nowadays → (1).

The bell tower is, by definition, a solo musical instrument and forms an orchestra with neighbouring bell towers. The desired hearing distance determines the height of the bell loft in the tower, which should be above surrounding buildings. The quality of the bell tone depends on the material and acoustic design of the building. The tower is insulated against structure-borne sound. In this respect, free-standing towers have advantages such as access hatches for installing and changing bells, and accident-proof access to the bell loft for maintenance (stairs instead of a ladder).

The bell loft is a resonance and mixing chamber and determines the musical quality of the radiated sound. The loft is completely closed apart from the sound openings → (7) + (8).

The sound openings are at right angles to the direction of the bell swing. A lot of small openings are better than a few large ones. The sound radiation angle should not be more than 30° from the horizontal to protect the neighbourhood. The striking of the clapper should not radiate. This should be taken into account when positioning the sound shutters. The total openings should be a maximum of 5% of the interior walls of the bell loft if the walls have a smooth surface, and a maximum of 10% if they have a rough surface. Concrete floors and ceilings can be covered with wood → (9) + (10).

pitch	bell diameter d (mm)	bell weight W (kN)	bell diameter d (mm)	bell weight W (kN)	bell diameter d (mm)	bell weight W (kN)
			walls			
	light		medium		heavy	
F°	2250	58	2320	71		
F° sh.	2120	48	2220	59		
G°	2000	40	2100	50		
G° sh. A° fl.	1880	34	2000	41		
A°	1780	28	1880	35		
A° sh. B°	1680	24	1760	29		
B°	1580	20	1660	24		
c'	1480	16	1570	20	1680	31
c' sh. d' fl.	1400	14	1475	17	1580	25
d'	1325	11	1390	14	1500	21
d' sh. e' fl.	1240	10	1310	12	1410	17
e'	1170	8.0	1240	10	1330	15
f'	1110	7.0	1170	8.0	1250	13
f' sh. g' fl.	1035	5.5	1100	7.2	1175	11
g'	980	4.6	1040	6.0	1110	9.0
g' sh. a' fl.	930	4.0	980	5.0	1040	7.2
a'	875	3.2	925	4.3	985	6.2
a' sh. b'	830	2.8	870	3.5	930	5.3
b'	780	2.3	820	3.0	880	4.3
c''	740	2.0	775	2.5	830	3.7
c'' sh. d'' fl.	690	1.6	730	2.1	780	3.2
d''	650	1.4	690	1.7	735	2.6
d'' sh. e'' fl.	600	1.1	645	1.5	690	2.1
e''	575	0.90	610	1.2	650	1.7
f''	550	0.80	580	1.0	620	1.5
f'' sh. g'' fl.	510	0.65	545	0.80	595	1.2
g''	480	0.55	510	0.70	550	1.0
g'' sh. a'' fl.	450	0.45	480	0.59	525	0.90
a''	425	0.38	455	0.50	495	0.75
a'' sh. b''	390	0.32	430	0.40	465	0.65
b''	370	0.25	405	0.35	440	0.50
c'''	350	0.20	380	0.30	415	0.43

(11) **Characteristic values of bells**

SYNAGOGUES

God's first commission for a sacred building, with exact technical and design specifications, can be found in the passage in the Bible describing the construction of the Tabernacle (Exodus 25–27).

The focal point in a synagogue is not an altar but a raised preaching rostrum (almemor) with seats for the rabbi and the cantor. Extracts from the Torah are read from here. The synagogue is sited to face Jerusalem. On the front wall is an ark in which the Torah scrolls are kept (Aron Hakodesh). The ark and its contents are the holiest features in the synagogue. It is in one single section in the 'Askenasi' part of the world (European Jews), and in three sections in Sephardic areas (oriental Jews). Between the almemor and the Aron Hakodesh is an aisle used for the ceremonial procession preceding the reading from the scrolls.

The plan of every new synagogue is an attempt to solve anew the problems of the locations of the spiritual focal point, which is the almemor (i.e. a more orthodox, centralised building), and the spatial focal point, which is the Aron Hakodesh (i.e. a more modern long hall). The symbolic elements of the star of David, the seven-branched candelabrum and the Decalogue given to Moses are also essential.

A pulpit has been included in some synagogue interiors since at least the fifth or sixth century, but they were not commonplace until the eighth century. It is used for reading texts less holy than those read at the bimah table, and for offering prayers. It is likely to be a modest piece of furniture with only occasional ornamentation.

A synagogue may be surrounded by other annexes and buildings. It may even be part of a multi-synagogue complex, as at the Great Synagogue courtyard in Vilnius. The synagogue is often part of a community centre, thus combining spaces for assembly and prayer. There is usually (at least symbolically) a separate space for women out of view of the men, often in a gallery. At the entrance there is a fountain or washstand for hand washing. The ritual bath (mikva), with immersion for women, is usually in the cellar. It should have natural running water which has not passed through metal pipes. Some liberal synagogues and Reform temples have organs, but they are never showpieces.

The decorations in a synagogue may not contain depictions of human beings; only plants or geometrical or calligraphic ornamentation is allowed.

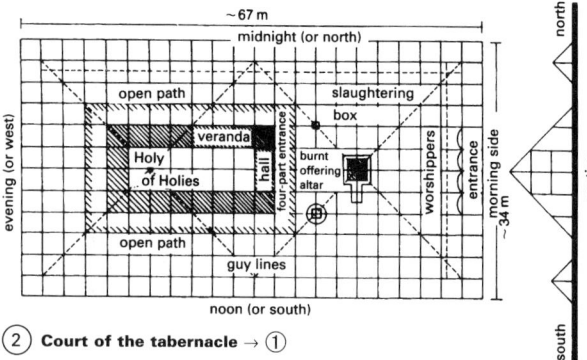

(1) Meeting tent (tabernacle): Jews' first place of worship

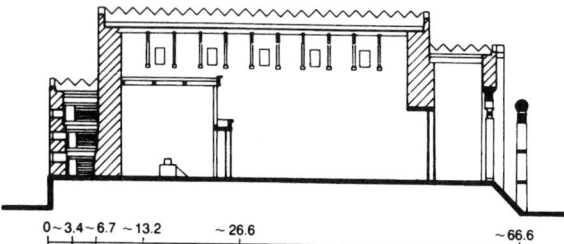

(2) Court of the tabernacle → (1)

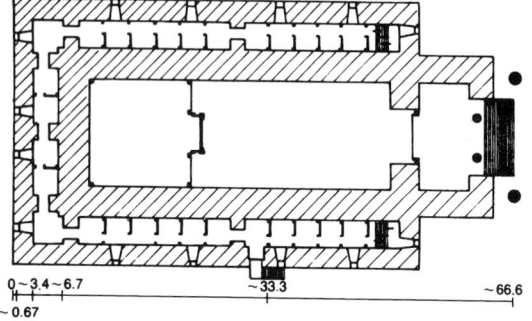

(3) Temple of Solomon, Jerusalem: longitudinal section → (4)

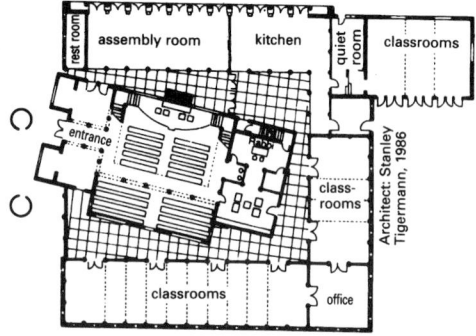

(4) Plan of the Temple

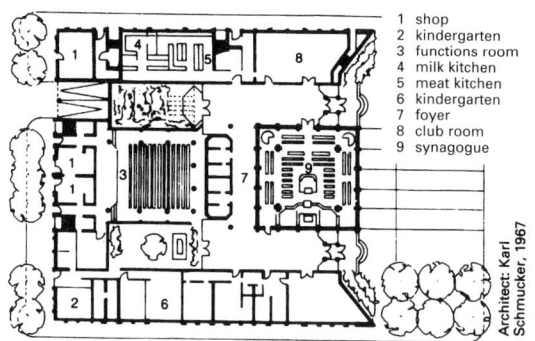

1 shop
2 kindergarten
3 functions room
4 milk kitchen
5 meat kitchen
6 kindergarten
7 foyer
8 club room
9 synagogue

(6) Mannheim, synagogue and community centre: plan

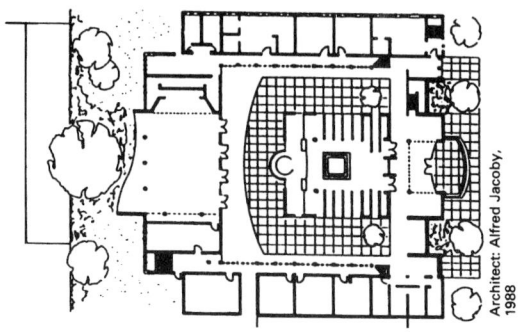

(7) Darmstadt, synagogue and community centre: ground floor plan

(5) Or Shalom Synagogue, Chicago: plan

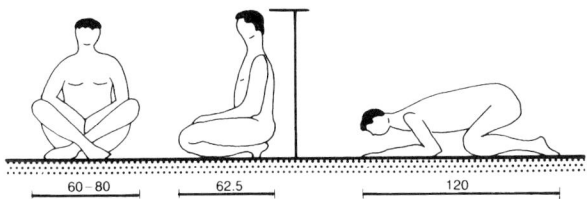

① **People at prayer**

60 – 80   62.5   120

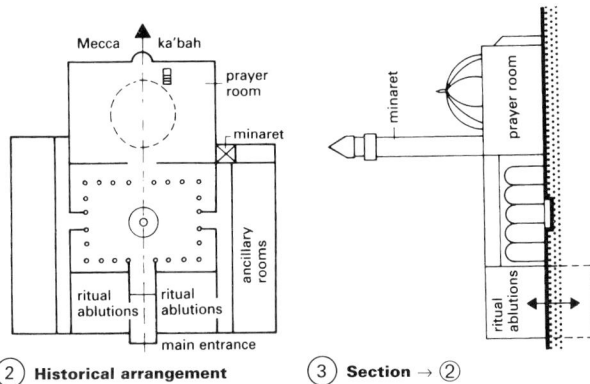

② **Historical arrangement**   ③ **Section → ②**

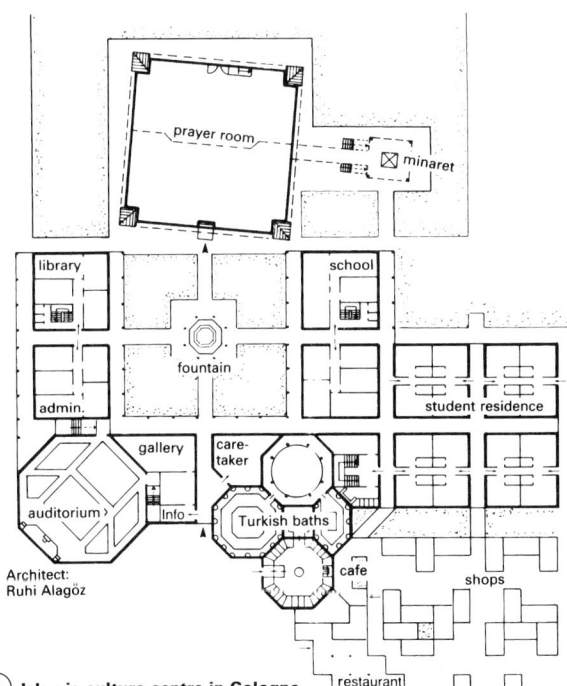

Architect:
Ruhi Alagöz

④ **Islamic culture centre in Cologne**

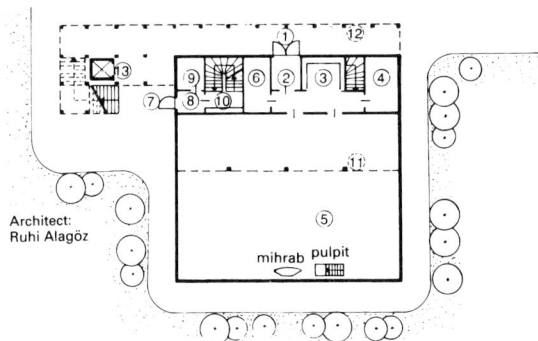

Architect:
Ruhi Alagöz

mihrab pulpit

⑤ **Islamic culture centre in Frankfurt**

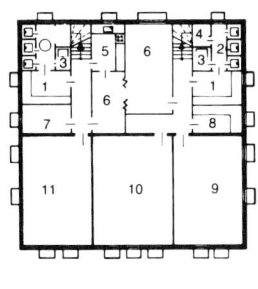

⑥ **Basement → ⑤**   ⑦ **Key → ⑤⑥**

Ground floor	Basement
1 entrance/men	1 rows of wash basins
2 draught lobby	2 WCs
3 shoe racks	3 shower
4 office/hodca	4 hoist
5 prayer room ground floor/ men	5 kitchen
6 information/ men	6 dining room
7 women's entrance	7 heating
8 draught lobby	8 hairdresser
9 information/ women	9 classroom/ men
10 shoe racks	10 library and lecture room
11 prayer room gallery/ women	11 classroom/ women
12 balcony	
13 minaret with lift	

MOSQUES

The five basic categories of mosque design occur in seven distinctive regional styles. In the Arabian heartland, Spain and North Africa there is a hypostyle hall and an open courtyard. In sub-Saharan West Africa the hypostyle hall is of mud-brick or rammed-earth construction. Iran and Central Asia have a bi-axial four-iwan style. On the Indian subcontinent there are triple domes and an extensive courtyard. In Anatolia there is always a massive central dome. The Chinese style has detached pavilions within a walled garden enclosure, and South-East Asia has a central pyramidal roof construction.

The mosque (masjid or jamih) is a house of prayer, a cultural centre, a place for social gatherings, a courthouse, a school and a university. (In Islam, the Quran is the central source of all rules for living and teaching, and for the pronouncements of law, religion etc.)

In Islamic countries the mosque is in the bazaar (souk), and thus in the centre of public life. In countries where the amenities of the bazaar (hairdressers, shops selling permitted foods, cafés etc.) do not exist, they should be included in the planning of the mosque.

Smaller mosques (masjid) rarely have a minaret (minare), whereas larger mosques (jamih) always do. There are neither bells nor organs in Islam. The muezzin's call to prayer can be heard five times a day resounding from the minaret, which has stairs or a lift leading to the upper ambulatory, which is usually covered. Nowadays the call to prayer is virtually always relayed by loudspeakers, although this is not permitted in some countries.

The size of the prayer hall is based on 0.85 m² praying space per person. It is usually rectangular or square, often with a central dome, and faces Mecca, the direction in which people pray (kibla). The prayer niche (mihrab) is set in the front wall (kibla) and next to it is the minbar (pulpit), which must always have an odd number of stairs. This is used by the prayer leader of the mosque (the Imam) in the Friday prayers. Men and women are segregated, sometimes purely symbolically, sometimes with the women in a gallery.

The entrance area has shelves for the school, and rooms for ritual ablutions and showers which must always have a flowing water supply. The WCs are usually squatting closets at right angles to the direction of Mecca. All these facilities often have separate entrances for men and women, including the stairs to the women's gallery.

Many mosques have a central courtyard the same size as the prayer hall, which can be used on holy days as an extension. It has a decorative fountain (tscheschme) for ritual ablutions. In hot countries, trees are planted in the courtyard in a geometrical pattern to provide shade.

Offices, a library, a lecture hall and classrooms, storerooms and apartments, at least for the imam and the muezzin, complete the accommodation.

Representational depictions of humans and animals is not allowed. Plants and geometrical ornamentation (arabesque), and verses from the Quran in Arabic calligraphy, are very popular and have been developed into a form of high culture.

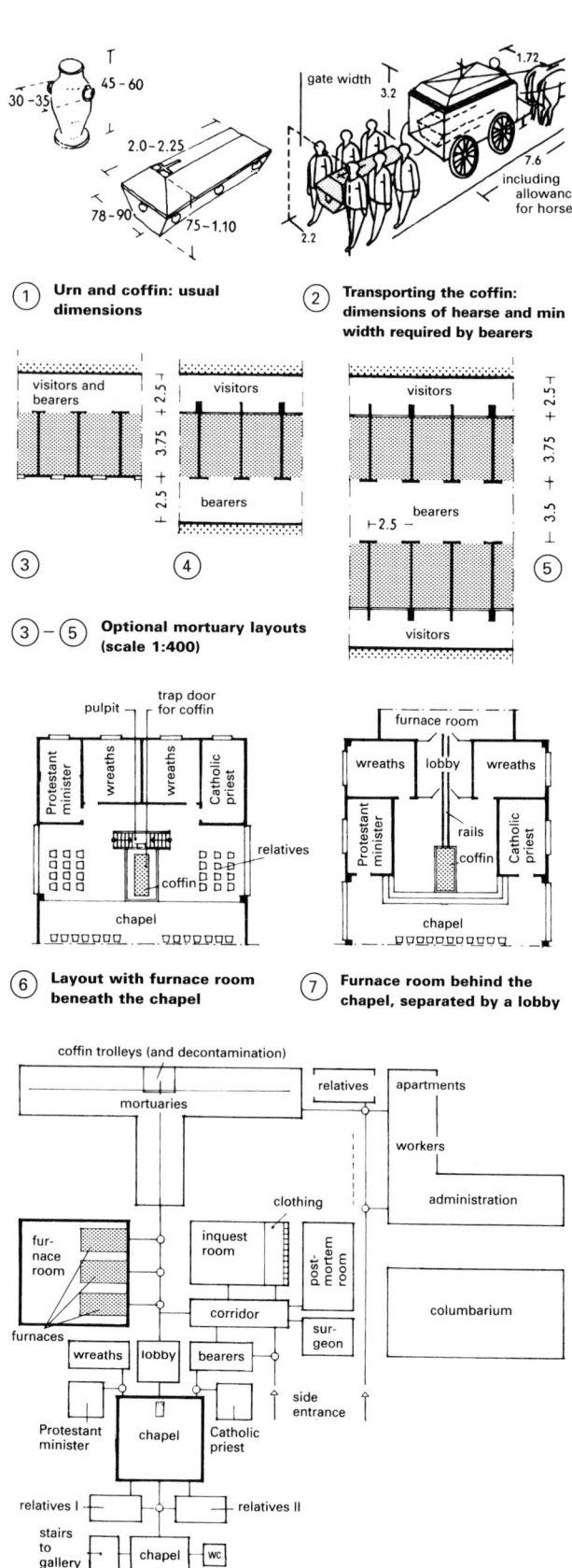

① Urn and coffin: usual dimensions

② Transporting the coffin: dimensions of hearse and min width required by bearers

③ – ⑤ Optional mortuary layouts (scale 1:400)

⑥ Layout with furnace room beneath the chapel

⑦ Furnace room behind the chapel, separated by a lobby

⑧ Spatial relationship in a mortuary with crematorium and ancillary rooms for a large cemetery

CEMETERIES AND CREMATORIA

Corpses are initially laid out in cubicles in a mortuary. These cubicles are separated by partitions to ensure privacy for mourning relatives, who can view the body through airtight glass panes up until the funeral. The linking gangway is generally for use by both the mourners and the bearers although in larger mortuaries separate gangways may be used → ③ – ⑤. Usual dimensions of cubicles are 2.20 × 3.50, 2.50 × 3.75 and 3.00 × 3.50 m.

The temperature in the mortuary should be maintained between 2° to 12°C and it must not be allowed to fall below the minimum figure because freezing would result in expansion of the internal moisture, possibly causing the corpses to burst. This temperature range must be maintained by central heating and cooling and constant ventilation, particularly in summer. Floors must be impervious, smooth and easy to clean; walls are best lime-washed and should be re-coated frequently.

Larger mortuaries also need a room for attendants and bearers (roughly 15–20 m² in size, including toilets and washing facilities) and space for the coffin trolleys should also be provided. Coffin sizes are variable, depending on the size of the corpse → ①, but the trolleys are generally 2.20 × 1.08 to 3.00 × 1.10 m in size. In city mortuaries a special room may be set aside for unidentified bodies, with storage for their clothing and an adjacent post-mortem room and doctor's surgery → ⑧.

The furnace room should either be on a floor below the chapel, with lift for coffins → ⑥ or behind the chapel and separated from it by a lobby → ⑦ + ⑧. Horizontal movement of coffins can easily be done by hand-operated winches. The door to the lobby or the floor trap should close slowly as the coffin gradually disappears through the opening.

In the furnace room the coffin is transferred from a trolley to the chamotte grating inside the furnace. A two-storey furnace is roughly 4.30 m high and may use either electricity (approximately 45 kW per cremation), coke or gas to carry out the combustion. Cremation is a completely dust-free and odourless process achieved by surrounding the body with dry air at 900–1000°C dry; flames do not touch the body. After the furnace has been pre-heated for 2–3 hours in advance, the cremation itself takes $1\frac{1}{4}$ to $1\frac{1}{2}$ hours and is monitored through peep-holes. The ashes are collected in an iron box before being transferred to an urn. The size of urns is often limited by cemetery regulations. Wall niches in columbaria are usually 38–40 cm wide and deep and 50–60 cm high.

These installations should if possible be behind the cemetery chapel, which is non-denominational. For this reason there are two rooms for clergy. The size of the chapel varies, but should seat at least 100 people and have standing room for a further 100. Around the chapel there will be a need for waiting rooms for relatives, administration rooms, coffin and equipment stores and, possibly, flats for the cemetery keeper and caretaker.

In Britain, crematoria are now being built by the private sector. They are always surrounded by a garden for the dispersal of ashes. Urns, niches and miniature graves are often available in a compact memorial garden to provide a temporary memorial (5–10 years).

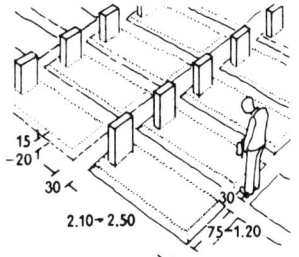

① **Grave arrangement head to foot in sections of 200–300 graves**

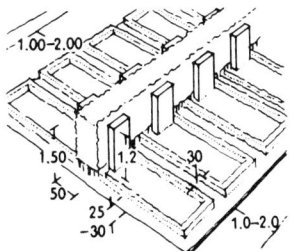

② **Head to head arrangement in narrow cemetery; separated by hedges; sunken path**

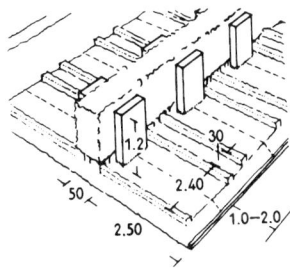

③ **Double graves; separated by hedges; uniform sunken path**

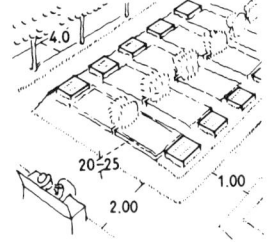

④ **Simple rows of graves with prescribed planting (proposed by H. Hartwig)**

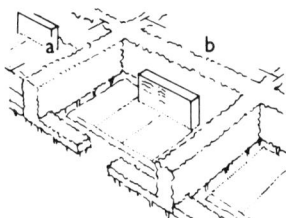

size	a	b	two behind each other a	two behind each other b
2 part	2.50	2.40	2.50	1.50
4 part	2.50	4.80	2.50	2.50
6 part	2.50	7.20	2.50	3.90

⑤ **Family graves**

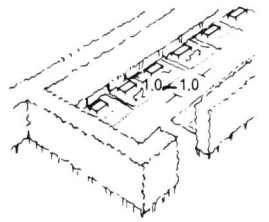

⑥ **Section for urns between hedges or in areas surrounded by trees, similar to ④**

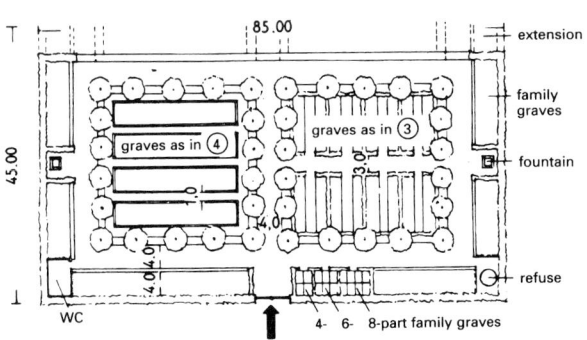

⑦ **Cemeteries for larger villages or land near a church, i.e. without cemetery chapel (proposed by H. Hartwig)**

CEMETERIES AND GRAVEYARDS

There is a distinction between churchyards and cemeteries. In Britain, for example, the growth of churchyards was slow and gradual; each year the graves of a few parishioners were added until the churchyard was exhausted. Burials were then made using old graves. Cemeteries, on the other hand, came into existence during the nineteenth century with the aim of solving problems caused by large numbers of people coming into towns and cities to find work. The need for new cemeteries is always dealt with by local authorities rather than the church and kept extremely simple for maintenance reasons.

The site should have soil that is easy to dig (clay or sandy) and be well drained, with a ground water level ≥ 2.50–3.00 m deep. If necessary, drainage should be provided. Attractive surroundings are preferable.

The space requirement is approximately 40 hectares, including paths and open spaces, per 100 000 inhabitants although many existing cemeteries are smaller than this, particularly in cities. Of this 50–65% is purely for graves and urns, the rest for buildings, paths and gardens. In Britain, roughly 70% of dead bodies are cremated; the rest are buried in graveyards. The size and length of use of graves as specified in cemetery regulations vary greatly.

Type of grave	size (cm)	space between graves (cm)	decomposition time/period of use (years)
1) row, for adults	210 × 75 – 250 × 120	30	20 – 25
2) row, for children up to 10 yrs	150 × 60 – 150 × 75	30	20
3) row, for children up to 3 yrs	100 × 60	30	15
purchased grave with hedges	300 × 150 – 350 × 150		40 – 100
crypt places	300 × 120 – 350 × 150		50 – 100
urn places	100 × 100 – 150 × 100	60	10 – 100
main places	150 × 150	100	30 – 100

Military or war cemeteries and memorials

These are usually reserved for the burial of servicemen and soldiers who die during the wars, and for their commemoration. Two examples of well-maintained military cemeteries in Britain are at Cambridge and Aldershot. At Cambridge, the American Government established its own cemetery for its servicemen who died in Europe during and after the Second World War. At Aldershot, British Soldiers have been buried since the middle of last century. The American cemetery is on flat ground, whereas Aldershot is on hilly ground, which gives it the look of a pleasant park.

Graveyards as parks

Many village churchyards and a few churchyards in the centres of towns have become small parks. They have benches, lawns and established trees to provide shade and a relaxing environment.

Gravestones

In any section of graves surrounded by a hedge the gravestones should all be flat or standing and as far as possible of uniform colour and size (see examples below).

Type of grave	height	width	thickness
simple	100 – 105	40 – 45	9 – 10
double with plants to rear	120 – 125	50 – 55	10 – 12
triple, at appropriate places	120	150	13 – 15

DRAUGHTING GUIDELINES

Atherton, Harry: Designs on your Desktop. *A Comprehensive Guide to Computer-Aided Design* (Wilmslow (England), Sigma Press, 1988)

Bell, R.J.: *SI: The International System of Units* (London, HMSO, 1993)

BSI: **BS 1192**: *Construction Drawing Practice* (London, British Standards Institution, 1984 and 1987)
BS 1192: **Part 1**: 1984 *Recommendations for General Principles*
BS 1192: **Part 2**: 1987 *Recommendations for Architectural and Engineering Drawings*
BS 1192: **Part 3**: 1987 *Recommendations for Symbols and Other Graphic Conventions*

Hawkes, Barry: *Succeeding with AutoCAD. A Full Course in 2D Drafting and 3D Modelling* (London, McGraw-Hill Book Company, 1995)

Hepler, Donald E. and Wallach Paul I.: *Architecture: Drafting and Design*, 4th edn (New York, McGraw-Hill Book Company, 1982)

PSA, Property Services Agency: *PSA Drawing Practice Manual*, 2nd edn (Croydon, DAS/HOP, May 1989)

Riley, Peter et al.: *Computer-Aided Engineering* (London, City and Guilds/Macmillan, 1994)

Rodriguez, Walter: *The Modeling of Design Ideas. Graphics and Visualization Techniques for Engineers* (New York, McGraw-Hill Book Company, 1992)

Yarwood, A.: *Technical Drawing with Design* (London, The Macmillan Press Ltd, 1994)

MEASUREMENT BASIS

Ching, Francis D.K.: *Architecture: Form, Space, Order* (New York, Van Nostrand Reinhold Company, 1979)

Le Corbusier, Charles-Edouard Jeanneret: *Modulor: A Harmonious Measure for the Human Scale* (London, Faber and Faber, 1954)

Le Corbusier, Charles-Edouard Jeanneret: *The Modulor II* (London, Faber and Faber, 1958)

Le Corbusier, Charles-Edouard Jeanneret: *Towards a New Architecture*, Translated by Frederick Etchells (London, William Clowes and Sons, 1970)

Lenclos, Jean Philippe, Graves, Michael and Crosby, Theo (Essays by): *The Color Compendium* (New York, Augustine Hope and Margaret Walch, Van Nostrand Reinhold, 1990)

Meiss, Piere Von: *Elements of Architecture from Form to Place*, Translated by Katherine Hanault (London, Van Noctrand Reinhold, 1990)

Morgan, Morris H.: *Vitruvius: The Ten Books of Architecture* (New York, Dover Publications Inc., 1960)

Murray, Peter: *The Architecture of the Italian Renaissance* (London, Thames and Hudson, 1991)

Parsons, K.C.: *Human Thermal Environments* (London, Taylor and Francis Ltd, 1993)

Rasmussen, Steen Eiler: *Experiencing Architecture* (Cambridge Massachusetts, The MIT Press, 1991)

Smith, Peter: *Architecture and the Principle and Harmony* (London, RIBA Publications, 1987)

Summerson, John: *The Classical Language of Architecture* (London, Thames and Hudson, 1991)

Taverne, Ed and Wagenhaar Cor (eds): *The Colour of the City* (Holland, V+K Publishing, 1992)

Tzonis, Alexander and Lefaivre, Liane: *Classical Architecture: The Poetic of Order* (Cambridge Massachusetts, MIT Press, 1986)

Wittkower, Rudolf: *Architectural Principles in the Age of Humanism* (London, Academy Editions, St Martin Press, 1988)

DESIGN

Cruz, Teddy and Boddington, Anne (eds): *Architecture of the Borderlands* (Chichester, Wiley, 1999)

Franck, Karen A.: *Architecture Inside Out* (Chichester, Wiley, 1999)

HMSO: *Accessible Thresholds in New Housing: Guidance for House Builders and Designers* (Norwich, The Stationery Office, 1999)

CONSTRUCTION MANAGEMENT

Cleland, David I.: *Project Management: Strategic Design and Implementation*, 3rd edn (New York, London, McGraw-Hill, 1999)

Finch, Edward: *Using the Internet in Building Design, Construction and Management* (London, Arnold, 1999)

Franks, James: *Building Procurement Systems: a Client's Guide*, 3rd edn (Harlow, Longman, 1998)

Halpin, Daniel W.: *Construction Management*, 2nd edn (New York, Chichester, Wiley, 1998)

Maylor, Harvey: *Project Management*, 2nd edn (London, Financial Times/Pitman, 1999)

BUILDING COMPONENTS

Blanc, Alan: *Internal Components* (Harlow, Longman Scientific & Technical, 1994)

BRE: *Building Components and Materials*, Building Research Establishment Digests, Part 2: (London, HMSO, 1983)

Everett, Alan: *Materials* (Essex, Longman Scientific & Technical, 1992)

McEvoy, Michael: *External Components* (Harlow, Longman Scientific & Technical, 1994)

Osbourn, Derek: *Components* (London, The Mitchell Publishing Company Limited, 1989)

HEATING AND VENTILATION

Havrella, Raymond A.: *Heating, Ventilating, and Air Conditioning Fundamentals* (New York, London, McGraw-Hill, 1981)

McQuiston, Faye C.: *Heating, Ventilating, and Air Conditioning: Analysis and Design*, 4th edn (New York, Chichester, Wiley, 1994)

Plumb, Derek: *Heating and Ventilating* (Cheltenham, Thornes, June 1980)

Porges, Fred: *Handbook of Heating, Ventilating and Air Conditioning*, 8th edn (London, Butterworths, 1982)

THERMAL AND SOUND INSULATION

BRE: *Sound Insulation: a Compilation of BRE Publications*, A Collection of BRE Digests, Defect Action Sheets and Information Papers, published between 1992 and 1994 (Watford, Building Research Establishment)

BRE: *Thermal Insulation: Avoiding Risks: a Good Practice Guide Supporting Building Regulations Requirements*, 2nd edn (Watford, Building Research Establishment, HMSO, 1994)

Burberry, Peter: *Environment and Services*, 8th edn (Harlow, Longman, 1997)

Diamant, Rudolph M.E.: *Thermal and Acoustic Insulation* (London, Butterworths, 1986)

Thomas, Randall, Fordham, Max & Partners: *Environmental Design. An Introduction for Architects and Engineers* (London, E. & F.N. Spon, 1996)

FIRE PROTECTION AND MEANS OF ESCAPE

Fire Protection for Structural Steel in Buildings. Prepared by the ASFPCM, the Fire Research Station and BSC Teeside Laboratories (Croydon, ASFPCM, Constrado, 1983)

Fire Safety in Health Care Premises; Fire alarm and detection systems. Department of Health and Social Security, Welsh Office Series Health technical memorandum 82 (London, HMSO, 1982)

Fire Safety in Health Care Premises; General fire precautions. Department of Health and Social Security, (and) Welsh Office Series Health technical memorandum no.83 (London, HMSO, 1982)

Billington, M.J.: *Means of Escape from Fire: An Illustrated Guide to the Law* (Oxford, Blackwell Science, 1993)

Department of the Environment: *The Building Regulations 1985: Mandatory Rules for Means of Escape in Case of Fire* (London, HMSO, 1985)

Jenkins and Potter: *Low Rise Domestic Construction in Brick.* Prepared for the Brick Development Association by Jenkins and Potter, consulting engineers and the National Building Agency. [2]: Means of escape Part [2] (Windsor, Brick Development Association, 1978)

Nowak, Andrzej S. and Galambos, Ted V. (eds): *Making Buildings Safer for People: During Hurricanes, Earthquakes, and Fires* (New York, Van Nostrand Reinhold, 1990)

Reid, Esmond: *Fire Safety Measures in Hotels.* A report prepared for the Commission of the European Communities, Directorate-General Environment, Consumer Protection and Nuclear Safety (Brussels, Bureau Européen des Unions de Consommateurs for the Commission of the European Communities, 1984)

Smith, E. and Harmathy, T.Z. (eds): *Design of Buildings for Fire Safety.* Symposium on Design of Buildings for Fire Safety, Boston, 1978 (Philadelphia, ASTM, 1979)

ARTIFICIAL LIGHTING AND DAYLIGHT

Guzowski, Mary: *Daylighting for Sustainable Design* (Boston Massachusetts, London, Irwin/McGraw-Hill, 1999)

Johnson, Glenn M.: *The Art of Illumination: Residential Lighting Design* (New York, London, McGraw-Hill, 1999)

Littlefair, P.J.: *Solar Shading of Buildings* (Garston, Construction Research Communications, 1999)

Palmer, Scott: *Essential Guide to Stage Management, Lighting and Sound* (London, Hodder & Stoughton, 1999)

Phillips, Derek: *Lighting Modern Buildings* (Oxford, Architectural, 1999)

Pritchard, David C.: *Lighting*, 6th edn (Harlow, Longman, 1999)

WINDOWS AND DOORS

Barker, Theodore Cardwell: *The Glassmakers. Pilkington: The Rise of an International Company, 1826-1976* (London, Weidenfeld and Nicolson, 1977)

Barker, Theodore Cardwell: *Pilkington. An Age of Glass: the Illustrated History* (London, Boxtree, 1994)

Barry, Robin: *The Construction of Buildings*, Vol. 2: Windows, Doors, Stairs, Fires, Stoves and Chimneys, Internal Finishes and External Rendering, 5th edn (Oxford, Blackwell Science, 1999)

Beckett, H.E. and Godfrey, J.A.: *Windows. Performance, Design and Installation* (London, Crosby Lockwood Staples, 1974)

BSI: **BS 4787:** *Internal and External Wood Doorsets, Door Leaves and Frames* (London, British Standards Institution, 1980)

   BS 4787: Part 1: 1980 [AMD 3] *Dimensional Requirements*

BSI: **BS 8213:** *Windows, Doors and Rooflights* (London, British Standards Institution, 1991)

   BS 8213: Part 1: 1991 *Code of Practice for Safety in Use and During Cleaning of Windows and Doors* (including Guidance on Cleaning Materials and Methods)

   BS 8213: Part 4: 1990 *Code of Practice for the Installation of Replacement Windows and Doorsets in Dwellings*

Caudle, James: *Doors, Windows and Blinds*, Specification 93, Technical, pp.239-311 (London, Emap Business Publishing, 1993)

Collin, Ian D. and Collins, Eric J.: *Window Selection. A Guide for Architects and Designers* (London, Newnes-Butterworths, 1977)

Hoffmann, Gretl: *Doors. Excellence in International Design* (London, George Godwin Ltd, 1977)

Turner, Denis Philip: *Window Glass Design Guide* (London, The Architectural Press Ltd, 1977)

STAIRS, ESCALATORS AND LIFTS

Blanc, Alan: *Stairs, Steps and Ramps* (Oxford, Butterworth Architecture, 1996)

BSI: **BS 5395:** *Stairs, Ladders and Walkways* (London, British Standards Institution)

BSI: **BS 5655:** *Lifts and Service Lifts* (London, British Standards Institution)

BSI: **BS EN 115:** 1995 *Safety rules for the construction and installation of escalators and passenger conveyors* (London, British Standards Institution)

BSI: **BS 5776:** 1996 *Powered stairlifts* (London, British Standards Institution)

BSI: **BS 5900:** 1999 *Specification for powered domestic lifts with partially enclosed cars and no lift-well enclosures* (London, British Standards Institution)

Lampugnani, Vittorio Magnago and Hartwig, Lutz (General eds): *Vertical, lift escalator paternoster: a cultural of vertical transport* (Berlin, Ernst and Sohn,1994)

Mannes, Willibald: *Designing Staircases* (New York, London, Van Nostrand Reinhold, 1982)

NHS Estates: *Lifts*, Design Considerations, Series Health technical memorandum no. 2024 (London, HMSO, 1995)

Stowe, Janet: *Guide to the Selection of Stairlifts* (Leeds, Rheumatology and Rehabilitation Research Unit, 1988)

Strakosch, George R.: *Vertical Transportation: Elevators and Escalators*, 2nd edn (New York, Chichester, Wiley, 1983)

Templer, John A.: *The Staircase, Studies of Hazards, Falls, and Safer Design* (London, MIT Press, 1992)

REFURBISHMENT, MAINTENANCE AND CHANGE OF USE

The Building Conservation Directory: a Guide to Specialist Suppliers, Consultants and Craftsmen in Traditional Building Conservation, Refurbishment and Design, (Tisbury, Cathedral Communications, 1999)

Re-roofing: a Guide to Flat Roof Maintenance and Refurbishment (Northwich, Euroroof Ltd, 1985)

Austin, Richard L.: *Adaptive Reuse. Issues and Case Studies in Building Preservation* (New York, Van Nostrand Reinhold Company, 1988)

Chandler, Ian: *Repair and Refurbishment of Modern Buildings* (London, Batsford, 1991)

Cunnington, Pamela: *Care for Old Houses* (Sherborne, Dorset, Prism Alpha, 1984)

Cunnington, Pamela: *Change of Use. The Conversion of Old Buildings* (London, Alphabooks, A & C Black, 1988)

Eley, Peter and Worthington, John: *Industrial Rehabilitation. The Use of Redundant Buildings for Small Enterprises* (London, The Architectural Press, 1984)

Highfield, David: *Rehabilitation and Re-use of Old Buildings* (London, E. & F.N. Spon, 1987)

Mack, Lorrie: *Homes by Design. Transforming Uncommon Properties into Stylish Homes* (London, Cassell, 1993)

ROADS AND STREETS

Making Ways for the Bicycle: a Guide to Traffic-free Path Construction (Bristol, Sustrans Ltd, 1994)

Walkways: Town Centre Factsheets 1-12 (London, Pedestrians Association, 1993)

The British Road Federation: *Old Roads to Green Roads: Improving the Environmental Performance of the Existing Road Network* (London, Landor Publishing, 1999). Based on a report by Hyder Consulting.

Burton, Anthony: *The Cotswold Way* (London, Aurum Press in association with the Ordnance Survey, 1995)

Great Britain Countryside Commission: *Paths, Routes and Trails, Policies and Priorities* (Cheltenham, Countryside Commission, 1989)

Hass-Klau, Carmen et al.: *Streets as Living Space: Helping Public Places Play Their Proper Role: Good Practice Guide with Examples From a Town Centre Study of European Pedestrian Behaviour* (London, Landor [for Environmental and Transport Planning], 1999)

Moughtin, J.C.: *Urban Design: Street and Square*, 2nd edn (Oxford, Architectural, 1999)

Sloman, Lynn: *Living Streets: a Guide to Cutting Traffic and Reclaiming Street Space* (London, Transport 2000, 1999)

GARDENS

Asensio Cerver, Francisco: *Spectacular Pools* (New York, Hearst, 1999)

Carr, Diane: *Paths and Patios* (London, Bloomsbury, 1994)

Littlewood, Michael: *Landscape Detailing*, Vol.3: Structures, 3rd edn (Oxford, Architectural Press, 1997)

Osmundson, Theodore H.: *Roof Gardens, History, Design and Construction* (W.W. Norton, May 97)

Watkin, David: *The English Vision: the Picturesque in Architecture, Landscape and Garden Design* (London, Murray, 1982)

HOUSES AND RESIDENTIAL BUILDINGS

Classic Homes [Videorecording – Programme 7]: The Terrace House Series (London, Channel 4, 1998)

Static Holiday Caravans and Chalets (London, English Tourist Board, 1973)

Borer, Pat: *The Whole House Book, Ecological Building Design and Materials* (Powys, Centre for Alternative Technology, 1998)

Centre on Environment for the Handicapped: *Designing Bathrooms for Disabled People*: Proceedings of a seminar held on 6 March 1985 at the King's Fund Centre, London (London, Centre on Environment for the Handicapped, 1985)

Colquhoun, Ian: *RIBA Book of 20th Century British Housing* (Oxford, Butterworth-Heinemann, 1999)

Department of Health and Social Security: *Laundry*, revised edn (London, HMSO, 1977)

Dibie, Pascal: *Ethnologie de la Chambre à Coucher* (Paris, B. Grasset, 1987)

Glendinning, Miles: *Tower Block: Modern Public Housing in England, Scotland, Wales and Northern Ireland* (New Haven, London: Yale University Press for The Paul Mellon Centre for Studies in British Art, 1994)

Hawkesworth, Rex: *Housing Design in the Private Sector: an Architect's View Towards a Design Philosophy*, Vol.2 (Portsmouth, Serious Graphics, University of Portsmouth Enterprise, 1998)

HMSO: *Accessible Thresholds in New Housing: Guidance for House Builders and Designers* (Norwich, The Stationery Office, 1999)

HMSO: *Laundry* (London, HMSO, 1994)

Hoffmann, Hubert: *One-family Housing: Solutions to an Urban Dilemma; Terrace Houses, Patio Houses, Linked Houses* (London, Thames & Hudson, 1967)

Horsey, Miles: *Tenements and Towers: Glasgow Working-class Housing 1890-1990* (Edinburgh: Royal Commission on the Ancient and Historical Monuments of Scotland, 1990)

IEA Solar Heating and Cooling (SHC) Programme: Task 20, Glazed balconies in building renovation (London, James & James, 1997)

Knevitt, Charles: *Shelter: Human Habitats from Around the World*; foreword by HRH the Prince of Wales (Streatley-on-Thames, Polymath Publishing, 1994)

Lincolnshire, Planning Department: *Development on the Lincolnshire Coast: [draft] Subject Plan: Holiday Accommodation, Informal Recreation, Reclamation* (Lincoln, Lincolnshire County Council, 1981)

Mazzurco, Philip: *Bath Design: Concepts, Ideas, and Projects* (London, Columbus, 1986)

Ministry of Housing and Local Government, Research and Development Group: *Designing a Low-rise Housing System: How the 5M System was Evolved: the pilot project at Sheffield* (London, HMSO, 1970)

Murphy, James D.: *The Semi-detached House: Its Place in Suburban Housing* (Dublin, Housing Research Unit, School of Architecture, University College, Dublin: Cement-Roadstone Holdings Ltd, 1977)

Pickles, Judith: *Housing for Varying Needs: a Design Guide*, Part 1: Houses and flats (Edinburgh, Stationery Office, 1998)

Pickles, Judith: *Housing for Varying Needs: a Design Guide*, Part 2: Housing with integral support (Edinburgh, Stationery Office, 1999)

Schild, Erich et al.: *Structural Failure in Residential Buildings*, Vol.1: Flat Roofs, Roof Terraces, Balconies; translated from the German by Sheila Bacon (London, Crosby Lockwood Staples, 1978)

Stallibrass, Chloe: *Seaside Resorts and the Holiday Accommodation Industry: a Case Study of Scarborough* (Oxford, Pergamon, 1980)

White, Gleeson: *A Note on Simplicity of Design in Furniture for Bedrooms with Special Reference to Some Recently Produced by Messrs Heal and Son* (London, Heal and Son, 1898)

Withers, Jane: Hot Water: *Bathing and the Contemporary Bathroom* (London, Quadrille, 1999)

OLD PEOPLE'S HOMES

Buildings Research Team, School of Architecture, Oxford Brookes University: *Buildings Design and the Delivery of Day Care Services to Elderly People* (London, HMSO, 1994)

Stoncham, Jane and Thoday, Peter: *Landscape Design for Elderly and Disabled People* (Chichester, Packard Publishing Limited, 1994)

Torrington, Judith: *Care Homes for Older People* (London, E. & F.N. Spon, 1996)

Valins, Martin: *Housing for Elderly People. A Guide for Architects and Clients* (London, The Architectural Press Ltd, 1988)

Weal, Francis and Francesca: *Housing the Elderly. Options and Design* (London, The Mitchell Publishing Company Ltd, 1988)

EDUCATIONAL AND RESEARCH FACILITIES

DfEE, Department for Education and Employment, Architects and Building Branch: *Area Guidelines for Schools*, Building Bulletin 82 (London, HMSO, 1996)

DfEE, Department for Education and Employment, Architects and Building Branch: *School Grounds. A Guide to Good Practice*, Building Bulletin 85 (London, HMSO, 1997)

Dudek, Mark: *Architecture of Schools and the New Learning Environment* (Oxford, Architectural, 1999)

Dudek, Mark: *Kindergarten Architecture: Space for the Imagination* (London, E. & F.N. Spon, 1996)

Galison, Peter and Thompson, Emily: *The Architecture of Science* (Cambridge Massachusetts, London, MIT, 1999)

Griffin, Brian: *Laboratory Design Guide* (Oxford, Architectural Press, 1998)

Hain, Walter: *Laboratories. A Briefing and Design Guide* (London, E. & F.N. Spon, 1995)

Mills, Edward D. (ed.): *Planning. Buildings for Education, Culture and Science* (London, Butterworth and Co Ltd, 1976)

Price, Barbara: *Technical Colleges and Colleges of Further Education* (London, B.T. Batsford Ltd, 1959)

LIBRARIES

Brawne, Michael et al.: *Library Builders* (London, Academy Editions, 1997)

Hargrave, R.: *Office Library Systems. A Guide for the Construction Industry* (London, The Architectural Press Ltd, 1987)

Harrison, Dean (ed.): *Library Buildings in the United Kingdom 1990-1994* (London, Library Services Limited, 1995)

Lushington, Nolan and Mills, Willis N. Jr.: *Libraries Designed for Users. A Planning Handbook* (Connecticut, Library Professional Publications, 1980)

Paulhans, Peters and Friedemann Wild (eds): *Libraries for Schools and Universities* (New York, Van Nostrand Reinhold Company, 1972)

St John Wilson, Colin: *The Design and Construction of the British* (London, British Library, 1998)

Taylor, Sue (ed.): *Building Libraries for the Information Age.* Based on the proceedings of a symposium on the Future of Higher Educational Libraries at the King's Manor, York 11-12 April 1994 (York, Institute of Advanced Architectural Studies, The University of York, May 1995)

Thompson, Godfrey: *Planning and Design of Library Buildings*, 3rd edn (Oxford, The Architectural Press Ltd, 1996)

MUSEUMS

Buzas, Stefen and Bryant, Richard: *Sir John Soane's Museum, London* (Tübingen/Berlin, Ernst Wasmuth Verlag, 1994)

Darragh, Joan and Snyder, James S.: *Museum Design. Planning and Building for Art* (Oxford, Oxford University Press, 1993)

Davis, Douglas: *The Museum Transformed* (New York, Abbeville Press Publishers, 1990)

Lord, Gail Dexter and Barry: *The Manual of Museum Planning* (London, HMSO, 1991)

Matthews, Geoff: *Museums and Art Galleries. Design and Development Guides* (Oxford, Butterworth Architecture, 1991)

Montaner, Josep Ma.: *New Museums* (London, Architecture Design and Technology Press, 1990)

Steele, James: *Museum Builders* (London, Academy Editions, 1994)

OFFICE BUILDINGS

Bailey, Stephen: *Offices: A Briefing and Design Guide* (London, Butterworth Architecture, 1990)

BCO, British Council for Offices: *Specification for Urban Offices* (Reading, Publishing Business Ltd, 1994)

Bennett, David: *Skyscrapers. The World's Tallest Buildings and How They Work* (London, Aurum Press Ltd, 1995)

Cox, Butler: *Information Technology and Buildings: A Practical Guide for Designers* (London, Butler Cox, 1990)

DBD, Directorate of Building Development: *Office Space: A Primer for Users and Designers* (London, HMSO, 1976)

Kleeman, Walter B. Jr.: *Interior Design of the Electronic Office: The Comfort and Productivity Payoff* (New York, Van Nostrand Reinhold, 1991)

Rayfield, Julie K.: *The Office Interior Design: An Introduction for Facilities Managers and Designers* (New York, John Wiley & Sons Inc., 1994)

Reid, Esmond: *Understanding Buildings: A Multidisciplinary Approach* (Essex, Longman Scientific & Technical, 1991)

Stocker, Paul and Howarth, Andrew: *Office Design and Planning* (London, CCTA, HMSO, 1992)

BANKS

Boddy, Martin: *The Building Societies* (London, The Macmillan Press Ltd, 1980)

Booker, John: *Temples of Mammon: The Architecture of Banking* (Edinburgh, Edinburgh University Press, 1990)

The Building Societies Association: *Building Society Fact Book 1987* (London, The Building Societies Association, July 1987)

The Building Societies Association: *The Future Constitution and Powers of Building Societies* (London, The Building Societies Association, January 1983)

Deilmann, Harald and Thomas: *Buildings for Banking and Insurance* (Stuttgart, Karl Krämer Verlag, 1978)

DOE, Department of the Environment: *Introduction to Energy Efficiency in Post Offices, Building Societies, Banks and Agencies* (Great Britain, Department of the Environment, March 1994)

Gough, T.G.: *The Economics of Building Societies* (London, The Macmillan Press Ltd, 1982)

Norkett, Paul: *Building Societies and Their Subsidiaries* (London, Routledge/Tekron Publications, 1989)

Parissien, Steven (ed.): *Banking on Change: A Current Account of Britain's Historic Banks* (Great Britain, The Georgian Group etc, 1992)

Sschumann-Bacia, Eva: *John Soane and the Bank of England* (London, Longman Group UK Ltd, 1991)

Weingarden, Lauren S.: *Louis H. Sullivan: The Banks* (Cambridge, Massachusetts, The MIT Press, 1987)

ARCADES

Geist, Johann Friedrich: *Arcades, the History of a Building Type* (Cambridge Massachusetts, MIT Press, 1983)

MacKeith, Margaret: *Shopping Arcades: a Gazetteer of Extant British Arcades, 1817-1939* (London, Mansell, 1985)

MacKeith, Margaret: *The History and Conservation of Shopping Arcades* (London, Mansell, 1986)

SHOPS

Fitch, Rodney and Knobel, Lance: *Fitch on Retail Design* (Oxford, Phaidon Press Ltd, 1990)

Green, William R.: *The Retail Store. Design and Construction*, 2nd edn (New York, Van Nostrand Reinhold, 1991)

Israel, Lawrence J.: *Store Planning/Design. History, Theory, Process* (New York, John Wiley & Sons, Inc., 1994)

Longstreth, Richard W.: *The Drive-in, the Supermarket, and the Transformation of Commercial Space in Los Angeles, 1914-1941* (Cambridge Massachusetts, London, MIT, 1999)

Mun, David: *Shops. A Manual of Planning and Design* (London, The Architectural Press Ltd, 1986)

Wawrowsky, Rhode Kellermann & Partners: *Architecture for the Retail Trade* (Basel, Birkhäuser Verlag, 1996)

White, Ken: *Bookstore. Planning and Design* (New York, McGraw-Hill, Inc., 1982)

WORKSHOPS AND INDUSTRIAL BUILDINGS

Planning Commitments for Industry, Warehousing, Offices and Shops, March 1984 (Reading, County Planning Department, 1984)

The Effects of Retail Warehousing on a Traditional Town Centre: a Study of Chichester City Centre and the Portfield Retail Warehouse Park (Chichester, West Sussex County Council, Planning Dept, 1992)

Ackermann, Kurt: *Building for Industry* (UK, Watermark Publications Ltd, 1991)

Bayliss, R.: *Carpentry and Joinery*, Book 1 (London, Hutchinson and Co. Ltd, 1981)

Drury, Jolyon: *Factories. Planning, Design and Modernisation* (London, The Architectural Press Ltd, 1986)

Eatwick-Field, John and Stillman, John: *The Design and Practice of Joinery* (London, The Architectural Press Ltd, 1973)

Falconer, Peter and Drury, Jolyon: *Building and Planning for Industrial Storage and Distribution* (London, The Architectural Press Ltd, 1987)

Grube, Oswald W.: *Industrial Buildings and Factories* (London, The Architectural Press Ltd, 1971)

Peters, Paulhans: *Design and Planning: Factories* (New York, Van Nostrand Reinhold Company, 1972)

Phillips, Alan: *The Best in Industrial Architecture* (London, B.T. Batsford Ltd, 1993)

Scott, Ian: *Retail Warehousing* (London, Fletcher King, 1989)

Tompkins, James A. et al: *Facilities Planning*, 2nd edn (New York, John Wiley & Sons, Inc., 1996)

Törnqvist, Anders and Ullmark, Peter: *When People Matter* (Stockholm, The Swedish Council for Building Research, 1989)

Wilkinson, Chris: *Supersheds. The Architecture of Long-Span, Large-Volume Buildings*, 2nd edn (London, The Architectural Press Ltd, 1995)

AGRICULTURAL BUILDINGS

Environment Agency: *Farm Pollution and How to Avoid It* (leaflet)

Environment Agency: *Farm Waste Management Plans* (leaflet)

Environment Agency: *Farm Waste Minimisation* (leaflet)

Environment Agency: *Farm Waste Regulations* (leaflet)

Lake, Jeremy: *Historic Farm Buildings* (London, Blandford Press, 1989)

Lytle, R.J.: *Farm Builder's Handbook*, 3rd edn (Farmington, Michigan, Structures Publishing Company, 1978)

Noton, Nicholas H.: *Farm Buildings* (Reading College of Estate Management, 1982)

Weller, John B.: *Farm Buildings. Techniques, Design, Profit*, Vol. 1 (London, Crosby Lockwood & Son Ltd, 1965)

Wiliam, Eurwyn: *The Historical Farm Buildings of Wales* (Edinburgh, John Donald Publishers Ltd, 1986)

RAILWAYS

European Transport Conference. Seminar A, 1999, Cambridge: *Operating Railways for Traffic Growth and Profit* (London, PTRC Education and Research Services on behalf of the Association for European Transport, 1999)

Railway Group Standard: *Structure Gauging and Clearances*, GC/RT5204, Issue 2 (London, Safety & Standard Directorate Railtrack Plc, November 1995)

Bertolini, Luca: *Cities on Rails, the Redevelopment of Railway Station areas* (London, E. & F.N. Spon, 1998)

Ross, Julian: *Railway Stations: Planning, Design and Management* (Oxford, Architectural, 1999)

CAR PARKS AND GARAGES

Multi-storey Car Parks in Shopping Centres and Office Blocks. Report of the British Parking Association seminar held in London, 28 October 1980 in conjunction with the Royal Institute of British Architects and of the Open Meeting held on 27 March 1980 (St Albans, British Parking Association, 1980)

Berwick-upon-Tweed (England), Borough Council: *Berwick-upon-Tweed Bus Station: Development Brief Approval*, 5 May 1994 (Berwick-upon-Tweed Borough Council, 1994)

Chrest, Anthony P.: *Parking Structures, Planning, Design, Construction, Maintenance, and Repair*, 2nd edn (New York, London, Chapman & Hall, 1996)

Institution of Structural Engineers: *Design Recommendations for Multi-storey and Underground Car Parks*. Revised report of a joint committee of the Institution of Structural Engineers and the Institution of Highways and Transportation, 2nd edn (London, Institution of Structural Engineers, 1984)

McCluskey, Jim: *Parking: a Handbook of Environmental Design* (London, E. & F.N. Spon, 1987)

Sedgwick, J.R.E.: *The Valuation and Development of Petrol Filling Stations* (1969)

Taylor, D. H.: *Bus Station Planning and Design* (Coventry, University of Warwick, 1977)

Wang, T.: *Workplace Parking Levy*, Prepared for the Chartered Institute of Transport and Royal Town Planning Institute (Crowthorne, Transport Research Laboratory, 1999)

AIRPORTS

Asensio Cerver, Francisco: *Stations and Terminals* (New York, Arco for Hearst Books, 1997)

Binney, Marcus: *Airport Builders* (London, Academy Editions, 1999)

Blow, Christopher J.: *Airport Terminals*, 2nd edn (Oxford, Architectural Press, 1997)

Bode, Steven et al. (eds): *Airport* (London, Photographers' Gallery, 1997)

Edwards, Brian: *The Modern Terminal. New Approaches to Airport Architecture* (London, E. & F.N. Spon, 1998)

RESTAURANTS

Abercrombie, Stanley: *Hospitality and Restaurant Design* (New York, Hearst, 1999)

Baraban, Regina S. and Durocher, Joseph F.: *Successful Restaurant Design* (New York, Van Nostrand Reinhold, 1989)

Casamassima, Christy: *Bar Excellence: Designs for Pubs and Clubs* (Glen Cove, New York, PBC International, 1999)

Dartford, James: *Architects' Data Sheets. Dining Spaces* (London, Architecture Design and Technology Press, 1990)

Entwistle, Jill: *Designing with Light: Bars and Restaurants* (Hove, RotoVision, 1999)

Lawson, Fred: *Restaurants, Clubs and Bars* (London, The Architectural Press, 1987)

HOTELS AND MOTELS

Architect's Journal (ed.): *Principles of Hotel Design* (London, The Architectural Press, 1970)

Bangert, Albrecht and Riewoldt, Otto: *New Hotel Design* (London, Laurence King Publishing, 1993)

Lawson, Fred R.: *Hotels and Resorts. Planning, Design and Refurbishment* (Oxford, Butterworth Architecture, 1995)

Lawson, Fred R.: *Hotels, Motels and Condominiums: Design, Planning and Maintenance* (London, The Architectural Press Ltd, 1976)

ZOOS AND AQUARIUMS

Guillery, Peter: *The Buildings of London Zoo* (London, The Royal Commission on the Historical Monuments of England, 1993)

Victorian Society: *Creature Comforts: The Problems of London Zoo*. Joint report issued by the Victorian Society and the Thirties Society, revised edn (London, Victorian Society, 1992)

Wylson, Anthony and Patricia: *Theme Parks, Leisure Centres, Zoos and Aquaria* (Essex, Longman Group UK Ltd, 1994)

THEATRES AND CINEMAS

Appleton, Ian: *Building for the Performing Arts. A Design and Development Guide* (Oxford, Butterworth Architecture, 1996)

Athanasopulos, Christos G.: *Contemporary Theater. Evolution and Design* (New York, John Wiley and Sons Inc., 1983)

Barron, Michael: *Auditorium Acoustics and Architectural Design* (London, E. & F.N. Spon, 1993)

Gray, Richard: *Cinemas in Britain. One Hundred Years of Cinema Architecture* (London, Lund Humphries Publishers, 1996)

Home Office/The Scottish Office: *Guide to Fire Precautions in Existing Places of Entertainment and Like Premises* (London, HMSO, 1990)

Izenour, George C.: *Theater Design* (New York, McGraw-Hill Book Company, 1977)

Valentine, Maggie: *The Show Starts on the Sidewalk. An Architectural History of the Movie Theatre* (New Haven, London, Yale University Press, 1994)

SPORT AND RECREATION

Konrath, Andrea: *Small Public Indoor Pools: Monitoring Report*, written by Andrea Konrath and Jenny King (London, Sports Council, 1994)

Marchaj, C.A.: *Sailing Theory and Practice*, revised edn (London, Granada Publishing, 1982)

The Sports Council, Guidance Notes: *Athletics – Outdoor* (London, Sports Council, March 1995)

The Sports Council, Guidance Notes: *Cricket* (London, Sports Council, November 1994)

The Sports Council, Guidance Notes: *Cricket – Indoor* (London, Sports Council, November 1994)

The Sports Council, Guidance Notes: *Floodlighting* (London, Sports Council, November 1994)

The Sports Council, Guidance Notes: *Shooting Ranges –Indoor* (London, Sports Council, November 1994)

The Sports Council, Guidance Notes: *Tennis – Indoor* (London, Sports Council, November 1994)

The Sports Council: *Handbook of Sports and Recreational Building Design, Vol. 1, Ice Rinks and Swimming Pools*. Edited by Geraint John and Helen Heard (London, Architectural Press Ltd, 1981)

The Sports Council: *Handbook of Sports and Recreational Building Design, Vol. 2, Indoor Sports*. Edited by Geraint John and Kit Campbell (Oxford, Butterworth Architecture, 1995)

The Sports Council: *Handbook of Sports and Recreational Building Design, Vol. 3, Outdoor Sports*. Edited by Geraint John and Helen Heard (London, Architectural Press Ltd, 1981)

The Sports Council: *Handbook of Sports and Recreational Building Design, Vol. 4, Sports Data*. Edited by Geraint John and Helen Heard (London, Architectural Press Ltd, 1981)

The Sports Council: *Small Public Indoor Pools: Technical Report* (London, Sports Council, 1993)

The Sports Council: *The Small Pool Package: a Gift for Anyone Wanting to Build a Small Public Indoor Pool* (London, Sports Council, 1995)

HEALTHCARE BUILDINGS

Hosking, Sarah: *Healing the Hospital Environment: Design, Management and Maintenance of Healthcare Premises* (London, New York, E. & F.N. Spon, 1999)

James, W. Paul and Tatton-Brown, William: *Hospitals. Design and Development* (London, Architectural Press Ltd, 1986)

NHS Estates: *Accommodation for Day Care. Day Surgery Unit*. Health Building Note 52, Vol. 1 (London, HMSO, 1993)

NHS Estates: *General Medical Practice Premises for the Provision of Primary Health Care Services*. Health Building Note 46 (London, HMSO, 1991)

NHS Estates: *Local Healthcare Facilities*. Health Building Note 36, Vol. 1 (London, HMSO, 1995)

Valins, Martin S.: *Primary Health Care Centres* (London, Longman Building Studies, 1993)

PLACES OF WORSHIP

de Breffny, Brian: *The Synagogue* (London, Weidenfeld and Nicolson, 1978)

Clowney, Paul and Tessa: *Exploring Churches* (Oxford, Lion Publishing Plc, 1993)

Davies, J.G.: *Temples, Churches and Mosques. A Guide to the Appreciation of Religious Architecture* (Oxford, Basil Blackwell, 1982)

Editors of Architectural Record Magazine: *Religious Buildings* (London, McGraw-Hill Book Company, 1979)

Frishman, Martin and Khan, Hasan-Uddin: *The Mosque. History, Architectural Development and Regional Diversity* (London, Thames and Hudson Ltd, 1994)

Gieselmann, Reinhard: *Contemporary Church Architecture* (London, Thames and Hudson Ltd, 1972)

Heathcote, Edwin and Spens, Iona: *Church Builders* (Chichester, Academy Editions, 1997)

Krinsky, Carol Herselle: *Synagogues of Europe. Architecture, History, Meaning* (New York, Cambridge Massachusetts, London, The Architectural History Foundation and the MIT Press, 1985)

Serageldin, Ismaïl and Steele, James: *Architecture of the Contemporary Mosque* (London, Academy Editions, 1996)

Wigoder, Geoffrey: *The Story of the Synagogue. A Diaspora Museum Book* (Jerusalem, The Domino Press, 1986)

CEMETERIES

Colvin, Howard: *Architecture and the After-Life* (New Haven, London, Yale University Press, 1991)

Curl, James Stevens: *A Celebration of Death* (London, B.T.Batsford Ltd, 1993)

Hudson, Kenneth: *Churchyards and Cemeteries* (London, The Bodley Head Ltd, 1984)

GENERAL

Adler, David (ed): *Metric Handbook. Planning and Design Data*, 2nd edn (Oxford, Architectural Press, 1999)

Jones, Vincent: *Neufert Architects' Data*, 2nd (International) English Edition (Oxford, Blackwell Science, 1995)

Powell-Smith, Vincent and Billington, M. J.: *The Building Regulations. Explained and Illustrated*, 9th edn (Oxford, Blackwell Science, 1992)

Williams, Alan (ed.): *Specification 93*, Technical (London, Emap Business Publishing, 1993)

DRAUGHTING GUIDELINES

BS ISO 128
Technical drawings – General principles of presentation
ISO 128-23 1999
Lines on construction drawings
BS ISO 536 1995 [AMD 1]
Paper and board – Determination of grammage
(Withdrawn, now known as BS EN ISO 536: 1997 (AMD 9309))
BS EN ISO 1660 1996
Technical drawings – Dimensioning and tolerancing of profiles
(Also known as BS 308: Section 2.3: 1996)
BS ISO 3534
Statistics – Vocabulary and symbols
ISO 3534-1 1993
Probability and general statistical terms
(Supersedes BS 5532: Part 1: 1978)
ISO 3534-2 1993
Statistical quality control
ISO 3534-3 1985
Design of experiments
(Previously known as BS 5532: Part 3: 1986)
BS EN ISO 3766 1999
Construction drawings – Simplified representation of concrete reinforcement
(With BS EN ISO 7518: 1999, supersedes BS 1192-3: 1987)
BS EN ISO 4157
Construction drawings – Designation systems
EN ISO 4157-1 1999
Buildings and parts of buildings
(Partially supersedes BS 1192-1: 1984)
EN ISO 4157-2 1999
Room names and numbers
EN ISO 4157-3 1999
Room identifiers
BS EN ISO 4172 1997
Technical drawings – Construction drawings – Drawings for the assembly of prefabricated structures
BS EN ISO 5261 1999
Technical drawings – Simplified representation of bars and profile sections
BS EN ISO 5456
Technical drawings – Projection methods
EN ISO 5456-1 1999
Synopsis
EN ISO 5456-2 1999
Orthographic representations
EN ISO 5456-3 1999
Axonometric representations
BS EN ISO 5457 1999
Technical product documentation – Sizes and layout of drawing sheets
(Supersedes BS 3429: 1984)

BS EN ISO 6284 1999
Construction drawings – Indication of limit deviations
(Partially supersedes BS 1192-1: 1984)
BS EN ISO 6412
Technical drawings – Simplified representation of pipelines
EN ISO 6412-1 1995
General rules and orthogonal representation
(Also known as BS 308: Section 4.6: 1995)
EN ISO 6412-2 1995
Isometric projection
(Also known as BS 308: Section 4.7: 1995)
EN ISO 6412-3 1996
Terminal features of ventilation and drainage systems
(Also known as BS 308: Section 4.8: 1996)
BS EN ISO 6413 1995
Technical drawings – Representations of spines and serrations
(Also known as BS 308: Section 1.9 1995 and part supersedes BS 308: Part 1)
BS EN ISO 6414 1995
Technical drawings for glassware
(Previously known as BS 2774: 1983)
BS EN ISO 6433 1995
Technical drawing – Item references
(Also known as BS 308: Section 1.8: 1995)
BS EN ISO 7437 1996
Technical drawings – Construction drawings – General rules for execution of production drawings for prefabricated structural components
BS EN ISO 7518 1999
Construction drawings – Simplified representation of demolition and rebuilding
(With BS EN ISO 3766: 1999, supersedes BS 1192-3: 1987)
BS EN ISO 7519 1997
Technical drawings – Construction drawings – General principles of presentation for general arrangement and assembly drawings
BS EN ISO 8560 1999
Construction drawings – Representation of modular sizes, lines and grids
(Partially supersedes BS 1192-1: 1984)
BS EN ISO 9431 1999
Construction drawings – Spaces for drawing and for text, and title blocks on drawing sheets
(Partially supersedes BS 1192-1: 1984)
BS ISO/IEC 9636
Information technology – Computer graphics – Interfacing techniques

for dialogues with graphical devices (CGI) – Functional specification
ISO/IEC 9636-1 1991
Overview, profiles, and conformance
ISO/IEC 9636-2 1991
Control
ISO/IEC 9636-3 1991
Output
ISO/IEC 9636-4 1991
Segments
ISO/IEC 9636-5 1991
Input and echoing
ISO/IEC 9636-6 1991
Raster
BS ISO/IEC 9637
Information technology – Computer graphics – Interfacing techniques for dialogues with graphical devices (CGI) – Data stream binding
ISO/IEC 9637-1 1994
Character encoding
ISO/IEC 9637-2 1992
Binary encoding
BS ISO/IEC 9638
Information technology – Computer graphics – Interfacing techniques for dialogues with graphical devices (CGI) – Language bindings
ISO/IEC 9638-3 1994
Ada
BS ISO/IEC 9646
Information technology – Open Systems Interconnection – Conformance testing methodology and framework
ISO/IEC 9646-1 1991 [AMD 0]
General concepts
(Also known as BS EN 29646-1: 1992)
BS EN ISO 11091 1999
Construction drawings – Landscape drawing practice
(Supersedes BS 1192-3: 1987 and BS 1192-4: 1984)
BS EN 60617
Graphical symbols for diagrams
EN 60617-2 1996
Symbol elements, qualifying symbols and other symbols having general application
(Supersedes BS 3939: Part 2: 1985)
EN 60617-11 1997
Architectural and topographical installation plans and diagrams
(Supersedes BS 3939: Part 11: 1985)
BS EN 81714
Design of graphical symbols for use in the technical documentation of products
EN 81714-2 1999
Specification for graphical symbols in a computer sensible form, including graphical symbols for a reference library, and requirements for their interchange

595

MEASUREMENT BASIS

BS EN ISO 7250 1998

Basic human body measurements for technological design

DESIGN

BS ISO 6243 1997

Climatic data for building design – Proposed system of symbols

CONSTRUCTION MANAGEMENT

BS EN 1325

Value management, value analysis, functional analysis vocabulary

EN 1325-1 1997

Value analysis and functional analysis

BS EN ISO 9000

Quality management and quality assurance standards

EN ISO 9000-1 1994

Guidelines for selection and use

(Previously known as BS 5750: Section 0.1: 1987)

BS EN 13290

Space project management – General requirements

EN 13290-1 1999

Policy and principles

BS EN ISO 14001 1996

Environmental management systems – Specification with guidance for use

(Supersedes BS 7750: 1994 which remains current)

BS EN ISO 14010 1996

Guidelines for environmental auditing – General principles

BS EN ISO 14011 1996

Guidelines for environmental auditing – Audit procedures – Auditing of environmental management systems

BS EN ISO 14012 1996

Guidelines for environmental auditing – Qualification criteria for environmental auditors

BS EN ISO 14040 1997

Environmental management – Life cycle assessment – Principles and framework

BS EN ISO 14041 1998

Environmental management – Life cycle assessment – Goal and scope definition and inventory analysis

TOOLS AND EQUIPMENT

BS EN 131

Ladders

EN 131-1 1993 [AMD 2]

Terms, types, functional sizes

(Incorporating Corrigendum No.1 (AMD 7873)

EN 131-2 1993

Requirements, testing, marking

(Incorporating Corrigendum No.1 (AMD 7874)

BS EN 204 1991

Classification of non-structural adhesives for joining of wood and derived timber products

(Supersedes DD 74: 1981)

BS EN 205 1991

Test methods for wood adhesives for non-structural applications – Determination of tensile shear strength of lap joints

(Supersedes DD 74: 1981)

BS EN 301 1992

Adhesives, phenolic and aminoplastic, for load-bearing timber structures: classification and performance requirements

(Supersedes BS 1204: Parts 1 and 2: 1979)

BS EN 302

Adhesives for load-bearing timber structures: test methods

EN 302-1 1992

Determination of bond strength in longitudinal tensile shear

(Supersedes BS 1204: Parts 1 and 2: 1979)

EN 302-2 1992 [AMD 1]

Determination of resistance to delamination (Laboratory method)

(Supersedes BS 1204: Parts 1 and 2: 1979)

EN 302-3 1992

Determination of the effect of acid damage to wood fibres by temperature and humidity cycling on the transverse tensile strength

(Supersedes BS 1204: Parts 1 and 2: 1979)

EN 302-4 1992

Determination of the effects of wood shrinkage on the shear strength

(Supersedes BS 1204: Parts 1 and 2: 1979)

BS EN 330 1993

Wood preservatives – Field test method for determining the relative protective effectiveness of a wood preservative for use under a coating and exposed out of ground contact: L-joint method

BS ISO 445 1996 [AMD 1]

Pallets for materials handling – Vocabulary

(Withdrawn, now known as BS EN ISO 445: 1999)

BS EN ISO 445 1999

Pallets for materials handling – Vocabulary

(Previously known as BS ISO 445: 1999)

BS EN 474

Earth-moving machinery – Safety

EN 474-1 1995 [AMD 2]

General requirements

EN 474-2 1996

Requirements for tractor-dozers

EN 474-3 1996

Requirements for loaders

EN 474-4 1996

Requirements for backhoe loaders

EN 474-5 1996 [AMD 1]

RELATED STANDARDS

Requirements for hydraulic excavators

EN 474-6 1997 [AMD 1]

Requirements for dumpers

EN 474-7 1998

Requirements for scrapers

EN 474-8 1998

Requirements for graders

EN 474-9 1998

Requirements for pipelayers

EN 474-10 1998

Requirements for trenchers

EN 474-11 1998

Requirements for earth and landfill compactors

BS ISO 509 1996

Pallet trucks – Principal dimensions

(Supersedes BS 4155: 1967)

BS EN 847

Tools for woodworking – Safety requirements

EN 847-1 1997

Milling tools and circular saw blades

BS EN 848

Safety of woodworking machines – One side moulding machines with rotating tool

EN 848-1 1999

Single spindle vertical moulding machines

EN 848-2 1999

Single spindle handfed/integrated fed routing machines

EN 848-3 1999

CNC woodworking machines

BS EN 859 1998

Safety of woodworking machines – Handfed surface planing machines

BS EN 860 1997

Safety of woodworking machines – One side thickness planing machines

BS EN 861 1998

Safety of woodworking machines – Surface planing and thicknessing machines

BS EN 873 1997

Light conveyor belts – Principal characteristics and applications

BS EN 940 1997

Safety of woodworking machines – Combined woodworking machines

PD 1000 1999

Universal Decimal Classification – Pocket Edition

BS EN 1493 1999

Vehicle lifts

(Supersedes BS AU 161-1b and BS AU 161-2: 1989)

BS EN 1495 1998

Lifting platforms – Mast climbing work platforms

BS EN 1554 1999

Conveyor belts – Drum friction testing

(Supersedes BS 490: Section 11.3: 1991)

BS EN 1570 1999
Safety requirements for lifting tables
(Supersedes BS 5323: 1980)
BS EN 1870
Safety of woodworking machines – Circular sawing machines
EN 1870-1 1999
Circular saw benches (with and without sliding table) and dimension saws
(Incorporating Corrigendum No.1)
EN 1870-2 1999
Horizontal beam panel saws and vertical panel saws
BS ISO 2328 1993
Fork lift trucks – Hook-on type fork arms and fork arm carriages – Mounting dimensions
BS ISO 2330 1995
Fork-lift trucks – Fork arms – Technical characteristics and testing
(Supersedes BS 5639: Part 4: 1978)
BS ISO 8566
Cranes – Cabins
ISO 8566-4 1998
Jib cranes
BS ISO 10972
Cranes – Requirements for mechanisms
ISO 10972-1 1998
General
BS ISO 11994 1997
Cranes – Availability – Vocabulary
BS EN 60417
Graphical symbols for use on equipment
EN 60417-1 1999
Overview and application
EN 60417-2 1999
Symbol originals
BS EN 61010
Safety requirements for electrical equipment for measurement, control and laboratory use

BUILDING COMPONENTS
BS EN 196
Methods of testing cement
EN 196-5 1995
Pozzolanicity test for pozzolanic cements
(Supersedes BS 4550: Part 2: 1970)
EN 196-6 1992
Determination of fineness
(Supersedes BS 4550: Sections 3.2 and 3.3: 1978)
EN 196-7 1992
Methods of taking and preparing samples of cement
(Supersedes BS 4550: Part 1: 1978)
EN 196-21 1992
Determination of the chloride, carbon dioxide and alkali content of cement
BS EN 233 1999
Wallcoverings in roll form – Specification for finished

wallpapers, wall vinyls and plastics wallcoverings
BS EN 234 1997
Wallcoverings in roll form – Specification for wallcoverings for subsequent decoration
(Supersedes BS 1248: Part 3: 1990)
BS EN 253 1995
Preinsulated bonded pipe systems for underground hot water networks – pipe assembly of steel service pipes, polyurethane thermal insulation and outer casing of polyethylene
(Supersedes BS 4508: Part 3: 1977)
BS EN 259 1997
Wallcoverings in roll form – Specification for heavy duty wallcoverings
(Supersedes BS EN 259: 1992)
BS EN 266 1992
Textile wallcoverings
BS EN 295
Vitrified clay pipes and fittings and pipe joints for drains and sewers
EN 295-5 1994 [AMD 1]
Requirements for perforated vitrified clay pipes and fittings
EN 295-6 1996
Requirements for vitrified clay manholes
EN 295-7 1996
Requirements for vitrified clay pipes and joints for pipe jacking
BS EN 300 1997
Oriented Strand Boards (OSB) – Definitions, classification and specifications
(Supersedes BS 5669: Part 3 which remains current)
BS EN 309 1992
Wood particleboards – Definition and classification
BS EN 310 1993
Wood based panels – Determination of modulus of elasticity in bending and of bending strength
BS EN 311 1992
Particleboards – Surface soundness of particleboards, test method
BS EN 312
Particleboards – Specifications
EN 312-1 1997
General requirements for all board types
(With BS EN 312-2, 3, 4, 5, 6, 7, supersedes BS 5669: Parts 1 and 2: 1989)
EN 312-2 1997
Requirements for general purpose boards for use in dry conditions
(With BS EN 312-1, 3, 4, 5, 6, 7, supersedes BS 5669: Parts 1 and 2: 1989)
EN 312-3 1997

Requirements for boards for interior fitments (including furniture) for use in dry conditions
(With BS EN 312-1, 2, 4, 5, 6, 7, supersedes BS 5669: Parts 1 and 2: 1989)
EN 312-4 1997
Requirements for load-bearing boards for use in dry conditions
(With BS EN 312-1, 2, 3, 5, 6, 7, supersedes BS 5669: Parts 1 and 2: 1989)
EN 312-5 1997
Requirements for load-bearing boards for use in humid conditions
(With BS EN 312-1 to -4 and -6, will supersede BS 5669: Part 2: 1989)
EN 312-6 1997
Requirements for heavy duty load-bearing boards for use in dry conditions
(With BS EN 312-1, 2, 3, 4, 5, 7 will supersede BS 5669: Parts 1 and 2: 1989)
EN 312-7 1997
Requirements for heavy-duty load-bearing boards for use in humid conditions
(With BS EN 312-1 to -6 will supersede BS 5669: Part 2: 1989)
BS EN 313
Plywood – Classification and terminology
EN 313-1 1996
Classification
EN 313-2 1995
Terminology
BS EN 314
Plywood – Bonding quality
EN 314-1 1993
Test methods
EN 314-2 1993
Requirements
BS EN 315 1993
Plywood – Tolerances for dimensions
BS EN 316 1999
Wood fibreboards – Definition, classification and symbols
BS EN 317 1993
Particleboards and fibreboards – Determination of swelling in thickness after immersion in water
BS EN 318 1993
Fibreboards – Determination of dimensional changes associated with changes in relative humidity
BS EN 319 1993
Particleboards and fibreboards – Determination of tensile strength perpendicular to the plane of the board
BS EN 320 1993
Fibreboards – Determination of resistance to axial withdrawal of screws
BS EN 321 1993 [AMD 1]
Fibreboards – Cyclic tests in

humid conditions

BS EN 322 1993
Wood based panels –
Determination of moisture content

BS EN 323 1993
Wood based panels –
Determination of density

BS EN 324
Wood based panels –
Determination of dimensions of
boards
EN 324-1 1993
Determination of thickness, width
and length
EN 324-2 1993
Determination of squareness and
edge straightness

BS EN 325 1993
Wood based panels –
Determination of dimensions of
test pieces

BS EN 326
Wood based panels – Sampling,
cutting and inspection
EN 326-1 1994
Sampling and cutting of test
pieces and expression of test
results
EN 326-3 1998
Inspection of a consignment of
panels

BS EN 336 1995 [AMD 1]
Structural timber – Coniferous and
poplar – Sizes – Permissible
deviations

BS EN 338 1995
Structural timber – Strength
classes

BS EN 380 1993
Timber structures – Test methods
– General principles for static load
testing

BS EN 382
Fibreboards – Determination of
surface absorption
EN 382-1 1993
Test method for dry process
fibreboards
EN 382-2 1994
Test method for hardboards

BS EN 383 1993
Timber structures – Test methods
– Determination of embedding
strength and foundation values
for dowel type fasteners

BS EN 384 1995
Structural timber – Determination
of characteristic properties and
density

BS EN 385 1995
Finger jointed structural timber –
Performance requirements and
minimum production
requirements
(Supersedes BS 5291: 1984)

BS EN 386 1995
Glue laminated timber –
Performance requirements and
minimum production
requirements

(Partially supersedes BS 4169:
1988)

BS EN 390 1995
Glued laminated timber – Sizes –
Permissible deviations

BS EN 391 1995
Glued laminated timber –
Delamination test of glue lines
(Partially supersedes BS 4169:
1988)

BS EN 392 1995
Glued laminated timber – Shear
test of glue lines
(Partially supersedes BS 4169:
1988)

BS EN 408 1995
Timber structures – Structural
timber and glued laminated
timber – Determination of some
physical and mechanical
properties
(Supersedes BS 5820: 1979)

BS EN 409 1993
Timber structures – Test methods
– Determination of the yield
moment of dowel-type fasteners –
Nails

BS EN 413
Masonry cement
EN 413-2 1995
Test methods

BS EN 423 1993
Resilient floor coverings –
Determination of the effect of
stains

BS EN 424 1993
Resilient floor coverings –
Determination of the effect of the
simulated movement of a
furniture leg

BS EN 425 1994
Resilient floor coverings –
Determination of the effect of a
castor chair

BS EN 426 1993
Resilient floor coverings –
Determination of width, length,
straightness and flatness of sheet
material

BS EN 427 1994
Resilient floor coverings –
Determination of the side length,
squareness and straightness of
tiles

BS EN 428 1993
Resilient floor coverings –
Determination of overall thickness

BS EN 429 1993
Resilient floor coverings –
Determination of the thickness of
layers

BS EN 430 1994
Resilient floor coverings –
Determination of mass per unit
area

BS EN 431 1994
Resilient floor coverings –
Determination of peel resistance

BS EN 432 1994
Resilient floor coverings –

Determination of shear force

BS EN 433 1994
Resilient floor coverings –
Determination of residual
indentation after static loading

BS EN 434 1994
Resilient floor coverings –
Determination of dimensional
stability and curling after
exposure to heat

BS EN 435 1994
Resilient floor coverings –
Determination of flexibility

BS EN 436 1994
Resilient floor coverings –
Determination of density

BS EN 459
Building lime
EN 459-2 1995
Test methods

BS EN 460 1994
Durability of wood and wood
based products – Natural
durability of solid wood – Guide
to the durability requirements for
wood to be used in hazard classes

BS EN 480
Admixtures for concrete, mortar
and grout – Test methods
EN 480-1 1998
Reference concrete and reference
mortar for testing
EN 480-2 1997
Determination of setting time
EN 480-4 1997
Determination of bleeding of
concrete
EN 480-5 1997
Determination of capillary absorp-
tion
EN 480-6 1997
Infrared analysis
EN 480-8 1997
Determination of the conventional
dry material content
EN 480-10 1997
Determination of water soluble
chloride content
EN 480-11 1999
Determination of air void
characteristics in hardened
concrete
EN 480-12 1998
Determination of the alkali content
of admixtures

BS EN 490 1994
Concrete roofing tiles and fittings
– Product specifications
(Supersedes BS 473, 550: 1990)

BS EN 491 1994
Concrete roofing tiles and fittings
– Test methods
(Supersedes BS 473, 550: 1990)

BS EN 492 1994 [AMD 3]
Fibre-cement slates and their
fittings for roofing – Product
specification and test methods
(Supersedes BS 690: Part 4: 1974)

BS EN 494 1994 [AMD 3]
Fibre-cement profiled sheets and

fittings for roofing – Product
specification and test methods
(Supersedes BS 690: Part 3: 1973,
Part 6, 1976 and BS 4624: Section
2: 1981)
BS EN 501 1994
Roofing products from metal
sheet – Specification for fully
supported roofing products of zinc
sheet
BS EN 516 1995
Prefabricated accessories for
roofing – Installations for roof
access – Walkways, treads and
steps
BS EN 517 1995
Prefabricated accessories for
roofing – Roof safety hooks
BS EN 518 1995
Structural timber – Grading –
Requirements for visual strength
grading standards
BS EN 519 1995
Structural timber – Grading –
Requirements for machine
strength graded timber and
grading machines
BS EN 538 1994
Clay roofing tiles for
discontinuous laying – Flexural
strength test
BS EN 539
Clay roofing tiles for discontinuous
laying – Determination of physical
characteristics
EN 539-1 1994
Impermeability test
EN 539-2 1998
Test for frost resistance
BS EN 548 1997
Resilient floor coverings –
Specification for plain and
decorative linoleum
BS EN 588
Fibre-cement pipes for sewers and
drains
EN 588-1 1997
Pipes, joints and fittings for
gravity systems
(Supersedes BS 3656: 1981)
BS EN 594 1996
Timber structures – Test methods
– Racking strength and stiffness of
timber frame wall panels
BS EN 595 1995
Timber structures – Test methods
– Test trusses for the
determination of strength and
deformation behaviour
EN ISO 595-2 1995
Design performance requirements
and tests
(Previously known as BS 1263:
Part 2: 1989)
BS EN 596 1995
Timber structures – Test methods
– Soft body impact test of timber
framed walls
BS EN 598 1995
Ductile iron pipes, fittings,

accessories and their joints for
sewerage applications –
Requirements and test methods
BS EN 607 1996
Eaves gutters and fittings made of
PVC-U – Definitions, requirements
and testing
(Partially supersedes BS 4576:
Part 1: 1989)
BS EN 612 1996 [AMD 1]
Eaves gutters and rainwater
downpipes of metal sheet –
Definitions, classifications and
requirements
(Supersedes BS 1431: 1969, BS
1091: Section 1:1: 1963, BS 2997:
Sections C and D:1958)
BS EN 622
Fibreboards – Specifications
EN 622-1 1997
General requirements
(Together with BS EN 622-2 to -5
partially supersedes BS 1142:
1989)
EN 622-2 1997
Requirements for hardboards
(With BS EN 622-1, -3 to -5, will
supersede BS 1142: 1989)
EN 622-3 1997
Requirements for medium boards
(With BS EN 622-1 and 2, and -4
to -5 partially supersedes BS 1142:
1989)
EN 622-4 1997
Requirements for softboards
(With BS EN 622-1 to -3 and -5
partially supersedes BS 1142:
1989)
EN 622-5 1997
Requirements for dry process
boards (MDF)
(With BS EN 622-1 to -4 partially
supersedes BS 1142: 1989)
BS EN 633 1994
Cement-bonded particleboards –
Definition and classification
BS EN 634
Cement-bonded particle-boards –
Specification
EN 634-1 1995
General requirements
EN 634-2 1997
Requirements for OPC bonded
particleboards for use in dry,
humid and exterior conditions
(Partially supersedes BS 5669:
Part 4: 1989)
BS EN 635
Plywood – Classification by
surface appearance
EN 635-1 1995
General
EN 635-2 1995 [AMD 1]
Hardwood
(Partially supersedes BS 6566:
Part 6: 1985)
EN 635-3 1995 [AMD 1]
Softwood
(Partially supersedes BS 6566:
Part 6: 1985)

EN 635-5 1999
Methods of measuring and
expressing characteristics and
defects
BS EN 636
Plywood – Specifications
EN 636-1 1997
Requirements for plywood for use
in dry conditions
EN 636-2 1997
Requirements for plywood for use
in humid conditions
EN 636-3 1997
Requirements for plywood for use
in exterior conditions
BS EN 637 1995
Plastics piping systems – Glass-
reinforced plastics components –
Determination of the amounts of
constituents using the gravimetric
method
(Incorporated in BS 2782: Part 12:
Method 1205A: 1995)
BS EN 649 1997
Resilient floor coverings –
Homogeneous and heterogeneous
polyvinyl chloride floor coverings
– Specification
(Supersedes BS 2592: 1973 and
BS 3261: Part 1: 1973)
BS EN 650 1997
Resilient floor coverings –
Polyvinyl chloride floor coverings
on jute backing or on polyester
felt backing or on polyester felt
with polyvinyl chloride backing –
Specification
(Supersedes BS 5085: Part 1:
1974)
BS EN 651 1997 [AMD 1]
Resilient floor coverings –
Polyvinyl chloride floor coverings
with foam layer – Specification
(Supersedes BS 5085: Part 2:
1976)
BS EN 652 1997
Resilient floor coverings –
Polyvinyl chloride floor coverings
with cork-based backing –
Specification
BS EN 653 1997
Resilient floor coverings –
Expanded (cushioned) polyvinyl
chloride floor coverings –
Specification
BS EN 654 1997
Resilient floor coverings – Semi-
flexible polyvinyl chloride tiles –
Specification
(Supersedes BS 3260:1969)
BS EN 655 1997
Resilient floor coverings – Tiles of
agglomerated composition cork
with polyvinyl chloride wear layer
– Specification
BS EN 660
Resilient floor coverings –
Determination of wear resistance
EN 660-1 1999
Stuttgart test

EN 660-2 1999
Frick-Taber test
BS EN 661 1995
*Resilient floor coverings –
Determination of the spreading of
water*
BS EN 662 1995
*Resilient floor coverings –
Determination of curling on
exposure to moisture*
BS EN 663 1995
*Resilient floor coverings –
Determination of conventional
pattern depth*
BS EN 664 1995
*Resilient floor coverings –
Determination of volatile loss*
BS EN 665 1995
*Resilient floor coverings –
Determination of exudation of
plasticizers*
BS EN 666 1995
*Resilient floor coverings –
Determination of gelling*
BS EN 669 1998
*Resilient floor coverings –
Determination of dimensional
stability of linoleum tiles caused
by changes in atmospheric
humidity*
BS EN 670 1998
*Resilient floor coverings –
Identification of linoleum and
determination of cement content
and ash residue*
BS EN 672 1997
*Resilient floor coverings –
Determination of apparent density
of agglomerated cork*
BS EN 678 1994
*Determination of the dry density
of autoclaved aerated concrete*
BS EN 679 1994
*Determination of the compressive
strength of autoclaved aerated
concrete*
BS EN 680 1994
*Determination of the drying
shrinkage of autoclaved aerated
concrete*
BS EN 685 1996
*Resilient floor coverings –
Classification*
BS EN 686 1997
*Resilient floor coverings –
Specification for plain and
decorative linoleum on a foam
backing*
BS EN 687 1997 [AMD 1]
*Resilient floor coverings –
Specification for plain and
decorative linoleum on a
corkment backing*
BS EN 688 1997
*Resilient floor coverings –
Specification for cork linoleum*
BS EN 695 1997
*Kitchen sinks – Connecting
dimensions*

BS EN 712 1995
*Thermoplastics piping systems –
End load bearing mechanical
joints between pressure pipes and
fittings – Test method for
resistance to pull-out under
constant longitudinal force*
(Also known as BS 2782: Method
112311: 1995)
BS EN 713 1995 [AMD 1]
*Plastics piping systems –
Mechanical joints between fittings
and polyolefin pressure pipes –
Test method for leak tightness
under internal pressure of
assemblies subjected to bending*
(Also known as BS 2782: Method
1123B: 1995)
BS EN 714 1995
*Thermoplastics piping systems –
Non-end load bearing elastomeric
sealing ring type joints between
pressure pipes and moulded
fittings – Test method for leak
tightness under internal hydrostatic
pressure without end thrust*
(Also known as BS 2782: Method
1123F: 1995)
BS EN 715 1995
*Thermoplastics piping systems –
End load bearing joints between
small diameter pressure pipes and
fittings – Test method for leak
tightness under internal water
pressure, including end thrust*
(Also known as BS 2782: Method
1123G: 1995)
BS EN 752
*Drains and sewer systems outside
buildings*
EN 752-1 1996
Generalities and definitions
(Supersedes BS 8005: Part 0: 1987
and clause 4 of BS 8301: 1985)
EN 752-2 1997
Performance requirements
EN 752-3 1997
Planning
EN 752-4 1998
*Hydraulic design and
environmental considerations*
(Supersedes BS 8005-1-5 and BS
8301: 1985)
EN 752-5 1998
Rehabilitation
EN 752-6 1998
Pumping installations
EN 752-7 1998
Maintenance and operations
(Incorporating Corrigendum No.1)
BS EN 772
Methods of test for masonry units
EN 772-2 1998
*Determination of percentage area
of voids in aggregate concrete
masonry units (by paper
indentation)*
EN 772-3 1998
Determination of net volume and

*percentage of voids of clay
masonry units by hydrostatic
weighing*
EN 772-4 1998
*Determination of real and bulk
density and of total and open
porosity for natural stone
masonry units*
EN 772-7 1998
*Determination of water absorption
of clay masonry damp proof
course units by boiling in water*
(Will partially supersede BS 3921:
1985)
EN 772-9 1998
*Determination of volume and
percentage of voids and net
volume of calcium silicate
masonry units by sand filling*
EN 772-10 1999
*Determination of moisture content
of calcium silicate and autoclaved
aerated concrete units*
BS EN 789 1996
*Timber structures – Test methods
– Determination of mechanical
properties of wood-based panels*
BS EN 877 1999
*Cast iron pipes and fittings, their
joints and accessories for the
evacuation of water from
buildings – Requirements, test
methods and quality assurance*
(Supersedes BS 416-2: 1990)
BS EN 911 1996
*Plastics piping systems –
Elastomeric sealing ring type
joints and mechanical joints for
thermoplastics pressure piping –
Test method for leak tightness
under external hydrostatic
pressure*
(Also known as BS 2782: Part 11:
Method 1123W: 1996)
BS EN 942 1996
*Timber in joinery – General
classification of timber quality*
(Supersedes BS 1186: Part 1:
1991)
BS EN 971
*Paints and varnishes – Terms and
definitions for coating materials*
EN 971-1 1996
General terms
(Supersedes some terms in BS
2015: 1992)
BS EN 975
*Sawn timber – Appearance
grading of hardwoods*
BS EN 989 1996
*Determination of the bond
behaviour between reinforcing
bars and autoclaved aerated
concrete by the 'push-out' test*
BS EN 990 1996
*Test methods for verification of
corrosion protection of
reinforcement in autoclaved
aerated concrete and lightweight*

aggregate concrete with open
structure

BS EN 991 1996

*Determination of the dimensions
of prefabricated reinforced
components made of autoclaved
aerated concrete, or lightweight
aggregate concrete with open
structure*

BS EN 1015

*Methods of test for mortar for
masonry*

EN 1015-1 1999

*Determination of particle size
distribution (by sieve analysis)*
(Will partially supersede BS 4551-
1: 1998)

EN 1015-2 1999

*Bulk sampling of mortars and
preparation of test mortars*
(Will partially supersede BS 4551-
1: 1998)

EN 1015-3 1999

*Determination of consistence of
fresh mortar (by flow table)*

EN 1015-4 1999

*Determination of consistence of
fresh mortar (by plunger
penetration)*
(Will partially supersede BS 4551-
1: 1998)

EN 1015-6 1999

*Determination of bulk density of
fresh mortar*
(Will partially supersede BS 4551-
1: 1998)

EN 1015-7 1999

*Determination of air content of
fresh mortar*
(Will partially supersede BS 4551-
1: 1998)

EN 1015-9 1999

*Determination of workable life
and correction time of fresh
mortar*

EN 1015-10 1999

*Determination of dry bulk density
of hardened mortar*

EN 1015-11 1999

*Determination of flexural and
compressive strength of hardened
mortar*

EN 1015-19 1999

*Determination of water vapour
permeability of hardened
rendering and plastering mortars*
(Partially supersedes BS 4551-1:
1998)

BS EN 1024 1997

*Clay roofing tiles for
discontinuous laying –
Determination of geometric
characteristics*

BS EN 1036 1999

*Glass in building – Mirrors from
silver-coated float glass for
internal use*

BS EN ISO 1043

Plastics – Symbols and

abbreviated terms

BS EN 1052

Methods of test for masonry

EN 1052-1 1999

*Determination of compressive
strength*
(Partially supersedes BS 5628-1:
1992)

EN 1052-2 1999

Determination of flexural strength

BS EN 1053 1996

*Plastics piping systems –
Thermoplastics piping systems for
non-pressure applications – Test
method for watertightness*
(Also known as BS 2782: Method
1112B: 1996, supersedes BS 2782:
Method 1112A: 1989)

BS EN 1054 1996

*Plastics piping systems –
Thermoplastics piping systems for
soil and waste discharge – Test
method for airtightness of joints*
(Also known as BS 2782: Method
1112C: 1996)

BS EN 1055 1996

*Plastics piping systems –
Thermoplastics piping systems for
soil and waste discharge inside
buildings – Test method for
resistance to elevated
temperature cycling*
(Also known as BS 2782: Method
1111A: 1996)

BS EN 1056 1996

*Plastics piping and ducting
systems – Plastics pipes and
fittings – Method for exposure to
direct (natural) weathering*
(Also known as BS 2782: Method
1107A: 1996)

BS EN 1058 1996

*Wood-based panels –
Determination of characteristic
values of mechanical properties
and density*

BS EN 1059 1999

*Timber structures – Product
requirements for prefabricated
trusses using punched metal plate
fasteners*

BS EN 1072 1995

*Plywood – Description of bending
properties for structural plywood*

BS EN 1091 1997

*Vacuum sewerage systems
outside buildings*

BS EN 1125 1997

*Building hardware – Panic exit
devices operated by a horizontal
bar – Requirements and test
methods*
(Replaces BS 5725: Part 1: 1981)

BS EN 1128 1996

*Cement-bonded particleboards –
Determination of hard body
impact resistance*

BS EN 1169 1999

Precast concrete products –

General rules for factory
production control of glass-fibre
reinforced cement

BS EN 1170

*Precast concrete products – Test
method for glass-fibre reinforced
cement*

EN 1170-1 1998

*Measuring the consistency of the
matrix – 'Slump test' method*
(With BS EN 1170: Parts 2-7
supersede BS 6432: 1984)

EN 1170-2 1998

*Measuring the fibre content in
fresh GRC, 'Wash out test'*

EN 1170-3 1998

*Measuring the fibre content of
sprayed GRC*
(With BS EN 1170: Parts 1, 2 and 4
to 7 supersedes BS 6432: 1984)

BS EN 1193 1998

*Timber structures – Structural
timber and glued laminated
timber – Determination of shear
strength and mechanical
properties perpendicular to the
grain*

BS EN 1194 1999

*Timber structures – Glued
laminated timber – Strength
classes and determination of
characteristic values*

BS EN 1195 1998 [AMD 1]

*Timber structures – Test methods
– Performance of structural floor
decking*

BS EN 1253

Gullies for buildings

EN 1253-1 1999

Requirements

EN 1253-2 1999

Test methods

EN 1253-3

Quality control

BS EN 1295

*Structural design of buried
pipelines under various conditions
of loading*

EN 1295-1 1998

General requirements

BS EN 1304 1998

*Clay roofing tiles for
discontinuous laying – Products
definitions and specifications*
(Supersedes BS 402-1: 1990)

BS EN 1307 1997

*Textile floor coverings –
Classification of pile carpets*
(Supersedes BS 7131: Part 1: 1989)

BS EN 1309

*Round and sawn timber – Method
of measurement of dimensions*

EN 1309-1 1997

Sawn timber

BS EN 1310 1997

*Round and sawn timber – Method
of measurement of features*

BS EN 1311 1997

Round and sawn timber – Method

of measurement of biological
degrade

BS EN 1312 1997
Round and sawn timber –
Determination of the batch
volume of sawn timber

BS EN 1313
Round and sawn timber –
Permitted deviations and
preferred sizes
EN 1313-1 1997
Softwood sawn timber
(Supersedes BS 4471: 1987)
EN 1313-2 1999
Hardwood sawn timber
(Supersedes BS 5450: 1977)

BS EN 1315
Dimensional classification
EN 1315-1 1997
Hardwood round timber
EN 1315-2 1997
Softwood round timber

BS EN 1316
Hardwood round timber –
Qualitative classification
EN 1316-1 1997
Oak and beech
EN 1316-2 1997
Poplar
EN 1316-3 1998
Ash and maples and sycamore

BS EN 1356 1997
Performance test for prefabricated
reinforced components of
autoclaved aerated concrete or
lightweight aggregate concrete
with open structure under
transverse load

BS EN 1380 1999
Timber structures – Test methods
– Load bearing nailed joints
(Together with BS EN 1381, 1382
and 1383: 1999, partially
supersedes BS 6948: 1989)

BS EN 1381 1999
Timber structures – Test methods
– Load bearing stapled joints
(Together with BS EN 1380, 1382
and 1383: 1999, partially
supersedes BS 6948: 1989)

BS EN 1383 1999
Timber structures – Test methods
– Pull-through resistance of timber
fasteners
(Together with BS EN 1380, 1381
and 1382: 1999, supersedes BS
6948: 1989)

BS EN 1399 1998
Resilient floor coverings –
Determination of resistance to
stubbed and burning cigarettes

BS EN 1401
Plastics piping systems for non-
pressure underground drainage
and sewerage – Unplasticized
poly(vinyl chloride) (PVC-U)
EN 1401-1 1998
Specifications for pipes, fittings
and the system

(Supersedes BS 5481: 1977 and
partially supersedes BS 4660: 1989)

BS EN 1438 1998
Symbols for timber and wood-
based products

BS EN 1443 1999
Chimneys – General requirements

BS EN 1457 1999
Chimneys – Clay/ceramic flue
liners – Requirements and test
methods
(Supersedes BS 1181: 1989, which
remains current)

BS EN 1470 1998
Textile floor coverings –
Classification of needled floor
coverings except for needled pile
floor coverings

BS EN 1504
Products and systems for the
protection and repair of concrete
structures – Definitions,
requirements, quality control and
evaluation of conformity
EN 1504-1 1998
Definitions

BS EN 1508 1999
Water supply – Requirements for
systems and components for the
storage of water

BS EN ISO 1513 1995
Paints and varnishes –
Examination and preparation of
samples testing
(Also known as BS 3900: Part A2:
1993)

BS EN ISO 1517 1995 [AMD 1]
Paints and varnishes – Surface-
drying test – Ballotini method
(Also known as BS 3900: Part C2:
1994)

BS EN 1521 1997
Determination of flexural strength
of lightweight aggregate concrete
with open structure

BS EN 1524
Copper and copper alloys –
Plumbing fittings

BS EN 1542 1999
Products and systems for the
protection and repair of concrete
structures – Test methods –
Measurement of bond strength by
pull-off

BS EN 1543 1998
Products and systems for the
protection and repair of concrete
structures – Test methods –
Determination of tensile strength
development for polymers

BS EN 1610 1998
Construction and testing of drains
and sewers

BS EN 1671 1997
Pressure sewerage systems
outside buildings

BS EN 1767 1999
Products and systems for the
protection and repair of concrete

structures – Test methods –
Infrared analysis

BS EN 1770 1998
Products and systems for the
protection and repair of concrete
structures – Test methods –
Determination of the coefficient of
thermal expansion

BS EN 1775 1998
Gas supply – Gas pipework in
buildings – Maximum operating
pressure ≤ 5 bar – Functional
recommendations

BS EN 1776 1999
Gas supply – Natural gas
measuring stations – Functional
requirements

BS EN 1799 1999
Products and systems for the
protection and repair of concrete
structures – Test methods – Tests
to measure the suitability of
structural bonding agents for
application to concrete surface

BS ISO 1803 1997
Building construction – Tolerances –
Expression of dimensional accuracy
– Principles and terminology

BS EN 1818 1999
Resilient floor coverings –
Determination of the effect of
loaded heavy duty castors

BS EN 1852
Plastics piping systems for non-
pressure underground drainage
and sewerage – Polypropylene
EN 1852-1 1998
Specifications for pipes, fittings
and the system

BS EN 1925 1999
Natural stone test methods –
Determination of water absorption
coefficient by capillarity

BS EN 1926 1999
Natural stone test methods –
Determination of compressive
strength

BS EN 1936 1999
Natural stone test methods –
Determination of real density and
apparent density, and of total and
open porosity

BS EN ISO 2812
Paints and varnishes –
Determination of resistance to
liquids
EN ISO 2812-1 1995 [AMD 1]
General methods
(Also known as BS 3900: Part G5:
1993)
EN ISO 2812-2 1995 [AMD 1]
Water immersion method
(Also known as BS 3900: Part G8:
1993)

BS EN ISO 2815 1998
Paints and varnishes – Buchholz
indentation test
(Also known as BS 3900: Part E9:
1976 (AMD 10176 October 1998))

BS EN ISO 3231 1998
*Paints and varnishes –
Determination of resistance to
humid atmosphere containing
sulphur dioxide*
(Also known as BS 3900: Part F8:
1993)
BS EN ISO 6708 1996
*Pipework components – Definition
and selection of DN (nominal size)*
BS EN ISO 6946 1997
*Building components and building
elements – Thermal resistance
and thermal transmittance –
Calculation method*
BS ISO 9047 1989 [AMD 1]
*Building construction – Sealants –
Determination of adhesion/
cohesion properties at variable
temperatures*
(Withdrawn, now known as BS EN
ISO 9074: 1998 (9870))
BS EN ISO 9047 1998
*Building construction – Sealants –
Determination of adhesion/
cohesion properties at variable
temperatures*
(Previously known as BS ISO
9047: 1989 (AMD 9870))
BS EN 10020 1991
*Definition and classification of
grades of steel*
(Supersedes BS 6562: Part 3:
1990)
BS EN 10027
Designation systems for steels
EN 10027-1 1992
Steel names, principal symbols
EN 10027-2 1992
Steel numbers
BS EN 10034 1993
*Structural steel I and H sections –
Tolerances on shape and
dimensions*
(Supersedes BS 4: Part 1: 1980)
BS EN 10056
*Structural steel equal and unequal
angles*
EN 10056-1 1999
Dimensions
(Supersedes BS 4848-4: 1972)
EN 10056-2 1993
*Tolerances on shape and
dimensions*
BS EN 10079 1993
Definition of steel products
(Supersedes BS 6562: Part 2:
1986)
BS EN 10088
Stainless steels
EN 10088-1 1995
List of stainless steels
(With BS EN 10088-2 and 3: 1995,
partially supersedes BS 970: Part
1: 1991)
BS EN 10155 1993
*Structural steels with improved
atmospheric corrosion resistance.
Technical delivery conditions*

(Partially supersedes BS 4360:
1990)
BS EN 10164 1993
*Steel products with improved
deformation properties perpen-
dicular to the surface of the
product – Technical delivery
conditions*
(Supersedes BS 6780: 1986)
BS EN 10208
*Steel pipes for pipelines for
combustible fluids – Technical
delivery conditions*
EN 10208-1 1998
Pipes of requirement class A
EN 10208-2 1997
Pipes of requirement class B
BS EN 10277
*Bright steel products – Technical
delivery conditions*
EN 10277-2 1999
*Steels for general engineering
purposes*
BS EN ISO 10545
Ceramic tiles
EN ISO 10545-1 1997
*Sampling and basis for
acceptance*
(Supersedes BS 6431: Part 23:
1986)
EN ISO 10545-2 1997
*Determinations of dimensions and
surface quality*
(Supersedes BS 6431: Part 10: 1984)
BS ISO 10563 1991
*Building construction – Sealants
for joints – Determination of
change in mass and volume*
(Withdrawn, now known as BS EN
ISO 10563: 1998)
BS EN ISO 10563 1998
*Building construction – Sealants
for joints – Determination of
change in mass and volume*
(Previously known as BS ISO
10563: 1991)
BS ISO 10590 1991
*Building construction – Sealants –
Determination of adhesion/
cohesion properties at maintained
extension after immersion in
water*
(Withdrawn, now known as BS EN
ISO 10590: 1998)
BS EN ISO 10590 1998
*Building construction – Sealants –
Determination of adhesion/
cohesion properties at maintained
extension after immersion in
water*
(Previously known as BS ISO
10590: 1991)
BS ISO 10591 [AMD 1]
*Building construction – Sealants –
Determination of adhesion/
cohesion properties after
immersion in water*
(Withdrawn, now known as BS EN
ISO 10591: 1998)

BS EN ISO 10591 1998
*Building construction – Sealants –
Determination of adhesion/
cohesion properties after
immersion in water*
(Previously known as BS ISO
10591: 1991 (AMD 9867))
BS ISO 11431 1993
*Building construction – Sealants –
Determination of adhesion/
cohesion properties after
exposure to artificial light through
glass*
BS ISO 11432 [AMD 1]
*Building construction – Sealants –
Determination of resistance to
compression*
(Withdrawn, now known as BS EN
ISO 11432: 1998)
BS EN ISO 11432 1998
*Building construction – Sealants –
Determination of resistance to
compression*
(Previously known as BS ISO
11432: 1993 (9866))
BS ISO 11600 1993
*Building construction – Sealants –
Classification and requirements*
BS EN 12103 1999
*Resilient floor coverings –
Agglomerated cork underlays –
Specification*
BS EN 12105 1998
*Resilient floor coverings –
Determination of moisture content
of agglomerated composition cork*
BS EN 12199 1998
*Resilient floor coverings –
Specifications for homogeneous
and heterogeneous relief rubber
floor coverings*
BS EN 12588 1999
*Lead and lead alloys – Rolled lead
sheet for building purposes*
(Supersedes BS 1178: 1982)
BS EN 12615 1999
*Products and systems for the
protection and repair of concrete
structures – Test methods –
Determination of slant shear
strength*
(Supersedes BS 6319-4: 1984)
BS EN ISO 12944
*Paints and varnishes – Corrosion
protection of steel structures by
protective paint systems*
BS EN 26927 1991
*Building construction – Jointing
products – Sealants – Vocabulary*
BS EN 27389 1991
*Building construction – Jointing
products – Determination of
elastic recovery*
BS EN 27390 1991
*Building construction – Jointing
products – Determination of
resistance to flow*
BS EN 28339 1991
Building construction – Jointing

products – Sealants –
Determination of tensile
properties
BS EN 28340 1991
Building construction – Jointing
products – Sealants –
Determination of tensile
properties at maintained
extension
BS EN 28394 1991
Building construction – Jointing
products – Determination of
extrudability of one-component
sealants
BS EN 29046 1991
Building construction – Sealants –
Determination of adhesion/
cohesion properties at constant
temperature
BS EN 29048 1991
Building construction – Jointing
products – Determination of
extrudability of sealants using
standardized apparatus
BS EN 61277 1998
Terrestrial photovoltaic (PV)
power generating systems –
General and guide

HEATING AND VENTILATION
BS EN 215
Thermostatic radiator valves
EN 215-1 1991
Requirements and test methods
BS EN 247 1997
Heat exchangers – Terminology
BS EN 255
Air conditioners, liquid chilling
packages and heat pumps with
electrically driven compressors –
Heating mode
EN 255-1 1997
Terms, definitions and
designations
EN 255-2 1997
Testing and requirements for
marking for space heating units
EN 255-3 1997
Testing and requirements for
marking for sanitary hot water
units
EN 255-4 1997
Requirements for space heating
and sanitary hot water units
BS EN 297 1994 [AMD 3]
Gas-fired central heating boilers –
Type B_{11} and B_{11BS} boilers fitted
with atmospheric burners of
nominal heat input not exceeding
70 kW
BS EN 303
Heating boilers
EN 303-1 1999
Heating boilers with forced
draught burners – Terminology,
general requirements, testing and
marking
EN 303-2 1999
Heating boilers with forced

draught burners – Special
requirements for boilers with
atomizing oil burners
EN 303-3 1999
Gas-fired central heating boilers –
Assembly comprising a boiler
body and a forced draught burner
EN 303-4 1999
Heating boilers with forced
draught burners – Special
requirements for boilers with
forced draught oil burners with
outputs up to 70 kW and a
maximum operating pressure of 3
bar – Terminology, special
requirements, testing and marking
(Partially supersedes BS 779: 1989
and BS 855: 1990)
EN 303-5 1999
Heating boilers for solid fuels,
hand and automatically fired,
nominal heat output of up to 300
kW – Terminology, requirements,
testing and marking
BS EN 304 1992 [AMD 1]
Heating boilers – Test code for
heating boilers for atomizing oil
burners
BS EN 442
Specification for radiators and
convectors
EN 442-1 1996
Technical specifications and
requirements
(With BS EN 442-2 will supersede
BS 3528: 1977)
EN 442-2 1997
Test methods and rating
EN 442-3 1997
Evaluation of conformity
(With BS EN 442-1 and -2
supersedes BS 3528: 1977)
BS EN 625 1996
Gas-fired central heating boilers –
Specific requirements for the
domestic hot water operation of
combination boilers of nominal
heat input not exceeding 70 kW
BS EN 778 1998
Domestic gas-fired forced
convection air heaters for space
heating not exceeding a net heat
input of 70 kW, without a fan to
assist transportation of combust-
ion air and/or combustion
products
(Supersedes BS 5258-4: 1987 and
BS 6332-5: 1986)
BS EN 779 1993 [AMD 1]
Particulate air filters for general
ventilation – Requirements,
testing, marking
(Supersedes BS 6540: Part 1: 1985)
BS EN 814
Air conditioners and heat pumps
with electrically driven
compressors – Cooling mode
EN 814-1 1997
Terms, definitions and

RELATED STANDARDS

designations
EN 814-2 1997
Testing requirements for marking
EN 814-3 1997
Requirements
BS EN 834 1995
Heat cost allocators for the
determination of the consumption
of room heating radiators –
Appliances with electrical energy
supply
BS EN 835 1995
Heat cost allocators for the
determination of the consumption
of room heating radiators –
Appliances without an electrical
energy supply, based on the
evaporation principle
BS EN 1264
Floor heating – Systems and
components
EN 1264-1 1998
Definitions and symbols
EN 1264-2 1998
Determination of the thermal
output
EN 1264-3 1998
Dimensioning
BS EN 1505 1998
Ventilation for buildings – Sheet
metal air ducts and fittings with
rectangular cross-section –
Dimensions
BS EN 1506 1998
Ventilation for buildings – Sheet
metal air ducts and fittings with
circular cross-section –
Dimensions
BS EN 1751 1999
Ventilation for buildings – Air
terminal devices – Aerodynamic
testing of dampers and valves
(Supersedes BS 6821: 1988)
BS EN 1886 1998
Ventilation for buildings – Air
handling units – Mechanical
performance
BS EN 12220 1998
Ventilation for buildings –
Ductwork – Dimensions of circular
flanges for general ventilation

THERMAL AND SOUND INSULATION
BS EN ISO 140
Acoustics – Measurement of
sound insulation in buildings and
of building elements
EN ISO 140-1 1998
Requirements for laboratory test
facilities with suppressed flanking
transmission
(Supersedes BS 2750: Part 1:
1980)
EN ISO 140-3 1995
Laboratory measurement of
airborne sound insulation of
building elements
(Supersedes BS 2750: Part 3:

1980. Also known as BS 2750: Part 3: 1995)

EN ISO 140-4 1998
Field measurements of airborne sound insulation between rooms
(Supersedes BS 2750-4: 1980)

EN ISO 140-5 1998
Field measurements of airborne sound insulation of façade elements and façades
(Supersedes BS 2750-5: 1980)

EN ISO 140-6 1998
Laboratory measurements of impact sound insulation of floors
(Supersedes BS 2750-6: 1980)

EN ISO 140-7 1998
Field measurements of impact sound insulation of floors
(Supersedes BS 2750-7: 1980)

EN ISO 140-8 1998
Laboratory measurements of the reduction of transmitted impact noise by floor coverings on a heavyweight standard floor
(Supersedes BS 2750: Part 8: 1980)

BS EN ISO 266 1997
Acoustics – Preferred frequencies
(Supersedes BS 3593: 1963)

BS EN ISO 717
Acoustics – Rating of sound insulation in buildings and of building elements

EN ISO 717-1 1997
Airborne sound insulation

EN 717-2 1995
Formaldehyde release by the gas analysis method

EN ISO 717-2 1997
Impact sound insulation

EN 717-3 1996
Formaldehyde release by the flask method

BS EN 822 1995
Thermal insulating products for building applications – Determination of length and width

BS EN 823 1995
Thermal insulating products for building applications – Determination of thickness

BS EN 824 1995
Thermal insulating products for building applications – Determination of squareness

BS EN 825 1995
Thermal insulating products for building applications – Determination of flatness

BS EN 826 1996
Thermal insulating products for building applications – Determination of compression behaviour

BS EN 832 1999
Thermal performance of buildings – Calculation of energy use for heating – Residential buildings

BS EN 1602 1997 [AMD 1]
Thermal insulating products for

building applications – Determination of the apparent destiny*

BS EN 1603 1997
Thermal insulating products for building applications – Determination of dimensional stability under constant normal laboratory conditions (23°C/50% relative humidity)

BS EN 1604 1997 [AMD 1]
Thermal insulating products for building applications – Determination of dimensional stability under specified temperature and humidity conditions

BS EN 1605 1997 [AMD 1]
Thermal insulating products for building applications – Determination of deformation under specified compressive load and temperature conditions

BS EN 1606 1997 [AMD 1]
Thermal insulating products for building applications – Determination of compressive creep

BS EN 1607 1997 [AMD 1]
Thermal insulating products for building applications – Determination of tensile strength perpendicular to faces

BS EN 1608 1997 [AMD 1]
Thermal insulating products for building applications – Determination of tensile strength parallel to faces

BS EN 1609 1997 [AMD 1]
Thermal insulating products for building applications – Determination of short term water absorption by partial immersion

BS EN 1934 1998
Thermal performance of buildings – Determination of thermal resistance by hot box method using heat flow meter – Masonry

BS EN 1946
Thermal performance of building products and components – Specific criteria for the assessment of laboratories measuring heat transfer properties

EN 1946-1 1999
Common criteria

EN 1946-2 1999
Measurements by guarded hot plate method

EN 1946-3 1999
Measurements by heat flow meter method

BS ISO 3743
Acoustics – Determination of sound power levels of noise sources using sound pressure – Engineering methods for small, movable sources in reverberant

fields*

ISO 3743-2 1994 [AMD 1]
Methods for special reverberation test rooms
(Now known as BS EN ISO 3743-2: 1997 (AMD 9426))

BS EN ISO 3743
Acoustics – Determination of sound power levels of noise sources using sound pressure – Engineering methods for small, movable sources in reverberant fields

EN ISO 3743-1 1995 [AMD 1]
Comparison for hard-walled test rooms
(Previously known as BS ISO 3743-1: 1994)

EN ISO 3743-2 1997
Methods for special reverberation test rooms
(Previously known as BS ISO 3743-2: 1994 (AMD 9426))

BS EN ISO 3744 1995 [AMD 1]
Acoustics – Determination of sound levels of noise sources using sound pressure – Engineering method in an essentially free field over a reflecting plane
(Previously known as BS ISO 3744: 1994)

BS EN ISO 3746 1996
Acoustics – Determination of sound power levels of noise sources using sound pressure – Survey method using an enveloping measurement surface over a reflecting plane
(Supersedes BS 4196: Part 5: 1981)

BS EN ISO 5135 1999
Acoustics – Determination of sound power levels of noise from air-terminal devices, air-terminal units, dampers and valves by measurement in a reverberation room
(Supersedes BS 4773-2: 1989)

BS EN ISO 7345 1996
Thermal insulation – Physical quantities and definitions

BS EN ISO 9251 1996
Thermal insulation – Heat transfer conditions and properties of materials – Vocabulary

BS EN ISO 9288 1996
Thermal insulation – Heat transfer by radiation – Physical quantities and definitions

BS EN ISO 9346 1996
Thermal insulation – Mass transfer – Physical quantities and definitions

BS ISO 9611 1996
Acoustics – Characterization of sources of structure-borne sound with respect to sound radiation from connected structures –

605

Measurement of velocity at the contact points of machinery when resiliently mounted

BS EN ISO 10211
Thermal bridges in building construction – Heat flows and surface temperatures

BS ISO 10551 1995
Ergonomics of the thermal environment – Assessment of the influence of the thermal environment using subjective judgement scales

BS ISO 11399 1995
Ergonomics of the thermal environment – Principles and application of relevant International Standards

BS EN ISO 11546
Acoustics – Determination of sound insulation performances of enclosures

EN ISO 11546-1 1996
Measurements under laboratory conditions (for declaration purposes)

EN ISO 11546-2 1996
Measurements in situ (for acceptance and verification purposes)

BS EN ISO 11654 1997
Acoustics – Sound absorbers for use in buildings – Rating of sound absorption

BS EN 12085 1997
Thermal insulating products for building applications – Determination of linear dimensions of test specimens

BS EN 12086 1997
Thermal insulating products for building applications – Determination of water vapour transmission properties

BS EN 12087 1997
Thermal insulating products for building applications – Determination of long term water absorption by immersion

BS EN 12088 1997
Thermal insulating products for building applications – Determination of long term water absorption diffusion

BS EN 12089 1997
Thermal insulating products for building applications – Determination of bending behaviour

BS EN 12090 1997
Thermal insulating products for building applications – Determination of shear behaviour

BS EN 12091 1997
Thermal insulating products for building applications – Determination of freeze-thaw resistance

BS EN 12429 1998
Thermal insulating products for

building applications – Conditioning to moisture equilibrium under specified temperature and humidity conditions

BS EN 12430 1998
Thermal insulating products for building applications – Determination of behaviour under point load

BS EN 12431 1998
Thermal insulating products for building applications – Determination of thickness for floating floor insulating products

BS EN 13187 1999
Thermal performance of buildings – Qualitative detection of thermal irregularities in building envelopes – Infrared method

BS EN ISO 13370 1998
Thermal performance of buildings – Heat transfer via the ground – Calculation methods

BS EN ISO 13786 1999
Thermal performance of building components – Dynamic thermal characteristics – Calculation methods

BS EN ISO 13789 1999
Thermal performance of buildings – Transmission heat loss coefficient – Calculation method

BS EN ISO 14683 1999
Thermal bridges in building construction – Linear thermal transmittance – Simplified methods and default values

BS EN 20140
Acoustics – Measurement of sound insulation in buildings and of building elements

EN 20140-2 1993
Determination, verification and application of precision data
(Also known as BS 2750: Part 2: 1993. Supersedes BS 2750: Part 2: 1980)

EN 20140-9 1994
Laboratory measurement of room-to-room airborne sound insulation of a suspended ceiling with a plenum above it
(Also known as BS 2750: Part 9: 1987)

EN 20140-10 1992
Laboratory measurement of airborne sound insulation of small building elements

BS EN 20354 1993 [AMD 2]
Acoustics – Measurement of sound absorption in a reverberation room
(Previously known as BS 3638: 1987)

BS EN 21683 1994
Acoustics – Preferred reference quantities for acoustic levels

BS EN 29052

RELATED STANDARDS

Acoustics – Method for the determination of dynamic stiffness

EN 29052-1 1992
Materials used under floating floors in dwellings

BS EN 29053 1993
Acoustics – Materials for acoustical applications – Determination of airflow resistance

FIRE PROTECTION AND MEANS OF ESCAPE

BS EN 54
Fire detection and fire alarm systems

EN 54-1 1996
Introduction
(Supersedes BS 5445: Part 1: 1977)

EN 54-2 1998
Control and indicating equipment
(With BS EN 54-4: 1997 supersedes BS 5839: Part 4: 1998 which remains current)

EN 54-4 1998
Power supply equipment
(With BS EN-54-2: 1997 supersedes BS 5839: Part 4: 1988 which remains current)

BS EN 179 1998
Building hardware – Emergency exit devices operated by a lever handle or push pad – Requirements and test methods

BS EN 615 1995
Fire protection – Fire extinguishing media – Specifications for powders (other than class D powders)
(Supersedes BS 6535: Part 3: 1989)

BS EN 1363
Fire resistance tests
EN 1363-1 1999
General requirements
EN 1363-2 1999
Alternative and additional procedures

BS EN 1364
Fire resistance tests for non-loadbearing elements
EN 1364-1 1999
Walls
EN 1364-2 1999
Ceilings

BS EN 1365
Fire resistance tests for loadbearing elements
EN 1365-1 1999
Walls
EN 1365-4 1999
Columns

BS EN 1366
Fire resistance tests for service installations
EN 1366-1 1999
Ducts

EN 1366-2 1999
Fire dampers
BS ISO TR 5925
*Fire tests – Smoke control door
and shutter assemblies*
ISO TR 5925-2 1997
*Commentary on test method and
test data application*
BS ISO 7203
*Fire extinguishing media – Foam
concentrates*
ISO 7203-1 1995
*Specification for low expansion
foam concentrates for top
application to water-immiscible
liquids*
ISO 7203-2 1995
*Specification for medium and
high expansion foam concentrates
for top application to water-
immiscible liquids*
BS ISO 10294
*Fire resistance tests – Fire
dampers for air distribution
systems*
ISO 10294-1 1996
Test method
ISO 10294-2 1999
*Classification, criteria and field of
application of test results*
ISO 10294-3 1999
Guidance on the test method
BS ISO 11925
*Reaction to fire tests – Ignitability
of building products subjected to
direct impingement of flame*
BS ISO TR 11925
*Reaction to fire tests – Ignitability
of building products subjected to
direct impingement of flame*
ISO TR 11925-1 1999
Guidance on ignitability
ISO 11925-2 1997 [AMD 1]
Single flame source test
ISO 11925-3 1997 [AMD 1]
Multi-source test
BS EN 12094
*Fixed firefighting systems –
Components for gas extinguishing
systems*
EN 12094-8 1998
*Requirements and test methods
for flexible connectors for CO_2
systems*
BS EN 12259
*Fixed fire fighting systems –
Components for sprinkler and
water spray systems*
EN 12259-1 1999
Sprinklers
EN 12259-2 1999
Wet alarm valve assemblies
BS ISO/TR 12470 1998
*Fire resistance tests – Guidance
on the application and
extenuation of results*
BS ISO TR 14697 1997
*Fire tests – Guidance on the
choice of substrates for building*

products
BS EN 25923 1994
*Fire protection – Fire
extinguishing media – Carbon
dioxide*
(Previously known as BS 6535:
Part 1: 1990)
BS EN 27201
*Fire protection – Fire extinguishing
media – Halogenated
hydrocarbons*
EN 27201-1 1994
Halon 1211 and halon 1301
(Previously known as BS 6535:
Section 2.1: 1990)
EN 27201-2 1994
*Code of practice for safe handling
and transfer procedures*
(Supersedes BS 6535: Section 2.2:
1989)
BS EN 50130
Alarm systems
EN 50130-4 1996 [AMD 1]
*Electromagnetic compatibility –
Product family standard:
Immunity requirements for
components of fire, intruder and
social alarm systems*
EN 50130-5 1999
Environmental test methods
BS EN 50131
*Alarm systems – Intrusion
systems*
EN 50131-1 1997 [AMD 1]
General requirements
EN 50131-6 1998 [AMD 1]
Power supplies
BS EN 50134
*Alarm systems – Social alarm
systems*
EN 50134-7 1996
Application guidelines
(Supersedes BS 6084: 1986)

ARTIFICIAL LIGHTING AND DAYLIGHT
BS EN 40
Lighting columns
EN 40-1 1992
Definitions and terms
(Supersedes BS 5649: Part 1:
1978)
BS EN 410 1998
*Glass in building – Determination
of luminous and solar
characteristics of glazing*
BS EN 572
*Glass in building – Basic soda
lime silicate glass products*
EN 572-1 1995
*Definitions and general physical
and mechanical properties*
EN 572-2 1995
Float glass
EN 572-3 1995
Polished wired glass
EN 572-4 1995
Drawn sheet glass
EN 572-5 1995

Patterned glass
EN 572-6 1995
Wired patterned glass
EN 572-7 1995
*Wired or unwired channel shaped
glass*
BS EN 673 1998
*Glass in building – Determination
of thermal transmittance (U value)
– Calculation method*
BS EN 674 1998
*Glass in building – Determination
of thermal transmittance (U value)
– Guarded hot plate method*
BS EN 675 1998
*Glass in building – Determination
of thermal transmittance (U value)
– Heat flow meter method*
BS EN 1096
Glass in building – Coated glass
EN 1096-1 1999
Definitions and classification
BS EN 1748
*Glass in building – Special basic
products*
EN 1748-1 1998
Borosilicate glasses
EN 1748-2 1998
Glass ceramics
BS EN ISO 12543
*Glass in building – Laminated
glass and laminated safety glass*
BS ISO 15469 1997
*Spatial distribution of daylight –
CIE standard overcast sky and
clear sky*
BS EN 60064 1996
*Tungsten filament lamps for
domestic and similar general
lighting purposes – Performance
requirements*
(Supersedes BS 161: 1990)
BS EN 60081 1998
*Double-capped fluorescent lamps
– Performance specifications*
BS EN 60432
*Safety specification for
incandescent lamps*
EN 60432-1 1995 [AMD 1]
*Tungsten filament lamps for
domestic and similar general
lighting purposes*
EN 60432-2 1995 [AMD 2]
*Tungsten halogen lamps for
domestic and similar general
lighting purposes*
BS EN 60598
Luminaires
EN 60598-1 1997 [AMD 1]
General requirements and tests
EN 60598-2
Particular requirements
EN 60598-2-2 1997
Recessed luminaires
(Supersedes BS 4533: Section
102.2: 1990 which remains
current)
EN 60598-2-3 1994 [AMD 2]
Luminaires for road and street

lighting
(Supersedes BS 4533: Section 102.3: 1990
EN 60598-2-4 1998
Portable general purpose luminaires
(Supersedes BS 4533: Section 102.4: 1990)
EN 60598-2-5 1998
Floodlights
(Incorporating Corrigendum No.1, supersedes BS 4533-102.5: 1990 which remains current)
EN 60598-2-6 1995 [AMD 1]
Luminaires with built-in transformers or converters for filament lamps
EN 60598-2-7 1997 [AMD 1]
Portable luminaires for garden use
(Incorporating Corrigendum No.1 (10563) Previously known as BS 4533: Section 102.7: 1990 (including AMD 1-3))
EN 60598-2-8 1997
Headlamps
EN 60598-2-18 1994 [AMD 1]
Luminaires for swimming pools and similar applications
(Supersedes BS 4533: Section 102.18: 1990)
EN 60598-2-20 1998 [AMD 1]
Lighting chains
(Incorporating Corrigendum No.1 (AMD 10561))
EN 60598-2-22 1999
Particular requirements – Luminaires for emergency lighting
(Incorporating Corrigendum No.1 supersedes BS 4533: Section 102.22: 1990, which remains current)
EN 60598-2-23 1997
Extra low voltage lighting systems for filament lamps
EN 60598-2-24 1999
Luminaires with limited surface temperatures
EN 60598-2-25 1995
Luminaires for use in clinical areas of hospitals and health care buildings
BS EN 60630 1999
Maximum lamp outlines for incandescent lamps
BS EN 61195 1994 [AMD 1]
Double-capped fluorescent lamps – Safety specifications
BS EN 61199 1994 [AMD 2]
Single-capped fluorescent lamps – Safety specifications
BS EN 61725 1997
Analytical expression for daily solar profiles

WINDOWS AND DOORS
BS EN 477 1999
Unplasticized polyvinylchloride (PVC-U) profiles for the fabrication

of windows and doors – Determination of the resistance to impact of main profiles by falling mass
BS EN 478 1999
Unplasticized polyvinylchloride (PVC-U) profiles for the fabrication of windows and doors – Appearance after exposure at 150 degrees centegrade – Test method
BS EN 479 1999
Unplasticized polyvinylchloride (PVC-U) profiles for the fabrication of windows and doors – Determination of heat reversion
BS EN 513 1999
Unplasticized polyvinylchloride (PVC-U) profiles for the fabrication of windows and doors – Determination of the resistance to artificial weathering
BS EN 947 1999
Hinged or pivoted doors – Determination of the resistance to vertical load
BS EN 948 1999
Hinged or pivoted doors – Determination of the resistance to static torsion
BS EN 949 1999
Windows and curtain walling, doors, blinds and shutters – Determination of the resistance to soft and heavy body impact for doors
BS EN 950 1999
Door leaves – Determination of the resistance to hard body impact
BS EN 951 1999
Door leaves – Method for measurement of height, width, thickness and squareness
BS EN 952 1999
Door leaves – General and local flatness – Measurement method
BS EN 1154 1997
Building hardware – Controlled door closing devices – Requirements and test methods
(Supersedes BS 6459: Part 1: 1984)
BS EN 1155 1997
Building hardware – Electrically powered hold-open devices for swing doors – Requirements and test methods
BS EN 1158 1997
Building hardware – Door coordinator devices – Requirements and test methods
BS EN 1522 1999
Windows, doors, shutters and blinds – Bullet resistance – Requirements and classification
BS EN 1523 1999
Windows, doors, shutters and blinds – Bullet resistance – Test method

RELATED STANDARDS
BS EN 1527 1998
Building hardware – Hardware for sliding doors and folding doors – Requirements and test methods

STAIRS, ESCALATORS AND LIFTS
BS EN 81
Safety rules for the construction and installation of lifts
EN 81-1 1998
Electric lifts
(Supersedes BS 5655-1: 1986)
EN 81-2 1998
Hydraulic lifts ((29))
(Supersedes BS 5655-2: 1988)
BS EN 115 1995 [AMD 1]
Safety rules for the construction and installation of escalators and passenger conveyors
(Supersedes BS 5656: 1983)
BS 5395:
Stairs, Ladders and Walkways
BS 5395: Part 1: 1977 [AMD 2]
Code of practice for the design of straight stairs
BS 5395: Part 2: 1984 [AMD 1]
Code of practice for the design of helical and spiral stairs
BS 5395: Part 3: 1985
Code of Practice for the design of industrial type stairs, permanent ladders and walkways
BS 5655:
Lifts and Service Lifts
BS 5655: Part 1: 1979 [AMD 2]
Safety rules for the construction and installation of electric lifts
(Remains current)
BS 5655: Part 1: 1986 [AMD 1]
Safety rules for the construction and installation of electric lifts
(Superseded by BS EN 81-1: 1998 but remains current)
PD 6500: 1986
Explanatory supplement to BS 5655: Part 1 Safety rules for the construction and installation of electric lifts (EN 81 Part 1)
(Withdrawn)
BS 5655: Part 2: 1988 [AMD 1]
Hydraulic lifts
(Withdrawn, superseded by BS EN 81-2: 1998 but remains current)
BS 5655: Part 3: 1989 [AMD 1]
Electric service lifts
BS 5655: Part 5: 1989
Dimensions of standard lift arrangement
BS 5655: Part 6: 1990
Code of practice for selection and installation
(Supersedes BS 2655: Part 2: 1959)
BS 5655: Part 7: 1983 [AMD 1]
Manual control devices, indicators and additional fittings

BS 5655: Part 8: 1983
Eyebolts for lift suspension
BS 5655: Part 9: 1985 [AMD 2]
Guide rails
BS 5655: Part 10: 1986
Testing and inspection of electric and hydraulic lifts
(Revised and replaces BS 2655: Part 7: 1970)
BS 5655: Subsection 10.1.1: 1995
Commissioning tests for new lifts
BS 5655: Subsection 10.2.1: 1995
Commissioning tests for new lifts
BS 5655: Part 11: 1989 [AMD 1]
Recommendations for the installation of new, and the modernization of, electric lifts in existing buildings
BS 5655: Part 12: 1989 [AMD 2]
Recommendations for the installation of new, and the modernization of, electric lifts in existing buildings
BS 5655: Part 13: 1995
Recommendations for vandal resistant lifts
(Supersedes DD 197:1990)
BS 5655: Part 14: 1995
Specification for hand-powered service lifts and platform hoists
BS EN 115: 1995
Safety rules for the construction and installation of escalators and passenger conveyors
BS 5776: 1996
Powered stairlifts
BS 5900: 1999
Specification for powered domestic lifts with partially enclosed cars and no lift-well enclosures

HOUSES AND RESIDENTIAL BUILDINGS
BS EN 1116 1996
Kitchen furniture – Co-ordinating sizes for kitchen furniture and kitchen appliances
(Supersedes BS 6222: Part 1: 1982)
BS EN 1153 1996
Kitchen furniture – Safety requirements and test methods for built-in and free standing kitchen cabinets and worktops
(Partially supersedes BS 6222: Part 2: 1992)
BS EN 12182 1999
Technical aids for disabled persons – General requirements and test methods

EDUCATIONAL AND RESEARCH FACILITIES
BS EN 1176
Playground equipment
EN 1176-1 1998
General safety requirements and

test methods
(Incorporating Corrigendum No.1.
Partially supersedes BS 5696-1: 1997 and BS 5696-1 and 2: 1986)
EN 1176-7 1997
Guidance on installation, inspection, maintenance and operation
(Partially supersedes BS 5696: Part 3: 1979)
BS EN 1177 1998
Impact absorbing playground surfacing – Safety requirements and test
(Partially supersedes BS 7188: 1989)

OFFICE BUILDINGS
BS EN 1023
Office furniture – Screens
EN 1023-1 1997
Dimensions
BS EN ISO 9241
Ergonomic requirements for office work with visual display terminals (VDTs)
EN ISO 9241-1 1997
General introduction
EN ISO 9241-4 1998
Keyboard requirements
(Supersedes BS 7179-4: 1990)
EN ISO 9241-5 1999
Workstation layout and postural requirements
(Supersedes BS 7179-5: 1990)
EN ISO 9241-7 1998
Requirements for display with reflections
EN ISO 9241-8 1998
Requirements for displayed colours
EN ISO 9241-10 1996
Dialogue principles
EN ISO 9241-11 1998 [AMD 1]
Guidance on usability
EN ISO 9241-12 1999
Presentation of information
EN ISO 9241-13 1999
User guidance
EN ISO 9241-15 1998
Command dialogues
EN ISO 9241-16 1999
Direct manipulation dialogues
EN ISO 9241-17 1998 [AMD 1]
Form-filling dialogues
BS ISO 9241
Ergonomic requirements for office work with visual display terminals (VDTs)
ISO 9241-14 1997
Menu dialogues
BS EN 29241
Ergonomic requirements for office work with visual display terminals (VDTs)
EN 29241-1 1993
General introduction
(Withdrawn, superseded by BS EN ISO 9241-1: 1997)

RELATED STANDARDS

EN 29241-2 1993
Guidance on task requirements
(Supersedes BS 7179: Part 2: 1990)
EN 29241-3 1993
Visual display requirements
(Supersedes BS 7179: Part 3: 1990)

SANITARY AND WASHING FACILITIES
BS 6465-1 1994
Sanitary Installations –
Part 1: Code of practice for scale of provision, selection and installation of sanitary appliances
BS 6465-2 1996
Sanitary Installations –
Part 2: Code of practice for space requirements for sanitary appliances
BS EN 31 1999
Pedestal wash basins – Connecting dimensions
(Supersedes BS 5506-1:1977
BS EN 32 1999
Wall-hung wash basins – Connecting dimensions
(Supersedes BS 5506-2:1977 which is withdrawn)
BS EN 33 1999
Pedestal WC pans with close-coupled flushing cistern – Connecting dimensions
(With BS EN 37:1999 supersedes BS 5503-1:1977)
BS EN 36 1999
Wall-hung bidets with over-rim supply – Connecting dimensions
(Supersedes BS 5505-2:1977)
BS EN 37 1999
Pedestal WC pans with independent water supply – Connecting dimensions
(With BS EN 33-1999 supersedes BS 5503-1:1977)
BS EN 111 1999
Wall-hung hand rinse basins – Connecting dimensions
(Supersedes BS 6731-1: 1988)
BS EN 200 1992
Sanitary tapware: General technical specifications for single taps and mixer taps (nominal size 1/2) PN 10: Minimum flow pressure of 0.05 Mpa (0.5 bar)
BS EN 232 1992
Baths – connecting dimensions
BS EN 246 1992
Sanitary tapware: General specifications for flow rate regulators
BS EN 251 1992
Shower trays – Connecting dimensions
BS EN 274 1993
Sanitary tapware – Waste fittings for basins, bidets and baths – General technical specifications

BS EN 329 1997
Sanitary tapware – Waste fittings for shower trays – general technical specifications
BS EN 411 1995
Sanitary tapware – Waste fittings for sinks – General technical specifications

PUBLIC TRANSPORT
BS EN 50125
Railway applications – Environmental conditions for equipment
EN 50125-1 1999
Equipment on board rolling stock
BS EN 50126 1999
Railway applications – The specification and demonstration of Reliability, Availability, Maintain-ability and Safety (RAMS)

RESTAURANTS
BS EN 203
Gas heated catering equipment
EN 203-1 1993 [AMD 2]
Safety requirements
(Supersedes BS 5314: Parts 1, 2, 3, 4, 5, 6, 7: 1976, 8, 9, 11, 12: 1979, 10, 13: 1982)
EN 203-1 1993 [AMD 1]
Specification for gas heated catering equipment
EN 203-2 1995
Rational use of energy

SPORT AND RECREATION
BS EN 748 1996 [AMD 2]
Playing field equipment – Football goals – Functional and safety requirements, test methods
BS EN 749 1996 [AMD 1]
Playing field equipment – Handball goals – Functional and safety requirements, test methods
BS EN 750 1996 [AMD 1]
Playing field equipment – Hockey goals – Functional and safety requirements, test methods
BS EN 913 1996
Gymnastic equipment – General safety requirements and test methods
(Supersedes BS 1892: Part 1: 1986)
BS EN 914 1996
Gymnastic equipment – Parallel bars and combination asymmetric /parallel bars – Functional and safety requirements, test methods
BS EN 915 1996
Gymnastic equipment – Asymmetric bars – Functional and safety requirements, test methods
(Supplement the general standard BS EN 913: 1996)

BS EN 916 1996
Gymnastic equipment – Vaulting boxes – Functional and safety requirements, test methods
(Supersedes BS 1892: Section 2.3: 1986)
BS EN 1270 1998
Playing field equipment – Basketball equipment – Functional and safety requirements, test methods
(Supersedes BS 1892-2.7: 1986)
BS EN 1271 1998
Playing field equipment – Volleyball equipment – Functional and safety requirements, test methods
BS EN 1509 1997
Playing field equipment – Badminton equipment – Functional and safety requirements, test methods
BS EN 1510 1997
Playing field equipment – Tennis equipment – Functional and safety requirements, test methods
BS EN 1516 1999
Surfaces for sports areas – Determination of resistance to indentation
(Incorporating Corrigendum No.1)
BS EN 1569 1999
Surfaces for sports areas – Determination of the behaviour under a rolling load
BS EN 12193 1999
Light and lighting – Sports lighting
BS EN 12196 1997
Gymnastics equipment – Horses and bucks – Functional and safety requirements, test methods
BS EN 12197 1997
Gymnastics equipment – Horizontal bars – Safety requirements and test methods
BS EN 12346 1999
Gymnastic equipment – Wall bars, lattice ladders and climbing frames – Safety requirements and test methods
BS EN 12432 1998
Gymnastic equipment – Balancing beams – Functional and safety requirements, test methods
BS EN 12655 1998
Gymnastic equipment – Hanging rings – Functional and safety requirements, test methods

CONVERSION OF UNITS
(pp. 611–27)

Conversion factors
Conversion tables

1 millimetres to inches
2 decimals of inch to millimetres
3 inches and fractions of inch to millimetres
4 feet and inches to metres
5 metres to feet
6 feet to metres
7 metres to yards
8 yards to metres
9 kilometres to miles
10 miles to kilometres
11 square centimetres to square inches
12 square inches to square centimetres
13 square metres to square feet
14 square feet to square metres
15 square metres to square yards
16 square yards to square metres
17 hectares to acres
18 acres to hectares
19 cubic centimetres to cubic inches
20 cubic inches to cubic centimetres
21 cubic metres to cubic feet
22 cubic feet to cubic metres
23 litres to cubic feet
24 cubic feet to litres
25 litres to imperial gallons
26 imperial gallons to litres
27 litres to US gallons
28 US gallons to litres
29 kilograms to pounds
30 pounds to kilograms
31 kilograms per cubic metre to pounds per cubic foot
32 pounds per cubic foot to kilograms per cubic metre
33 metres per second to miles per hour
34 miles per hour to metres per second
35 kilograms force per square centimetre to pounds force per square inch
36 pounds force per square inch to kilograms force per square centimetre
37 kilonewtons per square metre to pounds force per square inch
38 pounds force per square inch to kilonewtons per square metre
39 watts to British thermal units per hour
40 British thermal units per hour to watts
41 watts per square metre kelvin to British thermal units per square foot hour degree F
42 British thermal units per square foot hour degree F to watts per square metre kelvin

metric	'imperial'/US
length	
1.0 mm	0.039 in
25.4 mm (2.54 cm)	1 in
304.8 mm (30.48 cm)	1 ft
914.4 mm	1 yd
1 000.0 mm (1.0 m)	1 yd 3.4 in (1.093 yd)
20.117 m	1 chain
1 000.00 m (1 km)	0.621 mile
1 609.31 m	1 mile
area	
100 mm² (1.0 cm²)	0.155 in²
645.2 mm² (6.452 cm²)	1 in²
929.03 cm² (0.093 m²)	1 ft²'
0.836 m²	1 yd²
1.0 m²	1.196 yd² (10.764 ft²)
0.405 ha (4 046.9 m²)	1 acre
1.0 ha (10 000 m²)	2.471 acre
1.0 km²	0.386 mile²
2.59 km² (259 ha)	1 mile²
volume	
1000 mm³ (1.0 cm³; 1.0 ml)	0.061 in³
16387 mm³ (16.387 cm³; 0.0164 l; 16.387 ml)	1 in³
1.0 l (1.0 dm³; 1 000 cm³)	61.025 in³ (0.035 ft³)
0.028 m³ (28.32 l)	1 ft³
0.765 m³	1 yd³
1.0 m³	1.308 yd³ (35.314 ft³)
capacity	
1.0 ml	0.034 fl oz US
1.0 ml	0.035 fl oz imp
28.41 ml	1 fl oz imp
29.57 ml	1 fl oz US
0.473 litre	1 pint (liquid) US
0.568 litre	1 pint imp
1.0 litre	1.76 pint imp
1.0 litre	2.113 pint US
3.785 litre	1 gal US
4.546 litre	1 gal imp
100.0 litre	21.99 gal imp
100.0 litre	26.42 gal US
159.0 litre	1 barrel US
164.0 litre	1 barrel imp
mass	
1.0 g	0.035 oz (avoirdupois)
28.35 g	1 oz (avoirdupois)
454.0 g (0.454 kg)	1 lb
1 000.0 g (1 kg)	2.205 lb
45.36 kg	1 cwt US
50.8 kg	1 cwt imp
907.2 kg (0.907 t)	1 ton US
1 000.0 kg (1.0 t)	0.984 ton imp
1 000.0 kg (1.0 t)	1.102 ton US
1 016.0 kg (1.016 t)	1 ton imp
mass/unit length	
0.496 kg/m	1 lb/yd
0.564 kg/m (0.564 t/km)	1 ton US/mile
0.631 kg/m (0.631 t/km)	1 ton imp/mile
1.0 kg/m	0.056 lb/in (0.896 oz/in)
1.116 kg/m	1 oz/in
1.488 kg/m	1 lb/ft
17.86 kg/m	1 lb/in
length/unit mass	
1.0 m/kg	0.496 yd/lb
2.016 m/kg	1 yd/lb

metric	'imperial'/US
mass/unit area	
1.0 g/m²	0.003 oz/ft²
33.91 g/m²	1 oz/yd²
305.15 g/m²	1 oz/ft²
0.011 kg/m²	1 cwt US/acre
0.013 kg/m²	1 cwt imp/acre
0.224 kg/m²	1 ton US/acre
0.251 kg/m²	1 ton imp/acre
1.0 kg/m²	29.5 oz/yd²
4.882 kg/m²	1 lb/ft²
703.07 kg/m²	1 lb/in²
350.3 kg/km² (3.503 kg/ha; 0.35 g/m²)	1 ton US/mile²
392.3 kg/km² (3.923 kg/ha; 0.392 g/m²)	1 ton imp/mile²
density (mass/volume)	
0.593 kg/m³	1 lb/yd³
1.0 kg/m³	0.062 lb/ft³
16.02 kg/m³	1 lb/ft
1 186.7 kg/m³ (1.187 t/m³)	1 ton US/yd³
1 328.9 kg/m³ (1.329 t/m³)	1 ton imp/yd³
27 680.0 kg/m³ (27.68 t/m³; 27.68 g/cm³)	1 lb/in³
specific surface (area/unit mass)	
0.823 m²/t	1 yd²/ton
1.0 m²/kg	0.034 yd²/oz
29.493 m²/kg	1 yd²/oz
area/unit capacity	
0.184 m²/l	1 yd²/gal
1.0 m²/l	5.437 yd²/gal
concentration	
0.014 kg/m³	1 grain/gal imp
0.017 kg/m³	1 grain/gal US
1.0 kg/m³ (1.0 g/l)	58.42 grain/gal US
1.0 kg/m³ (1.0 g/l)	70.16 grain/gal imp
6.236 kg/m³	1 oz/gal imp
7.489 kg/m³	1 oz/gal US
mass rate of flow	
0.454 kg/s	1 lb/s
1.0 kg/s	2.204 lb/s
volume rate of flow	
0.063 l/s	1 gal US/minute
0.076 l/s	1 gal imp/minute
0.472 l/s	1 ft³/minute
1.0 l/s (86.4 m³/day)	13.2 gal imp/s
1.0 l/s	0.264 gal US/s
1.0 l/min	0.22 gal imp/min
1.0 l/min	0.264 gal US/min
3.785 l/s	1 gal US/s
4.546 l/s	1 gal imp/s
28.32 l/s	1 ft³/s
0.0038 m³/min	1 gal US/min
0.0045 m³/min	1 gal imp/min
1.0 m³/s	183.162 gal US/s
1.0 m³/s	219.969 gal imp/s
1.0 m³/h	35.31 ft³/h
0.0283 m³/s	1 ft³/s
velocity	
0.005 m/s	1 ft/minute
0.025 m/s	1 in/s
0.305 m/s	1 ft/s
1.0 m/s	3.28 ft/s
1 000.0 m/hr (1 km/hr)	0.621 mile/hr
1 609.0 m/hr (0.447 m/s)	1 mile/hr

611

metric	'imperial'/US
fuel consumption	
1.0 l/km	0.354 gal imp/mile
1.0 l/km	0.425 gal US/mile
2.352 l/km	1 gal US/mile
2.824 l/km	1 gal imp/mile
acceleration	
0.305 m/s²	1 ft/s²
1.0 m/s²	3.28 ft/s²
9.806 m/s² = g (standard acceleration due to gravity)	g = 32.172 ft/s²
temperature	
X°C	($^9/_5$X + 32) °F
$^5/_9$ × (X − 32) °C	X°F
temperature interval	
0.5556 K	1°F
1 K = 1°C	1.8°F
energy	
1.0 J	0.239 calorie
1.356 J	1 ft lbf
4.187 J	1.0 calorie
9.807 J (1 kgf m)	7.233 ft lbf
1055.06 J	1 Btu
3.6 MJ	1 kilowatt-hr
105.5 MJ	1 therm (100000 Btu)
power (energy/time)	
0.293 W	1 Btu/hr
1.0 W	0.738 ft lbf/s
1.163 W	1.0 kilocalorie/hr
1.356 W	1 ft lbf/s
4.187 W	1 calorie/s
1 kgf m/s (9.807 W)	7.233 ft lbf/s)
745.7 W	1 horsepower
1 metric horsepower (75 kgf m/s)	0.986 horsepower
intensity of heat flow rate	
1 W/m²	0.317 Btu/(ft² hr)
3.155 W/m²	1.0 Btu/(ft² hr)
thermal conductivity	
0.144 W/(m.K)	1 Btu in/(ft² hr °F)
1.0 W/(m.K)	6.933 Btu in/(ft² hr °F)
thermal conductance	
1.0 W/(m².K)	0.176 Btu/(ft² hr °F)
5.678 W/(m².K)	1.0 Btu/(ft² hr °F)
thermal registivity	
1.0 m K/W	0.144 ft² hr °F/(Btu in)
6.933 m K/W	1.0 ft² hr °F/(Btu in)
specific heat capacity	
1.0 kJ/(kg.K)	0.239 Btu/(lb °F)
4.187 kJ/(kg.K)	1.0 Btu/(lb °F)
1.0 kJ/(m³ K)	0.015 Btu/(ft³ °F)
67.07 kJ/(m³ K)	1.0 Btu/(ft³ °F)
specific energy	
1.0 kJ/kg	0.43 Btu/lb
2.326 kJ/kg	1.0 Btu/lb
1.0 kJ/m³ (1 kJ/l)	0.027 Btu/ft³
1.0 J/l	0.004 Btu/gal
232.1 J/l	1.0 Btu/gal

metric	'imperial'/US
refrigeration	
3.517 kW	12000 Btu/hr = 'ton of refrigeration'
illumination	
1 lx (1 lumen/m²)	0.093 ft-candle (0.093 lumen/ft²)
10.764 lx	1.0 ft-candle (1 lumen/ft²)
luminance	
0.3183 cd/m²	1 apostilb
1.0 cd/m²	0.000645 cd/ft²
10.764 cd/m²	1 cd/ft²
1550.0 cd/m²	1.0 cd/in²
force	
1.0 N	0.225 lbf
1.0 kgf (9.807 N; 1.0 kilopond)	2.205 lbf
4.448 kN	1.0 kipf (1000 lbf)
8.897 kN	1.0 tonf US
9.964 kN	1.0 tonf imp
force/unit length	
1.0 N/m	0.067 lbf/ft
14.59 N/m	1.0 lbf/ft
32.69 kN/m	1.0 tonf/ft
175.1 kN/m (175.1 N/mm)	1.0 lbf/in
moment of force (torque)	
0.113 Nm (113.0 Nmm)	1.0 lbf in
1.0 Nm	0.738 lbf ft
1.356 Nm	1.0 lbf ft
113.0 Nm	1.0 kipf in
253.1 Nm	1.0 tonf in
1356.0 Nm	1.0 kipf ft
3037.0 Nm	1.0 tonf ft
pressure	
1.0 Pa (1.0 N/m²)	0.021 lbf/ft²
1.0 kPa	0.145 lbf/in²
100.0 Pa	1.0 millibar
2.99 kPa	1 ft water
3.39 kPa	1 in mercury
6.9 kPa	1.0 lbf/in²
100.0 kPa	1.0 bar
101.33 kPa	1.0 standard atmosphere
107.25 kPa	1.0 tonf/ft²
15.44 MPa	1.0 tonf/in²

Length

1
millimetres
to inches

mm	0	1	2	3	4	5	6	7	8	9
	in									
0		0.04	0.08	0.11	0.16	0.2	0.24	0.28	0.31	0.35
10	0.39	0.43	0.47	0.51	0.55	0.59	0.63	0.67	0.71	0.75
20	0.79	0.83	0.87	0.91	0.94	0.98	1.02	1.06	1.1	1.14
30	1.18	1.22	1.25	1.3	1.34	1.38	1.41	1.46	1.5	1.57
40	1.57	1.61	1.65	1.69	1.73	1.77	1.81	1.85	1.89	1.93
50	1.97	2.00	2.05	2.09	2.13	2.17	2.21	2.24	2.28	2.32
60	2.36	2.4	2.44	2.48	2.52	2.56	2.6	2.64	2.68	2.72
70	2.76	2.8	2.83	2.87	2.91	2.95	3.0	3.03	3.07	3.11
80	3.15	3.19	3.23	3.27	3.31	3.35	3.39	3.42	3.46	3.5
90	3.54	3.58	3.62	3.66	3.7	3.74	3.78	3.82	3.86	3.9
100	3.94	3.98	4.02	4.06	4.09	4.13	4.17	4.21	4.25	4.29
110	4.33	4.37	4.41	4.45	4.49	4.53	4.57	4.61	4.65	4.69
120	4.72	4.76	4.8	4.84	4.88	4.92	4.96	5.0	5.04	5.08
130	5.12	5.16	5.2	5.24	5.28	5.31	5.35	5.39	5.43	5.47
140	5.51	5.55	5.59	5.63	5.67	5.71	5.75	5.79	5.83	5.87
150	5.91	5.94	5.98	6.02	6.06	6.1	6.14	6.18	6.22	6.26
160	6.3	6.34	6.38	6.42	6.46	6.5	6.54	6.57	6.61	6.65
170	6.69	6.73	6.77	6.81	6.85	6.89	6.93	6.97	7.01	7.05
180	7.09	7.13	7.17	7.21	7.24	7.28	7.32	7.36	7.4	7.44
190	7.48	7.52	7.56	7.6	7.64	7.68	7.72	7.76	7.8	7.83
200	7.87	7.91	7.95	7.99	8.03	8.07	8.11	8.15	8.19	8.23
210	8.27	8.31	8.35	8.39	8.43	8.46	8.5	8.54	8.58	8.62
220	8.66	8.7	8.74	8.78	8.82	8.86	8.9	8.94	8.98	9.02
230	9.06	9.09	9.13	9.17	9.21	9.25	9.29	9.33	9.37	9.41
240	9.45	9.49	9.53	9.57	9.61	9.65	9.69	9.72	9.76	9.8
250	9.84									

2
decimals of
inch to
millimetres

in	0.000	0.001	0.002	0.003	0.004	0.005	0.006	0.007	0.008	0.009
	mm									
0.0		0.0254	0.0508	0.0762	0.1016	0.127	0.1524	0.1778	0.2032	0.2286
0.01	0.254	0.2794	0.3048	0.3302	0.3556	0.381	0.4064	0.4318	0.4572	0.4826
0.02	0.508	0.5334	0.5588	0.5842	0.6096	0.635	0.6604	0.6858	0.7112	0.7366
0.03	0.762	0.7874	0.8128	0.8382	0.8636	0.889	0.9144	0.9398	0.9652	0.9906
0.04	1.016	1.0414	1.0668	1.0922	1.1176	1.143	1.1684	1.1938	1.2192	1.2446
0.05	1.27	1.2954	1.3208	1.3462	1.3716	1.397	1.4224	1.4478	1.4732	1.4986
0.06	1.524	1.5494	1.5748	1.6002	1.6256	1.651	1.6764	1.7018	1.7272	1.7526
0.07	1.778	1.8034	1.8288	1.8542	1.8796	1.905	1.9304	1.9558	1.9812	2.0066
0.08	2.032	2.0574	2.0828	2.1082	2.1336	2.159	2.1844	2.2098	2.2352	2.2606
0.09	2.286	2.3114	2.3368	2.3622	2.3876	2.413	2.4384	2.4638	2.4892	2.5146
0.1	2.54									

3
inches and
fractions of
inch to
millimetres

in	1/16	1/8	3/16	1/4	5/16	3/8	7/16	1/2	9/16	5/8	11/16	3/4	13/16	7/8	15/16
	mm														
		1.6	3.2	4.8	6.4	7.9	9.5	11.1	12.7	14.3	15.9	17.5	19.1	20.6	22.2	23.8
1	25.4	27.0	28.6	30.2	31.8	33.3	34.9	36.5	38.1	39.7	41.3	42.9	44.5	46.0	47.6	49.2
2	50.8	52.4	54.0	55.6	57.2	58.7	60.3	61.9	63.5	65.1	66.7	68.3	69.9	71.4	73.0	74.6
3	76.2	77.8	79.4	81.0	82.6	84.1	85.7	87.3	88.9	90.5	92.1	93.7	95.3	96.8	98.4	100.0
4	101.6	103.2	104.8	106.4	108.0	109.5	111.1	112.7	114.3	115.9	117.5	119.1	120.7	122.2	123.8	125.4
5	127.0	128.6	130.2	131.8	133.4	134.9	136.5	138.1	139.7	141.3	142.9	144.5	146.1	147.6	149.2	150.8
6	152.4	154.0	155.6	157.2	158.8	160.3	161.9	163.5	165.1	166.7	168.3	169.9	171.5	173.0	174.6	176.2
7	177.8	179.4	181.0	182.6	184.2	185.7	187.3	188.9	190.5	192.1	193.7	195.3	196.9	198.4	200.0	201.6
8	203.2	204.8	206.4	208.0	209.6	211.1	212.7	214.3	215.9	217.5	219.1	220.7	222.3	223.8	225.4	227.0
9	228.6	230.2	231.8	233.4	235.0	236.5	238.1	239.7	241.3	242.9	244.5	246.1	247.7	249.2	250.8	252.4
10	254.0	255.6	257.2	258.8	260.4	261.9	263.5	265.1	266.7	268.3	269.9	271.5	273.1	274.6	276.2	277.8

4
feet and
inches to
metres

	in											
	0	1	2	3	4	5	6	7	8	9	10	11
	m											
ft												
0		0.0254	0.0508	0.0762	0.1016	0.127	0.1524	0.1778	0.2032	0.2286	0.254	0.2794
1	0.3048	0.3302	0.3556	0.381	0.4064	0.4318	0.4572	0.4826	0.508	0.5334	0.5588	0.5842
2	0.6096	0.635	0.6604	0.6858	0.7112	0.7366	0.762	0.7874	0.8128	0.8382	0.8636	0.889
3	0.9144	0.9398	0.9652	0.9906	1.016	1.0414	1.0668	1.0922	1.1176	1.143	1.1684	1.1938
4	1.2192	1.2446	1.27	1.2954	1.3208	1.3462	1.3716	1.397	1.4224	1.4478	1.4732	1.4986
5	1.524	1.5494	1.5748	1.6002	1.6256	1.651	1.6764	1.7018	1.7272	1.7526	1.778	1.8034
6	1.8288	1.8542	1.8796	1.905	1.9304	1.9558	1.9812	2.0066	2.032	2.0574	2.0828	2.1082
7	2.1336	2.159	2.1844	2.2098	2.2352	2.2606	2.286	2.3114	2.3368	2.3622	2.3876	2.413
8	2.4384	2.4638	2.4892	2.5146	2.54	2.5654	2.5908	2.6162	2.6416	2.667	2.6924	2.7178
9	2.7432	2.7686	2.794	2.8194	2.8448	2.8702	2.8956	2.921	2.9464	2.9718	2.9972	3.0226
10	3.048											

5 metres to feet

m	0	1	2	3	4	5	6	7	8	9
	ft									
0		3.28	6.56	9.84	13.12	16.40	19.69	22.97	26.25	29.53
10	32.8	36.09	39.37	42.65	45.93	49.21	52.49	55.77	59.06	62.34
20	65.62	68.9	72.17	75.45	78.74	82.02	85.3	88.58	91.86	95.14
30	98.43	101.7	104.99	108.27	111.55	114.82	118.11	121.39	124.67	127.95
40	131.23	134.51	137.8	141.08	144.36	147.63	150.91	154.2	157.48	160.76
50	164.04	167.32	170.6	173.89	177.17	180.45	183.73	187.01	190.29	193.57
60	196.85	200.13	203.41	206.69	209.97	213.25	216.54	219.82	223.1	226.38
70	229.66	232.94	236.22	239.5	242.78	246.06	249.34	252.63	255.91	259.19
80	262.46	265.75	269.03	272.31	275.59	278.87	282.15	285.43	288.71	292.0
90	295.28	298.56	301.84	305.12	308.4	311.68	314.96	318.24	321.52	324.8
100	328.08	331.37	334.65	337.93	341.21	344.49	347.77	351.05	354.33	357.61
110	360.89	364.17	367.45	370.74	374.02	377.3	380.58	383.86	387.14	390.42
120	393.7	396.98	400.26	403.54	406.82	410.1	413.39	416.67	419.95	423.23
130	426.51	429.79	433.07	436.35	439.63	442.91	446.19	449.48	452.76	456.04
140	459.32	462.6	465.88	469.16	472.44	475.72	479.0	482.28	485.56	488.85
150	492.13	495.41	498.69	502.0	505.25	508.53	511.81	515.09	518.37	521.65
160	524.93	528.22	531.5	534.78	538.06	541.34	544.62	547.9	551.18	554.46
170	557.74	561.02	564.3	567.59	570.87	574.15	577.43	580.71	583.99	587.27
180	590.55	593.83	597.11	600.39	603.68	606.96	610.24	613.52	616.8	620.08
190	623.36	626.64	629.92	633.2	636.48	639.76	643.05	646.33	649.6	652.89
200	656.17	659.45	662.73	666.01	669.29	672.57	675.85	679.13	682.42	685.7
210	688.98	692.26	695.54	698.82	702.1	705.38	708.66	711.94	715.22	718.5
220	721.79	725.07	728.35	731.63	734.91	738.19	741.47	744.75	748.03	751.31
230	754.59	757.87	761.16	764.44	767.72	771.0	774.28	777.56	780.84	784.12
240	787.4	790.68	793.96	797.24	800.53	803.81	807.09	810.37	813.65	816.93
250	820.21									

7 metres to yards

m	0	1	2	3	4	5	6	7	8	9
	yd									
0		1.09	2.19	3.28	4.37	5.47	6.56	7.66	8.75	9.84
10	10.94	12.03	13.12	14.22	15.31	16.4	17.5	18.59	19.69	20.78
20	21.87	22.97	24.06	25.15	26.25	27.34	28.43	29.53	30.62	31.71
30	32.8	33.9	35.0	36.09	37.18	38.28	39.37	40.46	41.56	42.65
40	43.74	44.84	45.93	47.03	48.12	49.21	50.31	51.4	52.49	53.59
50	54.68	55.77	56.87	57.96	59.06	60.15	61.24	62.34	63.43	64.52
60	65.62	66.71	67.8	68.9	69.99	71.08	72.18	73.27	74.37	75.46
70	76.55	77.65	78.74	79.83	80.93	82.02	83.11	84.21	85.3	86.4
80	87.49	88.58	89.68	90.77	91.86	92.96	94.05	95.14	96.24	97.33
90	98.43	99.52	100.61	101.71	102.8	103.89	104.99	106.08	107.17	108.27
100	109.36	110.46	111.55	112.64	113.74	114.83	115.92	117.02	118.11	119.2
110	120.3	121.39	122.49	123.58	124.67	125.74	126.86	127.95	129.05	130.14
120	131.23	132.33	133.42	134.51	135.61	136.7	137.8	138.89	139.99	141.08
130	142.17	143.26	144.36	145.45	146.54	147.64	148.73	149.83	150.92	152.01
140	153.1	154.2	155.29	156.39	157.48	158.57	159.67	160.76	161.86	162.95
150	164.04	165.14	166.23	167.32	168.42	169.51	170.6	171.7	172.79	173.89
160	174.98	176.07	177.17	178.26	179.35	180.45	181.54	182.63	183.73	184.82
170	185.91	187.0	188.1	189.2	190.29	191.38	192.48	193.57	194.66	195.76
180	196.85	197.94	199.04	200.13	201.23	202.32	203.41	204.51	205.6	206.69
190	207.79	208.88	209.97	211.07	212.16	213.26	214.35	215.44	216.53	217.63
200	218.72	219.82	220.91	222.0	223.1	224.19	225.28	226.38	227.47	228.57
210	229.66	230.75	231.85	232.94	234.03	235.13	236.22	237.31	238.41	239.5
220	240.56	241.69	242.78	243.88	244.97	246.06	247.16	248.25	249.34	250.44
230	251.53	252.63	253.72	254.81	255.91	257.0	258.09	259.19	260.28	261.37
240	262.47	263.56	264.65	265.75	266.84	267.94	269.03	270.12	271.22	272.31
250	273.4									

9 kilometres to miles

km	0	1	2	3	4	5	6	7	8	9
	mile									
0		0.62	1.24	1.86	2.49	3.11	3.73	4.35	4.98	5.59
10	6.21	6.84	7.46	8.08	8.7	9.32	9.94	10.56	11.18	11.81
20	12.43	13.05	13.67	14.29	14.91	15.53	16.16	16.78	17.4	18.02
30	18.64	19.29	19.88	20.5	21.13	21.75	22.37	22.99	23.61	24.23
40	24.85	25.47	26.1	26.72	27.34	27.96	28.58	29.2	29.83	30.45
50	31.07	31.69	32.31	32.93	33.55	34.18	34.8	35.42	36.04	36.66
60	37.28	37.9	38.53	39.15	39.77	40.39	41.01	41.63	42.25	42.87
70	43.5	44.12	44.74	45.36	45.98	46.6	47.22	47.85	48.47	49.09
80	49.7	50.33	50.95	51.57	52.2	52.82	53.44	54.06	54.68	55.3
90	55.92	56.54	57.17	57.79	58.41	59.03	59.65	60.27	60.89	61.52
100	62.14									

6
feet to
metres

ft	0	1	2	3	4	5	6	7	8	9
	m									
0		0.31	0.6	0.91	1.22	1.52	1.83	2.13	2.44	2.74
10	3.05	3.35	3.66	3.96	4.27	4.57	4.88	5.18	5.49	5.79
20	6.1	6.4	6.71	7.01	7.31	7.62	7.92	8.23	8.53	8.84
30	9.14	9.45	9.75	10.06	10.36	10.67	10.97	11.28	11.58	11.89
40	12.19	12.5	12.80	13.1	13.41	13.72	14.02	14.36	14.63	14.94
50	15.24	15.54	15.85	16.15	16.46	16.76	17.07	17.37	17.68	17.98
60	18.29	18.59	18.9	19.2	19.58	19.81	20.12	20.42	20.73	21.03
70	21.33	21.64	21.95	22.25	22.56	22.86	23.16	23.47	23.77	24.08
80	24.38	24.69	24.99	25.3	25.6	25.91	26.21	26.52	26.82	27.13
90	27.43	27.74	28.04	28.35	28.65	28.96	29.26	29.57	29.87	30.18
100	30.48	30.78	31.09	31.39	31.7	32.0	32.31	32.61	32.92	33.22
110	33.53	33.83	34.14	34.44	34.75	35.05	35.37	35.67	36.0	36.3
120	36.58	36.88	37.19	37.49	37.8	38.1	38.41	38.7	39.01	39.32
130	39.62	39.93	40.23	40.54	40.84	41.15	41.45	41.76	42.06	42.37
140	42.67	42.98	43.28	43.59	43.89	44.2	44.5	44.81	45.11	45.46
150	45.72	46.02	46.33	46.63	46.94	47.24	47.55	47.85	48.16	48.46
160	48.77	49.07	49.38	49.68	49.99	50.29	50.6	50.9	51.21	51.51
170	51.82	52.12	52.43	52.73	53.04	53.34	53.64	53.95	54.25	54.56
180	54.86	55.17	55.47	55.78	56.08	56.39	56.69	57.0	57.3	57.61
190	57.91	58.22	58.52	58.83	59.13	59.44	59.74	60.05	60.35	60.66
200	60.96	61.26	61.57	61.87	62.18	62.48	62.79	63.09	63.4	63.7
210	64.01	64.31	64.62	64.92	65.23	65.53	65.84	66.14	66.45	66.75
220	67.06	67.36	67.67	67.97	68.28	68.58	68.89	69.19	69.49	69.79
230	70.1	70.41	70.71	71.02	71.32	71.63	71.93	72.24	72.54	72.85
240	73.15	73.46	73.76	74.07	74.37	74.68	74.98	75.29	75.59	75.9
250	76.2									

8
yards to
metres

yd	0	1	2	3	4	5	6	7	8	9
	m									
0		0.91	1.83	2.74	3.65	4.57	5.49	6.4	7.32	8.23
10	9.14	10.06	10.97	11.89	12.8	13.71	14.63	15.54	16.46	17.37
20	18.29	19.2	20.12	21.03	21.95	22.86	23.77	24.69	25.6	26.52
30	27.43	28.35	29.26	30.18	31.09	32.0	32.92	33.83	34.75	35.66
40	36.58	37.49	38.4	39.32	40.23	41.15	42.06	42.98	43.89	44.81
50	45.72	46.63	47.55	48.46	49.38	50.29	51.21	52.12	53.04	53.95
60	54.86	55.78	56.69	57.61	58.52	59.44	60.35	61.27	62.18	63.09
70	64.0	64.92	65.84	66.75	67.67	68.58	69.49	70.41	71.32	72.24
80	73.15	74.07	74.98	75.9	76.81	77.72	78.64	79.55	80.47	81.38
90	82.3	83.21	84.12	85.04	85.95	86.87	87.78	88.7	89.61	90.53
100	91.44	92.35	93.27	94.18	95.1	96.01	96.93	97.84	98.76	99.67
110	100.58	101.5	102.41	103.33	104.24	105.16	106.07	106.99	107.9	108.81
120	109.73	110.64	111.56	112.47	113.39	114.3	115.21	116.13	117.04	117.96
130	118.87	119.79	120.7	121.61	122.53	123.44	124.36	125.27	126.19	127.1
140	128.02	128.93	129.85	130.76	131.67	132.59	133.5	134.42	135.33	136.25
150	137.16	138.07	138.99	139.9	140.82	141.73	142.65	143.56	144.48	145.39
160	146.3	147.22	148.13	149.05	149.96	150.88	151.79	152.71	153.62	154.53
170	155.45	156.36	157.28	158.19	159.11	160.02	160.93	161.85	162.76	163.68
180	164.59	165.51	166.42	167.34	168.25	169.16	170.08	170.99	171.9	172.82
190	173.74	174.65	175.57	176.48	177.39	178.31	179.22	180.14	181.05	181.97
200	182.88	183.79	184.71	185.62	186.54	187.45	188.37	189.28	190.2	191.11
210	192.02	192.94	193.85	194.77	195.68	196.6	197.51	198.43	199.34	200.25
220	201.17	202.08	203.0	203.91	204.83	205.74	206.65	207.57	208.48	209.4
230	210.31	211.23	212.14	213.06	213.97	214.88	215.8	216.71	217.63	218.54
240	219.46	220.37	221.29	222.0	223.11	224.03	224.94	225.86	226.77	227.69
250	228.6									

10
miles to
kilometres

mile	0	1	2	3	4	5	6	7	8	9
	km									
0		1.61	3.22	4.83	6.44	8.05	9.66	11.27	12.87	14.48
10	16.09	17.7	19.31	20.92	22.53	24.14	25.75	27.36	28.97	30.58
20	32.19	33.8	35.41	37.01	38.62	40.23	41.84	43.45	45.06	46.67
30	48.28	49.89	51.5	53.11	54.72	56.33	57.94	59.55	61.16	62.76
40	64.37	65.98	67.59	69.2	70.81	72.42	74.03	75.64	77.25	78.86
50	80.47	82.08	83.69	85.3	86.9	88.51	90.12	91.73	93.34	94.95
60	96.56	98.17	99.78	101.39	103.0	104.61	106.22	107.83	109.44	111.05
70	112.65	114.26	115.87	117.48	119.09	120.7	122.31	123.92	125.53	127.14
80	128.75	130.36	131.97	133.58	135.19	136.79	138.4	140.01	141.62	143.23
90	144.84	146.45	148.06	149.67	151.28	152.89	154.5	156.11	157.72	159.33
100	160.93									

Area

11
square
centimetres
to square
inches

cm²	0	1	2	3	4	5	6	7	8	9
	in²									
0		0.16	0.31	0.47	0.62	0.78	0.93	1.09	1.24	1.4
10	1.6	1.71	1.86	2.02	2.17	2.33	2.48	2.64	2.79	2.95
20	3.1	3.26	3.41	3.57	3.72	3.88	4.03	4.19	4.34	4.5
30	4.65	4.81	4.96	5.12	5.27	5.43	5.58	5.74	5.9	6.05
40	6.2	6.36	6.51	6.67	6.82	6.98	7.13	7.29	7.44	7.6
50	7.75	7.91	8.06	8.22	8.37	8.53	8.68	8.84	9.0	9.15
60	9.3	9.46	9.61	9.77	9.92	10.08	10.23	10.39	10.54	10.7
70	10.85	11.01	11.16	11.32	11.47	11.63	11.78	11.94	12.09	12.25
80	12.4	12.56	12.71	12.87	13.02	13.18	13.33	13.49	13.64	13.8
90	13.95	14.11	14.26	14.42	14.57	14.73	14.88	15.04	15.19	15.35
100	15.5	15.66	15.81	15.97	16.12	16.28	16.43	16.59	16.74	16.9
110	17.05	17.21	17.36	17.52	17.67	17.83	17.98	18.14	18.29	18.45
120	18.6	18.76	18.91	19.07	19.22	19.38	19.53	19.69	19.84	20.0
130	20.15	20.31	20.46	20.62	20.77	20.93	21.08	21.24	21.39	21.55
140	21.7	21.86	22.01	22.17	22.32	22.48	22.63	22.79	22.94	23.1
150	23.25	23.41	23.56	23.72	23.87	24.03	24.18	24.34	24.49	24.65
160	24.8	24.96	25.11	25.27	25.42	25.58	25.73	25.89	26.04	26.2
170	26.35	26.51	26.66	26.82	26.97	27.13	27.28	27.44	27.59	27.75
180	27.9	28.06	28.21	28.37	28.52	28.68	28.83	28.99	29.14	29.3
190	29.45	29.61	29.76	29.92	30.07	30.23	30.38	30.54	30.69	30.85
200	31.0	31.16	31.31	31.47	31.62	31.78	31.93	32.09	32.24	32.4
210	32.55	32.71	32.86	33.02	33.17	33.33	33.48	33.64	33.79	33.95
220	34.1	34.26	34.41	34.57	34.72	34.88	35.03	35.19	35.34	35.5
230	35.65	35.81	35.96	36.12	36.27	36.43	36.58	36.75	36.89	37.05
240	37.20	37.36	37.51	37.67	37.82	37.98	38.13	38.29	38.44	38.6
250	38.75									

13
square
metres
to square
feet

m²	0	1	2	3	4	5	6	7	8	9
	ft²									
0		10.76	21.53	32.29	43.06	53.82	64.58	75.35	86.11	96.88
10	107.64	118.4	129.17	139.93	150.66	161.46	172.22	182.97	193.75	204.51
20	215.29	226.01	236.81	247.57	258.33	269.1	279.86	290.63	301.39	312.15
30	322.92	333.68	344.45	355.21	365.97	376.74	387.5	398.27	409.03	419.79
40	430.56	441.32	452.08	462.85	473.61	484.38	495.14	505.91	516.67	527.43
50	538.2	548.96	559.72	570.49	581.25	592.02	602.78	613.54	624.31	635.07
60	645.84	656.6	667.36	678.13	688.89	699.65	710.42	721.18	731.95	742.71
70	753.47	764.24	775.0	785.77	796.53	807.29	818.06	828.82	839.59	850.35
80	861.11	871.88	882.64	893.41	904.17	914.93	925.7	936.46	947.22	957.99
90	968.75	979.52	990.28	1 001.04	1 011.81	1 022.57	1 033.34	1 044.1	1 054.86	1 065.63
100	1 076.39	1 087.15	1 097.92	1 108.68	1 119.45	1 130.21	1 140.97	1 151.74	1 162.5	1 173.27
110	1 184.03	1 194.79	1 205.56	1 216.32	1 227.09	1 237.85	1 248.61	1 259.38	1 270.14	1 280.91
120	1 291.67	1 302.43	1 313.2	1 323.96	1 334.72	1 345.49	1 356.25	1 367.02	1 377.78	1 388.54
130	1 399.31	1 410.07	1 420.84	1 431.6	1 442.36	1 453.13	1 463.89	1 474.66	1 485.42	1 496.18
140	1 506.95	1 517.71	1 528.48	1 539.24	1 550.0	1 560.77	1 571.53	1 582.29	1 593.06	1 603.82
150	1 614.59	1 625.35	1 636.11	1 646.88	1 657.64	1 668.41	1 679.17	1 689.93	1 700.7	1 711.46
160	1 722.23	1 732.99	1 743.75	1 754.52	1 765.28	1 776.05	1 786.81	1 797.57	1 808.34	1 819.1
170	1 829.86	1 840.63	1 851.39	1 862.16	1 872.92	1 883.68	1 894.45	1 905.21	1 915.98	1 926.74
180	1 937.5	1 948.27	1 959.03	1 969.8	1 980.56	1 991.32	2 002.09	2 012.85	2 023.62	2 034.38
190	2 045.14	2 055.91	2 066.67	2 077.43	2 088.2	2 098.96	2 109.73	2 120.49	2 131.25	2 142.02
200	2 152.78	2 163.55	2 174.31	2 185.07	2 195.84	2 206.6	2 217.37	2 228.13	2 238.89	2 249.66
210	2 260.42	2 271.19	2 281.95	2 292.71	2 303.48	2 314.24	2 325.0	2 335.77	2 346.53	2 357.3
220	2 368.06	2 378.82	2 389.59	2 400.35	2 411.12	2 421.88	2 432.64	2 443.41	2 454.17	2 464.94
230	2 475.7	2 486.46	2 497.23	2 507.99	2 518.76	2 529.52	2 540.28	2 551.05	2 561.81	2 572.57
240	2 583.34	2 594.1	2 604.87	2 615.63	2 626.39	2 637.16	2 647.92	2 658.69	2 669.45	2 680.21
250	2 690.98	2 701.74	2 712.51	2 723.27	2 734.03	2 744.8	2 755.56	2 766.32	2 777.09	2 787.85
260	2 798.62	2 809.38	2 820.14	2 830.91	2 841.67	2 852.44	2 863.2	2 873.96	2 884.73	2 895.49
270	2 906.26	2 917.02	2 927.78	2 938.55	2 949.31	2 960.08	2 970.84	2 981.6	2 992.37	3 003.13
280	3 013.89	3 024.66	3 035.42	3 046.19	3 056.95	3 067.71	3 078.48	3 089.24	3 100.01	3 110.77
290	3 121.53	3 132.3	3 143.06	3 153.83	3 164.59	3 175.35	3 186.12	3 196.88	3 207.65	3 218.41
300	3 229.17	3 239.94	3 250.7	3 261.46	3 272.23	3 282.99	3 293.76	3 304.52	3 315.28	3 326.05
310	3 336.81	3 347.58	3 358.34	3 369.1	3 379.87	3 390.63	3 401.4	3 412.16	3 422.92	3 433.69
320	3 444.45	3 455.22	3 465.98	3 476.74	3 487.51	3 498.27	3 509.03	3 519.8	3 530.56	3 541.33
330	3 552.09	3 562.85	3 573.62	3 584.38	3 595.15	3 605.91	3 616.67	3 627.44	3 638.2	3 648.97
340	3 659.73	3 670.49	3 681.26	3 692.02	3 702.79	3 713.55	3 724.31	3 735.08	3 745.84	3 756.6
350	3 767.37	3 778.13	3 788.9	3 799.66	3 810.42	3 821.19	3 831.95	3 842.72	3 853.48	3 864.24
360	3 875.01	3 885.77	3 896.54	3 907.3	3 918.06	3 928.83	3 939.59	3 950.36	3 961.12	3 971.88
370	3 982.65	3 993.41	4 004.17	4 014.94	4 025.7	4 036.47	4 047.23	4 057.99	4 068.76	4 079.52
380	4 090.29	4 101.05	4 111.81	4 122.58	4 133.34	4 144.11	4 154.87	4 165.63	4 176.4	4 187.16
390	4 197.93	4 208.69	4 219.45	4 230.22	4 240.98	4 251.74	4 262.51	4 273.27	4 284.04	4 294.8
400	4 305.56	4 316.33	4 327.09	4 337.86	4 348.62	4 359.38	4 370.15	4 380.91	4 391.68	4 402.44
410	4 413.2	4 423.97	4 434.73	4 445.49	4 456.26	4 467.02	4 477.79	4 488.55	4 499.31	4 510.08
420	4 520.84	4 531.61	4 542.37	4 553.13	4 563.9	4 574.66	4 585.43	4 596.19	4 606.95	4 617.72
430	4 628.48	4 639.25	4 650.01	4 660.77	4 671.54	4 682.3	4 693.06	4 703.83	4 714.59	4 725.36
440	4 736.12	4 746.88	4 757.65	4 768.41	4 779.18	4 789.94	4 800.7	4 811.47	4 822.23	4 833.0
450	4 843.76	4 854.52	4 865.29	4 876.05	4 886.82	4 897.58	4 908.34	4 919.11	4 929.87	4 940.63
460	4 951.4	4 962.16	4 972.93	4 983.69	4 994.45	5 005.22	5 015.98	5 026.75	5 037.51	5 048.27
470	5 059.04	5 069.8	5 080.57	5 091.33	5 102.09	5 112.86	5 123.62	5 134.39	5 145.15	5 155.91
480	5 166.68	5 177.44	5 188.2	5 198.97	5 209.73	5 220.5	5 231.26	5 242.02	5 252.79	5 263.55
490	5 274.32	5 285.08	5 295.84	5 306.61	5 317.37	5 328.14	5 338.9	5 349.66	5 360.43	5 371.19
500	5 381.96									

CONVERSION TABLES

12 square inches to square centimetres

in²	0	1	2	3	4	5	6	7	8	9
	cm²									
0		6.45	12.9	19.36	25.81	32.26	38.71	45.16	51.61	58.06
10	64.52	70.97	77.41	83.87	90.32	96.77	103.23	109.68	116.13	122.58
20	129.03	135.48	141.94	148.39	154.84	161.29	167.74	174.19	180.65	187.1
30	193.55	200.0	206.45	212.9	219.35	225.8	232.26	238.71	245.16	251.61
40	258.06	264.52	270.97	277.42	283.87	290.32	296.77	303.23	309.68	316.13
50	322.58	329.03	335.48	341.94	348.4	354.84	361.29	367.74	374.19	380.64
60	387.1	393.55	400.0	406.45	412.91	419.35	425.81	432.26	438.71	445.16
70	451.61	458.06	464.52	470.97	477.42	483.87	490.32	496.77	503.23	509.68
80	516.13	522.58	529.03	535.48	541.93	548.39	554.84	561.29	567.74	574.19
90	580.64	587.1	593.55	600.0	606.45	612.91	619.35	625.81	632.26	638.71
100	645.16	651.61	658.06	664.51	670.97	677.42	683.87	690.32	696.77	703.22
110	709.6	716.13	722.58	729.03	735.48	741.93	748.39	754.84	761.29	767.74
120	774.19	780.64	787.1	793.55	800.0	806.45	812.9	819.35	825.81	832.26
130	838.71	845.16	851.61	858.06	864.51	870.97	877.42	883.87	890.32	896.77
140	903.22	909.68	916.13	922.58	929.03	935.48	941.93	948.39	954.84	961.29
150	967.74	974.19	980.64	987.1	993.55	1 000.00	1 006.45	1 012.9	1 019.35	1 025.8
160	1 032.26	1 038.71	1 045.16	1 051.61	1 058.06	1 064.51	1 070.97	1 077.42	1 083.87	1 090.32
170	1 096.77	1 103.22	1 109.68	1 116.13	1 122.58	1 129.03	1 135.48	1 141.93	1 148.38	1 154.84
180	1 161.29	1 167.74	1 174.19	1 180.64	1 187.09	1 193.55	1 200.0	1 206.45	1 212.9	1 219.35
190	1 225.8	1 232.26	1 238.71	1 245.16	1 251.61	1 258.06	1 264.51	1 270.97	1 277.42	1 283.87
200	1 290.32	1 296.77	1 303.22	1 309.67	1 316.13	1 322.58	1 329.03	1 335.48	1 341.93	1 348.38
210	1 354.84	1 361.29	1 367.74	1 374.19	1 380.64	1 387.09	1 393.55	1 400.0	1 406.45	1 412.9
220	1 419.35	1 425.8	1 432.26	1 438.71	1 445.16	1 451.61	1 458.06	1 464.51	1 470.96	1 477.42
230	1 483.87	1 490.32	1 496.77	1 503.22	1 509.67	1 516.13	1 522.58	1 529.03	1 535.48	1 541.93
240	1 548.38	1 554.84	1 561.29	1 567.74	1 574.19	1 580.64	1 587.09	1 593.55	1 600.0	1 606.45
250	1 612.9									

14 square feet to square metres

ft²	0	1	2	3	4	5	6	7	8	9
	m²									
0		0.09	0.19	0.28	0.37	0.46	0.56	0.65	0.74	0.84
10	0.93	1.02	1.11	1.21	1.3	1.39	1.49	1.58	1.67	1.77
20	1.86	1.95	2.04	2.14	2.23	2.32	2.42	2.51	2.6	2.69
30	2.79	2.88	2.97	3.07	3.16	3.25	3.34	3.44	3.53	3.62
40	3.72	3.81	3.9	3.99	4.09	4.18	4.27	4.37	4.46	4.55
50	4.65	4.74	4.83	4.92	5.02	5.11	5.2	5.3	5.39	5.48
60	5.57	5.67	5.76	5.85	5.95	6.04	6.13	6.22	6.32	6.41
70	6.5	6.6	6.69	6.78	6.87	6.97	7.06	7.15	7.25	7.34
80	7.43	7.53	7.62	7.71	7.8	7.9	7.99	8.08	8.18	8.27
90	8.36	8.45	8.55	8.64	8.73	8.83	8.92	9.01	9.1	9.2
100	9.29	9.38	9.48	9.57	9.66	9.75	9.85	9.94	10.03	10.13
110	10.22	10.31	10.41	10.5	10.59	10.68	10.78	10.87	10.96	11.06
120	11.15	11.24	11.33	11.43	11.52	11.61	11.71	11.8	11,89	11.98
130	12.08	12.17	12.26	12.36	12.45	12.54	12.63	12.73	12.82	12.91
140	13.01	13.1	13.19	13.29	13.38	13.47	13.56	13.66	13.75	13.84
150	13.94	14.03	14.12	14.21	14.31	14.4	14.49	14.59	14.68	14.77
160	14.86	14.96	15.05	15.14	15.24	15.33	15.42	15.51	15.61	15.7
170	15.79	15.89	15.98	16.07	16.17	16.26	16.35	16.44	16.54	16.63
180	16.72	16.82	16.91	17.0	17.09	17.19	17.28	17.37	17.47	17.56
190	17.65	17.74	17.84	17.93	18.02	18.12	18.21	18.3	18.39	18.49
200	18.58	18.67	18.77	18.86	18.95	19.05	19.14	19.23	19.32	19.42
210	19.51	19.6	19.7	19.79	19.88	19.97	20.07	20.16	20.25	20.35
220	20.44	20.53	20.62	20.72	20.81	20.9	21.0	21.09	21.18	21.27
230	21.37	21.46	21.55	21.65	21.74	21.83	21.93	22.02	22.11	22.2
240	22.3	22.39	22.48	22.58	22.67	22.76	22.85	22.95	23.04	23.13
250	23.23	23.32	23.41	23.5	23.6	23.69	23.78	23.88	23.97	24.06
260	24.15	24.25	24.34	24.43	24.53	24.62	24.71	24.81	24.9	24.99
270	25.08	25.18	25.27	25.36	25.46	25.55	25.64	25.73	25.83	25.92
280	26.01	26.11	26.2	26.29	26.38	26.48	26.57	26.66	26.76	26.85
290	26.94	27.03	27.13	27.22	27.31	27.41	27.5	27.59	27.69	27.78
300	27.87	27.96	28.06	28.15	28.24	28.34	28.43	28.52	28.61	28.71
310	28.8	28.89	28.99	29.08	29.17	29.26	29.36	29.45	29.54	29.64
320	29.73	29.82	29.91	30.01	30.1	30.19	30.29	30.38	30.47	30.57
330	30.66	30.75	30.84	30.94	31.03	31.12	31.22	31.31	31.4	31.49
340	31.59	31.68	31.77	31.87	31.96	32.05	32.14	32.24	32.33	32.42
350	32.52	32.61	32.7	32.79	32.89	32.98	33.07	33.17	33.26	33.35
360	33.45	33.54	33.63	33.72	33.82	33.91	34.0	34.1	34.19	34.28
370	34.37	34.47	34.56	34.65	34.75	34.84	34.93	35.02	35.12	35.21
380	35.3	35.4	35.49	35.58	35.67	35.77	35.86	35.95	36.05	36.14
390	36.23	36.33	36.42	36.51	36.6	36.7	36.79	36.88	36.98	37.07
400	37.16	37.25	37.35	37.44	37.53	37.63	37.72	37.81	37.9	38.0
410	38.09	38.18	38.28	38.37	38.46	38.55	38.65	38.74	38.83	38.93
420	39.02	39.11	39.21	39.3	39.39	39.48	39.58	39.67	39.76	39.86
430	39.95	40.04	40.13	40.23	40.32	40.41	40.51	40.6	40.69	40.78
440	40.88	40.97	41.06	41.16	41.25	41.34	41.43	41.53	41.62	41.71
450	41.81	41.9	41.99	42.09	42.18	42.27	42.36	42.46	42.55	42.64
460	42.74	42.83	42.92	43.01	43.11	43.2	43.29	43.39	43.48	43.57
470	43.66	43.76	43.85	43.94	44.04	44.13	44.22	44.31	44.41	44.5
480	44.59	44.69	44.78	44.87	44.97	45.06	45.15	45.24	45.34	45.43
490	45.52	45.62	45.71	45.8	45.89	45.99	46.08	46.17	46.27	46.36
500	46.45									

15
square
metres
to square
yards

m²	0	1	2	3	4	5	6	7	8	9
	yd²									
0		1.2	2.39	3.58	4.78	5.98	7.18	8.37	9.57	10.76
10	11.96	13.16	14.35	15.55	16.74	17.94	19.14	20.33	21.53	22.72
20	23.92	25.12	26.31	27.51	28.7	29.9	31.1	32.29	33.49	34.68
30	35.88	37.08	38.27	39.47	40.66	41.86	43.06	44.25	45.45	46.64
40	47.84	49.04	50.23	51.43	52.62	53.82	55.02	56.21	57.41	58.6
50	59.8	61.0	62.19	63.39	64.58	65.78	66.98	68.17	69.37	70.56
60	71.76	72.96	74.15	75.35	76.54	77.74	78.94	80.13	81.33	82.52
70	83.72	84.92	86.11	87.31	88.5	89.7	90.9	92.09	93.29	94.48
80	95.68	96.88	98.07	99.27	100.46	101.66	102.86	104.05	105.25	106.44
90	107.64	108.84	110.03	111.23	112.42	113.62	114.82	116.01	117.21	118.4
100	119.6	120.8	121.99	123.19	124.38	125.58	126.78	127.97	129.17	130.36
110	131.56	132.76	133.95	135.15	136.34	137.54	138.74	139.93	141.13	142.32
120	143.52	144.72	145.91	147.11	148.31	149.5	150.7	151.89	153.09	154.28
130	155.48	156.68	157.87	159.07	160.26	161.46	162.66	163.85	165.05	166.24
140	167.44	168.64	169.83	171.03	172.22	173.41	174.62	175.81	177.01	178.2
150	179.34	180.59	181.79	182.99	184.18	185.38	186.57	187.77	188.97	190.16
160	191.36	192.55	193.75	194.95	196.14	197.34	198.53	199.73	200.93	202.12
170	203.32	204.51	205.71	206.91	208.1	209.3	210.49	211.69	212.89	214.08
180	215.28	216.47	217.67	218.87	220.06	221.26	222.45	223.65	224.85	226.04
190	227.24	228.43	229.63	230.83	232.02	233.22	234.41	235.61	236.81	238.0
200	239.2	240.39	241.59	242.79	243.98	245.18	246.37	247.57	248.77	249.96
210	251.16	252.35	253.55	254.75	255.94	257.14	258.33	259.53	260.73	261.92
220	263.12	264.31	265.51	266.71	267.9	269.1	270.29	271.49	272.69	273.88
230	275.08	276.27	277.47	278.67	279.86	281.06	282.25	283.45	284.65	285.84
240	287.04	288.23	289.43	290.63	291.82	293.02	294.21	295.41	296.61	297.8
250	299.0	300.19	301.39	302.59	303.78	304.98	306.17	307.37	308.57	309.76
260	310.96	312.15	313.35	314.55	315.74	316.94	318.13	319.33	320.53	321.72
270	322.92	324.11	325.31	326.51	327.7	328.9	330.09	331.29	332.49	333.68
280	334.88	336.07	337.27	338.47	339.66	340.86	342.05	343.25	344.45	345.64
290	346.84	348.03	349.23	350.43	351.62	352.82	354.02	355.21	356.41	357.6
300	358.78	359.99	361.19	362.39	363.58	364.78	365.97	367.17	368.37	369.56
310	370.76	371.95	373.15	374.35	375.54	376.74	377.94	379.13	380.33	381.52
320	382.72	383.91	385.11	386.31	387.5	388.7	389.89	391.09	392.29	393.48
330	394.68	395.87	397.07	398.27	399.46	400.66	401.85	403.05	404.25	405.44
340	406.64	407.83	409.03	410.23	411.42	412.62	413.81	415.01	416.21	417.4
350	418.6	419.79	420.99	422.18	423.38	424.58	425.77	426.97	428.16	429.36
360	430.56	431.75	432.95	434.14	435.34	436.54	437.73	438.93	440.12	441.32
370	442.52	443.71	444.91	446.11	447.3	448.5	449.69	450.89	452.08	453.28
380	454.48	455.67	456.87	458.06	459.26	460.46	461.65	462.84	464.04	465.24
390	466.44	467.63	468.83	470.02	471.22	472.42	473.61	474.81	476.0	477.2
400	478.4	479.59	480.79	481.98	483.18	484.38	485.57	486.77	487.96	489.16
410	490.36	491.55	492.75	493.94	495.14	496.34	497.53	498.73	499.92	501.12
420	502.32	503.51	504.71	505.9	507.1	508.3	509.49	510.69	511.88	513.08
430	514.28	515.47	516.67	517.86	519.06	520.26	521.45	522.65	523.84	525.04
440	526.24	527.43	528.63	529.82	531.02	532.22	533.41	534.61	535.8	537.0
450	538.2	539.39	540.59	541.78	542.98	544.18	545.37	546.57	547.76	548.96
460	550.16	551.35	552.55	553.74	554.94	556.14	557.33	558.53	559.72	560.92
470	562.12	563.31	564.5	565.71	566.9	568.1	569.29	570.49	571.68	572.88
480	574.08	575.27	576.47	577.66	578.86	580.06	581.25	582.45	583.64	584.84
490	586.04	587.23	588.43	589.62	590.82	592.02	593.21	594.41	595.6	596.8
500	598.0									

17
hectares
to acres

ha	0	1	2	3	4	5	6	7	8	9
	acre									
		2.47	4.94	7.41	9.88	12.36	14.83	17.3	19.77	22.24

ha	0	10	20	30	40	50	60	70	80	90
	acre									
0		24.71	49.42	74.13	98.84	123.55	148.26	172.97	197.68	222.4
100	247.11	271.82	296.53	321.24	345.95	370.66	395.37	420.08	444.8	469.5
200	494.21	518.92	543.63	568.34	593.05	617.76	642.47	667.19	691.9	716.61
300	741.32	766.03	790.74	815.45	840.16	864.87	889.58	914.29	939.0	963.71
400	988.42	1 013.13	1 037.84	1 062.55	1 087.26	1 111.97	1 136.68	1 161.4	1 186.11	1 210.82
500	1 235.53	1 260.24	1 284.95	1 309.66	1 334.37	1 359.08	1 383.79	1 408.5	1 433.21	1 457.92
600	1 482.63	1 507.34	1 532.05	1 556.76	1 581.47	1 606.18	1 630.9	1 655.61	1 680.32	1 705.03
700	1 729.74	1 754.45	1 779.16	1 803.87	1 828.58	1 853.29	1 878.0	1 902.71	1 927.42	1 952.13
800	1 976.84	2 001.55	2 026.26	2 050.97	2 075.69	2 100.4	2 125.11	2 149.82	2 174.53	2 199.24
900	2 223.95	2 248.66	2 273.37	2 298.08	2 322.79	2 347.5	2 372.21	2 396.92	2 421.63	2 446.34
1 000	2 471.05									

16
square
yards
to square
metres

yd²	0	1	2	3	4	5	6	7	8	9
	m²									
0		0.84	1.67	2.51	3.34	4.18	5.02	5.85	6.69	7.53
10	8.36	9.2	10.03	10.87	11.71	12.54	13.38	14.21	15.05	15.89
20	16.72	17.56	18.39	19.23	20.07	20.9	21.74	22.58	23.41	24.25
30	25.08	25.92	26.76	27.59	28.43	29.26	30.1	30.94	31.77	32.61
40	33.45	34.28	35.12	35.95	36.79	37.63	38.46	39.3	40.13	40.97
50	41.81	42.64	43.48	44.31	45.15	45.99	46.82	47.66	48.5	49.33
60	50.17	51.0	51.84	52.68	53.51	54.35	55.18	56.02	56.86	57.69
70	58.53	59.37	60.2	61.04	61.87	62.71	63.55	64.38	65.22	66.05
80	66.89	67.7	68.56	69.3	70.23	71.07	71.9	72.74	73.5	74.4
90	75.25	76.09	76.92	77.76	78.6	79.43	80.27	81.10	81.94	82.78
100	83.61	84.45	85.29	86.12	86.96	87.79	88.62	89.47	90.3	91.14
110	91.97	92.81	93.65	94.48	95.32	96.15	96.99	97.83	98.66	99.5
120	100.34	101.17	102.0	102.84	103.68	104.52	105.35	106.19	107.02	107.86
130	108.7	109.53	110.37	111.21	112.04	112.88	113.71	114.55	115.39	116.22
140	117.06	117.89	118.73	119.57	120.41	121.24	122.08	122.91	123.75	124.58
150	125.42	126.26	127.09	127.93	128.76	129.6	130.44	131.27	132.11	132.94
160	133.78	134.62	135.45	136.29	137.13	137.96	138.8	139.63	140.47	141.31
170	142.14	142.98	143.81	144.65	145.49	146.32	147.16	148.0	148.83	149.67
180	150.5	151.34	152.18	153.01	153.85	154.68	155.52	156.36	157.19	158.03
190	158.86	159.7	160.54	161.37	162.21	163.05	163.88	164.72	165.55	166.39
200	167.23	168.06	168.9	169.73	170.57	171.41	172.24	173.08	173.91	174.75
210	175.59	176.42	177.26	178.1	178.93	179.77	180.61	181.44	182.28	183.11
220	183.95	184.78	185.62	186.46	187.29	188.13	188.97	189.80	190.64	191.47
230	192.31	193.15	193.98	194.82	195.65	196.49	197.33	198.16	199.0	199.83
240	200.67	201.51	202.34	203.18	204.02	204.85	205.69	206.52	207.36	208.2
250	209.03	209.87	210.7	211.54	212.38	213.21	214.1	214.89	215.72	216.56
260	217.39	218.3	219.07	219.9	220.74	221.57	222.41	223.25	224.08	224.92
270	225.75	226.59	227.43	228.26	229.1	229.94	230.77	231.61	232.44	233.28
280	234.12	234.95	235.79	236.62	237.46	238.3	239.13	239.97	240.81	241.64
290	242.48	243.31	244.15	244.99	245.82	246.66	247.49	248.33	249.17	250.0
300	250.84	251.67	252.51	253.35	254.18	255.02	255.86	256.69	257.53	258.36
310	259.2	260.04	260.87	261.71	262.54	263.38	264.22	265.05	265.89	266.73
320	267.56	268.4	269.23	270.07	270.91	271.74	272.58	273.41	274.25	275.09
330	275.92	276.76	277.59	278.43	279.27	280.11	280.94	281.78	282.61	283.45
340	284.28	285.12	285.96	286.79	287.63	288.46	289.3	290.14	290.97	291.81
350	292.65	293.48	294.32	295.15	295.99	296.83	297.66	298.5	299.33	300.17
360	301.0	301.84	302.68	303.51	304.35	305.19	306.02	306.86	307.7	308.53
370	309.37	310.2	311.04	311.88	312.71	313.55	314.38	315.22	316.06	316.89
380	317.73	318.57	319.4	320.24	321.07	321.91	322.75	323.58	324.42	325.25
390	326.09	326.93	327.76	328.6	329.43	330.27	331.11	331.94	332.78	333.62
400	334.45	335.29	336.12	336.96	337.8	338.63	339.47	340.31	341.14	341.98
410	342.81	343.65	344.48	345.32	346.16	346.99	347.83	348.67	349.51	350.34
420	351.17	352.01	352.85	353.68	354.52	355.35	356.19	357.03	357.86	358.7
430	359.54	360.37	361.21	362.04	362.88	363.72	364.55	365.39	366.22	367.06
440	367.9	368.73	369.57	370.41	371.24	372.08	372.91	373.75	374.59	375.42
450	376.26	377.09	377.93	378.77	379.6	380.44	381.27	382.11	382.95	383.78
460	384.62	385.46	386.29	387.13	387.96	388.8	389.64	390.47	391.31	392.14
470	392.98	393.82	394.65	395.49	396.32	397.16	398.0	398.83	399.67	400.51
480	401.34	402.18	403.01	403.85	404.69	405.52	406.36	407.19	408.03	408.87
490	409.7	410.54	411.38	412.21	413.05	413.88	414.72	415.56	416.39	417.23
500	418.0									

18
acres to
hectares

acre	0	1	2	3	4	5	6	7	8	9
	ha									
		0.4	0.81	1.21	1.62	2.02	2.42	2.83	3.23	3.64

acre	0	10	20	30	40	50	60	70	80	90
	ha									
0		4.05	8.09	12.14	16.19	20.23	24.28	28.33	32.37	36.42
100	40.47	44.52	48.56	52.6	56.66	60.71	64.75	68.8	72.84	76.89
200	80.94	84.98	89.03	93.08	97.12	101.17	105.22	109.26	113.31	117.36
300	121.41	125.46	129.5	133.55	137.59	141.64	145.69	149.73	153.78	157.83
400	161.87	165.92	169.97	174.02	178.06	182.11	186.16	190.20	194.25	198.3
500	202.34	206.39	210.44	214.48	218.53	222.58	226.62	230.67	234.71	238.77
600	242.81	246.86	250.91	254.95	259.0	263.05	267.09	271.14	275.19	279.23
700	283.28	287.33	291.37	295.42	299.47	303.51	307.56	311.61	315.66	319.7
800	323.75	327.8	331.84	335.84	339.94	343.98	348.03	352.07	356.12	360.17
900	364.22	368.26	372.31	376.36	380.41	384.45	388.5	392.55	396.59	400.64
1 000	404.69									

Volume

19
cubic
centimetres
to cubic
inches

cm³	0	1	2	3	4	5	6	7	8	9
in³										
		0.06	0.12	0.18	0.24	0.31	0.37	0.43	0.49	0.55

cm³	0	10	20	30	40	50	60	70	80	90
in³										
0		0.61	1.22	1.83	2.44	3.05	3.66	4.27	4.88	5.49
100	6.1	6.71	7.32	7.93	8.54	9.15	9.76	10.37	10.98	11.59
200	12.2	12.82	13.43	14.04	14.65	15.26	15.87	16.48	17.09	17.7
300	18.31	18.92	19.53	20.14	20.75	21.36	21.97	22.58	23.19	23.8
400	24.41	25.02	25.63	26.24	26.85	27.46	28.07	28.68	29.29	29.9
500	30.51	31.12	31.73	32.34	32.95	33.56	34.17	34.78	35.39	36.0
600	36.61	37.22	37.83	38.45	39.06	39.67	40.28	40.89	41.5	42.11
700	42.72	43.38	43.94	44.55	45.16	45.77	46.38	46.99	47.6	48.21
800	48.82	49.43	50.04	50.65	51.26	51.87	52.48	53.09	53.7	54.31
900	54.92	55.53	56.14	56.75	57.36	57.97	58.58	59.19	59.8	60.41
1 000	61.02									

21
cubic
metres to
cubic feet

m³	0	1	2	3	4	5	6	7	8	9
ft³										
0		35.31	70.63	105.94	141.26	176.57	211.89	247.2	282.52	317.83
10	353.15	388.46	423.78	459.09	494.41	592.72	565.04	600.35	635.67	670.98
20	706.29	741.61	776.92	812.24	847.55	882.87	918.18	953.5	988.81	1 024.13
30	1 059.44	1 094.75	1 130.07	1 165.38	1 200.7	1 236.01	1 271.33	1 306.64	1 341.96	1 377.27
40	1 412.59	1 447.9	1 483.22	1 518.53	1 553.85	1 589.16	1 624.47	1 659.79	1 695.1	1 730.42
50	1 765.73	1 801.05	1 836.36	1 871.68	1 906.99	1 942.31	1 977.62	2 012.94	2 048.25	2 083.57
60	2 118.88	2 154.19	2 189.51	2 224.82	2 260.14	2 295.45	2 330.77	2 366.08	2 401.4	2 436.71
70	2 472.03	2 507.34	2 542.66	2 577.97	2 613.29	2 648.6	2 683.91	2 719.23	2 754.54	2 789.86
80	2 825.17	2 860.49	2 895.8	2 931.12	2 966.43	3 001.75	3 037.06	3 072.38	3 107.69	3 143.01
90	3 178.32	3 213.63	3 248.95	3 284.26	3 319.58	3 354.89	3 390.21	3 425.52	3 460.84	3 496.15
100	3 531.47	3 566.78	3 602.1	3 637.41	3 672.73	3 708.04	3 743.35	3 778.67	3 813.98	3 849.3
110	3 884.61	3 919.93	3 955.24	3 990.56	4 025.87	4 061.19	4 096.5	4 131.82	4 167.13	4 202.45
120	4 237.76	4 273.07	4 308.39	4 343.7	4 379.02	4 414.33	4 449.65	4 484.96	4 520.28	4 555.59
130	4 590.91	4 626.22	4 661.54	4 696.85	4 732.17	4 767.48	4 802.79	4 838.11	4 873.42	4 908.74
140	4 944.05	4 979.37	5 014.68	5 050.0	5 085.31	5 120.63	5 155.94	5 191.26	5 226.57	5 261.89
150	5 297.2	5 332.51	5 367.83	5 403.14	5 438.46	5 473.77	5 509.09	5 544.4	5 579.72	5 615.03
160	5 650.35	5 685.66	5 720.98	5 756.29	5 791.61	5 826.92	5 862.23	5 897.55	5 932.86	5 968.18
170	6 003.49	6 038.81	6 074.12	6 109.44	6 144.75	6 180.07	6 215.38	6 250.7	6 286.01	6 321.33
180	6 356.64	6 391.95	6 427.27	6 462.58	6 497.9	6 533.21	6 568.53	6 603.84	6 639.16	6 674.47
190	6 709.79	6 745.1	6 780.42	6 815.73	6 851.05	6 886.36	6 921.67	6 956.99	6 992.3	7 027.62
200	7 062.93	7 098.25	7 133.56	7 168.88	7 204.19	7 239.51	7 274.82	7 310.14	7 345.45	7 380.77
210	7 416.08	7 451.39	7 486.71	7 522.02	7 557.34	7 592.65	7 627.97	7 663.28	7 698.6	7 733.91
220	7 769.23	7 804.54	7 839.86	7 875.17	7 910.49	7 945.8	7 981.11	8 016.43	8 051.74	8 087.06
230	8 122.37	8 157.69	8 193.0	8 228.32	8 263.63	8 298.95	8 334.26	8 369.58	8 404.89	8 440.21
240	8 475.52	8 510.83	8 546.15	8 581.46	8 616.78	8 652.09	8 687.41	8 722.72	8 758.04	8 793.35
250	8 828.67									

23
litres to
cubic feet

litre	0	1	2	3	4	5	6	7	8	9
ft³										
0		0.04	0.07	0.11	0.14	0.18	0.21	0.25	0.28	0.32
10	0.35	0.39	0.42	0.46	0.49	0.53	0.57	0.60	0.64	0.67
20	0.71	0.74	0.78	0.81	0.85	0.88	0.92	0.95	0.99	1.02
30	1.06	1.09	1.13	1.17	1.2	1.24	1.27	1.31	1.34	1.38
40	1.41	1.45	1.48	1.52	1.55	1.59	1.62	1.66	1.7	1.73
50	1.77	1.8	1.84	1.87	1.91	1.94	1.98	2.01	2.05	2.08
60	2.12	2.15	2.19	2.22	2.26	2.3	2.33	2.37	2.4	2.44
70	2.47	2.51	2.54	2.58	2.61	2.65	2.68	2.72	2.75	2.79
80	2.83	2.86	2.9	2.93	2.97	3.0	3.04	3.07	3.11	3.14
90	3.18	3.21	3.25	3.28	3.32	3.35	3.39	3.42	3.46	3.5
100	3.53									

in³	0	1	2	3	4	5	6	7	8	9	
	cm³										20
		16.39	32.77	49.16	65.55	81.94	98.32	114.71	131.1	147.48	cubic inches to cubic centimetres

in³	0	10	20	30	40	50	60	70	80	90
	cm³									
0		163.87	327.74	491.61	655.48	819.35	983.22	1 147.09	1 310.97	1 474.84
100	1 638.71	1 802.58	1 966.45	2 130.32	2 294.19	2 458.06	2 621.93	2 785.8	2 949.67	3 113.54
200	3 277.41	3 441.28	3 605.15	3 769.02	3 932.9	4 096.77	4 260.64	4 424.51	4 588.38	4 752.25
300	4 916.12	5 079.99	5 243.86	5 407.73	5 571.6	5 735.47	5 899.34	6 063.21	6 227.08	6 390.95
400	6 554.83	6 718.7	6 882.57	7 046.44	7 210.31	7 374.18	7 538.05	7 701.92	7 865.79	8 029.66
500	8 193.53	8 357.4	8 521.27	8 685.14	8 849.01	9 012.89	9 176.76	9 340.63	9 504.5	9 668.37
600	9 832.24	9 996.11	10 160.0	10 323.9	10 487.7	10 651.6	10 815.5	10 979.3	11 143.2	11 307.1
700	11 470.9	11 634.8	11 798.7	11 962.6	12 126.4	12 290.3	12 454.2	12 618.0	12 781.9	12 945.8
800	13 109.7	13 273.5	13 437.4	13 601.3	13 765.1	13 929.0	14 092.9	14 256.7	14 420.6	14 584.5
900	14 748.4	14 912.2	15 076.1	15 240.0	15 403.8	15 567.7	15 731.6	15 895.5	16 059.3	16 223.2
1 000	16 387.1									

ft³	0	1	2	3	4	5	6	7	8	9	
	m³										22
0		0.03	0.06	0.08	0.11	0.14	0.17	0.2	0.23	0.25	cubic feet to cubic metres
10	0.28	0.31	0.34	0.37	0.4	0.42	0.45	0.48	0.51	0.54	
20	0.57	0.59	0.62	0.65	0.68	0.71	0.74	0.77	0.79	0.82	
30	0.85	0.88	0.91	0.93	0.96	0.99	1.02	1.05	1.08	1.1	
40	1.13	1.16	1.19	1.22	1.25	1.27	1.3	1.33	1.36	1.39	
50	1.42	1.44	1.47	1.5	1.53	1.56	1.59	1.61	1.64	1.67	
60	1.7	1.73	1.76	1.78	1.81	1.84	1.87	1.9	1.93	1.95	
70	1.98	2.01	2.04	2.07	2.1	2.12	2.15	2.18	2.21	2.24	
80	2.27	2.29	2.32	2.35	2.38	2.41	2.44	2.46	2.49	2.52	
90	2.55	2.58	2.61	2.63	2.66	2.69	2.71	2.75	2.78	2.8	
100	2.83	2.86	2.89	2.92	2.94	2.97	3.01	3.03	3.06	3.09	
110	3.11	3.14	3.17	3.2	3.23	3.26	3.28	3.31	3.34	3.37	
120	3.4	3.43	3.46	3.48	3.51	3.54	3.57	3.6	3.62	3.65	
130	3.68	3.71	3.74	3.77	3.79	3.82	3.85	3.88	3.91	3.94	
140	3.96	4.0	4.02	4.05	4.08	4.11	4.13	4.16	4.19	4.22	
150	4.26	4.28	4.3	4.33	4.36	4.39	4.42	4.45	4.47	4.51	
160	4.53	4.56	4.59	4.62	4.64	4.67	4.7	4.73	4.76	4.79	
170	4.81	4.84	4.87	4.9	4.93	4.96	4.99	5.01	5.04	5.07	
180	5.1	5.13	5.15	5.18	5.21	5.24	5.27	5.3	5.32	5.35	
190	5.38	5.41	5.44	5.47	5.49	5.52	5.55	5.58	5.61	5.64	
200	5.66	5.69	5.72	5.75	5.78	5.8	5.83	5.86	5.89	5.92	
210	5.95	5.98	6.0	6.03	6.06	6.09	6.12	6.14	6.17	6.2	
220	6.23	6.26	6.29	6.31	6.34	6.37	6.4	6.43	6.46	6.48	
230	6.51	6.54	6.57	6.6	6.63	6.65	6.69	6.71	6.74	6.77	
240	6.8	6.82	6.85	6.88	6.91	6.94	6.97	6.99	7.02	7.05	
250	7.08										

ft³	0	1	2	3	4	5	6	7	8	9	
	litre										24
0		28.32	56.63	84.95	113.26	141.58	169.9	198.21	226.53	254.84	cubic feet to litres
10	283.16	311.48	339.79	368.11	396.42	424.74	453.06	481.37	509.69	538.01	
20	566.32	594.64	622.95	651.27	679.59	707.9	736.22	764.53	792.85	821.17	
30	849.48	877.8	906.11	934.43	962.75	991.06	1 019.38	1 047.69	1 076.01	1 104.33	
40	1 132.64	1 160.96	1 189.27	1 217.59	1 245.91	1 274.22	1 302.54	1 330.85	1 359.17	1 387.49	
50	1 415.8	1 444.12	1 472.43	1 500.75	1 529.07	1 557.38	1 585.7	1 614.02	1 642.33	1 670.65	
60	1 698.96	1 727.28	1 755.6	1 783.91	1 812.23	1 840.54	1 868.86	1 897.18	1 925.49	1 953.81	
70	1 982.12	2 010.44	2 038.76	2 067.07	2 095.39	2 123.7	2 152.02	2 180.34	2 208.65	2 236.97	
80	2 265.28	2 293.6	2 321.92	2 350.23	2 378.55	2 406.86	2 435.18	2 463.5	2 491.81	2 520.13	
90	2 548.44	2 576.76	2 605.08	2 633.39	2 661.71	2 690.03	2 718.34	2 746.66	2 774.97	2 803.29	
100	2 831.61										

25
litres to
imperial
gallons

litre	0	1	2	3	4	5	6	7	8	9
	gal imp									
0		0.22	0.44	0.66	0.88	1.1	1.32	1.54	1.76	1.98
10	2.2	2.42	2.64	2.86	3.08	3.3	3.52	3.74	3.96	4.18
20	4.4	4.62	4.84	5.06	5.28	5.5	5.72	5.94	6.16	6.38
30	6.6	6.82	7.04	7.26	7.48	7.7	7.92	8.14	8.36	8.58
40	8.8	9.02	9.24	9.46	9.68	9.9	10.12	10.34	10.56	10.78
50	11.0	11.22	11.44	11.66	11.88	12.1	12.32	12.54	12.76	12.98
60	13.2	13.42	13.64	13.86	14.08	14.3	14.52	14.74	14.96	15.18
70	15.4	15.62	15.84	16.06	16.28	16.5	16.72	16.94	17.16	17.38
80	17.6	17.82	18.04	18.26	18.48	18.7	18.92	19.14	19.36	19.58
90	19.8	20.02	20.24	20.46	20.68	20.9	21.12	21.34	21.56	21.78
100	22.0									

27
litres to
US gallons

litre	0	1	2	3	4	5	6	7	8	9
	gal US									
0		0.26	0.53	0.79	1.06	1.32	1.59	1.85	2.11	2.38
10	2.64	2.91	3.17	3.43	3.7	3.96	4.23	4.49	4.76	5.02
20	5.28	5.55	5.81	6.08	6.34	6.61	6.87	7.13	7.4	7.66
30	7.93	8.19	8.45	8.72	8.98	9.25	9.51	9.78	10.04	10.3
40	10.57	10.83	11.1	11.36	11.62	11.89	12.15	12.42	12.68	12.95
50	13.21	13.47	13.74	14.0	14.27	14.53	14.8	15.06	15.32	15.59
60	15.85	16.12	16.38	16.64	16.91	17.17	17.44	17.7	17.97	18.23
70	18.49	18.76	19.02	19.29	19.55	19.82	20.08	20.34	20.61	20.87
80	21.14	21.4	21.66	21.93	22.19	22.46	22.72	22.96	23.25	23.51
90	23.78	24.04	24.31	24.57	24.83	25.1	25.36	25.63	25.89	26.16
100	26.42									

Mass

29
kilograms
to pounds

kg	0	1	2	3	4	5	6	7	8	9
	lb									
0		2.21	4.41	6.61	8.82	11.02	13.23	15.43	17.64	19.84
10	22.05	24.25	26.46	28.66	30.86	33.07	35.27	37.47	39.68	41.89
20	44.09	46.3	48.5	50.71	52.91	55.12	57.32	59.52	61.73	63.93
30	66.14	68.34	70.55	72.75	74.96	77.16	79.37	81.57	83.78	85.98
40	88.18	90.39	92.59	94.8	97.0	99.2	101.41	103.61	105.82	108.03
50	110.23	112.44	114.64	116.85	119.05	121.25	123.46	125.66	127.87	130.07
60	132.28	134.48	136.69	138.89	141.1	143.3	145.51	147.71	149.91	152.12
70	154.32	156.53	158.73	160.94	163.14	165.35	167.55	169.76	171.96	174.17
80	176.37	178.57	180.78	182.98	185.19	187.39	189.6	191.8	194.01	196.21
90	198.42	200.62	202.83	205.03	207.24	209.44	211.64	213.85	216.05	218.26
100	220.46	222.67	224.87	227.08	229.28	231.49	233.69	235.9	238.1	240.3
110	242.51	244.71	246.92	249.12	251.33	253.53	255.74	257.94	260.15	262.35
120	264.56	266.76	268.96	271.17	273.37	275.58	277.78	279.99	282.19	284.4
130	286.6	288.81	291.01	293.22	295.42	297.62	299.83	302.03	304.24	306.44
140	308.65	310.85	313.06	315.26	317.47	319.67	321.88	324.08	326.28	328.49
150	330.69	332.9	335.1	337.31	339.51	341.72	343.92	346.13	348.33	350.54
160	352.74	354.94	357.15	359.35	361.56	363.76	365.97	368.17	370.38	372.58
170	374.79	377.0	379.2	381.4	383.6	385.81	388.01	390.22	392.42	394.68
180	396.83	399.04	401.24	403.45	405.65	407.86	410.06	412.26	414.47	416.67
190	418.88	421.08	423.29	425.49	427.68	429.9	432.11	434.31	436.52	438.72
200	440.93	443.13	445.33	447.54	449.74	451.95	454.15	456.36	458.56	460.77
210	462.97	465.18	467.38	469.59	471.79	473.99	476.2	478.4	480.61	482.81
220	485.02	487.22	489.43	491.63	493.84	496.04	498.25	500.45	502.65	504.86
230	507.06	509.2	511.47	513.6	515.88	518.0	520.29	522.4	524.7	526.9
240	529.1	531.31	533.5	535.72	537.9	540.13	542.3	544.54	546.7	548.9
250	551.16	553.36	555.57	557.77	559.97	562.18	564.38	566.59	568.79	571.0
260	573.2	575.41	577.61	579.82	582.02	584.23	586.43	588.63	590.84	593.04
270	595.25	597.45	599.66	601.86	604.07	606.27	608.48	610.68	612.89	615.09
280	617.29	619.5	621.7	623.91	626.11	628.32	630.52	632.73	634.93	637.14
290	639.34	641.55	643.75	645.95	648.16	650.36	652.57	654.77	656.98	659.18
300	661.39	663.59	665.8	668.0	670.21	672.41	674.62	676.82	679.02	681.23
310	683.43	685.64	687.84	690.05	692.25	694.46	696.66	698.87	701.07	703.28
320	705.48	707.68	709.89	712.09	714.3	716.5	718.71	720.91	723.12	725.32
330	727.53	729.73	731.93	734.14	736.34	738.55	740.75	742.96	745.16	747.37
340	749.57	751.78	753.98	756.19	758.39	760.6	762.8	765.0	767.21	769.41
350	771.62	773.82	776.03	778.23	780.44	782.64	784.85	787.05	789.26	791.46
360	793.66	795.87	798.07	800.28	802.48	804.69	806.89	809.1	811.31	813.51
370	815.71	817.92	820.12	822.32	824.53	826.73	828.94	831.14	833.35	835.55
380	837.76	839.96	842.17	844.37	846.58	848.78	850.98	853.19	855.39	857.6
390	859.8	862.0	864.21	866.41	868.62	870.8	873.03	875.2	877.44	879.64
400	881.85	884.05	886.26	888.46	890.67	892.87	895.08	897.28	899.49	901.69
410	903.9	906.1	908.31	910.51	912.71	914.92	917.12	919.33	921.53	923.74
420	925.94	928.15	930.35	932.56	934.76	936.97	939.17	941.37	943.58	945.78
430	947.99	950.19	952.4	954.6	956.81	959.01	961.22	963.42	965.63	967.83
440	970.03	972.24	974.44	976.65	978.85	981.06	983.26	985.47	987.67	989.88
450	992.08	994.29	996.49	998.69	1 000.9	1 003.1	1 005.31	1 007.51	1 009.72	1 011.92
460	1 014.13	1 016.33	1 018.54	1 020.74	1 022.94	1 025.15	1 027.35	1 029.56	1 031.76	1 033.97
470	1 036.17	1 038.38	1 040.58	1 042.79	1 044.99	1 047.2	1 049.4	1 051.6	1 053.81	1 056.01
480	1 058.22	1 060.42	1 062.63	1 064.83	1 067.04	1 069.24	1 071.45	1 073.65	1 075.86	1 078.06
490	1 080.27	1 082.47	1 084.67	1 086.88	1 089.08	1 091.29	1 093.49	1 095.7	1 097.9	1 100.11
500	1 102.31									

26
imperial
gallons
to litres

gal imp	0	1	2	3	4	5	6	7	8	9
	litre									
0		4.55	9.09	13.64	18.18	22.73	27.28	31.82	36.37	40.91
10	45.46	50.0	54.55	59.1	63.64	68.19	72.74	77.28	81.83	86.38
20	90.92	95.47	100.01	104.56	109.1	113.65	118.2	122.74	127.29	131.83
30	136.38	140.93	145.47	150.02	154.56	159.1	163.66	168.21	172.75	177.3
40	181.84	186.38	190.93	195.48	200.02	204.57	209.11	213.66	218.21	222.75
50	227.3	231.84	236.39	240.94	245.48	250.03	254.57	259.12	263.67	268.21
60	272.76	277.3	281.85	286.4	290.94	295.49	300.03	304.58	309.13	313.67
70	318.22	322.76	327.31	331.86	336.4	340.95	345.49	350.04	354.59	359.13
80	363.68	368.22	372.77	377.32	381.86	386.41	390.95	395.5	400.04	404.59
90	409.14	413.68	418.23	422.77	427.32	431.87	436.41	440.96	445.5	450.05
100	454.6									

28
US gallons
to litres

gal US	0	1	2	3	4	5	6	7	8	9
	litre									
0		3.79	7.57	11.36	15.14	18.93	22.71	26.5	30.28	34.07
10	37.85	41.64	45.42	49.21	52.99	56.78	60.56	64.35	68.13	71.92
20	75.7	79.49	83.27	87.06	90.84	94.63	98.41	102.2	105.98	109.77
30	113.55	117.34	121.12	124.91	128.69	132.48	136.26	140.05	143.83	147.62
40	151.40	155.19	158.97	162.76	166.54	170.33	174.11	177.9	181.68	185.47
50	189.25	193.04	196.82	200.61	204.39	208.18	211.96	215.75	219.53	223.32
60	227.1	230.89	234.67	238.46	242.24	246.03	249.81	253.6	257.38	261.17
70	264.95	268.74	272.52	276.31	280.09	283.88	287.66	291.45	295.23	299.02
80	302.81	306.59	310.37	314.16	317.94	321.73	325.51	329.3	333.08	336.87
90	340.65	344.44	348.22	352.01	355.79	359.58	363.36	367.14	370.93	374.72
100	378.51									

30
pounds to
kilograms

lb	0	1	2	3	4	5	6	7	8	9
	kg									
0		0.45	0.91	1.36	1.81	2.27	2.72	3.18	3.63	4.08
10	4.54	4.99	5.44	5.9	6.35	6.8	7.26	7.71	8.16	8.62
20	9.07	9.53	9.98	10.43	10.89	11.34	11.79	12.25	12.7	13.15
30	13.61	14.06	14.52	14.97	15.42	15.88	16.33	16.78	17.24	17.69
40	18.14	18.6	19.05	19.5	19.96	20.41	20.87	21.32	21.77	22.23
50	22.68	23.13	23.59	24.04	24.49	24.95	25.4	25.85	26.31	26.76
60	27.22	27.67	28.12	28.58	29.03	29.48	29.94	30.39	30.84	31.3
70	31.75	32.21	32.66	33.11	33.57	34.02	34.47	34.93	35.38	35.83
80	36.29	36.74	37.19	37.65	38.1	38.56	39.01	39.46	39.92	40.37
90	40.82	41.28	41.73	42.18	42.64	43.09	43.54	44.0	44.45	44.91
100	45.36	45.81	46.27	46.72	47.17	47.63	48.08	48.53	48.99	49.44
110	49.9	50.35	50.8	51.26	51.71	52.16	52.62	53.07	53.52	53.98
120	54.43	54.88	55.34	55.79	56.25	56.7	57.15	57.61	58.06	58.51
130	58.97	59.42	59.87	60.33	60.78	61.24	61.69	62.14	62.6	63.05
140	63.5	63.96	64.41	64.86	65.32	65.77	66.22	66.68	67.13	67.59
150	68.04	68.49	68.95	69.4	69.85	70.31	70.76	71.21	71.67	72.12
160	72.57	73.03	73.48	73.94	74.39	74.84	75.3	75.75	76.2	76.66
170	77.11	77.56	78.02	78.47	78.93	79.38	79.83	80.29	80.74	81.19
180	81.65	82.1	82.55	83.01	83.46	83.91	84.37	84.82	85.28	85.73
190	86.18	86.64	87.09	87.54	88.0	88.45	88.9	89.36	89.81	90.26
200	90.72	91.17	91.63	92.08	92.53	92.99	93.44	93.89	94.35	94.8
210	95.25	95.71	96.16	96.62	97 07	97.52	97.98	98.43	98.88	99.34
220	99.79	100.24	100.7	101.15	101.61	102.06	102.51	102.97	103.42	103.87
230	104.33	104.78	105.23	105.69	106.14	106.59	107.05	107.5	107.96	108.41
240	108 86	109.32	109.77	110.22	110.68	111.13	111.58	112.04	112.49	112.95
250	113.4	113.85	114.31	114.76	115.21	115.67	116.12	116.57	117.03	117 48
260	117.93	118.39	118.84	119.3	119.75	120.2	120.66	121.11	121.56	122.02
270	122.47	122.92	123.38	123.83	124.28	124.74	125.19	125.65	126.1	126.55
280	127.01	127.46	127.91	128.37	128.82	129.27	129.73	130.18	130.64	131.09
290	131.54	132.0	132.45	132.9	133.36	133.81	134.26	134.72	135.17	135.62
300	136.08	136.53	136.99	137.44	137.89	138.35	138.8	139.25	139.71	140.16
310	140.61	141.07	141.52	141.97	142.43	142.88	143.34	143.79	144.24	144.7
320	145.15	145.6	146.06	146.51	146.96	147.42	147.87	148.33	148.78	149.23
330	149.69	150.14	150.59	151.05	151.5	151.95	152.41	152.86	153.31	153.77
340	154.22	154.68	155.13	155.58	156.04	156.49	156.94	157.4	157.85	158.3
350	158.76	159.21	159.67	160.12	160.57	161.03	161.48	161.93	162.39	162.84
360	163.29	163.75	164.2	164.65	165.11	165.56	166.02	166.47	166.92	167.38
370	167.83	168.28	168.74	169.1	169.64	170.1	170.55	171.0	171.46	171.91
380	172.37	172.82	173.27	173.73	174.18	174.63	175.09	175.54	175.99	176.45
390	176.9	177.36	177.81	178.26	178.72	179.17	179.62	180.08	180.53	180.98
400	181.44	181.89	182.34	182.8	183.25	183.71	184.16	184.61	185.07	185.52
410	185.97	186.43	186.88	187.33	187.79	188.24	188.69	189.15	189.6	190.06
420	190.51	190.96	191.42	191.87	192.32	192.78	193.23	193.68	194.14	194.59
430	195.05	195.5	195.95	196.41	196.86	197.31	197.77	198.22	198.67	199.13
440	199.58	200.03	200.49	200.94	201.4	201.85	202.3	202.76	203.21	203.66
450	204.12	204.57	205.02	205.48	205.93	206.39	206.84	207.29	207.75	208.2
460	208.65	209.11	209.56	210.01	210.47	210.92	211.37	211.83	212.28	212.74
470	213.19	213.64	214.1	214.55	215.0	215.46	215.91	216.36	216.82	217.27
480	217.72	218.18	218.63	219.09	219.54	219.99	220.45	220.9	221.35	221.81
490	222.26	222.71	223.17	223.62	224.08	224.53	224.98	225.44	225.89	226.34
500	226.8									

Density (mass/ volume)

31 kilograms per cubic metre to pounds per cubic foot

kg/m³	0	10	20	30	40	50	60	70	80	90
	lb/ft³									
0		0.62	1.25	1.87	2.5	3.12	3.75	4.37	5.0	5.62
100	6.24	6.87	7.49	8.12	8.74	9.36	9.99	10.61	11.24	11.86
200	12.49	13.11	13.73	14.36	14.98	15.61	16.23	16.86	17.48	18.11
300	18.73	19.35	19.98	20.61	21.23	21.85	22.47	23.1	23.72	24.35
400	24.97	25.6	26.22	26.84	27.47	28.09	28.72	29.34	29.97	30.59
500	31.21	31.84	32.46	33.09	33.71	34.33	34.96	35.58	36.21	36.83
600	37.46	38.08	38.71	39.33	39.95	40.58	41.2	41.83	42.45	43.08
700	43.7	44.32	44.95	45.57	46.2	46.82	47.45	48.07	48.7	49.32
800	49.94	50.57	51.19	51.82	52.44	53.06	53.69	54.31	54.94	55.56
900	56.19	56.81	57.43	58.06	58.68	59.31	59.93	60.56	61.18	61.81
1 000	62.43									

Velocity

33 metres per second to miles per hour

m/s	0	1	2	3	4	5	6	7	8	9
	mile/hr									
0		2.24	4.47	6.71	8.95	11.18	13.42	15.66	17.9	20.13
10	22.37	24.61	26.84	29.08	31.32	33.55	35.79	38.03	40.26	42.51
20	44.74	46.96	49.21	51.45	53.69	55.92	58.16	60.4	62.63	64.87
30	67.11	69.35	71.58	73.82	76.06	78.29	80.53	82.77	85.0	87.24
40	89.48	91.71	93.95	96.19	98.43	100.66	102.9	105.13	107.37	109.61
50	111.85	114.08	116.32	118.56	120.8	123.03	125.27	127.5	129.74	131.98
60	134.22	136.45	138.69	140.93	143.16	145.4	147.64	149.88	152.11	154.34
70	156.59	158.82	161.06	163.3	165.53	167.77	170.0	172.24	174.48	176.72
80	178.96	181.19	183.43	185.67	187.9	190.14	192.38	194.61	196.85	199.09
90	201.32	203.56	205.8	208.04	210.27	212.51	214.75	216.98	219.22	221.46
100	223.69									

Pressure, stress

35 kilograms force per square centimetre to pounds force per square inch

kgf/cm²	0.0	0.1	0.2	0.3	0.4	0.5	0.6	0.7	0.8	0.9
	lbf/in²									
0		1.42	2.84	4.27	5.6	7.11	8.53	9.96	11.38	12.8
1	14.22	15.65	17.07	18.49	19.91	21.34	22.76	24.18	25.6	27.02
2	28.45	29.87	31.29	32.71	34.13	35.56	36.98	38.4	39.83	41.25
3	42.67	44.09	45.51	46.94	48.36	49.78	51.2	52.63	54.05	55.47
4	56.9	58.32	59.73	61.16	62.58	64.0	65.43	66.85	68.27	69.69
5	71.12	72.54	73.96	75.38	76.81	78.23	79.65	81.07	82.5	83.92
6	85.34	86.76	88.18	89.61	91.03	92.45	93.87	95.3	96.72	98.14
7	99.56	100.99	102.41	103.83	105.25	106.68	108.1	109.52	110.94	112.36
8	113.79	115.21	116.63	118.05	119.48	120.9	122.32	123.74	125.17	126.59
9	128.01	129.43	130.86	132.28	133.7	135.12	136.54	137.97	139.39	140.81
10	142.23									

37 kilonewtons per square metre to pounds force per square inch

kN/m² (k Pa)	0	10	20	30	40	50	60	70	80	90
	lbf/in²									
0		1.45	2.9	4.35	5.8	7.25	8.7	10.15	11.6	13.05
100	14.50	15.95	17.40	18.85	20.30	21.75	23.21	24.66	26.11	27.56
200	29.01	30.46	31.91	33.36	34.81	36.26	37.71	39.16	40.61	42.06
300	43.51	44.96	46.41	47.86	49.31	50.76	52.21	53.66	55.11	56.56
400	58.01	59.46	60.91	62.36	63.81	65.26	66.71	68.17	69.62	71.07
500	72.52	73.97	75.42	76.87	78.32	79.77	81.22	82.67	84.12	85.57
600	87.02	88.47	89.92	91.37	92.82	94.27	95.72	97.17	98.62	100.07
700	101.52	102.97	104.42	105.87	107.32	108.77	110.22	111.68	113.13	114.58
800	116.03	117.48	118.93	120.38	121.83	123.28	124.73	126.18	127.63	129.08
900	130.53	131.98	133.43	134.88	136.33	137.78	139.23	140.68	142.13	143.58
1 000	145.03									

lb/ft³	0	1	2	3	4	5	6	7	8	9
	kg/m³									
0		16.02	32.04	48.06	64.07	80.09	96.11	112.13	128.15	144.17
10	160.19	176.2	192.22	208.24	224.26	240.28	256.3	272.31	288.33	304.35
20	320.37	336.39	352.41	368.43	384.44	400.46	416.48	432.5	448.52	464.54
30	480.55	496.57	512.59	528.61	544.63	560.65	576.67	592.68	608.7	624.72
40	640.74	656.76	672.78	688.79	704.81	720.83	736.85	752.87	768.89	784.91
50	800.92	816.94	832.96	848.98	865.0	881.02	897.03	913.05	929.07	945.09
60	961.11	977.13	993.15	1 009.16	1 025.18	1 041.2	1 057.22	1 073.24	1 089.26	1 105.27
70	1 121.29	1 137.31	1 153.33	1 169.35	1 185.37	1 201.38	1 217.4	1 233.42	1 249.44	1 265.46
80	1 281.48	1 297.5	1 313.51	1 329.53	1 345.55	1 361.57	1 377.59	1 393.61	1 409.62	1 425.64
90	1 441.66	1 457.68	1 473.7	1 489.72	1 505.74	1 521.75	1 537.77	1 553.79	1 569.81	1 585.83
100	1 601.85									

32
pounds per cubic foot to kilograms per cubic metre

mile/hr	0	1	2	3	4	5	6	7	8	9
	m/s									
0		0.45	0.89	1.34	1.79	2.24	2.68	3.13	3.58	4.02
10	4.47	4.92	5.36	5.81	6.26	6.71	7.15	7.6	8.05	8.49
20	8.94	9.39	9.83	10.28	10.73	11.18	11.62	12.07	12.52	12.96
30	13.41	13.86	14.31	14.75	15.2	15.65	16.09	16.54	16.99	17.43
40	17.88	18.33	18.78	19.22	19.67	20.12	20.56	21.01	21.46	21.91
50	22.35	22.8	23.25	23.69	24.14	24.59	25.03	25.48	25.93	26.38
60	26.82	27.27	27.72	28.16	28.61	29.06	29.5	29.95	30.4	30.85
70	31.29	31.74	32.19	32.63	33.08	33.53	33.98	34.42	34.87	35.32
80	35.76	36.21	36.66	37.1	37.55	38.0	38.45	38.89	39.34	39.79
90	40.23	40.68	41.13	41.57	42.02	42.47	42.92	43.36	43.81	44.26
100	44.7									

34
miles per hour to metres per second

lbf/in²	0	1	2	3	4	5	6	7	8	9
	kgf/cm²									
0		0.07	0.14	0.21	0.28	0.35	0.42	0.49	0.56	0.63
10	0.7	0.77	0.84	0.91	0.98	1.05	1.12	1.2	1.27	1.34
20	1.41	1.48	1.55	1.62	1.69	1.76	1.83	1.9	1.97	2.04
30	2.11	2.18	2.25	2.32	2.39	2.46	2.53	2.6	2.67	2.74
40	2.81	2.88	2.95	3.02	3.09	3.16	3.23	3.3	3.37	3.45
50	3.52	3.59	3.66	3.73	3.8	3.87	3.94	4.01	4.08	4.15
60	4.22	4.29	4.36	4.43	4.5	4.57	4.64	4.71	4.78	4.85
70	4.92	4.99	5.06	5.13	5.2	5.27	5.34	5.41	5.48	5.55
80	5.62	5.69	5.77	5.84	5.91	5.98	6.05	6.12	6.19	6.26
90	6.33	6.4	6.47	6.54	6.61	6.68	6.75	6.82	6.89	6.96
100	7.03									

36
pounds force per square inch to kilograms force per square centimetre

lbf/in²	0	1	2	3	4	5	6	7	8	9
	kN/m² (k Pa)									
0		6.9	13.79	20.68	27.58	34.48	41.37	48.26	55.16	62.06
10	68.95	75.84	82.74	89.64	96.53	103.42	110.32	117.22	124.11	131.0
20	137.9	144.8	151.69	158.58	165.48	172.38	179.27	186.16	193.06	199.96
30	206.85	213.74	220.64	227.54	234.43	241.32	248.22	255.12	262.01	268.9
40	275.8	282.7	289.59	296.48	303.38	310.28	317.17	324.06	330.96	337.86
50	344.75	351.64	358.54	365.44	372.33	379.22	386.12	393.02	399.91	406.8
60	413.7	420.6	427.49	434.38	441.28	448.18	455.07	461.96	468.86	475.76
70	482.65	489.54	496.44	503.34	510.23	517.12	524.02	530.92	537.81	544.7
80	551.6	558.5	565.39	572.28	579.18	586.08	592.97	599.86	606.76	613.66
90	620.55	627.44	634.34	641.24	648.13	655.02	661.92	668.82	675.71	682.6
100	689.5									

38
pounds force per square inch to kilonewtons per square metre

Refrigeration

39
watts to
British
thermal
units per hour

W	0	1	2	3	4	5	6	7	8	9
	Btu/hr									
0		3.41	6.82	10.24	13.65	17.06	20.47	23.89	27.3	30.71
10	34.12	37.53	40.95	44.36	47.77	51.18	54.59	58.01	61.42	64.83
20	68.24	71.66	75.07	78.5	81.89	85.3	88.72	92.13	95.54	98.95
30	102.36	105.78	109.12	112.6	116.01	119.43	122.76	126.25	129.66	133.07
40	136.49	139.91	143.31	146.72	150.13	153.55	156.96	160.37	163.78	167.2
50	170.61	174.02	177.43	180.84	184.26	187.67	191.08	194.49	197.9	201.31
60	204.73	208.14	211.55	214.97	218.38	221.79	225.2	228.61	232.03	235.44
70	238.85	242.26	245.68	249.09	252.5	255.91	259.32	262.74	266.15	269.56
80	272.97	276.38	279.8	283.21	286.62	290.03	293.45	296.86	300.27	303.68
90	307.09	310.51	313.92	317.33	320.74	324.15	327.57	330.98	334.39	337.8
100	341.22									

Thermal conductance

41
watts per
square metre
kelvin to
British
thermal
units per
square foot
hour degree F

W/(m²K)	0.0	0.1	0.2	0.3	0.4	0.5	0.6	0.7	0.8	0.9
	Btu/(ft²hr°F)									
0.0		0.018	0.035	0.053	0.074	0.088	0.106	0.123	0.141	0.158
1.0	0.176	0.194	0.211	0.229	0.247	0.264	0.282	0.299	0.317	0.335
2.0	0.352	0.370	0.387	0.405	0.423	0.440	0.458	0.476	0.493	0.511
3.0	0.528	0.546	0.564	0.581	0.599	0.616	0.634	0.652	0.669	0.687
4.0	0.704	0.722	0.740	0.757	0.775	0.793	0.810	0.828	0.845	0.863
5.0	0.881	0.898	0.916	0.933	0.951	0.969	0.986	1.004	1.021	1.039
6.0	1.057	1.074	1.092	1.110	1.127	1.145	1.162	1.180	1.198	1.215
7.0	1.233	1.250	1.268	1.286	1.303	1.321	1.34	1.356	1.374	1.391
8.0	1.409	1.427	1.444	1.462	1.479	1.497	1.515	1.532	1.550	1.567
9.0	1.585	1.603	1.620	1.638	1.656	1.673	1.691	1.708	1.726	1.744
10.0	1.761									

Btu/hr	0	1	2	3	4	5	6	7	8	9
	W									
0		0.29	0.59	0.88	1.17	1.47	1.76	2.05	2.34	2.64
10	2.93	3.22	3.52	3.81	4.1	4.4	4.69	4.98	5.28	5.57
20	5.86	6.16	6.45	6.74	7.03	7.33	7.62	7.91	8.21	8.5
30	8.79	9.09	9.38	9.67	9.97	10.26	10.55	10.84	11.14	11.43
40	11.72	12.02	12.31	12.6	12.9	13.19	13.48	13.78	14.07	14.36
50	14.66	14.95	15.24	15.53	15.83	16.12	16.41	16.71	17.0	17.29
60	17.59	17.88	18.17	18.47	18.76	19.05	19.34	19.64	19.93	20.22
70	20.52	20.81	21.1	21.4	21.69	21.98	22.28	22.57	22.86	23.15
80	23.45	23.74	24.03	24.33	24.62	24.91	25.21	25.5	25.79	26.09
90	26.38	26.67	26.97	27.26	27.55	27.84	28.14	28.43	28.72	29.02
100	29.31									

40 British thermal units per hour to watts

Btu/(ft².hr°F)	0.00	0.01	0.02	0.03	0.04	0.05	0.06	0.07	0.08	0.09
	W/(m²K)									
0.0		0.057	0.114	0.17	0.227	0.284	0.341	0.397	0.454	0.511
0.1	0.568	0.624	0.681	0.738	0.795	0.852	0.908	0.965	1.022	1.079
0.2	1.136	1.192	1.249	1.306	1.363	1.42	1.476	1.533	1.59	1.647
0.3	1.703	1.76	1.817	1.874	1.931	1.987	2.044	2.101	2.158	2.214
0.4	2.271	2.328	2.385	2.442	2.498	2.555	2.612	2.669	2.725	2.782
0.5	2.839	2.896	2.953	3.009	3.066	3.123	3.18	3.236	3.293	3.35
0.6	3.407	3.464	3.52	3.577	3.634	3.691	3.747	3.804	3.861	3.918
0.7	3.975	4.031	4.088	4.145	4.202	4.258	4.315	4.372	4.429	4.486
0.8	4.542	4.599	4.656	4.713	4.77	4.826	4.883	4.94	4.997	5.053
0.9	5.11	5.167	5.224	5.281	5.337	5.394	5.451	5.508	5.564	5.621
1.0	5.678									

42 British thermal units per square foot hour degree F to watts per square metre kelvin

Abattoirs, 387
Absorption cooling, 106
Academic libraries, 327–9, 331–2
Access control systems, 190
Access corridors and decks, 296
Accident and emergency (A&E)
        departments, 571, 573
Acoustics, 319, 487, 489
        related publications and
                standards, 589, 604–606
        see also Sound
Administration rooms, hospitals, 571
Aerials, 140
After-school care centres, 325
Agricultural buildings, 405–21
        cattle sheds, 414–15
        facilities, 417–20
        for farm vehicles, 416
        pig sheds, 409–11
        poultry farms, 408
        related publications, 593
        small animal stalls, 405–7
        stables and horses, 412–13
        ventilation systems, 421
Agricultural glass, 170
Air conditioning, 105–8, 107, 120, 344,
        553
Airports, 446–51
        related publications, 593
Air supported structures, 86
Altars, 579
Amusement arcades, 540
Anaesthetics rooms, 552, 554
Anti-bandit glass, 168
Aprons, theatre, 448, 450
Aquariums, 473–4
Arcades, glazed, 363–7
        related publications, 592
Archery ranges, 525
Archives, 350, 571
Art galleries, 333–5
Articles of agreement, 44
Artrooms, 309
Athletics stadiums, 489, 500–3
Attack alarm systems, 189
Auditoriums, 478–80, 486
Automatic teller machines (ATMs),
        360, 362
Automation, office, 337, 340
Awnings, 86, 178, 398
Axis-field grid, 9
Axis spacing, 33

Babylon, hanging gardens of, 82
Badminton courts, 526
Baggage tables and racks, railway
        stations, 428
Bakeries, 368, 369, 385
Balconies, 295
Banked beds, 234, 235
Banked hedges, 236
Banks, 359–62
        related publications, 592
Bar charts, 46, 49
Barns, 417
Barrier-free living, 282, 301
Bathrooms
        domestic, 262–7
                disabled people, 301
                drainage connection values, 56, 57

renovation, 206
        sound insulation, 119
        ventilation, 70, 105
        hospitals, 560
        hotels, 465
        related standards, 609
Baths
        domestic, 262, 263, 265, 266, 267
        industrial buildings, 400
Bedrooms
        domestic, 257–61
        hotels, 465
Beds for flowers and plants, 234, 235
Beds for people
        hospitals, 543, 556, 568
        hotels, 465
        positioning, 259
        types and dimensions, 258, 259
        youth hostels, 470, 471
Bedsitting rooms, for nurses, 572
Behnisch, Günter, 88
Bells and bell towers, 583
Bicycle paths, 216, 219
Bicycles
        cyclecross/BMX, 523
        dimensions, 432
        parking, 218, 219, 529, 534
Bidets, 262
Billiard rooms, 527
Bills of quantities, 43, 44, 45, 48
Bistros, 460
Blast-resistant glass, 168
Blind people, 299
Blinds, 177, 178, 235, 351
Blocks
        glass, 171, 173
        masonry, 63–5
BMX, 523
Boathouses, 515
Boats, 512–16
Bobsleigh runs, 520
Boilers and boiler rooms, 95, 120
Bookshelves, libraries, 327, 328, 329
Boundary frequency, 117, 118
Boundary reference, 34
Bowling alleys, 528
Boxing rings, 526
Bracing walls, 63, 64
Breakfast bars, 256
Breakwaters, 514
Brechtel System, 54
Brewery products, cooling, 110
Bricks, 63–5
Brickwork dimensions, 32
Buffets, 459
Building biology, 21–3
Building societies, 359–62
Bullet-resistant glass, 168
Bunkers, hospitals, 570
Burglar alarm systems, 189, 190
Buses, dimensions and turning circles,
        432, 433
Bus stations, 430–1
Bus stops, 430
Butchers' shops, 369, 386, 387–8
Butter refrigeration, 109
Butt joints, 62, 73

Cabinets, office, 348, 349, 350
Cabins, ships', 269

Cable net structures, 87
CAD (computer-aided
        design/draughting), 10–11, 44, 45
CADD (computer-aided draughting
        and design), 10
Cafés, 459, 460
Cafeterias, 462, 463, 571
Caissons, 512, 514
Campers, 269, 432
Canopies, 86, 367
Caravans, 269
Car-parks, 437, 439–42
        bus stations, 430
        cinemas, 487
        motels, 469
        sports stadiums, 489
        swimming pools, 529, 534
        tennis courts, 506
Carpentry workshops, 375–8
Carports, 268
Cars
        dimensions, 432
        filling stations, 443–4
        repair shops and showrooms, 381–4
        service stations, 445
        turning and parking, 436–7, 439
Car washes, 443, 444
Cash dispensers, 360, 362
Cast glass, 170
Casualty departments, 571, 573
Cathedrals, 580
Cattle sheds and stalls, 414–15, 418
Ceilings
        offices, 343, 344
        sound insulation, 119, 123
        tennis courts, 507
Cellars, 59, 63
Cemeteries, 586–7
Central key systems, 188
Central position, non-modular
        components, 34
Ceramic floor tiles, 94
Chairs, office, 348, 349
        see also Seating
Change of use, 210–11
        related publications, 590
Changing rooms, 402, 461, 484, 530
Chapels, hospitals, 571
Check-outs, 368, 370, 373
Child daycare centres, 325–6
Children's homes, 305
Children's hospitals, 578
Chimneys, 68, 69, 139, 140
Churches, 579–83
Churchyards, 587
Cinemas, 106, 107, 486–8
        related publications, 594
Circarama, 487
Cladding, 36, 62
Clay pigeon shooting, 524, 525
Clean rooms, hospitals, 553
Clean room technology, 553
Climate, room, 19, 20
Climbing plants, 231, 232–3
Cloakrooms, 12, 308, 485, 492
Closed-plan offices, 342
Cobi golf, 509
Coffins, 586
Cold construction, flat roofs, 81, 84
Cold frames, 235

Cold storage rooms, 109–10
Cold stores, 250, 369
Collar roofs, 72, 73
Colleges, 107, 312, 314–20
    libraries, 327–9, 331–2
Colour, 26
    glass, 167
    light, 146
    rendering, 146, 159, 167
    reproduction, lamps, 145
Combination key systems, 188
Commentary boxes, 489
Common rooms, motels, 469
Communications centres, hospitals, 570
Composite walls, 119
Compression cooling systems, 106
Computer-aided design/draughting
    (CAD), 10–11, 44, 45
Computer-aided draughting and
    design (CADD), 10
Condensation, 112
Conditioning rooms, 504–5
Conference rooms, 456, 465
Confessionals, 579
Conservatories, 281
Construction drawings, 4–14, 43
Construction management, 43–50
    collaboration with client, 41
    communication records, 48
    planning, 43
    preparatory work, 41–2
    related publications and standards,
        589, 596
    supervision, 31, 45–50
Contiport system, 462
Contracts, 44–5, 47
Convector heaters, 96, 98
Conversions for disabled people, 300
Conveyor belts, 396, 567
Cookers, 252, 253
Cooling, air, 106, 109–10
Cooling towers, 106
Coordinate systems, modular, 34, 35
Copper roofs, 76
Corridors, 245
    access, 296
    disabled people, 298, 299
    fire protection measures, 135, 136, 137
    hospitals, 550, 552, 559
    hotels, 465
    offices, 343, 344
Counters, 349, 362, 368, 369, 371
Couple roofs, 72, 73
Courtyard houses, 275, 276, 279
CPM (critical path method), 46, 50
Cranes, 33, 396
Crawling boards, 69
Creches, 325
Crematoria, 586
Critical path method (CPM), 46, 50
Crossbow ranges, 525
Crossroads, 215
Crush barriers, 490
Cubicles, 264, 530
Cupboards
    fume, 322, 323
    hospitals, 559
    houses, 247, 248, 252, 257, 260–2
    offices, 349
Curling, 520–1

Curtains, 177, 186, 187, 495, 496
Cyclecross, 523
Cycle paths, 216, 219
Cycles, see Bicycles
Cylinder locks, 188

Damp-proofing, 59–61, 202
Daycare centres, 302, 325–6
Day clinics, 566
Daylight, 151–65
    global radiation, 155
    hospitals, 545, 548
    house orientation, 272
    insolation, 164–5
    libraries, 328, 329
    multistorey industrial buildings, 398
    office buildings, 338, 339, 346, 351
    related publications and standards,
        590, 607–608
    rooflighting, 162–3
Daylight factor, 157, 162
Decimal multipliers, 2
Decks, access, 296
Delannoy, François Jacques, 364
Demarcation areas, hospitals, 543, 555
Denmark, basic measurements, 33
Dental practices and treatment, 542, 565
Department stores, 371–2
Design issues
    colour, 24, 26
    construction management, 43
    form, 37–9
    functional use of materials, 36
    houses as expression of period, 39
    perception by observers, 24–6
    preparatory work, 41
    related publications and standards,
        589, 596
    working process, 40
Design method, 40
Desks, offices, 345, 348, 349
Detached houses, 280
D'Humy ramps, car parks, 441
Dialysis stations, 578
Dictation rooms, 553
Digitising tablets/digitisers, 10, 11
Dimensional co-ordination, hospitals,
    548–9
Dimensional relationships, 27–30
    application of Le Modulor, 30
Dining rooms and areas, 255–6, 310
Disabled people, building for, 298–301
    barrier-free living, 301
    bicycle parking, 218
    cash dispensers, 360
    child daycare centres, 325
    conversions, 300
    doors, 184, 298, 301
    gardens, 229, 234
    hospitals, 559, 565, 571
    hotels, 465
    houses and apartments, 299
    libraries, 327, 328
    lifts, 197, 198, 201, 301
    offices, 339
    old people's accommodation, 302–4
    parking spaces, 437
    primary healthcare centres, 542
    ramps, 194, 298, 301
    swimming pools, 530, 531

    travelators, 196
    WCs, industrial buildings, 399
    zoos, 473
Discharge lamps, 141
Dishwashers, 252, 253
Disks and disk drives, CAD, 10
Dispensaries, 567, 568
Diving facilities, 533
Documentation, 4–6, 31, 44–6, 47, 48
Domed structures, 86, 175
Doors
    disabled people, 184, 298, 301
    fire/smoke resisting, 130, 135–7
    frames, 184, 185
    garage, 187
    glass, 170
    hospitals, 550, 552, 559
    internal, 184
    locking systems, 188
    related publications and standards,
        590, 608
    renovation, 205
    revolving, 186
    riding facilities, 517
    sheep sheds, 407
    sizes, 184, 185
    sliding, 186
    sound insulation, 118
    strongrooms, 362
    supermarkets, 373
    warehouses, 187, 394
    workshops, 380, 382
Dormers, 74, 77
Dormitories, youth hostels, 470
Double glazing, 166–7, 169
Dovecotes, 405
Drach, A.V., 28
Drainage
    building and site, 55–8, 60–1
    guttering, 76
    pipes, 55–8, 60–1, 71, 76
    roof gardens, 84, 85
Draughting, see Construction drawings
Drawing boards, 7, 8, 320
Drawings, 4–14, 43–4
Drawing studios, 320
Drawing tables, 320
Drinking fountains, 400
Drive-in banks, 362
Drive-in cinemas, 488
Drive-in restaurants, 458
Ducting, ventilation, 70
Dust allergies, 98

Ear, nose and throat (ENT) treatment, 565
Earthworks, 53–4, 230
Ebensee system, 226
Echoes, 122, 123
Ecological building, houses, 66, 101, 284
Edge position, non-modular
    components, 34
Egg cooling, 110
Elderly people's accommodation,
    302–4, 305
Electrical repair shops, 386
Electrical services, 71, 96, 322, 344, 570
Electromagnetic spectrum, 151
Electromagnetism, SI units, 2
Elevators, see Lifts
Embankments, securing, 226, 229

Energy balance of buildings, 101
Energy conscious construction, 66, 101, 284
Entrance halls, 245, 571
Entrance screens, glass, 170
Equipment rooms, hospitals, 552
Erasers, 8
Escalators, 195, 196
Evaporative cooling, 106
Excavations, 51, 52
Experimental stations, 572
Extract fan units, 70
Extractor hoods, 252
Extractor systems, 127, 375, 382, 408
Eye treatment, 565

Farm buildings, see Agricultural buildings
Farm vehicles, 416
Fencing, 227–8, 394
Figure skating, 521
Filament lamps, 141
Filing cabinets, 348, 349, 350
Filling stations, 443–4
Filtering, 106
Fire
    detection, 125
    escape, means of, 133–6, 137
    extinguisher systems, 128–9
    plastics, 174
    protection, 130–2, 187
    related publications and standards, 590, 606–607
    safety
        car-parks, 442
        hospitals, 566, 570
        hotels, 465
        libraries, 328
        office buildings, 339, 353
        railways, 424
        roof gardens, 85
        transparent roofs and canopies, 367
        warehouses, 394
        youth hostels, 470
    smoke and heat extraction, 127
    spread, 126
Fire alarm systems, 125, 189
Fire appliances, 137, 433
Fire extinguisher systems
    CO$_2$ systems, 129
    foam systems, 129
    halon systems, 129
    powder systems, 129
    sprinkler systems, 128
Fireplaces, 68, 69
Fire-resistant glass, 130–1, 169, 172, 173
Fire stations, 452–4
First aid rooms, 489, 495
Fishmongers' shops, 369
Fish refrigeration, 109
Fitness rooms, 504–5
Fixed filter drainage, 60
Flat roofs, 79–81
    cold construction, 81, 84
    cultivation, 82–5
    warm construction, 80
Flats, 92, 93, 292–7
    related publications and standards, 591, 608
Floodlights, 147
Floor area requirements, offices, 337, 345–50

Floor heating systems, 98, 99
Flooring, 94
    agricultural buildings, 407, 410
    bathrooms, domestic, 266
    designs, 67, 94
    hospitals, 552
    mortuaries, 586
    offices, 343, 344
    renovation, 204–5, 206
    shops, 371
    sound insulation, 119, 123
    sports facilities, 493, 526
    suspended, 92, 93
    WCs, industrial buildings, 399
    workshops, 380, 382
Flower shops, 369
Flues, 68, 69
Fluorescent lamps, 148, 150
Fodder, 419
Fonts, 579
Food courts, retail outlets, 370
Footpaths, 216, 217, 229, 298
Foot-washing systems, 400, 530, 539
Föppl framework formula, 89
Forging workshops, 380
Forklift trucks, 434
Form, 37–9
Foster, Norman, 88
Foul water stacks, 58
Foundations structures, 51, 52, 53–4
Foyers, theatres, 485
Freezers, 253
Freight yards, 427
French drain, 60, 61
Front facing, 62
Frosted glass, 150
Fruit refrigeration, 109
Fruit shops, 369
Fume cupboards, 322, 323
Functional diagnosis facilities, 564
Functional use of materials, 36
Function rooms, 456
Furnace rooms, 586
Further education colleges, see Colleges

Game cooling and refrigeration, 110
Game shops, 369
Garages, 187, 301, 436–9, 440
Garden equipment, 239
Gardens, 229–38, 240–1, 417
    related publications, 591
    see also Roof gardens
Gas-fired heating systems, 95, 97
Gas heaters, 68, 97
'Gastronorm' system, 460
General practice premises, 541–2
Germany, 33, 75, 424
Glare, 146, 159, 160
Glass, 130–1, 150, 166–73, 201
Glazed arcades, 363–7
Glaziers' workshops, 377, 378
Global radiation, 155
Goat sheds, 406
Golden section, 20, 30
    theatres, 479
Golf courses, 508–11
Goods protection systems, 189
Goods sheds, 427
Grass turf, 226, 230
Gravestones and graveyards, 587
Greek alphabet, 3
Greengrocers' shops, 369

Greenhouses, 235
Gropius, W., 477
Ground compression piles, 53
Ground probes, 51
Ground water, 21, 51, 60–1
Group practices, 541–2
Guard rails, 193
GUM department store, Moscow, 365
Guttering, 76
Gymnasiums, 504–5, 565
Gymnastics halls and equipment, 492, 493, 494

Half-timbered houses, renovation, 203
Hallways, 246
Handrails, 193, 298, 302, 303, 550
Hanging gardens of Babylon, 82
Harbours, 514
Hay storage, 419
Healthcare buildings, 541–78
    see also Hospitals
Heat extraction systems, 127
Heating, 95–104, 106
    drive-in cinemas, 488
    hospitals, 569
    related publications and standards, 589, 604
    shops, 369
    swimming pools, 242
Heckmann Ecohouse, 66
Hedges, 236
Henhouses, 405, 408, 418
High-bay warehouses, 391, 392–5
High-pressure air conditioning systems, 108
Holiday homes, 269–70
Hopkins, Michael, 88
Horizontoscopes, 153
Horse boxes, 415
Horse stables/stalls, 413
Hospitals, 543–78
    A&E and outpatients departments, 573
    care areas, 557–60
    construction planning, 544
    corridors, doors, stairs and lifts, 550
    day clinics and outpatient surgery, 566
    demarcation, 543, 555
    dimensional co-ordination, 548–9
    forms of building, 546–7
    general areas, 571
    intensive care area, 556
    laboratories and functional diagnosis, 564
    laundry facilities, 305, 306
    maternity and neonatal care, 574
    mortuary, pathology and service yard, 575
    planning conception, 545
    post-operative facilities, 553
    related publications, 594
    special, 576–7
    special care area safety, 578
    supplementary disciplines, 565
    supplies areas, 567–70
    surgical department, 551, 552, 554
    teaching and research, 572
    treatment areas, 561–3
Hostels, 470–2
Hotels, 464–72
    kitchens, 459, 466, 467
    laundry facilities, 305, 306
    related publications, 594

Hotels (*cont.*)
  swimming pools, 242, 243
Houses
  bathrooms, 56, 57, 262–7
  bedrooms, 257–61
  carports, 268
  with conservatories, 281
  dining rooms/areas, 255–6
  dividing walls, 119
  ecological building, 66, 284
  as expression of period, 39
  kitchens, 251–4
  landings and hallways, 246
  multistorey, 92, 292–7
  orientation, 272
  pantries and larders, 250
  porches, entrance halls and
    corridors, 245
  related publications and standards,
    591, 608
  on slopes, 272, 274, 283, 288
  stone, 37
  storage space, 247, 250
  symbols, 12
  timber, 37, 271, 284
  types, 37, 273–80, 282–3, 285–7,
    288–91, 297
  utility rooms, 248–9
Human scale, 1, 15–19
Humidifying devices, 106
Humidity, 19, 20, 22, 105, 112, 242,
  328, 329
Hydraulic lifts, 200
Hydro-electric power stations, 404
Hypermarkets, 372, 374

Ice hockey, 521
Ice rinks, 520–1
Illuminance, *see* Daylight; Lighting
Impact sound insulation, 119
Imperial system, 31
  conversion factors, 611–12
Industrial buildings, 389–404
  related publications, 593
Inflatable structures, 86
Information technology, 337, 351
Insolation, 164–5
  see also Daylight
Intensive care areas, 556, 558
Interim Certificates, 48
Internal medicine treatment area, 562
Intersections, road, 215, 220
Isometry, 8
Isophonic maps, 225

Japan, 33, 159
Joiners' workshops, 375–8
Judo, 526
Junctions, road, 215, 220

KEBA joints, 91
Kerbstones, 217
Kindergartens, 325
Kitchens
  disabled people, 299, 301
  hospitals, 568, 569, 570
  hotels, 461, 467
  houses, 251–4
  large-scale catering, 462–3
  related standards, 609
  restaurants, 457, 459–61
  schools, 310

ventilation and air conditioning, 108
  youth hostels, 470
Kiwariho method, 33
Krainer walls, 226
Krupp–Montal® space frame, 91

Laboratories
  hospital, 564
  language, 308
  related publications, 592
  photographic, 309
  schools and colleges, 308, 321–4
Laminated glass, 131, 168
Lamps, 141–2
Landing bridges, 449
Landings, 192, 246
Language laboratories, 308
Larders, 250
Laundry facilities, 248, 305–6, 467, 469, 568
Laying nests, 405
Le Corbusier, 30, 82
Lecterns, 579, 580
Lecture theatres, 107, 315–19, 543
Lettering, 8
Letting of contracts, 44–5
Libraries, 310, 311, 327–32, 572
  related publications, 592
Lifts, 197–201
  disabled people, 201, 299, 301
  emergency systems, 190
  garages, 439
  hospitals, 550
  old people, 302
  related publications and standards,
    590, 608
  skyscrapers, 354
  sound insulation, 121
Lighting
  arrangement, 144–6
  art galleries, 333
  billiard rooms, 527
  density, 141
  drawing studios, 320
  hospitals, 552, 554, 557
  houses, 256, 257, 265
  intensity, 141
  lamps and fittings, 141–2
  lecture theatres, 319
  libraries, 329
  metalworking workshops, 380
  museums, 333
  natural, *see* Daylight
  offices, 346, 348, 351
  provision, 143
  redirection, 160
  related publications and standards,
    590, 607
  requirements, 147–50
  small animal stalls, 406
  tennis courts, 506
  theatres, 479
  warehouses, 394
  woodworking workshops, 375
Lightning protection, 138–9, 140
Light shelves, 160
Light transmittance, 167
Lignotrend, 66
Line diagrams, 46, 49
Line types and thicknesses, 9
Linked housing, 275, 276
Living rooms, 12, 118
Loading bays, 434–5

Lockers, 402, 428, 530, 559
Locking systems, 188, 218, 394
Loft space, 78, 180, 193
Log cabins, 270
Loggias, 295
Lorries, *see* Trucks
Luggage lockers, railway stations, 428
Luggage rooms, youth hostels, 470, 471
Luminous flux, 141, 147

Maintenance and restoration, 207–9
  related publications, 590
  see also Refurbishment of old
    buildings
Management, construction, 43–50
Manufacturer's information and
  specifications, 45
Marinas, 512–14
Martin, Pugh, 360
Masonry, 62–7
Master key systems, 188
Maternity care, 574
Mathematical symbols, 3
Measurement basis, 15–19, 27–35
  building biology, 21–23
  excavations, site and building
    measurements, 52
  human scale, 1, 15–18
  related publications and standards,
    589, 595
  room climate, 19–20
  units, 2–3, 6, 9
Meat cooling and refrigeration, 109, 110
Meat processing centres, 388
Media centres, schools, 310, 311
Mentally ill people, care of, 578
MERO space frame, 28, 90
Metalworking workshops, 379–80
Meteorological features, 154
Metra-potential method (MPM), 46, 50
Metric system, 31
Microfiche stations, 329
Military cemeteries/memorials, 587
Miniature golf, 508–9
Mirrors, 257, 399
Mirror-type glasses, 169
Modular system, 34, 35
  application of Le Modulor, 30
Moisture, SI units, 2
Monitoring system, 190
Mortar, 62
Mortuaries, 575, 586
Mosaic floors, 94
Mosques, 585
Motels, 469
Motorcycle dimensions, 432
Motorways, 220
Mountain slopes, house orientation, 272
Multistorey structures
  arcades, glazed, 363, 364
  car parks, 440, 441, 442
  housing, 92, 248, 266, 282, 292–7
  industrial buildings, 398
  office buildings, 352, 353–4, 358
  stairs, 192
  woodworking workshops, 375
Museums, 333–5
  related publications, 592
Music, 122, 123, 309

Natural stone, 22, 62, 94, 228, 229
Natural ventilation, 105

Nave, 580
Neonatal care, 574
Nesting boxes, 405
Networks, 46, 49–50
Night storage heating, 96
Noise, *see* Sound
Non-modular zone, 34
Northlight roofs, 75
Nursery schools, 325
Nurses, 553, 560
Nursing homes, old people, 302–4, 305

Obstetrics, 561, 574
Offers, 44
Office buildings, 336–62
    archives, 350
    banks and buildings societies, 359–62
    building technology, 344
    construction calculations, 343–51
    examples, 352–8
    floor area requirement, 345–50
    furniture, 348–9
    principles, 336–9
    related publications and standards, 592, 608
    sanitary facilities, 401
    typology, 340–2
    ventilation and air conditioning, 106, 107
    workstations with computers, 351
Oil-fired heating systems, 95
Oil storage tanks, 99, 100
Old people's accommodation, 302–4, 305
    related publications, 591
Open fires, 68
Open-plan banks and building societies, 360
Open-plan offices, 340, 341, 342
Open-plan schools, 313
Opera houses, 477, 478, 482–5
Operating theatres, 552, 553, 554
Organs, church, 581–2
Outpatients departments/surgery, 547, 566, 573

'Pachinko' gaming arcades, 540
Paint shops, 386
Pallets, 392, 394, 395, 396, 439
Pallet trucks, 434
Panorama masks, 153
Panoramic glass lifts, 201
Pantries, 250
Paper, sizes and folding, 4, 5, 7
Parallel motion rulers, 7
Park and ride systems, 430
Parking
    aircraft, 447, 450
    bicycle, 218, 219, 529, 534
    cars, 436–8; *see also* Car-parks
    fire engines, 453
    trucks, 436–8
Parks, graveyards as, 587
Parquet flooring, 94, 123
Partition curtains, 186, 495, 496
Pathology department, 575
Paths, 216, 217, 229, 298
Paving, 217, 229
Pencils and pens, architects', 7, 8
Perception and the eye, 24–7, 479
Performance specifications, 45
Pergolas, 229
Perspective drawing, 8

Perspective grids, 8
PERT (programme evaluation and review technique), 46
Petrol stations, 443–4
Pharmacies, hospitals, 553, 560, 567, 568
Photographic work and laboratories, 309
Photometric distance principle, 146
Physiological perception field, 479
Physiotherapy department, 565
Pigeons, 405
Pig sheds, 409–11, 418
Pile foundations, 53, 54
Piscator, E., 477
Pistol shooting, 524
Planning, construction, 43
Planting methods and plants, 231–2
Plant rooms, 107
Plan views, 6
Plaster rooms, 552
Plastics, 174
Platforms
    bus stations, 430
    railway stations, 424, 427, 429
Playgrounds, 326, 469, 474, 488
Plotters, 10, 11
Plunge pools, 539
Pneumatic roofing, 86
Ponds, garden, 237
Pontoons, 512, 514
Porches, 245
Poroton, 66
Post-operative facilities, 553
Potters, rooms for, 320
Poultry
    cooling and refrigeration, 110
    farms, 408
    shops, 369
    stalls, 405
Power stations, 403–4
Prayer rooms, 571
Press boxes, 489
Printers, 10, 11
Prisms, 160
Probes, ground, 51
Profiled glass, 172
Programme evaluation and review technique (PERT), 46
Projection rooms, 486, 488
Proportion, rules of, 1, 15, 24
Psychiatric care, 578
Public health offices, 573
Public houses, 458
Public libraries, 327, 330
Pucks, 10, 11
Pulpits, 579

Quick-set hedges, 236

Rabbit hutches, 406
Rack systems, warehouses, 394, 395
Radiation
    global, 155
    ground, 21–3
    solar, 154, 155–6
Radiators, 96, 114
Radiology departments, 562
Radiotherapy, 563, 578
Rafter roofs, 73
Raft foundations, 53
Railways
    European structure gauges and clearances, 424

freight yards, 427
related publications and standards 593, 609
restaurant cars, 457
stations, 428–9
track installations, 422–3
UK structure gauges and clearances, 425–6
urban light railways, 221, 223
Rainfall, 58, 238
Raised beds, 234
Ramps, 191, 194
    bus stations, 430
    car parks, 441, 442
    disabled people, 194, 298, 301
    drive-in cinemas, 488
    garden, 229
    loading, 434
    old people, 303
    shops, 371
Reading rooms, 327
Record books, 31
Recovery rooms, 553, 556
Redirection of light, 160
Reflections
    light, 146, 159
    sound, 120, 122, 123–4
Reflectors, 160
Refrigeration, cold storage rooms, 109–10
Refrigerators, 253
Refurbishment of old buildings, 202–6, 267
    related publications, 590
Refuse collection trucks, 433, 436
Regenerative energy, heating systems, 95
Rehearsal rooms, 485
Reilesch's perspective apparatus, 8
Reinforced masonry, 64, 65, 67
Remote control security systems, 190
Remote heating systems, 95
Research laboratories, 321–4, 564
Restaurant cars, 457
Restaurants, 305, 455–63, 466, 467
    related publications and standards, 593–609
Restoration, 207–9
    see also Refurbishment of old buildings
Retaining walls, 54, 226, 229
Reverberation time, 122, 124
Reversible offices, 341
Riding facilities, 517–18
Rifle shooting, 524
Ring drainage system, 60
Roads and streets, 212–25, 272, 450
    related publications, 591
Rogers, Richard, 88
Roller shutters, 187
Roller skating rinks, 521–2
Roller walls, 186
Roof gardens, 81, 82–5
    car-parks, 441, 442
Roof houses, 75
Rooflighting, 162–3, 175
Roofs, 72–85
    aerials, 140
    cattle stalls, 415
    chimneys, 69
    coverings, 75–6
    flat, 79–81, 84
    forms, 72–3, 75–6
    lightning protection, 138

Roofs (*cont.*)
    renovation, 204
    sheds, industrial, 397
    slopes, 33, 79, 83, 84
    sports stadiums, 490
    storage space, 247
    structures, 72–4
    tensile, 86
    thermal insulation, 114
    transparent, 367
    windows, 180; *see also* Rooflighting
    woodworking workshops, 375
Room climate, human factors, 19, 20
Roundabouts, 215
Rowing, 515
Royal boxes, 490
Runways, 448, 450
Rüter, E., 91

Sacristy, 580
Saddle rooms, 517
Safes, 359, 361
Safety deposit boxes, 359, 361
Safety glass, 168
Safety regulations, 394, 483, 563
    see also Fire safety
Sailing, 512–14
Sanitary installations, 401, 470, 471, 531
    see also Bathrooms; Showers; WCs
Sash windows, 105
Saunas, 537–9
Sawtooth roofs, 75, 138
Scales, 6
Scane space frame, 91
Schools, 307–13, 325, 326
Science libraries, 331
Science rooms, 309
Sculptors, rooms for, 320
Seating
    churches, 579
    cinemas, 487
    laboratories, 322
    lecture theatres, 318
    offices, 348, 349
    restaurants, 455–6, 458
    sports halls/stadiums, 490, 495
    theatres, 478, 479
Sectional drawings, 43
Security systems, 125, 188, 189–90
    banks and building societies, 361, 362
    libraries, 328
    offices, 349
    warehouses, 394
    see also Locking systems
Selectivity code, 167
Self-service restaurants, 459, 461
Semi-detached houses, 275, 276, 278
Serlio, Sebastiano, 476
Services
    connections, 71
    noise from, 120
Service stations, 445
Service yards, hospitals, 575
Set squares, 7
Sewage, farms, 420
Seward, Edwin, 364
Shadows and shading, 153, 159, 178, 235
Sheds
    agricultural, 406, 407, 409–11,
        414–15, 418
    garden, 270

goods, 427
    industrial, 397
Sheep sheds, 407
Sheet roofs, 76
Sheltered housing, 302
Shelving
    hospitals, 571
    libraries, 327, 328, 329
    metalworking workshops, 379
    offices, 350
    shops, 368, 371
    warehouses, 391, 394, 395
Shielding glass, 169
Ships' cabins, 269
Shooting ranges, 524–5
Shoplifting protection systems, 189
Shopping trolleys, 372, 373
Shops, 368–74
Showers
    domestic, 262–7
    hospitals, 558, 559
    industrial buildings, 400
    sports halls, 495
    swimming pools, 531, 534
Showrooms, vehicle, 381
Shutters, 178
Silos, 419
Sinks, 253
    see also Wash-basins
Site layouts, 6
Site measurements, 52
SI units, 2–3
Skateboarding, 522
Skating rinks, 520–2
Ski jumps, 519–20
Skittle alleys, 528
Skylights, 175
Skyscrapers, 354, 358
Slate roofs, 75
Slaughterhouses, 387
Sliding doors, 184, 186, 373
Slopes, houses on, 272, 274, 283, 288
Small animal stalls, 405–7
Small goods lifts, 199
Smoke extraction/venting systems,
    127, 175
Smoke hoods, 68
Snack-bars, 459, 460
Snorkel banks, 362
Soakaway, 60
Solar architecture, 101–3
Solar constant, 154
Solar control double glazing, 167
Solar electricity, 104
Solar energy, 101, 102, 104, 154, 155–6
    glass, 167
Solar heat, 104
Solar positions, 151–3, 164–5
Solar radiation, 154, 155–6
Solid fuel heating systems, 95
Solid masonry walling, 63, 65
Sound absorption, 120
Sound insulation, 117–24
    bathrooms, 266
    glass block walls, 173
    hospitals, 550
    related publications and standards,
        589, 604–606
    room acoustics, 122–4
    shooting ranges, 525
    traffic noise, 223, 225

    ventilation and air conditioning, 107
    vibration damping, 121
    windows, 118, 182
Sound-control glass, 169
Space frames, 89–91
Special care units, 558, 578
Specialist hospitals, 543, 576–7, 578
Specifications, 45, 48
Speech intelligibility, 122
Spiral ramp car-parks, 441, 442
Sport, related publications and
    standards, 594, 609–610
Sports halls, 491–6
Sports pitches, 497–9, 526–7
Sports stadiums, 489–90, 500–3
Squash courts, 527
Stables, 412–13, 517–18
Stages, theatre, 481–2
Stairlifts, 201, 299
Stairs, 191–4
    hospitals, 550
    offices, 353
    old people, 302
    related publications and standards,
        590, 608
    renovation, 206
    schools, 308
    sports stadiums, 489
    storage space under, 247
    symbols, 13
    theatres, 485
    youth hostels, 470
Standard Numbering System, 31–2, 33
Standing areas, sports stadiums, 490
Stargolf, 509
Stations, 428–9, 430–1
Steam jet cooling, 106
Stencils, lettering, 8
Stepped housing, 297
Steps, garden, 229
    see also Stairs
Stereographic projection of sun's path,
    152
Sterile goods rooms, 552
Sterilisation of hospital instruments,
    554, 567
Stone, natural, 23, 37, 62, 94, 228, 229
Storage
    bedrooms, 257, 260–1
    boats, 514
    CAD v. paper-based systems, 10
    cold storage rooms, 109–10
    freight yards, 427
    heating oil, 98, 99, 100
    hospitals, 571
    space, houses, 247, 250, 299
    sports halls, 492, 493
    theatres, 483
    warehouses, 391–5
Streets and roads, 212–25, 272, 450
Strip foundations, 53
Strongrooms, 359, 361–2
Structural glazing, 169
Stylus, 10, 11
Substerilisation rooms, 552
Summer houses, 270
Sunshine, 164–5
    see also Daylight
Supermarkets, 371–4
Supervision, construction, 45–50
Supplies areas, hospitals, 567–70

Supporting walls, 64, 65
Surgical departments and surgeries, 551–2, 553, 554, 566
Surveys, renovation of old buildings, 202
Suspended structures, 88, 92, 93
Sway factor, 354
Swimming pools, 240–4, 529–36
    roofs, 79, 81
    sound insulation, 120
    thermal insulation, 113, 114
Synagogues, 584

Tables, 348, 455, 456, 458
Table tennis, 527
Tableware, 255
Tailors' shops, 386
Tanking, 59–61
Teaching hospitals, 572
Tea rooms, 459
Technical colleges, see Colleges
Technical conditions, 45
Telecommuting, 337
Telescopic doors, 186, 187
Tempered glass, 168
Tender action, 44–5
Tennis facilities, 506–9
Tensioned structures, 86, 88
Tents, 269
Terminals, airport, 448–9, 450
Terraced houses, 275, 276, 277
Thatched roofs, 75, 138, 140
Theatres, 106, 107, 476–85
    related publications, 594
Thermal boundary layer resistance, 111
Thermal capacity, 111
Thermal conductance, 111, 181
Thermal conductivity, 111, 115–16
Thermal insulation
    drawing conventions, 14
    exterior walls and roofs, 66, 114–16
    flat roofs, 79
    floor heating systems, 99
    loft space, 78
    pig sheds, 410
    rabbit hutches, 406
    related publications and standards, 589, 605–606
    summertime, 156
    terminology and mechanisms, 111
    types of construction, 113
    ventilation, 105
    water vapour diffusion, 22, 112
Thermal resistance, 111, 114
Thermal resistivity, 111
Thermal transmittance, 111, 167
Thomsen, Kaj, 91
Three-level houses, 282
Throwing fields, 501
Ticket machines, railway stations, 428
Ticket offices, cinemas, 487, 488
Tile drain, 60
Tiled roofs, 75
Timber houses, 37, 203, 205, 270, 271, 284
Time and solar position, 152
Timetable display boards, railway stations, 428
'T' junctions, 215
Toboggan runs, 520
Toilets, see WCs
Topsoil, 230

Toughened glass, 168
Town houses, 275, 276
Tractors, 416
Traffic layout, 222–4
Traffic noise, 225
Training of plants, 231, 232
Trains, see Railways
Tramways, 221
Transfer lettering, 8
Transparent and translucent materials, 150
Travelators, 196
Trees, 236
Trellises, 231, 232
Trenches, 51
Triple glazing, 166
Trombé walls, 102
Trucks, 432, 433, 436, 438
T-squares, 7
Turf, 226, 230
Turning circles, 432, 435, 436–8

Ulm theatre, 480
Ultra-violet light-cooled glass, 169
United States of America, 33, 302, 338
Units, 2–3, 6, 9
Universities, 314–20
    hospitals, 543, 572
    lecture theatres, 107, 315–19
    libraries, 327–9, 331–2
    related publications and standards, 592. 608
Urban light railways, 221, 223
Urban planning, and disabled people, 298
Urinals, 263, 399
    see also WCs
Urns, 586, 587
Urological treatment, 565
Utility rooms, 248–9

Valuation example, 48
Vasari, Giorgio, 476
Vegetable refrigeration, 109
Vegetable shops, 369
Vehicles
    agricultural, 416
    dimensions, 430, 432
    loading bays, 434–5
    repair shops and showrooms, 381–4
    turning and parking, 432, 435, 436–8
Ventilation, 105–8
    agricultural buildings, 406, 408, 412, 415, 421
    bathrooms, 266
    bedroom cupboards, 260
    dome rooflights, 175
    ducting, 70
    greenhouses, 235
    hospitals, 563, 569, 574
    laboratories, 322
    libraries, 328, 329
    metalworking workshops, 380
    offices, 344, 346
    related publications and standards, 589, 604
    restaurant kitchens, 461
    shops, 369, 371
    sound insulation, 107, 120
    swimming pools, 242
    theatres, 478, 481
    WCs, industrial buildings, 399

windows, 105, 177
Venting, heat and smoke extraction, 127
Vibratory pressure process, 53
Video-conferencing, 337
Visual links, 158

Wagner, R., 477
Waiting rooms, 564, 565
Walls, 62–7
    glass blocks, 171, 173
    hospitals, 552, 559, 578
    low-energy construction, 66
    mortuaries, 586
    pig sheds, 410
    renovation, 206
    retaining, 54, 226, 229
    silos, 419
    sound insulation, 118, 119, 123
    tennis courts, 506
    thermal insulation, 114
    Trombé, 102
    types and thicknesses, 65
    WCs, industrial buildings, 399
    woodworking workshops, 375
War cemeteries/memorials, 587
Wardens, youth hostels, 470, 471
Wardrobes, 260–1, 469
Warehouse design, 187, 391–6
Warm construction, flat roofs, 80
Wash-basins, 262, 263, 399, 400, 559
Washing, air, 106
Washing facilities, industrial buildings, 400
Washrooms, hospitals, 552
Waste compaction units, 252
Waste disposal, 248
Waste water, farms, 420
Water
    consumption, 265, 569
    ground, 21, 51, 60–1
    rain, 58, 238
    waste, 420
Waterproofing membranes, 14, 85
Water sports, 516, 533
Water table, 51
Water vapour diffusion, 22, 112, 115–16
Wattle, 226, 230
WCs
    disabled people, 298
    hospitals, 553, 559
    houses, 262, 263, 264, 266, 267
    industrial buildings, 399, 401
    mosques, 585
    offices, 343, 401
    restaurants, 456, 461
    schools, 308
    sound insulation, 121
    sports halls, 492
    storage space, 247
    swimming pools, 531, 534
    theatres, 485
    ventilation, 70, 105
    youth hostels, 470
Weight-lifting, 526
Weinberg steps, 123
Welding workshops, 380
Wet cells, 558, 559
Wet rooms, 206, 264
Wheelchairs, 298
Wheelchair users, see Disabled people, building for

INDEX

Wholesale butchers, 387
Wind
    airports, 446, 450
    and chimney efficiency, 69
    farm facilities, 417
    harbours and marinas, 514
    house orientation, 272
    office buildings, 352, 354, 355
    porches, 245
Windows
    arrangement, 177
    cleaning, 183
    construction, 181–2
    daylight, 158
    glass, 166–70
    hospitals, 550, 553, 557
    lighting, 150
    loft, 77, 180
    multistorey industrial buildings, 398
    offices, 347, 348, 353

related publications and standards,
    590, 608
renovation, 205
restaurants, 456
riding facilities, 517
shading, 178
sizes, 176, 180
skylights and dome rooflights, 175
sound insulation, 118, 182
types and dimensions, 179
ventilation, 105, 177
woodworking workshops, 375
Woermann roofs, 81
Wood block paving, 94
Woodworking workshops, 375–8
Workshops, 375–88
    bakeries, 385
    hospitals, 570
    metalworking, 379–80
    related publications, 593

showrooms and vehicle repairs, 381–4
theatres, 484
wholesale butchers, 387, 388
woodworking, 375–8
Workstations, 336, 337
    construction calculations, 346, 347,
      349, 350, 351
    vehicle repair shops, 383
Wrestling, 526

X-ray department, 562

Yachts, 512–13, 514
Youth hostels, 470–2
Youth hotels, 471, 472

Zinco roof cultivation systems, 83
Zoos, 473–5
    related publications, 594